The Harper American Literature

Volume 1

▶ **Donald McQuade**
University of California, Berkeley
General Editor

▶ **Robert Atwan**
Seton Hall University

▶ **Martha Banta**
University of California at Los Angeles

▶ **Justin Kaplan**

▶ **David Minter**
Emory University

▶ **Cecelia Tichi**
Vanderbilt University

▶ **Helen Vendler**
Harvard University

Harper & Row, Publishers, New York
Cambridge, Philadelphia, San Francisco, Washington,
London, Mexico City, São Paulo, Singapore, Sydney

Cover Photo Thomas Cole,
Home in the Woods 1845.
Courtesy of Reynolda House
Museum of American Art,
Winston-Salem, N.C.

Sponsoring Editor
Phillip Leininger

Coordinating Editor
Jonathan Haber

Development Editor
Nat LaMar

Project Editor
Lenore Bonnie Biller

Text and Cover Design
Karen Salsgiver

Text Art
Vantage Art, Inc.

Production Manager
Jeanie Berke

Production Assistant
Brenda DeMartini

Compositor
*ComCom Division of Haddon
Craftsmen, Inc.*

Printer and Binder
R. R. Donnelley & Sons, Company

For permission to use copyrighted
material, grateful acknowledgment
is made to the copyright holders
listed on pp. 2417–2419, which
are hereby made part of this copyright page.

The Harper American Literature,
Volume 1

Copyright © 1987 by Harper &
Row, Publishers, Inc.

Library of Congress Cataloging in
Publication Data

The Harper American literature.

   Includes bibliographies and
indexes.
   1. American literature.
I. McQuade, Donald.
II. Harper & Row, Publishers.
PS507.H227 1987 810′.8 86-19412
ISBN 0-06-044372-3 (v. 1)
ISBN 0-06-044367-7 (pbk.: v. 1)
ISBN 0-06-044373-1 (v. 2)
ISBN 0-06-044368-5 (pbk.: v. 2)
ISBN 0-06-044374-x (Compact
Edition)
ISBN 0-06-044371-5 (pbk.: Com-
pact Edition)

8 9 9 8 7 6 5 4 3

Contents

---

1 The Literature of the New World: 1492–1620

93   # The Literature of Colonial America: 1620–1776

495   The Literature of the New Republic: 1776–1836

951 The Literature of the American Renaissance: 1836–1865

Preface

The Harper American Literature reaffirms and invigorates what is now a nearly 150-year-old tradition of multivolume collections of American literature. From the publication in 1855 of Evert A. and George L. Duyckinck's two-volume *Cyclopaedia of American Literature,* readers wanting to explore what the Duyckincks called "the literary biography of America" have had ready access to what each succeeding generation judged the literature most worthy of its collective attention. But *The Harper American Literature* realizes for the first time a goal announced in the Duyckincks' preface and subsequently endorsed by the editors of virtually every collection of American literature—"to bring together in one book convenient for perusal and reference . . . memorials and records of the writers of the country and their works, from the earliest period to the present day." What distinguishes *The Harper American Literature* from its predecessors is its commitment to presenting fully the richness of American literature, its thematic and stylistic range as well as its geographical and ethnic diversity. To this end, we have worked to extend the conventional boundaries of the American literary tradition.

Virtually all collections of American literature now in print begin either with a generous selection of Puritan writings or, in fewer instances, with Captain John Smith and his engaging account of the early years of the Virginia colony. Yet such beginnings ignore a great deal of compelling literature written in and about America long before the first settlements at either Roanoke Island or Plymouth Plantation—from Cabeza de Vaca's harrowing sixteenth century narrative of his struggles to survive along the southeast coast of what is now Texas to the compelling creation myths of Native Americans. To supplant the narrow, northeastern, Puritan bias of currently available texts, we begin with a wealth of presettlement writing. "The Literature of the New World, 1492–1620," maps out new approaches to the important cultural forces that have helped shape American life.

The Harper American Literature extends America's literary tradition in another significant direction. Its final section, "The Literature of Contemporary America, 1973–Present," gives unprecedented attention to our most recent—and eloquent—

writers of fiction, poetry, and drama, far beyond the mid-1960s boundaries set by editors of nearly all other collections. Sampling the work of such important contemporary writers of fiction as Raymond Carver and Bobbie Ann Mason, poets Louise Glück and Robert Pinsky, and playwright David Mamet—to name but a few of these many fresh and already celebrated voices—will enable readers to explore unexpected dimensions of American literature.

These unique sections, "The Literature of the New World" and "The Literature of Contemporary America," enlarge our presentation of the American literary scene. The earliest of our texts dates from 1492, the latest from 1986. We also reprint important but neglected works by classic writers, as well as important works by such neglected writers as Abigail Adams and Harriet Beecher Stowe. Throughout *The Harper American Literature,* the seven contributing editors aim to present the most comprehensive regathering and reassessment ever of America's literary tradition, including but extending beyond classic works. For example, we reprint as a separately bound supplement the centennial edition of *Adventures of Huckleberry Finn,* with a reconsideration of the novel's significance by the distinguished critic Hamlin Hill. At the same time, we include extensive portions of Twain's *Roughing It* as well as several of his tales, essays, and letters. Along with the most familiar sections of Washington Irving's *Sketch Book,* we include a representative chapter from his *History of the Life and Voyages of Christopher Columbus,* a rarely reprinted work that underscores both the continuity of American literature and the fascination of early nineteenth-century American writers with their distant past. To highlight the dramatic changes in Walt Whitman's poetic vision and accomplishments, we end our first volume with the 1855 edition of *Leaves of Grass,* reprinted in its entirety, and begin Volume Two with generous selections from the 1891 "Deathbed Edition" of his poems. Later in Volume Two, we give unprecedented attention to Gertrude Stein's role in the emergence of American modernism. By offering fresh perspectives on the work of America's literary masters, we provide evidence of the ways in which American literature helped shape, and in turn was influenced by, American culture during each period in its history. Throughout, we have taken special care to provide readers with ready access to unexpected and inviting selections without overburdening overcrowded reading schedules. We hope that inquisitive readers will be prompted to explore further the works, careers, and interconnections that give American literature its inexhaustible richness.

Committed to offering a broader range in the characteristic modes of America's most prominent literary figures, we established the following criteria to guide us in presenting the work of each writer: the literary merits of a particular selection, its significance in American literary history, its reflection of the range and depth of the writer's accomplishments, its connections to other themes and styles, and its power to document the literary values of the cultural context within which the writer works. Most often, we represent American writers by their most important work and by a sampling of other literary performances that show them engaging significant cultural issues.

A perennial problem of any collection of American literature is a structure that appears to isolate careers and periods without adequate attention to the interactions of these lives, works, and times. *The Harper American Literature* represents a concerted effort to weave selections, footnotes, author headnotes, and period introductions into a unified approach to American literature and the culture that informs it. In these two volumes, we seek not only to celebrate the classics of American literature and to locate neglected works of special literary merit, but also to suggest the many ways in which these works are enmeshed in a particular social and cultural context. We have designed the eleven period introductions to *The Harper American Literature* to show how major American writers were shaped by, how they were influential in, how they were responsive to their times—to offer a memorable view of the cultural immediacy of a period, what Gertrude Stein calls "the continuous present."

Each introduction focuses on the prevailing circumstances and competitions American writers faced in each period. What was it like for writers to work at different moments in American cultural history? Were writers peripheral or central figures in examining the major issues and crises of their eras? What major developments occurred in the related arts? What was the taste of the reading public in each period? What, more generally, was the state of language, literacy, and public discourse? The answers to these and similar questions create vivid images of what it was like for writers to live and work in their times.

Each period introduction highlights relevant American literary issues, cultural materials, and personalities. Brief "boxed inserts" include (but are not restricted to) selections from writers who otherwise may not warrant full representation, as well as literary and cultural documents. These literary and folk pieces, philosophical and historical statements, and illustrations add texture to the introductions. A short list of suggested further reading, arranged chronologically, follows each introduction.

A brief informative essay introduces each writer represented in *The Harper American Literature*. These headnote essays provide biographical details and the specific literary context for each writer's work. One major purpose of these headnotes is to show writers writing. In them, we trace the shape of an author's career and address the question of that writer's place in American literary history. We also consider how each writer feeds on, recoils from, or is in conflict with a particular literary, social, political, or cultural environment. At once biographical, contextual, and analytical, these essays counter the tendency to view writers in isolation from one another—by placing their contributions in the context of the main thematic and stylistic traditions of American literature. We designed the headnote essays to be informative enough to free our readers from the need to surround themselves with additional secondary sources before they read, but suggestions for further reading assist those who want to explore further the life and work of a particular author.

The Harper American Literature reprints virtually every recognized American literary classic. Yet we want these classics to reflect more than an attenuated literary tradition, one too often dismissed as elitist. We believe that America's literary classics can—and should—exemplify what the scholar Nathan Huggins calls a "pluralistic realism." No collection of American literature can be complete unless it includes a wide range of distinctive voices, including those of women, blacks, Asian-Americans, Mexican-Americans, and Native Americans. In our selections, headnote essays, and section introductions, we blend these works of literary and cultural merit with other, more traditional, selections so that these new voices can be heard as more than simply statistical responses or intellectual concessions to contemporary propriety.

The Harper American Literature broadens the restrictive notion of what constitutes an American classic. We include, for example, a representative selection of Native American oral and written literatures, stretching from the oral poetry of the sixteenth century to the fiction of such contemporary writers as N. Scott Momaday and Leslie Silko. In doing so, we seek to show how celebrated and less-heralded works of literature illumine each other and enable us to appreciate the diverse achievements that have shaped a distinctively American culture. For "major" and "minor" figures alike, our consistent editorial aim has been to preserve the writer's living complexity, his or her verbal struggles with the challenges of shaping a self, modifying a genre, extending a literary tradition, or enriching a cultural context—as these are reflected in individual acts of composition.

The Harper American Literature follows a simple chronological organization, established by the author's date of birth yet remaining responsive to such instructional clusters as "The Fiction of the Early Republic." We set no guidelines for the length of our selections, which vary from short poems to full-length novels *(The Scarlet Letter* and *Adventures of Huckleberry Finn)* and novellas—including Melville's *Benito Cereno* and *Billy Budd,* Henry James's *Daisy Miller* and *The Turn of the Screw,* Edith Wharton's *Summer,* Gertrude Stein's *The Gentle Lena,* and Saul Bellow's *Seize the Day*—as well as such extended works of nonfiction as Thoreau's *Walden.* We avoid excerpting whenever possible, but when a writer's most important work is principally in extended prose forms, we reprint self-contained chapters or passages. James Fenimore Cooper, for example, is represented by a chapter from each of *The Leather-Stocking Tales,* featuring the life and death of Natty Bumppo. Other selections, as in the case of Nabokov's *Lolita,* are justified by its author's having previously supervised publication of the material in an abbreviated format. Several authors, including Max Apple, Harold Brodkey, David Mamet, and Robert Stone, offered recommendations on which of their works to include.

We have taken great care to provide reliable and readable texts, editing or modernizing only as needed (principally in spelling and punctuation). We have aimed to maintain the flavor of the original while making it accessible to contemporary readers. We note special textual problems and give the date of first publication at the end of each selection, preceded by the date of composition, if known. Footnotes, which are kept to a judicious minimum, explain obscure references, biblical and classical allusions, foreign words, and phrases having special or archaic meanings. We avoid interpretive footnotes. We have tried in every way possible to create conditions for reading that will enable students to discover and develop the integrity of their own responses with the support of their instructors.

We present *The Harper American Literature* as the most comprehensive collection ever assembled for the purpose of understanding—and reconstructing— American literary history. But we also intend it to be a flexible instructional resource. Because it contains virtually all the primary and supporting material required for instructional use and leisurely reading, *The Harper American Literature* enables instructors and students to concentrate on the literary merits of major American writing. Readers will find in these pages new forms, subjects, themes, and styles—each the product of a distinctive American literary imagination.

Projects with the scope and complexity of *The Harper American Literature* are by interest and necessity collaborative intellectual enterprises. The seven contributing editors of this project met for extended periods to plan the project—to articulate the principles and procedures that would guide its development, decide on the features that would distinguish it from its predecessors, and agree on the authors and selections to be included. Within this collaborative context, several of the editors made selections and wrote headnote essays for writers in periods outside their areas of primary responsibility. And while the eleven period introductions are unified by common principles and purposes, each essay in *The Harper American Literature* remains an extended individual critical statement summarizing the literary and cultural distinctiveness of each period in American literary history. Robert Atwan is the author of the introduction to "The Literature of the New World, 1492–1620"; Cecelia Tichi of "The Literature of Colonial America, 1620–1776"; Donald McQuade of "The Literature of the New Republic, 1776–1836"; and Justin Kaplan of "The Literature of the American Renaissance, 1836–1865." For "The Literature of an Expanding Nation, 1865–1912," Justin Kaplan treated the decade following the Civil War, Martha Banta the next thirty years. David Minter wrote the introductions to "The Literature of Modernism: Prose, 1912–1940"; "The Literature of Post-War America: Prose, 1940–1973"; and "The Literature of Contemporary America: Prose, 1973–Present." Helen Vendler is the author of the introductions to "The Literature of Modernism: Poetry, 1912–1940"; "The Literature of Post-War America: Poetry, 1940–1973"; and "The Literature of Contemporary America: Poetry, 1973–Present."

Donald McQuade,
General Editor

Acknowledgments

The publication of *The Harper American Literature* represents the collaborative efforts of numerous professionals. In many ways its final shape challenges the accuracy of a century-old American adage, first recorded in Henry Ward Beecher's *Proverbs from Plymouth Pulpit* (1887): "It is not the going out of port, but the coming in, that determines the success of a voyage." As *The Harper American Literature* comes to completion, its seven contributing editors would like to acknowledge those who contributed to this ambitious undertaking at both ends.

The Harper American Literature could not have been launched without the intelligence and vision of John J. McDermott, Distinguished Professor of Philosophy at Texas A & M University, who helped articulate the need for a substantially different collection of American writing. His generous advice and rich understanding of American culture have proven invaluable throughout the project's development. Helene Brewer, Queens College, CUNY, served as a limitless resource during the early phases of shaping this collection. John Frederick Nims, University of Illinois at Chicago Circle, and Joseph F. Trimmer, Ball State University, made significant contributions to the project's development, especially during the first several rounds of extended conversations about its distinctive features. We are grateful for their continued support.

During the several years that the contributing editors developed *The Harper American Literature,* many of our colleagues across the country offered incisive readings of various drafts of the manuscript. For their thoughtful critiques and helpful suggestions, we would like to thank the following reviewers: Daniel Aaron, Harvard University; Maurice Bassan, San Francisco State University; Calvin Bedient, University of California at Los Angeles; Frank Bergon, Vassar College; Dennis Berthold, Texas A & M University; Lynn Z. Bloom, Virginia Commonwealth University; Virginia W. Brumbach, Eastfield College; Louis J. Budd, Duke University; Lawrence Buell, Oberlin College; Robert P. Burke, Joliet Junior College; Edwin H. Cady, Duke University; Bonnie Costello, Radcliffe College; Michael Dunne, Middle Tennessee State University; Kathy Early, Middlesex County College; Emory Elliott, Princeton University; Suzanne Ferguson, Ohio State University; Steven Fink, Ohio State University; Benjamin Franklin Fisher IV, University of Mississippi; Michael T. Gilmore, Brandeis University; James Goodwin, University of California at Los Angeles; Robert C. Grayson, Southeast Missouri State University; Malcolm Griffith, University of Washington; Phillip F. Gura, University of Colorado, Boulder; William Howarth, Princeton University; J. G. Jannsen, Arizona State University; Donald Kartiganer, University of Washington; Merrill Lewis, Western Washington University; John S. Mann, Western Illinois University; Terence Martin, Indiana University; Lee Mitchell, Princeton University; James Moore, Mount San Antonio College; Elsa Nettels, College of William and Mary; Sarah Emily Newton, California State University, Chico; John Frederick Nims, University of Illinois at Chicago Circle; Thornton H. Parsons, Syracuse University; David Perkins, Harvard University; Marjorie Perloff, University of Southern California; Robert L. Phillips, Mississippi State University; Donald Pizer, Tulane University; Joel Porte, Harvard University; Carolyn Porter, University of California, Berkeley; John Reardon, Miami University, Ohio; Louis D. Rubin, University of North Carolina at Chapel Hill; Henry M. Sayre, Oregon State University; Richard Schramm, University of Utah; Dorothy U. Seyler, Northern Virginia Community College; Frank Shuffelton, University of Rochester; Ellen Hurt Smith, Stetson University; Haskell Springer, University of Kansas; William T. Stafford, Purdue University; Eric J. Sundquist, University of California, Berkeley; David O. Tomlinson, U. S. Naval Academy; Darwin T. Turner, University of Iowa; Emily S. Watts, University of Illinois at Urbana–Champaign; Robert P. Weeks, University of Michigan; Michael West, University of Pittsburgh; Ann Woodlief, Virginia Commonwealth University; Larzer Ziff, Johns Hopkins University.

We are especially grateful to the following colleagues and friends for their many helpful suggestions and generous encouragement: Daniel Aaron, Harvard University; Max Apple, Rice University; Helene Atwan; Anne Bernays; Joe Cuomo, Queens College, CUNY; Joan Feinberg; Joseph A. Finder; Steven Fink, Ohio State University; Sally Fitzgerald; Bruce Forer, Queens College; William Howarth, Princeton University; Dennis Huston, Rice University; Walter Isle, Rice University; Betsy B. Kaufman, Queens College; Bridget Gellert Lyons, Rutgers University; Robert B. Lyons, Queens College; Rosemary Magee, Emory University; Wendy Martin, Queens College; Larry McMurtry; Susanne B. McQuade; Caroline Minter; Marie Ponsot, Queens College; Carolyn Porter, University of California, Berkeley; Edward Quinn, City College, CUNY; Harold Schechter, Queens College; Nancy Sommers, Rutgers University; Donald Stone, Queens College; Robert Towers, Columbia University; William Vesterman, Rutgers University; William P. Wilson, Queens College; and Thomas Wortham, University of California at Los Angeles. We are also indebted to Frederick Buell, Queens College, CUNY; his imaginative intelligence, critical acumen, and patient understanding made this a far more solid book than it otherwise would have been. William P. Kelly, Queens College, generously and repeatedly made his knowledge of American literature and culture available. Elissa Weaver, University of Chicago, provided what are at once highly reliable and readable new translations of materials relating to Columbus's voyages. Wallace Chafe, University of California at Santa Barbara; Russ Hall, Harper & Row; and William C. Sturtevant, Smithsonian Institution, helped strengthen our representation of Native American literature, as did the work of Paula Gunn Allen, University of California, Berkeley, and her colleagues on the Modern Language Association's Commission on the Languages and Literature of America. Sally McLendon, Hunter College, CUNY, contributed immeasurably to our efforts to call greater attention to the eloquence and significance of Native American oral and written literatures. H. Barbara Weinberg, Queens College, CUNY, served as an extraordinary resource for exploring the interrelations of American literature and art. Her command of American art history has made each volume of *The Harper American Literature* more attractive as well as more responsive to the interplay of artistic forces in our culture. We are grateful for her assistance.

   We would like to acknowledge the first-rate research and editorial assistance of Dianne Armstrong, University of California at Los Angeles; Stephanie Bobo, Boston University; Ruth Burke, University of California at Los Angeles; Carolyn Denard, Kennesaw College; JoEllen Fisherkeller, University of California, Berkeley; Ken Houghton, University of California at San Diego; Karen Johnson, Indiana University–Purdue University, Indianapolis; Laura Parkington, Seton Hall University; John Pearson, Boston University; and David Wheeler. Virginia, Marise, and Tara McDermott ingeniously prepared a chart of American literature that helped clarify our work. We would also like to acknowledge the special contributions of Trudy Baltz, who devoted great intelligence and energy to the project long before it took final shape, as well as of Michael Arnold and James Barszcz, both of Rutgers University, who offered incisive readings and excellent advice as the project neared completion. The preparation of this manuscript benefited greatly from the skillful and genial assistance of Nora Elias and

Jeannette Gilkison at the University of California at Los Angeles, as well as Sandy Qualls and Jo Taylor at Emory University.

We would also like to express our appreciation to the staffs at the libraries of Boston, Columbia, Emory, Harvard, Indiana, Princeton, and Seton Hall Universities; the University of California, Berkeley; the University of California at San Diego; Queens College; and the Maplewood and South Orange public libraries. In addition, we often relied on the expertise of Anthony Shipps, Indiana University; Elizabeth Smith, slide collection manager of the art history program, CUNY Graduate Center; and Errol Somay, New York Public Library.

Our continuing thanks go to the skillful and gracious professionals at Harper & Row. This project could not have been published without the support of Neale Sweet, vice-president and publisher. His commitment to *The Harper American Literature* and the principles underlying it has been exemplary. Lauren Bahr, director of development, kept the project on course with a masterful blend of energy, intelligence, and good will. Nat LaMar, development editor, quickly became an indispensable intellectual presence. His editorial insights and his knowledge of American literature are everywhere apparent to the contributing editors. We are also indebted to Jonathan Haber, who deftly coordinated the in-house editorial process with rare intelligence and excellent literary taste. Bonnie Biller, project editor, managed the flow of several thousand pages of manuscript and page proof with intelligent exactness and irrepressible good cheer. For the elegant look of these volumes, we would like to thank Karen Salsgiver. Claudia Kohner successfully guided the manuscript through its early development. Cara Tate proved to be an inexhaustible resource for solving every conceivable editorial and administrative problem; she helped make *The Harper American Literature* a better book to work on and read. George Blaine and Kathy Vuignier quietly contributed to the project with daily examples of efficiency. We would also like to thank Barbara Cinquegrani, Peter Coveney, Carole Knoeller, and Mira Schachne for their fine work.

Our greatest debt is to Phil Leininger, sponsoring editor. His expansive and detailed knowledge of American literature as well as his understanding and appreciation of this project's purpose made him a constant source of imaginative recommendations and useful advice. He helped us in every way to refine and realize our vision. Quite simply, *The Harper American Literature* would not exist without his having cultivated the commitment he shared with us to reexamine—and reconstruct—America's distinctive literary heritage.

We trust that all those who contributed to putting *The Harper American Literature* in print will endorse Ralph Waldo Emerson's notion that "the reward of a thing well done is to have it done."

The
Harper
American
Literature

Volume 1

John White,
Indians Fishing,
watercolor, ca. 1585.
British Museum, London.
Photograph: Bettmann Archive.

The Literature of the New World
1492–1620

The Discoveries of America

 America has had many discoverers. The first arrived
some 22,000 years ago, when emigrants from Asia
crossed the land bridge that is now the Bering Strait
to become the earliest inhabitants of the New World.
From these prehistoric migrations eventually grew
the great Aztec, Inca, and Mayan civilizations.
Recent archaeological evidence suggests that early in
the eleventh century A.D. the Vikings set up
campsites in Newfoundland and even made a few
unsuccessful attempts at colonization. It is also highly
probable that English fishing vessels routinely coasted
Canadian shores a decade or so before Christopher
Columbus set out on his momentous journey.

At 2:00 A.M., Friday, October 12, 1492, Columbus
undeniably made the first recorded discovery of
America. Yet his reputation as the discoverer of the
New World is somewhat tainted by the fact that he
never understood *what* it was he had actually found.
Like all early navigators, Columbus wanted to
discover a route, not a region. He ventured out with
the hope of finding a convenient sea passage to the
Orient, a trade route that would give Spain
commercial access to the opulent world Marco Polo
described so vividly in his famous thirteenth-century
account of an overland journey to the court of
Kublai Khan. From the moment Columbus first
spotted the island of Guanahaní—which he promptly
renamed San Salvador—he was certain that his grand
calculation had been correct: He had reached the east
by sailing west. He was so convinced of this that

throughout the four voyages he made to the New World between 1492 and 1502 he saw and interpreted everything—every plant, animal, mineral, place, and person he encountered—within the context of his having successfully reached Asia. To Washington Irving, Columbus was a man "predisposed to be deceived." The world he found was truly new, yet he persisted in seeing it as old.

Columbus's grand illusion derived ultimately from a mental picture of the earth that he pieced together from his reading of the prophetic books of the Bible, Marco Polo, and the famous ancient geographer Ptolemy. In brief, Columbus's dream of sailing directly west to Asia depended on what could be called the "small-earth theory." In his mathematically oriented *Geography* (ca. 150 A.D.), Ptolemy had grossly underestimated the size of the earth and had greatly extended Asia's eastern coast. This world image fitted in nicely with Marco Polo's speculations concerning the position of Japan, which Columbus—accepting Polo's location—estimated lay only 2,760 miles from Portugal. (The actual distance is well over 12,000 miles.) Columbus reinforced his calculations with quotations from the Old Testament prophets. In the apocryphal Book of Esdras (2:6) he read that the earth consists of six parts land and only one part water, a ratio that he believed would result in a short sea voyage. And in the Book of Ezekiel (5:5) he read that Jerusalem had been placed at the center of the world, a location that led him during his third voyage to conclude that he had approached the "Terrestrial Paradise," the original Garden of Eden.

Not only did Columbus derive an image of the world from the prophetic books, but he also wrote his own *Book of Prophecies*. In it he saw his career as the fulfillment of Isaiah 11:10–12: "And he shall set up an ensign for the nations." In 1502 Columbus wrote: "In carrying out this Enterprise of the Indies, neither reason, nor mathematics nor maps were any use to me: fully accomplished were the words of Isaiah." By his fourth voyage Columbus had sailed beyond geography into a vast, visionary world, wandering, as Irving put it, "in lands of his imagination." It was a geography in which every new observation, every new discovery, was made to fit into a single overarching theory—the belief that he had discovered a passage to India.

Credit for the discovery of America as a distinctly new region of the earth is often, though not without controversy, awarded to the Florentine navigator Amerigo Vespucci. In 1501, sailing to Brazil under the Portuguese flag, Vespucci noted that "we arrived at a new land which . . . we observed to be a continent." When his *Mundus Novus* (*The New World*) appeared in 1503, it received far wider circulation than anything Columbus had written. Vespucci was imbued with a deeper spirit of the Renaissance than Columbus, whose views in many respects resembled the views of such medieval travelers as Marco Polo. Vespucci doubted Ptolemy's accuracy. Like his family's friend Leonardo da Vinci, Vespucci maintained that observation was a more trustworthy guide than authority.

Vespucci secured his reputation as the discoverer of the New World by claiming in his next published work that he had found the South American continent during a 1497 voyage. Clearly he fabricated this early voyage to get around the fact that Columbus had set foot on—though not convincingly identified—the Paria peninsula of Venezuela on his third voyage in 1498. Thus Vespucci promoted himself not only as the first explorer to recognize the existence of a new world, but also as the first to discover its mainland.

"We Arri~

Now we come to the reasoning animals.
people completely nude, men as well as wc
They have bodies well proportioned, white in.
or no beard. I tried very hard to understand the.
27 days I ate and slept with them, and that which

They have no laws or faith, and live according to
recognize the immortality of the soul, they have among
property, because everything is common; they have no bot
and provinces, and no king! They obey nobody, each is lord
justice, no gratitude, which to them is unnecessary because it is
code. They live in common in houses made like very large cabins,
people who have no iron or other metal, it is possible to say that th.
are truly wonderful, for I have seen houses which are 200 *passi* long an.
wide and artfully made by craftsmen, and in one of these houses were 50t
perhaps 600 souls. They slept in nets [hammocks] woven of cotton, exposed
the air without any other covering; they eat seated on the ground; their food i.
roots of herbs and many good fruits, an infinity of fish and great quantities of
shellfish; crabs, oysters, lobsters, crayfish, and many other things which the sea
produces. The meat which they eat commonly is human flesh, as shall be told.
When they can have other flesh of animals and birds they eat that too but they
do not hunt for it much because they have no dogs and their land is very full
of woods which are filled with fierce wild beasts, so they do not ordinarily
enter the woods unless with a crowd of people.

Amerigo Vespucci (1502), on his first Brazilian voyage
(translated by S. E. Morison)

When an obscure German geographer, Martin Waldseemüller, came across
Vespucci's work while preparing an edition of Ptolemy, he decided that this new
land ought to bear the name of its founder: "[Europe, Africa, and Asia] have
been more widely explored, and another, fourth part has been discovered by
Americus Vesputius . . . , and I do not see why anyone should rightly forbid
naming it Amerigo, land of Americus as it were, after its discoverer Americus, a
man of acute genius, or America, inasmuch as both Europe and Asia have
received their names from women." The geographer then took the liberty of
writing the word *America* across the new territory on his 1507 world map.
Despite numerous objections (the Spanish and Portuguese continued to refer to
the New World as "the Indies" until the eighteenth century), and despite
Waldseemüller's own change of mind, the name stuck. Ralph Waldo Emerson
thought it "strange" that Vespucci had "managed in this lying world to supplant
Columbus and baptize half the earth with his own dishonest name."

Vespucci's writings and Waldseemüller's geography convinced Europeans that
something was drastically amiss with Columbus's version of the world. Here was
no string of Asian islands but a newly discovered continent, a fourth part of the
world. Ptolemy's influential map required serious revision; the world was not

supposed. As Vespucci cautiously admitted: "Let it be said in a
ience is certainly worth more than theory."

re of Experience

al issue of Renaissance thought, the conflict between experience and
etween modern observation and ancient authority, understandably left its
the literature of exploration. The discovery of the New World was
product of the Renaissance: Leonardo da Vinci drew his designs for a
machine in the same year Columbus claimed San Salvador for Spain.
rience became a key word of intellectual discourse: "To me it seems," da
ci wrote, "that all sciences are vain and full of errors that are not born of
xperience, mother of all certainty, and that are not tested by Experience." The
ension between experience and authority informed all of the arts and sciences of
the time. In geography the conflict was dramatized by two sorts of maps—the
theoretical maps of the entire world *(mappi mundi)* elaborately devised by learned
academicians and the practical cruising charts *(portolanos)* made from the direct
experience of working navigators. The early mariners and explorers constantly
found themselves confronted by a discrepancy between what the big maps led
them to expect and what was actually there.

By means of the *portolanos,* generations of mariners gradually pieced together a
precise outline of the known world, especially the heavily traveled
Mediterranean. Closely related to the practical coastal chart was the written
record of assorted observations and experiences navigators kept during a voyage.
Known in Greek as a *periplus* ("sailing around"), such navigational records go
back to the fifth century B.C. A *periplus* eventually came to signify the narrative
of a voyage round a coastline. Henry David Thoreau, a voluminous reader,
alludes in *Walden* to one of the most famous of these, *The Periplus of Hanno.*
The classical *periplus* clearly served as an important model of composition for the
early explorers of the New World and subsequently left its mark on the great
nineteenth-century voyage literature of Cooper, Poe, Thoreau, Twain, and
Melville. Ezra Pound in the *Cantos* also saw the form as a literary plunge into
direct experience: "periplum, not as land looks on a map / but as sea bord seen
by men sailing."

The attitude behind the *periplus*—that one's experiences be grounded in
personal observation and oriented to a specific location—would become a
conspicuous feature of American writing. "Nothing is so easy as to travel on a
map," wrote Crèvecoeur. "Our fingers smoothly glide over brooks and torrents
and mountains." Or as Melville put it in *Moby-Dick,* "It is not down in any
map; true places never are." Ernest Hemingway's version of the ancient *periplus*
involved a dialectical movement between detail and design in composition. In a
1924 letter he describes the literary method of his first collection of stories, *In
Our Time,* by using the language of exploration:

Finished the book of 14 stories with a chapter on *In Our Time* between each
story—that is the way they were meant to go—to give the picture of the whole
between examining it in detail. Like looking with your eye at something, say

a passing coast line, and then looking at it with 15 × binoculars. Or rather, maybe, looking at it and then going in and living in it—and then coming out and looking at it again.

Hemingway's method, as he reports it here, especially resembles James Fenimore Cooper's rhetorical procedure in *The Leatherstocking Tales,* where topographical description alternates continually between a "bird's-eye view" of a vast landscape and an extreme close-up of a particular spot.

One of the finest and most polished examples of coastal voyage writing is Giovanni da Verrazzano's "Letter to the King," the record of his 1524 journey up the North American seaboard from North Carolina to Maine. Verrazzano's, too, is primarily a voyage of confounded expectations. Like Columbus, he starts out theoretically: "My intention on this voyage was to reach Cathay and the extreme eastern coast of Asia." His experiences, however, forced him to recognize a new version of the globe. He concludes like a man of the Renaissance:

> But I did not expect to find such an obstacle of new land as I have found; and if for some reason I did expect to find it, I estimated there would be some strait to get through to the Eastern Ocean. This was the opinion of all the ancients, who certainly believed that our Western Ocean was joined to the Eastern Ocean of India without any land in between. Aristotle supports this theory by arguments of various analogies, but this opinion is quite contrary to that of the moderns, and has been proven false by experience. Nevertheless, land has been found by modern man which was unknown to the ancients.

Verrazzano's narrative prefigures one of the dominant themes of American literature and philosophy—the experiential challenge to an authoritative theoretical framework, or as the cultural philosopher John J. McDermott states it, "the dominance of the 'experience' over any conceptual anticipation of 'how things should be.' " As a method of *knowing,* the supremacy of experience to doctrine in American literature would be vividly dramatized in *Old Times on the Mississippi,* where a young Mark Twain learns to "read" the river, and in Faulkner's "The Bear," where the young Ike McCaslin learns how to "read" the woods.

Another feature of Verrazzano's narrative that would occupy a preeminent place in subsequent American literature is his emphasis on the idyllic landscape of the New World. Borrowing from the title of a popular Renaissance romance and ultimately from Virgil's *Eclogues,* Verrazzano baptized Virginia's Accomack peninsula "Arcadia." For Renaissance writers Arcadia represented a lovely natural landscape comfortably inhabited by shepherds who live—mainly for love and song—in hardy simplicity. This highly conventionalized ideal, known as the pastoral, evolved into a cultural attitude that not only shaped the American writer's response to the natural world but also led to a persistent devaluation of civilized society in favor of a return to simpler ways of life. As the critic Leo Marx noted in *The Machine in the Garden,* his study of the pastoral ideal in America, the central theme of a remarkably large number of books is the "withdrawal from society into an idealized landscape."

America and the Pastoral Ideal

Literary pastoral had long symbolized the European dream of a Golden Age, and with the discovery of the New World that dream seemed for a brief moment in history to have come true. It seemed, at last, that an actual physical world did indeed exist uncorrupted by man and resembling the original state of nature. Columbus on his third voyage thought that he had literally come near to the Terrestrial Paradise. Later explorers, possessing a less biblical sense of geography, would still see the primeval American landscape as offering the possibility for another earthly paradise. This view dominated most descriptions of the new land. Thus the great French essayist Montaigne would write of the inhabitants of America, "I think that what we have seen of these people with our own eyes surpasses not only the pictures with which poets have illustrated the golden age, and all their attempts to draw mankind in the state of happiness, but the ideas and the very aspirations of philosophers as well." In his "Ode to the Virginia Voyage" (ca. 1605), the English poet Michael Drayton succinctly expressed the general enthusiasm for the new Golden Age, calling Virginia "Earth's only paradise." One hundred years later the American writer Robert Beverley would say of the same region that it "did still seem to retain the virgin Purity and Plenty of the First Creation, and the People their Primitive Innocence."

For nearly all the early explorers, the vision of the Golden Age was also a vision of actual gold. All other motives for exploration—the investigation of new regions, the religious conversion of native populations, the discovery of previously unknown natural phenomena—were secondary compared to the acquisition of gold and silver. "We came here to serve God," said the conquistador Bernal Díaz, "and also to get rich." Columbus never ceased quizzing native chieftains about gold, and the repeated failure of all the first explorers to find precious metals severely dampened the initial European enthusiasm for the new land. After all, what good was this new world if it were poorer than the old one? What was the point in financing expedition after expedition if all that could be brought back were colorful birds, strange plants, and poor naked people? If no wealth could be found, then this entire New World amounted to no more than the "obstacle" Verrazzano found it to be—a vast and useless mass of land inconveniently blocking the way to the fabulous Indies. The search for gold, not geographical curiosity, stimulated the earliest penetrations into the North American wilderness.

During the period of inland exploration, the pastoral ideal had little to do with what we now think of as the wilderness. The conventional landscape of pastoral poetry and romance took the form of a gentle, bountiful, and orderly garden, the type of landscape the early explorers would have recognized as a standard feature of Renaissance painting. An appreciation of such landscapes was more the result of an acquired taste for certain picturesque configurations of natural scenery than of a direct encounter with vast and impenetrable forests. Verrazzano possessed a trained eye for the details of a landscape and could make careful discriminations among various "styles" of scenery. As he coasted north, he grew less enthusiastic about the land and its people. He found the northern forests too "dense" and—perhaps assuming some connection between environment and human nature—the inhabitants "barbarous."

For the first explorers and settlers, *wilderness* had highly pejorative connotations. The word conjured up medieval images of bestiality, malevolence, and the horrors of hell. From the deck of the *Mayflower* in 1620, William Bradford looked out on a "hideous and desolate wilderness, full of wild beasts and wild men." His was a landscape far removed from any comfortable pastoral ideal:

> For summer being done, all things stand upon them with a weatherbeaten face; and the whole country, full of woods and thickets, represented a wild and savage hue. If they looked behind them, there was the mighty ocean which they had passed, and was now as a main bar and gulf to separate them from all the civil parts of the world.

Nonetheless, by the end of the eighteenth century, the wilderness came to possess a decidedly positive value. By the era of Cooper and Thoreau, it would replace the cultivated garden as the ideal American landscape.

The New American Hero

Survival in the wilderness—the central action of so many exploration narratives—would become a recurring theme of both popular and classic American literature. Out of the confrontation with the wilderness emerged a new type of hero: tough, self-reliant, experienced, in contact with life at its most elemental levels. We can trace the origins of this new heroic personality in such early exploration texts as *The Narrative of Alvar Núñez Cabeza de Vaca* (1542), one of the great documents in the literature of human endurance. Cabeza de Vaca's story is the harrowing account of how four shipwrecked men managed to keep themselves alive while wandering for eight years through the hard country of the Texas Gulf. Like many American survival and captivity tales, Cabeza de Vaca's narrative culminates in a spiritual rebirth—the survivors in this case literally saving themselves by becoming faith healers among the various Indian communities that held them prisoner.

The connection between physical survival and spiritual rebirth is best expressed by the explorer who more than any other typified the new American hero—Captain John Smith. "It is a happy thing to be born to strength, wealth and honor," Smith wrote, "but that which is got by prowess and magnanimity is the truest luster; and those can the best distinguish content, that have escaped most honorable dangers; as if, out of every extremity, he found himself now born to a new life."

In Smith's vigorous writing, the idea of experience takes on new significance. Experience is important not only as a method of testing a theory but also as a supreme value in and for itself. Experiences become cumulative and hierarchical. The hero has many experiences—the more extreme the better.

Though Smith's numerous accounts of the New World contain a few Edenic overtones ("And then the Country of Massachusetts, which is the Paradise of all those parts"), his Arcadia is mainly a utilitarian utopia. His descriptions seem pastoral insofar as they are textured with an imagery of natural abundance. But even though the new land abounded with resources, it required, Smith continually emphasized, discipline and hard work to forge out of the raw resources an independent subsistence. The bitter experiences Smith eventually suffered in Virginia left him skeptical of the "golden promises" that made colonists "slaves in hopes of recompenses." Instead of the lure of gold, Smith held out to future settlers the lure of fish. Men, women, and children, he promised more extravagantly than usual, "with a small hook and line, by angling may take divers sorts of excellent fish at their pleasures; and is it not pretty sport to pull up two pense, six pense, and twelve pense, as fast as you can haul and vere [pay out] a line." Throughout his writing, Smith scornfully dismissed the possibility of gold and silver mines and underscored—in terms Benjamin Franklin a century later could hardly disagree with—the inevitable convertibility of labor into wealth.

The Sea Mark

Aloof, aloof; and come no near,
   the dangers do appear;
Which if my ruin had not been
   you had not seen:
I only lie upon this shelf
  to be a mark to all
  which on the same might fall,
That none may perish but myself.

If in or outward you be bound,
   do not forget to sound.
Neglect of that was cause of this
   to steer amiss.
The seas were calm, the wind was fair
  that made me so secure,
  that now I must endure
All weathers be they foul or fair.

The winter's cold, the summer's heat
   alternatively beat
Upon my bruised sides, that rue
   because too true
That no relief can ever come.
  But why should I despair
  being promised so fair
That there shall be a day of Doom.

Captain John Smith (ca. 1631)

Smith wrote his books and pamphlets primarily to attract potential colonists to America. Like such earlier promotional efforts as Thomas Hariot's *A brief and true report of the new found land of Virginia* (1588), Smith's writing stressed the "incredible abundance" of the New World. Smith, however, went a step further by promoting the land as a means to individual well-being, liberty, and improved social status. In his books we find the earliest formulations of what would become a prevailing image of America: an open society where someone without benefit of family connections, inheritance, or formal education can by virtue of hard work alone enjoy a happy, independent, and prosperous life. The role Smith played in the "invention" of America may be far more important than the part he played in its discovery.

Toward a Pluralistic Culture

With Captain John Smith, the English language and the American experience became inseparably united. For that reason Smith has often been called the first writer in American literature. Yet it is important to remember that initially the English participated only minimally in the colonization of the New World. While Smith struggled with a disorganized band of lazy colonists in Jamestown to erect a dingy fort, Spain and France had already created a New World literature. French influence extended throughout Canada, the Northeast, and the Midwest. By the mid-eighteenth century, Spain controlled everything west of the Mississippi and south of the Oregon country as well as Florida and territories south of Tennessee. The Dutch, too, made a considerable effort at colonizing the New World, controlling Manhattan Island along with the rich and beautiful Hudson valley.

A cultural pluralism characterized the New World from the start. Long before Smith reached Virginia, an African black named Estevan had journeyed far into the wilderness of New Mexico. And about the time Smith finally gave up on Jamestown, Santa Fe had become a successfully settled community. "We Americans," wrote Walt Whitman in a letter commemorating the anniversary of Santa Fe,

> have yet to really learn our own antecedents, and sort them, to unify them. They will be found ampler as has been supposed, and in widely different sources. Thus far, impress'd by New England writers and schoolmasters, we tacitly abandon ourselves to the notion that our United States have been fashioned from the British Islands only—which is a very great mistake."

Exploration writing did not end with Captain John Smith and Samuel de Champlain but evolved into an American literary tradition as men and women like William Bradford, Mary Rowlandson, William Byrd, Daniel Boone, Thomas Jefferson, and William Bartram conducted their various errands into the wilderness. America, as Thoreau reminds us in *The Maine Woods,* always seems in the process of being discovered. The sheer wonder of discovery, in fact, may be the Age of Exploration's most durable legacy to American literature. Steeped in the writings of the great discoverers and explorers, the major American authors, from Washington Irving and James Fenimore Cooper to Hart Crane and William Carlos Williams, repeatedly beheld a world that was excitingly and inexhaustibly new. The inescapable fact of that newness may be what is most essentially American about American literature.

Further Reading:

J. Fiske, *Discovery of America*, 2 vols., 1893.
F. J. Turner, *The Frontier in American History*, 1920.
H. N. Smith, *The Virgin Land*, 1950.
R. W. B. Lewis, *The American Adam*, 1955.
E. O'Gorman, *The Invention of America*, 1961.
C. L. Sanford, *The Quest for Paradise: Europe and the American Moral Imagination*, 1961.
L. Marx, *The Machine in the Garden: Technology and the Pastoral Ideal in America*, 1964.
H. M. Jones, *O Strange New World*, 1964.
J. J. McDermott, *The American Angle of Vision*, 1966.
R. Nash, *Wilderness and the American Mind*, 1967, 1973.

S. E. Morison, *The European Discovery of America: The Northern Voyages*, 1971, and *The Southern Voyages*, 1974.
E. Page, *American Genesis*, 1973.
R. Slotkin, *Regeneration Through Violence: The Mythology of the American Frontier, 1600–1860*, 1973.
J. Seelye, *Prophetic Waters: The River in Early American Life and Literature*, 1977.
W. Franklin, *Discoverers, Explorers, Settlers: The Diligent Writers of Early America*, 1979.
F. Turner, *Beyond Geography: The Western Spirit Against the Wilderness*, 1980.
T. Todorov, *The Conquest of America*, 1984.

Christopher Columbus
1451–1506

Between 1492 and 1502, Christopher Columbus, convinced that the world was much smaller than it is and that the Orient could be easily reached by sailing west, made four voyages to the New World. On the first journey, on October 12, 1492, he discovered the island of San Salvador, and from there he went on to find the Bahamas, Cuba, and Haiti (he named the island Hispaniola). Though he discovered none of the riches that Marco Polo had spoken about so glowingly, he nevertheless returned to Spain confident that he had indeed reached the East. He was so certain that he had found the Indies that he named the people of the islands "Indians."

During the voyage, Columbus kept a daily journal that, like so many other original documents of these expeditions, is now lost. Our information concerning the first voyage comes from an abstract made of Columbus's journal by the Spanish historian Bartolome de Las Casas. The abstract puts Columbus's observations into the third person, except when Las Casas thought the admiral's words should be left intact (these are noted by quotation marks). Otherwise, the abstract appears to retain all the essential facts of the journey.

Columbus set out on his second voyage in September 1493. Though he discovered Puerto Rico, Jamaica, parts of Cuba, the Virgin Islands, and the Lesser Antilles, the expedition proved to be a financial disaster: still no gold or silver, still no fabulous cities. Of this voyage there is neither a journal nor an abstract. An aristocratic friend of Columbus's, however, accompanied him on the expedition and left an informal account. Michele de Cuneo's record of the journey shows how quickly relations between the Europeans and the natives deteriorated. His cold-blooded narrative of the skirmish in which Columbus's crew surprised a band of Carib men and women near St. Croix represents the first recorded battle between the Old World and the New. It prefigures the many disastrous encounters that would occur between the two worlds for centuries.

On the third voyage, which departed in May 1498, Columbus discovered Trinidad and the Spanish Main and came very close to finding the Amazon. He set foot on the South American continent, but, believing it an island, sailed up to Cuba, which he ironically thought must be the mainland, the gateway to the land of the Great Khan. While sailing in the Gulf of Paria, off the coast of Venezuela, Columbus formed a fantastic theory, which he set out in his journals and in a formal letter to the queen and king of Spain. He imagined that the earth was not perfectly round but rather pear-shaped and that he had approached its highest point. Here was to be found the original Garden of Eden, the "Terrestrial Paradise."

A great navigator but a poor administrator, Columbus was eventually relieved of his governorship in the New World. He had not found riches, nor had he been able to establish a peaceful, successful colony. Arrested by a special delegation, Columbus was returned to Spain in chains. Frustrated, his mind turning more and more to visionary goals, he immersed himself in the prophetic books of the Bible and attempted to prove to the Crown that Spain was destined to liberate Jerusalem from Islam. To provide the finances for this religious goal, Columbus made yet another voyage to the New World, this time searching for a passage through the newly discovered islands. On this journey, though he discovered Honduras, Nicaragua, Costa Rica, Panama, and Colombia, he never found the illusory passage (none would exist until the opening of the Panama Canal in 1914). Throughout the trip, Columbus encountered fierce storms, smashed vessels, mutiny, and madness. He spent an entire year marooned in a small cove off Jamaica; physically ill and profoundly disillusioned, he dreamed of Cathay and recorded the voices he heard from heaven. He miraculously made it back to Spain in November 1504, and for the remaining year and a half of his life wrote report after report insisting on his great accomplishment—his discovery that the Malay peninsula could be reached by sailing west. He died never realizing the magnificence of what he actually did discover.

Further Reading:
W. Irving, *A History of the Life and Voyages of Christopher Columbus,* 1828.
S. E. Morison, *Admiral of the Ocean Sea: A Life of Christopher Columbus,* 1942.
B. Landstrom, *Columbus,* 1966.
E. Bradford, *Christopher Columbus,* 1973.

Text:
Journals and Other Documents on the Life and Voyages of Christopher Columbus, ed. S. E. Morison, 1963.

from The Journal of the First Voyage[*]

[The Discovery of the West Indies]
[October 12, 1492]

Friday, 12 October

At two hours after midnight appeared the land,[1] at a distance of 2 leagues. They handed all sails and set the *treo,* which is the mainsail without bonnets, and lay-to waiting for daylight Friday, when they arrived at an island of the Bahamas that was called in the Indians' tongue *Guanahaní.* Presently they saw naked people, and the Admiral went ashore in his barge, and Martín Alonso Pinzón and Vicente Yáñez, his brother, who was captain of the *Niña,* followed. The Admiral broke out the royal standard, and the captains [displayed] two banners of the Green Cross, which the Admiral flew on all the vessels as a signal, with an F and a Y,[2] one at one arm of the cross and the other on the other, and over each letter his or her crown.

Once ashore they saw very green trees, many streams, and fruits of different kinds. The Admiral called to the two captains and to the others who jumped ashore and to Rodrigo de Escobedo, secretary of the whole fleet, and to Rodrigo Sánchez of Segovia, and said that they should bear faith and witness how he before them all was taking, as in fact he took, possession of the said island for the King and Queen, their Lord and Lady, making the declarations that are required, as is set forth at length in the testimonies which were there taken down in writing. Presently there gathered many people of the island. What follows are the formal words of the Admiral, in his Book of the First Navigation and Discovery of these Indies:[3]

"I," says he, "in order that they might develop a very friendly disposition towards us, because I knew that they were a people who could better be freed and converted to our Holy Faith by love than by force, gave to some of them red caps and to others glass beads, which they hung on their necks, and many other things of slight value, in which they took much pleasure. They remained so much our [friends] that it was a marvel, later they came swimming to the ships' boats in which we were, and brought us parrots and cotton thread in skeins and darts and many other things, and we swopped them for other things that we gave them, such as little glass beads and hawks' bells.[4] Finally they traded and gave everything they had, with good will; but it appeared to me that these people were very poor in everything. They all go quite naked as their mothers bore them; and also the women, although I didn't see more than one really young girl. All that I saw were young men, none of them more than 30 years old, very well built, of very handsome bodies and very fine faces; the hair coarse, almost like the hair of a horse's tail, and short, the hair they wear over their eyebrows, except for a hank behind that they wear long and never cut. Some of them

---

[*] The first printed version of the *Journal* appeared in 1825. It was first translated into English in 1827. The present translation is by Samuel Eliot Morison.
[1] San Salvador.
[2] For Ferdinand and Isabella, the king and queen of Spain. (Isabella is spelled in Spanish with a Y.)
[3] Title of Columbus's original journal.
[4] Tiny bells used in falconry; these had proved, along with other trifles, popular with African natives.

paint themselves black (and they are of the color of the Canary Islanders, neither black nor white), and others paint themselves white, and some red, and others with what they find. And some paint their faces, others the body, some the eyes only, others only the nose. They bear no arms, nor know thereof; for I showed them swords and they grasped them by the blade and cut themselves through ignorance. They have no iron. Their darts are a kind of rod without iron, and some have at the end a fish's tooth and others, other things. They are generally fairly tall and good looking, well built. I saw some who had marks of wounds on their bodies, and made signs to them to ask what it was, and they showed me that people of other islands which are near came there and wished to capture them, and they defended themselves. And I believed and now believe that people do come here from the mainland to take them as slaves. They ought to be good servants and of good skill, for I see that they repeat very quickly whatever was said to them. I believe that they would easily be made Christians, because it seemed to me that they belonged to no religion. I, please Our Lord, will carry off six of them at my departure to Your Highnesses, that they may learn to speak. I saw no animal of any kind in this island, except parrots." All these are the words of the Admiral.

[October 13, 1492]

Saturday, 13 October
    At the time of daybreak there came to the beach many of these men, all young men, as I have said, and all of good stature, very handsome people. Their hair is not kinky but straight and coarse like horsehair; the whole forehead and head is very broad, more so than [in] any other race that I have yet seen, and the eyes very handsome and not small. They themselves are not at all black, but of the color of the Canary Islanders; nor should anything else be expected, because this is on the same latitude as the island of Ferro in the Canaries.[5] The legs of all, without exception, are very straight and [they have] no paunch, but are very well proportioned. They came to the ship in dug-outs which are fashioned like a long boat from the trunk of a tree, and all in one piece, and wonderfully made (considering the country), and so big that in some came 40 or 50 men, and others smaller, down to some in which but a single man came. They row with a thing like a baker's peel[6] and go wonderfully, and if they capsize all begin to swim and right it and bail it out with calabashes[7] that they carry. They brought skeins of spun cotton, and parrots, and darts, and other trifles that would be tedious to describe, and give all for whatever is given to them. And I was attentive and worked hard to know if there was any gold, and saw that some of them wore a little piece hanging from a thing like a needle case which they have in the nose; and by signs I could understand that, going to the S, or doubling the island to the S, there was a king there who had great vessels of it and possessed a lot. I urged them to go there, and later saw that they were not inclined to the journey. I decided to wait until tomorrow afternoon and then depart to the SW, since, as many of them informed me, there should be land to the S, SW, and NW, and that they of the NW

---

[5] Columbus accepted Aristotle's theory that people and things from the same latitude are similar.

[6] This was the first time that Europeans had seen canoe paddles.

[7] Gourds.

used to come to fight them many times; and so also to go to the SW to search for gold and precious stones. This island is very big[8] and very level; and the trees very green, and many bodies of water, and a very big lake in the middle, but no mountain, and the whole of it so green that it is a pleasure to gaze upon, and this people are very docile, and from their longing to have some of our things, and thinking that they will get nothing unless they give something, and not having it, they take what they can, and soon swim off. But all that they have, they give for whatever is given to them, even bartering for pieces of broken crockery and glass. I even saw 16 skeins of cotton given for three *ceitis* of Portugal, which is [equivalent to] a *blanca* of Castile,[9] and in them there was more than an *arroba*[10] of spun cotton. This I should have forbidden and would not have allowed anyone to take anything, except that I had ordered it all taken for Your Highnesses if there was any there in abundance. It is grown in this island; but from the short time I couldn't say for sure; and also here is found the gold that they wear hanging from the nose. But, to lose no time, I intend to go and see if I can find the Island of *Çipango*.[11] Now, as it was night, all went ashore in their dugouts.

[October 14, 1492]

Sunday, 14 October

"When day was breaking I ordered the ship's gig and the caravels' barges to be readied, and I went along the coast of the island to the NNE, to see the other side, which was the eastern side, what there was there, and also to see the villages; and soon I saw two or three, and the people who all came to the beach, shouting and giving thanks to God. Some brought us water, others, other things to eat. Others, when they saw that I didn't care to go ashore, plunged into the sea swimming, and came out, and we understood that they asked us if we had come from the sky. And one old man got into the boat, and others shouted in loud voices to all, men and women, 'Come and see the men who come from the sky, bring them food and drink.' Many came and many women, each with something, giving thanks to God, throwing themselves on the ground, they raised their hands to the sky, and then shouted to us to come ashore; but I was afraid to, from seeing a great reef of rocks which surrounded the whole of this island, and inside it was deep water and a harbor to hold all the ships in Christendom, and the entrance of it very narrow. It's true that inside this reef there are some shoal spots, but the sea moves no more than within a well. In order to see all this I kept going this morning, that I might give an account of all to Your Highnesses, and also [to see] where there might be a fortress; and I saw a piece of land which is formed like an island, although it isn't one (and on it there are six houses), the which could in two days be made an island, although I don't see that it would be necessary, because these people are very unskilled in arms, as Your Highnesses will see from the seven that I caused to be taken to carry them off to learn our language and return; unless Your Highnesses should order them all to be taken

---

[8] About 16 nautical miles long and 7 wide.
[9] Fractions of a cent.
[10] About 25 pounds.
[11] Japan; following Marco Polo's report,

Columbus thought the island of Japan was approximately 1,500 miles from the Asian continent.

to Castile or held captive in the same island, for with 50 men they could all be subjected and made to do all that one wished. And, moreover, next to said islet are groves of trees the most beautiful that I have seen, and as green and leafy as those of Castile in the months of April and May; and much water. I inspected all that harbor, and then returned to the ship and made sail, and saw so many islands that I could not decide where to go first; and those men whom I had captured made signs to me that they were so many that they could not be counted, and called by their names more than a hundred. Finally I looked for the biggest,[12] and decided to go there, and so I did, and it is probably distant from this island of San Salvador 5 leagues, and some of them more, some less. All are very level, without mountains, and very fertile, and all inhabited, and they make war on one another, although these are very simple people and very fine figures of men."

1492/1825

---

from Michele de Cuneo's Letter on Columbus's Second Voyage*

[October 28, 1495: The Cannibals]

In the name of Jesus and of his glorious mother Mary from whom all good things come. On the 25th of September, 1493, we left Cadiz under 17 sails and all in good order—15 square and 2 lateen sails—and on the 2nd of October we anchored at the Grand Canary Island; the following night we set sail and on the 5th we anchored at Gomera, one of the Canary Islands; and it would take too long to tell you about the glorious reception we were given, the rounds fired by cannons and flame-throwers, all ordered by the lady who governs the island and with whom our admiral was once somewhat in love.[1] Here we refreshed ourselves as much as we needed and on October 10th we set out on our voyage, but due to unfavorable weather we stayed around the Canary Islands three days. On the morning of October 13th, a Sunday, we left the Island of Ferro [Hierro], the last of the Canaries and we headed southwest. On the 25th of October, the eve of Saints Simon and Jude, at approximately 1600 we hit a storm of such force you wouldn't believe it and we thought our time was up. It lasted all night and 'til day and was so bad we couldn't see one another; at the end, as it pleased God, we found each other, and on November 3rd, a Sunday, we sighted land—five unknown islands. Our admiral named the first Santo Domingo since it was discovered on the Lord's day; the second he called Santa Maria la Gallante out of love for his ship, which was called Maria la Gallante. These two were not very large islands;

---

[12] Rum Cay.
* No official journal or abstract of the second voyage has survived. This account was written by Michele de Cuneo, an aristocratic friend who accompanied Columbus on the expedition. The translation here was prepared especially for this volume by Elissa Weaver.

[1] Although Cuneo is the only source of this information, Columbus apparently had fallen in love with the woman who ruled the island of Gomera.

nevertheless the admiral mapped them. If I remember correctly, it took us 22 days to get from the Island of Ferro to Santa Maria la Gallante, but I think one could well make the trip in 16 days of good wind.

On the island of Santa Maria la Gallante we got water and wood. The island is uninhabited even though it's full of trees and plains. We set sail from there that day and arrived at a large island inhabited by Cannibals,[2] who fled immediately to the mountains when they saw us. We landed on this island and stayed about 6 days since eleven of our men, who had banded together in order to steal, went 5 or 6 miles into the deserted area by such a route that when they wanted to return, they were unable to find their way, even though they were all sailors and could follow the sun, which they couldn't see well for the thick and full woods. When the admiral saw that these men had not returned and were nowhere to be found, he sent 200 men divided into 4 squadrons with trumpets, horns and lanterns, but even they were unable to find the lost men, and there was a time when we were more worried about the 200 men than the others before them. But, as it pleased God, the 200 returned with great difficulty and greater hunger; we judged that the eleven had been eaten by the Cannibals as they are wont to do. However, after 5 or 6 days, the eleven men, as it pleased God, when there remained little hope of ever finding them, built a fire on a cape; seeing the fire, we judged it to be them and we sent a boat and in that way recovered them. Had it not been that an old woman showed them the way back with gestures they'd have been done for since we had planned to set sail on the following day.

On that island we took 12 very beautiful and fat females about 15 or 16 years old and 2 boys of the same age whose genital member had been cut off down to their belly; and we judged that this had been done to keep them from mixing with their women or at least to fatten them and then eat them. These boys and girls had been picked by the Cannibals for us to send to Spain to the king as an exhibit. The admiral named this island Santa Maria di Guadalupe.[3]

We set sail from this island of Santa Maria di Guadalupe, the Island of Cannibals, on November 10th and on the 14th we reached another beautiful and fertile island[4] of Cannibals and we came to a very beautiful port. When the Cannibals caught sight of us they fled, as the others had, to the mountains and abandoned their houses where we went and took what we liked. In these few days we found many islands where we didn't disembark, but others where we did—for the night. When we didn't leave the ship we kept it tied, and this we did so we wouldn't travel on and out of fear of running aground. Because these islands were closely adjoining, the admiral called them the Eleven Thousand Virgins,[5] and the previous one, Santa Croce.

We had anchored and gone ashore one day when we saw, coming from a cape, a canoe, that is, a boat, for so it is called in their speech, and it was beating oars as though it were a well-armed brigantine. On it there were three or four male Cannibals with two female Cannibals and two captured Indian slaves—so the Cannibals call their other neighbors from those other islands; they had also just cut off their genital member down to their belly and so they were still sick. Since we had the captain's

---

[2] In the original manuscript the word is *Camballi*; it means either "Carib Indians" or "cannibals."
[3] Guadeloupe, named after the famous Spanish shrine.
[4] Now St. Croix.
[5] The Virgin Islands, named for the legend of St. Ursula and the 11,000 virgin martyrs of Cologne.

boat ashore with us, when we saw this canoe we quickly jumped into the boat and gave chase to the canoe. As we approached it, the Cannibals shot hard at us with their bows, and if we had not had our Pavian shields[6] we would have been half destroyed. I must also tell you that a companion who had a shield in his hand got hit by an arrow which went through the shield and into his chest 3 inches causing him to die within a few days. We captured this canoe with all the men. One Cannibal was wounded by a lance-blow and thinking him dead we left him in the sea. Suddenly we saw him begin to swim away; therefore we caught him and with a long hook we pulled him aboard where we cut off his head with an axe. We sent the other Cannibals together with the two slaves to Spain. When I was in the boat, I took a beautiful Cannibal girl and the admiral gave her to me. Having her in my room and she being naked as is their custom, I began to want to amuse myself with her. Since I wanted to have my way with her and she was not willing, she worked me over so badly with her nails that I wished I had never begun. To get to the end of the story, seeing how things were going, I got a rope and tied her up so tightly that she made unheard of cries which you wouldn't have believed. At the end, we got along so well that, let me tell you, it seemed she had studied at a school for whores. The admiral named the cape on that island the Cape of the Arrow for the man who was killed by the arrow.

On the 14th of November we set sail from the island in bad weather. On the 19th we anchored at a large and beautiful island of Indians called, in their language, Boluchen, which the admiral named St. John the Baptist.[7] As we sailed these 5 days both on the right and on the left we saw many islands all of which the admiral has had clearly mapped. At the island mentioned above we stopped to refresh ourselves and on the 21st we sailed; on the 25th, in the name of God, we anchored at Hispaniola,[8] an island discovered earlier by the admiral, where we went ashore at an excellent port called Monte Christo. In these few days we had more bad weather and we saw about 10 islands. We judged the distance from the island of Santo Domingo to Monte Christo to be 300 leagues. We were not able to keep a straight course for the shallows.

On the 27th of November we set sail to go to Monte Santo where the admiral on his last voyage left 38 men, and that same night we anchored at that very place.[9] On the 28th we went ashore, where we found all of our above-mentioned men dead and still stretched out there on the ground; their eyes were gone and we judged they had been eaten since when the Cannibals decapitate someone they immediately take out his eyes and eat them. They could have been dead 15 to 20 days. We were with the ruler of the place whose name was Goachanari, who, with tears running down his chest, and his men likewise, told us that the ruler of the mountain area named Goacanaboa had come with 3 thousand men and killed them together with some of their own people and robbed them out of spite. We found none of the things the admiral had left there, and having heard this story, we took it to be true. We spent 10 days on this business and on the 8th of December we left the place since it was not healthful because of its swamps, and we went to another place on the same island

---

[6] Large, rectangular shields from the northern Italian city of Pavia.
[7] Now Puerto Rico.
[8] The large island that Columbus called

Hispaniola is the present-day Haiti and the Dominican Republic.
[9] The fortress of Navidad, which Columbus had constructed on his first voyage.

to an excellent port where we went ashore. There we built 200 houses which are small, like the huts we build at home for hunting birds, and they are covered with grass.

When we had built the settlement[10] for ourselves, the inhabitants of the island, who lived between one and two leagues from us, came to visit, as though we were brothers, saying that we were men of God come down from the sky, and many stood in awe watching us. They brought us some of their food to eat and we gave them some of ours since they behaved like brothers. And here we arrive at the end of our voyage, although I will say more below of another voyage I made later with the admiral when he decided to find terra firma; but now we will speak of other things and first about the search for gold on the island of Hispaniola.

1495/1885

---

from Columbus's Letter to the Sovereigns on the Third Voyage[*]

[October 18, 1498: The Terrestrial Paradise]

When I sailed from Spain to the Indies I found immediately on passing 100 leagues west of the Azores a very considerable change in the sky and the stars, and in the temperature of the air and in the waters of the sea. I took great pains in putting this to the test. I found that, from north to south, passing the said islands by the said 100 leagues, the compass needles, which hitherto had varied northeasterly, now varied a full point to the NW. On reaching that line it was as if someone had transported a hill thither. Moreover, I found the sea full of a certain weed,[1] resembling little pine branches and heavily laden with fruit like that of the mastic. It is so thick that on the First Voyage I thought that it was a shoal and that the ship would run aground. But until we reached this line we did not come upon a single branch. When we got there, moreover, I found the sea very calm and smooth and although the wind was strong, it never got rough. Furthermore, beyond the said line, towards the west, I found the weather to be very mild and unchanging in character, winter or summer. When I was there I discovered that the North Star described a circle, with a diameter of 5°, and when the Guards are in the Right [E] Arm, the star is at its lowest elevation, and it continues to rise until it reaches Left [W] Arm; then it has 5° [elevation]. From that point it sinks until it once more returns to Right Arm.

On this [Third] Voyage . . . as soon as I succeeded in attaining this line [100 leagues W of the Azores] I immediately found the temperature very mild, and the further forward I went the more it increased; but I did not find the stars consistent with this. I found that, as night fell, I observed the North Star at an altitude of 5°, and then the Guards were at "head"; and afterwards at midnight I observed the Star 10° high, and at daybreak at 15° with the Guards at "feet." I found the smoothness of the sea conformed to this, but not the gulfweed. I was much amazed by this business of the

---

[10] Isabella, the first European attempt at a permanent settlement in the New World.

[*] The first printed version of this text appeared in 1825. It was printed again in 1892–1894. The latter is the version used as the basis for this translation by Samuel Eliot Morison.

[1] Gulfweed.

North Star, and hence for many nights I "shot" it with the quadrant very carefully. But I always found that the plumb-bob and line hit the same point [on the scale]. I regard this as something new, and mayhap it will be concluded that in this little space the sky changes so much.

I have always read that the world, both land and water, was spherical, as the authority and researches of Ptolemy and all the others who have written on this subject demonstrate and prove, as do the eclipses of the moon and other experiments that are made from east to west, and the elevation of the North Star from north to south. But I have seen this discrepancy, as I have said. I am compelled, therefore, to come to this view of the world: I have found that it does not have the kind of sphericity described by the authorities, but that it has the shape of a pear, which is all very round, except at the stem, which is rather prominent, or that it is as if one had a very round ball, on one part of which something like a woman's teat were placed, this part with the stem being the uppermost and nearest to the sky, lying below the equinoctial line in this ocean sea, at the end of the East. I mean by the end of the East the point where its land and islands terminate. To confirm this I cite all the arguments written above about the line which passes from north to south 100 leagues west of the Azores. For in crossing this to the westward the vessels keep rising gradually toward the sky and then enjoy milder weather; and the needle varied a point on account of this mildness. The farther and higher we went, the more the needle varied towards the NW. This elevation is responsible for the variation of the circle which the North Star describes with the Guards. The closer one comes to the equator, the higher they will rise and the greater the difference will be in the said stars and their orbits.

Ptolemy and the other scholars who have written about this world believed it spherical, thinking that this hemisphere was round like that in which they lived and which has its center in the island of Aryn,[2] which is below the equinoctial line between the Arabian Gulf and the Persian Gulf; the circle passes over Cape St. Vincent in Portugal in the west and by Cangara and the Seres[3] in the east. In that hemisphere I see nothing that stands in the way of its being round, as they claim. But as for this other hemisphere I maintain that it is like a half of a very round pear which had a long stem, as I have said, or like a woman's teat on a round ball. So neither Ptolemy nor the others who wrote about the world had any information about this half, for it was altogether unknown. They merely based their opinion on the hemisphere in which they lived, which is round, as I have said above. And now that Your Highnesses have ordered navigation and search and discovery it is revealed very clearly. For during this voyage when I was 20 degrees N of the equinoctial line I was there in the latitude of Arguin[4] and those other lands, and the people there are black and the land thoroughly scorched. After I went to Cape Verde Islands [I noticed] that the people in those regions are much darker, and the farther south they are the closer they approach the extreme; so, on the parallel of Sierra Leone, where I was when the North Star at nightfall had an elevation of 5°, the people are extremely black, and, after I sailed westward there, [I met] extreme heat. Once the line of which I spoke was passed, I found the climate increasingly mild, to such a degree that when I made the island

[2] In ancient and medieval geography, a sacred Asian city thought to be the "umbilical" of the world; it divided East from West.

[3] Ancient name for China.

[4] Island off the west coast of Africa.

of Trinidad, where the North Star at nightfall also had an elevation of 5°, I found the temperature there and in the land of Gracia very mild, the ground and the trees being very green and as beautiful as the orchards of Valencia in April. The people there are of very handsome build and whiter than any others I have seen in the Indies. Their hair is very long and smooth. The people are more intelligent and have more ability, and they are not cowards. The sun was then in Virgo, above our heads and theirs.

All this comes from the very mild temperature which prevails there, and this in turn comes from its being the highest land in the world and the closest to the sky. I therefore assert that the world is not spherical but that it has this other shape which I have already described, and which is in the hemisphere where the Indies end and the Ocean Sea [begins], and its extremity is below the equator. And this view is greatly supported by the fact that the sun, when Our Lord first created it, was at the first point of the East,[5] and the first light was here in the Orient, here where the world is highest. Although Aristotle was of the opinion that the Antarctic pole or the land beneath it is the highest part of the world and nearest the sky, other wise men opposed him, saying that the highest part is beneath the Arctic pole. By this reasoning it appears that they believed that one part of the world must be higher and closer to the sky than the other, and they did not hit upon this view that it is beneath the equator, for the reason I have stated. This is not surprising, for no sound knowledge was available about this hemisphere, but only very vague information of uncertain character, for no one had ever gone, or been sent, to check on it until now, when Your Highnesses gave orders that the sea and land be explored and discovered.

Holy Scripture testifies that Our Lord created the Terrestrial Paradise and planted in it the tree of life, and that a fountain sprang up there, from which flow the four principal rivers of the world: the Ganges in India, the Tigris and the Euphrates in [blank], which cut through a mountain range and form Mesopotamia and flow into Persia, and the Nile, which rises in Ethiopia and empties into the sea at Alexandria. I do not find and have never found any Latin or Greek work which definitely locates the Terrestrial Paradise in this world,[6] nor have I seen it securely placed on any world map on the basis of proof. Some put it at the sources of the Nile in Ethiopia, but others have visited all these countries without finding evidence of it in the mildness of the sky, or in its height towards the sky, by which it might be understood that it was there, or that the waters of the flood, which had risen above, had penetrated to it. Some gentiles attempted to argue that it was in the Fortunate Islands, which are the Canaries, etc. St. Isidore, Bede, Strabo, the Master of Scholastic History, St. Ambrose, Scotus, and all dependable theologians, agree that the Terrestrial Paradise is in the east, etc.

I return to my discussion of the land of Gracia and the river and lake I found there, so large that it may better be called sea than lake; for a lake is a place containing water and if it is large it is called a sea, as in the case of the Sea of Galilee and the Dead

---

[5] Aryn. (See footnote 2.)
[6] Columbus had assimilated a great deal of medieval thought concerning the exact location of the biblical Garden of Eden (i.e., the "Terrestrial Paradise").

Sea. I say that if this river does not originate in the Terrestrial Paradise, it comes and flows from a land of infinite size to the south, of which we have no knowledge as yet. But I am completely persuaded in my own mind that the Terrestrial Paradise is in the place I have described, and I rely upon the arguments and authorities above cited.

May it please Our Lord to grant Your Highnesses long life, health and leisure to be able to pursue this very noble Enterprise by which I think Our Lord is greatly served and Spain receives increase in dominion and all Christians are much consoled and pleased, for the name of Our Lord will here be preached. In all the lands which the vessels of Your Highnesses visit, and on every cape, I order a cross to be set up, and I inform all the people whom I find of the estate of Your Highnesses and how you are fixed in Spain. I tell them of our holy faith as best I can and of the dogma of our Holy Mother Church,[7] which has her members in the entire world: I tell them of the polity and nobility of all Christians, and of their faith in the Holy Trinity. May it please Our Lord to forgive the persons who reviled and do revile this most excellent Enterprise and who oppose and have opposed it so that it may not go forward, without considering how much honor and glory it is for the royal estate of Your Highnesses throughout the world. They know not what to say to malign it, except that it involves expense and that vessels have not been immediately dispatched laden with gold, without taking into account the shortness of time and the considerable difficulties that have been experienced here. They do not consider that in Castile, in the household of Your Highnesses, there are persons who each of them annually earn greater sums than it is necessary to expend on this enterprise. They likewise fail to note that no princes of Spain ever gained territory outside their borders save now, when Your Highnesses have an Other World here, by which our holy faith can be so greatly advanced and from which such great wealth can be drawn . . .

      Thanks be to God.

1492/1825

---

from Columbus's Letter to the Sovereigns on the Fourth Voyage[*]

[July 7, 1503: A Voice in Veragua[1]]

I returned again to the place[2] whence I had set forth with such heavy labor; and with the coming of the New Year, troubles began again. For, although the weather was fair for my voyage, my vessels were unseaworthy and my people dead or sick. On

[7] I.e., the Catholic church.
[*] The translation printed here is that of Dr. Milton Anastos in Samuel Eliot Morison, *Journals and Other Documents on* *the Life and Voyages of Christopher Columbus* (1963).
[1] Present-day Panama.
[2] Puerto Gordo, now Colon.

the day of Epiphany I reached Veragua[3] but the spirit had gone out of me. There Our Lord presented me with a river and a safe harbor, although there was only 10 *palmas*[4] of water in the entrance. There I put in with difficulty, and next day the tempest returned. If it had found me outside, I should not have been able to get in because of the sandbar. It rained without let-up until 14 February, so there was no opportunity to go ashore or improve my situation. Just when I believed myself safe, on 24 January, the river suddenly rose very high and turbulent, parting my cables and breastfasts,[5] and all but carried my vessels away; certainly they were in greater danger than I had ever seen them before. Our Lord came to my aid, as He has always done. I know not if any other man has ever suffered more. On 6 February, in the rain, I sent 70 men into the country, and they found many mines at a distance of five leagues. The Indians who accompanied them led them to a very high ridge. They pointed in every direction as far as the eye could reach and said that there was gold everywhere, and that the mines extended westward for 20 days' journey. They named the towns and villages, indicating where they were more or less numerous. I learned afterwards that the Quibián,[6] who had provided these Indians, had ordered them to indicate the distant mines, which belonged to someone else, his enemy, and that within his own lands a man could in ten days collect a *mozada*[7] of gold, whenever he wished. I have with me some Indians, his servants, who can testify to this. The boats can go as far as the place where he has his village. My brother returned with these people, all with gold they had gathered in four hours, the length of their stay in that place. The quantity is great, in view of the fact that none of them had ever seen mines, and very few had seen gold; most of them were mariners, and almost all ship's boys. I had plenty of building material and an abundance of supplies; I built a village and made many gifts to the Quibián, as they call the lord of that land. But I knew well that peace would not long endure. They are very wild, and our people very importunate, and I had sat down in his bailiwick. As soon as he saw the houses going up, and a lively trade going on, he decided to set fire to them and kill everyone. But his scheme miscarried. He was taken prisoner together with his women, his sons, and his servants, although his imprisonment was of short duration. The Quibián escaped from a trustworthy man into whose charge he had been given with a guard, and his sons escaped from a shipmaster to whose vessel they had been handed over for custody.

In January the mouth of the river became obstructed. In April, the vessels were all worm-eaten, and I could not keep them above water. At this time the river cut a channel, by which I brought out three empty ships with considerable difficulty. The boats went back into the river for salt and water. The sea rose high and furious and would not let them out again. The Indians were many and united and attacked them and in the end killed them. My brother and all the rest of the people were living on board a vessel which lay inside. I was outside very much alone, on this rude coast, with a high fever and very fatigued. There was no hope of escape. In this state, I climbed painfully to the highest part of the ship and cried out for help with a fearful voice, weeping, to Your Highnesses' war captains, in every direction; but none replied.

---

[3] Belen (Spanish for "Bethelem"), on the coast of Panama, where Columbus stayed from January 6 to April 16, 1503, and set up a trading post.
[4] About 90 inches.
[5] Large ropes or chains used to confine a ship's broadside to a wharf, quay, or another ship.

Here, it seems the breastfasts were tied to trees on the shore.
[6] The name the Indians of the region gave to their king.
[7] Probably, "as much as a boy could carry."

At length, groaning with exhaustion, I fell asleep, and heard a compassionate voice, saying, "O fool, and slow to believe and serve thy God, the God of every man! What more did He do for Moses or for David His servant than for thee? From thy birth He hath ever held thee in special charge. When He saw thee at man's estate, marvellously did He cause thy name to resound over the earth. The Indies, so rich a portion of the world, He gave thee for thine own, and thou hast divided them as it pleased thee. Of those barriers of the Ocean Sea, which were closed with such mighty chains, He hath given thee the keys.[8] Thou wast obeyed in so many lands, and thou hast won noble fame from Christendom. What more did He do for the people of Israel, when He carried them out of Egypt; or for David, whom from a shepherd He raised to be king over Judea? Turn thou to Him and acknowledge thy faults; His mercy is infinite; thine old age shall not hinder thee from performing mighty deeds, for many and vast heritages He holdeth. Abraham was past 100 when he begat Isaac, and Sarah was no young girl. Thou criest out for succor with a doubting heart. Reflect, who has afflicted thee so grievously and so often, God or the world? The privileges and promises which God bestows, He doth not revoke; nor doth He say, after having received service, that that was not His intention, and that it is to be understood differently. Nor doth He mete out suffering to make a show of His might. Whatever He promises He fulfils with interest; that is His way. Thus I have told thee what thy Creator hath done for thee and what He doth for all men. He hath now revealed to me a portion of the rewards for so many toils and dangers thou hast borne in the service of others."

I heard all this as in a swoon, but I had no answer to give in definite words; so true, only to weep for my transgressions. Whoever he was he finished by saying, "Fear not, but have trust. All these tribulations are written on tablets of marble, and not without cause."

I arose as soon as I could and at the end of nine days the weather turned fair, but not sufficient to move the ships out of the river. I rounded up the people who were on land and all the rest that I could, for there were not enough left both to remain on shore and to sail the vessels. I should like to have joined the others in keeping our village going if Your Highnesses had known about its existence, but fear that no vessels would ever put in there determined me, as well as the consideration that when it came to a question of providing succor, all hands should be taken care of.[9]

1503/1505

Giovanni da Verrazzano
1485?–1528

In the late spring and summer of 1524, Giovanni da Verrazzano, a Florentine navigator sailing under the French flag, explored the coast of North America from the present Cape Fear, in North Carolina, to the Maine shores, discovering

---

[8] Columbus alludes here to the prophecy in Seneca's *Medea* of the discovery of Western lands, a prophecy he always believed referred to him.

[9] Columbus omits the fact that his crew was forced out of Veragua by the Indians.

as he proceeded northward New York and Narragansett bays. Financed by a group of Italian bankers residing in France, Verrazzano's expedition studied the Atlantic coastline in the hope of finding the illusory Northwest Passage that would open a quick and profitable trade with the Orient. Upon his return to France, Verrazzano wrote the following letter to the king, outlining the course of his journey and describing the lands that he had seen. Gracefully composed and sprinkled with classical allusions, Verrazzano's official document stands as the earliest written account of the life and landscape along the northeastern seaboard of what would become the United States of America.

Verrazzano's voyage established a geographical fact that Columbus had not been able to face: The vast lovely region across the Atlantic was not the edge of the Orient but a completely new land, a world Europeans had not known existed. But Verrazzano was never given the opportunity to explore this "New World" further. Like all financial backers, his wanted immediate results. Verrazzano made several commercial voyages to South America, though always on the lookout for a passage to India, and in 1528 he met a grisly death. Exploring Guadaloupe, he was killed and then cannibalized by Caribs while his crew, anchoring offshore, helplessly watched. As one of the survivors of that tragic voyage recalled, "To so miserable an end came this valiant gentleman."

Further Readings:
J. Habert, *When New York Was Called Angoulême*, 1949.
S. E. Morison, *The European Discovery of America: The Northern Voyages*, 1971.

Text:
The Voyages of Giovanni da Verrazzano, 1524–1528, ed. L. Wroth, trans. S. Tarrow, 1970.

from Letter to the King*

[A New World]

Since the storm that we encountered in the northern regions, Most Serene King, I have not written to tell Your Majesty of what happened to the four ships which you sent out over the Ocean to explore new lands, as I thought that you had already been informed of everything—how we were forced by the fury of the winds to return in distress to Brittany with only the Normandy and the Dauphine, and that after undergoing repairs there, we began our voyage with these two ships, equipped for war, following the coasts of Spain, as Your Most Serene Majesty will have heard; and then according to our new plan, we continued the original voyage with only the Dauphine; now on our return from this voyage, I will tell Your Majesty of what we found.

* There are three manuscript versions of Verrazzano's letter. (The first English translation, by Richard Hakluyt, appeared in 1582.) The version reprinted here is based on the Cèllere-Morgan Codex, which was first published in 1910.

We set sail with the Dauphine from the deserted rock near the Island of Madeira, which belongs to the Most Serene King of Portugal on the XVII day of January last;[1] we had fifty men, and were provided with food for eight months, with arms and other articles of war, and naval munitions; we sailed westward on the gentle breath of a light easterly wind. In XXV days we covered eight hundred leagues. On the XXIIII day of February we went through a storm as violent as ever sailing man encountered. We were delivered from it with the divine help and goodness of the ship, whose glorious name and happy destiny enabled her to endure the violent waves of the sea. We continued on our westerly course, keeping rather to the north. In another XXV days we sailed more than four hundred leagues, where there appeared a new land which had never been seen before by any man, either ancient or modern. At first it appeared to be rather low-lying; having approached to within a quarter of a league, we realized that it was inhabited, for huge fires had been built on the seashore. We saw that the land stretched southward, and coasted along it in search of some port where we might anchor the ship and investigate the nature of the land, but in fifty leagues we found no harbor or place where we could stop with the ship. Seeing that the land continued to the south, we decided to turn and skirt it toward the north, where we found the land we had sighted earlier. So we anchored off the coast and sent the small boat in to land. We had seen many people coming to the seashore, but they fled when they saw us approaching; several times they stopped and turned around to look at us in great wonderment. We reassured them with various signs, and some of them came up, showing great delight at seeing us and marveling at our clothes, appearance, and our whiteness; they showed us by various signs where we could most easily secure the boat, and offered us some of their food. We were on land,[2] and I shall now tell Your Majesty briefly what we were able to learn of their life and customs.

They go completely naked except that around their loins they wear skins of small animals like martens, with a narrow belt of grass around the body, to which they tie various tails of other animals which hang down to the knees; the rest of the body is bare, and so is the head. Some of them wear garlands of birds' feathers. They are dark in color, not unlike the Ethiopians, with thick black hair, not very long, tied back behind the head like a small tail. As for the physique of these men, they are well proportioned, of medium height, a little taller than we are. They have broad chests, strong arms, and the legs and other parts of the body are well composed. There is nothing else, except that they tend to be rather broad in the face: but not all, for we saw many with angular faces. They have big black eyes, and an attentive and open look. They are not very strong, but they have a sharp cunning, and are agile and swift runners. From what we could tell from observation, in the last two respects they resemble the Orientals, particularly those from the farthest Sinarian regions.[3] We could not learn the details of the life and customs of these people because of the short time we spent on land, due to the fact that there were few men, and the ship was anchored on the high seas. Not far from these people, we found others on the shore whose way of life we think is similar. I will now tell Your Majesty about it, and describe the situation and nature of this land. The seashore is completely covered with

[1] In 1524.
[2] At or near the present-day Cape Fear, North Carolina. The probable sites of Verrazzano's landings are taken from Samuel Eliot Morison's *The European Discovery of America: The Northern*

Voyages (New York: Oxford University Press, 1971).
[3] Like Columbus, Verrazzano had studied Marco Polo's *Travels*.

fine sand xv feet deep, which rises in the form of small hills about fifty paces wide. After climbing farther, we found other streams and inlets from the sea which come in by several mouths, and follow the ins and outs of the shoreline. Nearby we could see a stretch of country much higher than the sandy shore, with many beautiful fields and plains full of great forests, some sparse and some dense; and the trees have so many colors, and are so beautiful and delightful that they defy description. And do not think, Your Majesty, that these forests are like the Hyrcanian Forest[4] or the wild wastelands of Scythia[5] and the northern countries, full of common trees; they are adorned and clothed with palms, laurel, cypress, and other varieties of tree unknown in our Europe. And these trees emit a sweet fragrance over a large area, the nature of which we could not examine for the reason stated above, not because we found it difficult to get through the forests—indeed, they are nowhere so dense as to be impenetrable. We think that they belong to the Orient by virtue of the surroundings, and that they are not without some kind of narcotic or aromatic liquor. There are other riches, like gold, which ground of such a color usually denotes. There is an abundance of animals, stags, deer, hares; and also of lakes and pools of running water with various types of bird, perfect for all the delights and pleasures of the hunt. . . .

. . . We left this place and continued to follow the coast, which we found veered to the east. All along it we saw great fires because of the numerous inhabitants; we anchored off the shore, since there was no harbor, and because we needed water we sent the small boat ashore with xxv men. The sea along the coast was churned up by enormous waves because of the open beach, and so it was impossible to put anyone ashore without endangering the boat. We saw many people on the beach making various friendly signs, and beckoning us ashore; and there I saw a magnificent deed, as Your Majesty will hear. We sent one of our young sailors swimming ashore to take the people some trinkets, such as little bells, mirrors, and other trifles, and when he came within four fathoms of them, he threw them the goods and tried to turn back, but he was so tossed about by the waves that he was carried up onto the beach half dead. Seeing this, the native people immediately ran up; they took him by the head, the legs, and arms and carried him some distance away. Whereupon the youth, realizing he was being carried away like this, was seized with terror, and began to utter loud cries. They answered him in their language to show him he should not be afraid. Then they placed him on the ground in the sun, at the foot of a small hill, and made gestures of great admiration, looking at the whiteness of his flesh and examining him from head to foot. They took off his shirt and shoes and hose, leaving him naked, then made a huge fire next to him, placing him near the heat. When the sailors in the boat saw this, they were filled with terror, as always when something new occurs, and thought the people wanted to roast him for food. After remaining with them for a while, he regained his strength, and showed them by signs that he wanted to return to the ship. With the greatest kindness, they accompanied him to the sea, holding him close and embracing him; and then to reassure him, they withdrew to a high hill and stood watching him until he was in the boat. The youth learned the following about these people: they are dark in color like the other [tribes], their skin is very glossy, they are of medium height, their faces are more clear-cut, their body and other limbs much more delicate and much less powerful, but they are

---

[4] Woods of central Germany.   [5] Region of Asia and central Europe.

more quick-witted. He saw nothing else. We left this place,[6] still following the coast which veered somewhat to the north, and after fifty leagues we reached another land[7] which seemed much more beautiful and full of great forests. We anchored there, and with xx men we penetrated about two leagues inland, to find that the people had fled in terror into the forests. Searching everywhere, we met with a very old woman and a young girl of xviii to xx years, who had hidden in the grass in fear. The old woman had two little girls whom she carried on her shoulders, and clinging to her neck a boy—they were all about eight years old. The young woman also had three children, but all girls. When we met them, they began to shout. The old woman made signs to us that the men had fled to the woods. We gave her some of our food to eat, which she accepted with great pleasure; the young woman refused everything and threw it angrily to the ground. We took the boy from the old woman to carry back to France, and we wanted to take the young woman, who was very beautiful and tall, but it was impossible to take her to the sea because of the loud cries she uttered. And as we were a long way from the ship and had to pass through several woods, we decided to leave her behind, and took only the boy. We found these people whiter than the previous ones; they were dressed in certain grasses that hang from the branches of the trees and which they weave with different threads of wild hemp. Their heads are bare and of the same shape as the others. On the whole they live on pulses,[8] which are abundant and different from ours in color and size, but are excellent and have a delicious taste; otherwise they live by hunting fish and birds, which they catch with bows and snares. They make [the bows] of hard wood, the arrows of reeds, and at the point they put the bones of fish and other animals. The wild animals here are much more ferocious than in Europe because they are continually being molested by hunters. We saw many of their little boats made out of a single tree, twenty feet long and four feet wide, which are put together without stone, iron, or any other kind of metal. For in the whole country, in the area of two hundred leagues that we covered, we did not see a single stone of any kind. They use the fourth element [fire] and burn the wood as much as necessary to hollow out the boat: they do the same for the stern and the prow so that when it sails it can plow through the waves of the sea. The land is like the previous one in situation, fertility, and beauty; the woods are sparse; the land is covered with different types of trees, but they are not so fragrant, since there it is more northern and cold. We saw there many vines growing wild, which climb up around the trees as they do in Cisalpine Gaul:[9] they would doubtless produce excellent wines if they were properly cultivated, for several times we found the dry fruit sweet and pleasant, not unlike our own. The people must value them, because wherever they grow, the bushes around them are removed so that the fruit can ripen better. We found wild roses, violets, and lilies, and many kinds of herbs and fragrant flowers different from ours. We did not find out about their houses, as they were in the interior of the country. We think from the many signs we saw that they are built of wood and grasses; we also think from various conjectures and signs that many of them who sleep in the country have nothing but the sky for cover. We learned nothing more of them. We think that all the others of the country we visited earlier live in the same way. After staying here for three days, anchored off the coast, we

---

[6] Most likely the Carolina Outer Banks.
[7] Probably Kitty Hawk, North Carolina.

[8] Beans.
[9] Lombardy, a region of northern Italy.

decided to leave because of the scarcity of ports, and we continued to follow the coast [which we baptized "Arcadia" on account of the beauty of the trees. In Arcadia we found a man who came to the shore to see who we were: he stood suspiciously and ready for flight. He watched us but would not come near. He was handsome, naked, with olive-colored skin, his hair fastened back in a knot. There were about xx of us ashore, and as we coaxed him, he approached to within about two fathoms of us, and showed us a burning stick, as if to offer us fire. And we made fire with powder and flint, and he trembled all over with fear as we fired a shot. He remained as if thunderstruck, and prayed, worshiping like a monk, pointing his finger to the sky, and indicating the sea and the ship, he appeared to bless (?) us.][10] to the northeast, sailing only during the day and casting anchor at night. . . .

. . . We reached another land[11] xv from the island, where we found an excellent harbor; before entering it, we saw about xx boats full of people who came around the ship uttering various cries of wonderment. They did not come nearer than fifty paces, but stopped to look at the structure of our ship, our persons, and our clothes; then all together they raised a loud cry which meant that they were joyful. We reassured them somewhat by imitating their gestures, and they came near enough for us to throw them a few little bells and mirrors and many trinkets, which they took and looked at, laughing, and then they confidently came on board ship. Among them were two kings, who were as beautiful of stature and build as I can possibly describe. The first was about xxxx years old, the other a young man of xxIIII, and they were dressed thus: the older man had on his naked body a stag skin, skillfully worked like damask with various embroideries; the head was bare, the hair tied back with various bands, and around the neck hung a wide chain decorated with many different-colored stones. The young man was dressed in almost the same way. These people are the most beautiful and have the most civil customs that we have found on this voyage. They are taller than we are; they are a bronze color, some tending more toward whiteness, others to a tawny color; the face is clear-cut; the hair is long and black, and they take great pains to decorate it; the eyes are black and alert, and their manner is sweet and gentle, very like the manner of the ancients. I shall not speak to Your Majesty of the other parts of the body, since they have all the proportions belonging to any well-built man. Their women are just as shapely and beautiful; very gracious, of attractive manner and pleasant appearance; their customs and behavior follow womanly custom as far as befits human nature; they go nude except for a stag skin embroidered like the men's, and some wear rich lynx skins on their arms; their bare heads are decorated with various ornaments made of braids of their own hair which hang down over their breasts on either side. Some have other hair arrangements such as the women of Egypt and Syria wear, and these women are older and have been joined in wedlock. Both men and women have various trinkets hanging from their ears as the Orientals do; and we saw that they had many sheets of worked copper which they prize more than gold. They do not value gold because of its color; they think it the most worthless of all, and rate blue and red above all other colors. The things we gave them that

[10] This passage is an addition, presumably Verrazzano's, to the original manuscript. "Arcadia" is an allusion to the pastoral landscape of Virgil's *Tenth Eclogue* and, more specifically, to an extremely popular Renaissance novel, Jacopo Sannazzaro's *Arcadia* (1504). The latter opens with a lyrical description of tall and wide-spreading trees in a wild and mountainous landscape.

[11] The present-day Newport, Rhode Island, harbor. The Indians were the Wampanoag, who a century later befriended the Pilgrims.

they prized the most were little bells, blue crystals, and other trinkets to put in the ear or around the neck. They did not appreciate cloth of silk and gold, nor even of any other kind, nor did they care to have them; the same was true for metals like steel and iron, for many times when we showed them some of our arms, they did not admire them, nor ask for them, but merely examined the workmanship. They did the same with mirrors; they would look at them quickly, and then refuse them, laughing. They are very generous and give away all they have. We made great friends with them, and one day before we entered the harbor with the ship, when we were lying at anchor one league out to sea because of unfavorable weather, they came out to the ship with a great number of their boats; they had painted and decorated their faces with various colors, showing us that it was a sign of happiness. They brought us some of their food, and showed us by signs where we should anchor in the port for the ship's safety, and then accompanied us all the way until we dropped anchor. We stayed there for xv days, taking advantage of the place to refresh ourselves. Every day the people came to see us on the ship, bringing their womenfolk. They are very careful with them, for when they come aboard and stay a long time, they make the women wait in the boats; and however many entreaties we made or offers of various gifts, we could not persuade them to let the women come on board ship. One of the two kings often came with the queen and many attendants for the pleasure of seeing us, and at first they always stopped on a piece of ground about two hundred paces away from us, and sent a boat to warn us of their arrival, saying they wanted to come and see the ship: they did this as a kind of precaution. And once they had a reply from us, they came immediately, and watched us for a while; but when they heard the irksome clamor of the crowd of sailors, they sent the queen and her maidens in a light little boat to wait on a small island about a quarter of a league from us. The king remained a long while, discussing by signs and gestures various fanciful notions, looking at all the ship's equipment, and asking especially about its uses; he imitated our manners, tasted our food, and then courteously took his leave of us. Sometimes when our men stayed on a small island near the ship for two or three days for their various needs, as is the custom of sailors, he would come with seven or eight of his attendants, watch our operations, and often ask us if we wanted to stay there any length of time, offering us all his help. Then he would shoot his bow and run and perform various games with his men to give us pleasure. We frequently went five to six leagues into the interior,[12] and found it as pleasant as I can possibly describe, and suitable for every kind of cultivation—grain, wine, or oil. For there the fields extend for xxv to xxx leagues; they are open and free of any obstacles or trees, and so fertile that any kind of seed would produce excellent crops. Then we entered the forests, which could be penetrated even by a large army; the trees there are oaks, cypresses, and others unknown in our Europe. We found Lucullian apples,[13] plums, and filberts, and many kinds of fruit different from ours. There is an enormous number of animals—stags, deer, lynx,[14] and other species; these people, like the others, capture them with snares and bows, which are their principal weapons. Their arrows are worked with great beauty, and they tip them not with iron but with emery, jasper, hard marble, and other sharp stones. They use the same kind of stone instead of iron for cutting trees, and make their little boats with a single log of wood, hollowed out

[12] Near Pawtucket, Rhode Island.
[13] Cherries.
[14] Wildcats.

with admirable skill; there is ample room in them for fourteen to xv men; they operate a short oar, broad at the end, with only the strength of their arms, and they go to sea without any danger, and as swiftly as they please. When we went farther inland we saw their houses, which are circular in shape, about XIIII to xv paces across, made of bent saplings; they are arranged without any architectural pattern, and are covered with cleverly worked mats of straw which protect them from wind and rain. There is no doubt that if they had the skilled workmen that we have, they would erect great buildings, for the whole maritime coast is full of various blue rocks, crystals, and alabaster, and for such a purpose it has an abundance of ports and shelter for ships. They move these houses from one place to another according to the richness of the site and the season. They need only carry the straw mats, and so they have new houses made in no time at all. In each house there lives a father with a very large family, for in some we saw xxv to xxx people. They live on the same food as the other people—pulse (which they produce with more systematic cultivation than the other tribes, and when sowing they observe the influence of the moon, the rising of the Pleiades, and many other customs derived from the ancients), and otherwise on game and fish. They live a long time, and rarely fall sick; if they are wounded, they cure themselves with fire without medicine; their end comes with old age. We consider them very compassionate and charitable toward their relatives, for they make great lamentations in times of adversity, recalling in their grief all their past happiness. At the end of their life, the relatives perform together the Sicilian lament, which is mingled with singing and lasts a long time. . . .

. . . Having supplied all our needs, we left this port on the sixth day of May and continued along the coast, never losing sight of land. We sailed one hundred and fifty leagues and found the land similar in nature, but somewhat higher, with several mountains which all showed signs of minerals. We did not land there because the weather was favorable and helped us in sailing along the coast: we think it resembles the other. The shore ran eastward. At a distance of fifty leagues, keeping more to the north, we found high country full of very dense forests,[15] composed of pines, cypresses, and similar trees which grow in cold regions. The people[16] were quite different from the others, for while the previous ones had been courteous in manner, these were full of crudity and vices, and were so barbarous that we could never make any communication with them, however many signs we made to them. They were clothed in skins of bear, lynx, sea-wolf and other animals. As far as we could judge from several visits to their houses, we think they live on game, fish, and several fruits which are a species of root which the earth produces itself. They have no pulse, and we saw no sign of cultivation, nor would the land be suitable for producing any fruit or grain on account of its sterility. If we wanted to trade with them for some of their things, they would come to the seashore on some rocks where the breakers were most violent, while we remained in the little boat, and they sent us what they wanted to give on a rope, continually shouting to us not to approach the land; they gave us the barter quickly, and would take in exchange only knives, hooks for fishing, and sharp metal. We found no courtesy in them, and when we had nothing more to exchange and left them, the men made all the signs of scorn and shame that any brute creature would make.[17] Against their wishes, we penetrated two or three leagues inland with xxv armed men,

---

[15] The coast of Maine.
[16] The Abnaki Indians.

[17] Verrazzano's(?) note: "such as showing their buttocks and laughing."

and when we disembarked on the shore, they shot at us with their bows and uttered loud cries before fleeing into the woods. We did not find anything of great value in this land, except for the vast forests and some hills which could contain some metal: for we saw many natives with "paternostri" beads of copper in their ears. We departed, skirting the coast in a northeasterly direction; we found the country more beautiful, open and bare of trees, with high mountains in the interior which slope down toward the seashore. In fifty leagues we discovered XXXII islands, all near the continent: they were small and pleasant in appearance, but high, and followed the curve of the land; some beautiful ports and channels were formed between them, such as those formed in the Adriatic Gulf in Illyria and Dalmatia.[18] We made no contact with the people and we think they were, like the others, devoid of manners and humanity. After sailing CL leagues in a northeasterly direction we approached the land which the Britons once found,[19] which lies in 50 degrees; and since we had exhausted all our naval stores and provisions, and had discovered seven hundred leagues or more of new land, we took on supplies of water and wood, and decided to return to France. Due to the lack of [a common] language, we were unable to find out by signs or gestures how much religious faith these people we found possess. We think they have neither religion nor laws, that they do not know of a First Cause or Author, that they do not worship the sky, the stars, the sun, the moon, or other planets, nor do they even practice any kind of idolatry; we do not know whether they offer any sacrifices or other prayers, nor are there any temples or churches of prayer among their peoples. We consider that they have no religion and that they live in absolute freedom, and that everything they do proceeds from Ignorance; for they are very easily persuaded, and they imitated everything that they saw us Christians do with regard to divine worship, with the same fervor and enthusiasm that we had. . . .

. . . My intention on this voyage was to reach Cathay and the extreme eastern coast of Asia, but I did not expect to find such an obstacle of new land as I have found; and if for some reason I did expect to find it, I estimated there would be some strait to get through to the Eastern Ocean. This was the opinion of all the ancients, who certainly believed that our Western Ocean was joined to the Eastern Ocean of India without any land in between. Aristotle supports this theory by arguments of various analogies, but this opinion is quite contrary to that of the moderns, and has been proven false by experience. Nevertheless, land has been found by modern man which was unknown to the ancients, another world with respect to the one they knew, which appears to be larger than our Europe, than Africa, and almost larger than Asia, if we estimate its size correctly. . . . and if the territorial area of this [new] land corresponds in size to its maritime shore, there is no doubt that it is larger than Asia. In this way we find that the extension of the land is much greater than the ancients believed, and contrary to the Mathematicians who considered that there was less land than water,[20] we have proven it by experience to be the reverse.

And as for the corporeal volume, we judge that there cannot be less land than water, as I hope to establish to Your Majesty at a better time by more reasoned and tried arguments.

---

[18] Western Yugoslavia, bordering the Adriatic.
[19] Apparently the eastern coast of Newfoundland.
[20] And contrary to the biblical reference in the

first book of the prophet Esdras, which claims that the ratio of earth to water is 6 to 1.

All this land or New World which we have described above is joined together, but is not linked with Asia or Africa (we know this for certain), but could be joined to Europe by Norway or Russia; this would be false according to the ancients, who declare that almost all the north has been navigated from the promontory of the Cimbri to the Orient, and affirm that they went around as far as the Caspian Sea itself. Therefore the continent would lie between two seas, to the east and west; but these two seas do not in fact surround either of the two continents, for beyond 54 degrees south from the Equator the New World extends eastward for a great distance, and to the north of the Equator it passes 66 degrees and continues eastward as far as 70 degrees. I hope that with Your Majesty's help we shall have more certain knowledge of this; may God Almighty prosper you in everlasting glory, so that we may see the perfect end to our cosmography, and that the sacred word of the gospel may be fulfilled: "their sound has gone out into every land."[21] In the ship "Dauphine" on the VIII day of July.

M.D. XXIIII.

Humble servant JANUS VERAZANUS.

1524/1556

Alvar Núñez Cabeza de Vaca
ca. 1490–ca. 1557

In 1528 Pánfilo de Narváez led an expedition to establish a conquistadorial regime on the west coast of Florida. Beaten by the Florida wilderness and the unyielding Apalachee Indians, the expedition—the first overland journey on future United States soil—tried to escape to Mexico, but a gulf storm wrecked the Spaniard's makeshift boats near Galveston Island, Texas. Starvation, exposure, disease, and exhaustion reduced the original party of three hundred to four men: Cabeza de Vaca, Alonzo del Castillo, Andrés Dorantes, and his Moroccan slave, Estevan (or Estevanico). For the next eight years they wandered the Gulf Coast, where they lived mainly on prickly pears and were periodically taken into captivity by various Indian tribes. The four apparently managed to survive by assuming the role—reluctantly at first—of medicine men or shamans and practicing faith healing. The grisly account of their journey is the subject of the first North American captivity tale, *The Narrative of Alvar Núñez Cabeza de Vaca* (1542).

Contemporary psychologists have observed that hostages may gradually come to identify with their captors. Because of his many favorable experiences, Cabeza de Vaca retained a sympathetic—though nonetheless politically superior—attitude to the Indians, which was far different from most other conquistadores. He argued that "to bring all these people to Christianity and subjection to Your Imperial Majesty, they must be won by kindness, the only certain way." At journey's end, Cabeza de Vaca assures the party of friendly Indians who had accompanied him to the Spanish outposts that they need fear no harm. He is deceived, and his profound disappointment with his own people results in a

---

[21] Romans 9:18.

dramatic psychological event that will recur throughout the literature of the New World: A tough-minded European explorer adrift in a vast alien land must suddenly confront not a mere loss of direction but a far more disorienting loss of identity.

Further Reading:
M. Bishop, *The Odyssey of Cabeza de Vaca,* 1933.
H. Long, *The Power Within Us,* 1944.

Text:
Spanish Explorers in the Southern United States 1528–1543, ed. F. W. Hodge, trans. B. Smith, 1907.

from The Narrative of Alvar Núñez Cabeza de Vaca[*]

[The Faith Healers]

That same night of our arrival,[1] some Indians came to Castillo and told him that they had great pain in the head, begging him to cure them. After he made over them the sign of the cross, and commended them to God, they instantly said that all the pain had left, and went to their houses bringing us prickly pears,[2] with a piece of venison, a thing to us little known. As the report of Castillo's performances spread, many came to us that night sick, that we should heal them, each bringing a piece of venison, until the quantity became so great we knew not where to dispose of it. We gave many thanks to God, for every day went on increasing his compassion and his gifts. After the sick were attended to, they began to dance and sing, making themselves festive, until sunrise; and because of our arrival, the rejoicing was continued for three days.

When these were ended, we asked the Indians about the country farther on, the people we should find in it, and of the subsistence there. They answered us, that throughout all the region prickly-pear plants abounded; but the fruit was now gathered and all the people had gone back to their houses. They said the country was very cold, and there were few skins. Reflecting on this, and that it was already winter, we resolved to pass the season with these Indians.

Five days after our arrival, all the Indians went off, taking us with them to gather more prickly pears, where there were other peoples speaking different tongues. After walking five days in great hunger, since on the way was no manner of fruit, we came to a river[3] and put up our houses. We then went to seek the product of certain trees, which is like peas. As there are no paths in the country, I was detained some time. The others returned, and coming to look for them in the dark I got lost. Thank God I found a burning tree, and in the warmth of it I passed the cold of that night. In the morning, loading myself with sticks, and taking two brands with me, I returned to seek them. In this manner I wandered five days, ever with my fire and load; for if the wood had failed me where none could be found, as many parts are without

---

[*] Cabeza de Vaca composed his narrative in 1536, after reaching Mexico; it was first published in Spain in 1542.
[1] In 1534.

[2] The spiny, edible fruit of the flat-stemmed cactus.
[3] Probably the San Antonio.

any, though I might have sought sticks elsewhere, there would have been no fire to kindle them. This was all the protection I had against cold, while walking naked as I was born. Going to the low woods near the rivers, I prepared myself for the night, stopping in them before sunset. I made a hole in the ground and threw in fuel which the trees abundantly afforded, collected in good quantity from those that were fallen and dry. About the whole I made four fires, in the form of a cross, which I watched and made up from time to time. I also gathered some bundles of the coarse straw that there abounds, with which I covered myself in the hole. In this way I was sheltered at night from cold. On one occasion while I slept, the fire fell upon the straw, when it began to blaze so rapidly that notwithstanding the haste I made to get out of it, I carried some marks on my hair of the danger to which I was exposed. All this while I tasted not a mouthful, nor did I find anything I could eat. My feet were bare and bled a good deal. Through the mercy of God, the wind did not blow from the north in all this time, otherwise I should have died.

At the end of the fifth day I arrived on the margin of a river,[4] where I found the Indians, who with the Christians, had considered me dead, supposing that I had been stung by a viper. All were rejoiced to see me, and most so were my companions. They said that up to that time they had struggled with great hunger, which was the cause of their not having sought me. At night, all gave me of their prickly pears, and the next morning we set out for a place where they were in large quantity, with which we satisfied our great craving, the Christians rendering thanks to our Lord that He had ever given us His aid. . . .

The next day morning, many Indians came, and brought five persons who had cramps and were very unwell. They came that Castillo might cure them. Each offered his bow and arrows, which Castillo received. At sunset he blessed them, commending them to God our Lord, and we all prayed to Him the best we could to send health; for that He knew there was no other means, than through Him, by which this people would aid us, so we could come forth from this unhappy existence. He bestowed it so mercifully, that, the morning having come, all got up well and sound, and were as strong as though they never had a disorder. It caused great admiration, and inclined us to render many thanks to God our Lord, whose goodness we now clearly beheld, giving us firm hopes that He would liberate and bring us to where we might serve Him. For myself I can say that I ever had trust in His providence that He would lead me out from that captivity, and thus I always spoke of it to my companions.

The Indians having gone and taken their friends with them in health, we departed for a place at which others were eating prickly pears. These people are called Cuthal-chuches[5] and Malicones, who speak different tongues. Adjoining them were others called Coayos and Susolas, who were on the opposite side, others called Atayos, who were at war with the Susolas, exchanging arrow shots daily. As through all the country they talked only of the wonders which God our Lord worked through us, persons came from many parts to seek us that we might cure them. At the end of the second day after our arrival, some of the Susolas came to us and besought Castillo that he would go to cure one wounded and others sick, and they said that among them was one very near his end. Castillo was a timid practitioner, most so in serious and

---

[4] Presumably, the same river where they had set up shelters.

[5] These two groups were apparently south Texas Indians.

dangerous cases, believing that his sins would weigh, and some day hinder him in performing cures. The Indians told me to go and heal them, as they liked me; they remembered that I had ministered to them in the walnut grove when they gave us nuts and skins, which occurred when I first joined the Christians. So I had to go with them, and Dorantes accompanied me with Estevanico. Coming near their huts, I perceived that the sick man we went to heal was dead. Many persons were around him weeping, and his house was prostrate, a sign that the one who dwelt in it is no more. When I arrived I found his eyes rolled up, and the pulse gone, he having all the appearances of death, as they seemed to me and as Dorantes said. I removed a mat with which he was covered, and supplicated our Lord as fervently as I could, that He would be pleased to give health to him, and to the rest that might have need of it. After he had been blessed and breathed upon many times, they brought me his bow, and gave me a basket of pounded prickly pears.

The natives took me to cure many others who were sick of a stupor, and presented me two more baskets of prickly pears, which I gave to the Indians who accompanied us. We then went back to our lodgings. Those to whom we gave the fruit tarried, and returned at night to their houses, reporting that he who had been dead and for whom I wrought before them, had got up whole and walked, had eaten and spoken with them and that all to whom I had ministered were well and much pleased. This caused great wonder and fear, and throughout the land the people talked of nothing else. All to whom the fame of it reached, came to seek us that we should cure them and bless their children.

When the Cuthalchuches, who were in company with our Indians, were about to return to their own country, they left us all the prickly pears they had, without keeping one: they gave us flints of very high value there, a palm and a half in length, with which they cut. They begged that we would remember them and pray to God that they might always be well, and we promised to do so. They left, the most satisfied beings in the world, having given us the best of all they had.

We remained with the Avavares eight months, reckoned by the number of moons. In all this time people came to seek us from many parts, and they said that most truly we were children of the sun. Dorantes and the negro[6] to this time had not attempted to practise; but because of the great solicitation made by those coming from different parts to find us, we all became physicians, although in being venturous and bold to attempt the performance of any cure, I was the most remarkable. No one whom we treated, but told us he was left well; and so great was the confidence that they would become healed if we administered to them, they even believed that whilst we remained none of them could die. These and the rest of the people behind, related an extraordinary circumstance, and by the way they counted, there appeared to be fifteen or sixteen years since it occurred.

They said that a man wandered through the country whom they called Badthing; he was small of body and wore beard, and they never distinctly saw his features. When he came to the house where they lived, their hair stood up and they trembled. Presently a blazing torch shone at the door, when he entered and seized whom he chose, and giving him three great gashes in the side with a very sharp flint, the width of the hand and two palms in length, he put his hand through them, drawing forth

---

[6] Estevan, or Estevanico, mentioned previously.

the entrails, from one of which he would cut off a portion more or less, the length of a palm, and throw it on the embers. Then he would give three gashes to an arm, the second cut on the inside of an elbow, and would sever the limb. A little after this, he would begin to unite it, and putting his hands on the wounds, these would instantly become healed. They said that frequently in the dance he appeared among them, sometimes in the dress of a woman, at others in that of a man; that when it pleased him he would take a buhío, or house, and lifting it high, after a little he would come down with it in a heavy fall. They also stated that many times they offered him victuals, but that he never ate: they asked him whence he came and where was his abiding place, and he showed them a fissure in the earth and said that his house was there below. These things they told us of, we much laughed at and ridiculed; and they seeing our incredulity, brought to us many of those they said he had seized; and we saw the marks of the gashes made in the places according to the manner they had described. We told them he was an evil one, and in the best way we could, gave them to understand, that if they would believe in God our Lord, and become Christians like us, they need have no fear of him, nor would he dare to come and inflict those injuries, and they might be certain he would not venture to appear while we remained in the land. At this they were delighted and lost much of their dread. They told us that they had seen the Asturian and Figueroa with people farther along the coast, whom we had called those of the figs.

They are all ignorant of time, either by the sun or moon, nor do they reckon by the month or year; they better know and understand the differences of the seasons, when the fruits come to ripen, where the fish resort, and the position of the stars, at which they are ready and practised. By these we were ever well treated. We dug our own food and brought our loads of wood and water. Their houses and also the things we ate, are like those of the nation from which we came, but they suffer far greater want, having neither maize, acorns, nor nuts. We always went naked like them, and covered ourselves at night with deer-skins.

Of the eight months we were among this people, six we supported in great want, for fish are not to be found where they are. At the expiration of the time, the prickly pears began to ripen,[7] and I and the negro went, without these Indians knowing it, to others farther on, a day's journey distant, called Maliacones. At the end of three days, I sent him to bring Castillo and Dorantes, and they having arrived, we all set out with the Indians who were going to get the small fruit of certain trees on which they support themselves ten or twelve days whilst the prickly pears are maturing. They joined others called Arbadaos, whom we found to be very weak, lank, and swollen, so much so as to cause us great astonishment. We told those with whom we came, that we wished to stop with these people, at which they showed regret and went back by the way they came; so we remained in the field near the houses of the Indians, which when they observed, after talking among themselves they came up together, and each of them taking one of us by the hand, led us to their dwellings. Among them we underwent greater hunger than with the others; we ate daily not more than two handfuls of the prickly pears, which were green and so milky they burned our mouths. As there was lack of water, those who ate suffered great thirst. In our extreme want we bought two dogs, giving in exchange some nets, with other things, and a skin I used to cover myself.

[7] I.e., in the summer of 1535.

I have already stated that throughout all this country we went naked, and as we were unaccustomed to being so, twice a year we cast our skins like serpents. The sun and air produced great sores on our breasts and shoulders, giving us sharp pain; and the large loads we had, being very heavy, caused the cords to cut into our arms. The country is so broken and thickset, that often after getting our wood in the forests, the blood flowed from us in many places, caused by the obstruction of thorns and shrubs that tore our flesh wherever we went. At times, when my turn came to get wood, after it had cost me much blood, I could not bring it out either on my back or by dragging. In these labors my only solace and relief were in thinking of the sufferings of our Redeemer, Jesus Christ, and in the blood He shed for me, in considering how much greater must have been the torment He sustained from the thorns, than that I there received.

I bartered with these Indians in combs that I made for them and in bows, arrows, and nets. We made mats, which are their houses, that they have great necessity for; and although they know how to make them, they wish to give their full time to getting food, since when otherwise employed they are pinched with hunger. Sometimes the Indians would set me to scraping and softening skins; and the days of my greatest prosperity there, were those in which they gave me skins to dress. I would scrape them a very great deal and eat the scraps, which would sustain me two or three days. When it happened among these people, as it had likewise among others whom we left behind, that a piece of meat was given us, we ate it raw; for if we had put it to roast, the first native that should come along would have taken it off and devoured it; and it appeared to us not well to expose it to this risk; besides we were in such condition it would have given us pain to eat it roasted, and we could not have digested it so well as raw. Such was the life we spent there; and the meagre subsistence we earned by the matters of traffic which were the work of our hands.

1536/1542

Pedro de Casteñeda
ca. 1510—ca. 1570

One of the earliest overland expeditions into the North American interior was conducted by a man who was neither European, Christian, white, nor free. Estevan (or, as he was called informally, Estevanico), a Moor from Morocco, accompanied his Spanish master, Andrés Dorante, to the New World as a member of the disastrous Narváez expedition that tried to take Florida in 1528. Nothing is known of Estevan's past, and had not the Narváez expedition failed, his life would have undoubtedly been lived out in the anonymity of slavery. But Estevan was one of the expedition's four survivors (see "The Narrative of Alvar Núñez Cabeza de Vaca"); after eight years of wandering and intermittent captivity, he managed to find his way to Mexico City.

As the four men crossed Texas, they heard stories about "populous towns" to the north. Spanish explorers, continually motivated by the fabulous, were already on the lookout for the mythic Seven Cities of Cíbola, and when the towns were brought to the attention of the viceroy of Mexico, he immediately planned a military expedition that would try to duplicate the riches Pizarro had wrested from the Incas during his conquest of Peru in 1533. In 1539 the viceroy sent an adventurous Italian friar, Marcos de Nizza, on a scouting mission to map out a route and gather information for a major expedition that Francisco de Coronado would undertake the following year. To lead the scouting party, the viceroy appointed Estevan, who knew the region and had presumably acquired skills in translation and diplomacy. Estevan and Marcos, however, made poor traveling companions; the friar disliked the Moor's arrogance and resented the caravan of Indian women Estevan had accumulated along the way. To ease tensions, Estevan went on ahead to the first of the reputed seven cities, Hawikuh, near the present New Mexico–Arizona border. There it seems that Estevan offended the Zuñi rulers, for he was put to death one May morning in 1539.

A terrified Marcos returned to Mexico with a handful of Indian survivors. His lavish descriptions of large and wealthy towns, however, encouraged Coronado's expedition in 1540 to the Colorado River region and the Great Plains. Though Coronado failed to find any precious metals and the most populous city turned out to be a village of a thousand inhabitants, his journey was the most extensive early foray into the interior of the present-day United States.

"The Death of the Negro Estevan" and "Coronado Discovers the Seven Cities of Gold" are recounted by a member of Coronado's army, Pedro de Casteñeda, in his memoirs, *The Narrative of the Expedition of Coronado* (ca. 1565).

Further Reading:
W. Lowery, *The Spanish Settlements Within the Present Limits of the United States*, 1901.
H. E. Bolton, *Coronado, Knight of Pueblos and Plains*, 1949.
J. U. Terrell, *Estevanico the Black*, 1968.

Text:
Spanish Explorers in the United States, 1528–1543, ed. F. Hodge, trans. G. P. Winship, 1907.

---

from The Narrative of the Expedition of Coronado[*]

[The Death of the Negro Estevan]

After Estevan had left the friars, he thought he could get all the reputation and honor himself, and that if he should discover those settlements with such famous high houses, alone, he would be considered bold and courageous. So he proceeded with the people who had followed him, and attempted to cross the wilderness which lies between the country he had passed through and Cibola. He was so far ahead of the friars that, when these reached Chichilticalli,[1] which is on the edge of the wilderness, he was already

[*] Casteñeda accompanied Coronado between 1540 and 1542 on his expeditions, and some 20 years later he recorded the *Narrative*. The earliest existing manuscript bears the date 1596.

[1] "Red house," so identified by the Aztec Indians because of its color. Probably located on or near the Rio Gila, near present-day Solomsville in southern Arizona.

at Cibola, which is eighty leagues beyond. It is 220 leagues from Culiacan[2] to the edge of the wilderness, and eighty across the desert, which makes 300, or perhaps ten more or less. As I said, Estevan reached Cibola loaded with the large quantity of turquoises they had given him and some beautiful women whom the Indians who followed him and carried his things were taking with them and had given him. These had followed him from all the settlements he had passed, believing that under his protection they could traverse the whole world without any danger. But as the people in this country were more intelligent than those who followed Estevan, they lodged him in a little hut they had outside their village, and the older men and the governors heard his story and took steps to find out the reason he had come to that country. For three days they made inquiries about him and held a council. The account which the negro gave them of two white men who were following him, sent by a great lord, who knew about the things in the sky, and how these were coming to instruct them in divine matters, made them think that he must be a spy or a guide from some nations who wished to come and conquer them, because it seemed to them unreasonable to say that the people were white in the country from which he came and that he was sent by them, he being black. Besides these other reasons, they thought it was hard of him to ask them for turquoises and women, and so they decided to kill him. They did this, but they did not kill any of those who went with him, although they kept some young fellows and let the others, about sixty persons, return freely to their own country. As these, who were badly scared, were returning in flight, they happened to come upon the friars in the desert sixty leagues from Cibola, and told them the sad news, which frightened them so much that they would not even trust these folks who had been with the negro, but opened the packs they were carrying and gave away everything they had except the holy vestments for saying mass. They returned from here by double marches, prepared for anything, without seeing any more of the country except what the Indians told them.

[Coronado Discovers the Seven Cities of Gold]

. . .After the general had crossed the inhabited region and came to Chichilticalli, where the wilderness begins, and saw nothing favorable, he could not help feeling somewhat downhearted, for, although the reports were very fine about what was ahead, there was nobody who had seen it except the Indians who went with the negro, and these had already been caught in some lies. Besides all this, he was much affected by seeing that the fame of Chichilticalli was summed up in one tumbledown house without any roof, although it appeared to have been a strong place at some former time when it was inhabited, and it was very plain that it had been built by a civilized and warlike race of strangers who had come from a distance. This building was made of red earth. From here they went on through the wilderness, and in fifteen days came to a river about eight leagues from Cibola which they called Red River,[3] because its waters were muddy and reddish. In this river they found mullets like those of Spain. The first Indians from that country were seen here—two of them, who ran away to give the news. During the night following the next day, about two leagues from the village, some Indians in a safe place yelled so that, although the men were ready for anything, some were

---

[2] San Miguel Culiacan in central Sinaloa. [3] Present-day Zuñi River in Arizona.

so excited that they put their saddles on hind-side before; but these were the new fellows. When the veterans had mounted and ridden round the camp, the Indians fled. None of them could be caught because they knew the country.

The next day they entered the settled country in good order, and when they saw the first village, which was Cibola, such were the curses that some hurled at Friar Marcos that I pray God may protect him from them.

It is a little, crowded village,[4] looking as if it had been crumpled all up together. There are haciendas[5] in New Spain which make a better appearance at a distance. It is a village of about two hundred warriors, is three and four stories high, with the houses small and having only a few rooms, and without a courtyard. One yard serves for each section. The people of the whole district had collected here, for there are seven villages in the province, and some of the others are even larger and stronger than Cibola. These folks waited for the army, drawn up by divisions in front of the village. When they refused to have peace on the terms the interpreters extended to them, but appeared defiant, the Santiago[6] was given, and they were at once put to flight. The Spaniards then attacked the village, which was taken with not a little difficulty, since they held the narrow and crooked entrance. During the attack they knocked the general down with a large stone, and would have killed him but for Don Garcia Lopez de Cardenas and Hernando de Alvarado, who threw themselves above him and drew him away, receiving the blows of the stones, which were not few. But the first fury of the Spaniards could not be resisted, and in less than an hour they entered the village and captured it. They discovered food there, which was the thing they were most in need of. After this the whole province was at peace.

ca. 1565/1596

Richard Hakluyt
ca. 1552–1616

California, like the Florida of Ponce de Leon, existed mythically long before it became a reliable designation on maps of the New World. According to the sixteenth-century Spanish historian António de Herrera, the conquistador who discovered California, Hernando Cortes, named it after an imaginary island of black Amazons he had read about in a popular chivalric romance, *Las Sergas del Virtuoso Cavallero Esplandian* (The adventures of the virtuous cavalier Esplandian). Explorers were familiar, too, with ancient legends concerning a western island inhabited solely by women. Cortes probably grafted these fictions together to fabricate yet another rich, exotic, and eminently exploitable kingdom.

[4] Hawikuh, located 15 miles southwest of present-day Zuñi near the Zuñi River in New Mexico; probably the village where Estevan lost his life.

[5] Large estates or farms.
[6] War cry or "loud invocation addressed to Saint James before engaging in battle with the Infidels" (from Captain John Stevens's *Dictionary*).

Cortes, however, did not travel far beyond his immediate discovery; he explored only a small section of the Baja peninsula. It was left to later Spanish explorers, most notably Juan Rodriguez Cabrillo, to conduct charting expeditions and landings farther north along the coast. Gradually, the Spanish, starting from Mexico, began organizing inland marches into the southern areas. But though Spanish vessels had reached the coastal waters of northern California, it was not until 1579, when the English navigator Sir Francis Drake dropped anchor apparently in what is now Drake's Bay,[1] that Europeans made their first contact with the region.

Drake and his crew, who had just given up their search for the Northwest Passage, stayed in northern California five weeks, preparing their weather-torn ship, the *Golden Hinde,* for the rest of its historic journey around the globe. The beautiful white cliffs along the bay reminded Drake of his native land, and envisioning a future English colony, he called the region "Nova Albion." (It was the first "New England.") Albion, the ancient name for the island of Britain, has been translated as "white land," a name the Romans thought referred to the famous white cliffs of Dover.

The following encounter between Drake's crew and the coastal Miwok Indians was reported in Richard Hakluyt's *The Principal Navigations, Voyages, Traffiques and Discoveries of the English Nation* (second edition, 1598–1600). A geographer, parson, and archivist, Hakluyt (pronounced "Haklet") served tirelessly as the unofficial publicist for early British navigation. He edited, translated, and compiled a mass of firsthand documents pertaining to the discovery, exploration, and colonization of the New World. His first book, *Divers Voyages Touching the Discovery of America,* dedicated to Sir Philip Sidney, was published in 1582. His major work, *The Principal Navigations,* which first appeared in 1589, has been called "the prose epic of [the] modern English nation." Based on several eyewitness reports, Hakluyt's account of Drake's circumnavigation figured prominently in his collection, but a need for secrecy kept it out of the first edition. A full-length account of Drake's voyage did not appear until 1628.

Further Reading:
H. R. Wagner, *Sir Francis Drake's Voyage Around the World: Its Aims and Achievements,* 1926.
R. F. Heizer, *Francis Drake and the California Indians,* 1947.
D. Wilson, *The World Encompassed: Francis Drake and His Great Voyage,* 1977.

Text:
The Principal Navigations, Voyages, Traffiques and Discoveries of the English Nation, 1598–1600, 2d ed., abridged and ed. J. Beeching, 1972.

[1] A great deal of controversy exists concerning the precise location of Drake's landing. One of the best authorities on the history of navigation, Samuel Eliot Morison, is "positive" Drake's Bay is the site, though others have made claims for Bodega Bay and San Francisco Bay.

from The Famous Voyage of Sir Francis Drake[1]

[The First "New England"]

The 5 day of June,[2] being in 43 degrees towards the pole Arctic, we found the air so cold, that our men being grievously pinched with the same, complained of the extremity thereof, and the further we went, the more the cold increased upon us. Whereupon we thought it best for that time to seek the land, and did so, finding it not mountainous, but low plain land, till we came within 38 degrees, it pleased God to send us into a fair and good bay, with a good wind to enter the same.

In this bay we anchored, and the people of the country having their houses close by the water's side, showed themselves unto us, and sent a present to our general.

When they came unto us, they greatly wondered at the things that we brought, but our general (according to his natural and accustomed humanity) courteously entreated them, and liberally bestowed on them necessary things to cover their nakedness, whereupon they supposed us to be gods, and would not be persuaded to the contrary.

Their houses are digged round about with earth, and have clefts of wood set upon them, joining close together at the top like a spire steeple, which by reason of that closeness are very warm.

Their beds is the ground with rushes strewed on it, and lying about the house, have the fire in the midst. The men go naked, the women take bulrushes, and comb them after the manner of hemp, and thereof make their loose garments, which being knit about their middles, hang down about their hips, having also about their shoulders a skin of deer, with the hair upon it. These women are very obedient and serviceable to their husbands.

After they were departed from us, they came and visited us the second time, and brought with them feathers and bags of tobacco for presents: and when they came to the top of the hill (at the bottom whereof we had pitched our tents) they stayed themselves: where one appointed for speaker wearied himself with making a long oration, which done, they left their bows upon the hill, and came down with their presents.

In the meantime the women remaining on the hill, tormented themselves lamentably, tearing their flesh from their cheeks,[3] whereby we perceived that they were about a sacrifice. In the meantime our general with his company went to prayer, and to reading of the Scriptures, at which exercise they were attentive, and seemed greatly to be affected with it.

The news of our being there spread through the country, the people that inhabited round about came down, and amongst them the king himself, a man of a goodly stature, and comely personage.

---

[1] The complete title of Hakluyt's account is *The Famous Voyage of Sir Francis Drake into the South Sea, and There Hence About the Whole Globe of the Earth, Begun in the Year of Our Lord, 1577.*

[2] In 1579.

[3] The significance of this self-laceration still puzzles ethnographers.

In the forefront was a man, who bore the sceptre or mace before the king, whereupon hanged two crowns, a lesser and a bigger, with three chains of a marvellous length: the crowns were made of knit work wrought artificially with feathers of divers colours: the chains were made of a bony substance, and few be the persons among them that are admitted to wear them. Next unto him, was the king himself, with his guard about his person, clad with coney skins, and other skins: after them followed the naked common sort of people, every one having his face painted, some with white, some with black, and other colours.

In the meantime our general gathered his men together, and marched within his fenced place, making against their approaching a very war-like show.

In coming towards our bulwarks and tents, the sceptre-bearer began a song observing his measures in a dance, and that with a stately countenance, whom the king with his guard, and every degree of persons following, did in like manner sing and dance, saving only the women, which danced and kept silence. The general permitted them to enter within our bulwark, where they continued their song and dance a reasonable time. They made signs to our general to sit down, to whom the king, and divers others made supplications, that he would take their province into his hand, and become their king, making signs that they would resign unto him their right and title of the whole land, and become his subjects.[4] In which, to persuade us the better, the king and the rest, with one consent, and with great reverence, joyfully singing a song, did set the crown upon his head, enriched his neck with all their chains: which thing our general thought not meet to reject, because he knew not what honour and profit it might be to our country. Wherefore in the name, and to the use of Her Majesty he took the sceptre, crown, and dignity of the said country into his hands.

Our necessary business being ended, our general with his company travelled up into the country to their villages, where we found herds of deer by 1,000 in a company, being most large, and fat of body.

Our general called this country Nova Albion, and that for two causes: the one in respect of the white cliffs, which lie towards the sea: and the other, because it might have some affinity with our country in name, which sometime was so called.

There is no part of earth here to be taken up, wherein there is not some probable show of gold or silver.

At our departure hence our general set up a monument of our being there, as also of Her Majesty's right and title to the same, namely a plate, nailed upon a fair great post, whereupon was engraved Her Majesty's name, the day and year of our arrival there, with the free giving up of the province and people into Her Majesty's hands, together with Her Highness' picture and arms, in a piece of six pence of current English money under the plate,[5] where under was also written the name of our general.

ca. 1589/1598–1600

---

[4] Or so Drake interpreted the signs.
[5] This plate was "found" in Marin County, California, in 1936 and was at the time authenticated by experts. It is now displayed at the entrance to the Bancroft Library at Berkeley. Other experts, however, including Samuel Eliot Morison, consider it a fake.

Michael Drayton
1563–1631

The first reports of Virginia emphasized the region's natural abundance and the pastoral simplicity of its inhabitants. One early English explorer, Arthur Barlowe, wrote glowingly in 1584 of a land of "incredible abundance," where the soil was "the most plentiful, sweet, fruitful and wholesome of all the world," and where the inhabitants were "most gentle, loving, and faithful, void of all guile, and treason, and such as lived after the manner of the Golden Age." So luxurious was this New World that even before reaching land, the traveler experienced a fragrance that seemed as though he "had been in the midst of some delicate garden, abounding with all kinds of odoriferous flowers."

Such Edenic imagery pervades Michael Drayton's "To the Virginia Voyage," a patriotic ode written to celebrate a 1606 expedition to the new colony. Drayton, a prolific poet now best known for his sonnets and odes (he introduced the Horatian ode into English verse), was apparently inspired by Hakluyt's stories of discovery to embark on a literary-historical exploration of his native realm. His most ambitious work, *Poly-Olbion* (1612, 1622), begins with the mythological founding of Britain and proceeds through thirty "songs" that cover the history, topography, and legends of a nation that not only was venturing into new worlds but was also in the process of discovering itself.

Further Reading:
C. L. Sanford, *The Quest for Paradise: Europe and the American Moral Imagination*, 1961.
H. Levin, *The Myth of the Golden Age in the Renaissance*, 1969.
H. Honour, *The New Golden Land: European Images of America from the Discoveries to the Present Time*, 1975.

Text:
Poems by Michael Drayton Esquyer, Collected into One Volume. With Sondry Peeces Inserted Never Before Imprinted, 1619. Spelling and punctuation have been changed to conform to modern usage.

To the Virginia Voyage

You brave heroic minds,
Worthy your country's name,
That honor still pursue,
Go and subdue,
Whilst loit'ring hinds[1]
Lurk here at home with shame.

5

[1] Female deer.

Britans, you stay too long;
Quickly aboard bestow you,
   And with a merry gale
   Swell your stretch'd sail,   10
With vows as strong
As the winds that blow you.

Your course securely steer
West and by south forth keep,
   Rocks, lee-shores, nor shoals,   15
   When Aeolus[2] scowls,
You need not fear,
So absolute the deep.

And cheerfully at sea,
Success you still entice,   20
   To get the pearl and gold,
   And ours to hold,
Virginia,
Earth's only paradise,

Where nature hath in store   25
Fowl, venison, and fish,
   And the fruitful'st soil
   Without your toil
Three harvests more,
All greater than your wish.   30

And the ambitious vine
Crowns with his purple mass,
   The cedar reaching high
   To kiss the sky,
The cypress, pine,   35
And useful sassafras.[3]

To those the golden age
Still nature's laws doth give,
   No other cares that tend,
   But them to defend   40
From winter's rage
That long there doth not live.

Whenas the luscious smell
Of that delicious land,

[2] In classical mythology, god of the winds.
[3] The plant was considered a remedy for many
illnesses, especially syphilis.

Above the seas that flows   45
The clear wind throws,
Your hearts to swell
Approaching the dear strand,

In kenning[4] of the shore,
Thanks to God first given,   50
    O you, the happi'st men,
    Be frolic then,
Let cannons roar,
Frighting the wide heaven.

And in regions far   55
Such heroes bring ye forth
    As those from whom we came,
    And plant our name
Under that star
Not known unto our north.   60

And as there plenty grows
Of laurel everywhere,
    Apollo's[5] sacred tree,
    You it may see
A poet's brows   65
To crown that may sing there.

Thy voyages attend,
Industrious Hakluyt,[6]
    Whose reading shall inflame
    Men to seek fame,   70
And much commend
To after times thy wit.

ca. 1605/1619

Thomas Hariot
1560–1621

In 1584 Sir Walter Raleigh, the English poet, historian, explorer, courtier, soldier, and entrepreneur, received from Queen Elizabeth an immense tract of land in the New World. After changing the name of the land from

---

[4] Seeing.
[5] Apollo: Greek god of light, music, poetry, healing, and prophecy.

[6] Richard Hakluyt (1552?–1616), English geographer and editor of explorers' narratives.

Windgandcon to Virginia, to honor the Virgin Queen who had bestowed it, Raleigh sent out an expedition headed by a gentleman soldier, Ralph Lane, to explore and colonize the region, which he hoped would soon become a profitable overseas empire.

Raleigh also sent along on this expedition, which landed on Roanoke Island in 1585, a prominent Oxford mathematician and astronomer, Thomas Hariot (sometimes spelled Harriot), to act as scientific observer and surveyor. When Hariot returned to London the following year, he began writing a scholarly treatise detailing the geography, natural resources, and civilization of the region. Raleigh's enormous political and financial problems, however, forced Hariot to set aside his projected book (unfortunately never finished) and to turn out instead an essentially promotional pamphlet. In *A briefe and true report of the new found land of Virginia* (1588), Hariot deliberately combined keen naturalistic observation with effective recruitment propaganda. It is the first published book about America written in English by an English eyewitness.

Raleigh commissioned as well a London artist, John White, to accompany Hariot and supply illustrations for his data. Because Hariot's major project was interrupted, White's magnificent watercolors never found their way into immediate publication. They did, however, inspire a Dutch engraver and bibliophile, Theodore De Bry, to make copies of them for inclusion in an extravagant, multilingual volume about the New World published in 1590. For generations, De Bry's *America* served as one of the most influential sources of information available to European readers about animal, botanical, and human life in the Americas.

Ralph Lane's Roanoke expedition, despite the important contributions it made to the knowledge of the region, was nearly a complete disaster. Though the new territory appeared to be one of great natural abundance, the English depended almost entirely on the Algonquian Indians for fish, meat, and grain. This irritating dependency—often repeated during the European explorations—was aggravated by earlier problems and, when combined with serious dissension among the colonists themselves, led to open conflict. Governor Lane's subsequent report to Raleigh contains information that Hariot's promotionally cautious account does not: the final confrontation with the Indians on the moonlit night of June 1, 1586. A few weeks later, the expedition was safely on its way back to London aboard one of Sir Francis Drake's ships, which had fortunately decided to make a stop at Roanoke Island.

The following year saw another attempt to colonize Roanoke. A more substantial endeavor, including women and children, this expedition also ended in failure—this time with the mysterious disappearance of all the colonists. Not until Captain John Smith's Jamestown settlement in 1607 would the English again undertake the risks of colonization. The New World, far from resembling an earthly paradise, was beginning to look inhospitable, unprofitable, and strange.

Further Reading:
M. C. Bradbrook, *The School of Night,* 1936.
M. Rukeyser, *The Traces of Thomas Hariot,*
1971.

Text:
A Briefe and True Report of the New Found Land of Virginia, 1588. Typography, spelling, and punctuation have been changed to conform to modern usage.

from A Briefe and True Report of the New Found Land of Virginia

[Of the Nature and Manners of the People]

It remains I speak a word or two of the natural inhabitants, their nature and manners . . . as that you may know how that they in respect of troubling our inhabiting and planting[1] are not to be feared; but that they shall have cause both to fear and love us that shall inhabit with them.

They are a people clothed with loose mantles made of deer skin, and aprons of the same round about their middle; all else naked; of such a difference of statures only as we in England; having no edge tools or weapons of iron or steel to offend us withal, neither know they how to make any. Those weapons that they have are only bows made of witch hazle and arrows of reed [and] flat-edged truncheons[2] also of wood about a yard long; neither have they anything to defend themselves but targets[3] made of bark and some armour made of sticks wickered together with thread.

Their towns are but small, and near the sea coast but few, some containing but 10 or 12 houses, some 20. The greatest that we have seen have been but of 30 houses. If they be walled it is only done with barks of trees made fast to stakes or else with poles only, fixed upright and close one by another.

Their houses are made of small poles made fast at the tops in round form after the manner as is used in many arbors in our gardens of England, [which are] in most towns covered with bark and in some with artificial mats made of long rushes [that extend] from the tops of the houses down to the ground. The length of them is commonly double to the breadth; in some places they are but 12 and 16 yards long, and in some others we have seen of four and twenty.

In some places of the country only one town belongs to the government of a *Wiroans* or chief Lord; in some others two or three, in some six, eight, and more. The greatest *Wiroans* that yet we had dealing with had but eighteen towns in his government, and [was] able to make not above seven or eight hundred fighting men at the most. The language of every government is different from any other, and the farther they are distant the greater is the difference.

Their manner of war amongst themselves is either by sudden surprising one another, most commonly about the dawning of the day or moonlight, or else by ambushes or some subtle devices. Set battles are very rare, except it fall out where there are many trees, where either party may have some hope of defence, after the delivery of every arrow, in leaping behind some or other.

If there fall out any war between us and them, what their fight is likely to be—we having advantages against them [in] so many manner of ways, as by our discipline, our strange weapons and other devices, [and] especially by ordinance[4] great and small—it may be easily imagined. By the experience we have had in some places, the turning up of their heels against us in running away was their best defence.

---

[1] I.e., colonizing.
[2] Clubs.
[3] Small shields.
[4] Artillery, both heavy and light.

With respect to us, they are a poor people and, for want of skill and judgment in the knowledge and use of our things, do esteem our trifles before things of greater value. Notwithstanding, in their proper manner considering the want[5] of such means as we have, they seem very ingenious. For although they have no such tools nor any such crafts, sciences and arts as we, yet in those things they do, they show excellency of wit.[6] And by how much they, upon due consideration, shall find our manner of knowledge and crafts to exceed theirs in perfection, and speed for doing or execution, by so much more it is probable that they should desire our friendship and love, and have the greater respect for pleasing and obeying us. Whereby [it] may be hoped, if means of good government be used, that they may in short time be brought to civility and the embracing of true religion.[7]

Some religion they have already, which, although it be far from the truth, yet being as it is, there is hope it may be the easier and sooner reformed.

They believe that there are many gods which they call *Montoac,* but of different sorts and degrees; [and] only one chief and great God, which has been from all eternity, [and] who, as they affirm, when he purposed to make the world, made first other gods of a principal order to be as means and instruments to be used in the creation and government to follow; and after[wards] the Sun, Moon, and Stars, as petty gods and the instruments of the other order more principal. First, they say, were made waters, out of which by the gods was made all diversity of creatures that are visible or invisible.

For mankind, they say, a woman was made first, which by the working of one of the gods, conceived and brought forth children. And in such sort they say they had their beginning.

But how many years or ages have passed since, they say they can make no relation, having no letters[8] nor other such means as we to keep records of the particularities of times past, but only tradition from father to son.

They think that all the gods are of human shape, and therefore they represent them by images in the form of men, which they call *Kewasowok* (one alone is called *Kewas*). These they place in houses appropriate or temples which they call *Machicomuck,* where they worship, pray, sing, and make many offerings unto them. In some *Machicomuck* we have seen but one Kewas, in some two, and in some other three. The common sort[9] think them to be also gods.

They believe also the immortality of the soul, that after this life, as soon as the soul is departed from the body, according to the works it has done, it is either carried to heaven, the habitation of gods, there to enjoy perpetual bliss and happiness; or else to a great pit or hole, which they think to be in the furthest part of their part of the world, toward the sunset, there to burn continually: the place they call *Popoqusso.*

For the confirmation of this opinion, they told me two stories of two men that had been lately dead and revived again. The one happened but [a] few years before our coming into the country to a wicked man which having been dead and buried, the next day the earth of the grave being seen to move, [he] was taken up again. [He] made declaration where his soul had been; that is to say, very near entering into

Popoqusso, had not one of the gods saved him and gave him leave to return again and teach his friends what they should do to avoid that terrible place of torment.

The other happened in the same year we were there but in a town that was threescore[10] miles from us. It was told me for strange news that one, being dead, buried and taken up again as the first, showed that, although his body had lain dead in the grave, yet his soul was alive and had traveled far in a long broad way, on both sides whereof grew most delicate and pleasant tress, bearing more rare and excellent fruit than ever he had seen before or was able to express. At length [he] came to most brave[11] and fair houses, near which he met his father, that had been dead before, who gave him great charge to go back again and show his friends what good they were to do to enjoy the pleasures of that place, which when he had done he should after[wards] come again.

What subtlety soever be in the Wiroances and Priests, this opinion works so much in many of the common and simple sort of people that it makes them have great respect for their Governors, and also [have] great care what they do to avoid torment after death and to enjoy bliss. Although notwithstanding there is punishment ordained for [such] malefactors as stealers, whoremongers,[12] and other sorts of wicked doers: some [are] punished with death, some with forfeitures, some with beating, according to the greatness of the facts.[13]

And this is the sum of their religion, which I learned by having special familiarity with some of their priests. Wherein they were not so sure grounded, nor gave such credit to their traditions and stories but through conversing with us they were brought into great doubts of their own [religion] and no small admiration of ours, with earnest desire in many to learn more than we had means (for want of perfect utterance in their language) to express.

Most things they saw with us—[such] as mathematical instruments, sea compasses, the virtue of the loadstone[14] in drawing iron, a perspective glass[15] whereby was shown many strange sights, burning glasses,[16] wildfire works,[17] guns, books, writing and reading, spring clocks[18] that seem to go of themselves, and many other things that we had—were so strange unto them and so far exceeded their capacities to comprehend the reason and means how they should be made and done that they thought they were rather the works of gods than of men, or at the least that they had been given and taught us of the gods. Which made many of them to have such opinion of us, as that if they knew not the truth of God and religion already, it was rather to be had from us, whom God so specially loved than from a people that were so simple, as they found themselves to be in comparison of us. Whereupon greater credit was given unto that we spoke of concerning such matters.

Many times and in every town where I came, according as I was able, I made declaration of the contents of the Bible: that therein was set forth the true and only GOD and his mighty works, [and] that therein was contained the true doctrine of salvation through Christ, with many particularities of Miracles and chief points of religion as I was able then to utter and thought fit for the time. And although I told

[10] Sixty.
[11] Excellent; admirable.
[12] Lechers or panderers.
[13] I.e., seriousness of the case.
[14] Magnet.
[15] Telescope.
[16] Magnifying glass that focuses the sun's rays.
[17] A highly combustible material used in warfare.
[18] Clocks that operate by means of a spring mechanism.

them the book materially and of itself was not of any such virtue as I thought they did conceive, but only the doctrine contained therein, yet would many be glad to touch it, to embrace it, to kiss it, to hold it to their breasts and heads, and stroke over all their bodies with it, to show their hungry desire of that knowledge which was spoken of.

The Wiroans with whom we dwelt [was] called Wingina, and many of his people would be glad many times to be with us at our prayers, and many times call upon us both in his own town, as also in others whither he sometimes accompanied us, to pray and sing Psalms, hoping thereby to be partaker of the same effects which we by that means also expected.

Twice this Wiroans was so grievously sick that he was like to die. And as he lay languishing, doubting of any help by his own priests and thinking he was in such danger for offending us and thereby our God, [he] sent for some of us to pray and be a means to our God that it would please Him either that he might live or after death dwell with Him in bliss. So likewise were the requests of many others in the like case.

On a time also when their corn began to wither by reason of a drought which happened extraordinarily—fearing that it had come to pass by reason that in some thing they had displeased us—many would come to us and desire us to pray to our God of England that He would preserve their corn, promising that when it was ripe we also should be partakers of the fruit.

There could at no time happen any strange sickness, losses, hurts, or any other cross unto them, but that they would impute to us the cause or means thereof for offending or not pleasing us.

One other rare and strange accident, leaving others, will I mention before I end, which moved the whole country that either knew or heard of us to have us in wonderful admiration.

There was no town where we had any subtle device[19] practiced against us (we leaving it unpunished or not revenged because we sought by all means possible to win them by gentleness) but that within a few days after our departure from every such town, the people began to die very fast and many in short space: in some towns about twenty, in some forty, in some sixty, and in one six score,[20] which in truth was very many in respect of their numbers. This happened in no place that we could learn but where we had been, where they used some practice[21] against us, and after such time. This disease [was] also so strange that they neither knew what it was nor how to cure it. The like, by report of the oldest men in the country, never happened before, time out of mind: a thing specially observed by us as also by the natural inhabitants themselves.

Insomuch that when some of the inhabitants which were our friends, and especially the *Wiroans Wingina,* had observed such effects in four or five towns to follow their[22] wicked practices, they were persuaded that it was the work of our God through our means, and that we by him might kill and slay whom we would without weapons and not come near them.

And thereupon when it had happened that they had understanding that any of their enemies had abused us in our journeys—hearing that we had wrought no revenge with

---

[19] Underhanded stratagem.
[20] One hundred twenty.

[21] Trick.
[22] I.e., the towns'.

our weapons, and fearing upon some cause the matter should so rest—[they] did come and entreat us that we would be a means to our God that they[23] as others that had dealt ill with us might in like sort die; alleging how much it would be for our credit and profit, as also theirs, and hoping furthermore that we would do so much at their request in respect of the friendship we profess them.

Whose entreaties although we showed that they were ungodly, affirming that our God would not subject Himself to any such prayers and requests of men—that indeed all things have been and were to be done according to his good pleasure as he had ordained—and that we to show our selves his true servants ought rather to make petition for the contrary: that they with them might live together with us, be made partakers of His truth and serve Him in righteousness. But notwithstanding in such sort, that we refer that as all other things, to be done according to His divine will and pleasure, and as by His wisdom he had ordained to be best.

Yet because the effect[24] fell out so suddenly and shortly after, according to their desires, they thought nevertheless it came to pass by our means, and that we, in using such speeches unto them, did but dissemble the matter. And [they] therefore came unto us to give us thanks in their manner that although we satisfied them not in promise, yet in deeds and effect we had fulfilled their desires.

This marvellous accident in all the country wrought so strange opinions of us, that some people could not tell whether to think us gods or men, and the rather because that all the space of their sickness, there was no man of ours known to die or that was specially sick. They noted also that we had no women amongst us [and] neither did we care for any of theirs.

Some therefore were of the opinion that we were not born of women, and therefore not mortal, but that we were men of an old generation many years past then risen again to immortality.

Some would likewise seem to prophesy that there were more of our generation yet to come, to kill theirs and take their places, as some thought the purpose was by that which was already done.

Those that were immediately to come after us they imagined to be in the air, yet invisible and without bodies, and that they by our entreaty and for the love of us did make the people to die in that sort as they did by shooting invisible bullets into them.

To confirm this opinion, their physicians to excuse their ignorance in curing the disease, would not be ashamed to say—but [would] earnestly make the simple people believe—that the strings of blood that they sucked out of the sick bodies were the strings wherewithal the invisible bullets were tied and cast.[25]

Some also thought that we shot them ourselves out of our pieces from the place where we dwelt and killed the people in any such town that had offended us as we liked—how far distant from us soever it were.

And some others said that it was the special work of God for our sakes, as we ourselves have cause in some sort to think no less, whatsoever some do or may imagine to the contrary, especially some Astrologers knowing of the Eclipse of the Sun, which

[23] I.e., their enemies.
[24] I.e., the disease.
[25] The mysterious disease, which puzzled both the Indians and Hariot, seems to have been some sort of pulmonary virus.

we saw the same year before in our voyage thither, which unto them appeared very terrible. And also of a Comet which began to appear but a few days before the beginning of the said sickness. But to conclude them from being the special causes of so special an accident, there are further reasons than I think fit at present to be alleged.

These their opinions I have set down the more at large[26] that it may appear unto you that there is good hope they may be brought through discreet dealing and government[27] to the embracing of the truth, and consequently to honor, obey, fear and love us.

And although some of our company towards the end of the year showed themselves too fierce in slaying some of the people in some towns, upon causes that on our part might easily enough have been born withal, yet notwithstanding because it was on their part justly deserved, the alteration of their opinions generally and for the most part concerning us is the less to be doubted. And whatsoever else they may be, by carefulness of ourselves need nothing at all to be feared.

The best nevertheless in this as in all actions besides is to be endeavored and hoped; and of the worst that may happen notice to be taken with consideration, and as much as may be eschewed.[28]

1588

Samuel de Champlain
ca. 1570–1635

Best known for his explorations of Canada, Samuel de Champlain nevertheless made several important expeditions within the present territory of the United States. Fifteen years before the Pilgrims landed at Plymouth, Champlain had sailed from Nova Scotia to Cape Cod and compiled the first detailed chart of the New England coast, including Martha's Vineyard and Plymouth Harbor. The French colony he subsequently founded in Quebec in 1608 was the second permanent European settlement in North America (Florida was the first).

In the spring of 1609, with only two of his men, Champlain agreed to join a combined force of Huron, Algonquian, and Montagnais Indians in a raid against their Iroquois enemies. His account of the confrontation, which occurred in the vicinity of what is now Fort Ticonderoga, is memorable for its grim introduction of European firearms into Indian warfare. Champlain's ill-advised participation in the bloody skirmish helped initiate a long-standing antagonism between French colonists and the politically important Iroquois nation.

The American historian Francis Parkman regarded Champlain as the first pioneer of the North American forests. Indeed, Champlain represents the beginnings of a new type of American hero—the frontiersman. Familiar with

[26] Extensively.
[27] Discipline.
[28] I.e., we should hope for the best and should regard the worst that could happen with due consideration and restraint.

Indian customs and wholly adapted to life in the woods, the frontiersmen (or *coureurs des bois* as they were known in French) dominated the North American wilderness from Hudson Bay to the Rockies and from the Great Lakes to the Gulf of Mexico. Tough, pragmatic, and self-reliant, this new breed of explorer would exert an enormous influence on the course of American culture.

Further Reading:
F. Parkman, *Pioneers of France in the New World,* 1865, rev. 1885.
M. Bishop, *Champlain: The Life of Fortitude,* 1948.
S. E. Morison, *Samuel de Champlain: Father of New France,* 1972.

Text:
The Voyages of Samuel de Champlain, 1604–1618, ed. W. L. Grant, trans. C. P. Otis, 1907.

---

from The Voyages of Samuel de Champlain, 1604–1618

The Voyages of 1608–1612

[An Encounter with the Iroquois]

We set out on the next day,[1] continuing our course in the river as far as the entrance of the lake. There are many pretty islands here, low, and containing very fine woods and meadows, with abundance of fowl and such animals of the chase as stags, fallow-deer, fawns, roe-bucks, bears, and others, which go from the main land to these islands. We captured a large number of these animals. There are also many beavers, not only in this river, but also in numerous other little ones that flow into it. These regions, although they are pleasant, are not inhabited by any savages, on account of their wars; but they withdraw as far as possible from the rivers into the interior, in order not to be suddenly surprised.

The next day we entered the lake,[2] which is of great extent, say eighty or a hundred leagues long, where I saw four fine islands, ten, twelve, and fifteen leagues long, which were formerly inhabited by the savages, like the River of the Iroquois; but they have been abandoned since the wars of the savages with one another prevail. There are also many rivers falling into the lake, bordered by many fine trees of the same kinds as those we have in France, with many vines finer than any I have seen in any other place; also many chestnut-trees on the border of this lake, which I had not seen before. There is also a great abundance of fish, of many varieties; among others, one called by the savages of the country *Chaousarou,*[3] which varies in length, the largest being, as the people told me, eight or ten feet long. I saw some five feet long, which were as large as my thigh; the head being as big as my two fists, with a snout two feet and a half long, and a double row of very sharp and dangerous teeth. Its body is, in shape, much like that of a pike; but it is armed with scales so strong that a poniard[4] could not pierce them. Its color is silver-gray. The extremity of its snout is like that of swine.

[1] July 13, 1609.
[2] Lake Champlain.
[3] "Garpike."
[4] Dagger.

This fish makes war upon all others in the lakes and rivers. It also possesses remarkable dexterity, as these people informed me, which is exhibited in the following manner. When it wants to capture birds, it swims in among the rushes, or reeds, which are found on the banks of the lake in several places, where it puts its snout out of water and keeps perfectly still: so that, when the birds come and light on its snout, supposing it to be only the stump of a tree, it adroitly closes it, which it had kept ajar, and pulls the birds by the feet down under water. The savages gave me the head of one of them, of which they make great account, saying that, when they have the headache, they bleed themselves with the teeth of this fish on the spot where they suffer pain, when it suddenly passes away.

Continuing our course over this lake on the western side, I noticed, while observing the country, some very high mountains[5] on the eastern side, on the top of which there was snow. I made inquiry of the savages whether these localities were inhabited, when they told me that the Iroquois dwelt there, and that there were beautiful valleys in these places, with plains productive in grain, such as I had eaten in this country, together with many kinds of fruit without limit. They said also that the lake extended near mountains, some twenty-five leagues distant from us, as I judge. I saw, on the south, other mountains,[6] no less high than the first, but without any snow. The savages told me that these mountains were thickly settled, and that it was there we were to find their enemies; but that it was necessary to pass a fall[7] in order to go there (which I afterwards saw), when we should enter another lake,[8] nine or ten leagues long. After reaching the end of the lake, we should have to go, they said, two leagues by land, and pass through a river[9] flowing into the sea on the Norumbegue coast, near that of Florida, whither it took them only two days to go by canoe, as I have since ascertained from some prisoners we captured, who gave me minute information in regard to all they had personal knowledge of, through some Algonquin interpreters, who understood the Iroquois language.

Now, as we began to approach within two or three days' journey of the abode of their enemies, we advanced only at night, resting during the day. But they did not fail to practise constantly their accustomed superstitions, in order to ascertain what was to be the result of their undertaking; and they often asked me if I had had a dream, and seen their enemies, to which I replied in the negative. Yet I did not cease to encourage them, and inspire in them hope. When night came, we set out on the journey until the next day, when we withdrew into the interior of the forest, and spent the rest of the day there. About ten or eleven o'clock, after taking a little walk about our encampment, I retired. While sleeping, I dreamed that I saw our enemies, the Iroquois, drowning in the lake near a mountain, within sight. When I expressed a wish to help them, our allies, the savages, told me we must let them all die, and that they were of no importance. When I awoke, they did not fail to ask me, as usual, if I had had a dream. I told them that I had, in fact, had a dream. This, upon being related, gave them so much confidence that they did not doubt any longer that good was to happen to them.

When it was evening, we embarked in our canoes to continue our course; and, as we advanced very quietly and without making any noise, we met on the 29th of the

---

[5] The Green Mountains of Vermont.
[6] The Adirondacks.
[7] Ticonderoga.

[8] Lake George.
[9] The Hudson.

month the Iroquois, about ten o'clock at evening, at the extremity of a cape[10] which extends into the lake on the western bank. They had come to fight. We both began to utter loud cries, all getting their arms in readiness. We withdrew out on the water, and the Iroquois went on shore, where they drew up all their canoes close to each other and began to fell trees with poor axes, which they acquire in war sometimes, using also others of stone. Thus they barricaded themselves very well.

Our forces also passed the entire night, their canoes being drawn up close to each other, and fastened to poles, so that they might not get separated, and that they might be all in readiness to fight, if occasion required. We were out upon the water, within arrow range of their barricades. When they were armed and in array, they despatched two canoes by themselves to the enemy to inquire if they wished to fight, to which the latter replied that they wanted nothing else: but they said that, at present, there was not much light, and that it would be necessary to wait for daylight, so as to be able to recognize each other; and that, as soon as the sun rose, they would offer us battle. This was agreed to by our side. Meanwhile, the entire night was spent in dancing and singing, on both sides, with endless insults and other talk; as, how little courage we had, how feeble a resistance we should make against their arms, and that, when day came, we should realize it to our ruin. Ours also were not slow in retorting, telling them they would see such execution of arms as never before, together with an abundance of such talk as is not unusual in the siege of a town. After this singing, dancing, and bandying words on both sides to the fill, when day came, my companions and myself continued under cover, for fear that the enemy would see us. We arranged our arms in the best manner possible, being, however, separated, each in one of the canoes of the savage Montagnais. After arming ourselves with light armor, we each took an arquebuse,[11] and went on shore. I saw the enemy go out of their barricade, nearly two hundred in number, stout and rugged in appearance. They came at a slow pace towards us, with a dignity and assurance which greatly amused me, having three chiefs at their head. Our men also advanced in the same order, telling me that those who had three large plumes were the chiefs, and that they had only these three, and that they could be distinguished by these plumes, which were much larger than those of their companions, and that I should do what I could to kill them. I promised to do all in my power, and said that I was very sorry they could not understand me, so that I might give order and shape to their mode of attacking their enemies, and then we should, without doubt, defeat them all; but that this could not now be obviated, and that I should be very glad to show them my courage and good-will when we should engage in the fight.

As soon as we had landed, they began to run for some two hundred paces towards their enemies, who stood firmly, not having as yet noticed my companions, who went into the woods with some savages. Our men began to call me with loud cries; and, in order to give me a passage-way, they opened in two parts, and put me at their head, where I marched some twenty paces in advance of the rest, until I was within about thirty paces of the enemy, who at once noticed me, and, halting, gazed at me, as I did also at them. When I saw them making a move to fire at us, I rested my musket against my cheek, and aimed directly at one of the three chiefs. With the same shot,

[10] Crown Point. The battle occurred at or near Ticonderoga.
[11] A small-caliber long gun operated by a matchlock or wheel-lock mechanism, dating from about 1400.

two fell to the ground; and one of their men was so wounded that he died some time after. I had loaded my musket with four balls. When our side saw this shot so favorable for them, they began to raise such loud cries that one could not have heard it thunder. Meanwhile, the arrows flew on both sides. The Iroquois were greatly astonished that two men had been so quickly killed, although they were equipped with armor woven from cotton thread, and with wood which was proof against their arrows. This caused great alarm among them. As I was loading again, one of my companions fired a shot from the woods, which astonished them anew to such a degree that, seeing their chiefs dead, they lost courage, and took to flight, abandoning their camp and fort, and fleeing into the woods, whither I pursued them, killing still more of them. Our savages also killed several of them, and took ten or twelve prisoners. The remainder escaped with the wounded. Fifteen or sixteen were wounded on our side with arrow-shots; but they were soon healed.

After gaining the victory, our men amused themselves by taking a great quantity of Indian corn and some meal from their enemies, also their armor, which they had left behind that they might run better. After feasting sumptuously, dancing and singing, we returned three hours after, with the prisoners. The spot where this attack took place is in latitude 43° and some minutes,[12] and the lake was called Lake Champlain.

1613

The Voyages of 1615–1618

[Lost in the Woods]

When they first went out hunting,[13] I lost my way in the woods, having followed a certain bird that seemed to me peculiar. It had a beak like that of a parrot, and was of the size of a hen. It was entirely yellow, except the head which was red, and the wings which were blue, and it flew by intervals like a partridge. The desire to kill it led me to pursue it from tree to tree for a very long time, until it flew away in good earnest. Thus losing all hope, I desired to retrace my steps, but found none of our hunters, who had been constantly getting ahead, and had reached the enclosure. While trying to overtake them, and going, as it seemed to me, straight to where the enclosure was, I found myself lost in the woods, going now on this side now on that, without being able to recognize my position. The night coming on, I was obliged to spend it at the foot of a great tree, and in the morning set out and walked until three o'clock in the afternoon, when I came to a little pond of still water. Here I noticed some game, which I pursued, killing three or four birds, which were very acceptable, since I had had nothing to eat. Unfortunately for me there had been no sunshine for three days, nothing but rain and cloudy weather, which increased my trouble. Tired and exhausted I prepared to rest myself and cook the birds in order to alleviate the hunger which I began painfully to feel, and which by God's favor was appeased.

When I had made my repast I began to consider what I should do, and to pray God to give me the will and courage to sustain patiently my misfortune if I should

---

[12] Minute: the sixtieth part of a degree.
[13] Champlain was in the company of a small band of Huron deerhunters somewhere north of Kingston, Ontario, in the late fall of 1615.

be obliged to remain abandoned in this forest without counsel or consolation except the Divine goodness and mercy, and at the same time to exert myself to return to our hunters. Thus committing all to His mercy I gathered up renewed courage, going here and there all day, without perceiving any foot-print or path, except those of wild beasts, of which I generally saw a good number. I was obliged to pass here this night also. Unfortunately I had forgotten to bring with me a small compass which would have put me on the right road, or nearly so. At the dawn of day, after a brief repast, I set out in order to find, if possible, some brook and follow it, thinking that it must of necessity flow into the river on the border of which our hunters were encamped. Having resolved upon this plan, I carried it out so well that at noon I found myself on the border of a little lake, about a league and a half in extent, where I killed some game, which was very timely for my wants; I had likewise remaining some eight or ten charges of powder, which was a great satisfaction.

I proceeded along the border of this lake to see where it discharged, and found a large brook, which I followed until five o'clock in the evening, when I heard a great noise, but on carefully listening failed to perceive clearly what it was. On hearing the noise, however, more distinctly, I concluded that it was a fall of water in the river which I was searching for. I proceeded nearer, and saw an opening, approaching which I found myself in a great and far-reaching meadow, where there was a large number of wild beasts, and looking to my right I perceived the river, broad and long. I looked to see if I could not recognize the place, and walking along on the meadow I noticed a little path where the savages carried their canoes. Finally, after careful observation, I recognized it as the same river, and that I had gone that way before.

I passed the night in better spirits than the previous ones, supping on the little I had. In the morning I re-examined the place where I was, and concluded from certain mountains on the border of the river that I had not been deceived, and that our hunters must be lower down by four or five good leagues. This distance I walked at my leisure along the border of the river, until I perceived the smoke of our hunters, where I arrived to the great pleasure not only of myself but of them, who were still searching for me, but had about given up all hopes of seeing me again. They begged me not to stray off from them any more, or never to forget to carry with me my compass, and they added: If you had not come, and we had not succeeded in finding, we should never have gone again to the French, for fear of their accusing us of having killed you. After this he was very careful of me when I went hunting, always giving me a savage as companion, who knew how to find again the place from which he started so well that it was something very remarkable.

1619

Native American Literature: First Encounters

In *Studies in Classic American Literature,* D. H. Lawrence points to the haunting presence of Native Americans in the nation's cultural consciousness: "A curious thing about the Spirit of Place is the fact that no place exerts its full influence upon a new-comer until the old inhabitant is dead or absorbed. So America." In the nearly five centuries that have passed since Christopher Columbus accidentally discovered America and opened unbounded vistas for the literature of the New World, the response of European emigrants to America to the people they found there has fluctuated greatly, often moving rapidly between the extremes of trying ruthlessly to eliminate or mindlessly to glorify the Native American population. Within these extremes, the colonists persisted in their efforts to assimilate each Native American group within their nation's cultural heritage.

Europeans found Columbus's discovery of the New World as bewildering as it was unexpected. Samuel Eliot Morison, the distinguished biographer of Columbus, notes that "when discovered it [America] was not wanted, and most of the exploration for the next fifty years was done in the hope of getting through or around it." Columbus's reports on his voyages, for example, underscore his conviction that he had accomplished what he had set out to do: discover a shorter route to the East Indies. And because he could not adjust his expectations to the reality he confronted in the New World, Columbus insisted on calling the people he found there Indians, as though they were the people of the Near East he had sailed west to find. Columbus had discovered America, but not its people.

Generations of European explorers and colonists repeated Columbus's efforts to reinvent America and its inhabitants. Europeans dealt with the unrelenting novelty of their experiences with this newfound land and the people who inhabited it by reconstituting those experiences according to a more readily accessible and familiar cultural framework. As the historian Edmundo O'Gorman has noted, "The native cultures of the newly found lands could not be recognized and respected in their own right, as an original way of realizing human ideals and values, but only for the meaning they might have in relation to Christian European culture." America was invented, O'Gorman suggests, "in the image of its inventor," by those who could not free themselves from inherited European cultural perspectives and values. As a result, the distinctive nature of Native American culture was, to use William Carlos Williams's terms (from *In the American Grain*), "lost in chaos of borrowed titles, many of them inappropriate, under which the true character lies hid." The pages that follow and later sections of *The Harper American Literature* try to present Native American literature in its own terms, to draw, as Williams notes, "from every source one thing, the strange phosphorus of the life, nameless under an old misappellation."

The most striking fact about Native American literature is the cultural diversity that it represents. At the time of Columbus's voyages, more than 350 distinct, mutually unintelligible Native American languages were spoken in the area that is now the United States—and nearly half of these languages are still spoken in contemporary America. Literally thousands of distinct political and social groups were spread across the land. Given this range of identities, no single image of the Native American people can accurately capture the complexity of their culture. Yet historically, convenient stereotypes have dominated the nation's view of Native Americans: naked, mysterious, gullible creatures or noble savages; cigar-store props and dime-novel caricatures on the warpath or resilient, loyal companions of white-horsed heroes; and, more recently, soft-spoken wise men with drug-induced access to fundamental knowledge. Over the course of five centuries, Native Americans have come to be isolated geographically and culturally, relegated to the lowly status of the "other," with relatively few opportunities to posit the richness and complexity of their individual and collective voices in the cultural consciousness of the nation within whose boundaries they live.

The literature of Native Americans has been transmitted primarily through the oral tradition. Skills in oratory are highly valued, in part because most North American tribes govern themselves through participatory democracy. Research conducted since the late nineteenth century reveals a number of highly developed oral literary forms—including ceremonial and popular songs, prayers, incantations, and mythic narratives—each with its own characteristic style and art in each Native American language. Yet because this literature is based on Native American cultural assumptions, it has traditionally been regarded as the province of anthropology rather than literary studies, much like Puritan sermons and explorers' narratives—texts that while culturally interesting have not been considered part of the belles lettres tradition. Closer examination suggests that the literary features of these Native American texts are consistent with the stylistic qualities, including repetition and rhythmic patterning, of the great oral tradition of European literature dating back to classical antiquity. Like its European counterpart, the Native American literary oral tradition has articulated important states of individual consciousness while helping to reinforce a sense of community within each language group.

The confrontation between European and Native American cultures in the New World is amply reported from colonial points of view. Spanish, English, and French explorers and missionaries have left graphic narratives of their efforts to "civilize" and convert the New World's population. Relatively few voices remain, however, to represent reliably the Native American perspective on these same events. Most eyewitness accounts survive through secondhand and thirdhand translations. Many suffer to an indeterminate extent by being "screened" by a colonial sensibility. Like Powhatan's speech printed here, the surviving text may well reflect more what their white audiences thought, or hoped, Native Americans had said than what they did in fact say. In other instances, such as Mayan responses to the Spanish conquest, Native American authors had to master the language of their conquerors in order to preserve the anguish of their people.

Since the late nineteenth century, an increasing amount of indigenous oral literature has been transcribed by Native Americans in their own languages as well as in English and is increasingly available to be read. As a result, accurate texts of Native American literature can be included in the American literary tradition with greater confidence and frequency. The texts presented here illustrate the varying forms of literature that distinguished the conquered from the conqueror in the New World. These texts help us appreciate not only how each side discovered the "other" that neither knew but also how vibrant the Native American oral tradition has remained.

Further Reading:

For comprehensive studies of the history and literature of Native Americans, see H. E. Driver, *Indians of North America*, 1961. W. T. Hagan, *American Indians*, 1961. R. H. Pearce, *The Savages of America: A Study of the Indian and the Idea of Civilization*, 2nd ed., 1965. D. McNickle, *Native American Tribalism*, 1973. W. E. Washburn, *The Indian in America*, 1975. *Handbook of North American Indians*, ed. W. C. Sturtevant, 20 vols. planned, 1978–. D. Hymes, *In Vain I Tried to Tell You: Essays in Native American Ethnopoetics*, 1981. K. Kroeber, *American Indian Literature: Texts and Interpretations*, 1981. A. Rosenstiel, *Red and White: Indian Views of the White Man, 1492–1982*, 1983. *Studies in American Indian Literature*, ed. Paula Gunn Allen, 1983. For Native American material in "The Literature of the New World," see E. O'Gorman, *The Invention of America*, 1961. D. Tedlock, *The Spoken Word and the Work of Interpretation*, 1983. T. Todorov, *The Conquest of America*, 1984. D. Buhane, *The Navajo Creation Story*, 1985.

A Bering Strait Eskimo Creation Myth

All Native American groups possess a body of narratives that can be called myths because of the central role they play in articulating religious experience and organizing ethical, moral, and social behavior. The myths also relate to Native American rituals and ceremonies. Just as the Christian mass or communion service reenacts a critical section of the Gospel (the Last Supper) and the Jewish Passover seder recalls central acts in the book of Exodus, Native American rituals and ceremonies frequently refer to and reenact important sections of myths.

Myths also had—and continue to have—an educational function, much as Bible stories are the basis of moral instruction in Christian Sunday schools. (In Native American societies, children's instruction took place primarily in the home, usually at night, and often during the winter season.)

In all their roles, Native American myths might best be understood as resembling dramatic performances. Virtually every component of the narrative includes direct speech, sometimes without apparent reason. In actual performance, the narrator would enact the scene, taking on different voices and gestures for different characters. Such a well-formed oral narrative may seem slow or awkward when written down in the form usually reserved for fiction, but in performance it would be absorbing. Moreover, like theater, the performance of oral literature can be expected to vary with the narrator, audience, setting, and time period.

Printed here are the beginning episodes of a Bering Strait Eskimo creation myth collected in Alaska between 1877 and 1881 by Edward William Nelson. The elderly man who told the tale remembered having learned the text from an old man who came from the Bering Strait. Nelson's source also remembered that when the man from Bering Strait "finished the tales on the third evening, he would pour a cup of water on the floor and say: 'Drink well, spirits of those of whom I have told.'"

The Bering Sea Eskimos occupy the lowland regions of western Alaska, between the Bering Straits and the Aleutian Islands. Unlike the Native Americans of the eastern Arctic and Greenland, Bering Strait Eskimos live in large, permanent villages with sizable log and sod houses during the winter and in plank houses during the summer. They eat a diet of stored fish, game, and berries, much like their Indian neighbors to the south on the Northwest coast. During the winter months they hold large festivals and dramatized ceremonies with masks and elaborate theatrical effects, the primary purpose of which is "to propitiate the spirits controlling the universe and bring success in hunting."

In their elegantly illustrated description of Bering Sea Eskimo life, William W. Fitzhugh and Susan A. Kaplan offer the following explanation of the cultural and religious importance of the Raven: "Spiritual transformation, symbolized by Man's first encounter with his maker, Raven, was at the heart of Bering Sea Eskimo life and culture. When an animal died its *inua* inhabited the form of an unborn animal of the same or similar species. Therefore, man needed to deal respectfully with animals and objects so as not to displease their *inuas*."

Further Reading:
W. W. Fitzhugh and S. A. Kaplan, *Inua: Spirit World of the Bering Sea Eskimos,* 1982. *Handbook of North American Indians,* gen. ed. W. C. Sturtevant, vol. 5, *Arctic,* ed. D. Damas, 1984.

Text:
18th Annual Report, Part 1, Bureau of American Ethnology, 1896–1897.

---

from The Time When There Were No People on the Earth Plain

It was in the time when there were no people on the earth plain. During four days the first man lay coiled up in the pod of a beach-pea. On the fifth day he stretched out his feet and burst the pod, falling to the ground, where he stood up, a full-grown man. He looked about him, and then moved his hands and arms, his neck and legs, and examined himself curiously. Looking back, he saw the pod from which he had fallen, still hanging to the vine, with a hole in the lower end, out of which he had dropped. Then he looked about him again and saw that he was getting farther away from his starting place, and that the ground moved up and down under his feet and seemed very soft. After a while he had an unpleasant feeling in his stomach, and he stooped down to take some water into his mouth from a small pool at his feet. The water ran down into his stomach and he felt better. When he looked up again he saw approaching, with a waving motion, a dark object which came on until just in front of him, when it stopped, and, standing on the ground, looked at him. This was a raven, and, as soon as it stopped, it raised one of its wings, pushed up its beak, like a mask, to the top of its head, and changed at once into a man. Before he raised his mask Raven had stared at the man, and after it was raised he stared more than ever, moving about from side to side to obtain a better view. At last he said: "What are you? Whence did you come? I have never seen anything like you." Then Raven looked at Man, and was still more surprised to find that this strange new being was so much like himself in shape.

Then he told Man to walk away a few steps, and in astonishment exclaimed again: "When did you come? I have never seen anything like you before." To this Man replied: "I came from the pea-pod." And he pointed to the plant from which he came. "Ah!" exclaimed Raven, "I made that vine, but did not know that anything like you would ever come from it. Come with me to the high ground over there; this ground I made later, and it is still soft and thin, but it is thicker and harder there."

In a short time they came to the higher land, which was firm under their feet. Then Raven asked Man if he had eaten anything. The latter answered that he had taken some soft stuff into him at one of the pools. "Ah!" said Raven, "you drank some water. Now wait for me here."

Then he drew down the mask over his face, changing again into a bird, and flew far up into the sky where he disappeared. Man waited where he had been left until the fourth day, when Raven returned, bringing four berries in his claws. Pushing up his mask, Raven became a man again and held out two salmonberries and two hearthberries, saying, "Here is what I have made for you to eat. I also wish them to be plentiful over the earth. Now eat them." Man took the berries and placed them in his mouth one after the other and they satisfied his hunger, which had made him feel uncomfortable. Raven then led Man to a small creek near by and left him while he went to the water's edge and molded a couple of pieces of clay into the form of a pair of mountain sheep, which he held in his hand, and when they became dry he called Man to show him what he had done. Man thought they were very pretty, and Raven told him to close his eyes. As soon as Man's eyes were closed Raven drew down his mask and waved his wings four times over the images, when they became endowed with life and bounded away as full-grown mountain sheep. Raven then raised his mask and told Man to look. When Man saw the sheep moving away, full of life, he cried out with pleasure. Seeing how pleased Man was, Raven said, "If these animals are numerous, perhaps people will wish very much to get them." And Man said he thought they would. "Well," said Raven, "it will be better for them to have their home among the high cliffs, so that every one can not kill them, and there only shall they be found."

Then Raven made two animals of clay which he endowed with life as before, but as they were dry only in spots when they were given life, they remained brown and white, and so originated the tame reindeer with mottled coat. Man thought these were very handsome, and Raven told him that they would be very scarce. In the same way a pair of wild reindeer were made and permitted to get dry and white only on their bellies, then they were given life; in consequence, to this day the belly of the wild reindeer is the only white part about it. Raven told Man that these animals would be very common, and people would kill many of them.

"You will be very lonely by yourself," said Raven. "I will make you a companion." He then went to a spot some distance from where he had made the animals, and looking now and then at Man, made an image very much like him. Then he fastened a lot of fine water grass on the back of the head for hair, and after the image had dried in his hands, he waved his wings over it as before and a beautiful young woman arose and stood beside Man. "There," cried Raven, "is a companion for you," and he led them back to a small knoll near by.

In those days there were no mountains far or near, and the sun never ceased shining brightly; no rain ever fell and no winds blew. When they came to the knoll, Raven showed the pair how to make a bed in the dry moss, and they slept there very warmly; Raven drew down his mask and slept near by in the form of a bird. Waking before the others, Raven went back to the creek and made a pair each of sticklebacks, graylings, and blackfish. When these were swimming about in the water, he called Man to see them. When the latter looked at them and saw the sticklebacks swim up the stream with a wriggling motion he was so surprised that he raised his hand suddenly and the fish darted away. Raven then showed him the graylings and told him that they would be found in clear mountain streams, while the sticklebacks would live along the seacoast and that both would be good for food. Next the shrew-mouse was made, Raven saying that it would not be good for food but would enliven the ground and prevent it from seeming barren and cheerless.

In this way Raven continued for several days making birds, fishes, and animals, showing them to Man, and explaining their uses. . . .

1899

A Navajo Evil-Chasing Chant

The Navajo, the largest contemporary American Indian population, have maintained their traditional beliefs and practices to a remarkable extent, considering that they were first contacted by European conquistadores in the sixteenth century. Central to Navajo beliefs are long, complex rituals, commonly referred to as chants. They combine prayer and song, along with the construction and use of ritually symbolic sand paintings within a traditional dwelling, the hogan, which has been ceremonially consecrated, as well as various ritual acts and objects. Each chant has a special relationship with certain supernatural beings, Holy People, whose participation is invoked by the correct performance of the rite. Most rituals can be performed in two, five, or nine nights. In *Language and Art in the Navajo Universe,* Gary Witherspoon notes:

> The primary purpose of Navajo ritual is to maintain or restore *hózhǫ́*. As discussed *hózhǫ́* is everything that is good, harmonious, orderly, happy, and beautiful. The opposite of *hózhǫ́* is *hóchxǫ'* which, of course, is the evil, the disorderly, and the ugly. Navajo rituals can be divided into three general kinds, depending on how they maintain, insure, or restore *hózhǫ́*. The first of these, the Blessingway rites *(Hózhǫ́ǫ́jí),* maintain and reinforce *hózhǫ́* by attracting and incorporating the goodness and power of benevolent Holy People. A second

general type of ritual, the Holyway rites *(Diyink'ehgo),* deals with Holy People who are potentially malevolent. These rites emphasize transformation; that is, transforming powers that are potentially malevolent and dangerous into benevolent powers. This is done by ritual control and compulsion, creating in the patient an immunity to the potential evil of the Holy Person thus controlled. A third general class of ritual, the Evilway rites *(Hóchxǫ'íjí),* emphasizes the exorcism of the evil powers of malevolent Holy People, thus eliminating *hóchxǫ'* and restoring *hózhǫ.*

"The Prayer of the First Night Male Shooting Chant Evil" is a ritual of this third type.

The prayer is central to a popular, living Navajo ritual, the shooting chant. This version was recorded sometime between 1930 and 1935 by Gladys Reichard from Miguelito (also known as Red Point). During the first night, the patient (who has previously gone through ritual purification) repeats this prayer, line by line, after the chanter, while holding symbolically significant offerings and seated on a buckskin on which a sand painting has been made. This repetition demands considerable concentration from both chanter and patient. "Although very long," Reichard notes, "it must be recited without error, repetition or hesitation, for only correct recitation compels the Holy People to participate, while mistakes may cause evil." Such prayers are transmitted and maintained entirely orally. Moreover, as Reichard notes, chanters learn prayers as wholes. "The teacher [recites] the prayer *in toto* and only in this form [can] the novice repeat it, never [can] he repeat, even to himself, parts on which his memory [is] weak."

Prayers are an important, formally distinct genre, characterized by elaborate formal structure and elliptical, highly contextual meanings, both among the Navajo and among most other Native American peoples. Navajo prayers have a well-developed "architecture." According to Reichard, they consist of "line and line-grouped repetitions" organized in three main parts: invocation, petition, and benediction. The more complex form consists of structured repetitions of these internally complex units. "The Prayer of the First Night Male Shooting Chant Evil" consists of five major units. Four consistently parallel units, each having an invocation, petition, and benediction and each addressed to a different Holy Person in a structured set of four (Holy Man, Holy Woman, Holy Boy, and Holy Girl), are followed by a fifth unit that provides a benediction for the whole prayer. The invocation includes the address to and description of the deity, including the reasons for the petition of the supernatural, while the petition consists, as Reichard notes, of "the lines which show what a patient wants" and the benediction "what he gets." As Reichard explains, all prayers "aim to identify the one-sung-over (the patient) with the supernaturals invoked. . . . Prayers to get a person out of danger . . . and those to deities most difficult of persuasion seem to have the greatest elaboration. They have the largest number of line repetitions and of great complicated clusters of such lines with precise modifications. . . . More effort is required to drive off evil than to attract good."

Further Reading:
F. J. Newcomb and G. A. Reichard,
Sandpaintings of the Navajo Shooting Chant, 1937,
1975.
G. A. Reichard, *Navajo Medicine Man:*
Sandpaintings and Legends of Miguelito, 1939.
G. A. Reichard, *Navajo Religion: A Study of*
Symbolism, 1950.
G. Witherspoon, *Language and Art in the Navajo*
Universe, 1977.
Handbook of North American Indians, gen. ed.
W. C. Sturtevant, vol. 10, *Southwest*, ed. A.
Ortiz, 1984.

Text:
G. A. Reichard, *Prayer: The Compulsive Word*,
1944.

---

from Prayer of the First Night Male Shooting Chant Evil

[Fourth Section]

At Rumbling Mountain,[1]
Holy Girl with the red-feathered arrow,
    This day I have become trustful
    This day I look to you
Rise up to protect me,   5
Stand before me to protect me,
With your strong feet rise up to protect me,
With your sturdy legs rise up to protect me,
With your strong body rise up to protect me,
With your healthy mind rise up to protect me,   10
With your powerful sound rise up to protect me,
With your fine head rise up to protect me,
You are the one who carries the dark bow with the red-feathered arrow,
    These you will carry before me to protect me,
    By means of these you have kept harm away from me.   15
    Thus in their shelter evil will pass me by.
    Thus in their shelter evil has passed me by.
    Thus in their shelter it has passed by.

---

[1] Navajo prayers and myths often contain ceremonial place names whose symbolism is an important part of the ritual. The collector of this text, Gladys A. Reichard, notes: "A satisfactory understanding of this geographical symbolism would involve exact knowledge of every rock and tree of the Navajo territory, a correlation of the numerous ceremonial names for each place, and an understanding of the mythological significance of each. This is not a mere matter of taking a chanter or two on a trip and getting his opinion of the terrain covered. No two agree about such matters since their perspective is based on ritual and each chanter's view is partially identified with his own locality."

Thus in their shelter it has passed by.
My mind being safe has been passed.   20
My mind being safe has been passed.
Ghost power of every kind with which I may be bothered,
    Surely this day to a point at the tips of my toes where it does not belong
      it moves out (in swelling fashion),
    From the tips of my body where it does not belong it moves out,
    From the tips of my fingers where it does not belong it moves out,   25
    From the tip of my speech where it does not belong it moves out.
Evil sorcery of every kind has gone away from me,
    To a point above it has gone
    Opposite it has gone
    To a place within it has gone.   30
Surely this day surviving you stand protecting me,
Surely this day surviving you stand protecting me,
    May you return protecting me.
As you are the ones at the very place where I tell you to be,
    May I be the one at the place where you tell me to be,   35
    May you be reciprocatingly dependable.
Surely this day invisible to the weapon of every kind of evil sorcery may I go
    about,
Surely this day you are the ones who put your feet down on it (cornmeal),
    So with it may I put my feet down.
Just as you are the ones who become evil,   40
    So may I become evil with it.
Just as you are the ones from whom evil is warned off with it,
    So may evil be warned away from me.
Just as evils swarm away from you because of it,
    So may evils swarm away from me.   45
The weapon of every kind of evil sorcery,
    From the tips of my toes where it does not belong may it move, I say.
    From the tips of my body where it does not belong may it move, I say.
    From the tips of my fingers where it does not belong may it move, I say.
    From the tip of my speech where it does not belong may it move, I say.   50
    Surely this day I shall be well again.
    Well I shall go about,
    Good health may I be,
    May my body be light,
    May my body be cool,   55
    May my feet be strong,
    May my legs be sturdy,
    May my body be whole,
    May my mind be clear,
    May my sound power be strong,   60
    May my head be dependable,
    May my gait be long,
    Surely this day happily I get up.

The weapon of every kind of evil sorcery,
 Away from me it has gone   65
 To a point above it has gone
 Opposite it has gone
 To the inside it has gone.
Evil power which has been mentioned, evil intention which has been
 mentioned,
 All have returned to normal.   70
 All have returned to normal.
Surely this day happily I go about, I say.
 May it be beautiful before me,
 May it be beautiful behind me,
 May it be beautiful under me,   75
 May it be beautiful above me,
 May all be beautiful around me,
 May my speech be controlled,
 Restoration-to-youth According-to-beauty I have become, I say.
 May all these things be so.   80

1944

An Onondaga Iroquois Creation Myth

"The Manner in Which It Established Itself" is an outstanding example of the long, richly complex performances characteristic of Iroquois myths in particular and Native American myths in general. Although myths are frequently said to take place in a time long before the present, the narrative action is usually associated with the known ethnographic details of the community in which it is told. Accordingly, in the Onondaga Iroquois creation myth printed here, the man-beings who dwell in the sky do so in long houses similar to the ones the Iroquois had traditionally lived in. The *Handbook of North American Indians* notes that these long houses had doors at either end and a raised platform running the length of each long wall. These platforms were divided by partitions into enclosed sleeping and seating areas for each nuclear family, with a fire shared by two facing enclosures in the walkway between. Presumably, too, an Iroquois audience would assume that such a house would be the residence of an extended family related matrilineally. The secluded ("down-fended") man and woman would thereby be expected to be members of the same matrilineage and not be available to each other as sexual partners.

 The version of the myth printed here was told in Onondaga in 1889 to the Tuscarora scholar John Naploeon Hewitt by John Buck, chief and fire-keeper of the League of the Iroquois. According to Hewitt, this creation myth was told in "the language of tradition and ceremony, which is formal, sometimes quaint, sometimes archaic, frequently mystical and largely metaphorical. But the figures of speech are made concrete by the elementary thought of the Iroquois, and the metaphor is regarded as fact." As Hewitt's observation suggests, although a myth is colloquially understood as something that is not true, these Native American narratives have the force of truth for those who tell and listen to them.

Further Reading:
Handbook of North American Indians, gen. ed.
W. C. Sturtevant, vol. 15, *Northeast,* ed. B. G.
Trigger, 1978.
F. Jennings, *The Ambiguous Iroquois Empire,*
1984.

Text:
Iroquoian Cosmology, Part 1, 21st Annual Report,
Bureau of American Ethnology, 1899–1900, ed. J.
N. Hewitt, 1903.

---

from The Manner in Which It Established Itself[*]

He who was my grandfather was wont to relate that, verily, he had heard the legend as it was customarily[1] told by five generations of grandsires, and this is what he himself was in the habit of telling. He customarily said: Man-beings[2] dwell in the sky, on the farther side of the visible sky [the ground separating this from the world above it].[3] The lodges they severally possess are customarily long. In the end of the lodges there are spread out strips of rough bark whereon lie the several mats (beds). There it is that, verily, all pass the night.

Early in the morning the warriors are in the habit of going to hunt and, as is their custom, they return every evening.

In that place there lived two persons, both down-fended,[4] and both persons of worth. Verily, one of these persons was a woman-being, a person of worth, and

---

[*] The full title of the myth is "The Manner in Which It Established Itself, in Which It Formed Itself, in Which, in Ancient Time, It Came About That the Earth Became Extant."

[1] The collector of this myth, John Napoleon Brinton Hewitt, here and following translates an Onondaga particle indicating that the action or state referred to occurred habitually.

[2] Hewitt's note: "The Iroquois term 'oñgwe'' . . . has both a singular and a collective denotation. It signifies 'mankind, man, human beings; a human being, a person.' But its original meaning was 'man-being' or 'primal being,' which signified collectively those beings who preceded man in existence and exceeded him in wisdom and effective power, the personified bodies and elements of nature, the gods and demi-gods of later myth and legend. . . . In this legend, when applied to times previous to the advent of man the word 'oñgwe'' usually denotes a man-being that is a

personification, one of the gods of the myths, one of that vague class of primal beings of which man was regarded by Iroquoian and other sages as a characteristic type."

[3] Bracketed and parenthetical insertions are Hewitt's clarifications.

[4] "Down-fended," secluded, an English term invented by Hewitt to translate the original Iroquoian word to reflect an Iroquoian custom: "Certain children should be strictly hidden from the sight of all persons save a trustee until they reached the age of puberty. The better to guard the ward from access the down of the cat-tail flag was carefully scattered about the place of concealment, so that no person could pass the forbidden place without first disturbing the down and so indicating invasion of the guarded precinct. . . . Persons so hidden were regarded as uncanny and endowed with an unusual measure of orenda, or magic potence."

down-fended; besides her there was a man-being, a person of worth, and down-fended.

In the end of the lodge there was a doorway. On the one side of it the woman-being abode, and on the other side of it the man-being abode.

Sometime afterward, then, this came to pass. As soon as all the man-beings had severally departed this woman-being came forth and went thither and, moreover, arrived at the place where the man-being abode, and she carried a comb with her. She said: "Do thou arise; let me disentangle thy hair." Now, verily, he arose, and then, moreover, she disentangled his hair, and straightened it out. It continued in this manner day after day.

Sometime afterward her kindred were surprised. It seems that the life of the maiden was now changed. Day after day it became more and more manifest that now she would give birth to a child. Now, moreover, her mother, the ancient one, became aware of it. Then, verily, she questioned her, saying to the maiden: "Moreover, what manner of person is to be joint parent with thee?" The maiden said nothing in reply. So, now, at that time, the man-being noticed that he began to be ill. For some time it continued thus, when, verily, his mother came to the place where he lay. She said: "Where is the place wherein thou art ill?" Then the man-being said in reply: "Oh, my mother! I will now tell thee that I, alas, am about to die." And his mother replied, saying: "What manner of thing is meant by thy saying 'I shall die?'"

It is said that they who dwelt there did not know what it is for one to say "I shall die." And the reason of it was that no one living there on the sky had ever theretofore died. At that time he said: "And, verily, this will come to pass when I die: My life will go forth. Moreover, my body will become cold. Oh, my mother! thus shalt thou do on my eyes: Thou must lay both thy hands on both sides. And, moreover, thou must keep thy eyes fixed thereon when thou thinkest that now he is [I am] nearly dead. So soon as thou seest that my breathing is being made to become less, then, and not till then, must thou think that now it is that he is about to die. And then, moreover, thou wilt place thy two hands on both my eyes. Now, I shall tell thee another thing. Ye must make a burial-case. When ye finish the task of making it, then, moreover, ye must place my body therein, and, moreover, ye must lay it up in a high place."

Now, verily, she, the ancient one, had her eyes fixed on him. So soon as she believed that now he was about to die, she placed both her hands on his eyes. Just so soon as she did this she began to weep. Moreover, all those who abode in the lodge were also affected in the same way; they all wept. Sometime after he had died they set themselves to work, making a burial-case. Moreover, so soon as they had finished their task they placed his body therein, and also laid it up in a high place.

Sometime after they had laid the burial-case in the high place, the maiden, now a woman-being, gave birth to a child, which was a female, a woman-being. Then the ancient one [elder one, the mother of the maiden] said: "Moreover, what manner of person is the father of the child?" The maiden said nothing in reply.

The girl child grew rapidly in size. It was not long after this that the girl child was running about. Suddenly, it seems, the girl child began to weep. It was impossible to stop her. Five are the number of days, it is said, that the girl child continued to weep. Then the elder one [her grandmother] said: "Do ye show her the burial-case lying there in the high place." Now, verily, they carried her person, and caused her to stand up high there. Then the girl child looked at it [the corpse], and then she ceased her weeping, and also she was pleased. It was a long time before they withdrew her; and it was not a long time before she again began to weep. Now, verily, they again carried her person, and, moreover, they caused her to stand there again. So, it continued thus, that, day after day, they were in the habit of carrying her, and causing her to stand there on the high place. It was not long before she by her own efforts was able to climb up to the place where lay the dead man-being. Thus it continued to be that she at all times went to view it.

Some time afterward it thus came to pass that she came down again bringing with her what was called an armlet, that being the kind of thing that the dead man-being had clasped about his arms, and, being of the wampum variety, it was, it is said, fine-looking. The elder one said: "What manner of thing caused thee to remove it?" The girl child replied, saying: "My father said: 'Do thou remove it. It will belong to thee. I, verily, am thy parent.'" The elder one said nothing more. It continued thus that customarily, as soon as another day came, she would again climb to the place where the burial-case lay. So, now, verily, all those who were in the lodge paid no more attention to her, merely watching her grow in size. Thus it continued that day after day, at all times, she continued to go to see it [the corpse]. They heard them conversing, it is said, and they also heard, it is told, what the two said. After a while she again came down bringing with her a necklace which the dead man-being had had around his neck, and which she had removed. She, it is reported, said: "Oh, my grandmother! My father gave this to me; that is the reason I removed it." So, it is reported, until the time she was full-grown, she was in the habit of going to view the place where lay the burial-case.

At that time, it is reported, her father said: "Now, my child, verily, thou hast grown to maturity. Moreover, I will decide upon the time when thou shalt marry." Some time afterward he said: "Thou must tell thy mother, saying: 'My father said to me, "Now thou must marry."'" Now, moreover, verily, thy mother must make loaves of bread, and it must fill a large forehead-strap-borne basket. Now, moreover, thou must make the bread, and thou must have it ready by the time it becomes night."

Truly, it thus came to pass. It became night, and, verily, the elder one had it all ready. She said: "I have now made it ready. The basket is even now full of bread." Now, the maiden again climbed up to the place where lay the burial-case. At that time they heard her say: "My mother has now made everything ready." He then replied: "To-morrow thou must depart; early in the morning thou must depart. The distance from here to the place where lives the one whom thou wilt marry is such that thou wilt spend one night on thy way thither. And he is a chief whom thou art to marry, and his name, by repute, is He-holds-the-earth."

Now the next day she dressed herself. As soon as she was ready she then again ran, going again to the place where lay the dead man-being. Then she told him, saying: "The time for me to depart has arrived." Now, at that time he told her, saying: "Do thou have courage. Thy pathway throughout its course is terrifying, and the reason that it is so is that many man-beings are traveling to and fro along this pathway. Do not, moreover, speak in reply if some person, whoever he may be, addresses words to thee. And when thou hast gone one half of thy journey, thou wilt come to a river there, and, moreover, the floating log whereon persons cross is maple. When thou dost arrive there, then thou wilt know that thou art half-way on thy journey. Then thou wilt cross the river, and also pass on. Thou must continue to travel without interruption. And thou wilt have traveled some time before thou arrivest at the place where thou wilt see a large field. Thou wilt see there, moreover, a lodge standing not far away. And there beside the lodge stands the tree that is called Tooth. Moreover, the blossoms this standing tree bears cause that world to be light, making it light for the man-beings dwelling there."

"Such, in kind, is the tree that stands beside the lodge. Just there is the lodge of the chief whom thou art to marry, and whom his people call He-holds-the-earth. When thou enterest the lodge, thou wilt look and see there in the middle of the lodge a mat spread, and there, on the mat, the chief lying down. Now, at that time, thou shalt lay thy basket down at his feet, and, moreover, thou shalt say: 'Thou and I marry.' He will say nothing. When it becomes night, he who is lying down will spread for thee a skin robe at the foot of his mat. There thou wilt stay over night. As soon as it is day again, he will say: 'Do thou arise; do thou work. Customarily one who lives in the lodge of her spouse works.' Then, verily, thou must work. He will lay down a string of corn ears and, moreover, he will say: 'Thou must soak the corn and thou must make mush.' At that time there will be a kettle of water set on the fire. As soon as it boils so that it is terrifying, thou must dissolve the meal therein. It must be boiling when thou makest the mush. He himself will speak, saying: 'Do you undress thyself.' Moreover, thou must there undress thyself. Thou must be in thy bare skin. Nowhere wilt thou have any garment on thy body. Now, the mush will be boiling, and the mush will be hot. Verily, on thy body will fall in places the spattering mush. He will say: 'Thou must not shrink back from it;' moreover, he will have his eyes fixed on thee there. Do not shrink back from it. So soon as it is cooked, thou shalt speak, saying: 'Now, verily, it is cooked; the mush is done.' He will arise, and, moreover, he will remove the kettle, and set it aside. Then, he will say: 'Do thou seat thyself on this side.' Now then, he will say: 'My slaves, ye dogs, do ye two come hither.' They two are very large. As soon as they two arrive he will say: 'Do ye two lick her body where the mush has fallen on it.' And their tongues are like rough bark. They will lick thee, going over thy whole body, all along thy body. Blood will drop from the places where they will lick. Do not allow thy body to flinch therefrom. As soon as they two finish this task he will say: 'Now, do thou again put on thy raiment.' Now, moreover, thou must again dress thyself completely. At that time he will take the basket and set it down, saying, moreover: 'Now, thou and I marry.' So now, so far as they are concerned, the dogs, his slaves, they two will eat." That is what the dead man-being told her.

It became night. Now, at that time, they verily laid their bodies down, and they slept. It became day, and the sun was present yonder when the maiden departed. She bore on her back by the forehead strap her basket of bread. Now, verily, she traveled with a rapid gait. It was not long before she was surprised to find a river. There beside the river she stood, thinking, verily, "I have lost my way." At that time she started back. Not long afterward those who abode in the home lodge were surprised that the maiden was returned. She said: "I believe I have lost my way." Now she laid her basket on the mat, and, moreover, she again ran thither and again climbed up to the place where lay the burial-case. So soon as she reached it she said: "Oh, father! I believe that I lost my way." He said: "What is the character of the land where thou believest that thou lost thy way?" "Where people habitually cross the river, then I returned," said the maiden. She told him everything. She said: "A maple log floats at the place where they habitually cross the river." He said: "Thou hast not lost thy way." She replied: "I think the distance to the place where the river is seems too short, and that is the reason that I think that I lost my way." At that time he said: "The place that I had indicated is far. But thy person is so endowed with magic potence, thou hast immanent in thee so much orenda[5] that it causes thy pace to be swift. Verily, so soon as thou arrivest at the river, thou shalt cross it and also shalt pass on." At that time the maiden said: "Oh, my father, now I depart." "So be it. Moreover, do thou take courage," said the dead man-being in reply. Now she again descended and again went into the lodge.

There then she placed her basket of bread on her back by means of the forehead strap. It was early in the morning when she departed. She had been traveling some time when she was surprised to hear a man-being speak to her, saying: "Do thou stand, verily." She did not stop. Aurora Borealis[6] it was who was talking. She had passed on some distance when she heard another man-being talking to her, saying: "I am thankful that thou hast now again returned home, my child. I am hungry, desiring to eat food." She did not stop. It was Fire Dragon of the Storm who was speaking to her. Sometime after she was again at the place where people customarily crossed the river. Now, at that place, he, the chief himself, stood, desiring to try her mind, saying: "Verily, thou shouldst stop here; verily, thou shouldst rest thyself." She did not stop. She only kept right on, and, moreover, she at once crossed the river there.

She traveled on for some time, and when the sun was at yonder height she was surprised that there was spread out there a large field. At that time, verily, she stopped beside the field. Now she looked, and there in the distance she saw a lodge—the lodge of the chief. Verily, she went thither. When she arrived there, she looked, and saw that it was true that beside the lodge stood the tree Tooth, whose flowers were the source of the light of the earth there present, and also of the man-beings dwelling there. Verily, she then entered the lodge. Then she looked, and saw that in the middle of the lodge a mat was spread, and that thereon, moreover, lay the chief. Now, at that time, she removed her pack-strap burden, and then she also set the basket before him, and then, moreover, she said: "Thou and I marry," and then, moreover, she handed the basket to him. He said nothing. When it became night, he spread a mat for her at the foot of his mat, and then, moreover, he said: "Verily, here thou wilt stay overnight." Moreover, it thus came to pass. Now, verily, they laid their bodies down and they slept.

When day came to them, the chief then said: "Do thou arise. Do thou work, moreover. It is customary for one to work who is living in the family of her spouse. Thou must soak corn. Thou must set a pot on the fire. And when it boils, then thou must put the corn therein. Moreover, when it boils, then thou must again remove the pot, and thou must wash the corn. As soon as thou finishest the task thou must then, moreover, pound it so that it will become meal. Now, moreover, thou must make mush. And during the time that it is boiling thou must continue to stir it; thou must do so without interruption after thou hast begun it. Moreover, do not allow thy body

---

[5] The word in the Onondaga original, *disaeñnoñ 'de'*, literally means "so thou art magical." This is a hypothetical Iroquoian term reconstructed by Hewitt from words meaning song, dance, power, and poison in the Iroquois language.
[6] The northern lights.

to shrink back when the mush spatters. That, moreover, will come to pass. Thou must undress thyself when thou workest. I, as to the rest, will say: 'Now it is cooked.' "

At that time he laid down there a string of corn earns, and the corn was white. So now, verily, she began her work. She undressed herself, and now, verily, she was naked. She soaked the corn, and she also washed the corn, and also pounded it, and she also made meal of it, and, now, moreover, in the pot she had set on the fire she made mush. She stirred it without interruption. But, nevertheless, it was so that she was suffering, for, verily, now there was nothing anywhere on her body. And now, moreover, it was evident that it was hot, as the mush spattered repeatedly. Some time after she was surprised that the chief said: "Now, verily, the mush which thou art making is cooked." At that time he arose to a standing position, and also removed the pot, and also set it on yonder side. At that time he said: "Do thou sit here." Now he went forward, and, taking up the basket, he took the bread therefrom, out of her basket. At that time he said: "Now, thou and I marry. Verily, so it seems, thou wert able to do it. Hitherto, no one from anywhere has been able to do it."

Now, at that time he shouted, saying: "My slaves, ye two dogs, do ye two come hither. It is necessary for me that ye two should lick this person abiding here clean of the mush that has fallen on her." Verily, she now looked and saw come forth two dogs, pure white in color and terrifying in size. So now, they two arrived at the place where she was. Now, verily, they two licked her entire body. The tongues of these two were like rough bark. So now, moreover, in whatsoever places they two licked over and along her body blood exuded therefrom. And the maiden did fortify her mind against it, and so she did not flinch from it. As soon as they two completed the task, then he himself took up sunflower oil, and with that, moreover, he anointed her body. As soon as he had finished this task he said: "Now, verily, do thou again dress thyself." Now she redressed herself entirely, and she was again clothed with raiment.

When it became night, he spread a mat for her at the foot of his mat. There they two passed two more nights. And the third day that came to them the chief said to her: "Now thou must again depart. Thou must go again to the place whence thou didst start." Then he took up the basket of the maiden and went then to the place where he kept meat of all kinds hanging in quarters. Now, verily, he took up the dried meat of the spotted fawn and put it into her basket. All the various kinds of meat he placed therein. As soon as the basket was full, he shook the basket to cause its contents to settle down. When he did shake it, there was seemingly just a little room left in it. Seven times, it is said, he shook the basket before he completely filled it. At that time he said: "Now thou must again depart. Do not, moreover, stand anywhere in the course of thy path homeward. And, moreover, when thou dost arrive there, thou must tell the people dwelling there that they, one and all, must remove the roofs from their several lodges. By and by it will become night and I will send that which is called corn. In so far as that thing is concerned, that is what man-beings will next in time live upon. This kind of thing will continue to be in existence for all time." At that time he took up the basket and also said: "Now, verily, thou shouldst bear it on thy back by means of the forehead strap." Now, at that time she departed.

Now again, as she traveled, she heard a man-being talking, saying: "Come, do thou stand." She did not stand. It was Aurora Borealis who was talking to her. She traveled on for some time, when she again heard a man-being talking, saying: "Verily, do thou stand. Now, verily, thou hast returned home. I am hungry. My child, I desire to eat food." She did not stop. In so far as he is concerned, it was White Fire Dragon who was talking to her. Now, she again arrived where she had crossed the river, and there again, beside the river, she stood. Now, moreover, she heard again a man-being saying: "Do thou stand. I desire that thou and I should converse together." She did not stop. It was the chief who was standing here seeking to tempt her mind. At once she crossed the river on the floating maple log. It was just midday when she again arrived at the place whence she departed, and she went directly into the lodge. As soon as she laid her burden down, she said: "Oh, my mother, now, hither I have returned." She, the elder one, spoke, saying: "I am thankful that thou hast arrived in peace." Then the maiden again spoke and said: "Ye severally must make preparations by severally removing the roofs from your lodges. There is an abundance of meat and corn also coming, as animals do come, when it becomes night, by and by." And at that time she at once went to the place where lay the burial-case of her dead father, and now, moreover, she again climbed up there. As soon as she reached the place, she said: "Oh, my father, I have now returned home." He said, in replying: "How fared it? Was he willing to do it?" She said: "He was willing." Now, again, he spoke, saying: "I am thankful that thou wast able to do it, as it seems. Thou art fortunate in this matter. And it seems, moreover, good, that thou shouldst, perhaps, at once return home, for the reason, verily, that the chief is immune to magic potence, that nothing can affect the orenda of Chief-who-has-the-standing-tree-called-Tooth, and whom some call He-holds-the-earth."

At that time all those who dwelt there undid their lodges by removing the roofs from all severally. Then, verily, when it became night, as soon as the darkness became settled, they heard the sounds made by the raining of corn, which fell in the lodges. Then they went to sleep. When it became day, they looked and saw that in the lodges corn lay piled up, quite filling them. Now, moreover, their chief said: "Do ye severally repair your lodges. And, moreover, ye must care for it and greatly esteem it; the thing has visited our village which He-who-has-the-standing-tree-called-Tooth has given you to share with him."

In a short time they were surprised, seemingly, that the maiden was nowhere to be found. She had again departed. They knew that she had again gone to the place where stood the lodge of the chief who was her consort. Now, verily, in reference to him he himself in turn was surprised to see her return home. When it became day again, the chief noticed that seemingly it appeared that the life of the maiden, his spouse, had changed. Thus it was that, day after day and night after night, he still considered the matter. The conditions were such that he did not know what thing was the cause that it [his spouse's condition] was thus, so he merely marveled that it had thus come to pass.

It is certain, it is said, that it formed itself there where they two conversed, where they two breathed together; that, verily, his breath is what the maiden caught, and it is that which was the cause of the change in the life of the maiden. And, moreover, that is the child to which she gave birth. And since then, from the time that he [her spouse] let man-beings go here on the earth, the manner in which man-beings are paired has transformed itself. This is the manner in which it will continue to be; this will be its manner of being done, whereby it will be possible for the man-beings dwelling on the earth to produce ohwachiras of posterity. Thus, too, it seems, it came to pass in regard to the beast-world, their bodies all shared in the change of the manner in which they would be able to produce ohwachiras of offspring here on the earth.

Thus it was that, without interruption, it became more and more evident that the maiden would give birth to a child. At that time the chief became convinced of it, and he said: "What is the matter that thy life has changed? Verily, thou art about to have a child. Never, moreover, have thou and I shared the same mat. I believe that it is not I who is the cause that thy life has changed. Dost thou thyself know who it is?" She did not understand the meaning of what he said.

Now, at that time, the chief began to be ill. Suddenly, it seems, she herself now became aware that her life had changed. Then she said, addressing the chief: "I believe that there is, perhaps, something the matter, as my life at the present time is not at all pleasant." He did not make any reply. Not long thereafter she again said: "My thoughts are not at all pleasant." Again he said nothing. So it continued thus that she did nothing but consider the matter, believing that something must be the matter, perhaps, that the condition of her body was such as it was. It became more and more evident that she was pregnant. Now it was evident that she was big with child.

Sometime afterward she again resolved to ask him still once more. She said: "As a matter of fact, there must be something the matter, perhaps, that my body is in this condition. And the thoughts of my mind are not at all pleasant. One would think that there can be no doubt that, seemingly, something is about to happen, because my life is so exceedingly unpleasant." Again he said nothing. When it became night, then, verily, they laid their bodies down and they slept. So now, verily, he there repeatedly considered the matter. Now, in so far as the maiden was concerned, she still did not understand what was about to take place from the changed condition of her body. Sometime afterward the chief spoke to her, saying: "As a matter of fact, a man-being (or rather woman-being) will arrive, and she is a man-being child, and thou must care for her. She will grow in size rapidly, and her name is Zephyrs."[7] The maiden said nothing, for the reason that she did not understand what her spouse told her. Not long afterward, then, verily, she gave birth to a child. She paid no attention to it. The only thing she did was to lay it on the place where the chief customarily passed the night. After ten days' time she again took it up therefrom.

Sometime afterward the chief became aware that he began to be ill. His suffering became more and more severe. All the persons dwelling in the village came to visit him. There he lay, and sang, saying: "Ye must pull up this standing tree that is called Tooth. The earth will be torn open, and there beside the abyss ye must lay me down. And moreover, there where my head lies, there must sit my spouse." That is what he, the Ancient One, sang. Then the man-beings dwelling there became aware that their chief was ill.

Now, verily, all came to visit him. They questioned him repeatedly, seeking to divine his Word, what thing, seemingly, was needful for him, what kind of thing, seemingly, he expected through a dream. Thus, day after day, it continued that they sought to find his Word. After a time the female man-being child was of fair size. She was then able to run about from place to place. But it thus continued that they kept on seeking to divine his Word. After a while, seemingly, one of the persons succeeded in finding his Word, and he said: "Now, perhaps, I myself have divined

[7] Hewitt's note: "This name Zephyrs merely approximates the meaning of the original, which signifies the warm springtide zephyrs that sometimes take the form of small whirlwinds or eddies of warm air."

the Word of him, the ordure, our chief." He who is called Aurora Borealis said this. And when he told the chief what manner of thing his soul craved, the chief was very pleased. And when he divined his Word, he said: "Is it not this that thy dream is saying, namely, that it is direful, if it so be that no person should divine thy Word, and that it will become still more direful? And yet, moreover, it is not certain that this is what thy soul craves; that its eyes may have seen thy standing tree, Tooth as to kind, pulled up, in order that the earth be torn open, and that there be an abyss that pierces the earth, and, moreover, that there beside the abyss one shall lay there, and at thy head thy spouse shall be seated with her legs hanging down into the abyss." At that time the chief said: "Ku".[8] I am thankful! Now, verily, the whole matter has been fulfilled by thy divining my Word."

During this time [the duration of the dream feast], a large body of man-beings,[9] paid a visit there. He, the Deer, paid a visit there. He, the Great-horned Deer [the Buck], paid a visit there. He, the Spotted Fawn, paid a visit, and was there seeking to divine the Word of the chief. He, the Bear, also paid a visit. Now, he also, the Beaver, paid a visit. And he, the Wind-who-moves-about-from-place-to-place, paid a visit also. And now, also, he, the Daylight, paid a visit. Now she also, the Night, the Thick Night, paid a visit. Now also she, the Star, paid a visit. Now, also, he, the Light-orb [the sun] paid a visit. And, too, the Water-of-springs, she paid a visit. Now, also, she, the Corn, paid a visit. Now, also, she, the Bean, paid a visit. Now, also, she, the Squash, paid a visit. Now, also, she, the Sunflower, paid a visit. Now, also, the Fire Dragon with the body of pure white color, he paid a visit. Now, also, the Rattle paid a visit. Now, also, he, the Red Meteor, paid a visit. Now, also, he, the Spring Wind, paid a visit. Now, also, he, the Great Turtle, paid a visit. Now, also, he, the Otter, paid a visit. Now, also, he, the Wolf, paid a visit. Now also, he, the Duck, paid a visit. Now, also, he, the Fresh Water, paid a visit. Now, also, he, the Yellowhammer, paid a visit. Now, also, he, the Medicine, paid a visit. Moreover, all things that are produced by themselves, that produce themselves, that is, the animals, and, next to them, the small animals, the flying things, of every species, all paid a visit. Now, sometime afterward, he, the Aurora Borealis, paid a visit. And, verily, he it was who divined the Word of the chief. Verily, he said: "The great standing tree, the Tooth, must be uprooted. And wherever it has a root there severally they must stand, and they must severally lay hold of each several root. And just then, and not before, shall they be able to uproot the standing tree. The earth will be torn open. Moreover, all persons must look therein. And there, beside the abyss, they must lay there. Now, moreover, there at thy head she with whom thou dost abide must sit with her legs hanging down into the abyss." Then, verily, the chief replied, saying: "Ku". I am thankful that ye have divined my word. Now all things have been fulfilled."

Verily, it did thus come to pass that they did uproot the standing tree, Tooth, that grew beside the lodge of the chief. And all the inhabitants of that place came thither with the intention of looking into the abyss. It did thus come to pass that everyone that dwelt there did look therein. At that time the chief then said, addressing his

[8] Hewitt's note: "Exclamation expressing gratification at having one's dream or vision divined and satisfied."
[9] Hewitt's note: "The relator of this version stated that there was a reputed connection between the visits of these different personages and the presence of their kinds in the new world beneath the sky land, but he had forgotten it."

spouse: "Now, too, let us two look into the abyss. Thou must bear her, Zephyrs, on thy back. Thou must wrap thyself with care." Now, moreover, he gave to her three ears of corn, and, next in order, the dried meat of the spotted fawn, and now, moreover, he said: "This ye two will have for provision." Now he also broke off three fagots of wood, which, moreover, he gave to her. She put them into her bosom, under her garments. Then, verily, they went thither to the place. They arrived at the spot where the earth was torn up, and then he said: "Do thou sit here." There, verily, she sat where the earth was broken off. There she hung both legs severally into the abyss. Now, in so far as he was concerned, he, the chief, was looking into the abyss, and there his spouse sat. Now, at that time he upraised himself, and said: "Do thou look hence into the abyss." Then she did in this manner, holding with her teeth her robe with its burden. Moreover, there along the edge of the abyss she seized with her hands, and, now, moreover, she bent over to look. He said: "Do thou bend much and plainly over." So she did do thus. As soon as she bent forward very much he seized the nape of her neck and pushed her into the abyss. Verily, now at that time she fell down thence. Now, verily, the man-being child and the man-being mother of it became one again. When she arrived on earth, the child was again born. At that time the chief himself arose and said, moreover: "Now, verily, I have become myself again; I am well again. Now, moreover, do ye again set up the tree."

And the chief was jealous, and that was the cause that he became ill. He was jealous of Aurora Borealis, and, in the next place, of the Fire Dragon with the pure white body. This latter gave him much mental trouble during the time that he, the chief, whom some call He-holds-the-earth, was married. . . .

1903

Native American Oral Poetry

The following two transcriptions of what were originally oral poems date back to the earliest years of contact between the Mayan people and the Spanish conquistadores. The Maya are natives of Central America; the majority settled in what is now the Yucatán, Guatemala, and western Honduras. They were able to maintain many aspects of their indigenous culture despite being forced to adapt to the influence of their conquerors. Soon after the Spanish conquest, for example, many Maya learned to translate their language into Spanish. They then proceeded to record Mayan history and culture in what quickly became the venerated Book of Chilam Balam of Chumayel, from which "The Beginning of Sickness" and "They Came from the East" are drawn.

"The Beginning of Sickness" uses the traditional repetition of Native American oral literature to contrast life before the arrival of the Spanish with the consequences of the conquistadores' presence in the New World. "They Came from the East" uses the same poetic device to express the Mayan willingness to accept the Christian conception of Dios (God) but not the persecution and deceit that accompanied such "conversion."

Further Reading:
The Book of Chilam Balam of Chumayel, trans.
R. Roys, 1933.
R. S. Chamberlain, *The Conquest and
Colonization of Yucatán*, 1949, 1966.
G. S. Morley, *Ancient Maya*, 1957.
J. Bierhorst, *In the Trail of the Wind*, 1971.

Text:
The Book of Chilam Balam of Chumayel, trans.
R. Roys, 1933.

The Beginning of Sickness

Then they adhered to their reason.
There was no sin;
in the holy faith[1] their lives were passed.
There was then no sickness;
they had then no aching bones;   5
they had then no high fever;
they had then no smallpox;
they had then no burning chest;
they had then no abdominal pains;
they had then no consumption;   10
they had then no headache.
At that time the course of humanity was orderly.
The foreigners made it otherwise when they arrived here.
They brought shameful things when they came . . .
this was the cause of our sickness also.   15
There were no more lucky days for us;
we had no sound judgment.
At the end of our loss of vision,
and of our shame,[2]
everything shall be revealed.   20

1933

---

[1] Retrospective reference to the Christian-like
virtue exhibited in pre-Columbian days.

[2] The excesses the Indians committed against their
own people.

They Came from the East

They came from the east when they arrived.
Then Christianity also began.
The fulfillment of its prophecy is ascribed to the east . . .
Then with the true God, the true *Dios,*
came the beginning of our misery. 5
It was the beginning of tribute,
the beginning of church dues,
the beginning of strife with purse-snatching,
the beginning of strife with blow-guns; 10
the beginning of strife by trampling on people,
the beginning of robbery with violence,
the beginning of forced debts,
the beginning of debts enforced by false testimony,
the beginning of individual strife, 15
a beginning of vexation.

1933

Powhatan
d. 1618

The early contacts between Native Americans and Europeans on the America's
East Coast duplicated the pattern on the West Coast—mistrust, violence, and
dispersion. The Algonquian Confederacy stretched across tidewater Virginia from
the Potomac River south to Albermarle Sound. For many years the leader of this
confederacy was Powhatan, also known as Wahunsonacock. Late in 1608 the
English colonists (including Captain John Smith) reluctantly followed the
instructions of the Virginia royal council in England and offered to crown
Powhatan a subject-king under James I as a gesture of recognition, friendship, and
peace. Powhatan insisted that the English come to his village at Weremoco (now
Gloucester County, Virginia), where he accepted a copper crown and gifts of a
woolen robe and an English bedstead. Powhatan's refusal to bow to the king of
England and his reciprocal gifts—his shoes and cloak—angered the English. This
awkward exchange began a period of strained relations between the colonists and
the Algonquians.

Captain John Smith made frequent trips up the Chicahominy River in the
Virginia colony to trade for Algonquian corn. On one of these expeditions,
Smith's party was attacked and captured by the Algonquians and taken to
Weremoco on the York River, where Powhatan delivered some version of the
speech printed here, transcribed by Smith. In it, Powhatan rebukes Smith and his

retinue for wishing "to conquer more than to trade" and for their excesses in dealing with the Native Americans.

There is, however, no compelling evidence to verify that John Smith spoke Powhatan's language or that Powhatan spoke English. In fact, it is highly unlikely that any individual would have been fluent in both languages at this point in Virginia's history. While the basis for Smith's transcription remains uncertain, Powhatan's speech might well represent Smith's best estimate of what Powhatan had said—or of what he hoped he had said.

A fragile peace between the English and the Algonquians was maintained for several years, mostly through the marriage of Powhatan's daughter, Pocahontas, to the Englishman John Rolfe. But by the mid-seventeenth century the British and the Indian tribes that had converted to Christianity defeated and disbanded the Algonquian Confederacy in a series of bloody encounters. The Algonquians are now extinct.

Further Reading:
G. Sagard, *The Long Journey to the Country of the Hurons*, 1632, ed. G. M. Wrong, 1939.
S. Smith, *Powhatan: A Metrical Romance*, 1841.
N. B. Wood, *Lives of Famous Indian Chiefs*, 1906.
R. W. Andrews, *Indian Leaders Who Helped Shape America*, 1971.
C. Feest, "Virginia Algonquians," in *Handbook of North American Indians*, gen. ed. W. C. Sturtevant, vol. 15, ed. B. G. Trigger, 1978.

Text:
S. G. Drake, *Biography and History of the Indians of North America*, 1841.

Letter to Captain John Smith

I am now grown old, and must soon die; and the succession must descend, in order, to my brothers, *Opitchapan, Opekankanough,* and *Catataugh,* and then to my two sisters, and their two daughters. I wish their experience was equal to mine; and that your love to us might not be less than ours to you. Why should you take by force that from us which you can have by love? Why should you destroy us, who have provided you with food? What can you get by war? We can hide our provisions, and fly into the woods; and then you must consequently famish by wronging your friends. What is the cause of your jealousy? You see us unarmed, and willing to supply your wants, if you will come in a friendly manner, and not with swords and guns, as to invade an enemy. I am not so simple, as not to know it is better to eat good meat, lie well, and sleep quietly with my women and children; to laugh and be merry with the English; and, being their friend, to have copper, hatchets, and whatever else I want, than to fly from all, to lie cold in the woods, feed upon acorns, roots, and such trash, and to be so hunted, that I cannot rest, eat, or sleep. In such circumstances, my men must watch, and if a twig should but break, all would cry out, "*Here comes*

Capt. Smith"; and so, in this miserable manner, to end my miserable life; and, Capt. Smith, this *might* be soon your fate too, through your rashness and unadvisedness. I, therefore, exhort you to peaceable councils; and, above all, I insist that the guns and swords, the cause of all our jealousy and uneasiness, be removed and sent away.

ca. 1609/1841

Captain John Smith
1580–1631

Captain John Smith entered the arena of North American exploration at a time when the romantic age of buccaneers and seadogs was giving way to the new, financially cautious policies of seventeenth-century colonization. Born into a moderately prosperous Lincolnshire family, Smith received a solid English grammar school education and, after a brief apprenticeship to a prominent merchant, enlisted at the age of fifteen to fight in the Netherlands. For ten years Smith pursued an adventurous military career that took him to Hungary, France, Germany, Spain, Austria, Rumania, Transylvania, Turkey, and North Africa. Toward the end of his life he wrote about these experiences in a brief autobiography, *The True Travels, Adventures, and Observations of Captain John Smith* (1630).

Upon his return to England, Smith—always eager for new adventures—joined the expedition that founded the Jamestown colony in 1607. An iron-willed disciplinarian, he tried almost single-handedly to keep a quarrelsome, inept, and frequently dissatisfied party intact. In his reports to his superiors Smith deplored the lack of skilled labor, complaining that too many of the colonists were "gentlemen" who found "not English cities, nor such fair houses, nor at their own wishes any of their accustomed dainties, with feather beds and down pillows, taverns and alehouses in every breathing place . . . For the country was to them a misery, a ruin, a death, a hell."

While at Jamestown, Smith conducted several short exploratory trips into the interior. During one of these journeys he was captured by Chesapeake Indians, who brought him to their king, Powhatan. As Smith many years later recounted the incident, he was condemned to death and then saved at the last minute by the timely intercession of Powhatan's favorite daughter, Pocahontas. Smith's failure to mention this dramatic episode in his first account of the Virginia expedition led a number of historians (beginning with Henry Adams) to consider the Pocahontas incident as mere fabricated afterthought. Yet, given Smith's promotional purposes at the time, it is quite possible that he wanted to omit any material that might scare off potential colonists. Whether true report or tall tale, Captain Smith's brief captivity and his hairbreadth escape have become one of the best-known passages in the literature of North American exploration.

Smith stayed on at Jamestown until the fall of 1609, when it was becoming clear that his efforts to bring effective management to the colony were futile. In 1614 he made another trip to North America, this time mapping out the coast of New England, a region he not only named but also fell so in love with that he ardently promoted its colonization in two important books, *A Description of New England* (1614) and *Advertisements for the Unexperienced Planters of New England, or Anywhere* (1631). The *Advertisements,* a list of "experienced memorandums" offering practical advice and theoretical suggestions on colonization, was addressed to the Puritan leaders who founded the Massachusetts Bay Colony in 1630. It was Smith's last work, and given the way he had been neglected during his final years, he would not have been surprised to find that most of his admonitions went unheeded.

Further Reading:
H. Adams, "Captain John Smith: Sometime Governour in Virginia and Admirall of New England," *North American Review,* January 1867.
B. Smith, *Captain John Smith: His Life and Legend,* 1953.
P. L. Barbour, *The Three Worlds of Captain John Smith,* 1964.
E. H. Emerson, *Captain John Smith,* 1971.
A. T. Vaughan, *American Genesis: Captain John Smith and the Founding of Virginia,* 1975.
F. Mossiker, *Pocahontas: The Life and Legend,* 1976.

Text:
Travels and Works of Captain John Smith, ed. E. Arber, 1884; reprinted with an introduction by A. G. Bradley, 2 vols., 1910. Spelling and punctuation have been changed to conform to modern usage.

from The Generall Historie of Virginia, New England, and the Summer Isles

from Book III

from Chapter II: [Captain Smith's Captivity]

But our comedies never endured long without a tragedy; some idle exceptions being muttered against Captain Smith[1] for not discovering the head of [the] Chickahominy river and [being] taxed by the Council to be too slow in so worthy an attempt. The next voyage he proceeded so far that with much labor by cutting of trees asunder he made his passage; but when his barge could pass no farther, he left her in a broad bay out of danger of shot, commanding none should go ashore till his return; himself with two English and two savages went up higher in a canoe. But he was not long absent but his men went ashore, whose want of government[2] gave both occasion and opportunity to the savages to surprise one George Cassen, whom they slew, and much failed not to have cut off the boat and all the rest.

Smith little dreaming of that accident, being got to the marshes at the river's head twenty miles in the desert,[3] had his two men slain (as is supposed) sleeping by the canoe, while himself by fowling sought them victual; who finding he was beset with

---

[1] The narrative is written in the third person. Smith often incorporated the official reports of others into his history; this section was written by Smith and several members of his party.

[2] Discipline.

[3] Wilderness.

200 savages, two of them he slew, still defending himself with the aid of a savage his guide, whom he bound to his arm with his garters and used him as a buckler,[4] yet he[5] was shot in his thigh a little, and had many arrows that stuck in his clothes but no great hurt, till at last they took him prisoner.

When this news came to Jamestown, much was their sorrow for his loss, few expecting what ensued.

Six or seven weeks[6] those barbarians kept him prisoner, many strange triumphs and conjurations they made of him, yet he so demeaned[7] himself amongst them as he not only diverted them from surprising the fort, but procured his own liberty, and got himself and his company such estimation amongst them, that those savages admired him more than their own *Quiyoughkasoucks*.[8]

The manner how they used and delivered him, is as follows.

The savages having drawn from George Cassen whither Captain Smith was gone, prosecuting that opportunity they followed him with 300 bowmen, conducted by the King of Pamunkey, who in divisions searching the turnings of the river found Robinson and Emry by the fireside; those they shot full of arrows and slew. Then finding the Captain, as is said, who used the savage that was his guide as his shield (three of them being slain and divers others so galled[9]) all the rest would not come near him. Thinking thus to have returned to his boat, regarding them, as he marched, more than his way, [he] slipped up to the middle in an oozy creek and his savage with him, yet durst they not come to him, till being near dead with cold, he threw away his arms. Then according to their composition[10] they drew him forth and led him to the fire where his men were slain. Diligently they chafed his benumbed limbs.

He demanding for their captain, they showed him Opechancanough, King of Pamunkey, to whom he gave a round ivory double compass dial. Much they marvelled at the playing of the fly[11] and needle, which they could see so plainly and yet not touch it because of the glass that covered them. But when he demonstrated by that globe-like jewel the roundness of the earth and skies, the sphere of the sun, moon, and stars, and how the sun did chase the night round about the world continually, the greatness of the land and sea, the diversity of nations, variety of complexions, and how we were to them antipodes,[12] and many other such like matters, they all stood as amazed with admiration.

Notwithstanding, within an hour after, they tied him to a tree, and as many as could stand about him prepared to shoot him; but the King holding up the compass in his hand, they all laid down their bows and arrows and in a triumphant manner led him to Orapakes,[13] where he was after their manner kindly feasted and well used.

Their order in conducting him was thus: Drawing themselves all in a file, the King in the midst had all their pieces and swords borne before him. Captain Smith was led

---

[4] Shield.
[5] Smith.
[6] Actually, approximately the three weeks from December 16, 1607, to January 8, 1608.
[7] Behaved; conducted.
[8] In Smith's own glossary of Indian words, the term is defined as "petty Gods, and their affinities."

[9] Harassed; annoyed.
[10] Habits.
[11] Compass face, indicating directional points.
[12] Opposite poles.
[13] An Indian village.

after him by three great savages holding him fast by each arm, and on each side six went in file with their arrows nocked.[14] But arriving at the town (which was but only thirty or forty hunting houses made of mats, which they remove as they please, as we our tents) all the women and children staring to behold him, the soldiers first all in file performed the form of a *bissone*[15] so well as could be, and on each flank, officers as sergeants to see them keep their orders. A good time they continued this exercise and then cast themselves in a ring, dancing in such several postures and singing and yelling out such hellish notes and screeches; being strangely painted, every one his quiver of arrows and at his back a club, on his arm a fox or an otter's skin or some such matter for his vambrace;[16] their heads and shoulders painted red with oil and pocones[17] mingled together, which scarlet-like color made an exceeding handsome show; each had his bow in his hand and the skin of a bird with her wings spread abroad,[18] dried, tied on his head, a piece of copper, a white shell, a long feather, with a small rattle growing at the tails of their snakes tied to it, or some such like toy.

All this while Smith and the King stood in the midst guarded, as before is said, and after three dances they all departed. Smith they conducted to a long house where thirty or forty tall fellows did guard him, and ere long more bread and venison was brought him than would have served twenty men. I think his stomach at that time was not very good; what he left they put in baskets and tied over his head. About midnight they set the meat again before him; all this time not one of them would eat a bit with him, till the next morning they brought him as much more, and then did they eat all the old and reserved the new as they had done the other, which made him think they would fat him to eat him. Yet in this desperate estate, to defend him from the cold, one Maocassater brought him his gown in requital of some beads and toys Smith had given him at his first arrival in Virginia.

Two days after, a man would have slain him (but that the guard prevented it) for the death of his son, to whom they conducted him to recover the poor man then breathing his last. Smith told them that at Jamestown he had a water[19] would do it, if they would let him fetch it, but they would not permit that, but made all the preparations they could to assault Jamestown, craving his advice, and for recompense he should have, life, liberty, land, and women. In part of a table book[20] he wrote his mind to them at the fort, what was intended, how they should follow that direction to affright the messengers, and without fail send him such things as he wrote for, and an inventory with them. The difficulty and danger he told the savages of, the mines, great guns, and other engines, exceedingly affrighted them, yet according to his request they went to Jamestown in as bitter weather as could be of frost and snow, and within three days returned with an answer.

But when they came to Jamestown, seeing men sally out as he had told them they would, they fled; yet in the night they came again to the same place where he had told them they should receive an answer and such things as he had promised them, which they found accordingly and with which they returned with no small expedi-

---

[14] Readied.
[15] A military maneuver.
[16] Forearm armor.
[17] Bloodroot.
[18] Spread out.
[19] A distilled alcoholic liquor, used medicinally.
[20] Notebook; tablet.

tion, to the wonder of them all that heard it, that he could either divine[21] or the paper could speak.

Then they led him to the Youghtanunds, the Mattapanients, the Payankatanks, the Nantaughtacunds, and Onawmanients upon the rivers of Rappahannock and Potomac, over all those rivers and back again by divers other several nations to the King's habitation at Pamunkey, where they entertained him with most strange and fearful conjurations:

As if near led to hell,
Amongst the devils to dwell.

Not long after, early in a morning, a great fire was made in a long house and a mat spread on the one side as on the other; on the one they caused him to sit, and all the guard went out of the house, and presently came skipping in a great grim fellow all painted over with coal mingled with oil, and many snakes' and weasels' skins stuffed with moss, and all their tails tied together so as they met on the crown of his head in a tassel, and round about the tassel was a coronet of feathers, the skins hanging round about his head, back, and shoulders and in a manner covered his face, with a hellish voice, and a rattle in his hand. With most strange gestures and passions he began his invocation and environed the fire with a circle of meal; which done, three more such like devils came rushing in with the like antique[22] tricks, painted half black, half red, but all their eyes were painted white and some red strokes like Mutchatos[23] along their cheeks; round about him those fiends danced a pretty while, and then came in three more as ugly as the rest, with red eyes and white strokes over their black faces; at last they all sat down right against him, three of them on the one hand of the chief priest and three on the other. Then all with their rattles began a song; which ended, the chief priest laid down five wheat corns; then, straining his arms and hands with such violence that he sweat and his veins swelled, he began a short oration; at the conclusion they all gave a short groan and then laid down three grains more. After that, began their song again, and then another oration, ever laying down so many corns as before till they had twice encircled the fire; that done, they took a bunch of little sticks prepared for that purpose, continuing still their devotion, and at the end of every song and oration they laid down a stick betwixt the divisions of corn. Till night, neither he nor they did either eat or drink, and then they feasted merrily with the best provisions they could make. Three days they used this ceremony; the meaning whereof, they told him, was to know if he intended them well or no. The circle of meal signified their country, the circles of corn the bounds of the sea, and the sticks his country. They imagined the world to be flat and round, like a trencher,[24] and they in the midst.

After this they brought him a bag of gunpowder, which they carefully preserved till the next spring, to plant as they did their corn, because they would be acquainted with the nature of that seed.

Opitchapam, the King's brother, invited him to his house, where, with as many platters of bread, fowl, and wild beasts as did environ him, he bid him welcome, but not any of them would eat a bit with him but put up all the remainder in baskets.

[21] Prophesy.
[22] Ancient.
[23] Mustaches.
[24] Platter.

At his return to Opechancanough's, all the King's women and their children flocked about him for their parts,[25] as a due by custom, to be merry with such fragments.

> But his waking mind in hideous dreams did
>> oft see wondrous shapes
> Of bodies strange, and huge in growth, and
>> of stupendous makes.

At last they brought him to Werowocomoco,[26] where was Powhatan, their Emperor. Here more than two hundred of those grim courtiers stood wondering at him, as [if] he had been a monster, till Powhatan and his train had put themselves in their greatest braveries.[27] Before a fire, upon a seat like a bedstead, he sat covered with a great robe made of Rarowcun[28] skins and all the tails hanging by. On either hand did sit a young wench of sixteen or eighteen years and along each side [of] the house, two rows of men and behind them as many women, with all their heads and shoulders painted red, many of their heads bedecked with the white down of birds; but every one with something, and a great chain of white beads about their necks.

At his entrance before the King, all the people gave a great shout. The Queen of Appomattoc[29] was appointed to bring him water to wash his hands, and another brought him a bunch of feathers, instead of a towel, to dry them; having feasted him after their best barbarous manner they could, a long consultation was held, but the conclusion was, two great stones were brought before Powhatan; then as many as could laid hands on him, dragged him to them, and thereon laid his head, and being ready with their clubs, to beat out his brains. Pocohontas, the King's dearest daughter, when no entreaty could prevail, got his head in her arms and laid her own upon his to save him from death,[30] whereat the Emperor was contented he should live to make him hatchets, and her bells, beads, and copper, for they thought him as well[31] of all occupations as themselves. For the King himself will make his own robes, shoes, bows, arrows, pots; plant, hunt, or do anything so well as the rest.

> They say he bore a pleasant show,
> But sure his heart was sad.
> For who can pleasant be, and rest,
> That lives in fear and dread:
> And having life suspected, doth
> It still suspected lead.

Two days after,[32] Powhatan, having disguised himself in the most fearfulest manner he could, caused Captain Smith to be brought forth to a great house in the woods and there upon a mat by the fire to be left alone. Not long after, from behind a mat that divided the house, was made the most dolefulest noise he ever heard; then

---

[25] Gifts.
[26] Chief's Town, Powhatan's home on the York River. This was on January 5, 1608.
[27] Costumes.
[28] Raccoon.
[29] Powhatan tribe on the James River.

[30] This may have been a custom among Indian women, who then had a claim over the person they rescued.
[31] Capable.
[32] On January 7, 1608.

Powhatan, more like a devil than a man, with some two hundred more as black as himself, came unto him and told him now they were friends, and presently he should go to Jamestown to send him two great guns and a grindstone for which he would give him the country of Capahowasick[33] and forever esteem him as his son Nantaquond.

So to Jamestown with twelve guides Powhatan sent him. That night they quartered in the woods, he still expecting (as he had done all this long time of his imprisonment) every hour to be put to one death or other, for all their feasting. But almighty God (by His divine providence) had mollified the hearts of those stern barbarians with compassion. The next morning betimes they came to the fort, where Smith having used the savages with what kindness he could, he showed Rawhunt, Powhatan's trusty servant, two demiculverins[34] and a millstone to carry [to] Powhatan; they found them somewhat too heavy, but when they did see him discharge them, being loaded with stones, among the boughs of a great tree loaded with icicles, the ice and branches came so tumbling down that the poor savages ran away half dead with fear. But at last we regained some conference with them and gave them such toys and sent to Powhatan, his women, and children such presents as gave them in general full content.

1624

---

from A Description of New England

[Growing Rich in the New World]

I have not been so ill bred, but I have tasted of plenty and pleasure, as well as want and misery; nor does necessity yet, or occasion of discontent, force me to these endeavors; nor am I ignorant what small thanks I shall have for my pains, or that many would have the world imagine them to be of great judgement, that can but blemish these my designs,[1] by their witty objections and detractions. Yet (I hope) my reasons with my deeds, will so prevail with some, that I shall not want employment in these affairs, to make the most blind see his own senselessness and incredulity, hoping that gain will make them affect that which religion, charity and the common good cannot. It were but a poor device in me to deceive myself, much more the King and State, my friends and country, with these inducements: which seeing His Majesty hath given permission, I wish all sorts of worthy, honest, industrious spirits would understand, and if they desire any further satisfaction, I will do my best to give it, not to persuade them to go only, but go with them; not leave them there, but live with them there.

I will not say, but by ill providing and undue managing, such courses may be taken [that] may make us miserable enough. But if I may have the execution of what I have projected; if they want to eat, let them eat or never digest[2] me. If I perform what I say, I desire but that reward out of the gains [which] may suit my pains, quality

---

[33] A neighboring tribe.
[34] Nine-foot cannon.

[1] I.e., his plans to colonize New England.
[2] Tolerate.

and condition. And if I abuse you with my tongue, take my head for satisfaction. If any dislike at the year's end, defraying their charge, by my consent they should freely return, if God please to bless me from such accidents as are beyond my power in reason to prevent. For I am not so simple to think that ever any other motive than wealth will ever erect there a commonwealth or draw company from their ease and humors[3] at home to stay in New England to effect my purposes.

And lest any should think the toil might be insupportable, though these things may be had by labor and diligence, I assure myself there are those who delight extremely in vain pleasure, that take much more pains in England to enjoy it than I should do here [in New England] to gain wealth sufficient. And yet I think they should not have half such sweet content for our pleasure here is still gains; in England charges and loss. Here nature and liberty afford us that freely which in England we want, or it costs us dearly. What pleasure can be more than (being tired with any occasion ashore, in planting vines, fruits, or herbs, in contriving their own grounds, to the pleasure of their own minds, their fields, gardens, orchards, buildings, ships, and other works, &c) to recreate themselves before their own doors, in their own boats upon the sea, where man, woman, and child, with a small hook and line, by angling may take divers sorts of excellent fish at their pleasures? And is it not pretty sport to pull up two pence, six pence, and twelve pence as fast as you can haul and veer[4] a line? He is a very bad fisher [that] cannot kill in one day, with his hook and line, one, two, or three hundred cods, which dressed and dried, if they be sold there for ten shilling the hundred [pounds], though in England they will give more than twenty, may not both the servant, the master, and merchant be well content with this gain? If a man work but three days in seven he may get more than he can spend, unless he will be excessive. Now that carpenter, mason, gardener, tailor, smith, sailor, forgers,[5] or what other, may they not make this a pretty recreation, though they fish but an hour in the day, to take more than they eat in a week? Or if they will not eat it, because there is so much better choice, yet [they may] sell it or change it with the fishermen or merchants for anything they want. And what sport does yield a more pleasing content and less hurt or charge than angling with a hook and crossing the sweet air from isle to isle, over the silent streams of a calm sea? Wherein the most curious may find pleasure, profit, and content.

Thus, though all men be not fishers, yet all men, whatsoever, may in other matters do as well. For necessity does in these cases so rule a commonwealth, and each in their several functions, as their labors in their qualities, may be as profitable because there is a necessary mutual use of all.

For gentlemen, what exercise should more delight them than ranging daily those unknown parts, using fowling and fishing, for hunting and hawking? And yet you shall see the wild hawks give you some pleasure, in seeing them stoop[6] (six or seven after one another) an hour or two together at the schools of fish in the fair harbors, as those ashore [do] at a fowl, and never trouble nor torment yourselves with watching, mewing,[7] feeding, and attending them, nor kill a horse and man with running and crying, "See you not a hawk?" For hunting also, the woods, lakes and

---

[3] Whims.
[4] Let out.
[5] Metal workers.

[6] Swoop.
[7] Keeping in cages.

rivers afford not only chase sufficient for any that delight in that kind of toil or pleasure but such beast to hunt that besides the delicacy of their bodies for food, their skins are so rich as may well recompense thy daily labor with a Captain's pay.

For laborers, if those [in England] that sow hemp, rape,[8] turnips, parsnips, carrots, cabbage, and such like, give twenty, thirty, forty, fifty shilling yearly for an acre of ground, and meat, drink, and wages to use it and yet grow rich, when better or at least as good ground may be had [in New England] and cost nothing but labor, it seems strange to me any such should there grow poor.

My purpose is not to persuade children from their parents, men from their wives, nor servants from their masters; only such as with free consent may be spared. But that each parish or village, in city or country, that will but apparel[9] their fatherless children of thirteen or fourteen years of age, or young married people that have small wealth to live on, here by their labor may live exceedingly well. Provided always that first there be a sufficient power to command them, houses to receive them, means to defend them, and meet[10] provisions for them; for any place may be overlain,[11] and it is most necessary to have a fortress (ere this grow to practice) and sufficient masters (as carpenters, masons, fishers, fowlers, gardeners, husbandmen,[12] sawyers,[13] smiths, spinners, tailors, weavers, and such like) to take ten, twelve, or twenty, or as there is occasion, for apprentices. The masters by this may quickly grow rich; these apprentices their trades themselves to do the like, to a general and an incredible benefit for king and country, master and servant.

1616

---

[8] Herb grown as a forage crop for hogs and sheep.

[9] Prepare.

[10] Suitable.

[11] Overthrown.

[12] Farmers.

[13] Those who saw timber.

Unknown artist,
Alice Mason,
oil on canvas, 1670.
Adams National Historic Site,
Quincy, Massachusetts.

John Hesselius,
Charles Calvert,
oil on canvas, 1761.
The Baltimore Museum of Art.
Gift of Alfred R. and Henry G. Riggs,
in memory of General Lawson Riggs.

The Literature of Colonial America 1620–1776

A "Citty upon a Hill"—New England

 In the seventeenth century a voluminous literature came from the New England colonists who first settled a rocky, sandy coastline that reaches into the Atlantic like a grappling hook. These Pilgrim and Puritan colonists aspired to be a "citty upon a hill," as the Massachusetts Puritan governor John Winthrop put it. Ideal city notwithstanding, they coped at first with primitive conditions. In the 1600s they "forsooke a fruitful land, stately buildings, goodly gardens, orchards, dear friends, and near relations" to seek God's way in the "desert wilderness" of the New World. In doing so, they also withdrew from the bitter religious controversy that threatened their livelihoods and their sense of spiritual and psychological well-being in England. In effect, King James I had carried out his threat against these religious dissenters: "I shall make them conform or I shall harry them out of the land."

The writings of the early explorers are multinational, but the literature of colonial America, north and south, is principally English, much of it motivated by religious commitment and the need to justify the radical act of uprooting households, voyaging over three thousand miles of heaving ocean, and starting life anew on a crudely mapped continent whose very existence had been verified only a century earlier. Much of the literature of colonial America can be traced directly to distress in the English families of such figures as William

Bradford and John Winthrop, Anne Bradstreet and Mary Rowlandson. Their lives were entwined in the tumultuous religious Reformation begun by Martin Luther (1483–1546) and spurred by the teachings of the French theologian John Calvin (1509–1564).

The Religious Background

In fact, important origins of our nation's literature lie in the Protestant Reformation, a part of the Renaissance that essentially changed the direction and definition of all forms of European and English culture, including music, visual arts, literature, philosophy, in the fourteenth and fifteenth centuries.

This ferment extended to religion. By the late Middle Ages numerous Christians felt that the vital center of human life, the church, had strayed from its original mission and become corrupt. To a humanist like Erasmus the New Testament teachings of the Gospel seemed to have become secondary to concern for elaborate ritual and to church hierarchy and politics. Such Protestant reformers as William Tyndale argued that Scripture, not an institution or its trappings, was the essence of the Christian life. The authority of the Pope came into question, and in 1543 King Henry VIII formed the Church of England, a Protestant national church independent of Roman Catholicism and the Pope. By English law citizens were required to obey its rules and observe its practices.

A fundamental issue in this period of religious struggle was disagreement over authority. In Roman Catholicism the Pope was the highest temporal authority; the state was subject to the church he led. Henry VIII reversed that relationship when he formed the Church of England. Thereafter the monarch became the temporal authority with the church subject to the state. Conformity—or nonconformity—to established authority was a hallmark of this struggle. Nonconformists, all of whom accepted biblical authority as ultimate, put either the believing community or the individual in charge of making crucial religious decisions. It is from this strain that developed a great individualist literature that characterizes America, north and south.

English religious controversy continued after Henry VIII formed the Church of England, for some people felt that the national church still held a "Romish taint." Eventually, through the reigns of Queens Mary (1553–1558) and Elizabeth (1558–1603) the controversy focused on whether such matters as ceremony, vestments, ornament, and church governance represented godly tradition or human and demonic corruption. Conservatives defended their use, while the nonconformists who worked to rid the church of them were called, scornfully at first, Puritans, for their efforts at purification. Some others, notably the Bradford group who migrated to Plymouth, Massachusetts, despaired of successful reforms and separated from the Church of England altogether. They took direction from the Bible (2 Corinthians): "Come out from among them and be ye separate, saith the Lord."

Meanwhile, Anglican Church officials and agents of King James I (1566–1625) and of Charles I (1625–1649) made life difficult for all dissenters. "Nothing but the wide ocean and savage deserts," wrote the poet John Milton, "could hide and shelter . . . numbers of faithful and freeborn Englishmen . . . from the fury of the bishops."

One such group of "faithful and freeborn Englishmen" were the Plymouth Pilgrims, who represented a new kind of resident in America. Unlike the Jamestown colonists, the Pilgrims had no ambitions for riches. And they knew better than to try subsisting as an Indian trading post or seasonal fishing camp. They understood that a successful colony needed a sound financial basis, that it had to feed and sustain itself and be able to conduct trade. Since 1608 the Bradford group had lived in Holland, which afforded them religious freedom but "Dutchified" their lives. Fearing the loss of their cultural identity and religious intensity, they persuaded the Virginia Company of London to finance their American colony and, despite delays and mishaps, set sail on the *Mayflower* on September 16, 1620, with 149 aboard, forty-seven of them crewmen and officers. Their grim toll in that first American winter, when half of them died, can be traced in part to the two-month voyage on a diet deficient in fresh produce and to the cold and barren land where they settled.

Americans cherish the Pilgrims of the tiny Plymouth colony largely because of William Bradford's compelling account of it in *Of Plymouth Plantation* (1856), which he may have written in one of three "carved chairs" left in his will and doubtless transported on the *Mayflower*. Much more of our colonial literature, however, comes from the far less radical Puritan immigrants who arrived in a so-called Great Migration to the Massachusetts Bay Colony (1628–1643). They clustered in towns around current-day Boston and then extended into Connecticut and other parts of New England. Wherever they went, they and their descendants kept records of their experience in prose and verse.

The Puritans, like all immigrants to America, hoped to build a better life, one they defined largely in spiritual terms. Deploring the intractable corruption of the Church of England, they decided to build a church as pure as was humanly possible in New England. God seemed to direct them to do so through providential signs of catastrophe in their native land. King Charles I ascended to the English throne in 1625, a year in which the plague threatened London. He pressured Parliament to impose new, heavy taxes in a time of general high inflation and, in some trades, depression. In 1629 the king dissolved Parliament, stripping the populace of legislative representation.

Puritans like John Winthrop of Suffolk experienced these events personally. An attorney and landholder of high principles, he was dismayed by dishonesty at court and, though previously successful in his family's cloth trade, saw it sink in depression as prices rose and heavier taxes loomed. Mysteriously, he lost his attorney's license (perhaps for Puritan beliefs) and saw two friends imprisoned for tax resistance. Winthrop, a landholder with acreage planted in wheat, rye, and barley, was also a landlord responsible for his tenants and household servants, and a husband and father of seven children. He read God's message in this convergence of dire events and took drastic action. Within a year he arranged to transport his household and family to America to help build the spiritually exemplary "citty upon a hill."

The Voyage; the Landfall

At first these colonial immigrants lived in squalor brightened spiritually by their religious devotion and physically by the furnishings they managed to ship with the Winthrop fleet at the cost of four English pounds sterling per ton (in addition to the passage cost of five pounds per adult). Items like William Bradford's "six leather chairs," "great beer bowle," court cupboard, pewter dishes, and "red Turkey grogram suit of clothes" took up space below decks with the colony's supplies of firearms and ammunition, tools and farming implements. In the Winthrop party, livestock (240 cattle, "about sixty horses") traveled in separate ships topside in open pens. Many animals died in the early-spring Atlantic storms that made the colonists' shipboard lives miserable as well.

The sea voyage was a grim initiation for colonial living, especially for Puritan immigrants like the poet Anne Dudley Bradstreet, who was accustomed to certain middle-class comforts of the day. For three tempestuous months she—and the women and children like her—slept in the stuffy "between-decks" area, with the main deck their roof, the ceiling of the cargo hold their floor. Bradstreet's husband and father, like the other men, slept in hammocks slung everywhere. The only heat came from the cooking stove, and because the threat of fire prevented the use of candles or lanterns, each day ended at sundown, when the passengers took to their beds. The "great cabin" in the ship's stern provided space for religious worship. Doubtless John Winthrop preached his sermon "A Model of Christian Charity" there, having written it and begun his diary in these stressful onboard conditions punctuated by monotonous meals of salt meat or fish, hard "biscuit," and the beer or "syder" that were at least drinkable. The hardship of the voyage and landing has engaged the imagination of twentieth-century American writers.

Landfall presented its own complications. The *Arbella,* the flagship of the fleet, dropped anchor off the tiny, year-old settlement of Salem, Massachusetts, on June 12, 1630. "Some gentlemen and some of the women" were rowed ashore in shallops, and the scene before them must have looked like their own bleak futures. For Salem Plantation had, at most, forty dwellings, of which about a dozen were recognizable houses framed in oak and covered with pine boards roughly sawed or hewn with axes. Others were thatch-roofed cottages of one or two rooms with chimneys of logs or of wattle and daub (woven twigs and plaster) and windows of greased paper. The one "faire house," that of the Salem governor, had four rooms and an attic, a great central chimney of brick and fieldstone, a shingled roof, and probably small leaded windows of hand-blown, diamond-shaped panes of colored glass brought from England. Civilization itself was doubtless symbolized in that one house.

Yet the poet Anne Bradstreet, the diarist (and governor) Winthrop, and the writer of a notable historical letter, Thomas Dudley, could only have been sobered to see the wretched hovels of the less prosperous Salem colonists who lived in hillside excavations or in "English wigwams," described by one minister as "verie little and homely, made with small poles prick't into the ground and so bended and fastened at the tops and on the side, they are matted with boughs and

Homage to Mistress Bradstreet

By the week we landed we were, most, used up.
Strange ships across us, after a fortnight's winds
unfavouring, frightened us;
bone-sad cold, sleet, scurvy; so were ill
many as one day we could have no sermons;
broils, quelled; a fatherless child unkennelled; vermin
crowding & waiting: waiting.

.   .   .   .

How long with nothing in the ruinous heat,
clams & acorns stomaching, distinction perishing,
at which my heart rose,
with brackish water, we would sing.
When whispers knew the Governor's last bread
was browning in his oven, we were discourag'd.
The Lady Arbella dying—
dyings—at which my heart rose, but I did submit.

                                   John Berryman (1953)

covered with sedge and old mats." From Salem colonists who honored the
newcomers with "a good venison pasty and good beer" came a grim story of
overcrowding, of provisions in short supply, of such household necessities as soap
produced by hand in the crudest fashion. No matter how spiritually elevated
these Puritan writers and their fellow colonists felt, they knew the "city upon a
hill" needed to do better. It was one thing for southern colonial writers a
century later to satirize colonists for "belly-aches" from eating unripe fruit or to
poke fun at their rustic lives in which "conversation's lost, and manners
drowned." But Massachusetts Bay colonists intending to build a new Jerusalem
hardly found such matters to be the grounds for humor. Salem, as Dudley
confided, "pleased us not."

For the first years, nonetheless, living conditions remained primitive. Dudley,
who was Anne Bradstreet's father, offers a valuable glimpse of the colonial writer
at work. "In the throng of domestic [and public] business" he wrote a newsletter
to the Lady Bridget, Countess of Lincoln, in March 1631 apologizing for written
work that he suspected might suffer from interruption, distraction, and crude
surroundings. "I have yet," he reported, "no table, nor other room to write in
than by the fireside upon my knee, in this sharp winter; to which my family
must have leave to resort, though they break good manners, and make me many
times forget what I would say, and say what I would not." Dudley was not the
only colonial writer to observe that as he wrote, the ink froze in his well.

Puritan Beliefs

What specific beliefs, we ask, could motivate these New England colonists in tasks so discouraging? What thoughts sustained them and moved so many to write the histories and verses, the sermons and autobiographies that went far to shape the national identity of the people and the place that became the United States of America?

These Puritans and Pilgrims held in common one set of unshakable beliefs, most of which sound perplexing and harsh to modern Americans. They believed, first, that because Adam and Eve disobeyed God and fell from grace, all their heirs were also fallen and predestined to eternal punishment—except for an elect group redeemed by the sufferings of Jesus Christ and chosen to be recipients of God's grace. They spoke of their doctrine in terms of covenants, the binding and solemn agreements made between two parties. In the Bible they discerned, first, a covenant of works made between God and Adam, who was to enjoy perpetual life in the Garden of Eden in return for total obedience to God. When Adam disobeyed, he committed the first or original sin, broke the covenant, fell from grace, and, together with Eve, was cast out of the Garden forever to toil in the world.

Later God made a second covenant, one of grace, with Abraham, whose children he promised to save unconditionally. The Puritans considered themselves descendants of Abraham, redeemed by Jesus Christ who was sent by God to show His mercy. These saved souls, an indeterminate but limited number called the elect, were to be brought to a full consciousness of their condition by the ministry of the biblical word. God extended His irresistible grace to them. Ultimately these elect souls would dwell with God in eternity.

No Puritan, however, felt that any action of one's own could change the unalterable will of God. All Puritans knew that their innate human depravity prevented them from "earning" salvation through good works or deeds or generous thoughts or any number of prayers or devotions. Yet every Puritan or Pilgrim worked to live an industrious, upright life in a useful trade or profession. The saints, as the regenerate Puritans called themselves, tried to love their neighbors and to obey their civil magistrates, as Cotton Mather's *Bonifacius* (1710) reveals. And they strove daily to open their hearts in order to ascertain God's disposition toward them. Those convinced they were favored with grace were considered reborn or regenerate. The phenomenon was, as a Puritan synod or council agreed, "evidently a supernatural work, most powerful and at the same time most delightful, astonishing, mysterious, and ineffable . . . so that all in whose hearts God works in this marvellous manner are . . . regenerated, and do actually believe."

The experience of saving grace, however, was not usually swift or instantaneous, but slow and agonizing. The soul first came into consciousness of its sin and worthlessness, often with the help of a minister's sermon, which some writers spoke of as verbal arrows piercing sin-hardened hearts. In sermons Puritan writers worked always for a simplicity and directness of style so that hearers could understand immediately and, they hoped, be moved. But an awareness did not necessarily come in a church or meetinghouse. One New England immigrant, Thomas Shepard, got "dead drunk" on a Saturday night at college, awoke late "that Sabbath" with a hangover, and then "in shame and confusion . . . went out into the cornfields . . . where the Lord . . . did meet me with much sadness of heart and troubled my soul."

Shepard, like all regenerate Puritans, made a slow and tortuous way to the conviction that he was sanctified in God's grace. Even years later as a prominent, influential minister in New England, he confided to his journal the haunting pangs of envy, anger, and vanity. "I saw," he wrote, "how apt my heart was to be like the sea. . . . It's blown with any wind. . . . If God's spirit breathes, it follows that; if Satan, it follows that."

From one day to the next no Puritan could relax from vigilant perseverance in faith. Absolute certainty of election was regarded as prideful, and thus a sin, so Puritans always felt a certain anxiety about their spiritual state even as they examined the conscience and recorded the findings in a diary or journal or, like the poet Edward Taylor, embodied them in poems. Even the most spiritually persevering of Puritans ran the risk of self-delusion and thus of hypocrisy, possibilities that were humbling in themselves. And some souls in quest of union with Christ never, in good conscience, felt the stirrings of His grace. A Mrs. Sparhawk "came to the [immigrant] ship thinking to get God" but in New England found her spiritual state unchanged. She "saw herself far from humiliation [God's humbling] and thought it was a shame." It is no exaggeration to say that a voluminous colonial literature arose from the private need to examine the inner life. The spiritual struggles—in essence the search for integrity —among so many individuals could only naturally lead to the public necessity to justify and explain the formation of Puritan society as a whole. These struggles have captured the interest of some twentieth-century American poets.

It is extremely difficult for modern readers to appreciate the attraction of such life and to understand why by 1642 some twenty thousand people had immigrated to New England to enter into colonial life dominated by Puritan practices. It is helpful, perhaps, to be reminded that in England Puritanism reformulated the terms of society. On the basis of biblical (which is to say God's) authority, Puritanism found one person to be as good as another, no matter what that person's earthly social station. Aristocracy might rule England, at least for the present, but Puritanism argued that the average man or woman might be one of God's elect and thus a spiritual aristocrat destined to inherit the heavens and the earth.

This message was conveyed in the early 1600s by a new breed of minister quite different from the merely custodial clergy from aristocratic English families. The new Puritan ministers, from middle-class or impoverished backgrounds and trained in certain colleges at Cambridge University, were idealistic, energetic, intellectual, and pastoral or caring. They reached out to a small but warmly responsive public. Some, like John Cotton, were so powerfully persuasive that large numbers of their congregations came with them to America.

Mr. Edwards and the Spider

I saw the spiders marching through the air,
Swimming from tree to tree that mildewed day
   In latter August when the hay
    Came creaking to the barn. But where
     The wind is westerly,
Where gnarled November makes the spiders fly
Into the apparitions of the sky,
  They purpose nothing but their ease and die
Urgently beating east to sunrise and the sea;

  What are we in the hands of the great God?
It was in vain you set up thorn and briar
   In battle array against the fire
    And treason crackling in your blood;
     For the wild thorns grow tame
And will do nothing to oppose the flame;
Your lacerations tell the losing game
  You play against a sickness past your cure.
How will the hands be strong? How will the heart endure?

  A very little thing, a little worm,
Or hourglass-blazoned spider, it is said,
   Can kill a tiger. Will the dead
    Hold up his mirror and affirm
     To the four winds the smell
And flash of his authority? It's well
If God who holds you to the pit of hell,
  Much as one holds a spider, will destroy,
Baffle and dissipate your soul. As a small boy

  On Windsor Marsh, I saw the spider die
When thrown into the bowels of fierce fire:
   There's no long struggle, no desire
    To get up on its feet and fly—
     It stretches out its feet
And dies. This is the sinner's last retreat;
Yes, and no strength exerted on the heat
  Then sinews the abolished will, when sick
And full of burning, it will whistle on a brick.

. . . .

Robert Lowell (1946)

These Puritans were not an other-worldly people. One article of faith especially connected their spiritual life to the work of colonization. Writings from William Bradford to Cotton Mather and beyond show the conviction that the apocalyptic prophecy of the New Testament Book of Revelation was about to be fulfilled. Within the scheme of Christian history, the Puritans believed, the final events of earthly time were coming to a close. They had a method for determining this. Martin Luther had shown them how. Luther argued that historical events on earth matched the symbols in Revelation. These symbols thus became guides to the past and to the future. The difficulty lay in correlating biblical and earthly events accurately. In theological study the ministers were trained to interpret such biblical symbols as the ten-horned beast, the grapes of wrath, the seven vials and to apply their meaning to such worldly events as war, plague, and royal oppression. To do so accurately was to know God's own timetable for the final events of human history. For according to Scripture, there would occur a period of severe earthly tumult and dissension, after which the Messiah, the Christ, would return to earth. At that point God would bind up Satan for one thousand years, the duration of the peaceful and harmonious Millennium, to be followed by one final great battle that signified the end of the world and the eternal peace of the elect with God.

These apocalyptic events were very much on the minds of the Puritan immigrants. The most popular work in their literature, Michael Wigglesworth's *Day of Doom* (1660), deals with that expectation as the final events of God's Judgment Day, including the rationale for human salvation and damnation, unfold in its stanzas. The subject of apocalypse recurs repeatedly in the literature of New England. The ideal of the peaceable kingdom of the millennium set a very high standard for the city on the hill. The new Jerusalem in America—as Cotton Mather put it, the *Theopolis Americana*—would have to be objectified in colonial life just as it was proclaimed in literature. Colonization itself, from felling trees to writing poems, was site preparation for the Christian millennium. Though the definition may have varied over the years, that may have been the first and deepest "American dream."

Colonial Life

That dream absorbed the daily energy of settlement, whose activities, terminology, and values also found their way into literature. What were those activities? How did these people live? As middle-class husbandmen and tradesmen, they brought English conventions to America, including belief in the great value of a permanent house and enclosed lands that kept the chaos of the dreaded wilderness out. During the first years of New England settlement, scouting parties of leading men surveyed inland areas for good soil, ample fresh water, timberlands, and natural meadows vital for feeding livestock. Returning to the coast, they got permission from the General Court (the legislature) to settle the area of their choice, then in good weather led their families, associates, and animals to it. Setting out in spring, they had at most eight months to settle before winter closed in.

On site a committee planned the house lots and fields based on English agriculture familiar to everyone. Each farmer needed several fields immediately— one for grain crops, another for pasture, and a third for meadow to yield hay for the winter feeding of livestock. No colonist had the time to clear picture-perfect fields. The charming stone fences of New England arose from the necessity to clear rocky fields so they could be tilled and planted, for the growing season was short and the harsh winters long. Well after the American Revolution, European travelers deplored the unsightly, scraggly fields in which crops grew among tall, charred stumps. But such visitors mistook necessity for slovenliness.

Providing shelter was a major undertaking. Northern colonists built heavy-timbered houses that began with the felling of entire trees whose trunks, intended for main supports, were hand-hewn and notched, then dragged with draft animals to the building site. Neighbors arrived on "raising day" to help push and fasten the structural timbers. The assembly was dangerous, its success a cause for prayers of thanks and celebration with food and perhaps "strong waters." The siding, usually of milled clapboards, and all the interior finishing were left to the occupant's family.

The colonial farmhouse in which many writers worked was divided into three areas: bedrooms, the hall or parlor for ceremonial occasions, and a kitchen, which became the center of activity. There the housewife, aided by older children and perhaps a serving girl or even a slave, smoked meats, dried herbs, put up fruits and vegetables, and ground grains. There she processed dairy products, dressed poultry, made soap from ashes, and carded and spun flax, wool, and cotton. Just outside, in the kitchen garden, she tended vegetables and a seasonal herb garden that was virtually the family's medicine chest. Chicory, for instance, soothed irritated eyes, mint aided women in childbirth, and thyme cured toothache. Anne Bradstreet and Mary Rowlandson would have known this lore and superintended these time-consuming tasks. Edward Taylor's "Huswifery" and other poems acknowledge his consciousness of them.

We must surmise that most colonial writers worked by candlelight after their very large households quieted down for the night. Those who were ministers doubtless had a certain family consent to withdraw to a quiet corner or, if they were city dwellers like Cotton Mather, to write sermons, verses, and diary entries in a private study off the streets "full of girls and boys sporting up and down," streets "full of good shops well furnished with all kinds of merchandise" and increasingly crowded with the specialized crafts and trades characteristic of the city.

The character of colonial New England life, however, was mainly rural. As each inland or coastal town was settled, the planning of house lots was crucial, since they were the tight nucleus of the society, which invited or "called" a minister and erected the all-important meetinghouse at the earliest opportunity. All roads radiated from the meetinghouse like the spokes of a wheel, for it was the hub of community life, attracting all but the sick for Sunday and Thursday sermons and, when death occurred, drawing the townspeople for funerals and burial in the graveyard adjacent to it. A few houses, including the parsonage, would be situated near the meetinghouse, in addition to a field sometimes called an artillery garden because the husbandmen-farmers gathered there regularly for militia exercises. Town magistrates were selected from the men of the community.

The meetinghouse, used for town meetings as well as for religious services, showed the Puritan congregation's fondness for color. As the center of religious and social life, townspeople contributed to its painting long before they could spare the expense of coloring their own houses. Favored shades were orange and chocolate, yellow, green, red, sky blue, and white. Such an accumulation might sound chaotic now, but at the time these colors signified a godly civil order in the wilderness.

Not surprisingly, some American innovation in agriculture proved necessary almost immediately. Predators and fierce winters forced colonists to build livestock shelters, and because native grasses were unsuited to grazing and haying, the settlers had to seed meadows in English grasses, which thrived. The ideal of the town as a corporation or commonwealth—an ideal recurrent in the literature —was objectified in cooperative "public works" projects such as bridges and livestock pounds, which required the hard work of fencing but kept the animals out of the arable fields. Stray livestock were a serious point of contention. In poems Anne Bradstreet lamented the absence of her husband on public business, but some of that business concerned lawsuits when, for example, a swine uprooted a farmer's field; once the Bradstreets' own mare was attacked by dogs and killed while eating hay on a neighbor's property.

Every New England housewife working to grind corn or wheat in a small hand mill looked forward to the day when her town had a miller. Every husbandman whose iron or steel tools needed repair anticipated the arrival of a blacksmith. Towns tried to lure these skilled craftsmen with promises of choice acreage and of a monopoly, for the mill and forge were considered public utilities. The sawmills, especially, proved welcome to colonists who dreaded the wilderness long before they saw it. These were people who brought to the New World a centuries-long European folkloric tradition that said that the unshaped land, or wilderness, was inhabited by unspeakable beasts. The sawmills that produced lumber for colonists' houses, and for export to Europe and the West Indies, also drove back the terrifying forest wilderness that harbored feral animals and satanic Indians.

Puritan Literature

From the beginnings of settlement the Puritan and Pilgrim writers labored to justify American innovations to an English audience. Men like Thomas Dudley and women like his daughter Anne or her confrere Mary Rowlandson did not have much leisure to sit writing before the fire, even with makeshift lapboards in the icy depths of winter. Their literary record reflects ideals and hardships. Historical literature like *Of Plymouth Plantation* (1856) and Winthrop's *Journal* (1853) and such sermons as Jonathan Edwards's "Sinners in the Hands of an Angry God" (1741) testify to the New Englanders' urgent justification of socioreligious practices.

Colonial writers also found ample subject matter in personal relations and in family life. To read the biographies of these writers is to see how vulnerable the women were to death in childbirth and how susceptible the children (and adults, for that matter) to mortal illness. Puritan writers' multiple marriages reflect the precariousness of colonial life and testify to their high regard for the sanctity of marriage, which they believed to be an ordinance of God.

The family and marriage, accordingly, became an important literary concern. It is evident, for example, in Cotton Mather's *Bonifacius, an Essay Upon the Good,* 1710, which deals with appropriate relations among family, neighbors, and community. Samuel Sewall's *Diary* shows a parent's anguish and joy, as does Anne Bradstreet's prose and verse. Marital love found expression in Bradstreet and in John Saffin.

The American experience provided colonial writers with some disquieting subject matter. Chattel slavery, customarily associated with the South, existed in New England and mocked Puritan aspirations; in the late 1600s the worldly Puritan diarist Samuel Sewall wrote an antislavery tract. The native Americans became another recurrent topic in colonial writing. Rhode Islander Roger Williams wrote a series of verses in which he used Indian traits to point up English barbarities. But orthodox Puritan writers could not regard Indians with objective interest, since a stated goal of colonization was the conversion of these heathen to Christianity. Squanto's help to the Pilgrims seemed to be God's providence at work in the initial encounter between the English and the Indians. But the "heathen" soon became alarmed by settlers' relentless encroachment on their lands, and two uprisings occurred, the Pequot War (1635–1636), which Puritans considered God's test of their mettle, and the severe King Philip's War (1675), which seriously threatened English settlement and suggested to some that their city on a hill was failing. Mary Rowlandson's narrative is an effort to redeem her experience in captivity—and implicitly the pilgrimage of all New Englanders—in that war.

Internal trials and dissension were another important concern to the colonial writers, who felt that God tried them even as Satan worked to subvert them. It was one thing to decree an orderly society based, as Winthrop said, on "justice and mercy" but another to organize and sustain it. Puritan-Pilgrim culture was prone to superstition and intolerant of dissent, and by our later standards it did not handle either well. Witchcraft and heresy were investigated and punished and were considered a legitimate preoccupation of writers seeking, in Puritan terms, to justify the ways of God to men, as Cotton Mather does within his biography of Sir William Phips, which includes episodes on the witch trials of the early 1690s.

New England literature shows Puritan intolerance of religious sects eager to coexist in the colony. Some Quakers learned this when they persisted in reentering the Puritans' jurisdiction after repeated expulsions. The Massachusetts Bay colonists denounced the "ranters and quakers," cropped the ears of three men, and hanged two men and one woman who returned to the Bay Colony repeatedly under penalty of death. The town of New Haven ruled that the "cursed sect of heretics" could finally be punished by imprisonment, whipping, forced labor, branding, and having "their tongues bored through with a hot iron."

Other troublesome dissidents were, so to speak, deported. When the Englishman Thomas Morton settled in Mount Wollaston (now Quincy,

Massachusetts) in 1625 to sell the Indians guns and to frolic with an assortment of traders, Indian maids, and former servants, Plymouth's Governor Bradford denounced the "riotous prodigallitie and profuse excess." Within three years several New England communities ousted the self-styled "Mine-Host of Merrymount," shipping him back to England. Morton's *New English Canaan* (1637) presents his side of the story, Bradford's *Of Plymouth Plantation* the other.

Dissension among the laity was especially painful for the Puritan community. Roger Williams, a "godly minister," as Winthrop called him, so insisted on overt separation of spiritual from temporal affairs that he threatened civil authority and was banished to Rhode Island. Williams's *The Bloody Tenet of Persecution* (1644) presents his view of the affair. Soon after he took up residence in Rhode Island, the Puritans were once again beset by internal dissension. In 1637 Anne Hutchinson, an influential parishioner of the prestigious Reverend John Cotton, proclaimed that the elect need not concern themselves with human law. Like Williams, she challenged the authenticity of civil and religious authority. One writer summarized the case against her: "The faithful ministers of Christ must have dung cast on their faces, and be no better than . . . opposers of Christ himself." Hutchinson's troubles were chronicled in Winthrop's *Journal*. She was brought to trial, found guilty, and, like Williams, banished from the Massachusetts Bay.

Subsequent generations have viewed her brutal slaying by Indians on Long Island as an indication of Puritan harshness and have seen the expulsion of Roger Williams and the execution and mutilation of Quakers in the same light. It is helpful to recall that the pluralistic America of the twentieth century was unlike anything the Puritans could have envisioned or desired. New Englanders fled a society they thought corrupted in spirit and circumstance and made tremendous personal sacrifices to live under what they understood to be God's direction. From their viewpoint, strict laws and orthodox practices were proper godly vigilance, not brutality, though it is understandable that a modern American might react negatively to them.

The colonists of the Great Migration and thereafter worked exhaustively to build their agricultural New Jerusalem. Some twenty years after the Winthrop group looked at Salem in dismay, one colonist could boast that "this remote, rocky, barren, bushy, wild-woody wilderness . . . now through the mercy of Christ [has] become a second England for fertilness. In so short a space," he added, "that is indeed the wonder of the world."

A "Vale of Plenty": The South

Southern colonists did not come to America to found a city upon a hill. Their American dream was quite different. Captain John Smith's expression "vale of plenty" captured the essence of the southern response to America. The vale or valley of plenty signified a fruitful garden, even a paradise, that could be attained with human effort. Two centuries of southern colonial writers saw their land as a natural paradise, not a howling wilderness. The Puritan might write of hardship on an improvised lapboard in winter, but the southerner reports no such discomfort. In 1665 Sir Robert Moray wrote an epistle describing life in the Carolinas:

In the American Grain

The result of that brave setting out of the Pilgrims has been an atavism that thwarts and destroys. The agonized spirit, that has followed like an idiot with undeveloped brain, governs with its great muscles, babbling in a text of the dead years. Here souls perish miserably, or, escaping, are bent into grotesque designs of violence and despair. It is an added strength thrown to a continent already too powerful for men. One had not expected that this seed of England would come to impersonate, and to marry, the very primitive itself; to creep into the very intestines of the settlers and turn them against themselves, to befoul the New World.

It has become "the most lawless country in the civilized world," a panorama of murders, perversions, a terrific ungoverned strength, excusable only because of the horrid beauty of its great machines. To-day it is a generation of gross know-nothingism, of blackened churches where hymns groan like chants from stupefied jungles, a generation universally eager to barter permanent values (the hope of an aristocracy) in return for opportunist material advantages, a generation hating those whom it obeys.

What prevented the normal growth? Was it England, the northern strain, the soil they landed on? It was, of course, the whole weight of the wild continent that made their condition of mind advantageous, forcing it to reproduce its own likeness, and no more.

William Carlos Williams (1925)

None can know the sweetness of it but he that tasts it. One ocular [visual] inspection, one aromatick smel of our woods, one hearing of the consert of our birds in those woods would affect them more than 1000 reported stories let the authors be never so readible.

Southern colonists conceived of the good life in terms of a fertile valley that, industriously cultivated, could realistically become an American dream come true —as Robert Beverley put it, a "paradise improved." These colonists came from English villages and from cities like London and Bristol. But they brought to America an ideal of English farm life and the Renaissance commitment to exploration and knowledge.

The colonial South included cultures of the Chesapeake Bay, Virginia, the Carolinas, and, in the eighteenth century, Georgia. The early southern writers were planters, merchants, artisans, and ministers, and they wrote in many forms, among them letters, personal journals, autobiographies, poems, sermons, and translations. Colonial southern writing enriched the national literature with satire, song, storytelling, and a spirit of exploration inherent in the English Renaissance. The southern ideal, expressed in literature and the fine arts, was that of country life. It was modeled on English farm life but intended to surpass it in the sylvan New World. Thus southern writers like Smith, Beverley, William Byrd II, and even the satirist Ebenezer Cooke elaborated the idea of America as a Canaan, a "vale" of plenty.

Southern colonists suffered the same shipboard travails as their counterparts in New England. Their justification for taking the land was similar to that of the Puritans. "We chanced in a lande," wrote Smith, "even as God made it, where we found only an idle, improvident, scattered people." Through two centuries the southerners negotiated treaties with that "scattered people" as they penetrated inland, cultivating the tobacco crop that depleted the richest soil, and which induced them to move on and to recruit workers—at first whites, then black slaves—for field cultivation. Southern colonists learned to expect killing winter frosts but knew they could look forward to very long summers whose growing season averaged six to nine months. Daily life could be conducted in the outdoors in forms not possible in the North. Thus in 1705 Beverley could observe that "all their drudgeries of cookery, washing, dairies, etc., are performed in offices detached from the dwelling-houses, which by this means are kept cool and sweet."

The southern colonists, like those in the North, first constructed dwellings of wattle and daub, though even in 1608 or 1609 a visitor to Jamestown noticed that beautifully woven Indian mats decorated colonists' walls. In Maryland, as elsewhere, early colonists ate and slept on shipboard while they constructed a framed timber fort and built cottages onshore. By the 1660s brick kilns were in use in Jamestown and Henrico, Virginia, and bricklayers were at work constructing houses. Later in that century, and throughout the next, brickwork became decorative in checkerboard and diagonal patterns that were popular throughout the South. The simple, versatile, quickly constructed log house, which was introduced to Englishmen by Germans and Scandinavians, probably first appeared in America in the Carolinas. By the end of the colonial period southern frontiersmen in western Virginia lived in it, as did some black slaves in "quarters" set at a distance from the main house.

Gardens complemented southern colonial houses at every socioeconomic level. They ranged from quadrangles of shrubs, flowers, and herbs to elaborate arrangements of terraces, mounds, ponds, and lakes modeled on English precedent but adapted to the new environment. Often decorative, edible, and medicinal vegetation was mixed together as ornamental gardens merged with the kitchen garden. And for some men and women interested in botany, medicine, and landscaping, the ornamental garden was a nursery and experiment station.

The legend of southern gracious living persists in twentieth-century movies and in the remaining eighteenth-century plantation houses and grounds open to tourists. Colonial texts document this quality of southern life as early as 1686, when a French traveler commented on his visit to Colonel William Fitzhugh's estate near Manassas, Virginia: "The Colonel's accommodations were . . . so ample that this company [of twenty] gave him no trouble at all; we were all supplied with beds. . . . Col. Fitzhugh showed us the largest hospitality. He had store of good wine and other things to drink, and a frolic ensued." Philip Fithian's *Journal* nearly a century later tells a comparable story. "The Ladies dined first," Fithian reports of a private ball in mid-1770s Virginia.

When they rose, each nimblest Fellow dined. . . . For drink, there were several sorts of Wine, good Lemon Punch, Toddy, Cyder, Porter, &c—About Seven the Ladies & Gentlemen begun to dance in the Ball-Room—first Minuets one

Round; Second Giggs; third Reels; And last of All Country-Dances. . . . The Ladies were Dressed Gay, and splendid, & when dancing, their Skirts & Brocades rustled and trailed behind them.

Though Fithian observes the wealthy at play, it must be remembered that good music and the fine arts were a part of life for many southerners, including yeoman farmers, apprentices, and merchants.

Southern colonial life assumed its own social forms. If it lacked the visible community focal point of the meetinghouse, southerners were nonetheless joined together by waterways and rounds of visits. The men mustered for militia exercises at appointed times and places and attended sessions of court. Many families sojourned to Anglican and other church services, and the roads themselves were at times the scene of social life, as owners raced horses on them and wagered on the outcome. "There are races at Williamsburg twice a year," wrote an Englishman named J. D. F. Smith, who visited the colonies in 1772, "also matches and sweepstakes very often, the inhabitants, almost to a man, being quite devoted to the diversion of horse-racing."

Yet most southern colonists, whether of modest holdings or vast acreage, were farmers vitally interested in weather, soil, seeds, crops, livestock, and the trades and crafts necessary to agrarian life. The cultivation of the principal money crop, tobacco, points up the degree of work required for the "vale of plenty." By 1618 tobacco was entrenched as a profitable crop, but colonial farmers worked hard to bring it to market. They first chose a site where the forest mold was virgin and in midwinter burned a pile of brush and logs to enrich the soil with ash and to clear it of potential weeds. The minuscule tobacco seeds (ten thousand to a teaspoon) were sown before winter's end. By late spring the seedlings were transplanted to prepared fields. In dry weather the crusts of mud had to be broken, and when the plants began to bud, the tops had to be nipped so that the leaves would grow desirably large. Insects and worms were, of course, removed by hand. At harvest time the leaves were finally cut, hung to dry in a protective enclosure, and finally packed in a barrel through which an axle was driven so it could be wheeled, sometimes many miles, to a shipping point on a tidewater wharf.

Southern colonial intellectual life in this agrarian culture was both broad and deep in spite of dispersed settlement patterns. Indian missionary work was one educational incentive, which John Brinsley, a Virginian, recognized in 1622 when he wrote that God had "ordained schooles of learning to be a principal means to reduce a barbarous people to civilitie." Formal education became a concern throughout the colonies. There were Jesuit schools in Catholic Maryland, a school for orphans founded in Georgia by the preacher George Whitefield, and a variety of private, parish, and tutorial schools elsewhere. The College of William and Mary, which Thomas Jefferson attended, was founded in 1693.

Schoolteachers were sometimes recruited like laborers and skilled craftsmen. As John Harrower confided to his diary in 1774, "This day I being reduced to the last shilling I hade I was obliged to engage to go [from London] to Virginia for four years as a schoolmaster for Bedd, Board, washing and five pound during the whole time." Harrower was hired by a Colonel Dangerfield of "Belvedere," near

Fredericksburg ("This morning about 8 A M the Colonel delivered his three sons to my Charge to teach them to read, write, and figure. His oldest son Edwin, 10 years of age, intred into two syllables in the spelling book, Bathurst his second son six years of age in the Alphabete and William his third son 4 years of age does not know the letters"). Indications are that tutors like Harrower often ran plantation schools for pupils numbering twenty or thirty. Students like his, the sons of wealthy southern colonists, were sometimes sent abroad to England for higher education, as William Byrd II was. The Virginian Hugh Jones complained in 1724 that in England such young men were kept "drudging on in what is of least use to them, in pedantick methods, too tedious for their volatile genius." Such young men, however, were able to enjoy the London cultural scene, including the drama, which Puritans abhorred but which the southern colonies appreciated and supported. This colonial linkage to the mother country has held the attention of the modern writer, who deliberately displays the stylistic richness of the southern colonial.

The Sot-Weed Factor

In the last years of the seventeenth century there was to be found among the fops and fools of the London coffee-houses one rangy, gangling flitch called Ebenezer Cooke, more ambitious than talented, and yet more talented than prudent, who, like his friends-in-folly, all of whom were supposed to be educating at Oxford or Cambridge, had found the sound of Mother English more fun to game with than her sense to labor over, and so rather than applying himself to the pains of scholarship, had learned the knack of versifying, and ground out quires of couplets after the fashion of the day, afroth with Joves and Jupiters, aclang with jarring rhymes, and string-taut with similes stretched to the snapping-point. . . .

[This] was his origin: Ebenezer was born American, though he'd not seen his birthplace since earliest childhood. His father, Andrew Cooke 2nd, of the Parish of St. Giles in the Fields, County of Middlesex—a red-faced, white-chopped, stout-winded old lecher with flinty eye and withered arm—had spent his youth in Maryland as agent for a British manufacturer, as had his father before him, and having a sharp eye for goods and a sharper for men, had added to the Cooke estate by the time he was thirty some one thousand acres of good wood and arable land on the Choptank River. The point on which this land lay he called Cooke's Point, and the small manor-house he built there, Malden. He married late in life and conceived twin children, Ebenezer and his sister Anna, whose mother (as if such an inordinate casting had cracked the mold) died bearing them. When the twins were but four Andrew returned to England, leaving Malden in the hands of an overseer, and thenceforth employed himself as a merchant, sending his own factors to the plantations. His affairs prospered, and the children were well provided for.

John Barth (1960)

Religious life was richly varied in the colonial South. During the seventeenth century the Anglican church (the Church of England) predominated, but Roman Catholics were appearing in all five southern colonies, as were other dissenters, including a few Puritans. With Lord Baltimore's founding of Maryland in 1634, Catholics had a colonial center. And Quaker missionaries were at work in Virginia in the mid-seventeenth century. After 1700, French and German Protestants, Lutherans, Baptists, and evangelical Presbyterians gained increasing religious influence in the South. They coexisted uneasily with the Anglican clergy, who overlooked the power of their evangelical fervor and so failed to take part in the religious movement known as the Great Awakening, a phenomenon in South and North alike.

Colonial writers of the South, like their northern counterparts, wrote much literature that was deliberately useful or purposeful. Such texts as Indian treaties, promotion tracts, sermons, and treatises on education or science or technology were intentionally utilitarian even though they all had aesthetic qualities. Yet an abundance of verse (elegies, pastoral poems, satires, ballads) and of journals, diaries, letters, essays, and autobiographies shows the powerful belletristic strain in writings of the region. It must be remembered as well that a literary tradition was in the making in the slave quarters. A growing population of black African slaves sang songs and kept alive the African folklore which, mingled with the slaves' experience in the New World, would eventually find its way into formal writing in the twentieth century. Though some slaves learned to read and write (using these very skills in the eighteenth century to petition for their freedom), slaves by law were kept illiterate in the South and therefore had no opportunity in the colonial era to give written expression to their oral traditions. That flowering would have to wait two hundred years. The record of extant southern literature of the seventeenth and eighteenth centuries is one of white writers.

It is a record of a complex and sophisticated intellectual and literary life. The Puritan Cotton Mather, an avid book collector, would have been surprised to learn that the only colonial American library larger than his own belonged to the Virginian aristocrat William Byrd II, a man of whom Mather could only have disapproved as licentious and ungodly. Ultimately the descendants of both men would join to unite the colonies in protest against British policy and, finally, in revolution. The Continental Congress and Declaration of Independence (1776) indicated the convergence of very different ways of life in the two regions. Southerners like William Byrd II and the Marylander Ebenezer Cooke were raconteurs and sharp observers of the American environment. When they joined their northern counterparts, the subjects congenial to them both were politics and the future of the colonies.

Toward the Revolution: The Eighteenth Century

In 1726 the English bishop, George Berkeley, wrote a verse which American colonists, including Benjamin Franklin, liked to quote because it nourished confidence in the growth of American culture:

Westward the course of empire takes its way;
    The first four acts already past,
A fifth shall close the drama with the day;
    Time's noblest offspring is the last.

Berkeley's "Verses on the Prospect of Planting Arts and Learning in America" expressed the patriotic idea of a progressively westward-moving culture. Through the eighteenth century the idea of westward empire began to coincide with the concept of nationhood. The European movement known as the Enlightenment began to transform American thought and writing and to make possible the political and literary unification of the thirteen very different colonies.

The Enlightenment

In the eighteenth century scientists and philosophers posed serious challenge to the seventeenth-century mind. Sir Isaac Newton (1642–1727) formulated the laws of gravity and motion, and John Locke (1633–1704) advanced the theory that knowledge is gained only by sensory perception. Newtonian thought embraced a pattern of ideas: that the universe is governed by immutable natural laws, that these laws constitute a harmonious system reflecting a benevolent and wise higher power, and that humankind desires to bring about a correspondingly harmonious, benevolent life on earth. Newton, a Christian, saw God as a cosmic geometrician. In so doing he inadvertently fostered the Enlightenment idea of Deism, which weakened the power of traditional religious authority.

The Deists, among them Benjamin Franklin, deduced the existence of God from the structure of the universe, not from the Bible. Surveying the numerous sects, each with its claims to unique divine revelation, they rejected revealed religion and looked instead to the "simplicity of nature," which signified the "established order, and course of natural things." The scientist Robert Boyle, a follower of Newton, wrote that mathematical and mechanical principles were "the alphabet in which God wrote the world." By implication, human beings could comprehend the laws of the universe and, by the application of reason, arrange human affairs in a correspondingly rational benevolent way. The Deists were less interested in theology than in the application of human reason to earthly problems. Concerns over human nature took precedence over such religious doctrines as the fall of man and the incarnation of Jesus Christ. John Locke reinforced this position by emphasizing that individuals are not born with innate ideas on good or evil but that each is a blank slate or *tabula rasa* upon which experience is inscribed to form character and personality. In eighteenth-century America, such Enlightenment ideas as the inevitability of progress, the efficacy of reason, and the perfectibility of man marked a distinct change in our literature. Concurrently, American writings were influenced by popular literary forms, including newspapers, and by social and religious patterns as well.

Living Conditions and Literacy

Living conditions in the colonies continued to vary in the eighteenth century. One Maryland colonist, a Dr. Hamilton, dined with a Susquehanna, Pennsylvania, family who had "neither knife, fork, spoon, plate, or napkin" and simply dug into a dirty wood dish, though in 1744 he observed that a New York City family owned such "superfluous things" as a "looking glass with a painted frame, half a dozen pewter spoons and as many plates, a set of stone tea dishes, and a tea pot." Such a family would be likely to read colonial newspapers, twenty-six of which had been published weekly by 1765. They were literary, attempting to imitate the sophisticated style of English periodicals, especially the essays of Joseph Addison and Richard Steele. William Park's *Virginia Gazette,* launched in Williamsburg in 1736, illustrates the compositional range of a successful early colonial newspaper. It contained a fair measure of poetry, a few mathematical puzzles, and a scattering of social announcements. It also featured serialized satirical pieces whose authors disguised their identity under such pen names as Miss Arabella Sly, Miss Amoret, and Miss Penelope Leer. Papers like the *Virginia Gazette* or Thomas Fleet's *Boston Evening Post* reached audiences of the gentry and professionals, as well as independent farmers, artisans, and schoolteachers. By the outbreak of the Revolutionary War, however, more papers began to adopt the principle of Isaiah Thomas, the Worcester, Massachusetts, editor-publisher who urged that journalism become a "popular" expression of "common sense in a common language."

Eighteenth-century booksellers, like many newspaper editors, depended on the professional classes for the bulk of their sales because books were terribly expensive. Personal libraries rarely exceeded twenty-five volumes and were dominated by what Cotton Mather called "devout and useful books," including the Bible, *The Pilgrim's Progress* (1678), sermons and tracts, almanacs, medical books, and practical and scientific treatises like *The Farmer's Companion* (1754) or Jared Eliot's *Essay on Field Husbandry* (1762).

Because the literacy rate was high (among white males, at least) in the South, the middle colonies, and especially New England, literary taste itself gradually became a value in colonial eighteenth-century America. Writers looked to the mother country for models, including those provided by Addison and Steele, John Dryden, Dr. Samuel Johnson, Jonathan Swift, and especially Alexander Pope, whose *Essay on Man* (1733–1734) went through forty-five American printings before the end of the century. Benjamin Franklin took full advantage of the exemplary lessons of these English figures. From an early age he equated good writing with a successful career, for Franklin sought the approval of the American reading public. His journalism, almanac wit, satirical essays, political pamphlets, scientific papers, and prolific correspondence cover virtually the full range of colonial writing, and do so in a crisp style that none of his American contemporaries could match.

Franklin exemplifies the secular concerns of a Deist in the American Enlightenment. His maxims ("Waste not, want not," for example) indicate paths toward self-improvement, and his numerous essays address human foibles, vices and virtues, and systematic programs by which the individual and society can be improved. Underlying much of his writing is a utilitarian premise. "I believe there is one supreme, most perfect Being, Author and Father of the Gods themselves," wrote Franklin, who went on to say that only the virtuous man could be happy. Consistently, his work addressed the subject of that virtue in a secular realm.

Jonathan Edwards and the Great Awakening

Religious life continued to be crucial to the colonial experience through the eighteenth century. Franklin's generation gave rise to a formidable theologian and metaphysician, Jonathan Edwards, whose thought and temperament so differed from Franklin's that it has become customary to view their careers as antithetical parts of the colonial mind. Both men originated in Puritan New England and were deeply influenced by the scientific and philosophical writing of Newton and Locke. In Franklin those influences found expression in a progress-oriented, public-spirited ideology based on the religious assumptions of Deism, the Newtonian view of a God who did not participate directly in human affairs. In Edwards, however, Enlightenment thought led to a reformulation of Puritanism, with emphasis on the authenticity of feelings or affections as indices of God's disposition toward the individual. Love, said Edwards, "is not only one of the affections but it is the first and chief . . . and the fountain of all the affections."

Edwards's stirring sermons placed him at the center of a series of religious revivals known as the Great Awakening, which was in large part a reaction against Deism and Newtonian science. Begun in the 1740s, this evangelical movement occurred in all colonies. It affected the Pennsylvania German Pietists, the Methodists, and the Baptists, Quakers, and Scotch-Irish Presbyterians in North Carolina, New Jersey, Connecticut, and Virginia. In several trips up and down the coast, the Methodist itinerant preacher George Whitefield (1714–1770) prayed that "grace in every heart might dwell," as the black versifier Phyllis Wheatley wrote in her elegy "On the Death of the Rev. Mr. George Whitefield, 1770": "Thy sermons in unequaled accents flowed, / And every bosom with devotion glowed." Whitefield was just one of the itinerant ministers who evoked evangelical religious feeling in the revival meetings. The Grand Itinerants, as Whitefield and his cohorts were called, made their way into remote settlements and released fervent emotional energies throughout the colonies.

In 1740 Whitefield brought his evangelistic energies to New England, traveling west from Boston to Jonathan Edwards's Northhampton, where he stayed with the Edwards family and preached in the parish church, moving Edwards to tears. Soon Edwards's own congregation—indeed the entire Holyoke Valley—was swept into the movement. Jonathan Edwards became its exponent. As a reader of John Locke in his student days, he understood the English philosopher's empiricism; but as a Puritan who had experienced the presence of God's grace in his early teens, Edwards felt that Locke's theories served to confine human life to the senses, even reduce it to the sensory level of beasts.

Yet Edwards saw in Lockean thought a potential antidote to the cold religiosity of reason, which he felt had gradually corrupted the Puritan mission in the eighteenth century. He used Lockean thought to reaffirm Puritan doctrine, especially that of predestination. Lockean psychology enabled Edwards to argue that the sovereignty of God is a phenomenon delightful to the senses. "I am bold to assert," he wrote in *A Treatise Concerning Religious Affections* (1746), "that there never was any considerable change wrought in the mind or conversation of any person, by any thing of a religious nature . . . who had not his affections moved," among them the "fear, hope, love, hatred, desire, joy, sorrow, gratitude, compassion, and zeal," all of which he thought were sanctioned in Scripture but neglected in a Deistic era.

The work of Edwards—in fact of all who participated in the Great Awakening—had significant implications for the American Revolution. The movement emphasized liberation from traditional authority and, in political terms, anticipated the eventual severance from England. Politically the Great Awakening can be read as a struggle between the values of a distant, established authority and those of individuals in remote communities. It bred intercolonial communications and fostered collective resistance toward distant, more orthodox opponents.

Settlers and Skirmishes

The eighteenth century saw marked demographic changes in the American colonies, deriving from the Treaty of Utrecht (1713) in which the monarchies of England, France, Spain, and Holland agreed to renounce claims to each other's thrones and entered into commercial pacts. Temporarily these pacts suppressed French and Spanish territorial designs and created a relatively stable Atlantic environment in which the colonies could undertake political and economic initiatives.

It is helpful to notice who lived where in the decades before the Revolution. In 1713 English colonists comprised ninety percent of the population. During the next fifty years that proportion declined to less than sixty percent even as the total colonial population increased fourfold. European colonists ventured to settle in the New World at a rate proportionally higher than at any previous time in American history. Germans found their way into Pennsylvania, western Maryland, Virginia, the Carolinas, and Georgia. Scotch-Irish settled from Maine to South Carolina in border areas, providing a buffer zone between settled habitations and the Indian-filled wilderness. By 1749 they accounted for nearly one quarter of Pennsylvania's population. The French Protestants, the Huguenots, settled in the southern and middle colonies, while the Dutch established elaborate feudal estates in New York's Hudson valley and controlled much of the colony's mercantile activity.

One-third to one-half of all white settlers who entered the New World before the Revolution arrived under contract ("indenture") for four to seven years' service in exchange for the costs of their transportation, food, clothing, and shelter. Most of these individuals and families fulfilled their contracts through work as field hands or household servants, though a few became artisans or teachers. A high mortality rate threatened this group, but they were, technically at least, "free," their period of bondage limited by a legally binding contract. Not so the increasing slave population, which rose to upwards of one-half million by 1770, ninety percent in the southern colonies. By the eve of the Revolution black slavery had developed into the "peculiar institution," with a century-long history of court cases that grappled with the contradictory views of slaves as property and as people. The virtues of freedom and of the freeholding of land in a pluralistic society entered American literature in the writings of Franklin and, after the Revolution, in Michel Guillaume Jean de Crèvecoeur's *Letters from an American Farmer.*

Intercolonial affairs did not proceed smoothly. The decades leading to the Revolution were fraught with tensions, even violence among the colonies and among ethnic and religious groups. For instance, fighting erupted between Connecticut and Pennsylvania in the 1750s over rival claims to Susquehanna land. And cities with large slave populations, like Charleston and New York, lived in continuous dread of riots and arson. Occasional labor insurrections, like that of the Greek and Italian immigrants in Florida in 1769, led to the virtual extinction of newly formed communities of the indentured. And Indian raids were a constant threat, especially during the French-Indian War (1756–1763).

The succession of wars against the French in North America established the British hegemony in North America and had far-reaching political and military consequences for the English colonists, including George Washington, who learned guerilla-type forest warfare and recognized that the British army was not invincible. When the French and Indians defeated General Braddock near Fort Duquesne (now Pittsburgh), Franklin noted that "the whole transaction gave us Americans the first suspicion that our exalted ideas of the prowess of British regulars had not been well founded."

In the decades leading up to the Revolutionary War, Britain found the colonists increasingly resistant to its policies, which often seemed capricious even to moderates. The Hat Act of 1732 and the Molasses Act of 1733, both unpopular measures to control colonial trade, had been countered with smuggling and commercial chicanery. The Stamp Act of 1765 met violent opposition. Tradesmen, artisans, and laborers joined in mass protests against the rather high tax levied on colonial newspapers, almanacs, advertisements, single-sheet or broadside publications, pamphlets, and legal documents. Colonial merchants agreed to boycott English goods, and the dissident "Sons of Liberty" intimidated or attacked British officials and destroyed their property.

Though Parliament repealed the Stamp Act within a year, the damage had been done. After 1765 newspapers scrutinized colonial affairs and assumed a major role in shaping anti-British sentiment, as did the more than two thousand pamphlets published between 1763 and 1776. Their authors were men like John Dickinson and Samuel and John Adams, whose names became synonymous with the literature of the Revolution. The pamphlets were a brilliant propaganda strategy, inexpensive to print and purchase, and both portable and durable. In the hands of a skilled rhetorician like Thomas Paine, the political pamphlet was a powerful armament for the colonists. It stirred sentiment and gave eloquent formal expression to strong feelings. Pamphlet literature reached colonists receptive to the contentious prose of political controversy and to an Enlightenment vocabulary of natural rights. Pamphlets hastened the formation of a revolutionary ideology. To overthrow British rule, one pamphlet declared, "nothing is wanted but your own Resolution, for great is the Authority and Power of the People."

Such sentiments were put to the test. When Parliament passed the Tea Act of 1773, colonial seaports united to prevent the unloading and sale of tea which, taxed by Britain, would still have been inexpensive to buy. The principle of unfair taxation, not the price of tea, was at issue when Samuel Adams's band of patriots disguised as Mohawks raided the British ships and dumped the tea chests into Boston Harbor. Immediately other colonies applauded the gesture and decided to stage "tea parties" of their own. By the following year, 1774, colonial relations with England had not improved, and the first of two Continental Congresses convened at Philadelphia. The colonists would soon hear rhetoric like Thomas Paine's: In January 1776 he wrote, "Of more worth is one honest man to society, and in the sight of God, than all the crowned ruffians that ever lived."

Within months Thomas Jefferson would codify those sentiments in the Declaration of Independence, a document thematically characteristic of a new body of American literature. In one sense the ideals of "life, liberty, and the pursuit of happiness" were characteristic of the American Enlightenment and so place Jefferson and the signers of the declaration fully in their contemporary moment.

Yet the ideology of the American Revolution has a long foreground in colonial American literature. Specific to its own cultural and historical moment, indebted to Enlightenment science and religion, the last and latest writings of the American colonists also hark back as far as Captain John Smith's Jamestown and William Bradford's Plymouth. Writings from the "vale of plenty" and from the Puritan "citty upon a hill" anticipate the literature of the American Revolution. Individual rights and the entitlement to liberty were values inscribed in the earliest colonial literature. If the "pursuit of happiness" is most congenial to the southern "vale of plenty" and if "liberty" itself required careful definition on the part of the Puritan, libertarian values nonetheless cut across geographic regions in writings dating from the early seventeenth century. Those values were embodied in a dazzling array of forms and genres, and they span the entire colonial period in literature, codifying the breadth and intensity of the American experience. Two centuries of colonial writing prepared the way for a subsequent literature of a libertarian nation-state. Thus Charles Pinckney of South Carolina could envision the "new country" of post-Revolutionary America when he said, "There will be few poor and few dependent" and "more equality of rank and fortune than in any other country in the world." Those ideals had their origins in the lives and writings of colonial America.

Further Reading:

S. Ahlstrom, *A Religious History of the American People*, 1972.

L. Ziff, *Puritanism in America: New Culture in a New World*, 1973.

H. May, *The Enlightenment in America*, 1976.

E. Emerson, *Puritanism in America, 1620–1750*, 1977.

S. Bercovitch, *The American Jeremiad*, 1978.

R. Davis, *The Intellectual Life of the Colonial South*, 3 vols., 1978.

J. Stilgoe, *Common Landscape of America, 1580 to 1845*, 1982.

William Bradford
1590–1657

William Bradford is the writer synonymous with the Pilgrims, the *Mayflower,* the first Thanksgiving. As a colonist, he was a governor engaged for over thirty years in religious, social, and economic problems. Yet he coauthored a geographical survey and wrote more than one thousand lines of verse. His history of the New England pilgrims, *Of Plymouth Plantation,* stands as one of the major works of colonial literature. In it Bradford recorded the struggles of the Plymouth, Massachusetts, Pilgrims in language he called "a plain style, with singular regard unto the simple truth in all things." Bradford's history tells its readers of the mutual love and affection of the *Mayflower* group. It commends the heroism of individuals and laments the inevitable weaknesses of bad judgment, cowardice, and greed. Central to the work is the very question of the colonists' survival in the New World.

Bradford called himself "a man of sorrows" and in retrospect may seem an unlikely candidate for a literary life. He was born in Austerfield, Yorkshire, of modestly prosperous parents. But after the boy's father died, Bradford's mother remarried, and William was raised by uncles and grandparents who taught him agriculture and animal husbandry. Unlike the numerous university-trained Puritan writers who moved in intellectual circles, Bradford prepared to become a farmer.

His plans changed in William's mid-teens, when he heard the sermons of Richard Clyfton, a nonconformist minister of a small congregation that met secretly at the home of William Brewster in Nottinghamshire. Bradford was so stirred by Clyfton's sermons that, to the dismay of his family and the "scoff" of his neighbors, he left home to join the Brewster group. As he put it in verse, "In dayes of Youth, / God did make known to me his Truth, / And call'd me from my Native place."

At the height of the Reformation, numerous groups like the one Bradford joined were gathering throughout England. But the Scrooby Pilgrims differed from most others on one crucial point. They believed that the Church of England was so thoroughly corrupted that they had no alternative but to separate from it. To reform or purify it, as the Puritans wished to do, seemed out of the question. The Scrooby group proposed instead to establish a "particular" church based on a formal covenant or pact agreed upon by the members, who swore allegiance to it in perpetuity. Their model was the Old Testament covenant made first with Adam and then with Abraham, in addition to the New Testament redemption of Christ. Scripture, in short, was their highest authority. But the Scrooby congregation broke English law when they separated from the national church. They committed treason and were thereafter an outlaw band.

The Scrooby Pilgrims' sojourn in the Netherlands may seem to be a detour on the way to America. In fact, they planned in 1607 to move to the Low Countries in order to find "freedom of religion for all men." Bradford went with them to Amsterdam in 1608 and on to Leyden in the following year. There they worshiped "God amongst themselves" while Bradford earned his living as a weaver and studied several languages, including Dutch, French, Latin, and Greek. But the Scrooby Pilgrims became disappointed that other English nonconformists did not join them, preferring "prisons in England rather than this liberty in Holland." Ten years passed, and the group saw itself aging and thinned by death. Fearful of dispersal, impoverished, and worried about the encroachment of Dutch ways into their lives and those of their children, the group decided to move again. "Weighty and solid reasons" prevailed over "newfangledness" or "giddy humour," Bradford assures us. But two conditions had to be met before the group could become colonists. They needed a charter from England authorizing them to settle on American land owned by the Virginia Company of London, and they needed financing, obtained when a group of "merchant adventurers" agreed to underwrite their expenses in exchange for return shipments of fish, furs, and minerals.

The Bradford party sailed on the *Mayflower* in September 1620 and reached Cape Cod, Massachusetts, after a two-month voyage in crowded conditions and stormy weather. At landfall they were considerably distant from the northernmost boundary of the Virginia territory, which extended approximately to the present site of New York City. But the Pilgrims were exhausted and reluctant to continue a wintry voyage. They decided to stay in New England. Because they lacked royal title to its land, however, they were vulnerable to charges that their officials lacked legal authority. The point was critical because a majority of the colonists were not Pilgrims but "strangers," fellow voyagers eager to remake their lives but uncommitted to church fellowship. The Bradford group thus formulated the Mayflower Compact, legitimating the "Civil Body Politick." It was the first New World document on democratic government. Bradford was one of the signers and soon became a colonial leader. Upon the death of John Carver, the Pilgrim governor, Bradford was elected to that office; he was reelected thirty times between 1621 and 1656.

When Bradford began, in 1630, to write *Of Plymouth Plantation,* the population of the Plymouth colony stood at some three hundred, three times its original number at landfall. Yet the census was less important to him than the quality of the spiritual life among the colonists he first called Pilgrims. They were more concerned for their spiritual wealth than their material expectations in America, which Bradford called a "roost" or "resting place." At several points he linked the Plymouth group to the Old Testament Israelites led by Moses. The Pilgrims, too, were a chosen people journeying through the wilderness in search of the promised land. They, like the Massachusetts Bay Puritans, anticipated the commencement of the Christian millennium, the harvest of the Lord characterized by "the Spirit of God and His grace" on earth. They understood the millennium to be a state of spiritual community and not a materialistic utopia. In this sense the "weather-beaten face" of a "wild and savage" Cape Cod landscape was relatively unimportant. But Bradford lived to see piety decline, worldly interests rise, and "wickedness . . . break forth." He thus wrote *Of Plymouth Plantation* to record God's providential work among the colonists and to remind readers that the Pilgrims must once again return to their original religious mission. Bradford's readers would surely have heard the language of Scripture in the rhythms and the references of his prose, for the Bible was his manual of style and rhetoric, as well as the record of God's truth.

Bradford began his history in 1630, leaving off in 1647. The manuscript was well known to other colonial historians, who used it as source material. In printed form, however, it was available only in the much-edited *New England's Memoriall,* prepared by Bradford's nephew. The original manuscript disappeared and was presumed lost after the Revolution but was discovered in the house of the bishop of London and published for the first time in 1856. It was returned to this country in 1897 and deposited in the Massachusetts State House in Boston. *Of Plymouth Plantation* remains vital because it is very much a human story embodied in a political and religious testament.

Further Reading:
S. E. Morison, *Builders of the Bay Colony,* 1930, 1958.
B. Smith, *Bradford of Plymouth,* 1951.
G. Langdon, *Pilgrim Colony,* 1966.
K. Caffrey, *The Mayflower,* 1974.

Text:
Of Plymouth Plantation, ed. S. E. Morison, 1952, 1959.

---

from Of Plymouth Plantation

And first of the occasion and inducements thereunto; the which, that I may truly unfold, I must begin at the very root and rise of the same. The which I shall endeavour to manifest in a plain style, with singular regard unto the simple truth in all things; at least as near as my slender judgment can attain the same.

Chapter I: [The Separatist Interpretation of the Reformation in England, 1550–1607]

It is well known unto the godly and judicious, how ever since the first breaking out of the light of the gospel in our honourable nation of England, (which was the first of nations whom the Lord adorned therewith after the gross darkness of popery which had covered and overspread the Christian world), what wars and oppositions ever since, Satan hath raised, maintained and continued against the Saints,[1] from time to time, in one sort or other. Sometimes by bloody death and cruel torments; other whiles imprisonments, banishments and other hard usages; as being loath his kingdom should go down, the truth prevail and the churches of God revert to their ancient purity and recover their primitive order, liberty and beauty.

But when he could not prevail by these means against the main truths of the gospel, but that they began to take rooting in many places, being watered with the blood of the martyrs and blessed from Heaven with a gracious increase; he then began to take him to his ancient stratagems, used of old against the first Christians. That when by the bloody and barbarous persecutions of the heathen emperors he could not stop and subvert the course of the gospel, but that it speedily overspread, with a wonderful

[1] Members of Pilgrim and Puritan churches.

celerity, the then best known parts of the world; he then began to sow errors, heresies and wonderful dissensions amongst the professors themselves, working upon their pride and ambition, with other corrupt passions incident to all mortal men, yea to the saints themselves in some measure, by which woeful effects followed. As not only bitter contentions and heartburnings, schisms, with other horrible confusions; but Satan took occasion and advantage thereby to foist in a number of vile ceremonies, with many unprofitable canons and decrees, which have since been as snares to many poor and peaceable souls even to this day.

So as in the ancient times, the persecutions by the heathen and their emperors was not greater than of the Christians one against other:—the Arians and other their complices against the orthodox and true Christians. As witnesseth Socrates in his second book.[2] His words are these:

> The violence truly (saith he) was no less than that of old practiced towards the Christians when they were compelled and drawn to sacrifice to idols; for many endured sundry kinds of torment, often rackings and dismembering of their joints, confiscating of their goods; some bereaved of their native soil, others departed this life under the hands of the tormentor, and some died in banishment and never saw their country again, etc.

The like method Satan hath seemed to hold in these later times, since the truth began to spring and spread after the great defection made by Antichrist, that man of sin.

For to let pass the infinite examples in sundry nations and several places of the world, and instance in our own, when as that old serpent could not prevail by those fiery flames and other his cruel tragedies, which he by his instruments put in ure[3] everywhere in the days of Queen Mary[4] and before, he then began another kind of war and went more closely to work; not only to oppugn but even to ruinate and destroy the kingdom of Christ by more secret and subtle means, by kindling the flames of contention and sowing the seeds of discord and bitter enmity amongst the professors and, seeming reformed, themselves. For when he could not prevail by the former means against the principal doctrines of faith, he bent his force against the holy discipline and outward regiment of the kingdom of Christ, by which those holy doctrines should be conserved, and true piety maintained amongst the saints and people of God.

Mr. Foxe[5] recordeth how that besides those worthy martyrs and confessors which were burned in Queen Mary's days and otherwise tormented, "Many (both students and others) fled out of the land to the number of 800, and became several congregations, at Wesel, Frankfort, Basel, Emden, Markpurge, Strasburg and Geneva, etc." Amongst whom (but especially those at Frankfort) began that bitter war of contention and persecution about the ceremonies and service book, and other popish and antichristian stuff, the plague of England to this day, which are like the high places in Israel which the prophets cried out against, and were their ruin. Which the better part

---

[2] Socrates Scholasticus (ca. fifth century A.D.), Greek historian. The passage is from *Ecclesiastical History* (London, 1577).
[3] I.e., into practice.
[4] Mary I (1516–1558), queen of England (1553–1558), attempted to restore Catholicism to England.
[5] John Foxe (1516–1587), English martyrologist.

sought, according to the purity of the gospel, to root out and utterly to abandon. And the other part (under veiled pretences) for their own ends and advancements, sought as stiffly to continue, maintain and defend. As appeareth by the discourse thereof published in print, anno 1575; a book that deserves better to be known and considered.

The one side laboured to have the right worship of God and discipline of Christ established in the church, according to the simplicity of the gospel, without the mixture of men's inventions; and to have and to be ruled by the laws of God's Word, dispensed in those offices, and by those officers of Pastors, Teachers and Elders, etc. according to the Scriptures. The other party, though under many colours and pretences, endeavoured to have the episcopal dignity (after the popish manner) with their large power and jurisdiction still retained; with all those courts, canons and ceremonies, together with all such livings, revenues and subordinate officers, with other such means as formerly upheld their antichristian greatness and enabled them with lordly and tyrannous power to persecute the poor servants of God. This contention was so great, as neither the honour of God, the common persecution, nor the mediation of Mr. Calvin and other worthies of the Lord in those places, could prevail with those thus episcopally minded; but they proceeded by all means to disturb the peace of this poor persecuted church, even so far as to charge (very unjustly and ungodlily yet prelatelike) some of their chief opposers with rebellion and high treason against the Emperor, and other such crimes.

And this contention died not with Queen Mary, nor was left beyond the seas. But at her death these people returning into England under gracious Queen Elizabeth, many of them being preferred to bishoprics and other promotions according to their aims and desires, that inveterate hatred against the holy discipline of Christ in His church hath continued to this day. Insomuch that for fear it should prevail, all plots and devices have been used to keep it out, incensing the Queen and State against it as dangerous for the commonwealth; and that it was most needful that the fundamental points of religion should be preached in those ignorant and superstitious times. And to win the weak and ignorant they might retain divers harmless ceremonies; and though it were to be wished that divers things were reformed, yet this was not a season for it. And many the like, to stop the mouths of the more godly, to bring them on to yield to one ceremony after another, and one corruption after another; by these wiles beguiling some and corrupting others till at length they began to persecute all the zealous professors in the land (though they knew little what this discipline meant) both by word and deed, if they would not submit to their ceremonies and become slaves to them and their popish trash, which have no ground in the Word of God, but are relics of that man of sin. And the more the light of the gospel grew, the more they urged their subscriptions to these corruptions. So as (notwithstanding all their former pretences and fair colours) they whose eyes God had not justly blinded might easily see whereto these things tended. And to cast contempt the more upon the sincere servants of God, they opprobriously and most injuriously gave unto and imposed upon them that name of Puritans, which is said the Novatians[6] out of pride did assume and take unto themselves. And lamentable it is to see the effects which have followed. Religion hath been disgraced, the godly grieved, afflicted, persecuted, and many exiled; sundry have lost their lives in prisons and other ways. On the other hand, sin

---

[6] Sect whose name, like that of Puritans, was originally a term of derision.

hath been countenanced; ignorance, profaneness and atheism increased, and the papists encouraged to hope again for a day.

This made that holy man Mr. Perkins[7] cry out in his exhortation to repentance, upon Zephaniah ii:

> of many, etc. Thus not profaneness nor wickedness but religion itself is a byword, a mockingstock, and a matter of reproach; so that in England at this day the man or woman that begins to profess religion and to serve God, must resolve with himself to sustain mocks and injuries even as though he lived amongst the enemies of religion.

And this, common experience hath confirmed and made too apparent. But that I may come more near my intendment.

When as by the travail and diligence of some godly and zealous preachers, and God's blessing on their labours, as in other places of the land, so in the North parts, many became enlightened by the Word of God and had their ignorance and sins discovered unto them, and began by His grace to reform their lives and make conscience of their ways; the work of God was no sooner manifest in them but presently they were both scoffed and scorned by the profane multitude; and the ministers urged with the yoke of subscription, or else must be silenced. And the poor people were so vexed with apparitors and pursuivants[8] and the commissary courts, as truly their affliction was not small. Which, notwithstanding, they bore sundry years with much patience, till they were occasioned by the continuance and increase of these troubles, and other means which the Lord raised up in those days, to see further into things by the light of the Word of God. How not only these base and beggarly ceremonies were unlawful, but also that the lordly and tyrannous power of the prelates ought not to be submitted unto; which thus, contrary to the freedom of the gospel, would load and burden men's consciences and by their compulsive power make a profane mixture of persons and things in the worship of God. And that their offices and callings, courts and canons, etc. were unlawful and antichristian; being such as have no warrant in the Word of God, but the same that were used in popery and still retained. Of which a famous author thus writeth in his Dutch commentaries,[9] at the coming of King James into England:

> The new king (saith he) found there established the reform religion according to the reformed religion of King Edward VI, retaining or keeping still the spiritual state of the bishops, etc. after the old manner, much varying and differing from the reformed churches in Scotland, France and the Netherlands, Emden, Geneva, etc., whose reformation is cut, or shapen much nearer the first Christian churches, as it was used in the Apostles' times.

So many, therefore, of these professors as saw the evil of these things in these parts, and whose hearts the Lord had touched with heavenly zeal for His truth, they shook

[7] William Perkins, seventeenth-century theologian at Emmanuel College, Cambridge University.
[8] Church of England officials whose duty it was to enforce conformity.
[9] Emanuel van Meteren, *General History of the Netherlands* (London, 1608).

off this yoke of antichristian bondage, and as the Lord's free people joined themselves (by a covenant of the Lord) into a church estate, in the fellowship of the gospel, to walk in all His ways made known, or to be made known unto them, according to their best endeavours, whatsoever it should cost them, the Lord assisting them. And that it cost them something this ensuing history will declare.

These people became two distinct bodies or churches, and in regard of distance of place did congregate severally; for they were of sundry towns and villages, some in Nottinghamshire, some of Lincolnshire, and some of Yorkshire where they border nearest together. In one of these churches (besides others of note) was Mr. John Smith, a man of able gifts and a good preacher, who afterwards was chosen their pastor. But these afterwards falling into some errours in the Low Countries, there (for the most part) buried themselves and their names.

But in this other church (which must be the subject of our discourse) besides other worthy men, was Mr. Richard Clyfton, a grave and reverend preacher, who by his pains and diligence had done much good, and under God had been a means of the conversion of many. And also that famous and worthy man Mr. John Robinson, who afterwards was their pastor for many years, till the Lord took him away by death. Also Mr. William Brewster a reverend man, who afterwards was chosen an elder of the church and lived with them till old age.

But after these things they could not long continue in any peaceable condition, but were hunted and persecuted on every side, so as their former afflictions were but as flea-bitings in comparison of these; which now came upon them. For some were taken and clapped up in prison, others had their houses beset and watched night and day, and hardly escaped their hands; and the most were fain to flee and leave their houses and habitations, and the means of their livelihood.

Yet these and many other sharper things which afterward befell them, were no other than they looked for, and therefore were the better prepared to bear them by the assistance of God's grace and Spirit.

Yet seeing themselves thus molested, and that there was no hope of their continuance there, by a joint consent they resolved to go into the Low Countries, where they heard was freedom of religion for all men; as also how sundry from London and other parts of the land had been exiled and persecuted for the same cause, and were gone thither, and lived at Amsterdam and in other places of the land. So after they had continued together about a year, and kept their meetings every Sabbath in one place or other, exercising the worship of God amongst themselves, notwithstanding all the diligence and malice of their adversaries, they seeing they could no longer continue in that condition, they resolved to get over into Holland as they could. Which was in the year 1607 and 1608; of which more at large in the next chapter.

Chapter IV: Showing the Reasons and Causes of Their Removal

After they had lived in this city about some eleven or twelve years (which is the more observable being the whole time of that famous truce between that state and the Spaniards) and sundry of them were taken away by death and many others began to be well stricken in years (the grave mistress of Experience having taught them many things), those prudent governors with sundry of the sagest members began both deeply to apprehend their present dangers and wisely to foresee the future and think of timely remedy. In the agitation of their thoughts, and much discourse of things hereabout, at length they began to incline to this conclusion: of removal to some other place. Not out of any newfangledness or other such like giddy humor by which men are oftentimes transported to their great hurt and danger, but for sundry weighty and solid reasons, some of the chief of which I will here briefly touch.

And first, they saw and found by experience the hardness of the place and country to be such as few in comparison would come to them, and fewer that would bide it out and continue with them. For many that came to them, and many more that desired to be with them, could not endure that great labour and hard fare, with other inconveniences which they underwent and were contented with. But though they loved their persons, approved their cause and honoured their sufferings, yet they left them as it were weeping, as Orpah did her mother-in-law Naomi,[10] or as those Romans did Cato in Utica who desired to be excused and borne with, though they could not all be Catos. For many, though they desired to enjoy the ordinances of God in their purity and the liberty of the gospel with them, yet (alas) they admitted of bondage with danger of conscience, rather than to endure these hardships. Yea, some preferred and chose the prisons in England rather than this liberty in Holland with these afflictions. But it was thought that if a better and easier place of living could be had, it would draw many and take away these discouragements. Yea, their pastor would often say that many of those who both wrote and preached now against them, if they were in a place where they might have liberty and live comfortably, they would then practice as they did.

Secondly. They saw that though the people generally bore all these difficulties very cheerfully and with a resolute courage, being in the best and strength of their years; yet old age began to steal on many of them; and their great and continual labours, with other crosses and sorrows, hastened it before the time. So as it was not only probably thought, but apparently seen, that within a few years more they would be in danger to scatter, by necessities pressing them, or sink under their burdens, or both. And therefore according to the divine proverb, that a wise man seeth the plague when it cometh, and hideth himself, Proverbs xxii.3, so they like skillful and beaten soldiers were fearful either to be entrapped or surrounded by their enemies so as they should neither be able to fight nor fly. And therefore thought it better to dislodge betimes to some place of better advantage and less danger, if any such could be found.

Thirdly. As necessity was a taskmaster over them so they were forced to be such, not only to their servants but in a sort to their dearest children, the which as it did not a little wound the tender hearts of many a loving father and mother, so it produced likewise sundry sad and sorrowful effects. For many of their children that were of best dispositions and gracious inclinations, having learned to bear the yoke in their youth and willing to bear part of their parents' burden, were oftentimes so oppressed with their heavy labours that though their minds were free and willing, yet their bodies bowed under the weight of the same, and became decrepit in their early youth, the vigour of nature being consumed in the very bud as it were. But that which was more lamentable, and of all sorrows most heavy to be borne, was that many of their children, by these occasions and the great licentiousness of youth in that country, and

[10] Ruth 1:14.

the manifold temptations of the place, were drawn away by evil examples into extravagant and dangerous courses, getting the reins off their necks and departing from their parents. Some became soldiers, others took upon them far voyages by sea, and others some worse courses tending to dissoluteness and the danger of their souls, to the great grief of their parents and dishonour of God. So that they saw their posterity would be in danger to degenerate and be corrupted.

Lastly (and which was not least), a great hope and inward zeal they had of laying some good foundation, or at least to make some way thereunto, for the propagating and advancing the gospel of the kingdom of Christ in those remote parts of the world; yea, though they should be but even as stepping-stones unto others for the performing of so great a work.

These and some other like reasons moved them to undertake this resolution of their removal; the which they afterward prosecuted with so great difficulties, as by the sequel will appear.

The place they had thoughts on was some of those vast and unpeopled countries of America, which are fruitful and fit for habitation, being devoid of all civil inhabitants, where there are only savage and brutish men which range up and down, little otherwise than the wild beasts of the same. This proposition being made public and coming to the scanning of all, it raised many variable opinions amongst men and caused many fears and doubts amongst themselves. Some, from their reasons and hopes conceived, laboured to stir up and encourage the rest to undertake and prosecute the same; others again, out of their fears, objected against it and sought to divert from it; alleging many things, and those neither unreasonable nor unprobable; as that it was a great design and subject to many unconceivable perils and dangers; as, besides the casualties of the sea (which none can be freed from), the length of the voyage was such as the weak bodies of women and other persons worn out with age and travail (as many of them were) could never be able to endure. And yet if they should, the miseries of the land which they should be exposed unto, would be too hard to be borne and likely, some or all of them together, to consume and utterly to ruinate them. For there they should be liable to famine and nakedness and the want, in a manner, of all things. The change of air, diet and drinking of water would infect their bodies with sore sicknesses and grievous diseases. And also those which should escape or overcome these difficulties should yet be in continual danger of the savage people, who are cruel, barbarous and most treacherous, being most furious in their rage and merciless where they overcome; not being content only to kill and take away life, but delight to torment men in the most bloody manner that may be; flaying some alive with the shells of fishes, cutting off the members and joints of others by piecemeal and broiling on the coals, eat the collops of their flesh in their sight whilst they live, with other cruelties horrible to be related.

And surely it could not be thought but the very hearing of these things could not but move the very bowels of men to grate within them and make the weak to quake and tremble. It was further objected that it would require greater sums of money to furnish such a voyage and to fit them with necessaries, than their consumed estates would amount to; and yet they must as well look to be seconded with supplies as presently to be transported. Also many precedents of ill success and lamentable miseries befallen others in the like designs were easy to be found, and not forgotten to be alleged; besides their own experience, in their former troubles and hardships in their removal into Holland, and how hard a thing it was for them to live in that strange place, though it was a neighbour country and a civil and rich commonwealth.

It was answered, that all great and honourable actions are accompanied with great difficulties and must be both enterprised and overcome with answerable courages. It was granted the dangers were great, but not desperate. The difficulties were many, but not invincible. For though there were many of them likely, yet they were not certain. It might be sundry of the things feared might never befall; others by provident care and the use of good means might in a great measure be prevented; and all of them, through the help of God, by fortitude and patience, might either be borne or overcome. True it was that such attempts were not to be made and undertaken without good ground and reason, not rashly or lightly as many have done for curiosity or hope of gain, etc. But their condition was not ordinary, their ends were good and honourable, their calling lawful and urgent; and therefore they might expect the blessing of God in their proceeding. Yea, though they should lose their lives in this action, yet might they have comfort in the same and their endeavours would be honourable. They lived here but as men in exile and in a poor condition, and as great miseries might possibly befall them in this place; for the twelve years of truce were now out and there was nothing but beating of drums and preparing for war, the events whereof are always uncertain. The Spaniard might prove as cruel as the savages of America, and the famine and pestilence as sore here as there, and their liberty less to look out for remedy.

After many other particular things answered and alleged on both sides, it was fully concluded by the major part to put this design in execution and to prosecute it by the best means they could.

Chapter IX: Of Their Voyage, and How They Passed the Sea; and of Their Safe Arrival at Cape Cod

September 6. These troubles being blown over, and now all being compact together in one ship, they put to sea again with a prosperous wind, which continued divers days together, which was some encouragement unto them; yet, according to the usual manner, many were afflicted with seasickness. And I may not omit here a special work of God's providence. There was a proud and very profane young man, one of the seamen, of a lusty, able body, which made him the more haughty; he would always be contemning the poor people in their sickness and cursing them daily with grievous execrations; and did not let to tell them that he hoped to help to cast half of them overboard before they came to their journey's end, and to make merry with what they had; and if he were by any gently reproved, he would curse and swear most bitterly. But it pleased God before they came half seas over, to smite this young man with a grievous disease, of which he died in a desperate manner, and so was himself the first that was thrown overboard. Thus his curses light on his own head, and it was an astonishment to all his fellows for they noted it to be the just hand of God upon him.

After they had enjoyed fair winds and weather for a season, they were encountered many times with cross winds and met with many fierce storms with which the ship was shroudly shaken, and her upper works made very leaky; and one of the main beams in the midships was bowed and cracked, which put them in some fear that the ship could not be able to perform the voyage. So some of the chief of the company, perceiving the mariners to fear the sufficiency of the ship as appeared by their mutterings, they entered into serious consultation with the master and other officers of the ship, to consider in time of the danger, and rather to return than to cast themselves into a desperate and inevitable peril. And truly there was great distraction and difference of opinion amongst the mariners themselves; fain would they do what could be done for their wages' sake (being now near half the seas over) and on the other hand they were loath to hazard their lives too desperately. But in examining of all opinions, the master and others affirmed they knew the ship to be strong and firm under water; and for the buckling of the main beam, there was a great iron screw the passengers brought out of Holland, which would raise the beam into his place; the which being done, the carpenter and master affirmed that with a post put under it, set firm in the lower deck and otherways bound, he would make it sufficient. And as for the decks and upper works, they would caulk them as well as they could, and though with the working of the ship they would not long keep staunch, yet there would otherwise be no great danger, if they did not overpress her with sails. So they committed themselves to the will of God and resolved to proceed.

In sundry of these storms the winds were so fierce and the seas so high, as they could not bear a knot of sail, but were forced to hull[11] for divers days together. And in one of them, as they thus lay at hull in a mighty storm, a lusty young man called John Howland, coming upon some occasion above the gratings was, with a seele[12] of the ship, thrown into sea; but it pleased God that he caught hold of the topsail halyards which hung overboard and ran out at length. Yet he held his hold (though he was sundry fathoms under water) till he was hauled up by the same rope to the brim of the water, and then with a boat hook and other means got into the ship again and his life saved. And though he was something ill with it, yet he lived many years after and became a profitable member both in church and commonwealth. In all this voyage there died but one of the passengers, which was William Butten, a youth, servant to Samuel Fuller, when they drew near the coast.

But to omit other things (that I may be brief) after long beating at sea they fell with that land which is called Cape Cod; the which being made and certainly known to be it, they were not a little joyful. After some deliberation had amongst themselves and with the master of the ship, they tacked about and resolved to stand for the southward (the wind and weather being fair) to find some place about Hudson's River for their habitation.[13] But after they had sailed that course about half the day, they fell amongst dangerous shoals and roaring breakers, and they were so far entangled therewith as they conceived themselves in great danger; and the wind shrinking upon them withal, they resolved to bear up again for the Cape and thought themselves happy to get out of those dangers before night overtook them, as by God's good providence they did. And the next day they got into the Cape Harbor where they rid in safety.

A word or two by the way of this cape. It was thus first named by Captain Gosnold and his company, Anno 1602, and after by Captain Smith was called Cape James; but

---

[11] To drift with the wind under short sail, typically in a storm.
[12] A roll or a pitch.
[13] The English were aware of Dutch claims to the area but did not honor those claims. The Pilgrims hoped to be the first to colonize the area, which the Dutch did not settle until six years later.

it retains the former name amongst seamen. Also, that point which first showed those dangerous shoals unto them they called Point Care, and Tucker's Terrour; but the French and Dutch to this day call it Malabar by reason of those perilous shoals and the losses they have suffered there.

Being thus arrived in a good harbor, and brought safe to land, they fell upon their knees and blessed the God of Heaven who had brought them over the vast and furious ocean, and delivered them from all the perils and miseries thereof, again to set their feet on the firm and stable earth, their proper element. And no marvel if they were thus joyful, seeing wise Seneca[14] was so affected with sailing a few miles on the coast of his own Italy, as he affirmed, that he had rather remain twenty years on his way by land than pass by sea to any place in a short time, so tedious and dreadful was the same unto him.

But here I cannot but stay and make a pause, and stand half amazed at this poor people's present condition; and so I think will the reader, too, when he well considers the same. Being thus passed the vast ocean, and a sea of troubles before in their preparation (as may be remembered by that which went before), they had now no friends to welcome them nor inns to entertain or refresh their weatherbeaten bodies; no houses or much less towns to repair to, to seek for succour. It is recorded in Scripture as a mercy to the Apostle and his shipwrecked company, that the barbarians showed them no small kindness in refreshing them, but these savage barbarians, when they met with them (as after will appear) were readier to fill their sides full of arrows than otherwise. And for the season it was winter, and they that know the winters of that country know them to be sharp and violent, and subject to cruel and fierce storms, dangerous to travel to known places, much more to search an unknown coast. Besides, what could they see but a hideous and desolate wilderness, full of wild beasts and wild men—and what multitudes there might be of them they knew not. Neither could they, as it were, go up to the top of Pisgah[15] to view from this wilderness a more goodly country to feed their hopes; for which way soever they turned their eyes (save upward to the heavens) they could have little solace or content in respect of any outward objects. For summer being done, all things stand upon them with a weather-beaten face, and the whole country, full of woods and thickets, represented a wild and savage hue. If they looked behind them, there was the mighty ocean which they had passed and was now as a main bar and gulf to separate them from all the civil parts of the world. If it be said they had a ship to succour them, it is true; but what heard they daily from the master and company? But that with speed they should look out a place (with their shallop) where they would be, at some near distance; for the season was such as he would not stir from thence till a safe harbor was discovered by them, where they would be, and he might go without danger; and that victuals consumed apace but he must and would keep sufficient for themselves and their return. Yea, it was muttered by some that if they got not a place in time, they would turn them and their goods ashore and leave them. Let it also be considered what weak hopes of supply and succour they left behind them, that might bear up their minds in this sad condition and trials they were under; and they could not but be very small. It

[14] Lucius Annaeus Seneca (ca. 4 B.C.–A.D. 65), Roman statesman and philosopher.
[15] Deuteronomy 33:34: "And Moses went up . . . to the top of Pisgah . . . and the Lord showed him all the land of Gilead . . . unto the utmost sea."

is true, indeed, the affections and love of their brethren at Leyden was cordial and entire towards them, but they had little power to help them or themselves; and how the case stood between them and the merchants at their coming away hath already been declared.

What could now sustain them but the Spirit of God and His grace? May not and ought not the children of these fathers rightly say: "Our fathers were Englishmen which came over this great ocean, and were ready to perish in this wilderness; but they cried unto the Lord, and He heard their voice and looked on their adversity,"[16] etc. "Let them therefore praise the Lord, because He is good: and His mercies endure forever." "Yea, let them which have been redeemed of the Lord, shew how He hath delivered them from the hand of the oppressor. When they wandered in the desert wilderness out of the way, and found no city to dwell in, both hungry and thirsty, their soul was overwhelmed in them. Let them confess before the Lord His loving-kindness and His wonderful works before the sons of men."[17]

Chapter X: Showing How They Sought Out a Place of Habitation; and What Befell Them Thereabout

Being thus arrived at Cape Cod the 11th of November, and necessity calling them to look out a place for habitation (as well as the master's and mariners' importunity); they having brought a large shallop with them out of England, stowed in quarters in the ship, they now got her out and set their carpenters to work to trim her up; but being much bruised and shattered in the ship with foul weather, they saw she would be long in mending. Whereupon a few of them tendered themselves to go by land and discover those nearest places, whilst the shallop was in mending; and the rather because as they went into that harbor there seemed to be an opening some two or three leagues off, which the master judged to be a river. It was conceived there might be some danger in the attempt, yet seeing them resolute, they were permitted to go, being sixteen of them well armed under the conduct of Captain Standish, having such instructions given them as was thought meet.

They set forth the 15th of November; and when they had marched about the space of a mile by the seaside, they espied five or six persons with a dog coming towards them, who were savages; but they fled from them and ran up into the woods, and the English followed them, partly to see if they could speak with them, and partly to discover if there might not be more of them lying in ambush. But the Indians seeing themselves thus followed, they again forsook the woods and ran away on the sands as hard as they could, so as they could not come near them but followed them by the track of their feet sundry miles and saw that they had come the same way. So, night coming on, they made their rendezvous and set out their sentinels, and rested in quiet that night; and the next morning followed their track till they had headed a great creek and so left the sands, and turned another way into the woods. But they still followed them by guess, hoping to find their dwellings; but they soon lost both them and themselves, falling into such thickets as were ready to tear their clothes and armor in pieces; but were most distressed for want of drink. But at length they found

[16] Deuteronomy 26:5, 7.   [17] Psalm 107:1-5, 8.

water and refreshed themselves, being the first New England water they drunk of, and was now in great thirst as pleasant unto them as wine or beer had been in foretimes.

Afterwards they directed their course to come to the other shore, for they knew it was a neck of land they were to cross over, and so at length got to the seaside and marched to this supposed river, and by the way found a pond of clear, fresh water, and shortly after a good quantity of clear ground where the Indians had formerly set corn, and some of their graves. And proceeding further they saw new stubble where corn had been set the same year; also they found where lately a house had been, where some planks and a great kettle was remaining, and heaps of sand newly paddled with their hands. Which, they digging up, found in them divers fair Indian baskets filled with corn, and some in ears, fair and good, of divers colours, which seemed to them a very goodly sight (having never seen any such before). This was near the place of that supposed river they came to seek, unto which they went and found it to open itself into two arms with a high cliff of sand in the entrance but more like to be creeks of salt water than any fresh, for aught they saw; and that there was good harborage for their shallop, leaving it further to be discovered by their shallop, when she was ready. So, their time limited them being expired, they returned to the ship lest they should be in fear of their safety; and took with them part of the corn and buried up the rest. And so, like the men from Eshcol, carried with them of the fruits of the land and showed their brethren; of which, and their return, they were marvelously glad and their hearts encouraged.

After this, the shallop being got ready, they set out again for the better discovery of this place, and the master of the ship desired to go himself. So there went some thirty men but found it to be no harbor for ships but only for boats. There was also found two of their houses covered with mats, and sundry of their implements in them, but the people were run away and could not be seen. Also there was found more of their corn and of their beans of various colours; the corn and beans they brought away, purposing to give them full satisfaction when they should meet with any of them as, about some six months afterward they did, to their good content.

And here is to be noted a special providence of God, and a great mercy to this poor people, that here they got seed to plant them corn the next year, or else they might have starved, for they had none nor any likelihood to get any till the season had been past, as the sequel did manifest. Neither is it likely they had had this, if the first voyage had not been made, for the ground was now all covered with snow and hard frozen; but the Lord is never wanting unto His in their greatest needs; let His holy name have all the praise.

The month of November being spent in these affairs, and much foul weather falling in, the 6th of December they sent out their shallop again with ten of their principal men and some seamen, upon further discovery, intending to circulate that deep bay of Cape Cod. The weather was very cold and it froze so hard as the spray of the sea lighting on their coats, they were as if they had been glazed. Yet that night betimes they got down into the bottom of the bay, and as they drew near the shore they saw some ten or twelve Indians very busy about something. They landed about a league or two from them, and had much ado to put ashore anywhere—it lay so full of flats. Being landed, it grew late and they made themselves a barricado with logs and boughs as well as they could in the time, and set out their sentinel and betook them to rest, and saw the smoke of the fire the savages made that night. When morning was come they divided their company, some to coast along the shore in the boat, and the rest marched through the woods to see the land, if any fit place might be for their dwelling. They came also to the place where they saw the Indians the night before, and found they had been cutting up a great fish like a grampus,[18] being some two inches thick of fat like a hog, some pieces whereof they had left by the way. And the shallop found two more of these fishes dead on the sands, a thing usual after storms in that place, by reason of the great flats of sand[19] that lie off.

So they ranged up and down all that day, but found no people, nor any place they liked. When the sun grew low, they hasted out of the woods to meet with their shallop, to whom they made signs to come to them into a creek hard by, the which they did at high water; of which they were very glad, for they had not seen each other all that day since the morning. So they made them a barricado as usually they did every night, with logs, stakes and thick pine boughs, the height of a man, leaving it open to leeward, partly to shelter them from the cold and wind (making their fire in the middle and lying round about it) and partly to defend them from any sudden assaults of the savages, if they should surround them; so being very weary, they betook them to rest. But about midnight they heard a hideous and great cry, and their sentinel called "Arm! arm!" So they bestirred them and stood to their arms and shot off a couple of muskets, and then the noise ceased. They concluded it was a company of wolves or such like wild beasts, for one of the seamen told them he had often heard such a noise in Newfoundland.

So they rested till about five of the clock in the morning; for the tide, and their purpose to go from thence, made them be stirring betimes. So after prayer they prepared for breakfast, and it being day dawning it was thought best to be carrying things down to the boat. But some said it was not best to carry the arms down, others said they would be the readier, for they had lapped them up in their coats from the dew; but some three or four would not carry theirs till they went themselves. Yet as it fell out, the water being not high enough, they laid them down on the bank side and came up to breakfast.

But presently, all on the sudden, they heard a great and strange cry, which they knew to be the same voices they heard in the night, though they varied their notes; and one of their company being abroad came running in and cried, "Men, Indians! Indians!" And withal, their arrows came flying amongst them. Their men ran with all speed to recover their arms, as by the good providence of God they did. In the meantime, of those that were there ready, two muskets were discharged at them, and two more stood ready in the entrance of their rendezvous but were commanded not to shoot till they could take full aim at them. And the other two charged again with all speed, for there were only four had arms there, and defended the barricado, which was first assaulted. The cry of the Indians was dreadful, especially when they saw their men run out of the rendezvous toward the shallop to recover their arms, the Indians wheeling about upon them. But some running out with coats of mail on, and cutlasses in their hands, they soon got their arms and let fly amongst them and quickly stopped their violence. Yet there was a lusty man, and no less valiant, stood behind a tree

[18] Large sea mammal related to whales, dolphins,   [19] I.e., sand bars
and porpoises.

within half a musket shot, and let his arrows fly at them; he was seen [to] shoot three arrows, which were all avoided. He stood three shots of a musket, till one taking full aim at him and made the bark or splinters of the tree fly about his ears, after which he gave an extraordinary shriek and away they went, all of them. They left some to keep the shallop and followed them about a quarter of a mile and shouted once or twice, and shot off two or three pieces, and so returned. This they did that they might conceive that they were not afraid of them or any way discouraged.

Thus it pleased God to vanquish their enemies and give them deliverance; and by His special providence so to dispose that not any one of them were either hurt or hit, though their arrows came close by them and on every side [of] them; and sundry of their coats, which hung up in the barricado, were shot through and through. Afterwards they gave God solemn thanks and praise for their deliverance, and gathered up a bundle of their arrows and sent them into England afterward by the master of the ship, and called that place the First Encounter.

From hence they departed and coasted all along but discerned no place likely for harbor; and therefore hasted to a place that their pilot (one Mr. Coppin who had been in the country before) did assure them was a good harbor, which he had been in, and they might fetch it before night; of which they were glad for it began to be foul weather.

After some hours' sailing it began to snow and rain, and about the middle of the afternoon the wind increased and the sea became very rough, and they broke their rudder, and it was as much as two men could do to steer her with a couple of oars. But their pilot bade them be of good cheer for he saw the harbor; but the storm increasing, and night drawing on, they bore what sail they could to get in, while they could see. But herewith they broke their mast in three pieces and their sail fell overboard in a very grown sea, so as they had like to have been cast away. Yet by God's mercy they recovered themselves, and having the flood with them, struck into the harbor. But when it came to, the pilot was deceived in the place, and said the Lord be merciful unto them for his eyes never saw that place before; and he and the master's mate would have run her ashore in a cove full of breakers before the wind. But a lusty seaman which steered bade those which rowed, if they were men, about with her or else they were all cast away; the which they did with speed. So he bid them be of good cheer and row lustily, for there was a fair sound before them, and he doubted not but they should find one place or other where they might ride in safety. And though it was very dark and rained sore, yet in the end they got under the lee of a small island and remained there all that night in safety. But they knew not this to be an island till morning, but were divided in their minds; some would keep the boat for fear they might be amongst the Indians, others were so wet and cold they could not endure but got ashore, and with much ado got fire (all things being so wet); and the rest were glad to come to them, for after midnight the wind shifted to the northwest and it froze hard.

But though this had been a day and night of much trouble and danger unto them, yet God gave them a morning of comfort and refreshing (as usually He doth to His children) for the next day was a fair, sunshining day, and they found themselves to be on an island secure from the Indians, where they might dry their stuff, fix their pieces and rest themselves; and gave God thanks for His mercies in their manifold deliverances. And this being the last day of the week, they prepared there to keep the Sabbath.

On Monday they sounded the harbor and found it fit for shipping, and marched into the land and found divers cornfields and little running brooks, a place (as they supposed) fit for situation. At least it was the best they could find, and the season and their present necessity made them glad to accept of it. So they returned to their ship again with this news to the rest of their people, which did much comfort their hearts.

On the 15th of December they weighed anchor to go to the place they had discovered, and came within two leagues of it, but were fain to bear up again; but the 16th day, the wind came fair, and they arrived safe in this harbor. And afterwards took better view of the place, and resolved where to pitch their dwelling; and the 25th day began to erect the first house for common use to receive them and their goods.

from **Chapter XI: The Remainder of Anno 1620**

[The Mayflower Compact]

I shall a little return back, and begin with a combination made by them before they came ashore; being the first foundation of their government in this place. Occasioned partly by the discontented and mutinous speeches that some of the strangers amongst them had let fall from them in the ship: That when they came ashore they would use their own liberty, for none had power to command them, the patent they had being for Virginia and not for New England, which belonged to another government, with which the Virginia Company had nothing to do. And partly that such an act by them done, this their condition considered, might be as firm as any patent, and in some respects more sure.

The form was as followeth:

IN THE NAME OF GOD, AMEN.
We whose names are underwritten, the loyal subjects of our dread Sovereign Lord King James, by the Grace of God of Great Britain, France, and Ireland King, Defender of the Faith, etc.

Having undertaken, for the Glory of God and advancement of the Christian Faith and Honour of our King and Country, a Voyage to plant the First Colony in the Northern Parts of Virginia, do by these presents solemnly and mutually in the presence of God and one of another, Covenant and Combine ourselves together into a Civil Body Politic, for our better ordering and preservation and furtherance of the ends aforesaid; and by virtue hereof to enact, constitute and frame such just and equal Laws, Ordinances, Acts, Constitutions and Offices, from time to time, as shall be thought most meet and convenient for the general good of the Colony, unto which we promise all due submission and obedience. In witness whereof we have hereunder subscribed our names at Cape Cod, the 11th of November, in the year of the reign of our Sovereign Lord King James, of England, France and Ireland the eighteenth, and of Scotland the fifty-fourth. Anno Domini 1620.

After this they chose, or rather confirmed, Mr. John Carver (a man godly and well approved amongst them) their Governor for that year. And after they had provided a place for their goods, or common store (which were long in unlading for want of boats, foulness of the winter weather and sickness of divers) and begun some small cottages for their habitation; as time would admit, they met and consulted of laws and orders, both for their civil and military government as the necessity of their condition did require, still adding thereunto as urgent occasion in several times, and as cases did require.

In these hard and difficult beginnings they found some discontents and murmurings arise amongst some, and mutinous speeches and carriages in other; but they were soon quelled and overcome by the wisdom, patience, and just and equal carriage of things, by the Governor and better part, which clave faithfully together in the main.

[The Starving Time]

But that which was most sad and lamentable was, that in two or three months' time half of their company died, especially in January and February, being the depth of winter, and wanting houses and other comforts; being infected with the scurvy and other diseases which this long voyage and their inaccommodate condition had brought upon them. So as there died some times two or three of a day in the foresaid time, that of 100 and odd persons, scarce fifty remained. And of these, in the time of most distress, there was but six or seven sound persons who to their great commendations, be it spoken, spared no pains night nor day, but with abundance of toil and hazard of their own health, fetched them wood, made them fires, dressed them meat, made their beds, washed their loathsome clothes, clothed and unclothed them. In a word, did all the homely and necessary offices for them which dainty and queasy stomachs cannot endure to hear named; and all this willingly and cheerfully, without any grudging in the least, showing herein their true love unto their friends and brethren; a rare example and worthy to be remembered. Two of these seven were Mr. William Brewster, their reverend Elder, and Myles Standish, their Captain and military commander, unto whom myself and many others were much beholden in our low and sick condition. And yet the Lord so upheld these persons as in this general calamity they were not at all infected either with sickness or lameness. And what I have said of these I may say of many others who died in this general visitation, and others yet living; that whilst they had health, yea, or any strength continuing, they were not wanting to any that had need of them. And I doubt not but their recompense is with the Lord.

But I may not here pass by another remarkable passage not to be forgotten. As this calamity fell among the passengers that were to be left here to plant, and were hasted ashore and made to drink water that the seamen might have the more beer, and one in his sickness desiring but a small can of beer, it was answered that if he were their own father he should have none. The disease began to fall amongst them also, so as almost half of their company died before they went away, and many of their officers and lustiest men, as the boatswain, gunner, three quartermasters, the cook and others. At which the Master was something strucken and sent to the sick ashore and told the Governor he should send for beer for them that had need of it, though he drunk water homeward bound.

But now amongst his company there was far another kind of carriage in this misery than amongst the passengers. For they that before had been boon companions in drinking and jollity in the time of their health and welfare, began now to desert one another in this calamity, saying they would not hazard their lives for them, they should be infected by coming to help them in their cabins; and so, after they came to lie by it, would do little or nothing for them but, "if they died, let them die." But such of the passengers as were yet aboard showed them what mercy they could, which made some of their hearts relent, as the boatswain (and some others) who was a proud young man and would often curse and scoff at the passengers. But when he grew weak, they had compassion on him and helped him; then he confessed he did not deserve it at their hands, he had abused them in word and deed. "Oh!" (saith he) "you, I now see, show your love like Christians indeed one to another, but we let one another lie and die like dogs." Another lay cursing his wife, saying if it had not been for her he had never come this unlucky voyage, and anon cursing his fellows, saying he had done this and that for some of them; he had spent so much and so much amongst them, and they were now weary of him and did not help him, having need. Another gave his companion all he had, if he died, to help him in his weakness; he went and got a little spice and made him a mess of meat once or twice. And because he died not so soon as he expected, he went amongst his fellows and swore the rogue would cozen him, he would see him choked before he made him any more meat; and yet the poor fellow died before morning.

[Indian Relations]

All this while the Indians came skulking about them, and would sometimes show themselves aloof off, but when any approached near them, they would run away; and once they stole away their tools where they had been at work and were gone to dinner. But about the 16th of March, a certain Indian came boldly amongst them and spoke to them in broken English, which they could well understand but marveled at it. At length they understood by discourse with him, that he was not of these parts, but belonged to the eastern parts where some English ships came to fish, with whom he was acquainted and could name sundry of them by their names, amongst whom he had got his language. He became profitable to them in acquainting them with many things concerning the state of the country in the east parts where he lived, which was afterwards profitable unto them; as also of the people here, of their names, number and strength, of their situation and distance from this place, and who was chief amongst them. His name was Samoset. He told them also of another Indian whose name was Squanto, a native of this place, who had been in England and could speak better English than himself.

Being, after some time of entertainment and gifts dismissed, a while after he came again, and five more with him, and they brought again all the tools that were stolen away before, and made way for the coming of their great Sachem, called Massasoit. Who, about four or five days after, came with the chief of his friends and other attendance, with the aforesaid Squanto. With whom, after friendly entertainment and some gifts given him, they made a peace with him (which hath now continued this 24 years) in these terms:

1. That neither he nor any of his should injure or do hurt to any of their people.

2. That if any of his did hurt to any of theirs, he should send the offender, that they might punish him.

3. That if anything were taken away from any of theirs, he should cause it to be restored; and they should do the like to his.

4. If any did unjustly war against him, they would aid him; if any did war against them, he should aid them.

5. He should send to his neighbours confederates to certify them of this, that they might not wrong them, but might be likewise comprised in the conditions of peace.

6. That when their men came to them, they should leave their bows and arrows behind them.

After these things he returned to his place called Sowams, some 40 miles from this place, but Squanto continued with them and was their interpreter and was a special instrument sent of God for their good beyond their expectation. He directed them how to set their corn, where to take fish, and to procure other commodities, and was also their pilot to bring them to unknown places for their profit, and never left them till he died. He was a native of this place, and scarce any left alive besides himself. He was carried away with divers others by one Hunt, a master of a ship, who thought to sell them for slaves in Spain. But he got away for England and was entertained by a merchant in London, and employed to Newfoundland and other parts, and lastly brought hither into these parts by one Mr. Dermer, a gentleman employed by Sir Ferdinando Gorges and others for discovery and other designs in these parts. Of whom I shall say something, because it is mentioned in a book set forth Anno 1622 by the President and Council for New England, that he made the peace between the savages of these parts and the English, of which this plantation, as it is intimated, had the benefit; but what a peace it was may appear by what befell him and his men.

This Mr. Dermer was here the same year that these people came, as appears by a relation written by him and given me by a friend, bearing date June 30, Anno 1620. And they came in November following, so there was but four months difference. In which relation to his honoured friend, he hath these passages of this very place:

> I will first begin (saith he) with that place from whence Squanto or Tisquantum, was taken away; which in Captain Smith's map is called Plymouth; and I would that Plymouth had the like commodities. I would that the first plantation might here be seated, if there come to the number of 50 persons, or upward. Otherwise, Charlton, because there the savages are less to be feared. The Pocanockets, which live to the west of Plymouth, bear an inveterate malice to the English, and are of more strength than all the savages from thence to Penobscot. Their desire of revenge was occasioned by an Englishman, who having many of them on board, made a greater slaughter with their murderers and small shot when as (they say) they offered no injury on their parts. Whether they were English or no it may be doubted; yet they believe they were, for the French have so possessed them. For which cause Squanto cannot deny but they would have killed me when I was at Namasket, had he not entreated hard for me.
>
> The soil of the borders of this great bay may be compared to most of the plantations which I have seen in Virginia. The land is of divers sorts, for Patuxet

is a hardy but strong soil; Nauset and Satucket are for the most part a blackish and deep mould much like that where groweth the best tobacco in Virginia. In the bottom of that great bay is store of cod and bass or mullet, etc. But above all he commends Pocanocket for the richest soil, and much open ground fit for English grain, etc.

Massachusetts is about nine leagues from Plymouth, and situated in the midst between both, is full of islands and peninsulas, very fertile for the most part.

With sundry such relations which I forbear to transcribe, being now better known than they were to him.

He was taken prisoner by the Indians at Manamoyick, a place not far from hence, now well known. He gave them what they demanded for his liberty, but when they had got what they desired, they kept him still, and endeavoured to kill his men. But he was freed by seizing on some of them and kept them bound till they gave him a canoe's load of corn. Of which, see *Purchas,* lib. 9, fol. 1778. But this was Anno 1619.

After the writing of the former relation, he came to the Isle of Capawack (which lies south of this place in the way to Virginia) and the aforesaid Squanto with him, where he going ashore amongst the Indians to trade, as he used to do, was betrayed and assaulted by them, and all his men slain, but one that kept the boat. But himself got aboard very sore wounded, and they had cut off his head upon the cuddy of the boat, had not the man rescued him with a sword. And so they got away and made shift to get into Virginia where he died, whether of his wounds or the diseases of the country, or both together, is uncertain. By all which it may appear how far these people were from peace, and with what danger this plantation was begun, save as the powerful hand of the Lord did protect them.

These things were partly the reason why they kept aloof and were so long before they came to the English. Another reason as after themselves made known was how about three years before, a French ship was cast away at Cape Cod, but the men got ashore and saved their lives, and much of their victuals and other goods. But after the Indians heard of it, they gathered together from these parts and never left watching and dogging them till they got advantage and killed them all but three or four which they kept, and sent from one sachem to another to make sport with, and used them worse than slaves. Of which the aforesaid Mr. Dermer redeemed two of them; and they conceived this ship was now come to revenge it.

Also, as after was made known, before they came to the English to make friendship, they got all the Powachs[20] of the country, for three days together in a horrid and devilish manner, to curse and execrate them with their conjurations, which assembly and service they held in a dark and dismal swamp.

But to return. The spring now approaching, it pleased God the mortality began to cease amongst them, and the sick and lame recovered apace, which put as [it] were new life into them, though they had borne their sad affliction with much patience and contentedness as I think any people could do. But it was the Lord which upheld them, and had beforehand prepared them; many having long borne the yoke, yea from their youth. Many other smaller matters I omit, sundry of them having been already

---

[20] Medicine men.

published in a journal made by one of the company, and some other passages of journeys and relations already published, to which I refer those that are willing to know them more particularly.

And being now come to the 25th of March, I shall begin the year 1621. . . .

from **Chapter XII: Anno Domini 1621**

[First Thanksgiving]

They began now to gather in the small harvest they had, and to fit up their houses and dwellings against winter, being all well recovered in health and strength and had all things in good plenty. For as some were thus employed in affairs abroad, others were exercised in fishing, about cod and bass and other fish, of which they took good store, of which every family had their portion. All the summer there was no want; and now began to come in store of fowl, as winter approached, of which this place did abound when they came first (but afterward decreased by degrees). And besides waterfowl there was great store of wild turkeys, of which they took many, besides venison, etc. Besides they had about a peck a meal a week to a person, or now since harvest, Indian corn to that proportion. Which made many afterwards write so largely of their plenty here to their friends in England, which were not feigned but true reports. . . .

from **Chapter XIX: Anno Domini 1628**

[Thomas Morton of Merrymount]

About some three or four years before this time, there came over one Captain Wollaston (a man of pretty parts) and with him three or four more of some eminency, who brought with them a great many servants, with provisions and other implements for to begin a plantation. And pitched themselves in a place within the Massachusetts which they called after their Captain's name, Mount Wollaston. Amongst whom was one Mr. Morton, who it should seem had some small adventure of his own or other men's amongst them, but had little respect amongst them, and was slighted by the meanest servants. Having continued there some time, and not finding things to answer their expectations nor profit to arise as they looked for, Captain Wollaston takes a great part of the servants and transports them to Virginia, where he puts them off at good rates, selling their time to other men; and writes back to one Mr. Rasdall (one of his chief partners and accounted their merchant) to bring another part of them to Virginia likewise, intending to put them off there as he had done the rest. And he, with the consent of the said Rasdall, appointed one Fitcher to be his Lieutenant and govern the remains of the Plantation till he or Rasdall returned to take further order thereabout. But this Morton abovesaid, having more craft than honesty (who had been a kind of pettifogger of Furnival's Inn) in the others' absence watches an opportunity (commons being but hard amongst them) and got some strong drink and other junkets and made them a feast; and after they were merry, he began to tell them he would give them good counsel. "You see," saith he, "that many of your fellows are carried to Virginia, and if you stay till this Rasdall return, you will also be carried away and sold for slaves with the rest. Therefore I would advise you to thrust out this Lieutenant

Fitcher, and I, having a part in the Plantation, will receive you as my partners and consociates; so may you be free from service, and we will converse, plant, trade, and live together as equals and support and protect one another," or to like effect. This counsel was easily received, so they took opportunity and thrust Lieutenant Fitcher out o'doors, and would suffer him to come no more amongst them, but forced him to seek bread to eat and other relief from his neighbours till he could get passage for England.

After this they fell to great licentiousness and led a dissolute life, pouring out themselves into all profaneness. And Morton became Lord of Misrule, and maintained (as it were) a School of Atheism. And after they had got some goods into their hands, and got much by trading with the Indians, they spent it as vainly in quaffing and drinking, both wine and strong waters in great excess (and, as some reported) £10 worth in a morning. They also set up a maypole, drinking and dancing about it many days together, inviting the Indian women for their consorts, dancing and frisking together like so many fairies, or furies, rather; and worse practices. As if they had anew revived and celebrated the feasts of the Roman goddess Flora, or the beastly practices of the mad Bacchanalians.[21] Morton likewise, to show his poetry composed sundry rhymes and verses, some tending to lasciviousness, and others to the detraction and scandal of some persons, which he affixed to this idle or idol maypole. They changed also the name of their place, and instead of calling it Mount Wollaston they call it Merry-mount, as if this jollity would have lasted ever. But this continued not long, for after Morton was sent for England (as follows to be declared) shortly after came over that worthy gentleman Mr. John Endecott, who brought over a patent under the broad seal for the government of the Massachusetts. Who, visiting those parts, caused that maypole to be cut down and rebuked them for their profaneness and admonished them to look there should be better walking. So they or others now changed the name of their place again and called it Mount Dagon.

Now to maintain this riotous prodigality and profuse excess, Morton, thinking himself lawless, and hearing what gain the French and fishermen made by trading of pieces, powder and shot to the Indians, he as the head of this consortship began the practice of the same in these parts. And first he taught them how to use them, to charge and discharge, and what proportion of powder to give the piece, according to the size or bigness of the same; and what shot to use for fowl and what for deer. And having thus instructed them, he employed some of them to hunt and fowl for him, so as they became far more active in that employment than any of the English, by reason of their swiftness of foot and nimbleness of body, being also quick-sighted and by continual exercise well knowing the haunts of all sorts of game. So as when they saw the execution that a piece would do, and the benefit that might come by the same, they became mad (as it were) after them and would not stick to give any price they could attain to for them; accounting their bows and arrows but baubles in comparison of them.

And here I may take occasion to bewail the mischief that this wicked man began in these parts, and which since, base covetousness prevailing in men that should know better, has now at length got the upper hand and made this thing common, notwithstanding any laws to the contrary. So as the Indians are full of pieces all over, both fowling pieces, muskets, pistols, etc. They have also their moulds to make shot of all

[21] Followers of the god of wine, Bacchus, and known for their drunken orgies.

sorts, as musket bullets, pistol bullets, swan and goose shot, and of smaller sorts. Yea some have seen them have their screw-plates to make screw-pins themselves when they want them, with sundry other implements, wherewith they are ordinarily better fitted and furnished than the English themselves. Yea, it is well known that they will have powder and shot when the English want it nor cannot get it; and that in a time of war or danger, as experience hath manifested, that when lead hath been scarce and men for their own defense would gladly have given a groat a pound, which is dear enough, yet hath it been bought up and sent to other places and sold to such as trade it with the Indians at 12*d* the pound. And it is like they give 3*s* or 4*s* the pound, for they will have it at any rate. And these things have been done in the same times when some of their neighbours and friends are daily killed by the Indians, or are in danger thereof and live but at the Indians' mercy. Yea some, as they have acquainted them with all other things, have told them how gunpowder is made, and all the materials in it, and that they are to be had in their own land; and I am confident, could they attain to make saltpeter, they would teach them to make powder.

O, the horribleness of this villainy! How many both Dutch and English have been lately slain by those Indians thus furnished, and no remedy provided; nay, the evil more increased, and the blood of their brethren sold for gain (as is to be feared) and in what danger all these colonies are in is too well known. O that princes and parliaments would take some timely order to prevent this mischief and at length to suppress it by some exemplary punishment upon some of these gain-thirsty murderers, for they deserve no better title, before their colonies in these parts be overthrown by these barbarous savages thus armed with their own weapons, by these evil instruments and traitors to their neighbours and country! But I have forgot myself and have been too long in this digression; but now to return.

This Morton having thus taught them the use of pieces, he sold them all he could spare, and he and his consorts determined to send for many out of England and had by some of the ships sent for above a score. The which being known, and his neighbours meeting the Indians in the woods armed with guns in this sort, it was a terror unto them who lived stragglingly and were of no strength in any place. And other places (though more remote) saw this mischief would quickly spread over all, if not prevented. Besides, they saw they should keep no servants, for Morton would entertain any, how vile soever, and all the scum of the country or any discontents would flock to him from all places, if this nest was not broken. And they should stand in more fear of their lives and goods in short time from this wicked and debased crew than from the savages themselves.

So sundry of the chief of the straggling plantations, meeting together, agreed by mutual consent to solicit those of Plymouth (who were then of more strength than them all) to join with them to prevent the further growth of this mischief, and suppress Morton and his consorts before they grew to further head and strength. Those that joined in this action, and after contributed to the charge of sending him for England, were from Piscataqua, Naumkeag, Winnisimmet, Wessagusset, Nantasket and other places where any English were seated. Those of Plymouth being thus sought to by their messengers and letters, and weighing both their reasons and the common danger, were willing to afford them their help though themselves had least cause of fear or hurt. So, to be short, they first resolved jointly to write to him, and in a friendly and neighbourly way to admonish him to forbear those courses, and sent a messenger with their letters to bring his answer.

But he was so high as he scorned all advice, and asked who had to do with him, he had and would trade pieces with the Indians, in despite of all, with many other scurrilous terms full of disdain. They sent to him a second time and bade him be better advised and more temperate in his terms, for the country could not bear the injury he did. It was against their common safety and against the King's proclamation. He answered in high terms as before; and that the King's proclamation was no law, demanding what penalty was upon it. It was answered, more than he could bear—His Majesty's displeasure. But insolently he persisted and said the King was dead and his displeasure with him, and many the like things. And threatened withal that if any came to molest him, let them look to themselves for he would prepare for them.

Upon which they saw there was no way but to take him by force; and having so far proceeded, now to give over would make him far more haughty and insolent. So they mutually resolved to proceed, and obtained of the Governor of Plymouth to send Captain Standish and some other aid with him, to take Morton by force. The which accordingly was done. But they found him to stand stiffly in his defense, having made fast his doors, armed his consorts, set divers dishes of powder and bullets ready on the table; and if they had not been over-armed with drink, more hurt might have been done. They summoned him to yield, but he kept his house and they could get nothing but scoffs and scorns from him. But at length, fearing they would do some violence to the house, he and some of his crew came out, but not to yield but to shoot; but they were so steeled with drink as their pieces were too heavy for them. Himself with a carbine, overcharged and almost half filled with powder and shot, as was after found, had thought to have shot Captain Standish; but he stepped to him and put by his piece and took him. Neither was there any hurt done to any of either side, save that one was so drunk that he ran his own nose upon the point of a sword that one held before him, as he entered the house; but he lost but a little of his hot blood.

Morton they brought away to Plymouth, where he was kept till a ship went from the Isle of Shoals for England, with which he was sent to the Council of New England, and letters written to give them information of his course and carriage. And also one was sent at their common charge to inform their Honours more particularly and to prosecute against him. But he fooled of the messenger, after he was gone from hence, and though he went for England yet nothing was done to him, not so much as rebuked, for aught was heard, but returned the next year. Some of the worst of the company were dispersed and some of the more modest kept the house till he should be heard from. But I have been too long about so unworthy a person, and bad a cause. . . .

from *Chapter XXIV: [Anno Domini 1633]*

[Mr. Roger Williams]

Mr. Roger Williams,[22] a man godly and zealous, having many precious parts but very unsettled in judgment, came over first to the Massachusetts; but upon some discontent left that place and came hither, where he was friendly entertained according to their

---

[22] Founder of Rhode Island.

poor ability, and exercised his gifts amongst them and after some time was admitted a member of the church. And his teaching well approved, for the benefit whereof I still bless God and am thankful to him even for his sharpest admonitions and reproofs so far as they agreed with truth. He this year began to fall into some strange opinions, and from opinion to practice, which caused some controversy between the church and him. And in the end some discontent on his part, by occasion whereof he left them something abruptly. Yet afterwards sued for his dismission to the church of Salem, which was granted, with some caution to them concerning him and what care they ought to have of him. But he soon fell into more things there, both to their and the government's trouble and disturbance. I shall not need to name particulars; they are too well known now to all, though for a time the church here went under some hard censure by his occasion from some that afterwards smarted themselves. But he is to be pitied and prayed for; and so I shall leave the matter and desire the Lord to show him his errors and reduce him into the way of truth and give him a settled judgment and constancy in the same, for I hope he belongs to the Lord, and that He will show him mercy. . . .

from Chapter XXXIII: Anno Domini 1643

[Longevity of the Pilgrim Fathers]

I cannot but here take occasion not only to mention but greatly to admire the marvelous providence of God! That notwithstanding the many changes and hardships that these people went through, and the many enemies they had and difficulties they met withal, that so many of them should live to very old age! It was not only this reverend man's condition (for one swallow makes no summer as they say) but many more of them did the like, some dying about and before this time and many still living, who attained to sixty years of age, and to sixty-five, divers to seventy and above, and some near eighty as he did. It must needs be more than ordinary and above natural reason, that so it should be. For it is found in experience that change of air, famine or unwholesome food, much drinking of water, sorrows and troubles, etc., all of them are enemies to health, causes of many diseases, consumers of natural vigour and the bodies of men, and shorteners of life. And yet of all these things they had a large part and suffered deeply in the same. They went from England to Holland, where they found both worse air and diet than that they came from; from thence, enduring a long imprisonment as it were in the ships at sea, into New England; and how it hath been with them here hath already been shown, and what crosses, troubles, fears, wants and sorrows they had been liable unto is easy to conjecture. So as in some sort they may say with the Apostle, 2 Corinthians xi.26, 27, they were "in journeyings often, in perils of waters, in perils of robbers, in perils of their own nation, in perils among the heathen, in perils in the wilderness, in perils in the sea, in perils among false brethren; in weariness and painfulness, in watching often, in hunger and thirst, in fasting often, in cold and nakedness."

What was it then that upheld them? It was God's visitation that preserved their spirits. Job x.12: "Thou hast given me life and grace, and thy visitation hath preserved my spirit." He that upheld the Apostle upheld them. "They were persecuted, but not forsaken, cast down, but perished not." "As unknown, and yet known; as dying, and behold we live; as chastened, and yet not killed"; 2 Corinthians vi.9.

God, it seems, would have all men to behold and observe such mercies and works of His providence as these are towards His people, that they in like cases might be encouraged to depend upon God in their trials, and also to bless His name when they see His goodness towards others. Man lives not by bread only, Deuteronomy viii.3. It is not by good and dainty fare, by peace and rest and heart's ease in enjoying the contentments and good things of this world only that preserves health and prolongs life; God in such examples would have the world see and behold that He can do it without them; and if the world will shut their eyes and take no notice thereof, yet He would have His people to see and consider it. Daniel could be better liking with pulse than others were with the king's dainties. Jacob, though he went from one nation to another people and passed through famine, fears and many afflictions, yet he lived till old age and died sweetly and rested in the Lord, as infinite others of God's servants have done and still shall do, through God's goodness, notwithstanding all the malice of their enemies, "when the branch of the wicked shall be cut off before his day" (Job xv.32) "and the bloody and deceitful men shall not live [out] half their days"; Psalm lv.23. . . .

from **Chapter XXXIV: Anno Domini 1644**

[Proposal to Remove to Nauset]

Mr. Edward Winslow was chosen Governor this year.

Many having left this place (as is before noted) by reason of the straitness and barrenness of the same and their finding of better accommodations elsewhere more suitable to their ends and minds; and sundry others still upon every occasion desiring their dismissions, the church began seriously to think whether it were not better jointly to remove to some other place than to be thus weakened and as it were insensibly dissolved. Many meetings and much consultation was held hereabout, and divers were men's minds and opinions. Some were still for staying together in this place, alleging men might here live if they would be content with their condition, and that it was not for want or necessity so much that they removed as for the enriching of themselves. Others were resolute upon removal and so signified that here they could not stay; but if the church did not remove, they must. Insomuch as many were swayed rather than there should be a dissolution, to condescend to a removal if a fit place could be found that might more conveniently and comfortably receive the whole, with such accession of others as might come to them for their better strength and subsistence; and some such-like cautions and limitations.

So as, with the aforesaid provisos, the greater part consented to a removal to a place called Nauset, which had been superficially viewed and the good will of the purchasers to whom it belonged obtained, with some addition thereto from the Court. But now they began to see their errour, that they had given away already the best and most commodious places to others, and now wanted themselves. For this place was about 50 miles from hence, and at an outside of the country remote from all society; also that it would prove so strait as it would not be competent to receive the whole body, much less be capable of any addition or increase; so as, at least in a short time, they should be worse there than they are now here. The which with sundry other like considerations and inconveniences made them change their resolutions. But such as were before resolved upon removal took advantage of this agreement and went on, notwithstanding; neither could the rest hinder them, they having made some beginning.

And thus was this poor church left, like an ancient mother grown old and forsaken of her children, though not in their affections yet in regard of their bodily presence and personal helpfulness; her ancient members being most of them worn away by death, and these of later time being like children translated into other families, and she like a widow left only to trust in God. Thus, she that had made many rich became herself poor. . . .

1856

John Winthrop
1588–1649

By birth and breeding, John Winthrop seems a man destined to have been a leader in Puritan colonial life. The son of an English country gentleman, Winthrop was at eighteen a married man acting as steward and justice of the peace on his father's estate at Groton, to which he had returned after two years of legal studies at Trinity College, Cambridge University. The Winthrops were Puritans, and though John wrote of his "wild and dissolute youth," he found "some peace and comfort in God and his wayes" in his late teens, and thereafter his faith strengthened by degrees.

Winthrop began to consider emigration to the New World when political and religious conditions worsened in England. Under the reign of Archbishop Laud, ministers who refused strict adherence to all Anglican practices fell under suspicion or were silenced. Openly a Puritan, Winthrop lost his attorneyship. Everywhere the dreaded Roman Catholicism seemed on the rise. By spring 1629, Winthrop feared that "God will bringe some heavye Affliction upon this lande" in the form of political reprisals or natural disasters such as the plague. Yet he trusted that the Lord would "provide a shelter & a hidinge place for us and others."

The Lord's instrument seemed to be the new Massachusetts Bay Company, which elected Winthrop its first governor in 1629. He sailed for America the following year on the *Arbella,* the flagship vessel of a fleet carrying some seven hundred persons in a "Great Migration" that would soon bring twenty thousand settlers to New England. At sea on board the *Arbella* Winthrop preached a now-classic sermon on the ideals of Christian charity that he felt must govern the colony in all its affairs. It was imperative, he argued, that the settlers form a commonwealth for the mutual benefit of all and that their society be able to withstand the scrutiny of a watchful world. In the Massachusetts Bay Winthrop acted as governor or deputy governor for nearly twenty years, upholding the standards set in his "Model of Christian Charity." In practice his leadership was sought in trials of settlement, trade, property disputes, economic hard times, Indian wars, and the religious controversies that threatened to split the colony into warring camps. Winthrop's *Journal* was the record of these events and became, over time, a record by which to measure how close colonial New England came to being that model "citty upon a hill."

One sequence of *Journal* entries outlines a grave internal threat to the colony. The so-called antinomian controversy came to a head in the trials of Mistress Anne Hutchinson, a woman whom subsequent generations have identified as a martyr to the cause of religious freedom and women's rights. Hutchinson, a housewife and the mother of twelve children, had been a parishioner of the Reverend John Cotton in Boston, England. One year after Cotton's departure for America, the Hutchinson family followed him. Mistress Hutchinson soon established herself as a valued nurse and midwife. In addition, as a devout and intellectually gifted woman she attracted a circle of some sixty women and men to "private conferences" on Mr. Cotton's sermons. Soon she broadened her discussions to include critical analyses of the teachings of other ministers.

As a partisan of Cotton and a sharp critic of his colleagues, Hutchinson put herself at the center of a theological controversy that concerned the part human beings could play in preparing their hearts to receive God's saving grace. The debate had already pitted Cotton against other powerful ministers, and the widespread publicity of Anne Hutchinson's meetings made her the focus of dissension.

Finally brought to trial on charges of sedition, Hutchinson testified that she had received special divine revelation. In Puritan theology this was heresy and carried political implications as well. The individual who received divine guidance directly from God would not need the teaching of the scriptural word (in Latin, *nomen*) from the ministers. Nor would public officials like Winthrop retain their authority, since they claimed that their power came from biblical injunctions. Hutchinson implicitly challenged the power of both church and state. Her minister, Cotton, joined all the others in condemning her.

She was banished by the Massachusetts General Court in November 1637 and moved to Rhode Island with a small band of her followers. When Hutchinson delivered a malformed infant, Winthrop described it in the *Journal* in excruciating detail, interpreting the deformity as a sign of God's judgment on the heretic and, of course, as the implicit vindication of Puritan governmental action. Yet Hutchinson remained in the American imagination. She was a major source for Hawthorne's character Hester in *The Scarlet Letter.* And her intellectual power anticipates that of Margaret Fuller, the mid-nineteenth century writer and great conversationalist who was sometimes as disturbing to Ralph Waldo Emerson as Anne Hutchinson was to John Winthrop.

Winthrop's *Journal* contains accounts of major Puritan controversies like that surrounding Hutchinson. It presents sharp glimpses of colonial life, like that of a townsman who lost his way "and wandered in the woods and swamps three days and two nights without taking any food" and "had torn his legs." Throughout, it emphasizes the working of God's providence in Puritan affairs. (God brought the disoriented townsman to the community of Scituate when he was "near spent" or exhausted.)

From an aesthetic viewpoint it is regrettable that Winthrop did not reshape the *Journal* into a finished narrative, as he intended to do. Yet it stands as a text revealing the Puritan commitment to contemporary history, which they believed would justify the ways of God to man.

Further Reading:
R. Winthrop, *Life and Letters of John Winthrop*, 1864–1867.
S. E. Morison, *Builders of the Bay Colony*, 1930.
E. Morgan, *The Puritan Dilemma*, 1958.
D. Rutman, *Winthrop's Boston*, 1965.
S. Bercovitch, *The Puritan Origins of the American Self*, 1975.

Texts:
"A Model of Christian Charity," *The Winthrop Papers*, ed. A. Forbes, 5 vols., 1929–1947.
The History of New England, ed. J. Savage, 2 vols., 1853, 1972.

---

from A Model of Christian Charity

Christian Charitie

A Modell Hereof

God Almightie in his most holy and wise providence hath soe disposed of the Condicion of mankinde, as in all times some must be rich some poore, some high and eminent in power and dignitie; others meane and in subjection.

The Reason Hereof

1. REAS: *First,* to hold conformity with the rest of his workes, being delighted to shewe forth the glory of his wisdome in the variety and differance of the Creatures and the glory of his power, in ordering all these differences for the preservacion and good of the whole, and the glory of his greatnes that as it is the glory of princes to have many officers, soe this great King will have many Stewards counting himselfe more honoured in dispencing his gifts to man by man, than if hee did it by his owne immediate hand.

2. REAS: *Secondly,* That he might have the more occasion to manifest the worke of his Spirit: first, upon the wicked in moderating and restraining them: soe that the riche and mighty should not eate up the poore, nor the poore, and despised rise up against their superiours, and shake off their yoake; 2ly in the regenerate in exercising His graces in them, as in the greate ones, their love mercy, gentlenes, temperance etc., in the poore and inferiour sorte, their faithe patience, obedience etc:

3. REAS: Thirdly, That every man might have need of other, and from hence they might be all knitt more nearly together in the Bond of brotherly affection: from hence

it appeares plainely that noe man is made more honourable than another or more wealthy etc., out of any particuler and singular respect to himselfe but for the glory of his Creator and the Common good of the Creature, Man; Therefore God still reserves the property of these gifts to himselfe as Ezek: 16. 17.[1] he there calls wealthe his gold and his silver etc. Prov: 3. 9.[2] he claimes their service as his due honour the Lord with thy riches etc. All men being thus (by divine providence) ranked into two sortes, riche and poore; under the first, are comprehended all such as are able to live comfortably by their owne meanes duly improved; and all others are poore according to the former distribution. There are two rules whereby wee are to walke one towards another: JUSTICE and MERCY. These are allways distinguished in their Act and in their obiect, yet may they both concurre in the same Subject in each respect; as sometimes there may be an occasion of shewing mercy to a rich man, in some sudden danger of distresse, and allso doing of meere Justice to a poor man in regard of some particuler contract etc. There is likewise a double Lawe by which wee are regulated in our conversacion one towardes another: in both the former respects, the lawe of nature and the lawe of grace, or the morrall lawe or the lawe of the gospell, to omit the rule of Justice as not properly belonging to this purpose otherwise then it may fall into consideracion in some particuler Cases: By the first of these lawes man as he was enabled soe withall is commaunded to love his neighbour as himselfe;[3] upon this ground stands all the precepts of the morrall lawe, which concernes our dealings with men. To apply this to the works of mercy this lawe requires two things: first that every man afford his help to another in every want or distresse; Secondly, That hee performe this out of the same affection, which makes him carefull of his owne good according to that of our Saviour (Math:[4] Whatsoever ye would that men should doe to you). This was practised by Abraham and Lott in entertaining the Angells and the old man of Gibea.[5]

The Lawe of Grace or the Gospell hath some differance from the former as in these respectes: first the lawe of nature was given to man in the estate of innocency; this of the gospell in the estate of regeneracy:[6] 2ly, the former propounds one man to another, as the same flesh and Image of God, this as a brother in Christ allso, and in the Communion of the same spirit and soe teacheth us to put a difference betweene Christians and others. Do good to all especially to the household of faith; upon this ground the Israelites were to put a difference betweene the brethren of such as were strangers though not of the Canaanites.[7] 3ly. The Lawe of nature could give noe rules for dealing with enemies for all are to be considered as friends in the estate of innocency, but the Gospell commaunds love to an enemy. Proofe. If thine Enemie hunger feede him; Love your Enemies, doe good to them that hate you (Math: 5. 44).

---

[1] "Thou hast also taken thy fair jewels given thee, and madest to thyself images of my gold and of my silver, which I had of men, and didst commit whoredom with them."

[2] "Honor the Lord with thy substance, and with the first fruits of all thine increase: So shall thy barns be filled with plenty, and thy presses burst out with new wine."

[3] Matthew 5:43; 19:19.

[4] Matthew 7:12.

[5] Abraham entertains the angels in Genesis 18:1–2. In Judges 19:16–21 an elderly man of Gilbeah shelters a Levite, a traveling priest, and defends him from enemies from a nearby city.

[6] Mankind is here held to have fallen to an unregenerate state after Adam and Eve sinned. Christ redeemed mankind through his suffering and crucifixion, and thereafter those who believe in him are saved or regenerate.

[7] Those who lived in the Promised Land, Canaan.

This Lawe of the Gospell propoundes likewise a difference of seasons and occasions; there is a time when a christian must sell all and give to the poore as they did in the Apostles times.[8] There is a tyme allso when a christian (though they give not all yet) must give beyond their abillity, as they of Macedonia. Cor: 2. 6.[9] Likewise community of perills calls for extraordinary liberallity and soe doth Community in some speciall service for the Churche. Lastly, when there is noe other meanes whereby our Christian brother may be relieved in this distresse, wee must help him beyond our ability, rather than tempt God, in putting him upon help by miraculous or extraordinary meanes. . . .

It rests now to make some applicacion of this discourse by the present design which gave the occasion of writing of it. Herein are 4 things to be propounded: first the persons, 2ly, the worke, 3ly, the end, 4ly the meanes.

1. For the persons, wee are a Company professing our selves fellow members of Christ, In which respect only though wee were absent from eache other many miles, and had our imploymentes as farr distant, yet wee ought to account our selves knit together by this bond of love, and live in the excercise of it, if wee would have comforte of our being in Christ; this was notorious in the practise of the Christians in former times, as is testified of the Waldenses[10] from the mouth of one of the adversaries Aeneas Syluius,[11] mutuo penè antequam norint, they use to love any of their owne religion even before they were acquainted with them.

2ly. for the worke wee have in hand, it is by a mutuall consent through a speciall overruling providence, and a more then an ordinary approbation of the Churches of Christ to seeke out a place of Cohabitation and Consorteship under a due forme of Goverment both civill and ecclesiasticall. In such cases as this the care of the public must oversway all private respects, by which not only conscience, but meer Civill pollicy doth binde us; for it is a true rule that particuler estates cannot subsist in the ruine of the public.

3ly. The end is to improve our lives to doe more service to the Lord the comforte and encrease of the body of christe whereof wee are members that our selves and posterity may be the better preserved from the Common corruptions of this evill world to serve the Lord and worke out our Salvacion under the power and purity of his holy Ordinances.

4ly for the meanes whereby this must be effected, they are 2fold: a Conformity with the worke and end wee aime at. These wee see are extraordinary, therefore wee must not content our selves with usuall ordinary meanes whatsoever wee did or ought to have done when wee lived in England, the same must wee do and more allso where wee goe: That which the most in their Churches maintain as a truth in profession only, wee must bring into familiar and constant practise, as in this duty of love wee must love brotherly without dissimulation, wee must love one another with a pure hearte fervently, wee must beare one anothers burthens, wee must not looke only on our owne things, but allso on the things of our brethren; neither must wee think that the lord will beare with such failings at our hands as hee dothe from those among whome wee have lived, and that for 3 Reasons.

[8] Luke 18:22: "Sell all that thou hast, and distribute unto the poor, and thou shalt have treasure in heaven."
[9] Actually 2 Corinthians 8:1–4.

[10] Followers of Pater Valdes, who rejected the authority of the pope and taught that the Bible was the sole authority in religion.
[11] Pope Pius II (1458–1464).

1. In regard of the more neare bond of mariage, betweene him and us, wherein he hath taken us to be his after a most strickt and peculiar manner which will make him the more Jealous of our love and obedience, soe he tells the people of Israell, you only have I knowne of all the families of the Earthe, therefore will I punish you for your Transgressions.

2ly, because the lord will be sanctified in them that come neare him. Wee know that there were many that corrupted the service of the Lord, some setting up Alters before his owne, others offering both strange fire and strange Sacrifices allso; yet there came noe fire from heaven, or other sudden Judgement upon them as did upon Nadab and Abihu,[12] who yet wee may thinke did not sinn presumptuously.

3ly When God gives a speciall Commission he lookes to have it strictly observed in every Article; when hee gave Saule a Commission to destroy Amaleck[13] hee indented with him upon certaine Articles, and because hee failed in one of the least, and that upon a faire pretence, it lost him the kingdome, which should have beene his reward, if hee had observed his Commission: Thus stands the cause betweene God and us, wee are entered into Covenant[14] with him for this worke, wee have taken out a Commission, the Lord hath given us leave to drawe our owne Articles, wee have professed to enterprise these Actions upon these and these ends, wee have hereupon besought him of favour and blessing: Now if the Lord shall please to heare us, and bring us in peace to the place wee desire, then hath hee ratified this Covenant and sealed our Commission, and will expect a strickt performance of the Articles contained in it, but if wee shall neglect the observacion of these Articles which are the ends wee have propounded, and dissembling with our God, shall fall to embrace this present world and prosecute our carnall intencions, seeking great things for our selves and our posterity, the Lord will surely break out in wrathe against us be revenged of such a perjured people and make us know the price of the breach of such a Covenant.

Now the only way to avoide this shipwracke and to provide for our posterity is to followe the Counsell of Micah,[15] to doe Justly, to love mercy, to walke humbly with our God; for this end, wee must be knit together in this worke as one man, wee must entertaine each other in brotherly Affection, wee must be willing to abridge our selves of our superfluities for the supply of others necessities, wee must uphold a familiar Commerce together in all meekness, gentleness, patience and liberallity, wee must delight in each other, make others Condicions our owne, rejoice together, mourne together, labour, and suffer together, allways haveing before our eyes our Commission and Community in the worke, our Community as members of the same body. Soe shall wee keepe the unity of the spirit in the bond of peace, the Lord will be our God and delight to dwell among us, as his owne people and will command a blessing upon us in all our ways, soe that wee shall see much more of his wisdom power goodnes and truth than formerly wee have beene acquainted with; wee shall finde that the God of Israell is among us, when ten of us shall be able to resist a thousand of our enemies, when hee shall make us a praise and glory, that men shall say of succeeding plantations: the lord make it like that of New England: for wee

---

[12] See Leviticus 10:1–2.

[13] In 1 Samuel 15:1–34, God instructed Saul to destroy the Amalekites and all their possessions. Because he spared their sheep and oxen, Saul disobeyed God.

[14] A legal contract in which God extends protection to the faithful, who promise to abide by his word.

[15] Micah 6:8: ". . .and what doth the Lord require of thee, but to do justly, and to love mercy, and to walk humbly with thy God?"

must Consider that wee shall be as a Citty upon a Hill,[16] the eyes of all people are uppon us; soe that if wee shall deale falsely with our god in this worke wee have undertaken and soe cause him to withdrawe his present help from us, wee shall be made a story and a by-word through the world, wee shall open the mouths of enemies to speake evill of the ways of god and all professours for Gods sake; wee shall shame the faces of many of gods worthy servants, and cause their prayers to be turned into Cursses upon us till wee be consumed out of the good land whether wee are going: And to shutt up this discourse with that exhortation of Moses that faithfull servant of the Lord in his last farewell to Israell (Deut. 30):[17] Beloved there is now set before us life, and good, death and evill in that wee are Commaunded this day to love the Lord our God, and to love one another to walk in his ways and to keepe his Commaundements and his Ordinance, and his lawes, and the Articles of our Covenant with him that wee may live and be multiplied, and that the Lord our God may blesse us in the land whether wee go to possesse it: But if our heartes shall turne away soe that wee will not obey, but shall be seduced and worship other Gods our pleasures, and proffitts, and serve them; it is propounded unto us this day, wee shall surely perish out of the good Land whither wee passe over this vast Sea to possess it;

Therefore lett us choose life,[18]
        that wee, and our Seede,
            may live; by obeyeing his
        voice, and cleaving to him,
            for hee is our life, and
                our prosperity.

1838

---

from The History of New England

[July 5, 1632]

At Watertown there was (in the view of divers witnesses) a great combat between a mouse and a snake; and, after a long fight, the mouse prevailed and killed the snake. The pastor of Boston, Mr. Wilson, a very sincere, holy man, hearing of it, gave this interpretation: That the snake was the devil; the mouse was a poor contemptible

---

[16] Matthew 5:14–15: "Ye are the light of the world. A city that is set on a hill cannot be hid. Neither do men light a candle, and put it under a bushel, but on a candlestick; and it giveth light unto all that are in the house."

[17] Deuteronomy 30:1–3: "And it shall come to pass, when all these things are come upon thee, the blessing and the curse, which I have set before thee, and thou shalt call them to mind among all the nations, whither the Lord thy God hath driven thee, And shalt return unto the Lord thy God, and shalt obey his voice

according to all that I command thee this day, thou and thy children, with all thine heart, and with all thy soul; That then the Lord thy God will turn thy captivity, and have compassion upon thee, and will return and gather thee from all the nations, whither the Lord thy God hath scattered thee."

[18] Deuteronomy 30:19: ". . . I have set before you life and death, blessing and cursing: therefore, choose life, that both thou and thy seed may live. . . ."

people, which God had brought hither, which should overcome Satan here, and dispossess him of his kingdom. Upon the same occasion, he told the Governor, that, before he was resolved to come into this country, he dreamed he was here, and that he saw a church arise out of the earth, which grew up and became a marvellous goodly church. . . .

[October 21, 1636]

One Mrs. Hutchinson,[1] a member of the church of Boston, a woman of a ready wit and bold spirit, brought over with her two dangerous errours: 1. That the person of the Holy Ghost dwells in a justified person; 2. That no sanctification can help to evidence to us our justification.—From these two grew many branches; as, 1. Our union with the Holy Ghost, so as a Christian remains dead to every spiritual action, and hath no gifts nor graces, other than such as are in hypocrites, nor any other sanctification but the Holy Ghost himself. . . .

The other ministers in the bay, hearing of these things, came to Boston at the time of a general court, and entered conference in private with them, to the end they might know the certainty of these things; that if need were, they might write to the church of Boston about them, to prevent (if it were possible) the dangers, which seemed hereby to hang over that and the rest of the churches. At this conference, Mr. Cotton was present, and gave satisfaction to them, so as he agreed with them all in the point of sanctification, and so did Mr. Wheelwright; so as they all did hold that sanctification did help to evidence justification. The same he had delivered plainly in public divers times; but, for the indwelling of the person of the Holy Ghost, he held that still, as some others of the ministers did, but not union with the person of the Holy Ghost, (as Mrs. Hutchinson and others did,) so as to amount to a personal union. . . .

[November 1, 1637]

The court also sent for Mrs. Hutchinson, and charged her with divers matters, as her keeping two publick lectures every week in her house, whereto sixty or eighty persons did usually resort, and for reproaching most of the ministers (viz. all except Mr. Cotton) for not preaching a covenant of free grace, and that they had not the seal of the Spirit, nor were able ministers of the New Testament; which were clearly proved against her, though she sought to shift it off. And, after many speeches to and fro, at last she was so full as she could not contain, but vented her revelations; amongst which this was one, that she had it revealed to her, that she should come into New England, and should here be persecuted, and that God would ruin us and our posterity, and the whole state, for the same. So the court proceeded and banished her; but, because it was winter, they committed her to a private house, where she was well provided, and her own friends and the elders permitted to go to her, but none else.

---

[1] Anne Hutchinson (1591–1643) taught that the elect, or chosen people, communicated directly with God and thus did not need clergymen's interpretations of Scripture or church doctrine. Her beliefs, called Antinomianism, threatened civil and religious leaders; as a consequence she was brought to trial, convicted of heresy, banished, and excommunicated. Her church minister was John Cotton (1584–1652).

The court called also Capt. Underhill, and some five or six more of the principal, whose hands were to the said petition; and because they stood to justify it, they were disfranchised, and such as had publick places were put from them.

The court also ordered that the rest, who had subscribed the petition, (and would not acknowledge their fault, and which near twenty of them did,) and some others, who had been chief stirrers in these contentions, &c. should be disarmed. This troubled some of them very much, especially because they were to bring them in themselves; but at last, when they saw no remedy, they obeyed.

All the proceedings of this court against these persons were set down at large, with the reasons and other observations, and were sent into England to be published there, to the end that all our godly friends might not be discouraged from coming to us, &c. . . .

[January 1638]

While Mrs. Hutchinson continued at Roxbury, divers of the elders and others resorted to her, and finding her to persist in maintaining those gross errours beforementioned, and many others, to the number of thirty or thereabout, some of them wrote to the church at Boston, offering to make proof of the same before the church, &c. 15; whereupon she was called, (the magistrates being desired to give her license to come,) and the lecture was appointed to begin at ten. (The general court being then at Newtown, the governour and the treasurer, being members of Boston, were permitted to come down, but the rest of the court continued at Newtown.) When she appeared, the errours were read to her. The first was, that the souls of men are mortal by generation, but, after, made immortal by Christ's purchase. This she maintained a long time; but at length she was so clearly convinced by reason and scripture, and the whole church agreeing that sufficient had been delivered for her conviction, that she yielded she had been in an errour. Then they proceeded to three other errours: 1. That there was no resurrection of these bodies, and that these bodies were not united to Christ, but every person united hath a new body, &c. These were also clearly confuted, but yet she held her own; so as the church (all but two of her sons) agreed she should be admonished, and because her sons would not agree to it, they were admonished also.

Mr. Cotton pronounced the sentence of admonition with great solemnity, and with much zeal and detestation of her errours and pride of spirit. The assembly continued till eight at night, and all did acknowledge the special presence of God's spirit therein; and she was appointed to appear again the next lecture day.

[March 22, 1638]

Mrs. Hutchinson appeared again; (she had been licensed by the court, in regard she had given hope of her repentance to be at Mr. Cotton's house, that both he and Mr. Davenport[2] might have the more opportunity to deal with her;) and the articles being again read to her, and her answer required, she delivered it in writing, wherein she made a retraction of near all, but with such explanations and circumstances as gave no satisfaction to the church; so as she was required to speak further to them. Then

[2] John Davenport (1597–1670), Puritan minister.

she declared, that it was just with God to leave her to herself, as he had done, for her slighting his ordinances, both magistracy and ministry; and confessed, that what she had spoken against the magistrates at the court (by way of revelation) was rash and ungrounded; and desired the church to pray for her. This gave the church good hope of her repentance; but when she was examined about some particulars, as that she had denied inherent righteousness, &c. she affirmed that it was never her judgment; and though it was proved by many testimonies, that she had been of that judgment, and so had persisted, and maintained it by argument against divers, yet she impudently persisted in her affirmation, to the astonishment of all the assembly. So that, after much time and many arguments had been spent to bring her to see her sin, but all in vain, the church, with one consent, cast her out. Some moved to have her admonished once more; but, it being for manifest evil in matter of conversation, it was agreed otherwise; and for that reason also the sentence was denounced by the pastor, matter of manners belonging properly to his place.

After she was excommunicated, her spirits, which seemed before to be somewhat dejected, revived again, and she gloried in her sufferings, saying, that it was the greatest happiness, next to Christ, that ever befell her. Indeed, it was a happy day to the churches of Christ here, and to many poor souls, who had been seduced by her, who, by what they heard and saw that day, were (through the grace of God) brought off quite from her errours, and settled again in the truth.

At this time the good providence of God so disposed, divers of the congregation (being the chief men of the party, her husband being one) were gone to Naragansett to seek out a new place for plantation, and taking liking of one in Plimouth patent, they went thither to have it granted them; but the magistrates there, knowing their spirit, gave them a denial, but consented they might buy of the Indians an island in the Naragansett Bay.[3]

After two or three days, the governour sent a warrant to Mrs. Hutchinson to depart this jurisdiction before the last of this month, according to the order of court, and for that end set her at liberty from her former constraint, so as she was not to go forth of her own house till her departure; and upon the 28th she went by water to her farm at the Mount, where she was to take water, with Mr. Wheelwright's wife and family, to go to Pascataquack; but she changed her mind, and went by land to Providence, and so to the island in the Naragansett Bay, which her husband and the rest of that sect had purchased of the Indians, and prepared with all speed to remove unto. For the court had ordered, that, except they were gone with their families by such a time, they should be summoned to the general court, &c. . . .

Mrs. Hutchinson, being removed to the Isle of Aquiday, in the Naragansett Bay, after her time was fulfilled, that she expected deliverance of a child, was delivered of a monstrous birth, which, being diversly related in the country, (and, in the open assembly at Boston, upon a lecture day, declared by Mr. Cotton to be twenty-seven several lumps of man's seed, without any alteration, or mixture of any thing from the woman, and thereupon gathered, that it might signify her errour in denying inherent righteousness, but that all was Christ in us, and nothing of ours in our faith, love, &c.) hereupon the governour wrote to Mr. Clarke, a physician and a preacher

---

[3] I.e., Rhode Island. In 1642 Anne Hutchinson moved to Long Island, New York, where she was killed in an Indian massacre one year later.

to those of the island, to know the certainty thereof, who returned him this answer: Mrs. Hutchinson, six weeks before her delivery, perceived her body to be greatly distempered, and her spirits failing, and in that regard doubtful of life, she sent to me, &c. and not long after . . . it was brought to light, and I was called to see it, where I beheld, first unwashed, (and afterwards in warm water,) several lumps, every one of them greatly confused, and if you consider each of them according to the representation of the whole, they were altogether without form; but if they were considered in respect of the parts of each lump of flesh, then there was a representation of innumerable distinct bodies in the form of a globe, not much unlike the swims of some fish, so confusedly knit together by so many several strings, (which I conceive were the beginning of veins and nerves,) so that it was impossible either to number the small round pieces in every lump, much less to discern from whence every string did fetch its original, they were so snarled one within another. The small globes I likewise opened, and perceived the matter of them (setting aside the membrane in which it was involved,) to be partly wind and partly water. Of these several lumps there were about twenty-six, according to the relation of those, who more narrowly searched into the number of them. I took notice of six or seven of some bigness; the rest were small; but all as I have declared, except one or two, which differed much from the rest both in matter and form; and the whole was like the [blank] of the liver, being similar and every where like itself. When I had opened it, the matter seemed to be blood congealed. The governour, not satisfied with this relation, spake after with the said Mr. Clarke, who thus cleared all the doubts: The lumps were twenty-six or twenty-seven, distinct and not joined together; there came no secundine after them; six of them were as great as his fist, and one as great as two fists; the rest each less than other, and the smallest about the bigness of the top of his thumb. The globes were round things, included in the lumps, about the bigness of a small Indian bean, and like the pearl in a man's eye. The two lumps, which differed from the rest, were like liver or congealed blood, and had no small globes in them, as the rest had. Mr. Cotton, next lecture day, acknowledged his errour, &c. and that he had his information by a letter from her husband, &c. . . .

[March 1640]

Many men began to inquire after the southern parts; and the great advantages supposed to be had in Virginia and the West Indies, &c. made this country to be disesteemed of many; and yet those countries (for all their great wealth) have sent hither, both this year and formerly, for supply of clothes and other necessaries; and some families have forsaken both Providence and other the Caribbee Islands and Virginia to come live here. And though our people saw what meagre, unhealthful countenances they brought hither, and how fat and well liking they became soon, yet they were so taken with the ease and plenty of those countries, as many of them sold their estates here to transport themselves to Providence; among whom the chief was John Humfrey, Esq. a gentleman of special parts of learning and activity, and a godly man, who had been one of the first beginners in the promoting of this plantation, and had laboured very much therein. He, being brought low in his estate, and having many children, and being well known to the lords of Providence, and offering himself to their service, was accepted to be the next governour. Whereupon he laboured much to draw men to join with him. This was looked at, both by the general court, and also by the elders, as an unwarrantable course; for though it was thought very needful to further plantation of churches in the West Indies, and all were willing to endeavour the same; yet to do it with disparagement of this country, (for they gave out that they could not subsist here,) caused us to fear, that the Lord was not with them in this way. And, withal, some considerations were propounded to them by the court, which diverted some of them, and made others to pause, upon three points especially: 1. How dangerous it was to bring up an ill report upon this good land, which God had found out and given to his people, and so to discourage the hearts of their brethren, &c. 2. To leave a place of rest and safety, to expose themselves, their wives and children, to the danger of a potent enemy, the Spaniard. 3. Their subjection to such governours as those in England shall set over them, &c. Notwithstanding these considerations, divers of them persisted in their resolutions, and went about to get some ship or bark to transport them; but they were still crossed by the hand of God. . . .

The sudden fall of land and cattle, and the scarcity of foreign commodities, and money, &c. with the thin access of people from England, put many into an unsettled frame of spirit, so as they concluded there would be no subsisting here, and accordingly they began to hasten away, some to the West Indies, others to the Dutch, at Long Island, &c. (for the governour there invited them by fair offers,) and others back for England. Among others who returned thither, there was one of the magistrates, Mr. Humfrey, and four ministers, and a schoolmaster. These would needs go against all advice, and had a fair and speedy voyage, till they came near England, all which time, three of the ministers, with the schoolmaster, spake reproachfully of the people and of the country, but the wind coming up against them, they were tossed up and down, (being in 10ber,[4]) so long till their provisions and other necessaries were near spent, and they were forced to strait allowance, yet at length the wind coming fair again, they got into the Sleeve, but then there arose so great a tempest at S. E. as they could bear no sail, and so were out of hope of being saved (being in the night also). Then they humbled themselves before the Lord, and acknowledged God's hand to be justly out against them for speaking evil of this good land and the Lord's people here, &c. Only one of them, Mr. Phillips of Wrentham, in England, had not joined with the rest, but spake well of the people, and of the country; upon this it pleased the Lord to spare their lives, and when they expected every moment to have been dashed upon the rocks, (for they were hard by the Needles,) he turned the wind so as they were carried safe to the Isle of Wight by St. Helen's: yet the Lord followed them on shore. Some were exposed to great straits and found no entertainment, their friends forsaking them. One had a daughter that presently ran mad, and two other of his daughters, being under ten years of age, were discovered to have been often abused by divers lewd persons, and filthiness in his family. The schoolmaster had no sooner hired an house, and gotten in some scholars, but the plague set in, and took away two of his own children.

Others who went to other places, upon like grounds, succeeded no better. They fled for fear of want, and many of them fell into it, even to extremity, as if they had hastened into the misery which they feared and fled from, besides the depriving themselves of the ordinances and church fellowship, and those civil liberties which they enjoyed here; whereas, such as staid in their places, kept their peace and ease, and enjoyed still the blessing of the ordinances, and never tasted of those troubles and

[4] I.e., October.

miseries, which they heard to have befallen those who departed. Much disputation there was about liberty of removing for outward advantages, and all ways were sought for an open door to get out at; but it is to be feared many crept out at a broken wall. For such as come together into a wilderness, where are nothing but wild beasts and beastlike men, and there confederate together in civil and church estate, whereby they do, implicitly at least, bind themselves to support each other, and all of them that society, whether civil or sacred, whereof they are members, how they can break from this without free consent, is hard to find, so as may satisfy a tender or good conscience in time of trial. Ask thy conscience, if thou wouldst have plucked up thy stakes, and brought thy family 3000 miles, if thou hadst expected that all, or most, would have forsaken thee there. Ask again, what liberty thou hast towards others, which thou likest not to allow others towards thyself; for if one may go, another may, and so the greater part, and so church and commonwealth may be left destitute in a wilderness, exposed to misery and reproach, and all for thy ease and pleasure, whereas these all, being now thy brethren, as near to thee as the Israelites were to Moses, it were much safer for thee, after his example, to choose rather to suffer affliction with thy brethren, than to enlarge thy ease and pleasure by furthering the occasion of their ruin. . . .

[August 15, 1648]

The synod[5] met at Cambridge by adjournment from the last. Mr. Allen of Dedham preached. . . .

It fell out, about the midst of his sermon, there came a snake into the seat, where many of the elders sate behind the preacher. It came in at the door where people stood thick upon the stairs. Divers of the elders shifted from it, but Mr. Thomson, one of the elders of Braintree, (a man of much faith,) trode upon the head of it, and so held it with his foot and staff with a small pair of grains,[6] until it was killed. This being so remarkable, and nothing falling out but by divine providence, it is out of doubt, the Lord discovered somewhat of his mind in it. The serpent is the devil; the synod, the representative of the churches of Christ in New England. The devil had formerly and lately attempted their disturbance and dissolution; but their faith in the seed of the woman overcame him and crushed his head. . . .

1826

Roger Williams
ca. 1603–1683

Americans have enshrined Roger Williams as a symbol of civil and religious freedom. As the founder of the Rhode Island colony in 1636, he upheld religious toleration, kept church and state separate, and advocated Indian rights. In his best-known writing, *The Bloody Tenent* (1644), he propounded the doctrine of "liberty for cause of conscience." Yet in his lifetime Williams's fellow New

---

[5] Meeting for discussions of church doctrine.   [6] Two-pronged spear.

England colonists thought him a threat to both religion and society. In fear, exasperation, and regret, they banished the gifted young minister beyond the southern borders of Massachusetts, leaving Williams to found the town of Providence and to pursue his relentless, isolated quest for God's truth.

Williams was a London tailor's son with the good fortune to be educated at Cambridge and to serve as chaplain in the household of a wealthy nobleman, where he married one of the housemaids. By 1629, in his mid-twenties, Williams had embraced Puritanism and the following year sailed with his wife in the "Great Migration" of Puritans to the newly chartered Massachusetts Bay Colony. Trouble began almost immediately after he arrived. Williams refused to accept the ministry at a Boston church because it had not officially separated from the corrupted mother church in England and was therefore tainted. Shuttling between Salem and Plymouth for the next two years, Williams continued to expound radical views on church-state separation. He argued that the royal charter did not give valid title to the land of the Massachusetts Bay Colony and that magistrates lacked the authority to punish violations of the first four of the Ten Commandments. He also insisted that the land was wrongfully taken from the Indians, whom most Puritans regarded as heathen or agents of Satan.

Williams's unorthodox positions came directly from his belief that Christianity was utterly opposed to affairs of the material world. He rejected all practices and even word usage that intermixed the "purity of Christ" with the contaminated world. For instance, he thought the term *Christendom,* often used as a synonym for the Western world, was a sacrilegious misnomer because so much of the population was sinful and damned.

The Puritan New England authorities quickly saw the implications of Williams's position. If, as he argued, all worldly institutions lay outside the true Christendom, Puritan magistrates would be powerless to invoke God's scriptural word as the source of their political and civil authority. The state could collapse in anarchy. Through their most eloquent spokesman, John Cotton, the Puritan establishment tried to persuade Williams of the error of his ways—as Governor William Bradford put it, of his "strange opinions" and "unsettled judgment." Failing to do so, they banished him in 1635. In their view Rhode Island was a catch basin of heretics, a "Rogue's Island," as it was later dubbed. But to Williams it was a haven where, for nearly half a century, he continued to be a seeker of God's way.

Constantly arguing to justify his positions, Williams wrote sermons, religious tracts, and documents on colonial affairs. In addition, he undertook a massive project in linguistics. As a Rhode Island farmer who also traded with the Indians, Williams learned the native language thoroughly. Williams's *A Key into the Language of America* (1643) was intended to "open" the language of the Narragansett Indians, whose culture he respected and who, in turn, so trusted Williams that he became an invaluable ally in times of the Indian Wars (1637, 1675–1676), mediating between settlers and natives throughout New England. Williams's *Key* includes a series of verses that hinges on the question of civilization and barbarism, on truth and falsehood. In all of them Williams exploits the characteristics of the English and the Indians to point up a moral or to raise a probing question. Politically Williams has been identified as a forerunner of the democratic spokesmen Jefferson and Andrew Jackson. In

American literature his intellectual questing and his challenge to the existing order anticipate the great searching works of Thoreau, Emerson, and Melville.

Further Reading:
S. Brockunier, *The Impossible Democrat: Roger Williams,* 1940.
P. Miller, *Roger Williams: His Contribution to the American Tradition,* 1953.
O. Winslow, *Master Roger Williams,* 1957.
E. Morgan, *Roger Williams: The Church and State,* 1967.
J. Teunissen and E. Hinz, "Roger Williams, Thomas More, and the Narragansett Utopia," *Early American Literature,* Winter 1976–1977, pp. 281–295.

Text:
The Complete Writings of Roger Williams, ed. J. Trumball et al., 7 vols., 1866–1874, 1963.

---

from A Key into the Language of America

[The Courteous Pagan shall condemn]

1.   The Courteous Pagan shall condemn
      Uncourteous Englishmen
    Who live like Foxes, Bears and Wolves,
      Or Lyon in his Den.

2.   Let none sing *blessings* to their soules,   5
      For that they Courteous are:
    The wild *Barbarians* with no more
      Then Nature, go so farre:

3.   If Natures Sons both *wild* and *tame,*
      Humane and Courteous be: 10
    How ill becomes it Sonnes of God
      To want Humanity?

1866

[What Habacuck once spake, mine eyes]

What *Habacuck*[1] once spake, mine eyes
    Have often seene most true,
The greater fishes devour the lesse,
    And cruelly pursue.

[1] Hebrew prophet of the seventh century B.C., and author of the Old Testament book of the same name.

Forcing them through Coves and Creekes,   5
To leape on driest sand,
To gaspe on earthie element, or die
By wildest *Indians* hand.

Christs little ones must hunted be
Devour'd; yet rise as Hee.   10
And eate up those which now a while
Their fierce devourers be.

1866

[Truth is a Native, naked Beauty; but]

Truth is a Native, naked Beauty; but
Lying Inventions are but *Indian* Paints,
Dissembling hearts their Beautie's but a Lye,
Truth is the proper Beauty of Gods Saints.

Fowle are the *Indians* Haire and painted Faces,   5
More foule such Haire, such Face in *Israel*.
England so calls her selfe, yet there's
Absoloms foule Haire and Face of *Jesabell*.

Paints will not bide Christ's washing Flames of fire,
Fained Inventions will not bide such stormes: 10
O that we may prevent him, that betimes,
Repentance Teares may wash of all such Formes.

1866

Anne Bradstreet
ca. 1612–1672

Anne Bradstreet was an English gentlewoman whose heart "rose" in revulsion at
the sight of the New World. Yet she became the first significant poet in
American literature precisely by capturing the essence of life as a Puritan and as a
woman under colonial conditions. She "submitted," as she put it, to the "new
world and new manners," though the transition was undeniably wrenching.

Anne Dudley was born in Northampton, England. Her father, Thomas, was
then a financial officer in the household of the Earl of Lincoln. Anne called him
her "guide," her "instructor," and "a magazine of history." Dudley evidently
took unusual care with the education of his daughter, perhaps following one
educator's advice to teach the "Abcie and primer" while "playing with [the little
children] at dinners and suppers, or as they sit by the fire." Anne reported that at
about age six or seven she was reading the Scriptures.

Young Anne Bradstreet's era was intellectually lively, as was her immediate environment in the household of the nobleman whose library was probably accessible to her. She evidently knew Sir Walter Raleigh's *History of the World* (1614), a study of the ancient kingdoms and dynasties emphasizing God's authority through every historical cycle. And she knew the poetry of Sir Philip Sidney, Edmund Spenser, and Michael Drayton, in addition to Robert Burton's *Anatomy of Melancholy* and Francis Bacon's *Essays*. She had probably read some Shakespeare, and she openly admired Joshua Sylvester's translation of Guillaume du Bartas's *Divine Weeks and Works.* In addition, Anne knew John Foxe's *Actes and Monuments,* a Protestant martyrology, and countless contemporary Puritan tracts and pamphlets. But the girl's education came only in part from books. Her mind was doubtless sharpened from listening to the household debate and discussion of a distinguished company of Puritan intellectuals in the thick of a religious controversy unequaled in intensity since that time.

In the late 1620s political conditions worsened for the Dudley family, Puritan employees of a Puritan nobleman increasingly in the king's disfavor. Charles I began to prosecute retainers of Lord Lincoln, and Anne's father fell under suspicion of harboring a fugitive. In 1630 the Dudley family sailed with the Winthrop party to Massachusetts.

Anne, at sixteen, voyaged not only as Dudley's daughter but also as the wife of Simon Bradstreet, a graduate of Emmanuel College, Cambridge, a university center of nonconformity. Anne had married the twenty-five-year-old steward, her father's assistant, about two years earlier. At the time of her wedding Anne was recuperating from smallpox; her convalescence was perhaps lengthened by her earlier childhood bouts of rheumatic fever, and for the remainder of her life Anne Bradstreet's health was tenuous. She was subject to lameness, fever, and fainting in a land rife with disease and death. It is understandable that the dominant images in her poems concern the human body, illness, and mortality.

The Bradstreets began Massachusetts life in Salem, then a settlement of forty dwellings, most no more than huts. Almost immediately the couple relocated in Charlestown, close to Boston's inner harbor. In a letter Anne's father wrote, "They who had health to labor fell to building, wherein many were interrupted with sickness, and many died weekly, yea, almost daily." Because Charlestown lacked an adequate water supply, the Bradstreets and their neighbors cast about once again for a suitable home and, in spring 1631, resettled in Newtown, now Cambridge, where both the Dudleys and the Bradstreets built sturdy houses. But following an acrimonious term as governor, father Dudley decided to move to Agawam (Ipswich), a remote settlement of the Bay Colony that "aboundeth with fish, and flesh of fowls and beasts, . . . plowing grounds, many good rivers and harbours and no rattle snakes."

The Bradstreets and their new infant son moved with the Dudleys to this town, which was settled by remarkably accomplished families. These Ipswich settlers in part transcended the horrific wilderness conditions by sustaining a vigorous cultural and intellectual life. It was here that Anne Bradstreet began to write Christian epic poetry. She reached her permanent home, however, only in 1645–1646, when her husband moved the family fifteen miles west to (North)

Andover, a farming settlement surrounded on every side by dense virgin woodland. (At the time the Bradstreets took up residence, Andover offered a generous bounty for wolves, and "25 wolf-hooks" were among Simon Bradstreet's possessions.) Town officials allotted the Bradstreets twenty acres, and they probably lived in a three-story, central-chimney saltbox house. At this point they had five of what would be eight children.

During the years of their marriage, Simon Bradstreet was often absent on colonial business. He was secretary to the Bay Company, its deputy governor, and in 1645 its governor. In 1661, with the restoration of the monarchy in England, he traveled there to renegotiate the charter of the Bay Company. Bradstreet's absences increased his wife's burdens.

Given her circumstances, it is astonishing that Anne Bradstreet could make time to write poetry and prose. The household relocations, the eight births and years of child rearing, domestic and social obligations, the sicknesses, cramped quarters, and the disapproval (as she recorded in one poem) of "each carping tongue / who says my hand a needle better fits"—any or all would have silenced a writer who was less driven than she. Yet she called poetry a "room of my own," and she worked at it until her death.

Bradstreet's writings fall into two groups. One is scholarly and monumental and concerns such subjects as the four elements and four humors (named for the ancient Greeks' belief that the world was composed of earth, air, fire, and water and that the human temperament was formed of warmth, cold, wet, and dry). Bradstreet likewise searched for cosmic themes when she wrote poetry of historical cycles she called the ages of man and the four monarchies. This work was both imitative and derivative of her reading. It caused a stir when, without her knowledge, Bradstreet's brother-in-law took some of these poems to England and had them published under the title *The Tenth Muse Lately Sprung Up in America . . .* (1650). The printer's errors embarrassed Mistress Bradstreet, but the work had historical distinction as the first published volume of poetry to be written by a New England colonist. In these four-part poems Anne Bradstreet most fully reveals her ambition to take her place among the English and French poets, all of them men.

Ironically, the second group of "domestic" poems and the *Contemplations* stand as Bradstreet's literary achievement. She is now most appreciated for the writings that convey her personal feelings about New England and family life. As a mother she writes of her "eight birds hatcht in one nest" and as a wife inscribes her love for Simon ("If ever man were lov'd by wife, then thee"). Her tone ranges from light irony, as when she calls the error-ridden text of *The Tenth Muse* an "ill-form'd offspring of my feeble brain," to the poignance of the poem occasioned by the burning of the Bradstreet house in 1666. Her elegies on the death of her grandchildren convey a deep sense of loss even as they evoke the solace of her religion. These poems exploit the tension between the individual's wishes and desires and the need to submit to God's will. Many of the poems were published in 1678, six years after her death.

Some modern readers appreciate Bradstreet as a covertly secular poet, but Puritanism is a rigorous constant in her work. In early childhood she wrote, "I began to make conscience of my wayes, and what I knew was sinful. . . . I could not rest 'till by prayer I had confest unto God." In later life, sensitive to the natural world that surrounded her in Andover, she used motifs of nature to express her struggle en route to the heavenly kingdom. She attempted to view all nature as expressive of God's glory, and in affliction she turned to her Puritan God for solace and direction. She observed poignantly that "buds" like her granddaughter are "new blown to have so short a date" but affirmed that it is "His hand alone that guides nature and fate."

Further Reading:
J. Piercy, *Anne Bradstreet,* 1965.
E. White, *Anne Bradstreet: The Tenth Muse,*
1971.
A. Stanford, *Anne Bradstreet: The Worldly
Puritan,* 1974.
W. Martin, *An American Triptych,* 1984.

Text:
The Works of Anne Bradstreet, ed. J. Hensley,
1967.

The Prologue

1

To sing of wars, of captains, and of kings,
Of cities founded, commonwealths begun,
For my mean pen are too superior things:
Or how they all, or each their dates have run
Let poets and historians set these forth,   5
My obscure lines shall not so dim their worth.

2

But when my wond'ring eyes and envious heart
Great Bartas'[1] sugared lines do but read o'er,
Fool I do grudge the Muses did not part
'Twixt him and me that overfluent store;   10
A Bartas can do what a Bartas will
But simple I according to my skill.

3

From schoolboy's tongue no rhet'ric we expect,
Nor yet a sweet consort from broken strings,
Nor perfect beauty where's a main defect: 15

---

[1] Guillaume du Bartas (1544–1590), French poet.

My foolish, broken, blemished Muse so sings,
And this to mend, alas, no art is able,
'Cause nature made it so irreparable.

4

Nor can I, like that fluent sweet tongued Greek,[2]
Who lisped at first, in future times speak plain.   20
By art he gladly found what he did seek,
A full requital of his striving pain.
Art can do much, but this maxim's most sure:
A weak or wounded brain admits no cure.

5

I am obnoxious to each carping tongue   25
Who says my hand a needle better fits,
A poet's pen all scorn I should thus wrong,
For such despite they cast on female wits:
If what I do prove well, it won't advance,
They'll say it's stol'n, or else it was by chance.   30

6

But sure the antique Greeks were far more mild
Else of our sex, why feigned they those nine
And poesy made Calliope's[3] own child;
So 'mongst the rest they placed the arts divine:
But this weak knot they will full soon untie,   35
The Greeks did nought, but play the fools and lie.

7

Let Greeks be Greeks, and women what they are
Men have precedency and still excel,
It is but vain unjustly to wage war;
Men can do best, and women know it well.   40
Preeminence in all and each is yours;
Yet grant some small acknowledgement of ours.

8

And oh ye high flown quills that soar the skies,
And ever with your prey still catch your praise,

[2] Demosthenes (385?–322 B.C.), Athenian orator.
[3] Calliope, the Muse of heroic poetry, was one of the nine Muses who presided over the arts and sciences.

If e'er you deign these lowly lines your eyes,   45
Give thyme or parsley wreath, I ask no bays;[4]
This mean and unrefined ore of mine
Will make your glist'ring gold but more to shine.
1650

The Author to Her Book

Thou ill-formed offspring of my feeble brain,
Who after birth didst by my side remain,
Till snatched from thence by friends, less wise
     than true,
Who thee abroad, exposed to public view,
Made thee in rags, halting to th' press to trudge,   5
Where errors were not lessened (all may judge).
At thy return my blushing was not small,
My rambling brat (in print) should mother call,
I cast thee by as one unfit for light,
Thy visage was so irksome in my sight;   10
Yet being mine own, at length affection would
Thy blemishes amend, if so I could:
I washed thy face, but more defects I saw,
And rubbing off a spot still made a flaw.
I stretched thy joints to make thee even feet,   15
Yet still thou run'st more hobbling than is meet;
In better dress to trim thee was my mind,
But nought save homespun cloth i' th' house I find.
In this array 'mongst vulgars may'st thou roam.
In critic's hands beware thou dost not come,   20
And take thy way where yet thou art not known;
If for thy father asked, say thou hadst none;
And for thy mother, she alas is poor,
Which caused her thus to send thee out of door.
1678

---

[4] Laurels.

Contemplations

[1]

Some time now past in the autumnal tide,
When Phoebus wanted but one hour to bed,
The trees all richly clad, yet void of pride,
Where gilded o'er by his rich golden head.
Their leaves and fruits seemed painted, but was true,   5
Of green, of red, of yellow, mixed hue;
Rapt were my senses at this delectable view.

2

I wist not what to wish, yet sure thought I,
If so much excellence abide below,
How excellent is He that dwells on high,   10
Whose power and beauty by his works we know?
Sure he is goodness, wisdom, glory, light,
That hath this under world so richly dight;
More heaven than earth was here, no winter and no night.

3

Then on a stately oak I cast mine eye,   15
Whose ruffling top the clouds seemed to aspire;
How long since thou wast in thine infancy?
Thy strength, and stature, more thy years admire,
Hath hundred winters past since thou wast born?
Or thousand since thou brakest thy shell of horn?   20
If so, all these as nought, eternity doth scorn.

4

Then higher on the glistering Sun I gazed,
Whose beams was shaded by the leavie tree;
The more I looked, the more I grew amazed,
And softly said, "What glory's like to thee?"   25
Soul of this world, this universe's eye,
No wonder some made thee a deity;
Had I not better known, alas, the same had I.

5

Thou as a bridegroom from thy chamber rushes,
And as a strong man, joys to run a race;   30
The morn doth usher thee with smiles and blushes;
The Earth reflects her glances in thy face.
Birds, insects, animals with vegative,
Thy heat from death and dullness doth revive,
And in the darksome womb of fruitful nature dive.   35

6

Thy swift annual and diurnal course,
Thy daily straight and yearly oblique path,
Thy pleasing fervor and thy scorching force,
All mortals here the feeling knowledge hath.
Thy presence makes it day, thy absence night,   40
Quaternal seasons caused by thy might:
Hail creature, full of sweetness, beauty, and delight.

7

Art thou so full of glory that no eye
Hath strength thy shining rays once to behold?
And is thy splendid throne erect so high,   45
As to approach it, can no earthly mould?
How full of glory then must thy Creator be,
Who gave this bright light luster unto thee?
Admired, adored for ever, be that Majesty.

8

Silent alone, where none or saw, or heard,   50
In pathless paths I lead my wand'ring feet,
My humble eyes to lofty skies I reared
To sing some song, my mazed Muse thought meet.
My great Creator I would magnify,
That nature had thus decked liberally;
But Ah, and Ah, again, my imbecility!   55

9

I heard the merry grasshopper then sing.
The black-clad cricket bear a second part;
They kept one tune and played on the same string,
Seeming to glory in their little art.
Shall creatures abject thus their voices raise   60

And in their kind resound their Maker's praise,
Whilst I, as mute, can warble forth no higher lays?

10

When present times look back to ages past,
And men in being fancy those are dead,   65
It makes things gone perpetually to last,
And calls back months and years that long since fled.
It makes a man more aged in conceit
Than was Methuselah, or's grandsire great,
While of their persons and their acts his mind doth treat.   70

11

Sometimes in Eden fair he seems to be,
Sees glorious Adam there made lord of all,
Fancies the apple, dangle on the tree,
That turned his sovereign to a naked thrall.
Who like a miscreant's driven from that place,   75
To get his bread with pain and sweat of face,
A penalty imposed on his backsliding race.

12

Here sits our grandame in retired place,
And in her lap her bloody Cain new-born;
The weeping imp oft looks her in the face,   80
Bewails his unknown hap and fate forlorn;
His mother sighs to think of Paradise,
And how she lost her bliss to be more wise,
Believing him that was, and is, father of lies.

13

Here Cain and Abel come to sacrifice,   85
Fruits of the earth and fatlings each do bring,
On Abel's gift the fire descends from skies,
But no such sign on false Cain's offering;
With sullen hateful looks he goes his ways,
Hath thousand thoughts to end his brother's days,   90
Upon whose blood his future good he hopes to raise.

14

There Abel keeps his sheep, no ill he thinks;
His brother comes, then acts his fratricide;

The virgin Earth of blood her first draught drinks,
But since that time she often hath been cloyed.   95
The wretch with ghastly face and dreadful mind
Thinks each he sees will serve him in his kind,
Though none on earth but kindred near then could he find.

15

Who fancies not his looks now at the bar,
His face like death, his heart with horror fraught,   100
Nor malefactor ever felt like war,
When deep despair with wish of life hath fought,
Branded with guilt and crushed with treble woes,
A vagabond to Land of Nod he goes.
A city builds, that walls might him secure from foes.   105

16

Who thinks not oft upon the father's ages,
Their long descent, how nephews' sons they saw,
The starry observations of those sages,
And how their precepts to their sons were law,
How Adam sighed to see his progeny,   110
Clothed all in his black sinful livery,
Who neither guilt nor yet the punishment could fly.

17

Our life compare we with their length of days
Who to the tenth of theirs doth now arrive?
And though thus short, we shorten many ways,   115
Living so little while we are alive;
In eating, drinking, sleeping, vain delight
So unawares comes on perpetual night,
And puts all pleasures vain unto eternal flight.

18

When I behold the heavens as in their prime,   120
And then the earth (though old) still clad in green,
The stones and trees, insensible of time,
Nor age nor wrinkle on their front are seen;
If winter come and greenness then do fade,
A spring returns, and they more youthful made;   125
But man grows old, lies down, remains where once he's laid.

19

By birth more noble than those creatures all,
Yet seems by nature and by custom cursed,
No sooner born, but grief and care makes fall
That state obliterate he had at first;   130
Nor youth, nor strength, nor wisdom spring again,
Nor habitations long their names retain,
But in oblivion to the final day remain.

20

Shall I then praise the heavens, the trees, the earth
Because their beauty and their strength last longer?   135
Shall I wish there, or never to had birth,
Because they're bigger, and their bodies stronger?
Nay, they shall darken, perish, fade and die,
And when unmade, so ever shall they lie,
But man was made for endless immortality.   140

21

Under the cooling shadow of a stately elm
Close sat I by a goodly river's side,
Where gliding streams the rocks did overwhelm,
A lonely place, with pleasures dignified.
I once that loved the shady woods so well,   145
Now thought the rivers did the trees excel,
And if the sun would ever shine, there would I dwell.

22

While on the stealing stream I fixt mine eye,
Which to the longed-for ocean held its course,
I marked, nor crooks, nor rubs that there did lie   150
Could hinder ought, but still augment its force.
"O happy flood," quoth I, "that holds thy race
Till thou arrive at thy beloved place,
Nor is it rocks or shoals that can obstruct thy pace,

23

Nor is't enough, that thou alone mayst slide,   155
But hundred brooks in thy clear waves do meet,
So hand in hand along with thee they glide
To Thetis' house,¹ where all embrace and greet.
Thou emblem true of what I count the best,

¹ The sea.

O could I lead my rivulets to rest,   160
So may we press to that vast mansion, ever blest."

24

Ye fish, which in this liquid region 'bide,
That for each season have your habitation,
Now salt, now fresh where you think best to glide
To unknown coasts to give a visitation,   165
In lakes and ponds you leave your numerous fry;
So nature taught, and yet you know not why,
You wat'ry folk that know not your felicity.

25

Look how the wantons frisk to taste the air,
Then to the colder bottom straight they dive;   170
Eftsoon to Neptune's glassy hall repair
To see what trade they great ones there do drive,
Who forage o'er the spacious sea-green field,
And take the trembling prey before it yield,
Whose armour is their scales, their spreading fins their shield.   175

26

While musing thus with contemplation fed,
And thousand fancies buzzing in my brain,
The sweet-tongued Philomel² perched o'er my head
And chanted forth a most melodious strain
Which rapt me so with wonder and delight,   180
I judged my hearing better than my sight,
And wished me wings with her a while to take my flight.

27

"O merry Bird," said I, "that fears no snares,
That neither toils nor hoards up in thy barn,
Feels no sad thoughts nor cruciating cares   185
To gain more good or shun what might thee harm.
Thy clothes ne'er wear, thy meat is everywhere,
Thy bed a bough, thy drink the water clear,
Reminds not what is past, nor what's to come dost fear."

---

² Nightingale.

28

"The dawning morn with songs thou dost prevent,   190
Sets hundred notes unto thy feathered crew,
So each one tunes his pretty instrument,
And warbling out the old, begin anew,
And thus they pass their youth in summer season,
Then follow thee into a better region,   195
Where winter's never felt by that sweet airy legion."

29

Man at the best a creature frail and vain,
In knowledge ignorant, in strength but weak,
Subject to sorrows, losses, sickness, pain,
Each storm his state, his mind, his body break,   200
From some of these he never finds cessation,
But day or night, within, without, vexation,
Troubles from foes, from friends, from dearest, near'st relation.

30

And yet this sinful creature, frail and vain,
This lump of wretchedness, of sin and sorrow,   205
This weatherbeaten vessel wracked with pain,
Joys not in hope of an eternal morrow;
Nor all his losses, crosses, and vexation,
In weight, in frequency and long duration
Can make him deeply groan for that divine translation.   210

31

The mariner that on smooth waves doth glide
Sings merrily and steers his bark with ease,
As if he had command of wind and tide,
And now become great master of the seas:
But suddenly a storm spoils all the sport,   215
And makes him long for a more quiet port,
Which 'gainst all adverse winds may serve for fort.

32

So he that saileth in this world of pleasure,
Feeding on sweets, that never bit of th' sour,
That's full of friends, of honour, and of treasure,   220
Fond fool, he takes this earth ev'n for heav'n's bower.
But sad affliction comes and makes him see

Here's neither honour, wealth, nor safety;
Only above is found all with security.

33

O Time the fatal wrack of mortal things,   225
That draws oblivion's curtains over kings;
Their sumptuous monuments, men know them not,
Their names without a record are forgot,
Their parts, their ports, their pomp's all laid in th' dust
Nor wit nor gold, nor buildings scape times rust;   230
But he whose name is graved in the white stone
Shall last and shine when all of these are gone.

1678

Before the Birth of One of Her Children

All things within this fading world hath end,
Adversity doth still our joys attend;
No ties so strong, no friends so dear and sweet,
But with death's parting blow is sure to meet.
The sentence past is most irrevocable,   5
A common thing, yet oh, inevitable.
How soon, my Dear, death may my steps attend,
How soon't may be thy lot to lose thy friend,
We both are ignorant, yet love bids me
These farewell lines to recommend to thee,   10
That when that knot's untied that made us one,
I may seem thine, who in effect am none.
And if I see not half my days that's due,
What nature would, God grant to yours and you;
The many faults that well you know I have   15
Let be interred in my oblivious grave;
If any worth or virtue were in me,
Let that live freshly in thy memory
And when thou feel'st no grief, as I no harms,
Yet love thy dead, who long lay in thine arms.   20
And when thy loss shall be repaid with gains
Look to my little babes, my dear remains.
And if thou love thyself, or loved'st me,

These O protect from step-dame's injury.
And if chance to thine eyes shall bring this verse,   25
With some sad sighs honour my absent hearse;
And kiss this paper for thy love's dear sake,
Who with salt tears this last farewell did take.

1867

To My Dear and Loving Husband

If ever two were one, then surely we.
If ever man were loved by wife, then thee;
If ever wife was happy in a man,
Compare with me, ye women, if you can.
I prize thy love more than whole mines of gold   5
Or all the riches that the East doth hold.
My love is such that rivers cannot quench,
Nor ought but love from thee, give recompense.
Thy love is such I can no way repay,
The heavens reward thee manifold, I pray.   10
Then while we live, in love let's so persevere
That when we live no more, we may live ever.

1867

A Letter to Her Husband, Absent upon Public Employment

My head, my heart, mine eyes, my life, nay, more,
My joy, my magazine of earthly store,
If two be one, as surely thou and I,
How stayest thou there, whilst I at Ipswich lie?
So many steps, head from the heart to sever,   5
If but a neck, soon should we be together.
I, like the Earth this season, mourn in black,
My Sun is gone so far in's zodiac,
Whom whilst I 'joyed, nor storms, nor frost I felt,
His warmth such frigid colds did cause to melt,   10

My chilled limbs now numbed lie forlorn;
Return, return, sweet Sol, from Capricorn;[1]
In this dead time, alas, what can I more
Than view those fruits which through thy heat I
   bore?
Which sweet contentment yield me for a space,   15
True living pictures of their father's face.
O strange effect! now thou art southward gone,
I weary grow the tedious day so long;
But when thou northward to me shalt return,
I wish my Sun may never set, but burn   20
Within the Cancer[2] of my glowing breast,
The welcome house of him my dearest guest.
Where ever, ever stay, and go not thence,
Till nature's sad decree shall call thee hence;
Flesh of thy flesh, bone of thy bone,   25
I here, thou there, yet both but one.

1867

Another [Letter to Her Husband, Absent upon Public Employment]

Phoebus make haste, the day's too long, be gone,
The silent night's the fittest time for moan;
But stay this once, unto my suit give ear,
And tell my griefs in either hemisphere.
(And if the whirling of thy wheels don't drown'd)   5
The woeful accents of my doleful sound,
If in thy swift carrier thou canst make stay,
I crave this boon, this errand by the way,
Commend me to the man more loved than life,
Show him the sorrows of his widowed wife;   10
My dumpish thoughts, my groans, my brakish tears
My sobs, my longing hopes, my doubting fears,
And if he love, how can he there abide?
My interest's more than all the world beside.
He that can tell the stars or ocean sand,   15
Or all the grass that in the meads do stand,
The leaves in th' woods, the hail, or drops of rain,

---

[1] I.e., Winter.
[2] I.e., Summer.

Or in a corn-field number every grain,
Or every mote that in the sunshine hops,
May count my sighs, and number all my drops.   20
Tell him the countless steps that thou dost trace,
That once a day thy spouse thou may'st embrace;
And when thou canst not treat by loving mouth,
Thy rays afar salute her from the south.
But for one month I see no day (poor soul)   25
Like those far situate under the pole,
Which day by day long wait for thy arise,
O how they joy when thou dost light the skies.
O Phoebus, hadst thou but thus long from thine
Restrained the beams of thy beloved shine,   30
At thy return, if so thou could'st or durst,
Behold a Chaos blacker than the first.
Tell him here's worse than a confused matter,
His little world's a fathom under water.
Nought but the fervor of his ardent beams   35
Hath power to dry the torrent of these streams.
Tell him I would say more, but cannot well,
Oppressed minds abruptest tales do tell.
Now post with double speed, mark what I say,
By all our loves conjure him not to stay.   40

1867

In Memory of My Dear Grandchild Elizabeth Bradstreet, Who Deceased August, 1665, Being a Year and Half Old

[1]

Farewell dear babe, my heart's too much content,
Farewell sweet babe, the pleasure of mine eye,
Farewell fair flower that for a space was lent,
Then ta'en away unto eternity.
Blest babe, why should I once bewail thy fate,   5
Or sigh thy days so soon were terminate,
Sith thou art settled in an everlasting state.

2

By nature trees do rot when they are grown,
And plums and apples thoroughly ripe do fall,
And corn and grass are in their season mown,   10
And time brings down what is both strong and tall.
But plants new set to be eradicate,
And buds new blown to have so short a date,
Is by His hand alone that guides nature and fate.

1867

Here Follows Some Verses
upon the Burning of Our House
July 10th, 1666

Copied Out of a Loose Paper

In silent night when rest I took
For sorrow near I did not look
I wakened was with thund'ring noise
And piteous shrieks of dreadful voice.
That fearful sound of "Fire!" and "Fire!"   5
Let no man know is my desire.
I, starting up, the light did spy,
And to my God my heart did cry
To strengthen me in my distress
And not to leave me succorless.   10
Then, coming out, beheld a space
The flame consume my dwelling place.
And when I could no longer look,
I blest His name that gave and took,
That laid my goods now in the dust.   15
Yea, so it was, and so 'twas just.
It was His own, it was not mine,
Far be it that I should repine;
He might of all justly bereft
But yet sufficient for us left.   20
When by the ruins oft I past
My sorrowing eyes aside did cast,
And here and there the places spy
Where oft I sat and long did lie:
Here stood that trunk, and there that chest,   25

There lay that store I counted best.
My pleasant things in ashes lie,
And them behold no more shall I.
Under thy roof no guest shall sit,
Nor at thy table eat a bit.   30
No pleasant tale shall e'er be told,
Nor things recounted done of old.
No candle e'er shall shine in thee,
Nor bridegroom's voice e'er heard shall be.
In silence ever shall thou lie,   35
Adieu, Adieu, all's vanity.
Then straight I 'gin my heart to chide,
And did thy wealth on earth abide?
Didst fix thy hope on mold'ring dust?
The arm of flesh didst make thy trust?   40
Raise up thy thoughts above the sky
That dunghill mists away may fly.
Thou hast an house on high erect,
Framed by that mighty Architect,
With glory richly furnished,   45
Stands permanent though this be fled.
It's purchased and paid for too
By Him who hath enough to do.
A price so vast as is unknown
Yet by His gift is made thine own;   50
There's wealth enough, I need no more,
Farewell, my pelf,[1] farewell my store.
The world no longer let me love,
My hope and treasure lies above.
1867

Meditations Divine and Moral

1

There is no object that we see, no action that we do, no good that we enjoy, no evil that we feel or fear, but we may make some spiritual advantage of all; and he that makes such improvement is wise as well as pious.

2

Many can speak well, but few can do well. We are better scholars in the theory than the practic part, but he is a true Christian that is a proficient in both.

---

[1] Disparaging term for money or riches.

3

Youth is the time of getting, middle age of improving and old age of spending; a negligent youth is usually attended by an ignorant middle age, and both by an empty old age. He that hath nothing to feed on but vanity and lies must needs lie down in the bed of sorrow.

4

A ship that bears much sail and little or no ballast is easily overset, and that man whose head hath great abilities and his heart little or no grace is in danger of foundering.

5

It is reported of the peacock that, priding himself in his gay feathers, he ruffles them up, but spying his black feet, he soon lets fall his plumes; so he that glories in his gifts and adornings should look upon his corruptions, and that will damp his high thoughts.

6

The finest bread hath the least bran, the purest honey the least wax, and the sincerest Christian the least self-love.

7

The hireling that labours all the day comforts himself that when night comes he shall both take his rest and receive his reward; the painful Christian that hath wrought hard in God's vineyard and hath born the heat and drought of the day, when he perceives his sun apace to decline and the shadows of his evening to be stretched out, lifts up his head with joy, knowing his refreshing is at hand.

8

Downy beds make drowsy persons, but hard lodging keeps the eyes open; a prosperous state makes a secure Christian, but adversity makes him consider.

9

Sweet words are like honey: a little may refresh, but too much gluts the stomach.

10

Diverse children have their different natures: some are like flesh which nothing but salt will keep from putrefaction, some again like tender fruits that are best preserved with sugar. Those parents are wise that can fit their nurture according to their nature.

11

That town which thousands of enemies without hath not been able to take hath been delivered up by one traitor within, and that man which all the temptations of Satan without could not hurt hath been foiled by one lust within.

12

Authority without wisdom is like a heavy axe without an edge: fitter to bruise than polish.

13

The reason why Christians are so loath to exchange this world for a better is because they have more sense than faith: they see what they enjoy; they do but hope for that which is to come.

14

If we had no winter, the spring would not be so pleasant; if we did not sometimes taste of adversity, prosperity would not be so welcome.

15

A low man can go upright under that door where a taller is glad to stoop; so a man of weak faith and mean abilities may undergo a cross more patiently than he that excels him both in gifts and graces.

16

That house which is not often swept makes the cleanly inhabitant soon loath it, and that heart which is not continually purifying itself is no fit temple for the spirit of God to dwell in.

17

Few men are so humble as not to be proud of their abilities, and nothing will abase them more than this: what hast thou, but what thou hast received? Come, give an account of thy stewardship.

18

He that will undertake to climb up a steep mountain with a great burden on his back will find it a wearisome if not an impossible task; so he that thinks to mount to heaven clogged with the cares and riches of this life, 'tis no wonder if he faint by the way.

19

Corn, till it have past through the mill and been ground to powder, is not fit for bread. God so deals with his servants: he grinds them with grief and pain till they turn to dust, and then are they fit manchet[1] for his mansion.

20

God hath suitable comforts and supports for His children according to their several conditions. If He will make His face to shine upon them, He then makes them lie down in green pastures and leads them besides the still waters. If they stick in deep mire and clay, and all His waves and billows go over their heads, He then leads them to the rock which is higher than they.

21

He that walks among briars and thorns will be very careful where he sets his foot, and he that passes through the wilderness of this world had need ponder all his steps.

22

Want of prudence as well as piety hath brought men into great inconveniences, but he that is well stored with both seldom is so ensnared.

23

The skillful fisher hath his several baits for several fish, but there is a hook under all; Satan, that great Angler, hath his sundry baits for sundry tempers of men, which they all catch greedily at, but few perceives the hook till it be too late.

24

There is no new thing under the sun: there is nothing that can be said or done, but either that or something like it hath been both done and said before.

25

An aching head requires a soft pillow, and a drooping heart a strong support.

26

A sore finger may disquiet the whole body, but an ulcer within destroys it; so an enemy without may disturb a commonwealth, but dissentions within overthrow it.

[1] Fine bread.

27

It is a pleasant thing to behold the light, but sore eyes are not able to look upon it; the pure in heart shall see God, but the defiled in conscience shall rather choose to be buried under rocks and mountains than to behold the presence of the Lamb.

28

Wisdom with an inheritance is good, but wisdom without an inheritance is better than an inheritance without wisdom.

29

Lightning doth usually precede thunder, and storms rain, and strokes do not often fall till after threatening.

30

Yellow leaves argue want of sap and gray hairs want of moisture; so dry and sapless performances are symptoms of little spiritual vigor.

31

Iron, till it be thoroughly heat, is uncapable to be wrought; so God sees good to cast some men into the furnace of affliction and then beats them on His anvil into what frame he pleases.

32

Ambitious men are like hops that never rest climbing so long as they have anything to stay upon, but take away their props, and they are of all the most dejected.

33

Much labour wearies the body, and many thoughts oppress the mind; man aims at profit by the one and content in the other, but often misses of both and finds nothing but vanity and vexation of spirit.

34

Dim eyes are the concomitants of old age, and shortsightedness in those that are eyes of a republic fortells a declining state.

35

We read in Scriptures of three sorts of arrows; the arrow of an enemy, the arrow of pestilence, and the arrow of a slanderous tongue. The two first kill the body, the last the good name; the two former leave a man when he is once dead, but the last mangles him in his grave.

36

Sore labourers have hard hands and old sinners have brawny consciences.

37

Wickedness comes to its height by degrees. He that dares say of a less sin "Is it not a little one?" will ere long say of a greater, "Tush, God regards it not."

38

Some children are hardly weaned; although the teat be rubbed with wormwood or mustard, they will either wipe it off, or else suck down sweet and bitter together. So is it with some Christians: let God embitter all the sweets of this life, that so they might feed upon more substantial food, yet they are so childishly sottish that they are still hugging and sucking these empty breasts that God is forced to hedge up their way with thorns or lay affliction on their loins that so they might shake hands with the world, before it bid them farewell.

39

A prudent mother will not cloth her little child with a long and cumbersome garment; she easily forsees what events it is like to produce, at the best, but falls and bruises or perhaps somewhat worse. Much more will the allwise God proportion His dispensations according to the stature and strength of the person He bestows them on. Large endowments of honour, wealth, or a healthful body would quite overthrow some weak Christian; therefore God cuts their garments short to keep them in such a trim that they might run the ways of His commandment.

40

The spring is a lively emblem of the resurrection: after a long winter we see the leafless trees and dry stocks (at the approach of the sun) to resume their former vigor and beauty in a more ample manner than what they lost in the autumn; so shall it be at that great day after a long vacation, when the Sun of righteousness shall appear; those dry bones shall arise in far more glory than that which they lost at their creation, and in this transcends the spring that their leaf shall never fail nor their sap decline.

41

A wise father will not lay a burden on a child of seven years old which he knows is enough for one of twice his strength; much less will our heavenly Father (who knows our mold) lay such afflictions upon his weak children as would crush them to the dust, but according to the strength he will proportion the load. As God hath

His little children, so He hath His strong men, such as are come to a full stature in Christ, and many times He imposes weighty burdens on their shoulders, and yet they go upright under them, but it matters not whether the load be more or less if God afford His help.

42

"I have seen an end of all perfection," said the royal prophet, but he never said, "I have seen an end of all sinning." What he did say may be easily said by many, but what he did not say cannot truly be uttered by any.

43

Fire hath its force abated by water, not by wind, and anger must be allayed by cold words and not by blustering threats.

44

A sharp appetite and a thorough concoction is a sign of a healthful body; so a quick reception and a deliberate cogitation argues a sound mind.

45

We often see stones hang with drops not from any innate moisture, but from a thick air about them; so may we sometime see marble-hearted sinners seem full of contrition, but it is not from any dew of grace within but from some black clouds that impends them, which produces these sweating effects.

46

The words of the wise, saith Solomon, are as nails and as goads, both used for contrary ends; the one holds fast, the other puts forward. Such should be the precepts of the wise masters of assemblies to their hearers, not only to bid them hold fast the form of sound doctrine, but also so to run that they might obtain.

47

A shadow in the parching sun and a shelter in a blustering storm are of all seasons the most welcome; so a faithful friend in time of adversity is of all other most comfortable.

48

There is nothing admits of more admiration than God's various dispensation of His gifts among the sons of men, betwixt whom He hath put so vast a disproportion that they scarcely seem made of the same lump or sprung out of the loins of one Adam, some set in the highest dignity that mortality is capable of, and some again so base that they are viler than the earth, some so wise and learned that they seem like angels among men, and some again so ignorant and sottish that they are more like beasts than men, some pious saints, some incarnate devils, some exceeding beautiful, and some extremely deformed, some so strong and healthful that their bones are full of marrow and their breasts of milk, and some again so weak and feeble that while they live they are accounted among the dead; and no other reason can be given of all this but so it pleased Him whose will is the perfect rule of righteousness.

49

The treasures of this world may well be compared to husks, for they have no kernal in them, and they that feed upon them may soon stuff their throats, but cannot fill their bellies. They may be choked by them, but cannot be satisfied with them.

50

Sometimes the sun is only shadowed by a cloud that we cannot see his luster although we may walk by his light, but when he is set, we are in darkness till he arise again. So God doth sometime veil His face but for a moment that we cannot behold the light of His countenance as at some other time, yet He affords so much light as may direct our way, that we may go forwards to the city of habitation, but when He seems to set and be quite gone out of sight, then must we needs walk in darkness and see no light; yet then must we trust in the Lord and stay upon our God, and when the morning (which is the appointed time) is come, the Sun of righteousness will arise with healing in His wings.

51

The eyes and the ears are the inlets or doors of the soul, through which innumerable objects enter; yet is not that spacious room filled, neither doth it ever say it is enough, but like the daughters of the horseleach, cries, "Give, give"; and which is most strange, the more it receives, the more empty it finds itself and sees an impossibility ever to be filled but by Him in whom all fullness dwells.

52

Had not the wisest of men taught us this lesson that all is vanity and vexation of spirit, yet our own experience would soon have spelled it out, for what do we obtain of all these things, but it is with labour and vexation? When we enjoy them it is vanity and vexation, and if we loose them, then they are less than vanity and more than vexation, so that we have good cause often to repeat that sentence: vanity of vanities, vanity of vanities, all is vanity.

53

He that is to sail into a far country, although the ship, cabin, and provision be all convenient and comfortable for him, yet he hath no desire to make that his place of residence, but longs to put in at that port where his business lies. A Christian is sailing through this world unto his heavenly country, and here he hath many conveniences and comforts, but he must beware of desiring to make this the place of his abode, lest he meet with such tossings that may cause him to long for shore before he sees land. We must, therefore, be here as strangers and pilgrims, that we may plainly declare that we seek a city above and wait all the days of our appointed time till our change shall come.

54

He that never felt what it was to be sick or wounded doth not much care for the company of the physician or surgeon, but if he perceive a malady that threatens him with death, he will gladly entertain him whom he slighted before; so he that never felt the sickness of sin, nor the wounds of a guilty conscience cares not how far he keeps from him that hath skill to cure it, but when he finds his diseases to disrest him, and that he must needs perish if he have no remedy, will unfeignedly bid him welcome that brings a plaster for his sore or a cordial for his fainting.

55

We read of ten lepers that were cleansed but of one that returned thanks; we are more ready to receive mercies than we are to acknowledge them. Men can use great importunity when they are in distresses and show great ingratitude after their successes, but he that ordereth his conversation aright will glorify him that heard him in the day of his trouble.

56

The remembrance of former deliverances is a great support in present distresses. "He that delivered me," saith David, "from the paw of the lion and the paw of the bear will deliver me from this uncircumcised Philistine," and "He that hath delivered me," saith Paul, "will deliver me." God is the same yesterday, today, and forever; we are the same that stand in need of Him, today as well as yesterday, and so shall forever.

57

Great receipts call for great returns; the more that any man is intrusted withal, the larger his accounts stands upon God's score. It therefore behoves every man so to improve his talents that when his great Master shall call him to reckoning, He may receive His own with advantage.

58

Sin and shame ever go together. He that would be freed from the last must be sure to shun the company of the first.

59

God doth many times both reward and punish for one and the same action, as we see in Jehu; he is rewarded with a kingdom to the fourth generation for taking vengeance on the house of Ahab; and "Yet a little while," said God, "and I will avenge the blood of Jezreel upon the house of Jehu." He was rewarded for the matter, and yet punished for the manner, which should warn him that doth any special service for God to fix his eye on the command and not on his own ends, lest he meet with Jehu's reward, which will end in punishment.

60

He that would be content with a mean condition must not cast his eye upon one that is in a far better estate than himself, but let him look upon him that is lower than he is, and if he see, that such a one bears poverty comfortably, it will help to quiet him, but if that will not do, let him look on his own unworthiness and that will make him say with Jacob: I am less than the least of Thy mercies.

61

Corn is produced with much labour (as the husbandman well knows), and some land asks much more pains than some other doth to be brought into tilth; yet all must be ploughed and harrowed. Some children (like sour land) are of so tough and morose a disposition that the plough of correction must make long furrows on their back and the harrow of discipline go often over them before they be fit soil to sow the seed of morality much less of grace in them. But when by prudent nurture they are brought into a fit capacity, let the seed of good instruction and exhortation be sown in the spring of their youth, and a plentiful crop may be expected in the harvest of their years.

62

As a man is called the little world, so his heart may be called the little commonwealth; his more fixed and resolved thoughts are like to inhabitants, his slight and flitting thoughts are like passengers that travel to and fro continually; here is also the great court of justice erected, which is alway kept by conscience, who is both accuser, excuser, witness, and judge, whom no bribes can pervert nor flattery cause to favour, but as he finds the evidence, so he absolves or condemns; yea, so absolute is this court of judicature that there is no appeal from it, no not to the court of heaven itself, for if our conscience condemn us, He also who is greater than our conscience will do it much more, but he that would have boldness to go to the throne of grace to be accepted there must be sure to carry a certificate from the court of conscience that he stands right there.

63

He that would keep a pure heart and lead a blameless life must set himself alway in the awful presence of God. The consideration of His all-seeing eye will be a bridle to restrain from evil and spur to quicken on to good duties. We certainly dream of some remoteness betwixt God and us, or else we should not so often fail in our whole course of life as we do, but he that with David sets the Lord alway in his sight will not sin against Him.

64

We see in orchards some trees so fruitful that the weight of their burden is the breaking of their limbs, some again are but meanly loaden, and some have nothing to show but leaves only, and some among them are dry stock; so is it in the church, which is God's orchard; there are some eminent Christians that are so frequent in good duties that many times, the weight thereof impairs both their bodies and estates, and there are some (and they sincere ones, too) who have not attained to that fruitfulness, although they aim at perfection, and again there are others that have nothing to commend them but only a gay profession, and these are but leavie[2] Christians which are in as much danger of being cut down as the dry stock, for both cumber the ground.

65

We see in the firmament there is but one sun among a multitude of stars and those stars also to differ much one from the other in regard of bigness and brightness, yet all receive their light from that one sun; so is it in the church both militant and triumphant: there is but one Christ, who is the sun of righteousness, in the midst of an unnumerable company of saints and angels; those saints have their degrees, even in this life: some are stars of the first magnitude, and some of a less degree, and others (and they indeed the most in number) but small and obscure, yet all receive their luster (be it more or less) from that glorious sun that enlightens all in all, and if some of them shine so bright while they move on earth, how transcendently splendid shall they be when they are fixt in their heavenly spheres!

66

Men that have walked very extravagantly and at last bethink themselves of turning to God, the first thing which they eye is how to reform their ways rather than to beg forgiveness for their sins. Nature looks more at a compensation than at a pardon, but he that will not come for mercy without money and without price, but bring his filthy rags to barter for it, shall meet with miserable disappointment, going away empty bearing the reproach of his pride and folly.

67

All the works and doings of God are wonderful, but none more awful than His great work of election and reprobation; when we consider how many good parents have had bad children, and again how many bad parents have had pious children, it should

---

[2] Light; lacking in seriousness.

make us adore the sovereignty of God, who will not be tied to time nor place, nor yet to persons, but takes and chooses, when and where and whom He pleases; it should also teach the children of godly parents to walk with fear and trembling, lest they through unbelief fall short of a promise; it may also be a support to such as have or had wicked parents, that if they abide not in unbelief, God is able to gaff[3] them in. The upshot of all should make us with the apostle to admire the justice and mercy of God and say how unsearchable are His ways and His footsteps past finding out.

68

The gifts that God bestows on the sons of men are not only abused but most commonly employed for a clean contrary end than that which they were given for, as health, wealth, and honour, which might be so many steps to draw men to God in consideration of His bounty towards them, but have driven them the further from Him that they are ready to say: we are lords, we will come no more at Thee. If outward blessings be not as wings to help us mount upwards, they will certainly prove clogs and weights that will pull us lower downward.

69

All the comforts of this life may be compared to the gourd of Jonah, that notwith-standing we take great delight for a season in them and find their shadow very comfortable, yet there is some worm or other, of discontent, of fear, or grief that lies at the root, which in great part withers the pleasure which else we should take in them, and well it is that we perceive a decay in their greenness, for were earthly comforts permanent, who would look for heavenly?

70

All men are truly said to be tenants at will, and it may as truly be said that all have a lease of their lives, some longer, some shorter, as it pleases our great Landlord to let. All have their bounds set, over which they cannot pass, and till the expiration of that time, no dangers, no sickness, no pains, nor troubles shall put a period to our days. The certainty that that time will come, together with the uncertainty, how, where, and when, should make us so to number our days as to apply our hearts to wisdom, that when we are put out of these houses of clay we may be sure of an everlasting habitation that fades not away.

71

All weak and diseased bodies have hourly mementos of their mortality, but the soundest of men, have likewise their nightly monitor by the emblem of death, which is their sleep (for so is death often called), and not only their death, but their grave is lively represented before their eyes by beholding their bed, the morning may mind them of the resurrection, and the sun approaching of the appearing of the Sun of

---

[3] Hook.

righteousness, at whose coming they shall all rise out of their beds, the long night shall fly away, and the day of eternity shall never end. Seeing these things must be, what manner of persons ought we to be, in all good conversation?

72

As the brands of a fire, if once severed, will of themselves go out although you use no other means to extinguish them, so distance of place together with length of time (if there be no intercourse) will cool the affections of intimate friends, though there should be no displeasance between them.

73

A good name is as a precious ointment, and it is a great favour to have a good repute among good men; yet it is not that which commends us to God, for by His balance we must be weighed, and by His judgment we must be tried, and as He passes the sentence, so shall we stand.

74

Well doth the apostle call riches "deceitful" riches, and they may truly be compared to deceitful friends who speak fair and promise much but perform nothing, and so leave those in the lurch that most relied on them; so is it with the wealth, honours, and pleasures of this world which miserably delude men and make them put great confidence in them, but when death threatens and distress lays hold upon them, they prove like the reeds of Egypt that pierce instead of supporting, like empty wells in the time of drought that those that go to find water in them return with their empty pitchers ashamed.

75

It is admirable to consider the power of faith, by which all things are (almost) possible to be done; it can remove mountains (if need were); it hath stayed the course of the sun, raised the dead, cast out devils, reversed the order of nature, quenched the violence of the fire, made the water become firm footing for Peter to walk on; nay, more than all these, it hath overcome the omnipotent Himself, as when Moses intercedes for the people, God saith to him, "Let me alone, that I may destroy them," as if Moses had been able by the hand of faith to hold the everlasting arms of the mighty God of Jacob. Yea Jacob himself when he wrestled with God face to face in Penuel, "Let me go," saith that Angel. "I will not let thee go," replies Jacob, "till thou bless me." Faith is not only thus potent but it is so necessary that without faith there is no salvation; therefore with all our seekings and gettings, let us above all seek to obtain this pearl of price.

76

Some Christians do by their lusts and corruptions as the Israelites did by the Canaanites, not destroy them but put them under tribute, for that they could do (as they thought) with less hazard and more profit; but what was the issue, they became a snare unto them, pricks in their eyes and thorns in their sides, and at last overcame them and kept them under slavery; so it is most certain that those that are disobedient to the command of God and endeavour not to the utmost to drive out all their accursed inmates but make a league with them, they shall at last fall into perpetual bondage under them unless the great deliverer Christ Jesus come to their rescue.

77

God hath by his providence so ordered that no one country hath all commodities within itself, but what it wants another shall supply that so there may be a mutual commerce through the world. As it is with countries so it is with men; there was never yet any one man that had all excellences, let his parts natural and acquired, spiritual and moral, be never so large, yet he stands in need of something which another man hath (perhaps meaner than himself) which shows us perfection is not below, as also that God will have us beholden one to another.

1867

To My Dear Children

This book by any yet unread,
I leave for you when I am dead,
That being gone, here you may find
What was your living mother's mind.
Make use of what I leave in love,
And God shall bless you from above.
                                        A. B.

My dear children,

I, knowing by experience that the exhortations of parents take most effect when the speakers leave to speak, and those especially sink deepest which are spoke latest, and being ignorant whether on my death bed I shall have opportunity to speak to any of you, much less to all, thought it the best, whilst I was able, to compose some short matters (for what else to call them I know not) and bequeath to you, that when I am no more with you, yet I may be daily in your remembrance (although that is the least in my aim in what I now do), but that you may gain some spiritual advantage by my experience. I have not studied in this you read to show my skill, but to declare the truth, not to set forth myself, but the glory of God. If I had minded the former, it had been perhaps better pleasing to you, but seeing the last is the best, let it be best pleasing to you.

The method I will observe shall be this: I will begin with God's dealing with me from my childhood to this day.

In my young years, about 6 or 7 as I take it, I began to make conscience of my ways, and what I knew was sinful, as lying, disobedience to parents, etc., I avoided it. If at any time I was overtaken with the like evils, it was as a great trouble, and I could not be at rest 'till by prayer I had confessed it unto God. I was also troubled at the neglect of private duties though too often tardy that way. I also found much comfort in reading the Scriptures, especially those places I thought most concerned my condition, and as I grew to have more understanding, so the more solace I took in them.

In a long fit of sickness which I had on my bed I often communed with my heart and made my supplication to the most High who set me free from that affliction.

But as I grew up to be about 14 or 15, I found my heart more carnal, and sitting loose from God, vanity and the follies of youth take hold of me.

About 16, the Lord laid His hand sore upon me and smote me with the smallpox. When I was in my affliction, I besought the Lord and confessed my pride and vanity, and He was entreated of me and again restored me. But I rendered not to Him according to the benefit received.

After a short time I changed my condition and was married, and came into this country, where I found a new world and new manners, at which my heart rose. But after I was convinced it was the way of God, I submitted to it and joined to the church at Boston.

After some time I fell into a lingering sickness like a consumption together with a lameness, which correction I saw the Lord sent to humble and try me and do me good, and it was not altogether ineffectual.

It pleased God to keep me a long time without a child, which was a great grief to me and cost me many prayers and tears before I obtained one, and after him gave me many more of whom I now take the care, that as I have brought you into the world, and with great pains, weakness, cares, and fears brought you to this, I now travail in birth again of you till Christ be formed in you.

Among all my experiences of God's gracious dealings with me, I have constantly observed this, that He hath never suffered me long to sit loose from Him, but by one affliction or other hath made me look home, and search what was amiss; so usually thus it hath been with me that I have no sooner felt my heart out of order, but I have expected correction for it, which most commonly hath been upon my own person in sickness, weakness, pains, sometimes on my soul, in doubts and fears of God's displeasure and my sincerity towards Him; sometimes He hath smote a child with a sickness, sometimes chastened by losses in estate, and these times (through His great mercy) have been the times of my greatest getting and advantage; yea, I have found them the times when the Lord hath manifested the most love to me. Then have I gone to searching and have said with David, "Lord, search me and try me, see what ways of wickedness are in me, and lead me in the way everlasting," and seldom or never but I have found either some sin I lay under which God would have reformed, or some duty neglected which He would have performed, and by His help I have laid vows and bonds upon my soul to perform His righteous commands.

If at any time you are chastened of God, take it as thankfully and joyfully as in greatest mercies, for if ye be His, ye shall reap the greatest benefit by it. It hath been no small support to me in times of darkness when the Almighty hath hid His face from me that yet I have had abundance of sweetness and refreshment after affliction and more circumspection in my walking after I have been afflicted. I have been with

God like an untoward child, that no longer than the rod has been on my back (or at least in sight) but I have been apt to forget Him and myself, too. Before I was afflicted, I went astray, but now I keep Thy statutes.

I have had great experience of God's hearing my prayers and returning comfortable answers to me, either in granting the thing I prayed for, or else in satisfying my mind without it, and I have been confident it hath been from Him, because I have found my heart through His goodness enlarged in thankfulness to Him.

I have often been perplexed that I have not found that constant joy in my pilgrimage and refreshing which I supposed most of the servants of God have, although He hath not left me altogether without the witness of His holy spirit, who hath oft given me His word and set to His seal that it shall be well with me. I have sometimes tasted of that hidden manna that the world knows not, and have set up my Ebenezer, and have resolved with myself that against such a promise, such tastes of sweetness, the gates of hell shall never prevail; yet have I many times sinkings and droopings, and not enjoyed that felicity that sometimes I have done. But when I have been in darkness and seen no light, yet have I desired to stay myself upon the Lord, and when I have been in sickness and pain, I have thought if the Lord would but lift up the light of His countenance upon me, although He ground me to powder, it would be but light to me; yea, oft have I thought were I in hell itself and could there find the love of God toward me, it would be a heaven. And could I have been in heaven without the love of God, it would have been a hell to me, for in truth it is the absence and presence of God that makes heaven or hell.

Many times hath Satan troubled me concerning the verity of the Scriptures, many times by atheism how I could know whether there was a God; I never saw any miracles to confirm me, and those which I read of, how did I know but they were feigned? That there is a God my reason would soon tell me by the wondrous works that I see, the vast frame of the heaven and the earth, the order of all things, night and day, summer and winter, spring and autumn, the daily providing for this great household upon the earth, the preserving and directing of all to its proper end. The consideration of these things would with amazement certainly resolve me that there is an Eternal Being. But how should I know He is such a God as I worship in Trinity, and such a Saviour as I rely upon? Though this hath thousands of times been suggested to me, yet God hath helped me over. I have argued thus with myself. That there is a God, I see. If ever this God hath revealed himself, it must be in His word, and this must be it or none. Have I not found that operation by it that no human invention can work upon the soul, hath not judgments befallen divers who have scorned and contemned it, hath it not been preserved through all ages maugre[1] all the heathen tyrants and all of the enemies who have opposed it? Is there any story but that which shows the beginnings of times, and how the world came to be as we see? Do we not know the prophecies in it fulfilled which could not have been so long foretold by any but God Himself?

When I have got over this block, then have I another put in my way, that admit this be the true God whom we worship, and that be his word, yet why may not the Popish religion be the right? They have the same God, the same Christ, the same word. They only interpret it one way, we another.

[1] Despite.

This hath sometimes stuck with me, and more it would, but the vain fooleries that are in their religion together with their lying miracles and cruel persecutions of the saints, which admit were they as they term them, yet not so to be dealt withal.

The consideration of these things and many the like would soon turn me to my own religion again.

But some new troubles I have had since the world has been filled with blasphemy and sectaries, and some who have been accounted sincere Christians have been carried away with them, that sometimes I have said, "Is there faith upon the earth?" and I have not known what to think; but then I have remembered the works of Christ that so it must be, and if it were possible, the very elect should be deceived. "Behold," saith our Saviour, "I have told you before." That hath stayed my heart, and I can now say, "Return, O my Soul, to thy rest, upon this rock Christ Jesus will I build my faith, and if I perish, I perish"; but I know all the Powers of Hell shall never prevail against it. I know whom I have trusted, and whom I have believed, and that He is able to keep that I have committed to His charge.

Now to the King, immortal, eternal and invisible, the only wise God, be honour, and glory for ever and ever, Amen.

This was written in much sickness and weakness, and is very weakly and imperfectly done, but if you can pick any benefit out of it, it is the mark which I aimed at.

1867

John Saffin
1626–1710

John Saffin was a colonial merchant-attorney who ventured profitably in salt, iron, lumber, fish, and slaves. His contemporaries probably did not know that he also kept a personal notebook containing over fifty of his own poems. Saffin came to America as a young child and settled with his family south of Boston in Scituate, Massachusetts, a seashore town proud to be founded by "the best class of English gentlemen of their day; men of education, many of them college graduates." The sophisticated atmosphere of the town may help to explain why Saffin, who never attended college, showed remarkable learning in his notebook and had a successful career in law. By 1660 he had "joyned" a Boston church and married Martha Willet, most beloved of his three wives. (Saffin was twice left a widower.) He was a litigious man of volatile temper and incurred the enmity of divers colonists, including Judge Samuel Sewall. Ensnarled in several lawsuits, he finally submitted to a sort of forced retirement in Bristol (now Rhode Island) in 1687–1688.

The poems in Saffin's notebook include elegies, satires, acrostics, and love poems. Just one or two were published during his lifetime, and the others came to light only around 1900, when one of his descendants gave the handwritten notebook to the Rhode Island Historical Society. A number of his verses are deeply personal and concern family life. The deaths of Saffin's eight sons elicited some of his tenderest lyrics. The love poem "Sweetly (my Dearest) I left thee asleep" was written for his first wife and shows Saffin to be a male counterpart of Anne Bradstreet.

Further Reading:
H. Jantz, *The First Century of New England Verse*, 1943, 1962.
Seventeenth-Century American Poetry, ed. H. Meserole, 1968.

Text:
John Saffin: His Book, 1928.

[Sweetly (my Dearest) I left thee asleep]

Sweetly (my Dearest) I left thee asleep
Which Silent parting made my heart to weep,
Faine would I wake her, but Love did Reply
O wake her not, So sweetly let her Lye.
But must I goe, O must I Leave her So,   5
So ill at Ease: involv'd in Slumbering wo
Must I goe hence: and thus my Love desert
Unknown to Her, O must I now Depart;
Thus was I hurried with such thoughts as these,
Yet loath to Rob thee of thy present Ease,   10
Or rather senceless payn: farewell thought I,
My Joy my Deare in whom I live or Dye
Farewell Content, farewell fare Beauty's light
And the most pleasing Object of my Sight;
I must begone, Adieu my Dear, Adieu   15
Heavens grant good Tideings I next heare from you
Thus in sad Silence I alone and mute,
My lips bad thee farewell, with a Salute.
And so went from thee; turning back againe
I thought one kiss to little then Stole twaine   20
And then another: but no more of this,
Count with your Self how many of them you miss.
And now my love soon let me from the heare
Of thy good health, that may my Spirits Cheare
Acquaint me with such passages as may   25
Present themselves since I am come away
And above all things let me thee Request
To be both Chearfull quiet and at Rest
In thine own Spirit, and let nothing move
Thee unto Discontent my Joy my Love.   30

Hopeing that all things shall at last conduce
Unto our Comfort and a Blessed use
Considering that those things are hardly gain'd
Are most Delightfull when they are Attain'd.
Gold Crowns are heavy: Idalian Burn's[1]   35
And Lovers Days are good, and bad by turn's
But yet the Consummation will Repay
The Debt that's due many a happy Day
Which that it may so be, Ile Heaven Implore
To grant the fame henceforth forever more   40
And so farewell, farewell fair Beautys light
Ten thousand times Adieu my Dear Delight.
    Your Ever loveing friend whilest Hee
    Desolved is: or Cease to bee.

1928

Michael Wigglesworth
1631–1705

Michael Wigglesworth was a minister, a physician, and the author of the most
popular literary work of Puritan New England. His *Day of Doom* (1662) so
stirred the public imagination that the text was literally read to pieces. No copy
of the first edition survives. Readers found this 224-stanza theological poem,
subtitled *The Poetical Description of the Great and Last Judgment,* to be thoroughly
familiar in its subject matter, its Calvinist doctrine, and its ballad verse form. It is
probable that the poem originated in a dream of the twenty-two-year-old
Wigglesworth, who saw God's blessed "sheep" separated from the sinful "goats"
in the "dreadful day of judgment." Yet this was a dream of all New England
Puritans, who expected the final events of human history to occur at any
moment. *Day of Doom* gave each reader the graphic and complete description of
apocalyptic events preceding the end of human history.

    Wigglesworth was the son of a Yorkshire businessman who of necessity turned
farmer when he emigrated from England and settled his family in the newest and
most remote colonial plantation, New Haven (Connecticut). Michael, a frail boy,
tried farming the family's allotted acreage, especially when injury lamed his
father. But he had shown scholarly promise, and with his father's encouragement
he prepared for Harvard, from which he graduated first in his class, staying on to
study for his M.A. Though he intended to become a physician, his experience of
God's saving grace led him to the ministry.

    Wigglesworth experienced severe pangs of conscience that were unusual even
for a devout, introspective Puritan. Virtually every line of his *Diary* (1653–1657)

---

[1] Idalium, in Cypress, was sacred to Aphrodite,
Greek goddess of love and beauty.

records self-confessed "slouth," "sapless spirits," "pride," or "ocean of deadly poyson in my heart." He was wracked by sexual guilt, the "unresistable torments of carnal lusts." The *Diary* suggests that Wigglesworth's spiritual torment was not allayed by the comfort other Puritans found in their religion. Yet in 1656 the young minister accepted a call to the church in Malden, Massachusetts, and wed Mary Reyner. Throughout his adult life Wigglesworth was sickly, in Cotton Mather's phrase "a feeble little shadow of a man." He nevertheless married three wives, fathered eight children, and lived into his seventy-fourth year.

Wigglesworth's education in logic, rhetoric, Greek, Hebrew, ethics, and metaphysics fitted him for subtle and learned discourse, but he intended *Day of Doom* to be accessible to a broad range of the population, including unschooled people apt to find theological subtleties baffling. The key to Wigglesworth's design for the poem may be his college oration (ca. 1650) on eloquence, which, he argued, enlivens and elevates the understanding "beyond its natural vigor" or normal state. "Eloquence," Wigglesworth added, can rouse the imagination from its "slumber" and "revive the things known." *Day of Doom,* if eloquent by this definition, would stir its readers to an intense, new emotional awareness of the very Puritan doctrines and ideas already intellectually familiar to them. In easily memorized "fourteeners," the meter of hymns, Wigglesworth cast his vision of God's Judgment Day come suddenly to an unsuspecting world. Throughout, the poem exemplifies the Puritan "plain style," free of the ornaments of historical or literary allusion. The scriptural references in the margins of the text were an ongoing reminder that *Day of Doom* was God's truth.

Wigglesworth wrote two other lengthy poems, *God's Controversy with New-England* and *Meat Out of the Eater,* but neither approached *Day of Doom* as a popular success. Recent critics have had some difficulty accounting for the public reception of a work that seems to some to be inexorable doggerel, not "eloquence." Here it is useful to recall that Puritans were ever mindful of the imminent apocalypse and that their literature was rife with apocalyptic themes. *Day of Doom* may have been so successful precisely because Wigglesworth offered readers a comprehensive vision of Judgment Day. The individual could find (and memorize) passages especially responsive to his or her particular visions of it. A reader energized either by love or by hate could be satisfied by Wigglesworth's images of "sabbath polluters," "blasphemers lewd," and a loving God embracing his saints or chosen people. *Day of Doom* read like God's high drama in the colonial wilds.

Further Reading:
R. Crowder, *No Featherbed in Heaven: A Biography of Michael Wigglesworth,* 1962.

Text:
Seventeenth-Century American Poetry, ed. H. Meserole, 1968.
See also *The Diary of Michael Wigglesworth,* ed. E. Morgan, 1951, 1965.

from The Day of Doom

1

*The Security of
the World
before Christ's
coming to
Judgment.
Luk.* 12: 19

Still was the night, Serene and Bright,
    when all Men sleeping lay;
Calm was the season, and carnal reason
    thought so 'twould last for ay.
Soul, take thine ease, let sorrow cease,   5
    much good thou hast in store:
This was their Song, their Cups among,
    the Evening before.

2

Wallowing in all kind of sin,
    vile wretches lay secure: 10
The best of men had scarcely then
Mat. 25: 5   their Lamps kept in good ure.[1]
Virgins unwise, who through disguise
    amongst the best were number'd,
Had clos'd their eyes; yea, and the wise   15
    through sloth and frailty slumber'd.

3

Like as of old, when Men grow bold
Mat. 24: 37, 38   Gods threatnings to contemn,
Who stopt their Ear, and would not hear,
    when Mercy warned them: 20
But took their course, without remorse,
    til God began to powre
Destruction the World upon
    in a tempestuous showre.

4

They put away the evil day,   25
    and drown'd their care and fears,
Till drown'd were they, and swept away
    by vengeance unawares:
I *Thes.* 5: 3   So at the last, whilst Men sleep fast

[1] Use.

in their security,   30
Surpriz'd they are in such a snare
   as cometh suddenly.

5

The Suddenness,
Majesty, and
Terror of Christ's
appearing
   Mat. 25: 6
   II Pet. 3: 10

For at midnight brake forth a Light,
   which turn'd the night to day,
And speedily an hideous cry   35
   did all the world dismay.
Sinners awake, their hearts do ake,
   trembling their loynes surprizeth;
Amaz'd with fear, by what they hear,
   each one of them ariseth.   40

6

They rush from Beds with giddy heads,
   and to their windows run,
Viewing this light, which shines more bright
Mat. 24: 29, 30   then doth the Noon-day Sun.
Straightway appears (they see't with tears)   45
   the Son of God most dread;
Who with his Train comes on amain
   To Judge both Quick and Dead.

7

Before his face the Heav'ns gave place,
II Pet. 3: 10   and Skies are rent asunder,   50
With mighty voice, and hideous noise,
   more terrible than Thunder.
His brightness damps heav'ns glorious lamps
   and makes them hide their heads,
As if afraid and quite dismay'd,   55
   they quit their wonted steads.

8

Ye sons of men that durst contemn
   the Threatnings of Gods Word,
How cheer you now? your hearts, I trow,
   are thrill'd with a sword.   60
Now Atheist blind, whose brutish mind
   a God could never see,
Dost thou perceive, dost now believe,
   that Christ thy Judge shall be?

9

Stout Courages, (whose hardiness   65
    could Death and Hell out-face)
Are you as bold now you behold
    your Judge draw near apace?
They cry, no, no: Alas! and wo!
    our Courage all is gone: 70
Our hardiness (fool hardiness)
    hath us undone, undone.

10

No heart so bold, but now grows cold
    and almost dead with fear:
Rev. 6: 16   No eye so dry, but now can cry,   75
    and pour out many a tear.
Earths Potentates and pow'rful States,
    Captains and Men of Might,
Are quite abasht, their courage dasht
    at this most dreadful sight.   80

11

Mean men lament, great men do rent
    their Robes, and tear their hair:
Mat. 24: 30   They do not spare their flesh to tear
    through horrible despair.
All Kindreds wail: all hearts do fail: 85
    horror the world doth fill
With weeping eyes, and loud out-cries,
    yet knows not how to kill.

12

Rev. 6: 15, 16   Some hide themselves in Caves and Delves,
    in places under ground: 90
Some rashly leap into the Deep,
    to scape by being drown'd:
Some to the Rocks (O sensless blocks!)
    and woody Mountains run,
That there they might this fearful sight,   95
    and dreaded Presence shun.

13

In vain do they to Mountains say,
    Fall on us, and us hide

From Judges ire, more hot than fire,
    for who may it abide?   100
No hiding place can from his Face,
    sinners at all conceal,
Whose flaming Eyes hid things doth 'spy,
    and darkest things reveal.

14

Mat. 25: 31

The Judge draws nigh, exhalted high   105
    upon a lofty Throne,
Amidst the throng of Angels strong,
    lo, Israel's Holy One!
The excellence of whose presence
    and awful Majesty,   110
Amazeth Nature, and every Creature,
    doth more than terrify.

15

Rev. 6: 14

The Mountains smoak, the Hills are shook,
    the Earth is rent and torn,
As if she should be clean dissolv'd,   115
    or from the Center born.
The Sea doth roar, forsakes the shore,
    and Shrinks away for fear;
The wild Beasts flee into the sea,
    so soon as he draws near.   120

16

Whose Glory bright, whose wondrous might
whose Power Imperial,
So far surpass whatever was
    in Realms Terrestrial;
That tongues of men (nor Angels pen)   125
    cannot the same express,
And therefore I must pass it by,
    lest speaking should transgress.

17

I Thes. 4: 16
Resurrection of
  the Dead.
John 5: 28,
  29

Before his Throne a Trump is blown,
    Proclaiming th' Day of Doom: 130
Forthwith he cries, *Ye Dead arise,*
    and unto Judgment come.
No sooner said, but 'tis obey'd;

Sepulchers open'd are:
Dead Bodies all rise at his call,   135
　　and's mighty power declare

18

Both Sea and Land, at his Command,
　　their Dead at once surrender:
The Fire and Air constrained are
　　also their dead to tender.   140
The mighty word of this great Lord
　　links Body and Soul together
Both of the Just, and the unjust,
　　to part no more forever.

19

The living　　The same translates, from mortal states   145
Changed.　　　　to Immortality,
All that survive, and be alive,
　　i' th' twinkling of an eye:
Luk. 20: 36　　That so they may abide for ay
I Cor. 15: 52　　to endles weal or woe;   150
Both the Renate[2] and reprobate
　　are made to dy no more.

20

All brought to　　His winged Hosts file through all Coasts,
Judgment.　　　　together gathering
Mat. 24: 31　　Both good and bad, both quick and dead,   155
　　and all to Judgment bring.
Out of their holes those creeping Moles,
　　that hid themselves for fear,
By force they take, and quickly make
　　before the Judge appear.   160

21

II Cor. 5: 10 *The*　　Thus every one before the Throne
Sheep Separated　　　of Christ the Judge is brought,
from the Goats.　　Both righteous and impious
Mat. 25: 32　　　that good or ill had wrought.
A separation, and diff'ring station   165
　　by Christ appointed is
(To sinners sad) 'twixt good and bad,
　　'twixt Heirs of woe and bliss.

---

[2] Reborn.

22

Who are Christ's Sheep.
Mat. 5: 10, 11

At Christ's right hand the Sheep do stand,
   his holy Martyrs, who   170
For his dear Name suffering shame,
   calamity and woe,
Like Champions stood, and with their Blood
   their testimony sealed;
Whose innocence without offence,   175
   to Christ their Judge appealed.

23

Heb. 12: 5, 6, 7

Next unto whom there find a room
   all Christ's afflicted ones,
Who being chastised, neither despised
   nor sank amidst their groans: 180
Who by the Rod were turn'd to God,
   and loved him the more,
Not murmuring nor quarrelling
   when they were chast'ned sore.

24

Luke 7: 41, 47

Moreover, such as loved much,   185
   that had not such a tryal,
As might constrain to so great pain,
   and such deep self-denyal:
Yet ready were the Cross to bear,
   when Christ them call'd thereto,   190
And did rejoyce to hear his voice,
   they're counted Sheep also.

25

Joh. 21:15
Mat. 19: 14
Joh. 3: 3

Christ's Flock of Lambs there also stands,
   whose Faith was weak, yet true;
All sound Believers (Gospel receivers)   195
   whose Grace was small, but grew:
And them among an Infant throng
   of Babes, for whom Christ dy'd;
Whom for his own, by wayes unknown
   to men, he sanctify'd.   200

26

Rev. 6: 11
Phil. 3: 21

All stand before their Saviour
   in long white Robes yclad,

Their countenance full of pleasance,
    appearing wondrous glad.
O glorious sight! Behold how bright   205
    dust heaps are made to shine,
Conformed so their Lord unto,
    whose Glory is Divine.

27

The Goats   At Christ's left hand the Goats do stand,
described or the   all whining hypocrites,   210
several sorts of   Who for self-ends did seem Christ's friends,
Reprobates on the   but foster'd guileful sprites;
left hand.   Who Sheep resembled, but they dissembled
Mat. 24: 51   (their hearts were not sincere);
                Who once did throng Christ's Lambs among,   215
                but now must not come near.

28

Luk. 11: 24, 26   Apostates and Run-awayes,
Heb. 6: 4, 5, 6   such as have Christ forsaken,
Heb. 10: 29   Of whom the Devil, with seven more evil,
                hath fresh possession taken: 220
                Sinners in grain, reserv'd to pain
                and torments most severe:
                Because 'gainst light they sinn'd with spight,
                are also placed there.

29

Luk. 12: 47   There also stand a num'rous band,   225
Prov. 1: 24, 26   that no Profession made
Joh. 3: 19   Of Godliness, nor to redress
                their wayes at all essay'd:
                Who better knew, but (sinful Crew)
                Gospel and Law despised;   230
                Who all Christ's knocks withstood like blocks
                and would not be advised.

30

                Moreover, there with them appear
                a number, numberless
Gal. 3: 10   Of great and small, vile wretches all,   235
I *Cor.* 6: 9   that did Gods Law transgress:
Rev. 21: 8   Idolaters, false worshippers,
                Prophaners of Gods Name,

Who not at all thereon did call,
　　or took in vain the same.   240

31

Blasphemers lewd, and Swearers shrewd,
　　Scoffers at Purity,
Exod. 20: 7
and 8
That hated God, contemn'd his Rod,
　　and lov'd Security;
Sabbath-polluters, Saints persecutors,   245
　　Presumptuous men and proud,
II *Thes.* 1: 6, 8,
9
Who never lov'd those that reprov'd;
　　all stand amongst this Crowd.

32

Heb. 13: 4
I *Cor.* 6: 10
Adulterers and Whoremongers
　　were there, with all unchast: 250
There Covetous, and Ravenous,
　　that Riches got too fast:
Who us'd vile ways themselves to raise
　　t' Estates and worldly wealth,
Oppression by, or Knavery,   255
　　by force, or fraud, or stealth.

. . . .

219

The Saints rejoyce
to see Judgment
executed upon the
wicked World.
Ps. 58: 10
Rev. 19: 1, 2, 3
The Saints behold with courage bold,
　　and thankful wonderment,
To see all those that were their foes
　　thus sent to punishment: 260
Then do they sing unto their King
　　a Song of endless Praise:
They praise his Name, and do proclaim
　　that just are all his ways.

220

They ascend with
Christ into
Heaven
triumphing.
Mat. 25: 46
I *Joh.* 3: 2
I *Cor.* 13: 12
Thus with great joy and melody   265
　　to Heav'n they all ascend,
Him there to praise with sweetest layes,
　　and Hymns that never end,
Where with long Rest they shall be blest,
　　and nought shall them annoy: 270
Where they shall see as seen they be,
　　and whom they love enjoy.

221

Their Eternal
happiness and
incomparable
Glory there.

O glorious Place! where face to face
  Jehovah may be seen,
By such as were sinners whilere³   275
  and no dark vail between.
Where the Sun shine, and light Divine,
  of Gods bright Countenance,
Doth rest upon them every one.   280
  with sweetest influence.

222

O blessed state of the Renate!
  O wondrous Happiness,
To which they're brought, beyond what thought
  can reach, or words express!
Rev. 21: 4   Grief's water-course, and sorrows sourse,   285
  are turn'd to joyful streams,
Their old distress and heaviness
  are vanished like dreams.

223

For God above in arms of love
  doth dearly them embrace,   290
Psal. 16: 11   And fills their sprights with such delights,
  and pleasures in his grace;
As shall not fail, nor yet grow stale
  through frequency of use:
Nor do they fear God's favour there,   295
  to forfeit by abuse.

224

Heb. 12: 23   For there the Saints are perfect Saints,
  and holy ones indeed,
From all the sin that dwelt within
  their mortal bodies freed: 300
Made Kings and Priests to God through Christs
Rev. 1: 6 and   dear loves transcendency,
22: 5   There to remain, and there to reign
  with him Eternally.

1661

³ Formerly.

Mary Rowlandson
ca. 1635–ca. 1678

Mary Rowlandson became a best-selling author from the trauma of Indian attack and captivity. At sunrise in February 1676 she and her family fell victim to rampaging Indians who had banded together throughout New England in "King Philip's War," a desperate effort to regain tribal lands. The story of Mrs. Rowlandson's gruesome, painful ordeal in captivity was written as an exercise in psychological purgation and Puritan piety. It became a phenomenon in American publishing history. Mrs. Rowlandson's one literary effort, *A Narrative of the Captivity and Restoration of Mrs. Mary Rowlandson* (1682), was reprinted so many times that it ranks as one of the great best-sellers in all of American literature.

Little is known of Mary Rowlandson's early life. Like many Puritans, she was probably brought to New England in childhood by her father, the wealthy landholder John White, who settled in Lancaster, Massachusetts. Around 1656 Mary wed the Reverend Joseph Rowlandson, and for twenty years thereafter she lived the demanding life of a frontier housewife and mother of three children. In early summer 1675, Indian assaults began against the Massachusetts colonists, initiated by the sachem (chief) Philip, three of whose tribesmen had been executed in Plymouth. Word of the Indian uprising spread through the colony. The Rowlandsons and their neighbors, fearing attack, fortified their dwellings, but the Rowlandson house was one of twelve hundred houses to be burned in King Philip's War, and the child they lost was among three hundred casualties suffered by colonial families before the war ended in August 1676. Mary was held captive of Indians for eleven weeks, then ransomed for twenty pounds and reunited with her husband and two surviving children. In the following year the family moved to Wethersfield, Connecticut, where Rev. Rowlandson—and then Mary—died within months.

In her own colonial era, the *Narrative* was religious in purpose. It reassured its author and her readers that God might sorely test them with "many trials and afflictions" but would ultimately redeem them. Puritan writers saw the Indians as "Dregs and Lees of the Earth"—at worst Satan's emissaries, at best heathen. But Indian hostility indicated God's attitude toward the colonists. They found in Mary Rowlandson's example the assurance that God's redemptive power worked beyond the atrocities of this Indian war, one that Puritans felt posed a serious threat to the English settlements in New England. Mrs. Rowlandson's captivity and release to freedom seemed to be an individual reenactment of the colonists' communal mission toward salvation. Its piety, heroism, and fortitude were exemplary.

Mrs. Rowlandson and her contemporaries would be horrified to know that her *Narrative* is the fountainhead of popular frontier and wild-west thrillers recycling the pattern of attack, captivity, and escape from exotic Indians in wild, unsettled country. She would also be puzzled to hear that her *Narrative* is a part of our literature of cross-cultural encounter, including the writings of James Fenimore Cooper, Herman Melville, and William Faulkner. The *Narrative* is the antecedent of an important American literary tradition in which individualism and nationalism merge.

Further Reading:
A. Keiser, *The Indian in American Literature,* 1933.
R. Pearce, *The Savages of America,* 1953.
R. Slotkin, *Regeneration Through Violence,* 1973.
A. Kolodny, *The Land Before Her,* 1984.

Text:
Original Narratives of Early American History: Narratives of Indian Wars, 1675–1699, vol. 14, ed. C. Lincoln, 1913.

from A Narrative of the Captivity and Restauration of Mrs. Mary Rowlandson

On the tenth of February 1675,[1] Came the Indians with great numbers upon Lancaster: Their first coming was about Sun-rising; hearing the noise of some Guns, we looked out; several Houses[2] were burning, and the Smoke ascending to Heaven. There were five persons[3] taken in one house, the Father, and the Mother and a sucking Child, they knockt on the head; the other two they took and carried away alive. Their were two others, who being out of their Garison upon some occasion were set upon; one was knockt on the head, the other escaped: Another their was who running along was shot and wounded, and fell down; he begged of them his life, promising them Money (as they told me) but they would not hearken to him but knockt him in head, and stript him naked, and split open his Bowels. Another seeing many of the Indians about his Barn, ventured and went out, but was quickly shot down. There were three others belonging to the same Garison[4] who were killed; the Indians getting up upon the roof of the Barn, had advantage to shoot down upon them over their Fortification. Thus these murtherous wretches went on, burning, and destroying before them.

At length they came and beset our own house, and quickly it was the dolefullest day that ever mine eyes saw. The House stood upon the edge of a hill; some of the Indians got behind the hill, others into the Barn, and others behind anything that could shelter them; from all which places they shot against the House, so that the Bullets seemed to fly like hail; and quickly they wounded one man among us, then another, and then a third, About two hours (according to my observation, in that amazing time) they had been about the house before they prevailed to fire it (which they did with Flax and Hemp, which they brought out of the barn, and there being no defence

---

[1] Thursday, February 10, 1675/76. This and all other footnotes to the selection are from the source edition: Charles H. Lincoln, ed., *Narratives of the Indian Wars* (New York: Charles Scribner's Sons, 1913.).
[2] The houses mentioned were those of John White, Thomas Sawyer, John Prescott, and the Rowlandson and Wheeler garrisons.
[3] The family of John Ball, the tailor.
[4] The garrison of Richard Wheeler, on the southern side of George Hill.

about the House, only two Flankers[5] at two opposite corners and one of them not finished) they fired it once and one ventured out and quenched it, but they quickly fired it again, and that took. Now is the dreadfull hour come, that I have often heard of (in time of War, as it was the case of others) but now mine eyes see it. Some in our house were fighting for their lives, others wallowing in their blood, the House on fire over our heads, and the bloody Heathen ready to knock us on the head, if we stirred out. Now might we hear Mothers and Children crying out for themselves, and one another, Lord, What shall we do? Then I took my Children (and one of my sisters, hers) to go forth and leave the house: but as soon as we came to the dore and appeared, the Indians shot so thick that the bulletts rattled against the House, as if one had taken an handfull of stones and threw them, so that we were fain to give back. We had six stout Dogs belonging to our Garrison, but none of them would stir, though another time, if any Indian had come to the door, they were ready to fly upon him and tear him down. The Lord hereby would make us the more to acknowledge his hand, and to see that our help is always in him. But out we must go, the fire increasing, and coming along behind us, roaring, and the Indians gaping before us with their Guns, Spears and Hatchets to devour us. No sooner were we out of the House, but my Brother in Law[6] (being before wounded, in defending the house, in or near the throat) fell down dead, wherat the Indians scornfully shouted, and hallowed, and were presently upon him, stripping off his cloaths, the bulletts flying thick, one went through my side, and the same (as would seem) through the bowels and hand of my dear Child in my arms. One of my elder Sisters Children, named William[7] had then his Leg broken, which the Indians perceiving, they knockt him on head. Thus were we butchered by those merciless Heathen, standing amazed, with the blood running down to our heels. My eldest Sister being yet in the House, and seeing those wofull sights, the Infidels haling Mothers one way, and Children another, and some wallowing in their blood: and her elder Son telling her that her Son William was dead, and myself was wounded, she said, And, Lord, let me dy with them; which was no sooner said, but she was struck with a Bullet, and fell down dead over the threshold. I hope she is reaping the fruit of her good labours, being faithfull to the service of God in her place. In her younger years she lay under much trouble upon spiritual accounts, till it pleased God to make that precious Scripture take hold of her heart, 2 Cor. 12. 9. *And he said unto me, my Grace is sufficient for thee.* More then twenty years after I have heard her tell how sweet and comfortable that place was to her. But to return: The Indians laid hold of us, pulling me one way, and the Children another, and said, Come go along with us; I told them they would kill me: they answered, If I were willing to go along with them, they would not hurt me.

Oh the dolefull sight that now was to behold at this house! *Come, behold the works of the Lord, what dissolations he has made in the Earth.*[8] Of thirty seven persons who were in this one house, none escaped either present death, or a bitter captivity, save only one,[9] who might say as he, Job 1. 15, *And I only am escaped alone to tell the News.*

---

[5] Flankers were projections from which blank walls (curtains) could be enfiladed [hung].
[6] John Divoll had married Hannah, the youngest sister of Mrs. Rowlandson.
[7] William Kerley was the son of Mrs. Rowlandson's sister Elizabeth White, who had married Henry Kerley.

[8] Psalm [46:8].
[9] The person escaping was Ephraim Roper. The size of the garrison as given by contemporary writers varies from 37 to 55, of whom three Kettle children escaped in some way unknown to Mrs. Rowlandson.

There were twelve killed, some shot, some stab'd with their Spears, some knock'd down with their hatchets. When we are in prosperity, Oh the little that we think of such dreadfull sights, and to see our dear Friends, and Relations ly bleeding out their heart-blood upon the ground. There was one who was chopt into the head with a Hatchet, and stript naked, and yet was crawling up and down. It is a solemn sight to see so many Christians lying in their blood, some here, and some there, like a company of Sheep torn by Wolves, All of them stript naked by a company of hell-hounds, roaring, singing, ranting and insulting, as if they would have torn our very hearts out; yet the Lord by his Almighty power preserved a number of us from death, for there were twenty-four of us taken alive and carried Captive.

I had often before this said, that if the Indians should come, I should chuse rather to be killed by them then taken alive but when it came to the tryal my mind changed; their glittering weapons so daunted my spirit, that I chose rather to go along with those (as I may say) ravenous Beasts, then that moment to end my dayes; and that I may the better declare what happened to me during that grievous Captivity, I shall particularly speak of the severall Removes we had up and down the Wilderness.

The First Remove

Now away we must go with those Barbarous Creatures, with our bodies wounded and bleeding, and our hearts no less than our bodies. About a mile we went that night, up upon a hill within sight of the Town,[10] where they intended to lodge. There was hard by a vacant house (deserted by the English before, for fear of the Indians). I asked them whither I might not lodge in the house that night to which they answered, what will you love English men still? this was the dolefullest night that ever my eyes saw. Oh the roaring, and singing and danceing, and yelling of those black creatures in the night, which made the place a lively resemblance of hell. And as miserable was the wast that was there made, of Horses, Cattle, Sheep, Swine, Calves, Lambs, Roasting Pigs, and Fowl (which they had plundered in the Town) some roasting, some lying and burning, and some boyling to feed our merciless Enemies; who were joyful enough though we were disconsolate. To add to the dolefulness of the former day, and the dismalness of the present night: my thoughts ran upon my losses and sad bereaved condition. All was gone, my Husband gone (at least separated from me, he being in the Bay;[11] and to add to my grief, the Indians told me they would kill him as he came homeward) my Children gone, my Relations and Friends gone, our House and home and all our comforts within door, and without, all was gone, (except my life) and I knew not but the next moment that might go too. There remained nothing to me but one poor wounded Babe, and it seemed at present worse than death that it was in such a pitiful condition, bespeaking Compassion, and I had no refreshing for it, nor suitable things to revive it. Little do many think what is the savageness and bruitishness of this barbarous Enemy, I[12] even those that seem to profess more than others among them, when the English have fallen into their hands.

[10] George Hill.
[11] "In the Bay" means at Massachusetts Bay, *i.e.,* at or near Boston. If Joseph Rowlandson was in Boston he may have heard the summons for defence given at midnight of February 9 by Job Kattenait in Cambridge. The summons resulted in an appeal to Captain Wadsworth at Marlborough, but was too late.
[12] Ay[e].

Those seven that were killed at Lancaster the summer before upon a Sabbath day,[13] and the one that was afterward killed upon a week day, were slain and mangled in a barbarous manner, by one-ey'd John, and Marlborough's Praying Indians,[14] in which Capt. Mosely brought to Boston, as the Indians told me.

The Second Remove[15]

But now, the next morning, I must turn my back upon the Town, and travel with them into the vast and desolate Wilderness, I knew not whither. It is not my tongue, or pen can express the sorrows of my heart, and bitterness of my spirit, that I had at this departure: but God was with me, in a wonderfull manner, carrying me along, and bearing up my spirit, that it did not quite fail. One of the Indians carried my poor wounded Babe upon a horse, it went moaning all along, I shall dy, I shall dy. I went on foot after it, with sorrow that cannot be exprest. At length I took it off the horse, and carried it in my armes till my strength failed, and I fell down with it: Then they set me upon a horse with my wounded Child in my lap, and there being no furniture upon the horse back, as we were going down a steep hill, we both fell over the horses head, at which they like inhumane creatures laught, and rejoyced to see it, though I thought we should there have ended our dayes, as overcome with so many difficulties. But the Lord renewed my strength still, and carried me along, that I might see more of his Power; yea, so much that I could never have thought of, had I not experienced it.

After this it quickly began to snow, and when night came on, they stopt: and now down I must sit in the snow, by a little fire, and a few boughs behind me, with my sick Child in my lap; and calling much for water, being now (through the wound) fallen into a violent Fever. My own wound also growing so stiff, that I could scarce sit down or rise up; yet so it must be, that I must sit all this cold winter night upon the cold snowy ground, with my sick Child in my armes, looking that every hour would be the last of its life; and having no Christian friend near me, either to comfort or help me. Oh, I may see the wonderfull power of God, that my Spirit did not utterly sink under my affliction: still the Lord upheld me with his gracious and mercifull Spirit, and we were both alive to see the light of the next morning.

The Third Remove[16]

The morning being come, they prepared to go on their way. One of the Indians got up upon a horse, and they set me up behind him, with my poor sick Babe in my lap. A very wearisome and tedious day I had of it; what with my own wound, and my Childs being so exceeding sick, and in a lamentable condition with her wound. It may be easily judged what a poor feeble condition we were in, there being not the least

[13] The seven victims of the defeat of August 22, 1675, were George Bennett, Jacob Farrar, Jr., William Flagg, Mordecai McLoud, Mrs. McLoud, and two children. Joseph Wheeler died later.

[14] One-eyed John was known also as Monoco and Apequinsah. "Marlborough's Praying Indians" means the settlement of Christianized Indians at Marlborough, Massachusetts.

[15] The second remove was to Princeton, Massachusetts, near Mount Wachusett.

[16] The third remove, February 12–27, ended at an Indian village, Menameset (Wenimesset), on the Ware River, in what is now New Braintree. Quabaug was Brookfield.

crumb of refreshing that came within either of our mouths, from Wednesday night to Saturday night, except only a little cold water. . . .

. . .Thus nine dayes I sat upon my knees, with my Babe in my lap, till my flesh was raw again; my Child being even ready to depart this sorrowfull world, they bade me carry it out to another Wigwam (I suppose because they would not be troubled with such spectacles) Whither I went with a very heavy heart, and down I sat with the picture of death in my lap. About two houres in the night, my sweet Babe like a Lambe departed this life, on Feb. 18, 1675. It being about six yeares, and five months old. It was nine dayes from the first wounding, in this miserable condition, without any refreshing of one nature or other, except a little cold water. I cannot, but take notice, how at another time I could not bear to be in the room where any dead person was, but now the case is changed; I must and could ly down by my dead Babe, side by side all the night after. I have thought since of the wonderfull goodness of God to me, in preserving me in the use of my reason and senses, in that distressed time, that I did not use wicked and violent means to end my own miserable life. In the morning, when they understood that my child was dead they sent for me home to my Masters Wigwam: (by my Master in this writing, must be understood Quanopin,[17] who was a Saggamore, and married King Phillips wives Sister; not that he first took me, but I was sold to him by another Narrhaganset Indian, who took me when first I came out of the Garison). I went to take up my dead child in my arms to carry it with me, but they bid me let it alone: there was no resisting, but goe I must and leave it. When I had been at my masters wigwam, I took the first opportunity I could get, to go look after my dead child: when I came I askt them what they had done with it? then they told me it was upon the hill: then they went and shewed me where it was, where I saw the ground was newly digged, and there they told me they had buried it: There I left that Child in the Wilderness, and must commit it, and my self also in this Wilderness-condition, to him who is above all. God having taken away this dear Child, I went to see my daughter Mary, who was at this same Indian Town, at a Wigwam not very far off, though we had little liberty or opportunity to see one another. She was about ten years old, and taken from the door at first by a Praying Ind and afterward sold for a gun. When I came in sight, she would fall a weeping; at which they were provoked, and would not let me come near her, but bade me be gone; which was a heart-cutting word to me. I had one Child dead, another in the Wilderness, I knew not where, the third they would not let me come near to: *Me* (as he said) *have ye bereaved of my Children, Joseph is not, and Simeon is not, and ye will take Benjamin also, all these things are against me.* I could not sit still in this condition, but kept walking from one place to another. And as I was going along, my heart was even overwhelm'd with the thoughts of my condition, and that I should have Children, and a Nation which I knew not ruled over them. Whereupon I earnestly entreated the Lord, that he would consider my low estate, and shew me a token for good, and if it were his blessed will, some sign and hope of some relief. And indeed quickly the Lord answered, in some measure, my poor prayers: for as I was going up and down mourning and lamenting my condition, my Son came to me, and asked me how I did; I had not seen him before, since the destruction of the Town, and I

[17] Quinnapin was the husband of Weetamoo, the widow of Alexander, already referred to as the Queen of Pocasset. Mrs. Rowlandson became a servant to this wife. He had as well two other squaws.

knew not where he was, till I was informed by himself, that he was amongst a smaller percel of Indians, whose place was about six miles off; with tears in his eyes, he asked me whether his Sister Sarah was dead; and told me he had seen his Sister Mary; and prayed me, that I would not be troubled in reference to himself. . . .

. . . I cannot but take notice of the wonderfull mercy of God to me in those afflictions, in sending me a Bible. One of the Indians that came from Medfield fight, had brought some plunder, came to me, and asked me, if I would have a Bible, he had got one in his basket. I was glad of it, and asked him, whether he thought the Indians would let me read? he answered, yes: So I took the Bible, and in that melancholy time, it came into my mind to read first the 28. Chap. of Deut.,[18] which I did, and when I had read it, my dark heart wrought on this manner, That there was no mercy for me, that the blessings were gone, and the curses come in their room, and that I had lost my opportunity. But the Lord helped me still to go on reading till I came to Chap. 30 the seven first verses, where I found, There was mercy promised again, if we would return to him by repentance; and though we were scattered from one end of the Earth to the other, yet the Lord would gather us together, and turn all those curses upon our Enemies. I do not desire to live to forget this Scripture, and what comfort it was to me. . . .

The Fourth Remove[19]

And now I must part with that little Company I had. Here I parted from my Daughter Mary, (whom I never saw again till I saw her in Dorchester, returned from Captivity), and from four little Cousins and Neighbours, some of which I never saw afterward: the Lord only knows the end of them. Amongst them also was that poor Woman before mentioned, who came to a sad end, as some of the company told me in my travel: She having much grief upon her Spirit, about her miserable condition, being so near her time, she would be often asking the Indians to let her go home; they not being willing to that, and yet vexed with her importunity, gathered a great company together about her, and strip her naked, and set her in the midst of them; and when they had sung and danced about her (in their hellish manner) as long as they pleased, they knockt her on head, and the child in her arms with her: when they had done that, they made a fire and put them both into it, and told the other Children that were with them, that if they attempted to go home, they would serve them in like manner: The Children said, she did not shed one tear, but prayed all the while. But to return to my own Journey; we travelled about half a day or little more, and came to a desolate place in the Wilderness, where there were no Wigwams or Inhabitants before; we came about the middle of the afternoon to this place, cold and wet, and snowy, and hungry, and weary, and no refreshing, for man, but the cold ground to sit on, and our poor Indian cheer.

Heart-aking thoughts here I had about my poor Children, who were scattered up and down among the wild beasts of the forrest: My head was light and dissey (either through hunger or hard lodging, or trouble or altogether) my knees feeble, my body

[18] Ch. 28 of Deuteronomy is occupied with a recital of blessings for obedience to God and curses for disobedience.

[19] The fourth remove occupied February 28 to March 3. The camp was between Ware River and Miller's River, at the Indian village of Nichewaug in modern Petersham.

raw by sitting double night and day, that I cannot express to man the affliction that lay upon my Spirit, but the Lord helped me at that time to express it to himself. I opened my Bible to read, and the Lord brought that precious Scripture to me, Jer. 31. 16. *Thus saith the Lord, refrain thy voice from weeping, and thine eyes from tears, for thy work shall be rewarded, and they shall come again from the land of the Enemy.* This was a sweet Cordial to me, when I was ready to faint, many and many a time have I sat down, and weept sweetly over this Scripture. At this place we continued about four dayes.

The Fifth Remove [20]

The occasion (as I thought) of their moving at this time, was, the English Army, it being near and following them: For they went, as if they had gone for their lives, for some considerable way, and then they made a stop, and chose some of their stoutest men, and sent them back to hold the English Army in play whilst the rest escaped. . . .

The first week of my being among them, I hardly ate any thing; the second week, I found my stomach grow very faint for want of something; and yet it was very hard to get down their filthy trash: but the third week, though I could think how formerly my stomach would turn against this or that, and I could starve and dy before I could eat such things, yet they were sweet and savoury to my taste. I was at this time knitting a pair of white cotton stockins for my mistriss; and had not yet wrought upon a Sabbath day; when the Sabbath came they bade me go to work; I told them it was the Sabbath day, and desired them to let me rest, and told them I would do as much more to morrow; to which they answered me, they would break my face. And here I cannot but take notice of the strange providence of God in preserving the heathen: They were many hundreds, old and young, some sick, and some lame, many had Papooses at their backs, the greatest number at this time with us, were Squaws, and they travelled with all they had, bag and baggage, and yet they got over this River aforesaid; and on Munday they set their Wigwams on fire, and away they went: On that very day came the English Army after them to this River, and saw the smoak of their Wigwams, and yet this River put a stop to them. God did not give them courage or activity to go over after us; we were not ready for so great a mercy as victory and deliverance; if we had been, God would have found out a way for the English to have passed this River, as well as for the Indians with their Squaws and Children, and all their Luggage. *Oh that my People had hearkened to me, and Israel had walked in my ways, I should soon have subdued their Enemies, and turned my hand against their Adversaries,* Psal. 81: 13. 14. . . .

The Seventh Remove

After a restless and hungry night there, we had a wearisome time of it the next day. The Swamp by which we lay, was, as it were, a deep Dungeon, and an exceeding high and steep hill before it. Before I got to the top of the hill, I thought my heart

---

[20] In the fifth remove, March 3–5, they crossed the Baquaug (Miller's) River in Orange. The "Army" following was composed of Massachusetts and Connecticut forces under Captain Thomas Savage.

and legs, and all would have broken, and failed me. What through faintness, and soreness of body, it was a grievous day of travel to me. As we went along, I saw a place where English Cattle had been: that was comfort to me, such as it was: quickly after that we came to an English Path, which so took with me, that I thought I could have freely lyen down and dyed. That day, a little after noon, we came to Squaukheag, where the Indians quickly spread themselves over the deserted English Fields, gleaning what they could find; some pickt up ears of Wheat that were crickled down, some found ears of Indian Corn, some found Ground-nuts, and others sheaves of Wheat that were frozen together in the shock, and went to threshing of them out. My self got two ears of Indian Corn, and whilst I did but turn my back, one of them was stolen from me, which much troubled me. There came an Indian to them at that time, with a basket of Horse-liver. I asked him to give me a piece: What, says he, can you eat Horse-liver? I told him, I would try, if he would give a piece, which he did, and I laid it on the coals to rost; but before it was half ready they got half of it away from me, so that I was fain to take the rest and eat it as it was, with the blood about my mouth, and yet a savoury bit it was to me: *For to the hungry Soul every bitter thing is sweet.* [21] . . .

The Eight Remove[22]

On the morrow morning we must go over the River, i.e. Connecticot, to meet with King Philip; two Cannoos full, they had carried over, the next Turn I my self was to go; but as my foot was upon the Cannoo to step in, there was a sudden out-cry among them, and I must step back; and instead of going over the River, I must go four or five miles up the River farther Northward. Some of the Indians ran one way, and some another. The cause of this rout was, as I thought, their espying some English Scouts, who were thereabout. In this travel up the River, about noon the Company made a stop, and sate down; some to eat, and others to rest them. As I sate amongst them, musing of things past, my Son Joseph unexpectedly came to me: we asked of each other's welfare, bemoaning our dolefull condition, and the change that had come upon uss. We had Husband and Father, and Children, and Sisters, and Friends, and Relations, and House, and Home, and many Comforts of this Life: but now we may say, as Job, *Naked came I out of my Mothers Womb, and naked shall I return: The Lord gave, and the Lord hath taken away, Blessed be the Name of the Lord.* . . .

. . . And here I may take occasion to mention one principall ground of my setting forth these Lines: even as the Psalmist sayes, To declare the Works of the Lord, and his wonderfull Power in carrying us along, preserving us in the Wilderness, while under the Enemies hand, and returning of us in safety again, And His goodness in bringing to my hand so many comfortable and suitable Scriptures in my distress. But to Return, We travelled on till night; and in the morning, we must go over the River to Philip's Crew. When I was in the Cannoo, I could not but be amazed at the numerous crew of Pagans that were on the Bank on the other side. When I came ashore, they gathered all about me, I sitting alone in the midst: I observed they asked

---

[21] Proverbs 27:7.
[22] The eighth remove was to Coasset in South Vernon, Vermont, where Mrs. Rowlandson seems to have met King Philip for the first time, as he was returning from New York to take up the campaign of 1676.

one another questions, and laughed, and rejoyced over their Gains and Victories. Then my heart began to fail: and I fell a weeping which was the first time to my remembrance, that I wept before them. Although I had met with so much Affliction, and my heart was many times ready to break, yet could I not shed one tear in their sight: but rather had been all this while in a maze, and like one astonished: but now I may say as, Psal. 137. 1. *By the Rivers of Babylon, there we sate down: yea, we wept when we remembered Zion.* There one of them asked me, why I wept, I could hardly tell what to say: yet I answered, they would kill me: No, said he, none will hurt you. Then came one of them and gave me two spoon-fulls of Meal to comfort me, and another gave me half a pint of Pease; which was more worth than many Bushels at another time. Then I went to see King Philip, he bade me come in and sit down, and asked me whether I woold smoke it (a usual Complement nowadayes amongst Saints and Sinners), but this no way suited me. For though I had formerly used Tobacco, yet I had left it ever since I was first taken. It seems to be a Bait, the Devil layes to make men loose their precious time: I remember with shame, how formerly, when I had taken two or three pipes, I was presently ready for another, such a bewitching thing it is: But I thank God, he has now given me power over it; surely there are many who may be better imployed than to ly sucking a stinking Tobacco-pipe. . . .

The Twelfth Remove

It was upon a Sabbath-day-morning, that they prepared for their Travel. This morning I asked my master whither he would sell me to my Husband; he answered me *Nux*, [23] which did much rejoyce my spirit. My mistriss, before we went, was gone to the burial of a Papoos, and returning, she found me sitting and reading in my Bible; she snatched it hastily out of my hand, and threw it out of doors; I ran out and catcht it up, and put it into my pocket, and never let her see it afterward. Then they packed up their things to be gone, and gave me my load: I complained it was too heavy, whereupon she gave me a slap in the face, and bade me go; I lifted up my heart to God, hoping the Redemption was not far off. . . .

. . . [they said] come in more than their own: I told them, I could not tell where to go, they bade me go look; I told them, if I went to another Wigwam they would be angry, and send me home again. Then one of the Company drew his sword, and told me he would run me thorough if I did not go presently. Then was I fain to stoop to this rude fellow, and to go out in the night, I knew not whither. Mine eyes have seen that fellow afterwards walking up and down Boston, under the appearance of a Friend-Indian, and severall others of the like Cut. I went to one Wigwam, and they told me they had no room. Then I went to another, and they said the same; at last an old Indian bade me come to him, and his Squaw gave me some Ground-nuts; she gave me also something to lay under my head, and a good fire we had: and through the good providence of God, I had a comfortable lodging that night. In the morning, another Indian bade me come at night, and he would give me six Ground-nuts, which I did. We were at this place and time about two miles from Connecticut River. We went in the morning to gather Ground-nuts, to the River, and went back again that

[23] Yes.

night. I went with a good load at my back (for they when they went, though but a little way, would carry all their trumpery with them) I told them the skin was off my back, but I had no other comforting answer from them than this, That it would be no matter if my head were off too. . . .

. . . I had not seen my son a pritty while, and here was an Indian of whom I made inquiry after him, and asked him when he saw him: he answered me, that such a time his master roasted him, and that himself did eat a piece of him, as big as his two fingers, and that he was very good meat: But the Lord upheld my Spirit, under this discouragement; and I considered their horrible addictedness to lying, and that there is not one of them that makes the least conscience of speaking of truth. In this place, on a cold night, as I lay by the fire, I removed a stick that kept the heat from me, a Squaw moved it down again, at which I lookt up, and she threw a handfull of ashes in mine eyes; I thought I should have been quite blinded, and have never seen more: but lying down, the water run out of my eyes, and carried the dirt with it, that by the morning, I recovered my sight again. Yet upon this, and the like occasions, I hope it is not too much to say with Job, *Have pitty upon me, have pitty upon me, O ye my Friends, for the Hand of the Lord has touched me.* [24] And here I cannot but remember how many times sitting in their Wigwams, and musing on things past, I should suddenly leap up and run out, as if I had been at home, forgetting where I was, and what my condition was: But when I was without, and saw nothing but Wilderness, and Woods, and a company of barbarous heathens, my mind quickly returned to me, which made me think of that, spoken concerning Sampson, who said, *I will go out and shake my self as at other times, but he wist not that the Lord was departed from him.* [25] About this time I began to think that all my hopes of Restoration would come to nothing. I thought of the English Army, and hoped for their coming, and being taken by them, but that failed. I hoped to be carried to Albany, as the Indians had discoursed before, but that failed also. I thought of being sold to my Husband, as my master spake, but instead of that, my master himself was gone, and I left behind, so that my Spirit was now quite ready to sink. I asked them to let me go out and pick up some sticks, that I might get alone, And poure out my heart unto the Lord. Then also I took my Bible to read, but I found no comfort here neither, which many times I was wont to find: So easie a thing it is with God to dry up the Streames of Scripture-comfort from us. Yet I can say, that in all my sorrows and afflictions, God did not leave me to have my impatience work towards himself, as if his wayes were unrighteous. But I knew that he laid upon me less then I deserved. Afterward, before this dolefull time ended with me, I was turning the leaves of my Bible, and the Lord brought to me some Scriptures, which did a little revive me, as that Isai. 55. 8, *For my thoughts are not your thoughts, neither are your wayes my ways, saith the Lord.* And also that, Psal. 37. 5, *Commit thy way unto the Lord, trust also in him, and he shal bring it to pass.* . . .

The Fifteenth Remove

We went on our Travel. I having got one handfull of Ground-nuts, for my support that day, they gave me my load, and I went on cheerfully (with the thoughts of going homeward) haveing my burden more on my back than my spirit: we came to Baquaug

---

[24] Job 19:21.   [25] Judges 16:20.

River again that day, near which we abode a few dayes. Sometimes one of them would give me a Pipe, another a little Tobacco, another a little Salt: which I would change for a little Victuals. I cannot but think what a Wolvish appetite persons have in a starving condition: for many times when they gave me that which was hot, I was so greedy, that I should burn my mouth, that it would trouble me hours after, and yet I should quickly do the same again. And after I was thoroughly hungry, I was never again satisfied. For though sometimes it fell out, that I got enough, and did eat till I could eat no more, yet I was as unsatisfied as I was when I began. And now could I see that Scripture verified (there being many Scriptures which we do not take notice of, or understand till we are afflicted) Mic. 6. 14. *Thou shalt eat and not be satisfied.* . . .

The Nineteenth Remove

They said, when we went out, that we must travel to Wachuset this day. But a bitter weary day I had of it, travelling now three dayes together, without resting any day between. At last, after many weary steps, I saw Wachuset hills, but many miles off. Then we came to a great Swamp, through which we travelled, up to the knees in mud and water, which was heavy going to one tyred before. Being almost spent, I thought I should have sunk down at last, and never gat out; but I may say, as in Psal. 94. 18, *When my foot slipped, thy mercy, O Lord, held me up.* Going along, having indeed my life, but little spirit, Philip, who was in the Company, came up and took me by the hand, and said, Two weeks more and you shall be Mistress again. I asked him, if he spake true? he answered, Yes, and quickly you shal come to your master again; who had been gone from us three weeks. After many weary steps we came to Wachuset, where he was: and glad I was to see him. He asked me, When I washt me? I told him not this month, then he fetcht me some water himself, and bid me wash, and gave me the Glass to see how I lookt; and bid his Squaw give me something to eat: so she gave me a mess of beans and meat, and a little Ground-nut Cake. I was wonderfully revived with this favour shewed me, Psal. 106. 46, *He made them also to be pittied, of all those that carried them Captives.* . . .

Then came Tom and Peter, with the second Letter from the Council, about the captives. Though they were Indians, I gat them by the hand, and burst out into tears; my heart was so full that I could not speak to them; but recovering my self, I asked them how my husband did, and all my friends and acquaintance? they said, They are all very well but melancholy. They brought me two Biskets, and a pound of Tobacco. The Tobacco I quickly gave away. . . .

The Twentieth Remove

It was their usual manner to remove, when they had done any mischief, lest they should be found out: and so they did at this time. We went about three or four miles, and there they built a great wigwam, big enough to hold an hundred Indians, which they did in preparation to a great day of Dancing. . . .

. . . The Indians now began to come from all quarters, against their merry dancing day. Among some of them came one Goodwife Kettle: I told her my heart was so heavy that it was ready to break: so is mine too said she, but yet said, I hope we shall hear some good news shortly. I could hear how earnestly my Sister desired to see me, and I as earnestly desired to see her: and yet neither of us could get an opportunity. My Daughter was also now about a mile off, and I had not seen her in nine or ten weeks, as I had not seen my Sister since our first taking. I earnestly desired them to let me go and see them: yea, I intreated, begged, and perswaded them, but to let me see my Daughter; and yet so hard hearted were they, that they would not suffer it. They made use of their tyrannical power whilst they had it: but through the Lords wonderfull mercy, their time was now but short.

On a Sabbath day, the Sun being about an hour high in the afternoon, came Mr. John Hoar (the Council permitting him, and his own foreward spirit inclining him) together with the two forementioned Indians, Tom and Peter, with their third Letter from the Council. . . .

But to return again to my going home, where we may see a remarkable change of Providence: At first they were all against it, except my Husband would come for me; but afterwards they assented to it, and seemed much to rejoyce in it; some askt me to send them some Bread, others some Tobacco, others shaking me by the hand, offering me a Hood and Scarfe to ride in; not one moving hand or tongue against it. Thus hath the Lord answered my poor desire, and the many earnest requests of others put up unto God for me. In my travels an Indian came to me, and told me, if I were willing, he and his Squaw would run away, and go home along with me: I told him No: I was not willing to run away, but desired to wait God's time, that I might go home quietly, and without fear. And now God hath granted me my desire. O the wonderfull power of God that I have seen, and the experience that I have had: I have been in the midst of those roaring Lyons, and Salvage Bears, that feared neither God, nor Man, nor the Devil, by night and day, alone and in company: sleeping all sorts together, and yet not one of them ever offered me the least abuse of unchastity to me, in word or action. Though some are ready to say, I speak it for my own credit; But I speak it in the presence of God, and to his Glory. Gods Power is as great now, and as sufficient to save, as when he preserved Daniel in the Lion's Den; or the three Children in the fiery Furnace. I may well say as his Psal. 107. 12, *Oh give thanks unto the Lord for he is good, for his mercy endureth for ever.* Let the Redeemed of the Lord say so, whom he hath redeemed from the hand of the Enemy, especially that I should come away in the midst of so many hundreds of Enemies quietly and peaceably, and not a Dog moving his tongue. So I took my leave of them, and in coming along my heart melted into tears, more then all the while I was with them, and I was almost swallowed up with the thoughts that ever I should go home again. About the Sun going down, Mr. Hoar, and myself, and the two Indians came to Lancaster, and a solemn sight it was to me. There had I lived many comfortable years amongst my Relations and Neighbours, and now not one Christian to be seen, nor one house left standing. We went on to a Farm house that was yet standing, where we lay all night: and a comfortable lodging we had, though nothing but straw to ly on. The Lord preserved us in safety that night, and raised us up again in the morning, and carried us along, that before noon, we came to Concord. Now was I full of joy, and yet not without sorrow: joy to see such a lovely sight, so many Christians together, and some of them my Neighbours: There I met with my Brother, and my Brother-in-Law, who asked me, if I knew where his Wife was? Poor heart! he had helped to bury her, and knew it not; she being shot down by the house was partly burnt: so that those who were at Boston at the desolation of the Town, and came back afterward, and buried the dead, did not know her. Yet I was not without sorrow, to think how many were looking and longing, and my own Children amongst the rest, to enjoy that deliverance that I had now received, and I did not know whither ever I should see them again. Being recruited with food and raiment we went to Boston that day, where I met with my dear Husband. . . .

Our Family being now gathered together[26] (those of us that were living) the South Church in Boston hired an House for us: Then we removed . . . where we continued about three quarters of a year: still the Lord went along with us, and provided graciously for us. I thought it somewhat strange to set up House-keeping with bare walls; but as Solomon sayes, *Mony answers all things,* and that we had through the benevolence of Christian-friends, some in this Town, and some in that, and others: And some from England, that in a little time we might look, and see the House furnished with love. The Lord hath been exceeding good to us in our low estate, in that when we had neither house nor home, nor other necessaries; the Lord so moved the hearts of these and those towards us, that we wanted neither food, nor raiment for our selves or ours, Prov. 18. 24. *There is a Friend which sticketh closer than a brother.* And how many such Friends have we found, and now living amongst? And truly such a Friend have we found him to be unto us, in whose house we lived, *viz.* Mr. James Whitcomb, a Friend unto us near hand, and afar off.

I can remember the time, when I used to sleep quietly without workings in my thoughts, whole nights together, but now it is other wayes with me. When all are fast about me, and no eye open, but his who ever waketh, my thoughts are upon things past, upon the awfull dispensation of the Lord towards us; upon his wonderfull power and might, in carrying of us through so many difficulties, in returning us in safety, and suffering none to hurt us. I remember in the night season, how the other day I was in the midst of thousands of enemies, and nothing but death before me: It is then hard work to perswade my self, that ever I should be satisfied with bread again. But now we are fed with the finest of the Wheat, and, as I may say, With honey out of the rock: Instead of the Husk, we have the fatted Calf: The thoughts of these things in the particulars of them, and of the love and goodness of God towards us, make it true of me, what David said of himself, Psal. 6:6. *I watered my Couch with my tears.* Oh! the wonderfull power of God that mine eyes have seen, affording matter enough for my thoughts to run in, that when others are sleeping mine eyes are weeping.

I have seen the extrem vanity of this World: One hour I have been in health, and wealth, wanting nothing: But the next hour in sickness and wounds, and death, having nothing but sorrow and affliction.

Before I knew what affliction meant, I was ready sometimes to wish for it. When I lived in prosperity, having the comforts of the World about me, my relations by me, my Heart chearfull, and taking little care for any thing; and yet seeing many, whom I preferred before my self, under many tryals and afflictions, in sickness, weakness, poverty, losses, crosses, and cares of the World, I should be sometimes jealous least I should have my portion in this life, and that Scripture would come to my mind, Heb. 12. 6. *For whom the Lord loveth he chasteneth, and scourgeth every Son whom he receiveth.* But now I see the Lord had his time to scourge and chasten me.

[26] The Rowlandsons' son and daughter, in the care of other families, were now reunited with their parents.

The portion of some is to have their afflictions by drops, now one drop and then another; but the dregs of the Cup, the Wine of astonishment, like a sweeping rain that leaveth no food, did the Lord prepare to be my portion. Affliction I wanted, and affliction I had, full measure (I thought) pressed down and running over; yet I see, when God calls a Person to any thing, and through never so many difficulties, yet he is fully able to carry them through and make them see, and say they have been gainers thereby. And I hope I can say in some measure, As David did, *It is good for me that I have been afflicted.* The Lord hath shewed me the vanity of these outward things. That they are the Vanity of vanities, and vexation of spirit; that they are but a shadow, a blast, a bubble, and things of no continuance. That we must rely on God himself, and our whole dependance must be upon him. If trouble from smaller matters begin to arise in me, I have something at hand to check my self with, and say, why am I troubled? It was but the other day that if I had had the world, I would have given it for my freedom, or to have been a Servant to a Christian. I have learned to look beyond present and smaller troubles, and to be quieted under them, as Moses said, Exod. 14. 13. *Stand still and see the salvation of the Lord.*

1682

Edward Taylor
ca. 1642–1729

Edward Taylor's poems were virtually hidden in a manuscript book for more than two centuries. Their discovery and publication in 1939 brought Taylor to light as colonial America's foremost poet, though information about his life remains incomplete.

Taylor was born in Sketchley, England, near Leicestershire, during the turmoil of the English Civil War. As a farmer's son educated by a nonconformist schoolmaster, he grew up during the rise of Oliver Cromwell, the defeat of the armies of King Charles I, who was put to death, and the establishment of the Puritan Holy Commonwealth. It is possible that Taylor attended Cambridge University for a time, though official records are lacking. Taylor became a schoolmaster, but his career was cut short by the restoration of the English monarch in 1660: Taylor's unwillingness to comply with the Act of Uniformity, which required annual acceptance of communion at the Anglican ceremony, forced him to forfeit his position. In 1668 Taylor sailed for America.

He brought letters of introduction to several prominent Puritans of the Massachusetts Bay Colony, including Increase Mather, the wealthy mintmaster John Hull, and President Chauncy of Harvard. Taylor was admitted to the college with advanced standing in the class of 1671. The roommate of the diarist Samuel Sewall, Taylor prepared for the ministry. On commencement day he declaimed, in verse, before the president and fellows of the college on the virtues of English over the classical languages and Hebrew.

Though Taylor considered remaining at Harvard for additional study, he accepted a call to the sparsely settled western Massachusetts community of Westfield. In 1671 it took him eight days on horseback to travel the one hundred miles southwest from Boston across the Connecticut River to the settlement, where he spent the remainder of his life and wrote the poetry his readers have admired.

Three years after arriving at Westfield, Taylor married the daughter of a Connecticut clergyman and, when she died, remarried. Altogether Taylor fathered fourteen children, five of whom he buried in infancy or early childhood. "Five babes thou tookst from me," he wrote, addressing the God who had taken Taylor's wife and the mother of those "babes" as well. "Thine arrows . . . do strike and stob me in the very heart," he said, seeking comfort in God's mercy.

The Indian attacks known as "King Philip's War" (1675–1676) delayed Taylor's ordination and the gathering of his church. Instead, Westfield prepared for assault like other outlying settlements such as Lancaster, from which Mary Rowlandson was abducted. As a frontier minister, Taylor doubtless provided leadership during the crisis. In times of peace he would necessarily raise crops and tend livestock. He also prepared two weekly sermons and sustained the scholarly life to which he was so deeply committed. His library contained over two hundred books and tracts, many copied by hand because he could not afford to buy them. Taylor also served as the community physician, and it is not surprising to find images of medicinal plants and herbs in his poems.

By 1679 Taylor had "gathered" his church in a ceremony that conferred membership only on those who could attest to the presence of God's saving grace in their souls. Weekly the minister offered members the sacrament of communion, which represented the redemption of Christ through God's grace. None of Taylor's parishioners, however, knew that their minister's spiritual preparation had taken an unusual turn. At age forty-two Taylor embarked on a series of intensely private poems, the *Preparatory Meditations,* each one an integral part of his preparation to receive and to administer the sacrament of communion. Though Taylor wrote over forty thousand lines of poetry during his life, these poems are considered to be his finest, in part because they show the tensions of a mind simultaneously feeling and thinking out the human relationship to the Creator in vivid figures of speech.

The literary origins of the *Preparatory Meditations* have become clear to modern readers. Though the only volume of poetry in Taylor's library was that of fellow New England poet Anne Bradstreet, he evidently was familiar with— and used—the metaphysical tradition of such poets as George Herbert, Francis Quarles, and the Catholic poet Richard Crashaw. Their work showed the forging of wit and passion. It emphasized playful language, such as puns, and elaborate imagery. For Taylor and other Puritans, God's messages could be divined in such wordplay. Taylor's poetic images come from several sources, first among them the Bible, especially the sensuous Song of Songs. But Taylor also used poetic figures from the activities of everyday life, such as the weaving and farming he knew from his English boyhood, and from the conditions of western Massachusetts, where, he wrote, "little save Rusticity is." Taylor's poetry has been called "wilderness baroque," bringing elements of the unexpected into an ordered and formal structure that elicits an "earthly enjoyment of things divine."

Apart from the *Preparatory Meditations,* Taylor wrote miscellaneous occasional poems whose images reveal his apprehension of detail and whose themes are those of an orthodox Puritan. His interest in natural science is evident in "Upon a

Spider Cathing a Fly," in which he carefully traces the movement of the satanic spider. Taylor's best-known long poem bears the lengthy title *Gods Determinations touching his Elect: and the Elects Combat in their Conversion and coming up to God in Christ together with the Comfortable Effects thereof.* Known simply as *Gods Determinations,* the poem is based in the medieval debate literature, including the morality plays that Taylor might have seen in boyhood. Taylor's divine drama opposes good and evil in military terms familiar to the poet from the Bible and from his youth amid events of the English Civil War. There is some possibility that *Gods Determinations* was Taylor's counterpart to Michael Wigglesworth's extremely popular *Day of Doom.* Although the work is uneven, parts of it represent Taylor at his best.

Taylor served as minister at Westfield until 1729, taking time away only to return to Harvard College at the age of seventy-eight for the conferral of his master's degree. He died in his eighty-eighth year, requesting his heirs not to publish his poetry. That request was honored, but in 1937 Taylor's leather manuscript book, containing some four hundred pages, was found in the Yale University Library. The publication of a substantial selection from that book in 1939 established Taylor, the poet of "wilderness baroque," as a major figure in colonial American literature.

Further Reading:
N. Grabo, *Edward Taylor,* 1962.
D. Stanford, *Edward Taylor,* 1965.
W. Scheick, *The Will and the Word: The Poetry of Edward Taylor,* 1974.
K. Keller, *The Example of Edward Taylor,* 1975.

Text:
The Poems of Edward Taylor, ed. D. Stanford, 1960.
See also *Edward Taylor's Christographia,* ed. N. Grabo, 1962.
The Diary of Edward Taylor, ed. F. Murphy, 1964.

from Preparatory Meditations

Meditation 6 (First Series): [Am I thy Gold? Or Purse, Lord, for thy Wealth]

Am I thy Gold? Or Purse, Lord, for thy Wealth;
    Whether in mine, or mint refinde for thee?
Ime counted so, but count me o're thyselfe,
    Lest gold washt face, and brass in Heart I bee.
I Feare my Touchstone[1] touches when I try   5
    Mee, and my Counted Gold too overly.

[1] Used to test the purity of gold and silver by the color of the streak produced on it by rubbing it with either metal.

Am I new minted by thy Stamp indeed?
        Mine Eyes are dim; I cannot clearly see.
Be thou my Spectacles that I may read
        Thine Image, and Inscription stampt on mee.   10
        If thy bright Image do upon me stand
        I am a Golden Angell² in thy hand.

Lord, make my Soule thy Plate: thine Image bright
        Within the Circle of the same enfoile.
And on its brims in golden Letters write   15
        Thy Superscription in an Holy style.
        Then I shall be thy Money, thou my Hord:
        Let me thy Angell bee, bee thou my Lord.

1939

Meditation 8 (First Series): [I kening through Astronomy Divine]

*Joh. 6.51. I am the
Living Bread.*

I kening³ through Astronomy Divine
        The World's bright Battlement, wherein I spy
A Golden Path my Pensill cannot line,
        From that bright Throne unto my Threshold ly.
        And while my puzzled thoughts about it pore   5
        I finde the Bread of Life in't at my doore.

When that this Bird of Paradise put in
        This Wicker Cage (my Corps) to tweedle praise
Had peckt the Fruite forbad: and so did fling
        Away its Food; and lost its golden dayes;   10
        It fell into Celestiall Famine sore:
        And never could attain a morsell more.

Alas! alas! Poore Bird, what wilt thou doe?
        The Creatures field no food for Souls e're gave.
And if thou knock at Angells dores they show   15
        An Empty Barrell: they no soul bread have.
        Alas! Poore Bird, the Worlds White Loafe is done.
        And cannot yield thee here the smallest Crumb.

In this sad state, Gods Tender Bowells⁴ run
        Out streams of Grace: And he to end all strife   20
The Purest Wheate in Heaven, his deare-dear Son
        Grinds, and kneads up into this Bread of Life.

---

² Gold coin.
³ Discovering.

⁴ The bowels were supposedly the seat of pity
and tenderness.

Which Bread of Life from Heaven down came and stands
 Disht on thy Table up by Angells Hands.

Did God mould up this Bread in Heaven, and bake,   25
 Which from his Table came, and to thine goeth?
Doth he bespeake thee thus, This Soule Bread take.
 Come Eate thy fill of this thy God's White Loafe?
 Its Food too fine for Angells, yet come, take
 And Eate thy fill. Its Heavens Sugar Cake.   30

What Grace is this knead in this Loafe? This thing
 Souls are but petty things it to admire.
Yee Angells, help: This fill would to the brim
 Heav'ns whelm'd-down Chrystall meele Bowle, yea and higher.
 This Bread of Life dropt in thy mouth, doth Cry.   35
 Eate, Eate me, Soul, and thou shalt never dy.

1939

Meditation 29 (First Series): [My shattred Phancy stole away from mee]

*Joh. 20.17. My Father,
and your Father, to my God,
and your God.*

My shattred Phancy stole away from mee,
 (Wits run a Wooling[5] over Edens Parke)
And in Gods Garden saw a golden Tree,
 Whose Heart was All Divine, and gold its barke.
 Whose glorious limbs and fruitfull branches strong   5
 With Saints, and Angells bright are richly hung.

Thou! thou! my Deare-Deare Lord, art this rich Tree
 The Tree of Life Within Gods Paradise.
I am a Withred Twig, dri'de fit to bee
 A Chat[6] Cast in thy fire, Writh[7] off by Vice.   10
 Yet if thy Milke white-Gracious Hand will take mee
 And grafft mee in this golden stock, thou'lt make mee.

Thou'lt make me then its Fruite, and Branch to spring.
 And though a nipping Eastwinde blow, and all
Hells Nymps[8] with spite their Dog's sticks thereat ding[9]   15
 To Dash the Grafft off, and it's fruits to fall,

[5] Daydreaming.   [8] Imps.
[6] Piece of kindling.   [9] Strike.
[7] Wrenched.

Yet I shall stand thy Grafft, and Fruits that are
Fruits of the Tree of Life thy Grafft shall beare.

I being grafft in thee there up do stand
   In us Relations all that mutuall are.   20
I am thy Patient, Pupill, Servant, and
     Thy Sister, Mother, Doove, Spouse, Son, and Heire.
     Thou art my Priest, Physician, Prophet, King,
     Lord, Brother, Bridegroom, Father, Ev'ry thing.

I being grafft in thee am graffted here   25
   Into thy Family, and kindred Claim
To all in Heaven, God, Saints, and Angells there.
     I thy Relations my Relations name.
     Thy Father's mine, thy God my God, and I
     With Saints, and Angells draw Affinity.   30

My Lord, what is it that thou dost bestow?
   The Praise on this account fills up, and throngs
Eternity brimfull, doth overflow
     The Heavens vast with rich Angelick Songs.
     How should I blush? how Tremble at this thing,   35
     Not having yet my Gam-Ut,[10] learnd to sing.
But, Lord, as burnish't Sun Beams forth out fly
   Let Angell-Shine forth in my Life out flame,
That I may grace thy gracefull Family
     And not to thy Relations be a Shame.   40
     Make mee thy Grafft, be thou my Golden Stock.
     Thy Glory then I'le make my fruits and Crop.

1939

Meditation 32 (First Series): [Thy Grace, Dear Lord's my golden Wrack, I finde]

1 Cor. 3.22. *Whether*
Paul or Apollos, or Cephas.

Thy Grace, Dear Lord's my golden Wrack, I finde
   Screwing my Phancy into ragged Rhimes,
Tuning thy Praises in my feeble minde
     Untill I come to strike them on my Chimes.
     Were I an Angell bright, and borrow could   5
     King Davids Harp, I would them play on gold.

---

[10] Musical scale.

But plung'd I am, my minde is puzzled,
 When I would spin my Phancy thus unspun,
In finest Twine of Praise I'm muzzled.
  My tazzled[11] Thoughts twirld into Snick-Snarls[12] run.   10
  Thy Grace, my Lord, is such a glorious thing,
  It doth Confound me when I would it sing.
Eternall Love an Object mean did smite
 Which by the Prince of Darkness was beguilde,
That from this Love it ran and sweld with spite   15
 And in the way with filth was all defilde
  Yet must be reconcild, cleansd, and begrac'te
  Or from the fruits of Gods first Love displac'te.

Then Grace, my Lord, wrought in thy Heart a vent,
 Thy Soft Soft hand to this hard worke did goe,   20
And to the Milke White Throne of Justice went
 And entred bond that Grace might overflow.
  Hence did thy Person to my Nature ty
  And bleed through humane Veans to satisfy.

Oh! Grace, Grace, Grace! this Wealthy Grace doth lay 25
 Her Golden Channells from thy Fathers throne,
Into our Earthen Pitchers to Convay
 Heavens Aqua Vitae[13] to us for our own.
  O! let thy Golden Gutters run into
  My Cup this Liquour till it overflow.   30

Thine Ordinances,[14] Graces Wine-fats[15] where
 Thy Spirits Walkes, and Graces runs doe ly
And Angells waiting stand with holy Cheere
 From Graces Conduite Head, with all Supply.
  These Vessells full of Grace are, and the Bowls 35
  In which their Taps do run, are pretious Souls.

Thou to the Cups dost say (that Catch this Wine,)
 This Liquour, Golden Pipes, and Wine-fats plain,
Whether Paul, Apollos, Cephas,[16] all are thine.
 Oh Golden Word! Lord speake it ore again.   40
  Lord speake it home to me, say these are mine.
  My Bells shall then thy Praises bravely chime.

1939

---

[11] Tangled and frizzy.
[12] Tangles.
[13] Literally, "water of life."
[14] Sacraments, especially Holy Communion and baptism.
[15] Wine vats.
[16] Jesus's name for his apostle Peter.

Meditation 39 (First Series):
[My Sin! my Sin, My God, these Cursed Dregs]

*1 Joh. 2.1. If any
man sin, we have an Advocate.*

My Sin! my Sin, My God, these Cursed Dregs,
    Green, Yellow, Blew streakt Poyson hellish, ranck,
Bubs[17] hatcht in natures nest on Serpents Eggs,
    Yelp, Cherp and Cry; they set my Soule a Cramp.
    I frown, Chide, strik and fight them, mourn and Cry   5
    To Conquour them, but cannot them destroy.

I cannot kill nor Coop them up: my Curb
    'S less than a Snaffle in their mouth: my Rains
They as a twine thrid,[18] snap: by hell they're spurd:
    And load my Soule with swagging loads of pains.   10
    Black Imps, young Divells, snap, bite, drag to bring
    And pick mee headlong hells dread Whirle Poole in.

Lord, hold thy hand: for handle mee thou may'st
    In Wrath: but, oh, a twinckling Ray of hope
Methinks I spie thou graciously display'st.   15
    There is an Advocate: a doore is ope.
    Sin's poyson swell my heart would till it burst,
    Did not a hope hence creep in't thus, and nurse't.

Joy, joy, Gods Son's the Sinners Advocate
    Doth plead the Sinner guiltless, and a Saint.   20
But yet Atturnies pleas spring from the State
    The Case is in: if bad its bad in plaint.
    My Papers do contain no pleas that do
    Secure mee from, but knock me down to, woe.

I have no plea mine Advocate to give: 25
    What now? He'l anvill Arguments greate Store
Out of his Flesh and Blood to make thee live.
    O Deare bought Arguments: Good pleas therefore.
    Nails made of heavenly Steel, more Choice than gold
    Drove home, Well Clencht, eternally will hold.   30

Oh! Dear bought Plea, Deare Lord, what buy't so deare?
    What with thy blood purchase thy plea for me?
Take Argument out of thy Grave t'appeare
    And plead my Case with, me from Guilt to free.

---

[17] Pustules.   [18] Thread.

These maule both Sins, and Divells, and amaze   35
Both Saints, and Angells; Wreath their mouths with praise.

What shall I doe, my Lord? what do, that I
    May have thee plead my Case? I fee thee will
With Faith, Repentance, and obediently
        Thy Service gainst Satanick Sins fulfill.   40
        I'l fight thy fields while Live I do, although
        I should be hackt in pieces by thy foe.

Make me thy Friend, Lord, be my Surety: I
    Will be thy Client, be my Advocate:
My Sins make thine, thy Pleas make mine hereby.   45
    Thou wilt mee save, I will thee Celebrate.
    Thou'lt kill my Sins that cut my heart within:
    And my rough Feet shall thy smooth praises sing.

1954

Meditation 1 (Second Series):
[Oh Leaden heeld. Lord, give, forgive I pray]

*Col. 2.17. Which are Shaddows of
things to come and the body is Christs.*

Oh Leaden heeld.[19] Lord, give, forgive I pray.
    Infire my Heart: it bedded is in Snow.
I Chide myselfe seing myselfe decay.
        In heate and Zeale to thee, I frozen grow.
        File my dull Spirits: make them sharp and bright: 5
        Them firbush[20] for thyselfe, and thy delight.

My Stains are such, and sinke so deep, that all
    The Excellency in Created Shells
Too low, and little is to make it fall
        Out of my leather Coate wherein it dwells.   10
        This Excellence is but a Shade to that
        Which is enough to make my Stains go back.

The glory of the world slickt up in types[21]
    In all Choise things chosen to typify,
His glory upon whom the worke doth light,   15
        To thine's a Shaddow, or a butterfly.
        How glorious then, my Lord, art thou to mee
        Seing to cleanse me, 's worke alone for thee.

---

[19] In this context, heavily weighed down with sin.
[20] Furbish or polish.
[21] Reference to typology, a system of thought in which persons, events, or objects in the Old Testament prefigure those in the New Testament.

The glory of all Types doth meet in thee.
    Thy glory doth their glory quite excell: 20
More than the Sun excells in its bright glee
      A nat, an Earewig, Weevill, Snaile, or Shell.
      Wonders in Crowds start up; your eyes may strut
      Viewing his Excellence, and's bleeding cut.

Oh! that I had but halfe an eye to view   25
    This excellence of thine, undazled: so
Therewith to give my heart a touch anew
      Untill I quickned am, and made to glow.
      All is too little for thee: but alass
      Most of my little all hath other pass.   30
Then Pardon, Lord, my fault: and let thy beams
    Of Holiness pierce through this Heart of mine.
Ope to thy Blood a passage through my veans.
      Let thy pure blood my impure blood refine.
      Then with new blood and spirits I will dub   35
      My tunes upon thy Excellency good.

1960

Meditation 3 (Second Series): [Like to the Marigold, I blushing close]

*Rom. 5.14. Who is the
Figure of Him that was to come.*

Like to the Marigold, I blushing close
    My golden blossoms when thy sun goes down:
Moist'ning my leaves with Dewy Sighs, half frose
    By the nocturnall Cold, that hoares my Crown.
      Mine Apples ashes are in apple shells[22]   5
      And dirty too: strange and bewitching spells!
When Lord, mine Eye doth spie thy Grace to beame
    Thy Mediatoriall glory in the shine
Out Spouted so from Adams typick streame
    And Emblemiz'd in Noahs pollisht shrine   10
      Thine theirs outshines so far it makes their glory
      In brightest Colours, seem a smoaky story.

But when mine Eye full of these beams, doth cast
    Its rayes upon my dusty essence thin
Impregnate with a Sparke Divine, defacde,   15
    All Candid o're with Leprosie of Sin,

---

[22] Apples of Sodom, which look fair on the tree
but which turn to smoke and ashes when
picked.

Such Influences on my Spirits light,
    Which them as bitter gall, or Cold ice smite.

My brissled sins hence do so horrid peare,
    None but thyselfe, (and thou deckt up must bee   20
In thy Transcendent glory sparkling cleare)
    A Mediator unto God for mee.
    So high they rise, Faith scarce can toss a Sight
    Over their head upon thyselfe to light.

Is't possible such glory, Lord, ere should   25
    Center its Love on me Sins Dunghill else?
My Case up take? make it its own? Who would
    Wash with his blood my blots out? Crown his shelfe
    Or Dress his golden Cupboard with such ware?
    This makes my pale facde Hope almost despare.   30

Yet let my Titimouses Quill suck in
    Thy Graces milk Pails some small drop: or Cart
A Bit, or Splinter of some Ray, the wing
    Of Grace's sun sprindgd out, into my heart:
    To build there Wonders Chappell where thy Praise   35
    Shall be the Psalms sung forth in gracious layes.

1939

Meditation 26 (Second Series): [Unclean, Unclean: My Lord, Undone, all vile]

*Heb. 9.13.14. How much more
shall the blood of Christ, etc.*

Unclean, Unclean: My Lord, Undone, all vile
    Yea all Defild: What shall thy Servant doe?
Unfit for thee: not fit for holy Soile,
    Nor for Communion of Saints below.
    A bag of botches, Lump of Loathsomeness:
    Defild by Touch, by Issue: Leproust flesh.

Thou wilt have all that enter do thy fold
    Pure, Cleane, and bright, Whiter than whitest Snow
Better refin'd than most refined Gold:
    I am not so: but fowle: What shall I doe?   10
    Shall thy Church Doors be shut, and shut out mee?
    Shall not Church fellowship my portion bee?

How can it be? Thy Churches do require
    Pure Holiness: I am all filth, alas!
Shall I defile them, tumbled thus in mire?   15

Or they mee cleanse before I current pass?
If thus they do, Where is the Niter bright
And Sope they offer mee to wash me White?

The Brisk Red heifer's Ashes, when calcin'd,[23]
    Mixt all in running Water, is too Weake   20
To wash away my Filth: The Dooves[24] assign'd
    Burnt, and Sin Offerings neer do the feate
    But as they Emblemize the Fountain Spring
    Thy Blood, my Lord, set ope to wash off Sin.

Oh! richest Grace! Are thy Rich Veans then tapt   25
    To ope this Holy Fountain (boundless Sea)
For Sinners here to lavor[25] off (all sapt
    With Sin) their Sins and Sinfulness away?
    In this bright Chrystall Crimson Fountain flows
    What washeth whiter, than the Swan or Rose.   30

Oh! wash mee, Lord, in this Choice Fountain, White
    That I may enter, and not sully here
Thy Church, whose floore is pav'de with Graces bright
    And hold Church fellowship with Saints most cleare.
    My Voice all sweet, with their melodious layes[26]   35
    Shall make sweet Musick blossom'd with thy praise.

1960

Meditation 83 (Second Series): [A Garden, yea a Paradise indeed]

*Can. 5.1. I am come into
my Garden, etc.*

A Garden, yea a Paradise indeed,
    Of all Delightfull Beauteous flowers and sweet,
(A Cloud of rich perfume hence did proceed
    From sweet breathd plants,) first Adam was to keep.
    But sinning here he's from this Farm exilde,   5
    And th'Farm, Lord, thou camst to, 's a Garden stylde

A Garden-Church, set with Choice Herbs and Flowers.
    Here Lign-Aloes. And th'Tree of Life.
Here trees of Frankincense and Myrrh up towers.
    Here's Sharons Rose and Lillie: Beauties Strife.   10

[23] I.e., made into soap.
[24] Doves.
[25] Wash.
[26] Songs.

Here's Cassia, Cinnamon, Cloves, Nut Megs, Mace.
Sweet Calamus: and all Heavens herbs of Grace.[27]

Here's Order Choice, Beds, Allies[28] all in print.
Here bud sweet blushing Blossoms, sparkling brave
And Beautifull rich, spangled Flowers bepinckt   15
    Which White, Red, Blushie, Cherry Cheek't Smiles have,
    Making Celestiall aire their Civit[29] Box
    Of Aromatick Vapors: Spirituall Drops.

This Garden, Lord, thy Church, this Paradise
    Thou comst into, with thy Choice Spirits Gales   20
Making all Plants of Grace gust out like Spice
    Their sweet perfumed breath that us assailes.
    And sacrifice their Spirits sweet upon
    Their Beauties Altar to thee, Holy One.

This Garden too's the Soule, of thy Redeem'd: 25
    When thou thy Spirits plants therein hast set
In their Conversion now most Choicely 'steemd
    Embeautified with Graces bracelet.
    If that my Soule thy Paradise once bee:
    Thou wilt emparadise it e're with thee.   30

Make mee thy Garden; Lord, thy Grace my plant:
    Make mee thy Vineyard, and my plants thy Vine:
Then come into thy Garden: View each ranck:
    And make my Grape bleed in thy Cup rich wine.
    When thou comest in, My Garden flowers will smile   35
    And blossom Aromatick Praise the while.

1960

---

from God's Determinations

The Preface

Infinity, when all things it beheld
In Nothing, and of Nothing all did build,
Upon what Base was fixt the Lath, wherein
He turn'd this Globe, and riggalld[1] it so trim?
Who blew the Bellows of his Furnace Vast?   5
Or held the Mould wherein the world was Cast?
Who laid its Corner Stone? Or whose Command?

---

[27] See Song of Solomon 1–8.
[28] Garden walkways; here, "avenues" to biblical imagery in the Old and New Testaments.
[29] Perfume from the civit cat.
[1] Made ringed marks.

Where stand the Pillars upon which it stands?
Who Lac'de and Fillitted the earth so fine,
With Rivers like green Ribbons Smaragdine?   10
Who made the Sea's its Selvedge,[2] and it locks
Like a Quilt Ball within a Silver Box?
Who Spread its Canopy? Or Curtains Spun?
Who in this Bowling Alley bowld the Sun?
Who made it always when it rises set   15
To go at once both down, and up to get?
Who th'Curtain rods made for this Tapistry?
Who hung the twinckling Lanthorns in the Sky?
Who? who did this? or who is he? Why, know
Its Onely Might Almighty this did doe.   20
His hand hath made this noble worke which Stands
His Glorious Handywork not made by hands.
Who spake all things from nothing; and with ease
Can speake all things to nothing, if he please.
Whose Little finger at his pleasure Can   25
Out mete ten thousand worlds with halfe a Span:
Whose Might Almighty can by half a looks
Root up the rocks and rock the hills by th'roots.
Can take this mighty World up in his hande,
And shake it like a Squitchen[3] or a Wand.   30
Whose single Frown will make the Heavens shake
Like as an aspen leafe the Winde makes quake.
Oh! what a might is this Whose single frown
Doth shake the world as it would shake it down?
Which All from Nothing fet,[4] from Nothing, All: 35
Hath All on Nothing set, lets Nothing fall.
Gave All to nothing Man indeed, whereby
Through nothing man all might him Glorify.
In Nothing then imbosst the brightest Gem
More pretious than all pretiousness in them.   40
But Nothing man did throw down all by Sin:
And darkened that lightsom Gem in him.
    That now his Brightest Diamond is grown
    Darker by far than any Coalpit Stone.

1939

The Souls Groan to Christ for Succour

Good Lord, behold this Dreadfull Enemy
    Who makes me tremble with his fierce
        assaults,
I dare not trust, yet feare to give the ly,

[2] Border.
[3] A slip of branch cut for grafting.
[4] Fetched.

For in my soul, my soul finds many faults.
And though I justify myselfe to's face: 5
I do Condemn myselfe before thy Grace.

He strives to mount my sins, and them advance
    Above thy Merits, Pardons, or Good Will
Thy Grace to lessen, and thy Wrath t'inhance
    As if thou couldst not pay the sinner's bill.   10
He Chiefly injures thy rich Grace, I finde
    Though I confess my heart to sin inclin'de.
Those Graces which thy Grace enwrought⁵ in mee,
    He makes as nothing but a pack of Sins.
He maketh Grace no grace, but Crueltie.   15
    Is Graces Honey Comb, a Comb of Stings?
This makes me ready leave thy Grace and run.
    Which if I do, I finde I am undone.

I know he is thy Cur, therefore I bee
    Perplexed lest I from thy Pasture stray.   20
He bayghs,⁶ and barks so veh'mently at mee.
    Come rate this Cur, Lord, breake his teeth I
        pray.
Remember me I humbly pray thee first.
    Then halter up this Cur that is so Curst.

1939

Christs Reply

Peace, Peace, my Hony, do not Cry,
My Little Darling, wipe thine eye,
    Oh Cheer, Cheer up, come see.
Is anything too deare,⁷ my Dove,
Is anything too good, my Love   5
    To get or give for thee?

If in the severall thou art
This Yelper fierce will at thee bark:
    That thou art mine this shows.
As Spot barks back the sheep again   10
Before they to the Pound are ta'ne,
    So he and hence 'way goes.

But yet this Cur that bayghs so sore
Is broken tootht, and muzzled sure,

---

⁵ Worked.   ⁷ Expensive.
⁶ I.e., bays.

Fear not, my Pritty Heart.   15
His barking is to make thee Cling
Close underneath thy Saviours Wing.
    Why did my sweeten[8] start?

And if he run an inch too far,
I'le Check his Chain, and rate[9] the Cur.   20
    My Chick, keep clost to mee.
The Poles shall sooner kiss, and greet
And Paralells shall sooner meet
    Than thou shalt harmed bee.

He seeks to aggrivate thy sin   25
And screw them to the highest pin,
    To make thy faith to quaile.
Yet mountain Sins like mites should show
And then these mites for naught should goe
    Could he but once prevaile.   30

I smote thy sins upon the Head.
They Dead'ned are, though not quite dead:
    And shall not rise again.
I'l put away the Guilt thereof,
And purge its Filthiness cleare off: 35
    My Blood doth out the stain.

And though thy judgment was remiss
Thy Headstrong Will too Wilfull is.
    I will Renew the same.
And though thou do too frequently   40
Offend as heretofore hereby
    I'l not severly blaim.

And though thy senses do inveagle
Thy Noble Soul to tend the Beagle,
    That t'hunt her games forth go.   45
I'le Lure her back to me, and Change
Those fond Affections that do range
    As yelping beagles doe.

Although thy sins increase their race,
And though when thou hast sought for Grace,   50
    Thou fallst more than before
If thou by true Repentence Rise,
And Faith makes me thy Sacrifice,
    I'l pardon all, though more.

[8] Beloved.
[9] Reprove.

Though Satan strive to block thy way   55
By all his Stratagems he may:
   Come, come though through the fire.
For Hell that Gulph of fire for sins,
Is not so hot as t'burn thy Shins.
   Then Credit not the Lyar.   60

Those Cursed Vermin Sins that Crawle
All ore thy Soul, both Greate, and small
   Are onely Satans own:
Which he in his Malignity
Unto thy Souls true Sanctity   65
   In at the doors hath thrown.

And though they be Rebellion high,
Ath'ism or Apostacy:
   Though blasphemy it bee:
Unto what Quality, or Sise   70
Excepting one, so e're it rise.
   Repent, I'le pardon thee.

Although thy Soule was once a Stall[10]
Rich hung with Satans nicknacks all;
   If thou Repent thy Sin,   75
A Tabernacle in't I'le place
Fild with Gods Spirit, and his Grace.
   Oh Comfortable thing!

I dare the World therefore to show
A God like me, to anger slow: 80
   Whose wrath is full of Grace.
Doth hate all Sins both Greate, and small:
Yet when Repented, pardons all.
   Frowns with a Smiling Face.

As for thy outward Postures each,   85
Thy Gestures, Actions, and thy Speech,
   I Eye and Eying spare,
If thou repent. My Grace is more
Ten thousand times still tribled ore
   Than thou canst want, or ware.   90

As for the Wicked Charge he makes,
That he of Every Dish first takes
   Of all thy holy things.

[10] Vendor's booth.

Its false, deny the same, and say,
That which he had he stool away   95
    Out of thy Offerings.

Though to thy Griefe, poor Heart, thou finde
In Pray're too oft a wandring minde,
    In Sermons' Spirits dull.
Though faith in firy furnace flags,   100
And Zeale in Chilly Seasons lags.
    Temptations powerfull.

These faults are his, and none of thine
So far as thou dost them decline.
    Come then receive my Grace.   105
And when he buffits thee therefore
If thou my aid, and Grace implore
    I'le shew a pleasant face.

But still look for Temptations Deep,
Whilst that thy Noble Sparke doth keep   110
    Within a Mudwald Cote."
These White Frosts and the Showers that fall
Are but to whiten thee withall.
    Not rot the Web they smote.

If in the fire where Gold is tride   115
Thy Soule is put, and purifide
    Wilt thou lament thy loss?
If silver-like this fire refine
Thy Soul and make it brighter shine:
    Wilt thou bewaile the Dross?   120

Oh! fight my Field: no Colours fear:
I'l be thy Front, I'l be thy reare.
    Fail not: my Battells fight.
Defy the Tempter, and his Mock.
Anchor thy heart on mee thy Rock.   125
    I do in thee Delight.

1939

" Cottage.

Huswifery

Make me, O Lord, thy Spining Wheele compleate.
  Thy Holy Worde my Distaff¹ make for mee.
Make mine Affections² thy Swift Flyers neate
  And make my Soule thy holy Spoole to bee.
  My Conversation make to be thy Reele   5
  And reele the yarn thereon spun of thy
    Wheele.

Make me thy Loome then, knit therein this Twine:
  And make thy Holy Spirit, Lord, winde quills:³
Then weave the Web thyselfe. The yarn is fine.
  Thine Ordinances make my Fulling Mills.⁴   10
  Then dy the same in Heavenly Colours
    Choice,
  All pinkt⁵ with Varnisht⁶ Flowers of Paradise.

Then cloath therewith mine Understanding, Will,
  Affections, Judgment, Conscience, Memory
My Words, and Actions, that their shine may fill   15
  My wayes with glory and thee glorify.
  Then mine apparell shall display before yee
  That I am Cloathd in Holy robes for glory.

1937

Upon a Wasp Child¹ with Cold

The Bare² that breaths the Northern blast
Did numb, Torpedo like,³ a Wasp
Whose stiffend limbs encrampt, lay bathing
In Sol's warm breath and shine as saving,
Which with her hands she chafes and stands   5
Rubbing her Legs, Shanks, Thighs, and hands.

---

¹ The distaff holds the fibers of wool, which are twisted into threads by the revolving flyers and then wound onto the spool.
² Religious feelings.
³ Bobbins to hold the thread.
⁴ Mills in which cloth is cleansed and stiffened.

⁵ Decorated.
⁶ Shining.
¹ Chilled.
² Ursa Major and Ursa Minor, northern constellations.
³ Like the torpedo fish, which stuns its victims.

Her petty toes, and fingers ends
Nipt with this breath, she out extends
Unto the Sun, in greate desire
To warm her digits at that fire.   10
Doth hold her Temples in this state
Where pulse doth beate, and head doth ake.
Doth turn, and stretch her body small,
Doth Comb her velvet Capitall.[4]
As if her little brain pan were   15
A Volume of Choice precepts cleare.
As if her sattin jacket hot
Contained Apothecaries Shop
Of Natures recepts,[5] that prevails
To remedy all her sad ailes,   20
As if her velvet helmet high
Did turret[6] rationality.
She fans her wing up to the Winde
As if her Pettycoate were lin'de,
With reasons fleece, and hoises sails   25
And hu'ming flies in thankfull gails
Unto her dun Curld[7] palace Hall
Her warm thanks offering for all.

Lord cleare my misted sight that I
May hence view thy Divinity.   30
Some sparkes whereof thou up dost hasp[8]
Within this little downy Wasp
In whose small Corporation[9] wee
A school and a schoolmaster see
Where we may learn, and easily finde   35
A nimble Spirit bravely minde
Her worke in e'ry limb: and lace
It up neate with a vitall grace,
Acting each part though ne'er so small
Here of this Fustian[10] animall.   40
Till I enravisht Climb into
The Godhead on this Lather doe.
Where all my pipes inspir'de upraise
An Heavenly musick furrd[11] with praise.

1943

---

[4] Head.
[5] Recipes.
[6] Enclose.
[7] Dark, curved.

[8] Close.
[9] Body.
[10] Cloth similar to corduroy.
[11] Trimmed.

Samuel Sewall
1652–1730

Until his *Diary* was published late in the nineteenth century, Judge Samuel Sewall was known as the hanging judge of the infamous Salem witchcraft trials of 1692. Yet history has redeemed him, in part because Sewall publicly recanted his part in the witchcraft proceedings (taking "the Blame and Shame of it") and also because he wrote one of the earliest American antislavery tracts, *The Selling of Joseph* (1710). But the work that sympathetically documents Sewall's life is the *Diary*, a rich potpourri of Puritan colonial social history. The *Diary* firmly establishes Sewall as the recording secretary of colonial Boston and its environs, inhabited by six thousand souls between 1674 and 1727.

Sewall came from a well-to-do English family who provisioned themselves most comfortably in New England, to which Samuel was brought as a nine-year-old. Later, at Harvard, his roommate was the poet Edward Taylor, and as a ministerial student he met Hannah Hull, his future wife and the daughter of the colony's treasurer and mintmaster, who "set her affections" on him. Alliance by marriage with the Hull family virtually determined his future as a merchant, exporter, and magistrate.

An orthodox Puritan, Sewall was a conservative who gave money and land to his alma mater and sponsored missionary work among the Indians, whose land he felt was unfairly wrested from them. In 1683 he was elected to the Massachusetts General Court and served as a member of the Governor's Council. When the colonial charter was revoked and then restored at the time of the "Glorious Revolution" in the late 1680s, Sewall traveled to England to represent the interests of Massachusetts before Parliament. As a figure at the center of all Massachusetts affairs, Sewall perhaps inevitably became a judge in the witchcraft trials. Of the seven judges, only he repented sending twenty persons to their deaths largely on the strength of "spectral" evidence, or evidence of ghostly phenomena.

Sewall's *Diary* is not solely one of the psychological, spiritual introspection characteristic of the Puritan mind. It freely, even indiscriminately, mixes worldly with spiritual affairs, often with an abruptness that startles the modern reader but did not trouble a man convinced of the essential unity of God's cosmos.

Several Samuel Sewalls emerge in the fifty years covered by the *Diary*. There is always the orthodox Puritan horrified by signs of Roman Catholic "popery" and scornful of Anglicans and Quakers alike. There is the sensuous Sewall relishing seasonal fruits, good wines, and a well-laid table even as he scans the heavens for God's message inscribed in clouds, a comet's path, hailstones, or the earth in a chicken-yard allegory. There is the colonist mindful of the precariousness of life as he attended the countless funerals whose pageantry he enhanced with the elegies he wrote and had printed for the occasion, fastening them to the coffins as the mourners received souvenir rings or scarves. And there is the cost-conscious widower courting a succession of women in late midlife, enticing them with "almonds and reasons" as he calculated the financial status of two merged estates. Sprinkled throughout the *Diary* are the names of so many friends and acquaintances that a reader feels the entire population of Boston is registered at some point over the half century. Above all, this *Diary* shows Samuel Sewall as a family man, proud and often in spiritual doubt, but caring deeply about his children. He grieved terribly when his little son Henry died and forever worried about the happiness of his troubled son Samuel, Jr. It is this paternal Sewall who is represented in the following selection.

Further Reading:
O. Winslow, *Samuel Sewall of Boston,* 1964.
T. Strandness, *Samuel Sewall: A Puritan Portrait,* 1967.

Text:
The Diary of Samuel Sewall, ed. M. Thomas, 1973.
See also *The Diary of Samuel Sewall,* ed. H. Wish, 1967.

---

from The Diary of Samuel Sewall

[January 13, 1677]

Jan. 13, 1676/7. Giving my chickens meat, it came to my mind that I gave them nothing save Indian corn and water, and yet they eat it and thrived very well, and that that food was necessary for them, how mean soever, which much affected me and convinced what need I stood in of spiritual food, and that I should not nauseat[1] daily duties of Prayer, &c.

[May 8, 1685]

Friday May 8th—past 6, even, Walk with the honored Governour [*Bradstreet*] up Hoar's Lane, so to the Alms House; then down the length of the Common to Mr. Dean's Pasture, then through Cowel's Lane to the New Garden, then to our House, then to our Pasture by Engs's, then I waited on his Honour to his Gate and so home. This day our old Red Cow is kill'd, and we have a new black one brought in the room, of about four years old and better, marked with a Crop and slit in the Left Ear, and a Crop off the right Ear, with a little hollowing in. As came with his Honour through Cowell's Lane, Sam. came running and call'd out a pretty way off and cried out the Cow was dead and by the Heels, meaning hang'd up by the Butcher. At which I was much startled, understanding him she had been dead upon a Hill or cast with her heels upward, and so had lost her; for I was then looking for her and 't was unexpected, Mother having partly bargained and the Butcher fetcht her away in the Night unknown. Had served this family above Ten years, above Nine since my dwelling in it.

[July 6, 1685]

Monday, July 6 th. I am taken with a Feverish Fit; yet go to Court in the Afternoon, the County Court, where was read Major Pynchon's Letter to the Council; which

---

[1] Feel disgusted by.

is that 5 Men came to one of the Houses of Westfield (I think) about midnight 28th June, knockt at the door, the Man bid him come in, so in they came all Armed with drawn Swords, and threatened to run the man and his wife through if they stirred: so plundered that House, and another in like manner: told they had 60 Men in their Company and that if they stirred out of door, they would kill them; so stayd in a great part of Monday, then when thought the Coast was clear told the Neighbours and some were sent to Search after them; at last found them: one of the 5 snapt and missed fire, another shot, then one of ours shot so as to shoot one of theirs dead: another of the 5 fought one of ours with his sword, till another of ours knockt him down. One or two that were taken are brought to Boston, one at least is escaped. Major Pynchon writes 'twill cost near an hundred Pounds.

An Indian was branded in Court and had a piece of his Ear cut off for Burglary.

[December 19, 1685]

Satterday Dec. 19. Mr. Willard Prayes with my little Henry, being very ill.

[December 20, 1685]

Sabbath-day, Dec. 20. Send Notes to Mr. Willard and Mr. Moodey to pray for my Child Henry.

Monday, about four in the Morn the faint and moaning noise of my child forces me up to pray for it.

[December 21, 1685]

21. Monday even Mr. Moodey calls. I get him to go up and Pray with my extream sick Son.

[December 22, 1685]

Tuesday Morn, Dec. 22. Child makes no noise save by a kind of snoaring as it breathed, and as it were slept.

Read the 16th of the first Chron. in the family. Having read to my Wife and Nurse out of John: the fourteenth Chapter fell now in course, which I read and went to Prayer: By that time had done, could hear little Breathing, and so about Sun-rise, or little after, he fell asleep, I hope in Jesus, and that a Mansion was ready for him in the Father's House. Died in Nurse Hill's Lap. Nurse Hill washes and layes him out: because our private Meeting hath a day of Prayer tomorrow, Thorsday Mr. Willard's Lecture, and the Child dying after Sunrise (wether cloudy), have determined to bury on Thorsday after Lecture. The Lord sanctify his Dispensation, and prepare me and mine for the coming of our Lord, in whatsoever way it be. Mr. Tho. Oakes our Physician for this Child. Read the 16th Chap. of the First Chronicles in the Family.

Tuesday night read the 15th Jno in the Chamber, out of which Mr. Willard took his Text the day Henry was baptized: in the Family, the 3d of Matthew, both requiring Fruit.

[December 23, 1685]

Wednesday, Dec. 23. Go to the privat Fast at Brother Williams's. Capt. Scottow begins and is enlarged and fervent in praying for the Church and Christ's Witnesses: Made me conclude. Sung part 137. Ps. But if I Jerusalem, &c. Just before I went, Brother Longfellow came in, which was some exercise to me, he being so ill conditioned and so outwardly shabby. The Lord humble me. As I remember, he came so before; either upon the funeral of my Father or Johnny.

[December 24, 1685]

Thursday, Decr 24th 1685. We follow Little Henry to his Grave: Governour and Magistrates of the County here, 8 in all, beside my Self, Eight Ministers, and Several Persons of note. Mr. Phillips of Rowley here. I led Sam., then Cous. Savage led Mother, and Cousin Dummer led Cous. Quinsey's wife, he not well. Midwife Weeden and Nurse Hill carried the Corps by turns, and so by Men in its Chesnut Coffin 'twas set into a Grave (The Tomb full of water) between 4 and 5. At Lecture the 21. Psalm was Sung from 8th to the end. The Lord humble me kindly in respect of all my Enmity against Him, and let his breaking my Image in my Son be a means of it. Considerable snow this night. At night little Hull had a sore Convulsion Fit.

[January 2, 1686]

Satterday, Jany 2^d Last night had a very unusual Dream; viz. That our Saviour in the dayes of his Flesh when upon Earth, came to Boston and abode here sometime, and moreover that He Lodged in that time at Father Hull's; upon which in my Dream had two Reflections, One was how much more Boston had to say than Rome boasting of Peter's being there. The other a sense of great Respect that I ought to have shewed Father Hull since Christ chose when in Town, to take up His Quarters at his House. Admired the goodness and Wisdom of Christ in coming hither and spending some part of His short Life here.

[September 3, 1986]

Friday, Septr 3. Mr. Shrimpton, Capt. Lidget and others come in a Coach from Roxbury about 9. aclock or past; singing as they come, being inflamed with Drink: At Justice Morgan's they stop and drink Healths, curse, swear, talk profanely and baudily to the great disturbance of the Town and grief of good people. Such high-handed wickedness has hardly been heard of before in Boston.

[September 13, 1686]

Monday, Septr 13, 1686. Mr. Cotton Mather preaches the Election Sermon for the Artillery, at Charlestown, from Ps. 144. 1. made a very good Discourse. President and

Deputy President there. As I went in the morn I had Sam. to the Latin School, which is the first time. Mr. Chiever received him gladly.[2] . . .

[July 26, 1687]

Tuesday, July 26, 1687. About Nine aclock my dear Son Stephen Sewall expires, just after the Judges coming to Town; died in his Grandmother's Bed-Chamber in Nurse Hill's Arms. Had two Teeth cut, no Convulsions. Mr. Willard pray'd with him in the Morning Mr. Moodey coming in when at Prayer.

[July 27, 1687]

Wednesday, July 27, 1687. Between 6 and 7. after Noon, The Body of my dear Son Stephen is carried to the Tomb by Jn Davie, Sam Willard, Joseph Eliot and Samuel Moodey. Samuel Clark and Solomon Rainsford put him into Tomb. Sam. had the head; Solomon's foot, on a loose brick, slipt, and he slid down the steps and let go the Coffin; but the end rested upon Jonny's stone set there to show the Entrance, and Sam. held his part steadily; so was only a little knock. I led my wife, Brother Stephen led Mother Hull, Sam. led Hannah, Billy Dummer led Betty, Cous. Quinsey led his wife, Cous. Savage and Dummer went together. Got home between 7. and 8. Mr. Torrey visited us but could not stay the Funeral. Sam. and his sisters cryed much coming home and at home, so that could hardly quiet them. It seems they look'd into Tomb, and Sam said he saw a great Coffin there, his Grandfathers.

[September 15, 1688]

Sept. 15, 1688. Corrected Sam. for breach of the 9th Commandment, saying he had been at the Writing School, when he had not.

[January 12, 1690]

Sabbath, Jan. 12. Richard Dummer, a flourishing youth of 9 years old, dies of the Small Pocks. I tell Sam. of it and what need he had to prepare for Death, and therefore to endeavour really to pray when he said over the Lord's Prayer: He seem'd not much to mind, eating an Apple; but when he came to say, Our father, he burst out into a bitter Cry, and when I askt what was the matter and he could speak, he burst out into a bitter Cry and said he was afraid he should die. I pray'd with him, and read Scriptures comforting against death, as, O death where is thy sting, &c. All things yours. Life and Immortality brought to light by Christ, &c. 'Twas at noon.

---

[2] Samuel Sewall, Jr., was nine. Before long it must have been apparent to (the schoolmaster) Ezekiel Cheever, that Sam was not going to follow in his father's footsteps, for we find May 14, 1688 that he had been put to Eliezer Moody to learn to write. Sam's adolescence was a difficult period and the family prayed more than once for guidance as to his calling. He finally became a bookseller. In 1702 he married Rebecca, daughter of Governor Joseph Dudley, and later built a house at Muddy River (Brookline), where he engaged in farming. [This footnote and the following three footnotes are from M. Halsey Thomas, ed., *The Diary of Samuel Sewall* (New York: Farrar, Straus, & Giroux, 1973), and are reprinted by permission.]

[from May 9, 1690]

May 9. Friday, Rid to Dedham and there refresh'd, so home by 12. or thereabouts. . . .

Found my Family all well, save Sam's sore in his neck, and Hannah droops as though would have the Small Pocks. *Note.* I have had great heaviness on my Spirit before, and in this journey; and I resolved that if it pleas'd God to bring me to my family again, I would endeavour to serve Him better in Self-denial, Fruitfullness, Not pleasing Men, open Conversation, not being solicitous to seem in some indifferent things what I was not, or at least to conceal what I was; Endeavouring to goe and come at God's call and not otherwise; Labouring more constantly and throwly to Examin my self before sitting down to the Lord's Table. Now the good Lord God of his infinite Grace help me to perform my Vows, and give me a filial Fear of Himself, and save me from the fear of Man that brings a Snare.

[May 28, 1690]

May 28. Small Pocks appear.

[June 1, 1690]

Sabbath, June 1. Betty and Joseph are taken. Betty very delirious. Mr. Moodey is known to have the Distemper.

[June 9, 1690]

Monday, June 9 th. Joseph hath a very bad night, as also the night before.

[June 10, 1690]

June 10 th. He grows better and the Small Pocks doe apparently dye away in his face.

[June 11, 1690]

Wednesday, June 11th. We put Sam. to Bed, having the Small Pocks come out upon him, as the Physician and we judge. Betty is so well as to Goe into Mother Hull's Chamber, and keep Jane Company, between 9 and 10. mane.

[June 17, 1690]

June 17 th Tuesday. Sam. rises and sits up a good while very hearty and strong. Blessed be God.

[October 25, 1691]

Sabbath, Oct. 25, 1691. Boston, N. E. I pray'd this morn that God would give me a pardon of my Sins under the Broad Seal of Heaven; and through God's goodness have receiv'd some Refreshment and Light; I hope I doe thirst after Christ; and sensible of my own folly and Loathsomness that I value Him no more, and am so backward to be married by Him.

[October 28, 1691]

Wednesday, Oct. 28, 1691. My wife is brought to Bed of a Daughter about 8. in the morning; Elisabeth Weeden, Midwife. Rose about 4. m.

[November 19, 1961]

Thursday, Nov. 19th 1691. Sam. goes to Cambridge with Mr. Henry Newman, who is to carry him to morrow Nov. 20. to Mr. Neh. Hobart's at New Cambridge.

[December 7, 1691]

Monday, Dec. 7th. I ride to New-Cambridge to see Sam. He could hardly speak to me, his affections were so mov'd, having not seen me for above a fortnight; his Cough is still very bad, much increas'd by his going to Cambridge on foot in the night.

[April 29, 1695]

Monday, April 29, 1695. The morning is very warm and Sunshiny; in the Afternoon there is Thunder and Lightening, and about 2 P.M. a very extraordinary Storm of Hail, so that the ground was made white with it, as with the blossoms when fallen; 'twas as bigg as pistoll and Musquet Bullets; It broke of the Glass of the new House about 480 Quarrels [squares] of the Front; of Mr. Sergeant's about as much; Col. Shrimpton, Major General, Govr Bradstreet, New Meetinghouse, Mr. Willard, &c. Mr. Cotton Mather dined with us, and was with me in the new Kitchen when this was; He had just been mentioning that more Ministers Houses than others proportionably had been smitten with Lightening; enquiring what the meaning of God should be in it. Many Hail-Stones broke throw the Glass and flew to the middle of the Room, or farther: People afterward Gazed upon the House to see its Ruins. I got Mr. Mather to pray with us after this awfull Providence; He told God He had broken the brittle part of our house, and prayd that we might be ready for the time when our Clay-Tabernacles should be broken. Twas a sorrowfull thing to me to see the house so far undon again before t'was finish'd. It seems at Milton on the one hand, and at Lewis's [the ordinary at Lynn] on the other, there was no Hail.

[July 15, 1695]

July 15. I discourse Capt. Sam Checkly about his taking Sam. to be his Prentice. He seems to incline to it; and in a manner all I mention it to encourage me. The good Lord direct and prosper.

[February 7, 1696]

Sixth-day, Feb. 7 th. Mrs. Alden is buried. Bearers were Mr. Chiever, Capt. Hill, Capt. Williams, Mr. Walley, Mr. Ballentine.

Capt. Frary was pass'd by, though there, which several took notice of. *Note*. Last night Sam. could not sleep because of my Brother's speaking to him of removing to some other place, mentioning Mr. Usher's. I put him to get up a little wood, and he even fainted, at which Brother was much startled, and advis'd to remove him forthwith and place him somewhere else, or send him to Salem and he would doe the best he could for him. Since, I have express'd doubtfullness to Sam. as to his staying there.

He mention'd to me Mr. Wadsworth's Sermon against Idleness, which was an Affliction to him. He said his was an idle Calling, and that he did more at home than there, take one day with another. And he mention'd Mr. Stoddard's words to me, that should place him with a good Master, and where had fullness of Imployment. It seems Sam. overheard him, and now alleged these words against his being where he was because of his idleness. Mention'd also the difficulty of the imployment by reason of the numerousness of Goods and hard to distinguish them, many not being marked; whereas Books, the price of them was set down, and so could sell them readily. I spake to Capt. Checkly again and again, and he gave me no encouragement that his being there would be to Sam's profit; and Mrs. Checkly always discouraging.

Mr. Willard's Sermon from those Words. What doest thou here Elijah? was an Occasion to hasten the Removal.

[February 10, 1696]

Feb. 10. Secund-day. I went to Mr. Willard to ask whether had best keep him at home to day. He said, No: but tell Capt. Checkly first; but when I came back, Sam was weeping and much discompos'd, and loth to goe because 'twas a little later than usual, so I thought twas hardly fit for him to go in that Case, and went to Capt. Checkly and told him how it was, and thank'd him for his kindness to Sam. Capt. Checkly desired Sam. might come to their house and not be strange there, for which I thank'd him very kindly. He presented his Service to my wife, and I to his who was in her Chamber. Capt. Checkly gave me Sam's Copy-book that lay in a drawer.

[October 16, 1696]

October 16. Pray for Sam. and my daughters Hannah and Eliza. and others of my Children.

[April 14, 1700]

Sabbath, Apr. 14. I saw and heard the Swallows proclaim the Spring.

[April 29, 1700]

Monday, Apr. 29, 1700. Sam. Sewall, Josiah Willard Jn° Bayly, Sam. Gaskill, and [blank] Mountfort goe into the Harbour a fishing in a small Boat. Seeing Richd Fifield coming in, some would needs meet the ship and see who it was: Ship had fresh way with a fair wind; when came neare, Capt. call'd to them to beware, order'd what they should doe. But they did the clear contrary, fell foul on the ship, which broke their Mast short off, fill'd the Boat with water, threw Willard and Gaskill into the River. Both which were very near drown'd; especially Gaskill, who could not swim. It pleas'd God Fifield's Boat was out, so he presently man'd it and took them in. Gaskill was under water, but discover'd by his Hat that swam atop as a Buoy. Sam, Jn° Bayly and Mountfort caught hold of the Ship and climbed on board in a miserable fright as having stared death in the face. This is the second time Sam has been near drown'd with Josiah Willard. Mother was against his going, and prevented Joseph, who pleaded earnestly to go. He sensibly acknowledged the Good Providence in his staying at home, when he saw the issue.

[June 19, 1700]

Fourth-day, June, 19. 1700. Having been long and much dissatisfied with the Trade of fetching Negros from Guinea; at last I had a strong Inclination to Write something about it; but it wore off. At last reading Bayne, Ephes.[3] about servants, who mentions Blackamoors; I began to be uneasy that I had so long neglected doing any thing. When I was thus thinking, in came Bro[r] Belknap to shew me a Petition he intended to present to the Gen Court for the freeing a Negro and his wife, who were unjustly held in Bondage. And there is a Motion by a Boston Committee to get a Law that all Importers of Negros shall pay 40[s] *per* head, to discourage the bringing of them. And Mr. C. Mather resolves to publish a sheet to exhort Masters to labour their Conversion. Which makes me hope that I was call'd of God to Write this Apology for them; Let his Blessing accompany the same.[4]

[July 20, 1702]

July, 20. Sam. visits Mrs. Rebecka Dudley.

[September 15, 1702]

Sept[r] 15. Mr. Nehemiah Walter marries Mr. Sam Sewall and Mrs. Rebekah Dudley, in the Dining Room Chamber about 8 aclock. Mr. Willard concluded with prayer, Sung the last part of the 103 Psalm.

[June 18, 1703]

Friday, June, 18. 1703. My sons House was Raised at Muddy-River;[5] The day very comfortable because dry, cloudy, windy, cool.

---

[3] Paul Baynes, *A Commentarie Vpon The First Chapter of the Epistle of Saint Pavl, written to the Ephesians* (London, 1618).
[4] Here Sewall is referring to his anti-slavery tract, "The Selling of Joseph," which was printed June 24, 1700.
[5] On November 21, 1702, the General Court passed Private Act (No. 14), An Act to Enable Samuel Sewall Esq. and Hannah his wife, to Settle Certain Lands at Muddy River in the County of Suffolke upon Samuel Sewall their Eldest Son (*Acts and Resolves*, VI, 43–44). This tract containing about three hundred acres.

[December 25, 1704]

Dec^r *25.*. Monday, a Storm of Snow, yet many Sleds come to Town, with Wood, Hoops, Coal &c as is usual.

[December 30, 1704]

Dec^r *30.* Satterday, Daughter Sewall of Brooklin is brought to Bed of a Daughter, Rebeka. 31. is baptised.

[January 11, 1705]

Thorsday, Jan^y *11*th The Govr and his Lady essaying to come from Charlestown to Boston in their Slay, 4 Horses, two Troopers riding before them; First the Troopers fell into the water, and then the Govr making a stand, his four Horses fell in, and the Two Horses behind were drown'd, the Slay pressing them down. They were pull'd up upon the Ice, and there lay dead, a sad Spectacle. Many came from Charlestown with Boards, planks, Ropes &c. and sav'd the other Horses. Tis a wonderful Mercy That the Govr, his Lady, Driver, Postilion, Troopers escaped all safe.

[January 19, 1705]

January, 19. 1704/5 The Govr coming to Town, the way being difficult by Banks of Snow, his Slay was turn'd upon one side against the Fence next Cambridge, and all in it thrown out, Governour's Wigg thrown off, his head had some hurt; and my Son's Elbow. The Horses went away with the foundation and left the Superstructure of the Slay and the Riders behind.

[January 26, 1705]

Jan^y *26.* Mr. Hirst and I went to Brooklin to see my Little Grand Daughter, Rebeka Sewall: He and I were on Horseback; in Simson's slay were Madam Willard, daughter Hirst, Hannah, and Mrs. Betty Hirst. Had some difficulty in going because of some deep descents between Banks of Snow. But went and came very well. Blessed be God. Din'd there. Before we came away, we sung the 113th Psalm.

[June 15, 1707]

Lord's Day, June, 15th I felt my self dull and heavy and Listless as to Spiritual Good; Carnal, Lifeless; I sigh'd to God, that he would quicken me.

[June 16, 1707]

June. 16. My House was broken open in two places, and about Twenty pounds worth of Plate stolen away, and some Linen; My Spoon, and Knife, and Neckcloth was taken: I said, Is not this an Answer of Prayer? Jane came up, and gave us the Alarm betime in the morn. I was helped to submit to Christ's stroke, and say, Wellcome CHRIST!

[October 1, 1707]

Octob' 1. 1707. I went to Brooklin, and chose some Apple-trees from which my Son is to send me Apples: Din'd with my Son and Daughter and little Grand-daughter;

[November 23, 1707]

Nov' 23. 1707. My Son Samuel has his Son Samuel Baptised by Mr. Walter at Roxbury.

[August 3, 1710]

Fifth-day, Aug' 3. 1710. Our little Grand-Daughter Rebekah Sewall, born xr. 30. 1704. at Brooklin, died about Eight or Nine this morn. We knew not of her being Sick, till Dr. Noyes, as he returned, told us she was dead. The Lord effectually awaken us by these awfull Surprising Providences. My son and daughter got thither before their Child dyed, and had Mr. Walter to pray with her. She was sensible to the last, catching her breath till she quite lost it.

[August 18, 1717]

Friday, 8' 18. My wife grows worse and exceedingly Restless. Pray'd God to look upon her. Ask'd not after my going to bed. Had the advice of Mr. Williams and Dr. Cutler.

[August 19, 1717]

7ᵗʰ day, 8' 19. Call'd Dr. C. Mather to pray, which he did excellently in the Dining Room, having Suggested good Thoughts to my wife before he went down. After, Mr. Wadsworth pray'd in the Chamber when 'twas suppos'd my wife took little notice. About a quarter of an hour past four, my dear Wife expired in the Afternoon, whereby the Chamber was fill'd with a Flood of Tears. God is teaching me a new Lesson; to live a Widower's Life. Lord help me to Learn; and be a Sun and Shield to me, now so much of my Comfort and Defense are taken away.

[August 20, 1717]

8' 20. I goe to the publick Worship forenoon and Afternoon. My Son has much adoe to read the Note I put up, being overwhelm'd with tears.

[August 21, 1717]

8' 21. Monday, My dear wife is embowelled and put in a Cere-Cloth, the Weather being more than ordinarily hot.

[August 23, 1717]

Midweek, 8ʳ 23. My dear Wife is inter'd. Bearers, Lᵗ Govʳ Dummer, Majʳ Genˡ Winthrop; Col. Elisha Hutchinson, Col. Townsend; Andrew Belcher esqr and Simeon Stoddard esqr. I intended Col. Taylor for a Bearer, but he was from home. Had very Comfortable weather. Broʳ Gerrish pray'd with us when return'd from the Tomb: I went into it. Govʳ had a Scarf and Ring, and the Bearers, Govʳ Dudley, Brother Sewall, Hirst, Gerrish. Was very destitute for want of the help of Son Hirst, and Cousin Jane Green. This was the first day of the Genˡ Court. Gave the Deputies Books. Allen's Alarm. They sent Mr. Isa. Tay and Capt. Wadsworth to me to Thank me.

[August 24, 1717]

8ʳ 24. Went to Lecture.

[August 25, 1717]

8ʳ 25. Went to see Mr. [Grove] Hirst whom I found very sick. He took Solemn Leave of his Father and me. Prayed me to forgive. I said, I doe it heartily; and pray'd him to forgive me, Defects, Excesses; in many things we all offend. Afterward I told him he was in a great degree the Stay and Comfort of my Life.

[October 19, 1728]

October, 19. 1728. Seeing this to be the same day of the week and Moneth that the Wife of my youth expired Eleven years agoe, it much affected me. I writ to my dear Son Mr. Joseph Sewall of it, desiring him to come and dine with me: or however that he would call some time to join my Condolence. He came about Noon and made an excellent Prayer in the East Chamber. Laus Deo.

1878–1882

Cotton Mather
1663–1728

Honor and duty were thrust upon Cotton Mather from earliest childhood. He was the grandson of the illustrious Massachusetts Bay founders Richard Mather and John Cotton, the apparent prince regent of a Puritan dynasty. Mather accepted the responsibility of his lineage. He wrote in filial piety of the founders and in anxiety lest their backsliding descendants evade his efforts to revitalize the waning Puritan mission.

The Boston-born Mather was the eldest of twelve children. He was intellectually and spiritually precocious, at fourteen fasting to bring himself closer to God by bodily discipline and at sixteen joining his father's church, convinced that he had experienced God's saving grace and was therefore one of the elect. Before his teens the carefully tutored Mather had learned Hebrew and classical languages, and he entered Harvard at twelve. His youth and the prominence of his family made him vulnerable to the taunts of his classmates, who made his life miserable. When a stutter jeopardized his plans to enter the ministry, Mather decided instead to study medicine. Though the speech impediment abated and permitted the young man to resume his ministerial plans, Cotton Mather never lost interest in medicine and in scientific developments, as can be seen in his pioneering support of smallpox inoculation.

Mather was active in secular as well as religious affairs. He graduated from Harvard with distinction and remained for a master's degree in 1681. He served for the next forty years as his father's assistant in Boston's Old North Church, in whose tower Paul Revere would later look for his signal. Mather prepared up to five sermons per week while also working for reforms, including improved jail conditions, adequate and guaranteed schooling for children, and the religious education (and eventual emancipation) of slaves. Though Mather never left New England, he corresponded with religious leaders and scientists worldwide. He was elected a fellow of the Royal Society of London and awarded an honorary doctorate of divinity by the University of Glasgow in 1710. He had the largest scholarly library in New England.

Mather's personal life, never disclosed in his writings, was an "uneasy Wilderness." At twenty-three he married "a lovely and worthy young gentlewoman." She was the first of two beloved wives who died. His third wife went insane. Mather was evidently a most affectionate parent, but of his fifteen children only two survived him. He suffered embarrassing financial difficulties and lived to see his detractors name their slaves after him.

Though he worked to strengthen Puritanism, Cotton Mather's writings reflect its decline and, to some degree, a new spirit of ecumenicism. His major work, the *Magnalia Christi Americana* (1702), combines history and biography to commemorate the dedication and exemplary piety of such New England founders as Governor William Bradford, who stands in the *Magnalia* as an allegorical figure of Puritan sainthood. Mather's "Life of His Excellency Sir William Phips, Knt." is, perhaps inadvertently, quite different. Mather attempted to offer a detailed account of a politically controversial governor whose appointment was favored by Mather's father, Increase. The Phips biography, however, shows the rise from humble beginnings to wealth and prominence and embodies the American myth of the self-made man, a myth enacted in the life and writings of Benjamin Franklin and subsequently restated in the popular novels of Horatio Alger, Jr.

Mather's life of Phips includes an account of the 1692 Salem witchcraft trials. Phips, as governor, appointed a court to "hear and determine" the evidence against some nineteen persons accused of witchcraft, a subject of lifelong interest to Mather. Most Christians of his time believed that witchcraft was the devil's effort to undermine the work of Christ. Intangible spectral or ghostly evidence, which today's reader might dismiss as fantasy or hallucination, was admissible in court. Mather felt that the "diabolical divinations" of witchcraft were acutely at work in New England, a country devoted especially to the "worship and service of the Lord Jesus Christ." Mather's Phips stands as a Christian hero bringing the devil's agents to justice.

The ecumenical side of Mather emerges in *Bonifacius, an Essay upon the Good,* written in 1710. This most popular of his writings transcended Puritan sectarianism as Mather sought to guide individuals, families, neighbors, communities, even nations in their proper relations with one another. These "essays to do good" hearken to the Puritan community ideals set forth seventy years earlier in John Winthrop's image of the shining city on a hill. Love, trust, fairness, and mutual responsibility are the recurrent themes of *Bonifacius.* Perhaps subconsciously Mather worked to transform his "uneasy Wilderness" of parental and domestic pain, and public humiliation, into an idealized realm of communal love and respect. In a growing population of practical-minded people, *Bonifacius* was a manual for self-improvement and remained in print in various editions until the mid-nineteenth century.

Mather intended his writings to glorify God and to revive Puritan zeal, hoping that America would become the millennial city, the *Theopolis Americana* of which he writes in rhapsodic prose. Historically the times were against him, and in certain ways his writings testify to a waning era, which Mather in part understood. He wrote in the *Magnalia,* "Whether New-England may live anywhere else or not, it must live in our history." If he sounds like the spiritual archivist of a passing age, Mather is nonetheless precocious in his epic vision of the American experience. In the *Magnalia* and elsewhere, Mather unfolds and asserts the meaning of the new yet predestined American nation in its comprehensiveness and multiplicity. In literature he thus anticipates the work of Walt Whitman and William Carlos Williams, figures of succeeding centuries who built upon the tradition he helped to found.

Further Reading:
B. Wendell, *Cotton Mather, The Puritan Priest,* 1891, 1963.
R. Middlekauff, *The Mathers: Three Generations of Puritan Intellectuals,* 1971.
S. Bercovitch, *The Puritan Origins of the American Self,* 1975.
D. Levin, *Cotton Mather,* 1978.
K. Silverman, *The Life and Times of Cotton Mather,* 1984.

Texts:
Magnalia Christi Americana, 2 vols., 1853–1855.
Theopolis Americana, 1710.
Bonifacius, an Essay upon the Good, ed. D. Levin, 1966.

from Magnalia Christi Americana

The Life of William Bradford, Esq.

*Omnium Somnos illius vigilantia defendit; omnium otium, illius
Labor; omnium Delitias, illius Industria; omnium vacationem, illius
occupatio.*[1]

1. It has been a matter of some observation, that although Yorkshire be one of the
largest shires in England; yet, for all the *fires* of martyrdom which were kindled in
the days of Queen Mary, it afforded no more *fuel* than one poor *Leaf;* namely, John
Leaf, an apprentice, who suffered for the doctrine of the Reformation at the same time
and stake with the famous John Bradford.[2] But when the reign of Queen Elizabeth
would not admit the Reformation of worship to proceed unto those degrees, which
were proposed and pursued by no small number of the faithful in those days,
Yorkshire was not the least of the shires in England that afforded suffering *witnesses*
thereunto. The Churches there gathered were quickly molested with such a raging
persecution, that if the spirit of separation in them did carry them unto a further
extream than it should have done, one blameable cause thereof will be found in the
extremity of that persecution. Their troubles made that *cold* country too *hot* for them,
so that they were under a necessity to *seek* a retreat in the Low Countries; and yet
the watchful malice and fury of their adversaries rendred it almost impossible for them
to *find* what they sought. For them to leave their native soil, their lands and their
friends, and go into a strange place, where they must hear foreign language, and live
meanly and hardly, and in other imployments than that of husbandry, wherein they
had been educated, *these* must needs have been such discouragements as could have
been conquered by none, save those who "sought first the kingdom of God, and the
righteousness thereof." But that which would have made these discouragements the
more unconquerable unto an ordinary faith, was the terrible zeal of their enemies to
guard all ports, and search all ships, that none of them should be carried off. I will
not relate the sad things of this kind then *seen* and *felt* by this people of God; but
only exemplifie those trials with one short story. Divers of this people having hired
a Dutchman, then lying at Hull, to carry them over to Holland, he promised faithfully
to take them in between Grimsly and Hull; but they coming to the place a day or
two too soon, the appearance of such a multitude alarmed the officers of the town
adjoining, who came with a great body of soldiers to seize upon them. Now it
happened that one boat full of men had been carried aboard, while the women were
yet in a bark that lay aground in a creek at low water. The Dutchman perceiving
the storm that was thus beginning ashore, swore by the sacrament that he would stay
no longer for any of them; and so taking the advantage of a fair wind then blowing,
he put out to sea for Zealand.[3] The women thus left near Grimsly-common, bereaved
of their husbands, who had been hurried from them, and forsaken of their neighbours,
of whom none durst in this fright stay with them, were a very rueful spectacle; some

---

[1] Latin: "His watchfulness guards others' slumbers;
his toil secures others' rest; / his diligence
protects others' enjoyments; his constant
application, others' leisure."

[2] John Bradford (1510?–1555), English theologian
and religious essayist.

[3] Island province of Holland.

crying for *fear,* some shaking for *cold,* all dragged by troops of armed and angry men from one Justice to another, till not knowing what to do with them, they even dismissed them to shift as well as they could for themselves. But by their singular *afflictions,* and by their Christian *behaviours,* the *cause* for which they exposed themselves did gain considerably. In the mean time, the men at sea found reason to be glad that their families were not with them, for they were surprized with an horrible tempest, which held them for fourteen days together, in seven whereof they saw not sun, moon or star, but were driven upon the coast of Norway. The mariners often despaired of life, and once with doleful shrieks gave over all, as thinking the vessel was foundred: but the vessel rose again, and when the mariners with sunk hearts often cried out, "We sink! we sink!" the passengers, without such distraction of mind, even while the water was running into their mouths and ears, would chearfully shout, "Yet, Lord, thou canst save! Yet, Lord, thou canst save!" And the Lord accordingly brought them at last safe unto their desired haven: and not long after helped their distressed relations thither after them, where indeed they found upon almost all accounts a *new world,* but a world in which they found that they must live like strangers and pilgrims.

2. Among those devout people was our William Bradford, who was born *Anno* 1588, in an obscure village called Ansterfield, where the people were as unacquainted with the Bible, as the Jews do seem to have been with *part* of it in the days of Josiah; a most ignorant and licentious *people,* and *like unto their priest.* Here, and in some other places, he had a comfortable inheritance left him of his honest parents, who died while he was yet a child, and cast him on the education, first of his grand parents, and then of his uncles, who devoted him, like his ancestors, unto the affairs of husbandry. Soon a long sickness kept him, as he would afterwards thankfully say, from the *vanities of youth,* and made him the fitter for what he was afterwards to undergo. When he was about a dozen years old, the reading of the Scriptures began to cause great impressions upon him; and those impressions were much assisted and improved, when he came to enjoy Mr. Richard Clifton's illuminating ministry, not far from his abode; he was then also further befriended, by being brought into the company and fellowship of such as were then called professors; though the young man that brought him into it did after become a prophane and wicked *apostate.* Nor could the wrath of his uncles, nor the scoff of his neighbours, now turned upon him, as one of the *Puritans,* divert him from his pious inclinations.

3. At last, beholding how fearfully the evangelical and apostolical *church-form,* whereinto the churches of the primitive times were cast by the good spirit of God, had been *deformed* by the apostacy of the succeeding times; and what little progress the Reformation had yet made in many parts of Christendom towards its recovery, he set himself by reading, by discourse, by prayer, to learn whether it was not his duty to withdraw from the communion of the parish-assemblies, and engage with some society of the faithful, that should keep close unto the *written word* of God, as the *rule* of their worship. And after many distresses of mind concerning it, he took up a very deliberate and understanding resolution, of doing so; which resolution he chearfully prosecuted, although the provoked rage of his friends tried all the ways imaginable to reclaim him from it, unto all whom his answer was:

> "Were I like to endanger my life, or consume my estate by any ungodly courses,
> your counsels to me were very seasonable; but you know that I have been
> diligent and provident in my calling, and not only desirous to augment what

I have, but also to enjoy it in your company; to part from which will be as great a cross as can befal me. Nevertheless, to keep a good conscience, and walk in such a way as God has prescribed in his Word, is a thing which I must prefer before you all, and above life it self. Wherefore, since 'tis for a good cause that I am like to suffer the disasters which you lay before me, you have no cause to be either angry with me, or sorry for me; yea, I am not only willing to part with every thing that is dear to me in this world for this cause, but I am also thankful that God has given me an heart to do, and will accept me so to suffer for him."

Some lamented him, some derided him, *all* disswaded him: nevertheless, the more they did it, the more fixed he was in his purpose to seek the ordinances of the gospel, where they should be dispensed with most of the *commanded purity;* and the sudden deaths of the chief relations which thus lay at him, quickly after convinced him what a folly it had been to have quitted his profession, in expectation of any satisfaction from them. So to Holland he attempted a removal.

4. Having with a great company of Christians hired a ship to transport them for Holland, the master perfidiously betrayed them into the hands of those persecutors, who rifled and ransacked their goods, and clapped their persons into prison at Boston,[4] where they lay for a month together. But Mr. Bradford being a young man of about eighteen, was dismissed sooner than the rest, so that within a while he had opportunity with some others to get over to Zealand, through *perils*, both by *land* and *sea* not inconsiderable; where he was not long ashore ere a viper seized on his hand—that is, an officer—who carried him unto the magistrates, unto whom an envious passenger had accused him as having *fled* out of England. When the magistrates understood the true cause of his coming thither, they were well satisfied with him; and so he repaired joyfully unto his brethren at Amsterdam, where the difficulties to which he afterwards stooped in learning and serving of a Frenchman at the working of silks, were abundantly compensated by the delight wherewith he sat under the shadow of our Lord, in his purely dispensed ordinances. At the end of two years, he did, being of age to do it, convert his estate in England into money; but setting up for himself, he found some of his designs by the *providence* of God frowned upon, which he judged a *correction* bestowed by God upon him for certain decays of *internal piety,* whereinto he had fallen; the consumption of his *estate* he thought came to prevent a consumption in his *virtue.* But after he had resided in Holland about half a score years, he was one of those who bore a part in that hazardous and generous enterprise of removing into New-England, with part of the English church at Leyden, where, at their first landing, his dearest consort accidentally falling overboard, was drowned in the harbour; and the rest of his days were spent in the services, and the temptations, of that American wilderness.

5. Here was Mr. Bradford, in the year 1621, unanimously chosen the governour of the plantation: the difficulties whereof were such, that if he had not been a person of more than ordinary piety, wisdom and courage, he must have sunk under them. He had, with a laudable industry, been laying up a treasure of experiences, and he had now occasion to use it: indeed, nothing but an *experienced* man could have been

---

[4] Boston, England.

suitable to the necessities of the people. The potent nations of the Indians, into whose country they were come, would have cut them off, if the blessing of God upon *his* conduct had not quelled them; and if his prudence, justice and moderation had not over-ruled them, they had been ruined by their own distempers. One specimen of his demeanour is to this day particularly spoken of. A company of young fellows that were newly arrived, were very unwilling to comply with the governour's order for working abroad on the publick account; and therefore on Christmas-day, when he had called upon them, they excused themselves, with a pretence that it was against their conscience to *work* such a day. The governour gave them no answer, only that he would spare them till they were better informed; but by and by he found them all at *play* in the street, sporting themselves with various diversions; whereupon commanding the instruments of their games to be taken from them, he effectually gave them to understand, *"That it was against his conscience that they should play whilst others were at work:* and that if they had any devotion to the day, they should show it at home in the exercises of religion, and not in the streets with pastime and frolicks;" and this gentle reproof put a final stop to all such disorders for the future.

6. For two years together after the beginning of the colony, whereof he was now governour, the poor people had a great experiment of "man's not living by bread alone;" for when they were left all together without one morsel of bread for many months one after another, still the good providence of God relieved them, and supplied them, and this for the most part out of the *sea.* In this low condition of affairs, there was no little exercise for the prudence and patience of the governour, who chearfully bore his part in all: and, that industry might not flag, he quickly set himself to settle *propriety* among the new-planters; foreseeing that while the whole country laboured upon a common stock, the husbandry and business of the plantation could not flourish, as Plato and others long since dreamed that it would, if a *community* were established. Certainly, if the spirit which dwelt in the old puritans, had not inspired these new-planters, they had sunk under the burden of these difficulties; but our Bradford had a double portion of that spirit.

7. The plantation was quickly thrown into a storm that almost overwhelmed it, by the unhappy actions of a minister sent over from England by the adventurers concerned for the plantation; but by the blessing of Heaven on the conduct of the governour, they weathered out that storm. Only the adventurers hereupon breaking to pieces, threw up all their concernments with the infant-colony; whereof they gave this as one reason, "That the planters dissembled with his Majesty and their friends in their petition, wherein they declared for a church-discipline, agreeing with the French and others of the reforming churches in Europe." Whereas 'twas now urged, that they had admitted into their communion a person who at his admission utterly renounced the Churches of England, (which person, by the way, was *that* very man who had made the complaints against them,) and therefore, though they denied the *name* of Brownists,[5] yet they were the thing. In answer hereunto, the very words written by the governour were these:

---

[5] Separatist sect named for Robert Browne, who believed discipline to be an essential mark of the true church.

"Whereas you tax us with dissembling about the *French discipline,* you do us wrong, for we both hold and practice the *discipline* of the French and other Reformed Churches (as they have published the same in the Harmony of Confessions) according to our means, in effect and substance. But whereas you would tie us up to the French *discipline* in every circumstance, you derogate from the *liberty* we have in Christ Jesus. The Apostle Paul would have none to *follow him* in any thing, but wherein he *follows* Christ; much less ought any Christian or church in the world to do it. The French may err, we may err, and other churches may err, and doubtless do in many *circumstances.* That honour therefore belongs only to the *infallible Word of God*, and *pure Testament of Christ*, to be propounded and followed as the only rule and pattern for direction herein to all churches and Christians. And it is too great arrogancy for any man or church to think that he or they have so sounded the Word of God unto the bottom, as precisely to set down the church's discipline without error in substance or circumstances, that no other without blame may digress or differ in any thing from the same. And it is not difficult to shew that the Reformed Churches differ in many *circumstances* among themselves."

By which words it appears how far he was free from that rigid spirit of separation, which broke to pieces the Separatists themselves in the Low Countries, unto the great scandal of the reforming churches. He was indeed a person of a well-tempered spirit, or else it had been scarce possible for him to have kept the affairs of Plymouth in so good a temper for thirty-seven years together; in every one of which he was chosen their governour, except the three years wherein Mr. Winslow, and the two years wherein Mr. Prince, at the choice of the people, took a turn with him.

8. The leader of a people in a wilderness had need be a Moses; and if a Moses had not led the people of Plymouth Colony, when this worthy person was their governour, the people had never with so much unanimity and importunity still called him to lead them. Among many instances thereof, let this one piece of self-denial be told for a memorial of him, wheresoever this History shall be considered: The Patent of the Colony was taken in his name, running in these terms: "To William Bradford, his heirs, associates, and assigns." But when the number of the freemen was much increased, and many new townships erected, the General Court there desired of Mr. Bradford, that he would make a surrender of the same into their hands, which he willingly and presently assented unto, and confirmed it according to their desire by his hand and seal, reserving no more for himself than was his proportion, with others, by agreement. But as he found the providence of Heaven many ways recompensing his many acts of self-denial, so he gave this testimony to the faithfulness of the divine promises: "That he had forsaken friends, houses and lands for the sake of the gospel, and the Lord gave them him again." Here he prospered in his estate; and besides a worthy son which he had by a former wife, he had also two sons and a daughter by another, whom he married in this land.

9. He was a person for study as well as action; and hence, notwithstanding the difficulties through which he passed in his youth, he attained unto a notable skill in languages: the Dutch tongue was become almost as vernacular to him as the English; the French tongue he could also manage; the Latin and the Greek he had mastered; but the Hebrew he most of all studied, "Because," he said, "he would see with his

own eyes the ancient oracles of God in their native beauty." He was also well skilled in History, in Antiquity, and in Philosophy; and for Theology he became so versed in it, that he was an irrefragable disputant against the *errors,* especially those of Anabaptism,[6] which with trouble he saw rising in his colony; wherefore he wrote some significant things for the confutation of those errors. But the *crown* of all was his holy, prayerful, watchful, and fruitful walk with God, wherein he was very exemplary.

10. At length he fell into an indisposition of body, which rendred him unhealthy for a whole winter; and as the spring advanced, his health yet more declined; yet he felt himself not what he counted sick, till one day; in the night after which, the God of heaven so filled his mind with ineffable consolations, that he seemed little short of Paul, rapt up unto the unutterable entertainments of Paradise. The next morning he told his friends, "That the good Spirit of God had given him a pledge of his happiness in another world, and the first-fruits of his eternal glory;" and on the day following he died, May 9, 1657, in the 69th year of his age—lamented by all the colonies of New-England, as a common blessing and father to them all.

O mihi si Similis Contingat Clausula Vitæ![7]

Plato's brief description of a governour, is all that I will now leave as his character, in an

EPITAPH.

Νομευς Τροφος ἀγελης ανθρωπινης.[8]

MEN are but FLOCKS: BRADFORD beheld their need,
And long did them at once both rule and feed.

from **The Life of His Excellency
Sir William Phips, Knt.**

[The Rise to Wealth]

2. So *obscure* was the *original* of that memorable person, whose actions I am going to relate, that I must, in a way of writing like that of Plutarch,[9] prepare my reader for the intended relation, by first searching the archives of antiquity for a parallel. Now, because we will not parallel him with Eumenes, who, though he were the son of a poor carrier, became a governour of mighty provinces; nor with Marius, whose mean parentage did not hinder his becoming a glorious defender of his country, and seven times the chief magistrate of the chiefest city in the universe; nor with Iphicrates,

[6] The characteristic belief of several Protestant sects that infant baptism is not valid.

[7] Latin: "If only a similar end to life might touch me!"

[8] Greek: "The Shepherd is the one who is the nurse of the human flock."

[9] Greek biographer (A.D. 46?–?120) who wrote *Parallel Lives.* Mather proceeds to disclaim parallels with Eumenes, secretary to Philip of Macedon and Alexander the Great (362–316 B.C.); Gaius Marius (155?–86 B.C.), Roman general and consul; Iphicrates (415–353 B.C.), Athenian general who campaigned against Sparta and Corinth; Diocletian (A.D. 284–305), Roman emperor; Bonosus (third century A.D.); Giulio Mazarini (1602–1661), Italian-born cardinal who was chief minister to Louis XIV of France.

who became a successful and renowned general of a great people, though his father were a cobler; nor with Dioclesian, the son of a poor scrivener; nor with Bonosus, the son of a poor school-master, who yet came to sway the scepter of the Roman empire; nor, lastly, will I compare him to the more late example of the celebrated Mazarini, who, though no gentleman by his extraction, and one so sorrily educated that he might have wrote *man* before he could write 'at all; yet ascended unto that grandeur, in the memory of many yet living, as to umpire the most important affairs of Christendom: we will decline looking any further in that hemisphere of the world, and make the "hue and cry" throughout the regions of America, the New World, which he that is becoming the subject of our history, by his nativity, belonged unto. And in America, the first that meets me is Francisco Pizarro,[10] who, though a *spurious offspring,* exposed when a babe in a church-porch, at a sorry village of Navarre, and afterwards employed while he was a boy in keeping of cattel, yet, at length, stealing into America, he so thrived upon his adventures there, that upon some discoveries, which with an handful of men he had in a desperate expedition made of Peru, he obtained the King of Spain's commission for the conquest of it, and at last so incredibly enriched himself by the conquest, that he was made the first Vice-roy of Peru, and created Marquess of Anatilla.

To the latter and highest part of that story, if any thing hindred his Excellency Sir WILLIAM PHIPS from affording of a *parallel,* it was not the want either of design, or of courage, or of conduct in himself, but it was the fate of a *premature mortality.* For my reader now being satisfied that a person's being obscure in his original is not always a just prejudice to an expectation of considerable matters from him, I shall now inform him that this our Phips was born February 2, A.D. 1650, at a despicable plantation on the river of Kennebeck, and almost the furthest village of the eastern settlement of New-England. And as the father of that man which was as great a blessing as England had in the age of that man was a smith,[11] so a gun-smith—namely, James Phips, once of Bristol—had the honour of being the father to him whom we shall presently see made by the God of Heaven as great a blessing to New-England as that country could have had, if they themselves had pleased. His fruitful mother, yet living, had no less than twenty-six children, whereof twenty-one were sons; but equivalent to them all was WILLIAM, one of the youngest, whom his father, dying, left young with his mother, and with her he lived, "keeping of sheep in the wilderness," until he was eighteen years old; at which time he began to feel some further dispositions of mind from that providence of God which "took him from the sheepfolds, from following the ewes great with young, and brought him to feed his people."[12] Reader, enquire no further who was his father? Thou shalt anon see that he was, as the Italians express it, "a son to his own labours!"

3. His friends earnestly solicited him to settle among them in a plantation of the east; but he had an unaccountable *impulse* upon his mind, perswading him, as he would privately hint unto some of them, "that he was born to greater matters." To come at those "greater matters," his first contrivance was to bind himself an apprentice unto a ship carpenter for four years; in which time he became a master of the trade that

---

[10] Spanish conqueror of Peru (1470?–1541).
[11] I.e., Thomas Cromwell, father of Oliver Cromwell (1599–1658), the Puritan English general.
[12] Psalm 78:71.

once, in a vessel of more than *forty thousand tuns,* repaired the ruins of the earth; Noah's, I mean; he then betook himself an hundred and fifty miles further a field, even to Boston, the chief town of New-England; which being a place of the most business and resort in those parts of the world, he expected there more commodiously to pursue the *Spes Majorum et Meliorum*[13]—hopes which had inspired him. At Boston, where it was that he now learned first of all to *read* and *write,* he followed his trade for about a year; and, by a laudable deportment, so recommended himself, that he married a young gentlewoman of good repute, who was the widow of one Mr. John Hull, a well-bred merchant, but the daughter of one Captain Roger Spencer, a person of good fashion, who, having suffered much damage in his estate, by some unkind and unjust actions, which he bore with such patience, that for fear of thereby injuring the publick, he would not seek satisfaction, posterity might afterward see the reward of his *patience,* in what Providence hath now done for one of his own *posterity.* Within a little while after his marriage, he indented with several persons in Boston to build them a ship at Sheeps-coat River, two or three leagues eastward of Kennebeck; where having launched the ship, he also provided a lading of lumber to bring with him, which would have been to the advantage of all concerned. But just as the ship was hardly finished, the barbarous Indians on that river broke forth into an open and cruel war upon the English; and the miserable people, surprized by so sudden a storm of blood, had no refuge from the infidels but the *ship* now finishing in the harbour. Whereupon he left his intended *lading* behind him, and, instead thereof, carried with him his old neighbours and their families, free of all charges to Boston; so the first *action* that he did, after he was his own man, was to save his father's house, with the rest of the neighbourhood, from ruin; but the disappointment which befel him from the loss of his other *lading,* plunged his affairs into greater embarrassments with such as had employed him.

4. But he was hitherto no more than beginning to make *scaffolds* for further and higher *actions!* He would frequently tell the gentlewoman his wife that he should yet be *captain of a King's ship;* that he should come to have the *command of better men* than he was now accounted himself; and that he should be owner of a *fair brick-house* in the Green-lane of North-Boston; and that, it may be, this would not be all that the providence of God would bring him to. She entertained these passages with a sufficient incredulity; but he had so *serious* and *positive* an expectation of them, that it is not easie to say what was the *original* thereof. He was of an enterprizing genius, and naturally disdained *littleness:* but his disposition for *business* was of the Dutch mould, where, with a little shew of *wit,* there is as much *wisdom* demonstrated, as can be shewn by any nation. His talent lay not in the *airs* that serve chiefly for the pleasant and sudden turns of conversation; but he might say, as Themistocles,[14] "Though he could not play upon a fiddle, yet he knew how to make a little city become a great one." He would prudently contrive a weighty undertaking, and then patiently pursue it unto the end. He was of an inclination cutting rather like a *hatchet* than like a *razor;* he would propose very considerable matters to himself, and then so *cut through* them, that no difficulties could put by the edge of his resolutions. Being thus of the true temper for doing of great things, he betakes himself to the *sea,* the right *scene* for

[13] Latin: "Hopes of greater and better things."
[14] Athenian commander (527–460 B.C.) who won the naval battle at Salamis.

such things; and upon advice of a Spanish wreck about the Bahamas, he took a voyage thither; but with little more success than what just served him a little to furnish him for a voyage to England; whither he went in a vessel, not much unlike that which the Dutchmen stamped on their first coin, with these words about it: *Incertum quo Fata ferant.*[15] Having first informed himself that there was another Spanish wreck, wherein was lost a mighty treasure, hitherto undiscovered, he had a strong impression upon his mind that *he* must be the discoverer; and he made such representations of his design at White-Hall, that by the year 1683 he became the *captain of a King's ship,* and arrived at New-England commander of the Algier-Rose, a frigot of eighteen guns and ninety-five men.

5. To relate all the dangers through which he passed, both by sea and land, and all the tiresome trials of his *patience,* as well as of his *courage,* while year after year the most vexing accidents imaginable delayed the success of his design, it would even tire the patience of the reader: for very great was the experiment that Captain Phips made of the Italian observation, "He that cannot suffer both good and evil, will never come to any great preferment." Wherefore I shall supersede all *journal* of his voyages to and fro, with reciting one instance of his conduct, that showed him to be a person of no contemptible capacity. While he was captain of the Algier-Rose, his men growing weary of their unsuccessful enterprize, made a mutiny, wherein they approached him on the quarter-deck, with drawn swords in their hands, and required him to join with them in running away with the ship, to drive a trade of piracy on the South Seas. Captain Phips, though he had not so much of a weapon as an ox-goad, or a jaw-bone in his hands, yet, like another Shamgar or Samson,[16] with a most undaunted fortitude, he rushed in upon them, and with the blows of his bare hands, *felled* many of them, and *quelled* all the rest. But this is not the instance which I intended: that which I intend is, that (as it has been related unto me) one day while his frigot lay *careening,*[17] at a desolate Spanish island, by the side of a rock, from whence they had laid a bridge to the shoar, the men, whereof he had about an hundred, went all but about eight or ten to divert themselves, as they pretended, in the *woods;* where they all entred into an *agreement,* which they signed in a ring, That about seven o'clock that evening they would seize the captain, and those eight or ten which they knew to be true unto him, and leave them to perish on this island, and so be gone away unto the South Sea to *seek their fortune.* Will the reader now imagine that Captain Phips, having advice of this plot but about an hour and half before it was to be put in execution, yet within *two hours* brought all these rogues down upon their knees to beg for their lives? But so it was! for these knaves considering that they should want a *carpenter* with them in their villanous expedition, sent a messenger to fetch unto them the carpenter, who was then at work upon the vessel; and unto him they shewed their *articles;* telling him what he must look for if he did not subscribe among them. The carpenter being an honest fellow, did with much importunity prevail for one half hour's time to consider of the matter; and returning to work upon

---

[15] Latin: "None can tell where Fate will bear me."
[16] The strong man Samson killed 1,000 Philistine men with the jawbone of an ass (Judges 15:13–16). Shamgar killed 600 Philistines with

an oxgoad, "and he too delivered Israel" (Judges 3:31).
[17] Lying on its side so that the hull could be cleaned and repaired.

the vessel, with a *spy* by them set upon him, he feigned himself taken with a fit of the cholick, for the relief whereof he suddenly run unto the captain in the great cabbin for a *dram;* where, when he came, his business was only, in brief, to tell the captain of the horrible distress which he was fallen into; but the captain bid him as briefly return to the rogues in the woods, and sign their articles, and leave *him* to provide for the rest. The carpenter was no sooner gone but Captain Phips, calling together the few friends (it may be seven or eight) that were left him aboard, whereof the gunner was one, demanded of them, whether they would stand by him in the extremity which he informed them was now come upon him; thereto they replied, "They would stand by him, if he could save them;" and he answered, "By the help of God he did not fear it." All their provisions had been carried ashoar to a tent, made for that purpose there; about which they had placed several great guns to defend it, in case of any assault from Spaniards, that might happen to come that way. Wherefore Captain Phips immediately ordered those guns to be silently drawned and turned; and so pulling up the bridge, he charged his great guns aboard, and brought them to bear on every side of the tent. By this time the *army of rebels* comes out of the woods; but as they drew near to the tent of provisions, they saw such a change of circumstances, that they cried out, "We are betrayed!" And they were soon confirmed in it, when they heard the captain with a stern fury call to them, "Stand off, ye wretches, at your peril!" He quickly saw them cast into a more than ordinary confusion, when they saw *him* ready to fire his great guns upon them, if they offered one step further than he permitted them: and when he had signified unto them his resolve to abandon them unto all the desolation which they had purposed for him, he caused the *bridge* to be again laid, and his men begun to take the provisions aboard. When the wretches beheld what was coming upon them, they fell to very humble entreaties; and at last fell down upon their knees, protesting, "That they never had any thing against him, except only his unwillingness to go away with the King's ship upon the South-Sea design: but upon all other accounts, they would chuse rather to live and die with him than with any man in the world: however, since they saw how much he was dissatisfied at it, they would insist upon it no more, and humbly begged his pardon." And when he judged that he had kept them on their *knees* long enough, he having first secured their *arms,* received them aboard; but he immediately weighed anchor, and arriving at Jamaica, he turned them off. Now, with a small company of other men he sailed from thence to Hispaniola,[18] where, by the policy of his address, he fished out of a very old Spaniard (or Portuguese) a little advice about the true spot where lay the wreck which he had been hitherto seeking, as unprosperously as the chymists have their *aurisick stone:* that it was upon a *reef of shoals,* a few leagues to the northward of Port de la Plata, upon Hispaniola, a port so called, it seems, from the landing of some of the *shipwrecked* company, with a boat full of plate, saved out of their sinking frigot: nevertheless, when he had searched very narrowly the spot, whereof the old Spaniard had advised him, he had not hitherto exactly lit upon it. Such thorns did vex his affairs while he was in the Rose-frigot; but none of all these things could retund the edge of his expectations to find the *wreck;* with such expectations he returned then into England, that he might there better furnish himself to prosecute

[18] Haiti.

a *new discovery;* for though he judged he might, by proceeding a little further, have come at the right *spot;* yet he found his present company too ill a crew to be confided in.

6. So *proper* was his behaviour, that the best noblemen in the kingdom now admitted him into their conversation; but yet he was opposed by powerful enemies, that clogged his affairs with such demurrages,[19] and such *disappointments,* as would have wholly discouraged his designs, if his patience had not been *invincible.* "He who can wait, hath what he desireth." Thus his indefatigable patience, with a proportionable *diligence,* at length overcame the difficulties that had been thrown in his way; and prevailing with the Duke of Albemarle, and some other persons of quality, to fit him out, he set sail for the *fishing-ground,* which had been so well *baited* half an hundred years before: and as he had already discovered his *capacity for business* in many considerable actions, he now added unto those discoveries, by not only *providing* all, but also by *inventing* many of the instruments necessary to the prosecution of his intended *fishery.* Captain Phips arriving with a ship and a tender at Port de la Plata, made a stout canoo of a stately cotton-tree, so large as to carry eight or ten oars, for the making of which *periaga*[20] (as they call it) he did, with the same industry that he did every thing else, imploy his own *hand* and *adse,*[21] and endure no little hardship, lying abroad in the woods many nights together. This periaga, with the tender, being anchored at a place convenient, the periaga kept busking to and again, but could only discover a *reef of rising shoals* thereabouts, called "The Boilers,"—which, rising to be within two or three foot of the surface of the sea, were yet so steep, that a ship striking on them, would immediately sink down, who could say how many fathom, into the ocean? Here they could get no other pay for their long *peeping* among the *boilers,* but only such as caused them to think upon returning to their captain with the bad news of their total disappointment. Nevertheless, as they were upon the return, one of the men looking over the side of the periaga, into the calm water, he spied a *sea feather,* growing, as he judged, out of a rock; whereupon they bad one of their Indians to dive, and fetch this feather, that they might, however, carry home *something* with them, and make, at least, as fair a triumph as Caligula's.[22] The diver bringing up the feather, brought therewithal a surprizing story, that he perceived a number of great guns in the *watery world* where he had found his feather; the *report* of which *great guns* exceedingly astonished the whole company; and at once turned their despondencies for their ill success into *assurances* that they had now lit upon the *true spot* of ground which they had been looking for; and they were further confirmed in these assurances, when, upon further diving, the Indian fetcht up a *sow,* as they stiled it, or a lump of silver worth perhaps two or three hundred pounds. Upon this they prudently *buoyed* the place, that they might readily find it again; and they went back unto their captain, whom for some while they distressed with nothing but such *bad news* as they formerly thought they must have carried him: nevertheless, they so slipt in the sow of silver on one side under the table, where they were now sitting with the captain, and hearing him express his resolutions to wait still patiently upon the

[19] Demurrage: detaining of a vessel.
[20] Piragua.
[21] Adz, a chisel-like tool for dressing timbers or planks.

[22] Caligula: Roman emperor (A.D. 37–41) who gathered seashells as souvenirs of an abandoned military campaign in Germany.

providence of God under these disappointments, that when he should look on one side, he might see that *odd thing* before him. At last he *saw* it; seeing it, he cried out with some agony, "Why! what is this? whence comes this?" And then, with changed countenances, they told him *how* and where they got it. "Then," said he, "thanks be to God! we are made;" and so away they went, all hands to work; wherein they had this one further piece of remarkable prosperity, that whereas if they had first fallen upon that part of the Spanish wreck where the pieces of eight had been stowed in bags among the ballast, they had seen a more laborious, and less enriching time of it; now, most happily, they first fell upon that room in the wreck where the bullion had been stored up; and they so prospered in this *new fishery,* that in a little while they had, without the loss of any man's life, brought up *thirty-two tuns* of silver; for it was now come to measuring of silver by *tuns.* Besides which, one Adderly, of Providence, who had formerly been very helpful to Captain Phips in the search of this wreck, did, upon former agreement, meet him now with a little vessel here; and *he,* with his few hands, took up about *six tuns* of silver; whereof, nevertheless, he made so little use, that in a year or two he died at Bermudas, and, as I have heard, he ran *distracted* some while before he died. Thus did there once again come into the light of the sun a treasure which had been half an hundred years *groaning under the waters:* and in this time there was grown upon the plate a crust like limestone, to the thickness of several inches; which crust being broken open by iron contrived for that purpose, they knocked out whole bushels of rusty pieces of eight which were grown thereinto. Besides that incredible treasure of plate in various forms, thus fetched up, from seven or eight fathom under water, there were vast riches of *gold,* and *pearls* and *jewels,* which they also lit upon; and, indeed, for a more comprehensive *invoice,* I must but summarily say, "All that a Spanish frigot uses to be enriched withal." Thus did they continue *fishing* till their provisions failing them, 'twas time to be gone; but before they went, Captain Phips caused Adderly and his folk to swear, that they would none of them discover[23] the place of the wreck, or come to the place any more till the next year, when he expected again to be there himself. And it was also remarkable, that though the sows came up still so fast, that on the very last day of their being there they took up twenty, yet it was afterwards found, that they had in a manner wholly cleared that room of the ship where those *massy things* were stowed.

But there was one extraordinary distress which Captain Phips now found himself plunged into: for his men were come out with him upon seamen's wages, at so much *per* month; and when they saw such vast litters of silver *sows* and *pigs,* as they called them, come on board them at the captain's call, they knew not how to bear it, that they should not *share* all among themselves, and be gone to lead "a short life and a merry," in a climate where the arrest of those that had hired them should not reach them. In this terrible distress he made his vows unto Almighty God, that if the Lord would carry him safe home to England with what *he* had now given him, "to suck of the abundance of the seas, and of the treasures hid in the sands,"[24] he would for ever devote himself unto the interests of the Lord Jesus Christ and of his people, especially in the country which he did himself originally belong unto. And he then used all the obliging arts imaginable to make his men true unto him, especially by assuring them that, besides their wages, they should have ample *requitals* made unto

---

[23] I.e., reveal or disclose.

[24] Deuteronomy 33:19.

them; which if the rest of his employers would not agree unto, he would himself distribute his *own share* among them. Relying upon the word of one whom they had ever found worthy of their *love,* and of their *trust,* they declared themselves *content;* but still keeping a most careful eye upon them, he hastened back for England with as much *money* as he thought he could then safely *trust* his vessel withal; not counting it safe to supply himself with necessary provisions at any nearer port, and so return unto the wreck, by which delays he wisely feared lest all might be lost, more ways than one. Though he also left so much behind him, that many from divers parts made very considerable voyages of *gleanings* after his *harvest;* which came to pass by certain Bermudians compelling of Adderly's boy, whom they *spirited* away with them, to tell them the exact place where the wreck was to be found. Captain Phips now coming up to London in the year 1687, with near *three hundred thousand pounds sterling* aboard him, did acquit himself with such an exemplary honesty, that partly by his fulfilling his assurances to the seamen, and partly by his exact and punctual care to have his employers defrauded of nothing that might conscientiously belong unto them, he had less than *sixteen thousand pounds* left unto himself; as an acknowledgment of which *honesty* in him, the Duke of Albemarle made unto his wife, whom he never saw, a present of a golden cup, near a thousand pound in value. The character of an *honest man* he had so merited in the whole course of his life, and especially in this last act of it, that this, in conjunction with his other serviceable qualities, procured him the favours of the greatest persons in the nation; and "he that had been so diligent in his business, must now stand before Kings, and not stand before mean men."[25] There were indeed certain mean men—if base, little, dirty tricks, will entitle men to meanness —who urged the King to seize his whole cargo, instead of the tenths, upon his first arrival; on this pretence, that he had not been rightly informed of the *true state of the case* when he granted the patent, under the protection whereof these particular men had made themselves masters of all this mighty treasure; but the King replied, that he had been rightly informed by Captain Phips of the whole matter, as it now proved; and that it was the slanders of one then present which had, unto his damage, hindred him from hearkning to the information; wherefore he would give them, he said, no disturbance; they might keep what they had got; but Captain Phips, he saw, was a person of that honesty, fidelity and ability, that he should not want his countenance. Accordingly the King, in consideration of the service done by him, in bringing such a treasure into the nation, conferred upon him the honour of knighthood; and if we now reckon him a *knight of the golden fleece,* the stile might pretend unto some circumstances that would justifie it. Or call him, if you please, "the knight of honesty;" for it was *honesty* with *industry* that raised him; and he became a mighty river, without the running in of muddy water to make him so. Reader, now make a pause, and behold *one raised by God!*

7. I am willing to employ the testimonies of others, as much as may be, to support the credit of my history: and therefore, as I have hitherto related no more than what there are others enough to avouch; thus I shall chuse the words of an ingenious person, printed at London some years ago, to express the sum of what remains, whose words are these:

[25] Proverbs 22:29.

"It has always been Sir William Phips' disposition to seek the *wealth* of his people with as great zeal and unweariedness, as our publicans use to seek their *loss* and *ruin*. At first it seems they were in hopes to gain this gentleman to their party, as thinking him good-natured, and easie to be flattered out of his understanding; and the more, because they had the advantage of some no very good treatment, that Sir William had formerly met with from the people and government of New-England. But Sir William soon shewed them that what they expected would be his temptation to lead them into their little tricks, he embraced as a glorious opportunity to shew his *generosity* and *greatness of mind;* for in imitation of the greatest worthies that have ever been, he rather chose to join in the defence of his country, with some persons who formerly were none of his friends, than become the head of a *faction,* to its ruin and desolation. It seems this noble disposition of Sir William, joined with that capacity and good success wherewith he hath been attended, in raising himself by such an occasion as it may be, all things considered, has *never happened to any before him,* makes these men apprehensive;—and it must needs heighten their trouble to see that he neither hath, nor doth spare himself, nor any thing that is near and dear unto him, in promoting the good of his native country."

When Sir William Phips was, *per ardua et aspera* ["along steep and rugged paths"], thus raised into an *higher orb,* it might easily be thought that he could not be without charming temptations to take the way on the left hand. But as the grace of God kept him, in the midst of none of the strictest company, unto which his affairs daily led him, from abandoning himself to the lewd vices of gaming, drinking, swearing, and whoring, which the men "that made England to sin" debauched so many of the gentry into, and he deserved the salutations of the Roman poet:

> Cum Tu, inter scabiem tantam et Contagia Lucri,
> Nil parvum sapias, et adhuc Sublimia cures.[26]

Thus he was worthy to pass among the instances of heroick vertue for that humility that still adorned him: he was *raised,* and though he prudently accommodated himself to the *quality* whereto he was now raised, yet none could perceive him to be *lifted up.* Or, if this were not *heroick,* yet I will relate one thing more of him that must certainly be accounted so. He had, in his own country of New-England, met with *provocations* that were enough to have alienated any man living, that had no more than flesh and blood in him, from the service of it; and some that were enemies to that country now lay hard at him to join with them in their endeavours to ravish away their ancient liberties. But this gentleman had studied another way to *revenge* himself upon his country, and that was to serve it, in all *its* interests, with all of *his,* even with his *estate,* his time, his care, his *friends,* and his very *life!* The old heathen vertue of PIETAS IN PATRIAM, or, Love to one's country, he turned into Christian; and so notably exemplified it, in all the rest of his life, that it will be an essential thread which is to be now interwoven into all that remains of his *history* and his *character.*

---

[26] Horace (65–68 B.C.): "That spreading leprosy, the Lust of Gain, / Thy nobler spirit dares not to pollute; / But wiser wishes in thy heart remain, / And dignify thy life's sublime pursuit."

Accordingly, though he had the offers of a very gainful place among the commissioners of the navy, with many other invitations to settle himself in England, nothing but a return to New-England would content him. . . .

Sir William Phips was now invested with a commission under the King's broad-seal to be captain-general and governour in chief over the province of the Massachuset-bay in New-England: nor do I know a person in the world that could have been proposed more acceptable to the body of the people throughout New-England, and on that score more likely and able to serve the King's interests among the people there. . . .

[The Witchcraft Trials in Salem]

16. About the time of our blessed Lord's coming to reside on earth, we read of so many "possessed with devils," that it is commonly thought the *number* of such miserable *energumens*[27] was then encreased above what has been usual in other ages; and the *reason* of that increase has been made a matter of some enquiry. Now, though the *devils* might herein design by *preternatural operations* to blast the *miracles* of our Lord Jesus Christ, which point they gained among the blasphemous Pharisees; and the devils might herein also design a villanous imitation of what was coming to pass in the *incarnation* of our Lord Jesus Christ, wherein God came to *dwell in flesh;* yet I am not without suspicion, that there may be something further in the conjecture of the learned Bartholinus[28] hereupon, who says, It was *Quod judæi præter modum, Artibus Magicis dediti Dæmonem Advocaverint*—the Jews, by the frequent use of *magical tricks,* called in the devils among them.

It is very certain, there were hardly any people in the world grown more fond of *sorceries* than that unhappy people: the *Talmuds*[29] tell us of the little *parchments* with words upon them, which were their common *amulets,* and of the *charms* which they muttered over *wounds,* and of the various *enchantments* which they used against all sorts of disasters whatsoever. It is affirmed in the Talmuds, that no less than twenty-four scholars in one school were killed by *witchcraft;* and that no less than fourscore persons were hanged for *witchcraft* by one judge in one day. The *gloss* adds upon it, "That the women of Israel had generally fallen to the practice of witchcrafts;" and therefore it was required, that there should be still chosen into the council one skilful in the *arts of sorcerers,* and able thereby to discover who might be guilty of those *black arts* among such as were accused before them.

Now, the arrival of Sir William Phips to the government of New-England, was at a time when a governour would have had occasion for all the skill in *sorcery* that was ever necessary to a Jewish Counsellor; a time when scores of poor people had newly fallen under a prodigious *possession of devils,* which it was then generally thought had been by witchcrafts introduced. It is to be confessed and bewailed, that many inhabitants of New-England, and young people especially, had been led away with little *sorceries,* wherein they "did secretly those things that were not right against the Lord their God;" they would often cure hurts with *spells,* and practice detestable

---

[27] Persons possessed by devils.
[28] Caspar Bartholin (1585–1629), Dutch medical scholar who wrote on anatomy and astrology.

[29] Collection of Jewish law and tradition.

conjurations with *sieves,* and *keys,* and *pease,* and *nails,* and *horse-shoes,* and other implements, to learn the things for which they had a forbidden and impious curiosity. Wretched books had stoln into the land, wherein fools were instructed how to become able fortune-tellers: among which, I wonder that a blacker brand is not set upon that fortune-telling wheel, which that sham-scribler that goes under the letters of R. B.[30] has promised in his *"Delights for the Ingenious,"* as an *honest and pleasant recreation;* and by these books, the minds of many had been so poisoned, that they studied this *finer witchcraft;* until 'tis well if some of them were not betrayed into what is grosser, and more sensible and capital. Although these *diabolical divinations* are more ordinarily committed perhaps all over the *whole world,* than they are in the country of New-England, yet, that being a country devoted unto the worship and service of the Lord JESUS CHRIST above the *rest of the world,* HE signalized his vengeance against these wickednesses, with such extraordinary dispensations as have not been often seen in other places.

The *devils* which had been so played withal, and, it may be, by some few criminals more explicitly engaged and imployed, now broke in upon the country, after as astonishing a manner as was ever heard of. Some scores of people, first about Salem, the centre and first-born of all the towns in the colony, and afterwards in several other places, were arrested with many *preternatural vexations* upon their bodies, and a variety of cruel torments, which were evidently inflicted from the *dæmons* of the *invisible world.* The people that were infected and infested with such dæmons, in a few days' time arrived unto such a *refining alteration* upon their eyes, that they could see their tormentors: they saw a *devil* of a little *stature,* and of a tawny *colour,* attended still with spectres that appeared in more humane circumstances.

These *tormentors* tendred unto the afflicted a *book,* requiring them to *sign* it, or to *touch* it at least, in token of their consenting to be listed in the service of the devil; which they refusing to do, the spectres under the command of that *blackman,* as they called him, would apply themselves to torture them with prodigious molestations.

The afflicted wretches were horribly *distorted* and *convulsed;* they were *pinched* black and blue: *pins* would be run every where in their flesh; they would be *scalded* until they had *blisters* raised on them; and a thousand other things before hundreds of witnesses were done unto them, evidently *preternatural:* for if it were *preternatural* to keep a rigid *fast* for *nine,* yea, for *fifteen* days together; or if it were *preternatural* to have one's hands *tyed* close together with a rope to be plainly seen, and then by *unseen hands* presently pulled up a great way from the earth before a croud of people; such *preternatural* things were endured by them.

But of all the preternatural things which befel these people, there were none more *unaccountable* than those wherein the prestigious dæmons would ever now and then cover the most *corporeal* things in the world with a *fascinating mist* of *invisibility.* As now; a person was cruelly assaulted by a spectre, that, she said, run at her with a *spindle,* though no body else in the room could see either the spectre or the spindle: at last, in her agonies, giving a snatch at the spectre, she pulled the *spindle* away; and it was no sooner got into her hand, but the other folks then present beheld that it was indeed a real, proper, iron spindle; which, when they locked up very safe, it was nevertheless by the *dæmons* taken away to do farther mischief.

[30] Pseudonym for Nathaniel Crouch.

Again, a person was haunted by a most abusive spectre, which came to her, she said, with a *sheet* about her, though seen to none but her self. After she had undergone a deal of teaze from the annoyance of the spectre, she gave a violent *snatch* at the sheet that was upon it; where-from she tore a corner, which in her hand immediately was beheld by all that were present, a palpable corner of a sheet: and her father, which was now holding of her, *catched,* that he might *keep* what his daughter had so strangely seized; but the spectre had like to have wrung his hand off, by endeavouring to wrest it from him; however, he still held it, and several times this odd accident was renewed in the family. There wanted not the *oaths* of good credible people to these particulars.

Also, it is well known, that these wicked spectres did proceed so far as to steal several quantities of money from divers people, part of which individual money was dropt sometimes out of the air, before sufficient *spectators,* into the hands of the afflicted, while the spectres were urging them to subscribe their *covenant with death.* Moreover, *poisons* to the standers-by, wholly *invisibly,* were sometimes forced upon the afflicted; which when they have with much reluctancy swallowed, they have *swoln* presently, so that the common medicines for poisons have been found necessary to relieve them: yea, sometimes the spectres, in the *struggles,* have so dropt the poisons, that the standers-by have smelt them, and viewed them, and beheld the pillows of the miserable stained with them.

Yet more: the miserable have complained bitterly of *burning rags* run into their forceably distended *mouths;* and though nobody could see any such *clothes,* or indeed any *fires* in the chambers, yet presently the *scalds* were seen plainly by every body on the mouths of the complainers, and not only the *smell,* but the *smoke* of the burning sensibly filled the chambers.

Once more: the miserable exclaimed extreamly of *branding irons* heating at the fire on the hearth to mark them. Now, though the standers-by could see no irons, yet they could see distinctly the print of them in the ashes, and *smell* them too as they were carried by the *not-seen furies* unto the poor creatures for whom they were intended; and those poor creatures were thereupon so *stigmatized* with them, that they will bear the *marks* of them to their dying day. Nor are these the *tenth part* of the *prodigies* that fell out among the inhabitants of New-England.

Flashy people may burlesque these things, but when hundreds of the most sober people in a country where they have as much *mother-wit* certainly as the rest of mankind, know them to be *true,* nothing but the absurd and froward spirit of Sadducism[31] can question them. I have not yet mentioned so much as one thing that will not be justified, if it be required by the *oaths* of more considerate persons than any that can ridicule these odd *phænomena.*

But the worst part of this astonishing tragedy is yet behind; wherein Sir William Phips, at last being dropt, as it were from the *machin of heaven,* was an instrument of easing the distresses of the land, now "so darkened by the wrath of the Lord of Hosts." There were very worthy men upon the spot where the *assault from hell* was first made, who apprehended themselves called from the God of heaven to sift the business unto the bottom of it; and, indeed, the continual *impressions,* which the outcries and the havocks of the *afflicted people* that lived nigh unto them caused on their minds, gave no little edge to this apprehension.

---

[31] Sadducees denied the existence of spirits.

The persons were men eminent for wisdom and virtue, and they went about their enquiry into the matter, as *driven* unto it by a conscience of duty to God and the world. They did in the first place take it for granted that there are *witches,* or wicked children of men, who upon *covenanting* with, and *commissioning* of *evil spirits,* are attended by their ministry to accomplish the things desired of them: to satisfie them in which perswasion, they had not only the *assertions* of the holy Scriptures—assertions which the witch-advocates cannot evade without shifts, too foolish for the *prudent,* or too profane for any *honest* man to use—and they had not only the well-attested *relations* of the gravest authors, from Bodin to Bovet, and from Binsfield to Brombal and Baxter—to deny all which, would be as reasonable as to turn the chronicles of all nations into romances of *"Don Quixote"*[32] and the *"Seven Champions;"*[33] but they had also an *ocular demonstration* in one who, a little before, had been executed for witchcraft, when Joseph Dudley, Esq. was the chief-judge. There was one whose *magical images* were found, and who, *confessing her deeds,* (when a jury of doctors returned her *compos mentis*) actually shewed the whole court by what *ceremonies* used unto them she directed her *familiar spirits* how and where to cruciate the objects of her malice; and the experiment being made over and over again before the whole court, the *effect* followed exactly in the hurts done to the people at a distance from her. The existence of such witches was now taken for granted by those good men, wherein so far the generality of reasonable men have thought *they ran well;*[34] and they soon received the *confessions* of some *accused* persons to confirm them in it: but then they took one thing more for granted, wherein 'tis now as generally thought they *went out of the way.* The afflicted people vehemently accused several persons in several places that the spectres which afflicted them, did exactly resemble them; until the importunity of the accusations did provoke the magistrates to examine them. When many of the *accused* came upon their examination, it was found that the *dæmons* then a thousand ways abusing of the poor afflicted people, had with a marvellous exactness *represented* them; yea, it was found, that many of the *accused,* but casting their eye on the *afflicted,* the *afflicted,* though their faces were never so much another way, would fall down and lye in a sort of a swoon, wherein they would continue, whatever hands were laid upon them, until the hands of the *accused* came to touch them, and *then* they would revive immediately; and it was found, that various kinds of *natural actions,* done by many of the *accused* in or to their own bodies, as leaning, bending, turning awry, or squeezing their hands, or the like, were presently attended with the like things *preternaturally* done upon the bodies of the *afflicted,* though they were so far asunder, that the afflicted could not at all observe the accused.

It was also found, that the flesh of the afflicted was often *bitten* at such a rate, that not only the *print of teeth* would be left on their flesh, but the very *slaver* of spittle too; and there would appear just such a *set of teeth* as was in the accused, even such as might be clearly distinguished from other peoples. And usually the afflicted went through a terrible deal of seeming difficulties from the tormenting spectres, and must be long waited on before they could get a breathing space from their *torments* to give in their testimonies.

[32] *Don Quixote de la Mancha* (1605) by Miguel de Cervantes.
[33] *The Famous History of the Seven Champions*
of Christendom (1596) by Richard Johnson.
[34] I.e., they were right.

Now, many good men took up an opinion, that the *providence* of God would not permit an innocent person to come under such a spectral representation; and that a concurrence of so many circumstances would prove an accused person to be in a *confederacy* with the dæmons thus afflicting of the neighbours; they judged that, except these things might amount unto a conviction, it would scarce be possible ever to *convict a witch:* and they had some *philosophical schemes of witchcraft,* and of the method and manner wherein *magical poisons* operate, which further supported them in their opinion.

Sundry of the accused persons were brought unto their trial, while this opinion was yet prevailing in the minds of the judges and the juries, and perhaps the most of the people in the country, then mostly suffering; and though against some of them that were tried there came in so much *other evidence* of their diabolical compacts, that some of the most *judicious,* and yet *vehement* opposers of the notions then in vogue, publickly declared, "Had they themselves been on the bench, they could not have acquitted them;" nevertheless, divers were condemned, against whom the *chief evidence* was founded in the *spectral exhibitions.*

And it happening that some of the accused coming to confess themselves *guilty,* their *shapes* were no more seen by any of the afflicted, though the confession had been kept never so secret, but instead thereof the accused themselves became in all vexations just like the afflicted; this yet more confirmed many in the opinion that had been taken up.

And another thing that quickened them yet more to act upon it, was, that the afflicted were frequently entertained with *apparitions* of *ghosts* at the same time that the *spectres* of the supposed *witches* troubled them; which *ghosts* always cast the beholders into far more consternation than any of the *spectres;* and when they exhibited themselves, they cried out of being *murdered* by the *witchcrafts,* or other violences of the persons represented in the *spectres.* Once or twice these apparitions were seen by others at the very same time that they shewed themselves to the afflicted; and seldom were they seen at all but when something unusual and suspicious had attended the death of the party thus appearing.

The *afflicted* people many times had never heard any thing before of the persons appearing in *ghost,* or the persons *accused* by the *apparitions;* and yet the accused upon examination have confessed the murders of those very persons, though these accused also knew nothing of the apparitions that had come in against them; and the afflicted persons likewise, without any private agreement or collusion, when successively brought into a room, have all asserted the same *apparitions* to be there before them: these murders did seem to call for an enquiry.

On the other part, there were many persons of great judgment, piety and experience, who from the beginning were very much dissatisfied at these proceedings; they feared lest the *devil* would get so far into the *faith* of the people, that for the sake of many *truths* which they might find him telling of them, they would come at length to believe all his *lies;* whereupon what a desolation of names—yea, and of lives also —would ensue, a man might, without much witchcraft, be able to prognosticate; and they feared, lest in such an extraordinary descent of wicked spirits from their high places upon us, there might such *principles* be taken up, as, when put into *practice,* would unavoidably cause the *righteous to perish with the wicked,* and procure the blood-shed of persons like the Gibeonites, whom some learned men suppose to be under a false pretence of witchcraft, by Saul exterminated.[35]

However uncommon it might be for *guiltless persons* to come under such unaccountable circumstances, as were on so many of the accused, they held "some things there are, which, if suffered to be common, would subvert government, and disband and ruin humane society, yet God sometimes may suffer such things to evene, that we may know thereby how much we are beholden to him for that restraint which he lays upon the infernal spirits, who would else reduce a world into a chaos." They had already known of one at the town of Groton hideously agitated by *devils,* who in her fits cried out much against a very godly woman in the town, and when that woman approached unto her, though the eyes of the creature were never so shut, she yet manifested a violent sense of her approach: but when the gracious woman thus impeached, had prayed earnestly with and for this creature, then, instead of crying out against her any more, she owned, that she had in all been deluded by the *devil.* They now saw, that the more the *afflicted* were hearkened unto, the more the number of the *accused* encreased; until at last many scores were *cried out* upon, and among them, some who, by the unblameableness—yea, and serviceableness—of their whole conversation, had obtained the just reputation of *good people* among all that were acquainted with them. The character of the afflicted likewise added unto the common distaste; for though some of *them* too were *good people,* yet others of them, and such of them as were most flippent at *accusing,* had a far other character.

In fine, the country was in a dreadful *ferment,* and wise men foresaw a long train of dismal and bloody consequences. Hereupon they first advised that the afflicted might be kept asunder in the closest privacy; and one particular person, (whom I have cause to know,) in pursuance of this advice, offered himself singly to provide accommodations for any six of them, that so the success of more than ordinary *prayer* with *fasting* might, with *patience,* be *experienced,* before any other courses were taken.

And Sir William Phips arriving to his government, after this *ensnaring horrible storm* was begun, did consult the neighbouring ministers of the province, who made unto his Excellency and the council a return, (drawn up at their desire by Mr. Mather the younger, as I have been informed) wherein they declared:

"We judge, that in the prosecution of these and all such *witchcrafts,* there is need of a very critical and exquisite caution: lest by too much credulity for things received only upon the *devil's authority,* there be a door opened for a long train of miserable consequences, and Satan get an advantage over us; for we should not be ignorant of his devices.

"As in complaints upon *witchcrafts,* there may be matters of *enquiry,* which do not amount unto matters of *presumption;* and there may be matters of *presumption,* which yet may not be reckoned matters of *conviction;* so 'tis necessary that all proceedings thereabout be managed with an *exceeding tenderness*

---

[35] 2 Samuel 21:1–6. Saul's reason for the execution of the Gibeonites is a matter of speculation.

towards those that may be complained of: especially if they have been persons formerly of an *unblemished reputation.*

"When the *first enquiry* is made into the circumstances of such as may lye under any just suspicion of *witchcrafts,* we could wish that there may be admitted as little as is possible of such *noise, company,* and *openness* as may too hastily expose them that are examined: and that there may nothing be used as a *test* for the trial of the suspected, the lawfulness whereof may be doubted among the people of God: but that the directions given by such judicious writers as Perkins and Bernard, be consulted in such a case.

"*Presumptions,* whereupon persons may be committed, and much more *convictions,* whereupon persons may be condemned as guilty of *witchcrafts,* ought certainly to be more considerable, than barely the *accused* person's being *represented* by a *spectre* to the afflicted: inasmuch as it is an undoubted and a notorious thing, that a dæmon may, by God's permission, appear even to ill purposes in the shape of an *innocent,* yea, and a *virtuous* man: nor can we esteem *alterations* made in the *sufferers,* by a *look* or *touch* of the accused, to be an infallible evidence of guilt: but frequently liable to be abused by the devil's *legerdemains.*[36]

"We know not whether some *remarkable affronts* given to the *devils,* by our dis-believing of those testimonies whose whole force and strength is from *them* alone, may not put a period unto the progress of a direful calamity begun upon us, in the *accusation* of so many persons, whereof, we hope, some are yet *clear from the great transgression* laid unto their charge."

The ministers of the province also being jealous lest this counsel should not be duly followed, requested the President of Harvard-Colledge to compose and publish (which he did) some *cases of conscience* referring to these difficulties: in which treatise he did, with demonstrations of incomparable *reason* and *reading,* evince it, that Satan may appear in the shape of an innocent and a virtuous person, to afflict those that suffer by the *diabolical molestations:* and that the *ordeal* of the *sight,* and the *touch,* is not a conviction of a *covenant* with the devil, but liable to great exceptions against the *lawfulness,* as well as the *evidence* of it: and that either a free and fair *confession* of the criminals, or the oath of two credible persons proving such things against the person accused, as none but such as have a familiarity with the devil can know, or do, is necessary to the proof of the crime. Thus,

Cum misit Natura Feras, et Monstra per Orbem,
Misit et Alciden qui fera Monstra domet.[37]

The Dutch and French ministers in the province of New-York, having likewise about the same time their judgment asked by the Chief Judge of that province, who was then a gentleman of New-England, they gave it in under their hands, that if we believe no *venefick witchcraft,* we must renounce the Scripture of God, and the *consent* of almost all the world; but that yet the *apparition* of a person afflicting another, is a very insufficient proof of a *witch;* nor is it inconsistent with the holy and righteous

---

[36] Sleight-of-hand magic.
[37] Latin: "Nature sent monsters throughout the world, / but she also sent Hercules to subjugate them."

government of God over men, to permit the affliction of the neighbours, by devils, in the *shape* of *good men;* and that a *good name,* obtained by a *good life,* should not be lost by meer *spectral accusations.*

Now, upon a deliberate review of these things, his Excellency first *reprieved,* and then *pardoned* many of them that had been condemned; and there fell out several strange things that caused the spirit of the country to run as vehemently upon the *acquitting* of all the accused, as it by mistake ran at first upon the *condemning* of them. Some that had been zealously of the mind, that the devils could not in the shapes of good men afflict other men, were terribly confuted, by having their own shapes, and the shapes of their most intimate and valued friends, thus abused. And though more than twice twenty had made such voluntary, and harmonious, and uncontroulable confessions, that if they were all *sham,* there was therein the greatest violation made by the efficacy of the *invisible world,* upon the *rules of understanding humane affairs,* that was ever seen since "God made man upon the earth," yet they did so recede from their confessions, that it was very clear, some of them had been hitherto, in a sort of a *preternatural dream,* wherein they had said *of themselves,* they *knew not what themselves.*

In fine, the last courts that sate upon this *thorny business,* finding that it was impossible to penetrate into the whole meaning of the things that had happened, and that so many *unsearchable cheats* were interwoven into the *conclusion* of a mysterious business, which perhaps had not crept thereinto at the *beginning* of it, they *cleared* the accused as fast as they *tried* them; and within a little while the afflicted were most of them delivered out of their troubles also; and the land had peace restored unto it, by the "God of peace, treading Satan under foot." Erasmus, among other historians, does tell us, that at a town in Germany, a dæmon appeared on the top of a chimney, threatned that he would set the town on fire, and at length scattering some ashes abroad, the whole town was presently and horribly burnt unto the ground.

Sir William Phips now beheld such dæmons hideously scattering *fire* about the country, in the exasperations which the minds of men were on these things rising unto; and therefore when he had well canvased a *cause,* which perhaps might have puzzled the wisdom of the wisest men on earth to have managed, without any *error* in their administrations, he thought, if it would be any *error* at all, it would certainly be the *safest* for him to put a stop unto all future prosecutions, as far as it lay in him to do it.

He did so, and for it he had not only the printed acknowledgments of the New-Englanders, who publickly thanked him, "As one of the tribe of Zebulun, raised up from among themselves, and *spirited* as well as *commissioned* to be the *steers-man* of a vessel befogged in the *mare mortuum* [38] of witchcraft, who now so happily steered her course, that she escaped shipwreck, and was safely again moored under the Cape of *Good Hope;* and cut asunder the Circæan knot of enchantment, more difficult to be dissolved than the famous Gordian one of old."[39]

But the Queen also did him the honour to write unto him those gracious letters, wherein her Majesty commended his conduct in these *inexplicable* matters. And I did

---

[38] Latin: "Dead Sea."
[39] In Greek myth, the enchantress Circe turned men into swine; the Gordian knot (tied by the ancient king Gordius of Phrygia) was cut rather than untied by Alexander the Great.

right in calling these matters *inexplicable.* For if, after the kingdom of Sweden (in the year 1669, and 1670,) had some hundreds of their children by night often carried away by *spectres* to an *hellish rendezvous,* where the monsters that so *spirited* them, did every way *tempt* them to associate with them; and the Judges of the kingdom, after extraordinary supplications to Heaven, upon a strict enquiry, were so satisfied with the confessions of more than twenty of the accused, agreeing exactly unto the depositions of the afflicted, that they put several scores of *witches* to death, whereupon the confusions came unto a period; yet after all, the chiefest persons in the kingdom would question whether there were any *witchcrafts* at all in the whole affair; it must not be wondered at, if the people of New-England are to this hour full of *doubts,* about the *steps* which were taken, while a *war* from the *invisible world* was terrifying of them; and whether they did not kill some of their *own side* in the *smoke* and *noise* of this dreadful war. And it will be yet less wondred at, if we consider, that we have seen the whole English nation alarumed with a *plot,* and both Houses of Parliament, upon good grounds, voting their sense of it, and many persons most justly *hanged, drawn,* and *quartered,* for their share in it: when yet there are enough who to this day will pretend that they cannot comprehend how much of it is to be accounted *credible.* However, having related these wonderful passages, whereof, if the *veracity* of the relator in any one point be contested, there are whole *clouds of witnesses* to vindicate it, I will take my leave of the matter with an wholesome caution of Lactantius, which, it may be, some other parts of the world besides New-England may have occasion to think upon: *Efficiunt Dæmones, ut quæ non sunt, sic tamen, quasi sint, conspicienda Hominibus exhibeant.*[40] . . .

[A Picture of Phips]

18. Reader, 'tis time for us to view a little more to the *life,* the *picture* of the person, the *actions* of whose *life* we have hitherto been looking upon. Know then, that for his *exterior,* he was one *tall,* beyond the common set of men, and *thick* as well as *tall,* and *strong* as well as *thick:* he was, in all respects, exceedingly *robust,* and able to conquer such difficulties of *diet* and of *travel,* as would have killed most men alive: nor did the *fat,* whereinto he grew very much in his later years, take away the vigour of his motions.

He was well set, and he was therewithal of a very *comely,* though a very *manly* countenance: a countenance where any true skill in *physiognomy* would have read the characters of a *generous mind.* Wherefore passing to his *interior,* the very first thing which there offered it self unto observation, was a most incomparable *generosity.*

And of this, besides the innumerable instances which he gave in his usual hatred of *dirty* or *little* tricks, there was one instance for which I must freely say, "I never saw three men in this world that equalled him:" this was his wonderfully *forgiving spirit.* In the vast variety of business, through which he raced in his time, he met with many and mighty *injuries:* but although I have heard all that the most venemous *malice* could ever *hiss* at his memory, I never did hear unto this hour that he did ever once deliberately *revenge an injury.*

[40] Lactantius (A.D. 240–320): "Evil spirits make men believe in illusions."

Upon certain *affronts* he has made sudden *returns* that have shewed *choler* enough, and he has by *blow,* as well as by *word,* chastised incivilities: he was, indeed, sufficiently impatient of being *put upon;* and when *base men,* surprizing him at some *disadvantages* (for else few men durst have done it) have sometimes drawn upon him, he has, without the *wicked madness* of a *formal duel,* made them feel that he knew how to *correct fools.* Nevertheless, he ever declined a deliberate revenge of a wrong done unto him; though few men upon earth have, in their vicissitudes, been furnished with such frequent opportunities of revenge as Heaven brought into the hands of this gentleman.

Under great provocations, he would commonly say, " 'Tis no matter; let them alone; some time or other they'll see their weakness and rashness, and have occasion for me to do them a kindness; and they shall then see I have quite forgotten all their baseness." Accordingly, 'twas remarkable to see it, that few men ever did *him* a *mischief,* but those men afterwards had occasion for him to do *them* a *kindness:* and he did the kindness with as forgetful a bravery, as if the mischief had never been done at all. The Emperor Theodosius himself could not be readier to forgive; so worthily did he verifie that observation:

> Quo quisque est major, magis est placabilis ira,
> Et faciles motus mens generosa capit.[41]

In those places of *power* whereto the providence of God by several *degrees* raised him, it still fell out so, that before his *rise* thereunto he underwent such things as he counted very hard *abuses,* from those very persons over whom the Divine Providence afterwards gave him the *ascendant.* . . .

Hence, upon frequent occasions of uneasiness in his government, he would chuse thus to express himself: "Gentlemen, were it not that I am to do service for the publick, I should be much easier in returning unto my broad-ax again!" And hence, according to the *affable* courtesie which he ordinarily used unto all sorts of persons, (quite contrary to the *asperity* which the old proverb expects in the *raised,*) he would particularly when sailing in sight of Kennebeck, with armies under his command, call the young soldiers and sailors upon deck, and speak to them after this fashion: "Young men, it was upon that hill that I kept sheep a few years ago; and since you see that Almighty God has brought me to something, do you learn to fear God, and be honest, and mind your business, and follow no bad courses, and you don't know what you may come to!" A temper not altogether unlike what the advanced *shepherd* had, when he wrote the twenty-third Psalm; or when he imprinted on the coin of his kingdom the remembrance of his old condition; for Christianus Gerson, a Christianized Jew, has informed us that on the one side of David's coin were to be seen his old pouch and crook, the instrument of shepherdy; on the other side were enstamped the towers of Zion.

1702

[41] Latin: "The noblest soul is never resentful long,
/ And with an easy instinct pardons wrong."

from Theopolis Americana

. . . I happen this very Day, among certain Papers in my Study, to take up a copy of a Letter sent from a Worthy Person here, to one in *England,* about Seventy years ago, in which Letter there is this remarkable *Passage: Here is a Temple built, more glorious than* Solomons; *not of Dead Stones, but Living Saints; which may tempt the greatest Queen of Sheba, to come and see, and allure, even Kings from far to come and Worship in.* ————We may allow for the *Rhetorick* of the passage, and yet say, The *Golden Work* of God in these His Churches, if we may *Mend* any part, in which we should go on to more of the *Kingdom* of *Heaven,* let us Humbly do it. But, Sirs, Do not *Spoil* it. Oh! *Destroy it not; There is a Blessing in it.*

PEOPLE of GOD, May these be your Cares. Then there will be fulfilled unto us that Word, Isa. 1:26: *Thou shalt be called, The City of Righteousness, The Faithful City.* A CITY of such a GOLDEN STREET, will be a *Strong City;* God will *appoint Salvation for Walls and bulwarks* unto it; while none but a *Righteous Nation, which keeps the Truth,* inhabits it. O NEW ENGLAND, Keep such a STREET, and *Sweep* it where it wants to be better kept. Then, there *will be no breaking in or going out;* there will be no *Complaining in our Street.* No, we shall be an *Happy People,* I say, *an Happy people,* for the LORD will be OUR GOD. I will say unto you, Joel 2.21: *Fear not, O Land, be glad, and rejoyce, for the* LORD *will do great things.* God will make our *Enimies* to be found *Lyars* and *Losers;* Our *Coast* will be under His Protection. There will none dare go up against the *Land of Unwalled Villages.* Our God will incline the Government of our Nation also, to Remember what a *Loyal People* we have always approv'd our selves, and to cherish these *Colonies* as *Daughters* to be highly accounted of. Yea, O *Holy City;* Thou shalt *Lay up Gold as Dust,* and *the Gold of Potosi*[1] *as the Stones of the Brooks: The Almighty shall be thy Defence, and thou shalt have a Plenty* of all that thou desirest.

I have been Surprised at the Reading of a Passage in a *Pagen* Writer, who flourished more than Fifteen Hundred years ago. Tis AElian,[2] a Grecian Writer, who says that in Times long preceding his, there was a Tradition that *Europe* and *Asia* and *Africa* were encompassed by the Ocean. But without and beyond the Ocean there was a *great Island,* as big as *They.* And in that Other World, there was an huge CITY, called Ευσεβυς, THE GODLY CITY. In that CITY, sayes he, they enjoy all possible *Peace* and *Health,* and *Plenty;* And, he Sayes, *They are without Controversy a very Righteous People*—So *Righteous,* that they have God marvellously coming down among them. I know not what well to make of a Tradition so very *Ancient,* and yet having Such an *American* Face upon it. All I will say, is thus much: There are many Arguments to perswade us, that our glorious LORD will have an HOLY CITY in AMERICA, a *City,* the STREET whereof will be *Pure* GOLD. We cannot imagine that the brave Countries and Gardens which fill the *American Hemisphere* were made for nothing but a *Place for Dragons.* We may not imagine that when the *Kingdom* of God is *come,* and His *Will is done on Earth as it is done in Heaven,* which we have

---

[1] City in Bolivia.
[2] Claudius AElian (fl. A.D. 200), author of *Historical Miscellanies.*

never been taught to Pray for, if it must not one day be accomplished, a *Ballancing Half of the Globe* shall remain in the Hands of the *Devil,* who is then to be *Chained up* from *deceiving the Nations.* Has it not been promised unto our Great Saviour? Psalm 2.8: *I will give thee the uttermost parts of the Earth for thy Possession.* And, Psal. 86.9: *All Nations whom thou hast made shall come and worship before thee, O Lord, and shall glorify thy Name. And has it not been promised?* Mal. 1.11: *From the Rising of the Sun even unto the going down of the same, my Name shall be great among the Gentiles.* AMERICA is Legible in these Promises. But if it be not here plainly enough expressed, what can be more plain than the Prophecy concerning the Kingdom of our Saviour? Dan. 2.44: *It shall break in pieces, and consume all these Kingdoms, and it shall stand for ever.* The Kingdom of our Saviour becoming *a Great Mountain, that must fill the* WHOLE EARTH, does particularly fill and Change and Bless those Countries, which belong to the *Ten Kingdoms of the Roman Empire,* in the Papal and Final Edition of it. Now, the *American* Countries do belong to some of those *Ten Kingdoms;* are become a considerable part of their *Dominions;* And therefore, tis most certain, the *Glorious Holy Mountain* will some of it stand in these Countries as well as in the *European.* There have been MARTYRS OF CHRIST in *America.* The Blood of the *Martyrs* here is an Omen that the Truths for which they Suffered are to Rise, and Live, and carry all before them in the Land that has been so *Marked* for the Lord. Such men as they will doubtless have some Glorious *Power over the Nations* where they have been such *Overcomers;* They that are to *Shine as the Stars,* will *turn many unto Righteousness;* bring many to believe on the *Sun of Righteousness,* in these *Goings down of the Sun.* Tho' *Austin* knew nothing of *America,* yet no *American* could have made a better Descant on the Mystery of our Lord's *Garments, made of Four Parts, to every Souldier a Part,* than his *Quadripartita Vestis Domini Jesu, quadripartitam figuravit Ejus Ecclesiam, toto Scilicet, qui quatuor partibus constat, terrarum Orbe diffisam.*[3] The World, says he, which does *consist of Four Parts,* will have the *Church* of our Lord JESUS in every Part. But O AMERICA, will no Share of the Lord's *Garments* and *Glories* and the *Righteousness of the Saints* fall to thee, who art a Part of the World singly almost as great as the *Other Three?* Yea, the Day is at hand when that Voice will be heard concerning *shee. Put on thy beautiful Garments, O America, the Holy City!* Certainly, It was never intended that the Church of our Lord should be confined always within the Dimensions of *Scrabo's* Cloak, and that *all the World* should always be no more than it was when *Augustus* taxed it. We are Sorry, we are Troubled, That the *Good Seed* of the WORD, falling on the other *Three Soyls,* has brought forst so little *Good Fruit,* and for so little a while. But our Glorious LORD will order that *Good Seed* ere long to be cast upon the Fertile Regions of *America,*[4] and it shall here find a *Good Ground* where it shall bring forth *Fruit* unto Astonishments, and unto Perpetuity! When our Lord uttered the Parable to which I have now alluded, we read, *He went into a Ship,* and from thence instructed the *Multitude that stood on the Shore.* I will believe that in this very *Action* there was a *Parable* and a *Prophesy.* By *Navigation* there will be brought the Word of a Glorious CHRIST unto a Multitude afar off, and as the *Ships cover the Sea, the Earth,* and thou, AMERICA, too, *Shall be filled with*

---

[3] According to St. Augustine (354–430), one of the early Church Fathers, the garments of Jesus were divided into four parts, prefiguring the four-part division of the Christian church.

[4] See the parable of the sower in Matthew 13:1–17 and Luke 8:11–15.

the knowledge of the glorious Lord. The Fall of Old Pagan *Babylon* was brought about by the Diversion of her *Euphrates* from her. The Fall of the New Popish *Babylon* will be accompanied with the Loss of her *American* Interest; but when 'tis diverted from her, certainly it will then serve the *City of God.* I will add this: When we critically Examine the *Accomplishment of the Prophecies* in the Judgments of the *Seven Trumpets,* whereof *Six* have done sounding, we shall find that by the SEA was meant *Portugal* and *Spain* and *France,* with the adjoyning *Islands* from the *Rhine* and the *Rhosne* to the Western Ocean, and the Peninsula of *Italy,* all which are almost wholly Encompassed with the *sea,* and mighty Rivers. I conceive we are now entring into the Dispensation of the *Seven Vials,*[5] one of the First whereof is *Poured out upon the Sea, and it becomes as the Blood of a Dead Man and every Living Soul dies in the Sea.* The most Obvious Application of it is to be trembled at!—But it is easy to draw Some *American* consequences. I wave them and only say, Tis thought by Some that *America* might be intended as a Place where the Worshippers of the Glorious JESUS may be Sheltered, while fearful Things are doing in the *European* World, and (as 'tis foretold it shall be!) *The Land shall be fearfully Emptied and Spoiled; The Curse will devour the Earth, and they that dwell therein will be desolate; the Inhabitants of the Earth will be burned, and few men will be left* (See the XXIV. of *Isaiah*). Whether it shall be so or no, we are sure there is a Day at hand, *When the Lord of Hosts will Reign among His Ancient People Gloriously.* In that Day, it will be impossible for the *Holy* People and the *Teachers* and *Rulers* of the *Reformed World* in the other *Hemisphere* to leave *America* unvisited. It will be impossible for a People so inspired from Heaven for the Propagation of true Christianity as will then be the *Stars* of that *Hemisphere,* to be unconcerned about *America,* and *all the Ends of the World that are to turn unto the Lord; all the Kindreds of the Nations that are to Worship before Him.* It will be impossible that the Effect of the Essayes used by Men filled with the SPIRIT of CHRIST, and able to do more than all that was done in the Primitive Times (For, *When He gives the Word, Great will be the Army of them that so Publish it!*), Should not be a conquest of *America,* ten thousand times more glorious than all that ever any *Cortez*[6] pretended unto. The *Kingdom* here will be *the Lord's,* and The Lord will be *Governour among the Nations.* When the Holy SPIRIT of God, that *River,* the *Streams* whereof are to *Make glad the City of God,* shall, as He will, Run down into and thorough the World, and make the World become a *Watered Garden* and an *Eden* for the *Lord from Heaven,* and *God shall dwell with men* by His Holy *Spirit* marvellously Possessing, and purifying, and Enlightening of them. Can you think that *America* shall be nothing but *Miery Places and Marshes, given to Salt?* By no means. O wide *Atlantick,* Thou shalt not stand in the way as any Hindrance of those Communications!

Verily, Our Glorious LORD will have Dominion from *Sea to Sea.* In those Days will the *Righteous flourish.* Then they who *dwell in the Wilderness* and even in *this* also *Shall bow before Him. They that are of the city* shall have something to do here for Him. O NEW ENGLAND, There is Room to hope That thou also shalt belong to the CITY. Thou hast already made a *Seihn* [sign] of *America,* on behalf of the Glorious LORD. It is in some sort His *Primier Seihn* [sign]. The *Seihn* [sign] *in Fact,* which the Son of GOD has taken of these *American* Territories is, we hope a *Seihn* [sign] *in Law* for all the rest. And certainly, Thou shalt not be cast off when He comes

[5] Reference to forthcoming Judgment Day. See Revelation 15:1–8; 16:2–21.

[6] Hernando Cortes (1485–1547), Spanish explorer and conqueror of Mexico.

into the *Actual Possession* of all the rest. Thy Name shall then be *Jehovah Shammah*, THE LORD IS THERE. And, *As we have heard, so shall we see, in the City of the Lord of Hosts, in the City of our God:* GOD *will establish it* for ever more.

The Design of my SERMON is To bespeak all possible *Anticipations* of this Felicity!

1710

---

from Bonifacius, an Essay upon the Good

[*from* **Chapter Three: Relative to Home and Neighborhood**]

11. The *useful man* may now with a very good grace, extend and enlarge the *sphere* of his consideration. My next PROPOSAL now shall be: Let every man consider the RELATION, wherein the Sovereign God has placed him, and let him *devise what good he may do,* that may render his *relatives,* the better for him. One great way to prove ourselves *really good,* is to be *relatively* good. By this, more than by anything in the world, it is, that we *adorn the doctrine of God our Saviour.* It would be an *excellent wisdom* in a man, to make the *interest* he has in the good opinion and affection of *anyone,* an *advantage* to do good service for God upon them: He that *has a friend* will show himself indeed *friendly,* if he thinks, "Such an one loves me, and will hearken to me; what good shall I take advantage hence to persuade him to?"

This will take place more particularly, where the endearing ties of *natural relation* do give us an *interest.* Let us call over our several *relations,* and let us have devices of something that may be called *heroical goodness,* in our discharging of them. Why should we not, at least once or twice in a *week,* make this *relational goodness,* the subject of our *inquiries,* and our *purposes?* Particularly, let us begin with our *domestic relations,* and *provide for those of our own house,* lest we deny some glorious rules and hopes of our Christian faith, in our negligence.

First, in the CONJUGAL RELATION, how agreeably may the *consorts* think on those words: "What knowest thou, O wife, whether thou shalt save thy husband?" Or, "How knowest thou, O man, whether thou shalt save thy wife?"

The HUSBAND will do well to think: "What shall I do, that my wife may have cause forever to bless God, for bringing her unto me?" And, "What shall I do that in my carriage towards my wife, the kindness of the blessed JESUS towards His Church, may be followed and resembled?" That this question may be the more perfectly answered, Sir, sometimes ask her to help you in the answer; ask her to tell you, what she would have you to do.

But then, the WIFE also will do well to think: "Wherein may I be to my husband, a wife of that character: she will do him good, and not evil, all the days of his life?" . . .

With my married people, I will particularly leave a good note, which I find in the Memorials of *Gervase Disney,* Esq. "Family passions, cloud faith, disturb duty, darken comfort." You'll do the more good unto one another, the more this note is thought upon. When the *husband* and *wife* are always contriving to be blessings unto one another, I will say with *Tertullian, Unde sufficiam ad enarrandam faelicitatem ejus matrimonii!*[1] O happy marriage!

PARENTS, Oh! how much ought you to be continually *devising,* and even *travailing,* for the *good* of your *children.* Often *devise:* how to make them *wise children;* how to carry on a desirable *education* for them; an *education* that shall render them desirable; how to render them lovely, and polite creatures, and *serviceable* in their generation. Often *devise,* how to enrich their minds with valuable *knowledge;* how to instill generous, and gracious, and heavenly *principles* into their minds; how to restrain and rescue them from the *paths of the Destroyer,* and fortify them against their *special temptations.* There is a world of *good,* that you have to do for them. You are without *bowels,* Oh! be not such *monsters!* if you are not in a continual agony to do for them all the *good* that ever you can. It was no mistake of *Pacatus Drepanius* in his panegyric to *Theodosius: Instituente natura plus fere filios quam nosmetipsos diligimus.*[2]

I will prosecute this matter, by transcribing a copy of PARENTAL RESOLUTIONS, which I have somewhere met withal.

I. "At the birth of my children, I would use all *explicit solemnity* in the *baptismal* dedication and consecration of them unto the LORD. I would present them to the BAPTISM of the Lord, not as a mere formality; but wondering at the grace of the infinite GOD, who will accept my children, as *His,* I would resolve to do all I can that they may be His. I would now actually give them up unto God; entreating, that the child may be a *child* of God the *Father,* a *subject* of God the *Son,* a temple of God the *Spirit,* and be rescued from the condition of a *child of wrath,* and be possessed and employed by the Lord as an everlasting instrument of His glory.

II. "My children are no sooner grown capable of minding the admonitions, but I would often, often admonish them to be sensible of their *baptismal engagements* to be the Lord's. Often tell them, of their *baptism,* and of what it binds 'em to: oftener far, and more times than there were *drops of water,* that were cast on the infant, upon that occasion!

"Often say to them, 'Child, you have been baptized; you were washed in the name of the great God; now you must not sin against Him; to sin is to do a dirty, a filthy thing.' Say, 'Child, you must every day cry to God that He would be your Father, and your Saviour, and your Leader; in your baptism He promised that He would be so, if you sought unto Him.' Say, 'Child, you must renounce the service of Satan, you must not follow the vanities of this world, you must lead a life of serious religion; in your baptism you were bound unto the service of your only Saviour.' Tell the child: 'What is your name; you must sooner forget this name, that was given you in your baptism, than forget that you are a servant of a glorious Christ whose name was put upon you in your baptism.'

III. "Let my *prayers* for my *children* be daily, with constancy, with fervency, with agony; yea, *by name* let me mention each one of them, every day before the Lord. I would importunately beg for all suitable blessings to be bestowed upon them: that God would *give them grace, and give them glory, and withhold no good thing from them;* that God would *smile on their education, and give His good angels the charge over them,*

---

[1] Latin: "How can I find words to describe the happiness of their marriage!"

[2] Latin: "Nature teaches us to love our children as ourselves."

and keep them from evil, that it may not grieve them; that when *their father and mother shall forsake them, the Lord may take them up.* With importunity I would plead that promise on their behalf: *the Heavenly Father will give the Holy Spirit unto them that ask Him.* Oh! happy children, if by *asking* I may obtain the *Holy Spirit* for them!

IV. "I would betimes entertain the children, with delightful *stories* out of the Bible. In the talk of the *table,* I would go through the *Bible,* when the *olive-plants about my table* are capable of being so *watered.* But I would always conclude the *stories* with some *lessons* of piety, to be inferred from them. . . .

VIII. "I would betimes do what I can, to beget a *temper of benignity* in my *children,* both towards one another, and towards all other people. I will instruct them how ready they should be to *communicate unto others,* a part of what they have; and they shall see, my encouragements, when they discover a *loving,* a *courteous,* an *helpful* disposition. I will give them now and then a piece of money, for them with their own little hands to dispense unto the poor. Yea, if any one has *hurt* them, or *vexed* them, I will not only forbid them all *revenge,* but also oblige them to do a *kindness* as soon as may be to the *vexatious* person. All *coarseness* of *language* or *carriage* in them, I will discountenance it.

IX. "I would be solicitous to have my *children* expert, not only at reading handsomely, but also at writing a fair hand. I will then assign them such *books* to *read,* as I may judge most agreeable and profitable; obliging them to give me some account of what they *read;* but keep a strict eye upon them, that they don't stumble on *the Devil's library,* and poison themselves with foolish *romances,* or *novels,* or *plays,* or *songs,* or *jests that are not convenient.* I will set them also, to *write* out such things, as may be of the greatest benefit unto them; and they shall have their blank books, neatly kept on purpose, to enter such passages as I advise them to. I will particularly require them now and then, to *write* a *prayer* of their own composing, and bring it unto me; that so I may discern, what sense they have of their own everlasting interests.

X. "I wish that my *children* may as soon as may be, feel the principles of *reason* and *honor,* working in them, and that I may carry on their education, very much upon those principles. Therefore, first, I will wholly avoid, that harsh, fierce, crabbed usage of the children, that would make them tremble, and abhor to come into my presence. I will so use them, that they shall *fear* to offend me, and yet mightily *love* to see me, and be glad of my coming home, if I have been abroad at any time. I would have it looked upon as a severe and awful *punishment* for a crime in the family, to be *forbidden for awhile to come into my presence.* I would raise in them, an high opinion of their father's *love* to them, and of his being *better able* to judge what is good for them, than they are for themselves. I would bring them to believe, *'tis best for them to be and do as I would have them.* Hereupon I would continually magnify the matter to them, what a brave thing 'tis to *know* the things that are excellent; and more brave to *do* the things that are virtuous. I would have them to propose it as a *reward* of their well-doing at any time, *I will now go to my father, and he will teach me something that I was never taught before.* I would have them afraid of doing any *base* thing, from an horror of the *baseness* in it. My first animadversion on a lesser fault in them, shall be a *surprise,* a *wonder,* vehemently expressed before them, that ever they should be guilty of doing so foolishly; a vehement *belief,* that they will never do the like again; a weeping resolution in them, that they will not. I will never dispense a *blow,* except it be for an atrocious crime, or for a lesser fault obstinately persisted in; either for an enormity, or for an *obstinacy.* I would ever *proportion* chastisements unto miscarriages; not smite bitterly for a very small piece of *childishness,* and only frown a little for some real *wickedness.* Nor shall my *chatisements* ever be dispensed in a *passion* and a *fury;* but with them, I will first show them the command of GOD, by transgressing whereof they have displeased me. The slavish, raving, fighting way of education too commonly used, I look upon it, as a considerable article in the wrath and curse of GOD, upon a miserable world.

XI. "As soon as we can, we'll get up to yet *higher principles.* I will often tell the *children,* what cause they have to *love* a glorious CHRIST, who has *died* for them. And, how much He will be *well-pleased* with their *well-doing.* And, what a noble thing, 'tis to follow His *example;* which *example* I will describe unto them. I will often tell them, that the *eye of God* is upon them; the great GOD knows all they do, and hears all they speak. I will often tell them, that there will be a time, when they must appear before the *Judgment-Seat* of the holy LORD; and they must *now* do nothing, that may *then* be a grief and shame unto them. I will set before them, the delights of that *Heaven* that is prepared for pious children; and the torments of that *Hell* that is prepared of old, for naughty ones. I will inform them, of the *good offices* which the *good angels* do for *little ones* that have the fear of God, and are afraid of sin. And, how the *devils* tempt them to do ill things; how they hearken to the *devils,* and are like *them,* when they do such things; and what mischiefs the *devils* may get leave to do them in this world, and what a sad thing 'twill be, to be among the devils in the *Place of Dragons.* I will cry to God, that He *will make them feel the power of these principles.*

XII. "When the *children* are of a fit age for it, I will sometimes *closet* them; have them with me *alone;* talk with them about the state of their souls; their *experiences,* their *proficiencies,* their *temptations;* obtain their declared consent unto every stroke in the *Covenant of Grace;* and then pray with them, and weep unto the Lord for His *grace,* to be bestowed upon them, and make them witnesses of the agony with which I am *travailing* to see the image of CHRIST formed in them. Certainly, they'll never forget such actions!

XIII. "I would be very watchful and cautious, about the *companions* of my *children.* I will be very inquisitive, what *company* they keep; if they are in hazard of being ensnared by any *vicious company,* I will earnestly pull them out of it, as *brands out of the burning.* I will find out, and procure, *laudable companions* for them.

XIV. "As in *catechizing* the children, so in the *repetition* of the public sermons, I would use this method. I will put every *truth* into a *question,* to be answered still, with *Yes,* or *No.* By this method, I hope to awaken their *attention* as well as enlighten their *understanding.* And thus I shall have an opportunity to ask, 'Do you desire such or such a grace of God?' and the like. Yea, I may have opportunity to demand, and perhaps to *obtain* their early, and frequent, and why not *sincere?,* consent unto the glorious articles of the *New Covenant.* The *Spirit of Grace* may fall upon them in this action; and they may be seized by Him, and held as His *temples,* through eternal ages.

XV. "When a Day of *Humiliation* arrives, I will make them know the *meaning* of the Day. And after time given them to consider of it, I will order them to tell me: *what special afflictions they have met withal?* And, *what good they hope to get by those afflictions?* On a Day of *Thanksgiving,* they shall also be made to know the *intent* of the Day. And after consideration, they shall tell me, *what mercies of God unto them they take special notice of:* And, *what duties to God, they confess and resolve, under such obligations?* Indeed, for something of this importance, to be pursued in my conversation with the children, I would not confine myself unto the *solemn Days,* which may occur too seldom for it. Very particularly, when the *birthdays* of the children anniversarily arrive to any of them, I would then take them aside, and mind them of the age, which *having obtained help from God* they are come unto; how *thankful* they should be for the mercies of God, which they have hitherto lived upon; how *fruitful* they should be in all goodness, that so they may still enjoy their mercies. And I would inquire of them, whether they have ever yet begun to mind the *work* which God sent them into the world upon; how far they understand the work; and what good strokes they have struck at it; and, how they design to spend the rest of their time, if God still continue them in the world.

XVI. "When the *children* are in any *trouble,* as, if they be *sick,* or *pained,* I will take advantage therefrom, to set before them the evil of *sin,* which brings all our *trouble;* and how fearful a thing it will be to be cast among the damned, who are in easeless and endless *trouble.* I will set before them the benefit of an interest in a CHRIST, by which their *trouble* will be sanctified unto them, and they will be prepared for *death,* and for fullness of joy in an happy eternity after *death.*

XVII. "I incline, that among all the points of a polite education which I would endeavor for my *children,* they may each of them, the *daughters* as well as the *sons,* have so much insight into some *skill,* which lies in the way of *gain* (the *limners',* or the *scriveners',* or the *apothecaries',* or some other *mystery,* to which their own inclination may most carry them) that they may be able to subsist themselves, and get something of a livelihood, in case the Providence of God should bring them into necessities. Why not they as well as *Paul the Tent-Maker!* The *children* of the best fashion, may have occasion to bless the parents, that make such a provision for them! The Jews have a saying; 'tis worth my remembering it: *Quicunque filium suum non docet opificium, perinde est ac si eum doceret latrocinium.*[3]

XVIII. "As soon as ever I can, I would make my children apprehensive of the main END, for which they are to *live;* that so they may as soon as may be, *begin to live;* and their *youth* not be nothing but *vanity.* I would show them, that their main END must be, *to acknowledge the great* GOD, *and His glorious* CHRIST; *and bring others to acknowledge Him:* and that they are never *wise* nor *well,* but when they are doing so. I would show them, what the *acknowledgments* are, and how they are to be made. I would make them able to answer the grand question, *why they live; and what is the end of the actions that fill their lives?* Teach them, how their *Creator* and *Redeemer* is to be obeyed in everything; and, how everything is to be done in *obedience* to Him; teach them, how even their *diversions,* and their *ornaments,* and the *tasks* of their education, must all be to fit them for the *further service* of Him, to whom I have devoted them; and how in these also, His commandments must be the rule of all they do. I would sometimes therefore surprise them with an inquiry, 'Child, what is this for? Give me a good account, why you do it?' How comfortably shall I see them *walking in the light,* if I may bring them *wisely* to answer this inquiry; and what *children of the light?*

---

[3] Latin: "He who does not teach his son a craft, teaches him theft."

XIX. "I would oblige the *children,* to retire sometimes, and ponder on that question: 'What shall I wish to have done, if I were now a-dying?' And report unto me, their *own answer* to the question; of which I would then take advantage, to inculcate the *lessons of godliness* upon them. I would also direct them and oblige them, at a proper time for it, seriously to realize, their own appearance before the awful *Judgment-Seat* of the Lord JESUS CHRIST, and consider, *what they have to plead, that they may not be sent away into everlasting punishment; what they have to plead, that they may be admitted into the Holy City.* I would instruct them, what *plea* to prepare; first, show them, how to get a part in the *righteousness* of Him that is to be their *Judge;* by receiving it with a thankful *faith,* as the *gift* of infinite grace unto the distressed and unworthy sinner: then, show them how to prove that their *faith* is not a counterfeit, by their continual endeavor to please Him in all things, who is to be their *Judge,* and to serve His Kingdom and interest in the world. And I would charge them, to make this preparation.

XX. "If I live to see the children *marriageable,* I would, before I consult with Heaven and earth for their best accommodation in the *married state,* endeavor the *espousal* of their souls unto their only *Saviour.* I would as plainly, and as fully as I can, propose unto them, the terms on which the glorious Redeemer would *espouse* them to Himself, *in righteousness and judgment, and favor, and mercies forever;* and solicit their consent unto His proposals and overtures. Then would I go on, to do what may be expected from a tender parent for them, in their *temporal circumstances.* . . .

MASTERS, yea, and MISTRESSES too, must have their *devices, how to do good unto their servants;* how to make them the *servants* of Christ, and the *children* of God. God whom you must remember to be *your Master in Heaven,* has brought them, and put them into your hands. Who can tell what *good* He has brought them for? How if they should be the *elect* of God, fetched from *Africa,* or the *Indies,* and brought into your families, on purpose, that by the means of their being *there,* they may be brought home unto the *Shepherd of Souls?* Oh! that the *souls* of our *slaves,* were of more account with us! that we gave a better demonstration that we *despise not our own souls,* by doing what we can for the *souls* of our *slaves,* and not using them as if they had no *souls!* that the poor *slaves* and *blacks,* which live with us, may by our means be made the *candidates* of the Heavenly life! How can we pretend unto *Christianity,* when we do no more to *Christianize* our *slaves!* Verily, you must give an *account* unto God, concerning *them.* If they be lost, through your negligence, what answer can you make unto *God the Judge of all!* Methinks, common principles of gratitude should incline you, to study the happiness of those, by whose obsequious labors, your lives are so much accommodated. Certainly, they would be the *better servants* to you, the more faithful, the more honest, the more industrious, and submissive *servants* to you, for your bringing them into the service of your *common Lord.*

But if any servant of God, may be so honored by Him, as to be made the successful instrument, of obtaining from a *British* Parliament, *an act for the Christianizing of the slaves in the Plantations;* then it may be hoped, something more may be done, than has yet been done, that the *blood of souls* may not be found in the *skirts* of our nation: a *controversy* of Heaven with our Colonies may be removed, and *prosperity* may be restored; or, however the honorable instrument, will have unspeakable *peace* and *joy,* in the remembrance of his endeavors. In the meantime, the *slave-trade* is a spectacle that shocks *humanity.*

The harmless natives basely they trepan,
And barter baubles for the *souls of men.*
The wretches they to Christian climes bring o'er
To serve worse heathens than they did before.

12. Methinks, this excellent zeal should be carried into our *neighborhood. Neighbors,*
you stand *related* unto one another; and you should be full of *devices,* that all the
neighbors may have cause to be glad of your being in the *neighborhood.* We read, "The
righteous is more excellent than his neighbor." But we shall scarce own him so, except
he be *more excellent* AS *a neighbor.* He must *excel* in the duties of *good neighborhood.*
Let that man be *better* than his *neighbor,* who labors to be a *better neighbor;* to do most
good unto *his neighbor.*

And here, first, the *poor* people that lie *wounded,* must have *wine* and *oil* poured
into their *wounds.* It was a charming stroke in the character with [which?] a modern
prince had given to him, *To be in distress, is to deserve his favor.* O good neighbor,
put on that princely, that more than royal quality. See who in the neighborhood may
deserve thy favor. We are told, *This is pure religion and undefiled* (a jewel, that neither
is a counterfeit, nor has any flaws in it): *to visit the fatherless and widows in their affliction.*
The *orphans* and the *widows,* and so all the children of *affliction* in the neighborhood,
must be *visited,* and relieved with all agreeable kindnesses.

Neighbors, be concerned, that the *orphans* and *widows* in your neighborhood, may
be well provided for. *They* meet with grievous difficulties; with unknown temptations. While their next *relatives* were yet living, they were, perhaps, but meanly
provided for. What must they now be in their more solitary condition? Their condition should be considered: and the result of the consideration should be that: *I
delivered the orphan, that had no helper, and I caused the heart of the widow to sing for joy.*

By consequence, all the afflicted in the neighborhood, are to be thought upon. Sirs,
would it be too much for you, at least *once in a week,* to think, "What neighbor is
reduced into a pinching and painful poverty? Or in any degree impoverished with
heavy losses?" Think, "What neighbor is languishing with sickness; especially if sick
with sore maladies, and of some continuance?" Think, "What neighbor is heartbroken
with sad bereavements; bereaved of desirable relatives?" And think: "What neighbor
has a soul buffeted, and buried with violent assaults of the Wicked one?" But then
think, "What shall be done for such neighbors?"

First, you will *pity* them. The evangelical precept is, *Have compassion one of another,
be pitiful.* It was of old, and ever will be, the just expectation, *To him that is afflicted,
pity should be shown.* And let our *pity* to them, flame out in our *prayer* for them. It
were a very lovely practice for you, in the *daily prayer* of your *closet* every evening,
to think, "What miserable object have I seen today, that I may do well now to
mention for the mercies of the Lord?"

But this is not all. 'Tis possible, 'tis probable, you may do well to *visit* them; and
when you *visit* them, *comfort* them. Carry them some *good word,* which may raise a
gladness, in an *heart stooping with heaviness.*

And lastly. Give them all the *assistances* that may answer their *occasions:* assist them
with *advice* to them; assist them with *address* to others for them. And if it be needful,
bestow your ALMS upon them; *deal thy bread to the hungry; bring to thy house the poor
that are cast out; when thou seest the naked, cover him. . . .*

In moving for the *devices of good neighborhood,* a principal motion which I have to make, is, that you consult the *spiritual* interests of your neighborhood, as well as the *temporal.* Be concerned, lest the *deceitfulness of sin* undo any of the neighbors. If there be any *idle persons* among them, I beseech you, cure them of their *idleness;* don't nourish 'em and harden 'em in that; but find *employment* for them. Find 'em *work;* set 'em to *work;* keep 'em to *work. Then,* as much of your other bounty to them, as you please.

If any *children* in the neighborhood, are under no education, don't allow 'em to continue so. Let care be taken, that they may be better educated; and be taught to read; and be taught their *Catechism;* and the truths and ways of their only Saviour.

Once more. If any in the neighborhood, are taking to *bad courses,* lovingly and faithfully admonish them. If any in the neighborhood are enemies to their own welfare, or their families; prudently dispense your admonitions unto them. If there are any *prayerless families,* never leave off entreating and exhorting of them, till you have persuaded them, to set up the *worship* of God. If there be any *service* of God, or of His people, to which any one may need to be excited, give him a tender excitation. Whatever *snare* you see any one in, be so kind, as to tell him of his danger to be *ensnared,* and save him from it. By putting of *good books* into the hands of your neighbors, and gaining of them a promise to *read the books,* who can tell what good you may do unto them! It is possible, you may in this way, with ingenuity, and with efficacy, administer those *reproofs,* which you may owe unto such neighbors, as are to be *reproved* for their miscarriages. The *books* will balk nothing, that is to be said, on the subjects, that you would have the neighbors advised upon.

Finally. If there be any *base houses,* which threaten to debauch, and poison, and confound the neighborhood, let your charity to your neighbors make you do all you can for the suppression of them.

That my PROPOSAL *To Do Good in the Neighborhood, and as a Neighbor,* may be more fully formed and followed; I will conclude it, with minding you, that a world of *self-denial* is to be exercised in the execution of it. You must be armed against *selfishness,* all *selfish* and *squinting* intentions, in your generous resolutions. . . .

1710

Robert Beverley
ca. 1673–1722

Robert Beverley's *History* couples his admiration for the explorers of Virginia with criticism of the gentlemen who colonized it. He hails the visionary "Learned and Valiant Sir Walter Raleigh" and scorns traders suffering "Belly-Ache" from eating green fruit and "unripe Trash." Beverley's *History and Present State of Virginia* (1705), a work of cultural analysis as well as history, combines close observation with a satiric tone.

Robert Beverley was born in Virginia and educated in England, probably in Yorkshire. He returned to America to accept a clerkship for a Virginian colonial official. After a series of such appointments, he was elected to the legislative House of Burgesses as a representative of Jamestown. Beverley inherited a plantation, to which he added another tract of some six thousand acres, which became known as Beverley Park. In 1697 he married, only to be widowed less than a year later at the birth of his son.

Robert Beverley was a litigious man often involved in disputes with Virginian officials. After a series of accusations during a sojourn in England in 1703, he was forced to retire to his plantation. In his later years he decided to compile the laws of Virginia and may have authored an anonymously published pamphlet entitled *An Essay upon the Government of the English Plantations on the Continent of America . . . By an American* (1701).

Beverley's literary reputation, however, rests on his *History.* According to the author, the work was conceived in irritation over the errors and misrepresentations in John Oldmixon's *The British Empire in America* (1708), which he saw in manuscript. But Beverley may have had another, utilitarian purpose in writing his own *History:* Owners of large plantations of the period were eager to attract foreign immigrants, including French Huguenots. The book, which presents numerous attractions of life in Virginia, may thus have been written for promotional purposes.

Beverley's *History* is significant in the development of American literature because the work is shaped by a deliberately American point of view. It accepts and asserts the normality of the New World garden and provides a secular counterbalance to the Puritan historians' New England Holy Commonwealth.

Further Reading:
L. Wright, introduction to *The History and Present State of Virginia,* 1968.
L. Simpson, *The Dispossessed Garden: Pastoral and History in Southern Literature,* 1975.

Text:
The History and Present State of Virginia, ed. L. Wright, 1968.

---

from The History and Present State of Virginia

from Book I

Chap. I: Shewing What Happen'd in the First Attempts to Settle Virginia, Before the Discovery of Chesapeak Bay

1. The Learned and Valiant Sir *Walter Raleigh*[1] having entertain'd some deeper and more serious Considerations upon the State of the Earth, than most other Men of his Time, as may sufficiently appear by his incomparable book, *The History of the World;* And having laid together the many Stories then in *Europe* concerning *America;* the Native Beauty, Riches, and Value of this Part of the World; and the immense Profits the *Spaniards* drew from a small Settlement or two thereon made; resolv'd upon an Adventure for further Discoveries.

---

[1] English explorer and writer (1552?–1618).

According to this Purpose, in the Year of our Lord, 1583, He got several Men of great Value and Estate to join with him in an Expedition of this Nature: And for their Incouragement obtain'd Letters Patents from Queen *Elizabeth,* bearing date the 25th of *March,* 1584, for turning their Discoveries to their own Advantage.

2. In *April* following they set out Two small vessels under the Command of Capt. *Philip Amidas,* and Capt. *Arthur Barlow,* who, after a prosperous Voyage, anchor'd at the Inlet by *Roenoke,* at present under the Government of North *Carolina.* They made good Profit of the *Indian* Truck, which they bought for Things of much inferior Value, and return'd. Being over-pleased with their Profits, and finding all Things there entirely new, and surprizing; they gave a very advantageous Account of Matters; by representing the Country so delightful and desirable; so pleasant, and plentiful; the Climate, and Air, so temperate, sweet, and wholsome; the Woods, and Soil, so charming, and fruitful; and all other Things so agreeable, that Paradice it self seem'd to be there, in its first Native Lustre.

They gave particular Accounts of the Variety of good Fruits, and some whereof they had never seen the Like before; but above all, that there were Grapes in such abundance, as was never known in the World; Stately tall large Oaks, and other Timber: Red Cedar, Cypress, Pines, and other Evergreens, and Sweetwoods; for tallness and largeness exceeding all they had ever heard of: Wild Fowl, Fish, Deer, and other Game in such Plenty, and Variety; that no Epicure could desire more than this New World did seem naturally to afford.

And, to make it yet more desirable, they reported the Native *Indians* (which were then the only Inhabitants) so affable, kind, and good-natur'd; so uncultivated in Learning, Trades, and Fashions; so innocent, and ignorant of all manner of Politicks, Tricks, and Cunning; and so desirous of the Company of the *English;* That they seem'd rather to be like soft Wax, ready to take any Impression, than any ways likely to oppose the Settling of the *English* near them. They represented it as a Scene laid open for the good and gracious Q. *Elizabeth,* to propagate the Gospel in, and extend her Dominions over: As if purposely reserv'd for her Majesty, by a peculiar Direction of Providence, that had brought all former Adventures in this Affair to nothing: And to give a further Taste of their Discovery, they took with them, in their Return for *England,* Two Men of the Native *Indians,* named *Wanchese* and *Manteo.*

3. Her Majesty accordingly took the Hint, and espoused the Project, as far as her present Engagements in War with *Spain* would let her; being so well pleased with the Account given, that as the greatest Mark of Honour she could do the Discovery, she call'd the Country by the Name of *Virginia;* as well, for that it was first discover'd in her Reign, a Virgin Queen; as that it did still seem to retain the Virgin Purity and Plenty of the first Creation, and the People their Primitive Innocence: For they seem'd not debauch'd nor corrupted with those Pomps and Vanities, which had depraved and inslaved the Rest of Mankind; neither were their Hands harden'd by Labour, nor their Minds corrupted by the Desire of hoarding up Treasure: They were without Boundaries to their Land, and without Property in Cattle; and seem'd to have escaped, or rather not to have been concern'd in the first Curse, *Of getting their Bread by the Sweat of their Brows:*[2] For, by their Pleasure alone, they supplied all their Necessities; namely, by Fishing, Fowling and Hunting; Skins being their only Cloathing; and these

---

[2] See Genesis 3:19, God's curse of Adam: "By the sweat of your face you shall eat bread. . . ."

too, Five-Sixths of the Year thrown by: Living without Labour, and only gathering the Fruits of the Earth when ripe, or fit for use: Neither fearing present Want, nor solicitous for the Future, but daily finding sufficient afresh for their Subsistance.

4. This Report was back'd, nay much advanc'd, by the vast Riches and Treasure mention'd in several Merchants Letters from *Mexico* and *Peru,* to their Correspondents in *Spain;* which Letters were taken with their Ships and Treasure, by some of ours in her Majesty's Service, in Prosecution of the *Spanish* Wars: This was Incouragement enough for a new Adventure, and set Peoples Invention at work, till they had satisfied themselves, and made sufficient Essays for the further Discovery of the Country. Pursuant whereunto Sir *Richard Greenvile,* the Chief of Sir *Walter Raleigh's* Associates, having obtain'd Seven Sail of Ships, well laden with Provision, Arms, Ammunition, and spare Men to make a Settlement, set out in Person with them early in the Spring of the succeeding Year, to make further Discoveries, taking back the Two *Indians* with him; and according to his Wish, in the latter End of *May,* arriv'd at the same Place, where the *English* had been the Year before; there he made a Settlement, sow'd Beans and Peas, which he saw come up and grow to Admiration while he staid, which was about Two Months, and having made some little Discoveries more in the *Sound* to the Southward, and got some Treasure in Skins, Furs, Pearl, and other Rarities of the Country, for Things of inconsiderable Value, he return'd for *England,* leaving One Hundred and Eight Men upon *Roenoke* Island, under the Command of Mr. *Ralph Lane,* to keep Possession.

5. As soon as Sir *Richard Greenvile* was gone, they, according to Order and their own Inclination, set themselves earnestly about discovering the Country, and ranged about a little too indiscreetly up the Rivers, and into the Land backward from the Rivers, which gave the *Indians* a Jealousie of their Meaning: For they cut off several Straglers of them, and had laid Designs to destroy the rest, but were happily prevented. This put the *English* upon the Precaution of keeping more within Bounds, and not venturing themselves too defenceless Abroad, who till then had depended too much upon the Natives Simplicity and Innocence.

After the *Indians* had done this Mischief, they never observ'd any real Faith towards those *English:* For being naturally suspicious and revengeful themselves, they never thought the *English* could forgive them; and so by this Jealousie, caus'd by the Cowardize of their Nature, they were continually doing Mischief.

The *English,* notwithstanding all this, continued their Discoveries, but more carefully than they had done before, and kept the *Indians* in some Awe, by threatening them with the Return of their Companions again with a greater Supply of Men and Goods: And, before the Cold of the Winter became uneasie, they had extended their Discoveries near an Hundred Miles along the Sea-Coast to the Northward; but not reaching the Southern Cape of *Chesapeak* Bay in *Virginia,* they had as yet found no good Harbour.

6. In this Condition they maintain'd their Settlement all the Winter, and till *August* following; but were much distress'd for Want of Provisions, not having learn'd to gather Food, as the *Indians* did, nor having Conveniencies like them of taking Fish and Fowl: Besides, being now fallen out with the *Indians,* they fear'd to expose themselves to their Contempt and Cruelty; because they had not received the Supply they talk'd of, and which had been expected in the Spring.

All they could do under these Distresses, and the Despair of the Recruits promised them this Year, was only to keep a good looking out to Seaward, if, perchance, they might find any Means of Escape, or Recruit. And, to their great Joy and Satisfaction, in *August* aforesaid, they happen'd to espy, and make themselves be seen to Sir *Francis Drake*'s[3] Fleet, consisting of Twenty Three Sail, who being sent by her Majesty upon the Coast of *America*, in Search of the *Spanish* Treasures, had Orders from her Majesty to take a View of this Plantation, and see what Assistance or Encouragement it wanted: Their first Petition to him was to grant them a fresh Supply of Men and Provisions, with a small Vessel, and Boats to attend them; that so if they should be put to Distress for want of Relief, they might imbark for *England.* This was as readily granted by Sir *Francis Drake* as ask'd by them; and a Ship was appointed them, which Ship they began immediately to fit up, and supply plentifully with all manner of Stores for a long Stay; but while they were a doing this, a great Storm arose, and drove that very Ship (with some others) from her Anchor to Sea, and so she was lost for that Occasion.

Sir *Francis* would have given them another Ship, but this Accident coming on the Back of so many Hardships which they had undergone, daunted them, and put them upon imagining that Providence was averse to their Designs; And now having given over, for that Year, the Expectation of their promised Supply from *England,* they consulted together, and agreed to desire Sir *Francis Drake* to take them along with him, which he did.

Thus their first Intention of Settlement fell, after discovering many Things of the natural Growth of the Country, useful for the Life of Man, and beneficial to Trade, they having observ'd a vast Variety of Fish, Fowl and Beasts; Fruits, Seeds, Plants, Roots, Timber-Trees, Sweet-Woods and Gums: They had likewise attain'd some little Knowledge in the Language of the *Indians,* their Religion, Manners, and Ways of Correspondence one with another; and been made sensible of their Cunning and Treachery towards themselves.

7. While these Things were thus acting in *America,* the Adventurers in *England* were providing, tho' too tediously, to send them Recruits. And tho' it was late before they could dispatch them (for they met with several Disappointments, and had many Squabbles among themselves.) However, at last they provided Four good Ships, with all manner of Recruits suitable for the Colony, and Sir *Walter Raleigh* designed to go in Person with them.

Sir *Walter* got his Ship ready first, and fearing the ill Consequence of a Delay, and the Discouragement it might be to those that were left to make a Settlement, he set Sail by himself. And a Fortnight after him Sir *Richard Greenvile* sail'd with the Three other Ships.

Sir *Walter* fell in with the Land at Cape *Hattoras,*[4] a little to the Southward of the Place, where the 108 Men had been settled, and after Search not finding them, he return'd: However, Sir *Richard,* with his Ships, found the Place where he had left the Men, but entirely deserted, which was at first a great Disheartening to him, thinking them all destroy'd, because he knew not that Sir *Francis Drake* had been there, and taken them off; but he was a little better satisfied by *Manteo*'s Report, that they were not cut off by the *Indians,* tho' he could give no good Account what was become

---

[3] Sir Francis Drake (1540?–1596), English admiral and explorer who sailed around the world from 1577 to 1580.

[4] Cape Hatteras, a promontory on an island on the east coast of North Carolina.

of them. However, notwithstanding this seeming Discouragement, he again left Fifty Men in the same Island of *Roenoke,* built them Houses necessary, gave them Two Years Provision, and return'd.

8. The next Summer, being *Anno* 1587. Three Ships more were sent, under the Command of Mr. *John White,* who himself was to settle there as Governour with more Men, and some Women, carrying also plentiful Recruits of Provisions.

In the latter End of *July* they arrived at *Roenoke* aforesaid, where they again encounter'd the uncomfortable News of the Loss of these Men also; who (as they were inform'd by *Manteo*) were secretly set upon by the *Indians,* some cut off, and the others fled, and not to be heard of, and their Place of Habitation now all grown up with Weeds. However, they repair'd the Houses on *Roenoke,* and sate down there again.

The 13th of *August* they christen'd *Manteo,* and stiled him Lord of *Dassamonpeak,* an *Indian* Nation so call'd, in Reward of the Fidelity he had shown to the *English* from the Beginning; who being the first *Indian* that was made a Christian in that Part of the World, I thought it not amiss to remember him.

On the same Occasion also may be mention'd the first Child there born of Christian Parentage, *viz.* a Daughter of Mr. *Ananias Dare.* She was born the 18th of the same *August* upon *Roenoke,* and, after the Name of the Country, was christen'd *Virginia.*

This seem'd to be a Settlement prosperously made, being carry'd on with much Zeal and Unanimity among themselves. The Form of Government consisted of a Governour and Twelve Councellors, incorporated by the name of the Governour and Assistants of the City of *Raleigh* in *Virginia.*

Many Nations of the *Indians* renew'd their Peace, and made firm Leagues with the Corporation: The chief Men of the *English* also were so far from being dishearten'd at the former Disappointments, that they disputed for the Liberty of remaining on the Spot; and by meer Constraint compell'd Mr. *White,* their Governour, to return for *England,* to negociate the Business of their Recruits and Supply, as a Man the most capable to manage that Affair, leaving at his Departure One Hundred and Fifteen in the Corporation.

9. It was above Two Years before Mr. *White* could obtain any Grant of Supplies; and then, in the latter End of the Year 1589, he set out from *Plimouth* with Three Ships, and sail'd round by the *Western* and *Carribbee* Islands, they having hitherto not found any nearer Way: For tho' they were skill'd in Navigation, and understood the Use of the Globes, yet did Example so much prevail upon them, that they chose to sail a Thousand Leagues about, rather than attempt a more direct Passage.

Towards the Middle of *August,* 1590. they arriv'd upon the Coast, at Cape *Hattoras,* and went to search upon Roenoke for the People; but found, by Letters on the Trees, that they were remov'd to *Croatan,* one of the islands forming the *Sound,* and Southward of Roenoke about Twenty Leagues, but no Sign of Distress. Thither they design'd to sail to them in their ships; but a Storm arising in the mean while, lay so hard upon them, that their Cables broke; they lost Three of their Anchors, were forced to Sea; and so return'd Home, without ever going near those poor People again for Sixteen Years following: And it is supposed, that the *Indians* seeing them forsaken by their Country, and unfurnish'd of their expected Supplies, cut them off; For to this Day they were never more heard of.

Thus, after all this vast Expence and Trouble, and the Hazard and Loss of so many

Lives, Sir *Walter Raleigh,* the great Projector and Furtherer of these Discoveries and Settlements, being under Trouble, all Thoughts of further prosecuting these Designs, lay dead for about Twelve Years following.

from **Chap. II: Containing an Account of the First Settlement of Chesapeak Bay, in Virginia, by the Corporation of London Adventurers, and Their Proceedings During Their Government by a President and Council Elective**

14. By Virtue of this Patent, Capt. *John Smith* was sent by the *London* Company in December, 1606, on his Voyage with Three small Ships; and a Commission was given to him, and to several other Gentlemen, to establish a Colony, and to govern by a President, to be chosen Annually, and Council, who should be invested with sufficient Authorities and Powers. And now all Things seem'd to promise a Plantation in good Earnest. . . .

17. In the Interval of these Ships returning from *England,* the *English* had a very advantageous Trade with the *Indians;* and might have made much greater Gains of it, and managed it both to the greater Satisfaction of the *Indians,* and the greater Ease and Security of themselves; if they had been under any Rule, or subject to any Method in Trade, and not left at Liberty to outvie or outbid one another; by which they not only cut short their own Profit, but created Jealousies and Disturbances among the *Indians,* by letting one have a better Bargain than another: For they being unaccustom'd to barter, such of them as had been hardest dealt by in their Commodities, thought themselves cheated and abused; and so conceiv'd a Grudge against the *English* in general, making it a National Quarrel: And this seems to be the original Cause of most of their subsequent Misfortunes by the *Indians.*

What also gave a greater Interruption to this Trade, was an Object that drew all their Eyes and Thoughts aside, even from taking the necessary Care for their Preservation, and for the Support of their Lives; which was this; They found in a Neck of Land, on the Back of *James-Town-Island,* a fresh Stream of Water springing out of a small Bank, which wash'd down with it a yellow sort of Dust-Isinglass, which being cleansed by the fresh streaming of the Water, lay shining in the Bottom of that limpid Element, and stirr'd up in them an unseasonable and inordinate Desire after Riches: For they, taking all to be Gold that glister'd, run into the utmost Distraction, neglecting both the necessary Defence of their Lives from the *Indians,* and the Support of their Bodies by securing of Provisions; absolutely relying, like *Midas,* upon the Almighty Power of Gold, thinking, that where this was in plenty nothing could be wanting: But they soon grew sensible of their Error; and found that if this gilded Dirt had been real Gold, it could have been of no Advantage to them. For, by their Negligence, they were reduced to an exceeding Scarcity of Provisions, and that little they had, was lost by the Burning of their Town, while all Hands were employ'd upon this imaginary Golden Treasure; so that they were forced to live for sometime upon the wild Fruits of the Earth, and upon Crabs, Muscles, and such like, not having a Day's Provision before-hand; as some of the laziest *Indians,* who have no Pleasure in Exercise, and won't be at the Pains to fish and hunt: And, indeed, not so well as they neither; For by this careless neglecting of their Defence against the *Indians,* many of 'em were destroy'd by that cruel People; and the Rest durst not venture abroad, but were forced to be content with what fell just into their Mouths.

18. In this Condition they were, when the first Ship of the Two before-mention'd came to their Assistance, but their Golden Dreams overcame all Difficulties: They spoke not, nor thought of any thing but Gold, and that was all the Lading that most of them were willing to take Care for; accordingly they put into this Ship all the yellow Dirt they had gathered, and what Skins and Furs they had trucked for; and filling her up with Cedar, sent her away.

After she was gone, the other Ship arrived, which they stow'd likewise with this supposed Gold-Dust, designing never to be poor again; filling her up with Cedar and Clap-board.

Those Two Ships being thus dispatched, they made several Discoveries in *James* River, and up *Chesapeak* Bay, by the Undertaking and Management of Capt. *John Smith;*[5] And the Year 1608 was the first Year in which they gather'd *Indian* Corn of their own planting.

While these Discoveries were making by Capt. *Smith,* Matters run again into Confusion in *James* Town; and several uneasie People, taking Advantage of his Absence, attempted to desert the Settlement, and run away with the small Vessel that was left to attend upon it; for Capt. *Smith* was the only Man among them that could manage the Discoveries with Success, and he was the only Man too that could keep the Settlement in Order. Thus the *English* continued to give themselves as much Perplexity by their own Distraction, as the *Indians* did by their Watchfulness and Resentments. . . .

26. *Anno* 1612, Two Ships more arriv'd with Supplies: And Capt. *Argall,* who commanded one of them, being sent in her to *Patowmeck* to buy Corn, he there met with *Pocahontas,* the Excellent Daughter of *Powhatan;* and having prevail'd with her to come Aboard to a Treat, he detain'd her Prisoner, and carried her to *James-Town,* designing to make Peace with her Father by her Release: But on the Contrary, that Prince resented the Affront very highly; and although he loved his Daughter with all imaginable Tenderness, yet he would not be brought to Terms by that unhandsome Treachery; till about Two Years after a Marriage being proposed between Mr. *John Rolfe,* an *English* Gentleman, and this Lady; which *Powhatan* taking to be a sincere Token of Friendship, he vouchsafed to consent to it, and to conclude a Peace.

Intermarriage had been indeed the Method proposed very often by the *Indians* in the Beginning, urging it frequently as a certain Rule, that the *English* were not their Friends, if they refused it. And I can't but think it would have been happy for that Country, had they embraced this Proposal: For, the Jealousie of the *Indians,* which I take to be the Cause of most of the Rapines and Murders they committed, would by this Means have been altogether prevented, and consequently the Abundance of Blood that was shed on both sides would have been saved; the great Extremities they were so often reduced to, by which so many died, would not have happened; the Colony, instead of all these Losses of Men on both Sides, would have been increasing in Children to its Advantage; the Country would have escaped the *Odium* which

[5] English adventurer and colonist of Virginia (1580–1631).

undeservedly fell upon it, by the Errors and Convulsions in the first Management; and, in all Likelihood, many, if not most, of the *Indians* would have been converted to Christianity by this kind Method; the Country would have been full of People, by the Preservation of the many *Christians* and *Indians* that fell in the Wars between them. Besides, there would have been a Continuance of all those Nations of *Indians* that are now dwindled away to nothing by their frequent Removals, or are fled to other Parts; not to mention the Invitation that so much Success and Prosperity would have been for others to have gone over and settled there, instead of the Frights and Terrors that were produced by all those Misfortunes that happen'd. . . .

45. *Anno,* 1622, Inferior Courts were first appointed by the General Assembly, under the Name of *County Courts,* for Tryal of Minute Causes; the Governour and Council still remaining Judges of the Supream Court of the Colony. In the mean time, by the great Increase of People, and the long Quiet they had enjoy'd among the *Indians,* since the Marriage of *Pocahontas,* and the Accession of *Oppechancanough* to the Imperial Crown; all Men were lull'd into a fatal Security, and became every where familiar with the *Indians,* Eating, Drinking and Sleeping amongst them; by which means they became perfectly acquainted with all our *English* Strength, and the Use of our Arms: Knowing at all Times, when and where to find our People; whether at Home, or in the Woods; in Bodies, or disperst; in Condition of Defence, or indefencible. This Exposing of their Weekness gave them Occasion to think more contemptibly of them, than otherwise, perhaps, they would have done; for which Reason they became more peevish, and more hardy to attempt any thing against them.

46. Thus upon the Loss of one of their leading Men, (a War Captain, as they call him,) who was likewise supposed to be justly kill'd, *Oppechancanough* took Affront, and in Revenge laid the Plot of a general Massacre of the *English,* to be executed on the 22d of *March,* 1622, a little before Noon, at a Time when our Men were all at Work abroad in their Plantations, disperst and unarm'd. This Hellish Contrivance was to take Effect upon all the several Settlements at one and the same Instant, except on the Eastern Shore, whither this Plot did not reach. The *Indians* had been made so familiar with the *English,* as to borrow their Boats and Canoes to cross the Rivers in, when they went to consult with their Neighbouring *Indians* upon this execrable Conspiracy. And, to colour their Design the better, they brought Presents of Deer, Turkies, Fish and Fruits to the *English* the Evening before. The very Morning of the Massacre, they came freely and unarm'd among them, eating with them, and behaving themselves with the same Freedom and Friendship as formerly, till the very Minute they were to put their Plot in Execution. Then they fell to Work all at once every where, knocking the *English* unawares on the Head, some with their Hatchets, which they call *Tommahauks,* others with the Hows and Axes of the *English* themselves, shooting at those who escap'd the Reach of their Hands; sparing neither Age nor Sex, but destroying Man, Woman and Child, according to their cruel Way of leaving none behind to bear Resentment. But whatever was not done by Surprize that Day, was left undone, and many that made early Resistance escap'd.

By the Account taken of the *Christians* murder'd that Morning, they were found to be Three Hundred Forty Seven, most of them falling by their own Instruments, and Working-Tools.

from **Book III: Of the Indians, Their Religion,
Laws, and Customs, in War and Peace**

Chap. I: Of the Persons of the Indians,
and Their Dress

1. The *Indians* are of the middling and largest stature of the *English:* They are straight and well proportion'd, having the cleanest and most exact Limbs in the World: They are so perfect in their outward frame, that I never heard of one single *Indian,* that was either dwarfish, crooked, bandy-legg'd, or otherwise misshapen. But if they have any such practice among them, as the *Romans* had, of exposing such Children till they dyed, as were weak and misshapen at their Birth, they are very shy of confessing it, and I could never yet learn that they had.

Their Colour, when they are grown up, is a Chesnut brown and tawny; but much clearer in their Infancy. Their Skin comes afterwards to harden and grow blacker, by greasing and Sunning themselves. They have generally coal-black Hair, and very black Eyes, which are most commonly grac'd with that sort of Squint which many of the *Jews* are observ'd to have. Their Women are generally Beautiful, possessing an uncommon delicacy of Shape and Features, and wanting no Charm, but that of a fair Complexion.

2. The Men wear their Hair cut after several fanciful Fashions, sometimes greas'd, and sometimes painted. The Great Men, or better sort, preserve a long Lock behind for distinction. They pull their Beards up by the roots with a Muscle-shell; and both Men and Women do the same by the other parts of their Body for Cleanliness sake. The Women wear the Hair of the Head very long, either hanging at their Backs, or brought before in a single Lock, bound up with a Fillet of Peak, or Beads; sometimes also they wear it neatly tyed up in a Knot behind. It is commonly greased, and shining black, but never painted.

The People of Condition of both Sexes, wear a sort of Coronet on their Heads, from 4 to 6 inches broad, open at the top, and composed of Peak, or Beads, or else of both interwoven together, and workt into Figures, made by a nice mixture of the Colours. Sometimes they wear a Wreath of Dyed Furrs; as likewise Bracelets on their Necks and Arms. The Common People go bareheaded, only sticking large shining Feathers about their Heads, as their fancies lead them.

from Chap. II: Of the Marriages Amongst the
Indians, and Management of Their Children

6. The *Indians* have their solemnities of Marriage, and esteem the Vows made at that time as most sacred and inviolable. Notwithstanding, they allow both the Man and the Wife to part upon disagreement; yet so great is the disreputation of a Divorce, that Marry'd people, to avoid the Character of Inconstant and Ungenerous, very rarely let their Quarrels proceed to a Separation. However, when it does so happen, they reckon all the ties of Matrimony dissolv'd, and each hath the liberty of marrying another. But Infidelity is accounted the most unpardonable of all Crimes in either of the Parties, as long as the Contract continues.

In these Separations, the Children go, according to the affection of the Parent, with the one or the other; for Children are not reckon'd a Charge among them, but rather Riches, according to the blessing of the Old Testament; and if they happen to differ about dividing their Children, their method is then, to part them equally, allowing the Man the first choice. . . .

8. The manner of the *Indians* treating their young Children is very strange, for instead of keeping them warm, at their first entry into the World, and wrapping them up, with I don't know how many Cloaths, according to our fond custom; the first thing they do, is to dip the Child over Head and Ears in cold Water, and then to bind it naked to a convenient Board, having a hole fitly plac'd for evacuation; but they always put Cotton, Wool, Furr, or other soft thing, for the Body to rest easy on, between the Child and the Board. In this posture they keep it several months, till the Bones begin to harden, the Joynts to knit, and the Limbs to grow strong; and then they let it loose from the Board, suffering it to crawl about, except when they are feeding, or playing with it.

While the Child is thus at the Board, they either lay it flat on its back, or set it leaning on one end, or else hang it up by a string fasten'd to the upper end of the Board for that purpose. The Child and Board being all this while carry'd about together. As our Women undress their Children to clean them and shift their Linnen, so they do theirs to wash and grease them. . . .

from Chap. III: Of the Towns, Buildings and Fortifications of the Indians

10. The manner the *Indians* have of building their Houses, is very slight and cheap; when they would erect a *Wigwang*, [6] which is the *Indian* name for a House, they stick Saplins into the ground by one end, and bend the other at the top, fastening them together by strings made of fibrous Roots, the rind of Trees, or of the green Wood of the white Oak, which will rive into Thongs. The smallest sort of these Cabbins are conical like a Bee-hive; but the larger are built in an oblong form, and both are cover'd with the Bark of Trees, which will rive off into great flakes. Their Windows are little holes left open for the passage of the Light, which in bad weather they stop with Shutters of the same Bark, opening the Leeward Windows for Air and Light. Their Chimney, as among the true-Born *Irish,* is a little hole in the top of the House, to let out the Smoak, having no sort of Funnel, or any thing within, to confine the Smoke from ranging through the whole Roof of the Cabbins, if the vent will not let it out fast enough. The Fire is always made in the middle of the Cabbin. Their Door is a Pendent Mat, when they are near home; but when they go abroad, they barricado it with great Logs of Wood set against the Mat, which are sufficient to keep out Wild Beasts. There's never more than one Room in a House, except in some Houses of State, or Religion, where the Partition is made only by Mats, and loose Poles.

11. Their Houses or Cabbins, as we call them, are by this ill method of Building, continually Smoaky, when they have Fire in them; but to ease that inconvenience, and to make the Smoak less troublesome to their Eyes, they generally burn Pine, or

[6] Wigwam.

Lightwood, (that is, the fat knots of dead Pine) the Smoak of which does not offend the Eyes, but smuts the Skin exceedingly, and is perhaps another occasion of the darkness of their Complexion. . . .

from Book IV, Part II: Of the Husbandry, and Improvements of Virginia

from Chap. XV: Of the People, Inhabitants of Virginia

65. I Can easily imagin with Sir *Josiah Child*,[7] that this, as well as all the rest of the Plantations, was for the most part at first peopled by Persons of low Circumstances, and by such as were willing to seek their Fortunes in a Foreign Country. Nor was it hardly possible it should be otherwise; for 'tis not likely that any Man of a plentiful Estate, should voluntarily abandon a happy Certainty, to roam after imaginary Advantages, in a New World. Besides which incertainty, he must have propos'd to himself to encounter the infinite Difficulties and Dangers, that attend a New Settlement. These Discouragements were sufficient to terrifie any Man, that could live easy in *England,* from going to provoke his Fortune in a strange Land. . . .

from Chap. XVI: Of the Buildings in Virginia

68. There are two fine Publick Buildings in this Country, which are the most Magnificent of any in *America;* One of which is the College before spoken of, and the other the Capitol or State-House, as it was formerly call'd: That is, the House for Convention of the General Assembly, for the Setting of the General Court, for the Meeting of the Council, and for keeping of their several Offices.

Not far from this, is also built the publick Prison of the Country, which is a large and convenient Structure, with Partitions for the different Sexes, and distinct Rooms for Petty-Offenders. To this is also annexed a convenient Yard to Air the Criminals in, for preservation of their Life and Health, till the time of their Trial.

These are all erected at Middle-Plantation, now nam'd *Williamsburgh,* where Land is laid out for a new Town. The College, and Capitol are both built of Brick, and cover'd with Shingle.

69. The Private Buildings are of late very much improved; several Gentlemen there, having built themselves large Brick Houses of many Rooms on a Floor, and several Stories high, as also some Stone-Houses: but they don't covet to make them lofty, having extent enough of Ground to build upon; and now and then they are visited by high Winds, which would incommode a towring Fabrick. They always contrive to have large Rooms, that they may be cool in Summer. Of late they have made their Stories much higher than formerly, and their Windows large, and sasht with Cristal Glass; and within they adorn their Apartments with rich Furniture.

All their Drudgeries of Cookery, Washing, Daries, &c. are perform'd in Offices detacht from the Dwelling-Houses, which by this means are kept more cool and Sweet.

[7] Author of *A New Discourse of Trade* (1698).

Their Tobacco-Houses are all built of Wood, as open and airy as is consistent with keeping out the Rain; which sort of Building, is most convenient for the curing of their Tobacco. . . .

Chap. XIX: Of the Temperature of the Climate, and the Inconveniencies Attending It

77. The Natural Temperature of the Inha[bit]ed part of the Country, is hot and moist: tho this Moisture I take to be occasion'd by the abundance of low Grounds, Marshes, Creeks, and Rivers, which are every where among their lower Settlements; but more backward in the Woods, where they are now Seating, and making new Plantations, they have abundance of high and dry Land, where there are only Crystal Streams of Water, which flow gently from their Springs, and divide themselves into innumerable Branches, to moisten and enrich the adjacent Lands.

78. The Country is in a very happy Situation, between the extreams of Heat and Cold, but inclining rather to the first. Certainly it must be a happy Climate, since it is very near of the same Latitude with the Land of Promise. Besides, As *Judæa* was full of Rivers, and Branches of Rivers; So is *Virginia:* As that was seated upon a great Bay and Sea, wherein were all the conveniences for Shipping and Trade; So is *Virginia.* Had that fertility of Soil? So has *Virginia,* equal to any Land in the known World. In fine, if any one impartially considers all the Advantages of this Country, as Nature made it; he must allow it to be as fine a Place, as any in the Universe; but I confess I am asham'd to say any thing of its Improvements, because I must at the same time reproach my Country-Men with a Laziness that is unpardonable. If there be any excuse for them in this Matter, 'tis the exceeding plenty of good things, with which Nature has blest them; for where God Almighty is so Merciful as to work for People, they never work for themselves.

All the Countries in the World, seated in or near the Latitude of *Virginia,* are esteem'd the Fruitfullest, and Pleasantest of all Clymates. As for Example, *Canaan, Syria, Persia,* great part of *India, China* and *Japan,* the *Morea, Spain, Portugal,* and the Coast of *Barbary,* none of which differ many Degrees of Latitude from *Virginia.* These are reckon'd the Gardens of the World, while *Virginia* is unjustly neglected by its own Inhabitants, and abus'd by other People.

79. That which makes this Country most unfortunate, is, that it must submit to receive its Character from the Mouths not only of unfit, but very unequal Judges; For, all its Reproaches happen after this manner.

Many of the Merchants and others that go thither from *England,* make no distinction between a cold, and a hot Country: but wisely go sweltering about in their thick Cloaths all the Summer, because they used to do so in their *Northern* Climate; and then unfairly complain of the heat of the Country. They greedily Surfeit with their delicious Fruits, and are guilty of great Intemperance, through the exceeding Generosity of the Inhabitants; by which means they fall Sick, and then unjustly complain of the unhealthiness of the Country. In the next place, the Sailers for want of Towns there, are put to the hardship of rowling most of the Tobacco, a Mile or more, to the Water-side; this Splinters their Hands sometimes, and provokes 'em to curse the Country. Such Exercise, and a bright Sun, makes them hot, and then they imprudently fall to drinking cold Water, or perhaps New Cyder, which in its Season, they find at every Planter's House; Or else they greedily devour all the green Fruit, and unripe

Trash they can meet with, and so fall into Fluxes, Fevers, and the Belly-Ach; and then, to spare their own Indiscretion, they in their Tarpawlin Language, cry, God D——the Country. This is the true State of the case, as to the Complaints of its being Sickly; For, by the most impartial Observation I can make, if People will be perswaded to be Temperate, and take due care of themselves, I believe it is as healthy a Country, as any under Heaven: but the extraordinary pleasantness of the Weather, and the goodness of the Fruit, lead People into many Temptations. The clearness and bright-ness of the Sky, add new vigour to their Spirits, and perfectly remove all Splenetick and sullen Thoughts. Here they enjoy all the benefits of a warm Sun, and by their shady Groves, are protected from its Inconvenience. Here all their Senses are enter-tain'd with an endless Succession of Native Pleasures. Their Eyes are ravished with the Beauties of naked Nature. Their Ears are Serenaded with the perpetual murmur of Brooks, and the thorow-base which the Wind plays, when it wantons through the Trees; the merry Birds too, join their pleasing Notes to this rural Consort, especially the Mock-birds, who love Society so well, that whenever they see Mankind, they will perch upon a Twigg very near them, and sing the sweetest wild Airs in the World: But what is most remarkable in these Melodious Animals, they will frequently fly at small distances before a Traveller, warbling out their Notes several Miles an end, and by their Musick, make a Man forget the Fatigues of his Journey. Their Taste is regaled with the most delicious Fruits, which without Art, they have in great Variety and Perfection. And then their smell is refreshed with an eternal fragrancy of Flowers and Sweets, with which Nature perfumes and adorns the Woods almost the whole year round.

Have you pleasure in a Garden? All things thrive in it, most surprisingly; you can't walk by a Bed of Flowers, but besides the entertainment of their Beauty, your Eyes will be saluted with the charming colours of the Humming Bird, which revels among the Flowers, and licks off the Dew and Honey from their tender Leaves, on which it only feeds. It's size is not half so large as an *English* Wren, and its colour is a glorious shining mixture of Scarlet, Green, and Gold. Colonel *Byrd,* in his Garden, which is the finest in that Country, has a Summer-House set round with the *Indian* Honey-Suckle, which all the Summer is continually full of sweet Flowers, in which these Birds delight exceedingly. Upon these Flowers, I have seen ten or a dozen of these Beautiful Creatures together, which sported about me so familiarly, that with their little Wings they often fann'd my Face.

1705

Ebenezer Cooke
1670–ca. 1732

Ebenezer Cooke's *The Sot-Weed Factor; or, A Voyage to Maryland* (1708) places its author in the tradition of the southern colonial writers who used satire, song, mock epic, and the like to convey their impressions of New World manners and mores. These writers were sometimes gentlemen or squires whose writings were free of immediate utilitarian purposes. Thus *The Sot-Weed Factor* ranges freely in biting wit and satiric observation of uncivil—in fact, barbarous—plantation life.

The details of Ebenezer Cooke's life have eluded researchers. In 1661 his grandfather obtained a grant of land "for trading with the Indians" on the eastern shore of Maryland's Chesapeake Bay. But for two generations the Cookes were absentee landlords who spent most of their time in England, where Ebenezer was probably raised after being born in Maryland. Scant records suggest that he may have prepared for a career in law, and it is probable that *The Sot-Weed Factor* was based on firsthand observation of Maryland colonial life.

A sotweed factor was usually an English merchant's representative. He would arrive in America along with a ship's cargo for trade to the planters. Because his were long-lasting or durable goods, the sotweed factor was in a favorable position to trade advantageously with the planters, who were forced to divest themselves of their crop eventually. Cooke uses the persona or mask of the sotweed factor to spoof Maryland plantation life and institutions. He employs the hudibrastic style, named for Samuel Butler's *Hudibras* (1663–1678), which was conspicuously humorous in its elements of burlesque, the mock epic, epigrams, and outrageous rhymes. Eventually in Cooke's poem the crafty colonists prove to be more than a match for the self-styled English sophisticates. And some readers feel that the real object of Cooke's satire is the arrogant English assumption that America was only a wilderness colonized by boors and rustics.

Apart from revised editions of *The Sot-Weed Factor* and a sequel entitled *Sotweed Redivivus* (1730), Cooke also wrote elegies, a few of which are extant. His work was known only to a few scholars until the American novelist John Barth published his comic novel *The Sot-Weed Factor* in 1960. Barth's own humor prepared a contemporary audience to appreciate the work of his eighteenth-century source.

Further Reading:
R. Arner, "Ebenezer Cooke's *The Sot-Weed Factor:* The Structure of Satire," *Southern Literary Journal* 4 (1971), pp. 33–47.
J. Lemay, *Men of Letters in Colonial Maryland*, 1972.
E. Cohen, *Ebenezer Cooke: The Sot-Weed Canon*, 1975.

Text:
The Sot-Weed Factor; or, A Voyage to Maryland, 1708.

---

from The Maryland Muse

from **The Sot-Weed Factor**[1]

Condemn'd by Fate, to wayward Curse
Of Friends unkind, and empty Purse,
Plagues worse than fill'd *Pandora's* Box,[2]
I took my Leave of *Albion's* Rocks,[3]
With heavy Heart, concern'd that I   5

[1] The tobacco merchant.
[2] In Greek myth, the box containing evils and disorders that were let loose to afflict the human race. The bearer of the box was Pandora, a woman fashioned by the gods.
[3] England.

Was forc'd my native Soil to fly,
And the old World must bid Good-b'ye:
But Heav'n ordain'd it shou'd be so,
And to repine is vain, we know.

Freighted with Fools, from *Plimouth* Sound,   10
To *Maryland* our Ship was bound;
Where we arriv'd, in dreadful Pain,
Shock'd by the Terrors of the Main;
For full Three Months our wav'ring Boat
Did thro' the surly Ocean float,   15
And furious Storms and threatning Blasts,
Both split our Sails, and sprung our Masts:
Weary'd, yet pleas'd we did escape
Such Ills, we achor'd at the *Cape;*[4]
But weighing[5] soon, we plow'd the *Bay,*   20
To cove it in *Piscataway.*[6]

Intending there to open Store,
I put myself and Goods on Shore,
Where soon repair'd a numerous Crew,
In Shirts and Draw'rs, of *Scotch*-cloth[7] blew,   25
With neither Stocking, Hat, nor Shoe:
These *Sotweed* Planters crowd the Shore,
In Hew as tawny as a *Moor;*
Figures, so strange, no God design'd
To be a Part of Human-kind: 30
But wanton Nature, void of Rest,
Moulded the brittle Clay in Jest.

    At last, a Fancy very odd,
Took me, This was *The Land of* Nod,
Planted at first when Vagrant *Cain*   35
His Brother had unjustly slain;[8]
Then, conscious of the Crime he'd done,
From Vengeance dire hither run,
And in a Hut supinely dwelt,
The first in *Furrs* and *Sotweed* dealt: 40
And ever since that Time, this Place
Has harbour'd a detested Race,
Who, when they could not thrive at Home;
For Refuge to these Worlds did roam,
In Hopes by Flight they might prevent   45
The Devil, and his fell Intent,

---

[4] Cooke's note: "The first land on the coast of Virginia and Maryland."
[5] I.e., weighing anchor.
[6] Cooke's note: "The Bay of Piscataway, the usual place where our ships come to anchor in Maryland."
[7] Blue linen.
[8] See Genesis 4:16.

Obtain from Tripple-Tree⁹ Reprieve,
And Heav'n and Hell alike deceive:
But e're their Manners I display,
I think it fit I open lay   50
My Entertainment by the Way,
That Strangers well may be aware on
What homely Diet they must fare on;
To see that Shore where no good sense is found,
But Conversation's lost, and Manners drown'd.   55

I cross'd unto the other Side
A River, whose impetuous Tide,
Those *Savage* Borders do divide,
In such a swimming odd Invension,
I scarce can give it's due Dimension,   60
The *Indians* call this watry Waggon,
Canoe, a Vessel none can brag on,
Cut from a Poplar Tree, or Pine,
And fashion'd like a Trough for Swine:
In this most noble Fishing-boat,   65
I boldly put my self afloat,
Standing erect, with Legs stretch'd wide,
We paddled to the other Side;
Where being landed safe by Hap,¹⁰
(As *Sol* fell into *Thetis'* Lap)¹¹   70
A ravenous Gang, bent on the Strowl,¹²
Of Wolves for Prey, began to howl:
This put me in a pannick Fright,
Lest I shou'd be devour'd quite:
But as I there a Musing stood,   75
And quite benighted in the Wood,
A Female Voice pierc'd thro' my Ears,
Crying, You Rogue drive home the Steers:
I listen'd¹³ that attractive Sound,
And streight a Herd of Cattle found,   80
Drove by a Youth, and homeward bound.
Cheer'd with the Sight, I streight thought fit
To ask, Where I a Bed might get?
The surly Peasant bid me stay,
And ask'd, From whom I'd run away?   85
Surpris'd at such a sawcy Word,
I instantly lugg'd out my Sword,

⁹ The gallows.
¹⁰ By chance.
¹¹ When the Roman sun god, Sol, fell into the
lap of Thetis, an ocean nymph from Greek
myth; i.e., at sunset.

¹² Stroll.
¹³ Listened to.

Swearing I was no Fugitive,
But from *Great Britain* did arrive,
In hopes I here might better thrive.   90
To which he mildly made Reply,
I beg your Pardon, Sir, that I
Shou'd talk to you unmannerly:
But if you please to go with me,
To yonder House you'll welcome be.   95

Encountring soon the smoaky Seat,
The Planter old did thus me greet.
Whether You're come from Goal,[14] *or College,*
You're Welcome, to my certain Knowlege,
And if You'll please all Night to stay,   100
My Son shall put You in the Way:
Which Offer I most kindly took,
And for a Seat did round me look,
When presently among the rest
He plac'd his unknown *English* Guest,   105
Who found 'em drinking, for a Whet,[15]
A Cask of Sider on the Fret:[16]
'Till Supper came upon the Table,
On which I fed whilst I was able;
So after hearty Entertainment,   110
Of Drink and Victuals, without Payment
For Planters Tables, you must know
Are free for all that come and go,
Whilst Pone,[17] with Milk and Mush well stor'd
In wooden Dishes grac'd the Board,   115
With Hominy[18] and Sider-Pap,
Which scarce an *English* Dog would lap,
Well stuff'd with Fat from Bacon fryd,
And with Melasses dulcify'd.
Then out our Landlord pulls his Pouch.   120
As greasy as the Leather Couch
On which he sat, and streight begun
To load with Weed his *Indian Gun,*[19]
In Length scarce longer than one's Finger
Or that for which the Ladies linger.   125
His Pipe smoak'd out, with awful Grace,
With Aspect grave and solemn Pace,
The Reverend Sir, walks to a Chest,
Of all his Furniture the best,

[14] Jail.
[15] Appetizer.
[16] Fermented.

[17] Cornbread.
[18] Hulled corn boiled in water or milk.
[19] Pipe.

Closely confin'd within a Room,   130
Which seldom felt the Weight of Broom
From thence he lugs a Cagg of Rum,
And nodding to me, thus begun:
I find, says he, *you don't much care*
For this our Indian *Country Fare;*   135
But let me tell you, Friend of mine,
You may be glad of it in Time,
Tho' now you're Stomach is so fine;
And if within this Land you stay,
You'll find it true what I do say: 140
This said, the Rundlet[20] up he threw,
And bending backwards strongly drew;
I pluck'd as stoutly, for my Part,
Altho' it made me sick at Heart,
And got so soon into my Head,   145
I scarce could find my Way to Bed;
Where I was instantly convey'd,
By one that pass'd for Chamber-Maid,
Tho' by her loose and sluttish Dress,
She rather seem'd a *Bedlam-Bess.*[21]   150
Curious to know from whence she came,
I press'd her to declare her Name?
She blushing, seem'd to hide her Eyes,
And thus in civil Terms replies:
In better Times, o'er to this Land   155
I was unhappily trepann'd,[22]
Perchance as well I did appear,
As any Gentlewoman here,
Not then a Slave for Twice Two Year;
My Cloaths were fashionably new,   160
Nor were my Shifts of Scotch *Cloth blew:*
But Things are chang'd: Now at the Hoe
I daily work, and barefoot go,
In weeding Corn, and feeding Swine,
I spend my melancholly Time;   165
Kidnapp'd and fool'd, I hither fled,
To shun a hated Nuptial Bed;
And to my Grief, already find
Worse Plagues than those I left behind.

Whate'er the Wand'rer did profess,   170
Good faith I cou'd not chuse but guess

---

[20] Small keg.   [22] Ensnared.
[21] Servant in a madhouse. Bedlam was a notorious
London asylum for the insane.

The Cause which brought her to this Place,[23]
Was Supping e're the Priest said Grace:
Quick as my Thoughts the Slave was fled,
Her Candle left to shew my Bed,   175
Which, made of Feathers soft and good,
Close in the Chimney-corner flood:
Laid me down, expecting Rest,
To be in Golden Slumbers blest;
But soon a Noise disturb'd my Quiet,   180
And plagu'd me with Nocturnal Riot:
A Puss,[24] which in the Ashes lay,
With grunting Pig, began a Fray,
And prudent Dog, that Feuds might cease,
Most sharply bark'd, to keep the Peace: 185
This Quarrel scarcely was decided
By Stick, that ready lay provided,
But *Reynard,*[25] arch and cunning Loon,
Crept into my Apartment soon,
In hot Pursuit of Ducks and Geese,   190
With full Intent the same to seize;
Their cackling 'Plaints with strange Surprise
Chas'd Sleep's thick Vapours from my Eyes;
Raging, I jump'd upon the Floor,
And like a drunken Sailor swore,   195
With Sword I fiercely laid about,
And soon dispers'd the feather'd Rout,
The Poultry out of Window flew,
And *Reynard* cautiously withdrew;
The Dogs who this Encounter heard,   200
Fiercely themselves to aid me rear'd,
And to the Place of Combat run,
Exactly as the Field was won,
Fretting and hot as roasted Capon,
And greasy as a Flitch of Bacon.[26]   205

I to the Orchard did repair,
To breathe the cool and open Air,
Impatient waiting for bright Day,
Extended on a Bank I lay;
But Fortune here, that sawcy Whore,   210
Disturb'd me worse, and plagu'd me more
Than she had done the Night before;
Hoarse croaking Frogs did round me ring,
Such Peals the Dead to Life wou'd bring,

---

[23] I.e., with child.
[24] Cat.

[25] Traditionally, a fox.
[26] Side of bacon.

A Noise might move their Wooden King:[27]   215
I stuff'd my Ears with Cotton white,
And curs'd the melancholly Night,
For fear of being deaf outright:
But soon my Vows I did recant,
And *Hearing* as a Blessing grant,   220
When a confounded *Rattle-Snake*
With Hissing made my Heart to ach,
Not knowing how to fly the Foe,
Or whither in the dark to go,
By strange good Luck I took a Tree,   225
Prepar'd by Fate to set me free,
Where, riding on a Limb astride,
Night and the Branches did me hide,
And I the De'el[28] and Snake defy'd.
Not yet from Plagues exempted quite,   230
The curs'd *Muschetoes*[29] did me bite;
'Til rising Morn, and blushing Day,
Drove both my Fears and Ills away,
And from Night's Terrors set me free,
Discharg'd from hospitable Tree.   235
    I did to Planter's Booth[30] repair,
And there at Breakfast nobly fare,
On Rasher[31] broil'd, of infant Bear;
I thought the Cubb delicious Meat,
Which ne'er did ought but Chesnuts eat,   240
Nor was young *Orson's* Flesh the worse,
Because he suck'd a *Pagan* Nurse:[32]
Our Breakfast done, the Planter stout,
Handed a Glass of Rum about.

    Pleas'd with the Treatment I did find,   245
I took my Leave of Host so kind.
Who, to oblige me, did provide
His eldest Son to be my Guide;
And lent me Horses of his own,
A skittish Colt and aged Roan,   250
The fourlegg'd Prop of his Wife *Joan.*
Steering our Course in Trott or Pace,
We sail'd directly for a Place,

[27] I.e., a wood idol. (See Isaiah 45:20.)
[28] Devil.
[29] Mosquitoes.
[30] A small, boxlike room.
[31] Portion.
[32] In *Valentine and Orson,* a French romance, the abandoned child Orson is nursed by a bear in the wilds.

In *MARYLAND* of high Renown;
Known by the Name of *Battle-Town:*   255
To view the Crowds did there resort,
Which Justice made, and Law, their Sport,
In their Sagacious County Court:
Scarce had we enter'd on the Way,
Which thro' the Woods and Marshes lay,   260
But *Indian* strange did soon appear
In hot Pursuit of wounded Deer;
No mortal Creature can express
His wild fantastick Air and Dress;
His painted Skin, in Colours dy'd,   265
His sable Hair, in Satchel ty'd,
Show'd *Savages* not free from Pride:
His tawny Thighs and Bosom bare,
Disdain'd an useless Coat to wear,
Scorn'd Summers Heat and Winters Air;   270
His manly Shoulders, such as please
Widows and Wives, were bath'd with Grease,
Of Cub and Bear, whose supple Oil,
Prepar'd his Limbs in Heat and Toil.
. . . .

   I then began to think with Care,   275
How I might sell my *British* Ware;
That with my Freight I might comply,
Did on my Charter-Party[33] lye:
To this Intent, with Guide before,
I tript it to the *Eastern* Shore;   280
Where riding near a Sandy Bay,
I met a Planter in my Way,
A pious, consciencious Rogue,
As e're wore Bonnet, Hat, or Brogue,[34]
Who neither swore, nor kept his Word,   285
But cheated in the Fear o' th' Lord;
And when his Debts he could not pay,
From trusting Fools he'd run away.

   With this sly Zealot, soon I struck
A Bargain, for my *English* Truck,   290
Agreeing for Ten Thousand Weight
Of *Sotweed* good, and fit for Freight:
Broad *Oronoko,*[35] bright and sound,

---

[33] Contract between merchants and shippers to guarantee safe arrival and sale of cargo.   [34] Shoe.
[35] Tobacco plant.

The Growth and Product of his Ground;
In Cask, that shou'd contain compleat   295
Five Hundred of Tobacco neat.

The Contract thus betwixt us made,
Not well acquainted with the Trade,
My Goods I trusted to the Cheat,
Whose Crop was then o'board the Fleet;   300
And going to receive my own,
I found the Bird was newly flown;
Cursing this execrable Slave,
This damn'd pretended Godly Knave,
On due Revenge and Justice bent,   305
I instantly to Council went;
Unto an ambodexter[36] Quack,
Who learnedly had got the Knack
Of giving Clysters,[37] making Pills,
Of filling Bonds, and forging Wills;   310
And with a Stock of Impudence,
Supply'd his want of Wit and Sence,
With Looks demure, amazing People
No wiser than a Daw[38] on Steeple:
My Anger flushing in my Face,   315
I stated the preceeding Case,
And of my Money was so free
That he'd have poison'd you or me,
And hang'd his Father on a Tree,
For such another tempting Fee.   320

Smiling, said he, the Cause is clear,
I'll manage him, you need not fear,
The Case is judg'd, good Sir, but look
In *Galen,* no, in my Lord Cook,[39]
I vow to G-d, I was mistook: 325
I'll take out a Provincial Writ.[40]
And trownce him for his knavish Wit,
Upon my Life, I'll win the Cause,
With as much Ease I cure the Yaws:[41]
Resolv'd to plague the Holy Brother,   330
I set one Rogue to catch another.

---

[36] Ambidextrous, meaning double-dealing. Cooke
wrote, "This fellow was an apothecary
[pharmacist] turned an attorney at law."
[37] Enemas.
[38] Crow.

[39] Galen: (129?–199) Greek physician; Cook: Sir
Edward Coke (1552–1634), author of *Institutes
of the Laws of England.*
[40] Restraining order.
[41] Skin disease.

To try the Cause then fully bent,
Up to *Annapolis* I went,
A City situate on a Plain,
Where scarce a House will keep out Rain;   335
The Buildings fram'd with Cypress rare,
Resembles much our *Southwark-Fair;*[42]
But Strangers there will scarcely meet,
With Market Place, Exchange, or Street;
And if the Truth I may report,   340
It's not so large as *Tottenham-Court.*[43]
St. *Mary's*[44] once was in Repute,
Now Here the Judges try the Suit,
And Lawyers twice a Year dispute.
As oft the Bench most gravely meet,   345
Some to get drink, and some to eat
A swinging Share of Country Treat:
But as for Justice write or wrong,
Not one amongst the numerous Throng
Knows what it means, or has the Heart,   350
To vindicate a Stranger's Part.

Now, Court being call'd by beat of Drum,
The Judges left their Punch and Rum;
When Pettifogging Doctor draws
His Papers forth, and opens Cause;   355
And lest I should the Better get,
Brib'd! Quack suppress'd his knavish Wit:
So Maid upon the downy Field,
Pretends a Rape, and fights to yield:
The byass'd Court without Delay,   360
Adjudg'd my Debt in Country Pay,
In Pipe Staves, Corn, or Flesh of Boar,[45]
Rare Cargo for the *English* Shore,
Raging with Grief, full Speed I ran,
To join the Fleet at *Kickatan:*[46]   365
And while I waited for a Wind,
This Wish proceeded from my Mind,

If any Youngster cross the Ocean,
To sell his Wares—may he with Caution

---

[42] London market fair.
[43] Section of London.
[44] Maryland settlement, founded in 1634.
[45] Cooke's note: "There is a law in this country [which says] the plaintiff may pay his debt in country pay, which consists in the produce of his plantation."
[46] Cooke's note: "The homeward bound fleet meets here."

> Before he pays, receive each Hogshead,　　　　　　　370
> Lest he be cheated by some Dogshead,
> Both of his Goods and his Tobacco;
> And then like me, he shall not lack-woe.
> 　　And may that Land where Hospitality
> Is every Planter's darling Quality,　　　　　　　375
> Be by each Trader kindly us'd,
> And may no Trader be abus'd;
> Then each of them shall deal with Pleasure,
> And each encrease the other's Treasure.
> *1708*

William Byrd II
1674–1744

William Byrd II was a witty sophisticate who thoroughly enjoyed his life as a Virginia aristocrat. Wealthy and well read, Byrd moved as easily in the drawing rooms of Georgian England as he did on the tobacco docks of his colonial plantation. He was a literary man within the tradition of the urbane dilettante and had a library of over 22,000 volumes, the largest in the American colonies.

Byrd's father inherited substantial Virginia acreage and profited from the Indian fur trade. He enlarged his estate through marriage and sent his four children to England for education suitable to a prosperous family with connections to the English gentry. At age seven William attended an Essex grammar school notable for the strength of its classical education, which Byrd clearly appreciated. He kept lifelong habits of reading classical authors upon waking. ("I rose about 6 o'clock and read two chapters in Hebrew and some Greek in Lucian. I said my prayers and ate boiled milk for breakfast.")

Byrd's father insisted that the boy learn the business practices necessary for plantation management and so installed him in the offices of the family's London tobacco merchant. In addition, young Byrd studied law at the Middle Temple, one of the Inns of Court that harbored writers and intellectuals as well as barristers. There Byrd made the acquaintance of the dramatists William Congreve and William Wycherly, as well as Nicholas Rowe, the biographer and editor of Shakespeare. Evidently Byrd had sufficient interest in science to use his connections to gain admission to the Royal Society. Throughout his fifteen years in England, Byrd gradually took his place as a gentleman and gallant in sophisticated London society.

Byrd readily readapted to Virginia plantation life, however, when his father called him home in 1696. He became active in Virginia politics and, because of his London connections, traveled back and forth several times. At his father's death in 1704 Byrd assumed full responsibility for the estate, which totaled more than 26,000 acres of land, including the present site of Richmond. Byrd married in 1706 and remarried several years after the death of his wife, all the while increasing the size of his estate until he held 179,000 acres, which he left, along with Westover, the manor house he built in brick for permanence, to his son.

Byrd's literary reputation is based on several writings. His diary is a miscellany of dietary practices, religious devotions, social and business intercourse, and sexual escapades that resemble the plays of his dramatist friends. ("Then I went to visit Mrs. A—l—n and committed uncleanness with the maid because the mistress was not at home. However when the mistress came I rogered her and about 12 o'clock went home and ate a plum cake for supper. I neglected my prayers, for which God forgive me.")

In 1728 Byrd accepted a commission to survey the disputed boundary between Virginia and North Carolina. He later developed the diary of that undertaking into his *History of the Dividing Line,* which circulated among his friends before finally being published in 1841. The *History* is anecdotal, at points ironic and sardonic. Byrd's voice is that of the observer-participant who never fails to be interested in all phenomena of the American environment. As a planter, he saw himself as "one of the patriarchs" in a secular colonial Canaan.

Further Reading:
R. Beatty, *William Byrd of Westover*, 1932.
P. Marambaud, *William Byrd of Westover,*
1674–1744, 1971.
The Correspondence of the Three William Byrds
of Westover, Virginia, 1684–1776, 2 vols., ed.
M. Tinling, 1977.

Text:
The Prose Works of William Byrd of Westover,
ed. L. Wright, 1966.

---

from The History of the Dividing Line

[The Great Dismal Swamp]

7. This morning the surveyors began to run the dividing line from the cedar post we had driven into the sand, allowing near three degrees for the variation. Without making this just allowance, we should not have obeyed His Majesty's order in running a due-west line. It seems the former commissioners had not been so exact, which gave our friends of Carolina but too just an exception to their proceedings. The line cut Dosier's Island, consisting only of a flat sand with here and there an humble shrub growing upon it. From thence it crossed over a narrow arm of the sound into Knott's Island and there split a plantation belonging to William Harding.

The day being far spent, we encamped in this man's pasture, though it lay very low and the season now inclined people to aguish distempers. He suffered us to cut cedar branches for our enclosure and other wood for firing, to correct the moist air and drive away the damps. Our landlady, in the days of her youth, it seems, had been a laundress in the Temple and talked over her adventures in that station with as much pleasure as an old soldier talks over his battles and distempers and, I believe, with as many additions to the truth.

The soil is good in many places of this island, and the extent of it pretty large. It lies in the form of a wedge: the south end of it is several miles over, but toward the north it sharpens into a point. It is a plentiful place for stock by reason of the wide marshes adjacent to it and because of its warm situation. But the inhabitants pay a little dear for this convenience by losing as much blood in the summer season by the infinite number of mosquitoes as all their beef and pork can recruit in the winter.

The sheep are as large as in Lincolnshire,[1] because they are never pinched by cold or hunger. The whole island was hitherto reckoned to lie in Virginia, but now our line has given the greater part of it to Carolina. The principal freeholder here is Mr. White, who keeps open house for all travelers that either debt or shipwreck happens to cast in his way.

8. By break of day we sent away our largest piragua[2] with the baggage round the south end of Knott's Island, with orders to the men to wait for us in the mouth of North River. Soon after, we embarked ourselves on board the smaller vessel, with intent, if possible, to find a passage round the north end of the island.

We found this navigation very difficult by reason of the continued shoals and often stuck fast aground; for though the sound spreads many miles, yet it is in most places extremely shallow and requires a skillful pilot to steer even a canoe safe over it. It was almost as hard to keep our temper as to keep the channel in this provoking situation. But the most impatient amongst us stroked down their choler[3] and swallowed their curses, lest, if they suffered them to break out, they might sound like complaining, which was expressly forbid as the first step to sedition.

At a distance we descried several islands to the northward of us, the largest of which goes by the name of Cedar Island. Our piragua stuck so often that we had a fair chance to be benighted in this wide water, which must certainly have been our fate had we not luckily spied a canoe that was giving a fortuneteller a cast from Princess Anne County over to North Carolina. But, as conjurers are sometimes mistaken, the man mistrusted we were officers of justice in pursuit of a young wench he had carried off along with him. We gave the canoe chase for more than an hour and when we came up with her threatened to make them all prisoners unless they would direct us into the right channel. By the pilotage of these people we rowed up an arm of the sound called the Back Bay till we came to the head of it. There we were stopped by a miry pocosin[4] full half a mile in breadth, through which we were obliged to daggle on foot, plunging now and then, though we picked our way, up to the knees in mud. At the end of this charming walk we gained the terra firma of Princess Anne County. In that dirty condition we were afterwards obliged to foot it two miles as far as John Heath's plantation, where we expected to meet the surveyors and the men who waited upon them.

While we were performing this tedious voyage, they had carried the line through the firm land of Knott's Island, where it was no more than half a mile wide. After that they traversed a large marsh, that was exceeding miry and extended to an arm of the Back Bay. They crossed that water in a canoe which we had ordered round for that purpose and then waded over another marsh that reached quite to the high land of Princess Anne. Both these marshes together make a breadth of five miles, in

---

[1] In England.
[2] Canoe.

[3] Anger.
[4] Swamp.

which the men frequently sank up to the middle without muttering the least complaint. On the contrary, they turned all these disasters into merriment.

It was discovered by this day's work that Knott's Island was improperly so called, being in truth no more than a peninsula. The northwest side of it is only divided from the main by the great marsh above-mentioned, which is seldom totally overflowed. Instead of that, it might by the labor of a few trenches be drained into firm meadow, capable of grazing as many cattle as Job in his best estate was master of. In the miry condition it now lies, it feeds great numbers in the winter, though when the weather grows warm they are driven from thence by the mighty armies of mosquitoes, which are the plague of the lower part of Carolina as much as the flies were formerly of Egypt (and some rabbis think those flies were no other than mosquitoes).

All the people in the neighborhood flocked to John Heath's to behold such rarities as they fancied us to be. The men left their beloved chimney corners, the good women their spinning wheels, and some, of more curiosity than ordinary, rose out of their sick beds to come and stare at us. They looked upon us as a troop of knights-errant who were running this great risk of our lives, as they imagined, for the public weal; and some of the gravest of them questioned much whether we were not all criminals condemned to this dirty work for offenses against the state. What puzzled them most was what could make our men so very light-hearted under such intolerable drudgery. "Ye have little reason to be merry, my masters," said one of them, with a very solemn face. "I fancy the pocosin you must struggle with tomorrow will make you change your note and try what metal you are made of. Ye are, to be sure, the first of human race that ever had the boldness to attempt it, and I dare say will be the last. If, therefore, you have any worldly goods to dispose of, my advice is that you make your wills this very night, for fear you die intestate tomorrow." But, alas, these frightful tales were so far from disheartening the men that they served only to whet their resolution.

9. The surveyors entered early upon their business this morning and ran the line through Mr. Eyland's plantation, as far as the banks of North River. They passed over it in the piragua and landed in Gibbs's marsh, which was a mile in breadth and tolerably firm. They trudged through this marsh without much difficulty as far as the high land, which promised more fertility than any they had seen in these lower parts. But this firm land lasted not long before they came upon the dreadful pocosin they had been threatened with. Nor did they find it one jot better than it had been painted to them. The beavers and otters had rendered it quite impassable for any creatures but themselves.

Our poor fellows had much ado to drag their legs after them in this quagmire, but, disdaining to be balked, they could hardly be persuaded from pressing forward by the surveyors, who found it absolutely necessary to make a traverse in the deepest place to prevent their sticking fast in the mire and becoming a certain prey to the turkey buzzards.

This horrible day's work ended two miles to the northward of Mr. Merchant's plantation, divided from Northwest River by a narrow swamp which is causewayed over. We took up our quarters in the open field not far from the house, correcting by a fire as large as a Roman funeral pile the aguish exhalations arising from the sunken grounds that surrounded us.

The neck of land included betwixt North River and Northwest River, with the adjacent marsh, belonged formerly to Governor Gibbs[5] but since his decrease to Colonel Bladen, in right of his first lady, who was Mr. Gibbs's daughter. It would be a valuable tract of land in any country but North Carolina, where, for want of navigation and commerce, the best estate affords little more than a coarse subsistence.

10. The Sabbath happened very opportunely, to give some ease to our jaded people, who rested religiously from every work but that of cooking the kettle. We observed very few cornfields in our walks and those very small, which seemed the stranger to us because we could see no other tokens of husbandry or improvement. But upon further inquiry we were given to understand people only made corn for themselves and not for their stocks, which know very well how to get their own living. Both cattle and hogs ramble into the neighboring marshes and swamps, where they maintain themselves the whole winter long and are not fetched home till the spring. Thus these indolent wretches during one half of the year lose the advantage of the milk of their cattle, as well as their dung, and many of the poor creatures perish in the mire, into the bargain, by this ill management. Some who pique themselves more upon industry than their neighbors will now and then, in compliment to their cattle, cut down a tree whose limbs are loaded with the moss afore-mentioned. The trouble would be too great to climb the tree in order to gather this provender, but the shortest way (which in this country is always counted the best) is to fell it, just like the lazy Indians, who do the same by such trees as bear fruit and so make one harvest for all. By this bad husbandry milk is so scarce in the winter season that were a big-bellied woman to long for it she would tax her longing. And, in truth, I believe this is often the case, and at the same time a very good reason why so many people in this province are marked with a custard complexion.

The only business here is raising of hogs, which is managed with the least trouble and affords the diet they are most fond of. The truth of it is, the inhabitants of North Carolina devour so much swine's flesh that it fills them full of gross humors. For want, too, of a constant supply of salt, they are commonly obliged to eat it fresh, and that begets the highest taint of scurvy. Thus, whenever a severe cold happens to constitutions thus vitiated, 'tis apt to improve into the yaws,[6] called there very justly the country distemper. This has all the symptoms of the pox, with this aggravation, that no preparation of mercury will touch it. First it seizes the throat, next the palate, and lastly shows its spite to the poor nose, of which 'tis apt in a small time treacherously to undermine the foundation. This calamity is so common and familiar here that it ceases to be a scandal, and in the disputes that happen about beauty the noses have in some companies much ado to carry it. Nay, 'tis said that once, after three good pork years, a motion had like to have been made in the House of Burgesses that a man with a nose should be incapable of holding any place of profit in the province; which extraordinary motion could never have been intended without some hopes of a majority.

Thus, considering the foul and pernicious effects of eating swine's flesh in a hot country, it was wisely forbid and made an abomination to the Jews, who lived much in the same latitude with Carolina.

---

[5] Although Philip Ludwell was appointed governor of North Carolina, John Gibbs claimed the title and refused to acknowledge the appointee's authority. Gibbs's heir, Martin Bladen, was married to Gibbs's daughter Mary.
[6] A skin disease.

11. We ordered the surveyors early to their business, who were blessed with pretty dry grounds for three miles together. But they paid dear for it in the next two, consisting of one continued frightful pocosin, which no creatures but those of the amphibious kind ever had ventured into before. This filthy quagmire did in earnest put the men's courage to a trial, and though I can't say it made them lose their patience, yet they lost their humor for joking. They kept their gravity like so many Spaniards, so that a man might then have taken his opportunity to plunge up to the chin without danger of being laughed at. However, this unusual composure of countenance could not fairly be called complaining.

Their day's work ended at the mouth of Northern's Creek, which empties itself into Northwest River; though we chose to quarter a little higher up the river near Mossy Point. This we did for the convenience of an old house to shelter our persons and baggage from the rain, which threatened us hard. We judged the thing right, for there fell an heavy shower in the night that drove the most hardy of us into the house. Though indeed our case was not much mended by retreating thither, because, that tenement having not long before been used as a pork store, the moisture of the air dissolved the salt that lay scattered on the floor and made it as wet withindoors as without. However, the swamps and marshes we were lately accustomed to had made such beavers and otters of us that nobody caught the least cold.

We had encamped so early that we found time in the evening to walk near half a mile into the woods. There we came upon a family of mulattoes that called themselves free, though by the shyness of the master of the house, who took care to keep least in sight, their freedom seemed a little doubtful. It is certain many slaves shelter themselves in this obscure part of the world, nor will any of their righteous neighbors discover them. On the contrary, they find their account in settling such fugitives on some out-of-the way corner of their land to raise stocks for a mean and inconsiderable share, well knowing their condition makes it necessary for them to submit to any terms. Nor were these worthy borderers content to shelter runaway slaves, but debtors and criminals have often met with the like indulgence. But if the government of North Carolina have encouraged this unneighborly policy in order to increase their people, it is no more than what ancient Rome did before them, which was made a city of refuge for all debtors and fugitives and from that wretched beginning grew up in time to be mistress of great part of the world. And, considering how Fortune delights in bringing great things out of small, who knows but Carolina may, one time or other, come to be the seat of some other great empire?

12. Everything had been so soaked with the rain that we were obliged to lie by a good part of the morning and dry them. However, that time was not lost, because it gave the surveyors an opportunity of platting off their work and taking the course of the river. It likewise helped to recruit the spirits of the men, who had been a little harassed with yesterday's march. Notwithstanding all this, we crossed the river before noon and advanced our line three miles. It was not possible to make more of it by reason good part of the way was either marsh or pocosin. The line cut two or three plantations, leaving part of them in Virginia and part of them in Carolina. This was a case that happened frequently, to the great inconvenience of the owners, who were therefore obliged to take out two patents and pay for a new survey in each government.

In the evening we took up our quarters in Mr. Ballance's pasture, a little above the bridge built over Northwest River. There we discharged the two piraguas, which in truth had been very serviceable in transporting us over the many waters in that dirty and difficult part of our business. Our landlord had a tolerable good house and clean furniture, and yet we could not be tempted to lodge in it. We chose rather to lie in the open field, for fear of growing too tender. A clear sky, spangled with stars, was our canopy, which, being the last thing we saw before we fell asleep, gave us magnificent dreams. The truth of it is, we took so much pleasure in that natural kind of lodging that I think at the foot of the account mankind are great losers by the luxury of feather beds and warm apartments.

The curiosity of beholding so new and withal so sweet a method of encamping brought one of the Senators of North Carolina to make us a midnight visit. But he was so very clamorous in his commendations of it that the sentinel, not seeing his quality either through his habit or behavior, had like to have treated him roughly. After excusing the unseasonableness of his visit and letting us know he was a parliament man, he swore he was so taken with our lodging that he would set fire to his house as soon as he got home and teach his wife and children to lie like us in the open field.

13. Early this morning our chaplain repaired to us with the men we had left at Mr. Wilson's. We had sent for them the evening before to relieve those who had the labor oar from Currituck Inlet. But to our great surprise, they petitioned not to be relieved, hoping to gain immortal reputation by being the first of mankind that ventured through the Great Dismal.[7] But the rest being equally ambitious of the same honor, it was but fair to decide their pretensions by lot. After Fortune had declared herself, those which she had excluded offered money to the happy persons to go in their stead. But Hercules would have as soon sold the glory of cleansing the Augean stables,[8] which was pretty near the same sort of work. No sooner was the controversy at an end but we sent those unfortunate fellows back to their quarters whom chance had condemned to remain upon firm land and sleep in a whole skin. In the meanwhile, the surveyors carried the line three miles, which was no contemptible day's work, considering how cruelly they were entangled with briers and gallbushes. The leaf of this last shrub bespeaks it to be of the alaternus family.

Our work ended within a quarter of a mile of the Dismal above-mentioned, where the ground began to be already full of sunken holes and slashes, which had, here and there, some few reeds growing in them. 'Tis hardly credible how little the bordering inhabitants were acquainted with this mighty swamp, notwithstanding they had lived their whole lives within smell of it. Yet, as great strangers as they were to it, they pretended to be very exact in their account of its dimensions and were positive it could not be above seven or eight miles wide, but knew no more of the matter than stargazers know of the distance of the fixed stars. At the same time, they were simple enough to amuse our men with idle stories of the lions, panthers, and alligators they were likely to encounter in that dreadful place. In short, we saw plainly there was no intelligence of this *Terra Incognita*[9] to be got but from our own experience. For that reason it was resolved to make the requisite dispositions to enter it next morning.

[7] I.e., the Great Dismal Swamp along the eastern boundary between Virginia and North Carolina.
[8] As one of twelve labors, each one an exercise in humility, Hercules was required to clean in one day the stables where the enormous herds of cattle owned by the King of Elis were housed.
[9] Latin: "Unexplored land."

We allotted every one of the surveyors for this painful enterprise, with twelve men to attend them. Fewer than that could not be employed in clearing the way, carrying the chain, marking the trees, and bearing the necessary bedding and provisions. Nor would the commissioners themselves have spared their persons on this occasion but for fear of adding to the poor men's burden, while they were certain they could add nothing to their resolution.

We quartered with our friend and fellow traveler, William Wilkins, who had been our faithful pilot to Currituck and lived about a mile from the place where the line ended. Everything looked so very clean and the furniture so neat that we were tempted to lodge withindoors. But the novelty of being shut up so close quite spoiled our rest, nor did we breathe so free by abundance as when we lay in the open air.

14. Before nine of the clock this morning the provisions, bedding, and other necessaries were made up into packs for the men to carry on their shoulders into the Dismal. They were victualed for eight days at full allowance, nobody doubting but that would be abundantly sufficient to carry them through that inhospitable place; nor indeed was it possible for the poor fellows to stagger under more. As it was, their loads weighed from sixty to seventy pounds, in just proportion to the strength of those who were to bear them. 'Twould have been unconscionable to have saddled them with burdens heavier than that, when they were to lug them through a filthy bog which was hardly practicable with no burden at all. Besides this luggage at their backs, they were obliged to measure the distance, mark the trees, and clear the way for the surveyors every step they went. It was really a pleasure to see with how much cheerfulness they undertook and with how much spirit they went through all this drudgery. For their greater safety, the commissioners took care to furnish them with Peruvian bark,[10] rhubarb, and ipecacuanha, in case they might happen, in that wet journey, to be taken with fevers or fluxes.

Although there was no need of example to inflame persons already so cheerful, yet to enter the people with the better grace, the author and two more of the commissioners accompanied them half a mile into the Dismal. The skirts of it were thinly planted with dwarf reeds and gallbushes, but when we got into the Dismal itself we found the reeds grew there much taller and closer and, to mend the matter, were so interlaced with bamboo briers that there was no scuffling through them without the help of pioneers. At the same time we found the ground moist and trembling under our feet like a quagmire, insomuch that it was an easy matter to run a ten-foot pole up to the head in it without exerting any uncommon strength to do it. Two of the men whose burdens were the least cumbersome had orders to march before with their tomahawks and clear the way in order to make an opening for the surveyors. By their assistance we made a shift to push the line half a mile in three hours and then reached a small piece of firm land about a hundred yards wide, standing up above the rest like an island. Here the people were glad to lay down their loads and take a little refreshment, while the happy man whose lot it was to carry the jug of rum began already, like Aesop's bread carriers, to find it grow a good deal lighter.

After reposing about an hour, the commissioners recommended vigor and constancy to their fellow travelers, by whom they were answered with three cheerful huzzas, in token of obedience. This ceremony was no sooner over but they took up

---

[10] Purported remedy for fever, especially malaria.

their burdens and attended the motion of the surveyors, who, though they worked with all their might, could reach but one mile farther, the same obstacles still attending them which they had met with in the morning. However small this distance may seem to such as are used to travel at their ease, yet our poor men, who were obliged to work with an unwieldy load at their backs, had reason to think it a long way; especially in a bog where they had no firm footing but every step made a deep impression which was instantly filled with water. At the same time they were laboring with their hands to cut down the reeds, which were ten feet high, their legs were hampered with briers. Besides, the weather happened to be warm, and the tallness of the reeds kept off every friendly breeze from coming to refresh them. And indeed it was a little provoking to hear the wind whistling among the branches of the white cedars, which grew here and there amongst the reeds, and at the same time not to have the comfort to feel the least breath of it.

In the meantime the three commissioners returned out of the Dismal the same way they went in and, having joined their brethren, proceeded that night as far as Mr. Wilson's. This worthy person lives within sight of the Dismal, in the skirts whereof his stocks range and maintain themselves all the winter, and yet he knew as little of it as he did of *Terra Australis Incognita.*[11] He told us a Canterbury tale of a North Briton whose curiosity spurred him a long way into this great desert, as he called it, near twenty years ago, but he, having no compass nor seeing the sun for several days together, wandered about till he was almost famished; but at last he bethought himself of a secret his countrymen make use of to pilot themselves in a dark day. He took a fat louse out of his collar and exposed it to the open day on a piece of white paper, which he brought along with him for his journal. The poor insect, having no eyelids, turned himself about till he found the darkest part of the heavens and so made the best of his way toward the North. By this direction he steered himself safe out and gave such a frightful account of the monsters he saw and the distresses he underwent that no mortal since has been hardy enough to go upon the like dangerous discovery.

15. The surveyors pursued their work with all diligence but still found the soil of the Dismal so spongy that the water oozed up into every footstep they took. To their sorrow, too, they found the reeds and briers more firmly interwoven than they did the day before. But the greatest grievance was from large cypresses which the wind had blown down and heaped upon one another. On the limbs of most of them grew sharp snags, pointing every way like so many pikes, that required much pains and caution to avoid. These trees, being evergreens and shooting their large tops very high, are easily overset by every gust of wind, because there is no firm earth to steady their roots. Thus many of them were laid prostrate, to the great encumbrance of the way. Such variety of difficulties made the business go on heavily, insomuch that from morning till night the line could advance no farther than one mile and thirty-one poles.

Never was rum, that cordial of life, found more necessary than it was in this dirty place. It did not only recruit the people's spirits, now almost jaded with fatigue, but served to correct the badness of the water and at the same time to resist the malignity of the air. Whenever the men wanted to drink, which was very often, they had

---

[11] Latin: "Unexplored land of Australia."

nothing more to do but make a hole and the water bubbled up in a moment. But it was far from being either clear or well tasted and had, besides, a physical effect from the tincture it received from the roots of the shrubs and trees that grew in the neighborhood.

While the surveyors were thus painfully employed, the commissioners discharged the long score they had with Mr. Wilson for the men and horses which had been quartered upon him during our expedition to Currituck. From thence we marched in good order along the east side of the Dismal and passed the long bridge that lies over the south branch of Elizabeth River. At the end of eighteen miles we reached Timothy Ivy's plantation, where we pitched our tent for the first time and were furnished with everything the place afforded. We perceived the happy effects of industry in this family, in which every one looked tidy and clean and carried in their countenances the cheerful marks of plenty. We saw no drones there, which are but too common, alas, in that part of the world. Though, in truth, the distemper of laziness seizes the men oftener much than the women. These last spin, weave, and knit, all with their own hands, while their husbands, depending on the bounty of the climate, are slothful in everything but getting of children, and in that only instance make themselves useful members of an infant colony.

There is but little wool in that province, though cotton grows very kindly and, so far south, is seldom nipped by the frost. The good women mix this with their wool for their outer garments; though, for want of fulling, that kind of manufacture is open and sleazy. Flax likewise thrives there extremely, being perhaps as fine as any in the world, and I question not might with a little care and pains be brought to rival that of Egypt; and yet the men are here so intolerably lazy they seldom take the trouble to propagate it.

16. The line was this day carried one mile and an half and sixteen poles. The soil continued soft and miry but fuller of trees, especially white cedars. Many of these, too, were thrown down and piled in heaps, high enough for a good Muscovite fortification. The worst of it was, the poor fellows began now to be troubled with fluxes, occasioned by bad water and moist lodging, but chewing of rhubarb kept that malady within bounds.

In the meantime, the commissioners decamped early in the morning and made a march of twenty-five miles, as far as Mr. Andrew Meade's, who lives upon Nansemond River. They were no sooner got under the shelter of that hospitable roof but it began to rain hard and continued so to do great part of the night. This gave them much pain for their friends in the Dismal, whose sufferings spoiled their taste for the good cheer wherewith they were entertained themselves. However, late that evening these poor men had the fortune to come upon another terra firma, which was the luckier for them because the lower ground, by the rain that fell, was made a fitter lodging for tadpoles than men. In our journey we remarked that the north side of this great swamp lies higher than either the east or the west, nor were the approaches to it so full of sunken grounds.

We passed by no less than two Quaker meetinghouses, one of which had an awkward ornament on the west end of it that seemed to ape a steeple. I must own I expected no such piece of foppery from a sect of so much outside simplicity. That persuasion prevails much in the lower end of Nansemond County, for want of ministers to pilot the people a decenter way to Heaven. The ill reputation of tobacco planted in those lower parishes makes the clergy unwilling to accept of them, unless it be such whose abilities are as mean as their pay. Thus, whether the churches be quite void or but indifferently filled, the Quakers will have an opportunity of gaining proselytes. 'Tis a wonder no popish missionaries are sent from Maryland to labor in this neglected vineyard, who we know have zeal enough to traverse sea and land on the meritorious errand of making converts. Nor is it less strange that some wolf in sheep's clothing arrives not from New England to lead astray a flock that has no shepherd. People uninstructed in any religion are ready to embrace the first that offers. 'Tis natural for helpless man to adore his Maker in some form or other, and were there any exception to this rule, I should suspect it to be among the Hottentots[12] of the Cape of Good Hope and of North Carolina.

There fell a great deal of rain in the night, accompanied with a strong wind. The fellow feeling we had for the poor Dismalites, on account of this unkind weather, rendered the down we laid upon uneasy. We fancied them half-drowned in their wet lodging, with the trees blowing down about their ears. These were the gloomy images our fears suggested, though 'twas so much uneasiness clear gains. They happened to come off much better, by being luckily encamped on the dry piece of ground afore-mentioned.

1841

Jonathan Edwards
1703–1758

Jonathan Edwards was a soft-spoken Puritan mystic and intellectual who ranged boldly in thought and writing; he is best known for a sermon that depicts sinners dangling by a spider's filament over "hell's wide gaping mouth." Edwards was born in East Windsor, Connecticut, the sole son among ten daughters of the Reverend Timothy Edwards and Esther Stoddard, herself the daughter of the renowned Puritan minister Solomon Stoddard. Tutored at home by his gifted parents, Edwards entered Yale at the age of thirteen. As his college diary shows, Edwards, like Benjamin Franklin, was determined to improve himself and "never to lose one moment of time." He graduated in 1720 and remained in New Haven for two additional years of theological study. Licensed to preach in 1722, Edwards served in a New York Presbyterian Church for two years, then returned to New Haven as a Yale tutor. The private writings of these student days show his youthful idealism, his deep concern for empirically gathered data, and his passionate involvement in religious experience.

In 1727, in his midtwenties, Edwards became his grandfather's assistant minister at the church in Northampton, Massachusetts. That July he married Sarah Pierrepont, the granddaughter of the illustrious Puritan minister Thomas Hooker. The young man doubtless looked forward to several years of a clerical apprenticeship, but Stoddard's death within two years left young Edwards the

---

[12] Natives of South Africa.

sole pastor of an important congregation. Situated at the northern part of the Connecticut River valley, Northampton was the home of many of the "river Gods," leading merchants and political figures of the valley who had grown accustomed to a liberal theology. Edwards's grandfather had presided over his congregation with a sense of the value of compromise.

Edwards proved to be very different from his predecessor, though initially he carried out his duties quietly. In 1731 he traveled to Boston to deliver an important lecture before an audience of prestigious ministers. Well aware of the contemporary ecumenical spirit of things, Edwards asserted that these newer "reasonable" moderations of Puritan doctrine were "repugnant to the design and tenor of the gospel." Edwards championed the orthodox Puritanism of the founders in the face of the new "free and catholick" temper of the times. His Northampton sermons and other writings over the next few years fortified that position. Above all, Edwards wished to move his congregation beyond a mere cerebral grasp of doctrine. His reading of the philosopher John Locke reinforced his belief that intellectual comprehension of religious ideas was insufficient. Instead, the individual must be moved actually to experience the doctrinal truth. It was the difference, Edwards wrote, between knowing the word *fire* and being burned. Edwards worked to make his Northampton congregation appreciate that difference and to yearn for religious experience. As Edwards wrote, "People do not need to have their heads stored so much as their hearts touched."

From 1735 the hearts of the Northampton congregation were indeed touched in an unusual religious revival in which Edwards played a vital part. The people of the town, he wrote, "seemed to be seized with a deep concern about their eternal salvation . . . in a truly wonderful and astonishing manner." Soon the revival spread throughout the Connecticut River valley, bringing much word-of-mouth attention to Edwards and his congregation. Though their revival ran its course in two years, the evangelical fervor of the Northampton awakening anticipated the much larger Great Awakening which preoccupied the American colonies from New England to Georgia in the 1740s.

Edwards grew increasingly interested in the psychology of religious conversion. He was familiar with the newer theories of sensate knowledge espoused by Locke and by the English philosopher George Berkeley, though his belief in the tenets of Puritanism was unshakable. Exploring the nature of religious experience, Edwards sought to reconcile his inherited Puritanism with the new theories, arguing that knowledge was acquired from sensory experience, not from innate powers of mind. His major work on this subject became *A Treatise Concerning Religious Affections* (1746). Edwards concluded that God's grace was experienced through the "affections," which were not merely emotions but the force that moved the individual toward affirmative possession or to repudiation. In Edwards's scheme of thought, love "is not only one of the affections but it is the first and chief . . . and the fountain of all the affections."

In large part Edwards's religious beliefs were the outcome of his mystical conversion experience in his youth. He later described it in his *Personal Narrative*, in terms so appreciative of the natural world that he sounds to some like a Romantic writer. Believing, however, in the absolute supremacy of God, Edwards saw revivalism as an opportunity to authenticate his faith and to restore

Puritanism to its original strength. To this end he delivered the sulphurous sermon titled "Sinners in the Hands of an Angry God," which remains the best-known sermon in American history. It was designed specifically to awaken the congregation to a sense of their sinfulness. In Puritan theology this intense, personal experience of depravity was the necessary first step toward conversion. "Sinners in the Hands of an Angry God" was just one of a handful of imprecatory sermons among the thousand extant from Edwards's twenty-four years at Northampton and from his years elsewhere, but it bears the stamp of his major concerns: that raised affections are visible signs, that mere human efforts to achieve salvation are futile, and that God alone is the omnipotent judge.

Edwards made Northampton a renowned center of orthodoxy and revived spirituality, but by the mid-1740s affairs between the minister and his congregation were moving toward crisis. A backlash developed over the excesses of the Great Awakening and its itinerant preachers, whose "beastly brayings" Edwards himself deplored. Yet some concurred with Edwards's ministerial opponent, Charles Chauncy, that Edwards was a "visionary enthusiast, and not to be minded." There was further squabbling over Edwards's propensity to trade with Boston merchants. There was trouble, too, when Edwards attempted to discipline some children of prominent families for circulating "bad books" (meaning a manual for midwives) and when Joseph Hawley, the son of a man who committed suicide during the Northampton revivals, rallied a faction against him. At last Edwards was forced to resign. Without public rancor he preached his farewell sermon in 1750.

In the following year Edwards assumed the duties of a frontier minister to whites and Indians in Stockbridge, a remote western Massachusetts mission. There Edwards wrote his greatest philosophical works, including *Freedom of the Will* (1754), *The Doctrine of Original Sin Defended* (1758), and *The Nature of True Virtue* (1765). These works examine the nature and place of free will in a predetermined universe and explore the relation between virtue and religious affections. The publication of these works brought Edwards renewed attention from scholars and intellectuals, who invited him to become the president of Princeton University. He arrived with his family amid an outbreak of smallpox. In 1758, after less than two months in office, Edwards died from an adverse reaction to a smallpox inoculation, for which he had volunteered. He is revered as an American philosopher of originality and a literary stylist of subtlety and power.

Further Reading:
T. H. Johnson, *The Printed Writings of Jonathan Edwards, 1703–1758,* 1940, 1970.
O. Winslow, *Jonathan Edwards,* 1940.
P. Miller, *Jonathan Edwards,* 1949.
A. Aldridge, *Jonathan Edwards,* 1964.
C. Cherry, *The Theology of Jonathan Edwards,* 1966.
E. Griffin, *Jonathan Edwards,* 1971.

Texts:
Images or Shadows of Divine Things, ed. P. Miller, 1948.
Remaining selections from *The Works of President Edwards,* 10 vols., ed. S. Dwight, 1829–1830.

Personal Narrative

I had a variety of concerns and exercises about my soul from my childhood; but had two more remarkable seasons of awakening,[1] before I met with that change by which I was brought to those new dispositions, and that new sense of things, that I have since had. The first time was when I was a boy, some years before I went to college, at a time of remarkable awakening in my father's congregation. I was then very much affected for many months, and concerned about the things of religion, and my soul's salvation; and was abundant in duties. I used to pray five times a day in secret, and to spend much time in religious talk with other boys; and used to meet with them to pray together. I experienced I know not what kind of delight in religion. My mind was much engaged in it, and had much self-righteous pleasure; and it was my delight to abound in religious duties. I with some of my schoolmates joined together, and built a booth in a swamp, in a very retired spot, for a place of prayer. And besides, I had particular secret places of my own in the woods, where I used to retire by myself; and was from time to time much affected. My affections[2] seemed to be lively and easily moved, and I seemed to be in my element when engaged in religious duties. And I am ready to think, many are deceived with such affections, and such a kind of delight as I then had in religion, and mistake it for grace.

But in process of time, my convictions and affections wore off; and I entirely lost all those affections and delights and left off secret prayer, at least as to any constant performance of it; and returned like a dog to his vomit,[3] and went on in the ways of sin. Indeed I was at times very uneasy, especially towards the latter part of my time at college, when it pleased God to seize me with the pleurisy, in which He brought me nigh to the grave, and shook me over the pit of hell. And yet, it was not long after my recovery, before I fell again into my old ways of sin. But God would not suffer me to go on with any quietness; I had great and violent inward struggles, till, after many conflicts with wicked inclinations, repeated resolutions, and bonds that I laid myself under by a kind of vows to God, I was brought wholly to break off all former wicked ways, and all ways of known outward sin; and to apply myself to seek salvation, and practice many religious duties; but without that kind of affection and delight which I had formerly experienced. My concern now wrought more by inward struggles and conflicts, and self-reflections. I made seeking my salvation the main business of my life. But yet, it seems to me I sought after a miserable manner; which has made me sometimes since to question, whether ever it issued in that which was saving; being ready to doubt, whether such miserable seeking ever succeeded. I was indeed brought to seek salvation in a manner that I never was before; I felt a spirit to part with all things in the world, for an interest in Christ. My concern continued and prevailed, with many exercising thoughts and inward struggles; but yet it never seemed to be proper to express that concern by the name of terror.

[1] Religious enlivening.
[2] Religious feelings.
[3] See Proverbs 26:11.

From my childhood up, my mind had been full of objections against the doctrine of God's sovereignty, in choosing whom He would to eternal life, and rejecting whom He pleased; leaving them eternally to perish, and be everlastingly tormented in hell. It used to appear like a horrible doctrine to me. But I remember the time very well, when I seemed to be convinced, and fully satisfied, as to this sovereignty of God, and His justice in thus eternally disposing of men, according to His sovereign pleasure. But I never could give an account how, or by what means, I was thus convinced, not in the least imagining at the time, nor a long time after, that there was any extraordinary influence of God's Spirit in it; but only that now I saw further, and my reason apprehended the justice and reasonableness of it. However, my mind rested in it; and it put an end to all those cavils and objections. And there has been a wonderful alteration in my mind, with respect to the doctrine of God's sovereignty, from that day to this; so that I scarce ever have found so much as the rising of an objection against it, in the most absolute sense, in God's showing mercy to whom He will show mercy, and hardening whom He will.[4] God's absolute sovereignty and justice, with respect to salvation and damnation, is what my mind seems to rest assured of, as much as of anything that I see with my eyes; at least it is so at times. But I have often, since that first conviction, had quite another kind of sense of God's sovereignty than I had then. I have often since had not only a conviction, but a delightful conviction. The doctrine has very often appeared exceeding pleasant, bright, and sweet. Absolute sovereignty is what I love to ascribe to God. But my first conviction was not so.

The first instance that I remember of that sort of inward, sweet delight in God and divine things that I have lived much in since, was on reading those words, 1 Timothy 1:17, *Now unto the King eternal, immortal, invisible, the only wise God, be honor and glory forever and ever, Amen.* As I read the words, there came into my soul, and was as it were diffused through it, a sense of the glory of the Divine Being; a new sense, quite different from anything I ever experienced before. Never any words of Scripture seemed to me as these words did. I thought within myself, how excellent a Being that was, and how happy I should be, if I might enjoy that God, and be rapt[5] up to him in heaven, and be as it were swallowed up in him forever! I kept saying, and as it were singing over these words of Scripture to myself; and went to pray to God that I might enjoy Him, and prayed in a manner quite different from what I used to do; with a new sort of affection. But it never came into my thought that there was anything spiritual, or of a saving nature, in this.

From about that time, I began to have a new kind of apprehensions and ideas of Christ, and the work of redemption, and the glorious way of salvation by Him. An inward, sweet sense of these things, at times, came into my heart; and my soul was led away in pleasant views and contemplations of them. And my mind was greatly engaged to spend my time in reading and meditating on Christ, on the beauty and excellency of His person, and the lovely way of salvation by free grace in Him. I found no books so delightful to me, as those that treated of these subjects. Those words, Canticles[6] 2:1, used to be abundantly with me, *I am the Rose of Sharon, and the lily of the valleys.* The words seemed to me sweetly to represent the loveliness and beauty

---

[4] See Romans 9:18.
[5] Lifted.

[6] The biblical Song of Solomon.

of Jesus Christ. The whole book of Canticles used to be pleasant to me, and I used to be much in reading it, about that time; and found, from time to time, an inward sweetness, that would carry me away, in my contemplations. This I know not how to express otherwise, than by a calm, sweet abstraction of soul from all the concerns of this world; and sometimes a kind of vision, or fixed ideas and imaginations, of being alone in the mountains, or some solitary wilderness, far from all mankind, sweetly conversing with Christ, and wrapped and swallowed up in God. The sense I had of divine things would often of a sudden kindle up, as it were, a sweet burning in my heart; an ardor of soul, that I know not how to express.

Not long after I first began to experience these things, I gave an account to my father of some things that had passed in my mind. I was pretty much affected by the discourse we had together; and when the discourse was ended, I walked abroad alone, in a solitary place in my father's pasture, for contemplation. And as I was walking there, and looking up on the sky and clouds, there came into my mind so sweet a sense of the glorious *majesty* and *grace* of God, that I know not how to express. I seemed to see them both in a sweet conjunction; majesty and meekness joined together; it was a sweet and gentle, and holy majesty; and also a majestic meekness; an awful sweetness; a high, and great, and holy gentleness.

After this my sense of divine things gradually increased, and became more and more lively, and had more of that inward sweetness. The appearance of every thing was altered; there seemed to be, as it were, a calm, sweet cast, or appearance of divine glory, in almost everything. God's excellency, His wisdom, His purity and love, seemed to appear in every thing; in the sun, and moon, and stars; in the clouds and blue sky; in the grass, flowers, trees; in the water, and all nature; which used greatly to fix my mind. I often used to sit and view the moon for a long time; and in the day spent much time in viewing the clouds and sky, to behold the sweet glory of God in these things; in the meantime, singing forth, with a low voice, my contemplations of the Creator and Redeemer. And scarce anything, among all the works of nature, was so sweet to me as thunder and lightning; formerly, nothing had been so terrible to me. Before, I used to be uncommonly terrified with thunder, and to be struck with terror when I saw a thunder storm rising; but now, on the contrary, it rejoiced me. I felt God, so to speak, at the first appearance of a thunder storm; and used to take the opportunity, at such times, to fix myself in order to view the clouds, and see the lightnings play, and hear the majestic and awful voice of God's thunder, which oftentimes was exceedingly entertaining, leading me to sweet contemplations of my great and glorious God. While thus engaged, it always seemed natural to me to sing, or chant forth my meditations; or, to speak my thoughts in soliloquies with a singing voice.

I felt then great satisfaction, as to my good state; but that did not content me. I had vehement longings of soul after God and Christ, and after more holiness, where-with my heart seemed to be full, and ready to break; which often brought to my mind the words of the Psalmist, Psalms 119:20: *My soul breaketh for the longing that it hath.* I often felt a mourning and lamenting in my heart, that I had not turned to God sooner, that I might have had more time to grow in grace. My mind was greatly fixed on divine things; almost perpetually in the contemplation of them. I spent most of my time in thinking of divine things, year after year; often walking alone in the woods, and solitary places, for meditation, soliloquy, and prayer, and converse with

God; and it was always my manner, at such times, to sing forth my contemplations. I was almost constantly in ejaculatory prayer, wherever I was. Prayer seemed to be natural to me, as the breath by which the inward burnings of my heart had vent. The delights which I now felt in the things of religion, were of an exceeding different kind from those before mentioned, that I had when a boy; and what I then had no more notion of, than one born blind has of pleasant and beautiful colors. They were of a more inward, pure, soul-animating and refreshing nature. Those former delights never reached the heart; and did not arise from any sight of the divine excellency of the things of God; or any taste of the soul-satisfying and life-giving good there is in them.

My sense of divine things seemed gradually to increase, until I went to preach at New York,[7] which was about a year and a half after they[8] began; and while I was there, I felt them, very sensibly, in a higher degree than I had done before. My longings after God and holiness were much increased. Pure and humble, holy and heavenly Christianity appeared exceedingly amiable to me. I felt a burning desire to be in everything a complete Christian; and conformed to the blessed image of Christ; and that I might live, in all things, according to the pure, sweet and blessed rules of the gospel. I had an eager thirsting after progress in these things; which put me upon pursuing and pressing after them. It was my continual strife day and night, and constant inquiry, how I should *be* more holy, and *live* more holily, and more becoming a child of God, and a disciple of Christ. I now sought an increase of grace and holiness, and a holy life, with much more earnestness, than ever I sought grace before I had it. I used to be continually examining myself, and studying and contriving for likely ways and means, how I should live holily, with far greater diligence and earnestness, than ever I pursued anything in my life; but yet with too great a dependence on my own strength; which afterwards proved a great damage to me. My experience had not then taught me, as it has done since, my extreme feebleness and impotence, every manner of way; and the bottomless depths of secret corruption and deceit there was in my heart. However, I went on with my eager pursuit after more holiness, and conformity to Christ.

The heaven I desired was a heaven of holiness; to be with God, and to spend my eternity in divine love, and holy communion with Christ. My mind was very much taken up with contemplations on heaven, and the enjoyments there; and living there in perfect holiness, humility, and love; and it used at that time to appear a great part of the happiness of heaven, that there the saints could express their love to Christ. It appeared to me a great clog and burden, that what I felt within, I could not express as I desired. The inward ardor of my soul seemed to be hindered and pent up, and could not freely flame out as it would. I used often to think, how in heaven this principle should freely and fully vent and express itself. Heaven appeared exceedingly delightful, as a world of love; and that all happiness consisted in living in pure, humble, heavenly, divine love.

I remember the thoughts I used then to have of holiness; and said sometimes to myself, "I do certainly know that I love holiness, such as the gospel prescribes." It appeared to me, that there was nothing in it but what was ravishingly lovely; the

---

[7] Edwards was minister of a church in New York City from August 1722 to May 1723.

[8] I.e., his sense of divine things.

highest beauty and amiableness—a *divine* beauty; far purer than anything here upon earth; and that everything else was like mire and defilement, in comparison of it.

Holiness, as I then wrote down some of my contemplations on it, appeared to me to be of a sweet, pleasant, charming, serene, calm nature; which brought an inexpressible purity, brightness, peacefulness and ravishment to the soul. In other words, that it made the soul like a field or garden of God, with all manner of pleasant flowers; all pleasant, delightful, and undisturbed; enjoying a sweet calm, and the gentle vivifying beams of the sun. The soul of a true Christian, as I then wrote my meditations, appeared like such a little white flower as we see in the spring of the year; low and humble on the ground, opening its bosom to receive the pleasant beams of the sun's glory; rejoicing as it were in a calm rapture; diffusing around a sweet fragrancy; standing peacefully and lovingly, in the midst of other flowers round about; all in like manner opening their bosoms, to drink in the light of the sun. There was no part of creature holiness, that I had so great a sense of its loveliness, as humility, brokenness of heart, and poverty of spirit; and there was nothing that I so earnestly longed for. My heart panted after this, to lie low before God, as in the dust; that I might be nothing, and that God might be ALL, that I might become as a little child.[9]

While at New York, I was sometimes much affected with reflections on my past life, considering how late it was before I began to be truly religious; and how wickedly I had lived till then; and once so as to weep abundantly, and for a considerable time together.

On *January* 12, 1723, I made a solemn dedication of myself to God, and wrote it down; giving up myself and all that I had to God; to be for the future, in no respect my own; to act as one that had no right to himself in any respect. And solemnly vowed to take God for my whole portion and felicity; looking on nothing else as any part of my happiness, nor acting as if it were; and His law for the constant rule of my obedience; engaging to fight with all my might, against the world, the flesh, and the devil,[10] to the end of my life. But I have reason to be infinitely humbled, when I consider how much I have failed of answering my obligation.

I had then abundance of sweet religious conversation in the family where I lived, with Mr. John Smith and his pious mother. My heart was knit in affection to those in whom were appearances of true piety; and I could bear the thoughts of no other companions but such as were holy, and the disciples of the blessed Jesus. I had great longings for the advancement of Christ's kingdom in the world; and my secret prayer used to be, in great part, taken up in praying for it. If I heard the least hint of anything that happened, in any part of the world, that appeared, in some respect or other, to have a favorable aspect on the interests of Christ's kingdom, my soul eagerly catched at it; and it would much animate and refresh me. I used to be eager to read public news letters, mainly for that end; to see if I could not find some news favorable to the interest of religion in the world.

I very frequently used to retire into a solitary place, on the banks of Hudson's river, at some distance from the city, for contemplation on divine things, and secret converse

---

[9] Mark 10:15: "Whosoever shall not receive the kingdom of God as a little child, he shall not enter therein."

[10] From the Litany in the Anglican Book of Common Prayer.

with God; and had many sweet hours there. Sometimes Mr. Smith and I walked there together, to converse on the things of God; and our conversation used to turn much on the advancement of Christ's kingdom in the world, and the glorious things that God would accomplish for his church in the latter days. I had then, and at other times, the greatest delight in the holy Scriptures, of any book whatsoever. Oftentimes in reading it, every word seemed to touch my heart. I felt a harmony between something in my heart, and those sweet and powerful words. I seemed often to see so much light exhibited by every sentence, and such a refreshing food communicated, that I could not get along in reading; often dwelling long on one sentence, to see the wonders contained in it; and yet almost every sentence seemed to be full of wonders.

I came away from New York in the month of April, 1723, and had a most bitter parting with Madam Smith and her son. My heart seemed to sink within me at leaving the family and city, where I had enjoyed so many sweet and pleasant days. I went from New York to Wethersfield,[11] by water, and as I sailed away, I kept sight of the city as long as I could. However, that night, after this sorrowful parting, I was greatly comforted in God at Westchester,[12] where we went ashore to lodge; and had a pleasant time of it all the voyage to Saybrook.[13] It was sweet to me to think of meeting dear Christians in heaven, where we should never part more. At Saybrook we went ashore to lodge, on Saturday, and there kept the Sabbath; where I had a sweet and refreshing season, walking alone in the fields.

After I came home to Windsor,[14] I remained much in a like frame of mind, as when at New York; only sometimes I felt my heart ready to sink with the thoughts of my friends at New York. My support was in contemplations on the heavenly state; as I find in my diary of May 1, 1723. It was a comfort to think of that state, where there is fulness of joy; where reigns heavenly, calm, and delightful love, without alloy; where there are continually the dearest expressions of love; where is the enjoyment of the persons loved, without ever parting; where those persons who appear so lovely in this world, will really be inexpressibly more lovely and full of love to us. And how sweetly will the mutual lovers join together to sing the praises of God and the Lamb![15] How will it fill us with joy to think, that this enjoyment, these sweet exercises will never cease, but will last to all eternity! I continued much in the same frame, in the general, as when at New York, till I went to New Haven as tutor to the college;[16] particularly once at Bolton,[17] on a journey from Boston, while walking out alone in the fields. After I went to New Haven I sunk in religion; my mind being diverted from my eager pursuits after holiness, by some affairs that greatly perplexed and distracted my thoughts.

In September, 1725, I was taken ill at New Haven, and while endeavoring to go home to Windsor, was so ill at the North Village, that I could go no further; where I lay sick for about a quarter of a year. In this sickness, God was pleased to visit me again with the sweet influences of His Spirit. My mind was greatly engaged there in divine, pleasant contemplations, and longings of soul. I observed that those who watched with me, would often be looking out wishfully for the morning; which

---

[11] In Connecticut.
[12] Westchester County, near New York City.
[13] In Connecticut.
[14] In Connecticut.
[15] I.e., the Lamb of God, the symbol of Christ (Revelation 15:3).

[16] Yale College, where Edwards became a tutor in 1724.
[17] In Connecticut.

brought to my mind those words of the Psalmist, and which my soul with delight made its own language, *My soul waiteth for the Lord, more than they that watch for the morning, I say, more than they that watch for the morning;*[18] and when the light of the day came in at the windows, it refreshed my soul from one morning to another. It seemed to be some image of the light of God's glory.

I remember, about that time, I used greatly to long for the conversion of some that I was concerned with; I could gladly honor them, and with delight be a servant to them, and lie at their feet, if they were but truly holy. But, some time after this, I was again greatly diverted in my mind with some temporal concerns that exceedingly took up my thoughts, greatly to the wounding of my soul; and went on through various exercises, that it would be tedious to relate, which gave me much more experience of my own heart, than ever I had before.

Since I came to this town,[19] I have often had sweet complacency in God, in views of His glorious perfections and the excellency of Jesus Christ. God has appeared to me a glorious and lovely Being, chiefly on the account of His holiness. The holiness of God has always appeared to me the most lovely of all His attributes. The doctrines of God's absolute sovereignty, and free grace, in showing mercy to whom He would show mercy; and man's absolute dependence on the operations of God's Holy Spirit, have very often appeared to me as sweet and glorious doctrines. These doctrines have been much my delight. God's sovereignty has ever appeared to me, a great part of His glory. It has often been my delight to approach God, and adore Him as a sovereign God, and ask sovereign mercy of Him.

I have loved the doctrines of the gospel; they have been to my soul like green pastures. The gospel has seemed to me the richest treasure; the treasure that I have most desired, and long that it might dwell richly in me. The way of salvation by Christ has appeared, in a general way, glorious and excellent, most pleasant and most beautiful. It has often seemed to me, that it would in a great measure spoil heaven, to receive it in any other way. That text has often been affecting and delightful to me. Isaiah 32:2, *A man shall be an hiding place from the wind, and a covert from the tempest,* &c.

It has often appeared to me delightful, to be united to Christ; to have Him for my head, and to be a member of His body; also to have Christ for my teacher and prophet. I very often think with sweetness, and longings, and pantings of soul, of being, a little child, taking hold of Christ, to be led by Him through the wilderness of this world. That text, Matthew 18:3, has often been sweet to me, *Except ye be converted and become as little children,* &c. I love to think of coming to Christ, to receive salvation of Him, poor in spirit, and quite empty of self, humbly exalting Him alone; cut off entirely from my own root, in order to grow into, and out of Christ; to have God in Christ to be all in all; and to live by faith on the son of God, a life of humble, unfeigned confidence in Him. That scripture has often been sweet to me, Psalms 115:1. *Not unto us, O Lord, not unto us, but unto thy name give glory, for thy mercy, and for thy truth's sake.* And those words of Christ, Luke 10:21. *In that hour Jesus rejoiced in spirit, and said, I thank thee, O Father, Lord of heaven and earth, that thou hast hid these things from the wise and prudent, and has revealed them unto babes: even so, Father; for so it seemed*

---

[18] See Psalm 130:6.
[19] Northampton, Massachusetts. In 1727 Edwards was appointed assistant minister there.

good in thy sight. That sovereignty of God which Christ rejoiced in, seemed to me worthy of such joy; and that rejoicing seemed to show the excellency of Christ, and of what spirit He was.

Sometimes, only mentioning a single word caused my heart to burn within me; or only seeing the name of Christ, or the name of some attribute of God. And God has appeared glorious to me, on account of the Trinity. It has made me have exalting thoughts of God, that He subsists in three persons; Father, Son, and Holy Ghost. The sweetest joys and delights I have experienced, have not been those that have arisen from a hope of my own good estate; but in a direct view of the glorious things of the gospel. When I enjoy this sweetness, it seems to carry me above the thoughts of my own estate; it seems at such times a loss that I cannot bear, to take off my eye from the glorious pleasant object I behold without me, to turn my eye in upon myself, and my own good estate.

My heart has been much on the advancement of Christ's kingdom in the world. The histories of the past advancement of Christ's kingdom have been sweet to me. When I have read histories of past ages, the pleasantest thing in all my reading has been, to read of the kingdom of Christ being promoted. And when I have expected, in my reading, to come to any such thing, I have rejoiced in the prospect, all the way as I read. And my mind has been much entertained and delighted with the Scripture promises and prophecies, which relate to the future glorious advancement of Christ's kingdom upon earth.

I have sometimes had a sense of the excellent fulness of Christ, and His meetness and suitableness as a Saviour, whereby He has appeared to me, far above all, the chief of ten thousands.[20] His blood and atonement have appeared sweet, and His righteousness sweet; which was always accompanied with ardency of spirit; and inward strugglings, and breathings, and groanings that cannot be uttered to be emptied of myself, and swallowed up in Christ.

Once as I rode out into the woods for my health, in 1737, having alighted from my horse in a retired place, as my manner commonly has been, to walk for divine contemplation and prayer, I had a view that for me was extraordinary, of the glory of the Son of God, as Mediator between God and man, and His wonderful, great, full, pure and sweet grace and love, and meek and gentle condescension. This grace that appeared so calm and sweet, appeared also great above the heavens. The person of Christ appeared ineffably excellent, with an excellency great enough to swallow up all thought and conception—which continued, as near as I can judge, about an hour; which kept me the greater part of the time in a flood of tears, and weeping aloud. I felt an ardency of soul to be, what I know not otherwise how to express, emptied and annihilated; to lie in the dust, and to be full of Christ alone; to love Him with a holy and pure love; to trust in Him; to live upon Him; to serve and follow Him; and to be perfectly sanctified and made pure, with a divine and heavenly purity. I have, several other times, had views very much of the same nature, and which have had the same effects.

I have many times had a sense of the glory of the third person in the Trinity, in His office of sanctifier; in His holy operations, communicating divine light and life

[20] Song of Solomon 5:10: "My beloved is . . . chiefest among ten thousand."

to the soul. God, in the communications of His Holy Spirit, has appeared as an infinite fountain of divine glory and sweetness; being full, and sufficient to fill and satisfy the soul; pouring forth itself in sweet communications; like the sun in its glory, sweetly and pleasantly diffusing light and life. And I have sometimes had an affecting sense of the excellency of the word of God, as the word of life; as the light of life; a sweet, excellent, life-giving word; accompanied with a thirsting after that word, that it might dwell richly in my heart.

Often, since I lived in this town, I have had very affecting views of my own sinfulness and vileness; very frequently to such a degree as to hold me in a kind of loud weeping, sometimes for a considerable time together; so that I have often been forced to shut myself up. I have had a vastly greater sense of my own wickedness, and the badness of my own heart, than ever I had before my conversion. It has often appeared to me, that if God should mark iniquity against me, I should appear the very worst of all mankind; of all that have been since the beginning of the world to this time; and that I should have by far the lowest place in hell. When others, that have come to talk with me about their soul concerns, have expressed the sense they have had of their own wickedness, by saying that it seemed to them, that they were as bad as the devil himself; I thought their expressions seemed exceedingly faint and feeble, to represent my wickedness.

My wickedness, as I am in myself, has long appeared to me perfectly ineffable, and swallowing up all thought and imagination; like an infinite deluge, or mountains over my head. I know not how to express better what my sins appear to me to be, than by heaping infinite upon infinite, and multiplying infinite by infinite. Very often, for these many years, these expressions are in my mind and in my mouth, "Infinite upon infinite—Infinite upon infinite!" When I look into my heart, and take a view of my wickedness, it looks like an abyss infinitely deeper than hell. And it appears to me, that were it not for free grace, exalted and raised up to the infinite height of all the fulness and glory of the great Jehovah, and the arm of His power and grace stretched forth in all the majesty of His power, and in all the glory of His sovereignty, I should appear sunk down in my sins below hell itself; far beyond the sight of everything, but the eye of sovereign grace, that can pierce even down to such a depth. And yet it seems to me that my conviction of sin is exceedingly small and faint; it is enough to amaze me, that I have no more sense of my sin. I know certainly, that I have very little sense of my sinfulness. When I have had turns of weeping for my sins, I thought I knew at the time that my repentance was nothing to my sin.

I have greatly longed of late, for a broken heart, and to lie low before God; and, when I ask for humility, I cannot bear the thoughts of being no more humble than other Christians. It seems to me, that though their degrees of humility may be suitable for them, yet it would be a vile self-exaltation in me, not to be the lowest in humility of all mankind. Others speak of their longing to be "humbled to the dust"; that may be a proper expression for them, but I always think of myself, that I ought, and it is an expression that has long been natural for me to use in prayer, "to lie infinitely low before God." And it is affecting to think, how ignorant I was, when a young Christian, of the bottomless, infinite depths of wickedness, pride, hypocrisy, and deceit, left in my heart.

I have a much greater sense of my universal, exceeding dependence on God's grace and strength, and mere good pleasure, of late, than I used formerly to have; and have experienced more of an abhorrence of my own righteousness. The very thought of any joy arising in me, on any consideration of my own amiableness, performances, or experiences, or any goodness of heart or life, is nauseous and detestable to me. And yet I am greatly afflicted with a proud and self-righteous spirit, much more sensibly than I used to be formerly. I see that serpent rising and putting forth its head continually, everywhere, all around me.

Though it seems to me, that, in some respects, I was a far better Christian, for two or three years after my first conversion, than I am now; and lived in a more constant delight and pleasure; yet, of late years, I have had a more full and constant sense of the absolute sovereignty of God, and a delight in that sovereignty; and have had more of a sense of the glory of Christ, as a Mediator revealed in the gospel. On one Saturday night, in particular, I had such a discovery of the excellency of the gospel above all other doctrines, that I could not but say to myself, "This is my chosen light, my chosen doctrine;" and of Christ, "This is my chosen Prophet." It appeared sweet, beyond all expression, to follow Christ, and to be taught, and enlightened, and instructed by Him; to learn of Him, and live to Him. Another Saturday night, (*January,* 1739) I had such a sense, how sweet and blessed a thing it was to walk in the way of duty; to do that which was right and meet to be done, and agreeable to the holy mind of God; that it caused me to break forth into a kind of loud weeping, which held me some time, so that I was forced to shut myself up, and fasten the doors. I could not but, as it were, cry out, "How happy are they which do that which is right in the sight of God! They are blessed indeed, they are the happy ones!" I had, at the same time, a very affecting sense, how meet and suitable it was that God should govern the world, and order all things according to His own pleasure; and I rejoiced in it, that God reigned, and that His will was done.

1765

---

from A Divine and Supernatural Light

Doctrine

That there is such a thing as a spiritual and divine light, immediately imparted to the soul by God, of a different nature from any that is obtained by natural means. And on this subject I would,

    I. Show what this divine light is.
    II. How it is given immediately by God, and not obtained by natural means.
    III. Show the truth of the doctrine.

And then conclude with a brief improvement.

    I. I would show what this spiritual and divine light is. And in order to it would show,

    First, In a few things, what it is not. And here,

    1. Those convictions that natural men may have of their sin and misery, is not this spiritual and divine light. Men, in a natural condition, may have convictions of the

guilt that lies upon them, and of the anger of God, and their danger of divine vengeance. Such convictions are from the light of truth. That some sinners have a greater conviction of their guilt and misery than others, is because some have more light, or more of an apprehension of truth than others. And this light and conviction may be from the Spirit of God; the Spirit convinces men of sin; but yet nature is much more concerned in it than in the communication of that spiritual and divine light that is spoken of in the doctrine; it is from the Spirit of God only as assisting natural principles, and not as infusing any new principles. Common grace differs from special, in that it influences only by assisting of nature; and not by imparting grace, or bestowing any thing above nature. The light that is obtained, is wholly natural, or of no superior kind to what mere nature attains to, though more of that kind be obtained than would be obtained, if men were left wholly to themselves; or, in other words, common grace only assists the faculties of the soul to do that more fully which they do by nature, as natural conscience or reason will by mere nature make a man sensible of guilt, and will accuse and condemn him when he has done amiss. Conscience is a principle natural to men; and the work that it doth naturally, or of itself, is to give an apprehension of right and wrong, and to suggest to the mind the relation that there is between right and wrong and a retribution. The Spirit of God, in those convictions which unregenerate men sometimes have, assists conscience to do this work in a further degree than it would do if they were left to themselves. He helps it against those things that tend to stupify it, and obstruct its exercise. But in the renewing and sanctifying work of the Holy Ghost, those things are wrought in the soul that are above nature, and of which there is nothing of the like kind in the soul by nature; and they are caused to exist in the soul habitually, and according to such a stated constitution or law, that lays such a foundation for exercises in a continued course, as is called a principle of nature. Not only are remaining principles assisted to do their work more freely and fully, but those principles are restored that were utterly destroyed by the fall; and the mind thenceforward habitually exerts those acts that the dominion of sin had made it as wholly destitute of as a dead body is of vital acts.

The Spirit of God acts in a very different manner in the one case, from what he doth in the other. He may, indeed, act upon the mind of a natural man, but he acts in the mind of a saint as an indwelling vital principle. He acts upon the mind of an unregenerate person as an extrinsic occasional agent; for, in acting upon them, he doth not unite himself to them: for, notwithstanding all his influences that they may possess, they are still sensual, having not the Spirit. Jude 19. But he unites himself with the mind of a saint, takes him for his temple, actuates and influences him as a new supernatural principle of life and action. There is this difference, that the Spirit of God, in acting in the soul of a godly man, exerts and communicates himself there in his own proper nature. Holiness is the proper nature of the Spirit of God. The Holy Spirit operates in the minds of the godly, by uniting himself to them, and living in them, and exerting his own nature in the exercise of their faculties. The Spirit of God may act upon a creature, and yet not in acting communicate himself. The Spirit of God may act upon inanimate creatures; as, *the Spirit moved upon the face of the waters,* in the beginning of the creation; so the Spirit of God may act upon the minds of men many ways, and communicate himself no more than when he acts upon an inanimate creature. For instance, he may excite thoughts in them, may assist their natural reason and understanding, or may assist other natural principles, and this without any union with the soul, but may act, as it were, upon an external object. But as he acts in his holy influences and spiritual operations, he acts in a way of peculiar communication of himself; so that the subject is thence denominated spiritual.

2. This spiritual and divine light does not consist in any impression made upon the imagination. It is no impression upon the mind, as though one saw any thing with the bodily eyes. It is no imagination or idea of an outward light or glory, or any beauty of form or countenance, or a visible lustre or brightness of any object. The imagination may be strongly impressed with such things; but this is not spiritual light. Indeed when the mind has a lively discovery of spiritual things, and is greatly affected with the power of divine light, it may, and probably very commonly doth, much affect the imagination; so that impressions of an outward beauty or brightness may *accompany* those spiritual discoveries. But spiritual light is not that impression upon the imagination, but an exceedingly different thing. Natural men may have lively impressions on their imaginations; and we cannot determine but that the devil, who transforms himself into an angel of light, may cause imaginations of an outward beauty, or visible glory, and of sounds and speeches, and other such things; but these are things of a vastly inferior nature to spiritual light.

3. This spiritual light is not the suggesting of any new truths or propositions not contained in the word of God. This suggesting of new truths or doctrines to the mind, independent of any antecedent revelations of those propositions, either in word or writing, is inspiration; such as the prophets and apostles had, and such as some enthusiasts pretend to. But this spiritual light that I am speaking of, is quite a different thing from inspiration. It reveals no new doctrine, it suggests no new proposition to the mind, it teaches no new thing of God, or Christ, or another world, not taught in the Bible, but only gives a due apprehension of those things that are taught in the word of God.

4. It is not every affecting view that men have of religious things that is this spiritual and divine light. Men by mere principles of nature are capable of being affected with things that have a special relation to religion as well as other things. A person by mere nature, for instance, may be liable to be affected with the story of Jesus Christ, and the sufferings he underwent, as well as by any other tragical story. He may be the more affected with it from the interest he conceives mankind to have in it. Yea, he may be affected with it without believing it; as well as a man may be affected with what he reads in a romance, or sees acted in a stage-play. He may be affected with a lively and eloquent description of many pleasant things that attend the state of the blessed in heaven, as well as his imagination be entertained by a romantic description of the pleasantness of fairy land, or the like. And a common belief of the truth of such things, from education or otherwise, may help forward their affection. We read in Scripture of many that were greatly affected with things of a religious nature, who yet are there represented as wholly graceless, and many of them very ill men. A person therefore may have affecting views of the things of religion, and yet be very destitute of spiritual light. Flesh and blood may be the author of this; one man may give another an affecting view of divine things with but common assistance; but God alone can give a spiritual discovery of them.—But I proceed to show,

Secondly, Positively what this spiritual and divine light is.

And it may be thus described: A true sense of the divine excellency of the things revealed in the word of God, and a conviction of the truth and reality of them thence arising. This spiritual light primarily consists in the former of these, *viz.* A real sense and apprehension of the divine excellency of things revealed in the word of God. A spiritual and saving conviction of the truth and reality of these things, arises from such a sight of their divine excellency and glory; so that this conviction of their truth is an effect and natural consequence of this sight of their divine glory. There is therefore in this spiritual light,

1. A true sense of the divine and superlative excellency of the things of religion; a real sense of the excellency of God and Jesus Christ, and of the work of redemption, and the ways and works of God revealed in the gospel. There is a divine and superlative glory in these things; an excellency that is of a vastly higher kind, and more sublime nature than in other things; a glory greatly distinguishing them from all that is earthly and temporal. He that is spiritually enlightened truly apprehends and sees it, or has a sense of it. He does not merely rationally believe that God is glorious, but he has a sense of the gloriousness of God in his heart. There is not only a rational belief that God is holy, and that holiness is a good thing, but there is a sense of the loveliness of God's holiness. There is not only a speculatively judging that God is gracious, but a sense how amiable God is on account of the beauty of this divine attribute.

There is a twofold knowledge of good of which God has made the mind of man capable. The first, that which is merely notional; as when a person only speculatively judges that any thing is, which, by the agreement of mankind, is called good or excellent, *viz.* that which is most to general advantage, and between which and a reward there is a suitableness,—and the like. And the other is, that which consists in the sense of the heart; as when the heart is sensible of pleasure and delight in the presence of the idea of it. In the former is exercised merely the speculative faculty, or the understanding, in distinction from the will or disposition of the soul. In the latter, the will, or inclination, or heart, are mainly concerned.

Thus there is a difference between having an *opinion,* that God is holy and gracious, and having a *sense* of the loveliness and beauty of that holiness and grace. There is a difference between having a rational judgment that honey is sweet, and having a sense of its sweetness. A man may have the former, that knows not how honey tastes; but a man cannot have the latter unless he has an idea of the taste of honey in his mind. So there is a difference between believing that a person is beautiful, and having a sense of his beauty. The former may be obtained by hearsay, but the latter only by seeing the countenance. When the heart is sensible of the beauty and amiableness of a thing, it necessarily feels pleasure in the apprehension. It is implied in a person's being heartily sensible of the loveliness of a thing, that the idea of it is pleasant to his soul; which is a far different thing from having a rational opinion that it is excellent.

2. There arises from this sense of the divine excellency of things contained in the word of God, a conviction of the truth and reality of them; and that, either indirectly or directly.

First, Indirectly, and that two ways:

1. As the prejudices of the heart, against the truth of divine things, are hereby removed; so that the mind becomes susceptive of the due force of rational arguments for their truth. The mind of man is naturally full of prejudices against divine truth.

It is full of enmity against the doctrines of the gospel; which is a disadvantage to those arguments that prove their truth, and causes them to lose their force upon the mind. But when a person has discovered to him the divine excellency of Christian doctrines, this destroys the enmity, removes those prejudices, sanctifies the reason, and causes it to lie open to the force of arguments for their truth.

Hence was the different effect that Christ's miracles had to convince the disciples, from what they had to convince the scribes and Pharisees. Not that they had a stronger reason, or had their reason more improved; but their reason was sanctified, and those blinding prejudices, that the Scribes and Pharisees were under, were removed by the sense they had of the excellency of Christ, and his doctrine.

It not only removes the hindrances of reason, but positively helps reason. It makes even the speculative notions more lively. It engages the attention of the mind, with more fixedness and intenseness to that kind of objects; which causes it to have a clearer view of them, and enables it more clearly to see their mutual relations, and occasions it to take more notice of them. The ideas themselves that other wise are dim and obscure, are by this means impressed with the greater strength, and have a light cast upon them; so that the mind can better judge of them. As he that beholds objects on the face of the earth, when the light of the sun is cast upon them, is under greater advantage to discern them in their true forms and natural relations, than he that sees them in a dim twilight.

The mind, being sensible of the excellency of divine objects, dwells upon them with delight; and the powers of the soul are more awakened and enlivened to employ themselves in the contemplation of them, and exert themselves more fully and much more to the purpose. The beauty of the objects draws on the faculties, and draws forth their exercises; so that reason itself is under far greater advantages for its proper and free exercises, and to attain its proper end, free of darkness and delusion.—But,

Secondly, A true sense of the divine excellency of the things of God's word doth more directly and immediately convince us of their truth; and that because the excellency of these things is so superlative. There is a beauty in them so divine and godlike, that it greatly and evidently distinguishes them from things merely human, or that of which men are the inventors and authors; a glory so high and great, that when clearly seen, commands assent to their divine reality. When there is an actual and lively discovery of this beauty and excellency, it will not allow of any such thought as that it is the fruit of men's invention. This is a kind of intuitive and immediate evidence. They believe the doctrines of God's word to be divine, because they see a divine, and transcendent, and most evidently distinguishing glory in them; such a glory as, if clearly seen, does not leave room to doubt of their being of God, and not of men.

Such a conviction of the truths of religion as this, arising from a sense of their divine excellency, is included in saving faith. And this original of it, is that by which it is most essentially distinguished from that common assent, of which unregenerate men are capable.

II. I proceed now to the *second* thing proposed, *viz.* To shew how this light is immediately given by God, and not obtained by natural means. And here,

1. It is not intended that the natural faculties are not used in it. They are the subject of this light: and in such a manner, that they are not merely passive, but active in

it. God, in letting in this light into the soul, deals with man according to his nature, and makes use of his rational faculties. But yet this light is not the less immediately from God for that; the faculties are made use of as the subject, and not as the cause. As the use we make of our eyes in beholding various objects, when the sun arises, is not the cause of the light that discovers those objects to us.

2. It is not intended that outward means have no concern in this affair. It is not in this affair, as in inspiration, where new truths are suggested; for, by this light is given only a due apprehension of the same truths that are revealed in the word of God: and therefore it is not given without the word. The gospel is employed in this affair. This light is the "light of the glorious gospel of Christ." 2 Cor. iv. 4. The gospel is as a glass, by which this light is conveyed to us. 1 Cor. xiii. 12. "Now we see through a glass."—But,

3. When it is said that this light is given immediately by God, and not obtained by natural means, hereby is intended, that it is given by God without making use of any means that operate by their own power or natural force. God makes use of means; but it is not as mediate causes to produce this effect. There are not truly any second causes of it; but it is produced by God immediately. The word of God is no proper cause of this effect; but is made use of only to convey to the mind the subject-matter of this saving instruction: And this indeed it doth convey to us by natural force or influence. It conveys to our minds these doctrines; it is the cause of a notion of them in our heads, but not of the sense of their divine excellency in our hearts. Indeed a person cannot have spiritual light without the word. But that does not argue, that the word properly causes that light. The mind cannot see the excellency of any doctrine, unless that doctrine be first in the mind; but seeing the excellency of the doctrine may be immediately from the Spirit of God; through the conveying of the doctrine, or proposition, itself, may be by the word. So that the notions which are the subject-matter of this light, are conveyed to the mind by the word of God; but that due sense of the heart, wherein this light formally consists, is immediately by the Spirit of God. as, for instance, the notion that there is a Christ, and that Christ is holy and gracious, is conveyed to the mind by the word of God: But the sense of the excellency of Christ, by reason of that holiness and grace, is, nevertheless, immediately the work of the Holy Spirit.—I come now,

III. To show the truth of the doctrine; that is, to show that there is such a thing as that spiritual light that has been described, thus immediately let into the mind by God. And here I would show, briefly, that this doctrine is both *scriptural* and *rational*.

First, It is scriptural. My text is not only full to the purpose, but it is a doctrine with which the Scripture abounds. . . .

Secondly, This doctrine is rational.

I will conclude with a very brief improvement of what has been said.

First, This doctrine may lead us to reflect on the goodness of God, that has so ordered it, that a saving evidence of the truth of the gospel is such, as is attainable by persons of mean capacities and advantages, as well as those that are of the greatest parts and learning. If the evidence of the gospel depended only on history, and such reasonings as learned men only are capable of, it would be above the reach of far the greatest part of mankind. But persons with an ordinary degree of knowledge, are capable, without a long and subtile train of reasoning, to see the divine excellency of the things of religion: they are capable of being taught by the Spirit of God, as well as learned men. The evidence that is this way obtained, is vastly better and more satisfying, than all that can be obtained by the arguings of those that are most learned, and greatest masters of reason. And babes are as capable of knowing these things, as the wise and prudent; and they are often hid from these, when they are revealed to those. 1 Cor. i. 26, 27. "For ye see your calling, brethren, how that not many wise men, after the flesh, not many mighty, not many noble, are called. But God hath chosen the foolish things of the world."—

Secondly. This doctrine may well put us upon examining ourselves, whether we have ever had this divine light let into our souls. If there be such a thing, doubtless it is of great importance whether we have thus been taught by the Spirit of God; whether the light of the glorious gospel of Christ, who is the image of God, hath shined unto us, giving us the light of the knowledge of the glory of God in the face of Jesus Christ; whether we have seen the Son, and believed on him, or have that faith of gospel doctrines which arises from a spiritual sight of Christ.

Thirdly. All may hence be exhorted, earnestly to seek this spiritual light. To influence and move to it, the following things may be considered.

1. This is the most excellent and divine wisdom that any creature is capable of. It is more excellent than any human learning; it is far more excellent than all the knowledge of the greatest philosophers or statesmen. Yea, the least glimpse of the glory of God in the face of Christ doth more exalt and ennoble the soul, than all the knowledge of those that have the greatest speculative understanding in divinity without grace. This knowledge has the most noble object that can be, *viz.* the divine glory and excellency of God and Christ. The knowledge of these objects is that wherein consists the most excellent knowledge of the angels, yea, of God himself.

2. This knowledge is that which is above all others sweet and joyful. Men have a great deal of pleasure in human knowledge, in studies of natural things; but this is nothing to that joy which arises from this divine light shining into the soul. This light gives a view of those things that are immensely the most exquisitely beautiful, and capable of delighting the eye of the understanding. This spiritual light is the dawning of the light of glory in the heart. There is nothing so powerful as this to support persons in affliction, and to give the mind peace and brightness in this stormy and dark world.

3. This light is such as effectually influences the inclination, and changes the nature of the soul. It assimilates our nature to the divine nature, and changes the soul into an image of the same glory that is beheld. 2 Cor. iii. 18. "But we all with open face, beholding as in a glass the glory of the Lord, are changed into the same image, from glory to glory, even as by the Spirit of the Lord." This knowledge will wean from the world, and raise the inclination to heavenly things. It will turn the heart to God as the fountain of good, and to choose him for the only portion. This light, and this only, will bring the soul to a saving close with Christ. It conforms the heart to the gospel, mortifies its enmity and opposition against the scheme of salvation therein revealed; it causes the heart to embrace the joyful tidings, and entirely to adhere to, and acquiesce in, the revelation of Christ as our Saviour; it causes the whole soul to accord and symphonize with it, admitting it with entire credit and respect, cleaving to it with full inclination and affection; and it effectually disposes the soul to give up itself entirely to Christ.

4. This light, and this only, has its fruit in an universal holiness of life. No merely notional or speculative understanding of the doctrines of religion will ever bring to this. But this light, as it reaches the bottom of the heart, and changes the nature, so it will effectually dispose to an universal obedience. It shows God as worthy to be obeyed and served. It draws forth the heart in a sincere love to God, which is the only principle of a true, gracious, and universal obedience: and it convinces of the reality of those glorious rewards that God has promised to them that obey him.

1734

Sinners in the Hands of an Angry God

Their foot shall slide in due time.
Deuteronomy 32:35

In this verse is threatened the vengeance of God on the wicked unbelieving Israelites, that were God's visible people, and lived under means of grace;[1] and that notwithstanding all God's wonderful works that He had wrought towards that people, yet remained, as is expressed verse 28, void of counsel, having no understanding in them; and that, under all the cultivations of heaven, brought forth bitter and poisonous fruit; as in the two verses next preceding the text.

The expression that I have chosen for my text, *their foot shall slide in due time,* seems to imply the following things relating to the punishment and destruction that these wicked Israelites were exposed to.

1. That they are always exposed to *destruction,* as one that stands or walks in slippery places is always exposed to fall. This is implied in the manner of their destruction's coming upon them, being represented by their foot's sliding. The same is expressed, Psalm 73:18: "Surely thou didst set them in slippery places: thou castedst them down into destruction."

2. It implies that they were always exposed to sudden, unexpected destruction. As he that walks in slippery places is every moment liable to fall, he cannot foresee one moment whether he shall stand or fall the next; and when he does fall, he falls at once, without warning, which is also expressed in that Psalm 73:18–19: "Surely thou didst set them in slippery places: thou castedst them down into destruction. How are they brought into desolation as in a moment."

3. Another thing implied is that they are liable to fall of *themselves,* without being thrown down by the hand of another, as he that stands or walks on slippery ground needs nothing but his own weight to throw him down.

---

[1] According to God's covenant with Abraham (Genesis 17–18), the chosen people would receive God's grace and be saved. In Puritan thought Jesus' atonement fulfilled the covenant with Abraham, which restored the possibility of salvation previously lost through the sin of Adam and Eve.

4. That the reason why they are not fallen already, and do not fall now, is only that God's appointed time is not come. For it is said that when that due time or appointed time comes, *their foot shall slide*. Then they shall be left to fall, as they are inclined by their own weight. God will not hold them up in these slippery places any longer but will let them go; and then, at that very instant, they shall fall into destruction; as he that stands on such slippery declining ground on the edge of a pit that he cannot stand alone, when he is let go he immediately falls and is lost.

The observation from the words that I would now insist upon is this.

There is nothing that keeps wicked men at any one moment out of hell, but the mere pleasure of God.

By the *mere* pleasure of God, I mean His *sovereign* pleasure, His arbitrary will, restrained by no obligation, hindered by no manner of difficulty, any more than if nothing else but God's mere will had in the least degree, or in any respect whatsoever, any hand in the preservation of wicked men one moment.

The truth of this observation may appear by the following considerations.

1. There is no want of *power* in God to cast wicked men into hell at any moment. Men's hands cannot be strong when God rises up: the strongest have no power to resist Him, nor can any deliver out of His hands.

He is not only able to cast wicked men into hell, but He can most easily do it. Sometimes an earthly prince meets with a great deal of difficulty to subdue a rebel that has found means to fortify himself and has made himself strong by the number of his followers. But it is not so with God. There is no fortress that is any defence against the power of God. Though hand join in hand, and vast multitudes of God's enemies combine and associate themselves, they are easily broken in pieces; they are as great heaps of light chaff before the whirlwind, or large quantities of dry stubble before devouring flames. We find it easy to tread on and crush a worm that we see crawling on the earth; so it is easy for us to cut or singe a slender thread that any thing hangs by; thus easy is it for God, when He pleases, to cast his enemies down to hell. What are we, that we should think to stand before Him, at whose rebuke the earth trembles and before Whom the rocks are thrown down!

2. They *deserve* to be cast into hell; so that divine justice never stands in the way, it makes no objection against God's using His power at any moment to destroy them. Yea, on the contrary, justice calls aloud for an infinite punishment of their sins. Divine justice says of the tree that brings forth such grapes of Sodom, "Cut it down, why cumbereth it the ground?" Luke 13:7. The sword of divine justice is every moment brandished over their heads, and it is nothing but the hand of arbitrary mercy, and God's mere will, that holds it back.

3. They are already under a sentence of *condemnation* to hell. They do not only justly deserve to be cast down thither, but the sentence of the law of God, that eternal and immutable rule of righteousness that God has fixed between Him and mankind, is gone out against them and stands against them, so that they are bound over already to hell: John 3:18, "He that believeth not is condemned already." So that every unconverted man properly belongs to hell; that is his place; from thence he is: John 8:23, "Ye are from beneath," and thither he is bound; it is the place that justice, and God's word, and the sentence of his unchangeable law, assign to him.

4. They are now the objects of that very same *anger* and wrath of God, that is expressed in the torments of hell; and the reason why they do not go down to hell

at each moment, is not because God, in whose power they are, is not then very angry with them, as angry as He is with many of those miserable creatures that He is now tormenting in hell, and do there feel and bear the fierceness of His wrath. Yea, God is a great deal more angry with great numbers that are now on earth, yea, doubtless, with many that are now in this congregation, that, it may be, are at ease and quiet, than He is with many of those that are now in the flames of hell.

So that it is not because God is unmindful of their wickedness, and does not resent it, that He does not let loose his hand and cut them off. God is not altogether such a one as themselves, though they may imagine Him to be so. The wrath of God burns against them; their damnation does not slumber; the pit is prepared; the fire is made ready; the furnace is now hot, ready to receive them; the flames do now rage and glow. The glittering sword is whet,[2] and held over them, and the pit hath opened its mouth under them.

5. The *devil* stands ready to fall upon them, and seize them as his own, at what moment God shall permit him. They belong to him; he has their souls in his possession, and under his dominion. The Scripture represents them as his goods, Luke 11:21. The devils watch them; they are ever by them, at their right hand; they stand waiting for them, like greedy hungry lions that see their prey, and expect to have it, but are for the present kept back; if God should withdraw His hand, by which they are restrained, they would in one moment fly upon their poor souls. The old serpent is gaping for them; hell opens its mouth wide to receive them; and if God should permit it, they would be hastily swallowed up and lost.

6. There are in the souls of wicked men those hellish *principles* reigning, that would presently kindle and flame out into hell-fire, if it were not for God's restraints. There is laid in the very nature of carnal men, a foundation for the torments of hell; there are those corrupt principles, in reigning power in them, and in full possession of them, that are the beginnings of hell-fire. These principles are active and powerful, exceeding violent in their nature, and if it were not for the restraining hand of God upon them, they would soon break out; they would flame out after the same manner as the same corruptions, the same enmity does in the hearts of damned souls, and would beget the same torments in them as they do in them. The souls of the wicked are in Scripture compared to the troubled sea, Isaiah 57:20. For the present, God restrains their wickedness by His mighty power, as He does the raging waves of the troubled sea, saying, "Hitherto shalt thou come, but no further;"[3] but if God should withdraw that restraining power, it would soon carry all before it. Sin is the ruin and misery of the soul; it is destructive in its nature; and if God should leave it without restraint, there would need nothing else to make the soul perfectly miserable. The corruption of the heart of man is a thing that is immoderate and boundless in its fury; and while wicked men live here, it is like fire pent up by God's restraints; whereas if it were let loose, it would set on fire the course of nature; and as the heart is now a sink of sin, so, if sin was not restrained, it would immediately turn the soul into a fiery oven or a furnace of fire and brimstone.

7. It is no security to wicked men for one moment, that there are no visible means of death at hand. It is no security to a natural man, that he is now in health, and that he does not see which way he should now immediately go out of the world by any

---

[2] Sharpened.   [3] Job 38:11.

accident, and that there is no visible danger in any respect in his circumstances. The manifold and continual experience of the world in all ages shows that this is no evidence that a man is not on the very brink of eternity and that the next step will not be into another world. The unseen, unthought of ways and means of persons going suddenly out of the world are innumerable and inconceivable. Unconverted men walk over the pit of hell on a rotten covering, and there are innumerable places in this covering so weak that they will not bear their weight, and these places are not seen. The arrows of death fly unseen at noonday;[4] the sharpest sight cannot discern them. God has so many different, unsearchable ways of taking wicked men out of the world and sending them to hell, that there is nothing to make it appear that God had need to be at the expense of a miracle, or go out of the ordinary course of His providence, to destroy any wicked man, at any moment. All the means that there are of sinners going out of the world, are so in God's hands and so absolutely subject to His power and determination, that it does not depend at all less on the mere will of God, whether sinners shall at any moment go to hell, than if means were never made use of or at all concerned in the case.

8. Natural men's *prudence* and *care* to preserve their own lives, or the care of others to preserve them, do not secure them a moment. This, divine providence and universal experience do also bear testimony to. There is this clear evidence that men's own wisdom is no security to them from death, that if it were otherwise we should see some difference between the wise and politic men of the world and others, with regard to their liableness to early and unexpected death; but how is it in fact? Ecclesiastes 2:16, "How dieth the wise man? As the fool."

9. All wicked men's *pains* and *contrivance* they use to escape hell, while they continue to reject Christ and so remain wicked men, do not secure them from hell one moment. Almost every natural man that hears of hell, flatters himself that he shall escape it; he depends upon himself for his own security; he flatters himself in what he has done, in what he is now doing, or what he intends to do; everyone lays out matters in his own mind how he shall avoid damnation and flatters himself that he contrives well for himself, and that his schemes will not fail. They hear indeed that there are but few saved and that the bigger part of men that have died heretofore are gone to hell; but each one imagines that he lays out matters better for his own escape than others have done; he does not intend to come to that place of torment; he says within himself that he intends to take care that shall be effectual and to order matters so for himself as not to fail.

But the foolish children of men do miserably delude themselves in their own schemes and in their confidence in their own strength and wisdom; they trust to nothing but a shadow. The greater part of those that heretofore have lived under the same means of grace, and are now dead, are undoubtedly gone to hell; and it was not because they were not as wise as those that are now alive; it was not because they did not lay out matters as well for themselves to secure their own escape. If it were so that we could come to speak with them, and could inquire of them, one by one,

---

[4] Psalm 91:5: "Thou shalt not be afraid for the terror by night; nor for the arrow that flieth by day."

whether they expected, when alive, and when they used to hear about hell, ever to be subjects of that misery, we, doubtless, should hear one and another reply, "No, I never intended to come here; I had laid out matters otherwise in my mind; I thought I should contrive well for myself; I thought my scheme good; I intended to take effectual care; but it came upon me unexpectedly; I did not look for it at that time, and in that manner; it came as a thief; death outwitted me; God's wrath was too quick for me; O my cursed foolishness! I was flattering myself and pleasing myself with vain dreams of what I would do hereafter; and when I was saying, peace and safety, then sudden destruction came upon me."

10. God has laid Himself under *no obligation,* by any promise, to keep any natural man out of hell one moment; God certainly has made no promises either of eternal life, or of any deliverance or preservation from eternal death, but what are contained in the covenant of grace, the promises that are given in Christ, in whom all the promises are yea and amen. But surely they have no interest in the promises of the covenant of grace that are not the children of the covenant, and that do not believe in any of the promises of the covenant, and have no interest in the Mediator of the covenant.

So that, whatever some have imagined and pretended about promises made to natural men's earnest seeking and knocking, it is plain and manifest that whatever pains a natural man takes in religion, whatever prayers he makes, till he believes in Christ, God is under no manner of obligation to keep him a moment from eternal destruction.

So that thus it is, that natural men are held in the hand of God, over the pit of hell; they have deserved the fiery pit and are already sentenced to it; and God is dreadfully provoked; His anger is as great towards them as to those that are actually suffering the executions of the fierceness of His wrath in hell, and they have done nothing in the least to appease or abate that anger; neither is God in the least bound by any promise to hold them up one moment; the devil is waiting for them; hell is gaping for them; the flames gather and flash about them, and would fain lay hold on them and swallow them up; the fire pent up in their own hearts is struggling to break out; and they have no interest in any Mediator; there are no means within reach that can be any security to them. In short, they have no refuge, nothing to take hold of; all that preserves them every moment is the mere arbitrary will and uncovenanted, unobliged forbearance of an incensed God.

Application

The use of this awful subject may be of awakening unconverted persons in this congregation. This that you have heard is the case of every one of you that are out of Christ. That world of mercy, that lake of burning brimstone, is extended abroad under you. There is the dreadful pit of the glowing flames of the wrath of God; there is hell's wide gaping mouth open; and you have nothing to stand upon, nor any thing to take hold of. There is nothing between you and hell but the air; it is only the power and mere pleasure of God that holds you up.

You probably are not sensible of this; you find you are kept out of hell but do not see the hand of God in it; but look at other things, as the good state of your bodily constitution, your care of your own life, and the means you use for your own preservation. But indeed these things are nothing; if God should withdraw His hand, they would avail no more to keep you from falling than the thin air to hold up a person that is suspended in it.

Your wickedness makes you, as it were, heavy as lead and to tend downwards with great weight and pressure towards hell; and if God should let you go, you would immediately sink and swiftly descend and plunge into the bottomless gulf, and your healthy constitution, and your own care and prudence, and best contrivance, and all your righteousness, would have no more influence to uphold you and keep you out of hell, than a spider's web would have to stop a falling rock. Were it not that so is the sovereign pleasure of God, the earth would not bear you one moment; for you are a burden to it; the creation groans with you; the creature is made subject to the bondage of your corruption, not willingly; the sun does not willingly shine upon you to give you light to serve sin and Satan; the earth does not willingly yield her increase to satisfy your lusts; nor is it willingly a stage for your wickedness to be acted upon; the air does not willingly serve you for breath to maintain the flame of life in your vitals while you spend your life in the service of God's enemies. God's creatures are good, and were made for men to serve God with, and do not willingly subserve to any other purpose, and groan when they are abused to purposes so directly contrary to their nature and end. And the world would spew you out, were it not for the sovereign hand of Him who hath subjected it in hope. There are the black clouds of God's wrath now hanging directly over your heads, full of the dreadful storm and big with thunder; and were it not for the restraining hand of God, it would immediately burst forth upon you. The sovereign pleasure of God, for the present, stays His rough wind; otherwise it would come with fury, and your destruction would come like a whirlwind, and you would be like the chaff of the summer threshing floor.

The wrath of God is like great waters that are dammed for the present; they increase more and more, and rise higher and higher, till an outlet is given; and the longer the stream is stopped, the more rapid and mighty is its course when once it is let loose. It is true that judgment against your evil works has not been executed hitherto; the floods of God's vengeance have been withheld; but your guilt in the meantime is constantly increasing, and you are every day treasuring up more wrath, the waters are continually rising and waxing more and more mighty; and there is nothing but the mere pleasure of God that holds the waters back that are unwilling to be stopped and press hard to go forward. If God should only withdraw His hand from the floodgate, it would immediately fly open, and the fiery floods of the fierceness and wrath of God would rush forth with inconceivable fury and would come upon you with omnipotent power; and if your strength were ten thousand times greater than it is, yea, ten thousand times greater than the strength of the stoutest, sturdiest devil in hell, it would be nothing to withstand or endure it.

The bow of God's wrath is bent, and the arrow made ready on the string, and justice bends the arrow at your heart and strains the bow, and it is nothing but the mere pleasure of God, and that of an angry God, without any promise or obligation at all, that keeps the arrow one moment from being made drunk with your blood.

Thus are all you that never passed under a great change of heart, by the mighty power of the Spirit of God upon your souls; all that were never born again, and made new creatures, and raised from being dead in sin, to a state of new, and before altogether unexperienced light and life (however you may have reformed your life in many things, and may have had religious affections, and may keep up a form of religion in your families, and closets, and in the houses of God, and may be strict in it), you are thus in the hands of an angry God; it is nothing but His mere pleasure that keeps you from being this moment swallowed up in everlasting destruction.

However unconvinced you may now be of the truth of what you hear, by and by you will be fully convinced of it. Those that are gone from being in the like circumstances with you, see that it was so with them; for destruction came suddenly upon most of them, when they expected nothing of it and while they were saying, "Peace and safety;" now they see that those things that they depended on for peace and safety were nothing but thin air and empty shadows.

The God that holds you over the pit of hell, much as one holds a spider, or some loathsome insect, over the fire, abhors you and is dreadfully provoked; His wrath towards you burns like fire; He looks upon you as worthy of nothing else but to be cast into the fire; He is of purer eyes than to bear to have you in His sight; you are ten thousand times more abominable in His eyes than the most hateful and venomous serpent is in ours. You have offended Him infinitely more than ever a stubborn rebel did his prince; and yet it is nothing but His hand that holds you from falling into the fire every moment; it is to be ascribed to nothing else, that you did not go to hell the last night, that you were suffered to awake again in this world, after you closed your eyes to sleep; and there is no other reason to be given, why you have not dropped into hell since you arose in the morning, but that God's hand has held you up; there is no other reason to be given why you have not gone to hell, since you have sat here in the house of God, provoking His pure eyes by your sinful, wicked manner of attending His solemn worship; yea, there is nothing else that is to be given as a reason why you do not this very moment drop down into hell.

O sinner! consider the fearful danger you are in; it is a great furnace of wrath, a wide and bottomless pit, full of the fire of wrath, that you are held over in the hand of that God, whose wrath is provoked and incensed as much against you, as against many of the damned in hell; you hang by a slender thread, with the flames of divine wrath flashing about it and ready every moment to singe it and burn it asunder; and you have no interest in any Mediator and nothing to lay hold of to save yourself, nothing to keep off the flames of wrath, nothing of your own, nothing that you ever have done, nothing that you can do to induce God to spare you one moment.

And consider here more particularly several things concerning that wrath that you are in such danger of.

1. *Whose* wrath it is. It is the wrath of the infinite God. If it were only the wrath of man, though it were of the most potent prince, it would be comparatively little to be regarded. The wrath of kings is very much dreaded, especially of absolute monarchs that have the possessions and lives of their subjects wholly in their power, to be disposed of at their mere will. Proverbs 20:2, "The fear of a king is as the roaring of a lion: whoso provoketh him to anger sinneth against his own soul." The subject that very much enrages an arbitrary prince is liable to suffer the most extreme torments that human art can invent or human power can inflict. But the greatest earthly potentates, in their greatest majesty and strength, and when clothed in their greatest terrors, are but feeble, despicable worms of the dust, in comparison of the great and almighty Creator and King of heaven and earth; it is but little that they can do, when

most enraged and when they have exerted the utmost of their fury. All the kings of the earth, before God, are as grasshoppers; they are nothing and less than nothing; both their love and their hatred is to be despised. The wrath of the great King of kings is as much more terrible than theirs, as His majesty is greater. Luke 12:4–5, "And I say unto you, my friends, Be not afraid of them that kill the body, and after that, have no more that they can do. But I will forewarn you whom ye shall fear: Fear him, which after he hath killed, hath power to cast into hell; yea, I say unto you, Fear him."

2. It is the *fierceness* of His wrath that you are exposed to. We often read of the fury of God; as in Isaiah 59:18: "According to their deeds, accordingly he will repay fury to his adversaries." So Isaiah 66:15, "For behold, the Lord will come with fire, and with his chariots like a whirlwind, to render his anger with fury, and his rebuke with flames of fire." And so in many other places. So Revelation 19:15. There we read of "the winepress of the fierceness and wrath of Almighty God." The words are exceedingly terrible; if it had only been said, "the wrath of God," the words would have implied that which is infinitely dreadful; but it is not only said so, but "the fierceness and wrath of God," the fury of God! the fierceness of Jehovah! Oh how dreadful must that be! Who can utter or conceive what such expressions carry in them! But it is also "the fierceness and wrath of Almighty God." As though there would be a very great manifestation of His almighty power in what the fierceness of His wrath should inflict, as though omnipotence should be, as it were, enraged and exerted, as men are wont to exert their strength in the fierceness of their wrath. Oh! then, what will be the consequence! What will become of the poor worm that shall suffer it! Whose hands can be strong! And whose heart endure! To what a dreadful, inexpressible, inconceivable depth of misery must the poor creature be sunk who shall be the subject of this!

Consider this, you that are here present, that yet remain in an unregenerate state. That God will execute the fierceness of His anger, implies that He will inflict wrath without any pity; when God beholds the ineffable extremity of your case, and sees your torment so vastly disproportioned to your strength, and sees how your poor soul is crushed and sinks down, as it were, into an infinite gloom, He will have no compassion upon you; He will not forbear the executions of his wrath or in the least lighten His hand; there shall be no moderation or mercy, nor will God then at all stay His rough wind; He will have no regard to your welfare, nor be at all careful lest you should suffer too much in any other sense, than only that you should not suffer beyond what strict justice requires; nothing shall be withheld because it is so hard for you to bear. Ezekiel 8:18, "Therefore will I also deal in fury: mine eye shall not spare, neither will I have pity: and though they cry in mine ears with a loud voice, yet will I not hear them." Now God stands ready to pity you; this is a day of mercy; you may cry now with some encouragement of obtaining mercy; but when once the day of mercy is past, your most lamentable and dolorous cries and shrieks will be in vain; you will be wholly lost and thrown away of God, as to any regard to your welfare; God will have no other use to put you to but to suffer misery; you shall be continued in being to no other end; for you will be a vessel of wrath fitted to destruction; and there will be no other use of this vessel but to be filled full of wrath; God will be so far from pitying you when you cry to him, that it is said he will only "laugh and mock," Proverbs 1:25–26, &c.

How awful are those words, Isaiah 63:3, which are the words of the great God: "I will tread them in mine anger, and trample them in my fury; and their blood shall be sprinkled upon my garments, and I will stain all my raiment." It is perhaps impossible to conceive of words that carry in them greater manifestations of these three things, viz., contempt, and hatred, and fierceness of indignation. If you cry to God to pity you, He will be so far from pitying you in your doleful case, or showing you the least regard or favor, that instead of that He will only tread you under foot; and though He will know that you cannot bear the weight of omnipotence treading upon you, He will not regard that, but He will crush you under His feet without mercy; He will crush out your blood and make it fly, and it shall be sprinkled on His garments, so as to stain all His raiment. He will not only hate you, but He will have you in the utmost contempt; no place shall be thought fit for you but under His feet, to be trodden down as the mire in the streets.

3. The *misery* you are exposed to is that which God will inflict to that end, that He might show what that wrath of Jehovah is. God hath had it on His heart to show to angels and men both how excellent His love is and also how terrible His wrath is. Sometimes earthly kings have a mind to show how terrible their wrath is, by the extreme punishments they would execute on those that provoke them. Nebuchadnezzar, that mighty and haughty monarch of the Chaldean empire, was willing to show his wrath when enraged with Shadrach, Meshech, and Abednego[5] and accordingly gave order that the burning fiery furnace should be heated seven times hotter than it was before; doubtless, it was raised to the utmost degree of fierceness that human art could raise it; but the great God is also willing to show His wrath and magnify His awful Majesty and mighty power in the extreme sufferings of His enemies. Romans 9:22, "What if God, willing to show his wrath, and to make his power known, endured with much long-suffering, the vessels of wrath fitted to destruction?" And seeing this is His design, and what He has determined, to show how terrible the unmixed, unrestrained wrath, the fury, and fierceness of Jehovah is, He will do it to effect. There will be something accomplished and brought to pass that will be dreadful with a witness. When the great and angry God hath risen up and executed His awful vengeance on the poor sinner and the wretch is actually suffering the infinite weight and power of his indignation, then will God call upon the whole universe to behold that awful majesty and mighty power that is to be seen in it. Isaiah 33:12–14, "And the people shall be as the burnings of lime: as thorns cut up shall they be burnt in the fire. Hear, ye that are afar off, what I have done; and ye that are near, acknowledge my might. The sinners in Zion are afraid; fearfulness hath surprised the hypocrites," &c.

Thus it will be with you that are in an unconverted state, if you continue in it; the infinite might, and majesty, and terribleness of the Omnipotent God shall be magnified upon you in the ineffable strength of your torments; you shall be tormented in the presence of holy angels, and in the presence of the Lamb; and when you shall be in this state of suffering, the glorious inhabitants of heaven shall go forth and look on the awful spectacle, that they may see what the wrath and fierceness of the Almighty is; and when they have seen it, they will fall down and adore that great power and majesty. Isaiah 66:23–24, "And it shall come to pass, that from one new

5 As described in Daniel 3:1–30.

moon to another, and from one Sabbath to another, shall all flesh come to worship before me, saith the Lord. And they shall go forth and look upon the carcasses of the men that have transgressed against me; for their worm shall not die, neither shall their fire be quenched; and they shall be an abhorring unto all flesh."

4. It is everlasting wrath. It would be dreadful to suffer this fierceness and wrath of Almighty God one moment; but you must suffer it to all eternity. There will be no end to this exquisite horrible misery. When you look forward, you shall see a long forever, a boundless duration before you, which will swallow up your thoughts, and amaze your soul; and you will absolutely despair of ever having any deliverance, any end, any mitigation, any rest at all. You will know certainly that you must wear out long ages, millions of millions of ages, in wrestling and conflicting with this almighty merciless vengeance; and then when you have so done, when so many ages have actually been spent by you in this manner, you will know that all is but a point to what remains. So that your punishment will indeed be infinite. Oh, who can express what the state of a soul in such circumstances is! All that we can possibly say about it gives but a very feeble, faint representation of it; it is inexpressible and inconceivable: For "who knows the power of God's anger?"[6]

How dreadful is the state of those that are daily and hourly in the danger of this great wrath and infinite misery! But this is the dismal case of every soul in this congregation that has not been born again, however moral and strict, sober and religious, they may otherwise be. Oh that you would consider it, whether you be young or old! There is reason to think that there are many in this congregation now hearing this discourse that will actually be the subjects of this very misery to all eternity. We know not who they are, or in what seats they sit, or what thoughts they now have. It may be they are now at ease, and hear all these things without much disturbance, and are now flattering themselves that they are not the persons, promising themselves that they shall escape. If they knew that there was one person, and but one, in the whole congregation, that was to be the subject of this misery, what an awful thing would it be to think of! If we knew who it was, what an awful sight would it be to see such a person! How might all the rest of the congregation lift up a lamentable and bitter cry over him! But, alas! instead of one, how many is it likely will remember this discourse in hell? And it would be a wonder, if some that are now present should not be in hell in a very short time, even before this year is out. And it would be no wonder if some persons, that now sit here, in some seats of this meetinghouse, in health, quiet and secure, should be there before tomorrow morning. Those of you that finally continue in a natural condition, that shall keep out of hell longest will be there in a little time! your damnation does not slumber; it will come swiftly, and, in all probability, very suddenly upon many of you. You have reason to wonder that you are not already in hell. It is doubtless the case of some whom you have seen and known, that never deserved hell more than you, and that heretofore appeared as likely to have been now alive as you. Their case is past all hope; they are crying in extreme misery and perfect despair; but here you are in the land of the living and in the house of God, and have an opportunity to obtain salvation. What would not those poor damned hopeless souls give for one day's opportunity such as you now enjoy!

[6] Psalm 90:11.

And now you have an extraordinary opportunity, a day wherein Christ has thrown the door of mercy wide open, and stands in calling and crying with a loud voice to poor sinners; a day wherein many are flocking to Him, and pressing into the kingdom of God. Many are daily coming from the east, west, north and south; many that were very lately in the same miserable condition that you are in, are now in a happy state, with their hearts filled with love to Him who has loved them and washed them from their sins in His own blood, and rejoicing in hope of the glory of God. How awful it is to be left behind at such a day! To see so many others feasting, while you are pining and perishing! To see so many rejoicing and singing for joy of heart, while you have cause to mourn for sorrow of heart and howl for vexation of spirit! How can you rest one moment in such a condition? Are not your souls as precious as the souls of the people at Suffield,[7] where they are flocking from day to day to Christ?

Are there not many here who have lived long in the world, and are not to this day born again? and so are aliens from the commonwealth of Israel, and have done nothing ever since they have lived, but treasure up wrath against the day of wrath? Oh, sirs, your case, in an especial manner, is extremely dangerous. Your guilt and hardness of heart is extremely great. Do you not see how generally persons of your years are passed over and left, in the present remarkable and wonderful dispensation of God's mercy? You had need to consider yourselves and awake thoroughly out of sleep. You cannot bear the fierceness and wrath of the infinite God. And you, young men and young women, will you neglect this precious season which you now enjoy, when so many others of your age are renouncing all youthful vanities and flocking to Christ? You especially have now an extraordinary opportunity; but if you neglect it, it will soon be with you as with those persons who spent all the precious days of youth in sin and are now come to such a dreadful pass in blindness and hardness. And you, children, who are unconverted, do not you know that you are going down to hell, to bear the dreadful wrath of that God who is now angry with you every day and every night? Will you be content to be the children of the devil, when so many other children in the land are converted and are become the holy and happy children of the King of kings?

And let every one that is yet of Christ, and hanging over the pit of hell, whether they be old men and women, or middle aged, or young people, or little children, now hearken to the loud calls of God's word and providence. This acceptable year of the Lord, a day of such great favors to some, will doubtless be a day of as remarkable vengeance to others. Men's hearts harden, and their guilt increases apace at such a day as this, if they neglect their souls; and never was there so great danger of such persons being given up to hardness of heart and blindness of mind. God seems now to be hastily gathering in His elect in all parts of the land; and probably the greater part of adult persons that ever shall be saved will be brought in now in a little time and that it will be as it was on the great out-pouring of the Spirit upon the Jews in the apostles' days; the election will obtain, and the rest will be blinded. If this should be the case with you, you will eternally curse this day, and will curse the day that ever you were born to see such a season of the pouring out of God's Spirit, and will wish that you had died and gone to hell before you had seen it. Now undoubtedly it is,

---

[7] Edwards's note: "A town in the neighborhood."

as it was in the days of John the Baptist, the axe is in an extraordinary manner laid at the root of the trees, that every tree which brings not forth good fruit may be hewn down and cast into the fire.[8]

Therefore, let every one that is out of Christ, now awake and fly from the wrath to come. The wrath of Almighty God is now undoubtedly hanging over a great part of this congregation: Let every one fly out of Sodom: "Haste and escape for your lives, look not behind you, escape to the mountain, lest you be consumed."[9]

1741

Letter to Rev. Dr. Benjamin Colman

[The History of the Great Awakening]

Northampton
Nov. 6, 1736

Rev. and Honored Sir,

Having seen your letter to my honored Uncle Williams' of Hatfield, of July 20 [1736], wherein you inform him of the notice taken by the Rev. Dr. Watts and Dr. Guyse of London, of the late wonderful work of God in this and some other towns of this county, and of their desire to be more perfectly informed of it; and at the same time signify your own desires that some of us would send you a full account, and that I would undertake it; I will therefore now do it in as just and faithful a manner as in me lies.

The people of the county in general, I suppose, are as sober, orderly and good sort of people as in any part of New England, and I believe they have been preserved the freest by far of any part in the country from error and variety of sect and opinions. Indeed there has been nothing of it till of late a small number of Baptists at Springfield. Our distance from the seaports, and being so far within the land, in the corner of the country, has doubtless been one reason why we have not been corrupted with vice, as most other parts. But without question the religion and good order of the county, and their purity in doctrine, has under God, been very much owing to the great abilities and eminent piety of my venerable and honored grandfather Stoddard. I suppose we have been the freest of any part of the land from unhappy divisions and quarrels in our ecclesiastical and religious affairs, till the late lamentable Springfield contention.[2]

The town of Northampton is of about eighty-two years' standing, and has now about two hundred families, which mostly dwell more compactly together than any town of such a bigness in these parts of the country; which probably has been some

---

[8] Luke 3:9.
[9] Genesis 19:17.
[1] William Williams (1665–1741), pastor at Hatfield, Massachusetts, 1685–1741.
[2] Robert Breck (1713–1784) was named pastor of

the church at Springfield in spite of the many protests of members of the Hampshire Ministers' Association that Breck was guilty of heterodoxy and misconduct.

occasion that both our corruption and reformation have been from time to time the more swiftly propagated through the town. In general the people seem as rational and understanding as any I have been acquainted with, and have ever from their beginning been noted for religion, and distinguished by their knowledge in things that relate to heart religion and Christian experience, and their great regard thereto.

I am the third minister that has been settled in the town. The Rev. Mr. Eleazar Mather, who was the first, was ordained in July 1661, and died July 1669.[3] His heart was much in his work, he was abundant in his labors for the good of precious souls, had the high esteem and love of his people, and was blessed with no small success. The Rev. Mr. Stoddard, who succeeded him, came to the town the November after his death, but was not ordained till September 11, 1672, and died February 11, 1728/9, so that he continued in the work of the ministry here near sixty years. And as he was renowned for his gifts and graces, so he was blessed from the beginning with extraordinary success, in the conversion of many. He had five harvests, as he called them; the first was about fifty-seven years ago, the second about fifty-three, the third about forty, the fourth about twenty-four, the fifth and last about eighteen years ago. Some of those times were much more remarkable than others, and the ingathering of souls more plentiful. In each of them, I have heard my grandfather say, that the bigger part of the young people of the town seemed to be mainly concerned for their eternal salvation.

After the last of these came a more degenerate time, at least among the young people, by far I suppose than had been ever before. Mr. Stoddard indeed had the comfort before he died of seeing no small moving among some, and a considerable ingathering of souls, even after I was settled with him in the ministry, which was about two years before his death. And I have reason to bless God for the great advantage I had by it. There were near twenty that Mr. Stoddard hoped were then savingly converted, but there was nothing of any general awakening.

After my grandfather's death, it seemed a time of extraordinary dullness in religion. Licentiousness had for many years too much prevailed among the youth of the town. It was the manner of too many of them to get together, in conventions of both sexes for mirth and jollity, which they called frolics; and they would spend the greater part of the night in them, without regard to order in the families they belonged to. And indeed family government did too much fail in the town. But within two or three years after Mr. Stoddard's death, there began to be a sensible amendment of these evils. The young people hearkened to counsel, and by degrees left off their frolicking, and grew observably more decent in their attendance on the public worship and manifested more of a religious concern.

At the latter end of the year 1733, there appeared a very unusual flexibleness and yielding to advice. It had been their manner to make the evening after the Sabbath,[4] and after our public lecture, the times of their mirth and company-keeping. A sermon was therefore preached the Lord's day before the lecture, to shew the evil tendency of the practice, and to persuade them to reform it. And it was urged on heads of families to agree to govern and restrain their households at those times; and withal it was more privately moved to them, to meet the next day in their several neighbor-

---

[3] Mather lived from 1637 to 1669.
[4] In the custom of some churches, including

Jonathan Edwards's, the Sabbath observance began and ended with evening.

hoods to know one another's minds; which was accordingly done, and the motion complied with throughout the town. But parents found little or no occasion for the exercise of government in the case; the young people declared themselves convinced by what they had heard from the pulpit, and there was a thorough reformation of these disorders, which has continued.

Presently after this, there began to appear a remarkable religious concern in a little village about three miles from the main body of the town, where a number of persons seemed to be savingly wrought upon. In the April following, *anno* 1734, there happened a very sudden and awful death of a young man in the bloom of life, which, with what was said publicly on that occasion, much affected many of our young people. This was followed also with another death, of a young married woman, who was in great distress in the beginning of her illness, but died full of comfort, with satisfying evidence of God's saving mercy to her; in a most earnest manner warning and counseling others, which seemed to contribute much to the solemnizing [of] the spirits of many.

In the fall of the year I moved to the young people that they would agree to spend the evenings after the lectures in social religion in various parts of the town, which was accordingly done; and those meetings have been since continued, and the example followed by elder people.

About this time began the noise which was in this part of the country about Arminianism,[5] which seemed to appear with a threatening aspect. The friends of vital piety trembled for fear of the issue, but contrary to their fears it was strangely overruled to the promoting of religion. A sermon concerning "Justification by Faith Alone" (though great fault was found with meddling with the controversy, and it was elsewhere ridiculed, yet) proved a word in season, and it was evidently attended with a remarkable blessing to the souls of the people in this town; giving them universal satisfaction about the main thing in question, which they had been in trembling concern about.

And then it was in the latter part of December that the Spirit of God began extraordinarily to set in, and wonderfully to work among us; so that there were, very suddenly, one after another, five or six persons that were to all appearance savingly converted; and some of them wrought upon in a remarkable manner. Among these, I was surprised with the relation of a young woman that had been one of the greatest company-keepers in the whole town, in whom there appeared evident a glorious work of God's infinite power and sovereign grace; a new and truly broken, sanctified heart. Yet I was filled with concern about the effect it might have on others, and was ready to conclude (though too rashly) that some would be hardened by it in carelessness and looseness of life, and would take occasion to reproach religion; but the event was the reverse to a wonderful degree. God made it, I suppose, the greatest occasion of awakening to others, of anything that ever came to pass in the town. I have had abundant opportunity to know the effect it had, by my private conversation with many. The news of it seemed as a flash of lightning upon the hearts, both of young people and others. The persons farthest from seriousness were greatly affected with it: many went to talk with her, to their great satisfaction. And presently upon this, a great and earnest concern about the great things of religion and the eternal world

---

[5] Disbelief in predestination.

became universal, in all parts of the town, and among persons of all degrees and ages. The noise among the dry bones waxed louder and louder. All other talk but about spiritual and eternal things was thrown by. All the conversation in all companies, and upon all occasions, was upon these things only; except so much as was necessary for people's carrying on their ordinary secular business. Other discourse, than of the things of God, would scarce be tolerated in any company. The minds of people were wonderfully taken off from the world: it was treated among us as a thing of very little consequence. Men seemed to follow their worldly business more as a part of duty, than from any disposition they had to it. The temptation now seemed to be on the other hand to neglect worldly affairs too much, and to spend too much time in the immediate exercises of religion: which thing was, however, misrepresented by reports spread in distant parts of the land, as though the people here had wholly thrown by all worldly business. Yet true it was, that religion was with all sorts the main concern, and the world only a thing by the bye. The only thing was to get the kingdom of heaven, and everyone appeared pressing into it. The engagedness of their hearts herein, could not be hid; it appeared in their very countenances. It was then a dreadful thing among us to be out of Christ; and in danger every day of dropping into hell. People were intent upon this, to escape for their lives, and to flee from the wrath to come. All eagerly laid hold of opportunities for their souls, and met often in private houses for religious exercises. There was scarce a single person in the town, old or young, left unconcerned. The vainest and loosest formerly, were now greatly awakened; and the work of conversion went on in an astonishing manner. Souls came as it were by flocks to Jesus Christ. For many months together from day to day, were evident instances of it.

In the spring and summer following, *anno* 1735, the town seemed to be full of the presence of God, full of love and joy so as never before, and yet full of distress. This was almost in every house, on the account of salvation being brought into them. Parents rejoiced over their children as newborn, and husbands and wives in each other; God's day was a delight, and his tabernacles amiable; our public assemblies indeed beautiful, and the congregation alive in God's service; everyone earnestly intent on the public worship, and eager to drink in the Word from the mouth of the minister; generally in tears while the Word was preached, some weeping with sorrow, others with joy and love, others with pity and concern for the souls of their neighbors. Our public praises were greatly enlivened, and God was served in our psalmody as in the beauties of holiness. There was scarce any part of divine worship wherein God's saints among us had grace so drawn forth, and their hearts so lifted up, as in singing the praises of God. Our congregation had excelled all that ever I knew in the external part of the duty before, generally carrying regularly and well three parts of music, and the women a part by themselves; but now they were evidently wont to sing with unusual elevations of heart and voice, which made the duty pleasant indeed. In all companies on other days, on whatsoever occasions persons were met together, Christ was to be heard of and seen in the midst of them. Our young people, when they met, were wont to spend their time in talking of the excellency of Jesus Christ, the gloriousness of the way of salvation, the wonderful free and sovereign grace of God, and his work in the conversion of a soul, the truth and certainty of God's Word, the sweetness of the views of his perfections, etc. And even at weddings, which were formerly occasions of mirth and jollity, there was now no discourse of anything but religion, and no appearance of any but spiritual mirth. The converted were greatly enlivened, and renewed as with fresh oil, though some much more than others, according to the measure of the gift of Christ; and many who had before labored under difficulties about their own state, had now their doubts removed by more clear discoveries to them of the love of God.

When this work of God first appeared, and was so extraordinarily carried on among us in the winter, others round about us seemed not to know what to make of it, and many scoffed at it; some compared our conversions to certain distempers. But it was very observable of many that occasionally came among us from abroad, with disregardful hearts, that what they saw here cured 'em of this temper of mind. Strangers were generally surprised to find things so much beyond what they had heard, and were wont to tell others that the state of the town could not be conceived by those that had not seen it. The notice taken of it when the Court set here in March was very observable, and so at our lectures, when many were remarkably affected. Many had their consciences smitten and awakened, and went home with wounded hearts, and with impressions that never wore off, but had hopefully a saving issue; and those that before had serious thoughts, had their convictions greatly increased. Others that came only on visits or business appeared to be savingly wrought upon, partook of the shower of blessing rained down on us, and went home rejoicing. Till at length the same work began openly to appear and prevail in several other towns of the county.

In the month of March the people of South Hadley began to be seized with deep concern about the things of religion, which very soon became universal: and it has been there not much if anything short of what it has been here, in proportion to the bigness of the place.

About the same time it began to break forth in the west part of Suffield, and soon spread into all the town, where it has also been very great. It next appeared at Sunderland and soon overspread the town; and for a season was no less remarkable there than here. About the same time it began in a part of Deerfield called Green River, and afterwards filled the town, where there had been a glorious work. It became manifest also in the south part of Hatfield, and in the second week of April the whole town seemed to be seized as it were at once, great numbers resorting to their minister for advice, and many have been added to the church. There has been also a very general awakening at West Springfield and Longmeadow; and at Enfield there was for a time a pretty general concern, observable among some that had been before very loose persons. At the same time, the Rev. Mr. Bull of Westfield informed me of a great alteration there, and that more had been done in one week than in seven years before. Something of this appeared also in the first precinct in Springfield, principally in the north and south extremes of the parish. And at Hadley Old Town there was gradually so much of a work of God upon souls, as at another time would have been thought worthy of much notice. For a short time there was also a very great and general concern of the like nature at Northfield. And wherever it appeared, it seemed not to be in vain, but in every place God brought saving blessings with him. It might well be said here from place to place, "Who are these that fly as a cloud, and as the doves to their windows?" [Isa. 60:8]. The continual news from town to town kept alive the talk of religion, and as it greatly quickened and rejoiced the hearts of good people, so it much awakened those that looked upon themselves as still left behind, and made them earnest to share in the great blessing that others had obtained.

This remarkable pouring out of the Spirit of God, which extended from one end of the county to the other, was not confined to it. Many places in Connecticut partook of the same mercy: as in the first parish in Windsor, under the pastoral care of the Rev. Mr. Marsh[6] while we had no knowledge of each other's circumstances. Afterwards, also in East Windsor, my honored father's parish, which has been in times past a place favored with like mercy, above any on this western side of New England, excepting Northampton, there having been four or five times of general awakening since my father's settlement among them. Last spring and summer the work of God was wonderful at Coventry, under the ministry of the Rev. Mr. Meacham.[7] At the same time it was great in a part of Lebanon, called The Crank, where Mr. Wheelock,[8] a young gentleman is lately settled. So at Durham, under the ministry of the Rev. Mr. Chauncy,[9] and in Stratford under the ministry of the Rev. Mr. Gold,[10] and in another parish called Ripton under the pastoral care of Mr. Mills.[11] A considerable revival of religion was also at New Haven, Old Town, as I have been informed by the Rev. Mr. Noyes there, and by others; which flourishing of religion there still continues and has lately much increased.

Mention is made of some other places by the Rev. Mr. Edwards, as Mansfield, Tolland, the North Parish in Preston, etc. And then he goes on to observe upon all:

That it seems a very extraordinary dispensation of Providence, beyond God's usual way of working, on the account of the universality of it, affecting all sorts, sober and vicious, high and low, wise and unwise, old and young; so that where anyone seemed to remain senseless, it would be spoken of as a strange thing. So also in the numbers of those on whom we hope it has had a saving effect. We have had about six hundred and twenty communicants, which include almost all our adults: the church was large before, but persons never thronged into it as now. Our sacraments are eight weeks asunder, and I received into our communion about an hundred before one sacrament, and fourscore of them at one time; whose appearance, when they presented themselves to make an open explicit profession of Christianity, was very affecting to the congregation. I took in near sixty before the next sacrament. But it is not the manner here, as in many other churches in the country, to make a relation of experience of a work of conversion. I am far from pretending to determine, but if I might be allowed to say what appears to me probable, more than three hundred souls were savingly brought home to Christ in this town, in the space of half a year, and about the same number of males as females, which was far from what has been usual here. Those of our young people who are here on other accounts most likely and considerable, are mostly, as I hope, truly pious and leading in the ways of religion. Those that were

---

[6] Jonathan Marsh (1685–1747), pastor at Windsor, Connecticut.

[7] Joseph Meacham (1686–1752), pastor at South Coventry, Connecticut.

[8] Eleazar Wheelock (1711–1779), pastor at Lebanon (now Columbia), Connecticut.

[9] Nathaniel Chauncy (1681–1756), pastor at Durham, Connecticut.

[10] Hezekiah Gold (1695–1761), pastor at Stratford, Connecticut.

[11] Jedediah Mills (1696–1776), pastor at Ripton (now Huntington), Connecticut.

formerly our looser young persons are generally to all appearance become lovers of God and Christ, and spiritual in their dispositions. And I hope that by far the greater part above sixteen years of age have the saving knowledge of Christ; and so by what I have heard, I suppose it is at some other places. I suppose there were [converted] upward of fifty persons in this town above forty years of age, and more than twenty of them above fifty, and ten above sixty and two above seventy. And I suppose near thirty were wrought upon between ten and fourteen, and two between nine and ten, and one about four years old; several Negroes also appeared to have been born again.

The Rev. writer goes on to speak of the hand of God visible in the quickness of the work, and in the degree of saving light, love and joy experienced by many; and is very large in the vast variety of manner wherein persons were wrought on. On this head he says:

As to the manner of persons being wrought upon, there is a vast variety, yet in many things there is a great analogy in all. Persons are first awakened with a sense of their miserable condition by nature, and the danger they are in of perishing eternally. Some are more suddenly seized with convictions, by something they hear in public or in private conference; their consciences are suddenly smitten as if their hearts were pierced through with a dart. Others have their awakenings more gradually; they are thoughtful that it is their wisest way to delay no longer, and set themselves seriously to meditate on those things that have the most awakening tendency, and their awakenings have increased, till a sense of their misery has (by the influence of God's Spirit) taken fast hold of them. Others that before this time had been something religious and concerned, have been made sensible that their slack and dull way of seeking was never like to attain their purpose, and have been roused up to a greater violence for the kingdom of heaven [cf. Matt. 11:12].

These awakenings when they first seized on persons have had two effects. First, they have been brought immediately to quit their sinful practices, and the looser sort to dread their former vices and extravagances. The other effect was, that it put them upon earnest application of themselves to the means of salvation; reading, prayer, meditation, the ordinances of God's house, and private conference.

There is a very great variety as to the degree of fear and trouble, before they obtain any comfortable evidences of pardon and acceptance with God. Some have had abundantly more encouragement and hope: others have had such a sense of the displeasure of God, and the great danger they were in of damnation, that they could not sleep; the thoughts of sleeping in such a condition have been frightful to them. Sometimes the distemper of melancholy is evidently mixed, of which, when it happens, Satan seems to make great advantage, as a great bar in the way of any good effect. One knows not how to deal with such persons, [for] they turn everything that is said to them the wrong way. But it has been very remarkable, that there has been far less of this now, than there was wont to be in persons under awakenings at other times. Some persons that had before for a long time been entangled with peculiar temptations and hurtful distresses, were soon helped over them; and they have been successfully carried on in the way of life. Yet there have been some instances of persons that have had as great a sense of their danger and misery, as their natures could subsist under; sometimes brought to the borders of despair, and it has looked as black as midnight to them, a little before the day-dawn in their souls.

Some few instances there have been of persons under such a sense of God's wrath for sin, that they have been overborne and made to cry out with amazement. But more commonly persons' distresses have not been to such a degree.

The design of the spirit of God in these legal terrors seems most evidently to be, to make way for, and to bring persons to a conviction of their absolute dependence upon his sovereign power and grace, and universal necessity of a Mediator, by leading them into a sense of their exceeding wickedness and guiltiness in his sight, the pollution and insufficiency of their own righteousness, that they can in no wise help themselves, and that God would be just and righteous in casting them off forever.

In those whose awakenings seem to issue in conversion, commonly the first thing that appears after their legal troubles, is a conviction of the justice of God in their condemnation; from a sense of their exceeding sinfulness and the vileness of all their performances. Others have the sins of their lives in an extraordinary manner set before them; multitudes of them coming then fresh to their remembrance, with their aggravations. Some have their minds especially fixed upon some particular wicked practice. Some are especially convinced by a sight of the corruption and wickedness of their hearts; or some particular corruption in the time of their awakening, whereby the enmity of their hearts against God has been manifested. Some are convinced by a sense of the greatness of the sin of unbelief, the opposition of their hearts to Christ, and obstinacy in rejecting him, etc.

Commonly persons' minds immediately before this discovery of God's justice are exceeding restless, and in a kind of struggle and tumult; and sometimes in a mere anguish. But generally as soon as they have this conviction, it immediately brings their minds to a calm and composure: and often they then come to a conclusion within themselves, that they will lie at God's foot, in hopes of mercy, and wait his time. And it is observable, that persons when they first have this sense of the justice of God, rarely in the time of it think anything of its being that humiliation which they have often heard insisted on, and whereby they are prepared for mercy.

After this legal humiliation and calm of spirit, in some persons it is some time before any special manifestations are made to their souls of the grace of God as revealed in the Gospel; but very often some comfortable and sweet view of a merciful God and an all-sufficient Saviour, or some of the great and joyful things of the Gospel immediately follow, or in a very little time. And in some, the first sight of their just desert of hell, and of God's sovereignty with respect to their salvation, and a discovery of all-sufficient grace, seem to be as it were together.

The discoveries that are given, whence the first special comforts are derived, are in some respects various; more frequently Christ is distinctly the object of the mind, in his sufficiency and willingness to save sinners; but some have their thoughts more especially fixed on God, in some of his sweet and glorious attributes. In some the truths of the Gospel in general, in some the certainty of some particular promises, etc.

There are many that have lately been converted, who have been accounted very knowing persons, especially in the things of religion, and could talk with more than common understanding of conversion, that declare that all their former wisdom is brought to nought, and that they appear to themselves to have been mere babes. And it has seemed to have been with delight that they have seen themselves thus brought down and become nothing; that free grace and divine power might be exalted in them.

It was very wonderful to see after what manner persons' affections were sometimes moved and wrought upon, when God did suddenly open their eyes and let into their minds a sense of his grace, and the fullness of Christ and his readiness to save; who before were broken with apprehensions of divine wrath, and sunk as into an abyss with a sense of guilt, which they were ready to think was beyond the mercy of God. Their joyful surprise has caused their hearts as it were to leap; tears issuing like a flood, intermingled with their joy; and sometimes they have not been able to forbear expressing with a loud voice their great admiration, and sometimes ready to faint.

The converting influences of God's Spirit very commonly bring an extraordinary conviction of the reality and certainty of the great things of religion. They have that sight and taste of the divinity and divine excellency of the things of the Gospel, that is more to convince them than reading of hundreds of volumes of arguments without it. It seems to me, in many instances amongst us, they have at such times been as far from doubting of the truth of them, as from doubting whether there be a sun, when their eyes behold it in a clear hemisphere.

Some persons have had so great a sense of the glory of God and the excellency of Christ, that nature and life has seemed almost to sink under it. I have seen some (and been in conversation with them) in such frames, who certainly have been perfectly sober, and very remote from anything like enthusiastic wildness, expressing themselves concerning the glory of God's perfections, the wonderfulness of his grace in Christ and their own unworthiness, in a manner that can't be expressed after them. Their sense of their exceeding littleness or vileness, and their disposition to debase themselves before God, has appeared to be great in proportion to their light and joy. Such persons amongst us as have been thus distinguished with most extraordinary discoveries of God, have commonly in no wise appeared with the assuming and self-conceited, and self-sufficient airs of enthusiasts; but exceedingly the contrary: and are eminent for a spirit of meekness, modesty, self-diffidence, and low opinion of themselves.

And those who have been thought to be converted amongst us, generally express an humbleness of mind desirous to lie in the dust before God: and very often speak of their sense of the excellency of the way of salvation by free and sovereign grace, through the righteousness of Christ alone, and how it is with delight they renounce their own righteousness.

There is a great difference among those that are converted, as to the hope and satisfaction they have of their own state. They generally have an awful apprehension of the dreadfulness of a false hope. And there has been observable in most a great caution lest in giving an account of their experiences they should say too much, or use too strong terms.

This is but a small and broken extract of what the Rev. writer says of the manner wherein souls were wrought on; and he adds a very particular exemplification of it in two instances, too large to be inserted in this appendix. Toward the close of his letter he adds:

After these things,[12] instances of conversion were rare in comparison of what had before been. Yet religion remained the main subject of conversation for several months

---

[12] Reference to the suicide of Joseph Hawley and the "enthusiastic delusions" of which he writes later.

after. But in general there was a gradual decline of that engaged lively spirit which had been before. Several things happened to give a diversion to people's minds, and turned their conversation to other things.

But as to those that have been thought to be converted among us in this time, the change in them seems abiding. They appear to have a new sense of things, new apprehensions and views of God, and the great things of the Gospel. They have a new sense of the truth of them, and they affect them in a new manner; though it is very far from being always alike with them, nor can they revive a sense of things when they please. Their hearts are often touched, and sometimes filled with new sweetnesses and delights. There seems to be an inward ardor and burning of heart which they express, of which they never experienced the like before. There are yet new kind of breathings and pantings and breakings of soul for the longings it hath.

Some that before were very rough in their temper and manner, seem to be remarkably softened and sweetened. And some have their souls exceedingly filled and overwhelmed with light, love, and comfort, long since the work of God has ceased to be so remarkable.

There is still a great deal of religious conversation maintained in the town, among young and old; and private religious meetings on Sabbath and lecture nights are still maintained; and many children still keep up such meetings among themselves. I know of no one young person in the town that has reverted to former ways of looseness and extravagance in any respect; but we still remain a reformed people, and God has evidently made us a new people. A great part of the country have not received favorable thoughts of this affair, and to this day retain a jealousy about it, and prejudice against it: yet so it has pleased God to work, and we are evidently a people blessed of him; and in this corner of the world God dwells and manifests his glory.

Thus, Rev. Sir, I have given a large and particular account of this remarkable affair, which I leave entirely with you to use as you think best; and if you please to send anything to the Rev. Dr. Guyse, I shall be glad to have it signified to him as my humble desire, that since he and his congregation have been pleased to take so much notice of us, they would still think of us at the throne of grace, and seek there for us that God would not forsake us, but enable us to bring forth fruits answerable to our profession and our mercies.

When I first heard of the notice which the Rev. Dr. Watts and Dr. Guyse took of God's mercies to us, I took occasion to inform our congregation of it in a discourse from those words, "A city set upon an hill cannot be hid" [Matt. 5:14]; and I have since read that part of your letter to my congregation, and labored as much as in me lay to enforce their duty from it; with which they were very sensibly moved and affected. I ask your prayers for this county and town, and a particular interest in them for him who is, with humble respect, Sir, your, etc.,

Jonathan Edwards.

1935

Benjamin Franklin
1706–1790

Eighteenth-century America produced a number of towering, versatile person-alities, but none with the creative range of Benjamin Franklin. A summary of his career reads like one of Walt Whitman's catalogs of occupations: printer, publisher, journalist, essayist, scientist, philosopher, merchant, educator, inventor, politician, diplomat. "Everything," remarked Herman Melville ironically, "but a poet." Franklin possessed the kind of energy that wishes to improve nearly every aspect of life, and he combined that energy with a restless, empirical, pragmatic mode of thinking that would in time become stereotypical of the national character. That he also raised himself, as he says in the opening paragraph of his *Autobiography,* from "poverty and obscurity" to "a state of affluence and some degree of celebrity in the world" further enhances the distinctive American quality of his astounding career.

Franklin was born in Boston in 1706, the fifteenth child of a soap and candle maker. The early "poverty" in which he claims to have been raised may be more accurate than the "obscurity." As a respected member of the Boston community and the prestigious Old South Church, Josiah Franklin numbered among his friends many leading Boston figures, including the illustrious Samuel Sewall, whom young Franklin met at home prayer meetings. Showing signs of precocity, Franklin was sent to the Boston Grammar School, where he characteristically rose to the head of his class. The expenses of the large Franklin family, however, prevented his continuing in a college preparatory curriculum, and he was removed to a private school established to teach future tradesmen the necessary skills of "writing and arithmetic." At ten Franklin left school altogether to help in the family business, but disliking it, was officially apprenticed two years later to his half brother James, who had recently set up a printing shop in Boston. Franklin made, as he says, "great progress" in this trade and particularly enjoyed the access it gave him to books and booksellers.

Although Franklin may have turned out to be "everything but a poet," he nevertheless began his literary career with "two occasional ballads" that he single-handedly penned, printed, and peddled. But after his father ridiculed these performances and informed him that "verse makers" were generally "beggars," Franklin prudently turned his efforts to the development of a prose style that he claims in his *Autobiography* "has been of great use to me in the course of my life and was a principal means of my advancement." In 1722, the year after his brother founded the iconoclastic *New England Courant*—a newspaper Sewall characterized as "impudent"—Franklin wrote a series of humorous essays in the vein of Addison and Steele's popular *Spectator Papers* and submitted them to the *Courant* under a pseudonym. The essays appeared over the name of a "Mrs. Silence Dogood," a play on Cotton Mather's popular *Bonifacius, an Essay upon the Good* (1710), a book whose solid moral advice Franklin later admitted influenced his career. After the fourteenth "Dogood" paper, Franklin let his brother in on the author's identity, but this disclosure added to a growing tension between master and apprentice. The relationship ended bitterly the next year;

Franklin violated the terms of indenture and ran off to begin a new life in Philadelphia.

He found work in Samuel Keimer's small, ill-equipped printing shop but did not stay for long. The governor of Pennsylvania, Sir William Keith, at the suggestion of Franklin's brother-in-law, decided to assist the young printer by sponsoring a trip to London, where he could master the trade, buy the latest equipment, and make important business contacts—all necessary if he were ever to run his own shop. When he reached London, Franklin learned that he could not rely on Keith's promises. Undiscouraged, he quickly found employment in a famous London printing house, where by day he perfected his craft and by evening made the acquaintance of some noted writers, scientists, and philosophers, including Hans Sloane and Bernard Mandeville. During this period he also wrote a brief metaphysical treatise, "A Dissertation on Liberty and Necessity, Pleasure and Pain." No Jonathan Edwards when it came to finely drawn speculation on freedom of the will, Franklin promptly disowned the work and later referred to it as one of the "errata" of his life.

Franklin returned to Philadelphia in 1726 and began working as a merchant's clerk. When his employer died the following year, he had little choice than go back to Keimer's printing shop. He determined to make a success of himself by adhering to a meticulous schedule of work and self-improvement and by methodically attending to every detail of daily existence with a rigor that would have pleased his Puritan forebears. Over the next three years Franklin purchased and revitalized a newspaper *(The Pennsylvania Gazette),* opened a stationer's shop, and was appointed public printer of Pennsylvania. In 1730 he married Deborah Read, whom he had first noticed the day he made his awkward entrance into Philadelphia as a runaway apprentice. Between 1733 and 1744 he founded a fire company, established America's first circulating library, was appointed deputy postmaster general of the colonies, launched a magazine, organized the American Philosophical Society, invented the popular Franklin stove, and drew up a proposal for what would become the University of Pennsylvania.

In 1732 Franklin began *Poor Richard's Almanac,* a somewhat parodic annual compendium of weather predictions, folk wisdom, poetic snippets, recipes, medical advice, proverbs, moral anecdotes, and useful information on how to make money and save time for people who had little of either. Franklin lifted domestic cost accounting to new heights: He worked unceasingly, always demanding of himself what he required in 1725 of the members of his "junto" for mutual improvement—that they "be serviceable to *mankind,* to their country, to their friends, or to themselves." Such a philosophy prompted D. H. Lawrence's famous reproach of Franklin's career: "All the qualities of a great man, and never more than a great citizen."

By 1748 Franklin had made enough money to leave the management of his various businesses in other hands so that he could concentrate his energies in two areas, science and politics, each of which earned for him an international reputation. He had begun conducting experiments in electricity in 1746, and five years later the first of many editions of *Experiments and Observations on Electricity* was published in London. Franklin had an eye for the theatrical side of science; in the summer of 1752 he performed his highly publicized kite experiments, which established the electrical nature of lightning and ensured his election to the

Royal Society of London. Not one to ignore the practical application of a theoretical insight, Franklin recommended in 1753 that "pointed rods" be used on buildings to prevent damage from lightning, a suggestion soon implemented throughout the world. For painters and poets of the late eighteenth century, the bolt of lightning served as an image of political liberty. As a result of his experiments, Franklin became the embodiment of human enlightenment. To Philip Freneau, Franklin was a revolutionary philosopher "Who seized from kings their sceptred pride, / And turned the lightning's darts aside."

From his proposal for colonial unification at the Albany Congress in 1754 to his stirring speech at the Constitutional Convention in 1787, Franklin played a pivotal role in the struggle for colonial independence and the building of a new nation. In 1755 and 1756 he lent his business skills to help General Braddock obtain transportation and supplies during the French and Indian War. As a colonel of militia, he supervised the construction of forts in Pennsylvania. Between 1757 and 1762 he served as agent for the Province of Pennsylvania in London. Upon Franklin's leaving England, the philosopher David Hume wrote: "I am very sorry that you intend soon to leave our hemisphere. America has sent us many good things,—gold, silver, sugar, tobacco, indigo, and so forth; but you are the first great man of letters, for whom we are beholden to her." Within two years Franklin was back in London—this time representing the colonies before the House of Commons to protest the Stamp Act.

Franklin returned to Philadelphia in 1775 to serve as a delegate to the Second Continental Congress and as a member of the committee appointed to draft the Declaration of Independence. Jefferson reportedly explained that Franklin was not asked to write the document because he could not have resisted the urge to include a few jokes. In 1776 Franklin sailed for Paris as a congressional minister to the Court of Louis XVI, where he secured crucial support for his homeland. He charmed Parisian society with his wit and warmth, unsuccessfully proposed marriage to Mme. Helvetius, a prominent widow (Franklin's wife had died in 1774), and printed on his small private press a series of graceful, amusing "bagatelles."

In 1781 Franklin was sent to France to negotiate a peace treaty with Great Britain, which he signed, with John Jay and John Adams, two years later. While in Paris he resumed his interest in science: He investigated the claims of Mesmer's experiments in animal magnetism, wrote *Maritime Observations* and *On the Causes and Cure of Smokey Chimneys,* and enthusiastically looked into the Montgolfier balloon ascensions. He resigned his diplomatic post in 1785 and returned to Philadelphia, where he served in the state government before being elected president of the Pennsylvanian Society for the Abolition of Slavery and a delegate to the Constitutional Convention. In 1788, "afflicted with almost constant and grievous pain," he retired altogether from public life.

On his second visit to England, during a leisurely week in August 1771, Franklin began his memoirs. He got as far as his marriage in 1730 when political responsibilities forced him to discontinue. He did not resume the task until urged by friends during his stay at Passy, a Paris suburb, to complete what one friend thought would be an "efficacious advertisement" for a new nation. Franklin complied, but this time he did not (as he had in the opening section of the memoirs) address his writing to his son William, who had since taken up the

Loyalist cause. Instead, he omitted family anecdotes and concentrated on his public career and the regimen he devised to ensure success and happiness. In 1788, back in Philadelphia, he completed another large installment and, just a few weeks before he died, added yet a fourth section, taking his career up until 1759. The uncompleted *Autobiography* passed through a number of unauthorized and unreliable editions until the original manuscript was discovered in France in 1868. Cotton Mather's "Life of Sir William Phips" (1697) had earlier used the paradigm of the self-made man in America, but Franklin's *Autobiography* transformed the rags-to-riches theme into world myth.

John Bunyan had always been one of Franklin's favorite authors, and it is not difficult to see his *Autobiography* as a kind of *Pilgrim's Progress* of the Enlightenment—a predominantly moral tale in which a "career" replaces a "calling." A secular pilgrim who never entirely relinquished his New England heritage, Franklin nevertheless permanently altered the meaning of *progress*.

Further Reading:
M. Twain. "The Late Benjamin Franklin," *Galaxy*, 1870.
C. Van Doren, *Benjamin Franklin*, 1938, 1973.
Benjamin Franklin and the American Character, ed. C. G. Sanford, 1955.
I. Cohen, *Franklin and Newton*, 1956.
A. O. Aldridge, *Franklin and His French Contemporaries*, 1957.
B. Granger, *Benjamin Franklin: An American Man of Letters*, 1964.
R. F. Sayre, *The Examined Life*, 1964.
A. O. Aldridge, *Benjamin Franklin: Philosopher and Man*, 1965.
R. Burlingame, *Benjamin Franklin: Envoy Extraordinary*, 1967.
C. Lopez and E. W. Herbert, *The Private Franklin: The Man and His Family*, 1975.
A. B. Tourtellot, *Benjamin Franklin: The Boston Years*, 1977.

Texts:
The Autobiography of Benjamin Franklin, ed. L. W. Labaree et al., 1964.
Other selections prior to 1773 are from *The Papers of Benjamin Franklin*, ed. L. W. Labaree et al., 21 vols., 1959–1978.
All remaining selections are from *The Writings of Benjamin Franklin*, ed. A. H. Smyth, 10 vols., 1905–1907.
(Some inconsistencies in spelling have been silently corrected.)

---

from The Autobiography

from Part One

Twyford,[1] at the Bishop of St. Asaph's 1771.

Dear Son,[2]

I have ever had a Pleasure in obtaining any little Anecdotes of my Ancestors. You may remember the Enquiries I made among the Remains of my Relations when you were with me in England; and the Journey I took for that purpose.[3] Now imagining

[1] Country home near Winchester, England, of Franklin's friend Jonathan Shipley, bishop of St. Asaph.

[2] William Franklin, later royal governor of New Jersey.

[3] During a tour of England in 1758, they searched out the home of their ancestors.

it may be equally agreeable to you to know the Circumstances of *my* Life, many of which you are yet unacquainted with; and expecting a Weeks uninterrupted Leisure in my present Country Retirement, I sit down to write them for you. To which I have besides some other Inducements. Having emerg'd from the Poverty and Obscurity in which I was born and bred, to a State of Affluence and some Degree of Reputation in the World, and having gone so far thro' Life with a considerable Share of Felicity, the conducing Means I made use of, which, with the Blessing of God, so well succeeded, my Posterity may like to know, as they may find some of them suitable to their own Situations, and therefore fit to be imitated. That Felicity, when I reflected on it, has induc'd me sometimes to say, that were it offer'd to my Choice, I should have no Objection to a Repetition of the same Life from its Beginning, only asking the Advantage Authors have in a second Edition to correct some Faults of the first. So would I if I might, besides corr[ectin]g the Faults, change some sinister Accidents and Events of it for others more favourable, but tho' this were deny'd, I should still accept the Offer. However, since such a Repetition is not to be expected, the next Thing most like living one's Life over again, seems to be a *Recollection* of that Life; and to make that Recollection as durable as possible, the putting it down in Writing. Hereby, too, I shall indulge the Inclination so natural in old Men, to be talking of themselves and their own past Actions, and I shall indulge it, without being troublesome to others who thro' respect to Age might think themselves oblig'd to give me a Hearing, since this may be read or not as any one pleases. And lastly, (I may as well confess it, since my Denial of it will be believ'd by no body) perhaps I shall a good deal gratify my own *Vanity*. Indeed I scarce ever heard or saw the introductory Words, *Without Vanity I may say,* &c. but some vain thing immediately follow'd. Most People dislike Vanity in others whatever Share they have of it themselves, but I give it fair Quarter wherever I meet with it, being persuaded that it is often productive of Good to the Possessor and to others that are within his Sphere of Action: And therefore in many Cases it would not be quite absurd if a Man were to thank God for his Vanity among the other Comforts of Life. . . .

And now I speak of thanking God, I desire with all Humility to acknowledge, that I owe the mention'd Happiness of my past Life to his kind Providence, which led me to the Means I us'd and gave them Success. My Belief of this, induces me to *hope,* tho' I must not *presume,* that the same Goodness will still be exercis'd towards me in continuing that Happiness, or in enabling me to bear a fatal Reverse, which I may experience as others have done, the Complexion of my future Fortune being known to him only: and in whose Power it is to bless to us even our Afflictions.

The Notes one of my Uncles (who had the same kind of Curiosity in collecting Family Anecdotes) once put into my Hands, furnish'd me with several Particulars relating to our Ancestors. From these Notes I learnt that the Family had liv'd in the same Village, Ecton in Northamptonshire, for 300 Years, and how much longer he knew not (perhaps from the Time when the Name *Franklin* that before was the Name of an Order of People,[4] was assum'd by them for a Surname, when others took Surnames all over the Kingdom). (Here a Note)[5] on a Freehold of about 30 Acres, aided by the Smith's Business which had continued in the Family till his Time, the

---

[4] In feudal England, *franklin* was a term for a middle-class property owner.

[5] Omitted by Franklin.

eldest Son being always bred to that Business. A Custom which he and my Father both followed as to their eldest Sons. When I search'd the Register at Ecton, I found an Account of their Births, Marriages and Burials, from the Year 1555 only, there being no Register kept in that Parish at any time preceding. By that Register I perceiv'd that I was the youngest Son of the youngest Son for 5 Generations back.

My Grandfather Thomas, who was born in 1598, lived at Ecton till he grew too old to follow Business longer, when he went to live with his Son John, a Dyer at Banbury in Oxfordshire, with whom my Father serv'd an Apprenticeship. There my Grandfather died and lies buried. We saw his Gravestone in 1758. His eldest Son Thomas liv'd in the House at Ecton, and left it with the Land to his only Child, a Daughter, who with her Husband, one Fisher of Wellingborough sold it to Mr. Isted, now Lord of the Manor there. My Grandfather had 4 Sons that grew up, viz. Thomas, John, Benjamin and Josiah. I will give you what Account I can of them at this distance from my Papers, and if they are not lost in my Absence, you will among them find many more Particulars. Thomas was bred a Smith under his Father, but being ingenious, and encourag'd in Learning (as all his Brothers like wise were) by an Esquire Palmer then the principal Gentleman in that Parish, he qualify'd for the Business of Scrivener,[6] became a considerable Man in the County Affairs, was a chief Mover of all publick Spirited Undertakings, for the County, or Town of Northampton and his own Village, of which many Instances were told us at Ecton and he was much taken Notice of and patroniz'd by the then Lord Halifax. He died in 1702, Jan. 6, old Stile, just 4 Years to a Day before I was born.[7] The Account we receiv'd of his Life and Character from some old People at Ecton, I remember struck you, as something extraordinary from its Similarity to what you knew of mine. Had he died on the same Day, you said one might have suppos'd a Transmigration.

John was bred a Dyer, I believe of Woollens. Benjamin, was bred a Silk Dyer, serving an Apprenticeship at London. He was an ingenious Man, I remember him well, for when I was a Boy he came over to my Father in Boston, and lived in the House with us some Years. He lived to a great Age. His Grandson Samuel Franklin now lives in Boston. He left behind him two Quarto Volumes, M.S. of his own Poetry, consisting of little occasional Pieces address'd to his Friends and Relations, of which the following sent to me, is a Specimen. (Here insert it.)[8] He had form'd a Shorthand of his own, which he taught me, but never practising it I have now forgot it. I was nam'd after this Uncle, there being a particular Affection between him and my Father. He was very pious, a great Attender of Sermons of the best Preachers, which he took down in his Shorthand and had with him many Volumes of them. He was also much of a Politician, too much perhaps for his Station. There fell lately into my Hands in London a Collection he had made of all the principal Pamphlets relating to Publick Affairs from 1641 to 1717. Many of the Volumes are wanting, as appears by the Numbering, but there still remains 8 Vols. Folio, and 24 in 4to and 8vo.[9] A Dealer in old Books met with them, and knowing me by my sometimes buying of him, he brought them to me. It seems my Uncle must have

---

[6] A professional writer, often responsible for legal documents.
[7] Because of astronomical inaccuracies, the Julian ("Old Style") calendar was replaced by the Gregorian ("New Style") calendar in 1752. An act of Parliament advanced the calendar 11 days, thus shifting Franklin's birth date from January 6, 1706, to January 17, 1706.
[8] Omitted by Franklin.
[9] Traditional designations of book sizes.

left them here when he went to America, which was above 50 Years since. There are many of his Notes in the Margins.

This obscure Family of ours was early in the Reformation, and continu'd Protestants thro' the Reign of Queen Mary,[10] when they were sometimes in Danger of Trouble on Account of their Zeal against Popery. They had got an English Bible, and to conceal and secure it, it was fastned open with Tapes under and within the Frame of a Joint Stool. When my Great Great Grandfather read in it to his Family, he turn'd up the Joint Stool upon his Knees, turning over the Leaves then under the Tapes. One of the Children stood at the Door to give Notice if he saw the Apparitor coming, who was an Officer of the Spiritual Court. In that Case the Stool was turn'd down again upon its feet, when the Bible remain'd conceal'd under it as before. This Anecdote I had from my Uncle Benjamin. The Family continu'd all of the Church of England till about the End of Charles the 2ds Reign,[11] when some of the Ministers that had been outed for Nonconformity,[12] holding Conventicles[13] in Northampton-shire, Benjamin and Josiah adher'd to them, and so continu'd all their Lives. The rest of the Family remain'd with the Episcopal Church.

Josiah, my Father, married young, and carried his Wife with three Children unto New England, about 1682.[14] The Conventicles having been forbidden by Law, and frequently disturbed, induced some considerable Men of his Acquaintance to remove to that Country, and he was prevail'd with to accompany them thither, where they expected to enjoy their Mode of Religion with Freedom. By the same Wife he had 4 Children more born there, and by a second Wife ten more, in all 17, of which I remember 13 sitting at one time at his Table, who all grew up to be Men and Women, and married. I was the youngest Son and the youngest Child but two, and was born in Boston, N. England.

My Mother the 2d Wife was Abiah Folger, a Daughter of Peter Folger, one of the first Settlers of New England,[15] of whom honourable mention is made by Cotton Mather, in his Church History of that Country, (entitled Magnalia Christi Americana) as a *godly learned Englishman,* if I remember the words rightly. I have heard that he wrote sundry small occasional Pieces, but only one of them[16] was printed which I saw now many Years since. It was written in 1675, in the homespun Verse of that Time and People, and address'd to those then concern'd in the Government there. It was in favour of Liberty of Conscience, and in behalf of the Baptists, Quakers, and other Sectaries, that had been under Persecution; ascribing the Indian Wars and other Distresses, that had befallen the Country to that Persecution, as so many Judgments of God, to punish so heinous an Offence; and exhorting a Repeal of those uncharitable Laws. The whole appear'd to me as written with a good deal of Decent Plainness and manly Freedom. The six last concluding Lines I remember, tho' I have forgotten the two first of the Stanza, but the Purport of them was that his Censures proceeded from *Goodwill,* and therefore he would be known as the Author,

---

[10] A Roman Catholic, she reigned from 1553 to 1558.
[11] Charles II ruled from 1660 to 1685.
[12] They were ousted from the Church of England for refusing to read the prayer book.
[13] Secret religious meetings.
[14] Actually, 1683.
[15] The Folgers were a prominent Nantucket, Massachusetts, family.
[16] *A Looking Glass for the Times, or the Former Spirit of New England Revived in This Generation* (Boston, 1676).

because to be a Libeller, (says he)
  I hate it with my Heart.
From Sherburne Town[17] where now I dwell,
  My Name I do put here,
Without Offence, your real Friend,
  It is Peter Folgier.

My elder Brothers were all put Apprentices to different Trades. I was put to the Grammar School at Eight Years of Age, my Father intending to devote me as the Tithe[18] of his Sons to the Service of the Church. My early Readiness in learning to read (which must have been very early, as I do not remember when I could not read) and the Opinion of all his Friends that I should certainly make a good Scholar, encourag'd him in this Purpose of his. My Uncle Benjamin too approv'd of it, and propos'd to give me all his Shorthand Volumes of Sermons I suppose as a Stock to set up with, if I would learn his Character.[19] I continu'd however at the Grammar School not quite one Year, tho' in that time I had risen gradually from the Middle of the Class of that Year to be the Head of it, and farther was remov'd into the next Class above it, in order to go with that into the third at the End of the Year. But my Father in the mean time, from a View of the Expence of a College Education which, having so large a Family, he could not well afford, and the mean Living many so educated were afterwards able to obtain, Reasons that he gave to his Friends in my Hearing, altered his first Intention, took me from the Grammar School, and sent me to a School for Writing and Arithmetic kept by a then famous Man, Mr. Geo. Brownell, very successful in his Profession generally, and that by mild encouraging Methods. Under him I acquired fair Writing pretty soon, but I fail'd in the Arithmetic, and made no Progress in it.

At Ten Years old, I was taken home to assist my Father in his Business, which was that of a Tallow Chandler and Sope-Boiler. A Business he was not bred to, but had assumed on his Arrival in New England and on finding his Dying Trade would not maintain his Family, being in little Request. Accordingly I was employed in cutting Wick for the Candles, filling the Dipping Mold, and the Molds for cast Candles, attending the Shop, going of Errands, &c. I dislik'd the Trade and had a strong Inclination for the Sea; but my Father declar'd against it; however, living near the Water, I was much in and about it, learnt early to swim well, and to manage Boats, and when in a Boat or Canoe with other Boys I was commonly allow'd to govern, especially in any case of Difficulty; and upon other Occasions I was generally a Leader among the Boys, and sometimes led them into Scrapes, of which I will mention one Instance, as it shows an early projecting public Spirit, tho' not then justly conducted. There was a Salt Marsh that bounded part of the Mill Pond, on the Edge of which at Highwater, we us'd to stand to fish for Minews. By much Trampling, we had made it a mere Quagmire. My Proposal was to build a Wharf there fit for us to stand upon, and I show'd my Comrades a large Heap of Stones which were intended for a new

---

[17] Franklin's note: "In the Island of Nantucket."
[18] A contribution of the tenth part of one's income to the church; Franklin was the tenth son.
[19] The shorthand method.

House near the Marsh, and which would very well suit our Purpose. Accordingly in the Evening when the Workmen were gone, I assembled a Number of my Playfellows, and working with them diligently like so many Emmets,[20] sometimes two or three to a Stone, we brought them all away and built our little Wharff. The next Morning the Workmen were surpriz'd at Missing the Stones; which were found in our Wharff; Enquiry was made after the Removers; we were discovered and complain'd of; several of us were corrected by our Fathers; and tho' I pleaded the Usefulness of the Work, mine convinc'd me that nothing was useful which was not honest.

I think you may like to know Something of his Person and Character. He had an excellent Constitution of Body, was of middle Stature, but well set and very strong. He was ingenious, could draw prettily, was skill'd a little in Music and had a clear pleasing Voice, so that when he play'd Psalm Tunes on his Violin and sung withal as he sometimes did in an Evening after the Business of the Day was over, it was extreamly agreable to hear. He had a mechanical Genius too, and on occasion was very handy in the Use of other Tradesmen's Tools. But his great Excellence lay in a sound Understanding, and solid Judgment in prudential Matters, both in private and publick Affairs. In the latter indeed he was never employed, the numerous Family he had to educate and the straitness of his Circumstances, keeping him close to his Trade, but I remember well his being frequently visited by leading People, who consulted him for his Opinion in Affairs of the Town or of the Church he belong'd to and show'd a good deal of Respect for his Judgment and Advice. He was also much consulted by private Persons about their Affairs when any Difficulty occur'd, and frequently chosen an Arbitrator between contending Parties. At his Table he lik'd to have as often as he could, some sensible Friend or Neighbour, to converse with, and always took care to start some ingenious or useful Topic for Discourse, which might tend to improve the Minds of his Children. By this means he turn'd our Attention to what was good, just, and prudent in the Conduct of Life; and little or no Notice was ever taken of what related to the Victuals on the Table, whether it was well or ill drest, in or out of season, of good or bad flavour, preferable or inferior to this or that other thing of the kind; so that I was bro't up in such a perfect Inattention to those Matters as to be quite Indifferent what kind of Food was set before me; and so unobservant of it, that to this Day, if I am ask'd I can scarce tell, a few Hours after Dinner, what I din'd upon. This has been a Convenience to me in travelling, where my Companions have been sometimes very unhappy for want of a suitable Gratification of their more delicate because better instructed Tastes and Appetites.

My Mother had likewise an excellent Constitution. She suckled all her 10 Children. I never knew either my Father or Mother to have any Sickness but that of which they dy'd, he at 89 and she at 85 Years of age. They lie buried together at Boston, where I some years since plac'd a Marble stone over their Grave with this Inscription

Josiah Franklin
And Abiah his Wife
Lie here interred.
They lived lovingly together in Wedlock

[20] Ants.

Fifty-five Years.
Without an Estate or any gainful Employment,
By constant labour and Industry,
With God's Blessing,
They maintained a large Family
Comfortably;
And brought up thirteen Children,
And seven Grand Children
Reputably.
From this Instance, Reader,
Be encouraged to Diligence in thy Calling,
And distrust not Providence.
He was a pious & prudent Man,
She a discreet and virtuous Woman.
Their youngest Son,
In filial Regard to their Memory,
Places this Stone.
J.F. born 1655—Died 1744. Ætat[21] 89
A.F. born 1667—died 1752—85

By my rambling Digressions I perceive my self to be grown old. I us'd to write more methodically. But one does not dress for private Company as for a publick Ball. 'Tis perhaps only Negligence.

To return. I continu'd thus employ'd in my Father's Business for two Years, that is till I was 12 Years old; and my Brother John, who was bred to that Business having left my Father, married and set up for himself at Rhodeisland, there was all Appearance that I was destin'd to supply his Place and be a Tallow Chandler. But my Dislike to the Trade continuing, my Father was under Apprehensions that if he did not find one for me more agreable, I should break away and get to Sea, as his Son Josiah had done to his great Vexation. He therefore sometimes took me to walk with him, and see Joiners, Bricklayers, Turners, Braziers, &c. at their Work, that he might observe my Inclination, and endeavour to fix it on some Trade or other on Land. It has ever since been a Pleasure to me to see good Workmen handle their Tools; and it has been useful to me, having learnt so much by it, as to be able to do little Jobs my self in my House, when a Workman could not readily be got; and to construct little Machines for my Experiments while the Intention of making the Experiment was fresh and warm in my Mind. My Father at last fix'd upon the Cutler's Trade, and my Uncle Benjamin's Son Samuel who was bred to that Business in London being about that time establish'd in Boston, I was sent to be with him some time on liking. But his Expectations of a Fee with me displeasing my Father, I was taken home again.

From a Child I was fond of Reading, and all the little Money that came into my Hands was ever laid out in Books. Pleas'd with the Pilgrim's Progress,[22] my first

---

[21] Latin: abbreviation for "Aged."
[22] John Bunyan's best-known work, published in 1678.

Collection was of John Bunyan's Works, in separate little Volumes. I afterwards sold them to enable me to buy R. Burton's[23] Historical Collections; they were small Chapmen's Books and cheap, 40 or 50 in all. My Father's little Library consisted chiefly of Books in polemic Divinity, most of which I read, and have since often regretted, that at a time when I had such a Thirst for Knowledge, more proper Books had not fallen in my Way, since it was now resolv'd I should not be a Clergyman. Plutarch's Lives[24] there was, in which I read abundantly, and I still think that time spent to great Advantage. There was also a Book of Defoe's, called an Essay on Projects,[25] and another of Dr. Mather's, call'd Essays to do Good[26] which perhaps gave me a Turn of Thinking that had an Influence on some of the principal future Events of my Life.

This Bookish Inclination at length determin'd my Father to make me a Printer, tho' he had already one Son, (James) of that Profession. In 1717 my Brother James return'd from England with a Press and Letters to set up his Business in Boston. I lik'd it much better than that of my Father, but still had a Hankering for the Sea. To prevent the apprehended Effect of such an Inclination, my Father was impatient to have me bound to my Brother. I stood out some time, but at last was persuaded and signed the Indentures, when I was yet but 12 Years old. I was to serve as an Apprentice till I was 21 Years of Age, only I was to be allow'd Journeyman's Wages during the last Year. In a little time I made great Proficiency in the Business, and became a useful Hand to my Brother. I now had Access to better Books. An Acquaintance with the Apprentices of Booksellers, enabled me sometimes to borrow a small one, which I was careful to return soon and clean. Often I sat up in my Room reading the greatest Part of the Night, when the Book was borrow'd in the Evening and to be return'd early in the Morning lest it should be miss'd or wanted. And after some time an ingenious Tradesman Mr. Matthew Adams who had a pretty Collection of Books, and who frequented our Printing House, took Notice of me, invited me to his Library, and very kindly lent me such Books as I chose to read. I now took a Fancy to Poetry, and made some little Pieces. My Brother, thinking it might turn to account encourag'd me, and put me on composing two occasional Ballads. One was called the *Light House Tragedy,* and contain'd an Account of the drowning of Capt. Worthilake with his Two Daughters; the other was a Sailor Song on the Taking of *Teach* or Blackbeard the Pirate.[27] They were wretched Stuff, in the Grubstreet Ballad Stile, and when they were printed he sent me about the Town to sell them. The first sold wonderfully, the Event being recent, having made a great Noise. This flatter'd my Vanity. But my Father discourag'd me, by ridiculing my Performances, and telling me Verse-makers were generally Beggars; so I escap'd being a Poet, most probably a very bad one. But as Prose Writing has been of great Use to me in the Course of my Life, and was a

---

[23] A pseudonym of Nathaniel Crouch, who "melted down the best . . . English histories into twelve penny books, which are filled with wonders, rarities, and curiosities" (*Dictionary of National Biography*).

[24] *Parallel Lives,* the Greek historian Plutarch's series of 46 paired biographies.

[25] Published in 1697, *Essay Upon Projects* suggested several civic and fiscal improvements.

[26] Published in 1710, *Bonifacius, an Essay upon the Good* inspired a number of Franklin's civic and moral endeavors.

[27] These two were written in November 1718. The full texts of Franklin's ballads have not been found.

principal Means of my Advancement, I shall tell you how in such a Situation I acquir'd what little Ability I have in that Way.

There was another Bookish Lad in the Town, John Collins by Name, with whom I was intimately acquainted. We sometimes disputed, and very fond we were of Argument, and very desirous of confuting one another. Which disputacious Turn, by the way, is apt to become a very bad Habit, making People often extreamly disagreeable in Company, by the Contradiction that is necessary to bring it into Practice, and thence, besides souring and spoiling the Conversation, is productive of Disgusts and perhaps Enmities where you may have occasion for Friendship. I had caught it by reading my Father's Books of Dispute about Religion. Persons of good Sense, I have since observ'd, seldom fall into it, except Lawyers, University Men, and Men of all Sorts that have been bred at Edinborough. A Question was once some how or other started between Collins and me, of the Propriety of educating the Female Sex in Learning, and their Abilities for Study. He was of Opinion that it was improper; and that they were naturally unequal to it. I took the contrary Side, perhaps a little for Dispute sake. He was naturally more eloquent, had a ready Plenty of Words, and sometimes as I thought bore me down more by his Fluency than by the Strength of his Reasons. As we parted without settling the Point, and were not to see one another again for some time, I sat down to put my Arguments in Writing, which I copied fair and sent to him. He answer'd and I reply'd. Three or four Letters of a Side had pass'd, when my Father happen'd to find my Papers, and read them. Without entring into the Discussion, he took occasion to talk to me about the Manner of my Writing, observ'd that tho' I had the Advantage of my Antagonist in correct Spelling and pointing[28] (which I ow'd to the Printing House) I fell far short in elegance of Expression, in Method and in Perspicuity, of which he convinc'd me by several Instances. I saw the Justice of his Remarks, and thence grew more attentive to the *Manner* in Writing, and determin'd to endeavour at Improvement.

About this time I met with an odd Volume of the Spectator.[29] It was the third. I had never before seen any of them. I bought it, read it over and over, and was much delighted with it. I thought the Writing excellent, and wish'd if possible to imitate it. With that View, I took some of the Papers, and making short Hints of the Sentiment in each Sentence, laid them by a few Days, and then without looking at the Book, try'd to compleat the Papers again, by expressing each hinted Sentiment at length and as fully as it had been express'd before, in any suitable Words, that should come to hand.

Then I compar'd my Spectator with the Original, discover'd some of my Faults and corrected them. But I found I wanted a Stock of Words or a Readiness in recollecting and using them, which I thought I should have acquir'd before that time, if I had gone on making Verses, since the continual Occasion for Words of the same Import but of different Length, to suit the Measure, or of different Sound for the Rhyme, would have laid me under a constant Necessity of searching for Variety, and also have tended to fix that Variety in my Mind, and make me Master of it. Therefore I took some of the Tales and turn'd them into Verse: And after a time, when I had pretty well forgotten the Prose, turn'd them back again. I also sometimes jumbled my

[28] Punctuating.
[29] An enormously influential London literary daily

(1711–1712) conducted by Joseph Addison and Richard Steele.

Collections of Hints into Confusion, and after some Weeks, endeavour'd to reduce them into the best Order, before I began to form the full Sentences, and compleat the Paper. This was to teach me Method in the Arrangement of Thoughts. By comparing my work afterwards with the original, I discover'd many faults and amended them; but I sometimes had the Pleasure of Fancying that in certain Particulars of small Import, I had been lucky enough to improve the Method or the Language and this encourag'd me to think I might possibly in time come to be a tolerable English Writer, of which I was extreamly ambitious.

My Time for these Exercises and for Reading, was at Night, after Work or before Work began in the Morning; or on Sundays, when I contrived to be in the Printing House alone, evading as much as I could the common Attendance on publick Worship, which my Father used to exact of me when I was under his Care: and which indeed I still thought a Duty; tho' I could not, as it seemed to me, afford the Time to practise it.

When about 16 Years of Age, I happen'd to meet with a Book, written by one Tryon, recommending a Vegetable Diet.[30] I determined to go into it. My Brother being yet unmarried, did not keep House, but boarded himself and his Apprentices in another Family. My refusing to eat Flesh occasioned an Inconveniency, and I was frequently chid for my singularity. I made my self acquainted with Tryon's Manner of preparing some of his Dishes, such as Boiling Potatoes or Rice, making Hasty Pudding, and a few others, and then propos'd to my Brother, that if he would give me Weekly half the Money he paid for my Board I would board my self. He instantly agreed to it, and I presently found that I could save half what he paid me. This was an additional Fund for buying Books: but I had another Advantage in it. My Brother and the rest going from the Printing House to their Meals, I remain'd there alone, and dispatching presently my light Repast, (which often was no more than a Bisket or a Slice of Bread, a Handful of Raisins or a Tart from the Pastry Cook's, and a Glass of Water) had the rest of the Time till their Return, for Study, in which I made the greater Progress from that greater Clearness of Head and quicker Apprehension which usually attend Temperance in Eating and Drinking. And now it was that being on some Occasion made asham'd of my Ignorance in Figures, which I had twice failed in learning when at School, I took Cocker's Book of Arithmetick,[31] and went thro' the whole by my self with great Ease. I also read Seller's and Sturmy's Books of Navigation,[32] and became acquainted with the little Geometry they contain, but never proceeded far in that Science. And I read about this Time Locke on Human Understanding, and the Art of Thinking by Messrs. du Port Royal.[33]

While I was intent on improving my Language, I met with an English Grammar (I think it was Greenwood's)[34] at the End of which there were two little Sketches of the Arts of Rhetoric and Logic, the latter finishing with a Specimen of a Dispute in the Socratic Method. And soon after I procur'd Xenophon's Memorable Things

---

[30] Thomas Tryon's *The Way to Health, Long Life and Happiness, or a Discourse of Temperance* (1691).

[31] Edward Cocker (1631–1675) wrote several books on arithmetic.

[32] John Seller's *An Epitome of the Art of Navigation* (1681); Samuel Sturmy's *The Mariner's Magazine; or Sturmy's Mathematical and Practical Arts* (1669).

[33] John Locke's *Essay Concerning Human Understanding* (1690) and *Logic: Or the Art of Thinking* by Antoine Arnauld and Pierre Nicole (1662; English trans. 1687).

[34] James Greenwood's *An Essay Towards a Practical English Grammar* (1711).

of Socrates,[35] wherein there are many Instances of the same Method. I was charm'd with it, adopted it, dropt my abrupt Contradiction, and positive Argumentation, and put on the humble Enquirer and Doubter. And being then, from reading Shaftsbury and Collins,[36] become a real Doubter in many Points of our Religious Doctrine, I found this Method safest for my self and very embarassing to those against whom I used it, therefore I took a Delight in it, practis'd it continually and grew very artful and expert in drawing People even of superior Knowledge into Concessions the Consequences of which they did not foresee, entangling them in Difficulties out of which they could not extricate themselves, and so obtaining Victories that neither my self nor my Cause always deserved.

I continu'd this Method some few Years, but gradually left it, retaining only the Habit of expressing my self in Terms of modest Diffidence, never using when I advance any thing that may possibly be disputed, the Words, *Certainly, undoubtedly,* or any others that give the Air of Positiveness to an Opinion; but rather say, I conceive, or I apprehend a Thing to be so or so, It appears to me, or I should think it so or so for such and such Reasons, or I imagine it to be so, or it is so if I am not mistaken. This Habit I believe has been of great Advantage to me, when I have had occasion to inculcate my Opinions and persuade Men into Measures that I have been from time to time engag'd in promoting. And as the chief Ends of Conversation are to *inform,* or to be *informed,* to *please* or to *persuade,* I wish wellmeaning sensible Men would not lessen their Power of doing Good by a Positive assuming Manner that seldom fails to disgust, tends to create Opposition, and to defeat every one of those Purposes for which Speech was given us, to wit, giving or receiving Information, or Pleasure: For if you would *inform,* a positive dogmatical Manner in advancing your Sentiments, may provoke Contradiction and prevent a candid Attention. If you wish Information and Improvement from the Knowledge of others and yet at the same time express your self as firmly fix'd in your present Opinions, modest sensible Men, who do not love Disputation, will probably leave you undisturb'd in the Possession of your Error; and by such a Manner you can seldom hope to recommend your self in *pleasing* your Hearers, or to persuade those whose Concurrence you desire. Pope says, judiciously,

> Men should be taught as if you taught them not,
> And things unknown propos'd as things forgot,

farther recommending it to us,

> To speak tho' sure, with seeming Diffidence.[37]

And he might have coupled with this Line that which he has coupled with another, I think less properly,

> For Want of Modesty is Want of Sense.

---

[35] Translated by Edward Bysshe (1712).
[36] Anthony Ashley Cooper, third earl of Shaftesbury (1671–1713); Anthony Collins (1676–1729).

[37] Alexander Pope (1688–1744), *An Essay on Criticism* (1711), ll. 574–575, 567.

If you ask why, *less properly,* I must repeat the Lines;

> Immodest Words admit of *no* Defence;
> *For* Want of Modesty is Want of Sense.[38]

Now is not *Want of Sense* (where a Man is so unfortunate as to want it) some Apology for his *Want of Modesty?* and would not the Lines stand more justly thus?

> Immodest Words admit *but this* Defence,
> That Want of Modesty is Want of Sense.

This however I should submit to better Judgments.

My Brother had in 1720 or 21, begun to print a Newspaper. It was the second that appear'd in America, and was called *The New England Courant.* The only one before it, was *the Boston News Letter.*[39] I remember his being dissuaded by some of his Friends from the Undertaking, as not likely to succeed, one Newspaper being in their Judgment enough for America. At this time 1771 there are not less than five and twenty. He went on however with the Undertaking, and after having work'd in composing the Types and printing off the Sheets I was employ'd to carry the Papers thro' the Streets to the Customers. He had some ingenious Men among his Friends who amus'd themselves by writing little Pieces for this Paper, which gain'd it Credit, and made it more in Demand; and these Gentlemen often visited us. Hearing their Conversations, and their Accounts of the Approbation their Papers were receiv'd with, I was excited to try my Hand among them. But being still a Boy, and suspecting that my Brother would object to printing any Thing of mine in his Paper if he knew it to be mine, I contriv'd to disguise my Hand, and writing an anonymous Paper I put it in at Night under the Door of the Printing House. It was found in the Morning and communicated to his Writing Friends when they call'd in as usual. They read it, commented on it in my Hearing, and I had the exquisite Pleasure, of finding it met with their Approbation, and that in their different Guesses at the Author none were named but Men of some Character among us for Learning and Ingenuity.

I suppose now that I was rather lucky in my Judges: And that perhaps they were not really so very good ones as I then esteem'd them. Encourag'd however by this, I wrote and convey'd in the same Way to the Press several more Papers,[40] which were equally approv'd, and I kept my Secret till my small Fund of Sense for such Performances was pretty well exhausted, and then I discovered it; when I began to be considered a little more by my Brother's Acquaintance, and in a manner that did not quite please him, as he thought, probably with reason, that it tended to make me too vain. And perhaps this might be one Occasion of the Differences that we frequently

---

[38] Franklin quotes, although inaccurately, from Wentworth Dillon, fourth earl of Roscommon (1633?–1685), *Essay on Translated Verse* (1684), ll. 113–114. These lines frequently were credited to Pope.

[39] *The New England Courant* was the fourth. *The Boston News Letter,* established April 24, 1704, was the first continuously published newspaper in the colonies. The earliest newspaper to appear, *Publick Occurrences* (September 25, 1690), lasted only one issue.

[40] Franklin's 14 letters, published under the pseudonym "Silence Dogood" in *The New England Courant* between April 12 and October 8, 1722.

had about this Time. Tho' a Brother, he considered himself as my Master, and me as his Apprentice; and accordingly expected the same Services from me as he would from another; while I thought he demean'd me too much in some he requir'd of me, who from a Brother expected more Indulgence. Our Disputes were often brought before our Father, and I fancy I was either generally in the right, or else a better Pleader, because the Judgment was generally in my favour: But my Brother was passionate and had often beaten me, which I took extreamly amiss; and thinking my Apprenticeship very tedious, I was continually wishing for some Opportunity of shortening it, which at length offered in a manner unexpected.[41]

One of the Pieces in our News-Paper, on some political Point which I have now forgotten, gave Offence to the Assembly. He was taken up, censur'd and imprison'd for a Month by the Speaker's Warrant, I suppose because he would not discover his Author. I too was taken up and examin'd before the Council; but tho' I did not give them any Satisfaction, they contented themselves with admonishing me, and dismiss'd me; considering me perhaps as an Apprentice who was bound to keep his Master's Secrets. During my Brother's Confinement, which I resented a good deal, notwithstanding our private Differences, I had the Management of the Paper, and I made bold to give our Rulers some Rubs in it, which my Brother took very kindly, while others began to consider me in an unfavourable Light, as a young Genius that had a Turn for Libelling and Satyr. My Brother's Discharge was accompany'd with an Order of the House, (a very odd one) *that James Franklin should no longer print the Paper called the New England Courant.* There was a Consultation held in our Printing House among his Friends what he should do in this Case. Some propos'd to evade the Order by changing the Name of the Paper; but my Brother seeing Inconveniences in that, it was finally concluded on as a better Way, to let it be printed for the future under the Name of *Benjamin Franklin.* And to avoid the Censure of the Assembly that might fall on him, as still printing it by his Apprentice, the Contrivance was, that my old Indenture should be return'd to me with a full Discharge on the Back of it, to be shown on Occasion; but to secure to him the Benefit of my Service I was to sign new Indentures for the Remainder of the Term, which were to be kept private. A very flimsy Scheme it was, but however it was immediately executed, and the Paper went on accordingly under my Name for several Months. At length a fresh Difference arising between my Brother and me, I took upon me to assert my Freedom, presuming that he would not venture to produce the new Indentures. It was not fair in me to take this Advantage, and this I therefore reckon one of the first Errata[42] of my Life: But the Unfairness of it weigh'd little with me, when under the Impressions of Resentment, for the Blows his Passion too often urg'd him to bestow upon me. Tho' he was otherwise not an ill-natur'd Man: Perhaps I was too saucy and provoking.

When he found I would leave him, he took care to prevent my getting Employment in any other Printing-House of the Town, by going round and speaking to every Master, who accordingly refus'd to give me Work. I then thought of going to New York as the nearest Place where there was a Printer: and I was the rather inclin'd to leave Boston, when I reflected that I had already made myself a little obnoxious to

---

[41] Franklin's note: "I fancy his harsh and tyrannical Treatment of me, might be a means of impressing me with that Aversion to arbitrary Power that has stuck to me thro' my whole Life."

[42] Plural of Latin *erratum*: "errors."

the governing Party; and from the arbitrary Proceedings of the Assembly in my Brother's Case it was likely I might if I stay'd soon bring myself into Scrapes; and farther that my indiscrete Disputations about Religion began to make me pointed at with Horror by good People, as an Infidel or Atheist. I determin'd on the Point: but my Father now siding with my Brother, I was sensible that if I attempted to go openly, Means would be used to prevent me. My Friend Collins therefore undertook to manage a little for me. He agreed with the Captain of a New York Sloop for my Passage, under the Notion of my being a young Acquaintance of his that had got a naughty Girl with Child, whose Friends would compel me to marry her, and therefore I could not appear or come away publickly. So I sold some of my Books to raise a little Money, Was taken on board privately, and as we had a fair Wind in three Days I found my self in New York near 300 Miles from home, a Boy of but 17, without the least Recommendation to or Knowledge of any Person in the Place, and with very little Money in my Pocket.

My Inclinations for the Sea, were by this time worne out, or I might now have gratify'd them. But having a Trade, and supposing my self a pretty good Workman, I offer'd my Service to the Printer of the Place, old Mr. Wm. Bradford,[43] (who had been the first Printer in Pensilvania, but remov'd from thence upon the Quarrel of Geo. Keith).[44] He could give me no Employment, having little to do, and Help enough already: But, says he, my Son[45] at Philadelphia has lately lost his principal Hand, Aquila Rose, by Death. If you go thither I believe he may employ you. Philadelphia was 100 Miles farther. I set out, however, in a Boat for Amboy, leaving my Chest and Things to follow me round by Sea. In crossing the Bay we met with a Squall that tore our rotten Sails to pieces, prevented our getting into the Kill,[46] and drove us upon Long Island. In our Way a drunken Dutchman, who was a Passenger too, fell over board; when he was sinking I reach'd thro' the Water to his shock Pate and drew him up so that we got him in again. His Ducking sober'd him a little, and he went to sleep, taking first out of his Pocket a Book which he desir'd I would dry for him. It prov'd to be my old favourite Author Bunyan's Pilgrim's Progress in Dutch, finely printed on good Paper with copper Cuts, a Dress better than I had ever seen it wear in its own Language. I have since found that it has been translated into most of the Languages of Europe, and suppose it has been more generally read than any other Book except perhaps the Bible. Honest John was the first that I know of who mix'd Narration and Dialogue, a Method of Writing very engaging to the Reader, who in the most interesting Parts finds himself as it were brought into the Company, and present at the Discourse. Defoe in his Cruso, his Moll Flanders, Religious Courtship, Family Instructor, and other Pieces, has imitated it with Success. And Richardson has done the same in his Pamela, &c.[47]

When we drew near the Island we found it was at a Place where there could be no Landing, there being a great Surff on the stony Beach. So we dropt Anchor and

---

[43] William Bradford (1663–1752), one of the chief printers in the colonies at the time.

[44] George Keith (1638–1716), a controversial Quaker leader.

[45] Andrew Bradford (1686–1742), who in 1719 published *The American Mercury*, the first newspaper printed in Pennsylvania.

[46] Narrow channel separating Staten Island, New York, from New Jersey.

[47] Samuel Richardson's *Pamela, or Virtue Rewarded* (1740) became the first novel published in the Colonies when Franklin reprinted it in 1744.

swung round towards the Shore. Some People came down to the Water Edge and hallow'd to us, as we did to them. But the Wind was so high and the Surff so loud, that we could not hear so as to understand each other. There were Canoes on the Shore, and we made Signs and hallow'd that they should fetch us, but they either did not understand us, or thought it impracticable. So they went away, and Night coming on, we had no Remedy but to wait till the Wind should abate, and in the mean time the Boatman and I concluded to sleep if we could, and so crouded into the Scuttle with the Dutchman who was still wet, and the Spray beating over the Head of our Boat, leak'd thro' to us, so that we were soon almost as wet as he. In this Manner we lay all Night with very little Rest. But the Wind abating the next Day, we made a Shift to reach Amboy before Night, having been 30 Hours on the Water without Victuals, or any Drink but a Bottle of filthy Rum: The Water we sail'd on being salt.

In the Evening I found my self very feverish, and went in to Bed. But having read somewhere that cold Water drank plentifully was good for a Fever, I follow'd the Prescription, sweat plentifully most of the Night, my Fever left me, and in the Morning crossing the Ferry, I proceeded on my Journey, on foot, having 50 Miles to Burlington,[48] where I was told I should find Boats that would carry me the rest of the Way to Philadelphia.

It rain'd very hard all the Day, I was thoroughly soak'd and by Noon a good deal tir'd, so I stopt at a poor Inn, where I staid all Night, beginning now to wish I had never left home. I cut so miserable a Figure too, that I found by the Questions ask'd me I was suspected to be some runaway Servant, and in danger of being taken up on that Suspicion. However I proceeded the next Day, and got in the Evening to an Inn within 8 or 10 Miles of Burlington, kept by one Dr. Brown.

He entred into Conversation with me while I took some Refreshment, and finding I had read a little, became very sociable and friendly. Our Acquaintance continu'd as long as he liv'd. He had been, I imagine, an itinerant Doctor, for there was no Town in England, or Country in Europe, of which he could not give a very particular Account. He had some Letters, and was ingenious, but much of an Unbeliever, and wickedly undertook some Years after to travesty the Bible in doggrel Verse as Cotton[49] had done Virgil. By this means he set many of the Facts in a very ridiculous Light, and might have hurt weak minds if his Work had been publish'd: but it never was. At his House I lay that Night, and the next Morning reach'd Burlington. But had the Mortification to find that the regular Boats were gone, a little before my coming, and no other expected to go till Tuesday, this being Saturday. Wherefore I return'd to an old Woman in the Town of whom I had bought Gingerbread to eat on the Water, and ask'd her Advice; she invited me to lodge at her House till a Passage by Water should offer: and being tired with my foot Travelling, I accepted the Invitation. She understanding I was a Printer, would have had me stay at that Town and follow my Business, being ignorant of the Stock necessary to begin with. She was very hospitable, gave me a Dinner of Ox Cheek with great Goodwill, accepting only of a Pot of Ale in return. And I tho't my self fix'd till Tuesday should come. However walking in the Evening by the Side of the River a Boat came by, which

[48] Town in western New Jersey.
[49] Charles Cotton (1630–1687), author of

Scarronides, or the First Book of Virgil Travestie (1664).

I found was going towards Philadelphia, with several People in her. They took me in, and as there was no Wind, we row'd all the Way; and about Midnight not having yet seen the City, some of the Company were confident we must have pass'd it, and would row no farther, the others knew not where we were, so we put towards the Shore, got into a Creek, landed near an old Fence with the Rails of which we made a Fire, the Night being cold, in October, and there we remain'd till Daylight. Then one of the Company knew the Place to be Cooper's Creek a little above Philadelphia, which we saw as soon as we got out of the Creek, and arriv'd there about 8 or 9 a Clock, on the Sunday morning, and landed at the Market street Wharff.[50]

I have been the more particular in this Description of my Journey, and shall be so of my first Entry into that City, that you may in your Mind compare such unlikely Beginnings with the Figure I have since made there. I was in my Working Dress, my best Cloaths being to come round by Sea. I was dirty from my Journey; my Pockets were stuff'd out with Shirts and Stockings; I knew no Soul, nor where to look for Lodging. I was fatigu'd with Travelling, Rowing and Want of Rest. I was very hungry, and my whole Stock of Cash consisted of a Dutch Dollar and about a Shilling in Copper. The latter I gave the People of the Boat for my Passage, who at first refus'd it on Account of my Rowing; but I insisted on their taking it, a Man being sometimes more generous when he has but a little Money than when he has plenty, perhaps thro' Fear of being thought to have but little.

Then I walk'd up the Street, gazing about, till near the Market House I met a Boy with Bread. I had made many a Meal on Bread, and inquiring where he got it, I went immediately to the Baker's he directed me to in second Street; and ask'd for Bisket, intending such as we had in Boston, but they it seems were not made in Philadelphia, then I ask'd for a threepenny Loaf, and was told they had none such: so not considering or knowing the Difference of Money and the greater Cheapness nor the Names of his Bread, I bad him give me three penny worth of any sort. He gave me accordingly three great Puffy Rolls. I was surpriz'd at the Quantity, but took it, and having no room in my Pockets, walk'd off, with a Roll under each Arm, and eating the other. Thus I went up Market Street as far as fourth Street, passing by the Door of Mr. Read, my future Wife's Father, when she standing at the Door saw me, and thought I made as I certainly did a most awkward ridiculous Appearance. Then I turn'd and went down Chestnut Street and part of Walnut Street, eating my Roll all the Way, and coming round found my self again at Market Street Wharff, near the Boat I came in, to which I went for a Draught of the River Water, and being fill'd with one of my Rolls, gave the other two to a Woman and her Child that came down the River in the Boat with us and were waiting to go farther. Thus refresh'd I walk'd again up the Street, which by this time had many clean dress'd People in it who were all walking the same Way; I join'd them, and thereby was led into the great Meeting House of the Quakers near the Market. I sat down among them, and after looking round a while and hearing nothing said, being very drowzy thro' Labour and want of Rest the preceding Night, I fell fast asleep, and continu'd so till the Meeting broke up, when one was kind enough to rouse me. This was therefore the first House I was in or slept in, in Philadelphia.

---

[50] The landing took place sometime in October 1723.

Walking again down towards the River, and looking in the Faces of People, I met a young Quaker Man whose Countenance I lik'd, and accosting him requested he would tell me where a Stranger could get Lodging. We were then near the Sign of the Three Mariners. Here, says he, is one Place that entertains Strangers, but it is not a reputable House; if thee wilt walk with me, I'll show thee a better. He brought me to the Crooked Billet in Water-Street. Here I got a Dinner. And while I was eating it, several sly Questions were ask'd me, as it seem'd to be suspected from my youth and Appearance, that I might be some Runaway. After Dinner my Sleepiness return'd: and being shown to a Bed, I lay down without undressing, and slept till Six in the Evening; was call'd to Supper; went to Bed again very early and slept soundly till the next Morning. Then I made my self as tidy as I could, and went to Andrew Bradford the Printer's. I found in the Shop the old Man his Father, whom I had seen at New York, and who travelling on horse back had got to Philadelphia before me. He introduc'd me to his Son, who receiv'd me civilly, gave me a Breakfast, but told me he did not at present want a Hand, being lately supply'd with one. But there was another Printer in town lately set up, one Keimer,[51] who perhaps might employ me; if not, I should be welcome to lodge at his House, and he would give me a little Work to do now and then till fuller Business should offer.

The old Gentleman said, he would go with me to the new Printer: and when we found him, Neighbour, says Bradford, I have brought to see you a young Man of your Business, perhaps you may want such a One. He ask'd me a few Questions, put a Composing Stick in my Hand to see how I work'd, and then said he would employ me soon, tho' he had just then nothing for me to do. And taking old Bradford whom he had never seen before, to be one of the Towns People that had a Good Will for him, enter'd into a Conversation on his present Undertaking and Prospects; while Bradford not discovering[52] that he was the other Printer's Father, on Keimer's saying he expected soon to get the greatest Part of the Business into his own Hands, drew him on by artful Questions and starting little Doubts, to explain all his Views, what interest he rely'd on, and in what manner he intended to proceed. I who stood by and heard all, saw immediately that one of them was a crafty old Sophister, and the other a mere Novice. Bradford left me with Keimer, who was greatly surpriz'd when I told him who the old Man was.

Keimer's Printing House I found, consisted of an old shatter'd Press, and one small worn-out Fount of English,[53] which he was then using himself, composing in it an Elegy on Aquila Rose before-mentioned, an ingenious young Man of excellent Character much respected in the Town, Clerk of the Assembly, and a pretty Poet. Keimer made Verses, too, but very indifferently. He could not be said to write them, for his Manner was to compose them in the Types directly out of his Head; so there being no Copy, but one Pair of Cases, and the Elegy likely to require all the Letter, no one could help him. I endeavour'd to put his Press (which he had not yet us'd, and of which he understood nothing) into Order fit to be work'd with; and promising

---

[51] Samuel Keimer (ca. 1688–1742) had deserted his wife in London and come to Philadelphia the year before in order to establish himself as a printer. At the time Franklin met him, Keimer was in his mid-thirties. After failing at the printer's trade, he left Philadelphia in 1730.

[52] Disclosing.

[53] A "fount," or font, of type contains the complete alphabet of single letters cast in the same size and design. "English" was an oversized, and hence cumbersome, typeface.

to come and print off his Elegy as soon as he should have got it ready, I return'd to Bradford's who gave me a little job to do for the present, and there I lodged and dieted. A few Days after Keimer sent for me to print off the Elegy.[54] And now he had got another Pair of Cases,[55] and a Pamphlet to reprint, on which he set me to work.

These two Printers I found poorly qualified for their Business. Bradford had not been bred to it, and was very illiterate; and Keimer tho' something of a Scholar, was a mere Compositor, knowing nothing of Presswork. He had been one of the French Prophets[56] and could act their enthusiastic Agitations. At this time he did not profess any particular Religion, but something of all on occasion; was very ignorant of the World, and had, as I afterwards found, a good deal of the Knave in his Composition. He did not like my Lodging at Bradford's while I work'd with him. He had a House indeed, but without Furniture, so he could not lodge me: But he got me a Lodging at Mr. Read's before-mentioned, who was the Owner of his House. And my Chest and Clothes being come by this time, I made rather a more respectable Appearance in the Eyes of Miss Read, than I had done when she first happen'd to see me eating my Roll in the Street.

I began now to have some Acquaintance among the young People of the Town, that were Lovers of Reading with whom I spent my Evenings very pleasantly and gaining Money by my Industry and Frugality, I lived very agreably, forgetting Boston as much as I could, and not desiring that any there should know where I resided, except my Friend Collins who was in my Secret, and kept it when I wrote to him. At length an Incident happened that sent me back again much sooner than I had intended.

I had a Brother-in-law, Robert Holmes,[57] Master of a Sloop, that traded between Boston and Delaware. He being at New Castle 40 Miles below Philadelphia, heard there of me, and wrote me a Letter, mentioning the Concern of my Friends in Boston at my abrupt Departure, assuring me of their Goodwill to me, and that every thing would be accommodated to my Mind if I would return, to which he exhorted me very earnestly. I wrote an Answer to his Letter, thank'd him for his Advice, but stated my Reasons for quitting Boston fully, and in such a Light as to convince him I was not so wrong as he had apprehended.

Sir William Keith Governor of the Province,[58] was then at New Castle, and Capt. Holmes happening to be in Company with him when my Letter came to hand, spoke to him of me, and show'd him the Letter. The Governor read it, and seem'd surpriz'd when he was told my Age. He said I appear'd a young Man of promising Parts, and therefore should be encouraged: The Printers at Philadelphia were wretched ones, and if I would set up there, he made no doubt I should succeed; for his Part, he would procure me the publick Business, and do me every other Service in his Power. This my Brother-in-Law afterwards told me in Boston. But I knew as yet nothing of it;

---

[54] A single-leaf broadside, sold by Keimer for twopence.
[55] Trays of type.
[56] Sect of French Protestant refugees in England in 1706. Subject to trances and revelations, its members proclaimed the imminent coming of a messianic kingdom.

[57] Holmes, married to Franklin's sister Mary, was captain of a ship.
[58] Sir William Keith (1680–1749) was governor of Pennsylvania from 1717 to 1726.

when one Day Keimer and I being at Work together near the Window, we saw the Governor and another Gentleman (which prov'd to be Col. French, of New Castle) finely dress'd, come directly across the Street to our House, and heard them at the Door. Keimer ran down immediately, thinking it a Visit to him. But the Governor enquir'd for me, came up, and with a Condescension and Politeness I had been quite unus'd to, made me many Compliments, desired to be acquainted with me, blam'd me kindly for not having made my self known to him when I first came to the Place, and would have me away with him to the Tavern where he was going with Col. French to taste as he said some excellent Madeira. I was not a little surpriz'd, and Keimer star'd like a Pig poison'd. I went however with the Governor and Col. French, to a Tavern the Corner of Third Street, and over the Madeira he propos'd my Setting up my Business, laid before me the Probabilities of Success, and both he and Col. French assur'd me I should have their Interest and Influence in procuring the Publick Business of both Governments. On my doubting whether my Father would assist me in it, Sir William said he would give me a Letter to him, in which he would state the Advantages, and he did not doubt of prevailing with him. So it was concluded I should return to Boston in the first Vessel with the Governor's Letter recommending me to my Father. In the mean time the Intention was to be kept secret, and I went on working with Keimer as usual, the Governor sending for me now and then to dine with him, a very great Honour I thought it, and conversing with me in the most affable, familiar, and friendly manner imaginable.

About the End of April 1724. a little Vessel offer'd for Boston. I took Leave of Keimer as going to see my Friends. The Governor gave me an ample Letter, saying many flattering things of me to my Father, and strongly recommending the Project of my setting up at Philadelphia, as a Thing that must make my Fortune. We struck on a Shoal in going down the Bay and sprung a Leak, we had a blustring time at Sea, and were oblig'd to pump almost continually, at which I took my Turn. We arriv'd safe however at Boston in about a Fortnight. I had been absent Seven Months and my Friends had heard nothing of me; for my Br. Holmes was not yet return'd; and had not written about me. My unexpected Appearance surpriz'd the Family; all were however very glad to see me and made me Welcome, except my Brother. I went to see him at his Printing-House: I was better dress'd than ever while in his Service, having a genteel new Suit from Head to foot, a Watch, and my Pockets lin'd with near Five Pounds Sterling in Silver. He receiv'd me not very frankly, look'd me all over, and turn'd to his Work again. The Journey-Men were inquisitive where I had been, what sort of a Country it was, and how I lik'd it? I prais'd it much, and the happy Life I led in it; expressing strongly my Intention of returning to it; and one of them asking what kind of Money we had there, I produc'd a handful of Silver and spread it before them, which was a kind of Raree-Show[59] they had not been us'd to, Paper being the Money of Boston. Then I took an Opportunity of letting them see my Watch: and lastly, (my Brother still grum and sullen) I gave them a Piece of Eight[60] to drink and took my Leave. This Visit of mine offended him extreamly. For when my Mother some time after spoke to him of a Reconciliation, and of her Wishes to see us on good Terms together, and that we might live for the future as

---

[59] Small street show.
[60] Spanish dollar. The term "piece of eight" has a parallel in the contemporary expression "two bits," meaning a quarter of a dollar.

Brothers, he said, I had insulted him in such a Manner before his People that he could never forget or forgive it. In this however he was mistaken.

My Father receiv'd the Governor's Letter with some apparent Surprize; but said little of it to me for some Days; when Capt. Holmes returning, he show'd it to him, ask'd if he knew Keith, and what kind of a Man he was: Adding his Opinion that he must be of small Discretion, to think of setting a Boy up in Business who wanted yet 3 Years of being at Man's Estate. Holmes said what he could in favour of the Project; but my Father was clear in the Impropriety of it; and at last gave a flat Denial to it. Then he wrote a civil Letter to Sir William thanking him for the Patronage he had so kindly offered me, but declining to assist me as yet in Setting up, I being in his Opinion too young to be trusted with the Management of a Business so important, and for which the Preparation must be so expensive.

My Friend and Companion Collins, who was a Clerk at the Post-Office, pleas'd with the Account I gave him of my new Country, determin'd to go thither also: And while I waited for my Fathers Determination,[61] he set out before me by Land to Rhodeisland, leaving his Books which were a pretty Collection of Mathematicks and Natural Philosophy, to come with mine and me to New York where he propos'd to wait for me. My Father, tho' he did not approve Sir William's Proposition was yet pleas'd that I had been able to obtain so advantageous a Character from a Person of such Note where I had resided, and that I had been so industrious and careful as to equip my self so handsomely in so short a time: therefore seeing no Prospect of an Accommodation between my Brother and me, he gave his Consent to my Returning again to Philadelphia, advis'd me to behave respectfully to the People there, endeavour to obtain the general Esteem, and avoid lampooning and libelling to which he thought I had too much Inclination; telling me, that by steady Industry and a prudent Parsimony, I might save enough by the time I was One and Twenty to set me up, and that if I came near the Matter he would help me out with the rest. This was all I could obtain, except some small Gifts as Tokens of his and my Mother's Love, when I embark'd again for New-York, now with their Approbation and their Blessing.

The Sloop putting in at Newport, Rhodeisland, I visited my Brother John, who had been married and settled there some Years. He received me very affectionately, for he always lov'd me. A Friend of his, one Vernon, having some Money due to him in Pensilvania, about 35 Pounds Currency, desired I would receive it for him, and keep it till I had his Directions what to remit it in. Accordingly he gave me an Order. This afterwards occasion'd me a good deal of Uneasiness. At Newport we took in a Number of Passengers for New York: Among which were two young Women, Companions, and a grave, sensible Matron-like Quaker-Woman with her Attendants. I had shown an obliging readiness to do her some little Services which impress'd her I suppose with a degree of Good-will towards me. Therefore when she saw a daily growing Familiarity between me and the two Young Women, which they appear'd to encourage, she took me aside and said, Young Man, I am concern'd for thee, as thou has no Friend with thee, and seems not to know much of the World, or of the Snares Youth is expos'd to; depend upon it those are very bad Women, I can see it in all their Actions, and if thee art not upon thy Guard, they will draw thee into some Danger: they are Strangers to thee, and I advise thee

[61] Decision.

in a friendly Concern for thy Welfare, to have no Acquaintance with them. As I seem'd at first not to think so ill of them as she did, she mention'd some Things she had observ'd and heard that had escap'd my Notice; but now convinc'd me she was right. I thank'd her for her kind Advice, and promis'd to follow it. When we arriv'd at New York, they told me where they liv'd, and invited me to come and see them: but I avoided it. And it was well I did: For the next Day, the Captain miss'd a Silver Spoon and some other Things that had been taken out of his Cabbin, and knowing that these were a Couple of Strumpets, he got a Warrant to search their Lodgings, found the stolen Goods, and had the Thieves punish'd. So tho' we had escap'd a sunken Rock which we scrap'd upon in the Passage, I thought this Escape of rather more Importance to me.

At New York I found my Friend Collins, who had arriv'd there some Time before me. We had been intimate from Children, and had read the same Books together. But he had the Advantage of more time for reading, and Studying and a wonderful Genius for Mathematical Learning in which he far outstript me. While I liv'd in Boston most of my Hours of Leisure for Conversation were spent with him, and he continu'd a sober as well as an industrious Lad; was much respected for his Learning by several of the Clergy and other Gentlemen, and seem'd to promise making a good Figure in Life: but during my Absence he had acquir'd a Habit of Sotting with Brandy; and I found by his own Account and what I heard from others, that he had been drunk every day since his Arrival at New York, and behav'd very oddly. He had gam'd too and lost his Money, so that I was oblig'd to discharge[62] his Lodgings, and defray his Expences to and at Philadelphia: Which prov'd extreamly inconvenient to me. The then Governor of N York, Burnet,[63] Son of Bishop Burnet hearing from the Captain that a young Man, one of his Passengers, had a great many Books, desired he would bring me to see him. I waited upon him accordingly, and should have taken Collins with me but that he was not sober. The Governor treated me with great Civility, show'd me his Library, which was a very large one, and we had a good deal of Conversation about Books and Authors. This was the second Governor who had done me the Honour to take Notice of me, which to a poor Boy like me was very pleasing.

We proceeded to Philadelphia. I received on the Way Vernon's Money, without which we could hardly have finish'd our Journey. Collins wish'd to be employ'd in some Counting House; but whether they discover'd his Dramming by his Breath, or by his Behaviour, tho' he had some Recommendations, he met with no Success in any Application, and continu'd Lodging and Boarding at the same House with me and at my Expence. Knowing I had that Money of Vernon's he was continually borrowing of me, still promising Repayment as soon as he should be in Business. At length he had got so much of it, that I was distress'd to think what I should do, in case of being call'd on to remit it. His Drinking continu'd about which we sometimes quarrel'd, for when a little intoxicated he was very fractious. Once in a Boat on the Delaware with some other young Men, he refused to row in his Turn: I will be row'd home, says he. We will not row you, says I. You must or stay all Night on the Water, says he, just as you please. The others said, Let us row; what signifies it? But my Mind

---

[62] Pay for.
[63] William Burnet (1688–1729) served as governor from 1720 to 1728.

being soured with his other Conduct, I continu'd to refuse. So he swore he would make me row, or throw me overboard; and coming along stepping on the Thwarts towards me, when he came up and struck at me I clapt my Hand under his Crutch,[64] and rising pitch'd him head-foremost into the River. I knew he was a good Swimmer, and so was under little Concern about him; but before he could get round to lay hold of the Boat, we had with a few Strokes pull'd her out of his Reach. And ever when he drew near the Boat, we ask'd if he would row, striking a few Strokes to slide her away from him. He was ready to die with Vexation, and obstinately would not promise to row; however seeing him at last beginning to tire, we lifted him in; and brought him home dripping wet in the Evening. We hardly exchang'd a civil Word afterwards; and a West India Captain who had a Commission to procure a Tutor for the Sons of a Gentleman at Barbadoes, happening to meet with him, agreed to carry him thither. He left me then, promising to remit me the first Money he should receive in order to discharge the Debt. But I never heard of him after.

The Breaking into this Money of Vernon's was one of the first great Errata of my Life. And this Affair show'd that my Father was not much out in his Judgment when he suppos'd me too young to manage Business of Importance. But Sir William, on reading his Letter, said he was too prudent. There was great Difference in Persons, and Discretion did not always accompany Years, nor was Youth always without it. And since he will not set you up, says he, I will do it my self. Give me an Inventory of the Things necessary to be had from England, and I will send for them. You shall repay me when you are able; I am resolv'd to have a good Printer here, and I am sure you must succeed. This was spoken with such an Appearance of Cordiality, that I had not the least doubt of his meaning what he said. I had hitherto kept the Proposition of my Setting up a Secret in Philadelphia, and I still kept it. Had it been known that I depended on the Governor, probably some Friend that knew him better would have advis'd me not to rely on him, as I afterwards heard it as his known Character to be liberal of Promises which he never meant to keep. Yet unsolicited as he was by me, how could I think his generous Offers insincere? I believ'd him one of the best Men in the World.

I presented him an Inventory of a little Printing House, amounting by my Computation to about £100 Sterling. He lik'd it, but ask'd me if my being on the Spot in England to chuse the Types and see that every thing was good of the kind, might not be of some Advantage. Then, says he, when there, you may make Acquaintances and establish Correspondencies in the Bookselling and Stationary Way. I agreed that this might be advantageous. Then says he, get yourself ready to go with Annis;[65] which was the annual Ship, and the only one at that Time usually passing between London and Philadelphia. But it would be some Months before Annis sail'd, so I continu'd working with Keimer, fretting about the Money Collins had got from me, and in daily Apprehensions of being call'd upon by Vernon, which however did not happen for some Years after.

I believe I have omitted mentioning that in my first Voyage from Boston, being becalm'd off Block Island,[66] our People set about catching Cod and hawl'd up a great

---

[64] Crotch.
[65] Captain Thomas Annis, master of the "annual Ship" that sailed between Philadelphia and England.

[66] Ten miles off the coast of Rhode Island.

many. Hitherto I had stuck to my Resolution of not eating animal Food; and on this Occasion, I consider'd with my Master Tryon, the taking every Fish as a kind of unprovok'd Murder, since none of them had or ever could do us any Injury that might justify the Slaughter. All this seem'd very reasonable. But I had formerly been a great Lover of Fish, and when this came hot out of the Frying Pan, it smelt admirably well. I balanc'd some time between Principle and Inclination: till I recollected, that when the Fish were opened, I saw smaller Fish taken out of their Stomachs: then thought I, if you eat one another, I don't see why we mayn't eat you. So I din'd upon Cod very heartily and continu'd to eat with other People, returning only now and then occasionally to a vegetable Diet. So convenient a thing it is to be a *reasonable Creature,* since it enables one to find or make a Reason for every thing one has a mind to do.

Keimer and I liv'd on a pretty good familiar Footing and agreed tolerably well: for he suspected nothing of my Setting up. He retain'd a great deal of his old Enthusiasms, and lov'd Argumentation. We therefore had many Disputations. I us'd to work him so with my Socratic Method, and had trapann'd[67] him so often by Questions apparently so distant from any Point we had in hand, and yet by degrees led to the Point, and brought him into Difficulties and Contradictions that at last he grew ridiculously cautious, and would hardly answer me the most common Question, without asking first, *What do you intend to infer from that?* However it gave him so high an Opinion of my Abilities in the Confuting Way, that he seriously propos'd my being his Colleague in a Project he had of setting up a new Sect. He was to preach the Doctrines, and I was to confound all Opponents. When he came to explain with me upon the Doctrines, I found several Conundrums which I objected to unless I might have my Way a little too, and introduce some of mine. Keimer wore his Beard at full Length, because somewhere in the Mosaic Law it is said, *thou shalt not mar the Corners of thy Beard.*[68] He likewise kept the seventh day Sabbath; and these two Points were Essentials with him. I dislik'd both, but agreed to admit them upon Condition of his adopting the Doctrine of using no animal Food. I doubt, says he, my Constitution will not bear that. I assur'd him it would, and that he would be the better for it. He was usually a great Glutton, and I promis'd my self some Diversion in half-starving him. He agreed to try the Practice if I would keep him Company. I did so and we held it for three Months. We had our Victuals dress'd and brought to us regularly by a Woman in the Neighbourhood, who had from me a List of 40 Dishes to be prepar'd for us at different times, in all which there was neither Fish Flesh nor Fowl, and the whim suited me the better at this time from the Cheapness of it, not costing us above 18*d.*[69] Sterling each, per Week. I have since kept several Lents most strictly, Leaving the common Diet for that, and that for the common, abruptly, without the least Inconvenience: So that I think there is little in the Advice of making those Changes by easy Gradations. I went on pleasantly, but poor Keimer suffer'd grievously, tir'd of the Project, long'd for the Flesh Pots of Egypt, and order'd a roast Pig. He invited me and two Women Friends to dine with him, but it being brought too soon upon table, he could not resist the Temptation, and ate it all up before we came.

---

67 Trapped.
68 Leviticus 19:27: "Ye shall not round the corners of your heads, neither shalt thou mar the corners of thy beard."

69 Small *d* is an abbreviation for the British penny (plural: pence).

I had made some Courtship during this time to Miss Read. I had a great Respect and Affection for her, and had some Reason to believe she had the same for me: but as I was about to take a long Voyage, and we were both very young, only a little above 18. it was thought most prudent by her Mother to prevent our going too far at present, as a Marriage if it was to take place would be more convenient after my Return, when I should be as I expected set up in my Business. Perhaps too she thought my Expectations not so wellfounded as I imagined them to be.

My chief Acquaintances at this time were, Charles Osborne, Joseph Watson, and James Ralph;[70] All Lovers of Reading. The two first were Clerks to an eminent Scrivener or Conveyancer[71] in the Town, Charles Brogden;[72] the other was Clerk to a Merchant. Watson was a pious sensible young Man, of great Integrity. The others rather more lax in their Principles of Religion, particularly Ralph, who as well as Collins had been unsettled by me, for which they both made me suffer. Osborne was sensible, candid, frank, sincere, and affectionate to his Friends; but in litterary Matters too fond of Criticising. Ralph, was ingenious, genteel in his Manners, and extreamly eloquent; I think I never knew a prettier Talker. Both of them great Admirers of Poetry, and began to try their Hands in little Pieces. Many pleasant Walks we four had together on Sundays into the Woods near Skuylkill,[73] where we read to one another and conferr'd on what we read.

Ralph was inclin'd to pursue the Study of Poetry, not doubting but he might become eminent in it and make his Fortune by it, alledging that the best Poets must when they first began to write, make as many Faults as he did. Osborne dissuaded him, assur'd him he had no Genius for Poetry, and advis'd him to think of nothing beyond the Business he was bred to; that in the mercantile way tho' he had no Stock, he might by his Diligence and Punctuality recommend himself to Employment as a Factor,[74] and in time acquire wherewith to trade on his own Account. I approv'd the amusing one's self with Poetry now and then, so far as to improve one's Language, but no farther. On this it was propos'd that we should each of us at our next Meeting produce a Piece of our own Composing, in order to improve by our mutual Observations, Criticisms and Corrections. As Language and Expression was what we had in View, we excluded all Considerations of Invention, by agreeing that the Task should be a Version of the 18th Psalm, which describes the Descent of a Deity. When the Time of our Meeting drew nigh, Ralph call'd on me first, and let me know his Piece was ready. I told him I had been busy, and having little Inclination had done nothing. He then show'd me his Piece for my Opinion; and I much approv'd it, as it appear'd to me to have great Merit. Now, says he, Osborne never will allow the least Merit in any thing of mine, but makes 1000 Criticisms out of mere Envy. He is not so jealous of you. I wish therefore you would take this Piece, and produce it as yours. I will pretend not to have had time, and so produce nothing: We shall then see what he will say to it. It was agreed, and I immediately transcrib'd it that it might appear in my own hand. We met. Watson's Performance was read: there were some Beauties in it: but many Defects. Osborne's was read: it was much better. Ralph did it Justice,

---

[70] James Ralph (d. 1762). A failure as a poet, Ralph achieved success as a political writer in England. Upon Franklin's return to London in 1757, Ralph helped him prepare propaganda for the colonies.

[71] One who drafts property deeds and leases.
[72] Charles Brockden.
[73] The Schuylkill River in Philadelphia.
[74] Business representative.

remark'd some Faults, but applauded the Beauties. He himself had nothing to produce. I was backward, seem'd desirous of being excus'd, had not had sufficient Time to correct; &c. but no Excuse could be admitted, produce I must. It was read and repeated; Watson and Osborne gave up the Contest; and join'd in applauding it immoderately. Ralph only made some Criticisms and propos'd some Amendments, but I defended my Text. Osborne was against Ralph, and told him he was no better a Critic than Poet; so he dropt the Argument. As they two went home together, Osborne express'd himself still more strongly in favour of what he thought my Production, having restrain'd himself before as he said, lest I should think it Flattery. But who would have imagin'd, says he, that Franklin had been capable of such a Performance; such Painting, such Force! such Fire! he has even improv'd the Original! In his common Conversation, he seems to have no Choice of Words; he hesitates and blunders; and yet, good God, how he writes! When we next met, Ralph discover'd the Trick, we had plaid him, and Osborne was a little laught at. This Transaction fix'd Ralph in his Resolution of becoming a Poet. I did all I could to dissuade him from it, but He continued scribbling Verses, till Pope cur'd him.[75] He became however a pretty good Prose Writer. More of him hereafter.

But as I may not have occasion again to mention the other two, I shall just remark here, that Watson died in my Arms a few Years after, much lamented, being the best of our Set. Osborne went to the West Indies, where he became an eminent Lawyer and made Money, but died young. He and I had made a serious Agreement, that the one who happen'd first to die, should if possible make a friendly Visit to the other, and acquaint him how he found things in that Separate State. But he never fulfill'd his Promise.

The Governor, seeming to like my Company, had me frequently to his House; and his setting me up was always mention'd as a fix'd thing. I was to take with me Letters recommendatory to a Number of his Friends, besides the Letter of Credit to furnish me with the necessary Money for purchasing the Press and Types, Paper, &c. For these Letters I was appointed to call at different times, when they were to be ready, but a future time was still named. Thus we went on till the Ship whose Departure too had been several times postponed was on the Point of sailing. Then when I call'd to take my Leave and Receive the Letters, his Secretary, Dr. Bard, came out to me and said the Governor was extreamly busy, in writing, but would be down at Newcastle[76] before the Ship, and there the Letters would be delivered to me.

Ralph, tho' married and having one Child, had determined to accompany me in this Voyage. It was thought he intended to establish a Correspondence, and obtain Goods to sell on Commission. But I found afterwards, that thro' some Discontent with his Wifes Relations, he purposed to leave her on their Hands, and never return again. Having taken leave of my Friends, and interchang'd some Promises with Miss Read, I left Philadelphia in the Ship, which anchor'd at Newcastle. The Governor was there. But when I went to his Lodging, the Secretary came to me from him with the civillest Message in the World, that he could not then see me being engag'd in Business of the utmost Importance; but should send the Letters to me on board, wish'd me heartily

[75] Ralph was attacked by Alexander Pope in the second edition of the *Dunciad* (III, 159–160): "Silence, ye Wolves! while Ralph to Cynthia howls, / And makes Night hideous—Answer him, ye Owls."
[76] In Delaware.

a good Voyage and a speedy Return, &c. I return'd on board, a little puzzled, but still not doubting.

Mr. Andrew Hamilton,[77] a famous Lawyer of Philadelphia, had taken Passage in the same Ship for himself and Son: and with Mr. Denham[78] a Quaker Merchant, and Messrs. Onion and Russel Masters of an Iron Work in Maryland, had engag'd the Great Cabin; so that Ralph and I were forc'd to take up with a Birth in the Steerage:[79] And none on board knowing us, were considered as ordinary Persons. But Mr. Hamilton and his Son (it was James, since Governor) return'd from New Castle to Philadelphia, the Father being recall'd by a great Fee to plead for a seized Ship. And just before we sail'd Col. French coming on board, and showing me great Respect, I was more taken Notice of, and with my Friend Ralph invited by the other Gentlemen to come into the Cabin, there being now Room. Accordingly we remov'd thither.

Understanding that Col. French had brought on board the Governor's Dispatches, I ask'd the Captain for those Letters that were to be under my Care. He said all were put into the Bag together; and he could not then come at them; but before we landed in England, I should have an Opportunity of picking them out. So I was satisfy'd for the present, and we proceeded on our Voyage. We had a sociable Company in the Cabin, and lived uncommonly well, having the Addition of all Mr. Hamilton's Stores, who had laid in plentifully. In this Passage Mr. Denham contracted a Friendship for me that continued during his Life. The voyage was otherwise not a pleasant one, as we had a great deal of bad Weather.

When we came into the Channel, the Captain kept his word with me, and gave me an Opportunity of examining the Bag for the Governor's Letters. I found none upon which my Name was put, as under my Care; I pick'd out 6 or 7 that by the Hand writing I thought might be the promis'd Letters, especially as one of them was directed to Basket the King's Printer, and another to some Stationer. We arriv'd in London the 24th of December, 1724. I waited upon the Stationer who came first in my way, delivering the Letter as from Gov. Keith. I don't know such a Person, says he: but opening the Letter, O, this is from Riddlesden,[80] I have lately found him to be a compleat Rascal, and I will have nothing to do with him, nor receive any Letters from him. So putting the Letter into my Hand, he turn'd on his Heel and left me to serve some Customer. I was surprized to find these were not the Governor's Letters. And after recollecting and comparing Circumstances, I began to doubt his Sincerity. I found my Friend Denham, and opened the whole Affair to him. He let me into Keith's Character, told me there was not the least Probability that he had written any Letters for me, that no one who knew him had the smallest Dependance on him, and he laught at the Notion of the Governor's giving me a Letter of Credit, having as he said no Credit to give. On my expressing some Concern about what I should do: he advis'd me to endeavour getting some Employment in the Way of my Business. Among the Printers here, says he, you will improve yourself; and when you return to America, you will set up to greater Advantage.

---

[77] Andrew Hamilton (ca. 1678–1741), father of James Hamilton (1710–1783), who served as governor of Pennsylvania four times between 1748 and 1773.

[78] Thomas Denham (d. 1728), Philadelphia merchant and later a benefactor to Franklin.

[79] Cheapest accommodations on a ship, located in the stern near the rudder.

[80] William Riddlesden, a well-known Maryland swindler and con artist.

We both of us happen'd to know, as well as the Stationer, that Riddlesden the attorney, was a very Knave. He had half ruin'd Miss Read's Father by drawing him in to be bound for him.[81] By his Letter it appear'd, there was a secret Scheme on foot to the Prejudice of Hamilton, (Suppos'd to be then coming over with us,) and that Keith was concern'd in it with Riddlesden. Denham, who was a Friend of Hamilton's, thought he ought to be acquainted with it. So when he arriv'd in England, which was soon after, partly from Resentment and Ill-Will to Keith and Riddlesden, and partly from Good Will to him: I waited on him, and gave him the Letter. He thank'd me cordially, the Information being of Importance to him. And from that time he became my Friend, greatly to my Advantage afterwards on many Occasions.

But what shall we think of a Governor's playing such pitiful Tricks, and imposing so grossly on a poor ignorant Boy! It was a Habit he had acquired. He wish'd to please every body; and having little to give, he gave Expectations. He was otherwise an ingenious sensible Man, a pretty good Writer, and a good Governor for the People, tho' not for his Constituents the Proprietaries, whose Instructions he sometimes disregarded. Several of our best Laws were of his Planning, and pass'd during his Administration.

Ralph and I were inseparable Companions. We took Lodgings together in Little Britain at 3s. 6d. per Week, as much as we could then afford. He found some Relations, but they were poor and unable to assist him. He now let me know his Intentions of remaining in London, and that he never meant to return to Philadelphia. He had brought no Money with him, the whole he could muster having been expended in paying his Passage. I had 15 Pistoles:[82] So he borrowed occasionally of me, to subsist while he was looking out for Business. He first endeavoured to get into the Playhouse, believing himself qualify'd for an Actor; but Wilkes,[83] to whom he apply'd, advis'd him candidly not to think of that Employment, as it was impossible he should succeed in it. Then he propos'd to Roberts, a Publisher in Paternoster Row,[84] to write for him a Weekly Paper like the Spectator, on certain Conditions, which Roberts did not approve. Then he endeavour'd to get Employment as a Hackney writer[85] to copy for the Stationers[86] and Lawyers about the Temple:[87] but could find no Vacancy.

I immediately got into Work at Palmer's then a famous Printing House in Bartholomew Close; and here I continu'd near a Year. I was pretty diligent; but spent with Ralph a good deal of my Earnings in going to Plays and other Places of Amusement. We had together consum'd all my Pistoles, and now just rubb'd on from hand to mouth. He seem'd quite to forget his Wife and Child, and I by degrees my Engagements with Miss Read, to whom I never wrote more than one Letter, and that was to let her know I was not likely soon to return. This was another of the great

[81] Read's "ruin" came about through a contract that held him legally responsible for Riddlesden's debts.
[82] Pistole: Spanish gold coin worth just under one English pound.
[83] Robert Wilks (1665?–1732), prominent London actor.
[84] Street that served as one of the centers for the London printing business.

[85] Hired writer who worked out of a horse-drawn cab called a "hackney." (The term *hack writer* derives therefrom.)
[86] Printers and sellers of legal forms.
[87] Group of buildings that comprised the center for the London legal profession.

Errata of my Life, which I should wish to correct if I were to live it over again. In fact, by our Expences, I was constantly kept unable to pay my Passage.

At Palmer's I was employ'd in composing for the second Edition of Woollaston's Religion of Nature.[88] Some of his Reasonings not appearing to me well-founded, I wrote a little metaphysical Piece, in which I made Remarks on them. It was entitled, *A Dissertation on Liberty and Necessity, Pleasure and pain.* I inscrib'd it to my Friend Ralph. I printed a small Number. It occasion'd my being more consider'd by Mr. Palmer, as a young Man of some Ingenuity, tho' he seriously expostulated with me upon the Principles of my Pamphlet which to him appear'd abominable. My printing this Pamphlet was another Erratum.[89]

While I lodg'd in Little Britain I made an Acquaintance with one Wilcox a Bookseller, whose Shop was at the next Door. He had an immense Collection of second-hand Books. Circulating Libraries were not then in Use; but we agreed that on certain reasonable Terms which I have now forgotten, I might take, read and return any of his Books. This I esteem'd a great Advantage, and I made as much use of it as I could.

My pamphlet by some means falling into the Hands of one Lyons, a Surgeon, Author of a Book intituled *The Infallibility of Human Judgment,* it occasioned an Acquaintance between us; he took great Notice of me, call'd on me often, to converse on those Subjects, carried me to the Horns a pale Ale-House in ——— Lane, Cheapside, and introduc'd me to Dr. Mandevile, Author of the Fable of the Bees[90] who had a Club there, of which he was the Soul, being a most facetious entertaining Companion. Lyons too introduc'd me, to Dr. Pemberton, at Batson's Coffee House,[91] who promis'd to give me an Opportunity some time or other of seeing Sir Isaac Newton, of which I was extreamly desirous; but this never happened.

I had brought over a few Curiosities among which the principal was a Purse made of the Asbestos, which purifies by Fire. Sir Hans Sloane heard of it, came to see me, and invited me to his House in Bloomsbury Square, where he show'd me all his Curiosities, and persuaded me to let him add that to the Number, for which he paid me handsomely.

In our House there lodg'd a young Woman; a Millener, who I think had a Shop in the Cloisters. She had been genteelly bred, was sensible and lively, and of most pleasing Conversation. Ralph read Plays to her in the Evenings, they grew intimate, she took another Lodging, and he follow'd her. They liv'd together some time, but he being still out of Business, and her Income not sufficient to maintain them with her Child, he took a Resolution of going from London, to try for a Country School, which he thought himself well qualify'd to undertake, as he wrote an excellent Hand, and was a Master of Arithmetic and Accounts. This however he deem'd a Business

---

[88] Actually the third edition of *The Religion of Nature Delineated* (1722), a treatise on morality as derived from observations of nature by the Anglican clergyman and schoolmaster William Wollaston.

[89] This pamphlet (1725) subjected Franklin to charges of atheism by its denial of the existence of vice and virtue. Franklin soon afterward burned all but one of the copies. Only four copies are known to exist today.

[90] Bernard Mandeville's *Fable of the Bees* (1714) argued that the greedy self-pursuits of the individual ultimately benefited society. Although the treatise was viciously attacked by moralists for its cynicism, it nevertheless was widely read and went through numerous reprints. Mandeville was an important source for James Madison's arguments in *The Federalist,* Number 10.

[91] A favorite meeting place of physicians.

below him, and confident of future better Fortune when he should be unwilling to have it known that he once was so meanly employ'd, he chang'd his Name, and did me the Honour to assume mine. For I soon after had a Letter from him, acquainting me, that he was settled in a small Village in Berkshire, I think it was, where he taught reading and writing to 10 or a dozen Boys at 6 pence each per Week, recommending Mrs. T. to my Care, and desiring me to write to him directing for Mr. Franklin Schoolmaster at such a Place. He continu'd to write frequently, sending me large Specimens of an Epic Poem, which he was then composing, and desiring my Remarks and Corrections. These I gave him from time to time, but endeavour'd rather to discourage his Proceeding. One of Young's Satires was then just publish'd. I copy'd and sent him a great Part of it, which set in a strong Light the Folly of pursuing the Muses with any Hope of Advancement by them.[92] All was in vain. Sheets of the Poem continu'd to come by every Post. In the mean time Mrs. T. having on his Account lost her Friends and Business, was often in Distresses, and us'd to send for me, and borrow what I could spare to help her out of them. I grew fond of her Company, and being at this time under no Religious Restraints, and presuming on my Importance to her, I attempted Familiarities, (another Erratum) which she repuls'd with a proper Resentment, and acquainted him with my Behaviour. This made a Breach between us, and when he return'd again to London, he let me know he thought I had cancel'd all the Obligations he had been under to me. So I found I was never to expect his Repaying me what I lent to him or advanc'd for him. This was however not then of much Consequence, as he was totally unable. And in the Loss of his Friendship I found my self reliev'd from a Burthen. I now began to think of getting a little Money beforehand; and expecting better Work, I left Palmer's to work at Watts's near Lincoln's Inn Fields, a still greater Printing House. Here I continu'd all the rest of my Stay in London.

At my first Admission into this Printing House, I took to working at Press, imagining I felt a Want of the Bodily Exercise I had been us'd to in America, where Presswork is mix'd with Composing. I drank only Water; the other Workmen, near 50 in Number, were great Guzzlers of Beer. On occasion I carried up and down Stairs a large Form of Types[93] in each hand, when others carried but one in both Hands. They wonder'd to see from this and several Instances that the Water-American as they call'd me was *stronger* than themselves who drank *strong* Beer. We had an Alehouse Boy who attended always in the House to supply the Workmen. My Companion at the Press, drank every day a Pint before Breakfast, a Pint at Breakfast with his Bread and Cheese; a Pint between Breakfast and Dinner; a Pint at Dinner; a Pint in the Afternoon about Six o'Clock, and another when he had done his Day's-Work. I thought it a detestable Custom. But it was necessary, he suppos'd, to drink *strong* Beer that he might be *strong* to labour. I endeavour'd to convince him that the Bodily Strength afforded by Beer could only be in proportion to the Grain or Flour of the Barley dissolved in the Water of which it was made; that there was more Flour in a Penny-worth of Bread, and therefore if he would eat that with a Pint of Water, it would give him more strength than a Quart of Beer. He drank on however, and

[92] This reference is probably to *Love of Fame, the Universal Passion* (1725), by Edward Young (1683–1765).

[93] Pages of type, set and secured in a metal frame or "chase."

had 4 or 5 Shillings to pay out of his Wages every Saturday Night for that muddling Liquor; an Expence I was free from. And thus these poor Devils keep themselves always under.

Watts after some Weeks desiring to have me in the Composing Room, I left the Pressmen. A new *Bienvenu*[94] or Sum for Drink, being 5s., was demanded of me by the Compositors. I thought it an Imposition, as I had paid below. The Master thought so too, and forbad my Paying it. I stood out two or three Weeks, was accordingly considered as an Excommunicate, and had so many little Pieces of private Mischief done me, by mixing my Sorts, transposing my Pages, breaking my Matter,[95] &c. &c. if I were ever so little out of the Room, and all ascrib'd to the Chapel Ghost, which they said ever haunted those not regularly admitted, that notwithstanding the Master's Protection, I found myself oblig'd to comply and pay the Money; convinc'd of the Folly of being on ill Terms with those one is to live with continually. I was now on a fair Footing with them, and soon acquir'd considerable Influence. I propos'd some reasonable Alterations in their Chapel[96] Laws, and carried them against all Opposition. From my Example a great Part of them, left their muddling Breakfast of Beer and Bread and Cheese, finding they could with me be supply'd from a neighbouring House with a large Porringer of hot Water-gruel, sprinkled with Pepper, crumb'd with Bread, and a Bit of Butter in it, for the Price of a Pint of Beer, viz, three halfpence. This was a more comfortable as well as cheaper Breakfast, and kept their Heads clearer. Those who continu'd sotting with Beer all day, were often, by not paying, out of Credit at the Alehouse, and us'd to make Interest with me to get Beer, *their Light,* as they phras'd it, *being out.* I watch'd the Pay table on Saturday Night, and collected what I stood engag'd for them, having to pay some times near Thirty Shillings a Week on their Accounts. This, and my being esteem'd a pretty good Riggite, that is a jocular verbal Satyrist, supported my Consequence in the Society. My constant Attendance, (I never making a St. Monday),[97] recommended me to the Master; and my uncommon Quickness at Composing, occasion'd my being put upon all Work of Dispatch which was generally better paid. So I went on now very agreably.

My Lodging in Little Britain being too remote, I found another in Duke-street opposite to the Romish[98] Chapel. It was two pair of Stairs backwards at an Italian Warehouse. A Widow Lady kept the House; she had a Daughter and a Maid Servant, and a Journeyman who attended the Warehouse, but lodg'd abroad. After sending to enquire my Character at the House where I last lodg'd, she agreed to take me in at the same Rate, 3s. 6d. per Week, cheaper as she said from the Protection she expected in having a Man lodge in the House. She was a Widow, an elderly Woman, had been bred a Protestant, being a Clergyman's Daughter, but was converted to the Catholic Religion by her Husband, whose Memory she much revered, had lived much among People of Distinction, and knew a 1000 Anecdotes of them as far back as the Times of Charles the Second. She was lame in her Knees with the Gout, and therefore seldom stirr'd out of her Room, so sometimes wanted Company; and hers was so highly amusing to me; that I was sure to spend an Evening with her whenever she desired it. Our Supper was only half an Anchovy each, on a very little Strip of Bread and

---

94 French: "welcome."
95 Sorts: letters from the same font or style of type; Matter: a body of lines set into pages.
96 Franklin's note: "A Printing House is always called a Chappel by the Workmen."

97 I.e., never absent from work on Monday because of weekend revelry or observance of a Saint's day (holiday).
98 Roman Catholic.

Butter, and half a Pint of Ale between us. But the Entertainment was in her Conversation. My always keeping good Hours, and giving little Trouble in the Family, made her unwilling to part with me; so that when I talk'd of a Lodging I had heard of, nearer my Business, for 2*s.* a week, which, intent as I now was on saving Money, made some difference; she bid me not think of it, for she would abate me two Shillings a Week for the future, so I remain'd with her at 1*s.* 6*d.* as long as I staid in London.

In a garret of her House there lived a Maiden Lady of 70 in the most retired Manner, of whom my Landlady gave me this Account, that she was a Roman Catholic, had been sent abroad when young and lodg'd in a Nunnery with an intent of becoming a Nun: but the Country not agreeing with her, she return'd to England, where there being no Nunnery, she had vow'd to lead the Life of a Nun as near as might be done in those Circumstances: Accordingly she had given all her Estate to charitable Uses, reserving only Twelve Pounds a Year to live on, and out of this Sum she still gave a great deal in Charity, living her self on Water-gruel only, and using no Fire but to boil it. She had lived many Years in that Garret, being permitted to remain there gratis by successive Catholic Tenants of the House below, as they deem'd it a blessing to have her there. A Priest visited her, to confess her every Day. I have ask'd her, says my Landlady, how she, as she liv'd, could possibly find so much Employment for a Confessor? O, says she, it is impossible to avoid *vain Thoughts.* I was permitted once to visit her: she was chearful and polite, and convers'd pleasantly. The room was clean, but had no other furniture than a matras, a Table with a Crucifix and Book, a Stool, which she gave me to sit on, and a Picture over the Chimney of St. Veronica, displaying her Handkerchief with the miraculous Figure of Christ's bleeding Face on it, which she explain'd to me with great Seriousness. She look'd pale, but was never sick, and I give it as another Instance on how small an Income Life and Health may be supported.

At Watts's Printinghouse I contracted an Acquaintance with an ingenious young Man, one Wygate, who having wealthy Relations, had been better educated than most Printers, was a tolerable Latinist, spoke French, and lov'd Reading. I taught him, and a Friend of his, to swim, at twice going into the River, and they soon became good Swimmers. They introduc'd me to some Gentlemen from the Country who went to Chelsea by Water to see the College and Don Saltero's Curiosities.[99] In our Return, at the Request of the Company, whose Curiosity Wygate had excited, I stript and leapt into the River, and swam from near Chelsea to Blackfryars,[100] performing on the Way many Feats of Activity both upon and under Water, that surpriz'd and pleas'd those to whom they were Novelties. I had from a Child been ever delighted with this Exercise, had studied and practis'd all Thevenot's Motions and Positions,[101] added some of my own, aiming at the graceful and easy, as well as the Useful. All these I took this Occasion of exhibiting to the Company, and was much flatter'd by their Admiration. And Wygate, who was desirous of becoming a Master, grew more and more attach'd to me, on that account, as well as from the Similarity of our Studies. He at length propos'd to me travelling all over Europe together, supporting ourselves everywhere by working at our Business. I was once inclin'd to it. But mentioning

---

[99] The College: probably, Chelsea Hospital, built by Christopher Wren in 1682 on the site of Chelsea College; Don Saltero's Curiosities: bogus religious relics assembled by James Salter, a Chelsea coffee house proprietor.

[100] A distance of about three miles.

[101] In Melchisédeck de Thévenot's *The Art of Swimming* (1699).

it to my good Friend Mr. Denham, with whom I often spent an Hour, when I had Leisure. He dissuaded me from it, advising me to think only of returning to Pensilvania, which he was now about to do.

I must record one Trait of this Good Man's Character. He had formerly been in Business at Bristol, but fail'd in Debt to a Number of People, compounded[102] and went to America. There, by a close Application to Business as a Merchant, he acquir'd a plentiful Fortune in a few Years. Returning to England in the Ship with me, He invited his old Creditors to an Entertainment, at which he thank'd them for the easy Composition[103] they had favour'd him with, and when they expected nothing but the Treat, every Man at the first Remove,[104] found under his Plate an Order on a Banker for the full Amount of the unpaid Remainder with Interest.

He now told me he was about to return to Philadelphia, and should carry over a great Quantity of Goods in order to open a Store there: He propos'd to take me over as his Clerk, to keep his Books (in which he would instruct me) copy his Letters, and attend the Store. He added, that as soon as I should be acquainted with mercantile Business he would promote me by sending me with a Cargo of Flour and Bread &c. to the West Indies, and procure me Commissions from others; which would be profitable, and if I manag'd well, would establish me handsomely. The Thing pleas'd me, for I was grown tired of London, remember'd with Pleasure the happy Months I had spent in Pennsylvania, and wish'd again to see it. Therefore I immediately agreed, on the Terms of Fifty Pounds a Year, Pensylvania Money; less indeed than my present Gettings as a Compostor,[105] but affording a better Prospect.

I now took Leave of Printing, as I thought for ever, and was daily employ'd in my new Business; going about with Mr. Denham among the Tradesmen, to purchase various Articles, and seeing them pack'd up, doing Errands, calling upon Workmen to dispatch, &c, and when all was on board, I had a few Days Leisure. On one of these Days I was to my Surprize sent for by a great Man I knew only by Name, a Sir William Wyndham[106] and I waited upon him. He had heard by some means or other of my Swimming from Chelsey to Blackfryars, and of my teaching Wygate and another young Man to swim in a few hours. He had two Sons about to set out on their Travels; he wish'd to have them first taught Swimming; and propos'd to gratify me handsomely if I would teach them. They were not yet come to Town and my Stay was uncertain, so I could not undertake it. But from this Incident I thought it likely, that if I were to remain in England and open a Swimming School, I might get a good deal of Money. And it struck me so strongly, that had the Overture been sooner made me, probably I should not so soon have returned to America. After many Years, you and I had something of more Importance to do with one of these Sons of Sir William Wyndham, become Earl of Egremont, which I shall mention in its Place.[107]

Thus I spent about 18 Months in London. Most Part of the Time, I work'd hard at my Business, and spent but little upon my self except in seeing Plays and in Books. My Friend Ralph had kept me poor. He owed me about 27 Pounds; which I was now never likely to receive; a great Sum out of my small Earnings. I lov'd him notwith-

---

[102] Paid some of his debts (so that he would not be prosecuted).
[103] Settlement.
[104] End of the first course of a meal.

[105] Compositor; one who sets type.
[106] Well-known English politician (1687–1740).
[107] There is no further mention of Wyndham in the *Autobiography*.

standing, for he had many amiable Qualities. Tho' I had by no means improv'd my Fortune. But I had pick'd up some very ingenious Acquaintance whose Conversation was of great Advantage to me, and I had read considerably.

We sail'd from Gravesend on the 23d of July 1726. For the Incidents of the Voyage, I refer you to my Journal, where you will find them all minutely related. Perhaps the most important Part of that Journal is the *Plan* to be found in it which I formed at Sea, for regulating my future Conduct in Life.[108] It is the more remarkable, as being form'd when I was so young, and yet being pretty faithfully adhered to quite thro' to old Age. We landed in Philadelphia the 11th of October, where I found sundry Alterations. Keith was no longer Governor, being superceded by Major Gordon:[109] I met him walking the Streets as a common Citizen. He seem'd a little asham'd at seeing me, but pass'd without saying any thing. I should have been as much asham'd at seeing Miss Read, had not her Friends, despairing with Reason of my Return, after the Receipt of my Letter, persuaded her to marry another, one Rogers, a Potter, which was done in my Absence. With him however she was never happy, and soon parted from him, refusing to cohabit with him, or bear his Name It being now said that he had another Wife. He was a worthless Fellow tho' an excellent Workman which was the Temptation to her Friends. He got into Debt, and ran away in 1727 or 28. Went to the West Indies, and died there. Keimer had got a better House, a Shop well supply'd with Stationary, plenty of new Types, a number of Hands tho' none good, and seem'd to have a great deal of Business.

Mr. Denham took a Store in Water Street, where we open'd our Goods. I attended the Business diligently, studied Accounts, and grew in a little Time expert at selling. We lodg'd and boarded together, he counsell'd me as a Father, having a sincere Regard for me: I respected and lov'd him: and we might have gone on together very happily: But in the beginning of Feby. 1726/7 when I had just pass'd my 21st Year, we both were taken ill. My Distemper was a Pleurisy, which very nearly carried me off: I suffered a good deal, gave up the Point in my own mind, and was rather disappointed when I found my Self recovering; regretting in some degree that I must now some time or other have all that disagreable Work to do over again. I forget what his Distemper was. It held him a long time, and at length carried him off. He left me a small Legacy in a nuncupative Will,[110] as a Token of his Kindness for me, and he left me once more to the wide World. For the Store was taken into the Care of his Executors, and my Employment under him ended: my Brother-in-law Holmes, being now at Philadelphia, advis'd my Return to my Business. And Keimer tempted me with an Offer of large Wages by the Year to come and take the Management of his Printing-House, that he might better attend his Stationer's Shop. I had heard a bad Character of him in London, from his Wife and her Friends, and was not fond of having any more to do with him. I try'd for farther Employment as a Merchant's Clerk; but not readily meeting with any, I clos'd[111] again with Keimer.

I found in *his* House these Hands; Hugh Meredith[112] a Welsh-Pensilvanian, 30 Years

---

108 Only the "Journal" of the voyage survives; the "Plan" has been lost.

109 Patrick Gordon (1644–1736), governor of Pennsylvania from 1726 to 1736.

110 A will that is made orally and never set down in writing.

111 Agreed on a contract.

112 Meredith (1696?–?1749) was later Franklin's business partner.

of Age, bred to Country Work: honest, sensible, had a great deal of solid Observation, was something of a Reader, but given to drink: Stephen Potts,[113] a young Country Man of full Age, bred to the Same: of uncommon natural Parts,[114] and great Wit and Humour, but a little idle. These he had agreed with at extream low Wages, per Week, to be rais'd a Shilling every 3 Months, as they would deserve by improving in their Business, and the Expectation of these High wages to come on hereafter was what he had drawn them in with. Meredith was to work at Press, Potts at Bookbinding, which he by Agreement, was to teach them, tho' he knew neither one nor t'other. John ———— a wild Irishman brought up to no Business, whose Service for 4 Years Keimer had purchas'd[115] from the Captain of a Ship. He too was to be made a Pressman. George Webb, an Oxford Scholar, whose Time for 4 Years he had likewise bought, intending him for a Compositor: of whom more presently. And David Harry, a Country Boy, whom he had taken Apprentice. I soon perceiv'd that the Intention of engaging me at Wages so much higher than he had been us'd to give, was to have these raw cheap Hands form'd thro' me, and as soon as I had instructed them, then, they being all articled[116] to him, he should be able to do without me. I went on however, very chearfully; put his Printing House in Order, which had been in great Confusion, and brought his Hands by degrees to mind their Business and to do it better.

It was an odd thing to find an Oxford Scholar in the Situation of a bought Servant. He was not more than 18 Years of Age, and gave me this Account of himself; that he was born in Gloucester, educated at a Grammar School there, had been distinguish'd among the Scholars for some apparent Superiority in performing his Part when they exhibited Plays; belong'd to the Witty Club there, and had written some Pieces in Prose and Verse which were printed in the Gloucester Newspapers. Thence he was sent to Oxford; there he continu'd about a Year, but not well-satisfy'd, wishing of all things to see London and become a Player. At length receiving his Quarterly Allowance of 15 Guineas, instead of discharging his Debts, he walk'd out of Town, hid his Gown in a Furz Bush, and footed it to London, where having no Friend to advise him, he fell into bad Company, soon spent his Guineas, found no means of being introduc'd among the Players, grew necessitous, pawn'd his Cloaths and wanted Bread. Walking the Street very hungry, and not knowing what to do with himself, a Crimp's Bill[117] was put into his Hand, offering immediate Entertainment and Encouragement to such as would bind themselves to serve in America. He went directly, sign'd the Indentures, was put into the Ship and came over; never writing a Line to acquaint his Friends what was become of him. He was lively, witty, good-natur'd, and a pleasant Companion, but idle, thoughtless and imprudent to the last Degree.

John the Irishman soon ran away. With the rest I began to live very agreably; for they all respected me, the more as they found Keimer incapable of instructing them, and that from me they learnt something daily. We never work'd on a Saturday, that being Keimer's Sabbath. So I had two Days for Reading. My Acquaintance with

---

[113] Stephen Potts (d. 1758), bookseller and tavern keeper.
[114] I.e., particularly intelligent.
[115] In payment for his passage.

[116] Contracted as a printer to work exclusively under Keimer.
[117] Offer to become an indentured servant in exchange for passage to America.

Ingenious People in the Town, increased. Keimer himself treated me with great Civility, and apparent Regard; and nothing now made me uneasy but my Debt to Vernon, which I was yet unable to pay being hitherto but a poor Oeconomist. He however kindly made no Demand of it.

Our Printing-House often wanted Sorts,[118] and there was no Letter Founder in America. I had seen Types cast at James's[119] in London, but without much Attention to the Manner: However I now contriv'd a Mould, made use of the Letters we had, as Puncheons,[120] struck the Matrices[121] in Lead, and thus supply'd in a pretty tolerable way all Deficiencies. I also engrav'd several Things on occasion. I made the Ink, I was Warehouse-man and every thing, in short quite a Factotum.[122]

But however serviceable I might be, I found that my Services became every Day of less Importance, as the other Hands improv'd in the Business. And when Keimer paid my second Quarter's Wages, he let me know that he felt them too heavy, and thought I should make an Abatement. He grew by degrees less civil, put on more of the Master, frequently found Fault, was captious and seem'd ready for an Outbreaking. I went on nevertheless with a good deal of Patience, thinking that his incumber'd Circumstances were partly the Cause. At length a Trifle snapt our Connexion. For a great Noise happening near the Courthouse, I put my Head out of the Window to see what was the Matter. Keimer being in the Street look'd up and saw me, call'd out to me in a loud Voice and angry Tone to mind my Business, adding some reproachful Words, that nettled me the more for their Publicity, all the Neighbours who were looking out on the same Occasion being Witnesses how I was treated. He came up immediately into the Printing-House, continu'd the Quarrel, high Words pass'd on both Sides, he gave me the Quarter's Warning we had stipulated, expressing a Wish that he had not been oblig'd to so long a Warning: I told him his Wish was unnecessary for I would leave him that Instant; and so taking my Hat walk'd out of Doors; desiring Meredith whom I saw below to take care of some Things I left, and bring them to my Lodging.

Meredith came accordingly in the Evening, when we talk'd my Affair over. He had conceiv'd a great Regard for me, and was very unwilling that I should leave the House while he remain'd in it. He dissuaded me from returning to my native Country[123] which I began to think of. He reminded me that Keimer was in debt for all he possess'd, that his Creditors began to be uneasy, that he kept his Shop miserably, sold often without Profit for ready Money, and often trusted without keeping Accounts. That he must therefore fail; which would make a Vacancy I might profit of. I objected my Want of Money. He then let me know, that his Father had a high Opinion of me, and from some Discourse that had pass'd between them, he was sure would advance Money to set us up, if I would enter into Partnership with him. My Time, says he, will be out with Keimer in the Spring. By that time we may have our Press and Types in from London: I am sensible I am no Workman. If you like it, Your Skill in the Business shall be set against the Stock I furnish; and we will share

---

[118] Used here in reference to the lack of a particular typeface. Thus a printer who was "out of sorts" was likely to become angry—hence the popular expression.

[119] The type foundry of Thomas James, London's largest.

[120] Tools for stamping.

[121] Molds into which hot lead is poured to make new pieces of type.

[122] Jack-of-all-trades.

[123] I.e., Boston.

the Profits equally. The Proposal was agreable, and I consented. His father was in Town, and approv'd of it, the more as he saw I had great Influence with his Son, had prevail'd on him to abstain long from Dramdrinking,[124] and he hop'd might break him of that wretched Habit entirely, when we came to be so closely connected. I gave an Inventory to the Father, who carry'd it to a Merchant; the Things were sent for; the Secret was to be kept till they should arrive, and in the mean time I was to get work if I could at the other Printing House. But I found no Vacancy there, and so remain'd idle a few Days, when Keimer, on a Prospect of being employ'd to print some Paper-money, in New Jersey, which would require Cuts and various Types that I only could supply, and apprehending Bradford might engage me and get the Jobb from him, sent me a very civil Message, that old Friends should not part for a few Words, the Effect of sudden Passion, and wishing me to return. Meredith persuaded me to comply, as it would give more Opportunity for his Improvement under my daily Instructions. So I return'd, and we went on more smoothly than for some time before. The New Jersey Jobb was obtain'd. I contriv'd a Copper-Plate Press for it, the first that had been seen in the Country. I cut several Ornaments and Checks for the Bills. We went together to Burlington,[125] where I executed the Whole to Satisfaction, and he received so large a Sum for the Work, as to be enabled thereby to keep his Head much longer above Water.

At Burlington I made an Acquaintance with many principal People of the Province. Several of them had been appointed by the Assembly a Committee to attend the Press, and take Care that no more Bills were printed than the Law directed. They were therefore by Turns constantly with us, and generally he who attended brought with him a Friend or two for Company. My Mind having been much more improv'd by Reading than Keimer's, I suppose it was for that Reason my Conversation seem'd to be more valu'd. They had me to their Houses, introduc'd me to their Friends and show'd me much Civility, while he, tho' the Master, was a little neglected. In truth he was an odd Fish, ignorant of common Life, fond of rudely opposing receiv'd Opinions, slovenly to extream dirtiness, enthusiastic[126] in some Points of Religion, and a little Knavish withal. We continu'd there near 3 Months, and by that time I could reckon among my acquired Friends, Judge Allen, Samuel Bustill, the Secretary of the Province, Isaac Pearson, Joseph Cooper and several of the Smiths, Members of Assembly, and Isaac Decow the Surveyor General. The latter was a shrewd sagacious old Man, who told me that he began for himself when young by wheeling Clay for the Brickmakers, learnt to write after he was of Age, carry'd the Chain for Surveyors, who taught him Surveying, and he had now by his Industry acquir'd a good Estate; and says he, I foresee, that you will soon work this Man out of his Business and make a Fortune in it at Philadelphia. He had not then the least Intimation of my Intention to set up there or any where. These Friends were afterwards of great Use to me, as I occasionally was to some of them. They all continued their Regard for me as long as they lived.

Before I enter upon my public Appearance in Business it may be well to let you know the then State of my Mind, with regard to my Principles and Morals, that you may see how far those influenc'd the future Events of my Life. My Parents had early

---

[124] Drinking small amounts of alcohol.
[125] Burlington, New Jersey.

[126] Overly zealous.

given me religious Impressions, and brought me through my Childhood piously in the Dissenting Way. But I was scarce 15 when, after doubting by turns of several Points as I found them disputed in the different Books I read, I began to doubt of Revelation it self. Some Books against Deism fell into my Hands; they were said to be the Substance of Sermons preached at Boyle's Lectures.[127] It happened that they wrought an Effect on me quite contrary to what was intended by them: For the Arguments of the Deists which were quoted to be refuted, appeared to me much stronger than the Refutations. In short I soon became a thorough Deist. My Arguments perverted some others, particularly Collins and Ralph: but each of them having afterwards wrong'd me greatly without the least Compunction and recollecting Keith's Conduct towards me, (who was another Freethinker) and my own towards Vernon and Miss Read which at Times gave me great Trouble, I began to suspect that this Doctrine tho' it might be true, was not very useful. My London Pamphlet, which had for its Motto those Lines of Dryden

—Whatever is, is right.—
Tho' purblind Man
Sees but a Part of the Chain, the nearest Link,
His Eyes not carrying to the equal Beam,
That poizes all, above.[128]

And from the Attributes of God, his infinite Wisdom, Goodness and Power concluded that nothing could possibly be wrong in the World, and that Vice and Virtue were empty Distinctions, no such Things existing: appear'd now not so clever a Performance as I once thought it; and I doubted whether some Error had not insinuated itself unperceiv'd into my Argument, so as to infect all that follow'd, as is common in metaphysical Reasonings. I grew convinc'd that *Truth, Sincerity and Integrity* in Dealings between Man and Man, were of the utmost Importance to the Felicity of Life, and I form'd written Resolutions, (which still remain in my Journal Book) to practice them ever while I lived. Revelation had indeed no weight with me as such; but I entertain'd an Opinion, that tho' certain Actions might not be bad *because* they were forbidden by it, or good *because* it commanded them; yet probably those Actions might be forbidden *because* they were bad for us, or commanded *because* they were beneficial to us, in their own Natures, all the Circumstances of things considered. And this Persuasion, with the kind hand of Providence, or some guardian Angel, or accidental favourable Circumstances and Situations, or all together, preserved me (thro' this dangerous Time of Youth and the hazardous Situations I was sometimes in among Strangers, remote from the Eye and Advice of my Father) without any *wilful* gross Immorality or Injustice that might have been expected from my Want of Religion. I say *wilful,* because the Instances I have mentioned, had something of *Necessity* in them, from my Youth, Inexperience, and the Knavery of

---

[127] Series of lectures defending Christianity against skeptics, established by the chemist Robert Boyle (1627–1691).
[128] The first line is not Dryden's but is from Alexander Pope's *Essay on Man* (1733), I, 284. The remaining lines are from Dryden's *Oedipus,* Act III, Sc. i, ll. 244–248.

others. I had therefore a tolerable Character to begin the World with, I valued it properly, and determin'd to preserve it.

We had not been long return'd to Philadelphia, before the New Types arriv'd from London. We settled with Keimer, and left him by his Consent before he heard of it. We found a House to hire near the Market, and took it. To lessen the Rent, (which was then but £24 a Year tho' I have since known it let for 70) we took in Tho' Godfrey a Glazier[129] and his Family, who were to pay a considerable Part of it to us, and we to board with them. We had scarce opened our Letters and put our Press in Order, before George House, an Acquaintance of Mine, brought a Country-man to us; whom he had met in the Street enquiring for a Printer. All our Cash was now expended in the Variety of Particulars we had been obliged to procure and this Countryman's Five Shillings being our first Fruits, and coming so seasonably, gave me more Pleasure than any Crown[130] I have since earn'd; and from the Gratitude I felt towards House, has made me often more ready than perhaps I should otherwise have been to assist young Beginners.

There are Croakers in every Country always boding its Ruin. Such a one then lived in Philadelphia, a Person of Note, an elderly Man, with a wise Look, and very grave Manner of speaking. His Name was Samuel Mickle. This Gentleman, a Stranger to me, stopt one Day at my Door, and asked me if I was the young Man who had lately opened a new Printing House: Being Answer'd in the Affirmative; he said he was sorry for me, because it was an expensive Undertaking and the Expence would be lost; for Philadelphia was a sinking[131] Place, the People already half Bankrupts or near being so; all Appearances of the contrary, such as new Buildings and the Rise of Rents being to his certain Knowledge fallacious, for they were in fact among the Things that would soon ruin us. And he gave me such a Detail of Misfortunes, now existing or that were soon to exist, that he left me half-melancholy. Had I known him before I engag'd in this Business, probably I never should have done it. This man continu'd to live in this decaying Place; and to declaim in the same Strain, refusing for many Years to buy a house there, because all was going to Destruction, and at last I had the Pleasure of seeing him give five times as much for one as he might have bought it for when he first began his Croaking.

I should have mention'd before, that in the Autumn of the preceding Year I had form'd most of my ingenious Acquaintance into a Club for mutual Improvement, which we call'd the Junto.[132] We met on Friday Evenings. The Rules I drew up requir'd that every Member in his Turn should produce one or more Queries on any Point of Morals, Politics or Natural Philosophy, to be discuss'd by the Company, and once in three Months produce and read an Essay of his own Writing on any Subject he pleased. Our Debates were to be under the Direction of a President, and to be conducted in the sincere Spirit of Enquiry after Truth, without Fondness for Dispute, or Desire of Victory; and to prevent Warmth all Expressions of Positiveness in Opinion, or of direct Contradiction, were after some time made contraband and prohibited under small pecuniary Penalties. The first Members were Joseph Brientnal, a Copyer of Deeds for the Scriveners; a good-natur'd friendly middle-ag'd Man, a great Lover of Poetry, reading all he could meet with, and writing some that was tolerable; very ingenious in many little Nicknackeries, and of sensible Conversation.

---

[129] One who sets glass panes in windows and doors.

[130] A five-shilling coin.

[131] Failing.

[132] Small group or clique (from the Spanish *junta*).

Thomas Godfrey, a self-taught Mathematician, great in his Way, and afterwards Inventor of what is now call'd Hadley's Quadrant.[133] But he knew little out of his way, and was not a pleasing Companion, as like most Great Mathematicians I have met with, he expected unusual Precision in every thing said, or was forever denying or distinguishing upon Trifles, to the Disturbance of all Conversation. He soon left us. Nicholas Scull, a Surveyor, afterwards Surveyor-General, Who lov'd Books, and sometimes made a few Verses. William Parsons, bred a Shoemaker, but loving Reading, had acquir'd a considerable Share of Mathematics, which he first studied with a View to Astrology that he afterwards laught at. He also became Surveyor General. William Maugridge, a Joiner, a most exquisite Mechanic and a solid sensible Man. Hugh Meredith, Stephen Potts, and George Webb, I have Characteris'd before. Robert Grace, a young Gentleman of some fortune, generous, lively and witty, a Lover of Punning and of his Friends. And William Coleman, then a Merchant's Clerk, about my Age, who had the coolest clearest Head, the best Heart, and the exactest Morals, of almost any Man I ever met with. He became afterwards a Merchant of great Note, and one of our Provincial Judges: Our Friendship continued without Interruption to his Death upwards of 40 Years.

And the club continu'd almost as long and was the best School of Philosophy, Morals and Politics that then existed in the Province; for our Queries which were read the Week preceding their Discussion, put us on Reading with Attention upon the several Subjects, that we might speak more to the purpose: and here too we acquired better Habits of Conversation, every thing being studied in our Rules which might prevent our disgusting each other. From hence the long Continuance of the Club, which I shall have frequent Occasion to speak farther of hereafter; But my giving this Account of it here, is to show something of the Interest I had, every one of these exerting themselves in recommending Business to us. Brientnal particularly procur'd us from the Quakers, the Printing 40 Sheets of their History, the rest being to be done by Keimer: and upon this we work'd exceeding hard, for the Price was low. It was a Folio, Pro Patria Size, in Pica with long Primer[134] Notes. I compos'd of it a Sheet a Day, and Meredith work'd it off at Press. It was often 11 at Night and sometimes later, before I had finish'd my Distribution[135] for the next days Work: for the little Jobbs sent in by our other Friends now and then put us back. But so determin'd I was to continue doing a Sheet a Day of the Folio, that one Night when having impos'd[136] my Forms, I thought my Days Work over, one of them by accident was broken and two Pages reduc'd to Pie,[137] I immediately distributed and compos'd it over again before I went to bed. And this Industry visible to our Neighbours began to give us Character and Credit; particularly I was told, that mention being made of the new Printing Office at the Merchants every-night-Club, the general Opinion was that it must fail, there being already two Printers in the Place, Keimer and Bradford; but Doctor Baird (whom you and I saw many Years after at his native Place, St. Andrews in Scotland) gave a contrary Opinion; for the Industry of that Franklin, says he, is superior to any thing I ever saw of the kind: I see him still at work when I

[133] Instrument for measuring the altitude above the horizon of celestial bodies.

[134] Folio: the printing sheet (folded, each sheet gave four book pages); Pro Patria: a size of printing sheet; Pica: type 12 points in size; Primer: type 10 points in size.

[135] Returning sorts and single letters of type to their designated places in the cases.

[136] Secured the type in its frame, ready for printing.

[137] A confusion; a mess.

go home from Club; and he is at Work again before his Neighbours are out of bed. This struck the rest, and we soon after had Offers from one of them to Supply us with Stationary. But as yet we did not chuse to engage in Shop Business.

I mention this Industry the more particularly and the more freely, tho' it seems to be talking in my own Praise, that those of my Posterity who shall read it, may know the Use of that Virtue, when they see its Effects in my Favour throughout this Relation.

George Webb, who had found a Female Friend that lent him wherewith to purchase his Time of Keimer, now came to offer himself as a Journeyman to us. We could not then imploy him, but I foolishly let him know, as a Secret, that I soon intended to begin a Newspaper, and might then have Work for him. My Hopes of Success as I told him were founded on this, that the then only Newspaper,[138] printed by Bradford was a paltry thing, wretchedly manag'd, and no way entertaining; and yet was profitable to him. I therefore thought a good Paper could scarcely fail of good Encouragement. I requested Webb not to mention it, but he told it to Keimer, who immediately, to be beforehand with me, published Proposals for Printing one himself, on which Webb was to be employ'd. I resented this, and to counteract them, as I could not yet begin our Paper, I wrote several Pieces of Entertainment for Bradford's Paper, under the Title of the Busy Body which Brientnal continu'd some Months.[139] By this means the Attention of the Publick was fix'd on that Paper, and Keimers Proposals which we burlesqu'd and ridicul'd, were disregarded. He began his Paper however, and after carrying it on three Quarters of a Year, with at most only 90 subscribers, he offer'd it to me for a Trifle, and I having been ready some time to go on with it, took it in hand directly, and it prov'd in a few Years extreamly profitable to me.[140]

I perceive that I am apt to speak in the singular Number, though our Partnership still continu'd. The Reason may be, that in fact the whole Management of the Business lay upon me. Meredith was no Compositor, a poor Pressman, and seldom sober. My Friends lamented my Connection with him, but I was to make the best of it.

Our first Papers made a quite different Appearance from any before in the Province, a better Type and better printed: but some spirited Remarks[141] of my Writing on the Dispute then going on between Govr. Burnet and the Massachusetts Assembly, struck the principal People, occasion'd the Paper and the Manager of it to be much talk'd of, and in a few Weeks brought them all to be our Subscribers. Their Example was follow'd by many, and our Number went on growing continually. This was one of the first good Effects of my having learnt a little to scribble. Another was, that the leading Men, seeing a News Paper now in the hands of one who could also handle a Pen, thought it convenient to oblige and encourage me. Bradford still printed the Votes and Laws and other Publick Business. He had printed an Address of the House to the Governor in a coarse blundering manner; We reprinted it elegantly and correctly, and sent one to every Member. They were sensible of the Difference, it

[138] *The American Weekly Mercury,* established December 22, 1719.

[139] Franklin wrote all of the first four issues and part of two others in this series.

[140] *The Universal Instructor in all Arts and Sciences: and Pennsylvania Gazette* was shortened to *The Pennsylvania Gazette* when Franklin and Meredith took the paper over in October 1729.

It subsequently became one of the finest newspapers in the colonies.

[141] Franklin first met Burnet in 1724 when he was governor of New York. Burnet had since become governor of Massachusetts and engaged in a dispute with the assembly over his salary. Franklin's "remarks" supported the Assembly's "ardent Spirit of Liberty."

strengthen'd the Hands of our Friends in the House, and they voted us their Printers for the Year ensuing.

Among my Friends in the House I must not forget Mr. Hamilton before mentioned, who was now returned from England and had a Seat in it.[142] He interested himself[143] for me strongly in that Instance, as he did in many others afterwards, continuing his Patronage till his Death. Mr. Vernon about this time put me in mind of the Debt I ow'd him: but did not press me. I wrote him an ingenuous Letter of Acknowledgments, crav'd his Forbearance a little longer which he allow'd me, and as soon as I was able I paid the Principal with Interest and many Thanks. So that *Erratum* was in some degree corrected.

But now another Difficulty came upon me, which I had never the least Reason to expect. Mr. Meredith's Father, who was to have paid for our Printing House according to the Expectations given me, was able to advance only one Hundred Pounds, Currency, which had been paid, and a Hundred more was due to the Merchant; who grew impatient and su'd us all. We gave Bail, but saw that if the Money could not be rais'd in time, the Suit must come to a Judgment and Execution,[144] and our hopeful Prospects must with us be ruined, as the Press and Letters must be sold for Payment, perhaps at half Price. In this Distress two true Friends whose Kindness I have never forgotten nor ever shall forget while I can remember any thing, came to me separately unknown to each other, and without any Application from me, offering each of them to advance me all the Money that should be necessary to enable me to take the whole Business upon my self if that should be practicable, but they did not like my continuing the Partnership with Meredith, who as they said was often seen drunk in the Streets, and playing at low Games in Alehouses, much to our Discredit. These two Friends were William Coleman and Robert Grace.[145] I told them I could not propose a Separation while any Prospect remain'd of the Merediths fulfilling their Part of our Agreement. Because I thought myself under great Obligations to them for what they had done and would do if they could. But if they finally fail'd in their Performance, and our Partnership must be dissolv'd, I should then think myself at Liberty to accept the assistance of my Friends.

Thus the matter rested for some time. When I said to my Partner, perhaps your Father is dissatisfied at the Part you have undertaken in this Affair of ours, and is unwilling to advance for you and me what he would for you alone: if that is the Case, tell me, and I will resign the whole to you and go about my Business. No says he, my Father has really been disappointed and is really unable; and I am unwilling to distress him farther. I see this is a Business I am not fit for. I was bred a Farmer, and it was a Folly in me to come to Town and put my Self at 30 Years of Age an Apprentice to learn a new Trade. Many of our Welsh People are going to settle in North Carolina where Land is cheap: I am inclin'd to go with them, and follow my old Employment. You may find Friends to assist you. If you will take the Debts of the Company upon you, return to my Father the hundred Pound he has advanc'd, pay my little personal Debts, and give me Thirty Pounds and a new Saddle, I will relinquish the Partnership and leave the whole in your Hands. I agreed to this

[142] Andrew Hamilton, Speaker of the Assembly.
[143] Franklin's note: "I got his son once £500."
[144] Legal order of seizure and sale of property.
[145] William Coleman (1704–1769) and Robert Grace (1709–1766) were original members of the junto. Later, Grace's ironworks manufactured the "Franklin stove."

Proposal. It was drawn up in Writing, sign'd and seal'd immediately. I gave him what he demanded and he went soon after to Carolina; from whence he sent me next Year two long Letters, containing the best Account that had been given of that Country, the Climate, Soil, Husbandry, &c. for in those Matters he was very judicious. I printed them in the Papers,[146] and they gave Grate Satisfaction to the Publick.

As soon as he was gone, I recurr'd to my two Friends; and because I would not give an unkind Preference to either, I took half what each had offered and I wanted, of one, and half of the other; paid off the Company Debts, and went on with the Business in my own Name, advertising that the Partnership was dissolved. I think this was in or about the Year 1729.[147]

About this Time there was a Cry among the People for more Paper-Money, only £15,000, being extant in the province and that soon to be sunk. The wealthy Inhabitants oppos'd any Addition, being against all Paper Currency, from an Apprehension that it would depreciate as it had done in New England to the Prejudice of all Creditors. We had discuss'd this Point in our Junto, where I was on the Side of an Addition, being persuaded that the first small Sum struck in 1723 had done much good, by increasing the Trade Employment, and Number of Inhabitants in the Province, since I now saw all the old Houses inhabited, and many new ones building, where as I remember'd well, that when I first walk'd about the Streets of Philadelphia, eating my Roll, I saw most of the Houses in Walnut street between Second and Front streets with Bills on their Doors, to be let; and many likewise in Chestnut street, and other Streets; which made me then think the Inhabitants of the City were one after another deserting it. Our Debates possess'd me so fully of the Subject, that I wrote and printed an anonymous Pamphlet on it, entituled, *The Nature and Necessity of a Paper Currency.* It was well receiv'd by the common People in general; but the Rich Men dislik'd it; for it increas'd and strengthen'd the Clamour for more Money; and they happening to have no Writers among them that were able to answer it, their Opposition slacken'd, and the Point was carried by a Majority in the House. My Friends there, who conceiv'd I had been of some Service, thought fit to reward me, by employing me in printing the Money, a very profitable Jobb, and a great Help to me.[148] This was another Advantage gain'd by my being able to write. The Utility of this Currency became by Time and Experience so evident, as never afterwards to be much disputed, so that it grew soon to £55000, and in 1739 to £80,000 since which it arose during War to upwards of £350,000. Trade, Building and Inhabitants all the while increasing. Tho' I now think there are Limits beyond which the Quantity may be hurtful.

I soon after obtain'd, thro' my Friend Hamilton, the Printing of the New Castle[149] Paper Money, another profitable Jobb, as I then thought it; small Things appearing great to those in small Circumstances. And these to me were really great Advantages, as they were great Encouragements. He procured me also the Printing of the Laws and Votes of that Government which continu'd in my Hands as long as I follow'd the Business.[150]

---

[146] *The Pennsylvania Gazette,* May 6 and 13, 1731.
[147] Actually July 14, 1730.
[148] Andrew Bradford was in fact given the 1729 contract to print £20,000. Franklin, however, did get the next contract, in 1731, to print £40,000.
[149] These counties, now part of Delaware, had the

same proprietary governor as did Pennsylvania. Andrew Hamilton was Speaker of the House in both Assemblies.
[150] Franklin began printing the yearly proceedings of the Delaware Assembly in 1734; he published the collected laws in 1741.

I now open'd a little Stationer's Shop.[151] I had in it Blanks of all Sorts the correctest that ever appear'd among us, being assisted in that by my friend Brientnal; I had also Paper, Parchment, Chapmen's Books, &c. One Whitemarsh a Compositor I had known in London, an excellent Workman now came to me and work'd with me constantly and diligently, and I took an Apprentice the Son of Aquila Rose. I began now gradually to pay off the Debt I was under for the Printing-House. In order to secure my Credit and Character as a Tradesman, I took care not only to be in *Reality* Industrious and frugal, but to avoid all *Appearances* of the Contrary. I drest plainly; I was seen at no Places of idle Diversion; I never went out a-fishing or shooting; a Book, indeed, sometimes debauch'd me from my Work; but that was seldom, snug, and gave no Scandal: and to show that I was not above my Business, I sometimes brought home the Paper I purchas'd at the Stores, thro' the Streets on a Wheelbarrow. Thus being esteem'd an industrious thriving young Man, and paying duly for what I bought, the Merchants who imported Stationary solicited my Custom, others propos'd supplying me with Books, and I went on swimmingly. In the mean time Keimer's Credit and Business declining daily, he was at last forc'd to sell his Printing-house to satisfy his Creditors. He went to Barbadoes, and there lived some Years, in very poor Circumstances.

His Apprentice David Harry, whom I had instructed while I work'd with him, set up in his Place at Philadelphia, having bought his Materials. I was at first apprehensive of a powerful Rival in Harry, as his Friends were very able, and had a good deal of Interest. I therefore propos'd a Partnership to him; which he, fortunately for me, rejected with Scorn. He was very proud, dress'd like a Gentleman, liv'd expensively, took much Diversion and Pleasure abroad, ran in debt, and neglected his Business, upon which all Business left him; and finding nothing to do, he follow'd Keimer to Barbadoes; taking the Printinghouse with him. There this Apprentice employ'd his former Master as a Journeyman. They quarrel'd often. Harry went continually behindhand, and at length was forc'd to sell his Types, and return to his Country Work in Pensilvania. The Person that bought them, employ'd Keimer to use them, but in a few years he died. There remain'd now no Competitor with me at Philadelphia, but the old one, Bradford, who was rich and easy, did a little Printing now and then by straggling Hands, but was not very anxious about the Business. However, as he kept the Post Office, it was imagined he had better Opportunities of obtaining News, his Paper was thought a better Distributer of Advertisements than mine, and therefore had many more, which was a profitable thing to him and a Disadvantage to me. For tho' I did indeed receive and send Papers by Post, yet the publick Opinion was otherwise; for what I did send was by Bribing the Riders who took them privately: Bradford being unkind enough to forbid it: which occasion'd some Resentment on my Part; and I thought so meanly of him for it, that when I afterwards came into his Situation,[152] I took care never to imitate it.

I had hitherto continu'd to board with Godfrey who lived in Part of my House with his Wife and Children, and had one Side of the Shop for his Glazier's Business, tho' he work'd little, being always absorb'd in his Mathematics. Mrs. Godfrey projected a Match for me with a Relation's Daughter, took Opportunities of bringing

---

[151] The earliest surviving account books indicate that Franklin opened this shop about July 1730.
[152] Franklin was appointed deputy postmaster general in 1753. Such a position was good fortune for anyone in the publishing business.

us often together, till a serious Courtship on my Part ensu'd, the Girl[153] being in herself very deserving. The old Folks encourag'd me by continual Invitations to Supper, and by leaving us together, till at length it was time to explain. Mrs. Godfrey manag'd our little Treaty. I let her know that I expected as much Money with their Daughter as would pay off my Remaining Debt for the Printinghouse, which I believe was not then above a Hundred Pounds. She brought me Word they had no such Sum to spare. I said they might mortgage their House in the Loan Office. The Answer to this after some Days was, that they did not approve the Match; that on Enquiry of Bradford they had been inform'd the Printing Business was not a profitable one, the Types would soon be worn out and more wanted, that S. Keimer and D. Harry had fail'd one after the other, and I should probably soon follow them; and therefore I was forbidden the House, and the Daughter shut up. Whether this was a real Change of Sentiment, or only Artifice, on a Supposition of our being too far engag'd in Affection to retract, and therefore that we should steal a Marriage, which would leave them at Liberty to give or withhold what they pleas'd, I know not: but I suspected the latter, resented it, and went no more. Mrs. Godfrey brought me afterwards some more favourable Accounts of their Disposition, and would have drawn me on again: but I declared absolutely my Resolution to have nothing more to do with that Family. This was resented by the Godfreys, we differed, and they removed, leaving me the whole House, and I resolved to take no more Inmates.

But this Affair having turn'd my Thoughts to Marriage, I look'd round me, and made Overtures of Acquaintance in other Places; but soon found that the Business of a Printer being generally thought a poor one, I was not to expect Money with a Wife[154] unless with such a one, as I should not otherwise think agreable. In the mean time, that hard-to-be-govern'd Passion of Youth, had hurried me frequently into Intrigues with low Women that fell in my Way, which were attended with some Expence and great Inconvenience, besides a continual Risque to my Health by a Distemper which of all Things I dreaded, tho' by great good Luck I escaped it.[155]

A friendly Correspondence as Neighbours and old Acquaintances, had continued between me and Mrs. Read's family, who all had a Regard for me from the time of my first Lodging in their House. I was often invited there and consulted in their Affairs, wherein I sometimes was of service. I pity'd poor Miss Read's unfortunate Situation, who was generally dejected, seldom chearful, and avoided Company. I consider'd my Giddiness and Inconstancy when in London as in a great degree the Cause of her Unhappiness; tho' the Mother was good enough to think the Fault more her own than mine, as she had prevented our Marrying before I went thither, and persuaded the other Match in my Absence. Our mutual Affection was revived, but there were now great Objections to our Union. That Match was indeed look'd upon as invalid, a preceding Wife being said to be living in England; but this could not easily be prov'd, because of the Distance. And tho' there was a Report of his Death, it was not certain. Then tho' it should be true, he had left many Debts which his Successor might be call'd on to pay. We ventured however, over all these

---

[153] The name of the girl is not known.
[154] During this time the financial considerations of a proposed marriage far outweighed romantic

ones. Hence, Franklin's monetary expectations were not out of the ordinary.
[155] Franklin is referring to syphilis.

Difficulties, and I [took] her to wife Sept. 1. 1730.[156] None of the inconveniencies happened that we had apprehended, she prov'd a good and faithful Helpmate, assisted me much by attending the Shop, we throve together, and have ever mutually endeavour'd to make each other happy. Thus I corrected that great *Erratum* as well as I could.

About this Time our Club Meeting, not at a Tavern, but in a little Room of Mr. Grace's set apart for that Purpose; a Proposition was made by me that since our Books were often referr'd to in our Disquisitions upon the Queries, it might be convenient to us to have them all together where we met, that upon Occasion they might be consulted; and by thus clubbing our Books to a common Library, we should, while we lik'd to keep them together, have each of us the Advantage of using the Books of all the other Members, which would be nearly as beneficial as if each owned the whole. It was lik'd and agreed to, and we fill'd one End of the Room with such Books as we could best spare. The Number was not so great as we expected; and tho' they had been of great Use, yet some Inconveniencies occurring for want of due Care of them, the Collection after about a Year was separated, and each took his Books home again.

And now I set on foot my first Project of a public Nature, that for a Subscription Library. I drew up the Proposals, got them put into Form by our great Scrivener Brockden, and by the help of my Friends in the Junto, procur'd Fifty Subscribers of 40s. each to begin with and 10s. a Year for 50 Years, the Term our Company was to continue. We afterwards obtain'd a Charter, the Company being increas'd to 100. This was the Mother of all the N American Subscription Libraries now so numerous.[157] It is become a great thing itself, and continually increasing. These Libraries have improv'd the general Conversation of the Americans, made the common Tradesmen and Farmers as intelligent as most Gentlemen from other Countries, and perhaps have contributed in some degree to the Stand so generally made throughout the Colonies in Defence of their Privileges.[158]

Thus far was written with the Intention express'd in the Beginning and therefore contains several little family Anecdotes of no Importance to others.[159] What follows was written many Years after in compliance with the Advice contain'd in these Letters, and accordingly intended for the Publick. The Affairs of the Revolution occasion'd the Interruption.

Letter from Mr. Abel James[160] with Notes of my Life, to be here inserted. Also

[156] Lacking evidence that her first husband, the missing John Rogers, was either dead or practicing bigamy, Deborah was legally still Rogers's spouse and could not remarry. (The punishment for bigamy was 39 lashes in public and life imprisonment.) However, Deborah's family and all their friends quickly recognized the "difficulties" of the situation and thereafter accepted this "common law" marriage as adequate, and the Franklin's two children were regarded as legitimate. In the absence of divorce or annulment laws, such arrangements were not uncommon. Deborah Read Franklin died in 1774.

[157] The Library Company of Philadelphia was the first subscription library in North America, although a good many public or semipublic collections (most of them small and oriented to religion) existed long before 1731.

[158] Franklin, writing in 1771, here refers to the growing colonial protests against British "tyranny," which were to culminate in revolution a few years later.

[159] Because of the Revolution, Franklin was now estranged from his Loyalist son William, to whom he had originally addressed the opening of the *Autobiography*.

[160] James (1726?–1790) was a Philadelphia Quaker merchant and an old friend of Franklin's.

Letter from Mr. Vaughan[161] to the same purpose

My dear and honored Friend.[162]

I have often been desirous of writing to thee, but could not be reconciled to the Thoughts that the Letter might fall into the Hands of the British, lest some Printer or Busy Body should publish some Part of the Contents and give our Friends Pain and myself Censure.

Some Time since there fell into my Hands to my great Joy about 23 Sheets in thy own hand-writing containing an Account of the Parentage and Life of thyself, directed to thy Son ending in the Year 1730 with which there were Notes likewise in thy writing,[163] a Copy of which I inclose in Hopes it may be a means if thou continuedst it up to a later period, that the first and latter part may be put together, and if it is not yet continued, I hope thou wilt not delay it, Life is uncertain as the Preacher tells us, and what will the World say if kind, humane and benevolent Ben Franklin should leave his Friends and the World deprived of so pleasing and profitable a Work, a Work which would be useful and entertaining not only to a few, but to millions.

The Influence Writings under that Class have on the Minds of Youth is very great, and has no where appeared so plain as in our public Friend's Journal. It almost insensibly leads the Youth into the Resolution of endeavouring to become as good and as eminent as the Journalist. Should thine for Instance when published, and I think it could not fail of it, lead the Youth to equal the Industry and Temperance of thy early Youth, what a Blessing with that Class would such a Work be. I know of no Character living nor many of them put together, who has so much in his Power as Thyself to promote a greater Spirit of Industry and early Attention to Business, Frugality and Temperance with the American Youth. Not that I think the Work would have no other Merit and Use in the World, far from it, but the first is of such vast Importance, that I know nothing that can equal it.   ABEL JAMES

The foregoing letter and the minutes accompanying it being shewn to a friend, I received from him the following:

Paris, January 31, 1783.

My dearest Sir,

When I had read over your sheets of minutes of the principal incidents of your life, recovered for you by your Quaker acquaintance; I told you I would send you a letter expressing my reasons why I thought it would be useful to complete and publish it as he desired. Various concerns have for some time past prevented this letter being written, and I do not know whether it was worth any expectation: happening to be at leisure however at present, I shall by writing at least interest and instruct myself; but as the terms I am inclined to use may tend to offend a person of your manners, I shall only tell you how I would address any other person, who was as good

---

[161] Benjamin Vaughan (1751–1835), English diplomat and editor of the first collection (1779) of Franklin's works.
[162] James's letter was probably written in 1782, after the last battle of the Revolution but before a formal peace agreement had been reached.

[163] Soon after he began to write, in 1771, Franklin made an outline for his autobiography. It contains various topics that he planned, but neglected, to cover.

and as great as yourself, but less diffident. I would say to him, sir, I *solicit* the history of your life from the following motives.

Your history is so remarkable, that if you do not give it, somebody else will certainly give it; and perhaps so as nearly to do as much harm, as your own management of the thing might do good.

It will moreover present a table of the internal circumstances of your country, which will very much tend to invite to its settlers of virtuous and manly minds. And considering the eagerness with which such information is sought by them, and the extent of your reputation, I do not know of a more efficacious advertisement than your Biography would give.

All that has happened to you is also connected with the detail of the manners and situation of *a rising* people; and in this respect I do not think that the writings of Caesar and Tacitus can be more interesting to a true judge of human nature and society.

But these, Sir, are small reasons in my opinion, compared with the chance which your life will give for the forming of future great men; and in conjunction with your Art of Virtue, (which you design to publish) of improving the features of private character, and consequently of aiding all happiness both public and domestic.

The two works I allude to, Sir, will in particular give a noble rule and example of *self-education*. School and other education constantly proceed upon false principles, and shew a clumsy apparatus pointed at a false mark; but your apparatus is simple, and the mark a true one; and while parents and young persons are left destitute of other just means of estimating and becoming prepared for a reasonable course in life, your discovery that the thing is in many a man's private power, will be invaluable!

Influence upon the private character late in life, is not only an influence late in life, but a weak influence. It is in *youth* that we plant our chief habits and prejudices; it is in youth that we take our party as to profession, pursuits, and matrimony. In youth therefore the turn is given; in youth the education even of the next generation is given; in youth the private and public character is determined; and the term of life extending but from youth to age, life ought to begin well from youth; and more especially *before* we take our party[164] as to our principal objects.

But your Biography will not merely teach self-education, but the education of *a wise man;* and the wisest man will receive lights and improve his progress, by seeing detailed the conduct of another wise man. And why are weaker men to be deprived of such helps, when we see our race has been blundering on in the dark, almost without a guide in this particular, from the farthest trace of time? Shew then, Sir, how much is to be done, *both to sons and fathers;* and invite all wise men to become like yourself; and other men to become wise.

When we see how cruel statesmen and warriors can be to the humble race, and how absurd distinguished men can be to their acquaintance, it will be instructive to observe the instances multiply of pacific acquiescing manners; and to find how compatible it is to be great and *domestic;* enviable and yet *good-humored.*

The little private incidents which you will also have to relate, will have considerable use, as we want above all things, *rules of prudence in ordinary affairs;* and it will be curious to see how you have acted in these. It will be so far a sort of key to life,

---

[164] Make our decisions.

and explain many things that all men ought to have once explained to them, to give them a chance of becoming wise by foresight.

The nearest thing to having experience of one's own, is to have other people's affairs brought before us in a shape that is interesting; this is sure to happen from your pen. Your affairs and management will have an air of simplicity or importance that will not fail to strike; and I am convinced you have conducted them with as much originality as if you had been conducting discussions in politics or philosophy; and what more worthy of experiments and system, (its importance and its errors considered) than human life!

Some men have been virtuous blindly, others have speculated fantastically, and others have been shrewd to bad purposes; but you, Sir, I am sure, will give under your hand, nothing but what is at the same moment, wise, practical, and good.

Your account of yourself (for I suppose the parallel I am drawing for Dr. Franklin, will hold not only in point of character but of private history), will shew that you are ashamed of no origin; a thing the more important, as you prove how little necessary all origin is to happiness, virtue, or greatness.

As no end likewise happens without a means, so we shall find, Sir, that even you yourself framed a plan by which you became considerable; but at the same time we may see that though the event is flattering, the means are as simple as wisdom could make them; that is, depending upon nature, virtue, thought, and habit.

Another thing demonstrated will be the propriety of every man's waiting for his time for appearing upon the stage of the world. Our sensations being very much fixed to the moment, we are apt to forget that more moments are to follow the first, and consequently that man should arrange his conduct so as to suit the *whole* of a life. Your attribution appears to have been applied to your *life,* and the passing moments of it have been enlivened with content and enjoyment, instead of being tormented with foolish impatience or regrets. Such a conduct is easy for those who make virtue and themselves their standard, and who try to keep themselves in countenance by examples of other truly great men, of whom patience is so often the characteristic.

Your Quaker correspondent, Sir, (for here again I will suppose the subject of my letter resembling Dr. Franklin,) praised your frugality, diligence, and temperance, which he considered as a pattern for all youth: but it is singular that he should have forgotten your modesty, and your disinterestedness, without which you never could have waited for your advancement, or found your situation in the mean time comfortable; which is a strong lesson to shew the poverty of glory, and the importance of regulating our minds.

If this correspondent had known the nature of your reputation as well as I do, he would have said; your former writings and measures would secure attention to your Biography and Art of Virtue; and your Biography and Art of Virtue, in return, would secure attention to them. This is an advantage attendant upon a various character, and which brings all that belongs to it into greater play; and it is the more useful, as perhaps more persons are at a loss for the *means* of improving their minds and characters, than they are for the time or the inclination to do it.

But there is one concluding reflection, Sir, that will shew the use of your life as a mere piece of biography. This style of writing seems a little gone out of vogue, and yet it is a very useful one; and your specimen of it may be particularly serviceable, as it will make a subject of comparison with the lives of various public cutthroats and intriguers, and with absurd monastic self-tormentors, or vain literary triflers. If it encourages more writings of the same kind with your own, and induces more men to spend lives fit to be written; it will be worth all Plutarch's Lives put together.

But being tired of figuring to myself a character of which every feature suits only one man in the world, without giving him the praise of it; I shall end my letter, my dear Dr. Franklin, with a personal application to your proper self.

I am earnestly desirous then, my dear Sir, that you should let the world into the traits of your genuine character, as civil broils may otherwise tend to disguise or traduce it. Considering your great age, the caution of your character, and your peculiar style of thinking, it is not likely that any one besides yourself can be sufficiently master of the facts of your life, or the intentions of your mind.

Besides all this, the immense revolution of the present period, will necessarily turn our attention towards the author of it; and when virtuous principles have been pretended in it, it will be highly important to shew that such have really influenced; and, as your own character will be the principal one to receive a scrutiny, it is proper (even for its effects upon your vast and rising country, as well as upon England and upon Europe), that it should stand respectable and eternal. For the furtherance of human happiness, I have always maintained that it is necessary to prove that man is not even at present a vicious and detestable animal; and still more to prove that good management may greatly amend him; and it is for much the same reason, that I am anxious to see the opinion established, that there are fair characters existing among the individuals of the race; for the moment that all men, without exception, shall be conceived abandoned, good people will cease efforts deemed to be hopeless, and perhaps think of taking their share in the scramble of life, or at least of making it comfortable principally for themselves.

Take then, my dear Sir, this work most speedily into hand: shew yourself good as you are good, temperate as you are temperate; and above all things, prove yourself as one who from your infancy have loved justice, liberty, and concord, in a way that has made it natural and consistent for you to have acted, as we have seen you act in the last seventeen years of your life. Let Englishmen be made not only to respect, but even to love you. When they think well of individuals in your native country, they will go nearer to thinking well of your country; and when your countrymen see themselves well thought of by Englishmen, they will go nearer to thinking well of England. Extend your views even further; do not stop at those who speak the English tongue, but after having settled so many points in nature and politics, think of bettering the whole race of men.

As I have not read any part of the life in question, but know only the character that lived it, I write somewhat at hazard. I am sure however, that the life, and the treatise I allude to (on the Art of Virtue), will necessarily fulfil the chief of my expectations; and still more so if you take up the measure of suiting these performances to the several views above stated. Should they even prove unsuccessful in all that a sanguine admirer of yours hopes from them, you will at least have framed pieces to interest the human mind; and whoever gives a feeling of pleasure that is innocent to man, has added so much to the fair side of a life otherwise too much darkened by anxiety, and too much injured by pain.

In the hope therefore that you will listen to the prayer addressed to you in this letter, I beg to subscribe myself, my dearest Sir, &c. &c.   BENJ. VAUGHAN.

1771–1784/1791

Part Two: Continuation of the Account of My Life.

Begun at Passy[165] 1784

It is some time since I receiv'd the above Letters, but I have been too busy till now to think of complying with the Request they contain. It might too be much better done if I were at home among my Papers, which would aid my Memory and help to ascertain Dates. But my Return being uncertain, and having just now a little Leisure, I will endeavour to recollect and write what I can; if I live to get home, it may there be corrected and improv'd.[166]

Not having any Copy here of what is already written, I know not whether an Account is given of the means I used to establish the Philadelphia publick Library, which from a small Beginning is now become so considerable, though I remember to have come down to near the Time of that Transaction, 1730. I will therefore begin here, with an Account of it, which may be struck out if found to have been already given.

At the time I establish'd my self in Pensylvania, there was not a good Bookseller's Shop in any of the Colonies to the Southward of Boston. In New-York and Philadelphia the Printers were indeed Stationers, they sold only Paper, &c., Almanacks, Ballads, and a few common School Books. Those who lov'd Reading were oblig'd to send for their Books from England. The Members of the Junto had each a few. We had left the Alehouse where we first met, and hired a Room to hold our Club in. I propos'd that we should all of us bring our Books to that Room, where they would not only be ready to consult in our Conferences, but become a common Benefit, each of us being at Liberty to borrow such as he wish'd to read at home. This was accordingly done, and for some time contented us. Finding the Advantage of this little Collection, I propos'd to render the Benefit from Books more common by commencing a Public Subscription Library. I drew a Sketch of the Plan and Rules that would be necessary, and got a skilful Conveyancer, Mr. Charles Brockden to put the whole in Form of Articles of Agreement to be subscribed; by which each Subscriber engag'd to pay a certain Sum down for the first Purchase of Books and an annual Contribution for encreasing them. So few were the Readers at that time in Philadelphia, and the Majority of us so poor, that I was not able with great Industry to find more than Fifty Persons, mostly young Tradesmen, willing to pay down for this purpose Forty Shillings each, and Ten Shillings per Annum. On this little Fund we began. The Books were imported. The Library was open one Day in the Week for lending them to the Subscribers, on their Promisory Notes to pay Double the Value if not duly returned. The Institution soon manifested its Utility, was imitated by other Towns and in other Provinces, the Librarys were augmented by Donations, Reading became fashionable, and our People having no publick Amusements to divert their Attention from Study became better acquainted with Books, and in a few Years

[165] Suburb of Paris where Franklin stayed while serving as negotiator for the United States during the writing of the Treaty of Paris.

[166] The Treaty of Peace with Britain was signed in Paris on September 3, 1783. Franklin asked Congress for leave to come home, but he remained as minister until succeeded by Thomas Jefferson in May 1785. He left Paris for America that July. Franklin was 78 years old when he wrote this part of the *Autobiography*.

were observ'd by Strangers to be better instructed and more intelligent than People of the same Rank generally are in other Countries.

When we were about to sign the above-mentioned Articles, which were to be binding on us, our Heirs, &c. for fifty Years, Mr Brockden, the Scrivener, said to us, "You are young Men, but it is scarce probable that any of you will live to see the Expiration of the Term fix'd in this Instrument." A Number of us, however, are yet living: But the Instrument was after a few Years rendered null by a Charter that incorporated and gave Perpetuity to the Company.

The Objections, and Reluctances I met with in Soliciting the Subscriptions, made me soon feel the Impropriety of presenting one's self as the Proposer of any useful Project that might be suppos'd to raise one's Reputation in the smallest degree above that of one's Neighbours, when one has need of their Assistance to accomplish that Project. I therefore put my self as much as I could out of sight, and stated it as a scheme of a *Number of Friends,* who had requested me to go about and propose it to such as they thought Lovers of Reading. In this way my Affair went on more smoothly, and I ever after practis'd it on such Occasions; and from my frequent Successes, can heartily recommend it. The present little Sacrifice of your Vanity will afterwards be amply repaid. If it remains a while uncertain to whom the Merit belongs, some one more vain than yourself will be encourag'd to claim it, and then even Envy will be dispos'd to do you Justice, by plucking those assum'd Feathers, and restoring them to their right Owner.

This Library afforded me the means of Improvement by constant Study, for which I set apart an Hour or two each Day; and thus repair'd in some Degree the Loss of the Learned Education my Father once intended for me. Reading was the only Amusement I allow'd my self. I spent no time in Taverns, Games, or Frolicks of any kind. And my Industry in my Business continu'd as indefatigable as it was necessary. I was in debt for my Printing-house, I had a young Family[167] coming on to be educated, and I had to contend with for business two Printers who were establish'd in the Place before me. My Circumstances however grew daily easier: my original Habits of Frugality continuing. And my Father having among his Instructions to me when a Boy, frequently repeated a Proverb of Solomon, *"Seest thou a Man diligent in his Calling, he shall stand before Kings, he shall not stand before mean Men."*[168] I from thence consider'd Industry as a Means of obtaining Wealth and Distinction, which encourag'd me, tho' I did not think that I should ever literally stand before Kings, which however has since happened.—for I have stood before five, and even had the honour of sitting down with one, the King of Denmark, to Dinner.

We have an English Proverb that says,

He that would thrive
Must ask his Wife;

it was lucky for me that I had one as much dispos'd to Industry and Frugality as my self. She assisted me chearfully in my Business, folding and stitching Pamphlets, tending Shop, purchasing old Linen Rags for the Paper-makers, &c. &c. We kept no

[167] Franklin's children were William (b. ca. 1731),   [168] Proverbs 22:29.
Francis (b. 1732), and Sarah (b. 1743).

idle Servants, our Table was plain and simple, our Furniture of the cheapest. For instance my Breakfast was a long time Bread and Milk, (no Tea) and I ate it out of a twopenny earthen Porringer[169] with a Pewter Spoon. But mark how Luxury will enter Families, and make a Progress, in Spite of Principle. Being call'd one Morning to Breakfast, I found it in a China Bowl with a Spoon of Silver. They had been bought for me without my Knowledge by my Wife, and had cost her the enormous Sum of three and twenty Shillings, for which she had no other Excuse or Apology to make, but that she thought her Husband deserv'd a Silver Spoon and China Bowl as well as any of his Neighbours. This was the first Appearance of Plate[170] and China in our House, which afterwards in a Course of Years as our Wealth encreas'd augmented gradually to several Hundred Pounds in Value.

I had been religiously educated as a Presbyterian; and tho' some of the Dogmas of that Persuasion, such as the Eternal Decrees of God, Election, Reprobation, &c. appear'd to me unintelligible, others doubtful, and I early absented myself from the Public Assemblies of the Sect, Sunday being my Studying-Day, I never was without some religious Principles; I never doubted, for instance, the Existance of the Deity, that he made the World, and govern'd it by his Providence; that the most acceptable Service of God was the doing Good to Man; that our Souls are immortal; and that all Crime will be punished and Virtue rewarded either here or hereafter; these I esteem'd the Essentials of every Religion, and being to be found in all the Religions we had in our Country I respected them all, tho' with different degrees of Respect as I found them more or less mix'd with other Articles which without any Tendency to inspire, promote or confirm Morality, serv'd principally to divide us and make us unfriendly to one another. This Respect to all, with an Opinion that the worst had some good Effects, induc'd me to avoid all Discourse that might tend to lessen the good Opinion another might have of his own Religion; and as our Province increas'd in People and new Places of worship were continually wanted, and generally erected by voluntary Contribution, my Mite for such purpose, whatever might be the Sect, was never refused.[171]

Tho' I seldom attended any Public Worship, I had still an Opinion of its Propriety, and of its Utility when rightly conducted, and I regularly paid my annual Subscription for the Support of the only Presbyterian Minister or Meeting we had in Philadelphia. He us'd to visit me sometimes as a Friend, and admonish me to attend his Administrations, and I was now and then prevail'd on to do so, once for five Sundays successively. Had he been, *in my Opinion,* a good Preacher perhaps I might have continued, notwithstanding the occasion I had for the Sunday's Leisure in my Course of Study: but his Discourses were chiefly either polemic Arguments, or Explications of the Peculiar Doctrines of our Sect, and were all to me very dry, uninteresting and unedifying, since not a single moral Principle was inculcated or enforc'd, their Aim seeming to be rather to make us Presbyterians than good Citizens. At length he took for his Text that Verse of the 4th Chapter of Philippians, *Finally, Brethren, Whatsoever Things are true, honest, just, pure, lovely, or of good report, if there be any virtue, or any praise, think on these Things;*[172] and I imagin'd in a

---

[169] Porridge bowl.
[170] Silver.
[171] In 1788 Franklin was one of the largest donors to the erection of a synagogue for the Jewish population of Philadelphia.
[172] Philippians 4:8.

Sermon on such a Text, we could not miss of having some Morality: but he confin'd himself to five Points only as meant by the Apostle, viz. 1. Keeping holy the Sabbath Day. 2. Being diligent in Reading the Holy Scriptures. 3. Attending duly the Publick Worship. 4. Partaking of the Sacrament. 5. Paying a due Respect to God's Ministers. These might be all good Things, but as they were not the kind of good Things that I expected from that Text, I despaired of ever meeting with them from any other, was disgusted, and attended his Preaching no more. I had some Years before compos'd a little Liturgy or Form of Prayer for my own private Use, viz, in 1728. entitled, *Articles of Belief and Acts of Religion.* I return'd to the Use of this, and went no more to the public Assemblies. My Conduct might be blameable, but I leave it without attempting farther to excuse it, my present purpose being to relate Facts, and not to make Apologies for them.

It was about this time that I conceiv'd the bold and arduous Project of arriving at moral Perfection.[173] I wish'd to live without committing any Fault at any time; I would conquer all that either Natural Inclination, Custom, or Company might lead me into. As I knew, or thought I knew, what was right and wrong, I did not see why I might not *always* do the one and avoid the other. But I soon found I had undertaken a Task of more Difficulty than I had imagined. While my *Attention was taken up* in guarding against one Fault, I was often surpriz'd by another. Habit took the Advantage of Inattention. Inclination was sometimes too strong for Reason. I concluded at length, that the mere speculative Conviction that it was our Interest to be compleatly virtuous, was not sufficient to prevent our Slipping, and that the contrary Habits must be broken and good ones acquired and established, before we can have any Dependance on a steady uniform Rectitude of Conduct. For this purpose I therefore contriv'd the following Method.

In the various Enumerations of the moral Virtues I had met with in my Reading, I found the Catalogue more or less numerous, as different Writers included more or fewer Ideas under the same Name. Temperance, for Example, was by some confin'd to Eating and Drinking, while by others it was extended to mean the moderating every other Pleasure, Appetite, Inclination or Passion, bodily or mental, even to our Avarice and Ambition. I propos'd to myself, for the sake of Clearness, to use rather more Names with fewer Ideas annex'd to each, than a few Names with more Ideas; and I included under Thirteen Names of Virtues all that at that time occurr'd to me as necessary or desirable, and annex'd to each a short Precept, which fully express'd the Extent I gave to its Meaning.

These Names of Virtues with their Precepts were

1. TEMPERANCE.

Eat not to Dulness. Drink not to Elevation.

2. SILENCE.

Speak not but what may benefit others or yourself. Avoid trifling Conversation.

---

[173] Franklin had at one time planned to write a
book on moral improvement.

3. Order.

Let all your Things have their Places. Let each Part of your Business have its Time.

4. Resolution.

Resolve to perform what you ought. Perform without fail what you resolve.

5. Frugality.

Make no Expence but to do good to others or yourself: i.e. Waste nothing.

6. Industry.

Lose no Time. Be always employ'd in something useful. Cut off all unnecessary Actions.

7. Sincerity.

Use no hurtful Deceit. Think innocently and justly; and, if you speak, speak accordingly.

8. Justice.

Wrong none, by doing Injuries or omitting the Benefits that are your Duty.

9. Moderation.

Avoid Extreams. Forbear resenting Injuries so much as you think they deserve.

10. Cleanliness.

Tolerate no Uncleanness in Body, Cloaths or Habitation.

11. Tranquility.

Be not disturbed at Trifles, or at Accidents common or unavoidable.

12. Chastity.

Rarely use Venery but for Health or Offspring; Never to Dulness, Weakness, or the Injury of your own or another's Peace or Reputation.

13. Humility.

Imitate Jesus and Socrates.

My Intention being to acquire the *Habitude* of all these Virtues, I judg'd it would be well not to distract my Attention by attempting the whole at once, but to fix it on one of them at a time, and when I should be Master of that, then to proceed to another, and so on till I should have gone thro' the thirteen. And as the previous Acquisition of some might facilitate the Acquisition of certain others, I arrang'd them with that View as they stand above. *Temperance* first, as it tends to procure that Coolness and Clearness of Head, which is so necessary where constant Vigilance was to be kept up, and Guard maintained, against the unremitting Attraction of ancient Habits, and the Force of perpetual Temptations. This being acquir'd and establish'd, *Silence* would be more easy, and my Desire being to gain Knowledge at the same time that I improv'd in Virtue, and considering that in Conversation it was obtain'd rather by the use of the Ears than of the Tongue, and therefore wishing to break a Habit I was getting into of Prattling, Punning and Joking, which only made me acceptable to trifling Company, I gave *Silence* the second Place. This, and the next, *Order,* I expected would allow me more Time for attending to my Project and my Studies; RESOLUTION, once become habitual, would keep me firm in my Endeavours to obtain all the subsequent Virtues; *Frugality* and *Industry,* by freeing me from my remaining Debt, and producing Affluence and Independance, would make more easy the Practice of *Sincerity* and *Justice,* &c. &c. Conceiving then that agreable to the Advice of Pythagoras[174] in his Golden Verses daily Examination would be necessary, I contriv'd the following Method for conducting that Examination.

I made a little Book in which I allotted a Page for each of the Virtues. I rul'd each Page with red Ink, so as to have seven Columns, one for each Day of the Week, marking each Column with a Letter for the Day. I cross'd these Columns with thirteen red Lines, marking the Beginning of each Line with the first Letter of one of the Virtues, on which Line and in its proper Column I might mark by a little black Spot every Fault I found upon Examination to have been committed respecting that Virtue upon that Day.

I determined to give a Week's strict Attention to each of the Virtues successively. Thus in the first Week my great Guard was to avoid every the least Offence against Temperance, leaving the other Virtues to their ordinary Chance, only marking every Evening the Faults of the Day. Thus if in the first Week I could keep my first Line marked T clear of Spots, I suppos'd the Habit of that Virtue so much strengthen'd and its opposite weaken'd, that I might venture extending my Attention to include the next, and for the following Week keep both Lines clear of Spots. Proceeding thus to the last, I could go thro' a Course compleat in Thirteen Weeks, and four Courses in a Year. And like him who having a Garden to weed, does not attempt to eradicate all the bad Herbs at once, which would exceed his Reach and his Strength, but works on one of the Beds at a time, and having accomplish'd the first proceeds to a Second; so I should have, (I hoped) the encouraging Pleasure of seeing on my Pages the Progress I made in Virtue, by clearing successively my Lines of their Spots, till in the End by a Number of Courses, I should be happy in viewing a clean Book after a thirteen Weeks daily Examination.

---

[174] Greek philosopher and mathematician (sixth century B.C.). Franklin intended to insert the appropriate verse: "Let sleep not close your eyes till you have thrice examined the transactions of the day: where have I strayed, what have I done, what good have I omitted?"

Form of the Pages

TEMPERANCE						
Eat not to Dulness.						
Drink not to Elevation.						

	S	M	T	W	T	F	S
T							
S	••	•		•		•	
O	•	•	•		•	•	•
R			•			•	
F		•				•	
I				•			
S							
J							
M							
Cl.							
T							
Ch.							
H							

This my little Book had for its Motto these Lines from Addison's *Cato;*

> Here will I hold: If there is a Pow'r above us,
> (And that there is, all Nature cries aloud
> Thro' all her Works) he must delight in Virtue,
> And that which he delights in must be happy.[175]

Another from Cicero.

> O Vitœ Philosophia Dux! O Virtutum indagatrix, expultrixque vitiorum!
> Unus dies bene, et ex preceptis tuis actus, peccanti immortalitati est anteponen-
> dus.[176]

Another from the Proverbs of Solomon speaking of Wisdom or Virtue;

> Length of Days is in her right hand, and in her Left Hand Riches and
> Honours; Her Ways are Ways of Pleasantness, and all her Paths are Peace.
> III, 16, 17.

And conceiving God to be the Fountain of Wisdom, I thought it right and
necessary to solicit his Assistance for obtaining it; to this End I form'd the following
little Prayer, which was prefix'd to my Tables of Examination; for daily Use.

> O Powerful Goodness! bountiful Father! merciful Guide! Increase in me that
> Wisdom which discovers my truest Interests; Strengthen my Resolutions to
> perform what that Wisdom dictates. Accept my kind Offices to thy other
> Children, as the only Return in my Power for thy continual Favours to me.

[175] Joseph Addison, *Cato, a Tragedy* (1713), Act V,
Sc. i, ll. 15–18.

[176] Marcus Tullius Cicero, *Tusculan Disputations,* V,
ii, 5: "O philosophy, guide of life! O seeker
out of virtues and expeller of vices! [Here
Franklin omitted several lines from the
original.] One day lived well, and according to
thy precepts, is to be preferred to an eternity of
sin."

I us'd also sometimes a little Prayer which I took from Thomson's Poems. viz

> Father of Light and Life, thou Good supreme,
> O teach me what is good, teach me thy self!
> Save me from Folly, Vanity and Vice,
> From every low Pursuit, and fill my Soul
> With Knowledge, conscious Peace, and Virtue pure,
> Sacred, substantial, neverfading Bliss![177]

The Precept of *Order* requiring that *every Part of my Business should have its allotted Time,* one Page in my little Book contain'd the following Scheme of Employment for the Twenty-four Hours of a natural Day,

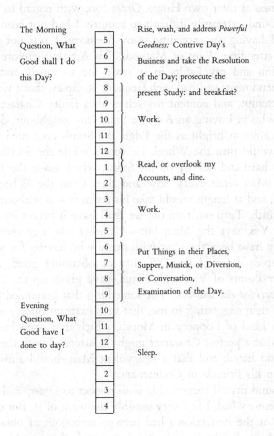

The Morning		
Question, What	5	Rise, wash, and address *Powerful*
Good shall I do	6	*Goodness*: Contrive Day's
this Day?	7	Business and take the Resolution of the Day; prosecute the present Study: and breakfast?
	8	
	9	
	10	Work.
	11	
	12	Read, or overlook my Accounts, and dine.
	1	
	2	
	3	Work.
	4	
	5	
	6	Put Things in their Places, Supper, Musick, or Diversion, or Conversation, Examination of the Day.
	7	
	8	
	9	
Evening	10	
Question, What	11	
Good have I	12	
done to day?	1	Sleep.
	2	
	3	
	4	

I enter'd upon the Execution of this Plan for Self Examination, and continu'd it with occasional Intermissions for some time. I was surpriz'd to find myself so much fuller of Faults than I had imagined, but I had the Satisfaction of seeing them diminish. To avoid the Trouble of renewing now and then my little Book, which

[177] James Thomson, *The Seasons* (1726), "Winter," ll. 218–223.

by scraping out the Marks on the Paper of old Faults to make room for new Ones in a new Course, became full of Holes: I transferr'd my Tables and Precepts to the Ivory Leaves of a Memorandum Book, on which the Lines were drawn with red Ink that made a durable Stain, and on those Lines I mark'd my Faults with a black Lead Pencil, which Marks I could easily wipe out with a wet Sponge. After a while I went thro' one Course only in a year, and afterwards only one in several Years, till at length I omitted them entirely, being employ'd in Voyages and Business abroad with a Multiplicity of Affairs, that interfered, but I always carried my little Book with me.

My Scheme of ORDER, gave me the most Trouble, and I found, that tho' it might be practicable where a Man's Business was such as to leave him the Disposition of his Time, that of a Journey-Man Printer for instance, it was not possible to be exactly observ'd by a Master, who must mix with the World, and often receive People of Business at their own Hours. *Order* too, with regard to Places for Things, Papers, &c. I found extreamly difficult to acquire. I had not been early accustomed to *Method,* and having an exceeding good Memory, I was not so sensible of the Inconvenience attending Want of Method. This Article therefore cost me so much painful Attention and my Faults in it vex'd me so much, and I made so little Progress in Amendment, and had such frequent Relapses, that I was almost ready to give up the Attempt, and content my self with a faulty Character in that respect. Like the Man who in buying an Ax of a Smith my neighbour, desired to have the whole of its Surface as bright as the Edge; the Smith consented to grind it bright for him if he would turn the Wheel. He turn'd while the Smith press'd the broad Face of the Ax hard and heavily on the Stone, which made the Turning of it very fatiguing. The Man came every now and then from the Wheel to see how the Work went on; and at length would take his Ax as it was without farther Grinding. No, says the Smith, Turn on, turn on; we shall have it bright by and by; as yet 'tis only speckled. Yes, says the Man; but—*I think I like a speckled Ax best.* And I believe this may have been the Case with many who having for want of some such Means as I employ'd found the Difficulty of obtaining good, and breaking bad Habits, in other Points of Vice and Virtue, have given up the Struggle, and concluded that *a speckled Ax was best.* For something that pretended to be Reason was every now and then suggesting to me, that such extream Nicety as I exacted of my self might be a kind of Foppery in Morals, which if it were known would make me ridiculous; that a perfect Character might be attended with the Inconvenience of being envied and hated; and that a benevolent Man should allow a few Faults in himself, to keep his Friends in Countenance.

In truth I found myself incorrigible with respect to *Order;* and now I am grown old, and my Memory bad, I feel very sensibly the want of it. But on the whole, tho' I never arrived at the Perfection I had been so ambitious of obtaining, but fell far short of it, yet I was by the Endeavour a better and a happier Man than I otherwise should have been, if I had not attempted it; As those who aim at perfect Writing by imitating the engraved Copies, tho' they never reach the wish'd for Excellence of those Copies, their Hand is mended by the Endeavour, and is tolerable while it continues fair and legible.

And it may be well my Posterity should be informed, that to this little Artifice, with the Blessing of God, their Ancestor ow'd the constant Felicity of his Life down to his 79th Year in which this is written. What Reverses may attend the Remainder is in the Hand of Providence: But if they arrive the Reflection on past Happiness enjoy'd ought to help his Bearing them with more Resignation. To *Temperance* he ascribes his long-continu'd Health, and what is still left to him of a good Constitution. To *Industry* and *Frugality* the early Easiness of his Circumstances, and Acquisition of his Fortune, with all that Knowledge which enabled him to be an useful Citizen, and obtain'd for him some Degree of Reputation among the Learned. To *Sincerity* and *Justice* the Confidence of his Country, and the honourable Employs it conferr'd upon him. And to the joint Influence of the whole Mass of the Virtues, even in the imperfect State he was able to acquire them, all that Evenness of Temper, and that Chearfulness in Conversation which makes his Company still sought for, and agreable even to his younger Acquaintance. I hope therefore that some of my Descendants may follow the Example and reap the Benefit.

It will be remark'd that, tho' my Scheme was not wholly without Religion there was in it no Mark of any of the distinguishing Tenets of any particular Sect. I had purposely avoided them; for being fully persuaded of the Utility and Excellency of my Method, and that it might be serviceable to People in all Religions, and intending some time or other to publish it, I would not have any thing in it that should prejudice any one of any Sect against it. I purposed writing a little Comment on each Virtue, in which I would have shown the Advantages of possessing it, and the Mischiefs attending its opposite Vice; and I should have called my Book the ART *of Virtue*, because it would have shown the *Means* and *Manner* of obtaining Virtue, which would have distinguish'd it from the mere Exhortation to be good, that does not instruct and indicate the Means; but is like the Apostle's Man of verbal Charity, who only, without showing to the Naked and the Hungry *how* or where they might get Cloaths or Victuals, exhorted them to be fed and clothed. *James* II, 15, 16.

But it so happened that my Intention of writing and publishing this Comment was never fulfilled. I did indeed, from time to time put down short Hints of the Sentiments, Reasonings, &c. to be made use of in it; some of which I have still by me: But the necessary close Attention to private Business in the earlier part of Life, and public Business since, have occasioned my postponing it. For it being connected in my Mind with a *great and extensive Project* that required the whole Man to execute, and which an unforeseen Succession of Employs prevented my attending to, it has hitherto remain'd unfinish'd.

In this Piece it was my Design to explain and enforce this Doctrine, that vicious Actions are not hurtful because they are forbidden, but forbidden because they are hurtful, the Nature of Man alone consider'd: That it was therefore every one's Interest to be virtuous, who wish'd to be happy even in this World. And I should from this Circumstance, there being always in the World a Number of rich Merchants, Nobility, States and Princes, who have need of honest Instruments for the Management of their Affairs, and such being so rare have endeavoured to convince young Persons, that no Qualities were so likely to make a poor Man's Fortune as those of Probity and Integrity.

My List of Virtues contain'd at first but twelve: But a Quaker Friend having kindly inform'd me that I was generally thought proud; that my Pride show'd itself frequently in Conversation; that I was not content with being in the right when discussing any Point, but was overbearing and rather insolent; of which he convinc'd me by mentioning several Instances; I determined endeavouring to cure myself if I could of this Vice or Folly among the rest, and I added *Humility* to my List, giving an extensive Meaning to the Word. I cannot boast of much Success in acquiring the *Reality* of this Virtue; but I had a good deal with regard to the *Appearance* of it. I made it a Rule to forbear all direct Contradiction to the Sentiments of others, and all positive Assertion of my own. I even forbid my self agreable to the old Laws of our Junto, the Use of every Word or Expression in the Language that imported a fix'd Opinion; such as *certainly, undoubtedly,* &c. and I adopted instead of them, *I conceive, I apprehend,* or *I imagine* a thing to be so or so, or it so appears to me at present. When another asserted something, that I thought an Error, I deny'd my self the Pleasure of contradicting him abruptly, and of showing immediately some Absurdity in his Proposition; and in answering I began by observing that in certain Cases or Circumstances his Opinion would be right, but that in the present case there appear'd or seem'd to me some Difference, &c. I soon found the Advantage of this Change in my Manners. The Conversations I engag'd in went on more pleasantly. The modest way in which I propos'd my Opinions, procur'd them a readier Reception and less Contradiction; I had less Mortification when I was found to be in the wrong, and I more easily prevail'd with others to give up their Mistakes and join with me when I happen'd to be in the right. And this Mode, which I at first put on, with some violence to natural Inclination, became at length so easy and so habitual to me, that perhaps for these Fifty Years past no one has ever heard a dogmatical Expression escape me. And to this Habit (after my Character of Integrity) I think it principally owing, that I had early so much Weight with my Fellow Citizens, when I proposed new Institutions, or Alterations in the old; and so much Influence in public Councils when I became a Member. For I was but a bad Speaker, never eloquent, subject to much Hesitation in my choice of Words, hardly correct in Language, and yet I generally carried my Points.

In reality there is perhaps no one of our natural Passions so hard to subdue as *Pride.* Disguise it, struggle with it, beat it down, stifle it, mortify it as much as one pleases, it is still alive, and will every now and then peep out and show itself. You will see it perhaps often in this History. For even if I could conceive that I had compleatly overcome it, I should probably by [be] proud of my Humility.

Thus far written at Passy 1784

1784/1818

Silence Dogood, No. 7[*]

Give me the Muse, whose generous Force,
Impatient of the Reins,
Pursues an unattempted Course,
Breaks all the Criticks Iron Chains.
Watts[1]

To the Author of the *New-England Courant.*

Sir,

It has been the Complaint of many Ingenious Foreigners, who have travell'd amongst us, *That good Poetry is not to be expected in New-England.* I am apt to Fancy, the Reason is, not because our Countreymen are altogether void of a Poetical Genius, nor yet because we have not those Advantages of Education which other Countries have, but purely because we do not afford that Praise and Encouragement which is merited, when any thing extraordinary of this Kind is produc'd among us: Upon which Consideration I have determined, when I meet with a Good Piece of New-England Poetry, to give it a suitable Encomium, and thereby endeavour to discover to the World some of its Beautys, in order to encourage the Author to go on, and bless the World with more, and more Excellent Productions.

There has lately appear'd among us a most Excellent Piece of Poetry, entituled, *An Elegy upon the much Lamented Death of Mrs. Mehitebell Kitel, Wife of Mr. John Kitel of Salem, &c.* It may justly be said in its Praise, without Flattery to the Author, that it is the most Extraordinary Piece that ever was wrote in New-England. The Language is so soft and Easy, the Expression so moving and pathetick, but above all, the Verse and Numbers so Charming and Natural, that it is almost beyond Comparison,

> The Muse disdains
> Those Links and Chains,
> Measures and Rules of vulgar Strains,
> And o'er the Laws of Harmony a Sovereign Queen she reigns.[2]

I find no English Author, Ancient or Modern, whose Elegies may be compar'd with this, in respect to the Elegance of Stile, or Smoothness of Rhime; and for the affecting Part, I will leave your Readers to judge, if ever they read any Lines, that would sooner make them *draw their Breath* and Sigh, if not shed Tears, than these following.

> Come let us mourn, for we have lost a Wife, a Daughter, and a Sister,
> Who has lately taken Flight, and greatly we have mist her.

In another Place,

---

[*] Published in *The New England Courant*, June 25, 1722.

[1] Isaac Watts, *The Adventurous Muse* (1709).
[2] Watts, *The Adventurous Muse.*

Some little Time before she yielded up her Breath,
She said, I ne'er shall hear one Sermon more on Earth.
She kist her Husband *some little Time* before she expir'd,
Then lean'd her Head the Pillow on, just out of Breath and tir'd.

But the Threefold Appellation in the first Line

a Wife, a Daughter, and a Sister,

must not pass unobserved. That Line in the celebrated Watts,

GUNSTON the Just, the Generous, and the Young,

is nothing Comparable to it. The latter only mentions three Qualifications of *one* Person who was deceased, which therefore could raise Grief and Compassion but for *One.* Whereas the former, *(our most excellent Poet)* gives his Reader a Sort of an Idea of the Death of *Three Persons,* viz.

a Wife, a Daughter, and a Sister,

which is *Three Times* as great a Loss as the Death of *One,* and consequently must raise *Three Times* as much Grief and Compassion in the Reader.

I should be very much straitned for Room, if I should attempt to discover even half the Excellencies of this Elegy which are obvious to me. Yet I cannot omit one Observation, which is, that the Author has (to his Honour) invented a new Species of Poetry, which wants a Name, and was never before known. His Muse scorns to be confin'd to the old Measures and Limits, or to observe the dull Rules of Criticks;

Nor Rapin gives her Rules to fly, nor Purcell Notes to sing. *Watts.*

Now 'tis Pity that such an Excellent Piece should not be dignify'd with a particular Name; and seeing it cannot justly be called, either *Epic, Sapphic, Lyric,* or *Pindaric,* nor any other Name yet invented, I presume it may, (in Honour and Remembrance of the Dead) be called the KITELIC. Thus much in the Praise of *Kitelic Poetry.*

It is certain, that those Elegies which are of our own Growth, (and our Soil seldom produces any other sort of Poetry) are by far the greatest part, wretchedly Dull and Ridiculous. Now since it is imagin'd by many, that our Poets are honest, well-meaning Fellows, who do their best, and that if they had but some Instructions how to govern Fancy with Judgment, they would make indifferent good Elegies; I shall here subjoin a Receipt for that purpose, which was left me as a Legacy, (among other valuable Rarities) by my Reverent Husband. It is as follows,

A RECEIPT to make a New-England Funeral ELEGY.

For the Title of your Elegy. Of these you may have enough ready made to your Hands; but if you should chuse to make it your self, you must be sure not to omit the Words *Aetatis Suae,*[3] which will Beautify it exceedingly.

---

[3] Latin: "Of His Age," a convention of Puritan elegies, usually abbreviated *Aet.*

For the Subject of your Elegy. Take one of your Neighbours who has lately departed this Life; it is no great matter at what Age the Party dy'd, but it will be best if he went away suddenly, being *Kill'd, Drown'd,* or *Froze to Death.*

Having chose the Person, take all his Virtues, Excellencies, &c. and if he have not enough, you may borrow some to make up a sufficient Quantity: To these add his last Words, dying Expressions, &c. if they are to be had; mix all these together, and be sure you *strain* them well. Then season all with a Handful or two of Melancholly Expressions, such as, *Dreadful, Deadly, cruel cold Death, unhappy Fate, weeping Eyes,* &c. Have mixed all these Ingredients well, put them into the empty Scull of some *young Harvard;* (but in Case you have ne'er a One at Hand, you may use your own,) there let them Ferment for the Space of a Fortnight, and by that Time they will be incorporated into a Body, which take out, and having prepared a sufficient Quantity of double Rhimes, such as, *Power, Flower; Quiver, Shiver; Grieve us, Leave us; tell you, excel you; Expeditions, Physicians; Fatigue him, Intrigue him;* &c. you must spread all upon Paper, and if you can procure a Scrap of Latin to put at the End, it will garnish it mightily; then having affixed your Name at the Bottom, with a *Mœstus Composuit,*[4] you will have an Excellent Elegy.

N.B. This Receipt will serve when a Female is the Subject of your Elegy, provided you borrow a greater Quantity of Virtues, Excellencies, &c. Sir, Your Servant,

SILENCE DOGOOD

1722/1722

A Witch Trial at Mount Holly[*]

BURLINGTON, Oct. 12. Saturday last at Mount-Holly, about 8 Miles from this Place,[1] near 300 People were gathered together to see an Experiment or two tried on some Persons accused of Witchcraft. It seems the Accused had been charged with making their Neighbours Sheep dance in an uncommon Manner, and with causing Hogs to speak, and sing Psalms, &c. to the great Terror and Amazement of the King's good and peaceable Subjects in this Province; and the Accusers being very positive that if the Accused were weighed in Scales against a Bible, the Bible would prove too heavy for them; or that, if they were bound and put into the River, they would swim; the said Accused desirous to make their Innocence appear, voluntarily offered to undergo the said Trials, if 2 of the most violent of their Accusers would be tried with them. Accordingly the Time and Place was agreed on, and advertised about the Country; The Accusers were 1 Man and 1 Woman; and the Accused the same. The Parties being met, and the People got together, a grand Consultation was held, before they proceeded to Trial; in which it was agreed to use the Scales first; and a Committee of

---

[4] Latin: "Sorrowfully Composed," another elegaic convention.
[*] Published in the *Pennsylvania Gazette,* October 22, 1730. Although no external evidence proves that Franklin wrote this hoax, it is traditionally included in his collected works.
[1] Franklin's note: "Burlington, New Jersey."

Men were appointed to search the Men, and a Committee of Women to search the Women, to see if they had any Thing of Weight about them, particularly Pins. After the Scrutiny was over, a huge great Bible belonging to the Justice of the Place was provided, and a Lane through the Populace was made from the Justices House to the Scales, which were fixed on a Gallows erected for that Purpose opposite to the House, that the Justices Wife and the rest of the Ladies might see the Trial, without coming amongst the Mob; and after the Manner of Moorfields, a large Ring was also made. Then came out of the House a grave tall Man carrying the Holy Writ before the supposed Wizard, &c. (as solemnly as the Sword-Bearer of London before the Lord Mayor) the Wizard was first put in the Scale, and over him was read a Chapter out of the Books of Moses, and then the Bible was put in the other Scale, (which being kept down before) was immediately let go; but to the great Surprize of the Spectators, Flesh and Bones came down plump, and outweighed that great good Book by abundance. After the same Manner, the others were served, and their Lumps of Mortality severally were too heavy for Moses and all the Prophets and Apostles. This being over, the Accusers and the rest of the Mob, not satisfied with this Experiment, would have the Trial by Water; accordingly a most solemn Procession was made to the Mill-pond; where both Accused and Accusers being stripp'd (saving only to the Women their Shifts) were bound Hand and Foot, and severally placed in the Water, lengthways, from the Side of a Barge or Flat, having for Security only a Rope about the Middle of each, which was held by some in the Flat. The Accuser Man being thin and spare, with some Difficulty began to sink at last; but the rest every one of them swam very light upon the Water. A Sailor in the Flat jump'd out upon the Back of the Man accused, thinking to drive him down to the Bottom, but the Person bound, without any Help, came up some time before the other. The Woman Accuser, being told that she did not sink, would be duck'd a second Time; when she swam again as light as before. Upon which she declared, That she believed the Accused had be-witched her to make her so light, and that she would be duck'd again a Hundred Times, but she would duck the devil out of her. The accused Man, being surpriz'd at his own Swimming, was not so confident of his Innocence as before, but said, *If I am a Witch, it is more than I know.* The more thinking Part of the Spectators were of Opinion, that any Person so bound and plac'd in the Water (unless they were mere Skin and Bones) would swim till their Breath was gone, and their Lungs fill'd with Water. But it being the general Belief of the Populace, that the Womens Shifts, and the Garters with which they were bound help'd to support them; it is said they are to be tried again the next warm Weather, naked.

1730

On Literary Style[*]

To the Printer of the *Gazette.*

There are few Men, of Capacity for making any considerable Figure in Life, who have not frequent Occasion to communicate their Thoughts to others in *Writing;* if not sometimes publickly as Authors, yet continually in the Management of their private Affairs, both of Business and Friendship: and since, when ill-express'd, the most proper Sentiments and justest Reasoning lose much of their native Force and Beauty, it seems to me that there is scarce any Accomplishment more necessary to a Man of Sense, than that of *Writing well* in his Mother Tongue: But as most other polite Acquirements, make a greater Appearance in a Man's Character, this however useful, is generally neglected or forgotten.

I believe there is no better Means of learning to write well, than this of attempting to entertain the Publick now and then in one of your Papers. When the Writer conceals himself, he has the Advantage of hearing the Censure both of Friends and Enemies, express'd with more Impartiality. And since, in some degree, it concerns the Credit of the Province, that such Things as are printed be performed tolerably well, mutual Improvement seems to be the Duty of all Lovers of Writing: I shall therefore frankly communicate the Observations I have made or collected on this Subject, and request those of others in Return.

I have thought in general, that whoever would write so as not to displease good Judges, should have particular Regard to these Three things, viz. That his Performance be *smooth, clear,* and *short:* For the contrary Qualities are apt to offend, either the Ear, the Understanding, or the Patience.

'Tis an Observation of Dr. Swift,[1] that modern Writers injure the Smoothness of our Tongue, by omitting Vowels wherever it is possible, and joining the harshest Consonants together with only an Apostrophe between; thus for *judged,* in it self not the smoothest of Words, they say *judg'd;* for *disturbed, disturb'd,* &c. It may be added to this, says another, that by changing *etb* into *s,* they have shortned one Syllable in a multitude of Words, and have thereby encreased, not only the *Hissing,* too offensive before, but also the great Number of Monosyllables, of which, without great Difficulty, a smooth Sentence cannot be composed. The Smoothness of a Period is also often Hurt by Parentheses, and therefore the best Writers endeavour to avoid them.

To write *clearly,* not only the most expressive, but the plainest Words should be chosen. In this, as well as in every other Particular requisite to Clearness,

---

[*] Published in the *Pennsylvania Gazette,* August 2, 1733. Franklin in 1727 "form'd most of [his] ingenious Acquaintances into a Club for mutual Improvement, which [they] called the Junto." The rules, as Franklin states in his *Autobiography,* "requir'd that every Member in his Turn should produce one or more Queries on any Point of Morals, Politics or Natural Philosophy, to be discuss'd by the Company, and once in three Months pronounce and read an Essay of his own Writing on any Subject he pleased." "On Literary Style" was one of Franklin's many contributions to the Junto Club.

[1] Jonathan Swift (1667–1745), Irish-born satirist and poet, who advocated a clear and cogent style of writing.

Dr. Tillotson[2] is an excellent Example. The Fondness of some Writers for such Words as carry with them an Air of Learning, renders them unintelligible to more than half their Countrymen. If a Man would that his Writings have an Effect on the Generality of Readers, he had better imitate that Gentleman, who would use no Word in his Works that was not well understood by his Cook-maid.

A too frequent Use of Phrases ought likewise to be avoided by him that would write clearly. They trouble the Language, not only rendring it extreamly difficult to Foreigners, but make the Meaning obscure to a great number of English Readers. Phrases, like learned Words, are seldom used without Affectation; when, with all true Judges, the simplest Stile is the most beautiful.

But supposing the most proper Words and Expressions chosen, the Performance may yet be weak and obscure, if it has not *Method.* If a Writer would *persuade,* he should proceed gradually from Things already allow'd, to those from which Assent is yet with-held, and make their Connection manifest. If he would *inform,* he must advance regularly from Things known to things unknown, distinctly without Confusion, and the lower he begins the better. It is a common Fault in Writers, to allow their Readers too much Knowledge: They begin with that which should be the Middle, and skipping backwards and forwards, 'tis impossible for any one but he who is perfect in the Subject before, to understand their Work, and such an one has no Occasion to read it. Perhaps a Habit of using good Method, cannot be better acquired, than by learning a little Geometry or Algebra.

Amplification, or the Art of saying Little in Much, should only be allowed to Speakers. If they preach, a Discourse of considerable Length is expected from them, upon every Subject they undertake, and perhaps they are not stock'd with naked Thoughts sufficient to furnish it out. If they plead in the Courts, it is of Use to speak abundance, tho' they reason little; for the Ignorant in a Jury, can scarcely believe it possible that a Man can talk so much and so long without being in the Right. Let them have the Liberty then, of repeating the same Sentences in other Words; let them put an Adjective to every Substantive, and double every Substantive with a Synonima; for this is more agreeable than hauking, spitting, taking Snuff, or any other Means of concealing Hesitation. Let them multiply Definitions, Comparisons, Similitudes and Examples. Permit them to make a Detail of Causes and Effects, enumerate all the Consequences, and express one Half by Metaphor and Circumlocution: Nay, allow the Preacher to tell us whatever a Thing is negatively, before he begins to tell us what it is affirmatively; and suffer him to divide and subdivide as far as *Two and fiftiethly.* All this is not intolerable while it is not written. But when a Discourse is to be bound down upon Paper, and subjected to the calm leisurely Examination of nice Judgment, every Thing that is needless gives Offence; and therefore all should be retrenched, that does not directly conduce to the End design'd. Had this been always done, many large and tiresome Folio's would have shrunk into Pamphlets, and many a Pamphlet into a single Period. However, tho' a multitude of Words obscure the Sense, and 'tis necessary to abridge a verbose Author in order to understand him; yet a Writer should take especial Care on the other Hand, that his Brevity doth not hurt his Perspicuity.

---

[2] John Tillotson (1630–1694), English archbishop, whose *Sermons* were collected between 1695 and 1704.

After all, if the Author does not intend his Piece for general Reading, he must exactly suit his Stile and Manner to the particular Taste of those he proposes for his Readers. Every one observes, the different Ways of Writing and Expression used by the different Sects of Religion; and can readily enough pronounce, that it is improper to use some of these Stiles in common, or to use the common Stile, when we address some of these Sects in particular.

To conclude, I shall venture to lay it down as a Maxim, *that no Piece can properly be called good, and well written, which is void of any Tendency to benefit the Reader, either by improving his Virtue or his Knowledge.* This Principle every Writer would do well to have in View, whenever he undertakes to write. All Performances done for meer Ostentation of Parts, are really contemptible; and withal far more subject to the Severity of Criticism, than those more meanly written, wherein the Author appears to have aimed at the Good of others. For when 'tis visible to every one, that a Man writes to show his Wit only, all his Expressions are sifted, and his Sense examined, in the nicest and most ill-natur'd manner; and every one is glad of an Opportunity to mortify him. But, what a vast Destruction would there be of Books, if they were to be saved or condemned on a Tryal by this Rule!

Besides, Pieces meerly humorous, are of all Sorts the hardest to succeed in. If they are not natural, they are stark naught; and there can be no real Humour in an Affectation of Humour.

Perhaps it may be said, that an ill Man is able to write an ill Thing well; that is, having an ill Design, and considering who are to be his Readers, he may use the properest Stile and Arguments to attain his Point. In this Sense, that is best wrote, which is best adapted to the Purpose of the Writer.

I am apprehensive, dear Readers, lest in this Piece, I should be guilty of every Fault I condemn, and deficient in every Thing I recommend; so much easier it is to offer Rules than to practise them. I am sure, however, of this, that I am Your very sincere Friend and Servant.

1733

---

from Poor Richard Improved, 1758[*]

[Father Abraham's Speech; or The Way to Wealth]

Courteous Reader,

I have heard that nothing gives an Author so great Pleasure, as to find his Works respectfully quoted by other learned Authors. This Pleasure I have seldom enjoyed; for tho' I have been, if I may say it without Vanity, an *eminent Author* of Almanacks

---

[*] Franklin's note from the *Autobiography,* Part III: "In 1732 I first published my Almanack, under the Name of *Richard Saunders;* it was continu'd by me about 25 Years, commonly call'd *Poor Richard's* Almanack. I endeavour'd to make it both entertaining and useful, and it accordingly came to be in such Demand that I reap'd considerable Profit from it, vending annually near ten Thousand. And observing that it was generally read, scarce any Neighbourhood in the

(continued)

annually now a full Quarter of a Century, my Brother Authors in the same Way, for what Reason I know not, have ever been very sparing in their Applauses; and no other Author has taken the least Notice of me, so that did not my Writings produce me some solid *Pudding,* the great Deficiency of *Praise* would have quite discouraged me.

I concluded at length, that the People were the best Judges of my Merit; for they buy my Works; and besides, in my Rambles, where I am not personally known, I have frequently heard one or other of my Adages repeated, with, *as Poor Richard says,* at the End on't; this gave me some Satisfaction, as it showed not only that my Instructions were regarded, but discovered likewise some Respect for my Authority; and I own, that to encourage the Practice of remembering and repeating those wise Sentences, I have sometimes *quoted myself* with great Gravity.

Judge then how much I must have been gratified by an Incident I am going to relate to you. I stopt my Horse lately where a great Number of People were collected at a Vendue of Merchant Goods. The Hour of Sale not being come, they were conversing on the Badness of the Times, and one of the Company call'd to a plain clean old Man, with white Locks, *Pray, Father Abraham, what think you of the Times? Won't these heavy Taxes quite ruin the Country? How shall we be ever able to pay them? What would you advise us to?*—Father Abraham stood up, and reply'd, If you'd have my Advice, I'll give it you in short, for a *Word to the Wise is enough,* and *many Words won't fill a Bushel,* as *Poor Richard says.* They join'd in desiring him to speak his Mind, and gathering round him, he proceeded as follows;

"Friends, says he, and Neighbours, the Taxes are indeed very heavy, and if those laid on by the Government were the only Ones we had to pay, we might more easily discharge them; but we have many others, and much more grievous to some of us. We are taxed twice as much by our *Idleness,* three times as much by our *Pride,* and four times as much by our *Folly,* and from these Taxes the Commissioners cannot ease or deliver us by allowing an Abatement. However let us hearken to good Advice,

Province being without it, I consider'd it as a proper Vehicle for conveying Instruction among the common People, who bought scarce any other Books. I therefore filled all the little Spaces that occurr'd between the Remarkable Days in the Calendar, with Proverbial Sentences, chiefly such as inculcated Industry and Frugality, as the Means of procuring Wealth and thereby securing Virtue, it being more difficult for a Man in Want to act always honestly, as (to use here one of those Proverbs) *it is hard for an empty Sack to stand upright.* These Proverbs, which contained the Wisdom of many Ages and Nations, I assembled and form'd into a connected Discourse prefix'd to the Almanack of 1757, as the Harangue of a wise old Man to the People attending an Auction. The bringing all these scatter'd Counsels thus into a Focus, enabled them to make greater Impression. The Piece being universally approved was copied in all the Newspapers of the Continent, reprinted in Britain on a Broadside to be stuck up in

Houses, two Translations were made of it in French, and great Numbers bought by the Clergy and Gentry to distribute gratis among their poor Parishioners and Tenants. In Pennsylvania, as it discouraged useless Expence in foreign Superfluities, some thought it had its share of Influence in producing that growing Plenty of Money which was observable for several Years after its Publication. . . ."

In 1748 Franklin enlarged his successful *Poor Richard's Almanack* and changed its title to *Poor Richard Improved.* For the 1758 edition, the twenty-sixth and last prepared under his supervision, Franklin invented the character Father Abraham, "a plain clean old Man, with white Locks," who in a long speech distills all of the aphoristic wisdom relating to hard work, prudence, and thrift contained in the earlier versions of the *Almanack.* This enormously popular preface, variously known as *Father Abraham's Speech* and *The Way to Wealth,* went through at least 145 printings before the end of the eighteenth century.

and something may be done for us; *God helps them that help themselves,* as Poor Richard says, in his Almanack of 1733.

It would be thought a hard Government that should tax its People one tenth Part of their *Time,* to be employed in its Service. But *Idleness* taxes many of us much more, if we reckon all that is spent in absolute *Sloth,* or doing of nothing, with that which is spent in idle Employments or Amusements, that amount to nothing. *Sloth,* by bringing on Diseases, absolutely shortens Life. *Sloth, like Rust, consumes faster than Labour wears, while the used Key is always bright,* as Poor Richard says. But *dost thou love Life, then do not squander Time, for that's the Stuff Life is made of,* as Poor Richard says. How much more than is necessary do we spend in Sleep! forgetting that *The sleeping Fox catches no Poultry,* and that *there will be sleeping enough in the Grave,* as Poor Richard says. If Time be of all Things the most precious, *wasting Time* must be, as Poor Richard says, *the greatest Prodigality,* since, as he elsewhere tells us, *Lost Time is never found again;* and what we call *Time-enough, always proves little enough:* Let us then be up and be doing, and doing to the Purpose; so by Diligence shall we do more with less Perplexity. *Sloth makes all Things difficult, but Industry all easy,* as Poor Richard says; and *He that riseth late, must trot all Day, and shall scarce overtake his Business at Night.* While *Laziness travels so slowly, that Poverty soon overtakes him,* as we read in Poor Richard, who adds, *Drive thy Business, let not that drive thee;* and *Early to Bed, and early to rise, makes a Man healthy, wealthy and wise.*

So what signifies *wishing* and *hoping* for better Times. We may make these Times better if we bestir ourselves. *Industry need not wish,* as Poor Richard says, and *He that lives upon Hope will die fasting. There are no Gains, without Pains;* then *Help Hands, for I have no Lands,* or if I have, they are smartly taxed. And, as Poor Richard likewise observes, *He that hath a Trade hath an Estate,* and *He that hath a Calling hath an Office of Profit and Honour;* but then the *Trade* must be worked at, and the *Calling* well followed, or neither the *Estate,* nor the *Office,* will enable us to pay our Taxes. If we are industrious we shall never starve; for, as Poor Richard says, *At the working Man's House Hunger looks in, but dares not enter.* Nor will the Bailiff nor the Constable enter, for *Industry pays Debts, while Despair encreaseth them,* says Poor Richard. What though you have found no Treasure, nor has any rich Relation left you a Legacy, *Diligence is the Mother of Good luck,* as Poor Richard says, and *God gives all Things to Industry.* Then *plough deep, while Sluggards sleep, and you shall have Corn to sell and to keep,* says Poor Dick. Work while it is called To-day, for you know not how much you may be hindered To-morrow, which makes Poor Richard say, *One To-day is worth two To-morrows;* and farther, *Have you somewhat to do To-morrow, do it To-day.* If you were a Servant, would you not be ashamed that a good Master should catch you idle? Are you then your own Master, *be ashamed to catch yourself idle,* as Poor Dick says. When there is so much to be done for yourself, your Family, your Country, and your gracious King, be up by Peep of Day; *Let not the Sun look down and say, Inglorious here he lies.* Handle your Tools without Mittens; remember that *the Cat in Gloves catches no Mice,* as Poor Richard says. 'Tis true there is much to be done, and perhaps you are weak handed, but stick to it steadily, and you will see great Effects, for *constant Dropping wears away Stones,* and by *Diligence and Patience the Mouse ate in two the Cable;* and *little Strokes fell great Oaks,* as Poor Richard says in his Almanack, the Year I cannot just now remember.

Methinks I hear some of you say, *Must a Man afford himself no Leisure?* I will tell thee, my Friend, what Poor Richard says, *Employ thy Time well if thou meanest to gain Leisure;* and, *since thou art not sure of a Minute, throw not away an Hour.* Leisure, is Time for doing something useful; this Leisure the diligent Man will obtain, but the lazy Man never; so that, as Poor Richard says, a *Life of Leisure and a Life of Laziness are two Things.* Do you imagine that Sloth will afford you more Comfort than Labour? No, for as Poor Richard says, *Trouble springs from Idleness, and grievous Toil from needless Ease. Many without Labour, would live by their WITS only, but they break for want of Stock.* Whereas Industry gives Comfort, and Plenty, and Respect: *Fly Pleasures, and they'll follow you. The diligent Spinner has a large Shift;*[1] and *now I have a Sheep and a Cow, every Body bids me Good morrow;* all which is well said by Poor Richard.

But with our Industry, we must likewise be *steady, settled* and *careful,* and oversee our own Affairs *with our own Eyes,* and not trust too much to others; for, as Poor Richard says,

> I never saw an oft removed Tree,
> Nor yet an oft removed Family,
> That throve so well as those that settled be.

And again, *Three Removes*[2] *is as bad as a Fire;* and again, *Keep thy Shop, and thy Shop will keep thee;* and again, *If you would have your Business done, go; If not, send.* And again,

> He that by the Plough would thrive,
> Himself must either hold or drive.

And again, *The Eye of a Master will do more Work than both his Hands;* and again, *Want of Care does us more Damage than Want of Knowledge;* and again, *Not to oversee Workmen, is to leave them your Purse open.* Trusting too much to others Care is the Ruin of many; for, as the Almanack says, *In the Affairs of this World, Men are saved, not by Faith, but by the Want of it;* but a Man's own Care is profitable; for, saith Poor Dick, *Learning is to the Studious,* and *Riches to the Careful,* as well as *Power to the Bold,* and *Heaven to the Virtuous.* And farther, *If you would have a faithful Servant, and one that you like, serve yourself.* And again, he adviseth to Circumspection and Care, even in the smallest Matters, because sometimes *a little Neglect may breed great Mischief;* adding, *For want of a Nail the Shoe was lost; for want of a Shoe the Horse was lost; and for want of a Horse the Rider was lost,* being overtaken and slain by the Enemy, all for want of Care about a Horse-shoe Nail.

So much for Industry, my Friends, and Attention to one's own Business; but to these we must add *Frugality,* if we would make our *Industry* more certainly successful. A Man may, if he knows not how to save as he gets, *keep his Nose all his Life to the Grindstone,* and die not worth a *Groat*[3] at last. *A fat Kitchen makes a lean Will,* as Poor Richard says; and,

---

[1] Wardrobe.
[2] Moves.
[3] About four pence.

Many Estates are spent in the Getting,
Since Women for Tea forsook Spinning and Knitting,
And Men for Punch forsook Hewing and Splitting.

If you would be wealthy, says he, in another Almanack, *think of Saving as well as of Getting: the Indies have not made Spain rich, because her* Outgoes *are greater than her* Incomes. Away then with your expensive Follies, and you will not have so much Cause to complain of hard Times, heavy Taxes, and chargeable Families; for, as Poor Dick says,

Women and Wine, Game and Deceit,
Make the Wealth small, and the Wants great.

And farther, *What maintains one Vice, would bring up two Children.* You may think perhaps, That a *little* Tea, or a *little* Punch now and then, Diet a *little* more costly, Clothes a *little* finer, and a *little* Entertainment now and then, can be no *great* Matter; but remember what Poor Richard says, *Many* a Little *makes a Mickle;*[4] and farther, *Beware of* little Expences; *a small Leak will sink a great Ship;* and again, *Who Dainties love, shall Beggars prove;* and moreover, *Fools make Feasts, and wise Men eat them.* Here you are all got together at this Vendue of *Fineries* and *Knicknacks.* You call them *Goods,* but if you do not take Care, they will prove *Evils* to some of you. You expect they will be sold *cheap,* and perhaps they may for less than they cost; but if you have no Occasion for them, they must be *dear* to you. Remember what Poor Richard says, *Buy what thou hast no Need of, and ere long thou shalt sell thy Necessaries.* And again, *At a great Pennyworth pause a while:* He means, that perhaps the Cheapness is *apparent* only, and not *real;* or the Bargain, by straitning thee in thy Business, may do thee more Harm than Good. For in another Place he says, *Many have been ruined by buying good Pennyworths.* Again, Poor Richard says, *'Tis foolish to lay out Money in a Purchase of Repentance;* and yet this Folly is practised every Day at Vendues, for want of minding the Almanack. *Wise Men,* as Poor Dick says, *learn by others Harms, Fools scarcely by their own;* but, *Felix quem faciunt aliena Pericula cautum.*[5] Many a one, for the Sake of Finery on the Back, have gone with a hungry Belly, and half starved their Families; *Silks and Sattins, Scarlet and Velvets,* as Poor Richard says, *put out the Kitchen Fire.* These are not the *Necessaries* of Life; they can scarcely be called the *Conveniencies,* and yet only because they look pretty, how many *want* to *have* them. The *artificial* Wants of Mankind thus become more numerous than the *natural;* and, as Poor Dick says, *For one* poor *Person, there are an hundred* indigent. By these, and other Extravagancies, the Genteel are reduced to Poverty, and forced to borrow of those whom they formerly despised, but who through *Industry* and *Frugality* have maintained their Standing; in which Case it appears plainly, that a *Ploughman on his Legs is higher than a Gentleman on his Knees,* as Poor Richard says. Perhaps they have had a small Estate left them, which they knew not the Getting of; they think *'tis Day, and will never be Night;* that a little to be spent out of *so much,* is not worth minding; (*a Child and a Fool,* as Poor Richard says, *imagine Twenty Shillings and Twenty Years*

---

[4] Lot.
[5] Latin: "They are fortunate who have been made wary by the misfortunes of others."

can never be spent) but, *always taking out of the Meal-tub, and never putting in, soon comes to the Bottom;* then, as Poor Dick says, *When the Well's dry, they know the Worth of Water.* But this they might have known before, if they had taken his Advice; *If you would know the Value of Money, go and try to borrow some;* for, *he that goes a borrowing goes a sorrowing;* and indeed so does he that lends to such People, when he goes *to get it in again.* Poor Dick farther advises, and says,

> Fond *Pride of Dress,* is sure a very Curse;
> E'er *Fancy* you consult, consult your Purse.

And again, *Pride is as loud a Beggar as Want, and a great deal more saucy.* When you have bought one fine Thing you must buy ten more, that your Appearance may be all of a Piece; but Poor Dick says, *'Tis easier to suppress the first Desire, than to satisfy all that follow it.* And 'tis as truly Folly for the Poor to ape the Rich, as for the Frog to swell, in order to equal the Ox.

> Great Estates may venture more,
> But little Boats should keep near Shore.

'Tis however a Folly soon punished; for *Pride that dines on Vanity sups on Contempt,* as Poor Richard says. And in another Place, *Pride breakfasted with Plenty, dined with Poverty, and supped with Infamy.* And after all, of what Use is this *Pride of Appearance,* for which so much is risked, so much is suffered? It cannot promote Health, or ease Pain; it makes no Increase of Merit in the Person, it creates Envy, it hastens Misfortune.

> What is a Butterfly? At best
> He's but a Caterpillar drest.
> The gaudy Fop's his Picture just,

as Poor Richard says.

But what Madness must it be to *run in Debt* for these Superfluities! We are offered, by the Terms of this Vendue, *Six Months Credit;* and that perhaps has induced some of us to attend it, because we cannot spare the ready Money, and hope now to be fine without it. But, ah, think what you do when you run in Debt; *You give to another Power over your Liberty.* If you cannot pay at the Time, you will be ashamed to see your Creditor; you will be in Fear when you speak to him; you will make poor pitiful sneaking Excuses, and by Degrees come to lose your Veracity, and sink into base downright lying; for, as Poor Richard says, *The second Vice is Lying, the first is running in Debt.* And again, to the same Purpose, *Lying rides upon Debt's Back.* Whereas a freeborn Englishman ought not to be ashamed or afraid to see or speak to any Man living. But Poverty often deprives a Man of all Spirit and Virtue: *'Tis hard for an empty Bag to stand upright,* as Poor Richard truly says. What would you think of that Prince, or that Government, who should issue an Edict forbidding you to dress like a Gentleman or a Gentlewoman, on Pain of Imprisonment or Servitude? Would you not say, that you are free, have a Right to dress as you please, and that such an Edict would be a Breach of your Privileges, and such a Government tyrannical? And yet you are about to put yourself under that Tyranny when you run in Debt for such

Dress! Your Creditor has Authority at his Pleasure to deprive you of your Liberty, by confining you in Goal for Life, or to sell you for a Servant, if you should not be able to pay him! When you have got your Bargain, you may, perhaps, think little of Payment; but *Creditors,* Poor Richard tells us, *have better Memories than Debtors;* and in another Place says, *Creditors are a superstitious Sect, great Observers of set Days and Times.* The Day comes round before you are aware, and the Demand is made before you are prepared to satisfy it. Or if you bear your Debt in Mind, the Term which at first seemed so long, will, as it lessens, appear extreamly short. *Time* will seem to have added Wings to his Heels as well as Shoulders. *Those have a short Lent,* saith Poor Richard, *who owe Money to be paid at Easter.* Then since, as he says, *The Borrower is a Slave to the Lender, and the Debtor to the Creditor,* disdain the Chain, preserve your Freedom; and maintain your Independency: Be *industrious* and *free;* be *frugal* and *free.* At present, perhaps, you may think yourself in thriving Circumstances, and that you can bear a little Extravagance without Injury; but,

For Age and Want, save while you may;
No Morning Sun lasts a whole Day,

as Poor Richard says. Gain may be temporary and uncertain, but ever while you live, Expence is constant and certain; and *'tis easier to build two Chimnies than to keep one in Fuel,* as Poor Richard says. So *rather go to Bed supperless than rise in Debt.*

Get what you can, and what you get hold;
'Tis the Stone that will turn all your Lead into Gold,

as Poor Richard says. And when you have got the Philosopher's Stone,[6] sure you will no longer complain of bad Times, or the Difficulty of paying Taxes.

This Doctrine, my Friends, is *Reason* and *Wisdom;* but after all, do not depend too much upon your own *Industry,* and *Frugality,* and *Prudence,* though excellent Things, for they may all be blasted without the Blessing of Heaven; and therefore ask that Blessing humbly, and be not uncharitable to those that at present seem to want it, but comfort and help them. Remember Job suffered, and was afterwards prosperous.

And now to conclude, *Experience keeps a dear School, but Fools will learn in no other, and scarce in that;* for it is true, *we may give Advice, but we cannot give Conduct,* as Poor Richard says: However, remember this, *They that won't be counselled, can't be helped,* as Poor Richard says: And farther, That *if you will not hear Reason, she'll surely rap your Knuckles.*

Thus the old Gentleman ended his Harangue. The People heard it, and approved the Doctrine, and immediately practised the contrary, just as if it had been a common Sermon; for the Vendue opened, and they began to buy extravagantly, notwithstanding all his Cautions, and their own Fear of Taxes. I found the good Man had thoroughly studied my Almanacks, and digested all I had dropt on those Topicks during the Course of Five-and-twenty Years. The frequent Mention he made of me must have tired any one else, but my Vanity was wonderfully delighted with it,

---

[6] In alchemy, the substance that was thought to turn base metals into gold.

though I was conscious that not a tenth Part of the Wisdom was my own which he ascribed to me, but rather the *Gleanings* I had made of the Sense of all Ages and Nations. However, I resolved to be the better for the Echo of it; and though I had at first determined to buy Stuff for a new Coat, I went away resolved to wear my old One a little longer. *Reader,* if thou wilt do the same, thy Profit will be as great as mine. I am, as ever, Thine to serve thee, RICHARD SAUNDERS.[7]
July 7, 1757.

1757/1758

The Sale of the Hessians[*]

From the Count de Schaumbergh to the Baron Hohendorf, commanding the Hessian troops in America.

Rome, February 18, 1777.

MONSIEUR LE BARON:—On my return from Naples, I received at Rome your letter of the 27th December of last year. I have learned with unspeakable pleasure the courage our troops exhibited at Trenton,[1] and you cannot imagine my joy on being told that of the 1,950 Hessians engaged in the fight, but 345 escaped. There were just 1,605 men killed, and I cannot sufficiently commend your prudence in sending an exact list of the dead to my minister in London. This precaution was the more necessary, as the report sent to the English ministry does not give but 1,455 dead. This would make 483,450 florins instead of 643,500 which I am entitled to demand under our convention. You will comprehend the prejudice which such an error would work in my finances, and I do not doubt you will take the necessary pains to prove that Lord North's[2] list is false and yours correct.

The court of London objects that there were a hundred wounded who ought not to be included in the list, nor paid for as dead; but I trust you will not overlook my

---

[7] Franklin used the name of a well-known seventeenth century London almanac writer.

[*] The date and place of the initial publication of this essay, one of Franklin's most successful burlesques, are not known. According to Moses Coit Tyler in *The Literary History of the American Revolution, 1763–1783:* "The Count de Schaumbergh's letter of instructions, seems to have been written by Franklin not long after his arrival in France in the latter part of 1776, and was intended to hold up to the execration of the civilized world both parties in the transaction by which the King of England bought of certain petty princes in Germany the troops with which to butcher his late American subjects. In some respects, this is the most powerful of all the satirical writings of Franklin. More, perhaps, than is the case with any other work of his, it displays, with marvelous subtlety and wit, that sort of genius which can reproduce with minute and perfect verisimilitude the psychological processes of some monstrous crime against human nature,—a crime which it thus portrays both to the horror and the derision of mankind."

[1] On Christmas night in 1776, Washington defeated a force of twelve hundred Hessians in the Battle of Trenton. Franklin exaggerates the report of Hessian casualties.

[2] Frederick North, British prime minister (1770–1782).

instructions to you on quitting Cassel, and that you will not have tried by human succor to recall the life of the unfortunates whose days could not be lengthened but by the loss of a leg or an arm. That would be making them a pernicious present, and I am sure they would rather die than live in a condition no longer fit for my service. I do not mean by this that you should assassinate them; we should be humane, my dear Baron, but you may insinuate to the surgeons with entire propriety that a crippled man is a reproach to their profession, and that there is no wiser course than to let every one of them die when he ceases to be fit to fight.

I am about to send to you some new recruits. Don't economize them. Remember glory before all things. Glory is true wealth. There is nothing degrades the soldier like the love of money. He must care only for honour and reputation, but this reputation must be acquired in the midst of dangers. A battle gained without costing the conqueror any blood is an inglorious success, while the conquered cover themselves with glory by perishing with their arms in their hands. Do you remember that of the 300 Lacedæmonians who defended the defile of Thermopylæ, not one returned? How happy should I be could I say the same of my brave Hessians!

It is true that their king, Leonidas, perished with them: but things have changed, and it is no longer the custom for princes of the empire to go and fight in America for a cause with which they have no concern. And besides, to whom should they pay the thirty guineas per man if I did not stay in Europe to receive them? Then, it is necessary also that I be ready to send recruits to replace the men you lose. For this purpose I must return to Hesse. It is true, grown men are becoming scarce there, but I will send you boys. Besides, the scarcer the commodity the higher the price. I am assured that the women and little girls have begun to till our lands, and they get on not badly. You did right to send back to Europe that Dr. Crumerus who was so successful in curing dysentery. Don't bother with a man who is subject to looseness of the bowels. That disease makes bad soldiers. One coward will do more mischief in an engagement than ten brave men will do good. Better that they burst in their barracks than fly in a battle, and tarnish the glory of our arms. Besides, you know that they pay me as killed for all who die from disease, and I don't get a farthing for runaways. My trip to Italy, which has cost me enormously, makes it desirable that there should be a great mortality among them. You will therefore promise promotion to all who expose themselves; you will exhort them to seek glory in the midst of dangers; you will say to Major Maundorff that I am not at all content with his saving the 345 men who escaped the massacre of Trenton. Through the whole campaign he has not had ten men killed in consequence of his orders. Finally, let it be your principal object to prolong the war and avoid a decisive engagement on either side, for I have made arrangements for a grand Italian opera, and I do not wish to be obliged to give it up. Meantime I pray God, my dear Baron de Hohendorf, to have you in his holy and gracious keeping.

n.d.

from Information to Those Who Would Remove to America[*]

Many Persons in Europe, having directly or by Letters, express'd to the Writer of this, who is well acquainted with North America, their Desire of transporting and establishing themselves in that Country; but who appear to have formed, thro' Ignorance, mistaken Ideas and Expectations of what is to be obtained there; he thinks it may be useful, and prevent inconvenient, expensive, and fruitless Removals and Voyages of improper Persons, if he gives some clearer and truer Notions of that part of the World, than appear to have hitherto prevailed.

He finds it is imagined by Numbers, that the Inhabitants of North America are rich, capable of rewarding, and dispos'd to reward, all sorts of Ingenuity; that they are at the same time ignorant of all the Sciences, and, consequently, that Strangers, possessing Talents in the Belles-Lettres, fine Arts, &c., must be highly esteemed, and so well paid, as to become easily rich themselves; that there are also abundance of profitable Offices to be disposed of, which the Natives are not qualified to fill; and that, having few Persons of Family among them, Strangers of Birth must be greatly respected, and of course easily obtain the best of those Offices, which will make all their Fortunes; that the Governments too, to encourage Emigrations from Europe, not only pay the Expence of personal Transportation, but give Lands gratis to Strangers, with Negroes to work for them, Utensils of Husbandry, and Stocks of Cattle. These are all wild Imaginations; and those who go to America with Expectations founded upon them will surely find themselves disappointed.

The Truth is, that though there are in that Country few People so miserable as the Poor of Europe, there are also very few that in Europe would be called rich; it is rather a general happy Mediocrity that prevails. There are few great Proprietors of the Soil, and few Tenants; most People cultivate their own Lands, or follow some Handicraft or Merchandise; very few rich enough to live idly upon their Rents or Incomes, or to pay the high Prices given in Europe for Paintings, Statues, Architecture, and the other Works of Art, that are more curious than useful. Hence the natural Geniuses, that have arisen in America with such Talents, have uniformly quitted that Country for Europe, where they can be more suitably rewarded. It is true, that Letters and Mathematical Knowledge are in Esteem there, but they are at the same time more common than is apprehended; there being already existing nine Colleges or Universities, viz. four in New England, and one in each of the Provinces of New York, New Jersey, Pensilvania, Maryland, and Virginia, all furnish'd with learned Professors; besides a number of smaller Academies; these educate many of their Youth in the Languages, and those Sciences that qualify men for the Professions of Divinity, Law, or Physick. Strangers indeed are by no means excluded from exercising those Professions; and the quick Increase of Inhabitants everywhere gives them a Chance of

---

[*] Title of pirated edition published in 1784. Franklin later that year published the pamphlet under the title *Advice to Such as Would Remove to America*.

Employ, which they have in common with the Natives. Of civil Offices, or Employments, there are few; no superfluous Ones, as in Europe; and it is a Rule establish'd
in some of the States, that no Office should be so profitable as to make it desirable.
The 36th Article of the Constitution of Pennsilvania, runs expressly in these Words;
"As every Freeman, to preserve his Independence, (if he has not a sufficient Estate)
ought to have some Profession, Calling, Trade, or Farm, whereby he may honestly
subsist, there can be no Necessity for, nor Use in, establishing Offices of Profit; the
usual Effects of which are Dependance and Servility, unbecoming Freemen, in the
Possessors and Expectants; Faction, Contention, Corruption, and Disorder among the
People. Wherefore, whenever an Office, thro' Increase of Fees or otherwise, becomes
so profitable, as to occasion many to apply for it, the Profits ought to be lessened by
the Legislature."

These Ideas prevailing more or less in all the United States, it cannot be worth any
Man's while, who has a means of Living at home, to expatriate himself, in hopes of
obtaining a profitable civil Office in America; and, as to military Offices, they are at
an End with the War, the Armies being disbanded. Much less is it adviseable for a
Person to go thither, who has no other Quality to recommend him but his Birth. In
Europe it has indeed its Value; but it is a Commodity that cannot be carried to a worse
Market than that of America, where people do not inquire concerning a Stranger,
What is he? but, *What can he do?* If he has any useful Art, he is welcome; and if he
exercises it, and behaves well, he will be respected by all that know him; but a mere
Man of Quality, who, on that Account, wants to live upon the Public, by some Office
or Salary, will be despis'd and disregarded. The Husbandman is in honor there, and
even the Mechanic, because their Employments are useful. The People have a saying,
that God Almighty is himself a Mechanic, the greatest in the Univers; and he is
respected and admired more for the Variety, Ingenuity, and Utility of his Handy-
works, than for the Antiquity of his Family. They are pleas'd with the Observation
of a Negro, and frequently mention it, that *Boccarorra* (meaning the White men) *make
de black man workee, make de Horse workee, make de Ox workee, make ebery ting workee;
only de Hog. He, de hog, no workee; he eat, he drink, he walk about, he go to sleep when
he please, he libb like a Gentleman.* According to these Opinions of the Americans, one
of them would think himself more oblig'd to a Genealogist, who could prove for him
that his Ancestors and Relations for ten Generations had been Ploughmen, Smiths,
Carpenters, Turners, Weavers, Tanners, or even Shoemakers, and consequently that
they were useful Members of Society; than if he could only prove that they were
Gentlemen, doing nothing of Value, but living idly on the Labour of others, mere
fruges consumere nati,[1] and otherwise *good for nothing,* till by their Death their Estates,
like the Carcass of the Negro's Gentleman-Hog, come to be *cut up.*

With regard to Encouragements for Strangers from Government, they are really
only what are derived from good Laws and Liberty. Strangers are welcome, because
there is room enough for them all, and therefore the old Inhabitants are not jealous
of them; the Laws protect them sufficiently, so that they have no need of the Patronage
of Great Men; and every one will enjoy securely the Profits of his Industry. But, if
he does not bring a Fortune with him, he must work and be industrious to live. One

[1] Franklin's note: "Born Merely to eat up the
corn.—Watts"

or two Years' residence gives him all the Rights of a Citizen; but the government does not at present, whatever it may have done in former times, hire People to become Settlers, by Paying their Passages, giving Land, Negroes, Utensils, Stock, or any other kind of Emolument whatsoever. In short, America is the Land of Labour, and by no means what the English call *Lubberland,* and the French *Pays de Cocagne,* where the streets are said to be pav'd with half-peck Loaves, the Houses til'd with Pancakes, and where the Fowls fly about ready roasted, crying, *Come eat me!*[2] . . .

1784

An Address to the Public;
from the Pennsylvania Society
for Promoting the Abolition of Slavery,
and the Relief of Free Negroes
Unlawfully Held in Bondage

It is with peculiar satisfaction we assure the friends of humanity, that, in prosecuting the design of our association, our endeavours have proved successful, far beyond our most sanguine expectations.

Encouraged by this success, and by the daily progress of that luminous and benign spirit of liberty, which is diffusing itself throughout the world, and humbly hoping for the continuance of the divine blessing on our labours, we have ventured to make an important addition to our original plan, and do therefore earnestly solicit the support and assistance of all who can feel the tender emotions of sympathy and compassion, or relish the exalted pleasure of beneficence.

Slavery is such an atrocious debasement of human nature, that its very extirpation, if not performed with solicitous care, may sometimes open a source of serious evils.

The unhappy man, who has long been treated as a brute animal, too frequently sinks beneath the common standard of the human species. The galling chains, that bind his body, do also fetter his intellectual faculties, and impair the social affections of his heart. Accustomed to move like a mere machine, by the will of a master, reflection is suspended; he has not the power of choice; and reason and conscience have but little influence over his conduct, because he is chiefly governed by the passion of fear. He is poor and friendless; perhaps worn out by extreme labour, age, and disease.

Under such circumstances, freedom may often prove a misfortune to himself, and prejudicial to society.

Attention to emancipated black people, it is therefore to be hoped, will become a branch of our national policy; but, as far as we contribute to promote this emancipation, so far that attention is evidently a serious duty incumbent on us, and which we mean to discharge to the best of our judgment and abilities.

---

[2] The text continues with a description of "the kind of Persons to whom an Emigration to America may be advantageous."

To instruct, to advise, to qualify those, who have been restored to freedom, for the exercise and enjoyment of civil liberty, to promote in them habits of industry, to furnish them with employments suited to their age, sex, talents, and other circumstances, and to procure their children an education calculated for their future situation in life; these are the great outlines of the annexed plan, which we have adopted, and which we conceive will essentially promote the public good, and the happiness of these our hitherto too much neglected fellow-creatures.

A plan so extensive cannot be carried into execution without considerable pecuniary resources, beyond the present ordinary funds of the Society. We hope much from the generosity of enlightened and benevolent freemen, and will gratefully receive any donations or subscriptions for this purpose, which may be made to our treasurer, James Starr, or to James Pemberton, chairman of our committee of correspondence.

Signed, by order of the Society,

B. FRANKLIN, *President.*

Philadelphia, 9th of
November, 1789.

1789/1789

Letters to Peter Collinson

[October 19, 1752: The Kite Experiment]*

Philadelphia, October 19

As frequent Mention is made in the News Papers from Europe, of the Success of the Philadelphia Experiment for drawing the Electric Fire from Clouds by Means of pointed Rods of Iron erected on high buildings, &c. it may be agreeable to the Curious to be inform'd, that the same Experiment has succeeded in Philadelphia, tho' made in a different and more easy Manner, which any one may try, as follows.

Make a small Cross of two light Strips of Cedar, the Arms so long as to reach to the four Corners of a large thin Silk Handkerchief when extended; tie the Corners of the Handkerchief to the Extremities of the Cross, so you have the Body of a Kite; which being properly accommodated with a Tail, Loop and String, will rise in the Air, like those made of Paper; but this being of Silk is fitter to bear the Wet and Wind of a Thunder Gust without tearing.[1] To the Top of the upright Stick of the Cross is to be fixed a very sharp pointed Wire, rising a Foot or more above the Wood.

---

* Published in the *Pennsylvania Gazette,* October 19, 1752. Reprinted in Joseph Priestley, *The History and Present State of Electricity, with Original Experiments* (London, 1767). This statement was sent to Franklin's friend Peter Collinson (1694–1768) and was read to the Royal Society on December 21, 1752. Collinson, an English Quaker, merchant, and noted botanist, maintained a long correspondence with Franklin and published Franklin's *Experiments and Observations on Electricity* (1751).

[1] This was not the first time that Franklin had experimented with kites. In a letter to Barbeu Dubourg (1773), Franklin nostalgically recalls a moment of childhood invention: "When I was a boy, I amused myself one day with flying a paper kite; and approaching the bank of a pond, which was near a mile broad, I tied the string to a stake, and the kite ascended to a very considerable height above the pond, while I was swimming. In a little time, being desirous of amusing myself with my kite, and enjoying at the same time the pleasure of swimming, I

To the End of the Twine, next the Hand, is to be tied a silk Ribbon, and where the Twine and the silk join, a Key may be fastened. This Kite is to be raised when a Thunder Gust appears to be coming on, and the Person who holds the String must stand within a Door, or Window, or under some Cover, so that the Silk Ribbon may not be wet; and Care must be taken that the Twine does not touch the Frame of the Door or Window. As soon as any of the Thunder Clouds come over the Kite, the pointed Wire will draw the Electric Fire from them, and the Kite, with all the Twine, will be electrified, and the loose Filaments of the Twine will stand out every Way, and be attracted by an approaching Finger. And when the Rain has wet the Kite and Twine, so that it can conduct the Electric Fire freely, you will find it stream out plentifully from the Key on the Approach of your Knuckle. At this Key the Phial may be charg'd; and from Electric Fire thus obtain'd, Spirits may be kindled, and all the other Electric Experiments be perform'd, which are usually done by the Help of a rubbed Glass Globe or Tube; and thereby the *Sameness* of the Electric Matter with that of Lightning compleatly demonstrated.

B. FRANKLIN

1752/1752

[August 25, 1755: Whirlwinds]

Dear Sir,   Philadelphia, Aug. 25, 1755.

As you have my former papers on Whirlwinds, &c. I now send you an account[2] of one which I had lately an opportunity of seeing and examining myself.

Being in Maryland, riding with Col. Tasker, and some other gentlemen to his country-seat, where I and my son were entertained by that amiable and worthy man, with great hospitality and kindness, we saw in the vale below us, a small whirlwind beginning in the road, and shewing itself by the dust it raised and contained. It appeared in the form of a sugar-loaf, spinning on its point, moving up the hill towards us, and enlarging as it came forward. When it passed by us, its smaller part near the ground, appeared not bigger than a common barrel, but widening upwards, it seemed, at 40 or 50 feet high, to be 20 or 30 feet in diameter. The rest of the company stood looking after it, but my curiosity being stronger, I followed it, riding close by its side, and observed its licking up, in its progress, all the dust that was under its smaller part. As it is a common opinion that a shot, fired through a water-spout, will break it, I tried to break this little whirlwind, by striking my whip frequently through it, but without any effect. Soon after, it quitted the road and took into the woods, growing every moment larger and stronger, raising, instead of dust, the old dry leaves with which the ground was thick covered, and making a great noise with them and the branches of the trees, bending some tall trees round in a circle swiftly and very surprizingly, though the progressive motion of the whirl was not so swift but that

returned; and, loosing from the stake the string with the little stick which was fastened to it, went again into the water, where I found, that, lying on my back and holding the stick in my hands, I was drawn along the surface of the water in a very agreeable manner."
[2] The incident Franklin recounts most likely occurred in April 1755 during a trip to Maryland. Along with his famous kite experiment, Franklin's "attack" on the whirlwind shows the combination of his scientific curiosity and his characteristic bravado in the face of dangerous natural phenomena.

a man on foot might have kept pace with it, but the circular motion was amazingly rapid. By the leaves it was now filled with, I could plainly perceive that the current of air they were driven by, moved upwards in a spiral line; and when I saw the trunks and bodies of large trees invelop'd in the passing whirl, which continued intire after it had left them, I no longer wondered that my whip had no effect on it in its smaller state. I accompanied it about three quarters of a mile, till some limbs of dead trees, broken off by the whirl, flying about, and falling near me, made me more apprehensive of danger; and then I stopped, looking at the top of it as it went on, which was visible, by means of the leaves contained in it, for a very great height above the trees. Many of the leaves, as they got loose from the upper and widest part, were scattered in the wind; but so great was their height in the air, that they appeared no bigger than flies. My son, who was, by this time, come up with me, followed the whirlwind till it left the woods, and crossed an old tobacco-field, where, finding neither dust nor leaves to take up, it gradually became invisible below as it went away over that field. The course of the general wind then blowing was along with us as we travelled, and the progressive motion of the whirlwind was in a direction nearly opposite, though it did not keep a strait line, nor was its progressive motion uniform, it making little sallies on either hand as it went, proceeding sometimes faster, and sometimes slower, and seeming sometimes for a few seconds almost stationary, then starting forwards pretty fast again. When we rejoined the company, they were admiring the vast height of the leaves, now brought by the common wind, over our heads. These leaves accompanied us as we travelled, some falling now and then round about us, and some not reaching the ground till we had gone near three miles from the place where we first saw the whirlwind begin. Upon my asking Col. Tasker if such whirlwinds were common in Maryland, he answered pleasantly, *No, not at all common; but we got this on purpose to treat Mr. Franklin.* And a very high treat it was, to Dear Sir, Your affectionate friend, and humble servant   B. F.

1755/1769

Letter to William Franklin

Passy, Aug. 16, 1784.

DEAR SON,

I received your Letter of the 22d past, and am glad to find that you desire to revive the affectionate Intercourse, that formerly existed between us. It will be very agreable to me; indeed nothing has ever hurt me so much and affected me with such keen Sensations, as to find myself deserted in my old Age by my only Son; and not only deserted, but to find him taking up Arms against me,[1] in a Cause, wherein my good

---

[1] William Franklin had taken up the Loyalist (British) cause during the Revolutionary War.

Fame, Fortune and Life were all at Stake. You conceived, you say, that your Duty to your King and Regard for your Country requir'd this. I ought not to blame you for differing in Sentiment with me in Public Affairs. We are Men, all subject to Errors. Our Opinions are not in our own Power; they are form'd and govern'd much by Circumstances, that are often as inexplicable as they are irresistible. Your Situation was such that few would have censured your remaining Neuter, *tho' there are Natural Duties which precede political ones, and cannot be extinguish'd by them.*

This is a disagreable Subject. I drop it. And we will endeavour, as you propose mutually to forget what has happened relating to it, as well as we can. I send your Son over to pay his Duty to you. You will find him much improv'd. He is greatly esteem'd and belov'd in this Country, and will make his Way anywhere. It is my Desire, that he should study the Law, as a necessary Part of Knowledge for a public Man, and profitable if he should have occasion to practise it. I would have you therefore put into his hands those Law-books you have, viz. Blackstone, Coke, Bacon, Viner, &c. He will inform you, that he received the Letter sent him by Mr. Galloway,[2] and the Paper it enclosed, safe.

On my leaving America, I deposited with that Friend for you, a Chest of Papers, among which was a Manuscript of nine or ten Volumes, relating to Manufactures, Agriculture, Commerce, Finance, etc., which cost me in England about 70 Guineas; eight Quire Books, containing the Rough Drafts of all my Letters while I liv'd in London. These are missing. I hope you have got them, if not, they are lost. Mr. Vaughan has publish'd in London a Volume of what he calls my Political Works. He proposes a second Edition; but, as the first was very incompleat, and you had many Things that were omitted, (for I used to send you sometimes the Rough Drafts, and sometimes the printed Pieces I wrote in London,) I have directed him to apply to you for what may be in your Power to furnish him with, or to delay his Publication till I can be at home again, if that may ever happen.

I did intend returning this year; but the Congress, instead of giving me Leave to do so, have sent me another Commission, which will keep me here at least a Year longer; and perhaps I may then be too old and feeble to bear the Voyage. I am here among a People that love and respect me, a most amiable Nation to live with; and perhaps I may conclude to die among them; for my Friends in America are dying off, one after another, and I have been so long abroad, that I should now be almost a Stranger in my own Country.

I shall be glad to see you when convenient, but would not have you come here at present. You may confide to your son the Family Affairs you wished to confer upon with me, for he is discreet. And I trust, that you will prudently avoid introducing him to Company, that it may be improper for him to be seen with. I shall hear from you by him and any letters to me afterwards, will come safe under Cover directed to Mr. Ferdinand Grand, Banker at Paris. Wishing you Health, and more Happiness than it seems you have lately experienced, I remain your affectionate father,

B. FRANKLIN.

1784/1907

[2] Joseph Galloway (ca. 1731–1803), a
Pennsylvania public figure who joined the
Loyalists.

Letter to Ezra Stiles[1]

Philad[a], March 9. 1790.

REVEREND AND DEAR SIR,

I received your kind Letter of Jan'y 28, and am glad you have at length received the portrait of Gov'r Yale[2] from his Family, and deposited it in the College Library. He was a great and good Man, and had the Merit of doing infinite Service to your Country by his Munificence to that Institution. The Honour you propose doing me by placing mine in the same Room with his, is much too great for my Deserts; but you always had a Partiality for me, and to that it must be ascribed. I am however too much obliged to Yale College, the first learned Society that took Notice of me and adorned me with its Honours,[3] to refuse a Request that comes from it thro' so esteemed a Friend. But I do not think any one of the Portraits you mention, as in my Possession, worthy of the Place and Company you propose to place it in. You have an excellent Artist lately arrived. If he will undertake to make one for you, I shall cheerfully pay the Expence; but he must not delay setting about it, or I may slip thro' his fingers, for I am now in my eighty-fifth year, and very infirm.[4]

I send with this a very learned Work, as it seems to me, on the antient Samaritan Coins, lately printed in Spain, and at least curious for the Beauty of the Impression. Please to accept it for your College Library. I have subscribed for the Encyclopædia[5] now printing here, with the Intention of presenting it to the College. I shall probably depart before the Work is finished, but shall leave Directions for its Continuance to the End. With this you will receive some of the first numbers.

You desire to know something of my Religion. It is the first time I have been questioned upon it. But I cannot take your Curiosity amiss, and shall endeavour in a few Words to gratify it. Here is my Creed. I believe in one God, Creator of the Universe. That he governs it by his Providence. That he ought to be worshipped. That the most acceptable Service we render to him is doing good to his other Children. That the soul of Man is immortal, and will be treated with Justice in another Life respecting its Conduct in this. These I take to be the fundamental Principles of all sound Religion, and I regard them as you do in whatever Sect I meet with them.

As to Jesus of Nazareth, my Opinion of whom you particularly desire, I think the System of Morals and his Religion, as he left them to us, the best the World ever saw or is likely to see; but I apprehend it has received various corrupting Changes, and I have, with most of the present Dissenters in England, some Doubts as to his Divinity; tho' it is a question I do not dogmatize upon, having never studied it, and think it needless to busy myself with it now, when I expect soon an Opportunity of knowing the Truth with less Trouble. I see no harm, however, in its being believed,

---

[1] Grandson of the Puritan poet Edward Taylor and president of Yale College, Stiles (1727–1795) had written Franklin for information about his religious "sentiments."
[2] Elihu Yale (1649–1721), for whom Yale College was named.

[3] Yale awarded Franklin an honorary degree in 1753.
[4] Franklin died a month later, on April 17.
[5] Franklin refers here to the third edition of the *Encyclopedia Britannica,* which was being printed in America for the first time.

if that Belief has the good Consequence, as probably it has, of making his Doctrines more respected and better observed; especially as I do not perceive, that the Supreme takes it amiss, by distinguishing the Unbelievers in his Government of the World with any peculiar Marks of his Displeasure.

I shall only add, respecting myself, that, having experienced the Goodness of that Being in conducting me prosperously thro' a long life, I have no doubt of its Continuance in the next, though without the smallest Conceit of meriting such Goodness. My Sentiments on this Head you will see in the Copy of an old Letter enclosed,[6] which I wrote in answer to one from a zealous Religionist, whom I had relieved in a paralytic case by electricity, and who, being afraid I should grow proud upon it, sent me his serious though rather impertinent Caution. I send you also the Copy of another Letter, which will shew something of my Disposition relating to Religion. With great and sincere Esteem and Affection, I am, Your obliged old Friend and most obedient humble Servant   B. FRANKLIN.

1790/1907

John Woolman
1720–1772

Raised in a small Quaker community some twenty miles from Philadelphia, John Woolman spent his earliest years in the midst of books, prayers, and entrepreneurs. By the age of sixteen, Woolman had received a traditionally disciplined religious education but had fallen prey, as he notes in the opening chapter of the *Journal,* to "wanton company" and to the "darkness, horror and amazement" of an undisclosed ailment. He sought comfort in the Scriptures and resolved that his "rebellious heart" would "bow down in spirit before the Lord." By the age of twenty-one, Woolman had moved the short distance to Mount Holly, New Jersey, to tend a retail store, serve as an apprentice tailor, and supplement his income with work as a scrivener, teacher, and surveyor.

Woolman's tailoring business prospered, but within two years he became disillusioned with the imbalance that success created in his life. He reaffirmed his religious commitments, renounced worldliness, and dedicated himself to a life of personal purity and public ministry. He first expressed his calling by speaking frequently at Quaker meetings in the area, and by the age of twenty-three he had set out on the first of what were to be more than thirty missionary excursions through New England and the middle colonies, traveling as far south as the Carolinas. These treks, mostly on foot, were impelled by both a missionary's zeal for rousing new converts and a social reformer's devotion to abolishing slavery and improving the lot of the poor. His ministry led him more often to urban centers of trade than to remote settlements in the rugged frontier landscape, and his approach remained one of friendly persuasion rather than emotional sermonizing.

[6] Probably written to Thomas Paine.

Traveling on behalf of the spiritual and social improvement of society, Woolman advocated a Thoreau-like commitment to simplicity as the basis for moral progress. He regarded wealth as a major source of corruption and, like Thoreau, measured the "cost" of a thing in terms of the amount of life required to be exchanged for it. A pacifist during the French and Indian Wars, Woolman also refused to underwrite the war effort with his taxes. His most famous essay, *A Plea for the Poor,* proposed a radical redistribution of wealth. Woolman taught that one should never benefit from the pain of others. His opposition to slavery, to what he called "that dark gloominess hanging over the land," was based on this pledge, as was his insistence on paying for his lodging when staying with Quaker slaveowners. Woolman's essays on the subject, most notably *Some Considerations on the Keeping of Negroes,* published by Benjamin Franklin in 1745, and a sequel, printed in 1762, argued that the children of both whites and blacks were being kept in bondage by the social and economic system of slavery. These tracts constitute some of America's earliest, most persuasive, and most prophetic abolitionist documents, statements that had considerable impact during the nineteenth-century debates on slavery. Woolman could point to both the plight of the oppressed and the spiritual predicament of the master when he solemnly intoned, "The seeds of great calamity and desolation are sown and growing fast on this continent."

Woolman deliberately composed rather than spontaneously kept his *Journal,* much in the manner of Jonathan Edwards's *Personal Narrative* and Benjamin Franklin's *Autobiography.* The passivity of his voice, its understatement, and the spare use of adjectives reflect Woolman's sacramental view of experience and his nearly selfless dedication to "leave some hints of my experience of the Goodness of God." Begun in Woolman's thirty-sixth year, the *Journal* traces the Divine Presence in his life from his childhood to what was to be his last voyage—in 1772, to England, where he died of a smallpox infection reportedly contracted while caring for the poor.

No testimony of an American Quaker's spiritual experience has evoked more praise than John Woolman's *Journal.* In England, the Romantic essayist Charles Lamb, despite his haughty announcement that it was the only book by an American that he had ever read more than once, urged his friends to learn Woolman "by heart." Lamb's contemporary, Crabb Robinson, judged the eighteenth-century Quaker "a beautiful soul. An illiterate tailor, he writes in a style of the most exquisite purity and grace." But more than the literary qualities, it was the moral attributes evident in the life of this New Jersey farmer's son that prompted Samuel Taylor Coleridge to observe, "I should almost despair of that man who could persue the life of John Woolman without an amelioration of heart." In a similar vein, the American poet John Greenleaf Whittier, writing in the introductory pages of his 1871 edition of the *Journal,* acclaimed the work "a classic of the inner life." William Ellery Channing, a pillar of the nineteenth-century Unitarian church, regarded the *Journal* as "the sweetest and purest autobiography in the language." But perhaps the most unreserved paean is tucked away in longhand on the back page of Ralph Waldo Emerson's personal copy of the *Journal:* "I find more wonderful wisdom in these pages than in any other book written since the days of the Apostles. There is a true philosophy—a clear insight—a right estimate of things." The influence of this Quaker mystic carried well into the twentieth century. Theodore Dreiser drew heavily on the *Journal* for his last novel, *The Bulwark* (1946), and Woolman's presence lingered on into the civil rights and antiwar movements of more recent years.

Further Reading:
J. Whitney, *John Woolman: American Quaker,* 1942.
E. Cady, *John Woolman,* 1965.
D. B. Shea, *Spiritual Autobiography in Early America,* 1968.
P. Rosenblatt, *John Woolman,* 1969.
John Woolman in England, ed. H. Cadbury, 1971.

Text:
The Journal and Major Essays of John Woolman, ed. P. P. Moulton, 1971.
See also *The Journal of John Woolman,* ed. J. G. Whittier, 1871.

---

from Journal

[Vocation]

I have often felt a motion of love to leave some hints in writing of my experience of the goodness of God, and now, in the thirty-sixth year of my age, I begin this work. I was born in Northampton, in Burlington County in West Jersey,[1] A.D. 1720, and before I was seven years old I began to be acquainted with the operations of divine love. Through the care of my parents, I was taught to read near as soon as I was capable of it, and as I went from school one Seventh Day,[2] I remember, while my companions went to play by the way, I went forward out of sight; and sitting down, I read the twenty-second chapter of the Revelations: "He showed me a river of water, clear as crystal, proceeding out of the throne of God and the Lamb, etc."[3] And in reading it my mind was drawn to seek after that pure habitation which I then believed God had prepared for his servants. The place where I sat and the sweetness that attended my mind remains fresh in my memory.

This and the like gracious visitations had that effect upon me, that when boys used ill language it troubled me, and through the continued mercies of God I was preserved from it. The pious instructions of my parents were often fresh in my mind when I happened amongst wicked children, and was of use to me. My parents, having a large family of children,[4] used frequently on First Days after meeting[5] to put us to read in the Holy Scriptures or some religious books, one after another, the rest sitting by without much conversation, which I have since often thought was a good practice. From what I had read and heard, I believed there had been in past ages people who walked in uprightness before God in a degree exceeding any that I knew, or heard

[1] Colonial New Jersey was divided into two provinces, East and West Jersey. The Woolman family lived near Mount Holly, a Quaker community 20 miles from Philadelphia.

[2] That is, on Saturday. In an effort to simplify their lives and to avoid celebrating the names of pagan gods ("Saturday" honors Saturn), the Quakers used numbers for the days of the week.

[3] Revelation 22:1–5 describes Paradise after Christ's triumph.

[4] John Woolman was the eldest in a family of seven boys and six girls.

[5] The simple "meetinghouse," not a formal church, served as the gathering place for Quaker worship.

of, now living; and the apprehension of there being less steadiness and firmness amongst people in this age than in past ages often troubled me while I was a child.

I had a dream about the ninth year of my age as follows: I saw the moon rise near the west and run a regular course eastward, so swift that in about a quarter of an hour she reached our meridian, when there descended from her a small cloud on a direct line to the earth, which lighted on a pleasant green about twenty yards from the door of my father's house (in which I thought I stood) and was immediately turned into a beautiful green tree. The moon appeared to run on with equal swiftness and soon set in the east, at which time the sun arose at the place where it commonly does in the summer, and shining with full radiance in a serene air, it appeared as pleasant a morning as ever I saw.

All this time I stood still in the door in an awful frame of mind,[6] and I observed that as heat increased by the rising sun, it wrought so powerfully on the little green tree that the leaves gradually withered; and before noon it appeared dry and dead. There then appeared a being, small of size, full of strength and resolution, moving swift from the north, southward, called a sun worm.[7]

Another thing remarkable in my childhood was that once, going to a neighbour's house, I saw on the way a robin sitting on her nest; and as I came near she went off, but having young ones, flew about and with many cries expressed her concern for them. I stood and threw stones at her, till one striking her, she fell down dead. At first I was pleased with the exploit, but after a few minutes was seized with horror, as having in a sportive way killed an innocent creature while she was careful for her young. I beheld her lying dead and thought those young ones for which she was so careful must now perish for want of their dam to nourish them; and after some painful considerations on the subject, I climbed up the tree, took all the young birds and killed them, supposing that better than to leave them to pine away and die miserably, and believed in this case that Scripture proverb was fulfilled, "The tender mercies of the wicked are cruel."[8] I then went on my errand, but for some hours could think of little else but the cruelties I had committed, and was much troubled.

Thus he whose tender mercies are over all his works hath placed a principle in the human mind which incites to exercise goodness toward every living creature; and this being singly attended to, people become tender-hearted and sympathizing, but being frequently and totally rejected, the mind shuts itself up in a contrary disposition.

About the twelfth year of my age, my father being abroad, my mother reproved me for some misconduct, to which I made an undutiful reply; and the next First Day as I was with my father returning from meeting, he told me he understood I had behaved amiss to my mother and advised me to be more careful in future. I knew myself blameable, and in shame and confusion remained silent. Being thus awakened to a sense of my wickedness, I felt remorse in my mind, and getting home I retired and prayed to the Lord to forgive me, and do not remember that I ever after that spoke unhandsomely to either of my parents, however foolish in other things.

Having attained the age of sixteen years, I began to love wanton company, and though I was preserved from profane language or scandalous conduct, still I perceived a plant in me which produced much wild grapes. Yet my merciful Father forsook

[6] I.e., full of awe.
[7] Imaginary sun snake.
[8] Proverbs 12:10: "A righteous man regardeth the life of his beast; but the tender mercies of the wicked are cruel."

me not utterly, but at times through his grace I was brought seriously to consider my ways, and the sight of my backsliding affected me with sorrow. But for want of rightly attending to the reproofs of instruction, vanity was added to vanity, and repentance to repentance; upon the whole my mind was more and more alienated from the Truth,[9] and I hastened toward destruction. While I meditate on the gulf toward which I travelled and reflect on my youthful disobedience, for these things I weep; mine eye runneth down with water.

Advancing in age the number of my acquaintance increased, and thereby my way grew more difficult. Though I had heretofore found comfort in reading the Holy Scriptures and thinking on heavenly things, I was now estranged therefrom. I knew I was going from the flock of Christ and had no resolution to return; hence serious reflections were uneasy to me and youthful vanities and diversions my greatest pleasure. Running in this road I found many like myself, and we associated in that which is reverse to true friendship.[10]

But in this swift race it pleased God to visit me with sickness, so that I doubted of recovering. And then did darkness, horror, and amazement with full force seize me, even when my pain and distress of body was very great. I thought it would have been better for me never to have had a being than to see the day which I now saw. I was filled with confusion, and in great affliction both of mind and body I lay and bewailed myself. I had not confidence to lift up my cries to God, whom I had thus offended, but in a deep sense of my great folly I was humbled before him, and at length that Word which is as a fire and a hammer broke and dissolved my rebellious heart. And then my cries were put up in contrition, and in the multitude of his mercies I found inward relief, and felt a close engagement that if he was pleased to restore my health, I might walk humbly before him.

After my recovery this exercise[11] remained with me a considerable time; but by degrees giving way to youthful vanities, they gained strength, and getting with wanton[12] young people I lost ground. The Lord had been very gracious and spoke peace to me in the time of my distress, and I now most ungratefully turned again to folly, on which account at times I felt sharp reproof but did not get low enough to cry for help. I was not so hardy as to commit things scandalous, but to exceed in vanity and promote mirth was my chief study. Still I retained a love and esteem for pious people, and their company brought an awe upon me.

My dear parents several times admonished me in the fear of the Lord, and their admonition entered into my heart and had a good effect for a season, but not getting deep enough to pray rightly, the tempter when he came found entrance. I remember once, having spent a part of the day in wantonness, as I went to bed at night there lay in a window near my bed a Bible, which I opened, and first cast my eye on the text, "We lie down in our shame, and our confusion covers us."[13] This I knew to be my case, and meeting with so unexpected a reproof, I was somewhat affected with it and went to bed under remorse of conscience, which I soon cast off again.

Thus time passed on; my heart was replenished with mirth and wantonness, while pleasing scenes of vanity were presented to my imagination till I attained the age of

---

[9] I.e., the ultimate spiritual reality.
[10] I.e., the reverse of the principles basic to the Quakers, who officially called themselves the Religious Society of Friends.

[11] Spiritual experience.
[12] Thoughtless; frivolous.
[13] Jeremiah 3:25.

eighteen years, near which time I felt the judgments of God in my soul like a consuming fire, and looking over my past life the prospect was moving. I was often sad and longed to be delivered from those vanities; then again my heart was strongly inclined to them, and there was in me a sore conflict. At times I turned to folly, and then again sorrow and confusion took hold of me. In a while I resolved totally to leave off some of my vanities, but there was a secret reserve in my heart of the more refined part of them, and I was not low enough to find true peace. Thus for some months I had great trouble, there remaining in me an unsubjected will which rendered my labours fruitless, till at length through the merciful continuance of heavenly visitations I was made to bow down in spirit before the Lord.

I remember one evening I had spent some time in reading a pious author, and walking out alone I humbly prayed to the Lord for his help, that I might be delivered from all those vanities which so ensnared me. Thus being brought low, he helped me; and as I learned to bear the cross I felt refreshment to come from his presence; but not keeping in that strength which gave victory, I lost ground again, the sense of which greatly affected me; and I sought deserts and lonely places and there with tears did confess my sins to God and humbly craved help of him. And I may say with reverence he was near to me in my troubles, and in those times of humiliation opened my ear to discipline.

I was now led to look seriously at the means by which I was drawn from the pure Truth, and learned this: that if I would live in the life which the faithful servants of God lived in, I must not go into company as heretofore in my own will, but all the cravings of sense must be governed by a divine principle. In times of sorrow and abasement these instructions were sealed upon me, and I felt the power of Christ prevail over selfish desires, so that I was preserved in a good degree of steadiness. And being young and believing at that time that a single life was best for me, I was strengthened to keep from such company as had often been a snare to me.

I kept steady to meetings, spent First Days after noon chiefly in reading the Scriptures and other good books, and was early convinced in my mind that true religion consisted in an inward life, wherein the heart doth love and reverence God the Creator and learn to exercise true justice and goodness, not only toward all men but also toward the brute creatures; that as the mind was moved on an inward principle to love God as an invisible, incomprehensible being, on the same principle it was moved to love him in all his manifestations in the visible world; that as by his breath the flame of life was kindled in all animal and sensitive creatures, to say we love God as unseen and at the same time exercise cruelty toward the least creature moving by his life, or by life derived from him, was a contradiction in itself.

I found no narrowness respecting sects and opinions, but believed that sincere, upright-hearted people in every Society who truly loved God were accepted of him.

As I lived under the cross[14] and simply followed the openings[15] of Truth, my mind from day to day was more enlightened; my former acquaintance was left to judge of me as they would, for I found it safest for me to live in private and keep these things sealed up in my own breast.

While I silently ponder on that change wrought in me, I find no language equal

---

[14] I.e., humbly and conscious of Christ's presence in his life.
[15] For the Quakers, "openings" were direct messages from God to those who lived in expectation of them.

to it nor any means to convey to another a clear idea of it. I looked upon the works of God in this visible creation and an awfulness covered me; my heart was tender and often contrite, and a universal love to my fellow creatures increased in me. This will be understood by such who have trodden in the same path. Some glances of real beauty may be seen in their faces who dwell in true meekness. There is a harmony in the sound of that voice to which divine love gives utterance, and some appearance of right order in their temper and conduct whose passions are fully regulated. Yet all these do not fully show forth that inward life to such who have not felt it, but this white stone and new name is known rightly to such only who have it.[16]

Now though I had been thus strengthened to bear the cross, I still found myself in great danger, having many weaknesses attending me and strong temptations to wrestle with, in the feeling whereof I frequently withdrew into private places and often with tears besought the Lord to help me, whose gracious ear was open to my cry.

All this time I lived with my parents and wrought on the plantation, and having had schooling pretty well for a planter, I used to improve in winter evenings and other leisure times. And being now in the twenty-first year of my age, a man in much business shopkeeping and baking asked me if I would hire with him to tend shop and keep books. I acquainted my father with the proposal, and after some deliberation it was agreed for me to go.

At home I had lived retired, and now having a prospect of being much in the way of company, I felt frequent and fervent cries in my heart to God, the Father of Mercies, that he would preserve me from all taint and corruption, that in this more public employ I might serve him, my gracious Redeemer, in that humility and self-denial with which I had been in a small degree exercised in a very private life.

The man who employed me furnished a shop in Mount Holly, about five miles from my father's house and six from his own, and there I lived alone and tended his shop. Shortly after my settlement here I was visited by several young people, my former acquaintance, who knew not but vanities would be as agreeable to me now as ever; and at these times I cried to the Lord in secret for wisdom and strength, for I felt myself encompassed with difficulties and had fresh occasion to bewail the follies of time past in contracting a familiarity with a libertine people. And as I had now left my father's house outwardly, I found my Heavenly Father to be merciful to me beyond what I can express.

By day I was much amongst people and had many trials to go through, but in evenings I was mostly alone and may with thankfulness acknowledge that in those times the spirit of supplication was often poured upon me under which I was frequently exercised and felt my strength renewed.

In a few months after I came here, my master bought several Scotch menservants[17] from on board a vessel and brought them to Mount Holly to sell, one of which was taken sick and died. The latter part of his sickness he, being delirious, used to curse and swear most sorrowfully, and after he was buried I was left to sleep alone the next night in the same chamber where he died. I perceived in me

---

[16] See Revelation 2:17: "To him that overcometh I will give . . . him a white stone, and in the stone a new name written, which no man knoweth saving he that receiveth it."

[17] I.e., bought their indentures, the legal agreements binding them to work for a specific period in payment for their passage to America. (Indentures could be bought, sold, and traded.)

a timorousness. I knew, however, I had not injured the man but assisted in taking care of him according to my capacity, and was not free to ask anyone on that occasion to sleep with me. Nature was feeble, but every trial was a fresh incitement to give myself up wholly to the service of God, for I found no helper like him in times of trouble.

After a while my former acquaintance gave over expecting me as one of their company, and I began to be known to some whose conversation was helpful to me. And now, as I had experienced the love of God through Jesus Christ to redeem me from many pollutions and to be a succour to me through a sea of conflicts, with which no person was fully acquainted, and as my heart was often enlarged in this heavenly principle, I felt a tender compassion for the youth who remained entangled in snares like those which had entangled me. From one month to another this love and tenderness increased, and my mind was more strongly engaged for the good of my fellow creatures.

I went to meetings in an awful frame of mind and endeavoured to be inwardly acquainted with the language of the True Shepherd. And one day being under a strong exercise of spirit, I stood up and said some words in a meeting, but not keeping close to the divine opening,[18] I said more than was required of me; and being soon sensible of my error, I was afflicted in mind some weeks without any light or comfort, even to that degree that I could take satisfaction in nothing. I remembered God and was troubled, and in the depth of my distress he had pity upon me and sent the Comforter. I then felt forgiveness for my offense, and my mind became calm and quiet, being truly thankful to my gracious Redeemer for his mercies. And after this, feeling the spring of divine love opened and a concern[19] to speak, I said a few words in a meeting, in which I found peace. This I believe was about six weeks from the first time, and as I was thus humbled and disciplined under the cross, my understanding became more strengthened to distinguish the language of the pure Spirit which inwardly moves upon the heart[20] and taught [me] to wait in silence sometimes many weeks together, until I felt that rise which prepares the creature to stand like a trumpet through which the Lord speaks to his flock.

From an inward purifying, and steadfast abiding under it, springs a lively operative desire for the good of others. All faithful people are not called to the public ministry, but whoever are, are called to minister of that which they have tasted and handled spiritually. The outward modes of worship are various, but wherever men are true ministers of Jesus Christ it is from the operation of his spirit upon their hearts, first purifying them and thus giving them a feeling sense of the conditions of others. This truth was early fixed in my mind, and I was taught to watch the pure opening and to take heed lest while I was standing to speak, my own will should get uppermost and cause me to utter words from worldly wisdom and depart from the channel of the true gospel ministry.

In the management of my outward affairs I may say with thankfulness I found Truth to be my support, and I was respected in my master's family, who came to live in Mount Holly within two year after my going there.

---

[18] I.e., rather than speaking about the religious truth that prompted him to stand and talk, he spoke about more worldly matters.

[19] A deeply felt conviction; what one is compelled to do, even against one's will.

[20] Quakers distinguish between selfish desire and an "inward light," which is marked by "disciplined understanding."

About the twenty-third year of my age, I had many fresh and heavenly openings in respect to the care and providence of the Almighty over his creatures in general, and over man as the most noble amongst those which are visible. And being clearly convinced in my judgment that to place my whole trust in God was best for me, I felt renewed engagements that in all things I might act on an inward principle of virtue and pursue worldly business no further than as Truth opened my way therein.

About the time called Christmas[21] I observed many people from the country and dwellers in town who, resorting to the public houses, spent their time in drinking and vain sports, tending to corrupt one another, on which account I was much troubled. At one house in particular there was much disorder, and I believed it was a duty laid on me to go and speak to the master of that house. I considered I was young and that several elderly Friends in town had opportunity to see these things, and though I would gladly have been excused, yet I could not feel my mind clear.

The exercise was heavy, and as I was reading what the Almighty said to Ezekiel respecting his duty as a watchman,[22] the matter was set home more clearly; and then with prayer and tears I besought the Lord for his assistance, who in loving-kindness gave me a resigned heart. Then at a suitable opportunity I went to the public house, and seeing the man amongst a company, I went to him and told him I wanted to speak with him; so we went aside, and there in the fear and dread of the Almighty I expressed to him what rested on my mind, which he took kindly, and afterward showed more regard to me than before. In a few years after, he died middle-aged, and I often thought that had I neglected my duty in that case it would have given me great trouble, and I was humbly thankful to my gracious Father, who had supported me herein.

My employer, having a Negro woman, sold her and directed me to write a bill of sale, the man being waiting who bought her. The thing was sudden, and though the thoughts of writing an instrument of slavery for one of my fellow creatures felt uneasy, yet I remembered I was hired by the year, that it was my master who directed me to do it, and that it was an elderly man, a member of our Society,[23] who bought her; so through weakness I gave way and wrote it, but at the executing it, I was so afflicted in my mind that I said before my master and the Friend that I believed slavekeeping to be a practice inconsistent with the Christian religion. This in some degree abated my uneasiness, yet as often as I reflected seriously upon it I thought I should have been clearer if I had desired to be excused from it as a thing against my conscience, for such it was. And some time after this a young man of our Society spake to me to write an instrument of slavery, he having lately taken a Negro into his house. I told him I was not easy to write it, for though many kept slaves in our Society, as in others, I still believed the practice was not right, and desired to be excused from writing [it]. I spoke to him in good will, and he told me that keeping slaves was not altogether agreeable to his mind, but that the slave being a gift made to his wife, he had accepted of her.

---

[21] Since the Quakers regarded every day as holy, they celebrated no special holidays.

[22] Ezekiel 3:17: "Son of man, I have made thee a watchman unto the house of Israel: therefore hear the word at my mouth, and give them warning from me."

[23] The Society of Friends. Woolman later became a leader of the effort to free the slaves of the Quakers.

[from **Travels Through North Carolina**]

About this time believing it good for me to settle, and thinking seriously about a companion, my heart was turned to the Lord with desires that he would give me wisdom to proceed therein agreeable to his will; and he was pleased to give me a well-inclined damsel, Sarah Ellis,[24] to whom I was married the 18th day, 8th month, 1749.

In the fall of the year 1750 died my father Samuel Woolman[25] with a fever, aged about sixty years. In his lifetime he manifested much care for us his children, that in our youth we might learn to fear the Lord, often endeavouring to imprint in our minds the true principles of virtue, and particularly to cherish in us a spirit of tenderness, not only toward poor people, but also towards all creatures of which we had the command.

After my return from Carolina I made some observations on keeping slaves, which I had some time before showed him, and he perused the manuscript,[26] proposed a few alterations, and appeared well satisfied that I found a concern on that account. And in his last sickness as I was watching with him one night, he being so far spent that there was no expectation of his recovery, but had the perfect use of his understanding, he asked me concerning the manuscript, whether I expected soon to offer it to the Overseers of the Press, and after some conversation thereon said, "I have all along been deeply affected with the oppression of the poor Negroes, and now at last my concern for them is as great as ever."

By his direction I had wrote his will in a time of health, and that night he desired me to read it to him, which I did, and he said it was agreeable to his mind. He then made mention of his end, which he believed was now near, and signified that though he was sensible[27] of many imperfections in the course of his life, yet his experience of the power of Truth and of the love and goodness of God from time to time, even till now, was such that he had no doubt but that in leaving this life he should enter into one more happy.

The next day his sister Elizabeth came to see him and told him of the decease of their sister Anne, who died a few days before. He then said, "I reckon sister Anne was free to leave this world." Elizabeth said she was. He then said, "I also am free to leave it," and being in great weakness of body said, "I hope I shall shortly go to rest." He continued in a weighty[28] frame of mind and was sensible till near the last.

2nd day, 9th month, 1751. Feeling drawings in my mind to visit Friends at the Great Meadows, in the upper part of West Jersey, with the unity of our Monthly Meeting I went there and had some searching laborious exercise amongst Friends in those parts, and found inward peace therein.

In the 9th month, 1753, in company with my well-esteemed friend John Sykes[29] and with the unity of Friends, we travelled about two weeks visiting Friends in Bucks County.[30] We laboured in the love of the gospel according to the measure received, and through the mercies of him who is strength to the poor who trust in him, we

---

[24] Woolman had known Sarah Ellis (1721–1787) since childhood.

[25] Samuel Woolman lived from 1690 to 1750.

[26] Woolman's essay entitled *Some Considerations on the Keeping of Negroes* (1754).

[27] Aware.

[28] Serious.

[29] Sykes (1682–1771) was a Quaker minister and frequent traveling companion of Woolman.

[30] In eastern Pennsylvania.

found satisfaction in our visit. And in the next winter, way opening to visit Friends' families within the compass of our Monthly Meeting, partly by the labours of two friends from Pennsylvania, I joined some in it, having had a desire some time that it might go forward amongst us.

About this time a person at some distance lying sick, his brother came to me to write his will. I knew he had slaves, and asking his brother, was told he intended to leave them slaves to his children. As writing is a profitable employ, as offending sober people is disagreeable to my inclination, I was straitened[31] in my mind; but as I looked to the Lord, he inclined my heart to his testimony, and I told the man that I believed the practice of continuing slavery to this people was not right and had a scruple in mind against doing writings of that kind: that though many in our Society kept them as slaves, still I was not easy to be concerned in it and desired to be excused from going to write the will. I spake to him in the fear of the Lord, and he made no reply to what I said, but went away; he also had some concerns in the practice, and I thought he was displeased with me.

In this case I had a fresh confirmation that acting contrary to present outward interest from a motive of divine love and in regard to truth and righteousness, and thereby incurring the resentments of people, opens the way to a treasure better than silver and to a friendship exceeding the friendship of men.

On the 7th day, 2nd month, 1754, at night, I dreamed that I was walking in an orchard, it appeared to be about the middle of the afternoon; when on a sudden I saw two lights in the east resembling two suns, but of a dull and gloomy aspect. The one appeared about the height of the sun at three hours high, and the other more northward and one-third lower. In a few minutes the air in the east appeared to be mingled with fire, and like a terrible storm coming westward the streams of fire reached the orchard where I stood, but I felt no harm. I then found one of my acquaintance standing near me, who was greatly distressed in mind at this unusual appearance. My mind felt calm, and I said to my friend, "We must all once die, and if it please the Lord that our death be in this way, it is good for us to be resigned." Then I walked to a house hard by, and going upstairs, saw people with sad and troubled aspects, amongst whom I passed into another room where the floor was only some loose boards. There I sat down alone by a window, and looking out I saw in the south three great red streams standing at equal distance from each other, the bottom of which appeared to stand on the earth and the top to reach above the region of the clouds. Across those three streams went less ones, and from each end of such small stream others extended in regular lines to the earth, all red and appeared to extend through the whole southern firmament. There then appeared on a green plain a great multitude of men in a military posture, some of whom I knew. They came near the house, and passing on westward some of them, looking up at me, expressed themselves in a scoffing, taunting way, to which I made no reply; soon after, an old captain of the militia came to me, and I was told these men were assembled to improve in the discipline of war. . . .

Until the year 1756 I continued to retail goods, besides following my trade as a

---

[31] Upset; distressed.

tailor, about which time I grew uneasy on account of my business growing too cumbersome. I began with selling trimmings for garments and from thence proceeded to sell clothes and linens, and at length having got a considerable shop of goods, my trade increased every year and the road to large business appeared open; but I felt a stop in my mind.

Through the mercies of the Almighty I had in a good degree learned to be content with a plain way of living. I had but a small family, that on serious consideration I believed Truth did not require me to engage in much cumbrous affairs. It had been my general practice to buy and sell things really useful. Things that served chiefly to please the vain mind in people I was not easy to trade in, seldom did it, and whenever I did I found it weaken me as a Christian.

The increase of business became my burden, for though my natural inclination was toward merchandise, yet I believed Truth required me to live more free from outward cumbers,[32] and there was now a strife in my mind between the two; and in this exercise my prayers were put up to the Lord, who graciously heard me and gave me a heart resigned to his holy will. Then I lessened my outward business, and as I had opportunity told my customers of my intentions that they might consider what shop to turn to, and so in a while wholly laid down merchandise, following my trade as a tailor, myself only, having no apprentice. I also had a nursery of apple trees, in which I employed some of my time—hoeing, grafting, trimming, and inoculating.

In merchandise it is the custom where I lived to sell chiefly on credit, and poor people often get in debt, and when payment is expected, not having wherewith to pay, their creditors often sue for it at law. Having often observed occurrences of this kind, I found it good for me to advise poor people to take such goods as were most useful and not costly.

In the time of trading, I had an opportunity of seeing that too liberal a use of spirituous liquors and the custom of wearing too costly apparel lead some people into great inconveniences, and these two things appear to be often connected one with the other. For by not attending to that use of things which is consistent with universal righteousness, there is an increase of labour which extends beyond what our Heavenly Father intends for us. And by great labour, and often by much sweating in the heat, there is even amongst such who are not drunkards a craving of some liquors to revive the spirits: that partly by the wanton, luxurious drinking of some, and partly by the drinkings of others led to it through immoderate labour, very great quantities of rum are every year expended in our colonies, the greater part of which we should have no need did we steadily attend to pure wisdom.

Where men take pleasure in feeling their minds elevated with strong drink and so indulge their appetite as to disorder their understandings, neglect their duty as members in a family or civil society, and cast off all pretense to religion, their case is much to be pitied. And where such whose lives are for the most part regular, and whose examples have a strong influence on the minds of others, adhere to some customs which strongly draw toward the use of more strong liquor than pure wisdom directs to the use of, this also, as it hinders the spreading of the spirit of

[32] Obstacles; encumbrances.

meekness and strengthens the hands of the more excessive drinkers, is a case to be lamented.

As the least degree of luxury hath some connection with evil, for those who profess to be disciples of Christ and are looked upon as leaders of the people, to have that mind in them which was also in him, and so stand separate from every wrong way, is a means of help to the weaker. As I have sometimes been much spent in the heat and taken spirits to revive me, I have found by experience that in such circumstance the mind is not so calm nor so fitly disposed for divine meditation as when all such extremes are avoided, and have felt an increasing care to attend to that Holy Spirit which sets right bounds to our desires and leads those who faithfully follow it to apply all the gifts of divine providence to the purposes for which they were intended. Did such who have the care of great estates attend with singleness of heart to this Heavenly Instructor, which so opens and enlarges the mind that men love their neighbours as themselves, they would have wisdom given them to manage without finding occasion to employ some people in the luxuries of life or to make it necessary for others to labour too hard. But for want of steadily regarding this principle of divine love, a selfish spirit takes place in the minds of people, which is attended with darkness and manifold confusions in the world.

In the course of my trading being somewhat troubled at the various law suits about collecting money which I saw going forward, on applying to a constable he gave me a list of his proceeding for one year as follows—to wit, served 267 warrants, 103 summonses, and 79 executions. As to writs served by the sheriff, I got no account of them.

I once had a warrant for an idle man who I believed was about to run away, which was the only time I applied to the law to recover money.

Though trading in things useful is an honest employ, yet through the great number of superfluities which are bought and sold and through the corruption of the times, they who apply to merchandise for a living have great need to be well experienced in that precept which the prophet Jeremiah laid down for his scribe: "Seekest thou great things for thyself? Seek them not."[33] . . .

A Friend of some note in Virginia, who hath slaves, told me that he being far from home on a lonesome journey had many serious thoughts about them, and that his mind was so impressed therewith that he believed that he saw a time coming when divine providence would alter the circumstance of these people respecting their condition as slaves.

From hence I went to Newbegun Creek[34] and sat a considerable time in much weakness. Then I felt Truth open the way to speak a little in much plainness and simplicity, till at length through the increase of divine love amongst us we had a seasoning opportunity. From thence to the head of Little River on a First Day, where was a crowded meeting and I believe was through divine goodness made profitable to some. Thence to the Old Neck, where I was led into a careful searching out the secret workings of the mystery of iniquity, which under a cover of religion exalts itself against that pure spirit which leads in the way of meekness and self-denial. From thence to Piney Woods; this was the last meeting I was at in Carolina and was large,

[33] See Jeremiah 45:5.   [34] In North Carolina.

and my heart being deeply engaged, I was drawn forth into a fervent labour amongst them.

When I was at Newbegin Creek, a Friend was there who laboured for his living, having no Negroes, and had been a minister many years. He came to me the next day, and as we rode together he signified that he wanted to talk with me concerning a difficulty he had been under, and related it near as follows, to wit: That as monies had of late years been raised by a tax to carry on the wars, he had a scruple in his mind in regard to paying it and chose rather to suffer distraint of goods than pay it. And as he was the only person who refused it in them parts and knew not that anyone else was in the like circumstance, he signified that it had been a heavy trial upon him, and the more so for that some of his brethren had been uneasy with his conduct in that case, and added that from a sympathy he felt with me yesterday in meeting, he found a freedom thus to open the matter in the way of querying concerning Friends in our parts; whereupon I told him the state of Friends amongst us as well as I was able, and also that I had for some time been under the like scruple. I believed him to be one who was concerned to walk uprightly before the Lord and esteemed it my duty to preserve this memorandum.

From hence I went back into Virginia and had a meeting near James Copeland's; it was a time of inward suffering, but through the goodness of the Lord I was made content. Then to another meeting where through the renewings of pure love we had a very comfortable meeting.

Travelling up and down of late, I have had renewed evidences that to be faithful to the Lord and content with his will concerning me is a most necessary and useful lesson for me to be learning, looking less at the effects of my labour than at the pure motion and reality of the concern as it arises from heavenly love. In the Lord Jehovah is everlasting strength, and as the mind by a humble resignation is united to him and we utter words from an inward knowledge that they arise from the heavenly spring, though our way may be difficult and require close attention to keep in it, and though the manner in which we may be led may tend to our own abasement, yet if we continue in patience and meekness, heavenly peace is the reward of our labours.

From hence I went to Curles Meeting, which, though small, was reviving to the honest-hearted. Thence to Black Creek and Caroline Meetings, from whence, accompanied by William Stanley[35] before-mentioned, we rode to Goose Creek, being much through the woods and about one hundred miles. We lodged the first night at a public house, the second in the woods, and the next day we reached a Friend's house at Goose Creek. In the woods we lay under some disadvantage, having no fireworks, nor bells for our horses, but we stopped some before night and let them feed on wild grass, which was plenty, we the meantime cutting with our knives a store against night, and then tied them; and gathering some bushes under an oak we lay down, but the mosquitoes being plenty and the ground damp, I slept but little.

Thus lying in the wilderness and looking at the stars, I was led to contemplate the condition of our first parents when they were sent forth from the garden, and

[35] Stanley (1729–1807) was from Cedar Creek, Virginia.

considered that they had no house, no tools for business, no garments but what their Creator gave them, no vessels for use, nor any fire to cook roots or herbs. But the Almighty, though they had been disobedient, was a father to them; way opened in process of time for all the conveniences of life. And he who by the gracious influence of his spirit illuminated their understanding and showed them what was acceptable to him and tended to their felicity as intelligent creatures, did also provide means for their happy living in this world as they attended to the manifestations of his wisdom.

To provide things relative to our outward living in the way of true wisdom is good, and the gift of improving in things useful is a good gift and comes from the Father of Lights. Many have had this gif[t] and from age to age there have been improvements of this kind made in the world. But some, not keeping to the pure gift, have in the creaturely cunning and self-exaltation sought out many inventions, which inventions of men, as distinct from that uprightness in which man was created, as in the first motion it was evil so the effects of it have been, and are, evil. That at this day it is as necessary for us constantly to attend on the heavenly gift to be qualified to use rightly the good things in this life amidst great improvements, as it was for our first parents, when they were without any improvements, without any friend or father but God only. . . .

[On Paying Taxes and Keeping Slaves]

One evening a Friend came to our lodgings who was a justice of the peace and in a friendly way introduced the subject of refusing to pay taxes to support wars, and perceiving that I was one who scrupled the payment, said he had wanted an opportunity with some in that circumstance; whereupon we had some conversation in a brotherly way on some texts of Scripture relating thereto, in the conclusion of which he said that according to our way of proceeding it would follow that whenever administration of government was ill, we must suffer distraint of goods rather than pay actively toward supporting it. To which I replied, "Men put in public stations are intended for good purposes, some to make good laws, others to take care that those laws are not broken. Now if those men thus set apart do not answer the design of their institution, our freely contributing to support them in that capacity when we certainly know that they are wrong is to strengthen them in a wrong way and tends to make them forget that it is so. But when from a clear understanding of the case we are really uneasy with the application of money, and in the spirit of meekness suffer distress to be made on our goods rather than to pay actively, this joined with an upright uniform life may tend to put men athinking about their own public conduct."

He said he would propose a medium: that is, where men in authority do not act agreeable to the mind of those who constituted them, he thought the people should rather remonstrate than refuse a voluntary payment of moneys so demanded, and added, "Civil government is an agreement of free men by which they oblige themselves to abide by certain laws as a standard, and to refuse to obey in that case is of like nature as to refuse to do any particular act which we had convenanted to do."

I replied that in making covenants it was agreeable to honesty and uprightness to take care that we do not foreclose ourselves from adhering strictly to true virtue in all occurrences relating thereto. But if I should unwarily promise to obey the orders of a certain man, or number of men, without any proviso, and he or they command me to assist in doing some great wickedness, I may then see my error in making such promise, and an active obedience in that case would be adding one evil to another; that though by such promise I should be liable to punishment for disobedience, yet to suffer rather than act to me appears most virtuous.

The whole of our conversation was in calmness and good will. And here it may be noted that in Pennsylvania, where there are many Friends under that scruple, a petition was presented to the Assembly by a large number of Friends, asking that no law might be passed to enjoin the payment of money for such uses which they as a peaceable people could not pay for conscience' sake.

The Monthly Meeting of Philadelphia having been under a concern on account of some Friends who this summer, 1758, had bought Negro slaves, the said meeting moved it in their Quarterly Meeting to have the minute reconsidered in the Yearly Meeting which was made last on that subject. And the said Quarterly Meeting appointed a committee to consider it and report to their next, which committee having met once and adjourned, and I, going to Philadelphia to meet a committee of the Yearly Meeting, was in town the evening on which the Quarterly Meeting's committee met the second time, and finding an inclination to sit with them, was admitted; and Friends had a weighty conference on the subject. And soon after their next Quarterly Meeting I heard that the case was coming to our Yearly Meeting, which brought a weighty exercise upon me, and under a sense of my own infirmities and the great danger I felt of turning aside from perfect purity, my mind was often drawn to retire alone and put up my prayers to the Lord that he would be graciously pleased to strengthen me, that setting aside all views of self-interest and the friendship of this world, I might stand fully resigned to his holy will.

In this Yearly Meeting several weighty matters were considered, and toward the last, that in relation to dealing with persons who purchase slaves. During the several sittings of the said meeting, my mind was frequently covered with inward prayer, and I could say with David that tears were my meat day and night.[36] The case of slavekeeping lay heavy upon me, nor did I find any engagement to speak directly to any other matter before the meeting. Now when this case was opened, several faithful Friends spake weightily thereto, with which I was comforted, and feeling a concern to cast in my mite, I said in substance as follows:

> In the difficulties attending us in this life, nothing is more precious than the mind of Truth inwardly manifested, and it is my earnest desire that in this weighty matter we may be so truly humbled as to be favoured with a clear understanding of the mind of Truth and follow it; this would be of more advantage to the Society than any mediums which are not in the clearness of divine wisdom. The case is difficult to some who have them, but if such set aside all self-interest and

[36] See Psalm 42:3.

come to be weaned from the desire of getting estates, or even from holding them together when Truth requires the contrary, I believe way will open that they will know how to steer through those difficulties.

Many Friends appeared to be deeply bowed under the weight of the work and manifested much firmness in their love to the cause of truth and universal righteousness in the earth. And though none did openly justify the practice of slavekeeping in general, yet some appeared concerned lest the meeting should go into such measures as might give uneasiness to many brethren, alleging that if Friends patiently continued under the exercise, the Lord in time to come might open a way for the deliverance of these people. And I, finding an engagement to speak, said:

> My mind is often led to consider the purity of the Divine Being and the justice of his judgments, and herein my soul is covered with awfulness. I cannot omit to hint of some cases where people have not been treated with the purity of justice, and the event hath been melancholy.
>
> Many slaves on this continent are oppressed, and their cries have reached the ears of the Most High! Such is the purity and certainty of his judgments that he cannot be partial in our favour. In infinite love and goodness he hath opened our understandings from one time to another concerning our duty toward this people, and it is not a time for delay.
>
> Should we now be sensible of what he requires of us, and through a respect to the private interest of some persons or through a regard to some friendships which do not stand on an immutable foundation, neglect to do our duty in firmness and constancy, still waiting for some extraordinary means to bring about their deliverance, it may be that by terrible things in righteousness God may answer us in this matter.

Many faithful brethren laboured with great firmness, and the love of Truth in a good degree prevailed. Several Friends who had Negroes expressed their desire that a rule might be made to deal with such Friends as offenders who bought slaves in future. To this it was answered that the root of this evil would never be effectually struck at until a thorough search was made into the circumstances of such Friends who kept Negroes, in regard to the righteousness of their motives in keeping them, that impartial justice might be administered throughout.

Several Friends expressed their desire that a visit might be made to such Friends who kept slaves, and many Friends declared that they believed liberty was the Negro's right, to which at length no opposition was made publicly, so that a minute was made more full on that subject than any heretofore and the names of several Friends entered who were free to join in a visit to such who kept slaves.

1756–1772/1774

Native American Literature:
The Myth of the Noble Savage

Our world has just discovered another world (and who will guarantee us that it is the last of its brothers, since the daemons, the sibyls, and we ourselves have up to now been ignorant of this one?) no less great, full, and well-limbed than itself, yet so new and so infantile that it is still being taught its A B C; not fifty years ago it knew neither letters, nor weights and measures, nor clothes, nor wheat, nor vines. It was still quite naked at the breast, and lived only on what its nursing mother provided. If we are right to infer the end of our world, and that poet is right about the youth of his own age, this other world will only be coming into the light when ours is leaving it. The universe will fall into paralysis; one member will be crippled, the other in full vigor.

I am much afraid that we shall have very greatly hastened the decline and ruin of this new world by our contagion, and that we will have sold it our opinions and our arts very dear. It was an infant world; yet we have not whipped it and subjected it to our discipline by the advantage of our natural valor and strength, nor won it over by our justice and goodness, nor subjugated it by our magnanimity. Most of the responses of these people and most of our dealings with them show that they were not at all behind us in natural brightness of mind and pertinence. . . .

How easy it would have been to make good use of souls so fresh, so famished to learn, and having, for the most part, such fine natural beginnings! On the contrary, we took advantage of their ignorance and inexperience to incline them the more easily toward treachery, lewdness, avarice, and every sort of inhumanity and cruelty, after the example and pattern of our ways. Who ever set the utility of commerce and trading at such a price? So many cities razed, so many nations exterminated, so many millions of people put to the sword, and the richest and most beautiful part of the world turned upside down, for the traffic in pearls and pepper! Base and mechanical victories! Never did ambition, never did public enmities, drive men against one another to such horrible hostilities and such miserable calamities.

Michel de Montaigne, "Of Coaches" (1585–1588)

Those that scaped the fire were slain with the sword, some hewed to pieces, others run through with their rapiers, so as they were quickly dispatched and very few escaped. It was conceived they thus destroyed about 400 at this time. It was a fearful sight to see them thus frying in the fire and the streams of blood quenching the same, and horrible was the stink and scent thereof; but the victory seemed a sweet sacrifice, and they gave the praise thereof to God, who had wrought so wonderfully for them, thus to enclose their enemies in their hands and give them so speedy a victory over so proud and insulting an enemy.

William Bradford, on the burning of a Pequot village,
Of Plymouth Plantation (1637)

I should think it requisite that convenient tracts of land should be set out to them; and that by plain and natural boundaries, as much as may be—as lakes, rivers, mountains, rocks—upon which for any Englishman to encroach should be accounted a crime.

Samuel Sewall, letter to Sir William Ashurst (May 3, 1700)

You will do well to try to inoculate the Indians by means of blankets in which smallpox patients have slept, as well as by every other method that can serve to extirpate this execrable race. I should be very glad if your scheme of hunting them down by dogs could take effect.

General Jeffrey Amherst, letter (1732)

Men no sooner began to set a Value upon each other and know what Esteem was, than each laid claim to it, and it was no longer safe for any Man to refuse it to another. Hence the first Duties of Civility and Politeness, even among Savages; and hence every voluntary Injury became an Affront, as besides the Mischief, which resulted from it as an Injury, the Party offended was sure to find in it a Contempt for his Person more intolerable than the Mischief itself. It is thus that every Man, punishing the Contempt expressed for him by others in proportion to the value set upon himself, the Effects of Revenge become terrible, and Men learned to be sanguinary and cruel. Such precisely was the Degree attained by most of the savage Nations with whom we are acquainted. And it is for want of sufficiently distinguishing Ideas, and observing at how great a Distance these People were from the first state of Nature, that so many Authors have hastily concluded that Man is naturally cruel, and requires a regular System of Police to be reclaimed; whereas nothing can be more gentle than him in his primitive State, when placed by Nature at an equal Distance from the Stupidity of Brutes, and the pernicious good Sense of civilized Man. . . .

The more we reflect on this State, the more convinced we shall be, that it was the least subject of any to Revolutions, the best for Man, and that nothing could have drawn him out of it but some fatal Accident, which, for the public good, should never have happened. The Example of the Savages, most of whom have been found in this Condition, seems to confirm that Mankind was formed ever to remain in it, that this Condition is the real Youth of the World, and that all ulterior Improvements have been so many Steps, in Appearance towards the Perfection of Individuals, but in Fact towards the Decrepitness of the Species.

Jean Jacques Rousseau, *Discourse upon the Origin and Foundation of the Inequality Among Mankind* (1755)

Unhappy people! to have lived in such times, and by such neighbors! We have seen that they would have been safer among the ancient heathens with whom the rites of hospitality were sacred. They would have been considered as guests of the public, and the religion of the country would have operated in their favor. But our frontier people call themselves Christians! They would have been safer if they had submitted to the Turks.

> Benjamin Franklin, *A Narrative of the Late Massacres in Lancaster County* (1764), [written soon after the murder of several Conestoga Indians by Scots-Irish settlers in Pennsylvania]

I have had frequent opportunities to observe moral dispositions in the men we call savages, that would do much honour to the most civilized European.

> Pierre Marie François De Pages, *Travels Round the World in the Years 1767–1771*

Seneca and Cherokee Oral History

No sooner had Europeans encountered coastal-dwelling Native Americans than many Indian people quickly ceased to exist. Within twenty years of Columbus's first having sighted America on October 12, 1492, the entire native population of Hispaniola (now Santo Domingo) was eliminated. Powhatan's Algonquin Confederacy had disappeared within fifty years of his speech to Captain John Smith.

Native American groups living considerably inland, such as the Iroquois, the Cherokee, and the Creek, were far more fortunate. Several generations passed before the number of European emigrants on the coast became so large that the adventurous were encouraged to strike out for the frontier. During this period of colonial expansion, several large inland groups of Native Americans had the opportunity to adjust physically to the new diseases the Europeans had carried with them (such as measles, smallpox, and whooping cough) as well as to adjust culturally, economically, and socially to the implications of permanent white settlement in North America. In addition, interior groups such as the Iroquois, the Cherokee, and the Creek were able to maintain a far more independent stance in response to the different European factions competing for dominance in the region. These Native Americans were able to play off the various European powers, especially the French and the English, against each other.

While the coastal Indians were alternately fighting off and trying to make peace with various European colonial groups, the inland tribes continued to be preoccupied with intertribal relations. But the introduction of European goods complicated matters. The Indians found themselves increasingly caught up in the fur trade in order to satisfy their initial desire, and subsequent need, for those goods. For example, the northern Iroquois tribes of the Five Nations, in what is now northern New York State, not only participated in the fur trade as primary suppliers but also served increasingly as brokers between neighboring Indian groups and the Europeans. They maintained this position through the political and military power of the Iroquois League. Before 1680 they had conquered all of the tribes on their immediate borders and aimed their military prowess against the more distant Illinois, Catawba, and Cherokee tribes. For nearly one hundred years the Iroquois and Cherokee continued to conduct small-scale raids on each other. As James Mooney notes in *Myths of the Cherokee,* "The great object of every Iroquois boy [was] to go against the Cherokee as soon as he was old enough to take the war path."

The journey from Iroquois country to the Cherokee frontier took more than five days "for a rapidly traveling war party" from what is now western New York State along "the Great Indian War Path" to Virginia, Kentucky, northern Tennessee, and North Carolina and on to the Creek territory in what is now Alabama. Mooney observes that "as the distance was too great for large expeditions, the war consisted chiefly of a series of individual exploits, a single Cherokee often going hundreds of miles to strike a blow, which was surely to be retaliated by the warriors to the north." The two narratives printed here offer different perspectives on such skirmishes and reveal something of the Native American ritual and folklore that surround war. The first selection represents Senecan oral history, the second Cherokee.

Cherokee oral tradition reports that the war was finally brought to an end by an Iroquois delegation sent to the Cherokee to propose a general alliance of southern and western tribes. A formal peace treaty was arranged by Sir William Johnson, the British agent for the Mohawk, in 1768.

Further Reading:
A. F. C. Wallace, *The Death and Rebirth of the Seneca,* 1970.
Handbook of North American Indians, gen. ed. W. C. Sturtevant, vol. 15, *Northeast,* ed. B. G. Trigger, 1978.

Text:
J. Mooney, *Myths of the Cherokees, 19th Annual Report of the Bureau of American Ethnology, Part 1, 1897–98,* 1900.

The Unseen Helpers

Ganogwioeoñ, a war chief of the Seneca, led a party against the Cherokee. When they came near the first town he left his men outside and went in alone. At the first house he found an old woman and her granddaughter. They did not see him, and he went into the house and hid himself under some wood. When darkness came on he heard the old woman say, "Maybe Ganogwioeoñ is near; I'll close the door." After a while he heard them going to bed. When he thought they were asleep he went into the house. The fire had burned down low, but the girl was still awake and saw him. She was about to scream, when he said, "I am Ganogwioeoñ. If you scream I'll kill you. If you keep quiet I'll not hurt you." They talked together, and he told her that in the morning she must bring the chief's daughter to him. She promised to do it, and told him where he should wait. Just before daylight he left the house.

In the morning the girl went to the chief's house and said to his daughter, "Let's go out together for wood." The chief's daughter got ready and went with her, and when they came to the place where Ganogwioeoñ was hiding he sprang out and killed her,[1] but did not hurt the other girl. He pulled off the scalp and gave such a loud scalp yell that all the warriors in the town heard it and came running out after him. He shook the scalp at them and then turned and ran. He killed the first one that came up, but when he tried to shoot the next one the bow broke and the Cherokee got him.

They tied him and carried him to the two women of the tribe who had the power to decide what should be done with him. Each of these women had two snakes tattooed on her lips, with their heads opposite each other, in such a way that when she opened her mouth the two snakes opened their mouths also. They decided to burn the soles of his feet until they were blistered, then to put grains of corn under the skin and to chase him with clubs until they had beaten him to death.

They stripped him and burnt his feet. Then they tied a bark rope around his waist, with an old man to hold the other end, and made him run between two lines of people, and with clubs in their hands. When they gave the word to start Ganogwioeoñ pulled the rope away from the old man and broke through the line and ran until he had left them all out of sight. When night came he crawled into a hollow log. He was naked and unarmed, with his feet in a pitiful condition, and thought he could never get away.

He heard footsteps on the leaves outside and thought his enemies were upon him. The footsteps came up to the log and some one said to another, "This is our friend." Then the stranger said to Ganogwioeoñ, "You think you are the same as dead, but it is not so. We will take care of you. Stick out your feet." He put out his feet from the log and felt something licking them. After a while the voice said, "I think we have licked his feet enough. Now we must crawl inside the log and lie on each side of him to keep him warm." They crawled in beside him. In the morning they crawled out and told him to stick out his feet again. They licked them again and then said to him, "Now we have done all we can do this time. Go on until you come to the place where you made a bark shelter a long time ago, and under the bark you will find something to help you." Ganogwioeoñ crawled out of the log, but they were gone. His feet were better now and he could walk comfortably. He went on until about noon, when he came to the bark shelter, and under it he found a knife, an awl, and a flint, that his men had hidden there two years before. He took them and started on again.

Toward evening he looked around until he found another hollow tree and crawled into it to sleep. At night he heard the footsteps and voices again. When he put out his feet again, as the strangers told him to do, they licked his feet as before and then crawled in and lay down on each side of him to keep him warm. Still he could not see them. In the morning after they went out they licked his feet again and said to him, "At noon you will find food." Then they went away.

[1] The Iroquois believed that killing a woman required greater courage because the attacker had to penetrate a village to do so.

Ganogwioeoñ crawled out of the tree and went on. At noon he came to a burning log, and near it was a dead bear, which was still warm, as if it had been killed only a short time before. He skinned the bear and found it very fat. He cut up the meat and roasted as much as he could eat or carry. While it was roasting he scraped the skin and rubbed rotten wood dust on it to clean it until he was tired. When night came he lay down to sleep. He heard the steps and the voices again and one said, "Well, our friend is lying down. He has plenty to eat, and it does not seem as if he is going to die. Let us lick his feet again." When they had finished they said to him, "You need not worry any more now. You will get home all right." Before it was day they left him.

When morning came he put the bearskin around him like a shirt, with the hair outside, and started on again, taking as much of the meat as he could carry. That night his friends came to him again. They said, "Your feet are well, but you will be cold," so they lay again on each side of him. Before daylight they left, saying, "About noon you will find something to wear." He went on and about midday he came to two young bears just killed. He skinned them and dressed the skins, then roasted as much meat as he wanted, and lay down to sleep. In the morning he made leggings of the skins, took some of the meat, and started on.

His friends came again the next night and told him that in the morning he would come upon something else to wear. As they said, about noon he found two fawns just killed. He turned the skins and made himself a pair of moccasins, then cut some of the meat, and traveled on until evening, when he made a fire and had supper.

That night again he heard the steps and voices, and one said, "My friend, very soon now you will reach home safely and find your friends all well. Now we will tell you why we have helped you. Whenever you went hunting you always gave the best part of the meat to us and kept only the smallest part for yourself. For that we are thankful and help you. In the morning you will see us and know who we are."[2]

In the morning when he woke up they were still there—two men as he thought —but after he had said the last words to them and started on, he turned again to look, and one was a white wolf and the other a black wolf. That day he reached home.

1900

Hemp-Carrier

On the southern slope of the ridge, along the trail from Robbinsville to Valley river, in Cherokee county, North Carolina, are the remains of a number of stone cairns. The piles are leveled now, but thirty years ago the stones were still heaped up into

[2] Ganogwioeoñ is apparently a member of the wolf clan, whose totemic figure protects him here. The Iroquois always left a portion of their hunting for their totemic animal. Thus the wolf protects him here.

pyramids, to which every Cherokee who passed added a stone. According to the tradition these piles marked the graves of a number of women and children of the tribe who were surprised and killed on the spot by a raiding party of the Iroquois shortly before the final peace between the two Nations. As soon as the news was brought to the settlements on Hiwassee and Cheowa[1] a party was made under Tâle´tanigi´skĭ, "Hemp-carrier," to follow and take vengeance on the enemy. Among others of the party was the father of the noted chief Tsunu´lăhûñ´skĭ, or Junaluska, who died on Cheowa about 1855.

For days they followed the trail of the Iroquois across the Great Smoky mountains, through forests and over rivers, until they finally tracked them to their very town in the far northern Seneca country. On the way they met another war party headed for the south, and the Cherokee killed them all and took their scalps. When they came near the Seneca town it was almost night, and they heard shouts in the townhouse, where the women were dancing over the fresh Cherokee scalps. The avengers hid themselves near the spring, and as the dancers came down to drink the Cherokee silently killed one and another until they had counted as many scalps as had been taken on Cheowa, and still the dancers in the townhouse never thought that enemies were near. Then said the Cherokee leader, "We have covered the scalps of our women and children. Shall we go home now like cowards, or shall we raise the war whoop and let the Seneca know that we are men?" "Let them come, if they will," said his men; and they raised the scalp yell of the Cherokee. At once there was an answering shout from the townhouse, and the dance came to a sudden stop. The Seneca warriors swarmed out with ready gun and hatchet, but the nimble Cherokee were off and away. There was a hot pursuit in the darkness, but the Cherokee knew the trails and were light and active runners, and managed to get away with the loss of only a single man. The rest got home safely, and the people were so well pleased with Hemp-carrier's bravery and success that they gave him seven wives.[2]

1900

Samson Occom
1723–1792

Missionaries conducted most of the training of Native Americans in English during the colonial period. Samson Occom was a product of such efforts and one of the first Native Americans to publish in English. A member of the Mohegan (or Mohican) tribe that, along with the Pequot, settled in southeastern Connecticut, Occom was one of the first students of the celebrated Congregational minister Eleazar Wheelock. In 1749 Occom moved to eastern Long Island to set up a church and school for the Montauk Indians. He was formally ordained in 1759. In 1766 he traveled to England to raise funds to establish what became Dartmouth College.

---

[1] Rivers running through Tennessee and North Carolina.

[2] Seven is the Cherokee ritual number.

On September 2, 1772, Samson Occom preached a sermon at the execution of Moses Paul, a thirty-year-old Mohegan who had been convicted of murder and sentenced to be hanged. Paul had served in the colonial militia and on board various frigates and commercial ships. In inviting Occom to preach at his execution, Moses Paul "earnestly wishes," Occom noted, "that his untimely End, may be a means of detering others, from following those sinful Practices, which has made him so public an Example for his Sin and Folly." The following excerpts from Occom's fiery sermon on "the wages of sin" and the self-inflicted frightful consequences of Indian drunkenness recall the religious and rhetorical traditions of Jonathan Edwards's "Sinners in the Hands of an Angry God" and also reveal Occom's self-consciousness about his audience—both the Indian Moses Paul and the white colonists who had come to witness his execution.

The sermon, the earliest extant by a Native American, quickly received widespread attention. Within a few years it had been reprinted nineteen times, making it a best-seller on the eve of the American Revolution and launching Occom's career as a noted public figure. Occom also composed a good deal of church music, much of which is gathered in his volume *A Choice Collection of Hymns and Spiritual Songs* (1774). A highly respected figure in both religious and educational circles, Samson Occom died in 1792, having devoted himself for years to the success of Dartmouth College.

Further Reading:
W. D. Love, *Samson Occom and the Christian Indians of New England*, 1899.
H. Blodgett, *Samson Occom*, 1935.

Text:
A Sermon Preached at the Execution of Moses Paul, an Indian, 1772.

---

from A Sermon, Preached at the Execution of Moses Paul, an Indian[*]

The Preface

The world is already full of books; and the people of God are abundantly furnished with excellent books upon divine subjects; and it seems, that every subject has been written upon over and over again: and the people in very deed have had precept upon precept, line upon line, here a little and there a little; and so in the whole, they have much, yea, very much, they have enough and more than enough. And when I come to consider these things, I am ready to say with myself, What folly and madness is it in me to suffer any thing of mine to appear in print, to expose my ignorance to the world.

It seems altogether unlikely that my performance will do any manner of service in the world, since the most excellent writings of worthy and learned men are

---

[*] The title page of the first edition reads: "A SERMON, Preached at the Execution of *Moses Paul*, An INDIAN, Who was executed at *New-Haven*, on the 2d of *September*, 1772, for the MURDER of Mr. MOSES COOK, Late of *Waterbury*, on the 7th of *December*, 1771. Preached at the Desire of said PAUL. By SAMSON OCCOM, Minister of the Gospel and Missionary to the INDIANS."

disregarded. But there are two or three considerations that have induced me to be willing, to suffer my broken hints to appear in the world. One is, that the books that are in the world are written in very high and refined language; and the sermons that are delivered every sabbath in general, are in a very high and lofty stile, so that the common people understand but little of them. But I think they can't help understanding my talk; it is common, plain, every day talk: little children may understand me. And poor Negroes may plainly and fully understand my meaning; and it may be of service to them. Again, it may in a particular manner be serviceable to my poor kindred the Indians. Further, as it comes from an uncommon quarter, it may induce people to read it, because it is from an Indian. Lastly, God works where and when he pleases, and by what instruments he sees fit, and he can and has used weak and unlikely instruments to bring about his great work.

It was a stormy and very uncomfortable day, when the following discourse was delivered, and about one half of it was not delivered, as it was written, and now it is a little altered and enlarged in some places.

Introduction

By the melancholy providence of God, and at the earnest desire and invitation of the poor condemned criminal, I am here before this great concourse of people at this time, to give the last discourse to the poor miserable object who is to be executed this day before your eyes, for the due reward of his folly and madness, and enormous wickedness. It is an unwelcome task to me to speak upon such an occasion; but since it is the desire of the poor man himself, who is to die a shameful death this day, in conscience I cannot deny him; I must endeavor to do the great work the dying man requests.

I conclude that this great concourse of people have come together to see the execution of justice upon this poor Indian, and I suppose the biggest part of you look upon yourselves christians, and as such I hope you will demean yourselves; and that you will have suitable commiseration towards this poor object. Tho' you can't in justice pray for his life to be continued in this world, yet you can pray earnestly for the salvation of his poor soul, consistently with the mind of God: Let this be therefore the fervent exercise of our souls: for this is the last day we have to pray for him. As for you, that don't regard religion, it cannot be expected, that you will put up one petition for this miserable creature: yet I would intreat you seriously to consider the frailty of corrupt nature, and behave yourselves as becomes rational creatures.

And in a word, let us all be suitably affected with the melancholy occasion of this day, knowing that we are all dying creatures, and accountable unto God. Though this poor condemned creature will in a few minutes know more than all of us, either in unutterable joy, or in inconceivable wo, yet we shall certainly know as much as he, in a few days.

The sacred words that I have chosen to speak from upon this undesirable occasion, are found written in the Epistle of St. PAUL to the

ROMANS VI. 23.

For the wages of sin is death, but the gift of God is eternal life through Jesus Christ our Lord.

[from **The Sermon**]

Death is called the King of Terrors, and it ought to be the subject of every man and woman's thoughts daily; because it is that unto which they are liable every moment of their lives: and therefore, it cannot be unseasonable to think, speak and hear of it at any time, and especially on this mournful occasion; for we must all come to it, how soon we cannot tell; whether we are prepared or not prepared, ready or not ready, whether death is welcome or not welcome, we must feel the force of it; whether we concern ourselves with death or not, it will concern itself with us. Seeing that this is the case with every one of us, what manner of persons ought we to be in all holy conversation, and godliness; how ought men to exert themselves in preparation for death continually for they know not what a day or an hour may bring forth, with respect to them. But, alas! according to the appearance of mankind in general, death is the least tho't of. They go on from day to day, as if they were to live here forever, as if this was the only life. They contrive, rack their inventions, disturb their rest, and even hazard their lives in all manner of dangers, both by sea and land; yea, they leave no stone unturned that they may live in the world, & at the same time have little or no contrivance to die well: God and their souls are neglected, and heaven & eternal happiness are disregarded; Christ and his religion are despised—yet most of these very men intend to be happy when they come to die, not considering that there must be great preparation in order to die well. Yea there is no [one] so fit to live as those that are fit to die; those that are not fit to die are not fit to live. Life & death are nearly connected; we generally own that it is a great and solemn thing to die. If this be true, then it is a great and solemn thing to live; for as we live, so we shall die. But I say again, how little do mankind realize these things? They are as busy about the things of this world as if there was no death before them. . . .

The next thing I shall consider, is the actual death of the body, or separation between soul and body. At the cessation of natural life, there is an end of all the enjoyments of this life; there is no more joy nor sorrow; no more hope nor fear, as to the body; no more contrivance and carrying on any business; no more merchandizing and trading; no more farming; no more buying and selling; no more building of any kind, no more contrivance at all to live in the world; no more flatteries nor frowns from the world; no more honour nor reproach; no more praise; no more good report, nor evil report; no more learning of any trades arts or sciences in the world; no more sinful pleasures, they are all at an end; recreations visiting, tavern hunting, music, and dancing, chambering, and carousing, playing at dice and cards, or any game whatsoever; cursing and swearing; and profaning the holy name of God, drunkenness, fighting, debauchery, lying and cheating, in this world must cease forever. Not only so, but they must bid an eternal farewell to all the world: bid farewell to all their beloved sins and pleasures; and the places and possessions, that knew them once, shall know them no more forever. And further, they must bid adieu to all sacred and divine things. They are obliged to leave the bible, and all the ordinances thereof; and to bid farewel to preachers, and all sermons and all christian people, and christian conversation; they must bid a long farewell to sabbaths and seasons, and opportunities to worship; yea, an eternal farewel to all mercy and all hope; an eternal farewel to God the Father, Son and Holy Ghost, and adieu to heaven and all happiness, to saints and all the inhabitants of the upper world. At your leisure please to read the destruction of Babylon; you will find it written in the 18th of the Revelations.

On the other hand, the poor departed soul must take up in lodging in sorrow, wo and misery, in the lake that burns with fire and brimstone, where the worm dieth not, and the fire is not quenched; where a multitude of frightful deformed devils dwell, and the damned ghosts of Adam's race; where darkness, horror and despair reigns, or where hope never comes, and where poor guilty naked souls will be tormented with exquisite torments, even the wrath of the Almighty poured out upon their damned souls; the smoke of their torments ascending up forever and ever; their mouths and nostrils streaming forth with living fire; and hellish groans, cries and shrieks all around them, and merciless devils upbraiding them for their folly and madness, and torment-ing them incessantly. And there they must endure the most unsatiable, fruitless desire, and the most overwhelming shame and confusion, and the most horrible fear, and the most doleful sorrow, and the most racking despair. When they call their flaming eyes to heaven, with Dives in torments, they behold an angry GOD, whose eyes are as a flaming fire, and they are struck with ten thousand darts of pain; and the sight of the happiness of the saints above, adds to their pains and aggravates their misery. And when they reflect upon their past folly and madness in neglecting the great salvation in their day, it will pierce them with ten thousand inconceivable torments: it will as it were enkindle their hell afresh; and it will cause them to curse themselves bitterly, and curse the day in which they were born, and curse their parents that were the instruments of their being in the world; yea, they will curse, bitterly curse, and with that very God that gave them their being, to be in the same condition with them in hell torments. This is what is called the second death, and it is the last death, and an eternal death to a guilty fool.

And O eternity, eternity, eternity! Who can measure it? Who can count the years thereof? Arithmetic must fail, the thoughts of men and angels are drowned in it; how shall we describe eternity? To what shall we compare it? Were it possible to employ a fly to carry off this globe by the small particles thereof, and to carry them to such a distance that it would return once in ten thousand years for another particle, and so continue till it has carried off all this globe, and framed them together in some unknown space, till it has made just such a world as this is: after all eternity would remain the same unexhausted duration. Thus must be the unavoidable portion of all impenitent sinners, let them be who they will, great or small, honorable or ignoble, rich or poor, bond or free. Negroes, Indians, English or of what nations soever, all that die in their sins, must go to hell together, for the wages of sin is death. . . .

I have now gone thro' what I proposed from my text. And I shall now make some application of the whole.

First on the criminal in particular and then to the auditory in general.

My poor unhappy brother MOSES;

As it was your own desire that I should preach to you this last discourse, so I shall speak plainly to you—You are the bone of my bone, and flesh of my flesh. You are an Indian, a despised creature, but you have despised yourself; yea you have despised God more; you have trodden under foot his authority; you have despised his com-mands and precepts: and now, as God says, be sure your sins will find you out. And now, poor Moses, your sins have found you out, and they have overtaken you this day; the day of your death is now come; the king of errors is at hand; you have but a very few moments to breathe in this world.——The just law of man and the holy laws of Jehovah, call aloud for the destruction of your mortal life; God says, "Whoso sheddeth man's blood, by man shall his blood be shed." This is the ancient decree of heaven, and it is to be executed by man; nor have you the least gleam of hope of escape, for the unalterable sentence is past; the terrible day of execution is come; the unwelcome guard is about you; and the fatal instruments of death are now made ready; your coffin and your grave, your last lodging are open ready to receive you.

Alas! poor Moses, now you know by sad, by woful experience, the living truth of our text, that the wages of sin is death. You have been already dead; yea, twice dead: by nature spiritually dead. And since the awful sentence of death has been passed upon you, you have been dead to all the pleasures of this life; or all the pleasures, lawful or unlawful, have been dead to you: And death, which is the wages of sin, is standing even on this side of your grave ready to put a final period to your mortal life; and just beyond the grave, eternal death awaits your poor soul, and devils are ready to drag your miserable soul down to their bottomless den, where everlasting wo and horror reigns; the place is filled with doleful shrieks, howls and groans of the damned. Oh! to what a miserable, forlorn, and wretched condition has your extravagant folly and wickedness bro't you! i.e. if you did in your sins. And O! what manner of repentance ought you to manifest! How ought your heart to bleed for what you have done! How ought you to prostrate your soul before a bleeding God! And under self-condemnation, cry out, Ah Lord, ah Lord, what have I done?——Whatever partiality, injustice and error there may be among the judges of the earth, remember that you have deferred a thousand deaths, and a thousand hells, by reason of your sins, at the hands of a holy God. Should God come out against you in strict justice, alas! what could you say for yourself? For you have been brought up under the bright sun-shine, and plain, and loud sound of the gospel; and you have had a good education; you can read and write well; and God has given you a good natural understanding: and therefore your sins are so much more aggravated.——You have not sinned in such an ignorant manner as others have done; but you have sinned with both your eyes open as it were, under the light even the glorious light of the gospel of the Lord Jesus Christ.——You have sinned against the light of your own conscience, against your knowledge and understanding; you have sinned against the pure and holy laws of God, and the just laws of men; you have sinned against heaven and earth; you have sinned against all the mercies and goodness of God; you have sinned against the whole bible, against the old and new testament; you have sinned against the blood of Christ, which is the blood of the everlasting covenant. O poor Moses, see what you have done! and now repent, repent, I say again repent; see how the blood you shed cries against you, and the Avenger of blood is at your heels. O fly, fly to the blood of the Lamp of God for the pardon of all your aggravated sins.

But let us now turn to a more pleasant theme.——Though you have been a great sinner, a heaven-daring sinner; yet hark and hear the joyful sound from heaven, even from the King of kings, and Lord of lords; that the gift of God is eternal life, through Jesus Christ our Lord.——It is a free gift, and offered to the greatest sinners, and upon their true repentance towards God and faith in the Lord Jesus Christ, they shall be welcome to the life which we have spoken of; it is offered upon free terms. He that hath no money may come; he that hath no righteousness, no goodness, may come;

the call is to poor undone sinners; the call is not to the righteous, but sinners calling them to repentance.—Hear the voice of the Sun of the Most High God, Come unto me all ye that labour and are heavy laden, and I will give you rest. This is a call, a gracious call to you poor Moses, under your present burdens and distresses. And Christ alone has a right to call sinners to himself. It would be presumptuous for a mighty angel to call a poor sinner in this manner; and were it possible for you to apply to all God's creatures, they would with one voice tell you, that it was not in them to help you. Go to all the means of grace, they would prove miserable helps without Christ himself. Yea, apply to all the ministers of the gospel in the world, they would all say, that it was not in them, but would only prove as indexes, to point out to you, the Lord Jesus Christ, the only Saviour of sinners of mankind. Yea, go to all the angels in heaven, they would do the same. Yes, go to God the father himself, without Christ, he cou'd not help you, to speak after the manner of men, he would also point to the Lord Jesus Christ, and say this is my beloved son, in whom I am well pleased, hear ye him. Thus you see, poor Moses that there is none in heaven, or on earth, that can help you, but Christ; he alone has power to save, and to give life.—God the eternal Father appointed him, chose him, authorized, and fully commissioned him to save sinners. He came down from heaven into this lower world, and became as one of us, and stood in our room. He was the second Adam. And as God demanded correct obedience of the first Adam; the second fulfil'd it; and as the first sinned, and incurred the wrath and anger of God, the second endured it; he suffered in our room. As he became sin for us, he was a man of sorrows, and acquainted with grief, all our strifes were laid upon him; yea, he was finally condemned, because we were under condemnation; and at last was executed and put to death, for our sins; was lifted up between the heaven and the earth, and was crucified on the accursed tree; his blessed hands and feet were fastened there;—there he died a shameful and ignominious death: there he finished the great work of our redemption: there his heart's blood was shed for our cleansing; there he fully satisfied the divine justice of God, for penitent, believing sinners, though they have been the chief of sinners—O Moses! this is good news to you, in this last day of your life; here is a crucified Saviour at hand for your sins; his blessed hands are out-stretched, all in a gore of blood for you. This is the only Saviour, an Almighty Saviour, just such as you stand in infinite and perishing need of. O, poor Moses! hear the dying prayer of a gracious Saviour on the accursed tree—Father forgive them for they know not what they do. This was a prayer for his enemies and murderers; and it is for you, if you will only repent and believe in him. O why will you die eternally, poor Moses, since Christ has died for sinners? Why will you go to hell from beneath a bleeding Saviour as it were? This is the day of your execution, yet it is the accepted time, it is the day of salvation if you will now believe in the Lord Jesus Christ. Must Christ follow you into the prison by his servants, and there intreat you to accept of eternal life, and will you refuse it? and must he follow you even to the gallows, and there beseech you to accept of him, and will you refuse him? Shall he be crucified by your gallows, as it were, and will you regard him not? O, poor Moses, now believe on the Lord Jesus Christ with all your heart, and thou shalt be saved eternally. Come just as you are with all your sins and abominations, with all your filthiness, with all your blood-guiltiness, with all your condemnation, and lay hold as the hope set before you this day. This is the last day of salvation with your soul; you will be beyond the bounds of mercy in a

few minutes more. O, what a joyful day would it be if you would now openly believe
in and receive the Lord Jesus Christ; it would be the beginning of heavenly days with
your poor soul; instead of a melancholy day, it would be a wedding day to your soul:
it would cause the very angels in heaven to rejoice, and the saints on earth to be glad;
it would cause the angels to come down from the realms above, and wait hovering
about your gallows, ready to convey your soul to the heavenly mansions, there to
take the possession of eternal glory and happiness, and join the heavenly choirs in
singing the songs of Moses and the Lamb: there to set down forever with Abraham,
Isaac and Jacob in the kingdom of God's glory; and your shame and guilt shall be
forever banished from the place, and all sorrow and fear forever fly away, and tears
be wip'd from your face; and there shall you forever admire the astonishing and
amazing and infinite mercy of God in Christ Jesus, in pardoning such a monstrous
sinner as you have been; there you will claim the highest note of praise, for the riches
of free grace in Christ Jesus. But if you will not accept of a Saviour so freely offered
to you in this last day of your life, you must make this very day bid farewell to God
the Father, Son and Holy Ghost, to heaven and all the saints and angels that are there;
and you must bid all the saints in this lower world an eternal farewell, and even the
whole world. And so I must leave you in the hands of God; and I must turn to the
whole auditory.

Sirs, We may plainly see, from what we have heard, and from the miserable object
before us, into what a doleful condition sin has brought mankind, even into a state
of death and misery. We are by nature as certainly under sentence of death from God,
as this miserable man is, by the just determination of man; and we are all dying
creatures, and we are, or ought to be sensible of it; and this is the dreadful fruit of
sin. O let us then fly from all appearance of sin; let us fight against it with all our
might; let us repent and turn to our God, and believe in the Lord Jesus Christ, that
we may live forever; let us all prepare for death for we know not how soon, nor how
suddenly we may be called out of the world. . . .

I shall now address myself to the Indians, my brethren and kindred according to
the flesh.

My poor kindred,

You see the woful consequences of sin, by freeing this our poor miserable countryman now before us, who is to die this day for his sins and great wickedness. And it
was the sin of drunkenness that has brought this destruction and untimely death upon
him. There is a dreadful ire denounced from the Almighty against drunkards; and it
is this sin, this abominable, this beastly and accursed sin of drunkenness, that has stript
us of every desirable comfort in this life; by this we are poor, miserable and wretched;
by this sin we have no name of credit in the world among polite nations; for this
sin we are despised in the world, and it is all right and just, for we despise ourselves
more; and if we don't regard ourselves, who will regard us? And it is for our sins
and especially for that accursed, that most devilish sin of drunkenness that we suffer
every day. For the love of strong drink we spend all that we have, and every thing
we can get. By this sin we can't have comfortable houses, nor any thing comfortable
in our houses; neither food nor raiment, nor decent utensils. We are obliged to put
up with any sort of shelter just to screen us from the severity of the weather; and
we go about with very mean, ragged and dirty clothes, almost naked. And we are

half-starved, for most of the time obliged to pick up any thing to eat.—And our poor children are suffering every day for want of the accessories of life; they are very often crying for want of food, and we have nothing to give them; and in the cold weather they are shivering and crying, being pinched with cold—All this for the love of strong drink. And this is not all the misery and evil we bring on ourselves in this world; but when we are intoxicated with strong drink, we drown our rational powers, by which we are distinguished from the brutal creation; we un-man ourselves, and bring ourselves not only level with the beasts of the field, but seven degrees beneath them; yea, we bring ourselves level with the devils; I don't know but we make ourselves worse than devils, for I never heard of drunken devils.

My poor kindred, do consider what a dreadful abominable sin drunkenness is. God made us men, and we chose to be beasts and devils; God made us rational creatures, and we chose to be fools. Do consider further, and behold a drunkard, and see how he looks, when he has drowned his reason; how deformed and shameful does he appear? He dis-figures every part of him, both soul and body, which was made after the image of God. He appears with awful deformity, and his whole visage is dis-figured; if he attempts to speak he cannot bring out his words distinct, so as to be understood, if he walks he reels and staggers to and for, and tumbles down. And see how he behaves, he is now laughing, and then he is crying; he is singing, and the next minute he is mourning; and is all love to every one, and soon he is raging, and for fighting, and killing all before him, even the nearest and the dearest relations and friends: Yes, nothing is too bad for a drunken man to do. He will do that, which we would not do for the world, in his right mind; he may lie with his own father or daughter as Lot did.

Further, when a person is drunk, he is just good for nothing in the world; he is of no service to himself, to his family, to his neighbors, or his country; and how much more unfit is he to serve God; yet he is just fit for the service of the devil.

Again, a man in drunkenness is in all manner of dangers, he may be killed by his fellow-man, by wild beasts, and tame beasts; he may fall into the fire, into the water, or into a ditch; or he may fall down as he walks along, and break his bones or his neck; and he may cut himself with edge-tools.—Further, if he has any money or any thing valuable, he may lose it all, or may be robb'd, or he may make a foolish bargain, and be cheated out of all he has.

I believe you know the truth of what I have just now said, many of you by sad experience; yet you will go on still in your drunkenness. Though you have been cheated over and over again, and you have lost your substance by drunkenness, yet you will venture to go on in this most destructive sin. O fools when will ye be wise? —We all know the truth of what I have been saying, by what we have seen and heard of drunken deaths. How many have been drowned in our rivers, and how many frozen to death in the winter seasons! yet drunkards go on without fear and consideration: Alas, alas! What will become of all such drunkards? Without doubt they must all go to hell, except they truly repent and turn to God. Drunkenness is so common amongst us, that even our young men, (and what is still more shocking) young women are not ashamed to get drunk. Our young men will get drunk as soon as they will eat when they are hungry.—It is generally esteemed amongst men, more abominable for a woman to be drunk than a man; and yet there is nothing more common amongst us than female drunkards. Women ought to be more modest than men; the holy scriptures recommend modesty to women in particular;—but drunken women have no modesty at all. It is more intolerable for a woman to get drunk. If we consider further, that she is in great danger of falling into the hands of the sons of Belial,[1] or wicked men, and being shamefully treated by them.

And here I cannot but observe, we find in sacred writ, a wo against men who put their bottles to their neighbours mouth to make them drunk, that they may see their nakedness: and no doubt there are such devilish men now in our days, as there were in the days of old.

And to conclude, consider my poor kindred, you that are drunkards, into what a miserable condition you have brought yourselves. There is a dreadful wo thundering against you every day, and the Lord says, That drunkards shall not inherit the kingdom of heaven.

And now let me exhort you all to break off from your drunkenness by a gospel repentance, and believe on the Lord Jesus and you shall be saved. Take warning by this doleful sight before us, and by all the dreadful judgments that have befallen poor drunkards. O let us all reform our lives, and live as becomes dying creatures, in time to come. Let us be persuaded that we are accountable creatures to God, and we must be called to an account in a few days. You that have been careless all your days, now awake to righteousness, and be concerned for your poor never-dying souls. Fight against all sins, and especially the sin that easily besets you, and behave in time to come as becomes rational creatures; and above all things, receive and believe on the Lord Jesus Christ, and you shall have eternal life; and when you come to die, your souls will be received into heaven, there to be with the Lord Jesus in eternal happiness, with all the saints in glory; which, GOD of his infinite mercy great, through Jesus Christ our Lord.

AMEN.

1772/1772

Logan
ca. 1725–1780

"I may challenge the whole orations of Demosthenes and Cicero, and of any more eminent orator, if Europe has furnished more eminent, to produce a single passage, superior to the speech of Logan, a Mingo chief, to Lord Dunmore, when governor of this state." So wrote Thomas Jefferson in *Notes on the State of Virginia* (1787), and thus began the controversy surrounding a Native American's noble eloquence.

Logan was the colonists' name for the Mingo (or Iroquois) chief Tachnechdorus, whose family was reported to have been among the many

---

[1] Satanic personification of wickedness and godliness; in John Milton's *Paradise Lost*, one of the fallen angels who rebelled against God.

murdered in retribution for Indian resistance to and robbery of white settlements along the Ohio River. After "shedding an abundance of tears," Logan is said to have made the following remarks in his own language. The translated message was then delivered to Lord Dunmore, the royal governor of Virginia, printed in the *Virginia Gazette,* and circulated widely both in the colonies and in Europe.

Long after Logan's death in 1780, Jefferson's political opponents attacked the speech's authenticity. Jefferson secured depositions from those who had heard the speech, but he did acknowledge that later research suggested that Logan's family may not have been among the original victims of the whites' retaliatory raids. In later editions of his *Notes,* Jefferson revised his account of the speech's circumstances but left the words intact. The speech continued to be widely reprinted throughout the nineteenth century and was featured in several editions of the enormously popular school text *McGuffey's Reader.* Yet the importance of the speech far exceeds its length. Whatever the circumstances of its composition, Logan's speech is a capsule reminder of the increasingly painful process of deteriorating Native American–white relations.

Further Reading:
N. B. Wood, *Lives of Famous Indian Chiefs,* 1906.
E. D. Seeber, "Critical Views on Logan's Speech," *Journal of American Folklore,* 1947.
W. Washburn, "Logan's Speech," in *An American Primer,* ed. D. J. Boorstin, 1966.
B. E. Johnson, *Forgotten Founders,* 1982.

Text:
Thomas Jefferson, *Notes on the State of Virginia,* 1787.

Speech at the End of Lord Dunmore's War

I appeal to any white to say, if ever he entered Logan's cabin hungry, and he gave him not meat: if ever he came cold and naked and he clothed him not.

During the course of the last long bloody war, Logan remained idle in his cabin, an advocate for peace. Such was my love for the whites, that my countrymen pointed as they passed, and said, "Logan is the friend of white men."

I had even thought to have lived with you, but for the injuries of one man. Col. Cresap[1] the last spring, in cold blood, and unprovoked, murdered all the relations of Logan; not even sparing my women and children.

There runs not a drop of my blood in the veins of any living creature. This called on me for revenge. I have sought it. I have killed many. I have fully glutted my

---

[1] Michael Cresap, later father-in-law of Luther Martin, a Maryland political opponent of Thomas Jefferson.

vengeance. For my country, I rejoice at the beams of peace. But do not harbor a thought that mine is the joy of fear. Logan never felt fear. He will not turn on his heel to save his life. Who is there to mourn for Logan?—Not one!

1774/1784

Phillis Wheatley
ca. 1754–1784

A frail but precious child who "had no other covering than a quantity of dirty carpet about her" stood among the "small Negroes" offered for sale in the following advertisement printed in the August 3, 1761, edition of the Boston *Evening Post:*

To Be Sold

A parcel of likely Negroes, imported from Africa, cheap for cash, or short credit; Enquire of John Avery, at his house next Door to the White-Horse, or at a Store adjoining to said Avery's Distill House, at the South End, near the South Market; Also, if any Persons have any Negro Men, strong and hearty, tho' not of the best moral character, which are proper Subjects for Transportation, may have an exchange for small Negroes.

Susannah Wheatley, the wife of a prosperous Boston tailor, purchased this young girl "for a trifle" and gave her, as was the custom, a Christian first name. Although her roots are obscure, Phillis Wheatley was judged "from the circumstance of shedding her front teeth" to be approximately seven years of age at the time of her sale, and more certainly to be the kidnap victim of slave traders who used northern cities to dispose of those Africans who remained after the "strong and hearty" were sold at more lucrative southern markets.

Phillis Wheatley quickly revealed "uncommon intelligence" and within sixteen months at the Wheatley house had mastered English, astronomy, geography, and history, as well as the most knotty passages from the Scriptures. The Wheatley family encouraged Phillis's formidable talents, tutored her in classical languages and literatures, exempted her from the usual domestic labors, removed her from the company of other blacks, and gradually turned her into a curiosity in New England's intellectual circles. A brilliant conversationalist, she frequently accompanied her owners on their social rounds of Boston but invariably declined "the seat offered her at their board, and, requesting that a side-table might be laid for her, dined modestly apart from the rest of the company." Given such circumstances, Phillis Wheatley spent most of her life complaisantly isolated from both blacks and whites, enthralled only by the companionship of British poetry, most notably Alexander Pope's heroic couplets.

Writing "originally for the Amusement of the Author," she filled all her leisure moments with poetry, published her first verse at thirteen, and soon won the praise of such prominent figures as Dr. Benjamin Rush and Thomas Hutchinson, the last colonial governor of Massachusetts. Fame followed the publication in 1770 of her widely reprinted broadside poem on the death of "the celebrated Divine, and eminent Servant of Jesus Christ, the late Reverend, and Pious George Whitefield," the preacher-missionary whose remarkable popularity during the Great Awakening Samuel Johnson attributed to the "peculiarity of his manner. He would be followed by crowds were he to wear a night-cap in the pulpit, or were he to preach from a tree."

In her nineteenth year, Phillis Wheatley crossed the Atlantic once more, but this time as a celebrated writer bound for London and a meeting with the Countess of Huntingdon, Whitefield's patron. This "sooty prodigy" from Boston soon became the "Sable Muse" of London. Voltaire acclaimed her, Franklin visited her, and the Lord Mayor of London and the Earl of Dartmouth honored her with special editions of *Paradise Lost* and Smollett's translation of *Don Quixote*. But in the midst of plans to present her to King George III, Phillis had to return to America to care for her sickly mistress. When she left London, Phillis Wheatley carried with her copies of her recently printed *Poems on Various Subjects, Religious and Moral* (1773), the first published volume by a black American. The circulation of a book of poems by a nineteen-year-old slave was regarded as so unusual that Wheatley's work, dedicated to the Countess of Huntingdon, had to be prefaced by the testimony of eighteen prestigious Bostonians, including John Hancock and the Reverend Mather Byles, certifying the poems' authenticity.

Written for a white audience and imitative of the prevailing Augustan poetic fashion, Wheatley's occasional verse reveals little of the self-consciousness that distinguishes much of later Afro-American literature. Yet, as Richard Wright, the twentieth-century black American novelist, reminds us, "Before the webs of slavery had so tightened as to snare nearly all Negroes in our land, one was freed by accident to give in clear, bell-like limpid cadence the hope of freedom in the New World."

At the onset of the American Revolution, Phillis fled with the Wheatley family to Providence, where she addressed a letter and poem "To His Excellency George Washington." Responding four months later, Washington apologized for the delay by citing "important occurrences, continually interposing to distract the mind and withdraw the attention." He hailed "this new instance" of Wheatley's "genius" and, at the risk of "imputation of vanity," sent the poem to Thomas Paine to be published in his *Pennsylvania Magazine*.

In the years following, Phillis Wheatley gained her freedom upon the death of the Wheatleys, married a free black, John Peters, and bore three children, all of whom died in childhood. Destitute, in failing health, and suffering from the unaccustomed burdens of menial work at "a common negro boarding-house," Wheatley tried to reverse her misfortune by advertising a three-hundred-page volume of "Poems & Letters on various subjects, dedicated to the Right Hon. Benjamin Franklin Esq." For want of subscribers, the project never appeared, and Phillis Wheatley, once the best-known colonial poet in England, died in obscurity in 1784.

Further Reading:
M. M. Odell, *Memoir,* 1834.
W. D. Jordan, *White over Black: American Attitudes Toward the Negro, 1550–1812,* 1968.
S. Graham, *The Story of Phillis Wheatley,* 1969.
M. A. Richmond, *Bid the Vassal Soar,* 1974.
W. Robinson, *Phillis Wheatley,* 1975.

Text:
The Poems of Phillis Wheatley, ed. J. D. Mason, 1966.

On the Death of the Rev. Mr. George Whitefield.[1] 1770

Hail, happy saint, on thine immortal throne,
Possest of glory, life, and bliss unknown;
We hear no more the music of thy tongue,
Thy wonted auditories cease to throng.
Thy sermons in unequall'd accents flow'd,   5
And ev'ry bosom with devotion glow'd;
Thou didst in strains of eloquence refin'd
Inflame the heart, and captivate the mind.
Unhappy we the setting sun deplore,
So glorious once, but ah! it shines no more.   10

Behold the prophet in his tow'ring flight!
He leaves the earth for heav'n's unmeasur'd height,
And worlds unknown receive him from our sight.
There *Whitefield* wings with rapid course his way,
And sails to *Zion*[2] through vast seas of day.   15
Thy pray'rs, great saint, and thine incessant cries
Have pierc'd the bosom of thy native skies.
Thou moon hast seen, and all the stars of light,
How he has wrestled with his God by night.
He pray'd that grace in ev'ry heart might dwell,   20
He long'd to see *America* excel;
He charg'd its youth that ev'ry grace divine
Should with full lustre in their conduct shine;
That Saviour, which his soul did first receive,
The greatest gift that ev'n a God can give,   25
He freely offer'd to the num'rous throng,
That on his lips with list'ning pleasure hung.

[1] Whitefield (1714–1770), an English disciple of John Wesley, was the most popular revivalist of the eighteenth century. Whitefield, who frequently visited the United States, died in Massachusetts. This, Wheatley's first published poem, brought her international acclaim.
[2] God's heavenly city.

"Take him, ye wretched, for your only good,
"Take him ye starving sinners, for your food;
"Ye thirsty, come to this life-giving stream,   30
"Ye preachers, take him for your joyful theme;
"Take him my dear *Americans,* he said,
"Be your complaints on his kind bosom laid:
"Take him, ye *Africans,* he longs for you,
"*Impartial Saviour* is his title due: 35
"Wash'd in the fountain of redeeming blood,
"You shall be sons, and kings, and priests to God."

Great *Countess,*[3] we *Americans* revere
Thy name, and mingle in thy grief sincere;
New England deeply feels, the *Orphans* mourn,   40
Their more than father will no more return.

But, though arrested by the hand of death,
Whitefield no more exerts his lab'ring breath,
Yet let us view him in th' eternal skies,
Let ev'ry heart to this bright vision rise;   45
While the tomb safe retains its sacred trust,
Till life divine re-animates his dust.

1770/1773

On Being Brought from Africa to America

'Twas mercy brought me from my *Pagan* land,
Taught my benighted soul to understand
That there's a God, that there's a *Saviour* too:
Once I redemption neither sought nor knew.
Some view our sable race with scornful eye,   5
"Their colour is a diabolic die."
Remember, *Christians, Negroes,* black as *Cain,*[1]
May be refin'd, and join th' angelic train.

1773/1773

---

[3] Selina Shirley Hastings (1707–1791), whom
Phillis Wheatley visited in 1773, was George
Whitefield's patron and an ardent member of
the Methodist church.

[1] Cain slew his brother, Abel, and for doing so
was marked by God (Genesis 4:1–15). This
mark is sometimes interpreted as the origin of
the Negro.

On Imagination

Thy various works, imperial queen, we see,
How bright their forms! how deck'd with pomp
  by thee!
Thy wond'rous acts in beauteous order stand,
And all attest how potent is thine hand.

From *Helicon's*[1] refulgent heights attend,   5
Ye sacred choir, and my attempts befriend:
To tell her glories with a faithful tongue,
Ye blooming graces, triumph in my song.

Now here, now there, the roving *Fancy* flies,
Till some lov'd object strikes her wand'ring eyes,   10
Whose silken fetters all the senses bind,
And soft captivity involves the mind.

Imagination! who can sing thy force?
Or who describe the swiftness of thy course?
Soaring through air to find the bright abode,   15
Th' empyreal palace of the thund'ring God,
We on thy pinions can surpass the wind,
And leave the rolling universe behind:
From star to star the mental optics rove,
Measure the skies, and range the realms above.   20
There in one view we grasp the mighty whole,
Or with new worlds amaze th' unbounded soul.

Though *Winter* frowns to *Fancy's* raptur'd eyes
The fields may flourish, and gay scenes arise;
The frozen deeps may break their iron bands,   25
And bid their waters murmur o'er the sands.
Fair *Flora*[2] may resume her fragrant reign,
And with her flow'ry riches deck the plain;
Sylvanus[3] may diffuse his honours round,
And all the forest may with leaves be crown'd: 30
Show'rs may descend, and dews their gems disclose,
And nectar sparkle on the blooming rose.

---

[1] In Greek mythology Mount Helicon is the home of the muses.
[2] In Roman legend, the goddess of flowers.
[3] Roman god of the forests.

Such is thy pow'r, nor are thine orders vain,
O thou the leader of the mental train:
In full perfection all thy works are wrought,   35
And thine the sceptre o'er the realms of thought.
Before thy throne the subject-passions bow,
Of subject-passions sov'reign ruler Thou,
At thy command joy rushes on the heart,
And through the glowing veins the spirits dart.   40

Fancy might now her silken pinions try
To rise from earth, and sweep th' expanse on high;
From *Tithon's* bed now might *Aurora*⁴ rise,
Her cheeks all glowing with celestial dies,
While a pure stream of light o'erflows the skies.   45
The monarch of the day I might behold,
And all the mountains tipt with radiant gold,
But I reluctant leave the pleasing views,
Which *Fancy* dresses to delight the *Muse;*
Winter austere forbids me to aspire,   50
And northern tempests damp the rising fire;
They chill the tides of *Fancy's* flowing sea,
Cease then, my song, cease the unequal lay.⁵

1773

To S. M.¹ A Young African Painter, on Seeing His Works

To show the lab'ring bosom's deep intent,
And thought in living characters to paint,
When first thy pencil did those beauties give,
And breathing figures learnt from thee to live,
How did those prospects give my soul delight,   5
A new creation rushing on my sight?
Still, wond'rous youth! each noble path pursue,
On deathless glories fix thine ardent view:
Still may the painter's and the poet's fire

---

⁴ Roman goddess of the dawn. In Greek myth Aurora's equivalent is Eos, who loved Tithonus.
⁵ Ballad or melody.

¹ Probably Scipio Moorhead, a Boston slave of the Reverend John Moorhead.

To aid thy pencil, and thy verse conspire!   10
And may the charms of each seraphic theme
Conduct thy footsteps to immortal fame!
High to the blissful wonders of the skies
Elate thy soul, and raise thy wishful eyes.
Thrice happy, when exalted to survey   15
That splendid city, crown'd with endless day,
Whose twice six gates[2] on radiant hinges ring:
Celestial *Salem*[3] blooms in endless spring.

Calm and serene thy moments glide along,
And may the muse inspire each future song!   20
Still, with the sweets of contemplation bless'd,
May peace with balmy wings your soul invest!
But when these shades of time are chas'd away,
And darkness ends in everlasting day,
On what seraphic pinions shall we move,   25
And view the landscapes in the realms above?
There shall thy tongue in heav'nly murmurs flow,
And there my muse with heav'nly transport glow:
No more to tell of *Damon's*[4] tender sighs,
Or rising radiance of *Aurora's*[5] eyes,   30
For nobler themes demand a nobler strain,
And purer language on th' ethereal plain.
Cease, gentle muse! the solemn gloom of night
Now seals the fair creation from my sight.

1773

To His Excellency General Washington[*]

SIR.

I Have taken the freedom to address your Excellency in the enclosed poem, and
entreat your acceptance, though I am not insensible of its inaccuracies. Your
being appointed by the Grand Continental Congress to be Generalissimo of the
armies of North America, together with the fame of your virtues, excite sensations not easy to suppress. Your generosity, therefore, I presume, will pardon the

---

[2] Revelation 21:12 represents the walls of
heavenly Jerusalem by 12 gates.
[3] Jerusalem (in heaven).
[4] Damon: in classical mythology, a shepherd
singer who pledged his life for his condemned
friend Pythias.

[5] Aurora: goddess of the dawn in Roman myth.
[*] Washington responded to Wheatley, praising
her poetical elegance and inviting her to visit
him in Cambridge, Massachusetts.

attempt. Wishing your Excellency all possible success in the great cause you are so generously engaged in. I am,

Your Excellency's most obedient humble servant,
PHILLIS WHEATLEY.

Providence, Oct. 26, 1775.
His Excellency Gen. Washington.

Celestial choir! enthron'd in realms of light,
  Columbia's¹ scenes of glorious toils I write.
While freedom's cause her anxious breast alarms,
She flashes dreadful in refulgent arms.
See mother earth her offspring's fate bemoan,   5
And nations gaze at scenes before unknown!
See the bright beams of heaven's revolving light
Involved in sorrows and the veil of night!
  The goddess comes, she moves divinely fair,
Olive and laurel binds her golden hair: 10
Wherever shines this native of the skies,
Unnumber'd charms and recent graces rise.
  Muse! bow propitious while my pen relates
How pour her armies through a thousand gates,
As when Eolus² heaven's fair face deforms,   15
Enwrapp'd in tempest and a night of storms;
Astonish'd ocean feels the wild uproar,
The refluent surges beat the sounding shore;
Or thick as leaves in Autumn's golden reign,
Such, and so many, moves the warrior's train.   20
In bright array they seek the work of war,
Where high unfurl'd the ensign waves in air.
Shall I to Washington their praise recite?
Enough thou know'st them in the fields of fight.
Thee, first in peace and honours,—we demand   25
The grace and glory of thy martial band.
Fam'd for thy valour, for thy virtues more,
Hear every tongue thy guardian aid implore!
  One century scarce perform'd its destined round,
When Gallic powers Columbia's fury found;³   30
And so may you, whoever dares disgrace
The land of freedom's heaven-defended race!
Fix'd are the eyes of nations on the scales,
For in their hopes Columbia's arm prevails.
Anon Britannia droops the pensive head,   35
While round increase the rising hills of dead.

---

¹ American poets had been referring to America as Columbia since 1761.
² In Roman myth Aeolus is god of the winds.
³ In the French and Indian War, which continued for nearly 50 years and which is said to have begun with King William's War (1689–1697) and Queen Anne's War (1702–1703).

Ah! cruel blindness to Columbia's state!
Lament thy thirst of boundless power too late.
   Proceed, great chief, with virtue on thy side,
Thy ev'ry action let the goddess guide.   40
A crown, a mansion, and a throne that shine,
   With gold unfading, WASHINGTON! be thine.

1775/1776

Black Petitions for Freedom

Plantation inventories, diaries, letters, legislation, newspaper advertisements, legal documents, and court records constitute the principal sources of information on the black experience in colonial America. Nearly all were written by whites. Frequent dislocations and general exclusion from education account in large measure for the scarcity of first-person reports. Given these circumstances, eighteenth-century black American culture was almost exclusively oral. It survives in fragments of such collective activity as songs and hymns, with only the rare personal testaments of fugitive slave narratives. For example, it was not until the eve of the Revolution that an appreciable amount of black literature—written mostly by the poet Phillis Wheatley—could gain the attention and respect of white colonists. *Freedom's Journal,* the nation's first newspaper edited for and by blacks, did not appear until 1827. The individual struggles and achievements of generations of black Americans thus remain essentially unrecorded.

At the same time as Samuel Adams was drafting polemic essays condemning Parliament's suppression of the colonists' "natural rights" and Thomas Paine was urging them to take up arms "to reap the blessings of freedom," an anonymous group of black slaves petitioned the Massachusetts governor and assembly to recognize their legal claims to freedom. The petitioners asserted that they too were a "freeborn Pepel and have never forfeited this Blessing by aney compact or agreement whatever." They appealed to the legislators' charity and humanitarian impulses by recapitulating the abuses they had suffered. These black petitions stand as eloquent briefs for personal freedom. Their call for a "Natural and Unaliable Right" to liberty and for the "privileges and immunities" of "free and natural born subjects" anticipates much of the language and sentiment of the Declaration of Independence.

Text:
Collections of the Massachusetts Historical Society
III, 5th series, 1877.

from Black Petitions for Freedom

To his Excellency Thomas Hutch[inson Gov]ernor of
said Prov[i]nce, to the Honorable his Majestys
Council, [and to the] Honourable House of
Representatives in General Court assembled
June 1773.

The Petition of us the subscribers in behalf of all thous who by divine Permission are held in a state of slavery, within the bowels of a free Country, Humbly
sheweth,—

That your Petitioners apprehend they have in comon with other men a naturel right
to be free and without molestation to injoy such Property as thay may acquire by
their industry, or by any other means not detrimetal to their fellow men and that no
person can have any just claim to their services unless. . . .

1773/1773

To his Excellency Thomas Gage Esq Captain General
and Governor in Chief in and over this Province.
To the Honourable his Majestys Council and the
Honourable House of Representatives in General
Court assembled may 25 177———[1]

The Petition of a Grate Number of Blackes of this Province who by divine permission
are held in a state of Slavery within the bowels of a free and christian Country
    Humbly Shewing
That your Petitioners apprehind we have in common with all other men a naturel
right to our freedoms without Being depriv'd of them by our fellow men as we are
a freeborn Pepel and have never forfeited this Blessing by aney compact or agreement
whatever. But we were unjustly dragged by the cruel hand of power from our dearest
frinds and sum of us stolen from the bosoms of our tender Parents and from a Populous
Pleasant and plentiful country and Brought hither to be made slaves for Life in a
Christian land. Thus are we deprived of every thing that hath a tendency to make
life even tolerable, the endearing ties of husband and wife we are strangers to for we
are no longer man and wife then our masters or mestreses thinkes proper marred or
onmarred. Our children are also taken from us by force and sent maney miles from
us wear we seldom or ever see them again there to be made slaves of for Life which
sumtimes is vere short by Reson of Being dragged from their mothers Breest Thus
our Lives are imbittered to us on these accounts By our deplorable situation we are
rendered incapable of shewing our obedience to Almighty God how can a slave
perform the duties of a husband to a wife or parent to his child How can a husband

---

[1] The last numeral has been changed several times
in the manuscript, but the date should be 1774.

10 Commandments
Christianity

leave master and work and cleave to his wife How can the wife submit themselves to there husbands in all things. How can the child obey thear parents in all things. There is a grat number of us sencear . . . members of the Church of Christ how can the master and the slave be said to fulfil that command Live in love let Brotherly Love contuner and abound Beare yea onenothers Bordenes How can the master be said to Beare my Borden when he Beares me down whith the Have chanes of slavery and operson against my will and how can we fulfill our parte of duty to him whilst in this condition and as we cannot searve our God as we ought whilst in this situation Nither can we reap an equal benefet from the laws of the Land which doth not justifi but condemns Slavery or if there had bin aney Law to hold us in Bondege we are Humbely of the Opinion ther never was aney to inslave our children for life when Born in a free Countrey. We therfor Bage your Excellency and Honours will give this its deu weight and consideration and that you will accordingly cause an act of the legislative to be pessed that we may obtain our Natural right our freedoms and our children be set at lebety at the yeare of Twenty one for whoues sekes more petequeley your Petitioners is in Duty ever to Pray.

1774/1774

To his Excellency Thomas Gage Governor:—
To the Honourable His Majesty's Council, and the
Honourable House of Representatives of the
Province of the Massachusetts Bay in General Court
assembled, June—Anno Domini 1774.

The Petition of us the Subscribers, in behalf of all those, who, by divine permission, are held in a State of *Slavery* within the Bowels of a Free Country.

Humbly Sheweth

That your petitioners apprehend, they have in common with other men, a natural right to be free, and without molestation, to enjoy such property, as they may acquire by their industry, or by any other means not detrimental to their fellow men; and that no person can have any just claim to their services unless by the laws of the land they have forfeited them, or by voluntary compact become servants; neither of which is our case; but we were dragged by the cruel hand of power, some of us from our dearest connections, and others stolen from the bosoms of tender parents and brought hither to be enslaved. Thus are we deprived of every thing that has a tendency to make life even tol[erable.]. . . . We are informed, there is no law of this Province, whereby our masters can claim our services, mere custom is the tyrant that keeps us in bondage, and deprives us of that use of the law, which our fellow men, who we believe under God are no better than us, are entitled to and do enjoy. We do not claim rigid justice, but as we are deserving like other men, of some compensation for all our toils and sufferings; we would therefore in addition to our prayer, that all of us, excepting such as are now infirm through age, or otherways unable to support themselves, may be liberated and made free men of this community, and be entitled to all the privileges and immunities of its free and natural born subjects. Further humbly ask that your Excellency and Honours would be pleased to give and grant to us some part of

Tyranny & Law

religion/law, am principles.

the unimproved land, belonging to the province, for a settlement, that each of us may there quietly sit down under his own fig tree [and enjoy] the fruits of his labour. . . .

1774/1774

To the Honorable Counsel & House of
[Representa]tives for the State of Massachusitte Bay
in General Court assembled, Jan. 13, 1777.

The petition of A Great Number of Blackes detained in a State of slavery in the Bowels of a free & Christian Country Humbly shuwith that your Petitioners apprehend that thay have in Common with all other men a Natural and Unaliable Right to that freedom which the Grat Parent of the Unavers hath Bestowed equalley on all menkind and which they have Never forfuted by any Compact or agreement whatever—but thay wher Unjustly Dragged by the hand of cruel Power from their Derest friends and sum of them Even torn from the Embraces of their tender Parents —from A popolous Pleasant and plentiful contry and in violation of Laws of Nature and off Nations and in defiance of all the tender feelings of humanity Brough hear Either to Be sold Like Beast of Burthen & Like them Condemnd to Slavery for Life —Among A People Profesing the mild Religion of Jesus A people Not Insensible of the Secrets of Rationable Being Nor without spirit to Resent the unjust endeavours of others to Reduce them to a state of Bondage and Subjection your honouer Need not to be informed that A Life of Slavery Like that of your petioners Deprived of Every social privilege of Every thing Requiset to Render Life Tolable is far worse then Nonexistance.

[In imitat]ion of the Lawdable Example of the Good People of these States your petiononers have Long and Patiently waited the Evnt of petition after petition By them presented to the Legislative Body of this state and cannot but with Grief Reflect that their Sucess hath ben but too similar they Cannot but express their Astonishment that It has Never Bin Consirdered that Every Principle from which Amarica has Acted in the Cours of their unhappy Deficultes with Great Briton Pleads Stronger than A thousand arguments in favowrs of your petioners they therfor humble Beseech your honours to give this petion its due weight & consideration and cause an act of the Legislatur to be past Wherby they may Be Restored to the Enjoyments of that which is the Naturel Right of all men—and their Children who wher Born in this Land of Liberty may not be heald as Slaves after they arive at the age of Twenty one years so may the Inhabitance of thes Stats No longer chargeable with the inconsistancey of acting themselves the part which they condem and oppose in others Be prospered in their present Glorious struggle for Liberty and have those Blessing to them, &c.

1777/1777

Washington Allston,
The Poor Author and the Rich Bookseller,
oil on canvas, 1811.
Courtesy, Museum of Fine Arts, Boston.
Bequest of Charles Sprague Sargent, 1927.

The Literature of the New Republic 1776–1836

 The Declaration of Independence proclaimed the political freedom of the American colonies and launched their self-conscious quest for a national identity. Americans quickly found themselves grappling with many momentous issues, not the least of them being, to borrow the title of St. Jean de Crèvecoeur's celebrated essay, "What is an American?" Along with that overarching question came several other related issues that were debated for the next century: Did America possess a unique, distinctive culture? Was there such a thing as an American language? Did an authentic American literature exist? That such issues were debated is not at all surprising given the colonies' newly won independence from England, but what is surprising is that they continued to be public concerns for many decades after the new nation had been founded.

The founding of the American republic hardly seemed auspicious in literary terms. Most literary historians have tended to dismiss the period between 1776 and 1836, as one put it, "as a sort of blank space between the Revolution and the mature work of Irving, Bryant and Cooper." Another judged the writers of the new republic "blind sailors navigating the Dead Sea of Federalist Pessimism." Yet important literary accomplishments *do* mark the period between 1776 and 1836. American writers expressed the essential features of a distinctive national literature during these years. For the first time, they consciously, though anxiously, asserted their autonomy, sought workable alternatives to servile imitation of English neoclassical models, and abandoned the traditional literary expressions of Enlightenment social consciousness in favor of greater individuality in more spontaneous forms commensurate with the powerful presence of the American landscape. This period also saw produced the early writings of such notable American literary figures as Edgar Allan Poe, Nathaniel Hawthorne, and Ralph Waldo Emerson, as well as the major works of Washington Irving, James Fenimore Cooper, and William Cullen Bryant.

More important, however, American writers in the years between 1776 and 1836 articulated the literary values that would define much of subsequent American literary history—indigenous values that would find their fullest expression in the years after 1836. The literature of the new republic constitutes this nation's first comprehensive attempt to establish an independent literary identity. Controversy, anxiety, false starts, numerous obstacles, and impressive accomplishments characterize this quest.

The Literature of Persuasion

"America must be as independent in *literature,*" wrote Noah Webster, "as she is in politics." Because the new nation had not yet created a literature free of English influence, Americans remained, to use Webster's phrase, "mental colonists." Just as the Revolution had fulfilled the nation's sense of political destiny, a distinctively national literature would express and fulfill America's cultural destiny. In this respect literature took on in the early years of the new republic both practical and almost religious functions. Once political independence had been achieved, developing an indigenous American literary tradition would be the next phase of America's quest to establish what the Puritans had called "a city on a hill." Yet establishing—and exercising— America's literary independence would take far longer than asserting it. Virtually every interested citizen recognized that the problems facing the new nation in its quest for literary autonomy were formidable; to some they appeared insurmountable. Patriotism could prove no substitute for talent and vision.

When the American colonists' grievances against British rule erupted into the Revolutionary War, the most widely circulated forms of colonial literature were travel narratives, religious journals, and political tracts, as well as poetry and occasional essays highly derivative in their structures and themes from British models. To be sure, a growing number of young writers—including Philip Freneau, Hugh Henry Brackenridge, Noah Webster, Joel Barlow, Timothy Dwight, and John Trumbull—sought to express what Freneau and Brackenridge called, in their 1771 Princeton University commencement ode, "the Rising Glory of America." Yet these same writers—and scores of less celebrated figures— postponed their literary ambitions and put their pens in the service of securing political independence. As the notable literary historian Moses Coit Tyler explained, the Revolutionary War "drove out the tranquil forms of literature and encouraged more aggressive and partisan literary efforts." Forms of public discourse better suited to more topical subjects quickly gained prominence. Philip Freneau described the literary mood of the period most succinctly when he wrote: "An age employ'd in steel, / Can no poetic rapture feel."

Writers seemed to be everywhere, aggressively addressing the pressing issues of the time. In no other period of American literary history would writers so passionately involve themselves with so strong a sense of public responsibility in such crucial public debates. As Thomas Paine noted in *The American Crisis,* writers had the power "to make a world happy—to teach mankind the art of being so—to exhibit, on the theater of the universe, a character hitherto unknown—and to have, as it were, a new creation entrusted to our hands." And with that power came a sense of moral leadership. The obligation of American writers, Joel Barlow argued, was to "excite emulation through the kingdoms of the earth, and meliorate the condition of the human race." With such noble goals, American writers posted their patriotic ballads and broadsides in the streets and recited or sang them in local taverns and meeting halls. Their satires on the political controversies and caricatures of the leading personalities on both sides of the Atlantic contended for the shrinking space in newspapers whose pulp and rag content had increasingly been diverted to support the escalating war.

Ethan Allen Captures Fort Ticonderoga

The garrison being asleep, except the sentries, we gave them three huzzas, which greatly surprised them. One of the sentries made a pass at one of my officers with a charged bayonet, and slightly wounded him. My first thought was to kill him with my sword; but, in an instant, I altered the design and fury of the blow to a slight cut on the side of the head, upon which he dropped his gun, and asked quarter, which I readily granted him. . . . I ordered the commander, Captain de la Place, to come forth instantly, or I would sacrifice the whole garrison; at which the Captain came immediately to the door, with his breeches in his hand, when I ordered him to deliver me the fort instantly; he asked me by what authority I demanded it: I answered him, *"In the name of the great Jehovah and the Continental Congress."* The authority of the Congress being very little known at that time, he began to speak again; but I interrupted him, and with my drawn sword over his head, again demanded an immediate surrender of the garrison; with which he then complied. . . . This surprise was carried into execution in the gray of the morning of the 10th of May, 1775. The sun seemed to rise that morning with a superior lustre, and Ticonderoga and its dependencies smiled to its conquerors, who tossed about the flowing bowl, and wished success to Congress, and the liberty and freedom of America.

Ethan Allen, *Narrative of Captivity* (1779)

The popular literature of the American Revolution consisted principally of first-hand narratives of legendary campaigns, of a raw recruit's heroic life at the end of a gun barrel or in a prisoner-of-war camp. Modeled to a large extent on the Indian captivity narratives popular in the late seventeenth and early eighteenth centuries, these often harrowing battle accounts invariably substituted patriotic lessons for the moral conclusions of their predecessors. Religious writing, especially sermons both from the pulpit and later in print, also played an important role in mustering resistance to the British. The influence of the clergy in the revolutionary cause became noticeable enough to prompt those loyal to the crown to label the ministers who supported the Revolution "the Black Regiment."

The most pervasive and influential form of writing during the Revolutionary period was the political pamphlet, and its master the redoubtable Thomas Paine. Political pamphlets and essays were so widely distributed that American writing immediately before, during, and after the war might well be called "the literature of persuasion." Pamphlets, however, gradually yielded to the increasing number of newspapers and magazines that appeared at the turn of the century, only to resurface in the mid-nineteenth century during the heated public debate over slavery and secession.

Making Thirteen Clocks Tick Together

Developing a distinctively American literary tradition was irrevocably tied in the early years of the new republic to efforts to establish a *national* political identity. But securing such an identity remained complicated by such formidable obstacles as economic and cultural dependency on England as well as domestic diversity and conflict. In the aftermath of America's Declaration of Independence and its defeat of the British in the Revolutionary War, many former colonists became extremely concerned about whether the newly formed confederation of thirteen states could ever properly be called a nation. Little *national* sentiment was evident among the "united" states. State allegiances seemed more important in determining self-identity than the notion of being an "American." Many years and a bloody civil war would pass before Americans developed the habit of saying "the United States is" rather than "the United States are."

By and large, for both rich and poor, to live in the newly formed United States was to live in an economically and culturally "underdeveloped" country, whose standards of living and cultural taste depended almost exclusively on British goods and styles—whether in business, clothing, household furnishings, painting, architecture, periodicals, or heroic couplets. Independently minded Americans repeatedly complained about the new nation's economic and cultural subservience. St. Jean de Crèvecoeur, the French aristocrat successfully transplanted to the American frontier, complained about the number of shops stocked with British products and calculated that at least "one fifth of all our labors every year is laid out in English commodities." Thomas Jefferson, even more bitterly, regarded his fellow Virginia planters as little more than "a species of property annexed to certain mercantile houses in London." In economic terms, the original thirteen states remained for many years more closely tied to England than to each other. The lure of materialism frequently tested America's commitment to idealistic principles. In matters of goods and services, most Americans subscribed, however reluctantly, to the notion that British is better.

Socially, the new nation could hardly be described as a homogeneous democracy replete with egalitarian impulses. A slowly emerging economic and social hierarchy was increasingly evident—in classes ranging from quasi-aristocratic landholders to slaves and indentured servants, and from artisans and merchants boosting profits in coastal commercial centers to resolutely self-sufficient men and women pushing the wilderness farther southward and westward. Sectional rivalries and prejudices also abounded. In 1813 John Adams wrote disconsolately to a friend, "How shall we cure that distemper of State vanity?" The difficulties of traveling from one region to another gradually transformed lack of information into misperception.

No religion or national system of education unified the citizenry. The variety of religious affiliations (including, among other sects, Catholics, Hugenots, Unitarians, Presbyterians, and Lutherans) only increased factionalism among Americans. Virtually every religious sect had chosen sides in the conflict between the traditional authority of the Protestant church and faith in natural rights and individual reason. In this predominantly Newtonian view of religion, known as Deism, God exists but does not participate directly in human affairs.

"The Intellectual Soil of America Is Sterile"

The causes, indeed, why the intellectual soil of America is so comparatively sterile are obvious. We do not cultivate it; nor, while we can resort to foreign fields, from whence all our wants are so easily and readily supplied, and which have been cultivated for ages, do we find sufficient inducement to labour in our own. We are united by language, manners, and taste, by the bonds of peace and commercial intercourse, with an enlightened nation, the centre of whose arts and population may be considered as much *our* centre, as much the fountain whence *we* draw light and knowledge through books, as that of the inhabitants of Wales and Cumberland. In relation to the British capital as the centre of English literature, arts, and science, the situation of *New* and *Old York* may be regarded as the same. It is only the gradual influence of time, that, by increasing our numbers and furnishing a ready market for the works of domestic hands and heads, will at length generate and continue a race of artists and authors, purely indigenous, and who may vie with those of Europe.

Charles Brockden Brown, Preface to *The American Review and Literary Journal* (1801)

Opposing political tendencies, regional interests, cultural diversity, and broad-based philosophical and religious tensions characterized much of the public life in the new nation. Nowhere were these traits more amply evident than in the debate over the function and powers of a central government. There was considerable concern about whether there would—or could—be an effective national government. As an expression of this crucial debate over whether a strong central government was at once indispensable to the new nation's survival as well as compatible with individual liberty, *The Federalist* constitutes the United States' first classic literary text.

In 1787 the thirteen states, some quite reluctantly, sent delegates to take up the matter of a constitution, a document that would define the fundamental principles of the new nation, determine the powers and duties of the government, guarantee certain rights to the people, and codify the laws of the land. Draft in hand, these representatives returned home to weigh public support for ratification. Many Americans could see no point in abandoning the Articles of Confederation— which had entrusted nearly total sovereignty to the states and claimed no political authority over individuals. An equally large number of Americans, having fought to free themselves from the restraints of one powerful central authority, were wary of establishing another of their own.

To promote the Constitution in New York and in other reluctant states, Alexander Hamilton of New York, James Madison of Virginia, and John Jay of New York published a series of eighty-five letters in a New York newspaper in 1787 and 1788 under the collective pseudonym "Publius." These letters, given the title *The Federalist* when they were first collected in a volume in 1788, endorsed the principle of an indivisible union of states coordinated by a strong central government. *The Federalist* served as a tough-minded argument that gave meaning and justification to the Constitution and helped ensure its adoption. Yet, in another sense, *The Federalist* also contributed significantly to developing a national literature. In its discussion of the distinctions between "federal" and "national" and its predisposition to expect the worst and demand the best from human nature, *The Federalist* also helped define the polarities of the American character, establishing themes and a tone central to much of later American literature.

Cultivating New Meanings

The debate over the nature and extent of a federal government's powers reverberated in virtually every aspect of American culture. One important example can be found in the concerted effort, led by the young Noah Webster, to purify and standardize the American language. Webster envisioned an America "peopled with a hundred millions of men, *all speaking the same language,*" and his *Dissertations on the English Language* (1789) attempted to establish a uniform set of principles "for the rules of pronunciation in our language," just as his speller had done so much to regularize American orthography. Webster hoped, in effect, to do for the English language what the Puritan experiment in the New World had attempted to do for religion—to set an American example for purifying what had become corrupt in Europe. "On examining the language, and comparing the practice of speaking among the yeomanry of this country, with the stile of Shakespear and Addison," Webster observed, "I am constrained to declare that the people of America, in particular the English descendants, speak the most pure English now known in the world. There is hardly a foreign idiom in their language; by which I mean, a phrase that has not been used by the best English writers from the time of Chaucer." As this passage suggests, Webster's interest in linguistic reform was decidedly conservative. "In the few instances in which I write words a little differently from the present usage," he explained, "I do *not* innovate, but *reject innovation.* When I write *fether, lether,* and *mold,* I do nothing more than reduce the words to their original orthography, no other being used in our earliest English books." Searching for what he called a "primitive etymological orthography" that would "call back the language to the purity of former times," Webster envisioned a language spoken and written in America that would set the standard for enlightened discourse at home and abroad.

Linguistic uniformity had already become one of the hallmarks of the new nation in the wake of the Revolution. As John Witherspoon, the Scottish-born president of Princeton University, noted, Americans spoke with greater uniformity than people in England "for a very obvious reason, viz. that being much more unsettled, and moving frequently from place to place, they are not so liable to local peculiarities either in accent or phraseology. There is a greater difference in dialect between one county and another in Britain, than there is between one state and another in America." American mobility, the absence of sharply drawn geographic and class boundaries, and what James Fenimore Cooper called "the inexhaustible activity of the population" were creating a democratic base for developing a language common to all the American people.

In his quest for linguistic purity and uniformity, Webster had seriously miscalculated the influence on the American vocabulary of territorial expansion (into the polyglot Louisiana and Northwest territories) as well as frontier life and immigration. In addition, as H. L. Mencken later noted in his classic three-volume study *The American Language* (1919; 1974), more "Americanisms" (a word coined by John Witherspoon in 1781) entered the language between the American Revolution and 1800 than at any other time before the mid-nineteenth century rush to the West. When Webster published his *American Dictionary of the English Language* in 1828, he had not fundamentally changed his position on the purity of the American language, but he had softened it considerably. He recognized that differences between American and British English were traceable less to local variations than to basic differences in the respective institutions and customs of each nation. In drawing on numerous examples from American writers for his definitions, Webster apparently had become satisfied with explaining such distinctions with the skill of a lexicographer rather than continuing to call for reforms in spelling and usage.

Yet the issues Webster had raised about orthography would persist in American literature well into the twentieth century, stretching well beyond his search for etymological purity to Walt Whitman's unusual spellings and usages, as well as to Emily Dickinson's pronunciation (implied by her rhyme schemes) and Ezra Pound's abbreviations ("sd" and "thro," for example). In a curious way, the efforts of these three writers proved consistent with Webster's original purpose: to make words look more like they were spoken, to emphasize, in effect, the *voice* in American literature. And each writer also helped define, as did Webster, the distinctive nature of an American literary voice.

The Quest for Literary Independence

The treaties of Paris (1783) and Ghent (1814) may have freed the new nation politically, but Americans remained extremely insecure both intellectually and culturally. The new nation's reliance on the English language and a lingering attraction to the cultural tradition deflated the initial and widespread expectation among Americans that their political freedom would result in an equally independent literary and cultural identity. Several other factors heightened the new nation's collective anxiety about its cultural identity both in the present and in the future. One highly controversial proposition, promoted by the French naturalist and theologian Georges Louis Le Clerc de Buffon (1707–1788), asserted that the human race had degenerated in the Western Hemisphere, an assertion rebuked by Thomas Jefferson in his *Notes on the State of Virginia* (1785) and attacked in a March 1787 editorial in *American Museum* magazine. The United States, the editors advised, ought "to explode the European creed, that we are infantile in our acquisitions, and savage in our manners, because we are inhabitants of a new world, lately occupied by a race of savages." More widespread—and accurate—was the conviction among many American writers that they could not establish an indigenous identity until they had developed both the language and the intellectual structures adequate to express the distinctive qualities of American experience.

Literature and Commerce

The spirit of our people is *commercial*. It has been said, and perhaps with some justice, that the *love of gain* peculiarly characterizes the inhabitants of the United States. The tendency of this spirit to discourage literature is obvious. In such a state of Society, men will not only be apt to bend their whole attention to the acquirement of property and neglect the cultivation of their minds as an affair of secondary moment, but letters and science will seldom be found in high estimation; the amount of wealth will be the principal test of influence; the learned will experience but little reward either of honour or emolument; and, of course, superficial education will be the prevailing character.

Samuel Miller, *A Brief Retrospect of the Eighteenth Century*
(1803)

Much of the nation's creative energy in its earliest years focused on securing economic and political stability. John Quincy Adams spoke for the vast majority when he noted how difficult it was "to be a man of business and a man of rime." More important, the United States lacked an audience sizable and interested enough to support writers and artists. Philip Freneau advised the would-be writer to "graft his authorship upon some other calling." Few writers in the early years of the new republic had the financial resources to devote themselves full-time to cultivating their art. Many, like Freneau and William Cullen Bryant, wrote for and edited newspapers; some, like John Trumbull, practiced law. Still others, like Noah Webster and Timothy Dwight, turned to teaching, lecturing, and training for the ministry. In 1816 John Pickering noted that books were written primarily "by men, who were obliged to depend upon other employments for their support, and who could devote to literary pursuits those few moments only, which their thirst for learning, stimulated them to snatch from their daily avocations." Several years later, Henry Wadsworth Longfellow's father urged his son to explore another calling because "there is not wealth and munificence enough in this country to afford sufficient encouragement and patronage to merely literary men." The sense of public responsibility and moral leadership that American writers had so vigorously exercised during the earliest years of the new nation was gradually yielding in the early decades of the nineteenth century to a sense of isolation, if not alienation. In this respect, the period between 1776 and 1836 reflects a growing anti-intellectual strain in American society that ever since has traditionally set writers apart from their fellow citizens.

Aspiring writers faced difficulties that loomed larger than personal sacrifice and distracted audiences. Cultural, political, and legal obstacles discouraged all but the resolute. Many cultivated citizens feared that the principles of democracy would reduce cultural standards to the least common denominator, thereby producing, in the reigning logic of the time, a mediocre literary tradition—a concern the influential magazine *Boston Anthology* bellowed in an 1807 editorial: "The spirit of democracy blasts everything beautiful in nature and corrodes everything in art." The lack of an adequate copyright law also discouraged native literary talent. Without enforceable protection for writers, American printers found it far easier to reprint, at far greater profit, already successful British books than to publish—at far greater risk—the works of American authors. John Adams remarked, for example, that American readers were "disposed to encourage a thousand foolish republications from Europe rather than one useful work of their own growth."

With American bookstores filled with English and continental models well into the second decade of the nineteenth century, American writers in the new republic continued to feel the pressure to imitate the prevailing forms of literary expression rather than to invent new ones to accommodate what was gradually being recognized as the unrelenting originality of American experience. The most notable writers during the first decades of the new nation—including Philip Freneau, Hugh Henry Brackenridge, Noah Webster, and especially Joel Barlow,

Timothy Dwight, and John Trumbull, who came to be known as the "Connecticut Wits"—adapted the major features of imported neoclassical forms to American subjects. In their shared interest in preserving literary decorum and restraint, working within traditional literary forms, especially those with epic and satiric purposes, and associating America with classical Greece and Rome, these writers strove to demonstrate that America was capable of inspiring its own versions of literary grandeur.

The predominance of neoclassical elements in the literature of the new republic also reflects both a lingering sense of American cultural inferiority among these writers and a concern that cultural anarchy might be a legacy of the American Revolution. Their reverence for tradition, their interest in learned rather than spontaneous forms of literary expression, and their readiness to conform artistically suggest that writers were quite willing—and prepared—to legislate national standards for both the new nation's political and literary experiences. They were eager advocates of an *orderly* search for national cultural identity and would willingly have assumed the role of moral monitors of the new nation's progress.

Given these predilections, these writers might seem at first to be anomalies in what eventually became the tradition of American literature that defined its essential features in the works of such later, and less predictable, figures as Emerson, Whitman, Dickinson, and Twain. Yet the Federalist writers' sense of moral superiority links them to the abolitionists and Transcendentalists of the next period, just as their interest in satire and social conservativism connects them to such writers as Longfellow, Thoreau, Whittier, and Lowell. And what places them in the mainstream of American literary tradition is their resolute belief in what the American historian Henry Adams, a descendant of a family more practiced in making history than in writing about it, called "the omnivorous ambition" of that time. Leaders like Thomas Jefferson, Adams observed, "might without extravagance count upon a coming time when diffused ease and education should bring the masses into familiar contact with higher forms of human achievement, and their vast creative power, turned toward a nobler culture, might rise to the level of that democratic genius which found expression in the Parthenon."

Westward the Course of Empire

At the center of American cultural development in the first few decades following the Revolution was a powerful, optimistic idea: the course of empire was inexorably moving westward. Many years after independence had been declared, John Adams could recall the pervasiveness of this cultural belief:

There is nothing . . . more ancient in my memory than the observation that the arts, sciences, and empire had travelled westward; and in conversation it was always added since I was a child, that their next leap would be over the Atlantic and in to America.

At the back of Adams's mind, no doubt, were the stately lines of George Berkeley's "Verses on the Prospect of Planting Arts and Learning in America."

Written in 1726, the poem both commemorated Berkeley's plans to establish a college in America and celebrated the next geographic "leap" in a centuries-old European concept:

Westward the course of empire takes its way;
   The first four acts already past,
A fifth shall close the drama of the day;
   Time's noblest offspring is the last.

Berkeley's poem went through a remarkable number of printings after its first appearance in America in 1752 and helped nourish confidence in the growth of an indigenous American culture. The patriotic idea of a progressively westward-moving culture would reverberate through virtually every aspect of the cultural life of the new nation.

When Yale president Ezra Stiles reiterated in 1783 the notion that "all the arts may be transplanted from Europe and Asia and flourish in America with an augmented lustre," he was thinking not only of the ennobling, humanistic disciplines (the "culture") Berkeley tried to cultivate in colonial America but also of the more utilitarian "arts" that would accelerate the new nation's growth and expansion. But there was little of an achieved "culture" that Stiles proudly could point to in 1783.

By any standard, the applied and imaginative arts in the early years of the new republic would have struck most cultivated Europeans as impoverished. From the English point of view, the United States could boast of no Addison and Steele; no Pope, Swift, Richardson, Johnson, Burke, or Hume; no Byron, Keats, or Shelley, who were the admired young writers of that time. Writing in his later years, Benjamin Franklin wondered why a "petty island" like England "should enjoy in every Neighbourhood, more sensible, virtuous, and elegant Minds, than we can collect in ranging one hundred Leagues in our vast Forests." Yet Franklin at least had patriotic convention on his side when he added: "But, 'tis said, the Arts delight to travel Westward." He did not dwell on the fact, however, that as the arts headed westward, a large percentage of American artistic and professional talent—painters, musicians, physicians, lawyers, and ministers— headed eastward to England and the continent for study and training. The two finest painters of the period, John Singleton Copley (1738–1815) and Benjamin West (1738–1820), both traveled from colonial America to England to secure their professional reputations.

Professional prospects seemed as dim for drama, playwrights, and actors in post-Revolutionary America. The first play written by an American and acted by a professional American company, Thomas Godfrey's *Prince of Parthia*, was not staged until 1767. Long afterward, New England still continued to legislate against plays as "dangerous to the soul" and as a "great and unnecessary" expense, a diversion that discouraged industry and frugality, and an entertainment which increased "immorality, impiety, and a contempt for religion." Actors discovered more receptive audiences in the southern states, where a few resident companies managed to earn a modest living in the more densely populated cities. And while a few English touring companies performed Shakespeare and Restoration drama for appreciative southern audiences, the population in most areas remained too scattered in the late eighteenth century to support residential theatrical groups.

What little American drama there was in the new nation consisted primarily of adaptations of European models reworked to satisfy American thematic interests. Royall Tyler's *The Contrast* (1787) is the best-known American play of this period. Its focus on the distinctions between native dignity and foreign affectation earned it a special place in the limited repertoire of American theater companies. Later, such writers as William Dunlap (1766–1839) and John Howard Payne (1791–1852) dramatized historical subjects and nationalistic sentiments to small but appreciative audiences, Dunlap in *André* (1798) and Payne in *Brutus* (1818). In the early decades of the new republic, the theater faced popular indifference and lacked institutional support.

Printing and the Reading Public

As a major industrial art, printing served as one of the clearest indications of the cultural lag that characterized the relationship of American and British arts, crafts, and trades into the early years of the nineteenth century. In 1776 well over one hundred printing presses were at work throughout the new nation. Yet a printing press in itself represented the merest beginning of a trade. It was in the best interests of British suppliers to continue the colonial policy of keeping Americans dependent on run-down, secondhand equipment and materials. Type, always difficult to obtain, remained prohibitively expensive after the Revolutionary War. Better quality paper and ink had never been available to the American colonists in sufficient amounts, and the Revolution did little to change that fact. The inadequacies of American printing were widely known and lamented. In 1779 the elderly Benjamin Franklin, serving as the American representative at the French court, wryly observed when sent a batch of Boston newspapers that the paper and typography were of such poor quality that "if you should ever have any secrets that you should wish to be well kept, get them printed in these papers."

The Contrast

Exult each patriotic heart!—this night is shewn
A piece, which we may fairly call our own;
Where the proud titles of "My Lord! Your Grace!"
To humble Mr and plain Sir give place.
Our Author pictures not from foreign climes
The fashions, or the follies of the times;
But has confin'd the subject of his work
To the gay scenes—the circles of New-York.
On native themes his Muse displays her pow'rs;
If ours the faults, the virtues too are ours.
Why should our thoughts to distant countries roam,
When each refinement may be found at home?

Royall Tyler, from the prologue to *The Contrast* (1787)

In the first several decades following the Revolution, newspapers continued as the staple of the American printing trade. As such, their cultural content continued to reflect the economic and literary dependencies of their printer-publishers. American newspapers tried to reproduce a sophisticated, English literary tone, one that remained directly imported from the enormously successful periodical essays of Addison and Steele. American newspaper editors in the new republic seemed determined to sound as polite, chatty, and witty as their British models. And the contents of most American newspapers left little doubt that a relatively small, affluent class of readers determined the papers' interests, style, tone, and subscription base.

Since newspapers provided one of the major outlets for the new republic's literary efforts, the space accorded literature in those pages was one reliable measure of their importance to the general public in the new nation. Newspapers contained a fair measure of poetry, a few occasional essays, and a scattering of literary reviews and notices. Yet newspaper columns in the new republic featured more profitable, less intellectually demanding enterprises: a scattering of social announcements, a generous sampling of political reports from local and congressional sources as well as foreign dispatches, a wealth of advertisements and lists of cargo arrivals, along with editorial commentary and thinly disguised satire. From their odes to their ads, most newspapers in the new republic were addressed to social groupings roughly designated in those presociology days as "the better sort" (the gentry and the upper ranks of professional classes) and "the middle sort" (independent farmers, artisans, schoolteachers, and the lower ranks of the professions). "The meaner sort" (laborers, seamen, and indentured servants), those whom Alexander Hamilton called "the great beast," did not find a place in the network of public communications until the introduction of the so-called "Penny Press" in the late 1820s and early 1830s.

After the Revolutionary War, more papers gradually began to adopt the principle advocated by Massachusetts printer Isaiah Thomas—that journalism ought to be "popular" and written in a style that would express "common sense in common language." Thomas promoted his own *Massachusetts Spy* (founded in 1770) as one that could be read by "mechanics and other classes of people who had not much time to spare from business." Thomas's confidence that newspapers could reach "the meaner sort" had been bolstered by an upward trend in reading and writing skills that moved closer to nearly universal literacy among American white males by the beginning of the nineteenth century. In New England the legacy of Calvinism, the policy of compulsory education, and the ideology of self-improvement resulted in the highest rate of literacy in the new republic. In the middle and southern colonies, the relatively high literacy rate among European immigrants counterbalanced the lower percentage of literate native white males and helped extend reading and writing skills beyond only the wealthy and socially prominent. Yet the spread of these "popular" forms of journalism reduced even further the number of ready outlets for publishing American writers.

The market for American newspapers developed rapidly in the early decades of the new republic. In 1785 approximately seventy-five newspapers were being printed in the United States. Five years later, that number had climbed to nearly one hundred. By 1820 technical improvements and the beginnings of industrialization had helped increase the total to 508. By 1830, such developments as steam and cylinder presses helped to more than double that number. Nearly every town in America—and several fairly remote frontier settlements—could boast of its own printing press. It seemed that Americans had become addicted to newsprint. But the ever-increasing number of newspapers in print was offset by the limited circulation of each. Even taking into account the rather high reader-per-copy ratio (estimated in the early years of the new nation to be well over twenty), the reading public for newspapers still represented in post-Revolutionary America a surprisingly small portion of the total reading public. The new nation was demonstrating a consistent cultural feature of modern societies: populations grow literate faster than they develop the habit of reading.

In many respects, the book market presented even greater problems for American printers than did newspaper circulations. Given the technical difficulties and production costs they continued to face after the Revolution, American printers could only occasionally afford to tie up their presses with books, and even then the quality of their products could hardly compete with the handsome editions routinely manufactured in England. But whether domestic or imported, books remained too expensive for most Americans' modest standard of living. A single volume of any writer's work would have cost an American laborer a sizable portion of a week's wages. Even for the fairly affluent, books were regarded as luxuries. With the introduction of such mechanical improvements as the Columbia iron press in 1807 and other more efficient printing methods, cheaper printed matter eventually found its way into the homes of the poor, but even then, as James Fenimore Cooper observed, such reading material usually consisted of little more than "a fragment of a Bible, *Pilgrim's Progress,* and an almanac that was four years old."

Regardless of their size and owner's profession, personal libraries in the first few decades following the Revolution were still dominated by the Puritan legacy of what Cotton Mather had called "devout and useful Books." The Bible, *Pilgrim's Progress, The Book of Common Prayer,* sermons, theological tracts, and such didactic staples as *The Practice of Piety* and *The Whole Duty of Man* lined many of the shelves in the growing number of bookshops squeezed into the bustling commercial districts of coastal cities. While Americans still seemed absorbed in reflection about their own spiritual welfare, they also seemed increasingly interested in broadening their experiences and cultivating the vast amount of untilled land that stretched farther and farther westward.

Frontiers of Literature

When Thomas Jefferson's purchase of the Louisiana Territory in 1803 doubled the area of the United States and opened the prospect of expansion to the Pacific, countless Americans were drawn by the large stretches of land available to anyone who wanted them. Not everyone, of course, could afford to develop this land or even, in some areas, to get to it; but many of those who could did so.

Successive waves of pioneers, settlers, farmers, speculators, townspeople, and managers of commerce explored the remote regions of the country in the first half of the nineteenth century. Eagerly they pursued visions of adventure, ownership, and economic self-sufficiency in settlements whose names expressed the new nation's collective hopes: Canaan, Valhalla, Arcadia, Paradise, El Dorado, Beulah. Yet these and other frontier settlements also quickly began to duplicate the distinguishing characteristics of the places the settlers had left. In effect, the American frontier would become the site for a cultural version of Eli Whitney's theory of interchangeable parts. With such names as Rome, Athens, Cambridge, Essex, and Plymouth, many American frontier towns would increasingly be built to reflect eastern and European specifications. Standardized building materials and prefabricated structures followed by the mid-nineteenth century. America's fascination with mobility and duplicative experience had begun to take on cultural as well as social and economic significance in American life and literature. Seen from a European perspective, America appeared to be, to use Thomas Babington Macaulay's phrase, "all sail and no anchor."

The Backwoodsman

The people in the Atlantic states have not yet recovered from the horror inspired by the term "backwoodsman." This prejudice is particularly strong in New England, and is more or less felt from Maine to Georgia. . . . But the backwoodsman of the west, as I have seen him, is generally an amiable and virtuous man. His general motive for coming here is to be a freeholder, to have plenty of rich land, and to be able to settle his children about him. It is a most virtuous motive. And I fully believe that nine in ten of the emigrants have come here with no other motive. You find, in truth, that he has vices and barbarisms peculiar to his situation. His manners are rough. He wears, it may be, a long beard. He has a great quantity of bear- and deerskins wrought into his household establishment, his furniture and dress. He carries a knife or a dirk in his bosom, and when in the woods has a rifle on his back and a pack of dogs at his heels. An Atlantic stranger, transferred directly from one of our cities to his door, would recoil from an encounter with him. But remember that his rifle and his dogs are among his chief means of support and profit. Remember that all his first days here were passed in the dread of the savages. Remember that he still encounters them, still meets bears and panthers. Enter his door and tell him you are benighted and wish the shelter of his cabin for the night. The welcome is indeed seemingly ungracious: "I reckon you can stay," or "I suppose we must let you stay." But this apparent ungraciousness is the harbinger of every kindness that he can bestow and every comfort that his cabin can afford. Good coffee, corn bread and butter, venison, pork, wild and tame fowls, are set before you. His wife, timid, silent, reserved, but constantly attentive to your comfort, does not sit at the table with you, but, like the wives of the patriarchs, stands and attends on you. You are shown to the best bed which the house can afford. When this kind of hospitality has been afforded you as long as you choose to stay, and when you depart and speak about your bill, you are most commonly told with some slight mark of resentment that they do not keep tavern.

Timothy Flint, *Recollections of the Last Ten Years* (1826)

Despite the uncertainty that characterized much of American life in the early nineteenth century, reflected in its as yet undetermined geographical and experiential boundaries, Americans found it relatively easy to be optimistic about the future of their new nation. With so much of its territory unsettled, and with a population so rich in individual and collective spontaneity, vision, and energy, the United States promised to be, to use the literary historian Perry Miller's phrase, "nature's nation." Space was rapidly replacing time as the single most crucial factor in American life, and it would soon dominate American literature as well. The land itself had become the new nation's most precious commodity and its greatest source for literary subjects and locations. The land, and the sense of "place" it engendered, had come to serve as the locus for American vision and aspiration.

Scores of early nineteenth century pioneer diaries and journals, most to this day without public recognition, recorded the dramatic nature of unprecedented experiences along the ever-expanding southern and western frontiers. Gradually, however, as settlers transformed freshly cut clearings into towns, Americans with more literary aspirations began to turn out with increasing frequency a newly appropriate subject for literature—personal accounts of life west of the Alleghenies. Timothy Flint's renditions of backwoods America helped chart what remains the most legendary part of our national consciousness and encouraged even more ambitious and extravagant literary efforts. More widely publicized literary excursions, including those of Washington Irving and James Fenimore Cooper, drew even greater attention to the American frontier, especially among readers in coastal cities. Broadening the nation's literary horizon had become a fact of cultural life in the new republic.

As new populations cleared more land and pushed the frontier farther southward and westward, the settlers' interest in the literature of the frontier remained secondary to their need for practical books. Guides to virtually every aspect of frontier life began to compete vigorously with political and religious titles. Backwoods peddlers had to create more places among their assorted wares for copies of various guides to farming and everyday life along the frontier. As white settlers pushed back the wilderness and displaced greater numbers of Native Americans, books about Indians also appeared with greater frequency, with such self-explanatory titles as *The American Savage: How He May Be Tamed by the Weapons of Civilization*. Yet at the same time that white settlers drove more and more Native Americans from their land and appropriated their knowledge of agriculture and medicine, the broader American reading public continued to be fascinated with what were known as captivity narratives—harrowing accounts of the narrator's capture, imprisonment, torture, and inevitable escape from Indian captors. Eventually these narratives gave way to the equally heroic exploits of such legendary frontier figures as Daniel Boone and Davy Crockett. The popularity of these frontier stories gave rise to what became the even more celebrated tradition of the tall tale and local color fiction in late nineteenth century American literature.

Davy Crockett's Legendary Shooting Match with Mike Fink

Mike was a boatman on the Mississip, but he had a little cabbin on the head of the Cumberland, and a horrid handsome wife, that loved him the wickedest that ever you see. Mike only worked enough to find his wife in rags, and himself in powder, and lead, and whiskey, and the rest of the time he spent in nocking over bar and turkeys, and bouncing deer, and sometimes drawing a lead on an injun. So one night I fell in with him in the woods, where him and his wife shook down a blanket for me in his wigwam. In the morning sez Mike to me, "I've got the handsomest wife, and the fastest horse, and the sharpest shooting iron in all Kentuck, and if any man dare doubt it, I'll be in his hair quicker than hell could scorch a feather." This put my dander up, and sez I, "I've nothing to say agin your wife, Mike, for it can't be denied she's a shocking handesome woman, and Mrs. Crockett's in Tennessee, and I've got no horses. Mike, I don't exactly like to tell you you lie about what you say about your rifle, but I'm d———d if you speak the truth, and I'll prove it. Do you see that are cat sitting on the top rail of your potato patch, about a hundred and fifty yards off? If she ever hears agin, I'll be shot if it shan't be without ears."

Sketches and Eccentricities of Col. David Crockett, of West Tennessee (1833)

Since land was now the new nation's principal commodity, and its cultivation a chief occupation, ownership disputes proved inevitable. Books on law were accordingly carted out to frontier settlements, where doctors, ministers, and occasionally the settlers themselves had to compensate for the shortage of lawyers in adjudicating conflicting claims. Even more specialized books dealing with, for example, medicine, agriculture, or horsemanship could be found nestled among the piles of outdated almanacs in backwoods cabins. The almanac undisputedly reigned as the new nation's best-seller and served as the chief instrument for reaching what one writer called "the solitary dwellings of the poor and illiterate, where the studied ingenuity of the learned writers never comes." Combined with the increasing sales of guides to domesticating the frontier, the almanac set what is still an enduring standard for America's dedication to self-made success.

Often there were not enough books to satisfy the American public's interest in self-improvement. Even if there were, many Americans could not afford them. The spread of subscription libraries offered one ingenious solution to this predicament. Beginning in 1731 when Benjamin Franklin organized the Library Company of Philadelphia, subscription libraries recruited members who paid fees to be put toward the purchase of books, which then circulated among the subscribers. At the outbreak of the Revolution, sixty-four subscription libraries, dedicated to "the promotion of knowledge and virtue," had been established, with the borrowing time sensibly determined by the length of the book, the user's distance from the library, and the fee charged. In the years following the Revolution, public circulating libraries flourished and exerted considerable influence on the cultural life of the new republic. In the preface to his novel *The Algerine Captive* (1797), Royall Tyler describes the libraries' impact on the changing literary consciousness of the nation:

> In our inland towns of consequence, social libraries had been constituted, composed of books designed to amuse rather than to instruct, and country bookshelves, fostering the new born taste of the people, had filled the whole land with modern Travels and Novels almost as incredible. The diffusion of a taste for any species of writing through all ranks, in so short a time, would appear impracticable to a European.

Reading was gradually becoming a democratic practice, no longer an activity restricted by virtue of education to the upper class in urban settings.

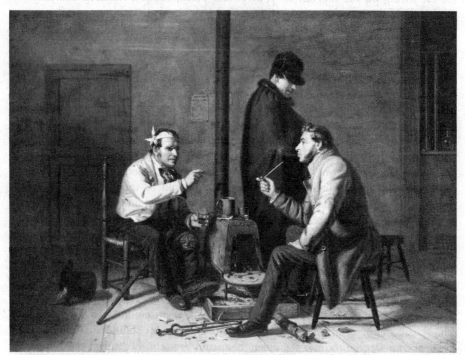

William Sidney Mount, The Long Story (Tough Story), *oil on panel, 1837 (© in the collection of The Corcoran Gallery of Art, Washington, D.C.).*

An American Education

The education we got was solid enough in some respects, and very superficial in others. In arithmetic, geometry, surveying, mechanics, and such solid and practical matters, we were earnest students, but our geography was chiefly American, and the United States was larger than all the universe beside. In the same way our history was American history, brief but glorious. We despised monarchial countries and governments too thoroughly to care much about their histories; and if we studied them, it was that we might contrast their despotisms with our own free and happy institutions. We were taught every day and in every way that ours was the freest, the happiest, and soon to be the greatest and most powerful country in the world. This is the religious faith of every American. He learns it in his infancy, and he can never forget it. . . .

Our education was adapted to intensify our self-esteem, and to make us believe that we were the most intelligent, the most enlightened, the freest, most Christian, and greatest people the sun ever shone upon. Ours was the model Government of the world; our institutions were the model institutions, our country the model Republic. I do not in the least exaggerate. We read it in our books and newspapers, heard it in sermons, speeches, and orations, thanked God for it in our prayers, and devoutly believed it always.

Thomas Low Nichols, *Forty Years of American Life* (1864)

The Prospects of an American Literature

Despite a formidable list of circumstances and problems that had impaired the development of a truly distinctive American literature, writers and readers in the early nineteenth century could find several reasons to be encouraged about the cultural prospects of the new republic. In his monumental nine-volume study of the period, *History of the United States of America During the Administrations of Jefferson and Madison* (1889), Henry Adams observed:

> The average American was more intelligent than the average European, and was becoming every year still more active-minded as the new movement of society caught him up and swept him through a life of more varied experiences. On all sides the national mind responded to its stimulants. Deficient as the American was in the machinery of higher instruction; remote and poor, unable by any exertion to acquire the training, the capital, or even the elementary textbooks he needed for a fair development of his natural powers—his native energy and ambition already responded to the spur applied to them.

Nowhere were these "varied experiences" and "native energy and ambition" more amply evident than in the scores of new magazines that appeared in the first few decades of the new republic. Frank Luther Mott, a respected historian of the trade, estimates that no fewer than seventy-one periodicals began publishing between 1786 and 1800, with "several hundred more" appearing between 1800 and 1830. Most were relatively brief (few exceeded sixty-four pages in length), and nearly all relied initially on material reprinted from British sources to fill their pages inexpensively. Yet their subtitles reveal the scope of their interests: the *Massachusetts Magazine* billed itself as a *Monthly Museum of Knowledge and Rational Entertainment. Containing, Poetry, Musick, Biography, History, Physick, Geography, Morality, Criticism, Philosophy, Mathematicks, Agriculture, Architecture, Chymistry, Novels, Tales, Romances, Translations, News, Marriages, Deaths, Meteorological Observations, &c.,&c.*

In addition to being compendiums, as one publication put it, of "useful knowledge of every kind," American periodicals also served as the principal forum for the debate over the prospects of developing a truly indigenous American literature. Each issue of the *North American Review,* founded in 1815 as the first American journal devoted exclusively to printing American material, resounded with calls for American writers to stop imitating British and continental literary models. The most vocal advocates of a distinctively national literature—including William Tudor, Walter Channing, and James Kirke Paulding—criticized the still prevailing preference among American writers for neoclassical forms and standards. These critics argued that American writers ought to concentrate instead on more immediate subjects and less studied forms for literary expression. Condemning what Channing called "the Literary Delinquency of America," these critics recognized in American scenery, history, and social relations suitable and untapped resources for literary distinction. Other critics, including R. H. Dana, Sr., and Francis Calley Gray, encouraged American literary independence, but at a much slower pace and without either excluding foreign examples or sacrificing literary standards.

James Kirke Paulding remained the most eloquent and hopeful voice among the periodical essayists' campaign for literary independence. In his essay "National Literature" (1819–1820), he noted that American writers had "debased the genius of this new world by making it the ape and the tributary of that of the old" and observed that the new nation had overlooked its own "rich resources, and sponged upon the exhausted treasury of our impoverished neighbors." American literary independence, Paulding claimed, would not be secure until the American writer freed himself

American Language and Literature

The whole external character of our country is totally unlike that of England. Our descriptions, of course, which must, if we ever have a poetry, be made in the language of another country, can never be distinctive. They can never possess the peculiar claims which those of native individuality teem with; which are more beautiful to a foreigner because he is willing in reading them to heighten the beauties of an obscure passage by lending it the aid of his own imagination. How tame will his language sound who would describe Niagara in language fitted for the falls at London bridge, or attempt the majesty of the Mississippi in that which was made for the Thames?

Walter Channing (1815)

from a habit of servile imitation; by daring to think and feel, and express his feelings; by dwelling on scenes and events connected with our pride and affections; by indulging in those little peculiarities of thought, feeling and expression which belong to every nation; by borrowing from nature, and not from those who disfigure or burlesque her. . . . These causes lead to the final establishment of a national literature. . . . This country is not destined to be always behind in the race of literary glory. The time will assuredly come, when that same freedom of thought and action which has given such a spur to our genius in other respects, will achieve similar wonders in literature.

With its attention to "those little peculiarities of thought, feeling, and expression which belong to every nation," its emphasis on an "air and character of originality," and its promotion of American history and nature as suitable literary subjects, Paulding's remarks anticipate the major themes of Ralph Waldo Emerson's celebrated essay "The American Scholar." The message was clear: American writers must fathom their own distinctive experiences before they could create a national literature equal to expressing those experiences in indigenous terms.

The Makings of American Literature

The basic ingredients of an independent national literature were in place: ambitious writers, suitable subjects, and an increasing number of printing presses, newspapers, magazines, book shops, schools, and libraries. All that remained was to make that literature distinctively American. "It does not follow because many books are written by persons born in America," Margaret Fuller cautioned several years later, "that there exists an American literature. Books which imitate or represent the thought and life of Europe do not constitute an American literature. Before such can exist, an original idea must animate this nation and fresh currents must call into life fresh thoughts along its shores."

By the late 1820s, Americans could point with pride to the publication of, among other notable works, Washington Irving's *Sketch Book* (1819–1820), William Cullen Bryant's *Poems* (1821), three of James Fenimore Cooper's "Leather-Stocking Tales" (*The Pioneers,* 1823; *The Last of the Mohicans,* 1826; and *The Prairie,* 1827), Edgar Allan Poe's *Tamerlane and Other Poems* (1827), and Noah Webster's *American Dictionary* (1828). Ample evidence of America's literary progress could also be seen in the increasing number of writers who devoted themselves exclusively to their craft as well as in the growing interest in literary theory and controversy. The prominence of the so-called Knickerbocker School, the most famous group of writers in the early decades of the new republic, added luster to the American literary scene and helped turn New York into the literary matrix of the early nineteenth century, outshining Philadelphia, just as that city had in turn overshadowed Boston. However, the writers identified with the Knickerbocker group—including, among others, James Kirke Paulding, Fitz-Greene Halleck, John Howard Payne, Washington Irving, and, for a time, William Cullen Bryant and James Fenimore Cooper—were closer geographically than in aesthetic principle. Yet however loosely associated, these writers did avow the same interest in exploring American subjects and themes.

Yet none of these responses would have met Paulding's and Fuller's challenge to create an independent national literature. As their remarks underscore, the most persistent problem facing writers who aspired to create a national literature in the early nineteenth century was the inadequacy—or, better, the inappropriateness— of European forms to express states of consciousness that were specifically American. The issue was not the lack of American material suitable for literary purposes but the resistance of that material to European methods of expression. Intent on being *American,* writers in the new republic had yet to discover how to do so.

Self-consciousness about the irrepressible novelty of American experience proved to be the new nation's greatest literary resource. With, as Timothy Dwight observed, no "ancient castles, ruined abbeys, and fine pictures" to re-create in literature, American writers sought new modes and styles to express their nation's unprecedented experiences in the natural world. The land and the limitless experiences it generated had become an "experiment," a word first used in an American context. "Men are like plants," Crèvecoeur observed; they are as different as "the peculiar soil and exposition in which they grow." And with no sense of failure to inhibit them, Americans in the early decades of the new republic were free to explore their indigenous experience. The extraordinary discoveries in botany recorded in William Bartram's *Travels Through North and South Carolina, Georgia, East and West Florida* (1791), for example, not only increased the nation's understanding of the natural world but also provided many prominent American poets of the time (including Philip Freneau and William Cullen Bryant) with reliable yet exotic views of American nature.

Novelty and experimentation, which were everywhere apparent in daily American experience, surfaced at first only intermittently in the nation's characteristic literary forms. Imitating imported literary methods still dominated poetic expression throughout the period, including the works of its two major poets, Philip Freneau and William Cullen Bryant. Both Freneau and the renowned Bryant, who vehemently denounced those who "do not praise a thing until [they] see the seal of transatlantic approbation upon it," found it far easier to admire indigenous American subjects than to render them in distinctively American terms. In this respect, their stately and powerful poetic voices seem more harbingers of than precedents for such fiercely original poetic imaginations as those of Walt Whitman and Emily Dickinson later in the nineteenth century.

The familiar essay met much the same fate as poetry in the hands of American writers during the early republic. Most newspapers featured essay series, many written under such delightful pseudonyms as "The Prompter" (Noah Webster), "Tomo Cheeki" and "Robert Slender" (Philip Freneau), "Oliver Oldstyle" (Joseph Dennie), and "Jonathan Oldstyle" (from the pen of the master of the genre, Washington Irving). Despite the essay's use as the principal means to decry British influence on American literature, most American writers regularly invoked Addison and Steele as their literary precedent, just as American reviewers relied on their English counterparts to set the standard for witty and incisive commentary on cultural and social affairs.

During this same period, however, two groups that had rarely posited their voices in colonial American literature began to express their individual and collective interests and sensibilities. Women and blacks made significant gains as writers and readers during the years between 1776 and 1836. For blacks, a class deliberately kept uneducated in the new republic, learning to read and write was largely a matter of fortitude, luck, or subterfuge. But in March 1827, John B. Russwurm, the first black American college graduate (Bowdoin, 1826), and Samuel Cornish founded *Freedom's Journal* in New York City. This, the nation's first newspaper owned and edited by blacks, aimed to serve both to inform "our brethren in the different states of this great confederacy" and to conciliate what the editors hoped would be a large white audience. In its attention to "useful knowledge of every kind," "moral and religious improvement," and "civil rights," *Freedom's Journal* succeeded admirably in its announced purpose: "to plead our own cause." It also contributed to the nature of the debate over abolition.

On Female Education

In calling on my patriotic countrymen, to effect so noble an object, the consideration of national glory, should not be overlooked. Ages have rolled away;—barbarians have trodden the weaker sex beneath their feet;—tyrants have robbed us of the present light of heaven, and fain would take its future also. Nations, calling themselves polite, have made us the fancied idols of ridiculous worship, and we have repaid them with ruin for their folly. But where is that wise and heroic country, which has considered, that our rights are sacred, though we cannot defend them? that tho' a weaker, we are an essential part of the body politic, whose corruption or improvement must affect the whole? and which, having thus considered, has sought to give us by education, that rank in the scale of being, to which our importance entitles us? History shows not that country. It shows many, whose legislatures have sought to improve their various vegetable productions, and their breeds of useful brutes; but none, whose public councils have made it an object of their deliberations, to improve the character of their women. Yet though history lifts not her finger to such a one, anticipation does. She points to a nation, which having thrown off the shackles of authority and precedent, shrinks not from schemes of improvement, because other nations have never attempted them; but, which, in its pride of independance, would rather lead than follow, in the march of human improvement: a nation, wise and magnanimous to plan, enterprising to undertake, and rich in resources to execute. Does not every American exult that this country is his own? And who knows how great and good a race of men, may yet arise from the forming hand of mothers, enlightened by the bounty of that beloved country, to defend her liberties, to plan her future improvement, and to raise her to unparalleled glory.

Emma Willard, "An Address to . . . the Legislature of New York Proposing a Plan for Improving Female Education" (1819)

Women had from childhood on traditionally been discriminated against educationally in colonial America, and despite the urgings of Abigail Adams and other prominent women, the Revolution and its aftermath did little to improve their lot. For women in the new nation, literacy continued to be determined principally by their class. Those who read, did, and mainly fiction. The development of the American novel depended to a large extent on a female readership.

Sentimental novels were among the most popular forms of fiction in the new republic. Highly didactic, these novels—including William Hill Brown's *Power of Sympathy* (1789) and Susannah Rowson's *Charlotte Temple: A Tale of Truth* (1791)—featured an epistolary style derived primarily from Samuel Richardson. The prefaces to these novels emphasized moral messages and disclaimers; Brown explained, for example, that he wrote *The Power of Sympathy* to "expose the dangerous Consequences of Seduction and to set forth the advantages of female Education." Yet such prominent figures as Thomas Jefferson, Timothy Dwight, and Noah Webster severely criticized American novelists in the new republic for corrupting impressionable young women with fanciful accounts of contemporary life. A fairly widespread belief held, in the words of one critic, that novels "lead onto a path of vice," "inflame the passions and corrupt the heart," "pollute the imaginations of young women and likewise give them false ideas of life."

Other popular fictional forms of the time were the historical romances influenced primarily by Sir Walter Scott and the satiric novel. *The Algerine Captive* (1797) by Royall Tyler and *Modern Chivalry* (1792) by Hugh Henry Brackenridge remain the best known, with Brackenridge among the first authors to incorporate American materials and current events into their work, including the Whiskey Rebellion, the American Constitution, and the French Revolution. Charles Brockden Brown's Gothic novels—including *Wieland* (1798), *Edgar Huntly* (1799), and *Arthur Mervyn* (1799–1800)—also enjoyed wide readership. The American writer must "examine objects with his own eyes," Brown exhorted. He must "employ European models merely for the improvement of his taste" and draw on "all that is genuine and peculiar in the scene before him" to create literature equivalent to his sources. The irony of Brown's work, like that of each of the other novelists in the new republic, is its dependence on English and continental sources. Yet these fictional forms also introduce characters, settings, and themes that would be developed more elaborately in the later fiction of Irving, Cooper, Poe, Hawthorne, and Melville.

European Models and the American Landscape

The careers of Washington Irving and James Fenimore Cooper span the period of America's self-conscious quest for an independent literary identity, and their writings most clearly illustrate the major tension in the literature of the new republic: eager but anxious responses to the lure of literary nationalism set off against assurances of working within traditional European models. Their writings also underscore the principal literary issues in the new republic: the writer's identity in a society preoccupied with material progress; the literary consequences of America's absorption in the present and the future and its neglect of the past; and, above all, the writer's need to create an *American* time and place where the imagination could flourish. For Irving this would be colonial Sleepy Hollow. For Cooper it was the unspoiled, dense woods of the frontier as well as the open stretches of the sea, the same regions depicted in the new American landscape painting led by Thomas Cole. Later writers, including Hawthorne, Thoreau, Twain, Crane, and Faulkner, created their own distinctive versions of a specifically American historical context, but Irving and Cooper first grappled with the issue in a way that made the nature of both the literary problem and its solution luminously clear.

Irving helped American writers discover the literary potential of the past by adapting Europe's rich cultural heritage to American settings. Cooper shared Irving's interest in the literary possibilities of history and opened two additional prospects for American literature: the frontier and life at sea. Cooper's "Leather-Stocking Tales" played a significant role in establishing the frontier as the principal shaping influence on nineteenth century and much of twentieth century American literature and turned Natty Bumppo into the American archetype of individual freedom and self-reliance. Cooper's backwoodsman served as the fictional forerunner of countless legendary mountain men and cowboys, America's purest examples of self-expression in the wilderness.

"A Fitting Place to Speak of God"

Perhaps the most impressive characteristic of American scenery is its wildness.

It is the most distinctive because in civilized Europe the primitive features of scenery have long since been destroyed or modified—the extensive forests that once overshadowed a great part of it have been felled—rugged mountains have been smoothed, and impetuous rivers turned from their courses to accommodate the tastes and necessities of a dense population—the once tangled wood is now a grassy lawn; the turbulent brook a navigable stream—crags that could not be removed have been crowned with towers, and the rudest valleys tamed by the plough.

And to this cultivated state our western world is fast approaching; but nature is still predominant, and there are those who regret that with the improvements of cultivation the sublimity of the wilderness should pass away: for those scenes of solitude from which the hand of nature has never been lifted, affect the mind with a more deep toned emotion than aught which the hand of man has touched. Amid them the consequent associations are of God the creator—they are his undefiled works, and the mind is cast into the contemplation of eternal things.

Thomas Cole, "Essay on American Scenery" (1835)

John Quidor, The Return of Rip Van Winkle, *oil on canvas, 1829 (National Gallery of Art, Washington, D.C., Andrew W. Mellon Collection).*

The irony of Cooper's and Irving's accomplishments is that in both cases they were nurtured principally during the authors' extended stays in Europe. Irving's and Cooper's familiar essays, stories, novels, and social criticism, adapted largely from European sources, form a compendium of American literary taste in the first half of the nineteenth century—moving in Irving's case from neoclassical wit and satire to Romantic interest in atmosphere and sentiment, and in the case of Cooper from an interest in the traditional novel of manners to the broader brushstrokes of painting mythic American landscapes populated with legendary characters. The diversity (their willingness to explore multiple aspects of experience), the dynamism (their constant growth as writers), and the organic unity of their writings (their interest in the whole as much as the part), along with their commitment to extolling a strong sense of individuality, independence, and introspection in the face of the powerful rawness of the American landscape, place Irving and Cooper at the beginning of what would become a long tradition of Romantic writing in American literature, a tradition that would have its fullest expression in the great flowering of the American Renaissance. At the end of "The American Scholar" (1837), Ralph Waldo Emerson proclaimed that Americans "will walk on our own feet; we will work with our own hands; we will speak our own minds." The writers of the new republic laid the foundation that enabled Emerson to declare the symbolic birth of a truly distinctive American literature with such confidence.

Further Reading:

H. Adams, *The History of the United States of America During the Administrations of Jefferson and Madison,* 8 vols., 1884–1901.

M. Ellis, *Joseph Dennie and His Circle,* 1915.

V. W. Brooks, *The Flowering of New England,* 1936.

L. Howard, *The Connecticut Wits,* 1943.

H. M. Jones, *O Strange New World: American Culture, the Formative Years,* 1952.

H. H. Clark, *Transitions in American Literary History,* 1953.

B. T. Spencer, *The Quest for Nationality,* 1957.

D. Boorstin, *The Americans: The Colonial Experience,* 1958.

M. Cunliffe, *The Nation Takes Shape,* 1959.

R. B. Nye, *The Cultural Life of the New Nation,* 1960.

L. P. Simpson, *The Federalist Literary Mind,* 1962.

C. L. Sanford, *Quest for America 1810–1824,* 1964.

D. Boorstin, *The Americans: The National Experience,* 1965.

G. Dangerfield, *The Awakening of American Nationalism, 1815–1828,* 1965.

W. Hedges, *Washington Irving: An American Study, 1802–1832,* 1965.

J. T. Main, *The Social Structure of Revolutionary America,* 1965.

P. Miller, *The Life of the Mind in America: From*

the Revolution to the Civil War, 1965.

R. E. Spiller, *The American Literary Revolution,* 1967.

W. Charvat, *The Profession of Authorship in America, 1800–1870,* ed. M. J. Bruccoli, 1968.

H. Petter, *The Early American Novel,* 1971.

L. Simpson, *The Man of Letters in New England and the South,* 1973.

L. J. Friedman, *Inventors of the Promised Land,* 1975.

H. F. May, *The Enlightenment in America,* 1976.

K. Silverman, *Cultural History of the American Revolution,* 1976.

S. Bercovitch, *The Puritan Origins of the American Self,* 1975.

M. Kammen, *A Season of Youth: The American Revolution and the Historical Imagination,* 1978.

J. Ellis, *After the Revolution,* 1979.

E. Elliott, *Revolutionary Writers: Literature and Authority in the New Republic, 1725–1810,* 1982.

J. Fliegelman, *Prodigals and Pilgrims: The American Revolution Against Patriarchal Authority,* 1982.

R. Ferguson, *Law and Letters in American Culture,* 1984.

R. H. Wiebe, *The Opening of American Society,* 1984.

L. Buell, *New England Literary Culture: From Revolution Through Renaissance,* 1986.

Thomas Jefferson
1743–1826

Thomas Jefferson's literary life is intertwined with his life as diplomat, statesman, architect, environmental planner, scientist, politician, and theorist of education. The versatile Jefferson is an awesome figure to later generations who proclaim the value and necessity of specialization. Jefferson embodies the eighteenth-century ideal of a gentleman, a "man of parts" who is worldly, learned, and proficient in numerous endeavors. Jefferson lived that ideal. More, he became an American paradox, an aristocrat who was also a democrat.

Jefferson was born in central Virginia near the future sites of Monticello and the University of Virginia. His father's estate, Shadwell, was at that time near the frontier, and Peter Jefferson, a farmer and surveyor, taught his son Indian lore and mapmaking, perhaps the basis for Jefferson's eventual interests in anthropological study and in design. At age five Jefferson was sent to an English school some fifty miles distant and at ten was enrolled in a Latin school for training in classical language and literature. In 1760 he entered the College of William and Mary, where he had the "great good fortune," as he put it, "to be instructed by Dr. William Small, then Professor of Mathematics, a man profound in most of the useful branches of science, with a happy talent of communication, correct and gentlemanly manners, and an enlarged and liberal mind." This teacher, Jefferson wrote, "probably fixed the destinies of my life."

Upon graduation in 1762, and with Small's guidance, Jefferson began to study law. Once again he found a mentor—George Wythe, a prominent attorney who also became Jefferson's "most affectionate friend through life." Under the influence of Small and Wythe, Jefferson gradually imbibed the principles of republicanism. He shed the orthodox, conservative Anglican heritage and embraced Deism, which provided the model of the Creator to be emulated in building a new republic. Through Dr. Small he became aware of the Scottish Common Sense school, from which he came to believe that the moral sense is one's highest faculty and is equally present to all, a view later expressed in the Declaration of Independence, which he drafted.

Jefferson was admitted to the bar in 1767 and practiced law while taking advantage of the cultural opportunities of Williamsburg, which was a colonial capital as well as a college town. He learned the violin, sometimes playing in string quartets with Governor Francis Fauquier, himself a member of the Royal Society and another of the father figures in the young man's life. Jefferson also attended theatrical performances and began collecting the books that proliferated into a library of about ten thousand volumes that later became the basis for the Library of Congress. He doubtless learned to participate in the polished, urbane conversation of the colonial aristocracy, though Jefferson never was skilled in public speaking.

Jefferson entered Virginia politics in 1769, when he was elected to the legislative House of Burgesses. In those years he also began the construction of Monticello (the estate would not be complete for some forty years). Jefferson was acutely sensitive to style and proportion in architecture. He thought the buildings of his college, William and Mary, "misshapen," like "brick-kilns," and the Williamsburg governor's palace "not handsome." The design for Monticello was Jefferson's own, and has been called classical with American elements. Jefferson's interest in design continued into his Presidential years, when he took part in the plan for the nation's Capitol, and into his so-called retirement, when he designed the campus and buildings (and the curriculum) of the University of Virginia at Charlottesville.

In 1772 Jefferson married Martha Wayles Skelton, a wealthy, slaveholding widow. Within a year their first child, a daughter, was born. The couple had six children, including a son, but only two daughters lived to adulthood. Jefferson was deeply bereaved when his wife died after ten years of marriage. His daughter wrote, "In those melancholy rambles [on horseback], I was his constant companion—a solitary witness to many a burst of grief." Jefferson never remarried.

Pre-Revolutionary politics proved irresistible. In 1773 Jefferson attended a meeting of the Virginia Committee of Correspondence, an intercolonial group that promoted the exchange of letters in opposition to harsh and arbitrary British policies. In 1774 Jefferson attended the newly formed Continental Congress and won respect for his clear style and moderate tone in a pamphlet that defended colonial rights, *A Summary View of the Rights of British America*. By 1776, with events of the Revolution moving swiftly, Jefferson was one of a committee appointed to draft a document announcing the severance of the colonies from England. Though the committee and the congress edited the draft, the Declaration of Independence was Jefferson's. His remarks on the Declaration are revealing. "I turned to neither book nor pamphlet while writing it," he said. "I did not consider it as any part of my charge to invent new ideas, but to place before mankind the common sense of the subject." He considered the Declaration of Independence "an expression of the American mind." The ideals of the Declaration were compatible with Jefferson's work in Virginia to establish religious freedom by law and thus to separate church and state. These two achievements meant so much to him that he included them, together with his fathering of the University of Virginia, in the epitaph he wrote and left behind at his death.

During the Revolutionary War years, Jefferson served as governor of Virginia, narrowly escaping British capture. In 1783 he was elected to Congress and became minister to France, where he served for five years. He was a member of Washington's Cabinet, Vice-President under John Adams, and then President for two terms beginning in 1801. Jefferson envisioned the United States as a self-sufficient, agrarian nation and enacted his vision of its future in the Louisiana Purchase (1803), persuading Congress to sponsor the expedition of Meriwether Lewis and William Clark to explore and map the new territory. Jefferson's Presidency marked the beginning of the democratic plain style in politics. The Chief Executive lived at a boardinghouse, rejected all outward signs of wealth or pomp (including ornamental shoe buckles), and was known to receive visitors in his slippers. After his Presidency he withdrew from public life. ("I am retired to Monticello, where, in the bosom of my family, and surrounded by my books, I enjoy a repose to which I have long been a stranger.")

Evidence suggests that the "bosom" of Jefferson's family included a thirty-eight-year relationship with a slave woman, Sally Hemings, who was a quadroon, the half sister of Jefferson's deceased wife. Social attitudes of the time would have made marital legitimation of the relationship impossible, no matter how much both parties might have wished otherwise. The affair, together with Jefferson's keeping of slaves, has raised charges of hypocrisy against him and has remained troubling to scholars and analysts. It must be pointed out, however, that Jefferson attempted to outlaw slavery in his original draft of the Declaration of Independence and that as President he worked successfully for the enactment of a law banning the further importation of slaves.

Jefferson's literary achievement is a part of his public life. His *Notes on Virginia* (1785), a work of natural science, was occasioned by a query by the Marquis de Barbé-Marois, who posed a set of questions concerning the geography, social history, and ecology of Virginia. Jefferson took the opportunity not only to respond to the questions but also to rebut the widely held European view that America was an unhealthy place that was causing the degeneration of its species. Jefferson's book won him the apology of the famous French naturalist Georges Louis Leclerc de Buffon.

In the years of his so-called retirement, Jefferson kept up a large correspondence. Fortunately, he had reconciled with his New England counterpart, former President John Adams, after a political rift of several years. The two resumed their friendship, and the letters on both sides deepened in reflection and outspokenness. Jefferson died within hours of his old friend Adams on the jubilee of the promulgation of the Declaration of Independence, July 4, 1826. He said, "I find friendship to be like wine, raw when new, ripened with age, the true old man's milk and restorative cordial."

Jefferson's splendid political legacy tends to obscure his achievement in literature. His style, however, and the rhetorical strategies evident in *Notes on Virginia,* in letters, and in the declaration evince the belletristic strain in Jefferson's intellect. His genres—from letters to political documents and geography—remind us that literature embraces wide-ranging forms that remain vital in the hands of a masterful practitioner.

Further Reading:
A. Koch, *The Philosophy of Thomas Jefferson,* 1943.
D. Malone, *Jefferson and His Time,* 5 vols., 1948–1974.
D. Boorstin, *The Lost World of Thomas Jefferson,* 1948.
M. Peterson, *Thomas Jefferson and the New Nation,* 1970.
F. Brodie, *Thomas Jefferson: An Intimate History,* 1974.
G. Wills, *Inventing America,* 1978.
W. Bottorff, *Thomas Jefferson,* 1979.

Texts:
"The Declaration of Independence," *Papers of Thomas Jefferson,* 18 vols., ed. J. Boyd., 1950–1971.
Notes on the State of Virginia, ed. W. Peden, 1955.
The Adams-Jefferson Letters, ed. L. Cappon, 1959.
Writings of Thomas Jefferson, 10 vols., ed. P. Ford, 1892–1899.

The Declaration of Independence as Adopted by Congress

In Congress July 4, 1776

The Unanimous Declaration of the Thirteen United States of America

When in the Course of human events, it becomes necessary for one people to dissolve the political bands which have connected them with another, and to assume among the powers of the earth, the separate and equal station to which the Laws of Nature and of Nature's God entitle them, a decent respect to the opinions of mankind requires that they should declare the causes which impel them to the separation. We hold these truths to be self-evident, that all men are created equal, that they are endowed by their Creator with certain unalienable Rights, that among these are Life, Liberty and the pursuit of Happiness. That to secure these rights, Governments are instituted among Men, deriving their just powers from the consent of the governed, That whenever any Form of Government becomes destructive of these ends, it is the Right of the People to alter or to abolish it, and to institute new Government, laying its foundation on such principles and organizing its powers in such form, as to them shall seem most likely to effect their Safety and Happiness. Prudence, indeed, will dictate that Governments long established should not be changed for light and transient causes; and accordingly all experience hath shewn, that mankind are more disposed to suffer, while evils are sufferable, than to right themselves by abolishing the forms to which they are accustomed. But when a long train of abuses and usurpations, pursuing invariably the same Object evinces a design to reduce them under absolute Despotism, it is their right, it is their duty, to throw off such Government, and to provide new Guards for their future security. Such has been the patient sufferance of these Colonies; and such is now the necessity which constrains them to alter their former Systems of Government. The history of the present King of Great Britain is a history of repeated injuries and usurpations, all having in direct object the establishment of an absolute Tyranny over these States. To prove this, let Facts be submitted to a candid world. He has refused his Assent to Laws, the most wholesome and necessary for the public good. He has forbidden his Governors to pass Laws of immediate and pressing importance, unless suspended in their operation till his Assent should be obtained; and when so suspended, he has utterly neglected to attend to them. He has refused to pass other Laws for the accommodation of large districts of people, unless those people would relinquish the right of Representation in the Legislature, a right inestimable to them and formidable to tyrants only. He has called together legislative bodies at places unusual, uncomfortable, and distant from the depository of their public Records, for the sole purpose of fatiguing them into compliance with his measures. He has dissolved Representative Houses repeatedly, for opposing with manly firmness his invasions on the rights of the people. He has refused for a long time, after such dissolutions, to cause others to be elected; whereby the Legislative powers, incapable of Annihilation, have returned to the People at large for their exercise; the State remaining in the mean time exposed to all the dangers of invasion from without, and convulsions within. He has endeavoured to prevent the population of these States; for that purpose obstructing the Laws for Naturalization of Foreigners; refusing to pass others to encourage their migrations hither, and raising the conditions of new Appropriations of Lands. He has obstructed the Administration of Justice, by refusing his Assent to Laws for establishing Judiciary powers. He has made Judges dependent on his Will alone, for the tenure of their offices, and the amount and payment of their salaries. He has erected a multitude of New Offices, and sent hither swarms of Officers to harrass our people, and eat out their substance. He has kept among us, in times of peace, standing Armies without the Consent of our legislatures. He has affected to render the Military independent of and superior to the Civil power. He has combined with others to subject us to a jurisdiction foreign to our constitution, and unacknowledged by our laws; giving his Assent to their Acts of pretended Legislation: For Quartering large bodies of armed troops among us: For protecting them, by a mock Trial, from punishment for any Murders which they should commit on the Inhabitants of these

States: For cutting off our Trade with all parts of the world: For imposing Taxes on us without our Consent: For depriving us in many cases of the benefits of Trial by Jury: For transporting us beyond Seas to be tried for pretended offences: For abolishing the free System of English Laws in a neighbouring Province, establishing therein an Arbitrary government, and enlarging its Boundaries so as to render it at once an example and fit instrument for introducing the same absolute rule into these Colonies: For taking away our Charters, abolishing our most valuable Laws, and altering fundamentally the Forms of our Governments: For suspending our own Legislatures, and declaring themselves invested with power to legislate for us in all cases whatsoever. He has abdicated Government here, by declaring us out of his Protection and waging War against us. He has plundered our seas, ravaged our Coasts, burnt our towns, and destroyed the Lives of our people. He is at this time transporting large Armies of foreign Mercenaries to compleat the works of death, desolation and tyranny, already begun with circumstances of Cruelty & perfidy scarcely paralleled in the most barbarous ages, and totally unworthy the Head of a civilized nation. He has constrained our fellow Citizens taken Captive on the high Seas to bear Arms against their Country, to become the executioners of their friends and Brethren, or to fall themselves by their Hands. He has excited domestic insurrections amongst us, and has endeavoured to bring on the inhabitants of our frontiers, the merciless Indian Savages, whose known rule of warfare, is an undistinguished destruction of all ages, sexes and conditions. In every stage of these Oppressions We have Petitioned for Redress in the most humble terms: Our repeated Petitions have been answered only by repeated injury. A Prince, whose character is thus marked by every act which may define a Tyrant, is unfit to be the ruler of a free people. Nor have We been wanting in attentions to our Brittish brethren. We have warned them from time to time of attempts by their legislature to extend an unwarrantable jurisdiction over us. We have reminded them of the circumstances of our emigration and settlement here. We have appealed to their native justice and magnanimity, and we have conjured them by the ties of our common kindred to disavow these usurpations, which, would inevitably interrupt our connections and correspondence. They too have been deaf to the voice of justice and of consanguinity. We must, therefore, acquiesce in the necessity, which denounces our Separation, and hold them, as we hold the rest of mankind, Enemies in War, in Peace Friends.

We, therefore, the Representatives of the united States of America, in General Congress, Assembled, appealing to the Supreme Judge of the world for the rectitude of our intentions, do, in the Name, and by Authority of the good People of these Colonies, solemnly publish and declare, That these United Colonies are, and of Right ought to be Free and Independent States; that they are Absolved from all Allegiance to the British Crown, and that all political connection between them and the State of Great Britain, is and ought to be totally dissolved; and that as Free and Independent States, they have full Power to levy War, conclude Peace, contract Alliances, establish Commerce, and to do all other Acts and Things which Independent States may of right do. And for the support of this Declaration, with a firm reliance on the protection of divine Providence, we mutually pledge to each other our Lives, our Fortunes and our sacred Honor.

1776

from Notes on the State of Virginia

from **Query IV: Mountains**

[Confluence of the Shenandoah and Potomac Rivers]

It is worthy notice, that our mountains are not solitary and scattered confusedly over the face of the country; but that they commence at about 150 miles from the sea-coast, are disposed in ridges one behind another, running nearly parallel with the sea-coast, though rather approaching it as they advance north-eastwardly. To the south-west, as the tract of country between the sea-coast and the Mississipi becomes narrower, the mountains converge into a single ridge, which, as it approaches the Gulph of Mexico, subsides into plain country, and gives rise to some of the waters of that Gulph, and particularly to a river called the Apalachicola, probably from the Apalachies, an Indian nation formerly residing on it. Hence the mountains giving rise to that river, and seen from its various parts, were called the Apalachian mountains, being in fact the end or termination only of the great ridges passing through the continent. European geographers however extended the name northwardly as far as the mountains extended; some giving it, after their separation into different ridges, to the Blue ridge, others to the North mountain, others to the Alleghaney, others to the Laurel ridge, as may be seen in their different maps. But the fact I believe is, that none of these ridges were ever known by that name to the inhabitants, either native or emigrant, but as they saw them so called in European maps. In the same direction generally are the veins of lime-stone, coal and other minerals hitherto discovered: and so range the falls of our great rivers. But the courses of the great rivers are at right angles with these. James and Patowmac penetrate through all the ridges of mountains eastward of the Alleghaney; that is broken by no watercourse. It is in fact the spine of the country between the Atlantic on one side, and the Missisipi and St. Laurence on the other. The passage of the Patowmac through the Blue ridge is perhaps one of the most stupendous scenes in nature. You stand on a very high point of land. On your right comes up the Shenandoah, having ranged along the foot of the mountain an hundred miles to seek a vent. On your left approaches the Patowmac, in quest of a passage also. In the moment of their junction they rush together against the mountain, rend it asunder, and pass off to the sea. The first glance of this scene hurries our senses into the opinion, that this earth has been created in time, that the mountains were formed first, that the rivers began to flow afterwards, that in this place particularly they have been dammed up by the Blue ridge of mountains, and have formed an ocean which filled the whole valley; that continuing to rise they have at length broken over at this spot, and have torn the mountain down from its summit to its base. The piles of rock on each hand, but particularly on the Shenandoah, the evident marks of their disrupture and avulsion from their beds by the most powerful agents of nature, corroborate the impression. But the distant finishing which nature has given to the picture is of a very different character. It is a true contrast to the fore-ground. It is as placid and delightful, as that is wild and tremendous. For the mountain being cloven asunder, she presents to your eye, through the cleft, a small catch of smooth blue horizon, at an infinite distance in the plain country, inviting you, as it were, from the riot and tumult roaring around, to pass through the breach and participate of the calm below. Here the eye ultimately composes itself; and that way too the road happens actually to lead. You cross the Patowmac above the junction, pass along its side through the base of the mountain for three miles, its terrible precipices hanging in fragments over you, and within about 20 miles reach Frederic town and the fine country around that. This scene is worth a voyage across the Atlantic. Yet here, as in the neighbourhood of the natural bridge, are people who have passed their lives within half a dozen miles, and have never been to survey these monuments of a war between rivers and mountains, which must have shaken the earth itself to its center. . . .

from **Query V: Cascades**

[Natural Bridge]

The *Natural bridge,* the most sublime of Nature's works, though not comprehended under the present head, must not be pretermitted.[1] It is on the ascent of a hill, which seems to have been cloven through its length by some great convulsion. The fissure, just at the bridge, is, by some admeasurements, 270 feet deep, by others only 205. It is about 45 feet wide at the bottom, and 90 feet at the top; this of course determines the length of the bridge, and its height from the water. Its breadth in the middle, is about 60 feet, but more at the ends, and the thickness of the mass at the summit of the arch, about 40 feet. A part of this thickness is constituted by a coat of earth, which gives growth to many large trees. The residue, with the hill on both sides, is one solid rock of limestone. The arch approaches the Semi-elliptical form; but the larger axis of the ellipsis, which would be the cord of the arch, is many times longer than the (semi-axis which gives its height.) Though the sides of this bridge are provided in some parts with a parapet of fixed rocks, yet few men have resolution to walk to them and look over into the abyss. You involuntarily fall on your hands and feet, creep to the parapet and peep over it. Looking down from this height about a minute, gave me a violent head ach. (This painful sensation is relieved by a short, but pleasing view of the Blue ridge along the fissure downwards, and upwards by that of the Short hills, which, with the Purgatory mountain is a divergence from the North ridge; and, descending then to the valley below, the sensation becomes delightful in the extreme. It is impossible for the emotions, arising from the sublime, to be felt beyond what they are here: so beautiful an arch, so elevated, so light, and springing, as it were, up to heaven, the rapture of the Spectator is really indiscribable! The fissure continues deep and narrow and, following the margin of the stream upwards about three eights of a mile you arrive at a limestone cavern, less remarkable, however, for height and extent than those before described. Its entrance into the hill is but a few feet above the bed of the stream.) This bridge is in the county of Rockbridge, to which it has given name, and affords a public and commodious passage over a valley, which cannot be crossed elsewhere for a considerable distance. The stream passing under it is called

---

[1] I.e., although not a cascade, the natural bridge must not be omitted.

Cedar creek. It is a water of James river, and sufficient in the driest seasons to turn a grist-mill, though its fountain is not more than two miles above.

from Query VI: Productions Mineral, Vegetable and Animal

[Rebuttal to Count Buffon]

The opinion advanced by the Count de Buffon,[2] is 1. That the animals common both to the old and new world, are smaller in the latter. 2. That those peculiar to the new, are on a smaller scale. 3. That those which have been domesticated in both, have degenerated in America: and 4. That on the whole it exhibits fewer species. And the reason he thinks is, that the heats of America are less; that more waters are spread over its surface by nature, and fewer of these drained off by the hand of man. In other words, that heat is friendly, and moisture adverse to the production and developement of large quadrupeds. . . .

Hitherto I have considered this hypothesis as applied to brute animals only, and not in its extension to the man of America, whether aboriginal or transplanted. It is the opinion of Mons. de Buffon that the former furnishes no exception to it: "Although the savage of the new world is about the same height as man in our world, this does not suffice for him to constitute an exception to the general fact that all living nature has become smaller on that continent. The savage is feeble, and has small organs of generation; he has neither hair nor beard, and no ardor whatever for his female; although swifter than the European because he is better accustomed to running, he is, on the other hand, less strong in body; he is also less sensitive, and yet more timid and cowardly; he has no vivacity, no activity of mind; the activity of his body is less an exercise, a voluntary motion, than a necessary action caused by want; relieve him of hunger and thirst, and you deprive him of the active principle of all his movements; he will rest stupidly upon his legs or lying down entire days. There is no need for seeking further the cause of the isolated mode of life of these savages and their repugnance for society: the most precious spark of the fire of nature has been refused to them; they lack ardor for their females, and consequently have no love for their fellow men; not knowing this strongest and most tender of all affections, their other feelings are also cold and languid; they love their parents and children but little; the most intimate of all ties, the family connection, binds them therefore but loosely together; between family and family there is no tie at all; hence they have no communion, no commonwealth, no state of society. Physical love constitues their only morality; their heart is icy, their society cold, and their rule harsh. They look upon their wives only as servants for all work, or as beasts of burden, which they load without consideration with the burden of their hunting, and which they compel without mercy, without gratitude, to perform tasks which are often beyond their strength. They have only few children, and they take little care of them. Everywhere

[2] Georges Louis Leclerc de Buffon (1707–1788), French author of the multivolume *Natural History,* which argued that the American environment was conducive to the degeneration of species and thus unsuited to civilized life.

the original defect appears: they are indifferent because they have little sexual capacity, and this indifference to the other sex is the fundamental defect which weakens their nature, prevents its development, and—destroying the very germs of life—uproots society at the same time. Man is here no exception to the general rule. Nature, by refusing him the power of love, has treated him worse and lowered him deeper than any animal." An afflicting picture indeed, which, for the honor of human nature, I am glad to believe has no original. Of the Indian of South America I know nothing; for I would not honor with the appelation of knowledge, what I derive from the fables published of them. These I believe to be just as true as the fables of Æsop. This belief is founded on what I have seen of man, white, red, and black, and what has been written of him by authors, enlightened themselves, and writing amidst an enlightened people. The Indian of North America being more within our reach, I can speak of him somewhat from my own knowledge, but more from the information of others better acquainted with him, and on whose truth and judgment I can rely. From these sources I am able to say, in contradiction to this representation, that he is neither more defective in ardor, nor more impotent with his female, than the white reduced to the same diet and exercise: that he is brave, when an enterprize depends on bravery; education with him making the point of honor consist in the destruction of an enemy by stratagem, and in the preservation of his own person free from injury; or perhaps this is nature; while it is education which teaches us to honor force more than finesse; that he will defend himself against an host of enemies, always chusing to be killed, rather than to surrender, though it be to the whites, who he knows will treat him well: that in other situations also he meets death with more deliberation, and endures tortures with a firmness unknown almost to religious enthusiasm with us: that he is affectionate to his children, careful of them, and indulgent in the extreme: that his affections comprehend his other connections, weakening, as with us, from circle to circle, as they recede from the center: that his friendships are strong and faithful to the uttermost extremity: that his sensibility is keen, even the warriors weeping most bitterly on the loss of their children, though in general they endeavour to appear superior to human events: that his vivacity and activity of mind is equal to ours in the same situation; hence his eagerness for hunting, and for games of chance. The women are submitted to unjust drudgery. This I believe is the case with every barbarous people. With such, force is law. The stronger sex therefore imposes on the weaker. It is civilization alone which replaces women in the enjoyment of their natural equality. That first teaches us to subdue the selfish passions, and to respect those rights in others which we value in ourselves. Were we in equal barbarism, our females would be equal drudges. The man with them is less strong than with us, but their woman stronger than ours; and both for the same obvious reason; because our man and their woman is habituated to labour, and formed by it. With both races the sex which is indulged with ease is least athletic. An Indian man is small in the hand and wrist for the same reason for which a sailor is large and strong in the arms and shoulders, and a porter in the legs and thighs.—They raise fewer children than we do. The causes of this are to be found, not in a difference of nature, but of circumstance. The women very frequently attending the men in their parties of war and of hunting, child-bearing becomes extremely inconvenient to them. It is said, therefore, that they have learnt the practice of procuring abortion by the use of some vegetable; and that it even extends to prevent conception for a considerable time after. During these parties they are exposed to numerous hazards, to excessive exertions, to the greatest extremities of hunger. Even at their homes the nation depends for food, through a certain part of every year, on the gleanings of the forest: that is, they experience a famine once in every year. With all animals, if the female be badly fed, or not fed at all, her young perish: and if both male and female be reduced to like want, generation becomes less active, less productive. To the obstacles then of want and hazard, which nature has opposed to the multiplication of wild animals, for the purpose of restraining their numbers within certain bounds, those of labour and of voluntary abortion are added with the Indian. No wonder then if they multiply less than we do. Where food is regularly supplied, a single farm will shew more of cattle, than a whole country of forests can of buffaloes. The same Indian women, when married to white traders, who feed them and their children plentifully and regularly, who exempt them from excessive drudgery, who keep them stationary and unexposed to accident, produce and raise as many children as the white women. Instances are known, under these circumstances, of their rearing a dozen children. . . .

Before we condemn the Indians of this continent as wanting genius,[3] we must consider that letters[4] have not yet been introduced among them. Were we to compare them in their present state with the Europeans North of the Alps, when the Roman arms and arts first crossed those mountains, the comparison would be unequal, because, at that time, those parts of Europe were swarming with numbers; because numbers produce emulation, and multiply the chances of improvement, and one improvement begets another. Yet I may safely ask, How many good poets, how many able mathematicians, how many great inventors in arts or sciences, had Europe North of the Alps then produced? And it was sixteen centuries after this before a Newton could be formed. I do not mean to deny, that there are varieties in the race of man, distinguished by their powers both of body and mind. I believe there are, as I see to be the case in the races of other animals. I only mean to suggest a doubt, whether the bulk and faculties of animals depend on the side of the Atlantic on which their food happens to grow, or which furnishes the elements of which they are compounded? Whether nature has enlisted herself as a Cis[5] or Trans-Atlantic partisan? I am induced to suspect, there has been more eloquence than sound reasoning displayed in support of this theory; that it is one of those cases where the judgment has been seduced by a glowing pen: and whilst I render every tribute of honor and esteem to the celebrated Zoologist, who has added, and is still adding, so many precious things to the treasures of science, I must doubt whether in this instance he has not cherished error also, by lending her for a moment his vivid imagination and bewitching language.

So far the Count de Buffon has carried this new theory of the tendency of nature to belittle her productions on this side of the Atlantic. Its application to the race of whites, transplanted from Europe, remained for the Abbé Raynal.[6] "One must be astonished (he says) that America has not yet produced one good poet, one able mathematician, one man of genius in a single art or a single science." "America has

---

[3] Mental capacity and ability.
[4] Learning or knowledge.
[5] On the near side (i.e., European).
[6] Guillaume Thomas François Raynal

(1713–1796), French writer who concurred with Buffon that the American environment was degenerate.

not yet produced one good poet." When we shall have existed as a people as long as the Greeks did before they produced a Homer, the Romans a Virgil, the French a Racine and Voltaire, the English a Shakespeare and Milton, should this reproach be still true, we will enquire from what unfriendly causes it has proceeded, that the other countries of Europe and quarters of the earth shall not have inscribed any name in the roll of poets. But neither has America produced "one able mathematician, one man of genius in a single art or a single science." In war we have produced a Washington, whose memory will be adored while liberty shall have votaries, whose name will triumph over time, and will in future ages assume its just station among the most celebrated worthies of the world, when that wretched philosophy shall be forgotten which would have arranged him among the degeneracies of nature. In physics we have produced a Franklin, than whom no one of the present age has made more important discoveries, nor has enriched philosophy with more, or more ingenious solutions of the phænomena of nature. We have supposed Mr. Rittenhouse[7] second to no astronomer living: that in genius he must be the first, because he is self-taught. As an artist he has exhibited as great a proof of mechanical genius as the world has ever produced. He has not indeed made a world; but he has by imitation approached nearer its Maker than any man who has lived from the creation to this day. As in philosophy and war, so in government, in oratory, in painting, in the plastic art, we might shew that America, though but a child of yesterday, has already given hopeful proofs of genius, as well of the nobler kinds, which arouse the best feelings of man, which call him into action, which substantiate his freedom, and conduct him to happiness, as of the subordinate, which serve to amuse him only. We therefore suppose, that this reproach is as unjust as it is unkind; and that, of the geniuses which adorn the present age, America contributes its full share. For comparing it with those countries, where genius is most cultivated, where are the most excellent models for art, and scaffoldings for the attainment of science, as France and England for instance, we calculate thus. The United States contain three millions of inhabitants; France twenty millions; and the British islands ten. We produce a Washington, a Franklin, a Rittenhouse. France then should have half a dozen in each of these lines, and Great-Britain half that number, equally eminent. It may be true, that France has: we are but just becoming acquainted with her, and our acquaintance so far gives us high ideas of the genius of her inhabitants. It would be injuring too many of them to name particularly a Voltaire, a Buffon, the constellation of Encyclopedists,[8] the Abbé Raynal himself, &c. &c. We therefore have reason to believe she can produce her full quota of genius. The present war having so long cut off all communication with Great-Britain, we are not able to make a fair estimate of the state of science in that country. The spirit in which she wages war is the only sample before our eyes, and that does not seem the legitimate offspring either of science or of civilization. The sun of her glory is fast descending to the horizon. Her philosophy has crossed the Channel, her freedom the Atlantic, and herself seems passing to that awful dissolution, whose issue is not given human foresight to scan.

---

[7] David Rittenhouse (1732–1796), American astronomer who built orreries, or models of the solar system.

[8] Such figures as Denis Diderot (1713–1784), who contributed to the French Encyclopédie (1751–1771).

from **Query XVIII: Manners**

[On Slavery]

It is difficult to determine on the standard by which the manners of a nation may be tried, whether *catholic,*[9] or *particular.* It is more difficult for a native to bring to that standard the manners of his own nation, familiarized to him by habit. There must doubtless be an unhappy influence on the manners of our people produced by the existence of slavery among us. The whole commerce between master and slave is a perpetual exercise of the most boisterous passions, the most unremitting despotism on the one part, and degrading submissions on the other. Our children see this, and learn to imitate it; for man is an imitative animal. This quality is the germ of all education in him. From his cradle to his grave he is learning to do what he sees others do. If a parent could find no motive either in his philanthropy or his self-love, for restraining the intemperance of passion towards his slave, it should always be a sufficient one that his child is present. But generally it is not sufficient. The parent storms, the child looks on, catches the lineaments of wrath, puts on the same airs in the circle of smaller slaves, gives a loose to his worst of passions, and thus nursed, educated, and daily exercised in tyranny, cannot but be stamped by it with odious peculiarities. The man must be a prodigy who can retain his manners and morals undepraved by such circumstances. And with what execration should the statesman be loaded, who permitting one half the citizens thus to trample on the rights of the other, transforms those into despots, and these into enemies, destroys the morals of the one part, and the amor patriæ[10] of the other. For if a slave can have a country in this world, it must be any other in preference to that in which he is born to live and labour for another: in which he must lock up the faculties of his nature, contribute as far as depends on his individual endeavours to the evanishment[11] of the human race, or entail[12] his own miserable condition on the endless generations proceeding from him. With the morals of the people, their industry also is destroyed. For in a warm climate, no man will labour for himself who can make another labour for him. This is so true, that of the proprietors of slaves a very small proportion indeed are ever seen to labour. And can the liberties of a nation be thought secure when we have removed their only firm basis, a conviction in the minds of the people that these liberties are of the gift of God? That they are not to be violated but with his wrath? Indeed I tremble for my country when I reflect that God is just: that his justice cannot sleep for ever: that considering numbers, nature and natural means only, a revolution of the wheel of fortune, an exchange of situation, is among possible events: that it may become probable by supernatural interference! The Almighty has no attribute which can take side with us in such a contest.—But it is impossible to be temperate and to pursue this subject through the various considerations of policy, of morals, of history natural and civil. We must be contented to hope they will force their way into every one's mind. I think a change already perceptible, since the origin of the present revolution. The spirit of the master is abating, that of the slave rising from the dust, his condition mollifying, the way I hope preparing, under the auspices of heaven, for a total

---

[9] Universal.
[10] Love of country; patriotism.

[11] Disappearance.
[12] Impose.

emancipation, and that this is disposed, in the order of events, to be with the consent of the masters, rather than by their extirpation.

from **Query XIX: Manufactures**

[American Agrarianism]

The political œconomists of Europe have established it as a principle that every state should endeavour to manufacture for itself: and this principle, like many others, we transfer to America, without calculating the difference of circumstance which should often produce a difference of result. In Europe the lands are either cultivated, or locked up against the cultivator. Manufacture must therefore be resorted to of necessity not of choice, to support the surplus of their people. But we have an immensity of land courting the industry of the husbandman. Is it best then that all our citizens should be employed in its improvement, or that one half should be called off from that to exercise manufactures and handicraft arts for the other? Those who labour in the earth are the chosen people of God, if ever he had a chosen people, whose breasts he has made his peculiar deposit for substantial and genuine virtue. It is the focus in which he keeps alive that sacred fire, which otherwise might escape from the face of the earth. Corruption of morals in the mass of cultivators is a phænomenon of which no age nor nation has furnished an example. It is the mark set on those, who not looking up to heaven, to their own soil and industry, as does the husbandman, for their subsistance, depend for it on the casualties and caprice of customers. Dependance begets subservience and venality, suffocates the germ of virtue, and prepares fit tools for the designs of ambition. This, the natural progress and consequence of the arts, has sometimes perhaps been retarded by accidental circumstances: but, generally speaking, the proportion which the aggregate of the other classes of citizens bears in any state to that of its husbandmen, is the proportion of its unsound to its healthy parts, and is a good-enough barometer whereby to measure its degree of corruption. While we have land to labour then, let us never wish to see our citizens occupied at a work-bench, or twirling a distaff.[13] Carpenters, masons, smiths, are wanting[14] in husbandry: but, for the general operations of manufacture, let our work-shops remain in Europe. It is better to carry provisions and materials to workmen there, than bring them to the provisions and materials, and with them their manners and principles. The loss by the transportation of commodities across the Atlantic will be made up in happiness and permanence of government. The mobs of great cities add just so much to the support of pure government, as sores do to the strength of the human body. It is the manners and spirit of a people which preserve a republic in vigour. A degeneracy in these is a canker which soon eats to the heart of its laws and constitution.

1785

---

[13] Spinning-wheel attachment.   [14] Lacking.

Letter to Nathaniel Burwell

MONTICELLO, March 14, 1818.

DEAR SIR,—Your letter of February 17th found me suffering under an attack of rheumatism, which has but now left me at sufficient ease to attend to the letters I have received. A plan of female education has never been a subject of systematic contemplation with me. It has occupied my attention so far only as the education of my own daughters occasionally required. Considering that they would be placed in a country situation, where little aid could be obtained from abroad, I thought it essential to give them a solid education, which might enable them, when become mothers, to educate their own daughters, and even to direct the course for sons, should their fathers be lost, or incapable, or inattentive. My surviving daughter accordingly, the mother of many daughters as well as sons, has made their education the object of her life, and being a better judge of the practical part than myself, it is with her aid and that of one of her *élèves*[1] that I shall subjoin a catalogue of the books for such a course of reading as we have practiced.

A great obstacle to good education is the inordinate passion prevalent for novels, and the time lost in that reading which should be instructively employed. When this poison infects the mind, it destroys its tone and revolts it against wholesome reading. Reason and fact, plain and unadorned, are rejected. Nothing can engage attention unless dressed in all the figments of fancy, and nothing so bedecked comes amiss. The result is a bloated imagination, sickly judgment, and disgust towards all the real businesses of life. This mass of trash, however, is not without some distinction; some few modelling their narratives, although fictitious, on the incidents of real life, have been able to make them interesting and useful vehicles of a sound morality. Such, I think, are Marmontel's[2] new moral tales, but not his old ones, which are really immoral. Such are the writings of Miss Edgeworth, and some of those of Madame Genlis.[3] For a like reason, too, much poetry should not be indulged. Some is useful for forming style and taste. Pope, Dryden, Thompson, Shakspeare, and of the French, Molière, Racine, the Corneilles,[4] may be read with pleasure and improvement.

The French language, become that of the general intercourse of nations, and from their extraordinary advances, now the depository of all science, is an indispensable part of education for both sexes. In the subjoined catalogue, therefore, I have placed the books of both languages indifferently, according as the one or the other offers what is best.

The ornaments too, and the amusements of life, are entitled to their portion of attention. These, for a female, are dancing, drawing, and music. The first is a healthy exercise, elegant and very attractive for young people. Every affectionate parent

---

[1] French: "students."

[2] Jean François Marmontel (1723–1799), French prose writer, essayist, and historian.

[3] Miss Edgeworth: Maria Edgeworth (1767–1849), English novelist; Madame Genlis: Stéphanie Félicité, comtesse de Genlis (1746–1830), French novelist.

[4] Alexander Pope (1688–1744), English poet; John Dryden (1631–1700), English poet, dramatist, and critic; James Thompson (1700–1748), English poet; William Shakespeare (1564–1616); Jean Baptiste Poquelin Molière (1622–1673), French actor and playwright; Jean Baptiste Racine (1639–1699), French dramatist; Pierre Corneille (1606–1684), French dramatist and poet.

would be pleased to see his daughter qualified to participate with her companions, and without awkwardness at least, in the circles of festivity, of which she occasionally becomes a part. It is a necessary accomplishment, therefore, although of short use, for the French rule is wise, that no lady dances after marriage. This is founded in solid physical reasons, gestation and nursing leaving little time to a married lady when this exercise can be either safe or innocent. Drawing is thought less of in this country than in Europe. It is an innocent and engaging amusement, often useful, and a qualification not to be neglected in one who is to become a mother and an instructor. Music is invaluable where a person has an ear. Where they have not, it should not be attempted. It furnishes a delightful recreation for the hours of respite from the cares of the day, and lasts us through life. The taste of this country, too, calls for this accomplishment more strongly than for either of the others.

I need say nothing of household economy, in which the mothers of our country are generally skilled, and generally careful to instruct their daughters. We all know its value, and that diligence and dexterity in all its processes are inestimable treasures. The order and economy of a house are as honorable to the mistress as those of the farm to the master, and if either be neglected, ruin follows, and children destitute of the means of living.

This, Sir, is offered as a summary sketch on a subject on which I have not thought much. It probably contains nothing but what has already occurred to yourself, and claims your acceptance on no other ground than as a testimony of my respect for your wishes, and of my great esteem and respect.

1904

Letters to Abigail Adams

[September 25, 1785]

Paris Sep. 25. 1785.

DEAR MADAM

Mr. Short's return the night before last availed me of your favour of Aug. 12. I immediately ordered the shoes you desired which will be ready tomorrow. I am not certain whether this will be in time for the departure of Mr. Barclay or of Colo. Franks, for it is not yet decided which of them goes to London. I have also procured for you three plateaux de dessert with a silvered ballustrade round them, and four figures of Biscuit. The former cost 192$^{\text{†t}}$, the latter 12$^{\text{†t}}$ each, making together 240 livres or 10. Louis. The merchant undertakes to send them by the way of Rouen through the hands of Mr. Garvey and to have them delivered in London. There will be some additional expences of packing, transportation and duties here. Those in England I imagine you can save. When I know the amount I will inform you of it, but there will be no occasion to remit it here. With respect to the figures I could only find three of those you named, matched in size. These were Minerva, Diana, and Apollo.[1] I was obliged to add a fourth, unguided by your choice. They offered me a fine

---

[1] In Roman myth, Minerva and Diana were, respectively, goddesses of wisdom and the arts, and of the moon and hunting. Apollo was the ancient Roman and Greek god of light, the arts, and manly beauty.

Venus;[2] but I thought it out of taste to have two at table at the same time. Paris and Helen[3] were presented. I conceived it would be cruel to remove them from their peculiar shrine. When they shall pass the Atlantic, it will be to sing a requiem over our freedom and happiness. At length a fine Mars[4] was offered, calm, bold, his faulchion not drawn, but ready to be drawn. This will do, thinks I, for the table of the American Minister in London, where those whom it may concern may look and learn that though Wisdom is our guide, and the Song and Chase our supreme delight, yet we offer adoration to that tutelar god also who rocked the cradle of our birth, who has accepted our infant offerings, and has shewn himself the patron of our rights and avenger of our wrongs. The groupe then was closed, and your party formed. Envy and malice will never be quiet. I hear it already whispered to you that in admitting Minerva to your table I have departed from the principle which made me reject Venus: in plain English that I have paid a just respect to the daughter but failed to the mother. No Madam, my respect to both is sincere. Wisdom, I know, is social. She seeks her fellows. But Beauty is jealous, and illy bears the presence of a rival—but, Allons,[5] let us turn over another leaf, and begin the next chapter. I receive by Mr. Short a budget of London papers. They teem with every horror of which human nature is capable. Assassinations, suicides, thefts, robberies, and, what is worse than assassination, theft, suicide or robbery, the blackest slanders! Indeed the man must be of rock, who can stand all this; to Mr. Adams it will be but one victory the more. It would have illy suited me. I do not love difficulties. I am fond of quiet, willing to do my duty, but irritable by slander and apt to be forced by it to abandon my post. These are weaknesses from which reason and your counsels will preserve Mr. Adams. I fancy it must be the quantity of animal food eaten by the English which renders their character insusceptible of civilisation. I suspect it is in their kitchens and not in their churches that their reformation must be worked, and that Missionaries of that description from hence would avail more than those who should endeavor to tame them by precepts of religion or philosophy. But what do the foolish printers of America mean by retailing all this stuff in our papers? As if it was not enough to be slandered by one's enemies without circulating the slanders among his friends also.

To shew you how willingly I shall ever receive and execute your commissions, I venture to impose one on you. From what I recollect of the diaper[6] and damask we used to import from England I think they were better and cheaper than here. You are well acquainted with those of both countries. If you are of the same opinion I would trouble you to send me two sets of table cloths and napkins for 20 covers each, by Colo. Franks or Mr. Barclay who will bring them to me. But if you think they can be better got here I would rather avoid the trouble this commission will give. I inclose you a specimen of what is offered me at 100. livres for the table cloth and 12 napkins. I suppose that, of the same quality, a table cloth 2. aunes wide and 4. aunes long, and 20 napkins of 1. aune each, would cost 7. guineas.—I shall certainly charge the publick my house rent and court taxes. I shall do more. I shall charge my outfit. Without this I can never get out of debt. I think it will be allowed. Congress is too reasonable to expect, where no imprudent expences are incurred, none but those which

---

[2] In Roman myth, goddess of love and beauty.
[3] According to Greek myth, Paris initiated the Greek-Trojan war when he abducted Helen of Troy.

[4] Roman god of war.
[5] French: "Let's go."
[6] Linen or cotton fabric with repeated woven figures.

are required by a decent respect to the mantle with which they cover the public servants, that such expences should be left as a burthen on our private fortunes. But when writing to you, I fancy myself at Auteuil, and chatter on till the last page of my paper awakes me from my reverie, and tells me it is time to assure you of the sincere respect and esteem with which I have the honour to be Dear Madam your most obedient and most humble servt.,

TH: JEFFERSON

P.S. The cask of wine at Auteuil, I take chearfully. I suppose the seller will apply to me for the price. Otherwise, as I do not know who he is, I shall not be able to find him out.

1904

[June 13, 1804]

Washington June 13.04

DEAR MADAM

The affectionate sentiments which you have had the goodness to express in your letter of May 20. towards my dear departed daughter, have awakened in me sensibilities natural to the occasion, and recalled your kindnesses to her which I shall ever remember with gratitude and friendship. I can assure you with truth they had made an indelible impression on her mind, and that, to the last, on our meetings after long separations, whether I had heard lately of you, and how you did, were among the earliest of her enquiries. In giving you this assurance I perform a sacred duty for her, and at the same time am thankful for the occasion furnished me of expressing my regret that circumstances should have arisen which have seemed to draw a line of separation between us. The friendship with which you honoured me has ever been valued, and fully reciprocated; and altho' events have been passing which might be trying to some minds, I never believed yours to be of that kind, nor felt that my own was. Neither my estimate of your character, nor the esteem founded in that, have ever been lessened for a single moment, although doubts whether it would be acceptable may have forbidden manifestations of it. Mr. Adams's friendship and mine began at an earlier date. It accompanied us thro' long and important scenes. The different conclusions we had drawn from our political reading and reflections were not permitted to lessen mutual esteem, each party being conscious they were the result of an honest conviction in the other. Like differences of opinion existing among our fellow citizens attached them to the one or the other of us, and produced a rivalship in their minds which did not exist in ours. We never stood in one another's way: for if either had been withdrawn at any time, his favorers would not have gone over to the other, but would have sought for some one of homogeneous opinions. This consideration was sufficient to keep down all jealousy between us, and to guard our friendship from any disturbance by sentiments of rivalship: and I can say with truth that one act of Mr. Adams's life, and one only, ever gave me a moment's personal displeasure. I did consider his last appointments to office as personally unkind.[7] They were from among

---

[7] The Judiciary Act, passed February 13, 1801, reduced the membership of the Supreme Court to five, increased the number of district judges, and relieved the Supreme Court justices from traveling the circuit. President Adams appointed Federalists to these new positions, to the discomfiture of his successor. The act was repealed by the Republican Congress of 1802. If the act was partisan in origin, it did provide some needed reforms.

my most ardent political enemies, from whom no faithful cooperation could ever be expected, and laid me under the embarrasment of acting thro' men whose views were to defeat mine; or to encounter the odium of putting others in their places. It seemed but common justice to leave a successor free to act by instruments of his own choice. If my respect for him did not permit me to ascribe the whole blame to the influence of others, it left something for friendship to forgive, and after brooding over it for some little time, and not always resisting the expression of it, I forgave it cordially, and returned to the same state of esteem and respect for him which had so long subsisted. Having come into life a little later than Mr. Adams, his career has preceded mine, as mine is followed by some other, and it will probably be closed at the same distance after him which time originally placed between us. I maintain for him, and shall carry into private life an uniform and high measure of respect and good will, and for yourself a sincere attachment. I have thus, my dear Madam, opened myself to you without reserve, which I have long wished an opportunity of doing; and, without knowing how it will be recieved, I feel relief from being unbosomed. And I have now only to entreat your forgiveness for this transition from a subject of domestic affliction to one which seems of a different aspect. But tho connected with political events, it has been viewed by me most strongly in it's unfortunate bearings on my private friendships. The injury these have sustained has been a heavy price for what has never given me equal pleasure. That you may both be favored with health, tranquility and long life, is the prayer of one who tenders you the assurances of his highest consideration and esteem.

TH: JEFFERSON

1904

Letters to John Adams

[from *January 21, 1812*]

Monticello Jan. 21. 1812.

DEAR SIR

I thank you before hand (for they are not yet arrived) for the specimens of homespun you have been so kind as to forward me by post. I doubt not their excellence, knowing how far you are advanced in these things in your quarter. Here we do little in the fine way, but in coarse and midling goods a great deal. Every family in the country is a manufactory within itself, and is very generally able to make within itself all the stouter and midling stuffs for it's own cloathing and household use. We consider a sheep for every person in the family as sufficient to clothe it, in addition to the cotton, hemp and flax which we raise ourselves. For fine stuff we shall depend on your Northern manufactures. Of these, that is to say, of company establishments, we have none. We use little machinery. The Spinning Jenny[1] and loom with the flying

---

[1] Early spinning machine, enabling one person to make several yarns at once.

shuttle can be managed in a family; but nothing more complicated. The economy and thriftiness resulting from our household manufactures are such that they will never again be laid aside; and nothing more salutary for us has ever happened than the British obstructions to our demands for their manufactures. Restore free intercourse when they will, their commerce with us will have totally changed its form, and the articles we shall in future want from them will not exceed their own consumption of our produce.

A letter from you calls up recollections very dear to my mind. It carries me back to the times when, beset with difficulties and dangers, we were fellow laborers in the same cause, struggling for what is most valuable to man; his right of self-government. Laboring always at the same oar, with some wave ever ahead threatening to over-whelm us and yet passing harmless under our bark, we knew not how, we rode through the storm with heart and hand, and made a happy port. Still we did not expect to be without rubs and difficulties; and we have had them. . . . and so we have gone on, and so we shall go on, puzzled and prospering beyond example in the history of man. And I do believe we shall continue to growl, [i.e., grow] to multiply and prosper until we exhibit an association, powerful, wise and happy, beyond what has yet been seen by men. As for France and England, with all their pre-eminence in science, the one is a den of robbers, and the other of pirates. And if science produces no better fruits than tyranny, murder, rapine and destitution of national morality, I would rather wish our country to be ignorant, honest and estimable as our neighboring savages are.

But whither is senile garrulity leading me? Into politics, of which I have taken final leave. I think little of them, and say less. I have given up newspapers in exchange for Tacitus and Thucydides, for Newton and Euclid;[2] and I find myself much the happier. Sometimes indeed I look back to former occurrences, in remembrance of our old friends and fellow laborers, who have fallen before us. Of the signers of the Declaration of Independence I see now living not more than half a dozen on your side of the Potomak, and, on this side, myself alone.[3] You and I have been wonderfully spared, and myself with remarkable health, and a considerable activity of body and mind. I am on horseback 3. or 4. hours of every day; visit 3. or 4. times a year a possession I have 90 miles distant,[4] performing the winter journey on horseback. I walk little however; a single mile being too much for me; and I live in the midst of my grandchildren, one of whom has lately promoted me to be a great grandfather.[5] I have heard with pleasure that you also retain good health, and a greater power of exercise in walking than I do. But I would rather have heard this from yourself, and that,

[2] Tacitus (55–120), Roman historian; Thucydides (460–400 B.C.), Greek historian; Isaac Newton (1642–1727), English mathematician who formulated the law of gravity; Euclid (fl. ca. 300 B.C.), Greek geometrician.
[3] Ten signers of the Declaration, including Adams and Jefferson, were alive in 1812: Elbridge Gerry (d. 1814) and Robert Treat Paine (d. 1814) of Massachusetts, William Ellery (d. 1820) of Rhode Island, William Floyd (d. 1821) of New York, Benjamin Rush (d. 1813) and George Clymer (d. 1813) of Pennsylvania,

Thomas McKean (d. 1817) of Delaware, and Charles Carroll (d. 1832) of Maryland.
[4] Poplar Forest, in Bedford County, Virginia, which Jefferson had acquired in 1774 from his father-in-law's estate. He built an octagonal house there while he was president.
[5] Jefferson's first great-grandchild was John Warner Bankhead (b. 1810), eldest child of Charles Lewis Bankhead and Anne Cary Randolph Bankhead, first-born of Thomas Mann Randolph and Martha Jefferson Randolph.

writing a letter, like mine, full of egotisms, and of details of your health, your habits, occupations and enjoyments, I should have the pleasure of knowing that, in the race of life, you do not keep, in it's physical decline, the same distance ahead of me which you have done in political honors and achievements. No circumstances have lessened the interest I feel in these particulars respecting yourself; none have suspended for one moment my sincere esteem for you; and I now salute you with unchanged affections and respect.

TH: JEFFERSON

1904

[from *July 5, 1814*]

Monticello July 5.14

DEAR SIR

Since mine of Jan. 24. yours of Mar. 14. was received. It was not acknoleged in the short one of May 18. by Mr. Rives, the only object of that having been to enable one of our most promising young men to have the advantage of making his bow to you. I learned with great regret the serious illness mentioned in your letter: and I hope Mr. Rives will be able to tell me you are entirely restored. But our machines have now been running for 70. or 80. years, and we must expect that, worn as they are, here a pivot, there a wheel, now a pinion, next a spring, will be giving way: and however we may tinker them up for awhile, all will at length surcease motion. Our watches, with works of brass and steel, wear out within that period. Shall you and I last to see the course the seven-fold wonders of the times will take? The Attila[6] of the age dethroned, the ruthless destroyer of 10. millions of the human race, whose thirst for blood appeared unquenchable, the great oppressor of the rights and liberties of the world, shut up within the circuit of a little island of the Mediterranean,[7] and dwindled to the condition of an humble and degraded pensioner on the bounty of those he had most injured. How miserably, how meanly, has he closed his inflated career! What a sample of the Bathos will his history present! He should have perished on the swords of his enemies, under the walls of Paris.

> 'Leon piagato a morte Cosi fra l'ire estrema
> Sente mancar la vita, rugge, minaccia, e freme,
> Guarda la sua ferita, Che fa tremar morendo
> Ne s'avilisce ancor. Tal volta il cacciator.'[8]
>   Metast Adriano.

But Bonaparte was a lion in the field only. In civil life a cold-blooded, calculating unprincipled Ursurper, without a virtue, no statesman, knowing nothing of com-

---

[6] I.e., Napoleon Bonaparte (1761–1821), emperor of France (1804–1815).
[7] Napoleon was banished to the island of Elba in 1814. He escaped on March 1, 1815, to lead the French armies during the Hundred Days until his final defeat at Waterloo on June 18.

[8] "The lion stricken to death / realizes that he is dying, / and looks at his wounds from which / he grows ever weaker and weaker. // Then with his final wrath / he roars, threatens, and screams, / which makes tremble at him dying / the hunter."

merce, political economy, or civil government, and supplying ignorance by bold presumption. I had supposed him a great man until his entrance into the Assembly.[9] From that date however I set him down as a great scoundrel only. To the wonders of his rise and fall, we may add that of a Czar of Muscovy dictating, *in Paris,* laws and limits to all the successors of the Caesars,[10] and holding even the balance in which the fortunes of this new world are suspended. I own that, while I rejoice, for the good of mankind, in the deliverance of Europe from the havoc which would have never ceased while Bonaparte should have lived in power, I see with anxiety the tyrant of the ocean remaining in vigor, and even participating in the merit of crushing his brother tyrant. While the world is thus turned up side down, on which side of it are we? . . .

I am just returned from one of my long absences, having been at my other home for five weeks past. Having more leisure there than here for reading, I amused myself with reading seriously Plato's[11] republic. I am wrong however in calling it amusement, for it was the heaviest task-work I ever went through. I had occasionally before taken up some of his other works, but scarcely ever had patience to go through a whole dialogue. While wading thro' the whimsies, the puerilities,[12] and unintelligible jargon of this work, I laid it down often to ask myself how it could have been that the world should have so long consented to give reputation to such nonsense as this? How the soi-disant[13] Christian world indeed should have done it, is a piece of historical curiosity. But how could the Roman good sense do it? And particularly how could Cicero[14] bestow such eulogies on Plato? Altho' Cicero did not wield the dense logic of Demosthenes,[15] yet he was able, learned, laborious, practised in the business of the world, and honest. He could not be the dupe of mere style, of which he was himself the first master in the world. With the Moderns, I think, it is rather a matter of fashion and authority. Education is chiefly in the hands of persons who, from their profession, have an interest in the reputation and the dreams of Plato. They give the tone while at school, and few, in their after-years, have occasion to revise their college opinions. But fashion and authority apart, and bringing Plato to the test of reason, take from him his sophisms, futilities, and incomprehensibilities, and what remains? In truth, he is one of the race of genuine Sophists,[16] who has escaped the oblivion of his brethren, first by the elegance of his diction, but chiefly by the adoption and incorporation of his whimsies into the body of artificial Christianity. His foggy mind, is forever presenting the semblances of objects which, half seen thro' a mist, can be defined neither in form or dimension. Yet this which should have consigned him to early

---

[9] The coup d'état of November 9, 1799, in which Bonaparte drove the legislative Council of 500 of the French Republic (the Directory) from its meeting place and proclaimed the Consulate (headed by three consuls) with himself as First Consul.

[10] I.e., in the "constitutional charter," issued in 1814 by Louis XVIII of the restored Bourbon dynasty, partly at the insistence of Tsar Alexander I.

[11] Plato (427–347 B.C.), Greek philosopher. The *Republic,* fashioned in numerous dialogues, argues that the idea or form of a thing is somewhat like our abstract sense of that thing

but has a real existence outside the material world. It is the unchanging reality behind the changing appearance and can only be understood by pure reason unaffected by sensation. Plato's supreme idea is that of the Good.

[12] Childish qualities.

[13] So-called.

[14] Marcus Tullius Cicero (106–43 B.C.), Roman orator and statesman.

[15] Athenian orator and statesman (383–322 B.C.).

[16] Ancient Greek teachers of philosophy noted for the ingenuity and speciousness of their arguments.

oblivion really procured him immortality of fame and reverence. The Christian priesthood, finding the doctrines of Christ levelled to every understanding, and too plain to need explanation, saw, in the mysticisms of Plato, materials with which they might build up an artificial system which might, from it's indistinctness, admit everlasting controversy, give employment for their order, and introduce it to profit, power and pre-eminence. The doctrines which flowed from the lips of Jesus himself are within the comprehension of a child; but thousands of volumes have not yet explained the Platonisms engrafted on them: and for this obvious reason that nonsense can never be explained. Their purposes however are answered. Plato is canonized; and it is now deemed as impious to question his merits as those of an Apostle of Jesus. He is peculiarly appealed to as an advocate of the immortality of the soul; and yet I will venture to say that were there no better arguments than his in proof of it, not a man in the world would believe it. It is fortunate for us that Platonic republicanism has not obtained the same favor as Platonic Christianity; or we should now have been all living, men, women and children, pell mell together, like beasts of the field or forest. Yet 'Plato is a great Philosopher,' said La Fontaine.[17] But says Fontenelle 'do you find his ideas very clear'? 'Oh no! he is of an obscurity impenetrable.' 'Do you not find him full of contradictions?' 'Certainly,' replied La Fontaine, 'he is but a Sophist.' Yet immediately after, he exclaims again, 'Oh Plato was a great Philosopher.' Socrates had reason indeed to complain of the misrepresentations of Plato; for in truth his dialogues are libels on Socrates.

But why am I dosing you with these Ante-diluvian[18] topics? Because I am glad to have some one to whom they are familiar, and who will not recieve them as if dropped from the moon. Our post-revolutionary youth are born under happier stars than you and I were. They acquire all learning in their mothers' womb, and bring it into the world ready-made. The information of books is no longer necessary; and all knolege which is not innate, is in contempt, or neglect at least. Every folly must run its round; and so, I suppose, must that of self-learning, and self sufficiency; of rejecting the knolege acquired in past ages, and starting on the new ground of intuition. When sobered by experience I hope our successors will turn their attention to the advantages of education. I mean of education on the broad scale, and not that of the petty *academies,* as they call themselves, which are starting up in every neighborhood, and where one or two men, possessing Latin, and sometimes Greek, a knolege of the globes, and the first six books of Euclid, imagine and communicate this as the sum of science. They commit their pupils to the theatre of the world with just taste enough of learning to be alienated from industrious pursuits, and not enough to do service in the ranks of science. We have some exceptions indeed. I presented one to you lately, and we have some others. But the terms I use are general truths. I hope the necessity will at length be seen of establishing institutions, here as in Europe, where every branch of science, useful at this day, may be taught in its highest degrees. Have you ever turned your thoughts to the plan of such an institution? I mean to a specification of the particular sciences of real use in human affairs, and how they might be so grouped as to require so many professors only as might bring them within the views of a just but enlightened economy? I should be happy in a communication of

[17] Jean de La Fontaine (1621–1695), French poet and fabulist.   [18] Before the Flood (i.e., ancient).

your ideas on this problem, either loose or digested. But to avoid my being run away with by another subject, and adding to the length and ennui of the present letter, I will here present to Mrs. Adams and yourself the assurance of my constant and sincere friendship and respect.

TH: JEFFERSON

1904

John Adams
1735–1826

Historically, John Adams has belonged more to American politics than to its literature. As the second President of the United States (1797–1801) and the author of a three-volume work on constitutions, Adams figures in discussions of American political history. Yet John Adams had many voices: satirist, polemicist, autobiographer, lover, and wit all emerge in Adams's diary and in his letters, especially those to his wife, Abigail, and to Thomas Jefferson. These writings show Adams to be a figure who deserves attention as a literary man in an age in which individual and national interests merged.

Adams was the son of a Braintree, Massachusetts, farmer and leather crafter active in local politics. His mother's family was sufficiently distinguished to have a coat of arms. Both parents were "fond of reading," and John's father was eager for his son to be well educated. After a boyhood of outdoor work and sports, John crammed for entrance to Harvard, where he claimed "a growing Curiosity, a Love of Books" and mastered the mid-eighteenth-century college curriculum of classical languages, logic, rhetoric, mathematics, and physics. Adams was invited to join a "play-reading Club" and grew proficient in dramatic speaking. As a self-styled boyhood "Church-going Animal" whose minister emphasized good works over Calvinist predestinarianism, Adams appreciated theological debate at Harvard and continued in the tradition of liberal Protestantism. He looked with suspicion on the evangelicism of the Great Awakening.

In 1755 Adams completed college and accepted a schoolmaster's post at Worcester, thirty miles west of Boston. In the following year he began to study law, which he called "human reason" for the "preservation of the . . . morals and liberties of millions of the human species." In 1758 he returned to Braintree to practice law. The literary side of him emerged at this time. He filled his diary with character sketches and began to write for Boston newspapers, including the *Evening Post,* which published his "Humphrey Ploughjogger" letters addressing rural problems in a humorous country dialect.

In 1764 Adams married Abigail Smith, following a courtship carried out in part in correspondence between "Lysander" and "Diana," the classical names they adopted. Abigail Adams's mind proved to be a match for her husband's. (Their descendant, the writer Henry Adams, wrote that "in the way of [American] letters there is nothing but my old great grandmother Abigail Adams's that are worth reading.") John Adams's marriage to Abigail prompted the rich, flourishing literary dialogue in correspondence during the long separations lying before them.

In the years prior to the Revolutionary War, John Adams enlarged his law practice and began to speak out against British colonial policy. In response to the Stamp Act he wrote a dissertation on law and authored anonymous "Whig" articles for Boston newspapers. Yet in 1770 he helped to defend the British soldiers who had shot and killed colonists in the Boston Massacre, saying that a "judgment of death against those soldiers would have been as foul a stain upon this country as the executions of the Quakers or witches." After 1774 the politically ambitious Adams represented Massachusetts in the Continental Congress, where he eventually proposed George Washington as the commander in chief of the newly formed Continental Army.

Adams spent the war years and those of the early republic abroad and in the new capital. In wartime he was emissary to France and then served as minister to Holland, finally engaging in the preliminary peace negotiations with the British. In 1784 Adams's family joined him at Auteuil, France, and became friendly with Jefferson and his daughter. In 1788 Adams returned to Braintree, only to depart within a year to serve as the first Vice-President of the United States (1789–1797), then as President. Thereafter he retired to Quincy, where he wrote newspaper articles, an autobiography, and letters that grew into a voluminous correspondence, especially with Jefferson, to whom he had become reconciled after some fifteen years of political and personal estrangement.

Abigail died in 1818. Adams and Jefferson died within hours of each other on July 4, 1826.

As a passionate, sometimes hot-headed man, Adams wrote such treatises as his preface to "Defense of the Constitutions" in closely argued, cerebral prose unrevealing of the author's temperament. But in personal correspondence with his wife and his son, John Quincy, Adams shows his powers of observation, his wit, even his malice. He was capable of irreverence toward so venerable a figure as Benjamin Franklin, who later also became the target of the wit of Herman Melville. Adams's letters most fully reveal his literary achievement, a point that the twentieth-century poet-critic Ezra Pound recognized when he called the Adams-Jefferson letters the literary masterpiece of the American Revolution.

Further Reading:
P. Smith, *John Adams*, 2 vols., 1962.
P. Shaw, *The Character of John Adams*, 1976.
R. A. East, *John Adams*, 1979.

Texts:
The Diary and Autobiography of John Adams, ed. L. Butterfield, 1961.
The Book of Abigail and John: Selected Letters of the Adams Family, 1762–1784, ed. L. H. Butterfield et al., 1975.
The Adams-Jefferson Letters, ed. L. Cappon, 1959.
"Defense of the Constitutions of Government in Massachusetts During the Revolution," *The Works of John Adams*, ed. C. Adams, 1851.

from Diary and Autobiography of John Adams

[from **February 11, 1765**]

... I always consider the settlement of America with Reverence and Wonder—as the Opening of a grand scene and Design in Providence, for the Illumination of the Ignorant and the Emancipation of the slavish Part of Mankind all over the Earth.

[from **December 18, 1765**]

Braintree Decr. 18th. 1765. Wednesday

The People, even to the lowest Ranks, have become more attentive to their Liberties, more inquisitive about them, and more determined to defend them, than they were ever before known or had occasion to be. Innumerable have been the Monuments of Wit, Humour, Sense, Learning, Spirit, Patriotism, and Heroism, erected in the several Colonies and Provinces, in the Course of this Year. Our Presses have groaned, our Pulpits have thundered, our Legislatures have resolved, our Towns have voted, The Crown Officers have every where trembled, and all their little Tools and Creatures, been afraid to Speak and ashamed to be seen. . . .

How long We are to remain in this languid Condition, this passive Obedience to the Stamp Act, is not certain. But such a Pause cannot be lasting. Debtors grow insolent. Creditors grow angry. And it is to be expected that the Public offices will very soon be forced open, unless such favourable Accounts should be received from England. . . .

[from **December 17, 1773**]

1773. Decr. 17th.

Last Night 3 Cargoes of Bohea Tea were emptied into the Sea. This Morning a Man-of-War sails.

This is the most magnificent Movement of all. There is a Dignity, a Majesty, a Sublimity, in this last Effort of the Patriots, that I greatly admire. The People should never rise, without doing something to be remembered—something notable And striking. This Destruction of the Tea is so bold, so daring, so firm, intrepid and inflexible, and it must have so important Consequences, and so lasting, that I can't but consider it as an Epocha in History. . . .

[from **May 27, 1778**]

May 27th. Wednesday. I must now, in order to explain and justify my own Conduct give an Account of that of my Colleague Dr. Franklin. . . .

I found that the Business of our Commission would never be done, unless I did it. My two Colleagues would agree in nothing. The Life of Dr. Franklin was a Scene of continual discipation. I could never obtain the favour of his Company in a Morning before Breakfast which would have been the most convenient time to read over the Letters and papers, deliberate on their contents, and decide upon the Substance of the Answers. It was late when he breakfasted, and as soon as Breakfast was over, a crowd of Carriges came to his Levee or if you like the term better to his Lodgings, with all Sorts of People; some Phylosophers, Accademicians and Economists; some of his small tribe of humble friends in the litterary Way whom he employed to translate some of his ancient Compositions, such as his Bonhomme Richard and for what I know his Polly Baker &c.; but by far the greater part were Women and Children, come to have the honour to see the great Franklin, and to have the pleasure of telling Stories about his Simplicity, his bald head and scattering strait hairs, among their Acquaintances. These Visitors occupied all the time, commonly, till it was time to dress to go to Dinner. He was invited to dine abroad every day and never declined unless when We had invited Company to dine with Us. I was always invited with him, till I found it necessary to send Apologies, that I might have some time to study the french Language and do the Business of the mission. Mr. Franklin kept a horn book always in his Pockett in which he minuted all his invitations to dinner, and Mr. Lee said it was the only thing in which he was punctual. It was the Custom in France to dine between one and two O'Clock: so that when the time came to dress, it was time for the Voiture[1] to be ready to carry him to dinner. Mr. Lee came daily to my Appartment to attend to Business, but we could rarely obtain the Company of Dr. Franklin for a few minutes, and often when I had drawn the Papers and had them fairly copied for Signature, and Mr. Lee and I had signed them, I was frequently obliged to wait several days, before I could procure the Signature of Dr. Franklin to them. He went according to his Invitation to his Dinner and after that went sometimes to the Play, sometimes to the Philosophers but most commonly to visit those Ladies who were complaisant enough to depart from the custom of France so far as to procure Setts of Tea Geer as it is called and make Tea for him. . . . After Tea the Evening was spent, in hearing the Ladies sing and play upon their Piano Fortes and other instruments of Musick, and in various Games as Cards, Chess, Backgammon, &c. &c. Mr. Franklin I believe however never play'd at any Thing but Chess or Checquers. In these Agreeable and important Occupations and Amusements, The Afternoon and Evening was spent, and he came home at all hours from Nine to twelve O'Clock at night. This Course of Life contributed to his Pleasure and I believe to his health and Longevity. He was now between Seventy and Eighty and I had so much respect and compassion for his Age, that I should have been happy to have done all the Business or rather all the Drudgery, if I could have been favoured with a few moments in a day to receive his Advice concerning the manner in which it ought to be done. But this condescention was not attainable. All that could be had was his Signature, after it was done, and this it is true he very rarely refused though he sometimes delayed.

[from *April 1–10, 1786*]

Stratford-upon-Avon is interesting as it is the Scæne of the Birth, Death and Sepulture of Shakespear. Three Doors from the Inn, is the House where he was born, as small and mean, as you can conceive. They shew Us an old Wooden Chair in the Chimney

---

[1] French: "carriage."

Corner, where He sat. We cutt off a Chip according to the Custom. A Mulberry Tree that he planted has been cutt down, and is carefully preserved for Sale. The House where he died has been taken down and the Spot is now only Yard or Garden. The Curse upon him who should remove his Bones, which is written on his Grave Stone, alludes to a Pile of some Thousands of human Bones, which lie exposed in that Church. There is nothing preserved of this great Genius which is worth knowing— nothing which might inform Us what Education, what Company, what Accident turned his Mind to Letters and the Drama. His name is not even on his Grave Stone. An ill-sculptured Head is sett up by his Wife, by the Side of his Grave in the Church. But paintings and Sculpture would be thrown away upon his Fame. His Wit, and Fancy, his Taste and Judgment, His Knowledge of Nature, of Life and Character, are immortal. . . .

1850–1856

Letters to Abigail Smith Adams

[April 14, 1764]

Saturday, Two O Clock

The Deacon and his Three Children are arrivd and the Operation has been performed, and all well. And now our Hospital[1] is full. There are Ten, of Us, under this Roof, now expecting to be sick. One, of Us, Mr. Wheat, begins to complain of a Pain Under his Arm and in his Knees, and about his Back, so that We expect within a few Hours to see the Course of the Eruption and of the fever that preeceeds and accompanies it.

Your Friends, Miss Paine and Miss Nicholson have been here, and are gone. I delivered your Letters. Arpasia asked me, if you was five feet and six Inches tall? I replyd I had not taken Measure as Yet. You know the Meaning of this Question. She is neither Tall, nor short, neither lean nor fat—pitted with the small Pox—a fine Bloom. Features somewhat like Esther Quincy's. An Eye, that indicates not only Vivacity, but Fire—not only Resolution, but Intrepidity. (Scandal protect me, Candor forgive me.) I cannot say that the Kindness, the softness, the Tenderness, that constitutes the Characteristick Excellence of your sex, and for the Want of which no Abilities can atone, are very conspicuous Either in her Face, Air or Behaviour.

Is it not insufferable thus to remark on a Lady whose face I have once only and then but just seen and with whom I have only exchangd two or three Words? Shes a Buxom Lass however, and I own I longed for a Game of Romps with her, and should infallibly have taken one, only I thought the Dress I was in, the Air I had breathd and especially the Medicine I had taken, would not very greatly please a Lady, a stranger, of much Delicacy. Poll Palmer and I shall unquestionably go to romping very soon.

[1] Adams was hospitalized for several days for inoculation against smallpox.

Perkins, Sprague and Lord, are the Physicians that attend this House. Each has a few Particulars in Point of Diet, in which he differs from the others, and Each has Pills and Powders, different from the others to administer, different at least in size, and shape and Colour. I like my own vastly the best, the Dr. Lord is really a Man of sense.

I fear I must write less than I have done. The Drs. don't approve it. They will allow of nothing scarcly but the Card Table, Chequer Bord, Flute, Violin, and singing, unless, Tittle Tattle, Roll and Tumble, shuttle Cock &c.

Pray write as often as you can to yr.

John Adams

1850–1856

[September 29, 1774]

Philadelphia Septr. 29. 1774

My Dear

Sitting down to write to you, is a Scene almost too tender for my State of Nerves. It calls up to my View the anxious, distress'd state you must be in, amidst the Confusions and Dangers, which surround you. I long to return, and administer all the Consolation in my Power, but when I shall have accomplished all the Business I have to do here, I know not, and if it should be necessary to stay here till Christmas, or longer, in order to effect our Purposes. I am determined patiently to wait.

Patience, Forbearance, Long Suffering, are the Lessons taught here for our Province, and at the same Time absolute and open Resistance to the new Government. I wish I could convince Gentlemen, of the Danger, or Impracticability of this as fully as I believe it myself.

The Art and Address, of Ambassadors from a dozen belligerent Powers of Europe, nay of a Conclave of Cardinals at the Election of a Pope, or of the Princes in Germany at the Choice of an Emperor, would not exceed the Specimens We have seen.—Yet the Congress all profess the same political Principles.

They all profess to consider our Province as suffering in the common Cause, and indeed they seem to feel for Us, as if for themselves. We have had as great Questions to discuss as ever engaged the Attention of Men, and an infinite Multitude of them.

I received a very kind Letter from Deacon Palmer, acquainting me with Mr. Cranch's designs of removing to Braintree, which I approve very much—and wish I had an House for every Family in Boston, and Abilities to provide for them, in the Country.

I submit it to you, my Dear, whether it would not be best to remove all the Books and Papers and Furniture in the Office at Boston up to Braintree. There will be no Business there nor any where, I suppose, and my young Friends can study there better than in Boston at present.

I shall be kill'd with Kindness, in this Place. We go to congress at Nine, and there We stay, most earnestly engaged in Debates upon the most abstruse Misteries of State untill three in the Afternoon, then We adjourn, and go to Dinner with some of the Nobles of Pensylvania, at four O Clock and feast upon ten thousand Delicacies, and sitt drinking Madeira, Claret and Burgundy till six or seven, and then go home, fatigued to death with Business, Company, and Care.—Yet I hold it out, surprizingly.

I drink no Cyder, but feast upon Phyladelphia Beer, and Porter. A Gentleman, one Mr. Hare, has lately set up in this City a Manufactory of Porter, as good as any that comes from London. I pray We may introduce it into the Massachusetts. It agrees with me, infinitely better than Punch, Wine, or Cyder, or any other Spirituous Liquor.—My Love to my dear Children one by one. My Compliments to Mr. Thaxter, and Rice and every Body else. Yours most affectionately,

John Adams

1850–1856

[May 2, 1775]

Hartford May 2d. 1775

My Dear

Mr. Eliot of Fairfield, is this Moment arrived in his Way to Boston. He read us a Letter from the Dr. his Father dated Yesterday Sennight being Sunday. The Drs. Description of the Melancholly of the Town, is enough to melt a Stone. The Tryals of that unhappy and devoted People are likely to be severe indeed. God grant that the Furnace of Affliction may refine them. God grant that they may be relieved from their present Distress.

It is Arrogance and Presumption in human Sagacity to pretend to penetrate far into the Designs of Heaven. The most perfect Reverence and Resignation becomes us. But, I cant help depending upon this, that the present dreadfull Calamity of that beloved Town is intended to bind the Colonies together in more indissoluble Bands, and to animate their Exertions, at this great Crisis in the Affairs of Mankind. It has this Effect, in a most remarkable Degree, as far as I have yet seen or heard. It will plead, with all America, with more irresistable Perswasion, than Angells trumpet tongued.

In a Cause which interests the whole Globe, at a Time, when my Friends and Country are in such keen Distress, I am scarcely ever interrupted, in the least Degree, by Apprehensions for my Personal Safety. I am often concerned for you and our dear Babes, surrounded as you are by People who are too timorous and too much susceptible of allarms. Many Fears and Jealousies and imaginary Dangers, will be suggested to you, but I hope you will not be impressed by them.

In Case of real Danger, of which you cannot fail to have previous Intimations, fly to the Woods with our Children. Give my tenderest Love to them, and to all.

1850–1856

[June 17, 1775]

June 17

I can now inform you that the Congress have made Choice of the modest and virtuous, the amiable, generous and brave George Washington Esqr., to be the General of the American Army, and that he is to repair as soon as possible to the Camp before Boston. This Appointment will have a great Effect, in cementing and securing the Union of these Colonies—The Continent is really in earnest in defending the Country. They have voted Ten Companies of Rifle Men to be sent from Pensylvania, Maryland and Virginia, to join the Army before Boston. These are an excellent Species of Light Infantry. They use a peculiar Kind of [. . . ca]ll'd a Rifle—it has circular or [...] Grooves within the Barrell, and carries a Ball, with great Exactness to great Distances. They are the most accurate Marksmen in the World.

I begin to hope We shall not sit all Summer.

I hope the People of our Province, will treat the General with all that Confidence and Affection, that Politeness and Respect, which is due to one of the most important Characters in the World. The Liberties of America, depend upon him, in a great Degree.

I have never been able to obtain from our Province, any regular and particular Intelligence since I left it. Kent, Swift, Tudor, Dr. Cooper, Dr. Winthrop, and others wrote me often, last Fall—not a Line from them this Time.

I have found this Congress like the last. When We first came together, I found a strong Jealousy of Us, from New England, and the Massachusetts in Particular. Suspicions were entertained of Designs of Independency—an American Republic—Presbyterian Principles—and twenty other Things. Our Sentiments were heard in Congress, with great Caution—and seemed to make but little Impression: but the longer We sat, the more clearly they saw the Necessity of pursuing vigorous Measures. It has been so now. Every Day We sit, the more We are convinced that the Designs against Us, are hostile and sanguinary, and that nothing but Fortitude, Vigour, and Perseverance can save Us.

But America is a great, unwieldy Body. Its Progress must be slow. It is like a large Fleet sailing under Convoy. The fleetest Sailors must wait for the dullest and slowest. Like a Coach and six—the swiftest Horses must be slackened and the slowest quickened, that all may keep an even Pace.

It is long since I heard from you. I fear you have been kept in continual Alarms. My Duty and Love to all. My dear Nabby, Johnny, Charly and Tommy come here and kiss me.

We have appointed a continental Fast. Millions will be upon their Knees at once before their great Creator, imploring his Forgiveness and Blessing, his Smiles on American Councils and Arms.

My Duty to your Uncle Quincy—your Papa, Mama and mine—my Brothers and sisters and yours.

Adieu.

1850–1856

[from *July 23, 1775*]

July 23 1775

My Dear

You have more than once in your Letters mentioned Dr. Franklin, and in one intimated a Desire that I should write you something concerning him.

Dr. Franklin has been very constant in his Attendance on Congress from the Beginning. His Conduct has been composed and grave and in the Opinion of many Gentlemen very reserved. He has not assumed any Thing, nor affected to take the lead; but has seemed to choose that the Congress should pursue their own Principles and sentiments and adopt their own Plans: Yet he has not been backward: has been very usefull, on many occasions, and discovered a Disposition entirely American. He does not hesitate at our boldest Measures, but rather seems to think us too irresolute, and backward. He thinks us at present in an odd State, neither in Peace nor War, neither dependent nor independent. But he thinks that We shall soon assume a Character more decisive.

He thinks, that We have the Power of preserving ourselves, and that even if We should be driven to the disagreable Necessity of assuming a total Independency, and set up a separate state, We could maintain it. The People of England, have thought that the Opposition in America, was wholly owing to Dr. Franklin: and I suppose their scribblers will attribute the Temper, and Proceedings of this Congress to him: but there cannot be a greater Mistake. He has had but little share farther than to cooperate and assist. He is however a great and good Man. I wish his Colleagues from this City[2] were All like him, particularly one, whose Abilities and Virtues, formerly trumpeted so much in America, have been found wanting. . . .

John Adams

1850–1856

[from July 3, 1776]

Philadelphia July 3d. 1776

Had a Declaration of Independency been made seven Months ago, it would have been attended with many great and glorious Effects. . . . We might before this Hour, have formed Alliances with foreign States.—We should have mastered Quebec and been in Possession of Canada. . . . You will perhaps wonder, how such a Declaration would have influenced our Affairs, in Canada, but if I could write with Freedom I could easily convince you, that it would, and explain to you the manner how.—Many Gentlemen in high Stations and of great Influence have been duped, by the ministerial Bubble of Commissioners to treat. . . . And in real, sincere Expectation of this Event, which they so fondly wished, they have been slow and languid, in promoting Measures for the Reduction of that Province. Others there are in the Colonies who really wished that our Enterprise in Canada would be defeated, that the Colonies might be brought into Danger and Distress between two Fires, and be thus induced to submit. Others really wished to defeat the Expedition to Canada, lest the Conquest of it, should elevate the Minds of the People too much to hearken to those Terms of Reconciliation which they believed would be offered Us. These jarring Views, Wishes and Designs, occasioned an opposition to many salutary Measures, which were proposed for the Support of that Expedition, and caused Obstructions, Embarrassments and studied Delays, which have finally, lost Us the Province.

All these Causes however in Conjunction would not have disappointed Us, if it had not been for a Misfortune, which could not be foreseen, and perhaps could not have been prevented, I mean the Prevalence of the small Pox among our Troops. . . . This fatal Pestilence compleated our Destruction.—It is a Frown of Providence upon Us, which We ought to lay to heart.

But on the other Hand, the Delay of this Declaration to this Time, has many great Advantages attending it.—The Hopes of Reconciliation, which were fondly entertained by Multitudes of honest and well meaning tho weak and mistaken People, have been gradually and at last totally extinguished.—Time has been given for the whole

---

[2] Philadelphia.

People, maturely to consider the great Question of Independence and to ripen their Judgments, dissipate their Fears, and allure their Hopes, by discussing it in News Papers and Pamphletts, by debating it, in Assemblies, Conventions, Committees of Safety and Inspection, in Town and County Meetings, as well as in private Conversations, so that the whole People in every Colony of the 13, have now adopted it, as their own Act. —This will cement the Union, and avoid those Heats and perhaps Convulsions which might have been occasioned, by such a Declaration Six Months ago.

But the Day is past. The Second Day of July 1776, will be the most memorable Epocha, in the History of America.—I am apt to believe that it will be celebrated, by succeeding Generations, as the great anniversary Festival. It ought to be commemorated, as the Day of Deliverance by solemn Acts of Devotion to God Almighty. It ought to be solemnized with Pomp and Parade, with Shews, Games, Sports, Guns, Bells, Bonfires and Illuminations from one End of this Continent to the other from this Time forward forever more.

You will think me transported with Enthusiasm but I am not.—I am well aware of the Toil and Blood and Treasure, that it will cost Us to maintain this Declaration, and support and defend these States.—Yet through all the Gloom I can see the Rays of ravishing Light and Glory. I can see that the End is more than worth all the Means. And that Posterity will tryumph in that Day's Transaction, even altho We should rue it, which I trust in God We shall not.

[August 14, 1776]

Philadelphia 14. August 1776

This is the Anniversary of a memorable day, in the History of America: a day when the Principle of American Resistance and Independence, was first asserted, and carried into Action. The Stamp Office fell before the rising Spirit of our Countrymen.—It is not impossible that the two *gratefull* Brothers[3] may make their grand Attack this very day: if they should, it is possible it may be more glorious for this Country, than ever: it is certain it will become more memorable.

Your Favours of August 1. and 5. came by Yesterdays Post. I congratulate you all upon your agreable Prospects. Even my pathetic little Hero Charles, I hope will have the Distemper finely. It is very odd that the Dr. can't put Infection enough into his Veigns, nay it is unaccountable to me that he has not taken it, in the natural Way before now. I am under little Apprehension, prepared as he is, if he should. I am concerned about you, much more. So many Persons about you, sick. The Children troublesome—your Mind perplexed—yourself weak and relaxed. The Situation must be disagreable. The Country Air, and Exercise however, will refresh you.

I am put upon a Committee to prepare a Device for a Golden Medal to commemorate the Surrender of Boston to the American Arms, and upon another to prepare Devices for a Great Seal for the confederated States. There is a Gentleman here of French Extraction, whose Name is Du Simitiere, a Painter by Profession whose Designs are very ingenious, and his Drawings well executed. He has been applied to

---

[3] Richard Howe (1726–1799), earl and British admiral; and William Howe, fifth viscount (1729–1814), British general.

for his Advice. I waited on him yesterday, and saw his Sketches. For the Medal he proposes Liberty with her Spear and Pileus, leaning on General Washington. The British Fleet in Boston Harbour, with all their Sterns towards the Town, the American Troops, marching in. For the Seal he proposes. The Arms of the several Nations from whence America has been peopled, as English, Scotch, Irish, Dutch, German &c. each in a Shield. On one side of them Liberty, with her Pileus, on the other a Rifler, in his Uniform, with his Rifled Gun in one Hand, and his Tomahauk, in the other. This Dress and these Troops with this Kind of Armour, being peculiar to America—unless the Dress was known to the Romans. Dr. F[ranklin] shewed me, yesterday, a Book, containing an Account of the Dresses of all the Roman Soldiers, one of which, appeared exactly like it.

This Mr. Du simitiere is a very curious Man. He has begun a Collection of Materials for an History of this Revolution. He begins with the first Advices of the Tea Ships. He cutts out of the Newspapers, every Scrap of Intelligence, and every Piece of Speculation, and pastes it upon clean Paper, arranging them under the Head of the State to which they belong and intends to bind them up in Volumes. He has a List of every Speculation and Pamphlet concerning Independence, and another of those concerning Forms of Government.

Dr. F. proposes a Device for a Seal. Moses lifting up his Wand, and dividing the Red Sea, and Pharaoh, in his Chariot overwhelmed with the Waters.—This Motto. Rebellion to Tyrants is Obedience to God.

Mr. Jefferson proposed. The Children of Israel in the Wilderness, led by a Cloud by day, and a Pillar of Fire by night, and on the other Side Hengist and Horsa, the Saxon Chiefs, from whom We claim the Honour of being descended and whose Political Principles and Form of Government We have assumed.

I proposed the Choice of Hercules, as engraved by Gribeline in some Editions of Lord Shaftsburys Works. The Hero resting on his Clubb. Virtue pointing to her rugged Mountain, on one Hand, and perswading him to ascend. Sloth, glancing at her flowery Paths of Pleasure, wantonly reclining on the Ground, displaying the Charms both of her Eloquence and Person, to seduce him into Vice. But this is too complicated a Group for a Seal or Medal, and it is not original.

I shall conclude by repeating my Request for Horses and a servant. Let the Horses be good ones. I cant ride a bad Horse, so many hundred Miles. If our Affairs had not been in so critical a state at N. York, I should have run away before now. But I am determined now to stay, untill some Gentleman is sent here in my Room, and until my Horses come. But the Time will be very tedious.

The whole Force is arrived at Staten Island.

1850–1856

[April 26, 1777]

Saturday Evening 26 April 1777

I have been lately more remiss, than usual in Writing to you. There has been a great Dearth of News. Nothing from England, nothing from France, Spain, or any other Part of Europe, nothing from the West Indies. Nothing from Howe, and his Banditti, nothing from General Washington.

There are various Conjectures that Lord How is dead, sick, or gone to England, as the Proclamations run in the Name of Will. Howe only, and nobody from New York can tell any Thing of his Lordship.

I am wearied out, with Expectations that the Massachusetts Troops would have arrived, e'er now, at Head Quarters.—Do our People intend to leave the Continent in the Lurch? Do they mean to submit? or what Fatality attends them? With the noblest Prize in View, that ever Mortals contended for, and with the fairest Prospect of obtaining it upon easy Terms, The People of the Massachusetts Bay, are dead.

Does our State intend to send only half, or a third of their Quota? Do they wish to see another, crippled, disastrous and disgracefull Campaign for Want of an Army? —I am more sick and more ashamed of my own Countrymen, than ever I was before. The Spleen, the Vapours, the Dismals, the Horrors, seem to have seized our whole State.

More Wrath than Terror, has seized me. I am very mad. The gloomy Cowardice of the Times, is intollerable in N. England.

Indeed I feel not a little out of Humour, from Indisposition of Body. You know, I cannot pass a Spring, or fall, without an ill Turn—and I have had one of these four or five Weeks—a Cold, as usual. Warm Weather, and a little Exercise, with a little Medicine, I suppose will cure me as usual. I am not confined, but moap about and drudge as usual, like a Gally Slave. I am a Fool if ever there was one to be such a Slave. I won't be much longer. I will be more free, in some World or other.

Is it not intollerable, that the opening Spring, which I should enjoy with my Wife and Children upon my little Farm, should pass away, and laugh at me, for labouring, Day after Day, and Month after Month, in a Conclave, Where neither Taste, nor Fancy, nor Reason, nor Passion, nor Appetite can be gratified?

Posterity! You will never know, how much it cost the present Generation, to preserve your Freedom! I hope you will make a good Use of it. If you do not, I shall repent in Heaven, that I ever took half the Pains to preserve it.

1850–1856

[*from February 13, 1779]*

Passy Feb. 13 1779

My dearest Friend

Yours of 15 Decr. was sent me Yesterday by the Marquiss[4] whose Praises are celebrated in all the Letters from America. You must be content to receive a short Letter, because I have not Time now to write a long one.—I have lost many of your Letters, which are invaluable to me, and you have lost a vast Number of mine. Barns, Niles, and many other Vessells are lost.

I have received Intelligence much more agreable, than that of a removal to Holland, I mean that of being reduced to a private Citizen which gives me more Pleasure, than you can imagine. I shall therefore soon present before you, your own good Man. Happy—happy indeed shall I be, once more to see our Fireside.

I have written before to Mrs. Warren and shall write again now.

---

[4] Marquis Lafayette (1757–1834), French soldier and statesman who served in the Revolutionary army.

Dr. J. is transcribing your scotch song, which is a charming one. Oh my leaping Heart.

I must not write a Word to you about Politicks, because you are a Woman. What an offence have I committed?—a Woman!

I shall soon make it up. I think Women better than Men in General, and I know that you can keep a Secret as well as any Man whatever. But the World dont know this. Therefore if I were to write any Secrets to you and the letter should be caught, and hitched into a Newspaper, the World would say, I was not to be trusted with a Secret.

I never had so much Trouble in my Life, as here, yet I grow fat. The Climate and soil agree with me—so do the Cookery and even the Manners of the People, of those of them at least that I converse with, Churlish Republican, as some of you, on your side the Water call me. The English have got at me in their News Papers. They make fine Work of me—fanatic—Bigot—perfect Cypher—not one Word of the Language—aukward Figure—uncouth dress—no Address—No Character—cunning hard headed Attorney. But the falsest of it all is, that I am disgusted with the Parisians —Whereas I declare I admire the Parisians prodigiously. They are the happiest People in the World, I believe, and have the best Disposition to make others so.

If I had your Ladyship and our little folks here, and no Politicks to plague me and an hundred Thousand Livres a Year Rent, I should be the happiest Being on Earth. . . .

1850–1856

[post May 12, 1780]

[Paris]

My dear Portia

The inclosed Dialogue in the Shades was written by Mr. Edmund Jennings now residing at Brussells, a Native of Maryland. I will send you the Rest when I can get it.

How I lament the Loss of my Packets by Austin! There were I suppose Letters from Congress of great Importance to me. I know not what I shall do without them. I suppose there was Authority to draw &c. Mr. T[haxter]'s Letter from his father, hints that Mr. L. is coming here. This will be excellent.

Since my Arrival this time I have driven about Paris, more than I did before. The rural Scenes around this Town are charming. The public Walks, Gardens, &c. are extreamly beautifull. The Gardens of the Palais Royal, the Gardens of the Tuilleries, are very fine. The Place de Louis 15, the Place Vendome or Place de Louis 14, the Place victoire, the Place royal, are fine Squares, ornamented with very magnificent statues. I wish I had time to describe these objects to you in a manner, that I should have done, 25 Years ago, but my Head is too full of Schemes and my Heart of Anxiety to use Expressions borrowed from you know whom.

To take a Walk in the Gardens of the Palace of the Tuilleries, and describe the Statues there, all in marble, in which the ancient Divinities and Heroes are represented with exquisite Art, would be a very pleasant Amusement, and instructive Entertainment, improving in History, Mythology, Poetry, as well as in Statuary. Another Walk in the Gardens of Versailles, would be usefull and agreable.—But to observe these

Objects with Taste and describe them so as to be understood, would require more time and thought than I can possibly Spare. It is not indeed the fine Arts, which our Country requires. The Usefull, the mechanic Arts, are those which We have occasion for in a young Country, as yet simple and not far advanced in Luxury, altho perhaps much too far for her Age and Character.

I could fill Volumes with Descriptions of Temples and Palaces, Paintings, Sculptures, Tapestry, Porcelaine, &c. &c. &c.—if I could have time. But I could not do this without neglecting my duty.—The Science of Government it is my Duty to study, more than all other Sciences: the Art of Legislation and Administration and Negotiation, ought to take Place, indeed to exclude in a manner all other Arts.—I must study Politicks and War that my sons may have liberty to study Mathematicks and Philosophy. My sons ought to study Mathematicks and Philosophy, Geography, natural History, Naval Architecture, navigation, Commerce and Agriculture, in order to give their Children a right to study Painting, Poetry, Musick, Architecture, Statuary, Tapestry and Porcelaine.

Adieu.

1850–1856

[January 22, 1783]

Paris Jan. 22. 1783

My dearest Friend

The Preliminaries of Peace and an Armistice, were signed at Versailles on the 20 and on the 21. We went again to pay our Respects to the King and Royal Family upon the Occasion. Mr. Jay was gone upon a little Excursion to Normandie and Mr. Laurens was gone to Bath, both for their health, so that the signature was made by Mr. Franklin and me.—I want an Excursion too.

Thus drops the Curtain upon this mighty Trajedy, it has unravelled itself happily for Us—and Heaven be praised. Some of our dearest Interests have been saved, thro many dangers. I have no News from my son, since the 8th. December, when he was at Stockholm, but hope every hour to hear of his Arrival at the Hague.

I hope to receive the Acceptance of my Resignation so as to come home in the Spring Ships.

I had written thus far when yours of 23 decr. was brought in. Its Contents have awakened all my sensibility, and shew in a stronger Light than ever the Necessity of my coming home. I confess I don't like the Subject at all. My Child is too young for such Thoughts, and I don't like your Word "Dissipation" at all. I don't know what it means—it may mean every Thing. There is not Modesty and Diffidence enough in the Traits you send me. My Child is a Model, as you represent her and as I know her, and is not to be the Prize, I hope of any, even reformed Rake. A Lawyer would be my Choice, but it must be a Lawyer who spends his Midnights as well as Evenings at his Age over his Books not at any Ladys Fire Side. I should have thought you had seen enough to be more upon your Guard than to write Billets upon such a subject to such a youth. A Youth who has been giddy enough to spend his Fortune or half his Fortune in Gaieties, is not the Youth for me, Let his Person, Family, Connections and Taste for Poetry be what they will. I am not looking out for a Poet, nor a Professor of belle Letters.

In the Name of all that is tender dont criticise Your Daughter for those qualities which are her greatest Glory, her Reserve, and her Prudence which I am amazed to hear you call Want of Sensibility. The more Silent She is in Company, the better for me in exact Proportion and I would have this observed as a Rule by the Mother as well as the Daughter.

You know moreover or ought to know my utter Inability to do any Thing for my Children, and you know the long dependence of young Gentlemen of the most promising Talents and obstinate Industry, at the Bar. My Children will have nothing but their Liberty and the Right to catch Fish, on the Banks of Newfoundland. This is all the Fortune that I have been able to make for myself or them.

I know not however, enough of this subject to decide any Thing.—Is he a Speaker at the Bar? If not he will never be any Thing. But above all I positively forbid any Connection between my Daughter and any Youth upon Earth, who does not totally eradicate every Taste for Gaiety and Expence. I never knew one who had it and indulged it, but what was made a Rascall by it, sooner or later.

This Youth has had a Brother in Europe, and a detestible Specimen he exhibited. Their Father had not all those nice sentiments which I wish, although an Honourable Man.

I think he and you have both advanced too fast, and I should advise both to retreat. Your Family as well as mine have had too much Cause to rue the Qualities which by your own Account have been in him. And if they were ever in him they are not yet out.

This is too serious a subject to equivocate about. I don't like this method of Courting Mothers. There is something too fantastical and affected in all this Business for me. It is not nature, modest, virtuous, noble nature. The Simplicity of Nature is the best Rule with me to judge of every Thing, in Love as well as State and War.

This is all between you and me.

I would give the World to be with you Tomorrow. But there is a vast Ocean. —No Ennemies.—But I have not yet Leave from my Masters. I dont love to go home in a Miff, Pet or Passion nor with an ill Grace, but I hope soon to have leave. I can never stay in Holland—the Air of that Country chills every drop of Blood in my Veins. If I were to stay in Europe another Year I would insist upon your coming with your daughter but this is not to be and I will come home to you.

Adieu ah ah Adieu.

1850–1856

Letters to John Quincy Adams

[May 14, 1781]

Amsterdam, May 14. 1781

My dear Son

I received yours of 13 this morning.

If you have not found a convenient Place to remove into, you may continue in your present Lodgings another Month.

I am glad you have finished Phædrus, and made Such Progress in Nepos, and in Greek.

Amidst your Ardour for Greek and Latin I hope you will not forget your mother Tongue. Read Somewhat in the English Poets every day. You will find them elegant, entertaining and instructive Companions, through your whole Life. In all the Disquisitions you have heard concerning the Happiness of Life, has it ever been recommended to you to read Poetry?

To one who has a Taste, the Poets serve to fill up Time which would otherwise pass in Idleness, Languor, or Vice. You will never be alone, with a Poet in your Poket. You will never have an idle Hour.

How many weary hours have been made alert, how many melancholly ones gay, how many vacant ones useful, to me, in the course of my Life, by this means?

Your Brother grows dayly better but is still weak and pale. He shall write to you, Soon.

Your affectionate Father,   J. Adams

1850–1856

[May 14, 1783]

Paris May 14. 1783

My dear Child

Mr. Hardouin has just now called upon me, and delivered me your Letter of the 6 Instant.

I find that, although, your hand Writing is distinct and legible, yet it has not engaged so much of your Attention as to be remarkably neat. I should advise you to be very carefull of it: never to write in a hurry, and never to let a slovenly Word or Letter go from you. If one begins at your Age, it is easier to learn to write well than ill, both in Characters and Style. There are not two prettier accomplishments than a handsome hand and Style, and these are only to be acquired in youth. I have suffered much, through my whole Life, from a Negligence of these Things in my young days, and I wish you to know it. Your hand and Style, are clear enough to shew that you may easily make them manly and beautifull, and when a habit is got, all is easy.

I see your Travells have been expensive, as I expected they would be: but I hope your Improvements have been worth the Money. Have you kept a regular Journal? If you have not, you will be likely to forget most of the Observations you have made. If you have omitted this Usefull Exercise, let me advise you to recommence it, immediately. Let it be your Amusement, to minute every day, whatever you may have seen or heard worth Notice. One contracts a Fondness of Writing by Use. We learn to write readily, and what is of more importance, We think, and improve our Judgments, by committing our Thoughts to Paper.

Your Exercises in Latin and Greek must not be omitted a single day, and you should turn your Mind a little to Mathematicks. There is among my Books a Fennings Algebra. Begin it immediately and go through it, by a small Portion every day. You will find it as entertaining as an Arabean Tale. The Vulgar Fractions with which it begins, is the best extant, and you should make yourself quite familiar with it.

A regular Distribution of your Time, is of great Importance. You must measure out your Hours, for Study, Meals, Amusements, Exercise and Sleep, and suffer nothing to divert you, at least from those devoted to study.

But above all Things, my Son, take Care of your Behaviour and preserve the Character you have acquired, for Prudence and Solidity. Remember your tender Years and treat all the World with Modesty, Decency and Respect.

The Advantage you have in Mr. Dumas's Attention to you is a very prescious one. He is himself a Walking Library, and so great a Master of Languages ancient and modern is very rarely seen. The Art of asking Questions is the most essential to one who wants to learn. Never be too wise to ask a Question.

Be as frugal as possible, in your Expences.

Write to your Mamma, Sister and Brothers, as often as you have Opportunity. It will be a Grief to me to loose a Spring Passage home, but although I have my fears I dont yet despair.

Every Body gives me a very flattering Character of your Sister, and I am well pleased with what I hear of you: The principal Satisfaction I can expect in Life, in future, will be in your good Behaviour and that of my other Children. My Hopes from all of you are very agreable. God grant, I may not be dissappointed.

Your affectionate Father,   John Adams

1850–1856

Letters to Thomas Jefferson

[from **February 3, 1812**]

Quincy February 3, 1812

DEAR SIR

Sitting at My Fireside with my Daughter Smith, on the first of February My Servant brought me a Bundle of Letters and Newspapers from the Post Office in this Town: one of the first Letters that struck my Eye had the Post Mark of Milton 23. Jany. 1812. Milton is the next Town to Quincy and the Post Office in it is but three Miles from my House. How could the Letter be so long in coming three miles? Reading the Superscription, I instantly handed the Letter to Mrs. Smith. Is that not Mr. Jeffersons hand? Looking attentively at it, she answered it is very like it. How is it possible a Letter from Mr. Jefferson, could get into the Milton Post office? Opening the Letter I found it, indeed from Monticello in the hand and with the Signature of Mr. Jefferson: but this did not much diminish my Surprize. How is it possible a Letter can come from Mr. Jefferson to me in seven or Eight days? I had no Expectation of an Answer, thinking the Distance so great and the Roads so embarrassed under two or three Months. This History would not be worth recording but for the Discovery it made of a Fact, very pleasing to me, vizt. that the Communication between Us is much easier, surer and may be more frequent than I had ever believed or suspected to be possible.

The Material of the Samples of American Manufacture which I sent you was not Wool nor Cotton, nor Silk nor Flax nor Hemp nor Iron nor Wood. They were spun from the Brain of John Quincy Adams and consist in two Volumes of his Lectures on Rhetorick and oratory, delivered when he was Professor of that Science in our University of Cambridge. A Relation of mine, a first Cousin of my ever honoured, beloved and revered Mother, Nicholas Boylston, a rich Merchant of Boston, bequeathed by his Will a Donation for establishing a Professorship, and John Quincy Adams, having in his Veins so much of the Blood of the Founder, was most earnestly solicited to become the first Professor. The Volumes I sent you are the Fruit of his Labour during the short time he held that office. But it ought to be remembered that he attended his Duty as a Senator of the United States during the same Period. It is with some Anxiety submitted to your Judgment.

Your Account of the flourishing State of Manufactures in Families in your Part of the Country is highly delightful to me. I wish the Spirit may spread and prevail through the Union. Within my Memory We were much in the same Way in New England: but in later Times We have run a gadding abroad too much to seek for Eatables, Drinkables and Wearables.

Your Life and mine for almost half a Century have been nearly all of a Piece, resembling in the whole, mine in The Gulph Stream, chaced by three British Frigates, in a Hurricane from the North East and a hideous Tempest of Thunder and Lightning, which cracked our Mainmast, struck three and twenty Men on Deck, wounded four and killed one. I do not remember that my Feelings, during those three days were very different from what they have been for fifty Years. . . .

Your Memoranda of the past, your Sense of the present and Prospect for the Future seem to be well founded, as far as I see. But the Latter i.e. the Prospect of the Future, will depend on the Union: and how is that Union to be preserved? Concordia Res parvae crescunt, Discordia Maximae dilabuntur.[1] Our Union is an immense Structure. In Russia, I doubt not, a Temple or Pallace might be erected of Wood, Brick or Marble, which should be cemented only with Ice. A sublime and beautiful Building it might be; surpassing St. Sophia, St. Peters, St. Pauls, Notre Dame or St. Genevieve. But the first Week, if not the first day of the *Debacle* would melt all the Cement and Tumble The Glass and Marble, the Gold and Silver, the Timber and the Iron into one promiscuous chaotic or anarchic heap.

I will not at present point out the precise Years Days and Months when; nor the Names of the Men by whom this Union has been put in Jeopardy. Your Recollection can be at no more loss than mine. . . .

The Union is still to me an Object of as much Anxiety as ever Independence was. To this I have sacrificed my Popularity in New England and yet what Treatment do I still receive from the Randolphs and Sheffeys of Virginia. By the Way are not these Eastern Shore Men? My Senectutal Loquacity has more than retaliated your "Senile Garrulity."

I have read Thucidides and Tacitus, so often, and at such distant Periods of my Life, that elegant, profound and enchanting as is their Style, I am weary of them. When I read them I seem to be only reading the History of my own Times and my own Life. I am heartily weary of both; i.e. of recollecting the History of both: for I am not weary of Living. Whatever a peevish Patriarch might say, I have never yet seen the day in which I could say I have had no Pleasure; or that I have had more Pain than Pleasure. . . .

JOHN ADAMS

P.S. I forgot to remark your Preference to Savage over civilized life. I have Something to say upon that Subject. If I am in an Error, you can set me Right, but

---

[1] Latin: "Small things grow in harmony, great things decay in disharmony."

by all I know of one or the other I would rather be the poorest Man in France or England, with sound health of Body and Mind, than the proudest King, Sachem or Warriour of any Tribe of Savages in America.

1850–1856

[from **May 6, 1816]**

Quincy May 6 1816

DEAR SIR

Neither Eyes Fingers or Paper held out, to dispatch all the Trifles I wished to write in my last Letter.

In your favour of April 8th, You "wonder for what good End the Sensations of Grief could be intended"? You ["]wish the Pathologists would tell Us, what the Use of Grief, in Our Œconomy, and of what good it is the Cause proximate or remote." When I approach such questions as this, I consider myself, like one of those little Eels in Vinaigre, or one of those Animalcules in black or red Peper or in the Horse radish Root, that bite our Tongues so cruelly, reasoning upon the το παν ["totality"]. Of what Use is this Sting upon the Tongue? Why might We not have the Benefit of these Stimulants, without the Sting? Why might We not have the fragrance and Beauty of the Rose without the Thorn?

In the first place, however, We know not the Connections between pleasure and Pain. They seem to be mechanical and inseperable. How can We conceive a strong Passion, a Sanguine Hope suddenly disappointed without producing Pain? or Grief? Swift at 70, recollected the Fish he had angled out of Water when a Boy, which broke loose from his hoock, and said I feel the disappointment at this Moment. A Merchant plans all his fortune and all his Credit, in a single India or China Ship. She Arrives at the Viniard with a Cargo worth a Million, in Order. Sailing round the Cape for Boston a sudden Storm wrecks her, Ship Cargo and Crew all lost. Is it possible that the Merchant ruined, bankrupt sent to Prison by his Creditors, his Wife and Children starving, should not grieve? Suppose a young Couple, with every Advant[a]ge of Persons, fortunes and Connection on the Point of an indissoluble Union. A flash of Lightening or any one of those millions of Accidents which are alloted to Humanity prove fatal to one of the Lovers. Is it possible that the other, and all the Friends of both should not grieve? It should seem that Grief, as a mere Passion must necesarily be in Proportion to Sensibility.

Did you ever see a Portrait or a Statue of a great Man, without perceiving strong Traits of Paine and Anxiety? These Furrows were all ploughed in the Countenance, by Grief. Our juvenile Oracle, Sir Edward Coke, thought that none were fit for Legislators and Magistrates, but *"Sad Men."* And Who were these sad Men? They were aged Men, who had been tossed and buffeted in the Vicissitudes of Life, forced upon profound Reflection by Grief and disappointments and taught to command their Passions and Prejudices.

But, All this, You will say, is nothing to the purpose. It is only repeating and exemplifying a Fact, which my question supposed to be well known, viz the Existence of Grief; and is no Answer to my Question, "What Are the Uses of Grief." This is very true, and you are very right: but may not the Uses of Grief be inferred, or at least suggested by such Exemplifications of known facts? Grief Compels the

India Merchant to think; to reflect upon the plan of his Voyage. "Have I not been rash, to trust my Fortune, my Family, my Liberty, to the Caprices of Winds and Waves in a single Ship? I will never again give a loose to my Imagination and Avarice." ["]It had been wiser and more honest to have traded on a smaller Scale upon my own Capital." The dessolated Lover and disappointed Connections, are compelled by their Grief to reflect on the Vanity of human Wishes and Expectations; to learn the essential Lesson of Resignation; to review their own Conduct towards the deceased; to correct any Errors or faults in their future Conduct towards their remaining friends and towards all Men; to recollect the Virtues of the lost Friend and resolve to imitate them; his Follies and Vices if he had any and resolve to avoid them. Grief drives Men into habits of serious Reflection sharpens the Understanding and softens the heart; it compells them to arrouse their Reason, to assert its Empire over their Passions Propensities and Prejudices; to elevate them to a Superiority over all human Events; to give them the Felicis Annimi immotan tranquilitatem ["the imperturbable tranquillity of a happy heart"]; in short to make them Stoicks and Christians.

After all, as Grief is a Pain, it stands in the Predicament of all other Evil and the great question Occurs what is the Origin and what the final cause of Evil. This perhaps is known only to Omnicience. We poor Mortals have nothing to do with it, but to fabricate all the good We can out of all inevitable Evils, and to avoid all that are avoidable, and many such there are, among which are our own unnecessary Apprehensions and imaginary Fears. Though Stoical Apathy is impossible, Yet Patience and Resignation and tranquility may be acquired by Consideration in a great degree, very much for the hapiness of Life. . . .

1850–1856

[from June 11, 1822]

Montezillo June 11th. 1822.

DEAR SIR,

Half an hour ago I received, and this moment have heard read for the third or fourth time, the best letter that ever was written by an Octogenearian, dated June the 1st. It is so excellent that I am almost under an invincible temptation to commit a breach of trust by lending it to a printer. My Son, Thomas Boylston, says it would be worth five hundred dollars to any newspaper in Boston, but I dare not betray your confidence.

I have not sprained my wrist, but both my Arms and hands are so over-strained that I cannot write a line. . . . I cannot mount my Horse, but I can walk three miles over a rugged rockey Mountain, and have done it within a Month. Yet I feel when setting in my chair, as if I could not rise out of it, and when risen, as if I could not walk across the room; my sight is very dim; hearing pritty good; memory poor enough.

I answer your question, Is Death an Evil? It is not an Evil. It is a blessing to the individual, and to the world. Yet we ought not to wish for it till life becomes insupportable; we must wait the pleasure and convenience of this great teacher. Winter is as terrible to me, as to you. I am almost reduced in it, to the life of a Bear or a torpid swallow. I cannot read, but my delight is to hear others read, and I tease all my friends most unmercifully and tyrannically, against their consent. The Ass has kicked in vain, all men say the dull animal has missed the mark.

This globe is a Theatre of War, its inhabitants are all heroes. I believe the little Eels in Vinegar and the animalcule in pepper water, I believe are quarrelsome. The Bees are as warlike as Romans, Russians, Britains, or Frenchmen. Ants or Caterpilars and Canker worms are the only tribes amongst whom I have not seen battles. And Heaven itself, if we believe Hindoos, Jews, and Christians, has not always been at peace. We need not trouble ourselves about these things nor fret ourselves because of Evil doers but safely trust the ruler with his skies. Nor need we dread the approach of dotage, let it come if it must. Thomson, it seems, still delights in his four stories. And Starke remembers to the last his Bennington, and exulted in his Glory. The worst of the Evil is that our friends will suffer more by our imbecility than we ourselves.

Diplomatic flickerings, it seemes, have not yet ceased. It seems as if a Council of Ambassadors could never agree.

In wishing for your health and happiness I am very selfish, for I hope for more letters; this is worth more than five hundred dollars to me, for it has already given me, and will continue to give me more pleasure than a thousand. Mr. Jay who is about your age I am told experiences more decay than you do. I am your old friend

JOHN ADAMS

1850–1856

---

from Defense of the Constitutions of Government in Massachusetts During the Revolution

from Preface

The arts and sciences, in general, during the three or four last centuries, have had a regular course of progressive improvement. The inventions in mechanic arts, the discoveries in natural philosophy, navigation, and commerce, and the advancement of civilization and humanity, have occasioned changes in the condition of the world, and the human character, which would have astonished the most refined nations of antiquity. A continuation of similar exertions is every day rendering Europe more and more like one community, or single family. Even in the theory and practice of government, in all the simple monarchies, considerable improvements have been made. The checks and balances of republican governments have been in some degree adopted at the courts of princes. By the erection of various tribunals, to register the laws, and exercise the judicial power—by indulging the petitions and remonstrances of subjects, until by habit they are regarded as rights—a control has been established over ministers of state, and the royal councils, which, in some degree, approaches the spirit of republics. Property is generally secure, and personal liberty seldom invaded. The press has great influence, even where it is not expressly tolerated; and the public opinion must be respected by a minister, or his place becomes insecure. Commerce begins to thrive; and if religious toleration were established, personal liberty a little more protected, by giving an absolute right to demand a public trial in a certain reasonable time, and the states were invested with a few more privileges, or rather restored to some that have been taken away, these governments would be brought to as great a degree of perfection, they would approach as near to the character of governments of laws and not of men, as their nature will probably admit of. In so general a refinement, or more properly a reformation of manners and improvement in science, is it not unaccountable that the knowledge of the principles and construction of free governments, in which the happiness of life, and even the further progress of improvement in education and society, in knowledge and virtue, are so deeply interested, should have remained at a full stand for two or three thousand years?

According to a story in Herodotus,[1] the nature of monarchy, aristocracy, and democracy, and the advantages and inconveniences of each, were as well understood at the time of the neighing of the horse of Darius,[2] as they are at this hour. A variety of mixtures of these simple species were conceived and attempted, with various success, by the Greeks and Romans. Representations, instead of collections, of the people; a total separation of the executive from the legislative power, and of the judicial from both; and a balance in the legislature, by three independent, equal branches, are perhaps the only three discoveries in the constitution of a free government, since the institution of Lycurgus.[3] Even these have been so unfortunate, that they have never spread: the first has been given up by all the nations, excepting one, which had once adopted it; and the other two, reduced to practice, if not invented, by the English nation, have never been imitated by any other, except their own descendants in America.

While it would be rash to say, that nothing further can be done to bring a free government, in all its parts, still nearer to perfection, the representations of the people are most obviously susceptible of improvement. The end to be aimed at, in the formation of a representative assembly, seems to be the sense of the people, the public voice. The perfection of the portrait consists in its likeness. Numbers, or property, or both, should be the rule; and the proportions of electors and members an affair of calculation. The duration should not be so long that the deputy should have time to forget the opinions of his constituents. Corruption in elections is the great enemy of freedom. Among the provisions to prevent it, more frequent elections, and a more general privilege of voting, are not all that might be devised. Dividing the districts, diminishing the distance of travel, and confining the choice to residents, would be great advances towards the annihilation of corruption. The modern aristocracies of Holland, Venice, Bern, &c., have tempered themselves with innumerable checks, by which they have given a great degree of stability to that form of government; and though liberty and life can never be there enjoyed so well as in a free republic, none is perhaps more capable of profound sagacity. We shall learn to prize the checks and balances of a free government, and even those of the modern aristocracies, if we recollect the miseries of Greece, which arose from its ignorance of them. The only balance attempted against the ancient kings was a body of nobles; and the consequences

---

[1] Herodotus (fifth century B.C.) was called by Cicero and others "the father of history."

[2] Darius (521–486 B.C.) consolidated and expanded the eastern Mediterranean empire.

[3] Distinguished Attic orator of noble character, who excelled in finance and carried out important public works projects (338–326 B.C.).

were perpetual alternations of rebellion and tyranny, and the butchery of thousands upon every revolution from one to the other. When kings were abolished, aristocracies tyrannized; and then no balance was attempted but between aristocracy and democracy. This, in the nature of things, could be no balance at all, and therefore the pendulum was forever on the swing.

It is impossible to read in Thucydides,[4] his account of the factions and confusions throughout all Greece, which were introduced by this want of an equilibrium, without horror. "During the few days that Eurymedon, with his troops, continued at Corcyra, the people of that city extended the massacre to all whom they judged their enemies. The crime alleged was, their attempt to overturn the democracy. Some perished merely through private enmity; some, by the hands of the borrower, on account of the money they had lent. Every kind of death, every dreadful act, was perpetrated. Fathers slew their children; some were dragged from altars, some were butchered at them; numbers, immured in temples, were starved. The contagion spread through the whole extent of Greece; factions raged in every city; the licentious many contending for the Athenians, and the aspiring few for the Lacedæmonians. The consequence was, seditions in cities, with all their numerous and tragical incidents."

"Such things ever will be," says Thucydides, "so long as human nature continues the same." But if this nervous historian had known a balance of three powers, he would not have pronounced the distemper so incurable, but would have added—*so long as parties in cities remain unbalanced.* He adds,—"Words lost their signification; brutal rashness was fortitude; prudence, cowardice; modesty, effeminacy; and being wise in every thing, to be good for nothing: the hot temper was manly valor; calm deliberation, plausible knavery; he who boiled with indignation, was trustworthy; and he who presumed to contradict, was ever suspected. Connection of blood was less regarded than transient acquaintance; associations were not formed for mutual advantage, consistent with law, but for rapine against all law; trust was only communication of guilt; revenge was more valued, than never to have suffered an injury; perjuries were master-pieces of cunning; the dupes only blushed, the villains most impudently triumphed."

"The source of all these evils was a thirst of power, from rapacious and ambitious passions. The men of large influence, some contending for the just equality of the democratical, and others for the fair decorum of aristocratical government, by artful sounds, embarrassed those communities, for their own private lucre, by the keenest spirit, the most daring projects, and most dreadful machinations. Revenge, not limited by justice or the public welfare, was measured only by such retaliation as was judged the sweetest; by capital condemnations, by iniquitous sentences, and by glutting the present rancor of their hearts with their own hands. The pious and upright conduct was on both sides disregarded; the moderate citizens fell victims to both. Seditions introduced every species of outrageous wickedness into the Grecian manners. Sincerity was laughed out of countenance; the whole order of human life was confounded; the human temper, too apt to transgress in spite of laws, now having gained the ascendant over law, seemed to glory that it was too strong for justice, and an enemy to all superiority."

---

[4] Thucydides (460–400 B.C.) was the historian of the Peloponnesian wars.

Mr. Hume[5] has collected, from Diodorus Siculus[6] alone, a few massacres which happened in only sixty of the most polished years of Greece:—"From Sybaris, 500 nobles banished; of Chians, 600 citizens; at Ephesus, 340 killed, 1000 banished; of Cyrenians, 500 nobles killed, all the rest banished; the Corinthians killed 120, banished 500; Phæbidas banished 300 Bœotians. Upon the fall of the Lacedæmonians, democracies were restored in many cities, and severe vengeance taken of the nobles; the banished nobles returning, butchered their adversaries at Phialæ, in Corinth, in Megara, in Phliasia, where they killed 300 of the people; but these again revolting, killed above 600 of the nobles, and banished the rest. In Arcadia, 1400 banished, besides many killed; the banished retired to Sparta and Pallantium, the latter were delivered up to their countrymen, and all killed. Of the banished from Argos and Thebes, there were 500 in the Spartan army. The people, before the usurpation of Agathocles, had banished 600 nobles; afterwards that tyrant, in concurrence with the people, killed 4000 nobles, and banished 6000; and killed 4000 people at Gela; his brother banished 8000 from Syracuse. The inhabitants of Ædgesta, to the number of 40,000, were killed, man, woman, and child, for the sake of their money; all the relations of the Libyan army, fathers, brothers, children, killed; 7000 exiles killed after capitulation. These numbers, compared with the population of those cities, are prodigious; yet Agathocles was a man of character, and not to be suspected of wanton cruelty, contrary to the maxims of his age."[7]

Such were the fashionable outrages of unbalanced parties. In the name of human and divine benevolence, is such a system as this to be recommended to Americans, in this age of the world? Human nature is as incapable now of going through revolutions with temper and sobriety, with patience and prudence, or without fury and madness, as it was among the Greeks so long ago. The latest revolution that we read of was conducted, at least on one side, in the Grecian style, with laconic energy; and with a little Attic salt, at least, without too much patience, foresight, and prudence, on the other. Without three orders, and an effectual balance between them, in every American constitution, it must be destined to frequent unavoidable revolutions; though they are delayed a few years, they must come in time. The United States are large and populous nations, in comparison with the Grecian commonwealths, or even the Swiss cantons; and they are growing every day more disproportionate, and therefore less capable of being held together by simple governments. Countries that increase in population so rapidly as the States of America did, even during such an impoverishing and destructive war as the last was, are not to be long bound with silken threads; lions, young or old, will not be bound by cobwebs. It would be better for America, it is nevertheless agreed, to ring all the changes with the whole set of bells, and go through all the revolutions of the Grecian States, rather than establish an absolute monarchy among them, notwithstanding all the great and real improvements which have been made in that kind of government.

The objection to it is not because it is supported by nobles, and a subordination of ranks; for all governments, even the most democratical, are supported by a subordi-

[5] David Hume (1711–1776), Scottish philosopher and political economist.
[6] Sicilian historian of Roman and world history (ca. 40 B.C.).

[7] From "On the Populousness of Ancient Nations" in Hume's *Essays.*

nation of offices, and of ranks too. None ever existed without it but in a state of anarchy and outrage, in a contempt of law and justice, no better than no government. But the nobles, in the European monarchies, support them more by opposing than promoting their ordinary views. The kings are supported by their armies; the nobles support the crown, as it is in full possession of the gift of all employments; but they support it still more by checking its ministers, and preventing them from running into abuses of power and wanton despotism; otherwise the people would be pushed to extremities and insurrections. It is thus that the nobles reconcile the monarchical authority to the obedience of the subjects; but take away the standing armies, and leave the nobles to themselves, and in a few years, they would overturn every monarchy in Europe, and erect aristocracies.

It is become a kind of fashion among writers, to admit, as a maxim, that if you could be always sure of a wise, active, and virtuous prince, monarchy would be the best of governments. But this is so far from being admissible, that it will forever remain true, that a free government has a great advantage over a simple monarchy. The best and wisest prince, by means of a freer communication with his people, and the greater opportunities to collect the best advice from the best of his subjects, would have an immense advantage in a free state over a monarchy. A senate consisting of all that is most noble, wealthy, and able in the nation, with a right to counsel the crown at all times, is a check to ministers, and a security against abuses, such as a body of nobles who never meet, and have no such right, can never supply. Another assembly, composed of representatives chosen by the people in all parts, gives free access to the whole nation, and communicates all its wants, knowledge, projects, and wishes to government; it excites emulation among all classes, removes complaints, redresses grievances, affords opportunities of exertion to genius, though in obscurity, and gives full scope to all the faculties of man; it opens a passage for every speculation to the legislature, to administration, and to the public; it gives a universal energy to the human character, in every part of the state, such as never can be obtained in a monarchy.

There is a third particular which deserves attention both from governments and people. In a simple monarchy, the ministers of state can never know their friends from their enemies; secret cabals undermine their influence, and blast their reputation. This occasions a jealousy ever anxious and irritated, which never thinks the government safe without an encouragement of informers and spies, throughout every part of the state, who interrupt the tranquillity of private life, destroy the confidence of families in their own domestics and in one another, and poison freedom in its sweetest retirements. In a free government, on the contrary, the ministers can have no enemies of consequence but among the members of the great or little council, where every man is obliged to take his side, and declare his opinion, upon every question. This circumstance alone, to every manly mind, would be sufficient to decide the preference in favor of a free government. Even secrecy, where the executive is entire in one hand, is as easily and surely preserved in a free government, as in a simple monarchy; and as to despatch, all the simple monarchies of the whole universe may be defied to produce greater or more numerous examples of it than are to be found in English history. An Alexander, or a Frederic,[8] possessed of the prerogatives only of a king of

---

[8] Alexander: Alexander III of Macedon (356–323 B.C.); Frederic: Frederick William II (1744–1797), king of Prussia.

England, and leading his own armies, would never find himself embarrassed or delayed in any honest enterprise. He might be restrained, indeed, from running mad, and from making conquests to the ruin of his nation, merely for his own glory; but this is no argument against a free government.

There can be no free government without a democratical branch in the constitution. Monarchies and aristocracies are in possession of the voice and influence of every university and academy in Europe. Democracy, simple democracy, never had a patron among men of letters. Democratical mixtures in government have lost almost all the advocates they ever had out of England and America. Men of letters must have a great deal of praise, and some of the necessaries, conveniences, and ornaments of life. Monarchies and aristocracies pay well and applaud liberally. The people have almost always expected to be served gratis, and to be paid for the honor of serving them; and their applauses and adorations are bestowed too often on artifices and tricks, on hypocrisy and superstition, on flattery, bribes, and largesses. It is no wonder then that democracies and democratical mixtures are annihilated all over Europe, except on a barren rock, a paltry fen, an inaccessible mountain, or an impenetrable forest. The people of England, to their immortal honor, are hitherto an exception; but, to the humiliation of human nature, they show very often that they are like other men. The people in America have now the best opportunity and the greatest trust in their hands, that Providence ever committed to so small a number, since the transgression of the first pair; if they betray their trust, their guilt will merit even greater punishment than other nations have suffered, and the indignation of Heaven. If there is one certain truth to be collected from the history of all ages, it is this; that the people's rights and liberties, and the democratical mixture in a constitution, can never be preserved without a strong executive, or, in other words, without separating the executive from the legislative power. If the executive power, or any considerable part of it, is left in the hands either of an aristocratical or a democratical assembly, it will corrupt the legislature as necessarily as rust corrupts iron, or as arsenic poisons the human body; and when the legislature is corrupted, the people are undone.

The rich, the well-born, and the able, acquire an influence among the people that will soon be too much for simple honesty and plain sense, in a house of representatives. The most illustrious of them must, therefore, be separated from the mass, and placed by themselves in a senate; this is, to all honest and useful intents, an ostracism. A member of a senate, of immense wealth, the most respected birth, and transcendent abilities has no influence in the nation, in comparison of what he would have in a single representative assembly. When a senate exists, the most powerful man in the state may be safely admitted into the house of representatives, because the people have it in their power to remove him into the senate as soon as his influence becomes dangerous. The senate becomes the great object of ambition; and the richest and the most sagacious wish to merit an advancement to it by services to the public in the house. When he has obtained the object of his wishes, you may still hope for the benefits of his exertions, without dreading his passions; for the executive power being in other hands, he has lost much of his influence with the people, and can govern very few votes more than his own among the senators.

It was the general opinion of ancient nations, that the Divinity alone was adequate to the important office of giving laws to men. The Greeks entertained this prejudice throughout all their dispersions; the Romans cultivated the same popular delusion; and modern nations, in the consecration of kings, and in several superstitious chimeras of divine right in princes and nobles, are nearly unanimous in preserving remnants of it. Even the venerable magistrates of Amersfort devoutly believe themselves God's vicegerents. Is it that obedience to the laws can be obtained from mankind in no other manner? Are the jealousy of power, and the envy of superiority, so strong in all men, that no considerations of public or private utility are sufficient to engage their submission to rules for their own happiness? Or is the disposition to imposture so prevalent in men of experience, that their private views of ambition and avarice can be accomplished only by artifice? It was a tradition in antiquity that the laws of Crete were dictated to Minos by the inspiration of Jupiter. This legislator and his brother Rhadamanthus were both his sons; once in nine years they went to converse with their father, to propose questions concerning the wants of the people; and his answers were recorded as laws for their government. The laws of Lacedæmon were communicated by Apollo to Lycurgus; and, lest the meaning of the deity should not have been perfectly comprehended, or correctly expressed, they were afterwards confirmed by his oracle at Delphos. Among the Romans, Numa was indebted for those laws which procured the prosperity of his country to his conversations with Egeria. The Greeks imported these mysteries from Egypt and the East, whose despotisms, from the remotest antiquity to this day, have been founded in the same solemn empiricism; their emperors and nobles being all descended from their gods. Woden and Thor were divinities too; and their posterity ruled a thousand years in the north by the strength of a like credulity. Manco Capac was the child of the sun, the visible deity of the Peruvians; and transmitted his divinity, as well as his earthly dignity and authority, through a line of incas. And the rudest tribes of savages in North America have certain families from which their leaders are always chosen, under the immediate protection of the god War. There is nothing in which mankind have been more unanimous; yet nothing can be inferred from it more than this, that the multitude have always been credulous, and the few are always artful.

The United States of America have exhibited, perhaps, the first example of governments erected on the simple principles of nature; and if men are now sufficiently enlightened to disabuse themselves of artifice, imposture, hypocrisy, and superstition, they will consider this event as an era in their history. Although the detail of the formation of the American governments is at present little known or regarded either in Europe or in America, it may hereafter become an object of curiosity. It will never be pretended that any persons employed in that service had interviews with the gods, or were in any degree under the inspiration of Heaven, more than those at work upon ships or houses, or laboring in merchandise or agriculture; it will forever be acknowledged that these governments were contrived merely by the use of reason and the senses, as Copley painted Chatham; West, Wolf; and Trumbull,[9] Warren and Montgomery; as Dwight, Barlow, Trumbull, and Humphries[10] composed their verse, and Belknap and Ramsay[11] history; as Godfrey invented his quadrant, and Rittenhouse his planetarium; as Boylston[12] practised inoculation, and Franklin electricity; as Paine

[9] John Singleton Copley (1738–1815), Benjamin West (1738–1820), and John Trumbull (1756–1843) were American painters.

[10] Timothy Dwight (1752–1817), Joel Barlow (1754–1812), and David Humphreys (1753–1818) were American poets.

[11] Jeremy Belknap (1744–1798) and David Ramsay (1749–1815) were historians of American regions.

[12] Thomas Godfrey (1704–1749), David Rittenhouse (1732–1796), and Zabdiel Boylston (1679–1766) were American men of science.

exposed the mistakes of Raynal, and Jefferson those of Buffon, so unphilosophically borrowed from the despicable dreams of De Pau. Neither the people, nor their conventions, committees, or sub-committees, considered legislation in any other light than as ordinary arts and sciences, only more important. Called without expectation, and compelled without previous inclination, though undoubtedly at the best period of time, both for England and America, suddenly to erect new systems of laws for their future government, they adopted the method of a wise architect, in erecting a new palace for the residence of his sovereign. They determined to consult Vitruvius, Palladio, and all other writers of reputation in the art; to examine the most celebrated buildings, whether they remain entire or in ruins; to compare these with the principles of writers; and to inquire how far both the theories and models were founded in nature, or created by fancy; and when this was done, so far as their circumstances would allow, to adopt the advantages and reject the inconveniences of all. Unembarrassed by attachments to noble families, hereditary lines and successions, or any considerations of royal blood, even the pious mystery of holy oil had no more influence than that other one of holy water. The people were universally too enlightened to be imposed on by artifice; and their leaders, or more properly followers, were men of too much honor to attempt it. Thirteen governments thus founded on the natural authority of the people alone, without a pretence of miracle or mystery, and which are destined to spread over the northern part of that whole quarter of the globe, are a great point gained in favor of the rights of mankind. The experiment is made, and has completely succeeded; it can no longer be called in question, whether authority in magistrates and obedience of citizens can be grounded on reason, morality, and the Christian religion, without the monkery of priests, or the knavery of politicians. As the writer was personally acquainted with most of the gentlemen in each of the states, who had the principal share in the first draughts, the following work was really written to lay before the public a specimen of that kind of reading and reasoning which produced the American constitutions.

It is not a little surprising that all this kind of learning should have been unknown to any illustrious philosopher and statesman, and especially one who really was, what he has been often called, "a well of science." But if he could be unacquainted with it, or it could have escaped his memory, we may suppose millions in America have occasion to be reminded of it. The writer has long seen with anxiety the facility with which philosophers of greatest name have undertaken to write of American affairs, without knowing any thing of them, and have echoed and reëchoed each other's visionary language. Having neither talents, leisure, nor inclination to meet such champions in the field of literary controversy, he little thought of venturing to propose to them any questions. Circumstances, however, have lately occurred which seem to require that some notice should be taken of one of them. If the publication of these papers should contribute any thing to turn the attention of the younger gentlemen of letters in America to this kind of inquiry, it will produce an effect of some importance to their country. The subject is the most interesting that can engage the understanding or the heart; for whether the end of man, in this stage of his existence, be enjoyment, or improvement, or both, it can never be attained so well in a bad government as a good one. . . .

1787

Abigail Adams
1744–1818

Abigail Smith Adams, in failing health and retired from a rigorous public life, reflected on her married life in a letter to her granddaughter dated October 26, 1814:

> Yesterday completes half a century since I entered the married state, then just your age. I have great cause of thankfulness, that I have lived so long and enjoyed so large a portion of happiness as has been my lot. The greatest source of unhappiness I have known in that period has arisen from the long and cruel separations which I was called, in a time of war and with a young family around me, to submit to.

These "long and cruel separations" attended her husband John's many years of public service: as a Massachusetts delegate to the Continental Congresses, as a negotiator of the Treaty of Paris, as the American joint commissioner at the court of France, as the nation's first vice-president, and as the second president of the United States. John Adams's frequent and prolonged absences resulted not only in Abigail's uncommon self-sufficiency but also in her voluminous, rich correspondence with her husband; with her son John Quincy, who later served as sixth president of the United States; and with numerous political leaders in the new republic. These letters constitute one of the most incisive private commentaries on the public events that crowded the new nation's history.

Abigail Smith Adams was the second of three daughters born to Reverend William Smith and Elizabeth Quincy, parents who could trace their distinguished lineages back through the pages of Cotton Mather's *Magnalia Christi Americana*. She entered, as did all eighteenth-century women, a world indifferent to the education of females. In a letter dated 1817, she observed:

> My early education did not partake of the opportunities which the present days offer, and which even our common country schools now afford. I never was sent to any school. I was always sick. Female education, in the best families, went no further than writing and arithmetic; in some few and rare instances, music and dancing.

Under the tutelage of her grandmother, who offered a "happy method of mixing instruction and amusement," young Abigail became a practiced letter writer early on and read widely among English poets and essayists, developing an especially high regard for Addison and Steele's *Spectator* papers.

In 1764 she married John Adams, despite some resistance from her family, who regarded this lawyer son of a small farmer as beneath their own social and professional standing. Within the next decade, Abigail Adams bore a daughter, Abby, and three sons, John Quincy, Thomas, and Charles. As her husband traveled more frequently to participate in the political controversies that led to the American Revolution, Abigail endured the prolonged silences of late eighteenth-century mail and took on increasingly more responsibility for her family's well-being. Her letters to John during this period reveal her many talents: cultivating a farm, managing the finances, ordering and selling goods from abroad, discussing current prices, and arguing over local and national politics.

Armed with an independent and imaginative intelligence, she vigorously expressed her ideas on a wide range of subjects, most particularly on women's rights. Her letters reveal her longing for an American declaration of independence, and she was one of the first Americans to perceive the implications of the Revolution for blacks and women. A lifelong advocate of black emancipation and education, Abigail Adams also repeatedly argued that women should be better educated than their colonial ancestors. She also insisted that wives ought to be freed from the absolute legal authority husbands held over their lives: "If particular care and attention is not paid to the ladies, we are determined to foment a rebellion, and will not hold ourselves bound by any laws in which we have no voice or representation." Abigail Adams remained steadfast in the counsel she offered her husband: She was determined to strengthen women's roles in American culture and politics. She once admonished her husband, "If you complain of education in sons, what shall I say in regard to daughters who every day experience the want of it? . . . If we mean to have heroes, statesmen, and philosophers, we should have learned women." Her own wide reading is evident in the many literary and biblical allusions that punctuate her correspondence, especially in her letters detailing the progress of the Revolutionary War while her husband was abroad. In this respect, she may well have been of more assistance to him than he to her.

Soon after the war, Abigail Adams joined her husband in Europe for the American trade negotiations. Her correspondence during this period is filled with trenchant observations on European manners and customs as well as revealing glimpses of the social behavior of some of the leading American representatives, including Benjamin Franklin and Thomas Jefferson. The Adams family returned to the United States in 1788 and to John Adams's election as vice-president. The presidency followed in 1797, and it was not until 1801 that the family settled permanently in their home at Braintree (now Quincy), Massachusetts, where Abigail lived in retirement until her death from typhoid fever in 1818.

Abigail Adams's letters document the personal costs of supporting public needs. Not until Franklin and Eleanor Roosevelt would America once again witness such a celebrated union of such dynamic individuals. Yet no other marriage of such visible figures in American life has so successfully wed public and private lives for so long.

Further Reading:
J. Whitney, *Abigail Adams*, 1947.
L. Withey, *Dearest Friend: A Life of Abigail Adams*, 1981.

Texts:
Letters of Mrs. Adams, the Wife of John Adams, ed. C. F. Adams, 2 vols., 1840.
Familiar Letters of John Adams and His Wife Abigail Adams, During the Revolution, ed. C. F. Adams, 1876.
The Book of Abigail and John: Selected Letters of the Adams Family, 1762–1784, ed. L. H. Butterfield et al., 1975.
See also *New Letters, 1788–1801*, ed. S. Mitchell, 1947.

Letters to John Adams

[May 9, 1764]

Weymouth May th 9 1764

Welcome, Welcome thrice welcome is Lysander[1] to Braintree, but ten times more so would he be at Weymouth, whither you are affraid to come.—Once it was not so. May not I come and see you, at least look thro a window at you? Should you not be glad to see your Diana?[2] I flatter myself you would.

Your Brother brought your Letter, tho he did not let me see him, deliverd it the Doctor from whom received it safe. I thank you for your Catalogue, but must confess I was so hardned as to read over most of my Faults with as much pleasure, as an other person would have read their perfections. And Lysander must excuse me if I still persist in some of them, at least till I am convinced that an alteration would contribute to his happiness. Especially may I avoid that Freedom of Behaviour which according to the plan given, consists in Voilations[3] of Decency, and which would render me unfit to Herd even with the Brutes. And permit me to tell you Sir, nor disdain to be a learner, that there is such a thing as Modesty without either Hypocricy or Formality.

As to a neglect of Singing, that I acknowledg to be a Fault which if posible shall not be complaind of a second time, nor should you have had occasion for it now, if I had not a voice harsh as the screech of a peacock.

The Capotal fault shall be rectified, tho not with any hopes of being lookd upon as a Beauty, to appear agreeable in the Eyes of Lysander, has been for Years past, and still is the height of my ambition.

The 5th fault, will endeavour to amend of it, but you know I think that a gentleman has no business to concern himself about the Leggs of a Lady, for my part I do not apprehend any bad effects from the practise, yet since you desire it, and that you may not for the future trouble Yourself so much about it, will reform.

The sixth and last can be cured only by a Dancing School.

But I must not write more. I borrow a hint from you, therefore will not add to my faults that of a tedious Letter—a fault I never yet had reason to complain of in you, for however long, they never were otherways than agreeable to your own

A Smith

1764/1963

[March 31, 1776]

Braintree March 31 1776

I wish you would ever write me a Letter half as long as I write you; and tell me if you may where your Fleet are gone? What sort of Defence Virginia can make against our common Enemy? Whether it is so situated as to make an able Defence?

---

[1] Male character in Shakespeare's *A Midsummer Night's Dream* (1595–1596). Lysander, in love with Hermia, plans their elopement to escape her father's decree that she follow his will or enter a nunnery.

[2] Virgin Roman goddess of the forest, the hunt, and the moon.

[3] There are numerous irregularities in spellings in Abigail Adams's letters, as here of *violations*. This number diminishes in later letters.

Are not the Gentery Lords and the common people vassals, are they not like the uncivilized Natives Brittain represents us to be? I hope their Riffel Men who have shewen themselves very savage and even Blood thirsty; are not a specimen of the Generality of the people.

I am willing to allow the Colony great merit for having produced a Washington but they have been shamefully duped by a Dunmore.[4]

I have sometimes been ready to think that the passion for Liberty cannot be Eaqually Strong in the Breasts of those who have been accustomed to deprive their fellow Creatures of theirs. Of this I am certain that it is not founded upon that generous and christian principal of doing to others as we would that others should do unto us.

Do not you want to see Boston; I am fearfull of the small pox, or I should have been in before this time. I got Mr. Crane[5] to go to our House and see what state it was in. I find it has been occupied by one of the Doctors of a Regiment, very dirty, but no other damage has been done to it. The few things which were left in it are all gone. Cranch[6] has the key which he never deliverd up. I have wrote to him for it and am determined to get it cleand as soon as possible and shut it up. I look upon it a new acquisition of property, a property which one month ago I did not value at a single Shilling, and could with pleasure have seen it in flames.

The Town in General is left in a better state than we expected, more oweing to a percipitate flight than any Regard to the inhabitants, tho some individuals discovered a sense of honour and justice and have left the rent of the Houses in which they were, for the owners and the furniture unhurt, or if damaged sufficent to make it good.

Others have committed abominable Ravages. The Mansion House of your President is safe and the furniture unhurt whilst both the House and Furniture of the Solisiter General have fallen a prey to their own merciless party. Surely the very Fiends feel a Reverential awe for Virtue and patriotism, whilst they Detest the paricide and traitor.

I feel very differently at the approach of spring to what I did a month ago. We knew not then whether we could plant or sow with safety, whether when we had toild we could reap the fruits of our own industery, whether we could rest in our own Cottages, or whether we should not be driven from the sea coasts to seek shelter in the wilderness, but now we feel as if we might sit under our own vine and eat the good of the land.

I feel a gaieti de Coar[7] to which before I was a stranger. I think the Sun looks brighter, the Birds sing more melodiously, and Nature puts on a more chearfull countanance. We feel a temporary peace, and the poor fugitives are returning to their deserted habitations.

Tho we felicitate ourselves, we sympathize with those who are trembling least the Lot of Boston should be theirs. But they cannot be in similar circumstances unless pusilanimity and cowardise should take possession of them. They have time and warning given them to see the Evil and shun it.—I long to hear that you have declared

---

[4] John, earl of Dunmore and colonial governor of Virginia, who favored the Loyalist cause. He later seized the supplies of the colonial arsenal at Williamsburg.

[5] Abigail Adams's agent in Boston.

[6] Most likely a slip of the pen that should read "Crane." Richard Cranch was Abigail's brother-in-law.

[7] *Gaieté du coeur*, French for "lightheartedness."

an independancy—and by the way in the new Code of Laws[8] which I suppose it will be necessary for you to make I desire you would Remember the Ladies, and be more generous and favourable to them than your ancestors. Do not put such unlimited power into the hands of the Husbands. Remember all Men would be tyrants if they could. If perticuliar care and attention is not paid to the Laidies we are determined to foment a Rebelion, and will not hold ourselves bound by any Laws in which we have no voice, or Representation.

That your Sex are Naturally Tyrannical is a Truth so thoroughly established as to admit of no dispute, but such of you as wish to be happy willingly give up the harsh title of Master for the more tender and endearing one of Friend. Why then, not put it out of the power of the vicious and the Lawless to use us with cruelty and indignity with impunity. Men of Sense in all Ages abhor those customs which treat us only as the vassals of your Sex. Regard us then as Beings placed by providence under your protection and in immitation of the Supreem Being make use of that power only for our happiness.

1776/1876

[July 13, 1776]

Boston July 13 1776

I must begin with apoligising to you for not writing since the 17 of June. I have really had so many cares upon my Hands and Mind, with a bad inflamation in my Eyes that I have not been able to write. I now date from Boston where I yesterday arrived and was with all 4 of our Little ones innoculated for the small pox. My unkle and Aunt[9] were so kind as to send me an invitation with my family. Mr. Cranch[10] and wife and family; My Sister Betsy and her Little Neice,[11] Cotton Tufts and Mr. Thaxter,[12] a maid who has had the Distemper and my old Nurse compose our family. A Boy too I should have added. 17 in all. My unkles maid with his Little daughter and a Negro Man are here. We had our Bedding &c. to bring. A Cow we have driven down from B[raintre]e and some Hay I have had put into the Stable, wood &c. and we have really commenced housekeepers here. The House was furnished with almost every article (except Beds) which we have free use of, and think ourselves much obliged by the fine accommodations and kind offer of our Friends. All our necessary Stores we purchase jointly. Our Little ones stood the opperation Manfully. Dr. Bulfinch is our Physician. Such a Spirit of innoculation never before took place; the Town and every House in it, are as full as they can hold. I believe there are not less than 30 persons from Braintree. Mrs. Quincy, Mrs. Lincoln, Miss Betsy and Nancy[13] are our near

[8] Abigail Adams's eager anticipation of what would become the Declaration of Independence and the Constitution.

[9] Cotton Tufts, Sr. (1732–1815), Abigail's maternal uncle, and his wife Lucy Quincy (d. 1785).

[10] Richard Cranch (1726–1811), married to Abigail's sister Mary (1741–1811). (They had three children.)

[11] Elizabeth Smith and presumably Louisa Catherine Smith, daughter of Abigail's only brother, William.

[12] Cotton Tufts, Jr. (1757–1833), Abigail's first cousin, and John Thaxter, Jr. (1755–1791), a clerk to John Adams and the latter's private secretary during his residence in Europe.

[13] Mrs. Quincy: Ann Marsh, the third wife of Colonel Josiah Quincy; Mrs. Lincoln: Hannah Quincy Lincoln, married daughter of the Quincys; Miss Betsy and Nancy: Elizabeth and Ann, daughters of the Quincys.

Neighbours. God Grant that we may all go comfortably thro the Distemper, the phisick part is bad enough I know. I knew your mind so perfectly upon the subject that I thought nothing, but our recovery would give you eaquel pleasure, and as to safety there was none. The Soldiers innoculated privately, so did many of the inhabitants and the paper curency spread it everywhere. I immediately determined to set myself about it, and get ready with my children. I wish it was so you could have been with us, but I submit.

I received some Letters from you last Saturday Night 26 of June. You mention a Letter of the 16 which I have never received, and I suppose must relate something to private affairs which I wrote about in May and sent by Harry.

As to News we have taken several fine prizes since I wrote you as you will see by the news papers. The present Report is of Lord Hows[14] comeing with unlimited powers. However suppose it is so, I believe he little thinks of treating with us as independant States. How can any person yet dreem of a settlement, accommodations &c. They have neither the spirit nor feeling of Men, yet I see some who never were call'd Tories, gratified with the Idea of Lord Hows being upon his passage with such powers.

1776/1876

[August 14, 1776]

August 14 1776

I wrote you to day by Mr. Smith[15] but as I suppose this will reach you sooner, I omitted mentioning any thing of my family in it.

Nabby[16] has enough of the small Pox for all the family beside. She is pretty well coverd, not a spot but what is so soar that she can neither walk sit stand or lay with any comfort. She is as patient as one can expect, but they are a very soar sort. If it was a disorder to which we could be subject more than once I would go as far as it was possible to avoid it. She is sweld a good deal. You will receive a perticuliar account before this reaches you of the uncommon manner in which the small Pox acts, it bafels the skill of the most Experience'd here. Billy Cranch[17] is now out with about 40, and so well as not to be detaind at Home an hour for it. Charlly[18] remains in the same state he did.

Your Letter of August 3 came by this days Post. I find it very conveniant to be so handy. I can receive a Letter at Night, sit down and reply to it, and send it of in the morning.

You remark upon the deficiency of Education in your Countrymen. It never I believe was in a worse state, at least for many years. The Colledge is not in the state one could wish, the Schollars complain that their professer in Philosophy is taken of by publick Business to their great detriment. In this Town I never saw so great a neglect of Education. The poorer sort of children are wholly neglected, and left to range the Streets without Schools, without Buisness, given up to all Evil. The Town is not as formerly divided into Wards. There is either too much Buisness left upon

[14] Admiral Richard Howe, sent on a conciliatory commission by Britain to the committee from the Continental Congress.

[15] Mr. B. Smith, a visitor from South Carolina.

[16] The Adamses' daughter Abigail.

[17] William Cranch, son of Richard and Mary Cranch.

[18] The Adamses' son Charles.

the hands of a few, or too little care to do it. We daily see the Necessity of a regular Government.—You speak of our Worthy Brother.[19] I often lament it that a Man so peculiarly formed for the Education of youth, and so well qualified as he is in many Branches of Litrature, excelling in Philosiphy and the Mathematicks, should not be imployd in some publick Station. I know not the person who would make half so good a Successor to Dr. Winthrope.[20] He has a peculiar easy manner of communicating his Ideas to Youth, and the Goodness of his Heart, and the purity of his morrals without an affected austerity must have a happy Effect upon the minds of Pupils.

If you complain of neglect of Education in sons, What shall I say with regard to daughters, who every day experience the want of it. With regard to the Education of my own children, I find myself soon out of my depth, and destitute and deficient in every part of Education.

I most sincerely wish that some more liberal plan might be laid and executed for the Benefit of the rising Generation, and that our new constitution may be distinguished for Learning and Virtue. If we mean to have Heroes, Statesmen and Philosophers, we should have learned women. The world perhaps would laugh at me, and accuse me of vanity, But you I know have a mind too enlarged and liberal to disregard the Sentiment. If much depends as is allowed upon the early Education of youth and the first principals which are instilld take the deepest root, great benifit must arise from litirary accomplishments in women.

Excuse me my pen has run away with me. I have no thoughts of comeing to P[hiladelphi]a. The length of time I have [and] shall be detain here would have prevented me, even if you had no thoughts of returning till December, but I live in daily Expectation of seeing you here. Your Health I think requires your immediate return. I expected Mr. Gerry[21] would have set off before now, but he finds it perhaps very hard to leave his Mistress[22]—I won't say harder than some do to leave their wives. Mr. Gerry stood very high in my Esteem—what is meat for one is not for an other —no accounting for fancy. She is a queer dame and leads people wild dances.

But hush—Post, dont betray your trust and loose my Letter.

Nabby is poorly this morning. The pock are near the turn, 6 or 7 hundred boils are no agreable feeling. You and I know not what a feeling it is. Miss Katy can tell. I had but 3 they were very clever and fill'd nicely. The Town instead of being clear of this distemper are now in the height of it, hundreds having it in the natural way through the deceitfulness of innoculation.

Adieu ever yours. Breakfast waits.

Portia[23]

1776/1876

[19] Probably Richard Cranch, who became a judge of the Court of the Common Pleas in Massachusetts.

[20] Dr. John Winthrope (d. 1779), Hollis Professor of Mathematics and Natural Philosophy at Harvard College.

[21] Elbridge Gerry (1744–1814), a signer of the Declaration of Independence, delegate to the Continental Congress in Philadelphia (1776–1781), and later vice-president of the United States (1813–1814).

[22] Catherine Hunt, whom Gerry did not marry because she had not been educated in reading or writing and subsequently could not respond to his letters.

[23] A signature Abigail adopted after marriage. The character Portia, in Shakespeare's *The Merchant of Venice* (1596–1597), aids her lover's best friend by her clever negotiations.

[April 10, 1782]

April 10th. 1782

My dearest Friend

How great was my joy to see the well known Signature of my Friend after a Melancholy Solicitude of many months in which my hopes and fears alternately preponderated.

It was January when Charles arrived. By him I expected Letters, but found not a line; instead of which the heavy tidings of your illness reachd me. I then found my Friends had been no strangers of what they carefully conceald from me. Your Letter to Charles dated in November was the only consolation I had; by that I found that the most dangerous period of your illness was pass'd, and that you considerd yourself as recovering tho feeble. My anxiety and apprehensions from that day untill your Letters arrived, which was near 3 months, conspired to render me unhappy. Capt. Trowbridge in the Fire Brand[24] arrived with your favours of October and December and in some measure dispeld the Gloom which hung heavy at my heart. How did it leap for joy to find I was not the misirable Being I sometimes feared I was. I felt that Gratitude to Heaven which great deliverences both demand and inspire. I will not distrust the providential Care of the supreem disposer of events, from whose Hand I have so frequently received distinguished favours. Such I call the preservation of my dear Friend and children from the uncertain Element upon which they have frequently embarked; their preservation from the hands of their enimies I have reason to consider in the same view, especially when I reflect upon the cruel and inhumane treatment experienced by a Gentleman of Mr. Laurences[25] age and respectable character.

The restoration of my dearest Friend from so dangerous a Sickness, demands all my gratitude, whilst I fail not to supplicate Heaven for the continuance of a Life upon which my temporal happiness rests, and deprived of which my own existance would become a burden. Often has the Question which you say staggerd your philosophy occured to me, nor have I felt so misirable upon account of my own personal Situation, when I considerd that according to the common course of Nature, more than half my days were allready passt, as for those in whom our days are renewed. Their hopes and prospects would vanish, their best prospects, those of Education, would be greatly diminished—but I will not anticipate those miseries which I would shun. Hope is my best Friend and kindest comforter; she assures me that the pure unabated affection, which neither time or absence can allay or abate, shall e'er long be crowned with the completion of its fondest wishes, in the safe return of the beloved object; the age of romance has long ago past, but the affection of almost Infant years has matured and strengthend untill it has become a vital principle, nor has the world any thing to bestow which could in the smallest degree compensate for the loss. Desire and Sorrow were denounced upon our Sex; as a punishment for the transgression of Eve. I have sometimes thought that we are formed to experience more exquisite Sensations than is the Lot of your Sex. More tender and susceptable by Nature of those impression[s] which create happiness or misiry, we Suffer and enjoy in a higher degree. I never wonderd at the philosopher who thanked the Gods that he was created a Man rather than a Woman.

[24] Captain Trowbridge commanded the merchant ship *Firebrand*.   [25] John Laurance (1750–1810), a judge who later served in the U. S. Senate (1797–1800).

I cannot say, but that I was dissapointed when I found that your return to your native land was a still distant Idea. I think your Situation cannot be so dissagreable as I feared it was, yet that dreadfull climate is my terror.—You mortify me indeed when you talk of sending Charles to Colledge, who it is not probable will be fit under three or four years. Surely my dear Friend fleeting as time is I cannot reconcile myself to the Idea of living in this cruel State of Seperation for [4?] or even three years to come. Eight years have already past, since you could call yourself an Inhabitant of this State. I shall assume the Signature of Penelope,[26] for my dear Ulysses[27] has already been a wanderer from me near half the term of years that, that Hero was encountering Neptune, Calipso, the Circes and Syrens.[28] In the poetical Language of Penelope I shall address you

"Oh! haste to me! A Little longer Stay
Will ev'ry grace, each fancy'd charm decay:
Increasing cares, and times resistless rage
Will waste my bloom, and wither it to age."[29]

You will ask me I suppose what is become of my patriotick virtue? It is that which most ardently calls for your return. I greatly fear that the climate in which you now reside will prove fatal to your Life, whilst your Life and usefullness might be many years of Service to your Country in a more Healthy climate. If the Essentials of her political system are safe, as I would fain hope they are, yet the impositions and injuries, to which she is hourly liable, and daily suffering, call for the exertions of her wisest and ablest citizens. You know by many years experience what it is to struggle with difficulties—with wickedness in high places—from thence you are led to covet a private Station as the post of Honour, but should such an Idea generally prevail, who would be left to stem the torrent?

Should we at this day possess those invaluable Blessings transmitted us by our venerable Ancestors, if they had not inforced by their example, what they taught by their precepts?

"While pride, oppression and injustice reign
the World will still demand her Catos[30] presence."[31]

Why should I indulge an Idea, that whilst the active powers of my Friend remain, they will not be devoted to the Service of his country?

Can I believe that the Man who fears neither poverty or dangers, who sees not

---

[26] Devoted wife of Odysseus (Latin: "Ulysses") in Homer's *Odyssey* (sixth century B.C.). Penelope was a model of domestic fidelity who endured twenty years of anxiety and grief during her husband's absence.

[27] In the *Odyssey,* king of Ithaca and Greek leader in the Trojan War who journeyed for ten years after the war before returning home.

[28] Neptune: Roman god of the sea; Calipso: the divine nymph with whom Odysseus lived for seven years after his ship foundered and he

washed ashore on her island; Circe: a sorceress who changed Odysseus' men to swine but was forced by Odysseus to change them back; Syrens: Greek mythic female creatures who lured mariners onto the rocks around their island with their singing.

[29] Abigail Adams's own verse.

[30] Probably either Cato the Elder (234–149 B.C.) or Cato the Younger (95–46 B.C.), Roman statesman and philosopher, respectively.

[31] The source of these lines is unknown.

charms sufficient either in Riches, power or places to tempt him in the least to swerve from the purest Sentiments of Honour and Delicacy; will retire, unnoticed, Fameless to a Rustick cottage there by dint of Labour to earn his Bread. I need not much examination of my Heart to say I would not willing[ly] consent to it.

Have not Cincinnatus and Regulus[32] been handed down to posterity, with immortal honour?

Without fortune it is more than probable we shall end our days, but let the well earned Fame of having Sacrificed those prospects, from a principal of universal Benevolence and good will to Man, descend as an inheritance to our ofspring. The Luxery of Foreign Nations may possibly infect them but they have not before them an example of it, so far as respects their domestick life. They are not Bred up with an Idea of possessing Hereditary Riches or Grandeur. Retired from the Capital, they see little of the extravagance or dissipation, which prevails there, and at the close of day, in lieu of the Card table, some usefull Book employs their leisure hours. These habits early fixed, and daily inculcated, will I hope render them usefull and ornamental Members of Society.—But we cannot see into futurity.—With Regard to politicks, it is rather a dull season for them, we are recruiting for the Army.

The Enemy make sad Havock with our Navigation. Mr. Lovell[33] is appointed continential Receiver of taxes and is on his way to this State.

It is difficult to get Gentlemen of abilities and Integrity to serve in congress, few very few are willing to Sacrifice their Interest as others have done before them.

Your favour of december 18th came by way of Philadelphia, but all those Letters sent by Capt. Reeler[34] were lost, thrown over Board. Our Friends are well and desire to be rememberd to you. Charles will write if he is able to, before the vessel sails, but he is sick at present, threatned I fear with a fever. I received one Letter from my young Russian to whom I shall write—and 2 from Mr. Thaxter.[35] If the vessel gives me time I shall write. We wait impatiently for the result of your demand. These slow slugish wheels move not in unison with our feelings.

Adieu my dear Friend. How gladly would I visit you and partake of your Labours and cares, sooth you to rest, and alleviate your anxieties were it given me to visit you even by moon Light, as the faries are fabled to do.

I cheer my Heart with the distant prospect. All that I can hope for at present, is to hear of your welfare which of all things lies nearest the Heart of Your ever affectionate

Portia

1782/1973

---

[32] Cincinnatus was appointed Roman dictator in 458 B.C. and was dispatched to rescue Minucius from the seige of Aequu. He freed Minucius, resigned his dictatorship, and returned to his farm beyond the Tiber. Regulus was in command of Roman troops on an African expedition when he was defeated and captured in Carthage. He was sent in 250 B.C. to Rome on parole to arrange an exchange of prisoners;

he then voluntarily returned to Carthage, where he was purportedly tortured to death.
[33] James Lovell (1737–1814), a delegate from Massachusetts to the General Congress.
[34] The Adamses' friend and commander of a merchant ship.
[35] John Thaxter, Abigail Adams's cousin and tutor to their son John Quincy Adams.

Letter to John Quincy Adams

[January 19, 1780]

Janry. 19 1780

My dear Son[1]

I hope you have had no occasion either from Enemies or the Dangers of the Sea to repent your second voyage to France. If I had thought your reluctance arose from proper deliberation, or that you was capable of judgeing what was most for your own benifit, I should not have urged you to have accompanied your Father and Brother when you appeared so averse to the voyage.

You however readily submitted to my advice, and I hope will never have occasion yourself, nor give me reason to Lament it. Your knowledge of the Language must give you greater advantages now, than you could possibly have reaped whilst Ignorant of it, and as you increase in years you will find your understanding opening and daily improveing.

Some Author that I have met with compares a judicious traveller, to a river that increases its stream the farther it flows from its source, or to certain springs which running through rich veins of minerals improve their qualities as they pass along. It will be expected of you my son that as you are favourd with superior advantages under the instructive Eye of a tender parent, that your improvements should bear some proportion to your advantages. Nothing is wanting with you, but attention, dilligence and steady application, Nature has not been deficient.

These are times in which a Genious would wish to live. It is not in the still calm of life, or the repose of a pacific station, that great characters are formed. Would Cicero have shone so distinguished an orator, if he had not been roused, kindled and enflamed by the Tyranny of Catiline, Millo, Verres and Mark Anthony.[2] The Habits of a vigorous mind are formed in contending with difficulties. All History will convince you of this, and that wisdom and penetration are the fruits of experience, not the Lessons of retirement and leisure.

Great necessities call out great virtues. When a mind is raised, and animated by scenes that engage the Heart, then those qualities which would otherways lay dormant, wake into Life, and form the Character of the Hero and the Statesman.

War, Tyrrany and Desolation are the Scourges of the Almighty, and ought no doubt to be deprecated. Yet it is your Lot my Son to be an Eye witness of these Calimities in your own Native land, and at the same time to owe your existance among a people who have made a glorious defence of their invaded Liberties, and who, aided by a generous and powerfull Ally, with the blessing of heaven will transmit this inheritance to ages yet unborn.

---

[1] John Quincy Adams accompanied his father and brother Charles on John Adams's trip to negotiate peace with Great Britain.

[2] The influence of Cicero (106–43 B.C.), patriotic Roman orator, in Caesar's senate secured the prosecution of Catiline for conspiracy and of Verres for extortion. Cicero also publicly denounced Mark Antony because of the latter's ruthless competition for the Roman dictatorship; and when Antony gained control, he had Cicero executed. However, Cicero had applauded Milo (Millo), who murdered Claudius, a competitor for Caesar's throne; hence the mention of Milo here appears inappropriate.

Nor ought it to be one of the least of your excitements towards exerting every power and faculty of your mind, that you have a parent who has taken so large and active a share in this contest, and discharged the trust reposed in him with so much satisfaction as to be honourd with the important Embassy, which at present calls him abroad.

I cannot fulfill the whole of my duty towards you, if I close this Letter, without reminding you of a failing which calls for a strict attention and watchfull care to correct. You must do it for yourself. You must curb that impetuosity of temper, for which I have frequently chid you, but which properly directed may be productive of great good. I know you capable of these exertions, with pleasure I observed my advice was not lost upon you. If you indulge yourself in the practise of any foible or vice in youth, it will gain strength with your years and become your conquerer.

The strict and invoilable regard you have ever paid to truth, gives me pleasing hopes that you will not swerve from her dictates, but add justice, fortitude, and every Manly Virtue which can adorn a good citizen, do Honour to your Country, and render your parents supreemly happy, particuliarly your ever affectionate Mother,

AA

1840

Letters to Thomas Jefferson

[February 11, 1786]

London, Grosvenor Square, Feb. 11th, 1786.[1]

Col. Humphries[2] talks of leaving us on Monday. It is with regret, I assure you, Sir, that we part with him. His visit here has given us an opportunity of becoming more acquainted with his real worth and merit, and our friendship for him has risen in proportion to our intimacy. The two American Secretaries of Legation would do honor to their country placed in more distinguished stations. Yet these missions abroad, circumscribed as they are in point of expenses, place the ministers of the United States in the lowest point of view of any envoy from any other Court; and in Europe every being is estimated, and every country valued, in proportion to their show and splendor. In a private station I have not a wish for expensive living, but, whatever my fair countrywomen may think, and I hear they envy my situation, I will most joyfully exchange Europe for America, and my public for a private life. I am really surfeited with Europe, and most heartily long for the rural cottage, the purer and honester manners of my native land, where domestic happiness reigns unrivalled, and virtue and honor go hand in hand. I hope one season more will give us an

---

[1] Abigail Adams wrote this letter from Great Britain, where her husband was then serving as U.S. Ambassador.

[2] David Humphreys (1752–1818), a military aide to George Washington and secretary to the Commercial Commission.

opportunity of making our escape. At present we are in the situation of Sterne's starling.[3]

Congress have by the last dispatches informed this Court that they expect them to appoint a minister. It is said (not officially) that Mr. Temple[4] is coldly received, that no Englishman has visited him, and the Americans are not very social with him. But as Colonel Humphries will be able to give you every intelligence, there can be no occasion for my adding any thing further than to acquaint you that I have endeavored to execute your commission agreeably to your directions. Enclosed you will find the memorandum. I purchased a small trunk, which I think you will find useful to you to put the shirts in, as they will not be liable to get rubbed on the journey. If the balance should prove in my favor, I will request you to send me 4 ells of cambric at about 14 livres per ell or 15, a pair of black lace lappets[5]—these are what the ladies wear at court—and 12 ells of black lace at 6 or 7 livres per ell. Some gentleman coming this way will be so kind as to put them in his pocket, and Mrs. Barclay,[6] I dare say, will take the trouble of purchasing them for me; for troubling you with such trifling matters is a little like putting Hercules to the distaff.[7]

My love to Miss Jefferson,[8] and compliments to Mr. Short.[9] Mrs. Siddons[10] is acting again upon the stage, and I hope Colonel Humphries will prevail with you to cross the Channel to see her. Be assured, dear Sir, that nothing would give more pleasure to your friends here than a visit from you, and in that number I claim the honor of subscribing myself.

A. ADAMS

4 pair of shoes for Miss Adams, by the person who made Mrs. A.'s, 2 of satin and 2 of spring silk, without straps, and of the most fashionable colors.

ENCLOSURE

Memorandum of purchases made for TJ reading as follows:

To 2 peices of Irish linen at 4s. pr. yd.	8£	14s.	od.
To making 12 Shirts at 3s per Shirt	1	16	0
To buttons thread silk	0	3	0
To Washing	0	3	6
A Trunk	1	1	0
	11	17	6

The Louis I parted with at 20 shillings

1871

[3] The reference to a caged starling appears in A Sentimental Journey by Laurence Sterne (1713–1768).

[4] Sir John Temple (1730–1798), native of Massachusetts and surveyor general of customs under King George III.

[5] Ell: former English unit of cloth length, measuring 45 inches; cambric: fine white linen fabric; livre: former French unit of value, replaced by the franc in 1795; lappets: streamers on a woman's headdress, usually hanging down on either side of the face.

[6] Presumably the wife of Thomas Barclay of Philadelphia, consul in France.

[7] Hercules: the son of Zeus and Alcmene, and a hero of extraordinary strength; distaff: staff that holds unspun flax or wool from which thread is drawn. Here the sense is that Hercules would be attending to traditional women's work.

[8] Mary Jefferson (d. 1804), daughter of Thomas.

[9] Thomas Jefferson's secretary.

[10] Mrs. Sarah Kemble Siddons (1755–1831), renowned English actress.

[July 6, 1787]

London july 6, 1787

MY DEAR SIR

If I had thought you would so soon have sent for your dear little Girl, I should have been tempted to have kept her arrival here, from you a secret. I am really loth to part with her, and she last evening upon Petit's[11] arrival, was thrown into all her former distresses, and bursting into Tears, told me it would be as hard to leave me as it was her Aunt Epps.[12] She has been so often deceived that she will not quit me a moment least she should be carried away. Nor can I scarcely prevail upon her to see Petit. Tho she says she does not remember you, yet she has been taught to consider you with affection and fondness, and depended upon your comeing for her. She told me this morning, that as she had left all her Friends in virginia to come over the ocean to see you, she did think you would have taken the pains to have come here for her, and not have sent a man whom she cannot understand. I express her own words. I expostulated with her upon the long journey you had been, and the difficulty you had to come and upon the care kindness and attention of Petit, whom I so well knew. But she cannot yet hear me. She is a child of the quickest sensibility, and the maturest understanding, that I have ever met with for her years. She had been 5 weeks at sea, and with men only, so that on the first day of her arrival, she was as rough as a little sailor, and then she been decoyed from the ship, which made her very angry, and no one having any Authority over her; I was apprehensive I should meet with some trouble. But where there are such materials to work upon as I have found in her, there is no danger. She listend to my admonitions, and attended to my advice and in two days, was restored to the amiable lovely Child which her Aunt had formed her. In short she is the favorite of every creature in the House, and I cannot but feel Sir, how many pleasures you must lose by committing her to a convent. Yet situated as you are, you cannot keep her with you. The Girl she has with her, wants more care than the child, and is wholy incapable of looking properly after her, without some superiour to direct her.

As both Miss Jefferson and the maid had cloaths only proper for the sea, I have purchased and made up for them, such things as I should have done had they been my own, to the amount of Eleven or 12 Guineys.[13] The particulars I will send by Petit.

Captain Ramsey has said that he would accompany your daughter to Paris provided she would not go without him, but this would be putting you to an expence that may perhaps be avoided by Petits staying a few days longer. The greatest difficulty in familiarizing her to him, is on account of the language. I have not the Heart to force her into a Carriage against her will and send her from me almost in a Frenzy; as I know will be the case, unless I can reconcile her to the thoughts of going and I have given her my word that Petit shall stay until I can hear again from you. Books are her delight, and I have furnishd her out a little library, and she reads to me by the hour with great distinctness, and comments on what she reads with much propriety.

[11] Petit: manservant to Thomas Jefferson.
[12] Elizabeth Wayles Eppes, Jefferson's maternal aunt.

[13] I.e., guineas (or, approximately, pounds).

Mrs. Smith desires to be remembered to you, and the little Boy[14] his Grandmama thinks is as fine a Boy as any in the Kingdom. I am my dear sir with Sentiments of Esteem Your Friend and Humble Servant,

A ADAMS

1955

[May 20, 1804]

Quincy May 20th 1804

SIR

Had you been no other than the private inhabitant of Monticello, I should e'er this time have addrest you, with that sympathy, which a recent event has awakend in my Bosom. But reasons of various kinds withheld my pen, untill the powerfull feelings of my heart, have burst through the restraint, and called upon me to shed the tear of sorrow over the departed remains, of your beloved and deserving daughter,[15] an event which I most sincerely mourn.

The attachment which I formed for her, when you committed her to my care: upon her arrival in a foreign Land: has remained with me to this hour, and the recent account of her death, which I read in a late paper, brought fresh to my remembrance the strong sensibility she discoverd, tho but a child of nine years of age at having been seperated from her Friends, and country, and brought, as she expressed it, "to a strange land amongst strangers." The tender scene of her seperation from me, rose to my recollection, when she clung around my neck and wet my Bosom with her tears, saying, "O! now I have learnt to Love you, why will they tear me from you"[16]

It has been some time since that I conceived of any event in this Life, which could call forth, feelings of mutual sympathy. But I know how closely entwined around a parents heart, are those chords which bind the filial to the parental Bosom, and when snaped assunder, how agonizing the pangs of separation.[17]

I have tasted the bitter cup, and bow with reverence, and humility before the great dispenser of it, without whose permission, and over ruling providence, not a sparrow falls to the ground. That you may derive comfort and consolation in this day of your sorrow and affliction, from that only source calculated to heal the wounded heart— a firm belief in the Being: perfections and attributes of God, is the sincere and ardent wish of her, who once took pleasure in subscribing Herself your Friend

ABIGAIL ADAMS

1871

---

[14] Mrs. Smith: Abigail Adams Smith (Mrs. William Stephen Smith) (1765–1813), Abigail Adams's daughter; the little boy: William Steuben Smith (b. 1787), Abigail Adams's grandson.
[15] Mary Jefferson Eppes (Mrs. John Wayles Eppes), who died April 17, 1804.

[16] See Abigail Adams's letter to Jefferson dated July 6, 1787.
[17] Charles Adams, Abigail's son, had died November 30, 1800.

Thomas Paine
1737–1809

Thomas Paine sailed to Philadelphia on the eve of the American Revolution, buoyed by a letter of introduction from Benjamin Franklin extolling his ingenuity and recommending his employment as "a clerk, or as assistant tutor in a school, or assistant surveyor." At the age of thirty-seven, Paine was determined to reverse his misfortune as a member of the English commercial class.

The son of a Thetford corsetmaker, Paine had twice fled the Quaker environment of his youth before settling in London, resuming his father's trade, and filling himself with all the science and political philosophy his considerable intellectual curiosity could gather. In 1760 Paine experienced the first in a series of adversities: the death of his wife in childbirth during the first year of their marriage. He was later fired twice from his job collecting excise taxes, worked briefly—and unhappily—as a teacher in Kensington, married someone with whom he apparently never lived, and took over her father's failing business. Before long, Paine was reduced to posting the following announcement in the local British newspaper:

> To be sold by auction, on Thursday the 14th of April, and following day, all the household furniture, stock in trade and other effects of Thomas Pain, grocer and tobacconist, near the West Gate in Lewes: Also a horse tobacco snuff mill, with all the utensils for cutting tobacco and grinding snuff; and two unopened crates of cream colored stoneware.

Such indignities would pursue Thomas Paine all his life. His own repeated misfortunes make more appreciable his fundamental commitment "to meliorate the situation of mankind."

Within six months of his arrival in America, Paine could proudly report to Franklin that, despite never having "published a syllable" in England, his numerous topical essays on slavery, unhappy marriages, dueling, inventions, and the rights of the "Female Sex" had helped nearly triple the circulation of the *Pennsylvania Magazine, or American Museum,* the journal he edited and gradually converted into an important popular advocate of independence. He had entered a new world of political turmoil, yet the populace's attachment to Britain was, as he noted, "obstinate." Like the majority of Americans, Paine regarded the dispute with England "as a kind of law suit, in which I supposed, the parties would find a way either to decide or settle it. I had no thoughts of independence or arms." But these sentiments shifted radically with the outbreak of hostilities at Lexington and Concord:

> The world could not then have persuaded me that I should be either a soldier or an author. If I had any talents for either, they were buried in me, and might ever have continued so, had not the necessity of the times dragged and driven them into action. I had formed my plan of life, and conceiving myself happy,

wished everybody else so. But when the country into which I had just set foot, was set on fire about my ears, it was time to stir. Those who had been long settled had something to defend; those who had just come had something to pursue; and the call was equal and universal.

On January 10, 1776, at the encouragement of Dr. Benjamin Rush, Paine published *Common Sense*. Within three months, the pamphlet had sold more than one hundred thousand copies, an extraordinary number in an age when most works were published by subscription, with sales averaging well below one thousand. Paine drew on the conversational idioms of taverns, coffeehouses, and street-corner oratory to create an incisive commentary on the source and function of government. His bold and simple argument rallied a scattered citizenry to the cause of freedom and exerted considerable influence on the new nation's emerging political philosophy.

Paine's conviction that "those who expect to reap the blessings of freedom must . . . undergo the fatigue of supporting it" led him to enlist in the Revolutionary forces, serving as aide-de-camp to General Nathanael Greene. Witnessing the loss of New York and joining the retreat to Newark, Paine wrote the first of the *American Crisis* letter-pamphlets ("These are the times that try men's souls"), a text that George Washington ordered read to all the troops. Over the next seven years, Paine published thirteen essays in the series, along with three supplementary pieces. Each helped bolster the sagging spirits of the ill-fitted troops and firm the resolve of an occasionally diffident population.

After a brief stint in western Pennsylvania soliciting the support of the Indians in the Revolutionary cause, Paine was elected secretary of the Congressional Committee on Foreign Affairs in April 1777. He held this post until disclosing secret information he knew would save Congress the expense of profiteering loans from France. Once again beset by dwindling finances, Paine drifted in and out of various jobs and causes. He supported Robert Morris's efforts to start what is now the Bank of America; he traveled to France to secure additional relief for the Continental Army; he drafted the first legislative act of emancipation while serving as clerk of the Pennsylvania Assembly. In 1783 he moved to Bordentown, New Jersey, and devoted himself to invention. He produced, among other items, a smokeless candle and developed a model for an iron bridge without piers. But in 1787, when he could not muster enough capital to finance his projects, he once again left for France.

Paine traveled frequently to England over the next few years and oversaw the construction of the first bridge built under the patent the British government had awarded him. He visited Paris in 1790 to observe the French Revolution and quickly became enmeshed in the political debate it inspired. In 1791 he drafted the first part of *The Rights of Man* as a defense of the French cause in response to Edmund Burke's *Reflections on the Late Revolution in France*. Paine defended what he called the "natural rights" of national independence, free discussion, personal freedom, and franchise. He also reaffirmed the belief Roger Williams had posited nearly one hundred years earlier—that these rights must be confirmed by each generation. In Paine's view, "every age and generation must be free to act for itself *in all cases* as the ages and generations which preceded it. The vanity and presumption of governing beyond the grave is the most ridiculous and insolent of all tyrannies." Charged with sedition in England, Paine fled to France in 1792, where he was made an honorary citizen, represented Calais at the French Convention, and helped draft that nation's constitution. But his opposition to the execution of Louis XVI landed him in prison for ten months. Before being led away, Paine gave to Joel Barlow, the American poet and journalist, the first part of *The Age of Reason,* a Deist tract that attacked Christianity and praised the virtues of both an impersonal God and the common people.

Paine was released from prison through the efforts of James Monroe, the American ambassador, in whose home Paine lived for the next eighteen months. In ill health and bitter about his neglect while in prison, Paine wrote the second part of *The Age of Reason,* published numerous essays denouncing the Federalists in America, and formulated "agrarian justice," a radical proposal for the democratization of wealth. Banished from England, imprisoned in France, and branded an "infidel" in America, Paine could take some solace in an earlier declaration:

> I speak an open and disinterested language, dictated by no passion but that of humanity. . . . Independence is my happiness, and I view things as they are, without regard to place or purpose; my country is the world, and my religion is to do good.

His altruistic sense of the world included humanitarian views of capital punishment, labor reform, and pensions. His vision culminated in the prospect of a league of nations to foster disarmament.

Thomas Paine returned to the United States in 1802 and spent his last seven years adjusting to new political and social circumstances. Insulted and harassed because of his religious writings, Paine suffered one final round of ignominy: He was not allowed to vote; he was humiliated on his deathbed by the local clergy and barred from burial in a Quaker cemetery. Ten years after his death, Paine's body was exhumed and returned to England to be displayed as a symbol of social reform. His bones, which eventually disappeared, were reported to have been auctioned off as a curiosity.

Paine's criticism of the Bible (Theodore Roosevelt called him a "filthy little atheist") long distracted readers from recognizing Paine's importance as a writer. His humanitarian impulses shaped much of the new nation's thinking about tyranny, justice, equality, and the natural rights of the individual. And his determination to offer a willing audience a plain, simple, vigorous, and forthright version of eighteenth-century liberal thought made Paine one of the most persuasive writers in America's struggle for independence.

Further Reading:
M. D. Conway, *The Life of Thomas Paine,* 2 vols., 1892.
J. Dos Passos, *The Living Thoughts of Thomas Paine,* 1940.
L. Gurko, *Tom Paine, Freedom's Apostle,* 1957.
A. O. Aldridge, *Man of Reason: The Life of Thomas Paine,* 1959.
D. Hawke, *Paine,* 1974.

Text:
The Writings of Thomas Paine, ed. M. D. Conway, 4 vols., 1894–1896.

An Occasional Letter on the Female Sex

> O Woman! lovely Woman!
> Nature made thee to temper man,
> We had been Brutes without you.
> Otway

If we take a survey of ages and of countries, we shall find the women, almost—without exception—at all times and in all places, adored and oppressed. Man, who has never neglected an opportunity of exerting his power, in paying homage to their beauty, has always availed himself of their weakness. He has been at once their tyrant and their slave.

Nature herself, in forming beings so susceptible and tender, appears to have been more attentive to their charms than to their happiness. Continually surrounded with griefs and fears, the women more than share all our miseries, and are besides subjected to ills which are peculiarly their own. They cannot be the means of life without exposing themselves to the loss of it; every revolution which they undergo, alters their health, and threatens their existence. Cruel distempers attack their beauty—and the hour, which confirms their release from those, is perhaps the most melancholy of their lives. It robs them of the most essential characteristic of their sex. They can then only hope for protection from the humiliating claims of pity, or the feeble voice of gratitude.

Society, instead of alleviating their condition, is to them the source of new miseries. More than one half of the globe is covered with savages; and among all these people women are completely wretched. Man, in a state of barbarity, equally cruel and indolent, active by necessity, but naturally inclined to repose, is acquainted with little more than the physical effects of love; and, having none of those moral ideas which only can soften the empire of force, he is led to consider it as his supreme law, subjecting to his despotism those whom reason had made his equal, but whose imbecility betrayed them to his strength. "Nothing" (says Professor Miller, speaking of the women of barbarous nations) "can exceed the dependence and subjection in which they are kept, or the toil and drudgery which they are obliged to undergo. The husband, when he is not engaged in some warlike exercise, indulges himself in idleness, and devolves upon his wife the whole burden of his domestic affairs. He disdains to assist her in any of those servile employments. She sleeps in a different bed, and is seldom permitted to have any conversation or correspondence with him."

The women among the Indians of America are what the Helots[1] were among the Spartans, a vanquished people, obliged to toil for their conquerors. Hence on the banks of the Oroonoko,[2] we have seen mothers slaying their daughters out of compassion, and smothering them in the hour of their birth. They consider this barbarous pity as a virtue.

---

[1] Class of serfs in ancient Sparta.   [2] Orinoco, a river in southeastern Venezuela.

"The men (says Commodore Byron, in his account of the inhabitants of South-America) exercise a most despotic authority over their wives, whom they consider in the same view they do any other part of their property, and dispose of them accordingly: Even their common treatment of them is cruel; for though the toil and hazard of procuring food lies entirely on the women, yet they are not suffered to touch any part of it till the husband is satisfied; and then he assigns them their portion, which is generally very scanty, and such as he has not a stomach for himself."

Among the nations of the East we find another kind of despotism and dominion prevail—the Seraglio,[3] and the domestic servitude of woman, authorised by the manners and established by the laws. In Turkey, in Persia, in India, in Japan, and over the vast empire of China, one half of the human species is oppressed by the other.

The excess of oppression in those countries springs from the excess of love.

All Asia is covered with prisons, where beauty in bondage waits the caprices of a master. The multitude of women there assembled have no will, no inclinations but his: Their triumphs are only for a moment; and their rivalry, their hate, and their animosities, continue till death. There the lovely sex are obliged to repay even their servitude with the most tender affections; or, what is still more mortifying, with the counterfeit of an affection, which they do not feel: There the most gloomy tyranny has subjected them to creatures, who, being of neither sex, are a dishonour to both: There, in short, their education tends only to debase them; their virtues are forced; their very pleasures are involuntary and joyless; and after an existence of a few years —till the bloom of youth is over—their period of neglect commences, which is long and dreadful. In the temperate latitude where the climates, giving less ardour to passion, leave more confidence in virtue, the women have not been deprived of their liberty, but a severe legislation has, at all times, kept them in a state of dependence. One while, they were confined to their own apartments, and debarred at once from business and amusement; at other times, a tedious guardianship defrauded their hearts, and insulted their understandings. Affronted in one country by polygamy, which gives them their rivals for their inseparable companions; inslaved in another by indissoluble ties, which often join the gentle to the rude, and sensibility to brutality: Even in countries where they may be esteemed most happy, constrained in their desires in the disposal of their goods, robbed of freedom of will by the laws, the slaves of opinion, which rules them with absolute sway, and construes the slightest appearances into guilt; surrounded on all sides by judges, who are at once tyrants and their seducers, and who, after having prepared their faults, punish every lapse with dishonour—nay, usurp the right of degrading them on suspicion! Who does not feel for the tender sex? Yet such, I am sorry to say, is the lot of woman over the whole earth. Man with regard to them, in all climates, and in all ages, has been either an insensible husband or an oppressor; but they have sometimes experienced the cold and deliberate oppression of pride, and sometimes the violent and terrible tyranny of jealousy. When they are not beloved they are nothing; and, when they are, they are tormented. They have almost equal cause to be afraid of indifference and of love. Over three quarters of the globe nature has placed them between contempt and misery.

[3] Large harem in a sultan's palace.

"The melting desires, or the fiery passions," says Professor Ferguson,[4] "which in one climate take place between the sexes, are, in another, changed into a sober consideration, or a patience of mutual disgust. This change is remarked in crossing the Mediterranean, in following the course of the Mississippi, in ascending the mountains of Caucasus, and in passing from the Alps and the Pyrenees to the shores of the Baltic.

"The burning ardours and torturing jealousies of the Seraglio and Harem, which have reigned so long in Asia and Africa, and which, in the southern parts of Europe, have scarcely given way to the differences of religion and civil establishments, are found, however, with an abatement of heat in the climate, to be more easily changed, in one latitude, into a temporary passion, which engrosses the mind without infeebling it, and which excites to romantic atchievments. By a farther progress to the north it is changed into a spirit of gallantry, which employs the wit and fancy more than the heart, which prefers intrigue to enjoyment, and substitutes affection and vanity where sentiment and desire have failed. As it departs from the sun, the same passion is farther composed into a habit of domestic connection, or frozen into a state of insensibility, under which the sexes at freedom scarcely choose to unite their society."

Even among people where beauty received the highest homage, we find men who would deprive the sex of every kind of reputation: "The most virtuous woman," says a celebrated Greek, "is she who is least talked of." That morose man, while he imposes duties upon women, would deprive them of the sweets of public esteem, and in exacting virtues from them, would make it a crime to aspire at honour.

If a woman were to defend the cause of her sex, she might address him in the following manner:

"How great is your injustice? If we have an equal right with you to virtue, why should we not have an equal right to praise? The public esteem ought to wait upon merit. Our duties are different from yours, but they are not therefore less difficult to fulfil, or of less consequence to society: They are the fountains of your felicity, and the sweetness of life. We are wives and mothers. 'T is we who form the union and the cordiality of families: 'T is we who soften that savage rudeness which considers everything as due to force, and which would involve man with man in eternal war. We cultivate in you that humanity which makes you feel for the misfortunes of others, and our tears forewarn you of your own danger. Nay, you cannot be ignorant that we have need of courage not less than you: More feeble in ourselves, we have perhaps more trials to encounter. Nature assails us with sorrow, law and custom press us with constraint, and sensibility and virtue alarm us with their continual conflict. Sometimes also the name of citizen demands from us the tribute of fortitude. When you offer your blood to the State think that it is ours. In giving it our sons and our husbands we give more than ourselves. You can only die on the field of battle, but we have the misfortune to survive those whom we love most. Alas! while your ambitious vanity is unceasingly labouring to cover the earth with statutes, with monuments, and with inscriptions to eternize, if possible,

---

[4] Adam Ferguson, professor of moral philosophy at the University of Edinburgh and author of *Essay on the History of Civil Society* (1767) and *Institutes of Moral Philosophy* (1769).

your names, and give yourselves an existence, when this body is no more, why must we be condemned to live and to die unknown? Would that the grave and eternal forgetfulness should be our lot. Be not our tyrants in all: Permit our names to be sometimes pronounced beyond the narrow circle in which we live: Permit friendship, or at least love, to inscribe its emblems on the tomb where our ashes repose; and deny us not that public esteem which, after the esteem of one's self, is the sweetest reward of well doing."

All men, however, it must be owned, have not been equally unjust to their fair companions. In some countries public honours have been paid to women. Art has erected them monuments. Eloquence has celebrated their virtues, and History has collected whatever could adorn their character.

1775

from Common Sense[*]

Introduction

Perhaps the sentiments contained in the following pages, are not *yet* sufficiently fashionable to procure them general Favor; a long Habit of not thinking a Thing *wrong,* gives it a superficial appearance of being *right,* and raises at first a formidable outcry in defence of Custom. But the Tumult soon subsides. Time makes more Converts than Reason.

As a long and violent abuse of power is generally the means of calling the right of it in question, (and in matters too which might never have been thought of, had not the sufferers been aggravated into the inquiry,) and as the King of England hath undertaken in his *own right,* to support the Parliament in what he calls *Theirs,* and as the good People of this Country are grievously oppressed by the Combination, they have an undoubted privilege to enquire into the Pretensions of both, and equally to reject the Usurpation of *either.*

In the following Sheets, the Author hath studiously avoided every thing which is personal among ourselves. Compliments as well as censure to individuals make no part thereof. The wise and the worthy need not the triumph of a Pamphlet; and those whose sentiments are injudicious or unfriendly will cease of themselves, unless too much pains is bestowed upon their conversions.

The cause of America is in a great measure the cause of all mankind. Many circumstances have, and will arise, which are not local, but universal, and through which the principles of all lovers of mankind are affected, and in the event of which their affections are interested. The laying a country desolate with fire and sword, declaring war against the natural rights of all mankind, and extirpating the defenders

---

[*] The complete title is *Common Sense: Addressed to the Inhabitants of America on the Following Interesting Subjects: viz.: I. Of the origin and design of government in general; with concise remarks on the English constitution. II. of* monarchy and hereditary succession. III. Thoughts on the present state of American affairs. IV. Of the present ability of America; with some miscellaneous reflections.

thereof from the face of the earth, is the concern of every man to whom nature hath given the power of feeling; of which class, regardless of party censure, is

THE AUTHOR.

Thoughts on the Present State of American Affairs

In the following pages I offer nothing more than simple facts, plain arguments, and common sense: and have no other preliminaries to settle with the reader, than that he will divest himself of prejudice and prepossession, and suffer his reason and his feelings to determine for themselves: that he will put on, or rather that he will not put off, the true character of a man, and generously enlarge his views beyond the present day.

Volumes have been written on the subject of the struggle between England and America. Men of all ranks have embarked in the controversy, from different motives, and with various designs; but all have been ineffectual, and the period of debate is closed. Arms as the last resource decide the contest; the appeal was the choice of the King, and the Continent has accepted the challenge.

It hath been reported of the late Mr. Pelham[1] (who tho' an able minister was not without his faults) that on his being attacked in the House of Commons on the score that his measures were only of a temporary kind, replied, *"they will last my time."* Should a thought so fatal and unmanly possess the Colonies in the present contest, the name of ancestors will be remembered by future generations with detestation.

The Sun never shined on a cause of greater worth. 'Tis not the affair of a City, a County, a Province, or a Kingdom; but of a Continent—of at least one eighth part of the habitable Globe. 'Tis not the concern of a day, a year, or an age; posterity are virtually involved in the contest, and will be more or less affected even to the end of time, by the proceedings now. Now is the seed-time of Continental union, faith and honour. The least fracture now will be like a name engraved with the point of a pin on the tender rind of a young oak; the wound would enlarge with the tree, and posterity read it in full grown characters.

By referring the matter from argument to arms, a new æra for politics is struck —a new method of thinking hath arisen. All plans, proposals, &c. prior to the nineteenth of April, *i.e.* to the commencement of hostilities,[2] are like the almanacks of the last year; which tho' proper then, are superceded and useless now. Whatever was advanced by the advocates on either side of the question then, terminated in one and the same point, viz. a union with Great Britain; the only difference between the parties was the method of effecting it; the one proposing force, the other friendship; but it hath so far happened that the first hath failed, and the second hath withdrawn her influence.

As much hath been said of the advantages of reconciliation, which, like an agreeable dream, hath passed away and left us as we were, it is but right that we should examine the contrary side of the argument, and enquire into some of the many material injuries which these Colonies sustain, and always will sustain, by being connected with and

[1] British prime minister (1743–1754).
[2] At Lexington, Massachusetts, the first armed conflict of the American Revolution began as the "minutemen" defended their ammunition stores against the British on April 19, 1775.

dependent on Great-Britain. To examine that connection and dependence, on the principles of nature and common sense, to see what we have to trust to, if separated, and what we are to expect, if dependant.

I have heard it asserted by some, that as America has flourished under her former connection with Great-Britain, the same connection is necessary towards her future happiness, and will always have the same effect. Nothing can be more fallacious than this kind of argument. We may as well assert that because a child has thrived upon milk, that it is never to have meat, or that the first twenty years of our lives is to become a precedent for the next twenty. But even this is admitting more than is true; for I answer roundly, that America would have flourished as much, and probably much more, had no European power taken any notice of her. The commerce by which she hath enriched herself are the necessaries of life, and will always have a market while eating is the custom of Europe.

But she has protected us, say some. That she hath engrossed us is true, and defended the Continent at our expense as well as her own, is admitted; and she would have defended Turkey from the same motive, *viz.* for the sake of trade and dominion.

Alas! we have been long led away by ancient prejudices and made large sacrifices to superstition. We have boasted the protection of Great Britain, without considering, that her motive was *interest* not *attachment;* and that she did not protect us from *our enemies* on *our account;* but from *her enemies* on *her own account,* from those who had no quarrel with us on any *other account,* and who will always be our enemies on the *same account.* Let Britain waive her pretensions to the Continent, or the Continent throw off the dependance, and we should be at peace with France and Spain, were they at war with Britain. The miseries of Hanover[3] last war ought to warn us against connections.

It hath lately been asserted in parliament, that the Colonies have no relation to each other but through the Parent Country, *i.e.* that Pennsylvania and the Jerseys,[4] and so on for the rest, are sister Colonies by the way of England; this is certainly a very roundabout way of proving relationship, but it is the nearest and only true way of proving enmity (or enemyship, if I may so call it.) France and Spain never were, nor perhaps ever will be, our enemies as *Americans,* but as our being the *subjects of Great Britain.*

But Britain is the parent country, say some. Then the more shame upon her conduct. Even brutes do not devour their young, nor savages make war upon their families; Wherefore, the assertion, if true, turns to her reproach; but it happens not to be true, or only partly so, and the phrase *parent* or *mother country* hath been jesuitically adopted by the King and his parasites, with a low papistical design of gaining an unfair bias on the credulous weakness of our minds. Europe, and not England, is the parent country of America. This new World hath been the asylum for the persecuted lovers of civil and religious liberty from *every part* of Europe. Hither have they fled, not from the tender embraces of the mother, but from the cruelty of the monster; and it is so far true of England, that the same tyranny which drove the first emigrants from home, pursues their descendants still.

---

[3] Britain's King George III was a descendant of the Prussian House of Hanover; here Paine refers to the Seven Years' War (1756–1763), which originally engaged Prussia and Austria and expanded to include all major European powers. Although Britain was favored in the war settlement, American losses in the French and Indian campaigns were severe.

[4] At the time the colony was sectioned into East and West Jersey.

In this extensive quarter of the globe, we forget the narrow limits of three hundred and sixty miles (the extent of England) and carry our friendship on a larger scale; we claim brotherhood with every European Christian, and triumph in the generosity of the sentiment.

It is pleasant to observe by what regular gradations we surmount the force of local prejudices, as we enlarge our acquaintance with the World. A man born in any town in England divided into parishes, will naturally associate most with his fellow parishioners (because their interests in many cases will be common) and distinguish him by the name of *neighbour;* if he meet him but a few miles from home, he drops the narrow idea of a street, and salutes him by the name of *townsman;* if he travel out of the county and meet him in any other, he forgets the minor divisions of street and town, and calls him *countryman, i.e. countyman:* but if in their foreign excursions they should associate in France, or any other part of *Europe,* their local remembrance would be enlarged into that of *Englishmen.* And by a just parity of reasoning, all Europeans meeting in America, or any other quarter of the globe, are *countrymen;* for England, Holland, Germany, or Sweden, when compared with the whole, stand in the same places on the larger scale, which the divisions of street, town, and county do on the smaller ones; Distinctions too limited for Continental minds. Not one third of the inhabitants, even of this province[5] are of English descent. Wherefore, I reprobate the phrase of Parent or Mother Country applied to England only, as being false, selfish, narrow and ungenerous.

But, admitting that we were all of English descent, what does it amount to? Nothing. Britain, being now an open enemy, extinguishes every other name and title: and to say that reconciliation is our duty, is truly farcical. The first king of England, of the present line (William the Conqueror) was a Frenchman, and half the peers of England are descendants from the same country; wherefore, by the same method of reasoning, England ought to be governed by France.

Much hath been said of the united strength of Britain and the Colonies, that in conjunction they might bid defiance to the world: But this is mere presumption; the fate of war is uncertain, neither do the expressions mean any thing; for this continent would never suffer itself to be drained of inhabitants, to support the British arms in either Asia, Africa, or Europe.

Besides, what have we to do with setting the world at defiance? Our plan is commerce, and that, well attended to, will secure us the peace and friendship of all Europe; because it is the interest of all Europe to have America a free port. Her trade will always be a protection, and her barrenness of gold and silver secure her from invaders.

I challenge the warmest advocate for reconciliation to show a single advantage that this continent can reap by being connected with Great Britain. I repeat the challenge; not a single advantage is derived. Our corn will fetch its price in any market in Europe, and our imported goods must be paid for by them where we will.

But the injuries and disadvantages which we sustain by that connection, are without number; and our duty to mankind at large, as well as to ourselves, instruct us to renounce the alliance: because, any submission to, or dependance on, Great Britain, tends directly to involve this Continent in European wars and quarrels, and set us at variance with nations who would otherwise seek our friendship, and against whom

[5] Pennsylvania.

we have neither anger nor complaint. As Europe is our market for trade, we ought to form no partial connection with any part of it. It is the true interest of America to steer clear of European contentions, which she never can do, while, by her dependance on Britain, she is made the makeweight in the scale of British politics.

Europe is too thickly planted with Kingdoms to be long at peace, and whenever a war breaks out between England and any foreign power, the trade of America goes to ruin, *because of her connection with Britain.* The next war may not turn out like the last,[6] and should it not, the advocates for reconciliation now will be wishing for separation then, because neutrality in that case would be a safer convoy than a man of war. Everything that is right or reasonable pleads for separation. The blood of the slain, the weeping voice of nature cries, 'TIS TIME TO PART. Even the distance at which the Almighty hath placed England and America is a strong and natural proof that the authority of the one over the other, was never the design of Heaven. The time likewise at which the Continent was discovered, adds weight to the argument, and the manner in which it was peopled, encreases the force of it. The Reformation was preceded by the discovery of America: As if the Almighty graciously meant to open a sanctuary to the persecuted in future years, when home should afford neither friendship nor safety.

The authority of Great Britain over this continent, is a form of government, which sooner or later must have an end: And a serious mind can draw no true pleasure by looking forward, under the painful and positive conviction that what he calls "the present constitution" is merely temporary. As parents, we can have no joy, knowing that this government is not sufficiently lasting to ensure any thing which we may bequeath to posterity: And by a plain method of argument, as we are running the next generation into debt, we ought to do the work of it, otherwise we use them meanly and pitifully. In order to discover the line of our duty rightly, we should take our children in our hand, and fix our station a few years farther into life; that eminence will present a prospect which a few present fears and prejudices conceal from our sight.

Though I would carefully avoid giving unnecessary offence, yet I am inclined to believe, that all those who espouse the doctrine of reconciliation, may be included within the following descriptions.

Interested men, who are not to be trusted, weak men who *cannot* see, prejudiced men who will not see, and a certain set of moderate men who think better of the European world than it deserves; and this last class, by an ill-judged deliberation, will be the cause of more calamities to this Continent than all the other three.

It is the good fortune of many to live distant from the scene of present sorrow; the evil is not sufficiently brought to their doors to make them feel the precariousness with which all American property is possessed. But let our imaginations transport us a few moments to Boston; that seat of wretchedness will teach us wisdom, and instruct us for ever to renounce a power in whom we can have no trust.[7] The inhabitants of that unfortunate city who but a few months ago were in ease and affluence, have now no other alternative than to stay and starve, or turn out to beg. Endangered by the fire of their friends if they continue within the city, and plundered by the soldiery

---

[6] At the conclusion of the Seven Years' War, Britain was given all the French territory in North America through the Treaty of Paris (1763).

[7] Boston was blockaded for six months under British military occupation.

if they leave it, in their present situation they are prisoners without the hope of redemption, and in a general attack for their relief they would be exposed to the fury of both armies.

Men of passive tempers look somewhat lightly over the offences of Great Britain, and, still hoping for the best, are apt to call out, *Come, come, we shall be friends again for all this.* But examine the passions and feelings of mankind: bring the doctrine of reconciliation to the touchstone of nature, and then tell me whether you can hereafter love, honour, and faithfully serve the power that hath carried fire and sword into your land? If you cannot do all these, then are you only deceiving yourselves, and by your delay bringing ruin upon posterity. Your future connection with Britain, whom you can neither love nor honour, will be forced and unnatural, and being formed only on the plan of present convenience, will in a little time fall into a relapse more wretched than the first. But if you say, you can still pass the violations over, then I ask, hath your house been burnt? Hath your property been destroyed before your face? Are your wife and children destitute of a bed to lie on, or bread to live on? Have you lost a parent or a child by their hands, and yourself the ruined and wretched survivor? If you have not, then you are not a judge of those who have. But if you have, and can still shake hands with the murderers, then are you unworthy the name of husband, father, friend, or lover, and whatever may be your rank or title in life, you have the heart of a coward, and the spirit of a sycophant.

This is not inflaming or exaggerating matters, but trying them by those feelings and affections which nature justifies, and without which we should be incapable of discharging the social duties of life, or enjoying the felicities of it. I mean not to exhibit horror for the purpose of provoking revenge, but to awaken us from fatal and unmanly slumbers, that we may pursue determinately some fixed object. 'Tis not in the power of Britain or of Europe to conquer America, if she doth not conquer herself by delay and timidity. The present winter is worth an age if rightly employed, but if lost or neglected the whole Continent will partake of the misfortune; and there is no punishment which that man doth not deserve, be he who, or what, or where he will, that may be the means of sacrificing a season so precious and useful.

'Tis repugnant to reason, to the universal order of things, to all examples from former ages, to suppose that this Continent can long remain subject to any external power. The most sanguine in Britain doth not think so. The utmost stretch of human wisdom cannot, at this time, compass a plan, short of separation, which can promise the continent even a year's security. Reconciliation is *now* a fallacious dream. Nature hath deserted the connection, and art cannot supply her place. For, as Milton wisely expresses, "never can true reconcilement grow where wounds of deadly hate have pierced so deep."[8]

A government of our own is our natural right: and when a man seriously reflects on the precariousness of human affairs, he will become convinced, that it is infinitely wiser and safer, to form a constitution of our own in a cool deliberate manner, while we have it in our power, than to trust such an interesting event to time and chance. If we omit it now, some Massanello[9] may hereafter arise, who, laying hold of popular

---

[8] John Milton, *Paradise Lost,* IV, 98–99.

[9] Paine's note: "Thomas Anello, otherwise Massanello, a fisherman of Naples who after spiriting up his countrymen in the public marketplace, against the oppression of the Spaniards, to whom the place was then subject, prompted them to revolt, and in the space of a day became King."

disquietudes, may collect together the desperate and the discontented, and by assuming to themselves the powers of government, finally sweep away the liberties of the Continent like a deluge. Should the government of America return again into the hands of Britain, the tottering situation of things will be a temptation for some desperate adventurer to try his fortune; and in such a case, what relief can Britain give? Ere she could hear the news, the fatal business might be done; and ourselves suffering like the wretched Britons under the oppression of the Conqueror. Ye that oppose independance now, ye know not what ye do: ye are opening a door to eternal tyranny, by keeping vacant the seat of government. There are thousands and tens of thousands, who would think it glorious to expel from the Continent, that barbarous and hellish power, which hath stirred up the Indians and the Negroes to destroy us; the cruelty hath a double guilt, it is dealing brutally by us, and treacherously by them.

To talk of friendship with those in whom our reason forbids us to have faith, and our affections wounded thro' a thousand pores instruct us to detest, is madness and folly. Every day wears out the little remains of kindred between us and them; and can there be any reason to hope, that as the relationship expires, the affection will encrease, or that we shall agree better when we have ten times more and greater concerns to quarrel over than ever?

Ye that tell us of harmony and reconciliation, can ye restore to us the time that is past? Can ye give to prostitution its former innocence? neither can ye reconcile Britain and America. The last cord now is broken, the people of England are presenting addresses against us. There are injuries which nature cannot forgive; she would cease to be nature if she did. As well can the lover forgive the ravisher of his mistress, as the Continent forgive the murders of Britain. The Almighty hath implanted in us these unextinguishable feelings for good and wise purposes. They are the Guardians of his Image in our hearts. They distinguish us from the herd of common animals. The social compact would dissolve, and justice be extirpated from the earth, or have only a casual existence were we callous to the touches of affection. The robber and the murderer would often escape unpunished, did not the injuries which our tempers sustain, provoke us into justice.

O! ye that love mankind! Ye that dare oppose not only the tyranny but the tyrant, stand forth! Every spot of the old world is overrun with oppression. Freedom hath been hunted round the Globe. Asia and Africa have long expelled her. Europe regards her like a stranger, and England hath given her warning to depart. O! receive the fugitive, and prepare in time an asylum for mankind.

1776

---

from The American Crisis

Number 1

These are the times that try men's souls. The summer soldier and the sunshine patriot will, in this crisis, shrink from the service of their country; but he that stands it *now*, deserves the love and thanks of man and woman. Tyranny, like hell, is not easily conquered; yet we have this consolation with us, that the harder the conflict, the more glorious the triumph. What we obtain too cheap, we esteem too lightly: it is dearness only that gives every thing its value. Heaven knows how to put a proper price upon its goods; and it would be strange indeed if so celestial an article as FREEDOM should not be highly rated. Britain, with an army to enforce her tyranny, has declared that she has a right (*not only to* TAX) but "to BIND *us in* ALL CASES WHATSOEVER,"[1] and if being *bound in that manner,* is not slavery, then is there not such a thing as slavery upon earth. Even the expression is impious; for so unlimited a power can belong only to God.

Whether the independence of the continent was declared too soon, or delayed too long, I will not now enter into as an argument; my own simple opinion is, that had it been eight months earlier, it would have been much better. We did not make a proper use of last winter, neither could we, while we were in a dependant state. However, the fault, if it were one, was all our own;[2] we have none to blame but ourselves. But no great deal is lost yet. All that Howe[3] has been doing for this month past, is rather a ravage than a conquest, which the spirit of the Jerseys,[4] a year ago, would have quickly repulsed, and which time and a little resolution will soon recover.

I have as little superstition in me as any man living, but my secret opinion has ever been, and still is, that God Almighty will not give up a people to military destruction, or leave them unsupportedly to perish, who have so earnestly and so repeatedly sought to avoid the calamities of war, by every decent method which wisdom could invent. Neither have I so much of the infidel in me, as to suppose that He has relinquished the government of the world, and given us up to the care of devils; and as I do not, I cannot see on what grounds the king of Britain can look up to heaven for help against us: a common murderer, a highwayman, or a house-breaker, has as good a pretence as he.

'Tis surprising to see how rapidly a panic will sometimes run through a country. All nations and ages have been subject to them: Britain has trembled like an ague at the report of a French fleet of flat bottomed boats; and in the fourteenth century[5] the whole English army, after ravaging the kingdom of France, was driven back like men petrified with fear; and this brave exploit was performed by a few broken forces collected and headed by a woman, Joan of Arc. Would that heaven might inspire some Jersey maid to spirit up her countrymen, and save her fair fellow sufferers from ravage and ravishment! Yet panics, in some cases, have their uses; they produce as much good as hurt. Their duration is always short; the mind soon grows through them, and acquires a firmer habit than before. But their peculiar advantage is, that they are the touchstones of sincerity and hypocrisy, and bring things and men to light, which might otherwise have lain forever undiscovered. In fact, they have the same effect on secret traitors, which an imaginary apparition would have upon a private murderer. They sift out the hidden thoughts of man, and hold them up in public to the world. Many a disguised tory has lately shown his head, that shall penitentially solemnize with curses the day on which Howe arrived upon the Delaware.

---

[1] The quotation is from an English parliamentary act of 1776.

[2] Paine's note, a quotation from his *Common Sense* (1776): "The present winter is worth an age, if rightly employed; but if lost or neglected, the whole continent will partake of the evil; and there is no punishment that man does not deserve, be he who, or what, or where he will, that may be the means of sacrificing a season so precious and useful."

[3] British general.

[4] The colony was composed of East Jersey and West Jersey.

[5] Actually the fifteenth century.

As I was with the troops at Fort Lee, and marched with them to the edge of Pennsylvania, I am well acquainted with many circumstances, which those who live at a distance know but little or nothing of. Our situation there was exceedingly cramped, the place being a narrow neck of land between the North River[6] and the Hackensack. Our force was inconsiderable, being not one fourth so great as Howe could bring against us. We had no army at hand to have relieved the garrison, had we shut ourselves up and stood on our defence. Our ammunition, light artillery, and the best part of our stores, had been removed, on the apprehension that Howe would endeavor to penetrate the Jerseys, in which case Fort Lee could be of no use to us; for it must occur to every thinking man, whether in the army or not, that these kind of field forts are only for temporary purposes, and last in use no longer than the enemy directs his force against the particular object, which such forts are raised to defend. Such was our situation and condition at Fort Lee on the morning of the 20th of November, when an officer arrived with information that the enemy with 200 boats had landed about seven miles above: Major General [Nathaniel] Green, who commanded the garrison, immediately ordered them under arms, and sent express to General Washington at the town of Hackensack, distant by the way of the ferry = six miles. Our first object was to secure the bridge over the Hackensack, which laid up the river between the enemy and us, about six miles from us, and three from them. General Washington arrived in about three quarters of an hour, and marched at the head of the troops towards the bridge, which place I expected we should have a brush for; however, they did not choose to dispute it with us, and the greatest part of our troops went over the bridge, the rest over the ferry, except some which passed at a mill on a small creek, between the bridge and the ferry, and made their way through some marshy grounds up to the town of Hackensack, and there passed the river. We brought off as much baggage as the wagons could contain, the rest was lost. The simple object was to bring off the garrison, and march them on till they could be strengthened by the Jersey or Pennsylvania militia, so as to be enabled to make a stand. We staid four days at Newark, collected our out-posts with some of the Jersey militia, and marched out twice to meet the enemy, on being informed that they were advancing, though our numbers were greatly inferior to theirs. Howe, in my little opinion, committed a great error in generalship in not throwing a body of forces off from Staten Island through Amboy, by which means he might have seized all our stores at Brunswick, and intercepted our march into Pennsylvania; but if we believe the power of hell to be limited, we must likewise believe that their agents are under some providential controul.

I shall not now attempt to give all the particulars of our retreat to the Delaware; suffice it for the present to say, that both officers and men, though greatly harassed and fatigued, frequently without rest, covering, or provision, the inevitable consequences of a long retreat, bore it with a manly and martial spirit. All their wishes centered in one, which was, that the country would turn out and help them to drive the enemy back. Voltaire has remarked that king William[7] never appeared to full advantage but in difficulties and in action; the same remark may be made on General

---

[6] The Hudson.

[7] William III, king of England from 1689 to 1702.

Washington, for the character fits him. There is a natural firmness in some minds which cannot be unlocked by trifles, but which, when unlocked, discovers a cabinet of fortitude; and I reckon it among those kind of public blessings, which we do not immediately see, that God hath blessed him with uninterrupted health, and given him a mind that can even flourish upon care.

I shall conclude this paper with some miscellaneous remarks on the state of our affairs; and shall begin with asking the following question, Why is it that the enemy have left the New-England provinces, and made these middle ones the seat of war? The answer is easy: New-England is not infested with tories, and we are. I have been tender in raising the cry against these men, and used numberless arguments to show them their danger, but it will not do to sacrifice a world either to their folly or their baseness. The period is now arrived, in which either they or we must change our sentiments, or one or both must fall. And what is a tory? Good God! what is he? I should not be afraid to go with a hundred whigs against a thousand tories, were they to attempt to get into arms. Every tory is a coward; for servile, slavish, self-interested fear is the foundation of toryism; and a man under such influence, though he may be cruel, never can be brave.

But, before the line of irrecoverable separation be drawn between us, let us reason the matter together: Your conduct is an invitation to the enemy, yet not one in a thousand of you has heart enough to join him. Howe is as much deceived by you as the American cause is injured by you. He expects you will all take up arms, and flock to his standard, with muskets on your shoulders. Your opinions are of no use to him, unless you support him personally, for 'tis soldiers, and not tories, that he wants.

I once felt all that kind of anger, which a man ought to feel, against the mean principles that are held by the tories: a noted one, who kept a tavern at Amboy, was standing at his door, with as pretty a child in his hand, about eight or nine years old, as I ever saw, and after speaking his mind as freely as he thought was prudent, finished with this unfatherly expression, *"Well! give me peace in my day."* Not a man lives on the continent but fully believes that a separation must some time or other finally take place, and a generous parent should have said, *"If there must be trouble, let it be in my day, that my child may have peace;"* and this single reflection, well applied, is sufficient to awaken every man to duty. Not a place upon earth might be so happy as America. Her situation is remote from all the wrangling world, and she has nothing to do but to trade with them. A man can distinguish himself between temper and principle, and I am as confident, as I am that God governs the world, that America will never be happy till she gets clear of foreign dominion. Wars, without ceasing, will break out till that period arrives, and the continent must in the end be conqueror; for though the flame of liberty may sometimes cease to shine, the coal can never expire.

America did not, nor does not want force; but she wanted a proper application of that force. Wisdom is not the purchase of a day, and it is no wonder that we should err at the first setting off. From an excess of tenderness, we were unwilling to raise an army, and trusted our cause to the temporary defence of a well-meaning militia. A summer's experience has now taught us better; yet with those troops, while they were collected, we were able to set bounds to the progress of the enemy, and, thank God! they are again assembling. I always considered militia as the best troops in the world for a sudden exertion, but they will not do for a long campaign. Howe, it is probable, will make an attempt on this city;[8] should he fail on this side the Delaware, he is ruined: if he succeeds, our cause is not ruined. He stakes all on his side against a part on ours; admitting he succeeds, the consequence will be, that armies from both ends of the continent will march to assist their suffering friends in the middle states; for he cannot go everywhere, it is impossible. I consider Howe as the greatest enemy the tories have; he is bringing a war into their country, which, had it not been for him and partly for themselves, they had been clear of. Should he now be expelled, I wish with all the devotion of a Christian, that the names of whig and tory may never more be mentioned; but should the tories give him encouragement to come, or assistance if he come, I as sincerely wish that our next year's arms may expel them from the continent, and the congress appropriate their possessions to the relief of those who have suffered in well-doing. A single successful battle next year will settle the whole. America could carry on a two years war by the confiscation of the property of disaffected persons, and be made happy by their expulsion. Say not that this is revenge, call it rather the soft resentment of a suffering people, who, having no object in view but the *good* of *all,* have staked their *own all* upon a seemingly doubtful event. Yet it is folly to argue against determined hardness; eloquence may strike the ear, and the language of sorrow draw forth the tear of compassion, but nothing can reach the heart that is steeled with prejudice.

Quitting this class of men, I turn with the warm ardor of a friend to those who have nobly stood, and are yet determined to stand the matter out: I call not upon a few, but upon all: not on *this* state or *that* state, but on *every* state: up and help us; lay your shoulders to the wheel; better have too much force than too little, when so great an object is at stake. Let it be told to the future world, that in the depth of winter, when nothing but hope and virtue could survive, that the city and the country, alarmed at one common danger, came forth to meet and to repulse it. Say not that thousands are gone, turn out your tens of thousands; throw not the burden of the day upon Providence, but *"show your faith by your works,"*[9] that God may bless you. It matters not where you live, or what rank of life you hold, the evil or the blessing will reach you all. The far and the near, the home counties and the back, the rich and the poor, will suffer or rejoice alike. The heart that feels not now, is dead: the blood of his children will curse his cowardice, who shrinks back at a time when a little might have saved the whole, and made *them* happy. I love the man that can smile in trouble, that can gather strength from distress, and grow brave by reflection. 'Tis the business of little minds to shrink; but he whose heart is firm, and whose conscience approves his conduct, will pursue his principles unto death. My own line of reasoning is to myself as straight and clear as a ray of light. Not all the treasures of the world, so far as I believe, could have induced me to support an offensive war, for I think it murder; but if a thief breaks into my house, burns and destroys my property, and kills or threatens to kill me, or those that are in it, and to *"bind me in all cases whatsoever"*[10] to his absolute will, am I to suffer it? What signifies it to me, whether he who does it is a king or a common man; my countryman or not my countryman; whether it be done by an individual villain, or an army of them? If we reason to the root of things we shall find no difference; neither can any just cause be assigned why

[8] Philadelphia.
[9] James 2:18.
[10] See footnote 1.

we should punish in the one case and pardon in the other. Let them call me rebel, and welcome, I feel no concern from it; but I should suffer the misery of devils, were I to make a whore of my soul by swearing allegiance to one whose character is that of a sottish, stupid, stubborn, worthless, brutish man. I conceive likewise a horrid idea in receiving mercy from a being, who at the last day shall be shrieking to the rocks and mountains to cover him, and fleeing with terror from the orphan, the widow, and the slain of America.

There are cases which cannot be overdone by language, and this is one. There are persons, too, who see not the full extent of the evil which threatens them; they solace themselves with hopes that the enemy, if he succeed, will be merciful. It is the madness of folly, to expect mercy from those who have refused to do justice; and even mercy, where conquest is the object, is only a trick of war; the cunning of the fox is as murderous as the violence of the wolf, and we ought to guard equally against both. Howe's first object is, partly by threats and partly by promises, to terrify or seduce the people to deliver up their arms and receive mercy. The ministry recommended the same plan to Gage,[11] and this is what the tories call making their peace, *"a peace which passeth all understanding" indeed!*[12] A peace which would be the immediate forerunner of a worse ruin than any we have yet thought of. Ye men of Pennsylvania, do reason upon these things! Were the back counties to give up their arms, they would fall an easy prey to the Indians, who are all armed: this perhaps is what some tories would not be sorry for. Were the home counties to deliver up their arms, they would be exposed to the resentment of the back counties, who would then have it in their power to chastise their defection at pleasure. And were any one state to give up its arms, *that* state must be garrisoned by all Howe's army of Britons and Hessians to preserve it from the anger of the rest. Mutual fear is the principal link in the chain of mutual love, and woe be to that state that breaks the compact. Howe is mercifully inviting you to barbarous destruction, and men must be either rogues or fools that will not see it. I dwell not upon the vapours of imagination; I bring reason to your ears, and, in language as plain as A, B, C, hold up truth to your eyes.

I thank God, that I fear not. I see no real cause for fear. I know our situation well, and can see the way out of it. While our army was collected, Howe dared not risk a battle; and it is no credit to him that he decamped from the White Plains, and waited a mean opportunity to ravage the defenceless Jerseys; but it is great credit to us, that, with a handful of men, we sustained an orderly retreat for near an hundred miles, brought off our ammunition, all our field pieces, the greatest part of our stores, and had four rivers to pass. None can say that our retreat was precipitate, for we were near three weeks in performing it, that the country[13] might have time to come in. Twice we marched back to meet the enemy, and remained out till dark. The sign of fear was not seen in our camp, and had not some of the cowardly and disaffected inhabitants spread false alarms through the country, the Jerseys had never been ravaged. Once more we are again collected and collecting; our new army at both ends of the continent is recruiting fast, and we shall be able to open the next campaign with sixty thousand men, well armed and clothed. This is our situation, and who will may know it. By perseverance and fortitude we have the prospect of a glorious issue;

---

[11] A commander of British forces from 1763 to 1775.

[12] A play on Philippians 4:7.

[13] I.e., local volunteers.

by cowardice and submission, the sad choice of a variety of evils—a ravaged country —a depopulated city—habitations without safety, and slavery without hope—our homes turned into barracks and bawdy-houses for Hessians, and a future race to provide for, whose fathers we shall doubt of. Look on this picture and weep over it! and if there yet remains one thoughtless wretch who believes it not, let him suffer it unlamented.

COMMON SENSE.

1776

---

from The Age of Reason

Chapter I: The Author's Profession of Faith

It has been my intention, for several years past, to publish my thoughts upon religion; I am well aware of the difficulties that attend the subject, and from that consideration, had reserved it to a more advanced period of life. I intended it to be the last offering I should make to my fellow-citizens of all nations, and that at a time when the purity of the motive that induced me to it could not admit of a question, even by those who might disapprove the work.

The circumstance that has now taken place in France,[1] of the total abolition of the whole national order of priesthood, and of everything appertaining to compulsive systems of religion, and compulsive articles of faith, has not only precipitated my intention, but rendered a work of this kind exceedingly necessary, lest, in the general wreck of superstition, of false systems of government, and false theology, we lose sight of morality, of humanity, and of the theology that is true.

As several of my colleagues, and others of my fellow-citizens of France, have given me the example of making their voluntary and individual profession of faith, I also will make mine; and I do this with all that sincerity and frankness with which the mind of man communicates with itself.

I believe in one God, and no more; and I hope for happiness beyond this life.

I believe in the equality of man, and I believe that religious duties consist in doing justice, loving mercy, and endeavouring to make our fellow-creatures happy.

But, lest it should be supposed that I believe many other things in addition to these, I shall, in the progress of this work, declare the things I do not believe, and my reasons for not believing them.

I do not believe in the creed professed by the Jewish church, by the Roman church, by the Greek church, by the Turkish church, by the Protestant church, nor by any church that I know of. My own mind is my own church.

All national institutions of churches, whether Jewish, Christian, or Turkish, appear to me no other than human inventions set up to terrify and enslave mankind, and monopolize power and profit.

---

[1] By 1792, the Catholic church in France had been disbanded by radical leaders of the French Revolution. Churches were closed, and the Christian calendar was abolished.

I do not mean by this declaration to condemn those who believe otherwise; they have the same right to their belief as I have to mine. But it is necessary to the happiness of man, that he be mentally faithful to himself. Infidelity does not consist in believing, or in disbelieving; it consists in professing to believe what he does not believe.

It is impossible to calculate the moral mischief, if I may so express it, that mental lying has produced in society. When a man has so far corrupted and prostituted the chastity of his mind, as to subscribe his professional belief to things he does not believe, he has prepared himself for the commission of every other crime. He takes up the trade of a priest for the sake of gain, and, in order to qualify himself for that trade, he begins with a perjury. Can we conceive anything more destructive to morality than this?

Soon after I had published the pamphlet COMMON SENSE, in America, I saw the exceeding probability that a revolution in the system of government would be followed by a revolution in the system of religion. The adulterous connection of church and state, wherever it had taken place, whether Jewish, Christian, or Turkish, had so effectually prohibited, by pains and penalties, every discussion upon established creeds, and upon first principles of religion, that until the system of government should be changed, those subjects could not be brought fairly and openly before the world; but that whenever this should be done, a revolution in the system of religion would follow. Human inventions and priest-craft would be detected; and man would return to the pure, unmixed, and unadulterated belief of one God, and no more.

Chapter II: Of Missions and Revelations

Every national church or religion has established itself by pretending some special mission from God, communicated to certain individuals. The Jews have their Moses; the Christians their Jesus Christ, their apostles and saints; and the Turks their Mahomet; as if the way to God was not open to every man alike.

Each of those churches shows certain books, which they call *revelation,* or the Word of God. The Jews say that their Word of God was given by God to Moses face to face; the Christians say, that their Word of God came by divine inspiration; and the Turks say, that their Word of God (the Koran) was brought by an angel from heaven. Each of those churches accuses the other of unbelief; and, for my own part, I disbelieve them all.

As it is necessary to affix right ideas to words, I will, before I proceed further into the subject, offer some observations on the word *revelation.* Revelation when applied to religion, means something communicated *immediately* from God to man.

No one will deny or dispute the power of the Almighty to make such a communication if he pleases. But admitting, for the sake of a case, that something has been revealed to a certain person, and not revealed to any other person, it is revelation to that person only. When he tells it to a second person, a second to a third, a third to a fourth, and so on, it ceases to be a revelation to all those persons. It is revelation to the first person only, and *hearsay* to every other, and, consequently, they are not obliged to believe it.

It is a contradiction in terms and ideas to call anything a revelation that comes to us at second hand, either verbally or in writing. Revelation is necessarily limited to the first communication. After this, it is only an account of something which that person says was a revelation made to him; and though he may find himself obliged to believe it, it cannot be incumbent on me to believe it in the same manner, for it was not a revelation made to *me,* and I have only his word for it that it was made to *him.*

When Moses told the children of Israel that he received the two tables of the commandments from the hand of God, they were not obliged to believe him, because they had no other authority for it than his telling them so; and I have no other authority for it than some historian telling me so, the commandments carrying no internal evidence of divinity with them. They contain some good moral precepts such as any man qualified to be a lawgiver or a legislator could produce himself, without having recourse to supernatural intervention.[2]

When I am told that the Koran was written in Heaven, and brought to Mahomet by an angel, the account comes to near the same kind of hearsay evidence and second hand authority as the former. I did not see the angel myself, and therefore I have a right not to believe it.

When also I am told that a woman, called the Virgin Mary, said, or gave out, that she was with child without any cohabitation with a man, and that her betrothed husband, Joseph, said that an angel told him so, I have a right to believe them or not: such a circumstance required a much stronger evidence than their bare word for it: but we have not even this; for neither Joseph nor Mary wrote any such matter themselves. It is only reported by others that *they said so.* It is hearsay upon hearsay, and I do not chuse to rest my belief upon such evidence.

It is, however, not difficult to account for the credit that was given to the story of Jesus Christ being the Son of God. He was born when the heathen mythology had still some fashion and repute in the world, and that mythology had prepared the people for the belief of such a story. Almost all the extraordinary men that lived under the heathen mythology were reputed to be the sons of some of their gods. It was not a new thing at that time to believe a man to have been celestially begotten; the intercourse of gods with women was then a matter of familiar opinion. Their Jupiter,[3] according to their accounts, had cohabited with hundreds; the story therefore had nothing in it either new, wonderful, or obscene; it was conformable to the opinions that then prevailed among the people called Gentiles, or mythologists, and it was those people only that believed it. The Jews, who had kept strictly to the belief of one God, and no more, and who had always rejected the heathen mythology, never credited the story.

It is curious to observe how the theory of what is called the Christian Church, sprung out of the tail of the heathen mythology. A direct incorporation took place in the first instance, by making the reputed founder to be celestially begotten. The trinity of gods that then followed was no other than a reduction of the former plurality, which was about twenty or thirty thousand. The statue of Mary succeeded the statue of Diana of Ephesus.[4] The deification of heroes changed into the canonization of saints. The Mythologists had gods for everything; the Christian Mythologists had saints for everything. The church became as crouded with the one, as the pantheon[5] had been with the other; and Rome was the place of both. The Christian theory is little else than the idolatry of the ancient mythologists, accommodated to the purposes

[2] Paine's note: "It is, however, necessary to accept the declaration which says that God *visits the sins of the fathers upon the children.* This is contrary to every principle of moral justice."
[3] Supreme god of Roman mythology.
[4] A temple at Ephesus in Asia Minor honors the Roman fertility goddess Diana. (See Acts 19:23–24.)
[5] Roman temple of all the gods.

of power and revenue; and it yet remains to reason and philosophy to abolish the amphibious fraud.

Chapter IV: Of the Bases of Christianity

It is upon this plain narrative of facts, together with another case I am going to mention, that the Christian mythologists, calling themselves the Christian Church, have erected their fable, which for absurdity and extravagance is not exceeded by anything that is to be found in the mythology of the ancients.

The ancient mythologists tell us that the race of giants made war against Jupiter, and that one of them threw a hundred rocks against him at one throw; that Jupiter defeated him with thunder, and confined him afterwards under Mount Etna;[6] and that every time the Giant turns himself, Mount Etna belches fire. It is here easy to see that the circumstance of the mountain, that of its being a volcano, suggested the idea of the fable; and that the fable is made to fit and wind itself up with that circumstance.

The Christian mythologists tell that their Satan made war against the Almighty, who defeated him, and confined him afterwards, not under a mountain, but in a pit. It is here easy to see that the first fable suggested the idea of the second; for the fable of Jupiter and the Giants was told many hundred years before that of Satan.

Thus far the ancient and the Christian mythologists differ very little from each other. But the latter have contrived to carry the matter much farther. They have contrived to connect the fabulous part of the story of Jesus Christ with the fable originating from Mount Etna; and, in order to make all the parts of the story tye together, they have taken to their aid the traditions of the Jews; for the Christian mythology is made up partly from the ancient mythology, and partly from the Jewish traditions.

The Christian mythologists, after having confined Satan in a pit, were obliged to let him out again to bring on the sequel of the fable. He is then introduced into the garden of Eden in the shape of a snake, or a serpent, and in that shape he enters into familiar conversation with Eve, who is no ways surprised to hear a snake talk; and the issue of this tête-à-tête is, that he persuades her to eat an apple, and the eating of that apple damns all mankind.

After giving Satan this triumph over the whole creation, one would have supposed that the church mythologists would have been kind enough to send him back again to the pit, or, if they had not done this, that they would have put a mountain upon him, (for they say that their faith can remove a mountain) or have put him under a mountain, as the former mythologists had done, to prevent his getting again among the women, and doing more mischief. But instead of this, they leave him at large, without even obliging him to give his parole. The secret of which is, that they could not do without him; and after being at the trouble of making him, they bribed him to stay. They promised him ALL the Jews, ALL the Turks by anticipation, nine-tenths of the world beside, and Mahomet into the bargain. After this, who can doubt the bountifulness of the Christian Mythology?

---

[6] Volcano in northeastern Sicily.

Having thus made an insurrection and a battle in heaven, in which none of the combatants could be either killed or wounded—put Satan into the pit—let him out again—given him a triumph over the whole creation—damned all mankind by the eating of an apple, these Christian mythologists bring the two ends of their fable together. They represent this virtuous and amiable man, Jesus Christ, to be at once both God and man, and also the Son of God, celestially begotten, on purpose to be sacrificed, because they say that Eve in her longing had eaten an apple.

1794

St. Jean de Crèvecoeur
1735–1813

"What then is the American, this new man?" With that question a Jesuit-trained, English-educated, aristocratic Frenchman who had adopted New York as his native ground began one of the earliest inquiries into a relatively new psychosocial phenomenon, the American identity.

The question suited the personality of the man who asked it. Himself an amalgam of identities, Michel Guillaume Jean de Crèvecoeur was born near Caen, in Normandy, in 1735. He received a Jesuit education, completed his studies in England, and then, at nineteen, left for Canada, where he served as an officer and cartographer under General Montcalm. After Wolfe defeated the French at Quebec in 1759, Crèvecoeur resigned his commission and traveled extensively through the British colonies. He finally settled down in New York, where in 1765 he took out citizenship papers, purchased a large farm in Orange County, married a woman from Yonkers, had three children, and immersed himself physically and philosophically in the role of "a simple American farmer." Presumably to assure himself of his new identity, he decided to go by the English name Hector St. John, though he was never consistent about what he called himself: "J. Hector St. John (a *Pennsylvanian* farmer)" appears on the title page of his first book, and throughout his career he used various combinations of his real and assumed names.

The American Revolution interrupted a pattern of life that Crèvecoeur rhapsodically described as one of idyllic agrarian self-sufficiency. Partisans are not noted for their tolerance of mixed identities during times of political crisis, and Crèvecoeur, who attempted to remain neutral, found himself suspected by both sides. His rural tranquility shattered by the war, his life in danger, he resolved to leave the country. After months of anxious waiting and a few more months in a British prison in New York City, Crèvecoeur obtained permission in 1780 to sail with one of his children for Europe. He took with him manuscripts he had worked on during his early travels and his farming days. In 1782 a London publisher brought out *Letters from an American Farmer*, a series of twelve epistolary essays, all but one of which Crèvecoeur had composed before the

Revolution. The *Letters* were an immediate success, and Crèvecoeur became a popular figure in Parisian literary circles, where, according to the fashionable primitivism of the time, he was referred to as "an American savage." An advertisement appended to the *Letters* promised a second series, but in 1783 Crèvecoeur accepted a position in New York City as French consul to New York, Connecticut, and New Jersey. The second series of letters remained unpublished until the 1920s, when they were rediscovered and brought out as *Sketches of Eighteenth-Century America.* Revealing more clearly than in previous writings his Tory leanings and advocating highly restrictive trade policies, the sequel of letters had probably been suppressed once Crèvecoeur had assumed his new diplomatic position.

When Crèvecoeur returned to America in 1783, he found his wife dead, his farm destroyed by an allied attack of Loyalists and Indians, and his children in the care of a Boston family. Recovering his children, he moved to New York City, where he established headquarters and worked at continuing friendly diplomatic relations between his two countries. He also contributed medical and agricultural articles to journals and is credited with having introduced alfalfa to the United States. He made another trip to Paris to prepare a second edition of the *Letters,* then, after serving as consul for three more years, left America permanently in 1790. In 1801 he published in French a three-volume travel book on America, *Le Voyage dans la haute Pennsylvanie et dans l'état de New-York,* which he camouflaged as merely his edited translation of an anonymous, deteriorated English manuscript discovered in Copenhagen. Crèvecoeur died in Normandy in 1813.

Like many late-eighteenth-century writers, Crèvecoeur wrote glowingly of nature and the values of an agrarian economy. His enticing descriptions of a simple rural life based on a domestic economy of "ample subsistence" had the unfortunate promotional effect of luring many people into frontier conditions that little resembled the author's Orange County plantation. "I used to admire my head off," said D. H. Lawrence of Crèvecoeur's world, "before I tiptoed into the Wilds and saw the shacks of the Homesteaders." But if Crèvecoeur sometimes cheats on the side of sentimentality when it comes to providing an accurate account of rural benefits and New World opportunities, he could, as *Sketches of Eighteenth-Century America* shows, also write quite convincingly of rural hardships and the ordinary tasks of agricultural life. The set of sketches collected as "Thoughts of an American Farmer on Various Rural Subjects" offers one of the most vivid accounts we have of everyday life in a small, late-eighteenth-century farm community.

Although Crèvecoeur wrote most effectively when he was being least promotional and least theoretical, he nevertheless remains best known for his investigations into the American character. He concludes his most famous essay with a case study (omitted here) of a single immigrant whose history answers the essay's central question, "What is an American?" Given Crèvecoeur's versatility, his pragmatic buoyancy, his capacity for multiple loyalties, and his self-reliance and self-inventiveness, he might just as well have appended his own biography as the answer to that still intriguing question.

Further Reading:
J. P. Mitchell, *St. Jean de Crèvecoeur*, 1916.
Thomas Philbrick, *St. John de Crèvecoeur*, 1970.

Texts:
Letters from an American Farmer, ed. W. B. Trent, 1904.
See also *Crèvecoeur's 18th-Century Travels in Pennsylvania and New York*, ed. P. G. Adams, 1962.
Letters from an American Farmer, ed. A. E. Stone, 1963.
Journey into Northern Pennsylvania and the State of New York, ed. C. S. Bostelmann, 1964.

from Letters from an American Farmer

from Letter III: What Is an American?

I wish I could be acquainted with the feelings and thoughts which must agitate the heart and present themselves to the mind of an enlightened Englishman, when he first lands on this continent. He must greatly rejoice that he lived at a time to see this fair country discovered and settled; he must necessarily feel a share of national pride, when he views the chain of settlements which embellishes these extended shores. When he says to himself, this is the work of my countrymen, who, when convulsed by factions, afflicted by a variety of miseries and wants, restless and impatient, took refuge here. They brought along with them their national genius, to which they principally owe what liberty they enjoy, and what substance they possess. Here he sees the industry of his native country displayed in a new manner, and traces in their works the embrios of all the arts, sciences, and ingenuity which flourish in Europe. Here he beholds fair cities, substantial villages, extensive fields, an immense country filled with decent houses, good roads, orchards, meadows, and bridges, where an hundred years ago all was wild, woody and uncultivated! What a train of pleasing ideas this fair spectacle must suggest; it is a prospect which must inspire a good citizen with the most heartfelt pleasure. The difficulty consists in the manner of viewing so extensive a scene. He is arrived on a new continent; a modern society offers itself to his contemplation, different from what he had hitherto seen. It is not composed, as in Europe, of great lords who possess every thing, and of a herd of people who have nothing. Here are no aristocratical families, no courts, no kings, no bishops, no ecclesiastical dominion, no invisible power giving to a few a very visible one; no great manufacturers employing thousands, no great refinements of luxury. The rich and the poor are not so far removed from each other as they are in Europe. Some few towns excepted, we are all tillers of the earth, from Nova Scotia to West Florida. We are a people of cultivators, scattered over an immense territory, communicating with each other by means of good roads and navigable rivers, united by the silken bands of mild government, all respecting the laws, without dreading their power, because they are equitable. We are all animated with the spirit of an industry which is unfettered and unrestrained, because each person works for himself. If he travels through our rural districts he views not the hostile castle, and the haughty mansion, contrasted with the clay-built hut and miserable cabbin, where cattle and men help to keep each other warm, and dwell in meanness, smoke, and indigence. A pleasing uniformity of decent competence appears throughout our habitations. The meanest of our log-houses is a dry and comfortable habitation. Lawyer or merchant are the fairest titles our towns afford; that of a farmer is the only appellation of the rural inhabitants of our country. It must take some time ere he can reconcile himself to our dictionary, which is but short in words of dignity, and names of honour. There, on a Sunday, he sees a congregation of respectable farmers and their wives, all clad in neat homespun, well mounted, or riding in their own humble waggons. There is not among them an esquire, saving the unlettered magistrate. There he sees a parson as simple as his flock, a farmer who does not riot on the labour of others. We have no princes, for whom we toil, starve, and bleed: we are the most perfect society now existing in the world. Here man is free as he ought to be; nor is this pleasing equality so transitory as many others are. Many ages will not see the shores of our great lakes replenished with inland nations, nor the unknown bounds of North America entirely peopled. Who can tell how far it extends? Who can tell the millions of men whom it will feed and contain? for no European foot has as yet travelled half the extent of this mighty continent!

The next wish of this traveller will be to know whence came all these people? they are a mixture of English, Scotch, Irish, French, Dutch, Germans, and Swedes. From this promiscuous breed, that race now called Americans have arisen. The eastern provinces must indeed be excepted, as being the unmixed descendents of Englishmen. I have heard many wish that they had been more intermixed also: for my part, I am no wisher, and think it much better as it has happened. They exhibit a most conspicuous figure in this great and variegated picture; they too enter for a great share in the pleasing perspective displayed in these thirteen provinces. I know it is fashionable to reflect on them, but I respect them for what they have done; for the accuracy and wisdom with which they have settled their territory; for the decency of their manners; for their early love of letters; their ancient college,[1] the first in this hemisphere; for their industry; which to me who am but a farmer, is the criterion of everything. There never was a people, situated as they are, who with so ungrateful a soil have done more in so short a time. Do you think that the monarchical ingredients which are more prevalent in other governments, have purged them from all foul stains? Their histories assert the contrary.

In this great American asylum, the poor of Europe have by some means met together, and in consequence of various causes; to what purpose should they ask one another what countrymen they are? Alas, two thirds of them had no country. Can a wretch who wanders about, who works and starves, whose life is a continual scene of sore affliction or pinching penury; can that man call England or any other kingdom his country? A country that had no bread for him, whose fields procured him no harvest, who met with nothing but the frowns of the rich, the severity of the laws, with jails and punishments; who owned not a single foot of the extensive surface of this planet? No! urged by a variety of motives, here they came. Every thing has tended to regenerate them; new laws, a new mode of living, a new social system; here they are become men: in Europe they were as so many useless plants, wanting vegetative mould, and refreshing showers; they withered, and were mowed down by want, hunger, and war; but now by the power of transplantation, like all other plants they

[1] Harvard, founded in 1636.

have taken root and flourished! Formerly they were not numbered in any civil lists of their country, except in those of the poor; here they rank as citizens. By what invisible power has the surprising metamorphosis been performed? By that of the laws and that of their industry. The laws, the indulgent laws, protect them as they arrive, stamping on them the symbol of adoption; they receive ample rewards for their labours; these accumulated rewards procure them lands; those lands confer on them the title of freemen, and to that title every benefit is affixed which men can possibly require. This is the great operation daily performed by our laws. From whence proceed these laws? From our government. Whence the government? It is derived from the original genius and strong desire of the people ratified and confirmed by the crown. This is the great chain which links us all, this is the picture which every province exhibits, Nova Scotia excepted. There the crown has done all;[2] either there were no people who had genius, or it was not much attended to: the consequence is, that the province is very thinly inhabited indeed; the power of the crown in conjunction with the musketos has prevented men from settling there. Yet some parts of it flourished once, and it contained a mild harmless set of people. But for the fault of a few leaders, the whole were banished. The greatest political error the crown ever committed in America, was to cut off men from a country which wanted nothing but men!

What attachment can a poor European emigrant have for a country where he had nothing? The knowledge of the language, the love of a few kindred as poor as himself, were the only cords that tied him: his country is now that which gives him land, bread, protection, and consequence: *Ubi panis ibi patria,*[3] is the motto of all emigrants. What then is the American, this new man? He is either an European, or the descendant of an European, hence that strange mixture of blood, which you will find in no other country. I could point out to you a family whose grandfather was an Englishmen, whose wife was Dutch, whose son married a French woman, and whose present four sons have now four wives of different nations. *He* is an American, who leaving behind him all his ancient prejudices and manners, receives new ones from the new mode of life he has embraced, the new government he obeys, and the new rank he holds. He becomes an American by being received in the broad lap of our great *Alma Mater.* Here individuals of all nations are melted into a new race of men, whose labours and posterity will one day cause great changes in the world. Americans are the western pilgrims, who are carrying along with them that great mass of arts, sciences, vigour, and industry which began long since in the east; they will finish the great circle. The Americans were once scattered all over Europe; here they are incorporated into one of the finest systems of population which has ever appeared, and which will hereafter become distinct by the power of the different climates they inhabit. The American ought therefore to love this country much better than that wherein either he or his forefathers were born. Here the rewards of his industry follow with equal steps the progress of his labour; his labour is founded on the basis of nature, *self-interest;* can it want a stronger allurement? Wives and children, who before in vain demanded of him a morsel of bread, now, fat and frolicsome, gladly help their father to clear those fields whence exuberant crops are to arise to feed and to clothe them all; without any

---

[2] In 1755 the English banished thousands of French settlers from Nova Scotia.

[3] Latin: "Where bread is, there is one's country."

part being claimed, either by a despotic prince, a rich abbot, or a mighty lord. Here religion demands but little of him; a small voluntary salary to the minister, and gratitude to God; can he refuse these? The American is a new man, who acts upon new principles; he must therefore entertain new ideas, and form new opinions. From involuntary idleness, servile dependence, penury, and useless labour, he has passed to toils of a very different nature, rewarded by ample subsistence.—This is an American.

British America is divided into many provinces, forming a large association, scattered along a coast 1500 miles extent and about 200 wide. This society I would fain examine, at least such as it appears in the middle provinces; if it does not afford that variety of tinges and gradations which may be observed in Europe, we have colours peculiar to ourselves. For instance, it is natural to conceive that those who live near the sea, must be very different from those who live in the woods; the intermediate space will afford a separate and distinct class.

Men are like plants; the goodness and flavour of the fruit proceeds from the peculiar soil and exposition in which they grow. We are nothing but what we derive from the air we breathe, the climate we inhabit, the government we obey, the system of religion we profess, and the nature of our employment. Here you will find but few crimes; these have acquired as yet no root among us. I wish I were able to trace all my ideas; if my ignorance prevents me from describing them properly, I hope I shall be able to delineate a few of the outlines, which are all I propose.

Those who live near the sea, feed more on fish than on flesh, and often encounter that boisterous element. This renders them more bold and enterprising; this leads them to neglect the confined occupations of the land. They see and converse with a variety of people; their intercourse with mankind becomes extensive. The sea inspires them with a love of traffic, a desire of transporting produce from one place to another; and leads them to a variety of resources which supply the place of labour. Those who inhabit the middle settlements, by far the most numerous, must be very different; the simple cultivation of the earth purifies them, but the indulgences of the government, the soft remonstrances of religion, the rank of independent freeholders, must necessarily inspire them with sentiments, very little known in Europe among people of the same class. What do I say? Europe has no such class of men; the early knowledge they acquire, the early bargains they make, give them a great degree of sagacity. As freemen they will be litigious; pride and obstinacy are often the cause of law suits; the nature of our laws and governments may be another. As citizens it is easy to imagine, that they will carefully read the newspapers, enter into every political disquisition, freely blame or censure governors and others. As farmers they will be careful and anxious to get as much as they can, because what they get is their own. As northern men they will love the chearful cup. As Christians, religion curbs them not in their opinions; the general indulgence leaves every one to think for themselves in spiritual matters; the laws inspect our actions, our thoughts are left to God. Industry, good living, selfishness, litigiousness, country politics, the pride of freemen, religious indifference, are their characteristics. If you recede still farther from the sea, you will come into more modern settlements; they exhibit the same strong lineaments, in a ruder appearance. Religion seems to have still less influence, and their manners are less improved.

Now we arrive near the great woods, near the last inhabited districts; there men seem to be placed still farther beyond the reach of government, which in some measure leaves them to themselves. How can it pervade every corner; as they were driven there by misfortunes, necessity of beginnings, desire of acquiring large tracks of land, idleness, frequent want of economy, ancient debts; the re-union of such people does not afford a very pleasing spectacle. When discord, want of unity and friendship; when either drunkenness or idleness prevail in such remote districts; contention, inactivity, and wretchedness must ensue. There are not the same remedies to these evils as in a long established community. The few magistrates they have, are in general little better than the rest; they are often in a perfect state of war; that of man against man, sometimes decided by blows, sometimes by means of the law; that of man against every wild inhabitant of these venerable woods, of which they are come to dispossess them. There men appear to be no better than carnivorous animals of a superior rank, living on the flesh of wild animals when they can catch them, and when they are not able, they subsist on grain. He who would wish to see America in its proper light, and have a true idea of its feeble beginnings and barbarous rudiments, must visit our extended line of frontiers where the last settlers dwell, and where he may see the first labours of settlement, the mode of clearing the earth, in all their different appearances; where men are wholly left dependent on their native tempers, and on the spur of uncertain industry, which often fails when not sanctified by the efficacy of a few moral rules. There, remote from the power of example, and check of shame, many families exhibit the most hideous parts of our society. They are a kind of forlorn hope, preceding by ten or twelve years the most respectable army of veterans which come after them. In that space, prosperity will polish some, vice and the law will drive off the rest, who uniting again with others like themselves will recede still farther; making room for more industrious people, who will finish their improvements, convert the loghouse into a convenient habitation, and rejoicing that the first heavy labours are finished, will change in a few years that hitherto barbarous country into a fine fertile, well regulated district. Such is our progress, such is the march of the Europeans toward the interior parts of this continent. In all societies there are off-casts; this impure part serves as our precursors or pioneers; my father himself was one of that class, but he came upon honest principles, and was therefore one of the few who held fast; by good conduct and temperance, he transmitted to me his fair inheritance, when not above one in fourteen of his contemporaries had the same good fortune.[4]

Forty years ago this smiling country was thus inhabited; it is now purged, a general decency of manners prevails throughout, and such has been the fate of our best countries.

Exclusive of those general characteristics, each province has its own, founded on the government, climate, mode of husbandry, customs, and peculiarity of circumstances. Europeans submit insensibly to these great powers, and become, in the course of a few generations, not only Americans in general, but either Pennsylvanians, Virginians, or provincials under some other name. Whoever traverses the continent must easily observe those strong differences, which will grow more evident in time. The inhabitants of Canada, Massachuset, the middle provinces, the southern ones will be as different as their climates; their only points of unity will be those of religion and language.

As I have endeavoured to shew you how Europeans become Americans; it may

---

[4] Part of Crèvecoeur's disguise; his father had
never been to America.

not be disagreeable to shew you likewise how the various Christian sects introduced, wear out, and how religious indifference becomes prevalent. When any considerable number of a particular sect happen to dwell contiguous to each other, they immediately erect a temple, and there worship the Divinity agreeably to their own peculiar ideas. Nobody disturbs them. If any new sect springs up in Europe, it may happen that many of its professors will come and settle in America. As they bring their zeal with them, they are at liberty to make proselytes if they can, and to build a meeting and to follow the dictates of their consciences; for neither the government nor any other power interferes. If they are peaceable subjects, and are industrious, what is it to their neighbours how and in what manner they think fit to address their prayers to the Supreme Being? But if the sectaries are not settled close together, if they are mixed with other denominations, their zeal will cool for want of fuel, and will be extinguished in a little time. Then the Americans become as to religion, what they are as to country, allied to all. In them the name of Englishman, Frenchman, and European is lost, and in like manner, the strict modes of Christianity as practised in Europe are lost also. This effect will extend itself still farther hereafter, and though this may appear to you as a strange idea, yet it is a very true one. I shall be able perhaps hereafter to explain myself better, in the meanwhile, let the following example serve as my first justification.

Let us suppose you and I to be travelling; we observe that in this house, to the right, lives a Catholic, who prays to God as he has been taught, and believes in transubstantiation; he works and raises wheat, he has a large family of children, all hale and robust; his belief, his prayers offend nobody. About one mile farther on the same road, his next neighbour may be a good honest plodding German Lutheran, who addresses himself to the same God, the God of all, agreeably to the modes he has been educated in, and believes in consubstantiation; by so doing he scandalizes nobody; he also works in his fields, embellishes the earth, clears swamps, &c. What has the world to do with his Lutheran principles? He persecutes nobody, and nobody persecutes him, he visits his neighbours, and his neighbours visit him. Next to him lives a seceder, the most enthusiastic of all sectaries; his zeal is hot and fiery, but separated as he is from others of the same complexion, he has no congregation of his own to resort to, where he might cabal and mingle religious pride with worldly obstinacy. He likewise raises good crops, his house is handsomely painted, his orchard is one of the fairest in the neighbourhood. How does it concern the welfare of the country, or of the province at large, what this man's religious sentiments are, or really whether he has any at all? He is a good farmer, he is a sober, peaceable, good citizen: William Penn himself would not wish for more. This is the visible character, the invisible one is only guessed at, and is nobody's business. Next again lives a Low Dutchman, who implicitly believes the rules laid down by the synod of Dort. He conceives no other idea of a clergyman than that of a hired man; if he does his work well he will pay him the stipulated sum; if not he will dismiss him, and do without his sermons, and let his church be shut up for years. But notwithstanding this coarse idea, you will find his house and farm to be the neatest in all the country; and you will judge by his waggon and fat horses, that he thinks more of the affairs of this world than of those of the next. He is sober and laborious, therefore he is all he ought to be as to the affairs of this life; as for those of the next, he must trust to the great Creator. Each of these people instruct their children as well as they can, but these instructions are feeble compared to those which are given to the youth of the poorest class in Europe. Their children will therefore grow up less zealous and more indifferent in matters of religion than their parents. The foolish vanity, or rather the fury of making Proselytes, is unknown here; they have no time, the seasons call for all their attention, and thus in a few years, this mixed neighbourhood will exhibit a strange religious medley, that will be neither pure Catholicism nor pure Calvinism. A very perceptible indifference even in the first generation, will become apparent; and it may happen that the daughter of the Catholic will marry the son of the seceder, and settle by themselves at a distance from their parents. What religious education will they give their children? A very imperfect one. If there happens to be in the neighbourhood any place of worship, we will suppose a Quaker's meeting; rather than not shew their fine clothes, they will go to it, and some of them may perhaps attach themselves to that society. Others will remain in a perfect state of indifference; the children of these zealous parents will not be able to tell what their religious principles are, and their grandchildren still less. The neighbourhood of a place of worship generally leads them to it, and the action of going thither, is the strongest evidence they can give of their attachment to any sect. The Quakers are the only people who retain a fondness for their own mode of worship; for be they ever so far separated from each other, they hold a sort of communion with the society, and seldom depart from its rules, at least in this country. Thus all sects are mixed as well as all nations; thus religious indifference is imperceptibly disseminated from one end of the continent to the other; which is at present one of the strongest characteristics of the Americans. Where this will reach no one can tell, perhaps it may leave a vacuum fit to receive other systems. Persecution, religious pride, the love of contradiction, are the food of what the world commonly calls religion. These motives have ceased here: zeal in Europe is confined; here it evaporates in the great distance it has to travel; there it is a grain of powder inclosed, here it burns away in the open air, and consumes without effect.

But to return to our back settlers. I must tell you, that there is something in the proximity of the woods, which is very singular. It is with men as it is with the plants and animals that grow and live in the forests; they are entirely different from those that live in the plains. I will candidly tell you all my thoughts but you are not to expect that I shall advance any reasons. By living in or near the woods, their actions are regulated by the wildness of the neighbourhood. The deer often come to eat their grain, the wolves to destroy their sheep, the bears to kill their hogs, the foxes to catch their poultry. This surrounding hostility, immediately puts the gun into their hands; they watch these animals, they kill some; and thus by defending their property, they soon become professed hunters; this is the progress; once hunters, farewell to the plough. The chase renders them ferocious, gloomy, and unsociable; a hunter wants no neighbour, he rather hates them, because he dreads the competition. In a little time their success in the woods makes them neglect their tillage. They trust to the natural fecundity of the earth, and therefore do little; carelessness in fencing, often exposes what little they sow to destruction; they are not at home to watch; in order therefore to make up the deficiency, they go oftener to the woods. That new mode of life brings along with it a new set of manners, which I cannot easily describe. These new manners being grafted on the old stock, produce a strange sort of lawless profligacy, the impressions of which are indelible. The manners of the Indian natives are respectable, compared with this European medley. Their wives and children live in sloth and inactivity; and having no proper pursuits, you may judge what education the latter receive. Their tender minds have nothing else to contemplate but the example of their parents; like them they grow up a mongrel breed, half civilized, half savage, except nature stamps on them some constitutional propensities. That rich, that voluptuous sentiment is gone that struck them so forcibly; the possession of their freeholds no longer conveys to their minds the same pleasure and pride. To all these reasons you must add, their lonely situation, and you cannot imagine what an effect on manners the great distances they live from each other has! Consider one of the last settlements in it's first view: of what is it composed? Europeans who have not that sufficient share of knowledge they ought to have, in order to prosper; people who have suddenly passed from oppression, dread of government, and fear of laws, into the unlimited freedom of the woods. This sudden change must have a very great effect on most men, and on that class particularly. Eating of wild meat, whatever you may think, tends to alter their temper; though all the proof I can adduce, is, that I have seen it: and having no place of worship to resort to, what little society this might afford, is denied them. The Sunday meetings, exclusive of religious benefits, were the only social bonds that might have inspired them with some degree of emulation in neatness. Is it then surprising to see men thus situated, immersed in great and heavy labours, degenerate a little? It is rather a wonder the effect is not more diffusive. The Moravians and the Quakers are the only instances in exception to what I have advanced. The first never settle singly, it is a colony of the society which emigrates; they carry with them their forms, worship, rules, and decency: the others never begin so hard, they are always able to buy improvements, in which there is a great advantage, for by that time the country is recovered from its first barbarity. Thus our bad people are those who are half cultivators and half hunters; and the worst of them are those who have degenerated altogether into the hunting state. As old ploughmen and new men of the woods, as Europeans and new made Indians, they contract the vices of both; they adopt the moroseness and ferocity of a native, without his mildness, or even his industry at home. If manners are not refined, at least they are rendered simple and inoffensive by tilling the earth; all our wants are supplied by it, our time is divided between labour and rest, and leaves none for the commission of great misdeeds. As hunters it is divided between the toil of the chase, the idleness of repose, or the indulgence of inebriation. Hunting is but a licentious idle life, and if it does not always pervert good dispositions; yet, when it is united with bad luck, it leads to want: want stimulates that propensity to rapacity and injustice, too natural to needy men, which is the fatal gradation. After this explanation of the effects which follow by living in the woods, shall we yet vainly flatter ourselves with the hope of converting the Indians? We should rather begin with converting our back-settlers; and now if I dare mention the name of religion, its sweet accents would be lost in the immensity of these woods. Men thus placed, are not fit either to receive or remember its mild instructions; they want temples and ministers, but as soon as men cease to remain at home, and begin to lead an erratic life, let them be either tawny or white, they cease to be its disciples.

Thus have I faintly and imperfectly endeavoured to trace our society from the sea to our woods! yet you must not imagine that every person who moves back, acts upon the same principles, or falls into the same degeneracy. Many families carry with them all their decency of conduct, purity of morals, and respect of religion; but these are scarce, the power of example is sometimes irresistible. Even among these back-settlers, their depravity is greater or less, according to what nation or province they belong. Were I to adduce proofs of this, I might be accused of partiality. If there happens to be some rich intervals, some fertile bottoms, in those remote districts, the people will there prefer tilling the land to hunting, and will attach themselves to it; but even on these fertile spots you may plainly perceive the inhabitants to acquire a great degree of rusticity and selfishness.

It is in consequence of this straggling situation, and the astonishing power it has on manners, that the back-settlers of both the Carolinas, Virginia, and many other parts, have been long a set of lawless people; it has been even dangerous to travel among them. Government can do nothing in so extensive a country, better it should wink at these irregularities, than that it should use means inconsistent with its usual mildness. Time will efface those stains: in proportion as the great body of population approaches them they will reform, and become polished and subordinate. Whatever has been said of the four New England provinces, no such degeneracy of manners has ever tarnished their annals; their back-settlers have been kept within the bounds of decency, and government, by means of wise laws, and by the influence of religion. What a detestable idea such people must have given to the natives of the Europeans! They trade with them, the worst of people are permitted to do that which none but persons of the best characters should be employed in. They get drunk with them, and often defraud the Indians. Their avarice, removed from the eyes of their superiors, knows no bounds; and aided by a little superiority of knowledge, these traders deceive them, and even sometimes shed blood. Hence those shocking violations, those sudden devastations which have so often stained our frontiers, when hundreds of innocent people have been sacrificed for the crimes of a few. It was in consequence of such behaviour, that the Indians took the hatchet against the Virginians in 1774. Thus are our first steps trod, thus are our first trees felled, in general, by the most vicious of our people; and thus the path is opened for the arrival of a second and better class, the true American freeholders; the most respectable set of people in this part of the world: respectable for their industry, their happy independence, the great share of freedom they possess, the good regulation of their families, and for extending the trade and the dominion of our mother country.

Europe contains hardly any other distinctions but lords and tenants; this fair country alone is settled by freeholders, the possessors of the soil they cultivate, members of the government they obey, and the framers of their own laws, by means of their representatives. This is a thought which you have taught me to cherish; our difference from Europe, far from diminishing, rather adds to our usefulness and consequence as men and subjects. Had our forefathers remained there, they would only have crouded it, and perhaps prolonged those convulsions which had shook it so long. Every industrious European who transports himself here, may be compared to a sprout growing at the foot of a great tree; it enjoys and draws but a little portion of sap; wrench it from the parent roots, transplant it, and it will become a tree bearing fruit also. Colonists are therefore entitled to the consideration due to the most useful subjects; a hundred families barely existing in some parts of Scotland, will here in six years, cause an annual exportation of 10,000 bushels of wheat: 100 bushels being but a common quantity for an industrious family to sell, if they cultivate good land. It is here then that the idle may be employed, the useless become useful, and the poor become rich; but by riches I do not mean gold and silver, we have but little of those metals; I mean a better sort of wealth, cleared lands, cattle, good houses, good cloaths, and an increase of people to enjoy them.

There is no wonder that this country has so many charms, and presents to Europeans so many temptations to remain in it. A traveller in Europe becomes a stranger as soon as he quits his own kingdom; but it is otherwise here. We know, properly speaking, no strangers; this is every person's country; the variety of our soils, situations, climates, governments, and produce, hath something which must please every body. No sooner does an European arrive, no matter of what condition, than his eyes are opened upon the fair prospect; he hears his language spoke, he retraces many of his own country manners, he perpetually hears the names of families and towns with which he is acquainted; he sees happiness and prosperity in all places disseminated; he meets with hospitality, kindness, and plenty every where; he beholds hardly any poor, he seldom hears of punishments and executions; and he wonders at the elegance of our towns, those miracles of industry and freedom. He cannot admire enough our rural districts, our convenient roads, good taverns, and our many accommodations; he involuntarily loves a country where every thing is so lovely. When in England, he was a mere Englishman; here he stands on a larger portion of the globe, not less than its fourth part, and may see the productions of the north, in iron and naval stores; the provisions of Ireland, the grain of Egypt, the indigo, the rice of China. He does not find, as in Europe, a crouded society, where every place is over-stocked; he does not feel that perpetual collision of parties, that difficulty of beginning, that contention which oversets so many. There is room for every body in America; has he any particular talent, or industry? he exerts it in order to procure a livelihood, and it succeeds. Is he a merchant? the avenues of trade are infinite; is he eminent in any respect? he will be employed and respected. Does he love a country life? pleasant farms present themselves; he may purchase what he wants, and thereby become an American farmer. Is he a labourer, sober and industrious? he need not go many miles, nor receive many informations before he will be hired, well fed at the table of his employer, and paid four or five times more than he can get in Europe. Does he want uncultivated lands? thousands of acres present themselves, which he may purchase cheap. Whatever be his talents or inclinations, if they are moderate, he may satisfy them. I do not mean that every one who comes will grow rich in a little time; no, but he may procure an easy, decent maintenance, by his industry. Instead of starving he will be fed, instead of being idle he will have employment; and these are riches enough for such men as come over here. The rich stay in Europe, it is only the middling and the poor that emigrate. Would you wish to travel in independent idleness, from north to south, you will find easy access, and the most chearful reception at every house; society without ostentation, good cheer without pride, and every decent diversion which the country affords, with little expence. It is no wonder that the European who has lived here a few years, is desirous to remain; Europe with all its pomp, is not to be compared to this continent, for men of middle stations, or labourers.

An European, when he first arrives, seems limited in his intentions, as well as in his views; but he very suddenly alters his scale; two hundred miles formerly appeared a very great distance, it is now but a trifle; he no sooner breathes our air than he forms schemes, and embarks in designs he never would have thought of in his own country. There the plenitude of society confines many useful ideas, and often extinguishes the most laudable schemes which here ripen into maturity. Thus Europeans become Americans.

But how is this accomplished in that croud of low, indigent people, who flock here every year from all parts of Europe? I will tell you; they no sooner arrive than they immediately feel the good effects of that plenty of provisions we possess: they fare on our best food, and are kindly entertained; their talents, character, and peculiar industry are immediately inquired into; they find countrymen every where disseminated, let them come from whatever part of Europe. Let me select one as an epitome of the rest; he is hired, he goes to work, and works moderately; instead of being employed by a haughty person, he finds himself with his equal, placed at the substantial table of the farmer, or else at an inferior one as good; his wages are high, his bed is not like that bed of sorrow on which he used to lie: if he behaves with propriety, and is faithful, he is caressed, and becomes as it were a member of the family. He begins to feel the effects of a sort of resurrection; hitherto he had not lived, but simply vegetated; he now feels himself a man, because he is treated as such; the laws of his own country had overlooked him in his insignificancy; the laws of this cover him with their mantle. Judge what an alteration there must arise in the mind and thoughts of this man; he begins to forget his former servitude and dependence, his heart involuntarily swells and glows; this first swell inspires him with those new thoughts which constitute an American. What love can he entertain for a country where his existence was a burthen to him; if he is a generous good man, the love of this new adoptive parent will sink deep into his heart. He looks around, and sees many a prosperous person, who but a few years before was as poor as himself. This encourages him much, he begins to form some little scheme, the first, alas, he ever formed in his life. If he is wise he thus spends two or three years, in which time he acquires knowledge, the use of tools, the modes of working the lands, felling trees, &c. This prepares the foundation of a good name, the most useful acquisition he can make. He is encouraged, he has gained friends; he is advised and directed, he feels bold, he purchases some land; he gives all the money he has brought over, as well as what he has earned, and trusts to the God of harvests for the discharge of the rest. His good name procures him credit. He is now possessed of the deed, conveying to him and his posterity the fee simple[5] and absolute property of two hundred acres of land, situated on such a river. What an epocha in this man's life! He is become a freeholder, from perhaps a German boor—he is now an American, a Pennsylvanian, an English subject. He is naturalized, his name is enrolled with those of the other citizens of the province. Instead of being a vagrant, he has a place of residence; he is called the inhabitant of such a county, or of such a district, and for the first time in his life counts for something; for hitherto he has been a cypher. I only repeat what I have heard many say, and no wonder their hearts should glow, and be agitated with a multitude of feelings, not easy to describe. From nothing to start into being; from a servant to the rank of a master; from being the slave of some despotic prince, to become a free man, invested with lands, to which every municipal blessing is annexed! What a change indeed! It is in consequence of that change that he becomes an American. This great metamorphosis has a double effect, it extinguishes all his European prejudices, he

---

[5] Full legal possession.

forgets that mechanism of subordination, that servility of disposition which poverty had taught him; and sometimes he is apt to forget too much, often passing from one extreme to the other. If he is a good man, he forms schemes of future prosperity, he proposes to educate his children better than he has been educated himself; he thinks of future modes of conduct, feels an ardor to labour he never felt before. Pride steps in and leads him to every thing that the laws do not forbid: he respects them; with a heart-felt gratitude he looks toward the east, toward that insular government from whose wisdom all his new felicity is derived, and under whose wings and protection he now lives. These reflections constitute him the good man and the good subject. Ye poor Europeans, ye, who sweat, and work for the great—ye, who are obliged to give so many sheaves to the church, so many to your lords, so many to your government, and have hardly any left for yourselves—ye, who are held in less estimation than favourite hunters or useless lap dogs—ye, who only breathe the air of nature, because it cannot be withheld from you; it is here that ye can conceive the possibility of those feelings I have been describing; it is here the laws of naturalization invite every one to partake of our great labours and felicity, to till unrented, untaxed lands! Many, corrupted beyond the power of amendment, have brought with them all their vices, and disregarding the advantages held to them, have gone on in their former career of iniquity, until they have been overtaken and punished by our laws. It is not every emigrant who succeeds; no, it is only the sober, the honest, and industrious: happy those to whom this transition has served as a powerful spur to labour, to prosperity, and to the good establishment of children, born in the days of their poverty; and who had no other portion to expect but the rags of their parents, had it not been for their happy emigration. Others again, have been led astray by this enchanting scene; their new pride, instead of leading them to the fields, has kept them in idleness; the idea of possessing lands is all that satisfies them—though surrounded with fertility, they have mouldered away their time in inactivity, misinformed husbandry, and ineffectual endeavours. How much wiser, in general, the honest Germans than almost all other Europeans; they hire themselves to some of their wealthy landsmen, and in that apprenticeship learn every thing that is necessary. They attentively consider the prosperous industry of others, which imprints in their minds a strong desire of possessing the same advantages. This forcible idea never quits them, they launch forth, and by dint of sobriety, rigid parsimony, and the most persevering industry, they commonly succeed. Their astonishment at their first arrival from Germany is very great—it is to them a dream; the contrast must be powerful indeed; they observe their countrymen flourishing in every place; they travel through whole counties where not a word of English is spoken; and in the names and the language of the people, they retrace Germany. They have been an useful acquisition to this continent, and to Pennsylvania in particular; to them it owes some share of its prosperity: to their mechanical knowledge and patience, it owes the finest mills in all America, the best teams of horses, and many other advantages. The recollection of their former poverty and slavery never quits them as long as they live.

The Scotch and the Irish might have lived in their own country perhaps as poor, but enjoying more civil advantages, the effects of their new situation do not strike them so forcibly, nor has it so lasting an effect. From whence the difference arises I know not, but out of twelve families of emigrants of each country, generally seven Scotch will succeed, nine German, and four Irish. The Scotch are frugal and laborious, but their wives cannot work so hard as German women, who on the contrary vie with their husbands, and often share with them the most severe toils of the field, which they understand better. They have therefore nothing to struggle against, but the common casualties of nature. The Irish do not prosper so well; they love to drink and to quarrel; they are litigious, and soon take to the gun, which is the ruin of every thing; they seem beside to labour under a greater degree of ignorance in husbandry than the others; perhaps it is that their industry had less scope, and was less exercised at home. I have heard many relate, how the land was parcelled out in that kingdom; their ancient conquest has been a great detriment to them, by over-setting their landed property. The lands possessed by a few, are leased down *ad infinitum,* and the occupiers often pay five guineas an acre. The poor are worse lodged there than any where else in Europe; their potatoes, which are easily raised, are perhaps an inducement to laziness: their wages are too low and their whisky too cheap.

There is no tracing observations of this kind, without making at the same time very great allowances, as there are every where to be found, a great many exceptions. The Irish themselves, from different parts of that kingdom, are very different. It is difficult to account for this surprising locality, one would think on so small an island an Irishman must be an Irishman: yet it is not so, they are different in their aptitude to, and in their love of labour.

The Scotch on the contrary are all industrious and saving; they want nothing more than a field to exert themselves in, and they are commonly sure of succeeding. The only difficulty they labour under is, that technical American knowledge which requires some time to obtain; it is not easy for those who seldom saw a tree, to conceive how it is to be felled, cut up, and split into rails and posts.

As I am fond of seeing and talking of prosperous families, I intend to finish this letter by relating to you the history of an honest Scotch Hebridean, who came here in 1774, which will shew you in epitome, what the Scotch can do, wherever they have room for the exertion of their industry. Whenever I hear of any new settlement, I pay it a visit once or twice a year, on purpose to observe the different steps each settler takes, the gradual improvements, the different tempers of each family, on which their prosperity in a great nature depends; their different modifications of industry, their ingenuity, and contrivance; for being all poor, their life requires sagacity and prudence. In an evening I love to hear them tell their stories, they furnish me with new ideas; I sit still and listen to their ancient misfortunes, observing in many of them a strong degree of gratitude to God, and the government. Many a well meant sermon have I preached to some of them. When I found laziness and inattention to prevail, who could refrain from wishing well to these new countrymen; after having undergone so many fatigues. Who could withhold good advice? What a happy change it must be, to descend from the high, sterile, bleak lands of Scotland, where every thing is barren and cold, to rest on some fertile farms in these middle provinces! Such a transition must have afforded the most pleasing satisfaction.

The following dialogue passed at an out-settlement, where I lately paid a visit:

Well, friend, how do you do now; I am come fifty odd miles on purpose to see you; how do you go on with your new cutting and slashing? Very well, good Sir, we learn the use of the axe bravely, we shall make it out; we have a belly full of victuals every day, our cows run about, and come home full of milk, our hogs get fat of themselves in the woods: Oh, this is a good country! God bless the king, and

William Penn; we shall do very well by and by, if we keep our healths. Your loghouse looks neat and light, where did you get these shingles? One of our neighbours is a New-England man, and he shewed us how to split them out of chestnut-trees. Now for a barn, but all in good time, here are fine trees to build with. Who is to frame it, sure you don't understand that work yet? A countryman of ours who has been in America these ten years, offers to wait for his money until the second crop is lodged in it. What did you give for your land? Thirty-five shillings per acre, payable in seven years. How many acres have you got? An hundred and fifty. That is enough to begin with; is not your land pretty hard to clear? Yes, Sir, hard enough, but it would be harder still if it was ready cleared, for then we should have no timber, and I love the woods much; the land is nothing without them. Have not you found out any bees yet? No, Sir; and if we had we should not know what to do with them. I will tell you by and by. You are very kind. Farewell, honest man, God prosper you; whenever you travel toward ————, enquire for J.S. he will entertain you kindly, provided you bring him good tidings from your family and farm. In this manner I often visit them, and carefully examine their houses, their modes of ingenuity, their different ways; and make them all relate all they know, and describe all they feel. These are scenes which I believe you would willingly share with me. I well remember your philanthropic turn of mind. Is it not better to contemplate under these humble roofs, the rudiments of future wealth and population, than to behold the accumulated bundles of litigious papers in the office of a lawyer? To examine how the world is gradually settled, how the howling swamp is converted into a pleasing meadow, the rough ridge into a fine field; and to hear the chearful whistling, the rural song, where there was no sound heard before, save the yell of the savage, the screech of the owl, or the hissing of the snake? Here an European, fatigued with luxury, riches, and pleasures, may find a sweet relaxation in a series of interesting scenes, as affecting as they are new. England, which now contains so many domes, so many castles, was once like this; a place woody and marshy; its inhabitants, now the favourite nation for arts and commerce, were once painted like our neighbours. The country will flourish in its turn, and the same observations will be made which I have just delineated. Posterity will look back with avidity and pleasure, to trace, if possible, the area of this or that particular settlement.

Pray, what is the reason that the Scots are in general more religious, more faithful, more honest, and industrious than the Irish? I do not mean to insinuate national reflections, God forbid! It ill becomes any man, and much less an American; but as I know men are nothing of themselves, and that they owe all their different modifications either to government or other local circumstances, there must be some powerful causes which constitute this great national difference.

Agreeable to the account which severale Scotchmen have given me of the north of Britain, of the Orkneys, and the Hebride Islands, they seem, on many accounts, to be unfit for the habitation of men; they appear to be calculated only for great sheep pastures. Who then can blame the inhabitants of these countries for transporting themselves hither? This great continent must in time absorb the poorest part of Europe; and this will happen in proportion as it becomes better known; and as war, taxation, oppression, and misery increase there. The Hebrides appear to be fit only for the residence of malefactors, and it would be much better to send felons there than either to Virginia or Maryland. What a strange compliment has our mother country paid to two of the finest provinces in America! England has entertained in that respect very mistaken ideas; what was intended as a punishment, is become the good fortune of several; many of those who have been transported as felons, are now rich, and strangers to the stings of those wants that urged them to violations of the law: they are become industrious, exemplary, and useful citizens. The English government should purchase the most northern and barren of those islands; it should send over to us the honest, primitive Hebrideans, settle them here on good lands, as a reward for their virtue and ancient poverty; and replace them with a colony of her wicked sons. The severity of the climate, the inclemency of the seasons, the sterility of the soil, the tempestuousness of the sea, would afflict and punish enough. Could there be found a spot better adapted to retaliate the injury it had received by their crimes? Some of those islands might be considered as the hell of Great Britain, where all evil spirits should be sent. Two essential ends would be answered by this simple operation. The good people, by emigration, would be rendered happier; the bad ones would be placed where they ought to be. In a few years the dread of being sent to that wintry region would have a much stronger effect, than that of transportation.—This is no place of punishment; were I a poor hopeless, breadless Englishman, and not restrained by the power of shame, I should be very thankful for the passage. It is of very little importance how, and in what manner an indigent man arrives; for if he is but sober, honest, and industrious, he has nothing more to ask of heaven. Let him go to work, he will have opportunities enough to earn a comfortable support, and even the means of procuring some land; which ought to be the utmost wish of every person who has health and hands to work. I knew a man who came to this country, in the literal sense of the expression, stark naked; I think he was a Frenchman, and a sailor on board an English man of war. Being discontented, he had stripped himself and swam ashore; where finding clothes and friends, he settled afterwards at Maraneck, in the county of Chester, in the province of New-York: he married and left a good farm to each of his sons. I knew another person who was but twelve years old when he was taken on the frontiers of Canada, by the Indians; at his arrival at Albany he was purchased by a gentleman, who generously bound him apprentice to a taylor. He lived to the age of ninety, and left behind him a fine estate and a numerous family, all well settled; many of them I am acquainted with.—Where is then the industrious European who ought to despair?

After a foreigner from any part of Europe is arrived, and become a citizen; let him devoutly listen to the voice of our great parent, which says to him, "Welcome to my shores, distressed European; bless the hour in which thou didst see my verdant fields, my fair navigable rivers, and my green mountains!—If thou wilt work, I have bread for thee; if thou wilt be honest, sober, and industrious, I have greater rewards to confer on thee—ease and independence. I will give thee fields to feed and cloath thee; a comfortable fire-side to sit by, and tell thy children by what means thou has prospered; and a decent bed to repose on. I shall endow thee beside with the immunities of a freeman. If thou wilt carefully educate thy children, teach them gratitude to God, and reverence to that government, that philanthropic government, which has collected here so many men and made them happy. I will also provide for thy progeny; and to every good man this ought to be the most holy, the most powerful, the most earnest wish he can possibly form, as well as the most consolatory prospect when he dies. Go thou and work and till; thou shalt prosper, provided thou be just, grateful and industrious." . . .

Letter IX: Description of Charles-Town;
Thoughts on Slavery; On Physical Evil;
A Melancholy Scene.

Charles-Town is, in the north, what Lima[6] is in the south; both are Capitals of the richest provinces of their respective hemispheres: you may therefore conjecture, that both cities must exhibit the appearances necessarily resulting from riches. Peru abounding in gold, Lima is filled with inhabitants who enjoy all those gradations of pleasure, refinement, and luxury, which proceed from wealth. Carolina produces commodities, more valuable perhaps than gold, because they are gained by greater industry; it exhibits also on our northern stage, a display of riches and luxury, inferior indeed to the former, but far superior to what are to be seen in our northern towns. Its situation is admirable, being built at the confluence of two large rivers, which receive in their course a great number of inferior streams; all navigable in the spring, for flat boats. Here the produce of this extensive territory concentres; here therefore is the seat of the most valuable exportation; their wharfs, their docks, their magazines,[7] are extremely convenient to facilitate this great commercial business. The inhabitants are the gayest in America; it is called the centre of our beau monde,[8] and is always filled with the richest planters of the province, who resort hither in quest of health and pleasure. Here are always to be seen a great number of valetudinarians[9] from the West-Indies, seeking for the renovation of health, exhausted by the debilitating nature of their sun, air, and modes of living. Many of these West-Indians have I seen, at thirty, loaded with the infirmities of old age; for nothing is more common in those countries of wealth, than for persons to lose the abilities of enjoying the comforts of life, at a time when we northern men just begin to taste the fruits of our labour and prudence. The round of pleasure, and the expences of those citizens' tables, are much superior to what you would imagine: indeed the growth of this town and province has been astonishingly rapid. It is pity that the narrowness of the neck on which it stands prevents it from increasing; and which is the reason why houses are so dear. The heat of the climate, which is sometimes very great in the interior parts of the country, is always temperate in Charles-Town; though sometimes when they have no sea breezes the sun is too powerful. The climate renders excesses of all kinds very dangerous, particularly those of the table; and yet, insensible or fearless of danger, they live on, and enjoy a short and a merry life: the rays of their sun seem to urge them irresistably to dissipation and pleasure: on the contrary, the women, from being abstemious, reach to a longer period of life, and seldom die without having had several husbands. An European at his first arrival must be greatly surprised when he sees the elegance of their houses, their sumptuous furniture, as well as the magnificence of their tables can he imagine himself in a country, the establishment of which is so recent?

The three principal classes of inhabitants are, lawyers, planters, and merchants; this is the province which has afforded to the first the richest spoils, for nothing can exceed their wealth, their power, and their influence. They have reached the *ne plus ultra*[10] of worldly felicity; no plantation is secured, no title is good, no will is valid, but what they dictate, regulate, and approve. The whole mass of provincial property is become

---

[6] Lima, Peru.
[7] Warehouses.
[8] French: "high society."

[9] Invalids.
[10] Latin: "the highest point."

tributary to this society; which, far above priests and bishops, disdain to be satisfied with the poor Mosaical portion of the tenth.[11] I appeal to the many inhabitants, who, while contending perhaps for their right to a few hundred acres, have lost by the mazes of the law their whole patrimony. These men are more properly law givers than interpreters of the law; and have united here, as well as in most other provinces, the skill and dexterity of the scribe with the power and ambition of the prince: who can tell where this may lead in a future day? The nature of our laws, and the spirit of freedom, which often tends to make us litigious, must necessarily throw the greatest part of the property of the colonies into the hands of these gentlemen. In another century, the law will possess in the north, what now the church possesses in Peru and Mexico.

While all is joy, festivity, and happiness in Charles-Town, would you imagine that scenes of misery overspread in the country? Their ears by habit are become deaf, their hearts are hardened; they neither see, hear, nor feel for the woes of their poor slaves, from whose painful labours all their wealth proceeds. Here the horrors of slavery, the hardship of incessant toils, are unseen; and no one thinks with compassion of those showers of sweat and of tears which from the bodies of Africans, daily drop, and moisten the ground they till. The cracks of the whip urging these miserable beings to excessive labour, are far too distant from the gay Capital to be heard. The chosen race eat, drink, and live happy, while the unfortunate one grubs up the ground, raises indigo, or husks the rice; exposed to a sun full as scorching as their native one; without the support of good food, without the cordials of any chearing liquor. This great contrast has often afforded me subjects of the most afflicting meditation. On the one side, behold a people enjoying all that life affords most bewitching and pleasurable, without labour, without fatigue, hardly subjected to the trouble of wishing. With gold, dug from Peruvian mountains, they order vessels to the coasts of Guinea; by virtue of that gold, wars, murders, and devastations are committed in some harmless, peaceable African neighbourhood, where dwelt innocent people, who even knew not but that all men were black. The daughter torn from her weeping mother, the child from the wretched parents, the wife from the loving husband; whole families swept away and brought through storms and tempests to this rich metropolis! There, arranged like horses at a fair, they are branded like cattle, and then driven to toil, to starve, and to languish for a few years on the different plantations of these citizens. And for whom must they work? For persons they know not, and who have no other power over them than that of violence; no other right than what this accursed metal has given them! Strange order of things! Oh, Nature, where art thou?—Are not these blacks thy children as well as we? On the other side, nothing is to be seen but the most diffusive misery and wretchedness, unrelieved even in thought or wish! Day after day they drudge on without any prospect of ever reaping for themselves; they are obliged to devote their lives, their limbs, their will, and every vital exertion to swell the wealth of masters; who look not upon them with half the kindness and affection with which they consider their dogs and horses. Kindness and affection are not the portion of those who till the earth, who carry the burdens, who convert the logs into useful boards. This reward, simple and natural as one would conceive it, would border on humanity; and planters must have none of it!

[11] I.e., the tithe of Old Testament (Mosaic) law.

If negroes are permitted to become fathers, this fatal indulgence only tends to increase their misery: the poor companions of their scanty pleasures are likewise the companions of their labours; and when at some critical seasons they could wish to see them relieved, with tears in their eyes they behold them perhaps doubly oppressed, obliged to bear the burden of nature—a fatal present—as well as that of unabated tasks. How many have I seen cursing the irresistible propensity, and regretting, that by having tasted of those harmless joys, they had become the authors of double misery to their wives. Like their masters, they are not permitted to partake of those ineffable sensations with which nature inspires the hearts of fathers and mothers; they must repel them all, and become callous and passive. This unnatural state often occasions the most acute, the most pungent of their afflictions; they have no time, like us, tenderly to rear their helpless offspring, to nurse them on their knees, to enjoy the delight of being parents. Their paternal fondness is embittered by considering, that if their children live, they must live to be slaves like themselves; no time is allowed them to exercise their pious office, the mothers must fasten them on their backs, and, with this double load, follow their husbands in the fields, where they too often hear no other sound than that of the voice or whip of the task-master, and the cries of their infants, broiling in the sun. These unfortunate creatures cry and weep like their parents, without a possibility of relief; the very instinct of the brute, so laudable, so irresistible, runs counter here to their master's interest; and to that god, all the laws of nature must give way. Thus planters get rich; so raw, so unexperienced am I in this mode of life, that were I to be possessed of a plantation, and my slaves treated as in general they are here, never could I rest in peace; my sleep would be perpetually disturbed by a retrospect of the frauds committed in Africa, in order to entrap them; frauds surpassing in enormity every thing which a common mind can possibly conceive. I should be thinking of the barbarous treatment they meet with on ship-board; of their anguish, of the despair necessarily inspired by their situation, when torn from their friends and relations; when delivered into the hands of a people differently coloured, whom they cannot understand; carried in a strange machine over an ever agitated element, which they had never seen before; and finally delivered over to the severities of the whippers, and the excessive labours of the field. Can it be possible that the force of custom should ever make me deaf to all these reflections, and as insensible to the injustice of that trade, and to their miseries, as the rich inhabitants of this town seem to be? What then is man; this being who boasts so much of the excellence and dignity of his nature, among that variety of unscrutable[12] mysteries, of unsolvable problems, with which he is surrounded? The reason why man has been thus created, is not the least astonishing! It is said, I know that they are much happier here than in the West-Indies; because land being cheaper upon this continent than in those islands, the fields allowed them to raise their subsistence from, are in general more extensive. The only possible chance of any alleviation depends on the humour of the planters, who, bred in the midst of slaves, learn from the example of their parents to despise them; and seldom conceive either from religion or philosophy, any ideas that tend to make their fate less calamitous; except some strong native tenderness of heart, some rays of philanthropy, overcome the obduracy contracted by habit.

I have not resided here long enough to become insensible of pain for the objects which I every day behold. In the choice of my friends and acquaintance, I always

---

[12] Crèvecoeur here obviously means *inscrutable*.

endeavour to find out those whose dispositions are somewhat congenial with my own. We have slaves likewise in our northern provinces; I hope the time draws near when they will be all emancipated: but how different their lot, how different their situation, in every possible respect! They enjoy as much liberty as their masters, they are as well clad, and as well fed; in health and sickness they are tenderly taken care of; they live under the same roof, and are, truly speaking, a part of our families. Many of them are taught to read and write, and are well instructed in the principles of religion; they are the companions of our labours, and treated as such; they enjoy many perquisites, many established holidays, and are not obliged to work more than white people. They marry where inclination leads them; visit their wives every week; are as decently clad as the common people; they are indulged in educating, cherishing, and chastising their children, who are taught subordination to them as to their lawful parents: in short, they participate in many of the benefits of our society, without being obliged to bear any of its burthens. They are fat, healthy, and hearty, and far from repining at their fate; they think themselves happier than many of the lower class whites: they share with their masters the wheat and meat provision they help to raise; many of those whom the good Quakers have emancipated, have received that great benefit with tears of regret, and have never quitted, though free, their former masters and benefactors.

But is it really true, as I have heard it asserted here, that those blacks are incapable of feeling the spurs of emulation, and the chearful sound of encouragement? By no means; there are a thousand proofs existing of their gratitude and fidelity: those hearts in which such noble dispositions can grow, are then like ours, they are susceptible of every generous sentiment, of every useful motive of action; they are capable of receiving lights,[13] of imbibing ideas that would greatly alleviate the weight of their miseries. But what methods have in general been made use of to obtain so desirable an end? None; the day in which they arrive and are sold, is the first of their labours; labours, which from that hour admit of no respite; for though indulged by law with relaxation on Sundays, they are obliged to employ that time which is intended for rest, to till their little plantations. What can be expected from wretches in such circumstances? Forced from their native country, cruelly treated when on board, and not less so on the plantations to which they are driven; is there any thing in this treatment but what must kindle all the passions, sow the seeds of inveterate resentment, and nourish a wish of perpetual revenge? They are left to the irresistible effects of those strong and natural propensities; the blows they receive are they conducive to extinguish them, or to win their affections? They are neither soothed by the hopes that their slavery will ever terminate but with their lives; or yet encouraged by the goodness of their food, or the mildness of their treatment. The very hopes held out to mankind by religion, that consolatory system, so useful to the miserable, are never presented to them; neither moral nor physical means are made use of to soften their chains; they are left in their original and untutored state; that very state where in the natural propensities of revenge and warm passions, are so soon kindled. Cheered by no one single motive that can impel the will, or excite their efforts; nothing but terrors and punishments are presented to them; death is denounced[14] if they run away; horrid delaceration[15] if they speak with their native freedom; perpetually awed by the terrible

---

[13] I.e., mental or spiritual illumination.
[14] I.e., a death sentence is pronounced.

[15] Tearing to pieces.

cracks of whips, or by the fear of capital punishments, while even those punishments often fail of their purpose.

A clergyman settled a few years ago at George-Town, and feeling as I do now, warmly recommended to the planters, from the pulpit, a relaxation of severity; he introduced the benignity of Christianity, and pathetically made use of the admirable precepts of that system to melt the hearts of his congregation into a greater degree of compassion toward their slaves than had been hitherto customary; "Sir (said one of his hearers) we pay you a genteel salary to read to us the prayers of the liturgy, and to explain to us such parts of the Gospel as the rule of the church directs; but we do not want you to teach us what we are to do with our blacks." The clergyman found it prudent to with-hold any farther admonition. Whence this astonishing right, or rather this barbarous custom, for most certainly we have no kind of right beyond that of force? We are told, it is true, that slavery cannot be so repugnant to human nature as we at first imagine, because it has been practised in all ages, and in all nations: the Lacedemonians[16] themselves, those great assertors of liberty, conquered the Helotes with the design of making them their slaves; the Romans, whom we consider as our masters in civil and military policy, lived in the exercise of the most horrid oppression; they conquered to plunder and to enslave. What a hideous aspect the face of the earth must then have exhibited! Provinces, towns, districts, often depopulated; their inhabitants driven to Rome, the greatest market in the world, and there sold by thousands! The Roman dominions were tilled by the hands of unfortunate people, who had once been, like their victors free, rich, and possessed of every benefit society can confer; until they became subject to the cruel right of war, and to lawless force. Is there then no superintending power who conducts the moral operations of the world, as well as the physical? The same sublime hand which guides the planets round the sun with so much exactness, which preserves the arrangement of the whole with such exalted wisdom and paternal care, and prevents the vast system from falling into confusion; doth it abandon mankind to all the errors, the follies, and the miseries, which their most frantic rage, and their most dangerous vices and passions can produce?

The history of the earth! doth it present any thing but crimes of the most heinous nature, committed from one end of the world to the other? We observe avarice, rapine, and murder, equally prevailing in all parts. History perpetually tells us, of millions of people abandoned to the caprice of the maddest princes, and of whole nations devoted to the blind fury of tyrants. Countries destroyed; nations alternately buried in ruins by other nations; some parts of the world beautifully cultivated, returned again to the pristine state; the fruits of ages of industry, the toil of thousands in a short time destroyed by a few! If one corner breathes in peace for a few years, it is, in turn subjected, torne, and levelled; one would almost believe the principles of action in man, considered as the first agent of this planet, to be poisoned in their most essential parts. We certainly are not that class of beings which we vainly think ourselves to be; man an animal of prey, seems to have rapine and the love of bloodshed implanted in his heart; nay, to hold it the most honourable occupation in society: we never speak of a hero of mathematics, a hero of knowledge of humanity; no, this illustrious appellation is reserved for the most successful butchers of the world. If Nature has given us a fruitful soil to inhabit, she has refused us such inclinations and

---

[16] Ancient Spartans.

propensities as would afford us the full enjoyment of it. Extensive as the surface of this planet is, not one half of it is yet cultivated, not half replenished; she created man, and placed him either in the woods or plains, and provided him with passions which must for ever oppose his happiness; every thing is submitted to the power of the strongest; men, like the elements, are always at war; the weakest yield to the most potent; force, subtilty, and malice, always triumph over unguarded honesty, and simplicity. Benignity, moderation, and justice, are virtues adapted only to the humble paths of life: we love to talk of virtue and to admire its beauty, while in the shade of solitude, and retirement; but when we step forth into active life, if it happen to be in competition with any passion or desire, do we observe it to prevail? Hence so many religious impostors have triumphed over the credulity of mankind, and have rendered their frauds the creeds of succeeding generations, during the course of many ages; until worne away by time, they have been replaced by new ones. Hence the most unjust war, if supported by the greatest force, always succeeds; hence the most just ones, when supported only by their justice, as often fail. Such is the ascendancy of power; the supreme arbiter of all the revolutions which we observe in this planet: so irresistible is power, that it often thwarts the tendency of the most forcible causes, and prevents their subsequent salutary effects, though ordained for the good of man by the Governor of the universe. Such is the perverseness of human nature; who can describe it in all its latitude?

   In the moments of our philanthropy we often talk of an indulgent nature, a kind parent, who for the benefit of mankind has taken singular pains to vary the genera of plants, fruits, grain, and the different productions of the earth; and has spread peculiar blessings in each climate. This is undoubtedly an object of contemplation which calls forth our warmest gratitude; for so singularly benevolent have those parental intentions been, that where barrenness of soil or severity of climate prevail, there she has implanted in the heart of man, sentiments which over-balance every misery, and supply the place of every want. She has given to the inhabitants of these regions, an attachment to their savage rocks and wild shores, unknown to those who inhabit the fertile fields of the temperate zone. Yet if we attentively view this globe, will it not appear rather a place of punishment, than of delight? And what misfortune! that those punishments should fall on the innocent, and its few delights be enjoyed by the most unworthy. Famine, diseases, elementary convulsions, human feuds, dissensions, &c. are the produce of every climate; each climate produces besides, vices, and miseries peculiar to its latitude. View the frigid sterility of the north, whose famished inhabitants hardly acquainted with the sun, live and fare worse than the bears they hunt: and to which they are superior only in the faculty of speaking. View the arctic and antarctic regions, those huge voids, where nothing lives; regions of eternal snow: where winter in all his horrors has established his throne, and arrested every creative power of nature. Will you call the miserable stragglers in these countries by the name of men? Now contrast this frigid power of the north and south with that of the sun; examine the parched lands of the torrid zone, replete with sulphureous exhalations; view those countries of Asia subject to pestilential infections which lay nature waste; view this globe often convulsed both from within and without; pouring forth from several mouths, rivers of boiling matter, which are imperceptibly leaving immense subterranean graves, wherein millions will one day perish! Look at the poisonous soil of the equator, at those putrid slimy tracks, teeming with horrid monsters, the enemies of the human race; look next at the sandy continent, scorched perhaps by the fatal approach of some ancient comet, now the abode of desolation. Examine the rains, the convulsive storms of those climates, where masses of sulphur, bitumen, and electrical fire, combining their dreadful powers, are incessantly hovering and bursting over a globe threatened with dissolution. On this little shell, how very few are the spots where man can live and flourish? even under those mild climates which seem to breathe peace and happiness, the poison of slavery, the fury of despotism, and the rage of superstition, are all combined against man! There only the few live and rule, whilst the many starve and utter ineffectual complaints: there, human nature appears more debased, perhaps than in the less favoured climates. The fertile plains of Asia, the rich low lands of Egypt and of Diarbeck,[17] the fruitful fields bordering on the Tigris and the Euphrates, the extensive country of the East-Indies in all its separate districts; all these must to the geographical eye, seem as if intended for terrestrial paradises: but though surrounded with the spontaneous riches of nature though her kindest favours seem to be shed on those beautiful regions with the most profuse hand; yet there in general we find the most wretched people in the world. Almost every where, liberty so natural to mankind, is refused, or rather enjoyed but by their tyrants; the word slave, is the appellation of every rank, who adore as a divinity, a being worse than themselves; subject to every caprice, and to every lawless rage which unrestrained power can give. Tears are shed, perpetual groans are heard, where only the accents of peace, alacrity, and gratitude should resound. There the very delirium of tyranny tramples on the best gifts of nature, and sports with the fate, the happiness, the lives of millions: there the extreme fertility of the ground always indicates the extreme misery of the inhabitants!

Every where one part of the human species are taught the art of shedding the blood of the other; of setting fire to their dwellings; of levelling the works of their industry: half of the existence of nations regularly employed in destroying other nations. What little political felicity is to be met with here and there, has cost oceans of blood to purchase; as if good was never to be the portion of unhappy man. Republics, kingdoms, monarchies, founded either on fraud or successful violence, increase by pursuing the steps of the same policy, until they are destroyed in their turn, either by the influence of their own crimes, or by more successful but equally criminal enemies.

If from this general review of human nature, we descend to the examination of what is called civilized society; there the combination of every natural and artificial want, makes us pay very dear for what little share of political felicity we enjoy. It is a strange heterogeneous assemblage of vices and virtues, and of a variety of other principles, for ever at war, for ever jarring for ever producing some dangerous, some distressing extreme. Where do you conceive then that nature intended we should be happy? Would you prefer the state of men in the woods, to that of men in a more improved situation? Evil preponderates in both; in the first they often eat each other for want of food, and in the other they often starve each other for want of room. For my part, I think the vices and miseries to be found in the latter, exceed those of the former; in which real evil is more scarce, more supportable, and less enormous. Yet we wish to see the earth peopled; to accomplish the happiness of kingdoms, which

[17] Southeast Turkey.

is said to consist in numbers. Gracious God! to what end is the introduction of so many beings into a mode of existence in which they must grope amidst as many errors, commit as many crimes, and meet with as many diseases, wants, and sufferings!

The following scene will I hope account for these melancholy reflections, and apologize for the gloomy thoughts with which I have filled this letter: my mind is, and always has been, oppressed since I became a witness to it. I was not long since invited to dine with a planter who lived three miles from ———, where he then resided. In order to avoid the heat of the sun, I resolved to go on foot, sheltered in a small path, leading through a pleasant wood. I was leisurely travelling along, attentively examining some peculiar plants which I had collected, when all at once I felt the air strongly agitated; though the day was perfectly calm and sultry. I immediately cast my eyes toward the cleared ground, from which I was but at a small distance, in order to see whether it was not occasioned by a sudden shower; when at that instant a sound resembling a deep rough voice, uttered, as I thought, a few inarticulate monosyllables. Alarmed and surprized, I precipitately looked all round, when I perceived at about six rods distance something resembling a cage, suspended to the limbs of a tree; all the branches of which appeared covered with large birds of prey, fluttering about, and anxiously endeavouring to perch on the cage. Actuated by an involuntary motion of my hands, more than by any design of my mind, I fired at them; they all flew to a short distance, with a most hideous noise: when, horrid to think and painful to repeat, I perceived a negro, suspended in the cage, and left there to expire! I shudder when I recollect that the birds had already picked out his eyes, his cheek bones were bare; his arms had been attacked in several places, and his body seemed covered with a multitude of wounds. From the edges of the hollow sockets and from the lacerations with which he was disfigured, the blood slowly dropped, and tinged the ground beneath. No sooner were the birds flown, than swarms of insects covered the whole body of this unfortunate wretch, eager to feed on his mangled flesh and to drink his blood. I found myself suddenly arrested by the power of affright and terror; my nerves were convulsed; I trembled, I stood motionless, involuntarily contemplating the fate of this negro, in all its dismal latitude. The living spectre, though deprived of his eyes, could still distinctly hear, and in his uncouth dialect begged me to give him some water to allay his thirst. Humanity herself would have recoiled back with horror; she would have balanced whether to lessen such reliefless distress, or mercifully with one blow to end this dreadful scene of agonizing torture! Had I had a ball in my gun, I certainly should have despatched him; but finding myself unable to perform so kind an office, I sought, though trembling, to relieve him as well as I could. A shell ready fixed to a pole, which had been used by some negroes, presented itself to me; I filled it with water, and with trembling hands I guided it to the quivering lips of the wretched sufferer. Urged by the irresistible power of thirst, he endeavoured to meet it, as he instinctively guessed its approach by the noise it made in passing through the bars of the cage. "Tankè, you whitè man, tankè you, putè somè poyson and givè me." How long have you been hanging there? I asked him. "Two days, and me no die; the birds, the birds; aaah me!" Oppressed with the reflections which this shocking spectacle afforded me, I mustered strength enough to walk away, and soon reached the house at which I intended to dine. There I heard that the reason for this slave being thus punished, was on account of his having killed the overseer of the plantation. They told me that the laws of

self-preservation rendered such executions necessary; and supported the doctrine of
slavery with the arguments generally made use of to justify the practice; with the
repetition of which I shall not trouble you at present.

Adieu.

1774–1781/1782

William Bartram
1739–1823

William Bartram was the son of the Pennsylvanian botanist, John Bartram, the
renowned self-educated scientist whom Linnaeus called "the greatest natural
botanist in the world." Raised in an atmosphere of Quaker piety and pacificism,
William extended the range of his father's researches and added substantially to
the classification of American plants and wildlife. Though he did not possess his
father's systematic rigor, William brought to their mutual studies a patient eye
for observation, an artistic talent, and an accomplished literary style.

Between 1773 and 1777 William, backed by an affluent London physician,
made a series of scientific expeditions to study the natural life of the largely
unexplored southeastern region of the colonies. Bartram fell in love with the
luxuriant, semitropical landscapes. The report of his journey, *Travels Through
North and South Carolina, Georgia, East and West Florida, the Cherokee Country,
Etc.*, published in Philadelphia in 1791, quickly became one of the most highly
acclaimed books of its time. Its rich and idyllic descriptions, its pantheistic strain,
and its dramatic renditions of nonhuman consciousness—such as the battle of
Florida alligators reprinted here—enthralled such European writers as
Chateaubriand, Southey, Wordsworth, and Coleridge.

The Florida territory had long had a reputation for mystery and violence.
Ponce de León had fought through its jungles searching for the miraculous
fountain that could rejuvenate male sexuality. The Spanish explorer Cabeza de
Vaca had seen his expedition devastated by the Florida wilderness and the
Apalachee Indians. By the middle of the eighteenth century Florida had become a
region of harsh juxtapositions: a newly formed Seminole nation clashed against a
two-hundred-year-old Spanish culture, and an inhospitable wilderness rubbed
against the seedy outposts of white traders.

Florida had become part of the English colonial system in 1763 as a result of
the treaty ending the French and Indian War. At the time, the region was still
one of those strange, vast, sparsely inhabited places known in spanish as
despoblados. Even its major city lay in ruins. Visiting St. Augustine, the oldest
European settlement in North America, William Bartram sadly observed that
soldiers had pulled down half the town for firewood and that the English had
drastically altered the fine old Spanish houses by driving chimneys through the
roofs and installing glass windows. Florida developed so slowly that by 1821,
when the territory officially became a part of the United States, the region
contained merely a few hundred European colonists.

On his travels Bartram meticulously observed not only flora and fauna but insects, soil conditions, waterways, geological formations, and Indian culture as well. Like Thoreau, he preferred to travel alone; rivers, wildlife, an occasional Indian or backwoodsman, and a notebook were his favorite companions. Unnecessary hunting, the exploitation of natural resources, and the prejudicial treatment of Indians never failed to distress him. Though he often idealized Indian life, he nonetheless understood and respected the intricate organization of Indian culture and society. When asked in 1789 by the newly formed American Ethnological Society which of the tribes he had visited seemed most civilized, Bartram pointedly rephrased the question to read "If adopting or imitating the manners and customs of white people is to be termed civilization" before going on to answer it.

Further Reading:
N. B. Fagin, *William Bartram: Interpreter of the American Landscape*, 1933.
E. Earnest, *John and William Bartram, Botanists and Explorers, 1699–1777, 1739–1823*, 1940.
John and William Bartram's America, ed. H. G. Cruickshank, 1957.

Text:
The Travels of William Bartram, ed. F. Harper, 1958.

---

from Travels Through North and South Carolina, Georgia, East and West Florida[1]

[from **The Alligators]**

The evening was temperately cool and calm. The crocodiles began to roar and appear in uncommon numbers along the shores and in the river. I fixed my camp in an open plain, near the utmost projection of the promontory, under the shelter of a large Live Oak, which stood on the highest part of the ground and but a few yards from my boat. From this open, high situation, I had a free prospect of the river, which was a matter of no trivial consideration to me, having good reason to dread the subtle attacks of the allegators,[2] who were crouding about my harbour. Having collected a good quantity of wood for the purpose of keeping up a light and smoke during the night, I began to think of preparing my supper, when, upon examining my stores, I found but a scanty provision, I thereupon determined, as the most expeditious way of supplying my necessities, to take my bob and try for some trout. About one

---

[1] The complete title is *Travels Through North and South Carolina, Georgia, East and West Florida, the Cherokee Country, the Extensive Territories of the Muscogulges, or Creek Confederacy, and the Country of the Chactaws, Containing an Account of the Soil of Those Regions, Together with* *Obsevations on the Manners of the Indians.* This celebrated passage recounts an incident at the entrance of St. John's River into Lake Dexter, Florida.

[2] Alligators. Bartram uses *crocodile* and *alligator* interchangeably.

hundred yards above my harbour, began a cove or bay of the river, out of which opened a large lagoon. The mouth or entrance from the river to it was narrow, but the waters soon after spread and formed a little lake, extending into the marshes, its entrance and shores within I observed to be verged with floating lawns of the Pistia and Nymphea[3] and other aquatic plants; these I knew were excellent haunts for trout.

The verges and islets of the lagoon were elegantly embellished with flowering plants and shrubs; the laughing coots with wings half spread were tripping over the little coves and hiding themselves in the tufts of grass; young broods of the painted summer teal, skimming the still surface of the waters, and following the watchful parent unconscious of danger, were frequently surprised by the voracious trout, and he in turn, as often by the subtle, greedy alligator. Behold him rushing forth from the flags and reeds. His enormous body swells. His plaited tail brandished high, floats upon the lake. The waters like a cataract descend from his opening jaws. Clouds of smoke issue from his dilated nostrils. The earth trembles with his thunder. When immediately from the opposite coast of the lagoon, emerges from the deep his rival champion. They suddenly dart upon each other. The boiling surface of the lake marks their rapid course, and a terrific conflict commences. They now sink to the bottom folded together in horrid wreaths. The water becomes thick and discoloured. Again they rise, their jaws clap together, re-echoing through the deep surrounding forests. Again they sink, when the contest ends at the muddy bottom of the lake, and the vanquished makes a hazardous escape, hiding himself in the muddy turbulent waters and sedge on a distant shore. The proud victor exulting returns to the place of action. The shores and forests resound his dreadful roar, together with the triumphing shouts of the plaited tribes around, witnesses of the horrid combat.

My apprehensions were highly alarmed after being a spectator of so dreadful a battle; it was obvious that every delay would but tend to encrease my dangers and difficulties, as the sun was near setting, and the alligators gathered around my harbour from all quarters; from these considerations I concluded to be expeditious in my trip to the lagoon, in order to take some fish. Not thinking it prudent to take my fusee[4] with me, lest I might lose it overboard in case of a battle, which I had every reason to dread before my return, I therefore furnished myself with a club for my defence, went on board, and penetrating the first line of those which surrounded my harbour, they gave way; but being pursued by several very large ones, I kept strictly on the watch, and paddled with all my might towards the entrance of the lagoon, hoping to be sheltered there from the multitude of my assailants; but ere I had half-way reached the place, I was attacked on all sides, several endeavouring to overset the canoe. My situation now became precarious to the last degree: two very large ones attacked me closely, at the same instant, rushing up with their heads and part of their bodies above the water, roaring terribly and belching floods of water over me. They struck their jaws together so close to my ears, as almost to stun me, and I expected every moment to be dragged out of the boat and instantly devoured, but I applied my weapons so effectually about me, though at random, that I was so successful as to beat them off a little; when, finding that they designed to renew the battle, I made for the shore, as the only means left me for my preservation, for, by keeping close to it, I should have my enemies on one side of me only, whereas I was before

---

[3] Pistia: water lettuce; Nymphea: water chestnut.   [4] Light musket.

surrounded by them, and there was a probability, if pushed to the last extremity, of saving myself, by jumping out of the canoe on shore, as it is easy to outwalk them on land, although comparatively as swift as lightning in the water. I found this last expedient alone could fully answer my expectations, for as soon as I gained the shore they drew off and kept aloof. This was a happy relief, as my confidence was, in some degree, recovered by it. On recollecting myself, I discovered that I had almost reached the entrance of the lagoon, and determined to venture in, if possible to take a few fish and then return to my harbour, while day-light continued; for I could now, with caution and resolution, make my way with safety along shore, and indeed there was no other way to regain my camp, without leaving my boat and making my retreat through the marshes and reeds, which, if I could even effect, would have been in a manner throwing myself away, for then there would have been no hopes of ever recovering my bark, and returning in safety to any settlements of men. I accordingly proceeded and made good my entrance into the lagoon, though not without opposition from the alligators, who formed a line across the entrance, but did not pursue me into it, nor was I molested by any there, though there were some very large ones in a cove at the upper end. I soon caught more trout than I had present occasion for, and the air was too hot and sultry to admit of their being kept for many hours, even though salted or barbecued. I now prepared for my return to camp, which I succeeded in with but little trouble, by keeping close to the shore, yet I was opposed upon re-entering the river out of the lagoon, and pursued near to my landing (though not closely attacked) particularly by an old daring one, about twelve feet in length, who kept close after me, and when I stepped on shore and turned about, in order to draw up my canoe, he rushed up near my feet and lay there for some time, looking me in the face, his head and shoulders out of water; I resolved he should pay for his temerity, and having a heavy load in my fusee, I ran to my camp, and returning with my piece, found him with his foot on the gunwale of the boat, in search of fish, on my coming up he withdrew sullenly and slowly into the water, but soon returned and placed himself in his former position, looking at me and seeming neither fearful or any way disturbed. I soon dispatched him by lodging the contents of my gun in his head, and then proceeded to cleanse and prepare my fish for supper, and accordingly took them out of the boat, laid them down on the sand close to the water, and began to scale them, when, raising my head, I saw before me, through the clear water, the head and shoulders of a very large alligator, moving slowly towards me; I instantly stepped back, when, with a sweep of his tail, he brushed off several of my fish. It was certainly most providential that I looked up at that instant, as the monster would probably, in less than a minute, have seized and dragged me into the river. This incredible boldness of the animal disturbed me greatly, supposing there could now be no reasonable safety for me during the night, but by keeping continually on the watch; I therefore, as soon as I had prepared the fish, proceeded to secure myself and effects in the best manner I could: in the first place, I hauled my bark upon the shore, almost clear out of the water, to prevent their oversetting or sinking her, after this every moveable was taken out and carried to my camp, which was but a few yards off; then ranging some dry wood in such order as was the most convenient, cleared the ground round about it, that there might be no impediment in my way, in case of an attack in the night, either from the water or the land; for I discovered by this time, that this small isthmus, from its remote situation and fruitfulness, was resorted to by bears and wolves. Having prepared myself in the best manner I could, I charged my gun and proceeded to reconnoitre my camp and the adjacent grounds; when I discovered that the peninsula and grove, at the distance of about two hundred yards from my encampment, on the land side, were invested by a Cypress swamp, covered with water, which below was joined to the shore of the little lake, and above to the marshes surrounding the lagoon, so that I was confined to an islet exceedingly circumscribed, and I found there was no other retreat for me, in case of an attack, but by either ascending one of the large Oaks, or pushing off with my boat.

It was by this time dusk, and the alligators had nearly ceased their roar, when I was again alarmed by a tumultuous noise that seemed to be in my harbour, and therefore engaged my immediate attention. Returning to my camp I found it undisturbed, and then continued on to the extreme point of the promontory, where I saw a scene, new and surprising, which at first threw my senses into such a tumult, that it was some time before I could comprehend what was the matter; however, I soon accounted for the prodigious assemblage of crocodiles at this place, which exceeded every thing of the kind I had ever heard of.

How shall I express myself so as to convey an adequate idea of it to the reader, and at the same time avoid raising suspicions of my want of veracity. Should I say, that the river (in this place) from shore to shore, and perhaps near half a mile above and below me, appeared to be one solid bank of fish, of various kinds, pushing through this narrow pass of St. Juans[5] into the little lake, on their return down the river, and that the alligators were in such incredible numbers, and so close together from shore to shore, that it would have been easy to have walked across on their heads, had the animals been harmless. What expressions can sufficiently declare the shocking scene that for some minutes continued, whilst this mighty army of fish were forcing the pass? During this attempt, thousands, I may say hundreds of thousands of them were caught and swallowed by the devouring alligators. I have seen an alligator take up out of the water several great fish at a time, and just squeeze them betwixt his jaws, while the tails of the great trout flapped about his eyes and lips, ere he had swallowed them. The horrid noise of their closing jaws, their plunging amidst the broken banks of fish, and rising with their prey some feet upright above the water, the floods of water and blood rushing out of their mouths, and the clouds of vapour issuing from their wide nostrils, were truly frightful. This scene continued at intervals during the night, as the fish came to the pass. After this sight, shocking and tremendous as it was, I found myself somewhat easier and more reconciled to my situation, being convinced that their extraordinary assemblage here, was owing to this annual feast of fish, and that they were so well employed in their own element, that I had little occasion to fear their paying me a visit. . . .

The alligator when full grown is a very large and terrible creature, and of prodigious strength, activity and swiftness in the water. I have seen them twenty feet in length, and some are supposed to be twenty-two or twenty-three feet; their body is as large as that of a horse; their shape exactly resembles that of a lizard, except their tail, which is flat or cuniform, being compressed on each side, and gradually diminishing from the abdomen to the extremity, which, with the whole body is covered with horny plates or squamae,[6] impenetrable when on the body of the live animal, even

---

[5] The St. Johns River.   [6] Scales.

to a rifle ball, except about their head and just behind their fore-legs or arms, where it is said they are only vulnerable. The head of a full grown one is about three feet, and the mouth opens nearly the same length, the eyes are small in proportion and seem sunk deep in the head, by means of the prominency of the brows; the nostrils are large, inflated and prominent on the top, so that the head in the water, resembles, at a distance, a great chunk of wood floating about. Only the upper jaw moves, which they raise almost perpendicular, so as to form a right angle with the lower one. In the fore part of the upper jaw, on each side, just under the nostrils, are two very large, thick, strong teeth or tusks, not very sharp, but rather the shape of a cone, these are as white as the finest polished ivory, and are not covered by any skin or lips, and always in sight, which gives the creature a frightful appearance; in the lower jaw are holes opposite to these teeth, to receive them; when they clap their jaws together it causes a surprising noise, like that which is made by forcing a heavy plank with violence upon the ground, and may be heard at a great distance.

But what is yet more surprising to a stranger, is the incredible loud and terrifying roar, which they are capable of making, especially in the spring season, their breeding time; it most resembles very heavy distant thunder, not only shaking the air and waters, but causing the earth to tremble; and when hundreds and thousands are roaring at the same time, you can scarcely be persuaded, but that the whole globe is violently and dangerously agitated.

An old champion, who is perhaps absolute sovereign of a little lake or lagoon (when fifty less than himself are obliged to content themselves with swelling and roaring in little coves round about) darts forth from the reedy coverts all at once, on the surface of the waters, in a right line; at first seemingly as rapid as lightning, but gradually more slowly until he arrives at the center of the lake, when he stops; he now swells himself by drawing in wind and water through his mouth, which causes a loud sonorous rattling in the throat for near a minute, but it is immediately forced out again through his mouth and nostrils, with a loud noise, brandishing his tail in the air, and the vapour ascending from his nostrils like smoke. At other times, when swollen to an extent ready to burst, his head and tail lifted up, he spins or twirls round on the surface of the water. He acts his part like an Indian chief when rehearsing his feats of war, and then retiring, the exhibition is continued by others who dare to step forth, and strive to excel each other, to gain the attention of the favourite female. . . .

1791

Gustavus Vassa (Oloudah Equiano)
1745–1801

Gustavus Vassa's *Narrative* reminds us that not all colonial American writings represent the New World as a pastoral Eden, as a New English Israel of the chosen people, or (in John Adams's term) as a "grand Design in Providence for the illumination of all mankind." Vassa's America is a slave state encountered through "the violence of the African trader, the pestilential stench of a Guinea [slave] ship, and the lash and lust of a brutal and unrelenting overseer." Vassa's *Narrative,* published in England, understandably was recognized on both sides of the Atlantic as a valuable antislavery polemic.

Vassa was born in Benin, west of the lower Niger River in western Africa. At age eleven he was kidnapped, enslaved, and sold repeatedly to different African tribal families. Reaching the coast, he saw "the sea and a slave ship" and succumbed to the most brutal treatment of his young life as a captive of "nominal Christians" transporting their human cargo to America. For a time Vassa served on a Virginia plantation; from there he was sold to a British naval officer, who helped to educate him. Subsequently he became the slave of a Philadelphia merchant and worked on vessels bound for the West Indies. His last owner helped him purchase his freedom, after which Vassa traveled as a ship's steward, became converted to Methodism, and settled permanently in England to work for the abolition of slavery. In 1790 Vassa presented to Parliament a petition calling for the end of the slave trade.

The Interesting Narrative of the Life of Oloudah Equiano, or Gustavus Vassa was published in two volumes in London in 1789. In the next five years, eight editions of this successful work appeared. In its own day the *Narrative* interested some readers as an exciting travel book, others as an antislavery tract. In American literature it is a minority report on human rights. Held for comparison against the Declaration of Independence and Paine's *Common Sense,* it becomes a scathing commentary on the gulf between American ideals and actualities.

Further Reading:
Equiano's Travels, ed. P. Edwards, 1966.
Cavalcade: Negro American Writing from 1760 to the Present, ed. A. Davis and S. Redding, 1971.

Text:
The Interesting Narrative of the Life of Oloudah Equiano, or Gustavus Vassa, 2 vols., 1789.

from The Interesting Narrative of the Life of Oloudah Equiano

[Chapter II:] Kidnapping and Enslavement

I hope the reader will not think I have trespassed on his patience in introducing myself to him, with some account of the manners and customs of my country. They had been implanted in me with great care, and made an impression on my mind which time could not erase, and which all the adversity and variety of fortune I have since experienced served only to rivet and record; for, whether the love of one's country be real or imaginary, or a lesson of reason, or an instinct of nature, I still look back with pleasure on the first scenes of my life, though that pleasure has been for the most part mingled with sorrow.

I have already acquainted the reader with the time and place of my birth. My father, besides many slaves, had a numerous family, of which seven lived to grow up, including myself and a sister, who was the only daughter. As I was the youngest of the sons, I became, of course, the greatest favorite with my mother, and was always with her; and she used to take particular pains to form my mind. I was trained up from my earliest years in the arts of agriculture and war: my daily exercise was shooting and throwing javelins; and my mother adorned me with emblems, after the manner of our greatest warriors. In this way I grew up till I was turned the age of eleven, when an end was put to my happiness in the following manner:—Generally, when the grown people in the neighborhood were gone far in the fields to labour, the children assembled together in some of the neighbors' premises to play; and commonly some of us used to get up a tree to look out for any assailant or kidnapper that might come upon us; for they sometimes took those opportunities of our parents' absence, to attack and carry off as many as they could seize. One day, as I was watching at the top of a tree in our yard, I saw one of those people come into the yard of our next neighbor but one, to kidnap, there being many stout young people in it. Immediately, on this, I gave the alarm of the rogue, and he was surrounded by the stoutest of them, who entangled him with cords, so that he could not escape till some of the grown people came and secured him.

But alas! ere long, it was my fate to be thus attacked, and to be carried off, when none of our grown people were nigh. One day, when all our people were gone out to their works as usual, and only I and my dear sister were left to mind the house, two men and a woman got over our walls, and in a moment seized us both; and without giving us time to cry out, or make resistance, they stopped our mouths and ran off with us into the nearest wood. Here they tied our hands, and continued to carry us as far as they could, till night came on, when we reached a small house, where the robbers halted for refreshment, and spent the night. We were then unbound, but were unable to take any food; and, being quite overpowered by fatigue and grief, our only relief was some sleep, which allayed our misfortune for a short time. The next morning we left the house, and continued traveling all the day. For a long time we had kept the woods, but at last we came into a road which I believed I knew. I now had some hopes of being delivered; for we had advanced but a little way when I discovered some people at a distance, on which I began to cry out for their assistance; but my cries had no other effect than to make them tie me faster and stop my mouth, and then they put me into a large sack. They also stopped my sister's mouth and tied her hands; and in this manner we proceeded till we were out of the sight of these people.—When we went to rest the following night they offered us some victuals, but we refused them; and the only comfort we had was in being in one another's arms all that night, and bathing each other with our tears.

But alas! we were soon deprived of even the small comfort of weeping together. The next day proved a day of greater sorrow than I had yet experienced; for my sister and I were then separated, while we lay clasped in each other's arms: it was in vain that we besought them not to part us; she was torn from me, and immediately carried away, while I was left in a state of distraction not to be described. I cried and grieved continually; and for several days did not eat any thing but what they forced into my mouth. At length, after many days traveling, during which I had often changed masters, I got into the hands of a chieftain, in a very pleasant country. This man had two wives and some children, and they all used me extremely well, and did all they could to comfort me; particularly the first wife, who was something like my mother. Although I was a great many days journey from my father's house, yet these people spoke exactly the same language with us. This first master of mine, as I may call him, was a smith, and my principal employment was working his bellows, which was the same kind as I had seen in my vicinity. They were in some respects not unlike the stoves here in gentlemen's kitchens; and were covered over with leather; and in the middle of that leather a stick was fixed, and a person stood up, and worked it, in the same manner as is done to pump water out of a cask with a hand pump. I believe it was gold he worked, for it was of a lovely bright yellow colour, and was worn by the women on their wrists and ancles. I was there I suppose about a month, and they at last used to trust me some little distance from the house. This liberty I used in embracing every opportunity to inquire the way to my own home: and I also sometimes, for the same purpose, went with the maidens, in the cool of the evenings, to bring pitchers of water from the springs for the use of the house.

I had also remarked where the sun rose in the morning, and set in the evening, as I had travelled along; and I had observed that my father's house was towards the rising of the sun. I therefore determined to seize the first opportunity of making my escape, and to shape my course for that quarter; for I was quite oppressed and weighed down by grief after my mother and friends; and my love of liberty, ever great, was strengthened by the mortifying circumstance of not daring to eat with the free-born children, although I was mostly their companion.—While I was projecting my escape one day, an unlucky event happened, which quite disconcerted my plan, and put an end to my hopes. I used to be sometimes employed in assisting an elderly woman slave to cook and take care of the poultry; and one morning while I was feeding some chickens, I happened to toss a small pebble at one of them, which hit it on the middle, and directly killed it. The old slave, having soon after missed the chicken, inquired after it; and on my relating the accident, (for I told her the truth, because my mother would never suffer me to tell a lie), she flew into a violent passion, threatened that I should suffer for it; and, my master being out, she immediately went and told her mistress what I had done. This alarmed me very much, and I expected an instant flogging, which to me was uncommonly dreadful; for I had seldom been beaten at home.

I therefore resolved to fly; and accordingly I ran into a thicket that was hard by, and hid myself in the bushes. Soon afterwards my mistress and the slave returned, and, not seeing me, they searched all the house, but not finding me, and I not making answer when they called to me, they thought I had run away, and the whole neighborhood was raised in the pursuit of me. In that part of the country (as well as ours) the houses and villages were skirted with woods or shrubberies, and the bushes were so thick, that a man could readily conceal himself in them, so as to elude the strictest search. The neighbors continued the whole day looking for me, and several times many of them came within a few yards of the place where I lay hid. I expected every moment, when I heard a rustling among the trees, to be found out, and punished by my master; but they never discovered me, though they were often so near that I even heard their conjectures as they were looking about for me; and I now learned from them that any attempt to return home would be hopeless. Most of them supposed I had fled towards home; but the distance was so great, and the way so intricate, that they thought I could never reach it, and that I should be lost in the woods. When I heard this I was seized with a violent panic, and abandoned myself to despair. Night too began to approach, and aggravated all my fears. I had before entertained hopes of getting home, and had determined when it should be dark to make the attempt; but I was now convinced that it was fruitless, and began to consider that, if possibly I could escape all other animals, I could not those of the human kind; and that, not knowing the way, I must perish in the woods.—Thus was I like the hunted deer:

—"Ev'ry leaf, and ev'ry whisp'ring breath
"Convey'd a foe, and ev'ry foe a death."

I heard frequent rustlings among the leaves; and being pretty sure they were snakes, I expected every instant to be stung by them.—This increased my anguish; and the horror of my situation became now quite insupportable. I at length quitted the thicket, very faint and hungry, for I had not eaten or drank anything all the day, and crept to my master's kitchen, from whence I set out at first, and which was an open shed, and laid myself down in the ashes with an anxious wish for death to relieve me from all my pains. I was scarcely awake in the morning, when the old woman slave, who was the first up, came to light the fire, and saw me in the fireplace. She was very much surprised to see me, and could scarcely believe her own eyes. She now promised to intercede for me, and went for her master, who soon after came, and having lightly reprimanded me, ordered me to be taken care of, and not ill treated.

Soon after this my master's only daughter and child by his first wife sickened and died, which affected him so much that for some time he was almost frantic, and really would have killed himself, had he not been watched and prevented. However, in a small time afterwards he recovered and I was again sold. I was now carried to the left of the sun's rising, through many dreary wastes and dismal woods, amidst the hideous roaring of wild beasts.—The people I was sold to used to carry me very often, when I was tired, either on their shoulders or on their backs. I saw many convenient well-built sheds along the road, at proper distances, to accommodate the merchants and travellers, who lay in those buildings along with their wives, who often accompany them; and they always go well armed.

From the time I left my own nation I always found somebody that understood me till I came to the sea coast. The languages of different nations did not totally differ, nor were they so copious as those of the Europeans, particularly the English. They were therefore easily learned; and while I was journeying thus through Africa, I acquired two or three different tongues. In this manner I had been travelling for a considerable time, when one evening to my great surprise, whom should I see brought to the house where I was but my dear sister? As soon as she saw me she gave a loud shriek, and ran into my arms. I was quite overpowered: neither of us could speak, but, for a considerable time, clung to each other in mutual embraces, unable to do anything but weep. Our meeting affected all who saw us; and indeed I must acknowledge, in honour of those sable destroyers of human rights, that I never met with any ill treatment, or saw any offered to their slaves, except tying them, when necessary to keep them from running away. When these people knew we were brother and sister, they indulged us to be together; and the man, to whom I supposed we belonged, lay with us, he in the middle, while she and I held one another by the hands across his breast all night; and thus for awhile we forgot our misfortunes in the joy of being together; but even this small comfort was soon to have an end; for scarcely had the fatal morning appeared, when she was again torn from me for ever! I was now more miserable, if possible, than before. The small relief which her presence gave me from pain was gone, and the wretchedness of my situation was redoubled by my anxiety after her fate, and my apprehensions lest her sufferings should be greater than mine, when I could not be with her to alleviate them. Yes, thou dear partner of my childish sports! thou sharer of my joys and sorrows! happy should I have ever esteemed myself to encounter every misery for you, and to procure your freedom by the sacrifice of my own! Though you were early forced from my arms, your image has been always rivetted in my heart, from which neither *time nor fortune* have been able to remove it: so that, while the thoughts of your suffering have dampened my prosperity, they have mingled with adversity and increased its bitterness.—To that Heaven which protects the weak from the strong, I commit the care of your innocence and virtues, if they have not already received their full reward, and if your youth and delicacy have not long since fallen victims to the violence of the African trader, the pestilential stench of a Guinea ship, the seasoning in the European colonies, or the lash and lust of a brutal and unrelenting overseer.

I did not long remain after my sister. I was again sold, and carried through a number of places, till after travelling a considerable time, I came to a town called Tinmah, in the most beautiful country I had yet seen in Africa. It was extremely rich, and there were many rivulets which flowed through it, and supplied a large pond in the centre of the town, where the people washed. Here I first saw and tasted cocoa nuts, which I thought superior to any nuts I had ever tasted before; and the trees which were loaded were also interspersed among the houses, which had commodious shades adjoining, and were in the same manner as ours, the insides being neatly plastered and whitewashed. Here I also saw and tasted for the first time, sugar cane. Their money consisted of little white shells, the size of the finger nail. I was sold here for one hundred and seventy-two of them, by a merchant who lived and brought me there. I had been about two or three days at his house, when a wealthy widow, a neighbor of his, came there one evening, and brought with her an only son, a young gentleman about my own age and size. Here they saw me; and having taken a fancy to me, I was bought of the merchant, and went home with them. Her house and premises were situated close to one of those rivulets I have mentioned, and were the finest I ever saw in Africa: they were very extensive, and she had a number of slaves to attend her. The next day I was washed and perfumed, and when meal time came, I was led into the presence of my mistress, and ate and drank before her with her son. This filled me with astonishment; and I could scarce help expressing my surprise that the young gentleman should suffer me, who was bound, to eat with him who was free; and not only so, but that he would not at any time either eat or drink till I had taken first, because I was the eldest, which was agreeable to our custom. Indeed, everything here, and all their treatment of me, made me forget that I was a slave. The language of these people resembled ours so nearly, that we understood each other perfectly. They had also the same customs as we. There were likewise slaves daily to attend us, while my young master and I, with other boys, sported with our darts and bows and arrows, as I had been used to do at home. In this resemblance to my former happy state, I passed about two months; and I now began to think I was to be adopted into the family, and was beginning to be reconciled to my situation, and to forget by degrees my misfortunes, when all at once the delusion vanished; for, without the least previous knowledge, one morning early, while my dear master and companion was still asleep, I was awakened out of my reverie to fresh sorrow, and hurried away even amongst the uncircumcised.[1]

Thus at the very moment I dreamed of the greatest happiness, I found myself most miserable; and it seemed as if fortune wished to give me this taste of joy only to render the reverse more poignant.——The change I now experienced, was as painful as it was sudden and unexpected. It was a change indeed, from a state of bliss to a scene which is inexpressible by me, as it discovered to me an element I had never before beheld, and till then had no idea of, and wherein such instances of hardship and cruelty occurred, as I can never reflect on but with horror.

All the nations and people I had hitherto passed through, resembled our own in their manners, customs and language; but I came at length to a country, the inhabitants of which differed from us in all those particulars. I was very much struck with this difference, especially when I came among a people who did not circumcise, and ate without washing their hands. They cooked also in iron pots, and had European cutlasses and cross bows, which were unknown to us, and fought with their fists among themselves. Their women were not so modest as ours, for they ate and drank, and slept with their men. But, above all, I was amazed to see no sacrifices or offerings among them. In some of these places the people ornamented themselves with scars, and likewise filed their teeth very sharp. They wanted sometimes to ornament me in the same manner, but I would not suffer them; hoping that I might some time be among a people who did not thus disfigure themselves, as I thought they did. At last I came to the banks of a large river which was covered with canoes, in which the people appeared to live with their household utensils, and provisions of all kinds. I was beyond measure astonished at this, as I had never before seen any water larger than a pond or a rivulet: and my surprise was mingled with no small fear when I was put into one of these canoes, and we began to paddle and move along the river. We continued going on thus till night, when we came to land, and made fires on the banks, each family by themselves; some dragged their canoes on shore, others stayed and cooked in theirs, and laid in them all night. Those on the land had mats, of which they made tents, some in the shape of little houses; in these we slept; and after the morning meal, we embarked again and proceeded as before. I was often very much astonished to see some of the women, as well as the men, jump into the water, dive to the bottom, come up again, and swim about.——Thus I continued to travel, sometimes by land, sometimes by water, through different countries and various nations, till, at the end of six or seven months after I had been kidnapped, I arrived at the sea coast. It would be tedious and uninteresting to relate all the incidents which befell me during this journey, and which I have not yet forgotten; of the various hands I passed through, and the manners and customs of all the different people among whom I lived. I shall therefore only observe, that in all the places where I was, the soil was exceedingly rich; the pumpkins, eadas, plaintains, yams, etc., were in great abundance, and of incredible size. There were also vast quantities of different gums, though not used for any purpose, and every where a great deal of tobacco. The cotton even grew quite wild, and there was plenty of red-wood. I saw no mechanics whatever in all

[1] I.e., he was treated as a person of low esteem.

the way, except such as I have mentioned. The chief employment in all these countries was agriculture, and both the males and females, as with us, were brought up to it, and trained in the arts of war.

The first object which saluted my eyes when I arrived on the coast, was the sea, and a slave ship, which was then riding at anchor, and waiting for its cargo. These filled me with astonishment, which was soon converted into terror, when I was carried on board. I was immediately handled, and tossed up to see if I were sound, by some of the crew; and I was now persuaded that I had gotten into a world of bad spirits, and that they were going to kill me. Their complexions, too, differing so much from ours, their long hair, and the language they spoke, (which was very different from any I had ever heard) united to confirm me in this belief. Indeed, such were the horrors of my views and fears at the moment, that, if ten thousand worlds had been my own, I would have freely parted with them all to have exchanged my condition with that of the meanest slave in my own country. When I looked round the ship too, and saw a large furnace of copper boiling, and a multitude of black people of every description chained together, every one of their countenances expressing dejection and sorrow, I no longer doubted of my fate; and quite overpowered with horror and anguish, I fell motionless on the deck and fainted. When I recovered a little, I found some black people about me, who I believed were some of those who had brought me on board, and had been receiving their pay; they talked to me in order to cheer me, but all in vain. I asked them if we were not to be eaten by those white men with horrible looks, red faces and long hair. They told me I was not: and one of the crew brought me a small portion of spirituous liquor in a wine glass, but, being afraid of him, I would not take it out of his hand. One of the blacks, therefore, took it from him and gave it to me, and I took a little down my palate, which, instead of reviving me, as they thought it would, threw me into the greatest consternation at the strange feeling it produced, having never tasted any such liquor before. Soon after this, the blacks who brought me on board went off, and left me abandoned to despair.

I now saw myself deprived of all chance of returning to my native country, or even the least glimpse of hope of gaining the shore, which I now considered as friendly; and I even wished for my former slavery in preference to my present situation, which was filled with horrors of every kind, still heightened by my ignorance of what I was to undergo. I was not long suffered to indulge my grief; I was soon put down under the decks, and there I received such a salutation in my nostrils as I had never experienced in my life: so that, with the loathsomeness of the stench and crying together, I became so sick and low that I was not able to eat, nor had I the least desire to taste any thing. I now wished for the last friend, death, to relieve me; but soon, to my grief, two of the white men offered me eatables; and, on my refusing to eat, one of them held me fast by the hands, and laid me across, I think the windlass, and tied my feet, while the other flogged me severely. I had never experienced any thing of this kind before, and although not being used to the water, I naturally feared that element the first time I saw it, yet, nevertheless, could I have got over the nettings, I would have jumped over the side, but I could not; and besides, the crew used to watch us very closely who were not chained down to the decks, lest we should leap into the water; and I have seen some of these poor African prisoners most severely cut, for attempting to do so, and hourly whipped for not eating. This indeed was often the case with myself. In a little time after, amongst the poor chained men, I found some of my own nation, which in a small degree gave ease to my mind. I inquired of these what was to be done with us? They gave me to understand, we were to be carried to these white people's country to work for them. I then was a little revived, and thought, if it were no worse than working, my situation was not so desperate; but still I feared I should be put to death, the white people looked and acted, as I thought, in so savage a manner; for I had never seen among any people such instances of brutal cruelty; and this not only shown towards us blacks, but also to some of the whites themselves. One white man in particular I saw, when we were permitted to be on deck, flogged so unmercifully with a large rope near the foremast, that he died in consequence of it; and they tossed him over the side as they would have done a brute. This made me fear these people the more; and I expected nothing less than to be treated in the same manner. I could not help expressing my fears and apprehensions to some of my countrymen; I asked them if these people had no country, but lived in this hollow place? (the ship) they told me they did not, but came from a distant one. "Then," said I, "how comes it in all our country we never heard of them?" They told me because they lived so very far off. I then asked where were their women? had they any like themselves? I was told they had. "And why," said I, "do we not see them?" They answered, because they were left behind. I asked how the vessel could go? they told me they could not tell; but that there was cloth put upon the masts by the help of the ropes I saw, and then the vessel went on; and the white men had some spell or magic they put in the water when they liked in order to stop the vessel. I was exceedingly amazed at this account, and really thought they were spirits. I therefore wished much to be from amongst them, for I expected they would sacrifice me; but my wishes were vain, for we were so quartered that it was impossible for any of us to make our escape.

While we stayed on the coast I was mostly on deck; and one day, to my great astonishment, I saw one of these vessels coming in with the sails up. As soon as the whites saw it, they gave a great shout, at which we were amazed; and the more so, as the vessel appeared larger by approaching nearer. At last, she came to an anchor in my sight, and when the anchor was let go, I and my countrymen who saw it, were lost in astonishment to observe the vessel stop—and were now convinced it was done by magic. Soon after this the other ship got her boats out, and they came on board of us, and the people of both ships seemed very glad to see each other.—Several of the strangers also shook hands with us black people, and made motions with their hands, signifying, I suppose, we were to go to their country, but we did not understand them.

At last, when the ship we were in, had got in all her cargo, they made ready with many fearful noises, and we were all put under deck, so that we could not see how they managed the vessel. But this disappointment was the least of my sorrow. The stench of the hold while we were on the coast was so intolerably loathsome, that it was dangerous to remain there for any time, and some of us had been permitted to stay on the deck for the fresh air; but now that the whole ship's cargo were confined together, it became absolutely pestilential. The closeness of the place, and the heat of the climate, added to the number in the ship, which was so crowded that each had scarcely room to turn himself, almost suffocated us. This produced copious perspirations, so that the air soon became unfit for respiration, from a variety of loathsome smells, and brought on a sickness among the slaves, of which many died—thus falling victims to the improvident avarice, as I may call it, of their purchasers. This wretched situation was again aggravated by the falling of the chains, now become insupportable; and the filth of the necessary tubs, into which the children often fell, and were almost suffocated. The shrieks of the women, and the groans of the dying, rendered the whole a scene of horror almost inconceivable. Happily perhaps, for myself, I was soon reduced so low here that it was thought necessary to keep me almost always on deck; and from my extreme youth I was not put in fetters. In this situation I expected every hour to share the fate of my companions, some of whom were almost daily brought upon the deck at the point of death, which I began to hope would soon put an end to my miseries. Often did I think many of the inhabitants of the deep much more happy than myself. I envied them the freedom they enjoyed, and as often wished I could change my condition for theirs. Every circumstance I met with, served only to render my state more painful, and heightened my apprehensions, and my opinion of the cruelty of the whites.

One day they had taken a number of fishes; and when they had killed and satisfied themselves with as many as they thought fit, to our astonishment, who were on deck, rather than give any of them to us to eat, as we expected, they tossed the remaining fish into the sea again, although we begged and prayed for some as well as we could, but in vain; and some of my countrymen, being pressed by hunger, took an opportunity, when they thought no one saw them, of trying to get a little privately; but they were discovered, and the attempt procured them some very severe floggings. One day, when we had a smooth sea and moderate wind, two of my wearied countrymen who were chained together, (I was near them at the time,) preferring death to such a life of misery, somehow made through the nettings and jumped into the sea: immediately, another quite dejected fellow, who, on account of his illness, was suffered to be out of irons, also followed their example; and I believe many more would very soon have done the same, if they had not been prevented by the ship's crew, who were instantly alarmed. Those of us that were the most active, were in a moment put down under the deck, and there was such a noise and confusion amongst the people of the ship as I never heard before, to stop her and get the boat out to go after the slaves. However, two of the wretched were drowned, but they got the other, and afterwards flogged him unmercifully, for thus attempting to prefer death to slavery. In this manner we continued to undergo more hardships than I can now relate, hardships which are inseparable from this accursed trade. Many a time we were near suffocation from the want of fresh air, which we were often without for whole days together. This and the stench of the necessary tubs, carried off many.

During our passage, I first saw flying fishes, which surprised me very much; they used frequently to fly across the ship, and many of them fell on the deck. I also now first saw the use of the quadrant; I had often with astonishment seen the mariners make observations with it, and I could not think what it meant. They at last took notice of my surprise; and one of them, willing to increase it, as well as to gratify my curiosity, made me one day look through it. The clouds appeared to me to be land, which disappeared as they passed along. This heightened my wonder; and I was now more persuaded than ever, that I was in another world, and that every thing about me was magic. At last, we came in sight of the island of Barbadoes, at which the whites on board gave a great shout, and made many signs of joy to us. We did not know what to think of this; but as the vessel drew nearer, we plainly saw the harbor, and other ships of different kinds and sizes, and we soon anchored amongst them, off Bridgetown. Many merchants and planters now came on board, though it was in the evening. They put us in separate parcels, and examined us attentively. They also made us jump, and pointed to the land, signifying we were to go there. We thought by this, we should be eaten by these ugly men, as they appeared to us; and, when soon after we were all put down under the deck again, there was much dread and trembling among us, and nothing but bitter cries to be heard all the night from these apprehensions, insomuch that at last the white people got some old slaves from the land to pacify us. They told us we were not to be eaten, but to work, and were soon to go on land, where we should see many of our country people. This report eased us much. And sure enough, soon after we were landed, there came to us Africans of all languages.

We were conducted immediately to the merchant's yard, where we were all pent up together, like so many sheep in a fold, without regard to sex or age. As every object was new to me, everything I saw filled me with surprise. What struck me first, was that the houses were built with bricks and stories, and in every other respect different from those I had seen in Africa; but I was still more astonished on seeing people on horseback. I did not know what this could mean; and, indeed, I thought these people were full of nothing but magical arts. While I was in this astonishment, one of my fellow-prisoners spoke to a countryman of his, about the horses, who said they were the same kind they had in their country. I understood them, though they were from a distant part of Africa; and I thought it odd I had not seen any horses there; but afterwards, when I came to converse with different Africans, I found they had many horses amongst them, and much larger than those I then saw.

We were not many days in the merchant's custody, before we were sold after their usual manner, which is this:—On a signal given, (as the beat of a drum,) the buyers rush at once into the yard where the slaves are confined, and make choice of that parcel they like best. The noise and clamor with which this is attended, and the eagerness visible in the countenance of the buyers, serve not a little to increase the apprehension of terrified Africans, who may well be supposed to consider them as the ministers of that destruction to which they think themselves devoted. In this manner, without scruple, are relations and friends separated, most of them never to see each other again. I remember in the vessel in which I was brought over, in the men's apartment, there were several brothers, who, in the sale, were sold in different lots; and it was very moving on this occasion, to see and hear their cries at parting. O, ye nominal Christians! might not an African ask you—Learned you this from your God, who says unto you, Do unto all men as you would men should do unto you? Is it not enough that we are torn from our country and friends, to toil for your luxury and lust of gain? Must every tender feeling be likewise sacrificed to your avarice? Are the dearest friends and relations, now rendered more dear by their separation from their kindred, still to be parted from each other, and thus prevented from cheering the gloom of slavery, with the small comfort of being together, and mingling their sufferings and sorrows? Why are parents to lose their children, brothers their sisters, or husbands their wives? Surely, this is a new refinement in cruelty, which, while it has no advantage to atone for it, thus aggravates distress, and adds fresh horrors even to the wretchedness of slavery.

1789

The Federalist

On October 27, 1787, a month after the Federal Convention presented for
individual state ratification a new constitution to replace the six-year-old Articles
of Confederation, the first of a series of eighty-five incisively argued political
essays defending the new document appeared in a New York newspaper. Signed
"Publius" and explicitly addressed "to the People of New York," the essay,
written by Alexander Hamilton (1757–1804), established immediately the topic
and tone of the series: to persuade the citizens of New York by means of careful
"deliberation" that their personal liberty and security as well as the future
prosperity of the entire country depended on a strong central government, which
only the immediate adoption of the proposed Constitution could provide.
Although the Constitution required only the approval of nine states for
ratification, its supporters felt that anything short of unanimity would cause a
serious breach among the states, one that would inevitably lead to dangerous
alliances among themselves and with foreign nations. Hamilton especially felt that
New York, led by its governor, George Clinton, a powerful advocate of local
sovereignty, represented a key state in the impending battle for ratification.

"Publius" became a collective pseudonym shortly after the first essay as
Hamilton enlisted the help of two other partisans: John Jay (1745–1829), the
affluent, conservative New York attorney who eventually served as a Supreme
Court Justice and later as governor of New York, and the young though
politically seasoned Virginian James Madison (1751–1836), who, more than any
other delegate to the convention, had been responsible for the overall design of
the Constitution and who would later serve as fourth president of the United
States. Since Jay had held the office of secretary of foreign affairs under the
Articles of Confederation and had helped negotiate the Treaty of Paris, his
diplomatic experiences lent impressive support to his essays on international
relations. Because of poor health, however, Jay was able to contribute only five
essays to the series; after the fifth paper it became, with one exception,
exclusively the labor of Hamilton and Madison.

A native of the West Indies, Alexander Hamilton completed his studies at
Columbia (then called King's College), served on Washington's staff during the
Revolution, and afterward established a highly successful law practice in New
York City. At the Constitutional Convention, which he attended sporadically,
Hamilton argued strenuously for an energetic central government headed by a
powerful executive. An outspoken proponent of business interests and
industrialization, Hamilton, as the first secretary of the Treasury, brilliantly
engineered a fiscal policy that gave the floundering new nation the foreign
credibility and domestic assurance it needed to survive. When in January 1790,
only a year and a half after the final *Federalist* essay went to press, Hamilton
submitted to Congress his "Report on the Public Credit," his chief political
opponent had become Publius's other half, James Madison. By then, the
Constitution ratified and the machinery of the new administration in operation,

Madison was thinking and acting more sectionally as a Virginian and less, as Hamilton liked to put it, "continentally" as an American.

But in 1787 Publius's "split personality" could be seen only in a few inconsistencies and disparate emphases, tensions forgivable and easily overlooked in the steadily accumulating output of penetrating political analysis. Composed hastily and under too much pressure, the papers could hardly offer systematic coverage of all the principles of constitutional government. Nevertheless, given the strains of collaboration and deadlines, Publius achieved a remarkably high-minded level of political discourse and an admirable degree of theoretical complexity. The man who would in a few years become Hamilton's fiercest enemy, Thomas Jefferson, considered *The Federalist* "the best commentary on the principles of government, which ever was written" and later made the book required reading for all students at the University of Virginia. What was conceived primarily as a popular series of campaign tracts to influence a relatively small group of voters eventually became, by virtue of its articulation and political discernment, one of the central documents of American government, a necessary supplement to all historical and judicial interpretation of the Constitution.

At the center of Publius's argument, as the opening paper makes clear, is the desire for a strong Union and the belief that a new constitution must supersede the totally inadequate Articles of Confederation. What may seem obvious today, it is important to remember, was not so obvious then. A country that had recently gone through a debilitating war to shake off the political and economic impositions of one strong government was hardly eager to adopt another to replace it. Many Americans naturally equated a strong central government with monarchy. They saw, furthermore, the Articles of Confederation as a perfectly respectable document that guaranteed nearly complete sovereignty to the separate states and, even better, claimed no political authority over individuals. And as Hamilton noted in the first paper, people holding positions in state government would understandably be reluctant to support any new confederation, loose or strong, that threatened the continuation of their offices or promised to diminish their authority. The Constitutional Convention itself, moreover, was viewed by many citizens (especially in New York and Virginia) as unauthorized and extralegal, a fairly open conspiracy among a small group of reactionary, propertied people who, in their enthusiasm to "form a more perfect union," would undoubtedly perpetuate an aristocracy of the wealthy and influential.

Another objection that serious, well-informed citizens raised against the Constitution was that no republic, certainly no democracy, could be maintained in a country as geographically diverse and extensive as their own. In general, objections to the Constitution varied according to the degree of local suspicions and local power. The main task Publius faced throughout the papers was to convince a skeptical public that a strong central government was not only possible and indispensable for security and survival but also that, more important, it was compatible with individual liberty.

In Publius's papers, as in all significant political discourse, definitions and distinctions play a crucial role. In fact, the very title given to the series after the individual essays had been collected in May 1788, *The Federalist,* caused considerable confusion. Those who supported the Articles of Confederation argued that *they* were the real Federalists and contended that Publius had coopted the term to disguise what was essentially a nationalist program. *National,* an explosive political word at the time, had been conscientiously eliminated from the Constitution. The term appears throughout the papers, especially in the thirty-ninth letter, where Madison, always apprehensive about nomenclature, maintains a delicately balanced argument as he moves back and forth between federal and national definitions, continually refining his distinctions as he demonstrates the inevitable interpenetration of both forms in the total operations of government. (Though neither Hamilton nor Madison seems nervous with the word, it is interesting that one of the most decisive reasons that could be offered today for the existence of a national state—a common cultural identity—is rarely appealed to as an argument for union.) In an earlier paper Madison had confronted another result of the "confusion of names," the important distinctions between a republic and a democracy. Language, he acknowledges in yet another paper, is a "cloudy medium" in which the science of politics and the complex institutions it attempts to delineate are continually being trapped in "obscurity."

For Hamilton and Madison, the intellectual confusions brought about by vague and inaccurate definitions and the emotional confusions resulting from "intemperance of expression" presented formidable obstacles to both good government and good writing. Political and literary style was best preserved by adhering to "cool and deliberate" thinking; Publius seldom indulges in rhetorical flourishes. In fact, the vocabulary of "passion" (one of the key words of *The Federalist*) is throughout the series closely associated with the "animosity," "violence," and "disease" generated by the "factions" that Madison examines in the celebrated tenth paper. Hamilton, in particular, was wary of political emotions and believed that the papers would help protect the public from "every sudden breeze of passion or every transient impulse." In their exacting style and dispassionate designs, Publius's essays, always lucid, often ironic, tough-mindedly predisposed to expect the worst and demand the best from human nature, represent the consummate expression of one of America's most consequential political programs and philosophies.

Further Reading:　　　　　　　　　　　**Text:**
G. Dietze, *The Federalist: A Classic on Federalism*　　*The Federalist,* ed. J. E. Cooke, 1961.
and Free Government, 1960.
J. C. Miller, *The Federalist Era,* 1960.

***from* The Federalist**

No. 1 [Alexander Hamilton]

October 27, 1787

To the People of the State of New York.

After an unequivocal experience of the inefficacy of the subsisting Federal Government, you are called upon to deliberate on a new Constitution for the United States of America. The subject speaks its own importance; comprehending in its consequences, nothing less than the existence of the Union, the safety and welfare of the parts of which it is composed, the fate of an empire, in many respects, the most interesting in the world. It has been frequently remarked, that it seems to have been reserved to the people of this country, by their conduct and example, to decide the important question, whether societies of men are really capable or not, of establishing good government from reflection and choice, or whether they are forever destined to depend, for their political constitutions, on accident and force. If there be any truth in the remark, the crisis, at which we are arrived, may with propriety be regarded as the era in which that decision is to be made; and a wrong election of the part we shall act, may, in this view, deserve to be considered as the general misfortune of mankind.

This idea will add the inducements of philanthropy to those of patriotism to heighten the solicitude, which all considerate and good men must feel for the event. Happy will it be if our choice should be directed by a judicious estimate of our true interests, unperplexed and unbiassed by considerations not connected with the public good. But this is a thing more ardently to be wished, than seriously to be expected. The plan offered to our deliberations, affects too many particular interests, innovates upon too many local institutions, not to involve in its discussion a variety of objects foreign to its merits, and of views, passions and prejudices little favourable to the discovery of truth.

Among the most formidable of the obstacles which the new Constitution will have to encounter, may readily be distinguished the obvious interest of a certain class of men in every State to resist all changes which may hazard a diminution of the power, emolument and consequence of the offices they hold under the State-establishments —and the perverted ambition of another class of men, who will either hope to aggrandise themselves by the confusions of their country, or will flatter themselves with fairer prospects of elevation from the subdivision of the empire into several partial confederacies, than from its union under one government.

It is not, however, my design to dwell upon observations of this nature. I am well aware that it would be disingenuous to resolve indiscriminately the opposition of any set of men (merely because their situations might subject them to suspicion) into interested or ambitious views: Candour will oblige us to admit, that even such men may be actuated by upright intentions; and it cannot be doubted that much of the opposition which has made its appearance, or may hereafter make its appearance, will spring from sources, blameless at least, if not respectable, the honest errors of minds led astray by preconceived jealousies and fears. So numerous indeed and so powerful are the causes, which serve to give a false bias to the judgment, that we upon many occasions, see wise and good men on the wrong as well as on the right side of questions, of the first magnitude to society. This circumstance, if duly attended to, would furnish a lesson of moderation to those, who are ever so much persuaded of their being in the right, in any controversy. And a further reason for caution, in this respect, might be drawn from the reflection, that we are not always sure, that those who advocate the truth are influenced by purer principles than their antagonists. Ambition, avarice, personal animosity, party opposition, and many other motives, not more laudable than these, are apt to operate as well upon those who support as upon those who oppose the right side of a question. Were there not even these inducements to moderation, nothing could be more illjudged than that intolerant spirit, which has, at all times, characterised political parties. For, in politics as in religion, it is equally absurd to aim at making proselytes by fire and sword. Heresies in either can rarely be cured by persecution.

And yet however just these sentiments will be allowed to be, we have already sufficient indications, that it will happen in this as in all former cases of great national discussion. A torrent of angry and malignant passions will be let loose. To judge from the conduct of the opposite parties, we shall be led to conclude that they will mutually hope to evince the justness of their opinions, and to increase the number of their converts by the loudness of their declamations, and by the bitterness of their invectives. An enlightened zeal for the energy and efficiency of government will be stigmatized, as the off-spring of a temper fond of despotic power and hostile to the principles of liberty. An overscrupulous jealousy of danger to the rights of the people, which is more commonly the fault of the head than of the heart, will be represented as mere pretence and artifice; the bait for popularity at the expence of public good. It will be forgotten, on the one hand, that jealousy is the usual concomitant of violent love, and that the noble enthusiasm of liberty is too apt to be infected with a spirit of narrow and illiberal distrust. On the other hand, it will be equally forgotten, that the vigour of government is essential to the security of liberty; that, in the contemplation of a sound and well informed judgment, their interest can never be separated; and that a dangerous ambition more often lurks behind the specious mask of zeal for the rights of the people, than under the forbidding appearance of zeal for the firmness and efficiency of government. History will teach us, that the former has been found a much more certain road to the introduction of despotism, than the latter, and that of those men who have overturned the liberties of republics the greatest number have begun their career, by paying an obsequious court to the people, commencing Demagogues and ending Tyrants.

In the course of the preceeding observations I have had an eye, my Fellow Citizens, to putting you upon your guard against all attempts, from whatever quarter, to influence your decision in a matter of the utmost moment to your welfare by any impressions other than those which may result from the evidence of truth. You will, no doubt, at the same time, have collected from the general scope of them that they proceed from a source not unfriendly to the new Constitution. Yes, my Countrymen, I own to you, that, after having given it an attentive consideration, I am clearly of opinion, it is your interest to adopt it. I am convinced, that this is the safest course for your liberty, your dignity, and your happiness. I effect not reserves, which I do not feel. I will not amuse you with an appearance of deliberation, when I have decided. I frankly acknowledge to you my convictions, and I will freely lay before you the reasons on which they are founded. The consciousness of good intentions disdains ambiguity. I shall not however multiply professions on this head. My motives must remain in the depository of my own breast: My arguments will be open to all, and may be judged of by all. They shall at least be offered in a spirit, which will not disgrace the cause of truth.

I propose in a series of papers to discuss the following interesting particulars—*The utility of the UNION to your political prosperity—The insufficiency of the present Confederation to preserve that Union—The necessity of a government at least equally energetic with the one proposed to the attainment of this object—The conformity of the proposed constitution to the true principles of republican government—Its analogy to your own state constitution* —and lastly, *The additional security, which its adoption will afford to the preservation of that species of government, to liberty and to property.*

In the progress of this discussion I shall endeavour to give a satisfactory answer to all the objections which shall have made their appearance that may seem to have any claim to your attention.

It may perhaps be thought superfluous to offer arguments to prove the utility of the UNION, a point, no doubt, deeply engraved on the hearts of the great body of the people in every state, and one, which it may be imagined has no adversaries. But the fact is, that we already hear it whispered in the private circles of those who oppose the new constitution, that the Thirteen States are of too great extent for any general system, and that we must of necessity resort to separate confederacies of distinct portions of the whole. This doctrine will, in all probability, be gradually propagated, till it has votaries enough to countenance an open avowal of it. For nothing can be more evident, to those who are able to take an enlarged view of the subject, than the alternative of an adoption of the new Constitution, or a dismemberment of the Union. It will therefore be of use to begin by examining the advantages of that Union, the certain evils and the probable dangers, to which every State will be exposed from its dissolution. This shall accordingly constitute the subject of my next address.

PUBLIUS.[1]

1787/1787

No. 10: [James Madison]

November 22, 1787

To the People of the State of New York.

Among the numerous advantages promised by a well constructed Union, none deserves to be more accurately developed than its tendency to break and control the violence of faction. The friend of popular governments, never finds himself so much alarmed for their character and fate, as when he contemplates their propensity to this dangerous vice. He will not fail therefore to set a due value on any plan which, without violating the principles to which he is attached, provides a proper cure for it. The instability, injustice and confusion introduced into the public councils, have

[1] "Publius" was the pseudonym of the writers of the *Federalist* and was known to be such by most eighteenth-century readers.

in truth been the mortal diseases under which popular governments have every where perished; as they continue to be the favorite and fruitful topics from which the adversaries to liberty derive their most specious declamations. The valuable improvements made by the American Constitutions on the popular models, both ancient and modern, cannot certainly be too much admired; but it would be an unwarrantable partiality, to contend that they have as effectually obviated the danger on this side as was wished and expected. Complaints are every where heard from our most considerate and virtuous citizens, equally the friends of public and private faith, and of public and personal liberty; that our governments are too unstable; that the public good is disregarded in the conflicts of rival parties; and that measures are too often decided, not according to the rules of justice, and the rights of the minor party; but by the superior force of an interested and over-bearing majority. However anxiously we may wish that these complaints had no foundation, the evidence of known facts will not permit us to deny that they are in some degree true. It will be found indeed, on a candid review of our situation, that some of the distresses under which we labor, have been erroneously charged on the operation of our governments; but it will be found, at the same time, that other causes will not alone account for many of our heaviest misfortunes; and particularly, for that prevailing and increasing distrust of public engagements, and alarm for private rights, which are echoed from one end of the continent to the other. These must be chiefly, if not wholly, effects of the unsteadiness and injustice, with which a factious spirit has tainted our public administrations.

By a faction I understand a number of citizens, whether amounting to a majority or minority of the whole, who are united and actuated by some common impulse of passion, or of interest, adverse to the rights of other citizens, or to the permanent and aggregate interests of the community.

There are two methods of curing the mischiefs of faction: the one, by removing its causes; the other, by controling its effects.

There are again two methods of removing the causes of faction: the one by destroying the liberty which is essential to its existence; the other, by giving to every citizen the same opinions, the same passions, and the same interests.

It could never be more truly said than of the first remedy, that it is worse than the disease. Liberty is to faction, what air is to fire, an aliment[2] without which it instantly expires. But it could not be a less folly to abolish liberty, which is essential to political life, because it nourishes faction, than it would be to wish the annihilation of air, which is essential to animal life, because it imparts to fire its destructive agency.

The second expedient is as impracticable, as the first would be unwise. As long as the reason of man continues fallible, and he is at liberty to exercise it, different opinions will be formed. As long as the connection subsists between his reason and his self-love, his opinions and his passions will have a reciprocal influence on each other; and the former will be objects to which the latter will attach themselves. The diversity in the faculties of men from which the rights of property originate, is not less an insuperable obstacle to a uniformity of interests. The protection of these faculties is the first object of Government. From the protection of different and unequal faculties of acquiring property, the possession of different degrees and kinds

[2] Nutriment.

of property immediately results: and from the influence of these on the sentiments and views of the respective proprietors, ensues a division of the society into different interests and parties.

The latent causes of faction are thus sown in the nature of man; and we see them every where brought into different degrees of activity, according to the different circumstances of civil society. A zeal for different opinions concerning religion, concerning Government and many other points, as well of speculation as of practice; an attachment to different leaders ambitiously contending for pre-eminence and power; or to persons of other descriptions whose fortunes have been interesting to the human passions, have in turn divided mankind into parties, inflamed them with mutual animosity, and rendered them much more disposed to vex and oppress each other, than to co-operate for their common good. So strong is this propensity of mankind to fall into mutual animosities, that where no substantial occasion presents itself, the most frivolous and fanciful distinctions have been sufficient to kindle their unfriendly passions, and excite their most violent conflicts. But the most common and durable source of factions, has been the various and unequal distribution of property. Those who hold, and those who are without property, have ever formed distinct interests in society. Those who are creditors, and those who are debtors, fall under a like discrimination. A landed interest, a manufacturing interest, a mercantile interest, a monied interest, with many lesser interests, grow up of necessity in civilized nations, and divide them into different classes, actuated by different sentiments and views. The regulation of these various and interfering interests forms the principal task of modern Legislation, and involves the spirit of party and faction in the necessary and ordinary operations of Government.

No man is allowed to be a judge in his own cause; because his interest would certainly bias his judgment, and, not improbably, corrupt his integrity. With equal, nay with greater reason, a body of men, are unfit to be both judges and parties, at the same time; yet, what are many of the most important acts of legislation, but so many judicial determinations, not indeed concerning the rights of single persons, but concerning the rights of large bodies of citizens; and what are the different classes of legislators, but advocates and parties to the causes which they determine? Is a law proposed concerning private debts? It is a question to which the creditors are parties on one side, and the debtors on the other. Justice ought to hold the balance between them. Yet the parties are and must be themselves the judges; and the most numerous party, or, in other words, the most powerful faction must be expected to prevail. Shall domestic manufactures be encouraged, and in what degree, by restrictions on foreign manufactures? are questions which would be differently decided by the landed and the manufacturing classes; and probably by neither, with a sole regard to justice and the public good. The apportionment of taxes on the various descriptions of property, is an act which seems to require the most exact impartiality; yet, there is perhaps no legislative act in which greater opportunity and temptation are given to a predominant party, to trample on the rules of justice. Every shilling with which they over-burden the inferior number, is a shilling saved to their own pockets.

It is in vain to say, that enlightened statesmen will be able to adjust these clashing interests, and render them all subservient to the public good. Enlightened statesmen will not always be at the helm: Nor, in many cases, can such an adjustment be made at all, without taking into view indirect and remote considerations, which will rarely prevail over the immediate interest which one party may find in disregarding the rights of another, or the good of the whole.

The inference to which we are brought, is, that the *causes* of faction cannot be removed; and that relief is only to be sought in the means of controling its *effects*.

If a faction consists of less than a majority, relief is supplied by the republican principle, which enables the majority to defeat its sinister views by regular vote: It may clog the administration, it may convulse the society; but it will be unable to execute and mask its violence under the forms of the Constitution. When a majority is included in a faction, the form of popular government on the other hand enables it to sacrifice to its ruling passion or interest, both the public good and the rights of other citizens. To secure the public good, and private rights, against the danger of such a faction, and at the same time to preserve the spirit and the form of popular government, is then the great object to which our enquiries are directed: Let me add that it is the great desideratum,[3] by which alone this form of government can be rescued from the opprobrium under which it has so long labored, and be recommended to the esteem and adoption of mankind.

By what means is this object attainable? Evidently by one of two only. Either the existence of the same passion or interest in a majority at the same time, must be prevented; or the majority, having such co-existent passion or interest, must be rendered, by their number and local situation, unable to concert and carry into effect schemes of oppression. If the impulse and the opportunity be suffered to coincide, we well know that neither moral nor religious motives can be relied on as an adequate control. They are not found to be such on the injustice and violence of individuals, and lose their efficacy in proportion to the number combined together; that is, in proportion as their efficacy becomes needful.

From this view of the subject, it may be concluded, that a pure Democracy, by which I mean, a Society, consisting of a small number of citizens, who assemble and administer the Government in person, can admit of no cure for the mischiefs of faction. A common passion or interest will, in almost every case, be felt by a majority of the whole; a communication and concert results from the form of Government itself; and there is nothing to check the inducements to sacrifice the weaker party, or an obnoxious individual. Hence it is, that such Democracies have ever been spectacles of turbulence and contention; have ever been found incompatible with personal security, or the rights of property; and have in general been as short in their lives, as they have been violent in their deaths. Theoretic politicians, who have patronized this species of Government, have erroneously supposed, that by reducing mankind to a perfect equality in their political rights, they would, at the same time, be perfectly equalized and assimilated in their possessions, their opinions, and their passions.

A Republic, by which I mean a Government in which the scheme of representation takes place, opens a different prospect, and promises the cure for which we are seeking. Let us examine the points in which it varies from pure Democracy, and we shall comprehend both the nature of the cure, and the efficacy which it must derive from the Union.

The two great points of difference between a Democracy and a Republic are, first, the delegation of the Government, in the latter, to a small number of citizens elected

---

[3] Necessary goal.

by the rest: secondly, the greater number of citizens, and greater sphere of country, over which the latter may be extended.

The effect of the first difference is, on the one hand to refine and enlarge the public views, by passing them through the medium of a chosen body of citizens, whose wisdom may best discern the true interest of their country, and whose patriotism and love of justice, will be least likely to sacrifice it to temporary or partial considerations. Under such a regulation, it may well happen that the public voice pronounced by the representatives of the people, will be more consonant to the public good, than if pronounced by the people themselves convened for the purpose. On the other hand, the effect may be inverted. Men of factious tempers, of local prejudices, or of sinister designs, may by intrigue, by corruption or by other means, first obtain the suffrages,[4] and then betray the interests of the people. The question resulting is, whether small or extensive Republics are most favorable to the election of proper guardians of the public weal:[5] and it is clearly decided in favor of the latter by two obvious considerations.

In the first place it is to be remarked that however small the Republic may be, the Representatives must be raised to a certain number, in order to guard against the cabals of a few; and that however large it may be, they must be limited to a certain number, in order to guard against the confusion of a multitude. Hence the number of Representatives in the two cases, not being in proportion to that of the Constituents, and being proportionally greatest in the small Republic, it follows, that if the proportion of fit characters, be not less, in the large than in the small Republic, the former will present a greater option, and consequently a greater probability of a fit choice.

In the next place, as each Representative will be chosen by a greater number of citizens in the large than in the small Republic, it will be more difficult for unworthy candidates to practise with success the vicious arts, by which elections are too often carried; and the suffrages of the people being more free, will be more likely to centre on men who possess the most attractive merit, and the most diffusive and established characters.

It must be confessed, that in this, as in most other cases, there is a mean, on both sides of which inconveniences will be found to lie. By enlarging too much the number of electors, you render the representative too little acquainted with all their local circumstances and lesser interests; as by reducing it too much, you render him unduly attached to these, and too little fit to comprehend and pursue great and national objects. The Federal Constitution forms a happy combination in this respect; the great and aggregate interests being referred to the national, the local and particular, to the state legislatures.

The other point of difference is, the greater number of citizens and extent of territory which may be brought within the compass of Republican, than of Democratic Government; and it is this circumstance principally which renders factious combinations less to be dreaded in the former, than in the latter. The smaller the society, the fewer probably will be the distinct parties and interests composing it; the fewer the distinct parties and interests, the more frequently will a majority be found of the same party; and the smaller the number of individuals composing a majority,

---

[4] Support of the voters.   [5] Well-being.

and the smaller the compass within which they are placed, the more easily will they concert and execute their plans of oppression. Extend the sphere, and you take in a greater variety of parties and interests; you make it less probable that a majority of the whole will have a common motive to invade the rights of other citizens; or if such a common motive exists, it will be more difficult for all who feel it to discover their own strength, and to act in unison with each other. Besides other impediments, it may be remarked, that where there is a consciousness of unjust or dishonorable purposes, communication is always checked by distrust, in proportion to the number whose concurrence is necessary.

Hence it clearly appears, that the same advantage, which a Republic has over a Democracy, in controling the effects of faction, is enjoyed by a large over a small Republic—is enjoyed by the Union over the States composing it. Does this advantage consist in the substitution of Representatives, whose enlightened views and virtuous sentiments render them superior to local prejudices, and to schemes of injustice? It will not be denied, that the Representation of the Union will be most likely to possess these requisite endowments. Does it consist in the greater security afforded by a greater variety of parties, against the event of any one party being able to outnumber and oppress the rest? In an equal degree does the encreased variety of parties, comprised within the Union, encrease this security. Does it, in fine, consist in the greater obstacles opposed to the concert and accomplishment of the secret wishes of an unjust and interested majority? Here, again, the extent of the Union gives it the most palpable advantage.

The influence of factious leaders may kindle a flame within their particular States, but will be unable to spread a general conflagration through the other States: a religious sect, may degenerate into a political faction in a part of the Confederacy: but the variety of sects dispersed over the entire face of it, must secure the national Councils against any danger from that source: a rage for paper money, for an abolition of debts, for an equal division of property, or for any other improper or wicked project, will be less apt to pervade the whole body of the Union, than a particular member of it; in the same proportion as such a malady is more likely to taint a particular county or district, than an entire State.

In the extent and proper structure of the Union, therefore, we behold a Republican remedy for the diseases most incident to Republican Government. And according to the degree of pleasure and pride, we feel in being Republicans, ought to be our zeal in cherishing the spirit, and supporting the character of Federalists.

PUBLIUS.

1787/1787

Philip Freneau
1752–1832

When Philip Freneau died in 1832 on the side of a snow-swept road in the rural stretches of New Jersey, he was far removed from the center of the political and ideological controversies that dominated the earliest years of the new republic. He had once been heralded as the most forceful literary voice in the American

Revolution. Later he was considered too radical for many political tastes and was finally regarded as simply unfashionable. With no appreciable audience for his acerbic wit and arcadian visions, Freneau could only lament: "To write was my sad destiny, / The worst of trades, we all agree." His disillusionment with the course of American politics and the drift of his own career ferried him back and forth between satire and solitude.

The son of a prosperous woman of Scottish ancestry and a French Hugenot émigré, Philip Freneau was born into comfortable circumstances in New York City on January 2, 1752. The eldest of five children, Freneau stayed behind to study the classics and the English poets when the family moved to Mount Pleasant, a thousand-acre tract in New Jersey modeled on an elaborate southern plantation and the site to which Freneau would intermittently retreat from economic misfortune and political combat. At the urging of his father, Freneau prepared for the ministry, and at the age of sixteen he enrolled as a second-year student at the College of New Jersey (later Princeton), where he was a classmate of James Madison and Hugh Henry Brackenridge and a friend of Aaron Burr. While there, Freneau alternately inveighed against the British program of colonial taxation and wrote fanciful, grandiloquent verses on such historical subjects as "The Prophet Jonah," "The Pyramids of Egypt," and "The Monument of Phaon." He also collaborated with Brackenridge on an unfinished novel, *Father Bombo's Pilgrimage to Mecca in Arabia,* and on "A Poem on the Rising Glory of America," read as the commencement ode in 1771. Freneau's commitment to a vision of America's future inspired him to record indigenous experiences, although ones that, at least for his generation, were best expressed in the forms of "heav'nly Pope" and "godlike Addison."

After college, Freneau worked first at education. He spent thirteen remarkably long days on Long Island teaching the children of "some bullies, some merchants, and other scoundrels." He later served for less than a year as Brackenridge's assistant at the Somerset Academy in Maryland. Commenting in a letter to Madison that teaching "by no means suits my 'giddy wandring brain,'" Freneau proceeded to study theology for two years before gravitating to New York, where he wrote a series of popular attacks on the British presence in the colonies. Discouraged by the political controversy his poetry had occasioned, Freneau left New York in 1776 for a two-year stay in the West Indies, during which he produced a fitting number of idyllic poems. But the increasing tempo of Revolutionary activities drew him home. He was captured and released by the British en route and joined the New Jersey militia when he reached the United States.

Freneau devoted himself completely to the Revolutionary cause. He ran supplies through British naval blockades and contributed patriotic verse to Brackenridge's newly formed *United States Magazine.* In 1780 Freneau was again captured at sea, but this time he was imprisoned aboard British ships in New York harbor. Within a year of his release, Freneau published "The Prison Ship," a popular broadside recording his mistreatment at the hands of his captors. He then traveled to Philadelphia to help edit the strongly anti-British *Freeman's Journal.*

After a brief stint as a postal clerk at the end of the war and a new round of disheartening squabbles in Pennsylvania politics, Freneau withdrew to the seclusion of nearly seven years of work at sea. He served as the captain of coastal vessels and published a great deal of satirical, fanciful, and humorous verse in the newspapers of the ports he plied. The growing popularity of his poetry lured him ashore, and in 1790 he settled in New York. There he helped edit the *Daily Advertiser,* married Eleanor Forman, and served as a translator for the State Department under Thomas Jefferson.

Inspired by the politics of Jefferson and the other prominent Republicans of the time, Freneau established the *National Gazette* in Philadelphia as a virulent response to the Federalist political and economic policies of Alexander Hamilton and John Adams. While Jefferson judged that Freneau had saved a nation "which was galloping fast into monarchy," George Washington had only scorn for "that rascal Freneau." Yale president Timothy Dwight regarded him as a "mere incendiary, or rather as a despicable tool of bigger incendiaries," and branded Freneau's newspaper "a public nuisance."

A yellow fever epidemic, poor advertising revenue, and unbridled attacks on his Republican editorials drove Freneau from Philadelphia in 1793. He retired to Mount Pleasant for nearly a year but returned to public life as publisher of another newspaper, the *Jersey Chronicle.* When that venture failed, he launched yet another, the *Time-Piece and Literary Companion,* which focused, he announced, on "literary amusements and an abridgment of the most interesting intelligence foreign and domestic." Despite an unusually large number of female contributors who "gave freely of their sentimental lyrics and sprightly letters," the journal overplayed Freneau's public-spirited but sneering editorials on the federal government and fell victim to the sedition law. Retreating once again to Mount Pleasant, Freneau penned a series of humorous essays for the Philadelphia *Aurora* in the guise of Robert Slender, a rustic sage far removed from political controversy. By 1800 Freneau had settled into discreet obscurity and returned to a life at sea. He surfaced again at the outbreak of the War of 1812, but with much of his vituperative energy drained.

Freneau published five volumes of poetry in his lifetime. In each, the intensity of his poems on the splendor of the American landscape often competed with self-conscious political satires on British subjects. Yet Freneau always maintained his commitment to explore native themes in colloquial terms. "The Wild Honeysuckle" (1786) and "The Indian Burying Ground" (1788), printed more than a decade before Wordsworth and Coleridge's *Lyrical Ballads,* are perhaps the best testaments to that interest.

The unpretentious characters that populate Freneau's essays and journalism ("The Pilgrim," "Tomo-Cheeki, the Creek Indian," and "Hezakiah Salem," the defrocked Yankee deacon) express his sensitivity to the philosophical, social, and economic issues that preoccupied American society in the first decades of the new nation. Freneau anticipated William Cullen Bryant's preoccupation with lush poetic landscapes, Ralph Waldo Emerson's insistent individualism, and Walt Whitman's embrace of the commonplace in America. Freneau's writing helped expand the field for American writers and introduced complexities into native themes.

Freneau's passion for the Revolution, when combined with his own career frustrations and his gradual alienation from the political management of the early republic, no doubt impelled him to construct mythopoetic versions of order and tranquillity, which ultimately reveal as much about Freneau's own consciousness as they do about the currents of political life in late-eighteenth-century America. Freneau turned politics into an image of himself, and he became the final victim of his own imagination.

Further Reading:
L. Leary, *That Rascal Freneau: A Study in Literary Failure*, 1941, 1964.
N. F. Adkins, *Philip Freneau and Cosmic Enigma: The Religious and Philosophical Speculations of an American Poet*, 1949.
J. Axelrad, *Philip Freneau: Champion of Democracy*, 1967.
P. Marsh, *The Works of Philip Freneau: A Critical Study*, 1968.
M. Bowden, *Philip Freneau*, 1976.
R. Vitzthum, *Land and Sea: The Lyric Poetry of Philip Freneau*, 1978.

Texts:
"On Mr. Paine's Rights of Man" and "On the Uniformity and Perfection of Nature" from *Poems of Freneau*, ed. H. H. Clark, 1929.
All others from *The Poems of Philip Freneau*, ed. F. L. Pattee, 3 vols., 1902–1907.

To the Memory of the Brave Americans[*]

Under General Greene in South Carolina who fell in the action of September 8, 1781

At Eutaw Springs the valiant died;
  Their limbs with dust are covered o'er—
Weep on, ye springs, your tearful tide;
  How many heroes are no more!

If in this wreck of ruin, they   5
  Can yet be thought to claim a tear,
O smite your gentle breast, and say
  The friends of freedom slumber here!

Thou, who shalt trace this bloody plain,
  If goodness rules thy generous breast,   10
Sigh for the wasted rural reign;
  Sigh for the shepherds, sunk to rest!

[*] The poem is based on the attack of General Nathanael Greene's forces upon the British garrison at Eutaw Springs on the Santee River between Charleston and Columbia, South Carolina. More than five hundred Americans were killed or wounded during the assault and the British counterattack.

Stranger, their humble graves adorn;
    You too may fall, and ask a tear;
'Tis not the beauty of the morn
    That proves the evening shall be clear.—   15

They saw their injured country's woe;
    The flaming town, the wasted field;
Then rushed to meet the insulting foe;
    They took the spear—but left the shield.   20

Led by thy conquering genius, Greene,
    The Britons they compelled to fly;
None distant viewed the fatal plain,
    None grieved, in such a cause to die—

But, like the Parthian,[1] famed of old,   25
    Who, flying, still their arrows threw,
These routed Britons, full as bold,
    Retreated, and retreating slew.

Now rest in peace, our patriot band;
    Though far from nature's limits thrown,   30
We trust they find a happier land,
    A brighter sunshine of their own.

1781

On the Emigration to America
And Peopling the Western Country

To western woods, and lonely plains,
Palemon[1] from the crowd departs,
Where Nature's wildest genius reigns,
To tame the soil, and plant the arts—
What wonders there shall freedom show,   5
What mighty states successive grow!

From Europe's proud, despotic shores
Hither the stranger takes his way,
And in our new found world explores
A happier soil, a milder sway,   10

---

[1] The warriors of Parthia, in ancient Persia, developed the tactic of feigning retreat and then turning back to battle when their enemies had dispersed.

[1] Character in Chaucer's "Knight's Tale" (in *The Canterbury Tales*) who has come to represent any person setting out on a journey.

Where no proud despot holds him down,
No slaves insult him with a crown.

What charming scenes attract the eye,
On wild Ohio's savage stream!
There Nature reigns, whose works outvie   15
The boldest pattern art can frame;
There ages past have rolled away,
And forests bloomed but to decay.

From these fair plains, these rural seats,
So long concealed, so lately known,   20
The unsocial Indian far retreats,
To make some other clime his own,
When other streams, less pleasing, flow,
And darker forests round him grow.

Great Sire[2] of floods! whose varied wave   25
Through climes and countries takes its way,
To whom creating Nature gave
Ten thousand streams to swell thy sway!
No longer shall they useless prove,
Nor idly through the forests rove;   30

Nor longer shall your princely flood
From distant lakes be swelled in vain,
Nor longer through a darksome wood
Advance, unnoticed, to the main,
Far other ends, the heavens decree—   35
And commerce plans new freights for thee.

While virtue warms the generous breast,
There heaven-born freedom shall reside,
Nor shall the voice of war molest,
Nor Europe's all-aspiring pride—   40
There Reason shall new laws devise,
And order from confusion rise.

Forsaking kings and regal state,
With all their pomp and fancied bliss,
The traveller owns, convinced though late,   45
No realm so free, so blest as this—
The east is half to slaves consigned,
Where kings and priests enchain the mind.

O come the time, and haste the day,
When man shall man no longer crush,   50

[2] Freneau's note: "Mississippi."

When Reason shall enforce her sway,
Nor these fair regions raise our blush,
Where still the African complains,
And mourns his yet unbroken chains.

Far brighter scenes a future age,   55
The muse predicts, these States will hail,
Whose genius may the world engage,
Whose deeds may over death prevail,
And happier systems bring to view,
Than all the eastern sages knew.   60

1784/1785

The Wild Honey Suckle

Fair flower, that dost so comely grow,
Hid in this silent, dull retreat,
Untouched thy honied blossoms blow,
Unseen thy little branches greet:
    No roving foot shall crush thee here,   5
    No busy hand provoke a tear.

By Nature's self in white arrayed,
She bade thee shun the vulgar eye,
And planted here the guardian shade,
And sent soft waters murmuring by;   10
    Thus quietly thy summer goes,
    Thy days declining to repose.

Smit with those charms, that must decay,
I grieve to see your future doom;
They died—nor were those flowers more gay,   15
The flowers that did in Eden bloom;
    Unpitying frosts, and Autumn's power
    Shall leave no vestige of this flower.

From morning suns and evening dews
At first thy little being came: 20
If nothing once, you nothing lose,
For when you die you are the same;
    The space between, is but an hour,
    The frail duration of a flower.

1786

The Indian Burying Ground

In spite of all the learned have said,
    I still my old opinion keep;
The posture, that we give the dead,
    Points out the soul's eternal sleep.

Not so the ancients of these lands—   5
    The Indian, when from life released,
Again is seated with his friends,
    And shares again the joyous feast.[1]

His imaged birds, and painted bowl,
    And venison, for a journey dressed,   10
Bespeak the nature of the soul,
    Activity, that knows no rest.

His bow, for action ready bent,
    And arrows, with a head of stone,
Can only mean that life is spent,   15
    And not the old ideas gone.

Thou, stranger, that shalt come this way,
    No fraud upon the dead commit—
Observe the swelling turf, and say
    They do not lie, but here they sit.   20

Here still a lofty rock remains,
    On which the curious eye may trace
(Now wasted, half, by wearing rains)
    The fancies of a ruder race.

Here still an aged elm aspires,   25
    Beneath whose far-projecting shade
(And which the shepherd still admires)
    The children of the forest played!

There oft a restless Indian queen
    (Pale Shebah,[2] with her braided hair)   30
And many a barbarous form is seen
    To chide the man that lingers there.

---

[1] Freneau's note: "The North American Indians bury their dead in a sitting posture; decorating the corpse with wampum, the images of birds, quadrupeds, &c: And (if that of a warrior) with bows, arrows, tomhawks [*sic*], and other military weapons."

[2] The Queen of Sheba, legendary for her beauty and wisdom. (See 1 Kings 10 and 2 Chronicles 9.)

By midnight moons, o'er moistening dews;
In habit for the chase arrayed,
The hunter still the deer pursues,   35
The hunter and the deer, a shade!

And long shall timorous fancy see
The painted chief, and pointed spear,
And Reason's self shall bow the knee
To shadows and delusions here.   40

1787

On Mr. Paine's Rights of Man[*]

Thus briefly sketched the sacred RIGHTS OF MAN,
How inconsistent with the ROYAL PLAN!
Which for itself exclusive honour craves,
Where some are masters born, and millions slaves.
With what contempt must every eye look down   5
On that base, childish bauble called a *crown,*
The gilded bait, that lures the crowd, to come,
Bow down their necks, and meet a slavish doom;
The source of half the miseries men endure,
The quack that kills them, while it seems to cure.   10
     Roused by the REASON of his manly page,
Once more shall PAINE a listening world engage:
From Reason's source, a bold reform he brings,
In raising up *mankind,* he pulls down *kings,*
Who, source of discord, patrons of all wrong,   15
On blood and murder have been fed too long:
Hid from the world, and tutored to be base,
The curse, the scourge, the ruin of our race,
Their's was the task, a dull designing few,
To shackle beings that they scarcely knew,   20
Who made this globe the residence of slaves,
And built their thrones on systems formed by
     knaves
—Advance, bright years, to work their final fall,
And haste the period that shall crush them all.

[*] Thomas Paine (1737–1809) had supported the
French Revolution in *The Rights of Man*
(1791).

Who, that has read and scann'd the historic page   25
But glows, at every line, with kindling rage,
To see by them the rights of men aspersed,
Freedom restrain'd, and Nature's law reversed,
Men, ranked with beasts, by monarchs *will'd* away,
And bound young fools, or madmen to obey: 30
Now driven to wars, and now oppressed at home,
Compelled in crowds o'er distant seas to roam,
From India's climes the plundered prize to bring
To glad the strumpet, or to glut the king.
    COLUMBIA,[1] hail! immortal be thy reign: 35
Without a king, we till the smiling plain;
Without a king, we trace the unbounded sea,
And traffic round the globe, through each degree;
Each foreign clime our honour'd flag reveres,
Which asks no monarch, to support the STARS: 40
Without a *king,* the laws maintain their sway,
While honour bids each generous heart obey.
Be ours the task the ambitious to restrain,
And this great lesson teach—that kings are vain;
That warring realms to certain ruin haste,   45
That kings subsist by war, and wars are waste:
So shall our nation, form'd on Virtue's plan,
Remain the guardian of the Rights of Man,
A vast Republic, famed through every clime,
Without a king, to see the end of time.   50

1791

To Crispin O'Conner
A Back-Woodsman

[supposed to be written by Hezekiah Salem]

Wise was your plan when twenty years ago
From Patrick's isle you first resolved to stray,
Where lords and knights, as thick as rushes grow,
And vulgar folks are in each other's way;

Where mother-country acts the step-dame's part,   5
Cuts off, by aid of hemp, each petty sinner,
And twice or thrice in every score of years
Hatches sad wars to make her brood the thinner.

[1] America.

How few aspire to quit the ungrateful soil
That starves the plant it had the strength to bear: 10
How many stay, to grieve, and fret, and toil,
And view the plenty that they must not share.

This you beheld, and westward set your nose,
Like some bold prow, that ploughs the Atlantic foam,
And left less venturous weights, like famished crows,—   15
To feed on hog-peas, hips, and haws, at home.

Safe landed here, not long the coast detained
Your wary steps:—but wandering on, you found
Far in the west, a paltry spot of land,
That no man envied, and that no man owned.   20

A woody hill, beside a dismal bog—
This was your choice; nor were you much to blame:
And here, responsive to the croaking frog,
You grubbed, and stubbed, and feared no landlord's claim.

An axe, an adze, a hammer, and a saw;   25
These were the tools, that built your humble shed:
A cock, a hen, a mastiff, and a cow:
These were your subjects, to this desert led.

Now times are changed—and labour's nervous hand
Bids harvests rise where briars and bushes grew;   30
The dismal bog, by lengthy sluices drained,
Supports no more hoarse captain Bull Frog's crew.—

Prosper your toil!—but, friend, had you remained
In lands, where starred and gartered nobles shine,
When you had, thus, to sixty years attained,   35
What different fate, 'Squire Crispin, had been thine!

Nine pence a day, coarse fare, a bed of boards,
The midnight loom, high rents, and excised beer;
Slave to dull squires, kings' brats, and huffish lords,
(Thanks be to Heaven) not yet in fashion here!   40
1792

To Sir Toby

A sugar planter in the interior parts of Jamaica near
the city of San Jago de la Vega, (Spanish town) 1784

"The motions of his spirit are black as night,
And his affections dark as Erebus."

Shakespeare.[1]

If there exists a hell—the case is clear—
Sir Toby's slaves enjoy that portion here:
Here are no blazing brimstone lakes—'tis true;
But kindled Rum too often burns as blue;
In which some fiend, whom nature must detest,   5
Steeps Toby's brand, and marks poor Cudjoe's breast.[2]
    Here whips on whips excite perpetual fears,
And mingled howlings vibrate on my ears:
Here nature's plagues abound, to fret and teaze,
Snakes, scorpions, despots, lizards, centipees[3]—   10
No art, no care escapes the busy lash;
All have their dues—and all are paid in cash—
The eternal driver keeps a steady eye
On a black herd, who would his vengeance fly,
But chained, imprisoned, on a burning soil,   15
For the mean avarice of a tyrant, toil!
The lengthy cart-whip guards this monster's reign—
And cracks, like pistols, from the fields of cane.
    Ye powers! who formed these wretched tribes, relate,
What had they done, to merit such a fate!   20
Why were they brought from Eboe's[4] sultry waste,
To see that plenty which they must not taste—
Food, which they cannot buy, and dare not steal;
Yams and potatoes—many a scanty meal!—
    One, with a gibbet[5] wakes his negro's fears,   25
One to the windmill nails him by the ears;
One keeps his slave in darkened dens, unfed,
One puts the wretch in pickle ere he's dead:
This, from a tree suspends him by the thumbs,
That, from his table grudges even the crumbs!   30
    O'er yond' rough hills a tribe of females go,

---

[1] From *The Merchant of Venice*, Act V, Sc. i, l.
79. Freneau substituted "black as night" for
"dull as night." Erebus, in Greek mythology, is
the dark area below the earth through which
the dead must pass before reaching Hades.
[2] Freneau's note: " 'Cudge' was a familiar term
for a slave. This passage refers to the West
India custom (sanctioned by law) of branding a
newly imported slave on the breast, with a red
hot iron, as an evidence of the purchaser's
property."
[3] Centipedes.
[4] Freneau's note: "A small negro kingdom near
the river Senegal."
[5] Gallows.

Each with her gourd, her infant, and her hoe;
Scorched by a sun that has no mercy here,
Driven by a devil, whom men call overseer—
In chains, twelve wretches to their labours haste;   35
Twice twelve I saw, with iron collars graced!—
   Are such the fruits that spring from vast domains?
Is wealth, thus got, Sir Toby, worth your pains!—
Who would your wealth on terms, like these, possess,
Where all we see is pregnant with distress—   40
Angola's[6] natives scourged by ruffian hands,
And toil's hard product shipp'd to foreign lands.
   Talk not of blossoms, and your endless spring;
What joy, what smile, can scenes of misery bring?—
Though Nature, here, has every blessing spread,   45
Poor is the labourer—and how meanly fed!—
   Here Stygian[7] paintings light and shade renew,
Pictures of hell, that Virgil's[8] pencil drew:
Here, surly Charons[9] make their annual trip,
And ghosts arrive in every Guinea ship,[10]   50
To find what beasts these western isles afford,
Plutonian[11] scourges, and despotic lords:—
   Here, they, of stuff determined to be free,
Must climb the rude cliffs of the Liguanee;[12]
Beyond the clouds, in sculking haste repair,   55
And hardly safe from brother traitors[13] there.—

1784/1792

On a Honey Bee

Drinking from a glass of wine and drowned therein

Thou, born to sip the lake or spring,
Or quaff the waters of the stream,
Why hither come on vagrant wing?—
Does Bacchus tempting seem—
Did he, for you, this glass prepare?—   5
Will I admit you to a share?

---

[6] Angola: a Portuguese province in West Africa.
[7] Resembling hell; derived from the Greek mythic river Styx, which souls must cross.
[8] Freneau's note: "See *Aeneid*, Book 6th.—and Fenelon's Telemachus, Book 18."
[9] Charon ferried the dead over the river Styx to Hades in Greek myth.
[10] I.e., slave ships from West Africa.
[11] Reference to Pluto, god of the underworld.
[12] Freneau's note: "The mountains northward of Kingston."
[13] Freneau's note: "Alluding to the Independent negroes in the blue mountains, who for a stipulated reward, deliver up every fugitive that falls into their hands, to the English Government."

Did storms harass or foes perplex,
Did wasps or king-birds bring dismay—
Did wars distress, or labours vex,
Or did you miss your way?—   10
A better seat you could not take
Than on the margin of this lake.

Welcome!—I hail you to my glass:
All welcome, here, you find;
Here, let the cloud of trouble pass,   15
Here, be all care resigned.—
This fluid never fails to please,
And drown the griefs of men or bees.

What forced you here, we cannot know,
And you will scarcely tell—   20
But cheery we would have you go
And bid a glad farewell:
On lighter wings we bid you fly,
Your dart will now all foes defy.

Yet take not, oh! too deep a drink,   25
And in this ocean die;
Here bigger bees than you might sink,
Even bees full six feet high.
Like Pharaoh,[1] then, you would be said
To perish in a sea of red.   30

Do as you please, your will is mine;
Enjoy it without fear—
And your grave will be this glass of wine,
Your epitaph—a tear—
Go, take your seat in Charon's boat,   35
We'll tell the hive, you died afloat.

1797

---

[1] Pharaoh's army drowned in the Red Sea while
pursuing the Israelites. (See Exodus 14:1–27.)

On the Uniformity and Perfection of Nature

On one fix'd point all nature moves,
Nor deviates from the track she loves;
Her system, drawn from reason's source,
She scorns to change her wonted course.

Could she descend from that great plan   5
To work unusual things for man,
To suit the insect of an hour—
This would betray a want of power,

Unsettled in its first design
And erring, when it did combine   10
The parts that form the vast machine,
The figures sketch'd on nature's scene.

Perfections of the great first cause
Submit to no contracted laws,
But all-sufficient, all-supreme,   15
Include no trivial views in them.

Who looks through nature with an eye
That would the scheme of heaven descry,
Observes her constant, still the same,
In all her laws, through all her frame.   20

No imperfection can be found
In all that is, above, around,—
All, nature made, in reason's sight
Is order all, and *all is right*.

1815

To a New-England Poet

Though skilled in latin and in greek,
And earning fifty cents a week,
Such knowledge, and the income, too,
Should teach you better what to do:
  The meanest drudges, kept in pay,   5
  Can pocket fifty cents a day.

Why stay in such a *tasteless land,*
Where ALL must on a *level* stand,
(Excepting people, *at their ease,*
Who choose the *level* where they please:)   10
See IRVING gone to Britain's court[1]
To people of *another sort,*
He will return, with wealth and fame,
While *Yankees* hardly know *your* name.

Lo! he has kissed a Monarch's—hand!   15
Before a PRINCE I see him stand,
And with the glittering nobles mix,
Forgetting *times* of seventy-six,[2]
While *you* with terror meet the frown
Of *Bank Directors* of the town,   20
  The home-made *nobles* of our times,
  Who hate the bard, and spurn his rhymes.

Why pause?—like IRVING, haste away,
To England your addresses pay;
And England will reward you well,   25
When you some pompous story tell
Of British feats, and British arms,
  The *maids* of honor, and their *charms.*

Dear Bard, I pray you, take the hint,
In England what you write and print,   30
Republished here in shop, or stall,
Will perfectly enchant us all:
  It will assume a different face,
  And post your name at every place,

---

[1] Freneau refers here to the international
reputation enjoyed by Washington Irving
(1783–1859).

[2] I.e., the American Revolution of 1776.

From splendid domes of first degree   35
Where *ladies* meet, to sip their tea;
From marble halls, where lawyers plead,
Or Congress-men talk loud, indeed,
To huts, where evening clubs appear,
And 'squires resort—to guzzle Beer.   40
1823

John Trumbull
1750–1831

During the Revolutionary period, a literary movement at Yale helped produce a number of talented, generally conservative, and highly ambitious writers determined to create an indigenous American literature by, oddly enough, following English literary models. The self-conscious imitative verse and prose of the Connecticut or Hartford Wits, as the group came to be called, though it dealt unswervingly with American themes and often attempted to give literary certification to American linguistic coinages (Noah Webster was a peripheral member of the group), demonstrated perhaps more than anything else that cultural independence from England would require more than a Declaration of Independence and a Constitution. Within a few decades the work even of the group's leading poets, John Trumbull, Timothy Dwight, and Joel Barlow, would drop completely out of fashion, most early nineteenth-century critics objecting, as did William Cullen Bryant, to "their artificial elevation of style" and "perpetual mannerism." This critical verdict has not been reversed, and the work of these poets, though frequently anthologized, has seldom been reedited and never been definitively collected.

The first of the Yale poets to make a name for himself, John Trumbull, was born into a prestigious Westbury, Connecticut, family in 1750. One of the most astonishing child prodigies in American history, Trumbull began to read at two, and before he was four he had completed Addison and Steele's *Spectator Papers* as well as the entire Bible. He claims in an autobiographical sketch that his interest in literature stemmed from "earliest infancy" and that by the time he was five he had "not only committed to memory most of the poetry" in his father's library "but was seized with an unaccountable ambition of composing verses himself." Latin and Greek presented few obstacles, and when he was seven, Trumbull passed Yale's admission examinations. His father, however, kept him at home, where he privately engaged in "a miscellaneous course of study" for six years before moving to New Haven.

Trumbull stayed at Yale for ten years as an undergraduate, graduate student, and tutor, writing occasional burlesques and elegies, which he circulated among friends but rarely published; starting a *Spectator*-like newspaper, *The Meddler;* and contributing satirical essays to the *Connecticut Courant.* With his friend and fellow tutor Timothy Dwight, he also tried to renovate the Yale curriculum by eliminating "learned languages, mathematics, logic, and scholastic theology," subjects Trumbull sarcastically thought were "dignified with the name of Solid Learning." The young men proposed to introduce in place of these outmoded studies "English poetry and the *belles-lettres.*" Out of this passion for educational reform came Trumbull's first significant production, *The Progress of Dulness* (1772–1773), a three-part verse satire composed in deliberately casual octosyllabic couplets borrowed from the English poetry of Swift, Butler, Churchill, and Prior.

Unlike his Yale colleagues Dwight and Barlow, whose "strong flight" and "Homeric fire" he praised, Trumbull never followed through on his epic ambitions. His talent was instinctively satiric, though throughout his career he did his best to pretend otherwise, often promoting himself as an incurably romantic poet of the sublime:

> That one must be born a Poet is an old adage, but that any one, tho' formed with the keenest sensibility, & the most extravagantly romantic feelings, should have an innate attention to the minutiae of Criticism, is perhaps uncommon. I was born the dupe of imagination. My satirical turn was not native. It was produced by the keen spirit of critical observation; operating on disappointed expectations and avenging itself on real or fancied wrongs.

Trumbull knew firsthand that satire inevitably makes enemies, but he also sensed that it was, as Edgar Allan Poe recognized, a mode particularly unsuited to the American social climate. After the first part of *The Progress of Dulness* (the "Tom Brainless" section) appeared, Trumbull found himself, as he had anticipated, with "a new set of Enemies," and his backing off from the controversy can be seen in the safer subjects he chose for the poem's next two installments: the conventional foibles of fops and coquettes.

In 1773 Trumbull resigned his tutorship at Yale and moved to Boston, where he studied law with John Adams and quickly became embroiled in Revolutionary politics: "An Elegy of the Times," a long, technically accomplished series of quatrains commemorating the political consequences of the Boston Tea Party, appeared in 1774. When Adams left for the Continental Congress in Philadelphia, Trumbull returned to New Haven to practice law and, after the solicitation of some of his friends in Congress, to begin the first canto of what was to be his most popular work, *M'Fingal*. Printed anonymously, as were all of his poems, *M'Fingal*, in four cantos of rapid-fire octosyllabic couplets, made slapstick fun of Tory diatribe and British colonial politics while it criticized less directly the "patriotic" rabble who violently implemented Whig policy. As Trumbull later put it, his intention had been "to satirize the follies and extravagances of my countrymen, as well as their enemies . . . with as much impartiality as possible." An enormously successful work that went through hundreds of unauthorized printings, *M'Fingal* maintained a rather remarkable political balance and epigrammatic flow, qualities that helped turn it into a stockpile of nasty quotations for both Whigs and Tories and, later, Republicans and Federalists.

Although successive editions of *M'Fingal* won Trumbull many honors and kept his name before the public, he wrote very little poetry after 1782. In 1789 he was appointed state's attorney for Hartford County and served in the state legislature in 1792 and 1800. A forceful Federalist, Trumbull continued to write anonymous satirical essays but abandoned political causes altogether in 1801 when he was appointed judge of the Superior Court of Connecticut. In 1819 he retired from public life and a few years later left Hartford to live with his daughter and son-in-law in Detroit, where he died in 1831.

As one of his last literary endeavors, he supervised in 1820 a collection of his poetry. Still trying to play down his satirical verse, Trumbull ignored the advice he received from friends and editors to print some of his early unpublished pieces and added instead to *The Progress of Dulness* and *M'Fingal* a number of elegant and elegiac poems that might have been written by "Tom Brainless" in his abstruser moments.

Further Reading:
V. L. Parrington, *The Connecticut Wits*, 1926.
A. Cowie, *John Trumbull: Connecticut Wit*, 1936.
L. Howard, *The Connecticut Wits*, 1943.

Texts:
The Poetical Works of John Trumbull, 2 vols., 1820.
The Satiric Poems of John Trumbull, ed. E. T. Bowden, 1962.

---

from The Progress of Dulness

Preface

"Pray what does the author mean?" is the first question most readers will ask, and the last they are able to answer. Therefore in a few words I will explain the subject and design of the following Poem.

The subject is the state of the times in regard to literature and religion. The author was prompted to write by a hope that it might be of use to point out, in a clear, concise, and striking manner, those general errors, that hinder the advantages of education, and the growth of piety. The subject is inexhaustible; nor is my design yet completed. This first part describes the principal mistakes in one course of life, and exemplifies the following well-known truth;— That to the frequent scandal, as well of religion, as learning, a fellow, without any share of genius, or application to study, may pass with credit through life, receive the honors of a liberal education, and be admitted to the right hand of fellowship among ministers of the gospel;— that except in one neighbouring province, ignorance wanders unmolested at our colleges, examinations are dwindled to meer form and ceremony, and after four years dozing there, no one is ever refused the honors of a degree, on account of dulness and insufficiency;—that the meer knowledge of antient languages, of the abstruser parts of mathematics, and the dark researches of metaphysics, is of little advantage in any business or profession in life;—that it would be more beneficial, in every place of public education, to take pains in teaching the elements of oratory, the grammar of the English tongue, and the elegancies of style, and composition;—that in numberless instances, sufficient care hath not been taken to exclude the ignorant and irreligious from the sacred desk;—that this tenderness to the undeserving tends to debase the dignity of the clergy, and to hinder many worthy men from undertaking the office of the ministry;—and that the virulent controversies of the present day concerning religious, or in many cases, meerly speculative opinions, savouring so highly of vanity and ostentation, and breathing a spirit so opposite to christian benevolence, have done more hurt to the cause of religion, than all the malice, the ridicule, and the folly of its enemies.

New Haven, August 1772.

from Part I: Or the Adventures of Tom Brainless

"Our Tom has grown a sturdy boy;
His progress fills my heart with joy;
A steady soul, that yields to rule,
And quite ingenious too, at school.
Our master says, (I'm sure he's right,)   5
There's not a lad in town so bright.
He'll cypher bravely, write and read,
And say his catechism and creed,
And scorns to hesitate or falter
In Primer, Spelling-book or Psalter.[1]   10
Hard work indeed, he does not love it;
His genius is too much above it.
Give him a good substantial teacher,
I'll lay he'd make a special preacher.
I've loved good learning all my life;   15
We'll send the lad to college, wife."
     Thus sway'd by fond and sightless passion,
His parents hold a consultation;
If on their couch, or round their fire,
I need not tell, nor you enquire.   20
     The point's agreed; the boy well pleased,
From country cares and labor eased;
No more to rise by break of day
To drive home cows, or deal out hay;
To work no more in snow or hail,   25
And blow his fingers o'er the flail,
Or mid the toils of harvest sweat
Beneath the summer's sultry heat,
Serene, he bids the farm, good-bye,
And quits the plough without a sigh.   30
Propitious to their constant friend,
The pow'rs of idleness attend.
     So to the priest in form he goes,
Prepared to study and to doze.
The parson, in his youth before,   35
Had run the same dull progress o'er;
His sole concern to see with care

---

[1] Psalm book.

His church and farm in good repair.
His skill in tongues, that once he knew,
Had bid him long, a last adieu;   40
Away his Latin rules had fled,
And Greek had vanish'd from his head.
    Then view our youth with grammar teazing,
Untaught in meaning, sense or reason;
Of knowledge e'er he gain his fill, he   45
Must diet long on husks of Lily,[2]
Drudge on for weary months in vain,
By mem'ry's strength, and dint of brain;
From thence to murd'ring Virgil's[3] verse,
And construing Tully[4] into farce,   50
Or lab'ring with his grave preceptor,
In Greek to blunder o'er a chapter.
The Latin Testament affords
The needed help of ready words;
At hand the Dictionary laid,   55
Gives up its page in frequent aid;
Hard by, the Lexicon and Grammar,
Those helps of mem'ry when they stammer;
The lesson's short; the priest contented;
His task to hear is sooner ended.   60
He lets him mind his own concerns,
Then tells his parents how he learns.
    Two years thus spent in gathering knowledge,
The lad sets forth t' unlade at college,
While down his sire and priest attend him,   65
To introduce and recommend him;
Or if detain'd, a letter's sent
Of much apocryphal content,
To set him forth, how dull soever,
As very learn'd and very clever;   70
A genius of the first emission,
With burning love for erudition;
So studious he'll outwatch the moon
And think the planets set too soon.
He had but little time to fit in;   75
Examination too must frighten.
Depend upon't he must do well,
He knows much more than he can tell;
Admit him, and in little space

[2] William Lily (ca. 1468–1522), English scholar and co-author of the famous Eton Latin grammar. Trumbull's note: "Lily's was the only Latin Grammar then in use."

[3] Virgil: Publius Vergilius Maro (70–19 B.C.),

Roman pastoral and epic poet; author of *The Aeneid*.

[4] Marcus Tullius Cicero (106–43 B.C.), Roman orator and author.

He'll beat his rivals in the race;　　　　　　80
His father's incomes are but small,
He comes now, if he come at all.
　So said, so done, at college now
He enters well, no matter how;
New scenes awhile his fancy please,　　　　85
But all must yield to love of ease.
In the same round condemn'd each day,
To study, read, recite and pray;
To make his hours of business double—
He can't endure th' increasing trouble;　　90
And finds at length, as times grow pressing,
All plagues are easier than his lesson.
With sleepy eyes and count'nance heavy,
With much excuse of *non paravi*,[5]
Much absence, *tardes* and *egresses*,　　　95
The college-evil on him seizes.
Then ev'ry book, which ought to please,
Stirs up the seeds of dire disease;
Greek spoils his eyes, the print's so fine,
Grown dim with study, or with wine;　　　100
Of Tully's latin much afraid,
Each page, he calls the doctor's aid;
While geometry, with lines so crooked,
Sprains all his wits to overlook it.
His sickness puts on every name,　　　　105
Its cause and uses still the same;
'Tis tooth-ache, cholic, gout or stone,
With phases various as the moon;
But though through all the body spread,
Still makes its cap'tal seat, the head.　　110
In all diseases, 'tis expected,
The weakest parts be most infected.
　Kind head-ache hail! thou blest disease,
The friend of idleness and ease;
Who mid the still and dreary bound　　　115
Where college walls her sons surround,
In spite of fears, in justice' spite,
Assumest o'er laws dispensing right,
Sett'st from his task the blunderer free,
Excused by dulness and by thee.　　　　120
Thy vot'ries bid a bold defiance
To all the calls and threats of science,

[5] Trumbull's note: "*Non paravi,* I have not prepared for recitation—an excuse commonly given; *tardes* and *egresses,* were terms used at college, for coming in late and going out before the conclusion of service."

Slight learning human and divine,
And hear no prayers, and fear no fine.
   And yet how oft the studious gain,   125
The dulness of a letter'd brain;
Despising such low things the while,
As English grammar, phrase and style;
Despising ev'ry nicer art,
That aids the tongue, or mends the heart;   130
Read ancient authors o'er in vain,
Nor taste one beauty they contain;
Humbly on trust accept the sense,
But deal for words at vast expense;
Search well how every term must vary   135
From Lexicon to Dictionary;
And plodding on in one dull tone,
Gain ancient tongues and lose their own,
Bid every graceful charm defiance,
And woo the skeleton of science.   140
   Come ye, who finer arts despise,
And scoff at verse as heathen lies;
In all the pride of dulness rage
At Pope, or Milton's deathless page;
Or stung by truth's deep-searching line,   145
Rave ev'n at rhymes as low as mine;
Say ye, who boast the name of wise,
Wherein substantial learning lies.
Is it, superb in classic lore,
To speak what Homer spoke before,   150
To write the language Tully wrote,
The style, the cadence and the note?
Is there a charm in sounds of Greek,
No language else can learn to speak;
That cures distemper'd brains at once,   155
Like Pliny's[6] rhymes for broken bones?
Is there a spirit found in Latin,
That must evap'rate in translating?
And say are sense and genius bound
To any vehicles of sound?   160
Can knowledge never reach the brains,
Unless convey'd in ancient strains?
While Homer sets before your eyes
Achilles' rage, Ulysses' lies,
Th' amours of Jove in masquerade,   165
And Mars entrapp'd by Phœbus' aid;

---

[6] Pliny: Caius Plinius Secundus (A.D. 23–79),
author of *Natural History*.

While Virgil sings, in verses grave,
His lovers meeting in a cave,
His ships turn'd nymphs, in pagan fables,
And how the Trojans eat their tables;   170
While half this learning but displays
The follies of the former days;
And for our linguists, fairly try them,
A tutor'd parrot might defy them.
   Go to the vulgar—'tis decreed,   175
There you must preach and write or plead;
Broach every curious Latin phrase
From Tully down to Lily's days:
All this your hearers have no share in,
Bate but their laughing and their staring.   180
Interpreters must pass between,
To let them know a word you mean.
   Yet could you reach that lofty tongue
Which Plato wrote and Homer sung;
Or ape the Latin verse and scanning,   185
Like Vida, Cowley or Buchanan;[7]
Or bear ten phrase-books[8] in your head;
Yet know, these languages are dead,
And nothing, e'er, by death, was seen
Improved in beauty, strength or mien,   190
Whether the sexton use his spade,
Or sorcerer wake the parted shade.
Think how would Tully stare or smile
At these wan spectres of his style,
Or Horace[9] in his jovial way   195
Ask what these babblers mean to say.
   Let modern Logic next arise
With newborn light to glad your eyes,
Enthroned on high in Reason's chair,
Usurp her name, assume her air,   200
Give laws, to think with quaint precision,
And deal out loads of definition.
   Sense, in dull syllogisms confined,
Scorns these weak trammels of the mind,
Nor needs t' enquire by logic's leave   205
What to reject and what receive;
Throws all her trifling bulwarks down,
Expatiates free; while from her frown

---

[7] Vida: Marco Girolamo Vida (ca. 1490–1566),
author of *Ars poetica*; Cowley: Abraham
Cowley (1618–1687), English poet; Buchanan:
George Buchanan (1506–1582), Scottish author.
All wrote Latin verses.

[8] Handy guides to idiomatic phrases and
expressions.
[9] Quintus Horatius Flaccus (65–8 B.C.),
immensely popular and influential Roman poet.

Alike the dunce and pedant smart,
The fool of nature, or of art.   210
    On books of Rhetorick turn your hopes,
Unawed by figures or by tropes.
What silly rules in pomp appear!
What mighty nothings stun the ear!
Athroismos, Mesoteleuton,   215
Symploce and *Paregmenon!* [10]
Thus, in such sounds high rumbling, run
The names of jingle and of pun;
Thus shall your pathos melt the heart,
And shame the Greek and Roman art.   220
    Say then, where solid learning lies
And what the toil that makes us wise!
Is it by mathematic's aid
To count the worlds in light array'd,
To know each star, that lifts its eye,   225
To sparkle in the midnight sky?
Say ye, who draw the curious line
Between the useful and the fine,
How little can this noble art
Its aid in human things impart,   230
Or give to life a cheerful ray,
And force our pains, and cares away.
    Is it to know whate'er was done
Above the circle of the sun?
Is it to lift the active mind   235
Beyond the bounds by heaven assign'd;
And leave our little world at home,
Through realms of entity to roam;
Attempt the secrets dark to scan,
Eternal wisdom hid from man;   240
And make religion but the sign
In din of battle when to join?
    Vain man, to madness still a prey,
Thy space a point, thy life a day,
A feeble worm, that aim'st to stride   245
In all the foppery of pride!
The glimmering lamp of reason's ray
Was given to guide thy darksome way.
Why wilt thou spread thy insect wings,
And strive to reach sublimer things?   250
Thy doubts confess, thy blindness own,

[10] Figures of speech in classical rhetoric. Trumbull
is making fun of the impressive-sounding Latin
names of such ordinary verbal operations.

Nor vex thy thoughts with scenes unknown.
Indulgent heaven to man below,
Hath all explain'd we need to know;
Hath clearly taught enough to prove   255
Content below, and bliss above.
Thy boastful wish how proud and vain,
While heaven forbids the vaunting strain!
For metaphysics rightly shown
But teach how little can be known: 260
Though quibbles still maintain their station,
Conjecture serves for demonstration,
Armies of pens draw forth to fight,
And **** and **** write.
   Oh! might I live to see that day,   265
When sense shall point to youths their way;
Through every maze of science guide;
O'er education's laws preside;
The good retain, with just discerning
Explode the quackeries of learning;   270
Give ancient arts their real due,
Explain their faults, and beauties too;
Teach where to imitate, and mend,
And point their uses and their end.
Then bright philosophy would shine,   275
And ethics teach the laws divine;
Our youths might learn each nobler art,
That shews a passage to the heart;
From ancient languages well known
Transfuse new beauties to our own;   280
With taste and fancy well refin'd,
Where moral rapture warms the mind,
From schools dismiss'ed, with lib'ral hand,
Spread useful learning o'er the land;
And bid the eastern world admire   285
Our rising worth, and bright'ning fire.
   But while through fancy's realms we roam,
The main concern is left at home;
Return'd, our hero still we find
The same, as blundering and as blind.   290
   Four years at college dozed away
In sleep, and slothfulness and play,
Too dull for vice, with clearest conscience,
Charged with no fault but that of nonsense,
And nonsense long, with serious air,   295
Has wander'd unmolested there,
He passes trial, fair and free,
And takes in form his first degree.

A scholar see him now commence
Without the aid of books or sense;   300
For passing college cures the brain,
Like mills to grind men young again.
The scholar-dress, that once array'd him,
The charm, *Admitto te ad gradum,* [11]
With touch of parchment can refine,   305
And make the veriest coxcomb shine,
Confer the gift of tongues at once,
And fill with sense the vacant dunce.
So kingly crowns contain quintessence
Of worship, dignity and presence;   310
Give learning, genius, virtue, worth,
Wit, valor, wisdom, and so forth;
Hide the bald pate, and cover o'er
The cap of folly worn before.
 Our hero's wit and learning now may   315
Be proved by token of diploma,
Of that diploma, which with speed
He learns to construe and to read;
And stalks abroad with conscious stride,
In all the airs of pedant pride,   320
With passport sign'd for wit and knowledge,
And current under seal of college.
 Few months now past, he sees with pain
His purse as empty as his brain;
His father leaves him then to fate,   325
And throws him off, as useless weight;
But gives him good advice, to teach
A school at first and then to preach.
. . . .

1772

Timothy Dwight
1752–1817

From the years following the Revolutionary War until his death in 1817,
Timothy Dwight reigned as the leading conservative figure in Connecticut
religion and politics. Staunchly orthodox and antidemocratic, Dwight combined
the vigorous Calvinism of Cotton Mather with the patriotic Federalism of

[11] Trumbull's note: *"Admitto te ad gradum,* I admit
you to a degree; part of the words used in
conferring the honours of college."

Alexander Hamilton. As a spokesman for a "regular, established society" that would foster among its members restraint and good conduct, Dwight continually attacked in prose and poetry the growing political enfranchisement of the ordinary citizen, the intellectual attitudes liberated by the French Revolution, and what he felt was the swelling tide of religious infidelity. An overbearing talker with a detached, authoritarian manner, he was known even among his friends as the "Protestant Pope of New England." To an unsympathetic twentieth-century critic, Vernon Parrington, "his mind was closed as tight as his study window in January." Yet for all of his conservatism, Dwight exhibited a remarkably inquisitive mind and never hesitated to entertain innovative ideas when convinced of their utility.

Born into a prominent New England family in Northampton, Massachusetts, the grandson of Jonathan Edwards and great-great-grandson of Solomon Stoddard, Dwight entered Yale at thirteen, where he met fellow prodigy John Trumbull. After graduation in 1769, he spent a few years teaching at a New Haven grammar school and then returned to Yale, where he acquired a reputation as an industrious and popular tutor who helped introduce contemporary literature into the undergraduate curriculum. In 1777, after being turned down for the presidency of Yale, he enlisted as a chaplain in the colonial army. He served for two years, gaining a reputation as a popular preacher and a successful composer of patriotic verse and songs. In 1779 family obligations forced him to return home and find employment: He conducted a school, which he staffed with former Yale classmates (including Joel Barlow), managed two farms, preached in neighboring villages, and represented his district for two terms in the Massachusetts legislature. In 1783 he was appointed pastor of the Congregational church at Greenfield Hill, Connecticut, where he also founded a distinguished coeducational academy. An untiring man who, like his hero Samuel Johnson, thought idleness one of the chief vices, Dwight managed during his busy pastorate to involve himself spiritedly in community affairs and write, besides numerous sermons, an eleven-book religious epic, *The Conquest of Canaan* (1785); an anti-Deist verse satire, *The Triumph of Infidelity* (1788); and a seven-part pastoral-topographical poem, *Greenfield Hill* (1794). The last of these, self-consciously imitative of Pope, Goldsmith, and Thomson, records Dwight's affectionate interest in the society, local history, landscape, and language of his native region and inaugurates in America a poetic tradition that would find twentieth-century urban expression in William Carlos Williams's epic celebration of the "local," *Paterson.*

In 1785 Dwight was elected president of Yale. Though as an educator he continually promoted his conservative blend of Calvinism and Federalism, he nevertheless helped modernize college study by bringing in prominent scholars and broadening the curriculum to include contemporary literature as well as American geography, chemistry, modern languages, and medicine. An indefatigable preacher, especially on the subject of "infidelity," his sermons were collected after his death in five volumes as *Theology, Explained and Defended* (1818–1819), an impressive transcript of what within a few years would become a completely outmoded religion and ideology.

During his presidency, Dwight also decided, for reasons of health as well as

curiosity, to study firsthand what seems, next to God, to be closest to his heart—
New England. Between 1795 and 1815 he made a series of excursions totaling
some 18,000 miles up, down, and across the New England countryside and into
New York. He looked into nearly every cultural and demographic phenomenon:
the terrain, weather variations, forestry, life expectancies, etymology of place
names, criminal codes, local history and scandals, schools, roads, canals, the
beauties of scenery as well as the state of religion, architecture, factories, Indian
culture, libraries, the American language, and whatever else attracted his highly
disciplined attention. His goal was to be "at once comprehensive and minute," to
provide "thorough information" for later generations about a region that, even
before the railroad and industrialization, he noticed was undergoing rapid and
unrecorded change. Composed in the form of letters to an imaginary English
gentleman, the journals are loosely organized around three of Dwight's
preoccupations: to show how a wilderness had been quickly transformed into a
largely prosperous civilization, to correct the misrepresentations of foreign visitors
to America, and to discredit the liberal ideology that taught that people would
be morally improved by living, as did the Indians, in an untrammeled state of
nature. His copious travel notes were published posthumously as *Travels in
New-England and New York* in four volumes in 1821 and 1822.

Further Reading:
L. Howard, *The Connecticut Wits*, 1943.
K. Silverman, *Timothy Dwight*, 1969.

Text:
Travels in New-England and New York, 4 vols.,
ed. B. M. Solomon, 1969.

---

from Travels in New-England and New York

Letter XLVIII: Fashionable Education

Dear Sir,

In a former letter I mentioned the attention generally given to education by the
inhabitants of Boston. I will now communicate to you some observations concerning
a mode of education adopted to some extent, as I believe, both here and in many other
places, particularly those which are wealthy and populous. In almost all instances
where it is pursued at all, it is chiefly confined to people of fashion.

The end proposed by the parents is to make their children objects of admiration.
The means, though not sanctioned, are certainly characterized by the end. That I have
not mistaken the end may be easily proved by a single resort to almost any genteel
company. To such company the children of the family are regularly introduced, and
the praise of the guests is administered to them as regularly as the dinner or the tea
is served up. Commendation is rung through all its changes; and you may hear, both
in concert and succession: "beautiful children," "fine children," "sweet children,"
"lovely children," "what a charming family!" "what a delightful family!" "You are
a fine little fellow." "You are a sweet little girl." "My son, can't you speak one of

your pieces before this good company?" "Caroline, where is your work?" "Susan, bring Miss Caroline's work and show it to that lady." "Susan, bring with you the picture which she finished last week;" with many other things of a similar nature. Were you to pass a twelve month in this country, and to believe all that you heard said by people not destitute of respectability, whatever opinion you might form of the parents, you would suppose that the children were a superior race of beings, both in person and mind; and that beauty, genius, grace, and loveliness had descended to this world in form and determined to make these states their future residence.

The means of effectuating this darling object are the communication of what are called accomplishments. The children are solicitously taught music, dancing, embroidery, ease, confidence, graceful manners, etc., etc. To these may be added what is called reading and traveling. You may very naturally ask me what fault I find in these branches of education. My objection lies originally to *the end which is proposed, and to the direction which it gives to the means,* in themselves harmless and capable of being useful. Children educated in the manner to which I refer soon learn that the primary end of their efforts, and even of their existence, is *appearance only. What they are,* they soon discern is of little consequence; but, *what they appear to be* is of importance inestimable. The whole force of the early mind is directed, therefore, to this object, and exhausted in acquiring the trifles of which it is composed.

The thoughts of a boy thus educated are spent upon the color, quality, and fashion of his clothes, and upon the several fashions to which his dress is to be successively conformed; upon his bow, his walk, his mode of dancing, his behavior in company, and his nice observance of the established rules of good breeding. To mingle without awkwardness or confusion in that empty, unmeaning chat, those mere vibrations of the tongue termed fashionable conversation, is the ultimate aim of his eloquence; and to comprehend and to discuss without impropriety the passing topics of the day, the chief object of his mental exertions. When he reads, he reads only to appear with advantage in such conversation. When he acts, he acts only to be admired by those who look on. Novels, plays, and other trifles of a similar nature are the customary subjects of his investigation. Voyages, travels, biography, and sometimes history limit his severe researches. By such a mind thinking will be loathed, and study regarded with terror. In the pursuits to which it is devoted, there is nothing to call forth, to try, or to increase its strength. Its powers, instead of being raised to new degrees of energy, are never exercised to the extent in which they already exist. His present capacity cannot be known for want of trial. What that capacity might become cannot be even conjectured. Destitute of that habit of laboring which alone can render labor pleasing, or even supportable, he dreads exertion as a calamity. The sight of a classic author gives him a chill; a lesson in Locke or Euclid, a mental ague.

Thus in a youth formed perhaps by nature for extensive views and manly efforts sloth of mind is generated, dandled, and nursed on the knee of parental indulgence. A soft, luxurious, and sickly character is spread over both the understanding and the affections, which forbids their growth, prevents their vigor, and ruins every hope of future eminence and future worth. The faculties of the mind, like those of the body, acquire strength only by exercise. To attain their greatest strength, both must be exercised daily, and often to the utmost. Had Goliath never exerted the powers of his body, he would have been an infant in strength; had Newton never exerted those of his mind, he would have been an infant in understanding. Genius in the abstract is a mere capacity for exertion. This is the gift of nature, and is all that she gives. The utmost of this capacity can never be conjectured until the mind has in a long-continued, habitual course made its most vigorous efforts.

If these observations are just, they furnish every parent an easy and sure directory for the intellectual education of his children. If he wishes them to possess the greatest strength of which they are capable, he must induce them to the most vigorous mental exertions. The reading education which I have described will never accomplish the purpose. Hard study, a thorough investigation of mathematical science, and a resolute attention to the most powerful efforts of distinguished logicians, in a word, an old-fashioned, rigid, academical education will ever be found indispensable to the youth who is destined to possess mental greatness.

On girls, this unfortunate system induces additional evils. Miss, the darling of her father and the pride of her mother, is taught from the beginning to regard her dress as a momentous concern. She is instructed in embroidery merely that she may finish a piece of work which from time to time is to be brought out to be seen, admired, and praised by visitors; or framed and hung up in the room to be still more frequently seen, admired, and praised. She is taught music only that she may perform a few times to excite the same admiration and applause for her skill on the pianoforte. She is taught to draw merely to finish a picture which, when richly framed and ornamented is hung up to become an altar for the same incense. Do not misunderstand me. I have no quarrel with these accomplishments. So far as they contribute to make the subject of them more amiable, useful, or happy, I admit their value. It is the *employment* of them which I censure, the sacrifice made by the parent of his property and his child at the shrine of vanity.

The reading of girls is regularly lighter than that of boys. When the standard of reading for boys is set too low, that for girls will be proportionally lowered. Where boys investigate books of sound philosophy and labor in mathematical and logical pursuits, girls read history, the higher poetry, and judicious discourses in morality and religion. When the utmost labor of boys is bounded by history, biography, and the pamphlets of the day, girls sink down to songs, novels, and plays.

Of this reading what, let me ask, are the consequences? By the first novel which she reads, she is introduced into a world literally new, a middle region between "this spot which men call earth" and that which is formed in Arabian tales. Instead of houses inhabited by mere men, women, and children, she is presented with a succession of splendid palaces and gloomy castles inhabited by tenants, half human and half angelic, or haunted by downright fiends. Everything in the character and circumstances of these beings comes at the wish or the call of the enchanter. Whatever can supply their wants, suit their wishes, or forward, or frustrate their designs is regularly at hand. The heroes are as handsome, as dignified, as brave, as generous, as affectionate, as faithful, and as accomplished as he supposes will satisfy the demands of his readers. At the same time, they have always a quantum sufficit of money; or, if not, some relation dies at the proper time and leaves them an ample supply. Every heroine is also a compound of all that is graceful and lovely. Her person is fashioned "by the hand of harmony." Her complexion outvies the snow and shames the rose. Her features are such as Milton's Eve might envy, and her mind is of the same class with those refined beings to whom this great poet in his list of the celestial orders gives the elegant names of virtues. With these delightful inhabitants of Utopia are contrasted iron-handed misers, profligate guardians, traitorous servants, and hags not excelled by those of Lapland itself. It ought not be omitted that in this sequestered region the fields and gardens are all secondhand copies of paradise. On them, whenever it is convenient, the morning beams with every tint of elegance and every ray of glory; and when Aurora has no further use for these fine things, her sister, Evening, puts them on herself and appears scarcely less splendid or less delightful.

With this ideal world the unfortunate girl corresponds so much and so long that she ultimately considers it as her own proper residence. With its inhabitants she converses so frequently and so habitually that they become almost her only familiar acquaintance.

But she must one day act in the real world. What can she expect after having resided so long in novels, but that fortunes, and villas, and Edens will spring up everywhere in her progress through life to promote her enjoyment. She has read herself into a heroine, and is fairly entitled to all the appendages of this character. If her imagination may be trusted, she is to be romantically rich and romantically happy. The mornings which dawn upon her are ever to be bright, the days serene, and the evenings fragrant and delightful. In a word, the curse pronounced upon mankind is to her to lose its gloomy influence, and sorrow and toil are to fly from the path in which she chooses to walk through life.

With these views, how disappointed must she be by the rugged course of nature? How untoward must be the progress of facts? How coarsely must the voice of truth grate upon her ear? How disgusted must she be to find herself surrounded not by trusty Johns and faithful Chloes, but by ordinary domestics, chilling her with rusticity, provoking her by their negligence, insulting her with their impudence, and leaving her service without even giving her warning. Must she not feel that it is a kind of impertinence in the days to be cloudy and wet, in the nights to be dark and chilly, in the streets to encumber her with mud or choke her with dust, and in the prospects to present nothing but the mere vulgar scenes of this vulgar world.

The very food which she eats, for eat she must, will disgust her by its coarse unlikeness to the viands on which her imagination has so often feasted. Her friends, even those most intimately connected with her, will lose all the amiableness with which they are invested by natural affection, because they differ so grossly in their persons, manners, and opinions from the fine forms of fancy, and from the poetical minds whose residence is a novel or a song. In a word, the world will become to her a solitude, and its inhabitants, strangers, because her taste for living has become too refined, too dainty, to relish anything found in real life.

If she is at all pleasing and amiable, she will be addressed. But by whom? Not by a Corydon, a Strephon, or even a Grandison.[1] At the best, her suitor will be a being formed of flesh and blood, who intends to live by business, and to acquire reputation by diligence, integrity, and good sense. He is in pursuit of a wife and, therefore, can hardly wish for an angel. It will be difficult for him to believe that a being so exalted would assume the marriage vow, do the honors of his table, direct the business of his family, or preside over the education of his children. He has hitherto spent his life

---

[1] Conventional pastoral names. Grandison is the hero of Samuel Richardson's last novel, *History of Sir Charles Grandison* (1753).

perhaps in acting vigorously in the counting room, contending strenuously at the bar, or pursuing with diligence some other business merely human. How can such a being frame his mouth to lisp the pretty things which alone can be in unison with so delicate an ear? Figure to yourself the disgust, the pain, the surprise of this silken existence even at the most refined language of honesty, and at the most honorable sentiments of affection obtruded on her by such a suitor.

Should some man of art and mischief happen to think the conquest worth obtaining, how easily might she become a victim to the very accomplishments in which she considers all excellence as involved?

Besides, this life is always in some degree a season of suffering and sorrow. In what manner can our heroine encounter either? To patience and fortitude, she has from her infancy been a stranger. With religion she is unacquainted. Principles such as religion approves, she has none. This world has daily blasted all her expectations; with the future world she has not begun a connection. Between the Bible and novels, there is a gulf fixed which few novel readers are willing to pass. The consciousness of virtue, the dignified pleasure of having performed our duty, the serene remembrance of an useful life, the hope of an interest in the Redeemer, and the promise of a glorious inheritance in the favor of God are never found in novels, and of course have never been found by her. A weary, distressed, bewildered voyager amid the billows of affliction, she looks around her in vain to find a pilot, a polestar, or a shore.

Under the influence of this education, persons of both sexes also are in extreme danger of becoming a voluntary prey to the modern philosophy and to the principles of enchantment and perdition which it so successfully holds out to minds destitute of sound principle and defensive prudence. Unaccustomed to think, they are pleased to find others willing to think for them. Unaccustomed to reason, their minds will be perplexed by every argument advanced against their opinions. The admission of truth, the comprehension of good sense, requires the toil of sober, vigorous thought. The admission of fiction, and of philosophical as truly as of poetical fiction, demands nothing but the luscious indulgence of fancy. To a soft and dainty mind, a taste fascinated by mental luxury, how much more congenial is the latter employment than the former. How improbable is it, how hopeless, that such a mind can fail to reject the dictates of sober truth and sound understanding, and from a self-indulgence by habit rendered indispensable imbibe the wretched doctrines created by the philosophists of the present day? How improbable is it that any mind which has once imbibed these doctrines can escape from absolute ruin?

I know that this education is expressly attempted with a view to superior refinement, but it is not a refinement of the taste, the understanding, or the heart. It is merely a refinement of the imagination, of an imagination already soft and sickly, of a sensibility already excessive, of a relish already fastidious. To a genuine perfection of taste it bears no more resemblance than the delicate white of decay to the native fairness of complexion, or than the blush of a hectic to the bloom of health.

It is not here intended that this mode of education prevails more in Boston than in other populous places on this continent. Perhaps it prevails less. That it actually exists in such places, that it is fashionable, and that this town has a share in the evil will not, I believe, be questioned. I have taken this occasion to enter my own protest against it. In every part of it the dictates of common sense are laid aside, that which is of the least importance is most regarded, and that which is of the greatest, most forgotten. To enable children to appear with such fashionable advantages as to gain admiration and applause is the sole concern. To enable them to be what they ought to be, wise, virtuous, and useful, is left out of the system. The mind, instead of being educated, is left to the care of accident and fashion. Dress, manners, and accomplishments are placed under expensive masters, and regulated with extreme solicitude. With this education, what can a son or a daughter become? Not a man, nor a woman, but a well-dressed bundle of accomplishments. Not a blessing, nor an heir of immortality, but a fribble or a doll.

I am, Sir, yours, etc.

1795–1815/1821–1822

Joel Barlow
1754–1812

Joel Barlow's career represents an unusual twist in the customary life cycle: He started out as a political and social conservative and ended as an outspoken radical. One of the youngest of the Yale group that became popularly known as the Connecticut or Hartford Wits, Barlow, of all his colleagues, underwent the most dramatic personal and professional changes. Born a Connecticut farmer's son, he died on an important diplomatic mission to Napoleon in Poland. At one time a prominent member of Hartford's close-knit conservative intelligentsia, he later befriended the radical Thomas Paine and converted to Jeffersonian Republicanism. A former contributor to an influential series of Federalist anti-insurrectionist satires, he became an impassioned defender of the French Revolution. Once a committed Congregationalist and an army chaplain, he turned to Deism and was frequently attacked as an atheist. A poet who originally inscribed his first important publication, *The Vision of Columbus*, to King Louis XVI, he dedicated its extensive, liberalized revision both to his country and especially to the American inventor Robert Fulton.

Barlow began his college studies at Dartmouth but soon transferred to Yale, where he met Noah Webster, John Trumbull, and Timothy Dwight. Distinguishing himself as a poet, he was invited to deliver the commencement poem at his graduation in 1778. He served for a brief time as an army chaplain and afterward settled in Hartford, where he edited and published a newspaper, the *American Mercury;* went into the printing and stationers business; and eventually decided to practice law. In 1787 he published *The Vision of Columbus,* a self-consciously correct, patriotic volume in the panoramic-vision genre that was then passing for "epic." During this period he also became involved in *The Anarchiad,* a newspaper series of Federalist satires, modeled after Pope's *The Dunciad* and designed to counteract what the Wits considered to be a growing drift toward "faction" and insurrection (see *Federalist Papers* No. 10). In 1788 Barlow traveled to France and England as a promoter for the Scioto Association, a land speculation agency from which Barlow promptly resigned when its extensive claims proved fraudulant.

For seventeen years Barlow remained in Europe, familiarizing himself with Continental social thought and immersing himself in London and Parisian radical politics. In 1792 he published *Advice to the Privileged Orders,* an "attack on monarchy, aristocracy, the clergy, and a rapidly growing trans-Atlantic militarism." In the same year he also wrote a satiric poem, *The Conspiracy of Kings,* and *A Letter to the National Convention,* for which he was awarded French citizenship. In 1793, while unsuccessfully running for office as Savoy delegate to the National Convention, he whimsically composed as a diversion the poem for which he is most often remembered, "The Hasty Pudding," a mock-heroic celebration of the blessings of plain New England cooking and living. From 1795 to 1797 he served in Algiers as a special minister with instructions to obtain the release of American prisoners being held by Barbary pirates. His mission accomplished, Barlow spent the next seven years in Paris, acquiring a fortune in securities speculation, participating in his friend Robert Fulton's steamboat and submarine experiments, and collaborating with him on a long, uncompleted philosophical poem about canal construction, as well as continuing his attacks on American anti-French foreign policy.

In 1804 Barlow and his wife (whom he had secretly married in 1781) returned to America and built Kalorama, a luxurious estate in Washington, D.C., where Barlow installed one of the finest libraries and wine cellars in the nation and graced republican society as a leading cosmopolite. He also revised considerably his early epic *The Vision of Columbus,* toning down its Federalism and Congregationalism by adding long libertarian stretches and by "Americanizing" its language:

> Our language is constantly and rapidly improving. The unexampled progress of the sciences and arts for the last thirty years has enriched it with a great number of new words, which are now become as necessary to the writer as his ancient mother tongue. The same progress which leads to further extensions of ideas will still extend the vocabulary; and our neology must and will keep pace with the advancement of our knowledge. Hence will follow a closer definition and more accurate use of words, with a stricter attention to their orthography.

Despite his embarrassment with "the atheistical principles" the new version contained, Noah Webster would write: "I like most of your neology—your new epithets and terms are mostly well formed—expressive—and a valuable addition to our language."

Barlow was at work in 1811 on a republican version of the American Revolution when President Madison prevailed upon him as friend and influential adviser to serve as minister plenipotentiary to Napoleon. After a frustrating year of negotiations in Paris, Barlow set off to meet personally with Napoleon at Vilna. But as Napoleon's invasion of Russia grew increasingly disastrous, Barlow's chances for an audience with the emperor deteriorated. They never met. In the midst of the retreat from Moscow, surrounded by "sickness, famine and frost," Barlow, who thought all his writings had enthusiastically endorsed George Berkeley's celebrated prophecy that "westward the course of empire takes its way," died of pneumonia sometime during Christmas week in Zarnowiec, a tiny village near Krakow, where he is still buried.

Further Reading:
C. B. Todd, *Life and Letters: Joel Barlow,* 1886.
T. A. Zunder, *The Early Days of Joel Barlow, a Connecticut Wit: His Life and Works from 1754 to 1787,* 1934.
L. Howard, *The Connecticut Wits,* 1943.
J. Woodress, *A Yankee's Odyssey: The Life of Joel Barlow,* 1958.

Texts:
The Hasty Pudding, 1796.
"On the Discoveries of Captain Lewis," *The Literary Magazine,* February 1807.
"Advice to a Raven in Russia," in Leon Howard, "Joel Barlow and Napoleon," *Huntington Library Quarterly,* October 1938.

The Hasty-Pudding*
A Poem, in Three Cantos

Written at Chambery in Savoy Jan. 1793

Omne tulit punctum qui miscuit utile dulci.[1]
He makes a good breakfast who mixes pudding with molasses.

To Mrs. Washington.

MADAM:—A simplicity in diet, whether it be considered with reference to the happiness of individuals or the prosperity of a nation, is of more consequence than we are apt to imagine. In recommending so great and necessary a virtue to the rational part of mankind, I wish it were in my power to do it in such a manner as would be likely to gain their attention. I am sensible that it is one of those subjects in which example has infinitely more power than the most convincing arguments, or the highest charms of poetry. Goldsmith's *Deserted Village,* though possessing these two advantages in a greater degree than any other work of the kind, has not prevented villages in England from being deserted. The apparent interest of the rich individuals, who form the taste as well as the laws in that country, has been against him; and with that interest it has been vain to contend.

The vicious habits which in this little piece I endeavor to combat, seem to me not so difficult to cure. No class of people has any interest in supporting them, unless it be the interest which certain families may feel in vying with each other in sumptuous entertainments. There may indeed be some instances of depraved appetites which no arguments will conquer; but these must be rare. There are very few persons but would always prefer a plain dish for themselves, and would prefer it likewise for their guests, if there were no risk of reputation in the case. This difficulty can only be removed

---

* Dr. Benjamin Rush observed in 1789 that nostalgia, or "home sickness," was a frequent "disease" in the Revolutionary army, especially among New Englanders. The "disease," which was to become an increasingly common theme in American poetry, inspired Joel Barlow when, shortly after being made a citizen of France, he was surprisingly served New England corn-meal mush at Chambery, in Savoy, near the French Alps.

The text is from the first New Haven edition of 1796. Because of Barlow's concern with orthography, the text has not been modernized.

[1] From *Ars Poetica* of the Roman poet Horace (65–8 B.C.): "He gains the approval of all who mixes the useful with the sweet."

by example; and the example should proceed from those whose situation enables them to take the lead in forming the manners of a nation. Persons of this description in America, I should hope, are neither above nor below the influence of truth and reason when conveyed in language suited to the subject.

Whether the manner I have chosen to address my arguments to them be such as to promise any success, is what I cannot decide. But I certainly had hopes of doing some good, or I should not have taken the pains of putting so many rhymes together; and much less should I have ventured to place your name at the head of these observations.

Your situation commands the respect and your character the affections of a numerous people. These circumstances impose a duty upon you, which I believe you discharge to your own satisfaction and that of others. The example of your domestic virtues has doubtless a great effect among your countrywomen. I only wish to rank *simplicity of diet* among the virtues. In that case it will certainly be cherished by you, and I should hope more esteemed by others than it is at present.

THE AUTHOR.

Canto I

Ye Alps audacious, thro' the Heavens that rise,
To cramp the day and hide me from the skies;
Ye Gallic flags,[2] that o'er their heights unfurl'd,
Bear death to kings, and freedom to the world,
I sing not you. A softer theme I chuse,   5
A virgin theme, unconscious of the Muse,
But fruitful, rich, well suited to inspire
The purest frenzy of poetic fire.
    Despise it not, ye Bards to terror steel'd,
Who hurl'd your thunders round the epic field;   10
Nor ye who strain your midnight throats to sing
Joys that the vineyard and the still-house[3] bring;
Or on some distant fair your notes employ,
And speak of raptures that you ne'er enjoy.
I sing the sweets I know, the charms I feel,   15
My morning incense, and my evening meal,
The sweets of Hasty-Pudding. Come, dear bowl,
Glide o'er my palate, and inspire my soul.
The milk beside thee, smoking from the kine,
Its substance mingled, married in with thine,   20
Shall cool and temper thy superior heat,
And save the pains of blowing while I eat.
    Oh! could the smooth, the emblematic song
Flow like thy genial juices o'er my tongue,
Could those mild morsels in my numbers chime,   25

---

[2] Barlow had recently written in support of Savoy's annexation to France.

[3] A distillery.

And, as they roll in substance, roll in rhyme,
No more thy aukward unpoetic name
Should shun the Muse, or prejudice thy fame;
But rising grateful to the accustom'd ear,
All Bards should catch it, and all realms revere! 30
    Assist me first with pious toil to trace
Thro' wrecks of time thy lineage and thy race;
Declare what lovely squaw, in days of yore,
(Ere great Columbus sought thy native shore)
First gave thee to the world; her works of fame 35
Have liv'd indeed, but liv'd without a name.
Some tawny Ceres,[4] goddess of her days,
First learn'd with stones to crack the well-dry'd maize,
Thro' the rough sieve to shake the golden show'r,
In boiling water stir the yellow flour. 40
The yellow flour, bestrew'd and stir'd with haste,
Swell in the flood and thickens to a paste,
    Then puffs and wallops,[5] rises to the brim,
Drinks the dry knobs[6] that on the surface swim:
The knobs at last the busy ladle breaks, 45
And the whole mass its true consistence takes.
    Could but her sacred name, unknown so long,
Rise like her labors, to the sons of song,
To her, to them, I'd consecrate my lays,
And blow her pudding with the breath of praise. 50
If 'twas Oella, whom I sang before,[7]
I here ascribe her one great virtue more.
Not thro' the rich Peruvian realms alone
The fame of Sol's sweet daughter should be known,
But o'er the world's wide climes should live secure, 55
Far as his rays extend, as long as they endure.
    Dear Hasty-Pudding, what unpromis'd joy
Expands my heart, to meet thee in Savoy!
Doom'd o'er the world thro' devious paths to roam,
Each clime my country, and each house my home, 60
My soul is sooth'd, my cares have found an end,
I greet my long-lost, unforgotten friend.
    For thee thro' Paris, that corrupted town,
How long in vain I wandered up and down,
Where shameless Bacchus,[8] with his drenching hoard 65
Cold from his cave usurps the morning board.
London is lost in smoke and steep'd in tea;

---

[4] Roman goddess of grain ("cereal") and agriculture.
[5] Boils with a noisy bubbling.
[6] Lumps.
[7] In his *Vision of Columbus* (1787), Barlow had sung of the mythological Peruvian princess, daughter of the Sun and goddess of household arts.
[8] God of wine in Greek mythology.

No Yankey there can lisp the name of thee:
The uncouth word, a libel on the town,
Would call a proclamation from the crown.[9]   70
For climes oblique, that fear the sun's full rays,
Chill'd in their fogs, exclude the generous maize;
A grain whose rich luxuriant growth requires
Short gentle showers, and bright etherial fires.

But here tho' distant from our native shore,   75
With mutual glee we meet and laugh once more,
The same! I know thee by that yellow face,
That strong complexion of true Indian race,
Which time can never change, nor soil impair,
Nor Alpine snows, nor Turkey's morbid air;   80
For endless years, thro' every mild domain,
Where grows the maize, there thou art sure to reign.

But man, more fickle, the bold licence claims,
In different realms to give thee different names.
Thee the soft nations round the warm Levant[10]   85
Palanta call, the French of course Polante;[11]
E'en in thy native regions, how I blush
To hear the Pennsylvanians call thee Mush!
On Hudson's banks, while men of Belgie spawn
Insult and eat thee by the name suppawn.[12]   90
All spurious appellations, void of truth:
I've better known thee from my earliest youth,
Thy name is Hasty-Pudding! thus our sires
Were wont to greet thee fuming from their fires;
And while they argu'd in thy just defence   95
With logic clear, they thus explained the sense:—
"In haste the boiling cauldron o'er the blaze,
"Receives and cooks the ready-powder'd maize;
"In haste 'tis serv'd, and then in equal haste,
"With cooling milk, we make the sweet repast.   100
"No carving to be done, no knife to grate
"The tender ear, and wound the stony plate;
"But the smooth spoon, just fitted to the lip,
"And taught with art the yielding mass to dip,
"By frequent journies to the bowl well stor'd,   105
"Performs the hasty honors of the board."
Such is thy name, significant and clear,
A name, a sound to every Yankey dear,
But most to me, whose heart and palate chaste

Preserve my pure hereditary taste.   110
There are who strive to stamp with disrepute
The luscious food, because it feeds the brute;
In tropes of high-strain'd wit, while gaudy prigs
Compare thy nursling man to pamper'd pigs;
With sovereign scorn I treat the vulgar jest,   115
Nor fear to share thy bounties with the beast.
What though the generous cow gives me to quaff
The milk nutritious; am I then a calf?
Or can the genius of the noisy swine,
Tho' nurs'd on pudding, thence lay claim to mine?   120
Sure the sweet song, I fashion to thy praise,
Runs more melodious than the notes they raise.
    My song resounding in its grateful glee,
No merit claims; I praise myself in thee.
My father lov'd thee through his length of days: 125
For thee his fields were shaded o'er with maize;
From thee what health, what vigour he possest,
Ten sturdy freemen sprung from him attest;
Thy constellation rul'd my natal morn,
And all my bones were made of Indian corn.   130
Delicious grain! whatever form it take,
To roast or boil, to smother or to bake,
In every dish 'tis welcome still to me,
But most, my Hasty-Pudding, most in thee.
    Let the green Succatash with thee contend,   135
Let beans and corn their sweetest juices blend,
Let butter drench them in its yellow tide,
And a long slice of bacon grace their side;
Not all the plate, how fam'd soe'er it be,
Can please my palate like a bowl of thee.   140
Some talk of Hoe-cake,[13] fair Virginia's pride,
Rich Johnny-cake[14] this mouth has often tri'd;
Both please me well, their virtues much the same;
Alike their fabric, as allied their fame,
Except in dear New-England, where the last   145
Receives a dash of pumpkin in the paste,
To give it sweetness and improve the taste.
But place them all before me, smoking hot,
The big round dumplin rolling from the pot;
The pudding of the bag, whose quivering breast,   150
With suet lin'd leads on the Yankey feast;
The Charlotte brown,[15] within whose crusty sides
A belly soft the pulpy apple hides;

[13] A thin corn-meal cake.   [15] A fruit pastry.
[14] Another version of corn cake.

The yellow bread, whose face like amber glows,
And all of Indian that the bake-pan knows—   155
You tempt me not—my fav'rite greets my eyes,
To that lov'd bowl my spoon by instinct flies.

Canto II

   To mix the food by vicious rules of art,
To kill the stomach and to sink the heart,
To make mankind, to social virtue sour,   160
Cram o'er each dish, and be what they devour;
For this the kitchen Muse first framed her book,
Commanding sweats to stream from every cook;
Children no more their antic gambols tried,
And friends to physic wonder'd why they died.   165
Not so the Yankey—his abundant feast,
With simples furnished, and with plainness drest,
A numerous offspring gathers round the board,
And cheers alike the servant and the lord;
Whose well-bought hunger prompts the joyous taste,   170
And health attends them from the short repast.
While the full pail rewards the milk-maid's toil,
The mother sees the morning cauldron boil;
To stir the pudding next demands their care,
To spread the table and the bowls prepare;   175
To feed the children, as their portions cool,
And comb their heads, and send them off to school.
   Yet may the simplest dish, some rules impart,
For nature scorns not all the aids of art.
E'en Hasty-Pudding, purest of all food,   180
May still be bad, indifferent, or good,
As sage experience the short process guides,
Or want of skill, or want of care presides.
Whoe'er would form it on the surest plan,
To rear the child and long sustain the man;   185
To shield the morals while it mends the size,
And all the powers of every food supplies,
Attend the lessons that the Muse shall bring,
Suspend your spoons, and listen while I sing.
But since, O man! thy life and health demand   190
Not food alone, but labour from thy hand,
First in the field, beneath the sun's strong rays,
Ask of thy mother earth the needful maize;
She loves the race that courts her yielding soil,
And gives her bounties to the sons of toil.   195
When now the ox, obedient to thy call,
Repays the loan that fill'd the winter stall,

Pursue his traces o'er the furrow'd plain,
And plant in measur'd hills the golden grain.
But when the tender germe begins to shoot,   200
And the green spire declares the sprouting root,
Then guard your nursling from each greedy foe,
Th' insidious worm, the all-devouring crow.
A little ashes, sprinkled round the spire,
Soon steep'd in rain, will bid the worm retire;   205
The feather'd robber with his hungry maw
Swift flies the field before your man of straw,
A frightful image, such as school boys bring
When met to burn the Pope,[16] or hang the King.
Thrice in the season, through each verdant row   210
Wield the strong plough-share and the faithful hoe;
The faithful hoe, a double task that takes,
To till the summer corn, and roast the winter cakes.
Slow springs the blade, while check'd by chilling rains,
Ere yet the sun the seat of Cancer[17] gains;   215
But when his fiercest fires emblaze the land,
Then start the juices, then the roots expand;
Then, like a column of Corinthian mould,[18]
The stalk struts upward, and the leaves unfold;
The bushy branches all the ridges fill,   220
Entwine their arms, and kiss from hill to hill.
Here cease to vex them, all your cares are done;
Leave the last labours to the parent sun;
Beneath his genial smiles the well-drest field,
When autumn calls, a plenteous crop shall yield.   225
Now the strong foliage bears the standards high,
And shoots the tall top-gallants[19] to the sky;
The suckling ears their silky fringes bend,
And pregnant grown, their swelling coats distend;
The loaded stalk, while still the burthen grows,   230
O'erhangs the space that runs between the rows;
High as a hop-field waves the silent grove,
A safe retreat for little thefts of love,
When the pledg'd roasting-ears invite the maid,
To meet her swain beneath the new-form'd shade;   235
His generous hand unloads the cumbrous hill,
And the green spoils her ready basket fill;
Small compensation for the two-fold bliss,
The promis'd wedding and the present kiss.

---

[16] Most likely Barlow is referring to Guy Fawkes
Day, an annual November celebration where a
Catholic conspirator against the king of
England is burned in effigy.
[17] A Zodiac sign, entered by the sun on June 21.

[18] The most ornate of Greek architectural
columns.
[19] Nautical term for the mast and sails above the
top mast.

Slight depredations these; but now the moon   240
Calls from his hollow tree the sly raccoon;
And while by night he bears the prize away,
The bolder squirrel labours through the day.
Both thieves alike, but provident of time,
A virtue, rare, that almost hides their crime.   245
Then let them steal the little stores they can,
And fill their gran'ries from the toils of man;
We've one advantage where they take no part,—
With all their wiles they ne'er have found the art
To boil the Hasty-Pudding; here we shine   250
Superior far to tenants of the pine;
This envied boon to man shall still belong,
Unshar'd by them in substance or in song.
At last the closing season browns the plain,
And ripe October gathers in the grain;   255
Deep loaded carts the spacious corn-house fill,
The sack distended marches to the mill;
The lab'ring mill beneath the burthen groans,
And show'rs the future pudding from the stones;
Till the glad house-wife greets the powder'd gold,   260
And the new crop exterminates the old.

Canto III

The days grow short; but tho' the falling sun
To the glad swain proclaims his day's work done,
Night's pleasing shades his various task prolong,
And yield new subjects to my various song.   265
For now, the corn-house fill'd, the harvest home,
Th' invited neighbours to the *Husking*[20] come;
A frolic scene, where work, and mirth, and play,
Unite their charms, to chace the hours away.
Where the huge heap lies center'd in the hall,   270
The lamp suspended from the cheerful wall,
Brown corn-fed nymphs, and strong hard-handed beaux,
Alternate rang'd, extend in circling rows,
Assume their seats, the solid mass attack;
The dry husks rustle, and the corn-cobs crack;   275
The song, the laugh, alternate notes resound,
And the sweet cider trips in silence round.
The laws of Husking ev'ry wight[21] can tell;
And sure no laws he ever keeps so well:

[20] Party for husking corn.   [21] Human being.

For each red ear a general kiss he gains,   280
With each smut[22] ear she smuts the luckless swains;
But when to some sweet maid a prize is cast,
Red as her lips, and taper as her waist,
She walks the round, and culls one favor'd beau,
Who leaps, the luscious tribute to bestow.   285
Various the sport, as are the wits and brains
Of well pleas'd lasses and contending swains:
Till the vast mound of corn is swept away,
And he that gets the last ear, wins the day.
Meanwhile the house-wife urges all her care,   290
The well-earn'd feast to hasten and prepare.
The sifted meal already waits her hand,
The milk is strain'd the bowls in order stand,
The fire flames high; and, as a pool (that takes
The headlong stream that o'er the mill-dam breaks)   295
Foams, roars and rages with incessant toils,
So the vext cauldron rages, roars and boils.
First with clean salt she seasons well the food,
Then strews the flour and thickens all the flood.
Long o'er the simmering fire she lets it stand: 300
To stir it well demands a stronger hand;
The husband takes his turn; and round and round
The ladle flies; at last the toil is crown'd;
When to the board the thronging huskers pour,
And take their seats as at the corn before.   305
I leave them to their feast. There still belong
More copious matters to my faithful song.
For rules there are, tho' ne'er unfolded yet,
Nice rules and wise, how pudding should be ate.
Some with molasses line the luscious treat,   310
And mix, like Bards, the useful with the sweet.
A wholesome dish, and well-deserving praise,
A great resource in those bleak wintry days,
When the chill'd earth lies buried deep in snow,
And raging Boreas[23] drives the shivering cow.   315
Blest cow! thy praise shall still my notes employ,
Great source of health, the only source of joy;[24]
How oft thy teats these pious hands have prest!
How oft thy bounties prove my only feast!
How oft I've fed thee with my fav'rite grain!   320

---

[22] Damaged by fungus.
[23] The north wind.
[24] In other editions the following couplet appears

next: "Mother of Egypt's God—but sure, for
one / Were I to leave my God, I'd worship
thee."

And roar'd, like thee, to find thy children slain!
Ye swains who know her various worth to prize,
Ah! house her well from Winter's angry skies.
Potatoes, Pumpkins, should her sadness cheer,
Corn from your crib, and mashes from your beer;   325
When Spring returns she'll well acquit the loan,
And nurse at once your infants and her own.
Milk then with pudding I should always chuse;
To this in future I confine my Muse,
Till she in haste some farther hints unfold,   330
Well for the young, nor useless to the old.
First in your bowl the milk abundant take,
Then drop with care along the silver lake
Your flakes of pudding; these at first will hide
Their little bulk beneath the swelling tide;   335
But when their growing mass no more can sink,
When the soft island looms above the brink,
Then check your hand: you've got the portion's due,
So taught our sires, and what they taught is true.
There is a choice in spoons. Tho' small appear   340
The nice distinction, yet to me 'tis clear,
The deep bowl'd Gallic spoon, contriv'd to scoop
In ample draughts the thin diluted soup,
Performs not well in those substantial things,
Whose mass adhesive to the metal clings;   345
Where the strong labial muscles must embrace,
The gentle curve, and sweep the hollow space.
With ease to enter and discharge the freight,
A bowl less concave but still more dilate,
Becomes the pudding best. The shape, the size,   350
A secret rests unknown to vulgar eyes.
Experienc'd feeders can alone impart
A rule so much above the lore of art.
These tuneful lips, that thousand spoons have tried,
With just precision could the point decide,   355
Tho' not in song; the muse but poorly shines
In cones, and cubes, and geometric lines.
Yet the true form, as near as she can tell,
Is that small section of a goose-egg-shell,
Which in two equal portions shall divide   360
The distance from the centre to the side.
Fear not to slaver; 'tis no deadly sin,
Like the free Frenchman, from your joyous chin
Suspend the ready napkin; or, like me,
Poise with one hand your bowl upon your knee;   365
Just in the zenith your wise head project,

Your full spoon, rising in a line direct,
Bold as a bucket, heeds no drops that fall,
The wide mouth'd bowl will surely catch them all.[25]
1793/1796

On the Discoveries of Captain Lewis[*]

Let the Nile cloak his head in the clouds, and defy
    The researches of science and time;
Let the Niger escape the keen traveller's eye,
    By plunging or changing his clime.

Columbus! not so shall thy boundless domain   5
    Defraud thy brave sons of their right:
Streams, midlands, and shorelands elude us in vain,
    We shall drag their dark regions to light.

Look down, sainted sage, from thy synod of Gods;
    See, inspired by thy venturous soul,   10
Mackenzie roll northward his earth-draining floods,
    And surge the broad waves to the pole.

With the same soaring genius thy Lewis ascends,
    And seizing the car of the sun,
O'er the sky-propping hills and high waters he bends   15
    And gives the proud earth a new zone.

---

[25] Note added by Barlow to later edition: "There are various ways of preparing and eating it; with molasses, butter, sugar, cream, and fried. Why so excellent a thing cannot be eaten alone? Nothing is perfect alone, even man who boasts of so much perfection is nothing without his fellow substance. In eating, beware of the lurking heat that lies deep in the mass; dip your spoon gently, take shallow dips and cool it by degrees. It is sometimes necessary to blow. This is indicated by certain signs which every experienced feeder knows. They should be taught to young beginners. I have known a child's tongue blistered for want of this attention, and then the school-dame would insist that the poor thing had told a lie. A mistake: the falsehood was in the faithless pudding. A prudent mother will cool it for her child with her own sweet breath. The husband, seeing this, pretends his own wants blowing too from the same lips. A sly deceit of love. She knows the cheat, but feigning ignorance, lends her pouting lips and gives a gentle blast, which warms the husband's heart more than it cools his pudding."

[*] Recited at a dinner given in Washington, D.C., on January 14, 1807, for Captain Meriwether Lewis, celebrating his return from the western journeys. The text is from *The Literary Magazine*, Vol VII (February 1807).

Potowmak, Ohio, Missouri had felt
   Half her globe in their cincture' comprest;
His long curving course has completed the belt,
   And tamed the last tide of the west.   20

Then hear the loud voice of the nation proclaim,
   And all ages resound the decree:
Let our occident stream² bear the young hero's name
   Who taught him his path to the sea.

These four brother floods, like a garland of flowers,   25
   Shall entwine all our states in a band,
Conform and confederate their wide spreading powers,
   And their wealth and their wisdom expand.

From Darien to Davis one garden shall bloom,
   Where war's wearied banners are furl'd,   30
And the far scenting breezes that waft its perfume,
   Shall settle the storms of the world.

Then hear the loud voice of the nation proclaim
   And all ages resound the decree:
Let our occident stream bear the young hero's name,   35
Who taught him his path to the sea.

1807/1807

Advice to a Raven in Russia*

      Black fool, why winter here? These frozen skies,
      Worn by your wings and deafen'd by your cries,
      Should warn you hence, where milder suns invite,
      And day alternates with his mother night.
         You fear perhaps your food will fail you there, 5
      Your human carnage, that delicious fare
      That lured you hither, following still your friend
      The great Napoleon to the world's bleak end.
      You fear, because the southern climes pour'd forth

---

¹ Belt or girdle.
² The Lewis River in the Cascade Mountains of southwest Washington.
* Dictated to his secretary a few weeks before his death in December 1812. Most of Barlow's poetry after *The Columbiad* focused bitterly on the devastation of the Napoleonic Wars. The text is from Leon Howard, "Joel Barlow and Napoleon," *Huntington Library Quarterly,* 2 (October 1938).

Their clustering nations to infest the north.   10
Bavarians, Austrians, those who Drink the Po
And those who skirt the Tuscan seas below,
With all Germania, Neustria,[1] Belgia, Gaul,
Doom'd here to wade thro slaughter to their fall,
You fear he left behind no wars, to feed   15
His feather'd canibals and nurse the breed.
     Fear not, my screamer, call your greedy train,
Sweep over Europe, hurry back to Spain,
You'll find his legions there; the valliant crew
Please best their master when they toil for you.   20
Abundant there they spread the country o'er
And taint the breeze with every nation's gore.
Iberian, Lussian,[2] British widely strown,
But still more wide and copious flows their own.
     Go where you will; Calabria, Malta, Greece,   25
Egypt and Syria still his fame increase,
Domingo's fatten'd isle and India's plains
Glow deep with purple drawn from Gallic veins.
No Raven's wing can stretch the flight so far
As the torn bandrols of Napoleon's war.   30
Choose then your climate, fix your best abode,
He'll make you deserts and he'll bring you blood.
     How could you fear a dearth? have not mankind,
Tho slain by millions, millions left behind?
Has not CONSCRIPTION still the power to weild   35
Her annual faulchion[3] o'er the human field?
A faithful harvester! or if a man
Escape that gleaner, shall he scape the BAN?
The triple BAN, that like the hound of hell
Gripes with three joles;[4] to hold his victim well. 40
     Fear nothing then, hatch fast your ravenous brood,
Teach them to cry to Bonaparte for food;
They'll be like you, of all his suppliant train,
The only class that never cries in vain.
For see what mutual benefits you lend!   45
(The surest way to fix the mutual friend)
While on his slaughter'd troops your tribes are fed,
You cleanse his camp and carry off his dead.
Imperial Scavenger! but now you know
Your work is vain amid these hills of snow.   50
His tentless troops are marbled thro with frost
And change to crystal when the breath is lost.

---

[1] Part of the Frankish Empire, comprising much
of the Seine and Loire valleys.
[2] Portuguese.
[3] Sword or sickle.
[4] Jaws.

Mere trunks of ice, tho limb'd like human frames
And lately warm'd with life's endearing flames,
They cannot taint the air, the world impest,   55
Nor can you tear one fiber from their breast.
No! from their visual sockets, as they lie,
With beak and claws you cannot pluck an eye.
The frozen orb, preserving still its form,
Defies your talons as it braves the storm,   60
But stands and stares to God, as if to know
In what curst hands he leaves his world below.
    Fly then, or starve; tho all the dreadful road
From Minsk to Moskow with their bodies strow'd
May count some Myriads, yet they can't suffice   65
To feed you more beneath these dreary skies.
Go back, and winter in the wilds of Spain;
Feast there awhile, and in the next campaign
Rejoin your master; for you'll find him then,
With his new million of the race of men,   70
Clothed in his thunders, all his flags unfurl'd,
Raging and storming o'er the prostrate world.
    War after war his hungry soul requires,
State after State shall sink beneath his fires,
Yet other Spains in victim smoke shall rise   75
And other Moskows suffocate the skies,
Each land lie reeking with its people's slain
And not a stream run bloodless to the main.
Till men resume their souls, and dare to shed
Earth's total vengeance on the monster's head.   80
Hurl from his blood-built throne this king of woes,
Dash him to dust, and let the world repose.

1812/1843

Noah Webster
1758–1843

Noah Webster's monumental work, *An American Dictionary of the English Language,* overshadows the extraordinary range of his achievements. With the energy and curiosity of Benjamin Franklin and the diligence and moral zeal of John Woolman, Webster mastered the intricacies of such vastly different disciplines as law, politics, history, linguistics, music, economics, medicine, journalism, education, and agriculture. Only his vigor outdistanced his accomplishments. Noah Webster's mind—and his pen—explored virtually every important facet of American life during the new nation's formative years.

Webster's roots ran deep in American history. He could trace his lineage

through the governorship of Connecticut to the founding of Hartford and as far
back as William Bradford of Plymouth Plantation. The fourth of five children,
he divided his childhood between working the family farm on the outskirts of
Hartford and disciplining himself in the precepts of the *New England Primer*. He
entered Yale in 1774 and, along with his classmate Joel Barlow, quickly came to
share the political and cultural attitudes of Yale's two most distinguished young
tutors, Timothy Dwight and John Trumbull. Literary historians later dubbed this
group "the Connecticut wits."

Webster participated briefly in the Revolutionary War before graduating from
Yale in 1778. Faced with no immediate means of support, he reluctantly took up
teaching and studied law on the side. In 1781 he opened a practice in Hartford
and earned a master's degree at Yale for a thesis titled "On the Universal
Diffusion of Literature as Introductory to the Universal Diffusion of
Christianity." Unable to secure steady work as a lawyer, Webster tried to reopen
the school he had so unceremoniously abandoned the year before. The
advertisement promoting the school emphasized the neglect of female education
and "the general inattention to the grammatical purity and elegance of our native
language"—a subject that absorbed him for the rest of his life.

Webster's work on language appeared at a time when Americans were still
inordinately dependent on English manners, customs, literature, and textbooks.
The American Spelling Book (1783) was only the first of his innumerable efforts to
define a distinctively American language. In it he proposed to strengthen national
unity by promoting a common language that would "extirpate the improprieties
and vulgarisms which were necessarily introduced by settlers from various parts
of Europe." He also intended to eliminate "those odious distinctions of provincial
dialects," to render the "acquisition of our language easy and the pronunciation
accurate and uniform," and to establish the democratic criterion of "general
custom" as the "rule of speaking." Webster's speller featured American place
names and a chronology of important events in American history aimed at
inspiring youth with a "love of virtue, patriotism, and religion."

The unprecedented success of *The American Spelling Book* (over 100 million
copies were sold before the text went out of general use in the twentieth
century) launched Webster on a lifelong series of promotional tours. At each stop
along the way, he indefatigably lectured local residents on the need for a national
identity:

> Unshackle your minds. You have an empire to raise and support by your
> exertions, and a national character to establish and extend by your wisdom and
> virtue. Every engine should be employed to render the people of this country
> national, to call their attachments home to their own country, and to inspire
> them with the pride of national character.

Such patriotic abstractions fueled Webster's enormous energy and ego and helped
gear the nation for federalism. But he rarely enjoyed the rewards of his labors.
Ever concerned about his own finances (he sent his son in the late 1830s to
Indiana to corner the textbook market in the western territories), he invariably
signed away most of his royalties to fund his next project.

Encouraged by the reception of his early patriotic ventures, Webster proposed more radical solutions to the major political, social, and educational controversies of the day. He wrote provocative editorials for two journals he financed: *The American Magazine* (1787–1788), New York's first monthly digest of news and opinion, and *American Minerva* (1793–1803), a pro-Federalist daily newspaper. In them, Webster vigorously endorsed such reforms as equal distribution of property, abolition of slavery, and religious tolerance. In addition, he demanded improvements in sanitation, disease control, and city planning as well as devised plans for unemployment insurance and forest conservation. Yet he had his greatest impact as an itinerant advocate of the Constitution, arguing agressively for a strong national union. He set out to convince the American public that the Revolution had not ended. In speeches, letters, essays, pamphlets, and books, he proselytized for a United States as independent in its language as in its politics and as famous for its arts as for its arms.

Benjamin Franklin had proposed a phonetic alphabet in 1768; Webster, twenty years later, judged the plan unworkable. With the support of his aging mentor, Webster announced a bold new plan that included eliminating all superfluous and silent letters from American language (*bread/bred, friend/frend, give/giv*), replacing vague or indeterminate sounds with definite ones *(mean/meen, grieve/greev)*, and eradicating all foreign influences on American spelling *(chorus/korus)*. Webster toured the country on behalf of his proposal and defended it at some length in an appendix to his *Dissertations on the English Language* (1789), a work he dedicated to Franklin. Severely criticized for what was regarded as his intransigent and angular vision, Webster withdrew to Hartford, where he practiced law with John Trumbull, rejoined the "wits" at the conservative Friendly Club, and took solace in the advice Dr. Benjamin Rush offered him in a letter written during the worst days of the yellow fever epidemic in Philadelphia: "That man will be egregiously disappointed who expects the rewards of patriotism or successful enterprises on this side of the grave. . . . Continue to do all the good you can by enlightening our country. *Expect* to be persecuted for doing good; and *Learn* to rejoice in persecution."

Disillusioned with politics, Webster resolved to cultivate his scholarly interests. Between 1802 and 1812 he completed *Elements of Useful Knowledge,* a four-volume textbook survey of United States history and science. But when his research convinced him that "popular errors proceeding from a misunderstanding of words are among the efficient causes of our political disorder," he pushed irrepressibly toward publishing an American dictionary as an instrument of national order.

A Compendious Dictionary of the English Language (1806) was the fourth dictionary compiled in the United States (three small volumes had appeared in 1798 and 1800), but the first to be so insistently American. Believing that "a national language is a bond of national union," Webster featured the vocabulary of America's "new circumstances, new modes of life, new laws, new ideas" and in the process contributed to the idea of progress—what he first was to call "the American way." A one-dollar abridgment, designed for school use, followed in 1807, along with advertisements soliciting support for a "complete Dictionary." Despite charges that he was a "thirsty reformer" who would "unsettle the whole of our admirable language," Webster resolutely continued his research, spending the next ten years preparing a synopsis of the affinities of the more than twenty languages he had mastered.

An American Dictionary of the English Language (1828) declared America's linguistic independence. The two-volume, seventy-thousand-word compilation also memorialized Webster's conversion to evangelical Protestantism some years earlier. In addition to drawing examples from such conventional sources as law and civil policy, Webster created scores of maxims and religious sentiments to illustrate his definitions. The *American Dictionary* was soon adopted as the legislative and judicial standard and enjoyed such immense popularity that Webster's name became synonymous with *dictionary*. Yet, despite frequent promotional tours, he earned little for his work and eventually had to mortgage his home to finance a second edition.

Webster was no less diligent in old age. Recognizing that newspapers and the Bible comprised the bulk of the reading done by most Americans, he published an American version called *The Holy Bible . . . with Amendments to the Language* (1833). He spent his last years revising his schoolbooks and preparing seven new ones, including *The Little Franklin: Teaching Children to Read What They Daily Speak, and to Learn What They Ought to Know* (1836). The role of a quiet, industrious sage never suited Webster. He participated energetically in public life, stoutly maintaining until his death in 1843 that he belonged to "no party but to the class of citizens who love their country and strive to promote its interests, political, moral, literary, and religious."

Further Reading:
Notes on the Life of Noah Webster, ed. E. Ford, 2 vols., 1912.
H. R. Warfel, *Noah Webster, Schoolmaster to America,* 1936.

Text:
An American Dictionary of the English Language, 1828.
See also *Letters of Noah Webster,* ed. H. R. Warfel, 1953.

---

from An American Dictionary of the English Language

Preface

In the year 1783, just at the close of the revolution, I published an elementary book for facilitating the acquisition of our vernacular tongue, and for correcting a vicious pronunciation, which prevailed extensively among the common people of this country. Soon after the publication of that work, I believe in the following year, that learned and respectable scholar, the Rev. Dr. Goodrich of Durham, one of the trustees of Yale College, suggested to me, the propriety and expediency of my compiling a dictionary, which should complete a system for the instruction of the citizens of this country in the language. At that time, I could not indulge the thought, much less the hope, of undertaking such a work; as I was neither qualified by research, nor had I the means of support, during the execution of the work, had I been disposed to undertake it. For many years therefore, though I considered such a work as very desirable, yet it appeared to me impracticable; as I was under the necessity of devoting my time to other occupations for obtaining subsistence.

About twenty-seven years ago, I began to think of attempting the compilation of a Dictionary. I was induced to this undertaking, not more by the suggestion of friends, than by my own experience of the want of such a work, while reading modern books of science. In this pursuit, I found almost insuperable difficulties, from the want of a dictionary, for explaining many new words, which recent discoveries in the physical sciences had introduced into use. To remedy this defect in part, I published my Compendious Dictionary in 1806; and soon after made preparations for undertaking a larger work.

My original design did not extend to an investigation of the origin and progress of our language; much less of other languages. I limited my views to the correcting of certain errors in the best English Dictionaries, and to the supplying of words in which they are deficient. But after writing through two letters of the alphabet, I determined to change my plan. I found myself embarrassed, at every step, for want of a knowledge of the origin of words, which Johnson, Bailey, Junius, Skinner[1] and some other authors do not afford the means of obtaining. Then laying aside my manuscripts, and all books treating of language, except lexicons and dictionaries, I endeavored, by a diligent comparison of words, having the same or cognate radical letters, in about twenty languages, to obtain a more correct knowledge of the primary sense of original words, of the affinities between the English and many other languages, and thus to enable myself to trace words to their source.

I had not pursued this course more than three or four years, before I discovered that I had to unlearn a great deal that I had spent years in learning, and that it was necessary for me to go back to the first rudiments of a branch of erudition, which I had before cultivated, as I had supposed, with success.

I spent ten years in this comparison of radical words, and in forming a synopsis of the principal words in twenty languages, arranged in classes, under their primary elements or letters. The result has been to open what are to me new views of language, and to unfold what appear to be the genuine principles on which these languages are constructed.

After completing this synopsis, I proceeded to correct what I had written of the Dictionary, and to complete the remaining part of the work. But before I had finished it, I determined on a voyage to Europe, with the view of obtaining some books and some assistance which I wanted; of learning the real state of the pronunciation of our language in England, as well as the general state of philology in that country; and of attempting to bring about some agreement or coincidence of opinions, in regard to unsettled points in pronunciation and grammatical construction. In some of these objects I failed; in others, my designs were answered.

It is not only important, but, in a degree necessary, that the people of this

---

[1] Samuel Johnson (1709–1784), Nathan Bailey (d. 1742), Franciscus Junius (1589–1677), and Stephen Skinner (1623–1667) were all noted contributors to the fields of lexicography and philology.

country, should have an *American Dictionary* of the English Language; for, although the body of the language is the same as in England, and it is desirable to
perpetuate that sameness, yet some differences must exist. Language is the expression of ideas; and if the people of one country cannot preserve an identity of ideas,
they cannot retain an identity of language. Now an identity of ideas depends materially upon a sameness of things or objects with which the people of the two
countries are conversant. But in no two portions of the earth, remote from each
other, can such identity be found. Even physical objects must be different. But the
principal differences between the people of this country and of all others, arise
from different forms of government, different laws, institutions and customs. Thus
the practice of hawking and hunting, the institution of heraldry, and the feudal
system of England originated terms which formed, and some of which now form,
a necessary part of the language of that country; but, in the United States, many
of these terms are no part of our present language,—and they cannot be, for the
things which they express do not exist in this country. They can be known to us
only as obsolete or as foreign words. On the other hand, the institutions in this
country which are new and peculiar, give rise to new terms or to new applications
of old terms, unknown to the people of England; which cannot be explained by
them and which will not be inserted in their dictionaries, unless copied from ours.
Thus the terms, *land-office; land-warrant; location of land; consociation* of churches;
regent of a university; *intendant* of a city; *plantation, selectmen, senate, congress, court,
assembly, escheat,* &c. are either words not belonging to the language of England,
or they are applied to things in this country which do not exist in that. No person
in this country will be satisfied with the English definitions of the words *congress,
senate* and *assembly, court,* &c. for although these are words used in England, yet
they are applied in this country to express ideas which they do not express in that
country. With our present constitutions of government, *escheat* can never have its
feudal sense in the United States.

But this is not all. In many cases, the nature of our governments, and of our civil
institutions, requires an appropriate language in the definition of words, even when
the words express the same thing, as in England. Thus the English Dictionaries inform
us that a *Justice* is one deputed by the *King* to do right by way of judgment—he is
a *Lord* by his office—Justices of the peace are appointed by the *King's commission*—
language which is inaccurate in respect to this officer in the United States. So
constitutionally is defined by Todd or Chalmers, *legally,* but in this country the
distinction between *constitution* and *law* requires a different definition. In the United
States, a *plantation* is a very different thing from what it is in England. The word
marshal, in this country, has one important application unknown in England or in
Europe.

A great number of words in our language require to be defined in a phraseology
accommodated to the condition and institutions of the people in these states, and the
people of England must look to an American Dictionary for a correct understanding
of such terms.

The necessity therefore of a Dictionary suited to the people of the United States
is obvious; and I should suppose that this fact being admitted, there could be no

difference of opinion as to the *time,* when such a work ought to be substituted for English Dictionaries.

There are many other considerations of a public nature, which serve to justify this attempt to furnish an American Work which shall be a guide to the youth of the United States. Most of these are too obvious to require illustration.

One consideration however which is dictated by my own feelings, but which I trust will meet with approbation in correspondent feelings in my fellow citizens, ought not to be passed in silence. It is this. "The chief glory of a nation," says Dr. Johnson, "arises from its authors." With this opinion deeply impressed on my mind, I have the same ambition which actuated that great man when he expressed a wish to give celebrity to Bacon, to Hooker, to Milton and to Boyle.

I do not indeed expect to add celebrity to the names of *Franklin, Washington, Adams, Jay, Madison, Marshall, Ramsay, Dwight, Smith, Trumbull, Hamilton, Belknap, Ames, Mason, Kent, Hare, Silliman, Cleaveland, Walsh, Irving,* and many other Americans distinguished by their writings or by their science; but it is with pride and satisfaction, that I can place them, as authorities, on the same page with those of *Boyle, Hooker, Milton, Dryden, Addison, Ray, Milner, Cowper, Davy, Thomson* and *Jameson.*

A life devoted to reading and to an investigation of the origin and principles of our vernacular language, and especially a particular examination of the best English writers, with a view to a comparison of their style and phraseology, with those of the best American writers, and with our colloquial usage, enables me to affirm with confidence, that the genuine English idiom is as well preserved by the unmixed English of this country, as it is by the best *English* writers. Examples to prove this fact will be found in the Introduction to this work. It is true, that many of our writers have neglected to cultivate taste, and the embellishments of style; but even these have written the language in its genuine *idiom.* In this respect, Franklin and Washington, whose language is their hereditary mother tongue, unsophisticated by modern grammar, present as pure models of genuine English, as Addison or Swift. But I may go farther, and affirm, with truth, that our country has produced some of the best models of composition. The style of President Smith; of the authors of the Federalist; of Mr. Ames; of Dr. Mason; of Mr. Harper; of Chancellor Kent; of Mr. Barlow; of the legal decisions of the Supreme Court of the United States; of the reports of legal decisions in some of the particular states; and many other writings; in purity, in elegance and in technical precision, is equaled only by that of the best British authors, and surpassed by that of no English compositions of a similar kind.

The United States commenced their existence under circumstances wholly novel and unexampled in the history of nations. They commenced with civilization, with learning, with science, with constitutions of free government, and with that best gift of God to man, the christian religion. Their population is now equal to that of England; in arts and sciences, our citizens are very little behind the most enlightened people on earth; in some respects, they have no superiors; and our language, within two centuries, will be spoken by more people in this country, than any other language on earth, except the Chinese, in Asia, and even that may not be an exception.

It has been my aim in this work, now offered to my fellow citizens, to ascertain the true principles of the language, in its orthography and structure; to purify it from some palpable errors, and reduce the number of its anomalies, thus giving it more regularity and consistency in its forms, both of words and sentences; and in this manner, to furnish a standard of our vernacular tongue, which we shall not be ashamed to bequeath to *three hundred millions of people,* who are destined to occupy, and I hope, to adorn the vast territory within our jurisdiction.

If the language can be improved in regularity, so as to be more easily acquired by our own citizens, and by foreigners, and thus be rendered a more useful instrument for the propagation of science, arts, civilization and christianity; if it can be rescued from the mischievous influence of sciolists and that dabbling spirit of innovation which is perpetually disturbing its settled usages and filling it with anomalies; if, in short, our vernacular language can be redeemed from corruptions, and our philology and literature from degradation; it would be a source of great satisfaction to me to be one among the instruments of promoting these valuable objects. If this object cannot be effected, and my wishes and hopes are to be frustrated, my labor will be lost, and this work must sink into oblivion.

This Dictionary, like all others of the kind, must be left, in some degree, imperfect; for what individual is competent to trace to their source, and define in all their various applications, popular, scientific and technical, *sixty* or *seventy thousand* words! It satisfies my mind that I have done all that my health, my talents and my pecuniary means would enable me to accomplish. I present it to my fellow citizens, not with frigid indifference, but with my ardent wishes for their improvement and their happiness; and for the continued increase of the wealth, the learning, the moral and religious elevation of character, and the glory of my country.

To that great and benevolent Being, who, during the preparation of this work, has sustained a feeble constitution, amidst obstacles and toils, disappointments, infirmities and depression; who has twice borne me and my manuscripts in safety across the Atlantic, and given me strength and resolution to bring the work to a close, I would present the tribute of my most grateful acknowledgments. And if the talent which he entrusted to my care, has not been put to the most profitable use in his service, I hope it has not been "kept laid up in a napkin," and that any misapplication of it may be graciously forgiven.

New Haven, 1828.

[A Sampling from An American Dictionary]

AUTHOR, n. [L. *auctor*; Ir. *ughdar*; W. *awdur*; Fr. *auteur*; Sp. *autor*; It. *autore*. The Latin word is from the root of *augeo,* to increase, or cause to enlarge. The primary sense is one who brings or causes to come forth.]

1. One who produces, creates, or brings into being; as, God is the *author* of the Universe.
2. The beginner, former, or first mover of any thing; hence, the efficient cause of a thing. It is appropriately applied to one who composes or writes a book, or original work, and in a more general sense, to one whose occupation is to compose and write books; opposed to compiler or translator. . . .

DU'TY, *n.* [from *due,* Fr. *d*] That which a person owes to another; that which a person is bound, by any natural, moral or legal obligation, to pay, do or perform. Obedience to princes, magistrates and the laws is the *duty* of every citizen and subject; obedience, respect and kindness to parents are *duties* of children; fidelity to friends is a *duty*; reverence, obedience and prayer to God are indispensable *duties*; the government and religious instruction of children are *duties* of parents which they cannot neglect without guilt.

2. Forbearance of that which is forbid by morality, law, justice or propriety. It is our *duty* to refrain from lewdness, intemperance, profaneness and injustice.

3. Obedience; submission.

4. Act of reverence or respect.

> They both did *duty* to their lady. *Spenser.*

5. The business of a soldier or marine on guard; as, the company is on *duty*. It is applied also to other services or labor.

6. The business of war; military service; as, the regiment did *duty* in Flanders.

7. Tax, toll, impost, or customs; excise; any sum of money required by government to be paid on the importation, exportation, or consumption of goods. An impost on land or other real estate, and on the stock of farmers, is not called a *duty*, but a *direct tax.* *U. States.* . . .

EDUCA'TION, *n.* [L. *educatio.*] The bringing up, as of a child; instruction; formation of manners. Education comprehends all that series of instruction and discipline which is intended to enlighten the understanding, correct the temper, and form the manners and habits of youth, and fit them for usefulness in their future stations. To give children a good *education* in manners, arts and science, is important; to give them a religious *education* is indispensable; and an immense responsibility rests on parents and guardians who neglect these duties. . . .

EXPE'RIENCE, *n.* [L. *experientia,* from *experior,* to try; *ex* and ant. *perior*; Gr. πειραω to attempt, whence *pirate*; G. *erfahren,* from *fahren,* to move, to go, to drive, to *ferry*; D. *ervaaren,* from *vaaren,* to go, to move, to sail; Sw. *forfara, fara*; Dan. *forfarer, farer*; Sax. and Goth. *faran*; Eng. to *fare*. The L. *periculum,* Eng. *peril,* are from the same root. We see the root of these words is to go, to *fare,* to drive, urge or press, to strain or stretch forward. See Class Br. No. 3. Ar. No. 4. 19. 23.]

1. Trial, or a series of trials or experiments; active effort or attempt to do or to prove something, or repeated efforts. A man attempts to raise wheat on moist or clayey ground; his attempt fails of success; *experience* proves that wheat will not flourish on such a soil. He repeats the trial, and his *experience* proves the same fact. A single trial is usually denominated an *experiment*; *experience* may be a series of trials, or the result of such trials.

2. Observation of a fact or of the same facts or events happening under like circumstances.

3. Trial from suffering or enjoyment; suffering itself; the use of the senses; as the *experience* we have of pain or sickness. We know the effect of light, of smell or of taste by *experience*. We learn the instability of human affairs by observation or by *experience*. We learn the value of integrity by *experience*. Hence,

4. Knowledge derived from trials, use, practice, or from a series of observations. . . .

FREE, *a.* [Sax. *frig, freoh,* free; *frigan, freogan,* to free; G. *frei*; D. *vry*; Dan. *fri*; Sw. *fri*; all contracted from *frig,* which corresponds with Heb. and Ch. פרק ; Syr. ܦܪܩ ; Sam. ; Ar. فرق , faraka, to *break,* to separate, to divide, to free, to redeem, &c. See *Frank.*]

1. Being at liberty; not being under necessity or restraint, physical or moral; a word of general application to the body, the will or mind, and to corporations.

2. In *government,* not enslaved; not in a state of vassalage or dependence; subject only to fixed laws, made by consent, and to a regular administration of such laws; not subject to the arbitrary will of a sovereign or lord; as a *free* state, nation or people.

3. Instituted by a free people, or by consent or choice of those who are to be subjects, and securing private rights and privileges by fixed laws and principles; not arbitrary or despotic; as a *free* constitution or government.

   There can be no *free* government without a democratical branch in the constitution.   *J. Adams.*

4. Not imprisoned, confined or under arrest; as, the prisoner is set *free.*

5. Unconstrained; unrestrained; not under compulsion or control. A man is *free* to pursue his own choice; he enjoys *free* will.

6. Permitted; allowed; open; not appropriated; as, places of honor and confidence are *free* to all; we seldom hear of a commerce perfectly *free.*

7. Not obstructed; as, the water has a *free* passage or channel; the house is open to a *free* current of air.

8. Licentious; unrestrained. The reviewer is very *free* in his censures.

9. Open; candid; frank; ingenuous; unreserved; as, we had a *free* conversation together.

   Will you be *free* and candid to your friend?   *Otway.*

10. Liberal in expenses; not parsimonious; as a *free* purse; a man is *free* to give to all useful institutions.

11. Gratuitous; not gained by importunity or purchase. He made him a *free* offer of his services. It is a *free* gift. The salvation of men is of *free* grace.

12. Clear of crime or offense; guiltless; innocent.

    My hands are guilty, but my heart is *free.*   *Dryden.*

13. Not having feeling or suffering; clear; exempt; with *from*; as *free from* pain or disease; *free from* remorse.

14. Not encumbered with; as *free* from a burden.

15. Open to all, without restriction or without expense; as a *free* school.

16. Invested with franchises; enjoying certain immunities; with *of*; as a man *free of* the city of London.

17. Possessing without vassalage or slavish conditions; as *free* of his farm. *Dryden.*

18. Liberated from the government or control of parents, or of a guardian or master. A son or an apprentice, when of age, is *free.*

19. Ready; eager; not dull; acting without spurring or whipping; as a *free* horse.

20. Genteel; charming.   [*Not in use.*] *Chaucer.*

IMPRÖVEMENT, *n.* improov'ment. Advancement in moral worth, learning, wisdom, skill or other excellence; as the *improvement* of the mind or of the heart by cultivation; *improvement* in classical learning, science or mechanical skill; *improvement* in music; *improvement* in holiness.

2. Melioration; a making or growing better, or more valuable; as the *improvement* of barren or exhausted land; the *improvement* of the roads; the *improvement* of the breed of horses or cattle.

3. A valuable addition; excellence added, or a change for the better; sometimes with *on*.

> The parts of Sinon, Camilla, and some few others, are *improvements on* the
> Greek poet.   *Addison*.

4. Advance or progress from any state to a better.

> There is a design of publishing the history of architecture, with its several
> *improvements* and decays.   *Addison*.

5. Instruction; growth in knowledge or refinement; edification.

> I look upon your city as the best place of *improvement*.   *South*.

6. Use or employment to beneficial purposes; a turning to good account; as the *improvement* of natural advantages or spiritual privileges.

> A good *improvement* of his reason.   *S. Clarke*.

7. Practical application; as the *improvement* of the doctrines and principles of a sermon.

> I shall make some *improvement* of this doctrine.   *Tillotson*.

Hence,

8. The part of a discourse intended to enforce and apply the doctrines, is called the *improvement*.

9. Use; occupancy.

10. *Improvements*, plu., valuable addictions or melioration, as buildings, clearings, drains, fences, &c., on a farm.   *Kent*.

LIB'ERTY, *n.* [L. *libertas*, from *liber*, free; Fr. *liberté;* It. *libertá;* Sp. *libertad.* Class Lb. No. 24. 27. 30. 31.]

1. Freedom from restraint, in a general sense, and applicable to the body, or to the will or mind. The body is at *liberty*, when not confined; the will or mind is at *liberty*, when not checked or controlled. A man enjoys *liberty*, when no physical force operates to restrain his actions or volitions.

2. *Natural liberty*, consists in the power of acting as one thinks fit, without any restraint or control, except from the laws of nature. It is a state of exemption from the control of others, and from positive laws and the institutions of social life. This liberty is abridged by the establishment of government.

3. *Civil liberty*, is the liberty of men in a state of society, or natural liberty, so far only abridged and restrained, as is necessary and expedient for the safety and interest of the society, state or nation. A restraint of natural liberty, not necessary or expedient for the public, is tyranny or oppression. Civil liberty is an exemption from the arbitrary will of others, which exemption is secured by established laws, which restrain every man from injuring or controlling another. Hence the restraints of law are essential to *civil liberty*.

> The *liberty* of one depends not so much on the removal of all restraint from
> him, as on the due restraint upon the *liberty* of others.   *Ames*.
> In this sentence, the latter word *liberty* denotes *natural liberty*.

4. *Political liberty*, is sometimes used as synonymous with *civil liberty*. But it more properly designates the *liberty of a nation*, the freedom of a nation or state from

all unjust abridgment of its rights and independence by another nation. Hence we often speak of the *political liberties* of Europe, or the nations of Europe.

5. *Religious liberty,* is the free right of adopting and enjoying opinions on religious subjects, and of worshiping the Supreme Being according to the dictates of conscience, without external control.

6. *Liberty,* in metaphysics, as opposed to *necessity,* is the power of an agent to do or forbear any particular action, according to the determination or thought of the mind, by which either is preferred to the other.   *Locke.*

    Freedom of the will; exemption from compulsion or restraint in willing or volition.

7. Privilege; exemption; immunity enjoyed by prescription or by grant; with a plural. Thus we speak of the *liberties* of the commercial cities of Europe.

8. Leave; permission granted. The witness obtained *liberty* to leave the court.

9. A space in which one is permitted to pass without restraint, and beyond which he may not lawfully pass; with a plural; as the *liberties* of a prison.

10. Freedom of action or speech beyond the ordinary bounds of civility or decorum. Females should repel all improper *liberties.*

To take the liberty to do or say any thing, to use freedom not specially granted.

To set at liberty, to deliver from confinement; to release from restraint.

To be at liberty, to be free from restraint.

Liberty of the press, is freedom from any restriction on the power to publish books; the free power of publishing what one pleases, subject only to punishment for abusing the privilege, or publishing what is mischievous to the public or injurious to individuals.   *Blackstone. . . .*

PAT'RIOTISM, *n.* Love of one's country; the passion which aims to serve one's country, either in defending it from invasion, or protecting its rights and maintaining its laws and institutions in vigor and purity. *Patriotism* is the characteristic of a good citizen, the noblest passion that animates a man in the character of a citizen. . . .

POLITI"CIAN, *a.* Cunning; using artifice. *Obs.*

POLITI"CIAN, *n.* [Fr. *politicien.*] One versed in the science of government and the art of governing; one skilled in politics.   *Dryden. Pope.*

2. A man of artifice or deep contrivance.   *South. . . .*

SAV'AGE, *n.* A human being in his native state of rudeness; one who is untaught, uncivilized or without cultivation of mind or manners. The *savages* of America, when uncorrupted by the vices of civilized men, are remarkable for their hospitality to strangers, and for their truth, fidelity and gratitude to their friends, but implacably cruel and revengeful towards their enemies. From this last trait of the savage character, the word came to signify,

2. A man of extreme, unfeeling, brutal cruelty; a barbarian.

3. The name of a genus of fierce voracious flies.   *Dict. Nat. Hist. . . .*

Native American Literature:
"Westward the Course
of Empire"

It may be regarded as certain, that not a foot of land will ever be taken from the Indians, without their own consent. The sacredness of their rights is felt by all thinking persons in America as much as in Europe.

Thomas Jefferson (1786)

The utmost good faith shall always be observed toward the Indians; their lands and property shall never be taken from them without their consent; and in their property, rights, and liberty they never shall be invaded or disturbed unless in just and lawful wars authorized by Congress; but laws founded in justice and humanity shall, from time to time, be made for preventing wrongs being done to them and for preserving peace and friendship with them.

Northwest Ordinance (July 13, 1787)

It is necessary that we should not lose sight of an important truth which continually receives new confirmations, namely, that the provisions heretofore made with a view to the protection of the Indians from the violences of the lawless part of our frontier inhabitants are insufficient. It is demonstrated that these violences can now be perpetrated with impunity, and it can need no argument to prove that, unless the murdering of Indians can be restrained by bringing the murderers to condign punishment, all the exertions of the Government to prevent destructive retaliations by the Indians will prove fruitless and all our present agreeable prospects illusory. The frequent destruction of innocent women and children, who are chiefly the victims of retaliation, must continue to shock humanity.

President George Washington, Message to Congress (1795)

The tribes which occupied the countries now constituting the Eastern states were annihilated or have melted away to make room for the whites. The waves of population and civilization are rolling to the westward, and we now propose to acquire the countries occupied by the red men of the South and West by a fair exchange, and, at the expense of the United States, to send them to a land where their existence may be prolonged and perhaps made perpetual.

President Andrew Jackson, Message to Congress (December 6, 1830)

In the whole history of the incipient settlement of our country, not one solitary instance of an attempt to settle an unoccupied tract, claimed by the natives, is to be found, which was not succeeded by all the revolting details of Indian warfare. It is of little importance to inquire, which party was the aggressor. The natives were not sufficient civilians to distinguish between the right of empire and the right of soil. Beside a repulsion of nature, an incompatibility of character and pursuit, they constantly saw in every settler a new element to effect their expulsion from their native soul. Our industry, fixed residences, modes, laws, institutions, schools, religion, rendered an union with them as incompatible as with animals of another nature. The crime of aggression, force, and final extinction, charged upon the whites, in relation to the natives, and discussed on the narrow principles of crimination and recrimination, has only been discussed hitherto in a manner worthy of congress wranglers, and in a style of narrow puerility. In the unchangeable order of things, two such races can not exist together, each preserving its co-ordinate identity. Either this great continent, in the order of Providence, should have remained in the occupancy of half a million of savages, engaged in everlasting conflicts of their peculiar warfare with each other, or it must have become, as it has, the domain of civilized millions. It is in vain to charge upon the latter race results, which grew out of the laws of nature, and the universal march of human events. Let the same occupancy of the American wilderness by the municipal European be repeated, if it could be, under the control of the most philanthropic eulogists of the savages, and every reasoning mind will discover, that in the gradual ascendency of the one race, the decline of the other must have been a consequence, and that substantially the same annals would be repeated, as the dark and revolting incidents which we have to record.

Timothy Flint, Indian Wars of the West (1833)

A crime is projected that confounds our understandings by its magnitude—a crime that really deprives us as well as the Cherokees of a country, for how could we call the conspiracy that should crush these poor Indians our government, or the land that was cursed by their parting and dying imprecations our country, any more? You, sir, will bring down that renowned chair in which you sit into infamy if your seal is set to this instrument of perfidy; and the name of this nation, hitherto the sweet omen of religion and liberty, will stink to the world.

Ralph Waldo Emerson, letter to President Martin Van Buren
on the removal of the Cherokee Indians (April 23, 1838)

It is too often the case, that civilized beings sojourning among savages soon come to regard them with disdain and contempt. But though in many cases this feeling is almost natural, it is not defensible; and it is wholly wrong. Why should we contemn them? Because we are better than they? Assuredly not; for herein we are rebuked by the story of the Publican and the Pharisee. Because, then, that in many things we are happier? But this should be ground for commiseration, not disdain. Xavier and Elliot despised not the savages; and had Newton or Milton dwelt among them they would not have done so. When we affect to contemn savages, we should remember that by so doing we asperse our own progenitors; for they were savages also. Who can swear, that among the naked British barbarians sent to Rome to be stared at more than 1500 years ago, the ancestor of Bacon might not have been found? Why, among the very Thugs of India, or the bloody Dyaks of Borneo, exists the germ of all that is intellectually elevated and grand. We are all of us—Anglo-Saxons, Dyaks, and Indians—sprung from one head, and made in one image. And if we regret this brotherhood now, we shall be forced to join hands hereafter. A misfortune is not a fault; and good luck is not meritorious. The savage is born a savage; and the civilized being but inherits his civilization, nothing more.

Let us not disdain, then, but pity. And wherever we recognize the image of God, let us reverence it, though it hung from the gallows.

> Herman Melville, review of Francis Parkman's *The California and Oregon Trail* (1849)

Tecumseh
1768–1813

From the earliest contacts between Native Americans and white settlers, the principal source of tension and conflict remained the colonists' encroachment on Native American lands. With the founding of the new republic, that expansion became government policy, expressed most frequently either in drafting extremely advantageous treaties with the Native Americans or driving them farther into the frontier. One of the most bitterly contested agreements was the Treaty of Fort Wayne (1809), in which a group of Shawnee ceded sizable tracts of land to the American government, represented by, among others, General William Harrison.

Tecumseh (or Tecumtha), the legendary Shawnee orator and warrior, led the opposition to this treaty. From his village on the Wabash River, near the mouth of the Tippecanoe (in what is now Indiana), Tecumseh made several long trips on horseback through the Midwest and South in the years prior to the War of 1812 seeking the support of other tribes in his cause. He argued that the white settlers and the U.S. government were "never contented, but always encroaching. The way, and the only way to check and stop this evil, is, for all the red men to unite in claiming a common and equal right in land, as it was at first, and should be yet; for it was never divided, but belongs to all, for the use of each." In the speech printed here, Tecumseh tries to enlist the support of the Osage, who had originally settled in the Ohio Valley but had been forced to move to what is now Missouri.

Although Tecumseh ventured beyond the Mississippi and into Canada to urge other Native Americans to regain the lands they had lost in a series of ill-advised treaties, he never succeeded in establishing that coalition of tribes. At the outbreak of the War of 1812 he left for Canada, where the British made him a brigadier general. He died in battle on Ontario's Thames River on October 5, 1813.

Tecumseh's speech underscores that many of the outstanding extant examples of Native American oratory focus on relations with whites—even, as is the case here, in addresses to other Native Americans.

Further Reading:
J. M. Oskison, *Tecumseh and His Times: The Story of a Great Indian*, 1938.
G. Tucker, *Tecumseh: Vision of Glory*, 1956.
Tecumseh, Fact and Fiction in Early Records: A Book of Primary Source Materials, ed. C. F. Klinch, 1961.
B. Drake, *Life of Tecumseh*, 1969.
W. C. Vanderwerth, *Indian Oratory*, 1971.
R. D. Edmunds, *The Shawnee Prophet*, 1983.

Text:
J. D. Hunter, "Memoirs of a Captivity Among the Indians of North America," 1924, in *Native American Testimony*, ed. P. Nabokov, 1978.

"We All Belong to One Family"*

Brothers—We all belong to one family; we are all children of the Great Spirit; we walk in the same path; slake our thirst at the same spring; and now affairs of the greatest concern lead us to smoke the pipe around the same council fire!

Brothers—We are friends; we must assist each other to bear our burdens. The blood of many of our fathers and brothers has run like water on the ground, to satisfy the avarice of the white men. We, ourselves, are threatened with a great evil; nothing will pacify them but the destruction of all the red men.

Brothers—When the white men first set foot on our grounds, they were hungry; they had no place on which to spread their blankets, or to kindle their fires. They were feeble; they could do nothing for themselves. Our fathers commiserated their distress, and shared freely with them whatever the Great Spirit had given his red children. They gave them food when hungry, medicine when sick, spread skins for them to sleep on, and gave them grounds, that they might hunt and raise corn.

Brothers—The white people are like poisonous serpents: when chilled, they are feeble, and harmless, but invigorate them with warmth, and they sting their benefactors to death.

The white people came among us feeble; and now we have made them strong, they wish to kill us, or drive us back, as they would wolves and panthers.

Brothers—The white men are not friends to the Indians: at first, they only asked for land sufficient for a wigwam; now, nothing will satisfy them but the whole of our hunting grounds, from the rising to the setting sun.

---

* Tecumseh hoped to establish a coalition of tribes who would fight to regain the land they had lost in the Ohio Valley through a series of ill-advised treaties with William H. Harrison, the American governor of the Indiana Territory. Tecumseh here tries to enlist the support of the Osage Indians.

Brothers—The white men want more than our hunting grounds; they wish to kill our warriors; they would even kill our old men, women, and little ones.

Brothers—Many winters ago, there was no land; the sun did not rise and set: all was darkness. The Great Spirit made all things. He gave the white people a home beyond the great waters. He supplied these grounds with game, and gave them to his red children; and he gave them strength and courage to defend them.

Brothers—My people wish for peace; the red men all wish for peace; but where the white people are, there is no peace for them, except it be on the bosom of our mother.

Brothers—The white men despise and cheat the Indians; they abuse and insult them; they do not think the red men sufficiently good to live.

The red men have borne many and great injuries; they ought to suffer them no longer. My people will not; they are determined on vengeance; they have taken up the tomahawk; they will make it fat with blood; they will drink the blood of the white people.

Brothers—My people are brave and numerous; but the white people are too strong for them alone. I wish you to take up the tomahawk with them. If we all unite, we will cause the rivers to stain the great waters with their blood.

Brothers—If you do not unite with us, they will first destroy us, and then you will fall an easy prey to them. They have destroyed many nations of red men because they were not united, because they were not friends to each other.

Brothers—The white people send runners amongst us; they wish to make us enemies, that they may sweep over and desolate our hunting grounds, like devastating winds, or rushing waters.

Brothers—Our Great Father[1] over the great waters is angry with the white people, our enemies. He will send his brave warriors against them; he will send us rifles, and whatever else we want—he is our friend, and we are his children.

Brothers—Who are the white people that we should fear them? They cannot run fast, and are good marks to shoot at: they are only men; our fathers have killed many of them; we are not squaws, and we will stain the earth red with their blood.

Brothers—The Great Spirit is angry with our enemies; he speaks in thunder, and the earth swallows up villages, and drinks up the Mississippi. The great waters will cover their lowlands; their corn cannot grow; and the Great Spirit will sweep those who escape to the hills from the earth with his terrible breath.

Brothers—We must be united; we must smoke the same pipe; we must fight each other's battles; and more than all, we must love the Great Spirit; he is for us; he will destroy our enemies, and make his red children happy.

1810/1924

---

[1] I.e., King George III of England (1760–1820).

William Apes
b. 1798

In May 1833 the Mashpee tribal council presented a series of unequivocal resolutions to the Massachusetts state government declaring their right both to rule themselves and to drive out any white trespassers from their land. The driving force behind those resolutions was William Apes, preacher, social reformer, and defender of Native American rights. Several generations were to find inspiration in the story of Apes's life. In his struggles they recognized the possibility of Native American dignity and accomplishment in a period when all signs pointed to the removal of their peoples from the new nation's culture, its conscience, and its future.

William Apes was abandoned by his Native American mother and half-white father soon after the family moved from his birthplace near Colrain, Massachusetts, to the two small Pequot reservations near Colchester, Connecticut. By the age of five, William had been beaten so often and so severely by his alcoholic grandfather that his recovery depended on the town's charity for a year. From the age of six he was "bound out" to successive sets of foster parents, the first Baptists, the second Presbyterians. They provided him with six years of formal schooling but left him no freer from verbal and physical abuse than before.

At the age of fifteen Apes fled from his latest guardians and wandered between New York and New England before joining the U.S. Army, on a drunken whim, as a drummer boy. Reclassified as an infantry soldier during the War of 1812, Apes deserted. Quickly recaptured, he served for more than two years along the Canadian border under the threat of "Indian torture."

At the end of the War of 1812 Apes began several years' work at odd jobs in northern New York State and Canada before returning to the Pequot reservation near Groton, Connecticut, where he spent the next few years hiring himself out to local farmers. Apes had discovered Methodist revival meetings at age fifteen. He now grew ever more confident about his religious calling. By the early 1820s Apes was regularly preaching the Gospel to Native American and white audiences. His success apparently angered the local preachers, and he soon found himself what he called an "outcast from society." He married an older mulatto woman, and over the next few years supported his wife and several children by farming and working as a tavern keeper. Gradually he returned to preaching and between 1826 and 1829 traveled throughout New England ministering to Native American, black, and white church groups.

Apes published a brief autobiography, *A Son of the Forest*, in 1829. A second, enlarged edition, in 1831, gave increasing room to Apes's belief that Christ had died for *all* people. "If black or red skins, or any other skin of color is disgraceful to God, it appears that [God] has disgraced himself a great deal—for he has made fifteen colored people to one white, and placed them upon the earth." His autobiography also includes an impassioned brief for the use of the term *Native Americans.* According to Kim McQuaid, the author of the fullest biographical account of Apes, *A Son of the Forest* is "the first such narrative published in book form by an American Indian." It set the standard for many Native American autobiographies later in the nineteenth century.

Apes also published several sermons and human rights tracts, including *The Increase in the Kingdom of Christ: A Sermon* (1831) and *The Experiences of Five Christian Indians: Or, The Indians' Looking Glass for the White Man* (1833). These argued on behalf of equality among Native Americans, blacks, and whites at a time when Indian removal had hardened into national policy. By the mid-1830s, Apes had become a celebrated preacher, an advocate of Indian rights, and a social reformer, especially among the Mashpee tribe of southeastern Massachusetts, among whom he and his family had settled. In 1836 he published a comprehensive study of the rights of Native Americans and their relations with white Americans, titled *Eulogy on King Philip* in honor of the legendary seventeenth-century Native American hero who had driven white settlers from tribal lands in New England. Within a few years of the book's controversial publication, Apes had withdrawn from public view, ironically an example himself of the "vanishing race" that he so vigorously defended and that he helped to remain a vibrant part of American culture.

Further Reading:
E. S. Bates, "William Apes," *Dictionary of American Biography,* vol. 1, 1928.
F. P. Prucha, *American Indian Policy in the Formative Years, 1790–1834,* 1962.
K. McQuaid, "William Apes, Pequot: An Indian Reformer in the Jackson Era," *New England Quarterly,* 1977.

Text:
A Son of the Forest, 1829.

---

from A Son of the Forest

from Chapter 1

William Apes, the author of the following narrative, was born in the town of Colereign, Massachusetts, on the thirty-first of January, in the year of our Lord seventeen hundred and ninety-eight. My grandfather was a white man, and married a female attached to the royal family of Philip,[1] king of the Pequod tribe of Indians, so well known in that part of American history, which relates to the wars between the whites and the natives. My grandmother was, if I am not misinformed, the king's granddaughter, and a fair and beautiful woman. This statement is given not with a view of appearing great, in the estimation of others—what I would ask, is *royal* blood —the blood of a king is no better than that of the subject—we are in fact but one family; we are all the descendants of one great progenitor—Adam. I would not boast of my extraction, as I consider myself nothing more than a worm of the earth.

I have given the above account of my origin, with the simple view of narrating

[1] King Philip, the son of Massasoit and chief of the Wampanoag Indians. The reference here is to King Philip's War (1675–1676), the most deadly of Indian conflicts in New England. The Pequot Indians are an Algonquin tribe of southeastern Connecticut.

the truth as I have received it; and under the settled conviction that I must render an account at the last day, to the sovereign Judge of all men, for every word contained in this little book. . . .

from **Chapter 2**

. . . I thought it disgraceful to be called an Indian;[2] it was considered as a slur upon an oppressed and scattered nation, and I have often been led to inquire where the whites received this word, which they so often threw as an opprobrious epithet at the sons of the forest. I could not find it in the bible, and therefore concluded, that it was a word imported for the special purpose of degrading us. At other times I thought it was derived from the term in-gen-uity. But the proper term which ought to be applied to our nation, to distinguish it from the rest of the human family, is that of *"Natives"*—and I humbly conceive that the natives of this country are the only people under heaven who have a just title to the name, inasmuch as we are the only people who retain the original complexion of our father Adam. Notwithstanding my thoughts on this matter, so completely was I weaned from the interests and affections of my brethren, that a mere threat of being sent away among the Indians into the dreary woods, had a much better effect in making me obedient to the commands of my superiors, than any corporeal punishment that they ever inflicted. I had received a lesson in the unnatural treatment of my own relations, which could not be effaced; and I thought that if those who should have loved and protected me, treated me with such unkindness, surely I had no reason to expect mercy or favour at the hands of those who knew me in no other relation than that of a cast-off member of the tribe. A threat, of the kind alluded to, invariably produced obedience on my part, so far as I understood the nature of the command.

I cannot perhaps give a better idea of the dread which prevaded my mind on seeing any of my brethren of the forest, than by relating the following occurrence. One day several of the family went into the woods to gather berries, taking me with them. We had not been out long before we fell in with a company of white females, on the same errand—their complexion was, to say, the least, as *dark* as that of the natives. This circumstance filled my mind with terror, and I broke from the party with my utmost speed, and I could not muster courage enough to look behind until I had reached home. By this time my imagination had pictured out a tale of blood, and as soon as I regained breath sufficient to answer the questions which my master asked, I informed him that we had met a body of the natives in the woods, but what had become of the party I could not tell. Notwithstanding the manifest incredibility of my tale of terror, Mr. Furman was agitated; my very appearance was sufficient to convince him that I had been terrified by something, and summoning the remainder of the family, he sallied out in quest of the absent party, whom he found searching for me among the bushes. The whole mystery was soon unravelled. It may be proper for me here to remark, that the great fear I entertained of my brethren, was occasioned by the many stories I had heard of their cruelty towards the whites—how they were in the habit of killing and scalping men, women and children. But the whites did not

---

[2] Apes, whose father was of mixed blood, was brought up among Europeans—first by his white grandfather, a drinker who physically abused his grandchildren, then by the Furmans, a poor laboring couple.

tell me that they were in a great majority of instances the aggressors—that they had imbrued their hands in the life blood of my brethren, driven them from their once peaceful and happy homes—that they introduced among them the fatal and exterminating diseases of civilized life. If the whites had told me how cruel they had been to the "poor Indian," I should have apprehended as much harm from them.

Shortly after this occurrence I relapsed into my former bad habits—was fond of the company of the boys, and in a short time lost in a great measure that spirit of obedience which had made me the favourite of my mistress. I was easily led astray, and, once in particular, I was induced by a boy, (my senior by five or six years) to assist him in his depredations on a water melon patch belonging to one of the neighbours. But we were found out, and my companion in wickedness led me deeper in sin, by persuading me to deny the crime laid to our charge. I obeyed him to the very letter, and when accused, flatly denied knowing any thing of the matter. The boasted courage of the boy, however, began to fail as soon as he saw danger thicken, and he confessed it as strongly as he had denied it. The man from whom we had pillaged the melons threatened to send us to Newgate, but he relented. The story shortly afterward reached the ears of the good Mrs. Furman, who talked seriously to me about it. She told me that I could be sent to prison for it—that I had done wrong, and gave me a great deal of wholesome advice. This had a much better effect than forty floggings—it sunk so deep into my mind that the impression can never be effaced.

I now went on without difficulty for a few months, when I was assailed by fresh and unexpected troubles. One of the girls belonging to the house had taken some offence at me, and declared she would be revenged. The better to effect this end, she told Mr. Furman that I had not only threatened to kill her, but had actually pursued her with a knife, whereupon he came to the place where I was working and began to whip me severely. I could not tell for what. I told him I had done no harm, to which he replied, "I will learn you, you Indian dog, how to chase people with a knife." I told him I had not, but he would not believe me, and continued to whip me for a long while. But the poor man soon found out his error, as *after* he had flogged me, he undertook to investigate the matter, when to his amazement he discovered it was nothing but fiction, as all the children assured him that I did no such thing. He regretted being so hasty—but I saw wherein the great difficulty consisted, if I had not denied the melon affair, he would have believed me, but as I had uttered an untruth about that, it was natural for him to think that the person who will tell one lie, will not scruple at two. For a long while after this circumstance transpired, I did not associate with my companions.

1829

John Ridge
1803–1839

By the European standards adopted by late-eighteenth-century Americans, the Cherokee Nation was the most "civilized" of the Native American tribes. After nearly two centuries of contact with missionaries and white traders and several

generations of intermarriage with whites, the Cherokee had assimilated many of
the values and beliefs of the new republic. They developed, for example, large,
profitable plantations and accumulated scores of slaves. From all accounts, they
cultivated highly refined lives in much of the area that is now Georgia,
Tennessee, and western North Carolina. Yet their prosperity proved to be
short-lived.

In 1802 Georgia agreed to cede to the United States its western lands, which
are now Alabama and Mississippi, in exchange for the federal government's
pledge to remove all Native Americans from Georgia "as soon as it could be
done peacefully and upon favorable terms." In 1817 approximately one-third of
the Cherokee nation agreed to relinquish their lands in Georgia in exchange for
territory in what is now Arkansas. But the overwhelming majority of the
Cherokee refused to move. Georgia's political leaders responded by enacting a
series of stringent laws designed to force their removal. Gradually, an increasingly
influential, although small, group of Cherokee became convinced that their
nation's own hope for survival lay in yielding to the pressures to move west and
reunite with those who had resettled earlier. Along with his father, Major Ridge,
and his cousins Elias Boudinot and Stand Watie, John Ridge led the effort to
reunite the Cherokee Nation.

John Ridge and Elias Boudinot (the founding editor of the *Cherokee Phoenix*)
attended school in Cornwall, Connecticut, where both eventually married into
prominent white families. After brief service in Washington in the mid-1820s as a
liaison between tribal delegations and government officials, Ridge returned with
his wife to Cherokee country and quickly settled into a prosperous life
combining law practice, plantation ownership, political controversy, and tribal
leadership. Against the wishes of the majority of the so-called East Cherokee,
Ridge, along with his father and his cousins Boudinot and Watie, signed the
Treaty of New Echoton with the U.S. government. The terms of the agreement
included exchanging Cherokee land east of the Mississippi for $4.5 million and
800,000 acres in what is now Kansas and Oklahoma. The U.S. Senate quickly
ratified the treaty, and by 1838 the Cherokee removal had begun on what
quickly became known as the "Trail of Tears." Ridge is reported to have said, "I
know that in signing this treaty I have signed my own death warrant."

Four years later Ridge, his father, and Boudinot were murdered, thereby
dividing the Cherokee Nation into two hostile camps and bringing it close to the
brink of civil war. In 1846 the feuding factions agreed to a treaty settling their
differences. Following a few years of relative tranquillity, the Cherokee Nation
was once again divided, this time into proslavery and antislavery factions that
would fight with great distinction on opposing sides of the Civil War. By then,
many of the Cherokee had abandoned their Oklahoma reservation and headed
west, seeking prosperity in the California gold rush. One of these fortune seekers
was Ridge's son, John Rollin Ridge, later a celebrated newspaper editor and the
author of *The Life and Adventures of Joaquín Murieta* (1854).

During John Ridge's relatively brief stay in Washington in the mid-1820s, he
met Albert Gallatin, who was then living in Baltimore and collecting
vocabularies of various Indian languages. (In 1842 Gallatin founded the Bureau of
American Ethnology.) Dubbed the "Linnaeus . . . of systematic philogy relating
to the North American Indians," Gallatin enlisted John Ridge's help in collecting

data and later urged Ridge, through an intermediary, to write "a sketch of the progress made in the civilization of the Cherokees." Such an essay, Gallatin argued, would generate a "favourable effect . . . on public opinion both here and abroad" and would also provide "an opportunity to Mr. Ridge to obtain a general reputation which he may not again meet with." The following essay complies with Gallatin's request that Ridge write "a short account of the Cherokee nation particularly as relates to their civilisation and how it was introduced."

Further Reading:
E. E. Dale and G. Litton, *Cherokee Cavaliers: Forty Years of Cherokee History as Told in the Correspondence of the Ridge-Watie-Boudinot Family*, 1939.
T. Wilkins, *Cherokee Tragedy: The Story of the Ridge Family and the Decimation of a People*, 1970.

Text:
William C. Sturtevant, "John Ridge on Cherokee Civilization in 1826," *Journal of Cherokee Studies*, 1982.

Essay on Cherokee Civilization

Washington City March 10th 1826

Hon. Albert Gallatin[1]
Sir

In attempting to comply with your request—that of giving you a short account of the Cherokee Nation, its present state of Civilization, and the manner of its introduction, I take the liberty to observe, that in the absence of Chronology and official papers of my Nation, and at a distance from it, where I least expected to undertake an object of this kind, my observations will be confined to facts that have transpired within my own knowledge except so far as relates to the first period when our civilization as a people began to shew it has been effected.

The Cherokee nation is bounded on the North by East Tennessee & North Carolina, east by Georgia, south by the Creek Nation and State of Alabama—and west by West Tennessee. Its extreme length may be upwards of two hundred miles, & extreme breadth about one hundred and thirty—rough conjecture suppose it to contain about ten million Acres of Land. This territory is divided by Law into eight Districts or Counties, the boundaries of which are regularly designated and defined. A correct Census of the Nation was taken last year (1825) by order of the National Council to ascertain the amount of property & taxable individuals within the Nation. The result proved to be 13.583 native Citizens—147 white men married with Indians & 73 white women d[itt]o & African Slaves 1.277 to which if we add 400 Cherokees who took Reservations in North Carolina & not included in the Census, and who

---

[1] American financier and statesman (1761–1849).

have since merged again among us—the Cherokee Nation will contain 15.280 inhabitants. There are a few instances of African Mixture with Cherokee blood & wherever it is seen is considered in the light of misfortune & disgrace but that of the white may be as 1 to 4—occasioned by intermarriage which has been increasing in proportion to the march of civilization. This population is dispersed over the face of the Country on separate farms; & villages or a community possessing one fence, and local laws to govern the labour of the Citizens who acted in concert in cultivating their patches have disappeared long since and to my knowledge there is but one of this Character at Coosawattie the inhabitants of which are gradually diminishing by migration to the woods where they prefer to clear the forests and govern their own plantations. In this view of their location it readily appears that they are farmers and herdsmen, which is their real character. Personal distinctions and gradation in property has been and will be a primary feature in the character of Nations, from the rudest tribes that roam the forest, to those who have ascended to the pinnacle of highest grandeur and intellect. So it is with us, but it happily operates as a stimulous for emulation which gives force and accelerates the wheels of our improvements.

Our Country is well adapted for the growth of Indian Corn, wheat, Rye, Oats, Irish and Sweet Potatoes, which are cultivated by our people. Cotton is universally raised for domestic consumption, & a few have grown it for Market, and have realized very good profits. I take pleasure to state that there is not to my knowledge a solitary Cherokee to be found who depends upon the Chase for subsistence. Every head of a family has his own farm and House. The hardest portion of manual labor is performed by the men & women occasionally lend a hand in the field more by choice & necessity than anything else. Justice is due to the females of the poorer class of whom I now speak. Duties assigned them by nature as Mothers or Wives are well attended to and cheerfully do they prepare our meals, & for the family they sew, they spin and weave and are in fact a valuable portion of our Citizens. The African Slaves are mostly held by half breeds & full blooded Indians of talents. The valuable portion of property is retained in this Class. They have a few framed and brick Houses, but their Houses are usually constructed of hewed logs with brick chimnies & shingled Roofs. Their furniture is better than the exterior of their buildings would induce a stranger to believe. Servants attend at their meals, & the same rules and etiquette is observed at table as in the first families of the whites. Every family in the Nation possesses Hogs, Cattle & Horses, and a respectable number have begun to pay attention to the introduction of Sheep, which are increasing very fast. The Horse is in general use for purposes of riding, drawing the plough or waggon. I am sorry that I have not with me the estimate of the respective number of live property & their value, as well as the number of ploughs, looms, waggons, Saw and grist mills &tc. in the Nation.

The females were the first who were induced to undertake domestic manufactures, and they are still confined to them. These consist of white and striped homespun, coarse woollen Blankets, and in many instances of very valuable and comfortable twilled and figured coverlets. Woollen and Cotton Stockings are manufactured in every family for domestic use. A great portion of Cherokee clothing is furnished from our own people; and fancy goods such as silks, calicoes, cambrics handkerchiefs & Shawls etc.—are introduced by native Merchants from the adjoining States. The principal portion of our trade consists in Hogs and horned Cattle. Skins formerly were sold in respectable quantities, but that kind of trade is fast declining and becomes less reputable. Cherokees on the Tennessee River have already commenced to trade in Cotton and grow it on large plantations for which they have experienced flattering profit. Preparation is making by all those in good circumstances, to cultivate the Cotton for market which will soon be a Staple commodity of traffic for the Nation.

In giving you a view of the nature of our Government you will be better able to ascertain the State of our improvement. Having been honored with a seat in its National Councils I have better acquaintance with this branch of your inquiry than any other. All Indian Nations are divided into tribes, distinguished by different names. These are again subdivided into Towns. In each of these Tribes and Towns are some men prominent for humanity, wisdom, and valor. The Assembly of such men forms their "Council fire." They are a standing body of Chieftans, who are first in the social Circle, and foremost in the deadly fight. They possess within themselves Legislative judicial and executive powers. The first law of Nature and of Indians is against murder. Retaliation and revenge is the prerogative of the tribe to whom the victim belongs and the friends and relatives of the aggressor are compelled by law to remain neuter. This was a principle of Government in the worst of Shapes of our people. Our Chiefs were numerous and their accountability was small. Lands could then be obtained at a price most convenient to the United States as their Commissioners with the assistance of the Agent could always procure a majority for a Cession, and when this was done the patriotic Chiefs yielded to secure their shares for the trifling equivalent. Savage ignorance saw its own folly by the effect which presented itself in a shape not to be misunderstood. The tide of white population was advancing on all sides & the Indians poor in goods, but well supplied with the vices of their neighbors were retreating to a given point where they would eventually be crushed in the folds of the encroaching Serpent! The Remedy was within themselves and this could only be supplied successfully in the amendment of their Government. Useless members were stricken off. A National seat of their Government was selected, and a State House was built and the Chiefs organized themselves into a standing body of legislators who annually meet in October. They are composed of two departments, the National Committee and the Representative Council. The former consist of 13 Members, including their President, and have a Clerk to record their proceedings—they control and regulate their funds —they have power to inspect the books of their Treasurer, & acknowledge claims and Legislature & negative or concur with the proceedings in the other branch of the Legislature. The Representatives have legislative powers to fill vacancies in the National Committee, concur with or reject their acts, and in conjunction with the Committee elect their Head Chiefs or executive, or expel them for misconduct. Laws of course are passed in the usual way of the adjoining States, which are at present written in the English Language, and commerce in the style to wit—"Be it resolved by the National Committee and Council of the Cherokee Nation"—The members of our Legislative Council are chosen to represent the eight Districts satisfactorily as possible as circumstances will allow. Our Judiciary having less obstacles to encounter in rendering it so is more perfect than our Legislature. It is independent. Possesses power to bring any Chief of any grade before its tribunal, by all causes, pass sentence, and enforce it. Every District has a Court of Justice, over which the district Judge and circuit Judge presides the latter having Jurisdiction over two districts. A Jury is attached to each Court, but are liable to substitution, in case a reasonable objection is made either by the plaintiff or defendant. The Officers of the District, such as Sherifs, Marshalls, and Constables are compelled to attend these Courts. All appeals are finally decided by the Supreme Court of the Nation, which meets at every Session of the National Council at the same place, and has power to exact costs—which is not allowed to the District Courts.

As we are yet destitute of Prisons, justice is quickly inflicted. A thief as soon as convicted and sentence passed, is tied to the next tree, and on the naked skin is impressed his receipt for release. We have not as yet many written laws, it being the policy of our Government to regulate itself to the capacity and state of improvement of our Citizens. Most of the adjudications are founded in the Spirit of Natural Law or Common Sense. A sketch of a few of the Laws are as follow.

1st. Law to regulate our Citizens agreeable to the intercourse laws of the United States for the purpose of securing peace on on the Frontier.

2d. Prohibiting the introduction of ardent Spirits by the whites. Penalty—confiscation.

3d. Regulating intermarriages with the whites, which makes it necessary for a white man to obtain a license and be married by a Gospel minister, or some authorised person.

4th. Against Murder.—5th. Against stealing.

6th. Against renting land and introducing white people without a special written permission of the Legislative Council—Penalty expulsion of the whites so introduced as intruders, and a fine of $500 on the aggressor and one hundred stripes on the naked back.

7th. Giving indefensible title to Lands improved, the houses etc. to the Citizens with power to sell or transfer them among each other, but not to Citizens of the adjoining States.

8th. Regulating taxes & defining the duties of Collectors.

9th. Prohibiting the sale of any more Lands to the United States except it be done by and with the concurrence of the National Committee & Council, or a Delegation authorised by them—Penalty—disgrace & death.

10th. A law to protect the Orphan and Widow to the father's or husband's property after death.

11th. Regulating the Salary of the two head Chiefs, Treasurer, Judges, and pay of the members of the National Council, & their Clerks during actual Service, and officers of the Nation generally.

12th. Regulating the Judicial Courts of the Nation, & defining their powers.

13th. Defining the powers of the Chiefs, and that only to be exercised in a body in their legislative capacity at the times appointed by law—and in the recess to be on a level with private Citizens.

The above laws are written and are well understood, respected and enforced. It is needless to say that all the people are well satisfied with their Government & Laws —and it is a universal care with us, to secure these blessings as an inheritance to Posterity. The laws of our Nation from time immemorial recognizes a separate property in the wife and husband, and this principle is universally cherished among the less informed Class and in fact in every grade of intelligence—If they are so disposed, the law secures to the Ladies, the control of their own property. Rules and regulations in the transfer of property, in the absence of written laws on this subject, are adopted from the adjoining States, and are respected in our Courts. Property descends from Parents equally to the children—if none, to the next blood relatives, on either side, but if a Will is made, it is respected to the fullest extent, and every person possessed of property is entitled to dispose of it in this way.

Superstition is the portion of all uncivilized Nations and Idolatry is only engendered in the brain of rudeness. The Cherokees in their most savage state never worshipped the work of their own hands, neither the elements of water or fire, nor any one a portion of the splendid lights that adorn Heaven's canopy above. They had a rational belief of a great first Cause or Spirit—as the author of all good—and in a bad Spirit as the Author of all evil. These they conceived were at variance and waged perpetual war—and supposed the good Spirit as superior to the bad one. These immortal Beings had on both sides numerous intelligent beings of analogous dispositions to their Chieftans. They had a Heaven which consisted of a visible World to those only who had passed from death to immortality. It was adorned with all the beauties which a savage imagination could conceive. An open Forest, yet various, giving light and shade, & fruit of every kind. Sweet smelling flowers, of various hues, exquisite to the eye. Game of all kinds in great abundance, enough of feasts and plenty of dances; to crown the whole the most cheerful enchanting beautiful women, prepared and adorned by the great Spirit for every individual Indian—who by wisdom, hospitality and bravery, was introduced to this happy and immortal region. The bad place or Hell was the reverse of this, & was situated in the vicinity of the good place, where the wretched, compelled to live in hunger, hostility and darkness, could hear the rejoicings of those in the blissful state, without the possibility of reaching its shores. Witches and Wizards were in existence and pretended to possess supernatural powers and to have intercourse with the infernal Spirits, and were supposed capable of transforming themselves into the shape of beasts of the forest and fowls of the air, and take their nocturnal excursions in pursuit of human victims, particularly those suffering from disease, which compelled the unfortunate friends of the invalids to employ witch shooters to protect them. They were the dread of the Land, and many a time have I trembled at the croaking of a Frog, the hooting of an Owl, or guttural hoarseness of the Raven in the night, in my younger days. After the people became more courageous the poor witches experienced a sad reverse of fortune—they were often butchered or tomahawked on suspicion by the enraged friends of the deceased, particularly in unexpected cases of death, occasioned by indisposition of short duration. The severity of Revenge fell most principally on the grey hairs of aged persons of both sexes, and on children who were supposed to inherit such powers of noted parents who had retired from the Stage of life long ago. To stop this evil it was necessary to pass a law considering all slaughters of this kind in the light of Murder, which has effected the desired remedy. There are yet among us who pretend to possess powers of milder character, such as making rain, allaying storms or whirlwinds, playing with thunder, and foretelling future events, with many other insignificant pretences not worth mentioning. They are monuments of folly and ridicule in the eye of intelligent Indians, and are only listened to in few dark spots of gross ignorance in the Nation.

The Standard of Religion is advancing with a steady march in different parts of the Nation—and the Gospel is preached in eight organised churches at the Missionary Stations, by Presbyterians, Baptists, Moravians, & Methodists, each of whom have a respectable number of Indian Christians of exemplary characters attached to them. The Sabbath is known by all the Cherokees, and many observe it with respect and attend meetings of religious worship. Religion has a powerful effect on the Indians whenever it is professed by them. There is no vice of any kind which it does not expel. Drunkenness and habits of Idleness fall before it, & I know of individuals who were a public nuisance who have become useful and good Citizens. We have no law regulating Marriage—and Polygamy is still allowed to native Cherokees. This last vestige of our ignorance is not respected by our people, & increase of intelligence and morality is fast consuming it. An attempt was made to discountenance Polygamy by law, but failed not from its popularity, but by a feeling of delicacy to a number of our old Chiefs who had married under older customs. Time will effect the desired change, and it is worthy of mention, even now in the advance of law, & unrequired, the better class of our females, prefer to be united in Marriage attended by the solemnities of the Christian mode.

In regard to the love of revenge the Indians have been represented in the grossest colours. I never could have the audacity to ascribe inconsistancy to any portion of God's creation. The various Nations of the Earth were created for noble purposes, endowed with sensibility to feel their own wrongs and sympathize for another's woe. Education alone makes distinction in the refinement of the heart. Savages of the human race are not like the beasts of the Forests, which even trained to live contented in the yard, retain in full vigor an Instinct of indiscriminate cruelty.

Intemperance like Love, is found in the Halls of the great and in the wig wam of the Indian—with this difference—"Indians consider it no harm to drink, but the whites do, and drink notwithstanding"—Nations cannot be civilized unless they renounce every inducement that tends to their deterioration. As a whole, I cannot call the Cherokees a civilized people and perhaps in this respect it would baffle our expectations if we were to look for it, in any Nation on the face of the Earth.

But then I am far from acknowledging that we are a Nation of Drunkards. Our young men are too fond of their popularity among the other sex to yield to it. Among our old Chiefs are many that dance in frolic and sing over the Whiskey bottle—But these are on the decline in number and in fame. Confidence will always be placed in Chiefs whose faculties are under no such control—four years ago our highest Chiefs were seen drunk near the Council fire—but now not one would be so lost to shame as thus to appear & be expelled from his seat. In our Country, females aspire to gain sober men for husbands and mankind must yield to the tender sex. Woman civilized man or makes him barbarous at her pleasure. If Ladies gave us universally the smiles of approbation in our extravagancies we would be extravagant—if in murder, we would delight to kill—if in cruelty we would be cruel—

There are about thirteen Schools in the Nation—and may contain about two hundred and fifty Students—and are entirely supported by humane Societies in different part of the United States.

The Nation itself has not yet actively engaged in aiding education, but have & is making preparation to lend a hand in this laudable work. Twelve miles square of Land is reserved in a treaty with J.C. Calhoun in 1819, who was then Secretary of War, in which the President is authorized to sell the land & invest the proceeds, to draw Interest and apply it for the education of Cherokee youth as he shall think best. This tract has not been sold owing as I have understood to the unfavorable condition of the market at this time. A Law has been passed for establishing a National Academy of a high order at our Seat of Government, where it is intended the youth who have deservedly gone through their Studies in the common Schools, to finish their educations.

It is in contemplation to obtain an able gentleman from the North to preside over it as President, but the Assistants & Trustees of the School will be native Cherokees. The edifice will be of brick, forty feet square, well furnished with Seats and Desks for the Students. Besides this many of our youth are educated in the adjoining States at the expense of their friends. Two young Ladies have recently finished their Studies in the Salem Academy in North Carolina. Their cultivation and appearance is such, that they will bear the test of comparison with those of any Class in the United States. Their Father has purchased a costly Piano for their use. I am acquainted with others who are preparing for an admission into that excellent Institution. I suppose that there are one third of our people who are able to read & write in the English Language. In the Cherokee Language, there is a large majority who read and write in George Guess' syllabic character. Mr. Guess is an Indian unacquainted with the English Language—but an untutored Philosopher, who has succeeded in a few months as it were to educate a Nation. In making his System he was ridiculed and discountenanced by his friends who were considered competent to judge. He persevered however, and gained the attention of the ignorant, to whom he explained his invention & proceeded to teach them. Among those unacquainted with the English it is very much esteemed —Portions of the bible are translated & read and Hymns are sung in that character. With the Cherokees of the Arkansas they correspond regularly by letter in Guess' character. It is in contemplation to establish a printing press composed of the English and Cherokee types at our Seat of Government, and a weekly paper will be edited in both languages at the same place. For this object $15.00 were appropriated by our Council last Fall, and other regulations adopted to carry the object into effect. We have also a Society organized called the Moral and Literary Society of the Cherokee Nation. Col. Walter S. Adair a Cherokee of fine education is President of it. A library is attached to it.

Having given a view of the present State of civilization of the Cherokee Nation it may not be amiss to relate the time and manner of its introduction. About the year 1795 missionaries were sent by the United Brethren to the Cherokees and established a Station called Spring place in the Centre of the Nation. At or about that time Col. Silas Dinsmore was appointed to the Agency of the nation by Genl. Washington who from the Indian Testimony itself laboured indefatigably to induce the Indians to lead a domestic life by distributing hoes and ploughs among the men, and cotton cards, spinning wheels and Looms to the women. It appears when this change of Hunter life for a civilized one was proposed by the Agent in Council, that the Chiefs unanimously laughed at him, for attempting to introduce white people's customs among Indians created to pursue the chase. Not discouraged here, he turned to individuals, and succeeded to gain some to pay attention to his plan by way of experiments which succeeded. An anecdote is related of a Chief who was opposed to the views of the Agent. It was customary for the Indians to hunt at certain Seasons, and before this Chief started, came to the Agent and said, that he was going on a Hunt, should be gone six Moons, and hoped during his absence he would not mention to his family his new plan; that it would do for white people, but not for Indians. While this Chief was absent, the Agent prevailed on his wife and daughters to spin and weave cloth, and it was done to that extent, as to be more valuable than the Chief's Hunt at his return. Pleasantly disappointed he immediately came to the Agent and accused him for making his women better Hunters and requested a plough, which was given to him, and from that time he became a farmer. In the mean time the Moravians opened a School for the Indians—cleared a farm—cultivated a garden—& planted an Orchard. The venerable Mr. Gambold and his aimiable wife were a visible monument of industry, goodness & friendship to the Indians, and as far as it was in their power they converted "the Wilderness to bud and blossom as the rose." The boys and girls were taught the rudiments of education and were occasionally required to labor in the Garden & in the Field. Here they were first taught to sing and pray to their Creator, and here Gospel Worship was first established in our Nation. Never can I forget father & Mother Gambold who dispersed the clouds of ignorance that encircled me round and opened my eyes to behold the light of civilization. My Intellect expanded and took a wider range—my Superstition vanished, and I began to reason correctly.

"Curious to view the Kings of ancient days
The mighty dead, that live in endless praise."

I might indulge in sad review of the past, and point to Nations once powerful, that as Lords of the creation roamed America's Forests. The sun of our glory is set, and we are left the Shadow of what once was a reality! Powerful in war & sage in peace, our Chiefs now sleep with their heroic deeds in the bosom of the Earth! It was not their destiny to become great. Had they concentrated their Council fires, their empire might have stood like a Pyramid, for ages yet unborn to admire. It was for Strangers to effect this, and necessity now compels the last remnant to look to it for protection. It is true, we enjoy self Government, but we live in fear, and uncertainty foretells our Fall. Strangers urge our removal, they point to the west and there they say we can live happy. Our National existence is suspended on the faith and honor of the United States alone. We are in the paw of a Lion—convenience may induce him [to] crush and with a faint Struggle we may cease to be! But all Nations have experienced change. Mutability is stamped on every thing that walks the Earth. Even now we are forced by natural causes to a Channel that will mingle the blood of our race with the white.

In the lapse of half a Century if Cherokee blood is not destroyed it will run its courses in the veins of fair complexions who will read that their Ancestors under the Stars of adversity, and curses of their enemies became a civilized Nation.

I am Sir
Respectfully your friend
John Ridge

1826/1982

Cherokee Oral Tradition

Representatives of three continents—Europeans, Africans, and Native Americans —came into repeated contact in the American Southeast throughout the colonial period and well into the late nineteenth century. Frequent cultural and especially linguistic and folklore exchanges marked these contacts. For example, the folk hero Brer Rabbit made famous by Joel Chandler Harris was, according to James Mooney, the renowned anthropologist who collected the tales printed here, an African-European analogue of "the Great White Rabbit—the hero-god, trickster, and wonder-worker of all the tribes east of the Mississippi from Hudson Bay to the Gulf." The two versions of "The Rabbit and Tar Wolf" printed here demonstrate that both the trickster figure and the specific plots attached to him were distributed among members of all three groups. The different versions of this same tale also highlight the kinds of changes narrators traditionally make in reciting such tales.

The first version was collected by Mooney in 1891 from among the western Cherokee, who had been forcibly removed to Oklahoma by the U.S. government in violation of their rights. It was collected from James D. Wafford, who was born in the old Cherokee Nation near the site of present-day Clarkesville, Georgia, in 1806. Mooney quotes Wafford as saying that he had "repeatedly heard it in boyhood about Valley river, in the old nation from Cherokee who spoke no English." According to Mooney, "In the course of his long life [Wafford] filled many positions of trust and honor among his people." He was one of the two commanders of the largest detachment of emigrants at the time of the removal and was also listed as a member of the council for the western nation in the Cherokee Almanac of 1846.

The second version was printed in the *Cherokee Advocate* on December 18, 1845. The *Advocate* was first published in 1844, a few years after the removal of the Cherokee to the west, with William P. Ross as editor. It continues to be published under the auspices of the Cherokee Nation. It appears in both Cherokee and English and is distributed free among all the Cherokee, an unparalleled example of government interest in an informed citizenry.

Further Reading:
J. C. Harris, *Nights with Uncle Remus,* 1883, and *Uncle Remus, His Songs and His Sayings,* 1886. F. Boas, "Dissemination of Tales Among the Natives of North America," *Journal of American Folklore,* 1891, and "The Growth of Indian Mythologies," *Journal of American Folklore,* 1896.

Text:
J. Mooney, *Myths of the Cherokees, 19th Annual Report of the Bureau of American Ethnology, Part 1, 1897–98,* 1900.

The Rabbit and the Tar Wolf

[First Version]

Once there was such a long spell of dry weather that there was no more water in the creeks and springs, and the animals held a council to see what to do about it. They decided to dig a well, and all agreed to help except the Rabbit, who was a lazy fellow, and said, "I don't need to dig for water. The dew on the grass is enough for me." The others did not like this, but they went to work together and dug their well.

They noticed that the Rabbit kept sleek and lively, although it was still dry weather and the water was getting low in the well. They said, "That tricky Rabbit steals our water at night," so they made a wolf of pine gum and tar and set it up by the well to scare the thief. That night the Rabbit came, as he had been coming every night, to drink enough to last him all next day. He saw the queer black thing by the well and said, "Who's there?" but the tar wolf said nothing. He came nearer, but the wolf never moved, so he grew braver and said, "Get out of my way or I'll strike you." Still the wolf never moved and the Rabbit came up and struck it with his paw, but the gum held his foot and it stuck fast. Now he was angry and said, "Let me go or I'll kick you." Still the wolf said nothing. Then the Rabbit struck again with his hind foot, so hard that it was caught in the gum and he could not move, and there he stuck until the animals came for water in the morning. When they found who the thief was they had great sport over him for a while and then got ready to kill him, but as soon as he was unfastened from the tar wolf he managed to get away.

[Second Version]

Once upon a time there was such a severe drought that all streams of water and all lakes were dried up. In this emergency the beasts assembled together to devise means to procure water. It was proposed by one to dig a well. All agreed to do so except the hare. She refused because it would soil her tiny paws. The rest, however, dug their well and were fortunate enough to find water. The hare beginning to suffer and thirst, and having no right to the well, was thrown upon her wits to procure water. She determined, as the easiest way, to steal from the public well. The rest of the animals, surprised to find that the hare was so well supplied with water, asked her where she got it. She replied that she arose betimes in the morning and gathered the dewdrops. However the wolf and the fox suspected her of theft and hit on the following plan to detect her:

They made a wolf of tar and placed it near the well. On the following night the hare came as usual after her supply of water. On seeing the tar wolf she demanded who was there. Receiving no answer she repeated the demand, threatening to kick the wolf if he did not reply. She receiving no reply kicked the wolf, and by this means adhered to the tar and was caught. When the fox and wolf got hold of her they consulted what it was best to do with her. One proposed cutting her head off. This the hare protested would be useless, as it had often been tried without hurting her. Other methods were proposed for dispatching her, all of which she said would be useless. At last it was proposed to let her loose to perish in a thicket. Upon this the hare affected great uneasiness and pleaded hard for life. Her enemies, however, refused to listen and she was accordingly let loose. As soon, however, as she was out of reach of her enemies she gave a whoop, and bounding away she exclaimed: 'This is where I live.'—

1900

Gadigwanahsti
d. ca. 1870

The North American Indians inhabited a world with spiritual values and practices quite different from those of European culture. Among the Native Americans of the Southeast, religion and medicine traditionally have not been separate, as they are in white European and American societies. Folk medicine continues to be practiced by native doctors using old, highly revered practices.

The following sacred love formula for fixing the affections was originally written in the Cherokee language using the syllabary invented by Sequoyah. Its author is a North Carolina Cherokee doctor and Baptist minister named Gadigwanahsti.

Further Reading:
J. Mooney, *The Sacred Formulas of the Cherokees,
7th Annual Report of the Bureau of American
Ethnology,* 1891.

Text:
"Southeastern Indian Formulas," W. C.
Sturtevant, in *Native North American Spirituality
of the Eastern Woodlands: Sacred Myths, Dreams,
Visions, Speeches, Healing Formulas, Rituals and
Ceremonials,* ed. E. Tooker, 1979.

To Fix the Affections*
[A Cherokee Sacred Love Formula]

Yu! Ha! Now the souls have come together.
You are of the Deer clan.
Your name is Ayasta.
I am of the Wolf clan.
Your body, I take it, I eat it.   5

---

* Originally written in the Sequoyah syllabary by Gadigwanahsti and translated by James Mooney in *The Sacred Formulas of the Cherokees, Seventh Annual Report of the Bureau of American Ethnology* (Washington, 1891). In Gadigwanahsti's original, the personal and clan names were omitted, with X's and O's indicating where they should be inserted. Mooney added the names and clans for Gadigwanahsti and Ayasta, his wife. Mooney's translation has been slightly rearranged by W. C. Sturtevant.

Yu! Ha! Now the souls have come together.
You are of the Deer clan.
Your name is Ayasta.
I am of the Wolf clan.
Your flesh I take, I eat. Yu!¹   10

Yu! Ha! Now the souls have come together.
You are of the Deer clan.
Your name is Ayasta.
I am of the Wolf clan.
Your spittle I take, I eat. I! Yu!   15

Yu! Ha! Now the souls have come together.
You are of the Deer clan.
Your name is Ayasta.
I am of the Wolf clan.
Your heart I take, I eat. Yu!   20

Listen! "Ha! Now the souls have met, never to part," you have said, O Ancient
    One above.
O Black Spider, you have been brought down from on high.
You have let down your web.
She is of the Deer clan; her name is Ayasta.
Her soul you have trapped in your web.   25
There where the people of the seven clans² are continually coming in sight and
    again disappearing,
There was never any feeling of loneliness.

Listen! Ha! But now you have covered her over with loneliness.
Her eyes have faded; her eyes have come to fasten themselves on one alone.
Whither can her soul escape?   30
Let her be sorrowing as she goes along, and not for one night alone.
Let her become an aimless wanderer, whose trail may never be followed.
O Black Spider, may you hold her soul in your web so that it shall never get
    through the meshes.
What is the name of the soul? They two have come together. It is mine!

Listen! Ha! And now you have hearkened, O Ancient Red.³   35
Your grandchildren⁴ have come to the edge of your body.⁵
You hold them yet more firmly in your grasp,
Never to let go your hold.
O Ancient One, we have become as one.

---

¹ Device to mark the end of a stanza.
² Figurative term for the entire Cherokee nation,
also occasionally used for the entire world.
³ God of fire.

⁴ I.e., the more important deities.
⁵ I.e., the performer has warmed his hands over a
fire.

The woman has put her soul into our hands.   40
We shall never let it go! Yu!

And this also is just for the same purpose.[6] It must be done by stealth at night when
they are asleep. One must put the hand on the middle of the breast and rub on spittle
with the hand, they say. The other formula is equally good.

1979

William Ralganal Benson
ca. 1863–1936

There are few reliable accounts of what actually transpired during the early years
of contact between Native Americans and western settlers. Official government
documents usually branded Native American resistance to the settlers' occupation
of their lands an uprising or massacre whenever settlers' lives were lost. So too,
most early white efforts to defend Native American behavior depended on
sentimental distortions of the Indians' beliefs, rights, and culture. William
Ralganal Benson's account of the Stone and Kelsey "massacre" on the shores of
northern California's Clear Lake in 1849 is limited by neither predisposition. As
an informant and interpreter of Native American experience and lore for the
anthropologists who worked in the Clear Lake region in the early twentieth
century, Benson was well known for his integrity. From all indications, his
narrative is at once one of the most reliable reports of the early conflicts between
white settlers and Native Americans and one of the most insightful and
compelling views of Native American attitudes toward the settlers who
eventually crowded them off their lands.

William Ralganal Benson was born about 1863 in what were then still the
remote stretches of Lake County, California. His mother was descended from a
long line of Pomo chiefs; his father, a white settler named Addison Benson, had
renounced his former life and taken up permanent residence among the Pomo
tribe. He died when his son was fairly young, leaving Ralganal, the Pomo word
for "wampum gatherer," with little knowledge of English. Over the years,
William Ralganal Benson taught himself to read and write mostly by ear, and
much of the text printed here reflects his practice with phonetic spelling. Benson
also taught himself to type, and the unusual punctuation in this text reflects his
deliberate efforts to preserve the oral tradition of retelling his story. Each period,
for example, is meant to indicate an emphasis or a fairly long pause in the
narrative.

Benson's story serves to counterbalance the official versions of the incident
recorded in local histories. One such account of the "massacre" consists of the
following brief entry:

---

[6] Reference to the preceding love chant in the
original manuscript.

In the fall of 1849, when Stone and Kelsey were away with the vaqueros, attending to their cattle one day, Augustine's squaw poured water into their guns. The next morning some of the Indians made a charge on the house. Kelsey was killed outright with an arrow shot through the window. Stone escaped upstairs and on the Indians rushing up against him, jumped out of an upper window, ran to the creek and hid in a clump of willows. . . . An old Indian found him and killed him with a blow of a rock on the head.

But even these "official" renditions of what happened at Kelseyville acknowledge, in the words of another report, that "the consensus of opinion is that the deed was justified by the harsh and unjust treatment given the Indians by these two frontiersmen."

Benson's narrative does fuse events that took place nearly a year apart. Stone and Kelsey were killed in the fall of 1849, after gold had been discovered and Kelsey had impressed several of the Pomo tribe into joining his failed search for instant wealth. The second episode, the retaliatory raid against the Pomo tribe, occurred almost a year later. Although not an eyewitness, Benson nonetheless takes us closer to the state of mind of the Native Americans who were no longer willing to endure the abuses of greedy settlers.

Further Reading:
The official versions of what occurred at Kelseyville may be found in C. A. Menifee, *Historical and Descriptive Sketch Book of Napa, Sonoma, Lake and Mendocino Counties*, 1879, *History of Napa and Lake Counties*, 1881, and A. O. Carpenter and P. H. Millberry, *History of Mendocino and Lake Counties*, 1910.

Text:
California Historical Society Quarterly, 1932.

The Stone and Kelsey "Massacre"

The Facts Of Stone and Kelsey Massacre. in Lake County California.[1] As it was stated to me by the five indians who went to stone and kelseys house purpose to kill the two white men. after debateing all night. Shuk and Xasis.[2] these two men were the instigators of the massacre. it was not because Shuk and Xasis had any Ill feeling torge the two white men. there were two indian villages. one on west side and one on the east side.[3] the indians in both of these camps were starveing, stone or kelsey would not let them go out hunting or fishing. Shuk and Xasis was stone and kelsey headriders looking out for stock. cattle horses and hogs. the horses and cattle were all along the lake on the west side and some in bachelors valley. also in upper lake. so it took 18

---

[1] Located in northern California.
[2] Members of the Pomo tribe, as are the other Indian namenes that follow.

[3] I.e., of Clear Lake.

indian herdsman to look after the stock in these places. Shuk and Xasis was foremans for the herds. and only those herds got anything to eat. each one of these herders got 4 cups of wheat for a days work. this cup would hold about one and ahalf pint of water. the wheat was boiled before it was given to the herders. and the herders shire with thir famlys. the herders who had large famlys were also starveing. about 20 old people died during the winter from starvetion. from severe whipping 4 died. a nephew of an indian lady who were liveing with stone was shoot to deth by stone. the mother of this young man was sick and starveing. this sick woman told her son to go over to stones wife or the sick womans sister. tell your aunt that iam starveing and sick tell her that i would like to have a handfull of wheat. the young man lost no time going to stones house. the young man told the aunt what his mother said. the lady then gave the young man 5 cups of wheat and tied it up in her apron and the young man started for the camp. stone came about that time and called the young man back. the young man stoped stone who was horse back. rode up to the young man took the wheat from him and then shoot him. the young man died two days after. such as whipping and tieing their hands togather with rope, the rope then thrown over a limb of a tree and then drawn up untell the indians toes barly touchs the ground and let them hang there for hours. this was common punishment. when a father or mother of young girl. was asked to bring the girl to his house. by stone or kelsey. if this order was not obeyed. he or her would be whipped or hung by the hands. such punishment occurred two or three times a week. and many of the old men and woman died from fear and starvetion.

these two white men had the indians to build a high fence around thir villages. and the head riders were to see that no indian went out side of this fence after dark. if any one was caught out side of this fence after dark was taken to stones and kelseys house and there was tied both hands and feet and placed in a room and kept there all night. the next day was taken to a tree and was tied down. then the strongs man was chosen to whippe the prisoner. the village on the west side was the Qu-Lah-Na-Poh[4] tribes the village on the east side. Xa-Bah-Na-Poh.[5] tribes.

the starvetion of the indians was the cause of the massacre of stone and kelsey. the indians who was starving hired a man by the name of Shuk and a nother man by the name of Xasis. to kill a beef for them. Shuk and Xasis agreed to go out and kill a beef for them. the two men then plan to go out that nigth and kill a beef for them. thir plan then was to take the best horsses in the barn. stones horse which was the best lasso horse. so between the two men. they agreed to take both stones and kelseys horses. so the two men went to stone and kelseys house to see if they had went to bed. it was raining a little. moonligth now and then they found stone and kelsey had went to bed so they went to the barn and took stone and kelseys horses and saddles. Shuk wanted to do the job in the day time but Xasis said stone or kelsey would sure find them and would kill the both of them. Shuk said then somebody is going to get killed on this job so any how they went out west they knew where a larg band was feeding they soon rounded the band up and Shuk was to make the first lasso Xasis

---

[4] One of the two pre-contact villages (Quuhlá-Naapó in contemporary Eastern Pomo practical orthography) in Big Valley; it was located on the west side of Clear Lake in northern California.

[5] The second of the two Pomo villages (Xaabé-Naapó in contemporary Eastern Pomo practical orthography), this one located on the eastern side of Clear Lake.

was good on lassing the foot of anox so he was to do the foot lassing. Shuk said to Xasis get redy i see large one hear hurry and come on. Shuk got a chance and threwed the rope on the large or Xasis came as quick as he could the band then begin to stampede. the ox also started with the band. the ground was wet and slippery and raining. and before Xasis could get his rope on. Shuks horse fell to the ground. the horse and the ox got away. Xasis tried to lass the horse but could not get near it to throw the rope on. the horse soon found the other horses and it was then much harder to get the horse. so the chase was given up. the two went back to the camp and reported to the people who hired them. told them the bad luck they had. Xasis then took the horse he had back to the barn which was kelseys horse. all the men who hired Shuk and Xasis was gathered in Xasiss house, here they debated all night. Shuk and Xasis wanted to kill stone and kelsey. they said stone and kelsey would kill them as soon as they would find out that the horses was taken with out them known; one man got up and suggested that the tribe give stone and kelsey forty sticks of beades which means 16000 beads or 100 dollars. no one agreed. another man suggested that he or Shuk. tell stoneor kelsey that the horse was stolen. no one agreed, and another man suggested that the other horse should be turned out and tell stone and kelsey both horses were stlen. no one agreed. every thing looks bad for Shuk and Xasis. no one agreed with Shuk and Xasis to kill the two white men. at daylight one man agreed to go with Shuk and Xasis. his indian name. Ba-Tus, was known by the whites as Busi. and alittle while later Kra-nas agreed. and as the four men started out another man joined the Shuk and Xasis band: Ma-Laxa-Qe-Tu. while this Debateing was going on the hired or servants boys and girls of stones and kelseys were told by Shuk and Xasis to carrie out allthe guns. bows and arrows. knives and every thing like weapon was taken out of the house by these girls and boys so the two white men was helpless in defense. so Shuk and Xasis knew the white man, did not have any thing to defen themselfs with and they were sure of their victims. so the five men went to the house where stone and kelsey were liveing. at daylight were to the place where stone always built a fire under a large pot in which he boiled wheat for the indian herders.about 16 of them. these five men waited around this pot untell stone came out to build the fire. Stone came out with pot full of fire which was taken from the fireplace. and said to the indians. whats the matter boys you came Early this morning. some thing rong; the indians said. O nothing me hungry thats all. Qka-Nas: or cayote Jim as he was known by the whites: Qka-Nas said to the men. I thought you men came to kill this man; give me these arrows and bow. He jerk the bow and the arrows away from Shuk and drew it and as he did.Stone rose quickly and turned to Qka-Nas and said what are you trying to do Jim, and as Stone said it. the indian cut loose. the arrow. struck the victimpith of the stomach. the victim mediately pull the arrow out and ran for the house. fighting his way. he broke one mans arm with the pot he had. and succeeded in geting in the house and locked the door after him. little later Kelsey came and opened the door and noticed the blood on the doorstep. the indians advanced. Kelsey seen that the indians ment business. he said to them. no matar kelsey. kelsey bueno hombre para vosotros.[6] the indians charged and two of the indians caught kelsey and the fight began. in this fight kelsey was stabed twice in the back. kelsey managed to brake loose. he ran for the creek and the indians after him.

[6] Spanish: "a good man for us."

a man by the name of Xa-sis or blind Jose, as he was known by the whites. who was in pursuit. shot kelsey in the back. kelsey manage to pull the arrow out jest as he got to the creek and jumped in the water and dove under and came out on the other side of the creek. where several indians were waiting. there was one man kelsey knew well. he thought who would save him. this man was Joe sefeis, indian name. Ju-Luh. he beged Joe to save him. Joe he could not save him from being killed. Joe said to kelsey. its too late kelsey; if I attempt to save you. I allso will be killed. I can not save you kelsey; kelsey was geting weak from loss of blood. Big Jim and Joe had kelsey by the arms. Big Jim said to his wife. this is a man who killed our son. take this spear. now you have the chance to take revenge. Big Jim's wife took the spear and stabed the white man in the hart. this womans name was Da-Pi-Tauo. the body was left laying there for the cayotes. this hapend on the east side of the creek. while this was going on. Xasis and Qra-Nas was trailing the blood up stairs and for a hour allmost. Qra-Nas said they crawled up stairs breathless thinking that stone was yet alive. they opend the door of a wheat bend and saw stones foot Qra-Nas drew his arrow across the bow. redy to cut loose. for a moment they watch the lifeless body. Xa-sis discovered that the body was dead. they then took the body and threw it out the window. and then they called all the people to come and take what wheat and corn they could pack and go to-a hiding place. where they could not be found by the whites. so the indian of both villages came and took all the wheat and corn they could gather in the place. and then went to hide themselfs. some went to Fishels point and somewent to scotts valley. the men went out to kill cattle for their use and every man who was able to ride caught himself a horse. in around the valley and upper lake and bachelor valley. there was about one thousand head of horses. and about four thousand head of cattles. so the indians lived fat for a while. Qra-Nas and Ma-Laq-Qe-Tou was chosen to watch the trail that came in from lower lake. and Shuk and Xasis was watching the trail on the west side of the valley. yom-mey-nah and ge-we-leh were watching the trail that came from eight mile valley. two—or three weeks had pass. no white man were seen on eather trail. one day. Qra-nas and ma-Laq-Qe-Tou seen two white men on horse back came over the hill. they stoped on top of the hill. they saw nothing staring around stone and kelseys place. no indians in the village. Qra-nas and Ma-Laq-Tou. went around behind a small hill to cut the white man off. the white man saw the indians trying to go around behind them. the whites turned and went back before the indians got in back of them. so three or four days went by. no more white man was seen. one day the lake watchers saw a boat came around the point. som news coming. they said to each others. two of the men went to the landing. to see what the news were. they were told that the white warriors had came to kill all the indians around the lake. so hide the best you can. the whites are making boats and with that they are coming up the lake. so we are told by the people down there. so they had two men go up on top of uncle sam mountain. the north peak. from there they watch the lower lake. for three days they watch the lake. one morning they saw a long boat came up the lake with pole on the bow with red cloth. and several of them came. every one of the boats had ten to fifteen men. the smoke signal was given by the two watchmen. every indian around the lake knew the soldiers were coming up the lake. and how many of them. and those who were watching the trail saw the infantrys coming over the hill from lower lake. these two men were watching from ash hill. they went to stones and kelseys house. from there the horsemen went down torge the lake and the soldiers went across the valley torge lakeport. they went on to scotts valley. shoot afew shoots with their big gun and went on to upper lake and camped on Emmerson hill. from there they saw the indian camp on the island. the next morning the white warriors went across in their long dugouts. the indians said they would met them in peace.so when the whites landed the indians went to wellcom them.but the white man was determined to kill them. Ge-Wi-Lih said he threw up his hands and said no harm me good man. but the white man fired and shoot him in the arm and another shoot came and hit a man staning along side of him and was killed.so they had to run and fight back; as they ran back in the tules and hed under the water; four or five of them gave alittle battle and another man was shoot in the shoulder. some of them jumped in the water and hed in the tuleys. many women and children were killed on around this island. one old lady a (indian) told about what she saw while hiding under abank,in under aover hanging tuleys. She said she saw two white man coming with their guns up in the air and on their guns hung a little girl. they brought it to the creek and threw it in the water. and alittle while later, two more men came in the same manner. this time they had a little boy on the end of their guns and also threw it in the water. alittle ways from her she, said layed awoman shoot through the shoulder. she held her little baby in her arms. two white men came running torge the woman and baby, they stabed the woman and the baby and, and threw both of them over the bank in to the water. she said she heared the woman say, O my baby; she said when they gathered the dead, they found all the little ones were killed by being stabed, and many of the woman were also killed stabing. she said it took them four or five days to gather up the dead. and the dead were all burnt on the east side by the creek. they called it the sailand creek. (Ba-Don-Bi-Da-Meh). this old lady also told about the whites hung aman on Emerson sailand this indian was met by the soldiers while marching from scotts valley to upper lake. the indian was hung and alarge fire built under the hanging indian. and another indian was caught near Emerson hill. this one was tied to atree and burnt to death.

the next morning the soldiers started for mendocino county.[7] and there killed many indians. the camp was on the ranch now known as Ed Howell ranch. the solders made camp a little ways below, bout one half mile from the indian camp. the indians wanted to surrender, but the solders did not give them time, the solders went in the camp and shoot them down as tho if they were dogs. som of them escaped by going down a little creek leading to the river. and som of them hed in the brush. and those who hed in the brush most of them were killed. and those who hed in the water was over looked. they killed mostly woman and children.

the solders caught two boys age about 14 or 15. the solders took them to lower lake, and then turned them loose, when the solders started the two boys back, they loded them with meat and hard bread, one said as soon as they got out of site, they threw the meat away and som of the bread also. he said they went on a dog trot for dear life. thinking all the time that the solders would follow them and kill them. he said they would side tract once and awhile and get up on a high peak to see if the solders were coming he said when they got back that night they could nothing but crying. he said all the dead had been taken across to a large dance house had been and was cremated. wetness, Bo-Dom, or Jeo Beatti, and Krao Lah, indian-name.an

---

[7] County north of San Francisco.

old lady said her further dug a large hole in abank of the river and they hed in the hole. one old man said that he was aboy at the time he said the solders shoot his mother, she fell to the ground with her baby in her arms, he said his mother told him to climb high up in the tree.so he did and from there he said he could see the solders running about the camp and shooting the men and woman and stabing boys and girls. he said mother was not yet dead and was telling him to keep quit. two of the solders heard her talking and ran up to her and stabed her and child. and a little ways from his mother, he said laid a man dieing, holding his boy in his arms the solders also stabed him, but did not kill the boy, they took the boy to the camp, crying, they gave it every thing they could find in camp but the little boy did not quit crying. it was aboy about three years of age, when the solders were geting redy to move camp, they raped the boy up in ablanket and lief the little boy seting by the fire raped up in a blanket and was stell crying, and that boy is live today, his name is bill ball, now lives in Boonville; One Old man told me about the solders killing the indiuns in this same camp. he said young man.from the description he gave. he must have been about 18 or 20 years of age. he said he and another boy about the same age was taken by the soldurs and.he said there were two solders in charge of them. one would walk ahead and one behind them. he said the solders took him and the other boy. they both were bearfooted he said when they begin to climb the mountain between mendocino and lake country. he said they were made to keep up with the solders. thir feet were geting sore but they had to keep up with the solders. when they were climbing over the bottlerock mountain.thir feet were cutup by the rocks and thir feet were bleeding and they could not walk up with the solders. the man behind would jab them with the sharp knife fixed on the end of the gun. he said one of the solders came and looked at thir feet and went to abox opened it took a cup and diped something out of asack and brought it to them and told them both of them to hold their foots on a log near by. the solder took ahand full of the stuff and rubed it in the cuts on the bottom of their feet. he said he noticed that the stuff the solder put on their feet look like salt. sureenough it was salt. the solder tied clouth over their feet and told them not to take them off.he said the tears were roling down his cheeks. he said all the solders came and stood around them laughing. he said they roled and twested for about two hours. and they also rubed salt in the wounds on their seats and backs wher they jabed them with the solders big knife.as he call it. two or three days later the chife solder told them they could go back. they was then gaven meat and bread, all they could pack. he said they started on thir back journey. he said it was all most difficult for them to walk but raped alot of cloth around thir feet and by doing so made thir way all right. he said the meat and bread got too heavy for fast traveling so they threw the meat and some of the bread away. looking back all the time thinking that the solders would follow them and kill them. now and then they would side tract. and look back to see if the solders were following them. after seen no solders following them they would start out for another run. he said they traveled in such manner untell they got to thir home. he said to himself. hear Iam not to see my mother and sister but to see thir blood scattered over the ground like water and thir bodys for coyotes to devour. he said he sat down under a tree and cryed all day.

1932

Fiction of the Early Republic

In June 1788, a socially prominent thirty-seven-year-old Hartford woman
mysteriously took a room by herself at the Bell Tavern in Danvers,
Massachusetts. A month later she gave birth to a stillborn child and within a few
days was herself dead of puerperal fever. The sad, furtive death of Elizabeth
Whitman, a cousin of the poet John Trumbull and a close friend of Joel Barlow,
immediately inspired an endless stream of prurient gossip, abetted by New
England newspapers, which printed, along with their moral assessments,
appropriate samples of her poetry. Her grave—happily for the owners of the Bell
Tavern—was promptly elevated to the status of tourist site, and even into the
early twentieth century, books appeared containing fetishistic illustrations of
Elizabeth Whitman's tombstone, her writing desk, wallpaper from the room in
which she died, a spoon with which she supposedly ate. A classic victim of
seduction and betrayal, she became one of the earliest casualties of unprincipled
male behavior to enter American folklore.

As a cult figure, however, Elizabeth Whitman represented more than an
innocent, spirited woman undone by smooth talk and a cozening smile. She
became an example of what can happen to impressionable young (and not so
young) ladies who waste their time reading fiction and forming inadequate,
romanticized notions of life. Her destiny, commentators agreed, would have been
far happier had she spent more time with Dr. Johnson and less with Fanny
Burney, immersed herself more frequently in instructive essays and less in what
John Trumbull called "the amorous follies of romances." To moralists, the lesson
seemed clear: Elizabeth Whitman was a victim of literature, seduced not so much
by the deceitfulness of men as by the equally powerful deceits of fiction. Her fate
served as yet another late-eighteenth-century rallying point against the
perniciousness of novel reading.

The novel, as developed and perfected by such English writers as Richardson
(his *Pamela*, reprinted in 1744 by Benjamin Franklin, was the first novel
published in America), Defoe, Fielding, Smollett, and Sterne, met with more
cultural resistance in America than it did in England. In general, two factors
contributed to this late-eighteenth-century American resistance to fiction: first, a
continuing Puritanical hostility toward any literature produced and consumed
chiefly for entertainment, and second, a prevailing commonsense philosophy that
distrusted any thinking (or writing) that deviated from a tough-minded,
empirical relationship to the actual world. But neither theological nor
metaphysical censorship could in the long run stop the fictional enticements daily
crowding the shelves of bookstores and the new "slopshops of literature," the
circulating libraries. Between the publication of Franklin's edition of *Pamela* and
the first genuinely American novel, William Hill Brown's *The Power of
Sympathy*, in 1789, only fifty-six foreign novels were reprinted in this country. In
the eleven years between 1789 and 1800, however, American publishers released
thirty-seven domestic titles and reprinted over 350 foreign works of fiction.

Early American novelists, because of the critical opposition to fiction, learned
to be cagey about constructing their imagined worlds. Anticipating critical and

moral hostility from the press and pulpit (neither editors nor preachers welcomed additional prose competition), they tried to disarm criticism by promoting their novels as virtuous works of instruction depicting characters and events derived from real life. To advertise their authenticity, many early American novels paraded such subtitles as "A Tale Founded upon Truth," "Based upon Recent Facts," or "Founded on Incidents in Real Life." Many also played the tricky, though in this case hardly risky, game of having the characters themselves disavow the specious pleasures and moral hazards of novel reading: "Many fine girls have been ruined by reading Novels," argues a character in *The Power of Sympathy,* a novel that claimed to be "Founded in Truth" and that, less than a year after her death, dragged in the sad tale of Elizabeth Whitman to serve as a poignant illustrative commentary on the insidiousness of fiction.

Most of the fiction devised during this first burst of the domestically produced novel was clearly calculated to appeal to the female consumer—the "ladies," the "sex," or the "American fair." Book advertisements throughout the 1790s increasingly zeroed in on this new audience with such headlines as "To the Ladies: Novels for Winter Evening Amusements." Dedications, prefaces, notes, apologies, and an occasional direct address within the text left no doubt as to the intended readership: William Hill Brown not only dedicated *The Power of Sympathy* "To the Young Ladies of United Columbia" but also, in a nervous preface, assures his audience that "novels have ever met with a ready reception into the libraries of the ladies." In another fictional transmutation—this time thinly disguised as the melancholy adventures of Eliza Wharton—the story of Elizabeth Whitman as told by Hannah W. Foster in *The Coquette* becomes a tale composed "for the sake of my sex in general" in which "the American fair learn to reject with disdain every insinuation derogatory to their true dignity and honor."

A new industry was emerging in the 1790s, featuring a new ("novel"), well-advertised commodity designed to attract a new kind of "consumer" (the modern use of that word is, incidentally, contemporaneous with the beginnings of the novel). Writers, publishers, and booksellers discovered that the selling power of fiction largely depended on the formation and sustenance of a vigorous market of heroine addicts, readers always gratified by "virtue rewarded" so long as the rewards did not come too easily or too soon.

Among the most aggressive opponents of fiction were men and women dedicated to improving the quality of education. As satirically portrayed in John Trumbull's *The Progress of Dulness* (1772–1773), the education of a Tom Brainless, no matter how ridiculous, was still superior to that of a Harriet Simper, whose "reading is confin'd / To books that poison all the mind." "Fashionable education," according to Timothy Dwight, did incalculable harm to the social fabric by replacing the classics and the tougher studies with novels and romances, books especially dangerous in the hands of young women because girls had been denied the advantages of a solid education and were consequently too easily seduced by the "delightful inhabitants of Utopia." Novels demanded no serious mental effort and, worse, left their impressionable readers victims not of a great but of a rude awakening: An actual husband would be no match for the perfect husband of the imagination. So allied for educational reasons against prose fiction was the influential Yale group of poets and essayists (Noah Webster: "A hundred volumes of modern novels may be read without acquiring a new idea") that William Hill Brown was especially careful in *The Power of Sympathy* to endorse the accomplishments of Dwight, Barlow, and Webster and in addition to recommend his own novel as upholding the "advantages of female education." Brown followed *The Power of Sympathy* with another novel, but Hannah W. Foster was perhaps more sincere in her detestation, for after the huge success of *The Coquette* she expiated her guilt with *The Boarding School* (1798), a serious, pedagogical work that allowed her to complain that "novels are the favorite, and the most dangerous kind of reading, now adopted by the generality of young ladies." In their prefaces, most authors relied on a single strategy: "Novels are bad, but not this one."

Sentimental, melodramatic, artistically clumsy, devoted to quests for self-fulfillment, and bristling with violence, the novels of the late eighteenth and early nineteenth centuries established a direction and a market for American fiction. By virtue of the kinds of criticism they had to circumvent, they also helped fashion the socio-aesthetic context in which future novelists would work. Though period styles change, tales based on the verifiable data of actual experiences would always appeal to the American reading public more than highly imaginative versions of reality. A density of fact—as Melville in *Moby-Dick* (1851) and Pynchon in *Gravity's Rainbow* (1973) understood—would persuade any skeptical person that the time spent reading "mere" fiction can be justified in terms of sheer information acquired. Authors of popular novels too, have instinctively known that a combination of fictional devices and informative "facticity" helps sell books. Readers expect to be entertained and instructed, to be taken in by a good yarn but not fleeced along the way.

In her concluding remarks to *Uncle Tom's Cabin,* (1852), Harriet Beecher Stowe claims that she had often been asked "whether this narrative is a true one"; she then proceeds to demonstrate that every character and event in the novel had a counterpart in reality. When in a similar venture Alex Haley in 1976 defended his method of blending fact and fiction by referring to *Roots* as "faction," he was, consciously or not, acknowledging procedures that have been indispensable to American writing from the time the earliest novelists discovered—through trial, error, and subterfuge—the narrative requirements of a pragmatic reading public.

Further Reading:
H. R. Brown, *The Sentimental Novel in America, 1789–1860,* 1940.
J. D. Hart, *The Popular Book: A History of* *America's Literary Taste,* 1950.
T. Martin, *The Instructed Vision,* 1961.
H. Petter, *The Early American Novel,* 1971.

William Hill Brown
1765–1793

On January 22, 1789, a Boston newspaper ran the following advertisement:

This Day Published
THE POWER OF SYMPATHY, or
THE TRIUMPH OF NATURE
The First American Novel.

But despite the fanfare, this anonymously issued, epistolary novel never achieved popularity and was seldom mentioned, even in passing, in discussions of American literature until the end of the nineteenth century, when its authorship was finally attributed to William Hill Brown.

A Boston poet, dramatist, and essayist, Brown was a frequent contributor to the new magazines and reviews that had just begun to play an essential part in the new republic's machinery of literary production. In *The Power of Sympathy*, written when he was twenty-four, Brown attempted in a nearly paralyzing self-conscious fashion to transport the popular sentimental-seduction-suicide fiction of Richardson and Goethe to American soil. In so doing, he managed to produce, however synthetic the article, a work one critic has called "a morbid, nasty book" and another "a literate . . . and an ambitious" one.

In the following selection from *The Power of Sympathy*, the "sensible" Mrs. Holmes describes to a younger friend a recent discussion on novel reading and its place in female education. To bring the conversation closer to home, Brown appended a long footnote recounting the misfortunes of Elizabeth Whitman. No evidence exists, however, that Brown knew Whitman personally or that she actually was "a great reader of novels and romances," though her poetry does disclose a rather painful literary vulnerability.

Further Reading:
Leslie Fiedler, *Love and Death in the American Novel*, 1966.

Text:
The Power of Sympathy, 1789.

---

from The Power of Sympathy

Preface

Novels have ever met with a ready reception into the Libraries of the Ladies, but this species of writing hath not been received with universal approbation: Futility is not the only charge brought against it. Any attempt, therefore, to make these studies more advantageous, has at least a claim upon the patience and candour of the publick.

In Novels which *expose* no particular Vice, and which *recommend* no particular Virtue, the fair Reader, though she may find amusement, must finish them without being impressed with any particular idea: So that if they are harmless, they are not beneficial.

Of the Letters before us, it is necessary to remark, that this errour on each side has been avoided—the dangerous Consequences of Seduction are exposed, and the Advantages of Female Education set forth and recommended.

Letter XI: Mrs. Holmes to Myra Belleview

I sit down to give you, my dear Myra, some account of the visitants of today, and their conversation. We are not always *distinguished* by such company, but perhaps it is sometimes necessary; and as it is a relaxation from thought, it serves to give us more pleasure in returning to the conversation of people of ideas.

Mrs. Bourn assumes a higher rank in life than she pretended to seven years ago. —She then walked on foot—she now, by good fortune, rides in a chariot. Placed, however, in a situation with which her education does not altogether comport, she has nothing disagreeable but her over assiduity to please—this is sometimes disgusting, for one cannot feast heartily upon honey: It is an errour which a candid mind easily forgives. She sometimes appears solicitous to display her mental accomplishments, and desirous to improve those of her daughter; but it is merely apparent. Notwithstanding a temporary wish may arise towards the attainment of this point, a habitual vacancy nips it in the bud.

Miss Bourn is about the age of fourteen—genteel, with a tolerable share of beauty, but not striking—her dress was elegant, but might have been adjusted to more advantage—not altogether aukward in her manners, nor yet can she be called graceful —she has a peculiar air of *drollery* which takes her by fits, and for this reason, perhaps, does not avail herself of every opportunity of displaying the modesty of her sex— she has seen much company, but instead of polishing her manners, it has only increased her assurance.

Thus much of the characters of our *company*. After some small chat which passed as we took a turn in the garden, we entered the Temple.

"What books would you recommend to put into the hands of my daughter?" said Mrs. Bourn, as she walked into the library—"it is a matter of some importance." "It is a matter of *more* importance," answered Worthy, "than is generally imagined, for unless a proper selection is made, one would do better never to read at all:—Now, Madam, as much depends on the choice of books, care should be taken not to put those in the way of young persons, which might leave on their minds any disagreeable prejudices, or which has a tendency to corrupt their morals."—"As obvious as your remark is," added Mr. Holmes, "it is evidently overlooked in the common course of education. We wisely exclude those persons from our conversation, whose characters are bad, whose manners are depraved, or whose morals are impure; but if they are excluded from an apprehension of contaminating our minds, how much more dangerous is the company of those books, where the strokes aimed at virtue are redoubled, and the poison of vice, by repeatedly reading the same thing, indelibly distains the young mind?"

"We all agree," rejoined Worthy, "that it is as great a matter of virtue and prudence to be circumspect in the selection of our books, as in the choice of our company.—But, Sir, the best things may be subverted to an ill use. Hence we may possibly trace the cause of the ill tendency of many of the Novels extant."

"Most of the Novels," interrupted my father, "with which our female libraries are overrun, are built on a foundation not always placed on strict morality, and in the pursuit of objects not always probable or praiseworthy.—Novels, not regulated on the chaste principles of true friendship, rational love, and connubial duty, appear to me totally unfit to form the minds of women, of friends, or of wives."

"But, as most young people read," says Mrs. Bourn—"what rule can be *hit upon* to make study always terminate to advantage?"

"Impossible," cried Miss, "for I read as much as any body, and, though it may afford amusement, while I am employed, I do not remember a single word, when I lay down the book."

"This confirms what I say of Novels," cried Mr. Holmes, addressing Worthy in a jocular manner, "just calculated to kill time—to attract the attention of the reader for an hour, but leave not one idea on the mind."

"I am far from condemning every production in the gross," replied Worthy; "general satire against any particular class, or order of men, may be viewed in the same light as a satire against the species—it is the same with books—If there are corrupt or mortified members, it is hardly fair to destroy the whole body. Now I grant some Novels have a bad tendency, yet there are many which contain excellent sentiments—let these receive their deserved reward—let those be discountenanced; and if it is impossible "to smite them with an apoplexy, there is a moral certainty of their dying of a consumption."—But, as Mrs. Bourn observes, most young persons read, I will therefore recommend to those who wish to mingle instruction with entertainment, method and regularity in reading. To *dip* into *any book* burthens the mind with unnecessary lumber, and may rather be called a disadvantage, than a benefit —The record of memory is so scrawled and blotted with imperfect ideas, that not one legible character can be traced."

"Were I to throw my thoughts on this subject," said my good father-in-law, as he began to enter more warmly into the debates—drawing his chair opposite Worthy, and raising his hand with a poetical enthusiasm—"Were I to throw my thoughts on this subject into an Allegory, I would describe the human mind as an extensive plain, and knowledge as the river that should water it. If the course of the river be properly directed, the plain will be fertilized and cultivated to advantage; but if books, which are the sources that feed this river, rush into it from every quarter, it will overflow its banks, and the plain will become inundated: When, therefore, knowledge flows on in its proper channel, this extensive and valuable field, the mind, instead of being covered with stagnant waters, is cultivated to the utmost advantage, and blooms luxuriantly into a general efflorescence—for a river properly restricted by high banks, is necessarily progressive."

The old gentleman brought down his hand with great solemnity, and we complimented him on his poetical exertion. "I cannot comprehend the meaning of this matter," said the penetrative Miss Bourn. "I will explain it to you, my little dear," said he, with great good nature—"If you read with any design to improve your mind in virtue and every amiable accomplishment, you should be careful to read methodically, which will enable you to form an estimate of the various topicks discussed in

company, and to bear a part in all those conversations which belong to your sex—
you see, therefore, how necessary general knowledge is—what would you think of
a woman advanced in life, who has no other store of knowledge, than what she has
obtained from experience?"

"I think she would have a sorry time of it;" answered Miss.

"To prevent it in yourself," said Mrs. Bourn to her daughter, "be assiduous to lay
in a good stock of this knowledge, while your mind is yet free from prejudice and
care."

"How shall I *go to work,* Madam," enquired the delicate daughter.

Mrs. Bourn turned towards Mr. Holmes, which was hint enough for the good old
man to proceed.

"There is a medium to be observed, continued he, in a lady's reading; she is not
to receive everything she finds, even in the best books, as invariable lessons of conduct;
in books written in an easy, flowing style, which excel in description and the
luxuriance of fancy, the imagination is apt to get heated—she ought, therefore, to
discern with an eye of judgment, between the superficial and the penetrating—the
elegant and the tawdry—what may be merely amusing, and what may be useful.
General reading will not teach her a true knowledge of the world.

"In books she finds recorded the faithfulness of friendship—the constancy of *true
love,* and even that honesty is the best policy. If virtue is represented carrying its
reward with it, she too easily persuades herself that mankind have adopted this plan:
Thus she finds, when, perhaps, it is too late, that she has entertained wrong notions
of human nature; that her friends are deceitful—her lovers false—and that men
consult interest oftener than honesty.

"A young lady who has imbibed her ideas of the world from desultory reading,
and placed confidence on the virtue of others, will bring back disappointment, when
she expected gratitude. Unsuspicious of deceit, she is easily deceived—from the purity
of her own thoughts, she trusts the faith of mankind, until experience convinces her
of her errour—she falls a sacrifice to her credulity, and her only consolation is the
simplicity and goodness of her heart.

"The story of Miss Whitman[1] is an emphatical illustration of the truth of these
observations. An inflated fancy, not restricted by judgment, leads too often to *disappointment* and repentance. Such will be the fate of those who become (to use her own
words)

"Lost in the magick of that sweet employ,
"To build *gay scenes* and fashion *future joy.*"

"With a good heart she possessed a poetical imagination, and an unbounded thrift
for novelty; but these airy talents, not counterpoised with judgment, or perhaps serious
reflection, instead of adding to her happiness, were the cause of her ruin."

"I conclude from your reasoning," said I, "and it is, besides, my own opinion, that
many fine girls have been ruined by reading Novels."

[1] Brown here included a long and detailed note
about Elizabeth Whitman along with the text
of one of her poems.

"And I believe," added Mrs. Bourn "we may trace from hence the causes of spleen in many persons advanced in life."

"You mean old maids, Madam," cries the sagacious Miss, "like my aunt Deborah —she calls all the men deceitful, and most women, with her, are no better than they should be."

"Well said!" exclaimed Worthy, "the recollection of chagrin and former disappointment, sours one's temper and mortifies the heart—disappointment will be more or less severe in proportion as we elevate our expectations; for the most *sanguine tempers* are the soonest discouraged; as the highest building is in the most danger of falling."

"It appears from what I have said," resumed Mr. Holmes, "that those books which teach us a knowledge of the world are useful to form the minds of females, and ought therefore to be studied."

I mentioned Rochefoucault's maxims.—

"Do they not degrade human nature?" enquired my father.

"This little book," answered Worthy, "contains much truth—and those short sketches traced by the hand of judgment, present to us the leading features of mankind." "But," replied my father, "that *interest should assume all shapes,* is a doctrine, which, in my mind, represents a caricature rather than a living picture." "It is the duty of a painter to produce a likeness," said Worthy.—"And a skilful one," cried my father, continuing the metaphor, "will bring the amiable qualities of the heart to light; and throw those which disgrace humanity into the shade." "I doubt," rejoined Worthy, "whether this flattery will answer the purpose you aim to accomplish—You entertain a high opinion of *the dignity of human nature,* and are displeased at the author who advances any thing derogatory to that dignity. Swift, in speaking of these maxims, in one of his best poems, affirms,

"They argue no corrupted mind
"In him—the fault is in mankind."

"As I began this subject," added I, "it shall be ended by one observation—As these maxims give us an idea of the manners and characters of men, among whom a young person is soon to appear; and as it is necessary to her security and happiness that she be made acquainted with them—they may be read to advantage."

"There is another medium," said Mr. Holmes, assenting to my observation, "to be noticed in the study of a lady—she takes up a book, either for instruction or entertainment; the medium lies in knowing when to put it down. Constant application becomes labour—it sours the temper—gives an air of thoughtfulness, and frequently of absence. By *immoderate reading* we hoard up opinions and become insensibly attached to them; this miserly conduct sinks us to affectation, and disgustful pedantry; *conversation* only can remedy this dangerous evil, strengthen the judgment, and make reading really useful. They mutually depend upon, and assist each other.

"A knowledge of history which exhibits to us in one view the rise, progress and decay of nations—which points out the advancement of the mind in society, and the improvements in the arts which adorn human nature, comes with propriety under the notice of a lady. To observe the origin of civilization—the gradual progress of society, and the refinements of manners, policy, morality and religion—to observe the progression of mankind from simplicity to luxury, from luxury to effeminacy, and the gradual steps of the decline of empire, and the dissolution of states and kingdoms, must blend that happy union of instruction and entertainment, which never fails to win our attention to the pursuit of all subjects.

"Poetry claims her due from the ladies. Poetry enlarges and strengthens the mind, refines the taste and improves the judgment. It has been asserted that women have no business with *satire*—now satire is but a branch of poetry. I acknowledge, however, much false wit is sent into the world, under this general title; but no critick with whom I am acquainted ever called satire false wit—for so long as vice and folly continue to predominate in the human heart, the satirist will be considered as a useful member of society. I believe Addison calls him an auxiliary to the pulpit. Suffer me to enlarge on this *new idea*. Satire is the correction of the vices and follies of the human heart; a woman may, therefore, read it to advantage. What I mean by enforcing this point, is, to impress the minds of females with a principle of self correction; for among all kinds of knowledge which arise from reading, the duty of self knowledge is a very eminent one; and is at the same time, the most useful and important.

Our ordinary intercourse with the world, will present to us in a very clear point of view, the fallacious ideas we sometimes entertain of our own self knowledge.—We are blinded by pride and self love, and will not observe our own imperfections, which we blame with the greatest acrimony in other people, and seem to detest with the greatest abhorrence; so that it often happens, while we are branding our neighbour for some foible, or vanity, we ourselves are equally guilty.

"Ridiculous as this conduct must appear in the eyes of all judicious people, it is too frequently practised to escape observation.

"I will drop this piece of morality, with a charge to the fair reader, that whenever she discovers a satire, ridiculing or recriminating the follies or crimes of mankind, that she look into her own heart, and compare the strictures on the conduct of others with her own feeling."

1789

Susanna Haswell Rowson
1762–1824

An actress, businesswoman, journalist, editor, and educator, Susanna Rowson began her career as an English novelist and ended it as an American one. Her most famous book, *Charlotte Temple: A Tale of Truth,* first published in England in 1791, appeared three years later in the United States, where it went through three editions before 1800 and by 1810 had sold over fifty thousand copies. It is estimated that overall the novel has gone through some two hundred editions, taking both its own and its heroine's physical appearance through a spectrum of styles as period sensibilities changed: One late-nineteenth-century pulp edition featured Charlotte as "the Fastest Girl in New York."

In her preface to the novel, Mrs. Rowson insists on her tale's authenticity and didactic intentions, providing another early example of what was rapidly becoming a fixture of American fiction. Like Hannah Foster, she later founded an academy for young ladies, but unlike her sister novelist, she continued to write fiction that, as she notes throughout the prefaces to her many novels, never embarrassed her. In one of these prefaces (to *Trials of the Human Heart*) she writes:

> Though many a leisure hour has been amused and many a sorrowful one beguiled whilst, giving fancy the reins, I have applied myself to the pen, and it has ever been my pride that I never yet wrote a line that might tend to mislead the untutored judgment, or corrupt the inexperienced heart, and heaven forbid that I should suffer aught to escape my pen that might well call a blush to the cheek of innocence or deserve a glance of displeasure from the eye of the most rigid moralist.

Such good intentions did not prevent scores of tearful young admirers of Mrs. Rowson's heroine from visiting the "Charlotte Temple" gravesite in New York City and perhaps only confirm D. H. Lawrence's famous dictum that the "old American artists were hopeless liars," who, when they set out "to point a moral or adorn a tale," discovered that the tale had a tendency to point "the other way."

Further Reading:
W. Martin, "Profile: Susanna Rowson, Early American Novelist," *Women's Studies*, 1974.

Text:
Charlotte Temple: A Tale of Truth, 1897.

---

from Charlotte Temple: A Tale of Truth

The Author's Preface

For the perusal of the young and thoughtless of the fair sex this Tale of Truth is designed; and I could wish my fair readers to consider it as not merely the effusion of Fancy, but as a reality. The circumstances on which I have founded this novel were related to me some little time since by an old lady who had personally known Charlotte, tho she concealed the real names of the characters and likewise the place where the unfortunate scenes were acted: yet, as it was impossible to offer a relation to the public in such an imperfect state, I have thrown over the whole a slight veil of fiction, and substituted names and places according to my own fancy. The principal characters in this little tale are now consigned to the silent tomb: it can therefore hurt the feelings of no one, and may, I flatter myself, be of service to some who are so unfortunate as to have neither friends to advise or understanding to direct them through the various and unexpected evils that attend a young and unprotected woman in her first entrance into life.

While the tear of compassion still trembled in my eye for the fate of the unhappy Charlotte, I may have children of my own, said I, to whom this recital may be of use, and if to your own children, said Benevolence, why not to the many daughters of Misfortune who, deprived of natural friends or spoilt by a mistaken education, are thrown on an unfeeling world without the least power to defend themselves from the snares, not only of the other sex, but from the more dangerous arts of the profligate of their own?

Sensible as I am that a novel writer, at a time when such a variety of works are ushered into the world under that name, stands but a poor chance for fame in the annals of literature, but conscious that I wrote with a mind anxious for the happiness of that sex whose morals and conduct have so powerful an influence on mankind in general; and convinced that I have not wrote a line that conveys a wrong idea to the head, or a corrupt wish to the heart, I shall rest satisfied in the purity of my own intentions, and if I merit not applause, I feel that I dread not censure.

If the following tale should save one hapless fair one from the errors which ruined poor Charlotte, or rescue from impending misery the heart of one anxious parent, I shall feel a much higher gratification in reflecting on this trifling performance than could possibly result from the applause which might attend the most elegant, finished piece of literature whose tendency might deprave the heart or mislead the understanding.

1791

Royall Tyler
1757–1826

A lawyer and Chief Justice of the Supreme Court of Vermont (1807–1813), Royall Tyler was one of the first American writers to test the possibilities of a literary career in the new republic. He wrote on a wide variety of subjects for a number of newspapers and periodicals. His play *The Contrast,* produced in New York City in 1787, stimulated an independent American drama by featuring authentic native types who spoke in recognizable regional dialects. Between 1794 and 1811, Tyler collaborated with the editor and literary journalist Joseph Dennie (the "American Addison") on a satirical series of essays on American taste, style, and manners, written from a Federalist viewpoint, that claimed to originate from the "Shop of Colon and Spondee." In the midst of a successful legal career, Tyler found time to compose a great number of miscellaneous essays; literary, political, and social criticism; poems; fiction; and an autobiography.

In the following preface from *The Algerine Captive* (1797), a satirical novel that Tyler hoped would "display a portrait of New England, hitherto unattempted," the author observes the expanding domestic market for fiction and stresses the need for more "homespun" products.

Further Reading:
The Prose of Royall Tyler, ed. M. B. Péladeau, 1972.

Text:
The Algerine Captive, 1802.

---

from The Algerine Captive

Preface

One of the first observations the author of the following sheets made upon his return to his native country, after an absence of seven years, was the extreme avidity with which books of mere amusement were purchased and perused by all ranks of his countrymen. When he left New England, books of biography, travels, novels, and modern romances, were confined to our sea-ports; or, if known in the country, were read only in the families of clergymen, physicians, and lawyers: while certain funeral discourses, the last words and dying speeches of Bryan Shaheen, and Levi Ames, and some dreary somebody's Day of Doom, formed the most diverting part of the farmer's library. On his return from captivity, he found a surprising alteration in the public taste. In our inland towns of consequence, social libraries had been instituted, composed of books designed to amuse rather than to instruct; and country booksellers, fostering the new-born taste of the people, had filled the whole land with modern travels, and novels almost as incredible. The diffusion of a taste for any species of writing through all ranks, in so short a time, would appear impracticable to an European. The peasant of Europe must first be taught to read, before he can acquire a taste in letters. In New England, the work is half completed. In no other country are there so many people, who, in proportion to its numbers, can read and write; and, therefore, no sooner was a taste for amusing literature diffused, than all orders of country life, with one accord, forsook the sober sermons and practical pieties of their fathers, for the gay stories and splendid impieties of the traveller and the novelist. The worthy farmer no longer fatigued himself with Bunyan's Pilgrim up the 'hill of difficulty' or through the 'slough of despond,' but quaffed wine with Brydone in the hermitage of Vesuvius, or sported with Bruce on the fairy-land of Abyssinia:[1] while Dolly the dairy maid, and Jonathan the hired man, threw aside the ballad of the cruel step-mother, over which they had so often wept in concert, and now amused themselves into so agreeable a terror with the haunted houses and hobgoblins of Mrs. Ratcliffe,[2] that they were both afraid to sleep alone.

Although a love of literature, however frivolous, may be pleasing to the man of letters, yet there are two things to be deplored in it. The first is, that, while so many books are vended, they are not of our own manufacture. If our wives and daughters will wear gauze and ribbands, it is a pity they are not wrought in our own looms. The second misfortune is, that novels, being the picture of the times, the New England reader is insensibly taught to admire the levity, and often the vices, of the parent country. While the fancy is enchanted, the heart is corrupted. The farmer's daughter, while she pities the misfortune of some modern heroine, is exposed to the attacks of vice, from which her ignorance would have formed her surest shield. If the English novel does not inculcate vice, it at least impresses on the young female mind an erroneous idea of the world in which she is to live. It paints the manners, customs,

---

[1] Two examples of popular eighteenth-century travel books.
[2] Ann W. Radcliffe (1764–1823), English author of popular gothic fiction; her *Mysteries of Udolpho* appeared in 1794.

and habits, of a strange country; excites a fondness for false splendor; and renders the homespun habits of her own country disgusting.

There are two things wanted, said a friend to the author: that we write our own books of amusement, and that they exhibit our own manners. Why then do you not write the history of your own life? The first part of it, if not highly interesting, would at least display a portrait of New England manners, hitherto unattempted. Your captivity among the Algerines, with some notices of the manners of that ferocious race, so dreaded by commercial powers, and so little known in our country, would at least be interesting; and I see no advantage which the novel writer can have over you, unless your readers should be of the sentiment of the young lady mentioned by Addison in his Spectator, who, as he informs us, borrowed Plutarch's lives, and, after reading the first volume with infinite delight, supposing it to be a novel, threw aside the others with disgust, because a man of letters had inadvertently told her the work was founded on FACT.

1797

Hugh Henry Brackenridge
1748–1816

From the inception of the Republic, Americans have been lucky in the social critics who pull them up by their mental bootstraps. Many have been warm of temper, cool of brain, witty of tongue, and utterly devoted to exposing the follies of "the American way" of power politics. Hugh Henry Brackenridge was one of the first of our critic-humorists. Although far less well known than later writers in the same tradition, Brackenridge was a worthy precursor of Henry David Thoreau and Mark Twain. Like them, he claimed the job of needling his compatriots—getting them to ask whether they had the good sense life in the United States demands of its citizens. He performed this salutary task by concocting the six volumes of *Modern Chivalry* that hiccuped their way into print between 1792 and 1815. But before Brackenridge was ready to relate the adventures of his hero, Captain Farrago, he himself had to undergo many wanderings and a variety of experiences in the young country.

Brackenridge was born in Scotland in 1748. In 1753 he emigrated with his family to the frontier of Pennsylvania, where he shared the toil of other Scots-Irish pioneer-farmers. In his early teens he was studying Latin and Greek with local clergymen and trying his hand at writing humorous verse. By the time he was fifteen, he was teaching in his own school. In 1768, at twenty, he entered Princeton, where he was a classmate of Philip Freneau and James Madison. He formed an especially firm friendship with Freneau, who joined him in writing satires and fictional narratives. The commencement day poem Brackenridge composed with Freneau in 1771, "The Rising Glory of America," was a serious celebration of the future greatness of the American colonies. When it appeared in print in 1772, it caused little stir; the public was more concerned about the agitated state of political affairs with Great Britain than about encouraging talented young poets in its midst.

Between graduation from Princeton with a B.A. in 1771 and the start of the Revolutionary War, Brackenridge taught in a preparatory school, studied for the ministry, and wrote two patriotic plays. From 1776 to 1778 he served as a nonordained chaplain with the Continental Army. In 1778 he left the army and went to Philadelphia with great plans for starting a monthly magazine, but he lost his high hopes—and his savings—when *The United States Magazine* folded within the year.

At thirty-three Brackenridge left the city for the woods—the frontier village of Pittsburgh, where he practiced law, wrote for Freneau's *Freeman's Journal,* became a member of the state assembly, began the *Pittsburgh Gazette,* opened the town's first bookstore, and helped to found what later became the local university. This record of achievements might make Brackenridge's life appear to match Benjamin Franklin's as a model American success story—the self-made man whose vigor and intelligence become indispensable to his community. This was not the case. Franklin had the popular touch; at certain crucial moments in his career, Brackenridge did not. Franklin managed without offending his public to point up what happens when irresponsible citizens fail in their social duties. Brackenridge had the uncharming habit of calling people fools.

As his reputation grew, his political fortunes declined. A frontier people listened to the sarcastic critic of the unschooled, unwashed, unprincipled masses and heard only contempt for the voter. Branded a Federalist, an Easterner, and an elitist, Brackenridge left politics to concentrate on his faltering law practice and newspaper. It was many years before he regained public esteem, mended his finances, and was named to the state's supreme court. Brackenridge is still known to many who have not studied his writings as an enemy of the common citizen. Yet he was a true Jeffersonian democrat. His critics were unable to see that he detested fools whatever their social and economic class.

The disillusionment about the balance of power in American society that Mark Twain was to express a century later runs throughout *Modern Chivalry.* Its dominant theme, to be echoed in the work of James Fenimore Cooper, Henry David Thoreau, and William Faulkner, is the confrontation between the natural aristocrat and the plebians. Brackenridge was present at the very beginnings of the American political system; from the start he addressed the problems that arise when a government based on the popular will receives less than the full measure of the people's common sense and common decency. But rather than sermonize, Brackenridge had his own literary strategy. He presented his views through the observations of a testy yet amiable, somewhat naive yeoman farmer named Captain Farrago. Self-educated, opinionated, and idealistic, Farrago journeys through the countryside accompanied by his shrewd, opportunistic Irish servant, Teague O'Regan.

The narrative plan of *Modern Chivalry*—easygoing, unstructured, and episodic —allows Brackenridge to comment colloquially and whimsically on a wealth of events throughout a young America. Later Huckleberry Finn would find similar fools and rapscallions on a similar ramble through high and low places in the antebellum South. Like Huck in the middle of the coming century,

Brackenridge's Captain Farrago found that "modern chivalry" in the United States falls far short of the ideal. His accounts of American social and political fumbling after perfection remind us of the benefits of having native humorists with strong social consciences—of whom Henry Brackenridge was among the first.

Further Reading:
C. M. Newlin, *The Life and Writings of Hugh Henry Brackenridge*, 1932.
D. Marder, *Hugh Henry Brackenridge*, 1967.

Text:
Modern Chivalry, 1792.

from Modern Chivalry[*]

from **Chapter I**

John Farrago, was a man of about fifty-three years of age, of good natural sense, and considerable reading; but in some things whimsical, owing perhaps to his greater knowledge of books than of the world; but, in some degree, also, to his having never married, being what they call an old batchelor, a characteristic of which is, usually, singularity and whim. He had the advantage of having had in early life, an academic education; but having never applied himself to any of the learned professions, he had lived the greater part of his life on a small farm, which he cultivated with servants[¹] or hired hands, as he could conveniently supply himself with either. The servant that he had at this time, was an Irishman, whose name was Teague Oregan. I shall say nothing of the character of this man, because the very name imports what he was.

A strange idea came into the head of Captain Farrago about this time; for, by the bye, I had forgot to mention that having been chosen captain of a company of militia in the neighbourhood, he had gone by the name of Captain ever since; for the rule is, once a captain, and always a captain; but, as I was observing, the idea had come in to his head, to saddle an old horse that he had, and ride about the world a little, with his man Teague at his heels, to see how things were going on here and there, and to observe human nature. For it is a mistake to suppose, that a man cannot learn man by reading him in a corner, as well as on the widest space of transaction. At any rate, it may yield amusement. . . .

Chapter III

The Captain rising early next morning, and setting out on his way, had now arrived at a place where a number of people were convened, for the purpose of electing persons to represent them in the legislature of the state. There was a weaver who was a candidate to this appointment, and seemed to have a good deal of interest among

---

[*] From Volume I, published together with Volume II in 1792. Volumes III and IV came out in 1793 and 1797, respectively. Part II was published in 1804–1805.

[¹] I.e., indentured persons bound to service for a specified period of time.

the people. But another, who was a man of education, was his competitor. Relying on some talent of speaking which he thought he possessed, he addressed the multitude.

Said he, Fellow citizens, I pretend not to any great abilities; but am conscious to myself that I have the best good will to serve you. But it is very astonishing to me, that this weaver should conceive himself qualified for the trust. For though my acquirements are not great, yet his are still less. The mechanical business which he pursues, must necessarily take up so much of his time, that he cannot apply himself to political studies. I should therefore think it would be more answerable to your dignity, and conducive to your interest, to be represented by a man at least of some letters, than by an illiterate handicraftsman like this. It will be more honourable for himself, to remain at his loom and knot threads, than to come forward in a legislative capacity: because, in the one case, he is in the sphere where God and nature has placed him; in the other, he is like a fish out of water, and must struggle for breath in a new element.

Is it possible he can understand the affairs of government, whose mind has been concentered to the small object of weaving webs; to the price by the yard, the grist of the thread, and such like matters as concern a manufacturer of cloths? The feet of him who weaves, are more occupied than the head, or at least as much; and therefore the whole man must be, at least, but in half accustomed to exercise his mental powers. For these reasons, all other things set aside, the chance is in my favour, with respect to information. However, you will decide, and give your suffrages to him or to me, as you shall judge expedient.

The Captain hearing these observations, and looking at the weaver, could not help advancing, and undertaking to subjoin something in support of what had been just said. Said he, I have no prejudice against a weaver more than another man. Nor do I know any harm in the trade; save that from the sedentary life in a damp place, there is usually a paleness of the countenance: but this is a physical, not a moral evil. Such usually occupy subterranean apartments; not for the purpose, like Demosthenes,[2] of shaving their heads, and writing over eight times the history of Thucydides,[3] and perfecting a stile of oratory; but rather to keep the thread moist; or because this is considered but as an inglorious sort of trade, and is frequently thrust away into cellars, and damp outhouses, which are not occupied for a better use.

But to rise from the cellar to the senate house, would be an unnatural hoist. To come from counting threads, and adjusting them to the splits of a reed, to regulate the finances of a government, would be preposterous; there being no congruity in the case. There is no analogy between knotting threads and framing laws. It would be a reversion of the order of things. Not that a manufacturer of linen or woolen, or other stuff, is an inferior character, but a different one, from that which ought to be employed in affairs of state. It is unnecessary to enlarge on this subject; for you must all be convinced of the truth and propriety of what I say. But if you will give me leave to take the manufacturer aside a little, I think I can explain to him my ideas on the subject; and very probably prevail with him to withdraw his pretensions. The people seeming to acquiesce, and beckoning to the weaver, they drew aside, and the Captain addressed him in the following words:

Mr. Traddle, said he, for that was the name of the manufacturer, I have not the

---

[2] Famous orator of ancient Athens (384–322 B.C.).
[3] Athenian historian (ca. 460–400 B.C.) who wrote an account of the Peloponnesian War that set the standard for later histories.

smallest idea of wounding your sensibility; but it would seem to me, it would be more your interest to pursue your occupation, than to launch out into that of which you have no knowledge. When you go to the senate house, the application to you will not be to warp a web; but to make laws for the commonwealth. Now, suppose that the making these laws, requires a knowledge of commerce, or of the interests of agriculture, or those principles upon which the different manufactures depend, what service could you render. It is possible you might think justly enough; but could you speak? You are not in the habit of public speaking. You are not furnished with those common place ideas, with which even very ignorant men can pass for knowing something. There is nothing makes a man so ridiculous as to attempt what is above his sphere. You are no tumbler for instance; yet should you give out that you could vault upon a man's back; or turn head over heels, like the wheels of a cart; the stiffness of your joints would encumber you; and you would fall upon your backside to the ground. Such a squash as that would do you damage. The getting up to ride on the state is an unsafe thing to those who are not accustomed to such horsemanship. It is a disagreeable thing for a man to be laughed at, and there is no way of keeping ones self from it but by avoiding all affectation.

While they were thus discoursing, a bustle had taken place among the croud. Teague hearing so much about elections, and serving the government, took it into his head, that he could be a legislator himself. The thing was not displeasing to the people, who seemed to favour his pretensions; owing, in some degree, to there being several of his countrymen among the croud; but more especially to the fluctuation of the popular mind, and a disposition to what is new and ignoble. For though the weaver was not the most elevated object of choice, yet he was still preferable to this tatter-demalion, who was but a menial servant, and had so much of what is called the brogue on his tongue, as to fall far short of an elegant speaker.

The Captain coming up, and finding what was on the carpet, was greatly chagrined at not having been able to give the multitude a better idea of the importance of a legislative trust; alarmed also, from an apprehension of the loss of his servant. Under these impressions he resumed his address to the multitude. Said he, This is making the matter still worse, gentlemen: this servant of mine is but a bog-trotter;[4] who can scarcely speak the dialect in which your laws ought to be written; but certainly has never read a single treatise on any political subject; for the truth is, he cannot read at all. The young people of the lower class, in Ireland, have seldom the advantage of a good education; especially the descendants of the ancient Irish, who have most of them a great assurance of countenance, but little information, or literature. This young man, whose family name is Oregan, has been my servant for several years. And, except a too great fondness for women, which now and then brings him into scrapes, he has demeaned himself in a manner tolerable enough. But he is totally ignorant of the great principles of legislation; and more especially, the particular interests of the government. A free government is a noble possession to a people: and this freedom consists in an equal right to make laws, and to have the benefit of the laws when made. Though doubtless, in such a government, the lowest citizen may become chief magistrate; yet it is sufficient to possess the right; not absolutely necessary to exercise it. Or even if you should think proper, now and then, to shew your privilege, and exert, in a signal manner, the democratic prerogative, yet is it not descending too low

---

[4] Pejorative term for an Irish immigrant.

to filch away from me a hireling, which I cannot well spare, to serve your purpose. You are surely carrying the matter too far, in thinking to make a senator of this hostler; to take him away from an employment to which he has been bred, and put him to another, to which he has served no apprenticeship: to set those hands which have been lately employed in currying my horse, to the draughting bills, and preparing business for the house.

The people were tenacious of their choice, and insisted on giving Teague their suffrages; and by the frown upon their brows, seemed to indicate resentment at what has been said; as indirectly charging them with want of judgment; or calling in question their privilege to do what they thought proper. It is a very strange thing, said one of them, who was a speaker for the rest, that after having conquered Burgoyne[5] and Cornwallis,[6] and got a government of our own, we cannot put in it whom we please. This young man may be your servant, or another man's servant; but if we chuse to make him a delegate, what is that to you. He may not be yet skilled in the matter, but there is a good day a-coming. We will impower him; and it is better to trust a plain man like him, than one of your high flyers, that will make laws to suit their own purposes.

Said the Captain, I had much rather you would send the weaver, though I thought that improper, than to invade my household, and thus detract from me the very person that I have about me to brush my boots, and clean my spurs. The prolocutor of the people gave him to understand that his surmises were useless, for the people had determined on the choice, and Teague they would have, for a representative.

Finding it answered no end to expostulate with the multitude, he requested to speak a word with Teague by himself. Stepping aside, he said to him, composing his voice, and addressing him in a soft manner; Teague, you are quite wrong in this matter they have put into your head. Do you know what it is to be a member of a deliberate body? What qualifications are necessary? Do you understand any thing of geography? If a question should be, to make a law to dig a canal in some part of the state, can you describe the bearing of the mountains, and the course of the rivers? Or if commerce is to be pushed to some new quarter, by the force of regulations, are you competent to decide in such a case? There will be questions of law, and astronomy on the carpet. How you must gape and stare like a fool, when you come to be asked your opinion on these subjects? Are you acquainted with the abstract principles of finance; with the funding public securities; the ways and means of raising the revenue; providing for the discharge of the public debts, and all other things which respect the economy of the government? Even if you had knowledge, have you a facility of speaking. I would suppose you would have too much pride to go to the house just to say, Ay, or No. This is not the fault of your nature, but of your education; having been accustomed to dig turf[7] in your early years, rather than instructing yourself in the classics, or common school books.

When a man becomes a member of a public body, he is like a racoon, or other

---

[5] General John Burgoyne (1722–1792), known as Gentleman Johnny, the noted British military leader defeated in the Battle of Saratoga during the American Revolution.

[6] Charles Cornwallis (1735–1805), made the first marquis Cornwallis for his achievements as a general and statesman; he commanded the British army during the American Revolution but was forced to surrender to General George Washington after the Battle of Yorktown in 1781, which signaled the end of the war.

[7] The Irish traditionally use turf dug from bogs as fuel for their hearth-fires.

beast that climbs up the fork of a tree; the boys pushing at him with pitch-forks, or throwing stones, or shooting at him with an arrow, the dogs barking in the mean time. One will find fault with your not speaking; another with your speaking, if you speak at all. They will have you in the newspapers, and ridicule you as a perfect beast. There is what they call the caricatura; that is, representing you with a dog's head, or a cat's claw. As you have a red head, they will very probably make a fox of you, or a sorrel horse, or a brindled cow. It is the devil in hell to be exposed to the squibs and crackers of the gazette wits and publications. You know no more about these matters than a goose; and yet you would undertake rashly, without advice, to enter on the office; nay, contrary to advice. For I would not for a thousand guineas, though I have not the half of it to spare, that the breed of the Oregans should come to this; bringing on them a worse stain than stealing sheep; to which they are addicted. You have nothing but your character, Teague, in a new country to depend upon. Let it never be said, that you quitted an honest livelihood, the taking care of my horse, to follow the new fangled whims of the times, and to be a statesman.

Teague was moved chiefly with the last part of the address, and consented to give up the object.

The Captain, glad of this, took him back to the people, and announced his disposition to decline the honour which they had intended him.

Teague acknowledged that he had changed his mind, and was willing to remain in a private station.

The people did not seem well pleased with the Captain; but as nothing more could be said about the matter, they turned their attention to the weaver, and gave him their suffrages.

Chapter IV

Captain Farrago leaving this place, proceeded on his way; and at the distance of a mile or two, met a man with a bridle in his hand; who had lost a horse, and had been at a conjurer's to make enquiry, and recover his property.

It struck the mind of the Captain to go to this conjuring person, and make a demand of him, what was the cause that the multitude were so disposed to elevate the low to the highest station. He had rode but about a mile, when the habitation of the conjurer, by the direction and description of the man who had lost the horse had given, began to be in view. Coming up to the door, and enquiring if that was not where conjurer Kolt lived, they were answered Yes. Accordingly alighting, and entering the domicile, all those things took place which usually happen, or are described in cases of this nature, viz. there was the conjurer's assistant, who gave the Captain to understand that master had withdrawn a little, but would be in shortly.

In the mean time, the assistant endeavoured to draw from him some account of the occasion of his journey; which the other readily communicated; and the conjurer, who was listening through a crack in the partition, overheard. Finding it was not a horse or a cow, or a piece of linen that was lost, but an abstract question of political philosophy which was to be put, he came from his lurking place, and entered, as if not knowing that any person had been waiting for him.

After mutual salutations, the Captain gave him to understand the object which he had in view by calling on him.

Said the conjurer, This lies not at all in my way. If it had been a dozen of spoons, or a stolen watch, that you had to look for, I could very readily, by the assistance of my art, have assisted you in the recovery; but as to this matter of man's imaginations and attachments in political affairs, I have no more understanding than another man.

It is very strange, said the Captain, that you who can tell by what means a thing is stolen, and the place where it is deposited, though at a thousand miles distance, should know so little of what is going on in the breast of man, as not to be able to develope his secret thoughts, and the motives of his actions.

It is not of our business, said the other; but should we undertake it, I do not see that it would be very difficult to explain all that puzzles you at present. There is no need of a conjurer to tell why it is that the common people are more disposed to trust one of their own class, than those who may affect to be superior. Besides, there is a certain pride in man, which leads him to elevate the low, and pull down the high. There is a kind of creating power exerted in making a senator of an unqualified person; which when the author has done, he exults over the work, and like the Creator himself when he made the world, sees that "it is very good." Moreover, there is in every government a patrician class, against whom the spirit of the multitude naturally militates: And hence a perpetual war; the aristocrats endeavouring to detrude the people, and the people contending to obtrude themselves. And it is right it should be so; for by this fermentation, the spirit of democracy is kept alive.

The Captain, thanking him for his information, asked him what was to pay; at the same time pulling out half a crown from a green silk purse which he had in his breeches pocket. The conjurer gave him to understand, that as the solution of these difficulties was not within his province, he took nothing for it. The Captain expressing his sense of his disinterested service, bade him adieu.

Chapter V: Containing Reflections

A democracy is beyond all question the freest government: because under this, every man is equally protected by the laws, and has equally a voice in making them. But I do not say an equal voice; because some men have stronger lungs than others, and can express more forcibly their opinions of public affairs. Others, though they may not speak very loud, yet have a faculty of saying more in a short time; and even in the case of others, who speak little or none at all, yet what they do say containing good sense, comes with greater weight; so that all things considered, every citizen, has not, in this sense of the word, an equal voice. But the right being equal, what great harm if it is unequally exercised? is it necessary that every man should become a statesman? No more than that every man should become a poet or a painter. The sciences, are open to all; but let him only who has taste and genius pursue them. If any man covets the office of a bishop, says St. Paul, he covets a good work. But again, he adds this caution, Ordain not a novice, lest being lifted up with pride, he falls into the condemnation of the devil. It is indeed making a devil of a man to lift him up to a state to which he is not suited. A ditcher is a respectable character, with his over-alls on, and a spade in his hand; but put the same man to those offices which require the head whereas he has been accustomed to impress with his foot, and there appears a contrast between the individual and the occupation.

There are individuals in society, who prefer honour to wealth or cultivate political studies as a branch of literary pursuits; and offer themselves to serve public bodies, in order to have an opportunity of discovering their knowledge, and exercising their judgment. It must be chagrining to these, and hurtful to the public, to see those who have no talent this way, and ought to have no taste, preposterously obtrude themselves upon the government. It is the same as if a brick-layer should usurp the office of a taylor and come with his square and perpendicular, to take the measure of a pair of breeches.

It is proper that those who cultivate oratory, should go to the house of orators. But for an Ay and No man to be ambitious of that place, is to sacrifice his credit to his vanity.

I would not mean to insinuate that legislators are to be selected from the more wealthy of the citizens, yet a man's circumstances ought to be such as afford him leisure for study and reflection. There is often wealth without taste or talent. I have no idea, that because a man lives in a great house and has a cluster of bricks or stones about his backside, that he is therefore fit for a legislator. There is so much pride and arrogance with those who consider themselves the first in a government, that it deserves to be checked by the populace, and the evil most usually commences on this side. Men associate with their own persons, the adventitious circumstances of birth and fortune: So that a fellow blowing with fat and repletion, conceives himself superior to the poor lean man, that lodges in an inferior mansion. But as in all cases, so in this, there is a medium. Genius and virtue are independent of rank and fortune; and it is neither the opulent, nor the indigent, but the man of ability and integrity that ought to be called forth to serve his country: and while, on the one hand, the aristocratic part of the government, arrogates a right to represent; on the other hand, the democratic contends the point; and from this conjunction and opposition of forces, there is produced a compound resolution, which carries the object in an intermediate direction. When we see therefore, a Teague Oregan lifted up, the philosopher will reflect, that it is to balence some purse-proud fellow, equally as ignorant, that comes down from the sphere of aristocratic interest.

But every man ought to consider for himself, whether it is his use to be this draw-back, on either side. For as when good liquor is to be distilled, you throw in some material useless in itself to correct the effervescence of the spirit; so it may be his part to act as a sedative. For though we commend the effect, yet still the material retains but its original value.

But as the nature of things is such, let no man who means well to the common-wealth, and offers to serve it, be hurt in his mind when some one of meaner talents is preferred. The people are a sovereign, and greatly despotic; but, in the main, just.

I have a great mind, in order to elevate the composition, to make quotations from the Greek and Roman history. And I am conscious to myself, that I have read the writers on the government of Italy and Greece, in ancient, as well as in modern times. But I have drawn a great deal more from reflection on the nature of things, than from all the writings I have ever read. Nay, the history of the election, which I have just given, will afford a better lesson to the American mind, than all that is to be found in other examples. We have seen here, a weaver a favoured candidate, and in the next instance, a bog-trotter superseding him. Now it may be said, that this is fiction; but fiction, or no fiction, the nature of the thing will make it a reality. But I return to the adventures of the Captain, whom I have upon my hands; and who, as far as I can yet discover, is a good honest man; and means what is benevolent and useful; though his ideas may not comport with the ordinary manner of thinking, in every particular.

1792

Charles Brockden Brown
1771–1810

While traveling across the United States in 1879, Robert Louis Stevenson noted:

> In this society, more than any other that ever I was in, it was the narrator alone who seemed to enjoy the narrative. It was rarely that anyone listened for the listening. If he lent an ear to another man's story, it was because he was in immediate want of a hearer for one of his own.

Had he been reading Charles Brockden Brown's fiction during his trip, Stevenson would have found ample literary confirmation of his social observation. Certainly, few novelists have relied so heavily as Brown on the monologues of obsessive storytellers: "It was impossible to be incommunicative," claims a character in defense of his own loquacity. In a Brown novel, moreover, nearly every character has a stake in the total narrative since each has an urgent tale that must be told. At times, narrative and life force seem identical: As the narrator of *Weiland* says, "When I lay down the pen the taper of life will expire; my existence will terminate with my tale." Tales generate more tales, all of which eventually wrap around each other so mysteriously that the reader occasionally loses both the direction of the narrative and the identity of the narrator. In Brown's most ambitious novel, *Arthur Mervyn,* the original narrator soon gives way to a second, who in the course of his own story soon drifts into the autobiography of a third. In such a fictional world, the problems of narrative reliability become all-engrossing as characters move disconcertingly back and forth between the roles of narrators and listeners.

Brown's bewildering narratives result partly from artistic intention, partly from inexperience, carelessness, and insecurity. He thought of himself as making an original contribution to fiction ("calling forth the passions and engaging the sympathy of the reader, by means hitherto unemployed") and was conscious that he lacked literary models for what he wanted to accomplish. He wrote most of his fiction at an incredible speed (four novels published within a year), and by working on more than one novel at a time he inadvertently allowed characters and events from one book to filter into another. Also, as an early American novelist attempting to win the approval of a largely unidentified reading public to whom fiction seemed merely a matter of straightforward seduction stories for young ladies, Brown naturally felt a great deal of insecurity about his role. Never sure of his audience, he anxiously—following the lead of epistolary novelists—created along with his compulsive narrators a reassuring number of compulsive listeners.

Born into a Philadelphia Quaker family in 1771, Brown attended the prestigious Friends' Latin School and at sixteen took up the study of law, which he abandoned a few years later for a far more precarious career in literature. To the American literary historian Van Wyck Brooks, Brown represented "the first American writer who made a profession of letters and never turned aside from the path he had chosen." After making a small name for himself in Philadelphia literary circles as the young author of a series of stilted essays entitled "The Rhapsodist," he traveled to New York, where he met a number of influential Federalist writers, including Timothy Dwight and one of the Yale president's favorite pupils, Elihu Hubbard Smith, a physician and the editor of America's first poetry anthology. He also met his future biographer, William Dunlap, the highly versatile dramatist, painter, and art historian, who introduced him to German theater and poetry. In 1798, sharing rooms in New York City with Elihu Smith, Brown survived a yellow fever epidemic but never forgot the experience of watching his close friend die of the disease.

Brown had also survived the disastrous outbreak of yellow fever in Philadelphia in 1793, a historical moment to which he gives compelling fictional shape in the first part of *Arthur Mervyn,* which he brought out in 1798. Yellow fever fascinated Brown, both as a representation of senseless malignity and as a grisly experience of urban life. As a theme, the plague worked perfectly with the strains of gothic horror and scientific realism that Brown, anticipating Edgar Allen Poe, tried to fuse in his fiction. In 1798 he also published *Alcuin,* a dialogue on women's rights arguing for greater sexual freedom and the overhaul of obsolete marriage laws, radical views he would later exchange for more conservative notions. In this year too appeared his tightest, most successful novel, *Weiland,* an eerie tale of religious delusion and mass murder based on newspaper accounts of an ugly incident on the New York frontier. In the following year Brown issued two more novels, *Ormond,* a story of masculine monomania defeated by feminist bravery, and *Edgar Huntly,* a tale of sleepwalking, murder, and dehumanization which introduced into American fiction the wilderness theme that James Fenimore Cooper would later turn into myth.

With the publication of the second half of *Arthur Mervyn* in 1800, Brown seemed to have burned himself out as a novelist. Sick, exhausted, penniless, acutely sensitive to his lack of American readers, he tossed off in 1801 his last two novels, *Clara Howard* and *Jane Talbot,* desperately trying to find his way into the growing market for sentimental women's fiction—the market about which Hawthorne, Melville, and James would eventually grumble and rage. Finally, except for a few scattered tales, he gave up on fiction altogether and began to devote himself exclusively to magazine editing.

He had started in 1799 *The Monthly Magazine and American Review,* but that had folded before the year was out. In 1803 he discovered a talent for political controversy by bringing out pamphlets arguing passionately in favor of the Louisiana Purchase and American claims to the Mississippi. That year he also began publication of *The Literary Magazine and American Register,* a periodical he maintained until 1806, when he launched the semiannual *American Register, or General Repository of History, Politics, and Science,* which he edited almost single-handedly until his death in 1810. In his last years Brown turned more and more to writing history. Had he lived longer, he would undoubtedly have joined the ranks of Henry Adams, and it is not surprising that one of the earliest biographic appreciations of his career was prepared by one of America's most eminent historians, William H. Prescott.

For all his stylistic and structural faults—and they can be formidable—Brown nevertheless produced in a very short time a solid amount of powerful and compelling fiction. He took the American novel into new geographic and moral territories, and his genius, commended by Shelley for its humanitarian sympathies and by Keats for its "accomplish'd horror," presided over the future course of American fiction. To read his four chief novels and the handful of tales is to venture into a hallucinatory landscape inhabited by sleepwalkers, ventriloquists, prostitutes, plague victims, murderers, imposters, counterfeiters, pietists, harmless lunatics, dangerous monomaniacs, and crazed visionaries. In this psychological landscape, Franklin's morally perfectible creature continually clashes with Edwards's "loathsome insect over the fire." Our attempts to do good as often as not backfire, producing far greater misery than they had ever intended to alleviate. Men and women sincerely motivated by benevolence and schemes of social justice learn, as does Clara Weiland, that "ideas exist in our minds that can be accounted for by no established laws."

Further Reading:
H. R. Warfel, *Charles Brockden Brown: American Gothic Novelist*, 1949.
D. A. Ringe, *Charles Brockden Brown*, 1966.
A. Axelrod, *Charles Brockden Brown: An American Tale*, 1983.

Text:
Edgar Huntly; or Memoirs of a Sleepwalker, ed. David Stineback, 1973.
See also *Charles Brockden Brown's Novels*, 6 vols., 1963.

from Edgar Huntly; or Memoirs of a Sleepwalker

To the Public.

The flattering reception that has been given, by the public, to Arthur Mervyn, has prompted the writer to solicit a continuance of the same favor, and to offer to the world a new performance.

America has opened new views to the naturalist and politician, but has seldom furnished themes to the moral painter. That new springs of action and new motives to curiosity should operate,—that the field of investigation, opened to us by our own country, should differ essentially from those which exist in Europe,—may be readily conceived. The sources of amusement to the fancy and instruction to the heart, that are peculiar to ourselves, are equally numerous and inexhaustible. It is the purpose of this work to profit by some of these sources; to exhibit a series of adventures, growing out of the condition of our country and connected with one of the most common and most wonderful diseases or affections of the human frame.

One merit the writer may at least claim: that of calling forth the passions and engaging the sympathy of the reader by means hitherto unemployed by preceding authors. Puerile superstition and exploded manners, Gothic castles and chimeras, are the materials usually employed for this end. The incidents of Indian hostility and the perils of the Western wilderness are far more suitable; and for a native of America to overlook these would admit of no apology. These, therefore, are, in part, the ingredients of this tale, and these he has been ambitious of depicting in vivid and faithful colors. The success of his efforts must be estimated by the liberal and candid reader.

C.B.B.

XVI: [In the Cave]¹

Here, my friend, thou must permit me to pause. The following incidents are of a kind to which the most ardent invention has never conceived a parallel. Fortune, in her most wayward mood, could scarcely be suspected of an influence like this. The scene was pregnant with astonishment and horror. I cannot, even now, recall it without reviving the dismay and confusion which I then experienced.

Possibly, the period will arrive when I shall look back without agony on the perils I have undergone. That period is still distant. Solitude and sleep are now no more than the signals to summon up a tribe of ugly phantoms. Famine, and blindness, and death, and savage enemies, never fail to be conjured up by the silence and darkness of the night. I cannot dissipate them by any efforts of reason. My cowardice requires the perpetual consolation of light. My heart droops when I mark the decline of the sun, and I never sleep but with candle burning at my pillow. If, by any chance, I should awake and find myself immersed in darkness, I know not what act of desperation I might be suddenly impelled to commit.

I have delayed this narrative longer than my duty to my friend enjoined. Now that I am able to hold a pen, I will hasten to terminate that uncertainty with regard to my fate in which my silence has involved thee. I will recall that series of unheard-of and disastrous vicissitudes which has constituted the latest portion of my life.

I am not certain, however, that I shall relate them in an intelligible manner. One image runs into another; sensations succeed in so rapid a train, that I fear I shall be unable to distribute and express them with sufficient perspicuity. As I look back, my heart is sore, and aches with my bosom. I am conscious to a kind of complex sentiment of distress and forlornness that cannot be perfectly portrayed by words; but I must do as well as I can. In the utmost vigor of my faculties, no eloquence that I possess would do justice to the tale. Now, in my languishing and feeble state, I shall furnish thee with little more than a glimpse of the truth. With these glimpses, transient and faint as they are, thou must be satisfied.

I have said that I slept. My memory assures me of this; it informs me of the previous circumstances of my laying aside my clothes, of placing the light upon a chair within reach of my pillow, of throwing myself upon the bed, and of gazing on the rays of the moon reflected on the wall and almost obscured by those of the candle. I remember my occasional relapses into fits of incoherent fancies, the harbingers of sleep. I

---

¹ The narrative takes the form of a letter to Huntly's fiancée. The setting is rural Pennsylvania. The narrator, Edgar Huntly, has been obsessively pursuing a deranged Irish immigrant he suspects murdered his fiancée's brother. In the following episode, which Brown had originally published separately, Huntly, a sleepwalker, has just awakened in the pit of a cave. Thus begins a series of grisly adventures in which he confronts his most elemental instincts.

remember, as it were, the instant when my thoughts ceased to flow and my senses were arrested by the leaden wand of forgetfulness.

My return to sensation and to consciousness took place in no such tranquil scene. I emerged from oblivion by degrees so slow and so faint, that their succession cannot be marked. When enabled at length to attend to the information which my senses afforded, I was conscious for a time of nothing but existence. It was unaccompanied with lassitude or pain, but I felt disinclined to stretch my limbs or raise my eyelids. My thoughts were wildering and mazy, and, though consciousness was present, it was disconnected with the locomotive or voluntary power.

From this state a transition was speedily effected. I perceived that my posture was supine, and that I lay upon my back. I attempted to open my eyes. The weight that oppressed them was too great for a slight exertion to remove. The exertion which I made cost me a pang more acute than any which I ever experienced. My eyes, however, were opened; but the darkness that environed me was as intense as before.

I attempted to rise, but my limbs were cold, and my joints had almost lost their flexibility. My efforts were repeated, and at length I attained a sitting posture. I was now sensible of pain in my shoulders and back. I was universally in that state to which the frame is reduced by blows of a club, mercilessly and endlessly repeated; my temples throbbed, and my face was covered with clammy and cold drops; but that which threw me into deepest consternation was my inability to see. I turned my head to different quarters; I stretched my eyelids, and exerted every visual energy, but in vain. I was wrapped in the murkiest and most impenetrable gloom.

The first effort of reflection was to suggest the belief that I was blind; that disease is known to assail us in a moment and without previous warning. This, surely, was the misfortune that had now befallen me. Some ray, however fleeting and uncertain, could not fail to be discerned, if the power of vision were not utterly extinguished. In what circumstances could I possibly be placed, from which every particle of light should, by other means, be excluded?

This led my thoughts into a new train. I endeavored to recall the past; but the past was too much in contradiction to the present, and my intellect was too much shattered by external violence, to allow me accurately to review it.

Since my sight availed nothing to the knowledge of my condition, I betook myself to other instruments. The element which I breathed was stagnant and cold. The spot where I lay was rugged and hard. I was neither naked nor clothed: a shirt and trousers composed my dress, and the shoes and stockings, which always accompanied these, were now wanting. What could I infer from this scanty garb, this chilling atmosphere, this stony bed?

I had awakened as from sleep. What was my condition when I fell asleep? Surely it was different from the present. Then I inhabited a lightsome chamber and was stretched upon a down bed; now I was supine upon a rugged surface and immersed in palpable obscurity. Then I was in perfect health; now my frame was covered with bruises and every joint was racked with pain. What dungeon or den had received me, and by whose command was I transported hither?

After various efforts I stood upon my feet. At first I tottered and staggered. I stretched out my hands on all sides, but met only with vacuity. I advanced forward. At the third step my foot moved something which lay upon the ground: I stooped and took it up, and found, on examination, that it was an Indian tomahawk. This incident afforded me no hint from which I might conjecture my state.

Proceeding irresolutely and slowly forward, my hands at length touched a wall. This, like the flooring, was of stone, and was rugged and impenetrable. I followed this wall. An advancing angle occurred at a short distance, which was followed by similar angles. I continued to explore this clue, till the suspicion occurred that I was merely going round the walls of a vast and irregular apartment.

The utter darkness disabled me from comparing directions and distances. This discovery, therefore, was not made on a sudden, and was still entangled with some doubt. My blood recovered some warmth, and my muscles some elasticity; but in proportion as my sensibility returned, my pains augmented. Overpowered by my fears and my agonies, I desisted from my fruitless search, and sat down, supporting my back against the wall.

My excruciating sensations for a time occupied my attention. These, in combination with other causes, gradually produced a species of delirium. I existed, as it were, in a wakeful dream. With nothing to correct my erroneous perceptions, the images of the past occurred in capricious combinations and vivid hues. Methought I was the victim of some tyrant who had thrust me into a dungeon of his fortress, and left me no power to determine whether he intended I should perish with famine, or linger out a long life in hopeless imprisonment. Whether the day was shut out by insuperable walls, or the darkness that surrounded me was owing to the night and to the smallness of those crannies through which daylight was to be admitted, I conjectured in vain.

Sometimes I imagined myself buried alive. Methought I had fallen into seeming death, and my friends had consigned me to the tomb, from which a resurrection was impossible. That, in such a case, my limbs would have been confined to a coffin, and my coffin to a grave, and that I should instantly have been suffocated, did not occur to destroy my supposition. Neither did this supposition overwhelm me with terror or prompt my efforts at deliverance. My state was full of tumult and confusion, and my attention was incessantly divided between my painful sensations and my feverish dreams.

There is no standard by which time can be measured but the succession of our thoughts and the changes that take place in the external world. From the latter I was totally excluded. The former made the lapse of some hours appear like the tediousness of weeks and months. At length, a new sensation recalled my rambling meditations, and gave substance to my fears. I now felt the cravings of hunger, and perceived that, unless my deliverance were speedily effected, I must suffer a tedious and lingering death.

I once more tasked my understanding and my senses to discover the nature of my present situation and the means of escape. I listened to catch some sound. I heard an unequal and varying echo, sometimes near and sometimes distant, sometimes dying away and sometimes swelling into loudness. It was unlike anything I had before heard, but it was evident that it arose from wind sweeping through spacious halls and winding passages. These tokens were incompatible with the result of the examinations I had made. If my hands were true, I was immured between walls through which there was no avenue.

I now exerted my voice, and cried as loud as my wasted strength would admit. Its echoes were sent back to me in broken and confused sounds and from above. This effort was casual, but some part of that uncertainty in which I was involved was instantly dispelled by it. In passing through the cavern on the former day, I have mentioned the verge of the pit at which I arrived. To acquaint me as far as was possible with the dimensions of the place, I had hallooed with all my force, knowing that sound is reflected according to the distance and relative positions of the substances from which it is repelled.

The effect produced by my voice on this occasion resembled, with remarkable exactness, the effect which was then produced. Was I, then, shut up in the same cavern? Had I reached the brink of the same precipice and been thrown headlong into that vacuity? Whence else could arise the bruises which I had received, but from my fall? Yet all remembrance of my journey hither was lost. I had determined to explore this cave on the ensuing day, but my memory informed me not that this intention had been carried into effect. Still, it was only possible to conclude that I had come hither on my intended expedition, and had been thrown by another, or had, by some ill chance, fallen, into the pit.

This opinion was conformable to what I had already observed. The pavement and walls were rugged like those of the footing and sides of the cave through which I had formerly passed.

But if this were true, what was the abhorred catastrophe to which I was now reserved? The sides of this pit were inaccessible; human footsteps would never wander into these recesses. My friends were unapprised of my forlorn state. Here I should continue till wasted by famine. In this grave should I linger out a few days in unspeakable agonies, and then perish forever.

The inroads of hunger were already experienced; and this knowledge of the desperateness of my calamity urged me to frenzy. I had none but capricious and unseen fate to condemn. The author of my distress, and the means he had taken to decoy me hither, were incomprehensible. Surely my senses were fettered or depraved by some spell. I was still asleep, and this was merely a tormenting vision; or madness had seized me, and the darkness that environed and the hunger that afflicted me existed only in my own distempered imagination.

The consolation of these doubts could not last long. Every hour added to the proof that my perceptions were real. My hunger speedily became ferocious. I tore the linen of my shirt between my teeth and swallowed the fragments. I felt a strong propensity to bite the flesh from my arm. My heart overflowed with cruelty, and I pondered on the delight I should experience in rending some living animal to pieces, and drinking its blood and grinding its quivering fibers between my teeth.

This agony had already passed beyond the limits of endurance. I saw that time, instead of bringing respite or relief, would only aggravate my wants, and that my only remaining hope was to die before I should be assaulted by the last extremes of famine. I now recollected that a tomahawk was at hand, and rejoiced in the possession of an instrument by which I could so effectually terminate my sufferings.

I took it in my hand, moved its edge over my fingers, and reflected on the force that was required to make it reach my heart. I investigated the spot where it should enter, and strove to fortify myself with resolution to repeat the stroke a second or third time, if the first should prove insufficient. I was sensible that I might fail to inflict a mortal wound, but delighted to consider that the blood which would be made to flow would finally release me, and that meanwhile my pains would be alleviated by swallowing this blood.

You will not wonder that I felt some reluctance to employ so fatal though indispensable a remedy. I once more ruminated on the possibility of rescuing myself by other means. I now reflected that the upper termination of the wall could not be an immeasurable distance from the pavement. I had fallen from a height; but if that height had been considerable, instead of being merely bruised, should I not have been dashed into pieces?

Gleams of hope burst anew upon my soul. Was it not possible, I asked, to reach the top of this pit? The sides were rugged and uneven. Would not their projectures and abruptnesses serve me as steps by which I might ascend in safety? This expedient was to be tried without delay. Shortly my strength would fail, and my doom would be irrevocably sealed.

I will not enumerate my laborious efforts, my alternations of despondency and confidence, the eager and unwearied scrutiny with which I examined the surface, the attempts which I made, and the failures which, for a time, succeeded each other. A hundred times, when I had ascended some feet from the bottom, I was compelled to relinquish my undertaking by the *untenable* smoothness of the spaces which remained to be gone over. A hundred times I threw myself, exhausted by fatigue and my pains, on the ground. The consciousness was gradually restored that, till I had attempted every part of the wall, it was absurd to despair, and I again drew my tottering limbs and aching joints to that part of the wall which had not been surveyed.

At length, as I stretched my hand upward, I found somewhat that seemed like a recession in the wall. It was possible that this was the top of the cavity, and this might be the avenue to liberty. My heart leaped with joy, and I proceeded to climb the wall. No undertaking could be conceived more arduous than this. The space between this verge and the floor was nearly smooth. The verge was higher from the bottom than my head. The only means of ascending that were offered me were by my hands, with which I could draw myself upward so as, at length, to maintain my hold with my feet.

My efforts were indefatigable, and at length I placed myself on the verge. When this was accomplished, my strength was nearly gone. Had I not found space enough beyond this brink to stretch myself at length, I should unavoidably have fallen backward into the pit, and all my pains had served no other end than to deepen my despair and hasten my destruction.

What impediments and perils remained to be encountered I could not judge. I was now inclined to forebode the worst. The interval of repose which was necessary to be taken, in order to recruit my strength, would accelerate the ravages of famine, and leave me without the power to proceed.

In this state, I once more consoled myself that an instrument of death was at hand. I had drawn up with me the tomahawk, being sensible that, should this impediment be overcome, others might remain that would prove insuperable. Before I employed it, however, I cast my eyes wildly and languidly around. The darkness was no less intense than in the pit below, and yet two objects were distinctly seen.

They resembled a fixed and obscure flame. They were motionless. Though lustrous themselves, they created no illumination around them. This circumstance, added to others, which reminded me of similar objects noted on former occasions, immediately explained the nature of what I beheld. These were the eyes of a panther.

Thus had I struggled to obtain a post where a savage was lurking and waited only till my efforts should place me within reach of his fangs. The first impulse was to arm myself against this enemy. The desperateness of my condition was, for a moment, forgotten. The weapon which was so lately lifted against my own bosom was now raised to defend my life against the assault of another.

There was no time for deliberation and delay. In a moment he might spring from his station and tear me to pieces. My utmost speed might not enable me to reach him where he sat, but merely to encounter his assault. I did not reflect how far my strength was adequate to save me. All the force that remained was mustered up and exerted in a throw.

No one knows the powers that are latent in his constitution. Called forth by imminent dangers, our efforts frequently exceed our most sanguine belief. Though tottering on the verge of dissolution, and apparently unable to crawl from this spot, a force was exerted in this throw probably greater than I had ever before exerted. It was resistless and unerring. I aimed at the middle space between those glowing orbs. I penetrated the skull, and the animal fell, struggling and shrieking, on the ground.

My ears quickly informed me when his pangs were at an end. His cries and his convulsions lasted for a moment and then ceased. The effect of his voice, in these subterranean abodes, was unspeakably rueful.

The abruptness of this incident, and the preternatural exertion of my strength, left me in a state of languor and sinking, from which slowly and with difficulty I recovered. The first suggestion that occurred was to feed upon the carcass of this animal. My hunger had arrived at that pitch where all fastidiousness and scruples are at an end. I crept to the spot. I will not shock you by relating the extremes to which dire necessity had driven me. I review this scene with loathing and horror. Now that it is past I look back upon it as on some hideous dream. The whole appears to be some freak of insanity. No alternative was offered, and hunger was capable of being appeased even by a banquet so detestable.

If this appetite has sometimes subdued the sentiments of nature, and compelled the mother to feed upon the flesh of her offspring, it will not excite amazement that I did not turn from the yet warm blood and reeking fibers of a brute.

One evil was now removed, only to give place to another. The first sensations of fullness had scarcely been felt when my stomach was seized by pangs, whose acuteness exceeded all that I ever before experienced. I bitterly lamented my inordinate avidity. The excruciations of famine were better than the agonies which this abhorred meal had produced.

Death was now impending with no less proximity and certainty, though in a different form. Death was a sweet relief for my present miseries, and I vehemently longed for its arrival. I stretched myself on the ground. I threw myself into every posture that promised some alleviation of this evil. I rolled along the pavement of the cavern, wholly inattentive to the dangers that environed me. That I did not fall into the pit whence I had emerged must be ascribed to some miraculous chance.

How long my miseries endured, it is not possible to tell. I cannot even form a plausible conjecture. Judging by the lingering train of my sensations, I should conjecture that some days elapsed in this deplorable condition; but nature could not have so long sustained a conflict like this.

Gradually my pains subsided, and I fell into a deep sleep. I was visited by dreams of a thousand hues. They led me to flowing streams and plenteous banquets, which, though placed within my view, some power forbade me to approach. From this sleep I recovered to the fruition of solitude and darkness, but my frame was in a state less feeble than before. That which I had eaten had produced temporary distress, but on the whole had been of use. If this food had not been provided for me, I should scarcely have avoided death. I had reason, therefore, to congratulate myself on the danger that had lately occurred.

I had acted without foresight, and yet no wisdom could have prescribed more salutary measures. The panther was slain, not from a view to the relief of my hunger, but from the self-preserving and involuntary impulse. Had I foreknown the pangs to which my ravenous and bloody meal would give birth, I should have carefully abstained; and yet these pangs were a useful effort of nature to subdue and convert to nourishment the matter I had swallowed.

I was now assailed by the torments of thirst. My invention and my courage were anew bent to obviate this pressing evil. I reflected that there was some recess from this cavern, even from the spot where I now stood. Before, I was doubtful whether in this direction from this pit any avenue could be found; but, since the panther had come hither, there was reason to suppose the existence of some such avenue.

I now likewise attended to a sound, which, from its invariable tenor, denoted somewhat different from the whistling of a gale. It seemed like the murmur of a running stream. I now prepared to go forward and endeavor to move along in that direction in which this sound apparently came.

On either side, and above my head, there was nothing but vacuity. My steps were to be guided by the pavement, which, though unequal and rugged, appeared, on the whole, to ascend. My safety required that I should employ both hands and feet in exploring my way.

I went on thus for a considerable period. The murmur, instead of becoming more distinct, gradually died away. My progress was arrested by fatigue, and I began once more to despond. My exertions produced a perspiration, which, while it augmented my thirst, happily supplied me with imperfect means of appeasing it.

This expedient would, perhaps, have been accidentally suggested; but my ingenuity was assisted by remembering the history of certain English prisoners in Bengal,[2] whom their merciless enemy imprisoned in a small room, and some of whom preserved themselves alive merely by swallowing the moisture that flowed from their bodies. This experiment I now performed with no less success.

This was slender and transitory consolation. I knew that, wandering at random, I might never reach the outlet of this cavern, or might be disabled, by hunger and fatigue, from going farther than the outlet. The cravings which had lately been satiated would speedily return, and my negligence had cut me off from the resource which had recently been furnished. I thought not till now that a second meal might be indispensable.

To return upon my footsteps to the spot where the dead animal lay was a heartless project. I might thus be placing myself at a hopeless distance from liberty. Besides, my track could not be retraced. I had frequently deviated from a straight direction for the sake of avoiding impediments. All of which I was sensible was that I was travelling up an irregular acclivity. I hoped some time to reach the summit, but had no reason for adhering to one line of ascent in preference to another.

To remain where I was was manifestly absurd. Whether I mounted or descended,

[2] In 1756 a large group of Europeans was imprisoned in Calcutta in such a small guardhouse that most died of suffocation. Huntly recalls the famous account of one of the survivors of the "Black Hole" of Calcutta.

a change of place was most likely to benefit me. I resolved to vary my direction, and, instead of ascending, keep along the side of what I accounted a hill. I had gone some hundred feet when the murmur, before described, once more saluted my ear.

This sound, being imagined to proceed from a running stream, could not but light up joy in the heart of one nearly perishing with thirst. I proceeded with new courage. The sound approached no nearer, nor became more distinct; but, as long as it died not away, I was satisfied to listen and to hope.

I was eagerly observant if any the least glimmering of light should visit this recess. At length, on the right hand, a gleam, infinitely faint, caught my attention. It was wavering and unequal. I directed my steps towards it. It became more vivid and permanent. It was of that kind, however, which proceeded from a fire, kindled with dry sticks, and not from the sun. I now heard the crackling of flames.

This sound made me pause, or, at least, to proceed with circumspection. At length the scene opened, and I found myself at the entrance of a cave. I quickly reached a station, when I saw a fire burning. At first no other object was noted, but it was easy to infer that the fire was kindled by men, and that they who kindled it could be at no great distance.

XVII

Thus was I delivered from my prison, and restored to the enjoyment of the air and the light. Perhaps the chance was almost miraculous that led me to this opening. In any other direction, I might have involved myself in an inextricable maze and rendered my destruction sure; but what now remained to place me in absolute security? Beyond the fire I could see nothing; but, since the smoke rolled rapidly away, it was plain that on the opposite side the cavern was open to the air.

I went forward, but my eyes were fixed upon the fire; presently, in consequence of changing my station, I perceived several feet, and the skirts of blankets. I was somewhat startled at these appearances. The legs were naked, and scored into uncouth figures. The moccasins which lay beside them, and which were adorned in a grotesque manner, in addition to other incidents, immediately suggested the suspicion that they were Indians. No spectacle was more adapted than this to excite wonder and alarm. Had some mysterious power snatched me from the earth, and cast me, in a moment, into the heart of the wilderness? Was I still in the vicinity of my parental habitation, or was I thousands of miles distant?

Were these the permanent inhabitants of this region, or were they wanderers and robbers? While in the heart of the mountain, I had entertained a vague belief that I was still within the precincts of Norwalk. This opinion was shaken for a moment by the objects which I now beheld, but it insensibly returned; yet how was this opinion to be reconciled to appearances so strange and uncouth, and what measure did a due regard to my safety enjoin me to take?

I now gained a view of four brawny and terrific figures, stretched upon the ground. They lay parallel to each other, on their left sides, in consequence of which their faces were turned from me. Between each was an interval where lay a musket. Their right hands seemed placed upon the stocks of their guns, as if to seize them on the first moment of alarm.

The aperture through which these objects were seen was at the back of the cave, and some feet from the ground. It was merely large enough to suffer a human body to pass. It was involved in profound darkness, and there was no danger of being suspected or discovered as long as I maintained silence and kept out of view.

It was easily imagined that these guests would make but a short sojourn in this spot. There was reason to suppose that it was now night, and that, after a short repose, they would start up and resume their journey. It was my first design to remain shrouded in this covert till their departure, and I prepared to endure imprisonment and thirst somewhat longer.

Meanwhile my thoughts were busy in accounting for this spectacle. I need not tell thee that Norwalk is the termination of a sterile and narrow tract which begins in the Indian country. It forms a sort of rugged and rocky vein, and continues upwards of fifty miles. It is crossed in a few places by narrow and intricate paths, by which a communication is maintained between the farms and settlements on the opposite sides of the ridge.

During former Indian wars, this rude surface was sometimes traversed by the red men, and they made, by means of it, frequent and destructive inroads into the heart of the English settlements. During the last war, notwithstanding the progress of population, and the multiplied perils of such an expedition, a band of them had once penetrated into Norwalk, and lingered long enough to pillage and murder some of the neighboring inhabitants.

I have reason to remember that event. My father's house was placed on the verge of this solitude. Eight of these assassins assailed it at the dead of night. My parents and an infant child were murdered in their beds; the house was pillaged, and then burnt to the ground. Happily, myself and my two sisters were abroad upon a visit. The preceding day had been fixed for our return to our father's house; but a storm occurred, which made it dangerous to cross the river, and, by obliging us to defer our journey, rescued us from captivity or death.

Most men are haunted by some species of terror or antipathy, which they are, for the most part, able to trace to some incident which befell them in their early years. You will not be surprised that the fate of my parents, and the sight of the body of one of this savage band, who, in the pursuit that was made after them, was overtaken and killed, should produce lasting and terrific images in my fancy. I never looked upon or called up the image of a savage without shuddering.

I knew that, at this time, some hostilities had been committed on the frontier; that a long course of injuries and encroachments had lately exasperated the Indian tribes; that an implacable and exterminating war was generally expected. We imagined ourselves at an inaccessible distance from the danger; but I could not but remember that this persuasion was formerly as strong as at present, and that an expedition which had once succeeded might possibly be attempted again. Here was every token of enmity and bloodshed. Each prostrate figure was furnished with a rifled musket, and a leathern bag tied round his waist, which was, probably, stored with powder and ball.

From these reflections, the sense of my own danger was revived and enforced; but I likewise ruminated on the evils which might impend over others. I should, no doubt, be safe by remaining in this nook; but might not some means be pursued to warn others of their danger? Should they leave this spot without notice of their approach being given to the fearless and pacific tenants of the neighboring district, they might commit, in a few hours, the most horrid and irreparable devastation.

The alarm could only be diffused in one way. Could I not escape unperceived, and without alarming the sleepers, from this cavern? The slumber of an Indian is broken by the slightest noise; but, if all noise be precluded, it is commonly profound. It was possible, I conceived, to leave my present post, to descend into the cave, and issue forth without the smallest signal. Sleep usually comes at their bidding, and if, perchance, they should be wakeful at an unseasonable moment, they always sit upon their haunches, and, leaning their elbows on their knees, consume the tedious hours in smoking. My peril would be great. Accidents which I could not foresee, and over which I had no command, might occur to awaken someone at the moment I was passing the fire. Should I pass in safety, I might issue forth into a wilderness, of which I had no knowledge, where I might wander till I perished with famine, or where my footsteps might be noted and pursued and overtaken by these implacable foes. These perils were enormous and imminent; but I likewise considered that I might be at no great distance from the habitations of men, and that my escape might rescue them from the most dreadful calamities. I determined to make this dangerous experiment without delay.

I came nearer to the aperture, and had, consequently, a larger view of this recess. To my unspeakable dismay, I now caught a glimpse of one seated at the fire. His back was turned towards me, so that I could distinctly survey his gigantic form and fantastic ornaments.

My project was frustrated. This one was probably commissioned to watch and to awaken his companions when a due portion of sleep had been taken. That he would not be unfaithful or remiss in the performance of the part assigned to him was easily predicted. To pass him without exciting his notice (and the entrance could not otherwise be reached) was impossible. Once more I shrunk back, and revolved with hopelessness and anguish the necessity to which I was reduced.

This interval of dreary foreboding did not last long. Some motion in him that was seated by the fire attracted my notice. I looked, and beheld him rise from his place and go forth from the cavern. This unexpected incident led my thoughts into a new channel. Could not some advantage be taken of his absence? Could not this opportunity be seized for making my escape? He had left his gun and hatchet on the ground. It was likely, therefore, that he had not gone far, and would speedily return. Might not these weapons be seized, and some provision be thus made against the danger of meeting him without, or of being pursued?

Before a resolution could be formed, a new sound saluted my ear. It was a deep groan, succeeded by sobs that seemed struggling for utterance but were vehemently counteracted by the sufferer. This low and bitter lamentation apparently proceeded from someone within the cave. It could not be from one of this swarthy band. It must, then, proceed from a captive, whom they had reserved for torment or servitude, and who had seized the opportunity afforded by the absence of him that watched to give vent to his despair.

I again thrust my head forward, and beheld, lying on the ground, apart from the rest and bound hand and foot, a young girl. Her dress was the coarse russet garb of the country, and bespoke her to be some farmer's daughter. Her features denoted the last degree of fear and anguish, and she moved her limbs in such a manner as showed that the ligatures by which she was confined produced, by their tightness, the utmost degree of pain.

My wishes were now bent not only to preserve myself and to frustrate the future attempts of these savages, but likewise to relieve this miserable victim. This could only be done by escaping from the cavern and returning with seasonable aid. The sobs of the girl were likely to rouse the sleepers. My appearance before her would prompt her to testify her surprise by some exclamation or shriek. What could hence be predicted but that the band would start on their feet and level their unerring pieces at my head?

I know not why I was insensible to these dangers. My thirst was rendered by these delays intolerable. It took from me, in some degree, the power of deliberation. The murmurs which had drawn me hither continued still to be heard. Some torrent or cascade could not be far distant from the entrance of the cavern, and it seemed as if one draught of clear water was a luxury cheaply purchased by death itself. This, in addition to considerations more disinterested, and which I have already mentioned, impelled me forward.

The girl's cheek rested on the hard rock, and her eyes were dim with tears. As they were turned towards me, however, I hoped that my movements would be noticed by her gradually and without abruptness. This expectation was fulfilled. I had not advanced many steps before she discovered me. This moment was critical beyond all others in the course of my existence. My life was suspended, as it were, by a spider's thread. All rested on the effect which this discovery should make upon this feeble victim.

I was watchful of the first movement of her eye which should indicate a consciousness of my presence. I labored, by gestures and looks, to deter her from betraying her emotion. My attention was, at the same time, fixed upon the sleepers, and an anxious glance was cast toward the quarter whence the watchful savage might appear.

I stooped and seized the musket and hatchet. The space beyond the fire was, as I expected, open to the air. I issued forth with trembling steps. The sensations inspired by the dangers which environed me, added to my recent horrors, and the influence of the moon, which had now gained the zenith, and whose lustre dazzled my long-benighted senses, cannot be adequately described.

For a minute, I was unable to distinguish objects. This confusion was speedily corrected, and I found myself on the verge of a steep. Craggy eminences arose on all sides. On the left hand was a space that offered some footing, and hither I turned. A torrent was below me, and this path appeared to lead to it. It quickly appeared in sight, and all foreign cares were, for a time, suspended.

This water fell from the upper regions of the hill, upon a flat projecture which was continued on either side, and on part of which I was now standing. The path was bounded on the left by an inaccessible wall, and on the right terminated, at the distance of two or three feet from the wall, in a precipice. The water was eight or ten paces distant, and no impediment seemed likely to rise between us. I rushed forward with speed.

My progress was quickly checked. Close to the falling water, seated on the edge, his back supported by the rock, and his legs hanging over the precipice, I now beheld the savage who left the cave before me. The noise of the cascade and the improbability of interruption, at least from this quarter, had made him inattentive to my motions.

I paused. Along this verge lay the only road by which I could reach the water, and by which I could escape. The passage was completely occupied by this antagonist. To advance toward him, or to remain where I was, would produce the same effect.

I should, in either case, be detected. He was unarmed; but his outcries would instantly summon his companions to his aid. I could not hope to overpower him and pass him in defiance of his opposition. But, if this were effected, pursuit would be instantly commenced. I was unacquainted with the way. The way was unquestionably difficult. My strength was nearly annihilated; I should be overtaken in a moment, or their deficiency in speed would be supplied by the accuracy of their aim. Their bullets, at least, would reach me.

There was one method of removing this impediment. The piece which I held in my hand was cocked. There could be no doubt that it was loaded. A precaution of this kind would never be omitted by a warrior of this hue. At a greater distance than this, I should not fear to reach the mark. Should I not discharge it, and, at the same moment, rush forward to secure the road which my adversary's death would open to me?

Perhaps you will conceive a purpose like this to have argued a sanguinary and murderous disposition. Let it be remembered, however, that I entertained no doubts about the hostile designs of these men. This was sufficiently indicated by their arms, their guise, and the captive who attended them. Let the fate of my parents be, likewise, remembered. I was not certain but that these very men were the assassins of my family, and were those who had reduced me and my sisters to the condition of orphans and dependants. No words can describe the torments of my thirst. Relief to these torments, and safety to my life, were within view. How could I hesitate?

Yet I did hesitate. My aversion to bloodshed was not to be subdued but by the direst necessity. I knew, indeed, that the discharge of a musket would only alarm the enemies who remained behind; but I had another and a better weapon in my grasp. I could rive the head of my adversary, and cast him headlong, without any noise which should be heard, into the cavern.

Still I was willing to withdraw, to re-enter the cave, and take shelter in the darksome recesses from which I had emerged. Here I might remain, unsuspected, till these detested guests should depart. The hazards attending my re-entrance were to be boldly encountered, and the torments of unsatisfied thirst were to be patiently endured, rather than imbrue my hands in the blood of my fellowmen. But this expedient would be ineffectual if my retreat should be observed by this savage. Of that I was bound to be incontestably assured. I retreated, therefore, but kept my eye fixed at the same time upon the enemy.

Some ill fate decreed that I should not retreat unobserved. Scarcely had I withdrawn three paces when he started from his seat, and, turning towards me, walked with a quick pace. The shadow of the rock, and the improbability of meeting an enemy here, concealed me for a moment from his observation. I stood still. The slightest motion would have attracted his notice. At present, the narrow space engaged all his vigilance. Cautious footsteps, and attention to the path, were indispensable to his safety. The respite was momentary, and I employed it in my own defense.

How otherwise could I act? The danger that impended aimed at nothing less than my life. To take the life of another was the only method of averting it. The means were in my hand, and they were used. In an extremity like this, my muscles would have acted almost in defiance of my will.

The stroke was quick as lightning, and the wound was mortal and deep. He had not time to descry the author of his fate, but, sinking on the path, expired without a groan. The hatchet buried itself in his breast, and rolled with him to the bottom of the precipice.

Never before had I taken the life of a human creature. On this head I had, indeed, entertained somewhat of religious scruples. These scruples did not forbid me to defend myself, but they made me cautious and reluctant to decide. Though they could not withhold my hand when urged by a necessity like this, they were sufficient to make me look back upon the deed with remorse and dismay.

I did not escape all compunction in the present instance, but the tumult of my feelings was quickly allayed. To quench my thirst was a consideration by which all others were supplanted. I approached the torrent, and not only drank copiously, but laved my head, neck, and arms in this delicious element.

1799

Washington Irving
1783–1859

Washington Irving's life spans virtually all of American history and culture from the Revolution to the Civil War. Celebrated both at home and abroad as the dean of American letters, Irving lived to see his writings translated into twelve languages and printed in more than fifty different editions. His essays and sketches earned the respect of Europe's leading intellectuals and the praise of such prominent English writers as Coleridge, Byron, Scott, and Dickens. The influential London *Athenaeum* credited Irving with having declared America's literary independence. He was universally regarded, in the words of the Victorian novelist William Makepeace Thackeray, as "the first Ambassador whom the New World of Letters sent to the Old." Irving's immense popularity reflected his mastery of the leading aesthetic assumptions of the times. The Neoclassical wit and satire of his early essays and the Romantic interest in atmosphere and sentiment of his later sketches constitute a compendium of American literary taste in the first half of the nineteenth century. His anxieties as a writer offer an enlightening introduction to the cultural preoccupations of the new republic, and his accomplishments remain a harbinger of the literary achievements of the American Renaissance.

Washington Irving was born in New York's lower Manhattan in April 1783, a few days before Congress ratified the preliminary treaty ending the Revolutionary War; he was named after the war's most prominent hero. The youngest of eleven children, Irving grew up in a home bristling with Federalist sentiments and Calvinist principles; his father, a Scottish hardware merchant, is said to have "led the children to believe all pleasures were wicked." Although the New York of Irving's youth was hardly the bustling metropolis Walt Whitman would celebrate in *Leaves of Grass* (1855), the city's abundant supply of Dutch and British cultural traditions did provide this frail child with a great deal of fascinating folklore to explore. His relatively brief formal schooling took place in the city's private academies, but his more enduring education occurred along the city's streets and piers listening to merchants and seamen weave homespun tales of adventure and romance.

Washington Irving took a very early interest in writing and, much like Benjamin Franklin before him, modeled his first work on the familiar essays of Addison and Steele's *Spectator,* also publishing them under a pseudonym in the newspaper his brother edited. His first published writing, a series of nine essays written at the age of nineteen and printed over the signature "Jonathan, Oldstyle, Gent.," lightly satirizes American political, social, and literary provincialism and earned Irving modest critical attention. The pseudonym Irving used in these essays —a combination of the British nickname for American patriots and the name of the calendar abandoned by England and the colonies in 1752—reflects the lifelong tension he felt between the lure of literary nationalism and a reliance on European cultural forms.

Irving had studied law, but in 1803 he eagerly interrupted his work as a law clerk (he assisted the judge who had tried Aaron Burr for treason) to travel through the frontier of upper New York State and eastern Canada. The threat of tuberculosis prompted Irving's family to send him to Europe in 1804. In Rome he met the American painter Washington Allston and flirted with the idea of taking up art. His notebooks from this two-year tour reveal a burgeoning interest in writing and contain a wealth of material to be used later in his essays and sketches. He returned to the United States not only in better health but also with greater sensitivity to American provincialism. He was admitted to the New York bar in 1806, but, like such later distinguished American literary figures as James Russell Lowell and Sidney Lanier, Irving practiced in a desultory fashion, preferring to spend his time cultivating his interests in current political and cultural affairs and nurturing his friendships with several like-minded young professionals. This group, loosely assembled under such names as the Nine Worthies, the Ancient Club of New York, and (Irving's own favorite) the Lads of Kilkenny, consisted of well-to-do and well-read bachelors intent on displaying their wit and sophistication in New York's taverns and literary circles.

The spirit of this group is best represented in Irving's first major literary venture, *Salmagundi; or, the Whim-Whams and Opinions of Launcelot Langstaff, Esq., and Others* (1807–1808). Published in collaboration with his brother William and James Kirke Paulding, this series of twenty pocket-sized pamphlets was lightheartedly addressed to "critics, amateurs, dilettanti, and cognoscenti" and intended "to instruct the young, reform the old, correct the town, and castigate the age." They named their magazine after a spicy hash and developed it into a delightful intellectual potpourri of social criticism, literary reviews, and lampoons of the latest trends in politics and the theater. Yet each issue also contained a healthy measure of self-parody; the editors recognized they could be as naive and sentimental about progress as the people they ridiculed.

The immediate success of *Salmagundi* drew the attention of numerous writers. It quickly became the gravitational center of a literary circle that eventually became known as the Knickerbocker school. This group included such writers as Fitz-Greene Halleck, Joseph Rodman Drake, Samuel Woodworth, and the authors of such American popular classics as "Home, Sweet Home" (John Howard Payne) and "A Visit from St. Nicholas" (Clement Clark Moore).

William Cullen Bryant and James Fenimore Cooper were also identified with this "school." In virtually every case, however, the association of these writers was more geographic than aesthetic. But as soon as Washington Irving had published Diedrich Knickerbocker's *History of New York* (1809), the label would prove hard to escape.

A History of New York, from the Beginning of the World to the End of the Dutch Dynasty, by Diedrich Knickerbocker was intended as a burlesque of the methods of contemporary historians, more particularly those of Dr. Samuel Mitchell in his *Pictures of New York; or the Traveller's Guide through the Commercial Metropolis of the United States* (1807). The eight books of Irving's *History* provide a caustic view of New York's Dutch colonial history, interspersed with satiric portraits of current politics and literature, including Thomas Jefferson's vision of democracy and Joel Barlow's and Timothy Dwight's efforts to create epic poetry for the new republic. The book brought Irving extraordinary financial success, earning several thousand dollars in royalties at a time when nearly all authors had to underwrite the costs of publishing their work. Irving also enjoyed international acclaim; Sir Walter Scott praised the work in what undoubtedly were then extravagant terms: "I have never read anything so closely resembling the style of Dean Swift, as the annals of Diedrich Knickerbocker."

Irving remained a Federalist in politics and culture throughout his life. His critics accused him of being a dandy and an Anglophile whose American identity as a writer was more a matter of birth than sensibility. Yet Irving's early work had dealt directly—and most often satirically—with the issue most central to an American writer's identity, the absence of a native cultural tradition. Having exhausted what he saw as the possibilities of cultural satire, Irving lapsed into nearly a ten-year lull as a writer.

His prolonged literary silence is generally attributed to the psychological malaise that attended the death of his young fiancée, Matilda Hoffman, but more particularly it well may be the lingering result of what he viewed as the cultural vacuum in America. Irving filled these ten years with numerous, although irregular, activities. He traveled among the social circles of New York, Philadelphia, and Washington; he signed on as a partner in a brother's cutlery firm; he saw brief service as a staff adjutant in the War of 1812; he edited— anonymously—Philadelphia's *Analectic* magazine, in which he printed both excerpts from British periodicals and commissioned occasional essays.

What might be called the second phase of Irving's career began in 1815 with his second trip to Europe. He remained there for the next seventeen years. Ostensibly, Irving had traveled to Europe to help manage the Liverpool office of his family's importing business, but he may also have been seeking circumstances more conducive to his literary interests. Within three years, the family business had collapsed into bankruptcy and Irving had decided to gamble on making a living as a writer.

Irving's years in Europe regenerated his creative energies. Encouraged by Scott, Irving discovered the literary potential of the English countryside in the works of the Romantic poets. He resolved to adapt Europe's rich cultural heritage to American settings. The principal expression of this interest was *The Sketch Book* (1819–1820), a compendium of gracefully written familiar essays nostalgically surveying the traditions of English life ("The Christmas Dinner," "A Sunday in London," "Westminster Abbey"), along with six chapters on American scenes, including an essay on "Traits of Indian Character" and two Americanized renditions of European folktales, "Rip Van Winkle" and "The Legend of Sleepy Hollow." Published in several installments, *The Sketch Book* captured unprecedented attention for an American work. Irving had become the first American to command an international audience. As Geoffrey Crayon, the pseudonym he used in writing *The Sketch Book,* Irving had also become a literary celebrity. Although he was viewed slightly condescendingly by the English (as an American who writes as though he were English), he was lionized as a figure of national pride in the United States. *The Sketch Book* had answered one British critic's challenge: "In the four quarters of the globe, who reads an American book?"

Irving's accomplishments in *The Sketch Book* transcend his use of picturesque Hudson Valley local color to create a realistic context for stories adapted from European sources. "Rip Van Winkle" and "The Legend of Sleepy Hollow" also highlight concerns fundamental to appreciating American literary history: the role of the imagination in a society devoted to material progress, the marginal identity of the artist in American life, the sense of loss implicit in America's commitment to the present and future while neglecting the past, and the urgent need to establish a specifically American historical context. At the same time, *The Sketch Book* expresses the American writer's need to create what the critic Richard Poirier has called "a world elsewhere," a place (in this case Sleepy Hollow) where and a time (colonial America) when the imagination might flourish. Later American writers would locate this "world" in colonial Salem (Nathaniel Hawthorne), Walden Pond (Henry David Thoreau), the boundless ocean (Herman Melville), the splendid Mississippi (Mark Twain), and Yoknapatawpha County (William Faulkner), to name but a few.

Washington Irving spent the early 1820s searching the Continent for additional literary material, all the while enjoying the the literary status afforded him in London, Paris, Dresden, and Vienna. His next work, *Bracebridge Hall* (1822), an account of life in preindustrial England, contained little of the thematic focus and the stylistic energy of *The Sketch Book,* but it was equally well received. After collaborating with J. H. Payne on writing and producing several plays in France, Irving published—to uniformly discouraging reviews—*Tales of a Traveller* (1824), an unsuccessful blend of German and American folklore. Two unproductive years followed in France before he served as a diplomatic attaché in Spain (1826–1829). There he began translating Martin Fernández de Navarette's life of Columbus, recognizing in Columbus's life a predicament quite similar to his own as a figure torn between the Old World and the New. He soon abandoned the translation, immersed himself in archival records, and produced an erudite but popular *History of the Life and Voyages of Christopher Columbus* (1828), followed by *A Chronicle of the Conquest of Granada* (1829) and *The Alhambra* (1832), which the American historian William Hickling Prescott judged "a beautiful Spanish Sketch-Book." Before returning to the United States in 1832, Irving served for nearly three years as secretary to the American legation in London.

When challenged to explain whether his protracted absence from the United

States indicated that he had renounced his native land, Irving replied, "I am endeavouring to serve my country. Whatever I have written has been written with the feelings and published as the writing of an American. Is that renouncing my country? How else am I to serve my country—by coming home and begging an office of it: which I should not have the kind of talent or the business habits requisite to fill?—If I can do any good in this world it is with my pen." Irving's sense of dislocation, if not alienation, during his seventeen years in Europe anticipates the experiences of later American writers, including Henry James and the prominent figures in what has come to be known as the "Lost Generation": Ezra Pound, T. S. Eliot, Gertrude Stein, and Ernest Hemingway.

The final phase of Irving's career began with his triumphant return to the United States. He brought with him an honorary degree from Oxford, the medal of the Royal Society of Literature, and an international reputation unprecedented for an American writer. Soon after his arrival, he set out for a tour of the American South and West. The diary of his adventurous experiences on the Oklahoma frontier formed the basis for his autobiographical narrative *A Tour of the Prairies*, printed as the first volume of *The Crayon Miscellany* (1835). The book marks another significant shift in Irving's work, from the detached cynicism of Jonathan Oldstyle and the reserve of Geoffrey Crayon to direct authorial participation in *A Tour*. As Irving moves farther into the Plains, he gradually sheds his storyteller's distance and interest in romance and recounts each successive primitive incident with far less ironic detachment. The later portions of *A Tour* may be seen as Irving's own dramatic initiation into what are often the violent rituals of establishing a distinctively American identity.

Irving settled in New York for the decade following his western tour. He published two additional books based on this trip: *Astoria* (1836), an account of John Jacob Astor's fur-trading empire, and *The Adventures of Captain Bonneville, U.S.A.* (1837). He also cultivated his interests in antiquarian subjects and American biography. He declined invitations to run for election as mayor of New York City and later to serve as secretary of the navy under President Van Buren. But Irving did return to Europe in 1842 as minister to Spain, the first in a line of literary figures—including James Russell Lowell, Nathaniel Hawthorne, Bret Harte, and William Dean Howells—to serve their country as foreign ministers. After three years in Spain, Irving spent a year in London negotiating a diplomatic resolution to the Oregon question. He returned to the United States in 1846 and spent his last years at Sunnyside, his country retreat near Tarrytown, New York, to enjoy his literary preeminence and to continue writing.

Preoccupied with biography during his final years, Irving published a study of the English writer Oliver Goldsmith in 1840 and the two-volume *Mahomet and His Successors* in 1849 and 1850. In 1859, the year he died, Irving completed a massive five-volume biography of George Washington. He planned the biography as early as 1825 and had been absorbed in the details of Washington's life ever since. He recognized in Washington's life the instructive paradigm for the American experience that he judged the new nation needed. He regarded the project as something of a prose epic and as an opportunity for America to re-create a distinguished past for itself worthy of its imagined future greatness.

Washington Irving's career as a writer paralleled the new nation's as a culture.

His literary career reflects both the cultural anxiety of the new republic and its growing self-assurance in the years immediately preceding the Civil War. In this respect, Irving's work illustrates with striking clarity the early struggle of American culture to establish its autonomy. Many prominent American writers in the nineteenth century, from James Fenimore Cooper to Henry James, claimed that America lacked subject matter suitable for literature. Yet, as Irving's work suggests, the problem was not as much the paucity of American experience as it was that such experience was resistant to the European forms imposed on it. As Irving eventually discovered, the literary models available to American writers in the early decades of the nineteenth century were inappropriate—or inadequate— to the experiences they were expected to transform. This problem often left the literature of the new republic either fragmented or derivative. Irving's struggles with this problem illustrate rather than resolve America's efforts to establish cultural independence. Years before James Fenimore Cooper, Nathaniel Hawthorne, and Henry James investigated the nature of the American identity, Washington Irving recognized the artistic problems implicit in forging a distinctively new American prespective from inherited English traditions. Despite the derivative nature of a good deal of Irving's writing, he helped develop the American short story and secured the legitimacy of American authorship. Irving's work remains not only a hallmark of the new nation's literary tastes but also a projection of new patterns of vision responsive to a new cultural context.

Further Reading:
V. W. Brooks, *The World of Washington Irving*, 1944.
S. T. Williams, *Biography of Washington Irving*, 1935, 1979.
E. Wagenknecht, *Washington Irving: Moderation Displayed*, 1962.
L. Leary, *Irving*, 1963.
W. L. Hedges, *Washington Irving: An American Study, 1802–1832*, 1965.
D. Ringe, *The Pictorial Mode: Space and Time in the Art of Bryant, Irving, and Cooper*, 1971.
A. B. Myer, *Washington Irving: A Tribute*, 1972.
M. Roth, *Comedy and America: The Lost World of Washington Irving*, 1976.
A. B. Myer, *A Century of Commentary on the Works of Washington Irving*, 1976.
H. Springer, *Washington Irving: A Reference Guide*, 1976.

Text:
The Works of Washington Irving, 1860.
A definitive edition of Washington Irving's writing, under the general editorship of Richard Dilworth Rust, is scheduled for completion shortly.

from The Sketch Book[*]

The Author's Account of Himself

*"I am of this mind with Homer, that as the snaile that crept
out of her shel was turned eftsoons into a toad, and thereby was
forced to make a stoole to sit on; so the traveller that stragleth from
his owne country is in a short time transformed into so monstrous
a shape, that he is faine to alter his mansion with his manners,
and to live where he can, not where he would."*

Lyly's *Euphues*[1]

I was always fond of visiting new scenes, and observing strange characters and
manners. Even when a mere child I began my travels, and made many tours of
discovery into foreign parts and unknown regions of my native city, to the frequent
alarm of my parents, and the emolument of the town-crier. As I grew into boyhood,
I extended the range of my observations. My holiday afternoons were spent in rambles
about the surrounding country. I made myself familiar with all its places famous in
history or fable. I knew every spot where a murder or robbery had been committed,
or a ghost seen. I visited the neighboring villages, and added greatly to my stock of
knowledge, by noting their habits and customs, and conversing with their sages and
great men. I even journeyed one long summer's day to the summit of the most distant
hill, whence I stretched my eye over many a mile of terra incognita,[2] and was
astonished to find how vast a globe I inhabited.

This rambling propensity strengthened with my years. Books of voyages and
travels became my passion, and in devouring their contents, I neglected the regular
exercises of the school. How wistfully would I wander about the pierheads in fine
weather, and watch the parting ships, bound to distant climes—with what longing
eyes would I gaze after their lessening sails, and waft myself in imagination to the
ends of the earth!

Further reading and thinking, though they brought this vague inclination into
more reasonable bounds, only served to make it more decided. I visited various parts
of my own country; and had I been merely a lover of fine scenery, I should have felt
little desire to seek elsewhere its gratification, for on no country have the charms of
nature been more prodigally lavished. Her mighty lakes, like oceans of liquid silver;
her mountains, with their bright aerial tints; her valleys, teeming with wild fertility;
her tremendous cataracts, thundering in their solitudes; her boundless plains, waving
with spontaneous verdure; her broad deep rivers, rolling in solemn silence to the ocean;
her trackless forests, where vegetation puts forth all its magnificence; her skies,

---

[*] This essay and two others were originally
published in 1819–1820 as *The Sketch Book of
Geoffrey Crayon, Gent.,* which incorporates an
adopted pseudonym for Irving. *The Sketch Book*
was later revised and expanded to include 32
tales and sketches.

[1] From *Euphues and his England* (1580), a prose
romance by John Lyly (1554?–1606).
[2] Latin: "unknown land."

kindling with the magic of summer clouds and glorious sunshine;—no, never need an American look beyond his own country for the sublime and beautiful of natural scenery.

But Europe held forth the charms of storied and poetical association. There were to be seen the masterpiece of art, the refinements of highly-cultivated society, the quaint peculiarities of ancient and local custom. My native country was full of youthful promise: Europe was rich in the accumulated treasures of age. Her very ruins told the history of times gone by, and every mouldering stone was a chronicle. I longed to wander over the scenes of renowned achievement—to tread, as it were, in the footsteps of antiquity—to loiter about the ruined castle—to meditate on the falling tower—to escape, in short, from the common-place realities of the present, and lose myself among the shadowy grandeurs of the past.

I had, beside all this, an earnest desire to see the great men of the earth. We have, it is true, our great men in America: not a city but has an ample share of them. I have mingled among them in my time, and been almost withered by the shade into which they cast me; for there is nothing so baleful to a small man as the shade of a great one, particularly the great man of a city. But I was anxious to see the great men of Europe; for I had read in the works of various philosophers, that all animals degenerated in America, and man among the number.[3] A great man of Europe, thought I, must therefore be as superior to a great man of America, as a peak of the Alps to a highland of the Hudson; and in this idea I was confirmed, by observing the comparative importance and swelling magnitude of many English travellers among us, who, I was assured, were very little people in their own country. I will visit this land of wonders, thought I, and see the gigantic race from which I am degenerated.

It has been either my good or evil lot to have my roving passion gratified. I have wandered through different countries, and witnessed many of the shifting scenes of life. I cannot say that I have studied them with the eye of a philosopher; but rather with the sauntering gaze with which humble lovers of the picturesque stroll from the window of one print-shop to another; caught sometimes by the delineations of beauty, sometimes by the distortions of caricature, and sometimes by the loveliness of landscape. As it is the fashion for modern tourists to travel pencil in hand, and bring home their portfolios filled with sketches, I am disposed to get up a few for the entertainment of my friends. When, however, I look over the hints and memorandums I have taken down for the purpose, my heart almost fails me at finding how my idle humor has led me aside from the great objects studied by every regular traveller who would make a book. I fear I shall give equal disappointment with an unlucky landscape painter, who had travelled on the continent, but, following the bent of his vagrant inclination, had sketched in nooks, and corners, and by-places. His sketch-book was accordingly crowded with cottages, and landscapes, and obscure ruins; but he had neglected to paint St. Peter's, or the Coliseum; the cascade of Terni,[4] or the bay of Naples; and had not a single glacier or volcano in his whole collection.

---

[3] Georges Louis Leclerc de Buffon (1707–1788), a French naturalist, concluded that the American environment would cause the physical degeneration of European emigrants.

[4] Famous waterfalls in central Italy.

Rip Van Winkle[5]

A posthumous writing of Diedrich Knickerbocker

By Woden,[6] God of Sacons,
From whence comes Wensday, that is Wodensday.
Truth is a thing that ever I will keep
Unto thylke day in which I creep into
My sepulchre—
          Cartwright[7]

[The following Tale was found among the papers of the late Diedrich Knickerbocker, an old gentleman of New York, who was very curious in the Dutch history of the province, and the manners of the descendants from its primitive settlers. His historical researches, however, did not lie so much among books as among men; for the former are lamentably scanty on his favorite topics; whereas he found the old burghers, and still more their wives, rich in that legendary lore, so invaluable to true history. Whenever, therefore, he happened upon a genuine Dutch family, snugly shut up in its low-roofed farmhouse, under a spreading sycamore, he looked upon it as a little clasped volume of black-letter,[8] and studied it with the zeal of a book-worm.

The result of all these researches was a history of the province during the reign of the Dutch governors, which he published some years since. There have been various opinions as to the literary character of his work, and, to tell the truth, it is not a whit better than it should be. Its chief merit is its scrupulous accuracy, which indeed was a little questioned on its first appearance, but has since been completely established; and it is now admitted into all historical collections, as a book of unquestionable authority.

The old gentleman died shortly after the publication of his work, and now that he is dead and gone, it cannot do much harm to his memory to say that his time might have been much better employed in weightier labors. He, however, was apt to ride his hobby his own way; and though it did now and then kick up the dust a little in the eyes of his neighbors, and grieve the spirit of some friends, for whom he felt the truest deference and affection; yet his errors and follies are remembered "more in sorrow than in anger,"[9] and it begins to be suspected, that he never intended to injure or offend. But however his memory may be appreciated by critics, it is still held dear by many folk, whose good opinion is well worth having; particularly by certain biscuit-bakers, who have gone so far as to imprint his likeness on their new-year cakes; and have thus given him a chance for immortality, almost equal to the being stamped on a Waterloo Medal,[10] or a Queen Anne's Farthing.][11]

Whoever has made a voyage up the Hudson must remember the Kaatskill[12] mountains. They are a dismembered branch of the great Appalachian family, and are seen

---

[5] "Rip Van Winkle" and "The Legend of Sleepy Hollow" are adaptations of German folk legends.
[6] In Norse mythology, supreme god and creator.
[7] From *The Ordinary* (1651) by English playwright William Cartwright (1611–1643).
[8] Typeface used in early printed books, now called Gothic or Old English.
[9] Shakespeare's *Hamlet*, Act I, Sc. ii, l. 232.
[10] The Waterloo Medal was minted after the British defeat of Napoleon in 1815.
[11] Farthing: English coin of small value.
[12] The Catskills in southeastern New York.

away to the west of the river, swelling up to a noble height, and lording it over the surrounding country. Every change of season, every change of weather, indeed, every hour of the day, produces some change in the magical hues and shapes of these mountains, and they are regarded by all the good wives, far and near, as perfect barometers. When the weather is fair and settled, they are clothed in blue and purple, and print their bold outlines on the clear evening sky; but, sometimes, when the rest of the landscape is cloudless, they will gather a hood of gray vapors about their summits, which, in the last rays of the setting sun, will glow and light up like a crown of glory.

At the foot of these fairy mountains, the voyager may have descried the light smoke curling up from a village, whose shingle-roofs gleam among the trees, just where the blue tints of the upland melt away into the fresh green of the nearer landscape. It is a little village, of great antiquity, having been founded by some of the Dutch colonists, in the early times of the province, just about the beginning of the government of the good Peter Stuyvesant,[13] (may he rest in peace!) and there were some of the houses of the original settlers standing within a few years, built of small yellow bricks brought from Holland, having latticed windows and gable fronts, surmounted with weather-cocks.

In that same village, and in one of these very houses (which, to tell the precise truth, was sadly time-worn and weather-beaten), there lived many years since, while the country was yet a province of Great Britain, a simple good-natured fellow, of the name of Rip Van Winkle. He was a descendant of the Van Winkles who figured so gallantly in the chivalrous days of Peter Stuyvesant, and accompanied him to the siege of Fort Christina.[14] He inherited, however, but little of the martial character of his ancestors. I have observed that he was a simple good-natured man; he was, moreover, a kind neighbor, and an obedient hen-pecked husband. Indeed, to the latter circumstance might be owing that meekness of spirit which gained him such universal popularity; for those men are most apt to be obsequious and conciliating abroad, who are under the discipline of shrews at home. Their tempers, doubtless, are rendered pliant and malleable in the fiery furnace of domestic tribulation; and a curtain lecture[15] is worth all the sermons in the world for teaching the virtues of patience and long-suffering. A termagant wife may, therefore, in some respects, be considered a tolerable blessing; and if so, Rip Van Winkle was thrice blessed.

Certain it is, that he was a great favorite among all the good wives of the village, who, as usual, with the amiable sex, took his part in all family squabbles; and never failed, whenever they talked those matters over in their evening gossipings, to lay all the blame on Dame Van Winkle. The children of the village, too, would shout with joy whenever he approached. He assisted at their sports, made their playthings, taught them to fly kites and shoot marbles, and told them long stories of ghosts, witches, and Indians. Whenever he went dodging about the village, he was surrounded by a troop of them, hanging on his skirts, clambering on his back, and playing a thousand

---

[13] Last governor of the Dutch province of New Netherlands (1647–1664).

[14] Peter Stuyvesant (1592–1672) led Dutch forces in defeating the Swedish colonists at Fort Christina on the Delaware in 1655.

[15] Tirade delivered by an angry wife from behind her bed curtains.

tricks on him with impunity; and not a dog would bark at him throughout the neighborhood.

The great error in Rip's composition was an insuperable aversion to all kinds of profitable labor. It could not be from the want of assiduity or perseverance; for he would sit on a wet rock, with a rod as long and heavy as a Tartar's lance, and fish all day without a murmur, even though he should not be encouraged by a single nibble. He would carry a fowling-piece on his shoulder for hours together, trudging through woods and swamps, and up hill and down dale, to shoot a few squirrels or wild pigeons. He would never refuse to assist a neighbor even in the roughest toil, and was a foremost man at all country frolics for husking Indian corn, or building stone-fences; the women of the village, too, used to employ him to run their errands, and to do such little odd jobs as their less obliging husbands would not do for them. In a word Rip was ready to attend to anybody's business but his own; but as to doing family duty, and keeping his farm in order, he found it impossible.

In fact, he declared it was of no use to work on his farm; it was the most pestilent little piece of ground in the whole country; every thing about it went wrong, and would go wrong, in spite of him. His fences were continually falling to pieces; his cow would either go astray, or get among the cabbages; weeds were sure to grow quicker in his fields than anywhere else; the rain always made a point of setting in just as he had some out-door work to do; so that though his patrimonial estate had dwindled away under his management, acre by acre, until there was little more left than a mere patch of Indian corn and potatoes, yet it was the worst conditioned farm in the neighborhood.

His children, too, were as ragged and wild as if they belonged to nobody. His son Rip, an urchin begotten in his own likeness, promised to inherit the habits, with the old clothes of his father. He was generally seen trooping like a colt at his mother's heels, equipped in a pair of his father's cast-off galligaskins, which he had much ado to hold up with one hand, as a fine lady does her train in bad weather.

Rip Van Winkle, however, was one of those happy mortals, of foolish, well-oiled dispositions, who take the world easy, eat white bread or brown, whichever can be got with least thought or trouble, and would rather starve on a penny than work for a pound. If left to himself, he would have whistled life away in perfect contentment; but his wife kept continually dinning in his ears about his idleness, his carelessness, and the ruin he was bringing on his family. Morning, noon, and night, her tongue was incessantly going, and every thing he said or did was sure to produce a torrent of household eloquence. Rip had but one way of replying to all lectures of the kind, and that, by frequent use, had grown into a habit. He shrugged his shoulders, shook his head, cast up his eyes, but said nothing. This, however, always provoked a fresh volley from his wife; so that he was fain to draw off his forces, and take to the outside of the house—the only side which, in truth, belongs to a hen-pecked husband.

Rip's sole domestic adherent was his dog Wolf, who was as much hen-pecked as his master; for Dame Van Winkle regarded them as companions in idleness, and even looked upon Wolf with an evil eye, as the cause of his master's going so often astray. True it is, in all points of spirit befitting an honorable dog, he was as courageous an animal as ever scoured the woods—but what courage can withstand the everduring and all-besetting terrors of a woman's tongue? The moment Wolf entered the house his crest fell, his tail drooped to the ground, or curled between his legs, he sneaked about with a gallows air, casting many a sidelong glance at Dame Van Winkle, and at the least flourish of a broomstick or ladle, he would fly to the door with yelping precipitation.

Times grew worse and worse with Rip Van Winkle as years of matrimony rolled on; a tart temper never mellows with age, and a sharp tongue is the only edged tool that grows keener with constant use. For a long while he used to console himself, when driven from home, by frequenting a kind of perpetual club of the sages, philosophers, and other idle personages of the village; which held its sessions on a bench before a small inn, designated by a rubicund portrait of His Majesty George the Third. Here they used to sit in the shade through a long lazy summer's day, talking listlessly over village gossip, or telling endless sleepy stories about nothing. But it would have been worth any statesman's money to have heard the profound discussions that sometimes took place, when by chance an old newspaper fell into their hands from some passing traveller. How solemnly they would listen to the contents, as drawled out by Derrick Van Bummel, the schoolmaster, a dapper learned little man, who was not to be daunted by the most gigantic word in the dictionary; and how sagely they would deliberate upon public events some months after they had taken place.

The opinions of this junto[16] were completely controlled by Nicholas Vedder, a patriarch of the village, and landlord of the inn, at the door of which he took his seat from morning till night, just moving sufficiently to avoid the sun and keep in the shade of a large tree; so that the neighbors could tell the hour by his movements as accurately as by a sun-dial. It is true he was rarely heard to speak, but smoked his pipe incessantly. His adherents, however (for every great man has his adherents), perfectly understood him, and knew how to gather his opinions. When any thing that was read or related displeased him, he was observed to smoke his pipe vehemently, and to send forth short, frequent and angry puffs; but when pleased, he would inhale the smoke slowly and tranquilly, and emit it in light and placid clouds; and sometimes, taking the pipe from his mouth, and letting the fragrant vapor curl about his nose, would gravely nod his head in token of perfect approbation.

From even this stronghold the unlucky Rip was at length routed by his termagant wife, who would suddenly break in upon the tranquillity of the assemblage and call the members all to naught; nor was that august personage, Nicholas Vedder himself, sacred from the daring tongue of this terrible virago, who charged him outright with encouraging her husband in habits of idleness.

Poor Rip was at last reduced almost to despair; and his only alternative, to escape from the labor of the farm and clamor of his wife, was to take gun in hand and stroll away into the woods. Here he would sometimes seat himself at the foot of a tree, and share the contents of his wallet[17] with Wolf, with whom he sympathized as a fellow-sufferer in persecution. "Poor Wolf," he would say, "thy mistress leads thee a dog's life of it; but never mind, my lad, whilst I live thou shalt never want a friend to stand by thee!" Wolf would wag his tail, look wistfully in his master's face, and if dogs can feel pity I verily believe he reciprocated the sentiment with all his heart.

In a long ramble of the kind on a fine autumnal day, Rip had unconsciously scrambled to one of the highest parts of the Kaatskill mountains. He was after his favorite sport of squirrel shooting, and the still solitudes had echoed and reechoed with the reports of his gun. Panting and fatigued, he threw himself, late in the afternoon,

---

[16] Committee or caucus.   [17] Here, knapsack.

on a green knoll, covered with mountain herbage, that crowned the brow of a precipice. From an opening between the trees he could overlook all the lower country for many a mile of rich woodland. He saw at a distance the lordly Hudson, far, far below him, moving on its silent but majestic course, with the reflection of a purple cloud, or the sail of a lagging bark, here and there sleeping on its glassy bosom, and at last losing itself in the blue highlands.

On the other side he looked down into a deep mountain glen, wild, lonely, and shagged, the bottom filled with fragments from the impending cliffs, and scarcely lighted by the reflected rays of the setting sun. For some time Rip lay musing on this scene; evening was gradually advancing; the mountains began to throw their long blue shadows over the valleys; he saw that it would be dark long before he could reach the village, and he heaved a heavy sigh when he thought of encountering the terrors of Dame Van Winkle.

As he was about to descend, he heard a voice from a distance, hallooing, "Rip Van Winkle! Rip Van Winkle!" He looked round, but could see nothing but a crow winging its solitary flight across the mountain. He thought his fancy must have deceived him, and turned again to descend, when he heard the same cry ring through the still evening air; "Rip Van Winkle! Rip Van Winkle!"—at the same time Wolf bristled up his back, and giving a low growl, skulked to his master's side, looking fearfully down into the glen. Rip now felt a vague apprehension stealing over him; he looked anxiously in the same direction, and perceived a strange figure slowly toiling up the rocks, and bending under the weight of something he carried on his back. He was surprised to see any human being in this lonely and unfrequented place, but supposing it to be some one of the neighborhood in need of his assistance, he hastened down to yield it.

On nearer approach he was still more surprised at the singularity of the stranger's appearance. He was a short square-built old fellow, with thick bushy hair, and a grizzled beard. His dress was of the antique Dutch fashion—a cloth jerkin strapped round the waist—several pair of breeches, the outer one of ample volume, decorated with rows of buttons down the sides, and bunches at the knees. He bore on his shoulder a stout keg, that seemed full of liquor, and made signs for Rip to approach and assist him with the load. Though rather shy and distrustful of this new acquaintance, Rip complied with his usual alacrity; and mutually relieving one another, they clambered up a narrow gully, apparently the dry bed of a mountain torrent. As they ascended, Rip every now and then heard long rolling peals, like distant thunder, that seemed to issue out of a deep ravine, or rather cleft, between lofty rocks, toward which their rugged path conducted. He paused for an instant, but supposing it to be the muttering of one of those transient thunder-showers which often take place in mountain heights, he proceeded. Passing through the ravine, they came to a hollow, like a small amphitheatre, surrounded by perpendicular precipices, over the brinks of which impending trees shot their branches, so that you only caught glimpses of the azure sky and the bright evening cloud. During the whole time Rip and his companion had labored on in silence; for though the former marvelled greatly what could be the object of carrying a keg of liquor up this wild mountain, yet there was something strange and incomprehensible about the unknown, that inspired awe and checked familiarity.

On entering the amphitheatre, new objects of wonder presented themselves. On a level spot in the centre was a company of odd-looking personages playing at nine-pins. They were dressed in a quaint outlandish fashion; some wore short doublets, others jerkins, with long knives in their belts, and most of them had enormous breeches, of similar style with that of the guide's. Their visages, too, were peculiar: one had a large beard, broad face, and small piggish eyes: the face of another seemed to consist entirely of nose, and was surmounted by a white sugar-loaf hat, set off with a little red cock's tail. They all had beards, of various shapes and colors. There was one who seemed to be the commander. He was a stout old gentleman, with a weather-beaten countenance; he wore a laced doublet, broad belt and hanger,[18] high crowned hat and feather, red stockings, and high-heeled shoes, with roses[19] in them. The whole group reminded Rip of the figures in an old Flemish painting, in the parlor of Dominic[20] Van Shaick, the village parson, and which had been brought over from Holland at the time of the settlement.

What seemed particularly odd to Rip was, that though these folks were evidently amusing themselves, yet they maintained the gravest faces, the most mysterious silence, and were, withal, the most melancholy party of pleasure he had ever witnessed. Nothing interrupted the stillness of the scene but the noise of the balls, which, whenever they were rolled, echoed along the mountains like rumbling peals of thunder.

As Rip and his companion approached them, they suddenly desisted from their play, and stared at him with such fixed statue-like gaze, and such strange, uncouth, lack-lustre countenances, that his heart turned within him, and his knees smote together. His companion now emptied the contents of the keg into large flagons, and made signs to him to wait upon the company. He obeyed with fear and trembling; they quaffed the liquor in profound silence, and then returned to their game.

By degrees Rip's awe and apprehension subsided. He even ventured, when no eye was fixed upon him, to taste the beverage, which he found had much of the flavor of excellent Hollands.[21] He was naturally a thirsty soul, and was soon tempted to repeat the draught. One taste provoked another; and he reiterated his visits to the flagon so often that at length his senses were overpowered, his eyes swam in his head, his head gradually declined, and he fell into a deep sleep.

On waking, he found himself on the green knoll whence he had first seen the old man of the glen. He rubbed his eyes—it was a bright sunny morning. The birds were hopping and twittering among the bushes, and the eagle was wheeling aloft, and breasting the pure mountain breeze. "Surely," thought Rip, "I have not slept here all night." He recalled the occurrences before he fell asleep. The strange man with a keg of liquor—the mountain ravine—the wild retreat among the rocks—the wobegone party at nine-pins—the flagon—"Oh! that flagon! that wicked flagon!" thought Rip—"what excuse shall I make to Dame Van Winkle!"

He looked round for his gun, but in place of the clean well-oiled fowling-piece, he found an old firelock lying by him, the barrel incrusted with rust, the lock falling off, and the stock worm-eaten. He now suspected that the grave roysters of the mountain had put a trick upon him, and, having dosed him with liquor, had robbed him of his gun. Wolf, too, had disappeared, but he might have strayed away after a squirrel or partridge. He whistled after him and shouted his

---

[18] Short, curved sword worn at the side.   [20] Pastor.
[19] Rosettes.   [21] Dutch gin.

name, but all in vain; the echoes repeated his whistle and shout, but no dog was to be seen.

He determined to revisit the scene of the last evening's gambol, and if he met with any of the party, to demand his dog and gun. As he rose to walk, he found himself stiff in the joints, and wanting in his usual activity. "These mountain beds do not agree with me," thought Rip, "and if this frolic should lay me up with a fit of the rheumatism, I shall have a blessed time with Dame Van Winkle." With some difficulty he got down into the glen: he found the gully up which he and his companion had ascended the preceding evening; but to his astonishment a mountain stream was now foaming down it, leaping from rock to rock, and filling the glen with babbling murmurs. He, however, made shift to scramble up its sides, working his toilsome way through thickets of birch, sassafras, and witch-hazel, and sometimes tripped up or entangled by the wild grapevines that twisted their coils or tendrils from tree to tree, and spread a kind of network in his path.

At length he reached to where the ravine had opened through the cliffs to the amphitheatre; but no traces of such opening remained. The rocks presented a high impenetrable wall over which the torrent came tumbling in a sheet of feathery foam, and fell into a broad deep basin, black from the shadows of the surrounding forest. Here, then, poor Rip was brought to a stand. He again called and whistled after his dog; he was only answered by the cawing of a flock of idle crows, sporting high in air about a dry tree that overhung a sunny precipice; and who, secure in their elevation, seemed to look down and scoff at the poor man's perplexities. What was to be done? the morning was passing away, and Rip felt famished for want of his breakfast. He grieved to give up his dog and gun; he dreaded to meet his wife; but it would not do to starve among the mountains. He shook his head, shouldered the rusty firelock, and, with a heart full of trouble and anxiety, turned his steps homeward.

As he approached the village he met a number of people, but none whom he knew, which somewhat surprised him, for he had thought himself acquainted with every one in the country round. Their dress, too, was of a different fashion from that to which he was accustomed. They all stared at him with equal marks of surprise, and whenever they cast their eyes upon him, invariably stroked their chins. The constant recurrence of this gesture induced Rip, involuntarily, to do the same, when, to his astonishment, he found his beard had grown a foot long!

He had now entered the skirts of the village. A troop of strange children ran at his heels, hooting after him, and pointing at his gray beard. The dogs, too, not one of which he recognized for an old acquaintance, barked at him as he passed. The very village was altered; it was larger and more populous. There were rows of houses which he had never seen before, and those which had been his familiar haunts had disappeared. Strange names were over the doors—strange faces at the windows—every thing was strange. His mind now misgave him; he began to doubt whether both he and the world around him were not bewitched. Surely this was his native village, which he had left but the day before. There stood the Kaatskill mountains—there ran the silver Hudson at a distance—there was every hill and dale precisely as it had always been—Rip was sorely perplexed—"That flagon last night," thought he, "has addled my poor head sadly!"

It was with some difficulty that he found the way to his own house, which he approached with silent awe, expecting every moment to hear the shrill voice of Dame Van Winkle. He found the house gone to decay—the roof fallen in, the windows shattered, and the doors off the hinges. A half-starved dog that looked like Wolf was sulking about it. Rip called him by name, but the cur snarled, showed his teeth, and passed on. This was an unkind cut indeed—"My very dog," sighed poor Rip, "has forgotten me!"

He entered the house, which, to tell the truth, Dame Van Winkle had always kept in neat order. It was empty, forlorn, and apparently abandoned. This desolateness overcame all his connubial fears—he called loudly for his wife and children—the lonely chambers rang for a moment with his voice, and then all again was silence.

He now hurried forth, and hastened to his old resort, the village inn—but it too was gone. A large rickety wooden building stood in its place, with great gaping windows, some of them broken and mended with old hats and petticoats, and over the door was painted, "the Union Hotel, by Jonathan Doolittle." Instead of the great tree that used to shelter the quiet little Dutch inn of yore, there now was reared a tall naked pole, with something on the top that looked like a red night-cap, and from it was fluttering a flag, on which was a singular assemblage of stars and stripes—all this was strange and incomprehensible.[22] He recognized on the sign, however, the ruby face of King George, under which he had smoked so many a peaceful pipe; but even this was singularly metamorphosed. The red coat was changed for one of blue and buff,[23] a sword was held in the hand instead of a sceptre, the head was decorated with a cocked hat, and underneath was painted in large characters, GENERAL WASHINGTON.

There was, as usual, a crowd of folk about the door, but none that Rip recollected. The very character of the people seemed changed. There was a busy, bustling, disputatious tone about it, instead of the accustomed phlegm and drowsy tranquillity. He looked in vain for the sage Nicholas Vedder, with his broad face, double chin, and fair long pipe, uttering clouds of tobacco-smoke instead of idle speeches; or Van Bummel, the schoolmaster, doling forth the contents of an ancient newspaper. In place of these, a lean, bilious-looking fellow, with his pockets full of handbills, was haranguing vehemently about rights of citizens—elections—members of congress— liberty—Bunker's Hill—heroes of seventy-six—and other words, which were a perfect Babylonish jargon[24] to the bewildered Van Winkle.

The appearance of Rip, with his long grizzled beard, his rusty fowling-piece, his uncouth dress, and an army of women and children at his heels, soon attracted the attention of the tavern politicians. They crowded around him, eyeing him from head to foot with great curiosity. The orator bustled up to him, and, drawing him partly aside, inquired "on which side he voted?" Rip stared in vacant stupidity. Another short but busy little fellow pulled him by the arm, and, rising on tiptoe, inquired in his ear, "Whether he was Federal or Democrat?"[25] Rip was equally at a loss to comprehend the question; when a knowing, self-important old gentleman, in a sharp cocked hat, made his way through the crowd, putting them to the right and left with his elbows as he passed, and planting himself before Van Winkle, with one arm akimbo, the other resting on his cane, his keen eyes and sharp hat penetrating, as it were, into his very soul, demanded in an austere tone, "what brought him to the election with a gun on his shoulder, and a mob at his heels, and whether he meant

---

[22] The liberty cap and liberty pole were adopted as symbols of freedom during the French and American revolutions.
[23] Colors of the American army uniforms.

[24] Reference to the "Confusion of Tongues" at the Tower of Babel (Genesis 11:1–9).
[25] Political parties of early America, respectively conservative and liberal.

to breed a riot in the village?"—"Alas! gentlemen," cried Rip, somewhat dismayed, "I am a poor quiet man, a native of the place, and a loyal subject of the king, God bless him!"

Here a general shout burst from the by-standers—"A tory! a tory! a spy! a refugee! hustle him! away with him!" It was with great difficulty that the self-important man in the cocked hat restored order; and, having assumed a tenfold austerity of brow, demanded again of the unknown culprit, what he came there for, and whom he was seeking? The poor man humbly assured him that he meant no harm, but merely came there in search of some of his neighbors, who used to keep about the tavern.

"Well—who are they?—name them."

Rip bethought himself a moment, and inquired, "Where's Nicholas Vedder?"

There was a silence for a little while, when an old man replied, in a thin piping voice, "Nicholas Vedder! why, he is dead and gone these eighteen years! There was a wooden tombstone in the church-yard that used to tell all about him, but that's rotten and gone too."

"Where's Brom Dutcher?"

"Oh, he went off to the army in the beginning of the war; some say he was killed at the storming of Stony Point—others say he was drowned in a squall at the foot of Antony's Nose.[26] I don't know—he never came back again."

"Where's Van Bummel, the schoolmaster?"

"He went off to the wars too, was a great militia general, and is now in congress."

Rip's heart died away at hearing of these sad changes in his home and friends, and finding himself thus alone in the world. Every answer puzzled him too, by treating of such enormous lapses of time, and of matters which he could not understand: war —congress—Stony Point;—he had no courage to ask after any more friends, but cried out in despair, "Does nobody here know Rip Van Winkle?"

"Oh, Rip Van Winkle!" exclaimed two or three, "Oh, to be sure! that's Rip Van Winkle yonder, leaning against the tree."

Rip looked, and beheld a precise counterpart of himself, as he went up to the mountain: apparently as lazy, and certainly as ragged. The poor fellow was now completely confounded. He doubted his own identity, and whether he was himself or another man. In the midst of his bewilderment, the man in the cocked hat demanded who he was, and what was his name?

"God knows," exclaimed he, at his wit's end; "I'm not myself—I'm somebody else —that's me yonder—no—that's somebody else got into my shoes—I was myself last night, but I fell asleep on the mountain, and they've changed my gun, and every thing's changed, and I'm changed, and I can't tell what's my name, or who I am!"

The by-standers began now to look at each other, nod, wink significantly, and tap their fingers against their foreheads. There was a whisper, also, about securing the gun, and keeping the old fellow from doing mischief, at the very suggestion of which the self-important man in the cocked hat retired with some precipitation. At this critical moment a fresh comely woman pressed through the throng to get a peep at the gray-bearded man. She had a chubby child in her arms, which, frightened at his looks, began to cry. "Hush, Rip," cried she, "hush, you little fool; the old man won't hurt you." The name of the child, the air of the mother, the tone of her voice, all awakened

[26] Mountain near West Point on the Hudson River.

a train of recollections in his mind. "What is your name, my good woman?" asked he.

"Judith Gardenier."

"And your father's name?"

"Ah, poor man, Rip Van Winkle was his name, but it's twenty years since he went away from home with his gun, and never has been heard of since—his dog came home without him; but whether he shot himself, or was carried away by the Indians, nobody can tell. I was then but a little girl."

Rip had but one question more to ask; but he put it with a faltering voice: "Where's your mother?"

"Oh, she too had died but a short time since; she broke a blood-vessel in a fit of passion at a New-England peddler."

There was a drop of comfort, at least, in this intelligence. The honest man could contain himself no longer. He caught his daughter and her child in his arms. "I am your father!" cried he—"Young Rip Van Winkle once—old Rip Van Winkle now! —Does nobody know poor Rip Van Winkle?"

All stood amazed, until an old woman, tottering out from among the crowd, put her hand to her brow, and peering under it in his face for a moment, exclaimed, "Sure enough! it is Rip Van Winkle—it is himself! Welcome home again, old neighbor —Why, where have you been these twenty long years?"

Rip's story was soon told, for the whole twenty years had been to him but as one night. The neighbors stared when they heard it; some were seen to wink at each other, and put their tongues in their cheeks: and the self-important man in the cocked hat, who, when the alarm was over, had returned to the field, screwed down the corners of his mouth, and shook his head—upon which there was a general shaking of the head throughout the assemblage.

It was determined, however, to take the opinion of old Peter Vanderdonk, who was seen slowly advancing up the road. He was a descendant of the historian of that name,[27] who wrote one of the earliest accounts of the province. Peter was the most ancient inhabitant of the village, and well versed in all the wonderful events and traditions of the neighborhood. He recollected Rip at once, and corroborated his story in the most satisfactory manner. He assured the company that it was a fact, handed down from his ancestor the historian, that the Kaatskill mountains had always been haunted by strange beings. That it was affirmed that the great Hendrick Hudson,[28] the first discoverer of the river and country, kept a kind of vigil there every twenty years, with his crew of the Half-moon; being permitted in this way to revisit the scenes of his enterprise, and keep a guardian eye upon the river, and the great city called by his name.[29] That his father had once seen them in their old Dutch dresses playing at nine-pins in a hollow of the mountain; and that he himself had heard, one summer afternoon, the sound of their balls, like distant peals of thunder.

To make a long story short, the company broke up, and returned to the more important concerns of the election. Rip's daughter took him home to live with her;

[27] Adriaen Van Der Donck (1620?–1655), Dutch lawyer and author of a history of New Netherlands (Amsterdam, 1655).
[28] English navigator Henry Hudson (d. 1611),

employed by the Dutch to explore the river that now bears his name.
[29] The town of Hudson, New York.

she had a snug, well-furnished house, and a stout cheery farmer for a husband, whom Rip recollected for one of the urchins that used to climb upon his back. As to Rip's son and heir, who was the ditto of himself, seen leaning against the tree, he was employed to work on the farm; but evinced an hereditary disposition to attend to any thing else but his business.

Rip now resumed his old walks and habits; he soon found many of his former cronies, though all rather the worse for the wear and tear of time; and preferred making friends among the rising generation, with whom he soon grew into great favor.

Having nothing to do at home, and being arrived at that happy age when a man can be idle with impunity, he took his place once more on the bench at the inn door, and was reverenced as one of the patriarchs of the village, and a chronicle of the old times "before the war." It was some time before he could get into the regular track of gossip, or could be made to comprehend the strange events that had taken place during his torpor. How that there had been a revolutionary war—that the country had thrown off the yoke of old England—and that, instead of being a subject of his Majesty George the Third, he was now a free citizen of the United States. Rip, in fact, was no politician; the changes of states and empires made but little impression on him; but there was one species of despotism under which he had long groaned, and that was—petticoat government. Happily that was at an end; he had got his neck out of the yoke of matrimony, and could go in and out whenever he pleased, without dreading the tyranny of Dame Van Winkle. Whenever her name was mentioned, however, he shook his head, shrugged his shoulders, and cast up his eyes; which might pass either for an expression of resignation to his fate, or joy at his deliverance.

He used to tell his story to every stranger that arrived at Mr. Doolittle's hotel. He was observed, at first, to vary on some points every time he told it, which was, doubtless, owing to his having so recently awaked. It at last settled down precisely to the tale I have related, and not a man, woman, or child in the neighborhood, but knew it by heart. Some always pretended to doubt the reality of it, and insisted that Rip had been out of his head, and that this was one point on which he always remained flighty. The old Dutch inhabitants, however, almost universally gave it full credit. Even to this day they never hear a thunderstorm of a summer afternoon about the Kaatskill, but they say Hendrick Hudson and his crew are at their game of nine-pins; and it is a common wish of all henpecked husbands in the neighborhood, when life hangs heavy on their hands, that they might have a quieting draught out of Rip Van Winkle's flagon.

Note

The foregoing Tale, one would suspect, had been suggested to Mr. Knickerbocker by a little German superstition about the Emperor Frederick *der Rothbart*,[30] and the Kyphaüser mountain: the subjoined note, however, which he had appended to the tale, shows that it is an absolute fact, narrated with his usual fidelity:

[30] Frederick Barbarossa (1123–1190), emperor of the Holy Roman Empire (1152–1190). Legend maintains that he is resting in a cave in the Kyffhauser Mountain in Germany until his country needs his rule. (*Barbarossa* and *der Rothbart* mean "red beard" in Latin and German, respectively.)

"The story of Rip Van Winkle may seem incredible to many, but nevertheless I give it my full belief, for I know the vicinity of our old Dutch settlements to have been very subject to marvellous events and appearances. Indeed, I have heard many stranger stories than this, in the villages along the Hudson; all of which were too well authenticated to admit of a doubt. I have even talked with Rip Van Winkle myself, who, when last I saw him, was a very venerable old man, and so perfectly rational and consistent on every other point, that I think no conscientious person could refuse to take this into the bargain; may, I have seen a certificate on the subject taken before a country justice and signed with a cross, in the justice's own handwriting. The story, therefore, is beyond the possibility of doubt.

D.K."

Traits of Indian Character

"I appeal to any white man if ever he entered Logan's cabin hungry, and he gave him not to eat; if ever he came cold and naked, and he clothed him not."
Speech of an Indian chief

There is something in the character and habits of the North American savage, taken in connection with the scenery over which he is accustomed to range, its vast lakes, boundless forests, majestic rivers, and trackless plains, that is, to my mind, wonderfully striking and sublime. He is formed for the wilderness, as the Arab is for the desert. His nature is stern, simple, and enduring; fitted to grapple with difficulties, and to support privations. There seems but little soil in his heart for the support of the kindly virtues; and yet, if we would but take the trouble to penetrate through that proud stoicism and habitual taciturnity, which lock up his character from casual observation, we should find him linked to his fellow-man of civilized life by more of those sympathies and affections than are usually ascribed to him.

It has been the lot of the unfortunate aborigines of America, in the early periods of colonization, to be doubly wronged by the white men. They have been dispossessed of their hereditary possessions by mercenary and frequently wanton warfare: and their characters have been traduced by bigoted and interested writers. The colonist often treated them like beasts of the forest; and the author has endeavored to justify him in his outrages. The former found it easier to exterminate than to civilize; the latter to vilify than to discriminate. The appellations of savage and pagan were deemed sufficient to sanction the hostilities of both; and thus the poor wanderers of the forest were persecuted and defamed, not because they were guilty, but because they were ignorant.

The rights of the savage have seldom been properly appreciated or respected by the white man. In peace he has too often been the dupe of artful traffic; in war he has been regarded as a ferocious animal, whose life or death was a question of mere precaution and convenience. Man is cruelly wasteful of life when his own safety is endangered, and he is sheltered by impunity; and little mercy is to be expected from him, when he feels the sting of the reptile and is conscious of the power to destroy.

The same prejudices, which were indulged thus early, exist in common circulation at the present day. Certain learned societies have, it is true, with laudable diligence, endeavored to investigate and record the real characters and manners of the Indian tribes; the American government, too, has wisely and humanely exerted itself to inculcate a friendly and forbearing spirit towards them, and to protect them from fraud and injustice.[31] The current opinion of the Indian character, however, is too apt to be formed from the miserable hordes which infest the frontiers, and hang on the skirts of the settlements. These are too commonly composed of degenerate beings, corrupted and enfeebled by the vices of society, without being benefited by its civilization. That proud independence, which formed the main pillar of savage virtue, has been shaken down, and the whole moral fabric lies in ruins. Their spirits are humiliated and debased by a sense of inferiority, and their native courage cowed and daunted by the superior knowledge and power of their enlightened neighbors. Society has advanced upon them like one of those withering airs that will sometimes breed desolation over a whole region of fertility. It has enervated their strength, multiplied their diseases, and superinduced upon their original barbarity the low vices of artificial life. It has given them a thousand superfluous wants, whilst it has diminished their means of mere existence. It has driven before it the animals of the chase, who fly from the sound of the axe and the smoke of the settlement, and seek refuge in the depths of remoter forests and yet untrodden wilds. Thus do we too often find the Indians on our frontiers to be the mere wrecks and remnants of once powerful tribes, who have lingered in the vicinity of the settlements, and sunk into precarious and vagabond existence. Poverty, repining and hopeless poverty, a canker of the mind unknown in savage life, corrodes their spirits, and blights every free and noble quality of their natures. They become drunken, indolent, feeble, thievish, and pusillanimous. They loiter like vagrants about the settlements, among spacious dwellings replete with elaborate comforts, which only render them sensible of the comparative wretchedness of their own condition. Luxury spreads its ample board before their eyes; but they are excluded from the banquet. Plenty revels over the fields; but they are starving in the midst of its abundance: the whole wilderness has blossomed into a garden; but they feel as reptiles that infest it.

How different was their state while yet the undisputed lords of the soil! Their wants were few, and the means of gratification within their reach. They saw every one around them sharing the same lot, enduring the same hardships, feeding on the same aliments, arrayed in the same rude garments. No roof then rose, but was open to the homeless stranger; no smoke curled among the trees, but he was welcome to sit down by its fire, and join the hunter in his repast. "For," says an old historian of New England, "their life is so void of care, and they are so loving also, that they make use of those things they enjoy as common goods, and are therein so compassionate, that rather than one should starve through want, they would starve all; thus they pass their time merrily, not regarding our pomp, but are better content with their own, which some men esteem so meanly of." Such were the Indians, whilst in the pride and energy of their primitive natures: they resembled those wild plants, which thrive best in the shades of the forest, but shrink from the hand of cultivation, and perish beneath the influence of the sun.

[31] Irving's note: "The American government has been indefatigable in its exertions to ameliorate the situation of the Indians, and to introduce among them the arts of civilization, and civil and religious knowledge. To protect them from the frauds of the white traders, no purchase of land from them by individuals is permitted; nor is any person allowed to receive lands from them as a present, without the express sanction of government. These precautions are strictly enforced."

In discussing the savage character, writers have been too prone to indulge in vulgar prejudice and passionate exaggeration, instead of the candid temper of true philosophy. They have not sufficiently considered the peculiar circumstances in which the Indians have been placed, and the peculiar principles under which they have been educated. No being acts more rigidly from rule than the Indian. His whole conduct is regulated according to some general maxims early implanted in his mind. The moral laws that govern him are, to be sure, but few; but then he conforms to them all;—the white man abounds in laws of religion, morals, and manners, but how many does he violate?

A frequent ground of accusation against the Indians is their disregard of treaties, and the treachery and wantonness with which, in time of apparent peace, they will suddenly fly to hostilities. The intercourse of the white men with the Indians, however, is too apt to be cold, distrustful, oppressive, and insulting. They seldom treat them with that confidence and frankness which are indispensable to real friendship; nor is sufficient caution observed not to offend against those feelings of pride or superstition, which often prompts the Indian to hostility quicker than mere considerations of interest. The solitary savage feels silently, but acutely. His sensibilities are not diffused over so wide a surface as those of the white man; but they run in steadier and deeper channels. His pride, his affections, his superstitions, are all directed towards fewer objects; but the wounds inflicted on them are proportionably severe, and furnish motives of hostility which we cannot sufficiently appreciate. Where a community is also limited in number, and forms one great patriarchal family, as in an Indian tribe, the injury of an individual is the injury of the whole; and the sentiment of vengeance is almost instantaneously diffused. One council fire is sufficient for the discussion and arrangement of a plan of hostilities. Here all the fighting men and sages assemble. Eloquence and superstition combine to inflame the minds of the warriors. The orator awakens their martial ardor, and they are wrought up to a kind of religious desperation, by the visions of the prophet and the dreamer.

An instance of one of those sudden exasperations, arising from a motive peculiar to the Indian character, is extant in an old record of the early settlement of Massachusetts. The planters of Plymouth had defaced the monuments of the dead at Passonagessit, and had plundered the grave of the Sachem's[32] mother of some skins with which it had been decorated. The Indians are remarkable for the reverence which they entertain for the sepulchres of their kindred. Tribes that have passed generations exiled from the abodes of their ancestors, when by chance they have been travelling in the vicinity, have been known to turn aside from the highway, and, guided by wonderfully accurate tradition, have crossed the country for miles to some tumulus, buried perhaps in woods, where the bones of their tribe were anciently deposited; and there have passed hours in silent meditation. Influenced by this sublime and holy feeling, the Sachem, whose mother's tomb had been violated, gathered his men together, and addressed them in the following beautifully simple and pathetic harangue; a curious specimen of Indian eloquence, and an affecting instance of filial piety in a savage.

"When last the glorious light of all the sky was underneath this globe, and birds grew silent, I began to settle, as my custom is, to take repose. Before mine eyes were fast closed, methought I saw a vision, at which my spirit was much troubled; and

---

[32] Sachem: chief of several North American Indian tribes.

trembling at that doleful sight, a spirit cried aloud, 'Behold, my son, whom I have cherished, see the breasts that gave thee suck, the hands that lapped thee warm, and fed thee oft. Canst thou forget to take revenge of those wild people who have defaced my monument in a despiteful manner, disdaining our antiquities and honorable customs? See, now, the Sachem's grave lies like the common people, defaced by an ignoble race. Thy mother doth complain, and implores thy aid against this thievish people, who have newly intruded on our land. If this be suffered, I shall not rest quiet in my everlasting habitation.' This said, the spirit vanished, and I, all in a sweat, not able scarce to speak, began to get some strength, and recollect my spirits that were fled, and determined to demand your counsel and assistance."

I have adduced this anecdote at some length, as it tends to show how these sudden acts of hostility, which have been attributed to caprice and perfidy, may often arise from deep and generous motives, which our inattention to Indian character and customs prevents our properly appreciating.

Another ground of violent outcry against the Indians is their barbarity to the vanquished. This had its origin partly in policy and partly in superstition. The tribes, though sometimes called nations, were never so formidable in their numbers, but that the loss of several warriors was sensibly felt; this was particularly the case when they had been frequently engaged in warfare; and many an instance occurs in Indian history, where a tribe, that had long been formidable to its neighbors, has been broken up and driven away, by the capture and massacre of its principal fighting men. There was a strong temptation, therefore, to the victor to be merciless; not so much to gratify any cruel revenge, as to provide for future security. The Indians had also the superstitious belief, frequent among barbarous nations, and prevalent also among the ancients, that the manes of their friends who had fallen in battle were soothed by the blood of the captives. The prisoners, however, who are not thus sacrificed, are adopted into their families in the place of the slain, and are treated with the confidence and affection of relatives and friends; nay, so hospitable and tender is their entertainment, that when the alternative is offered them, they will often prefer to remain with their adopted brethren, rather than return to the home and the friends of their youth.

The cruelty of the Indians towards their prisoners has been heightened since the colonization of the whites. What was formerly a compliance with policy and superstition, has been exasperated into a gratification of vengeance. They cannot but be sensible that the white men are the usurpers of their ancient dominion, the cause of their degradation, and the gradual destroyers of their race. They go forth to battle, smarting with injuries and indignities which they have individually suffered, and they are driven to madness and despair by the wide-spreading desolation, and the over-whelming ruin of European warfare. The whites have too frequently set them an example of violence, by burning their villages, and laying waste their slender means of subsistence: and yet they wonder that savages do not show moderation and magnanimity towards those who have left them nothing but mere existence and wretchedness.

We stigmatize the Indians, also, as cowardly and treacherous, because they use stratagem in warfare, in preference to open force; but in this they are fully justified by their rude code of honor. They are early taught that stratagem is praiseworthy; the bravest warrior thinks it no disgrace to lurk in silence, and take every advantage of his foe: he triumphs in the superior craft and sagacity by which he has been enabled to surprise and destroy an enemy. Indeed, man is naturally more prone to subtilty than open valor, owing to his physical weakness in comparison with other animals. They are endowed with natural weapons of defense: with horns, with tusks, with hoofs, and talons; but man has to depend on his superior sagacity. In all his encounters with these, his proper enemies, he resorts to stratagem; and when he perversely turns his hostility against his fellow-man, he at first continues the same subtle mode of warfare.

The natural principle of war is to do the most harm to our enemy with the least harm to ourselves; and this of course is to be effected by stratagem. That chivalrous courage which induces us to despise the suggestions of prudence, and to rush in the face of certain danger, is the offspring of society, and produced by education. It is honorable, because it is in fact the triumph of lofty sentiment over an instinctive repugnance to pain, and over those yearnings after personal ease and security, which society has condemned as ignoble. It is kept alive by pride and the fear of shame; and thus the dread of real evil is overcome by the superior dread of an evil which exists but in the imagination. It has been cherished and stimulated also by various means. It has been the theme of spirit-stirring song and chivalrous story. The poet and minstrel have delighted to shed round it the splendors of fiction; and even the historian has forgotten the sober gravity of narration, and broken forth into enthusiasm and rhapsody in its praise. Triumphs and gorgeous pageants have been its reward: monuments, on which art has exhausted its skill, and opulence its treasures, have been erected to perpetuate a nation's gratitude and admiration. Thus artificially excited, courage has risen to an extraordinary and factitious degree of heroism: and arrayed in all the glorious "pomp and circumstance of war," this turbulent quality has even been able to eclipse many of those quiet, but invaluable virtues, which silently ennoble the human character, and swell the tide of human happiness.

But if courage intrinsically consists in the defiance of danger and pain, the life of the Indian is a continual exhibition of it. He lives in a state of perpetual hostility and risk. Peril and adventure are congenial to his nature; or rather seem necessary to arouse his faculties and to give an interest to his existence. Surrounded by hostile tribes, whose mode of warfare is by ambush and surprisal, he is always prepared for fight, and lives with his weapons in his hands. As the ship careers in fearful singleness through the solitudes of ocean;—as the bird mingles among clouds and storms, and wings its way, a mere speck, across the pathless fields of air;—so the Indian holds his course, silent, solitary, but undaunted, through the boundless bosom of the wilderness. His expeditions may vie in distance and danger with the pilgrimage of the devotee, or the crusade of the knight-errant. He traverses vast forests, exposed to the hazards of lonely sickness, of lurking enemies, and pining famine. Stormy lakes, those great inland seas, are no obstacles to his wanderings: in his light canoe of bark he sports, like a feather, on their waves, and darts, with the swiftness of an arrow, down the roaring rapids of the rivers. His very subsistence is snatched from the midst of toil and peril. He gains his food by the hardships and dangers of the chase: he wraps himself in the spoils of the bear, the panther, and the buffalo, and sleeps among the thunders of the cataract.

No hero of ancient or modern days can surpass the Indian in his lofty contempt of death, and the fortitude with which he sustains its cruellest infliction. Indeed we here behold him rising superior to the white man, in consequence of his peculiar education. The latter rushes to glorious death at the cannon's mouth; the former calmly contemplates its approach, and triumphantly endures it, amidst the varied torments of surrounding foes and the protracted agonies of fire. He even takes a pride in taunting his persecutors, and provoking their ingenuity of torture; and as the devouring flames prey on his very vitals, and the flesh shrinks from the sinews, he raises his last song of triumph, breathing the defiance of an unconquered heart, and invoking the spirits of his fathers to witness that he dies without a groan.

Notwithstanding the obloquy with which the early historians have overshadowed the characters of the unfortunate natives, some bright gleams occasionally break through, which throw a degree of melancholy lustre on their memories. Facts are occasionally to be met with in the rude annals of the eastern provinces, which, though recorded with the coloring of prejudice and bigotry, yet speak for themselves; and will be dwelt on with applause and sympathy, when prejudice shall have passed away.

In one of the homely narratives of the Indian wars in New England, there is a touching account of the desolation carried into the tribe of the Pequod Indians.[33] Humanity shrinks from the cold-blooded detail of indiscriminate butchery. In one place we read of the surprisal of an Indian fort in the night, when the wigwams were wrapped in flames, and the miserable inhabitants shot down and slain in attempting to escape, "all being despatched and ended in the course of an hour." After a series of similar transactions, "our soldiers," as the historian piously observes, "being resolved by God's assistance to make a final destruction of them," the unhappy savages being hunted from their homes and fortresses, and pursued with fire and sword, a scanty, but gallant band, the sad remnant of the Pequod warriors, with their wives and children, took refuge in a swamp.

Burning with indignation, and rendered sullen by despair; with hearts bursting with grief at the destruction of their tribe, and spirits galled and sore at the fancied ignominy of their defeat, they refused to ask their lives at the hands of an insulting foe, and preferred death to submission.

As the night drew on they were surrounded in their dismal retreat, so as to render escape impracticable. Thus situated, their enemy "plied them with shot all the time, by which means many were killed and buried in the mire." In the darkness and fog that preceded the dawn of day some few broke through the besiegers and escaped into the woods: "the rest were left to the conquerors, of which many were killed in the swamp, like sullen dogs who would rather, in their self-willedness and madness, sit still and be shot through, or cut to pieces," then implore for mercy. When the day broke upon this handful of forlorn but dauntless spirits, the soldiers, we are told, entering the swamp, "saw several heaps of them sitting close together, upon whom they discharged their pieces, laden with ten or twelve pistol bullets at a time, putting the muzzles of the pieces under the boughs, within a few yards of them; so as, besides those that were found dead, many more were killed and sunk into the mire, and never were minded more by friend or foe."

Can any one read this plain unvarnished tale, without admiring the stern resolution, the unbending pride, the loftiness of spirit, that seemed to nerve the hearts of these self-taught heroes, and to raise them above the instinctive feelings of human nature? When the Gauls laid waste the city of Rome, they found the senators clothed in their robes, and seated with stern tranquillity in their curule chairs; in this manner they suffered death without resistance or even supplication. Such conduct was, in them, applauded as noble and magnanimous; in the hapless Indian it was reviled as obstinate

---

[33] The Pequots, an Indian tribe who controlled eastern Connecticut, were virtually destroyed by the English in 1637.

and sullen! How truly are we the dupes of show and circumstance! How different is virtue, clothed in purple and enthroned in state, from virtue, naked and destitute, and perishing obscurely in a wilderness!

But I forbear to dwell on these gloomy pictures. The eastern tribes have long since disappeared; the forests that sheltered them have been laid low, and scarce any traces remain of them in the thickly-settled states of New England, excepting here and there the Indian name of a village or a stream. And such must, sooner or later, be the fate of those other tribes which skirt the frontiers, and have occasionally been inveigled from their forests to mingle in the wars of white men. In a little while, and they will go the way that their brethren have gone before. The few hordes which still linger about the shores of Huron and Superior, and the tributary streams of the Mississippi, will share the fate of those tribes that once spread over Massachusetts and Connecticut, and lorded it along the proud banks of the Hudson; of that gigantic race said to have existed on the borders of the Susquehanna;[34] and of those various nations that flourished about the Potomac and the Rappahannock,[35] and that peopled the forests of the vast valley of Shenandoah.[36] They will vanish like a vapor from the face of the earth; their very history will be lost in forgetfulness; and "the places that now know them will know them no more for ever." Or if, perchance, some dubious memorial of them should survive, it may be in the romantic dreams of the poet, to people in imagination his glades and groves, like the fauns and satyrs and sylvan deities[37] of antiquity. But should he venture upon the dark story of their wrongs and wretchedness; should he tell how they were invaded, corrupted, despoiled, driven from their native abodes and the sepulchres of their fathers, hunted like wild beasts about the earth, and sent down with violence and butchery to the grave, posterity will either turn with horror and incredulity from the tale, or blush with indignation at the inhumanity of their forefathers.—"We are driven back," said an old warrior, "until we can retreat no farther—our hatchets are broken, our bows are snapped, our fires are nearly extinguished:—a little longer, and the white man will cease to persecute us—for we shall cease to exist!"

The Legend of Sleepy Hollow

Found among the papers of the late Diedrich
Knickerbocker

A pleasing land of drowsy head it was,
Of dreams that wave before the half-shut eye;
And of gay castles in the clouds that pass,
For ever flushing round a summer sky.
Castle of Indolence[38]

In the bosom of one of those spacious coves which indent the eastern shore of the Hudson, at that broad expansion of the river denominated by the ancient Dutch navigators the Tappan Zee,[39] and where they always prudently shortened sail, and

[34] River in Pennsylvania.
[35] River in Virginia.
[36] Region in Virginia.
[37] Spirits of the woodlands in Greek myth.

[38] By James Thomson (1700–1748), Scottish poet.
[39] Expanse in the Hudson River in Tarrytown, New York.

implored the protection of St. Nicholas when they crossed, there lies a small market-town or rural port, which by some is called Greensburgh, but which is more generally and properly known by the name of Tarry Town. This name was given, we are told, in former days, by the good housewives of the adjacent country, from the inveterate propensity of their husbands to linger about the village tavern on market days. Be that as it may, I do not vouch for the fact, but merely advert to it, for the sake of being precise and authentic. Not far from this village, perhaps about two miles, there is a little valley, or rather lap of land, among high hills, which is one of the quietest places in the whole world. A small brook glides through it, with just murmur enough to lull one to repose; and the occasional whistle of a quail, or tapping of a woodpecker, is almost the only sound that ever breaks in upon the uniform tranquillity.

I recollect that, when a stripling, my first exploit in squirrel-shooting was in a grove of tall walnut-trees that shades one side of the valley. I had wandered into it at noon time, when all nature is peculiarly quiet, and was startled by the roar of my own gun, as it broke the Sabbath stillness around, and was prolonged and reverberated by the angry echoes. If ever I should wish for a retreat, whither I might steal from the world and its distractions, and dream quietly away the remnant of a troubled life, I know of none more promising than this little valley.

From the listless repose of the place, and the peculiar character of its inhabitants, who are descendants from the original Dutch settlers, this sequestered glen has long been known by the name of Sleepy Hollow,[40] and its rustic lads are called the Sleepy Hollow Boys throughout all the neighboring country. A drowsy, dreamy influence seems to hang over the land, and to pervade the very atmosphere. Some say that the place was bewitched by a high German[41] doctor, during the early days of the settlement; others, that an old Indian chief, the prophet or wizard of his tribe, held his powwows there before the country was discovered by Master Hendrick Hudson.[42] Certain it is, the place still continues under the sway of some witching power, that holds a spell over the minds of the good people, causing them to walk in a continual reverie. They are given to all kinds of marvellous beliefs; are subject to trances and visions; and frequently see strange sights, and hear music and voices in the air. The whole neighborhood abounds with local tales, haunted spots, and twilight superstitions; stars shoot and meteors glare oftener across the valley than in any other part of the country, and the nightmare, with her whole nine fold,[43] seems to make it the favorite scene of her gambols.

The dominant spirit, however, that haunts this enchanted region, and seems to be commander-in-chief of all the powers of the air, is the apparition of a figure on horseback without a head. It is said by some to be the ghost of a Hessian trooper,[44] whose head had been carried away by a cannon-ball, in some nameless battle during the revolutionary war; and who is ever and anon seen by the country folk, hurrying along in the gloom of night, as if on the wings of the wind. His haunts are not confined to the valley, but extend at times to the adjacent roads, and especially to the vicinity of a church at no great distance. Indeed, certain of the most authentic historians of

---

[40] At Tarrytown.
[41] High German: from southern Germany.
[42] Henry Hudson.
[43] The demonic nightmare of folk legend had nine foals or imps.

[44] Mercenary from Hesse, Germany, hired by the British to fight in the American revolution.

those parts, who have been careful in collecting and collating the floating facts concerning this spectre, allege that the body of the trooper, having been buried in the church-yard, the ghost rides forth to the scene of battle in nightly quest of his head; and that the rushing speed with which he sometimes passes along the Hollow, like a midnight blast, is owing to his being belated, and in a hurry to get back to the church-yard before daybreak.[45]

Such is the general purport of this legendary superstition, which has furnished materials for many a wild story in that region of shadows; and the spectre is known, at all the country firesides, by the name of the Headless Horseman of Sleepy Hollow.

It is remarkable that the visionary propensity I have mentioned is not confined to the native inhabitants of the valley, but is unconsciously imbibed by every one who resides there for a time. However wide awake they may have been before they entered that sleepy region, they are sure, in a little time, to inhale the witching influence of the air, and begin to grow imaginative—to dream dreams, and see apparitions.

I mention this peaceful spot with all possible laud; for it is in such little retired Dutch valleys, found here and there embosomed in the great State of New-York, that population, manners, and customs, remain fixed; while the great torrent of migration and improvement, which is making such incessant changes in other parts of this restless country, sweeps by them unobserved. They are like those little nooks of still water which border a rapid stream; where we may see the straw and bubble riding quietly at anchor, or slowly revolving in their mimic harbor, undisturbed by the rush of the passing current. Though many years have elapsed since I trod the drowsy shades of Sleepy Hollow, yet I question whether I should not still find the same trees and the same families vegetating in its sheltered bosom.

In this by-place of nature, there abode, in a remote period of American history, that is to say, some thirty years since, a worthy wight of the name of Ichabod Crane; who sojourned, or, as he expressed it, "tarried," in Sleepy Hollow, for the purpose of instructing the children of the vicinity. He was a native of Connecticut; a State which supplies the Union with pioneers for the mind as well as for the forest, and sends forth yearly its legions of frontier woodsmen and country schoolmasters. The cognomen of Crane was not inapplicable to his person. He was tall, but exceedingly lank, with narrow shoulders, long arms and legs, hands that dangled a mile out of his sleeves, feet that might have served for shovels, and his whole frame most loosely hung together. His head was small, and flat at top, with huge ears, large green glassy eyes, and a long snipe nose, so that it looked like a weather-cock, perched upon his spindle neck, to tell which way the wind blew. To see him striding along the profile of a hill on a windy day, with his clothes bagging and fluttering about him, one might have mistaken him for the genius of famine descending upon the earth, or some scarecrow eloped from a cornfield.

His school-house was a low building of one large room, rudely constructed of logs; the windows partly glazed, and partly patched with leaves of old copy-books. It was most ingeniously secured at vacant hours, by a withe twisted in the handle of the door, and stakes set against the window shutters; so that, though a thief might get in with

---

[45] Reference to the superstition that spirits must return to their graves before dawn.

perfect ease, he would find some embarrassment in getting out; an idea most probably borrowed by the architect, Yost Van Houten, from the mystery of an eel-pot.[46] The school-house stood in a rather lonely but pleasant situation, just at the foot of a woody hill, with a brook running close by, and a formidable birch tree growing at one end of it. From hence the low murmur of his pupils' voices, conning over their lessons, might be heard in a drowsy summer's day, like the hum of a bee-hive; interrupted now and then by the authoritative voice of the master, in the tone of menace or command; or, peradventure, by the appalling sound of the birch, as he urged some tardy loiterer along the flowery path of knowledge. Truth to say, he was a conscientious man, and ever bore in mind the golden maxim, "Spare the rod and spoil the child."[47]—Ichabod Crane's scholars certainly were not spoiled.

I would not have it imagined, however, that he was one of those cruel potentates of the school, who joy in the smart[48] of their subjects; on the contrary, he administered justice with discrimination rather than severity; taking the burthen off the backs of the weak, and laying it on those of the strong. Your mere puny stripling, that winced at the least flourish of the rod, was passed by with indulgence; but the claims of justice were satisfied by inflicting a double portion on some little, tough, wrong-headed, broad-skirted Dutch urchin, who sulked and swelled and grew dogged and sullen beneath the birch. All this he called "doing his duty by their parents;" and he never inflicted a chastisement without following it by the assurance, so consolatory to the smarting urchin, that "he would remember it, and thank him for it the longest day he had to live."

When school hours were over, he was even the companion and playmate of the larger boys; and on holiday afternoons would convoy some of the smaller ones home, who happened to have pretty sisters, or good housewives for mothers, noted for the comforts of the cupboard. Indeed it behooved him to keep on good terms with his pupils. The revenue arising from his school was small, and would have been scarcely sufficient to furnish him with daily bread, for he was a huge feeder, and though lank, had the dilating powers of an anaconda;[49] but to help out his maintenance, he was, according to country custom in those parts, boarded and lodged at the houses of the farmers, whose children he instructed. With these he lived successively a week at a time; thus going the rounds of the neighborhood, with all his worldly effects tied up in a cotton handkerchief.

That all this might not be too onerous on the purses of his rustic patrons, who are apt to consider the costs of schooling a grievous burden, and schoolmasters as mere drones, he had various ways of rendering himself both useful and agreeable. He assisted the farmers occasionally in the lighter labors of their farms; helped to make hay; mended the fences; took the horses to water; drove the cows from pasture; and cut wood for the winter fire. He laid aside, too, all the dominant dignity and absolute sway with which he lorded it in his little empire, the school, and became wonderfully gentle and ingratiating. He found favor in the eyes of the mothers, by petting the

---

[46] Eel trap.

[47] From *Hudibras* (1664) by English poet Samuel Butler (1612–1680). The passage originates in Proverbs 13:24: "He that spareth his rod, hateth his son."

[48] Pain.

[49] Species of large snake capable of swallowing animals whole.

children, particularly the youngest; and like the lion bold, which whilom[50] so magnanimously the lamb did hold,[51] he would sit with a child on one knee, and rock a cradle with his foot for whole hours together.

In addition to his other vocations, he was the singing-master of the neighborhood, and picked up many bright shillings by instructing the young folks in psalmody. It was a matter of no little vanity to him, on Sundays, to take his station in front of the church gallery, with a band of chosen singers; where, in his own mind, he completely carried away the palm from the parson. Certain it is, his voice resounded far above all the rest of the congregation; and there are peculiar quavers still to be heard in that church, and which may even be heard half a mile off, quite to the opposite side of the mill-pond, on a still Sunday morning, which are said to be legitimately descended from the nose of Ichabod Crane. Thus, by divers little makeshifts in that ingenious way which is commonly denominated "by hook and by crook,"[52] the worthy pedagogue got on tolerably enough, and was thought, by all who understood nothing of the labor of headwork, to have a wonderfully easy life of it.

The schoolmaster is generally a man of some importance in the female circle of a rural neighborhood; being considered a kind of idle gentlemanlike personage, of vastly superior taste and accomplishments to the rough country swains, and, indeed, inferior in learning only to the parson. His appearance, therefore, is apt to occasion some little stir at the tea-table of a farmhouse, and the addition of a supernumerary dish of cakes or sweetmeats, or, peradventure, the parade of a silver tea-pot. Our man of letters, therefore, was peculiarly happy in the smiles of all the country damsels. How he would figure among them in the churchyard, between services on Sundays! gathering grapes for them from the wild vines that overrun the surrounding trees; reciting for their amusement all the epitaphs on the tombstones; or sauntering, with a whole bevy of them, along the banks of the adjacent mill-pond; while the more bashful country bumpkins hung sheepishly back, envying his superior elegance and address.

From his half itinerant life, also, he was a kind of travelling gazette, carrying the whole budget of local gossip from house to house; so that his appearance was always greeted with satisfaction. He was, moreover, esteemed by the women as a man of great erudition, for he had read several books quite through, and was a perfect master of Cotton Mather's[53] history of New England Witchcraft, in which, by the way, he most firmly and potently believed.

He was, in fact, an odd mixture of small shrewdness and simple credulity. His appetite for the marvellous, and his powers of digesting it, were equally extraordinary; and both had been increased by his residence in this spellbound region. No tale was too gross or monstrous for his capacious swallow. It was often his delight, after his school was dismissed in the afternoon, to stretch himself on the rich bed of clover,

---

[50] Formerly.

[51] The *New England Primer* represents the letter *L* with a lion and a lamb and the rhyme "The Lion Bold / The Lamb doth hold" (from Isaiah 11:6–9).

[52] From "Colyn Cloute" (1519?) by John Skelton (1460?–1529), English poet.

[53] Cotton Mather (1663–1728), author of *Memorable Providences Relating to Witchcraft* (1689) and *The Wonders of the Invisible World* (1693).

bordering the little brook that whimpered by his school-house, and there con over old Mather's direful tales, until the gathering dusk of the evening made the printed page a mere mist before his eyes. Then, as he wended his way, by swamp and stream and awful woodland, to the farmhouse where he happened to be quartered, every sound of nature, at that witching hour, fluttered his excited imagination: the moan of the whip-poor-will[54] from the hill-side; the boding cry of the tree-toad, that harbinger of storm; the dreary hooting of the screech-owl, or the sudden rustling in the thicket of birds frightened from their roost. The fire-flies, too, which sparkled most vividly in the darkest places, now and then startled him, as one of uncommon brightness would stream across his path; and if, by chance, a huge blockhead of a beetle came winging his blundering flight against him, the poor varlet was ready to give up the ghost, with the idea that he was struck with a witch's token. His only resource on such occasions, either to drown thought, or drive away evil spirits, was to sing psalm tunes;—and the good people of Sleepy Hollow, as they sat by their doors of an evening, were often filled with awe, at hearing his nasal melody, "in linked sweetness long drawn out,"[55] floating from the distant hill, or along the dusky road.

Another of his sources of fearful pleasure was to pass long winter evenings with the old Dutch wives, as they sat spinning by the fire, with a row of apples roasting and spluttering along the hearth, and listen to their marvellous tales of ghosts and goblins, and haunted fields, and haunted brooks, and haunted bridges, and haunted houses, and particularly of the headless horseman, or galloping Hessian of the Hollow, as they sometimes called him. He would delight them equally by his anecdotes of witchcraft, and of the direful omens and portentous sights and sounds in the air, which prevailed in the earlier times of Connecticut; and would frighten them wofully with speculations upon comets and shooting stars; and with the alarming fact that the world did absolutely turn round, and that they were half the time topsy-turvy!

But if there was a pleasure in all this, while snugly cuddling in the chimney corner of a chamber that was all of a ruddy glow from the crackling wood fire, and where, of course, no spectre dared to show his face, it was dearly purchased by the terrors of his subsequent walk homewards. What fearful shapes and shadows beset his path amidst the dim and ghastly glare of a snowy night!—With what wistful look did he eye every trembling ray of light streaming across the waste fields from some distant window!—How often was he appalled by some shrub covered with snow, which, like a sheeted spectre, beset his very path!—How often did he shrink with curdling awe at the sound of his own steps on the frosty crust beneath his feet; and dread to look over his shoulder, lest he should behold some uncouth being tramping close behind him!—and how often was he thrown into complete dismay by some rushing blast, howling among the trees, in the idea that it was the Galloping Hessian on one of his nightly scourings!

All these, however, were mere terrors of the night, phantoms of the mind that walk in darkness; and though he had seen many spectres in his time, and been more than once beset by Satan in divers shapes, in his lonely perambulations, yet daylight put

---

[54] Irving's note: "The whip-poor-will is a bird which is only heard at night. It receives its name from its note, which is thought to resemble those words."

[55] From "L'Allegro" (1632) by John Milton (1608–1674), English poet.

an end to all these evils; and he would have passed a pleasant life of it, in despite of the devil and all his works, if his path had not been crossed by a being that causes more perplexity to mortal man than ghosts, goblins, and the whole race of witches put together, and that was—a woman.

Among the musical disciples who assembled, one evening in each week, to receive his instructions in psalmody, was Katrina Van Tassel, the daughter and only child of a substantial Dutch farmer. She was a blooming lass of fresh eighteen; plump as a partridge; ripe and melting and rosy cheeked as one of her father's peaches, and universally famed, not merely for her beauty, but her vast expectations. She was withal a little of a coquette, as might be perceived even in her dress, which was a mixture of ancient and modern fashions, as most suited to set off her charms. She wore the ornaments of pure yellow gold, which her great-great-grandmother had brought over from Saardam;[56] the tempting stomacher[57] of the olden time; and withal a provokingly short petticoat, to display the prettiest foot and ankle in the country round.

Ichabod Crane had a soft and foolish heart towards the sex; and it is not to be wondered at, that so tempting a morsel soon found favor in his eyes; more especially after he had visited her in her paternal mansion. Old Baltus Van Tassel was a perfect picture of a thriving, contented, liberal-hearted farmer. He seldom, it is true, sent either his eyes or his thoughts beyond the boundaries of his own farm; but within those every thing was snug, happy, and well-conditioned. He was satisfied with his wealth, but not proud of it; and piqued himself upon the hearty abundance, rather than the style in which he lived. His stronghold was situated on the banks of the Hudson, in one of those green, sheltered, fertile nooks, in which the Dutch farmers are so fond of nestling. A great elm-tree spread its broad branches over it; at the foot of which bubbled up a spring of the softest and sweetest water, in a little well, formed of a barrel; and then stole sparkling away through the grass, to a neighboring brook, that bubbled along among alders and dwarf willows. Hard by the farmhouse was a vast barn, that might have served for a church; every window and crevice of which seemed bursting forth with the treasures of the farm; the flail was busily resounding within it from morning to night; swallows and martins skimmed twittering about the eaves; and rows of pigeons, some with one eye turned up, as if watching the weather, some with their heads under their wings, or buried in their bosoms, and others swelling, and cooing, and bowing about their dames, were enjoying the sunshine on the roof. Sleek unwieldy porkers were grunting in the repose and abundance of their pens; whence sallied forth, now and then, troops of sucking pigs, as if to snuff the air. A stately squadron of snowy geese were riding in an adjoining pond, convoying whole fleets of ducks; regiments of turkeys were gobbling through the farmyard, and guinea fowls fretting about it, like ill-tempered housewives, with their peevish discontented cry. Before the barn door strutted the gallant cock, that pattern of a husband, a warrior, and a fine gentleman, clapping his burnished wings, and crowing in the pride and gladness of his heart—sometimes tearing up the earth with his feet, and then generously calling his ever-hungry family of wives and children to enjoy the rich morsel which he had discovered.

---

[56] Modern Zaandam, near Amsterdam.
[57] Decorated centerpiece of the bodice or waistband of a dress.

The pedagogue's mouth watered, as he looked upon this sumptuous promise of luxurious winter fare. In his devouring mind's eye, he pictured to himself every roasting-pig running about with a pudding in his belly, and an apple in his mouth; the pigeons were snugly put to bed in a comfortable pie, and tucked in with a coverlet of crust; the geese were swimming in their own gravy; and the ducks pairing cosily in dishes, like snug married couples, with a decent competency of onion sauce. In the porkers he saw carved out the future sleek side of bacon, and juicy relishing ham; not a turkey but he beheld daintily trussed up, with its gizzard under its wing, and, peradventure, a necklace of savory sausages; and even bright chanticleer himself lay sprawling on his back, in a side-dish, with uplifted claws, as if craving that quarter[58] which his chivalrous spirit disdained to ask while living.

As the enraptured Ichabod fancied all this, and as he rolled his great green eyes over the fat meadow-lands, the rich fields of wheat, of rye, of buckwheat, and Indian corn, and the orchards burthened with ruddy fruit, which surrounded the warm tenement of Van Tassel, his heart yearned after the damsel who was to inherit these domains, and his imagination expanded with the idea, how they might be readily turned into cash, and the money invested in immense tracts of wild land, and shingle palaces in the wilderness. Nay, his busy fancy already realized his hopes, and presented to him the blooming Katrina, with a whole family of children, mounted on the top of a wagon loaded with household trumpery, with pots and kettles dangling beneath; and he beheld himself bestriding a pacing mare, with a colt at her heels, setting out for Kentucky, Tennessee, or the Lord knows where.

When he entered the house the conquest of his heart was complete. It was one of those spacious farmhouses, with high-ridged, but lowly-sloping roofs, built in the style handed down from the first Dutch settlers; the low projecting eaves forming a piazza along the front, capable of being closed up in bad weather. Under this were hung flails, harness, various utensils of husbandry, and nets for fishing in the neighboring river. Benches were built along the sides for summer use; and a great spinning-wheel at one end, and a churn at the other, showed the various uses to which this important porch might be devoted. From this piazza the wondering Ichabod entered the hall, which formed the centre of the mansion and the place of usual residence. Here, rows of resplendent pewter, ranged on a long dresser, dazzled his eyes. In one corner stood a huge bag of wool ready to be spun; in another a quantity of linsey-woolsey just from the loom; ears of Indian corn, and strings of dried apples and peaches, hung in gay festoons along the walls, mingled with the gaud of red peppers; and a door left ajar gave him a peep into the best parlor, where the claw-footed chairs, and dark mahogany tables, shone like mirrors; and irons, with their accompanying shovel and tongs, glistened from their covert of asparagus tops; mock-oranges and conch-shells decorated the mantel-piece; strings of various colored birds' eggs were suspended above it: a great ostrich egg was hung from the centre of the room, and a corner cupboard, knowingly left open, displayed immense treasures of old silver and well-mended china.

From the moment Ichabod laid his eyes upon these regions of delight, the peace of his mind was at an end, and his only study was how to gain the affections of the peerless daughter of Van Tassel. In this enterprise, however, he had more real difficul-

[58] Clemency.

ties than generally fell to the lot of a knight-errant of yore, who seldom had any thing but giants, enchanters, fiery dragons, and such like easily-conquered adversaries, to contend with; and had to make his way merely through gates of iron and brass, and walls of adamant, to the castle keep, where the lady of his heart was confined; all which he achieved as easily as a man would carve his way to the centre of a Christmas pie; and then the lady gave him her hand as a matter of course. Ichabod, on the contrary, had to win his way to the heart of a country coquette, beset with a labyrinth of whims and caprices, which were for ever presenting new difficulties and impediments; and he had to encounter a host of fearful adversaries of real flesh and blood, the numerous rustic admirers, who beset every portal to her heart; keeping a watchful and angry eye upon each other, but ready to fly out in the common cause against any new competitor.

Among these the most formidable was a burly, roaring, roystering blade, of the name of Abraham, or, according to the Dutch abbreviation, Brom Van Brunt, the hero of the country round, which rang with his feats of strength and hardihood. He was broad-shouldered and double-jointed, with short curly black hair, and a bluff, but not unpleasant countenance, having a mingled air of fun and arrogance. From his Herculean frame and great powers of limb, he had received the nickname of BROM BONES, by which he was universally known. He was famed for great knowledge and skill in horsemanship, being as dexterous on horseback as a Tartar.[59] He was foremost at all races and cock-fights; and, with the ascendency which bodily strength acquires in rustic life, was the umpire in all disputes, setting his hat on one side, and giving his decisions with an air and tone admitting of no gainsay or appeal. He was always ready for either a fight or a frolic; but had more mischief than ill-will in his composition; and, with all his overbearing roughness, there was a strong dash of waggish good humor at bottom. He had three or four boon companions, who regarded him as their model, and at the head of whom he scoured the country, attending every scene of feud or merriment for miles round. In cold weather he was distinguished by a fur cap, surmounted with a flaunting fox's tail; and when the folks at a country gathering descried this well-known crest at a distance, whisking about among a squad of hard riders, they always stood by for a squall. Sometimes his crew would be heard dashing along past the farmhouses at midnight, with whoop and halloo, like a troop of Don Cossacks;[60] and the old dames, startled out of their sleep, would listen for a moment till the hurry-scurry had clattered by, and then exclaim, "Ay, there goes Brom Bones and his gang!" The neighbors looked upon him with a mixture of awe, admiration, and good will; and when any madcap prank, or rustic brawl, occurred in the vicinity, always shook their heads, and warranted Brom Bones was at the bottom of it.

This rantipole[61] hero had for some time singled out the blooming Katrina for the object of his uncouth gallantries, and though his amorous toyings were something like the gentle caresses and endearments of a bear, yet it was whispered that she did not altogether discourage his hopes. Certain it is, his advances were signals for rival candidates to retire, who felt no inclination to cross a lion in his amours; insomuch, that when his horse was seen tied to Van Tassel's paling, on a Sunday night, a sure

---

[59] Violent Asian warrior.
[60] Russian cavalry of the Don River area.
[61] Wild and reckless.

sign that his master was courting, or, as it is termed, "sparking," within, all other suitors passed by in despair, and carried the war into other quarters.

Such was the formidable rival with whom Ichabod Crane had to contend, and, considering all things, a stouter man than he would have shrunk from the competition, and a wiser man would have despaired. He had, however, a happy mixture of pliability and perseverance in his nature; he was in form and spirit like a supple-jack[62] —yielding, but tough; though he bent, he never broke; and though he bowed beneath the slightest pressure, yet, the moment it was away—jerk! he was as erect, and carried his head as high as ever.

To have taken the field openly against his rival would have been madness; for he was not a man to be thwarted in his amours, any more than that stormy lover, Achilles.[63] Ichabod, therefore, made his advances in a quiet and gently-insinuating manner. Under cover of his character of singing-master, he made frequent visits at the farmhouse; not that he had any thing to apprehend from the meddlesome interference of parents, which is so often a stumbling-block in the path of lovers. Balt Van Tassel was an easy indulgent soul; he loved his daughter better even than his pipe, and, like a reasonable man and an excellent father, let her have her way in every thing. His notable little wife, too, had enough to do to attend to her housekeeping and manage her poultry; for, as she sagely observed, ducks and geese are foolish things, and must be looked after, but girls can take care of themselves. Thus while the busy dame bustled about the house, or plied her spinning-wheel at one end of the piazza, honest Balt would sit smoking his evening pipe at the other, watching the achievements of a little wooden warrior, who, armed with a sword in each hand, was most valiantly fighting the wind on the pinnacle of the barn. In the mean time, Ichabod would carry on his suit with the daughter by the side of the spring under the great elm, or sauntering along in the twilight, that hour so favorable to the lover's eloquence.

I profess not to know how women's hearts are wooed and won. To me they have always been matters of riddle and admiration. Some seem to have but one vulnerable point, or door of access; while others have a thousand avenues, and may be captured in a thousand different ways. It is a great triumph of skill to gain the former, but a still greater proof of generalship to maintain possession of the latter, for the man must battle for his fortress at every door and window. He who wins a thousand common hearts is therefore entitled to some renown; but he who keeps undisputed sway over the heart of a coquette, is indeed a hero. Certain it is, this was not the case with the redoubtable Brom Bones; and from the moment Ichabod Crane made his advances, the interests of the former evidently declined; his horse was no longer seen tied at the palings on Sunday nights, and a deadly feud gradually arose between him and the preceptor of Sleepy Hollow.

Brom, who had a degree of rough chivalry in his nature, would fain have carried matters to open warfare, and have settled their pretensions to the lady, according to the mode of those most concise and simple reasoners, the knights-errant of yore— by single combat; but Ichabod was too conscious of the superior might of his adversary to enter the lists against him: he had overheard a boast of Bones, that he would "double the schoolmaster up, and lay him on a shelf of his own school-house;" and he was

---

[62] A woody vine with strong, pliant stems.
[63] In Homer's *Iliad* Achilles became furious when his captive love, Briseis, was taken from him by King Agamemnon.

too wary to give him an opportunity. There was something extremely provoking in this obstinately pacific system; it left Brom no alternative but to draw upon the funds of rustic waggery in his disposition, and to play off boorish practical jokes upon his rival. Ichabod became the object of whimsical persecution to Bones, and his gang of rough riders. They harried his hitherto peaceful domains; smoked out his singing school, by stopping up the chimney; broke into the school-house at night, in spite of its formidable fastenings of withe and window stakes, and turned every thing topsy-turvy: so that the poor schoolmaster began to think all the witches in the country held their meetings there. But what was still more annoying, Brom took all opportunities of turning him into ridicule in presence of his mistress, and had a scoundrel dog whom he taught to whine in the most ludicrous manner, and introduced as a rival of Ichabod's to instruct her in psalmody.

In this way matters went on for some time, without producing any material effect on the relative situation of the contending powers. On a fine autumnal afternoon, Ichabod, in pensive mood, sat enthroned on the lofty stool whence he usually watched all the concerns of his little literary realm. In his hand he swayed a ferule, that sceptre of despotic power; the birch of justice reposed on three nails, behind the throne, a constant terror to evil doers; while on the desk before him might be seen sundry contraband articles and prohibited weapons, detected upon the persons of idle urchins; such as half-munched apples, popguns, whirligigs, fly-cages, and whole legions of rampant little paper game-cocks. Apparently there had been some appalling act of justice recently inflicted, for his scholars were all busily intent upon their books, or slyly whispering behind them with one eye kept upon the master; and a kind of buzzing stillness reigned throughout the school-room. It was suddenly interrupted by the appearance of a negro, in tow-cloth jacket and trowsers, a round-crowned fragment of a hat, like the cap of Mercury,[64] and mounted on the back of a ragged, wild, half-broken colt, which he managed with a rope by way of halter. He came clattering up to the school door with an invitation to Ichabod to attend a merry-making or "quilting frolic," to be held that evening at Mynheer Van Tassel's; and having delivered his message with that air of importance, and effort at fine language, which a negro is apt to display on petty embassies of the kind, he dashed over the brook, and was seen scampering away up the hollow, full of the importance and hurry of his mission.

All was now bustle and hubbub in the late quiet school-room. The scholars were hurried through their lessons, without stopping at trifles; those who were nimble skipped over half with impunity, and those who were tardy, had a smart application now and then in the rear, to quicken their speed, or help them over a tall word. Books were flung aside without being put away on the shelves, inkstands were overturned, benches thrown down, and the whole school was turned loose an hour before the usual time, bursting forth like a legion of young imps, yelping and racketing about the green, in joy at their early emancipation.

The gallant Ichabod now spent at least an extra half hour at his toilet, brushing and furbishing up his best, and indeed only suit of rusty black, and arranging his looks by a bit of broken looking-glass, that hung up in the school-house. That he might

---

[64] The winged hat of Mercury, Roman messenger of the gods, is a symbol of speed.

make his appearance before his mistress in the true style of a cavalier, he borrowed a horse from the farmer with whom he was domiciliated, a choleric old Dutchman, of the name of Hans Van Ripper, and, thus gallantly mounted, issued forth, like a knight-errant in quest of adventures. But it is meet I should, in the true spirit of romantic story, give some account of the looks and equipments of my hero and his steed. The animal he bestrode was a broken-down plough-horse, that had outlived almost every thing but his viciousness. He was gaunt and shagged, with a ewe neck and a head like a hammer; his rusty mane and tail were tangled and knotted with burrs; one eye had lost its pupil, and was glaring and spectral; but the other had the gleam of a genuine devil in it. Still he must have had fire and mettle in his day, if we may judge from the name he bore of Gunpowder. He had, in fact, been a favorite steed of his master's, the choleric Van Ripper, who was a furious rider, and had infused, very probably, some of his own spirit into the animal; for, old and broken-down as he looked, there was more of the lurking devil in him than in any young filly in the country.

Ichabod was a suitable figure for such a steed. He rode with short stirrups, which brought his knees nearly up to the pommel of the saddle; his sharp elbows stuck out like grasshoppers'; he carried his whip perpendicularly in his hand, like a sceptre, and, as his horse jogged on, the motion of his arms was not unlike the flapping of a pair of wings. A small wool hat rested on the top of his nose, for so his scanty strip of forehead might be called; and the skirts of his black coat fluttered out almost to the horse's tail. Such was the appearance of Ichabod and his steed, as they shambled out of the gate of Hans Van Ripper, and it was altogether such an apparition as is seldom to be met with in broad daylight.

It was, as I have said, a fine autumnal day, the sky was clear and serene, and nature wore that rich and golden livery which we always associate with the idea of abundance. The forests had put on their sober brown and yellow, while some trees of the tenderer kind had been nipped by the frosts into brilliant dyes of orange, purple, and scarlet. Streaming files of wild ducks began to make their appearance high in the air; the bark of the squirrel might be heard from the groves of beech and hickory nuts, and the pensive whistle of the quail at intervals from the neighboring stubble-field.

The small birds were taking their farewell banquets. In the fulness of their revelry, they fluttered, chirping and frolicking, from bush to bush, and tree to tree, capricious from the very profusion and variety around them. There was the honest cock-robin, the favorite game of stripling sportsmen, with its loud querulous note; and the twittering blackbirds flying in sable clouds; and the golden-winged woodpecker, with his crimson crest, his broad black gorget,[65] and splendid plumage; and the cedar bird, with its red-tipt wings and yellow-tipt tail, and its little monteiro cap of feathers;[66] and the blue jay, that noisy coxcomb, in his gay light-blue coat and white under-clothes; screaming and chattering, nodding and bobbing and bowing, and pretending to be on good terms with every songster of the grove.

As Ichabod jogged slowly on his way, his eye, ever open to every symptom of culinary abundance, ranged with delight over the treasures of jolly autumn. On all

---

[65] Throat.
[66] I.e., a feathered plume resembling a hunting cap with flaps.

sides he beheld vast store of apples; some hanging in oppressive opulence on the trees; some gathered into baskets and barrels for the market; others heaped up in rich piles for the cider-press. Farther on he beheld great fields of Indian corn, with its golden ears peeping from their leafy coverts, and holding out the promise of cakes and hasty pudding; and the yellow pumpkins lying beneath them, turning up their fair round bellies to the sun, and giving ample prospects of the most luxurious of pies; and anon he passed the fragrant buckwheat fields, breathing the odor of the bee-hive, and as he beheld them, soft anticipations stole over his mind of dainty slapjacks, well buttered, and garnished with honey or treacle, by the delicate little dimpled hand of Katrina Van Tassel.

Thus feeding his mind with many sweet thoughts and "sugared suppositions," he journeyed along the sides of a range of hills which look out upon some of the goodliest scenes of the mighty Hudson. The sun gradually wheeled his broad disk down into the west. The wide bosom of the Tappan Zee lay motionless and glassy, excepting that here and there a gentle undulation waved and prolonged the blue shadow of the distant mountain. A few amber clouds floated in the sky, without a breath of air to move them. The horizon was of a fine golden tint, changing gradually into a pure apple green, and from that into the deep blue of the midheaven. A slanting ray lingered on the woody crests of the precipices that overhung some parts of the river, giving greater depth to the dark-gray and purple of their rocky sides. A sloop was loitering in the distance, dropping slowly down with the tide, her sail hanging uselessly against the mast; and as the reflection of the sky gleamed along the still water, it seemed as if the vessel was suspended in the air.

It was toward evening that Ichabod arrived at the castle of the Heer Van Tassel, which he found thronged with the pride and flower of the adjacent country. Old farmers, a spare leathern-faced race, in homespun coats and breeches, blue stockings, huge shoes, and magnificent pewter buckles. Their brisk withered little dames, in close crimped caps, long-waisted shortgowns, homespun petticoats, with scissors and pin-cushions, and gay calico pockets hanging on the outside. Buxom lasses, almost as antiquated as their mothers, excepting where a straw hat, a fine ribbon, or perhaps a white frock, gave symptoms of city innovation. The sons, in short square-skirted coats with rows of stupendous brass buttons, and their hair generally queued in the fashion of the times, especially if they could procure an eel-skin for the purpose, it being esteemed, throughout the country, as a potent nourisher and strengthener of the hair.

Brom Bones, however, was the hero of the scene, having come to the gathering on his favorite steed Daredevil, a creature, like himself, full of mettle and mischief, and which no one but himself could manage. He was, in fact, noted for preferring vicious animals, given to all kinds of tricks, which kept the rider in constant risk of his neck, for he held a tractable well-broken horse as unworthy of a lad of spirit.

Fain would I pause to dwell upon the world of charms that burst upon the enraptured gaze of my hero, as he entered the state parlor of Van Tassel's mansion. Not those of the bevy of buxom lasses, with their luxurious display of red and white; but the ample charms of a genuine Dutch country tea-table, in the sumptuous time of autumn. Such heaped-up platters of cakes of various and almost indescribable kinds, known only to experienced Dutch housewives! There was the doughty dough-nut, the tenderer oly koek,[67] and the crisp and crumbling cruller; sweet cakes and short cakes, ginger cakes and honey cakes, and the whole family of cakes. And then there were apple pies and peach pies and pumpkin pies; besides slices of ham and smoked beef; and moreover delectable dishes of preserved plums, and peaches, and pears, and quinces; not to mention broiled shad and roasted chickens; together with bowls of milk and cream, all mingled higgledy-piggledy, pretty much as I have enumerated them, with the motherly tea-pot sending up its clouds of vapor from the midst— Heaven bless the mark! I want breath and time to discuss this banquet as it deserves, and am too eager to get on with my story. Happily, Ichabod Crane was not in so great a hurry as his historian, but did ample justice to every dainty.

He was a kind and thankful creature, whose heart dilated in proportion as his skin was filled with good cheer; and whose spirits rose with eating as some men's do with drink. He could not help, too, rolling his large eyes round him as he ate, and chuckling with the possibility that he might one day be lord of all this scene of almost unimaginable luxury and splendor. Then, he thought, how soon he'd turn his back upon the old school-house; snap his fingers in the face of Hans Van Ripper, and every other niggardly patron, and kick any itinerant pedagogue out of doors that should dare to call him comrade!

Old Baltus Van Tassel moved about among his guests with a face dilated with content and good humor, round and jolly as the harvest moon. His hospitable attentions were brief, but expressive, being confined to a shake of the hand, a slap on the shoulder, a loud laugh, and a pressing invitation to "fall to, and help themselves."

And now the sound of the music from the common room, or hall, summoned to the dance. The musician was an old grayheaded negro, who had been the itinerant orchestra of the neighborhood for more than half a century. His instrument was as old and battered as himself. The greater part of the time he scraped on two or three strings, accompanying every movement of the bow with a motion of the head; bowing almost to the ground, and stamping with his foot whenever a fresh couple were to start.

Ichabod prided himself upon his dancing as much as upon his vocal powers. Not a limb, not a fibre about him was idle; and to have seen his loosely hung frame in full motion, and clattering about the room, you would have thought Saint Vitus[68] himself, that blessed patron of the dance, was figuring before you in person. He was the admiration of all the negroes; who, having gathered, of all ages and sizes, from the farm and the neighborhood, stood forming a pyramid of shining black faces at every door and window, gazing with delight at the scene, rolling their white eye-balls, and showing grinning rows of ivory from ear to ear. How could the flogger of urchins be otherwise than animated and joyous? the lady of his heart was his partner in the dance, and smiling graciously in reply to all his amorous oglings; while Brom Bones, sorely smitten with love and jealousy, sat brooding by himself in one corner.

When the dance was at an end, Ichabod was attracted to a knot of the sager folks,

---

[67] "Oil cake," a delicate pastry fried in oil.
[68] Early Christian martyr invoked by victims of nervous disorders.

who, with old Van Tassel, sat smoking at one end of the piazza, gossiping over former times, and drawing out long stories about the war.

This neighborhood, at the time of which I am speaking, was one of those highly-favored places which abound with chronicle and great men. The British and American line had run near it during the war; it had, therefore, been the scene of marauding, and infested with refugees, cow-boys,[69] and all kinds of border chivalry. Just sufficient time had elapsed to enable each story-teller to dress up his tale with a little becoming fiction, and, in the indistinctness of his recollection, to make himself the hero of every exploit.

There was the story of Doffue Martling, a large blue-bearded Dutchman, who had nearly taken a British frigate with an old iron nine-pounder[70] from a mud breastwork, only that his gun burst at the sixth discharge. And there was an old gentleman who shall be nameless, being too rich a mynheer to be lightly mentioned, who, in the battle of Whiteplains,[71] being an excellent master of defence, parried a musket ball with a small sword, insomuch that he absolutely felt it whiz round the blade, and glance off at the hilt: in proof of which, he was ready at any time to show the sword, with the hilt a little bent. There were several more that had been equally great in the field, not one of whom but was persuaded that he had a considerable hand in bringing the war to a happy termination.

But all these were nothing to the tales of ghosts and apparitions that succeeded. The neighborhood is rich in legendary treasures of the kind. Local tales and superstitions thrive best in these sheltered long-settled retreats; but are trampled under foot by the shifting throng that forms the population of most of our country places. Besides, there is no encouragement for ghosts in most of our villages, for they have scarcely had time to finish their first nap, and turn themselves in their graves, before their surviving friends have travelled away from the neighborhood; so that when they turn out at night to walk their rounds, they have no acquaintance left to call upon. This is perhaps the reason why we so seldom hear of ghosts except in our long-established Dutch communities.

The immediate cause, however, of the prevalence of supernatural stories in these parts, was doubtless owing to the vicinity of Sleepy Hollow. There was a contagion in the very air that blew from that haunted region; it breathed forth an atmosphere of dreams and fancies infecting all the land. Several of the Sleepy Hollow people were present at Van Tassel's, and, as usual, were doling out their wild and wonderful legends. Many dismal tales were told about funeral trains, and mourning cries and wailings heard and seen about the great tree where the unfortunate Major André[72] was taken, and which stood in the neighborhood. Some mention was made also of the woman in white, that haunted the dark glen at Raven Rock, and was often heard to shriek on winter nights before a storm, having perished there in the snow. The chief part of the stories, however, turned upon the favorite spectre of Sleepy Hollow, the headless horseman, who had been heard several times of late, patrolling the country; and, it was said, tethered his horse nightly among the graves in the churchyard.

[69] Bands of pro-British guerillas operating near New York during the Revolution.
[70] Small cannon.
[71] Scene of George Washington's defeat by the British near New York City in 1776.

[72] John André (1751–1780), captured and executed as a British spy.

The sequestered situation of this church seems always to have made it a favorite haunt of troubled spirits. It stands on a knoll, surrounded by locust-trees and lofty elms, from among which its decent whitewashed walls shine modestly forth, like Christian purity beaming through the shades of retirement. A gentle slope descends from it to a silver sheet of water, bordered by high trees, between which, peeps may be caught at the blue hills of the Hudson. To look upon its grass-grown yard, where the sunbeams seem to sleep so quietly, one would think that there at least the dead might rest in peace. On one side of the church extends a wide woody dell, along which raves a large brook among broken rocks and trunks of fallen trees. Over a deep black part of the stream, not far from the church, was formerly thrown a wooden bridge; the road that led to it, and the bridge itself, were thickly shaded by overhanging trees, which cast a gloom about it, even in the daytime; but occasioned a fearful darkness at night. This was one of the favorite haunts of the headless horseman; and the place where he was most frequently encountered. The tale was told of old Brouwer, a most heretical disbeliever in ghosts, how he met the horseman returning from his foray into Sleepy Hollow, and was obliged to get up behind him; how they galloped over bush and brake, over hill and swamp, until they reached the bridge; when the horseman suddenly turned into a skeleton, threw old Brouwer into the brook, and sprang away over the tree-tops with a clap of thunder.

This story was immediately matched by a thrice marvellous adventure of Brom Bones, who made light of the galloping Hessian as an arrant jockey.[73] He affirmed that, on returning one night from the neighboring village of Sing Sing,[74] he had been overtaken by this midnight trooper; that he had offered to race with him for a bowl of punch, and should have won it too, for Daredevil beat the goblin horse all hollow, but, just as they came to the church-bridge, the Hessian bolted, and vanished in a flash of fire.

All these tales, told in that drowsy undertone with which men talk in the dark, the countenances of the listeners only now and then receiving a casual gleam from the glare of a pipe, sank deep in the mind of Ichabod. He repaid them in kind with large extracts from his invaluable author, Cotton Mather, and added many marvellous events that had taken place in his native State of Connecticut, and fearful sights which he had seen in his nightly walks about Sleepy Hollow.

The revel now gradually broke up. The old farmers gathered together their families in their wagons, and were heard for some time rattling along the hollow roads, and over the distant hills. Some of the damsels mounted on pillions behind their favorite swains, and their light-hearted laughter, mingling with the clatter of hoofs, echoed along the silent woodlands, sounding fainter and fainter until they gradually died away—and the late scene of noise and frolic was all silent and deserted. Ichabod only lingered behind, according to the custom of country lovers, to have a te-à-te with the heiress, fully convinced that he was now on the high road to success. What passed at this interview I will not pretend to say, for in fact I do not know. Something, however, I fear me, must have gone wrong, for he certainly sallied forth, after no very great interval, with an air quite desolate and chop-fallen.—Oh these women! these women! Could that girl have been playing off any of her coquettish tricks?— Was her encouragement of the poor pedagogue all a mere sham to secure her conquest

[73] Fraud or cheat.   [74] Now known as Ossining, New York.

of his rival?—Heaven only knows, not I!—Let it suffice to say, Ichabod stole forth with the air of one who had been sacking a hen-roost, rather than a fair lady's heart. Without looking to the right or left to notice the scene of rural wealth, on which he had so often gloated, he went straight to the stable, and with several hearty cuffs and kicks, roused his steed most uncourteously from the comfortable quarters in which he was soundly sleeping, dreaming of mountains of corn and oats, and whole valleys of timothy and clover.

It was the very witching time of night[75] that Ichabod, heavy-hearted and crest-fallen, pursued his travel homewards, along the sides of the lofty hills which rise above Tarry Town, and which he had traversed so cheerily in the afternoon. The hour was as dismal as himself. Far below him, the Tappan Zee spread its dusky and indistinct waste of waters, with here and there the tall mast of a sloop, riding quietly at anchor under the land. In the dead hush of midnight, he could even hear the barking of the watch dog from the opposite shore of the Hudson; but it was so vague and faint as only to give an idea of his distance from this faithful companion of man. Now and then, too, the long-drawn crowing of a cock, accidentally awakened, would sound far, far off, from some farmhouse away among the hills—but it was like a dreaming sound in his ear. No signs of life occurred near him, but occasionally the melancholy chirp of a cricket, or perhaps the guttural twang of a bull-frog, from a neighboring marsh, as if sleeping uncomfortably, and turning suddenly in his bed.

All the stories of ghosts and goblins that he had heard in the afternoon, now came crowding upon his recollection. The night grew darker and darker; the stars seemed to sink deeper in the sky, and driving clouds occasionally hid them from his sight. He had never felt so lonely and dismal. He was, moreover, approaching the very place where many of the scenes of the ghost stories had been laid. In the centre of the road stood an enormous tulip-tree, which towered like a giant above all the other trees of the neighborhood, and formed a kind of landmark. Its limbs were gnarled, and fantastic, large enough to form trunks for ordinary trees, twisting down almost to the earth, and rising again into the air. It was connected with the tragical story of the unfortunate André, who had been taken prisoner hard by; and was universally known by the name of Major André's tree. The common people regarded it with a mixture of respect and superstition, partly out of sympathy for the fate of its ill-starred namesake, and partly from the tales of strange sights and doleful lamentations told concerning it.

As Ichabod approached this fearful tree, he began to whistle: he thought his whistle was answered—it was but a blast sweeping sharply through the dry branches. As he approached a little nearer, he thought he saw something white, hanging in the midst of the tree—he paused and ceased whistling; but on looking more narrowly, perceived that it was a place where the tree had been scathed by lightning, and the white wood laid bare. Suddenly he heard a groan—his teeth chattered and his knees smote against the saddle: it was but the rubbing of one huge bough upon another, as they were swayed about by the breeze. He passed the tree in safety, but new perils lay before him.

About two hundred yards from the tree a small brook crossed the road, and ran

[75] As described in Shakespeare's *Hamlet,* Act III, Sc. ii, l. 406.

into a marshy and thickly-wooded glen, known by the name of Wiley's swamp. A few rough logs, laid side by side, served for a bridge over this stream. On that side of the road where the brook entered the wood, a group of oaks and chestnuts, matted thick with wild grapevines, threw a cavernous gloom over it. To pass this bridge was the severest trial. It was at this identical spot that the unfortunate André was captured, and under the covert of those chestnuts and vines were the sturdy yoemen concealed who surprised him. This has ever since been considered a haunted stream, and fearful are the feelings of the schoolboy who has to pass it alone after dark.

As he approached the stream his heart began to thump; he summoned up, however, all his resolution, gave his horse half a score of kicks in the ribs, and attempted to dash briskly across the bridge; but instead of starting forward, the perverse old animal made a lateral movement, and ran broadside against the fence. Ichabod, whose fears increased with the delay, jerked the reins on the other side, and kicked lustily with the contrary foot: it was all in vain; his steed started, it is true, but it was only to plunge to the opposite side of the road into a thicket of brambles and alder bushes. The schoolmaster now bestowed both whip and heel upon the starveling ribs of old Gunpowder, who dashed forward, snuffling and snorting, but came to a stand just by the bridge, with a suddenness that had nearly sent his rider sprawling over his head. Just at this moment a plashy tramp by the side of the bridge caught the sensitive ear of Ichabod. In the dark shadow of the grove, on the margin of the brook, he beheld something huge, misshapen, black and towering. It stirred not, but seemed gathered up in the gloom, like some gigantic monster ready to spring upon the traveller.

The hair of the affrighted pedagogue rose upon his head with terror. What was to be done? To turn and fly was now too late; and besides, what chance was there of escaping ghost or goblin, if such it was, which could ride upon the wings of the wind? Summoning up, therefore, a show of courage, he demanded in stammering accents—"Who are you?" He received no reply. He repeated his demand in a still more agitated voice. Still there was no answer. Once more he cudgelled the sides of the inflexible Gunpowder, and, shutting his eyes, broke forth with involuntary fervor into a psalm tune. Just then the shadowy object of alarm put itself in motion, and, with a scramble and a bound, stood at once in the middle of the road. Though the night was dark and dismal, yet the form of the unknown might now in some degree be ascertained. He appeared to be a horseman of large dimensions, and mounted on a black horse of powerful frame. He made no offer of molestation or sociability, but kept aloof on one side of the road, jogging along on the blind side of old Gunpowder, who had now got over his fright and waywardness.

Ichabod, who had no relish for this strange midnight companion, and bethought himself of the adventure of Brom Bones with the Galloping Hessian, now quickened his steed, in hopes of leaving him behind. The stranger, however, quickened his horse to an equal pace. Ichabod pulled up, and fell into a walk, thinking to lag behind— the other did the same. His heart began to sink within him; he endeavored to resume his psalm tune, but his parched tongue clove to the roof of his mouth, and he could not utter a stave. There was something in the moody and dogged silence of this pertinacious companion, that was mysterious and appalling. It was soon fearfully accounted for. On mounting a rising ground, which brought the figure of his fellow-traveller in relief against the sky, gigantic in height, and muffled in a cloak, Ichabod was horror-struck, on perceiving that he was headless!—but his horror was still more increased, on observing that the head, which should have rested on his shoulders, was carried before him on the pommel of the saddle: his terror rose to desperation; he rained a shower of kicks and blows upon Gunpowder, hoping, by a sudden movement, to give his companion the slip—but the spectre started full jump with him. Away then they dashed, through thick and thin; stones flying, and sparks flashing at every bound. Ichabod's flimsy garments fluttered in the air, as he stretched his long lank body away over his horse's head, in the eagerness of his flight.

They had now reached the road which turns off to Sleepy Hollow; but Gunpowder, who seemed possessed with a demon, instead of keeping up it, made an opposite turn, and plunged headlong down hill to the left. This road leads through a sandy hollow, shaded by trees for about a quarter of a mile, where it crosses the bridge famous in goblin story, and just beyond swells the green knoll on which stands the whitewashed church.

As yet the panic of the steed had given his unskilful rider an apparent advantage in the chase; but just as he had got half way through the hollow, the girths of the saddle gave way, and he felt it slipping from under him. He seized it by the pommel, and endeavored to hold it firm, but in vain; and had just time to save himself by clasping old Gunpowder round the neck, when the saddle fell to the earth, and he heard it trampled under foot by his pursuer. For a moment the terror of Hans Van Ripper's wrath passed across his mind—for it was his Sunday saddle; but this was no time for petty fears; the goblin was hard on his haunches; and (unskilful rider that he was!) he had much ado to maintain his seat; sometimes slipping on one side, sometimes on another, and sometimes jolted on the high ridge of his horse's back-bone, with a violence that he verily feared would cleave him asunder.

An opening in the trees now cheered him with the hopes that the church bridge was at hand. The wavering reflection of a silver star in the bosom of the brook told him that he was not mistaken. He saw the walls of the church dimly glaring under the trees beyond. He recollected the place where Brom Bones's ghostly competitor had disappeared. "If I can but reach that bridge," thought Ichabod, "I am safe."[76] Just then he heard the black steed panting and blowing close behind him; he even fancied that he felt his hot breath. Another convulsive kick in the ribs, and old Gunpowder sprang upon the bridge; he thundered over the resounding planks; he gained the opposite side; and now Ichabod cast a look behind to see if his pursuer should vanish, according to rule, in a flash of fire and brimstone. Just then he saw the goblin rising in his stirrups, and in the very act of hurling his head at him. Ichabod endeavored to dodge the horrible missile, but too late. It encountered his cranium with a tremendous crash—he was tumbled headlong into the dust, and Gunpowder, the black steed, and the goblin rider, passed by like a whirlwind.

The next morning the old horse was found without his saddle, and with the bridle under his feet, soberly cropping the grass at his master's gate. Ichabod did not make his appearance at breakfast—dinner-hour came, but no Ichabod. The boys assembled at the school-house, and strolled idly about the banks of the brook; but no schoolmaster. Hans Van Ripper now began to feel some uneasiness about the fate of poor Ichabod, and his saddle. An inquiry was set on foot, and after diligent investigation

[76] Superstition maintained that evil spirits could not cross water.

they came upon his traces. In one part of the road leading to the church was found the saddle trampled in the dirt; the tracks of horses' hoofs deeply dented in the road, and evidently at furious speed, were traced to the bridge, beyond which, on the bank of a broad part of the brook, where the water ran deep and black, was found the hat of the unfortunate Ichabod, and close beside it a shattered pumpkin.

The brook was searched, but the body of the schoolmaster was not to be discovered. Hans Van Ripper, as executor of his estate, examined the bundle which contained all his worldly effects. They consisted of two shirts and a half; two stocks[77] for the neck; a pair or two of worsted stockings; an old pair of corduroy small-clothes; a rusty razor; a book of psalm tunes, full of dogs' ears; and a broken pitchpipe. As to the books and furniture of the school-house, they belonged to the community, excepting Cotton Mather's History of Witchcraft, a New England Almanac, and a book of dreams and fortune-telling; in which last was a sheet of foolscap much scribbled and blotted in several fruitless attempts to make a copy of verses in honor of the heiress of Van Tassel. These magic books and the poetic scrawl were forthwith consigned to the flames by Hans Van Ripper; who from that time forward determined to send his children no more to school; observing, that he never knew any good come of this same reading and writing. Whatever money the schoolmaster possessed, and he had received his quarter's pay but a day or two before, he must have had about his person at the time of his disappearance.

The mysterious event caused much speculation at the church on the following Sunday. Knots of gazers and gossips were collected in the churchyard, at the bridge, and at the spot where the hat and pumpkin had been found. The stories of Brouwer, of Bones, and a whole budget of others, were called to mind; and when they had diligently considered them all, and compared them with the symptoms of the present case, they shook their heads, and came to the conclusion that Ichabod had been carried off by the galloping Hessian. As he was a bachelor, and in nobody's debt, nobody troubled his head any more about him. The school was removed to a different quarter of the hollow, and another pedagogue reigned in his stead.

It is true, an old farmer, who had been down to New York on a visit several years after, and from whom this account of the ghostly adventure was received, brought home the intelligence that Ichabod Crane was still alive; that he had left the neighborhood, partly through fear of the goblin and Hans Van Ripper, and partly in mortification at having been suddenly dismissed by the heiress; that he had changed his quarters to a distant part of the country; had kept school and studied law at the same time, had been admitted to the bar, turned politician, electioneered, written for the newspapers, and finally had been made a justice of the Ten Pound Court.[78] Brom Bones too, who shortly after his rival's disappearance conducted the blooming Katrina in triumph to the altar, was observed to look exceedingly knowing whenever the story of Ichabod was related, and always burst into a hearty laugh at the mention of the pumpkin; which led some to suspect that he knew more about the matter than he chose to tell.

The old country wives, however, who are the best judges of these matters, maintain to this day that Ichabod was spirited away by supernatural means; and it is a favorite story often told about the neighborhood round the winter evening fire. The bridge became more than ever an object of superstitious awe, and that may be the reason why

---

[77] Stock: scarf or cravat.   [78] Limited to cases involving no more than £10.

the road has been altered of late years, so as to approach the church by the border of the mill-pond. The school-house being deserted, soon fell to decay, and was reported to be haunted by the ghost of the unfortunate pedagogue; and the ploughboy, loitering homeward of a still summer evening, has often fancied his voice at a distance, chanting a melancholy psalm tune among the tranquil solitudes of Sleepy Hollow.

Postscript Found in the Handwriting of Mr. Knickerbocker.

The preceding Tale is given, almost in the precise words in which I heard it related at a Corporation meeting of the ancient city of Manhattoes,[79] at which were present many of its sagest and most illustrious burghers. The narrator was a pleasant, shabby, gentlemanly old fellow, in pepper-and-salt clothes, with a sadly humorous face; and one whom I strongly suspected of being poor,—he made such efforts to be entertaining. When his story was concluded, there was much laughter and approbation, particularly from two or three deputy aldermen, who had been asleep the greater part of the time. There was, however, one tall, dry-looking old gentleman, with beetling eyebrows, who maintained a grave and rather severe face throughout: now and then folding his arms, inclining his head, and looking down upon the floor, as if turning a doubt over in his mind. He was one of your wary men, who never laugh, but upon good grounds—when they have reason and the law on their side. When the mirth of the rest of the company had subsided, and silence was restored, he leaned one arm on the elbow of his chair, and, sticking the other akimbo, demanded, with a slight but exceedingly sage motion of the head, and contraction of the brow, what was the moral of the story, and what it went to prove?

The story-teller, who was just putting a glass of wine to his lips, as a refreshment after his toils, paused for a moment, looked at his inquirer with an air of infinite deference, and, lowering the glass slowly to the table, observed, that the story was intended most logically to prove:—

"That there is no situation in life but has its advantages and pleasures—provided we will but take a joke as we find it:

"That, therefore, he that runs races with goblin troopers is likely to have rough riding of it.

"Ergo, for a country schoolmaster to be refused the hand of a Dutch heiress, is a certain step to high preferment in the state."

The cautious old gentleman knit his brows tenfold closer after this explanation, being sorely puzzled by the ratiocination of the syllogism; while, methought, the one in pepper-and-salt eyed him with something of a triumphant leer. At length, he observed, that all this was very well, but still he thought the story a little on the extravagant—there were one or two points on which he had his doubts.

"Faith, sir," replied the story-teller, "as to that matter, I don't believe one-half of it myself."

D.K.

1819–1820

---

[79] I.e., New York City.

from A History of the Life and Voyages of Christopher Columbus

from Book IV

Chapter I: First Landing of Columbus in the New World

It was on Friday morning, the 12th of October, that Columbus first beheld the New World. As the day dawned he saw before him a level island, several leagues in extent, and covered with trees like a continual orchard. Though apparently uncultivated, it was populous, for the inhabitants were seen issuing from all parts of the woods and running to the shore. They were perfectly naked, and, as they stood gazing at the ships, appeared by their attitudes and gestures to be lost in astonishment. Columbus made signal for the ships to cast anchor, and the boats to be manned and armed. He entered his own boat, richly attired in scarlet, and holding the royal standard; whilst Martin Alonzo Pinzon, and Vincent Jañez his brother, put off in company in their boats; each with a banner of the enterprise emblazoned with a green cross, having on either side the letters F. and Y., the initials of the Castilian monarchs Fernando and Ysabel, surmounted by crowns.

As he approached the shore, Columbus, who was disposed for all kinds of agreeable impressions, was delighted with the purity and suavity of the atmosphere, the crystal transparency of the sea, and the extraordinary beauty of the vegetation. He beheld, also, fruits of an unknown kind upon the trees which overhung the shores. On landing he threw himself on his knees, kissed the earth, and returned thanks to God with tears of joy. His example was followed by the rest, whose hearts indeed overflowed with the same feelings of gratitude. Columbus then rising drew his sword, displayed the royal standard, and assembling round him the two captains, with Rodrigo de Escobedo, notary of the armament, Rodrigo Sanchez, and the rest who had landed, he took solemn possession in the name of the Castilian sovereigns, giving the island the name of San Salvador. Having complied with the requisite forms and ceremonies, he called upon all present to take the oath of obedience to him, as admiral and viceroy, representing the persons of the sovereigns.

The feelings of the crew now burst forth in the most extravagant transports. They had recently considered themselves devoted men, hurrying forward to destruction; they now looked upon themselves as favorites of fortune, and gave themselves up to the most unbounded joy. They thronged around the admiral with overflowing zeal, some embracing him, others kissing his hands. Those who had been most mutinous and turbulent during the voyage, were now most devoted and enthusiastic. Some begged favors of him, as if he had already wealth and honors in his gift. Many abject spirits, who had outraged him by their insolence, now crouched at his feet, begging pardon for all the trouble they had caused him, and promising the blindest obedience for the future.

The natives of the island, when, at the dawn of day, they had beheld the ships hovering on their coast, had supposed them monsters which had issued from the deep during the night. They had crowded to the beach, and watched their movements with awful anxiety. Their veering about, apparently without effort, and the shifting and furling of their sails, resembling huge wings, filled them with astonishment. When they beheld their boats approach the shore, and a number of strange beings clad in glittering steel, or raiment of various colors, landing upon the beach, they fled in affright to the woods. Finding, however, that there was no attempt to pursue nor molest them, they gradually recovered from their terror, and approached the Spaniards with great awe; frequently prostrating themselves on the earth, and making signs of adoration. During the ceremonies of taking possession, they remained gazing in timid admiration at the complexion, the beards, the shining armor, and splendid dress of the Spaniards. The admiral particularly attracted their attention, from his commanding height, his air of authority, his dress of scarlet, and the deference which was paid him by his companions; all which pointed him out to be the commander. When they had still further recovered from their fears, they approached the Spaniards, touched their beards, and examined their hands and faces, admiring their whiteness. Columbus was pleased with their gentleness and confiding simplicity, and suffered their scrutiny with perfect acquiescence, winning them by his benignity. They now supposed that the ships had sailed out of the crystal firmament which bounded their horizon, or had descended from above on their ample wings, and that these marvelous beings were inhabitants of the skies.

The natives of the island were no less objects of curiosity to the Spaniards, differing, as they did, from any race of men they had ever seen. Their appearance gave no promise of either wealth or civilization, for they were entirely naked, and painted with a variety of colors. With some it was confined merely to a part of the face, the nose, or around the eyes; with others it extended to the whole body, and gave them a wild and fantastic appearance. Their complexion was of a tawny or copper hue, and they were entirely destitute of beards. Their hair was not crisped, like the recently-discovered tribes of the African coast, under the same latitude, but straight and coarse, partly cut short above the ears, but some locks were left long behind and falling upon their shoulders. Their features, though obscured and disfigured by paint, were agreeable; they had lofty foreheads and remarkably fine eyes. They were of moderate stature and well-shaped; most of them appeared to be under thirty years of age: there was but one female with them, quite young, naked like her companions, and beautifully formed.

As Columbus supposed himself to have landed on an island at the extremity of India, he called the natives by the general appellation of Indians, which was universally adopted before the true nature of his discovery was known, and has since been extended to all the aboriginals of the New World.

The islanders were friendly and gentle. Their only arms were lances, hardened at the end by fire, or pointed with a flint, or the teeth or bone of a fish. There was no iron to be seen, nor did they appear acquainted with its properties; for, when a drawn sword was presented to them, they unguardedly took it by the edge.

Columbus distributed among them colored caps, glass beads, hawks' bells, and other trifles, such as the Portuguese were accustomed to trade with among the nations of the gold coast of Africa. They received them eagerly, hung the beads round their necks, and were wonderfully pleased with their finery, and with the sound of the bells. The Spaniards remained all day on shore refreshing themselves after their anxious voyage amidst the beautiful groves of the island; and returned on board late in the evening, delighted with all they had seen.

On the following morning, at break of day, the shore was thronged with the natives; some swam off to the ships, others came in light barks which they called canoes, formed of a single tree, hollowed, and capable of holding from one man to the number of forty or fifty. These they managed dextrously with paddles, and, if overturned, swam about in the water with perfect unconcern, as if in their natural element, righting their canoes with great facility, and baling them with calabashes.[1]

They were eager to procure more toys and trinkets, not, apparently, from any idea of their intrinsic value, but because every thing from the hands of the strangers possessed a supernatural virtue in their eyes, as having been brought from heaven; they even picked up fragments of glass and earthenware as valuable prizes. They had but few objects to offer in return, except parrots, of which great numbers were domesticated among them, and cotton yarn, of which they had abundance, and would exchange large balls of five and twenty pounds' weight for the merest trifle. They brought also cakes of a kind of bread called cassava,[2] which constituted a principal part of their food, and was afterwards an important article of provisions with the Spaniards. It was formed from a great root called yuca, which they cultivated in fields. This they cut into small morsels, which they grated or scraped, and strained in a press, making a broad thin cake, which was afterwards dried hard, and would keep for a long time, being steeped in water when eaten. It was insipid, but nourishing, though the water strained from it in the preparation was a deadly poison. There was another kind of yuca destitute of this poisonous quality, which was eaten in the root, either boiled or roasted.

The avarice of the discoverers was quickly excited by the sight of small ornaments of gold, worn by some of the natives in their noses. These the latter gladly exchanged for glass beads and hawks' bells; and both parties exulted in the bargain, no doubt admiring each other's simplicity. As gold, however, was an object of royal monopoly in all enterprises of discovery, Columbus forbade any traffic in it without his express sanction; and he put the same prohibition on the traffic for cotton, reserving to the crown all trade for it, wherever it should be found in any quantity.

He inquired of the natives where this gold was procured. They answered him by signs, pointing to the south, where, he understood them, dwelt a king of such wealth that he was served in vessels of wrought gold. He understood, also, that there was land to the south, the southwest, and the northwest; and that the people from the last mentioned quarter frequently proceeded to the southwest in quest of gold and precious stones, making in their way descents upon the islands, and carrying off the inhabitants. Several of the natives showed him scars of wounds received in battles with these invaders. It is evident that a great part of this fancied intelligence was self-delusion on the part of Columbus; for he was under a spell of the imagination, which gave its own shapes and colors to every object. He was persuaded that he had arrived among the islands described by Marco Polo, as lying opposite Cathay, in the Chinese sea, and

---

[1] Gourds that served as containers.
[2] The fleshy rootstocks of the cassava plant yielded a nutritious starch or flour.

he construed every thing to accord with the account given of those opulent regions. Thus the enemies which the natives spoke of as coming from the northwest, he concluded to be the people of the mainland of Asia, the subjects of the great Khan of Tartary, who were represented by the Venetian traveler as accustomed to make war upon the islands, and to enslave their inhabitants. The country to the south, abounding in gold, could be no other than the famous island of Cipango; and the king who was served out of vessels of gold, must be the monarch whose magnificent city and gorgeous palace, covered with plates of gold, had been extolled in such splendid terms by Marco Polo.

The island where Columbus had thus, for the first time, set his foot upon the New World, was called by the natives, Guanahanè. It still retains the name of San Salvador, which he gave to it, though called by the English, Cat Island. The light which he had seen the evening previous to his making land, may have been on Watling's Island, which lies a few leagues to the east. San Salvador is one of the great cluster of the Lucayos, or Bahama Islands, which stretch southeast and northwest, from the coast of Florida to Hispaniola, covering the northern coast of Cuba.

On the morning of the 14th of October, the admiral set off at daybreak with the boats of the ships to reconnoitre the island, directing his course to the northeast. The coast was surrounded by a reef of rocks, within which there was depth of water and sufficient harbor to receive all the ships in Christendom. The entrance was very narrow; within there were several sand-banks, but the water was as still as in a pool.

The island appeared throughout to be well wooded, with streams of water, and a large lake in the centre. As the boats proceeded, they passed two or three villages, the inhabitants of which, men as well as women, ran to the shores, throwing themselves on the ground, lifting up their hands and eyes, either giving thanks to Heaven, or worshiping the Spaniards as supernatural beings. They ran along parallel to the boats, calling after the Spaniards, and inviting them by signs to land, offering them various fruits and vessels of water. Finding, however, that the boats continued on their course, many threw themselves into the sea and swam after them, and others followed in canoes. The admiral received them all with kindness, giving them glass beads and other trifles, which were received with transport as celestial presents, for the invariable idea of the savages was, that the white men had come from the skies.

In this way they pursued their course, until they came to a small peninsula, which with two or three days' labor might be separated from the main-land and surrounded with water, and was therefore specified by Columbus as an excellent situation for a fortress. On this were six Indian cabins, surrounded by groves and gardens as beautiful as those of Castile. The sailors being wearied with rowing, and the island not appearing to the admiral of sufficient importance to induce colonization, he returned to the ships, taking seven of the natives with him, that they might acquire the Spanish language and serve as interpreters.

Having taken in a supply of wood and water, they left the island of San Salvador the same evening, the admiral being impatient to arrive at the wealthy country to the south, which he flattered himself would prove the famous island of Cipango.

1828

from A Tour on the Prairies

Chapter VII: News of the Rangers—The Count and His Indian Squire—Halt in the Woods— Woodland Scene—Osage Village—Osage Visitors at Our Evening Camp

In the morning early, (Oct. 12,) the two Creeks who had been sent express by the commander of Fort Gibson, to stop the company of rangers, arrived at our encampment on their return. They had left the company encamped about fifty miles distant, in a fine place on the Arkansas, abounding in game, where they intended to await our arrival. This news spread animation throughout our party, and we set out on our march at sunrise, with renewed spirit.

In mounting our steeds, the young Osage attempted to throw a blanket upon his wild horse. The fine, sensitive animal took fright, reared and recoiled. The attitudes of the wild horse and the almost naked savage, would have formed studies for a painter or a statuary.

I often pleased myself in the course of our march, with noticing the appearance of the young Count and his newly-enlisted follower, as they rode before me. Never was preux chevalier[1] better suited with an esquire. The Count was well mounted, and as I have before observed, was a bold and graceful rider. He was fond, too, of caracoling[2] his horse, and dashing about in the buoyancy of youthful spirits. His dress was a gay Indian hunting frock of dressed deer skin, setting well to the shape, dyed of a beautiful purple, and fancifully embroidered with silks of various colors; as if it had been the work of some Indian beauty, to decorate a favorite chief. With this he wore leathern pantaloons and moccasons, a foraging cap, and a double-barrelled gun slung by a bandoleer[3] athwart his back: so that he was quite a picturesque figure as he managed gracefully his spirited steed.

The young Osage would ride close behind him on his wild and beautifully mottled horse, which was decorated with crimson tufts of hair. He rode with his finely shaped head and bust naked; his blanket being girt round his waist. He carried his rifle in one hand, and managed his horse with the other, and seemed ready to dash off at a moment's warning, with his youthful leader, on any madcap foray or scamper. The Count, with the sanguine anticipations of youth, promised himself many hardy adventures and exploits in company with his youthful "brave," when we should get among the buffaloes, in the Pawnee hunting grounds.

After riding some distance, we crossed a narrow, deep stream, upon a solid bridge, the remains of an old beaver dam; the industrious community which had constructed it had all been destroyed. Above us, a streaming flight of wild geese, high in air, and making a vociferous noise, gave note of the waning year.

About half past ten o'clock we made a halt in a forest, where there was abundance of the pea-vine.[4] Here we turned the horses loose to graze. A fire was made, water

---

[1] French: "gallant horseman."
[2] Somewhat theatrical zigzag turn made in horsemanship.

[3] Broad belt worn over the shoulder.
[4] Prairie plant that bears peas.

procured from an adjacent spring, and in a short time our little Frenchman, Tonish, had a pot of coffee prepared for our refreshment. While partaking of it, we were joined by an old Osage, one of a small hunting party who had recently passed this way. He was in search of his horse, which had wandered away, or been stolen. Our half-breed, Beatte, made a wry face on hearing of Osage hunters in this direction. "Until we pass those hunters," said he, "we shall see no buffaloes. They frighten away every thing like a prairie on fire."

The morning repast being over, the party amused themselves in various ways. Some shot with their rifles at a mark, others lay asleep half buried in the deep bed of foliage, with their heads resting on their saddles; others gossiped round the fire at the foot of a tree, which sent up wreaths of blue smoke among the branches. The horses banqueted luxuriously on the pea-vines, and some lay down and rolled amongst them.

We were overshadowed by lofty trees, with straight, smooth trunks, like stately columns; and as the glancing rays of the sun shone through the transparent leaves, tinted with the many-colored hues of autumn, I was reminded of the effect of sunshine among the stained windows and clustering columns of a Gothic cathedral. Indeed there is a grandeur and solemnity in our spacious forests of the West, that awaken in me the same feeling I have experienced in those vast and venerable piles, and the sound of the wind sweeping through them, supplies occasionally the deep breathings of the organ.

About noon the bugle sounded to horse, and we were again on the march, hoping to arrive at the encampment of the rangers before night; as the old Osage had assured us it was not above ten or twelve miles distant. In our course through a forest, we passed by a lonely pool, covered with the most magnificent water-lilies I had ever beheld; among which swam several wood-ducks, one of the most beautiful of water-fowl, remarkable for the gracefulness and brilliancy of its plumage.

After proceeding some distance farther, we came down upon the banks of the Arkansas, at a place where tracks of numerous horses, all entering the water, showed where a party of Osage hunters had recently crossed the river on their way to the buffalo range. After letting our horses drink in the river, we continued along its bank for a space, and then across prairies, where we saw a distant smoke, which we hoped might proceed from the encampment of the rangers. Following what we supposed to be their trail, we came to a meadow in which were a number of horses grazing: they were not, however, the horses of the troop. A little farther on, we reached a straggling Osage village, on the banks of the Arkansas. Our arrival created quite a sensation. A number of old men came forward and shook hands with us all severally; while the women and children huddled together in groups, staring at us wildly, chattering and laughing among themselves. We found that all the young men of the village had departed on a hunting expedition, leaving the women and children and old men behind. Here the Commissioner made a speech from on horseback; informing his hearers of the purport of his mission, to promote a general peace among the tribes of the West, and urging them to lay aside all warlike and bloodthirsty notions, and not to make any wanton attacks upon the Pawnees. This speech being interpreted by Beatte, seemed to have a most pacifying effect upon the multitude, who promised faithfully that, as far as in them lay, the peace should not be disturbed; and indeed their age and sex gave some reason to trust that they would keep their word.

Still hoping to reach the camp of the rangers before nightfall, we pushed on until twilight, when we were obliged to halt on the borders of a ravine. The rangers bivouacked under trees, at the bottom of the dell, while we pitched our tent on a rocky knoll near a running stream. The night came on dark and overcast, with flying clouds, and much appearance of rain. The fires of the rangers burnt brightly in the dell, and threw strong masses of light upon the robber-looking groups that were cooking, eating and drinking around them. To add to the wildness of the scene, several Osage Indians, visitors from the village we had passed, were mingled among the men. Three of them came and seated themselves by our fire. They watched every thing that was going on round them in silence, and looked like figures of monumental bronze. We gave them food, and, what they most relished, coffee; for the Indians partake in the universal fondness for this beverage which pervades the West. When they had made their supper, they stretched themselves, side by side, before the fire, and began a low nasal chant, drumming with their hands upon their breasts, by way of accompaniment. Their chant seemed to consist of regular staves, every one terminating, not in a melodious cadence, but in the abrupt interjection huh! uttered almost like a hiccup. This chant, we were told by our interpreter, Beatte, related to ourselves, our appearance, our treatment of them, and all that they knew of our plans. In one part they spoke of the young Count, whose animated character and eagerness for Indian enterprise had struck their fancy, and they indulged in some waggery about him and the young Indian beauties, that produced great merriment among our half-breeds.

This mode of improvising is common throughout the savage tribes; and in this way, with a few simple inflections of the voice, they chant all their exploits in war and hunting, and occasionally indulge in a vein of comic humor and dry satire, to which the Indians appear to me much more prone than is generally imagined.

In fact, the Indians that I have had an opportunity of seeing in real life, are quite different from those described in poetry. They are by no means the stoics that they are represented; taciturn, unbending, without a tear or a smile. Taciturn they are, it is true, when in company with white men, whose good-will they distrust, and whose language they do not understand; but the white man is equally taciturn under like circumstances. When the Indians are among themselves, however, there cannot be greater gossips. Half their time is taken up in talking over their adventures in war and hunting, and in telling whimsical stories. They are great mimics and buffoons, also, and entertain themselves excessively at the expense of the whites with whom they have associated, and who have supposed them impressed with profound respect for their grandeur and dignity. They are curious observers, noting every thing in silence, but with a keen and watchful eye; occasionally exchanging a glance or a grunt with each other, when any thing particularly strikes them: but reserving all comments until they are alone. Then it is that they give full scope to criticism, satire, mimicry, and mirth.

In the course of my journey along the frontier, I have had repeated opportunities of noticing their excitability and boisterous merriment at their games; and have occasionally noticed a group of Osages sitting round a fire until a late hour of the night, engaged in the most animated and lively conversation; and at times making the woods resound with peals of laughter. As to tears, they have them in abundance, both real and affected; at times they make a merit of them. No one weeps more bitterly or profusely at the death of a relative or friend: and they have stated times when they repair to howl and lament at their graves. I have heard doleful wailings at daybreak, in the neighboring Indian villages, made by some of the inhabitants, who go out at that hour into the fields, to mourn and weep for the dead: at such times, I am told, the tears will stream down their cheeks in torrents.

As far as I can judge, the Indian of poetical fiction is like the shepherd of pastoral romance, a mere personification of imaginary attributes.

The nasal chant of our Osage guests gradually died away; they covered their heads with their blankets and fell fast asleep, and in a little while all was silent, excepting the pattering of scattered rain-drops upon our tent.

In the morning our Indian visitors breakfasted with us, but the young Osage who was to act as esquire to the Count in his knight-errantry on the prairies, was nowhere to be found. His wild horse, too, was missing, and, after many conjectures, we came to the conclusion that he had taken "Indian leave" of us in the night. We afterwards ascertained that he had been persuaded so to do by the Osages we had recently met with; who had represented to him the perils that would attend him in an expedition to the Pawnee hunting grounds, where he might fall into the hands of the implacable enemies of his tribe: and, what was scarcely less to be apprehended, the annoyances to which he would be subjected from the capricious and overbearing conduct of the white men; who, as I have witnessed in my own short experience, are prone to treat the poor Indians as little better than brute animals. Indeed, he had had a specimen of it himself in the narrow escape he made from the infliction of "Lynch's law,"[5] by the hard-winking worthy of the frontier, for the flagitious[6] crime of finding a stray horse.

The disappearance of the youth was generally regretted by our party, for we had all taken a great fancy to him from his handsome, frank, and manly appearance, and the easy grace of his deportment. He was indeed a native-born gentleman. By none, however, was he so much lamented as by the young Count, who thus suddenly found himself deprived of his esquire. I regretted the departure of the Osage for his own sake, for we should have cherished him throughout the expedition, and I am convinced, from the munificent spirit of his patron, he would have returned to his tribe laden with wealth of beads and trinkets and Indian blankets.

Chapter IX: A Bee Hunt

The beautiful forest in which we were encamped abounded in bee-trees; that is to say, trees in the decayed trunks of which wild bees had established their hives. It is surprising in what countless swarms the bees have overspread the Far West, within but a moderate number of years. The Indians consider them the harbinger of the white man, as the buffalo is of the red man; and say that, in proportion as the bee advances, the Indian and buffalo retire. We are always accustomed to associate the hum of the bee-hive with the farmhouse and flower-garden, and to consider those industrious little animals as connected with the busy haunts of man, and I am told that the wild bee is seldom to be met with at any great distance from the frontier. They have been the heralds of civilization, steadfastly preceding it as it advanced from the Atlantic borders, and some of the ancient settlers of the West pretend to give the very year when the honey-bee first crossed the Mississippi. The Indians with surprise found the mouldering trees of their forests suddenly teeming with ambrosial sweets, and nothing,

---

[5] I.e., justice without due process of law.   [6] Shameful; egregious.

I am told, can exceed the greedy relish with which they banquet for the first time upon this unbought luxury of the wilderness.

At present the honey-bee swarms in myriads, in the noble groves and forests which skirt and intersect the prairies, and extend along the alluvial bottoms of the rivers. It seems to me as if these beautiful regions answer literally to the description of the land of promise, "a land flowing with milk and honey;" for the rich pasturage of the prairies is calculated to sustain herds of cattle as countless as the sands upon the sea-shore, while the flowers with which they are enamelled render them a very paradise for the nectar-seeking bee.

We had not been long in the camp when a party set out in quest of a bee-tree; and, being curious to witness the sport, I gladly accepted an invitation to accompany them. The party was headed by a veteran bee-hunter, a tall lank fellow in home-spun garb that hung loosely about his limbs, and a straw hat shaped not unlike a bee-hive; a comrade, equally uncouth in garb, and without a hat, straddled along at his heels, with a long rifle on his shoulder. To these succeeded half a dozen others, some with axes and some with rifles, for no one stirs far from the camp without his firearms, so as to be ready either for wild deer or wild Indian.

After proceeding some distance we came to an open glade on the skirts of the forest. Here our leader halted, and then advanced quietly to a low bush, on the top of which I perceived a piece of honey-comb. This I found was the bait or lure for the wild bees. Several were humming about it, and diving into its cells. When they had laden themselves with honey they would rise into the air, and dart off in a straight line, almost with the velocity of a bullet. The hunters watched attentively the course they took, and then set off in the same direction, stumbling along over twisted roots and fallen trees, with their eyes turned up to the sky. In this way they traced the honey-laden bees to their hive, in the hollow trunk of a blasted oak, where, after buzzing about for a moment, they entered a hole about sixty feet from the ground.

Two of the bee-hunters now plied their axes vigorously at the foot of the tree to level it with the ground. The mere spectators and amateurs, in the meantime, drew off to a cautious distance, to be out of the way of the falling of the tree and the vengeance of its inmates. The jarring blows of the axe seemed to have no effect in alarming or disturbing this most industrious community. They continued to ply at their usual occupations, some arriving full freighted into port, others sallying forth on new expeditions, like so many merchantmen in a money-making metropolis, little suspicious of impending bankruptcy and downfall. Even a loud crack which announced the disrupture of the trunk, failed to divert their attention from the intense pursuit of gain; at length down came the tree with a tremendous crash, bursting open from end to end, and displaying all the hoarded treasures of the commonwealth.

One of the hunters immediately ran up with a whisp of lighted hay as a defence against the bees. The latter, however, made no attack and sought no revenge; they seemed stupefied by the catastrophe and unsuspicious of its cause, and remained crawling and buzzing about the ruins without offering us any molestation. Every one of the party now fell to, with spoon and hunting knife, to scoop out the flakes of honey-comb with which the hollow trunk was stored. Some of them were of old date and a deep brown color, others were beautifully white, and the honey in their cells was almost limpid. Such of the combs as were entire were placed in camp kettles to be conveyed to the encampment; those which had been shivered in the fall were devoured upon the spot. Every stark bee-hunter was to be seen with a rich morsel in his hand, dripping about his fingers, and disappearing as rapidly as a cream tart before the holiday appetite of a schoolboy.

Nor was it the bee-hunters alone that profited by the downfall of this industrious community; as if the bees would carry through the similitude of their habits with those of laborious and gainful man, I beheld numbers from rival hives, arriving on eager wing, to enrich themselves with the ruins of their neighbors. These busied themselves as eagerly and cheerfully as so many wreckers on an Indiaman that has been driven on shore; plunging into the cells of the broken honey-combs, banqueting greedily on the spoil, and then winging their way full freighted to their homes. As to the poor proprietors of the ruin, they seemed to have no heart to do any thing, not even to taste the nectar that flowed around them; but crawled backwards and forwards, in vacant desolation, as I have seen a poor fellow with his hands in his pockets, whistling vacantly and despondingly about the ruins of his house that had been burnt.

It is difficult to describe the bewilderment and confusion of the bees of the bankrupt hive who had been absent at the time of the catastrophe, and who arrived from time to time, with full cargoes from abroad. At first they wheeled about in the air, in the place where the fallen tree had once reared its head, astonished at finding it all a vacuum. At length, as if comprehending their disaster, they settled down in clusters on a dry branch of a neighboring tree, whence they seemed to contemplate the prostrate ruin, and to buzz forth doleful lamentations over the downfall of their republic. It was a scene on which the "melancholy Jacques"[7] might have moralized by the hour.

We now abandoned the place, leaving much honey in the hollow of the tree. "It will all be cleared off by varmint," said one of the rangers. "What vermin?" asked I. "Oh, bears, and skunks, and racoons, and 'possums. The bears is the knowingest varmint for finding out a bee-tree in the world. They'll gnaw for days together at the trunk till they make a hole big enough to get in their paws, and then they'll haul out honey, bees and all."

Chapter XXIX: The Grand Prairie— A Buffalo Hunt

After proceeding about two hours in a southerly direction, we emerged towards mid-day from the dreary belt of the Cross Timber, and to our infinite delight beheld "the great Prairie," stretching to the right and left before us. We could distinctly trace the meandering course of the Main Canadian, and various smaller streams, by the strips of green forest that bordered them. The landscape was vast and beautiful. There is always an expansion of feeling in looking upon these boundless and fertile wastes; but I was doubly conscious of it after emerging from our "close dungeon of innumerous boughs."

From a rising ground Beatte pointed out the place where he and his comrades had killed the buffaloes; and we beheld several black objects moving in the distance, which he said were part of the herd. The Captain determined to shape his course to a woody bottom about a mile distant, and to encamp there for a day or two, by way of having

---

[7] In Shakespeare's *As You Like It.*

a regular buffalo hunt, and getting a supply of provisions. As the troop defiled along the slope of the hill towards the camping ground, Beatte proposed to my messmates and myself, that we should put ourselves under his guidance, promising to take us where we should have plenty of sport. Leaving the line of march, therefore, we diverged towards the prairie; traversing a small valley, and ascending a gentle swell of land. As we reached the summit, we beheld a gang of wild horses about a mile off. Beatte was immediately on the alert, and no longer thought of buffalo hunting. He was mounted on his powerful half-wild horse, with a lariat coiled at the saddle-bow, and set off in pursuit; while we remained on a rising ground watching his manœuvres with great solicitude. Taking advantage of a strip of woodland, he stole quietly along, so as to get close to them before he was perceived. The moment they caught sight of him a grand scamper took place. We watched him skirting along the horizon like a privateer in full chase of a merchantman; at length he passed over the brow of a ridge, and down into a shallow valley; in a few moments he was on the opposite hill, and close upon one of the horses. He was soon head and head, and appeared to be trying to noose his prey; but they both disappeared again below the hill, and we saw no more of them. It turned out afterwards, that he had noosed a powerful horse, but could not hold him, and had lost his lariat in the attempt.

While we were waiting for his return, we perceived two buffalo bulls descending a slope, towards a stream, which wound through a ravine fringed with trees. The young Count and myself endeavored to get near them under covert of the trees. They discovered us while we were yet three or four hundred yards off; and turning about, retreated up the rising ground. We urged our horses across the ravine, and gave chase. The immense weight of head and shoulders causes the buffalo to labor heavily up hill; but it accelerates his descent. We had the advantage, therefore, and gained rapidly upon the fugitives, though it was difficult to get our horses to approach them, their very scent inspiring them with terror. The Count, who had a double-barrelled gun loaded with ball, fired, but it missed. The bulls now altered their course, and galloped down hill with headlong rapidity. As they ran in different directions, we each singled one and separated. I was provided with a brace of veteran brass-barrelled pistols, which I had borrowed at Fort Gibson, and which had evidently seen some service. Pistols are very effective in buffalo hunting, as the hunter can ride up close to the animal, and fire at it while at full speed; whereas the long heavy rifles used on the frontier, cannot be easily managed, nor discharged with accurate aim from horseback. My object, therefore, was to get within pistol shot of the buffalo. This was no very easy matter. I was well mounted on a horse of excellent speed and bottom, that seemed eager for the chase, and soon overtook the game; but the moment he came nearly parallel, he would keep sheering off, with ears forked and pricked forward, and every symptom of aversion and alarm. It was no wonder. Of all animals, a buffalo, when close pressed by the hunter, has an aspect the most diabolical. His two short black horns, curve out of a huge frontlet of shaggy hair; his eyes glow like coals; his mouth is open, his tongue parched and drawn up into a half crescent; his tail is erect, and tufted and whisking about in the air, he is a perfect picture of mingled rage and terror.

It was with difficulty I urged my horse sufficiently near, when, taking aim, to my chagrin, both pistols missed fire. Unfortunately the locks of these veteran weapons were so much worn, that in the gallop, the priming had been shaken out of the pans. At the snapping of the last pistol I was close upon the buffalo, when, in his despair, he turned round with a sudden snort and rushed upon me. My horse wheeled about as if on a pivot, made a convulsive spring, and, as I had been leaning on one side with pistol extended, I came near being thrown at the feet of the buffalo.

Three or four bounds of the horse carried us out of the reach of the enemy; who, having merely turned in desperate self-defence, quickly resumed his flight. As soon as I could gather in my panic-stricken horse, and prime the pistols afresh, I again spurred in pursuit of the buffalo, who had slackened his speed to take breath. On my approach he again set off full tilt, heaving himself forward with a heavy rolling gallop, dashing with headlong precipitation through brakes and ravines, while several deer and wolves, startled from their coverts by his thundering career, ran helter-skelter to right and left across the waste.

A gallop across the prairies in pursuit of game, is by no means so smooth a career as those may imagine, who have only the idea of an open level plain. It is true, the prairies of the hunting ground are not so much entangled with flowering plants and long herbage as the lower prairies, and are principally covered with short buffalo grass; but they are diversified by hill and dale, and where most level, are apt to be cut up by deep rifts and ravines, made by torrents after rains; and which, yawning from an even surface, are almost like pitfalls in the way of the hunter, checking him suddenly, when in full career, or subjecting him to the risk of limb and life. The plains, too, are beset by burrowing holes of small animals, in which the horse is apt to sink to the fetlock,[8] and throw both himself and his rider. The late rain had covered some parts of the prairie, where the ground was hard, with a thin sheet of water, through which the horse had to splash his way. In other parts there were innumerable shallow hollows, eight or ten feet in diameter, made by the buffaloes, who wallow in sand and mud like swine. These being filled with water, shone like mirrors, so that the horse was continually leaping over them or springing on one side. We had reached, too, a rough part of the prairie, very much broken and cut up; the buffalo, who was running for life, took no heed to his course, plunging down break-neck ravines, where it was necessary to skirt the borders in search of a safer descent. At length we came to where a winter stream had torn a deep chasm across the whole prairie, leaving open jagged rocks, and forming a long glen bordered by steep crumbling cliffs of mingled stone and clay. Down one of these the buffalo flung himself, half tumbling, half leaping, and then scuttled along the bottom; while I, seeing all further pursuit useless, pulled up, and gazed quietly after him from the border of the cliff, until he disappeared amidst the windings of the ravine.

Nothing now remained but to turn my steed and rejoin my companions. Here at first was some little difficulty. The ardor of the chase had betrayed me into a long, heedless gallop. I now found myself in the midst of a lonely waste, in which the prospect was bounded by undulating swells of land, naked and uniform, where, from the deficiency of landmarks and distinct features, an inexperienced man may become bewildered, and lose his way as readily as in the wastes of the ocean. The day, too, was overcast, so that I could not guide myself by the sun; my only mode was to retrace the track my horse had made in coming, though this I would often lose sight of, where the ground was covered with parched herbage.

---

[8] Cushiony tuft of hair on the back of the leg just above the hoof of a horse.

To one unaccustomed to it, there is something inexpressibly lonely in the solitude of a prairie. The loneliness of a forest seems nothing to it. There the view is shut in by trees, and the imagination is left free to picture some livelier scene beyond. But here we have an immense extent of landscape without a sign of human existence. We have the consciousness of being far, far beyond the bounds of human habitation; we feel as if moving in the midst of a desert world. As my horse lagged slowly back over the scenes of our late scamper, and the delirium of the chase had passed away, I was peculiarly sensible to these circumstances. The silence of the waste was now and then broken by the cry of a distant flock of pelicans, stalking like spectres about a shallow pool; sometimes by the sinister croaking of a raven in the air, while occasionally a scoundrel wolf would scour off from before me; and, having attained a safe distance, would sit down and howl and whine with tones that gave a dreariness to the surrounding solitude.

After pursuing my way for some time, I descried a horseman on the edge of a distant hill, and soon recognized him to be the Count. He had been equally unsuccessful with myself; we were shortly after rejoined by our worthy comrade, the Virtuoso, who, with spectacles on nose, had made two or three ineffectual shots from horseback.

We determined not to seek the camp until we had made one more effort. Casting our eyes about the surrounding waste, we descried a herd of buffalo about two miles distant, scattered apart, and quietly grazing near a small strip of trees and bushes. It required but little stretch of fancy to picture them so many cattle grazing on the edge of a common, and that the grove might shelter some lowly farmhouse.

We now formed our plan to circumvent the herd, and by getting on the other side of them, to hunt them in the direction where we knew our camp to be situated: otherwise, the pursuit might take us to such a distance as to render it impossible to find our way back before nightfall. Taking a wide circuit therefore, we moved slowly and cautiously, pausing occasionally, when we saw any of the herd desist from grazing. The wind fortunately set from them, otherwise they might have scented us and have taken the alarm. In this way, we succeeded in getting round the herd without disturbing it. It consisted of about forty head, bulls, cows and calves. Separating to some distance from each other, we now approached slowly in a parallel line, hoping by degrees to steal near without exciting attention. They began, however, to move off quietly, stopping at every step or two to graze, when suddenly a bull that, unobserved by us, had been taking his siesta under a clump of trees to our left, roused himself from his lair, and hastened to join his companions. We were still at a considerable distance, but the game had taken the alarm. We quickened our pace, they broke into a gallop, and now commenced a full chase.

As the ground was level, they shouldered along with great speed, following each other in a line; two or three bulls bringing up the rear, the last of whom, from his enormous size and venerable frontlet, and beard of sunburnt hair, looked like the patriarch of the herd; and as if he might long have reigned the monarch of the prairie.

There is a mixture of the awful and the comic in the look of these huge animals, as they bear their great bulk forwards, with an up and down motion of the unwieldy head and shoulders; their tail cocked up like the cue of Pantaloon in a pantomime, the end whisking about in a fierce yet whimsical style, and their eyes glaring venomously with an expression of fright and fury.

For some time I kept parallel with the line, without being able to force my horse within pistol shot, so much had he been alarmed by the assault of the buffalo in the preceding chase. At length I succeeded, but was again balked by my pistols missing fire. My companions, whose horses were less fleet, and more way-worn, could not overtake the herd; at length Mr. L., who was in the rear of the line, and losing ground, levelled his double-barrelled gun, and fired a long raking shot. It struck a buffalo just above the loins, broke its back-bone, and brought it to the ground. He stopped and alighted to dispatch his prey, when borrowing his gun, which had yet a charge remaining in it, I put my horse to his speed, again overtook the herd which was thundering along, pursued by the Count. With my present weapon there was no need of urging my horse to such close quarters; galloping along parallel, therefore, I singled out a buffalo, and by a fortunate shot brought it down on the spot. The ball had struck a vital part; it could not move from the place where it fell, but lay there struggling in mortal agony, while the rest of the herd kept on their headlong career across the prairie.

Dismounting, I now fettered my horse to prevent his straying, and advanced to contemplate my victim. I am nothing of a sportsman; I had been prompted to this unwonted exploit by the magnitude of the game, and the excitement of an adventurous chase. Now that the excitement was over, I could not but look with commiseration upon the poor animal that lay struggling and bleeding at my feet. His very size and importance, which had before inspired me with eagerness, now increased my compunction. It seemed as if I had inflicted pain in proportion to the bulk of my victim, and as if there were a hundred-fold greater waste of life than there would have been in the destruction of an animal of inferior size.

To add to these after-qualms of conscience, the poor animal lingered in his agony. He had evidently received a mortal wound, but death might be long in coming. It would not do to leave him here to be torn piecemeal, while yet alive, by the wolves that had already snuffed his blood, and were sulking and howling at a distance, and waiting for my departure; and by the ravens that were flapping about, croaking dismally in the air. It became now an act of mercy to give him his quietus,[9] and put him out of his misery. I primed one of the pistols, therefore, and advanced close up to the buffalo. To inflict a wound thus in cold blood, I found a totally different thing from firing in the heat of the chase. Taking aim, however, just behind the fore-shoulder, my pistol for once proved true; the ball must have passed through the heart, for the animal gave one convulsive throe and expired.

While I stood meditating and moralizing over the wreck I had so wantonly produced, with my horse grazing near me, I was rejoined by my fellow-sportsman, the Virtuoso; who, being a man of universal adroitness, and withal, more experienced and hardened in the gentle art of "venerie,"[10] soon managed to carve out the tongue of the buffalo, and delivered it to me to bear back to the camp as a trophy.

1835

___

[9] Final release from life.   [10] Hunting.

James Fenimore Cooper
1789–1851

James Fenimore Cooper's life spans America's cultural transformation—from the new nation's anxious efforts to establish a distinctive cultural identity to its confident expression of a truly distinguished literary tradition in the mid-nineteenth-century "renaissance." In 1789, the year of Cooper's birth, American writers self-consciously struggled with the lag between the new republic's political and cultural independence. "The first was accomplished in about seven years," Philip Freneau wrote half humorously; "the latter will not be completely effected, perhaps, in as many centuries." In 1851, the year of Cooper's death, American readers had already seen the publication of most of Ralph Waldo Emerson's essays and poems, Edgar Allan Poe's tales and verse, Nathaniel Hawthorne's *The Scarlet Letter* (1850) and *House of the Seven Gables* (1851), and Herman Melville's *Moby-Dick* (1851). Henry David Thoreau's *Walden* (1854) and Walt Whitman's *Leaves of Grass* (1855) would follow within a few years of Cooper's death.

James Fenimore Cooper played a primary role in America's early literary development. Writing in 1831 as an author celebrated both in the United States and abroad, Cooper proposed a literary ambition that he had little difficulty satisfying: America's "mental independence is my object, and if I can go down to the grave with the reflection that I have done a little towards it, I shall have the consolation of knowing that I have not been useless in my generation." Cooper's accomplishments far exceeded his literary aims. He was the first American novelist to explore and define native themes, settings, and characters. He launched several distinct genres in American fiction: the American novel of manners, the sea novel, the European-American novel, and, in the "Leather-Stocking" series, the novel of the mythic frontier. Cooper also helped establish what has become the American writer's traditional role as a social and cultural critic.

Within fourteen months of their son's birth in Burlington, New Jersey, in 1789, Cooper's parents moved their family to the several-thousand-acre tract they owned on the shores of Otsego Lake in central New York State. Cooperstown, founded and named by his father, provided both the setting for much of Cooper's childhood and the source for his aristocratic view of the frontier and its inhabitants. Cooper's father, Judge William Cooper, a prominent political leader (a two-term member of Congress) as well as a wealthy merchant and landowner, passed on his ardent Federalist beliefs to his son. Trained from birth to be a country gentleman, James Cooper prepared for college by studying with an English tutor. He entered Yale at age thirteen, steeped in Shakespeare and the major eighteenth-century English poets. Within two years, Cooper had been summarily dismissed by Timothy Dwight, then the president, for rowdy behavior and dangerous pranks. Family tradition has it that young Cooper had set off a small explosion in another student's room by jamming a rag full of powder into the keyhole and igniting it.

Sent to sea by his father after his dismissal from Yale, Cooper served for two years as a deckhand on a merchant ship before being commissioned a midshipman in the navy, where he labored—without distinction or disruption—for the next three years. He resigned his commission in 1811 shortly after his marriage to Susan Augusta De Lancey, the daughter of a wealthy New York family with lingering Tory sentiments. His father died soon after—from a blow to the head received during a political dispute. Cooper's inheritance included more than fifty thousand dollars as well as his father's political and social conservatism. Quickly settled into a life as a country gentleman, Cooper revealed little initial interest in pursuing a career as a writer.

Cooper never freed himself completely from the legacy of his accomplished and strong-willed father. Their relationship in many respects previews the persistent tension evident both in Cooper's writing and in his nation's culture—the conflicting lures of the desire for personal and cultural originality and the attraction toward established forms and inherited contexts. This dual anxiety is most readily felt in Cooper's—and his nation's—attitudes toward the future: at once a celebratory anticipation and an overarching fear that undisciplined originality would lead to chaos. These contradictory impulses took on greater importance as the amount of Cooper's inheritance steadily dwindled.

Cooper plunged into a literary career at age thirty, when his wife urged him to act on his claim that he could write a better novel than the sentimental tale of rural English life he had been reading aloud to her. In her *Family Memoirs,* Cooper's daughter Susan recounts the episode that changed the course of her father's life:

> My mother was not well, she was lying on the sofa, and he was reading this newly imported novel to her; it must have been very trashy; after a chapter or two he threw it aside exclaiming, "I could write you a better book myself." Our mother laughed at the idea as at the height of absurdity—he who disliked writing even a letter, that he should write a book! He persisted in his declarations, however, and almost immediately wrote the first pages of a tale not yet named, the scene laid in England as a matter of course.

Impatient with his own efforts, Cooper destroyed those first pages but soon completed a full-length manuscript, *Precaution* (1820). A novel of manners in the tradition of Jane Austen, *Precaution* proved his point and left him with a lifelong urge to write.

Cooper's second novel, *The Spy: A Tale of the Neutral Ground* (1821), was yet another—although not immediate—product of that family incident. As Cooper later explained in *A Letter to His Countrymen* (1834):

> Accident first made me a writer, and the same accident gave a direction to my pen. Ashamed to have fallen into the track of imitation, I endeavored to repair the wrong done to my own views, by producing a work that should be purely American, and of which love of country should be the theme.

With the Revolutionary War as a backdrop, *The Spy* demonstrated Cooper's belief that American history could be a suitable setting for fiction. The novel quickly became a best-seller in the United States and in Europe. Within a year, it was reprinted in several editions, turned into a play, and translated into several languages. Cooper had suddenly become the most popular American writer in Europe.

The frontier of his childhood provided the setting for his third novel, *The Pioneers; or, The Sources of the Susquehanna*. Set in the Otsego Lake region during the decade following the Revolutionary War, *The Pioneers* also became an immediate best-seller and the first in what would become a series of five "Leather-Stocking Tales": *The Pioneers* (1823), *The Last of the Mohicans* (1826), *The Prairie* (1827), *The Pathfinder* (1840), and *The Deerslayer* (1841). (In relation to plot, the sequence is *The Deerslayer, The Last of the Mohicans, The Pathfinder, The Pioneers,* and *The Prairie*.) Deriving their collective title from their hero's nickname (based on his habit of wearing long deerskin leggings), the "Leather-Stocking Tales" trace the life, adventures, and death of Natty Bumppo and his Indian companions, most notably the chieftain Chingachgook. A simple character whose love of the wilderness and dislike of civilization's restraints remain consistent—and uncompromised—throughout the series, Natty Bumppo possesses the moral resolve, generosity, and resourcefulness that set the standard for American fictional heroes well into the twentieth century.

Following the publication of *The Pioneers,* Cooper's attention to American settings and characters promptly shifted from the wilderness to the sea. In *The Pilot* (1823), he set out to prove that he could draw on his own experience to create a more accurate and appealing rendition of life at sea than the English novelist Walter Scott had provided in his novel *The Pirate* (1823). The first of what would be Cooper's eleven sea novels, *The Pilot* blended technical detail, memorable characters (such as Long Tom Coffin), and patriotic appeal to create yet another enormously successful novel—a fictional precedent whose influence Herman Melville and Joseph Conrad would later generously acknowledge.

In the short span of three years, Cooper had opened three new territories for American fiction: the nation's past, its frontier, and its life at sea. The three settings of Cooper's fiction—and the characters who populated them—became the precursors of everything from the renegade heroes in the novels of such classic American writers as Melville, Twain, and Faulkner to the rugged western stereotypes in American dime novels and their celluloid counterparts in popular films and television.

By the mid-1820s, James Fenimore Cooper (he added his mother's maiden name in 1826) had established a formidable reputation in American literary circles. He moved to New York City, where he founded the Bread and Cheese Club, which included such notable literary figures as the poets Fitz-Greene Halleck and William Cullen Bryant and such celebrated painters as Asher Durand and Samuel F. B. Morse. To commemorate each of the thirteen original states and to strengthen his reputation as America's leading novelist, Cooper projected a series of novels on national themes. He completed only *Lionel Lincoln* (1825), a romantic tale of Boston during the Revolution.

The success of *The Pioneers* prompted Cooper to resume his account of the adventures of the frontier scout Natty Bumppo in *The Last of the Mohicans* (1826) and *The Prairie* (1827), completing the latter while traveling in Europe.

Initially drawn to the Continent because of his own poor health, his interest in introducing his daughters to Italian and French culture, and his eagerness to protect his royalties abroad, Cooper spent the next seven years there, based primarily in Lyons, where he served, often rather casually, as the American consul. During this period he also wrote several more novels, three of which— *The Red Rover* (1827), *The Wept of Wishton-Wish* (1829), and *The Water Witch* (1830)—focus on American history and life at sea.

While abroad, Cooper unhesitatingly defended American culture and democracy from attacks by cynical British commentators. Cooper responded to these critics in *Notions of the Americans* (1828), a series of fictional letters from a sophisticated European traveler to a member of a geographic society. The book, however, pleased neither the Americans, who were increasingly alienated both by Cooper's long absence and by his association with European aristocracy, nor the English, who preferred the America depicted in *The Pioneers*. Cooper returned to fiction in *The Bravo* (1831), *The Heidenmauer* (1832), and *The Headsman* (1833). This trilogy, published as a response to Sir Walter Scott's idealized treatment of medieval England, focused on the limits of European social standards by tracing their development out of feudal abuses. Cooper's seven years in Europe also marked a serious shift in his writing—from his early, largely optimistic writing to his later, more broad-ranging and highly critical work. The moral champion of American life would soon become one of its fiercest critics. And literature would become his means for proposing social reforms.

Cooper had set out for Europe during the presidency of John Quincy Adams. He returned to a far different place, Jacksonian America. Repulsed by what he regarded as President Jackson's vulgar and narrow version of frontier democracy, Cooper argued strenuously for a return to American life led by an elite minority, principally the Christian agrarian gentlemen of his youth. He was quickly judged a reactionary by the same Americans he had idealized while living abroad; he received neither the warm reception nor the privileged treatment afforded Washington Irving when he had returned from Europe the year before. Sorely disappointed by what he considered the mediocrity of Jacksonian democracy, Cooper launched a series of polemic salvos at American behavior and belief. *A Letter to His Countrymen* (1834), *The Monikins* (1835), four volumes of *Gleanings in Europe* (1837–1838), and *The American Democrat* (1838) express his social and political criticism as well as his aristocratic ideals. *Homeward Bound* (1838) and *Home as Found* (1838) render these same concerns in fictional terms.

Cooper's repudiation of the faults of the American society he returned to was neither cranky nor negative but reformist in character and intention. He returned to America hoping that he would find an independent culture equal to any in Europe; what he discovered was a nation whose excesses in the name of democracy were exacerbated by the mediocrity of its lowest-common-denominator approach to national issues and values. During what had become a fractious period in American history, Cooper hoped to unify American social and cultural principles and opinions. "It is high time," he wrote in *Gleanings in Europe,* "not only for the respectability, but for the *safety* of the American people, that they should promulgate a set of principles that are more in harmony with their facts." Cooper's purpose in writing had become as much to exert moral leadership as to set aesthetic standards.

Cooper envisioned an America in which democratic gentlemen would provide the leadership necessary to explore the full potential of the New World. These paragons would combine a respect for tradition with a commitment to democratic values and reasoned change. Their position would be achieved by merit rather than birth, by manifest quality rather than privilege. For Cooper, moderation and balance were cardinal virtues. In his vision, America would embody neither the common excesses of frontier democracy nor the traditional arrogance of European aristocracy. America would mature into a democracy in which the access afforded by social mobility would elevate the best people to positions of power. Yet if Cooper had served as the progenitor of American social criticism, he would also eventually become its victim.

There is both a hopeful exuberance and a mounting sadness in Cooper's social criticism. *Notions of the Americans* expressed his belief in his nation's unbounded possibilities, yet he steadily lost that faith as he realized that power in America had become the province of those he regarded as demagogues rather than of the Jeffersonian gentry like himself. Cooper feared the mediocrity that conformity inevitably produced.

Charged by the press with being a Tory renegade, Cooper spent a good deal of the rest of his life defending himself in public and suing his detractors for libel. More often than not, he won. He spent a good portion of each year in Cooperstown, where he enjoyed the companionship and support of his daughter Susan, who also served as his amanuensis. But he eventually became embroiled in controversy there as well. He sided with the rural landlords in their disputes with tenant farmers, a debate that erupted into violence in the "Anti-rent War" of the 1840s. The trilogy known as "The Littlepage Manuscripts"—*Satanstoe* (1845), *The Chainbearer* (1845), and *The Redskins* (1846)—traces three generations of the Littlepage family through the decades that led to the Anti-rent War.

During these years, Cooper's prodigious talents had also produced a controversial *History of the Navy* (1839), several biographies of naval officers and a former shipmate, and a book, *Mercedes of Castile* (1840), focusing on Columbus's first voyage to the New World. Other notable works included *Wyandotte* (1843), on the early days of the Revolution in New York; *Le Mouchoir* (1843), reissued as *Autobiography of a Pocket-Handkerchief*, a brief romantic sketch of New York's class distinctions; *Afloat and Ashore* (1844) and a sequel, *Miles Wallingford* (1844), which contains Cooper's fictional self-portrait; *The Crater* (1848), a utopian social allegory; and *Jack Tier* (1848), *The Oak Openings* (1848), and *Sea Lions* (1848), each a fast-paced historical romance. *The Ways of the Hour* (1850), Cooper's last novel, helped refine the nature of the mystery tale.

Despite the extraordinary range of his literary interests and accomplishments, Cooper's fame in his own day and his importance in American cultural history depended primarily, he realized, on the reception of his "Leather-Stocking Tales." He resumed the series with the publication of the fourth volume, *The Pathfinder*, in 1840 and concluded his treatment of Natty Bumppo in *The Deerslayer* (1841), which recounts the earliest exploits of his mythic hero in the years before the French and Indian Wars. The popularity of the "Leather-Stocking" series, their articulation of an American mythos, their movement from old age to youth (what D. H. Lawrence called "the true myth of America"), their progressive departure from overt social engagement, and their definition of the frontier as the primary fact of American history truly distinguished these novels as classics in American literature. Yet later generations of American writers, most notably Mark Twain in his widely read essay "Fenimore Cooper's Literary Offenses," ridiculed Cooper's handling of language, syntax, dialogue, plot, narrative pace, and characterization—especially his portrayal of women. As James Russell Lowell wryly noted in *A Fable for Critics* (1848): "The women he draws from one model don't vary, / All sappy as maples and flat as a prairie." Such criticism reduced the "Leather-Stocking" series to the status of elementary school texts by the turn of the twentieth century. Renewed attention to Cooper's social criticism in the 1920s gradually led to a reassessment of the "Leather-Stocking" novels.

Although Cooper did have considerable difficulty developing a style to express adequately the distinctiveness of his American subject matter in the "Leather-Stocking Tales," he did unfold several themes that quickly took on mythic importance in American literary history. Cooper used some of the major thematic concerns of the series—advancing a sense of both temporal order and the past's continued presence—to help give shape to American history at a time when our nation's historical consciousness seemed precarious and ephemeral. The "Leather-Stocking" series also helped define the American preoccupation with the landscape. Cooper had recognized quite early that space was—and remains—*the* fundamental reality of American life. And his depiction of the American land— and more particularly his ability to envision personal freedom in the unencumbered space stretching beyond the confines of institutional life—enabled his "Leather-Stocking Tales" to transcend the creakiness of his plots and the clumsiness of his language. As a cultural mediator between civilization and the wilderness, Natty Bumppo served as the metaphor for all that Cooper achieved— an image of an ideal, balanced existence that receded ceaselessly into the past. As Cooper explained in his preface to the "Leather-Stocking Tales," Natty Bumppo was "a fit subject to represent the better qualities of both conditions, without pushing either to extremes." As such, Natty Bumppo is a prototypical American hero, an antecedent of, for example, Melville's Ishmael, Twain's Huck Finn, Faulkner's Ike McCaslin, and Hemingway's protagonists.

The sense of loss that increasingly dominates each of the "Leather-Stocking" novels illustrated—much like Cooper's social criticism—the shifting national views on America's direction and destiny in the first half of the nineteenth century. The pervasive melancholy of late-eighteenth- and early-nineteenth-century literature, which essentially shaped Cooper's writing, ceased to be merely a borrowed rhetorical device in the course of the "Leather-Stocking" series and became instead a way to conceptualize a recurring image in American writing—a gradual diminution of an impossible vision of the land, one that nonetheless remained a powerful *imagined* alternative to material progress.

James Fenimore Cooper died on September 14, 1851, in Cooperstown, New York. Less than two weeks later a memorial service was held in New York City, at which Washington Irving presided and Daniel Webster and William Cullen Bryant spoke. In his eulogy, Bryant praised Cooper's achievements and noted:

He wrote not for the fastidious, the over-refined, the morbidly delicate . . . but he wrote . . . for men and women in the ordinary healthful state of feeling—

and in their admiration he found his reward. It is for this class that public libraries are obliged to provide themselves with an extraordinary number of copies of his works. . . . Hence it is that he has earned a fame wider, I think, than any author of modern times.

Cooper's life and work had already taken on mythic dimensions. The breadth of his interests and the range of his accomplishments set the standards for nineteenth-century American writers. He was the first American novelist to create an extensive body of work. His social criticism helped define issues central to American identity—qualities of leadership, standards of excellence, measures for minority and majority voices, and the like. In this respect, Cooper might be regarded, to use D. H. Lawrence's phrase, as a saint with a gun. And just as the "Leather-Stocking Tales" had returned American culture to a pristine origin that defined all that was to follow, so too did Cooper's writing create a foundation for the careers of later writers and the directions of our nation's literary canon.

Cooper's primacy in American literary history, then, is not as much a matter of historical accident as it is the result of his visionary power. He articulated a compelling sense of the literary potential of American history—of the possibilities implicit in its past, of the tensions and contradictions inherent in its present, of the pressures exerted by its uncertain and unprecedented future. Cooper helped accelerate America's literary development by formulating thematic patterns, narrative structures, and prototypical characters and situations that later writers would return to again and again in their own efforts to come to terms with America's distinctive cultural identity.

Further Reading:
W. C. Bryant, "Discourse on the Life and Genius of Cooper," in *Memorial of James Fenimore Cooper,* 1852.
S. F. Cooper, *The Cooper Gallery,* 1865.
D. H. Lawrence, *Studies in Classic American Literature,* 1923.
H. W. Boynton, *James Fenimore Cooper,* 1931.
R. E. Spiller, *Fenimore Cooper: Critic of His Times,* 1931.
V. W. Brooks, *The World of Washington Irving,* 1950.
J. Grossman, *James Fenimore Cooper,* 1947, 1967.
H. N. Smith, *Virgin Land,* 1957.
M. Bewley, *The Eccentric Design,* 1959.
D. A. Ringe, *James Fenimore Cooper,* 1962.
L. Fiedler, *Love and Death in the American Novel,* 1966.
R. Slotkin, *Regeneration Through Violence: The Mythology of the American Frontier, 1600–1860,* 1973.
H. D. Peck, *A World by Itself: The Pastoral Moment in Cooper's Fiction,* 1977.
S. Railton, *Fenimore Cooper: A Study of His Life and Imagination,* 1979.
W. Franklin, *The New World of James Fenimore Cooper,* 1982.
W. P. Kelly, *Plotting America's Past: Fenimore Cooper and the Leatherstocking Tales,* 1984.

Texts:
Notions of the Americans: Picked Up by a Travelling Bachelor, 1828.
The American Democrat, with an introduction by H. L. Mencken, 1956.
Cooper's Novels, 1859–1861.
A 48-volume edition of the works of James Fenimore Cooper is being prepared by the State University of New York Press.
See also *The Letters and Journals of James Fenimore Cooper,* ed. J. F. Beard, 6 vols., 1960–1968.

from Notions of the Americans

Picked Up by a Travelling Bachelor

To the Abbate Giromachi, &c. &c.

Florence

Washington, ⸺

You ask me to write freely on the subject of the literature and the arts of the United States. The subjects are so meagre as to render it a task that would require no small portion of the talents necessary to figure in either, in order to render them of interest. Still, as the request has come in so urgent a form, I shall endeavour to oblige you.

The Americans have been placed, as respects moral and intellectual advancement, different from all other infant nations. They have never been without the wants of civilization, nor have they ever been entirely without the means of a supply. Thus pictures, and books, and statuary, and every thing else which appertains to elegant life, have always been known to them in an abundance, and of a quality exactly proportioned to their cost. Books, being the cheapest, and the nation having great leisure and prodigious zest for information, are not only the most common, as you will readily suppose, but they are probably more common than among any other people. I scarcely remember ever to have entered an American dwelling, however humble, without finding fewer or more books. As they form the most essential division of the subject, not only on account of their greater frequency, but on account of their far greater importance, I shall give them the first notice in this letter.

Unlike the progress of the two professions in the countries of our hemisphere, in America the printer came into existence before the author. Reprints of English works gave the first employment to the press. Then came almanacks, psalm-books, religious tracts, sermons, journals, political essays, and even rude attempts at poetry. All these preceded the revolution. The first journal was established in Boston at the commencement of the last century. There are several original polemical works of great originality and power that belong to the same period. I do not know that more learning and talents existed at that early day in the states of New England than in Virginia, Maryland and the Carolinas, but there was certainly a stronger desire to exhibit them.

The colleges or universities, as they were somewhat prematurely called, date very far back in the brief history of the country. There is no stronger evidence of the intellectual character, or of the judicious ambition of these people, than what this simple fact furnishes. Harvard College, now the university of Cambridge—(it better deserves the title at this day)—was founded in 1638; within less than *twenty years* after the landing of the first settlers in New England! Yale (in Connecticut) was founded in 1701. Columbia (in the city of New York) was founded in 1754. Nassau Hall (in New Jersey) in 1738; and William and Mary (in Virginia) as far back as 1691. These are the oldest literary institutions in the United States, and all but the last are in flourishing conditions to the present hour. The first has given degrees to about five thousand graduates, and rarely has less than three hundred and fifty or four hundred students. Yale is about as well attended. The others contain from a hundred and fifty to two hundred under-graduates. But these are not a moiety of the present colleges, or universities, (as they all aspire to be called,) existing in the country. There is no state, except a few of the newest, without at least one, and several have two or three.

Less attention is paid to classical learning here than in Europe; and, as the term of residence rarely exceeds four years, profound scholars are by no means common. This country possesses neither the population nor the endowments to maintain a large class of learned idlers, in order that one man in a hundred may contribute a mite to the growing stock of general knowledge. There is a luxury in this expenditure of animal force, to which the Americans have not yet attained. The good is far too problematical and remote, and the expense of man too certain, to be prematurely sought. I have heard, I will confess, an American legislator quote Horace and Cicero; but it is far from being the humour of the country. I thought the taste of the orator questionable. A learned quotation is rarely of any use in an argument, since few men are fools enough not to see that the application of any maxim to politics is liable to a thousand practical objections, and, nine times in ten, they are evidences of the want of a direct, natural, and vigorous train of thought. They are the affectations, but rarely the ebullitions[1] of true talent. When a man feels strongly, or thinks strongly, or speaks strongly, he is just as apt to do it in his native tongue as he is to laugh when he is tickled, or to weep when in sorrow. The Americans are strong speakers and acute thinkers, but no great quoters of the morals and axioms of a heathen age, because they happen to be recorded in Latin.

The higher branches of learning are certainly on the advance in this country. The gentlemen of the middle and southern states, before the revolution, were very generally educated in Europe, and they were consequently, in this particular, like our own people. Those who came into life during the struggle, and shortly after, fared worse. Even the next generation had little to boast of in the way of instruction. I find that boys entered the colleges so late as the commencement of the present century, who had read a part of the Greek Testament, and a few books of Cicero and Virgil, with perhaps a little of Horace. But great changes have been made, and are still making, in the degree of previous qualification.

Still, it would be premature to say that there is any one of the American universities where classical knowledge, or even science is profoundly attained, even at the present day. Some of the professors push their studies, for a life, certainly; and you well know, after all, that little short of a life, and a long one too, will make any man a good general scholar. In 1820, near eight thousand graduates of the twelve oldest colleges of this country (according to their catalogues) were then living. Of this number, 1,406 were clergymen. As some of the catalogues consulted were several years old, this number was, of necessity, greatly within the truth. Between the years 1800 and 1810, it is found that of 2,792 graduates, four hundred and fifty-three became clergymen. Here is pretty good evidence that religion is not neglected in America, and that its ministers are not, as a matter of course, absolutely ignorant.

But the effects of the literary institutions of the United States are somewhat peculiar. Few men devote their lives to scholarship. The knowledge that is actually acquired, is perhaps quite sufficient for the more practical and useful pursuits. Thousands of young men, who have read the more familiar classics, who have gone through

---

[1] Vigorous displays.

enough of mathematics to obtain a sense of their own tastes, and of the value of precision, who have cultivated *belles lettres* to a reasonable extent, and who have been moderately instructed in the arts of composition, and in the rules of taste, are given forth to the country to mingle in its active employments. I am inclined to believe that a class of American graduates carries away with it quite as much general and diversified knowledge, as a class from one of our own universities. The excellence in particular branches is commonly wanting; but the deficiency is more than supplied by variety of information. The youth who has passed four years within the walls of a college, goes into the office of a lawyer for a few more. The profession of the law is not subdivided in America. The same man is counsellor, attorney, and conveyancer.[2] Here the student gets a general insight into the principles, and a familiarity with the practice of the law, rather than an acquaintance with the study as a science. With this instruction he enters the world as a practitioner. Instead of existing in a state of dreaming retrospection, lost in a maze of theories, he is at once turned loose into the jostlings of the world. If perchance he encounters an antagonist a little more erudite than himself, he seizes the natural truth for his sheet anchor, and leaves precedent and quaint follies to him who has made them his study and delight. No doubt he often blunders, and is frequently, of necessity, defeated. But in the course of this irreverent treatment, usages and opinions, which are bottomed in no better foundation than antiquity, and which are as inapplicable to the present state of the world, as the present state of the world is, or ought to be, unfavourable to all feudal absurdities, come to receive their death warrants. In the mean time, by dint of sheer experience, and by the collision of intellects, the practitioner gets a stock of learning, that is acquired in the best possible school; and, what is of far more importance, the laws themselves get a dress which brings them within the fashions of the day. This same man becomes a legislator perhaps, and, if particularly clever, he is made to take an active part in the framing of laws that are not to harmonize with the other parts of an elaborate theory, but which are intended to make men comfortable and happy. Now, taken with more or less qualification, this is the history of thousands in this country, and it is also an important part of the history of the country itself.

In considering the course of instruction in the United States, you are always to commence at the foundation. The common schools, which so generally exist, have certainly elevated the population above that of any other country, and are still elevating it higher, as they improve and increase in numbers. Law is getting every day to be more of a science, but it is a science that is forming rules better adapted to the spirit of the age. Medicine is improving, and in the cities it is, perhaps now, in point of practice, quite on a level with that of Europe. Indeed, the well-educated American physician very commonly enjoys an advantage that is little known in Europe. After obtaining a degree in his own country, he passes a few years in London, Edinburgh, Paris, and frequently in Germany, and returns with his gleanings from their several schools. This is not the case with one individual, but with many, annually. Indeed, there is so much of a fashion in it, and the custom is attended by so many positive advantages, that its neglect would be a serious obstacle to any very eminent success. Good operators are by no means scarce, and as surgery and medicine are united

---

[2] Lawyer specializing in properties and real estate.

in the same person, there is great judgment in their practice. Human life is something more valuable in America than in Europe, and I think a critical attention to patients more common here than with us, especially when the sufferer belongs to an inferior condition in life. The profession is highly respectable; and in all parts of the country the better sort of its practitioners mingle, on terms of perfect equality, with the highest classes of society. There are several physicians in congress, and a great many in the different state legislatures.

Of the ministry it is unnecessary to speak. The clergy are of all denominations, and they are educated, or not, precisely as they belong to sects which consider the gift of human knowledge of any importance. You have already seen how large a proportion of the graduates of some of the colleges enter the desk.

As respects authorship, there is not much to be said. Compared to the books that are printed and read, those of native origin are few indeed. The principal reason of this poverty of original writers, is owing to the circumstance that men are not yet driven to their wits for bread. The United States are the first nation that possessed institutions, and, of course, distinctive opinions of its own, that was ever dependent on a foreign people for its literature. Speaking the same language as the English, and long in the habit of importing their books from the mother country, the revolution effected no immediate change in the nature of their studies, or mental amusements. The works were reprinted, it is true, for the purposes of economy, but they still continued English. Had the latter nation used this powerful engine with tolerable address, I think they would have secured such an ally in this country as would have rendered their own decline not only more secure, but as illustrious as had been their rise. There are many theories entertained as to the effect produced in this country by the falsehoods and jealous calumnies which have been undeniably uttered in the mother country, by means of the press, concerning her republican descendant. It is my own opinion that, like all other ridiculous absurdities, they have defeated themselves, and that they are now more laughed at and derided, even here, than resented. By all that I can learn, twenty years ago, the Americans were, perhaps, far too much disposed to receive the opinions and to adopt the prejudices of their relatives; whereas, I think it is very apparent that they are now beginning to receive them with singular distrust. It is not worth our while to enter further into this subject, except as it has had, or is likely to have, an influence on the national literature.[3]

It is quite obvious, that, so far as taste and forms alone are concerned, the literature of England and that of America must be fashioned after the same models. The authors, previously to the revolution, are common property, and it is quite idle to say that the American has not just as good a right to claim Milton, and Shakespeare, and all the old masters of the language, for his countrymen, as an Englishman. The Americans having continued to cultivate, and to cultivate extensively, an acquaintance with the writers of the mother country, since the separation, it is evident they must have kept pace with the trifling changes of the day. The only peculiarity that can, or ought to

[3] Cooper's note: "The writer might give, in proof of this opinion, one fact. He is led to believe that, so lately as within ten years, several English periodical works were re-printed, and much read in the United States, and that now they patronize their own, while the former are far less sought, though the demand, by means of the increased population, should have been nearly doubled. Some of the works are no longer even re-printed."

be expected in their literature, is that which is connected with the promulgation of their distinctive political opinions. They have not been remiss in this duty, as any one may see, who chooses to examine their books. But we will devote a few minutes to a more minute account of the actual condition of American literature.

The first, and the most important, though certainly the most familiar branch of this subject, is connected with the public journals. It is not easy to say how many newspapers are printed in the United States. The estimated number varies from six hundred to a thousand. In the State of New York there are more than fifty counties. Now, it is rare that a county, in a state as old as that of New York (especially in the more northern parts of the country), does not possess one paper at least. The cities have many. The smaller towns sometimes have three or four, and very many of the counties four or five. There cannot be many less than one hundred and fifty journals in the state of New York alone. Pennsylvania is said to possess eighty. But we will suppose that these two states publish two hundred journals. They contain about 3,000,000 of inhabitants. As the former is an enlightened state, and the latter rather below the scale of the general intelligence of the nation, it may not be a very bad average of the whole population. This rate would give eight hundred journals for the United States, which is probably something within the truth. I confess, however, this manner of equalizing estimates in America, is very uncertain in general, since a great deal, in such a question, must depend on the progress of society in each particular section of the country.

As might be expected, there is nearly every degree of merit to be found in these journals. No one of them has the benefit of that collected talent which is so often enlisted in the support of the more important journals of Europe. There is not often more than one editor to the best; but he is usually some man who has seen, in his own person, enough of men and things to enable him to speak with tolerable discretion on passing events. The usefulness of the American journals, however, does not consist in their giving the tone to the public mind, in politics and morals, but in imparting facts. It is certain that, could the journals agree, they might, by their united efforts, give a powerful inclination to the common will. But, in point of fact, they do not agree on any one subject or set of subjects, except, perhaps, on those which directly affect their own interests. They, consequently, counteract, instead of aiding each other, on all points of disputed policy; and it is in the bold and sturdy discussions that follow, that men arrive at the truth. The occasional union in their own favour, is a thing too easily seen through to do either good or harm. So far, then, from the journals succeeding in leading the public opinion astray, they are invariably obliged to submit to it. They serve to keep it alive, by furnishing the means for its expression, but they rarely do more. Of course, the influence of each particular press is in proportion to the constancy and the ability with which it is found to support what is thought to be sound principles; but those principles must be in accordance with the private opinions of men, or most of their labour is lost.

The public press in America is rather more decent than that of England, and less decorous than that of France. The tone of the nation, and the respect for private feelings, which are, perhaps, in some measure, the consequence of a less artificial state of society, produce the former; and the liberty, which is a necessary attendant of fearless discussion, is, I think, the cause of the latter. The affairs of an individual are rarely touched upon in the journals of this country; never, unless it is thought they have a direct connection with the public interests, or from a wish to do him good. Still there is a habit, getting into use in America, no less than in France, that is borrowed from the English, which proves that the more unworthy feelings of our nature are common to men under all systems, and only need opportunity to find encouragement. I allude to the practice of repeating the proceedings of the courts of justice, in order to cater to a vicious appetite for amusement in the public.

It is pretended that, as a court of justice is open to the world, there can be no harm in giving the utmost publicity to its proceedings. It is strange the courts should act so rigidly on the principle, that it is better a dozen guilty men should go free, than that one innocent man should suffer, and yet permit the gross injustice that is daily done by means of this practice. One would think, that if a court of justice is so open to the world, that it should be the business of the people of the world to enter it, in order that they might be certain that the information they crave should be without colouring or exaggeration. It is idle to say that the reports are accurate, and that he who reads is enabled to do justice to the accused, by comparing the facts that are laid before him. A reporter may give the expression of the tongue; but can he convey that of the eye, of the countenance, or of the form?—without regarding all of which no man is perfectly master of the degree of credibility that is due to any witness of whose character he is necessarily ignorant. But every man has an infallible means of assuring himself of the value of these reports. Who has ever read a dozen of them without meeting with one (or perhaps more), in which the decision of the court and jury is to him a matter of surprise? It is true he assumes, that those who were present knew best, and as he has no great interest in the matter, he is commonly satisfied. But how is it with the unfortunate man who is wrongfully brought out of his retirement to repel an unjust attack against his person, his property, or his character? If he be a man of virtue, he is a man of sensibility; and not only he, but, what is far worse, those tender beings, whose existence is wrapped up in his own, are to be wounded daily and hourly, for weeks at a time, in order that a depraved appetite should be glutted. It is enough for justice that her proceedings should be so public as to prevent the danger of corruption; but we pervert a blessing to a curse, in making that which was intended for our protection, the means of so much individual misery. It is an unavoidable evil of the law that it necessarily works some wrong, in order to do much good; but it is cruel that even the acquittal of a man should be unnecessarily circulated, in a manner to make all men remember that he had been accused. We have proof of the consequences of this practice in England. Men daily shrink from resistance to base frauds, rather than expose themselves to the observations and comments of those who enliven their breakfasts by sporting with these exhibitions of their fellow creatures. There are, undoubtedly, cases of that magnitude which require some sacrifice of private feelings, in order that the community should reap the advantage; but the regular books are sufficient for authorities—the decisions of the courts are sufficient for justice—and the utmost possible oblivion should prove as nearly sufficient as may be to serve the ends of a prudent and a righteous humanity.

Nothing can be more free than the press of this country, on all subjects connected with politics. Treason cannot be written, unless by communicating with an open enemy. There is no other protection to a public man than that which is given by an independent jury, which punishes, of course, in proportion to the dignity and importance of the injured party. But the utmost lenity is always used in construing the right of the press to canvass the public acts of public men. Mere common place charges defeat themselves, and get into discredit so soon as to be lost, while graver accusations are met by grave replies. There is no doubt that the complacency of individuals is sometimes disturbed by these liberties; but they serve to keep the officers of the government to their work, while they rarely do any lasting, or even temporary injury. Serious and criminal accusations against a public man, if groundless, are, by the law of reason, a crime against the community, and, as such, they are punished. The general principle observed in these matters is very simple. If A. accuse B. of an act that is an offence against law, he may be called on for his proof, and if he fail he must take the consequences. But an editor of a paper, or any one else, who should bring a criminal charge, no matter how grave, against the president, and who could prove it, is just as certain of doing it with impunity, as if he held the whole power in his own hands. He would be protected by the invincible shield of public opinion, which is not only in consonance with the law, but which, in this country, makes law.

Actions for injuries done by the press, considering the number of journals, are astonishingly rare in America. When one remembers the usual difficulty of obtaining legal proof, which is a constant temptation, even to the guilty, to appeal to the courts; and, on the other hand, the great freedom of the press, which is a constant temptation to abuse the trust, this fact, in itself, furnishes irresistible evidence of the general tone of decency which predominates in this nation. The truth is, that public opinion, among its other laws, has imperiously prescribed that, amidst the utmost latitude of discussion, certain limits shall not be passed; and public opinion, which is so completely the offspring of a free press, must be obeyed in this, as well as in other matters.

Leaving the journals, we come to those publications which make their appearance periodically. Of these there are a good many, some few of which are well supported. There are several scientific works, that are printed monthly, or quarterly, of respectable merit, and four or five reviews. Magazines of a more general character are not much encouraged. England, which is teeming with educated men, who are glad to make their bread by writing for these works, still affords too strong a competition for the success of any American attempts, in this species of literature. Though few, perhaps no English magazine is actually republished in America, a vast number are imported and read in the towns, where the support for any similar original production must first be found.

The literature of the United States has, indeed, too powerful obstacles to conquer before (to use a mercantile expression) it can ever enter the markets of its own country on terms of perfect equality with that of England. Solitary and individual works of genius may, indeed, be occasionally brought to light, under the impulses of the high feeling which has conceived them; but, I fear, a good, wholesome, profitable, and continued pecuniary support is the applause that talent most craves. The fact, that an American publisher can get an English work without money, must, for a few years longer (unless legislative protection shall be extended to their own authors), have a tendency to repress a national literature. No man will pay a writer for an epic, a tragedy, a sonnet, a history, or a romance, when he can get a work of equal merit for nothing. I have conversed with those who are conversant on the subject, and, I confess, I have been astonished at the information they imparted.

A capital American publisher has assured me that there are not a dozen writers in this country, whose works he should feel confidence in publishing at all, while he reprints hundreds of English books without the least hesitation. This preference is by no means so much owing to any difference in merit, as to the fact that, when the price of the original author is to be added to the uniform hazard which accompanies all literary speculations, the risk becomes too great. The general taste of the reading world in this country is better than that of England.[4] The fact is both proved and explained by the circumstance that thousands of works that are printed and read in the mother country, are not printed and read here. The publisher on this side of the Atlantic has the advantage of seeing the reviews of every book he wishes to print, and, what is of far more importance, he knows, with the exception of books that he is sure of selling, by means of a name, the decision of the English critics before he makes his choice. Nine times in ten, popularity, which is all he looks for, is a sufficient test of general merit. Thus, while you find every English work of character, or notoriety, on the shelves of an American bookstore, you may ask in vain for most of the trash that is so greedily devoured in the circulating libraries of the mother country, and which would be just as eagerly devoured here, had not a better taste been created by a compelled abstinence. That taste must now be overcome before such works could be sold at all.

When I say that books are not rejected here, from any want of talent in the writers, perhaps I ought to explain. I wish to express something a little different. Talent is sure of too many avenues to wealth and honours, in America, to seek, unnecessarily, an unknown and hazardous path. It is better paid in the ordinary pursuits of life, than it would be likely to be paid by an adventure in which an extraordinary and skillful, because practised, foreign competition is certain. Perhaps high talent does not often make the trial with the American bookseller; but it is precisely for the reason I have named.

The second obstacle against which American literature has to contend is in the poverty of materials. There is scarcely an ore which contributes to the wealth of the author, that is found, here, in veins as rich as in Europe. There are no annals for the historian; no follies (beyond the most vulgar and common place) for the satirist; no manners for the dramatist; no obscure fictions for the writer of romance; no gross and hardy offences against decorum for the moralist; nor any of the rich artificial auxiliaries of poetry. The weakest hand can extract a spark from the flint, but it would baffle the strength of a giant to attempt kindling a flame with a pudding stone.[5] I very well know there are theorists who assume that the society and institutions of this country are, or ought to be, particularly favourable to novelties and variety. But the experience of one month, in these states, is sufficient to show any observant man the falsity of their position. The effect of a promiscuous assemblage any where, is to create a standard of deportment; and great liberty permits every one to aim at its attainment. I have never seen a nation so much alike in my life, as the people of the United States, and what is more, they are not only like each other, but they are remarkably like that which common sense tells them they ought to resemble. No doubt, traits of character that are a little peculiar, without, however, being either very poetical, or very rich,

---

[4] Cooper's note: "The writer does not mean that the best taste of America is better than that of England; perhaps it is not quite so good; but, as a whole, the American reading world requires better books than the whole of the English reading world."

[5] Sedimentary rock composed of pebbles of varying sizes and mineral contents.

are to be found in remote districts; but they are rare, and not always happy exceptions. In short, it is not possible to conceive a state of society in which more of the attributes of plain good sense, or fewer of the artificial absurdities of life, are to be found, than here. There is no costume for the peasant, (there is scarcely a peasant at all,) no wig for the judge, no baton for the general, no diadem for the chief magistrate. The darkest ages of their history are illuminated by the light of truth; the utmost efforts of their chivalry are limited by the laws of God; and even the deeds of their sages and heroes are to be sung in a language that would differ but little from a version of the ten commandments. However useful and respectable all this may be in actual life, it indicates but one direction to the man of genius.

It is very true there are a few young poets now living in this country, who have known how to extract sweets from even these wholesome, but scentless native plants. They have, however, been compelled to seek their inspiration in the universal laws of nature, and they have succeeded, precisely in proportion as they have been most general in their application. Among these gifted young men, there is one (Halleck)[6] who is remarkable for an exquisite vein of ironical wit, mingled with a fine, poetical, and, frequently, a lofty expression. This gentleman commenced his career as a satirist in one of the journals of New York. Heaven knows, his materials were none of the richest; and yet the melody of his verse, the quaintness and force of his comparisons, and the exceeding humour of his strong points, brought him instantly into notice. He then attempted a general satire, by giving the history of the early days of a *belle*.[7] He was again successful, though every body, at least every body of any talent, felt that he wrote in leading-strings. But he happened, shortly after the appearance of the little volume just named (Fanny),[8] to visit England. Here his spirit was properly excited, and, probably on a rainy day, he was induced to try his hand at a *jeu d'esprit*,[9] in the mother country. The result was one of the finest semi-heroic ironical descriptions to be found in the English language.[10] This simple fact, in itself, proves the truth of a great deal of what I have just been writing, since it shews the effect a superiority of material can produce on the efforts of a man of true genius.

Notwithstanding the difficulties of the subject, talent has even done more than in the instance of Mr. Halleck. I could mention several other young poets of this country of rare merit. By mentioning Bryant, Percival, and Sprague,[11] I shall direct your attention to the names of those whose works would be most likely to give you pleasure. Unfortunately they are not yet known in Italian, but I think even you would not turn in distaste from the task of translation which the best of their effusions will invite.

The next, though certainly an inferior branch of imaginative writing, is fictitious composition. From the facts just named, you cannot expect that the novelists, or romance writers of the United States, should be very successful. The same reason will be likely, for a long time to come, to repress the ardour of dramatic genius. Still, tales and plays are no novelties in the literature of this country. Of the former, there are

---

[6] Fitz-Greene Halleck (1790–1867).
[7] French: "young woman."
[8] *Fanny* (1821), a satire on local politics and fashions in the form of Byron's *Don Juan*.
[9] French: "a play of the wit"; here meaning a witty composition.

[10] Cooper's note: "This little *morceau* [French: 'piece'] of pleasant irony is called Alnwick Castle." The latter was published in 1827.
[11] William Cullen Bryant (1794–1878), James Gates Percival (1795–1856), and Charles Sprague (1791–1875).

many as old as soon after the revolution; and a vast number have been published within the last five years. One of their authors of romance, who curbed his talents by as few allusions as possible to actual society, is distinguished for power and comprehensiveness of thought. I remember to have read one of his books (Wieland)[12] when a boy, and I take it to be a never-failing evidence of genius, that, amid a thousand similar pictures which have succeeded, the images it has left still stand distinct and prominent in my recollection. This author (Mr. Brockden Brown)[13] enjoys a high reputation among his countrymen, whose opinions are sufficiently impartial, since he flattered no particular prejudice of the nation in any of his works.

The reputation of Irving is well known to you. He is an author distinguished for a quality (humour) that has been denied his countrymen; and his merit is the more rare, that it has been shewn in a state of society so cold and so restrained. Besides these writers, there are many others of a similar character, who enjoy a greater or less degree of favour in their own country. The works of two or three have even been translated (into French) in Europe, and a great many are reprinted in England. Though every writer of fiction in America has to contend against the difficulties I have named, there is a certain interest in the novelty of the subject, which is not without its charm. I think, however, it will be found that they have all been successful, or the reverse, just as they have drawn warily, or freely, on the distinctive habits of their own country. I now speak of their success purely as writers of romance. It certainly would be possible for an American to give a description of the manners of his own country, in a book that he might choose to call a romance, which should be read, because the world is curious on the subject, but which would certainly never be read for that nearly indefinable poetical interest which attaches itself to a description of manners less bald and uniform. All the attempts to blend history with romance in America, have been comparative failures, (and perhaps fortunately,) since the subjects are too familiar to be treated with the freedom that the imagination absolutely requires. Some of the descriptions of the progress of society on the borders, have had a rather better success, since there is a positive, though no very poetical, novelty in the subject; but, on the whole, the books which have been best received, are those in which the authors have trusted most to their own conceptions of character, and to qualities that are common to the rest of the world and to human nature. This fact, if its truth be admitted, will serve to prove that the American writer must seek his renown in the exhibition of qualities that are general, while he is confessedly compelled to limit his observations to a state of society that has a wonderful tendency not only to repress passion, but to equalize humours.

The Americans have always been prolific writers on polemics and politics. Their sermons and fourth of July orations are numberless. Their historians, without being very classical or very profound, are remarkable for truth and good sense. There is not, perhaps, in the language a closer reasoner in metaphysics than Edwards;[14] and their

---

[12] *Wieland; or the Transformation,* which appeared in 1798.
[13] Considered the "father of the American novel," Charles Brockden Brown (1771–1810) wrote six novels that remain cornerstones of early American fiction. The most popular of these, *Wieland* (1798), *Arthur Mervyn* (1798–1800),

Ormond (1799), and *Edgar Huntly* (1801), are all macabre in conception, containing events that border on the supernatural without exceeding the bounds of plausibility.
[14] Jonathan Edwards (1703–1758), American theologian and philosopher.

theological writers find great favour among the sectarians of their respective schools.

The stage of the United States is decidedly English. Both plays and players, with few exceptions, are imported. Theatres are numerous, and they are to be found in places where a traveller would little expect to meet them. Of course they are of all sizes and of every degree of decoration and architectural beauty known in Europe, below the very highest. The façade of the principal theatre in Philadelphia is a chaste specimen in marble, of the Ionic, if my memory is correct. In New York, there are two theatres about as large as the Théâtre Français (in the interior), and not much inferior in embellishments. Besides these, there is a very pretty little theatre, where lighter pieces are performed, and another with a vast stage for melo-dramas. There are also one or two other places of dramatic representation in this city, in which horses and men contend for the bays.

The Americans pay well for dramatic talent. Cooke,[15] the greatest English tragedian of our age, died on this side of the Atlantic; and there are few players of eminence in the mother country who are not tempted, at some time or other, to cross the ocean. Shakespeare, is of course, the great author of America, as he is of England, and I think he is quite as well relished here as there. In point of taste, if all the rest of the world be any thing against England, that of America is the best, since it unquestionably approaches nearest to that of the continent of Europe. Nearly one half of the theatrical taste of the English is condemned by their own judgments, since the stage is not much supported by those who have had an opportunity of seeing any other. You will be apt to ask me how it happens, then, that the American taste is better? Because the people, being less exaggerated in their habits, are less disposed to tolerate caricatures, and because the theatres are not yet sufficiently numerous (though that hour is near) to admit of a representation that shall not be subject to the control of a certain degree of intelligence. I have heard an English player complain that he never saw such a dull audience as the one before which he had just been exhibiting; and I heard the same audience complain that they never listened to such dull jokes. Now, there was talent enough in both parties; but the one had formed his taste in a coarse school, and the others had formed theirs under the dominion of common sense. Independently of this peculiarity, there is a vast deal of acquired, travelled taste in this country. English tragedy, and high English comedy, both of which, you know, are excellent, never fail here, if well played; that is, they never fail under the usual limits of all amusement. One will cloy of sweets. But the fact of the taste and judgment of these people, in theatrical exhibitions, is proved by the number of their good theatres, compared to their population.

Of dramatic writers there are none, or next to none. The remarks I have made in respect to novels apply with double force to this species of composition. A witty and successful American comedy could only proceed from extraordinary talent. There would be less difficulty, certainly, with a tragedy; but still, there is rather too much foreign competition, and too much domestic employment in other pursuits, to invite genius to so doubtful an enterprise. The very baldness of ordinary American life is in deadly hostility to scenic representation. The character must be supported solely by its intrinsic power. The judge, the footman, the clown, the lawyer, the belle, or

---

[15] George Frederick Cooke (1756–1811), British Shakespearean actor.

the beau, can receive no great assistance from dress. Melo-dramas, except the scene should be laid in the woods, are out of the question. It would be necessary to seek the great clock, which is to strike the portentous twelve blows, in the nearest church; a vaulted passage would degenerate into a cellar; and, as for ghosts, the country was discovered, since their visitations have ceased. The smallest departure from the incidents of ordinary life would do violence to every man's experience; and, as already mentioned, the passions which belong to human nature must be delineated, in America, subject to the influence of that despot—common sense.

Notwithstanding the overwhelming influence of British publications, and all the difficulties I have named, original books are getting to be numerous in the United States. The impulses of talent and intelligence are bearing down a thousand obstacles. I think the new works will increase rapidly, and that they are destined to produce a powerful influence on the world. We will pursue this subject another time.—Adieu.

1828

---

from The American Democrat

Introduction by the Author

This little work has been written, in consequence of its author's having had many occasions to observe the manner in which principles that are of the last importance to the happiness of the community, are getting to be confounded in the popular mind. Notions that are impracticable, and which if persevered in, cannot fail to produce disorganization, if not revolution, are widely prevalent, and while many seem disposed to complain, few show a disposition to correct them. In those instances in which efforts are made to resist or to advance the innovations of the times, the writers take the extremes of the disputed points, the one side looking as far behind it, over ground that can never be retrod, as the other looks ahead, in the idle hope of substituting a fancied perfection for the ills of life. It is the intention of this book to make a commencement towards a more just discrimination between truth and prejudice. With what success the task has been accomplished, the honest reader will judge for himself.

The Americans are obnoxious to the charge of tolerating gross personalities, a state of things that encourages bodies of men in their errors while it oppresses individuals, and which never produced good of any sort, at the very time they are nationally irritable on the subject of common failings. This is reversing the case as it exists in most civilized countries, where personalities excite disgust, and society is deemed fair game. This weakness in the American character might easily be accounted for, but, the object being rather to amend than to explain, the body of the work is referred to for examples.

Power always has most to apprehend from its own illusions. Monarchs have incurred more hazards from the follies of their own that have grown up under the adulation of parasites, than from the machinations of their enemies; and, in a democracy, the delusion that would elsewhere be poured into the ears of the prince, is poured into those of the people. It is hoped that this work, while free from the spirit of partizanship, will be thought to be exempt from this imputation.

The writer believes himself to be as good a democrat as there is in America. But his democracy is not of the impracticable school. He prefers a democracy to any other system, on account of its comparative advantages, and not on account of its perfection. He knows it has evils; great and increasing evils, and evils peculiar to itself; but he believes that monarchy and aristocracy have more. It will be very apparent to all who read this book, that he is not a believer in the scheme of raising men very far above their natural propensities.

A long absence from home, has, in a certain degree, put the writer in the situation of a foreigner in his own country; a situation probably much better for noting peculiarities, than that of one who never left it. Two things have struck him painfully on his return; a disposition in the majority to carry out the opinions of the system to extremes, and a disposition in the minority to abandon all to the current of the day, with the hope that this current will lead, in the end, to radical changes. Fifteen years since, all complaints against the institutions were virtually silenced, whereas now it is rare to hear them praised, except by the mass, or by those who wish to profit by the favors of the mass.

In the midst of these conflicting opinions, the voice of simple, honest, and what, in a country like this, ought to be fearless, truth, is nearly smothered; the one party effecting its ends by fulsome, false and meretricious eulogiums,[1] in which it does not itself believe, and the other giving utterance to its discontent in useless and unmanly complaints. It has been the aim of the writer to avoid both these errors also.

No attempt has been made to write very profound treatises on any of the subjects of this little book. The limits and objects of the work forbade it; the intention being rather to present to the reader those opinions that are suited to the actual condition of the country, than to dwell on principles more general. A work of the size of this might be written on the subject of "Instruction" alone, but it has been the intention to present reasons and facts to the reader, that are peculiarly American, rather than to exhaust the subjects.

Had a suitable compound offered, the title of this book would have been something like "Anti-Cant,"[2] for such a term expresses the intention of the writer, better, perhaps, than the one he has actually chosen. The work is written more in the spirit of censure than of praise, for its aim is correction; and virtues bring their own reward, while errors are dangerous.

On American Equality

The equality of the United States is no more absolute than that of any other country. There may be less inequality in this nation than in most others, but inequality exists, and, in some respects, with stronger features than it is usual to meet with in the rest of christendom.

The rights of property being an indispensable condition of civilization, and its quiet possession every where guaranteed, equality of condition is rendered impossible. One man must labor, while another may live luxuriously on his means; one has leisure and opportunity to cultivate his tastes, to increase his information, and to refine his habits,

---

[1] Pompous oratory.

[2] Cooper's own coinage, roughly meaning

straightforward talk unencumbered by specialized jargon.

while another is compelled to toil, that he may live. One is reduced to serve, while another commands, and, of course, there can be no equality in their social conditions.

The justice and relative advantage of these differencies, as well as their several duties, will be elsewhere considered.

By the inequality of civil and political rights that exists in certain parts of the Union, and the great equality that exists in others, we see the necessity of referring the true character of the institutions to those of the states, without a just understanding of which, it is impossible to obtain any general and accurate ideas of the real polity of the country.

The same general exceptions to civil and political equality, that are found in other free countries, exist in this, though under laws peculiar to ourselves. Women and minors are excluded from the suffrage, and from maintaining suits at law, under the usual provisions, here as well as elsewhere. None but natives of the country can fill many of the higher offices, and paupers, felons and all those who have not fixed residences, are also excluded from the suffrage. In a few of the states property is made the test of political rights, and, in nearly half of them, a large portion of the inhabitants, who are of a different race from the original European occupants of the soil, are entirely excluded from all political, and from many of the civil rights, that are enjoyed by those who are deemed citizens. A slave can neither choose, nor be chosen to office, nor, in most of the states, can even a free man, unless a white man. A slave can neither sue nor be sued; he can not hold property, real or personal, nor can he, in many of the states be a witness in any suit, civil or criminal.

It follows from these facts, that absolute equality of condition, of political rights, or of civil rights, does not exist in the United States, though they all exist in a much greater degree in some states than in others, and in some of the states, perhaps, to as great a degree as is practicable. In what are usually called the free states of America, or those in which domestic slavery is abolished, there is to be found as much equality in every respect as comports with safety, civilization and the rights of property. This is also true, as respects the white population, in those states in which domestic slavery does exist; though the number of the bond is in a large proportion to that of the free.

As the tendency of the institutions of America is to the right, we learn in these truths, the power of facts, every question of politics being strictly a question of practice. They who fancy it possible to frame the institutions of a country, on the pure principles of abstract justice, as these principles exist in theories, know little of human nature, or of the restraints that are necessary to society. Abuses assail us in a thousand forms, and it is hopeless to aspire to any condition of humanity, approaching perfection. The very necessity of a government at all, arises from the impossibility of controlling the passions by any other means than that of force.

The celebrated proposition contained in the declaration of independence is not to be understood literally. All men are not "created equal," in a physical, or even in a moral sense, unless we limit the signification to one of political rights. This much is true, since human institutions are a human invention, with which nature has had no connection. Men are not born equals, physically, since one has a good constitution, another a bad; one is handsome, another ugly; one white, another black. Neither are men born equals morally, one possessing genius, or a natural aptitude, while his brother is an idiot. As regards all human institutions men are born equal, no sophistry being able to prove that nature intended one should inherit power and wealth, another slavery and want. Still artificial inequalities are the inevitable consequences of artificial ordinances, and in founding a new governing principle for the social compact, the American legislators instituted new modes of difference.

The very existence of government at all, infers inequality. The citizen who is preferred to office becomes the superior of those who are not, so long as he is the repository of power, and the child inherits the wealth of the parent as a controlling law of society. All that the great American proposition, therefore, can mean, is to set up new and juster notions of natural rights than those which existed previously, by asserting, in substance, that God has not instituted political inequalities, as was pretended by the advocates of the Jus Divinum,[3] and that men possessed a full and natural authority to form such social institutions as best suited their necessities.

There are numerous instances in which the social inequality of America may do violence to our notions of abstract justice, but the compromise of interests under which all civilized society must exist, renders this unavoidable. Great principles seldom escape working injustice in particular things, and this so much the more, in establishing the relations of a community, for in them many great, and frequently conflicting principles enter, to maintain the more essential features of which sacrifices of parts become necessary. If we would have civilization and the exertion indispensable to its success, we must have property; if we have property, we must have its rights; if we have the rights of property, we must take those consequences of the rights of property which are inseparable from the rights themselves.

The equality of rights in America, therefore, after allowing for the striking exception of domestic slavery, is only a greater extension of the principle than common, while there is no such thing as an equality of condition. All that can be said of the first, is that it has been carried as far as a prudent discretion will at all allow, and of the last, that the inequality is the simple result of civilization, unaided by any of those factitious plans that have been elsewhere devised in order to augment the power of the strong, and to enfeeble the weak.

Equality is no where laid down as a governing principle of the institutions of the United States, neither the word, nor any inference that can be fairly deduced from its meaning, occurring in the constitution. As respect the states, themselves, the professions of an equality of rights are more clear, and slavery excepted, the intention in all their governments is to maintain it, as far as practicable, though equality of condition is no where mentioned, all political economists knowing that it is unattainable, if, indeed, it be desirable. Desirable in practice, it can hardly be, since the result would be to force all down to the level of the lowest.

All that a good government aims at, therefore, is to add no unnecessary and artificial aid to the force of its own unavoidable consequences, and to abstain from fortifying and accumulating social inequality as a means of increasing political inequalities.

On Liberty

Liberty, like equality, is a word more used than understood. Perfect and absolute liberty is as incompatible with the existence of society, as equality of condition. It

[3] Latin: "Divine Law."

is impracticable in a state of nature even, since, without the protection of the law, the strong would oppress and enslave the weak. We are then to understand by liberty, merely such a state of the social compact as permits the members of a community to lay no more restraints on themselves, than are required by their real necessities, and obvious interests. To this definition may be added, that it is a requisite of liberty, that the body of a nation should retain the power to modify its institutions, as circumstances shall require.

The natural disposition of all men being to enjoy a perfect freedom of action, it is a common error to suppose that the nation which possesses the mildest laws, or laws that impose the least personal restraints, is the freest. This opinion is untenable, since the power that concedes this freedom of action, can recall it. Unless it is lodged in the body of the community itself, there is, therefore, no pledge for the continuance of such a liberty. A familiar, supposititious case will render this truth more obvious.

A slave holder in Virginia is the master of two slaves: to one he grants his liberty, with the means to go to a town in a free state. The other accompanies his old associate clandestinely. In this town, they engage their services voluntarily, to a common master, who assigns to them equal shares in the same labor, paying them the same wages. In time, the master learns their situation, but, being an indulgent man, he allows the slave to retain his present situation. In all material things, these brothers are equal; they labor together, receive the same wages, and eat of the same food. Yet one is bond, and the other free, since it is in the power of the master, or of his heir, or of his assignee, at any time, to reclaim the services of the one who was not legally manumitted,[4] and reduce him again to the condition of slavery. One of these brothers is the master of his own acts, while the other, though temporarily enjoying the same privileges, holds them subject to the will of a superior.

This is an all important distinction in the consideration of political liberty, since the circumstances of no two countries are precisely the same, and all municipal regulations ought to have direct reference to the actual condition of a community. It follows, that no country can properly be deemed free, unless the body of the nation possess, in the last resort, the legal power to frame its laws according to its wants. This power must also abide in the nation, or it becomes merely an historical fact, for he that was once free is not necessarily free always, any more than he that was once happy, is to consider himself happy in perpetuity.

This definition of liberty is new to the world, for a government founded on such principles is a novelty. Hitherto, a nation has been deemed free, whose people were possessed of a certain amount of franchises, without any reference to the general repository of power. Such a nation may not be absolutely enslaved, but it can scarcely be considered in possession of an affirmative political liberty, since it is not the master of its own fortunes.

Having settled what is the foundation of liberty, it remains to be seen by what process a people can exercise this authority over themselves. The usual course is to refer all matters of choice to the decision of majorities. The common axiom of democracies, however, which says that "the majority must rule," is to be received with many limitations. Were the majority of a country to rule without restraint, it is probable as much injustice and oppression would follow, as are found under the

---

[4] Freed from slavery.

dominion of one. It belongs to the nature of men to arrange themselves in parties, to lose sight of truth and justice in partizanship and prejudice, to mistake their own impulses for that which is proper, and to do wrong because they are indisposed to seek the right. Were it wise to trust power, unreservedly, to majorities, all fundamental and controlling laws would be unnecessary, since they might, as occasion required, emanate from the will of numbers. Constitutions would be useless.

The majority rules in prescribed cases, and in no other. It elects to office, it enacts ordinary laws, subject however to the restrictions of the constitution, and it decides most of the questions that arise in the primitive meetings of the people; questions that do not usually effect any of the principal interests of life.

The majority does not rule in settling fundamental laws, under the constitution; or when it does rule in such cases, it is with particular checks produced by time and new combinations; it does not pass judgment in trials at law, or under impeachment, and it is impotent in many matters touching vested rights. In the state of New York, the majority is impotent, in granting corporations, and in appropriating money for local purposes.

Though majorities often decide wrong, it is believed that they are less liable to do so than minorities. There can be no question that the educated and affluent classes of a country, are more capable of coming to wise and intelligent decisions in affairs of state, than the mass of a population. Their wealth and leisure afford them opportunities for observation and comparison, while their general information and greater knowledge of character, enable them to judge more accurately of men and measures. That these opportunities are not properly used, is owing to the unceasing desire of men to turn their advantages to their own particular benefit, and to their passions. All history proves, when power is the sole possession of a few, that it is perverted to their sole advantage, the public suffering in order that their rulers may prosper. The same nature which imposes the necessity of governments at all, seems to point out the expediency of confiding its control, in the last resort, to the body of the nation, as the only lasting protection against gross abuses.

We do not adopt the popular polity because it is perfect, but because it is less imperfect than any other. As man, by his nature, is liable to err, it is vain to expect an infallible whole that is composed of fallible parts. The government that emanates from a single will, supposing that will to be pure, enlightened, impartial, just and consistent, would be the best in the world, were it attainable for men. Such is the government of the universe, the result of which is perfect harmony. As no man is without spot in his justice, as no man has infinite wisdom, or infinite mercy, we are driven to take refuge in the opposite extreme, or in a government of many.

It is common for the advocates of monarchy and aristocracy to deride the opinions of the mass, as no more than the impulses of ignorance and prejudices. While experience unhappily shows that this charge has too much truth, it also shows that the educated and few form no exemption to the common rule of humanity. The most intelligent men of every country in which there is liberty of thought and action, yielding to their interests or their passions, are always found taking the opposite extremes of contested questions, thus triumphantly refuting an arrogant proposition, that of the exclusive fitness of the few to govern, by an unanswerable fact. The minority of a country is never known to agree, except in its efforts to reduce and oppress the majority. Were this not so, parties would be unknown in all countries but democracies, whereas the factions of aristocracies have been among the fiercest and least governable of any recorded in history.

Although real political liberty can have but one character, that of a popular base, the world contains many modifications of governments that are, more or less, worthy to be termed free. In most of these states, however, the liberties of the mass, are of the negative character of franchises, which franchises are not power of themselves, but merely an exemption from the abuses of power. Perhaps no state exists, in which the people, either by usage, or by direct concessions from the source of authority, do not possess some of these franchises; for, if there is no such thing, in practice, as perfect and absolute liberty, neither is there any such thing, in practice, as total and unmitigated slavery. In the one case, nature has rendered man incapable of enjoying freedom without restraint, and in the other, incapable of submitting, entirely without resistance, to oppression. The harshest despots are compelled to acknowledge the immutable principles of eternal justice, affecting necessity and the love of right, for their most ruthless deeds.

England is a country in which the franchises of the subject are more than usually numerous. Among the most conspicuous of these are the right of trial by jury, and that of the *habeas corpus*. Of the former it is unnecessary to speak, but as the latter is a phrase that may be unintelligible to many, it may be well to explain it.

The literal signification of *Habeas Corpus* is, "thou may'st have the body." In arbitrary governments, it is much the usage to oppress men, under the pretence of justice, by causing them to be arrested on false, or trivial charges, and of subjecting them to long and vexatious imprisonments, by protracting, or altogether evading the day of trial. The issue of a writ of *Habeas Corpus,* is an order to bring the accused before an impartial and independent judge, who examines into the charge, and who orders the prisoner to be set at liberty, unless there be sufficient legal ground for his detention.

This provision of the English law has been wisely retained in our system, for without some such regulation, it would be almost as easy to detain a citizen unjustly, under a popular government, as to detain the subject of a monarchy; the difference in favor of the first, consisting only in the greater responsibility of its functionaries.

By comparing the privileges of the *Habeas Corpus,* where it exists alone, and as a franchise, with those of the citizen who enjoys it merely as a provision of his own, against the abuses of ordinances that he had a voice in framing, we learn the essential difference between real liberty and franchises. The Englishman can appeal to a tribunal, against the abuse of an existing law, but if the law be not with him, he has no power to evade it, however unjust, or oppressive. The American has the same appeal against the abuse of a law, with the additional power to vote for its repeal, should the law itself be vicious. The one profits by a franchise to liberate his person only, submitting to his imprisonment however, if legality has been respected; while the other, in addition to this privilege, has a voice in getting rid of the obnoxious law, itself, and in preventing a recurrence of the wrong.

Some countries have the profession of possessing a government of the people, because an ancient dynasty has been set aside in a revolution, and a new one seated on the throne, either directly by the people, or by a combination that has been made to assume the character of a popular decision. Admitting that a people actually had an agency in framing such a system, and in naming their ruler, they cannot claim to be free, since they have parted with the power they did actually possess. No proposition can be clearer than that he who has given away a thing is no longer its master.

Of this nature is the present government of France. In that country the ancient dynasty has been set aside by a combination of leaders, through the agency of a few active spirits among the mass, and a prince put upon the throne, who is virtually invested with all the authority of his predecessor. Still, as the right of the last sovereign is clearly derived from a revolution, which has been made to assume the appearance of popular will, his government is termed a government of the people. This is a fallacy that can deceive no one of the smallest reflection. Such a system may be the best that France can now receive, but it is a mystification to call it by any other than its proper name. It is not a government of consultation, but one of pure force as respects a vast majority of Frenchmen.

A good deal of the same objection lies against the government of Great Britain, which, though freer in practice than that of France, is not based on a really free system. It may be said that both these governments are as free as comports with discretion, as indeed may be said of Turkey, since men get to be disqualified for the possession of any advantage in time; but such an admission is only an avowal of unfitness, and not a proof of enjoyment.

It is usual to maintain, that in democracies the tyranny of majorities is a greater evil than the oppression of minorities in narrow systems. Although this evil is exaggerated, since the laws being equal in their action it is not easy to oppress the few without oppressing all, it undeniably is the weak side of a popular government. To guard against this, we have framed constitutions, which point out the cases in which the majority shall decide, limiting their power, and bringing that they do possess within the circle of certain general and just principles. It will be elsewhere shown that it is a great mistake for the American citizen to take sides with the public, in doubtful cases affecting the rights of individuals, as this is the precise form in which oppression is the most likely to exhibit itself in a popular government.

Although it is true, that no genuine liberty can exist without being based on popular authority in the last resort, it is equally true that it can not exist when thus based, without many restraints on the power of the mass. These restraints are necessarily various and numerous. A familiar example will show their action. The majority of the people of a state might be in debt to its minority. Were the power of the former unrestrained, circumstances might arise in which they would declare depreciated bank notes a legal tender, and thus clear themselves of their liabilities, at the expense of their creditors. To prevent this, the constitution orders that nothing shall be made a legal tender but the precious metals, thus limiting the power of majorities in a way that the government is not limited in absolute monarchies, in which paper is often made to possess the value of gold and silver.

Liberty therefore may be defined to be a controlling authority that resides in the body of a nation, but so restrained as only to be exercised on certain general principles that shall do as little violence to natural justice, as is compatible with the peace and security of society.

Advantages of a Democracy

The principal advantage of a democracy, is a general elevation in the character of the people. If few are raised to a very great height, few are depressed very low. As a consequence, the average of society is much more respectable than under any other form of government. The vulgar charge that the tendency of democracies is to levelling, meaning to drag all down to the level of the lowest, is singularly untrue, its real tendency being to elevate the depressed to a condition not unworthy of their manhood. In the absence of privileged orders, entails and distinctions, devised permanently to separate men into social castes, it is true none are great but those who become so by their acts, but, confining the remark to the upper classes of society, it would be much more true to say that democracy refuses to lend itself to unnatural and arbitrary distinctions, than to accuse it of a tendency to level those who have a just claim to be elevated. A denial of a favor, is not an invasion of a right.

Democracies are exempt from the military charges, both pecuniary and personal, that become necessary in governments in which the majority are subjects, since no force is required to repress those who, under other systems, are dangerous to the state, by their greater physical power.

As the success of democracies is mainly dependent on the intelligence of the people, the means of preserving the government are precisely those which most conduce to the happiness and social progress of man. Hence we find the state endeavoring to raise its citizens in the scale of being, the certain means of laying the broadest foundation of national prosperity. If the arts are advanced in aristocracies, through the taste of patrons, in democracies, though of slower growth, they will prosper as a consequence of general information; or as a superstructure reared on a wider and more solid foundation.

Democracies being, as nearly as possible, founded in natural justice, little violence is done to the sense of right by the institutions, and men have less occasion than usual, to resort to fallacies and false principles in cultivating the faculties. As a consequence, common sense is more encouraged, and the community is apt to entertain juster notions of all moral truths, than under systems that are necessarily sophisticated. Society is thus a gainer in the greatest element of happiness, or in the right perception of the different relations between men and things.

Democracies being established for the common interests, and the public agents being held in constant check by the people, their general tendency is to serve the whole community, and not small portions of it, as is the case in narrow governments. It is as rational to suppose that a hungry man will first help his neighbor to bread, when master of his own acts, as to suppose that any but those who feel themselves to be truly public servants, will first bethink themselves of the public, when in situations of public trust. In a government of one, that one and his parasites will be the first and best served; in a government of a few, the few; and in a government of many, the many. Thus the general tendency of democratical institutions is to equalize advantages, and to spread its blessings over the entire surface of society.

Democracies, other things being equal, are the cheapest form of government, since little money is lavished in representation, and they who have to pay the taxes, have also, directly or indirectly, a voice in imposing them.

Democracies are less liable to popular tumults than any other polities, because the people, having legal means in their power to redress wrongs, have little inducement to employ any other. The man who can right himself by a vote, will seldom resort to a musket. Grievances, moreover, are less frequent, the most corrupt representatives of a democratic constituency generally standing in awe of its censure.

As men in bodies usually defer to the right, unless acting under erroneous impressions, or excited by sudden resentments, democracies pay more respect to abstract justice, in the management of their foreign concerns, than either aristocracies or monarchies, an appeal always lying against abuses, or violations of principle, to a popular sentiment, that, in the end, seldom fails to decide in favor of truth.

In democracies, with a due allowance for the workings of personal selfishness, it is usually a motive with those in places of trust, to consult the interests of the mass, there being little doubt, that in this system, the entire community has more regard paid to its wants and wishes, than in either of the two others.

On the Disadvantages of Democracy

Democracies are liable to popular impulses, which, necessarily arising from imperfect information, often work injustice from good motives. Tumults of the people are less apt to occur in democracies than under any other form of government, for, possessing the legal means of redressing themselves, there is less necessity to resort to force, but, public opinion constituting, virtually, the power of the state, measures are more apt to be influenced by sudden mutations of sentiment, than under systems where the rulers have better opportunities and more leisure for examination. There is more feeling and less design in the movements of masses than in those of small bodies, except as design emanates from demagogues and political managers.

The efforts of the masses that are struggling to obtain their rights, in monarchies and aristocracies, however, are not to be imputed to democracy; in such cases, the people use their natural weapon, force, merely because they are denied any participation in the legal authority.

When democracies are small, these impulses frequently do great injury to the public service, but in large states they are seldom of sufficient extent to produce results before there is time to feel the influence of reason. It is, therefore, one of the errors of politicians to imagine democracies more practicable in small than in large communities, an error that has probably arisen from the fact that, the ignorance of masses having hitherto put men at the mercy of the combinations of the affluent and intelligent, democracies have been permitted to exist only in countries insignificant by their wealth and numbers.

Large democracies, on the other hand, while less exposed to the principal evil of this form of government, than smaller, are unable to scrutinize and understand character with the severity and intelligence that are of so much importance in all representative governments, and consequently the people are peculiarly exposed to become the dupes of demagogues and political schemers, most of the crimes of democracies arising from the faults and designs of men of this character, rather than from the propensities of the people, who, having little temptation to do wrong, are seldom guilty of crimes except through ignorance.

Democracies are necessarily controlled by public opinion, and failing of the means of obtaining power more honestly, the fraudulent and ambitious find a motive to mislead, and even to corrupt the common sentiment, to attain their ends. This is the greatest and most pervading danger of all large democracies, since it is sapping the foundations of society, by undermining its virtue. We see the effects of this baneful influence, in the openness and audacity with which men avow improper motives and improper acts, trusting to find support in a popular feeling, for while vicious influences are perhaps more admitted in other countries, than in America, in none are they so openly avowed.

It may also be urged against democracies, that, nothing being more corrupting than the management of human affairs, which are constantly demanding sacrifices of permanent principles to interests that are as constantly fluctuating, their people are exposed to assaults on their morals from this quarter, that the masses of other nations escape. It is probable, however, that this evil, while it ought properly to be enumerated as one of the disadvantages of the system, is more than counterbalanced by the main results, even on the score of morals.

The constant appeals to public opinion in a democracy, though excellent as a corrective of public vices, induce private hypocrisy, causing men to conceal their own convictions when opposed to those of the mass, the latter being seldom wholly right, or wholly wrong. A want of national manliness is a vice to be guarded against, for the man who would dare to resist a monarch, shrinks from opposing an entire community. That the latter is quite often wrong, however, is abundantly proved by the fact, that its own judgments fluctuate, as it reasons and thinks differently this year, or this month even, from what it reasoned and thought the last.

The tendency of democracies is, in all things, to mediocrity, since the tastes, knowledge and principles of the majority form the tribunal of appeal. This circumstance, while it certainly serves to elevate the average qualities of a nation, renders the introduction of a high standard difficult. Thus do we find in literature, the arts, architecture and in all acquired knowledge, a tendency in America to gravitate towards the common center in this, as in other things; lending a value and estimation to mediocrity that are not elsewhere given. It is fair to expect, however, that a foundation so broad, may in time sustain a superstructure of commensurate proportions, and that the influence of masses will in this, as in the other interests, have a generally beneficial effect. Still it should not be forgotten that, with the exception of those works, of which, as they appeal to human sympathies or the practices of men, an intelligent public is the best judge, the mass of no community is qualified to decide the most correctly on any thing, which, in its nature, is above its reach.

It is a besetting vice of democracies to substitute public opinion for law. This is the usual form in which masses of men exhibit their tyranny. When the majority of the entire community commits this fault it is a sore grievance, but when local bodies, influenced by local interests, pretend to style themselves the public, they are assuming powers that properly belong to the whole body of the people, and to them only under constitutional limitations. No tyranny of one, nor any tyranny of the few, is worse than this. All attempts in the public, therefore, to do that which the public has no right to do, should be frowned upon as the precise form in which tyranny is the most apt to be displayed in a democracy.

Democracies, depending so much on popular opinion are more liable to be influenced to their injury, through the management of foreign and hostile nations, than other governments. It is generally known that, in Europe, secret means are resorted to, to influence sentiment in this way, and we have witnessed in this country open appeals to the people, against the acts of their servants, in matters of foreign relations, made by foreign, not to say, hostile agents. Perhaps no stronger case can be cited of this weakness on the part of democracies, than is shown in this fact, for here we find men sufficiently audacious to build the hope of so far abusing opinion, as to persuade a people to act directly against their own dignity and interests.

The misleading of public opinion in one way or another, is the parent of the principal disadvantages of a democracy, for in most instances it is first corrupting a community in order that it may be otherwise injured. Were it not for the counteracting influence of reason, which, in the end, seldom, perhaps never fails to assert its power, this defect would of itself, be sufficient to induce all discreet men to decide against this form of government. The greater the danger, the greater the necessity that all well-intentioned and right-minded citizens should be on their guard against its influence.

It would be hazardous, however, to impute all the peculiar faults of American character, to the institutions, the country existing under so many unusual influences. If the latter were overlooked, one might be induced to think frankness and sincerity of character were less encouraged by popular institutions than was formerly supposed, close observers affirming that these qualities are less frequent here, than in most other countries. When the general ease of society is remembered, there is unquestionably more deception of opinion practised than one would naturally expect, but this failing is properly to be imputed to causes that have no necessary connection with democratical institutions, though men defer to public opinion, right or wrong, quite as submissively as they defer to princes. Although truths are not smothered altogether in democracies, they are often temporarily abandoned under this malign influence, unless there is a powerful motive to sustain them at the moment. While we see in our own democracy this manifest disposition to defer to the wrong, in matters that are not properly subject to the common sentiment, in deference to the popular will of the hour, there is a singular boldness in the use of personalities, as if men avenged themselves for the restraints of the one case by a licentiousness that is without hazard.

The base feelings of detraction and envy have more room for exhibition, and perhaps a stronger incentive in a democracy, than in other forms of government, in which the people get accustomed to personal deference by the artificial distinctions of the institutions. This is the reason that men become impatient of all superiority in a democracy, and manifest a wish to prefer those who affect a deference to the public, rather than those who are worthy.

An Aristocrat and a Democrat

We live in an age, when the words aristocrat and democrat are much used, without regard to the real significations. An aristocrat is one of a few, who possess the political power of a country; a democrat, one of the many. The words are also properly applied to those who entertain notions favorable to aristocratical, or democratical forms of government. Such persons are not, necessarily, either aristocrats, or democrats in fact, but merely so in opinion. Thus a member of a democratical government may have an aristocratical bias, and *vice versa*.

To call a man who has the habits and opinions of a gentleman, an aristocrat, from that fact alone, is an abuse of terms, and betrays ignorance of the true principles of government, as well as of the world. It must be an equivocal freedom, under which every one is not the master of his own innocent acts and associations, and he is a sneaking democrat indeed, who will submit to be dictated to, in those habits over which neither law nor morality assumes a right of control.

Some men fancy that a democrat can only be one who seeks the level, social, mental and moral, of the majority, a rule that would at once exclude all men of refinement, education and taste from the class. These persons are enemies of democracy, as they at once render it impracticable. They are usually great sticklers for their own associations and habits, too, though unable to comprehend any of a nature that are superior. They are, in truth, aristocrats in principle, though assuming a contrary pretension; the ground work of all their feelings and arguments being self. Such is not the intention of liberty, whose aim is to leave every man to be the master of his own acts; denying hereditary honors, it is true, as unjust and unnecessary, but not denying the inevitable consequences of civilization.

The law of God is the only rule of conduct, in this, as in other matters. Each man should do as he would be done by. Were the question put to the greatest advocate of indiscriminate association, whether he would submit to have his company and habits dictated to him, he would be one of the first to resist the tyranny; for they, who are the most rigid in maintaining their own claims, in such matters, are usually the loudest in decrying those whom they fancy to be better off than themselves. Indeed, it may be taken as a rule in social intercourse, that he who is the most apt to question the pretensions of others, is the most conscious of the doubtful position he himself occupies; thus establishing the very claims he affects to deny, by letting his jealousy of it be seen. Manners, education and refinement, are positive things, and they bring with them innocent tastes which are productive of high enjoyments; and it is as unjust to deny their possessors their indulgence, as it would be to insist on the less fortunate's passing the time they would rather devote to athletic amusements, in listening to operas for which they have no relish, sung in a language they do not understand.

All that democracy means, is as equal a participation in rights as is practicable; and to pretend that social equality is a condition of popular institutions, is to assume that the latter are destructive of civilization, for, as nothing is more self-evident than the impossibility of raising all men to the highest standard of tastes and refinement, the alternative would be to reduce the entire community to the lowest. The whole embarrassment on this point exists in the difficulty of making men comprehend qualities they do not themselves possess. We can all perceive the difference between ourselves and our inferiors, but when it comes to a question of the difference between us and our superiors, we fail to appreciate merits of which we have no proper conceptions. In face of this obvious difficulty, there is the safe and just governing rule, already mentioned, or that of permitting every one to be the undisturbed judge of his own habits and associations, so long as they are innocent, and do not impair the rights of others to be equally judges for themselves. It follows, that social intercourse must regulate itself, independently of institutions, with the exception that the latter, while they withhold no natural, bestow no factitious advantages beyond those which are inseparable from the rights of property, and general civilization.

In a democracy, men are just as free to aim at the highest attainable places in society, as to obtain the largest fortunes; and it would be clearly unworthy of all noble sentiment to say, that the grovelling competition for money shall alone be free, while that which enlists all the liberal acquirements and elevated sentiments of the race, is denied the democrat. Such an avowal would be at once, a declaration of the inferiority of the system, since nothing but ignorance and vulgarity could be its fruits.

The democratic gentleman must differ in many essential particulars, from the aristocratical gentleman, though in their ordinary habits and tastes they are virtually identical. Their principles vary; and, to a slight degree, their deportment accordingly. The democrat, recognizing the right of all to participate in power, will be more liberal in his general sentiments, a quality of superiority in itself; but, in conceding this much to his fellow man, he will proudly maintain his own independence of vulgar domination, as indispensable to his personal habits. The same principles and manliness that would induce him to depose a royal despot, would induce him to resist a vulgar tyrant.

There is no more capital, though more common error, than to suppose him an aristocrat who maintains his independence of habits; for democracy asserts the control of the majority, only, in matters of law, and not in matters of custom. The very object of the institution is the utmost practicable personal liberty, and to affirm the contrary, would be sacrificing the end to the means.

An aristocrat, therefore, is merely one who fortifies his exclusive privileges by positive institutions, and a democrat, one who is willing to admit of a free competition, in all things. To say, however, that the last supposes this competition will lead to nothing, is an assumption that means are employed without any reference to an end. He is the purest democrat who best maintains his rights, and no rights can be dearer to a man of cultivation, than exemptions from unseasonable invasions on his time, by the coarse-minded and ignorant.

On Civilization

Civilization means a condition of society that is the opposite of the savage, or barbarous state. In other languages this term is more strictly applied to the arts of life, than in the English, in which we are more apt to associate with it the moral condition of a country.

England stands at the head of modern civilization, as a whole, although many countries surpass her in particular parts. The higher tastes of England are not as refined and cultivated, perhaps, as those of Italy and France, but the base of society is infinitely more advanced.

America occupies a middle place in the scale, wanting most of the higher tastes, and excelling in that species of civilization which marks ease and improvement in the middling and lower classes. There is one feature connected with the civilization of this country that is peculiar; for while the people have long been accustomed to the habits of England, they have not been possessed of those arts by which the different objects of the comforts they have enjoyed are produced. For a long time articles as humble as hats, shovels and hoes, were not fabricated in the country, though the time never has been when the Anglo-Americans were unaccustomed to their use.

Although there is a difference between the civilization of the towns, and that of the country, in America, it is less marked than in Europe. The disparity between the refinement, mental cultivation and the elegances of life, is much less apparent than usual, as between an American capital and an American village, though the localities, of course, make some distinctions. As a whole, civilization, while it is less perfect in this country than in the European nations, is more equally diffused throughout the entire community. Still it better becomes the American people to strive to advance their condition than to manifest a weak, unmanly and provincial sensibility to the faults that are occasionally commented on, nations, like individuals, merely betraying a consciousness of their own demerits, by meeting admonition with insult and anger.

The Americans are deficient on many points of civilization, solely for the want of physical force in given places, the practice of covering large surfaces unavoidably retarding the improvements of the nation. This is rather the subject of regret, than a matter of reproach. They are almost ignorant of the art of music, one of the most elevating, innocent and refining of human tastes, whose influence on the habits and morals of a people is of the most beneficial tendency. This taste and knowledge are not only wanting to the people, but an appreciation of their importance. They are also wanting in most of the high tastes, and consequently in the high enjoyments, that accompany a knowledge of all the fine arts in general, and in much that depends on learning, research, and familiarity with the world.

The Americans excel in humanity, in the ordinary comforts, though inferior to the English in this respect, in general civility, in the means of motion while confined to great routes, in shipping and most of the facilities of trade, in common instruction and an aptitude to ordinary pursuits, and in an absence of the sophisms[5] that beset older and more artificial systems. It is, however, to be regretted, that as the nation recedes from the struggle that created the present system, the truths that came uppermost in the collision, are gradually yielding to a new set of sophisms, more peculiar to the present order of things.

There is a familiar and too much despised branch of civilization, of which the population of this country is singularly and unhappily ignorant; that of cookery. The art of eating and drinking, is one of those on which more depends, perhaps, than on any other, since health, activity of mind, constitutional enjoyments, even learning, refinement, and, to a certain degree, morals, are all, more or less, connected with our diet. The Americans are the grossest feeders of any civilized nation known. As a nation, their food is heavy, coarse, ill prepared and indigestible, while it is taken in the least artificial forms that cookery will allow. The predominance of grease in the American kitchen, coupled with the habits of hasty eating and of constant expectoration,[6] are the causes of the diseases of the stomach so common in America. The science of the table extends far beyond the indulgence of our appetites, as the school of manners includes health and morals, as well as that which is agreeable. Vegetable diet is almost converted into an injury in America, from an ignorance of the best modes of preparation, while even animal food is much abused, and loses half its nutriment.

The same is true as respects liquors. The heating and exciting wines, the brandies, and the coarser drinks of the laboring classes, all conspire to injure the physical and the moral man, while they defeat their own ends.

These are points of civilization on which this country has yet much to learn, for while the tables of the polished and cultivated partake of the abundance of the country, and wealth has even found means to introduce some knowledge of the kitchen, there is not perhaps on the face of the globe, the same number of people among whom the good things of the earth are so much abused, or ignorantly wasted, as among the

---

[5] Subtly fallacious arguments intended to deceive.   [6] Coughing and spitting.

people of the United States. National character is, in some measure, affected by a knowledge of the art of preparing food, there being as good reason to suppose that man is as much affected by diet as any other animal, and it is certain that the connection between our moral and physical qualities is so intimate as to cause them to react on each other.

Conclusion

The inferences to be drawn from the foregoing reasons and facts, admitting both to be just, may be briefly summed up as follows.

No expedients can equalize the temporal lots of men; for without civilization and government, the strong would oppress the weak, and, with them, an inducement to exertion must be left, by bestowing rewards on talents, industry and success. All that the best institutions, then, can achieve, is to remove useless obstacles, and to permit merit to be the artisan of its own fortune, without always degrading demerit to the place it ought naturally to fill.

Every human excellence is merely comparative, there being no good without alloy. It is idle therefore to expect a system that shall exhibit faultlessness, or perfection.

The terms liberty, equality, right and justice, used in a political sense, are merely terms of convention, and of comparative excellence, there being no such thing, in practice, as either of these qualities being carried out purely, according to the abstract notions of theories.

The affairs of life embrace a multitude of interests, and he who reasons on any one of them, without consulting the rest, is a visionary unsuited to control the business of the world.

There is a prevalent disposition in the designing to forget the means in the end, and on the part of the mass to overlook the result in the more immediate agencies. The first is the consequence of cupidity; the last of short-sightedness, and frequently of the passions. Both these faults need be vigilantly watched in a democracy, as the first unsettles principles while it favors artifice, and the last is substituting the transient motives of a day, for the deliberate policy and collected wisdom of ages.

Men are the constant dupes of names, while their happiness and well-being mainly depend on things. The highest proof a community can give of its fitness for self government, is its readiness in distinguishing between the two; for frauds, oppression, flattery and vice, are the offspring of the mistakes.

It is a governing principle of nature, that the agency which can produce most good, when perverted from its proper aim, is most productive of evil. It behooves the well-intentioned, therefore, vigilantly to watch the tendency of even their most highly prized institutions, since that which was established in the interests of the right, may so easily become the agent of the wrong.

The disposition of all power is to abuses, nor does it at all mend the matter that its possessors are a majority. Unrestrained political authority, though it be confided to masses, cannot be trusted without positive limitations, men in bodies being but an aggregation of the passions, weaknesses and interests of men as individuals.

It is as idle to expect what is termed gratitude, in a democracy, as from any other repository of power. Bodies of men, though submitting to human impulses generally, and often sympathetic as well as violent, are seldom generous. In matters that touch the common feeling, they are avaricious of praise, and they usually visit any want of success in a public man, as a personal wrong. Thus it is that we see a dozen victories forgotten in a single defeat, an irritable vanity in the place of a masculine pride, and a sensitiveness to opinion, instead of a just appreciation of acts.

Under every system it is more especially the office of the prudent and candid to guard against the evils peculiar to that particular system, than to declaim against the abuses of others. Thus, in a democracy, instead of decrying monarchs and aristocrats, who are impotent, it is wiser to look into the sore spots of the only form of government that can do any practical injury, and to apply the necessary remedies, than to be glorifying ourselves at the expense of charity, common sense, and not unfrequently of truth.

Life is made up of positive things, the existence of which it is not only folly, but which it is often unsafe to deny. Nothing is gained by setting up impracticable theories, but alienating opinion from the facts under which we live, all the actual distinctions that are inseparable from the possession of property, learning, breeding, refinement, tastes and principles, existing as well in one form of government, as in another; the only difference between ourselves and other nations, in this particular, lying in the fact that there are no other artificial distinctions than those that are inseparable from the recognised principles and indispensable laws of civilization.

There is less real inequality in the condition of men than outward circumstances would give reason to believe. If refinement brings additional happiness, it also adds point to misery. Fortunately, the high consolations of religion, in which lies the only lasting and true relief from the cares and seeming injustice of the world, are equally attainable, or, if there be a disadvantage connected with this engrossing interest, it is against those whose lots are vulgarly supposed to be the most desirable.

1838

Preface to *The Leather-Stocking Tales**

This series of Stories, which has obtained the name of "The Leather-Stocking Tales," has been written in a very desultory and inartificial manner. The order in which the several books appeared was essentially different from that in which they would have been presented to the world, had the regular course of their incidents been consulted. In "The Pioneers," the first of the series written, the Leather-Stocking is represented as already old, and driven from his early haunts in the forest, by the sound of the axe and the smoke of the settler. "The Last of the Mohicans," the next book in the order of publication, carried the readers back to a much earlier period in the history

---

* Written especially for a complete edition of
The Leather-Stocking Tales that appeared in
1850.

of our hero, representing him as middle-aged, and in the fullest vigor of manhood. In "The Prairie," his career terminates, and he is laid in his grave. There, it was originally the intention to leave him, in the expectation that, as in the case of the human mass, he would soon be forgotten. But a latent regard for this character induced the author to resuscitate him in "The Pathfinder," a book that was not long after succeeded by "The Deerslayer," thus completing the series as it now exists.

While the five books that have been written were originally published in the order just mentioned, that of the incidents insomuch as they are connected with the career of their principal character, is, as has been stated, very different. Taking the life of the Leather-Stocking as a guide, "The Deerslayer" should have been the opening book, for in that work he is seen just emerging into manhood; to be succeeded by "The Last of the Mohicans," "The Pathfinder," "The Pioneers," and "The Prairie." This arrangement embraces the order of events, though far from being that in which the books at first appeared. "The Pioneers" was published in 1822;[1] "The Deerslayer" in 1841; making the interval between them nineteen years. Whether these progressive years have had a tendency to lessen the value of the last-named book, by lessening the native fire of its author, or of adding somewhat in the way of improved taste and a more matured judgment, is for others to decide.

If anything from the pen of the writer of these romances is at all to outlive himself, it is, unquestionably, the series of "The Leather-Stocking Tales." To say this is not to predict a very lasting reputation for the series itself, but simply to express the belief it will outlast any, or all, of the works from the same hand.

It is undeniable that the desultory manner in which "The Leather-Stocking Tales" were written has, in a measure, impaired their harmony, and otherwise lessened their interest. This is proved by the fate of the two books last published, though probably the two most worthy an enlightened and cultivated reader's notice. If the facts could be ascertained, it is probable the result would show that of all those (in America, in particular) who have read the three first books of the series, not one in ten has a knowledge of the existence even of the two last. Several causes have tended to produce this result. The long interval of time between the appearance of "The Prairie" and that of "The Pathfinder" was itself a reason why the later books of the series should be overlooked. There was no longer novelty to attract attention, and the interest was materially impaired by the manner in which events were necessarily anticipated, in laying the last of the series first before the world. With the generation that is now coming on the stage this fault will be partially removed by the edition contained in the present work, in which the several tales will be arranged solely in reference to their connection with each other.

The author has often been asked if he had any original in his mind, for the character of Leather-Stocking. In a physical sense, different individuals known to the writer in early life certainly presented themselves as models, through his recollections; but in a moral sense this man of the forest is purely a creation. The idea of delineating a character that possessed little of civilization but its highest principles as they are exhibited in the uneducated, and all of savage life that is not incompatible with these great rules of conduct, is perhaps natural to the situation in which Natty was placed.

---

[1] *The Pioneers* did not appear until February 1823.

He is too proud of his origin to sink into the condition of the wild Indian, and too much a man of the woods not to imbibe as much as was at all desirable from his friends and companions. In a moral point of view it was the intention to illustrate the effect of seed scattered by the wayside. To use his own language, his "gifts" were "white gifts," and he was not disposed to bring on them discredit. On the other hand, removed from nearly all the temptations of civilized life, placed in the best associations of that which is deemed savage, and favorably disposed by nature to improve such advantages, it appeared to the writer that his hero was a fit subject to represent the better qualities of both conditions, without pushing either to extremes.

There was no violent stretch of the imagination, perhaps, in supposing one of civilized associations in childhood retaining many of his earliest lessons amid the scenes of the forest. Had these early impressions, however, not been sustained by continued though casual connection with men of his own color, if not of his own caste, all our information goes to show he would soon have lost every trace of his origin. It is believed that sufficient attention was paid to the particular circumstances in which this individual was placed, to justify the picture of his qualities that has been drawn. The Delawares early attracted the attention of the missionaries, and were a tribe unusually influenced by their precepts and example. In many instances they became Christians, and cases occurred in which their subsequent lives gave proof of the efficacy of the great moral changes that had taken place within them.

A leading character in a work of fiction has a fair right to the aid which can be obtained from a poetical view of the subject. It is in this view, rather than in one more strictly circumstantial, that Leather-Stocking has been drawn. The imagination has no great task in portraying to itself a being removed from the every-day induce-ments to err which abound in civilized life, while he retains the best and simplest of his early impressions; who sees God in the forest; hears him in the winds; bows to him in the firmament that o'ercanopies all; submits to his sway in a humble belief of his justice and mercy—in a word, a being who finds the impress of the Deity in all the works of nature, without any of the blots produced by the expedients, and passion, and mistakes of man. This is the most that has been attempted in the character of Leather-Stocking. Had this been done without any of the drawbacks of humanity, the picture would have been, in all probability, more pleasing than just. In order to preserve the *vraisemblable,* [2] therefore, traits derived from the prejudices, tastes, and even the weaknesses of his youth, have been mixed up with these higher qualities and longings, in a way, it is hoped, to represent a reasonable picture of human nature, without offering to the spectator a "monster of goodness."

It has been objected to these books that they give a more favorable picture of the red man than he deserves. The writer apprehends that much of this objection arises from the habits of those who have made it. One of his critics, on the appearance of the first work in which Indian character was portrayed, objected that its "characters were Indians of the school of Heckewelder, [3] rather than of the school of nature." These words quite probably contain the substance of the true answer to the objection. Heckewelder was an ardent, benevolent missionary, bent on the good of the red man, and seeing in him one who had the soul, reason, and characteristics of a fellow-being.

---

[2] French: "verisimilitude." In a literary sense, realism.

[3] John Gottlieb Heckewelder (1743–1823), pioneer Moravian missionary among the Indians.

The critic is understood to have been a very distinguished agent of the government, one very familiar with Indians, as they are seen at the councils to treat for the sale of their lands, where little or none of their domestic qualities come in play, and where, indeed, their evil passions are known to have the fullest scope. As just would it be to draw conclusions of the general state of American society from the scenes of the capital, as to suppose that the negotiating of one of these treaties is a fair picture of Indian life.

It is the privilege of all writers of fiction, more particularly when their works aspire to the elevation of romances, to present the *beau-idéal*[4] of their characters to the reader. This it is which constitutes poetry, and to suppose that the red man is to be represented only in the squalid misery or in the degraded moral state that certainly more or less belongs to his condition, is, we apprehend, taking a very narrow view of an author's privileges. Such criticism would have deprived the world of even Homer.

1850

---

from The Deerslayer

Chapter VII

> *"Clear, placid Leman! Thy contrasted lake*
> *With the wild world I dwelt in, is a thing*
> *Which warns me, with its stillness, to forsake*
> *Earth's troubled waters for a purer spring.*
> *This quiet sail is as a noiseless wing*
> *To waft me from distraction: once I loved*
> *Torn ocean's roar, but thy soft murmuring*
> *Sounds sweet as if a sister's voice reproved,*
> *   That I with stern delights should e'er have been so*
> *moved."*[1]
> Byron.

Day had fairly dawned before the young man, whom we have left in the situation described in the last chapter, again opened his eyes. This was no sooner done than he started up and looked about him with the eagerness of one who suddenly felt the importance of accurately ascertaining his precise position. His rest had been deep and undisturbed; and when he awoke, it was with a clearness of intellect and a readiness of resources that were much needed at that particular moment. The sun had not risen, it is true, but the vault of heaven was rich with the winning softness that "brings and shuts the day," while the whole air was filled with the carols of birds, the hymns of the feathered tribe. These sounds first told Deerslayer the risks he ran. The air—for wind it could scarce be called—was still light, it is true, but it had increased a little in the course of the night, and as the canoes were mere feathers on the water, they

---

[4] French: "highest form of beauty."
[1] *Childe Harold's Pilgrimage* (Canto III, stanza 85), by George Gordon, Lord Byron (1788–1824).

had drifted twice the expected distance; and, what was still more dangerous, had approached so near the base of the mountain, that here rose precipitously from the eastern shore, as to render the carols of the birds plainly audible. This was not the worst. The third canoe had taken the same direction, and was slowly drifting toward a point where it must inevitably touch, unless turned aside by a shift of wind or human hands. In other respects, nothing presented itself to attract attention or to awaken alarm. The castle stood on its shoal, nearly abreast of the canoes, for the drift had amounted to miles in the course of the night, and the ark lay fastened to its piles, as both had been left so many hours before.

As a matter of course, Deerslayer's attention was first given to the canoe ahead. It was already quite near the point, and a very few strokes of the paddle sufficed to tell him that it must touch before he could possibly overtake it. Just at this moment, too, the wind inopportunely freshened, rendering the drift of the light craft much more rapid and certain. Feeling the impossibility of preventing a contact with the land, the young man wisely determined not to heat himself with unnecessary exertions; but first looking to the priming of his piece, he proceeded slowly and warily toward the point, taking care to make a little circuit, that he might be exposed on only one side as he approached.

The canoe adrift, being directed by no such intelligence, pursued its proper way and grounded on a small sunken rock, at the distance of three or four yards from the shore. Just at that moment, Deerslayer had got abreast of the point and turned the bows of his own boat to the land; first casting loose his tow, that his movements might be unencumbered. The canoe hung an instant on the rock; then it rose a hair's-breadth on an almost imperceptible swell of the water, swung round, floated clear, and reached the strand. All this the young man noted, but it neither quickened his pulses nor hastened his hand. If any one had been lying in wait for the arrival of the waif, he must be seen, and the utmost caution in approaching the shore became indispensable; if no one was in ambush, hurry was unnecessary. The point being nearly diagonally opposite to the Indian encampment, he hoped the last, though the former was not only possible, but probable; for the savages were prompt in adopting all the expedients of their particular modes of warfare, and quite likely had many scouts searching the shores for craft to carry them off to the castle. As a glance at the lake from any height or projection would expose the smallest object on its surface, there was little hope that either of the canoes could pass unseen; and Indian sagacity needed no instruction to tell which way a boat or a log would drift, when the direction of the wind was known. As Deerslayer drew nearer and nearer to the land, the stroke of his paddle grew slower, his eye became more watchful, and his ears and nostrils almost dilated with the effort to detect any lurking danger. 'Twas a trying moment for a novice, nor was there the encouragement which even the timid sometimes feel, when conscious of being observed and commended. He was entirely alone, thrown on his own resources, and was cheered by no friendly eye, emboldened by no encouraging voice. Notwithstanding all these circumstances, the most experienced veteran in forest warfare could not have behaved better. Equally free from recklessness and hesitation, his advance was marked by a sort of philosophical prudence, that appeared to render him superior to all motives but those which were best calculated to effect his purpose. Such was the commencement of a career in forest exploits, that afterward rendered this man, in his way, and under the limits of his habits and opportunities, as renowned as many a hero whose name has adorned the pages of works more celebrated than legends simple as ours can ever become.

When about a hundred yards from the shore, Deerslayer rose in the canoe, gave three or four vigorous strokes with the paddle, sufficient of themselves to impel the bark to land, and then quickly laying aside the instrument of labor, he seized that of war. He was in the very act of raising the rifle, when a sharp report was followed by the buzz of a bullet that passed so near his body as to cause him involuntarily to start. The next instant Deerslayer staggered and fell his whole length in the bottom of the canoe. A yell—it came from a single voice—followed, and an Indian leaped from the bushes upon the open area of the point, bounding toward the canoe. This was the moment the young man desired. He rose on the instant and levelled his own rifle at his uncovered foe; but his finger hesitated about pulling the trigger on one whom he held at such a disadvantage. This little delay, probably, saved the life of the Indian, who bounded back into the cover as swiftly as he had broken out of it. In the mean time Deerslayer had been swiftly approaching the land, and his own canoe reached the point just as his enemy disappeared. As its movements had not been directed, it touched the shore a few yards from the other boat; and though the rifle of his foe had to be loaded, there was not time to secure his prize and to carry it beyond danger before he would be exposed to another shot. Under the circumstances, therefore, he did not pause an instant, but dashed into the woods and sought a cover.

On the immediate point there was a small open area, partly in native grass and partly beach, but a dense fringe of bushes lined its upper side. This narrow belt of dwarf vegetation passed, one issued immediately into the high and gloomy vaults of the forest. The land was tolerably level for a few hundred feet, and then it rose precipitously in a mountain-side. The trees were tall, large, and so free from under-brush that they resembled vast columns, irregularly scattered, upholding a dome of leaves. Although they stood tolerably close together, for their ages and size, the eye could penetrate to considerable distances; and bodies of men, even, might have engaged beneath their cover with concert and intelligence.

Deerslayer knew that his adversary must be employed in reloading, unless he had fled. The former proved to be the case, for the young man had no sooner placed himself behind a tree than he caught a glimpse of the arm of the Indian, his body being concealed by an oak, in the very act of forcing the leathered bullet home. Nothing would have been easier than to spring forward and decide the affair by a close assault on his unprepared foe; but every feeling of Deerslayer revolted at such a step, although his own life had just been attempted from a cover. He was yet unpractised in the ruthless expedients of savage warfare, of which he knew nothing except by tradition and theory, and it struck him as an unfair advantage to assail an unarmed foe. His color had heightened, his eye frowned, his lips were compressed, and all his energies were collected and ready; but, instead of advancing to fire, he dropped his rifle to the usual position of a sportsman in readiness to catch his aim, and muttered to himself, unconscious that he was speaking:

"No, no—that may be red-skin warfare, but it's not a Christian's gifts. Let the miscreant charge, and then we'll take it out like men; for the canoe he *must* not and *shall* not have. No, no; let him have time to load, and God will take care of the right!"

All this time the Indian had been so intent on his own movements that he was even ignorant that his enemy was in the wood. His only apprehension was, that the canoe would be recovered and carried away before he might be in readiness to prevent it. He had sought the cover from habit, but was within a few feet of the fringe of bushes, and could be at the margin of the forest in readiness to fire in a moment. The distance between him and his enemy was about fifty yards, and the trees were so arranged by nature that the line of sight was not interrupted, except by the particular trees behind which each party stood.

His rifle was no sooner loaded than the savage glanced around him, and advanced incautiously as regarded the real, but stealthily as respected the fancied position of his enemy, until he was fairly exposed. Then Deerslayer stepped from behind his own cover and hailed him.

"This-a-way, red-skin; this-a-way, if you're looking for me," he called out. "I'm young in war, but not so young as to stand on an open beach to be shot down like an owl by daylight. It rests on yourself whether it's peace or war atween us; for my gifts are white gifts, and I'm not one of them that thinks it valiant to slay human mortals singly in the woods."

The savage was a good deal startled by this sudden discovery of the danger he ran. He had a little knowledge of English, however, and caught the drift of the other's meaning. He was also too well schooled to betray alarm, but, dropping the butt of his rifle to the earth with an air of confidence, he made a gesture of lofty courtesy. All this was done with the ease and self-possession of one accustomed to consider no man his superior. In the midst of this consummate acting, however, the volcano that raged within caused his eyes to glare and his nostrils to dilate like those of some wild beast that is suddenly prevented from taking the fatal leap.

"Two canoe," he said, in the deep guttural tones of his race, holding up the number of fingers he mentioned, by way of preventing mistakes; "one for you—one for me."

"No, no, Mingo,[2] that will never do. You own neither; and neither shall you have, as long as I can prevent it. I know it's war atween your people and mine, but that's no reason why human mortals should slay each other like savage creatur's that meet in the woods; go your way, then, and leave me to go mine. The world is large enough for us both; and when we meet fairly in battle, why, the Lord will order the fate of each of us."

"Good!" exclaimed the Indian; "my brother missionary—great talk; all about Manitou."[3]

"Not so—not so, warrior. I'm not good enough for the Moravians,[4] and am too good for most of the other vagabonds that preach about in the woods. No, no, I'm only a hunter, as yet, though afore the peace is made, 'tis like enough there'll be occasion to strike a blow at some of your people. Still, I wish it to be done in fair fight, and not in a quarrel about the ownership of a miserable canoe."

"Good! My brother very young—but he very wise. Little warrior—great talker. Chief, sometimes, in council."

"I don't know this, nor do I say it, Injin," returned Deerslayer, coloring a little at the ill-concealed sarcasm of the other's manner; "I look forward to a life in the woods, and I only hope it may be a peaceable one. All young men must go on the war-path when there's occasion, but war isn't needfully massacre. I've seen enough

---

[2] Slang term for an Iroquois or Sioux brave.
[3] One of the great spirits that rule nature.

[4] Early sect of devout European missionaries who preached among the Indians.

of the last, this very night, to know that Providence frowns on it; and I now invite you to go your own way, while I go mine; and hope that we may part fri'nds."

"Good! My brother has two scalp—grey hair under t'other. Old wisdom—young tongue."

Here the savage advanced with confidence, his hand extended, his face smiling, and his whole bearing denoting amity and respect. Deerslayer met his offered friendship in a proper spirit, and they shook hands cordially, each endeavoring to assure the other of his sincerity and desire to be at peace.

"All have his own," said the Indian; "my canoe, mine; your canoe, your'n. Go look; if your'n, you keep; if mine, I keep."

"That's just, red-skin; though you must be wrong in thinking the canoe your property. Howsever, seein' is believin', and we'll go down to the shore, where you may look with your own eyes; for it's likely you'll object to trustin' altogether to mine."

The Indian uttered his favorite exclamation of "good!" and then they walked side by side toward the shore. There was no apparent distrust in the manner of either, the Indian moving in advance, as if he wished to show his companion that he did not fear turning his back to him. As they reached the open ground the former pointed toward Deerslayer's boat, and said emphatically:

"No mine—pale-face canoe. *This* red-man's. No want other man's canoe—want his own."

"You're wrong, red-skin, you're altogether wrong. This canoe was left in old Hutter's keeping, and is his'n according to all law, red or white, till its owner comes to claim it. Here's the seats and the stitching of the bark to speak for themselves. No man ever know'd an Injin to turn off such work."

"Good! My brother little ole—big wisdom. Injin no make him. White man's work."

"I'm glad you think so, for holding out to the contrary might have made ill blood atween us; every one having a right to take possession of his own. I'll just shove the canoe out of reach of dispute at once, as the quickest way of settling difficulties."

While Deerslayer was speaking he put a foot against the end of the light boat, and giving a vigorous shove, he sent it out into the lake a hundred feet or more, where, taking the true current, it would necessarily float past the point and be in no further danger of coming ashore. The savage started at this ready and decided expedient, and his companion saw that he cast a hurried and fierce glance at his own canoe, or that which contained the paddles. The change of manner, however, was but momentary, and then the Iroquois resumed his air of friendliness and a smile of satisfaction.

"Good!" he repeated, with stronger emphasis than ever. "Young head, old mind. Know how to settle quarrel. Farewell, brother. He go to house in water—muskrat house—Injin go to camp; tell chiefs no find canoe."

Deerslayer was not sorry to hear this proposal, for he felt anxious to join the females, and he took the offered hand of the Indian very willingly. The parting words were friendly, and, while the red-man walked calmly toward the wood, with the rifle in the hollow of his arm, without once looking back in uneasiness or distrust, the white man moved toward the remaining canoe, carrying his piece in the same pacific manner, it is true, but keeping his eyes fastened on the movements of the other. This distrust, however, seemed to be altogether uncalled for, and as if ashamed to have entertained it, the young man averted his look and stepped carelessly up to his boat. Here he began to push the canoe from the shore and to make his other preparations for departing. He might have been thus employed a minute, when, happening to turn his face toward the land, his quick and certain eye told him at a glance the imminent jeopardy in which his life was placed. The black, ferocious eyes of the savage were glancing on him, like those of the crouching tiger, through a small opening in the bushes, and the muzzle of his rifle seemed already to be opening in a line with his own body.

Then, indeed, the long practice of Deerslayer, as a hunter, did him good service. Accustomed to fire with the deer on the bound, and often when the precise position of the animal's body had in a manner to be guessed at, he used the same expedients here. To cock and poise his rifle were the acts of a single moment and a single motion; then, aiming almost without sighting, he fired into the bushes where he knew a body ought to be, in order to sustain the appalling countenance which alone was visible. There was not time to raise the piece any higher or to take a more deliberate aim. So rapid were his movements that both parties discharged their pieces at the same instant, the concussions mingling in one report. The mountains, indeed, gave back but a single echo. Deerslayer dropped his piece and stood, with head erect, steady as one of the pines in the calm of a June morning, watching the result; while the savage gave the yell that has become historical for its appalling influence leaped through the bushes and came bounding across the open ground, flourishing a tomahawk. Still Deerslayer moved not, but stood with his unloaded rifle fallen against his shoulders, while, with a hunter's habits, his hands were mechanically feeling for the powder-horn and charger. When about forty feet from his enemy, the savage hurled his keen weapon; but it was with an eye so vacant and a hand so unsteady and feeble that the young man caught it by the handle as it was flying past him. At that instant the Indian staggered and fell his whole length on the ground.

"I know'd it—I know'd it!" exclaimed Deerslayer, who was already preparing to force a fresh bullet into his rifle; "I know'd it must come to this, as soon as I had got the range from the creatur's eyes. A man sights suddenly and fires quick when his own life's in danger; yes, I know'd it would come to this. I was about the hundredth part of a second too quick for him, or it might have been bad for me! The riptyle's bullet has just grazed my side—but, say what you will for or ag'in 'em, a red-skin is by no means as sartain with powder and ball as a white man. Their gifts don't seem to lie that-a-way. Even Chingachgook,[5] great as he is in other matters, isn't downright deadly with the rifle."

By this time the piece was reloaded, and Deerslayer, after tossing the tomahawk into the canoe, advanced to his victim, and stood over him, leaning on his rifle, in melancholy attention. It was the first instance in which he had seen a man fall in battle —it was the first fellow-creature against whom he had ever seriously raised his own hand. The sensations were novel; and regret, with the freshness of our better feelings, mingled with his triumph. The Indian was not dead, though shot directly through the body. He lay on his back motionless, but his eyes, now full of consciousness,

---

[5] A young Mohican chief of the larger Delaware tribe, he is also Deerslayer's Indian "blood-brother." Natty Bumppo was orphaned at an early age and was partially raised by the Delaware Indians. Chingachgook plays a significant role in both *The Deerslayer* and *The Last of the Mohicans*.

watched each action of his victor—as the fallen bird regards the fowler—jealous of every movement. The man probably expected the fatal blow which was to precede the loss of his scalp; or perhaps he anticipated that this latter act of cruelty would precede his death. Deerslayer read his thoughts; and he found a melancholy satisfaction in relieving the apprehensions of the helpless savage.

"No, no, red-skin," he said; "you've nothing more to fear from me. I am of a Christian stock, and scalping is not of my gifts. I'll just make sartain of your rifle and then come back and do you what service I can. Though here I can't stay much longer, as the crack of three rifles will be apt to bring some of your devils down upon me."

The close of this was said in a sort of a soliloquy, as the young man went in quest of the fallen rifle. The piece was found where its owner had dropped it, and was immediately put into the canoe. Laying his own rifle at its side, Deerslayer then returned and stood over the Indian again.

"All inmity atween you and me's at an ind, red-skin," he said; "and you may set your heart at rest on the score of the scalp or any further injury. My gifts are white, as I've told you; and I hope my conduct will be white also!"

Could looks have conveyed all they meant, it is probable Deerslayer's innocent vanity on the subject of color would have been rebuked a little; but he comprehended the gratitude that was expressed in the eyes of the dying savage, without in the least detecting the bitter sarcasm that struggled with the better feeling.

"Water!" ejaculated the thirsty and unfortunate creature; "give poor Injun water."

"Aye, water you shall have, if you drink the lake dry. I'll just carry you down to it, that you may take your fill. This is the way, they tell me, with all wounded people—water is their greatest comfort and delight."

So saying, Deerslayer raised the Indian in his arms, and carried him to the lake. Here he first helped him to take an attitude in which he could appease his burning thirst; after which he seated himself on a stone and took the head of his wounded adversary in his own lap and endeavored to soothe his anguish in the best manner he could.

"It would be sinful in me to tell you your time hadn't come, warrior," he commenced, "and therefore I'll not say it. You've passed the middle age already, and, considerin' the sort of lives ye lead, your days have been pretty well filled. The principal thing now is to look forward to what comes next. Neither red-skin nor pale-face, on the whole, calculates much on sleepin' forever; but both expect to live in another world. Each has his gifts, and will be judged by 'em, and, I suppose, you've thought these matters over enough, not to stand in need of sarmons when the trial comes. You'll find your happy hunting-grounds, if you've been a just Injin; if an onjust, you'll meet your desarts in another way. I've my own idees about these things; but you're too old and exper'enced to need any explanations from one as young as I."

"Good!" ejaculated the Indian, whose voice retained its depth even as life ebbed away; "young head—ole wisdom!"

"It's sometimes a consolation, when the ind comes, to know that them we've harmed, or *tried* to harm, forgive us. I suppose natur' seeks this relief, by way of getting a pardon on 'arth; as we never can know whether He pardons, who is all in all, till judgment itself comes. It's soothing to know that *any* pardon at such times; and that, I conclude, is the secret. Now, as for myself, I overlook altogether your designs ag'in my life; first, because no harm came of 'em; next, because it's your gifts and natur' and trainin', and I ought not to have trusted you at all; and, finally and chiefly, because I can bear no ill-will to a dying man, whether heathen or Christian. So put your heart at ease, so far as I'm consarned; you know best what other matters ought to trouble you, or what ought to give you satisfaction in so trying a moment."

It is probable that the Indian had some of the fearful glimpses of the unknown state of being which God in mercy seems at times to afford to all the human race; but they were necessarily in conformity with his habits and prejudices. Like most of his people, and like too many of our own, he thought more of dying in a way to gain applause among those he left than to secure a better state of existence hereafter. While Deerslayer was speaking, his mind was a little bewildered, though he felt that the intention was good; and when he had done, a regret passed over his spirit that none of his own tribe were present to witness his stoicism under extreme bodily suffering, and the firmness with which he met his end. With the high innate courtesy that so often distinguishes the Indian warrior before he becomes corrupted by too much intercourse with the worst class of the white men, he endeavored to express his thankfulness for the other's good intentions, and to let him understand that they were appreciated.

"Good!" he repeated, for this was an English word much used by the savages— "good—young head; young *heart,* too. *Old* heart tough; no shed tear. Hear Indian when he die, and no want to lie—what he call him?"

"Deerslayer is the name I bear now, though the Delawares have said that when I get back from this war-path, I shall have a more manly title, provided I can 'arn one."

"That good name for boy—poor name for warrior. He get better quick. No fear *there*"—the savage had strength sufficient, under the strong excitement he felt, to raise a hand and tap the young man on his breast—"eye sartain—finger lightning—aim, death—great warrior soon. No Deerslayer—Hawkeye—Hawkeye—Hawkeye. Shake hand."

Deerslayer—or Hawkeye, as the youth was then first named, for in after years he bore the appellation throughout all that region—Deerslayer took the hand of the savage, whose last breath was drawn in that attitude, gazing in admiration at the countenance of a stranger, who had shown so much readiness, skill, and firmness, in a scene that was equally trying and novel. When the reader remembers it is the highest gratification an Indian can receive to see his enemy betray weakness, he will be better able to appreciate the conduct which had extorted so great a concession at such a moment.

"His spirit has fled!" said Deerslayer, in a suppressed, melancholy voice. "Ah's me! Well, to this we must all come, sooner or later; and he is happiest, let his skin be of what color it may, who is best fitted to meet it. Here lies the body of no doubt a brave warrior, and the soul is already flying toward its heaven or hell, whether that be a happy hunting-ground, a place scant of game; regions of glory, according to Moravian doctrine, or flames of fire! So it happens, too, as regards other matters! Here have old Hutter and Hurry Harry got themselves into difficulty, if they hav'n't got themselves into torment and death, and all for a bounty that luck offers to me in what many would think a lawful and suitable manner. But not a farthing of such money shall cross my hand. White I was born, and white will I die; clinging to color to the last, even though the King's Majesty, his governors, and all his councils, both at home and in the Colonies, forget from what they come, and where they hope to go, and all for a little advantage in warfare. No, no—warrior, hand of mine shall never molest your scalp, and so your soul may rest in peace on the p'int of making a decent appearance, when the body comes to join it, in your own land of spirits."

Deerslayer arose as soon as he had spoken. Then he placed the body of the dead man in a sitting posture, with its back against the little rock, taking the necessary care to prevent it from falling or in any way settling into an attitude that might be thought unseemly by the sensitive, though wild, notions of a savage. When this duty was performed, the young man stood gazing at the grim countenance of his fallen foe, in a sort of melancholy abstraction. As was his practice, however, a habit gained by living so much alone in the forest, he then began again to give utterance to his thoughts and feelings aloud.

"I didn't wish your life, red-skin," he said, "but you left me no choice atween killing or being killed. Each party acted according to his gifts, I suppose, and blame can light on neither. You were treacherous, according to your natur' in war, and I was a little oversightful, as I'm apt to be in trusting others. Well, this is my first battle with a human mortal, though it's not likely to be the last. I have fou't most of the creatur's of the forest, such as bears, wolves, painters,[6] and catamounts,[7] but this is the beginning with the red-skins. If I was Injin born, now, I might tell of this, or carry in the scalp, and boast of the expl'ite afore the whole tribe; or, if my inimy had only been even a bear, 'twould have been nat'ral and proper to let everybody know what had happened; but I don't well see how I'm to let even Chingachgook into this secret, so long as it can be done only by boasting with a white tongue. And why should I wish to boast of it a'ter all? It's slaying a human, although he was a savage; and how do I know that he was a just Injin; and that he has not been taken away suddenly to anything but happy hunting-grounds. When it's onsartain whether good or evil has been done, the wisest way is not to be boastful—still, I *should* like Chingachgook to know that I haven't discredited the Delawares or my training!"

Part of this was uttered aloud, while part was merely muttered between the speaker's teeth; his more confident opinions enjoying the first advantage, while his doubts were expressed in the latter mode. Soliloquy and reflection received a startling interruption, however, by the sudden appearance of a second Indian on the lake shore, a few hundred yards from the point. This man, evidently another scout, who had probably been drawn to the place by the reports of the rifles, broke out of the forest with so little caution that Deerslayer caught a view of his person before he was himself discovered. When the latter event did occur, as was the case a moment later, the savage gave a loud yell, which was answered by a dozen voices from different parts of the mountain-side. There was no longer any time for delay; in another minute the boat was quitting the shore under long and steady sweeps of the paddle.

As soon as Deerslayer believed himself to be at a safe distance, he ceased his efforts, permitting the little bark to drift, while he leisurely took a survey of the state of things. The canoe first sent adrift was floating before the air, quite a quarter of a mile above him, and a little nearer to the shore than he wished, now that he knew more of the savages were so near at hand. The canoe shoved from the point was within a few yards of him, he having directed his own course toward it on quitting the land. The dead Indian lay in grim quiet where he had left him, the warrior who had shown

[6] Panthers.   [7] Lynxes or cougars.

himself from the forest had already vanished, and the woods themselves were as silent and seemingly deserted as the day they came fresh from the hands of their great Creator. This profound stillness, however, lasted but a moment. When time had been given to the scouts of the enemy to reconnoitre, they burst out of the thicket upon the naked point, filling the air with yells of fury at discovering the death of their companion. These cries were immediately succeeded by shouts of delight when they reached the body and clustered eagerly around it. Deerslayer was a sufficient adept in the usages of the natives to understand the reason of the change. The yell was the customary lamentation at the loss of a warrior, the shout a sign of rejoicing that the conqueror had not been able to secure the scalp; the trophy without which a victory is never considered complete. The distance at which the canoes lay probably prevented any attempts to injure the conqueror, the American Indian, like the panther of his own woods, seldom making any effort against his foe unless tolerably certain it is under circumstances that may be expected to prove effective.

As the young man had no longer any motive to remain near the point, he prepared to collect his canoes, in order to tow them off to the castle. That nearest was soon in tow, when he proceeded in quest of the other, which was all this time floating up the lake. The eye of Deerslayer was no sooner fastened on this last boat, than it struck him that it was nearer to the shore than it would have been had it merely followed the course of the gentle current of air. He began to suspect the influence of some unseen current in the water, and he quickened his exertions, in order to regain possession of it before it could drift into a dangerous proximity to the woods. On getting nearer, he thought that the canoe had a perceptible motion through the water, and, as it lay broadside to the air, that this motion was taking it toward the land. A few vigorous strokes of the paddle carried him still nearer, when the mystery was explained. Something was evidently in motion on the off-side of the canoe or that which was furthest from himself, and closer scrutiny showed that it was a naked human arm. An Indian was lying in the bottom of the canoe, and was propelling it slowly, but certainly, to the shore, using his hand as a paddle. Deerslayer understood the whole artifice at a glance. A savage had swum off to the boat while he was occupied with his enemy on the point, got possession, and was using these means to urge it to the shore.

Satisfied that the man in the canoe could have no arms, Deerslayer did not hesitate to dash close alongside of the retiring boat, without deeming it necessary to raise his own rifle. As soon as the wash of the water, which he made in approaching, became audible to the prostrate savage, the latter sprang to his feet, and uttered an exclamation that proved how completely he was taken by surprise.

"If you've enj'yed yourself enough in that canoe, redskin," Deerslayer coolly observed, stopping his own career in sufficient time to prevent an absolute collision between the two boats—"if you've enj'yed yourself enough in that canoe, you'll do a prudent act by taking to the lake ag'in. I'm reasonable in these matters, and don't crave your blood, though there's them about that would look upon you more as a due-bill for the bounty than a human mortal.[8] Take to the lake this minute, afore we get to hot words."

The savage was one of those who did not understand a word of English, and he

---

[8] At the time, the British were offering an attractive premium for Indian scalps.

was indebted to the gestures of Deerslayer, and to the expression of an eye that did not often deceive, for an imperfect comprehension of his meaning. Perhaps, too, the sight of the rifle that lay so near the hand of the white man quickened his decision. At all events, he crouched like a tiger about to take his leap, uttered a yell, and the next instant his naked body disappeared in the water. When he rose to take breath, it was at the distance of several yards from the canoe, and the hasty glance he threw behind him denoted how much he feared the arrival of a fatal messenger from the rifle of his foe. But the young man made no indication of any hostile intention. Deliberately securing the canoe to the others, he began to paddle from the shore; and by the time the Indian reached the land, and had shaken himself, like a spaniel on quitting the water, his dreaded enemy was already beyond rifle-shot on his way to the castle. As was so much his practice, Deerslayer did not fail to soliloquize on what had just occurred, while steadily pursuing his course toward the point of destination.

"Well, well"—he commenced—" 'twould have been wrong to kill a human mortal without an object. Scalps are of no account with me, and life is sweet, and ought not to be taken marcilessly by them that have white gifts. The savage was a Mingo, it's true; and I make no doubt he is, and will be as long as he lives, a ra'al riptyle and vagabond; but that's no reason I should forget my gifts and color. No, no—let him go; if ever we meet ag'in, rifle in hand, why then 'twill be seen which has the stoutest heart and the quickest eye. Hawkeye! That's not a bad name for a warrior, sounding much more manful and valiant than Deerslayer! 'Twouldn't be a bad title to begin with, and it has been fairly 'arned. If 'twas Chingachgook, now, he might go home and boast of his deeds, and the chiefs would name him Hawkeye in a minute; but it don't become white blood to brag, and 'tisn't easy to see how the matter can be known unless I do. Well, well—everything is in the hands of Providence; this affair as well as another; I'll trust to that for getting my desarts in all things."

Having thus betrayed what might be termed his weak spot, the young man continued to paddle in silence, making his way diligently, and as fast as his tows would allow him, toward the castle. By this time the sun had not only risen, but it had appeared over the eastern mountains, and was shedding a flood of glorious light on this as yet unchristened sheet of water. The whole scene was radiant with beauty; and no one unaccustomed to the ordinary history of the woods would fancy it had so lately witnessed incidents so ruthless and barbarous. As he approached the building of old Hutter, Deerslayer thought, or rather *felt,* that its appearance was in singular harmony with all the rest of the scene. Although nothing had been consulted but strength and security, the rude, massive logs, covered with their rough bark, the projecting roof, and the form, would contribute to render the building picturesque in almost any situation, while its actual position added novelty and piquancy to its other points of interest.

When Deerslayer drew nearer to the castle, however, objects of interest presented themselves that at once eclipsed any beauties that might have distinguished the scenery of the lake, and the site of the singular edifice. Judith and Hetty stood on the platform before the door, Hurry's door-yard, awaiting his approach with manifest anxiety; the former, from time to time, taking a survey of his person and of the canoes through the old ship's spy-glass that has been already mentioned. Never probably did this girl seem more brilliantly beautiful than at that moment; the flush of anxiety and alarm increasing her color to its richest tints, while the softness of her eyes, a charm that even poor Hetty shared with her, was deepened by intense concern. Such, at least, without pausing or pretending to analyze motives, or to draw any other very nice distinctions between cause and effect, were the opinions of the young man, as his canoes reached the side of the ark, where he carefully fastened all three before he put his foot on the platform.

1841

---

from The Last of the Mohicans

Chapter XIII

"I'll seek a readier path."[1]
Parnell

The route taken by Hawk-eye lay across those sandy plains, relieved by occasional valleys and swells of land, which had been traversed by their party on the morning of the same day, with the baffled Magua for their guide. The sun had now fallen low toward the distant mountains; and as their journey lay through the interminable forest, the heat was no longer oppressive. Their progress, in consequence, was proportionate; and long before the twilight gathered about them, they had made good many toilsome miles on their return.

The hunter, like the savage whose place he filled, seemed to select among the blind signs of their wild route, with a species of instinct, seldom abating his speed, and never pausing to deliberate. A rapid and oblique glance at the moss on the trees, with an occasional upward gaze toward the setting sun, or a steady but passing look at the direction of the numerous watercourses, through which he waded, were sufficient to determine his path, and remove his greatest difficulties. In the mean time, the forest began to change its hues, losing that lively green which had embellished its arches, in the graver light which is the usual precursor of the close of day.

While the eyes of the sisters were endeavoring to catch glimpses through the trees of the flood of golden glory which formed a glittering halo around the sun, tingeing here and there with ruby streaks, or bordering with narrow edgings of shining yellow, a mass of clouds that lay piled at no great distance above the western hills, Hawk-eye turned suddenly, and pointing upward toward the gorgeous heavens, he spoke—

"Yonder is the signal given to man to seek his food and natural rest," he said; "better and wiser would it be, if he could understand the signs of nature, and take a lesson from the fowls of the air, and the beasts of the fields! Our night, however, will soon be over; for, with the moon, we must be up and moving again. I remember to have fou't the Maquas, hereaways, in the first war in which I ever drew blood from man; and we threw up a work of blocks, to keep the ravenous varments from handling

[1] From the poem "A Night-Piece on Death" by Thomas Parnell (1679–1718).

our scalps. If my marks do not fail me, we shall find the place a few rods further to our left."

Without waiting for an assent, or, indeed, for any reply, the sturdy hunter moved boldly into a dense thicket of young chestnuts, shoving aside the branches of the exuberant shoots which nearly covered the ground, like a man who expected, at each step, to discover some object he had formerly known. The recollection of the scout did not deceive him. After penetrating through the brush, matted as it was with briers, for a few hundred feet, he entered an open space, that surrounded a low, green hillock, which was crowned by the decayed block-house in question. This rude and neglected building was one of those deserted works, which, having been thrown up on an emergency, had been abandoned with the disappearance of danger, and was now quietly crumbling in the solitude of the forest, neglected, and nearly forgotten, like the circumstances which had caused it to be reared. Such memorials of the passage and struggles of man are yet frequent throughout the broad barrier of wilderness which once separated the hostile provinces, and form a species of ruins that are intimately associated with the recollections of colonial history, and which are in appropriate keeping with the gloomy character of the surrounding scenery. The roof of bark had long since fallen, and mingled with the soil; but the huge logs of pine, which had been hastily thrown together, still preserved their relative positions, though one angle of the work had given way under the pressure, and threatened a speedy downfall to the remainder of the rustic edifice. While Heyward and his companions hesitated to approach a building so decayed, Hawk-eye and the Indians entered within the low walls, not only without fear, but with obvious interest. While the former surveyed the ruins, both internally and externally, with the curiosity of one whose recollections were reviving at each moment, Chingachgook related to his son, in the language of the Delawares, and with the pride of a conqueror, the brief history of the skirmish which had been fought, in his youth, in that secluded spot. A strain of melancholy, however, blended with his triumph, rendering his voice, as usual, soft and musical.

In the mean time, the sisters gladly dismounted, and prepared to enjoy their halt in the coolness of the evening, and in a security which they believed nothing but the beasts of the forest could invade.

"Would not our resting-place have been more retired, my worthy friend," demanded the more vigilant Duncan, perceiving that the scout had already finished his short survey, "had we chosen a spot less known, and one more rarely visited than this?"

"Few live who know the block-house was ever raised," was the slow and musing answer, " 'tis not often that books are made, and narratives written, of such a skrimmage as was here fou't atween the Mohicans and the Mohawks,[2] in a war of their own waging. I was then a younker, and went out with the Delawares, because I know'd they were a scandalized and wronged race. Forty days and forty nights did the imps crave our blood around this pile of logs, which I designed and partly reared, being, as you'll remember, no Indian myself, but a man without a cross. The Delawares lent themselves to the work, and we made it good, ten to twenty, until our numbers

[2] The Mohicans and Mohawks were rival groups within the Algonquin tribe. The Mohicans, a considerably smaller group occupying the upper Hudson River area, were eventually eliminated by the Mohawks.

were nearly equal, and then we sallied out upon the hounds, and not a man of them ever got back to tell the fate of his party. Yes, yes; I was then young, and new to the sight of blood; and not relishing the thought that creatures who had spirits like myself should lay on the naked ground, to be torn asunder by beasts, or to bleach in the rains, I buried the dead with my own hands, under that very little hillock where you have placed yourselves; and no bad seat does it make neither, though it be raised by the bones of mortal men."

Heyward and the sisters arose, on the instant, from the grassy sepulchre; nor could the two latter, notwithstanding the terrific scenes they had so recently passed through, entirely suppress an emotion of natural horror, when they found themselves in such familiar contact with the grave of the dead Mohawks. The gray light, the gloomy little area of dark grass, surrounded by its border of brush, beyond which the pines rose, in breathing silence, apparently, into the very clouds, and the deathlike stillness of the vast forest, were all in unison to deepen such a sensation.

"They are gone, and they are harmless," continued Hawk-eye, waving his hand, with a melancholy smile, at their manifest alarm: "they'll never shout the war-whoop nor strike a blow with the tomahawk again! And of all those who aided in placing them where they lie, Chingachgook and I only are living. The brothers and family of the Mohican formed our war-party; and you see before you all that are now left of his race."

The eyes of the listeners involuntarily sought the forms of the Indians, with a compassionate interest in their desolate fortune. Their dark persons were still to be seen within the shadows of the block-house, the son listening to the relation of his father with that sort of intenseness which would be created by a narrative that redounded so much to the honor of those whose names he had long revered for their courage and savage virtues.

"I had thought the Delawares a pacific people," said Duncan, "and that they never waged war in person; trusting the defence of their lands to those very Mohawks that you slew!"

"'Tis true in part," returned the scout, "and yet, at the bottom, 'tis a wicked lie. Such a treaty was made in ages gone by, through the deviltries of the Dutchers, who wished to disarm the natives that had the best right to the country, where they had settled themselves. The Mohicans, though a part of the same nation having to deal with the English, never entered into the silly bargain, but kept to their manhood; as in truth did the Delawares, when their eyes were opened to their folly. You see before you a chief of the great Mohican Sagamores! Once his family could chase their deer over tracts of country wider than that which belongs to the Albany Patteroon, without crossing brook or hill that was not their own; but what is left to their descendant! He may find his six feet of earth when God chooses, and keep it in peace perhaps, if he has a friend who will take the pains to sink his head so low, that the ploughshares cannot reach it!"

"Enough!" said Heyward, apprehensive that the subject might lead to a discussion that would interrupt the harmony so necessary to the preservation of his fair companions: "we have journeyed far, and few among us are blessed with forms like that of yours, which seems to know neither fatigue nor weakness."

"The sinews and bones of a man carry me through it all," said the hunter, surveying his muscular limbs with a simplicity that betrayed the honest pleasure the compliment afforded him: "there are larger and heavier men to be found in the settlements, but you might travel many days in a city before you could meet one able to walk fifty miles without stopping to take breath, or who has kept the hounds within hearing during a chase of hours. However, as flesh and blood are not always the same, it is quite reasonable to suppose that the gentle ones are willing to rest, after all they have seen and done this day. Uncas, clear out the spring, while your father and I make a cover for their tender heads of these chestnut shoots, and a bed of grass and leaves."

The dialogue ceased, while the hunter and his companions busied themselves in preparations for the comfort and protection of those they guided. A spring, which many long years before had induced the natives to select the place for their temporary fortification, was soon cleared of leaves, and a fountain of crystal gushed from the bed, diffusing its waters over the verdant hillock. A corner of the building was then roofed in such a manner as to exclude the heavy dew of the climate, and piles of sweet shrubs and dried leaves were laid beneath it for the sisters to repose on.

While the diligent woodsmen were employed in this manner, Cora and Alice partook of that refreshment which duty required much more than inclination prompted them to accept. They then retired within the walls, and first offering up their thanksgivings for past mercies, and petitioning for a continuance of the Divine favor throughout the coming night, they laid their tender forms on the fragrant couch, and in spite of recollections and forebodings, soon sank into those slumbers which nature so imperiously demanded, and which were sweetened by hopes for the morrow. Duncan had prepared himself to pass the night in watchfulness near them, just without the ruin, but the scout, perceiving his intention, pointed toward Chingachgook, as he cooly disposed his own person on the grass, and said—

"The eyes of a white man are too heavy and too blind for such a watch as this! The Mohican will be our sentinel, therefore let us sleep."

"I proved myself a sluggard on my post during the past night," said Heyward, "and have less need of repose than you, who did more credit to the character of a soldier. Let all the party seek their rest, then, while I hold the guard."

"If we lay among the white tents of the 60th, and in front of an enemy like the French, I could not ask for a better watchman," returned the scout; "but in the darkness and among the signs of the wilderness your judgment would be like the folly of a child, and your vigilance thrown away. Do then, like Uncas and myself, sleep, and sleep in safety."

Heyward perceived, in truth, that the younger Indian had thrown his form on the side of the hillock while they were talking, like one who sought to make the most of the time allotted to rest, and that his example had been followed by David, whose voice literally "clove to his jaws" with the fever of his wound, heightened, as it was, by their toilsome march. Unwilling to prolong a useless discussion, the young man affected to comply, by posting his back against the logs of the block-house, in a half-recumbent posture, though resolutely determined, in his own mind, not to close an eye until he had delivered his precious charge into the arms of Munro himself. Hawk-eye, believing he had prevailed, soon fell asleep, and a silence as deep as the solitude in which they had found it pervaded the retired spot.

For many minutes Duncan succeeded in keeping his senses on the alert, and alive to every moaning sound that arose from the forest. His vision became more acute as the shades of evening settled on the place; and even after the stars were glimmering above his head, he was able to distinguish the recumbent forms of his companions, as they lay stretched on the grass, and to note the person of Chingachgook, who sat upright and motionless as one of the trees which formed the dark barrier on every side of them. He still heard the gentle breathings of the sisters, who lay within a few feet of him, and not a leaf was ruffled by the passing air, of which his ear did not detect the whispering sound. At length, however, the mournful notes of a whip-poor-will became blended with the moanings of an owl; his heavy eyes occasionally sought the bright rays of the stars, and then he fancied he saw them through the fallen lids. At instants of momentary wakefulness he mistook a bush for his associate sentinel; his head next sank upon his shoulder, which, in its turn, sought the support of the ground; and, finally, his whole person became relaxed and pliant, and the young man sank into a deep sleep, dreaming that he was a knight of ancient chivalry, holding his midnight vigils before the tent of a recaptured princess, whose favor he did not despair of gaining, by such a proof of devotion and watchfulness.

How long the tired Duncan lay in this insensible state he never knew himself, but his slumbering visions had been long lost in total forgetfulness, when he was awakened by a light tap on the shoulder. Aroused by this signal, slight as it was, he sprang upon his feet with a confused recollection of the self-imposed duty he had assumed with the commencement of the night—

"Who comes?" he demanded, feeling for his sword, at the place where it was usually suspended. "Speak! friend or enemy?"

"Friend," replied the low voice of Chingachgook; who, pointing upward at the luminary which was shedding its mild light through the opening in the trees, directly on their bivouac, immediately added, in his rude English, "moon comes, and white man's fort far—far off; time to move, when sleep shuts both eyes of the Frenchman!"

"You say true! call up your friends, and bridle the horses, while I prepare my own companions for the march!"

"We are awake, Duncan," said the soft, silvery tones of Alice within the building, "and ready to travel very fast, after so refreshing a sleep; but you have watched through the tedious night in our behalf, after having endured so much fatigue the livelong day!"

"Say, rather, I would have watched, but my treacherous eyes betrayed me; twice have I proved myself unfit for the trust I bear."

"Nay, Duncan, deny it not," interrupted the smiling Alice, issuing from the shadows of the building into the light of the moon, in all the loveliness of her freshened beauty; "I know you to be a heedless one, when self is the object of your care, and but too vigilant in favor of others. Can we not tarry here a little longer, while you find the rest you need? Cheerfully, most cheerfully, will Cora and I keep the vigils, while you, and all these brave men, endeavor to snatch a little sleep!"

"If shame could cure me of my drowsiness, I should never close an eye again," said the uneasy youth, gazing at the ingenuous countenance of Alice, where, however, in its sweet solicitude, he read nothing to confirm his half-awakened suspicion. "It is but too true, that after heading you into danger by my heedlessness, I have not even the merit of guarding your pillows as should become a soldier."

"No one but Duncan himself should accuse Duncan of such a weakness. Go, then, and sleep; believe me, neither of us, weak girls as we are, will betray our watch."

The young man was relieved from the awkwardness of making any further protestations of his own demerits, by an exclamation from Chingachgook, and the attitude of riveted attention assumed by his son.

"The Mohicans hear an enemy!" whispered Hawk-eye, who, by this time, in common with the whole party, was awake and stirring. "They scent danger in the wind!"

"God forbid!" exclaimed Heyward. "Surely we have had enough of bloodshed."

While he spoke, however, the young soldier seized his rifle, and advancing toward the front, prepared to atone for his venial remissness, by freely exposing his life in defence of those he attended.

" 'Tis some creature of the forest prowling around us in quest of food," he said, in a whisper, as soon as the low, and apparently distant sounds, which had startled the Mohicans, reached his own ears.

"Hist!" returned the attentive scout; " 'tis man; even I can now tell his tread, poor as my senses are when compared to an Indian's! That scampering Huron has fallen in with one of Montcalm's outlying parties, and they have struck upon our trail. I shouldn't like, myself, to spill more human blood in this spot," he added, looking around with anxiety in his features, at the dim objects by which he was surrounded; "but what must be, must! Lead the horses into the block-house, Uncas; and, friends, do you follow to the same shelter. Poor and old as it is, it offers a cover, and has rung with the crack of a rifle afore to-night!"

He was instantly obeyed, the Mohicans leading the Narragansets within the ruin, whither the whole party repaired, with the most guarded silence.

The sounds of approaching footsteps were now too distinctly audible, to leave any doubts as to the nature of the interruption. They were soon mingled with voices calling to each other in an Indian dialect, which the hunter, in a whisper, affirmed to Heyward was the language of the Hurons. When the party reached the point where the horses had entered the thicket which surrounded the block-house, they were evidently at fault, having lost those marks which, until that moment, had directed their pursuit.

It would seem by the voices that twenty men were soon collected at that one spot, mingling their different opinions and advice in noisy clamor.

"The knaves know our weakness," whispered Hawk-eye, who stood by the side of Heyward, in deep shade, looking through an opening in the logs, "or they wouldn't indulge their idleness in such a squaw's march. Listen to the reptiles! each man among them seems to have two tongues, and but a single leg."

Duncan, brave as he was in the combat, could not, in such a moment of painful suspense, make any reply to the cool and characteristic remark of the scout. He only grasped his rifle more firmly, and fastened his eyes upon the narrow opening, through which he gazed upon the moonlight view with increasing anxiety. The deeper tones of one who spoke as having authority were next heard, amid a silence that denoted the respect with which his orders, or rather advice, was received. After which, by the rustling of leaves, and cracking of dried twigs, it was apparent the savages were separating in pursuit of the lost trail. Fortunately for the pursued, the light of the moon, while it shed a flood of mild lustre upon the little area around the ruin, was not sufficiently strong to penetrate the deep arches of the forest, where the objects still lay in deceptive shadow. The search proved fruitless; for so short and sudden had been the passage from the faint path the travellers had journeyed into the thicket, that every trace of their footsteps was lost in the obscurity of the woods.

It was not long, however, before the restless savages were heard beating the brush, and gradually approaching the inner edge of that dense border of young chestnuts which encircled the little area.

"They are coming," muttered Heyward, endeavoring to thrust his rifle through the chink in the logs; "let us fire on their approach."

"Keep everything in the shade," returned the scout; "the snapping of a flint, or even the smell of a single karnel of the brimstone, would bring the hungry varlets upon us in a body. Should it please God that we must give battle for the scalps, trust to the experience of men who know the ways of the savages, and who are not often backward when the war-whoop is howled."

Duncan cast his eyes behind him, and saw that the trembling sisters were cowering in the far corner of the building, while the Mohicans stood in the shadow, like two upright posts, ready, and apparently willing, to strike, when the blow should be needed. Curbing his impatience, he again looked out upon the area, and awaited the result in silence. At that instant the thicket opened, and a tall and armed Huron advanced a few paces into the open space. As he gazed upon the silent block-house, the moon fell full upon his swarthy countenance, and betrayed its surprise and curiosity. He made the exclamation which usually accompanies the former emotion in an Indian, and, calling in a low voice, soon drew a companion to his side.

These children of the woods stood together for several moments pointing at the crumbling edifice, and conversing in the unintelligible language of their tribe. They then approached, though with slow and cautious steps, pausing every instant to look at the building, like startled deer, whose curiosity struggled powerfully with their awakened apprehensions for the mastery. The foot of one of them suddenly rested on the mound, and he stopped to examine its nature. At this moment, Heyward observed that the scout loosened his knife in its sheath, and lowered the muzzle of his rifle. Imitating these movements, the young man prepared himself for the struggle, which now seemed inevitable.

The savages were so near, that the least motion in one of the horses, or even a breath louder than common, would have betrayed the fugitives. But, in discovering the character of the mound, the attention of the Hurons appeared directed to a different object. They spoke together, and the sounds of their voices were low and solemn, as if influenced by a reverence that was deeply blended with awe. Then they drew wearily back, keeping their eyes riveted on the ruin, as if they expected to see the apparitions of the dead issue from its silent walls, until having reached the boundary of the area, they moved slowly into the thicket, and disappeared.

Hawk-eye dropped the breech of his rifle to the earth, and drawing a long, free breath, exclaimed in an audible whisper—

"Ay! they respect the dead, and it has this time saved their own lives, and it may be, the lives of better men too."

Heyward lent his attention, for a single moment, to his companion, but without replying, he again turned toward those who just then interested him more. He heard the two Hurons leave the bushes, and it was soon plain that all the pursuers were gathered about them, in deep attention to their report. After a few minutes of earnest and solemn dialogue, altogether different from the noisy clamor with which they had first collected about the spot, the sounds grew fainter and more distant, and finally were lost in the depths of the forest.

Hawk-eye waited until a signal from the listening Chingachgook assured him that every sound from the retiring party was completely swallowed by the distance, when he motioned to Heyward to lead forth the horses, and to assist the sisters into their saddles. The instant this was done, they issued through the broken gateway, and stealing out by a direction opposite to the one by which they had entered, they quitted the spot, the sisters casting furtive glances at the silent grave and crumbling ruin, as they left the soft light of the moon, to bury themselves in the gloom of the woods.
1826

---

from The Pathfinder

Chapter XVIII

> *It is to be all made of sighs and tears;—*
> *It is to be all made of faith and service:—*
> *It is to be all made of fantasy—*
> *All made of passion, and all made of wishes:*
> *All adoration, duty, an observance;*
> *All humbleness, all patience, and impatience,*
> *All purity, all trial, all observance.*"[1]
> Shakespeare

It was near noon when the gale broke; and then its force abated as suddenly as its violence had arisen. In less than two hours after the wind fell, the surface of the lake, though still agitated, was no longer glittering with foam; and in double that time the entire sheet presented the ordinary scene of disturbed water, that was unbroken by the violence of a tempest. Still the waves came rolling incessantly toward the shore, and the lines of breakers remained, though the spray had ceased to fly: the combing of the swells was more moderate, and all that there was of violence proceeded from the impulsion of wind that had abated.

As it was impossible to make head against the sea that was still up, with the light opposing air that blew from the eastward, all thoughts of getting under way that afternoon were abandoned. Jasper, who had now quietly resumed the command of the Scud, busied himself, however, in heaving up to the anchors, which were lifted in succession. The kedges that backed them were weighed, and everything was got in readiness for a prompt departure, as soon as the state of the weather would allow. In the mean time, they who had no concern with those duties sought such means of amusement as their peculiar circumstances allowed.

As is common with those who are unused to the confinement of a vessel, Mabel

---

[1] *As You Like It,* Act V, Sc. ii, ll. 83, 88, 93–97.

cast wistful eyes toward the shore; nor was it long before she expressed a wish that it were possible to land. The Pathfinder was near her at the time, and he assured her that nothing would be easier, as they had a bark canoe on deck, which was the best possible mode of conveyance to go through a surf. After the usual doubts and misgivings, the sergeant was appealed to: his opinion proved to be favorable, and preparations to carry the whim into effect were immediately made.

The party that was to land consisted of Sergeant Dunham, his daughter, and the Pathfinder. Accustomed to the canoe, Mabel took her seat in the centre with great steadiness, her father was placed in the bows, while the guide assumed the office of conductor, by steering in the stern. There was little need of impelling the canoe by means of the paddle, for the rollers sent it forward, at moments, with a violence that set every effort to govern its movements at defiance. More than once, ere the shore was reached, Mabel repented of her temerity, but Pathfinder encouraged her, and really manifested so much self-possession, coolness, and strength of arm himself that even a female might have hesitated about owning all her apprehensions. Our heroine was no coward, and while she felt the novelty of her situation, she also experienced a fair proportion of its wild delight. At moments, indeed, her heart was in her mouth, as the bubble of a boat floated on the very crest of a foaming breaker, appearing to skim the water like a swallow, and then she flushed and laughed, as, left by the glancing element, they appeared to linger behind, ashamed of having been outdone in the headlong race. A few minutes sufficed for this excitement, for, though the distance between the cutter and the land considerably exceeded a quarter of a mile, the intermediate space was passed in a very few minutes.

On landing, the sergeant kissed his daughter kindly, for he was so much of a soldier as always to feel more at home on terra-firma[2] than when afloat, and, taking his gun, he announced his intention to pass an hour in quest of game.

"Pathfinder will remain near you, girl, and no doubt he will tell you some of the traditions of this part of the world or some of his own experiences with the Mingos."

The guide laughed, promised to have a care of Mabel, and in a few minutes the father had ascended a steep acclivity, and disappeared in the forest. The others took another direction, which, after a few minutes of sharp ascent also, brought them to a small naked point on the promontory, where the eye overlooked an extensive and very peculiar panorama. Here Mabel seated herself on a fragment of fallen rock, to recover her breath and strength, while her companion, on whose sinews no personal exertion seemed to make any impression, stood at her side, leaning in his own and not ungraceful manner on his long rifle. Several minutes passed, and neither spoke; Mabel, in particular, being lost in admiration of the view.

The position the two had attained was sufficiently elevated to command a wide reach of the lake, which stretched away toward the northeast in a boundless sheet, glittering beneath the rays of an afternoon's sun, and yet betraying the remains of that agitation which it had endured while tossed by the late tempest. The land set bounds to its limits, in a huge crescent, disappearing in distance toward the southeast and the north. Far as the eye could reach, nothing but forest was visible, not even a solitary sign of civilization breaking in upon the uniform and grand magnificence of nature. The gale had driven the Scud beyond the line of those forts with which the French

---

[2] Latin: "solid ground."

were then endeavoring to gird the English North American possessions; for, following the channels of communication between the great lakes, their posts were on the banks of the Niagara, while our adventurers had reached a point many leagues westward of that celebrated strait. The cutter rode at single anchor, without the breakers, resembling some well-imagined and accurately executed toy, that was intended rather for a glass case than for the struggles with the elements which she had so lately gone through; while the canoe lay on the narrow beach, just out of reach of the waves that came booming upon the land, a speck upon the shingles.

"We are very far, here, from human habitations!" exclaimed Mabel, when, after a long and musing survey of the scene, its principal peculiarities forced themselves on her active and ever-brilliant imagination: "this is, indeed, being on a frontier!"

"Have they more sightly scenes than this nearer the sea, and around their large towns?" demanded Pathfinder, with an interest he was apt to discover in such a subject.

"I will not say that; there is more to remind one of his fellow-beings there than here; less, perhaps, to remind one of God."

"Ay, Mabel, that is what my own feelings say. I am but a poor hunter, I know; untaught and unl'arned; but God is as near me, in this my home, as he is near the king in his royal palace."

"Who can doubt it?" returned Mabel, looking from the view up into the hard-featured but honest face of her companion, though not without surprise at the energy of his manner. "One feels nearer to God, in such a spot, I think, than when the mind is distracted by the objects of the towns."

"You say all I wish to say myself, Mabel, but in so much plainer speech that you make me ashamed of wishing to let others know what I feel on such matters. I have coasted this lake in s'arch of skins, afore the war, and have been here already; not at this very spot, for we landed yonder, where you may see the blasted oak that stands above the cluster of hemlocks——"

"How! Pathfinder, can you remember all these trifles so accurately?"

"These are our streets and houses; our churches and palaces. Remember them, indeed! I once made an appointment with the Big Sarpent, to meet at twelve o'clock at noon near the foot of a certain pine, at the end of six months, when neither of us was within three hundred miles of the spot. The tree stood and stands still, unless the judgment of Providence has lighted on that too, in the midst of the forest, fifty miles from any settlement, but in a most extraordinary neighborhood for beaver."

"And did you meet at that very spot and hour?"

"Does the sun rise and set? When I reached the tree, I found the Sarpent leaning against its trunk, with torn leggings and muddied moccasins. The Delaware had got into a swamp, and it worried him not a little to find his way out of it; but, as the sun which comes over the eastern hills in the morning goes down behind the western at night, so was he true to time and place. No fear of Chingachgook when there is either a friend or an enemy in the case. He is equally sartain with each."

"And where is the Delaware now—why is he not with us to-day?"

"He is scouting on the Mingo trail, where I ought to have been too, but for a great human infirmity."

"You seem above, beyond, superior to all infirmity, Pathfinder; I never yet met with a man who appeared to be so little liable to the weaknesses of nature."

"If you mean in the way of health and strength, Mabel, Providence has been kind to me; though I fancy the open air, long hunts, active scoutings, forest fare, and the sleep of a good conscience may always keep the doctors at a distance. But I am human arter all; yes, I find I'm very human in some of my feelin's.''

Mabel looked surprised, and it would be no more than delineating the character of her sex if we added that her sweet countenance expressed a good deal of curiosity, too, though her tongue was more discreet.

"There is something bewitching in this wild life of yours, Pathfinder," she exclaimed, a tinge of enthusiasm mantling her cheeks. "I find I'm fast getting to be a frontier girl, and am coming to love all this grand silence of the woods. The towns seem tame to me; and, as my father will probably pass the remainder of his days here, where he has already lived so long, I begin to feel that I should be happy to continue with him, and not return to the seashore."

"The woods are never silent, Mabel, to such as understand their meaning. Days at a time have I travelled them alone, without feeling the want of company; and, as for conversation, for such as can comprehend their language, there is no want of rational and instructive discourse."

"I believe you are happier when alone, Pathfinder, than when mingling with your fellow-creatures."

"I will not say that—I will not say exactly that! I have seen the time when I have thought that God was sufficient for me in the forest, and that I craved no more than his bounty and his care. But other feelin's have got uppermost, and I suppose natur' will have its way. All other creatur's mate, Mabel, and it was intended man should do so, too."

"And have you never bethought you of seeking a wife, Pathfinder, to share your fortunes?" inquired the girl, with the directness and simplicity that the pure of heart and the undesigning are the most apt to manifest, and with that feeling of affection which is inbred in her sex. "To me, it seems, you only want a home to return to, from your wanderings, to render your life completely happy. Were I a man, it would be my delight to roam through these forests at will or to sail over this beautiful lake."

"I understand you, Mabel; and God bless you for thinking of the welfare of men as humble as we are. We have our pleasures, it is true, as well as our gifts, but we might be happier; yes, I do think we might be happier."

"Happier! in what way, Pathfinder? In this pure air, with these cool and shaded forests to wander through, this lovely lake to gaze at and sail upon, with clear consciences, and abundance for all the real wants, men ought to be nothing less than as perfectly happy as their infirmities will allow."

"Every creatur' has its gifts, Mabel, and men have theirn," answered the guide, looking stealthily at his beautiful companion, whose cheeks had flushed and eyes brightened under the ardor of feelings excited by the novelty of her striking situation; "and all must obey them. Do you see yonder pigeon that is just alightin' on the beech, —here in a line with the fallen chestnut?"

"Certainly; it is the only thing stirring with life in it, besides ourselves, that is to be seen in this vast solitude."

"Not so, Mabel, not so; Providence makes nothing that lives to live quite alone. Here is its mate, just rising on the wing; it has been feedin' near the other beech, but it will not long be separated from its companion."

"I understand you, Pathfinder," returned Mabel, smiling sweetly, though as calmly as if the discourse was with her father. "But a hunter may find a mate, even in this wild region. The Indian girls are affectionate and true, I know, for such was the wife of Arrowhead, to a husband who oftener frowned than smiled."

"That would never do, Mabel, and good would never come of it. Kind must cling to kind, and country to country, if one would find happiness. If, indeed, I could meet with one like you, who would consent to be a hunter's wife, and who would not scorn my ignorance and rudeness, then, indeed, would all the toil of the past appear like the sporting of the young deer, and all the future like sunshine!"

"One like me!—A girl of my years and indiscretion would hardly make a fit companion for the boldest scout and surest hunter on the lines!"

"Ah! Mabel, I fear me that I have been improving a red-skin's gifts with a pale-face's natur'! Such a character would insure a wife, in an Injin village."

"Surely, surely, Pathfinder, you would not think of choosing one as ignorant, as frivolous, as vain, and as inexperienced as I, for your wife!" Mabel would have added, "and as young," but an instinctive feeling of delicacy repressed the words.

"And why not, Mabel? If you are ignorant of frontier usages, you know more than all of us of pleasant anecdotes and town customs; as for frivolous, I know not what it means, but if it signifies beauty, ah's me! I fear it is no fault in my eyes. Vain you are not, as is seen by the kind manner in which you listen to all my idle tales about scoutings and trails; and as for experience, that will come with years. Besides, Mabel, I fear men think little of these matters, when they are about to take wives, I do."

"Pathfinder—your words—your looks—surely all this is meant in trifling—you speak in pleasantry!"

"To me it is always agreeable to be near you, Mabel, and I should sleep sounder this blessed night than I have done for a week past, could I think that you find such discourse as pleasant as I do."

We shall not say that Mabel Dunham had not believed herself a favorite with the guide. This her quick feminine sagacity had early discovered, and perhaps she had occasionally thought there had mingled with his regard and friendship some of that manly tenderness which the ruder sex must be coarse indeed not to show, on occasions, to the gentler; but the idea that he seriously sought her for his wife had never before crossed the mind of the spirited and ingenuous girl. Now, however, a gleam of something like the truth broke in upon her imagination, less induced by the words of her companion, perhaps, than by his manner. Looking earnestly into the rugged, honest countenance of the scout, Mabel's own features became concerned and grave, and when she spoke again, it was with a gentleness of manner that attracted him to her even more powerfully than the words themselves were calculated to repel.

"You and I should understand each other, Pathfinder," she said, with an earnest sincerity, "nor should there be any cloud between us. You are too upright and frank to meet with anything but sincerity and frankness in return. Surely—surely, all this means nothing—has no other connection with your feelings than such a friendship as one of your wisdom and character would naturally feel for a girl like me!"

"I believe it's all as nat'ral, Mabel; yes, I do; the sergeant tells me he had such feelings toward your own mother, and I think I've seen something like it in the young people I have, from time to time, guided through the wilderness. Yes, yes—I dare say it's all nat'ral enough, and that makes it come so easy, and is a great comfort to me."

"Pathfinder, your words make me uneasy! Speak plainer, or change the subject forever. You do not—cannot mean that—you—cannot wish me to understand—" Even the tongue of the spirited Mabel faltered, and she shrank with maiden shame from adding what she wished so earnestly to say. Rallying her courage, however, and determined to know all as soon and as plainly as possible, after a moment's hesitation she continued: "I mean, Pathfinder, that you do not wish me to understand that you seriously think of me as a wife?"

"I do, Mabel; that's it—that's just it, and you have put the matter in a much better point of view than I, with my forest gifts and frontier ways, would ever be able to do. The sargeant and I have concluded on the matter, if it is agreeable to you, as he thinks is likely will be the case, though I doubt my own power to please one who deserves the best husband America can produce."

Mabel's countenance changed from uneasiness to surprise, and then, by a transition still quicker, from surprise to pain.

"My father!" she exclaimed. "My dear father has thought of my becoming your wife, Pathfinder!"

"Yes, he has, Mabel; he has indeed. He has even thought such a thing might be agreeable to you, and has almost encouraged me to fancy it might be true."

"But you, yourself—you certainly can care nothing whether this singular expectation shall ever be realized or not?"

"Anan?"

"I mean, Pathfinder, that you have talked of this match more to oblige my father than anything else; that your feelings are no way concerned, let my answer be what it may?"

The scout looked earnestly into the beautiful face of Mabel, which had flushed with the ardor and novelty of her sensations, and it was impossible to mistake the intense admiration that betrayed itself in every lineament of his ingenuous countenance.

"I have often thought myself happy, Mabel, when ranging the woods, on a successful hunt, breathing the pure air of the hills, and filled with vigor and health, but I now feel that it has all been idleness and vanity compared with the delight it would give me to know that you thought better of me than you think of most others."

"Better of you!—I do indeed think better of you, Pathfinder, than of most others —I am not certain that I do not think better of you than of any other; for your truth, honesty, simplicity, justice, and courage are scarcely equalled by any of earth."

"Ah! Mabel!—These are sweet and encouraging words from you, and the sargeant, a'ter all, was not as near wrong as I feared."

"Nay, Pathfinder—in the name of all that is sacred and just, do not let us misunderstand each other, in a matter of so much importance. While I esteem, respect—nay, reverence you, almost as much as I reverence my own dear father, it is impossible that I should ever become your wife—that I—"

The change in her companion's countenance was so sudden and so great that the moment the effect of what she had uttered became visible in the face of the Pathfinder Mabel arrested her own words, notwithstanding her strong desire to be explicit, the reluctance with which she could at any time cause pain being sufficient of itself to induce the pause. Neither spoke for some time, the shade of disappointment that crossed the rugged lineaments of the hunter amounting so nearly to anguish as to frighten his companion, while the sensation of choking became so strong in the

Pathfinder that he fairly griped his throat, like one who sought physical relief for physical suffering. The convulsive manner in which his fingers worked actually struck the alarmed girl with a feeling of awe.

"Nay, Pathfinder," Mabel eagerly added, the instant she could command her voice —"I may have said more than I mean, for all things of this nature are possible, and women, they say, are never sure of their own minds. What I wish you to understand is, that it is not likely that you and I should ever think of each other as man and wife ought to think of each other."

"I do not—I shall never think in that way again, Mabel," gasped forth the Pathfinder, who appeared to utter his words like one just raised above the pressure of some suffocating substance. "No—no—I shall never think of you, or any one else, again, in that way."

"Pathfinder—dear Pathfinder—understand me—do not attach more meaning to my words than I do myself—a match like that would be unwise—unnatural, perhaps."

"Yes, unnat'ral—ag'in natur'; and so I told the sargeant, but he *would* have it otherwise."

"Pathfinder!—Oh! this is worse than I could have imagined—take my hand, excellent Pathfinder, and let me see that you do not hate me. For God's sake, smile upon me again!"

"Hate you, Mabel!—Smile upon you!—Ah's me!"

"Nay, give me your hand; your hardy, true, and manly hand—both, both, Pathfinder, for I shall not be easy until I feel certain that we are friends again, and that all this has been a mistake."

"Mabel," said the guide, looking wistfully into the face of the generous and impetuous girl, as she held his two hard and sunburnt hands in her own pretty and delicate fingers, and laughing in his own silent and peculiar manner, while anguish gleamed over lineaments which seemed incapable of deception, even while agitated with emotions so conflicting, "Mabel, the sargeant was wrong!"

The pent-up feelings could endure no more, and the tears rolled down the cheeks of the scout like rain. His fingers again worked convulsively at his throat, and his breast heaved, as if it possessed a tenant of which it would be rid, by any effort, however desperate.

"Pathfinder!—Pathfinder!" Mabel almost shrieked,—"anything but this—anything but this. Speak to me, Pathfinder,—smile again—say one kind word—anything to prove you can forgive me."

"The sargeant was wrong!" exclaimed the guide, laughing amid his agony, in a way to terrify his companion by the unnatural mixture of anguish and light-heartedness. "I knew it—I knew it, and said it; yes, the sargeant was wrong, a'ter all."

"We can be friends, though we cannot be man and wife," continued Mabel, almost as much disturbed as her companion, scarce knowing what she said; "we can always be friends, and always will."

"I thought the sargeant was mistaken," resumed the Pathfinder, when a great effort had enabled him to command himself, "for I did not think my gifts were such as would please the fancy of a town-bred gal. It would have been better, Mabel, had he not over-persuaded me into a different notion; and it might have been better, too, had you not been so pleasant and friendly, like; yes, it would."

"If I thought any error of mine had raised false expectations in you, Pathfinder, however unintentionally on my part, I should never forgive myself; for, believe me, I would rather endure pain in my own feelings than you should suffer."

"That's just it, Mabel; that's just it. These speeches and opinions, spoken in so soft a voice, and in a way I'm so unused to in the woods, have done the mischief. But I now see plainly, and begin to understand the difference between us better, and will strive to keep down thought, and to go abroad ag'in as I used to do, looking for the game and the inimy. Ah's me! Mabel, I have indeed been on a false trail since we met!"

"But you will now travel on the true one. In a little while you will forget all this, and think of me as a friend who owes you her life."

"This may be the way in the towns, but I doubt if it's nat'ral to the woods. With us, when the eye sees a lovely sight, it is apt to keep it long in view, or when the mind takes in an upright and proper feeling, it is loath to part with it."

"But it is not a proper feeling that you should love me, nor am I a lovely sight. You will forget it all, when you come seriously to recollect that I am altogether unsuited to be your wife."

"So I told the sargeant—but he would have it otherwise. I knew you was too young and beautiful for one of middle age, like myself, and who never was comely to look at, even in youth; and then your ways have not been my ways, nor would a hunter's cabin be a fitting place for one who was edicated among chiefs, as it were. If I were younger and comelier, though, like Jasper Eau-douce—"

"Never mind Jasper Eau-douce," interrupted Mabel, impatiently; "we can talk of something else."

"Jasper is a worthy lad, Mabel; ay, and a comely," returned the guileless guide, looking earnestly at the girl, as if he distrusted her judgment in speaking slightingly of his friend. "Were I only half as comely as Jasper Western, my misgivings in this affair would not have been so great, and they might not have been so true."

"We will not talk of Jasper Western," repeated Mabel, the color mounting to her temples; "he may be good enough in a gale or on the lake, but he is not good enough to talk of here."

"I fear me, Mabel, he is better than the man who is likely to be your husband, though the sargeant says that never can take place. But the sargeant was wrong once, and he may be wrong twice."

"And who is likely to be my husband, Pathfinder? This is scarcely less strange than what has just passed between us!"

"I know it is nat'ral for like to seek like, and for them that have consorted much with officers' ladies to wish to be officers' ladies themselves. But, Mabel, I may speak plainly to you, I know, and I hope my words will not give you pain, for, now I understand what it is to be disappointed in such feelings, I wouldn't wish to cause even a Mingo sorrow on this head. But happiness is not always to be found in a marquee, any more than in a tent; and though the officers' quarters may look more tempting than the rest of the barracks, there is often great misery between husband and wife inside of their doors."

"I do not doubt it in the least, Pathfinder; and did it rest with me to decide, I would sooner follow you to some cabin in the woods, and share your fortune, whether it might be better or worse, than go inside the door of any officer I know, with an intention of remaining there as its master's wife."

"Mabel, this is not what Lundie hopes or Lundie thinks!"

"And what care I for Lundie? He is major of the 55th, and may command his men to wheel and march about as he pleases, but he cannot compel me to wed the greatest or the meanest of his mess: besides, what can you know of Lundie's wishes on such a subject?"

"From Lundie's own mouth. The sargeant had told him that he wished me for a son-in-law; and the major being an old and a true friend, conversed with me on the subject: he put it to me plainly, whether it would not be more ginerous in me to let an officer succeed than to strive to make you share a hunter's fortune. I owned the truth, I did; and that was that I thought it might; but when he told me that the quartermaster would be his choice, I would not abide by the conditions. No—no—Mabel; I know Davy Muir well, and though he may make you a lady, he can never make you a happy woman, or himself a gentleman. I say this honestly, I do; for I now plainly see that the sargeant has been wrong."

"My father has been very wrong if he has said or done aught to cause you sorrow, Pathfinder; and so great is my respect for you, so sincere my friendship, that were it not for one—I mean that no person need fear Lieutenant Muir's influence with me. I would rather remain as I am to my dying day than become a lady at the cost of being his wife."

"I do not think you would say that which you do not feel, Mabel," returned Pathfinder, earnestly.

"Not at such a moment, on such a subject, and least of all to you. No; Lieutenant Muir may find wives where he can—my name shall never be on his catalogue."

"Thank you—thank you for that, Mabel; for though there is no longer any hope for me, I could never be happy were you to take to the quartermaster. I feared the commission might count for something, I did, and I know the man. It is not jealousy that makes me speak in this manner, but truth, for I know the man. Now, were you to fancy a desarving youth, one like Jasper Western, for instance—"

"Why always mention Jasper Eau-douce, Pathfinder? he can have no concern with our friendship; let us talk of yourself, and of the manner in which you intend to pass the winter."

"Ah's me!—I'm little worth at the best, Mabel, unless it may be on a trail, or with the rifle; and less worth now that I've discovered the sargeant's mistake. There is no need, therefore, of talking of me. It has been very pleasant to me to be near you so long, and even to fancy that the sargeant was right, but that is all over now. I shall go down the lake with Jasper, and then there will be business to occupy us, and that will keep useless thoughts out of the mind."

"And you will forget this—forget me—no, not forget me either, Pathfinder; but you will resume your old pursuits, and cease to think a girl of sufficient importance to disturb your peace?"

"I never know'd it afore, Mabel, but girls, as you call them, though gals is the name I've been taught to use, are of more account in this life than I could have believed. Now, afore I know'd you, the new-born babe did not sleep more sweetly than I used to could; my head was no sooner on the root, or the stone, or mayhap on the skin, than all was lost to the senses, unless it might be to go over in the night the business of the day, in a dream like; and there I lay till the moment came to be stirring, and the swallows were not more certain to be on the wing with the light than I to be afoot at the moment I wished to be. All this seemed a gift, and might be calculated on, even in the midst of a Mingo camp; for I've been outlying, in my time, in the very villages of the vagabonds."

"And all this will return to you, Pathfinder; for one so upright and sincere will never waste his happiness on a mere fancy. You will dream again of your hunts, of the deer you have slain, and of the beaver you have taken."

"Ah's me, Mabel, I wish never to dream again! Before we met I had a sort of pleasure in following up the hounds, in fancy, as it might be; and even in striking a trail of the Iroquois—nay, I've been in skrimmages and ambushments in thought, like, and found satisfaction in it according to my gifts; but all those things have lost their charms since I've made acquaintance with you. Now, I think no longer of anything rude in my dreams, but the very last night we stayed in the garrison I imagined I had a cabin in a grove of sugar maples, and at the root of every tree was a Mabel Dunham, while the birds that were among the branches sang ballads, instead of the notes that natur' gave, and even the deer stopped to listen. I tried to shoot a fa'an, but Killdeer missed fire, and the creatur' laughed in my face, as pleasantly as a young girl laughs in her merriment, and then it bounded away, looking back as if expecting me to follow."

"No more of this, Pathfinder—we'll talk no more of these things," said Mabel, dashing the tears from her eyes; for the simple, earnest manner in which this hardy woodsman betrayed the deep hold she had taken of his feelings nearly proved too much for her own generous heart. "Now let us look for my father; he cannot be distant, as I heard his gun quite near."

"The sargeant was wrong—yes, he was wrong, and it's of no use to attempt to make the dove consort with the wolf."

"Here comes my dear father," interrupted Mabel; "let us look cheerful and happy, Pathfinder, as such good friends ought to look, and keep each other's secrets."

A pause succeeded; the sargeant's foot was heard crushing the dried twigs hard by, and then his form appeared shoving aside the bushes of a copse quite near. As he issued into the open ground the old soldier scrutinized his daughter and her companion, and speaking good-naturedly, he said:

"Mabel, child, you are young and light of foot—look for a bird I've shot that fell just beyond the thicket of young hemlocks on the shore; and as Jasper is showing signs of an intention of getting under way, you need not take the trouble to clamber up this hill again, but we will meet you on the beach in a few minutes."

Mabel obeyed, bounding down the hill with the elastic step of youth and health. But, notwithstanding the lightness of her steps, the heart of the girl was heavy, and no sooner was she hid from observation by the thicket than she threw herself on the root of a tree and wept as if her heart would break. The sargeant watched her until she disappeared, with a father's pride, and then turned to his companion with a smile as kind and as familiar as his habits would allow him to use toward any.

"She has her mother's lightness and activity, my friend, with somewhat of her father's force," he said. "Her mother was not quite as handsome, I think myself; but the Dunhams were always thought comely, whether men or women. Well, Pathfinder, I take it for granted you've not overlooked the opportunity, but have spoken plainly to the girl? Women like frankness in matters of this sort."

"I believe Mabel and I understand each other, at last, sargeant," returned the other, looking another way to avoid the soldier's face.

"So much the better. Some people fancy that a little doubt and uncertainty make love all the livelier, but I am one of those who think the plainer the tongue speaks the easier the mind will comprehend. Was Mabel surprised?"

"I fear she was, sargeant; I fear she was taken quite by surprise—yes, I do."

"Well, well, surprises in love are like an ambush in war, and quite as lawful; though it is not as easy to tell when a woman is surprised as to tell when it happens to an enemy. Mabel did not run away, my worthy friend, did she?"

"No, sargeant, Mabel did not try to escape; *that* I can say with a clear conscience."

"I hope the girl was not too willing, neither! Her mother was shy and coy for a month, at least—but frankness, after all, is a recommendation in man or woman."

"That it is—that it is—and judgment, too."

"You are not to look for too much judgment in a young creature of twenty, Pathfinder, but it will come with experience. A mistake in you, or in me, for instance, might not be so easily overlooked, but in a girl of Mabel's years one is not to strain at a gnat lest they swallow a camel."

The muscles of the listener's face twitched as the sargeant was thus delivering his sentiments, though the former had now recovered a portion of that stoicism which formed so large a part of his character, and which he had probably imbibed from long association with the Indians. His eyes rose and fell, and once a gleam shot athwart his hard features, as if he were about to indulge in his peculiar laugh; but the joyous feeling, if it really existed, was as quickly lost in a look allied to anguish. It was this unusual mixture of wild and keen mental agony with native, simple joyousness that had most struck Mabel, who, in the interview just related, had a dozen times been on the point of believing that her suitor's heart was only lightly touched, as images of happiness and humor gleamed over a mind that was almost infantine in its simplicity and nature; an impression, however, that was soon driven away by the discovery of emotions so painful and so deep that they seemed to harrow the very soul. Indeed, in this respect, the Pathfinder was a mere child: unpractised in the ways of the world, he had no idea of concealing a thought of any kind, and his mind received and reflected each emotion with the pliability and readiness of that period of life; the infant scarcely yielding its wayward imagination to the passing impression with greater facility than this man, so simple in all his personal feelings, so stern, stoical, masculine, and severe in all that touched his ordinary pursuits.

"You say true, sargeant," Pathfinder answered—"a mistake in one like you is a more serious matter."

"You will find Mabel sincere and honest in the end, give her but a little time."

"Ah's me, sargeant!"

"A man of your merits would make an impression on a rock, give him time, Pathfinder."

"Sargeant Dunham, we are old fellow-campaigners—that is, as campaigns are carried on here in the wilderness; and we have done so many kind acts to each other that we can afford to be candid—what has caused you to believe that a girl like Mabel could ever fancy one as rude as I am?"

"What?—why, a variety of reasons, and good reasons, too, my friend. Those same acts of kindness, perhaps, and the campaigns you mention; moreover, you are my sworn and tried comrade."

"All this sounds well, so far as you and I be consarned, but they do not touch the

"Which is more than his share. A man may marry twice, without offence to good morals and decency, I allow, but four times is an aggravation."

"I should think even marrying once what Master Cap calls a circumstance," put in Pathfinder, laughing in his quiet way, for by this time his spirits had recovered some of their buoyancy.

"It is indeed, my friend, and a most solemn circumstance too. If it were not that Mabel is to be your wife, I would advise you to remain single. But here is the girl herself, and discretion is the word."

"Ah's me! sargeant, I fear you are mistaken!"

1840

from The Pioneers

Chapter XXXIII

Fetch here the stocks, ho!
You stubborn ancient knave, you reverend braggart,
We'll teach you![1]
            Lear

The long days and early sun of July allowed time for a gathering of the interested, before the little bell of the academy announced that the appointed hour had arrived for administering right to the wronged, and punishment to the guilty. Ever since the dawn of day, the highways and woodpaths that, issuing from the forests, and winding along the sides of the mountains, centered in Templeton, had been thronged with equestrians and footmen, bound to the haven of justice. There was to be seen a well-clad yeoman, mounted on a sleek, switch-tailed steed, ambling along the highway, with his red face elevated in a manner that said, "I have paid for my land, and fear no man;" while his bosom was swelling with the pride of being one of the grand inquest for the county. At his side rode a companion, his equal in independence of feeling, perhaps, but his inferior in thrift, as in property and consideration. This was a professed dealer in lawsuits,—a man whose name appeared in every calendar,— whose substance, gained in the multifarious expedients of a settler's changeable habits, was wasted in feeding the harpies[2] of the courts. He was endeavoring to impress the mind of the grand juror with the merits of a cause now at issue. Along with these was a pedestrian, who, having thrown a rifle frock over his shirt, and placed his best wool hat above his sunburnt visage, had issued from his retreat in the woods by a footpath, and was striving to keep company with the others, on his way to hear and to decide the disputes of his neighbors, as a petit juror.[3] Fifty similar little knots of countrymen might have been seen, on that morning, journeying toward the shire-town on the same errand.

---

[1] Shakespeare's *King Lear*, Act II, Sc. ii, ll. 129–131.
[2] Mythological predatory monsters having the heads and torsos of women and the tails, wings, and talons of birds.
[3] Member of a civil jury.

By ten o'clock the streets of the village were filled with busy faces; some talking of their private concerns, some listening to a popular expounder of political creeds; and others gaping in at the open stores, admiring the finery, or examining scythes, axes, and such other manufactures as attracted their curiosity or excited their admiration. A few women were in the crowd, most carrying infants, and followed, at a lounging, listless gait, by their rustic lords and masters. There was one young couple, in whom connubial love was yet fresh, walking at a respectful distance from each other; while the swain directed the timid steps of his bride, by a gallant offering of a thumb!

At the first stroke of the bell, Richard issued from the door of the "Bold Dragoon," flourishing a sheathed sword, that he was fond of saying his ancestors had carried in one of Cromwell's victories, and crying, in an authoritative tone, to "clear the way for the court." The order was obeyed promptly, though not servilely, the members of the crowd nodding familiarly to the members of the procession as it passed. A party of constables with their staves followed the Sheriff, preceding Marmaduke, and four plain, grave-looking yeomen, who were his associates on the bench. There was nothing to distinguish these subordinate judges from the better part of the spectators, except gravity, which they affected a little more than common, and that one of their number was attired in an old-fashioned military coat, with skirts that reached no lower than the middle of his thighs, and bearing two little silver epaulettes, not half so big as a modern pair of shoulder-knots. This gentleman was a colonel of the militia, in attendance on a courtmartial, who found leisure to steal a moment from his military to attend to his civil jurisdiction; but this incongruity excited neither notice nor comment. Three or four clean-shaved lawyers followed, as meekly as if they were lambs going to the slaughter. One or two of their number had contrived to obtain an air of scholastic gravity by wearing spectacles. The rear was brought up by another posse of constables, and the mob followed the whole into the room where the court held its sittings.

The edifice was composed of a basement of squared logs, perforated here and there with small grated windows, through which a few wistful faces were gazing at the crowd without. Among the captives were the guilty, downcast countenances of the counterfeiters, and the simple but honest features of the Leather-stocking. The dungeons were to be distinguished, externally, from the debtors' apartments only by the size of the apertures, the thickness of the grates, and by the heads of the spikes that were driven into the logs as a protection against the illegal use of edge-tools. The upper story was of framework, regularly covered with boards, and contained one room decently fitted up for the purposes of justice. A bench, raised on a narrow platform to the height of a man above the floor, and protected in front by a light railing, ran along one of its sides. In the centre was a seat, furnished with rude arms, that was always filled by the presiding judge. In front, on a level with the floor of the room, was a large table covered with green baize, and surrounded by benches; and at either of its ends were rows of seats, rising one over the other, for jury boxes. Each of these divisions was surrounded by a railing. The remainder of the room was an open square, appropriated to the spectators.

When the judges were seated, the lawyers had taken possession of the table, and the noise of moving feet had ceased in the area, the proclamations were made in the usual form, the jurors were sworn, the charge was given, and the court proceeded to hear the business before them.

We shall not detain the reader with a description of the captious discussions that occupied the court for the first two hours. Judge Temple had impressed on the jury, in his charge, the necessity for despatch on their part, recommending to their notice, from motives of humanity, the prisoners in the jail, as the first objects of their attention. Accordingly, after the period we have mentioned had elapsed, the cry of the officer to "clear the way for the grand jury," announced the entrance of that body. The usual forms were observed, when the foreman handed up to the bench two bills, on both of which the Judge observed, at the first glance of his eye, the name of Nathaniel Bumppo. It was a leisure moment with the court; some low whispering passed between the bench and the Sheriff, who gave a signal to his officers, and in a very few minutes the silence that prevailed was interrupted by a general movement in the outer crowd; when presently the Leather-Stocking made his appearance, ushered into the criminal's bar under the custody of two constables. The hum ceased, the people closed into the open space again, and the silence soon became so deep, that the hard breathing of the prisoner was audible.

Natty was dressed in his buckskin garments, without his coat, in place of which he wore only a shirt of coarse linen-check, fastened at his throat by the sinew of a deer, leaving his red neck and weather-beaten face exposed and bare. It was the first time that he had ever crossed the threshold of a court of justice, and curiosity seemed to be strongly blended with his personal feelings. He raised his eyes to the bench, thence to the jury-boxes, the bar, and the crowd without, meeting everywhere looks fastened on himself. After surveying his own person, as searching the cause of this unusual attraction, he once more turned his face around the assemblage, and opened his mouth in one of his silent and remarkable laughs.

"Prisoner, remove your cap," said Judge Temple.

The order was either unheard or unheeded.

"Nathaniel Bumppo, be uncovered," repeated the Judge.

Natty started at the sound of his name, and raising his face earnestly toward the bench, he said—

"Anan!"

Mr. Lippet arose from his seat at the table, and whispered in the ear of the prisoner; when Natty gave him a nod of assent, and took the deerskin covering from his head.

"Mr. District Attorney," said the Judge, "the prisoner is ready; we wait for the indictment."

The duties of public prosecutor were discharged by Dirck Van der School, who adjusted his spectacles, cast a cautious look around him at his brethren of the bar, which he ended by throwing his head aside so as to catch one glance over the glasses, when he proceeded to read the bill aloud. It was the usual charge for an assault and battery on the person of Hiram Doolittle, and was couched in the ancient language of such instruments, especial care having been taken by the scribe not to omit the name of a single offensive weapon known to the law. When he had done, Mr. Van der School removed his spectacles, which he closed and placed in his pocket, seemingly for the pleasure of again opening and replacing them on his nose. After this revolution was repeated once or twice, he handed the bill over to Mr. Lippet, with a cavalier air, that said as much as "Pick a hole in that if you can."

Natty listened to the charge with great attention, leaning forward toward the reader with an earnestness that denoted his interest; and when it was ended, he raised his tall body to the utmost, and drew a long sigh. All eyes were turned to the prisoner, whose voice was vainly expected to break the stillness of the room.

"You have heard the presentment that the grand jury have made, Nathaniel Bumppo," said the Judge; "what do you plead to the charge?"

The old man dropped his head for a moment in a reflecting attitude, and then raising it, he laughed before he answered—

"That I handled the man a little rough or so, is not to be denied; but that there was occasion to make use of all the things that the gentleman has spoken of, is downright untrue. I am not much of a wrestler, seeing that I'm getting old; but I was out among the Scotch-Irishers[4]—let me see—it must have been as long ago as the first year of the old war—"

"Mr. Lippet, if you are retained for the prisoner," interrupted Judge Temple, "instruct your client how to plead; if not, the court will assign him counsel."

Aroused from studying the indictment by this appeal, the attorney got up, and after a short dialogue with the hunter in a low voice, he informed the court that they were ready to proceed.

"Do you plead guilty or not guilty?" said the Judge.

"I may say not guilty with a clean conscience," returned Natty; "for there's no guilt in doing what's right; and I'd rather died on the spot, than had him put foot in the hut at that moment."

Richard started at this declaration, and bent his eyes significantly on Hiram, who returned the look with a slight movement of his eyebrows.

"Proceed to open the cause, Mr. District Attorney," continued the Judge. "Mr. Clerk, enter the plea of not guilty."

After a short opening address from Mr. Van der School, Hiram was summoned to the bar to give his testimony. It was delivered to the letter, perhaps, but with all that moral coloring which can be conveyed under such expressions as, "thinking no harm," "feeling it my bounden duty as a magistrate," and "seeing that the constable was back'ard in the business." When he had done, and the district attorney declined putting any further interrogatories, Mr. Lippet arose, with an air of keen investigation, and asked the following questions:

"Are you a constable of this county, sir?"

"No, sir," said Hiram, "I'm only a justice-peace."

"I ask you, Mr. Doolittle, in the face of this court, putting it to your conscience and your knowledge of the law, whether you had any right to enter that man's dwelling?"

"Hem!" said Hiram, undergoing a violent struggle between his desire for vengeance and his love of legal fame; "I do suppose—that in—that is—strict law—that

[4] Group of early settlers of mixed Scottish and Irish lineage who fought in the British-Indian wars.

supposing—maybe I hadn't a real—lawful right;—but as the case was—and Billy was so back'ard—I thought I might come for'ard in the business."

"I ask you again, sir," continued the lawyer, following up his success, "whether this old, this friendless old man, did or did not repeatedly forbid your entrance?"

"Why, I must say," said Hiram, "that he was considerable cross-grained; not what I call clever, seeing that it was only one neighbor wanting to go into the house of another."

"Oh! then you own it was only meant for a neighborly visit on your part, and without the sanction of law. Remember, gentlemen, the words of the witness, 'one neighbor wanting to enter the house of another.' Now, sir, I ask you if Nathaniel Bumppo did not again and again order you not to enter?"

"There was some words passed between us," said Hiram, "but I read the warrant to him aloud."

"I repeat my question; did he tell you not to enter his habitation?"

"There was a good deal passed betwixt us—but I've the warrant in my pocket; maybe the court would wish to see it?"

"Witness," said Judge Temple, "answer the question directly; did or did not the prisoner forbid your entering his hut?"

"Why, I some think—"

"Answer without equivocation," continued the Judge, sternly.

"He did."

"And did you attempt to enter after this order?"

"I did; but the warrant was in my hand."

"Proceed, Mr. Lippet, with your examination."

But the attorney saw that the impression was in favor of his client, and, waving his hand with a supercilious manner, as if unwilling to insult the understanding of the jury with any further defence, he replied—

"No, sir; I leave it for your honor to charge; I rest my case here."

"Mr. District Attorney," said the Judge, "have you anything to say?"

Mr. Van der School removed his spectacles, folded them, and replacing them once more on his nose, eyed the other bill which he held in his hand, and then said, looking at the bar over the top of his glasses—

"I shall rest the prosecution here, if the court please."

Judge Temple arose and began the charge.

"Gentlemen of the jury," he said, "you have heard the testimony, and I shall detain you but a moment. If an officer meet with resistance in the execution of a process he has an undoubted right to call any citizen to his assistance; and the acts of such assistant come within the protection of the law. I shall leave you to judge, gentlemen, from the testimony, how far the witness in this prosecution can be so considered, feeling less reluctance to submit the case thus informally to your decision, because there is yet another indictment to be tried, which involves heavier charges against the unfortunate prisoner."

The tone of Marmaduke was mild and insinuating, and as his sentiments were given with such apparent impartiality, they did not fail of carrying due weight with the jury. The grave-looking yeomen who composed this tribunal, laid their heads together for a few minutes, without leaving the box, when the foreman arose, and after the forms of the court were duly observed, he pronounced the prisoner to be—

"Not guilty."

"You are acquitted of this charge, Nathaniel Bumppo," said the Judge.

"Anan!" said Natty.

"You are found not guilty of striking and assaulting Mr. Doolittle."

"No, no, I'll not deny but that I took him a little roughly by the shoulders," said Natty, looking about him with great simplicity, "and that I—"

"You are acquitted," interrupted the Judge, "and there is nothing further to be said or done in the matter."

A look of joy lighted up the features of the old man, who now comprehended the case, and placing his cap eagerly on his head again, he threw up the bar of his little prison, and said feelingly—

"I must say this for you, Judge Temple, that the law has not been so hard on me as I dreaded. I hope God will bless you for the kind things you've done to me this day."

But the staff of the constable was opposed to his egress, and Mr. Lippet whispered a few words in his ear, when the aged hunter sank back into his place, and, removing his cap, stroked down the remnants of his gray and sandy locks, with an air of mortification mingled with submission.

"Mr. District Attorney," said Judge Temple, affecting to busy himself with his minutes, "proceed with the second indictment."

Mr. Van der School took great care that no part of the presentment, which he now read, should be lost on his auditors. It accused the prisoner of resisting the execution of a search-warrant, by force of arms, and particularized, in the vague language of the law, among a variety of other weapons, the use of the rifle. This was indeed a more serious charge than an ordinary assault and battery, and a corresponding degree of interest was manifested by the spectators in its result. The prisoner was duly arraigned, and his plea again demanded. Mr. Lippet had anticipated the answers of Natty, and in a whisper advised him how to lead. But the feelings of the old hunter were awakened by some of the expressions of the indictment, and, forgetful of his caution, he exclaimed—

" 'Tis a wicked untruth; I crave no man's blood. Them thieves, the Iroquois, won't say it to my face, that I ever thirsted after man's blood. I have fou't as a soldier that feared his Maker and his officer, but I never pulled trigger on any but a warrior that was up and awake. No man can say that I ever struck even a Mingo in his blanket. I believe there's some who thinks there's no God in a wilderness!"

"Attend to your plea, Bumppo," said the Judge; "you hear that you are accused of using your rifle against an officer of justice? are you guilty or not guilty?"

By this time the irritated feelings of Natty had found vent; and he rested on the bar for a moment, in a musing posture, when he lifted his face, with his silent laugh, and, pointing to where the wood-chopper stood, he said—

"Would Billy Kirby be standing there, d'ye think, if I had used the rifle?"

"Then you deny it," said Mr. Lippet; "you plead not guilty?"

"Sartain," said Natty; "Billy knows that I never fired at all. Billy, do you remember the turkey last winter? ah! me! that was better than common firing; but I can't shoot as I used to could."

"Enter the plea of not guilty," said Judge Temple, strongly affected by the simplicity of the prisoner.

Hiram was again sworn, and his testimony given on the second charge. He had discovered his former error, and proceeded more cautiously than before. He related very distinctly, and for the man, with amazing terseness, the suspicion against the hunter, the complaint, the issuing of the warrant, and the swearing in of Kirby; all of which, he affirmed, were done in due form of law. He then added the manner in which the constable had been received; and stated distinctly, that Natty had pointed the rifle at Kirby, and threatened his life, if he attempted to execute his duty. All this was confirmed by Jotham, who was observed to adhere closely to the story of the magistrate. Mr. Lippet conducted an artful cross-examination of these two witnesses, but after consuming much time, was compelled to relinquish the attempt to obtain any advantage, in despair.

At length the district attorney called the wood-chopper to the bar. Billy gave an extremely confused account of the whole affair, although he evidently aimed at the truth, until Mr. Van der School aided him, by asking some direct questions:—

"It appears from examining the papers, that you demanded admission into the hut legally; so you were put in bodily fear by his rifle and threats?"

"I didn't mind them that, man," said Billy, snapping his fingers; "I should be a poor stick to mind old Leather-Stocking."

"But I understood you to say (referring to your previous words (as delivered here in court) in the commencement of your testimony) that you thought he meant to shoot you?"

"To be sure I did; and so would you too, squire, if you had seen the chap dropping a muzzle that never misses, and cocking an eye that has a natural squint by long practice. I thought there would be a dust on't, and my back was up at once; but Leather-Stocking gi'n up the skin, and so the matter ended."

"Ah! Billy," said Natty, shaking his head, "'twas a lucky thought in me to throw out the hide, or there might have been blood spilt; and I'm sure, if it had been yourn, I should have mourn'd it sorely the little while I have to stay."

"Well, Leather-Stocking," returned Billy, facing the prisoner with a freedom and familiarity that utterly disregarded the presence of the court, "as you are on the subject, it may be that you've no—"

"Go on with your examination, Mr. District Attorney."

That gentleman eyed the familiarity between his witness and the prisoner with manifest disgust, and indicated to the court that he was done.

"Then you didn't feel frightened, Mr. Kirby?" said the counsel for the prisoner.

"Me! no," said Billy, casting his eyes over his own huge frame with evident self-satisfaction; "I'm not to be skeared so easy."

"You look like a hardy man; where were you born, sir?"

"Varmount state; 'tis a mountaynious place, but there's a stiff soil, and it's pretty much wooded with beech and maple."

"I have always heard so," said Mr. Lippet, soothingly. "You have been used to the rifle yourself, in that country?"

"I pull the second best trigger in this county. I knock under to Natty Bumppo there, sin' he shot the pigeon."

Leather-Stocking raised his head, and laughed again, when he abruptly thrust out a wrinkled hand, and said—

"You're young yet, Billy, and hav'n't seen the matches that I have; but here's my hand; I bear no malice to you, I don't."

Mr. Lippet allowed this conciliatory offering to be accepted, and judiciously paused, while the spirit of peace was exercising its influence over the two; but the Judge interposed his authority.

"This is an improper place for such dialogues," he said.

"Proceed with your examination of this witness, Mr. Lippet, or I shall order the next."

The attorney started, as if unconscious of any impropriety, and continued—

"So you settled the matter with Natty amicably on the spot, did you?"

"He gi'n me the skin, and I didn't want to quarrel with an old man; for my part, I see no such mighty matter in shooting a buck!"

"And you parted friends? and you would never have thought of bringing the business up before a court, hadn't you been subpœnaed?"

"I don't think I should; he gi'n the skin, and I didn't feel a hard thought, though Squire Doolittle got some affronted."

"I have done, sir," said Mr. Lippet, probably relying on the charge of the Judge, as he again seated himself, with the air of a man who felt that his success was certain.

When Mr. Van der School arose to address the jury, he commenced by saying—

"Gentlemen of the jury, I should have interrupted the leading questions put by the prisoner's counsel (by leading questions I mean telling him what to say), did I not feel confident that the law of the land was superior to any advantages (I mean legal advantages) which he might obtain by his art. The counsel for the prisoner, gentlemen, has endeavored to persuade you, in opposition to your own good sense, to believe that pointing a rifle at a constable (elected or deputed) is a very innocent affair; and that society (I mean the commonwealth, gentlemen) shall not be endangered thereby. But let me claim your attention, while we look over the particulars of this heinous offence." Here Mr. Van der School favored the jury with an abridgment of the testimony, recounted in such a manner as utterly to confuse the faculties of his worthy listeners. After this exhibition he closed as follows:—"And now, gentlemen, having thus made plain to your senses the crime of which this unfortunate man has been guilty (unfortunate both on account of his ignorance and his guilt), I shall leave you to your own consciences; not in the least doubting that you will see the importance (notwithstanding the prisoner's counsel (doubtless relying on your former verdict) wishes to appear so confident of success) of punishing the offender, and asserting the dignity of the laws."

It was now the duty of the Judge to deliver his charge. It consisted of a short, comprehensive summary of the testimony, laying bare the artifice of the prisoner's counsel, and placing the facts in so obvious a light, that they could not well be misunderstood. "Living as we do, gentlemen," he concluded, "on the skirts of society, it becomes doubly necessary to protect the ministers of the law. If you believe the witnesses, in their construction of the acts of the prisoner, it is your duty to convict him; but if you believe that the old man, who this day appears before you, meant not to harm the constable, but was acting more under the influence of habit than by the instigations of malice, it will be your duty to judge him, but to do it with lenity."

As before, the jury did not leave their box; but, after a consultation of some little time, their foreman arose, and pronounced the prisoner—

"Guilty."

There was but little surprise manifested in the court room at this verdict, as the testimony, the greater part of which we have omitted, was too clear and direct to be passed over. The judges seemed to have anticipated this sentiment, for a consultation was passing among them also, during the deliberation of the jury, and the preparatory movements of the "bench" announced the coming sentence.

"Nathaniel Bumppo," commenced the Judge, making the customary pause.

The old hunter, who had been musing again, with his head on the bar, raised himself, and cried, with a prompt, military tone—

"Here."

The Judge waved his hand for silence, and proceeded—

"In forming their sentence, the court have been governed as much by the consideration of your ignorance of the laws, as by a strict sense of the importance of punishing such outrages as this of which you have been found guilty. They have therefore passed over the obvious punishment of whipping on the bare back, in mercy to your years; but as the dignity of the law requires an open exhibition of the consequences of your crime, it is ordered, that you be conveyed from this room to the public stocks, where you are to be confined for one hour; that you pay a fine to the state of one hundred dollars; and that you be imprisoned in the jail of this county for one calendar month, and furthermore, that your imprisonment do not cease until the said fine shall be paid. I feel it my duty, Nathaniel Bumppo—"

"And where should I get the money?" interrupted the Leather-Stocking, eagerly; "where should I get the money? you'll take away the bounty on the painters,[5] because I cut the throat of a deer; and how is an old man to find so much gold or silver in the woods? No, no, judge: think better of it, and don't talk of shutting me up in a jail for the little time I have to stay."

"If you have anything to urge against the passing of the sentence, the court will yet hear you," said the Judge, mildly.

"I have enough to say ag'in it," cried Natty, grasping the bar on which his fingers were working with a convulsed motion. "Where am I to get the money? Let me out into the woods and hills, where I've been used to breathe the clear air, and though I'm threescore and ten, if you've left game enough in the country, I'll travel night and day but I'll make you up the sum afore the season is over. Yes, yes—you see the reason of the thing, and the wickedness of shutting up an old man, that has spent his days, as one may say, where he could always look into the windows of heaven."

"I must be governed by the law—"

"Talk not to me of law, Marmaduke Temple," interrupted the hunter. "Did the beast of the forest mind your laws, when it was thirsty and hungering for the blood of your own child! She was kneeling to her God for a greater favor than I ask, and he heard her; and if you now say no to my prayers, do you think he will be deaf?"

"My private feelings must not enter into—"

"Hear me, Marmaduke Temple," interrupted the old man, with melancholy earnestness, "and hear reason. I've travelled these mountains when you was no judge, but an infant in your mother's arms; and I feel as if I had a right and a privilege to travel them ag'in afore I die. Have you forgot the time that you come on to the lake-shore, when there wasn't even a jail to lodge in; and didn't I give you my own bear-skin to sleep on, and the fat of a noble buck to satisfy the cravings of your hunger? Yes, yes—you thought it no sin then to kill a deer! And this I did, though I had no reason

---

[5] Panthers.

to love you, for you had never done anything but harm to them that loved and sheltered me. And now, will you shut me up in your dungeons to pay me for my kindness? A hundred dollars! where should I get the money? No, no—there's them that says hard things of you, Marmaduke Temple, but you an't so bad as to wish to see an old man die in a prison, because he stood up for the right. Come, friend, let me pass; it's long sin' I've been used to such crowds, and I crave to be in the woods ag'in. Don't fear me, Judge—I bid you not to fear me; for if there's beaver enough left on the streams, or the buckskins will sell for a shilling a-piece, you shall have the last penny of the fine. Where are ye, pups! come away, dogs! come away! we have a grievous toil to do for our years, but it shall be done—yes, yes, I've promised it, and it shall be done!"

It is unnecessary to say, that the movement of the Leather-Stocking was again intercepted by the constable; but before he had time to speak, a bustling in the crowd, and a loud hem, drew all eyes to another part of the room.

Benjamin had succeeded in edging his way through the people, and was now seen balancing his short body, with one foot in a window and the other on a railing of the jurybox. To the amazement of the whole court, the steward was evidently preparing to speak. After a good deal of difficulty, he succeeded in drawing from his pocket a small bag, and then found utterance.

"If-so-be," he said, "that your honor is agreeable to trust the poor fellow out on another cruise among the beasts, here's a small matter that will help to bring down the risk, seeing that there's just thirty-five of your Spaniards[6] in it; and I wish, from the bottom of my heart, that they was raal British guineas,[7] for the sake of the old boy. But 'tis as it is; and if Squire Dickens will just be so good as to overhaul this small bit of an account, and take enough from the bag to settle the same, he's welcome to hold on upon the rest, till such time as the Leather-Stocking can grapple with them said beaver, or, for that matter, forever, and no thanks asked."

As Benjamin concluded, he thrust out the wooden register of his arrears to the "Bold Dragon" with one hand, while he offered his bag of dollars with the other. Astonishment at this singular interruption produced a profound stillness in the room, which was only interrupted by the Sheriff, who struck his sword on the table, and cried—

"Silence!"

"There must be an end to this," said the Judge, struggling to overcome his feelings. "Constable, lead the prisoner to the stocks. Mr. Clerk, what stands next on the calendar?"

Natty seemed to yield to his destiny, for he sank his head on his chest, and followed the officer from the court-room in silence. The crowd moved back for the passage of the prisoner, and when his tall form was seen descending from the outer door, a rush of the people to the scene of his disgrace followed.

1823

---

[6] Spanish dollars.   [7] Guinea: British coin worth about £1.

from The Prairie

Chapter XXXIV

—Methought I heard a voice.[1]
Shakespeare

The watercourses were at their height, and the boat went down the swift current like a bird. The passage proved prosperous and speedy. In less than a third of the time that would have been necessary for the same journey by land, it was accomplished by the favor of those rapid rivers. Issuing from one stream into another, as the veins of the human body communicate with the larger channels of life, they soon entered the grand artery of the western waters, and landed safely at the very door of the father of Inez.

The joy of Don Augustin, and the embarrassment of the worthy father Ignatius, may be imagined. The former wept and returned thanks to Heaven; the latter returned thanks and did not weep. The mild provincials were too happy to raise any questions on the character of so joyful a restoration; and, by a sort of general consent, it soon became to be an admitted opinion that the bride of Middleton had been kidnapped by a villain, and that she was restored to her friends by human agency. There were, as respects this belief, certainly a few sceptics, but then they enjoyed their doubts in private, with that species of sublimated and solitary gratification that a miser finds in gazing at his growing, but useless hoards.

In order to give the worthy priest something to employ his mind, Middleton made him the instrument of uniting Paul and Ellen. The former consented to the ceremony, because he found that all his friends laid great stress on the matter; but shortly after, he led his bride into the plains of Kentucky, under the pretence of paying certain customary visits to sundry members of the family of Hover. While there, he took occasion to have the marriage properly solemnized by a justice of the peace of his acquaintance, in whose ability to forge the nuptial chain he had much more faith than in that of all the gownsmen[2] within the pale of Rome. Ellen, who appeared conscious that some extraordinary preventives might prove necessary to keep one of so erratic a temper as her partner, within the proper matrimonial boundaries, raised no objections to these double knots, and all parties were content.

The local importance Middleton had acquired, by his union with the daughter of so affluent a proprietor as Don Augustin, united to his personal merit, attracted the attention of the government. He was soon employed in various situations of responsibility and confidence, which both served to elevate his character in the public estimation, and to afford the means of patronage. The bee-hunter was among the first of those to whom he saw fit to extend his favor. It was far from difficult to find situations suited to the abilities of Paul, in the state of society that existed three-and-twenty years ago in those regions. The efforts of Middleton and Inez, in behalf of her husband, were warmly and sagaciously seconded by Ellen, and they succeeded, in process of time, in working a great and beneficial change in his character. He soon became a landholder, then a prosperous cultivator of the soil, and shortly after a town-officer.

[1] *Macbeth*, Act II, Sc. ii, l. 35.   [2] I.e., ministers or priests.

By that progressive change in fortunes, which in the republic is often seen to be so singularly accompanied by a corresponding improvement in knowledge and self-respect, he went on, from step to step, until his wife enjoyed the maternal delight of seeing her children placed far beyond the danger of returning to that state from which both their parents had issued. Paul is actually at this moment a member of the lower branch of the legislature of the State where he has long resided; and he is even notorious for making speeches that have a tendency to put that deliberative body in good humor, and which, as they are based on great practical knowledge suited to the condition of the country, possess a merit that is much wanted in many more subtle and fine-spun theories, that are daily heard in similar assemblies, to issue from the lips of certain instinctive politicians. But all these happy fruits were the results of much care, and of a long period of time. Middleton, who fills, with a credit better suited to the difference in their educations, a seat in a far higher branch of legislative authority, is the source from which we have derived most of the intelligence necessary to compose our legend. In addition to what he has related of Paul, and of his own continued happiness, he has added a short narrative of what took place on a subsequent visit to the prairies, with which, as we conceive it a suitable termination to what has gone before, we shall judge it wise to conclude our labors.

In the autumn of the year that succeeded the season in which the preceding events occurred, the young man, still in the military service, found himself on the waters of the Missouri, at a point not far remote from the Pawnee towns. Released from any immediate calls of duty, and strongly urged to the measure by Paul, who was in his company, he determined to take horse, and cross the country to visit the partisan, and to inquire into the fate of his friend the trapper. As his train was suited to his functions and rank, the journey was effected, with the privations and hardships that are the accompaniments to all travelling in a wild, but without any of those dangers and alarms that marked his former passage through the same regions. When within a proper distance, he despatched an Indian runner, belonging to a friendly tribe, to announce the approach of himself and party, continuing his route at a deliberate pace, in order that the intelligence might, as was customary, precede his arrival. To the surprise of the travellers, their message was unanswered. Hour succeeded hour, and mile after mile was passed, without bringing either the signs of an honorable reception, or the more simple assurances of a friendly welcome. At length the cavalcade, at whose head rode Middleton and Paul, descended from the elevated plain, on which they had long been journeying, to a luxuriant bottom, that brought them to the level of the village of the Loups. The sun was beginning to fall, and a sheet of golden light was spread over the placid plain, lending to its even surface those glorious tints and hues, that the human imagination is apt to conceive, form the embellishment of still more imposing scenes. The verdure of the year yet remained, and herds of horses and mules were grazing peacefully in the vast natural pasture, under the keeping of vigilant Pawnee boys. Paul pointed out among them the well-known form of Asinus, sleek, fat, and luxuriating in the fulness of content, as he stood with reclining ears and closed eyelids, seemingly musing on the exquisite nature of his present indolent enjoyment.

The route of the party led them at no great distance from one of those watchful youths who was charged with a trust heavy as the principal wealth of his tribe. He heard the trampling of the horses, and cast his eye aside, but instead of manifesting curiosity or alarm, his look instantly returned whence it had been withdrawn, to the spot where the village was known to stand.

"There is something remarkable in all this," muttered Middleton, half offended at what he conceived to be not only a slight to his rank, but offensive to himself personally; "yonder boy has heard of our approach, or he would not fail to notify his tribe; and yet he scarcely deigns to favor us with a glance. Look to your arms, men; it may be necessary to let these savages feel our strength."

"Therein, Captain, I think you're in an error," returned Paul: "if honesty is to be met on the prairies at all, you will find it in our old friend Hard-Heart; neither is an Indian to be judged of by the rules of a white. See! we are not altogether slighted, for here comes a party at last to meet us, though it is a little pitiful as to show and numbers."

Paul was right in both particulars. A group of horsemen were at length seen wheeling round a little copse, and advancing across the plain directly toward them. The advance of this party was slow and dignified. As it drew nigh, the partisan of the Loups was seen at its head, followed by a dozen younger warriors of his tribe. They were all unarmed, nor did they even wear any of those ornaments or feathers, which are considered testimonials of respect to the guest an Indian receives, as well as evidence of his own importance.

The meeting was friendly, though a little restrained on both sides. Middleton, jealous of his own consideration, no less than of the authority of his government, suspected some undue influence on the part of the agents of the Canadas; and, as he was determined to maintain the authority of which he was the representative, he felt himself constrained to manifest a hauteur[3] that he was far from feeling. It was not so easy to penetrate the motives of the Pawnees. Calm, dignified, and yet far from repulsive, they set an example of courtesy, blended with reserve, that many a diplomatist of the most polished court might have striven in vain to imitate.

In this manner the two parties continued their course to the town. Middleton had time during the remainder of the ride, to revolve in his mind all the probable reasons which his ingenuity could suggest for this strange reception. Although he was accompanied by a regular interpreter, the chiefs made their salutations in a manner that dispensed with his services. Twenty times the Captain turned his glance on his former friend, endeavoring to read the expression of his rigid features. But every effort and all conjectures proved equally futile. The eye of Hard-Heart was fixed, composed, and a little anxious; but as to every other emotion, impenetrable. He neither spoke himself, nor seemed willing to invite discourse in his visitors: it was therefore necessary for Middleton to adopt the patient manners of his companions, and to await the issue for the explanation.

When they entered the town, its inhabitants were seen collected in an open space, where they were arranged with the customary deference to age and rank. The whole formed a large circle, in the centre of which were perhaps a dozen of the principal chiefs. Hard-Heart waved his hand as he approached, and, as the mass of bodies opened he rode through, followed by his companions. Here they dismounted; and as the beasts were led apart, the strangers found themselves environed by a thousand grave, composed, but solicitous faces.

---

[3] Haughtiness.

Middleton gazed about him in growing concern, for no cry, no song, no shout welcomed him among a people, from whom he had so lately parted with regret. His uneasiness, not to say apprehensions, was shared by all his followers. Determination and stern resolution began to assume the place of anxiety in every eye, as each man silently felt for his arms, and assured himself that his several weapons were in a state for service. But there was no answering symptom of hostility on the part of their hosts. Hard-Heart beckoned for Middleton and Paul to follow, leading the way toward the cluster of forms that occupied the centre of the circle. Here the visitors found a solution of all the movements which had given them so much reason for apprehension.

The trapper was placed on a rude seat, which had been made, with studied care, to support his frame in an upright and easy attitude. The first glance of the eye told his former friends, that the old man was at length called upon to pay the last tribute of nature. His eye was glazed, and apparently as devoid of sight as of expression. His features were a little more sunken and strongly marked than formerly; but there, all change, so far as exterior was concerned, might be said to have ceased. His approaching end was not to be ascribed to any positive disease, but had been a gradual and mild decay of the physical powers. Life, it is true, still lingered in his system; but it was as if at times entirely ready to depart, and then it would appear to reanimate the sinking form, reluctant to give up the possession of a tenement that had never been corrupted by vice or undermined by disease. It would have been no violent fancy to have imagined that the spirit fluttered about the placid lips of the old woodsman, reluctant to depart from a shell that had so long given it an honest and honorable shelter.

His body was placed so as to let the light of the setting sun fall full upon the solemn features. His head was bare, the long, thin locks of gray fluttering lightly in the evening breeze. His rifle lay upon his knee, and the other accoutrements of the chase were placed at his side, within reach of his hand. Between his feet lay the figure of a hound, with its head crouching to the earth, as if it slumbered; and so perfectly easy and natural was its position, that a second glance was necessary to tell Middleton he saw only the skin of Hector, stuffed, by Indian tenderness and ingenuity, in a manner to represent the living animal. His own dog was playing at a distance with the child of Tachechana and Mahtoree. The mother herself stood at hand, holding in her arms a second offspring, that might boast of a parentage no less honorable than that which belonged to the son of Hard-Heart. Le Balafré was seated nigh the dying trapper, with every mark about his person that the hour of his own departure was not far distant. The rest of those immediately in the centre were aged men, who had apparently drawn near in order to observe the manner in which a just and fearless warrior would depart on the greatest of his journeys.

The old man was reaping the rewards of a life remarkable for temperance and activity, in a tranquil and placid death. His vigor in a manner endured to the very last. Decay, when it did occur, was rapid, but free from pain. He had hunted with the tribe in the spring, and even throughout most of the summer; when his limbs suddenly refused to perform their customary offices. A sympathizing weakness took possession of all his faculties; and the Pawnees believed that they were going to lose, in this unexpected manner, a sage and counsellor whom they had begun both to love and respect. But, as we have already said, the immortal occupant seemed unwilling to desert its tenement. The lamp of life flickered, without becoming extinguished. On the morning of the day on which Middleton arrived, there was a general reviving of the powers of the whole man. His tongue was again heard in wholesome maxims, and his eye from time to time recognized the persons of his friends. It merely proved to be a brief and final intercourse with the world, on the part of one who had already been considered, as to mental communion, to have taken his leave of it forever.

When he had placed his guests in front of the dying man, Hard-Heart, after a pause, that proceeded as much from sorrow as decorum, leaned a little forward, and demanded—

"Does my father hear the words of his son?"

"Speak," returned the trapper, in tones that issued from his chest, but which were rendered awfully distinct by the stillness that reigned in the place. "I am about to depart from the village of the Loups, and shortly shall be beyond the reach of your voice."

"Let the wise chief have no cares for his journey," continued Hard-Heart, with an earnest solicitude that led him to forget, for the moment, that others were waiting to address his adopted parent; "a hundred Loups shall clear his path from briers."

"Pawnee, I die, as I have lived, a Christian man!" resumed the trapper, with a force of voice that had the same startling effect on his hearers as is produced by the trumpet, when its blast rises suddenly and freely on the air, after its obstructed sounds have been heard struggling in the distance: "as I came into life so will I leave it. Horses and arms are not needed to stand in the presence of the Great Spirit of my people. He knows my color, and according to my gifts will He judge my deeds."

"My father will tell my young men how many Mingoes he has struck, and what acts of valor and justice he has done, that they may know how to imitate him."

"A boastful tongue is not heard in the heaven of a white man!" solemnly returned the old man. "What I have done He has seen. His eyes are always open. That which has been well done will He remember; wherein I have been wrong will He not forget to chastise, though He will do the same in mercy. No, my son; a Pale-face may not sing his own praises, and hope to have them acceptable before his God!"

A little disappointed, the young partisan stepped modestly back, making way for the recent comers to approach. Middleton took one of the meagre hands of the trapper, and struggling to command his voice, he succeeded in announcing his presence.

The old man listened like one whose thoughts were dwelling on a very different subject; but when the other had succeeded in making him understand that he was present, an expression of joyful recognition passed over his faded features.

"I hope you have not so soon forgotten those whom you so materially served!" Middleton concluded. "It would pain me to think my hold on your memory was so light."

"Little that I have ever seen is forgotten," returned the trapper; "I am at the close of many weary days, but there is not one among them all that I could wish to overlook. I remember you, with the whole of your company; ay, and your gran'ther, that went before you. I am glad that you have come back upon these plains, for I had need of one who speaks the English, since little faith can be put in the traders of these regions. Will you do a favor to an old and dying man?"

"Name it," said Middleton; "it shall be done."

"It is a far journey to send such trifles," resumed the old man, who spoke at short intervals, as strength and breath permitted, "a far and weary journey is the same; but kindnesses and friendships are things not to be forgotten. There is a settlement among the Otsego hills—"

"I know the place," interrupted Middleton, observing that he spoke with increasing difficulty; "proceed to tell me what you would have done."

"Take this rifle, and pouch, and horn, and send them to the person whose name is graven on the plates of the stock,—a trader cut the letters with his knife,—for it is long that I have intended to send him such a token of my love!"

"It shall be so. Is there more that you could wish?"

"Little else have I to bestow. My traps I give to my Indian son; for honestly and kindly has he kept his faith. Let him stand before me."

Middleton explained to the chief what the trapper had said, and relinquished his own place to the other.

"Pawnee," continued the old man, always changing his language to suit the person he addressed, and not unfrequently according to the ideas he expressed, "it is a custom of my people for the father to leave his blessing with the son before he shuts his eyes forever. This blessing I give to you; take it; for the prayers of a Christian man will never make the path of a just warrior to the blessed prairies either longer or more tangled. May the God of a white man look on your deeds with friendly eyes, and may you never commit an act that shall cause Him to darken His face. I know not whether we shall ever meet again. There are many traditions concerning the place of Good Spirits. It is not for one like me, old and experienced though I am, to set up my opinion against a nation's. You believe in the blessed prairies, and I have faith in the sayings of my fathers. If both are true our parting will be final; but if it should prove that the same meaning is hid under different words, we shall yet stand together, Pawnee, before the face of your Wahcondah, who will then be no other than my God. There is much to be said in favor of both religions, for each seems suited to its own people, and no doubt it was so intended. I fear I have not altogether followed the gifts of my color, inasmuch as I find it a little painful to give up forever the use of the rifle, and the comforts of the chase. But then the fault has been my own, seeing that it could not have been His. Ay, Hector," he continued, leaning forward a little, and feeling for the ears of the hound, "our parting has come at last, dog, and it will be a long hunt. You have been an honest, and a bold, and a faithful hound. Pawnee, you cannot slay the pup on my grave, for where a Christian dog falls there he lies forever; but you can be kind to him after I am gone, for the love you bear his master."

"The words of my father are in my ears," returned the young partisan, making a grave and respectful gesture of assent.

"Do you hear what the chief has promised, dog?" demanded the trapper, making an effort to attract the notice of the insensible effigy of his hound. Receiving no answering look, nor hearing any friendly whine, the old man felt for the mouth, and endeavored to force his hand between the cold lips. The truth then flashed upon him, although he was far from perceiving the whole extent of the deception. Falling back in his seat, he hung his head, like one who felt a severe and unexpected shock. Profiting by this momentary forgetfulness, two young Indians removed the skin with the same delicacy of feeling that had induced them to attempt the pious fraud.

"The dog is dead!" muttered the trapper, after a pause of many minutes; "a hound has his time as well as a man; and well has he filled his days! Captain," he added, making an effort to wave his hand for Middleton, "I am glad you have come; for though kind, and well meaning according to the gifts of their color, these Indians are not the men to lay the head of a white man in his grave. I have been thinking, too, of this dog at my feet; it will not do to set forth the opinion that a Christian can expect to meet his hound again; still there can be little harm in placing what is left of so faithful a servant nigh the bones of his master."

"It shall be as you desire."

"I'm glad you think with me in this matter. In order, then, to save labor, lay the pup at my feet; or for that matter, put him side by side. A hunter need never be ashamed to be found in company with his dog!"

"I charge myself with your wish."

The old man made a long, and apparently a musing pause. At times he raised his eyes wistfully, as if he would again address Middleton, but some innate feeling appeared always to suppress his words. The other, who observed his hesitation, inquired in a way most likely to encourage him to proceed whether there was aught else that he could wish to have done.

"I am without kith or kin in the wide world!" the trapper answered: "when I am gone there will be an end of my race. We have never been chiefs; but honest, and useful in our way I hope it cannot be denied we have always proved ourselves. My father lies buried near the sea, and the bones of his son will whiten on the prairie—"

"Name the spot, and your remains shall be placed by the side of your father," interrupted Middleton.

"Not so, not so, Captain. Let me sleep where I have lived—beyond the din of the settlements! Still I see no need why the grave of an honest man should be hid, like a Red-skin in his ambushment. I paid a man in the settlements to make and put a graven stone at the head of my father's resting-place. It was of the value of twelve beaverskins, and cunningly and curiously was it carved! Then it told to all comers that the body of such a Christian lay beneath; and it spoke of his manner of life, of his years, and of his honesty. When we had done with the Frenchers in the old war I made a journey to the spot, in order to see that all was rightly performed, and glad I am to say, the workman had not forgotten his faith."

"And such a stone you would have at your grave?"

"I! no, no, I have no son but Hard-Heart, and it is little that an Indian knows of white fashions and usages. Besides, I am his debtor already, seeing it is so little I have done since I have lived in his tribe. The rifle might bring the value of such a thing —but then I know it will give the boy pleasure to hang the piece in his hall, for many is the deer and the bird that he has seen it destroy. No, no, the gun must be sent to him whose name is graven on the lock!"

"But there is one who would gladly prove his affection in the way you wish; he who owes you not only his own deliverance from so many dangers, but who inherits a heavy debt of gratitude from his ancestors. The stone shall be put at the head of your grave."

The old man extended his emaciated hand, and gave the other a squeeze of thanks.

"I thought you might be willing to do it, but I was backward in asking the favor," he said, "seeing that you are not of my kin. Put no boastful words on the same, but just the name, the age, and the time of the death, with something from the holy book; no more, no more. My name will then not be altogether lost on 'arth; I need no more."

Middleton intimated his assent, and then followed a pause that was only broken by distant and broken sentences from the dying man. He appeared now to have closed his accounts with the world, and to await merely for the final summons to quit it. Middleton and Hard-Heart placed themselves on the opposite sides of his seat, and watched with melancholy solicitude, the variations of his countenance. For two hours there was no very sensible alteration. The expression of his faded and time-worn features was that of a calm and dignified repose. From time to time he spoke, uttering some brief sentence in the way of advice, or asking some simple questions concerning those in whose fortunes he took a friendly interest. During the whole of that solemn and anxious period each individual of the tribe kept his place, in the most self-restrained patience. When the old man spoke, all bent their heads to listen; and when his words were uttered, they seemed to ponder on their wisdom and usefulness.

As the flame drew nigher to the socket his voice was hushed, and there were moments when his attendants doubted whether he still belonged to the living. Middleton, who watched each wavering expression of his weather-beaten visage, with the interest of a keen observer of human nature, softened by the tenderness of personal regard, fancied he could read the workings of the old man's soul in the strong lineaments of his countenance. Perhaps what the enlightened soldier took for the delusion of mistaken opinion did actually occur—for who has returned from that unknown world to explain by what forms, and in what manner, he was introduced into its awful precincts? Without pretending to explain what must ever be a mystery to the quick, we shall simply relate facts as they occurred.

The trapper had remained nearly motionless for an hour. His eyes alone had occasionally opened and shut. When opened, his gaze seemed fastened on the clouds which hung around the western horizon, reflecting the bright colors, and giving form and loveliness to the glorious tints of an American sunset. The hour—the calm beauty of the season—the occasion, all conspired to fill the spectators with solemn awe. Suddenly, while musing on the remarkable position in which he was placed, Middleton felt the hand which he held grasp his own with incredible power, and the old man, supported on either side by his friends, rose upright to his feet. For a moment he looked about him, as if to invite all in presence to listen (the lingering remnant of human frailty), and then, with a fine military elevation of the head, and with a voice that might be heard in every part of that numerous assembly, he pronounced the word—

"Here!"

A movement so entirely unexpected, and the air of grandeur and humility which were so remarkably united in the mien of the trapper, together with the clear and uncommon force of his utterance, produced a short period of confusion in the faculties of all present. When Middleton and Hard-Heart, each of whom had involuntarily extended a hand to support the form of the old man, turned to him again, they found that the subject of their interest was removed forever beyond the necessity of their care. They mournfully placed the body in its seat, and Le Balafré arose to announce the termination of the scene to the tribe. The voice of the old Indian seemed a sort of echo from that invisible world to which the meek spirit of the trapper had just departed.

"A valiant, a just, and a wise warrior, has gone on the path which will lead him to the blessed grounds of his people!" he said. "When the voice of the Wahcondah called him, he was ready to answer. Go, my children; remember the just chief of the Pale-faces, and clear your own tracks from briers!"

The grave was made beneath the shade of some noble oaks. It has been carefully watched to the present hour by the Pawnees of the Loup, and is often shown to the traveller and the trader as a spot where a just white man sleeps. In due time the stone was placed at its head, with the simple inscription which the trapper had himself requested. The only liberty taken by Middleton was to add—*"May no wanton hand ever disturb his remains!"*

1827

William Cullen Bryant
1794–1878

William Cullen Bryant's popular image haunts his poetry. The classroom portrait of this legendary patriarch of American verse, with a chiseled old face and deep-set eyes peering out from behind bushy eyebrows and a long, flowing white beard, solemnly oversaw generations of American schoolchildren dutifully reciting "Thanatopsis" and "To a Waterfowl." Not until Robert Frost in the mid-twentieth century would there be another American poet with as venerable a public reputation.

Few American writers have had longer—or more visible—literary careers than Bryant. His publications span the administrations of seventeen presidents, from Thomas Jefferson to Rutherford B. Hayes. Yet the definitive edition of Bryant's poems consists of but two relatively small volumes. And few American poets have expressed a more consistent vision of the world: meditative, restrained, full of dignified serenity and pleasure in nature. Bryant's early work reveals few youthful flaws, his last efforts few signs of his eighty-three years.

William Cullen Bryant was born in Cummington, a small town in western Massachusetts's Berkshire Mountains. His mother, a hardy Calvinist descendant of the Pilgrim John Alden, made the following brief entry in her diary for November 3, 1794: "Stormy, wind N.E. Churned. Seven in the evening a son was born." His father, a doctor, encouraged him to read widely in the family's modest but well-chosen library of English and classical literature. The following passage from Bryant's fragment of an autobiography recalls the importance of his youth:

I was always from my earliest years a delighted observer of external nature— the splendors of a winter daybreak over the wide waste of snow seen from our windows, the glories of the autumnal woods, the gloomy approaches of the thunderstorm, and its departure amid sunshine and rainbows, the return of spring, with its flowers, and the first snowfall of winter. The poets fostered this taste in me, and though at the time I rarely heard such things spoken of, it was none the less cherished in my secret mind.

Privately educated by country ministers, as was the custom in rural New England, Bryant began writing poetry at eight years of age and, supported by his father, had his first work published as an anonymous "Youth of Thirteen." *The Embargo; or, Sketches of the Times* (1808) is a Federalist satire on the policies of President Jefferson, whom Bryant came to admire years later. The poem's vitriolic couplets testify both to Bryant's youthful poetic tendencies and to the still reigning influence of Alexander Pope on American verse. At fifteen, Bryant entered Williams College as a sophomore, but financial difficulties prevented him from transferring to Yale for his junior year. He studied law privately instead and was admitted to the Massachusetts bar in 1814. He wrote a great deal of poetry during those early years of practicing law, and he also served as town clerk of Great Barrington, where in 1821 he married Fanny Fairchild. His *Poems* were published in the same year. Bryant was eager to settle in Boston, but his father discouraged him, noting that there were too many lawyers there already. Poetry provided no alternative as a livelihood. Four years after the publication of his poems, the volume had earned him a meager $14.21.

In 1825 Bryant moved to New York, where he edited a magazine, the *New York Review,* and became part of a literary group that came to be known as the Knickerbocker School and included Washington Irving and James Fenimore Cooper. In 1826 he signed on as the assistant editor of the New York *Evening Post,* and from 1829 to his death in 1878 he served as its editor in chief. An inveterate traveler, Bryant made several trips to Europe and the American frontier (to visit his pioneer brothers) and lengthy visits to Canada, Mexico, and the Caribbean. But New York remained his home and writing his central activity for the rest of his life.

Although Bryant spent more than fifty years there, New York seems to have had little impact on either his character or his poetry. Never quite as urbane as Washington Irving, Bryant maintained the austerity of a New England winter in his life and work. He rarely allowed himself, as he notes in "The Poet," the luxury of "burning words" or "impassioned thought." One early biographer claimed that this predilection may have stemmed from "the fact that when he was a child his parents, becoming alarmed at the unnaturally large size of his head, used to soak it in cold water, sometimes breaking the ice to do so. Bryant never quite got this chill out of his style." A less apocryphal explanation might be Bryant's lifelong interest in the classics and his familiarity with the leading eighteenth-century Neoclassical English poets who wrote on nature and melancholy, especially those in the "Graveyard school," most notably Thomson, Blair, Young, and Gray. This influence is never more apparent than in "Thanatopsis," first published in the newly established *North American Review* in 1817. Recalling the circumstances, one of the editors, Richard Henry Dana, Sr., later wrote:

> Going into town one day while assisting E. T. Channing (now Professor) in the *North American Review* [1817], he read to me a couple of pieces of poetry which had just been sent to the *Review*— the "Thanatopsis" and "The Inscription for the Entrance to a Wood." While C—— was reading one of them, I broke out, saying, "That was never written on this side of the water"—and naturally enough, considering what American poetry had been up to that moment.

Bryant, like many of his contemporaries, was absorbed in the issues surrounding American literary nationalism. He vigorously opposed the lingering tendency of many Americans who "do not praise a thing until [they] see the seal of transatlantic approbation upon it." He insisted that America was "a rich and varied field for literature." Yet, like his counterparts in the art world, particularly his "kindred spirits" in what came to be known as the Hudson River school, Bryant was more successful at introducing indigenous American subjects than in treating them in distinctively American terms.

His literary criticism, however, stands as one of the earliest efforts in the new nation to study poetry systematically. From his *Lectures on Poetry* (delivered in 1825 but published posthumously in 1884) to his essay "Poets and Poetry of the English Language" (printed as the introduction to his anthology, *A Library of Poetry and Song,* in 1871), Bryant consistently focused on the original, imaginative, moral, and didactic properties of poetry. Bryant sought "a luminous style" in his verse, and in reading him we ought to keep in mind his own guidelines for writing it:

> The elements of poetry lie in natural objects, in the vicissitudes of human life, in the emotions of the human heart, and the relations of man to man. He who can present them in combinations and lights which at once affect the mind with a deep sense of their truth and beauty is the poet for his own age and the ages that succeed him. . . . The metaphysician, the subtle thinker, the dealer in abstruse speculations, whatever his skill in versification, misapplies it when he abandons the more convenient form of prose, and perplexes himself with the attempt to express his ideas in poetic numbers.

More than two-thirds of Bryant's poems focus on the natural world. In this respect, his repeated reading of Wordsworth as a youth had a profound impact on his verse. Dana describes the nature of the influence:

> I never shall forget with what feeling my friend Bryant, some years ago, described to me the effect produced upon him by his meeting for the first time with Wordsworth's ballads. He said that, upon opening the book, a thousand springs seemed to gush up at once in his heart, and the face of Nature, of a sudden, to change into a strange freshness and life.

Bryant's enthusiasm for Wordsworth's verse had waned noticeably by the time they finally met in England in 1845. Yet Bryant's vision of nature, like Wordsworth's, remains stately; both write with considerable self-control, emotional distance, and purity of line. And, revealing the influence of Wordsworth, Bryant is the first major American poet to celebrate what would soon become the Romantic tradition of recognizing divine splendor in nature's beauty and taking personal solace from it. In this respect, Bryant spent much of his life using nature and poetry as tools to create a religion to sustain himself. Yet Bryant's calm and powerful poetic voice remains a harbinger rather than an example of the more daring and fiercely independent literary imaginations that would soon demand the attention of mid-nineteenth-century audiences.

Nearly all of Bryant's poetry that claims our attention was written before

1840, when the pressures of editing a major newspaper in one of the nation's largest cities allowed him little time to write verse. Responding to his friend Dana's urging that he leave more time for poetry, Bryant wistfully noted:

> I should be glad of an opportunity to attempt something in the way I like best, and am, perhaps, fittest for; but here I am a draught-horser, harnessed to a daily drag. I have so much to do with my legs and hoofs, struggling and pulling and kicking, that, if there is anything of the Pegasus in me, I am too much exhausted to use my wings.

Bryant knew that there was but a small audience for poetry in the early decades of nineteenth-century America and that, as he told Dana, "no man makes money by it. . . . The taste for it is something old-fashioned; the march of the age is in another direction; mankind are occupied with politics, railroads, and steamboats." Not surprisingly, Bryant's became one of the most respected voices in nineteenth-century American journalism, and his incisive editorials tackled virtually every important issue of the the time. His opinions counted in every public cause, and his presence was felt in innumerable acts of community planning and service.

Bryant's literary efforts in his last few decades focused primarily on translating the *Iliad* (1870) and the *Odyssey* (1872), editing Shakespeare, celebrating American history and literature, and eulogizing the deaths of the nation's leading writers. The most revealing appraisal of Bryant's later life and work is implicit in Nathaniel Hawthorne's description of meeting him in Italy in 1858:

> There was a weary look in his face, as if he were tired of seeing things and doing things, though with certainly enough still to do and see. . . . His manners and whole aspect are particularly plain, though not affectedly so; but it seems as if in the decline of life, and the security of his position, he had put off whatever artificial polish he may heretofore have had, and resumed the simpler habits and deportment of his early New England breeding. . . . He is a man of refinement, who has seen the world, and is well aware of his own place in it.

Bryant remained an extremely popular poet, despite the long intervals between his volumes. By the time of his death in 1878, Bryant had become such a prominent figure in New York intellectual and political circles that the city's flags flew at half mast, its shops draped in black.

Bryant's importance in American literature can be considered in the appraisals of his more distinguished contemporaries. Edgar Allan Poe called Bryant "full of the aristocracy of intellect." Ralph Waldo Emerson praised Bryant as "always original—a true painter of the face of the country, and of the sentiment of his own people. . . . It is his proper praise that he first, and he only, made known to mankind our northern landscape—its summer splendor, its autumn russet, its winter lights and glooms." But it is Walt Whitman who offers the most expansive version of Bryant's achievement:

Bryant pulsing the first interior verse-throbs of a mighty world—bard of the river and the wood, ever conveying a taste of open air . . . always lurkingly fond of threnodies—beginning and ending his long career with chants of death . . . touching the highest universal truth, enthusiasms, duties—morals as grim and eternal, if not as stormy and fateful, as anything in Aeschylus.

Further Reading:
P. Godwin, *The Life and Works of William Cullen Bryant,* 2 vols., 1883.
J. Bigelow, *William Cullen Bryant,* 1890.
W. A. Bradley, *William Cullen Bryant,* 1905.
A. Nevins, *The Evening Post: A Century of Journalism,* 1922.
Bryant, ed. T. McDowell, 1935.
H. H. Peckham, *Gotham Yankee: A Biography of William Cullen Bryant,* 1950.
C. S. Johnson, *Politics and a Bellyful: The Journalistic Career of William Cullen Bryant,* 1962.
A. McLean, *William Cullen Bryant,* 1964.
C. Brown, *William Cullen Bryant,* 1972.

Text:
The Poetical Works of William Cullen Bryant, ed. P. Godwin, 2 vols., 1883.

Thanatopsis[1]

To him who in the love of Nature holds
Communion with her visible forms, she speaks
A various language; for his gayer hours
She has a voice of gladness, and a smile
And eloquence of beauty, and she glides   5
Into his darker musings, with a mild
And healing sympathy, that steals away
Their sharpness, ere he is aware. When thoughts
Of the last bitter hour come like a blight
Over thy spirit, and sad images   10
Of the stern agony, and shroud, and pall,
And breathless darkness, and the narrow house,
Make thee to shudder, and grow sick at heart;—
Go forth, under the open sky, and list
To Nature's teachings, while from all around—   15
Earth and her waters, and the depths of air—
Comes a still voice.—

                  Yet a few days, and thee
The all-beholding sun shall see no more

[1] Greek: "Meditation on Death."

In all his course; nor yet in the cold ground,
Where thy pale form was laid, with many tears,   20
Nor in the embrace of ocean, shall exist
Thy image. Earth, that nourished thee, shall claim
Thy growth, to be resolved to earth again,
And, lost each human trace, surrendering up
Thine individual being, shalt thou go   25
To mix for ever with the elements,
To be a brother to the insensible rock
And to the sluggish clod, which the rude swain
Turns with his share,[2] and treads upon. The oak
Shall send his roots abroad, and pierce thy mould.   30

    Yet not to thine eternal resting-place
Shalt thou retire alone, nor couldst thou wish
Couch more magnificent. Thou shalt lie down
With patriarchs of the infant world—with kings,
The powerful of the earth—the wise, the good,   35
Fair forms, and hoary seers of ages past,
All in one mighty sepulchre. The hills
Rock-ribbed and ancient as the sun,—the vales
Stretching in pensive quietness between;
The venerable woods—rivers that move   40
In majesty, and the complaining brooks
That make the meadows green; and, poured round all,
Old Ocean's gray and melancholy waste,—
Are but the solemn decorations all
Of the great tomb of man. The golden sun,   45
The planets, all the infinite host of heaven,
Are shining on the sad abodes of death,
Through the still lapse of ages. All that tread
The globe are but a handful to the tribes
That slumber in its bosom.—Take the wings   50
Of morning, pierce the Barcan wilderness,[3]
Or lose thyself in the continuous woods
Where rolls the Oregon,[4] and hears no sound,
Save his own dashings—yet the dead are there:
And millions in those solitudes, since first   55
The flight of years began, have laid them down
In their last sleep—the dead reign there alone.
So shalt thou rest, and what if thou withdraw
In silence from the living, and no friend
Take note of thy departure? All that breathe   60
Will share thy destiny. The gay will laugh
When thou art gone, the solemn brood of care

---

[2] Plowshare.
[3] The desert of Barca in northeast Libya.

[4] Indian name for what is now the Columbia River.

Plod on, and each one as before will chase
His favorite phantom; yet all these shall leave
Their mirth and their employments, and shall come   65
And make their bed with thee. As the long train
Of ages glides away, the sons of men,
The youth in life's fresh spring, and he who goes
In the full strength of years, matron and maid,
The speechless babe, and the gray-headed man—   70
Shall one by one be gathered to thy side,
By those, who in their turn shall follow them.

So live, that when thy summons comes to join
The innumerable caravan, which moves
To that mysterious realm, where each shall take   75
His chamber in the silent halls of death,
Thou go not, like the quarry-slave at night,
Scourged to his dungeon, but, sustained and soothed
By an unfaltering trust, approach thy grave,
Like one who wraps the drapery of his couch   80
About him, and lies down to pleasant dreams.

ca. 1814/1817; 1821

Inscription for the Entrance to a Wood

Stranger, if thou hast learned a truth which needs
No school of long experience, that the world
Is full of guilt and misery, and hast seen
Enough of all its sorrows, crimes, and cares,
To tire thee of it, enter this wild wood   5
And view the haunts of Nature. The calm shade
Shall bring a kindred calm, and the sweet breeze
That makes the green leaves dance, shall waft a balm
To thy sick heart. Thou wilt find nothing here
Of all that pained thee in the haunts of men,   10
And made thee loathe thy life. The primal curse[1]
Fell, it is true, upon the unsinning earth,
But not in vengeance. God hath yoked to guilt
Her pale tormentor, misery. Hence, these shades

---

[1] The curse of God placed on all creatures of the
earth upon the exile of Adam and Eve from
the Garden of Eden. (See Genesis 3.)

Are still the abodes of gladness; the thick roof   15
Of green and stirring branches is alive
And musical with birds, that sing and sport
In wantonness of spirit; while below
The squirrel, with raised paws and form erect,
Chirps merrily. Throngs of insects in the shade   20
Try their thin wings and dance in the warm beam
That waked them into life. Even the green trees
Partake the deep contentment; as they bend
To the soft winds, the sun from the blue sky
Looks in and sheds a blessing on the scene.   25
Scarce less the cleft-born wild-flower seems to enjoy
Existence than the wingèd plunderer
That sucks its sweets. The mossy rocks themselves,
And the old and ponderous trunks of prostrate trees
That lead from knoll to knoll a causey[2] rude   30
Or bridge the sunken brook, and their dark roots,
With all their earth upon them, twisting high,
Breathe fixed tranquillity. The rivulet
Sends forth glad sounds, and tripping o'er its bed
Of pebbly sands, or leaping down the rocks,   35
Seems, with continuous laughter, to rejoice
In its own being. Softly tread the marge,[3]
Lest from her midway perch thou scare the wren
That dips her bill in water. The cool wind,
That stirs the stream in play, shall come to thee,   40
Like one that loves thee nor will let thee pass
Ungreeted, and shall give its light embrace.
1817

To a Waterfowl

Whither, midst falling dew,
    While glow the heavens with the last steps of day,
Far, through their rosy depths, dost thou pursue
    Thy solitary way?

    Vainly the fowler's eye   5
Might mark thy distant flight to do thee wrong,
As, darkly painted on the crimson sky,
    Thy figure floats along.

[2] Obsolete term for causeway.   [3] Archaic: border or edge.

Seek'st thou the plashy brink
Of weedy lake, or marge of river wide,   10
Or where the rocking billows rise and sink
    On the chafed ocean-side?

There is a Power whose care
Teaches thy way along that pathless coast—
The desert and illimitable air—   15
    Lone wandering, but not lost.

All day thy wings have fanned,
At that far height, the cold, thin atmosphere,
Yet stoop not, weary, to the welcome land,
    Though the dark night is near.   20

And soon that toil shall end;
Soon shalt thou find a summer home, and rest,
And scream among thy fellows; reeds shall bend,
    Soon, o'er thy sheltered nest.

Thou'rt gone, the abyss of heaven   25
Hath swallowed up thy form; yet, on my heart
Deeply has sunk the lesson thou hast given,
    And shall not soon depart.

He who, from zone to zone,
Guides through the boundless sky thy certain flight,   30
In the long way that I must tread alone,
    Will lead my steps aright.

1815/1818; 1821

The Yellow Violet

When beechen buds begin to swell,
    And woods the blue-bird's warble know,
The yellow violet's modest bell
    Peeps from the last year's leaves below.

Ere russet fields their green resume,   5
    Sweet flower, I love, in forest bare,
To meet thee, when thy faint perfume
    Alone is in the virgin air.

Of all her train, the hands of Spring
    First plant thee in the watery mould,   10
And I have seen thee blossoming
    Beside the snow-bank's edges cold.

Thy parent sun, who bade thee view
    Pale skies, and chilling moisture sip,
Has bathed thee in his own bright hue,   15
    And streaked with jet thy glowing lip.

Yet slight thy form, and low thy seat,
    And earthward bent thy gentle eye,
Unapt the passing view to meet,
    When loftier flowers are flaunting nigh.   20

Oft, in the sunless April day,
    Thy early smile has stayed my walk;
But midst the gorgeous blooms of May,
    I passed thee on thy humble stalk.

So they, who climb to wealth, forget   25
    The friends in darker fortunes tried.
I copied them—but I regret
    That I should ape the ways of pride.

And when again the genial hour
    Awakes the painted tribes of light.   30
I'll not o'erlook the modest flower
    That made the woods of April bright.

1814/1821

A Forest Hymn

The groves were God's first temples. Ere man learned
To hew the shaft, and lay the architrave,
And spread the roof above them—ere he framed
The lofty vault, to gather and roll back
The sound of anthems; in the darkling wood,   5
Amid the cool and silence, he knelt down,
And offered to the Mightiest solemn thanks
And supplication. For his simple heart
Might not resist the sacred influence

Which, from the stilly twilight of the place,   10
And from the gray old trunks that high in heaven
Mingled their mossy boughs, and from the sound
Of the invisible breath that swayed at once
All their green tops, stole over him, and bowed
His spirit with the thought of boundless power   15
And inaccessible majesty. Ah, why
Should we, in the world's riper years, neglect
God's ancient sanctuaries, and adore
Only among the crowd, and under roofs
That our frail hands have raised? Let me, at least,   20
Here, in the shadow of this aged wood,
Offer one hymn—thrice happy, if it find
Acceptance in His ear.

                    Father, thy hand
Hath reared these venerable columns, thou
Didst weave this verdant roof. Thou didst look down   25
Upon the naked earth, and, forthwith, rose
All these fair ranks of trees. They, in thy sun,
Budded, and shook their green leaves in thy breeze,
And shot toward heaven. The century-living crow
Whose birth was in their tops, grew old and died   30
Among their branches, till, at last, they stood,
As now they stand, massy, and tall, and dark,
Fit shrine for humble worshipper to hold
Communion with his Maker. These dim vaults,
These winding aisles, of human pomp or pride   35
Report not. No fantastic carvings show
The boast of our vain race to change the form
Of thy fair works. But thou art here—thou fill'st
The solitude. Thou art in the soft winds
That run along the summit of these trees   40
In music; thou art in the cooler breath
That from the inmost darkness of the place
Comes, scarcely felt; the barky trunks, the ground,
The fresh moist ground, are all instinct with thee.
Here is continual worship;—Nature, here,   45
In the tranquillity that thou dost love,
Enjoys thy presence. Noiselessly, around,
From perch to perch, the solitary bird
Passes; and yon clear spring, that, midst its herbs,
Wells softly forth and wandering steeps the roots   50
Of half the mighty forest, tells no tale
Of all the good it does. Thou hast not left
Thyself without a witness, in the shades,
Of thy perfections. Grandeur, strength, and grace

Are here to speak of thee. This mighty oak— 55
By whose immovable stem I stand and seem
Almost annihilated—not a prince,
In all that proud old world beyond the deep,
E'er wore his crown as loftily as he
Wears the green coronal of leaves with which 60
Thy hand has graced him. Nestled at his root
Is beauty, such as blooms not in the glare
Of the broad sun. That delicate forest flower,
With scented breath and look so like a smile,
Seems, as it issues from the shapeless mould, 65
An emanation of the indwelling Life,
A visible token of the upholding Love,
That are the soul of this great universe.

   My heart is awed within me when I think
Of the great miracle that still goes on, 70
In silence, round me—the perpetual work
Of thy creation, finished, yet renewed
Forever. Written on thy works I read
The lesson of thy own eternity.
Lo! all grow old and die—but see again, 75
How on the faltering footsteps of decay
Youth presses—ever gay and beautiful youth
In all its beautiful forms. These lofty trees
Wave not less proudly that their ancestors
Moulder beneath them. Oh, there is not lost 80
One of earth's charms: upon her bosom yet,
After the flight of untold centuries,
The freshness of her far beginning lies
And yet shall lie. Life mocks the idle hate
Of his arch-enemy Death—yea, seats himself 85
Upon the tyrant's throne—the sepulchre,
And of the triumphs of his ghastly foe
Makes his own nourishment. For he came forth
From thine own bosom, and shall have no end.

   There have been holy men who hid themselves 90
Deep in the woody wilderness, and gave
Their lives to thought and prayer, till they outlived
The generation born with them, nor seemed
Less aged than the hoary trees and rocks
Around them;—and there have been holy men 95
Who deemed it were not well to pass life thus.
But let me often to these solitudes
Retire, and in thy presence reassure
My feeble virtue. Here its enemies,
The passions, at thy plainer footsteps shrink 100

And tremble and are still. O God! when thou
Dost scare the world with tempests, set on fire
The heavens with falling thunderbolts, or fill,
With all the waters of the firmament,
The swift dark whirlwind that uproots the woods   105
And drowns the villages; when, at thy call,
Uprises the great deep and throws himself
Upon the continent, and overwhelms
Its cities—who forgets not, at the sight
Of these tremendous tokens of thy power,   110
His pride, and lays his strifes and follies by?
Oh, from these sterner aspects of thy face
Spare me and mine, nor let us need the wrath
Of the mad unchained elements to teach
Who rules them. Be it ours to meditate,   115
In these calm shades, thy milder majesty,
And to the beautiful order of thy works
Learn to conform the order of our lives.

1825

To Cole, the Painter, Departing for Europe*

Thine eyes shall see the light of distant skies;
    Yet, COLE! thy heart shall bear to Europe's strand
    A living image of our own bright land,
Such as upon thy glorious canvas lies;
Lone lakes—savannas where the bison roves—   5
    Rocks rich with summer garlands—solemn streams—
    Skies, where the desert eagle wheels and screams—
Spring bloom and autumn blaze of boundless groves.
Fair scenes shall greet thee where thou goest—fair,
    But different—everywhere the trace of men,   10
    Paths, homes, graves, ruins, from the lowest glen
To where life shrinks from the fierce Alpine air.
    Gaze on them, till the tears shall dim thy sight,
    But keep that earlier, wilder image bright.

1829/1830

* Addressed to Bryant's friend Thomas Cole
(1801–1848), English-born painter of naturalist
American landscapes.

To the Fringed Gentian

Thou blossom bright with autumn dew,
And colored with the heaven's own blue,
That openest when the quiet light
Succeeds the keen and frosty night.

Thou comest not when violets lean   5
O'er wandering brooks and springs unseen,
Or columbines, in purple dressed,
Nod o'er the ground-bird's hidden nest.

Thou waitest late and com'st alone,
When woods are bare and birds are flown,   10
And frosts and shortening days portend
The aged year is near his end.

Then doth thy sweet and quiet eye
Look through its fringes to the sky,
Blue—blue—as if that sky let fall   15
A flower from its cerulean wall.

I would that thus, when I shall see
The hour of death draw near to me,
Hope, blossoming within my heart,
May look to heaven as I depart.   20

1829/1832

The Prairies[*]

These are the gardens of the Desert,[1] these
The unshorn fields, boundless and beautiful,
For which the speech of England has no name[2]—
The Prairies. I behold them for the first,
And my heart swells, while the dilated sight   5

---

[*] Written after Bryant's first view of the prairies of Illinois in 1832.

[1] In the early nineteenth century, the Great Plains of the American West were considered the "Great American Desert."

[2] The word *prairie* was adopted from the French explorers' term *la prairie*, meaning "meadow."

Takes in the encircling vastness. Lo! they stretch,
In airy undulations, far away,
As if the ocean, in his gentlest swell,
Stood still, with all his rounded billows fixed,
And motionless forever.—Motionless?—   10
No—they are all unchained again. The clouds
Sweep over with their shadows, and, beneath,
The surface rolls and fluctuates to the eye;
Dark hollows seem to glide along and chase
The sunny ridges. Breezes of the South!   15
Who toss the golden and the flame-like flowers,
And pass the prairie-hawk that, poised on high,
Flaps his broad wings, yet moves not—ye have played
Among the palms of Mexico and vines
Of Texas, and have crisped the limpid brooks   20
That from the fountains of Sonora[3] glide
Into the calm Pacific—have ye fanned
A nobler or a lovelier scene than this?
Man hath no power in all this glorious work:
The hand that built the firmament hath heaved   25
And smoothed these verdant swells, and sown their slopes
With herbage, planted them with island groves,
And hedged them round with forests. Fitting floor
For this magnificent temple of the sky—
With flowers whose glory and whose multitude   30
Rival the constellations! The great heavens
Seem to stoop down upon the scene in love,—
A nearer vault, and of a tenderer blue,
Than that which bends above our eastern hills.

As o'er the verdant waste I guide my steed,   35
Among the high rank grass that sweeps his sides
The hollow beating of his footstep seems
A sacrilegious sound. I think of those
Upon whose rest he tramples. Are they here—
The dead of other days?—and did the dust   40
Of these fair solitudes once stir with life
And burn with passion? Let the mighty mounds[4]
That overlook the rivers, or that rise
In the dim forest crowded with old oaks,
Answer. A race, that long has passed away,   45
Built them;—a disciplined and populous race
Heaped, with long toil, the earth, while yet the Greek
Was hewing the Pentelicus[5] to forms

[3] State in northwest Mexico.
[4] Indian burial earthworks ascribed to a vanished
race of ancient "mound builders."

[5] Greek Mt. Pentelikon, the site from which
marble was quarried for the Parthenon.

Of symmetry, and rearing on its rock
The glittering Parthenon. These ample fields   50
Nourished their harvests, here their herds were fed,
When haply by their stalls the bison lowed,
And bowed his manèd shoulder to the yoke.
All day this desert murmured with their toils,
Till twilight blushed, and lovers walked, and wooed   55
In a forgotten language, and old tunes,
From instruments of unremembered form,
Gave the soft winds a voice. The red man came—
The roaming hunter tribes, warlike and fierce,
And the mound-builders vanished from the earth.   60
The solitude of centuries untold
Has settled where they dwelt. The prairie-wolf
Hunts in their meadows, and his fresh-dug den
Yawns by my path. The gopher mines the ground
Where stood their swarming cities. All is gone;   65
All—save the piles of earth that hold their bones,
The platforms where they worshipped unknown gods,
The barriers which they builded from the soil
To keep the foe at bay—till o'er the walls
The wild beleaguerers broke, and, one by one,   70
The strongholds of the plain were forced, and heaped
With corpses. The brown vultures of the wood
Flocked to those vast uncovered sepulchres,
And sat unscared and silent at their feast.
Haply some solitary fugitive,   75
Lurking in marsh and forest, till the sense
Of desolation and of fear became
Bitterer than death, yielded himself to die.
Man's better nature triumphed then. Kind words
Welcomed and soothed him; the rude conquerors   80
Seated the captive with their chiefs; he chose
A bride among their maidens, and at length
Seemed to forget—yet ne'er forgot—the wife
Of his first love, and her sweet little ones,
Butchered, amid their shrieks, with all his race.   85

   Thus change the forms of being. Thus arise
Races of living things, glorious in strength,
And perish, as the quickening breath of God
Fills them, or is withdrawn. The red man, too,
Has left the blooming wilds he ranged so long,   90
And, nearer to the Rocky Mountains, sought
A wilder hunting-ground. The beaver builds
No longer by these streams, but far away,
On waters whose blue surface ne'er gave back
The white man's face—among Missouri's springs,   95

And pools whose issues swell the Oregon[6]—
He rears his little Venice. In these plains
The bison feeds no more. Twice twenty leagues
Beyond remotest smoke of hunter's camp,
Roams the majestic brute, in herds that shake   100
The earth with thundering steps—yet here I meet
His ancient footprints stamped beside the pool.

    Still this great solitude is quick with life.
Myriads of insects, gaudy as the flowers
They flutter over, gentle quadrupeds,   105
And birds, that scarce have learned the fear of man,
Are here, and sliding reptiles of the ground,
Startlingly beautiful. The graceful deer
Bounds to the wood at my approach. The bee,
A more adventurous colonist than man,   110
With whom he came across the eastern deep,
Fills the savannas with his murmurings,
And hides his sweets, as in the golden age,
Within the hollow oak. I listen long
To his domestic hum, and think I hear   115
The sound of that advancing multitude
Which soon shall fill these deserts. From the ground
Comes up the laugh of children, the soft voice
Of maidens, and the sweet and solemn hymn
Of Sabbath worshippers. The low of herds   120
Blends with the rustling of the heavy grain
Over the dark brown furrows. All at once
A fresher wind sweeps by, and breaks my dream,
And I am in the wilderness alone.

1832/1833

The Poet

Thou, who wouldst wear the name
    Of poet mid thy brethren of mankind,
And clothe in words of flame
    Thoughts that shall live within the general mind!
Deem not the framing of a deathless lay   5
    The pastime of a drowsy summer day.

[6] The Columbia River.

But gather all thy powers,
    And wreak them on the verse that thou dost
      weave,
And in thy lonely hours,
    At silent morning or at wakeful eve,   10
While the warm current tingles through thy veins,
Set forth the burning words in fluent strains.

No smooth array of phrase,
    Artfully sought and ordered though it be,
Which the cold rhymer lays   15
    Upon his page with languid industry,
Can wake the listless pulse to livelier speed,
Or fill with sudden tears the eyes that read.

The secret wouldst thou know
    To touch the heart or fire the blood at will?   20
Let thine own eyes o'erflow;
    Let thy lips quiver with the passionate thrill;
Seize the great thought, ere yet its power be past,
And bind, in words, the fleet emotion fast.

Then, should thy verse appear   25
    Halting and harsh, and all unaptly wrought,
Touch the crude line with fear,
    Save in the moment of impassioned thought;
Then summon back the original glow, and mend
The strain with rapture that with fire was penned.   30

Yet let no empty gust
    Of passion find an utterance in thy lay,
A blast that whirls the dust
    Along the howling street and dies away;
But feelings of calm power and mighty sweep,   35
Like currents journeying through the windless deep.

Seek'st thou, in living lays,
    To limn the beauty of the earth and sky?
Before thine inner gaze
    Let all that beauty in clear vision lie;   40
Look on it with exceeding love, and write
The words inspired by wonder and delight.

Of tempests wouldst thou sing,
    Or tell of battles—make thyself a part
Of the great tumult; cling   45
    To the tossed wreck with terror in thy heart;

Scale, with the assaulting host, the rampart's height,
And strike and struggle in the thickest fight.

So shalt thou frame a lay
    That haply may endure from age to age,   50
And they who read shall say:
    "What witchery hangs upon this poet's page!
What art is his the written spells to find
That sway from mood to mood the willing mind!"
1863/1864

Abraham Lincoln*

Oh, slow to smite and swift to spare,
    Gentle and merciful and just!
Who, in the fear of God, didst bear
    The sword of power, a nation's trust!

In sorrow by thy bier we stand,   5
    Amid the awe that hushes all,
And speak the anguish of a land
    That shook with horror at thy fall.

Thy task is done; the bond are free;
    We bear thee to an honored grave,   10
Whose proudest monument shall be
    The broken fetters of the slave.

Pure was thy life; its bloody close
    Hath placed thee with the sons of light,
Among the noble host of those   15
    Who perished in the cause of Right.
1865

---

* Written following the assassination of Lincoln on April 14, 1865, and read to a crowd of mourners gathered at New York's Union Square on April 24, 1865.

George Caleb Bingham,
Daniel Boone Escorting Settlers Through the Cumberland Gap,
oil on canvas, 1851–1852.
Collection, Washington University Gallery of Art, St. Louis.

The Literature of the American Renaissance 1836–1865

"Who Reads an American Book?"

 Could literature and art, as defined by colonial standards, thrive in the new nation? Were they at all appropriate to the special political, social, and economic conditions Americans found and in turn created? How could the language and literary models of England be naturalized to these conditions? Was there a cultural counterpart to political independence? These were some of the issues confronting the men and women who became the writers of the American Renaissance.

"We have no distinct class of literati in our country," Thomas Jefferson had noted. "Every man is engaged in some industrious pursuit. . . . Few therefore of those who are qualified have leisure to write." Former President John Quincy Adams declared "that literature was, and in its nature must always be, aristocratic; that democracy of numbers and literature were self-contradictory." Democratic nations, said Alexis de Tocqueville after visiting Jacksonian America in 1831, "will habitually prefer the useful to the beautiful, and they will require that the beautiful should be useful." Americans were newspaper readers, he said, and they relied on newspapers to "maintain civilization." "The universal equality of conditions spreads a monotonous tint over all society," said his traveling companion, the novelist Gustave de Beaumont; he warned Europeans not to "look for poetry, literature, or fine arts in this country." When one of the proprietors of the *North*

American Review first read young William Cullen Bryant's blank verse, Wordsworthian "Thanatopsis" (1817), a poem subsequently hailed as the finest yet written in America, he assumed the author was British: "No one on this side of the Atlantic is capable of writing such verse."

Washington Irving and James Fenimore Cooper, both successful professional men of letters, believed they had overcome cultural and economic obstacles likely to discourage other native writers. Americans were supposedly too busy making money and taming the wilderness to have leisure for literary reading, but with a few notable exceptions, chiefly the work of Irving and Cooper, most of the books they did read were written in England. This was partly due to a shortsighted Copyright Act, passed by the First Congress in 1790, that granted protection only to citizens or residents of the United States. All others were fair game for "pirates," publishers of unauthorized editions. The act's implicit rejection of international copyright encouraged American book, magazine, and newspaper publishers to favor foreign authors, whose work they could get for nothing and bring out cheaply, thereby neglecting or exploiting native authors, to whom they had to pay royalties or fees. ("Who will give two dollars a volume for Prescott," asked the author of *The Conquest of Peru,* "when they can buy Macaulay for seventy-five cents?") Established authors like Irving and Cooper brought out their own books and paid publishers a commission to distribute them, while untested American authors simply took their chances. Harper & Brothers paid Richard Henry Dana, Jr., a total of $250 for the copyright on his *Two Years Before the Mast* (1840), a best-seller that earned them about $50,000 before their license ran out. Outspoken opponents of international copyright, Harper & Brothers soon became the largest publisher in the world, with over fifteen hundred titles in print by midcentury.

After 1836 Charles Dickens succeeded Sir Walter Scott as the most popular author of both hemispheres and, consequently, chief victim of the pirates. "Dickens' *American Notes* were received by us at eight o'clock on Sunday evening," the publishers of the weekly *New World* announced on November 12, 1842. "We printed them complete in a double extra number . . . and issued them at one o'clock on Monday—being precisely seventeen hours from the time 'the copy was put in hand.'" They predicted a sale of 400,000 copies, not one of which would earn Dickens a penny. "There must be an international copyright agreement," he had argued on his visit to the United States earlier that year. "It becomes the character of a great country; firstly, because it is justice; secondly, because without it you can never have, and keep, a literature of your own." (Half a century later an International Copyright Law finally stood on the statute books.)

As yet without the annals, traditions, and associations that nurtured Old World writers, the United States offered its own a "poverty of materials," Cooper said. "The weakest hand can extract a spark from the flint, but it would baffle the strength of a giant to attempt kindling a flame with a pudding-stone." Yet Cooper had a shrewd sense of the future. "The literature of the United States is a subject of the highest interest to the civilized world," he wrote, "for when it does begin to be felt, it will be felt with a force, a directness, and a common sense in its application, that has never yet been known. . . . I think the time for the experiment is getting near."

John L. O'Sullivan launched his grandly titled *United States Magazine and Democratic Review* in 1837 with a declaration of purpose: "The vital principle of our literature must be democracy. . . . All history is to be rewritten; political science and the whole scope of moral truth have to be reconsidered in the light of the democratic principle." Following its "manifest destiny," a resounding slogan that O'Sullivan coined, messianic "Young America" was "to overspread the continent allotted by Providence for the free development of our yearly multiplying millions" and also lead the world to salvation by the road of republicanism. In ideology as well as religion this was an evangelical age. "We Americans are the peculiar, chosen people—the Israel of our times," Herman Melville wrote in 1850. "We bear the ark of the liberties of the world. . . . In our youth is our strength; in our inexperience, our wisdom." Writing in praise of Hawthorne's *Mosses from an Old Manse,* he declared that "men not very much inferior to Shakespeare are this day being born on the banks of the Ohio."

Similar spread-eagle sentiments were voiced all through the period. They were undoubtedly good for morale, but they were not necessarily good for literature and criticism. "It is now the fashion to extol everything American," Cooper observed. "The country is filled, today, with the most profound provincial self-admiration." "We are becoming boisterous and arrogant in the pride of a too speedily assumed literary freedom," said Poe. "We get up a hue and cry about the necessity of encouraging native writers of merit—we blindly fancy that we can accomplish this by indiscriminate puffing of good, bad, and indifferent . . . and thus often find ourselves involved in the gross paradox of liking a stupid book the better, because, sure enough, its stupidity is American." Poe was a universalist rather than a nationalist. He developed a body of literary theory that drew upon many European sources, and he enjoyed a considerable reputation in England and Europe, particularly among Charles Baudelaire and the French Symbolists. As editor he anticipated the great magazine-reading audience that arrived in full force only after the Civil War. As poet and fiction writer he courted the public's favor—and from time to time won it to a spectacular degree. During the later 1840s Poe's raven, the dusky phantom of his most popular poem, was so celebrated that it vied with the eagle for the title of national bird.

In *Kavanagh: A Tale* (1849), Longfellow satirized the rant of the "Young America" movement. "We want a national literature commensurate with our mountains and rivers," one of his characters announces. "We want a national literature altogether shaggy and unshorn, that shall shake the earth, like a herd of buffaloes, thundering over the prairies!" It was clear that something more than bluster and false analogies was called for if the country were to have a culture in keeping with its political character. "It does not follow because many books are written by persons born in America that there exists an American literature," Margaret Fuller wrote in 1846. "Before such can exist, an original idea must animate this nation and fresh currents of life must call into life fresh thoughts along its shores."

There were several main issues in this ongoing discussion. One, whether America provided a favorable cultural climate for writers, artists, and intellectuals, was to be debated again and again, after the Civil War and especially during the 1920s. But a second issue, whether America was capable of making a literature of its own fit to stand with the literatures of the Old World, simply ceased to exist. In retrospect one has only to point to two native poetic geniuses flourishing around midcentury, Walt Whitman and Emily Dickinson (her poems, written mainly during the early 1860s, were not published until several years after her death in 1886). As for broad popularity, Harriet Beecher Stowe and Henry Wadsworth Longfellow alone offered a sufficient rejoinder to the English wit Sydney Smith's gibe, "In the four quarters of the globe, who reads an American book?" London bookshops in 1852 displayed twenty different editions of *Uncle Tom's Cabin.* By 1856 this novel had sold nearly a million copies in the British Isles, had been translated into every European language, and was on its way to achieving a global popularity second only to that of the Bible. As for Longfellow, "No other poet has anything like your vogue," Hawthorne wrote to him from England in 1855, when Longfellow brought out *The Song of Hiawatha,* a long poem dealing with a native theme but treating it in accordance with the conventions of Norse epic. On publication day in 1858, Londoners bought some ten thousand copies of Longfellow's *The Courtship of Miles Standish,* another excursion into national legend. His reputation collapsed in the twentieth century, but his sculptured portrait, installed in the Poets' Corner at Westminster Abbey in 1884, two years after his death, continues to keep company with Chaucer, Spenser, and Shakespeare.

A wondrous half decade, 1850–1855, saw the publication of Hawthorne's *The Scarlet Letter* and *The House of the Seven Gables,* Melville's *Moby-Dick* and *Pierre,* Thoreau's *Walden,* and Whitman's *Leaves of Grass.* Together their short-term sales may not have exceeded that of any single now-forgotten domestic novel of the 1850s (Susan Warner's *The Wide, Wide World,* for example, or Mrs. E. D. E. N. Southworth's *The Curse of Clifton*). Most of these American classics, as they are now seen to be, did not begin to receive their full due until the 1920s. Like all significant and lasting art, they are autonomous, self-contained, self-justifying, and even to some extent self-generated. Still, neither Hawthorne's books nor those of Melville, Thoreau, and Whitman could have emerged from any other country in any other century, nor did they happen overnight or in a vacuum. "It takes a great deal of history to produce a little literature," Henry James was to say. "It needs a complex social machinery to set a writer in motion."

"The Infinitude of the Private Man"

"There are always two parties," Emerson wrote, "the party of the Past and the party of the Future; the Establishment and the Movement." He and the Reverend Theodore Parker, another prominent spokesman for Transcendentalism, claimed it was not a concerted party or movement at all but a loose confederation of compatible souls. Having imbibed a distillate of Kant, Goethe, Coleridge, Wordsworth, Carlyle, and other philosophical and literary idealists, the Transcendentalists set about their business in a characteristically self-reliant way. Embroiled in a doctrinal controversy over Holy Communion, Emerson went through a personal crisis and resigned from the Unitarian ministry to follow a career as writer and lecturer. Parker continued in the ministry but exhausted himself in debates and reforms. Margaret Fuller published the first major

American feminist treatise, *Woman in the Nineteenth Century,* in 1845; the following year she went to Europe as foreign correspondent for Horace Greeley's *New York Tribune* and committed herself to the cause of Italian nationalism. Thoreau built his hut at Walden Pond, was jailed for refusing to pay a poll tax, and preached civil disobedience.

Transcendentalism had only a scant organizational existence. It began as an informal "club," first convened in 1836. It generated *The Dial,* a quarterly journal of "literature, philosophy, and religion," edited by Fuller and Emerson, which lasted only four years (1840–1844), never reached a circulation of over three hundred, and was frequently ridiculed for unballasted flights into the empyrean. And it inspired two experiments in cooperative living and high thinking near Boston: Brook Farm (1841–1847) and Fruitlands (1843). Yet, out of all proportion to these evidences, Transcendentalism, especially as channeled through Emerson, generated a significant reexamination of values even in those who derided it. Reversing the European historical order, the Transcendental "reformation," announcing a gospel of spiritual self-sufficiency, came before the literary "renaissance," an awakening, maturation, and release of radical energies.

The Transcendentalists set themselves against what they considered to be the materialism, rationalism, conformity, and played-out liberalism of American religion and society. The social reformer William Henry Channing recalled the movement as inspiring "a vague yet exalting conception of the godlike nature of the human spirit" and "a pilgrimage from the idolatrous world of creeds and rituals to the temple of the Living God in the soul." Ideas of God, right and wrong, and immortality were not matters of doctrine or theology but, according to Parker, "facts of consciousness given by the instinctive action of human nature itself." The Transcendentalists contemplated the actualities of life in the street, the mill, the farmhouse, and the marketplace and aimed to restore to the humblest persons and pursuits a measure of poetry, religious impulse, mystery, surprise, joy, and dread and a sense of wonder and oneness with the universe. "I have taught

---

Letter to the Church in Purchase Street

There is a class of persons who desire a reform in the prevailing philosophy of the day. These are called Transcendentalists, because they believe in an order of truths which transcends the sphere of the external sense. Their leading idea is the supremacy of mind over matter. Hence they maintain that the truth of religion does not depend on tradition, nor historical facts, but has an unerring witness in the soul. There is a light, they believe, which enlighteneth every man that cometh into the world; there is a faculty in all—the most degraded, the most ignorant, the most obscure—to perceive spiritual truth when distinctly presented; and the ultimate appeal on all moral questions is not to a jury of scholars, a hierarchy of divines, or the prescriptions of a creed, but to the common sense of the human race.

George Ripley (1840)

one doctrine," Emerson said, "the infinitude of the private man." "All Souls' Day" had dawned: Each and every person was at once priest, church, and Bible, "a part of eternity and immensity, a god walking in flesh." "So we saunter toward the Holy Land," Thoreau wrote, "till one day the sun shall shine more brightly than ever he has done, shall perchance shine into our minds and hearts, and light up our whole lives with a great awakening light, as warm and serene and golden as on a bankside in autumn."

Transcendentalism arrived as social and religious protest. The conservative theologian Andrews Norton denounced it as "the latest form of infidelity," an unassisted and therefore arrogant attempt to attain assurance "concerning the unseen, the eternal, the great objects of religion." By the 1870s much of Transcendentalism's radical force had become diluted, dissipated, and factional. Emerson's particular brand ended up buttressing the cult of success. "Money is, in its effects and laws, as beautiful as roses," he said. "Property keeps the accounts of the world, and is always moral." After the Civil War, princes of industry and finance quoted his advice, "Hitch your wagon to a star," and installed him in the pantheon of American practical philosophers along with Benjamin Franklin. But Transcendentalism, as Emerson articulated it during the 1830s and 1840s, deplored materialism. A religious, ethical, and aesthetic response to nationalism, a homegrown counterpart of European romanticism with elements drawn from Eastern philosophy, this "latest form of infidelity" proved to be the animating force without which, as Margaret Fuller said, there could be no "American literature."

Responses to *The American Scholar*

Out of the West comes a clear utterance, clearly recognizable as a *man's* voice, and I *have* a kinsman and brother: God be thanked for it! I could have *wept* to read that speech; the clear high melody of it went tingling through my heart. . . . My brave Emerson!

Thomas Carlyle (1837)

This grand oration was our intellectual Declaration of Independence. . . . No listener ever forgot that Address, and among all the noble utterances of the speaker it may be questioned if one ever contained more truth in language more like that of immediate inspiration.

Oliver Wendell Holmes (1885)

We were socially and intellectually moored to English thought, till Emerson cut the cable and gave us a chance at the dangers and glories of blue water. . . . His oration before the Phi Beta Kappa Society at Cambridge, some thirty years ago, was an event without any former parallel in our literary annals.

James Russell Lowell (1871)

> It is good to be shifty in a new country.
>
> J. J. Hooper, *Some Adventures of Captain Simon Suggs, Late of the Tallapoosa Volunteers* (1845)

Three decisive Emerson statements—*Nature* (1836), *The American Scholar* (1837), and his 1838 address to the Harvard Divinity School—served as a Declaration of Independence for the spirit, intellect, and imagination. The homeliest trifle bristled with the polarity of material and spiritual truth; the writer was seer and sayer, "eye" and "I"; language was the hinge of the seen and the unseen, and all the world was a text to be read, studied, and rewritten. "Oregon and Texas are yet unsung," said Emerson. He awaited the arrival of native geniuses possessing "nerve and dagger" and a "tyrannous" command of "our incomparable materials." "America is a poem in our eyes; its ample geography dazzles the imagination, and it will not wait long for metres." Eventually Whitman had the last word in the debate over nationalism and culture. "The United States themselves," he announced in 1855, "are essentially the greatest poem."

In major respects, the literature of the American Renaissance was "a language experiment," as Whitman once described *Leaves of Grass,* a grappling with the transcendency of words. But it was also a series of inspired explorations of the theme of solitude and, correspondingly, of society. Tocqueville had warned, "Not only does democracy make each man forget his ancestors, but it hides his descendants and separates his contemporaries from them; it throws him back upon himself alone and threatens in the end to confine him entirely within the solitude of his own heart." "Instead of the social existence which all shared, was now separation," Emerson said. "Every one for himself; driven to find all his resources, hopes, rewards, society and deity within himself." This was as true of Thoreau in his cabin at Walden as it was of Melville's Ishmael aboard the *Pequod.* As Poe recognized, solitude also generated claustrophobia.

"Incomparable Materials"

The period of the American Renaissance is framed by two upheavals, the Panic of 1837 and the Civil War, and by two political leaders, Andrew Jackson and Abraham Lincoln, each of whom was widely perceived as representing the will of the people and the spirit of the frontier. The saturnalia of Jackson's first inauguration in 1829, a riot of drunkenness, bloody noses, and broken crystal and china, seemed to mark an end to patrician Presidency. The "great democratic God," Melville wrote in *Moby-Dick,* had plucked Old Hickory from the backwoods of Tennessee, hurled him upon a warhorse, and thundered him "higher than a throne." Yet for all the swirl, boil, and social ferment associated with Jacksonian democracy, to some contemporary observers the 1830s seemed peculiarly prosaic, a falling-off from the heroic age of the founders. A revolutionary nation was becoming middle-class. "Public and private avarice make the air we breathe thick and fat," Emerson said. "The mind of this country, taught to aim at low objects, eats upon itself." The celebrated "age of the common man" saw growing concentrations of wealth in the hands of a tiny percentage of the population. It was also an age of urban slums, wage slavery, and other inequities connected with the shift from an agrarian to an industrial economy. At New Orleans in 1815, Jackson defeated the British. In the White House two decades later, the first of the log-cabin Presidents, he defeated the Eastern banking interests only to see the country plunge into business failures and unemployment. The Panic of 1837 initiated the worst depression the United States had yet known.

Abraham Lincoln exercised unprecedented executive authority during a civil war far bloodier and longer than anyone had foreseen. Midway through the war, Whitman described Lincoln:

> He has a face like a hoosier Michael Angelo, so awful ugly it becomes beautiful, with its strange mouth, its deep cut, cris-cross lines, and its doughnut complexion. . . . He has shown, I sometimes think, an almost supernatural tact in keeping the ship afloat at all, with head steady, not only not going down, and now certain not to, but with proud and resolute spirit, and flag flying in sight of the world, menacing and high as ever.

Lincoln's "idiomatic western genius," as Whitman called it, was above all conspicuous in his spoken and written prose, a supple middle style that was lofty and colloquial, beautiful and homely, and always got to the point. Lincoln's prose showed that the basic forms of American humor, including the tall tale and the anecdote, were appropriate in statecraft as well as in literature. For the thirty-year-old Mark Twain, Lincoln's "With malice toward none" address proved that simplicity was one of the secrets of eloquence.

In the years between these two Presidencies, the face, form, and fiber of the United States underwent enormous change. Pushed by poverty and overcrowding at home and pulled by the promise of limitless opportunity in America, great waves of newcomers arrived from Ireland, Western Europe, and Scandinavia to settle in the cities, clear the wilderness, work the farms, build the canals and railroads. They created new opportunities and new labor needs that in turn attracted other immigrants. Meanwhile, especially in New York and New England in the 1840s and after, a riptide of movement from the country to the city, from the barn to the mill, drained villages and townships. Farmhouses stood empty, cleared land reverted to forest, and some regions, as Melville noted, looked as if they had been "depopulated by plague and war." When Jackson left office in 1837 the population was sixteen million. By 1865 it was thirty-six million, having grown by about thirty-five percent each decade. (Had that growth rate continued, the population of the United States today would be greater than China's.) What sorts of readers would these new millions be, and what sorts of writers could meet their needs? Whitman believed that "to have great poets, there must be great audiences, too."

"Self-made or Never Made"

The abolition of slavery was the most vigorous and portentous reform issue of the period. It drew militant support from other reform causes, notably the women's rights movement, given official identity in 1848 at the Seneca Falls (New York) Convention. The Quaker poet John Greenleaf Whittier told his fellow abolitionists, the southerners Sarah and Angelina Grimké, he feared "the cause of the poor and miserable slave" was being weakened by its association with women's rights, which he described as "a selfish crusade against some paltry grievance of your own." Nevertheless, the alliance was powerful evidence of an improving spirit that affected nearly every aspect of American life, from the care of the blind, the deaf, and the insane to municipal sanitation, the prevention of drunkenness, and the salvation of souls.

In 1837, the year of a great financial panic, Massachusetts established America's first state board of education and appointed as its secretary Horace Mann. He believed that the public elementary school, "the greatest discovery ever made by man," could prevent life in the open society from becoming a series of "gladiatorial contests." Under Mann and other reformers in the field, public education, a democratic dream that had appeared to be fading because it was expensive to provide as a service and humiliating to receive as a charity, became a significant cause. Until the results of normal-school training made themselves felt, elementary education remained largely a matter of the three R's administered by amateurs. One thrifty pedagogical system, devised by an English Quaker, Joseph Lancaster, employed hierarchies of student monitors to distribute rote learning along with fundamental moral precepts. In principle Lancaster's system separated children from ignorance the way Eli Whitney's cotton gin separated fibers from seeds. Standard school texts, William H. McGuffey's six *Eclectic Readers* (1836–1857), provided the same emphasis on the moral education of the young, morality here being understood as a worldly, materialistic, and thoroughly middle-class amalgam of religious principles and laissez-faire capitalism. The McGuffey *Readers,* which sold an estimated 122 million copies during the century, established canons of standard authors and literary decorum.

By midcentury, attendance in public systems that went from the infant grades through high school was growing faster than the population as a whole. Higher education, however, remained beyond the reach of all but a relative few (the estimated college enrollment was 27,000 in 1850, 56,000 in 1860). Along with a literacy rate significantly higher that that of the British Isles came a familiarity with certain basic texts (the Bible, Shakespeare, Dickens, and John Bunyan's *Pilgrim's Progress,* for example) that would seem quite remarkable today. Even the Mississippi valley "lunkheads" Mark Twain portrayed in *Huckleberry Finn* felt comfortable with the Bard's "histrionic muse" and possessed a considerable vocabulary of allusion.

The Teacher's Manual

We have been told of a teacher, who frequently relaxed discipline to such a degree, that the whole school was in an uproar. Awakened thus from his stupor, he would seize his cane, and belabor all round, till order was completely restored. This state of quiet, however, would last but a short time. The universal silence would soon be broken by a low whispering, which, remaining unnoticed, gradually increased in intensity, ending, finally, in loud talk, laughter, and jumping across the benches, which, of course, brought about the same round of general whipping, universal silence, &c. This picture is probably highly exaggerated; but there are few, who have not seen schools managed, more or less, on the same principles.

Thomas H. Palmer (1840)

For the developing readership of the period, the debating society and the lyceum were available, potent agencies of higher education. Benjamin Franklin's Junto Club, organized at Philadelphia in 1727, was the first of many debating and social societies that were to serve Americans as gymnasiums for mental exercise. Debaters in cities, towns, and villages addressed themselves to such topics as the pros and cons of slavery, capital punishment, and unrestricted immigration; the role of the arts and sciences in a democracy and of genetic and social factors in the formation of character; the achievements of Napoleon Bonaparte; and the relative merits of Queen Elizabeth and Mary, Queen of Scots. Tocqueville noted that the habit of public argument acquired in these societies left its mark on the native character: "An American cannot converse, but he can discuss. He speaks to you as if he was addressing a meeting."

The New Englander Josiah Holbrook described the lyceum system (which he founded in 1826) as a national network of "associations of Adults for Mutual Education." Arriving in remote settlements with the locomotive and the depot, lyceum lecture courses took their place in the civic order alongside the church, the schoolhouse, the courtroom, the saloon, and the jail. Citizens bought series or single tickets to hear evening talks on the North American Indian, the lives of Mohammed and Oliver Cromwell, the productive cycle of the honeybee, causes of the American Revolution, the sun, the education of children, and the capacity of the human mind for culture and improvement. "There was the real impression," Edward Everett Hale recalled, "that the kingdom of heaven was to be brought in by teaching people what were the relations of acids to alkalies, and what was the derivation of the word 'cordwainer.' If only we knew enough, it was thought, we should be wise enough to keep out of the fire, and we should not be burned." Lyceum lectures also served a social purpose in towns that lacked other secular entertainments: They enabled young men and women to mingle in semidarkened halls.

Emerson the Lecturer

In what other country, on sleety winter nights, would provincial and bucolic populations have gone forth in hundreds for the cold comfort of a literary discourse? The distillation anywhere else would certainly have appeared too thin, the appeal too special. But for many years the American people of the middle regions, outside of a few cities, had in the most rigorous seasons no other recreation. A gentleman, grave or gay, in a bare room, with a manuscript, before a desk, offered the reward of toil, the refreshment of pleasure, to the young, the middle-aged and the old of both sexes.

Henry James, *Partial Portraits* (1888)

By the end of the Civil War period, Holbrook's high-minded scheme began to give way to entertainment, box office, and the star system. But during its heyday as a distinctive institution of American life, the lyceum educated a generation and a half of readers, offered a forum for debate on such important reform issues as women's rights, temperance, and the abolition of slavery, and also provided writers and intellectuals with a source of income. For over thirty years Emerson, a preeminently popular figure on the lyceum circuit, endured the hardships of winter travel and made his living from lecture fees.

An era of self-trust, self-improvement, and perfectionism in general offered many other attractive ways of bringing in the kingdom of heaven. In the nineteenth as well as the twentieth century, the United States was world haven not only for immigrants and refugees from European oppression but also for schemes promising social and individual happiness, among them phrenology, or the science of mind, a European import. One of its founders, Johann Kaspar Spurzheim, was hailed as a messiah when he arrived in America in 1832 and was mourned accordingly when he was buried there the same year. His truth, such as it was, marched on for three decades.

In the phrenological scheme of things, each intellectual faculty had a specific location in the brain and could be measured by corresponding bumps on the skull; "secretiveness," "amativeness," "benevolence," and other traits were as palpable and distinct as onions, turnips, and potatoes in a sack. These homely propositions had an electrifying corollary. In the words of Orson Squire Fowler, the leading American popularizer of phrenology, "the exercise of particular mental faculties . . . causes the exercise, and consequent enlargement, of corresponding portions of the brain." One could "elevate" faculties that had been diagnosed deficient, "depress" those that were too prominent, and presumably arrive near, if not at, a state of perfection in personality, temperament, and ability. Fowler's motto was "self-made or never made."

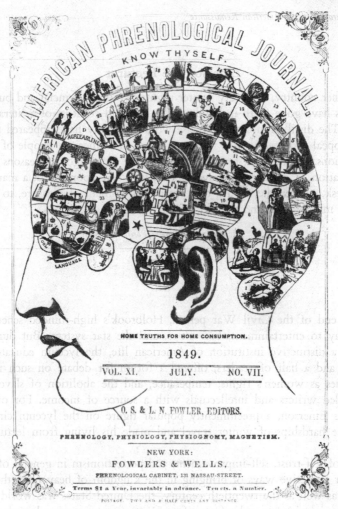

American Phrenological Journal (July 1949). Photograph courtesy of the Harvard College Library.

"The Peripatetic Phrenologist"

One of the most frequent arrivals in our village of Hannibal was the peripatetic phrenologist and he was popular and always welcome. . . . It is not at all likely, I think, that the traveling expert ever got any villager's character quite right, but it is a safe guess that he was always wise enough to furnish his clients character-charts that would compare favorably with George Washington's. It was a long time ago and I think I still remember that no phrenologist ever came across a skull in our town that fell much short of the Washington standard. This general and close approach to perfection ought to have roused suspicion, perhaps, but I do not remember that it did. It is my impression that the people admired phrenology and believed in it and that the voice of the doubter was not heard in the land.

Mark Twain (1906)

Phrenology turned out to be a benevolent, infinitely attractive fantasy, with no footing in either fact or theory, and in the hands of shabby practitioners plying their trade along the frontier it eventually declined into simple quackery. But when faith was strong the great science of mind offered the promise, Theodore Parker said, of "leading men to study the constitution of man more wisely than before." Poe claimed phrenology had achieved "the majesty of a science, and as a science ranks among the most important which can engage the attention of thinking beings." Horace Mann, as wholly serious as when confronting slavery, ignorance, profanity, or drunkenness, said phrenology was "the guide of philosophy, and the handmaid of Christianity," an opinion shared by Horace Greeley, William Cullen Bryant, Henry Ward Beecher, and others of comparable eminence. Emerson and Webster had their bumps read; so did Whitman, who was thereby confirmed in his mission to become the poet of America. Even in his old age he said, "I probably have not got by the phrenology stage yet."

In its heyday phrenology also energized a variety of other approaches to self-improvement and well-being. "Hydropathy," or water cure, offered an avenue to sobriety, moderation, personal cleanliness, and relief from bodily ills. Holistic regimens like those of Sylvester Graham, known then as the "Peristaltic Persuader" and memorialized now in the cracker that bears his name, prescribed unsifted whole-wheat flour, boiled vegetables, doses of cold water, and sexual abstinence. Mesmerists dealt in "animal magnetism," an "irradiating power" that worked on principles supposedly resembling those of the magnetic telegraph and accounted for telepathy, clairvoyance, and two-way communication with the dead. Spiritualism, epidemic after 1848 when the Fox sisters reported mysterious rappings and knockings in their upstate New York cottage, appeared to make heaven as democratic and accessible as the county courthouse. Among millions of believers in animal magnetism and related phenomena were Cooper, Irving, Poe, Hawthorne, Longfellow, Whittier, Greeley, and the Reverend Thomas Wentworth Higginson, who said that the discovery of "spiritual electricity" was as momentous as that of steam.

The word *spiritual* had deeper and more far-reaching meanings in a period of religious revivalism, another Great Awakening and evangelical renewal of faith. Especially along the frontier, the characteristic expression of this awakening was the camp meeting, a great outdoor assembly of the faithful and the repentant who came to pray and to be exhorted. "There is no country in the world where the Christian religion retains a greater influence over the souls of men than in America," Tocqueville wrote, adding that, despite the constitutional principle of separation of church and state, "the sovereign authority is religious." In certain sectors the religious revival tended to scant what might be seen as the moral contradiction of Christianity and slavery; it provoked outbreaks of virulent nativism and anti-Catholicism, and it resulted in an extraordinary proliferation of schisms and sectarian rivalries, as Emerson noted in his account of the Chardon Street Convention in Boston (1840–1841), an ad hoc ecumenical congress: "If the assembly was disorderly, it was picturesque. Madmen, madwomen, men with beards, Dunkers, Muggletonians, Come-outers, Groaners, Agrarians, Seventh-day Baptists, Quakers, Abolitionists, Calvinists, Unitarians, and Philosophers,—all came successively to the top, and seized their moment, if not their *hour,* wherein to chide, or pray, or preach, or protest." It seemed almost that the entire country was one vast camp meeting dedicated to the final eradication of sin and the redemption of the individual and scheduled to remain in session until the Second Coming. The same indigenous spiritual boil that generated Transcendentalism, Emersonian idealism, and much of the literature of the American Renaissance also generated two world religions, Joseph Smith's Church of Jesus Christ of Latter-Day Saints (1830) and Mary Baker Eddy's Church of Christ, Scientist (1879). Emily Dickinson wrote in hymn meters; Whitman's free verse was shaped by biblical cadences, and he envisioned the poet's role as that of prophet and priest.

Gold Rush

Between 1840 and 1860, expansion, conquest, and purchase increased the land area of the United States from 1.8 million to 3 million square miles. The Treaty of Guadalupe Hidalgo, concluding the war with Mexico in 1848, added the areas of present-day Texas, California, Arizona, New Mexico, and Utah, along with parts of Colorado and Wyoming—altogether an acquisition of over 500,000 square miles that was second in size only to the Louisiana Purchase. Five years later, the Gadsden Purchase completed the continental boundaries of the United States. Nevertheless, as Whitman wrote after the Civil War, expansionists continued to "reach north for Canada and south for Cuba." Their imaginations fired by explorers' reports like those of John C. Frémont, the most effective publicist of the trans-Mississippi West, thousands of young men left city and farm jobs, packed up their families, and set out along the Santa Fe, Oregon, and California trails.

Continental space, seemingly limitless, shaped the vision of writers and artists by demanding corresponding qualities of amplitude, grandeur, and reverence. But the fulfillment of manifest destiny also raised questions about where America was going. Whitman said, "It is as if we were somehow being endow'd with a vast and more and more thoroughly-appointed body, and then left with little or no soul." Reflecting on the war with Mexico, the New York diarist Philip Hone said that *Annexation* is now the greatest word in the American vocabulary. 'Veni-vidi-vici!' is inscribed on the banners of every Caesar who leads a straggling band of American adventurers across the prairies, over the mountains, up the rivers, and into the chaparral of a territory which an unprovoked war has given them the right to invade."

"Great Deeds Away out Yonder"

I fancied I could see Frémont's men, hauling the cannon up the savage battlements of the Rocky Mountains, flags in the air, Frémont at the head, waving his sword, his horse neighing wildly in the mountain wind, with unknown and unnamed empires on every hand. . . . I began to be inflamed with a love for action, adventure, glory, and great deeds away out yonder under the path of the setting sun.

Joaquin Miller, *Overland in a Covered Wagon: An Autobiography* (1930)

"The Abundance of Gold"

It was known that mines of the precious metals existed to a considerable extent in California at the time of its acquisition. Recent discoveries render it probable that these mines are more extensive and valuable than was anticipated. The accounts of the abundance of gold in that territory are of such an extraordinary character as would scarcely command belief, were they not corroborated by the authentic reports of officers in the public service, who have visited the mineral district, and derived the facts which they detail from personal observation. . . . The effects produced by the discovery of these rich mineral deposits, and the success which has attended the labours of those who have resorted to them, have produced a surprising change in the state of affairs in California. Labour commands a most exorbitant price, and all other pursuits but that of searching for the precious metal are abandoned. Nearly the whole of the male population of the country have gone to the gold districts. Ships arriving on the coast are deserted by their crews, and their voyages suspended for want of sailors.

President James K. Polk, message to Congress
(December 5, 1848)

The discovery of California gold in January 1848, just nine days before the signing of the Treaty of Guadalupe Hidalgo, appeared to many patriots to be something more than Yankee luck. It was a providential event, a confirmation of national grace and mission. Although this gold lay under their feet and ready to their hands, patriotic logic ran, it had not been revealed to the Indians, Spaniards, and Mexicans who occupied the land for two centuries before it became a part of Protestant America. ("In the hands of an enterprising people," Dana had said of California in 1840, "what a country this might be!") Now the existence of a great treasure had been discovered, quite accidentally, by a man from New Jersey, James Marshall, overseeing the construction of a sawmill on the south fork of the American River. "My eye was caught by something shining in the bottom of a ditch. . . . I reached my hand down and picked it up; it made my heart thump, for I was certain it was gold. The piece was about half the size and shape of a pea. Then I saw another." After President Polk verified the extent of the finds in his 1848 message to Congress, California gold fever supplanted the "Oregon fever" of a few years earlier, and a new wave of emigrants traveled west by way of Cape Horn (a fifteen-thousand-mile voyage), the Isthmus of Panama, and the overland trails. Many of them believed, as a paper in Ithaca, New York, reported, that all they had to do when they reached the Sacramento valley was "select a suitable location, erect cabins, and proceed to rake in the dust."

"Instead of being rich, I am ruined," said John Sutter, on whose property Marshall made his find. Marauders and squatters killed Sutter's cattle; his workers ran off to become prospectors while his wheat rotted in the fields and his tannery and mills stood idle; strangers preempted his mining claims. "By this sudden discovery of the gold, all my great plans were destroyed. Had I succeeded with my mills and manufactories for a few years before the gold was discovered, I should have been the richest citizen on the Pacific shore; but it had to be different." Marshall was another casualty and ended up working as a gardener. For him and Sutter, as well as for the many thousand prospectors who never struck it rich and were happy just to return home alive, the Gold Rush (like B. Traven's novel and John Huston's film, *The Treasure of the Sierra Madre*) proved to be a native version of Chaucer's tale about three revelers who quarreled over gold and killed one another. But the Gold Rush was also a peculiarly apt fable of America in transition. "I know of no more startling development of the morality of trade and all the modes of getting a living than the rush to California affords," Thoreau wrote in his journal. "Of what significance is . . . a world that will rush to the lottery of California gold-digging—to live by luck, to get the means of commanding the labor of others less lucky, *i.e.* slaveholding, without contributing any value to society? . . . Going to California. It is only three thousand miles nearer to hell." "The Californian rush for wealth in '49," Mark Twain was to recall, "introduced the change and begot the lust for money which is the rule of life to-day, and the hardness and cynicism which is the spirit of to-day." "And where are they now?" he wondered about the forty-niners. "Scattered to the ends of the earth—or prematurely aged and decrepit—or shot or stabbed in street affrays—or dead of disappointed hopes and broken hearts—all gone, or nearly all—victims devoted upon the altar of the golden calf."

Railroad Iron

California promoters had invoked the preclassical example of Jason's Argonauts and the Golden Fleece to suggest that the Gold Rush was a return to an Arcadian age of adventure. Thoreau, Mark Twain, and other social critics thought of the Gold Rush as a dividing line between America's own Arcadian age—in idealized retrospect a time of pastoral peace, agrarian self-sufficiency, and communal rectitude—and the industrial age of cities and machines, steam, electricity, steel, and big business. Gone was what the English journalist Harriet Martineau had called "a sweet temper diffused like sunshine over the land." For a glorious year and a half (April 1860–October 1861) Pony Express riders, buckskin-clad heroes armed with Colt six-shooters and eighteen-inch knives, carried mail nearly two thousand miles in eight days between Sacramento, California, and St. Joseph, Missouri, but the entire venture was little more than a romantic rear-guard action, "a flash of unreal fantasy," in Mark Twain's words. Outmoded by the telegraph and steam locomotive, the age's most conspicuous symbols and agencies of change, the Pony Express passed into American folklore. By the end of the 1860s, travelers rode coast-to-coast in the sleeping and dining luxury of George Pullman's Palace Cars.

"Railroad iron is a magician's rod in its power to evoke the sleeping energies of land and water," Emerson said. "Readers of poetry see the factory-village and the railway, and fancy that the poetry of the landscape is broken up by these; for these works of art are not yet consecrated in their reading; but the poet sees them fall within the great Order not less than the beehive or the spider's geometrical web." By the end of the period, the number of miles of track in operation

(35,000) had grown by a factor of twenty-six, and the prairies were opened for agricultural use; railroading was America's first billion-dollar industry and the pattern for other gigantic concentrations of capital. Literature and the facts of industry may have been compatible, as Emerson claimed, but what did these facts mean?

"Railroad iron" opened the wilderness but also preserved it by putting up obstacles to agriculture along the right-of-way. "Punctual as a Star," the locomotive was, in Emily Dickinson's words, both "docile and omnipotent"; its "horrid, hooting stanza" broke the primal silence, interrupted meditation, and itself became the subject of meditation. Hawthorne described the locomotive as looking "much more like a sort of mechanical demon, that would hurry us to the infernal regions, than a laudable contrivance for smoothing our way to the Celestial City." "I will not have my eyes put out and my ears spoiled by its smoke and steam and hissing," Thoreau wrote in Concord. Even on the empty Pacific, sailing toward his destruction while his country sailed toward civil war, Captain Ahab read his fate in the landscape of the steam locomotive: "The path to my fixed purpose is laid with iron rails, whereon my soul is grooved to run. Over unsounded gorges, through the rifled hearts of mountains, under torrents' beds, unerringly I rush! Naught's an obstacle, naught's an angle to the iron way!"

Impending Crisis

Whether the new industrial age represented progress or destruction was one of several ambiguities writers of the period had to confront. They were as divided here as they were in their responses to the other contradictions—social, economic, political, and moral—of American life around the middle of the century. The freest nation on earth, inspired by dreams of a just and perfect society, maintained the institution of slavery, denied women the vote and other legal rights, and harried its aboriginal population toward extinction through chicanery, forced removals, and broken treaties.

Torn between humanitarian and expedient principles, many Americans detested slavery but at the same time despaired of finding a fair or peaceful way of putting an end to it. Frederick Law Olmsted, travel writer, landscape architect, and subsequently designer (with architect Calvert Vaux) of New York's Central Park, journeyed extensively through the South during the 1850s. In *The Cotton Kingdom* (1861), a collection of his travel writings, he presented what is still respected as an informed picture of the wretchedness of slavery and slaveholding society. But for the most part, the writers of New England and the Middle States had as muddled a comprehension of the South, based on little or no firsthand experience, as their southern counterparts had of the North. Each group accused the other of fanaticism and monomania and fell back on unexamined stereotypes: The South was a violent, backward, culturally barren region ruled by King Cotton and his Lords of the Lash, while the North was culturally tyrannical, obsessed with trade and stirring up blood violence between slaves and masters. Moreover, within each loosely defined opposed faction there were, in turn, differences almost as extreme as those existing between the factions themselves.

At one end of the northern spectrum stood the abolitionist poet John Greenleaf Whittier. His single-mindedness was tempered by Quaker pacifism, while William Lloyd Garrison's abolitionist zeal—he denounced the U.S. Constitution as a "Covenant with Death and an Agreement with Hell"—made him as ardent a secessionist as the most fire-eating southerner. During the 1830s and 1840s, Emerson remained evasive on the great issue of the day: "What right have I to speak of slavery? Are we not *all* slaves?" (This meshed with the antiabolitionist argument that the white wage slaves—the indentured servants—of the North and industrialized England were infinitely worse off than the black chattel slaves of the Cotton Kingdom.) Hawthorne and Melville (despite the marked sympathy for blacks the latter showed in his novels) shunned reform causes and mass initiatives in general. Not a joiner either, Thoreau, before the Mexican War and the passage of the Fugitive Slave Law, nevertheless wrote in support of the antislavery movement and held an abolitionist meeting at Walden. Longfellow withdrew into genial isolation.

The historian Francis Parkman represented the other extreme of northern opinion and spoke for many southerners as well: "For my part, I would see every slave knocked on the head before I would see the Union go to pieces, and would include in the sacrifice as many abolitionists as could be conveniently brought together." This was the fundamental position that Lowell, a hot abolitionist earlier, arrived at just before the war and that Whitman, self-annointed bard of the Union and democracy, maintained even during the war.

Writers in the South, less visible as a group, in part because of their dependence on northern readers and publishing outlets, were also less vocal as a group, but they were spread along the same broad spectrum of opinion. The Charleston romancer William Gilmore Simms, the most prolific and popular writer of the South, and James De Bow, professor of political economy at the University of Louisiana, shared the familiar antebellum dream that a great civilization, like that of ancient Greece, could be raised on a foundation of human bondage. "The negro slaves of the South are the happiest, and in some sense, the freest people in the world," wrote the Virginia lawyer George Fitzhugh, author of *Sociology for the South; or, The Failure of Free Society* (1854) and *Cannibals All! or, Slaves Without Masters* (1857). "The children and the aged and infirm work not at all, and yet have all the comforts and necessities of life provided for them. They enjoy liberty, because they are oppressed neither by care nor labor. . . . Free laborers have not a thousandth part of the rights and liberties of negro slaves. Indeed, they have not a single right or a single liberty, unless it be the right or liberty to die." Neither a racist nor a secessionist, Fitzhugh believed that in a wicked world southern slavery was not quite so wicked as northern capitalism.

Meanwhile, Hinton Rowan Helper of North Carolina, a failed prospector in the Gold Rush who had become an out-and-out negrophobe, was urging abolition on the grounds that black slavery depressed the market for white labor and kept the South poor and backward. His populist, superficially progressive, but bitterly racist tract, *The Impending Crisis of the South* (1857), suppressed in some slave states and widely circulated by abolitionists in the North, may have been as effective in arousing sectional antagonism as *Uncle Tom's Cabin*. Fierce and uncompromising, the fire-eating Simms tried to promote his antithetic gospel of slavery to northern lecture audiences in 1856. Another Charlestonian, the poet Henry Timrod, was an apologist for slavery and "the laureate of the Confederacy" only with the utmost reluctance—he had tried to stay above sectional issues. Maryland novelist and politician John Pendleton Kennedy, Poe's friend and patron, wrote and lectured against secession. Like that of the North, the southern literary and intellectual community did not speak with one voice on the underlying issues of the Civil War.

The Missouri Compromise (1820), an attempt to establish geographical and political balance between free states and slave states, had offered the promise of domestic tranquillity while evading the basic moral issue involved. Nevertheless, Jefferson heard in its terms "a fire-bell" tolling "the knell of the Union." After half a generation of silence this bell began to toll again with increasing frequency. In November 1837, two months after Emerson called on "the American scholar" to speak his own mind and look to self-trust, a mob in Alton, Illinois, murdered Elijah Lovejoy, editor of the *Observer,* an abolitionist newspaper. The antislavery cause had its first martyr in a line that would end with Captain John Brown. Wendell Phillips's tribute to Lovejoy at a public meeting in Boston's Faneuil Hall belonged in a tradition of abolitionist oratory that eventually included Theodore Parker, Senator Charles Sumner, the Reverend Henry Ward Beecher, Frederick Douglass, and Henry Thoreau. The slavery issue surfaced again in the Mexican war, "essentially a war of false pretenses," Lowell said at the time, which would result in "widening the boundaries and so prolonging the life of slavery." "I call it murder," said Lowell's cracker-barrel Yankee, Hosea Biglow:

> They jest want this Californy
> So's to lug new slave-States in
> To abuse ye, an' to scorn ye,
> An' to plunder ye like sin. ....
> Chaps that make black slaves o' niggers
> Want to make wite slaves o' you.

The Impending Crisis of the South: How to Meet It

The causes which have impeded the progress and prosperity of the South, which have dwindled our commerce, and other similar pursuits, into the most contemptible insignificance; sunk a large majority of our people in galling poverty and ignorance, rendered a small minority conceited and tyrannical, and driven the rest away from their homes; entailed upon us a humiliating dependence on the Free States; disgraced us in the recesses of our own souls, and brought us under reproach in the eyes of all civilized and enlightened nations— may all be traced to one common source, and there find solution in the most hateful and horrible word, that was ever incorporated into the vocabulary of human economy—*Slavery!*

Hinton Rowan Helper (1857)

The Wilmot Proviso (1846), an attempt to outlaw slavery in any territory acquired from Mexico, revealed the peculiarly complex and contradictory makeup of the Free Soil movement, an amalgam of conscience, self-interest, and racism. "As if by magic," said a Whig paper in Boston, "it brought to a head the great question which is about to divide the American people." The author of the proviso, David Wilmot, a hitherto inconspicuous Democratic member of Congress from Pennsylvania, had "no morbid sympathy for the slave," he said, only a desire to protect white men from "the disgrace which association with negro slavery brings upon free labor." His position scarcely differed from Helper's.

On these issues Whitman exemplifies the hesitancies that afflicted other writers of the period. An ardent Free-Soiler, editor and publisher of the Brooklyn *Freeman,* a weekly newspaper dedicated to opposing "under all circumstances the addition to the Union, in future, of a single inch of *slave land,"* Whitman denounced abolitionism because it was fanatical, defied the law of the land, and, at a time when "United States" was still a plural noun, as in "these United States," jeopardized the sacred constitutional pact. (When the war came, Whitman maintained, as Lincoln did, that it was fought over the issue of the Union, not slavery, although without slavery the war might not have been fought at all.) Like Emerson, Thoreau, Parker, and many other writers (with the conspicuous exception of Melville) who accepted "scientific" doctrines of the day, Whitman also believed that blacks were genetically unsuited for assimilation into American life. "Nature has set an impassable seal against it," he declared in an 1850s editorial. His day-to-day social policy and conduct were no different from those of most northerners, abolitionists included, who deplored slavery but at the same time denied free blacks the most rudimentary civil rights. "You loathe them as you would a snake or a toad, yet you are indignant at their wrongs," St. Clare, a Louisiana planter, says to his New England cousin in Harriet Beecher Stowe's novel, *Uncle Tom's Cabin.* "You would not have them abused; but you don't want to have anything to do with them yourselves. You would send them to Africa, out of your sight and smell, and then send a missionary or two to do up all the self-denial of elevating them compendiously." Like her brother Henry Ward Beecher, Theodore Parker, and other antislavery radicals, Mrs. Stowe believed that the ultimate solution to an intolerable race problem was black colonization in a more tropical part of the world than the North American continent.

Bitter congressional debates over Henry Clay's "Omnibus Bill" (1850) and the Kansas-Nebraska Act (1854) created further dismay and confusion for northern liberals. Among their deposed heroes was Daniel Webster, a man of outstanding intellect and character; according to the phrenologists, his skull (twenty-five inches around) was to common skulls "what the great dome of St. Peter's is to the small cupolas at its side." On the Senate floor in March 1850, Webster, faced, as he believed, with the momentous choice of preserving the Union or countenancing secession, threw his support to Clay's compromise resolutions. In the bitter aftermath of Webster's speech, Parker said, "There is no such life of crime long enough to prepare a man for such a pitch of depravity." "When faith is lost, when honor dies, / The man is dead": In Whittier's poem, Webster is the biblical Ichabod, a name meaning, "the glory is departed."

"I Would Save the Union"

I would save the Union. I would save it the shortest way under the Constitution. The sooner the national authority can be restored; the nearer the Union will be "the Union as it was." If there be those who would not save the Union, unless they could at the same time *save* slavery, I do not agree with them. If there be those who would not save the Union unless they could at the same time *destroy* slavery, I do not agree with them. My paramount object in this struggle *is* to save the Union, and is *not* either to save or destroy slavery.

Abraham Lincoln, letter to Horace Greeley (August 22, 1862)

The most inflammatory of the compromise measures that Webster supported, the Fugitive Slave Law made the federal government the enforcing agency of southern property claims and created a corps of federal slave catchers to penetrate the asylums and underground railroads of the North. "This filthy enactment," Emerson wrote in his journal, "was made in the nineteenth century by men who could read and write. I will not obey it, by God." The Fugitive Slave Law triggered Mrs. Stowe's famous novel. President Franklin Pierce dispatched a government cutter and federal troops, armed with loaded rifles and fixed bayonets, to Boston in June 1854 to ensure the return of Anthony Burns, a runaway slave, to his owner in Virginia. The rendition of Burns left Thoreau "with the sense of having suffered a vast and indefinite loss," he said in his July 4 address, *Slavery in Massachusetts.* "I did not know at first what ailed me. At last it occurred to me that what I had lost was a country. . . . We have used up all our inherited freedom. If we would save our lives, we must fight for them." This was his version of the same "higher law" that Captain John Brown invoked in October 1859 when, hoping to raise a black insurrection in Virginia, he led his attack on the federal arsenal at Harpers Ferry and again, a month and a half later, when he mounted the scaffold to die "for God's eternal truth." Devoutly antislavery northerners believed, as Emerson put it, that Brown made "the gallows glorious like the Cross." "He is not Old Brown any longer," Thoreau said; "he is an angel of light." For Melville and Whitman, Brown's execution was also a "meteor" that aroused "forebodings," "portent" of a cataclysmic four-year civil war.

"I saw an open field," Ulysses Grant was to write of the Battle of Shiloh (April 6–7, 1862), "over which the Confederates had made repeated charges the day before, so covered with dead that it would have been possible to walk across the clearing, in any direction, without a foot touching the ground." Until Shiloh, Grant, "as well as thousands of other citizens, believed that the rebellion against the Government would collapse suddenly and soon."

Further Reading:
V. W. Brooks, *The Flowering of New England,*
1815–1865, 1936.
F. O. Matthiessen, *American Renaissance,* 1941.
V. W. Brooks, *The Times of Melville and*
Whitman, 1947.
The Transcendentalists, ed. P. Miller, 1950.
H. N. Smith, *Virgin Land,* 1950.
R. W. B. Lewis, *The American Adam,* 1955.
C. Bode, *The Anatomy of Popular Culture,*
1840–1861, 1959.
E. Wilson, *Patriotic Gore,* 1962.
L. Marx, *The Machine in the Garden,* 1964.
D. Boorstin, *The Americans: The National*
Experience, 1965.
J. A. Hawgood, *America's Western Frontiers,*

1967.
D. Aaron, *The Unwritten War,* 1973.
L. Buell, *Literary Transcendentalism,* 1973.
P. Miller, *The Raven and the Whale,* 1973.
R. B. Nye, *Society and Culture in America,*
1830–1860, 1974.
G. B. Forgie, *Patricide in the House Divided,*
1979.
B. Novak, *Nature and Culture: American*
Landscape and Painting, 1825–1875, 1980.
J. S. Holliday, *The World Rushed In: The*
California Gold Rush Experience, 1981.
L. Ziff, *Literary Democracy,* 1981.
J. R. Stilgoe, *Metropolitan Corridor,* 1983.
A. Kazin, *An American Procession,* 1984.

Ralph Waldo Emerson
1803–1882

Ralph Waldo Emerson has been such an original and pervasive presence in nineteenth- and twentieth-century American culture that most Americans know something about the spirit and substance of his writing, even if they have never deliberately read a line of his work. In voluminous journals, lectures, essays, and poems, Emerson articulated principles that have become central to defining traditional American values: self-reliance, individual authority and responsibility, a resolute optimism, moral idealism, the veneration of experience, and a worshipful return to nature. Emerson's expression of these fundamental principles in America's collective identity has been quoted, endorsed, and adapted by so many generations of writers and public figures that their familiarity may well reduce our appreciation of just how original these ideas were when Emerson expressed them. As the inheritors of a literary legacy nourished on a schoolroom diet of Emerson's most epigrammatic lines, contemporary readers must rediscover the range, freshness, complexity, and elasticity of his writing. The challenge in reading Emerson is to recover the originality of his now-familiar ideas.

From all accounts, Ralph Waldo Emerson was an intellectual radical who led a private and public life imbued with tradition and convention. Emerson was born in 1803 and grew up in a family whose heritage included nine successive generations of notable New England ministers. Religious custom and social ritual pervaded his life both at home and in Boston. His father, a well-known Unitarian preacher, died when Waldo was eight, leaving him, his mother, and four brothers with little more than pride in a family name that filled several chapters in local church history. With the encouragement of his resilient and inventive mother, Ruth Haskins, the support of his Puritanical step-grandfather, the Reverend Ezra Ripley, and the stern guidance of his strong-willed aunt, Mary Moody Emerson, Waldo entered Harvard at the age of 14. There he began keeping what quickly became extensive journals. In one early entry he succinctly summarized his childhood: "My recollections of early life are not very pleasant."

Emerson's performance at Harvard was not particularly distinguished. He graduated in 1821, thirty-ninth in a class of fifty-nine. After several unsettling years teaching, Emerson enrolled in the Harvard Divinity School and prepared to carry on the family tradition by studying to be a Unitarian minister. A liberal movement that first flourished in the eighteenth century as a rejection of the Calvinist legacy of Jonathan Edwards and the Great Awakening, Unitarianism shifted the emphasis in religious experience from the individual's depravity to one's moral capabilities and prospects for salvation. In effect, Unitarian belief substituted the principle of a moral democracy for the Puritan concept of a moral aristocracy. But by the time Emerson was "approbated to preach" in 1826, Unitarianism had taken on all of the trappings of the reigning orthodoxy at the Harvard Divinity School. Emerson's studies, interrupted by spells of weak eyesight and his own unconventional thinking, proceeded slowly. As he dispassionately noted some years later, "Had they examined me, they would never have passed me."

Within a few years, however, Emerson had married an aspiring poet, Ellen Tucker, and had settled into a successful life as the pastor of Boston's Second Church, where Increase and Cotton Mather had preached more than a century earlier. There he attracted considerable attention for his eloquent and unorthodox sermons. This period of what he called "uninterrupted prosperity" included an honorary membership in Phi Beta Kappa, appointment as chaplain of the Massachusetts Senate, and election to the Boston School Committee. But this period of contentment was short-lived. By 1831 his wife had died, his brother Edward's health had deteriorated rapidly, and his doubts about his own ministry had increased greatly. Impatient with the ceremonial rituals and institutional structures and pressures of the church, Emerson began to seek more direct and immediate access to religious experience. His journal entry for June 1832 summarizes his state of mind: "I have sometimes thought that in order to be a good minister it was necessary to leave the ministry. The profession is antiquated. In an altered age, we worship the dead forms of our forefathers." In Emerson's view, the Unitarian church had become far too negative and rational— "corpse-cold," as he called it. Advocating greater attention to the emotional and subjective elements of faith, Emerson sought more intuitive, personally revelatory religious experiences. In late October 1832 Emerson resigned his pastorate, having decided that he could no longer in good conscience administer Communion. "I find this amazing revelation of my immediate relation to God a solution to all the doubts that oppressed me," he wrote.

On Christmas Day in 1832 Emerson sailed for Europe and spent the next 10 months on the Continent and in England reading, recovering his health, and meeting such influential writers as William Wordsworth, Samuel Taylor Coleridge, and Thomas Carlyle, the latter of whom became a lifelong friend. Emerson returned to Massachusetts in 1833 and began a lecture series in Boston and its surrounding communities with such titles as "Human Life," "The Present Age," and "Human Culture." While his reputation as an orator earned him considerable attention, his $1,200 annual income from Ellen Tucker's estate—

approximately two-thirds of his earnings as a minister—freed him from the financial concerns that had afflicted him and his family since childhood. After the death of his brother Edward in 1834, Emerson moved to Concord, Massachusetts, where he briefly took up residence at the "Old Manse," the home of his Puritan ancestors and later of Nathaniel Hawthorne.

After a brief courtship filled with the "most agreeable recollections," Emerson married Lydia Jackson in 1835 and settled into a comfortable life in a large plain white frame house ("Coolidge Castle," or "Bush," as it came to be known), where they remained until fire destroyed it in 1872. Soon after their marriage, Emerson began a lifelong practice of calling his wife "Lidian," to avoid the New England pronunciation that slips an r sound between words that end and begin with a vowel. Nestled in the domestic quiet of a town filled with Revolutionary history, Emerson cultivated the simple pleasures of country living and worked on his writing. Occasionally, he traveled in the Northeast and out to the western frontier to lecture.

Only rarely did Emerson draw the same large crowds that came to hear the most popular politicians, reformers, phrenologists, and mesmerists of the mid-nineteenth century. Yet he always cut an imposing figure behind the lectern. He was tall, but years of poor health had worn at his body, sloped his shoulders, and made him appear slightly gaunt. Emerson had a chiseled look—a long, narrow, weathered face beneath a furrowed brow and thick brown hair, with deeply recessed blue eyes set off by a prominent nose and an angular chin. He had a broad mouth, but one unaccustomed to laughter. There was always something highly serious, almost lofty, even ethereal, about him. The calm dignity of his voice exuded the polished cadences of an eloquent preacher, and the practiced rhythm of his intonation created an air of oracular authority for his provocative statements.

Emerson the lecturer was as ambitious as he was dynamic. "A lecture is a new literature," he noted in his journals, "which leaves aside all tradition, time, place, circumstance, & addresses an assembly as mere human beings. . . . It has never been done well. It is an organ of sublime power." Emerson prepared rigorously for his lectures. He drew primarily on his extensive journals (his "savings bank," as he called them) for both subjects and phrasing. Although he did not make daily entries, his journals did serve as an invaluable compendium of his comments on the controversies of the time; descriptions of friends, neighbors, and public figures; musings about himself, his family, and his community; and reports on his reading, along with notes on the issues provoked by it. Once Emerson had settled on a subject for a lecture, he would work through his journals (he created an index for easier reference) in search of appropriate entries. Characteristically, he then rewrote these entries and blended them into a final draft. He later recast the most successful of his lectures into essays. In effect, Emerson used his lectures to field-test his ideas before committing them to print.

Emerson's first major publication was Nature (1836). The sizable first printing (1,500 copies) sold out within a few months, earning him a modest profit and considerable attention in the United States and abroad. Nature provides the theoretical underpinnings for developing what became an indigenous American literature in the nineteenth century. The essay is Emerson's most dramatic effort to reject the Old World and build anew: "Embosomed for a season in nature, whose floods of life stream around and through us, . . . why should we grope among the dry bones of the past?" Emerson determined that the imagination, set loose in the natural world, offered the best prospects to discover, as he declared, "an original relation to the universe."

Emerson's efforts to define the word *nature* remain far more than an exercise in semantics or philosophical speculation. He builds into his essay a strikingly bold proposition: to substitute nature for what was generally regarded to be the new nation's lack of a distinctive cultural heritage. In Emerson's view, nature— the land itself—should be the source for articulating and developing a unique American cultural identity. He would have nature become the gravitational field for defining American experience. Like his counterparts in art—most notably the painter Thomas Cole, who figured so prominently in the Hudson River school— Emerson revered nature and saw in America the finest expression of what has been called "Nature's nation." In contrast to the many Americans who viewed nature as something to exploit in their relentless push westward, Emerson and Cole venerated nature not for the economic but for the spiritual and artistic opportunities inherent in it. For Emerson and Cole, nature would replace the Bible as the greatest spiritual text, capable of being read by anyone. As Emerson noted in a later essay, "Circles": "We can never see christianity from the catechism;—from the pasture, from a boat in the pond, from amidst the songs of wood-birds we possibly may." Or, as he put it even more succinctly in a journal entry dated a few months before the publication of *Nature:* "Make your own Bible."

Emerson returned to Harvard in 1837 as the keynote speaker on Phi Beta Kappa Day. His address on that occasion, "The American Scholar," urged his audience to break with the past and to concentrate on recognizing and developing the enormous cultural potential of their own experience. Emerson hoped to formulate a set of distinctive principles for American experience, a forward-looking philosophy based on spontaneous action, creative intuition, and self-reliance. Like most of his writing, "The American Scholar" is explicitly inspirational. To be the representative American, the scholar must be self-reliant —full enough of self-trust to be open to any experience and patient enough to "relinquish display and immediate fame." The "true scholar," Emerson declared, doesn't lead a repetitive, derivative life but looks insistently and carefully at the present; refusing to be cut off from the world of action, the scholar relies on the creative power of intuition rather than on the treatises of others to map out the "resounding tumult" of experience.

Toward the end of "The American Scholar," Emerson underscored his revolutionary call for distinctively American experience and culture:

> I ask not for the great, the remote, the romantic, what is doing in Italy or Arabia; what is Greek art, or Provencal ministrelsy; I embrace the common, I explore and sit at the feet of the familiar, the low. Give me insight into to-day, and you may have the antique and future worlds.

It is through experience, the instincts, and "things near" that we may discover the unity of the world—the "one design," he noted, that "unites and animates the farthest pinnacle and the lowest trench." Emerson closed by proclaiming America's literary independence: "We have listened too long to the courtly muses of Europe. . . . We shall walk on our own feet, we will work with our own hands, we will speak our own minds."

"The American Scholar" produced, according to Emerson's close friend Bronson Alcott, a mixture of "confusion, consternation, surprise, and wonder." For Oliver Wendell Holmes, then a prominent young physician, the address represented nothing less than America's "intellectual Declaration of Independence." The distinguished literary critic James Russell Lowell, recalling his undergraduate days at Harvard, offered perhaps the most comprehensive view of the lecture's significance:

> The Puritan revolt had made us ecclesiastically and the Revolution politically independent, but we were socially and intellectually moored to English thought, till Emerson cut the cable and gave us a chance at the dangers and glories of blue water. . . . His oration before the Phi Beta Kappa Society at Cambridge, some thirty years ago, was an event without any former parallel in our literary annals.

Emerson broadened the nation's cultural horizons by encouraging the scholar to explore the aesthetic potential of what had previously been ignored—to recognize the potential majesty in the immediate, to see the ultimate lurking in the ordinary. No longer, Emerson asserted, would there be a hierarchy of meaning. No longer would "quality" be abstract. For Emerson, quality resided in the texture of experience. The scholar's—everyone's—task, then, would be to explore the implicitness of experience. In this respect, much of late-nineteenth- and twentieth-century literature, art, and popular culture can be said to have its symbolic birth in "The American Scholar." Consider, for example, Emerson's influence on the work of such divergent figures as Walt Whitman, William James, Robert Frost, William Carlos Williams, F. Scott Fitzgerald, Willa Cather, Gertrude Stein, A. R. Ammons, Frederick Law Olmsted, Louis Sullivan, Frank Lloyd Wright, and innumerable others.

Emerson's increasing reputation as a lecturer put him at the center of a small group of disaffected intellectuals who met frequently—though not on any regular schedule—to exchange ideas. Dubbed the "Transcendentalists" by their detractors (principally because they were reported to have spent so much time discussing Immanuel Kant's "transcendental" philosophy), the group included, among others, Margaret Fuller, Theodore Parker, Orestes Brownson, Bronson Alcott, Elizabeth Peabody, George Ripley, Frederic Henry Hedge, and Christopher Cranch. Mostly young and Boston bred, these feisty radical thinkers tackled the most pressing issues of the time and endorsed, with varying degrees of zeal, the major efforts at moral reform—most notably abolition, the temperance movement, and women's rights.

The first gathering of the Transcendentalists took place in September 1836, a few days after Emerson's *Nature* was published. The most appreciable public result of their discussions was *The Dial*, an intellectual miscellany published between 1840 and 1844 and edited at various times by Margaret Fuller, George

Ripley, and Emerson. Although *The Dial* had a relatively small circulation, it called attention to the Transcendentalists and gave them a public forum for expressing their characteristically liberal views of religious and social matters.

Because more than half the participants in the Transcendentalists' conversations had trained for the Unitarian ministry, their discussions naturally drifted toward the religious controversies of the day. These occasions invariably provided Emerson with frequent opportunities to test his own ideas about religion. Emerson firmly believed that the individual could experience God firsthand and was unequivocally opposed to the forms and ceremonies of any church. During one of these meetings, Emerson is known to have said:

> The Puritans came here in revolt against forms. Why should they have kept any, then? . . . Is *any* form necessary? Do we need any gift or foreign force? Can we not be self-sustaining? See this divinity of daisies around us. Can we not be level to them? What need is there of miracles? That Jesus lived purely was his strong argument.

These are substantially the same points that Emerson developed in a controversial address to the senior class at the Harvard Divinity School in the summer of 1838, a lecture that dramatically affected the remainder of his life.

The Divinity School address argued that religion is practiced by America's ministers "as if God were dead." Emerson challenged the church's assumption that "the age of inspiration is dead." He identified Jesus and the prophets as "holy bards," discounted the importance of miracles, redefined *good* and *evil,* and urged these fledgling ministers to cast aside conformity, to free themselves from the authority of the church. They must help their parishioners "to love God without mediator or veil." Hoping to stir these ministers to recognize that their preaching had to be "rammed with life," Emerson instead was roundly condemned as a heretic by the Divinity School faculty and effectively banned from speaking at Harvard for the next 30 years. In a journal entry dated April 1840, Emerson recalled the lecture and the furor it had caused:

> In all my lectures, I have taught one doctrine, namely, the infinitude of the private man. This the people accept readily enough, and even with loud commendation, as long as I call the lecture Art, or Politics, or Literature, or the Household; but the moment I call it Religion, they are shocked, though it only be the application of the same truth which they receive everywhere else, to a new class of facts.

The Divinity School address made Emerson a public figure of considerable importance. Some said it made him infamous. But perhaps Bronson Alcott's observation best summarizes this phase of Emerson's life: "Emerson's church consists of one member—himself."

Emerson's two volumes of essays, published in 1841 and 1844, respectively, provide ample evidence with which to trace his distinctively American mind. Yet his ideas grew and changed over the span of nearly fifty years of lecturing and writing. He often modified his thinking and occasionally shifted it dramatically. In his later years, for example, he tempered much of his earlier, occasionally extravagant optimism. Recursive in his early essays, his thinking tended to be linear in later ones. Throughout his essays, however, Emerson steadfastly resisted the complacency of attaching himself to any single, narrow, categorical view of experience; "to define is to confine," he noted. His thinking is characteristically provisional. It has a democratic ring to it—open to any influence, receptive to change and growth. Emerson's ideas can develop over the course of a single essay or over the length of his career precisely because he resists fixing or even limiting the significance of a thought. In this respect, reading Emerson may well be akin to listening to someone think aloud. Flashes of truth and moments of insight encourage a sense of surprise and intellectual discovery in his readers.

Emerson envisions an ideal for himself as a thinker and a writer wherein he can approximate in his essays the fluidity he ascribes to nature. He seeks to make the movement of thought in each of his sentences and paragraphs analogous to the flow of the natural world—to the point where the mind "insures an order of expression which is the order of nature itself." Thinking and writing are organic for Emerson; his essays characteristically proceed by association rather than by logic. They reflect the way his mind actually works: moving from impression to impression, from association to association, always enlarging the context and broadening the range of experience. Ideas often spiral out in many directions, usually without being drawn together in some sort of unifying statement or conclusion. As Emerson's mind moves in a tangled web of observation, discovery, allusion, aphorism, and quotation, his essays become aggregates of sentences and paragraphs—a collection of insights. In this respect, a sentence in Emerson's essays generally carries the weight of what in other writers would be a paragraph. Often he seems to leap from one sentence to the next with little regard for transitions. Like nineteenth-century American culture itself, Emerson's essays seem to have little patience with a single idea. Emerson recognized the need to create at least a provisional order for writing. "The maker of a sentence," he notes, "launches out into the infinite and builds a road into chaos and old night, and is followed by those who hear him with something of a wild creative delight." But Emerson's road is rarely either straight or narrow.

By the mid-1840s Emerson was spending more and more of his time on the road as one of the most respected members of what was known as the Lyceum movement, an association formed to offer general instruction to adults through a network of lectures and concerts. He was by no means successful everywhere he lectured. In the West, especially, he found difficult traveling conditions, primitive lodgings, and cantankerous and occasionally rowdy audiences more accustomed to humorous tall tales than to intellectual speculation. Yet Emerson's lectures, despite occasionally confused or unflattering responses, drew large audiences virtually everywhere. And his addresses on democratic self-reliance, repeated in nearly every section of the nation, became an unofficial national anthem for the integrity of the individual mind. The moral and personal values Emerson advocated—

especially the basic belief that each individual has "a greater possibility"—had enormous appeal to the average American in the 1840s.

Emerson lectured extensively in England in 1847 and 1848, spent more time with his friend Carlyle, and took copious notes for what became *Representative Men* (1850) and *English Traits* (1856), the latter a detailed, witty, insightful, and occasionally startled look at British culture. These works suggest just how empirical and skeptical Emerson had grown in the years following his first two collections of essays. The death of his six-year-old son, Waldo, in 1842 had deeply affected him, and although he had tried to "justify" the child's death in his essay "Experience" and in the poem "Threnody," Emerson clearly had begun to moderate his optimism. By the late 1840s he seemed willing to accept the painful realities of particular places, times, and events. He had also become slightly more aristocratic, even fateful, about the average American's potential. By the time he published *English Traits,* Emerson's style had become more factual and reportorial. He now observed the world from a more detached point of view.

A renowned international figure by the 1850s, Emerson spent much of his time resisting involvement in the public controversies of the day. "I do not often speak to public questions," he announced. "They are odious and hurtful, and it seems like meddling or leaving your work." He preferred to cultivate the interior landscape of what Thoreau called "home cosmography." There were exceptions, of course: He opposed racial and social injustice, slavery, the removal of the Cherokee Nation from Georgia in the late 1830s, United States involvement in the Mexican War, and the Fugitive Slave Law. The epigraph to his journal for 1837 puts his views on public issues most succinctly: "I write the laws, / Not plead a cause."

The Emerson house in Concord became a port of call for virtually every major American writer of the time. His last years were devoted to being "the representative American." Too old to participate in the Civil War, Emerson became absorbed in the rhetoric surrounding it and wrote movingly about the Emancipation Proclamation and the death of Lincoln. Regarded as a sage in the United States and abroad, Emerson spent much of his time lecturing and trying to compensate for what he believed was America's "bad name for superficialness." In the years following the Civil War he grew increasingly impatient with his own failing health and eventually needed the help of both his daughter, Ellen, and James Cabot, his authorized biographer and literary executor, to see him through his lecturing and publishing commitments. It may well have been the accidental burning of "Coolidge House" in 1872 that precipitated Emerson's decline. Facing the loss of important papers and the disarray of so many others, he began to lose his memory and slipped into senility. His memory gone and his ability to perform publicly irreparably impaired, Emerson slowly settled into dying. On April 27, 1882, Concord's church bells rang 79 times, proclaiming his life and announcing his death.

Perhaps the most appropriate epitaph for Emerson's life had been offered unceremoniously years before his death. In the early summer of 1848, near the end of his very successful—and controversial—lecture tour of Great Britain, a letter from a disconsolate reader appeared in a London newspaper, requesting that the admission price of Emerson's lectures be reduced so that the poorer classes could hear him speak. "Emerson," the letter writer observed, "is a phenomenon whose like is not in the world, and to miss him is to lose an important part of the Nineteenth century."

Further Reading:

O. W. Holmes, *Ralph Waldo Emerson*, 1885.
J. Cabot, *A Memoir of Ralph Waldo Emerson*, 2 vols., 1887.
V. W. Brooks, *The Life of Emerson*, 1932.
R. Rusk, *The Life of Ralph Waldo Emerson*, 1949, 1957.
V. Hopkins, *Spires of Form*, 1951.
S. Paul, *Emerson's Angle of Vision*, 1952.
F. Carpenter, *The Emerson Handbook*, 1953.
S. Whicher, *Freedom and Fate*, 1953, 1959.
Emerson's Workshop: An Analysis of His Reading in Periodicals Through 1836, ed. K. W. Cameron, 1964.
R. Poirier, *A World Elsewhere*, 1966.
Emerson Among His Contemporaries, ed. K. W. Cameron, 1967.
W. Harding, *Emerson's Library*, 1967.
J. Porte, *Emerson and Thoreau: Transcendentalists in Conflict*, 1967.
L. Buell, *Literary Transcendentalism*, 1973.
H. H. Waggoner, *Emerson as Poet*, 1974.
S. Bercovitch, *The Puritan Origins of the American Self*, 1975.
D. Porter, *Emerson and Literary Change*, 1978.
R. A. Yoder, *Emerson and the Orphic Poet in America*, 1978.
J. Porte, *Representative Man: Ralph Waldo Emerson in His Time*, 1979.
G. W. Allen, *Waldo Emerson*, 1981.
B. Packer, *Emerson's Fall*, 1982.
D. Robinson, *Apostle of Culture: Emerson as Preacher and Lecturer*, 1982.
D. Yannela, *Ralph Waldo Emerson*, 1982.
J. McAleer, *Ralph Waldo Emerson: Days of Encounter*, 1984.

Texts:

"Nature," "The American Scholar," the Divinity School address, "Self-reliance," and "The Over-soul" from *The Collected Works of Ralph Waldo Emerson*, vol. 1, ed. R. E. Spiller and A. R. Ferguson, 1971, and vol. 2, ed. J. Slater, A. R. Ferguson, and J. F. Carr, 1979. See also *The Early Lectures of Ralph Waldo Emerson*, 3 vols., ed. S. Whicher et al., 1959–1971.
"Circles" and all poetry from *The Complete Works of Ralph Waldo Emerson*, ed. E. W. Emerson, 1903–1904.
"The Poet" and "Experience" from *Essays, Second Series*, 1844.
"Fate" and "Illusions" from *The Conduct of Life*, 1860.
Journal entries from *Emerson in His Journals*, ed. J. Porte, 1982.
See also *The Journals of Ralph Waldo Emerson*, 10 vols., ed. E. W. Emerson and W. Forbes, 1909–1914, and *The Journals and Miscellaneous Notebooks of Ralph Waldo Emerson*, ed. W. Gilman, 16 vols., 1960–1982.
Letters from *The Correspondence of Emerson and Carlyle*, ed. J. Slater, 1964, and *The Letters of Ralph Waldo Emerson*, 6 vols., ed. R. L. Rusk, 1939, 1957.
See also *Emerson's Literary Criticism*, ed. E. W. Carlson, 1979.

Nature[*]

A subtle chain of countless rings
The next unto the farthest brings;
The eye reads omens where it goes,
And speaks all languages the rose;
And, striving to be man, the worm
Mounts through all the spires of form.[1]

Introduction

Our age is retrospective. It builds the sepulchres of the fathers. It writes biographies, histories, and criticism. The foregoing generations beheld God and nature face to face; we, through their eyes. Why should not we also enjoy an original relation to the universe? Why should not we have a poetry and philosophy of insight and not of tradition, and a religion by revelation to us, and not the history of theirs? Embosomed for a season in nature, whose floods of life stream around and through us, and invite us, by the powers they supply, to action proportioned to nature, why should we grope among the dry bones of the past, or put the living generation into masquerade out of its faded wardrobe? The sun shines to-day also. There is more wool and flax in the fields. There are new lands, new men, new thoughts. Let us demand our own works and laws and worship.

Undoubtedly we have no questions to ask which are unanswerable. We must trust the perfection of the creation so far as to believe that whatever curiosity the order of things has awakened in our minds, the order of things can satisfy. Every man's condition is a solution in hieroglyphic to those inquiries he would put. He acts it as life, before he apprehends it as truth. In like manner, nature is already, in its forms and tendencies, describing its own design. Let us interrogate the great apparition that shines so peacefully around us. Let us inquire, to what end is nature?

All science has one aim, namely, to find a theory of nature. We have theories of races and of functions, but scarcely yet a remote approach to an idea of creation. We are now so far from the road to truth, that religious teachers dispute and hate each other, and speculative men are esteemed unsound and frivolous. But to a sound judgment, the most abstract truth is the most practical. Whenever a true theory appears, it will be its own evidence. Its test is, that it will explain all phenomena. Now many are thought not only unexplained but inexplicable; as language, sleep, madness, dreams, beasts, sex.

Philosophically considered, the universe is composed of Nature and the Soul. Strictly speaking, therefore, all that is separate from us, all which Philosophy distinguishes as the NOT ME, that is, both nature and art, all other men and my own body,

---

[*] Emerson's first major work and the first proclamation of New England Transcendentalism.

[1] The first edition of "Nature" in 1836 had as its motto a quote from the Roman philosopher Plotinus: "Nature is but an image or imitation of wisdom, the last thing of the soul; nature being a thing which doth only do, but not know." In the 1849 edition, Emerson's epigraphic poem was substituted, supporting Darwin's concept of evolutionary progress.

must be ranked under this name, NATURE. In enumerating the values of nature and casting up their sum, I shall use the word in both senses—in its common and in its philosophical import. In inquiries so general as our present one, the inaccuracy is not material; no confusion of thought will occur. *Nature,* in the common sense, refers to essences unchanged by man; space, the air, the river, the leaf. *Art* is applied to the mixture of his will with the same things, as in a house, a canal, a statue, a picture. But his operations taken together are so insignificant, a little chipping, baking, patching, and washing, that in an impression so grand as that of the world on the human mind, they do not vary the result.

I

To go into solitude, a man needs to retire as much from his chamber as from society. I am not solitary whilst I read and write, though nobody is with me. But if a man would be alone, let him look at the stars. The rays that come from those heavenly worlds will separate between him and what he touches. One might think the atmosphere was made transparent with this design, to give man, in the heavenly bodies, the perpetual presence of the sublime. Seen in the streets of cities, how great they are! If the stars should appear one night in a thousand years, how would men believe and adore; and preserve for many generations the remembrance of the city of God which had been shown! But every night come out these envoys of beauty, and light the universe with their admonishing smile.

The stars awaken a certain reverence, because though always present, they are inaccessible; but all natural objects make a kindred impression, when the mind is open to their influence. Nature never wears a mean appearance. Neither does the wisest man extort her secret, and lose his curiosity by finding out all her perfection. Nature never became a toy to a wise spirit. The flowers, the animals, the mountains, reflected the wisdom of his best hour, as much as they had delighted the simplicity of his childhood.

When we speak of nature in this manner, we have a distinct but most poetical sense in the mind. We mean the integrity of impression made by manifold natural objects. It is this which distinguishes the stick of timber of the wood-cutter from the tree of the poet. The charming landscape which I saw this morning is indubitably made up of some twenty or thirty farms. Miller owns this field, Locke that, and Manning the woodland beyond. But none of them owns the landscape. There is a property in the horizon which no man has but he whose eye can integrate all the parts, that is, the poet. This is the best part of these men's farms, yet to this their warranty-deeds give no title.

To speak truly, few adult persons can see nature. Most persons do not see the sun. At least they have a very superficial seeing. The sun illuminates only the eye of the man, but shines into the eye and the heart of the child. The lover of nature is he whose inward and outward senses are still truly adjusted to each other; who has retained the spirit of infancy even into the era of manhood. His intercourse with heaven and earth becomes part of his daily food. In the presence of nature a wild delight runs through the man, in spite of real sorrows. Nature says—he is my creature, and maugre all his impertinent griefs, he shall be glad with me. Not the sun or the summer alone, but every hour and season yields its tribute of delight; for every hour and change corresponds to and authorizes a different state of the mind, from breathless noon to grimmest midnight. Nature is a setting that fits equally well a comic or a mourning piece. In good health, the air is a cordial of incredible virtue. Crossing a bare common, in snow puddles, at twilight, under a clouded sky, without having in my thoughts any occurrence of special good fortune, I have enjoyed a perfect exhilaration. I am glad to the brink of fear. In the woods, too, a man casts off his years, as the snake his slough, and at what period soever of life is always a child. In the woods is perpetual youth. Within these plantations of God, a decorum and sanctity reign, a perennial festival is dressed, and the guest sees not how he should tire of them in a thousand years. In the woods, we return to reason and faith. There I feel that nothing can befall me in life—no disgrace, no calamity (leaving me my eyes), which nature cannot repair. Standing on the bare ground—my head bathed by the blithe air and uplifted into infinite space—all mean egotism vanishes. I become a transparent eyeball; I am nothing; I see all; the currents of the Universal Being circulate through me; I am part or parcel of God. The name of the nearest friend sounds then foreign and accidental: to be brothers, to be acquaintances, master or servant, is then a trifle and a disturbance. I am the lover of uncontained and immortal beauty. In the wilderness, I find something more dear and connate than in streets or villages. In the tranquil landscape, and especially in the distant line of the horizon, man beholds somewhat as beautiful as his own nature.

The greatest delight which the fields and woods minister is the suggestion of an occult relation between man and the vegetable. I am not alone and unacknowledged. They nod to me, and I to them. The waving of the boughs in the storm is new to me and old. It takes me by surprise, and yet is not unknown. Its effect is like that of a higher thought or a better emotion coming over me, when I deemed I was thinking justly or doing right.

Yet it is certain that the power to produce this delight does not reside in nature, but in man, or in a harmony of both. It is necessary to use these pleasures with great temperance. For nature is not always tricked[2] in holiday attire, but the same scene which yesterday breathed perfume and glittered as for the frolic of the nymphs is overspread with melancholy to-day. Nature always wears the colors of the spirit. To a man laboring under calamity, the heat of his own fire hath sadness in it. Then there is a kind of contempt of the landscape felt by him who has just lost by death a dear friend. The sky is less grand as it shuts down over less worth in the population.

II: Commodity

Whoever considers the final cause of the world will discern a multitude of uses that enter as parts into that result. They all admit of being thrown into one of the following classes: Commodity; Beauty; Language; and Discipline.

Under the general name of commodity, I rank all those advantages which our senses owe to nature. This, of course, is a benefit which is temporary and mediate,[3] not ultimate, like its service to the soul. Yet although low, it is perfect in its kind, and is the only use of nature which all men apprehend. The misery of man appears like childish petulance, when we explore the steady and prodigal provision that has been

---

[2] Clad.   [3] In between.

made for his support and delight on this green ball which floats him through the heavens. What angels invented these splendid ornaments, these rich conveniences, this ocean of air above, this ocean of water beneath, this firmament of earth between? this zodiac of lights, this tent of dropping clouds, this striped coat of climates, this fourfold year? Beasts, fire, water, stones, and corn serve him. The field is at once his floor, his work-yard, his play-ground, his garden, and his bed.

"More servants wait on man
   Than he'll take notice of."[4]

Nature, in its ministry to man, is not only the material, but is also the process and the result. All the parts incessantly work into each other's hands for the profit of man. The wind sows the seed; the sun evaporates the sea; the wind blows the vapor to the field; the ice, on the other side of the planet, condenses rain on this; the rain feeds the plant; the plant feeds the animal; and thus the endless circulations of the divine charity nourish man.

The useful arts are reproductions or new combinations by the wit of man, of the same natural benefactors. He no longer waits for favoring gales, but by means of steam, he realizes the fable of Aeolus's bag,[5] and carries the two and thirty winds in the boiler of his boat. To diminish friction, he paves the road with iron bars,[6] and, mounting a coach with a ship-load of men, animals, and merchandise behind him, he darts through the country, from town to town, like an eagle or a swallow through the air. By the aggregate of these aids, how is the face of the world changed, from the era of Noah to that of Napoleon! The private poor man hath cities, ships, canals, bridges, built for him. He goes to the post-office, and the human race run on his errands; to the book-shop, and the human race read and write of all that happens for him; to the court-house, and nations repair his wrongs. He sets his house upon the road, and the human race go forth every morning, and shovel out the snow, and cut a path for him.

But there is no need of specifying particulars in this class of uses. The catalogue is endless, and the examples so obvious, that I shall leave them to the reader's reflection, with the general remark, that this mercenary benefit is one which has respect to a farther good. A man is fed, not that he may be fed, but that he may work.

III: Beauty

A nobler want of man is served by nature, namely, the love of Beauty.

The ancient Greeks called the world χόσμος,[7] beauty. Such is the constitution of all things, or such the plastic power of the human eye, that the primary forms, as the sky, the mountain, the tree, the animal, give us a delight *in and for themselves;* a pleasure arising from outline, color, motion, and grouping. This seems partly owing to the eye itself. The eye is the best of artists. By the mutual action of its structure

---

[4] From "Man" by the English poet George Herbert (1593–1633).

[5] Aeolus, a god in Homer's *Odyssey,* gave Odysseus "a mighty bag" of bottled winds. Inquisitive sailors opened this bag and released a tumultuous storm.

[6] Railroad tracks.

[7] Greek: "beauty" in the sense of the complexity of the universe expressed as orderly and harmonious.

and of the laws of light, perspective is produced, which integrates every mass of objects, of what character soever, into a well colored and shaded globe, so that where the particular objects are mean and unaffecting, the landscape which they compose is round and symmetrical. And as the eye is the best composer, so light is the first of painters. There is no object so foul that intense light will not make beautiful. And the stimulus it affords to the sense, and a sort of infinitude which it hath, like space and time, make all matter gay. Even the corpse has its own beauty. But besides this general grace diffused over nature, almost all the individual forms are agreeable to the eye, as is proved by our endless imitations of some of them, as the acorn, the grape, the pine-cone, the wheat-ear, the egg, the wings and forms of most birds, the lion's claw, the serpent, the butterfly, sea-shells, flames, clouds, buds, leaves, and the forms of many trees, as the palm.

For better consideration, we may distribute the aspects of Beauty in a threefold manner.

1.   First, the simple perception of natural forms is a delight. The influence of the forms and actions in nature is so needful to man, that, in its lowest functions, it seems to lie on the confines of commodity and beauty. To the body and mind which have been cramped by noxious work or company, nature is medicinal and restores their tone. The tradesman, the attorney comes out of the din and craft of the street and sees the sky and the woods, and is a man again. In their eternal calm, he finds himself. The health of the eye seems to demand a horizon. We are never tired, so long as we can see far enough.

But in other hours, Nature satisfies by its loveliness, and without any mixture of corporeal benefit. I see the spectacle of morning from the hilltop over against my house, from daybreak to sunrise, with emotions which an angel might share. The long slender bars of cloud float like fishes in the sea of crimson light. From the earth, as a shore, I look out into that silent sea. I seem to partake its rapid transformations; the active enchantment reaches my dust, and I dilate and conspire with the morning wind. How does Nature deify us with a few and cheap elements! Give me health and a day, and I will make the pomp of emperors ridiculous. The dawn is my Assyria;[8] the sunset and moonrise my Paphos,[9] and unimaginable realms of faerie; broad noon shall be my England of the senses and the understanding; the night shall be my Germany of mystic philosophy and dreams.[10]

Not less excellent, except for our less susceptibility in the afternoon, was the charm, last evening, of a January sunset. The western clouds divided and subdivided themselves into pink flakes modulated with tints of unspeakable softness, and the air had so much life and sweetness that it was a pain to come within doors. What was it that nature would say? Was there no meaning in the live repose of the valley behind the mill, and which Homer or Shakspeare could not re-form for me in words? The leafless trees become spires of flame in the sunset, with the blue east for their background, and the stars of the dead calices[11] of flowers, and every withered stem and stubble rimed with frost, contribute something to the mute music.

The inhabitants of cities suppose that the country landscape is pleasant only half

---

8 Ancient Near Eastern empire, emblematic of magnificence.
9 Ancient city of Cyprus, distinguished for its worship of Aphrodite, Greek goddess of love and beauty.

10 The rational empiricism of English philosophers, such as Hume, and the "common sense" school of thought are contrasted to the idealism of German philosophers, such as Kant.
11 External, leafy parts of flowers.

the year. I please myself with the graces of the winter scenery, and believe that we are as much touched by it as by the genial influences of summer. To the attentive eye, each moment of the year has its own beauty, and in the same field, it beholds, every hour, a picture which was never seen before and which shall never be seen again. The heavens change every moment, and reflect their glory or gloom on the plains beneath. The state of the crop in the surrounding farms alters the expression of the earth from week to week. The succession of native plants in the pastures and roadsides, which make the silent clock by which time tells the summer hours, will make even the divisions of the day sensible to a keen observer. The tribes of birds and insects, like the plants punctual to their time, follow each other, and the year has room for all. By watercourses, the variety is greater. In July, the blue pontederia or pickerel-weed blooms in large beds in the shallow parts of our pleasant river,[12] and swarms with yellow butterflies in continual motion. Art cannot rival this pomp of purple and gold. Indeed the river is a perpetual gala, and boasts each month a new ornament.

But this beauty of Nature which is seen and felt as beauty, is the least part. The shows of day, the dewy morning, the rainbow, mountains, orchards in blossom, stars, moonlight, shadows in still water, and the like, if too eagerly hunted, become shows merely, and mock us with their unreality. Go out of the house to see the moon, and 't is mere tinsel; it will not please as when its light shines upon your necessary journey. The beauty that shimmers in the yellow afternoons of October, who ever could clutch it? Go forth to find it, and it is gone; 't is only a mirage as you look from the windows of diligence.

2. The presence of a higher, namely, of the spiritual element is essential to its perfection. The high and divine beauty which can be loved without effeminacy, is that which is found in combination with the human will. Beauty is the mark God sets upon virtue. Every natural action is graceful. Every heroic act is also decent, and causes the place and the bystanders to shine. We are taught by great actions that the universe is the property of every individual in it. Every rational creature has all nature for his dowry and estate. It is his, if he will. He may divest himself of it; he may creep into a corner, and abdicate his kingdom, as most men do, but he is entitled to the world by his constitution. In proportion to the energy of his thought and will, he takes up the world into himself. "All those things for which men plough, build, or sail, obey virtue;" said Sallust.[13] "The winds and waves," said Gibbon, "are always on the side of the ablest navigators."[14] So are the sun and moon and all the stars of heaven. When a noble act is done—perchance in a scene of great natural beauty; when Leonidas[15] and his three hundred martyrs consume one day in dying, and the sun and moon come each and look at them once in the steep defile of Thermopylae; when Arnold Winkelried,[16] in the high Alps, under the shadow of the avalanche, gathers in his side a sheaf of Austrian spears to break the line for his comrades; are not these heroes entitled to add the beauty of the scene to the beauty of the deed? When the

---

[12] The Concord River.

[13] From *The Conspiracy of Catiline* by the Roman historian Gaius Sallustius Crispus (86–35 B.C.).

[14] From *The Decline and Fall of the Roman Empire* (1788) by Edward Gibbon (1737–1794), English historian.

[15] King Leonidas and 300 fellow Spartans died

while defending the pass at Thermopylae against the Persian army in 480 B.C.

[16] Swiss hero who exposed himself to the spears of the Austrians in the Battle of Sempach (1386). When the Austrians had exhausted their supply, Winkelried defeated them and proclaimed Swiss independence.

bark of Columbus nears the shore of America; before it the beach lined with savages, fleeing out of all their huts of cane; the sea behind; and the purple mountains of the Indian Archipelago around, can we separate the man from the living picture? Does not the New World clothe his form with her palm-groves and savannahs as fit drapery? Ever does natural beauty steal in like air, and envelop great actions. When Sir Harry Vane[17] was dragged up the Tower-hill,[18] sitting on a sled, to suffer death as the champion of the English laws, one of the multitude cried out to him, "You never sate on so glorious a seat!" Charles II, to intimidate the citizens of London, caused the patriot Lord Russell[19] to be drawn in an open coach through the principal streets of the city on his way to the scaffold. "But," his biographer says, "the multitude imagined they saw liberty and virtue sitting by his side." In private places, among sordid objects, an act of truth or heroism seems at once to draw to itself the sky as its temple, the sun as its candle. Nature stretches out her arms to embrace man, only let his thoughts be of equal greatness. Willingly does she follow his steps with the rose and the violet, and bend her lines of grandeur and grace to the decoration of her darling child. Only let his thoughts be of equal scope, and the frame will suit the picture. A virtuous man is in unison with her works, and makes the central figure of the visible sphere. Homer, Pindar, Socrates, Phocion,[20] associate themselves fitly in our memory with the geography and climate of Greece. The visible heavens and earth sympathize with Jesus. And in common life whosoever has seen a person of powerful character and happy genius, will have remarked how easily he took all things along with him—the persons, the opinions, and the day, and nature became ancillary to a man.

3.   There is still another aspect under which the beauty of the world may be viewed, namely, as it becomes an object of the intellect. Beside the relation of things to virtue, they have a relation to thought. The intellect searches out the absolute order of things as they stand in the mind of God, and without the colors of affection. The intellectual and the active powers seem to succeed each other, and the exclusive activity of the one generates the exclusive activity of the other. There is something unfriendly in each to the other, but they are like the alternate periods of feeding and working in animals; each prepares and will be followed by the other. Therefore does beauty, which, in relation to actions, as we have seen, comes unsought, and comes because it is unsought, remain for the apprehension and pursuit of the intellect; and then again, in its turn, of the active power. Nothing divine dies. All good is eternally reproductive. The beauty of nature re-forms itself in the mind, and not for barren contemplation, but for new creation.

All men are in some degree impressed by the face of the world; some men even to delight. This love of beauty is Taste. Others have the same love in such excess, that, not content with admiring, they seek to embody it in new forms. The creation of beauty is Art.

---

[17] English Puritan (1613–1662) executed for opposing the restoration of Charles II.
[18] Hill next to the Tower of London where executions for treason took place.
[19] William Russell (1639–1683), executed for cooperating with a plot to overthrow Charles II.

[20] Homer: Greek epic poet (fl. 850? B.C.); Pindar: Greek poet (522?–443 B.C.); Socrates: Greek philosopher (470?–399 B.C.); Phocion: Athenian general and statesman (402?–317 B.C.).

The production of a work of art throws a light upon the mystery of humanity. A work of art is an abstract or epitome of the world. It is the result or expression of nature, in miniature. For although the works of nature are innumerable and all different, the result or the expression of them all is similar and single. Nature is a sea of forms radically alike and even unique. A leaf, a sunbeam, a landscape, the ocean, make an analogous impression on the mind. What is common to them all—that perfectness and harmony, is beauty. The standard of beauty is the entire circuit of natural forms—the totality of nature; which the Italians expressed by defining beauty "il più nell' uno."[21] Nothing is quite beautiful alone; nothing but is beautiful in the whole. A single object is only so far beautiful as it suggests this universal grace. The poet, the painter, the sculptor, the musician, the architect, seek each to concentrate this radiance of the world on one point, and each in his several work to satisfy the love of beauty which stimulates him to produce. Thus is Art a nature passed through the alembic of man. Thus in art does Nature work through the will of a man filled with the beauty of her first works.

The world thus exists to the soul to satisfy the desire of beauty. This element I call an ultimate end. No reason can be asked or given why the soul seeks beauty. Beauty, in its largest and profoundest sense, is one expression for the universe. God is the all-fair. Truth, and goodness, and beauty, are but different faces of the same All. But beauty in nature is not ultimate. It is the herald of inward and eternal beauty, and is not alone a solid and satisfactory good. It must stand as a part, and not as yet the last or highest expression of the final cause of Nature.

IV: Language

Language is a third use which Nature subserves to man. Nature is the vehicle of thought, and in a simple, double, and three-fold degree.

1. Words are signs of natural facts.
2. Particular natural facts are symbols of particular spiritual facts.
3. Nature is the symbol of spirit.

1. Words are signs of natural facts. The use of natural history is to give us aid in supernatural history; the use of the outer creation, to give us language for the beings and changes of the inward creation. Every word which is used to express a moral or intellectual fact, if traced to its root, is found to be borrowed from some material appearance. *Right* means *straight; wrong* means *twisted; Spirit* primarily means *wind; transgression,* the crossing of a *line; supercilious,* the *raising of the eyebrow.* We say the *heart* to express emotion, the *head* to denote thought; and *thought* and *emotion* are words borrowed from sensible things, and now appropriated to spiritual nature. Most of the process by which this transformation is made, is hidden from us in the remote time when language was framed; but the same tendency may be daily observed in children. Children and savages use only nouns or names of things, which they convert into verbs, and apply to analogous mental acts.

2. But this origin of all words that convey a spiritual import—so conspicuous a fact in the history of language—is our least debt to nature. It is not words only that are emblematic; it is things which are emblematic. Every natural fact is a symbol of some spiritual fact. Every appearance in nature corresponds to some state of the

---

[21] Italian: "the many in one."

mind, and that state of the mind can only be described by presenting that natural appearance as its picture. An enraged man is a lion, a cunning man is a fox, a firm man is a rock, a learned man is a torch. A lamb is innocence; a snake is subtle spite; flowers express to us the delicate affections. Light and darkness are our familiar expression for knowledge and ignorance; and heat for love. Visible distance behind and before us, is respectively our image of memory and hope.

Who looks upon a river in a meditative hour and is not reminded of the flux of all things? Throw a stone into the stream, and the circles that propagate themselves are the beautiful type of all influence. Man is conscious of a universal soul within or behind his individual life, wherein, as in a firmament, the natures of Justice, Truth, Love, Freedom, arise and shine. This universal soul he calls Reason: it is not mine, or thine, or his, but we are its; we are its property and men. And the blue sky in which the private earth is buried, the sky with its eternal calm, and full of everlasting orbs, is the type of Reason. That which intellectually considered we call Reason, considered in relation to nature, we call Spirit. Spirit is the Creator. Spirit hath life in itself. And man in all ages and countries embodies it in his language as the FATHER.

It is easily seen that there is nothing lucky or capricious in these analogies, but that they are constant, and pervade nature. These are not the dreams of a few poets, here and there, but man is an analogist, and studies relations in all objects. He is placed in the centre of beings, and a ray of relation passes from every other being to him. And neither can man be understood without these objects, nor these objects without man. All the facts in natural history taken by themselves, have no value, but are barren, like a single sex. But marry it to human history, and it is full of life. Whole floras, all Linnæus' and Buffon's[22] volumes, are dry catalogues of facts; but the most trivial of these facts, the habit of a plant, the organs, or work, or noise of an insect, applied to the illustration of a fact in intellectual philosophy, or in any way associated to human nature, affects us in the most lively and agreeable manner. The seed of a plant —to what affecting analogies in the nature of man is that little fruit made use of, in all discourse, up to the voice of Paul, who calls the human corpse a seed—"It is sown a natural body; it is raised a spiritual body."[23] The motion of the earth round its axis and round the sun, makes the day and the year. These are certain amounts of brute light and heat. But is there no intent of an analogy between man's life and the seasons? And do the seasons gain no grandeur or pathos from that analogy? The instincts of the ant are very unimportant considered as the ant's; but the moment a ray of relation is seen to extend from it to man, and the little drudge is seen to be a monitor, a little body with a mighty heart, then all its habits, even that said to be recently observed, that it never sleeps, become sublime.

Because of this radical correspondence between visible things and human thoughts, savages, who have only what is necessary, converse in figures. As we go back in history, language becomes more picturesque, until its infancy, when it is all poetry; or all spiritual facts are represented by natural symbols. The same symbols are found to make the original elements of all languages. It has moreover been observed, that the idioms of all languages approach each other in passages of the greatest eloquence

[margin annotation: codependent]

---

[22] Linnæus: Carolus Linnæus (1707–1778), Swedish botanist; Buffon: Georges Louis Leclerc, comte de Buffon (1707–1788), French naturalist.   [23] See 1 Corinthians 15:44.

and power. And as this is the first language, so is it the last. This immediate dependence of language upon nature, this conversion of an outward phenomenon into a type of somewhat in human life, never loses its power to affect us. It is this which gives that piquancy to the conversation of a strong-natured farmer or backwoodsman, which all men relish.

A man's power to connect his thought with its proper symbol, and so to utter it, depends on the simplicity of his character, that is, upon his love of truth and his desire to communicate it without loss. The corruption of man is followed by the corruption of language. When simplicity of character and the sovereignty of ideas is broken up by the prevalence of secondary desires—the desire of riches, of pleasure, of power, and of praise—and duplicity and falsehood take place of simplicity and truth, the power over nature as an interpreter of the will is in a degree lost; new imagery ceases to be created, and old words are perverted to stand for things which are not; a paper currency is employed, when there is no bullion in the vaults. In due time the fraud is manifest, and words lose all power to stimulate the understanding or the affections. Hundreds of writers may be found in every long-civilized nation who for a short time believe and make others believe that they see and utter truths, who do not of themselves clothe one thought in its natural garment, but who feed unconsciously on the language created by the primary writers of the country, those, namely, who hold primarily on nature.

But wise men pierce this rotten diction and fasten words again to visible things; so that picturesque language is at once a commanding certificate that he who employs it is a man in alliance with truth and God. The moment our discourse rises above the ground line of familiar facts and is inflamed with passion or exalted by thought, it clothes itself in images. A man conversing in earnest, if he watch his intellectual processes, will find that a material image more or less luminous arises in his mind, contemporaneous with every thought, which furnishes the vestment of the thought. Hence, good writing and brilliant discourse are perpetual allegories. This imagery is spontaneous. It is the blending of experience with the present action of the mind. It is proper creation. It is the working of the Original Cause through the instruments he has already made.

These facts may suggest the advantage which the country-life possesses, for a powerful mind, over the artificial and curtailed life of cities. We know more from nature than we can at will communicate. Its light flows into the mind evermore, and we forget its presence. The poet, the orator, bred in the woods, whose senses have been nourished by their fair and appeasing changes, year after year, without design and without heed—shall not lose their lesson altogether, in the roar of cities or the broil of politics. Long hereafter, amidst agitation and terror in national councils— in the hour of revolution—these solemn images shall reappear in their morning lustre, as fit symbols and words of the thoughts which the passing events shall awaken. At the call of a noble sentiment, again the woods wave, the pines murmur, the river rolls and shines, and the cattle low upon the mountains, as he saw and heard them in his infancy. And with these forms, the spells of persuasion, the keys of power are put into his hands.

3.   We are thus assisted by natural objects in the expression of particular meanings. But how great a language to convey such pepper-corn[24] informations! Did it need

[24] Unimportant.

such noble races of creatures, this profusion of forms, this host of orbs in heaven, to furnish man with the dictionary and grammar of his municipal speech? Whilst we use this grand cipher to expedite the affairs of our pot and kettle, we feel that we have not yet put it to its use, neither are able. We are like travellers using the cinders of a volcano to roast their eggs. Whilst we see that it always stands ready to clothe what we would say, we cannot avoid the question whether the characters are not significant of themselves. Have mountains, and waves, and skies, no significance but what we consciously give them when we employ them as emblems of our thoughts? The world is emblematic. Parts of speech are metaphors, because the whole of nature is a metaphor of the human mind. The laws of moral nature answer to those of matter as face to face in a glass. "The visible world and the relation of its parts, is the dial plate of the invisible."[25] The axioms of physics translate the laws of ethics. Thus, "the whole is greater than its part;" "reaction is equal to action;" "the smallest weight may be made to lift the greatest, the difference of weight being compensated by time;" and many the like propositions, which have an ethical as well as physical sense. These propositions have a much more extensive and universal sense when applied to human life, than when confined to technical use.

In like manner, the memorable words of history and the proverbs of nations consist usually of a natural fact, selected as a picture or parable of a moral truth. Thus: A rolling stone gathers no moss; A bird in the hand is worth two in the bush; A cripple in the right way will beat a racer in the wrong; Make hay while the sun shines; 'T is hard to carry a full cup even; Vinegar is the son of wine; The last ounce broke the camel's back; Long-lived trees make roots first—and the like. In their primary sense these are trivial facts, but we repeat them for the value of their analogical import. What is true of proverbs, is true of all fables, parables, and allegories.

This relation between the mind and matter is not fancied by some poet, but stands in the will of God, and so is free to be known by all men. It appears to men, or it does not appear. When in fortunate hours we ponder this miracle, the wise man doubts if at all other times he is not blind and deaf;

> "Can such things be,
> And overcome us like a summer's cloud,
> Without our special wonder?"[26]

for the universe becomes transparent, and the light of higher laws than its own shines through it. It is the standing problem which has exercised the wonder and the study of every fine genius since the world began; from the era of the Egyptians and the Brahmins to that of Pythagoras, of Plato, of Bacon, of Leibnitz, of Swedenborg.[27] There sits the Sphinx[28] at the road-side, and from age to age, as each prophet comes

---

[25] Quoted from the philosopher Emanuel Swedenborg (1688–1772) (see note 27 below).

[26] Shakespeare's *Macbeth*, Act III, Sc. iv, ll. 110–112.

[27] Teachings that influenced Emerson's interpretations of the universe. Egyptian and Brahmin mystics taught transmigration of the soul. Pythagoras (sixth century B.C.) believed in the infinite recurrence of phenomena. Plato (428–347 B.C.) fostered the idealism of Western

philosophy. Francis Bacon (1561–1626), British founder of inductive science, believed in religious mysticism. Gottfried Wilhelm von Leibnitz (1646–1716) was a German mathematician and idealist philosopher. Emanuel Swedenborg (1688–1772) was the Swedish religious mentor whom Emerson characterized as "the mystic" in *Representative Men.*

[28] According to Greek mythology, this monster killed anyone who failed to answer her riddle.

by, he tries his fortune at reading her riddle. There seems to be a necessity in spirit to manifest itself in material forms; and day and night, river and storm, beast and bird, acid and alkali, preëxist in necessary Ideas in the mind of God, and are what they are by virtue of preceding affections in the world of spirit. A Fact is the end or last issue of spirit. The visible creation is the terminus or the circumference of the invisible world. "Material objects," said a French philosopher,[29] "are necessarily kinds of *scoriæ*[30] of the substantial thoughts of the Creator, which must always preserve an exact relation to their first origin; in other words, visible nature must have a spiritual and moral side."

This doctrine is abstruse, and though the images of "garment," "scoriæ," "mirror," etc., may stimulate the fancy, we must summon the aid of subtler and more vital expositors to make it plain. "Every scripture is to be interpreted by the same spirit which gave it forth,"[31] is the fundamental law of criticism. A life in harmony with Nature, the love of truth and of virtue, will purge the eyes to understand her text. By degrees we may come to know the primitive sense of the permanent objects of nature, so that the world shall be to us an open book, and every form significant of its hidden life and final cause.

A new interest surprises us, whilst, under the view now suggested, we contemplate the fearful extent and multitude of objects; since "every object rightly seen, unlocks a new faculty of the soul."[32] That which was unconscious truth, becomes, when interpreted and defined in an object, a part of the domain of knowledge—a new weapon in the magazine of power.

V: Discipline

In view of the significance of nature, we arrive at once at a new fact, that nature is a discipline. This use of the world includes the preceding uses, as parts of itself.

Space, time, society, labor, climate, food, locomotion, the animals, the mechanical forces, give us sincerest lessons, day by day, whose meaning is unlimited. They educate both the Understanding and the Reason. Every property of matter is a school for the understanding—its solidity or resistance, its inertia, its extension, its figure, its divisibility. The understanding adds, divides, combines, measures, and finds nutriment and room for its activity in this worthy scene. Meantime, Reason transfers all these lessons into its own world of thought, by perceiving the analogy that marries Matter and Mind.

1. Nature is a discipline of the understanding in intellectual truths. Our dealing with sensible objects is a constant exercise in the necessary lessons of difference, of likeness, of order, of being and seeming, of progressive arrangement; of ascent from particular to general; of combination to one end of manifold forces. Proportioned to the importance of the organ to be formed, is the extreme care with which its tuition is provided—a care pretermitted in no single case. What tedious training, day after day, year after year, never ending, to form the common sense; what continual reproduction of annoyances, inconveniences, dilemmas; what rejoicing over us of little

---

[29] Guillaume Oegger in *The True Messiah* (1829).
[30] Slag from the melting of metals.
[31] Quoted from the English Quaker George Fox (1624–1691).

[32] From a compendium of literary criticism and philosophy, *Aids to Reflection* (1825), by Samuel Taylor Coleridge (1772–1834).

men; what disputing of prices, what reckonings of interest—and all to form the Hand of the mind—to instruct us that "good thoughts are no better than good dreams, unless they be executed!"[33]

The same good office is performed by Property and its filial systems of debt and credit. Debt, grinding debt, whose iron face the widow, the orphan, and the sons of genius fear and hate—debt, which consumes so much time, which so cripples and disheartens a great spirit with cares that seem so base, is a preceptor whose lessons cannot be foregone, and is needed most by those who suffer from it most. Moreover, property, which has been well compared to snow—"if it fall level to-day, it will be blown into drifts to-morrow," is the surface action of internal machinery, like the index on the face of a clock. Whilst now it is the gymnastics of the understanding, it is hiving, in the foresight of the spirit, experience in profounder laws.

The whole character and fortune of the individual are affected by the least inequalities in the culture of the understanding; for example, in the perception of differences. Therefore is Space, and therefore Time, that man may know that things are not huddled and lumped, but sundered and individual. A bell and a plough have each their use, and neither can do the office of the other. Water is good to drink, coal to burn, wool to wear; but wool cannot be drunk, nor water spun, nor coal eaten. The wise man shows his wisdom in separation, in gradation, and his scale of creatures and of merits is as wide as nature. The foolish have no range in their scale, but suppose every man is as every other man. What is not good they call the worst, and what is not hateful, they call the best.

In like manner, what good heed Nature forms in us! She pardons no mistakes. Her yea is yea, and her nay, nay.

The first steps in Agriculture, Astronomy, Zoölogy (those first steps which the farmer, the hunter, and the sailor take), teach that Nature's dice are always loaded; that in her heaps and rubbish are concealed sure and useful results.

How calmly and genially the mind apprehends one after another the laws of physics! What noble emotions dilate the mortal as he enters into the councils of the creation, and feels by knowledge the privilege to BE! His insight refines him. The beauty of nature shines in his own breast. Man is greater that he can see this, and the universe less, because Time and Space relations vanish as laws are known.

Here again we are impressed and even daunted by the immense Universe to be explored. "What we know is a point to what we do not know."[34] Open any recent journal of science, and weigh the problems suggested concerning Light, Heat, Electricity, Magnetism, Physiology, Geology, and judge whether the interest of natural science is likely to be soon exhausted.

Passing by many particulars of the discipline of nature, we must not omit to specify two.

The exercise of the Will, or the lesson of power, is taught in every event. From the child's successive possession of his several senses up to the hour when he saith, "Thy will be done!"[35] he is learning the secret that he can reduce under his will not only

---

[33] From "Of Great Place" in the *Essays* (1625) of Sir Francis Bacon (1561–1626).
[34] Quotation attributed to English theologian and moralist Bishop Joseph Butler (1692–1752).
[35] Matthew 6:10; 26:42.

particular events but great classes, nay, the whole series of events, and so conform all facts to his character. Nature is thoroughly mediate. It is made to serve. It receives the dominion of man as meekly as the ass on which the Saviour rode.[36] It offers all its kingdoms to man as the raw material which he may mould into what is useful. Man is never weary of working it up. He forges the subtile and delicate air into wise and melodious words, and gives them wing as angels of persuasion and command. One after another his victorious thought comes up with and reduces all things, until the world becomes at last only a realized will—the double of the man.

2. Sensible objects conform to the premonitions of Reason and reflect the conscience. All things are moral; and in their boundless changes have an unceasing reference to spiritual nature. Therefore is nature glorious with form, color, and motion; that every globe in the remotest heaven, every chemical change from the rudest crystal up to the laws of life, every change of vegetation from the first principle of growth in the eye of a leaf, to the tropical forest and antediluvian coal-mine, every animal function from the sponge up to Hercules, shall hint or thunder to man the laws of right and wrong, and echo the Ten Commandments. Therefore is Nature ever the ally of Religion: lends all her pomp and riches to the religious sentiment. Prophet and priest, David, Isaiah, Jesus, have drawn deeply from this source. This ethical character so penetrates the bone and marrow of nature, as to seem the end for which it was made. Whatever private purpose is answered by any member or part, this is its public and universal function, and is never omitted. Nothing in nature is exhausted in its first use. When a thing has served an end to the uttermost, it is wholly new for an ulterior service. In God, every end is converted into a new means. Thus the use of commodity, regarded by itself, is mean and squalid. But it is to the mind an education in the doctrine of Use, namely, that a thing is good only so far as it serves; that a conspiring of parts and efforts to the production of an end is essential to any being. The first and gross manifestation of this truth is our inevitable and hated training in values and wants, in corn and meat.

It has already been illustrated, that every natural process is a version of a moral sentence. The moral law lies at the centre of nature and radiates to the circumference. It is the pith and marrow of every substance, every relation, and every process. All things with which we deal, preach to us. What is a farm but a mute gospel? The chaff and the wheat, weeds and plants, blight, rain, insects, sun—it is a sacred emblem from the first furrow of spring to the last stack which the snow of winter overtakes in the fields. But the sailor, the shepherd, the miner, the merchant, in their several resorts, have each an experience precisely parallel, and leading to the same conclusion: because all organizations are radically alike. Nor can it be doubted that this moral sentiment which thus scents the air, grows in the grain, and impregnates the waters of the world, is caught by man and sinks into his soul. The moral influence of nature upon every individual is that amount of truth which it illustrates to him. Who can estimate this? Who can guess how much firmness the sea-beaten rock has taught the fisherman? How much tranquillity has been reflected to man from the azure sky, over whose unspotted deeps the winds forevermore drive flocks of stormy clouds, and leave no wrinkle or stain? How much industry and providence and affection we have caught from the

---

[36] Matthew 21:5: "Behold thy king cometh unto thee, meek, and sitting upon an ass."

pantomime of brutes? What a searching preacher of self-command is the varying phenomenon of Health!

Herein is especially apprehended the unity of Nature—the unity in variety—which meets us everywhere. All the endless variety of things make an identical impression. Xenophanes[37] complained in his old age, that, look where he would, all things hastened back to Unity. He was weary of seeing the same entity in the tedious variety of forms. The fable of Proteus[38] has a cordial truth. A leaf, a drop, a crystal, a moment of time, is related to the whole, and partakes of the perfection of the whole. Each particle is a microcosm, and faithfully renders the likeness of the world.

Not only resemblances exist in things whose analogy is obvious, as when we detect the type of the human hand in the flipper of the fossil saurus,[39] but also in objects wherein there is great superficial unlikeness. Thus architecture is called "frozen music," by De Staël and Goethe.[40] Vitruvius[41] thought an architect should be a musician. "A Gothic church," said Coleridge,[42] "is a petrified religion." Michael Angelo maintained, that, to an architect, a knowledge of anatomy is essential. In Haydn's oratorios,[43] the notes present to the imagination not only motions, as of the snake, the stag, and the elephant, but colors also; as the green grass. The law of harmonic sounds reappears in the harmonic colors. The granite is differenced in its laws only by the more or less of heat from the river that wears it away. The river, as it flows, resembles the air that flows over it; the air resembles the light which traverses it with more subtle currents; the light resembles the heat which rides with it through Space. Each creature is only a modification of the other; the likeness in them is more than the difference, and their radical law is one and the same. A rule of one art, or a law of one organization, holds true throughout nature. So intimate is this Unity, that, it is easily seen, it lies under the undermost garment of Nature, and betrays its source in Universal Spirit. For it pervades Thought also. Every universal truth which we express in words, implies or supposes every other truth. *Omne verum vero consonat.*[44] It is like a great circle on a sphere, comprising all possible circles; which, however, may be drawn and comprise it in like manner. Every such truth is the absolute Ens[45] seen from one side. But it has innumerable sides.

The central Unity is still more conspicuous in actions. Words are finite organs of the infinite mind. They cannot cover the dimensions of what is in truth. They break, chop, and impoverish it. An action is the perfection and publication of thought. A right action seems to fill the eye, and to be related to all nature. "The wise man, in doing one thing, does all; or, in the one thing he does rightly, he sees the likeness of all which is done rightly."[46]

Words and actions are not the attributes of brute nature. They introduce us to the

---

[37] Greek philosopher of the sixth century B.C.

[38] God of Greek fable who could assume various forms.

[39] Extinct reptiles.

[40] De Staël: French writer Anne Louise Germaine (1766–1817), baronne de Staël; Goethe: German poet Johann Wolfgang von Goethe (1749–1832).

[41] Roman architect Marcus Vitruvius Pollio (first century B.C.).

[42] From "A Lecture on the General Characteristics of the Gothic Mind in the Middle Ages" in *Literary Remains* (1836) by Samuel Taylor Coleridge.

[43] Choral music of Austrian composer Franz Joseph Haydn (1732–1809).

[44] Latin: "Every truth agrees with every other truth."

[45] A name for "abstract being" in Latin philosophy.

[46] Quote from Goethe's *Wilhelm Meister's Travels* (1821, 1829).

human form, of which all other organizations appear to be degradations. When this appears among so many that surround it, the spirit prefers it to all others. It says, "From such as this have I drawn joy and knowledge; in such as this have I found and beheld myself; I will speak to it; it can speak again; it can yield me thought already formed and alive." In fact, the eye—the mind—is always accompanied by these forms, male and female; and these are incomparably the richest informations of the power and order that lie at the heart of things. Unfortunately every one of them bears the marks as of some injury; is marred and superficially defective. Nevertheless, far different from the deaf and dumb nature around them, these all rest like fountain-pipes on the unfathomed sea of thought and virtue whereto they alone, of all organizations, are the entrances.

It were a pleasant inquiry to follow into detail their ministry to our education, but where would it stop? We are associated in adolescent and adult life with some friends, who, like skies and waters, are coextensive with our idea; who, answering each to a certain affection of the soul, satisfy our desire on that side; whom we lack power to put at such focal distance from us, that we can mend or even analyze them. We cannot choose but love them. When much intercourse with a friend has supplied us with a standard of excellence, and has increased our respect for the resources of God who thus sends a real person to outgo our ideal; when he has, moreover, become an object of thought, and, whilst his character retains all its unconscious effect, is converted in the mind into solid and sweet wisdom—it is a sign to us that his office is closing, and he is commonly withdrawn from our sight in a short time.

VI: Idealism

Thus is the unspeakable but intelligible and practicable meaning of the world conveyed to man, the immortal pupil, in every object of sense. To this one end of Discipline, all parts of nature conspire.

A noble doubt perpetually suggests itself—whether this end be not the Final Cause of the Universe; and whether nature outwardly exists. It is a sufficient account of that Appearance we call the World, that God will teach a human mind, and so makes it the receiver of a certain number of congruent sensations, which we call sun and moon, man and woman, house and trade. In my utter impotence to test the authenticity of the report of my senses, to know whether the impressions they make on me correspond with outlying objects, what difference does it make, whether Orion[47] is up there in heaven, or some god paints the image in the firmament of the soul? The relations of parts and the end of the whole remaining the same, what is the difference, whether land and sea interact, and worlds revolve and intermingle without number or end— deep yawning under deep, and galaxy balancing galaxy, throughout absolute space —or whether, without relations of time and space, the same appearances are inscribed in the constant faith of man? Whether nature enjoy a substantial existence without, or is only in the apocalypse of the mind, it is alike useful and alike venerable to me. Be it what it may, it is ideal to me so long as I cannot try the accuracy of my senses.

The frivolous make themselves merry with the Ideal theory, as if its consequences were burlesque; as if it affected the stability of nature. It surely does not. God never

[47] Constellation of stars.

jests with us, and will not compromise the end of nature by permitting any inconsequence in its procession. Any distrust of the permanence of laws would paralyze the faculties of man. Their permanence is sacredly respected, and his faith therein is perfect. The wheels and springs of man are all set to the hypothesis of the permanence of nature. We are not built like a ship to be tossed, but like a house to stand. It is a natural consequence of this structure, that so long as the active powers predominate over the reflective, we resist with indignation any hint that nature is more short-lived or mutable than spirit. The broker, the wheelwright, the carpenter, the tollman, are much displeased at the intimation.

But whilst we acquiesce entirely in the permanence of natural laws, the question of the absolute existence of nature still remains open. It is the uniform effect of culture on the human mind, not to shake our faith in the stability of particular phenomena, as of heat, water, azote; but to lead us to regard nature as phenomenon, not a substance; to attribute necessary existence to spirit; to esteem nature as an accident and an effect.

To the senses and the unrenewed understanding, belongs a sort of instinctive belief in the absolute existence of nature. In their view man and nature are indissolubly joined. Things are ultimates, and they never look beyond their sphere. The presence of Reason mars this faith. The first effort of thought tends to relax this despotism of the senses which binds us to nature as if we were a part of it, and shows us nature aloof, and, as it were, afloat. Until this higher agency intervened, the animal eye sees, with wonderful accuracy, sharp outlines and colored surfaces. When the eye of Reason opens, to outline and surface are at once added grace and expression. These proceed from imagination and affection, and abate somewhat of the angular distinctness of objects. If the Reason be stimulated to more earnest vision, outlines and surfaces become transparent, and are no longer seen; causes and spirits are seen through them. The best moments of life are these delicious awakenings of the higher powers, and the reverential withdrawing of nature before its God.

Let us proceed to indicate the effects of culture.

1. Our first institution in the Ideal philosophy is a hint from Nature herself.

Nature is made to conspire with spirit to emancipate us. Certain mechanical changes, a small alteration in our local position, apprizes us of a dualism. We are strangely affected by seeing the shore from a moving ship, from a balloon, or through the tints of an unusual sky. The least change in our point of view gives the whole world a pictorial air. A man who seldom rides, needs only to get into a coach and traverse his own town, to turn the street into a puppet-show. The men, the women —talking, running, bartering, fighting—the earnest mechanic, the lounger, the beggar, the boys, the dogs, are unrealized at once, or, at least, wholly detached from all relation to the observer, and seen as apparent, not substantial beings. What new thoughts are suggested by seeing a face of country quite familiar, in the rapid movement of the railroad car! Nay, the most wonted objects (make a very slight change in the point of vision), please us most. In a camera obscura,[48] the butcher's cart, and the figure of one of our own family amuse us. So a portrait of a well-known face gratifies us. Turn the eyes upside down, by looking at the landscape through your

---

[48] Chamber into which an image is projected onto a wall; forerunner of the modern camera.

legs, and how agreeable is the picture, though you have seen it any time these twenty years!

In these cases, by mechanical means, is suggested the difference between the observer and the spectacle—between man and nature. Hence arises a pleasure mixed with awe; I may say, a low degree of the sublime is felt, from the fact, probably, that man is hereby apprized that whilst the world is a spectacle, something in himself is stable.

2.   In a higher manner the poet communicates the same pleasure. By a few strokes he delineates, as on air, the sun, the mountain, the camp, the city, the hero, the maiden, not different from what we know them, but only lifted from the ground and afloat before the eye. He unfixes the land and the sea, makes them revolve around the axis of his primary thought, and disposes them anew. Possessed himself by a heroic passion, he uses matter as symbols of it. The sensual man conforms thoughts to things; the poet conforms things to his thoughts. The one esteems nature as rooted and fast; the other, as fluid, and impresses his being thereon. To him, the refractory world is ductile and flexible; he invests dust and stones with humanity, and makes them the words of the Reason. The Imagination may be defined to be the use which the Reason makes of the material world. Shakspeare possesses the power of subordinating nature for the purposes of expression, beyond all poets. His imperial muse tosses the creation like a bauble from hand to hand, and uses it to embody any caprice of thought that is uppermost in his mind. The remotest spaces of nature are visited, and the farthest sundered things are brought together, by a subtile spiritual connection. We are made aware that magnitude of material things is relative, and all objects shrink and expand to serve the passion of the poet. Thus in his sonnets, the lays of birds, the scents and dyes of flowers he finds to be the *shadow* of his beloved; time, which keeps her from him, is his *chest;* the suspicion she has awakened, is her *ornament;*

> The ornament of beauty is Suspect,
> A crow which flies in heaven's sweetest air.[49]

His passion is not the fruit of chance; it swells, as he speaks, to a city, or a state.

> No, it was builded far from accident;
> It suffers not in smiling pomp, nor falls
> Under the brow of thralling discontent;
> It fears not policy, that heretic,
> That works on leases of short numbered hours,
> But all alone stands hugely politic.[50]

In the strength of his constancy, the Pyramids seem to him recent and transitory. The freshness of youth and love dazzles him with its resemblance to morning;

> Take those lips away
> Which so sweetly were forsworn;
> And those eyes,—the break of day,
> Lights that do mislead the morn.[51]

[49] Shakespeare, *Sonnets,* LXX, ll. 3–4.
[50] Shakespeare, *Sonnets,* CXXIV, ll. 5–11.
[51] Shakespeare, *Measure for Measure,* Act IV, Sc. i, ll. 1–4.

The wild beauty of this hyperbole, I may say in passing, it would not be easy to match in literature.

This transfiguration which all material objects undergo through the passion of the poet—this power which he exerts to dwarf the great, to magnify the small—might be illustrated by a thousand examples from his Plays. I have before me the Tempest, and will cite only these few lines.

> ARIEL. The strong based promontory
> Have I made shake, and by the spurs plucked up
> The pine and cedar.

Prospero calls for music to soothe the frantic Alonzo, and his companions;

> A solemn air, and the best comforter
> To an unsettled fancy, cure thy brains
> Now useless, boiled within thy skull.

Again;

> The charm dissolves apace,
> And, as the morning steals upon the night,
> Melting the darkness, so their rising senses
> Begin to chase the ignorant fumes that mantle
> Their clearer reason.
>   Their understanding
> Begins to swell: and the approaching tide
> Will shortly fill the reasonable shores
> That now lie foul and muddy.[52]

The perception of real affinities between events (that is to say, of *ideal* affinities, for those only are real), enables the poet thus to make free with the most imposing forms and phenomena of the world, and to assert the predominance of the soul.

3.   Whilst thus the poet animates nature with his own thoughts, he differs from the philosopher only herein, that the one proposes Beauty as his main end; the other Truth. But the philosopher, not less than the poet, postpones the apparent order and relations of things to the empire of thought. "The problem of philosophy," according to Plato, "is, for all that exists conditionally, to find a ground unconditioned and absolute."[53] It proceeds on the faith that a law determines all phenomena, which being known, the phenomena can be predicted. That law, when in the mind, is an idea. Its beauty is infinite. The true philosopher and the true poet are one, and a beauty, which is truth, and a truth, which is beauty, is the aim of both. Is not the charm of one of Plato's or Aristotle's definitions strictly like that of the Antigone of Sophocles? It is, in both cases, that a spiritual life has been imparted to nature; that the solid seeming

---

[52] Shakespeare, *The Tempest,* Act V, Sc. i, ll. 46–48, 58–60, 64–68, 79–82. Prospero, not Ariel, speaks the opening lines.

[53] Quotation from Plato's *Republic,* Book V. Emerson uses an abridged rendering from Coleridge's *The Friend* (1818).

block of matter has been pervaded and dissolved by a thought; that this feeble human being has penetrated the vast masses of nature with an informing soul, and recognized itself in their harmony, that is, seized their law. In physics, when this is attained, the memory disburthens itself of its cumbrous catalogues of particulars, and carries centuries of observation in a single formula.

Thus even in physics, the material is degraded before the spiritual. The astronomer, the geometer, rely on their irrefragable analysis, and disdain the results of observation. The sublime remark of Euler[54] on his law of arches, "This will be found contrary to all experience, yet is true;" had already transferred nature into the mind, and left matter like an outcast corpse.

4.   Intellectual science has been observed to beget invariably a doubt of the existence of matter. Turgot[55] said, "He that has never doubted the existence of matter, may be assured he has no aptitude for metaphysical inquiries." It fastens the attention upon immortal necessary uncreated natures, that is, upon Ideas; and in their presence we feel that the outward circumstance is a dream and a shade. Whilst we wait in this Olympus of gods, we think of nature as an appendix to the soul. We ascend into their region, and know that these are the thoughts of the Supreme Being. "These are they who were set up from everlasting, from the beginning, or ever the earth was. When he prepared the heavens, they were there; when he established the clouds above, when he strengthened the fountains of the deep. Then they were by him, as one brought up with him. Of them took he counsel."[56]

Their influence is proportionate. As objects of science they are accessible to few men. Yet all men are capable of being raised by piety or by passion, into their region. And no man touches these divine natures, without becoming, in some degree, himself divine. Like a new soul, they renew the body. We become physically nimble and lightsome; we tread on air; life is no longer irksome, and we think it will never be so. No man fears age or misfortune or death in their serene company, for he is transported out of the district of change. Whilst we behold unveiled the nature of Justice and Truth, we learn the difference between the absolute and the conditional or relative. We apprehend the absolute. As it were, for the first time, *we exist*. We become immortal, for we learn that time and space are relations of matter; that with a perception of truth or a virtuous will they have no affinity.

5.   Finally, religion and ethics, which may be fitly called the practice of ideas, or the introduction of ideas into life, have an analogous effect with all lower culture, in degrading nature and suggesting its dependence on spirit. Ethics and religion differ herein; that the one is the system of human duties commencing from man; the other, from God. Religion includes the personality of God; Ethics does not. They are one to our present design. They both put nature under foot. The first and last lesson of religion is, "The things that are seen, are temporal; the things that are unseen, are eternal."[57] It puts an affront upon nature. It does that for the unschooled, which philosophy does for Berkeley and Viasa.[58] The uniform language that may be heard

---

[54] Swiss mathematician Leonhard Euler (1707–1783).
[55] French statesman and economist Robert Jacques Turgot (1727–1781).
[56] Abbreviated version of Proverbs 8:23, 27, 28, 30.

[57] See 2 Corinthians 4:18.
[58] Berkeley: George Berkeley (1685–1753), English churchman and philosophical idealist; Viyasa: proverbial Hindu philosopher.

in the churches of the most ignorant sects is—"Contemn the unsubstantial shows of the world; they are vanities, dreams, shadows, unrealities; seek the realities of religion." The devotee flouts nature. Some theosophists have arrived at a certain hostility and indignation towards matter, as the Manichean[59] and Plotinus.[60] They distrusted in themselves any looking back to these flesh-pots of Egypt.[61] Plotinus was ashamed of his body. In short, they might all say of matter, what Michael Angelo said of external beauty, "It is the frail and weary weed, in which God dresses the soul which he has called into time."[62]

It appears that motion, poetry, physical and intellectual science, and religion, all tend to affect our convictions of the reality of the external world. But I own there is something ungrateful in expanding too curiously the particulars of the general proposition, that all culture tends to imbue us with idealism. I have no hostility to nature, but a child's love to it. I expand and live in the warm day like corn and melons. Let us speak her fair. I do not wish to fling stones at my beautiful mother, nor soil my gentle nest. I only wish to indicate the true position of nature in regard to man, wherein to establish man all right education tends; as the ground which to attain is the object of human life, that is, of man's connection with nature. Culture inverts the vulgar view of nature, and brings the mind to call that apparent which it uses to call real, and that real which it uses to call visionary. Children, it is true, believe in the external world. The belief that it appears only, is an afterthought, but with culture this faith will as surely arise on the mind as did the first.

The advantage of the ideal theory over the popular faith is this, that it presents the world in precisely that view which is most desirable to the mind. It is, in fact, the view which Reason, both speculative and practical, that is, philosophy and virtue, take. For seen in the light of thought, the world always is phenomenal; and virtue subordinates it to the mind. Idealism sees the world in God. It beholds the whole circle of persons and things, of actions and events, of country and religion, not as painfully accumulated, atom after atom, act after act, in an aged creeping Past, but as one vast picture which God paints on the instant eternity for the contemplation of the soul. Therefore the soul holds itself off from a too trivial and microscopic study of the universal tablet. It respects the end too much to immerse itself in the means. It sees something more important in Christianity than the scandals of ecclesiastical history or the niceties of criticism; and, very incurious concerning persons or miracles, and not at all disturbed by chasms of historical evidence, it accepts from God the phenomenon, as it finds it, as the pure and awful form of religion in the world. It is not hot and passionate at the appearance of what it calls its own good or bad fortune, at the union or opposition of other persons. No man is its enemy. It accepts whatsoever befalls, as part of its lesson. It is a watcher more than a doer, and it is a doer, only that it may the better watch.

---

[59] A disciple of Manes, third-century Christian sage who theorized that the evil of the body exists in duality with the goodness of the soul.

[60] Roman Neoplatonic philosopher (205?–?270).
[61] See Exodus 16:2–3.
[62] Michelangelo, *Sonnet* 51.

VII: Spirit

It is essential to a true theory of nature and of man, that it should contain[63] somewhat progressive. Uses that are exhausted or that may be, and facts that end in the statement, cannot be all that is true of this brave lodging wherein man is harbored, and wherein all his faculties find appropriate and endless exercise. And all the uses of nature admit of being summed in one, which yields the activity of man an infinite scope. Through all its kingdoms, to the suburbs and outskirts of things, it is faithful to the cause whence it had its origin. It always speaks of Spirit. It suggests the absolute. It is a perpetual effect. It is a great shadow pointing always to the sun behind us.

The aspect of Nature is devout. Like the figure of Jesus, she stands with bended head, and hands folded upon the breast. The happiest man is he who learns from nature the lesson of worship.

Of that ineffable essence which we call Spirit, he that thinks most, will say least. We can foresee God in the coarse, and, as it were, distant phenomena of matter; but when we try to define and describe himself, both language and thought desert us, and we are as helpless as fools and savages. That essence refuses to be recorded in propositions, but when man has worshipped him intellectually, the noblest ministry of nature is to stand as the apparition of God. It is the organ through which the universal spirit speaks to the individual, and strives to lead back the individual to it.

When we consider Spirit, we see that the views already presented do not include the whole circumference of man. We must add some related thoughts.

Three problems are put by nature to the mind: What is matter? Whence is it? and Whereto? The first of these questions only, the ideal theory answers. Idealism saith: matter is a phenomenon, not a substance. Idealism acquaints us with the total disparity between the evidence of our own being and the evidence of the world's being. The one is perfect; the other, incapable of any assurance; the mind is a part of the nature of things; the world is a divine dream, from which we may presently awake to the glories and certainties of day. Idealism is a hypothesis to account for nature by other principles than those of carpentry and chemistry. Yet, if it only deny the existence of matter, it does not satisfy the demands of the spirit. It leaves God out of me. It leaves me in the splendid labyrinth of my perceptions, to wander without end. Then the heart resists it, because it balks the affections in denying substantive being to men and women. Nature is so pervaded with human life that there is something of humanity in all and in every particular. But this theory makes nature foreign to me, and does not account for that consanguinity which we acknowledge to it.

Let it stand then, in the present state of our knowledge, merely as a useful introductory hypothesis, serving to apprize us of the eternal distinction between the soul and the world.

But when, following the invisible steps of thoughts, we come to inquire, Whence is matter? and Whereto? many truths arise to us out of the recesses of consciousness. We learn that the highest is present to the soul of man; that the dread universal essence, which is not wisdom, or love, or beauty, or power, but all in one, and each entirely, is that for which all things exist, and that by which they are; that spirit creates; that behind nature, throughout nature, spirit is present; one and not compound it does not

[63] Remain.

act upon us from without, that is, in space and time, but spiritually, or through ourselves: therefore, that spirit, that is, the Supreme Being, does not build up nature around us, but puts it forth through us, as the life of the tree puts forth new branches and leaves through the pores of the old. As a plant upon the earth, so a man rests upon the bosom of God; he is nourished by unfailing fountains, and draws at his need inexhaustible power. Who can set bounds to the possibilities of man? Once inhale the upper air, being admitted to behold the absolute natures of justice and truth, and we learn that man has access to the entire mind of the Creator, is himself the creator in the finite. This view, which admonishes me where the sources of wisdom and power lie, and points to virtue as to

> "The golden key
> Which opes the palace of eternity,"[64]

carries upon its face the highest certificate of truth, because it animates me to create my own world through the purification of my soul.

The world proceeds from the same spirit as the body of man. It is a remoter and inferior incarnation of God, a projection of God in the unconscious. But it differs from the body in one important respect. It is not, like that, now subjected to the human will. Its serene order is inviolable by us. It is, therefore, to us, the present expositor of the divine mind. It is a fixed point whereby we may measure our departure. As we degenerate, the contrast between us and our house is more evident. We are as much strangers in nature as we are aliens from God. We do not understand the notes of birds. The fox and the deer run away from us; the bear and tiger rend us. We do not know the uses of more than a few plants, as corn and the apple, the potato and the vine. Is not the landscape, every glimpse of which hath a grandeur, a face of him? Yet this may show us what discord is between man and nature, for you cannot freely admire a noble landscape if laborers are digging in the field hard by. The poet finds something ridiculous in his delight until he is out of the sight of men.

VIII: Prospects

In inquiries respecting the laws of the world and the frame of things, the highest reason is always the truest. That which seems faintly possible, it is so refined, is often faint and dim because it is deepest seated in the mind among the eternal verities. Empirical science is apt to cloud the sight, and by the very knowledge of functions and processes to bereave the student of the manly contemplation of the whole. The savant becomes unpoetic. But the best read naturalist who lends an entire and devout attention to truth, will see that there remains much to learn of his relation to the world, and that it is not to be learned by any addition or subtraction or other comparison of known quantities, but is arrived at by untaught sallies of the spirit, by a continual self-recovery, and by entire humility. He will perceive that there are far more excellent qualities in the student than preciseness and infallibility; that a guess is often more fruitful than an indisputable affirmation, and that a dream may let us deeper into the secret of nature than a hundred concerted experiments.

[64] John Milton, *Comus*, ll. 13–14.

For the problems to be solved are precisely those which the physiologist and the naturalist omit to state. It is not so pertinent to man to know all the individuals of the animal kingdom, as it is to know whence and whereto is this tyrannizing unity in his constitution, which evermore separates and classifies things, endeavoring to reduce the most diverse to one form. When I behold a rich landscape, it is less to my purpose to recite correctly the order and superposition of the strata, than to know why all thought of multitude is lost in a tranquil sense of unity. I cannot greatly honor minuteness in details, so long as there is no hint to explain the relation between things and thoughts; no ray upon the *metaphysics* of conchology, of botany, of the arts, to show the relation of the forms of flowers, shells, animals, architecture, to the mind, and build science upon ideas. In a cabinet of natural history,[65] we become sensible of a certain occult recognition and sympathy in regard to the most unwieldy and eccentric form of beast, fish, and insect. The American who has been confined, in his own country, to the sight of buildings designed after foreign models, is surprised on entering York Minster[66] or St. Peter's at Rome, by the feeling that these structures are imitations also—faint copies of an invisible archetype. Nor has science sufficient humanity, so long as the naturalist overlooks that wonderful congruity which subsists between man and the world; of which he is lord, not because he is the most subtile inhabitant, but because he is its head and heart, and finds something of himself in every great and small thing, in every mountain stratum, in every new law of color, fact of astronomy, or atmospheric influence which observation or analysis lays open. A perception of this mystery inspires the muse of George Herbert, the beautiful psalmist of the seventeenth century. The following lines are part of his little poem on Man.

> Man is all symmetry,
> Full of proportions, one limb to another,
>   And all to all the world besides.
>   Each part may call the farthest, brother;
> For head with foot hath private amity,
>   And both with moons and tides.
>
>   Nothing hath got so far
> But man hath caught and kept it as his prey;
>   His eyes dismount the highest star:
>   He is in little all the sphere.
> Herbs gladly cure our flesh, because that they
>   Find their acquaintance there.
>
>   For us, the winds do blow,
> The earth doth rest, heaven move, and fountains flow;
>   Nothing we see, but means our good,
>   As our delight, or as our treasure;
> The whole is either our cupboard of food,
>   Or cabinet of pleasure.

---

[65] I.e., display case of biological specimens.   [66] Stately cathedral at York, England.

The stars have us to bed:
Night draws the curtain; which the sun withdraws.
Music and light attend our head.
All things unto our flesh are kind,
In their descent and being; to our mind,
In their ascent and cause.

More servants wait on man
Than he'll take notice of. In every path,
He treads down that which doth befriend him
When sickness makes him pale and wan.
Oh mighty love! Man is one world, and hath
Another to attend him.[67]

The perception of this class of truths makes the attraction which draws men to science, but the end is lost sight of in attention to the means. In view of this half-sight of science, we accept the sentence of Plato, that "poetry comes nearer to vital truth than history." Every surmise and vaticination of the mind is entitled to a certain respect, and we learn to prefer imperfect theories, and sentences which contain glimpses of truth, to digested systems which have no one valuable suggestion. A wise writer will feel that the ends of study and composition are best answered by announcing undiscovered regions of thought, and so communicating, through hope, new activity to the torpid spirit.

I shall therefore conclude this essay with some traditions of man and nature, which a certain poet[68] sang to me; and which, as they have always been in the world, and perhaps reappear to every bard, may be both history and prophecy.

"The foundations of man are not in matter, but in spirit. But the element of spirit is eternity. To it, therefore, the longest series of events, the oldest chronologies are young and recent. In the cycle of the universal man, from whom the nown individuals proceed, centuries are points, and all history is but the epoch of one degradation.

"We distrust and deny inwardly our sympathy with nature. We own and disown our relation to it, by turns. We are like Nebuchadnezzar, dethroned, bereft of reason, and eating grass like an ox.[69] But who can set limits to the remedial force of spirit?

"A man is a god in ruin. When men are innocent, life shall be longer, and shall pass into the immortal as gently as we awake from dreams. Now, the world would be insane and rabid, if these disorganizations should last for hundreds of years. It is kept in check by death and infancy. Infancy is the perpetual Messiah, which comes into the arms of fallen men, and pleads with them to return to paradise.

"Man is the dwarf of himself. Once he was permeated and dissolved by spirit. He filled nature with his overflowing currents. Out from him sprang the sun and moon; from man the sun, from woman the moon. The laws of his mind, the periods of his actions externized themselves into day and night, into the year and the seasons. But,

[67] Stanzas 1–4 and 6 of "Man" (1633) by George Herbert (1593–1633), English poet.
[68] Perhaps Emerson himself, or Bronson Alcott (1799–1888), New England Transcendentalist and author of *Orphic Sayings* (1840).
[69] See Daniel 4:24–33. Nebuchadnezzar became irrational, "was driven from men, and did eat grass as oxen."

having made for himself this huge shell, his waters retired; he no longer fills the veins and veinlets; he is shrunk to a drop. He sees that the structure still fits him, but fits him colossally. Say, rather, once it fitted him, now it corresponds to him from far and on high. He adores timidly his own work. Now is man the follower of the sun, and woman the follower of the moon. Yet sometimes he starts in his slumber, and wonders at himself and his house, and muses strangely at the resemblance betwixt him and it. He perceives that if his law is still paramount, if still he have elemental power, if his word is sterling yet in nature, it is not conscious power, it is not inferior but superior to his will. It is instinct." Thus my Orphic[70] poet sang.

At present, man applies to nature but half his force. He works on the world with his understanding alone. He lives in it and masters it by a penny-wisdom; and he that works most in it is but a half-man, and whilst his arms are strong and his digestion good, his mind is imbruted, and he is a selfish savage. His relation to nature, his power over it, is through the understanding, as by manure; the economic use of fire, wind, water, and the mariner's needle; steam, coal, chemical agriculture; the repairs of the human body by the dentist and the surgeon. This is such a resumption of power as if a banished king should buy his territories inch by inch, instead of vaulting at once into his throne. Meantime, in the thick darkness, there are not wanting gleams of a better light—occasional examples of the action of man upon nature with his entire force—with reason as well as understanding. Such examples are, the traditions of miracles in the earliest antiquity of all nations; the history of Jesus Christ; the achievements of a principle, as in religious and political revolutions, and in the abolition of the slave-trade; the miracles of enthusiasm,[71] as those reported of Swedenborg, Hohenlohe, and the Shakers;[72] many obscure and yet contested facts, now arranged under the name of Animal Magnetism;[73] prayer; eloquence; self-healing; and the wisdom of children. These are examples of Reason's momentary grasp of the sceptre; the exertions of a power which exists not in time or space, but an instantaneous in-streaming causing power. The difference between the actual and the ideal force of man is happily figured by the schoolmen, in saying, that the knowledge of man is an evening knowledge, *vespertina cognitio,* but that of God is a morning knowledge, *matutina cognitio.*[74]

The problem of restoring to the world original and eternal beauty is solved by the redemption of the soul. The ruin or the blank that we see when we look at nature, is in our own eye. The axis of vision is not coincident with the axis of things, and so they appear not transparent but opaque. The reason why the world lacks unity, and lies broken and in heaps, is because man is disunited with himself. He cannot be a naturalist until he satisfies all the demands of the spirit. Love is as much its demand as perception. Indeed, neither can be perfect without the other. In the uttermost

---

[70] I.e., characteristic of mystic doctrines ascribed to Orpheus, poet of Greek mythology.
[71] Divine hysteria.
[72] Swedenborg: see note 27 above; Hohenlohe: Leopold Emmerich, German prince of Hohenlohe-Waldenberg-Schillingfurst (1794–1849), Catholic bishop and writer; Shakers: those affiliated with the millenial church, which had its inception in England in 1747 and which was renowned for its frenzied dancing and prophetic manifestations in services.
[73] Hypnosis.
[74] Latin phrases attributable to academic philosophers of the Middle Ages, particularly St. Augustine and St. Thomas Aquinas.

meaning of the words thought is devout, and devotion is thought. Deep calls unto deep.[75] But in actual life, the marriage is not celebrated. There are innocent men who worship God after the tradition of their fathers, but their sense of duty has not yet extended to the use of all their faculties. And there are patient naturalists, but they freeze their subject under the wintry light of the understanding. Is not prayer also a study of truth—a sally of the soul into the unfound infinite? No man ever prayed heartily without learning something. But when a faithful thinker, resolute to detach every object from personal relations and see it in the light of thought, shall, at the same time, kindle science with the fire of the holiest affections, then will God go forth anew into the creation.

It will not need, when the mind is prepared for study, to search for objects. The invariable mark of wisdom is to see the miraculous in the common. What is a day? What is a year? What is summer? What is woman? What is a child? What is sleep? To our blindness, these things seem unaffecting. We make fables to hide the baldness of the fact and conform it, as we say, to the higher law of the mind. But when the fact is seen under the light of an idea, the gaudy fable fades and shrivels. We behold the real higher law. To the wise, therefore, a fact is true poetry, and the most beautiful of fables. These wonders are brought to our own door. You also are a man. Man and woman and their social life, poverty, labor, sleep, fear, fortune, are known to you. Learn that none of these things is superficial, but that each phenomenon has its roots in the faculties and affections of the mind. Whilst the abstract question occupies your intellect, nature brings it in the concrete to be solved by your hands. It were a wise inquiry for the closet, to compare, point by point, especially at remarkable crises in life, our daily history with the rise and progress of ideas in the mind.

So shall we come to look at the world with new eyes. It shall answer the endless inquiry of the intellect—What is truth? and of the affections—What is good? by yielding itself passive to the educated Will. Then shall come to pass what my poet said: "Nature is not fixed but fluid. Spirit alters, moulds, makes it. The immobility or bruteness of nature is the absence of spirit; to pure spirit it is fluid, it is volatile, it is obedient. Every spirit builds itself a house, and beyond its house a world, and beyond its world a heaven. Know then that the world exists for you. For you is the phenomenon perfect. What we are, that only can we see. All that Adam had, all that Cæsar could, you have and can do. Adam called his house, heaven and earth; Cæsar called his house, Rome; you perhaps call yours, a cobbler's trade; a hundred acres of ploughed land; or a scholar's garret. Yet line for line and point for point your dominion is as great as theirs, though without fine names. Build therefore your own world. As fast as you conform your life to the pure idea in your mind, that will unfold its great proportions. A correspondent revolution in things will attend the influx of the spirit. So fast will disagreeable appearances, swine, spiders, snakes, pests, mad-houses, prisons, enemies, vanish; they are temporary and shall be no more seen. The sordor and filths of nature, the sun shall dry up and the wind exhale. As when the summer comes from the south the snow-banks melt and the face of the earth becomes green before it, so shall the advancing spirit create its ornaments along its path, and carry with it the beauty it visits and the song which enchants it; it shall draw beautiful

[75] Psalm 42:7.

faces, warm hearts, wise discourse, and heroic acts, around its way, until evil is no more seen. The kingdom of man over nature, which cometh not with observation —a dominion such as now is beyond his dream of God—he shall enter without more wonder than the blind man feels who is gradually restored to sight."

1836

The American Scholar*

MR. PRESIDENT AND GENTLEMEN:
I greet you on the recommencement of our literary year.[1] Our anniversary is one of hope, and, perhaps, not enough of labor. We do not meet for games of strength or skill, for the recitation of histories, tragedies, and odes, like the ancient Greeks; for parliaments of love and poesy, like the Troubadours;[2] nor for the advancement of science, like our contemporaries in the British and European capitals. Thus far, our holiday has been simply a friendly sign of the survival of the love of letters amongst a people too busy to give to letters any more. As such it is precious as the sign of an indestructible instinct. Perhaps the time is already come when it ought to be, and will be, something else; when the sluggard intellect of this continent will look from under its iron lids and fill the postponed expectation of the world with something better than the exertions of mechanical skill. Our day of dependence, our long apprenticeship to the learning of other lands, draws to a close. The millions that around us are rushing into life, cannot always be fed on the sere remains of foreign harvests. Events, actions arise, that must be sung, that will sing themselves. Who can doubt that poetry will revive and lead in a new age, as the star in the constellation Harp,[3] which now flames in our zenith, astronomers announce, shall one day be the polestar[4] for a thousand years?

In this hope I accept the topic which not only usage but the nature of our association seem to prescribe to this day—the AMERICAN SCHOLAR. Year by year we come up hither to read one more chapter of his biography. Let us inquire what light new days and events have thrown on his character and his hopes.

It is one of those fables which out of an unknown antiquity convey an unlooked-for wisdom, that the gods, in the beginning, divided Man into men, that he might be more helpful to himself;[5] just as the hand was divided into fingers, the better to answer its end.

---

* This essay was first printed as a pamphlet entitled *Man Thinking: An Oration Delivered Before the Phi Beta Kappa Society, at Cambridge, August 31, 1837.* Emerson retitled it "The American Scholar" in *Essays* (1841) in order to address all students and anyone else committed to thought.

[1] The customary college year, beginning in September.

[2] Courtly poets of southern France in the twelfth and thirteenth centuries.

[3] The constellation referred to is Lyra, which includes the bright star Vega.

[4] The earth's axis points toward the North Star.

[5] The fable recalled by Emerson is from Plato's *Symposium.*

The old fable covers a doctrine ever new and sublime; that there is One Man—present to all particular men only partially, or through one faculty; and that you must take the whole society to find the whole man. Man is not a farmer, or a professor, or an engineer, but he is all. Man is priest, and scholar, and statesman, and producer, and soldier. In the *divided* or social state these functions are parcelled out to individuals, each of whom aims to do his stint of the joint work, whilst each other performs his. The fable implies that the individual, to possess himself, must sometimes return from his own labor to embrace all the other laborers. But, unfortunately, this original unit, this fountain of power, has been so distributed to multitudes, has been so minutely subdivided and peddled out, that it is spilled into drops, and cannot be gathered. The state of society is one in which the members have suffered amputation from the trunk, and strut about so many walking monsters—a good finger, a neck, a stomach, an elbow, but never a man.

Man is thus metamorphosed into a thing, into many things. The planter, who is Man sent out into the field to gather food, is seldom cheered by any idea of the true dignity of his ministry. He sees his bushel and his cart, and nothing beyond, and sinks into the farmer, instead of Man on the farm. The tradesman scarcely ever gives an ideal worth to his work, but is ridden by the routine of his craft, and the soul is subject to dollars. The priest becomes a form; the attorney a statute-book; the mechanic a machine; the sailor a rope of the ship. Think Actively, not passively.

In this distribution of functions the scholar is the delegated intellect. In the right state he is *Man Thinking*. In the degenerate state, when the victim of society, he tends to become a mere thinker, or still worse, the parrot of other men's thinking.

In this view of him, as Man Thinking, the theory of his office is contained. Him Nature solicits with all her placid, all her monitory pictures; him the past instructs; him the future invites. Is not indeed every man a student, and do not all things exist for the student's behoof? And, finally, is not the true scholar the only true master? But the old oracle said, "All things have two handles: beware of the wrong one." In life, too often, the scholar errs with mankind and forfeits his privilege. Let us see him in his school, and consider him in reference to the main influences he receives.

I.   The first in time and the first in importance of the influences upon the mind is that of nature. Every day, the sun; and, after sunset, Night and her stars. Ever the winds blow; ever the grass grows. Every day, men and women, conversing—beholding and beholden. The scholar is he of all men whom this spectacle most engages. He must settle its value in his mind. What is nature to him? There is never a beginning, there is never an end, to the inexplicable continuity of this web of God, but always circular power returning into itself. Therein it resembles his own spirit, whose beginning, whose ending, he never can find—so entire, so boundless. Far too as her splendors shine, system on system shooting like rays, upward, downward, without centre, without circumference—in the mass and in the particle, Nature hastens to render account of herself to the mind. Classification begins. To the young mind every thing is individual, stands by itself. By and by, it finds how to join two things and see in them one nature; then three, then three thousand; and so, tyrannized over by its own unifying instinct, it goes on tying things together, diminishing anomalies, discovering roots running under ground whereby contrary and remote things cohere and flower out from one stem. It presently learns that since the dawn of history there has been a constant accumulation and classifying of facts. But what is classification but the perceiving that these objects are not chaotic, and are not foreign, but have a law which is also a law of the human mind? The astronomer discovers that geometry, a pure abstraction of the human mind, is the measure of planetary motion. The chemist finds proportions and intelligible method throughout matter; and science is nothing but the finding of analogy, identity, in the most remote parts. The ambitious soul sits down before each refractory fact; one after another reduces all strange constitutions, all new powers, to their class and their law, and goes on forever to animate the last fibre of organization, the outskirts of nature, by insight.

Thus to him, to this schoolboy under the bending dome of day, is suggested that he and it proceed from one root; one is leaf and one is flower; relation, sympathy, stirring in every vein. And what is that root? Is not that the soul of his soul? A thought too bold; a dream too wild. Yet when this spiritual light shall have revealed the law of more earthly natures—when he has learned to worship the soul, and to see that the natural philosophy that now is, is only the first gropings of its gigantic hand, he shall look forward to an ever expanding knowledge as to a becoming creator. He shall see that nature is the opposite of the soul, answering to it part for part. One is seal and one is print. Its beauty is the beauty of his own mind. Its laws are the laws of his own mind. Nature then becomes to him the measure of his attainments. So much of nature as he is ignorant of, so much of his own mind does he not yet possess. And, in fine, the ancient precept, "Know thyself," and the modern precept, "Study nature," become at last one maxim.

II. The next great influence[6] into the spirit of the scholar is the mind of the Past —in whatever form, whether of literature, of art, of institutions, that mind is inscribed. Books are the best type of the influence of the past, and perhaps we shall get at the truth—learn the amount of this influence more conveniently—by considering their value alone.

The theory of books is noble. The scholar of the first age received into him the world around; brooded thereon; gave it the new arrangement of his own mind, and uttered it again. It came into him life; it went out from him truth. It came to him shortlived actions; it went out from him immortal thoughts. It came to him business; it went from him poetry. It was dead fact; now, it is quick[7] thought. It can stand, and it can go. It now endures, it now flies, it now inspires. Precisely in proportion to the depth of mind from which it issued, so high does it soar, so long does it sing.

Or, I might say, it depends on how far the process had gone, of transmuting life into truth. In proportion to the completeness of the distillation, so will the purity and imperishableness of the product be. But none is quite perfect. As no air-pump can by any means make a perfect vacuum, so neither can any artist entirely exclude the conventional, the local, the perishable from his book, or write a book of pure thought, that shall be as efficient, in all respects, to a remote posterity, as to contemporaries, or rather to the second age. Each age, it is found, must write its own books; or rather, each generation for the next succeeding. The books of an older period will not fit this.

Yet hence arises a grave mischief. The sacredness which attaches to the act of creation, the act of thought, is transferred to the record. The poet chanting was felt

[6] Inflowing, from the Latin verb *influere*.   [7] Active or living.

to be a divine man: henceforth the chant is divine also. The writer was a just and wise spirit: henceforward it is settled the book is perfect; as love of the hero corrupts into worship of his statue. Instantly the book becomes noxious: the guide is a tyrant. The sluggish and perverted mind of the multitude, slow to open to the incursions of Reason, having once so opened, having once received this book, stands upon it, and makes an outcry if it is disparaged. Colleges are built on it. Books are written on it by thinkers, not by Man Thinking; by men of talent, that is, who start wrong, who set out from accepted dogmas, not from their own sight of principles. Meek young men grow up in libraries, believing it their duty to accept the views which Cicero, which Locke, which Bacon[8] have given; forgetful that Cicero, Locke, and Bacon were only young men in libraries when they wrote these books.

Hence, instead of Man Thinking, we have the bookworm. Hence the book-learned class, who value books, as such; not as related to nature and the human constitution, but as making a sort of Third Estate[9] with the world and the soul. Hence the restorers of readings, the emendators, the bibliomaniacs of all degrees.

Books are the best of things, well used; abused, among the worst. What is the right use? What is the one end which all means go to effect? They are for nothing but to inspire. I had better never see a book than to be warped by its attraction clean out of my own orbit, and made a satellite instead of a system. The one thing in the world, of value, is the active soul. This every man is entitled to; this every man contains within him, although in almost all men obstructed and as yet unborn. The soul active sees absolute truth and utters truth, or creates. In this action it is genius; not the privilege of here and there a favorite, but the sound estate of every man. In its essence it is progressive. The book, the college, the school of art, the institution of any kind, stop with some past utterance of genius. This is good, say they—let us hold by this. They pin me down. They look backward and not forward. But genius looks forward: the eyes of man are set in his forehead, not in his hindhead: man hopes: genius creates. Whatever talents may be, if the man create not, the pure efflux of the Deity is not his; cinders and smoke there may be, but not yet flame. There are creative manners, there are creative actions, and creative words; manners, actions, words, that is, indicative of no custom or authority, but springing spontaneous from the mind's own sense of good and fair.

On the other part, instead of being its own seer, let it receive from another mind its truth, though it were in torrents of light, without periods of solitude, inquest, and self-recovery, and a fatal disservice is done. Genius is always sufficiently the enemy of genius by over-influence. The literature of every nation bears me witness. The English dramatic poets have Shakspearized now for two hundred years.

Undoubtedly there is a right way of reading, so it be sternly subordinated. Man Thinking must not be subdued by his instruments. Books are for the scholar's idle times. When he can read God directly, the hour is too precious to be wasted in other men's transcripts of their readings. But when the intervals of darkness come, as come

[8] Cicero: Marcus Tullius Cicero (106–43 B.C.), Roman statesman and orator; Locke: John Locke (1632–1704), English philosopher and political thinker; Bacon: Sir Francis Bacon (1561–1626), English statesman and pioneer of inductive science.

[9] Analogous to the third of three separate estates or classes that feudal Europe acknowledged: the clergy, the nobility, and the common people.

they must—when the sun is hid and the stars withdraw their shining—we repair to the lamps which were kindled by their ray, to guide our steps to the East again, where the dawn is. We hear, that we may speak. The Arabian proverb says, "A fig tree, looking on a fig tree, becometh fruitful."

It is remarkable, the character of the pleasure we derive from the best books. They impress us with the conviction that one nature wrote and the same reads. We read the verses of one of the great English poets, of Chaucer, of Marvell, of Dryden, with the most modern joy—with a pleasure, I mean, which is in great part caused by the abstraction of all *time* from their verses. There is some awe mixed with the joy of our surprise, when this poet, who lived in some past world, two or three hundred years ago, says that which lies close to my own soul, that which I also had well-nigh thought and said. But for the evidence thence afforded to the philosophical doctrine of the identity of all minds, we should suppose some preëstablished harmony, some foresight of souls that were to be, and some preparation of stores for their future wants, like the fact observed in insects, who lay up food before death for the young grub they shall never see.

I would not be hurried by any love of system, by any exaggeration of instincts, to underrate the Book. We all know, that as the human body can be nourished on any food, though it were boiled grass and the broth of shoes, so the human mind can be fed by any knowledge. And great and heroic men have existed who had almost no other information than by the printed page. I only would say that it needs a strong head to bear that diet. One must be an inventor to read well. As the proverb says, "He that would bring home the wealth of the Indies, must carry out the wealth of the Indies." There is then creative reading as well as creative writing. When the mind is braced by labor and invention, the page of whatever book we read becomes luminous with manifold allusion. Every sentence is doubly significant, and the sense of our author is as broad as the world. We then see, what is always true, that as the seer's hour of vision is short and rare among heavy days and months, so is its record, perchance, the least part of his volume. The discerning will read, in his Plato or Shakspeare, only that least part—only the authentic utterances of the oracles; all the rest he rejects, were it never so many times Plato's and Shakspeare's.

Of course there is a portion of reading quite indispensable to a wise man. History and exact science he must learn by laborious reading. Colleges, in like manner, have their indispensable office—to teach elements. But they can only highly serve us when they aim not to drill, but to create; when they gather from far every ray of various genius to their hospitable halls, and by the concentrated fires, set the hearts of their youth on flame. Thought and knowledge are natures in which apparatus and pretension avail nothing. Gowns and pecuniary foundations, though of towns of gold, can never countervail the least sentence or syllable of wit. Forget this, and our American colleges will recede in their public importance, whilst they grow richer every year.

III. There goes in the world a notion that the scholar should be a recluse, a valetudinarian—as unfit for any handiwork or public labor as a penknife for an axe. The so-called "practical men" sneer at speculative men, as if, because they speculate or *see,* they could do nothing. I have heard it said that the clergy—who are always, more universally than any other class, the scholars of their day—are addressed as women; that the rough, spontaneous conversation of men they do not hear, but only a mincing and diluted speech. They are often virtually disfranchised; and indeed there are advocates for their celibacy. As far as this is true of the studious classes, it is not just and wise. Action is with the scholar subordinate, but it is essential. Without it he is not yet man. Without it thought can never ripen into truth. Whilst the world hangs before the eye as a cloud of beauty, we cannot even see its beauty. Inaction is cowardice, but there can be no scholar without the heroic mind. The preamble of thought, the transition through which it passes from the unconscious to the conscious, is action. Only so much do I know, as I have lived. Instantly we know whose words are loaded with life, and whose not.

The world—this shadow of the soul, or *other me*—lies wide around. Its attractions are the keys which unlock my thoughts and make me acquainted with myself. I run eagerly into this resounding tumult. I grasp the hands of those next me, and take my place in the ring to suffer and to work, taught by an instinct that so shall the dumb abyss be vocal with speech. I pierce its order; I dissipate its fear; I dispose of it within the circuit of my expanding life. So much only of life as I know by experience, so much of the wilderness have I vanquished and planted, or so far have I extended my being, my dominion. I do not see how any man can afford, for the sake of his nerves and his nap, to spare any action in which he can partake. It is pearls and rubies to his discourse. Drudgery, calamity, exasperation, want, are instructors in eloquence and wisdom. The true scholar grudges every opportunity of action past by, as a loss of power. It is the raw material out of which the intellect moulds her splendid products. A strange process too, this by which experience is converted into thought, as a mulberry leaf is converted into satin.[10] The manufacture goes forward at all hours.

The actions and events of our childhood and youth are now matters of calmest observation. They lie like fair pictures in the air. Not so with our recent actions—with the business which we now have in hand. On this we are quite unable to speculate. Our affections as yet circulate through it. We no more feel or know it than we feel the feet, or the hand, or the brain of our body. The new deed is yet a part of life—remains for a time immersed in our unconscious life. In some contemplative hour it detaches itself from the life like a ripe fruit, to become a thought of the mind. Instantly it is raised, transfigured; the corruptible has put on incorruption.[11] Henceforth it is an object of beauty, however base its origin and neighborhood. Observe too the impossibility of antedating this act. In its grub state, it cannot fly, it cannot shine, it is a dull grub. But suddenly, without observation, the selfsame thing unfurls beautiful wings, and is an angel of wisdom. So is there no fact, no event, in our private history, which shall not, sooner or later, lose its adhesive, inert form, and astonish us by soaring from our body into the empyrean. Cradle and infancy, school and playground, the fear of boys, and dogs, and ferrules, the love of little maids and berries, and many another fact that once filled the whole sky, are gone already; friend and relative, profession and party, town and country, nation and world, must also soar and sing.

Of course, he who has put forth his total strength in fit actions has the richest return of wisdom. I will not shut myself out of this globe of action, and transplant an oak into a flowerpot, there to hunger and pine; nor trust the revenue of some single faculty, and exhaust one vein of thought, much like those Savoyards,[12] who, getting

---

[10] I.e., silk, which is produced by silkworms feeding on mulberry leaves.
[11] 1 Corinthians 15:53: "For this corruptible must put on incorruption, and this mortal must put on immortality."
[12] Residents of Savoy, now a province of France.

their livelihood by carving shepherds, shepherdesses, and smoking Dutchmen,[13] for all Europe, went out one day to the mountain to find stock, and discovered that they had whittled up the last of their pine trees. Authors we have, in numbers, who have written out their vein, and who, moved by a commendable prudence, sail for Greece or Palestine, follow the trapper into the prairie, or ramble round Algiers, to replenish their merchantable stock.

If it were only for a vocabulary, the scholar would be covetous of action. Life is our dictionary. Years are well spent in country labors; in town; in the insight into trades and manufactures; in frank intercourse with many men and women; in science; in art; to the one end of mastering in all their facts a language by which to illustrate and embody our perceptions. I learn immediately from any speaker how much he has already lived, through the poverty or the splendor of his speech. Life lies behind us as the quarry from whence we get tiles and copestones for the masonry of to-day. This is the way to learn grammar. Colleges and books only copy the language which the field and the work-yard made.

But the final value of action, like that of books, and better than books, is that it is a resource. That great principle of Undulation in nature, that shows itself in the inspiring and expiring of the breath; in desire and satiety; in the ebb and flow of the sea; in day and night; in heat and cold; and, as yet more deeply ingrained in every atom and every fluid, is known to us under the name of Polarity—these "fits of easy transmission and reflection," as Newton[14] called them, are the law of nature because they are the law of spirit.

The mind now thinks, now acts, and each fit reproduces the other. When the artist has exhausted his materials, when the fancy no longer paints, when thoughts are no longer apprehended and books are a weariness—he has always the resources to *live*. Character is higher than intellect. Thinking is the function. Living is the functionary. The stream retreats to its source. A great soul will be strong to live, as well as strong to think. Does he lack organ or medium to impart his truths? He can still fall back on this elemental force of living them. This is a total act. Thinking is a partial act. Let the grandeur of justice shine in his affairs. Let the beauty of affection cheer his lowly roof. Those "far from fame," who dwell and act with him, will feel the force of his constitution in the doings and passages of the day better than it can be measured by any public and designed display. Time shall teach him that the scholar loses no hour which the man lives. Herein he unfolds the sacred germ of his instinct, screened from influence. What is lost in seemliness is gained in strength. Not out of those on whom systems of education have exhausted their culture, comes the helpful giant to destroy the old or to build the new, but out of unhandselled[15] savage nature; out of terrible Druids and Berserkers[16] come at last Alfred[17] and Shakspeare.

I hear therefore with joy whatever is beginning to be said of the dignity and necessity of labor to every citizen. There is virtue yet in the hoe and the spade, for learned as well as for unlearned hands. And labor is everywhere welcome; always we

---

[13] I.e., pipes.
[14] From *Optics* by Sir Isaac Newton (1642–1727), English mathematician and philosopher.
[15] Ungrateful.
[16] Respectively, barbaric Celts and uncivilized warriors of Norse mythology.

[17] Alfred (849–901), king of the West Saxons, who instituted English laws and fostered literacy.

are invited to work; only be this limitation observed, that a man shall not for the sake of wider activity sacrifice any opinion to the popular judgments and modes of action.

I have now spoken of the education of the scholar by nature, by books, and by action. It remains to say somewhat of his duties.

They are such as become Man Thinking. They may all be comprised in self-trust. The office of the scholar is to cheer, to raise, and to guide men by showing them facts amidst appearances. He plies the slow, unhonored, and unpaid task of observation. Flamsteed and Herschel,[18] in their glazed observatories, may catalogue the stars with the praise of all men, and the results being splendid and useful, honor is sure. But he, in his private observatory, cataloguing obscure and nebulous stars of the human mind, which as yet no man has thought of as such—watching days and months sometimes for a few facts; correcting still his old records; must relinquish display and immediate fame. In the long period of his preparation he must betray often an ignorance and shiftlessness in popular arts, incurring the disdain of the able who shoulder him aside. Long he must stammer in his speech; often forego the living for the dead. Worse yet, he must accept—how often!—poverty and solitude. For the ease and pleasure of treading the old road, accepting the fashions, the education, the religion of society, he takes the cross of making his own, and, of course, the self-accusation, the faint heart, the frequent uncertainty and loss of time, which are the nettles and tangling vines in the way of the self-relying and self-directed; and the state of virtual hostility in which he seems to stand to society, and especially to educated society. For all this loss and scorn, what offset? He is to find consolation in exercising the highest functions of human nature. He is one who raises himself from private considerations and breathes and lives on public and illustrious thoughts. He is the world's eye. He is the world's heart. He is to resist the vulgar prosperity that retrogrades ever to barbarism, by preserving and communicating heroic sentiments, noble biographies, melodious verse, and the conclusions of history. Whatsoever oracles the human heart, in all emergencies, in all solemn hours, has uttered as its commentary on the world of actions—these he shall receive and impart. And whatsoever new verdict Reason from her inviolable seat pronounces on the passing men and events of to-day—this he shall hear and promulgate.

These being his functions, it becomes him to feel all confidence in himself, and to defer never to the popular cry. He and he only knows the world. The world of any moment is the merest appearance. Some great decorum, some fetish of a government, some ephemeral trade, or war, or man, is cried up by half mankind and cried down by the other half, as if all depended on this particular up or down. The odds are that the whole question is not worth the poorest thought which the scholar has lost in listening to the controversy. Let him not quit his belief that a popgun is a popgun, though the ancient and honorable of the earth affirm it to be the crack of doom. In silence, in steadiness, in severe abstraction, let him hold by himself; add observation to observation, patient of neglect, patient of reproach, and bide his own time—happy enough if he can satisfy himself alone that this day he has seen something truly. Success

---

[18] John Flamsteed (1646–1719) and Sir Frederick William Herschel (1738–1822), prominent English astronomers.

treads on every right step. For the instinct is sure, that prompts him to tell his brother what he thinks. He then learns that in going down into the secrets of his own mind he has descended into the secrets of all minds. He learns that he who has mastered any law in his private thoughts, is master to that extent of all men whose language he speaks, and of all into whose language his own can be translated. The poet, in utter solitude remembering his spontaneous thoughts and recording them, is found to have recorded that which men in crowded cities find true for them also. The orator distrusts at first the fitness of his frank confessions, his want of knowledge of the persons he addresses, until he finds that he is the complement of his hearers; that they drink his words because he fulfils for them their own nature; the deeper he dives into his privatest, secretest presentiment, to his wonder he finds this is the most acceptable, most public, and universally true. The people delight in it; the better part of every man feels, This is my music; this is myself.

In self-trust all the virtues are comprehended. Free should the scholar be—free and brave. Free even to the definition of freedom, "without any hindrance that does not arise out of his own constitution." Brave; for fear is a thing which a scholar by his very function puts behind him. Fear always springs from ignorance. It is a shame to him if his tranquillity, amid dangerous times, arise from the presumption that like children and women his is a protected class; or if he seek a temporary peace by the diversion of his thoughts from politics or vexed questions, hiding his head like an ostrich in the flowering bushes, peeping into microscopes, and turning rhymes, as a boy whistles to keep his courage up. So is the danger a danger still; so is the fear worse. Manlike let him turn and face it. Let him look into its eye and search its nature, inspect its origin—see the whelping of this lion—which lies no great way back; he will then find in himself a perfect comprehension of its nature and extent; he will have made his hands meet on the other side, and can henceforth defy it and pass on superior. The world is his who can see through its pretension. What deafness, what stone-blind custom, what overgrown error you behold is there only by sufferance—by your sufferance. See it to be a lie, and you have already dealt it its mortal blow.

Yes, we are the cowed—we the trustless. It is a mischievous notion that we are come late into nature; that the world was finished a long time ago. As the world was plastic and fluid in the hands of God, so it is ever to so much of his attributes as we bring to it. To ignorance and sin, it is flint. They adapt themselves to it as they may; but in proportion as a man has any thing in him divine, the firmament flows before him and takes his signet and form. Not he is great who can alter matter, but he who can alter my state of mind. They are the kings of the world who give the color of their present thought to all nature and all art, and persuade men by the cheerful serenity of their carrying the matter, that this thing which they do is the apple which the ages have desired to pluck, now at last ripe, and inviting nations to the harvest. The great man makes the great thing. Wherever Macdonald sits, there is the head of the table.[19] Linnaeus makes botany the most alluring of studies, and wins it from the farmer and the herb-woman; Davy, chemistry; and Cuvier,[20] fossils. The day is always his who works in it with serenity and great aims. The unstable estimates of men crowd

---

[19] Emerson's version of a proverb of the time.
[20] Linnaeus: Swedish botanist Carolus Linnaeus (1707–1778); Davy: English chemist Sir

Humphrey Davy (1778–1829); Cuvier: French naturalist Georges Cuvier (1769–1832).

to him whose mind is filled with a truth, as the heaped waves of the Atlantic follow the moon.

For this self-trust, the reason is deeper than can be fathomed—darker than can be enlightened. I might not carry with me the feeling of my audience in stating my own belief. But I have already shown the ground of my hope, in adverting to the doctrine that man is one. I believe man has been wronged; he has wronged himself. He has almost lost the light that can lead him back to his prerogatives. Men are become of no account. Men in history, men in the world of to-day, are bugs, are spawn, and are called "the mass" and "the herd." In a century, in a millennium, one or two men; that is to say, one or two approximations to the right state of every man. All the rest behold in the hero or the poet their own green and crude being—ripened; yes, and are content to be less, so *that* may attain to its full stature. What a testimony, full of grandeur, full of pity, is borne to the demands of his own nature, by the poor clansman, the poor partisan, who rejoices in the glory of his chief. The poor and the low find some amends to their immense moral capacity, for their acquiescence in a political and social inferiority. They are content to be brushed like flies from the path of a great person, so that justice shall be done by him to that common nature which it is the dearest desire of all to see enlarged and glorified. They sun themselves in the great man's light, and feel it to be their own element. They cast the dignity of man from their downtrod selves upon the shoulders of a hero, and will perish to add one drop of blood to make that great heart beat, those giant sinews combat and conquer. He lives for us, and we live in him.

Men, such as they are, very naturally seek money or power; and power because it is as good as money—the "spoils," so called, "of office." And why not? for they aspire to the highest, and this, in their sleep-walking, they dream is highest. Wake them and they shall quit the false good and leap to the true, and leave governments to clerks and desks. This revolution is to be wrought by the gradual domestication of the idea of Culture. The main enterprise of the world for splendor, for extent, is the upbuilding of a man. Here are the materials strewn along the ground. The private life of one man shall be a more illustrious monarchy, more formidable to its enemy, more sweet and serene in its influence to its friend, than any kingdom in history. For a man, rightly viewed, comprehendeth the particular natures of all men. Each philosopher, each bard, each actor has only done for me, as by a delegate, what one day I can do for myself. The books which once we valued more than the apple of the eye, we have quite exhausted. What is that but saying that we have come up with the point of view which the universal mind took through the eyes of one scribe; we have been that man, and have passed on. First, one, then another, we drain all cisterns, and waxing greater by all these supplies, we crave a better and more abundant food. The man has never lived that can feed us ever. The human mind cannot be enshrined in a person who shall set a barrier on any one side to this unbounded, unboundable empire. It is one central fire, which, flaming now out of the lips of Etna,[21] lightens the capes of Sicily, and now out of the throat of Vesuvius,[22] illuminates the towers and vineyards of Naples. It is one light which beams out of a thousand stars. It is one soul which animates all men.

But I have dwelt perhaps tediously upon this abstraction of the Scholar. I ought

[21] Active volcano in Sicily.　　[22] Volcano in Italy.

not to delay longer to add what I have to say of nearer reference to the time and to this country.

Historically, there is thought to be a difference in the ideas which predominate over successive epochs, and there are data for marking the genius of the Classic, of the Romantic, and now of the Reflective or Philosophical age. With the views I have intimated of the oneness or the identity of the mind through all individuals, I do not much dwell on these differences. In fact, I believe each individual passes through all three. The boy is a Greek; the youth, romantic; the adult, reflective. I deny not, however, that a revolution in the leading idea may be distinctly enough traced.

Our age is bewailed as the age of Introversion. Must that needs be evil? We, it seems, are critical; we are embarrassed with second thoughts; we cannot enjoy any thing for hankering to know whereof the pleasure consists; we are lined with eyes; we see with our feet; the time is infected with Hamlet's unhappiness—

"Sicklied o'er with the pale cast of thought."[23]

It is so bad then? Sight is the last thing to be pitied. Would we be blind? Do we fear lest we should outsee nature and God, and drink truth dry? I look upon the discontent of the literary class as a mere announcement of the fact that they find themselves not in the state of mind of their fathers, and regret the coming state as untried; as a boy dreads the water before he has learned that he can swim. If there is any period one would desire to be born in, is it not the age of Revolution; when the old and the new stand side by side and admit of being compared; when the energies of all men are searched by fear and by hope; when the historic glories of the old can be compensated by the rich possibilities of the new era? This time, like all times, is a very good one, if we but know what to do with it.

I read with some joy of the auspicious signs of the coming days, as they glimmer already through poetry and art, through philosophy and science, through church and state.

One of these signs is the fact that the same movement which effected the elevation of what was called the lowest class in the state, assumed in literature a very marked and as benign an aspect. Instead of the sublime and beautiful, the near, the low, the common, was explored and poetized. That which had been negligently trodden under foot by those who were harnessing and provisioning themselves for long journeys into far countries, is suddenly found to be richer than all foreign parts. The literature of the poor, the feelings of the child, the philosophy of the street, the meaning of household life, are the topics of the time. It is a great stride. It is a sign—is it not? —of new vigor when the extremities are made active, when currents of warm life run into the hands and the feet. I ask not for the great, the remote, the romantic; what is doing in Italy or Arabia; what is Greek art, or Provencal minstrelsy;[24] I embrace the common, I explore and sit at the feet of the familiar, the low. Give me insight into to-day, and you may have the antique and future worlds. What would we really know the meaning of? The meal in the firkin; the milk in the pan; the ballad in the

[23] Shakespeare's *Hamlet,* Act III, Sc. i, l. 85.
[24] The troubadors of the late Middle Ages established Provence in southeast France as a cultural center.

street; the news of the boat; the glance of the eye; the form and the gait of the body; show me the ultimate reason of these matters; show me the sublime presence of the highest spiritual cause lurking, as always it does lurk, in these suburbs and extremities of nature; let me see every trifle bristling with the polarity that ranges it instantly on an eternal law; and the shop, the plough, and the ledger referred to the like cause by which light undulates and poets sing; and the world lies no longer a dull miscellany and lumber-room,[25] but has form and order; there is no trifle, there is no puzzle, but one design unites and animates the farthest pinnacle and the lowest trench.

This idea has inspired the genius of Goldsmith, Burns, Cowper, and, in a newer time, of Goethe, Wordsworth, and Carlyle. This idea they have differently followed and with various success. In contrast with their writing, the style of Pope, of Johnson, of Gibbon, looks cold and pedantic. This writing is blood-warm. Man is surprised to find that things near are not less beautiful and wondrous than things remote. The near explains the far. The drop is a small ocean. A man is related to all nature. This perception of the worth of the vulgar is fruitful in discoveries. Goethe, in this very thing the most modern of the moderns, has shown us, as none ever did, the genius of the ancients.

There is one man of genius who has done much for this philosophy of life, whose literary value has never yet been rightly estimated; I mean Emanuel Swedenborg.[26] The most imaginative of men, yet writing with the precision of a mathematician, he endeavored to engraft a purely philosophical Ethics on the popular Christianity of his time. Such an attempt of course must have difficulty which no genius could surmount. But he saw and showed the connection between nature and the affections of the soul. He pierced the emblematic or spiritual character of the visible, audible, tangible word. Especially did his shade-loving muse hover over and interpret the lower parts of nature; he showed the mysterious bond that allies moral evil to the foul material forms, and has given in epical parables a theory of insanity, of beasts, of unclean and fearful things.

Another sign of our times, also marked by an analogous political movement, is the new importance given to the single person. Every thing that tends to insulate the individual—to surround him with barriers of natural respect, so that each man shall feel the world is his, and man shall treat with man as a sovereign state with a sovereign state—tends to true union as well as greatness. "I learned," said the melancholy Pestalozzi,[27] "that no man in God's wide earth is either willing or able to help any other man." Help must come from the bosom alone. The scholar is that man who must take up into himself all the ability of the time, all the contributions of the past, all the hopes of the future. He must be an university of knowledges. If there be one lesson more than another which should pierce his ear, it is, The world is nothing, the man is all; in yourself is the law of all nature, and you know not yet how a globule of sap ascends; in yourself slumbers the whole of Reason; it is for you to know all; it is for you to dare all. Mr. President and Gentlemen, this confidence in the unsearched might of man belongs, by all motives, by all prophecy, by all preparation, to the American Scholar. We have listened too long to the courtly muses of Europe. The spirit of the American free-man is already suspected to be timid, imitative, tame.

[25] Room for storage.
[26] Swedish scientist and theologian (1688–1772).
[27] Swiss educational theorist Johann Heinrich Pestalozzi (1746–1826).

Public and private avarice make the air we breathe thick and fat. The scholar is decent, indolent, complaisant. See already the tragic consequence. The mind of this country, taught to aim at low objects, eats upon itself. There is no work for any but the decorous and the complaisant. Young men of the fairest promise, who begin life upon our shores, inflated by the mountain winds, shined upon by all the stars of God, find the earth below not in unison with these, but are hindered from action by the disgust which the principles on which business is managed inspire, and turn drudges, or die of disgust, some of them suicides. What is the remedy? They did not yet see, and thousands of young men as hopeful now crowding to the barriers for the career do not yet see, that if the single man plant himself indomitably on his instincts, and there abide, the huge world will come round to him. Patience—patience; with the shades of all the good and great for company; and for solace the perspective of your own infinite life; and for work the study and the communication of principles, the making those instincts prevalent, the conversion of the world. Is it not the chief disgrace in the world, not to be an unit; not to be reckoned one character; not to yield that peculiar fruit which each man was created to bear, but to be reckoned in the gross, in the hundred, or the thousand, of the party, the section, to which we belong; and our opinion predicted geographically, as the north, or the south? Not so, brothers and friends—please God, ours shall not be so. We will walk on our own feet; we will work with our own hands; we will speak our own minds. The study of letters shall be no longer a name for pity, for doubt, and for sensual indulgence. The dread of man and the love of man shall be a wall of defence and a wreath of joy around all. A nation of men will for the first time exist, because each believes himself inspired by the Divine Soul which also inspires all men.

1837

An Address*

In this refulgent summer, it has been a luxury to draw the breath of life. The grass grows, the buds burst, the meadow is spotted with fire and gold in the tint of flowers. The air is full of birds, and sweet with the breath of the pine, the balm-of-Gilead,[1] and the new hay. Night brings no gloom to the heart with its welcome shade. Through the transparent darkness the stars pour their almost spiritual rays. Man under them seems a young child, and his huge globe a toy. The cool night bathes the world as with a river, and prepares his eyes again for the crimson dawn. The mystery of nature was never displayed more happily. The corn and the wine have been freely dealt to all creatures, and the never-broken silence with which the old bounty goes forward

---

* Soon after it was delivered, Emerson's lecture was published as *An Address Delivered Before the Senior Class in Divinity College, Cambridge, Sunday Evening 15 July 1838.* His criticism of traditional Christianity so offended the religious establishment at Harvard that he was not invited to speak there again for 30 years.

[1] Fragrant evergreen tree.

has not yielded yet one word of explanation. One is constrained to respect the perfection of this world in which our senses converse. How wide; how rich; what invitation from every property it gives to every faculty of man! In its fruitful soils; in its navigable sea; in its mountains of metal and stone; in its forests of all woods; in its animals; in its chemical ingredients; in the powers and path of light, heat, attraction and life, it is well worth the pith and heart of great men to subdue and enjoy it. The planters, the mechanics, the inventors, the astronomers, the builders of cities, and the captains, history delights to honor.

But when the mind opens and reveals the laws which traverse the universe and make things what they are, then shrinks the great world at once into a mere illustration and fable of this mind. What am I? and What is? asks the human spirit with a curiosity new-kindled, but never to be quenched. Behold these outrunning laws, which our imperfect apprehension can see tend this way and that, but not come full circle. Behold these infinite relations, so like, so unlike; many, yet one. I would study, I would know, I would admire forever. These works of thought have been the entertainments of the human spirit in all ages.

A more secret, sweet, and overpowering beauty appears to man when his heart and mind open to the sentiment of virtue. Then he is instructed in what is above him. He learns that his being is without bound; that to the good, to the perfect, he is born, low as he now lies in evil and weakness. That which he venerates is still his own, though he has not realized it yet. *He ought.* He knows the sense of that grand word, though his analysis fails to render account of it. When in innocency or when by intellectual perception he attains to say—"I love the Right; Truth is beautiful within and without for evermore. Virtue, I am thine; save me; use me; thee will I serve, day and night, in great, in small, that I may be not virtuous, but virtue;" then is the end of the creation answered, and God is well pleased.

The sentiment of virtue is a reverence and delight in the presence of certain divine laws. It perceives that this homely game of life we play, covers, under what seem foolish details, principles that astonish. The child amidst his baubles is learning the action of light, motion, gravity, muscular force; and in the game of human life, love, fear, justice, appetite, man, and God, interact. These laws refuse to be adequately stated. They will not be written out on paper, or spoken by the tongue. They elude our persevering thought; yet we read them hourly in each other's faces, in each other's actions, in our own remorse. The moral traits which are all globed into every virtuous act and thought—in speech we must sever, and describe or suggest by painful enumeration of many particulars. Yet, as this sentiment is the essence of all religion, let me guide your eye to the precise objects of the sentiment, by an enumeration of some of those classes of facts in which this element is conspicuous.

The intuition of the moral sentiment is an insight of the perfection of the laws of the soul. These laws execute themselves. They are out of time, out of space, and not subject to circumstance. Thus in the soul of man there is a justice whose retributions are instant and entire. He who does a good deed is instantly ennobled. He who does a mean deed is by the action itself contracted. He who puts off impurity, thereby puts on purity. If a man is at heart just, then in so far is he God; the safety of God, the immortality of God, the majesty of God do enter into that man with justice. If a man dissemble, deceive, he deceives himself, and goes out of acquaintance with his own being. A man in the view of absolute goodness, adores, with total humility.

Every step so downward, is a step upward. The man who renounces himself, comes to himself.

See how this rapid intrinsic energy worketh everywhere, righting wrongs, correcting appearances, and bringing up facts to a harmony with thoughts. Its operation in life, though slow to the senses, is at last as sure as in the soul. By it a man is made the Providence to himself, dispensing good to his goodness, and evil to his sin. Character is always known. Thefts never enrich; alms never impoverish; murder will speak out of stone walls. The least admixture of a lie—for example, the taint of vanity, any attempt to make a good impression, a favorable appearance—will instantly vitiate the effect. But speak the truth, and all nature and all spirits help you with unexpected furtherance. Speak the truth, and all things alive or brute are vouchers, and the very roots of the grass underground there do seem to stir and move to bear you witness. See again the perfection of the Law as it applies itself to the affections, and becomes the law of society. As we are, so we associate. The good, by affinity, seek the good; the vile, by affinity, the vile. Thus of their own volition, souls proceed into heaven, into hell.

These facts have always suggested to man the sublime creed that the world is not the product of manifold power, but of one will, of one mind; and that one mind is everywhere active, in each ray of the star, in each wavelet of the pool; and whatever opposes that will is everywhere balked and baffled, because things are made so, and not otherwise. Good is positive. Evil is merely privative, not absolute: it is like cold, which is the privation of heat. All evil is so much death or nonentity. Benevolence is absolute and real. So much benevolence as a man hath, so much life hath he. For all things proceed out of this same spirit, which is differently named love, justice, temperance, in its different applications, just as the ocean receives different names on the several shores which it washes. All things proceed out of the same spirit, and all things conspire with it. Whilst a man seeks good ends, he is strong by the whole strength of nature. In so far as he roves from these ends, he bereaves himself of power, or auxiliaries; his being shrinks out of all remote channels, he becomes less and less, a mote, a point, until absolute badness is absolute death.

The perception of this law of laws awakens in the mind a sentiment which we call the religious sentiment, and which makes our highest happiness. Wonderful is its power to charm and to command. It is a mountain air. It is the embalmer of the world. It is myrrh and storax, and chlorine and rosemary. It makes the sky and the hills sublime, and the silent song of the stars is it. By it is the universe made safe and habitable, not by science or power. Thought may work cold and intransitive in things, and find no end or unity; but the dawn of the sentiment of virtue on the heart, gives and is the assurance that Law is sovereign over all natures; and the worlds, time, space, eternity, do seem to break out into joy.

This sentiment is divine and deifying. It is the beatitude of man. It makes him illimitable. Through it, the soul first knows itself. It corrects the capital mistake of the infant man, who seeks to be great by following the great, and hopes to derive advantages *from another*—by showing the fountain of all good to be in himself, and that he, equally with every man, is an inlet into the deeps of Reason. When he says, "I ought;" when love warms him; when he chooses, warned from on high, the good and great deed; then, deep melodies wander through his soul from Supreme Wisdom. Then he can worship, and be enlarged by his worship; for he can never go behind this sentiment. In the sublimest flights of the soul, rectitude is never surmounted, love is never outgrown.

This sentiment lies at the foundation of society, and successively creates all forms of worship. The principle of veneration never dies out. Man fallen into superstition, into sensuality, is never quite without the visions of the moral sentiment. In like manner, all the expressions of this sentiment are sacred and permanent in proportion to their purity. The expressions of this sentiment affect us more than all other compositions. The sentences of the oldest time, which ejaculate this piety, are still fresh and fragrant. This thought dwelled always deepest in the minds of men in the devout and contemplative East; not alone in Palestine, where it reached its purest expression, but in Egypt, in Persia, in India, in China. Europe has always owed to oriental genius its divine impulses. What these holy bards said, all sane men found agreeable and true. And the unique impression of Jesus upon mankind, whose name is not so much written as ploughed into the history of this world, is proof of the subtle virtue of this infusion.

Meantime, whilst the doors of the temple stand open, night and day, before every man, and the oracles of this truth cease never, it is guarded by one stern condition; this, namely, it is an intuition. It cannot be received at second hand. Truly speaking, it is not instruction, but provocation, that I can receive from another soul. What he announces, I must find true in me, or reject; and on his word, or as his second, be he who he may, I can accept nothing. On the contrary, the absence of this primary faith is the presence of degradation. As is the flood, so is the ebb. Let this faith depart, and the very words it spake and the things it made become false and hurtful. Then falls the church, the state, art, letters, life. The doctrine of the divine nature being forgotten, a sickness infects and dwarfs the constitution. Once man was all; now he is an appendage, a nuisance. And because the indwelling Supreme Spirit cannot wholly be got rid of, the doctrine of it suffers this perversion, that the divine nature is attributed to one or two persons, and denied to all the rest, and denied with fury. The doctrine of inspiration is lost; the base doctrine of the majority of voices usurps the place of the doctrine of the soul. Miracles, prophecy, poetry, the ideal life, the holy life, exist as ancient history merely; they are not in the belief, nor in the aspiration of society; but, when suggested, seem ridiculous. Life is comic or pitiful as soon as the high ends of being fade out of sight, and man becomes near-sighted, and can only attend to what addresses the senses.

These general views, which, whilst they are general, none will contest, find abundant illustration in the history of religion, and especially in the history of the Christian church. In that, all of us have had our birth and nurture. The truth contained in that, you, my young friends, are now setting forth to teach. As the Cultus, or established worship of the civilized world, it has great historical interest for us. Of its blessed words, which have been the consolation of humanity, you need not that I should speak. I shall endeavor to discharge my duty to you on this occasion, by pointing out two errors in its administration, which daily appear more gross from the point of view we have just now taken.

Jesus Christ belonged to the true race of prophets. He saw with open eye the mystery of the soul. Drawn by its severe harmony, ravished with its beauty, he lived in it, and had his being there. Alone in all history he estimated the greatness of man. One man was true to what is in you and me. He saw that God incarnates himself in man, and evermore goes forth anew to take possession of his World. He said, in this

We can all be Jesus in a way. He was the one person that lived up to that relation & understood his idea; this was distorted by tradition.

jubilee of sublime emotion, 'I am divine. Through me, God acts; through me, speaks. Would you see God, see me; or see thee, when thou also thinkest as I now think.' But what a distortion did his doctrine and memory suffer in the same, in the next, and the following ages! There is no doctrine of the Reason which will bear to be taught by the Understanding.[2] The understanding caught this high chant from the poet's lips, and said, in the next age, 'This was Jehovah come down out of heaven. I will kill you, if you say he was a man.' The idioms of his language and the figures of his rhetoric have usurped the place of his truth; and churches are not built on his principles, but on his tropes. Christianity became a Mythus,[3] as the poetic teaching of Greece and of Egypt, before. He spoke of miracles; for he felt that man's life was a miracle, and all that man doth, and he knew that this daily miracle shines as the character ascends. But the word Miracle, as pronounced by Christian churches, gives a false impression; it is Monster. It is not one with the blowing clover and the falling rain.

He felt respect for Moses and the prophets, but no unfit tenderness at postponing their initial revelations to the hour and the man that now is; to the eternal revelation in the heart. Thus was he a true man. Having seen that the law in us is commanding, he would not suffer it to be commanded. Boldly, with hand, and heart, and life, he declared it was God. Thus is he, as I think, the only soul in history who has appreciated the worth of man.

1. In this point of view we become sensible of the first defect of historical Christianity. Historical Christianity has fallen into the error that corrupts all attempts to communicate religion. As it appears to us, and as it has appeared for ages, it is not the doctrine of the soul, but an exaggeration of the personal, the positive, the ritual. It has dwelt, it dwells, with noxious exaggeration about the *person* of Jesus. The soul knows no persons. It invites every man to expand to the full circle of the universe, and will have no preferences but those of spontaneous love. But by this eastern monarchy of a Christianity, which indolence and fear have built, the friend of man is made the injurer of man. The manner in which his name is surrounded with expressions which were once sallies of admiration and love, but are now petrified into official titles, kills all generous sympathy and liking. All who hear me, feel that the language that describes Christ to Europe and America is not the style of friendship and enthusiasm to a good and noble heart, but is appropriated and formal—paints a demigod, as the Orientals or the Greeks would describe Osiris or Apollo.[4] Accept the injurious impositions of our early catechetical instruction,[5] and even honesty and self-denial were but splendid sins, if they did not wear the Christian name. One would rather be

"A pagan, suckled in a creed outworn,"[6]

[2] Throughout his works, Emerson uses "Reason" to mean knowledge derived from intuition and "Understanding" to mean knowledge derived from logic.
[3] Deliberately promoted cult.
[4] Osiris: Egyptian fertility god; Apollo: Greek god of the sun.

[5] Technique of religious instruction employing dogmatic questions and answers.
[6] From the sonnet "The World Is Too Much with Us" (1807) by William Wordsworth (1770–1850).

than to be defrauded of his manly right in coming into nature and finding not names and places, not land and professions, but even virtue and truth foreclosed and monopolized. You shall not be a man even. You shall not own the world; you shall not dare and live after the infinite Law that is in you, and in company with the infinite Beauty which heaven and earth reflect to you in all lovely forms; but you must subordinate your nature to Christ's nature; you must accept our interpretations, and take his portrait as the vulgar draw it.

That is always best which gives me to myself. The sublime is excited in me by the great stoical doctrine, Obey thyself. That which shows God in me, fortifies me. That which shows God out of me, makes me a wart and a wen. There is no longer a necessary reason for my being. Already the long shadows of untimely oblivion creep over me, and I shall decrease forever.

The divine bards are the friends of my virtue, of my intellect, of my strength. They admonish me that the gleams which flash across my mind are not mine, but God's; that they had the like, and were not disobedient to the heavenly vision.[7] So I love them. Noble provocations go out from them, inviting me to resist evil; to subdue the world; and to Be. And thus, by his holy thoughts, Jesus serves us, and thus only. To aim to convert a man by miracles is a profanation of the soul. A true conversion, a true Christ, is now, as always, to be made by the reception of beautiful sentiments. It is true that a great and rich soul, like his, falling among the simple, does so preponderate, that, as his did, it names the world. The world seems to them to exist for him, and they have not yet drunk so deeply of his sense as to see that only by coming again to themselves, or to God in themselves, can they grow for evermore. It is a low benefit to give me something; it is a high benefit to enable me to do somewhat of myself. The time is coming when all men will see that the gift of God to the soul is not a vaunting, overpowering, excluding sanctity, but a sweet, natural goodness, a goodness like thine and mine, and that so invites thine and mine to be and to grow.

The injustice of the vulgar tone of preaching is not less flagrant to Jesus than to the souls which it profanes. The preachers do not see that they make his gospel not glad, and shear him of the locks of beauty and the attributes of heaven. When I see a majestic Epaminondas,[8] or Washington; when I see among my contemporaries a true orator, an upright judge, a dear friend; when I vibrate to the melody and fancy of a poem; I see beauty that is to be desired. And so lovely, and with yet more entire consent of my human being, sounds in my ear the severe music of the bards that have sung of the true God in all ages. Now do not degrade the life and dialogues of Christ out of the circle of this charm, by insulation and peculiarity. Let them lie as they befell, alive and warm, part of human life and the landscape and the cheerful day.

2. The second defect of the traditionary and limited way of using the mind of Christ is a consequence of the first; this, namely; that the Moral Nature, that Law of laws whose revelations introduce greatness—yea, God himself—into the open soul, is not explored as the fountain of the established teaching in society. Men have come to speak of the revelation as somewhat long ago given and done, as if God were dead.

---

[7] See Acts 26:19: "I was not disobedient unto the heavenly vision."

[8] Greek statesman and general instrumental in ending Sparta's dominance in Greece.

The injury to faith throttles the preacher; and the goodliest of institutions becomes an uncertain and inarticulate voice.

It is very certain that it is the effect of conversation with the beauty of the soul, to beget a desire and need to impart to others the same knowledge and love. If utterance is denied, the thought lies like a burden on the man. Always the seer is a sayer. Somehow his dream is told; somehow he publishes it with solemn joy: sometimes with pencil on canvas, sometimes with chisel on stone, sometimes in towers and aisles of granite, his soul's worship is builded; sometimes in anthems of indefinite music; but clearest and most permanent, in words.

The man enamored of this excellency becomes its priest or poet. The office is coeval with the world. But observe the condition, the spiritual limitation of the office. The spirit only can teach. Not any profane man, not any sensual, not any liar, not any slave can teach, but only he can give, who has; he only can create, who is. The man on whom the soul descends, through whom the soul speaks, alone can teach. Courage, piety, love, wisdom, can teach; and every man can open his door to these angels, and they shall bring him the gift of tongues. But the man who aims to speak as books enable, as synods use, as the fashion guides, and as interest commands, babbles. Let him hush.

To this holy office you propose to devote yourselves. I wish you may feel your call in throbs of desire and hope. The office is the first in the world. It is of that reality that it cannot suffer the deduction of any falsehood. And it is my duty to say to you that the need was never greater of new revelation than now. From the views I have already expressed, you will infer the sad conviction, which I share, I believe, with numbers, of the universal decay and now almost death of faith in society. The soul is not preached. The Church seems to totter to its fall, almost all life extinct. On this occasion, any complaisance would be criminal which told you, whose hope and commission it is to preach the faith of Christ, that the faith of Christ is preached.

It is time that this ill-suppressed murmur of all thoughtful men against the famine of our churches; this moaning of the heart because it is bereaved of the consolation, the hope, the grandeur that come alone out of the culture of the moral nature—should be heard through the sleep of indolence, and over the din of routine. This great and perpetual office of the preacher is not discharged. Preaching is the expression of the moral sentiment in application to the duties of life. In how many churches, by how many prophets, tell me, is man made sensible that he is an infinite Soul; that the earth and heavens are passing into his mind; that he is drinking forever the soul of God? Where now sounds the persuasion, that by its very melody imparadises my heart, and so affirms its own origin in heaven? Where shall I hear words such as in elder ages drew men to leave all and follow—father and mother, house and land, wife and child?[9] Where shall I hear these august laws of moral being so pronounced as to fill my ear, and I feel ennobled by the offer of my uttermost action and passion? The test of the true faith, certainly, should be its power to charm and command the soul, as the laws of nature control the activity of the hands—so commanding that we find pleasure and honor in obeying. The faith should blend with the light of rising and of setting suns,

---

9 See Matthew 19:28–29: "And Jesus said unto them, . . . every one that hath forsaken houses, or brethren, or sisters, or father, or mother, or wife, or children, or lands, for my name's sake, shall receive an hundredfold, and shall inherit everlasting life."

with the flying cloud, the singing bird, and the breath of flowers. But now the priest's Sabbath has lost the splendor of nature; it is unlovely; we are glad when it is done; we can make, we do make, even sitting in our pews, a far better, holier, sweeter, for ourselves.

Whenever the pulpit is usurped by a formalist, then is the worshipper defrauded and disconsolate. We shrink as soon as the prayers begin, which do not uplift, but smite and offend us. We are fain to wrap our cloaks about us, and secure, as best we can, a solitude that hears not. I once heard a preacher who sorely tempted me to say I would go to church no more. Men go, thought I, where they are wont to go, else had no soul entered the temple in the afternoon. A snow-storm was falling around us. The snow-storm was real, the preacher merely spectral, and the eye felt the sad contrast in looking at him, and then out of the window behind him into the beautiful meteor of the snow. He had lived in vain. He had no one word intimating that he had laughed or wept, was married or in love, had been commended, or cheated, or chagrined. If he had ever lived and acted, we were none the wiser for it. The capital secret of his profession, namely, to convert life into truth, he had not learned. Not one fact in all his experience had he yet imported into his doctrine. This man had ploughed and planted and talked and bought and sold; he had read books; he had eaten and drunken; his head aches, his heart throbs; he smiles and suffers; yet was there not a surmise, a hint, in all the discourse, that he had ever lived at all. Not a line did he draw out of real history. The true preacher can be known by this, that he deals out to the people his life—life passed through the fire of thought. But of the bad preacher, it could not be told from his sermon what age of the world he fell in; whether he had a father or a child; whether he was a freeholder or a pauper; whether he was a citizen or a countryman; or any other fact of his biography. It seemed strange that the people should come to church. It seemed as if their houses were very unentertaining, that they should prefer this thoughtless clamor. It shows that there is a commanding attraction in the moral sentiment, that can lend a faint tint of light to dulness and ignorance coming in its name and place. The good hearer is sure he has been touched sometimes; is sure there is somewhat to be reached, and some word that can reach it. When he listens to these vain words, he comforts himself by their relation to his remembrance of better hours, and so they clatter and echo unchallenged.

I am not ignorant that when we preach unworthily, it is not always quite in vain. There is a good ear, in some men, that draws supplies to virtue out of very indifferent nutriment. There is poetic truth concealed in all the commonplaces of prayer and of sermons, and though foolishly spoken, they may be wisely heard; for each is some select expression that broke out in a moment of piety from some stricken or jubilant soul, and its excellency made it remembered. The prayers and even the dogmas of our church are like the zodiac of Denderah[10] and the astronomical monuments of the Hindoos, wholly insulated from anything now extant in the life and business of the people. They mark the height to which the waters once rose. But this docility is a check upon the mischief from the good and devout. In a large portion of the community, the religious service gives rise to quite other thoughts and emotions. We

[10] Ancient city in Egypt and place of worship of
the goddess Hathor, where a zodiacal table is
displayed in an ancient ruined temple.

need not chide the negligent servant. We are struck with pity, rather, at the swift retribution of his sloth. Alas for the unhappy man that is called to stand in the pulpit, and *not* give bread of life. Everything that befalls, accuses him. Would he ask contributions for the missions, foreign or domestic? Instantly his face is suffused with shame, to propose to his parish that they should send money a hundred or a thousand miles, to furnish such poor fare as they have at home and would do well to go the hundred or the thousand miles to escape. Would he urge people to a godly way of living; and can he ask a fellow-creature to come to Sabbath meetings, when he and they all know what is the poor uttermost they can hope for therein? Will he invite them privately to the Lord's Supper?[11] He dares not. If no heart warm this rite, the hollow, dry, creaking formality is too plain, than that he can face a man of wit and energy and put the invitation without terror. In the street, what has he to say to the bold village blasphemer? The village blasphemer sees fear in the face, form, and gait of the minister.

Let me not taint the sincerity of this plea by any oversight of the claims of good men. I know and honor the purity and strict conscience of numbers of the clergy. What life the public worship retains, it owes to the scattered company of pious men, who minister here and there in the churches, and who, sometimes accepting with too great tenderness the tenet of the elders, have not accepted from others, but from their own heart, the genuine impulses of virtue, and so still command our love and awe, to the sanctity of character. Moreover, the exceptions are not so much to be found in a few eminent preachers, as in the better hours, the truer inspirations of all—nay, in the sincere moments of every man. But, with whatever exception, it is still true that tradition characterizes the preaching of this country; that it comes out of the memory, and not out of the soul; that it aims at what is usual, and not at what is necessary and eternal; that thus historical Christianity destroys the power of preaching, by withdrawing it from the exploration of the moral nature of man; where the sublime is, where are the resources of astonishment and power. What a cruel injustice it is to that Law, the joy of the whole earth, which alone can make thought dear and rich; that Law whose fatal sureness the astronomical orbits poorly emulate; that it is travestied and depreciated, that it is behooted and behowled, and not a trait, not a word of it articulated. The pulpit in losing sight of this Law, loses its reason, and gropes after it knows not what. And for want of this culture the soul of the community is sick and faithless. It wants nothing so much as a stern, high, stoical, Christian discipline, to make it know itself and the divinity that speaks through it. Now man is ashamed of himself; he skulks and sneaks through the world, to be tolerated, to be pitied, and scarcely in a thousand years does any man dare to be wise and good, and so draw after him the tears and blessings of his kind.

Certainly there have been periods when, from the inactivity of the intellect on certain truths, a greater faith was possible in names and persons. The Puritans in England and America found in the Christ of the Catholic Church and in the dogmas inherited from Rome, scope for their austere piety and their longings for civil freedom. But their creed is passing away, and none arises in its room. I think no man can go with his thoughts about him into one of our churches, without feeling that

---

[11] In 1832 Emerson decided to resign as minister of the Second Church of Boston after losing faith in the special graces of the sacrament of Holy Communion.

what hold the public worship had on men is gone, or going. It has lost its grasp on the affection of the good and the fear of the bad. In the country, neighborhoods, half parishes are *signing off,* to use the local term. It is already beginning to indicate character and religion to withdraw from the religious meetings. I have heard a devout person, who prized the Sabbath, say in bitterness of heart, "On Sundays, it seems wicked to go to church." And the motive that holds the best there is now only a hope and a waiting. What was once a mere circumstance, that the best and the worst men in the parish, the poor and the rich, the learned and the ignorant, young and old, should meet one day as fellows in one house, in sign of an equal right in the soul, has come to be a paramount motive for going thither.

My friends, in these two errors, I think, I find the causes of a decaying church and a wasting unbelief. And what greater calamity can fall upon a nation than the loss of worship? Then all things go to decay. Genius leaves the temple to haunt the senate or the market. Literature becomes frivolous. Science is cold. The eye of youth is not lighted by the hope of other worlds, and age is without honor. Society lives to trifles, and when men die we do not mention them.

And now, my brothers, you will ask, What in these desponding days can be done by us? The remedy is already declared in the ground of our complaint of the Church. We have contrasted the Church with the Soul. In the soul then let the redemption be sought. Wherever a man comes, there comes revolution. The old is for slaves. When a man comes, all books are legible, all things transparent, all religions are forms. He is religious. Man is the wonderworker. He is seen amid miracles. All men bless and curse. He saith yea and nay, only. The stationariness of religion; the assumption that the age of inspiration is past, that the Bible is closed; the fear of degrading the character of Jesus by representing him as a man; indicate with sufficient clearness the falsehood of our theology. It is the office of a true teacher to show us that God is, not was; that He speaketh, not spake. The true Christianity—a faith like Christ's in the infinitude of men—is lost. None believeth in the soul of man, but only in some man or person old and departed. Ah me! no man goeth alone. All men go in flocks to this saint or that poet, avoiding the God who seeth in secret. They cannot see in secret; they love to be blind in public. They think society wiser than their soul, and know not that one soul, and their soul, is wiser than the whole world. See how nations and races flit by on the sea of time and leave no ripple to tell where they floated or sunk, and one good soul shall make the name of Moses, or of Zeno, or of Zoroaster,[12] reverend forever. None assayeth the stern ambition to be the Self of the nation and of nature, but each would be an easy secondary to some Christian scheme, or sectarian connection, or some eminent man. Once leave your own knowledge of God, your own sentiment, and take secondary knowledge, as St. Paul's, or George Fox's, or Swedenborg's,[13] and you get wide from God with every year this secondary form lasts, and if, as now, for centuries—the chasm yawns to that breadth, that men can scarcely be convinced there is in them anything divine.

Let me admonish you, first of all, to go alone; to refuse the good models, even

---

[12] Zeno: Greek philosopher Zeno of Citium (ca. 334–262 B.C.), founder of Stoicism; Zoroaster: religious reformer of ancient Persia (ca. 628–552 B.C.) and founder of Zoroastrianism.

[13] George Fox: English founder (1624–1691), of the Society of Friends (Quakers); Swedenborg: Emanuel Swedenborg (1688–1722), Swedish philosopher and theologian.

those which are sacred in the imagination of men, and dare to love God without mediator or veil. Friends enough you shall find who will hold up to your emulation Wesleys and Oberlins,[14] Saints and Prophets. Thank God for these good men, but say, 'I also am a man.' Imitation cannot go above its model. The imitator dooms himself to hopeless mediocrity. The inventor did it because it was natural to him, and so in him it has a charm. In the imitator something else is natural, and he bereaves himself of his own beauty, to come short of another man's.

Yourself a newborn bard of the Holy Ghost, cast behind you all conformity, and acquaint men at first hand with Deity. Look to it first and only, that fashion, custom, authority, pleasure, and money, are nothing to you—are not bandages over your eyes, that you cannot see—but live with the privilege of the immeasurable mind. Not too anxious to visit periodically all families and each family in your parish connection —when you meet one of these men or women, be to them a divine man; be to them thought and virtue; let their timid aspirations find in you a friend; let their trampled instincts be genially tempted out in your atmosphere; let their doubts know that you have doubted, and their wonder feel that you have wondered. By trusting your own heart, you shall gain more confidence in other men. For all our penny-wisdom, for all our soul-destroying slavery to habit, it is not to be doubted that all men have sublime thoughts; that all men value the few real hours of life; they love to be heard; they love to be caught up into the vision of principles. We mark with light in the memory the few interviews we have had, in the dreary years of routine and of sin, with souls that made our souls wiser; that spoke what we thought; that told us what we knew; that gave us leave to be what we inly were. Discharge to men the priestly office, and, present or absent, you shall be followed with their love as by an angel.

And, to this end, let us not aim at common degrees of merit. Can we not leave, to such as love it, the virtue that glitters for the commendation of society, and ourselves pierce the deep solitudes of absolute ability and worth? We easily come up to the standard of goodness in society. Society's praise can be cheaply secured, and almost all men are content with those easy merits; but the instant effect of conversing with God will be to put them away. There are persons who are not actors, not speakers, but influences; persons too great for fame, for display; who disdain eloquence; to whom all we call art and artist, seems too nearly allied to show and by-ends, to the exaggeration of the finite and selfish, and loss of the universal. The orators, the poets, the commanders encroach on us only as fair women do, by our allowance and homage. Slight them by preoccupation of mind, slight them, as you can well afford to do, by high and universal aims, and they instantly feel that you have right, and that it is in lower places that they must shine. They also feel your right; for they with you are open to the influx of the all-knowing Spirit, which annihilates before its broad noon the little shades and gradations of intelligence in the compositions we call wiser and wisest.

In such high communion let us study the grand strokes of rectitude: a bold benevolence, an independence of friends, so that not the unjust wishes of those who love us shall impair our freedom, but we shall resist for truth's sake the freest flow

---

[14] Wesley: English preacher John Wesley (1703–1791) or his brother Charles (1707–1788), founders of Methodism; Oberlin: Lutheran preacher Jean Frederic Oberlin (1740–1826), innovator in children's education.

of kindness, and appeal to sympathies far in advance; and—what is the highest form in which we know this beautiful element—a certain solidity of merit, that has nothing to do with opinion, and which is so essentially and manifestly virtue, that it is taken for granted that the right, the brave, the generous step will be taken by it, and nobody thinks of commending it. You would compliment a coxcomb doing a good act, but you would not praise an angel. The silence that accepts merit as the most natural thing in the world, is the highest applause. Such souls, when they appear, are the Imperial Guard of Virtue, the perpetual reserve, the dictators of fortune. One needs not praise their courage—they are the heart and soul of nature. O my friends, there are resources in us on which we have not drawn. There are men who rise refreshed on hearing a threat; men to whom a crisis which intimidates and paralyzes the majority—demanding not the faculties of prudence and thrift but comprehension, immovableness, the readiness of sacrifice—comes graceful and beloved as a bride. Napoleon said of Massena,[15] that he was not himself until the battle began to go against him; then, when the dead began to fall in ranks around him, awoke his powers of combination, and he put on terror and victory as a robe. So it is in rugged crises, in unweariable endurance, and in aims which put sympathy out of question that the angel is shown. But these are heights that we can scarce remember and look up to without contrition and shame. Let us thank God that such things exist.

And now let us do what we can to rekindle the smouldering, nigh quenched fire on the altar. The evils of the church that now is are manifest. The question returns, What shall we do? I confess, all attempts to project and establish a Cultus with new rites and forms, seem to me vain. Faith makes us, and not we it, and faith makes its own forms. All attempts to contrive a system are as cold as the new worship introduced by the French to the goddess of Reason—to-day, pasteboard and filigree, and ending to-morrow in madness and murder. Rather let the breath of new life be breathed by you through the forms already existing. For if once you are alive, you shall find they shall become plastic and new. The remedy to their deformity is first, soul, and second, soul, and evermore, soul. A whole popedom[16] of forms one pulsation of virtue can uplift and vivify. Two inestimable advantages Christianity has given us; first the Sabbath, the jubilee of the whole world, whose light dawns welcome alike into the closet of the philosopher, into the garret of toil, and into prison-cells, and everywhere suggests, even to the vile, the dignity of spiritual being. Let it stand forevermore, a temple, which new love, new faith, new sight shall restore to more than its first splendor to mankind. And secondly, the institution of preaching—the speech of man to men—essentially the most flexible of all organs, of all forms. What hinders that now, everywhere, in pulpits, in lecture-rooms, in houses, in fields, wherever the invitation of men or your own occasions lead you, you speak the very truth, as your life and conscience teach it, and cheer the waiting, fainting hearts of men with new hope and new revelation?

I look for the hour when that supreme Beauty which ravished the souls of those Eastern men, and chiefly of those Hebrews, and through their lips spoke oracles to all time, shall speak in the West also. The Hebrew and Greek Scriptures contain

---

[15] André Massena (1758–1817), marshal of Napoleon's empire.

[16] I.e., inflexible hierarchy.

immortal sentences, that have been bread of life to millions. But they have no epical integrity; are fragmentary; are not shown in their order to the intellect. I look for the new Teacher that shall follow so far those shining laws that he shall see them come full circle; shall see their rounding complete grace; shall see the world to be the mirror of the soul; shall see the identity of the law of gravitation with purity of heart; and shall show that the Ought, that Duty, is one thing with Science, with Beauty, and with Joy.

1838

Self-Reliance

"Ne te quæsiveris extra."[1]

"Man is his own star; and the soul that can
Render an honest and a perfect man,
Commands all light, all influence, all fate;
Nothing to him falls early or too late.
Our acts our angels are, or good or ill,
Our fatal shadows that walk by us still."
Epilogue to Beaumont and Fletcher's
Honest Man's Fortune[2]

Cast the bantling[3] *on the rocks,*
Suckle him with the she-wolf's teat;
Wintered with the hawk and fox,
Power and speed be hands and feet.[4]

I read the other day some verses written by an eminent painter[5] which were original and not conventional. The soul always hears an admonition in such lines, let the subject be what it may. The sentiment they instil is of more value than any thought they may contain. To believe your own thought, to believe that what is true for you in your private heart, is true for all men,—that is genius. Speak your latent conviction and it shall be the universal sense; for the inmost in due time becomes the outmost, —and our first thought is rendered back to us by the trumpets of the Last Judgment. Familiar as the voice of the mind is to each, the highest merit we ascribe to Moses, Plato, and Milton, is that they set at naught books and traditions, and spoke not what men wrote but what they thought. A man should learn to detect and watch that gleam of light which flashes across his mind from within, more than the lustre of the firmament of bards and sages. Yet he dismisses without notice his thought, because it is his. In every work of genius we recognize our own rejected thoughts: they come back to us with a certain alienated majesty. Great works of art have no more affecting lesson for us than this. They teach us to abide by our spontaneous impression with

---

[1] Latin: "Do not seek outside yourself."
[2] Elizabethan playwrights Francis Beaumont (1584–1616) and John Fletcher (1579–1625) were authors of *Honest Man's Fortune* (1647).
[3] Infant.
[4] Emerson's own verses.
[5] Most likely the American painter and poet Washington Allston (1779–1843).

good-humored inflexibility then most when the whole cry of voices is on the other side. Else, to-morrow a stranger will say with masterly good sense precisely what we have thought and felt all the time, and we shall be forced to take with shame our own opinion from another.

There is a time in every man's education when he arrives at the conviction that envy is ignorance; that imitation is suicide; that he must take himself for better, for worse, as his portion; that though the wide universe is full of good, no kernel of nourishing corn can come to him but through his toil bestowed on that plot of ground which is given to him to till. The power which resides in him is new in nature, and none but he knows what that is which he can do, nor does he know until he has tried. Not for nothing one face, one character, one fact makes much impression on him, and another none. This sculpture in the memory is not without preëstablished harmony. The eye was placed where one ray should fall, that it might testify of that particular ray. We but half express ourselves, and are ashamed of that divine idea which each of us represents. It may be safely trusted as proportionate and of good issues, so it be faithfully imparted, but God will not have his work made manifest by cowards. A man is relieved and gay when he has put his heart into his work and done his best; but what he has said or done otherwise, shall give him no peace. It is a deliverance which does not deliver. In the attempt his genius deserts him; no muse befriends; no invention, no hope.

Trust thyself: every heart vibrates to that iron string. Accept the place the divine Providence has found for you; the society of your contemporaries, the connexion of events. Great men have always done so and confided themselves childlike to the genius of their age, betraying their perception that the absolutely trustworthy was seated at their heart, working through their hands, predominating in all their being. And we are now men, and must accept in the highest mind the same transcendent destiny; and not minors and invalids in a protected corner, not cowards fleeing before a revolution, but guides, redeemers, and benefactors, obeying the Almighty effort, and advancing on Chaos and the Dark.

What pretty oracles nature yields us on this text in the face and behavior of children, babes and even brutes. That divided and rebel mind, that distrust of a sentiment because our arithmetic has computed the strength and means opposed to our purpose, these have not. Their mind being whole, their eye is as yet unconquered, and when we look in their faces, we are disconcerted. Infancy conforms to nobody: all conform to it, so that one babe commonly makes four or five out of the adults who prattle and play to it. So God has armed youth and puberty and manhood no less with its own piquancy and charm, and made it enviable and gracious and its claims not to be put by, if it will stand by itself. Do not think the youth has no force because he cannot speak to you and me. Hark! in the next room his voice is sufficiently clear and emphatic. It seems he knows how to speak to his contemporaries. Bashful or bold, then, he will know how to make us seniors very unnecessary.

The nonchalance of boys who are sure of a dinner, and would disdain as much as a lord to do or say aught to conciliate one, is the healthy attitude of human nature. A boy is in the parlour what the pit[6] is in the playhouse; independent, irre-

---

[6] Least expensive section of older theaters, where the audience was often clamorous and unrestrained.

sponsible, looking out from his corner on such people and facts as pass by, he tries and sentences them on their merits, in the swift summary way of boys, as good, bad, interesting, silly, eloquent, troublesome. He cumbers himself never about consequences, about interests: he gives an independent, genuine verdict. You must court him: he does not court you. But the man is, as it were, clapped into jail by his consciousness. As soon as he has once acted or spoken with eclat, he is a committed person, watched by the sympathy or the hatred of hundreds whose affections must now enter into his account. There is no Lethe[7] for this. Ah, that he could pass again into his neutrality! Who can thus avoid all pledges, and having observed, observe again from the same unaffected, unbiassed, unbribable, unaffrighted innocence, must always be formidable. He would utter opinions on all passing affairs, which being seen to be not private but necessary, would sink like darts into the ear of men, and put them in fear.

These are the voices which we hear in solitude, but they grow faint and inaudible as we enter into the world. Society everywhere is in conspiracy against the manhood of every one of its members. Society is a joint-stock company in which the members agree for the better securing of his bread to each shareholder, to surrender the liberty and culture of the eater. The virtue in most request is conformity. Self-reliance is its aversion. It loves not realities and creators, but names and customs.

Whoso would be a man must be a nonconformist. He who would gather immortal palms must not be hindered by the name of goodness, but must explore if it be goodness. Nothing is at last sacred but the integrity of your own mind. Absolve you to yourself, and you shall have the suffrage of the world. I remember an answer which when quite young I was prompted to make to a valued adviser who was wont to importune me with the dear old doctrines of the church. On my saying, What have I to do with the sacredness of traditions, if I live wholly from within? my friend suggested—"But these impulses may be from below, not from above." I replied, "They do not seem to me to be such; but if I am the Devil's child, I will live then from the Devil." No law can be sacred to me but that of my nature. Good and bad are but names very readily transferable to that or this; the only right is what is after my constitution, the only wrong what is against it. A man is to carry himself in the presence of all opposition as if everything were titular and ephemeral but he. I am ashamed to think how easily we capitulate to badges and names, to large societies and dead institutions. Every decent and well-spoken individual affects and sways me more than is right. I ought to go upright and vital, and speak the rude truth in all ways. If malice and vanity wear the coat of philanthropy, shall that pass? If an angry bigot assumes this bountiful cause of Abolition, and comes to me with his last news from Barbadoes,[8] why should I not say to him, "Go love thy infant; love thy wood-chopper: be good-natured and modest: have that grace; and never varnish your hard, uncharitable ambition with this incredible tenderness for black folk a thousand miles off. Thy love afar is spite at home." Rough and graceless would be such greeting, but truth is handsomer than the affectation of love. Your goodness must have some edge to it —else it is none. The doctrine of hatred must be preached as the counteraction of the doctrine of love when that pules and whines. I shun father and mother and wife and

---

[7] River in Greek mythology that causes forgetfulness.

[8] In 1834 slavery was officially abolished on this island (Barbados) in the British West Indies.

brother, when my genius calls me. I would write on the lintels of the door-post, *Whim.*[9] I hope it is somewhat better than whim at last, but we cannot spend the day in explanation. Expect me not to show cause why I seek or why I exclude company. Then, again, do not tell me, as a good man did to-day, of my obligation to put all poor men in good situations. Are they *my* poor? I tell thee, thou foolish philanthropist, that I grudge the dollar, the dime, the cent I give to such men as do not belong to me and to whom I do not belong. There is a class of persons to whom by all spiritual affinity I am bought and sold; for them I will go to prison, if need be; but your miscellaneous popular charities; the education at college of fools; the building of meeting-houses to the vain end to which many now stand; alms to sots; and the thousandfold Relief Societies;—though I confess with shame I sometimes succumb and give the dollar, it is a wicked dollar which by and by I shall have the manhood to withhold.

Virtues are in the popular estimate rather the exception than the rule. There is the man *and* his virtues. Men do what is called a good action, as some piece of courage or charity, much as they would pay a fine in expiation of daily non-appearance on parade. Their works are done as an apology or extenuation of their living in the world, —as invalids and the insane pay a high board. Their virtues are penances. I do not wish to expiate, but to live. My life is for itself and not for a spectacle. I much prefer that it should be of a lower strain, so it be genuine and equal, than that it should be glittering and unsteady. I wish it to be sound and sweet, and not to need diet and bleeding.[10] I ask primary evidence that you are a man, and refuse this appeal from the man to his actions. I know that for myself it makes no difference whether I do or forbear those actions which are reckoned excellent. I cannot consent to pay for a privilege where I have intrinsic right. Few and mean as my gifts may be, I actually am, and do not need for my own assurance or the assurance of my fellows any secondary testimony.

What I must do, is all that concerns me, not what the people think. This rule, equally arduous in actual and in intellectual life, may serve for the whole distinction between greatness and meanness. It is the harder, because you will always find those who think they know what is your duty better than you know it. It is easy in the world to live after the world's opinion; it is easy in solitude to live after our own; but the great man is he who in the midst of the crowd keeps with perfect sweetness the independence of solitude.

The objection to conforming to usages that have become dead to you, is, that it scatters your force. It loses your time and blurs the impression of your character. If you maintain a dead church, contribute to a dead Bible-Society, vote with a great party either for the Government or against it, spread your table like base housekeepers, —under all these screens, I have difficulty to detect the precise man you are. And, of course, so much force is withdrawn from your proper life. But do your work, and I shall know you. Do your work, and you shall reinforce yourself. A man must consider what a blindman's-buff is this game of conformity. If I know your sect, I

---

[9] I.e., for rejecting a family in order to obey a divine command (Matthew 10:34–37). See Exodus 12:17, in which God tells Moses to mark the "upper door post" and "two side posts" with blood so that God would not include those inside when he came to "smite all the firstborn in the land of Egypt, both man and beast."

[10] Bloodletting.

anticipate your argument. I hear a preacher announce for his text and topic the expediency of one of the institutions of his church. Do I not know beforehand that not possibly can he say a new and spontaneous word? Do I not know that with all this ostentation of examining the grounds of the institution, he will do no such thing? Do I not know that he is pledged to himself not to look but at one side,—the permitted side, not as a man, but as a parish minister? He is a retained attorney, and these airs of the bench are the emptiest affectation. Well, most men have bound their eyes with one or another handkerchief, and attached themselves to some one of these communities of opinion. This conformity makes them not false in a few particulars, authors of a few lies, but false in all particulars. Their every truth is not quite true. Their two is not the real two, their four not the real four: so that every word they say chagrins us, and we know not where to begin to set them right. Meantime nature is not slow to equip us in the prison-uniform of the party to which we adhere. We come to wear one cut of face and figure, and acquire by degrees the gentlest asinine expression. There is a mortifying experience in particular which does not fail to wreck itself also in the general history; I mean "the foolish face of praise,"[11] the forced smile which we put on in company where we do not feel at ease in answer to conversation which does not interest us. The muscles, not spontaneously moved, but moved by a low usurping wilfulness, grow tight about the outline of the face with the most disagreeable sensation.

For nonconformity the world whips you with its displeasure. And therefore a man must know how to estimate a sour face. The bystanders look askance on him in the public street or in the friend's parlor. If this aversation had its origin in contempt and resistance like his own, he might well go home with a sad countenance; but the sour faces of the multitude, like their sweet faces, have no deep cause, but are put on and off as the wind blows, and a newspaper directs. Yet is the discontent of the multitude more formidable than that of the senate and the college. It is easy enough for a firm man who knows the world to brook the rage of the cultivated classes. Their rage is decorous and prudent, for they are timid as being very vulnerable themselves. But when to their feminine rage the indignation of the people is added, when the ignorant and the poor are aroused, when the unintelligent brute force that lies at the bottom of society is made to growl and mow,[12] it needs the habit of magnanimity and religion to treat it godlike as a trifle of no concernment.

The other terror that scares us from self-trust is our consistency; a reverence for our past act or word, because the eyes of others have no other data for computing our orbit than our past acts, and we are loath to disappoint them.

But why should you keep your head over your shoulder? Why drag about this corpse of your memory, lest you contradict somewhat you have stated in this or that public place? Suppose you should contradict yourself; what then? It seems to be a rule of wisdom never to rely on your memory alone, scarcely even in acts of pure memory, but to bring the past for judgment into the thousand-eyed present, and live ever in a new day. In your metaphysics you have denied personality to the Deity: yet when

[11] Alexander Pope, "Epistle to Dr. Arbuthnot," l. 212.   [12] Archaic for "grimace."

the devout motions of the soul come, yield to them heart and life, though they should clothe God with shape and color. Leave your theory as Joseph his coat in the hand of the harlot,[13] and flee.

A foolish consistency is the hobgoblin of little minds, adored by little statesmen and philosophers and divines. With consistency a great soul has simply nothing to do. He may as well concern himself with his shadow on the wall. Speak what you think now in hard words, and to-morrow speak what to-morrow thinks in hard words again, though it contradict every thing you said to-day.—'Ah, so you shall be sure to be misunderstood.'—Is it so bad then to be misunderstood? Pythagoras[14] was misunderstood, and Socrates, and Jesus, and Luther, and Copernicus,[15] and Galileo,[16] and Newton, and every pure and wise spirit that ever took flesh. To be great is to be misunderstood.

I suppose no man can violate his nature. All the sallies of his will are rounded in by the last of his being as the inequalities of Andes and Himmaleh[17] are insignificant in the curve of the sphere. Nor does it matter how you gauge and try him. A character is like an acrostic or Alexandrian stanza;[18]—read it forward, backward, or across, it still spells the same thing. In this pleasing contrite wood-life which God allows me, let me record day by day my honest thought without prospect or retrospect, and, I cannot doubt, it will be found symmetrical, though I mean it not, and see it not. My book should smell of pines and resound with the hum of insects. The swallow over my window should interweave that thread or straw he carried in his bill into my web also. We pass for what we are. Character teaches above our wills. Men imagine that they communicate their virtue or vice only by overt actions and do not see that virtue or vice emit a breath every moment.

There will be an agreement in whatever variety of actions, so they be each honest and natural in their hour. For of one will, the actions will be harmonious, however unlike they seem. These varieties are lost sight of at a little distance, at a little height of thought. One tendency unites them all. The voyage of the best ship is a zigzag line of a hundred tacks. See the line from a sufficient distance, and it straightens itself to the average tendency. Your genuine action will explain itself and will explain your other genuine actions. Your conformity explains nothing. Act singly, and what you have already done singly, will justify you now. Greatness appeals to the future. If I can be firm enough to-day to do right and scorn eyes, I must have done so much right before, as to defend me now. Be it how it will, do right now. Always scorn appearances, and you always may. The force of character is cumulative. All the foregone days of virtue work their health into this. What makes the majesty of the heroes of the senate and the field, which so fills the imagination? The consciousness of a train of great days and victories behind. They shed an united light on the

---

[13] In Genesis 39:12, Potiphar's wife tempted Joseph by grabbing his garment and asking him to sleep with her, whereupon Joseph fled, leaving the garment behind.

[14] Greek mathematician (sixth century B.C.) and mystic philosopher.

[15] Polish astronomer (1473–1543) who proposed the current theory of the solar system, which was rejected in his lifetime.

[16] Galileo Galilei (1564–1642), Italian astronomer and physicist who endorsed Copernicus's theories and as a result was tried by the Inquisition of the Catholic church.

[17] Mountains in Asia bordering China and India (now Himalayas).

[18] Palindrome, or statement that can be read the same forward and backward.

advancing actor. He is attended as by a visible escort of angels. That is it which throws thunder into Chatham's[19] voice, and dignity into Washington's[20] port,[21] and America into Adams's[22] eye. Honor is venerable to us because it is no ephemeris. It is always ancient virtue. We worship it to-day, because it is not of to-day. We love it and pay it homage, because it is not a trap for our love and homage, but is self-dependent, self-derived, and therefore of an old immaculate pedigree, even if shown in a young person.

I hope in these days we have heard the last of conformity and consistency. Let the words be gazetted[23] and ridiculous henceforward. Instead of the gong for dinner, let us hear a whistle from the Spartan fife.[24] Let us never bow and apologize more. A great man is coming to eat at my house. I do not wish to please him: I wish that he should wish to please me. I will stand here for humanity, and though I would make it kind, I would make it true. Let us affront and reprimand the smooth mediocrity and squalid contentment of the times, and hurl in the face of custom, and trade, and office, the fact which is the upshot of all history, that there is a great responsible Thinker and Actor working wherever a man works; that a true man belongs to no other time or place, but is the centre of things. Where he is, there is nature. He measures you, and all men, and all events. Ordinarily every body in society reminds us of somewhat else or of some other person. Character, reality, reminds you of nothing else; it takes place of the whole creation. The man must be so much that he must make all circumstances indifferent. Every true man is a cause, a country, and an age; requires infinite spaces and numbers and time fully to accomplish his design; —and posterity seem to follow his steps as a train of clients. A man Cæsar is born, and for ages after, we have a Roman Empire. Christ is born, and millions of minds so grow and cleave to his genius, that he is confounded with virtue and the possible of man. An institution is the lengthened shadow of one man; as, Monachism, of the Hermit Antony; the Reformation, of Luther; Quakerism of Fox; Methodism, of Wesley; Abolition, of Clarkson.[25] Scipio,[26] Milton called "the height of Rome;" and all history resolves itself very easily into the biography of a few stout and earnest persons.

Let a man then know his worth, and keep things under his feet. Let him not peep or steal, or skulk up and down with the air of a charity-boy, a bastard, or an interloper, in the world which exists for him. But the man in the street finding no worth in himself which corresponds to the force which built a tower or sculptured a marble god, feels poor when he looks on these. To him a palace, a statue, or a costly book have an alien and forbidding air, much like a gay equipage, and seem to say like that, "Who are you, sir?" Yet they all are his, suitors for his notice, petitioners to his

---

[19] Chatham: William Pitt (1708–1778), earl of Chatham, English orator and statesman.

[20] Washington: George Washington (1732–1799), first American president.

[21] Demeanor.

[22] Adams: Revolutionary War patriot Samuel Adams (1722–1803); John Adams (1735–1826), second president; John Quincy Adams (1767–1848), sixth president.

[23] I.e., let an announcement be made of their public dismissal.

[24] The Spartans were noted for their strict discipline.

[25] Antony: St. Anthony (ca. 250–350) originated Christian monasticism; Fox: George Fox (1624–1691) founded the Society of Friends in England; Wesley: John Wesley (1703–1791) fostered Methodism; Clarkson: Thomas Clarkson (1760–1846) advocated abolition in England.

[26] Roman general (237–183 B.C.) who conquered Carthage.

faculties that they will come out and take possession. The picture waits for my verdict: it is not to command me, but I am to settle its claims to praise. That popular fable of the sot who was picked up dead drunk in the street, carried to the duke's house, washed and dressed and laid in the duke's bed, and, on his waking, treated with all obsequious ceremony like the duke, and assured that he had been insane, owes its popularity to the fact, that it symbolizes so well the state of man, who is in the world a sort of sot, but now and then wakes up, exercises his reason, and finds himself a true prince.

Our reading is mendicant and sycophantic. In history, our imagination plays us false. Kingdom and lordship, power and estate are a gaudier vocabulary than private John and Edward in a small house and common day's work: but the things of life are the same to both: the sum total of both is the same. Why all this deference to Alfred, and Scanderbeg, and Gustavus?[27] Suppose they were virtuous: did they wear out virtue? As great a stake depends on your private act to-day, as followed their public and renowned steps. When private men shall act with original views, the lustre will be transferred from the actions of kings to those of gentlemen.

The world has been instructed by its kings, who have so magnetized the eyes of nations. It has been taught by this colossal symbol the mutual reverence that is due from man to man. The joyful loyalty with which men have everywhere suffered the king, the noble, or the great proprietor to walk among them by a law of his own, make his own scale of men and things, and reverse theirs, pay for benefits not with money but with honor, and represent the Law in his person, was the hieroglyphic by which they obscurely signified their consciousness of their own right and comeliness, the right of every man.

The magnetism which all original action exerts is explained when we inquire the reason of self-trust. Who is the Trustee? What is the aboriginal Self on which a universal reliance may be grounded? What is the nature and power of that science-baffling star, without parallax,[28] without calculable elements, which shoots a ray of beauty even into trivial and impure actions, if the least mark of independence appear? The inquiry leads us to that source, at once the essence of genius, of virtue, and of life, which we call Spontaneity or Instinct. We denote this primary wisdom as Intuition, whilst all later teachings are tuitions. In that deep force, the last fact behind which analysis cannot go, all things find their common origin. For the sense of being which in calm hours rises, we know not how, in the soul, is not diverse from things, from space, from light, from time, from man, but one with them, and proceeds obviously from the same source whence their life and being also proceed. We first share the life by which things exist, and afterwards see them as appearances in nature, and forget that we have shared their cause. Here is the fountain of action and of thought. Here are the lungs of that inspiration which giveth man wisdom, and which cannot be denied without impiety and atheism. We lie in the lap of immense intelligence, which makes us receivers of its truth and organs of its activity. When we discern justice, when we discern truth, we do nothing of ourselves, but allow a

[27] Alfred: Alfred the Great (849–899), king of England; Scanderbeg: national hero of Albania (1403?–1468); Gustavus: Gustavus Adolphus (1594–1632), king of Sweden.
[28] Apparent change in the direction of an object caused by a change in the position from which it is seen. Emerson may well be using "without parallax" to mean "without an observational position."

passage to its beams. If we ask whence this comes, if we seek to pry into the soul that causes, all philosophy is at fault. Its presence or its absence is all we can affirm. Every man discriminates between the voluntary acts of his mind, and his involuntary perceptions, and knows that to his involuntary perceptions a perfect faith is due. He may err in the expression of them, but he knows that these things are so, like day and night, not to be disputed. My wilful actions and acquisitions are but roving;— the idlest reverie, the faintest native emotion, command my curiosity and respect. Thoughtless people contradict as readily the statement of perceptions as of opinions, or rather much more readily; for, they do not distinguish between perception and notion. They fancy that I choose to see this or that thing. But perception is not whimsical, but fatal. If I see a trait, my children will see it after me, and in course of time, all mankind,—although it may chance that no one has seen it before me. For my perception of it is as much a fact as the sun.

The relations of the soul to the divine spirit are so pure that it is profane to seek to interpose helps. It must be that when God speaketh, he should communicate not one thing, but all things; should fill the world with his voice; should scatter forth light, nature, time, souls, from the centre of the present thought; and new date and new create the whole. Whenever a mind is simple, and receives a divine wisdom, old things pass away,—means, teachers, texts, temples fall; it lives now and absorbs past and future into the present hour. All things are made sacred by relation to it,—one as much as another. All things are dissolved to their centre by their cause, and in the universal miracle petty and particular miracles disappear. If, therefore, a man claims to know and speak of God, and carries you backward to the phraseology of some old mouldered nation in another country, in another world, believe him not. Is the acorn better than the oak which is its fullness and completion? Is the parent better than the child into whom he has cast his ripened being? Whence then this worship of the past? The centuries are conspirators against the sanity and authority of the soul. Time and space are but physiological colors which the eye makes, but the soul is light; where it is, is day; where it was, is night; and history is an impertinence and an injury, if it be anything more than a cheerful apologue or parable of my being and becoming.

Man is timid and apologetic; he is no longer upright; he dares not say 'I think,' 'I am,' but quotes some saint or sage. He is ashamed before the blade of grass or the blowing rose. These roses under my window make no reference to former roses or to better ones; they are for what they are; they exist with God to-day. There is no time to them. There is simply the rose; it is perfect in every moment of its existence. Before a leaf-bud has burst, its whole life acts; in the full-blown flower, there is no more; in the leafless root, there is no less. Its nature is satisfied, and it satisfies nature, in all moments alike. But man postpones or remembers; he does not live in the present, but with reverted eye laments the past, or, heedless of the riches that surround him, stands on tiptoe to foresee the future. He cannot be happy and strong until he too lives with nature in the present, above time.

This should be plain enough. Yet see what strong intellects dare not yet hear God himself, unless he speak the phraseology of I know not what David, or Jeremiah, or Paul.[29] We shall not always set so great a price on a few texts, on a few lives. We are like children who repeat by rote the sentences of grandames and tutors, and, as

---

[29] The three biblical authors.

they grow older, of the men of talents and character they chance to see,—painfully recollecting the exact words they spoke; afterwards, when they come into the point of view which those had who uttered these sayings, they understand them, and are willing to let the words go; for, at any time, they can use words as good, when occasion comes. If we live truly, we shall see truly. It is as easy for the strong man to be strong, as it is for the weak to be weak. When we have new perception, we shall gladly disburden the memory of its hoarded treasures as old rubbish. When a man lives with God, his voice shall be as sweet as the murmur of the brook and the rustle of the corn.

And now at last the highest truth on this subject remains unsaid; probably, cannot be said; for all that we say is the far off remembering of the intuition. That thought, by what I can now nearest approach to say it, is this. When good is near you, when you have life in yourself, it is not by any known or accustomed way; you shall not discern the foot-prints of any other; you shall not see the face of man; you shall not hear any name;—the way, the thought, the good shall be wholly strange and new. It shall exclude example and experience. You take the way from man, not to man. All persons that ever existed are its forgotten ministers. Fear and hope are alike beneath it. There is somewhat low even in hope. In the hour of vision, there is nothing that can be called gratitude, nor properly joy. The soul raised over passion beholds identity and eternal causation, perceives the self-existence of Truth and Right, and calms itself with knowing that all things go well. Vast spaces of nature, the Atlantic Ocean, the South Sea,—long intervals of time, years, centuries,—are of no account. This which I think and feel underlay every former state of life and circumstances, as it does underlie my present, and what is called life, and what is called death.

Life only avails, not the having lived. Power ceases in the instant of repose; it resides in the moment of transition from a past to a new state, in the shooting of the gulf, in the darting to an aim. This one fact the world hates, that the soul *becomes;* for, that forever degrades the past, turns all riches to poverty, all reputation to a shame, confounds the saint with the rogue, shoves Jesus and Judas equally aside. Why then do we prate of self-reliance? Inasmuch as the soul is present, there will be power not confident but agent. To talk of reliance, is a poor external way of speaking. Speak rather of that which relies, because it works and is. Who has more obedience than I, masters me, though he should not raise his finger. Round him I must revolve by the gravitation of spirits. We fancy it rhetoric when we speak of eminent virtue. We do not yet see that virtue is Height, and that a man or a company of men plastic and permeable to principles, by the law of nature must overpower and ride all cities, nations, kings, rich men, poets, who are not.

This is the ultimate fact which we so quickly reach on this as on every topic, the resolution of all into the ever blessed ONE. Self-existence is the attribute of the Supreme Cause, and it constitutes the measure of good by the degree in which it enters into all lower forms. All things real are so by so much virtue as they contain. Commerce, husbandry, hunting, whaling, war, eloquence, personal weight, are some-what, and engage my respect as examples of its presence and impure action. I see the same law working in nature for conservation and growth. Power is in nature the essential measure of right. Nature suffers nothing to remain in her kingdoms which cannot help itself. The genesis and maturation of a planet, its poise and orbit, the bended tree recovering itself from the strong wind, the vital resources of every animal and vegetable, are demonstrations of the self-sufficing, and therefore self-relying soul.

Thus all concentrates; let us not rove; let us sit at home with the cause. Let us stun and astonish the intruding rabble of men and books and institutions by a simple declaration of the divine fact. Bid the invaders take the shoes from off their feet, for God is here within.[30] Let our simplicity judge them, and our docility to our own law demonstrate the poverty of nature and fortune beside our native riches.

But now we are a mob. Man does not stand in awe of man, nor is his genius admonished to stay at home, to put itself in communication with the internal ocean, but it goes abroad to beg a cup of water of the urns of other men. We must go alone. I like the silent church before the service begins, better than any preaching. How far off, how cool, how chaste the persons look, begirt each one with a precinct or sanctuary. So let us always sit. Why should we assume the faults of our friend, or wife, or father, or child, because they sit around our hearth, or are said to have the same blood? All men have my blood, and I have all men's. Not for that will I adopt their petulance or folly, even to the extent of being ashamed of it. But your isolation must not be mechanical, but spiritual, that is, must be elevation. At times the whole world seems to be in conspiracy to importune you with emphatic trifles. Friend, client, child, sickness, fear, want, charity, all knock at once at thy closet door and say,—"Come out unto us." But keep thy state; come not into their confusion. The power men possess to annoy me, I give them by a weak curiosity. No man can come near me but through my act. "What we love that we have, but by desire we bereave ourselves of the love."

If we cannot at once rise to the sanctities of obedience and faith, let us at least resist our temptations; let us enter into the state of war, and wake Thor and Woden,[31] courage and constancy, in our Saxon breasts. This is to be done in our smooth times by speaking the truth. Check this lying hospitality and lying affection. Live no longer to the expectation of these deceived and deceiving people with whom we converse. Say to them, O father, O mother, O wife, O brother, O friend, I have lived with you after appearances hitherto. Henceforward I am the truth's. Be it known unto you that henceforward I obey no law less than the eternal law. I will have no covenants but proximities. I shall endeavor to nourish my parents, to support my family, to be the chaste husband of one wife,—but these relations I must fill after a new and unprecedented way. I appeal from your customs. I must be myself. I cannot break myself any longer for you, or you. If you can love me for what I am, we shall be the happier. If you cannot, I will still seek to deserve that you should. I will not hide my tastes or aversions. I will so trust that what is deep is holy, that I will do strongly before the sun and moon whatever inly rejoices me, and the heart appoints. If you are noble, I will love you; if you are not, I will not hurt you and myself by hypocritical attentions. If you are true, but not in the same truth with me, cleave to your companions; I will seek my own. I do this not selfishly, but humbly and truly. It is alike your interest and mine and all men's, however long we have dwelt in lies, to live in truth. Does this sound harsh to-day? You will soon love what is dictated by your nature as well as mine, and if we follow the truth, it will bring us out safe at last.—But so you may give these friends pain. Yes, but I cannot sell my liberty

---

[30] See Exodus 3:5, in which God says to Moses: "Put off thy shoes from off thy feet, for the place whereon thou standest is holy ground."

[31] Thor and Woden (Odin) are gods of preeminent power in Norse mythology.

and my power, to save their sensibility. Besides, all persons have their moments of reason when they look out into the region of absolute truth; then will they justify me and do the same thing.

The populace think that your rejection of popular standards is a rejection of all standard, and mere antinomianism;[32] and the bold sensualist will use the name of philosophy to gild his crimes. But the law of consciousness abides. There are two confessionals, in one or the other of which we must be shriven. You may fulfil your round of duties by clearing yourself in the *direct,* or, in the *reflex* way. Consider whether you have satisfied your relations to father, mother, cousin, neighbor, town, cat, and dog; whether any of these can upbraid you. But I may also neglect this reflex standard, and absolve me to myself. I have my own stern claims and perfect circle. It denies the name of duty to many offices that are called duties. But if I can discharge its debts, it enables me to dispense with the popular code. If any one imagines that this law is lax, let him keep its commandment one day.

And truly it demands something godlike in him who has cast off the common motives of humanity, and has ventured to trust himself for a taskmaster. High be his heart, faithful his will, clear his sight, that he may in good earnest be doctrine, society, law to himself, that a simple purpose may be to him as strong as iron necessity is to others.

If any man consider the present aspects of what is called by distinction *society,* he will see the need of these ethics. The sinew and heart of man seem to be drawn out, and we are become timorous desponding whimperers. We are afraid of truth, afraid of fortune, afraid of death, and afraid of each other. Our age yields no great and perfect persons. We want men and women who shall renovate life and our social state, but we see that most natures are insolvent, cannot satisfy their own wants, have an ambition out of all proportion to their practical force, and do lean and beg day and night continually. Our housekeeping is mendicant, our arts, our occupations, our marriages, our religion we have not chosen, but society has chosen for us. We are parlor soldiers. We shun the rugged battle of fate, where strength is born.

If our young men miscarry in their first enterprizes, they lose all heart. If the young merchant fails, men say he is *ruined.* If the finest genius studies at one of our colleges, and is not installed in an office within one year afterwards in the cities or suburbs of Boston or New York, it seems to his friends and to himself that he is right in being disheartened and in complaining the rest of his life. A sturdy lad from New Hampshire or Vermont, who in turn tries all the professions, who *teams it, farms it, peddles,* keeps a school, preaches, edits a newspaper, goes to Congress, buys a township, and so forth, in successive years, and always, like a cat, falls on his feet, is worth a hundred of these city dolls. He walks abreast with his days, and feels no shame in not 'studying a profession,' for he does not postpone his life, but lives already. He has not one chance, but a hundred chances. Let a Stoic[33] open the resources of man, and tell men they are not leaning willows, but can and must detach themselves; that with the exercise of self-trust, new powers shall appear; that a man is the word made flesh,[34] born to shed

---

[32] Resistance to religious and moral laws.
[33] Ancient Greek philosophers who professed passionless independence and submission to natural law.

[34] John 1:14: "And the word was made flesh, and dwelt among us . . . full of grace and truth."

healing to the nations, that he should be ashamed of our compassion, and that the moment he acts from himself, tossing the laws, the books, idolatries, and customs out of the window, we pity him no more but thank and revere him,—and that teacher shall restore the life of man to splendor, and make his name dear to all History.

It is easy to see that a greater self-reliance must work a revolution in all the offices and relations of men; in their religion; in their education; in their pursuits; their modes of living; their association; in their property; in their speculative views.

1. In what prayers do men allow themselves! That which they call a holy office, is not so much as brave and manly. Prayer looks abroad and asks for some foreign addition to come through some foreign virtue, and loses itself in endless mazes of natural and supernatural, and mediatorial and miraculous. Prayer that craves a particular commodity,—any thing less than all good,—is vicious. Prayer is the contemplation of the facts of life from the highest point of view. It is the soliloquy of a beholding and jubilant soul. It is the spirit of God pronouncing his works good.[35] But prayer as a means to effect a private end, is meanness and theft. It supposes dualism and not unity in nature and consciousness. As soon as the man is at one with God, he will not beg. He will then see prayer in all action. The prayer of the farmer kneeling in his field to weed it, the prayer of the rower kneeling with the stroke of his oar, are true prayers heard throughout nature, though for cheap ends. Caratach, in Fletcher's Bonduca,[36] when admonished to inquire the mind of the god Audate, replies,—

"His hidden meaning lies in our endeavors,
Our valors are our best gods."

Another sort of false prayers are our regrets. Discontent is the want of self-reliance: it is infirmity of will. Regret calamities, if you can thereby help the sufferer; if not, attend your own work, and already the evil begins to be repaired. Our sympathy is just as base. We come to them who weep foolishly, and sit down and cry for company, instead of imparting to them truth and health in rough electric shocks, putting them once more in communication with their own reason. The secret of fortune is joy in our hands. Welcome evermore to gods and men is the self-helping man. For him all doors are flung wide: him all tongues greet, all honors crown, all eyes follow with desire. Our love goes out to him and embraces him, because he did not need it. We solicitously and apologetically caress and celebrate him, because he held on his way and scorned our disapprobation. The gods love him because men hated him. "To the persevering mortal," said Zoroaster,[37] "the blessed Immortals are swift."

As men's prayers are a disease of the will, so are their creeds a disease of the intellect. They say with those foolish Israelites, "Let not God speak to us, lest we die. Speak thou, speak any man with us, and we will obey."[38] Everywhere I am hindered of meeting God in my brother, because he has shut his own temple doors, and recites fables merely of his brother's, or his brother's brother's God. Every new mind is a new classification. If it prove a mind of uncommon activity and power, a Locke, a

---

[35] Genesis 1:31: "And God saw everything that he had made, and, behold, *it was* very good."

[36] Drama by Elizabethan playwright John Fletcher (1579–1625). The lines Emerson cites are slightly misquoted.

[37] Persian prophet of the sixth century B.C.

[38] Anxious words of the Hebrews to Moses, after God had given him the Ten Commandments. (See Exodus 20:19.)

Lavoisier, a Hutton, a Bentham, a Fourier,[39] it imposes its classification on other men, and lo! a new system. In proportion to the depth of the thought, and so to the number of the objects it touches and brings within reach of the pupil, is his complacency. But chiefly is this apparent in creeds and churches, which are also classifications of some powerful mind acting on the elemental thought of Duty, and man's relation to the Highest. Such is Calvinism, Quakerism, Swedenborgianism. The pupil takes the same delight in subordinating every thing to the new terminology, as a girl who has just learned botany in seeing a new earth and new seasons thereby. It will happen for a time, that the pupil will find his intellectual power has grown by the study of his master's mind. But in all unbalanced minds, the classification is idolized, passes for the end, and not for a speedily exhaustible means, so that the walls of the system blend to their eye in the remote horizon with the walls of the universe; the luminaries of heaven seem to them hung on the arch their master built. They cannot imagine how you aliens have any right to see,—how you can see; "It must be somehow that you stole the light from us." They do not yet perceive, that light, unsystematic, indomitable, will break into any cabin, even into theirs. Let them chirp awhile and call it their own. If they are honest and do well, presently their neat new pinfold[40] will be too strait and low, will crack, will lean, will rot and vanish, and the immortal light, all young and joyful, million-orbed, million-colored, will beam over the universe as on the first morning.

2. It is for want of self-culture that the superstition of Travelling, whose idols are Italy, England, Egypt, retains its fascination for all educated Americans. They who made England, Italy, or Greece venerable in the imagination, did so by sticking fast where they were, like an axis of the earth. In manly hours, we feel that duty is our place. The soul is no traveller: the wise man stays at home, and when his necessities, his duties, on any occasion call him from his house, or into foreign lands, he is at home still, and shall make men sensible by the expression of his countenance, that he goes the missionary of wisdom and virtue, and visits cities and men like a sovereign, and not like an interloper or a valet.

I have no churlish objection to the circumnavigation of the globe, for the purposes of art, of study, and benevolence, so that the man is first domesticated, or does not go abroad with the hope of finding somewhat greater than he knows. He who travels to be amused, or to get somewhat which he does not carry, travels away from himself, and grows old even in youth among old things. In Thebes, in Palmyra,[41] his will and mind have become old and dilapidated as they. He carries ruins to ruins.

Travelling is a fool's paradise. Our first journeys discover to us the indifference of places. At home I dream that at Naples, at Rome, I can be intoxicated with beauty, and lose my sadness. I pack my trunk, embrace my friends, embark on the sea, and at last wake up in Naples, and there beside me is the stern Fact, the sad self, unrelenting, identical, that I fled from. I seek the Vatican, and the palaces. I affect to be intoxicated

---

[39] Locke: John Locke (1632–1704), English philosopher who heralded a theory of knowledge; Lavoisier: Antoine Laurent Lavoisier (1743–1794), who initiated advances in chemistry; Hutton: James Hutton (1726–1797), pioneer in geology; Bentham: Jeremy Bentham (1748–1832), who originated practical doctrines for law and government; Fourier: François Marie Charles Fourier (1772–1837), who pioneered in sociology.

[40] Fenced yard for holding animals.

[41] Thebes; Palmyra: ancient cities in Egypt and Syria, respectively.

with sights and suggestions, but I am not intoxicated. My giant goes with me wherever I go.

3. But the rage of travelling is a symptom of a deeper unsoundness affecting the whole intellectual action. The intellect is vagabond, and our system of education fosters restlessness. Our minds travel when our bodies are forced to stay at home. We imitate; and what is imitation but the travelling of the mind? Our houses are built with foreign taste; our shelves are garnished with foreign ornaments; our opinions, our tastes, our faculties, lean, and follow the Past and the Distant. The soul created the arts wherever they have flourished. It was in his own mind that the artist sought his model. It was an application of his own thought to the thing to be done and the conditions to be observed. And why need we copy the Doric or the Gothic model? Beauty, convenience, grandeur of thought, and quaint expression are as near to us as to any, and if the American artist will study with hope and love the precise thing to be done by him, considering the climate, the soil, the length of the day, the wants of the people, the habit and form of the government, he will create a house in which all these will find themselves fitted, and taste and sentiment will be satisfied also.

Insist on yourself; never imitate. Your own gift you can present every moment with the cumulative force of a whole life's cultivation; but of the adopted talent of another, you have only an extemporaneous, half possession. That which each can do best, none but his Maker can teach him. No man yet knows what it is, nor can, till that person has exhibited it. Where is the master who could have taught Shakspeare? Where is the master who could have instructed Franklin, or Washington, or Bacon, or Newton? Every great man is a unique. The Scipionism[42] of Scipio is precisely that part he could not borrow. Shakspeare will never be made by the study of Shakspeare. Do that which is assigned you, and you cannot hope too much or dare too much. There is at this moment for you an utterance brave and grand as that of the colossal chisel of Phidias,[43] or trowel of the Egyptians, or the pen of Moses, or Dante, but different from all these. Not possibly will the soul all rich, all eloquent, with thousand-cloven tongue, deign to repeat itself; but if you can hear what these patriarchs say, surely you can reply to them in the same pitch of voice: for the ear and the tongue are two organs of one nature. Abide in the simple and noble regions of thy life, obey thy heart, and thou shalt reproduce the Foreworld again.

4. As our Religion, our Education, our Art look abroad, so does our spirit of society. All men plume themselves on the improvement of society, and no man improves.

Society never advances. It recedes as fast on one side as it gains on the other. It undergoes continual changes: it is barbarous, it is civilized, it is christianized, it is rich, it is scientific; but this change is not amelioration. For every thing that is given, something is taken. Society acquires new arts and loses old instincts. What a contrast between the well-clad, reading, writing, thinking American, with a watch, a pencil, and a bill of exchange in his pocket, and the naked New Zealander, whose property is a club, a spear, a mat, and an undivided twentieth of a shed to sleep under. But compare the health of the two men, and you shall see that the white man has lost

---

[42] I.e., Scipio's essence.
[43] Renowned Greek sculptor of the fifth century B.C.

his aboriginal strength. If the traveller tell us truly, strike the savage with a broad axe, and in a day or two the flesh shall unite and heal as if you struck the blow into soft pitch, and the same blow shall send the white to his grave.

The civilized man has built a coach, but has lost the use of his feet. He is supported on crutches, but lacks so much support of muscle. He has a fine Geneva watch, but he fails of the skill to tell the hour by the sun. A Greenwich nautical almanac he has, and so being sure of the information when he wants it, the man in the street does not know a star in the sky. The solstice he does not observe; the equinox he knows as little; and the whole bright calendar of the year is without a dial in his mind. His note-books impair his memory; his libraries overload his wit; the insurance office increases the number of accidents; and it may be a question whether machinery does not encumber; whether we have not lost by refinement some energy, by a christianity entrenched in establishments and forms, some vigor of wild virtue. For every stoic was a stoic; but in Christendom where is the Christian?

There is no more deviation in the moral standard than in the standard of height or bulk. No greater men are now than ever were. A singular equality may be observed between the great men of the first and of the last ages; nor can all the science, art, religion and philosophy of the nineteenth century avail to educate greater men than Plutarch's[44] heroes, three or four and twenty centuries ago. Not in time is the race progressive. Phocion, Socrates, Anaxagoras, Diogenes, are great men, but they leave no class.[45] He who is really of their class will not be called by their name, but will be his own man, and, in his turn the founder of a sect. The arts and inventions of each period are only its costume, and do not invigorate men. The harm of the improved machinery may compensate its good. Hudson and Behring accomplished so much in their fishing-boats, as to astonish Parry and Franklin, whose equipment exhausted the resources of science and art.[46] Galileo, with an opera-glass, discovered a more splendid series of celestial phenomena than any one since. Columbus found the New World in an undecked boat. It is curious to see the periodical disuse and perishing of means and machinery which were introduced with loud laudation, a few years or centuries before. The great genius returns to essential man. We reckoned the improvements of the art of war among the triumphs of science, and yet Napoleon conquered Europe by the Bivouac, which consisted of falling back on naked valor, and disencumbering it of all aids. The Emperor held it impossible to make a perfect army, says Las Cases,[47] "without abolishing our arms, magazines, commissaries, and carriages, until in imitation of the Roman custom, the soldier should receive his supply of corn, grind it in his hand-mill, and bake his bread himself."

Society is a wave. The wave moves onward, but the water of which it is composed, does not. The same particle does not rise from the valley to the ridge. Its unity is only phenomenal. The persons who make up a nation to-day, next year die, and their experience with them.

---

[44] Plutarch: Greek biographer (46?–?120) who recorded the lives of famous Romans and Greeks.

[45] All "great men" cited here were Greek philosophers of the third and fourth centuries B.C.

[46] Hudson: English navigator Henry Hudson

(d. 1611); Behring: Dutch navigator Vitus Jonassen Bering (1680–1741); Parry and Franklin: English arctic explorers Sir William Edward Parry (1790–1855) and Sir John Franklin (1786–1847).

[47] French historian Comte Emmanuel Augustin de las Cases (1766–1842).

And so the reliance on Property, including the reliance on governments which protect it, is the want of self-reliance. Men have looked away from themselves and at things so long, that they have come to esteem the religious, learned, and civil institutions, as guards of property, and they deprecate assaults on these, because they feel them to be assaults on property. They measure their esteem of each other, by what each has, and not by what each is. But a cultivated man becomes ashamed of his property, out of new respect for his nature. Especially he hates what he has, if he see that it is accidental,—came to him by inheritance, or gift, or crime; then he feels that it is not having; it does not belong to him, has no root in him, and merely lies there, because no revolution or no robber takes it away. But that which a man is, does always by necessity acquire, and what the man acquires is living property, which does not wait the beck of rulers, or mobs, or revolutions, or fire, or storm, or bankruptcies, but perpetually renews itself wherever the man breathes. "Thy lot or portion of life," said the Caliph Ali,[48] "is seeking after thee; therefore be at rest from seeking after it." Our dependence on these foreign goods leads us to our slavish respect for numbers. The political parties meet in numerous conventions; the greater the concourse, and with each new uproar of announcement, The delegation from Essex![49] The Democrats from New Hampshire! The Whigs of Maine! the young patriot feels himself stronger than before by a new thousand of eyes and arms. In like manner the reformers summon conventions, and vote and resolve in multitude. Not so, O friends! will the God deign to enter and inhabit you, but by a method precisely the reverse. It is only as a man puts off all foreign support, and stands alone, that I see him to be strong and to prevail. He is weaker by every recruit to his banner. Is not a man better than a town? Ask nothing of men, and in the endless mutation, thou only firm column must presently appear the upholder of all that surrounds thee. He who knows that power is inborn, that he is weak because he has looked for good out of him and elsewhere, and so perceiving, throws himself unhesitatingly on his thought, instantly rights himself, stands in the erect position, commands his limbs, works miracles; just as a man who stands on his feet is stronger than a man who stands on his head.

So use all that is called Fortune. Most men gamble with her, and gain all, and lose all, as her wheel rolls. But do thou leave as unlawful these winnings, and deal with Cause and Effect, the chancellors of God. In the Will work and acquire, and thou hast chained the wheel of Chance, and shalt sit hereafter out of fear from her rotations. A political victory, a rise of rents, the recovery of your sick, or the return of your absent friend, or some other favorable event, raises your spirits, and you think good days are preparing for you. Do not believe it. Nothing can bring you peace but yourself. Nothing can bring you peace but the triumph of principles.

1841

---

[48] Ali-ibn-abn-Talib (600?–661), fourth Moslem caliph of Mecca.
[49] County in Massachusetts.

The Over-Soul[1]

"But souls that of his own good life partake,
He loves as his own self; dear as his eye
They are to Him: He'll never them forsake:
When they shall die, then God himself shall die:
They live, they live in blest eternity."

Henry More

Space is ample, east and west,
But two cannot go abreast,
Cannot travel in it two:
Yonder masterful cuckoo
Crowds every egg out of the nest,
Quick or dead, except its own;
A spell is laid on sod and stone,
Night and Day were tampered with,
Every quality and pith
Surcharged and sultry with a power
That works its will on age and hour.

There is a difference between one and another hour of life, in their authority and subsequent effect. Our faith comes in moments; our vice is habitual. Yet there is a depth in those brief moments, which constrains us to ascribe more reality to them than to all other experiences. For this reason, the argument, which is always forthcoming to silence those who conceive extraordinary hopes of man, namely, the appeal to experience, is forever invalid and vain. We give up the past to the objector, and yet we hope. He must explain this hope. We grant that human life is mean; but how did we find out that it was mean? What is the ground of this uneasiness of ours; of this old discontent? What is the universal sense of want and ignorance, but the fine innuendo by which the soul makes its enormous claim? Why do men feel that the natural history of man has never been written, but he is always leaving behind what you have said of him, and it becomes old, and books of metaphysics worthless? The philosophy of six thousand years has not searched the chambers and magazines of the soul. In its experiments there has always remained, in the last analysis, a residuum it could not resolve. Man is a stream whose source is hidden. Our being is descending into us from we know not whence. The most exact calculator has no prescience that somewhat incalculable may not baulk the very next moment. I am constrained every moment to acknowledge a higher origin for events than the will I call mine.

As with events, so is it with thoughts. When I watch that flowing river, which, out of regions I see not, pours for a season its streams into me, I see that I am a pensioner; not a cause, but a surprised spectator of this ethereal water; that I desire and look up, and put myself in the attitude of reception, but from some alien energy the visions come.

---

[1] Emerson offers a definition of this term in the third paragraph of the essay. In his *Journals* (Vol. 7, p. 412), Emerson partially defines the term as "The Highest Thow Always Unknown." Henry More (1614–1687) was an English philosopher.

The Supreme Critic on the errors of the past and the present, and the only prophet of that which must be, is that great nature in which we rest, as the earth lies in the soft arms of the atmosphere; that Unity, that Over-Soul, within which every man's particular being is contained and made one with all other; that common heart, of which all sincere conversation is the worship, to which all right action is submission; that overpowering reality which confutes our tricks and talents, and constrains every one to pass for what he is, and to speak from his character and not from his tongue, and which evermore tends and aims to pass into our thought and hand, and become wisdom, and virtue, and power, and beauty. We live in succession, in division, in parts, in particles. Meantime within man is the soul of the whole; the wise silence; the universal beauty, to which every part and particle is equally related; the eternal ONE. And this deep power in which we exist, and whose beatitude is all accessible to us, is not only self-sufficing and perfect in every hour, but the act of seeing and the thing seen, the seer and the spectacle, the subject and the object, are one. We see the world piece by piece, as the sun, the moon, the animal, the tree; but the whole, of which these are the shining parts, is the soul. Only by the vision of that Wisdom can the horoscope of the ages be read, and by falling back on our better thoughts, by yielding to the spirit of prophecy which is innate in every man, we can know what it saith. Every man's words, who speaks from that life, must sound vain to those who do not dwell in the same thought on their own part. I dare not speak for it. My words do not carry its august sense; they fall short and cold. Only itself can inspire whom it will, and behold! their speech shall be lyrical, and sweet, and universal as the rising of the wind. Yet I desire, even by profane words, if I may not use sacred, to indicate the heaven of this deity, and to report what hints I have collected of the transcendent simplicity and energy of the Highest Law.

If we consider what happens in conversation, in reveries, in remorse, in times of passion, in surprises, in the instructions of dreams wherein often we see ourselves in masquerade,—the droll disguises only magnifying and enhancing a real element, and forcing it on our distinct notice,—we shall catch many hints that will broaden and lighten into knowledge of the secret of nature. All goes to show that the soul in man is not an organ, but animates and exercises all the organs; is not a function, like the power of memory, of calculation, of comparison, but uses these as hands and feet; is not a faculty, but a light; is not the intellect of the will, but the master of the intellect and the will; is the background of our being, in which they lie,—an immensity not possessed and that cannot be possessed. From within or from behind, a light shines through us upon things, and makes us aware that we are nothing, but the light is all. A man is the façade of a temple wherein all wisdom and all good abide. What we commonly call man, the eating, drinking, planting, counting man, does not, as we know him, represent himself, but misrepresents himself. Him we do not respect, but the soul, whose organ he is, would he let it appear through his action, would make our knees bend. When it breathes through his intellect, it is genius; when it breathes through his will, it is virtue; when it flows through his affection, it is love. And the blindness of the intellect begins, when it would be something of itself. The weakness of the will begins when the individual would be something of himself. All reform aims, in some one particular, to let the soul have its way through us; in other words, to engage us to obey.

Of this pure nature every man is at some time sensible. Language cannot paint it with his colors. It is too subtle. It is undefinable, unmeasurable, but we know that it pervades and contains us. We know that all spiritual being is in man. A wise old proverb says, "God comes to see us without bell:" that is, as there is no screen or ceiling between our heads and the infinite heavens, so is there no bar or wall in the soul where man, the effect, ceases, and God, the cause, begins. The walls are taken away. We lie open on one side to the deeps of spiritual nature, to all the attributes of God. Justice we see and know, Love, Freedom, Power. These natures no man ever got above, but they tower over us, and most in the moment when our interests tempt us to wound them.

The sovereignty of this nature whereof we speak, is made known by its independency of those limitations which circumscribe us on every hand. The soul circumscribes all things. As I have said, it contradicts all experience. In like manner it abolishes time and space. The influence of the senses has, in most men, overpowered the mind to that degree, that the walls of time and space have come to look real and insurmountable; and to speak with levity of these limits, is, in the world, the sign of insanity. Yet time and space are but inverse measures of the force of the soul. The spirit sports with time—

"Can crowd eternity into an hour,
  Or stretch an hour to eternity."[2]

We are often made to feel that there is another youth and age than that which is measured from the year of our natural birth. Some thoughts always find us young and keep us so. Such a thought is the love of the universal and eternal beauty. Every man parts from that contemplation with the feeling that it rather belongs to ages than to mortal life. The least activity of the intellectual powers redeems us in a degree from the conditions of time. In sickness, in languor, give us a strain of poetry or a profound sentence, and we are refreshed; or produce a volume of Plato, or Shakspeare, or remind us of their names, and instantly we come into a feeling of longevity. See how the deep, divine thought reduces centuries, and millenniums,[3] and makes itself present through all ages. Is the teaching of Christ less effective now than it was when first his mouth was opened? The emphasis of facts and persons in my thought has nothing to do with time. And so, always, the soul's scale is one; the scale of the senses and the understanding is another. Before the revelations of the soul, Time, Space and Nature shrink away. In common speech, we refer all things to time, as we habitually refer the immensely sundered stars to one concave sphere. And so we say that the Judgment is distant or near, that the Millennium approaches, that a day of certain political, moral, social reforms is at hand, and the like, when we mean, that in the nature of things, one of the facts we contemplate is external and fugitive, and the other is permanent and connate with the soul. The things we now esteem fixed, shall, one by one, detach themselves, like ripe fruit, from our experience, and fall. The wind

---

[2] An adaptation of "to see a world in a grain of sand / and a heaven in a wild flower, / hold infinity in the palm of your hand / and eternity in an hour," from William Blake's "Auguries of Innocence."
[3] Reference to the prophesied thousand-year

period in which Satan will be subdued and Jesus will rule on earth (Revelation 20:2). At the time of this essay, the American preacher William Miller had incited public hysteria with his prediction that the second coming of Jesus would occur in 1843.

shall blow them none knows whither.[4] The landscape, the figures, Boston, London, are facts as fugitive as any institution past, or any whiff of mist or smoke, and so is society, and so is the world. The soul looketh steadily forwards, creating a world before her, leaving worlds behind her. She has no dates, nor rites, nor persons, nor specialties, nor men. The soul knows only the soul; the web of events is the flowing robe in which she is clothed.

After its own law and not by arithmetic is the rate of its progress to be computed. The soul's advances are not made by gradation, such as can be represented by motion in a straight line; but rather by ascension of state, such as can be represented by metamorphosis,—from the egg to the worm, from the worm to the fly. The growths of genius are of a certain *total* character, that does not advance the elect individual first over John, then Adam, then Richard, and give to each the pain of discovered inferiority, but by every throe of growth, the man expands there where he works, passing, at each pulsation, classes, populations of men. With each divine impulse the mind rends the thin rinds of the visible and finite, and comes out into eternity, and inspires and expires its air. It converses with truths that have always been spoken in the world, and becomes conscious of a closer sympathy with Zeno and Arrian,[5] than with persons in the house.

This is the law of moral and of mental gain. The simple rise as by specific levity, not into a particular virtue, but into the region of all the virtues. They are in the spirit which contains them all. The soul requires purity, but purity is not it; requires justice, but justice is not that; requires beneficence, but is somewhat better: so that there is a kind of descent and accommodation felt when we leave speaking of moral nature, to urge a virtue which it enjoins. To the well-born child, all the virtues are natural, and not painfully acquired. Speak to his heart, and the man becomes suddenly virtuous.

Within the same sentiment is the germ of intellectual growth, which obeys the same law. Those who are capable of humility, of justice, of love, of aspiration, stand already on a platform that commands the sciences and arts, speech and poetry, action and grace. For whoso dwells in this moral beatitude already anticipates those special powers which men prize so highly. The lover has no talent, no skill, which passes for quite nothing with his enamored maiden, however little she may possess of related faculty; and the heart which abandons itself to the Supreme Mind finds itself related to all its works and will travel a royal road to particular knowledges and powers. In ascending to this primary and aboriginal sentiment, we have come from our remote station on the circumference instantaneously to the centre of the world, where, as in the closet of God, we see causes, and anticipate the universe, which is but a slow effect.

One mode of the divine teaching is the incarnation of the spirit in a form,—in forms, like my own. I live in society; with persons who answer to thoughts in my own mind, or express a certain obedience to the great instincts to which I live. I see its presence to them. I am certified of a common nature; and these other souls, these separated selves, draw me as nothing else can. They stir in me the new emotions we call passion; of love, hatred, fear, admiration, pity; thence comes conversation, compe-

---

[4] John 3:8: "The wind bloweth where it listeth, and thou hearest the sound thereof, but canst not tell whence it cometh, and wither it goeth: so is every one that is born of the spirit."

[5] Zeno: Greek founder of Stoicism (third century B.C.); Arrian: biographer of Epictetus, a Stoic.

tition, persuasion, cities, and war. Persons are supplementary to the primary teaching of the soul. In youth we are mad for persons. Childhood and youth see all the world in them. But the larger experience of man discovers the identical nature appearing through them all. Persons themselves acquaint us with the impersonal. In all conversation between two persons, tacit reference is made as to a third party, to a common nature. That third party or common nature is not social; it is impersonal; is God. And so in groups where debate is earnest, and especially on high questions, the company become aware that the thought rises to an equal level in all bosoms, that all have a spiritual property in what was said, as well as the sayer. They all become wiser than they were. It arches over them like a temple, this unity of thought, in which every heart beats with nobler sense of power and duty, and thinks and acts with unusual solemnity. All are conscious of attaining to a higher self-possession. It shines for all. There is a certain wisdom of humanity which is common to the greatest men with the lowest, and which our ordinary education often labors to silence and obstruct. The mind is one, and the best minds who love truth for its own sake, think much less of property in truth. They accept it thankfully everywhere, and do not label or stamp it with any man's name, for it is theirs long beforehand, and from eternity. The learned and the studious of thought have no monopoly of wisdom. Their violence of direction in some degree disqualifies them to think truly. We owe many valuable observations to people who are not very acute or profound, and who say the thing without effort, which we want and have long been hunting in vain. The action of the soul is oftener in that which is felt and left unsaid, than in that which is said in any conversation. It broods over every society, and they unconsciously seek for it in each other. We know better than we do. We do not yet possess ourselves, and we know at the same time that we are much more. I feel the same truth how often in my trivial conversation with my neighbors, that somewhat higher in each of us overlooks this by-play, and Jove nods to Jove from behind each of us.

Men descend to meet. In their habitual and mean service to the world, for which they forsake their native nobleness, they resemble those Arabian Sheikhs, who dwell in mean houses and affect an external poverty, to escape the rapacity of the Pacha, and reserve all their display of wealth for their interior and guarded retirements.

As it is present in all persons, so it is in every period of life. It is adult already in the infant man. In my dealing with my child, my Latin and Greek, my accomplishments and my money, stead me nothing; but as much soul as I have avails. If I am wilful, he sets his will against mine, one for one, and leaves me, if I please, the degradation of beating him by my superiority of strength. But if I renounce my will, and act for the soul, setting that up as umpire between us two, out of his young eyes looks the same soul; he reveres and loves with me.

The soul is the perceiver and revealer of truth. We know truth when we see it, let skeptic and scoffer say what they choose. Foolish people ask you, when you have spoken what they do not wish to hear, "How do you know it is truth, and not an error of your own?" We know truth when we see it, from opinion, as we know when we are awake that we are awake. It was a grand sentence of Emanuel Swedenborg,[6] which would alone indicate the greatness of that man's perception,—"It is no proof of a man's understanding to be able to confirm whatever he pleases; but to be able to discern that what is true is true, and that what is false is false, this is the mark and

[6] Swedish statesman and theologian (1688–1772).

character of intelligence." In the book I read, the good thought returns to me, as every truth will, the image of the whole soul. To the bad thought which I find in it, the same soul becomes a discerning, separating sword and lops it away. We are wiser than we know. If we will not interfere with our thought, but will act entirely, or see how the thing stands in God, we know the particular thing, and every thing, and every man. For, the Maker of all things and all persons, stands behind us, and casts his dread omniscience through us over things.

But beyond this recognition of its own in particular passages of the individual's experience, it also reveals truth. And here we should seek to reinforce ourselves by its very presence, and to speak with a worthier, loftier strain of that advent. For the soul's communication of truth is the highest event in nature, since it then does not give somewhat from itself, but it gives itself, or passes into and becomes that man whom it enlightens; or in proportion to that truth he receives, it takes him to itself.

We distinguish the announcements of the soul, its manifestations of its own nature, by the term *Revelation*. These are always attended by the emotion of the sublime. For this communication is an influx of the Divine mind into our mind. It is an ebb of the individual rivulet before the flowing surges of the sea of life. Every distinct apprehension of this central commandment agitates men with awe and delight. A thrill passes through all men at the reception of new truth, or at the performance of a great action, which comes out of the heart of nature. In these communications, the power to see, is not separated from the will to do, but the insight proceeds from obedience, and the obedience proceeds from a joyful perception. Every moment when the individual feels himself invaded by it, is memorable. By the necessity of our constitution, a certain enthusiasm attends the individual's consciousness of that divine presence. The character and duration of this enthusiasm varies with the state of the individual, from an extasy and trance and prophetic inspiration,—which is its rarer appearance, —to the faintest glow of virtuous emotion, in which form it warms, like our household fires, all the families and associations of men, and makes society possible. A certain tendency to insanity has always attended the opening of the religious sense in men, as if they had been "blasted with excess of light."[7] The trances of Socrates, the "union" of Plotinus, the vision of Porphyry, the conversion of Paul, the aurora of Behmen, the convulsions of George Fox and his Quakers, the illumination of Swedenborg, are of this kind.[8] What was in the case of these remarkable persons a ravishment, has, in innumerable instances in common life, been exhibited in less striking manner. Everywhere the history of religion betrays a tendency to enthusiasm. The rapture of the Moravian and Quietist; the opening of the internal sense of the Word, in the language of the New Jerusalem Church; the *revival* of the Calvinistic churches; the *experiences* of the Methodists,[9] are varying forms of that shudder of awe and delight with which the individual soul always mingles with the universal soul.

[7] From *The Progress of Poesy*, III, ii, 7, by English poet Thomas Gray (1716–1771).
[8] Plotinus and Porphyry: Neoplatonic Greek philosophers of the early Christian era; Paul: the apostle; Behmen: Jakob Behmen, German theosophist (1575–1624); George Fox: seventeenth-century English founder of Quakerism; Swedenborg: Emanuel Swedenborg, Swedish mystic and statesman (1688–1772).
[9] Moravians: Czechoslovakian exiles and affiliates of a Protestant sect in Saxony in the eighteenth century; Quietists: condemned as heretics by the Roman Catholic church in the seventeenth century for belief in salvation through the quiescence of the soul; New Jerusalem Church: followers of Swedenborg; Calvinistic churches included the Presbyterian and Congregational churches; Methodists: an offshoot of the Church of England.

The nature of these revelations is the same; they are perceptions of the absolute law. They are solutions of the soul's own questions. They do not answer the questions which the understanding asks. The soul answers never by words, but by the thing itself that is inquired after.

Revelation is the disclosure of the soul. The popular notion of a revelation, is, that it is a telling of fortunes. In past oracles of the soul, the understanding seeks to find answers to sensual questions, and undertakes to tell from God how long men shall exist, what their hands shall do, and who shall be their company, adding names, and dates, and places. But we must pick no locks. We must check this low curiosity. An answer in words is delusive; it is really no answer to the questions you ask. Do not require a description of the countries towards which you sail. The description does not describe them to you, and to-morrow you arrive there, and know them by inhabiting them. Men ask concerning the immortality of the soul, the employments of heaven, the state of the sinner, and so forth. They even dream that Jesus has left replies to precisely these interrogatories. Never a moment did that sublime spirit speak in their *patois.* [10] To truth, justice, love, the attributes of the soul, the idea of immutableness is essentially associated. Jesus, living in these moral sentiments, heedless of sensual fortunes, heeding only the manifestations of these, never made the separation of the idea of duration from the essence of these attributes, nor uttered a syllable concerning the duration of the soul. It was left to his disciples to sever duration from the moral elements and to teach the immortality of the soul as a doctrine, and maintain it by evidences. The moment the doctrine of the immortality is separately taught, man is already fallen. In the flowing of love, in the adoration of humility, there is no question of continuance. No inspired man ever asks this question, or condescends to these evidences. For the soul is true to itself, and the man in whom it is shed abroad, cannot wander from the present, which is infinite, to a future, which would be finite.

These questions which we lust to ask about the future, are a confession of sin. God has no answer for them. No answer in words can reply to a question of things. It is not in an arbitrary "decree of God," but in the nature of man that a veil shuts down on the facts of to-morrow: for the soul will not have us read any other cipher than that of cause and effect. By this veil, which curtains events, it instructs the children of men to live in to-day. The only mode of obtaining an answer to these questions of the senses, is, to forego all low curiosity, and, accepting the tide of being which floats us into the secret of nature, work and live, work and live, and all unawares, the advancing soul has built and forged for itself a new condition, and the question and the answer are one.

By the same fire, vital, consecrating, celestial, which burns until it shall dissolve all things into the waves and surges of an ocean of light, we see and know each other, and what spirit each is of. Who can tell the grounds of his knowledge of the character of the several individuals in his circle of friends? No man. Yet their acts and words do not disappoint him. In that man, though he knew no ill of him, he put no trust. In that other, though they had seldom met, authentic signs had yet passed, to signify that he might be trusted as one who had an interest in his own character. We know each other very well,—which of us has been just to himself, and whether that which we teach or behold, is only an aspiration, or is our honest effort also.

---

[10] Dialect or vernacular.

We are all discerners of spirits. That diagnosis lies aloft in our life or unconscious power. The intercourse of society,—its trade, its religion, its friendships, its quarrels, —is one wide, judicial investigation of character. In full court, or in small committee, or confronted face to face, accuser and accused, men offer themselves to be judged. Against their will they exhibit those decisive trifles by which character is read. But who judges? and what? Not our understanding. We do not read them by learning or craft. No; the wisdom of the wise man consists herein, that he does not judge them; he lets them judge themselves, and merely reads and records their own verdict.

By virtue of this inevitable nature, private will is overpowered, and, maugre our efforts, or our imperfections, your genius will speak from you, and mine from me. That which we are, we shall teach, not voluntarily, but involuntarily. Thoughts come into our minds by avenues which we never left open, and thoughts go out of our minds through avenues which we never voluntarily opened. Character teaches over our head. The infallible index of true progress is found in the tone the man takes. Neither his age, nor his breeding, nor company, nor books, nor actions, nor talents, nor all together, can hinder him from being deferential to a higher spirit than his own. If he have not found his home in God, his manners, his forms of speech, the turn of his sentences, the build, shall I say, of all his opinions will involuntarily confess it, let him brave it out how he will. If he have found his centre, the Deity will shine through him, through all the disguises of ignorance, of ungenial temperament, of unfavorable circumstance. The tone of seeking, is one, and the tone of having is another.

The great distinction between teachers sacred or literary,—between poets like Herbert, and poets like Pope,[11]—between philosophers like Spinoza, Kant, and Coleridge, and philosophers like Locke, Paley, Mackintosh, and Stewart,[12]—between men of the world, who are reckoned accomplished talkers, and here and there a fervent mystic, prophesying, half-insane under the infinitude of his thought,—is, that one class speak *from within,* or from experience, as parties and possessors of the fact; and the other class, *from without,* as spectators merely, or perhaps as acquainted with the fact, on the evidence of third persons. It is of no use to preach to me from without. I can do that too easily myself. Jesus speaks always from within, and in a degree that transcends all others. In that, is the miracle. I believe beforehand that it ought so to be. All men stand continually in the expectation of the appearance of such a teacher. But if a man do not speak from within the veil, where the word is one with that it tells of, let him lowly confess it.

The same Omniscience flows into the intellect, and makes what we call genius. Much of the wisdom of the world is not wisdom, and the most illuminated class of men are no doubt superior to literary fame, and are not writers. Among the multitude of scholars and authors, we feel no hallowing presence; we are sensible of a knack

---

[11] Herbert: George Herbert (1593–1633), English religious poet; Pope: Alexander Pope (1688–1744), English neoclassical poet.
[12] *Spinoza: Baruch (Benedict) Spinoza* (1632–1677), Dutch philosopher and theologian; Kant: Immanuel Kant (1724–1804), German philosopher; Coleridge: Samuel Taylor Coleridge (1772–1834), English philosopher-poet; Locke: John Locke (1632–1704), English writer and philosopher; Paley: William Paley (1743–1805), English writer; Mackintosh: Sir James Mackintosh (1765–1832), Scottish philosopher and utilitarian; Stewart: Dugald Stewart (1753–1828), member of the Scottish "common sense" school of philosophy.

and skill rather than of inspiration; they have a light, and know not whence it comes, and call it their own; their talent is some exaggerated faculty, some overgrown member, so that their strength is a disease. In these instances, the intellectual gifts do not make the impression of virtue, but almost of vice; and we feel that a man's talents stand in the way of his advancement in truth. But genius is religious. It is a larger imbibing of the common heart. It is not anomalous, but more like, and not less like other men. There is in all great poets, a wisdom of humanity, which is superior to any talents they exercise. The author, the wit, the partisan, the fine gentleman, does not take place of the man. Humanity shines in Homer, in Chaucer, in Spenser, in Shakspeare, in Milton. They are content with truth. They use the positive degree. They seem frigid and phlegmatic to those who have been spiced with the frantic passion and violent coloring of inferior, but popular writers. For, they are poets by the free course which they allow to the informing soul, which through their eyes beholds again, and blesses the things which it hath made. The soul is superior to its knowledge; wiser than any of its works. The great poet makes us feel our own wealth, and then we think less of his compositions. His best communication to our mind, is, to teach us to despise all he has done. Shakspeare carries us to such a lofty strain of intelligent activity, as to suggest a wealth which beggars his own; and we then feel that the splendid works which he has created, and which in other hours, we extol as a sort of self-existent poetry, take no stronger hold of real nature than the shadow of a passing traveller on the rock. The inspiration which uttered itself in Hamlet and Lear, could utter things as good from day to day, forever. Why then should I make account of Hamlet and Lear, as if we had not the soul from which they fell as syllables from the tongue?

This energy does not descend into individual life, on any other condition than entire possession. It comes to the lowly and simple; it comes to whomsoever will put off what is foreign and proud; it comes as insight; it comes as serenity and grandeur. When we see those whom it inhabits, we are apprized of new degrees of greatness. From that inspiration the man comes back with a changed tone. He does not talk with men, with an eye to their opinion. He tries them. It requires of us to be plain and true. The vain traveller attempts to embellish his life by quoting my Lord, and the Prince, and the Countess, who thus said or did to *him*. The ambitious vulgar, show you their spoons, and brooches, and rings, and preserve their cards and compliments. The more cultivated, in their account of their own experience, cull out the pleasing poetic circumstance,—the visit to Rome, the man of genius they saw, the brilliant friend they know; still further on, perhaps, the gorgeous landscape, the mountain lights, the mountain thoughts, they enjoyed yesterday,—and so seek to throw a romantic color over their life. But the soul that ascends to worship the great God, is plain and true; has no rose-color, no fine friends, no chivalry, no adventures; does not want admiration, dwells in the hour that now is, in the earnest experience of the common day,—by reason of the present moment and the mere trifle having become porous to thought, and bibulous of the sea of light.

Converse with a mind that is grandly simple, and literature looks like word-catching. The simplest utterances are worthiest to be written, yet are they so cheap, and so things of course, that in the infinite riches of the soul, it is like gathering a few pebbles off the ground, or bottling a little air in a phial, when the whole earth, and the whole atmosphere are ours. Nothing can pass there, or make you one of the circle, but the casting aside your trappings, and dealing man to man in naked truth, plain confession and omniscient affirmation.

Souls, such as these, treat you as gods would; walk as gods in the earth, accepting without any admiration, your wit, your bounty, your virtue even,—say rather your act of duty, for your virtue they own as their proper blood, royal as themselves, and over-royal, and the father of the gods. But what rebuke that plain fraternal bearing casts on the mutual flattery with which authors solace each other, and wound themselves! These flatter not. I do not wonder that these men go to see Cromwell, and Christina, and Charles II., and James I., and the Grand Turk. For they are in their own elevation, the fellows of kings, and must feel the servile tone of conversation in the world. They must always be a godsend to princes, for they confront them, a king to a king without ducking or concession, and give a high nature the refreshment and satisfaction of resistance, of plain humanity, of even companionship, and of new ideas. They leave them wiser and superior men. Souls like these make us feel that sincerity is more excellent than flattery. Deal so plainly with man and woman, as to constrain the utmost sincerity, and destroy all hope of trifling with you. It is the highest compliment you can pay. Their "highest praising," said Milton, "is not flattery, and their plainest advice is a kind of praising."[13]

Ineffable is the union of man and God in every act of the soul. The simplest person, who in his integrity worships God, becomes God; yet forever and ever the influx of this better and universal self is new and unsearchable. It inspires awe and astonishment. How dear, how soothing to man, arises the idea of God, peopling the lonely place, effacing the scars of our mistakes and disappointments! When we have broken our god of tradition, and ceased from our god of rhetoric, then may God fire the heart with his presence. It is the doubling of the heart itself, nay, the infinite enlargement of the heart with a power of growth to a new infinity on every side. It inspires in man an infallible trust. He has not the conviction, but the sight that the best is the true, and may in that thought easily dismiss all particular uncertainties and fears, and adjourn to the sure revelation of time, the solution of his private riddles. He is sure that his welfare is dear to the heart of being. In the presence of law to his mind, he is overflowed with a reliance so universal, that it sweeps away all cherished hopes and the most stable projects of mortal condition in its flood. He believes that he cannot escape from his good. The things that are really for thee, gravitate to thee. You are running to seek your friend. Let your feet run, but your mind need not. If you do not find him, will you not acquiesce that it is best you should not find him? for there is a power, which, as it is in you, is in him also, and could therefore very well bring you together, if it were for the best. You are preparing with eagerness to go and render a service to which your talent and your taste invite you, the love of men, and the hope of fame. Has it not occurred to you, that you have no right to go, unless you are equally willing to be prevented from going? O believe, as thou livest, that every sound that is spoken over the round world, which thou oughtest to hear, will vibrate on thine ear. Every proverb, every book, every byword that belongs to thee for aid or comfort, shall surely come home through open or winding passages. Every friend whom not thy fantastic will, but the great and tender heart in thee craveth, shall lock thee in his embrace. And this, because the heart in thee is the heart of all; not a valve,

---

[13] Adapted from John Milton's *Areopagitica* (1644).

not a wall, not an intersection is there anywhere in nature, but one blood rolls uninterruptedly, an endless circulation through all men, as the water of the globe is all one sea, and, truly seen, its tide is one.

Let man then learn the revelation of all nature, and all thought to his heart; this, namely; that the Highest dwells with him; that the sources of nature are in his own mind, if the sentiment of duty is there. But if he would know what the great God speaketh, he must "go into his closet and shut the door," as Jesus said.[14] God will not make himself manifest to cowards. He must greatly listen to himself, withdrawing himself from all the accents of other men's devotion. Even their prayers are hurtful to him, until he have made his own. Our religion vulgarly stands on numbers of believers. Whenever the appeal is made,—no matter how indirectly,—to numbers, proclamation is then and there made, that religion is not. He that finds God a sweet, enveloping thought to him, never counts his company. When I sit in that presence, who shall dare to come in? When I rest in perfect humility, when I burn with pure love,—what can Calvin or Swedenborg say?

It makes no difference whether the appeal is to numbers or to one. The faith that stands on authority is not faith. The reliance on authority measures the decline of religion, the withdrawal of the soul. The position men have given to Jesus, now for many centuries of history, is a position of authority. It characterizes themselves. It cannot alter the eternal facts. Great is the soul, and plain. It is no flatterer, it is no follower; it never appeals from itself. It believes in itself. Before the immense possibilities of man, all mere experience, all past biography, however spotless and sainted, shrinks away. Before that heaven which our presentiments foreshow us, we cannot easily praise any form of life we have seen or read of. We not only affirm that we have few great men, but absolutely speaking, that we have none; that we have no history, no record of any character or mode of living, that entirely contents us. The saints and demigods whom history worships, we are constrained to accept with a grain of allowance. Though in our lonely hours, we draw a new strength out of their memory, yet pressed on our attention, as they are by the thoughtless and customary, they fatigue and invade. The soul gives itself alone, original, and pure, to the Lonely, Original and Pure, who, on that condition, gladly inhabits, leads, and speaks through it. Then is it glad, young, and nimble. It is not wise, but it sees through all things. It is not called religious, but it is innocent. It calls the light its own, and feels that the grass grows, and the stone falls by a law inferior to, and dependent on its nature. Behold, it saith, I am born into the great, the universal mind. I the imperfect, adore my own Perfect. I am somehow receptive of the great soul, and thereby I do overlook the sun and the stars, and feel them to be the fair accidents and effects which change and pass. More and more the surges of everlasting nature enter into me, and I become public and human in my regards and actions. So come I to live in thoughts, and act with energies which are immortal. Thus revering the soul, and learning, as the ancient said, that "its beauty is immense," man will come to see that the world is the perennial miracle which the soul worketh, and be less astonished at particular wonders; he will learn that there is no profane history; that all history is sacred; that the universe is

---

[14] Matthew 6:6: "But thou, when thou prayest, enter into thy closet, and when thou hast shut the door, pray to thy father which is in secret; and thy father which seeth in secret shall reward thee openly."

represented in an atom, in a moment of time. He will weave no longer a spotted life of shreds and patches, but he will live with a divine unity. He will cease from what is base and frivolous in his life, and be content with all places and with any service he can render. He will calmly front the morrow in the negligency of that trust which carries God with it, and so hath already the whole future in the bottom of the heart.

1841

Circles

Nature centres into balls,
And her proud ephemerals,
Fast to surface and outside,
Scan the profile of the sphere;
Knew they what that signified,
A new genesis were here.[1]

The eye is the first circle; the horizon which it forms is the second; and throughout nature this primary figure is repeated without end. It is the highest emblem in the cipher of the world. St. Augustine described the nature of God as a circle whose centre was everywhere and its circumference nowhere.[2] We are all our lifetime reading the copious sense of this first of forms. One moral we have already deduced in considering the circular or compensatory character of every human action. Another analogy we shall now trace, that every action admits of being outdone. Our life is an apprenticeship to the truth that around every circle another can be drawn; that there is no end in nature, but every end is a beginning; that there is always another dawn risen on mid-noon, and under every deep a lower deep opens.

This fact, as far as it symbolizes the moral fact of the Unattainable, the flying Perfect, around which the hands of man can never meet, at once the inspirer and the condemner of every success, may conveniently serve us to connect many illustrations of human power in every department.

There are no fixtures in nature. The universe is fluid and volatile. Permanence is but a word of degrees. Our globe seen by God is a transparent law, not a mass of facts. The law dissolves the fact and holds it fluid. Our culture is the predominance of an idea which draws after it this train of cities and institutions. Let us rise into another idea; they will disappear. The Greek sculpture is all melted away, as if it had been statues of ice; here and there a solitary figure or fragment remaining, as we see flecks and scraps of snow left in cold dells and mountain clefts in June and July. For

---

[1] Emerson's own verses.

[2] Although St. Augustine wrote about the nature of God and circles, this metaphor is taken from *An Essay Towards the Theory of the Ideal or Intelligible World* (1701–1704) by John Norris, which refers to a God "whose center is everywhere and whose circumference is nowhere." Emerson copied this passage into his journal immediately before some "admirable passages" that Norris had "quoted from St. Augustine" about the City of God (*Journals and Miscellaneous Notebooks*, Vol. V, p. 57), and Emerson may well have confused the juxtaposition.

the genius that created it creates now somewhat else. The Greek letters last a little longer, but are already passing under the same sentence and tumbling into the inevitable pit which the creation of new thought opens for all that is old. The new continents are built out of the ruins of an old planet; the new races fed out of the decomposition of the foregoing. New arts destroy the old. See the investment of capital in aqueducts, made useless by hydraulics; fortifications, by gunpowder; roads and canals, by railways; sails, by steam; steam by electricity.

You admire this tower of granite, weathering the hurts of so many ages. Yet a little waving hand built this huge wall, and that which builds is better than that which is built. The hand that built can topple it down much faster. Better than the hand and nimbler was the invisible thought which wrought through it; and thus ever, behind the coarse effect, is a fine cause, which, being narrowly seen, is itself the effect of a finer cause. Everything looks permanent until its secret is known. A rich estate appears to women a firm and lasting fact; to a merchant, one easily created out of any materials, and easily lost. An orchard, good tillage, good grounds, seem a fixture, like a gold mine, or a river, to a citizen; but to a large farmer, not much more fixed than the state of the crop. Nature looks provokingly stable and secular, but it has a cause like all the rest; and when once I comprehend that, will these fields stretch so immovably wide, these leaves hang so individually considerable? Permanence is a word of degrees. Every thing is medial. Moons are no more bounds to spiritual power than bat-balls.

The key to every man is his thought. Sturdy and defying though he look, he has a helm which he obeys, which is the idea after which all his facts are classified. He can only be reformed by showing him a new idea which commands his own. The life of man is a self-evolving circle, which, from a ring imperceptibly small, rushes on all sides outwards to new and larger circles, and that without end. The extent to which this generation of circles, wheel without wheel, will go, depends on the force or truth of the individual soul. For it is the inert effort of each thought, having formed itself into a circular wave of circumstance—as for instance an empire, rules of an art, a local usage, a religious rite—to heap itself on that ridge and to solidify and hem in the life. But if the soul is quick and strong it bursts over that boundary on all sides and expands another orbit on the great deep, which also runs up into a high wave, with attempt again to stop and to bind. But the heart refuses to be imprisoned; in its first and narrowest pulses it already tends outward with a vast force and to immense and innumerable expansions.

Every ultimate fact is only the first of a new series. Every general law only a particular fact of some more general law presently to disclose itself. There is no outside, no inclosing wall, no circumference to us. The man finishes his story—how good! how final! how it puts a new face on all things! He fills the sky. Lo! on the other side rises also a man and draws a circle around the circle we had just pronounced the outline of the sphere. Then already is our first speaker not man, but only a first speaker. His only redress is forthwith to draw a circle outside of his antagonist. And so men do by themselves. The result of to-day, which haunts the mind and cannot be escaped, will presently be abridged into a word, and the principle that seemed to explain nature will itself be included as one example of a bolder generalization. In the thought of to-morrow there is a power to upheave all thy creed, all the creeds, all the literatures of the nations, and marshal thee to a heaven which no epic dream has yet depicted. Every man is not so much a workman in the world as he is a suggestion of that he should be. Men walk as prophecies of the next age.

Step by step we scale this mysterious ladder; the steps are actions, the new prospect is power. Every several result is threatened and judged by that which follows. Every one seems to be contradicted by the new; it is only limited by the new. The new statement is always hated by the old, and, to those dwelling in the old, comes like an abyss of scepticism. But the eye soon gets wonted to it, for the eye and it are effects of one cause; then its innocency and benefit appear, and presently, all its energy spent, it pales and dwindles before the revelation of the new hour.

Fear not the new generalization. Does the fact look crass and material, threatening to degrade thy theory of spirit? Resist it not; it goes to refine and raise thy theory of matter just as much.

There are no fixtures to men, if we appeal to consciousness. Every man supposes himself not to be fully understood; and if there is any truth in him, if he rests at last on the divine soul, I see not how it can be otherwise. The last chamber, the last closet, he must feel was never opened; there is always a residuum unknown, unanalyzable. That is, every man believes that he has a greater possibility.

Our moods do not believe in each other. To-day I am full of thoughts and can write what I please. I see no reason why I should not have the same thought, the same power of expression, to-morrow. What I write, whilst I write it, seems the most natural thing in the world; but yesterday I saw a dreary vacuity in this direction in which now I see so much; and a month hence, I doubt not, I shall wonder who he was that wrote so many continuous pages. Alas for this infirm faith, this will not strenuous, this vast ebb of a vast flow! I am God in nature; I am a weed by the wall.

The continual effort to raise himself above himself, to work a pitch above his last height, betrays itself in a man's relations. We thirst for approbation, yet cannot forgive the approver. The sweet of nature is love; yet if I have a friend I am tormented by my imperfections. The love of me accuses the other party. If he were high enough to slight me, then could I love him, and rise by my affection to new heights. A man's growth is seen in the successive choirs of his friends. For every friend whom he loses for truth, he gains a better. I thought as I walked in the woods and mused on my friends, why should I play with them this game of idolatry? I know and see too well, when not voluntarily blind, the speedy limits of persons called high and worthy. Rich, noble and great they are by the liberality of our speech, but truth is sad. O blessed Spirit, whom I forsake for these, they are not thou! Every personal consideration that we allow costs us heavenly state. We sell the thrones of angels for a short and turbulent pleasure.

How often must we learn this lesson? Men cease to interest us when we find their limitations. The only sin is limitation. As soon as you once come up with a man's limitations, it is all over with him. Has he talents? has he enterprise? has he knowledge? It boots not. Infinitely alluring and attractive was he to you yesterday, a great hope, a sea to swim in; now, you have found his shores, found it a pond, and you care not if you never see it again.

Each new step we take in thought reconciles twenty seemingly discordant facts, as expressions of one law. Aristotle and Plato are reckoned the respective heads of two schools. A wise man will see that Aristotle platonizes. By going one step farther back in thought, discordant opinions are reconciled by being seen to be two extremes of one principle, and we can never go so far back as to preclude a still higher vision.

Beware when the great God lets loose a thinker on this planet. Then all things are at risk. It is as when a conflagration has broken out in a great city, and no man knows what is safe, or where it will end. There is not a piece of science but its flank may be turned to-morrow; there is not any literary reputation, not the so-called eternal names of fame, that may not be revised and condemned. The very hopes of man, the thoughts of his heart, the religion of nations, the manners and morals of mankind are all at the mercy of a new generalization. Generalization is always a new influx of the divinity into the mind. Hence the thrill that attends it.

Valor consists in the power of self-recovery, so that a man cannot have his flank turned, cannot be out-generalled, but put him where you will, he stands. This can only be by his preferring truth to his past apprehension of truth, and his alert acceptance of it from whatever quarter; the intrepid conviction that his laws, his relations to society, his Christianity, his world, may at any time be superseded and decease.

There are degrees in idealism. We learn first to play with it academically, as the magnet was once a toy. Then we see in the heyday of youth and poetry that it may be true, that it is true in gleams and fragments. Then its countenance waxes stern and grand, and we see that it must be true. It now shows itself ethical and practical. We learn that God IS; that he is in me; and that all things are shadows of him. The idealism of Berkeley[3] is only a crude statement of the idealism of Jesus, and that again is a crude statement of the fact that all nature is the rapid efflux of goodness executing and organizing itself. Much more obviously is history and the state of the world at any one time directly dependent on the intellectual classification then existing in the minds of men. The things which are dear to men at this hour are so on account of the ideas which have emerged on their mental horizon, and which cause the present order of things, as a tree bears its apples. A new degree of culture would instantly revolutionize the entire system of human pursuits.

Conversation is a game of circles. In conversation we pluck up the *termini*[4] which bound the common of silence on every side. The parties are not to be judged by the spirit they partake and even express under this Pentecost.[5] Tomorrow they will have receded from this high-water mark. To-morrow you shall find them stooping under the old pack-saddles. Yet let us enjoy the cloven flame whilst it glows on our walls. When each new speaker strikes a new light, emancipates us from the oppression of the last speaker to oppress us with the greatness and exclusiveness of his own thought, then yields us to another redeemer, we seem to recover our rights, to become men. O, what truths profound and executable only in ages and orbs, are supposed in the announcement of every truth! In common hours, society sits cold and statuesque. We all stand waiting, empty—knowing, possibly, that we can be full, surrounded by mighty symbols which are not symbols to us, but prose and trivial toys. Then cometh the god and converts the statues into fiery men, and by a flash of his eye burns up the veil which shrouded all things, and the meaning of the very furniture, of cup and saucer, of chair and clock and tester, is manifest. The facts which loomed so large in the fogs of yesterday—property, climate, breeding, personal beauty and the like, have strangely changed their proportions. All that we reckoned settled shakes and rattles;

---

[3] George Berkeley (1685–1753), English philosophical idealist.
[4] Latin: "ends."

[5] Christian celebration marking the descent of the Holy Ghost upon the apostles.

and literatures, cities, climates, religions, leave their foundations and dance before our eyes. And yet here again see the swift circumscription! Good as is discourse, silence is better, and shames it. The length of the discourse indicates the distance of thought betwixt the speaker and the hearer. If they were at a perfect understanding in any part, no words would be necessary thereon. If at one in all parts, no words would be suffered.

Literature is a point outside of our hodiernal[6] circle through which a new one may be described. The use of literature is to afford us a platform whence we may command a view of our present life, a purchase by which we may move it. We fill ourselves with ancient learning, install ourselves the best we can in Greek, in Punic,[7] in Roman houses, only that we may wiselier see French, English and American houses and modes of living. In like manner we see literature best from the midst of wild nature, or from the din of affairs, or from a high religion. The field cannot be well seen from within the field. The astronomer must have his diameter of the earth's orbit as a base to find the parallax of any star.

Therefore we value the poet. All the argument and all the wisdom is not in the encyclopædia, or the treatise on metaphysics, or the Body of Divinity, but in the sonnet or the play. In my daily work I incline to repeat my old steps, and do not believe in remedial force, in the power of change and reform. But some Petrarch or Ariosto,[8] filled with the new wine of his imagination, writes me an ode or a brisk romance, full of daring thought and action. He smites and arouses me with his shrill tones, breaks up my whole chain of habits, and I open my eye on my own possibilities. He claps wings to the sides of all the solid old lumber of the world, and I am capable once more of choosing a straight path in theory and practice.

We have the same need to command a view of the religion of the world. We can never see Christianity from the catechism—from the pastures, from a boat in the pond, from amidst the songs of wood-birds we possibly may. Cleansed by the elemental light and wind, steeped in the sea of beautiful forms which the field offers us, we may chance to cast a right glance back upon biography. Christianity is rightly dear to the best of mankind; yet was there never a young philosopher whose breeding had fallen into the Christian church by whom that brave text of Paul's was not specially prized: "Then shall also the Son be subject unto Him who put all things under him, that God may be all in all."[9] Let the claims and virtues of persons be never so great and welcome, the instinct of man presses eagerly onward to the impersonal and illimitable, and gladly arms itself against the dogmatism of bigots with this generous word out of the book itself.

The natural world may be conceived of as a system of concentric circles, and we now and then detect in nature slight dislocations which apprise us that this surface on which we now stand is not fixed, but sliding. These manifold tenacious qualities, this chemistry and vegetation, these metals and animals, which seem to stand there for their own sake, are means and methods only—are words of God, and as fugitive as other words. Has the naturalist or chemist learned his craft, who has explored the gravity of atoms and the elective affinities, who has not yet discerned the deeper law whereof this is only a partial or approximate statement, namely that like draws to

---

[6] Of or belonging to the present day.
[7] Ancient civilization of Carthage.
[8] Petrarch; Ariosto: Francesco Petrarch

(1304–1374) and Lodovico Ariosto (1474–1533), Italian poets.
[9] 1 Corinthians 15:28.

like, and that the goods which belong to you gravitate to you and need not be pursued with pains and cost? Yet is that statement approximate also, and not final. Omnipresence is a higher fact. Not through subtle subterranean channels need friend and fact be drawn to their counterpart, but, rightly considered, these things proceed from the eternal generation of the soul. Cause and effect are two sides of one fact.

The same law of eternal procession ranges all that we call the virtues, and extinguishes each in the light of a better. The great man will not be prudent in the popular sense; all his prudence will be so much deduction from his grandeur. But it behooves each to see, when he sacrifices prudence, to what god he devotes it; if to ease and pleasure, he had better be prudent still; if to a great trust, he can well spare his mule and panniers who has a winged chariot instead. Geoffrey draws on his boots to go through the woods, that his feet may be safer from the bite of snakes; Aaron never thinks of such a peril. In many years neither is harmed by such an accident. Yet it seems to me that with every precaution you take against such an evil you put yourself into the power of the evil. I suppose that the highest prudence is the lowest prudence. Is this too sudden a rushing from the centre to the verge of our orbit? Think how many times we shall fall back into pitiful calculations before we take up our rest in the great sentiment, or make the verge of to-day the new centre. Besides, your bravest sentiment is familiar to the humblest men. The poor and the low have their way of expressing the last facts of philosophy as well as you. "Blessed be nothing" and "The worse things are, the better they are" are proverbs which express the transcendentalism of common life.

One man's justice is another's injustice; one man's beauty another's ugliness; one man's wisdom another's folly; as one beholds the same objects from a higher point. One man thinks justice consists in paying debts, and has no measure in his abhorrence of another who is very remiss in this duty and makes the creditor wait tediously. But that second man has his own way of looking at things; asks himself Which debt must I pay first, the debt to the rich, or the debt to the poor? the debt of money, or the debt of thought to mankind, of genius to nature? For you, O broker, there is no other principle but arithmetic. For me, commerce is of trivial import; love, faith, truth of character, the aspiration of man, these are sacred; nor can I detach one duty, like you, from all other duties, and concentrate my forces mechanically on the payment of moneys. Let me live onward; you shall find that, though slower, the progress of my character will liquidate all these debts without injustice to higher claims. If a man should dedicate himself to the payment of notes, would not this be injustice? Does he owe no debt but money? And are all claims on him to be postponed to a landlord's or a banker's?

There is no virtue which is final; all are initial. The virtues of society are vices of the saint. The terror of reform is the discovery that we must cast away our virtues, or what we have always esteemed such, into the same pit that has consumed our grosser vices:—

"Forgive his crimes, forgive his virtues too,
   Those smaller faults, half converts to the right."[10]

[10] From *The Complaint; or Night Thoughts*, IX, 2316–2317, by Edward Young.

It is the highest power of divine moments that they abolish our contritions also. I accuse myself of sloth and unprofitableness day by day; but when these waves of God flow into me I no longer reckon lost time. I no longer poorly compute my possible achievement by what remains to me of the month or the year; for these moments confer a sort of omnipresence and omnipotence which asks nothing of duration, but sees that the energy of the mind is commensurate with the work to be done, without time.

And thus, O circular philosopher, I hear some reader exclaim, you have arrived at a fine Pyrrhonism,[11] at an equivalence and indifferency of all actions, and would fain teach us that *if we are true,* forsooth, our crimes may be lively stones out of which we shall construct the temple of the true God!

I am not careful to justify myself. I own I am gladdened by seeing the predominance of the saccharine principle throughout vegetable nature, and not less by beholding in morals that unrestrained inundation of the principle of good into every chink and hole that selfishness has left open, yea into selfishness and sin itself; so that no evil is pure, nor hell itself without its extreme satisfactions. But lest I should mislead any when I have my own head and obey my whims, let me remind the reader that I am only an experimenter. Do not set the least value on what I do, or the least discredit on what I do not, as if I pretended to settle any thing as true or false. I unsettle all things. No facts are to me sacred; none are profane; I simply experiment, an endless seeker with no Past at my back.

Yet this incessant movement and progression which all things partake could never become sensible to us but by contrast to some principle of fixture or stability in the soul. Whilst the eternal generation of circles proceeds, the eternal generator abides. That central life is somewhat superior to creation, superior to knowledge and thought, and contains all its circles. Forever it labors to create a life and thought as large and excellent as itself, but in vain, for that which is made instructs how to make a better.

Thus there is no sleep, no pause, no preservation, but all things renew, germinate and spring. Why should we import rags and relics into the new hour? Nature abhors the old, and old age seems the only disease; all others run into this one. We call it by many names—fever, intemperance, insanity, stupidity and crime; they are all forms of old age; they are rest, conservatism, appropriation, inertia; not newness, not the way onward. We grizzle[12] every day. I see no need of it. Whilst we converse with what is above us, we do not grow old, but grow young. Infancy, youth, receptive, aspiring, with religious eye looking upward, counts itself nothing and abandons itself to the instruction flowing from all sides. But the man and woman of seventy assume to know all, they have outlived their hope, they renounce aspiration, accept the actual for the necessary and talk down to the young. Let them then become organs of the Holy Ghost; let them be lovers; let them behold truth; and their eyes are uplifted, their wrinkles smoothed, they are perfumed again with hope and power. This old age ought not to creep on a human mind. In nature every moment is new; the past is always swallowed and forgotten; the coming only is sacred. Nothing is secure but life,

---

[11] Pyrrho of Elis (360–270 B.C.) taught a theory of radical skepticism which held that truth was unattainable and that all external circumstances must be disregarded.

[12] Become gray-haired; grow old.

transition, the energizing spirit. No love can be bound by oath or covenant to secure it against a higher love. No truth so sublime but it may be trivial to-morrow in the light of new thoughts. People wish to be settled; only as far as they are unsettled is there any hope for them.

Life is a series of surprises. We do not guess to-day the mood, the pleasure, the power of to-morrow, when we are building up our being. Of lower states, of acts of routine and sense, we can tell somewhat; but the masterpieces of God, the total growths and universal movements of the soul, he hideth; they are incalculable. I can know that truth is divine and helpful; but how it shall help me I can have no guess, for *so to be* is the sole inlet of *so to know*. The new position of the advancing man has all the powers of the old, yet has them all new. It carries in its bosom all the energies of the past, yet is itself an exhalation of the morning. I cast away in this new moment all my once hoarded knowledge, as vacant and vain. Now for the first time seem I to know any thing rightly. The simplest words—we do not know what they mean except when we love and aspire.

The difference between talents and character is adroitness to keep the old and trodden round, and power and courage to make a new road to new and better goals. Character makes an overpowering present; a cheerful, determined hour, which fortifies all the company by making them see that much is possible and excellent that was not thought of. Character dulls the impression of particular events. When we see the conqueror we do not think much of any one battle or success. We see that we had exaggerated the difficulty. It was easy to him. The great man is not convulsible or tormentable; events pass over him without much impression. People say sometimes, 'See what I have overcome; see how cheerful I am; see how completely I have triumphed over these black events.' Not if they still remind me of the black event. True conquest is the causing the calamity to fade and disappear as an early cloud of insignificant result in a history so large and advancing.

The one thing which we seek with insatiable desire is to forget ourselves, to be surprised out of our propriety, to lose our sempiternal memory and to do something without knowing how or why; in short to draw a new circle. Nothing great was ever achieved without enthusiasm. The way of life is wonderful; it is by abandonment. The great moments of history are the facilities of performance through the strength of ideas, as the works of genius and religion. "A man," said Oliver Cromwell, "never rises so high as when he knows not whither he is going."[13] Dreams and drunkenness, the use of opium and alcohol are the semblance and counterfeit of this oracular genius, and hence their dangerous attraction for men. For the like reason they ask the aid of wild passions, as in gaming and war, to ape in some manner these flames and generosities of the heart.

1841

---

[13] According to Clarendon's *History of the Rebellion and Civil Wars in England*, Oliver Cromwell (1599–1628), English general and statesman, made this remark to Bellieure, the French minister.

The Poet

A moody child and wildly wise
Pursued the game with joyful eyes,
Which chose, like meteors, their way,
And rived the dark with private ray:
They overleapt the horizon's edge,
Searched with Apollo's privilege;
Through man, and woman, and sea, and star,
Saw the dance of nature forward far;
Through worlds, and races, and terms, and times,
Saw musical order, and pairing rhymes.[1]

Olympian bards who sung
Divine ideas below,
Which always find us young,
And always keep us so.[2]

Those who are esteemed umpires of taste, are often persons who have acquired some knowledge of admired pictures or sculptures, and have an inclination for whatever is elegant; but if you inquire whether they are beautiful souls, and whether their own acts are like fair pictures, you learn that they are selfish and sensual. Their cultivation is local, as if you should rub a log of dry wood in one spot to produce fire, all the rest remaining cold. Their knowledge of the fine arts is some study of rules and particulars, or some limited judgment of color or form, which is exercised for amusement or for show. It is a proof of the shallowness of the doctrine of beauty, as it lies in the minds of our amateurs, that men seem to have lost the perception of the instant dependence of form upon soul. There is no doctrine of forms in our philosophy. We were put into our bodies, as fire is put into a pan, to be carried about; but there is no accurate adjustment between the spirit and the organ, much less is the latter the germination of the former. So in regard to other forms, the intellectual men do not believe in any essential dependence of the material world on thought and volition. Theologians think it a pretty air-castle to talk of the spiritual meaning of a ship or a cloud, of a city or a contract, but they prefer to come again to the solid ground of historical evidence; and even the poets are contented with a civil and conformed manner of living, and to write poems from the fancy, at a safe distance from their own experience. But the highest minds of the world have never ceased to explore the double meaning, or, shall I say, the quadruple, or the centuple, or much more manifold meaning, of every sensuous fact: Orpheus, Empedocles, Heraclitus, Plato, Plutarch, Dante, Swedenborg,[3] and the masters of sculpture, picture, and poetry. For we are not pans and barrows, nor even porters of the fire and torch-bearers, but children of the fire, made of it, and only the same divinity transmuted, and at two or three removes, when we know least about it. And this hidden truth, that the fountains when all this river of Time, and its creatures, floweth, are intrinsically ideal

---

[1] From Emerson's unfinished poem "The Poet," published posthumously.
[2] From Emerson's "Ode to Beauty."
[3] Emerson refers here, respectively, to a mythical Greek poet, Greek philosophers of the fifth, sixth, and fourth centuries B.C., a Greek biographer of the first century, an Italian poet of the Middle Ages, and a Swedish mystical scientist of the eighteenth century.

and beautiful, draws us to the consideration of the nature and functions of the Poet, or the man of Beauty, to the means and materials he uses, and to the general aspect of the art in the present time.

The breadth of the problem is great, for the poet is representative. He stands among partial men for the complete man, and apprises us not of his wealth, but of the commonwealth. The young man reveres men of genius, because, to speak truly, they are more himself than he is. They receive of the soul as he also receives, but they more. Nature enhances her beauty, to the eye of loving men, from their belief that the poet is beholding her shows at the same time. He is isolated among his contemporaries, by truth and by his art, but with this consolation in his pursuits, that they will draw all men sooner or later. For all men live by truth, and stand in need of expression. In love, in art, in avarice, in politics, in labor, in games, we study to utter our painful secret. The man is only half himself, the other half is his expression.

Notwithstanding this necessity to be published, adequate expression is rare. I know not how it is that we need an interpreter; but the great majority of men seem to be minors, who have not yet come into possession of their own, or mutes, who cannot report the conversation they have had with nature. There is no man who does not anticipate a supersensual utility in the sun, and stars, earth, and water. These stand and wait to render him a peculiar service. But there is some obstruction, or some excess of phlegm in our constitution, which does not suffer them to yield the due effect. Too feeble fall the impressions of nature on us to make us artists. Every touch should thrill. Every man should be so much an artist, that he could report in conversation what had befallen him. Yet, in our experience, the rays or appulses[4] have sufficient force to arrive at the senses, but not enough to reach the quick, and compel the reproduction of themselves in speech. The poet is the person in whom these powers are in balance, the man without impediment, who sees and handles that which others dream of, traverses the whole scale of experience, and its representatives of man, in virtue of being the largest power to receive and to impart.

For the Universe has three children, born at one time, which reappear, under different names, in every system of thought, whether they be called cause, operation, and effect; or, more poetically, Jove, Pluto, Neptune; or, theologically, the Father, the Spirit, and the Son; but which we will call here, the Knower, the Doer, and the Sayer. These stand respectively for the love of truth, for the love of good, and for the love of beauty. These three are equal. Each is that which he is essentially, so that he cannot be surmounted or analyzed, and each of these three has the power of the others latent in him, and his own patent.

The poet is the sayer, the namer, and represents beauty. He is a sovereign, and stands on the centre. For the world is not painted, or adorned, but is from the beginning beautiful; and God has not made some beautiful things, but Beauty is the creator of the universe. Therefore the poet is not any permissive potentate, but is emperor in his own right. Criticism is infested with a cant of materialism, which assumes that manual skill and activity is the first merit of all men, and disparages such as say and do not, overlooking the fact, that some men, namely, poets, are natural sayers, sent into the world to the end of expression, and confounds them with those whose province is action, but who quit it to imitate the sayers. But Homer's words are as costly and admirable to Homer, as Agamemnon's victories are to Agamemnon. The

[4] Potent energies.

poet does not wait for the hero or the sage, but, as they act and think primarily, so he writes primarily what will and must be spoken, reckoning the others, though primaries also, yet, in respect to him, secondaries and servants; as sitters or models in the studio of a painter, or as assistants who bring building materials to an architect.

For poetry was all written before time was, and whenever we are so finely organized that we can penetrate into that region where the air is music, we hear those primal warblings, and attempt to write them down, but we lose ever and anon a word, or a verse, and substitute something of our own, and thus miswrite the poem. The men of more delicate ear write down these cadences more faithfully, and these transcripts, though imperfect, become the songs of the nations. For nature is as truly beautiful as it is good, or as it is reasonable, and must as much appear, as it must be done, or be known. Words and deeds are quite indifferent modes of the divine energy. Words are also actions, and actions are a kind of words.

The sign and credentials of the poet are, that he announces that which no man foretold. He is the true and only doctor;[5] he knows and tells; he is the only teller of news, for he was present and privy to the appearance which he describes. He is a beholder of ideas, and an utterer of the necessary and causal. For we do not speak now of men of poetical talents, or of industry and skill in metre, but of the true poet. I took part in a conversation the other day, concerning a recent writer of lyrics, a man of subtle mind, whose head appeared to be a music-box of delicate tunes and rhythms, and whose skill, and command of language, we could not sufficiently praise. But when the question arose, whether he was not only a lyrist, but a poet, we were obliged to confess that he is plainly a contemporary, not an eternal man. He does not stand out of our low limitations, like a Chimborazo[6] under the line, running up from the torrid base through all the climates of the globe, with belts of the herbage of every latitude on its high and mottled sides; but this genius is the landscape-garden of a modern house, adorned with fountains and statues, with well-bred men and women standing and sitting in the walks and terraces. We hear, through all the varied music, the ground-tone of conventional life. Our poets are men of talents who sing, and not the children of music. The argument is secondary, the finish of the verses is primary.

For it is not metres, but a metre-making argument, that makes a poem,—a thought so passionate and alive, that, like the spirit of a plant or an animal, it has an architecture of its own, and adorns nature with a new thing. The thought and the form are equal in the order of time, but in the order of genesis the thought is prior to the form. The poet has a new thought: he has a whole new experience to unfold; he will tell us how it was with him, and all men will be the richer in his fortune. For, the experience of each new age requires a new confession, and the world seems always waiting for its poet. I remember, when I was young, how much I was moved one morning by tidings that genius had appeared in a youth who sat near me at table. He had left his work, and gone rambling none knew whither, and had written hundreds of lines, but could not tell whether that which was in him was therein told: he could tell nothing but that all was changed,—man, beast, heaven, earth, and sea. How gladly we listened! how credulous! Society seemed to be compromised. We sat in the aurora of a sunrise which was to put out all the stars. Boston seemed to be at twice the distance it had

---

[5] In the traditional Latin sense, teacher.
[6] Mountain in Ecuador located below the equator.

the night before, or was much farther than that. Rome,—what was Rome? Plutarch and Shakspeare were in the yellow leaf,[7] and Homer no more should be heard of. It is much to know that poetry has been written this very day, under this very roof, by your side. What! that wonderful spirit has not expired! these stony moments are still sparkling and animated! I had fancied that the oracles were all silent, and nature had spent her fires, and behold! all night, from every pore, these fine auroras have been streaming. Every one has some interest in the advent of the poet, and no one knows how much it may concern him. We know that the secret of the world is profound, but who or what shall be our interpreter, we know not. A mountain ramble, a new style of face, a new person, may put the key into our hands. Of course, the value of genius to us is in the veracity of its report. Talent may frolic and juggle; genius realizes and adds. Mankind, in good earnest, have availed so far in understanding themselves and their work, that the foremost watchman on the peak announces his news. It is the truest word ever spoken, and the phrase will be the fittest, most musical, and the unerring voice of the world for that time.

All that we call sacred history attests that the birth of a poet is the principal event in chronology. Man, never so often deceived, still watches for the arrival of a brother who can hold him steady to a truth, until he has made it his own. With what joy I begin to read a poem, which I confide in as an inspiration! And now my chains are to be broken; I shall mount above these clouds and opaque airs in which I live,— opaque, though they seem transparent,—and from the heaven of truth I shall see and comprehend my relations. That will reconcile me to life, and renovate nature, to see trifles animated by a tendency, and to know what I am doing. Life will no more be a noise; now I shall see men and women, and know the signs by which they may be discerned from fools and satans. This day shall be better than my birth-day: then I became an animal: now I am invited into the science of the real. Such is the hope, but the fruition is postponed. Oftener it falls, that this winged man, who will carry me into the heaven, whirls me into the clouds, then leaps and frisks about with me from cloud to cloud, still affirming that he is bound heavenward; and I, being myself a novice, am slow in perceiving that he does not know the way into the heavens, and is merely bent that I should admire his skill to rise, like a fowl or a flying fish, a little way from the ground or the water; but the all-piercing, all-feeding, and ocular air of heaven, that man shall never inhabit. I tumble down again soon into my old nooks, and lead the life of exaggerations as before, and have lost my faith in the possibility of any guide who can lead me thither where I would be.

But leaving these victims of vanity, let us, with new hope, observe how nature, by worthier impulses, has ensured the poet's fidelity to his office of announcement and affirming, namely, by the beauty of things, which becomes a new, and higher beauty, when expressed. Nature offers all her creatures to him as a picture-language. Being used as a type, a second wonderful value appears in the object, far better than its old value, as the carpenter's stretched cord, if you hold your ear close enough, is musical in the breeze. "Things more excellent than every image," says Jamblichus,[8] "are expressed through images." Things admit of being used as symbols, because nature is a symbol, in the whole, and in every part. Every line we can draw in the sand,

---

[7] *Macbeth*, Act V, Sc. iii, ll. 22–23: "I have lived long enough. My way of life is fallen into the sere, the yellow leaf."

[8] Philosopher of the fourth century who advocated Neoplatonism, a religious mysticism drawing on elements of Greek philosophy.

has expression; and there is no body without its spirit or genius. All form is an effect of character; all condition, of the quality of the life; all harmony, of health; (and, for this reason, a perception of beauty should be sympathetic, or proper only to the good.) The beautiful rests on the foundations of the necessary. The soul makes the body, as the wise Spenser teaches:—

> "So every spirit, as it is most pure,
> And hath in it the more of heavenly light,
> So it the fairer body doth procure
> To habit in, and it more fairly dight,
> With cheerful grace and amiable sight.
> For, of the soul, the body form doth take,
> For soul is form, and doth the body make."[9]

Here we find ourselves, suddenly, not in a critical speculation, but in a holy place, and should go very warily and reverently. We stand before the secret of the world, there where Being passes into Appearance, and Unity into Variety.

The Universe is the externalisation of the soul. Wherever the life is, that bursts into appearance around it. Our science is sensual, and therefore superficial. The earth, and the heavenly bodies, physics, and chemistry, we sensually treat, as if they were self-existent; but these are the retinue of that Being we have. "The mighty heaven," said Proclus,[10] "exhibits, in its transfigurations, clear images of the splendor of intellectual perceptions; being moved in conjunction with the unapparent periods of intellectual natures." Therefore, science always goes abreast with the just elevation of the man, keeping step with religion and metaphysics; or, the state of science is an index of our self-knowledge. Since everything in nature answers to a moral power, if any phenomenon remains brute and dark, it is that the corresponding faculty in the observer is not yet active.

No wonder, then, if these waters be so deep, that we hover over them with a religious regard. The beauty of the fable proves the importance of the sense; to the poet, and to all others; or, if you please, every man is so far a poet as to be susceptible of these enchantments of nature: for all men have the thoughts whereof the universe is the celebration. I find that the fascination resides in the symbol. Who loves nature? Who does not? Is it only poets, and men of leisure and cultivation, who live with her? No; but also hunters, farmers, grooms, and butchers, though they express their affection in their choice of life, and not in their choice of words. The writer wonders what the coachman or the hunter values in riding, in horses, and dogs. It is not superficial qualities. When you talk with him, he holds these at as slight a rate as you. His worship is sympathetic; he has no definitions, but he is commanded in nature, by the living power which he feels to be there present. No imitation, or playing of these things, would content him; he loves the earnest of the northwind, of rain, of stone, and wood, and iron. A beauty not explicable, is dearer than a beauty which we can see to the end of. It is nature the symbol, nature certifying the supernatural, body overflowed by life, which he worships, with coarse, but sincere rites.

The inwardness, and mystery, of this attachment, drives men of every class to the

---

[9] From "An Hymn in Honor of Beauty" (1596)   [10] Greek Neoplatonic philosopher (411–485).
by English poet Edmund Spenser (1552?–1599).

use of emblems. The schools of poets, and philosophers, are not more intoxicated with their symbols, than the populace with theirs. In our political parties, compute the power of badges and emblems. See the great ball which they roll from Baltimore to Bunker hill![11] In the political processions, Lowell goes in a loom, and Lynn in a shoe, and Salem in a ship.[12] Witness the cider-barrel, the log-cabin, the hickory-stick, the palmetto, and all the cognizances of party. See the power of national emblems. Some stars, lilies, leopards, a crescent, a lion, an eagle, or other figure, which came into credit God knows how, on an old rag of bunting, blowing in the wind, on a fort, at the ends of the earth, shall make the blood tingle under the rudest, or the most conventional exterior. The people fancy they hate poetry, and they are all poets and mystics!

Beyond this universality of the symbolic language, we are apprised of the divineness of this superior use of things, whereby the world is a temple, whose walls are covered with emblems, pictures, and commandments of the Deity, in this, that there is no fact in nature which does not carry the whole sense of nature; and the distinctions which we make in events, and in affairs, of low and high, honest and base, disappear when nature is used as a symbol. Thought makes every thing fit for use. The vocabulary of an omniscient man would embrace words and images excluded from polite conversation. What would be base, or even obscene, to the obscene, becomes illustrious, spoken in a new connexion of thought. The piety of the Hebrew prophets purges their grossness. The circumcision is an example of the power of poetry to raise the low and offensive. Small and mean things serve as well as great symbols. The meaner the type by which a law is expressed, the more pungent it is, and the more lasting in the memories of men: just as we choose the smallest box, or case, in which any needful utensil can be carried. Bare lists of words are found suggestive, to an imaginative and excited mind; as it is related of Lord Chatham,[13] that he was accustomed to read in Bailey's Dictionary, when he was preparing to speak in Parliament. The poorest experience is rich enough for all the purposes of expressing thought. Why covet a knowledge of new facts? Day and night, house and garden, a few books, a few actions, serve us as well as would all trades and all spectacles. We are far from having exhausted the significance of the few symbols we use. We can come to use them yet with a terrible simplicity. It does not need that a poem should be long. Every word was once a poem. Every new relation is a new word. Also, we use defects and deformities to a sacred purpose, so expressing our sense that the evils of the world are such only to the evil eye. In the old mythology, mythologists observe, defects are ascribed to divine natures, as lameness to Vulcan, blindness to Cupid, and the like, to signify exuberances.

For, as it is dislocation and detachment from the life of God, that makes things ugly, the poet, who re-attaches things to nature and the Whole,—re-attaching even artificial things, and violations of nature, to nature, by a deeper insight,—disposes very easily of the most disagreeable facts. Readers of poetry see the factory-village, and the railway, and fancy that the poetry of the landscape is broken up by these; for these works of art are not yet consecrated in their reading; but the poet sees them fall within the great Order not less than the bee-hive, or the spider's geometrical web. Nature

---

[11] Allusion to a political gimmick used by the 1840 campaign supporters of W. H. Harrison: "Keep the ball a-rolling."
[12] The towns of Lowell, Lynn, and Salem,

Massachusetts, are represented by their major products.
[13] William Pitt (1708–1778), earl of Chatham, was a powerfully eloquent English statesman.

adopts them very fast into her vital circles, and the gliding train of cars she loves like her own. Besides, in a centred mind, it signifies nothing how many mechanical inventions you exhibit. Though you add millions, and never so surprising, the fact of mechanics has not gained a grain's weight. The spiritual fact remains unaltered, by many or by few particulars; as no mountain is of any appreciable height to break the curve of the sphere. A shrewd country-boy goes to the city for the first time, and the complacent citizen is not satisfied with his little wonder. It is not that he does not see all the fine houses, and know that he never saw such before, but he disposes of them as easily as the poet finds place for the railway. The chief value of the new fact, is to enhance the great and constant fact of Life, which can dwarf any and every circumstance, and to which the belt of wampum, and the commerce of America, are alike.

The world being thus put under the mind for verb and noun, the poet is he who can articulate it. For, though life is great, and fascinates, and absorbs,—and though all men are intelligent of the symbols through which it is named,—yet they cannot originally use them. We are symbols, and inhabit symbols; workman, work, and tools, words and things, birth and death, all are emblems; but we sympathize with the symbols, and, being infatuated with the economical uses of things, we do not know that they are thoughts. The poet, by an ulterior intellectual perception, gives them a power which makes their old use forgotten, and puts eyes, and a tongue, into every dumb and inanimate object. He perceives the independence of the thought on the symbol, the stability of the thought, the accidency and fugacity of the symbol. As the eyes of Lyncæus[14] were said to see through the earth, so the poet turns the world to glass, and shows us all things in their right series and procession. For, through that better perception, he stands one step nearer to things, and sees the flowing or metamorphosis; perceives that thought is multiform; that within the form of every creature is a force impelling it to ascend into a higher form; and, following with his eyes the life, uses the forms which express that life, and so his speech flows with the flowing of nature. All the facts of the animal economy, sex, nutriment, gestation, birth, growth, are symbols of the passage of the world into the soul of man, to suffer there a change, and reappear, a new and higher fact. He uses forms according to the life, and not according to the form. This is true science. The poet alone knows astronomy, chemistry, vegetation, and animation, for he does not stop at these facts, but employs them as signs. He knows why the plain, or meadow of space, was strown with these flowers we call suns, and moons, and stars; why the great deep is adorned with animals, with men, and gods; for, in every word he speaks he rides on them as the horses of thought.

By virtue of this science the poet is the Namer, or Language-maker, naming things sometimes after their appearance, sometimes after their essence, and giving to every one its own name and not another's, thereby rejoicing the intellect, which delights in detachment or boundary. The poets made all the words, and therefore language is the archives of history, and, if we must say it, a sort of tomb of the muses. For, though the origin of most of our words is forgotten, each word was at first a stroke of genius, and obtained currency, because for the moment it symbolized the world to the first speaker and to the hearer. The etymologist finds the deadest word to have

---

[14] In Greek myth, the sailor with the keenest eye.

been once a brilliant picture. Language is fossil poetry. As the limestone of the continent consists of infinite masses of the shells of animalcules, so language is made up of images, or tropes, which now, in their secondary use, have long ceased to remind us of their poetic origin. But the poet names the thing because he sees it, or comes one step nearer to it than any other. This expression, or naming, is not art, but a second nature, grown out of the first, as a leaf out of a tree. What we call nature, is a certain self-regulated motion, or change; and nature does all things by her own hands, and does not leave another to baptise her, but baptises herself; and this through the metamorphosis again. I remember that a certain poet[15] described it to me thus:

Genius is the activity which repairs the decays of things, whether wholly or partly of a material and finite kind. Nature, through all her kingdoms, insures herself. Nobody cares for planting the poor fungus: so she shakes down from the gills of one agaric countless spores, any one of which, being preserved, transmits new billions of spores to-morrow or next day. The new agaric of this hour has a chance which the old one had not. This atom of seed is thrown into a new place, not subject to the accidents which destroyed its parent two rods off. She makes a man; and having brought him to ripe age, she will no longer run the risk of losing this wonder at a blow, but she detaches from him a new self, that the kind may be safe from accidents to which the individual is exposed. So when the soul of the poet has come to ripeness of thought, she detaches and sends away from it its poems or songs,—a fearless, sleepless, deathless progeny, which is not exposed to the accidents of the weary kingdom of time: a fearless, vivacious offspring, clad with wings (such was the virtue of the soul out of which they came), which carry them fast and far, and infix them irrecoverably into the hearts of men. These wings are the beauty of the poet's soul. The songs, thus flying immortal from their mortal parent, are pursued by clamorous flights of censures, which swarm in far greater numbers, and threaten to devour them; but these last are not winged. At the end of a very short leap they fall plump down, and rot, having received from the souls out of which they came no beautiful wings. But the melodies of the poet ascend, and leap, and pierce into the deeps of infinite time.

So far the bard taught me, using his freer speech. But nature has a higher end, in the production of new individuals, than security, namely, *ascension,* or, the passage of the soul into higher forms. I knew, in my younger days, the sculptor who made the statue of the youth which stands in the public garden. He was, as I remember, unable to tell directly, what made him happy, or unhappy, but by wonderful indirections he could tell. He rose one day, according to his habit, before the dawn, and saw the morning break, grand as the eternity out of which it came, and, for many days after, he strove to express this tranquillity, and, lo! his chisel had fashioned out of marble the form of a beautiful youth, Phosphorus,[16] whose aspect is such, that, it is said, all persons who look on it become silent. The poet also resigns himself to his mood, and that thought which agitated him is expressed, but

---

[15] Presumably this is a droll reference to Emerson himself.

[16] "Light-bearing," a mythical Greek god associated with the morning star.

alter idem, [17] in a manner totally new. The expression is organic, or, the new type which things themselves take when liberated. As, in the sun, objects paint their images on the retina of the eye, so they, sharing the aspiration of the whole universe, tend to paint a far more delicate copy of their essence in his mind. Like the metamorphosis of things into higher organic forms, is their change into melodies. Over everything stands its dæmon, or soul, and, as the form of the thing is reflected by the eye, so the soul of the thing is reflected by a melody. The sea, the mountain-ridge, Niagara, and every flower-bed, pre-exist, or super-exist, in pre-cantations, [18] which sail like odors in the air, and when any man goes by with an ear sufficiently fine, he overhears them, and endeavors to write down the notes, without diluting or depraving them. And herein is the legitimation of criticism, in the mind's faith, that the poems are a corrupt version of some text in nature, with which they ought to be made to tally. A rhyme in one of our sonnets should not be less pleasing than the iterated nodes of a sea-shell, or the resembling difference of a group of flowers. The pairing of the birds is an idyl, not tedious as our idyls are; a tempest is a rough ode, without falsehood or rant: a summer, with its harvest sown, reaped, and stored, is an epic song, subordinating how many admirably executed parts. Why should not the symmetry and truth that modulate these, glide into our spirits, and we participate the invention of nature?

This insight, which expresses itself by what is called Imagination, is a very high sort of seeing, which does not come by study, but by the intellect being where and what it sees, by sharing the path, or circuit of things through forms, and so making them translucid to others. The path of things is silent. Will they suffer a speaker to go with them? A spy they will not suffer; a lover, a poet, is the transcendency of their own nature,—him they will suffer. The condition of true naming, on the poet's part, is his resigning himself to the divine aura which breathes through forms, and accompanying that.

It is a secret which every intellectual man quickly learns, that, beyond the energy of his possessed and conscious intellect, he is capable of a new energy (as of an intellect doubled on itself), by abandonment to the nature of things; that, beside his privacy of power as an individual man, there is a great public power, on which he can draw, by unlocking, at all risks, his human doors, and suffering the ethereal tides to roll and circulate through him: then he is caught up into the life of the Universe, his speech is thunder, his thought is law, and his words are universally intelligible as the plants and animals. The poet knows that he speaks adequately, then, only when he speaks somewhat wildly, or, "with the flower of the mind;" not with the intellect, used as an organ, but with the intellect released from all service, and suffered to take its direction from its celestial life; or, as the ancients were wont to express themselves, not with intellect alone, but with the intellect inebriated by nectar. As the traveller who has lost his way, throws his reins on his horse's neck, and trusts to the instinct of the animal to find his road, so must we do with the divine animal who carries us through this world. For if in any manner we can stimulate this instinct, new passages are opened for us into nature, the mind flows into and through things hardest and highest, and the metamorphosis is possible.

This is the reason why bards love wine, mead, narcotics, coffee, tea, opium, the fumes of sandal-wood and tobacco, or whatever other species of animal exhilaration. All men avail themselves of such means as they can, to add this extraordinary power

---

[17] Latin: "the same yet not identical."   [18] Incantations that are foretelling.

to their normal powers; and to this end they prize conversation, music, pictures, sculpture, dancing, theatres, travelling, war, mobs, fires, gaming, politics, or love, or science, or animal intoxication, which are several coarser or finer *quasi*-mechanical substitutes for the true nectar, which is the ravishment of the intellect by coming nearer to the fact. These are auxiliaries to the centrifugal tendency of a man, to his passage out into free space, and they help him to escape the custody of that body in which he is pent up, and of that jail-yard of individual relations in which he is enclosed. Hence a great number of such as were professionally expressors of Beauty, as painters, poets, musicians, and actors, have been more than others wont to lead a life of pleasure and indulgence; all but the few who received the true nectar; and, as it was a spurious mode of attaining freedom, as it was an emancipation not into the heavens, but into the freedom of baser places, they were punished for that advantage they won, by a dissipation and deterioration. But never can any advantage be taken of nature by a trick. The spirit of the world, the great calm presence of the creator, comes not forth to the sorceries of opium or of wine. The sublime vision comes to the pure and simple soul in a clean and chaste body. That is not an inspiration which we owe to narcotics, but some counterfeit excitement and fury. Milton says, that the lyric poet may drink wine and live generously, but the epic poet, he who shall sing of the gods, and their descent unto men, must drink water out of a wooden bowl.[19] For poetry is not 'Devil's wine,' but God's wine. It is with this as it is with toys. We fill the hands and nurseries of our children with all manner of dolls, drums, and horses, withdrawing their eyes from the plain face and sufficing objects of nature, the sun, and moon, the animals, the water, and stones, which should be their toys. So the poet's habit of living should be set on a key so low and plain, that the common influences should delight him. His cheerfulness should be the gift of the sunlight; the air should suffice for his inspiration, and he should be tipsy with water. That spirit which suffices quiet hearts, which seems to come forth to such from every dry knoll of sere grass, from every pine-stump, and half-imbedded stone, on which the dull March sun shines, comes forth to the poor and hungry, and such as are of simple taste. If thou fill thy brain with Boston and New York, with fashion and covetousness, and wilt stimulate thy jaded senses with wine and French coffee, thou shalt find no radiance of wisdom in the lonely waste of the pinewoods.

If the imagination intoxicates the poet, it is not inactive in other men. The metamorphosis excites in the beholder an emotion of joy. The use of symbols has a certain power of emancipation and exhilaration for all men. We seem to be touched by a wand, which makes us dance and run about happily, like children. We are like persons who come out of a cave or cellar into the open air. This is the effect on us of tropes, fables, oracles, and all poetic forms. Poets are thus liberating gods. Men have really got a new sense, and found within their world, another world, or nest of worlds; for, the metamorphosis once seen, we divine that it does not stop. I will not now consider how much this makes the charm of algebra and the mathematics, which also have their tropes, but it is felt in every definition; as, when Aristotle defines *space* to be an immovable vessel, in which things are contained;—or, when Plato defines a *line* to be a flowing point; or, *figure* to be bound of solid; and many the like. What a joyful sense of freedom we have, when Vitruvius[20] announces the old opinion of

---

[19] Restated from "Sixth Latin Elegy," a poem by John Milton.   [20] Roman architect and writer.

artists, that no architect can build any house well, who does not know something of anatomy. When Socrates, in Charmides,[21] tells us that the soul is cured of its maladies by certain incantations, and that these incantations are beautiful reasons, from which temperance is generated in souls; when Plato calls the world an animal; and Timæus[22] affirms that the plants also are animals; or affirms a man to be a heavenly tree, growing with his root, which is his head, upward; and, as George Chapman, following him, writes,—

> "So in our tree of man, whose nervie root
>   Springs in his top;"[23]

when Orpheus speaks of hoariness as "that white flower which marks extreme old age;" when Proclus calls the universe the statue of the intellect; when Chaucer, in his praise of "Gentilesse,"[24] compares good blood in mean condition to fire, which, though carried to the darkest house betwixt this and the mount of Caucasus, will yet hold its natural office, and burn as bright as if twenty thousand men did it behold, when John saw, in the apocalypse, the ruin of the world through evil, and the stars fall from heaven, as the figtree casteth her untimely fruit;[25] when Æsop reports the whole catalogue of common daily relations through the masquerade of birds and beasts;—we take the cheerful hint of the immortality of our essence, and its versatile habit and escapes, as when the gypsies say, "it is in vain to hang them, they cannot die."

The poets are thus liberating gods. The ancient British bards had for the title of their order, "Those who are free throughout the world." They are free, and they make free. An imaginative book renders us much more service at first, by stimulating us through its tropes, than afterward, when we arrive at the precise sense of the author. I think nothing is of any value in books, excepting the transcendental and extraordinary. If a man is inflamed and carried away by his thought, to that degree that he forgets the authors and the public, and heeds only this one dream, which holds him like an insanity, let me read his paper, and you may have all the arguments and histories and criticism. All the value which attaches to Pythagoras, Paracelsus, Cornelius Agrippa, Cardan, Kepler, Swedenborg, Schelling, Oken,[26] or any other who introduces questionable facts into his cosmogony, as angels, devils, magic, astrology, palmistry, mesmerism, and so on, is the certificate we have of departure from routine, and that here is a new witness. That also is the best success in conversation, the magic of liberty, which puts the world, like a ball, in our hands. How cheap even the liberty then seems; how mean to study, when an emotion communicates to the intellect the power to sap and upheave nature: how great the perspective! nations, times, systems, enter and disappear, like threads in tapestry of large figure and many colors; dream

---

[21] Dialogue of Plato.
[22] Another dialogue of Plato.
[23] Excerpt from George Chapman's (1559?–?1634) dedication to his translation of Homer.
[24] In "The Wife of Bath's Tale" by Geoffrey Chaucer.
[25] See Revelation 6:13.
[26] All of the following were dedicated to theoretical speculation. Pythagoras: Greek mathematician and mystic philosopher (sixth century B.C.); Paracelsus: Swiss alchemist

Philippus Paracelsus (1493–1541); Cornelius Agrippa: German physician (1486?–1535); Cardan: Italian mathematician Jerome Cardan (1501–1576); Kepler: German astronomer Johannes Kepler (1571–1630); Swedenborg: Swedish philosopher and religious writer Emanuel Swedenborg (1688–1772); Schelling: German philosopher Freidrich von Schelling (1775–1854); Oken: German naturalist Lorenz Oken (1779–1851).

delivers us to dream, and, while the drunkenness lasts, we will sell our bed, our philosophy, our religion, in our opulence.

There is good reason why we should prize this liberation. The fate of the poor shepherd, who, blinded and lost in the snowstorm, perishes in a drift within a few feet of his cottage door, is an emblem of the state of man. On the brink of the waters of life and truth, we are miserably dying. The inaccessibleness of every thought but that we are in, is wonderful. What if you come near to it,—you are as remote, when you are nearest, as when you are farthest. Every thought is also a prison; every heaven is also a prison. Therefore we love the poet, the inventor, who in any form, whether in an ode, or in an action, or in looks and behavior, has yielded us a new thought. He unlocks our chains, and admits us to a new scene.

This emancipation is dear to all men, and the power to impart it, as it must come from greater depth and scope of thought, is a measure of intellect. Therefore all books of the imagination endure, all which ascend to that truth, that the writer sees nature beneath him, and uses it as his exponent. Every verse or sentence, possessing this virtue, will take care of its own immortality. The religions of the world are the ejaculations of a few imaginative men.

But the quality of the imagination is to flow, and not to freeze. The poet did not stop at the color, or the form, but read their meaning; neither may he rest in this meaning, but he makes the same objects exponents of his new thought. Here is the difference betwixt the poet and the mystic, that the last nails a symbol to one sense, which was a true sense for a moment, but soon becomes old and false. For all symbols are fluxional; all language is vehicular and transitive, and is good, as ferries and horses are, for conveyance, not as farms and houses are, for homestead. Mysticism consists in the mistake of an accidental and individual symbol for an universal one. The morning-redness happens to be the favorite meteor to the eyes of Jacob Behmen,[27] and comes to stand to him for truth and faith; and he believes should stand for the same realities to every reader. But the first reader prefers as naturally the symbol of a mother and child, or a gardener and his bulb, or a jeweller polishing a gem. Either of these, or of a myriad more, are equally good to the person to whom they are significant. Only they must be held lightly, and be very willingly translated into the equivalent terms which others use. And the mystic must be steadily told,—All that you say is just as true without the tedious use of that symbol as with it. Let us have a little algebra, instead of this trite rhetoric,—universal signs, instead of these village symbols, —and we shall both be gainers. The history of hierarchies seems to show, that all religious error consisted in making the symbol too stark and solid, and, at last, nothing but an excess of the organ of language.

Swedenborg, of all men in the recent ages, stands eminently for the translator of nature into thought. I do not know the man in history to whom things stood so uniformly for words. Before him the metamorphosis continually plays. Everything on which his eye rests, obeys the impulses of moral nature. The figs become grapes whilst he eats them. When some of his angels affirmed a truth, the laurel twig which they held blossomed in their hands. The noise which, at a distance, appeared like gnashing and thumping, on coming nearer was found to be the voice of disputants. The men, in one of his visions, seen in heavenly light, appeared like dragons, and seemed in darkness; but, to each other, they appeared as men, and, when the light from

---

[27] German theosophist and mystic (1575–1624).

heaven shone into their cabin, they complained of the darkness, and were compelled to shut the window that they might see.

There was this perception in him, which makes the poet or seer, an object of awe and terror, namely, that the same man, or society of men, may wear one aspect to themselves and their companions, and a different aspect to higher intelligences. Certain priests, whom he describes as conversing very learnedly together, appeared to the children, who were at some distance, like dead horses: and many the like misappearances. And instantly the mind inquires, whether these fishes under the bridge, yonder oxen in the pasture, those dogs in the yard, are immutably fishes, oxen, and dogs, or only so appear to me, and perchance to themselves appear upright men; and whether I appear as a man to all eyes. The Bramins and Pythagoras propounded the same question, and if any poet has witnessed the transformation, he doubtless found it in harmony with various experiences. We have all seen changes as considerable in wheat and caterpillars. He is the poet, and shall draw us with love and terror, who sees, through the flowing vest, the firm nature, and can declare it.

I look in vain for the poet whom I describe. We do not, with sufficient plainness, or sufficient profoundness, address ourselves to life, nor dare we chaunt our own times and social circumstance. If we filled the day with bravery, we should not shrink from celebrating it. Time and nature yield us many gifts, but not yet the timely man, the new religion, the reconciler, whom all things await. Dante's praise is, that he dared to write his autobiography in colossal cipher, or into universality. We have yet had no genius in America, with tyrannous eye, which knew the value of our incomparable materials, and saw, in the barbarism and materialism of the times, another carnival of the same gods whose picture he so much admires in Homer; then in the middle age; then in Calvinism. Banks and tariffs, the newspaper and caucus, methodism and unitarianism, are flat and dull to dull people, but rest on the same foundations of wonder as the town of Troy, and the temple of Delphos, and are as swiftly passing away. Our logrolling, our stumps[28] and their politics, our fisheries, our Negroes, and Indians, our boats, and our repudiations, the wrath of rogues, and the pusillanimity of honest men, the northern trade, the southern planting, the western clearing, Oregon, and Texas, are yet unsung. Yet America is a poem in our eyes; its ample geography dazzles the imagination, and it will not wait long for metres. If I have not found that excellent combination of gifts in my countrymen which I seek, neither could I aid myself to fix the idea of the poet by reading now and then in Chalmers's[29] collection of five centuries of English poets. These are wits, more than poets, though there have been poets among them. But when we adhere to the ideal of the poet, we have our difficulties even with Milton and Homer. Milton is too literary, and Homer too literal and historical.

But I am not wise enough for a national criticism, and must use the old largeness a little longer, to discharge my errand from the muse to the poet concerning his art.

Art is the path of the creator to his work. The paths, or methods, are ideal and eternal, though few men ever see them, not the artist himself for years, or for a lifetime, unless he come into the conditions. The painter, the sculptor, the composer, the epic rhapsodist, the orator, all partake one desire, namely, to express themselves symmetrically and abundantly, not dwarfishly and fragmentarily. They found or put

[28] Political deceptions; public speaking.
[29] Scottish journalist and biographer Alexander

Chalmers (1759–1834) compiled an extensive collection of English poetry (1810).

themselves in certain conditions, as, the painter and sculptor before some impressive human figures; the orator, into the assembly of the people; and the others, in such scenes as each has found exciting to his intellect; and each presently feels the new desire. He hears a voice, he sees a beckoning. Then he is apprised, with wonder, what herds of dæmons hem him in. He can no more rest; he says, with the old painter, "By God, it is in me, and must go forth of me." He pursues a beauty, half seen, which flies before him. The poet pours out verses in every solitude. Most of the things he says are conventional, no doubt; but by and by he says something which is original and beautiful. That charms him. He would say nothing else but such things. In our way of talking, we say, "That is yours, this is mine;" but the poet knows well that it is not his; that it is as strange and beautiful to him as to you; he would fain hear the like eloquence at length. Once having tasted this immortal ichor, he cannot have enough of it, and, as an admirable creative power exists in these intellections, it is of the last importance that these things get spoken. What a little of all we know is said! What drops of all the sea of our science are baled up! and by what accident it is that these are exposed, when so many secrets sleep in nature! Hence the necessity of speech and song; hence these throbs and heart-beatings in the orator, at the door of the assembly, to the end, namely, that thought may be ejaculated as Logos, or Word.

Doubt not, O poet, but persist. Say, "It is in me, and shall out." Stand there, baulked and dumb, stuttering and stammering, hissed and hooted, stand and strive, until, at last, rage draw out of thee that *dream*-power which every night shows thee is thine own; a power transcending all limit and privacy, and by virtue of which a man is the conductor of the whole river of electricity. Nothing walks, or creeps, or grows, or exists, which must not in turn arise and walk before him as exponent of his meaning. Comes he to that power, his genius is no longer exhaustible. All the creatures, by pairs and by tribes, pour into his mind as into a Noah's ark, to come forth again to people a new world. This is like the stock of air for our respiration, or for the combustion of our fireplace, not a measure of gallons, but the entire atmosphere if wanted. And therefore the rich poets, as Homer, Chaucer, Shakspeare, and Raphael, have obviously no limits to their works, except the limits of their lifetime, and resemble a mirror carried through the street, ready to render an image of every created thing.

O poet! a new nobility is conferred in groves and pastures, and not in castles, or by the sword-blade, any longer. The conditions are hard, but equal. Thou shalt leave the world, and know the muse only. Thou shalt not know any longer the times, customs, graces, politics, or opinions of men, but shalt take all from the muse. For the time of towns is tolled from the world by funereal chimes, but in nature the universal hours are counted by succeeding tribes of animals and plants, and by growth of joy on joy. God wills also that thou abdicate a manifold and duplex life, and that thou be content that others speak for thee. Others shall be thy gentlemen, and shall represent all courtesy and worldly life for thee; others shall do the great and resounding actions also. Thou shalt lie close hid with nature, and canst not be afforded to the Capitol or the Exchange. The world is full of renunciations and apprenticeships, and this is thine: thou must pass for a fool and a churl for a long season. This is the screen and sheath in which Pan[30] has protected his well-beloved flower, and thou shalt

[30] God of the woods and fields in Greek mythology.

be known only to thine own, and they shall console thee with tenderest love. And thou shalt not be able to rehearse the names of thy friends in thy verse, for an old shame before the holy ideal. And this is the reward: that the ideal shall be real to thee, and the impressions of the actual world shall fall like summer rain, copious, but not troublesome, to thy invulnerable essence. Thou shalt have the whole land for thy park and manor, the sea for thy bath and navigation, without tax and without envy; the woods and the rivers thou shalt own; and thou shalt possess that wherein others are only tenants and boarders. Thou true land-lord! sea-lord! air-lord! Wherever snow falls, or water flows, or birds fly, wherever day and night meet in twilight, wherever the blue heaven is hung by clouds, or sown with stars, wherever are forms with transparent boundaries, wherever are outlets into celestial space, wherever is danger, and awe, and love, there is Beauty, plenteous as rain, shed for thee, and though thou shouldest walk the world over, thou shalt not be able to find a condition inopportune or ignoble.

1844

Experience*

The lords of life, the lords of life,—
I saw them pass,
In their own guise,
Like and unlike,
Portly and grim,
Use and Surprise,
Surface and Dream,
Succession swift, and spectral Wrong,
Temperament without a tongue,
And the inventor of the game
Omnipresent without name;—
Some to see, some to be guessed,
They marched from east to west:
Little man, least of all,
Among the legs of his guardians tall,
Walked about with puzzled look:—
Him by the hand dear nature took;
Dearest nature, strong and kind,
Whispered, "Darling, never mind!
Tomorrow they will wear another face,
The founder thou! these are thy race!"[1]

Where do we find ourselves? In a series[2] of which we do not know the extremes, and believe that it has none. We wake and find ourselves on a stair; there are stairs below us, which we seem to have ascended; there are stairs above us, many a one, which

---

* This essay appeared in January 1842, shortly after the death of Emerson's young son Waldo.

[1] The epigraph is Emerson's.

[2] In mathematics, a sequence of terms.

go upward and out of sight. But the Genius[3] which, according to the old belief, stands at the door by which we enter, and gives us the lethe[4] to drink, that we may tell no tales, mixed the cup too strongly, and we cannot shake off the lethargy now at noonday. Sleep lingers all our lifetime about our eyes, as night hovers all day in the boughs of the fir-tree. All things swim and glitter. Our life is not so much threatened as our perception. Ghost-like we glide through nature, and should not know our place again. Did our birth fall in some fit of indigence and frugality in nature, that she was so sparing of her fire and so liberal of her earth, that it appears to us that we lack the affirmative principle, and though we have health and reason, yet we have no superfluity of spirit for new creation? We have enough to live and bring the year about, but not an ounce to impart or to invest. Ah that our Genius were a little more of a genius! We are like millers on the lower levels of a stream, when the factories above them have exhausted the water. We too fancy that the upper people must have raised their dams.

If any of us knew what we were doing, or where we are going, then when we think we best know! We do not know today whether we are busy or idle. In times when we thought ourselves indolent, we have afterwards discovered, that much was accomplished, and much was begun in us. All our days are so unprofitable while they pass, that 'tis wonderful where or when we ever got anything of this which we call wisdom, poetry, virtue. We never got it on any dated calendar day. Some heavenly days must have been intercalated somewhere, like those that Hermes won with dice of the Moon, that Osiris[5] might be born. It is said, all martyrdoms looked mean when they were suffered. Every ship is a romantic object, except that we sail in. Embark, and the romance quits our vessel, and hangs on every other sail in the horizon. Our life looks trivial, and we shun to record it. Men seem to have learned of the horizon the art of perpetual retreating and reference. "Yonder uplands are rich pasturage, and my neighbor has fertile meadow, but my field," says the querulous farmer, "only holds the world together." I quote another man's saying; unluckily, that other withdraws himself in the same way, and quotes me. 'Tis the trick of nature thus to degrade today; a good deal of buzz, and somewhere a result slipped magically in. Every roof is agreeable to the eye, until it is lifted; then we find tragedy and moaning women, and hard-eyed husbands, and deluges of lethe, and the men ask, "What's the news?" as if the old were so bad. How many individuals can we count in society? how many actions? how many opinions? So much of our time is preparation, so much is routine, and so much retrospect, that the pith of each man's genius contracts itself to a very few hours. The history of literature—take the net result of Tiraboschi, Warton, or Schlegel,[6]—is a sum of very few ideas, and of very few original tales,—all the rest being variation of these. So in this great society wide lying around us, a critical analysis would find very few spontaneous actions. It is almost all custom and gross sense. There

---

[3] Personal guardian spirit.

[4] Water from Lethe, the mythic river of forgetfulness.

[5] In Plutarch's *Morals,* the mythological sun god Cronus declared that his wife, Rhea, could not give birth to her lover's child on any day of the year. Because Hermes won five new days for the calendar by shooting dice with the

Moon, Rhea was nevertheless able to deliver Osiris, the highest Egyptian divinity.

[6] All literary historians. Tiraboschi: Italian Girolamo Tiraboschi (1731–1794); Warton: British Thomas Warton (1728–1790); Schlegel: German philosopher Friedrich von Schlegel (1772–1829) or his brother August Wilhelm von Schlegel (1767–1845).

are even few opinions, and these seem organic in the speakers, and do not disturb the universal necessity.

What opium is instilled into all disaster! It shows formidable as we approach it, but there is at last no rough rasping friction, but the most slippery sliding surfaces. We fall soft on a thought. *Ate Dea*[7] is gentle,

> "Over men's heads walking aloft,
>   With tender feet treading so soft."[8]

People give and bemoan themselves, but it is not half so bad with them as they say. There are moods in which we court suffering, in the hope that here, at least, we shall find reality, sharp peaks and edges of truth. But it turns out to be scene-painting and counterfeit. The only thing grief has taught me, is to know how shallow it is. That, like all the rest, plays about the surface, and never introduces me into the reality, for contact with which, we would even pay the costly price of sons and lovers. Was it Boscovich[9] who found out that bodies never come in contact? Well, souls never touch their objects. An innavigable sea washes with silent waves between us and the things we aim at and converse with. Grief too will make us idealists. In the death of my son, now more than two years ago, I seem to have lost a beautiful estate,—no more. I cannot get it nearer to me. If tomorrow I should be informed of the bankruptcy of my principal debtors, the loss of my property would be a great inconvenience to me, perhaps, for many years; but it would leave me as it found me,—neither better nor worse. So is it with this calamity: it does not touch me: some thing which I fancied was a part of me, which could not be torn away without tearing me, nor enlarged without enriching me, falls off from me, and leaves no scar. It was caducous. I grieve that grief can teach me nothing, nor carry me one step into real nature. The Indian who was laid under a curse, that the wind should not blow on him, nor water flow to him, nor fire burn him,[10] is a type of us all. The dearest events are summer-rain, and we the Para coats[11] that shed every drop. Nothing is left us now but death. We look to that with a grim satisfaction, saying, there at least is reality that will not dodge us.

I take this evanescence and lubricity of all objects, which lets them slip through our fingers then when we clutch hardest, to be the most unhandsome part of our condition. Nature does not like to be observed, and likes that we should be her fools and playmates. We may have the sphere for our cricket-ball, but not a berry for our philosophy. Direct strokes she never gave us power to make; all our blows glance, all our hits are accidents. Our relations to each other are oblique and casual.

Dream delivers us to dream, and there is no end to illusion. Life is a train of moods like a string of beads, and, as we pass through them, they prove to be many-colored lenses which paint the world their own hue, and each shows only what lies in its focus. From the mountain you see the mountain. We animate what we can, and we see only

---

[7] Greek goddess of mischief and reckless folly.
[8] Homer's *Iliad,* XIX, 92–93.
[9] Ruggiero Giuseppe Boscovich (1711–1787), Italian physicist who developed a molecular theory of matter.

[10] See *The Curse of Kehama* (1810) by English poet Robert Southey (1774–1843).
[11] Then a term for rubber coats.

what we animate. Nature and books belong to the eyes that see them. It depends on the mood of the man, whether he shall see the sunset or the fine poem. There are always sunsets, and there is always genius; but only a few hours so serene that we can relish nature or criticism. The more or less depends on structure or temperament. Temperament is the iron wire on which the beads are strung. Of what use is fortune or talent to a cold and defective nature? Who cares what sensibility or discrimination a man has at some time shown, if he falls asleep in his chair? or if he laugh and giggle? or if he apologize? or is affected with egotism? or thinks of his dollar? or cannot go by food? or has gotten a child in his boyhood? Of what use is genius, if the organ is too convex or too concave, and cannot find a focal distance within the actual horizon of human life? Of what use, if the brain is too cold or too hot, and the man does not care enough for results, to stimulate him to experiment, and hold him up in it? or if the web is too finely woven, too irritable by pleasure and pain, so that life stagnates from too much reception, without due outlet? Of what use to make heroic vows of amendment, if the same old law-breaker is to keep them? What cheer can the religious sentiment yield, when that is suspected to be secretly dependent on the seasons of the year, and the state of the blood? I knew a witty physician who found theology in the biliary duct, and used to affirm that if there was disease in the liver, the man became a Calvinist, and if that organ was sound, he became a Unitarian.[12] Very mortifying is the reluctant experience that some unfriendly excess or imbecility neutralizes the promise of genius. We see young men who owe us a new world, so readily and lavishly they promise, but they never acquit the debt; they die young and dodge the account: or if they live, they lose themselves in the crowd.

Temperament also enters fully into the system of illusions, and shuts us in a prison of glass which we cannot see. There is an optical illusion about every person we meet. In truth, they are all creatures of given temperament, which will appear in a given character, whose boundaries they will never pass: but we look at them, they seem alive, and we presume there is impulse in them. In the moment it seems impulse; in the year, in the lifetime, it turns out to be a certain uniform tune which the revolving barrel of the music-box must play. Men resist the conclusion in the morning, but adopt it as the evening wears on, that temper prevails over everything of time, place, and condition, and is inconsumable in the flames of religion. Some modifications the moral sentiment avails to impose, but the individual texture holds its dominion, if not to bias the moral judgments, yet to fix the measure of activity and of enjoyment.

I thus express the law as it is read from the platform of ordinary life, but must not leave it without noticing the capital exception. For temperament is a power which no man willingly hears any one praise but himself. On the platform of physics, we cannot resist the contracting influences of so-called science. Temperament puts all divinity to rout. I know the mental proclivity of physicians. I hear the chuckle of the phrenologists. Theoretic kidnappers and slave-drivers, they esteem each man the victim of another, who winds him round his finger by knowing the law of his being, and by such cheap signboards as the color of his beard, or the slope of his occiput, reads the inventory of his fortunes and character. The grossest ignorance does not disgust like this impudent knowingness. The physicians say, they are not materialists;

---

[12] The Calvinist interpretation of Original Sin is viewed here as the psychosomatic display of a bodily disease. Unitarians do not believe that humankind is damned eternally but instead hold that we have spiritual autonomy.

but they are:—Spirit is matter reduced to an extreme thinness: O *so* thin!—But the definition of *spiritual* should be, *that which is its own evidence.* What notions do they attach to love! what to religion! One would not willingly pronounce these words in their hearing, and give them the occasion to profane them. I saw a gracious gentleman who adapts his conversation to the form of the head of the man he talks with! I had fancied that the value of life lay in its inscrutable possibilities; in the fact that I never know, in addressing myself to a new individual, what may befall me. I carry the keys of my castle in my hand, ready to throw them at the feet of my lord, whenever and in what disguise soever he shall appear. I know he is in the neighborhood hidden among vagabonds. Shall I preclude my future, by taking a high seat, and kindly adapting my conversation to the shape of heads? When I come to that, the doctors shall buy me for a cent.—"But, sir, medical history; the report to the Institute; the proven facts!"—I distrust the facts and the inferences. Temperament is the veto or limitation-power in the constitution, very justly applied to restrain an opposite excess in the constitution, but absurdly offered as a bar to original equity. When virtue is in presence, all subordinate powers sleep. On its own level, or in view of nature, temperament is final. I see not, if one be once caught in this trap of so-called sciences, any escape for the man from the links of the chain of physical necessity. Given such an embryo, such a history must follow. On this platform, one lives in a sty of sensualism, and would soon come to suicide. But it is impossible that the creative power should exclude itself. Into every intelligence there is a door which is never closed, through which the creator passes. The intellect, seeker of absolute truth, or the heart, lover of absolute good, intervenes for our succor, and at one whisper of these high powers, we awake from ineffectual struggles with this nightmare. We hurl it into its own hell, and cannot again contract ourselves to so base a state.

The secret of the illusoriness is in the necessity of a succession of moods or objects. Gladly we would anchor, but the anchorage is quicksand. This onward trick of nature is too strong for us: *Pero si muove.*[13] When, at night, I look at the moon and stars, I seem stationary, and they to hurry. Our love of the real draws us to permanence, but health of body consists in circulation, and sanity of mind in variety or facility of association. We need change of objects. Dedication to one thought is quickly odious. We house with the insane, and must humor them; then conversation dies out. Once I took such delight in Montaigne,[14] that I thought I should not need any other book; before that, in Shakspeare; then in Plutarch;[15] then in Plotinus;[16] at one time in Bacon;[17] afterwards in Goethe;[18] even in Bettine;[19] but now I turn the pages of either of them languidly, whilst I still cherish their genius. So with pictures; each will bear an emphasis of attention once, which it cannot retain, though we fain would continue to be pleased in that manner. How strongly I have felt of pictures, that when you have seen one well, you must take your leave of it; you shall never see it again. I have had good lessons from pictures, which I have since seen without emotion or remark. A deduction must be made from the opinion, which even the wise express

[13] Italian: "Still, it moves." Galileo's response after the Roman Catholic church forced him to retract his theory that the earth revolves around the sun.
[14] French essayist Michel de Montaigne (1533–1592).
[15] Greek biographer (A.D. 46?–?120).
[16] Roman philosopher (A.D. 205?–?270)
[17] English literary statesman (1561–1626).
[18] German poet and dramatist (1749–1832).
[19] German author Elizabeth ("Bettine") von Arnim (1785–1859).

of a new book or occurrence. Their opinion gives me tidings of their mood, and some vague guess at the new fact, but is nowise to be trusted as the lasting relation between that intellect and that thing. The child asks, "Mamma, why don't I like the story as well as when you told it me yesterday?" Alas, child, it is even so with the oldest cherubim of knowledge. But will it answer thy question to say, Because thou wert born to a whole, and this story is a particular? The reason of the pain this discovery causes us (and we make it late in respect to works of art and intellect), is the plaint of tragedy which murmurs from it in regard to persons, to friendship and love.

That immobility and absence of elasticity which we find in the arts, we find with more pain in the artist. There is no power of expansion in men. Our friends early appear to us as representatives of certain ideas, which they never pass or exceed. They stand on the brink of the ocean of thought and power, but they never take the single step that would bring them there. A man is like a bit of Labrador spar,[20] which has no lustre as you turn it in your hand, until you come to a particular angle; then it shows deep and beautiful colors. There is no adaptation or universal applicability in men, but each has his special talent, and the mastery of successful men consists in adroitly keeping themselves where and when that turn shall be oftenest to be practised. We do what we must, and call it by the best names we can, and would fain have the praise of having intended the result which ensues. I cannot recall any form of man who is not superfluous sometimes. But is not this pitiful? Life is not worth the taking, to do tricks in.

Of course, it needs the whole society, to give the symmetry we seek. The parti-colored wheel must revolve very fast to appear white. Something is learned too by conversing with so much folly and defect. In fine, whoever loses, we are always of the gaining party. Divinity is behind our failures and follies also. The plays of children are nonsense, but very educative nonsense. So it is with the largest and solemnest things, with commerce, government, church, marriage, and so with the history of every man's bread, and the ways by which he is to come by it. Like a bird which alights nowhere, but hops perpetually from bough to bough, is the Power which abides in no man and in no woman, but for a moment speaks from this one, and for another moment from that one.

But what help from these fineries or pedantries? What help from thought? Life is not dialectics. We, I think, in these times, have had lessons enough of the futility of criticism. Our young people have thought and written much on labor and reform, and for all that they have written, neither the world nor themselves have got on a step. Intellectual tasting of life will not supersede muscular activity. If a man should consider the nicety of the passage of a piece of bread down his throat, he would starve. At Education-Farm,[21] the noblest theory of life sat on the noblest figures of young men and maidens, quite powerless and melancholy. It would not rake or pitch a ton of hay; it would not rub down a horse; and the men and maidens it left pale and hungry. A political orator wittily compared our party promises to western roads, which opened stately enough, with planted trees on either side, to tempt the traveller, but soon became narrow and narrower, and ended in a squirrel-track, and ran up a

[20] Crystalline rock.
[21] Transcendentalist commune, more widely known as Brook Farm.

tree. So does culture with us; it ends in head-ache. Unspeakably sad and barren does life look to those, who a few months ago were dazzled with the splendor of the promise of the times. "There is now no longer any right course of action, nor any self-devotion left among the Iranis."[22] Objections and criticism we have had our fill of. There are objections to every course of life and action, and the practical wisdom infers an indifferency, from the omnipresence of objection. The whole frame of things preaches indifferency. Do not craze yourself with thinking, but go about your business anywhere. Life is not intellectual or critical, but sturdy. Its chief good is for well-mixed people who can enjoy what they find, without question. Nature hates peeping, and our mothers speak her very sense when they say, "Children, eat your victuals, and say no more of it." To fill the hour,—that is happiness; to fill the hour, and leave no crevice for a repentance or an approval. We live amid surfaces, and the true art of life is to skate well on them. Under the oldest mouldiest conventions, a man of native force prospers just as well as in the newest world, and that by skill of handling and treatment. He can take hold anywhere. Life itself is a mixture of power and form, and will not bear the least excess of either. To finish the moment, to find the journey's end in every step of the road, to live the greatest number of good hours, is wisdom. It is not the part of men, but of fanatics, or of mathematicians, if you will, to say, that, the shortness of life considered, it is not worth caring whether for so short a duration we were sprawling in want, or sitting high. Since our office is with moments, let us husband them. Five minutes of today are worth as much to me, as five minutes in the next millennium. Let us be poised, and wise, and our own, today. Let us treat the men and women well: treat them as if they were real: perhaps they are. Men live in their fancy, like drunkards whose hands are too soft and tremulous for successful labor. It is a tempest of fancies, and the only ballast I know, is a respect to the present hour. Without any shadow of doubt, amidst this vertigo of shows and politics, I settle myself ever the firmer in the creed, that we should not postpone and refer and wish, but do broad justice where we are, by whomsoever we deal with, accepting our actual companions and circumstances, however humble or odious, as the mystic officials to whom the universe has delegated its whole pleasure for us. If these are mean and malignant, their contentment, which is the last victory of justice, is a more satisfying echo to the heart, than the voice of poets and the casual sympathy of admirable persons. I think that however a thoughtful man may suffer from the defects and absurdities of his company, he cannot without affectation deny to any set of men and women, a sensibility to extraordinary merit. The coarse and frivolous have an instinct of superiority, if they have not a sympathy, and honor it in their blind capricious way with sincere homage.

The fine young people despise life, but in me, and in such as with me are free from dyspepsia, and to whom a day is a sound and solid good, it is a great excess of politeness to look scornful and to cry for company. I am grown by sympathy a little eager and sentimental, but leave me alone, and I should relish every hour and what it brought me, the potluck of the day, as heartily as the oldest gossip in the bar-room. I am thankful for small mercies. I compared notes with one of my friends who expects everything of the universe, and is disappointed when anything is less than the best, and I found that I begin at the other extreme, expecting nothing, and am always full

---

[22] From *Desatir,* ancient Persian writings attributed to Zoroaster (sixth century B.C.).

of thanks for moderate goods. I accept the clangor and jangle of contrary tendencies. I find my account in sots and bores also. They give a reality to the circumjacent picture, which such a vanishing meteorous appearance can ill spare. In the morning I awake, and find the old world, wife, babes, and mother, Concord and Boston, the dear old spiritual world, and even the dear old devil not far off. If we will take the good we find, asking no questions, we shall have heaping measures. The great gifts are not got by analysis. Everything good is on the highway. The middle region of our being is the temperate zone. We may climb into the thin and cold realm of pure geometry and lifeless science, or sink into that of sensation. Between these extremes is the equator of life, of thought, of spirit, of poetry,—a narrow belt. Moreover, in popular experience, everything good is on the highway. A collector peeps into all the picture-shops of Europe, for a landscape of Poussin, a crayon-sketch of Salvator;[23] but the Transfiguration, the Last Judgment, the Communion of St. Jerome,[24] and what are as transcendent as these, are on the walls of the Vatican, the Uffizi,[25] or the Louvre, where every footman may see them; to say nothing of nature's pictures in every street, of sunsets and sunrises every day, and the sculpture of the human body never absent. A collector recently bought at public auction, in London, for one hundred and fifty-seven guineas,[26] an autograph of Shakspeare: but for nothing a school-boy can read Hamlet, and can detect secrets of highest concernment yet unpublished therein. I think I will never read any but the commonest books,—the Bible, Homer, Dante, Shakspeare, and Milton. Then we are impatient of so public a life and planet, and run hither and thither for nooks and secrets. The imagination delights in the woodcraft of Indians, trappers, and bee-hunters. We fancy that we are strangers, and not so intimately domesticated in the planet as the wild man, and the wild beast and bird. But the exclusion reaches them also; reaches the climbing, flying, gliding, feathered and four-footed man. Fox and woodchuck, hawk and snipe, and bittern, when nearly seen, have no more root in the deep world than man, and are just such superficial tenants of the globe. Then the new molecular philosophy shows astronomical inter-spaces betwixt atom and atom, shows that the world is all outside: it has no inside.

The mid-world is best. Nature, as we know her, is no saint. The lights of the church, the ascetics, Gentoos[27] and Grahamites,[28] she does not distinguish by any favor. She comes eating and drinking and sinning. Her darlings, the great, the strong, the beautiful, are not children of our law, do not come out of the Sunday School, nor weigh their food, nor punctually keep the commandments. If we will be strong with her strength, we must not harbor such disconsolate consciences, borrowed too from the consciences of other nations. We must set up the strong present tense against all the rumors of wrath, past or to come. So many things are unsettled which it is of the first importance to settle,—and, pending their settlement, we will do as we do. Whilst the debate goes forward on the equity of commerce, and will not be closed for a century or two, New and Old England may keep shop. Law of copyright and

---

[23] Poussin: French classical painter Nicholas Poussin (1594–1665); Salvator: Italian painter Salvator Rosa (1615–1673), renowned for his exotic landscapes.
[24] Respectively, paintings of Raphael, Michelangelo, and Domenichino.
[25] Renowned museum in Florence.

[26] Guinea: British coin worth slightly more than one pound.
[27] Hindu sect.
[28] Vegetarian followers of Sylvester Graham (1794–1851), whose food faddism is paid tribute in the Graham cracker.

international copyright is to be discussed,[29] and, in the interim, we will sell our books for the most we can. Expediency of literature, reason of literature, lawfulness of writing down a thought, is questioned; much is to say on both sides, and, while the fight waxes hot, thou, dearest scholar, stick to thy foolish task, add a line every hour, and between whiles add a line. Right to hold land, right of property, is disputed, and the conventions convene, and before the vote is taken, dig away in your garden, and spend your earnings as a waif or godsend to all serene and beautiful purposes. Life itself is a bubble and a skepticism, and a sleep within a sleep. Grant it, and as much more as they will,—but thou, God's darling! heed thy private dream: thou wilt not be missed in the scorning and skepticism: there are enough of them: stay there in thy closet, and toil, until the rest are agreed what to do about it. Thy sickness, they say, and thy puny habit, require that thou do this or avoid that, but know that thy life is a flitting state, a tent for a night, and do thou, sick or well, finish that stint. Thou art sick, but shalt not be worse, and the universe, which holds thee dear, shall be the better.

Human life is made up of the two elements, power and form, and the proportion must be invariably kept, if we would have it sweet and sound. Each of these elements in excess makes a mischief as hurtful as its defect. Everything runs to excess: every good quality is noxious, if unmixed, and, to carry the danger to the edge of ruin, nature causes each man's peculiarity to superabound. Here, among the farms, we adduce the scholars as examples of this treachery. They are nature's victims of expression. You who see the artist, the orator, the poet, too near, and find their life no more excellent than that of mechanics or farmers, and themselves victims of partiality, very hollow and haggard, and pronounce them failures,—not heroes, but quacks,—conclude very reasonably, that these arts are not for man, but are disease. Yet nature will not bear you out. Irresistible nature made men such, and makes legions more of such, every day. You love the boy reading in a book, gazing at a drawing, or a cast: yet what are these millions who read and behold, but incipient writers and sculptors? Add a little more of that quality which now reads and sees, and they will seize the pen and chisel. And if one remembers how innocently he began to be an artist, he perceives that nature joined with his enemy. A man is a golden impossibility. The line he must walk is a hair's breadth. The wise through excess of wisdom is made a fool.

How easily, if fate would suffer it, we might keep forever these beautiful limits, and adjust ourselves, once for all, to the perfect calculation of the kingdom of known cause and effect. In the street and in the newspapers, life appears so plain a business, that manly resolution and adherence to the multiplication-table through all weathers, will insure success. But ah! presently comes a day, or is it only a half-hour, with its angel-whispering,—which discomfits the conclusions of nations and of years! Tomorrow again, everything looks real and angular, the habitual standards are reinstated, common sense is as rare as genius,—is the basis of genius, and experience is hands and feet to every enterprise;—and yet, he who should do his business on this understanding, would be quickly bankrupt. Power keeps quite another road than the turnpikes of choice and will, namely, the subterranean and invisible tunnels and channels of life.

---

[29] The United States Congress passed an international copyright law in 1891.

It is ridiculous that we are diplomatists, and doctors, and considerate people: there are no dupes like these. Life is a series of surprises, and would not be worth taking or keeping, if it were not. God delights to isolate us every day, and hide from us the past and the future. We would look about us, but with grand politeness he draws down before us an impenetrable screen of purest sky, and another behind us of purest sky. "You will not remember," he seems to say, "and you will not expect." All good conversation, manners, and action, come from a spontaneity which forgets usages, and makes the moment great. Nature hates calculators; her methods are saltatory and impulsive. Man lives by pulses; our organic movements are such; and the chemical and ethereal agents are undulatory and alternate; and the mind goes antagonizing on, and never prospers but by fits. We thrive by casualties. Our chief experiences have been casual. The most attractive class of people are those who are powerful obliquely, and not by the direct stroke: men of genius, but not yet accredited: one gets the cheer of their light, without paying too great a tax. Theirs is the beauty of the bird, or the morning light, and not of art. In the thought of genius there is always a surprise; and the moral sentiment is well called "the newness," for it is never other; as new to the oldest intelligence as to the young child,—"the kingdom that cometh without observation."[30] In like manner, for practical success, there must not be too much design. A man will not be observed in doing that which he can do best. There is a certain magic about his properest action, which stupefies your powers of observation, so that though it is done before you, you wist not of it. The art of life has a pudency, and will not be exposed. Every man is an impossibility, until he is born; every thing impossible, until we see a success. The ardors of piety agree at last with the coldest skepticism,—that nothing is of us or our works,—that all is of God. Nature will not spare us the smallest leaf of laurel. All writing comes by the grace of God, and all doing and having. I would gladly be moral, and keep due metes and bounds, which I dearly love, and allow the most to the will of man, but I have set my heart on honesty in this chapter, and I can see nothing at last, in success or failure, than more or less of vital force supplied from the Eternal. The results of life are uncalculated and uncalculable. The years teach much which the days never know. The persons who compose our company, converse, and come and go, and design and execute many things, and somewhat comes of it all, but an unlooked for result. The individual is always mistaken. He designed many things, and drew in other persons as coadjutors, quarrelled with some or all, blundered much, and something is done; all are a little advanced, but the individual is always mistaken. It turns out somewhat new, and very unlike what he promised himself.

The ancients, struck with this irreducibleness of the elements of human life to calculation, exalted Chance into a divinity, but that is to stay too long at the spark, —which glitters truly at one point,—but the universe is warm with the latency of the same fire. The miracle of life which will not be expounded, but will remain a miracle, introduces a new element. In the growth of the embryo, Sir Everard Home,[31] I think, noticed that the evolution was not from one central point, but coactive from three or more points. Life has no memory. That which proceeds in succession might be remembered, but that which is coexistent, or ejaculated from a

---

[30] See Luke 17:20.

[31] Scottish surgeon (1756–1832).

deeper cause, as yet far from being conscious, knows not its own tendency. So is it with us, now skeptical, or without unity, because immersed in forms and effects all seeming to be of equal yet hostile value, and now religious, whilst in the reception of spiritual law. Bear with these distractions, with this coetaneous growth of the parts: they will one day be *members,* and obey one will. On that one will, on that secret cause, they nail our attention and hope. Life is hereby melted into an expectation or a religion. Underneath the inharmonious and trivial particulars, is a musical perfection, the Ideal journeying always with us, the heaven without rent or seam. Do but observe the mode of our illumination. When I converse with a profound mind, or if at any time being alone I have good thoughts, I do not at once arrive at satisfactions, as when, being thirsty, I drink water, or go to the fire, being cold: no! but I am at first apprised of my vicinity to a new and excellent region of life. By persisting to read or to think, this region gives further sign of itself, as it were in flashes of light, in sudden discoveries of its profound beauty and repose, as if the clouds that covered it parted at intervals, and showed the approaching traveller the inland mountains, with the tranquil eternal meadows spread at their base, whereon flocks graze, and shepherds pipe and dance. But every insight from this realm of thought is felt as initial, and promises a sequel. I do not make it; I arrive there, and behold what was there already. I make! O no! I clap my hands in infantine joy and amazement, before the first opening to me of this august magnificence, old with the love and homage of innumerable ages, young with the life of life, the sunbright Mecca of the desert. And what a future it opens! I feel a new heart beating with the love of the new beauty. I am ready to die out of nature, and be born again into this new yet unapproachable America I have found in the West.

> "Since neither now nor yesterday began
> These thoughts, which have been ever, nor yet can
> A man be found who their first entrance knew."[32]

If I have described life as a flux of moods, I must now add, that there is that in us which changes not, and which ranks all sensations and states of mind. The consciousness in each man is a sliding scale, which identifies him now with the First Cause, and now with the flesh of his body; life above life, in infinite degrees. The sentiment from which it sprung determines the dignity of any deed, and the question ever is, not, what you have done or forborne, but, at whose command you have done or forborne it.

Fortune, Minerva,[33] Muse, Holy Ghost,—these are quaint names, too narrow to cover this unbounded substance. The baffled intellect must still kneel before this cause, which refuses to be named,—ineffable cause, which every fine genius has essayed to represent by some emphatic symbol, as, Thales by water, Anaximenes by air, Anaxagoras[34] by (Νους) thought, Zoroaster[35] by fire, Jesus and the moderns by love: and the metaphor of each has become a national religion. The Chinese Mencius[36] has not been the least successful in his generalization. "I fully understand language," he said,

---

[32] Translation of lines 455–457 from Sophocles' *Antigone.*
[33] Roman goddess of wisdom.
[34] Thales, Anaximenes, and Anaxagoras, respectively, were Greek philosophers of the seventh, sixth, and fifth centuries B.C.

[35] In sixth-century Persia, Zoroaster preached fire or light worship.
[36] Confucian philosopher Meng-Tse (third century B.C.).

"and nourish well my vast-flowing vigor."—"I beg to ask what you call vast-flowing vigor?"—said his companion. "The explanation," replied Mencius, "is difficult. This vigor is supremely great, and in the highest degree unbending. Nourish it correctly, and do it no injury, and it will fill up the vacancy between heaven and earth. This vigor accords with and assists justice and reason, and leaves no hunger."—In our more correct writing, we give to this generalization the name of Being, and thereby confess that we have arrived as far as we can go. Suffice it for the joy of the universe, that we have not arrived at a wall, but at interminable oceans. Our life seems not present, so much as prospective; not for the affairs on which it is wasted, but as a hint of this vast-flowing vigor. Most of life seems to be mere advertisement of faculty: information is given us not to sell ourselves cheap; that we are very great. So, in particulars, our greatness is always in a tendency or direction, not in an action. It is for us to believe in the rule, not in the exception. The noble are thus known from the ignoble. So in accepting the leading of the sentiments, it is not what we believe concerning the immortality of the soul, or the like, but *the universal impulse to believe,* that is the material circumstance, and is the principal fact in the history of the globe. Shall we describe this cause as that which works directly? The spirit is not helpless or needful of mediate organs. It has plentiful powers and direct effects. I am explained without explaining, I am felt without acting, and where I am not. Therefore all just persons are satisfied with their own praise. They refuse to explain themselves, and are content that new actions should do them that office. They believe that we communicate without speech, and above speech, and that no right action of ours is quite unaffecting to our friends, at whatever distance; for the influence of action is not to be measured by miles. Why should I fret myself, because a circumstance has occurred, which hinders my presence where I was expected? If I am not at the meeting, my presence where I am, should be as useful to the commonwealth of friendship and wisdom, as would be my presence in that place. I exert the same quality of power in all places. Thus journeys the mighty Ideal before us; it never was known to fall into the rear. No man ever came to an experience which was satiating, but his good is tidings of a better. Onward and onward! In liberated moments, we know that a new picture of life and duty is already possible; the elements already exist in many minds around you, of a doctrine of life which shall transcend any written record we have. The new statement will comprise the skepticisms, as well as the faiths of society, and out of unbeliefs a creed shall be formed. For, skepticisms are not gratuitous or lawless, but are limitations of the affirmative statement, and the new philosophy must take them in, and make affirmations outside of them, just as much as it must include the oldest beliefs.

It is very unhappy, but too late to be helped, the discovery we have made, that we exist. That discovery is called the Fall of Man. Ever afterwards, we suspect our instruments. We have learned that we do not see directly, but mediately, and that we have no means of correcting these colored and distorting lenses which we are, or of computing the amount of their errors. Perhaps these subject-lenses have a creative power; perhaps there are no objects. Once we lived in what we saw; now, the rapaciousness of this new power, which threatens to absorb all things, engages us. Nature, art, persons, letters, religions,—objects, successively tumble in, and God is but one of its ideas. Nature and literature are subjective phenomena; every evil and every good thing is a shadow which we cast. The street is full of humiliations to the proud.

As the fop contrived to dress his bailiffs in his livery, and make them wait on his guests at table, so the chagrins which the bad heart gives off as bubbles, at once take form as ladies and gentlemen in the street, shopmen or barkeepers in hotels, and threaten or insult whatever is threatenable and insultable in us. 'Tis the same with our idolatries. People forget that it is the eye which makes the horizon, and the rounding mind's eye which makes this or that man a type or representative of humanity with the name of hero or saint. Jesus the "providential man," is a good man on whom many people are agreed that these optical laws shall take effect. By love on one part, and by forbearance to press objection on the other part, it is for a time settled, that we will look at him in the centre of the horizon, and ascribe to him the properties that will attach to any man so seen. But the longest love or aversion has a speedy term. The great and crescive self, rooted in absolute nature, supplants all relative existence, and ruins the kingdom of mortal friendship and love. Marriage (in what is called the spiritual world) is impossible, because of the inequality between every subject and every object. The subject is the receiver of Godhead, and at every comparison must feel his being enhanced by that cryptic might. Though not in energy, yet by presence, this magazine[37] of substance cannot be otherwise than felt: nor can any force of intellect attribute to the object the proper deity which sleeps or wakes forever in every subject. Never can love make consciousness and ascription equal in force. There will be the same gulf between every me and thee, as between the original and the picture. The universe is the bride of the soul. All private sympathy is partial. Two human beings are like globes, which can touch only in a point, and, whilst they remain in contact, all other points of each of the spheres are inert; their turn must also come, and the longer a particular union lasts, the more energy of appetency[38] the parts not in union acquire.

Life will be imaged, but cannot be divided nor doubled. Any invasion of its unity would be chaos. The soul is not twin-born, but the only begotten, and though revealing itself as child in time, child in appearance, is of a fatal and universal power, admitting no co-life. Every day, every act betrays the ill-concealed deity. We believe in ourselves, as we do not believe in others. We permit all things to ourselves, and that which we call sin in others, is experiment for us. It is an instance of our faith in ourselves, that men never speak of crime as lightly as they think: or, every man thinks a latitude safe for himself, which is nowise to be indulged to another. The act looks very differently on the inside, and on the outside; in its quality, and in its consequences. Murder in the murderer is no such ruinous thought as poets and romancers will have it; it does not unsettle him, or fright him from his ordinary notice of trifles: it is an act quite easy to be contemplated, but in its sequel, it turns out to be a horrible jangle and confounding of all relations. Especially the crimes that spring from love, seem right and fair from the actor's point of view, but, when acted, are found destructive of society. No man at last believes that he can be lost, nor that the crime in him is as black as in the felon. Because the intellect qualifies in our own case the moral judgments. For there is no crime to the intellect. That is antinomian or hypernomian,[39] and judges law as well as fact. "It is worse than a crime, it is a blunder," said Napoleon, speaking the language of the intellect. To it, the world is a problem in mathematics or the science of quantity, and it leaves out praise and blame, and all

---

[37] Stored supply.
[38] Being propelled toward unity.
[39] Against or above the control of law.

weak emotions. All stealing is comparative. If you come to absolutes, pray who does not steal? Saints are sad, because they behold sin, (even when they speculate,) from the point of view of the conscience, and not of the intellect; a confusion of thought. Sin seen from the thought, is a diminution or *less:* seen from the conscience or will, it is pravity or *bad.* The intellect names it shade, absence of light, and no essence. The conscience must feel it as essence, essential evil. This it is not: it has an objective existence, but no subjective.

Thus inevitably does the universe wear our color, and every object fall successively into the subject itself. The subject exists, the subject enlarges; all things sooner or later fall into place. As I am, so I see; use what language we will, we can never say anything but what we are; Hermes, Cadmus,⁴⁰ Columbus, Newton, Buonaparte; are the mind's ministers. Instead of feeling a poverty when we encounter a great man, let us treat the new comer like a travelling geologist, who passes through our estate, and shows us good slate, or limestone, or anthracite, in our brush pasture. The partial action of each strong mind in one direction, is a telescope for the objects on which it is pointed. But every other part of knowledge is to be pushed to the same extravagance, ere the soul attains her due sphericity. Do you see that kitten chasing so prettily her own tail? If you could look with her eyes, you might see her surrounded with hundreds of figures performing complex dramas, with tragic and comic issues, long conversations, many characters, many ups and downs of fate,—and meantime it is only puss and her tail. How long before our masquerade will end its noise of tamborines, laughter, and shouting, and we shall find it was a solitary performance?—A subject and an object, —it takes so much to make the galvanic circuit complete, but magnitude adds nothing. What imports it whether it is Kepler⁴¹ and the sphere; Columbus and America; a reader and his book; or puss with her tail?

It is true that all the muses and love and religion hate these developments, and will find a way to punish the chemist, who publishes in the parlor the secrets of the laboratory. And we cannot say too little of our constitutional necessity of seeing things under private aspects, or saturated with our humors. And yet is the God the native of these bleak rocks. That need makes in morals the capital virtue of self-trust. We must hold hard to this poverty, however scandalous, and by more vigorous self-recoveries, after the sallies of action, possess our axis more firmly. The life of truth is cold, and so far mournful; but it is not the slave of tears, contritions, and perturbations. It does not attempt another's work, nor adopt another's facts. It is a main lesson of wisdom to know your own from another's. I have learned that I cannot dispose of other people's facts; but I possess such a key to my own, as persuades me against all their denials, that they also have a key to theirs. A sympathetic person is placed in the dilemma of a swimmer among drowning men, who all catch at him, and if he give so much as a leg or a finger, they will drown him. They wish to be saved from the mischiefs of their vices, but not from their vices. Charity would be wasted on this poor waiting on the symptoms. A wise and hardy physician will say, *Come out of that,* as the first condition of advice.

In this our talking America, we are ruined by our good nature and listening on

⁴⁰ Creative pioneers: Hermes, Greek god who invented the lyre; Cadmus, mythic founder of the Thebans, who brought the alphabet to Greece.

⁴¹ German physicist and astronomer Johannes Kepler (1571–1630), who pioneered the discovery of the laws of planetary motion.

all sides. This compliance takes away the power of being greatly useful. A man should not be able to look other than directly and forthright. A preoccupied attention is the only answer to the importunate frivolity of other people: an attention, and to an aim which makes their wants frivolous. This is a divine answer, and leaves no appeal, and no hard thoughts. In Flaxman's[42] drawing of the Eumenides of Æschylus, Orestes supplicates Apollo, whilst the Furies sleep on the threshold. The face of the god expresses a shade of regret and compassion, but calm with the conviction of the irreconcilableness of the two spheres. He is born into other politics, into the eternal and beautiful. The man at his feet asks for his interest in turmoils of the earth, into which his nature cannot enter. And the Eumenides there lying express pictorially this disparity. The god is surcharged with his divine destiny.

Illusion, Temperament, Succession, Surface, Surprise, Reality, Subjectiveness,—these are threads on the loom of time, these are the lords of life. I dare not assume to give their order, but I name them as I find them in my way. I know better than to claim any completeness for my picture. I am a fragment, and this is a fragment of me. I can very confidently announce one or another law, which throws itself into relief and form, but I am too young yet by some ages to compile a code. I gossip for my hour concerning the eternal politics. I have seen many fair pictures not in vain. A wonderful time I have lived in. I am not the novice I was fourteen, nor yet seven years ago. Let who will ask, where is the fruit? I find a private fruit sufficient. This is a fruit, —that I should not ask for a rash effect from meditations, counsels, and the hiving of truths. I should feel it pitiful to demand a result on this town and county, an overt effect on the instant month and year. The effect is deep and secular as the cause. It works on periods in which mortal lifetime is lost. All I know is reception; I am and I have: but I do not get, and when I have fancied I had gotten anything, I found I did not. I worship with wonder the great Fortune. My reception has been so large, that I am not annoyed by receiving this or that superabundantly. I say to the Genius, if he will pardon the proverb, *In for a mill, in for a million.* When I receive a new gift, I do not macerate my body to make the account square, for, if I should die, I could not make the account square. The benefit overran the merit the first day, and has overran the merit ever since. The merit itself, so-called, I reckon part of the receiving.

Also, that hankering after an overt or practical effect seems to me an apostasy. In good earnest, I am willing to spare this most unnecessary deal of doing. Life wears to me a visionary face. Hardest, roughest action is visionary also. It is but a choice between soft and turbulent dreams. People disparage knowing and the intellectual life, and urge doing. I am very content with knowing, if only I could know. That is an august entertainment, and would suffice me a great while. To know a little, would be worth the expense of this world. I hear always the law of Adrastia,[43] "that every soul which had acquired any truth, should be safe from harm until another period."[44]

I know that the world I converse with in the city and in the farms, is not the world

---

[42] Flaxman: British artist John Flaxman (1755–1826), illustrator of the scene mentioned from *The Eumenides* by Aeschylus (525–456 B.C.).

[43] Nemesis, Greek goddess of retribution or destiny.

[44] From Plato's *Phaedrus.*

I *think*. I observe that difference, and shall observe it. One day, I shall know the value
and law of this discrepance. But I have not found that much was gained by manipular
attempts to realize the world of thought. Many eager persons successively make an
experiment in this way, and make themselves ridiculous. They acquire democratic
manners, they foam at the mouth, they hate and deny. Worse, I observe, that, in the
history of mankind, there is never a solitary example of success,—taking their own
tests of success. I say this polemically, or in reply to the inquiry, why not realize your
world? But far be from me the despair which prejudges the law by a paltry empiricism,
—since there never was a right endeavor, but it succeeded. Patience and patience, we
shall win at the last. We must be very suspicious of the deceptions of the element
of time. It takes a good deal of time to eat or to sleep, or to earn a hundred dollars,
and a very little time to entertain a hope and an insight which becomes the light of
our life. We dress our garden, eat our dinners, discuss the household with our wives,
and these things make no impression, are forgotten next week; but in the solitude to
which every man is always returning, he has a sanity and revelations, which in his
passage into new worlds he will carry with him. Never mind the ridicule, never mind
the defeat: up again, old heart!—it seems to say,—there is victory yet for all justice;
and the true romance which the world exists to realize, will be the transformation
of genius into practical power.

1844

Fate[*]

> *Delicate omens traced in air,*
> *To the lone bard true witness bare;*
> *Birds with auguries on their wings*
> *Chanted undeceiving things,*
> *Him to beckon, him to warn;*
> *Well might then the poet scorn*
> *To learn of scribe or courier*
> *Hints writ in vaster character;*
> *And on his mind, at dawn of day,*
> *Soft shadows of the evening lay.*
> *For the prevision is allied*
> *Unto the thing so signified;*
> *Or say, the foresight that awaits*
> *Is the same Genius that creates.*[1]

It chanced during one winter a few years ago, that our cities were bent on discussing
the theory of the Age. By an odd coincidence, four or five noted men were each
reading a discourse to the citizens of Boston or New York, on the Spirit of the Times.

---

[*] This essay was first presented on December 22,
1851, in Boston as part of a lecture series, "The
Conduct of Life."

[1] Emerson's verses.

It so happened that the subject had the same prominence in some remarkable pamphlets and journals issued in London in the same season.[2] To me, however, the question of the times resolved itself into a practical question of the conduct of life. How shall I live? We are incompetent to solve the times. Our geometry cannot span the huge orbits of the prevailing ideas, behold their return and reconcile their opposition. We can only obey our own polarity. 'T is fine for us to speculate and elect our course, if we must accept an irresistible dictation.

In our first steps to gain our wishes we come upon immovable limitations. We are fired with the hope to reform men. After many experiments we find that we must begin earlier,—at school. But the boys and girls are not docile; we can make nothing of them. We decide that they are not of good stock. We must begin our reform earlier still,—at generation: that is to say, there is Fate, or laws of the world.

But if there be irresistible dictation, this dictation understands itself. If we must accept Fate, we are not less compelled to affirm liberty, the significance of the individual, the grandeur of duty, the power of character. This is true, and that other is true. But our geometry cannot span these extreme points and reconcile them. What to do? By obeying each thought frankly, by harping, or, if you will, pounding on each string, we learn at last its power. By the same obedience to other thoughts we learn theirs, and then comes some reasonable hope of harmonizing them. We are sure that, though we know not how, necessity does comport with liberty, the individual with the world, my polarity with the spirit of the times. The riddle of the age has for each a private solution. If one would study his own time, it must be by this method of taking up in turn each of the leading topics which belong to our scheme of human life, and by firmly stating all that is agreeable to experience on one, and doing the same justice to the opposing facts in the others, the true limitations will appear. Any excess of emphasis on one part would be corrected, and a just balance would be made.

But let us honestly state the facts. Our America has a bad name for superficialness. Great men, great nations, have not been boasters and buffoons, but perceivers of the terror of life, and have manned themselves to face it. The Spartan, embodying his religion in his country, dies before its majesty without a question. The Turk, who believes his doom is written on the iron leaf in the moment when he entered the world, rushes on the enemy's sabre with undivided will. The Turk, the Arab, the Persian, accepts the foreordained fate:—

> "On two days, it steads not to run from thy grave,
>   The appointed, and the unappointed day;
> On the first, neither balm nor physician can save,
>   Nor thee, on the second, the Universe slay."[3]

The Hindoo under the wheel is as firm. Our Calvinists[4] in the last generation had something of the same dignity. They felt that the weight of the Universe held them

---

[2] In the three decades preceding this essay's delivery, such notable English writers as William Hazlitt, R. H. Horne, Chandos Leigh, and John Stuart Mill had published works on this subject.

[3] Emerson's translation of a German version of a Persian poem attributed to the poet Pindar of Rei in Kuhistan. (See Emerson's *Journals,* Vol. 11, p. 103.)

[4] Colonial Calvinists believed, through the doctrine of election, that God arbitrarily decided a person's destiny.

down to their place. What could *they* do? Wise men feel that there is something which cannot be talked or voted away,—a strap or belt which girds the world:—

"The Destinee, ministre general,
    That executeth in the world over al,
    The purveiance that God hath seen beforne,
    So strong it is, that though the world had sworne
    The contrary of a thing by yea or nay,
    Yet sometime it shall fallen on a day
    That falleth not oft in a thousand yeer;
    For certainly, our appetités here,
    Be it of warre, or pees, or hate, or love,
    All this is ruled by the sight above."
        CHAUCER: *The Knighte's Tale*[5]

The Greek Tragedy expressed the same sense. "Whatever is fated that will take place. The great immense mind of Jove is not to be transgressed."[6]

Savages cling to a local god of one tribe or town. The broad ethics of Jesus were quickly narrowed to village theologies, which preach an election or favoritism. And now and then an amiable parson, like Jung Stilling or Robert Huntington,[7] believes in a pistareen-Providence, which, whenever the good man wants a dinner, makes that somebody shall knock at his door and leave a half-dollar. But Nature is no sentimentalist,—does not cosset or pamper us. We must see that the world is rough and surly, and will not mind drowning a man or a woman, but swallows your ship like a grain of dust. The cold, inconsiderate of persons, tingles your blood, benumbs your feet, freezes a man like an apple. The diseases, the elements, fortune, gravity, lightning, respect no persons. The way of Providence is a little rude. The habit of snake and spider, the snap of the tiger and other leapers and bloody jumpers, the crackle of the bones of his prey in the coil of the anaconda,—these are in the system, and our habits are like theirs. You have just dined, and however scrupulously the slaughter-house is concealed in the graceful distance of miles, there is complicity, expensive races,—race living at the expense of race. The planet is liable to shocks from comets, perturbations from planets, rendings from earthquake and volcano, alterations of climate, precessions of equinoxes. Rivers dry up by opening of the forest. The sea changes its bed. Towns and counties fall into it. At Lisbon an earthquake killed men like flies. At Naples three years ago ten thousand persons were crushed in a few minutes. The scurvy at sea, the sword of the climate in the west of Africa, at Cayenne, at Panama, at New Orleans, cut off men like a massacre. Our western prairie shakes with fever and ague. The cholera, the small-pox, have proved as mortal to some tribes as a frost to the crickets, which, having filled the summer with noise, are silenced by a fall

[5] Emerson's slightly altered version of lines 805–814.
[6] Aeschylus, *The Suppliants*, ll. 1047–1049.
[7] Jung Stilling: German mystic and physician Johann H. Jung-Stilling (1740–1817); Robert

Huntington: English eccentric minister William Huntington (1745–1813). The pistareen, a Spanish coin, circulated in the United States at a debased value.

of the temperature of one night. Without uncovering what does not concern us, or counting how many species of parasites hang on a bombyx,[8] or groping after intestinal parasites or infusory biters,[9] or the obscurities of alternate generation,—the forms of the shark, the *labrus,*[10] the jaw of the sea-wolf paved with crushing teeth, the weapons of the grampus,[11] and other warriors hidden in the sea, are hints of ferocity in the interiors of nature. Let us not deny it up and down. Providence has a wild, rough, incalculable road to its end, and it is of no use to try to whitewash its huge, mixed instrumentalities, or to dress up that terrific benefactor in a clean shirt and white neckcloth of a student in divinity.

Will you say, the disasters which threaten mankind are exceptional, and one need not lay his account for cataclysms every day? Aye, but what happens once may happen again, and so long as these strokes are not to be parried by us they must be feared.

But these shocks and ruins are less destructive to us than the stealthy power of other laws which act on us daily. An expense of ends to means is fate;—organization tyrannizing over character. The menagerie, or forms and powers of the spine, is a book of fate; the bill of the bird, the skull of the snake, determines tyrannically its limits. So is the scale of races, of temperaments;[12] so is sex; so is climate; so is the reaction of talents imprisoning the vital power in certain directions. Every spirit makes its house; but afterwards the house confines the spirit.

The gross lines are legible to the dull; the cabman is phrenologist so far, he looks in your face to see if his shilling is sure. A dome of brow denotes one thing, a pot-belly another; a squint, a pug-nose, mats of hair, the pigment of the epidermis, betray character. People seem sheathed in their tough organization. Ask Spurzheim, ask the doctors, ask Quetelet if temperaments decide nothing?—or if there be anything they do not decide?[13] Read the description in medical books of the four temperaments and you will think you are reading your own thoughts which you had not yet told. Find the part which black eyes and which blue eyes play severally in the company. How shall a man escape from his ancestors, or draw off from his veins the black drop which he drew from his father's or his mother's life? It often appears in a family as if all the qualities of the progenitors were potted in several jars,—some ruling quality in each son or daughter of the house; and sometimes the unmixed temperament, the rank unmitigated elixir, the family vice is drawn off in a separate individual and the others are proportionally relieved. We sometimes see a change of expression in our companion and say his father or his mother comes to the windows of his eyes, and sometimes a remote relative. In different hours a man represents each of several of his ancestors, as if there were seven or eight of us rolled up in each man's skin,—seven or eight ancestors at least; and they constitute the variety of notes for that new piece of music which his life is. At the corner of the street you read the possibility of each passenger in the facial angle, in the complexion, in the depth of his eye. His parentage determines it. Men are what their mothers made them. You may as well ask a loom which weaves

---

[8] Silkworm moth.
[9] Microscopic marine creatures.
[10] Predatory fish.
[11] The killer whale.
[12] According to ancient and medieval physiology, various mixtures of the four humors (blood,

phlegm, choler, and melancholy) determined a person's temperament.
[13] Spurzheim: Johann Spurzheim (1776–1832), German popularizer of phrenology; Quetelet: Belgian mathematician Lambert Quetelet (1796–1874), creator of the science of statistics.

huckabuck[14] why it does not make cashmere, as expect poetry from this engineer, or a chemical discovery from that jobber. Ask the digger in the ditch to explain Newton's laws; the fine organs of his brain have been pinched by overwork and squalid poverty from father to son for a hundred years. When each comes forth from his mother's womb, the gate of gifts closes behind him. Let him value his hands and feet, he has but one pair. So he has but one future, and that is already predetermined in his lobes and described in that little fatty face, pig-eye, and squat form. All the privilege and all the legislation of the world cannot meddle or help to make a poet or a prince of him.

Jesus said, "When he looketh on her, he hath committed adultery."[15] But he is an adulterer before he has yet looked on the woman, by the superfluity of animal and the defect of thought in his constitution. Who meets him, or who meets her, in the street, sees that they are ripe to be each other's victim.

In certain men digestion and sex absorb the vital force, and the stronger these are, the individual is so much weaker. The more of these drones perish, the better for the hive. If, later, they give birth to some superior individual, with force enough to add to this animal a new aim and a complete apparatus to work it out, all the ancestors are gladly forgotten. Most men and most women are merely one couple more. Now and then one has a new cell or camarilla opened in his brain,—an architectural, a musical, or a philological knack; some stray taste or talent for flowers, or chemistry, or pigments, or story-telling; a good hand for drawing, a good foot for dancing, an athletic frame for wide journeying, etc.—which skill nowise alters rank in the scale of nature, but serves to pass the time; the life of sensation going on as before. At last these hints and tendencies are fixed in one or in a succession. Each absorbs so much food and force as to become itself a new centre. The new talent draws off so rapidly the vital force that not enough remains for the animal functions, hardly enough for health; so that in the second generation, if the like genius appear, the health is visibly deteriorated and the generative force impaired.

People are born with the moral or with the material bias;—uterine brothers with this diverging destination; and I suppose, with high magnifiers, Mr. Frauenhofer or Dr. Carpenter[16] might come to distinguish in the embryo, at the fourth day,—this is a Whig, and that a Free-Soiler.[17]

It was a poetic attempt to lift this mountain of Fate, to reconcile this despotism of race with liberty, which led the Hindoos to say, "Fate is nothing but the deeds committed in a prior state of existence."[18] I find the coincidence of the extremes of Eastern and Western speculation in the daring statement of Schelling,[19] "There is in every man a certain feeling that he has been what he is from all eternity, and by no

[14] Coarse linen used as a towel.
[15] Matthew 5:28: "But I say unto you, that whosoever looketh on a woman to lust after her hath committed adultery with her already in his heart."
[16] The German optician Joseph von Frauenhofer (1787–1826) improved on the telescope; the English biologist William B. Carpenter (1813–1885) wrote on the functions of the microscope.
[17] At the time this lecture was delivered, "Whig"

and "Free-Soiler" represented the Anti-Democratic party and the antislavery faction of the Democratic party, respectively.
[18] This is probably a précis of the concept of karma rather than an accurate quote.
[19] German philosopher Friedrich Wilhelm Joseph von Schelling (1775–1854). The quote may well be from Schelling's *Philosophical Search for the Ways of Human Happiness,* translated by Elliot Cabot.

means became such in time." To say it less sublimely,—in the history of the individual is always an account of his condition, and he knows himself to be a party to his present estate.

A good deal of our politics is physiological. Now and then a man of wealth in the heyday of youth adopts the tenet of broadest freedom. In England there is always some man of wealth and large connection, planting himself, during all his years of health, on the side of progress, who, as soon as he begins to die, checks his forward play, calls in his troops and becomes conservative. All conservatives are such from personal defects. They have been effeminated by position or nature, born halt and blind, through luxury of their parents, and can only, like invalids, act on the defensive. But strong natures, backwoodsmen, New Hampshire giants, Napoleons, Burkes, Broughams, Websters, Kossuths,[20] are inevitable patriots, until their life ebbs and their defects and gout, palsy and money, warp them.

The strongest idea incarnates itself in majorities and nations, in the healthiest and strongest. Probably the election goes by avoirdupois weight, and if you could weigh bodily the tonnage of any hundred of the Whig and the Democratic party in a town on the Dearborn balance,[21] as they passed the hay-scales, you could predict with certainty which party would carry it. On the whole it would be rather the speediest way of deciding the vote, to put the selectmen or the mayor and aldermen at the hay-scales.

In science we have to consider two things: power and circumstance. All we know of the egg, from each successive discovery, is, *another vesicle;* and if, after five hundred years you get a better observer or a better glass, he finds, within the last observed, another. In vegetable and animal tissue it is just alike, and all that the primary power or spasm operates is still vesicles, vesicles. Yes,—but the tyrannical Circumstance! A vesicle in new circumstances, a vesicle lodged in darkness, Oken[22] thought, became animal; in light, a plant. Lodged in the parent animal, it suffers changes which end in unsheathing miraculous capability in the unaltered vesicle, and it unlocks itself to fish, bird, or quadruped, head and foot, eye and claw. The Circumstance is Nature. Nature is what you may do. There is much you may not. We have two things,— the circumstance, and the life. Once we thought positive power was all. Now we learn that negative power, or circumstance, is half. Nature is the tyrannous circumstance, the thick skull, the sheathed snake, the ponderous, rock-like jaw; necessitated activity; violent direction; the conditions of a tool, like the locomotive, strong enough on its track, but which can do nothing but mischief off of it; or skates, which are wings on the ice but fetters on the ground.

The book of Nature is the book of Fate. She turns the gigantic pages,—leaf after leaf,—never re-turning one. One leaf she lays down, a floor of granite; then a thousand ages, and a bed of slate; a thousand ages, and a measure of coal; a thousand ages, and a layer of marl and mud: vegetable forms appear; her first misshapen animals, zoöphyte, trilobium, fish; then, saurians,—rude forms, in which she has only blocked her future statue, concealing under these unwieldy monsters the fine type of her

---

[20] The exemplars here are British statesman Edmund Burke (1729–1797); English political leader Henry Brougham (1778–1868); Massachusetts politician Daniel Webster (1782–1852), leader of the Whig party;

Hungarian patriot Lajos Kossuth (1802–1894), leader of a struggle for freedom in 1848.
[21] Spring balance invented by Henry Dearborn.
[22] German naturalist Lorenz Oken (1779–1851), who posited that all organisms arise from cells.

coming king. The face of the planet cools and dries, the races meliorate, and man is born. But when a race has lived its term, it comes no more again.

The population of the world is a conditional population; not the best, but the best that could live now; and the scale of tribes, and the steadiness with which victory adheres to one tribe and defeat to another, is as uniform as the superposition of strata. We know in history what weight belongs to race. We see the English, French, and Germans planting themselves on every shore and market of America and Australia, and monopolizing the commerce of these countries. We like the nervous and victorious habit of our own branch of the family. We follow the step of the Jew, of the Indian, of the Negro. We see how much will has been expended to extinguish the Jew, in vain. Look at the unpalatable conclusions of Knox,[23] in his Fragment of Races; —a rash and unsatisfactory writer, but charged with pungent and unforgetable truths. "Nature respects race, and not hybrids." "Every race has its own *habitat.*" "Detach a colony from the race, and it deteriorates to the crab."[24] See the shades of the picture. The German and Irish millions, like the Negro, have a great deal of guano[25] in their destiny. They are ferried over the Atlantic and carted over America, to ditch and to drudge, to make corn cheap and then to lie down prematurely to make a spot of green grass on the prairie.

One more fagot of these adamantine bandages is the new science of Statistics. It is a rule that the most casual and extraordinary events, if the basis of population is broad enough, become matter of fixed calculation. It would not be safe to say when a captain like Bonaparte, a singer like Jenny Lind, or a navigator like Bowditch[26] would be born in Boston; but, on a population of twenty or two hundred millions, something like accuracy may be had.[27]

'T is frivolous to fix pedantically the date of particular inventions. They have all been invented over and over fifty times. Man is the arch machine of which all these shifts drawn from himself are toy models. He helps himself on each emergency by copying or duplicating his own structure, just so far as the need is. 'T is hard to find the right Homer, Zoroaster, or Menu;[28] harder still to find the Tubal Cain, or Vulcan, or Cadmus, or Copernicus, or Fust, or Fulton;[29] the indisputable inventor. There are scores and centuries of them. "The air is full of men." This kind of talent so abounds,

[23] Robert Knox (1791–1862), Scottish ethnologist, anatomist, and author of *The Races of Men, A Fragment* (1850). Knox tried to justify racial prejudice by noting biological and cultural differences.

[24] Reference to the way apple trees degenerate to crabapples when not tended.

[25] Dung of sea birds and bats, used as a fertilizer.

[26] Jenny Lind: British coloratura soprano (1820–1887); Bowditch: American mathematician and astronomer Nathaniel Bowditch (1773–1838), who authored the *New American Practical Navigator* (1802).

[27] Emerson's note: " 'Everything which pertains to the human species, considered as a whole, belongs to the order of physical facts. The greater the number of individuals, the more does the influence of the individual will disappear, leaving predominance to a series of general facts dependent on causes by which society exists, and is preserved.'—Quetelet."

[28] Homer: Greek poet and author of the *Iliad* and the *Odyssey;* Zoroaster: Persian religious leader of the sixth century B.C.; Menu: credited as author of the Hindu laws of *Manu.*

[29] Tubal-Cain: "an instructor of every artificer in brass and iron" (Genesis 4:22); Vulcan: Roman god of metalworking; Cadmus: mythical Phoenician prince who slew a dragon and scattered its teeth on the ground, from which an army rose up; Copernicus: Polish astronomer Nicolaus Copernicus (1473–1543), who discovered that the sun, not Earth, was the center of the planetary system; Fust: Johann Fust, German printer (1400?–?1466) associated with the invention of movable type; Fulton: American inventor Robert Fulton (1765–1815), who conceived plans for early steamboats.

this constructive tool-making efficiency, as if it adhered to the chemic atoms; as if the air he breathes were made of Vaucansons, Franklins, and Watts.[30]

Doubtless in every million there will be an astronomer, a mathematician, a comic poet, a mystic. No one can read the history of astronomy without perceiving that Copernicus, Newton, Laplace,[31] are not new men, or a new kind of men, but that Thales, Anaximenes, Hipparchus, Empedocles, Aristarchus, Pythagoras, Œnipodes[32] had anticipated them; each had the same tense geometrical brain, apt for the same vigorous computation and logic; a mind parallel to the movement of the world. The Roman mile probably rested on a measure of a degree of the meridian. Mahometan and Chinese know what we know of leap-year, of the Gregorian calendar, and of the precession of the equinoxes. As in every barrel of cowries brought to New Bedford there shall be one *orangia,*[33] so there will, in a dozen millions of Malays and Mahometans, be one or two astronomical skulls. In a large city, the most casual things, and things whose beauty lies in their casualty, are produced as punctually and to order as the baker's muffin for breakfast. Punch[34] makes exactly one capital joke a week; and the journals contrive to furnish one good piece of news every day.

And not less work the laws of repression, the penalities of violated functions. Famine, typhus, frost, war, suicide and effete races must be reckoned calculable parts of the system of the world.

These are pebbles from the mountain, hints of the terms by which our life is walled up, and which show a kind of mechanical exactness, as of a loom or mill in what we call casual or fortuitous events.

The force with which we resist these torrents of tendency looks so ridiculously inadequate that it amounts to little more than a criticism or protest made by a minority of one, under compulsion of millions. I seemed in the height of a tempest to see men overboard struggling in the waves, and driven about here and there. They glanced intelligently at each other, but 't was little they could do for one another; 't was much if each could keep afloat alone. Well, they had a right to their eye-beams, and all the rest was Fate.

We cannot trifle with this reality, this cropping-out in our planted gardens of the core of the world. No picture of life can have any veracity that does not admit the odious facts. A man's power is hooped in by a necessity which, by many experiments, he touches on every side until he learns its arc.

The element running through entire nature, which we popularly call Fate, is known to us as limitation. Whatever limits us we call Fate. If we are brute and

---

[30] I.e., men like French mathematician Jacques de Vaucanson (1709–1782), inventor of automata; American literary statesman and scientist Benjamin Franklin (1706–1790); and Scottish engineer James Watt (1736–1819), inventor of the modern steam engine.

[31] Copernicus: see footnote 29 above; Newton: English mathematician Sir Isaac Newton (1642–1727), who developed the theory of gravity; Laplace: French mathematician and astronomer Pierre Simon, marquis de Laplace (1749–1827).

[32] Thales: Greek philosopher and geometrician

(640?–546 B.C.) who believed in the roundness of the earth and held that the moon reflected the sun's rays; Anaximenes: Greek philosopher (sixth century B.C.) who proposed that air composes the soul; Hipparchus: Greek astronomer (second century B.C.); Pythagoras: Greek philosopher (sixth century B.C.) who was in contention with Oenopides of Chios concerning the discovery of the divergence of the ecliptic.

[33] Exquisite tropical seashell of the cowrie type.

[34] Satirical British weekly magazine.

barbarous, the fate takes a brute and dreadful shape. As we refine, our checks become finer. If we rise to spiritual culture, the antagonism takes a spiritual form. In the Hindoo fables, Vishnu follows Maya[35] through all her ascending changes, from insect and crawfish up to elephant; whatever form she took, he took the male form of that kind, until she became at last woman and goddess, and he a man and a god. The limitations refine as the soul purifies, but the ring of necessity is always perched at the top.

When the gods in the Norse heaven were unable to bind the Fenris Wolf[36] with steel or with weight of mountains,—the one he snapped and the other he spurned with his heel,—they put round his foot a limp band softer than silk or cobweb, and this held him; the more he spurned it the stiffer it drew. So soft and so stanch is the ring of Fate. Neither brandy, nor nectar, nor sulphuric ether, nor hell-fire, nor ichor,[37] nor poetry, nor genius, can get rid of this limp band. For if we give it the high sense in which the poets use it, even thought itself is not above Fate; that too must act according to eternal laws, and all that is wilful and fantastic in it is in opposition to its fundamental essence.

And last of all, high over thought, in the world of morals, Fate appears as vindicator, levelling the high, lifting the low, requiring justice in man, and always striking soon or late when justice is not done. What is useful will last, what is hurtful will sink. "The doer must suffer," said the Greeks; "you would soothe a Deity not to be soothed." "God himself cannot procure good for the wicked," said the Welsh triad. "God may consent, but only for a time," said the bard of Spain.[38] The limitation is impassable by any insight of man. In its last and loftiest ascensions, insight itself and the freedom of the will is one of its obedient members. But we must not run into generalizations too large, but show the natural bounds or essential distinctions, and seek to do justice to the other elements as well.

Thus we trace Fate in matter, mind, and morals; in race, in retardations of strata, and in thought and character as well. It is everywhere bound or limitation. But Fate has its lord; limitation its limits,—is different seen from above and from below, from within and from without. For though Fate is immense, so is Power, which is the other fact in the dual world, immense. If Fate follows and limits Power, Power attends and antagonizes Fate. We must respect Fate as natural history, but there is more than natural history. For who and what is this criticism that pries into the matter? Man is not order of nature, sack and sack, belly and members,[39] link in a chain, nor any ignominious baggage; but a stupendous antagonism, a dragging together of the poles of the Universe. He betrays his relation to what is below him,—thick-skulled, small-brained, fishy, quadrumanous,[40] quadruped ill-disguised, hardly escaped into biped,—and has paid for the new powers by loss of some of the old ones. But the lightning which explodes and fashions planets, maker of planets and suns, is in him. On one side elemental order, sandstone and granite, rock-ledges, peat-bog, forest, sea

---

[35] Vishnu: preserver of humankind in the Hindu divine trinity; Maya: Hindu goddess of illusion.

[36] In Norse mythology, a monster who was detained by fragile bindings and thus whose wrath seems imminent.

[37] The rarefied fluid in the veins of the gods.

[38] The source of these sayings is unidentified.

[39] See Shakespeare's *Coriolanus*, Act I, Sc. i, ll. 99–150.

[40] Possessing four feet with opposable first digits, as in primates other than humans.

and shore; and on the other part thought, the spirit which composes and decomposes nature,—here they are, side by side, god and devil, mind and matter, king and conspirator, belt and spasm, riding peacefully together in the eye and brain of every man.

Nor can he blink the freewill. To hazard the contradiction,—freedom is necessary. If you please to plant yourself on the side of Fate, and say, Fate is all; then we say, a part of Fate is the freedom of man. Forever wells up the impulse of choosing and acting in the soul. Intellect annuls Fate. So far as a man thinks, he is free. And though nothing is more disgusting than the crowing about liberty by slaves, as most men are, and the flippant mistaking for freedom of some paper preamble like a Declaration of Independence or the statute right to vote, by those who have never dared to think or to act,—yet it is wholesome to man to look not at Fate, but the other way: the practical view is the other. His sound relation to these facts is to use and command, not to cringe to them. "Look not on Nature, for her name is fatal," said the oracle. The too much contemplation of these limits induces meanness. They who talk much of destiny, their birth-star, etc., are in a lower dangerous plane, and invite the evils they fear.

I cited the instinctive and heroic races as proud believers in Destiny. They conspire with it; a loving resignation is with the event. But the dogma makes a different impression when it is held by the weak and lazy. 'T is weak and vicious people who cast the blame on Fate. The right use of Fate is to bring up our conduct to the loftiness of nature. Rude and invincible except by themselves are the elements. So let man be. Let him empty his breast of his windy conceits, and show his lordship by manners and deeds on the scale of nature. Let him hold his purpose as with the tug of gravitation. No power, no persuasion, no bribe shall make him give up his point. A man ought to compare advantageously with a river, an oak, or a mountain. He shall have not less the flow, the expansion, and the resistance of these.

'T is the best use of Fate to teach a fatal courage. Go face the fire at sea, or the cholera in your friend's house, or the burglar in your own, or what danger lies in the way of duty,—knowing you are guarded by the cherubim of Destiny. If you believe in Fate to your harm, believe it at least for your good.

For if Fate is so prevailing, man also is part of it, and can confront fate with fate. If the Universe have these savage accidents, our atoms are as savage in resistance. We should be crushed by the atmosphere, but for the reaction of the air within the body. A tube made of a film of glass can resist the shock of the ocean if filled with the same water. If there be omnipotence in the stroke, there is omnipotence of recoil.

1. But Fate against Fate is only parrying and defence: there are also the noble creative forces. The revelation of Thought takes man out of servitude into freedom. We rightly say of ourselves, we were born and afterward we were born again, and many times. We have successive experiences so important that the new forgets the old, and hence the mythology of the seven or the nine heavens. The day of days, the great day of the feast of life, is that in which the inward eye opens to the Unity in things, to the omnipresence of law:—sees that what is must be and ought to be, or is the best. This beatitude dips from on high down on us and we see. It is not in us so much as we are in it. If the air come to our lungs, we breathe and live; if not,

we die. If the light come to our eyes, we see; else not. And if truth come to our mind we suddenly expand to its dimensions, as if we grew to worlds. We are as lawgivers; we speak for Nature; we prophesy and divine.

This insight throws us on the party and interest of the Universe, against all and sundry; against ourselves as much as others. A man speaking from insight affirms of himself what is true of the mind: seeing its immortality, he says, I am immortal; seeing its invincibility, he says, I am strong. It is not in us, but we are in it. It is of the maker, not of what is made. All things are touched and changed by it. This uses and is not used. It distances those who share it from those who share it not. Those who share it not are flocks and herds. It dates from itself; not from former men or better men, gospel, or constitution, or college, or custom. Where it shines, Nature is no longer intrusive, but all things make a musical or pictorial impression. The world of men show like a comedy without laughter: populations, interests, government, history; 't is all toy figures in a toy house. It does not overvalue particular truths. We hear eagerly every thought and word quoted from an intellectual man. But in his presence our own mind is roused to activity, and we forget very fast what he says, much more interested in the new play of our own thought than in any thought of his. 'T is the majesty into which we have suddenly mounted, the impersonality, the scorn of egotisms, the sphere of laws, that engage us. Once we were stepping a little this way and a little that way; now we are as men in a balloon, and do not think so much of the point we have left, or the point we would make, as of the liberty and glory of the way.

Just as much intellect as you add, so much organic power. He who sees through the design, presides over it, and must will that which must be. We sit and rule, and, though we sleep, our dream will come to pass. Our thought, though it were only an hour old, affirms an oldest necessity, not to be separated from thought, and not to be separated from will. They must always have coexisted. It apprises us of its sovereignty and godhead, which refuse to be severed from it. It is not mine or thine, but the will of all mind. It is poured into the souls of all men, as the soul itself which constitutes them men. I know not whether there be, as is alleged, in the upper region of our atmosphere, a permanent westerly current which carries with it all atoms which rise to that height, but I see that when souls reach a certain clearness of perception they accept a knowledge and motive above selfishness. A breath of will blows eternally through the universe of souls in the direction of the Right and Necessary. It is the air which all intellects inhale and exhale, and it is the wind which blows the worlds into order and orbit.

Thought dissolves the material universe by carrying the mind up into a sphere where all is plastic. Of two men, each obeying his own thought, he whose thought is deepest will be the strongest character. Always one man more than another represents the will of Divine Providence to the period.

2. If thought makes free, so does the moral sentiment. The mixtures of spiritual chemistry refuse to be analyzed. Yet we can see that with the perception of truth is joined the desire that it shall prevail; that affection is essential to will. Moreover, when a strong will appears, it usually results from a certain unity of organization, as if the whole energy of body and mind flowed in one direction. All great force is real and

elemental. There is no manufacturing a strong will. There must be a pound to balance a pound. Where power is shown in will, it must rest on the universal force. Alaric[41] and Bonaparte must believe they rest on a truth, or their will can be bought or bent. There is a bribe possible for any finite will. But the pure sympathy with universal ends is an infinite force, and cannot be bribed or bent. Whoever has had experience of the moral sentiment cannot choose but believe in unlimited power. Each pulse from that heart is an oath from the Most High. I know not what the word *sublime* means, if it be not the intimations, in this infant, of a terrific force. A text of heroism, a name and anecdote of courage, are not arguments but sallies of freedom. One of these is the verse of the Persian Hafiz,[42] " 'T is written on the gate of Heaven, 'Woe unto him who suffers himself to be betrayed by Fate!' " Does the reading of history make us fatalists? What courage does not the opposite opinion show! A little whim of will to be free gallantly contending against the universe of chemistry.

But insight is not will, nor is affection will. Perception is cold, and goodness dies in wishes. As Voltaire[43] said, 't is the misfortune of worthy people that they are cowards; "un des plus grands malheurs des honnêtes gens c'est qu'ils sont des lâches." There must be a fusion of these two to generate the energy of will. There can be no driving force except through the conversion of the man into his will, making him the will, and the will him. And one may say boldly that no man has a right perception of any truth who has not been reacted on by it so as to be ready to be its martyr.

The one serious and formidable thing in nature is a will. Society is servile from want of will, and therefore the world wants saviours and religions. One way is right to go; the hero sees it, and moves on that aim, and has the world under him for root and support. He is to others as the world. His approbation is honor; his dissent, infamy. The glance of his eye has the force of sunbeams. A personal influence towers up in memory only worthy, and we gladly forget numbers, money, climate, gravitation, and the rest of Fate.

We can afford to allow the limitation, if we know it is the meter of the growing man. We stand against Fate, as children stand up against the wall in their father's house and notch their height from year to year. But when the boy grows to man, and is master of the house, he pulls down that wall and builds a new and bigger. 'T is only a question of time. Every brave youth is in training to ride and rule this dragon. His science is to make weapons and wings of these passions and retarding forces. Now whether, seeing these two things, fate and power, we are permitted to believe in unity? The bulk of mankind believe in two gods. They are under one dominion here in the house, as friend and parent, in social circles, in letters, in art, in love, in religion; but in mechanics, in dealing with steam and climate, in trade, in politics, they think they come under another; and that it would be a practical blunder to transfer the method and way of working of one sphere into the other. What good, honest, generous men at home, will be wolves and foxes on 'Change![44] What pious men in the parlor will vote for what reprobates at the polls! To a certain point, they believe themselves the

---

[41] King of the Visigoths and conquerer (in 410) of Rome (370?–410).
[42] Fourteenth-century Persian poet.

[43] Pseudonym for the French writer François Marie Arouet (1694–1778).
[44] The stock exchange.

care of a Providence. But in a steamboat, in an epidemic, in war, they believe a malignant energy rules.

But relation and connection are not somewhere and sometimes, but everywhere and always. The divine order does not stop where their sight stops. The friendly power works on the same rules in the next farm and the next planet. But where they have not experience they run against it and hurt themselves. Fate then is a name for facts not yet passed under the fire of thought; for causes which are unpenetrated.

But every jet of chaos which threatens to exterminate us is convertible by intellect into wholesome force. Fate is unpenetrated causes. The water drowns ship and sailor like a grain of dust. But learn to swim, trim your bark, and the wave which drowned it will be cloven by it and carry it like its own foam, a plume and a power. The cold is inconsiderate of persons, tingles your blood, freezes a man like a dew-drop. But learn to skate, and the ice will give you a graceful, sweet, and poetic motion. The cold will brace your limbs and brain to genius, and make you foremost men of time. Cold and sea will train an imperial Saxon race, which nature cannot bear to lose, and after cooping it up for a thousand years in yonder England, gives a hundred Englands, a hundred Mexicos. All the bloods it shall absorb and domineer: and more than Mexicos, the secrets of water and steam, the spasms of electricity, the ductility of metals, the chariot of the air, the ruddered balloon are awaiting you.

The annual slaughter from typhus far exceeds that of war; but right drainage destroys typhus. The plague in the sea-service from scurvy is healed by lemon juice and other diets portable or procurable; the depopulation by cholera and small-pox is ended by drainage and vaccination; and every other pest is not less in the chain of cause and effect, and may be fought off. And whilst art draws out the venom, it commonly extorts some benefit from the vanquished enemy. The mischievous torrent is taught to drudge for man; the wild beasts he makes useful for food, or dress, or labor; the chemic explosions are controlled like his watch. These are now the steeds on which he rides. Man moves in all modes, by legs of horses, by wings of wind, by steam, by gas of balloon, by electricity, and stands on tiptoe threatening to hunt the eagle in his own element. There's nothing he will not make his carrier.

Steam was till the other day the devil which we dreaded. Every pot made by any human potter or brazier had a hole in its cover, to let off the enemy, lest he should lift pot and roof and carry the house away. But the Marquis of Worcester,[45] Watt, and Fulton bethought themselves that where was power was not devil, but was God; that it must be availed of, and not by any means let off and wasted. Could he lift pots and roofs and houses so handily? He was the workman they were in search of. He could be used to lift away, chain and compel other devils far more reluctant and dangerous, namely, cubic miles of earth, mountains, weight or resistance of water, machinery, and the labors of all men in the world; and time he shall lengthen, and shorten space.

It has not fared much otherwise with higher kinds of steam. The opinion of the

[45] Edward Somerset, marquis of Worcester (1601–1667), eager student of mechanics and author of a book describing a machine akin to the steam engine.

million was the terror of the world, and it was attempted either to dissipate it, by amusing nations, or to pile it over with strata of society,—a layer of soldiers, over that a layer of lords, and a king on the top; with clamps and hoops of castles, garrisons, and police. But sometimes the religious principle would get in and burst the hoops and rive every mountain laid on top of it. The Fultons and Watts of politics, believing in unity, saw that it was a power, and by satisfying it (as justice satisfies everybody), through a different disposition of society,—grouping it on a level instead of piling it into a mountain,—they have contrived to make of this terror the most harmless and energetic form of a State.

Very odious, I confess, are the lessons of Fate. Who likes to have a dapper phrenologist pronouncing on his fortunes? Who likes to believe that he has, hidden in his skull, spine, and pelvis, all the vices of a Saxon or Celtic race, which will be sure to pull him down,—with what grandeur of hope and resolve he is fired,—into a selfish, huckstering, servile, dodging animal? A learned physician tells us the fact is invariable with the Neapolitan, that when mature he assumes the forms of the unmistakable scoundrel. That is a little overstated,—but may pass.

But these are magazines[46] and arsenals. A man must thank his defects, and stand in some terror of his talents. A transcendent talent draws so largely on his forces as to lame him; a defect pays him revenues on the other side. The sufferance which is the badge of the Jew, has made him, in these days, the ruler of the rulers of the earth.[47] If Fate is ore and quarry, if evil is good in the making, if limitation is power that shall be, if calamities, oppositions, and weights are wings and means,—we are reconciled.

Fate involves the melioration. No statement of the Universe can have any soundness which does not admit its ascending effort. The direction of the whole and of the parts is toward benefit, and in proportion to the health. Behind every individual closes organization; before him opens liberty,—the Better, the Best. The first and worse races are dead. The second and imperfect races are dying out, or remain for the maturing of higher. In the latest race, in man, every generosity, every new perception, the love and praise he extorts from his fellows, are certificates of advance out of fate into freedom. Liberation of the will from the sheaths and clogs of organization which he has outgrown, is the end and aim of this world. Every calamity is a spur and valuable hint; and where his endeavors do not yet fully avail, they tell as tendency. The whole circle of animal life—tooth against tooth, devouring war, war for food, a yelp of pain and a grunt of triumph, until at last the whole menagerie, the whole chemical mass is mellowed and refined for higher use—pleases at a sufficient perspective.

But to see how fate slides into freedom and freedom into fate, observe how far the roots of every creature run, or find if you can a point where there is no thread of connection. Our life is consentaneous and far-related. This knot of nature is so well tied that nobody was ever cunning enough to find the two ends. Nature is intricate, overlapped, interweaved and endless. Christopher Wren[48] said of the beautiful King's College chapel, that "if anybody would tell him where to lay the first stone, he would

---

[46] Storehouses.
[47] I.e., by dominating certain banks.
[48] English architect (1632–1723) who designed the renowned King's College Chapel at Cambridge University.

build such another." But where shall we find the first atom in this house of man, which is all consent, inosculation and balance of parts?

The web of relation is shown in *habitat,* shown in hibernation. When hibernation was observed, it was found that whilst some animals became torpid in winter, others were torpid in summer: hibernation then was a false name. The *long sleep* is not an effect of cold, but is regulated by the supply of food proper to the animal. It becomes torpid when the fruit or prey it lives on is not in season, and regains its activity when its food is ready.

Eyes are found in light; ears in auricular air; feet on land; fins in water; wings in air; and each creature where it was meant to be, with a mutual fitness. Every zone has its own *Fauna.* There is adjustment between the animal and its food, its parasite, its enemy. Balances are kept. It is not allowed to diminish in numbers, nor to exceed. The like adjustments exist for man. His food is cooked when he arrives; his coal in the pit; the house ventilated; the mud of the deluge dried; his companions arrived at the same hour, and awaiting him with love, concert, laughter and tears. These are coarse adjustments, but the invisible are not less. There are more belongings to every creature than his air and his food. His instincts must be met, and he has predisposing power that bends and fits what is near him to his use. He is not possible until the invisible things are right for him, as well as the visible. Of what changes then in sky and earth, and in finer skies and earths, does the appearance of some Dante[49] or Columbus apprise us!

How is this effected? Nature is no spendthrift, but takes the shortest way to her ends. As the general says to his soldiers, "If you want a fort, build a fort," so nature makes every creature do its own work and get its living,—is it planet, animal or tree. The planet makes itself. The animal cell makes itself;—then, what it wants. Every creature, wren or dragon, shall make its own lair. As soon as there is life, there is self-direction and absorbing and using of material. Life is freedom,—life in the direct ratio of its amount. You may be sure the new-born man is not inert. Life works both voluntarily and supernaturally in its neighborhood. Do you suppose he can be estimated by his weight in pounds, or that he is contained in his skin,—this reaching, radiating, jaculating[50] fellow? The smallest candle fills a mile with its rays, and the papillæ of a man run out to every star.

When there is something to be done, the world knows how to get it done. The vegetable eye makes leaf, pericarp, root, bark, or thorn, as the need is; the first cell converts itself into stomach, mouth, nose, or nail, according to the want; the world throws its life into a hero or a shepherd, and puts him where he is wanted. Dante and Columbus were Italians, in their time; they would be Russians or Americans to-day. Things ripen, new men come. The adaptation is not capricious. The ulterior aim, the purpose beyond itself, the correlation by which planets subside and crystallize, then animate beasts and men,—will not stop but will work into finer particulars, and from finer to finest.

The secret of the world is the tie between person and event. Person makes event, and event person. The "times," "the age," what is that but a few profound persons and a few active persons who epitomize the times?—Goethe, Hegel, Metternich,

[49] Italian poet Dante Alighieri (1265–1321), author of the *Divine Comedy.*   [50] Propelling.

Adams, Calhoun, Guizot, Peel, Cobden, Kossuth, Rothschild, Astor, Brunel,[51] and the rest. The same fitness must be presumed between a man and the time and event, as between the sexes, or between a race of animals and the food it eats, or the inferior races it uses. He thinks his fate alien, because the copula is hidden. But the soul contains the event that shall befall it; for the event is only the actualization of its thoughts, and what we pray to ourselves for is always granted. The event is the print of your form. It fits you like your skin. What each does is proper to him. Events are the children of his body and mind. We learn that the soul of Fate is the soul of us, as Hafiz[52] sings,—

> "Alas! till now I had not known,
> My guide and fortune's guide are one."

All the toys that infatuate men and which they play for,—houses, land, money, luxury, power, fame, are the selfsame thing, with a new gauze or two of illusion overlaid. And of all the drums and rattles by which men are made willing to have their heads broke, and are led out solemnly every morning to parade,—the most admirable is this by which we are brought to believe that events are arbitrary and independent of actions. At the conjuror's, we detect the hair by which he moves his puppet, but we have not eyes sharp enough to descry the thread that ties cause and effect.

Nature magically suits the man to his fortunes, by making these the fruit of his character. Ducks take to the water, eagles to the sky, waders to the sea margin, hunters to the forest, clerks to counting-rooms, soldiers to the frontier. Thus events grow on the same stem with persons; are sub-persons. The pleasure of life is according to the man that lives it, and not according to the work or the place. Life is an ecstasy. We know what madness belongs to love,—what power to paint a vile object in hues of heaven. As insane persons are indifferent to their dress, diet, and other accommodations, and as we do in dreams, with equanimity, the most absurd acts, so a drop more of wine in our cup of life will reconcile us to strange company and work. Each creature puts forth from itself its own condition and sphere, as the slug sweats out its slimy house on the pear-leaf, and the woolly aphides on the apple perspire their own bed, and the fish its shell. In youth we clothe ourselves with rainbows and go as brave as the zodiac. In age we put out another sort of perspiration,—gout, fever, rheumatism, caprice, doubt, fretting and avarice.

[51] Goethe: German dramatist and poet Johann Wolfgang von Goethe (1749–1832); Hegel: German philosopher George Wilhelm Friedrich Hegel (1770–1831); Metternich: Austrian statesman Prince Kemens von Metternich (1773–1859); Adams: second president of the United States, John Adams (1735–1826); Calhoun: vice-president of the United States (1825–1832), John C. Calhoun (1782–1850); Guizot: French statesman and historian François Guizot (1787–1874); Peel: British prime minister (1834–1835 and 1841–1846) Robert Peel (1788–1850); Cobden: British economist and politician Richard Cobden (1804–1865); Kossuth: see footnote 20 above; Rothschild: German-Jewish banker Meyer Rothschild (1743–1812); Astor: American fur trader John Jacob Astor (1763–1848); Brunel: Isambard Brunel (1806–1859), designer of the first Atlantic steamer.

[52] See footnote 42.

A man's fortunes are the fruit of his character. A man's friends are his magnetisms. We go to Herodotus and Plutarch[53] for examples of Fate; but we are examples. *"Quisque suos patimur manes."*[54] The tendency of every man to enact all that is in his constitution is expressed in the old belief that the efforts which we make to escape from our destiny only serve to lead us into it: and I have noticed a man likes better to be complimented on his position, as the proof of the last or total excellence, than on his merits.

A man will see his character emitted in the events that seem to meet, but which exude from and accompany him. Events expand with the character. As once he found himself among toys, so now he plays a part in colossal systems, and his growth is declared in his ambition, his companions and his performance. He looks like a piece of luck, but is a piece of causation; the mosaic, angulated and ground to fit into the gap he fills. Hence in each town there is some man who is, in his brain and performance, an explanation of the tillage, production, factories, banks, churches, ways of living and society of that town. If you do not chance to meet him, all that you see will leave you a little puzzled; if you see him it will become plain. We know in Massachusetts who built New Bedford, who built Lynn, Lowell, Lawrence, Clinton, Fitchburg, Holyoke, Portland, and many another noisy mart. Each of these men, if they were transparent, would seem to you not so much men as walking cities, and wherever you put them they would build one.

History is the action and reaction of these two,—Nature and Thought; two boys pushing each other on the curbstone of the pavement. Everything is pusher or pushed; and matter and mind are in perpetual tilt and balance, so. Whilst the man is weak, the earth takes up him. He plants his brain and affections. By and by he will take up the earth, and have his gardens and vineyards in the beautiful order and productiveness of his thought. Every solid in the universe is ready to become fluid on the approach of the mind, and the power to flux it is the measure of the mind. If the wall remain adamant, it accuses the want of thought. To a subtle force it will stream into new forms, expressive of the character of the mind. What is the city in which we sit here, but an aggregate of incongruous materials which have obeyed the will of some man? The granite was reluctant, but his hands were stronger, and it came. Iron was deep in the ground and well combined with stone, but could not hide from his fires. Wood, lime, stuffs, fruits, gums, were dispersed over the earth and sea, in vain. Here they are, within reach of every man's day-labor,—what he wants of them. The whole world is the flux of matter over the wires of thought to the poles or points where it would build. The races of men rise out of the ground preoccupied with a thought which rules them, and divided into parties ready armed and angry to fight for this metaphysical abstraction. The quality of the thought differences the Egyptian and the Roman, the Austrian and the American. The men who come on the stage at one period are all found to be related to each other. Certain ideas are in the air. We are all impressionable, for we are made of them; all impressionable, but some more than others, and these first express them. This explains the curious contemporaneousness of

---

[53] Herodotus: Greek historian (fifth century B.C.); Plutarch: Greek biographer (A.D. 46?–?120).   [54] Virgil's *Aeneid,* VI, 743: "Each person undergoes his special penalty."

inventions and discoveries. The truth is in the air, and the most impressionable brain will announce it first, but all will announce it a few minutes later. So women, as most susceptible, are the best index of the coming hour. So the great man, that is, the man most imbued with the spirit of the time, is the impressionable man;—of a fibre irritable and delicate, like iodine to light. He feels the infinitesimal attractions. His mind is righter than others because he yields to a current so feeble as can be felt only by a needle delicately poised.

The correlation is shown in defects. Möller,[55] in his Essay on Architecture, taught that the building which was fitted accurately to answer its end would turn out to be beautiful though beauty had not been intended. I find the like unity in human structures rather virulent and pervasive; that a crudity in the blood will appear in the argument; a hump in the shoulder will appear in the speech and handiwork. If his mind could be seen, the hump would be seen. If a man has a see-saw in his voice, it will run into his sentences, into his poem, into the structure of his fable, into his speculation, into his charity. And as every man is hunted by his own dæmon, vexed by his own disease, this checks all his activity.

So each man, like each plant, has his parasites. A strong, astringent, bilious nature has more truculent enemies than the slugs and moths that fret my leaves. Such an one has curculios, borers, knife-worms; a swindler ate him first, then a client, then a quack, then smooth, plausible gentlemen, bitter and selfish as Moloch.[56]

This correlation really existing can be divined. If the threads are there, thought can follow and show them. Especially when a soul is quick and docile, as Chaucer sings:—

"Or if the soule of proper kind
Be so parfite as men find,
That it wot what is to come,
And that he warneth all and some
Of everiche of hir aventures,
By avisions or figures;
But that our flesh hath no might
To understand it aright
For it is warned too derkely."[57]

Some people are made up of rhyme, coincidence, omen, periodicity, and presage: they meet the person they seek; what their companion prepares to say to them, they first say to him; and a hundred signs apprise them of what is about to befall.

Wonderful intricacy in the web, wonderful constancy in the design this vagabond life admits. We wonder how the fly finds its mate, and yet year after year, we find two men, two women, without legal or carnal tie, spend a great part of their best time within a few feet of each other. And the moral is that what we seek we shall

---

[55] German architect Georg Möller (1784–1852), author of *Essay on the Origin and Progress of Gothic Architecture* (1825).

[56] Mythical Phoenician god to whom children were sacrificed by fire.

[57] From Geoffrey Chaucer's "The House of Fame," ll. 43–51.

find;[58] what we flee from flees from us; as Goethe said, "what we wish for in youth, comes in heaps on us in old age,"[59] too often cursed with the granting of our prayer: and hence the high caution, that since we are sure of having what we wish, we beware to ask only for high things.

One key, one solution to the mysteries of human condition, one solution to the old knots of fate, freedom, and foreknowledge, exists; the propounding, namely, of the double consciousness. A man must ride alternately on the horses of his private and his public nature as the equestrians in the circus throw themselves nimbly from horse to horse, or plant one foot on the back of one and the other foot on the back of the other. So when a man is the victim of his fate, has sciatica in his loins and cramp in his mind; a club-foot and a club in his wit; a sour face and a selfish temper; a strut in his gait and a conceit in his affection; or is ground to powder by the vice of his race;—he is to rally on his relation to the Universe, which his ruin benefits. Leaving the dæmon who suffers, he is to take sides with the Deity who secures universal benefit by his pain.

To offset the drag of temperament and race, which pulls down, learn this lesson, namely, that by the cunning co-presence of two elements, which is throughout nature, whatever lames or paralyzes you draws in with it the divinity, in some form, to repay. A good intention clothes itself with sudden power. When a god wishes to ride, any chip or pebble will bud and shoot out winged feet and serve him for a horse.

Let us build altars to the Blessed Unity which holds nature and souls in perfect solution, and compels every atom to serve an universal end. I do not wonder at a snow-flake, a shell, a summer landscape, or the glory of the stars; but at the necessity of beauty under which the universe lies; that all is and must be pictorial; that the rainbow and the curve of the horizon and the arch of the blue vault are only results from the organism of the eye. There is no need for foolish amateurs to fetch me to admire a garden of flowers, or a sun-gilt cloud, or a waterfall, when I cannot look without seeing splendor and grace. How idle to choose a random sparkle here or there, when the indwelling necessity plants the rose of beauty on the brow of chaos, and discloses the central intention of Nature to be harmony and joy.

Let us build altars to the Beautiful Necessity. If we thought men were free in the sense that in a single exception one fantastical will could prevail over the law of things, it were all one as if a child's hand could pull down the sun. If in the least particular one could derange the order of nature,—who would accept the gift of life?

Let us build altars to the Beautiful Necessity, which secures that all is made of one piece; that plaintiff and defendant, friend and enemy, animal and planet, food and eater are of one kind. In astronomy is vast space but no foreign system; in geology, vast time but the same laws as to-day. Why should we be afraid of Nature, which is no other than "philosophy and theology embodied"? Why should we fear to be crushed by savage elements, we who are made up of the same elements? Let us build to the Beautiful Necessity, which makes man brave in believing that he cannot shun a danger that is appointed, nor incur one that is not; to the Necessity which rudely or softly

---

[58] Paraphrase of Matthew 7:7.
[59] From Goethe's epigraph to the second section of *Poetry and Truth*.

educates him to the perception that there are no contingencies; that Law rules throughout existence; a Law which is not intelligent but intelligence;—not personal nor impersonal—it disdains words and passes understanding; it dissolves persons; it vivifies nature; yet solicits the pure in heart to draw on all its omnipotence.

1860

Illusions

Flow, flow the waves hated,
Accursed, adored,
The waves of mutation:
No anchorage is.
Sleep is not, death is not;
Who seem to die live.
House you were born in,
Friends of your spring-time,
Old man and young maid,
Day's toil and its guerdon,
They are all vanishing,
Fleeing to fables,
Cannot be moored.
See the stars through them,
Through treacherous marbles.
Know, the stars yonder,
The stars everlasting,
Are fugitive also,
And emulate, vaulted,
The lambent heat-lightning,
And fire-fly's flight.

When thou dost return
On the wave's circulation,
Beholding the shimmer,
The wild dissipation,
And, out of endeavor
To change and to flow,
The gas become solid,
And phantoms and nothings
Return to be things,
And endless imbroglio
Is law and the world,—
Then first shalt thou know,
That in the wild turmoil,
Horsed on the Proteus,
Thou ridest to power,
And to endurance.

Some years ago, in company with an agreeable party, I spent a long summer day in exploring the Mammoth Cave in Kentucky. We traversed, through spacious galleries affording a solid masonry foundation for the town and county overhead, the six or eight black miles from the mouth of the cavern to the innermost recess which tourists visit,—a niche or grotto made of one seamless stalactite, and called, I believe, Serena's Bower. I lost the light of one day. I saw high domes and bottomless pits; heard the voice of unseen waterfalls; paddled three quarters of a mile in the deep Echo River, whose waters are peopled with the blind fish; crossed the streams "Lethe" and "Styx;" plied with music and guns the echoes in these alarming galleries; saw every form of stalagmite and stalactite in the sculptured and fretted chambers;—icicle, orange-flower, acanthus, grapes and snowball. We shot Bengal lights into the vaults and groins of the sparry cathedrals and examined all the masterpieces which the four combined engineers, water, limestone, gravitation and time, could make in the dark.

The mysteries and scenery of the cave had the same dignity that belongs to all natural objects, and which shames the fine things to which we foppishly compare them. I remarked especially the mimetic habit with which nature, on new instruments, hums her old tunes, making night to mimic day, and chemistry to ape vegetation. But I then took notice and still chiefly remember that the best thing which the cave had to offer was an illusion. On arriving at what is called the "Star-Chamber," our lamps were taken from us by the guide and extinguished or put aside, and, on looking upwards, I saw or seemed to see the night heaven thick with stars glimmering more or less brightly over our heads, and even what seemed a comet flaming among them. All the party were touched with astonishment and pleasure. Our musical friends sung with much feeling a pretty song, "The stars are in the quiet sky," etc., and I sat down on the rocky floor to enjoy the serene picture. Some crystal specks in the black ceiling high overhead, reflecting the light of a half-hid lamp, yielded this magnificent effect.

I own I did not like the cave so well for eking out its sublimities with this theatrical trick. But I have had many experiences like it, before and since; and we must be content to be pleased without too curiously analyzing the occasions. Our conversation with nature is not just what it seems. The cloud-rack, the sunrise and sunset glories, rainbows and Northern Lights are not quite so spheral as our childhood thought them, and the part our organization plays in them is too large. The senses interfere everywhere and mix their own structure with all they report of. Once we fancied the earth a plane, and stationary. In admiring the sunset we do not yet deduct the rounding, coördinating, pictorial powers of the eye.

The same interference from our organization creates the most of our pleasure and pain. Our first mistake is the belief that the circumstance gives the joy which we give to the circumstance. Life is an ecstasy. Life is sweet as nitrous oxide; and the fisherman dripping all day over a cold pond, the switchman at the railway intersection, the farmer in the field, the negro in the rice-swamp, the fop in the street, the hunter in the woods, the barrister with the jury, the belle at the ball, all ascribe a certain pleasure to their employment, which they themselves give it. Health and appetite impart the sweetness to sugar, bread and meat. We fancy that our civilization has got on far, but we still come back to our primers.

We live by our imaginations, by our admirations, by our sentiments. The child walks amid heaps of illusions, which he does not like to have disturbed. The boy, how sweet to him is his fancy! how dear the story of barons and battles! What a hero he is, whilst he feeds on his heroes! What a debt is his to imaginative books! He has no better friend or influence than Scott, Shakspeare, Plutarch and Homer.[1] The man lives to other objects, but who dare affirm that they are more real? Even the prose of the streets is full of refractions. In the life of the dreariest alderman, fancy enters into all details and colors them with rosy hue. He imitates the air and actions of people whom he admires, and is raised in his own eyes. He pays a debt quicker to a rich man than to a poor man. He wishes the bow and compliment of some leader in the state or in society; weighs what he says; perhaps he never comes nearer to him for that, but dies at last better contented for this amusement of his eyes and his fancy.

The world rolls, the din of life is never hushed. In London, in Paris, in Boston, in San Francisco, the carnival, the masquerade is at its height. Nobody drops his domino. The unities, the fictions of the piece it would be an impertinence to break. The chapter of fascinations is very long. Great is paint; nay, God is the painter; and we rightly accuse the critic who destroys too many illusions. Society does not love its unmaskers. It was wittily if somewhat bitterly said by D'Alembert,[2] *"qu'un état de vapeur était un état très fâcheux, parcequ'il nous faisait voir les choses comme elles sont."*[3] I find men victims of illusion in all parts of life. Children, youths, adults and old men, all are led by one bawble or another. Yoganidra, the goddess of illusion, Proteus, or Momus, or Gylfi's Mocking,[4]—for the Power has many names,—is stronger than the Titans, stronger than Apollo. Few have overheard the gods or surprised their secret. Life is a succession of lessons which must be lived to be understood. All is riddle, and the key to a riddle is another riddle. There are as many pillows of illusion as flakes in a snow-storm. We wake from one dream into another dream. The toys to be sure are various, and are graduated in refinement to the quality of the dupe. The intellectual man requires a fine bait; the sots are easily amused. But everybody is drugged with his own frenzy, and the pageant marches at all hours, with music and banner and badge.

Amid the joyous troop who give in to the charivari, comes now and then a sad-eyed boy whose eyes lack the requisite refractions to clothe the show in due glory, and who is afflicted with a tendency to trace home the glittering miscellany of fruits and flowers to one root. Science is a search after identity, and the scientific whim is lurking in all corners. At the State Fair a friend of mine complained that all the varieties of fancy pears in our orchards seem to have been selected by somebody who had a whim for a particular kind of pear, and only cultivated such as had that perfume; they were all alike. And I remember the quarrel of another youth with the confectioners, that when he racked his wit to choose the best comfits in the shops, in all the endless varieties of sweetmeat he could find only three flavors, or two. What then? Pears and cakes are good for something; and because you unluckily have an eye or nose too keen, why need you spoil the comfort which the rest of us find in them? I knew a humorist who in a good deal of rattle had a grain or two of sense. He shocked the company

---

[1] Scott: Sir Walter Scott (1771–1832), Scottish writer; Plutarch: Greek biographer of the first century A.D.; Homer: author (fl. 850? B.C.) of ancient Greek poems the *Iliad* and the *Odyssey*.
[2] French mathematician and philosopher Jean le Rond D'Alembert (1717?–1783).
[3] French: "that vertigo was distressing because it induced an actual perception of reality."

[4] Yoganidra: another name for Durga, meaning literally "sleep in the form of time"; Proteus: Greek god of the sea who could transform his appearance; Momus: Greek god of mockery and accusation; Gylfi: Swedish king renowned for guile and magic.

by maintaining that the attributes of God were two,—power and risibility, and that it was the duty of every pious man to keep up the comedy. And I have known gentlemen of great stake in the community, but whose sympathies were cold,—presidents of colleges and governors and senators,—who held themselves bound to sign every temperance pledge, and act with Bible societies and missions and peace-makers, and cry *Hist-a-boy!*[5] to every good dog. We must not carry comity too far, but we all have kind impulses in this direction. When the boys come into my yard for leave to gather horse-chestnuts, I own I enter into nature's game, and affect to grant the permission reluctantly, fearing that any moment they will find out the imposture of that showy chaff. But this tenderness is quite unnecessary; the enchantments are laid on very thick. Their young life is thatched with them. Bare and grim to tears is the lot of the children in the hovel I saw yesterday; yet not the less they hung it round with frippery romance, like the children of the happiest fortune, and talked of "the dear cottage where so many joyful hours had flown." Well, this thatching of hovels is the custom of the country. Women, more than all, are the element and kingdom of illusion. Being fascinated, they fascinate. They see through Claude-Lorraines.[6] And how dare any one, if he could, pluck away the *coulisses,* stage effects and ceremonies, by which they live? Too pathetic, too pitiable, is the region of affection, and its atmosphere always liable to *mirage.*

We are not very much to blame for our bad marriages. We live amid hallucinations; and this especial trap is laid to trip up our feet with, and all are tripped up first or last. But the mighty Mother who had been so sly with us, as if she felt that she owed us some indemnity, insinuates into the Pandora-box of marriage some deep and serious benefits and some great joys. We find a delight in the beauty and happiness of children that makes the heart too big for the body. In the worst-assorted connections there is ever some mixture of true marriage. Teague[7] and his jade get some just relations of mutual respect, kindly observation, and fostering of each other; learn something, and would carry themselves wiselier if they were now to begin.

'T is fine for us to point at one or another fine madman, as if there were any exempts. The scholar in his library is none. I, who have all my life heard any number of orations and debates, read poems and miscellaneous books, conversed with many geniuses, am still the victim of any new page; and if Marmaduke, or Hugh, or Moosehead,[8] or any other, invent a new style or mythology, I fancy that the world will be all brave and right if dressed in these colors, which I had not thought of. Then at once I will daub with this new paint; but it will not stick. 'T is like the cement which the peddler sells at the door; he makes broken crockery hold with it, but you can never buy of him a bit of the cement which will make it hold when he is gone.

Men who make themselves felt in the world avail themselves of a certain fate in their constitution which they know how to use. But they never deeply interest us unless they lift a corner of the curtain, or betray, never so slightly, their penetration of what is behind it. 'T is the charm of practical men that outside of their practicality are a certain poetry and play, as if they led the good horse Power by the bridle, and

---

[5] Exclamation used to urge an animal on.
[6] Claude Lorrain (1600–1682), French landscape painter.
[7] American deprecatory colloquialism for a lower-class Irishman; the term is derived from a character in the American novel *Modern Chivalry* (1792–1815) by H. H. Brackenridge (1748–1816).
[8] Marmaduke, . . . Moosehead: whimsical alternative to "Tom, Dick, and Harry."

preferred to walk, though they can ride so fiercely. Bonaparte is intellectual, as well as Cæsar; and the best soldiers, sea-captains and railway men have a gentleness when off duty, a good-natured admission that there are illusions, and who shall say that he is not their sport? We stigmatize the cast-iron fellows who cannot so detach themselves, as "dragon-ridden," "thunder-stricken," and fools of fate, with whatever powers endowed.

Since our tuition is through emblems and indirections, it is well to know that there is method in it, a fixed scale and rank above rank in the phantasms. We begin low with coarse masks and rise to the most subtle and beautiful. The red men told Columbus "they had an herb which took away fatigue;" but he found the illusion of "arriving from the east at the Indies" more composing to his lofty spirit than any tobacco. Is not our faith in the impenetrability of matter more sedative than narcotics? You play with jackstraws, balls, bowls, horse and gun, estates and politics; but there are finer games before you. Is not time a pretty toy? Life will show you masks that are worth all your carnivals. Yonder mountain must migrate into your mind. The fine star-dust and nebulous blur in Orion, "the portentous year of Mizar and Alcor," must come down and be dealt with in your household thought. What if you shall come to discern that the play and playground of all this pompous history are radiations from yourself, and that the sun borrows his beams? What terrible questions we are learning to ask! The former men believed in magic, by which temples, cities and men were swallowed up, and all trace of them gone. We are coming on the secret of a magic which sweeps out of men's minds all vestige of theism and beliefs which they and their fathers held and were framed upon.

There are deceptions of the senses, deceptions of the passions, and the structural, beneficent illusions of sentiment and of the intellect. There is the illusion of love, which attributes to the beloved person all which that person shares with his or her family, sex, age or condition, nay, with the human mind itself. 'T is these which the lover loves, and Anna Matilda[9] gets the credit of them. As if one shut up always in a tower, with one window through which the face of heaven and earth could be seen, should fancy that all the marvels he beheld belonged to that window. There is the illusion of time, which is very deep; who has disposed of it?—or come to the conviction that what seems the *succession* of thought is only the distribution of wholes into causal series? The intellect sees that every atom carries the whole of nature; that the mind opens to omnipotence; that, in the endless striving and ascents, the metamorphosis is entire, so that the soul doth not know itself in its own act when that act is perfected. There is illusion that shall deceive even the elect. There is illusion that shall deceive even the performer of the miracle. Though he make his body, he denies that he makes it. Though the world exist from thought, thought is daunted in presence of the world. One after the other we accept the mental laws, still resisting those which follow, which however must be accepted. But all our concessions only compel us to new profusion. And what avails it that science has come to treat space and time as simply forms of thought, and the material world as hypothetical, and withal our pretension of *property* and even of self-hood are fading with the rest, if, at last, even our thoughts are not finalities, but the incessant flowing and ascension reach these also, and each thought which yesterday was a finality, to-day is yielding to a larger generalization?

[9] I.e., any woman who is loved.

With such volatile elements to work in, 't is no wonder if our estimates are loose and floating. We must work and affirm, but we have no guess of the value of what we say or do. The cloud is now as big as your hand, and now it covers a county. That story of Thor, who was set to drain the drinking-horn in Asgard and to wrestle with the old woman and to run with the runner Lok,[10] and presently found that he had been drinking up the sea, and wrestling with Time, and racing with Thought, —describes us, who are contending, amid these seeming trifles, with the supreme energies of nature. We fancy we have fallen into bad company and squalid condition, low debts, shoe-bills, broken glass to pay for, pots to buy, butcher's meat, sugar, milk and coal. 'Set me some great task, ye gods! and I will show my spirit.' 'Not so,' says the good Heaven; 'plod and plough, vamp your old coats and hats, weave a shoestring; great affairs and the best wine by and by.' Well, 't is all phantasm; and if we weave a yard of tape in all humility and as well as we can, long hereafter we shall see it was no cotton tape at all but some galaxy which we braided, and that the threads were Time and Nature.

We cannot write the order of the variable winds. How can we penetrate the law of our shifting moods and susceptibility? Yet they differ as all and nothing. Instead of the firmament of yesterday, which our eyes require, it is to-day an egg-shell which coops us in; we cannot even see what or where our stars of destiny are. From day to day the capital facts of human life are hidden from our eyes. Suddenly the mist rolls up and reveals them, and we think how much good time is gone that might have been saved had any hint of these things been shown. A sudden rise in the road shows us the system of mountains, and all the summits, which have been just as near us all the year, but quite out of mind. But these alternations are not without their order, and we are parties to our various fortune. If life seem a succession of dreams, yet poetic justice is done in dreams also. The visions of good men are good; it is the undisciplined will that is whipped with bad thoughts and bad fortunes. When we break the laws, we lose our hold on the central reality. Like sick men in hospitals, we change only from bed to bed, from one folly to another; and it cannot signify much what becomes of such castaways, wailing, stupid, comatose creatures, lifted from bed to bed, from the nothing of life to the nothing of death.

In this kingdom of illusions we grope eagerly for stays and foundations. There is none but a strict and faithful dealing at home and a severe barring out of all duplicity or illusion there. Whatever games are played with us, we must play no games with ourselves, but deal in our privacy with the last honesty and truth. I look upon the simple and childish virtues of veracity and honesty as the root of all that is sublime in character. Speak as you think, be what you are, pay your debts of all kinds. I prefer to be owned as sound and solvent, and my word as good as my bond, and to be what cannot be skipped, or dissipated, or undermined, to all the *éclat* in the universe. This reality is the foundation of friendship, religion, poetry and art. At the top or at the bottom of all illusions, I set the cheat which still leads us to work and live for appearances; in spite of our conviction, in all sane hours, that it is what we really are that avails with friends, with strangers, and with fate or fortune.

One would think from the talk of men that riches and poverty were a great matter;

---

[10] Thor: Norse god of weather, thunder, and harvest; Asgard: home of the Norse gods; Lok: Loki, Norse god of mischief and malevolence.

and our civilization mainly respects it. But the Indians say that they do not think the white man, with his brow of care, always toiling, afraid of heat and cold, and keeping within doors, has any advantage of them. The permanent interest of every man is never to be in a false position, but to have the weight of nature to back him in all that he does. Riches and poverty are a thick or thin costume; and our life—the life of all of us—identical. For we transcend the circumstance continually and taste the real quality of existence; as in our employments, which only differ in the manifestations but express the same laws; or in our thoughts, which wear no silks and taste no ice-creams. We see God face to face every hour, and know the savor of nature.

The early Greek philosophers Heraclitus and Xenophanes[11] measured their force on this problem of identity. Diogenes of Apollonia[12] said that unless the atoms were made of one stuff, they could never blend and act with one another. But the Hindoos, in their sacred writings, express the liveliest feeling, both of the essential identity and of that illusion which they conceive variety to be. "The notions, '*I am,*' and '*This is mine,*' which influence mankind, are but delusions of the mother of the world. Dispel, O Lord of all creatures! the conceit of knowledge which proceeds from ignorance." And the beatitude of man they hold to lie in being freed from fascination.

The intellect is stimulated by the statement of truth in a trope, and the will by clothing the laws of life in illusions. But the unities of Truth and of Right are not broken by the disguise. There need never be any confusion in these. In a crowded life of many parts and performers, on a stage of nations, or in the obscurest hamlet in Maine or California, the same elements offer the same choices to each new comer, and, according to his election, he fixes his fortune in absolute Nature. It would be hard to put more mental and moral philosophy than the Persians have thrown into a sentence,—

"Fooled thou must be, though wisest of the wise:
Then be the fool of virtue, not of vice."

There is no chance and no anarchy in the universe. All is system and gradation. Every god is there sitting in his sphere. The young mortal enters the hall of the firmament; there is he alone with them alone, they pouring on him benedictions and gifts, and beckoning him up to their thrones. On the instant, and incessantly, fall snow-storms of illusions. He fancies himself in a vast crowd which sways this way and that and whose movement and doings he must obey: he fancies himself poor, orphaned, insignificant. The mad crowd drives hither and thither, now furiously commanding this thing to be done, now that. What is he that he should resist their will, and think or act for himself? Every moment new changes and new showers of deceptions to baffle and distract him. And when, by and by, for an instant, the air clears and the cloud lifts a little, there are the gods still sitting around him on their thrones,—they alone with him alone.

1860

---

[11] Heraclitus: Greek philosopher of the fifth century B.C.; Xenophanes: fifth-century B.C. Greek historian and biographer.

[12] Greek philosopher of the fifth century B.C.

Concord Hymn*

Sung at the completion of the Battle Monument,
July 4, 1837

By the rude bridge that arched the flood,
   Their flag to April's breeze unfurled,
Here once the embattled farmers stood
   And fired the shot heard round the world.

The foe long since in silence slept;   5
   Alike the conqueror silent sleeps;
And Time the ruined bridge has swept
   Down the dark stream which seaward creeps.

On this green bank, by this soft stream,
   We set to-day a votive stone;   10
That memory may their deed redeem,
   When, like our sires, our sons are gone.

Spirit, that made those heroes dare
   To die, and leave their children free,
Bid Time and Nature gently spare   15
   The shaft we raise to them and thee.

1837

The Rhodora[1]

On being asked, whence is the flower?

In May, when sea-winds pierced our solitudes,
I found the fresh Rhodora in the woods,
Spreading its leafless blooms in a damp nook,
To please the desert and the sluggish brook.
The purple petals, fallen in the pool,   5
Made the black water with their beauty gay;

---

* This poem was first printed in a pamphlet
distributed at the dedication of the monument
commemorating the battles of Lexington and
Concord (April 19, 1775) in the American
Revolutionary War.

[1] Shrub similar to the rhododendron found in
New England.

Here might the red-bird come his plumes to cool,
And court the flower that cheapens his array.
Rhodora! if the sages ask thee why
This charm is wasted on the earth and sky,   10
Tell them, dear, that if eyes were made for seeing,
Then Beauty is its own excuse for being:
Why thou wert there, O rival of the rose!
I never thought to ask, I never knew:
But, in my simple ignorance, suppose   15
The self-same Power that brought me there brought you.
1834/1839

Each and All

Little thinks, in the field, yon red-cloaked clown[1]
Of thee from the hill-top looking down;
The heifer that lows in the upland farm,
Far-heard, lows not thine ear to charm;
The sexton, tolling his bell at noon,   5
Deems not that great Napoleon
Stops his horse, and lists with delight,
Whilst his files sweep round yon Alpine height;
Nor knowest thou what argument
Thy life to thy neighbor's creed has lent.   10
All are needed by each one;
Nothing is fair or good alone.
I thought the sparrow's note from heaven,
Singing at dawn on the alder bough;
I brought him home, in his nest, at even;   15
He sings the song, but it cheers not now,
For I did not bring home the river and sky;—
He sang to my ear,—they sang to my eye.
The delicate shells lay on the shore;
The bubbles of the latest wave   20
Fresh pearls to their enamel gave,
And the bellowing of the savage sea
Greeted their safe escape to me.
I wiped away the weeds and foam,
I fetched my sea-born treasures home;   25

[1] Rustic; peasant.

But the poor, unsightly, noisome things
Had left their beauty on the shore
With the sun and the sand and the wild uproar.
The lover watched his graceful maid,
As 'mid the virgin train she strayed,   30
Nor knew her beauty's best attire
Was woven still by the snow-white choir.
At last she came to his hermitage,
Like the bird from the woodlands to the cage;—
The gay enchantment was undone,   35
A gentle wife, but fairy none.
Then I said, 'I covet truth;
Beauty is unripe childhood's cheat;
I leave it behind with the games of youth:'—
As I spoke, beneath my feet   40
The ground-pine curled its pretty wreath,
Running over the club-moss burrs;
I inhaled the violet's breath;
Around me stood the oaks and firs;
Pine-cones and acorns lay on the ground;   45
Over me soared the eternal sky,
Full of light and of deity;
Again I saw, again I heard,
The rolling river, the morning bird;—
Beauty through my senses stole;   50
I yielded myself to the perfect whole.

1839

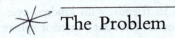 ## The Problem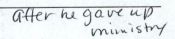

after he gave up ministry

I like a church; I like a cowl;
I love a prophet of the soul;
And on my heart monastic aisles
Fall like sweet strains, or pensive smiles;
Yet not for all his faith can see   5
Would I that cowlèd churchman be.

Why should the vest[1] on him allure,
Which I could not on me endure?

---

[1] Vestment.

Not from a vain or shallow thought
His awful Jove young Phidias[2] brought;   10
Never from lips of cunning fell
The thrilling Delphic oracle;[3]
Out from the heart of nature rolled
The burdens of the Bible old;
The litanies of nations came,   15
Like the volcano's tongue of flame,
Up from the burning core below,—
The canticles of love and woe:
The hand[4] that rounded Peter's dome
And groined the aisles of Christian Rome   20
Wrought in a sad sincerity;
Himself from God he could not free;
He builded better than he knew;—
The conscious stone to beauty grew.

Know'st thou what wove yon woodbird's nest   25
Of leaves, and feathers from her breast?
Or how the fish outbuilt her shell,
Painting with morn each annual cell?
Or how the sacred pine-tree adds
To her old leaves new myriads?   30
Such and so grew these holy piles,
Whilst love and terror laid the tiles.
Earth proudly wears the Parthenon,
As the best gem upon her zone,
And Morning opes with haste her lids   35
To gaze upon the Pyramids;
O'er England's abbeys bends the sky,
As on its friends, with kindred eye;
For out of Thought's interior sphere
These wonders rose to upper air;   40
And Nature gladly gave them place,
Adopted them into her race,
And granted them an equal date
With Andes and with Ararat.[5]

These temples grew as grows the grass;   45
Art might obey, but not surpass.
The passive Master lent his hand

---

[2] Greek sculptor, fifth century B.C.
[3] Prophetess at the Temple of Apollo at Delphos in ancient Greece.
[4] Reference to Michelangelo (1475–1564), who became the principal architect of St. Peter's Cathedral in Rome.

[5] Andes: mountain range in South America; Ararat: mountain in Asia Minor where Noah's ark landed after the flood.

To the vast soul that o'er him planned;
And the same power that reared the shrine
Bestrode the tribes that knelt within.   50
Ever the fiery Pentecost[6]
Girds with one flame the countless host,
Trances the heart through chanting choirs,
And through the priest the mind inspires.
The word unto the prophet spoken   55
Was writ on tables yet unbroken;
The word by seers or sibyls told,
In groves of oak, or fanes[7] of gold,
Still floats upon the morning wind,
Still whispers to the willing mind.   60
One accent of the Holy Ghost
The heedless world hath never lost.
I know what say the fathers wise,—
The Book itself before me lies,
Old *Chrysostom*,[8] best Augustine,[9]   65
And he who blent both in his line,
The younger *Golden Lips* or mines,
Taylor,[10] the Shakspeare of divines.
His words are music in my ear,
I see his cowlèd portrait dear;   70
And yet, for all his faith could see,
I would not the good bishop be.

1840

The Snow-storm

Announced by all the trumpets of the sky,
Arrives the snow, and, driving o'er the fields,
Seems nowhere to alight: the whited air
Hides hills and woods, the river, and the heaven,
And veils the farm-house at the garden's end.   5
The sled and traveller stopped, the courier's feet

---

[6] The Holy Spirit, who descended upon the apostles. (See Acts 2.)
[7] Temples.
[8] St. John of Antioch (A.D. 345?–407), called "Golden Lips" (Greek: *Chrysostom*) for his eloquence.

[9] St. Augustine (A.D. 354–430), author of *Confessions* and *The City of God*.
[10] Jeremy Taylor (1613–1667), English theologian.

Delayed, all friends shut out, the housemates sit
Around the radiant fireplace, enclosed
In a tumultuous privacy of storm.

　　Come see the north wind's masonry.　　　　　　10
Out of an unseen quarry evermore
Furnished with tile, the fierce artificer
Curves his white bastions with projected roof
Round every windward stake, or tree, or door.
Speeding, the myriad-handed, his wild work　　　15
So fanciful, so savage, nought cares he
For number or proportion. Mockingly,
On coop or kennel he hangs Parian[1] wreaths;
A swan-like form invests the hidden thorn;
Fills up the farmer's lane from wall to wall,　　20
Maugre the farmer's sighs; and at the gate
A tapering turret overtops the work.
And when his hours are numbered, and the world
Is all his own, retiring, as he were not,
Leaves, when the sun appears, astonished Art　　25
To mimic in slow structures, stone by stone,
Built in an age, the mad wind's night-work,
The frolic architecture of the snow.
1835/1841

Grace

How much, preventing God, how much I owe
To the defences thou hast round me set;
Example, custom, fear, occasion slow,—
These scorned bondmen were my parapet.
I dare not peep over this parapet　　　　　　　5
To gauge with glance the roaring gulf below,
The depths of sin to which I had descended,
Had not these me against myself defended.
1842

---

[1] I.e., like white marble quarried from the island
Paros, used by Greek sculptors.

Blight

Give me truths;
For I am weary of the surfaces,
And die of inanition. If I knew
Only the herbs and simples of the wood,
Rue, cinquefoil, gill, vervain and agrimony,   5
Blue-vetch and trillium, hawkweed, sassafras,
Milkweeds and murky brakes, quaint pipes and
    sun-dew,
And rare and virtuous roots, which in these woods
Draw untold juices from the common earth,
Untold, unknown, and I could surely spell   10
Their fragrance, and their chemistry apply
By sweet affinities to human flesh,
Driving the foe and stablishing the friend,—
O, that were much, and I could be a part
Of the round day, related to the sun   15
And planted world, and full executor
Of their imperfect functions.
But these young scholars, who invade our hills,
Bold as the engineer who fells the wood,
And travelling often in the cut he makes,   20
Love not the flower they pluck, and know it not,
And all their botany is Latin names.
The old men studied magic in the flowers,
And human fortunes in astronomy,
And an omnipotence in chemistry,   25
Preferring things to names, for these were men,
Were unitarians of the united world,
And, wheresoever their clear eye-beams fell,
They caught the footsteps of the SAME. Our eyes
Are armed, but we are strangers to the stars,   30
And strangers to the mystic beast and bird,
And strangers to the plant and to the mine.
The injured elements say, 'Not in us;'
And night and day, ocean and continent,
Fire, plant and mineral say, 'Not in us;'   35
And haughtily return us stare for stare.
For we invade them impiously for gain;
We devastate them unreligiously,
And coldly ask their pottage, not their love.
Therefore they shove us from them, yield to us   40
Only what to our griping toil is due;
But the sweet affluence of love and song,

The rich results of the divine consents
Of man and earth, of world beloved and lover,
The nectar and ambrosia, are withheld;   45
And in the midst of spoils and slaves, we thieves
And pirates of the universe, shut out
Daily to a more thin and outward rind,
Turn pale and starve. Therefore, to our sick eyes,
The stunted trees look sick, the summer short,   50
Clouds shade the sun, which will not tan our hay,
And nothing thrives to reach its natural term;
And life, shorn of its venerable length,
Even at its greatest space is a defeat,
And dies in anger that it was a dupe;   55
And, in its highest noon and wantonness,
Is early frugal, like a beggar's child;
Even in the hot pursuit of the best aims
And prizes of ambition, checks its hand,
Like Alpine cataracts frozen as they leaped,   60
Chilled with a miserly comparison
Of the toy's purchase with the length of life.
  1844

Fable

The mountain and the squirrel
Had a quarrel,
And the former called the latter 'Little Prig;'
Bun replied,
'You are doubtless very big;   5
But all sorts of things and weather
Must be taken in together,
To make up a year
And a sphere.
And I think it no disgrace   10
To occupy my place.
If I'm not so large as you,
You are not so small as I,
And not half so spry.
I'll not deny you make   15
A very pretty squirrel track;
Talents differ; all is well and wisely put;
If I cannot carry forests on my back,
Neither can you crack a nut.'
  1846

Uriel[1]

It fell in the ancient periods
  Which the brooding soul surveys,
Or ever the wild Time coined itself
  Into calendar months and days.

This was the lapse of Uriel,   5
  Which in Paradise befell.
Once, among the Pleiads[2] walking,
  Seyd[3] overheard the young gods talking;
And the treason, too long pent,
  To his ears was evident.   10
The young deities discussed
  Laws of form, and metre just,
Orb, quintessence, and sunbeams,
  What subsisteth, and what seems.
One, with low tones that decide,   15
  And doubt and reverend use defied,
With a look that solved the sphere,
  And stirred the devils everywhere,
Gave his sentiment divine
  Against the being of a line.   20
'Line in nature is not found;
  Unit and universe are round;
In vain produced, all rays return;
  Evil will bless, and ice will burn.'
As Uriel spoke with piercing eye,   25
  A shudder ran around the sky;
The stern old war-gods shook their heads,
  The seraphs frowned from myrtle-beds;
Seemed to the holy festival
  The rash word boded ill to all;   30
The balance-beam of Fate was bent;
  The bounds of good and ill were rent;
Strong Hades[4] could not keep his own,
  But all slid to confusion.

A sad self-knowledge, withering, fell   35
  On the beauty of Uriel;
In heaven once eminent, the god

---

[1] Name ascribed to the god of light in John
Milton's *Paradise Lost* (1667).
[2] Cluster of seven stars named for the seven
daughters of Atlas and Pleione in Greek myth.

[3] The thirteenth-century Persian poet Saadi.
[4] Another name for Pluto, ruler of the
underworld in Greek myth.

Withdrew, that hour, into his cloud;
Whether doomed to long gyration
In the sea of generation,   40
Or by knowledge grown too bright
To hit the nerve of feebler sight.
Straightway, a forgetting wind
Stole over the celestial kind,
And their lips the secret kept,   45
If in ashes the fire-seed slept.
But now and then, truth-speaking things
Shamed the angels' veiling wings;
And, shrilling from the solar course,
Or from fruit of chemic force,   50
Procession of a soul in matter,
Or the speeding change of water,
Or out of the good of evil born,
Came Uriel's voice of cherub scorn,
And a blush tinged the upper sky,   55
And the gods shook, they knew not why.

1847

Hamatreya[1]

Bulkeley, Hunt, Willard, Hosmer, Meriam, Flint,[2]
Possessed the land which rendered to their toil
Hay, corn, roots, hemp, flax, apples, wool and wood.
Each of these landlords walked amidst his farm,
Saying, ' 'T is mine, my children's and my name's.   5
How sweet the west wind sounds in my own trees!
How graceful climb those shadows on my hill!
I fancy these pure waters and the flags[3]
Know me, as does my dog: we sympathize;
And, I affirm, my actions smack of the soil.'   10

Where are these men? Asleep beneath their grounds:
And strangers, fond as they, their furrows plough.
Earth laughs in flowers, to see her boastful boys
Earth-proud, proud of the earth which is not theirs;

---

[1] A derivation of *Maitreya*, the Hindu god named
in the sacred *Vishnu Purana*. Also possibly a
Greek interpretation of "earth-mother."

[2] Family names of the first settlers of Concord,
Massachusetts.

[3] Wild irises.

Who steer the plough, but cannot steer their feet   15
Clear of the grave.
They added ridge to valley, brook to pond,
And sighed for all that bounded their domain;
'This suits me for a pasture; that's my park;
We must have clay, lime, gravel, granite-ledge,   20
And misty lowland, where to go for peat.
The land is well,—lies fairly to the south.
'T is good, when you have crossed the sea and back,
To find the sitfast acres where you left them.'
Ah! the hot owner sees not Death, who adds   25
Him to his land, a lump of mould the more.
Hear what the Earth says:—

EARTH-SONG

'Mine and yours;
Mine, not yours.
Earth endures;
Stars abide—   30
Shine down in the old sea;
Old are the shores;
But where are old men?
I who have seen much,
Such have I never seen.   35

'The lawyer's deed
Ran sure,
In tail,⁴
To them, and to their heirs
Who shall succeed,   40
Without fail,
Forevermore.

'Here is the land,
Shaggy with wood,
With its old valley,   45
Mound and flood.
But the heritors?—

Fled like the flood's foam.
The lawyer, and the laws,
And the kingdom,   50
Clean swept herefrom.

---

⁴ As in *entail*, the legal designation of an
inheritance to specific descendants.

'They called me theirs,
Who so controlled me;
Yet every one
Wished to stay, and is gone,   55
How am I theirs,
If they cannot hold me,
But I hold them?'

When I heard the Earth-song
I was no longer brave;   60
My avarice cooled
Like lust in the chill of the grave.

1847

Ode

Inscribed to W. H. Channing[1]

Though loath to grieve
The evil time's sole patriot,
I cannot leave
My honied thought
For the priest's cant,   5
Or statesman's rant.

If I refuse
My study for their politique,
Which at the best is trick,
The angry Muse   10
Puts confusion in my brain.

But who is he that prates
Of the culture of mankind,
Of better arts and life?
Go, blindworm, go,   15
Behold the famous States
Harrying Mexico
With rifle and with knife![2]

Or who, with accent bolder,
Dare praise the freedom-loving mountaineer?   20

---

[1] William Henry Channing (1810–1884),
Unitarian clergyman, Transcendentalist,
abolitionist, and nephew of William Ellery
Channing (1780–1842), Unitarian leader.

[2] Emerson opposed the Mexican War
(1846–1848), which he regarded as an effort to
extend slavery.

I found by thee, O rushing Contoocook![3]
And in thy valleys, Agiochook![4]
The jackals of the negro-holder.

The God who made New Hampshire
Taunted the lofty land   25
With little men;
Small bat and wren
House in the oak:
If earth-fire cleave
The upheaved land, and bury the folk,   30
The southern crocodile would grieve.
Virtue palters; Right is hence;
Freedom praised, but hid;
Funeral eloquence
Rattles the coffin-lid.   35

What boots thy zeal,
O glowing friend,
That would indignant rend
The northland from the south?
Wherefore? to what good end?   40
Boston Bay and Bunker Hill
Would serve things still;
Things are of the snake.

The horseman serves the horse,
The neatherd[5] serves the neat,   45
The merchant serves the purse,
The eater serves his meat;
'T is the day of the chattel,
Web to weave, and corn to grind;
Things are in the saddle,   50
And ride mankind.

There are two laws discrete,
Not reconciled—
Law for man, and law for thing;
The last builds town and fleet,   55
But it runs wild,
And doth the man unking.

'T is fit the forest fall,
The steep be graded,

---

[3] River in New Hampshire.   [5] Cowherd.
[4] The White Mountains of New Hampshire, a
state that had voted the Democratic, or
proslavery, ticket at the time.

The mountain tunnelled,   60
The sand shaded,
The orchard planted,
The glebe[6] tilled,
The prairie granted,
The stamer built.   65

Let man serve law for man;
Live for friendship, live for love,
For truth's and harmony's behoof;
The state may follow how it can,
As Olympus follows Jove.[7]   70

    Yet do not I implore
The wrinkled shopman to my sounding woods,
Nor bid the unwilling senator
Ask votes of thrushes in the solitudes.
Every one to his chosen work;   75
Foolish hands may mix and mar;
Wise and sure the issues are.
Round they roll till dark is light,
Sex to sex, and even to odd;
The over-god   80
Who marries Right to Might,
Who peoples, unpeoples,
He who exterminates
Races by stronger races,
Black by white faces,   85
Knows to bring honey
Out of the lion;[8]
Grafts gentlest scion
On pirate and Turk.

The Cossack eats Poland,[9]   90
Like stolen fruit;
Her last noble is ruined,
Her last poet mute:
Straight, into double band
The victors divide;   95
Half for freedom strike and stand;
The astonished Muse finds thousands at her side.

1847

---

[6] Soil.
[7] Another name for Zeus, or Jupiter, father of the Olympian deities in Greek myth.
[8] See Judges 14:8. Samson found the carcass of a lion in which bees had made honey: "Out of the eater came forth meat, and out of the strong came forth sweetness."
[9] Poland had been divided three times in the late eighteenth century, with Russia ("the Cossack") getting the most territory.

Give All to Love

Give all to love;
Obey thy heart;
Friends, kindred, days,
Estate, good-fame,
Plans, credit and the Muse,—   5
Nothing refuse.

'T is a brave master;
Let it have scope:
Follow it utterly,
Hope beyond hope: 10
High and more high
It dives into noon,
With wing unspent,
Untold intent;
But it is a god,   15
Knows its own path
And the outlets of the sky.

It was never for the mean;
It requireth courage stout.
Souls above doubt,   20
Valor unbending,
It will reward,—
They shall return
More than they were,
And ever ascending.   25

Leave all for love;
Yet, hear me, yet,
One word more thy heart behoved,
One pulse more of firm endeavor,—
Keep thee to-day,   30
To-morrow, forever,
Free as an Arab
Of thy beloved.

Cling with life to the maid;
But when the surprise,   35
First vague shadow of surmise
Flits across her bosom young,
Of a joy apart from thee,

Free be she, fancy-free;
Nor thou detain her vesture's hem,   40
Nor the palest rose she flung
From her summer diadem.

Though thou loved her as thyself,
As a self of purer clay,
Though her parting dims the day,   45
Stealing grace from all alive;
Heartily know,
When half-gods go,
The gods arrive.
1847

The Apology

Think me not unkind and rude
    That I walk alone in grove and glen;
I go to the god of the wood
    To fetch his word to men.

Tax not my sloth that I   5
    Fold my arms beside the brook;
Each cloud that floated in the sky
    Writes a letter in my book.

Chide me not, laborious band,
    For the idle flowers I brought;   10
Every aster in my hand
    Goes home loaded with a thought.

There was never mystery
    But 't is figured in the flowers;
Was never secret history   15
    But birds tell it in the bowers.

One harvest from thy field
    Homeward brought the oxen strong;
A second crop thine acres yield,
    Which I gather in a song.   20
1847

Merlin[1]

I

Thy trivial harp will never please
Or fill my craving ear;
Its chords should ring as blows the breeze,
Free, peremptory, clear.
No jingling serenader's art,   5
Nor tinkle of piano strings,
Can make the wild blood start
In its mystic springs.
The kingly bard
Must smite the chords rudely and hard,   10
As with hammer or with mace;
That they may render back
Artful thunder, which conveys
Secrets of the solar track,
Sparks of the supersolar blaze.   15
Merlin's blows are strokes of fate,
Chiming with the forest tone,
When boughs buffet boughs in the wood;
Chiming with the gasp and moan
Of the ice-imprisoned flood;   20
With the pulse of manly hearts;
With the voice of orators;
With the din of city arts;
With the cannonade of wars;
With the marches of the brave;   25
And prayers of might from martyrs' cave.

Great is the art,
Great be the manners, of the bard.
He shall not his brain encumber
With the coil of rhythm and number;   30
But, leaving rule and pale forethought,
He shall aye[2] climb
For his rhyme.
'Pass in, pass in,' the angels say,
'In to the upper doors,   35
Nor count compartments of the floors,

[1] In this poem, a legendary Welsh bard rather   [2] Always.
than the magician of Arthurian legend.

But mount to paradise
By the stairway of surprise.'

Blameless master of the games,
King of sport that never shames,   40
He shall daily joy dispense
Hid in song's sweet influence.
Forms more cheerly live and go,
What time the subtle mind
Sings aloud the tune whereto   45
Their pulses beat,
And march their feet,
And their members are combined.

By Sybarites[3] beguiled,
He shall no task decline;   50
Merlin's mighty line
Extremes of nature reconciled,—
Bereaved a tyrant of his will,
And made the lion mild.
Songs can the tempest still,   55
Scattered on the stormy air,
Mould the year to fair increase,
And bring in poetic peace.

He shall not seek to weave,
In weak, unhappy times,   60
Efficacious rhymes;
Wait his returning strength.
Bird that from the nadir's floor
To the zenith's top can soar,—
The soaring orbit of the muse exceeds that journey's
   length.   65
Nor profane affect to hit
Or compass that, by meddling wit,
Which only the propitious mind
Publishes when 't is inclined.
There are open hours   70
When the God's will sallies free,
And the dull idiot might see
The flowing fortunes of a thousand years;—
Sudden, at unawares,
Self-moved, fly-to the doors,   75
Nor sword of angels could reveal
What they conceal.

---

[3] Inhabitants of Sybaris, Greek city in Italy
famous for its wealth and hedonism.

II

The rhyme of the poet
Modulates the king's affairs;
Balance-loving Nature   80
Made all things in pairs.
To every foot its antipode;
Each color with its counter glowed;
To every tone beat answering tones,
Higher or graver;   85
Flavor gladly blends with flavor;
Leaf answers leaf upon the bough;
And match the paired cotyledons.[4]
Hands to hands, and feet to feet,
In one body grooms and brides;   90
Eldest rite, two married sides
In every mortal meet.
Light's far furnace shines,
Smelting balls and bars,
Forging double stars,   95
Glittering twins and trines.
The animals are sick with love,
Lovesick with rhyme;
Each with all propitious Time
Into chorus wove.   100

Like the dancers' ordered band,
Thoughts come also hand in hand;
In equal couples mated,
Or else alternated;
Adding by their mutual gage,   105
One to other, health and age.
Solitary fancies go
Short-lived wandering to and fro,
Most like to bachelors,
Or an ungiven maid,   110
Not ancestors,
With no posterity to make the lie afraid,
Or keep truth undecayed.
Perfect-paired as eagle's wings,
Justice is the rhyme of things;   115
Trade and counting use
The self-same tuneful muse;
And Nemesis,[5]
Who with even matches odd,

---

[4] First two leaves of a plant sprouted from a seed.   [5] Greek goddess of retribution and fate.

Who athwart space redresses 120
The partial wrong,
Fills the just period,
And finishes the song.

Subtle rhymes, with ruin rife,
Murmur in the house of life, 125
Sung by the Sisters[6] as they spin;
In perfect time and measure they
Build and unbuild our echoing clay.
As the two twilights of the day
Fold us music-drunken in. 130

1847

Days

Daughters of Time, the hypocritic Days,
Muffled and dumb like barefoot dervishes,
And marching single in an endless file,
Bring diadems and fagots in their hands.
To each they offer gifts after his will, 5
Bread, kingdoms, stars, and sky that holds them all.
I, in my pleached garden, watched the pomp,
Forgot my morning wishes, hastily
Took a few herbs and apples, and the Day
Turned and departed silent. I, too late, 10
Under her solemn fillet saw the scorn.

1857

Brahma[1]

If the red slayer[2] think he slays,
   Or if the slain think he is slain,
They know not well the subtle ways
   I keep, and pass, and turn again,

[6] The three fates in Greek mythology.
[1] In Hindu belief, the supreme spirit of the universe.

[2] Death.

Far or forgot to me is near;
    Shadow and sunlight are the same;
The vanished gods to me appear;
    And one to me are shame and fame.

They reckon ill who leave me out;
    When me they fly, I am the wings;   10
I am the doubter and the doubt,
    And I the hymn the Brahmin sings.

The strong gods[3] pine for my abode,
    And pine in vain the sacred Seven;[4]
But thou, meek lover of the good!   15
    Find me, and turn thy back on heaven.

1856/1857

Two Rivers

Thy summer voice, Musketaquit,[1]
Repeats the music of the rain;
But sweeter rivers pulsing flit
Through thee, as thou through Concord Plain.

Thou in thy narrow banks art pent: 5
The stream I love unbounded goes
Through flood and sea and firmament;
Through light, through life, it forward flows.

I see the inundation sweet,
I hear the spending of the stream   10
Through years, through men, through Nature fleet,
Through love and thought, through power and dream.

Musketaquit, a goblin strong,
Of shard and flint makes jewels gay;
They lose their grief who hear his song,   15
And where he winds is the day of day.

[3] Agni, god of fire; Indra, god of the sky; and
Yama, god of death.

[4] The seven high saints of Hinduism.
[1] The Concord River.

So forth and brighter fares my stream,—
Who drink it shall not thirst again;[2]
No darkness stains its equal gleam,
And ages drop in it like rain.   20

1858

Terminus[1]

It is time to be old,
To take in sail:—
The god of bounds,
Who sets to seas a shore,
Came to me in his fatal rounds,   5
And said: 'No more!
No farther shoot
Thy broad ambitious branches, and thy root.
Fancy departs: no more invent;
Contract thy firmament   10
To compass of a tent.
There's not enough for this and that,
Make thy option which of two;
Economize the failing river,
Not the less revere the Giver,   15
Leave the many and hold the few.
Timely wise accept the terms,
Soften the fall with wary foot;
A little while
Still plan and smile,   20
And,—fault of novel germs,—
Mature the unfallen fruit.
Curse, if thou wilt, thy sires,
Bad husbands of their fires,
Who, when they gave thee breath,   25
Failed to bequeath
The needful sinew stark as once,
The Baresark[2] marrow to thy bones,
But left a legacy of ebbing veins,
Inconstant heat and nerveless reins,—   30

---

[2] John 4:14: "Whosoever drinketh of the water
that I shall give him shall never thirst."
[1] Roman deity of boundaries.

[2] As in *berserk;* derived from the practice of
ancient Germanic warriors who battled without
armor, or "bare of shirt."

Amid the Muses, left thee deaf and dumb,
Amid the gladiators, halt and numb.'

    As the bird trims her to the gale,
I trim myself to the storm of time,
I man the rudder, reef the sail,   35
Obey the voice at eve obeyed at prime:
'Lowly faithful, banish fear,
Right onward drive unharmed;
The port, well worth the cruise, is near,
And every wave is charmed.'   40
1867

The Bohemian Hymn

In many forms we try
To utter God's infinity,
But the boundless hath no form,
And the Universal Friend
Doth as far transcend   5
An angel as a worm.

The great Idea baffles wit,
Language falters under it,
It leaves the learned in the lurch;
Nor art, nor power, nor toil can find   10
The measure of the eternal Mind,
Nor hymn, nor prayer, nor church.
1884

---

from Journals

[*from* April 18, 1824]

I am beginning my professional studies. In a month I shall be *legally* a man. And I deliberately dedicate my time, my talents, & my hopes to the Church. Man is an animal that looks before & after; and I should be loth to reflect at a remote period that I took so solemn a step in my existence without some careful examination of my past & present life. Since I cannot alter I would not repent the resolution I have made & this page must be witness to the latest year of my life whether I have good grounds to warrant my determination.

I cannot dissemble that my abilities are below my ambition. And I find that I judged by a false criterion when I measured my powers by my ability to understand & to criticise the intellectual character of another. For men graduate their respect not by the secret wealth but by the outward use; not by the power to understand, but by the power to act. I have or had a strong imagination & consequently a keen relish for the beauties of poetry. The exercise which the practice of composition gives to this faculty is the cause of my immoderate fondness for writing, which has swelled these pages to a voluminous extent. My reasoning faculty is proportionately weak, nor can I ever hope to write a Butler's Analogy or an Essay of Hume.[1] Nor is it strange that with this confession I should choose theology, which is from everlasting to everlasting 'debateable Ground.' For, the highest species of reasoning upon divine subjects is rather the fruit of a sort of moral imagination, than of the 'Reasoning Machines' such as Locke & Clarke[2] & David Hume. Dr. Channing's Dudleian Lecture[3] is the model of what I mean, and the faculty which produced this is akin to the higher flights of the fancy. I may add that the preaching most in vogue at the present day depends chiefly on imagination for its success, and asks those accomplishments which I believe are most within my grasp. I have set down little which can gratify my vanity, and I must further say that every comparison of myself with my mates that six or seven, perhaps sixteen or seventeen, years have made has convinced me that there exists a signal defect of character which neutralizes in great part the just influence my talents ought to have. Whether that defect be in the *address,* in the fault of good forms, which Queen Isabella[4] said were like perpetual letters commendatory, or deeper seated in an absence of common *sympathies,* or even in a levity of the understanding, I cannot tell. But its bitter fruits are a sore uneasiness in the company of most men & women, a frigid fear of offending & jealousy of disrespect, an inability to lead & an unwillingness to follow the current conversation, which contrive to make me second with all those among whom chiefly I wish to be first. . . .

But in Divinity I hope to thrive. I inherit from my sire[5] a formality of manner & speech, but I derive from him or his patriotic parent[6] a passionate love for the strains of eloquence. I burn after the 'aliquid immensum infinitumque'[7] which Cicero[8] desired. What we ardently love we learn to imitate. My understanding venerates & my heart loves that Cause which is dear to God & man—the laws of Morals, the Revelations which sanction, & the blood of martyrs & triumphant suffering of the

---

[1] Joseph Butler (1692–1752), English philosopher and bishop, wrote *Analogy of Religion* (1736), in which he tried to reconcile revelation and reason. David Hume (1711–1766), Scottish philosopher, wrote *Philosophical Essays* (1748).

[2] John Locke (1632–1704), English philosopher and author of *An Essay Concerning Human Understanding* (1690); Samuel Clarke (1675–1729), English philosopher, theologian, and author of *A Demonstration of the Being and Attributes of God* (1705).

[3] William Ellery Channing (1780–1842) delivered

a lecture entitled "The Evidence of Revealed Religion" on March 14, 1821.

[4] The allusion to Queen Isabella remains unclear.

[5] Emerson's father, William Emerson (1769–1811).

[6] Emerson's grandfather, Reverend William Emerson (1743–1776), a minister at Concord during the early Revolutionary period.

[7] Emerson's note: "Something great and immeasurable."

[8] Marcus Tullius Cicero (106–43 B.C.), Roman orator and political leader.

saints which seal them. In my better hours, I am the believer (if not the dupe) of brilliant promises, and can respect myself as the possessor of those powers which command the reason & passions of the multitude. The office of a clergyman is twofold; public preaching & private influence. Entire success in the first is the lot of few, but this I am encouraged to expect. If however the individual himself lack that moral worth which is to secure the last, his studies upon the first are idly spent. The most prodigious genius, a seraph's eloquence will shamefully defeat its own end, if it has not first won the heart of the defender to the cause he defends, but the coolest reason cannot censure my choice when I oblige myself *professionally* to a life which all wise men freely & advisedly adopt. I put no great restraint on myself & can therefore claim little merit in a manner of life which chimes with inclination & habit. . . .

I have mentioned a defect of character; perhaps it is not one, but many. Every wise man aims at an entire conquest of himself. We applaud as possessed of extraordinary good sense, one who never makes the slightest mistake in speech or action; one in whom not only every important step of life, but every passage of conversation, every duty of the day, even every movement of every muscle—hands, feet, & tongue, are measured & dictated by deliberate reason. I am not assuredly that excellent creature. A score of words & deeds issue from me daily, of which I am not the master. They are begotten of weakness & born of shame. I cannot assume the elevation I ought—but lose the influence I should exert among those of meaner or younger understanding, for want of sufficient *bottom* in my nature, for want of that confidence of manner which springs from an erect mind which is without fear & without reproach. In my frequent humiliation, even before women & children I am compelled to remember the poor boy who cried, "I told you, Father, they would find me out." Even those feelings which are counted noble & generous, take in me the taint of frailty. For my strong propensity to friendship, instead of working out its manly ends, degenerates to a fondness for particular casts of feature perchance not unlike the doting of old King James.[9] Stateliness & silence hang very like Mokannah's suspicious silver veil,[10] only concealing what is best not shewn. What is called a warm heart, I have not.

The stern accuser Conscience cries that the Catalogue of Confessions is not yet full. I am a lover of indolence, & of the belly. And the good have a right to ask the Neophyte who wears this garment of scarlet sin, why he comes where all are apparelled in white? Dares he hope that some patches of pure & generous feeling, some bright fragments of lofty thought, it may be of divine poesy shall charm the eye away from all the particoloured shades of his Character? And when he is clothed in the vestments of the priest, & has inscribed on his forehead 'Holiness to the Lord', & wears on his breast the breastplate of the tribes, then can the Ethiopian change his skin & the unclean be pure? Or how shall I strenuously enforce on men the duties & habits to which I am a stranger? Physician, heal thyself.[11] I need not go far for an answer to so natural a question. I am young in my everlasting existence. I already discern

---

[9] King James I (1566–1625) of England wrote on demonology.

[10] In Thomas Moore's *Lalla Rookh*, a popular early nineteenth-century Romantic poem, Hashim ibn-Hakim al-Mokanna wears a veil to hide his feigned divinity.

[11] In Luke 4:23, Jesus says to the people of Nazareth: "Ye will surely say unto me this proverb, Physician, heal Thyself: whatsoever we have done in Capernaum, do also here in thy country."

the deep dye of elementary errors, which threaten to colour its infinity of duration. And I judge that if I devote my nights & days *in form,* to the service of God & the War against Sin—I shall soon be prepared to do the same *in substance.*

I cannot accurately estimate my chances of success, in my profession, & in life. Were it just to judge the future from the past, they would be very low. In my case I think it is not. I have never expected success in my present employment. My scholars are carefully instructed, my money is faithfully earned, but the instructor is little wiser. & the duties were never congenial with my disposition. Thus far the dupe of hope I have trudged on with my bundle at my back, and my eye fixed on the distant hill where my burden would fall. It may be I shall write *dupe* a long time to come & the end of life shall intervene betwixt me & the release. My trust is that my profession shall be my regeneration of mind, manners, inward & outward estate; or rather my starting point, for I have hoped to put on eloquence as a robe, and by goodness and zeal and the awfulness of virtue to press & prevail over the false judgments, the rebel passions & corrupt habits of men. We blame the past, we magnify & gild the future and are not wiser for the multitude of days. Spin on, Ye of the adamantine spindle, spin on, my fragile thread.

[June 2, 1832]

I have sometimes thought that in order to be a good minister it was necessary to leave the ministry. The profession is antiquated. In an altered age, we worship in the dead forms of our forefathers. Were not a Socratic paganism better than an effete super-annuated Christianity?

[from *July 15, 1832, White Mountains*][12]

A few low mountains, a great many clouds always covering the great peaks, a circle of woods to the horizon, a peacock on the fence or in the yard, & two travellers no better contented than myself in the plain parlor of this house make up the whole picture of this unsabbatized Sunday. But the hours pass on—creep or fly—& bear me and my fellows to the decision of questions of duty; to the crises of our fate; and to the solution of this mortal problem. . . .

The hour of decision. It seems not worth while for them who charge others with exalting forms above the moon to fear forms themselves with extravagant dislike. I am so placed that my aliquid ingenii[13] may be brought into useful action. Let me not bury my talent in the earth in my indignation at this windmill. But though the thing may be useless & even pernicious, do not destroy what is good & useful in a high degree rather than comply with what is hurtful in a small degree. The Communicant celebrates on a foundation either of authority or of tradition an ordinance which has been the occasion to thousands—I hope to thousands of thousands—of contrition, of gratitude, of prayer, of faith, of love, & of holy living. Far be it from any of my friends—God forbid it be in my heart—to interrupt any occasion thus blessed of God's influences upon the human mind. I will not, because we may not all think alike

---

[12] Range of mountains in northern New Hampshire. [13] Emerson's note: "Something of a genius."

of the means, fight so strenuously against the means, as to miss of the end which we all value alike. I think Jesus did not mean to institute a perpetual celebration, but that a commemoration of him would be useful. Others think that Jesus did establish this one. We are agreed that one is useful, & we are agreed I hope in the way in which it must be made useful, viz, by each one's making it an original Commemoration.

I know very well that it is a bad sign in a man to be too conscientious, & stick at gnats. The most desperate scoundrels have been the over refiners. Without accomodation society is impracticable. But this ordinance is esteemed the most sacred of religious institutions & I cannot go habitually to an institution which they esteem holiest with indifference & dislike.

[October 1, 1832]

Has the doctrine ever been fairly preached of man's moral nature? The whole world holds on to formal Christianity, & nobody teaches the essential truth, the heart of Christianity for fear of shocking &c. Every teacher when once he finds himself insisting with all his might upon a great truth turns up the ends of it at last with a cautious showing *how* it is agreeable to the life & teaching of Jesus—as if that was any recommendation. As if the blessedness of Jesus' life & teaching were not because they were agreeable to the truth. Well this cripples his teaching. It bereaves the truth he inculcates of more than half its force by representing it as something secondary that can't stand alone. The truth of truth consists in this, that it is selfevident, selfsubsistent. It is light. You don't get a candle to see the sun rise. Instead of making Christianity a vehicle of truth you make truth only a horse for Christianity. It is a very operose way of making people good. You must be humble because Christ says, 'Be humble'. 'But why must I obey Christ?' 'Because God sent him.' But how do I know God sent him? 'Because your own heart teaches the same thing he taught.' Why then shall I not go to my own heart at first?

[September 1, 1833, Liverpool]

I thank the great God who has led me through this European scene, this last school-room in which he has pleased to instruct me from Malta's isle, thro' Sicily, thro' Italy, thro' Switzerland, thro' France, thro' England, thro' Scotland, in safety & pleasure & has now brought me to the shore & the ship that steers westward. He has shown me the men I wished to see—Landor, Coleridge, Carlyle, Wordsworth[14]—he has thereby comforted & confirmed me in my convictions. Many things I owe to the sight of these men. I shall judge more justly, less timidly, of wise men forevermore. To be sure not one of these is a mind of the very first class, but what the intercourse with each of these suggests is true of intercourse with better men, that they never *fill the ear*—fill the mind—no, it is an *idealized* portrait which always we draw of them. Upon an intelligent man, wholly a stranger to their names, they would make in conversation no deep impression—none of a world-filling fame—they would be remembered as sensible well read earnest men—not more. Especially are they all

---

[14] English poets and essayists Walter Savage Landor (1775–1864), Samuel Taylor Coleridge (1772–1834), Thomas Carlyle (1795–1881), and William Wordsworth (1770–1850).

deficient all these four—in different degrees but all deficient—in insight into religious truth. They have no idea of that species of moral truth which I call the first philosophy. (Peter Hunt[15] is as wise a talker as either of these men. Don't laugh.)

The comfort of meeting men of genius such as these is that they talk sincerely. They feel themselves to be so rich that they are above the meanness of pretending to knowledge which they have not & they frankly tell you what puzzles them. But Carlyle. Carlyle is so amiable that I love him. But I am very glad my travelling is done. A man not old feels himself too old to be a vagabond. The people at their work, the people whose avocations I interrupt by my letters of introduction accuse me by their looks for leaving my business to hinder theirs.

These men make you feel that fame is a conventional thing & that man is a sadly 'limitary' spirit. You speak to them as to children or persons of inferior capacity whom it is necessary to humor; adapting our tone & remarks to their known prejudices & not to our knowledge of the truth.

I believe in my heart it is better to admire too rashly, as I do, than to be admired too rashly as the great men of this day are. They miss by their premature canonization a great deal of necessary knowledge, & one of these days must begin the world again (as to their surprize they will find needful) poor. I speak now in general & not of these individuals. God save a great man from a little circle of flatterers. I know it is sweet, very sweet, rats bane.

[September 6, 1833]

Fair fine wind, still in the Channel—off the coast of Ireland but not in sight of land. This morning 37 sail in sight.

I like my book about nature & wish I knew where & how I ought to live. God will show me. I am glad to be on my way home yet not so glad as others & my way to the bottom I could find perchance with less regret for I think it would not hurt me, that is the ducking or drowning.

[November–December 1833]

This Book is my Savings Bank. I grow richer because I have somewhere to deposit my earnings; and fractions are worth more to me because corresponding fractions are waiting here that shall be made integers by their addition.

[from *November 15, 1834*]

Hail to the quiet fields of my fathers! Not wholly unattended by supernatural friendship & favor let me come hither. Bless my purposes as they are simple & virtuous. . . . Henceforth I design not to utter any speech, poem, or book that is not entirely & peculiarly my work. I will say at Public Lectures & the like, those things which I have meditated for their own sake & not for the first time with a view to that occasion. If otherwise you select a new subject & labor to make a good appearance on the appointed day, it is so much lost time to you & lost time to your hearer. It

---

[15] Student of Emerson's in 1825.

is a parenthesis in your genuine life. You are your own dupe. & for the sake of conciliating your audience you have failed to edify them & winning their ear you have really lost their love and gratitude.

[May 26, 1837]

Who shall define to me an Individual? I behold with awe & delight many illustrations of the One Universal Mind. I see my being imbedded in it. As a plant in the earth so I grow in God. I am only a form of him. He is the soul of Me. I can even with a mountainous aspiring say, *I am God,* by transferring my *Me* out of the flimsy & unclean precincts of my body, my fortunes, my private will, & meekly retiring upon the holy austerities of the Just & the Loving—upon the secret fountains of Nature. That thin & difficult ether, I also can breathe. The mortal lungs & nostrils burst & shrivel, but the soul itself needeth no organs—it is all element & all organ. Yet why not always so? How came the Individual thus armed & impassioned to parricide, thus murderously inclined ever to traverse & kill the divine life? Ah wicked Manichee![16] Into that dim problem I cannot enter. A believer in Unity, a seer of Unity, I yet behold two.

I behold; I bask in beauty; I await; I wonder; Where is my Godhead now? This is the Male & Female principle in Nature. One Man, male & female created he him. Hard as it is to describe God, it is harder to describe the Individual.

A certain wandering light comes to me which I instantly perceive to be the Cause of Causes. It transcends all proving. It is itself the ground of being; and I see that it is not one & I another, but this is the life of my life. That is one fact, then; that in certain moments I have known that I existed directly from God, and am, as it were, his organ. And in my ultimate consciousness Am He. Then, secondly, the contradictory fact is familiar, that I am a surprised spectator & learner of all my life. This is the habitual posture of the mind—beholding. But whenever the day dawns, the great day of truth on the soul, it comes with awful invitation to me to accept it, to blend with its aurora.

Cannot I conceive the Universe without a contradiction?

[August 31, 1838]

Yesterday at ΦBK[17] anniversary. Steady, steady. I am convinced that if a man will be a true scholar, he shall have perfect freedom. The young people & the mature hint at odium, & aversion of faces to be presently encountered in society. I say no: I fear it not. No scholar need fear it. For if it be true that he is merely an observer, a dispassionate reporter, no partisan, a singer merely for the love of music, his is a position of perfect immunity: to him no disgusts can attach; he is invulnerable. The vulgar think he would found a sect & would be installed & made much of. He knows better & much prefers his melons & his woods. Society has no bribe for me, neither

---

[16] Manichean: one who follows the dualistic religious philosophy taught by the Persian prophet Manes (ca. third century B.C.).

[17] Phi Beta Kappa, the national honor society of college students and graduates chosen on the basis of high academic standing. (See Emerson's essay "The American Scholar.")

in politics, nor church, nor college, nor city. My resources are far from exhausted. If they will not hear me lecture, I shall have leisure for my book which wants me. Beside, it is an universal maxim worthy of all acceptation that a man may have that allowance which he takes. Take the place & attitude to which you see your unquestionable right, & all men acquiesce. Who are these murmurers, these haters, these revilers? Men of no knowledge, & therefore no stability. The scholar on the contrary is sure of his point, is fast-rooted, & can securely predict the hour when all this roaring multitude shall roar *for* him. Analyze the chiding opposition & it is made up of such timidities, uncertainties, & no opinions, that it is not worth dispersing.

It is one of the blessings of old friends that you can afford to be stupid with them.

[from *October 26, 1838*]

Every word, every striking word that occurs in the pages of an original genius will provoke attack & be the subject of twenty pamphlets & a hundred paragraphs. Should he be so duped as to stop & listen? Rather, let him know that the page he writes today will contain a new subject for the pamphleteers, & that which he writes tomorrow, more. Let him not be misled to give it any more than the notice due from him, viz. just that which it had in his first page, before the controversy. The exaggeration of the notice is right for them, false for him. Every word that he quite naturally writes is as prodigious & offensive. So write on, & by & by will come a reader and an age that will justify all your context. Do not even look behind. Leave that bone for them to pick & welcome.

Let me study & work contentedly & faithfully, I do not remember my critics. I forget them—I depart from them by every step I take. If I think then of them, it is a bad sign. . . .

[*November 3, 1838*]

I should not dare to tell all my story. A great deal of it I do not yet understand. How much of it is incomplete. In my strait & decorous way of living, native to my family & to my country, & more strictly proper to me, is nothing extravagant or flowing. I content myself with moderate, languid actions, & never transgress the staidness of village manners. Herein I consult the poorness of my powers. More culture would come out of great virtues & vices perhaps, but I am not up to that. Should I obey an irregular impulse, & establish every new relation that my fancy prompted with the men & women I see, I should not be followed by my faculties; they would play me false in making good their very suggestions. They delight in inceptions, but they warrant nothing else.

I told Jones Very[18] that I had never suffered, & that I could scarce bring myself to feel a concern for the safety & life of my nearest friends that would satisfy them: that I saw clearly that if my wife, my child, my mother, should be taken from me, I should still remain whole with the same capacity of cheap enjoyment from all things. I should not grieve enough, although I love them. But could I make them feel what I feel—the boundless resources of the soul—remaining entire when particular threads

---

[18] Religious sonneteer (1813–1880).

of relation are snapped—I should then dismiss forever the little remains of uneasiness I have in regard to them.

[May 28, 1839]

There is no history: There is only Biography. The attempt to perpetuate, to fix a thought or principle, fails continually. You can only live for yourself: Your action is good only whilst it is alive—whilst it is in you. The awkward imitation of it by your child or your disciple, is not a repetition of it, is not the same thing but another thing. The new individual must work out the whole problem of science, letters, & theology for himself, can owe his fathers nothing. There is no history; only biography.

[September 14, 1839]

An education in things is not: we all are involved in the condemnation of words, an Age of words. We are shut up in schools & college recitation rooms for ten or fifteen years & come out at last with a bellyfull of words & do not know a thing. We cannot use our hands or our legs or our eyes or our arms. We do not know an edible root in the woods. We cannot tell our course by the stars nor the hour of the day by the sun. It is well if we can swim & skate. We are afraid of a horse, of a cow, of a dog, of a cat, of a spider. Far better was the Roman rule to teach a boy nothing that he could not learn standing. Now here are my wise young neighbors who instead of getting like the workmen into a railroad-car where they have not even the activity of holding the reins, have got into a boat which they have built with their own hands, with sails which they have contrived to serve as a tent by night, & gone up the river Merrimack[19] to live by their wits on the fish of the stream & the berries of the wood. My worthy neighbor Dr Bartlett expressed a true parental instinct when he desired to send his boy with them to learn something. The farm, the farm is the right school. The reason of my deep respect for the farmer is that he is a realist & not a dictionary. The farm is a piece of the world, the School house is not. The farm by training the physical rectifies & invigorates the metaphysical & moral nature.

[September 14–17, 1839]

I hate preaching whether in pulpits or Teachers' meetings. Preaching is a pledge & I wish to say what I think & feel today with the proviso that tomorrow perhaps I shall contradict it all. Freedom boundless I wish. I will not pledge myself not to drink wine, not to drink ink, not to lie, & not to commit adultery lest I hanker tomorrow to do these very things by reason of my having tied my hands. Besides Man is so poor he cannot afford to part with any advantages or bereave himself of the functions even of one hair. I do not like to speak to the Peace Society if so I am to restrain me in so extreme a privilege as the use of the sword & bullet. For the peace of the man who has forsworn the use of the bullet seems to me not quite peace, but a canting

[19] River flowing from central New Hampshire
through northeastern Massachusetts to the
Atlantic Ocean.

impotence: but with knife & pistol in my hands, if I, from greater bravery & honor, cast them aside, then I know the glory of peace.

The mob are always interesting. We hate editors, preachers, & all manner of scholars, and fashionists. A blacksmith, a truckman, a farmer we follow into the barroom & watch with eagerness what they shall say, for such as they, do not speak because they are expected to, but because they have somewhat to say.

It seems as if the present age of words should naturally be followed by an age of silence when men shall speak only through facts & so regain their health. We die of words. We are hanged, drawn, & quartered by dictionaries. We walk in the vale of shadows. It is an age of hobgoblins. Public Opinion is a hobgoblin, Christianity a hobgoblin, the God of popular worship a hobgoblin. When shall we attain to be real & be born into the new heaven & earth of nature & truth?

It is a disgrace to remember as we do. All our life is the pitifullest remembering. Memory is an indigestion, a flatulency of mind which eats over again its dinner all night with feverish disgust. Each man does but six or seven new things in all his lifetime; the smith, the joiner, the farmer repeat every day the same manipulations. The singer repeats his old song, the preacher his old sermon, the talker his old fact.

It is not good sense to repeat an old story to the same child. Yet the pulpit[20] thinks there is some piquancy or rag of meat in his paragraph about the traitor Judas or the good Samaritan.

[from *December 22–23, 1839*]

Every thing should be treated poetically—law, politics, housekeeping, money. A judge and a banker must drive their craft poetically as well as a dancer or a scribe. That is, they must exert that higher vision which causes the object to become fluid & plastic. Then they are inventive, they detect its capabilities. If they do not this they have nothing that can be called success, but the work & the workman become blockish & near the point of everlasting congelation. All human affairs need the perpetual intervention of this elastic principle to preserve them supple & alive as the earth needs the presence of caloric through its pores to resist the tendency to absolute solidity. If you would write a code or logarithms or a cook-book you cannot spare the poetic impulse. We must not only have hydrogen in balloons and steel springs under coaches but we must have fire under the Andes at the core of the world. . . .

[October 7, 1840]

I have been writing with some pains Essays on various matters as a sort of apology to my country for my apparent idleness. But the poor work has looked poorer daily as I strove to end it. My genius seemed to quit me in such a mechanical work, a seeming wise—a cold exhibition of dead thoughts. When I write a letter to any one whom I love, I have no lack of words or thoughts: I am wiser than myself & read my paper with the pleasure of one who receives a letter, but what I write to fill up the gaps of a chapter is hard & cold, is grammar & logic; there is no magic in it; I do not wish to see it again. Settle with yourself your accusations of me. If I do not please you, ask me not to please you, but please yourself. What you call my indolence,

[20] I.e., the preacher.

nature does not accuse; the twinkling leaves, the sailing fleets of waterflies, the deep sky like me well enough and know me for their own. With them I have no embarrassments, diffidences, or compunctions: with them I mean to stay. You think it is because I have an income which exempts me from your day-labor, that I waste (as you call it) my time in sungazing & stargazing. You do not know me. If my debts, as they threaten, should consume what money I have, I should live just as I do now: I should eat worse food & wear a coarser coat and should wonder in a potato patch instead of in the wood—but it is I & not my Twelve Hundred dollars a year, that love God.

[October 17, 1840]

Yesterday George & Sophia Ripley, Margaret Fuller & Alcott[21] discussed here the new social plans.[22] I wished to be convinced, to be thawed, to be made nobly mad by the kindlings before my eye of a new dawn of human piety. But this scheme was arithmetic & comfort; this was a hint borrowed from the Tremont House & U.S. Hotel;[23] a rage in our poverty & politics to live rich & gentlemanlike, an anchor to leeward against a change of weather; a prudent forecast on the probable issue of the great questions of pauperism & property. And not once could I be inflamed—but sat aloof & thoughtless, my voice faltered & fell. It was not the cave of persecution which is the palace of spiritual power, but only a room in the Astor House hired for the Transcendentalists. I do not wish to remove from my present prison to a prison a little larger. I wish to break all prisons. I have not yet conquered my own house. It irks & repents me. Shall I raise the siege of this hencoop & march baffled away to a pretended siege of Babylon? It seems to me that so to do were to dodge the problem I am set to solve, & to hide my impotency in the thick of a crowd. I can see too afar that I should not find myself more than now—no, not so much, in that select, but not by me selected, fraternity. Moreover to join this body would be to traverse all my long trumpeted theory, and the instinct which spoke from it, that one man is a counterpoise to a city—that a man is stronger than a city, that his solitude is more prevalent & beneficent than the concert of crowds.

[from May 6, 1841]

I doubt if the interior & spiritual history of New England could be truelier told than through the exhibition of family history such as this, the picture of this group of M.M.E. & the boys, mainly Charles.[24] The genius of that woman, the key to her life, is in the conflict of the new & the old ideas in New England. The heir of whatever was rich & profound & efficient in thought & emotion in the old religion which planted & peopled this land, she strangely united to this passionate piety the fatal gift of penetration, a love of philosophy, an impatience of words,

---

[21] George Ripley (1802–1880), his wife Sophia, Margaret Fuller (1810–1850), and Amos Bronson Alcott (1799–1888). (See note 37 below.)

[22] I.e., plans for Brook Farm, a utopian community.

[23] The Tremont House (opened in 1829) and the

U.S. Hotel (opened in 1840) were famous hotels in Boston. The Astor House (opened in 1836) was a famous luxury hotel in New York.

[24] Mary Moody Emerson, Ralph Waldo's aunt, and his brothers William, Edward, Bulkeley, and Charles.

and was thus a religious skeptic. She held on with both hands to the faith of the past generation as to the palladium of all that was good & hopeful in the physical & metaphysical worlds, and in all companies, & on all occasions, & especially with these darling nephews of her hope & pride, extolled & poetised this beloved Calvinism.[25] Yet all the time she doubted & denied it, & could not tell whether to be more glad or sorry to find that these boys were irremediably born to the adoption & furtherance of the new ideas. . . . These combined traits in M.M.E.'s character gave the new direction to her hope; that these boys should be richly & holily qualified & bred to purify the old faith of what narrowness & error adhered to it & import all its fire into the new age—such a gift should her Prometheus[26] bring to men. She hated the poor, low, thin, unprofitable, unpoetical Humanitarians as the devastators of the Church & robbers of the soul & never wearies with piling on them new terms of slight & weariness. "Ah!" she said, "what a poet would Byron[27] have been, if he had been born & bred a Calvinist!"

[September(?) 1841]

I told H.T.[28] that his freedom is in the form, but he does not disclose new matter. I am very familiar with all his thoughts—they are my own quite originally drest. But if the question be, what new ideas has he thrown into circulation, he has not yet told what that is which he was created to say. I said to him what I often feel, I only know three persons who seem to me fully to see this law of reciprocity or compensation —himself, Alcott,[29] & myself: and 'tis odd that we should all be neighbors, for in the wide land or the wide earth I do not know another who seems to have it as deeply & originally as these three Gothamites.[30]

[January 28, 1842]

Yesterday night at 15 minutes after eight my little Waldo[31] ended his life.

[January 30, 1842]

What he looked upon is better, what he looked not upon is insignificant. The morning of Friday I woke at 3 oclock, & every cock in every barnyard was shrilling with the most unnecessary noise. The sun went up the morning sky with all his light, but the landscape was dishonored by this loss. For this boy in whose remembrance I have both slept & awaked so oft, decorated for me the morning star, & the evening cloud, how much more all the particulars of daily economy; for he had touched with his lively curiosity every trivial fact & circumstance in the household, the hard coal & the soft

---

[25] The religious doctrines of John Calvin (1509–1564), French-born Swiss theologian and reformer. Calvinism emphasized the supremacy of the Scriptures in the revelation of truth, the omnipotence of God, the innate depravity of humankind, the salvation of the elect by God's grace alone, and a rigid moral code.

[26] In Greek mythology, Prometheus, a Titan, stole fire from Olympus and gave it to humankind.

[27] George Gordon, Lord Byron (1788–1824), English poet of the Romantic period.

[28] Henry David Thoreau (1817–1862), then Emerson's neighbor and a resident at Walden Pond.

[29] Amos Bronson Alcott (see note 37 below).

[30] City dwellers.

[31] Emerson's son Waldo (1836–1842), who died of scarlet fever.

coal which I put into my stove; the wood of which he brought his little quota for grandmother's fire, the hammer, the pincers, & file, he was so eager to use; the microscope, the magnet, the little globe, & every trinket & instrument in the study; the loads of gravel on the meadow, the nests in the henhouse and many & many a little visit to the doghouse and to the barn—For every thing he had his own name & way of thinking, his own pronunciation & manner. And every word came mended from that tongue. A boy of early wisdom, of a grave & even majestic deportment, of a perfect gentleness.

Every tramper that ever tramped is abroad but the little feet are still.

He gave up his little innocent breath like a bird.

He dictated a letter to his cousin Willie[32] on Monday night to thank him for the Magic Lantern[33] which he had sent him, and said I wish you would tell Cousin Willie that I have so many presents that I do not need that he should send me any more unless he wishes to very much.

The boy had his full swing in this world. Never I think did a child enjoy more. He had been thoroughly respected by his parents & those around him & not interfered with; and he had been the most fortunate in respect to the influences near him for his Aunt Elizabeth[34] had adopted him from his infancy & treated him ever with that plain & wise love which belongs to her and, as she boasted, had never given him sugar plums.[35] So he was won to her & always signalized her arrival as a visit to him & left playmates playthings & all to go to her. Then Mary Russell had been his friend & teacher for two summers with true love & wisdom. Then Henry Thoreau had been one of the family for the last year, & charmed Waldo by the variety of toys whistles boats popguns & all kinds of instruments which he could make & mend; & possessed his love & respect by the gentle firmness with which he always treated him. Margaret Fuller & Caroline Sturgis[36] had also marked the boy & caressed & conversed with him whenever they were here. Meantime every day his Grandmother gave him his reading lesson & had by patience taught him to read & spell; by patience & by love for she loved him dearly.

Sorrow makes us all children again, destroys all differences of intellect. The wisest knows nothing.

[from **March–April 1842**]

Here prepares now the good A B Alcott[37] to go to England after so long & strict acquaintance as I have had with him for seven years. I saw him for the first time in Boston in 1835. What shall we say of him to the wise Englishman? . . .

He delights in speculation, in nothing so much and is very well endowed & weaponed for that work with a copious, accurate, & elegant vocabulary; I may say poetic; so that I know no man who speaks such good English as he, and is so inventive

[32] William Emerson (1835–1864), Ralph Waldo's nephew.

[33] Light-projecting toy of the period.

[34] Elizabeth Hoar, who had been engaged to Ralph Waldo's now-dead brother Charles.

[35] I.e., had never pampered him.

[36] Margaret Fuller and Caroline Sturgis (Mrs.

William Tappan) were two of Emerson's young women friends.

[37] Amos Bronson Alcott (1799–1888), reformer, educator, father of Louisa May Alcott, and friend of Emerson and Thoreau; Alcott was celebrated for his conversations.

withal. He speaks truth truly; or the expression is adequate. Yet he knows only this one language. He hardly needs an antagonist—he needs only an intelligent ear. Where he is greeted by loving & intelligent persons his discourse soars to a wonderful height, so regular, so lucid, so playful, so new & disdainful of all boundaries of tradition & experience, that the hearers seem no longer to have bodies or material gravity, but almost they can mount into the air at pleasure, or leap at one bound out of this poor solar system. I say this of his speech exclusively, for when he attempts to write, he loses, in my judgment, all his power, & I derive more pain than pleasure from the perusal. The Boston Post expressed the feeling of most readers in its rude joke when it said of his Orphic Sayings[38] that they "resembled a train of 15 railroad cars with one passenger." . . .

It must be conceded that it is speculation which he loves & not action. Therefore he dissatisfies everybody & disgusts many. When the conversation is ended, all is over. He lives tomorrow as he lived today for further discourse, not to begin, as he seemed pledged to do, a New Celestial life. The ladies fancied that he loved cake; very likely; most people do. Yet in the last two years he has changed his way of living which was perhaps a little easy & selfindulgent for such a Zeno,[39] so far as to become ascetically temperate. He has no vocation to labor, and, although he strenuously preached it for a time, & made some efforts to practise it, he soon found he had no genius for it, and that it was a cruel waste of his time. It depressed his spirits even to tears. . . .

Another circumstance marks this extreme love of speculation. He carries all his opinions & all his condition & manner of life in his hand, &, whilst you talk with him, it is plain he has put out no roots, but is an air-plant, which can readily & without any ill consequence be transported to any place. He is quite ready at any moment to abandon his present residence & employment, his country, nay, his wife & children, on very short notice, to put any new dream into practice which has bubbled up in the effervescence of discourse. If it is so with his way of living, much more so is it with his opinions. He never remembers. He never affirms anything today because he has affirmed it before. You are rather astonished, having left him in the morning with one set of opinions, to find him in the evening totally escaped from all recollection of them, as confident of a new line of conduct, & heedless of his old advocacy. . . .

His vice, an intellectual vice, grew out of this constitution, & was that to which almost all spiritualists have been liable—a certain brooding on the private thought which produces monotony in the conversation, & egotism in the character. Steadily subjective himself, the variety of facts which seem necessary to the health of most minds, yielded him no variety of meaning, & he quickly quitted the play on objects, to come to *the Subject,* which was always the same, viz. *Alcott in reference to the World of Today.* . . .

Unhappily, his conversation never loses sight of his own personality. He never quotes; he never refers; his only illustration is his own biography. His topic yesterday

---

[38] Charming, esoteric principles set forth in the work ascribed to Orpheus, legendary Thracian poet.

[39] Greek philosopher (342?–?270 B.C.), and founder of Stoicism.

is Alcott on the 17 October; today, Alcott on the 18 October; tomorrow, on the 19th. So will it be always. The poet rapt into future times or into deeps of nature admired for themselves, lost in their law, cheers us with a lively charm; but this noble genius discredits genius to me. I do not want any more such persons to exist. Part of this egotism in him is a certain comparing eye which seems to sour his view of persons prosperously placed, & to make his conversation often accusing & minatory. He is not selfsufficing & serene.

[from July–October 1851]

H. T.[40] will not stick—he is not practically renovator. He is a boy, & will be an old boy. Pounding beans is good to the end of pounding Empires, but not, if at the end of years, it is only beans.

I fancy it an inexcusable fault in him that he is insignificant here in the town. He speaks at Lyceum or other meeting but somebody else speaks & his speech falls dead & is forgotten. He rails at the town doings & ought to correct & inspire them.

America is the idea of emancipation.

Abolish kingcraft, Slavery, feudalism, blackletter monopoly, pull down gallows, explode priestcraft, tariff, open the doors of the sea to all emigrants. Extemporize government, California, Texas, Lynch Law. All this covers selfgovernment. All proceeds on the belief that as the people have made a govt. they can make another, that their Union & law is not in their memory but in their blood. If they unmake the law they can easily make it again.

These thirty nations are equal to any work. They are to become 50 millions presently & should achieve something just & generous. Let them trample out this mischief before it has trampled out them. For the future of slavery is not inviting. But the destinies of nations are too great for our spanning & what are the instruments no policy can show, whether Liberia, whether flax, cotton, whether the working them out by Irish & Germans none can tell; or by what scourges God has guarded his law. But one thing is imperative, not to do unjustly, not to steal a man, or help steal him, or to call stealing honest.

S. Ward[41] thinks 'Twill do for Carolina to be unreasonable & nullify.[42] But not so with Massachusetts, which is the head: the toe may nullify, but the head must not nullify.

We are glad at last to get a clear case, one on which no shadow of doubt can hang. This is not meddling with other people's affairs—this is other people meddling with us. This is not going crusading after slaves who it is alleged are very happy & comfortable where they are: all that amiable argument falls to the ground, but

---

[40] Henry David Thoreau.
[41] Samuel Gray Ward (1814–1884), lobbyist in Washington for financial interests.
[42] I.e., nullify the Fugitive Slave Law (1850).

defending a human being who has taken the risks of being shot or burned alive, or cast into the sea, or starved to death or suffocated in a wooden box—taken all this risk to get away from his driver & recover the rights of man. And this man the Statute says, you men of Massachusetts shall kidnap & send back again a thousand miles across the sea to the dog-hutch he fled from. And this filthy enactment was made in the 19th Century, by people who could read & write.

I will not obey it, by God.

[from July 1852]

I live a good while & acquire as much skill in literature as an old carpenter does in wood. It occurs, then, what pity, that now, when you know something, have at least learned so much good omission, your organs should fail you; your eyes, health, fire & zeal of work, should decay daily. Then I remember that it is the mind of the world which is the good carpenter, the good scholar, sailor, or blacksmith, thousand-handed, versatile, all-applicable. . . . In you, this rich soul has peeped, despite your horny muddy eyes, at books & poetry. Well, it took you up, & showed you something to the purpose; that there was something there. Look, look, old mole! there, straight up before you, is the magnificent Sun. If only for the instant, you see it. Well, in this way it educates the youth of the Universe; in this way, warms, suns, refines every particle; then it drops the little channel or canal, through which the Life rolled beatific —like a fossil to the ground—thus touched & educated by a moment of sunshine, to be the fairer material for future channels & canals, through which the old Glory shall dart again, in new directions, until the Universe shall have been shot through & through, *tilled* with light.

[from Spring 1859(?)]

I am a natural reader, & only a writer in the absence of natural writers. In a true time, I should never have written. . . .

I have now for more than a year, I believe, ceased to write in my Journal, in which I formerly wrote almost daily. I see few intellectual persons, & even those to no purpose, & sometimes believe that I have no new thoughts, and that my life is quite at an end. But the magnet that lies in my drawer for years, may believe it has no magnetism, and, on touching it with steel, it shows the old virtue; and, this morning, came by a man with knowledge & interests like mine, in his head, and suddenly I had thoughts again.

Why do I hide in a library, read books, or write them, & skulk in the woods, & not dictate to these fellows, who, you say, dictate to me, as they should not? Why? but because in my bones is none of the magnetism which flows in theirs. They inundate all men with their streams. I have a reception & a perception, which they have not, but it is rare & casual, and yet drives me forth to watch these workers, if so be I may derive from their performance a new insight for mine. But there are no equal terms for me & them. They all unwittingly perform for me the part of the gymnotus on the fish.

The number of conceited people is so great, that it must subserve great uses in nature, like sexual passion.

1. You shall be somebody.
2. You shall have catholicity.
3. You shall know the power of the imagination.

You shall come from the Azure.

You shall be intellectual.

[November 1862]

In art, they have got that far, the rage for Saints & crucifixions & pietàs[43] is past, and landscape & portrait, & history, & *genres* have come in. It is significant enough of the like advance in religion.

There never was a nation great except through trial. A religious revolution cuts sharpest, & tests the faith & endurance. A civil war sweeps away all the false issues on which it begun, & arrives presently at real & lasting questions.

When we build, our first care is to find good foundation. If the surface be loose, or sandy, or springy, we clear it away, & dig down to the hard pan, or, better, to the living rock, & bed our courses in that. So will we do with the state. The War[44] is serving many good purposes. It is no respecter of respectable persons or of worn out party platforms. War is a realist, shatters everything flimsy & shifty, sets aside all false issues, & breaks through all that is not real as itself, comes to organise opinions & parties, resting on the necessities of man, like its own cannonade comes crushing in through party walls that have stood fifty or sixty years as if they were solid. The screaming of leaders, the votes by acclamation of conventions, are all idle wind. They cry for mercy but they cry to one who never knew the word. He is the Arm of the Fates and as has been said "nothing prevails against God but God." Everything must perish except that which must live.

Well, this is the task before us, to accept the benefit of the War: it has not created our false relations, they have created it. It simply demonstrates the rottenness it found. We watch its course as we did the cholera, which goes where predisposition already existed, took only the susceptible, set its seal on every putrid spot, & on none other, followed the limestone, & left the granite. So the War. Anxious Statesmen try to rule it, to slacken it here & let it rage there, to not exasperate, to

---

[43] Paintings or sculptures of the Virgin Mary holding and mourning the dead Jesus.   [44] The Civil War.

keep the black man out of it; to keep it well in hand, nor let it ride over old party lines, nor much molest trade, and to confine it to the frontier of the 2 sections. Why need Cape Cod, why need Casco Bay, why need Lake Superior, know any thing of it? But the Indians have been bought, & they come down on Lake Superior; Boston & Portland are threatened by the pirate; more than that, Secession unexpectedly shows teeth in Boston; our parties have just shown you that the war is already in Massachusetts, as in Richmond.

Let it search, let it grind, let it overturn, &, like the fire when it finds no more fuel, it burns out. The war will show, as all wars do, what wrong is intolerable, what wrong makes & breeds all this bad blood. I suppose that it shows two incompatible states of society, freedom & slavery. If a part of this country is civilized up to a clear insight of freedom, & of its necessity, and another part is not so far civilized, then I suppose that the same difficulties will continue; the war will not be extinguished; no treaties, no peace, no Constitutions can paper over the lips of that red crater.

Only when, at last, so many parts of the country as can combine on an equal & moral contract—not to protect each other in polygamy, or in kidnapping, or in eating men, but in humane & just activities—only so many can combine firmly & durably.

I speak the speech of an idealist. I say let the rule be right. If the theory is right, it is not so much matter about the facts. If the plan of your fort is right it is not so much matter that you have got a rotten beam or a cracked gun somewhere, they can by & by be replaced by better without tearing your fort to pieces. But if the plan is wrong, then all is rotten, & every step adds to the ruin. Then every screw is loose, and all the machine crazy. The question stands thus, reconstruction is no longer matter of doubt. All our action now is new & unconstitutional, & necessarily so. To bargain or treat at all with the rebels, to make arrangements with them about exchange of prisoners or hospitals, or truces to bury the dead, all unconstitutional & enough to drive a strict constructionist out of his wits. Much more in our future action touching peace, any & every arrangement short of forcible subjugation of the rebel country, will be flat disloyalty, on our part.

Then how to reconstruct. I say, this time, go to work right. Go down to the pan, see that your works turn on a jewel. Do not make an impossible mixture.

Do not lay your cornerstone on a shaking morass that will let down the superstructure into a bottomless pit again.

Leave slavery out. Since (unfortunately as some may think) God is God, & nothing satisfies all men but justice, let us have that, & let us stifle our prejudices against commonsense & humanity, & agree that every man shall have what he honestly earns, and, if he is a sane & innocent man, have an equal vote in the state, and a fair chance in society.

And I, speaking in the interest of no man & no party, but simply as a geometer of his forces, say that the smallest beginning, so that it is just, is better & stronger than the largest that is not quite just.

This time, no compromises, no concealments, no crimes that cannot be called by name, shall be tucked in under another name, like, "persons held to labor," meaning persons stolen, & "held", meaning held by hand-cuffs, when they are not under whips.

Now the smallest state so formed will & must be strong, the interest & the affection of every man will make it strong by his entire strength, and it will mightily persuade every other man, & every neighboring territory to make it larger, and it will not reach its limits until it comes to people who think that they are a little cunninger than the maker of this world & of the consciences of men.

[from June 1863]

In reading Henry Thoreau's Journal, I am very sensible of the vigor of his constitution. That oaken strength which I noted whenever he walked or worked or surveyed wood lots, the same unhesitating hand with which a field-laborer accosts a piece of work which I should shun as a waste of strength, Henry shows in his literary task. He has muscle, & ventures on & performs feats which I am forced to decline. In reading him, I find the same thought, the same spirit that is in me, but he takes a step beyond, & illustrates by excellent images that which I should have conveyed in a sleepy generality. 'Tis as if I went into a gymnasium, & saw youths leap, climb, & swing with a force unapproachable—though their feats are only continuations of my initial grapplings & jumps.

[May 24, 1864]

Yesterday, 23 May, we buried Hawthorne in Sleepy Hollow, in a pomp of sunshine & verdure, & gentle winds. James F. Clarke[45] read the service in the Church & at the grave. Longfellow, Lowell, Holmes, Agassiz, Hoar, Dwight, Whipple, Norton, Alcott, Hillard, Fields, Judge Thomas, & I, attended the hearse as pall bearers.[46] Franklin Pierce[47] was with the family. The church was copiously decorated with white flowers delicately arranged. The corpse was unwillingly shown—only a few moments to this company of his friends. But it was noble & serene in its aspect—nothing amiss —a calm & powerful head. A large company filled the church, & the grounds of the cemetery. All was so bright & quiet, that pain or mourning was hardly suggested, & Holmes said to me, that it looked like a happy meeting.

Clarke in the church said, that Hawthorne had done more justice than any other to the shades of life, shown a sympathy with the crime in our nature, &, like Jesus, was the friend of sinners.

I thought there was a tragic element in the event, that might be more fully rendered —in the painful solitude of the man—which, I suppose, could not longer be endured, & he died of it.

---

[45] James Freeman Clarke (1810–1888), who had officiated at Nathaniel Hawthorne's marriage to Sophia Peabody.

[46] Many of the pallbearers at Hawthorne's funeral were, along with Emerson, members of the Saturday Club, which gathered the last Saturday of each month at the Parker House in Boston. Henry Wadsworth Longfellow (1807–1882), and James Russell Lowell (1819–1891), prominent poets; Oliver Wendell Holmes (1809–1894), physician and author; Louis Agassiz (1807–1873), Swiss immigrant and scientist at Harvard; Ebenezer Rockwood Hoar

(1816–1895), brother of Charles Emerson's fiancee Elizabeth Hoar; John S. Dwight (1813–1893), music critic; Edwin Percy Whipple (1819–1886), literary critic; Charles Eliot Norton (1827–1908), writer; Amos Bronson Alcott (1799–1888), educator and Transcendentalist; George Hillard (1808–1879), writer and lawyer; James T. Fields (1817–1881), Hawthorne's publisher; and B. F. Thomas (1813–1878), Boston judge.

[47] Franklin Pierce (1804–1869) had served as president of the United States from 1853 to 1857.

I have found in his death a surprise & disappointment. I thought him a greater man than any of his works betray, that there was still a great deal of work in him, & that he might one day show a purer power.

Moreover I have felt sure of him in his neighborhood, & in his necessities of sympathy & intelligence, that I could well wait his time—his unwillingness & caprice —and might one day conquer a friendship. It would have been a happiness, doubtless to both of us, to have come into habits of unreserved intercourse. It was easy to talk with him—there were no barriers—only, he said so little, that I talked too much, & stopped only because—as he gave no indications—I feared to exceed. He showed no egotism or self-assertion, rather a humility, &, at one time, a fear that he had written himself out. One day, when I found him on the top of his hill, in the woods, he paced back the path to his house, & said, *"this path is the only remembrance of me that will remain."* Now it appears that I waited too long.

Lately, he had removed himself the more by the indignation his perverse politics & unfortunate friendship for that paltry Franklin Pierce awaked—though it rather moved pity for Hawthorne, & the assured belief that he would outlive it, & come right at last.

I have forgotten in what year (Sept. 27, 1842), but it was whilst he lived in the Manse,[48] soon after his marriage, that I said to him, "I shall never see you in this hazardous way; we must take a long walk together. Will you go to Harvard & visit the Shakers?"[49] He agreed, & we took a June day, & walked the twelve miles, got our dinner from the Brethren, slept at the Harvard Inn, & returned home by another road the next day. It was a satisfactory tramp; we had good talk on the way, of which I set down some record in my journal.

[Date Uncertain: Probably from the 1870s]

But of one thing I am well aware, that it is comparatively of little importance that I praise books to you. You will not read them the more that I should, nor the less if I held my peace. A better orator than I pleads for them with some of you, & to some of you a stronger dissuasion than I or any man could attempt, debars you from their use. I mean that some men are born to read, & must & will read at whatever cost, & others are born to work & executive skills, that take tyrannical possession of the man, & so absorb him that he has no ears or eyes for those pursuits which constitute the chief happiness of other souls. Books only put him to sleep. I surrender such willingly to the Fates—I hope, in each case, noble ones—that wait for them at the door.

1824–1870s(?)/1909

---

[48] Hawthorne had lived in the Emerson house, the Old Manse, in Concord.

[49] Religious sect that practiced communal living and celibacy.

Letter to Lydia Jackson[*]

[February 1, 1835]

Concord, 1 February

One of my wise masters, Edmund Burke, said, "A wise man will speak the truth with temperance that he may speak it the longer."[1] In this new sentiment that you awaken in me, my Lydian Queen,[2] what might scare others pleases me, its quietness, which I accept as a pledge of permanence. I delighted myself on Friday with my quite domesticated position & the good understanding that grew all the time, yet I went & came without one vehement word—or one passionate sign. In this was nothing of design, I merely surrendered myself to the hour & to the facts. I find a sort of grandeur in the modulated expressions of a love in which the individuals, & what might seem even reasonable personal expectations, are steadily postponed to a regard for truth & the universal love. Do not think me a metaphysical[3] lover. I am a man & hate & suspect the over refiners, & do sympathize with the homeliest pleasures & attractions by which our good foster mother Nature draws her children together. Yet am I well pleased that between us the most permanent ties should be the first formed & thereon should grow whatever others human nature will.

My Mother rejoices very much & asks me all manner of questions about you, many of which I cannot answer. I dont know whether you sing, or read French, or Latin, or where you have lived, & much more. So you see there is nothing for it but that you should come here & on the Battle-Ground stand the fire of her catechism.

Under this morning's severe but beautiful light I thought dear friend that hardly should I get away from Concord. I must win you to love it. I am born a poet, of a low class without doubt yet a poet. That is my nature & vocation. My singing be sure is very "husky," & is for the most part in prose. Still am I a poet in the sense of a perceiver & dear lover of the harmonies that are in the soul & in matter, & specially of the correspondences between these & those. A sunset, a forest, a snow storm, a certain river-view, are more to me than many friends & do ordinarily divide my day with my books. Wherever I go therefore I guard & study my rambling propensities with a care that is ridiculous to people, but to me is the care of my high calling. Now Concord is only one of a hundred towns in which I could find these necessary objects but Plymouth I fear is not one.[4] Plymouth is streets; I live in the wide champaign.[5]

Time enough for this however. If I succeed in preparing my lecture on Michel

---

[*] This may be the earliest extant letter to Lydia Jackson, whom Emerson married the following September.

[1] Freely quoted from the letters of Edmund Burke (1729–1797), British political theorist and philosopher.

[2] Emerson here playfully names Lydia Jackson queen of Lydia, an ancient Aegean country of Asia Minor.

[3] Allusion to the seventeenth-century English

poets of the school of John Donne, whose verse is characterized by complex, abstract imagery and an abundance of conceits.

[4] Subsequent letters reveal that Emerson was unyielding in his preference for Concord rather than Plymouth, Massachusetts, as a town suitable for a poet.

[5] In this context, level and open country; a plain.

Angelo Buonaroti this week for Thursday,[6] I will come to Plymouth on Friday. If I do not succeed—do not attain unto the Idea of that man—I shall read of Luther, Thursday & then I know not when I shall steal a visit.—

Dearest forgive the egotism of all this letter Say they not 'The more love the more egotism.' Repay it by as much & more. Write, write to me. And please dear Lidian take that same low counsel & leave thinking for the present & let the winds of heaven blow away your dyspepsia.

Waldo E.

1835/1939

Letters to Thomas Carlyle[*]

[from *May 10, 1838*]

Concord, 10 May, 1838

My dear friend,

Yesterday I had your letter of March. It quickens my purpose (always all but ripe) to write to you. If it had come earlier, I should have been confirmed in my original purpose of publishing "Select Miscellanies of T. C."[1] As it is, we are far on in the printing of the two first volumes (to make 900 pp.) of the papers as they stand in your list. And, now I find, we shall only get as far as the 17th or 18th article. I regret it, because this book will not embrace those papers I chiefly desire to provide people with; and it may be some time, in these years of bankruptcy & famine, before we shall think it prudent to publish two volumes more. But Loring[2] is a good man & thinks that many desire to see the sources of Nile.[3] I, for my part, fancy that to meet the taste of the readers we should publish *from the last,* backwards, beginning with the paper on Scott,[4] which has had the best reception ever known. Carlyleism is becoming so fashionable that the most austere Seniors are glad to qualify their reprobation by applauding this review. I have agreed with the bookseller publishing the Miscellanies, that he is to guarantee to you on every copy he sells, $1.00; and you are to have the total profit on every copy subscribed for. The retail price to be $2.50; the cost of the work is not yet precisely ascertained. The work will probably appear

---

[6] The *Boston Daily Advertiser* (January 29–February 26, 1835) had announced an introductory lecture, with no title for January 29 and lectures on Michelangelo (February 5), Martin Luther (February 12), John Milton (February 20), and George Fox (February 26), all to be held in Boston at the Society for the Diffusion of Useful Knowledge.

[*] Emerson served as an agent for the American publication of Carlyle's *The French Revolution* (1839).

[1] I.e., Thomas Carlyle.

[2] Emerson's friend George Bailey Loring.

[3] Emerson reports here Loring's opinion that Carlyle's papers should be published from the beginning. In his essay "New England Reformers" (1844), Emerson would write, "Caesar, just before the battle of Pharsalia, discourses with the Egyptian priest concerning the fountains of the Nile, and offers to quit the army, the empire, and Cleopatra, if he will show him those mysterious sources." The story itself is drawn from Lucan's *De Bello Civili,* Book X.

[4] Sir Walter Scott (1771–1832), Scottish historical novelist.

in six or seven weeks. We print 1000 copies. So whenever it is sold, you shall have 1000 dollars.

The French Revolution[5] continues to find friends & purchasers. It has gone to New Orleans, to Nashville, to Vicksburg. I have not been in Boston lately, but have determined that nearly or quite 800 copies should be gone. On the 1 July I shall make up accounts with the booksellers, & I hope to make you the most favorable returns. I shall use the advice of Barnard, Adams, & Co in regard to remittances.

When you publish your next book I think you must send it out to me in sheets, & let us print it here contemporaneously with the English Edition. The eclat[6] of so new a book would help the sale very much. But a better device would be, that you should embark in the Victoria steamer, & come in a fortnight to New York, & in 24 hours more, to Concord. Your study armchair, fireplace & bed long vacant auguring expect you. Then you shall revise your proofs & dictate wit & learning to the New World. Think of it in good earnest. In aid of your friendliest purpose, I will set down some of the facts. I occupy or *improve,* as we Yankees say, two acres only of God's earth, on which is my house, my kitchen-garden, my orchard of thirty young trees, my empty barn. My house is now a very good one for comfort, & abounding in room. Besides my house, I have, I believe, $22 000. whose income in ordinary years is 6 per cent. I have no other tithe or glebe[7] except the income of my winter lectures which was last winter 800 dollars. Well, with this income, here at home, I am a rich man. I stay at home and go abroad at my own instance. I have food, warmth, leisure, books, friends. Go away from home,—I am rich no longer. I never have a dollar to spend on a fancy. As no wise man, I suppose ever was rich in the sense of *freedom to spend,* because of the inundation of claims, so neither am I, who am not wise. But at home I am rich,—rich enough for ten brothers. My wife Lidian is an incarnation of Christianity,—I call her Asia[8]—& keeps my philosophy from Antinomianism.[9] My mother—whitest,[10] mildest, most conservative of ladies, whose only exception to her universal preference of old things is her son; my boy, a piece of love & sunshine, well worth my watching from morning to night; these & three domestic women who cook & sew & run for us, make all my household. Here I sit & read & write with very little system & as far as regards composition with the most fragmentary result: paragraphs incompressible each sentence an infinitely repellent particle. In summer with the aid of a neighbor, I manage my garden; & a week ago I set out on the west side of my house forty young pine trees to protect me or my son from the wind of January. The ornament of the place is the occasional presence of some ten or twelve persons good & wise who visit us in the course of the year. —But my story is too long already. God grant that you will come & bring that blessed wife, whose protracted illness we heartily grieve to learn, & whom a voyage & my

---

[5] Carlyle's *The French Revolution,* published in England in 1837 and in the United States in 1839.
[6] French: "brightness" or "flash"; in this context, "effect."
[7] Land given a minister as part of the assets of his service.
[8] This nickname for Lydia Jackson, Emerson's second wife, may well derive, as F. I. Carpenter notes in *Emerson and Asia* (1930), from

Emerson's sense that Asia represented "the passive, the religious, the contemplative, . . . the land where only the elemental questions of life are important." Emerson also called his wife "Lydian" and "Lidian."
[9] The belief that salvation could be secured personally and without the mediating presence of organized religion.
[10] I.e., purest, most guileless.

wifes & my mothers nursing would in less than a twelvemonth restore to blooming health. My wife sends to her this message; "Come, & I will be to you a sister." What have you to do with Italy? Your genius tendeth to the New, to the West. Come & live with me a year, & if you do not like New England well enough to stay, one of these years (when the History[11] has passed its ten editions & been translated into as many languages) I will come & dwell with you. . . .

1838/1883

[October 17, 1838]

Concord, 17 October, 1838

My dear friend,

I am quite uneasy that I do not hear from you. On the 21 July, I wrote to you & enclosed a remittance of £50 by a bill of exchange on Baring & Brothers, drawn by Chandler, Howard, & Co. which was sent in the steamer *Royal William*. On the 2 August, I received your letter of inquiry respecting our edition of the *Miscellanies*,[12] & wrote a few days later in reply; that we could send you out two or three hundred copies of our two first volumes, in sheets, at 89 cents per copy of two vols., & the small additional price of the new title-page. I said also that I would wait until I heard from you before commencing the printing of the two last volumes of the Miscellanies, and, if you desired it, would print any number of copies, with a title-page for London. This letter went in a steamer, the *Great Western*[13] probably,—about the 10 or 12 Augt. I have heard nothing from you since. I trust my letters have not miscarried. (A third was sent also by another channel, enclosing a duplicate of the bill of Exchange.) With more fervency, I trust that all goes well in the house of my friend;—and I suppose that you are absent on some salutary errand of repairs & recreation. Use, I pray you, your earliest hour in certifying me of the facts.

One word more in regard to business. I believe I expressed some surprise, in the July letter, that the book sellers should have no greater balance for us, at this settlement. I have since studied the account better, & see that we shall not be disappointed in the year of obtaining at least the sum first promised, $760.00; but the whole expense of the edition is paid out of the copies first sold, & our profits depend on the last sales. The edition is almost gone, & you shall have an account at the end of the year.

In a letter within a twelvemonth I have urged you to pay us a visit in America, & in Concord. I have believed that you would come, one day, & do believe it. But if, on your part, you have been generous & affectionate enough to your friends here —or curious enough concerning our society to wish to come, I think you must postpone, for the present, the satisfaction of your friendship & your curiosity. At this moment, I would not have you here, on any account. The publication of my "Address to the Divinity College,"[14] (copies of which I sent you) has been the occasion of an

---

[11] Carlyle's book *The French Revolution*.

[12] Another of Carlyle's works, published in America under Emerson's editorship.

[13] About the names of the two ships, *Royal William* and *Great Western*, Emerson noted in the margin of the letter: "Perhaps I

misremember the names. The first shd be last."

[14] Delivered as a lecture to the senior class at the Harvard Divinity School on July 15, 1838, and published as a pamphlet soon afterward in Boston.

outcry in all our leading local newspapers against my "infidelity," "pantheism," & "atheism." The writers warn all & sundry against me, & against whatever is supposed to be related to my connexion of opinion, &c; against Transcendentalism, Goethe & *Carlyle.*[15] I am heartily sorry to see this last aspect of the storm in our washbowl. For, as Carlyle is nowise guilty, & has unpopularities of his own, I do not wish to embroil him in my parish–differences. You were getting to be a great favorite with us all here, and are daily a greater, with the American public, but just now, *in Boston,* where I am known as your editor, I fear you lose by the association. Now it is indispensable to your right influence here, that you should never come before our people as one of a clique, but as a detached, that is, universally associated man; so I am happy, as I could not have thought, that you have not yet yielded yourself to my entreaties. Let us wait a little until this foolish clam[or] be overblown. My position is fortunately such as to put me quite out of the reach of any real inconvenience from the panic strikers or the panic struck; &, indeed, so far as this uneasiness is a necessary result of mere inaction of mind, it seems very clear to me that, if I live, my neighbors must look for a great many more shocks, & perhaps harder to bear. The article on German Religious Writers in the last Foreign Q. R. suits our meridian as well as yours; as is plainly signified by the circumstance that our newspapers copy into their columns the opening tirade *& no more.*[16] Who wrote that paper? And who wrote the paper on Montaigne in the Westminster?[17] I read with great satisfaction the Poems & Thoughts of Archaeus in Blackwood: "The Sexton's daughter" is a beautiful poem: and I recognize in them all, *the* Soul, with joy & love.[18] Tell me of the author's health & welfare; or will not he love me so much as to write me a letter with his own hand? —And tell me of yourself,—what task of love & wisdom the muses impose: & what happiness the good God sends to you & yours. I hope your wife has not forgotten me.

  Yours affectionately,

           R. W. Emerson

The Miscellanies Vols I & II are a popular book. About 500 copies have been sold. The second article on Jean Paul works with might on the inner man of young men. I hate to write you letters on business & facts like this. There are so few Friends that I think some time I shall meet you nearer, for I love you more than is fit to say. W. H. Channing[19] has written a Critique on you, which I suppose he has sent you in the Boston Review.

1838/1883

---

[15] Emerson refers here to the criticism and hostility prompted by the Divinity School Address. More particularly, Andrews Norton had published an anonymous article, "The New School in Literature and Religion," in the *Boston Daily Advertiser* on August 27, 1838, attacking Transcendentalism, Goethe, Emerson, and "that hyper-Germanized Englishman, Carlyle."

[16] In the *Foreign Quarterly Review,* July 1838. The first three paragraphs of the article criticized German mysticism and skepticism but were followed by a more even-handed treatment of German evangelism and the conclusion that

German theology and philosophy ought to be studied. The Boston *Courier* of September 24, 1838, reprinted only the first three paragraphs.

[17] John Sterling's "Montaigne and His Writings" in the *London and Westminster Review,* August 1838.

[18] Writing as "Archaeus," John Sterling had published a long poem, "The Sexton's Daughter," and a prose piece, "Thoughts and Images," in the July issue of *Blackwood.*

[19] William Henry Channing (1810–1884), clergyman, writer, and coeditor of the *Western Messenger.*

[from **May 6, 1856***]*

Concord, 6 May, 1856

Dear Carlyle,

There is no escape from the forces of time & life, & we do not write letters to the gods or to our friends, but only to attorneys landlords & tenants. But the planes or platforms on which all stand remain the same, & we are ever expecting the descent of the heavens, which is to put us into familiarity with the first named. When I ceased to write to you for a long time, I said to myself,—If any thing really good should happen here,—any stroke of good sense or virtue in our politics, or of great sense in a book,—I will send it on the instant to the formidable man; but I will not repeat to him every month, that there are no news. Thank me for my resolution, & for keeping it through the long night. One book, last summer, came out in New York, a nondescript monster which yet has terrible eyes & buffalo strength, & was indisputably American,—which I thought to send you; but the book throve so badly with the few to whom I showed it, & wanted good morals so much, that I never did. Yet I believe now again, I shall. It is called "Leaves of Grass,"—was written & printed by a journeyman printer in Brooklyn, N. Y. named Walter Whitman; and after you have looked into it, if you think, as you may, that it is only an auctioneer's inventory of a warehouse, you can light your pipe with it. . . .

1856/1883

---

from Letter to Henry Ware, Jr.[*]

[October 8, 1838]

October 8, 1838

. . . It strikes me very oddly and even a little ludicrously that the good and great men of Cambridge should think of raising me into an object of criticism. I have always been from my very incapacity of methodical writing a chartered libertine, free to worship and free to rail, lucky when I was understood but never esteemed near enough to the institutions and mind of society to deserve the notice of the masters of literature and religion. I have appreciated fully the advantage of my position, for I well knew that there was no scholar less willing or less able to be a polemic. I could not give account of myself if challenged. I could not possibly give you one of the "arguments" on which, as you cruelly hint, any position of mine stands. For I do not know, I confess, what arguments mean in reference to any expression of a thought. I delight in telling what I think, but if you ask me how I dare say so or why it is so I am the most helpless of mortal men; I see not even that either of these questions admit of an answer. So that in the present droll posture of my affairs, when I see myself

[*] Written in response to Ware's sermon "The Personality of the Deity."

suddenly raised into the importance of a heretic, I am very uneasy if I advert to the supposed duties of such a personage, who is expected to make good his thesis against all comers. I therefore tell you plainly I shall do no such thing. I shall read what you and other good men write as I have always done, glad when you speak my thought and skipping the page that has nothing for me. I shall go on just as before, seeing whatever I can and telling what I see, and I suppose with the same fortune as has hitherto attended me, the joy of finding that my abler and better brothers, who work with the sympathy of society and love it, unexpectedly confirm my perceptions, and find my nonsense is only their own thought in motley.[1]

1838/1939

---

from Letter to Oliver Wendell Holmes

[March 1856]

March, 1856

. . . I have not seen a true report of your speech[1] and confess to have drawn my sad thoughts about it from the comments of the journals. I am relieved to know that they misreported you, and the more they misreported or the wider you are from their notion of you, the better I shall be pleased. I divide men as aspirants and desperants. A scholar need not be cynical to feel that the vast multitude are almost on all fours; that the rich always vote after their fears; that cities, churches, colleges all go for the quadruped interest: and it is against this coalition that the pathetically small minority of disengaged or thinking men stand for the ideal right, for man as he should be, and (what is essential to any sane maintenance of his own right) for the right of every other as for his own. When masses then as cities or churches go for things as they are, we take no note of it; we expected as much. We leave them to the laws of repression, to the checks nature puts on beasts of prey, as mutual destruction, blind staggers, delirium tremens, or whatever else; but when a scholar (or disengaged man) seems to throw himself on the dark a cry of grief is heard from the aspirants' side exactly proportioned in its intensity to his believed spiritual rank. . . .

The cant of Union, like the cant of extending the area of liberty by the annexing Texas and Mexico, is too transparent for its most impudent repeater to hope to deceive you. And for the Union with Slavery no manly person will suffer a day to go by without discrediting, disintegrating and finally exploding it. The "Union" they talk of is dead and rotten. The real union, that is, the will to keep and renew union, is like the will to keep and renew life, and this alone gives any tension to the dead letter and . . . when we have broken every several inch of the old wooden hoop will still hold us staunch.

1856/1939

---

[1] I.e., in different, discordant forms.
[1] Holmes was quoted in the December 22, 1855, issue of the *Boston Daily Advertiser* as having

"denounced the abolitionists of New England in good round terms as 'traitors of the Union.'"

Margaret Fuller
1810–1850

Margaret Fuller's life and work transcended virtually every stereotype American women had to endure in the first half of the nineteenth century. She matured intellectually at a very early age yet married very late. She was a feminist pioneer in East Coast literary circles at a time when women pioneers were more apt to be leading wagon trains to the West Coast. She wrote first-rate—and controversial—journalism as well as social and literary criticism when women were expected to be preoccupied with insuring domestic tranquillity. She read the leading writers of her time and was vilified by many of them. Nine years after her death, Nathaniel Hawthorne poured out his dislike of her in his notebooks. He called her a "great humbug," a woman with a "strong, heavy, unpliable, and in many respects defective and evil nature." Even her friend, the English poet Elizabeth Barrett Browning, who knew her when both were living in Italy, cautioned potential readers: "If I wished anyone to do her justice, I should say, as I have said, 'Never read what she has written.' " Henry James concluded early on that Margaret Fuller had "left nothing behind her, her written utterance being naught." Yet recent scholarship suggests that Margaret Fuller did produce an impressive body of work. An accomplished teacher, translator, editor, columnist, poet, critic, and feminist theorist and advocate, as well as a social and political activist, Fuller became an articulate and influential voice in America's struggle to come to terms with its literary identity and social conscience.

Sarah Margaret Fuller was born in Cambridgeport, Massachusetts, on May 23, 1810, the first of Margaret and Timothy Fuller's five children. Her mother, having to contend with poor health, struggled continually to raise the family. Her father, a Harvard-trained lawyer and member of Congress, compensated for his wife's frailty by dominating the children's lives with an almost ruthless passion that apparently he alone considered affection. Recognizing young Margaret's intellectual bent, he decided to cultivate it as quickly and as fully as possible by designing a highly rigorous education for her. He was, as she later explained, "a severe teacher, both from his habits of mind and his ambitions for me." A stern disciplinarian and a dogmatic educational theorist, Timothy Fuller trained his daughter to read the classics by age six, Shakespeare by eight. Thereafter, he schooled her in modern languages, especially German, as well as in ancient and modern history, biblical scholarship, and English literature.

Reading and writing served as the principal activities of Margaret Fuller's early years. A prodigious letter writer, she repeatedly punctuated her youthful correspondence with the anxious intellectual ranklings of one who had been denied the pleasures of a peaceful childhood. Her father's intense and deliberate tutelage resulted, as she later noted, in a "premature development of the brain, that made me a 'youthful prodigy' by day, and by night a victim of spectral illusions," the most recurrent of which was a nightmare in which horses galloped across her head. The intellectual independence her father demanded of her prompted Margaret Fuller to regard herself as clearly out of place in a society that established homemaking and etiquette as high priorities in the training of young women.

After an unsettling year attending the Misses Prescott's school in rural Groton, Massachusetts (where for a time she sat next to Oliver Wendell Holmes), Margaret Fuller returned home in 1824 and resumed the course of study her father had so carefully laid out for her. For nearly the next decade she led a rather isolated, although intellectually high-charged, life. From all accounts, her education was far more rigorous than the instruction nearby Harvard University still denied to women of that time. Only occasionally did she venture out into the elite, male conversational world to which her father introduced her. Of the daring young liberal clergymen and writers she met during the late 1820s and early 1830s, Margaret Fuller developed lasting friendships with but a few, most notably James Freeman Clarke and W. H. Channing, who, along with Ralph Waldo Emerson, would prepare her *Memoirs* after her death. Yet even these few opportunities for intellectual companionship were denied her in 1833 when she moved with her family to Groton, where she was expected to concentrate on educating the four younger children in the family.

When Margaret Fuller's father died unexpectedly in 1835, responsibility for supporting the family fell to her. She did this principally through teaching at various schools for several years, including Boston's experimental Temple School, directed by the Transcendentalist Bronson Alcott. During this same period she intensified her study of German with the assistance of Dr. William Ellery Channing, the longtime minister at Boston's Federal Street Church. Reading Goethe would influence the course of both her thinking and teaching and prepare her for her first two book-length publications, translations titled *Eckermann's Conversations with Goethe* (1839) and *Correspondence of Franklin Günderode with Bettina von Arnim* (1842). Within a few years after her father's death, Margaret Fuller had expanded her once meager conversational network to include such soon-to-be celebrated cultural figures as Ralph Waldo Emerson (whom she first had visited in Concord in 1836), Henry David Thoreau, Frederic Henry Hedge, and most of the other liberal thinkers who came to be known as the Transcendentalists. In a letter dated November 16, 1837, to Caroline Sturgis, the intellectually energetic daughter of a Boston merchant, Fuller presented her own particularly insightful, if somewhat defensive and ironic, view of her own association with Transcendentalism:

As to transcendentalism and the nonsense which is talked by so many about it—I do not know what is meant. For myself, I should say that if it is meant that I have an active mind frequently busy with large topics, I hope it is so— if it is meant that I am honoured by the friendship of Mr. Emerson, Mr. Ripley, or Mr. Alcott, I hope it is so—but if it is meant that I cherish any opinions which interfere with domestic duties, cheerful carriage and judgment in the practical affairs of life, I challenge any or all in the little world which knows me to prove such deficiency from any acts of mine since I came to woman's estate.

Her "active mind" would indeed be "busy with large topics" in the years to come, both in her participation in the occasional meetings of the Transcendentalist Club and in her more frequent gatherings of Boston's most distinguished women.

Margaret Fuller assembled Boston's most intellectually powerful women at weekly "Conversations" at the home of the eminent teacher Elizabeth Peabody. Fuller orchestrated discussions of topics in such wide-ranging fields as mythology, education, philosophy, theology, and the fine arts, and she encouraged the group to consider contemporary social and ethical issues. Her intellectual leadership at these meetings was rarely challenged, and many sessions were reported to have ended when she lapsed into trancelike silences, broken only by the occasional rumbling of some indecipherable words. Her prominence in Boston's intellectual life seemed assured, if rather flamboyant.

In 1840 Fuller agreed to serve as the unsalaried editor of *The Dial,* the principal journal of Transcendentalist thought, and in July of that year she saw the first issue into print. For the next two years, she energetically tried to fulfill her hopes for this quarterly publication, described in a March 1840 letter to her friend W. H. Channing:

> A perfectly free organ is to be offered for the expression of individual thought and character. There are no party measures to be carried, no particular standard to be set up. A fair calm tone, I hope will pervade the essays in every form[.] I hope there will neither be a spirit of dogmatism nor of compromise. That this periodical will not aim at leading public opinion, but at stimulating each man to think for himself, to think more deeply and nobly by letting them see how some minds are keep alive by wise self-trust.

In addition to her literary reviews, which helped promote European Romanticism among America's young intellectuals, Fuller contributed several essays to *The Dial,* the most important of which was her important statement on women's rights, "The Great Lawsuit: Man Versus Men. Woman Versus Women." This essay established Fuller as a pioneer in women's rights. During the fall of 1844 she expanded the essay to book-length form and published it in 1845 under the title *Woman in the Nineteenth Century.* The original *Dial* essay, reprinted here, is a more tightly argued and powerful version of her hortatory invocation to free men and women from the social roles in which they have been trapped, although it lacks many of the book's scholarly allusions to women in history, mythology, and poetry. In both versions, however, Fuller uses what was even then the conventional analogy between the woman and the slave. At a time when the moral fervor surrounding abolition had increased dramatically, such rhetorical strategies proved particularly effective, if also controversial. Fuller's writing on women's issues helped inspire the reforms and clarify the agenda for political action proposed at the Seneca Falls conference on that subject in 1848.

Fuller resigned as the sole editor of *The Dial* after the July 1842 issue, but she continued to help Emerson edit the journal until it ceased publication in April 1844. Fuller's increasingly ambivalent attitude toward what she regarded as the inconsistent positions of the Transcendentalists was reflected in her changing attitude toward Emerson. Despite her considerable affection for him, she came to realize, for example, that his commitment to developing the self should have led him to be more interested in current social and political issues. And while she praised Emerson's "high tendency, absolute purity," and his seemingly effortless ability to "summon the freedom and infinite graces of an intellect cultivated much beyond any I had known," she also recognized the limitations of their relationship. "I was, indeed, always called on to be worthy," she said. "He absolutely distrusted me in every region of my life with which he was unacquainted. The same trait I detected in his relations with others. He had faith in the Universal, but not in the Individual Man; he met men, not as a brother, but as a critic."

Emerson's view of their relationship was equally ambivalent. He wrote of his "strange, cold-warm, attractive-repelling" conversations with her. And while he respected the intelligence and conviction that distinguished her life, he also groused, as he reports in the *Memoirs* of her life he helped prepare, that "she looked upon herself as a living statue, which should always stand on a polished pedestal, with rich accessories, and under the most fitting lights." Emerson apparently could not free himself from the female archetype he saw in her, at once an emotionally charged and intellectually arrogant woman.

Her contemporaries contempuously referred to her "mountainous me," a phrase derived from Emerson's well-circulated (and perhaps apocryphal) account of her own self-estimate: "I now know all the people worth knowing in America, and I find no intellect comparable to my own." Emerson, like many of his contemporaries, failed to remember that Margaret Fuller was a brilliant, feisty woman struggling for intellectual recognition in the male-dominated literary world of mid-nineteenth-century America. At a time when women were hardly encouraged to develop an active role in the new nation's culture, she was repeatedly made to think that the problem was hers and not the culture's.

Margaret Fuller's perspective on American culture broadened considerably when she accompanied her friend James Freeman Clarke and his wife, Sarah, on a trip to the Midwest in 1843. Her journal entries during that excursion form the basis for *Summer on the Lakes* (1844). The book is an intellectual miscellany, consisting of sketches, poetry, and brief translations, as well as excerpts from the books she had been reading, along with a critical commentary on each. The book's commercial failure was somewhat offset by the modest praise it earned. The newspaper publisher and editor Horace Greeley called it "one of the best works in the department ever issued from the American press." It also provided Henry David Thoreau with a convenient model for a similar compilation, *A Week on the Concord and Merrimack Rivers* (1849).

Horace Greeley's appreciation of *Summer on the Lakes* prompted him to offer Fuller a job as the literary critic for his newspaper, the *New York Tribune*. In December 1844 Fuller moved to New York to work as the first female writer on that prominent newspaper's staff. The reflective pace of editing *The Dial* quickly yielded to daily deadlines, and the small circle of readers who debated the contents of the Boston quarterly were subsumed within the collective identity of the masses who read the *Tribune.* Yet Fuller took great pleasure in her work; it provided her, she noted, with "a more various view of life than any I ever before was in."

Fuller wrote literary criticism distinguished by her breadth of learning and her uncompromising standards. Her unfavorable reviews of such figures as James Russell Lowell and Henry Wadsworth Longfellow offended Boston's literary Brahmins and caused Lowell to satirize her severely in "A Fable for Critics." Yet her essays on the most durable features of the literature of that time gained her the respect of most other writers and readers, including Edgar Allan Poe, who praised her intellectual rigor and freedom from partisanship, although he, like many others, criticized her syntactic and stylistic faults. As more of Fuller's literary criticism has been reprinted, she has come to be increasingly ranked with Poe as one of America's first two major literary critics.

The focus of her work gradually shifted from literary reviews to social criticism. Fuller tackled controversial public issues with great verve, exposing, for example, official neglect of such mid-nineteenth-century misfits as the blind and the insane; she also called attention to the abuses of female prisoners in New York. In 1846 she published *Papers on Literature and Art,* a collection of essays hastily assembled in the weeks preceding her eagerly anticipated departure for Europe, where she would serve as a foreign correspondent for Greeley's *Tribune.*

Soon after her arrival in Europe, Fuller met Thomas Carlyle, the renowned English writer, who judged her in a journal entry "a strange, lilting, lean old maid, not nearly such a bore as I expected." Carlyle added that Fuller's was "a truly heroic mind, altogether unique, so far as I know among the writing women of this generation." Before leaving London, Fuller also met Giuseppe Mazzini, the Italian patriot and republican revolutionary, who sparked her interest in political action. In Paris she met the novelist George Sand and Adam Mickiewicz, a Polish émigré writer who espoused revolutionary causes. Attracted to the revolutionary ferment sweeping across Europe, Fuller traveled in 1847 to Italy, then a very unsteady alignment of independent as well as papal and Austrian-controlled states. She regularly dispatched reports to the *Tribune* on the unification efforts of Mazzini and Giuseppe Garibaldi.

In the midst of this fast-paced period in Italy, Margaret Fuller met—and eventually married—Giovanni Angelo Ossoli, an aristocratic Italian (a marquis) sympathetic to the revolutionary effort. Ossoli seemed to prefer the elegant tempo of Rome's local cafés to the intense discussions of social and political issues from which his wife gained so much intellectual sustenance. She gave birth to a son, Angelo, in September 1848, but her writing and political action continued unabated.

By her own account, Fuller's stay in Europe helped her recognize the limitations of her liberal social conscience. At the same time that the *Communist Manifesto* was being published in London, Fuller was acting on her newly articulated belief that socialism would change the world and fulfill the promise of American democracy. Within a few months of Garibaldi's arrival in Rome and his declaration of the Roman Republic, France lay siege to the city on behalf of papal interests. Fuller served as the director of a hospital on an island in the Tiber River. When Rome fell to the French on July 4, 1849, she led her family to Florence, where, with the encouragement of Robert and Elizabeth Barrett Browning, Fuller began gathering information and anecdotes and drafting a history of the Italian revolution. That work was never completed. In dire need of money, Margaret Fuller, her husband, and son boarded a ship bound for the United States. On July 19, 1850, that ship sank off the Long Island coast at Fire Island, and all three perished.

Margaret Fuller's life and work offer ample evidence of the "cost," to use Thoreau's term, of being a productive woman in mid-nineteenth-century America. Unable to control what Hawthorne had described as her "unpliable" nature when she was among them, Fuller's friends reinterpreted her life in her *Memoirs.* The highly bowdlerized life recreated by James Freeman Clarke, W. H. Channing, and Ralph Waldo Emerson buried the aspects of her past that they regarded as radical. Only recently has scholarship begun to recover the complexities of her identity and work. She faced, for example, the conflict between being a woman and a writer at a time when American culture had not reconciled the two identities. She talked of the anguish of being regarded as "either a genius or a character. . . . I love but to be a woman; but womanhood is at present too strait-bounded to give me scope. At hours, I live truly as a woman; at others, I should stifle; as, on the other hand, I should palsy, when I would play the artist." One of the ironies of Margaret Fuller's life is that she did not discover herself fully as either an American woman or a writer until she moved to Europe.

Her work expresses one of the nation's most articulate early views of women's rights, and her literary criticism helped identify and clarify the strengths and weaknesses of American writing of her time. Hers was an original and influential voice in American literature. Soon after her death, Emerson confided to his journal that "I have lost in her my audience." Henry James acknowledged in his later years that Margaret Fuller "still unmistakably walks the passages" of his novels. And, given the recent interest in her prose, the real extent of her influence may well surface in the next generations of writers who read her work.

Further Reading:
W. H. Channing, J. F. Clarke, and R. W. Emerson, *Memoirs of Margaret Fuller Ossoli,* 1852.
M. Wade, *Margaret Fuller, Whetstone of Genius,* 1940.
M. B. Stern, *The Life of Margaret Fuller,* 1942.
J. J. Deiss, *The Roman Years of Margaret Fuller,* 1969.
B. G. Chevigny, *The Woman and the Myth: Margaret Fuller's Life and Writings,* 1976.
J. Myerson, *Margaret Fuller: An Annotated Bibliography,* 1977.
M. V. Allen, *The Achievement of Margaret Fuller,* 1979.
M. O. Urbanski, *Margaret Fuller's* Woman of the Nineteenth Century: *A Literary Study of Form and Content, of Sources and Influences,* 1980.
J. Myerson, *Critical Essays on Margaret Fuller,* 1980.

Texts:
"The Great Lawsuit" from *The Dial,* 1843.
"American Literature. Its Position in the Present Time, and Prospects for the Future" from *Papers on Literature and Art,* 1846.
See also *Letters of Margaret Fuller,* ed. R. N. Hudspeth, 1983–.

The Great Lawsuit[*]

Man Versus Men. Woman Versus Women

This great suit has now been carried on through many ages, with various results. The decisions have been numerous, but always followed by appeals to still higher courts. How can it be otherwise, when the law itself is the subject of frequent elucidation, constant revision? Man has, now and then, enjoyed a clear, triumphant hour, when some irresistible conviction warmed and purified the atmosphere of his planet. But, presently, he sought repose after his labors, when the crowd of pigmy adversaries bound him in his sleep. Long years of inglorious imprisonment followed, while his enemies revelled in his spoils, and no counsel could be found to plead his cause, in the absence of that all-promising glance, which had, at times, kindled the poetic soul to revelation of his claims, of his rights.

Yet a foundation for the largest claim is now established. It is known that his inheritance consists in no partial sway, no exclusive possession, such as his adversaries desire. For they, not content that the universe is rich, would, each one for himself, appropriate treasure; but in vain! The many-colored garment, which clothed with honor an elected son, when rent asunder for the many, is a worthless spoil. A band of robbers cannot live princely in the prince's castle; nor would he, like them, be content with less than all, though he would not, like them, seek it as fuel for riotous enjoyment, but as his principality, to administer and guard for the use of all living things therein. He cannot be satisfied with any one gift of the earth, any one department of knowledge, or telescopic peep at the heavens. He feels himself called to understand and aid nature, that she may, through his intelligence, be raised and interpreted; to be a student of, and servant to, the universe-spirit; and only king of his planet, that, as an angelic minister, he may bring it into conscious harmony with the law of that spirit.

Such is the inheritance of the orphan prince, and the illegitimate children of his family will not always be able to keep it from him, for, from the fields which they sow with dragon's teeth, and water with blood, rise monsters, which he alone has power to drive away.

---

[*] Fuller first published *The Great Lawsuit* in *The Dial* (July 1843). She expanded the work in 1844 and reprinted it under the title *Woman in the Nineteenth Century*. Her preliminary footnote to the 1844 edition clarifies the intention of the earlier title: "Objections having been made to the former title, as not sufficiently easy to be understood, the present has been substituted as expressive of the main purpose of the essay: though, by myself, the other is preferred, partly for the reason others do not like it.—that is, that it requires some thought to see what it means, and might thus prepare the reader to meet me on my own ground. Besides, it offers a larger scope, and is, in that way, more just to my desire. I meant by that title to intimate the fact that, while it is the destiny of Man, in the course of the ages, to ascertain and fulfill the law of his being, so that his wife shall be seen, as a whole, to be that of an angel or messenger, the action of prejudices and passions which attend, in the day, the growth of the individual, is continually obstructing the holy work that is to make earth a part of heaven. By Men I mean both man and woman; these are the two halves of one thought. I lay no especial stress on the welfare of either. I believe that the development of the one cannot be effected without that of the other. My highest wish is that this truth should be distinctly and rationally apprehended, and the conditions of life and freedom recognized as the same for the daughters and sons of time; twin exponents of a divine thought."

But it is not the purpose now to sing the prophecy of his jubilee. We have said that, in clear triumphant moments, this has many, many times been made manifest, and those moments, though past in time, have been translated into eternity by thought. The bright signs they left hang in the heavens, as single stars or constellations, and, already, a thickly-sown radiance consoles the wanderer in the darkest night. Heroes have filled the zodiac of beneficent labors, and then given up their mortal part[1] to the fire without a murmur. Sages and lawgivers have bent their whole nature to the search for truth, and thought themselves happy if they could buy, with the sacrifice of all temporal ease and pleasure, one seed for the future Eden. Poets and priests have strung the lyre with heart-strings, poured out their best blood upon the altar which, reared anew from age to age, shall at last sustain the flame which rises to highest heaven. What shall we say of those who, if not so directly, or so consciously, in connection with the central truth, yet, led and fashioned by a divine instinct, serve no less to develop and interpret the open secret of love passing into life, the divine energy creating for the purpose of happiness;—of the artist, whose hand, drawn by a preexistent harmony to a certain medium, moulds it to expressions of life more highly and completely organized than are seen elsewhere, and, by carrying out the intention of nature, reveals her meaning to those who are not yet sufficiently matured to divine it; of the philosopher, who listens steadily for causes, and, from those obvious, infers those yet unknown; of the historian, who, in faith that all events must have their reason and their aim, records them, and lays up archives from which the youth of prophets may be fed. The man of science dissects the statement, verifies the facts, and demonstrates connection even where he cannot its purpose.

Lives, too, which bear none of these names, have yielded tones of no less significance. The candlestick, set in a low place, has given light as faithfully, where it was needed, as that upon the hill.[2] In close alleys, in dismal nooks, the Word has been read as distinctly, as when shown by angels to holy men in the dark prison. Those who till a spot of earth, scarcely larger than is wanted for a grave, have deserved that the sun should shine upon its sod till violets answer.

So great has been, from time to time, the promise, that, in all ages, men have said the Gods themselves came down to dwell with them; that the All-Creating wandered on the earth to taste in a limited nature the sweetness of virtue, that the All-Sustaining incarnated himself, to guard, in space and time, the destinies of his world; that

---

[1] Fuller's note: "Ovid, Apotheosis of Hercules, translated into clumsy English by Mr. Gay, as follows: 'Jove said,
    Be all your fears forborne,
Th' Œtean fires do thou, great hero, scorn;
Who vanquished all things, shall subdue the flame;
The part alone of gross *maternal* frame,
Fire shall devour, while that from me he drew
Shall live immortal, and its force renew;
That, when he's dead, I'll raise to realms above,
May all the powers the righteous act approve.

If any God dissent, and judge too great
The sacred honors of the heavenly seat,
Even he shall own his deeds deserve the sky,
Even he, reluctant, shall at length comply.
Th' assembled powers assent.'"

[2] Matthew 5:15–16 (Sermon on the Mount): "Neither do men light a candle, and put it under a bushel, but on a candlestick; and it giveth light unto all that are in the house. Let your light so shine before men, that they may see your good works, and glorify your Father which is in heaven."

heavenly genius dwelt among the shepherds, to sing to them and teach them how to sing. Indeed,

"Der stets den Hirten gnädig sich bewies."
"He has constantly shown himself favorable to shepherds."

And these dwellers in green pastures and natural students of the stars, were selected to hail, first of all, the holy child, whose life and death presented the type of excellence, which has sustained the heart of so large a portion of mankind in these later generations.

Such marks have been left by the footsteps of man, whenever he has made his way through the wilderness of men. And whenever the pygmies stepped in one of these, they felt dilate within the breast somewhat that promised larger stature and purer blood. They were tempted to forsake their evil ways, to forsake the side of selfish personal existence, of decrepit skepticism, and covetousness of corruptible possessions. Conviction flowed in upon them. They, too, raised the cry; God is living, all is his, and all created beings are brothers, for they are his children. These were the triumphant moments; but as we have said, man slept and selfishness awoke.

Thus he is still kept out of his inheritance, still a pleader, still a pilgrim. But his reinstatement is sure. And now, no mere glimmering consciousness, but a certainty, is felt and spoken, that the highest ideal man can form of his own capabilities is that which he is destined to attain. Whatever the soul knows how to seek, it must attain. Knock, and it shall be opened; seek, and ye shall find. It is demonstrated, it is a maxim. He no longer paints his proper nature in some peculiar form and says, "Prometheus[3] had it," but "Man must have it." However disputed by many, however ignorantly used, or falsified, by those who do receive it, the fact of an universal, unceasing revelation, has been too clearly stated in words, to be lost sight of in thought, and sermons preached from the text, "Be ye perfect,"[4] are the only sermons of a pervasive and deep-searching influence.

But among those who meditate upon this text, there is great difference of view, as to the way in which perfection shall be sought.

Through the intellect, say some; Gather from every growth of life its seed of thought; look behind every symbol for its law. If thou canst *see* clearly, the rest will follow.

Through the life, say others; Do the best thou knowest to-day. Shrink not from incessant error, in this gradual, fragmentary state. Follow thy light for as much as it will show thee, be faithful as far as thou canst, in hope that faith presently will lead to sight. Help others, without blame that they need thy help. Love much, and be forgiven.

It needs not intellect, needs not experience, says a third. If you took the true way, these would be evolved in purity. You would not learn through them, but express through them a higher knowledge. In quietness, yield thy soul to the casual soul. Do not disturb its teachings by methods of thine own. Be still, seek not, but wait in obedience. Thy commission will be given.

---

[3] In Greek myth this Titan gave the stolen gift of fire to humans and was punished by Zeus.

[4] Matthew 5:48: "Be ye therefore perfect, even as your father which is in heaven is perfect."

Could we, indeed, say what we want, could we give a description of the child that is lost, he would be found. As soon as the soul can say clearly, that a certain demonstration is wanted, it is at hand. When the Jewish prophet described the Lamb, as the expression of what was required by the coming era, the time drew nigh.[5] But we say not, see not, as yet, clearly, what we would. Those who call for a more triumphant expression of love, a love that cannot be crucified, show not a perfect sense of what has already been expressed. Love has already been expressed, that made all things new, that gave the worm its ministry as well as the eagle; a love, to which it was alike to descend into the depths of hell, or to sit at the right hand of the Father.[6]

Yet, no doubt, a new manifestation is at hand, a new hour in the day of man. We cannot expect to see him a completed being, when the mass of men lie so entangled in the sod, or use the freedom of their limbs only with wolfish energy. The tree cannot come to flower till its root be freed from the cankering worm, and its whole growth open to air and light. Yet something new shall presently be shown of the life of man, for hearts crave it now, if minds do not know how to ask it.

Among the strains of prophecy, the following, by an earnest mind of a foreign land, written some thirty years ago, is not yet outgrown; and it has the merit of being a positive appeal from the heart, instead of a critical declaration what man shall *not* do.

"The ministry of man implies, that he must be filled from the divine fountains which are being engendered through all eternity, so that, at the mere name of his Master, he may be able to cast all his enemies into the abyss; that he may deliver all parts of nature from the barriers that imprison them; that he may purge the terrestrial atmosphere from the poisons that infect it; that he may preserve the bodies of men from the corrupt influences that surround, and the maladies that afflict them; still more, that he may keep their souls pure from the malignant insinuations which pollute, and the gloomy images that obscure them; that we may restore its serenity to the Word, which false words of men fill with mourning and sadness; that he may satisfy the desires of the angels, who await from him the development of the marvels of nature; that, in fine, his world may be filled with God, as eternity is."[7]

Another attempt we will give, by an obscure observer of our own day and country, to draw some lines of the desired image. It was suggested by seeing the design of Crawford's Orpheus,[8] and connecting with the circumstance of the American, in his garret at Rome, making choice of this subject, that of Americans here at home, showing such ambition to represent the character, by calling their prose and verse,

[5] "Ask thee a sign of the Lord thy God; ask it either in the depth, or in the height above" (Isaiah 7:11). In this chapter God announces to Ahaz and Isaiah the coming of Jesus.

[6] In Mark 16:19, after Jesus was crucified, he rose from his tomb and came to preach to his disciples. Then "he was received up into heaven, and sat on the right hand of God."

[7] From *The Ministry of Man and Spirit* (1802) by

the French philosopher Louis Claude de Saint-Martin (1743–1803).

[8] In Greek myth the music of Orpheus' lyre so mesmerized Hades that Orpheus almost retrieved his dead wife Eurydice from the underworld. Fuller saw the statue of Orpheus by Thomas Crawford (1814–1857) in 1839 at the Allston Gallery in Boston. Subsequently she wrote the poem that follows in this essay.

Orphic sayings, Orphics. Orpheus was a lawgiver by theocratic commission. He understood nature, and made all her forms move to his music. He told her secrets in the form of hymns, nature as seen in the mind of God. Then it is the prediction, that to learn and to do, all men must be lovers, and Orpheus was, in a high sense, a lover. His soul went forth towards all beings, yet could remain sternly faithful to a chosen type of excellence. Seeking what he loved, he feared not death nor hell, neither could any presence daunt his faith in the power of the celestial harmony that filled his soul.

It seemed significant of the state of things in this country, that the sculptor should have chosen the attitude of shading his eyes. When we have the statue here, it will give lessons in reverence.

> Each Orpheus must to the depths descend,
> For only thus the poet can be wise
>   Must make the sad Persephone[9] his friend,
> And buried love to second life arise;
>   Again his love must lose through too much love,
> Must lose his life by living life too true,
>   For what he sought below is passed above,
> Already done is all that he would do;
>   Must tune all being with his single lyre,
> Must melt all rocks free from their primal pain,
>   Must search all nature with his one soul's fire,
> Must bind anew all forms in heavenly chain.
>   If he already sees what he must do,
> Well may he shade his eyes from the far-shining view.[10]

Meanwhile, not a few believe, and men themselves have expressed the opinion, that the time is come when Euridice is to call for an Orpheus, rather than Orpheus for Euridice; that the idea of man, however imperfectly brought out, has been far more so than that of woman, and that an improvement in the daughters will best aid the reformation of the sons of this age.

It is worthy of remark, that, as the principle of liberty is better understood and more nobly interpreted, a broader protest is made in behalf of woman. As men become aware that all men have not had their fair chance, they are inclined to say that no women have had a fair chance. The French revolution, that strangely disguised angel, bore witness in favor of woman, but interpreted her claims no less ignorantly than those of man. Its idea of happiness did not rise beyond outward enjoyment, unobstructed by the tyranny of others. The title it gave was Citoyen, Citoyenne,[11] and it is not unimportant to woman that even this species of equality was awarded her. Before, she could be condemned to perish on the scaffold for treason, but not as a citizen, but a subject. The right, with which this title then invested a human being, was that of bloodshed and license. The Goddess of Liberty was impure. Yet truth was prophesied in the ravings of that hideous fever induced by long ignorance and abuse. Europe is conning a valued lesson from the blood-stained page. The same tendencies, farther unfolded, will bear good fruit in this country.

[9] In Greek myth, queen of the underworld.
[10] Fuller's own lines.
[11] French: "citizen" (male and female, respectively, and legally equal).

Yet, in this country, as by the Jews, when Moses was leading them to the promised land; everything has been done that inherited depravity could, to hinder the promise of heaven from its fulfilment. The cross, here as elsewhere, has been planted only to be blasphemed by cruelty and fraud. The name of the Prince of Peace has been profaned by all kinds of injustice towards the Gentile whom he said he came to save. But I need not speak of what has been done towards the red man, the black man. These deeds are the scoff of the world; and they have been accompanied by such pious words, that the gentlest would not dare to intercede with, "Father forgive them, for they know not what they do."[12]

Here, as elsewhere, the gain of creation consists always in the growth of individual minds, which live and aspire, as flowers bloom and birds sing, in the midst of morasses; and in the continual development of that thought, the thought of human destiny, which is given to eternity to fulfil, and which ages of failure only seemingly impede. Only seemingly, and whatever seems to the contrary, this country is as surely destined to elucidate a great moral law, as Europe was to promote the mental culture of man.

Though the national independence be blurred by the servility of individuals; though freedom and equality have been proclaimed only to leave room for a monstrous display of slave dealing and slave keeping; though the free American so often feels himself free, like the Roman, only to pamper his appetites and his indolence through the misery of his fellow beings, still it is not in vain, that the verbal statement has been made, "All men are born free and equal."[13] There it stands, a golden certainty, wherewith to encourage the good, to shame the bad. The new world may be called clearly to perceive that it incurs the utmost penalty, if it reject the sorrowful brother. And if men are deaf, the angels hear. But men cannot be deaf. It is inevitable that an external freedom, such as has been achieved for the nation, should be so also for every member of it. That, which has once been clearly conceived in the intelligence, must be acted out. It has become a law, irrevocable as that of the Medes[14] in their ancient dominion. Men will privately sin against it, but the law so clearly expressed by a leading mind of the age,

"Tutti fatti a sembianza d' un Solo;
  Figli tutti d' un solo riscatto,
  In qual ora, in qual parte del suolo
  Trascorriamo quest' aura vital,
  Siam fratelli, siam stretti ad un patto;
  Maladetto colui che lo infrange,
  Che s' innalza sul fiacco che piange,
  Che contrista uno spirto immortal."[15]

"All made in the likeness of the One,
  All children of one ransom,
  In whatever hour, in whatever part of the soil
  We draw this vital air,

---

[12] Words of Jesus regarding the Roman soldiers who crucified him (Luke 23:34).

[13] Paraphrase from the Declaration of Independence ("that all men are created equal").

[14] Media, part of modern Iran.

[15] From the Italian poet Alessandro Manzoni (1785–1873).

We are brothers, we must be bound by one compact,
Accursed he who infringes it,
Who raises himself upon the weak who weep,
Who saddens an immortal spirit."

cannot fail of universal recognition.

We sicken no less at the pomp than at the strife of words. We feel that never were lungs so puffed with the wind of declamation, on moral and religious subjects, as now. We are tempted to implore these "word-heroes," these word-Catos,[16] word-Christs, to beware of cant above all things; to remember that hypocrisy is the most hopeless as well as the meanest of crimes, and that those must surely be polluted by it, who do not keep a little of all this morality and religion for private use.[17] We feel that the mind may "grow black and rancid in the smoke" even of altars. We start up from the harangue to go into our closet and shut the door. But, when it has been shut long enough, we remember that where there is so much smoke, there must be some fire; with so much talk about virtue and freedom must be mingled some desire for them; that it cannot be in vain that such have become the common topics of conversation among men; that the very newspapers should proclaim themselves Pilgrims, Puritans, Heralds of Holiness.[18] The king that maintains so costly a retinue cannot be a mere Count of Carabbas[19] fiction. We have waited here long in the dust; we are tired and hungry, but the triumphal procession must appear at last.

Of all its banners, none has been more steadily upheld, and under none has more valor and willingness for real sacrifices been shown, than that of the champions of the enslaved African. And this band it is, which, partly in consequence of a natural following out of principles, partly because many women have been prominent in that cause, makes, just now, the warmest appeal in behalf of woman.

Though there has been a growing liberality on this point, yet society at large is not so prepared for the demands of this party, but that they are, and will be for some time, coldly regarded as the Jacobins[20] of their day.

"Is it not enough," cries the sorrowful trader, "that you have done all you could to break up the national Union, and thus destroy the prosperity of our country, but now you must be trying to break up family union, to take my wife away from the cradle, and the kitchen hearth, to vote at polls, and preach from a pulpit? Of course, if she does such things, she cannot attend to those of her own sphere. She is happy enough as she is. She has more leisure than I have, every means of improvement, every indulgence."

"Have you asked her whether she was satisfied with these indulgences?"

"No, but I know she is. She is too amiable to wish what would make me unhappy, and too judicious to wish to step beyond the sphere of her sex. I will never consent to have our peace disturbed by any such discussions."

[16] I.e., political reformers, such as Marcus Porcius Cato (234–149 B.C.).
[17] Fuller's note: "Dr. Johnson's one piece of advice should be written on every door; 'Clear your mind of cant.' But Byron, to whom it was so acceptable, in clearing away the noxious vine shook down the building too. Stirling's emendation is noteworthy, 'Realize your cant, not cast it off.' "
[18] Popular names for newspapers in Fuller's time.
[19] Typical name for a nobleman who takes pride in his wealth.
[20] Radical political group formed in 1789 during the French Revolution.

" 'Consent'—you? it is not consent from you that is in question, it is assent from your wife."

"Am I not the head of my house?"

"You are not the head of your wife. God has given her a mind of her own."

"I am the head and she the heart."

"God grant you play true to one another then. If the head represses no natural pulse of the heart, there can be no question as to your giving your consent. Both will be of one accord, and there needs but to present any question to get a full and true answer. There is no need of precaution, of indulgence, or consent. But our doubt is whether the heart consents with the head, or only acquiesces in its decree; and it is to ascertain the truth on this point, that we propose some liberating measures."

Thus vaguely are these questions proposed and discussed at present. But their being proposed at all implies much thought, and suggests more. Many women are considering within themselves what they need that they have not, and what they can have, if they find they need it. Many men are considering whether women are capable of being and having more than they are and have, and whether, if they are, it will be best to consent to improvement in their condition.

The numerous party, whose opinions are already labelled and adjusted too much to their mind to admit of any new light, strive, by lectures on some model-woman of bridal-like beauty and gentleness, by writing or lending little treatises, to mark out with due precision the limits of woman's sphere, and woman's mission, and to prevent other than the rightful shepherd from climbing the wall, or the flock from using any chance gap to run astray.

Without enrolling ourselves at once on either side, let us look upon the subject from that point of view which to-day offers. No better, it is to be feared, than a high house-top. A high hill-top, or at least a cathedral spire, would be desirable.

It is not surprising that it should be the Anti-Slavery party that pleads for woman, when we consider merely that she does not hold property on equal terms with men; so that, if a husband dies without a will, the wife, instead of stepping at once into his place as head of the family, inherits only a part of his fortune, as if she were a child, or ward only, not an equal partner.

We will not speak of the innumerable instances, in which profligate or idle men live upon the earnings of industrious wives; or if the wives leave them and take with them the children, to perform the double duty of mother and father, follow from place to place, and threaten to rob them of the children, if deprived of the rights of a husband, as they call them, planting themselves in their poor lodgings, frightening them into paying tribute by taking from them the children, running into debt at the expense of these otherwise so overtasked helots. Though such instances abound, the public opinion of his own sex is against the man, and when cases of extreme tyranny are made known, there is private action in the wife's favor. But if woman be, indeed, the weaker party, she ought to have legal protection, which would make such oppression impossible.

And knowing that there exists, in the world of men, a tone of feeling towards women as towards slaves, such as is expressed in the common phrase, "Tell that to women and children;" that the infinite soul can only work through them in already ascertained limits; that the prerogative of reason, man's highest portion, is allotted to them in a much lower degree; that it is better for them to be engaged in active labor, which is to be furnished and directed by those better able to think, &c. &c.; we need not go further, for who can review the experience of last week, without recalling words which imply, whether in jest or earnest, these views, and views like these? Knowing this, can we wonder that many reformers think that measures are not likely to be taken in behalf of women, unless their wishes could be publicly represented by women?

That can never be necessary, cry the other side. All men are privately influenced by women; each has his wife, sister, or female friends, and is too much biased by these relations to fail of representing their interests. And if this is not enough, let them propose and enforce their wishes with the pen. The beauty of home would be destroyed, the delicacy of the sex be violated, the dignity of halls of legislation destroyed, by an attempt to introduce them there. Such duties are inconsistent with those of a mother; and then we have ludicrous pictures of ladies in hysterics at the polls, and senate chambers filled with cradles.

But if, in reply, we admit as truth that woman seems destined by nature rather to the inner circle, we must add that the arrangements of civilized life have not been as yet such as to secure it to her. Her circle, if the duller, is not the quieter. If kept from excitement, she is not from drudgery. Not only the Indian carries the burdens of the camp, but the favorites of Louis the Fourteenth accompany him in his journeys, and the washerwoman stands at her tub and carries home her work at all seasons, and in all states of health.

As to the use of the pen, there was quite as much opposition to woman's possessing herself of that help to free-agency as there is now to her seizing on the rostrum or the desk; and she is likely to draw, from a permission to plead her cause that way, opposite inferences to what might be wished by those who now grant it.

As to the possibility of her filling, with grace and dignity, any such position, we should think those who had seen the great actresses, and heard the Quaker preachers of modern times, would not doubt, that woman can express publicly the fulness of thought and emotion, without losing any of the peculiar beauty of her sex.

As to her home, she is not likely to leave it more than she now does for balls, theatres, meetings for promoting missions, revival meetings, and others to which she flies, in hope of an animation for her existence, commensurate with what she sees enjoyed by men. Governors of Ladies' Fairs are no less engrossed by such a charge, than the Governor of the State by his; presidents of Washingtonian societies,[21] no less away from home than presidents of conventions. If men look straitly to it, they will find that, unless their own lives are domestic, those of the women will not be. The female Greek, of our day, is as much in the street as the male, to cry, What news? We doubt not it was the same in Athens of old. The women, shut out from the market-place, made up for it at the religious festivals. For human beings are not so constituted, that they can live without expansion; and if they do not get it one way, must another, or perish.

And, as to men's representing women fairly, at present, while we hear from men who owe to their wives not only all that is comfortable and graceful, but all that is wise in the arrangement of their lives, the frequent remark, "You cannot reason with

---

[21] Organizations similar to the present-day Daughters of the American Revolution.

a woman," when from those of delicacy, nobleness, and poetic culture, the contemptuous phrase, "Women and children," and that in no light sally of the hour, but in works intended to give a permanent statement of the best experiences, when not one man in the million, shall I say, no, not in the hundred million, can rise above the view that woman was made *for man,* when such traits as these are daily forced upon the attention, can we feel that man will always do justice to the interests of woman? Can we think that he takes a sufficiently discerning and religious view of her office and destiny, ever to do her justice, except when prompted by sentiment; accidentally or transiently, that is, for his sentiment will vary according to the relations in which he is placed. The lover, the poet, the artist, are likely to view her nobly. The father and the philosopher have some chance of liberality; the man of the world, the legislator for expediency, none.

Under these circumstances, without attaching importance in themselves to the changes demanded by the champions of woman, we hail them as signs of the times. We would have every arbitrary barrier thrown down. We would have every path laid open to woman as freely as to man. Were this done, and a slight temporary fermentation allowed to subside, we believe that the Divine would ascend into nature to a height unknown in the history of past ages, and nature, thus instructed, would regulate the spheres not only so as to avoid collision, but to bring forth ravishing harmony.

Yet then, and only then, will human beings be ripe for this, when inward and outward freedom for woman, as much as for man, shall be acknowledged as a right, not yielded as a concession. As the friend of the negro assumes that one man cannot, by right, hold another in bondage, should the friend of woman assume that man cannot, by right, lay even well-meant restrictions on woman. If the negro be a soul, if the woman be a soul, apparelled in flesh, to one master only are they accountable. There is but one law for all souls, and, if there is to be an interpreter of it, he comes not as man, or son of man, but as Son of God.

Were thought and feeling once so far elevated that man should esteem himself the brother and friend, but nowise the lord and tutor of woman, were he really bound with her in equal worship, arrangements as to function and employment would be of no consequence. What woman needs is not as a woman to act or rule, but as a nature to grow, as an intellect to discern, as a soul to live freely, and unimpeded to unfold such powers as were given her when we left our common home. If fewer talents were given her, yet, if allowed the free and full employment of these, so that she may render back to the giver his own with usury, she will not complain, nay, I dare to say she will bless and rejoice in her earthly birth-place, her earthly lot.

Let us consider what obstructions impede this good era, and what signs give reason to hope that it draws near.

I was talking on this subject with Miranda,[22] a woman, who, if any in the world, might speak without heat or bitterness of the position of her sex. Her father was a man who cherished no sentimental reverence for woman, but a firm belief in the equality of the sexes. She was his eldest child, and came to him at an age when he needed a companion. From the time she could speak and go alone, he addressed her not as a plaything, but as a living mind. Among the few verses he ever wrote were

[22] "Miranda" reflects Fuller's own experience.

a copy addressed to this child, when the first locks were cut from her head, and the reverence expressed on this occasion for that cherished head he never belied. It was to him the temple of immortal intellect. He respected his child, however, too much to be an indulgent parent. He called on her for clear judgment, for courage, for honor and fidelity, in short for such virtues as he knew. In so far as he possessed the keys to the wonders of this universe, he allowed free use of them to her, and by the incentive of a high expectation he forbade, as far as possible, that she should let the privilege lie idle.

Thus this child was early led to feel herself a child of the spirit. She took her place easily, not only in the world of organized being, but in the world of mind. A dignified sense of self-dependence was given as all her portion, and she found it a sure anchor. Herself securely anchored, her relations with others were established with equal security. She was fortunate, in a total absence of those charms which might have drawn to her bewildering flatteries, and of a strong electric nature, which repelled those who did not belong to her, and attracted those who did. With men and women her relations were noble; affectionate without passion, intellectual without coldness. The world was free to her, and she lived freely in it. Outward adversity came, and inward conflict, but that faith and self-respect had early been awakened, which must always lead at last to an outward serenity, and an inward peace.

Of Miranda I had always thought as an example, that the restraints upon the sex were insuperable only to those who think them so, or who noisily strive to break them. She had taken a course of her own, and no man stood in her way. Many of her acts had been unusual, but excited no uproar. Few helped, but none checked her; and the many men, who knew her mind and her life, showed to her confidence as to a brother, gentleness as to a sister. And not only refined, but very coarse men approved one in whom they saw resolution and clearness of design. Her mind was often the leading one, always effective.

When I talked with her upon these matters, and had said very much what I have written, she smilingly replied, And yet we must admit that I have been fortunate, and this should not be. My good father's early trust gave the first bias, and the rest followed of course. It is true that I have had less outward aid, in after years, than most women, but that is of little consequence. Religion was early awakened in my soul, a sense that what the soul is capable to ask it must attain, and that, though I might be aided by others, I must depend on myself as the only constant friend. This self-dependence, which was honored in me, is deprecated as a fault in most women. They are taught to learn their rule from without, not to unfold it from within.

This is the fault of man, who is still vain, and wishes to be more important to woman than by right he should be.

Men have not shown this disposition towards you, I said.

No, because the position I early was enabled to take, was one of self-reliance. And were all women as sure of their wants as I was, the result would be the same. The difficulty is to get them to the point where they shall naturally develop self-respect, the question how it is to be done.

Once I thought that men would help on this state of things more than I do now. I saw so many of them wretched in the connections they had formed in weakness and vanity. They seemed so glad to esteem women whenever they could!

But early I perceived that men never, in any extreme of despair, wished to be women. Where they admired any woman they were inclined to speak of her as above her sex. Silently I observed this, and feared it argued a rooted skepticism, which for ages had been fastening on the heart, and which only an age of miracles could eradicate.

Ever I have been treated with great sincerity; and I look upon it as a most signal instance of this, that an intimate friend of the other sex said in a fervent moment, that I deserved in some star to be a man. Another used as highest praise, in speaking of a character in literature, the words "a manly woman."

It is well known that of every strong woman they say she has a masculine mind.[23]

This by no means argues a willing want of generosity towards woman. Man is as generous towards her, as he knows how to be.

Wherever she has herself arisen in national or private history, and nobly shone forth in any ideal of excellence, men have received her, not only willingly, but with triumph. Their encomiums indeed are always in some sense mortifying, they show too much surprise.

In every-day life the feelings of the many are stained with vanity. Each wishes to be lord in a little world, to be superior at least over one; and he does not feel strong enough to retain a life-long ascendant over a strong nature. Only a Brutus would rejoice in a Portia.[24] Only Theseus could conquer before he wed the Amazonian Queen.[25] Hercules wished rather to rest from his labors with Dejanira, and received the poisoned robe, as a fit guerdon.[26] The tale should be interpreted to all those who seek repose with the weak.

But not only is man vain and fond of power, but the same want of development, which thus affects him morally in the intellect, prevents his discerning the destiny of woman. The boy wants no woman, but only a girl to play ball with him, and mark his pocket handkerchief.

Thus in Schiller's Dignity of Woman,[27] beautiful as the poem is, there is no "grave and perfect man," but only a great boy to be softened and restrained by the influence of girls. Poets, the elder brothers of their race, have usually seen further; but what can you expect of every-day men, if Schiller was not more prophetic as to what women must be? Even with Richter[28] one foremost thought about a wife was that she would "cook him something good."

The sexes should not only correspond to and appreciate one another, but prophesy to one another. In individual instances this happens. Two persons love in one another the future good which they aid one another to unfold. This is very imperfectly done as yet in the general life. Man has gone but little way, now he is waiting to see whether woman can keep step with him, but instead of calling out like a good brother; You can do it if you only think so, or impersonally; Any one can do what he tries to do, he often discourages with school-boy brag; Girls cant do that, girls cant play ball. But

---

[23] The 1844 version of this essay indicates that this is Miranda's last sentence.

[24] Brutus's wife. (See Shakespeare's *Julius Caesar*.)

[25] Theseus, a war hero in Greek myth, married the Amazonian queen known as Hippolyte or Orethyia.

[26] To win back his love, Dejanira sent Hercules a shirt that she thought was permeated with a love potion when in fact the garment contained a deadly poison that consumed his flesh.

[27] Poem by Johann Friedrich von Schiller (1759–1805).

[28] German novelist Jean Paul Richter (1763–1825), author of *Levana or The Doctrine of Education* (1807).

let any one defy their taunts, break through, and be brave and secure, they rend the air with shouts.

No! man is not willingly ungenerous. He wants faith and love, because he is not yet himself an elevated being. He cries with sneering skepticism; Give us a sign. But if the sign appears, his eyes glisten, and he offers not merely approval, but homage.

The severe nation[29] which taught that the happiness of the race was forfeited through the fault of a woman, and showed its thought of what sort of regard man owed her, by making him accuse her on the first question to his God, who gave her to the patriarch as a handmaid, and, by the Mosaical law, bound her to allegiance like a serf, even they greeted, with solemn rapture, all great and holy women as heroines, prophetesses, nay judges in Israel; and, if they made Eve listen to the serpent, gave Mary to the Holy Spirit. In other nations it has been the same down to our day. To the woman, who could conquer, a triumph was awarded. And not only those whose strength was recommended to the heart by association with goodness and beauty, but those who were bad, if they were steadfast and strong, had their claims allowed. In any age a Semiramis, an Elizabeth of England, a Catharine of Russia[30] makes her place good, whether in a large or small circle.

How has a little wit, a little genius, always been celebrated in a woman! What an intellectual triumph was that of the lonely Aspasia,[31] and how heartily acknowledged! She, indeed, met a Pericles. But what annalist, the rudest of men, the most plebeian of husbands, will spare from his page one of the few anecdotes of Roman women?—Sappho, Eloisa![32] The names are of thread-bare celebrity. The man habitually most narrow towards women will be flushed, as by the worst assault on Christianity, if you say it has made no improvement in her condition. Indeed, those most opposed to new acts in her favor are jealous of the reputation of those which have been done.

We will not speak of the enthusiasm excited by actresses, improvisatrici,[33] female singers, for here mingles the charm of beauty and grace, but female authors, even learned women, if not insufferably ugly and slovenly, from the Italian professor's daughter, who taught behind the curtain, down to Mrs. Carter and Madame Dacier,[34] are sure of an admiring audience, if they can once get a platform on which to stand.

But how to get this platform, or how to make it of reasonably easy access is the difficulty. Plants of great vigor will almost always struggle into blossom, despite impediments. But there should be encouragement, and a free, genial atmosphere for those of more timid sort, fair play for each in its own kind. Some are like the little, delicate flowers, which love to hide in the dripping mosses by the sides of mountain torrents, or in the shade of tall trees. But others require an open field, a rich and loosened soil, or they never show their proper hues.

---

[29] I.e., the Jews.
[30] Semiramis: legendary founder of Babylon; Elizabeth: queen of England (1558–1603); Catharine: empress of Russia (1762–1796).
[31] Prominent figure (470?–410 B.C.) in Greek literary and intellectual circles and later mistress to Pericles (495–429 B.C.), an Athenian statesman.
[32] Sappho: Greek lyric poet of the seventh century

B.C.; Eloisa: Eloise, French abbess (1101–1164) famous for her love and correspondence with Abelard (1079–1142), French philosopher and theologian.
[33] Female dancers or singers who improvise.
[34] Mrs. Carter: English poet Elizabeth Carter (1717–1806), a translator of the classics; Madame Dacier: French scholar Anne LeFevre Dacier (1654–1720), also a translator of the classics.

It may be said man does not have his fair play either; his energies are repressed and distorted by the interposition of artificial obstacles. Aye, but he himself has put them there; they have grown out of his own imperfections. If there *is* a misfortune in woman's lot, it is in obstacles being interposed by men, which do *not* mark her state, and if they express her past ignorance, do not her present needs. As every man is of woman born, she has slow but sure means of redress, yet the sooner a general justness of thought makes smooth the path, the better.

Man is of woman born, and her face bends over him in infancy with an expression he can never quite forget. Eminent men have delighted to pay tribute to this image, and it is a hackneyed observation, that most men of genius boast some remarkable development in the mother. The rudest tar brushes off a tear with his coat-sleeve at the hallowed name. The other day I met a decrepit old man of seventy, on a journey, who challenged the stage-company to guess where he was going. They guessed aright, "To see your mother." "Yes," said he, "she is ninety-two, but has good eye-sight still, they say. I've not seen her these forty years, and I thought I could not die in peace without." I should have liked his picture painted as a companion piece to that of a boisterous little boy, whom I saw attempt to declaim at a school exhibition.

"O that those lips had language! Life has passed
  With me but roughly since I heard thee last."[35]

He got but very little way before sudden tears shamed him from the stage.

Some gleams of the same expression which shone down upon his infancy, angelically pure and benign, visit man again with hopes of pure love, of a holy marriage. Or if not before, in the eyes of the mother of his child they again are seen, and dim fancies pass before his mind, that woman may not have been born for him alone, but have come from heaven, a commissioned soul, a messenger of truth and love.

In gleams, in dim fancies, this thought visits the mind of common men. It is soon obscured by the mists of sensuality, the dust of routine, and he thinks it was only some meteor or ignis fatuus[36] that shone. But, as a Rosicrucian lamp, it burns unwearied,[37] though condemned to the solitude of tombs. And, to its permanent life, as to every truth, each age has, in some form, borne witness. For the truths, which visit the minds of careless men only in fitful gleams, shine with radiant clearness into those of the poet, the priest, and the artist.

Whatever may have been the domestic manners of the ancient nations, the idea of woman was nobly manifested in their mythologies and poems, where she appeared as Sita in the Ramayana, a form of tender purity, in the Egyptian Isis, of divine wisdom never yet surpassed.[38] In Egypt, too, the Sphinx, walking the earth with lion tread, looked out upon its marvels in the calm, inscrutable beauty of a virgin's face,

---

[35] From "On the Receipt of My Mother's Picture" by English poet William Cowper (1731–1800).

[36] Latin: "foxfire" or "will-o'-the-wisp."

[37] The eternally blazing lamp was a practice of the Rosicrucians, a religious order prominent in the seventeenth and eighteenth centuries.

[38] In the Sanskrit epic poem of India, the *Ramayana* or *Life of Rama* (ca. 300 B.C.), Sita, the daughter of King Janaka, is rescued by the god Rama after being kidnapped; Isis is goddess of fertility in Egyptian mythology.

and the Greek could only add wings to the great emblem. In Greece, Ceres and Proserpine,[39] significantly termed "the great goddesses," were seen seated, side by side. They needed not to rise for any worshipper or any change; they were prepared for all things, as those initiated to their mysteries knew. More obvious is the meaning of those three forms, the Diana, Minerva, and Vesta.[40] Unlike in the expression of their beauty, but alike in this,—that each was self-sufficing. Other forms were only accessories and illustrations, none the complement to one like these. Another might indeed be the companion, and the Apollo and Diana set off one another's beauty. Of the Vesta, it is to be observed, that not only deep-eyed deep-discerning Greece, but ruder Rome, who represents the only form of good man (the always busy warrior) that could be indifferent to woman, confided the permanence of its glory to a tutelary goddess, and her wisest legislator spoke of Meditation as a nymph.

In Sparta, thought, in this respect as all others, was expressed in the characters of real life, and the women of Sparta were as much Spartans as the men. The Citoyen, Citoyenne, of France, was here actualized. Was not the calm equality they enjoyed well worth the honors of chivalry? They intelligently shared the ideal life of their nation.

Generally, we are told of these nations, that women occupied there a very subordinate position in actual life. It is difficult to believe this, when we see such range and dignity of thought on the subject in the mythologies, and find the poets producing such ideals as Cassandra, Iphigenia, Antigone, Macaria,[41] (though it is not unlike our own day, that men should revere those heroines of their great princely houses at theatres from which their women were excluded,) where Sibylline priestesses[42] told the oracle of the highest god, and he could not be content to reign with a court of less than nine Muses.[43] Even Victory[44] wore a female form.

But whatever were the facts of daily life, I cannot complain of the age and nation, which represents its thought by such a symbol as I see before me at this moment. It is a zodiac of the busts of gods and goddesses, arranged in pairs. The circle breathes the music of a heavenly order. Male and female heads are distinct in expression, but equal in beauty, strength, and calmness. Each male head is that of a brother and a king, each female of a sister and a queen. Could the thought, thus expressed, be lived out, there would be nothing more to be desired. There would be unison in variety, congeniality in difference.

Coming nearer our own time, we find religion and poetry no less true in their revelations. The rude man, but just disengaged from the sod, the Adam, accuses woman to his God, and records her disgrace to their posterity. He is not ashamed to write that he could be drawn from heaven by one beneath him. But in the same nation, educated by time, instructed by successive prophets, we find woman in as high a

---

[39] Ceres: goddess of agriculture; Proserpine: Ceres' daughter, and goddess of the underworld (also known as Persephone).

[40] Roman goddesses of the moon and hunting, wisdom and invention, and home and hearth, respectively.

[41] All from Greek mythology. Cassandra: the disbelieved prophetess of Troy; Iphigenia: daughter of Agamemnon, rescued from sacrifice for her father by the goddess Artemis;

Antigone: princess of Thebes, put to death because she buried her brother's corpse against her uncle's orders; Macaria: daughter of Hercules, who sacrificed herself to save Athens.

[42] Worshipers of Apollo who delivered the divine messages to the Delphic oracle.

[43] The nine sisters of Greek myth who presided over the arts and sciences.

[44] The statue popularly entitled *Victory of Samothrace* or *Winged Victory*.

position as she has ever occupied. And no figure, that has ever arisen to greet our eyes, has been received with more fervent reverence than that of the Madonna. Heine[45] calls her the Dame du Comptoir of the Catholic Church, and this jeer well expresses a serious truth.

And not only this holy and significant image was worshipped by the pilgrim, and the favorite subject of the artist, but it exercised an immediate influence on the destiny of the sex. The empresses, who embraced the cross, converted sons and husbands.[46] Whole calendars of female saints, heroic dames of chivalry, binding the emblem of faith on the heart of the best beloved, and wasting the bloom of youth in separation and loneliness, for the sake of duties they thought it religion to assume, with innumerable forms of poesy, trace their lineage to this one. Nor, however imperfect may be the action, in our day, of the faith thus expressed, and though we can scarcely think it nearer this ideal than that of India or Greece was near their ideal, is it in vain that the truth has been recognised, that woman is not only a part of man, bone of his bone and flesh of his flesh, born that men might not be lonely, but in themselves possessors of and possessed by immortal souls. This truth undoubtedly received a greater outward stability from the belief of the church, that the earthly parent of the Saviour of souls was a woman.

The Assumption of the Virgin,[47] as painted by sublime artists, Petrarch's Hymn to the Madonna, cannot have spoken to the world wholly without result, yet oftentimes those who had ears heard not.

Thus, the Idea of woman has not failed to be often and forcibly represented. So many instances throng on the mind, that we must stop here, lest the catalogue be swelled beyond the reader's patience.

Neither can she complain that she has not had her share of power. This, in all ranks of society, except the lowest, has been hers to the extent that vanity could crave, far beyond what wisdom would accept. In the very lowest, where man, pressed by poverty, sees in woman only the partner of toils and cares, and cannot hope, scarcely has an idea of a comfortable home, he maltreats her, often, and is less influenced by her. In all ranks, those who are amiable and uncomplaining, suffer much. They suffer long, and are kind; verily they have their reward. But wherever man is sufficiently raised above extreme poverty, or brutal stupidity, to care for the comforts of the fireside, or the bloom and ornament of life, woman has always power enough, if she choose to exert it, and is usually disposed to do so in proportion to her ignorance and childish vanity. Unacquainted with the importance of life and its purposes, trained to a selfish coquetry and love of petty power, she does not look beyond the pleasure of making herself felt at the moment, and governments are shaken and commerce broken up to gratify the pique of a female favorite. The English shopkeeper's wife does not vote, but it is for her interest that the politician canvasses by the coarsest flattery. France suffers no woman on her throne, but her proud nobles kiss the dust at the feet of Pompadour and Dubarry, for such flare in the lighted foreground where

[45] Heinrich Heine (1797–1856), German lyric poet and satirist, whose "jeer" translates roughly from the French as "Lady of the Counting House" or "Lady Chancellor of the Exchequer."

[46] Reference to the renowned discoverer of Jesus'

cross, Helena (A.D. 248?–328), mother of the Roman emperor Constantine the Great.

[47] Catholic doctrine describes the taking up of the Virgin Mary's body to heaven. Petrarch: Italian poet Francesco Petrarca.

a Roland would modestly aid in the closet.[48] Spain shuts up her women in the care of duennas,[49] and allows them no book but the Breviary;[50] but the ruin follows only the more surely from the worthless favorite of a worthless queen.

It is not the transient breath of poetic incense, that women want; each can receive that from a lover. It is not life-long sway; it needs but to become a coquette, a shrew, or a good cook to be sure of that. It is not money, nor notoriety, nor the badges of authority, that men have appropriated to themselves. If demands made in their behalf lay stress on any of these particulars, those who make them have not searched deeply into the need. It is for that which at once includes all these and precludes them; which would not be forbidden power, lest there be temptation to steal and misuse it; which would not have the mind perverted by flattery from a worthiness of esteem. It is for that which is the birthright of every being capable to receive it,—the freedom, the religious, the intelligent freedom of the universe, to use its means, to learn its secret as far as nature has enabled them, with God alone for their guide and their judge.

Ye cannot believe it, men; but the only reason why women ever assume what is more appropriate to you, is because you prevent them from finding out what is fit for themselves. Were they free, were they wise fully to develop the strength and beauty of woman, they would never wish to be men, or manlike. The well-instructed moon flies not from her orbit to seize on the glories of her partner. No; for she knows that one law rules, one heaven contains, one universe replies to them alike. It is with women as with the slave.

> "Vor dem Sklaven, wenn er die Kette bricht,
>   Vor dem freien Menschen erzittert nicht."

Tremble not before the free man, but before the slave who has chains to break.

In slavery, acknowledged slavery, women are on a par with men. Each is a work-tool, an article of property,—no more! In perfect freedom, such as is painted in Olympus, in Swedenborg's[51] angelic state, in the heaven where there is no marrying nor giving in marriage,[52] each is a purified intelligence, an enfranchised soul,—no less!

> Jene himmlische Gestalten
> Sie fragen nicht nach Mann und Weib,
>   Und keine Kleider, keine Falten
> Umgeben den verklärten Leib.[53]

---

[48] Pompadour: Jeanne Antoinette Poisson, marquise de Pompadour (1721–1764), lover of Louis XV of France; Dubarry: Marie Jeanne Beçu, comtesse du Barry (1743–1793) and final mistress of Louis XV, put to death during the French Revolution; Roland: Marie Jeanne Roland (1754–1793), Jacobin wife of Jean Marie Roland (1734–1793), who committed suicide on discovering that she had been guillotined.

[49] Duenna: usually an older governess and escort to the daughter of a Spanish or Portuguese family.

[50] Book containing hymns, prayers, and offices.

[51] Swedish statesman and mystic Emanuel Swedenborg (1688–1772) was author of *Heaven and Hell*.

[52] In Matthew 22:30, Jesus spoke to the Sadduces: "For in the resurrection they neither marry nor are given in marriage but are as the angels of God in Heaven."

[53] From *Wilhelm Meister's Apprenticeship* by Johann Wolfgang von Goethe (1749–1832). Just before her death Mignon sings: "Yonder heavenly Forms / They ask not whether one be Man or Woman / And no Garments, no Folds / Enclose the transfigured Body."

The child who sang this was a prophetic form, expressive of the longing for a state of perfect freedom, pure love. She could not remain here, but was transplanted to another air. And it may be that the air of this earth will never be so tempered, that such can bear it long. But, while they stay, they must bear testimony to the truth they are constituted to demand.

That an era approaches which shall approximate nearer to such a temper than any has yet done, there are many tokens, indeed so many that only a few of the most prominent can here be enumerated.

The reigns of Elizabeth of England and Isabella of Castile[54] foreboded this era. They expressed the beginning of the new state, while they forwarded its progress. These were strong characters, and in harmony with the wants of their time. One showed that this strength did not unfit a woman for the duties of a wife and mother; the other, that it could enable her to live and die alone. Elizabeth is certainly no pleasing example. In rising above the weakness, she did not lay aside the weaknesses ascribed to her sex; but her strength must be respected now, as it was in her own time.

We may accept it as an omen for ourselves, that it was Isabella who furnished Columbus with the means of coming hither. This land must pay back its debt to woman, without whose aid it would not have been brought into alliance with the civilized world.

The influence of Elizabeth on literature was real, though, by sympathy with its finer productions, she was no more entitled to give name to an era than Queen Anne.[55] It was simply that the fact of having a female sovereign on the throne affected the course of a writer's thoughts. In this sense, the presence of a woman on the throne always makes its mark. Life is lived before the eyes of all men, and their imaginations are stimulated as to the possibilities of woman. "We will die for our King, Maria Theresa,"[56] cry the wild warriors, clashing their swords, and the sounds vibrate through the poems of that generation. The range of female character in Spenser alone might content us for one period. Britomart and Belphoebe have as much room in the canvass as Florimel; and where this is the case, the haughtiest Amazon will not murmur that Una should be felt to be the highest type.[57]

Unlike as was the English Queen to a fairy queen, we may yet conceive that it was the image of a queen before the poet's mind, that called up this splendid court of women.

Shakspeare's range is also great, but he has left out the heroic characters, such as the Macaria of Greece,[58] the Britomart of Spenser. Ford and Massinger[59] have, in this respect, shown a higher flight of feeling than he. It was the holy and heroic woman they most loved, and if they could not paint an Imogen, a Desdemona, a Rosalind,[60] yet in those of a stronger mould, they showed a higher ideal, though with so much

---

[54] Elizabeth: 1558–1603; Isabella: 1474–1504.
[55] Queen of England from 1702 to 1714.
[56] Queen of Hungary and Bohemia from 1717 to 1780 and wife of the Emperor Francis I.
[57] In Edmund Spenser's *Faerie Queene* (1590), Britomart is a female knight who represents Chastity; Belphoebe is a huntress who resembles Queen Elizabeth I; Florimel is a witch; Una is the embodiment of Truth.

[58] Hercules' daughter, who sacrificed herself.
[59] As in the English plays *The Broken Heart* by John Ford (1586–1640) and *The Duke of Milan* by Philip Massinger (1583–1640).
[60] Imogen: in Shakespeare's *Cymbeline,* the abused but gallant wife; Desdemona: the impeccably loyal wife in *Othello*; Rosalind: the spirited and confident heroine of *As you Like It.*

less poetic power to represent it, than we see in Portia or Isabella.[61] The simple truth of Cordelia,[62] indeed, is of this sort. The beauty of Cordelia is neither male nor female; it is the beauty of virtue.

The ideal of love and marriage rose high in the mind of all the Christian nations who were capable of grave and deep feeling. We may take as examples of its English aspect, the lines,

> "I could not love thee, dear, so much,
>   Loved I not honor more."[63]

The address of the Commonwealth's man to his wife as she looked out from the Tower window to see him for the last time on his way to execution. "He stood up in the cart, waved his hat, and cried, 'To Heaven, my love, to Heaven! and leave you in the storm!' "

Such was the love of faith and honor, a love which stopped, like Colonel Hutchinson's, "on this side idolatry," because it was religious.[64] The meeting of two such souls Donne describes as giving birth to an "abler soul."[65]

Lord Herbert wrote to his love,

> "Were not our souls immortal made,
>   Our equal loves can make them such."[66]

In Spain the same thought is arrayed in a sublimity, which belongs to the sombre and passionate genius of the nation. Calderon's Justina resists all the temptation of the Demon, and raises her lover with her above the sweet lures of mere temporal happiness.[67] Their marriage is vowed at the stake, their souls are liberated together by the martyr flame into "a purer state of sensation and existence."

In Italy, the great poets wove into their lives an ideal love which answered to the highest wants. It included those of the intellect and the affections, for it was a love of spirit for spirit. It was not ascetic and superhuman, but interpreting all things, gave their proper beauty to details of the common life, the common day; the poet spoke of his love not as a flower to place in his bosom, or hold carelessly in his hand, but as a light towards which he must find wings to fly, or "a stair to heaven." He delighted to speak of her not only as the bride of his heart, but the mother of his soul, for he saw that, in cases where the right direction has been taken, the greater delicacy of her frame, and stillness of her life, left her more open to spiritual influx than man is. So

---

[61] Portia: either the clever heiress in *The Merchant of Venice* or the ideal Roman wife in *Julius Caesar*; Isabella: the resourceful heroine of *Measure for Measure*.

[62] The purely loving daughter in *King Lear*.

[63] From "To Lucasta Going to the Wars" by Richard Lovelace (1618–1657), English poet.

[64] Reference to Colonel John Hutchison (1615–1664), who supported the Commonwealth in the English Civil War; in his *Memoirs*, his widow Lucy Hutchison wrote about their mutual devotion. The poet and playwright Ben Johnson (ca. 1573–1637), in *Timber*, wrote of Shakespeare: "I loved the

man, and do honor his memory (on this side idolatry) as much as any."

[65] From line 43 of "The Ecstasy" by John Donne (ca. 1572–1631).

[66] From "An Ode upon a Question Moved Whether Love Should Continue for Ever" by Edward, Lord Herbert of Cherbury (1583–1648).

[67] Pedro Calderon de la Barca (1600–1681) wrote *El Magico Prodigioso (The Mighty Magician)*, in which Justina, daughter of a Christian during the Roman persecution in Antioch, makes an extraordinary appeal to Jesus to save herself from Lucifer.

he did not look upon her as betwixt him and earth, to serve his temporal needs, but rather betwixt him and heaven, to purify his affections and lead him to wisdom through her pure love. He sought in her not so much the Eve as the Madonna.

In these minds the thought, which glitters in all the legends of chivalry, shines in broad intellectual effulgence, not to be misinterpreted. And their thought is reverenced by the world, though it lies so far from them as yet, so far, that it seems as though a gulf of Death lay between.

Even with such men the practice was often widely different from the mental faith. I say mental, for if the heart were thoroughly alive with it, the practice could not be dissonant. Lord Herbert's was a marriage of convention, made for him at fifteen;[68] he was not discontented with it, but looked only to the advantages it brought of perpetuating his family on the basis of a great fortune. He paid, in act, what he considered a dutiful attention to the bond; his thoughts travelled elsewhere, and, while forming a high ideal of the companionship of minds in marriage, he seems never to have doubted that its realization must be postponed to some other stage of being. Dante, almost immediately after the death of Beatrice,[69] married a lady chosen for him by his friends.

Centuries have passed since, but civilized Europe is still in a transition state about marriage, not only in practice, but in thought. A great majority of societies and individuals are still doubtful whether earthly marriage is to be a union of souls, or merely a contract of convenience and utility. Were woman established in the rights of an immortal being, this could not be. She would not in some countries be given away by her father, with scarcely more respect for her own feelings than is shown by the Indian chief, who sells his daughter for a horse, and beats her if she runs away from her new home. Nor, in societies where her choice is left free, would she be perverted, by the current of opinion that seizes her, into the belief that she must marry, if it be only to find a protector, and a home of her own.

Neither would man, if he thought that the connection was of permanent importance, enter upon it so lightly. He would not deem it a trifle, that he was to enter into the closest relations with another soul, which, if not eternal in themselves, must eternally affect his growth.

Neither, did he believe woman capable of friendship, would he, by rash haste, lose the chance of finding a friend in the person who might, probably, live half a century by his side. Did love to his mind partake of infinity, he would not miss his chance of its revelations, that he might the sooner rest from his weariness by a bright fireside, and have a sweet and graceful attendant, "devoted to him alone." Were he a step higher, he would not carelessly enter into a relation, where he might not be able to do the duty of a friend, as well as a protector from external ill, to the other party, and have a being in his power pining for sympathy, intelligence, and aid, that he could not give.

Where the thought of equality has become pervasive, it shows itself in four kinds.

The household partnership. In our country the woman looks for a "smart but kind" husband, the man for a "capable, sweet-tempered" wife.

The man furnishes the house, the woman regulates it. Their relation is one of

---

[68] Herbert was married in 1599.
[69] The woman, perhaps Beatrice Portinari (1266–1290), who inspired Dante Alighieri

(1265–1321) to write *The New Life*. Dante later characterized her as his guide through Paradise in his poem *The Divine Comedy*.

mutual esteem, mutual dependence. Their talk is of business, their affection shows itself by practical kindness. They know that life goes more smoothly and cheerfully to each for the other's aid; they are grateful and content. The wife praises her husband as a "good provider," the husband in return compliments her as a "capital housekeeper." This relation is good as far as it goes.

Next comes a closer tie which takes the two forms, either of intellectual companionship, or mutual idolatry. The last, we suppose, is to no one a pleasing subject of contemplation. The parties weaken and narrow one another; they lock the gate against all the glories of the universe that they may live in a cell together. To themselves they seem the only wise, to all others steeped in infatuation, the gods smile as they look forward to the crisis of cure, to men the woman seems an unlovely syren, to women the man an effeminate boy.

The other form, of intellectual companionship, has become more and more frequent. Men engaged in public life, literary men, and artists have often found in their wives companions and confidants in thought no less than in feeling. And, as in the course of things the intellectual development of woman has spread wider and risen higher, they have, not unfrequently, shared the same employment. As in the case of Roland and his wife, who were friends in the household and the nation's councils, read together, regulated home affairs, or prepared public documents together indifferently.

It is very pleasant, in letters begun by Roland and finished by his wife, to see the harmony of mind and the difference of nature, one thought, but various ways of treating it.

This is one of the best instances of a marriage of friendship. It was only friendship, whose basis was esteem; probably neither party knew love, except by name.

Roland was a good man, worthy to esteem and be esteemed, his wife as deserving of admiration as able to do without it. Madame Roland is the fairest specimen we have yet of her class, as clear to discern her aim, as valiant to pursue it, as Spenser's Britomart, austerely set apart from all that did not belong to her, whether as woman or as mind. She is an antetype of a class to which the coming time will afford a field, the Spartan matron, brought by the culture of a book-furnishing age to intellectual consciousness and expansion.

Self-sufficing strength and clear-sightedness were in her combined with a power of deep and calm affection. The page of her life is one of unsullied dignity.

Her appeal to posterity is one against the injustice of those who committed such crimes in the name of liberty. She makes it in behalf of herself and her husband. I would put beside it on the shelf a little volume, containing a similar appeal from the verdict of contemporaries to that of mankind, that of Godwin in behalf of his wife, the celebrated, the by most men detested Mary Wolstonecraft.[70] In his view it was an appeal from the injustice of those who did such wrong in the name of virtue.

Were this little book interesting for no other cause, it would be so for the generous affection evinced under the peculiar circumstances. This man had courage to love and honor this woman in the face of the world's verdict, and of all that was repulsive

[70] William Godwin (1756–1836) wrote *Memoirs of the Author of "A Vindication of the Rights of Woman"* in 1798, just after his wife Mary Wollstonecraft (1759–1797) had died in childbirth.

in her own past history. He believed he saw of what soul she was, and that the thoughts she had struggled to act out were noble. He loved her and he defended her for the meaning and intensity of her inner life. It was a good fact.

Mary Wolstonecraft, like Madame Dudevant[71] (commonly known as George Sand) in our day, was a woman whose existence better proved the need of some new interpretation of woman's rights, than anything she wrote. Such women as these, rich in genius, of most tender sympathies, and capable of high virtue and a chastened harmony, ought not to find themselves by birth in a place so narrow, that in breaking bonds they become outlaws. Were there as much room in the world for such, as in Spenser's poem for Britomart, they would not run their heads so wildly against its laws. They find their way at last to purer air, but the world will not take off the brand it has set upon them. The champion of the rights of woman found in Godwin one who plead her own cause like a brother. George Sand smokes, wears male attire, wishes to be addressed as Mon frère;[72] perhaps, if she found those who were as brothers indeed, she would not care whether she were brother or sister.

We rejoice to see that she, who expresses such a painful contempt for men in most of her works, as shows she must have known great wrong from them, in La Roche Mauprat[73] depicting one raised, by the workings of love, from the depths of savage sensualism to a moral and intellectual life. It was love for a pure object, for a steadfast woman, one of those who, the Italian said, could make the stair to heaven.

Women like Sand will speak now, and cannot be silenced; their characters and their eloquence alike foretell an era when such as they shall easier learn to lead true lives. But though such forebode, not such shall be the parents of it. Those who would reform the world must show that they do not speak in the heat of wild impulse; their lives must be unstained by passionate error; they must be severe lawgivers to themselves. As to their transgressions and opinions, it may be observed, that the resolve of Eloisa to be only the mistress of Abelard, was that of one who saw the contract of marriage a seal of degradation.[74] Wherever abuses of this sort are seen, the timid will suffer, the bold protest. But society is in the right to outlaw them till she has revised her law, and she must be taught to do so, by one who speaks with authority, not in anger and haste.

If Godwin's choice of the calumniated authoress of the "Rights of Woman," for his honored wife, be a sign of a new era, no less so is an article of great learning and eloquence, published several years since in an English review, where the writer, in doing full justice to Eloisa, shows his bitter regret that she lives not now to love him, who might have known better how to prize her love than did the egotistical Abelard.

These marriages, these characters, with all their imperfections, express an onward tendency. They speak of aspiration of soul, of energy of mind, seeking clearness and freedom. Of a like promise are the tracts now publishing by Goodwyn Barmby[75] (the European Pariah as he calls himself) and his wife Catharine. Whatever we may think of their measures, we see them in wedlock, the two minds are wed by the only contract that can permanently avail, of a common faith, and a common purpose.

---

[71] French romantic novelist Amandine Aurore Lucile Dudevant (1804–1876), admired as a crusader for the liberation of women.
[72] French: literally "my brother." More broadly, "old friend" or "comrade."
[73] Drama by George Sand.
[74] Had Eloise married Abelard, he would have been forced by church laws to give up teaching theology.
[75] Minor British publisher.

We might mention instances, nearer home, of minds, partners in work and in life, sharing together, on equal terms, public and private interests, and which have not on any side that aspect of offence which characterizes the attitude of the last named; persons who steer straight onward, and in our freer life have not been obliged to run their heads against any wall. But the principles which guide them might, under petrified or oppressive institutions, have made them warlike, paradoxical, or, in some sense, Pariahs. The phenomenon is different, the law the same, in all these cases. Men and women have been obliged to build their house from the very foundation. If they found stone ready in the quarry, they took it peaceably, otherwise they alarmed the country by pulling down old towers to get materials.

These are all instances of marriage as intellectual companionship. The parties meet mind to mind, and a mutual trust is excited which can buckler them against a million. They work together for a common purpose, and, in all these instances, with the same implement, the pen.

A pleasing expression in this kind is afforded by the union in the names of the Howitts.[76] William and Mary Howitt we heard named together for years, supposing them to be brother and sister; the equality of labors and reputation, even so, was auspicious, more so, now we find them man and wife. In his late work on Germany, Howitt mentions his wife with pride, as one among the constellation of distinguished English women, and in a graceful, simple manner.

In naming these instances we do not mean to imply that community of employment is an essential to union of this sort, more than to the union of friendship. Harmony exists no less in difference than in likeness, if only the same key-note govern both parts. Woman the poem, man the poet; woman the heart, man the head; such divisions are only important when they are never to be transcended. If nature is never bound down, nor the voice of inspiration stifled, that is enough. We are pleased that women should write and speak, if they feel the need of it, from having something to tell; but silence for a hundred years would be as well, if that silence be from divine command, and not from man's tradition.

While Goetz von Berlichingen[77] rides to battle, his wife is busy in the kitchen; but difference of occupation does not prevent that community of life, that perfect esteem, with which he says,

"Whom God loves, to him gives he such a wife!"

Manzoni thus dedicates his Adelchi.[78]

"To his beloved and venerated wife, Enrichetta Luigia Blondel, who, with conjugal affections and maternal wisdom, has preserved a virgin mind, the author dedicates this Adelchi, grieving that he could not, by a more splendid and more durable monument, honor the dear name and the memory of so many virtues."

---

[76] British authors and translators Mary Howitt (1799–1888) and William Howitt (1792–1879).
[77] German knight (1481–1562) whom Fuller recognizes from Goethe's play *Goetz von Berlichingen*.

[78] The Italian writer Alessandro Manzoni (1785–1873) was author of the tragedy *Adelchi* (1822).

The relation could not be fairer, nor more equal, if she too had written poems. Yet the position of the parties might have been the reverse as well; the woman might have sung the deeds, given voice to the life of the man, and beauty would have been the result, as we see in pictures of Arcadia[79] the nymph singing to the shepherds, or the shepherd with his pipe allures the nymphs, either makes a good picture. The sounding lyre requires not muscular strength, but energy of soul to animate the hand which can control it. Nature seems to delight in varying her arrangements, as if to show that she will be fettered by no rule, and we must admit the same varieties that she admits.

I have not spoken of the higher grade of marriage union, the religious, which may be expressed as pilgrimage towards a common shrine. This includes the others; home sympathies, and household wisdom, for these pilgrims must know how to assist one another to carry their burdens along the dusty way; intellectual communion, for how sad it would be on such a journey to have a companion to whom you could not communicate thoughts and aspirations, as they sprang to life, who would have no feeling for the more and more glorious prospects that open as we advance, who would never see the flowers that may be gathered by the most industrious traveler. It must include all these. Such a fellow pilgrim Count Zinzendorf[80] seems to have found in his countess of whom he thus writes.

"Twenty-five years' experience has shown me that just the help-mate whom I have is the only one that could suit my vocation. Who else could have so carried through my family affairs? Who lived so spotlessly before the world? Who so wisely aided me in my rejection of a dry morality? Who so clearly set aside the Pharisaism[81] which, as years passed, threatened to creep in among us? Who so deeply discerned as to the spirits of delusion which sought to bewilder us? Who would have governed my whole economy so wisely, richly, and hospitably when circumstances commanded? Who have taken indifferently the part of servant or mistress, without on the one side affecting an especial spirituality, on the other being sullied by any worldly pride? Who, in a community where all ranks are eager to be on a level, would, from wise and real causes, have known how to maintain inward and outward distinctions? Who, without a murmur, have seen her husband encounter such dangers by land and sea? Who undertaken with him and sustained such astonishing pilgrimages? Who amid such difficulties always held up her head, and supported me? Who found so many hundred thousands and acquitted them on her own credit? And, finally, who, of all human beings, would so well understand and interpret to others my inner and outer being as this one, of such nobleness in her way of thinking, such great intellectual capacity, and free from the theological perplexities that enveloped me?"

---

[79] Peloponnesian pastoral region in Greece, symbolic of tranquility and simplicity.

[80] Nikolas Ludwig, Count von Zinzendorf (1700–1760), German head of the Bohemian Brethren, or the Moravian church, a Protestant sect founded in Bohemia in 1457.

[81] Hypocritical members of the Jewish sect, whom Jesus denounced in Matthew 23:27: " . . . which indeed appear beautiful outward, but are within full of dead men's bones, and of all uncleanness."

An observer[82] adds this testimony.

"We may in many marriages regard it as the best arrangement, if the man has so much advantage over his wife that she can, without much thought of her own, be, by him, led and directed, as by a father. But it was not so with the Count and his consort. She was not made to be a copy; she was an original; and, while she loved and honored him, she thought for herself on all subjects with so much intelligence, that he could and did look on her as a sister and friend also."

Such a woman is the sister and friend of all beings, as the worthy man is their brother and helper.

Another sign of the time is furnished by the triumphs of female authorship. These have been great and constantly increasing. They have taken possession of so many provinces for which men had pronounced them unfit, that though these still declare there are some inaccessible to them, it is difficult to say just *where* they must stop.

The shining names of famous women have cast light upon the path of the sex, and many obstructions have been removed. When a Montague[83] could learn better than her brother, and use her lore to such purpose afterwards as an observer, it seemed amiss to hinder women from preparing themselves to see, or from seeing all they could when prepared. Since Somerville[84] has achieved so much, will any young girl be prevented from attaining a knowledge of the physical sciences, if she wishes it? De Stael's[85] name was not so clear of offence; she could not forget the woman in the thought; while she was instructing you as a mind, she wished to be admired as a woman. Sentimental tears often dimmed the eagle glance. Her intellect, too, with all its splendor, trained in a drawing room, fed on flattery, was tainted and flawed; yet its beams make the obscurest school house in New England warmer and lighter to the little rugged girls, who are gathered together on its wooden bench. They may never through life hear her name, but she is not the less their benefactress.

This influence has been such that the aim certainly is, how, in arranging school instruction for girls, to give them as fair a field as boys. These arrangements are made as yet with little judgment or intelligence, just as the tutors of Jane Grey,[86] and the other famous women of her time, taught them Latin and Greek, because they knew nothing else themselves, so now the improvement in the education of girls is made by giving them gentlemen as teachers, who only teach what has been taught themselves at college, while methods and topics need revision for those new cases, which could better be made by those who had experienced the same wants. Women are often at the head of these institutions, but they have as yet seldom been thinking women, capable to organize a new whole for the wants of the time, and choose persons to officiate in the departments. And when some portion of education is got of a good sort from the school, the tone of society, the much larger proportion received from the world, contradicts its purport. Yet books have not been furnished, and a little

---

[82] August Gotlieb Spangenberg (1704–1792), who succeeded Count Zinzendorf as bishop of the Moravian church.

[83] Lady Mary Wortley Montague (1689–1762), a renowned letter writer.

[84] Mary Somerville (1789–1872), British scientific writer.

[85] French author and critic Madame de Staël (1766–1817), noted for her literary-political salons and love affairs.

[86] Lady Jane Grey (1537–1554), crowned queen of England in 1553 after Edward VI's death.

elementary instruction been given in vain. Women are better aware how large and rich the universe is, not so easily blinded by the narrowness and partial views of a home circle.

Whether much or little has or will be done, whether women will add to the talent of narration, the power of systematizing, whether they will carve marble as well as draw, is not important. But that it should be acknowledged that they have intellect which needs developing, that they should not be considered complete, if beings of affection and habit alone, is important.

Yet even this acknowledgment, rather obtained by woman than proffered by man, has been sullied by the usual selfishness. So much is said of women being better educated that they may be better companions and mothers *of men!* They should be fit for such companionship, and we have mentioned with satisfaction instances where it has been established. Earth knows no fairer, holier relation than that of a mother. But a being of infinite scope must not be treated with an exclusive view to any one relation. Give the soul free course, let the organization be freely developed, and the being will be fit for any and every relation to which it may be called. The intellect, no more than the sense of hearing, is to be cultivated, that she may be a more valuable companion to man, but because the Power who gave a power by its mere existence signifies that it must be brought out towards perfection.

In this regard, of self-dependence and a greater simplicity and fulness of being, we must hail as a preliminary the increase of the class contemptuously designated as old maids.

We cannot wonder at the aversion with which old bachelors and old maids have been regarded. Marriage is the natural means of forming a sphere, of taking root on the earth: it requires more strength to do this without such an opening, very many have failed of this, and their imperfections have been in every one's way. They have been more partial, more harsh, more officious and impertinent than others. Those, who have a complete experience of the human instincts, have a distrust as to whether they can be thoroughly human and humane, such as is hinted at in the saying, "Old maids' and bachelors' children are well cared for," which derides at once their ignorance and their presumption.

Yet the business of society has become so complex, that it could now scarcely be carried on without the presence of these despised auxiliaries, and detachments from the army of aunts and uncles are wanted to stop gaps in every hedge. They rove about, mental and moral Ishmaelites,[87] pitching their tents amid the fixed and ornamented habitations of men.

They thus gain a wider, if not so deep, experience. They are not so intimate with others, but thrown more upon themselves, and if they do not there find peace and incessant life, there is none to flatter them that they are not very poor and very mean.

A position, which so constantly admonishes, may be of inestimable benefit. The person may gain, undistracted by other relationships, a closer communion with the One. Such a use is made of it by saints and sibyls. Or she may be one of the lay sisters of charity, or more humbly only the useful drudge of all men, or the intellectual interpreter of the varied life she sees.

Or she may combine all these. Not "needing to care that she may please a husband," a frail and limited being, all her thoughts may turn to the centre, and by steadfast

---

[87] Noted for their transience. (See Genesis 15–25.)

contemplation enter into the secret of truth and love, use it for the use of all men, instead of a chosen few, and interpret through it all the forms of life.

Saints and geniuses have often chosen a lonely position, in the faith that, if undisturbed by the pressure of near ties they could give themselves up to the inspiring spirit, it would enable them to understand and reproduce life better than actual experience could.

How many old maids take this high stand, we cannot say; it is an unhappy fact that too many of those who come before the eye are gossips rather, and not always good-natured gossips. But, if these abuse, and none make the best of their vocation, yet, it has not failed to produce some good fruit. It has been seen by others, if not by themselves, that beings likely to be left alone need to be fortified and furnished within themselves, and education and thought have tended more and more to regard beings as related to absolute Being, as well as to other men. It has been seen that as the loss of no bond ought to destroy a human being, so ought the missing of none to hinder him from growing. And thus a circumstance of the time has helped to put woman on the true platform. Perhaps the next generation will look deeper into this matter, and find that contempt is put on old maids, or old women at all, merely because they do not use the elixir which will keep the soul always young. No one thinks of Michael Angelo's Persican Sibyl, or St. Theresa, or Tasso's Leonora, or the Greek Electra as an old maid,[88] though all had reached the period in life's course appointed to take that degree.

Even among the North American Indians, a race of men as completely engaged in mere instinctive life as almost any in the world, and where each chief, keeping many wives as useful servants, of course looks with no kind eye on celibacy in woman, it was excused in the following instance mentioned by Mrs. Jameson.[89] A woman dreamt in youth that she was betrothed to the sun. She built her a wigwam apart, filled it with emblems of her alliance and means of an independent life. There she passed her days, sustained by her own exertions, and true to her supposed engagement.

In any tribe, we believe, a woman, who lived as if she was betrothed to the sun, would be tolerated, and the rays which made her youth blossom sweetly would crown her with a halo in age.

There is on this subject a nobler view than heretofore, if not the noblest, and we greet improvement here, as much as on the subject of marriage. Both are fertile themes, but time permits not here to explore them.

If larger intellectual resources begin to be deemed necessary to woman, still more is a spiritual dignity in her, or even the mere assumption of its listened to with respect. Joanna Southcote, and Mother Anne Lee are sure of a band of disciples; Ecstatica, Dolorosa,[90] of enraptured believers who will visit them in their lowly huts, and wait for hours to revere them in their trances. The foreign noble traverses land and sea to hear a few words from the lips of the lowly peasant girl, whom he believes specially

[88] Persican Sibyl: one of the five ancient prophetesses depicted by Michelangelo in the Sistine Chapel; Saint Theresa (of Avila): Spanish Carmelite nun (1515–1582); Leonora (D'Este): guardian of Torquato Tasso, Italian poet, who was allegedly in love with her; Electra: in the Greek tragedy *Electra* by Aeschylus (525–456 B.C.), she and her brother Orestes avenge their father's murder.

[89] English writer Anna Brownell Jameson (1794–1860), author of *Winter Studies and Summer Rambles.*

[90] Joanna Southcote (1750–1814): English religious enthusiast; Mother Anne Lee (1736–1784): English founder of the Shaker movement; Ecstatica and Dolorosa: presumably model names for religious zealots.

visited by the Most High. Very beautiful in this way was the influence of the invalid of St. Petersburg, as described by De Maistre.[91]

To this region, however misunderstood, and ill-developed, belong the phenomena of Magnetism, or Mesmerism, as it is now often called, where the trance of the Ecstatica purports to be produced by the agency of one human being on another, instead of, as in her case, direct from the spirit.

The worldling has his sneer here as about the services of religion. "The churches can always be filled with women." "Show me a man in one of your magnetic states, and I will believe."

Women are indeed the easy victims of priestcraft, or self-delusion, but this might not be, if the intellect was developed in proportion to the other powers. They would then have a regulator and be in better equipoise, yet must retain the same nervous susceptibility, while their physical structure is such as it is.

It is with just that hope, that we welcome everything that tends to strengthen the fibre and develop the nature on more sides. When the intellect and affections are in harmony, when intellectual consciousness is calm and deep, inspiration will not be confounded with fancy.

The electrical, the magnetic element in woman has not been fairly developed at any period. Everything might be expected from it; she has far more of it than man. This is commonly expressed by saying, that her intuitions are more rapid and more correct.

But I cannot enlarge upon this here, except to say that on this side is highest promise. Should I speak of it fully, my title should be Cassandra, my topic the Seeress of Prevorst, the first, or the best observed subject of magnetism in our times, and who, like her ancestresses at Delphos, was roused to ecstacy or phrenzy by the touch of the laurel.[92]

In such cases worldlings sneer, but reverent men learn wondrous news, either from the person observed, or by the thoughts caused in themselves by the observation. Fenelon learns from Guyon,[93] Kerner from his Seeress what we fain would know. But to appreciate such disclosures one must be a child, and here the phrase, "women and children," may perhaps be interpreted aright, that only little children shall enter into the kingdom of heaven.[94]

All these motions of the time, tides that betoken a waxing moon, overflow upon our own land. The world at large is readier to let woman learn and manifest the capacities of her nature than it ever was before, and here is a less encumbered field, and freer air than anywhere else. And it ought to be so; we ought to pay for Isabella's jewels.[95]

---

[91] Joseph De Maistre (1754–1821), French philosopher, mystic, and author of *Soirées de St. Petersbourg.*

[92] Cassandra: prophetess and daughter of Priam, king of Troy; Seeress of Prevorst: in *Summer on the Lakes,* Fuller discusses the metaphysical allegations of Justinus Kerner's *Seherin von Prevorst*; ancestresses at Delphos: the classical Greek oracles of Delphi, loyal followers of Apollo who predicted the future to entreating mortals (the prophetesses chewed laurel leaves during their rituals).

[93] French Archbishop François Fenelon (1651–1715) studied quietism with Jeanne Guyon (1648–1717).

[94] Mark 10:14–15: "Suffer the little children to come unto me, and forbid them not: for of such is the kingdom of God."

[95] Isabella I (1451–1504), queen of Castile, sold her jewels in order to finance Columbus's expedition.

The names of nations are feminine. Religion, Virtue, and Victory are feminine. To those who have a superstition as to outward signs, it is not without significance that the name of the Queen of our mother-land should at this crisis be Victoria. Victoria the First. Perhaps to us it may be given to disclose the era there outwardly presaged.

Women here are much better situated than men. Good books are allowed with more time to read them. They are not so early forced into the bustle of life, nor so weighed down by demands for outward success. The perpetual changes, incident to our society, make the blood circulate freely through the body politic, and, if not favorable at present to the grace and bloom of life, they are so to activity, resource, and would be to reflection but for a low materialist tendency, from which the women are generally exempt.

They have time to think, and no traditions chain them, and few conventionalities compared with what must be met in other nations. There is no reason why the fact of a constant revelation should be hid from them, and when the mind once is awakened by that, it will not be restrained by the past, but fly to seek the seeds of a heavenly future.

Their employments are more favorable to the inward life than those of the men.

Woman is not addressed religiously here, more than elsewhere. She is told to be worthy to be the mother of a Washington, or the companion of some good man. But in many, many instances, she has already learnt that all bribes have the same flaw; that truth and good are to be sought for themselves alone. And already an ideal sweetness floats over many forms, shines in many eyes.

Already deep questions are put by young girls on the great theme, What shall I do to inherit eternal life?[96]

Men are very courteous to them. They praise them often, check them seldom. There is some chivalry in the feelings towards "the ladies," which gives them the best seats in the stage-coach, frequent admission not only to lectures of all sorts, but to courts of justice, halls of legislature, reform conventions. The newspaper editor "would be better pleased that the Lady's Book[97] were filled up exclusively by ladies. It would, then, indeed, be a true gem, worthy to be presented by young men to the mistresses of their affections." Can gallantry go farther?

In this country is venerated, wherever seen, the character which Goethe spoke of as an Ideal. "The excellent woman is she, who, if the husband dies, can be a father to the children." And this, if rightly read, tells a great deal.

Women who speak in public, if they have a moral power, such as has been felt from Angelina Grimke and Abby Kelly;[98] that is, if they speak for conscience' sake, to serve a cause which they hold sacred, invariably subdue the prejudices of their hearers, and excite an interest proportionate to the aversion with which it had been the purpose to regard them.

A passage in a private letter so happily illustrates this, that I take the liberty to make use of it, though there is not opportunity to ask leave either of the writer or owner

---

[96] Question posed to Jesus in Matthew 19:16: "Good master, what good thing shall I do, that I may have eternal life?"

[97] An extremely popular magazine of the period, *Godey's Lady's Book.*

[98] Angelina Grimke: abolitionist (1805–1879) and author of *Appeal to the Christian Women of the South* (1836); Abby Kelly: Quaker (1811–1887) and first woman to lecture on abolition before male *and* female audiences.

of the letter. I think they will pardon me when they see it in print; it is so good, that as many as possible should have the benefit of it.

Abby Kelly in the Town-House of ————

"The scene was not unheroic,—to see that woman, true to humanity and her own nature, a centre of rude eyes and tongues, even gentlemen feeling licensed to make part of a species of mob around a female out of her sphere. As she took her seat in the desk amid the great noise, and in the throng full, like a wave, of something to ensue. I saw her humanity in a gentleness and unpretension, tenderly open to the sphere around her, and, had she not been supported by the power of the will of genuineness and principle, she would have failed. It led her to prayer, which, in woman especially, is childlike; sensibility and will going to the side of God and looking up to him; and humanity was poured out in aspiration.

"She acted like a gentle hero, with her mild decision and womanly calmness. All heroism is mild and quiet and gentle, for it is life and possession, and combativeness and firmness show a want of actualness. She is as earnest, fresh, and simple as when she first entered the crusade. I think she did much good, more than the men in her place could do, for woman feels more as being and reproducing; this brings the subject more into home relations. Men speak through and mostly from intellect, and this addresses itself in others, which creates and is combative."

Not easily shall we find elsewhere, or before this time, any written observations on the same subject, so delicate and profound.

The late Dr. Channing,[99] whose enlarged and tender and religious nature shared every onward impulse of his time, though his thoughts followed his wishes with a deliberative caution, which belonged to his habits and temperament, was greatly interested in these expectations for women. His own treatment of them was absolutely and thoroughly religious. He regarded them as souls, each of which had a destiny of its own, incalculable to other minds, and whose leading it must follow, guided by the light of a private conscience. He had sentiment, delicacy, kindness, taste, but they were all pervaded and ruled by this one thought, that all beings had souls, and must vindicate their own inheritance. Thus all beings were treated by him with an equal, and sweet, though solemn courtesy. The young and unknown, the woman and the child, all felt themselves regarded with an infinite expectation, from which there was no reaction to vulgar prejudice. He demanded of all he met, to use his favorite phrase, "great truths."

His memory, every way dear and reverend, is by many especially cherished for this intercourse of unbroken respect.

At one time when the progress of Harriet Martineau through this country, An-

---

[99] William Ellery Channing (1780–1842), clergyman and one of the founders of Unitarianism.

gelina Grimke's appearance in public, and the visit of Mrs. Jameson[100] had turned his thoughts to this subject he expressed high hopes as to what the coming era would bring to woman. He had been much pleased with the dignified courage of Mrs. Jameson in taking up the defence of her sex, in a way from which women usually shrink, because, if they express themselves on such subjects with sufficient force and clearness to do any good, they are exposed to assaults whose vulgarity makes them painful. In intercourse with such a woman, he had shared her indignation at the base injustice, in many respects, and in many regions done to the sex; and been led to think of it far more than ever before. He seemed to think that he might some time write upon the subject. That his aid is withdrawn from the cause is a subject of great regret, for on this question, as on others, he would have known how to sum up the evidence and take, in the noblest spirit, middle ground. He always furnished a platform on which opposing parties could stand, and look at one another under the influence of his mildness and enlightened candor.

Two younger thinkers, men both, have uttered noble prophecies, auspicious for woman. Kinmont, all whose thoughts tended towards the establishment of the reign of love and peace, thought that the inevitable means of this would be an increased predominance given to the idea of woman. Had he lived longer to see the growth of the peace party, the reforms in life and medical practice which seek to substitute water for wine and drugs, pulse for animal food, he would have been confirmed in his view of the way in which the desired changes are to be effected.

In this connection I must mention Shelley,[101] who, like all men of genius, shared the feminine development, and, unlike many, knew it. His life was one of the first pulse-beats in the present reform-growth. He, too, abhorred blood and heat, and, by his system and his song, tended to reinstate a plant-like gentleness in the development of energy. In harmony with this his ideas of marriage were lofty, and of course no less so of woman, her nature, and destiny.

For woman, if by a sympathy as to outward condition, she is led to aid the enfranchisement of the slave, must no less so, by inward tendency, to favor measures which promise to bring the world more thoroughly and deeply into harmony with her nature. When the lamb takes place of the lion as the emblem of nations, both women and men will be as children of one spirit, perpetual learners of the word and doers thereof, not hearers only.

A writer in a late number of the New York Pathfinder, in two articles headed "Femality," has uttered a still more pregnant word than any we have named. He views woman truly from the soul, and not from society, and the depth and leading of his thoughts is proportionably remarkable. He views the feminine nature as a harmonizer of the vehement elements, and this has often been hinted elsewhere; but what he expresses most forcibly is the lyrical, the inspiring and inspired apprehensiveness of her being.

Had I room to dwell upon this topic, I could not say anything so precise, so near the heart of the matter, as may be found in that article; but, as it is, I can only indicate, not declare, my view.

---

[100] Harriet Martineau, British author of *Illustrations of Political Economy,* toured the United States in 1835; Angelina Grimke's appearance was during the late 1830s; and Anna Brownell Jameson traveled through the Northeast on her way to Canada in 1836.

[101] English poet Percy Bysshe Shelley (1792–1822).

There are two aspects of woman's nature, expressed by the ancients as Muse and Minerva.[102] It is the former to which the writer in the Pathfinder looks. It is the latter which Wordsworth has in mind, when he says,

> "With a placid brow,
> Which woman ne'er should forfeit, keep thy vow."[103]

The especial genius of woman I believe to be electrical in movement, intuitive in function, spiritual in tendency. She is great not so easily in classification, or re-creation, as in an instinctive seizure of causes, and a simple breathing out of what she receives that has the singleness of life, rather than the selecting or energizing of art.

More native to her is it to be the living model of the artist, than to set apart from herself any one form in objective reality; more native to inspire and receive the poem than to create it. In so far as soul is in her completely developed, all soul is the same; but as far as it is modified in her as woman, it flows, it breathes, it sings, rather than deposits soil, or finishes work, and that which is especially feminine flushes in blossom the face of earth, and pervades like air and water all this seeming solid globe, daily renewing and purifying its life. Such may be the especially feminine element, spoken of as Femality. But it is no more the order of nature that it should be incarnated pure in any form, than that the masculine energy should exist unmingled with it in any form.

Male and female represent the two sides of the great radical dualism. But, in fact, they are perpetually passing into one another. Fluid hardens to solid, solid rushes to fluid. There is no wholly masculine man, no purely feminine woman.

History jeers at the attempts of physiologists to bind great original laws by the forms which flow from them. They make a rule; they say from observation what can and cannot be. In vain! Nature provides exceptions to every rule. She sends women to battle, and sets Hercules spinning; she enables women to bear immense burdens, cold, and frost; she enables the man, who feels maternal love, to nourish his infant like a mother. Of late she plays still gayer pranks. Not only she deprives organizations, but organs, of a necessary end. She enables people to read with the top of the head, and see with the pit of the stomach. Presently she will make a female Newton, and a male Syren.[104]

Man partakes of the feminine in the Apollo, woman of the Masculine as Minerva.

Let us be wise and not impede the soul. Let her work as she will. Let us have one creative energy, one incessant revelation. Let it take what form it will, and let us not bind it by the past to man or woman, black or white. Jove sprang from Rhea, Pallas from Jove.[105] So let it be.

If it has been the tendency of the past remarks to call woman rather to the Minerva side,—if I, unlike the more generous writer, have spoken from society no less than the soul,—let it be pardoned. It is love that has caused this, love for many incarcerated

---

[102] Muse: goddess of an art or science; Minerva: goddess of wisdom.
[103] Altered from William Wordsworth's *Liberty: Sequel to the Preceding* (1835).
[104] Newton: Sir Isaac Newton (1642–1727), English mathematician; Syren: in Greek myth, one of

the sirens, or sea nymphs, who coaxed mariners into shipwreck on the rocks around their island.
[105] Rhea: mother of Jove; Pallas Athena: daughter of Jove, who burst from his head fully grown and completely armed.

souls, that might be freed could the idea of religious self-dependence be established in them, could the weakening habit of dependence on others be broken up.

Every relation, every gradation of nature, is incalculably precious, but only to the soul which is poised upon itself, and to whom no loss, no change, can bring dull discord, for it is in harmony with the central soul.

If any individual live too much in relations, so that he becomes a stranger to the resources of his own nature, he falls after a while into a distraction, or imbecility, from which he can only be cured by a time of isolation, which gives the renovating fountains time to rise up. With a society it is the same. Many minds, deprived of the traditionary or instinctive means of passing a cheerful existence, must find help in self-impulse or perish. It is therefore that while any elevation, in the view of union, is to be hailed with joy, we shall not decline celibacy as the great fact of the time. It is one from which no vow, no arrangement, can at present save a thinking mind. For now the rowers are pausing on their oars, they wait a change before they can pull together. All tends to illustrate the thought of a wise contemporary. Union is only possible to those who are units. To be fit for relations in time, souls, whether of man or woman, must be able to do without them in the spirit.

It is therefore that I would have woman lay aside all thought, such as she habitually cherishes, of being taught and led by men. I would have her, like the Indian girl, dedicate herself to the Sun, the Sun of Truth, and go no where if his beams did not make clear the path. I would have her free from compromise, from complaisance, from helplessness, because I would have her good enough and strong enough to love one and all beings, from the fulness, not the poverty of being.

Men, as at present instructed, will not help this work, because they also are under the slavery of habit. I have seen with delight their poetic impulses. A sister is the fairest ideal, and how nobly Wordsworth, and even Byron, have written of a sister.[106]

There is no sweeter sight than to see a father with his little daughter. Very vulgar men become refined to the eye when leading a little girl by the hand. At that moment the right relation between the sexes seems established, and you feel as if the man would aid in the noblest purpose, if you ask him in behalf of his little daughter. Once two fine figures stood before me, thus. The father of very intellectual aspect, his falcon eye softened by affection as he looked down on his fair child, she the image of himself, only more graceful and brilliant in expression. I was reminded of Southey's Kehama,[107] when lo, the dream was rudely broken. They were talking of education, and he said.

"I shall not have Maria brought too forward. If she knows too much, she will never find a husband; superior women hardly ever can."

"Surely," said his wife, with a blush, "you wish Maria to be as good and wise as she can, whether it will help her to marriage or not."

"No," he persisted, "I want her to have a sphere and a home, and some one to protect her when I am gone."

It was a trifling incident, but made a deep impression. I felt that the holiest relations fail to instruct the unprepared and perverted mind. If this man, indeed, would have looked at it on the other side, he was the last that would have been willing to have

<hr />

[106] Reference to the literary tributes paid by William Wordsworth to his sister Dorothy, and by Lord Byron to his half-sister Augusta Leigh.

[107] *The Curse of Kehama* (1810) by Robert Southey (1774–1843).

been taken himself for the home and protection he could give, but would have been much more likely to repeat the tale of Alcibiades with his phials.

But men do *not* look at both sides, and women must leave off asking them and being influenced by them, but retire within themselves, and explore the groundwork of being till they find their peculiar secret. Then when they come forth again, renovated and baptized, they will know how to turn all dross to gold, and will be rich and free though they live in a hut, tranquil, if in a crowd. Then their sweet singing shall not be from passionate impulse, but the lyrical overflow of a divine rapture, and a new music shall be elucidated from this many-chorded world.

Grant her then for a while the armor and the javelin.[108] Let her put from her the press of other minds and meditate in virgin loneliness. The same idea shall reappear in due time as Muse, or Ceres,[109] the all-kindly, patient Earth-Spirit.

I tire every one with my Goethean illustrations. But it cannot be helped.

Goethe, the great mind which gave itself absolutely to the leadings of truth, and let rise through him the waves which are still advancing through the century, was its intellectual prophet. Those who know him, see, daily, his thought fulfilled more and more, and they must speak of it, till his name weary and even nauseate, as all great names have in their time. And I cannot spare the reader, if such there be, his wonderful sight as to the prospects and wants of women.

As his Wilhelm grows in life and advances in wisdom, he becomes acquainted with women of more and more character, rising from Mariana to Macaria.[110]

Macaria, bound with the heavenly bodies in fixed revolutions, the centre of all relations, herself unrelated, expresses the Minerva side.

Mignon, the electrical, inspired lyrical nature.

All these women, though we see them in relations, we can think of as unrelated. They all are very individual, yet seem nowhere restrained. They satisfy for the present, yet arouse an infinite expectation.

The economist Theresa, the benevolent Natalia, the fair Saint, have chosen a path, but their thoughts are not narrowed to it. The functions of life to them are not ends, but suggestions.

Thus to them all things are important, because none is necessary. Their different characters have fair play, and each is beautiful in its minute indications, for nothing is enforced or conventional, but everything, however slight, grows from the essential life of the being.

Mignon and Theresa wear male attire when they like, and it is graceful for them to do so, while Macaria is confined to her arm chair behind the green curtain, and the Fair Saint could not bear a speck of dust on her robe.

All things are in their places in this little world because all is natural and free, just as "there is room for everything out of doors." Yet all is rounded in by natural harmony which will always arise where Truth and Love are sought in the light of freedom.

Goethe's book bodes an era of freedom like its own, of "extraordinary generous

---

[108] Armor and the javelin were traditional accompaniments of Athena, goddess of wisdom in Greek mythology.
[109] Roman goddess of agriculture.

[110] Female characters in Goethe's *Wilhelm Meister's Apprenticeship.* Others from the same work are mentioned in following paragraphs.

seeking," and new revelations. New individualities shall be developed in the actual world, which shall advance upon it as gently as the figures come out upon his canvass.

A profound thinker has said "no married woman can represent the female world, for she belongs to her husband. The idea of woman must be represented by a virgin."

But that is the very fault of marriage, and of the present relation between the sexes, that the woman does belong to the man, instead of forming a whole with him. Were it otherwise there would be no such limitation to the thought.

Woman, self-centred, would never be absorbed by any relation; it would be only an experience to her as to man. It is a vulgar error that love, *a* love to woman is her whole existence; she also is born for Truth and Love in their universal energy. Would she but assume her inheritance, Mary would not be the only Virgin Mother. Not Manzoni[III] alone would celebrate in his wife the virgin mind with the maternal wisdom and conjugal affections. The soul is ever young, ever virgin.

And will not she soon appear? The woman who shall vindicate their birthright for all women; who shall teach them what to claim, and how to use what they obtain? Shall not her name be for her era Victoria, for her country and her life Virginia? Yet predictions are rash; she herself must teach us to give her the fitting name.

1843

American Literature

Its Position in the Present Time, and Prospects for the Future

Some thinkers may object to this essay, that we are about to write of that which has as yet no existence.

For it does not follow because many books are written by persons born in America that there exists an American literature. Books which imitate or represent the thoughts and life of Europe do not constitute an American literature. Before such can exist, an original idea must animate this nation and fresh currents of life must call into life fresh thoughts along its shores.

We have no sympathy with national vanity. We are not anxious to prove that there is as yet much American literature. Of those who think and write among us in the methods and of the thoughts of Europe, we are not impatient; if their minds are still best adapted to such food and such action. If their books express life of mind and character in graceful forms, they are good and we like them. We consider them as colonists and useful schoolmasters to our people in a transition state; which lasts rather longer than is occupied in passing bodily the ocean which separates the New from the Old World.

We have been accused of an undue attachment to foreign continental literature, and it is true that in childhood we had well nigh "forgotten our English" while constantly reading in other languages. Still what we loved in the literature of conti-

III Allusion to the preface to *Adelchi* (see note 78 above).

nental Europe was the range and force of ideal manifestation in forms of national and individual greatness. A model was before us in the great Latins of simple masculine minds seizing upon life with unbroken power. The stamp both of nationality and individuality was very strong upon them; their lives and thoughts stood out in clear and bold relief. The English character has the iron force of the Latins, but not the frankness and expansion. Like their fruits, they need a summer sky to give them more sweetness and a richer flavor. This does not apply to Shakespeare, who has all the fine side of English genius, with the rich coloring and more fluent life of the Catholic countries. Other poets of England also are expansive more or less, and soar freely to seek the blue sky, but take it as a whole, there is in English literature, as in English character, a reminiscence of walls and ceilings, a tendency to the arbitrary and conventional that repels a mind trained in admiration of the antique spirit. It is only in later days that we are learning to prize the peculiar greatness which a thousand times outweighs this fault, and which has enabled English genius to go forth from its insular position and conquer such vast dominion in the realms both of matter and of mind.

Yet there is often between child and parent a reaction from excessive influence having been exerted, and such a one we have experienced in behalf of our country against England. We use her language and receive in torrents the influence of her thought, yet it is in many respects uncongenial and injurious to our constitution. What suits Great Britain, with her insular position and consequent need to concentrate and intensify her life, her limited monarchy and spirit of trade, does not suit a mixed race continually enriched with new blood from other stocks the most unlike that of our first descent, with ample field and verge enough to range in and leave every impulse free, and abundant opportunity to develop a genius wide and full as our rivers, flowery, luxuriant, and impassioned as our vast prairies, rooted in strength as the rocks on which the Puritan fathers landed.

That such a genius is to rise and work in this hemisphere we are confident; equally so that scarce the first faint streaks of that day's dawn are yet visible. It is sad for those that foresee, to know they may not live to share its glories, yet it is sweet, too, to know that every act and word uttered in the light of that foresight may tend to hasten or ennoble its fulfillment.

That day will not rise till the fusion of races among us is more complete. It will not rise till this nation shall attain sufficient moral and intellectual dignity to prize moral and intellectual no less highly than political freedom, not till the physical resources of the country being explored, all its regions studded with towns, broken by the plow, netted together by railways and telegraph lines, talent shall be left at leisure to turn its energies upon the higher department of man's existence. Nor then shall it be seen till from the leisurely and yearning soul of that riper time national ideas shall take birth, ideas craving to be clothed in a thousand fresh and original forms.

Without such ideas all attempts to construct a national literature must end in abortions like the monster of Frankenstein, things with forms and the instincts of forms, but soulless and therefore revolting. We cannot have expression till there is something to be expressed.

The symptoms of such a birth may be seen in a longing felt here and there for the sustenance of such ideas. At present it shows itself, where felt, in sympathy with the prevalent tone of society by attempts at external action, such as are classed under the head of social reform. But it needs to go deeper before we can have poets, needs to penetrate beneath the springs of action, to stir and remake the soil as by the action of fire.

Another symptom is the need felt by individuals of being even sternly sincere. This is the one great means by which alone progress can be essentially furthered. Truth is the nursing mother of genius. No man can be absolutely true to himself, eschewing cant, compromise, servile imitation, and complaisance, without becoming original, for there is in every creature a fountain of life which, if not choked back by stones and other dead rubbish, will create a fresh atmosphere and bring to life fresh beauty. And it is the same with the nation as with the individual man.

The best work we do for the future is by such truth. By use of that in whatever way, we harrow the soil and lay it open to the sun and air. The winds from all quarters of the globe bring seed enough, and there is nothing wanting but preparation of the soil and freedom in the atmosphere, for ripening of a new and golden harvest.

We are sad that we cannot be present at the gathering-in of this harvest. And yet we are joyous too, when we think that though our name may not be writ on the pillar of our country's fame, we can really do far more towards rearing it than those who come at a later period and to a seemingly fairer task. *Now,* the humblest effort, made in a noble spirit and with religious hope, cannot fail to be even infinitely useful. Whether we introduce some noble model from another time and clime to encourage aspiration in our own, or cheer into blossom the simplest wood-flower that ever rose from the earth, moved by the genuine impulse to grow, independent of the lures of money or celebrity; whether we speak boldly when fear or doubt keep others silent, or refuse to swell the popular cry upon an unworthy occasion, the spirit of truth, purely worshiped, shall turn our acts and forbearances alike to profit, informing them with oracles which the latest time shall bless.

Under present circumstances the amount of talent and labor given to writing ought to surprise us. Literature is in this dim and struggling state, and its pecuniary results exceedingly pitiful. From many well-known causes it is impossible for ninety-nine out of the hundred who wish to use the pen to ransom by its use the time they need. This state of things will have to be changed in some way. No man of genius writes for money; but it is essential to the free use of his powers that he should be able to disembarrass his life from care and perplexity. This is very difficult here; and the state of things gets worse and worse, as less and less is offered in pecuniary meed for works demanding great devotion of time and labor (to say nothing of the ether engaged) and the publisher, obliged to regard the transaction as a matter of business, demands of the author to give him only what will find an immediate market, for he cannot afford to take anything else. This will not do! When an immortal poet was secure only of a few copyists to circulate his works, there were princes and nobles to patronize literature and the arts. Here is only the public, and the public must learn how to cherish the nobler and rarer plants, and to plant the aloe, able to wait a hundred years for its bloom, or its garden will contain presently nothing but potatoes and pot-herbs. We shall have in the course of the next two or three years a convention of authors to inquire into the causes of this state of things and propose measures for its remedy. Some have already been thought of that look promising, but we shall not announce them till the time be ripe; that date is not distant, for the difficulties increase from day to day in consequence of the system of cheap publication on a great scale.

The ranks that led the way in the first half century of this republic were far better situated than we, in this respect. The country was not so deluged with the dingy page reprinted from Europe, and patriotic vanity was on the alert to answer the question, "Who reads an American book?" And many were the books written as worthy to be read as any out of the first class in England. They were, most of them, except in their subject matter, English books.

The list is large, and in making some cursory comments we do not wish to be understood as designating *all* who are worthy of notice, but only those who present themselves to our minds with some special claims.

In the department of ethics and philosophy we may inscribe two names as likely to live and be blessed and honored in the later time. These are the names of Channing[1] and of Emerson.

Dr. Channing had several leading thoughts which corresponded with the wants of his time, and have made him in it a father of thought. His leading idea of the "dignity of human nature" is one of vast results, and the peculiar form in which he advocated it had a great work to do in this new world. The spiritual beauty of his writings is very great; they are all distinguished for sweetness, elevation, candor, and a severe devotion to truth. On great questions he took middle ground and sought a panoramic view; he wished also to stand high, yet never forgot what was above more than what was around and beneath him. He was not well acquainted with man on the impulsive and passionate side of his nature, so that his view of character was sometimes narrow, but it was always noble. He exercised an expansive and purifying power on the atmosphere, and stands a godfather at the baptism of this country.

The Sage of Concord[2] has a very different mind, in everything except that he has the same disinterestedness and dignity of purpose, the same purity of spirit. He is a profound thinker. He is a man of ideas, and deals with causes rather than effects. His ideas are illustrated from a wide range of literary culture and refined observation, and embodied in a style whose melody and subtle fragrance enchant those who stand stupefied before the thoughts themselves, because their utmost depths do not enable them to sound his shallows. His influence does not yet extend over a wide space; he is too far beyond his place and his time to be felt at once or in full, but it searches deep, and yearly widens its circles. He is a harbinger of the better day. His beautiful elocution has been a great aid to him in opening the way for the reception of his written word.

In that large department of literature which includes descriptive sketches, whether of character or scenery, we are already rich. Irving,[3] a genial and fair nature, just what he ought to be and would have been at any time of the world, has drawn the scenes amid which his youth was spent in their primitive lineaments, with all the charms of his graceful jocund humor. He has his niche and need never be deposed; it is not one that another could occupy.

---

[1] William Ellery Channing (1780–1842), clergyman and founder of Unitarianism.
[2] Title bestowed on Ralph Waldo Emerson as a resident of Concord, Massachusetts.

[3] Washington Irving (1783–1859), American writer.

The first enthusiasm about Cooper[4] having subsided, we remember more his faults than his merits. His ready resentment and way of showing it in cases which it is the wont of gentlemen to pass by in silence or meet with a good-humored smile have caused unpleasant associations with his name, and his fellow-citizens, in danger of being tormented by suits for libel if they spoke freely of him, have ceased to speak of him at all. But neither these causes, nor the baldness of his plots, shallowness of thought, and poverty in the presentation of character, should make us forget the grandeur and originality of his sea-sketches, nor the redemption from oblivion of our forest-scenery, and the noble romance of the hunter-pioneer's life. Already, but for him, this fine page of life's romance would be almost forgotten. He has done much to redeem these irrevocable beauties from the corrosive acid of a semi-civilized invasion.

What shall we say of the poets? The list is scanty; amazingly so, for there is nothing in the causes that paralyze other kinds of literature that could affect lyrical and narrative poetry. Men's hearts beat, hope, and suffer always, and they must crave such means to vent them; yet of the myriad leaves garnished with smooth, stereotyped rhymes that issue yearly from our press, you will not find, one time in a million, a little piece written from any such impulse or with the least sincerity or sweetness of tone. They are written for the press in the spirit of imitation or vanity, the paltriest offspring of the human brain, for the heart disclaims, as the ear is shut against them. This is the kind of verse which is cherished by the magazines as a correspondent to the tawdry pictures of smiling milliners' dolls in the frontispiece. Like these they are only a fashion, a fashion based on no reality of love or beauty. The inducement to write them consists in a little money, or more frequently the charm of seeing an anonymous name printed at the top in capitals.

At their head Mr. Bryant[5] stands alone. His range is not great, nor his genius fertile. But his poetry is purely the language of his inmost nature, and the simple lovely garb in which his thoughts are arranged, a direct gift from the Muse. He has written nothing that is not excellent, and the atmosphere of his verse refreshes and composes the mind, like leaving the highway to enter some green lovely fragrant wood.

---

[4] James Fenimore Cooper (1789–1851). The following is Fuller's note: "Since writing the above we have read some excellent remarks by Mr. W.G. Simms on the writings of Cooper. We think the reasons are given for the powerful interest excited by Hawkeye and the Pilot, with great discrimination and force. 'They both think and feel, with a highly individual nature, that has been taught, by constant contemplation, in scenes of solitude. The vast unbroken ranges of forest to its one lonely occupant press upon the mind with the same sort of solemnity which one feels condemned to a life of partial isolation upon the ocean. Both are permitted that degree of commerce with their fellow beings, which suffices to maintain in strength the sweet and sacred sources of their humanity. . . . The very isolation to which, in the most successful of his stories, Mr. Cooper subjects his favorite personages, is, alone, a proof of his strength and genius. While the ordinary writer, the man of mere talent, is compelled to look around him among masses for his material, he contents himself with one man, and flings him upon the wilderness. The picture, then, which follows, must be one of intense individuality. Out of this one man's nature, his moods and fortunes, he spins his story. The agencie and dependencies are few. With self-reliance which is only found in true genius, he goes forward into the wilderness, whether of land or ocean; and the vicissitudes of either region, acting upon the natural resources of one man's mind, furnish the whole material of his work-shop. This mode of performance is highly dramatic, and thus it is that his scout, his trapper, his hunter, his pilot, all live to our eyes and thoughts, the perfect ideals of moral individuality.'"

[5] William Cullen Bryant (1794–1878).

Longfellow[6] is artificial and imitative. He borrows incessantly, and mixes what he borrows, so that it does not appear to the best advantage. He is very faulty in using broken or mixed metaphors. The ethical part of his writing has a hollow, secondhand sound. He has, however, elegance, a love of the beautiful, and a fancy for what is large and manly, if not a full sympathy with it. His verse breathes at times much sweetness; and if not allowed to supersede what is better, may promote a taste for good poetry. Though imitative, he is not mechanical.

We cannot say as much for Lowell,[7] who, we must declare it, though to the grief of some friends and the disgust of more, is absolutely wanting in the true spirit and tone of poesy. His interest in the moral questions of the day has supplied the want of vitality in himself; his great facility at versification has enabled him to fill the ear with a copious stream of pleasant sound. But his verse is stereotyped; his thought sounds no depth; and posterity will not remember him.

R. W. Emerson, in melody, in subtle beauty of thought and expression, takes the highest rank upon this list. But his poems are mostly philosophical, which is not the truest kind of poetry. They want the simple force of nature and passion, and while they charm the ear and interest the mind, fail to wake far-off echoes in the heart. The imagery wears a symbolical air, and serves rather as illustration than to delight us by fresh and glowing forms of life.

Meanwhile the most important part of our literature, while the work of diffusion is still going on, lies in the journals which monthly, weekly, daily send their messages to every corner of this great land, and form at present the only efficient instrument for the general education of the people.

Among these, the magazines take the lowest rank. Their object is principally to cater for the amusement of vacant hours, and as there is not a great deal of wit and light talent in this country, they do not even this to much advantage. More wit, grace, and elegant trifling embellish the annals of literature in one day of France than in a year of America.

The reviews are more able. If they cannot compare on equal terms with those of France, England, and Germany, where if genius be rare, at least a vast amount of talent and culture is brought to bear upon all the departments of knowledge, they are yet very creditable to a new country where so large a portion of manly ability must be bent on making laws, making speeches, making railroads and canals. They are, however, much injured by a partisan spirit and the fear of censure from their own public. This last is always slow death to a journal; its natural and only safe position is to *lead;* if instead it bows to the will of the multitude, it will find the ostracism of democracy far more dangerous than the worst censure of a tyranny could be. It is not half so dangerous to a man to be immured in a dungeon alone with God and his own clear conscience as to walk the streets fearing the scrutiny of a thousand eyes, ready to veil with anxious care whatever may not suit the many-headed monster in its momentary mood. Gentleness is dignified but caution is debasing; only a noble fearlessness can give wings to the mind, with which to soar beyond the common ken and learn what may be of use to the crowd below. Writers have nothing to do but to love truth fervently, seek justice according to their ability, and then express what is in the mind; they have nothing to do with consequences, God will take care of those.

---

[6] Henry Wadsworth Longfellow (1807–1882).   [7] James Russell Lowell (1819–1891).

The want of such noble courage, such faith in the power of truth and good desire, paralyzes mind greatly in this country. Publishers are afraid; authors are afraid; and if a worthy resistance is not made by religious souls, there is danger that all the light will soon be put under bushels, lest some wind should waft from it a spark that may kindle dangerous fire.

For want of such faith, and the catholic spirit that flows from it, we have no great leading review. The *North American* was once the best. While under the care of Edward Everett,[8] himself a host in extensive knowledge, grace and adroitness in applying it, and the power of enforcing grave meanings by a light and flexible satire that tickled while it wounded, it boasted more force, more life, a finer scope of power. But now though still exhibiting ability and information upon special points, it is entirely deficient in great leadings and the *vivida vis,*[9] but ambles and jogs at an old gentlemanly pace along a beaten path that leads to no important goal.

Several other journals have more life, energy, and directness than this, but there is none which occupies a truly great and commanding position, a beacon-light to all who sail that way. In order to do this, a journal must know how to cast aside all local and temporary considerations when new convictions command, and allow free range in its columns to all kinds of ability and all ways of viewing subjects. That would give it a life rich, bold, various.

The life of intellect is becoming more and more determined to the weekly and daily papers, whose light leaves fly so rapidly and profusely over the land. Speculations are afloat as to the influence of the electric telegraph upon their destiny, and it seems obvious that it should raise their character by taking from them in some measure the office of gathering and dispersing the news, and requiring of them rather to arrange and interpret it.

This mode of communication is susceptible of great excellence in the way of condensed essay, narrative, criticism, and is the natural receptacle for the lyrics of the day. That so few good ones deck the poet's corner, is because the indifference or unfitness of editors as to choosing and refusing makes this place at present undesirable to the poet. It might be otherwise.

The means which this organ affords of diffusing knowledge and sowing the seeds of thought where they may hardly fail of an infinite harvest, cannot be too highly prized by the discerning and benevolent. Minds of the first class are generally indisposed to this kind of writing; what must be done on the spur of the occasion and cast into the world so incomplete, as the hurried offspring of a day or hour's labor must generally be, cannot satisfy their judgment or do justice to their powers. But he who looks to the benefit of others and sees with what rapidity and ease instruction and thought are assimilated by men, when they come thus as it were on the wings of the wind, may be content, as an unhonored servant to the grand purposes of Destiny, to work in such a way at the Pantheon[10] which the ages shall complete, on which his name may not be inscribed but which will breathe the life of his soul.

The confidence in uprightness of intent and the safety of truth is still more needed here than in the more elaborate kinds of writing, as meanings cannot be fully explained nor expressions revised. Newspaper-writing is next door to conversation, and should be conducted on the same principles. It has this advantage: we address not our

---

[8] Everett (1794–1865) was editor of *The North American Review* (1815–1821).

[9] Latin: "living force."

[10] Greek or Roman temple of the gods.

neighbor, who forces us to remember his limitations and prejudices, but the ideal presence of human nature as we feel it ought to be and trust it will be. We address America rather than Americans.

We see we have omitted honored names in this essay. We have not spoken of Brown,[11] as a novelist by far our first in point of genius and instruction as to the soul of things. Yet his works have fallen almost out of print. It is their dark deep gloom that prevents their being popular, for their very beauties are grave and sad. But we see that *Ormond* is being republished at this moment. The picture of Roman character, of the life and resources of a single noble creature, of Constantia alone, should make that book an object of reverence. All these novels should be republished; if not favorites, they should at least not be lost sight of, for there will always be some who find in such powers of mental analysis the only response to their desires.

We have not spoken of Hawthorne,[12] the best writer of the day, in a similar range with Irving, only touching many more points and discerning far more deeply. But we have omitted many things in this slight sketch, for the subject even in this stage lies as a volume in our mind, and cannot be unrolled in completeness unless time and space were more abundant. Our object was to show that although by a thousand signs the existence is foreshown of those forces which are to animate an American literature, that faith, those hopes are not yet alive which shall usher it into a homogeneous or fully organized state of being. The future is glorious with certainties for those who do their duty in the present, and larklike, seeking the sun, challenge its eagles to an earthward flight, where their nests may be built in our mountains, and their young raise their cry of triumph unchecked by dullness in the echoes.

1846

Henry David Thoreau
1817–1862

Thoreau was a determined man. He may not have always recognized exactly what form his life would take, but he knew that he was meant to serve. As an avid student of what words signify once one cuts through the surface, he responded fully to the demands placed on him by "vocation"—the voice that calls someone out of the crowd to perform a sacred duty to the world.

To trace Thoreau's life and his writing career is to realize what "growing up in Concord" meant in the fertile, fervid years prior to the Civil War, particularly to one of the young people who had been born, as Emerson put it, with "knives in their brains." Thoreau spent his forty-four years listening to the sounds of the voice that led him toward his destiny. This attentiveness made him kin to a number of his New England contemporaries, especially those loosely grouped under the label Transcendentalists. But Thoreau felt compelled to follow a somewhat different drummer than the one followed by Ralph Waldo Emerson, Bronson Alcott, William Ellery Channing, or Margaret Fuller.

Any review of the checkered annals of Thoreau's aspirations, disappointments,

---

[11] Charles Brockden Brown (1771–1810), American novelist.   [12] Nathaniel Hawthorne (1804–1864).

and achievements makes clear how this man failed in the sight of many of his contemporaries, those relative few who had even heard of him. Such a review of his life also suggests why he is now considered one of America's major literary figures; it indicates that the myth of the man in the woods—the lonely rebel of Walden Pond—is less interesting and provocative than the reality that lies behind that misty cult figure.

Thoreau was born and raised in Concord, Massachusetts, the only hometown boy among the band of men and women later associated with that small but enormously influential New England village. In the parlance of the success stories that have piqued the American imagination since Benjamin Franklin's *Autobiography,* the Thoreau family was "poor but honest." One of the ways the Thoreaus got along was by making lead pencils in a family-circle factory, the kind of work that was being eased out of existence by the Industrial Revolution. The talent for entrepreneurship that made Thoreau an adroit maker of good pencils gave him pause once when he realized how easy it would be for him to corner the local cranberry market and become not so poor or so honest. His experiences in basic economics helped spur him to try other experiments in spiritual coinage. It became urgent for him to discover alternatives to the habits of buying and selling that he believed would ruin the American character.

But first Thoreau had to educate himself. Like Benjamin Franklin, Herman Melville, and Mark Twain (to name a few of the self-educated men of American literature), Thoreau learned that true education meant immersion in the world, whether or not he always liked what he found there. Thoreau started out, however, as a Harvard man. At the age of sixteen, he became one of the poor but diligent young men who, like Emerson a few years before, worked their way through the college. Thoreau's student essays are dutiful and a bit plodding, but they show early signs of his talent for seeing things from his distinctive point of view, one that would continue to puzzle conventional minds throughout his lifetime. Upon graduation in 1837, he returned to Concord—as he always did after forays away from home. He taught briefly but soon resigned that post rather than do what was expected of local schoolmasters: inflict bodily punishment on erring students. Four years of running a private school with his older brother John followed. John's illness and death put an end to Thoreau's interest in teaching in the institutional sense. He would remain a teacher all his days, but he had to find other ways to instruct, just as he had to find other means of working so that he could live well, rather than living wretchedly in order to work.

Emerson's house and mind were good places for Thoreau to continue his tutelage in the demands of the spirit. Between 1841 and 1843 he lived with the Emerson family as a handyman. He also lived with the ideas Emerson provided the Transcendentalist Club, a group that met to talk about social and personal reforms. However, the most crucial event in Thoreau's life occurred in 1845, the year he moved two miles out of Concord to live in a one-room hut erected beside Walden Pond on land Emerson had loaned him. But experiences other than Harvard and the Emersons had been readying Thoreau for that maturing time by the pond. They helped him to decide which voices he must use to persuade his listeners to the message of challenge and joy he felt compelled to declare.

Speaking in a classroom had not sufficed for Thoreau. His contemporaries found ready audiences for their ideas by lecturing before local groups, so he began to try his hand at this popular form of public address. Thoreau's audiences wanted either to be instructed with the kind of nature lore he drew from the walks in the woods he had been making since he was a child or to be amused by familiar Yankee wit, the kind that was simultaneously exaggeration and understatement. Thoreau provided both the lore and the wit in his lectures, but also something more, and this was not so readily accepted. His audiences did not care to be told that they were fools for having resigned themselves to living stupid, wasted lives, but this was precisely what Thoreau most wanted to tell them. Somehow he had to find ways to make his often harsh home truths palatable to the people he most wished to affect.

By the mid-1840s Thoreau had found a means to win over his audiences. He told them of his travels through the New England landscape, offered them brief essays on a life lived honestly and close to the nub, shucked free of the unnecessary "thingness" that weighed down their materialistic society. Out of a two-week canoe excursion that Thoreau and his brother had taken in 1839 came the experiences of the book *A Week on the Concord and Merrimack Rivers.* Thoreau's only previous experience at writing had been the essays and poems that Emerson printed in *The Dial,* the journal that he and Margaret Fuller edited, along with a piece placed in a Boston journal and "Paradise (to Be) Regained" and "The Landlord," both of which he sold to New York editors during his brief stay on Staten Island in 1843 while tutoring the children of Emerson's brother. These events came in quick succession, and the early 1840s were busy and instructive years for Thoreau's career. Just at this point, Thoreau walked out of Concord to the hut by Walden Pond and set up housekeeping; it was a day he considered symbolically apt for his first major undertaking as a writer: Independence Day, 1845.

Thoreau went into the woods to live the Walden life; while there, he stored up thoughts and experiences he would use when he left the pond in the early autumn of 1847 to begin the long process of writing his masterwork, *Walden.* But the initial reason he settled into the hut was to write *A Week on the Concord and Merrimack Rivers.* Recent scholarship indicates that not only did Thoreau consistently attempt throughout his career to adjust the specialness of his ideas and his literary manner to the expectations of potential reading audiences, but also that *A Week* was itself an important venture in the conversion of his ideas into a literary style that would have the greatest possible appeal.

Framed by the narrated events of a seven-day river trip, *A Week* is a mélange of nature observations, histories of the region through which the brothers pass in their little boat, and glimpses of contemporary scenes where the natural inhabitants are sometimes seen in abrasive contact with the human encroachments of factories and mills lining the banks. But Thoreau brought to *A Week* more than the notes he took in 1839 and the observations he had been keeping in journals since his college days; he brought into the narrative all his bookishness— the intellectual equipment common to well-read aspirants to literary fame in Thoreau's generation.

The chapters of *A Week* flow from day to day, veering from objects to ideas and from one literary style to another. There are poems, gazette histories, recountings of early Indian captivities, excerpts from Chaucer and the bardic epics, comparisons between the Greek, Oriental, and Christian versions of the best life, amiable encounters and a few head-on confrontations with wayfarers met along the way, pleasant ruminations about water, fish, and fishing, and serious considerations of the nature of true friendship. A grab-bag affair whose parts constitute less than a discernible whole, *A Week* was Thoreau's calculated effort to please as wide a reading audience as possible while winning them to a new way of thinking about the diverse worlds, both natural and mental, they had the power to make their own. Of the thousand copies of the book Thoreau had printed in 1849, approximately two hundred were sold. Writing *A Week* at Walden Pond was a failed experiment in the most obvious sense. But what Thoreau learned about addressing his audience from that failure was of the utmost value when it came time to write his next full-length book.

Walden: or, Life in the Woods, published in 1854, is what we remember best about Thoreau. The book was slow in coming into its final form. Thoreau spent five years reworking the material he had gathered into his journals during the Walden years of 1845 to 1847. He tinkered and copied, rewrote and recopied. With extreme consciousness of effort, he mastered a language of spontaneity. With great seriousness, he pointed up the wit of his observations concerning the absurdities of the country's social conditions. When at last the book was published, his friends responded to its several levels of mysticism and social theory. Too many took Thoreau's remarks too literally. *Walden* was liked, but not greatly, and it received relatively little critical attention. Thoreau's masterwork, so many years in the making, had to wait almost eighty years more—until the 1930s—before people recognized how advanced his program for the good life was.

Thoreau left Walden Pond in 1847 because he had "several more lives to live and could not spare any more for that one." Those other lives, of involvement with social and literary matters, together with "that one" of the man "on vacation" at Walden, resulted in the activities that occupied him through the fifteen years he had yet to live, giving him the ideas and energies he expended on the writing that lay ahead.

Thoreau said he scorned the need to travel far. Unlike the young Richard Henry Dana, Herman Melville, or the men who were just then setting out for the California gold fields, Thoreau insisted that the best traveling is done while staying home, exploring the cosmography of the imagination. Yet Thoreau made three forays into Maine, where he encountered forests and mountains far rawer than anything he could see in the gentler areas around Concord. Parts of the Maine experiences with Indians, moose, and mountains were published in magazines during his lifetime. *The Maine Woods,* the book version, appeared in 1864. Four trips to Cape Cod, one to Canada, and a long trip to Minnesota the year before his death also occurred during the years after he left Walden Pond. (Like many of the Transcendentalists, he was not averse to contradicting himself at times. Journeys to California were despicable; trips north or to Minnesota were worthy endeavors.) Each of these excursions, except the Minnesota trip, resulted in a book published posthumously: *Cape Cod* (1865) and *A Yankee in Canada* (1866).

Thoreau dealt with the life of the spirit, but he also kept close account of events that were shaking the American social and political system to its foundation: the Fugitive Slave Act, utopian reform plans for communal living and socialistic societies, the Mexican-American War, John Brown's raid on the Harpers Ferry arsenal, the underground railroad, the effects of the new telegraph and increased newspaper circulation, the coming to New England of the Irish immigrants and the changes in the landscape caused by the railroads they were hired to construct, the marketing of everything from blocks of pond ice for chilling the drinks of urban Bostonians to the wild berries whose flavor vanished the moment they were picked for shipment from their native hillsides. Thoreau took note of these events, wrote about them all, and participated directly in several: calling his neighbors together after John Brown's capture to read them his lecture in praise of the man's heroic acts on behalf of the slaves, conveying blacks over the underground railroad on their run toward freedom, and refusing to pay local taxes that supported the Mexican-American War effort.

Thoreau said he was happiest alone, yet he was frequently in contact with the Concord-Boston group that included Emerson, Fuller, Hawthorne, Alcott, and Ellery Channing. He made a special trip to New Jersey to meet Walt Whitman; he visited with others on his walks through the woods and to the surrounding farms, such as the Canadian woodcutter Alek Therion. He spent many hours as "servant to Admetus" (an allusion to the Greek myth of the poet-god Apollo, who lived among mortals by doing menial tasks for a local ruler), and he earned the wealth of his observations. Thoreau was also in touch with newspaper editors and book publishers whom he tried to interest in his works, as well as with the men who arranged his lecturing engagements that took him as far afield as Philadelphia and Bangor. Thoreau lived so busy a life, filled with so many activities that kept him in almost constant give-and-take with the everyday world, that it might seem surprising he had time for solitary meditations on the simplified life dedicated to contemplating eternal and universal truths.

Thoreau's health began to decline as early as 1855. By May 1862 he was dead of tuberculosis. Emerson stood over his grave outside Concord and delivered a eulogy that praised Thoreau's exceptional character but also lamented that he had failed to be all he should have been. These comments were based on Emerson's own expectations, colored by the on-again, off-again relationship of admiration and disappointment shared by the older man and his prickly younger friend. That scene by Thoreau's graveside represents what continued to happen in the years following his death as his status was taken under consideration by some of the more influential reputation makers of the period. John Greenleaf Whittier, Oliver Wendell Holmes, and James Russell Lowell, among others, sniped at Thoreau for having been surly, self-conscious, antagonistic, and without humor; that is, for personality traits that assumed more importance in their minds than the form his life's work as a writer had taken.

Thoreau's personal force had not been totally ignored during his lifetime, either as a writer or a thinker. The abrasive urgency of his self-appointed role as prophet and the pawky intelligence of his writing style made it impossible for his essays to be met altogether by silence or dismissal. Immediately after his death, however, it was easier to give approval to Thoreau by taming him, by reducing him to the pupil who had stood in the shadow cast by Emerson. Some tried to convert him into a nature writer who provided nice descriptions of woodland walks. Others turned him into the anecdotist of quaint bits of New England history. By the end of the century, however, Thoreau was taken up as a social reformer by the English Fabians and by Mahatma Ghandi in India, who focused on the same lessons in passive resistance that Martin Luther King, Jr., was to use in the American civil rights struggles. By the 1960s and 1970s Thoreau's image had been reshaped yet again. Many elected to make him the defiant loner and social anarchist, the mindless nature boy, or the dedicated environmentalist. The general effect of these manipulations continued to be reductive. Those who used Thoreau for their own purposes were often incapable of recognizing the critical eye and the sharp tongue he would have turned on their own slack minds and wayward doings.

Recent scholarship has reassessed the quality of Thoreau's prose style and analyzed the conscious adjustments he made in his writing so that what he wanted to say could be brought into line with what his audiences wanted to read. Older and continuing views of Thoreau as naturalist, social philosopher, and—inevitably—grist for psychobiographies are now being supplemented by appraisals of his forceful literary imagination. Hitherto neglected writings— including the journals, *A Week,* and such essays as "Wild Apples"—are the subject of the appraisals they deserve.

None of these newer evaluations threatens the place of *Walden.* It remains secure as one of the American masterworks. What is gained, however, in going beyond the conventional views of Thoreau is a better appreciation of how exactly he responded to the "voice" that pointed him toward his special vocation as a writer. The recent emphasis in the criticism points up the literary means he used to present the fact that we live perilously and paradoxically between heaven and earth—between "the higher laws" and "brute neighbors."

The many discrepancies Thoreau found in the world parallel his own nature. Both as a man and as a writer, he tried to convert the jagged connections of the world of human society into the seamless cosmic whole of nature's universe. He portrayed the aspirations of our dual selves, which go to the bottom of ponds and to the heights of stars. Thoreau realized the hazardous terms by which our duality comes into conjunction with the universe. We are instructed to live in the exact nick of time, lest we fall outside the fateful rhythms set up for our lives. We must be fully awake in order to escape the seep of the spirit into the dead weight of an exclusively material system. We have to simplify the acts of our daily doings while relishing the array of meanings that lie in the sacred "texts" found in the natural world. We are encouraged to go to inner frontiers where facts are "confronted"—traveling far while staying home.

But if Thoreau discovered means that save the soul, he did not fully know how to bring his discoveries to bear upon his own existence, or—most crucial to him as a writer—exactly how to make convincing contact with readers who are indifferent to the dangers surrounding them. However, in *Walden, A Week,* and other works, we find Thoreau working hard to convert into a confident prose style the anxieties we all feel in the face of universal paradoxes. Thoreau's writings provide a list of all the things he believed we must be concerned with because they were what mattered the most to him: how, without "marriage," to have the perfect friendship between one person and another or between the dual selves that lie within each person's nature; how to evoke the sense of social crisis without singing an ode of dejection; how to appeal to religious sensibilities while keeping free of the accepted Christian conventions of doctrine; how to achieve self-pride in the midst of self-doubts; how to attempt to live a model life without appearing to be an egoist and how to write in the autobiographical mode even when the facts make one seem the village fool; how to balance the carnal, "woodchuck" needs of our physical nature with a desire for chastity of spirit; how to insist on the primacy of the present and the value of the future; how to replace the past while using the wisdom of ancient scriptures; how to convey common sense by the uncommon means of language; and, most of all, how to celebrate the unique attributes of the true American democrat who must aspire to live in the heavens yet acknowledge the muddy depths and demands of the everyday world.

Further Reading:
J. Atkinson, *Henry Thoreau, The Cosmic Yankee*, 1927.
H. Canby, *Thoreau*, 1939, 1968.
J. Krutch, *Henry David Thoreau*, 1948.
R. Cook, *Passage to Walden*, 1949.
H. Hough, *Thoreau of Walden*, 1956.
Thoreau: A Century of Criticism, ed.
W. Harding, 1954.
L. Shanley, *The Making of Walden*, 1957.
S. Paul, *The Shores of America: Thoreau's Inward Exploration*, 1958.
W. Harding, *Thoreau Handbook*, 1959, revised 1980.
A. Derluth, *Concord Rebel: A Life of Henry David Thoreau*, 1962.
W. Harding and M. Meltzer, *A Thoreau Profile*, 1962.
Thoreau: A Collection of Critical Essays, ed.
S. Paul, 1962.
W. Harding, *The Days of Henry Thoreau*, 1965.
J. Porte, *Emerson and Thoreau, Transcendentalists in Conflict*, 1966.
C. Anderson, *The Magic Circle of Walden*, 1968.
J. G. Murray, *Henry David Thoreau*, 1968.
R. F. Stowell, *A Thoreau Gazetteer*, 1970, 1974.
S. Cavell, *The Senses of Walden*, 1972.
J. McIntosh, *Thoreau as Romantic Naturalist*, 1974.
R. C. Tuerk, *Central Still*, 1975.
M. Meyer, *Several More Lives to Live*, 1977.
F. Garber, *Thoreau's Redemptive Imagination*, 1977.
R. Lebeaux, *Young Man Thoreau*, 1977.
R. F. Sayre, *Thoreau and the American Indians*, 1977.
M. E. Moller, *Thoreau in the Human Community*, 1980.
R. Bridgman, *Dark Thoreau*, 1982.
W. Howarth, *The Book of Concord*, 1982.
Thoreau's Psychology, ed. R. D. Gozzi, 1983.
R. Lebeaux, *Thoreau's Seasons*, 1984.

Texts:
"Paradise (to Be) Regained," *Walden, The Maine Woods, A Week on the Concord and Merrimack Rivers*, "Resistance to Civil Government," and "Plea for Captain John Brown" from *The Writings of Henry D. Thoreau*, 25 vols. projected, ed. W. Harding, 1971–.
"Wild Apples," letter to H. G. O. Blake, and the journals from *The Writings of Henry David Thoreau* (Walden edition), 20 vols., 1906.
See also *Collected Poems of Henry Thoreau*, ed. C. Bode, 1943, 1964, 1974.
The Correspondence of Henry David Thoreau, ed. C. Bode and W. Harding, 1958.
Consciousness in Concord: Thoreau's Lost Journal (1840–1841), ed. P. Miller, 1958.
The Journal of Henry D. Thoreau, 2 vols., 1962.

Paradise (to Be) Regained

We learn that Mr. Etzler[1] is a native of Germany, and originally published his book in Pennsylvania, ten or twelve years ago; and now a second English edition, from the original American one, is demanded by his readers across the water, owing, we suppose, to the recent spread of Fourier's doctrines.[2] It is one of the signs of the times. We confess that we have risen from reading this book with enlarged ideas, and grander conceptions of our duties in this world. It did expand us a little. It is worth attending to, if only that it entertains large questions. Consider what Mr. Etzler proposes:[3]

"Fellow Men! I promise to show the means of creating a paradise within ten years, where everything desirable for human life may be had by every man in superabundance, without labor, and without pay; where the whole face of nature shall be changed into the most beautiful forms, and man may live in the most magnificent palaces, in all imaginable refinements of luxury, and in the most delightful gardens; where he may accomplish, without labor, in one year, more than hitherto could be done in thousands of years; may level mountains, sink valleys, create lakes, drain lakes and swamps, and intersect the land everywhere with beautiful canals, and roads for transporting heavy loads of many thousand tons, and for travelling one thousand miles in twenty-four hours; may cover the ocean with floating islands movable in any desired direction with immense power and celerity, in perfect security, and with all comforts and luxuries, bearing gardens and palaces, with thousands of families, and provided with rivulets of sweet water; may explore the interior of the globe, and travel from pole to pole in a fortnight; provide himself with means, unheard of yet, for increasing his knowledge of the world, and so his intelligence; lead a life of continual happiness, of enjoyments yet unknown; free himself from almost all the evils that afflict mankind, except death, and even put death far beyond the common period of human life, and finally render it less afflicting. Mankind may thus live in and enjoy a new world, far superior to the present, and raise themselves far higher in the scale of being."

---

[1] John Adolphus Etzler, author of *The Paradise Within the Reach of All Men, Without Labor, by Powers of Nature and Machinery* (1833). Etzler immigrated to the United States in 1831 as a member of the Emigration Society, led by John Augustus Roebling (the man who later built New York's Brooklyn Bridge). Etzler published other utopian tracts between 1841 and 1844, giving further expression to his millennial visions of the power of the machine to redeem the American landscape.

[2] The social theories of Jean-Baptiste Fourier (1768–1830), French mathematician, physicist,

and socialist reformer, were well received in the United States by utopian thinkers who sought to reorganize society along communal lines. One of the most famous Fourieristic "one-family" social experiments took place at Brook Farm in Massachusetts. Hawthorne lived there for a brief time before leaving in disappointment, but Emerson and Thoreau spurned the idea from the start as being too collectivist for their own principles of self-reliance and individualism.

[3] Thoreau both quotes and revises Etzler's wording.

It would seem from this and various indications beside, that there is a transcendentalism in mechanics as well as in ethics. While the whole field of the one reformer lies beyond the boundaries of space, the other is pushing his schemes for the elevation of the race to its utmost limits. While one scours the heavens, the other sweeps the earth. One says he will reform himself, and then nature and circumstances will be right. Let us not obstruct ourselves, for that is the greatest friction. It is of little importance though a cloud obstruct the view of the astronomer compared with his own blindness. The other will reform nature and circumstances, and then man will be right. Talk no more vaguely, says he, of reforming the world—I will reform the globe itself. What matters it whether I remove this humor out of my flesh, or the pestilent humor from the fleshy part of the globe? Nay, is not the latter the more generous course? At present the globe goes with a shattered constitution in its orbit. Has it not asthma, and ague, and fever, and dropsy, and flatulence, and pleurisy, and is it not afflicted with vermin? Has it not its healthful laws counteracted, and its vital energy which will yet redeem it? No doubt the simple powers of nature properly directed by man would make it healthy and paradise; as the laws of man's own constitution but wait to be obeyed, to restore him to health and happiness. Our panaceas cure but few ails, our general hospitals are private and exclusive. We must set up another Hygeian[4] than is now worshipped. Do not the quacks even direct small doses for children, larger for adults, and larger still for oxen and horses? Let us remember that we are to prescribe for the globe itself.

This fair homestead has fallen to us, and how little have we done to improve it, how little have we cleared and hedged and ditched! We are too inclined to go hence to a "better land," without lifting a finger, as our farmers are moving to the Ohio soil; but would it not be more heroic and faithful to till and redeem this New-England soil of the world? The still youthful energies of the globe have only to be directed in their proper channel. Every gazette brings accounts of the untutored freaks of the wind—shipwrecks and hurricanes which the mariner and planter accept as special or general providences; but they touch our consciences, they remind us of our sins. Another deluge would disgrace mankind. We confess we never had much respect for that antediluvian race. A thorough-bred business man cannot enter heartily upon the business of life without first looking into his accounts. How many things are now at loose ends. Who knows which way the wind will blow to-morrow? Let us not succumb to nature. We will marshal the clouds and restrain the tempests; we will bottle up pestilent exhalations, we will probe for earthquakes, grub them up; and give vent to the dangerous gases; we will disembowel the volcano, and extract its poison, take its seed out. We will wash water, and warm fire, and cool ice, and underprop the earth. We will teach birds to fly, and fishes to swim, and ruminants to chew the cud. It is time we had looked into these things.

And it becomes the moralist, too, to inquire what man might do to improve and beautify the system; what to make the stars shine more brightly, the sun more cheery and joyous, the moon more placid and content. Could he not heighten the tints of flowers and the melody of birds? Does he perform his duty to the inferior races? Should he not be a god to them? What is the part of magnanimity to the whale and the beaver? Should we not fear to exchange places with them for a day, lest by their

---

[4] Greek goddess of health, Hygeia.

behavior they should shame us? Might we not treat with magnanimity the shark and the tiger, not descend to meet them on their own level, with spears of sharks' teeth and bucklers of tiger's skin? We slander the hyena; man is the fiercest and cruelest animal. Ah! he is of little faith; even the erring comets and meteors would thank him, and return his kindness in their kind.

How meanly and grossly do we deal with nature! Could we not have a less gross labor? What else do these fine inventions suggest,—magnetism,[5] the daguerreotype, electricity? Can we not do more than cut and trim the forest,—can we not assist in its interior economy, in the circulation of the sap? Now we work superficially and violently. We do not suspect how much might be done to improve our relation with animated nature; what kindness and refined courtesy there might be.

There are certain pursuits which, if not wholly poetic and true, do at least suggest a nobler and finer relation to nature than we know. The keeping of bees, for instance, is a very slight interference. It is like directing the sunbeams. All nations, from the remotest antiquity, have thus fingered nature. There are Hymettus and Hybla,[6] and how many bee-renowned spots beside? There is nothing gross in the idea of these little herds,—their hum like the faintest low of kine in the meads. A pleasant reviewer has lately reminded us that in some places they are led out to pasture where the flowers are most abundant. "Columella[7] tells us," says he, "that the inhabitants of Arabia sent their hives into Attica to benefit by the later-blowing flowers." Annually are the hives, in immense pyramids, carried up the Nile in boats, and suffered to float slowly down the stream by night, resting by day, as the flowers put forth along the banks; and they determine the richness of any locality, and so the profitableness of delay, by the sinking of the boat in the water. We are told, by the same reviewer, of a man in Germany, whose bees yielded more honey than those of his neighbors, with no apparent advantage; but at length he informed them that he had turned his hives one degree more to the east, and so his bees, having two hours the start in the morning, got the first sip of honey. True, there is treachery and selfishness behind all this; but these things suggest to the poetic mind what might be done.

Many examples there are of a grosser interference, yet not without their apology. We saw last summer, on the side of a mountain, a dog employed to churn for a farmer's family, travelling upon a horizontal wheel, and though he had sore eyes, an alarming cough, and withal a demure aspect, yet their bread did get buttered for all that. Undoubtedly, in the most brilliant successes, the first rank is always sacrificed. Much useless travelling of horses, *in extenso*,[8] has of late years been improved for man's behoof, only two forces being taken advantage of,—the gravity of the horse, which is the centripetal, and his centrifugal inclination to go a-head. Only these two elements in the calculation. And is not the creature's whole economy better economized thus? Are not all finite beings better pleased with motions relative than absolute? And what is the great globe itself but such a wheel,—a larger tread-mill, —so that our horse's freest steps over prairies are oftentimes balked and rendered of no avail by the earth's motion on its axis? But here he is the central agent and

[5] Branch of physics that studies magnets and magnetic phenomena.
[6] Hymettus, mountain near Athens, and Hybla, town in Sicily, are famous for the honey produced in their areas.

[7] Lucius Junius Moderatus Columella (first century A.D.), Roman writer on agriculture. *De Re Rustica* is his best-known work.
[8] Extensively.

motive power; and, for variety of scenery, being provided with a window in front, do not the ever-varying activity and fluctuating energy of the creature himself work the effect of the most varied scenery on a country road? It must be confessed that horses at present work too exclusively for men, rarely men for horses; and the brute degenerates in man's society.

It will be seen that we contemplate a time when man's will shall be law to the physical world, and he shall no longer be deterred by such abstractions as time and space, height and depth, weight and hardness, but shall indeed be the lord of creation. "Well," says the faithless reader, " 'life is short, but art is long;' where is the power that will effect all these changes?" This it is the very object of Mr. Etzler's volume to show. At present, he would merely remind us that there are innumerable and immeasurable powers already existing in nature, unimproved on a large scale, or for generous and universal ends, amply sufficient for these purposes. He would only indicate their existence, as a surveyor makes known the existence of a water-power on any stream; but for their application he refers us to a sequel to this book, called the "Mechanical System." A few of the most obvious and familiar of these powers are, the Wind, the Tide, the Waves, the Sunshine. Let us consider their value.

First, there is the power of the Wind, constantly exerted over the globe. It appears from observation of a sailing-vessel, and from scientific tables, that the average power of the wind is equal to that of one horse for every one hundred square feet. "We know," says our author—

"that ships of the first class carry sails two hundred feet high; we may, therefore, equally, on land, oppose to the wind surfaces of the same height. Imagine a line of such surfaces one mile, or about 5,000 feet, long; they would then contain 1,000,000 square feet. Let these surfaces intersect the direction of the wind at right angles, by some contrivance, and receive, consequently, its full power at all times. Its average power being equal to one horse for every 100 square feet, the total power would be equal to 1,000,000 divided by 100, or 10,000 horses' power. Allowing the power of one horse to equal that of ten men, the power of 10,000 horses is equal to 100,000 men. But as men cannot work uninterruptedly, but want about half the time for sleep and repose, the same power would be equal to 200,000 men. . . . We are not limited to the height of 200 feet; we might extend, if required, the application of this power to the height of the clouds, by means of kites."

But we will have one such fence for every square mile of the globe's surface, for, as the wind usually strikes the earth at an angle of more than two degrees, which is evident from observing its effect on the high sea, it admits of even a closer approach. As the surface of the globe contains about 200,000,000 square miles, the whole power of the wind on these surfaces would equal 40,000,000,000,000 men's power, and "would perform 80,000 times as much work as all the men on earth could effect with their nerves."

If it should be objected that this computation includes the surface of the ocean and uninhabitable regions of the earth, where this power could not be applied for our purposes, Mr. Etzler is quick with his reply—"But, you will recollect," says he, "that

I have promised to show the means for rendering the ocean as inhabitable as the most fruitful dry land; and I do not exclude even the polar regions."

The reader will observe that our author uses the fence only as a convenient formula for expressing the power of the wind, and does not consider it a necessary method of its application. We do not attach much value to this statement of the comparative power of the wind and horse, for no common ground is mentioned on which they can be compared. Undoubtedly, each is incomparably excellent in its way, and every general comparison made for such practical purposes as are contemplated, which gives a preference to the one, must be made with some unfairness to the other. The scientific tables are, for the most part, true only in a tabular sense. We suspect that a loaded wagon, with a light sail, ten feet square, would not have been blown so far by the end of the year, under equal circumstances, as a common racer or dray horse would have drawn it. And how many crazy structures on our globe's surface, of the same dimensions, would wait for dry-rot if the traces of one horse were hitched to them, even to their windward side? Plainly, this is not the principle of comparison. But even the steady and constant force of the horse may be rated as equal to his weight at least. Yet we should prefer to let the zephyrs and gales bear, with all their weight, upon our fences, than that Dobbin, with feet braced, should lean ominously against them for a season.

Nevertheless, here is an almost incalculable power at our disposal, yet how trifling the use we make of it. It only serves to turn a few mills, blow a few vessels across the ocean, and a few trivial ends besides. What a poor compliment do we pay to our indefatigable and energetic servant!

"If you ask, perhaps, why this power is not used, if the statement be true, I have to ask in return, why is the power of steam so lately come to application? so many millions of men boiled water every day for many thousand years; they must have frequently seen that boiling water, in tightly closed pots or kettles, would lift the cover or burst the vessel with great violence. The power of steam was, therefore, as commonly known down to the least kitchen or wash-woman, as the power of wind; but close observation and reflection were bestowed neither on the one nor the other."

Men having discovered the power of falling water, which after all is comparatively slight, how eagerly do they seek out and improve these *privileges?* Let a difference of but a few feet in level be discovered on some stream near a populous town, some slight occasion for gravity to act, and the whole economy of the neighborhood is changed at once. Men do indeed speculate about and with this power as if it were the only privilege. But meanwhile this aerial stream is falling from far greater heights with more constant flow, never shrunk by drought, offering mill-sites wherever the wind blows; a Niagara in the air, with no Canada side;—only the application is hard.

There are the powers too of the Tide and Waves, constantly ebbing and flowing, lapsing and relapsing, but they serve man in but few ways. They turn a few tide mills, and perform a few other insignificant and accidental services only. We all perceive the effect of the tide; how imperceptibly it creeps up into our harbors and rivers, and raises the heaviest navies as easily as the lightest ship. Everything that floats must yield to it. But man, slow to take nature's constant hint of assistance, makes slight and irregular use of this power, in careening ships and getting them afloat when aground.

The following is Mr. Etzler's calculation on this head: To form a conception of the power which the tide affords, let us imagine a surface of 100 miles square, or 10,000 square miles, where the tide rises and sinks, on an average, 10 feet; how many men would it require to empty a basin of 10,000 square miles area, and 10 feet deep, filled with sea-water, in 6 1/4 hours and fill it again in the same time? As one man can raise 8 cubic feet of sea-water per minute, and in 6 1/4 hours 3,000, it would take 1,200,000,000 men, or as they could work only half the time, 2,400,000,000, to raise 3,000,000,000,000 cubic feet, or the whole quantity required in the given time.

This power may be applied in various ways. A large body, of the heaviest materials that will float, may first be raised by it, and being attached to the end of a balance reaching from the land, or from a stationary support, fastened to the bottom, when the tide falls, the whole weight will be brought to bear upon the end of the balance. Also when the tide rises it may be made to exert a nearly equal force in the opposite direction. It can be employed whenever a *point d'appui*[9] can be obtained.

"However, the application of the tide being by establishments fixed on the ground, it is natural to begin with them near the shores in shallow water, and upon sands, which may be extended gradually further into the sea. The shores of the continent, islands, and sands, being generally surrounded by shallow water, not exceeding from 50 to 100 fathoms in depth, for 20, 50, or 100 miles and upward. The coasts of North America, with their extensive sand-banks, islands, and rocks, may easily afford, for this purpose, a ground about 3,000 miles long, and, on an average, 100 miles broad, or 300,000 square miles, which, with a power of 240,000 men per square mile, as stated, at 10 feet tide, will be equal to 72,000 millions of men, or for every mile of coast, a power of 24,000,000 men."

"Rafts, of any extent, fastened on the ground of the sea, along the shore, and stretching far into the sea, may be covered with fertile soil, bearing vegetables and trees, of every description, the finest gardens, equal to those the firm land may admit of, and buildings and machineries, which may operate, not only on the sea, where they are, but which also, by means of mechanical connections, may extend their operations for many miles into the continent. (Etzler's Mechanical System, page 24.) Thus this power may cultivate the artificial soil for many miles upon the surface of the sea, near the shores, and, for several miles, the dry land, along the shore, in the most superior manner imaginable; it may build cities along the shore, consisting of the most magnificent palaces, every one surrounded by gardens and the most delightful sceneries; it may level the hills and unevennesses, or raise eminences for enjoying open prospect into the country and upon the sea; it may cover the barren shore with fertile soil, and beautify the same in various ways; it may clear the sea of shallows, and make easy the approach to the land, not merely of vessels, but of large floating islands, which may come from, and go to distant parts of the world, islands that have every commodity and security for their inhabitants which the firm land affords."

"Thus may a power, derived from the gravity of the moon and the ocean,

---

[9] Fulcrum or point of support.

hitherto but the objects of idle curiosity to the studious man, be made eminently subservient for creating the most delightful abodes along the coasts, where men may enjoy at the same time all the advantages of sea and dry land; the coasts may hereafter be continuous paradisiacal skirts between land and sea, everywhere crowded with the densest population. The shores and the sea along them will be no more as raw nature presents them now, but everywhere of easy and charming access, not even molested by the roar of waves, shaped as it may suit the purposes of their inhabitants; the sea will be cleared of every obstruction to free passage every-where, and its productions in fishes, etc., will be gathered in large, appropriate receptacles, to present them to the inhabitants of the shores and of the sea."

Verily, the land would wear a busy aspect at the spring and neap tide, and these island ships—these *terræ infirmæ*[10]—which realise the fables of antiquity, affect our imagination. We have often thought that the fittest locality for a human dwelling was on the edge of the land, that there the constant lesson and impression of the sea might sink deep into the life and character of the landsman, and perhaps impart a marine tint to his imagination. It is a noble word, that *mariner*—one who is conversant with the sea. There should be more of what it signifies in each of us. It is a worthy country to belong to—we look to see him not disgrace it. Perhaps we should be equally mariners and terreners,[11] and even our Green Mountains need some of that sea-green to be mixed with them.

The computation of the power of the waves is less satisfactory. While only the average power of the wind, and the average height of the tide, were taken before now, the extreme height of the waves is used, for they are made to rise ten feet above the level of the sea, to which, adding ten more for depression, we have twenty feet, or the extreme height of a wave. Indeed, the power of the waves, which is produced by the wind blowing obliquely and at disadvantage upon the water, is made to be, not only three thousand times greater than that of the tide, but one hundred times greater than that of the wind itself, meeting its object at right angles. Moreover, this power is measured by the area of the vessel, and not by its length mainly, and it seems to be forgotten that the motion of the waves is chiefly undulatory, and exerts a power only within the limits of a vibration, else the very continents, with their extensive coasts, would soon be set adrift.

Finally, there is the power to be derived from sunshine, by the principle on which Archimedes[12] contrived his burning mirrors, a multiplication of mirrors reflecting the rays of the sun upon the same spot, till the requisite degree of heat is obtained. The principal application of this power will be to the boiling of water and production of steam.

"How to create rivulets of sweet and wholesome water, on floating islands, in the midst of the ocean, will be no riddle now. Sea-water changed into steam, will distil into sweet water, leaving the salt on the bottom. Thus the steam engines on floating islands, for their propulsion and other mechanical purposes,

---

[10] Floating islands.
[11] Landsmen.

[12] Greek mathematician and physicist (287?–212 B.C.).

will serve, at the same time, for the distillery of sweet water, which, collected in basins, may be led through channels over the island, while, where required, it may be refrigerated by artificial means, and changed into cool water, surpassing, in salubrity, the best spring water, because nature hardly ever distils water so purely, and without admixture of less wholesome matter."

So much for these few and more obvious powers, already used to a trifling extent. But there are innumerable others in nature, not described nor discovered. These, however, will do for the present. This would be to make the sun and the moon equally our satellites. For, as the moon is the cause of the tides, and the sun the cause of the wind, which, in turn, is the cause of the waves, all the work of this planet would be performed by these far influences.

"But as these powers are very irregular and subject to interruptions; the next object is to show how they may be converted into powers that operate continually and uniformly for ever, until the machinery be worn out, or, in other words, into perpetual motions." . . . "Hitherto the power of the wind has been applied immediately upon the machinery for use, and we have had to wait the chances of the wind's blowing; while the operation was stopped as soon as the wind ceased to blow. But the manner, which I shall state hereafter, of applying this power, is to make it operate only for collecting or storing up power, and then to take out of this store, at any time, as much as may be wanted for final operation upon the machines. The power stored up is to react as required, and may do so long after the original power of the wind has ceased. And though the wind should cease for intervals of many months, we may have by the same power a uniform perpetual motion in a very simple way."

"The weight of a clock being wound up gives us an image of reaction. The sinking of this weight is the reaction of winding it up. It is not necessary to wait till it has run down before we wind up the weight, but it may be wound up at any time, partly or totally; and if done always before the weight reaches the bottom, the clock will be going perpetually. In a similar, though not in the same way, we may cause a reaction on a larger scale. We may raise, for instance, water by the immediate application of wind or steam to a pond upon some eminence, out of which, through an outlet, it may fall upon some wheel or other contrivance for setting machinery a going. Thus we may store up water in some eminent pond, and take out of this store, at any time, as much water through the outlet as we want to employ, by which means the original power may react for many days after it has ceased." . . . "Such reservoirs of moderate elevation or size need not be made artificially, but will be found made by nature very frequently, requiring but little aid for their completion. They require no regularity of form. Any valley with lower grounds in its vicinity, would answer the purpose. Small crevices may be filled up. Such places may be eligible for the beginning of enterprises of this kind."

The greater the height, of course the less water required. But suppose a level and dry country; then hill and valley, and "eminent pond," are to be constructed by main force; or if the springs are unusually low, then dirt and stones may be used, and the disadvantage arising from friction will be counterbalanced by their greater gravity. Nor shall a single rood of dry land be sunk in such artificial ponds as may be wasted, but their surfaces "may be covered with rafts decked with fertile earth, and all kinds of vegetables which may grow here as well anywhere else."

And finally, by the use of thick envelopes retaining the heat, and other contrivances, "the power of steam caused by sunshine may react at will, and thus be rendered perpetual, no matter how often or how long the sunshine may be interrupted. (Etzler's Mechanical System)."

Here is power enough, one would think, to accomplish somewhat. These are the powers below. Oh ye millwrights, ye engineers, ye operatives and speculators of every class, never again complain of a want of power; it is the grossest form of infidelity. The question is not how we shall execute, but what. Let us not use in a niggardly manner what is thus generously offered.

Consider what revolutions are to be effected in agriculture. First, in the new country, a machine is to move along taking out trees and stones to any required depth, and piling them up in convenient heaps; then the same machine, "with a little alteration," is to plane the ground perfectly, till there shall be no hills nor valleys, making the requisite canals, ditches and roads, as it goes along. The same machine, "with some other little alterations," is then to sift the ground thoroughly, supply fertile soil from other places if wanted, and plant it; and finally, the same machine "with a little addition," is to reap and gather in the crop, thresh and grind it, or press it to oil, or prepare it any way for final use. For the description of these machines we are referred to "Etzler's Mechanical System, pages 11 to 27." We should be pleased to see that "Mechanical System," though we have not been able to ascertain whether it has been published, or only exists as yet in the design of the author. We have great faith in it. But we cannot stop for applications now.

"Any wilderness, even the most hideous and sterile, may be converted into the most fertile and delightful gardens. The most dismal swamps may be cleared of all their spontaneous growth, filled up and levelled, and intersected by canals, ditches and aqueducts, for draining them entirely. The soil, if required, may be meliorated, by covering or mixing it with rich soil taken from distant places, and the same be mouldered to fine dust, levelled, sifted from all roots, weeds and stones, and sowed and planted in the most beautiful order and symmetry, with fruit trees and vegetables of every kind that may stand the climate."

New facilities for transportation and locomotion are to be adopted:

"Large and commodious vehicles, for carrying many thousand tons, running over peculiarly adapted level roads, at the rate of forty miles per hour, or one thousand miles per day, may transport men and things, small houses, and whatever may serve for comfort and ease, by land. Floating islands, constructed of logs, or of woodenstuff prepared in a similar manner, as is to be done with stone, and of live trees, which may be reared so as to interlace one another, and strengthen the whole, may be covered with gardens and palaces, and propelled by powerful engines, so as to run at an equal rate through seas and oceans. Thus, man may move, with the celerity of a bird's flight, in terrestrial paradises, from one climate to another, and see the world in all its variety, exchanging, with distant nations, the surplus of productions. The journey from one pole to another may be performed in a fortnight; the visit to a transmarine country in a week or two; or a journey round the world in one or two months by land and water. And why pass a dreary winter every year while there is yet room enough on the globe where nature is blessed with a perpetual summer, and with a far greater variety and luxuriance of vegetation? More than one-half the surface of the globe has no winter. Men will have it in their power to remove and prevent all bad influences of climate, and to enjoy, perpetually, only that temperature which suits their constitution and feeling best."

Who knows but by accumulating the power until the end of the present century, using meanwhile only the smallest allowance, reserving all that blows, all that shines, all that ebbs and flows, all that dashes, we may have got such a reserved accumulated power as to run the earth off its track into a new orbit, some summer, and so change the tedious vicissitude of the seasons? Or, perchance, coming generations will not abide the dissolution of the globe, but, availing themselves of future inventions in aerial locomotion, and the navigation of space, the entire race may migrate from the earth, to settle some vacant and more western planet, it may be still healthy, perchance unearthy, not composed of dirt and stones, whose primary strata only are strewn, and where no weeds are sown. It took but little art, a simple application of natural laws, a canoe, a paddle, and a sail of matting, to people the isles of the Pacific, and a little more will people the shining isles of space. Do we not see in the firmament the lights carried along the shore by night, as Columbus did? Let us not despair nor mutiny.

"The dwellings also ought to be very different from what is known, if the full benefit of our means is to be enjoyed. They are to be of a structure for which we have no name yet. They are to be neither palaces, nor temples, nor cities, but a combination of all, superior to whatever is known. Earth may be baked into bricks, or even vitrified stone by heat,—we may bake large masses of any size and form into stone and vitrified substance of the greatest durability, lasting even thousands of years, out of clayey earth, or of stones ground to dust, by the application of burning mirrors. This is to be done in the open air, without other preparation than gathering the substance, grinding and mixing it with water and cement, moulding or casting it, and bringing the focus of the burning mirrors of proper size upon the same. The character of the architecture is to be quite different from what it ever has been hitherto; large solid masses are to be baked or cast in one piece, ready shaped in any form that may be desired. The building may, therefore, consist of columns two hundred feet high and upwards, of proportionate thickness, and of one entire piece of vitrified substance; huge pieces are to be moulded so as to join and hook on to each other firmly, by proper joints and folds, and not to yield in any way without breaking."
"Foundries, of any description, are to be heated by burning mirrors, and will require no labor, except the making of the first moulds and the superintendence for gathering the metal and taking the finished articles away."

Alas, in the present state of science, we must take the finished articles away; but think not that man will always be a victim of circumstances.
The countryman who visited the city and found the streets cluttered with bricks

and lumber, reported that it was not yet finished, and one who considers the endless repairs and reforming of our houses, might well wonder when they will be done. But why may not the dwellings of men on this earth be built once for all of some durable material, some Roman or Etruscan masonry which will stand, so that time shall only adorn and beautify them? Why may we not finish the outward world for posterity, and leave them leisure to attend to the inner? Surely, all the gross necessities and economies might be cared for in a few years. All might be built and baked and stored up, during this, the term-time of the world, against the vacant eternity, and the globe go provisioned and furnished like our public vessels, for its voyage through space, as through some Pacific ocean, while we would "tie up the rudder and sleep before the wind,"[13] as those who sail from Lima to Manilla.

But, to go back a few years in imagination, think not that life in these crystal palaces is to bear any analogy to life in our present humble cottages. Far from it. Clothed, once for all, in some "flexible stuff," more durable than George Fox's suit of leather,[14] composed of "fibres of vegetables," "glutinated" together by some "cohesive substances," and made into sheets, like paper, of any size or form, man will put far from him corroding care and the whole host of ills.

"The twenty-five halls[15] in the inside of the square are to be each two hundred feet square and high; the forty corridors, each one hundred feet long and twenty wide; the eighty galleries, each from 1,000 to 1,250 feet long; about 7,000 private rooms, the whole surrounded and intersected by the grandest and most splendid colonnades imaginable; floors, ceilings, columns with their various beautiful and fanciful intervals, all shining, and reflecting to infinity all objects and persons, with splendid lustre of all beautiful colors, and fanciful shapes and pictures. All galleries, outside and within the halls, are to be provided with many thousand commodious and most elegant vehicles, in which persons may move up and down, like birds, in perfect security, and without exertion. Any member may procure himself all the common articles of his daily wants, by a short turn of some crank, without leaving his apartment; he may, at any time, bathe himself in cold or warm water, or in steam, or in some artificially prepared liquor for invigorating health. He may, at any time, give to the air in his apartment that temperature that suits his feeling best. He may cause, at any time, an agreeable scent of various kinds. He may, at any time, meliorate his breathing air,—that main vehicle of vital power. Thus, by a proper application of the physical knowledge of our days, man may be kept in a perpetual serenity of mind, and if there is no incurable disease or defect in his organism, in constant vigor of health, and his life be prolonged beyond any parallel which present times afford."

"One or two persons are sufficient to direct the kitchen business. They have nothing else to do but to superintend the cookery, and to watch the time of

---

[13] Paraphrase from *Christian Morals* by Sir Thomas Browne (1605–1682), English physician whose observations on metaphysical subjects were prized by a number of the New England writers of the day.

[14] Fox (1624–1691), English theologian and founder of the Society of Friends (known as the Quakers), advocated sensible, long-wearing clothes for his followers.

[15] Beginning here, Thoreau joins together a number of passages from Etzler's text without bothering to indicate the extent of his adaptations.

the victual being done, and then to remove them, with the table and vessels, into the dining-hall, or to the respective private apartments, by a slight motion of the hand at some crank. Any extraordinary desire of any person may be satisfied by going to the place where the thing is to be had; and anything that requires a particular preparation in cooking or baking, may be done by the person who desires it."

This is one of those instances in which the individual genius is found to consent, as indeed it always does, at last, with the universal. These last sentences have a certain sad and sober truth, which reminds us of the scripture of all nations. All expression of truth does at length take the deep ethical form. Here is hint of a place the most eligible of any in space, and of a servitor, in comparison with whom, all other helps dwindle into insignificance. We hope to hear more of him anon, for even crystal palace would be deficient without his invaluable services.

And as for the environs of the establishment,

"There will be afforded the most enrapturing views to be fancied, cut of the private apartments, from the galleries, from the roof, from its turrets and cupolas,—gardens as far as the eye can see, full of fruits and flowers, arranged in the most beautiful order, with walks, colonnades, aqueducts, canals, ponds, plains, amphitheatres, terraces, fountains, sculptural works, pavilions, gondolas, places for public amusement, etc., to delight the eye and fancy, the taste and smell." . . . "The walks and roads are to be paved with hard vitrified, large plates, so as to be always clean from all dirt in any weather or season. . . . The channels being of vitrified substance, and the water perfectly clear, and filtrated or distilled if required, may afford the most beautiful scenes imaginable, while a variety of fishes is seen clear down to the bottom playing about, and the canals may afford at the same time, the means of gliding smoothly along between various sceneries of art and nature, in beautiful gondolas, while their surface and borders may be covered with fine land and aquatic birds. The walks may be covered with porticos adorned with magnificent columns, statues and sculptural works; all of vitrified substance, and lasting for ever, while the beauties of nature around heighten the magnificence and deliciousness."

"The night affords no less delight to fancy and feelings. An infinite variety of grand, beautiful and fanciful objects and sceneries, radiating with crystalline brilliancy, by the illumination of gas-light; the human figures themselves, arrayed in the most beautiful pomp fancy may suggest, or the eye desire, shining even with brilliancy of stuffs and diamonds, like stones of various colors, elegantly shaped and arranged around the body; all reflected a thousand-fold in huge mirrors and reflectors of various forms; theatrical scenes of a grandeur and magnificence, and enrapturing illusions, unknown yet, in which any person may be either a spectator or actor; the speech and the songs reverberating with increased sound, rendered more sonorous and harmonious than by nature, by vaultings that are moveable into any shape at any time; the sweetest and most impressive harmony of music, produced by song and instruments partly not known yet, may thrill through the nerves and vary with other amusements and delights."

"At night the roof, and the inside and outside of the whole square, are illuminated by gas-light, which in the mazes of many-colored crystal-like colonnades and vaultings, is reflected with a brilliancy that gives to the whole a lustre of precious stones, as far as the eye can see,—such are the future abodes of men." . . . "Such is the life reserved to true intelligence, but withheld from ignorance, prejudice, and stupid adherence to custom." . . . "Such is the domestic life to be enjoyed by every human individual that will partake of it. Love and affection may there be fostered and enjoyed without any of the obstructions that oppose, diminish, and destroy them in the present state of men." . . . "It would be as ridiculous, then, to dispute and quarrel about the means of life, as it would be now about water to drink along mighty rivers, or about the permission to breathe air in the atmosphere, or about sticks in our extensive woods."

Thus is Paradise to be Regained, and that old and stern decree at length reversed. Man shall no more earn his living by the sweat of his brow. All labor shall be reduced to "a short turn of some crank," and "taking the finished article away." But there is a crank,—oh, how hard to be turned! Could there not be a crank upon a crank, —an infinitely small crank?—we would fain inquire. No,—alas! not. But there is a certain divine energy in every man, but sparingly employed as yet, which may be called the crank within,—the crank after all,—the prime mover in all machinery,— quite indispensable to all work. Would that we might get our hands on its handle! In fact no work can be shirked. It may be postponed indefinitely, but not infinitely. Nor can any really important work be made easier by co-operation or machinery. Not one particle of labor now threatening any man can be routed without being per- formed. It cannot be hunted out of the vicinity like jackals and hyenas. It will not run. You may begin by sawing the little sticks, or you may saw the great sticks first, but sooner or later you must saw them both.

We will not be imposed upon by this vast application of forces. We believe that most things will have to be accomplished still by the application called Industry. We are rather pleased after all to consider the small private, but both constant and accumulated force, which stands behind every spade in the field. This it is that makes the valleys shine, and the deserts really bloom. Sometimes, we confess, we are so degenerate as to reflect with pleasure on the days when men were yoked like cattle, and drew a crooked stick for a plough. After all, the great interests and methods were the same.

It is a rather serious objection to Mr. Etzler's schemes, that they require time, men, and money, three very superfluous and inconvenient things for an honest and well- disposed man to deal with. "The whole world," he tells us, "might therefore be really changed into a paradise, within less than ten years, commencing from the first year of an association for the purpose of constructing and applying the machinery." We are sensible of a startling incongruity when time and money are mentioned in this connection. The ten years which are proposed would be a tedious while to wait, if every man were at his post and did his duty, but quite too short a period, if we are to take time for it. But this fault is by no means peculiar to Mr. Etzler's schemes. There is far too much hurry and bustle, and too little patience and privacy, in all our methods, as if something were to be accomplished in centuries. The true reformer does not want time, nor money, nor co-operation, nor advice. What is time but the stuff delay is made of? And depend upon it, our virtue will not live on the interest of our money. He expects no income but our outgoes; so soon as we begin to count the cost the cost begins. And as for advice, the information floating in the atmosphere of society is as evanescent and unserviceable to him as gossamer for clubs of Hercules.[16] There is absolutely no common sense; it is common nonsense. If we are to risk a cent or a drop of our blood, who then shall advise us? For ourselves, we are too young for experience. Who is old enough? We are older by faith than by experience. In the unbending of the arm to do the deed there is experience worth all the maxims in the world.

"It will now be plainly seen that the execution of the proposals is not proper for individuals. Whether it be proper for government at this time, before the subject has become popular, is a question to be decided; all that is to be done, is to step forth, after mature reflection, to confess loudly one's conviction, and to constitute societies. Man is powerful but in union with many. Nothing great, for the improvement of his own condition, or that of his fellow men, can ever be effected by individual enterprise."

Alas! this is the crying sin of the age, this want of faith in the prevalence of a man. Nothing can be effected but by one man. He who wants help wants everything. True, this is the condition of our weakness, but it can never be the means of our recovery. We must first succeed alone, that we may enjoy our success together. We trust that the social movements which we witness indicate an aspiration not to be thus cheaply satisfied. In this matter of reforming the world, we have little faith in corporations; not thus was it first formed.

But our author is wise enough to say, that the raw materials for the accomplishment of his purposes, are "iron, copper, wood, earth chiefly, and a union of men whose eyes and understanding are not shut up by preconceptions." Aye, this last may be what we want mainly,—a company of "odd fellows" indeed.

"Small shares of twenty dollars will be sufficient,"—in all, from "200,000 to 300,000,"—"to create the first establishment for a whole community of from 3000 to 4000 individuals"—at the end of five years we shall have a principal of 200 millions of dollars, and so paradise will be wholly regained at the end of the tenth year. But, alas, the ten years have already elapsed, and there are no signs of Eden yet, for want of the requisite funds to begin the enterprise in a hopeful manner. Yet it seems a safe investment. Perchance they could be hired at a low rate, the property being mortgaged for security, and, if necessary, it could be given up in any stage of the enterprise, without loss, with the fixtures.

Mr. Etzler considers this "Address as a touchstone, to try whether our nation is in any way accessible to these great truths, for raising the human creature to a superior state of existence, in accordance with the knowledge and the spirit of the most cultivated minds of the present time." He has prepared a constitution, short and concise, consisting of twenty-one articles, so that wherever an association may spring up, it may go into operation without delay; and the editor informs us that "Communi-

---

[16] In Greek myth Hercules was the strongest of mortals and a powerful wielder of clubs in his physical confrontations.

cations on the subject of this book may be addressed to C. F. Stollmeyer, No. 6, Upper Charles street, Northampton square, London."

But we see two main difficulties in the way. First, the successful application of the powers by machinery, (we have not yet seen the "Mechanical System,") and, secondly, which is infinitely harder, the application of man to the work by faith. This it is, we fear, which will prolong the ten years to ten thousand at least. It will take a power more than "80,000 times greater than all the men on earth could effect with their nerves," to persuade men to use that which is already offered them. Even a greater than this physical power must be brought to bear upon that moral power. Faith, indeed, is all the reform that is needed; it is itself a reform. Doubtless, we are as slow to conceive of Paradise as of Heaven, of a perfect natural as of a perfect spiritual world. We see how past ages have loitered and erred; "Is perhaps our generation free from irrationality and error? Have we perhaps reached now the summit of human wisdom, and need no more to look out for mental or physical improvement?" Undoubtedly, we are never so visionary as to be prepared for what the next hour may bring forth.

Μέλλει τὸ θεῖον δ'ἐστι τοιοῦτον φύσει.[17]

The Divine is about to be, and such is its nature. In our wisest moments we are secreting a matter, which, like the lime of the shell fish, incrusts us quite over, and well for us, if, like it, we cast our shells from time to time, though they be pearl and of fairest tint. Let us consider under what disadvantages science has hitherto labored before we pronounce thus confidently on her progress.

"There was never any system in the productions of human labor; but they came into existence and fashion as chance directed men." "Only a few professional men of learning occupy themselves with teaching natural philosophy, chemistry, and the other branches of the sciences of nature, to a very limited extent, for very limited purposes, with very limited means." "The science of mechanics is but in a state of infancy. It is true, improvements are made upon improvements, instigated by patents of government; but they are made accidentally or at hap-hazard. There is no general system of this science, mathematical as it is, which developes its principles in their full extent, and the outlines of the application to which they lead. There is no idea of comparison between what is explored and what is yet to be explored in this science. The ancient Greeks placed mathematics at the head of their education. But we are glad to have filled our memory with notions, without troubling ourselves much with reasoning about them."

Mr. Etzler is not one of the enlightened practical men, the pioneers of the actual, who move with the slow deliberate tread of science, conserving the world; who execute the dreams of the last century, though they have no dreams of their own; yet he deals in the very raw but still solid material of all inventions. He has more of the practical than usually belongs to so bold a schemer, so resolute a dreamer. Yet his

[17] A slightly altered line from *Orestes* by Euripides, Greek dramatist of the fifth century B.C. "He is always on the verge of doing so: such is the nature of the divine."

success is in theory, and not in practice, and he feeds our faith rather than contents our understanding. His book wants order, serenity, dignity, everything,—but it does not fail to impart what only man can impart to man of much importance, his own faith. It is true his dreams are not thrilling nor bright enough, and he leaves off to dream where he who dreams just before the dawn begins. His castles in the air fall to the ground, because they are not built lofty enough; they should be secured to heaven's roof. After all, the theories and speculations of men concern us more than their puny execution. It is with a certain coldness and languor that we loiter about the actual and so called practical. How little do the most wonderful inventions of modern times detain us. They insult nature. Every machine, or particular application, seems a slight outrage against universal laws. How many fine inventions are there which do not clutter the ground? We think that those only succeed which minister to our sensible and animal wants, which bake or brew, wash or warm, or the like. But are those of no account which are patented by fancy and imagination, and succeed so admirably in our dreams that they give the tone still to our waking thoughts? Already nature is serving all those uses which science slowly derives on a much higher and grander scale to him that will be served by her. When the sunshine falls on the path of the poet, he enjoys all those pure benefits and pleasures which the arts slowly and partially realize from age to age. The winds which fan his cheek waft him the sum of that profit and happiness which their lagging inventions supply.

The chief fault of this book is, that it aims to secure the greatest degree of gross comfort and pleasure merely. It paints a Mahometan's[18] heaven, and stops short with singular abruptness when we think it is drawing near to the precincts of the Christian's, —and we trust we have not made here a distinction without a difference. Undoubtedly if we were to reform this outward life truly and thoroughly, we should find no duty of the inner omitted. It would be employment for our whole nature; and what we should do thereafter would be as vain a question as to ask the bird what it will do when its nest is built and its brood reared. But a moral reform must take place first, and then the necessity of the other will be superseded, and we shall sail and plough by its force alone. There is a speedier way than the Mechanical System can show to fill up marshes, to drown the roar of the waves, to tame hyenas, secure agreeable environs, diversify the land, and refresh it with "rivulets of sweet water," and that is by the power of rectitude and true behavior. It is only for a little while, only occasionally, methinks, that we want a garden. Surely a good man need not be at the labor to level a hill for the sake of a prospect, or raise fruits and flowers, and construct floating islands, for the sake of a paradise. He enjoys better prospects than lie behind any hill. Where an angel travels it will be paradise all the way, but where Satan travels it will be burning marl and cinders. What says Veeshnoo Sarma?[19] "He whose mind is at ease is possessed of all riches. Is it not the same to one whose foot is enclosed in a shoe, as if the whole surface of the earth were covered with leather?"

He who is conversant with the supernal powers will not worship these inferior deities of the wind, the waves, tide, and sunshine. But we would not disparage the importance of such calculations as we have described. They are truths in physics,

---

[18] Mohammedan's.
[19] In Hindu theology Veeshnoo, or Vishnu, the second member of the sacred trinity, is known as the Preserver. From *The Heetopades of Veeshnoo-Sarma,* translated by Charles Wilkins (1787).

because they are true in ethics. The moral powers no one would presume to calculate. Suppose we could compare the moral with the physical, and say how many horse-power the force of love, for instance, blowing on every square foot of a man's soul, would equal. No doubt we are well aware of this force; figures would not increase our respect for it; the sunshine is equal to but one ray of its heat. The light of the sun is but the shadow of love. "The souls of men loving and fearing God," says Raleigh,[20] "receive influence from that divine light itself, whereof the sun's clarity, and that of the stars, is by Plato called but a shadow. *Lumen est umbra Dei, Deus est Lumen Luminis.* Light is the shadow of God's brightness, who is the light of light," and, we may add, the heat of heat. Love is the wind, the tide, the waves, the sunshine. Its power is incalculable; it is many horse power. It never ceases, it never slacks; it can move the globe without a resting-place; it can warm without fire; it can feed without meat; it can clothe without garments; it can shelter without roof; it can make a paradise within which will dispense with a paradise without. But though the wisest men in all ages have labored to publish this force, and every human heart is, sooner or later, more or less, made to feel it, yet how little is actually applied to social ends. True, it is the motive power of all successful social machinery; but, as in physics, we have made the elements do only a little drudgery for us, steam to take the place of a few horses, wind of a few oars, water of a few cranks and hand-mills; as the mechanical forces have not yet been generously and largely applied to make the physical world answer to the ideal, so the power of love has been but meanly and sparingly applied, as yet. It has patented only such machines as the almshouses, the hospital, and the Bible Society,[21] while its infinite wind is still blowing, and blowing down these very structures, too, from time to time. Still less are we accumulating its power, and preparing to act with greater energy at a future time. Shall we not contribute our shares to this enterprise, then?

1843

Walden[*]

Economy

When I wrote the following pages, or rather the bulk of them, I lived alone, in the woods, a mile from any neighbor, in a house which I had built myself, on the shore of Walden Pond, in Concord, Massachusetts, and earned my living by the labor of my hands only. I lived there two years and two months. At present I am a sojourner in civilized life again.

---

[20] In the opening chapter of *The History of the World* (1614) by Sir Walter Raleigh (1552?–1618).

[21] As the result of a movement begun in 1804, Bible societies were organized for the purpose of making the Scriptures available throughout the country.

[*] *Walden* was published in 1854, seven years after Thoreau left his hut by the pond. While living at Walden Pond, Thoreau wrote *A Week on the Concord and Merrimack Rivers* and portions of *Walden*. He continued revising the latter between 1849 and 1854.

I should not obtrude my affairs so much on the notice of my readers if very particular inquiries had not been made by my townsmen concerning my mode of life, which some would call impertinent, though they do not appear to me at all impertinent, but, considering the circumstances, very natural and pertinent. Some have asked what I got to eat; if I did not feel lonesome; if I was not afraid; and the like. Others have been curious to learn what portion of my income I devoted to charitable purposes; and some, who have large families, how many poor children I maintained. I will therefore ask those of my readers who feel no particular interest in me to pardon me if I undertake to answer some of these questions in this book. In most books, the *I*, or first person, is omitted; in this it will be retained; that, in respect to egotism, is the main difference. We commonly do not remember that it is, after all, always the first person that is speaking. I should not talk so much about myself if there were any body else whom I knew as well. Unfortunately, I am confined to this theme by the narrowness of my experience. Moreover, I, on my side, require of every writer, first or last, a simple and sincere account of his own life, and not merely what he has heard of other men's lives; some such account as he would send to his kindred from a distant land; for if he has lived sincerely, it must have been in a distant land to me. Perhaps these pages are more particularly addressed to poor students. As for the rest of my readers, they will accept such portions as apply to them. I trust that none will stretch the seams in putting on the coat, for it may do good service to him whom it fits.

I would fain say something, not so much concerning the Chinese and Sandwich Islanders[1] as you who read these pages, who are said to live in New England; something about your condition, especially your outward condition or circumstances in this world, in this town, what it is, whether it is necessary that it be as bad as it is, whether it cannot be improved as well as not. I have travelled a good deal in Concord; and every where, in shops, and offices, and fields, the inhabitants have appeared to me to be doing penance in a thousand remarkable ways. What I have heard of Brahmins[2] sitting exposed to four fires and looking in the face of the sun; or hanging suspended, with their heads downward, over flames; or looking at the heavens over their shoulders "until it becomes impossible for them to resume their natural position, while from the twist of the neck nothing but liquids can pass into the stomach;" or dwelling, chained for life, at the foot of a tree; or measuring with their bodies, like caterpillars, the breadth of vast empires; or standing on one leg on the tops of pillars,—even these forms of conscious penance are hardly more incredible and astonishing than the scenes which I daily witness. The twelve labors of Hercules[3] were trifling in comparison with those which my neighbors have undertaken; for they were only twelve, and had an end; but I could never see that these men slew or captured any monster or finished any labor. They have no friend Iolas to burn with a hot iron the root of the hydra's head, but as soon as one head is crushed, two spring up.

I see young men, my townsmen, whose misfortune it is to have inherited farms,

---

[1] Natives of what are now the Hawaiian Islands.
[2] Hindus of the highest caste.
[3] In classic myth, the hero Hercules was set to perform twelve arduous tasks. Among these was the slaying of the nine-headed monster Hydra, which he was able to do with the help of his companion Iolas. Iolas seared the stumps of each of Hydra's heads as Hercules cut them off, so they could not grow back.

houses, barns, cattle, and farming tools; for these are more easily acquired than got rid of. Better if they had been born in the open pasture and suckled by a wolf, that they might have seen with clearer eyes what field they were called to labor in. Who made them serfs of the soil? Why should they eat their sixty acres, when man is condemned to eat only his peck of dirt? Why should they begin digging their graves as soon as they are born? They have got to live a man's life, pushing all these things before them, and get on as well as they can. How many a poor immortal soul have I met well nigh crushed and smothered under its load, creeping down the road of life, pushing before it a barn seventy-five feet by forty, its Augean stables[4] never cleansed, and one hundred acres of land, tillage, mowing, pasture, and wood-lot! The portionless, who struggle with no such unnecessary inherited encumbrances, find it labor enough to subdue and cultivate a few cubic feet of flesh.

But men labor under a mistake. The better part of the man is soon ploughed into the soil for compost. By a seeming fate, commonly called necessity, they are employed, as it says in an old book, laying up treasures which moth and rust will corrupt and thieves break through and steal.[5] It is a fool's life, as they will find when they get to the end of it, if not before. It is said that Deucalion and Pyrrha[6] created men by throwing stones over their heads behind them:—

Inde genus durum sumus, experiensque laborum,
Et documenta damus quâ simus origine nati.[7]

Or, as Raleigh rhymes it in his sonorous way,—

"From thence our kind hard-hearted is, enduring pain and care,
Approving that our bodies of a stony nature are."[8]

So much for a blind obedience to a blundering oracle, throwing the stones over their heads behind them, and not seeing where they fell.

Most men, even in this comparatively free country, through mere ignorance and mistake, are so occupied with the factitious cares and superfluously coarse labors of life that its finer fruits cannot be plucked by them. Their fingers, from excessive toil, are too clumsy and tremble too much for that. Actually, the laboring man has not leisure for a true integrity day by day; he cannot afford to sustain the manliest relations to men; his labor would be depreciated in the market. He has no time to be any thing but a machine. How can he remember well his ignorance—which his growth requires—who has so often to use his knowledge? We should feed and clothe him gratuitously sometimes, and recruit him with our cordials, before we judge of him. The finest qualities of our nature, like the bloom on fruits, can be preserved only by the most delicate handling. Yet we do not treat ourselves nor one another thus tenderly.

---

[4] Stables in which 3,000 oxen had been kept for 30 years by King Augeas; it was one of Hercules' labors to clean them.
[5] Thoreau paraphrases from Matthew 6:19, from "the old book (the Bible)."
[6] Survivors of a great flood, Deucalion and Pyrrha in classic myth repopulated the earth by

throwing stones over their shoulders which were transformed into men and women.
[7] *Metamorphoses*, Book I, by Ovid (43 B.C.–A.D. 17?).
[8] From *The History of the World* (1614) by Sir Walter Raleigh (1552?–1618), English explorer, historian, poet, and courtier.

Some of you, we all know, are poor, find it hard to live, are sometimes, as it were, gasping for breath. I have no doubt that some of you who read this book are unable to pay for all the dinners which you have actually eaten, or for the coats and shoes which are fast wearing or are already worn out, and have come to this page to spend borrowed or stolen time, robbing your creditors of an hour. It is very evident what mean and sneaking lives many of you live, for my sight has been whetted by experience; always on the limits,[9] trying to get into business and trying to get out of debt, a very ancient slough, called by the Latins, *æs alienum,* another's brass,[10] for some of their coins were made of brass; still living, and dying, and buried by this other's brass; always promising to pay, promising to pay, to-morrow, and dying to-day, insolvent; seeking to curry favor, to get custom, by how many modes, only not state-prison offences; lying, flattering, voting, contracting yourselves into a nut-shell of civility, or dilating into an atmosphere of thin and vaporous generosity, that you may persuade your neighbor to let you make his shoes, or his hat, or his coat, or his carriage, or import his groceries for him; making yourselves sick, that you may lay up something against a sick day, something to be tucked away in an old chest, or in a stocking behind the plastering, or, more safely, in the brick bank; no matter where, no matter how much or how little.

I sometimes wonder that we can be so frivolous, I may almost say, as to attend to the gross but somewhat foreign form of servitude called Negro Slavery, there are so many keen and subtle masters that enslave both north and south. It is hard to have a southern overseer; it is worse to have a northern one; but worst of all when you are the slave-driver of yourself. Talk of a divinity in man! Look at the teamster on the highway, wending to market by day or night; does any divinity stir within him? His highest duty to fodder and water his horses! What is his destiny to him compared with the shipping interests? Does not he drive for Squire Make-a-stir? How godlike, how immortal, is he? See how he cowers and sneaks, how vaguely all the day he fears, not being immortal nor divine, but the slave and prisoner of his own opinion of himself, a fame won by his own deeds. Public opinion is a weak tyrant compared with our own private opinion. What a man thinks of himself, that it is which determines, or rather indicates, his fate. Self-emancipation even in the West Indian provinces of the fancy and imagination,—what Wilberforce[11] is there to bring that about? Think, also, of the ladies of the land weaving toilet[12] cushions against the last day, not to betray too green an interest in their fates! As if you could kill time without injuring eternity.

The mass of men lead lives of quiet desperation. What is called resignation is confirmed desperation. From the desperate city you go into the desperate country, and have to console yourself with the bravery of minks and muskrats. A stereotyped but unconscious despair is concealed even under what are called the games and amusements of mankind. There is no play in them, for this comes after work. But it is a characteristic of wisdom not to do desperate things.

When we consider what, to use the words of the catechism,[13] is the chief end of

---

[9] In matters of credit.
[10] Someone else's money.
[11] William Wilberforce (1759–1833), English philanthropist and abolitionist.
[12] Boudoir, dressing room.

[13] The Westminster Catechism, printed in the *New England Primer,* the book of instruction for children in the New England colonies, stated that the chief purpose of human existence "is to glorify God and to enjoy him forever."

man, and what are the true necessaries and means of life, it appears as if men had deliberately chosen the common mode of living because they preferred it to any other. Yet they honestly think there is no choice left. But alert and healthy natures remember that the sun rose clear. It is never too late to give up our prejudices. No way of thinking or doing, however ancient, can be trusted without proof. What every body echoes or in silence passes by as true to-day may turn out to be falsehood to-morrow, mere smoke of opinion, which some had trusted for a cloud that would sprinkle fertilizing rain on their fields. What old people say you cannot do you try and find that you can. Old deeds for old people, and new deeds for new. Old people did not know enough once, perchance, to fetch fresh fuel to keep the fire a-going; new people put a little dry wood under a pot,[14] and are whirled round the globe with the speed of birds, in a way to kill old people, as the phrase is. Age is no better, hardly so well, qualified for an instructor as youth, for it has not profited so much as it has lost. One may almost doubt if the wisest man has learned any thing of absolute value by living. Practically, the old have no very important advice to give the young, their own experience has been so partial, and their lives have been such miserable failures, for private reasons, as they must believe; and it may be that they have some faith left which belies that experience, and they are only less young than they were. I have lived some thirty years on this planet, and I have yet to hear the first syllable of valuable or even earnest advice from my seniors. They have told me nothing, and probably cannot tell me any thing, to the purpose. Here is life, an experiment to a great extent untried by me; but it does not avail me that they have tried it. If I have any experience which I think valuable, I am sure to reflect that this my Mentors said nothing about.

One farmer says to me, "You cannot live on vegetable food solely, for it furnishes nothing to make bones with;" and so he religiously devotes a part of his day to supplying his system with the raw material of bones; walking all the while he talks behind his oxen, which, with vegetable-made bones, jerk him and his lumbering plough along in spite of every obstacle. Some things are really necessaries of life in some circles, the most helpless and diseased, which in others are luxuries merely, and in others still are entirely unknown.

The whole ground of human life seems to some to have been gone over by their predecessors, both the heights and the valleys, and all things to have been cared for. According to Evelyn,[15] "the wise Solomon prescribed ordinances for the very distances of trees; and the Roman prætors have decided how often you may go into your neighbor's land to gather the acorns which fall on it without trespass, and what share belongs to that neighbor." Hippocrates[16] has even left directions how we should cut our nails; that is, even with the ends of the fingers, neither shorter nor longer. Undoubtedly the very tedium and ennui which presume to have exhausted the variety and the joys of life are as old as Adam. But man's capacities have never been measured; nor are we to judge of what he can do by any precedents, so little has been tried. Whatever have been thy failures hitherto, "be not afflicted, my child, for who shall assign to thee what thou hast left undone?"[17]

---

[14] Locomotive steam boiler.

[15] John Evelyn (1620–1706), best known for his diaries, but also the author of *Sylva* (1644), a book on the growing of trees.

[16] Greek physician (460?–377 B.C.).

[17] From the *Vishnu Purana*, a Hindu sacred text.

We might try our lives by a thousand simple tests; as, for instance, that the same sun which ripens my beans illumines at once a system of earths like ours. If I had remembered this it would have prevented some mistakes. This was not the light in which I hoed them. The stars are the apexes of what wonderful triangles! What distant and different beings in the various mansions of the universe are contemplating the same one at the same moment! Nature and human life are as various as our several constitutions. Who shall say what prospect life offers to another? Could a greater miracle take place than for us to look through each other's eyes for an instant? We should live in all the ages of the world in an hour; ay, in all the worlds of the ages. History, Poetry, Mythology!—I know of no reading of another's experience so startling and informing as this would be.

The greater part of what my neighbors call good I believe in my soul to be bad, and if I repent of any thing, it is very likely to be my good behavior. What demon possessed me that I behaved so well? You may say the wisest thing you can, old man, —you who have lived seventy years, not without honor of a kind,—I hear an irresistible voice which invites me away from all that. One generation abandons the enterprises of another like stranded vessels.

I think that we may safely trust a good deal more than we do. We may waive just so much care of ourselves as we honestly bestow elsewhere. Nature is as well adapted to our weakness as to our strength. The incessant anxiety and strain of some is a well nigh incurable form of disease. We are made to exaggerate the importance of what work we do; and yet how much is not done by us! or, what if we had been taken sick? How vigilant we are! determined not to live by faith if we can avoid it; all the day long on the alert, at night we unwillingly say our prayers and commit ourselves to uncertainties. So thoroughly and sincerely are we compelled to live, reverencing our life, and denying the possibility of change. This is the only way, we say; but there are as many ways as there can be drawn radii from one centre. All change is a miracle to contemplate; but it is a miracle which is taking place every instant. Confucius[18] said, "To know that we know what we know, and that we do not know what we do not know, that is true knowledge." When one man has reduced a fact of the imagination to be a fact to his understanding, I foresee that all men will at length establish their lives on that basis.

Let us consider for a moment what most of the trouble and anxiety which I have referred to is about, and how much it is necessary that we be troubled or, at least, careful. It would be some advantage to live a primitive and frontier life, though in the midst of an outward civilization, if only to learn what are the gross necessaries of life and what methods have been taken to obtain them; or even to look over the old daybooks of the merchants, to see what it was that men most commonly bought at the stores, what they stored, that is, what are the grossest groceries. For the improvements of ages have had but little influence on the essential laws of man's existence; as our skeletons, probably, are not to be distinguished from those of our ancestors.

By the words, *necessary of life,* I mean whatever, of all that man obtains by his own

---

[18] From *The Analects,* II, 17, by the Chinese philosopher Confucius (ca. 551–479 B.C.).

exertions, has been from the first, or from long use has become, so important to human life that few, if any, whether from savageness, or poverty, or philosophy, ever attempt to do without it. To many creatures there is in this sense but one necessary of life, Food. To the bison of the prairie it is a few inches of palatable grass, with water to drink; unless he seeks the Shelter of the forest or the mountain's shadow. None of the brute creation requires more than Food and Shelter. The necessaries of life for man in this climate may, accurately enough, be distributed under the several heads of Food, Shelter, Clothing, and Fuel; for not till we have secured these are we prepared to entertain the true problems of life with freedom and a prospect of success. Man has invented, not only houses, but clothes and cooked food; and possibly from the accidental discovery of the warmth of fire, and the consequent use of it, at first a luxury, arose the present necessity to sit by it. We observe cats and dogs acquiring the same second nature. By proper Shelter and Clothing we legitimately retain our own internal heat; but with an excess of these, or of Fuel, that is, with an external heat greater than our own internal, may not cookery properly be said to begin? Darwin, the naturalist, says of the inhabitants of Tierra del Fuego,[19] that while his own party, who were well clothed and sitting close to a fire, were far from too warm, these naked savages, who were farther off, were observed, to his great surprise, "to be streaming with perspiration at undergoing such a roasting." So, we are told, the New Hollander[20] goes naked with impunity, while the European shivers in his clothes. Is it impossible to combine the hardiness of these savages with the intellectualness of the civilized man? According to Liebig,[21] man's body is a stove, and food the fuel which keeps up the internal combustion in the lungs. In cold weather we eat more, in warm less. The animal heat is the result of a slow combustion, and disease and death take place when this is too rapid; or for want of fuel, or from some defect in the draught, the fire goes out. Of course the vital heat is not to be confounded with fire; but so much for analogy. It appears, therefore, from the above list, that the expression, *animal life,* is nearly synonymous with the expression, *animal heat;* for while Food may be regarded as the Fuel which keeps up the fire within us,—and Fuel serves only to prepare that Food or to increase the warmth of our bodies by addition from without, —Shelter and Clothing also serve only to retain the *heat* thus generated and absorbed.

The grand necessity, then, for our bodies, is to keep warm, to keep the vital heat in us. What pains we accordingly take, not only with our Food, and Clothing, and Shelter, but with our beds, which are our night-clothes, robbing the nests and breasts of birds to prepare this shelter within a shelter, as the mole has its bed of grass and leaves at the end of its burrow! The poor man is wont to complain that this is a cold world; and to cold, no less physical than social, we refer directly a great part of our ails. The summer, in some climates, makes possible to man a sort of Elysian life.[22] Fuel, except to cook his Food, is then unnecessary; the sun is his fire, and many of the fruits are sufficiently cooked by its rays; while Food generally is more various, and more

---

[19] Charles Darwin (1809–1882) described this archipelago near the southern tip of South America in his *Journal of Researches* (1839).
[20] Aboriginal Australian.
[21] The German chemist Justus von Liebig (1803–1873).

[22] I.e., as fine a life as that enjoyed by the inhabitants of the paradise described in Greek myth.

easily obtained, and Clothing and Shelter are wholly or half unnecessary. At the present day, and in this country, as I find by my own experience, a few implements, a knife, an axe, a spade, a wheelbarrow, & c., and for the studious, lamplight, stationery, and access to a few books, rank next to necessaries, and can all be obtained at a trifling cost. Yet some, not wise, go to the other side of the globe, to barbarous and unhealthy regions, and devote themselves to trade for ten or twenty years, in order that they may live,—that is, keep comfortably warm,—and die in New England at last. The luxuriously rich are not simply kept comfortably warm, but unnaturally hot;[23] as I implied before, they are cooked, of course *à la mode.*[24]

Most of the luxuries, and many of the so called comforts of life, are not only not indispensable, but positive hinderances to the elevation of mankind. With respect to luxuries and comforts, the wisest have ever lived a more simple and meager life than the poor. The ancient philosophers, Chinese, Hindoo, Persian, and Greek, were a class than which none has been poorer in outward riches, none so rich in inward. We know not much about them. It is remarkable that *we* know so much of them as we do. The same is true of the more modern reformers and benefactors of their race. None can be an impartial or wise observer of human life but from the vantage ground of what *we* should call voluntary poverty. Of a life of luxury the fruit is luxury, whether in agriculture, or commerce, or literature, or art. There are nowadays professors of philosophy, but not philosophers. Yet it is admirable to profess because it was once admirable to live. To be a philosopher is not merely to have subtle thoughts, nor even to found a school, but so to love wisdom as to live according to its dictates, a life of simplicity, independence, magnanimity, and trust. It is to solve some of the problems of life, not only theoretically, but practically. The success of great scholars and thinkers is commonly a courtier-like success, not kingly, not manly. They make shift to live merely by conformity, practically as their fathers did, and are in no sense the progenitors of a nobler race of men. But why do men degenerate ever? What makes families run out? What is the nature of the luxury which enervates and destroys nations? Are we sure that there is none of it in our own lives? The philosopher is in advance of his age even in the outward form of his life. He is not fed, sheltered, clothed, warmed, like his contemporaries. How can a man be a philosopher and not maintain his vital heat by better methods than other men?

When a man is warmed by the several modes which I have described, what does he want next? Surely not more warmth of the same kind, as more and richer food, larger and more splendid houses, finer and more abundant clothing, more numerous incessant and hotter fires, and the like. When he has obtained those things which are necessary to life, there is another alternative than to obtain the superfluities; and that is, to adventure on life now, his vacation from humbler toil having commenced. The soil, it appears, is suited to the seed, for it has sent its radicle[25] downward, and it may now send its shoot upward also with confidence. Why has man rooted himself thus firmly in the earth, but that he may rise in the same proportion into the heavens above? —for the nobler plants are valued for the fruit they bear at last in the air and light, far from the ground, and are not treated like the humbler esculents, which, though

---

[23] With central heating.
[24] In high style.

[25] Root.

they may be biennials, are cultivated only till they have perfected their root, and often cut down at top for this purpose, so that most would not know them in their flowering season.

I do not mean to prescribe rules to strong and valiant natures, who will mind their own affairs whether in heaven or hell, and perchance build more magnificently and spend more lavishly than the richest, without ever impoverishing themselves, not knowing how they live,—if, indeed, there are any such, as has been dreamed; nor to those who find their encouragement and inspiration in precisely the present condition of things, and cherish it with the fondness and enthusiasm of lovers,—and, to some extent, I reckon myself in this number; I do not speak to those who are well employed, in whatever circumstances, and they know whether they are well employed or not; —but mainly to the mass of men who are discontented, and idly complaining of the hardness of their lot or of the times, when they might improve them. There are some who complain most energetically and inconsolably of any, because they are, as they say, doing their duty. I also have in my mind that seemingly wealthy, but most terribly impoverished class of all, who have accumulated dross, but know not how to use it, or get rid of it, and thus have forged their own golden or silver fetters.

If I should attempt to tell how I have desired to spend my life in years past, it would probably surprise those of my readers who are somewhat acquainted with its actual history; it would certainly astonish those who know nothing about it. I will only hint at some of the enterprises which I have cherished.

In any weather, at any hour of the day or night, I have been anxious to improve the nick of time, and notch it on my stick too; to stand on the meeting of two eternities, the past and future, which is precisely the present moment; to toe that line. You will pardon some obscurities, for there are more secrets in my trade than in most men's, and yet not voluntarily kept, but inseparable from its very nature. I would gladly tell all that I know about it, and never paint "No Admittance" on my gate.

I long ago lost a hound, a bay horse, and a turtledove, and am still on their trail. Many are the travellers I have spoken concerning them, describing their tracks and what calls they answered to. I have met one or two who had heard the hound, and the tramp of the horse, and even seen the dove disappear behind a cloud, and they seemed as anxious to recover them as if they had lost them themselves.

To anticipate, not the sunrise and the dawn merely, but, if possible, Nature herself! How many mornings, summer and winter, before yet any neighbor was stirring about his business, have I been about mine! No doubt, many of my townsmen have met me returning from this enterprise, farmers starting for Boston in the twilight, or woodchoppers going to their work. It is true, I never assisted the sun materially in his rising, but, doubt not, it was of the last importance only to be present at it.

So many autumn, ay, and winter days, spent outside the town, trying to hear what was in the wind, to hear and carry it express! I well-nigh sunk all my capital in it, and lost my own breath into the bargain, running in the face of it. If it had concerned either of the political parties, depend upon it, it would have appeared in the Gazette[26] with the earliest intelligence.[27] At other times watching from the observatory of some cliff or tree, to telegraph any new arrival; or waiting at evening on the hill-tops for

[26] The weekly newspaper of Concord.   [27] News.

the sky to fall, that I might catch something, though I never caught much, and that, manna-wise,[28] would dissolve again in the sun.

For a long time I was reporter to a journal,[29] of no very wide circulation, whose editor has never yet seen fit to print the bulk of my contributions, and, as is too common with writers, I got only my labor for my pains. However, in this case my pains were their own reward.

For many years I was self-appointed inspector of snow storms and rain storms, and did my duty faithfully; surveyor, if not of highways, then of forest paths and all across-lot routes, keeping them open, and ravines bridged and passable at all seasons, where the public heel had testified to their utility.

I have looked after the wild stock of the town, which give a faithful herdsman a good deal of trouble by leaping fences; and I have had an eye to the unfrequented nooks and corners of the farm; though I did not always know whether Jonas or Solomon worked in a particular field to-day; that was none of my business. I have watered the red huckleberry, the sand cherry and the nettle tree, the red pine and the black ash, the white grape and the yellow violet, which might have withered else in dry seasons.

In short, I went on thus for a long time, I may say it without boasting, faithfully minding my business, till it became more and more evident that my townsmen would not after all admit me into the list of town officers, nor make my place a sinecure with a moderate allowance. My accounts, which I can swear to have kept faithfully, I have, indeed, never got audited, still less accepted, still less paid and settled. However, I have not set my heart on that.

Not long since, a strolling Indian went to sell baskets at the house of a well-known lawyer in my neighborhood. "Do you wish to buy any baskets?" he asked. "No, we do not want any," was the reply. "What!" exclaimed the Indian as he went out the gate, "do you mean to starve us?" Having seen his industrious white neighbors so well off,—that the lawyer had only to weave arguments, and by some magic wealth and standing followed, he had said to himself; I will go into business; I will weave baskets; it is a thing which I can do. Thinking that when he had made the baskets he would have done his part, and then it would be the white man's to buy them. He had not discovered that it was necessary for him to make it worth the other's while to buy them, or at least make him think that it was so, or to make something else which it would be worth his while to buy. I too had woven a kind of basket of a delicate texture, but I had not made it worth any one's while to buy them. Yet not the less, in my case, did I think it worth my while to weave them, and instead of studying how to make it worth men's while to buy my baskets, I studied rather how to avoid the necessity of selling them. The life which men praise and regard as successful is but one kind. Why should we exaggerate any one kind at the expense of the others?

Finding that my fellow-citizens were not likely to offer me any room in the court house, or any curacy or living any where else, but I must shift for myself, I turned my face more exclusively than ever to the woods, where I was better known. I

[28] Exodus 16 recounts the time that manna, a food given to the Israelites on their journey out of Egypt, melted in the sun.
[29] Thoreau wrote on different occasions for *The*

Dial, The Democratic Review, and other magazines, and at all times faithfully "reported" his activities and thoughts to his own journals.

determined to go into business at once, and not wait to acquire the usual capital, using such slender means as I had already got. My purpose in going to Walden Pond was not to live cheaply nor to live dearly there, but to transact some private business[30] with the fewest obstacles; to be hindered from accomplishing which for want of a little common sense, a little enterprise and business talent, appeared not so sad as foolish.

I have always endeavored to acquire strict business habits; they are indispensable to every man. If your trade is with the Celestial Empire,[31] then some small counting house on the coast, in some Salem harbor, will be fixture enough. You will export such articles as the country affords, purely native products, much ice and pine timber and a little granite, always in native bottoms. These will be good ventures. To oversee all the details yourself in person; to be at once pilot and captain, and owner and underwriter; to buy and sell and keep the accounts; to read every letter received, and write or read every letter sent; to superintend the discharge of imports night and day; to be upon many parts of the coast almost at the same time;—often the richest freight will be discharged upon a Jersey shore;[32]—to be your own telegraph, unweariedly sweeping the horizon, speaking all passing vessels bound coastwise; to keep up a steady despatch of commodities, for the supply of such a distant and exorbitant market; to keep yourself informed of the state of the markets, prospects of war and peace every where, and anticipate the tendencies of trade and civilization,—taking advantage of the results of all exploring expeditions, using new passages and all improvements in navigation;—charts to be studied, the position of reefs and new lights and buoys to be ascertained, and ever, and ever, the logarithmic tables to be corrected, for by the error of some calculator the vessel often splits upon a rock that should have reached a friendly pier,—there is the untold fate of La Perouse;[33]—universal science to be kept pace with, studying the lives of all great discoverers and navigators, great adventurers and merchants, from Hanno and the Phœnicians[34] down to our day; in fine, account of stock to be taken from time to time, to know how you stand. It is a labor to task the faculties of a man,—such problems of profit and loss, of interest, of tare and tret,[35] and gauging of all kinds in it, as demand a universal knowledge.

I have thought that Walden Pond would be a good place for business, not solely on account of the railroad and the ice trade; it offers advantages which it may not be good policy to divulge; it is a good port and a good foundation. No Neva[36] marshes to be filled; though you must every where build on piles of your own driving. It is said that a flood-tide, with a westerly wind, and ice in the Neva, would sweep St. Petersburg from the face of the earth.

As this business was to be entered into without the usual capital, it may not be easy to conjecture where those means, that will still be indispensable to every such undertaking, were to be obtained. As for Clothing, to come at once to the practical part

---

[30] To complete his first book, *A Week on the Concord and Merrimack Rivers* (1849).
[31] China.
[32] New Jersey.
[33] Jean François de Gallup, count de la Perouse (1741–1788), French explorer lost somewhere in the South Pacific.

[34] Hanno was a Carthaginian explorer of the fifth century B.C.; the ancient Phoenicians were also famous for their voyages into uncharted waters.
[35] Calculations of weight.
[36] River in Russia near the site of St. Petersburg, now Leningrad.

of the question, perhaps we are led oftener by the love of novelty, and a regard for the opinions of men, in procuring it, than by a true utility. Let him who has work to do recollect that the object of clothing is, first, to retain the vital heat, and secondly, in this state of society, to cover nakedness, and he may judge how much of any necessary or important work may be accomplished without adding to his wardrobe. Kings and queens who wear a suit but once, though made by some tailor or dress-maker to their majesties, cannot know the comfort of wearing a suit that fits. They are no better than wooden horses to hang the clean clothes on. Every day our garments become more assimilated to ourselves, receiving the impress of the wearer's character, until we hesitate to lay them aside, without such delay and medical appliances and some such solemnity even as our bodies. No man ever stood the lower in my estimation for having a patch in his clothes; yet I am sure that there is greater anxiety, commonly, to have fashionable, or at least clean and unpatched clothes, than to have a sound conscience. But even if the rent is not mended, perhaps the worst vice betrayed is improvidence. I sometimes try my acquaintances by such tests as this;—who could wear a patch, or two extra seams only, over the knee? Most behave as if they believed that their prospects for life would be ruined if they should do it. It would be easier for them to hobble to town with a broken leg than with a broken pantaloon. Often if an accident happens to a gentleman's legs, they can be mended; but if a similar accident happens to the legs of his pantaloons, there is no help for it; for he considers, not what is truly respectable, but what is respected. We know but few men, a great many coats and breeches. Dress a scarecrow in your last shift, you standing shiftless by, who would not soonest salute the scarecrow? Passing a cornfield the other day, close by a hat and coat on a stake, I recognized the owner of the farm. He was only a little more weather-beaten than when I saw him last. I have heard of a dog that barked at every stranger who approached his master's premises with clothes on, but was easily quieted by a naked thief. It is an interesting question how far men would retain their relative rank if they were divested of their clothes. Could you, in such a case, tell surely of any company of civilized men, which belonged to the most respected class? When Madam Pfeiffer,[37] in her adventurous travels round the world, from east to west, had got so near home as Asiatic Russia, she says that she felt the necessity of wearing other than a travelling dress, when she went to meet the authorities, for she "was now in a civilized country, where —— people are judged of by their clothes." Even in our democratic New England towns the accidental possession of wealth, and its manifestation in dress and equipage alone, obtain for the possessor almost universal respect. But they who yield such respect, numerous as they are, are so far heathen, and need to have a missionary sent to them. Beside, clothes introduced sewing, a kind of work which you may call endless; a woman's dress, at least, is never done.

A man who has at length found something to do will not need to get a new suit to do it in; for him the old will do, that has lain dusty in the garret for an indeterminate period. Old shoes will serve a hero longer than they have served his valet,—if a hero ever has a valet—bare feet are older than shoes, and he can make

[37] Ida Reyer Pfeiffer (1797–1858), Austrian writer of travel books, such as *A Woman's Journey Round the World* (1852).

them do. Only they who go to soirées and legislative halls must have new coats, coats to change as often as the man changes in them. But if my jacket and trousers, my hat and shoes, are fit to worship God in, they will do; will they not? Who ever saw his old clothes,—his old coat, actually worn out, resolved into its primitive elements, so that it was not a deed of charity to bestow it on some poor boy, by him perchance to be bestowed on some poorer still, or shall we say richer, who could do with less? I say, beware of all enterprises that require new clothes, and not rather a new wearer of clothes. If there is not a new man, how can the new clothes be made to fit? If you have any enterprise before you, try it in your old clothes. All men want, not something to *do with,* but something to *do,* or rather something to *be.* Perhaps we should never procure a new suit, however ragged or dirty the old, until we have so conducted, so enterprised or sailed in some way, that we feel like new men in the old, and that to retain it would be like keeping new wine in old bottles.[38] Our moulting season, like that of the fowls, must be a crisis in our lives. The loon retires to solitary ponds to spend it. Thus also the snake casts its slough, and the caterpillar its wormy coat, by an internal industry and expansion; for clothes are but our outmost cuticle and mortal coil. Otherwise we shall be found sailing under false colors, and be inevitably cashiered at last by our own opinion, as well as that of mankind.

We don garment after garment, as if we grew like exogenous plants by addition without. Our outside and often thin and fanciful clothes are our epidermis or false skin, which partakes not of our life, and may be stripped off here and there without fatal injury; our thicker garments, constantly worn, are our cellular integument, or cortex; but our shirts are our liber or true bark, which cannot be removed without girdling and so destroying the man. I believe that all races at some seasons wear something equivalent to the shirt. It is desirable that a man be clad so simply that he can lay his hands on himself in the dark, and that he live in all respects so compactly and preparedly, that, if an enemy take the town, he can, like the old philosopher, walk out the gate empty-handed without anxiety. While one thick garment is, for most purposes, as good as three thin ones, and cheap clothing can be obtained at prices really to suit customers; while a thick coat can be bought for five dollars, which will last as many years, thick pantaloons for two dollars, cowhide boots for a dollar and a half a pair, a summer hat for a quarter of a dollar, and a winter cap for sixty-two and a half cents, or a better be made at home at a nominal cost, where is he so poor that, clad in such a suit, *of his own earning,* there will not be found wise men to do him reverence?

When I ask for a garment of a particular form, my tailoress tells me gravely, "They do not make them so now," not emphasizing the "They" at all, as if she quoted an authority as impersonal as the Fates,[39] and I find it difficult to get made what I want, simply because she cannot believe that I mean what I say, that I am so rash. When I hear this oracular sentence, I am for a moment absorbed in thought, emphasizing to myself each word separately that I may come at the meaning of it, that I may find out by what degree of consanguinity *They* are related to *me,* and what authority they may have in an affair which affects me so nearly; and, finally, I am inclined to answer her with equal mystery, and without any more emphasis of

---

[38] Allusion to Matthew 9:17.
[39] In classic myth, the goddesses who determine men's destinies.

the "they,"—"It is true, they did not make them so recently, but they do now." Of what use this measuring of me if she does not measure my character, but only the breadth of my shoulders, as it were a peg to hang the coat on? We worship not the Graces,[40] nor the Parcæ,[41] but Fashion. She spins and weaves and cuts with full authority. The head monkey[42] at Paris puts on a traveller's cap, and all the monkeys in America do the same. I sometimes despair of getting any thing quite simple and honest done in this world by the help of men. They would have to be passed through a powerful press first, to squeeze their old notions out of them, so that they would not soon get upon their legs again, and then there would be some one in the company with a maggot in his head, hatched from an egg deposited there nobody knows when, for not even fire kills these things, and you would have lost your labor. Nevertheless, we will not forget that some Egyptian wheat is said to have been handed down to us by a mummy.[43]

On the whole, I think that it cannot be maintained that dressing has in this or any country risen to the dignity of an art. At present men make shift to wear what they can get. Like shipwrecked sailors, they put on what they can find on the beach, and at a little distance, whether of space or time, laugh at each other's masquerade. Every generation laughs at the old fashions, but follows religiously the new. We are amused at beholding the costume of Henry VIII., or Queen Elizabeth,[44] as much as if it was that of the King and Queen of the Cannibal Islands. All costume off a man is pitiful or grotesque. It is only the serious eye peering from and the sincere life passed within it, which restrain laughter and consecrate the costume of any people. Let Harlequin be taken with a fit of the colic and his trappings will have to serve that mood too. When the soldier is hit by a cannon ball rags are as becoming as purple.

The childish and savage taste of men and women for new patterns keeps how many shaking and squinting through kaleidoscopes that they may discover the particular figure which this generation requires to-day. The manufacturers have learned that this taste is merely whimsical. Of two patterns which differ only by a few threads more or less of a particular color, the one will be sold readily, the other lie on the shelf, though it frequently happens that after the lapse of a season the latter becomes the most fashionable. Comparatively, tattooing is not the hideous custom which it is called. It is not barbarous merely because the printing is skin-deep and unalterable.

I cannot believe that our factory system is the best mode by which men may get clothing. The condition of the operatives is becoming every day more like that of the English; and it cannot be wondered at, since, as far as I have heard or observed, the principal object is, not that mankind may be well and honestly clad, but, unquestionably, that the corporations may be enriched. In the long run men hit only what they aim at. Therefore, though they should fail immediately, they had better aim at something high.

As for a Shelter, I will not deny that this is now a necessary of life, though there are instances of men having done without it for long periods in colder countries than this.

---

[40] Greek deities of beauty, happiness, and brilliance.
[41] Roman goddesses of destiny.
[42] Dictator of fashion.

[43] I.e., sprung from seeds sealed within an Egyptian tomb.
[44] Tudor king (1509–1547) and queen (1558–1603) of England.

Samuel Laing[45] says that "The Laplander in his skin dress, and in a skin bag which he puts over his head and shoulders, will sleep night after night on the snow—— in a degree of cold which would extinguish the life of one exposed to it in any woollen clothing." He had seen them asleep thus. Yet he adds, "They are not hardier than other people." But, probably, man did not live long on the earth without discovering the convenience which there is in a house, the domestic comforts, which phrase may have originally signified the satisfactions of the house more than of the family; though these must be extremely partial and occasional in those climates where the house is associated in our thoughts with winter or the rainy season chiefly, and two thirds of the year, except for a parasol, is unnecessary. In our climate, in the summer, it was formerly almost solely a covering at night. In the Indian gazettes a wigwam was the symbol of a day's march, and a row of them cut or painted on the bark of a tree signified that so many times they had camped. Man was not made so large limbed and robust but that he must seek to narrow his world, and wall in a space such as fitted him. He was at first bare and out of doors; but though this was pleasant enough in serene and warm weather, by daylight, the rainy season and the winter, to say nothing of the torrid sun, would perhaps have nipped his race in the bud if he had not made haste to clothe himself with the shelter of a house. Adam and Eve, according to the fable, wore the bower before other clothes. Man wanted a home, a place of warmth, or comfort, first of physical warmth, then the warmth of the affections.

We may imagine a time when, in the infancy of the human race, some enterprising mortal crept into a hollow in a rock for shelter. Every child begins the world again, to some extent, and loves to stay out of doors, even in wet and cold. It plays house, as well as horse, having an instinct for it. Who does not remember the interest with which when young he looked at shelving rocks, or any approach to a cave? It was the natural yearning of that portion of our most primitive ancestor which still survived in us. From the cave we have advanced to roofs of palm leaves, of bark and boughs, of linen woven and stretched, of grass and straw, of boards and shingles, of stones and tiles. At last, we know not what it is to live in the open air, and our lives are domestic in more senses than we think. From the hearth to the field is a great distance. It would be well perhaps if we were to spend more of our days and nights without any obstruction between us and the celestial bodies, if the poet did not speak so much from under a roof, or the saint dwell there so long. Birds do not sing in caves, nor do doves cherish their innocence in dovecots.

However, if one designs to construct a dwelling house, it behooves him to exercise a little Yankee shrewdness, lest after all he find himself in a workhouse, a labyrinth without a clew, a museum, an almshouse, a prison, or a splendid mausoleum instead. Consider first how slight a shelter is absolutely necessary. I have seen Penobscot Indians,[46] in this town, living in tents of thin cotton cloth, while the snow was nearly a foot deep around them, and I thought that they would be glad to have it deeper to keep out the wind. Formerly, when how to get my living honestly, with freedom left for my proper pursuits, was a question which vexed me even more than it does

45 In his book *Journal of a Residence in Norway* (1837).

46 Thoreau visited northern Maine and became acquainted with members of the Penobscot tribe at that time.

now, for unfortunately I am become somewhat callous, I used to see a large box by the railroad, six feet long by three wide, in which the laborers locked up their tools at night, and it suggested to me that every man who was hard pushed might get such a one for a dollar, and, having bored a few auger holes in it, to admit the air at least, get into it when it rained and at night, and hook down the lid, and so have freedom in his love, and in his soul be free. This did not appear the worst, nor by any means a despicable alternative. You could sit up as late as you pleased, and, whenever you got up, go abroad without any landlord or house-lord dogging you for rent. Many a man is harassed to death to pay the rent of a larger and more luxurious box who would not have frozen to death in such a box as this. I am far from jesting. Economy is a subject which admits of being treated with levity, but it cannot so be disposed of. A comfortable house for a rude and hardy race, that lived mostly out of doors, was once made here almost entirely of such materials as Nature furnished ready to their hands. Gookin,[47] who was superintendent of the Indians subject to the Massachusetts Colony, writing in 1674, says, "The best of their houses are covered very neatly, tight and warm, with barks of trees, slipped from their bodies at those seasons when the sap is up, and made into great flakes, with pressure of weighty timber, when they are green. . . . The meaner sort are covered with mats which they make of a kind of bulrush, and are also indifferently tight and warm, but not so good as the former. . . . Some I have seen, sixty or a hundred feet long and thirty feet broad. . . . I have often lodged in their wigwams, and found them as warm as the best English houses." He adds, that they were commonly carpeted and lined within with well-wrought embroidered mats, and were furnished with various utensils. The Indians had advanced so far as to regulate the effect of the wind by a mat suspended over the hole in the roof and moved by a string. Such a lodge was in the first instance constructed in a day or two at most, and taken down and put up in a few hours; and every family owned one, or its apartment in one.

In the savage state every family owns a shelter as good as the best, and sufficient for its coarser and simpler wants; but I think that I speak within bounds when I say that, though the birds of the air have their nests, and the foxes their holes,[48] and the savages their wigwams, in modern civilized society not more than one half the families own a shelter. In the large towns and cities, where civilization especially prevails, the number of those who own a shelter is a very small fraction of the whole. The rest pay an annual tax for this outside garment of all, become indispensable summer and winter, which would buy a village of Indian wigwams, but now helps to keep them poor as long as they live. I do not mean to insist here on the disadvantage of hiring compared with owning, but it is evident that the savage owns his shelter because it costs so little, while the civilized man hires his commonly because he cannot afford to own it; nor can he, in the long run, any better afford to hire. But, answers one, by merely paying this tax the poor civilized man secures an abode which is a palace compared with the savage's. An annual rent of from twenty-five to a hundred dollars, these are the country rates, entitles him to the benefit of the improvements of centuries, spacious apartments, clean paint and paper, Rumford fireplace,[49] back plastering,[50]

---

[47] Daniel Gookin (1612–1687) wrote *Historical Collections of the Indians in New England.*
[48] Reference to Matthew 8:20.

[49] Smokeless stove invented by Count Rumford (1753–1814).
[50] Insulation.

Venetian blinds, copper pump, spring lock, a commodious cellar, and many other things. But how happens it that he who is said to enjoy these things is so commonly a *poor* civilized man, while the savage, who has them not, is rich as a savage? If it is asserted that civilization is a real advance in the condition of man,—and I think that it is, though only the wise improve their advantages,—it must be shown that it has produced better dwellings without making them more costly; and the cost of a thing is the amount of what I will call life which is required to be exchanged for it, immediately or in the long run. An average house in this neighborhood costs perhaps eight hundred dollars, and to lay up this sum will take from ten to fifteen years of the laborer's life, even if he is not encumbered with a family;—estimating the pecuniary value of every man's labor at one dollar a day, for if some receive more, others receive less;—so that he must have spent more than half his life commonly before *his* wigwam will be earned. If we suppose him to pay a rent instead, this is but a doubtful choice of evils. Would the savage have been wise to exchange his wigwam for a palace on these terms?

It may be guessed that I reduce almost the whole advantage of holding this superfluous property as a fund in store against the future, so far as the individual is concerned, mainly to the defraying of funeral expenses. But perhaps a man is not required to bury himself. Nevertheless this points to an important distinction be-tween the civilized man and the savage; and, no doubt, they have designs on us for our benefit, in making the life of a civilized people an *institution*, in which the life of the individual is to a great extent absorbed, in order to preserve and perfect that of the race. But I wish to show at what a sacrifice this advantage is at present obtained, and to suggest that we may possibly so live as to secure all the advantage without suffering any of the disadvantage. What mean ye by saying that the poor ye have always with you, or that the fathers have eaten sour grapes, and the chil-dren's teeth are set on edge?[51]

"As I live, saith the Lord God, ye shall not have occasion any more to use this proverb in Israel."

"Behold all souls are mine; as the soul of the father, so also the soul of the son is mine: the soul that sinneth it shall die."[52]

When I consider my neighbors, the farmers of Concord, who are at least as well off as the other classes, I find that for the most part they have been toiling twenty, thirty, or forty years, that they may become the real owners of their farms, which commonly they have inherited with encumbrances, or else bought with hired money, —and we may regard one third of that toil as the cost of their houses,—but commonly they have not paid for them yet. It is true, the encumbrances sometimes outweigh the value of the farm, so that the farm itself becomes one great encumbrance, and still a man is found to inherit it, being well acquainted with it, as he says. On applying to the assessors, I am surprised to learn that they cannot at once name a dozen in the town who own their farms free and clear. If you would know the history of these homesteads, inquire at the bank where they are mortgaged. The man who has actually paid for his farm with labor on it is so rare that every neighbor can point to him. I doubt if there are three such men in Concord. What has been said of the merchants, that a very large majority, even ninety-seven in a hundred, are sure to fail, is equally

---

51 Reference to John 12:8 and Ezekiel 18:2.   52 Ezekiel 18:3–4.

true of the farmers. With regard to the merchants, however, one of them says pertinently that a great part of their failures are not genuine pecuniary failures, but merely failures to fulfil their engagements, because it is inconvenient; that is, it is the moral character that breaks down. But this puts an infinitely worse face on the matter, and suggests, beside, that probably not even the other three succeed in saving their souls, but are perchance bankrupt in a worse sense than they who fail honestly. Bankruptcy and repudiation are the spring-boards from which much of our civilization vaults and turns its somersets, but the savage stands on the unelastic plank of famine. Yet the Middlesex Cattle Show[53] goes off here with *éclat* annually, as if all the joints of the agricultural machine were suent.[54]

The farmer is endeavoring to solve the problem of livelihood by a formula more complicated than the problem itself. To get his shoestrings he speculates in herds of cattle. With consummate skill he has set his trap with a hair spring to catch comfort and independence, and then, as he turned away, got his own leg into it. This is the reason he is poor; and for a similar reason we are all poor in respect to a thousand savage comforts, though surrounded by luxuries. As Chapman sings,—

"The false society of men—
—for earthly greatness
All heavenly comforts rarefies to air."[55]

And when the farmer has got his house, he may not be the richer but the poorer for it, and it be the house that has got him. As I understand it, that was a valid objection urged by Momus[56] against the house which Minerva[57] made, that she "had not made it movable, by which means a bad neighborhood might be avoided;" and it may still be urged, for our houses are such unwieldy property that we are often imprisoned rather than housed in them; and the bad neighborhood to be avoided is our own scurvy selves. I know one or two families, at least, in this town, who, for nearly a generation, have been wishing to sell their houses in the outskirts and move into the village, but have not been able to accomplish it, and only death will set them free.

Granted that the *majority* are able at last either to own or hire the modern house with all its improvements. While civilization has been improving our houses, it has not equally improved the men who are to inhabit them. It has created palaces, but it was not so easy to create noblemen and kings. And *if the civilized man's pursuits are no worthier than the savage's, if he is employed the greater part of his life in obtaining gross necessaries and comforts merely, why should he have a better dwelling than the former?*

But how do the poor *minority* fare? Perhaps it will be found, that just in proportion as some have been placed in outward circumstances above the savage, others have been degraded below him. The luxury of one class is counterbalanced by the indigence of another. On the one side is the palace, on the other are the almshouse and "silent poor."[58] The myriads who built the pyramids to be the tombs of the Pharaohs were fed on garlic, and it may be were not decently buried themselves. The mason who

---

[53] Annual agricultural fair held in Concord.
[54] Properly functioning.
[55] From *Caesar and Pompey* (1631), Act V, Sc. i, ll. 210, 212–213, by George Chapman, English poet, dramatist, and translator (1559?–1634).

[56] God of mockery in classic myth.
[57] Handicrafts was one of the skills for which the Greek goddess acted as patron.
[58] Those who conceal their poverty.

finishes the cornice of the palace returns at night perchance to a hut not so good as a wigwam. It is a mistake to suppose that, in a country where the usual evidences of civilization exist, the condition of a very large body of the inhabitants may not be as degraded as that of savages. I refer to the degraded poor, not now to the degraded rich. To know this I should not need to look farther than to the shanties which every where border our railroads, that last improvement in civilization; where I see in my daily walks human beings living in sties, and all winter with an open door, for the sake of light, without any visible, often imaginable, wood pile, and the forms of both old and young are permanently contracted by the long habit of shrinking from cold and misery, and the development of all their limbs and faculties is checked. It certainly is fair to look at that class by whose labor the works which distinguish this generation are accomplished. Such too, to a greater or less extent, is the condition of the operatives of every denomination in England, which is the great workhouse of the world. Or I could refer you to Ireland,[59] which is marked as one of the white or enlightened spots on the map. Contrast the physical condition of the Irish with that of the North American Indian, or the South Sea Islander, or any other savage race before it was degraded by contact with the civilized man. Yet I have no doubt that that people's rulers are as wise as the average of civilized rulers. Their condition only proves what squalidness may consist with civilization. I hardly need refer now to the laborers in our Southern States who produce the staple exports of this country, and are themselves a staple production of the South. But to confine myself to those who are said to be in *moderate* circumstances.

Most men appear never to have considered what a house is, and are actually though needlessly poor all their lives because they think that they must have such a one as their neighbors have. As if one were to wear any sort of coat which the tailor might cut out for him, or, gradually leaving off palmleaf hat or cap of woodchuck skin, complain of hard times because he could not afford to buy him a crown! It is possible to invent a house still more convenient and luxurious than we have, which yet all would admit that man could not afford to pay for. Shall we always study to obtain more of these things, and not sometimes to be content with less? Shall the respectable citizen thus gravely teach, by precept and example, the necessity of the young man's providing a certain number of superfluous glow-shoes,[60] and umbrellas, and empty guest chambers for empty guests, before he dies? Why should not our furniture be as simple as the Arab's or the Indian's? When I think of the benefactors of the race, whom we have apotheosized as messengers from heaven, bearers of divine gifts to man, I do not see in my mind any retinue at their heels, any car-load of fashionable furniture. Or what if I were to allow—would it not be a singular allowance?—that our furniture should be more complex than the Arab's, in proportion as we are morally and intellectually his superiors! At present our houses are cluttered and defiled with it, and a good housewife would sweep out the greater part into the dust hole, and not leave her morning's work undone. Morning work! By the blushes of Aurora[61] and the music of Memnon,[62] what should be man's *morning work* in this world? I had three pieces of limestone on my desk, but I was terrified to find that they required

---

[59] That is, Ireland in the grip of the potato famine of the 1840s.
[60] Overshoes.
[61] Goddess of dawn in classic myth.

[62] Gigantic statue of an ancient Egyptian king that emitted musical sounds when struck by the morning light.

to be dusted daily, when the furniture of my mind was all undusted still, and I threw them out the window in disgust. How, then, could I have a furnished house? I would rather sit in the open air, for no dust gathers on the grass, unless where man has broken ground.

It is the luxurious and dissipated who set the fashions which the herd so diligently follow. The traveller who stops at the best houses, so called, soon discovers this, for the publicans presume him to be a Sardanapalus,[63] and if he resigned himself to their tender mercies he would soon be completely emasculated. I think that in the railroad car we are inclined to spend more on luxury than on safety and convenience, and it threatens without attaining these to become no better than a modern drawing room, with its divans, and ottomans, and sunshades, and a hundred other oriental things, which we are taking west with us, invented for the ladies of the harem and the effeminate natives of the Celestial Empire, which Jonathan[64] should be ashamed to know the names of. I would rather sit on a pumpkin and have it all to myself, than be crowded on a velvet cushion. I would rather ride on earth in an ox cart with a free circulation, than go to heaven in the fancy car of an excursion train and breathe a *malaria* all the way.

The very simplicity and nakedness of man's life in the primitive ages imply this advantage at least, that they left him still but a sojourner in nature. When he was refreshed with food and sleep he contemplated his journey again. He dwelt, as it were, in a tent in this world, and was either threading the valleys, or crossing the plains, or climbing the mountain tops. But lo! men have become the tools of their tools. The man who independently plucked the fruits when he was hungry is become a farmer; and he who stood under a tree for shelter, a housekeeper. We now no longer camp as for a night, but have settled down on earth and forgotten heaven. We have adopted Christianity merely as an improved method of *agri-*culture. We have built for this world a family mansion, and for the next a family tomb. The best works of art are the expression of man's struggle to free himself from this condition, but the effect of our art is merely to make this low state comfortable and that higher state to be forgotten. There is actually no place in this village for a work of *fine* art, if any had come down to us, to stand, for our lives, our houses and streets, furnish no proper pedestal for it. There is not a nail to hang a picture on, nor a shelf to receive the bust of a hero or a saint. When I consider how our houses are built and paid for, or not paid for, and their internal economy managed and sustained, I wonder that the floor does not give way under the visitor while he is admiring the gewgaws upon the mantel-piece, and let him through into the cellar, to some solid and honest though earthy foundation. I cannot but perceive that this so called rich and refined life is a thing jumped at, and I do not get on in the enjoyment of the *fine* arts which adorn it, my attention being wholly occupied with the jump; for I remember that the greatest genuine leap, due to human muscles alone, on record, is that of certain wandering Arabs, who are said to have cleared twenty-five feet on level ground. Without factitious support, man is sure to come to earth again beyond that distance. The first question which I am tempted to put to the proprietor of such great impropriety is, Who bolsters you? Are you one of the ninety-seven who fail? or of the three who

[63] Ruler of Assyria, whose kingdom was destroyed [64] A Yankee or American.
in the ninth century B.C.; known for his
immorality and decadent behavior.

succeed? Answer me these questions, and then perhaps I may look at your bawbles and find them ornamental. The cart before the horse is neither beautiful nor useful. Before we can adorn our houses with beautiful objects the walls must be stripped, and our lives must be stripped, and beautiful housekeeping and beautiful living be laid for a foundation: now, a taste for the beautiful is most cultivated out of doors, where there is no house and no housekeeper.

Old Johnson,[65] in his "Wonder-Working Providence," speaking of the first settlers of this town, with whom he was contemporary, tells us that "they burrow themselves in the earth for their first shelter under some hillside, and, casting the soil aloft upon timber, they make a smoky fire against the earth, at the highest side." They did not "provide them houses," says he, "till the earth, by the Lord's blessing, brought forth bread to feed them," and the first year's crop was so light that "they were forced to cut their bread very thin for a long season." The secretary of the Province of New Netherland,[66] writing Dutch, in 1650, for the information of those who wished to take up land there, states more particularly, that "those in New Netherland, and especially in New England, who have no means to build farm houses at first according to their wishes, dig a square pit in the ground, cellar fashion, six or seven feet deep, as long and as broad as they think proper, case the earth inside with wood all round the wall, and line the wood with the bark of trees or something else to prevent the caving in of the earth; floor this cellar with plank, and wainscot it overhead for a ceiling, raise a roof of spars clear up, and cover the spars with bark or green sods, so that they can live dry and warm in these houses with their entire families for two, three, and four years, it being understood that partitions are run through those cellars which are adapted to the size of the family. The wealthy and principal men in New England, in the beginning of the colonies, commenced their first dwelling houses in this fashion for two reasons; firstly, in order not to waste time in building, and not to want food the next season; secondly, in order not to discourage poor laboring people whom they brought over in numbers from Fatherland. In the course of three or four years when the country became adapted to agriculture, they built themselves handsome houses, spending on them several thousands."

In this course which our ancestors took there was a show of prudence at least, as if their principle were to satisfy the more pressing wants first. But are the more pressing wants satisfied now? When I think of acquiring for myself one of our luxurious dwellings, I am deterred, for, so to speak, the country is not yet adapted to *human* culture, and we are still forced to cut our *spiritual* bread far thinner than our forefathers did their wheaten. Not that all architectural ornament is to be neglected even in the rudest periods; but let our houses first be lined with beauty, where they come in contact with our lives, like the tenement of the shellfish, and not overlaid with it. But, alas! I have been inside one or two of them, and know what they are lined with.

Though we are not so degenerate but that we might possibly live in a cave or a wigwam or wear skins today, it certainly is better to accept the advantages, though so dearly bought, which the invention and industry of mankind offer. In such a

---

[65] Edward Johnson (1598–1672), author of *Wonder-Working Providence of Sion's Saviour in New England* (1654), account of early Puritan settlement.

[66] Later the colony of New York. The quotation that follows is taken from *The Documentary History of the State of New York* (1951).

neighborhood as this, boards and shingles, lime and bricks, are cheaper and more easily obtained than suitable caves, or whole logs, or bark in sufficient quantities, or even well-tempered clay or flat stones. I speak understandingly on this subject, for I have made myself acquainted with it both theoretically and practically. With a little more wit we might use these materials so as to become richer than the richest now are, and make our civilization a blessing. The civilized man is a more experienced and wiser savage. But to make haste to my own experiment.

Near the end of March, 1845, I borrowed an axe and went down to the woods by Walden Pond, nearest to where I intended to build my house, and began to cut down some tall arrowy white pines, still in their youth, for timber. It is difficult to begin without borrowing, but perhaps it is the most generous course thus to permit your fellow-men to have an interest in your enterprise. The owner of the axe, as he released his hold on it, said that it was the apple of his eye; but I returned it sharper than I received it. It was a pleasant hillside where I worked, covered with pine woods, through which I looked out on the pond, and a small open field in the woods where pines and hickories were springing up. The ice in the pond was not yet dissolved, though there were some open spaces, and it was all dark colored and saturated with water. There were some slight flurries of snow during the days that I worked there; but for the most part when I came out on to the railroad, on my way home, its yellow sand heap stretched away gleaming in the hazy atmosphere, and the rails shone in the spring sun, and I heard the lark and pewee and other birds already come to commence another year with us. They were pleasant spring days, in which the winter of man's discontent[67] was thawing as well as the earth, and the life that had lain torpid began to stretch itself. One day, when my axe had come off and I had cut a green hickory for a wedge, driving it with a stone, and had placed the whole to soak in a pond hole in order to swell the wood, I saw a striped snake run into the water, and he lay on the bottom, apparently without inconvenience, as long as I staid there, or more than a quarter of an hour; perhaps because he had not yet fairly come out of the torpid state. It appeared to me that for a like reason men remain in their present low and primitive condition; but if they should feel the influence of the spring of springs arousing them, they would of necessity rise to a higher and more ethereal life. I had previously seen the snakes in frosty mornings in my path with portions of their bodies still numb and inflexible, waiting for the sun to thaw them. On the 1st of April it rained and melted the ice, and in the early part of the day, which was very foggy, I heard a stray goose groping about over the pond and cackling as if lost, or like the spirit of the fog.

So I went on for some days cutting and hewing timber, and also studs and rafters, all with my narrow axe, not having many communicable or scholar-like thoughts, singing to myself,—

Men say they know many things;
But lo! they have taken wings,—
The arts and sciences,
And a thousand appliances;

[67] Paraphrase from *Richard III*, Act I, Sc. i, l. 1,
Shakespeare's history play.

The wind that blows
Is all that any body knows.[68]

I hewed the main timbers six inches square, most of the studs on two sides only, and the rafters and floor timbers on one side, leaving the rest of the bark on, so that they were just as straight and much stronger than sawed ones. Each stick was carefully mortised or tenoned by its stump, for I had borrowed other tools by this time. My days in the woods were not very long ones; yet I usually carried my dinner of bread and butter, and read the newspaper in which it was wrapped, at noon, sitting amid the green pine boughs which I had cut off, and to my bread was imparted some of their fragrance, for my hands were covered with a thick coat of pitch. Before I had done I was more the friend than the foe of the pine tree, though I had cut down some of them, having become better acquainted with it. Sometimes a rambler in the wood was attracted by the sound of my axe, and we chatted pleasantly over the chips which I had made.

By the middle of April, for I made no haste in my work, but rather made the most of it, my house was framed and ready for the raising. I had already bought the shanty of James Collins, an Irishman who worked on the Fitchburg Railroad, for boards. James Collins' shanty was considered an uncommonly fine one. When I called to see it he was not at home. I walked about the outside, at first unobserved from within, the window was so deep and high. It was of small dimensions, with a peaked cottage roof, and not much else to be seen, the dirt being raised five feet all around as if it were a compost heap. The roof was the soundest part, though a good deal warped and made brittle by the sun. Door-sill there was none, but a perennial passage for the hens under the door board. Mrs. C. came to the door and asked me to view it from the inside. The hens were driven in by my approach. It was dark, and had a dirt floor for the most part, dank, clammy, and aguish, only here a board and there a board which would not bear removal. She lighted a lamp to show me the inside of the roof and the walls, and also that the board floor extended under the bed, warning me not to step into the cellar, a sort of dust hole two feet deep. In her own words, they were "good boards overhead, good boards all around, and a good window,"—of two whole squares originally, only the cat had passed out that way lately. There was a stove, a bed, and a place to sit, an infant in the house where it was born, a silk parasol, gilt-framed looking-glass, and a patent new coffee mill nailed to an oak sapling, all told. The bargain was soon concluded, for James had in the mean while returned. I to pay four dollars and twenty-five cents to-night, he to vacate at five tomorrow morning, selling to nobody else meanwhile: I to take possession at six. It were well, he said, to be there early, and anticipate certain indistinct but wholly unjust claims on the score of ground rent and fuel. This he assured me was the only encumbrance. At six I passed him and his family on the road. One large bundle held their all,—bed, coffee-mill, looking-glass, hens,—all but the cat, she took to the woods and became a wild cat, and, as I learned afterward, trod in a trap set for woodchucks, and so became a dead cat at last.

I took down this dwelling the same morning, drawing the nails, and removed it to the pond side by small cartloads, spreading the boards on the grass there to bleach

[68] Thoreau's own verses.

and warp back again in the sun. One early thrush gave me a note or two as I drove along the woodland path. I was informed treacherously by a young Patrick[69] that neighbor Seeley, an Irishman, in the intervals of the carting, transferred the still tolerable, straight, and drivable nails, staples, and spikes to his pocket, and then stood when I came back to pass the time of day, and look freshly up, unconcerned, with spring thoughts, at the devastation; there being a dearth of work, as he said. He was there to represent spectatordom, and help make this seemingly insignificant event one with the removal of the gods of Troy.[70]

I dug my cellar in the side of a hill sloping to the south, where a woodchuck had formerly dug his burrow, down through sumach and blackberry roots, and the lowest stain of vegetation, six feet square by seven deep, to a fine sand where potatoes would not freeze in any winter. The sides were left shelving, and not stoned; but the sun having never shone on them, the sand still keeps its place. It was but two hours' work. I took particular pleasure in this breaking of ground, for in almost all latitudes men dig into the earth for an equable temperature. Under the most splendid house in the city is still to be found the cellar where they store their roots as of old, and long after the superstructure has disappeared posterity remark its dent in the earth. The house is still but a sort of porch at the entrance of a burrow.

At length, in the beginning of May, with the help of some of my acquaintances, rather to improve so good an occasion for neighborliness than from any necessity, I set up the frame of my house. No man was ever more honored in the character of his raisers than I. They are destined, I trust, to assist at the raising of loftier structures one day. I began to occupy my house on the 4th of July, as soon as it was boarded and roofed, for the boards were carefully feather-edged and lapped, so that it was perfectly impervious to rain; but before boarding I laid the foundation of a chimney at one end, bringing two cartloads of stones up the hill from the pond in my arms. I built the chimney after my hoeing in the fall, before a fire became necessary for warmth, doing my cooking in the mean while out of doors on the ground, early in the morning: which mode I still think is in some respects more convenient and agreeable than the usual one. When it stormed before my bread was baked, I fixed a few boards over the fire, and sat under them to watch my loaf, and passed some pleasant hours in that way. In those days, when my hands were much employed, I read but little, but the least scraps of paper which lay on the ground, my holder, or tablecloth, afforded me as much entertainment, in fact answered the same purpose as the Iliad.[71]

It would be worth the while to build still more deliberately than I did, considering, for instance, what foundation a door, a window, a cellar, a garret, have in the nature of man, and perchance never raising any superstructure until we found a better reason for it than our temporal necessities even. There is some of the same fitness in a man's building his own house that there is in a bird's building its own nest. Who knows but if men constructed their dwellings with their own hands, and provided food for

---

[69] Irishman.
[70] In Greek legend, Troy was safe as long as the statue of the goddess Pallas Athena remained in her temple; during the Trojan War the Greeks stole the statue, supposedly making their later victory possible.
[71] Homer's epic poem about the fall of Troy.

themselves and families simply and honestly enough, the poetic faculty would be universally developed, as birds universally sing when they are so engaged? But alas! we do like cowbirds and cuckoos, which lay their eggs in nests which other birds have built, and cheer no traveller with their chattering and unmusical notes. Shall we forever resign the pleasure of construction to the carpenter? What does architecture amount to in the experience of the mass of men? I never in all my walks came across a man engaged in so simple and natural an occupation as building his house. We belong to the community. It is not the tailor alone who is the ninth part of a man;[72] it is as much the preacher, and the merchant, and the farmer. Where is this division of labor to end? and what object does it finally serve? No doubt another *may* also think for me; but it is not therefore desirable that he should do so to the exclusion of my thinking for myself.

True, there are architects so called in this country, and I have heard of one at least possessed with the idea of making architectural ornaments have a core of truth, a necessity, and hence a beauty, as if it were a revelation to him. All very well perhaps from his point of view, but only a little better than the common dilettantism. A sentimental reformer in architecture, he began at the cornice, not at the foundation. It was only how to put a core of truth within the ornaments, that every sugar plum in fact might have an almond or caraway seed in it,—though I hold that almonds are most wholesome without the sugar,—and not how the inhabitant, the indweller, might build truly within and without, and let the ornaments take care of themselves. What reasonable man ever supposed that ornaments were something outward and in the skin merely,—that the tortoise got his spotted shell, or the shellfish its mother-o'-pearl tints, by such a contract as the inhabitants of Broadway their Trinity Church?[73] But a man has no more to do with the style of architecture of his house than a tortoise with that of its shell: nor need the soldier be so idle as to try to paint the precise *color* of his virtue on his standard. The enemy will find it out. He may turn pale when the trial comes. This man seemed to me to lean over the cornice and timidly whisper his half truth to the rude occupants who really knew it better than he. What of architectural beauty I now see, I know has gradually grown from within outward, out of the necessities and character of the indweller, who is the only builder,—out of some unconscious truthfulness, and nobleness, without ever a thought for the appearance; and whatever additional beauty of this kind is destined to be produced will be preceded by a like unconscious beauty of life. The most interesting dwellings in this country, as the painter knows, are the most unpretending, humble log huts and cottages of the poor commonly; it is the life of the inhabitants whose shells they are, and not any peculiarity in their surfaces merely, which makes them *picturesque;* and equally interesting will be the citizen's suburban box, when his life shall be as simple and as agreeable to the imagination, and there is as little straining after effect in the style of his dwelling. A great proportion of architectural ornaments are literally hollow, and a September gale would strip them off, like borrowed plumes, without injury to the substantials. They can do without *architecture* who have no olives nor wines in the cellar. What if an equal ado were made about the ornaments of style

---

[72] According to the old saying, which recognizes that those who make our clothes contribute to our being.

[73] Ornate Gothic-style church built in New York City (1839–1846).

in literature, and the architects of our bibles spent as much time about their cornices as the architects of our churches do? So are made the *belles-lettres* and the *beaux-arts* and their professors. Much it concerns a man, forsooth, how a few sticks are slanted over him or under him, and what colors are daubed upon his box. It would signify somewhat, if, in any earnest sense, *he* slanted them and daubed it; but the spirit having departed out of the tenant, it is of a piece with constructing his own coffin,—the architecture of the grave, and "carpenter" is but another name for "coffin-maker." One man says, in his despair or indifference to life, take up a handful of the earth at your feet, and paint your house that color. Is he thinking of his last and narrow house?[74] Toss up a copper[75] for it as well. What an abundance of leisure he must have! Why do you take up a handful of dirt? Better paint your house your own complexion; let it turn pale or blush for you. An enterprise to improve the style of cottage architecture! When you have got my ornaments ready I will wear them.

Before winter I built a chimney, and shingled the sides of my house, which were already impervious to rain, with imperfect and sappy shingles made of the first slice of the log, whose edges I was obliged to straighten with a plane.

I have thus a tight shingled and plastered house, ten feet wide by fifteen long, and eight-feet posts, with a garret and a closet, a large window on each side, two trap doors, one door at the end, and a brick fireplace opposite. The exact cost of my house, paying the usual price for such materials as I used, but not counting the work, all of which was done by myself, was as follows; and I give the details because very few are able to tell exactly what their houses cost, and fewer still, if any, the separate cost of the various materials which compose them:—

Boards,	$8 03 1/2,	mostly shanty boards.
Refuse shingles for roof and sides,	4 00	
Laths,	1 25	
Two second-hand windows with glass,	2 43	
One thousand old brick,	4 00	
Two casks of lime,	2 40	That was high.
Hair,	0 31	More than I needed.
Mantle-tree iron,	0 15	
Nails,	3 90	
Hinges and screws,	0 14	
Latch,	0 10	
Chalk,	0 01	
Transportation,	1 40	I carried a good part on my back.
In all,	$28 12 1/2	

[74] I.e., coffin.
[75] Coin used in payment to Charon, who ferried the dead across the river Styx in classic myth.

These are all the materials excepting the timber stones and sand, which I claimed by squatter's right. I have also a small wood-shed adjoining, made chiefly of the stuff which was left after building the house.

I intend to build me a house which will surpass any on the main street in Concord in grandeur and luxury, as soon as it pleases me as much and will cost me no more than my present one.

I thus found that the student who wishes for a shelter can obtain one for a lifetime at an expense not greater than the rent which he now pays annually. If I seem to boast more than is becoming, my excuse is that I brag for humanity rather than for myself; and my shortcomings and inconsistencies do not affect the truth of my statement. Notwithstanding much cant and hypocrisy,—chaff which I find it difficult to separate from my wheat, but for which I am as sorry as any man,—I will breathe freely and stretch myself in this respect, it is such a relief to both the moral and physical system; and I am resolved that I will not through humility become the devil's attorney.[76] I will endeavor to speak a good word for the truth. At Cambridge College[77] the mere rent of a student's room, which is only a little larger than my own, is thirty dollars each year, though the corporation had the advantage of building thirty-two side by side and under one roof, and the occupant suffers the inconvenience of many and noisy neighbors, and perhaps a residence in the fourth story. I cannot but think that if we had more true wisdom in these respects, not only less education would be needed, because, forsooth, more would already have been acquired, but the pecuniary expense of getting an education would in a great measure vanish. Those conveniences which the student requires at Cambridge or elsewhere cost him or somebody else ten times as great a sacrifice of life as they would with proper management on both sides. Those things for which the most money is demanded are never the things which the student most wants. Tuition, for instance, is an important item in the term bill, while for the far more valuable education which he gets by associating with the most cultivated of his contemporaries no charge is made. The mode of founding a college is, commonly, to get up a subscription of dollars and cents, and then following blindly the principles of a division of labor to its extreme, a principle which should never be followed but with circumspection,—to call in a contractor who makes this a subject of speculation, and he employs Irishmen or other operatives actually to lay the foundations, while the students that are to be are said to be fitting themselves for it; and for these oversights successive generations have to pay. I think that it would be *better than this,* for the students, or those who desire to be benefited by it, even to lay the foundation themselves. The student who secures his coveted leisure and retirement by systematically shirking any labor necessary to man obtains but an ignoble and unprofitable leisure, defrauding himself of the experience which alone can make leisure fruitful. "But," says one, "you do not mean that the students should go to work with their hands instead of their heads?" I do not mean that exactly, but I mean something which he might think a good deal like that; I mean that they should not *play* life, or *study* it merely, while the community supports them at this expensive game, but earnestly *live* it from beginning to end. How could youths better learn to

[76] Official appointed to Roman Catholic courts to probe any weaknesses in the cases of persons put forward for sainthood.

[77] Harvard College; Thoreau was a graduate in 1837.

live than by at once trying the experiment of living? Methinks this would exercise their minds as much as mathematics. If I wished a boy to know something about the arts and sciences, for instance, I would not pursue the common course, which is merely to send him into the neighborhood of some professor, where any thing is professed and practised but the art of life;—to survey the world through a telescope or a microscope, and never with his natural eye; to study chemistry, and not learn how his bread is made, or mechanics, and not learn how it is earned; to discover new satellites to Neptune, and not detect the motes in his eyes, or to what vagabond he is a satellite himself; or to be devoured by the monsters that swarm all around him, while contemplating the monsters in a drop of vinegar. Which would have advanced the most at the end of a month,—the boy who had made his own jack-knife from the ore which he had dug and smelted, reading as much as would be necessary for this,—or the boy who had attended the lectures on metallurgy at the Institute in the mean while, and had received a Rodgers' penknife[78] from his father? Which would be most likely to cut his fingers?—To my astonishment I was informed on leaving college that I had studied navigation!—why, if I had taken one turn down the harbor I should have known more about it. Even the *poor* student studies and is taught only *political* economy, while that economy of living which is synonymous with philosophy is not even sincerely professed in our colleges. The consequence is, that while he is reading Adam Smith, Ricardo, and Say,[79] he runs his father in debt irretrievably.

As with our colleges, so with a hundred "modern improvements"; there is an illusion about them; there is not always a positive advance. The devil goes on exacting compound interest to the last for his early share and numerous succeeding investments in them. Our inventions are wont to be pretty toys, which distract our attention from serious things. They are but improved means to an unimproved end, an end which it was already but too easy to arrive at; as railroads lead to Boston or New York. We are in great haste to construct a magnetic telegraph from Maine to Texas; but Maine and Texas, it may be, have nothing important to communicate. Either is in such a predicament as the man who was earnest to be introduced to a distinguished deaf woman, but when he was presented, and one end of her ear trumpet was put into his hand, had nothing to say. As if the main object were to talk fast and not to talk sensibly. We are eager to tunnel under the Atlantic and bring the old world some weeks nearer to the new; but perchance the first news that will leak through into the broad, flapping American ear will be that the Princess Adelaide[80] has the whooping cough. After all, the man whose horse trots a mile in a minute does not carry the most important messages; he is not an evangelist, nor does he come round eating locusts and wild honey.[81] I doubt if Flying Childers[82] ever carried a peck of corn to mill.

One says to me, "I wonder that you do not lay up money; you love to travel; you might take the cars and go to Fitchburg[83] to-day and see the country." But I

---

[78] Made by Joseph Rodgers, cutlery maker from Sheffield, England.

[79] Adam Smith, David Ricardo, and Jean Baptiste Léon Say, eighteenth-century economists.

[80] Sister of Louis-Phillipe, king of France, she lived 1771–1847.

[81] What sustained John the Baptist while living in the wilderness (Matthew 3:4).

[82] Well-known racehorse of the eighteenth century.

[83] Small town near Concord; end of the railroad line that passed by Walden Pond.

am wiser than that. I have learned that the swiftest traveller is he that goes afoot. I say to my friend, Suppose we try who will get there first. The distance is thirty miles; the fare ninety cents. That is almost a day's wages. I remember when wages were sixty cents a day for laborers on this very road. Well, I start now on foot, and get there before night; I have travelled at that rate by the week together. You will in the mean while have earned your fare, and arrive there some time to-morrow, or possibly this evening, if you are lucky enough to get a job in season. Instead of going to Fitchburg, you will be working here the greater part of the day. And so, if the railroad reached round the world, I think that I should keep ahead of you; and as for seeing the country and getting experience of that kind, I should have to cut your acquaintance altogether.

Such is the universal law, which no man can ever outwit, and with regard to the railroad even we may say it is as broad as it is long. To make a railroad round the world available to all mankind is equivalent to grading the whole surface of the planet. Men have an indistinct notion that if they keep up this activity of joint stocks and spades long enough all will at length ride somewhere, in next to no time, and for nothing; but though a crowd rushes to the depot, and the conductor shouts "All aboard!" when the smoke is blown away and the vapor condensed, it will be perceived that a few are riding, but the rest are run over,—and it will be called, and will be, "A melancholy accident." No doubt they can ride at last who shall have earned their fare, that is, if they survive so long, but they will probably have lost their elasticity and desire to travel by that time. This spending of the best part of one's life earning money in order to enjoy a questionable liberty during the least valuable part of it, reminds me of the Englishman who went to India to make a fortune first, in order that he might return to England and live the life of a poet. He should have gone up garret at once. "What!" exclaim a million Irishmen starting up from all the shanties in the land, "is not this railroad which we have built a good thing?" Yes, I answer, *comparatively* good, that is, you might have done worse; but I wish, as you are brothers of mine, that you could have spent your time better than digging in this dirt.

Before I finished my house, wishing to earn ten or twelve dollars by some honest and agreeable method, in order to meet my unusual expenses, I planted about two acres and a half of light and sandy soil near it chiefly with beans, but also a small part with potatoes, corn, peas, and turnips. The whole lot contains eleven acres, mostly growing up to pines and hickories, and was sold the preceding season for eight dollars and eight cents an acre. One farmer said that it was "good for nothing but to raise cheeping squirrels on." I put no manure on this land, not being the owner, but merely a squatter, and not expecting to cultivate so much again, and I did not quite hoe it all once. I got out several cords of stumps in ploughing, which supplied me with fuel for a long time, and left small circles of virgin mould, easily distinguishable through the summer by the greater luxuriance of the beans there. The dead and for the most part unmerchantable wood behind my house, and the driftwood from the pond, have supplied the remainder of my fuel. I was obliged to hire a team and a man for the ploughing, though I held the plough myself. My farm outgoes for the first season were, for implements, seed, work, &c., $14 72 1/2. The seed corn was given me. This never costs any thing to speak of, unless you plant more than enough. I got twelve bushels of beans, and eighteen bushels of potatoes, beside some peas and sweet corn. The yellow corn and turnips were too late to come to any thing. My whole income from the farm was

$23 44.

Deducting the outgoes, ... 14 72 1/2

there are left, ... $ 8 71 1/2,

beside produce consumed and on hand at the time this estimate was made of the value of $4 50,—the amount on hand much more than balancing a little grass which I did not raise. All things considered, that is, considering the importance of a man's soul and of to-day, notwithstanding the short time occupied by my experiment, nay, partly even because of its transient character, I believe that that was doing better than any farmer in Concord did that year.

The next year I did better still, for I spaded up all the land which I required, about a third of an acre, and I learned from the experience of both years, not being in the least awed by many celebrated works on husbandry, Arthur Young[84] among the rest, that if one would live simply and eat only the crop which he raised, and raise no more than he ate, and not exchange it for an insufficient quantity of more luxurious and expensive things, he would need to cultivate only a few rods of ground, and that it would be cheaper to spade up that than to use oxen to plough it, and to select a fresh spot from time to time than to manure the old, and he could do all his necessary farm work as it were with his left hand at odd hours in the summer; and thus he would not be tied to an ox, or horse, or cow, or pig, as at present. I desire to speak impartially on this point, and as one not interested in the success or failure of the present economical and social arrangements. I was more independent than any farmer in Concord, for I was not anchored to a house or farm, but could follow the bent of my genius, which is a very crooked one, every moment. Beside being better off than they already, if my house had been burned or my crops had failed, I should have been nearly as well off as before.

I am wont to think that men are not so much the keepers of herds as herds are the keepers of the men, the former are so much the freer. Men and oxen exchange work; but if we consider necessary work only, the oxen will be seen to have greatly the advantage, their farm is so much the larger. Man does some of his part of the exchange work in his six weeks of haying, and it is no boy's play. Certainly no nation that lived simply in all respects, that is, no nation of philosophers, would commit so great a blunder as to use the labor of animals. True, there never was and is not likely soon to be a nation of philosophers, nor am I certain it is desirable that there should be. However, *I* should never have broken a horse or bull and taken him to board for any work he might do for me, for fear I should become a horse-man or a herds-man merely; and if society seems to be the gainer by so doing, are we certain that what is one man's gain is not another's loss, and that the stable-boy has equal cause with his master to be satisfied? Granted that some public works would not have been constructed without this aid, and let man share the glory of such with the ox and horse;

[84] English author (1741–1820) of works on husbandry.

does it follow that he could not have accomplished works yet more worthy of himself in that case? When men begin to do, not merely unnecessary or artistic, but luxurious and idle work, with their assistance, it is inevitable that a few do all the exchange work with the oxen, or, in other words, become the slaves of the strongest. Man thus not only works for the animal within him, but, for a symbol of this, he works for the animal without him. Though we have many substantial houses of brick or stone, the prosperity of the farmer is still measured by the degree to which the barn overshadows the house. This town is said to have the largest houses for oxen cows and horses hereabouts, and it is not behindhand in its public buildings; but there are very few halls for free worship or free speech in this county. It should not be by their architecture, but why not even by their power of abstract thought, that nations should seek to commemorate themselves? How much more admirable the Bhagvat-Geeta[85] than all the ruins of the East! Towers and temples are the luxury of princes. A simple and independent mind does not toil at the bidding of any prince. Genius is not a retainer to any emperor, nor is its material silver, or gold, or marble, except to a trifling extent. To what end, pray, is so much stone hammered? In Arcadia,[86] when I was there, I did not see any hammering stone. Nations are possessed with an insane ambition to perpetuate the memory of themselves by the amount of hammered stone they leave. What if equal pains were taken to smooth and polish their manners? One piece of good sense would be more memorable than a monument as high as the moon. I love better to see stones in place. The grandeur of Thebes was a vulgar grandeur. More sensible is a rod of stone wall that bounds an honest man's field than a hundred-gated Thebes[87] that has wandered farther from the true end of life. The religion and civilization which are barbaric and heathenish build splendid temples; but what you might call Christianity does not. Most of the stone a nation hammers goes toward its tomb only. It buries itself alive. As for the Pyramids, there is nothing to wonder at in them so much as the fact that so many men could be found degraded enough to spend their lives constructing a tomb for some ambitious booby, whom it would have been wiser and manlier to have drowned in the Nile, and then given his body to the dogs. I might possibly invent some excuse for them and him, but I have no time for it. As for the religion and love of art of the builders, it is much the same all the world over, whether the building be an Egyptian temple or the United States Bank. It costs more than it comes to. The mainspring is vanity, assisted by the love of garlic and bread and butter. Mr. Balcom, a promising young architect, designs it on the back of his Vitruvius,[88] with hard pencil and ruler, and the job is let out to Dobson & Sons, stonecutters. When the thirty centuries begin to look down on it, mankind begin to look up at it. As for your high towers and monuments, there was a crazy fellow once in this town who undertook to dig through to China, and he got so far that, as he said, he heard the Chinese pots and kettles rattle; but I think that I shall not go out of my way to admire the hole which he made. Many are concerned about the monuments of the West and the East,—to know who built them.

---

[85] A sacred text of the Hindus, the *Bhagavad Gita.*
[86] Region in Greek myth where men supposedly lived in pastoral happiness. (Thoreau visited it only by means of his imagination.)
[87] City in ancient Egypt whose walls had 100 gates.
[88] Roman writings on architecture by Vitruvius (first century B.C.).

For my part, I should like to know who in those days did not build them,—who were above such trifling. But to proceed with my statistics.

By surveying, carpentry, and day-labor of various other kinds in the village in the mean while, for I have as many trades as fingers, I had earned $13 34. The expense of food for eight months, namely, from July 4th to March 1st, the time when these estimates were made, though I lived there more than two years,—not counting potatoes, a little green corn, and some peas, which I had raised, nor considering the value of what was on hand at the last date, was

Rice, ...	$1 73 1/2	
Molasses, ...	1 73	Cheapest form of the saccharine.
Rye meal, ...	1 04 3/4	
Indian meal, ...	0 99 3/4	Cheaper than rye.
Pork, ...	0 22	
Flour	0 88	} Costs more than Indian meal, both money and trouble.
Sugar, ...	0 80	
Lard, ...	0 65	
Apples, ...	0 25	
Dried apple, ...	0 22	
Sweet potatoes, ...	0 10	
One pumpkin, ...	0 6	
One watermelon, ...	0 2	
Salt, ...	0 3	

All experiments which failed.

Yes, I did eat $8 74, all told; but I should not thus unblushingly publish my guilt, if I did not know that most of my readers were equally guilty with myself, and that their deeds would look no better in print. The next year I sometimes caught a mess of fish for my dinner, and once I went so far as to slaughter a woodchuck which ravaged my bean-field,—effect his transmigration, as a Tartar[89] would say,—and devour him, partly for experiment's sake; but though it afforded me a momentary enjoyment, notwithstanding a musky flavor, I saw that the longest use would not make that a good practice, however it might seem to have your woodchucks ready dressed by the village butcher.

Clothing and some incidental expenses within the same dates, though little can be inferred from this item, amounted to

$8 40 3/4

Oil and some household utensils, ... 2 00

So that all the pecuniary outgoes, excepting for washing and mending, which for the most part were done out of the house, and their bills have not yet been received,

---

[89] Native of Russian Asia; the Tartars held that after death their souls passed into other bodies.

—and these are all and more than all the ways by which money necessarily goes out in this part of the world,—were

House, ...	$28 12½
Farm one year, ...	14 72½
Food eight months, ...	8 74
Clothing, &c., eight months, ...	8 40¾
Oil, &c., eight months, ...	2 00
In all, ...	$61 99¾

I address myself now to those of my readers who have a living to get. And to meet this I have for farm produce sold

	$23 44
Earned by day-labor, ...	13 34
In all, ...	$36 78,

which subtracted from the sum of the outgoes leaves a balance of $25 21 3/4 on the one side,—this being very nearly the means with which I started, and the measure of expenses to be incurred,—and on the other, beside the leisure and independence and health thus secured, a comfortable house for me as long as I choose to occupy it.

These statistics, however accidental and therefore uninstructive they may appear, as they have a certain completeness, have a certain value also. Nothing was given me of which I have not rendered some account. It appears from the above estimate, that my food alone cost me in money about twenty-seven cents a week. It was, for nearly two years after this, rye and Indian meal without yeast, potatoes, rice, a very little salt pork, molasses, and salt, and my drink water. It was fit that I should live on rice, mainly, who loved so well the philosophy of India. To meet the objections of some inveterate cavillers, I may as well state, that if I dined out occasionally, as I always had done, and I trust shall have opportunities to do again, it was frequently to the detriment of my domestic arrangements. But the dining out, being, as I have stated, a constant element, does not in the least affect a comparative statement like this.

I learned from my two years' experience that it would cost incredibly little trouble to obtain one's necessary food, even in this latitude; that a man may use as simple a diet as the animals, and yet retain health and strength. I have made a satisfactory dinner, satisfactory on several accounts, simply off a dish of purslane *(Portulaca oleracea)* which I gathered in my cornfield, boiled and salted. I give the Latin on account of the savoriness of the trivial name. And pray what more can a reasonable man desire, in peaceful times, in ordinary noons, than a sufficient number of ears of green sweet-corn boiled, with the addition of salt? Even the little variety which I used was a yielding to the demands of appetite, and not of health. Yet men have come to such a pass that they frequently starve, not for want of necessaries, but for want of luxuries; and I know a good woman who thinks that her son lost his life because he took to drinking water only.

The reader will perceive that I am treating the subject rather from an economic than a dietetic point of view, and he will not venture to put my abstemiousness to the test unless he has a well-stocked larder.

Bread I at first made of pure Indian meal and salt, genuine hoe-cakes, which I baked before my fire out of doors on a shingle or the end of a stick of timber sawed off in building my house; but it was wont to get smoked and to have a piny flavor. I tried flour also; but have at last found a mixture of rye and Indian meal most convenient and agreeable. In cold weather it was no little amusement to bake several small loaves of this in succession, tending and turning them as carefully as an Egyptian his hatching eggs. They were a real cereal fruit which I ripened, and they had to my senses a fragrance like that of other noble fruits, which I kept in as long as possible by wrapping them in cloths. I made a study of the ancient and indispensable art of bread-making, consulting such authorities as offered, going back to the primitive days and first invention of the unleavened kind, when from the wildness of nuts and meats men first reached the mildness and refinement of this diet, and travelling gradually down in my studies through that accidental souring of the dough which, it is supposed, taught the leavening process, and through the various fermentations thereafter, till I came to "good, sweet, wholesome bread," the staff of life. Leaven, which some deem the soul of bread, the *spiritus*[90] which fills its cellular tissue, which is religiously preserved like the vestal fire,[91]—some precious bottle-full, I suppose, first brought over in the May-flower, did the business for America, and its influence is still rising, swelling, spreading, in cerealian[92] billows over the land,—this seed I regularly and faithfully procured from the village, till at length one morning I forgot the rules, and scalded my yeast; by which accident I discovered that even this was not indispensable, —for my discoveries were not by the synthetic but analytic process,—and I have gladly omitted it since, though most housewives earnestly assured me that safe and wholesome bread without yeast might not be, and elderly people prophesied a speedy decay of the vital forces. Yet I find it not to be an essential ingredient, and after going without it for a year am still in the land of the living; and I am glad to escape the trivialness of carrying a bottle-full in my pocket, which would sometimes pop and discharge its contents to my discomfiture. It is simpler and more respectable to omit it. Man is an animal who more than any other can adapt himself to all climates and circumstances. Neither did I put any sal soda, or other acid or alkali, into my bread. It would seem that I made it according to the recipe which Marcus Porcius Cato[93] gave about two centuries before Christ. "Panem depsticium sic facito. Manus mortari-umque bene lavato. Farinam in mortarium indito, aquæ paulatim addito, subigitoque pulchre. Ubi bene subegeris, defingito, coquitoque sub testu." Which I take to mean —"Make kneaded bread thus. Wash your hands and trough well. Put the meal into the trough, add water gradually, and knead it thoroughly. When you have kneaded it well, mould it, and bake it under a cover," that is, in a baking-kettle. Not a word about leaven. But I did not always use this staff of life. At one time, owing to the emptiness of my purse, I saw none of it for more than a month.

---

[90] Latin: "breath of life."
[91] Sacred flame of the ancient Romans.
[92] Wordplay in reference to *cerulean,* the color blue.

[93] Roman statesman (234–149 B.C.), from whose *De Agricultura* the recipe is taken.

Every New Englander might easily raise all his own breadstuffs in this land of rye and Indian corn, and not depend on distant and fluctuating markets for them. Yet so far are we from simplicity and independence that, in Concord, fresh and sweet meal is rarely sold in the shops, and hominy and corn in a still coarser form are hardly used by any. For the most part the farmer gives to his cattle and hogs the grain of his own producing, and buys flour, which is at least no more wholesome, at a greater cost, at the store. I saw that I could easily raise my bushel or two of rye and Indian corn, for the former will grow on the poorest land, and the latter does not require the best, and grind them in a hand-mill, and so do without rice and pork; and if I must have some concentrated sweet, I found by experiment that I could make a very good molasses either of pumpkins or beets, and I knew that I needed only to set out a few maples to obtain it more easily still, and while these were growing I could use various substitutes beside those which I have named, "For," as the Forefathers sang,—

> "we can make liquor to sweeten our lips
> Of pumpkins and parsnips and walnut-tree chips."

Finally, as for salt, that grossest of groceries, to obtain this might be a fit occasion for a visit to the seashore, or, if I did without it altogether, I should probably drink the less water. I do not learn that the Indians ever troubled themselves to go after it.

Thus I could avoid all trade and barter, so far as my food was concerned, and having a shelter already, it would only remain to get clothing and fuel. The pantaloons which I now wear were woven in a farmer's family,—thank Heaven there is so much virtue still in man; for I think the fall from the farmer to the operative as great and memorable as that from the man to the farmer;—and in a new country fuel is an encumbrance. As for a habitat, if I were not permitted still to squat, I might purchase one acre at the same price for which the land I cultivated was sold—namely, eight dollars and eight cents. But as it was, I considered that I enhanced the value of the land by squatting on it.

There is a certain class of unbelievers who sometimes ask me such questions as, if I think that I can live on vegetable food alone; and to strike at the root of the matter at once,—for the root is faith,—I am accustomed to answer such, that I can live on board nails. If they cannot understand that, they cannot understand much that I have to say. For my part, I am glad to hear of experiments of this kind being tried; as that a young man tried for a fortnight to live on hard, raw corn on the ear, using his teeth for all mortar. The squirrel tribe tried the same and succeeded. The human race is interested in these experiments, though a few old women who are incapacitated for them, or who own their thirds in mills,[94] may be alarmed.

My furniture, part of which I made myself, and the rest cost me nothing of which I have not rendered an account, consisted of a bed, a table, a desk, three chairs, a looking-glass three inches in diameter, a pair of tongs and andirons, a kettle, a skillet, and a frying-pan, a dipper, a wash-bowl, two knives and forks, three plates, one cup,

---

[94] Toothless old women or those who own the traditional third of the estate left them upon their husbands' deaths and have invested in mills that do their grinding for them.

one spoon, a jug for oil, a jug for molasses, and a japanned lamp. None is so poor that he need sit on a pumpkin. That is shiftlessness. There is a plenty of such chairs as I like best in the village garrets to be had for taking them away. Furniture! Thank God, I can sit and I can stand without the aid of a furniture warehouse. What man but a philosopher would not be ashamed to see his furniture packed in a cart and going up country exposed to the light of heaven and the eyes of men, a beggarly account of empty boxes? That is Spaulding's furniture. I could never tell from inspecting such a load whether it belonged to a so called rich man or a poor one; the owner always seemed poverty-stricken. Indeed, the more you have of such things the poorer you are. Each load looks as if it contained the contents of a dozen shanties; and if one shanty is poor, this is a dozen times as poor. Pray, for what do we *move* ever but to get rid of our furniture, our *exuviæ;*[95] at last to go from this world to another newly furnished, and leave this to be burned? It is the same as if all these traps were buckled to a man's belt, and he could not move over the rough country where our lines are cast without dragging them,—dragging his trap. He was a lucky fox that left his tail in the trap. The muskrat will gnaw his third leg off to be free. No wonder man has lost his elasticity. How often he is at a dead set![96] "Sir, if I may be so bold, what do you mean by a dead set?" If you are a seer, whenever you meet a man you will see all that he owns, ay, and much that he pretends to disown, behind him, even to his kitchen furniture and all the trumpery which he saves and will not burn, and he will appear to be harnessed to it and making what headway he can. I think that the man is at a dead set who has got through a knot hole or gateway where his sledge load of furniture cannot follow him. I cannot but feel compassion when I hear some trig,[97] compact-looking man, seemingly free, all girded and ready, speak of his "furniture," as whether it is insured or not. "But what shall I do with my furniture?" My gay butterfly is entangled in a spider's web then. Even those who seem for a long while not to have any, if you inquire more narrowly you will find have some stored in somebody's barn. I look upon England to-day as an old gentleman who is travelling with a great deal of baggage, trumpery which has accumulated from long housekeeping, which he has not the courage to burn; great trunk, little trunk, bandbox and bundle. Throw away the first three at least. It would surpass the powers of a well man nowadays to take up his bed and walk, and I should certainly advise a sick one to lay down his bed and run. When I have met an immigrant tottering under a bundle which contained his all,—looking like an enormous wen which had grown out of the nape of his neck,—I have pitied him, not because that was his all, but because he had all *that* to carry. If I have got to drag my trap, I will take care that it be a light one and do not nip me in a vital part. But perchance it would be wisest never to put one's paw into it.

I would observe, by the way, that it costs me nothing for curtains, for I have no gazers to shut out but the sun and moon, and I am willing that they should look in. The moon will not sour milk nor taint meat of mine, nor will the sun injure my furniture or fade my carpet, and if he is sometimes too warm a friend, I find it still better economy to retreat behind some curtain which nature has provided, than to add a single item to the details of housekeeping. A lady once offered me a mat, but

---

[95] Latin: "discards."
[96] At a dead end; immobile.
[97] Spruce.

as I had no room to spare within the house, nor time to spare within or without to shake it, I declined it, preferring to wipe my feet on the sod before my door. It is best to avoid the beginnings of evil.

Not long since I was present at the auction of a deacon's effects, for his life had not been ineffectual:—

"The evil that men do lives after them."[98]

As usual, a great proportion was trumpery which had begun to accumulate in his father's day. Among the rest was a dried tapeworm. And now, after lying half a century in his garret and other dust holes, these things were not burned; instead of a *bonfire,* or purifying destruction of them, there was an *auction,*[99] or increasing of them. The neighbors eagerly collected to view them, bought them all, and carefully transported them to their garrets and dust holes, to lie there till their estates are settled, when they will start again. When a man dies he kicks the dust.

The customs of some savage nations might, perchance, be profitably imitated by us, for they at least go through the semblance of casting their slough annually; they have the idea of the thing, whether they have the reality or not. Would it not be well if we were to celebrate such a "busk," or "feast of first fruits," as Bartram[100] describes to have been the custom of the Mucclasse Indians? "When a town celebrates the busk," says he, "having previously provided themselves with new clothes, new pots, pans, and other household utensils and furniture, they collect all their worn out clothes and other despicable things, sweep and cleanse their houses, squares, and the whole town, of their filth, which with all the remaining grain and other old provisions they cast together into one common heap, and consume it with fire. After having taken medicine, and fasted for three days, all the fire in the town is extinguished. During this fast they abstain from the gratification of every appetite and passion whatever. A general amnesty is proclaimed; all malefactors may return to their town.—"

"On the fourth morning, the high priest, by rubbing dry wood together, produces new fire in the public square, from whence every habitation in the town is supplied with the new and pure flame."

They then feast on the new corn and fruits and dance and sing for three days, "and the four following days they receive visits and rejoice with their friends from neighboring towns who have in like manner purified and prepared themselves."

The Mexicans also practised a similar purification at the end of every fifty-two years, in the belief that it was time for the world to come to an end.

I have scarcely heard of a truer sacrament, that is, as the dictionary defines it, "outward and visible sign of an inward and spiritual grace," than this, and I have no doubt that they were originally inspired directly from Heaven to do thus, though they have no biblical record of the revelation.

For more than five years I maintained myself thus solely by the labor of my hands, and I found, that by working about six weeks in a year, I could meet all the expenses

---

[98] From Shakespeare's *Julius Caesar,* Act III, Sc. ii, l. 81.

[99] The original Latin meant "an increase"; modern usage applies to the raising of the cost of an item by bidding.

[100] William Bartram (1739–1823), American naturalist and travel writer.

of living. The whole of my winters, as well as most of my summers, I had free and clear for study. I have thoroughly tried school-keeping, and found that my expenses were in proportion, or rather out of proportion, to my income, for I was obliged to dress and train, not to say think and believe, accordingly, and I lost my time into the bargain. As I did not teach for the good of my fellow-men, but simply for a livelihood, this was a failure. I have tried trade; but I found that it would take ten years to get under way in that, and that then I should probably be on my way to the devil. I was actually afraid that I might by that time be doing what is called a good business. When formerly I was looking about to see what I could do for a living, some sad experience in conforming to the wishes of friends being fresh in my mind to tax my ingenuity, I thought often and seriously of picking huckleberries; that surely I could do, and its small profits might suffice,—for my greatest skill has been to want but little,—so little capital it required, so little distraction from my wonted moods, I foolishly thought. While my acquaintances went unhesitatingly into trade or the professions, I contemplated this occupation as most like theirs; ranging the hills all summer to pick the berries which came in my way, and thereafter carelessly dispose of them; so, to keep the flocks of Admetus.[101] I also dreamed that I might gather the wild herbs, or carry evergreens to such villagers as loved to be reminded of the woods, even to the city, by hay-cart loads. But I have since learned that trade curses every thing it handles; and though you trade in messages from heaven, the whole curse of trade attaches to the business.

As I preferred some things to others, and especially valued my freedom, as I could fare hard and yet succeed well, I did not wish to spend my time in earning rich carpets or other fine furniture, or delicate cookery, or a house in the Grecian or the Gothic style just yet. If there are any to whom it is no interruption to acquire these things, and who know how to use them when acquired, I relinquish to them the pursuit. Some are "industrious," and appear to love labor for its own sake, or perhaps because it keeps them out of worse mischief; to such I have at present nothing to say. Those who would not know what to do with more leisure than they now enjoy, I might advise to work twice as hard as they do,—work till they pay for themselves, and get their free papers.[102] For myself I found that the occupation of a day-laborer was the most independent of any, especially as it required only thirty or forty days in a year to support one. The laborer's day ends with the going down of the sun, and he is then free to devote himself to his chosen pursuit, independent of his labor; but his employer, who speculates from month to month, has no respite from one end of the year to the other.

In short, I am convinced, both by faith and experience, that to maintain one's self on this earth is not a hardship but a pastime, if we will live simply and wisely; as the pursuits of the simpler nations are still the sports of the more artificial. It is not necessary that a man should earn his living by the sweat of his brow, unless he sweats easier than I do.

One young man of my acquaintance, who has inherited some acres, told me that he thought he should live as I did, *if he had the means.* I would not have any one adopt *my* mode of living on any account; for, beside that before he has fairly learned it I may have found out another for myself, I desire that there may be as many different persons in the world as possible; but I would have each one be very careful to find

---

[101] To pass a time of servitude, as the god Apollo once did in the service of King Admetus.

[102] To end their period of indenturedness by working off their debts.

out and pursue *his own* way, and not his father's or his mother's or his neighbor's instead. The youth may build or plant or sail, only let him not be hindered from doing that which he tells me he would like to do. It is by a mathematical point only that we are wise, as the sailor or the fugitive slave keeps the polestar[103] in his eye; but that is sufficient guidance for all our life. We may not arrive at our port within a calculable period, but we would preserve the true course.

Undoubtedly, in this case, what is true for one is truer still for a thousand, as a large house is not more expensive than a small one in proportion to its size, since one roof may cover, one cellar underlie, and one wall separate several apartments. But for my part, I preferred the solitary dwelling. Moreover, it will commonly be cheaper to build the whole yourself than to convince another of the advantage of the common wall; and when you have done this, the common partition, to be much cheaper, must be a thin one, and that other may prove a bad neighbor, and also not keep his side in repair. The only coöperation which is commonly possible is exceedingly partial and superficial; and what little true coöperation there is, is as if it were not, being a harmony inaudible to men. If a man has faith he will coöperate with equal faith every where; if he has not faith, he will continue to live like the rest of the world, whatever company he is joined to. To coöperate, in the highest as well as the lowest sense, means *to get our living together.* I heard it proposed lately that two young men should travel together over the world, the one without money, earning his means as he went, before the mast and behind the plough, the other carrying a bill of exchange in his pocket. It was easy to see that they could not long be companions or coöperate, since one would not *operate* at all. They would part at the first interesting crisis in their adventures. Above all, as I have implied, the man who goes alone can start today; but he who travels with another must wait till that other is ready, and it may be a long time before they get off.

But all this is very selfish, I have heard some of my townsmen say. I confess that I have hitherto indulged very little in philanthropic enterprises. I have made some sacrifices to a sense of duty, and among others have sacrificed this pleasure also. There are those who have used all their arts to persuade me to undertake the support of some poor family in the town; and if I had nothing to do,—for the devil finds employment for the idle,—I might try my hand at some such pastime as that. However, when I have thought to indulge myself in this respect, and lay their Heaven under an obligation by maintaining certain poor persons in all respects as comfortably as I maintain myself, and have even ventured so far as to make them the offer, they have one and all unhesitatingly preferred to remain poor. While my townsmen and women are devoted in so many ways to the good of their fellows, I trust that one at least may be spared to other and less humane pursuits. You must have a genius for charity as well as for any thing else. As for Doing-good, that is one of the professions which are full. Moreover, I have tried it fairly, and, strange as it may seem, am satisfied that it does not agree with my constitution. Probably I should not consciously and deliberately forsake my particular calling to do the good which society demands of me, to save the universe from annihilation; and I believe that a like but infinitely

---

[103] The North Star, which guides him toward freedom in Canada.

greater steadfastness elsewhere is all that now preserves it. But I would not stand between any man and his genius; and to him who does this work, which I decline, with his whole heart and soul and life, I would say, Persevere, even if the world call it doing evil, as it is most likely they will.

I am far from supposing that my case is a peculiar one; no doubt many of my readers would make a similar defence. At doing something,—I will not engage that my neighbors shall pronounce it good,—I do not hesitate to say that I should be a capital fellow to hire; but what that is, it is for my employer to find out. What *good* I do, in the common sense of that word, must be aside from my main path, and for the most part wholly unintended. Men say, practically, Begin where you are and such as you are, without aiming mainly to become of more worth, and with kindness aforethought go about doing good. If I were to preach at all in this strain, I should say rather, Set about being good. As if the sun should stop when he had kindled his fires up to the splendor of a moon or a star of the sixth magnitude, and go about like a Robin Goodfellow,[104] peeping in at every cottage window, inspiring lunatics, and tainting meats, and making darkness visible, instead of steadily increasing his genial heat and beneficence till he is of such brightness that no mortal can look him in the face, and then, and in the mean while too, going about the world in his own orbit, doing it good, or rather, as a truer philosophy has discovered, the world going about him getting good. When Phaeton,[105] wishing to prove his heavenly birth by his beneficence, had the sun's chariot but one day, and drove out of the beaten track, he burned several blocks of houses in the lower streets of heaven, and scorched the surface of the earth, and dried up every spring, and made the great desert of Sahara, till at length Jupiter hurled him headlong to the earth with a thunderbolt, and the sun, through grief at his death, did not shine for a year.

There is no odor so bad as that which arises from goodness tainted. It is human, it is divine, carrion. If I knew for a certainty that a man was coming to my house with the conscious design of doing me good, I should run for my life, as from that dry and parching wind of the African deserts called the simoom, which fills the mouth and nose and ears and eyes with dust till you are suffocated, for fear that I should get some of his good done to me,—some of its virus mingled with my blood. No, —in this case I would rather suffer evil the natural way. A man is not a good *man* to me because he will feed me if I should be starving, or warm me if I should be freezing, or pull me out of a ditch if I should ever fall into one. I can find you a Newfoundland dog that will do as much. Philanthropy is not love for one's fellow-man in the broadest sense. Howard[106] was no doubt an exceedingly kind and worthy man in his way, and has his reward; but, comparatively speaking, what are a hundred Howards to *us,* if their philanthropy do not help *us* in our best estate, when we are most worthy to be helped? I never heard of a philanthropic meeting in which it was sincerely proposed to do any good to me, or the like of me.

The Jesuits[107] were quite balked by those Indians who, being burned at the stake, suggested new modes of torture to their tormentors. Being superior to physical

---

[104] In folklore, the elf who plays tricks; associated with Puck.
[105] Apollo's son, and thereby the son of the Sun.
[106] John Howard (1726?–1790), English leader in prison reform.

[107] Roman Catholic religious order, the Society of Jesus; one of its concerns was to convert Indians to Christianity.

suffering, it sometimes chanced that they were superior to any consolation which the missionaries could offer; and the law to do as you would be done by fell with less persuasiveness on the ears of those, who, for their part, did not care how they were done by, who loved their enemies after a new fashion, and came very near freely forgiving them all they did.

Be sure that you give the poor the aid they most need, though it be your example which leaves them far behind. If you give money, spend yourself with it, and do not merely abandon it to them. We make curious mistakes sometimes. Often the poor man is not so cold and hungry as he is dirty and ragged and gross. It is partly his taste, and not merely his misfortune. If you give him money, he will perhaps buy more rags with it. I was wont to pity the clumsy Irish laborers who cut ice on the pond, in such mean and ragged clothes, while I shivered in my more tidy and somewhat more fashionable garments, till, one bitter cold day, one who had slipped into the water came to my house to warm him, and I saw him strip off three pairs of pants and two pairs of stockings ere he got down to the skin, though they were dirty and ragged enough, it is true, and that he could afford to refuse the *extra* garments which I offered him, he had so many *intra* ones.[108] This ducking was the very thing he needed. Then I began to pity myself, and I saw that it would be a greater charity to bestow on me a flannel shirt than a whole slop-shop on him. There are a thousand hacking at the branches of evil to one who is striking at the root, and it may be that he who bestows the largest amount of time and money on the needy is doing the most by his mode of life to produce that misery which he strives in vain to relieve. It is the pious slave-breeder devoting the proceeds of every tenth slave[109] to buy a Sunday's liberty for the rest. Some show their kindness to the poor by employing them in their kitchens. Would they not be kinder if they employed themselves there? You boast of spending a tenth part of your income in charity; may be you should spend the nine tenths so, and done with it. Society recovers only a tenth part of the property then. Is this owing to the generosity of him in whose possession it is found, or to the remissness of the officers of justice?

Philanthropy is almost the only virtue which is sufficiently appreciated by mankind. Nay, it is greatly overrated; and it is our selfishness which overrates it. A robust poor man, one sunny day here in Concord, praised a fellow-townsman to me, because, as he said, he was kind to the poor; meaning himself. The kind uncles and aunts of the race are more esteemed than its true spiritual fathers and mothers. I once heard a reverend lecturer on England, a man of learning and intelligence, after enumerating her scientific, literary, and political worthies, Shakspeare, Bacon, Cromwell, Milton, Newton, and others, speak next of her Christian heroes, whom, as if his profession required it of him, he elevated to a place far above all the rest, as the greatest of the great. They were Penn, Howard, and Mrs. Fry.[110] Every one must feel the falsehood and cant of this. The last were not England's best men and women; only, perhaps, her best philanthropists.

I would not subtract any thing from the praise that is due to philanthropy, but

---

[108] *Extra:* "outer"; *intra:* "inner."
[109] In the custom of the tithe, churchgoers give one tenth of their income to support the church's good works.

[110] Like John Howard, the Quakers William Penn (1644–1718) and Elizabeth Fry (1780–1845) were active reformers of social ills.

merely demand justice for all who by their lives and works are a blessing to mankind. I do not value chiefly a man's uprightness and benevolence, which are, as it were, his stem and leaves. Those plants of whose greenness withered we make herb tea for the sick, serve but a humble use, and are most employed by quacks. I want the flower and fruit of a man; that some fragrance be wafted over from him to me, and some ripeness flavor our intercourse. His goodness must not be a partial and transitory act, but a constant superfluity, which costs him nothing and of which he is unconscious. This is a charity that hides a multitude of sins. The philanthropist too often surrounds mankind with the remembrance of his own cast-off griefs as an atmosphere, and calls it sympathy. We should impart our courage, and not our despair, our health and ease, and not our disease, and take care that this does not spread by contagion. From what southern plains[111] comes up the voice of wailing? Under what latitudes reside the heathen to whom we would send light? Who is that intemperate and brutal man whom we would redeem? If any thing ail a man, so that he does not perform his functions, if he have a pain in his bowels even,—for that is the seat of sympathy,[112] —he forthwith sets about reforming—the world. Being a microcosm himself, he discovers, and it is a true discovery, and he is the man to make it,—that the world has been eating green apples; to his eyes, in fact, the globe itself is a great green apple, which there is danger awful to think of that the children of men will nibble before it is ripe; and straightway his drastic philanthropy seeks out the Esquimaux[113] and the Patagonian,[114] and embraces the populous Indian and Chinese villages; and thus, by a few years of philanthropic activity, the powers in the mean while using him for their own ends, no doubt, he cures himself of his dyspepsia, the globe acquires a faint blush on one or both of its cheeks, as if it were beginning to be ripe, and life loses its crudity and is once more sweet and wholesome to live. I never dreamed of any enormity greater than I have committed. I never knew, and never shall know, a worse man than myself.

I believe that what so saddens the reformer is not his sympathy with his fellows in distress, but, though he be the holiest son of God, is his private ail. Let this be righted, let the spring come to him, the morning rise over his couch, and he will forsake his generous companions without apology. My excuse for not lecturing against the use of tobacco is, that I never chewed it; that is a penalty which reformed tobacco-chewers have to pay; though there are things enough I have chewed, which I could lecture against. If you should ever be betrayed into any of these philanthropies, do not let your left hand know what your right hand does, for it is not worth knowing.[115] Rescue the drowning and tie your shoe-strings. Take your time, and set about some free labor.

Our manners have been corrupted by communication with the saints. Our hymn-books resound with a melodious cursing of God and enduring him forever. One would say that even the prophets and redeemers had rather consoled the fears than confirmed the hopes of man. There is nowhere recorded a simple and irrepressible satisfaction with the gift of life, any memorable praise of God. All health and success does me good, however far off and withdrawn it may appear; all disease and failure

---

[111] Slave states.
[112] That compassion found its source in the bowels was an age-old notion.
[113] Eskimo.
[114] From the nethermost region of South America.
[115] See Matthew 6:3.

helps to make me sad and does me evil, however much sympathy it may have with me or I with it. If, then, we would indeed restore mankind by truly Indian, botanic, magnetic, or natural means, let us first be as simple and well as Nature ourselves, dispel the clouds which hang over our own brows, and take up a little life into our pores. Do not stay to be an overseer of the poor, but endeavor to become one of the worthies of the world.

I read in the Gulistan, or Flower Garden, of Sheik Sadi of Shiraz,[116] that "They asked a wise man, saying; Of the many celebrated trees which the Most High God has created lofty and umbrageous, they call none azad, or free, excepting the cypress, which bears no fruit; what mystery is there in this? He replied; Each has its appropriate produce, and appointed season, during the continuance of which it is fresh and blooming, and during their absence dry and withered; to neither of which states is the cypress exposed, being always flourishing; and of this nature are the azads, or religious independents.—Fix not thy heart on that which is transitory; for the Dijlah, or Tigris, will continue to flow through Bagdad after the race of caliphs is extinct: if thy hand has plenty, be liberal as the date tree; but if it affords nothing to give away, be an azad, or free man, like the cypress."

Complemental Verses

The Pretensions of Poverty[117]

"Thou dost presume too much, poor needy wretch,
　　To claim a station in the firmament,
Because thy humble cottage, or thy tub,
　　Nurses some lazy or pedantic virtue
In the cheap sunshine or by shady springs,
With roots and pot-herbs; where thy right hand,
Tearing those humane passions from the mind,
Upon whose stocks fair blooming virtues flourish,
Degradeth nature, and benumbeth sense,
And, Gorgon-like, turns active men to stone.
We not require the dull society
　　Of your necessitated temperance,
Or that unnatural stupidity
That knows nor joy nor sorrow; nor your forc'd
Falsely exalted passive fortitude
Above the active. This low abject brood,
That fix their seats in mediocrity,
Become your servile minds; but we advance
Such virtues only as admit excess,
Brave, bounteous acts, regal magnificence,

[116] Persian poet of the thirteenth century.
[117] The English poet Thomas Carew (1595?–1645)

wrote this poem, which was included in *Coelum Brittannicum* (1661). Thoreau added the title.

All-seeing prudence, magnanimity
That knows no bound, and that heroic virtue
For which antiquity hath left no name,
But patterns only, such as Hercules,
Achilles, Theseus. Back to thy loath'd cell;
And when thou seest the new enlightened sphere,
Study to know but what those worthies were."

T. CAREW

Where I Lived, and What I Lived For

At a certain season of our life we are accustomed to consider every spot as the possible site of a house. I have thus surveyed the country on every side within a dozen miles of where I live. In imagination I have bought all the farms in succession, for all were to be bought, and I knew their price. I walked over each farmer's premises, tasted his wild apples, discoursed on husbandry with him, took his farm at his price, at any price, mortgaging it to him in my mind; even put a higher price on it,—took every thing but a deed of it,—took his word for his deed, for I dearly love to talk,—cultivated it, and him too to some extent, I trust, and withdrew when I had enjoyed it long enough, leaving him to carry it on. This experience entitled me to be regarded as a sort of real-estate broker by my friends. Wherever I sat, there I might live, and the landscape radiated from me accordingly. What is a house but a *sedes,* a seat?—better if a country seat. I discovered many a site for a house not likely to be soon improved, which some might have thought too far from the village, but to my eyes the village was too far from it. Well, there I might live, I said; and there I did live, for an hour, a summer and a winter life; saw how I could let the years run off, buffet the winter through, and see the spring come in. The future inhabitants of this region, wherever they may place their houses, may be sure that they have been anticipated. An afternoon sufficed to lay out the land into orchard woodlot and pasture, and to decide what fine oaks or pines should be left to stand before the door, and whence each blasted tree could be seen to the best advantage; and then I let it lie, fallow perchance, for a man is rich in proportion to the number of things which he can afford to let alone.

My imagination carried me so far that I even had the refusal of several farms,— the refusal was all I wanted,—but I never got my fingers burned by actual possession. The nearest that I came to actual possession was when I bought the Hollowell Place, and had begun to sort my seeds, and collected materials with which to make a wheelbarrow to carry it on or off with; but before the owner gave me a deed of it, his wife—every man has such a wife—changed her mind and wished to keep it, and he offered me ten dollars to release him. Now, to speak the truth, I had but ten cents in the world, and it surpassed my arithmetic to tell, if I was that man who had ten cents, or who had a farm, or ten dollars, or all together. However, I let him keep the ten dollars and the farm too, for I had carried it far enough; or rather, to be generous, I sold him the farm for just what I gave for it, and, as he was not a rich man, made him a present of ten dollars, and still had my ten cents, and seeds, and materials for a wheelbarrow left. I found thus that I had been a rich man without any damage to my poverty. But I retained the landscape, and I have since annually carried off what it yielded without a wheelbarrow. With respect to landscapes,—

"I am monarch of all I *survey,*
    My right there is none to dispute."[118]

I have frequently seen a poet withdraw, having enjoyed the most valuable part of a farm, while the crusty farmer supposed that he had got a few wild apples only. Why, the owner does not know it for many years when a poet has put his farm in rhyme, the most admirable kind of invisible fence, has fairly impounded it, milked it, skimmed it, and got all the cream, and left the farmer only the skimmed milk.

The real attractions of the Hollowell farm, to me, were; its complete retirement, being about two miles from the village, half a mile from the nearest neighbor, and separated from the highway by a broad field; its bounding on the river, which the owner said protected it by its fogs from frosts in the spring, though that was nothing to me; the gray color and ruinous state of the house and barn, and the dilapidated fences, which put such an interval between me and the last occupant; the hollow and lichen-covered apple trees, gnawed by rabbits, showing what kind of neighbors I should have; but above all, the recollection I had of it from my earliest voyages up the river, when the house was concealed behind a dense grove of red maples, through which I heard the house-dog bark. I was in haste to buy it, before the proprietor finished getting out some rocks, cutting down the hollow apple trees, and grubbing up some young birches which had sprung up in the pasture, or, in short, had made any more of his improvements. To enjoy these advantages I was ready to carry it on; like Atlas,[119] to take the world on my shoulders,—I never heard what compensation he received for that,—and do all those things which had no other motive or excuse but that I might pay for it and be unmolested in my possession of it; for I knew all the while that it would yield the most abundant crop of the kind I wanted if I could only afford to let it alone. But it turned out as I have said.

All that I could say, then, with respect to farming on a large scale, (I have always cultivated a garden,) was, that I had had my seeds ready. Many think that seeds improve with age. I have no doubt that time discriminates between the good and the bad; and when at last I shall plant, I shall be less likely to be disappointed. But I would say to my fellows, once for all, As long as possible live free and uncommitted. It makes but little difference whether you are committed to a farm or the county jail.

Old Cato, whose "De Re Rusticâ"[120] is my "Cultivator," says, and the only translation I have seen makes sheer nonsense of the passage, "When you think of getting a farm, turn it thus in your mind, not to buy greedily; nor spare your pains to look at it, and do not think it enough to go round it once. The oftener you go

---

[118] Thoreau, a part-time surveyor, chose to emphasize the word *survey* when quoting from "Verses Supposed to be Written by Alexander Selkirk" by William Cowper (1731–1800).

[119] In classic myth, the giant who bore the world on his shoulders.

[120] Marcus Porcius Cato (234–149 B.C.), author of a work on agriculture (160? B.C.) that is sometimes given this name.

there the more it will please you, if it is good." I think I shall not buy greedily, but go round and round it as long as I live, and be buried in it first, that it may please me the more at last.

The present was my next experiment of this kind, which I purpose to describe more at length; for convenience, putting the experience of two years into one. As I have said, I do not propose to write an ode to dejection, but to brag as lustily as chanticleer in the morning, standing on his roost, if only to wake my neighbors up.

When first I took up my abode in the woods, that is, began to spend my nights as well as days there, which, by accident, was on Independence Day, or the fourth of July, 1845, my house was not finished for winter, but was merely a defence against the rain, without plastering or chimney, the walls being of rough weather-stained boards, with wide chinks, which made it cool at night. The upright white hewn studs and freshly planed door and window casings gave it a clean and airy look, especially in the morning, when its timbers were saturated with dew, so that I fancied that by noon some sweet gum would exude from them. To my imagination it retained throughout the day more or less of this auroral character, reminding me of a certain house on a mountain which I had visited the year before. This was an airy and unplastered cabin, fit to entertain a travelling god, and where a goddess might trail her garments. The winds which passed over my dwelling were such as sweep over the ridges of mountains, bearing the broken strains, or celestial parts only, of terrestrial music. The morning wind forever blows, the poem of creation is uninterrupted; but few are the ears that hear it. Olympus[121] is but the outside of the earth every where.

The only house I had been the owner of before, if I except a boat, was a tent, which I used occasionally when making excursions in the summer, and this is still rolled up in my garret; but the boat, after passing from hand to hand, has gone down the stream of time. With this more substantial shelter about me, I had made some progress toward settling in the world. This frame, so slightly clad, was a sort of crystallization around me, and reacted on the builder. It was suggestive somewhat as a picture in outlines. I did not need to go out doors to take the air, for the atmosphere within had lost none of its freshness. It was not so much within doors as behind a door where I sat, even in the rainiest weather. The Harivansa[122] says, "An abode without birds is like a meat without seasoning." Such was not my abode, for I found myself suddenly neighbor to the birds; not by having imprisoned one, but having caged myself near them. I was not only nearer to some of those which commonly frequent the garden and the orchard, but to those wilder and more thrilling songsters of the forest which never, or rarely, serenade a villager,—the wood-thrush, the veery, the scarlet tanager, the field-sparrow, the whippoorwill, and many others.

I was seated by the shore of a small pond, about a mile and a half south of the village of Concord and somewhat higher than it, in the midst of an extensive wood between that town and Lincoln, and about two miles south of that our only field known to fame, Concord Battle Ground;[123] but I was so low in the woods that the opposite shore, half a mile off, like the rest, covered with wood, was my most distant

[121] Mountain abode of the Greek gods.
[122] Fifth century Hindu religious epic.
[123] Where one of the opening battles of the
American Revolution was fought, on April 19, 1775.

horizon. For the first week, whenever I looked out on the pond it impressed me like a tarn high up on the side of a mountain, its bottom far above the surface of other lakes, and, as the sun arose, I saw it throwing off its nightly clothing of mist, and here and there, by degrees, its soft ripples, or its smooth reflecting surface was revealed, while the mists, like ghosts, were stealthily withdrawing in every direction into the woods, as at the breaking up of some nocturnal conventicle. The very dew seemed to hang upon the trees later into the day than usual, as on the sides of mountains.

This small lake was of most value as a neighbor in the intervals of a gentle rain storm in August, when, both air and water being perfectly still, but the sky overcast, mid-afternoon had all the serenity of evening, and the wood-thrush sang around, and was heard from shore to shore. A lake like this is never smoother than at such a time; and the clear portion of the air above it being shallow and darkened by clouds, the water, full of light and reflections, becomes a lower heaven itself so much the more important. From a hill top near by, where the wood had been recently cut off, there was a pleasing vista southward across the pond, through a wide indentation in the hills which form the shore there, where their opposite sides sloping toward each other suggested a stream flowing out in that direction through a wooded valley, but stream there was none. That way I looked between and over the near green hills to some distant and higher ones in the horizon, tinged with blue. Indeed, by standing on tiptoe I could catch a glimpse of some of the peaks of the still bluer and more distant mountain ranges in the north-west, those true-blue coins from heaven's own mint, and also of some portion of the village. But in other directions, even from this point, I could not see over or beyond the woods which surrounded me. It is well to have some water in your neighborhood, to give buoyancy to and float the earth. One value even of the smallest well is, that when you look into it you see that earth is not continent but insular. This is as important as that it keeps butter cool. When I looked across the pond from this peak toward the Sudbury meadows, which in time of flood I distinguished elevated perhaps by a mirage in their seething valley, like a coin in a basin, all the earth beyond the pond appeared like a thin crust insulated and floated even by this small sheet of intervening water, and I was reminded that this on which I dwelt was but *dry land.*

Though the view from my door was still more contracted, I did not feel crowded or confined in the least. There was pasture enough for my imagination. The low shrub-oak plateau to which the opposite shore arose, stretched away toward the prairies of the West and the steppes of Tartary,[124] affording ample room for all the roving families of men. "There are none happy in the world but beings who enjoy freely a vast horizon,"—said Damodara,[125] when his herds required new and larger pastures.

Both place and time were changed, and I dwelt nearer to those parts of the universe and to those eras in history which had most attracted me. Where I lived was as far off as many a region viewed nightly by astronomers. We are wont to imagine rare and delectable places in some remote and more celestial corner of the system, behind the constellation of Cassiopeia's Chair, far from noise and disturbance. I discovered

---

[124] In Russian Asia.
[125] Hindu god mentioned in the *Harivansa;* another name for Krishna.

that my house actually had its site in such a withdrawn, but forever new and unprofaned, part of the universe. If it were worth the while to settle in those parts near to the Pleiades or the Hyades, to Aldebaran or Altair,[126] then I was really there, or at an equal remoteness from the life which I had left behind, dwindled and twinkling with as fine a ray to my nearest neighbor, and to be seen only in moonless nights by him. Such was that part of creation where I had squatted;—

> "There was a shepherd that did live,
> And held his thoughts as high
> As were the mounts whereon his flocks
> Did hourly feed him by."

What should we think of the shepherd's life if his flocks always wandered to higher pastures than his thoughts?

Every morning was a cheerful invitation to make my life of equal simplicity, and I may say innocence, with Nature herself. I have been as sincere a worshipper of Aurora[127] as the Greeks. I got up early and bathed in the pond; that was a religious exercise, and one of the best things which I did. They say that characters were engraven on the bathing tub of king Tching-thang[128] to this effect: "Renew thyself completely each day; do it again, and again, and forever again." I can understand that. Morning brings back the heroic ages. I was as much affected by the faint hum of a mosquito making its invisible and unimaginable tour through my apartment at earliest dawn, when I was sitting with door and windows open, as I could be by any trumpet that ever sang of fame. It was Homer's requiem; itself an Iliad and Odyssey in the air, singing its own wrath and wanderings. There was something cosmical about it; a standing advertisement, till forbidden, of the everlasting vigor and fertility of the world. The morning, which is the most memorable season of the day, is the awakening hour. Then there is least somnolence in us; and for an hour, at least, some part of us awakes which slumbers all the rest of the day and night. Little is to be expected of that day, if it can be called a day, to which we are not awakened by our Genius, but by the mechanical nudgings of some servitor, are not awakened by our own newly-acquired force and aspirations from within, accompanied by the undulations of celestial music, instead of factory bells, and a fragrance filling the air—to a higher life than we fell asleep from; and thus the darkness bear its fruit, and prove itself to be good, no less than the light. That man who does not believe that each day contains an earlier, more sacred, and auroral hour than he has yet profaned, has despaired of life, and is pursuing a descending and darkening way. After a partial cessation of his sensuous life, the soul of man, or its organs rather, are reinvigorated each day, and his Genius[129] tries again what noble life it can make. All memorable events, I should say, transpire in morning time and in a morning atmosphere. The Vedas[130] say, "All intelligences awake with the morning." Poetry and art, and the fairest and most memorable of the actions of men, date from such an hour. All poets and heroes, like

---

[126] Stars and constellations.
[127] Although Thoreau refers to Aurora as a Greek goddess (of the dawn), that was the Roman name for her.
[128] The lines, taken from the tub of the Chinese monarch who founded the Shang dynasty (1766–1122 B.C.), are from a gloss of Confucius' *The Great Learning.*
[129] Guardian spirit.
[130] Religious text of the Hindus.

Memnon, are the children of Aurora, and emit their music at sunrise. To him whose elastic and vigorous thought keeps pace with the sun, the day is a perpetual morning. It matters not what the clocks say or the attitudes and labors of men. Morning is when I am awake and there is a dawn in me. Moral reform is the effort to throw off sleep. Why is it that men give so poor an account of their day if they have not been slumbering? They are not such poor calculators. If they had not been overcome with drowsiness they would have performed something. The millions are awake enough for physical labor; but only one in a million is awake enough for effective intellectual exertion, only one in a hundred millions to a poetic or divine life. To be awake is to be alive. I have never yet met a man who was quite awake. How could I have looked him in the face?

We must learn to reawaken and keep ourselves awake, not by mechanical aids, but by an infinite expectation of the dawn, which does not forsake us in our soundest sleep. I know of no more encouraging fact than the unquestionable ability of man to elevate his life by a conscious endeavor. It is something to be able to paint a particular picture, or to carve a statue, and so to make a few objects beautiful; but it is far more glorious to carve and paint the very atmosphere and medium through which we look, which morally we can do. To affect the quality of the day, that is the highest of arts. Every man is tasked to make his life, even in its details, worthy of the contemplation of his most elevated and critical hour. If we refused, or rather used up, such paltry information as we get, the oracles would distinctly inform us how this might be done.

I went to the woods because I wished to live deliberately, to front only the essential facts of life, and see if I could not learn what it had to teach, and not, when I came to die, discover that I had not lived. I did not wish to live what was not life, living is so dear; nor did I wish to practise resignation, unless it was quite necessary. I wanted to live deep and suck out all the marrow of life, to live so sturdily and Spartanlike as to put to rout all that was not life, to cut a broad swath and shave close, to drive life into a corner, and reduce it to its lowest terms, and, if it proved to be mean, why then to get the whole and genuine meanness of it, and publish its meanness to the world; or if it were sublime, to know it by experience, and be able to give a true account of it in my next excursion. For most men, it appears to me, are in a strange uncertainty about it, whether it is of the devil or of God, and have *somewhat hastily* concluded that it is the chief end of man here to "glorify God and enjoy him forever."

Still we live meanly, like ants; though the fable tells us that we were long ago changed into men;[131] like pygmies we fight with cranes;[132] it is error upon error, and clout upon clout, and our best virtue has for its occasion a superfluous and evitable wretchedness. Our life is frittered away by detail. An honest man has hardly need to count more than his ten fingers, or in extreme cases he may add his ten toes, and lump the rest. Simplicity, simplicity, simplicity! I say, let your affairs be as two or three, and not a hundred or a thousand; instead of a million count half a dozen, and keep your accounts on your thumb nail. In the midst of this chopping sea of civilized life, such are the clouds and storms and quicksands and thousand-and-one items to be allowed for, that a man has to live, if he would not founder and go to the bottom

---

[131] In a classic myth Zeus transformed ants into men for the purpose of repopulating a plague-devastated land.

[132] The Trojans were likened to cranes that fought with pygmies in the *Iliad*, Book III.

and not make his port at all, by dead reckoning,[133] and he must be a great calculator indeed who succeeds. Simplify, simplify. Instead of three meals a day, if it be necessary eat but one; instead of a hundred dishes, five; and reduce other things in proportion. Our life is like a German Confederacy,[134] made up of petty states, with its boundary forever fluctuating, so that even a German cannot tell you how it is bounded at any moment. The nation itself, with all its so called internal improvements, which, by the way, are all external and superficial, is just such an unwieldy and overgrown establishment, cluttered with furniture and tripped up by its own traps, ruined by luxury and heedless expense, by want of calculation and a worthy aim, as the million households in the land; and the only cure for it as for them is in a rigid economy, a stern and more than Spartan simplicity of life and elevation of purpose. It lives too fast. Men think that it is essential that the *Nation* have commerce, and export ice, and talk through a telegraph, and ride thirty miles an hour, without a doubt, whether *they* do or not; but whether we should live like baboons or like men, is a little uncertain. If we do not get our sleepers,[135] and forge rails, and devote days and nights to the work, but go to tinkering upon our *lives* to improve *them,* who will build railroads? And if railroads are not built, how shall we get to heaven in season? But if we stay at home and mind our business, who will want railroads? We do not ride on the railroad; it rides upon us. Did you ever think what those sleepers are that underlie the railroad? Each one is a man, an Irish-man, or a Yankee man. The rails are laid on them, and they are covered with sand, and the cars run smoothly over them. They are sound sleepers, I assure you. And every few years a new lot is laid down and run over; so that, if some have the pleasure of riding on a rail, others have the misfortune to be ridden upon. And when they run over a man that is walking in his sleep, a supernumerary sleeper in the wrong position, and wake him up, they suddenly stop the cars, and make a hue and cry about it, as if this were an exception. I am glad to know that it takes a gang of men for every five miles to keep the sleepers down and level in their beds as it is, for this is a sign that they may sometime get up again.

Why should we live with such hurry and waste of life? We are determined to be starved before we are hungry. Men say that a stitch in time saves nine, and so they take a thousand stitches to-day to save nine to-morrow. As for *work,* we haven't any of any consequence. We have the Saint Vitus' dance, and cannot possibly keep our heads still. If I should only give a few pulls at the parish bell-rope, as for a fire, that is, without setting the bell,[136] there is hardly a man on his farm in the outskirts of Concord, notwithstanding that press of engagements which was his excuse so many times this morning, nor a boy, nor a woman, I might almost say, but would forsake all and follow that sound, not mainly to save property from the flames, but, if we will confess the truth, much more to see it burn, since burn it must, and we, be it known, did not set it on fire,—or to see it put out, and have a hand in it, if that is done as handsomely; yes, even if it were the parish church itself. Hardly a man takes a half hour's nap after dinner, but when he wakes he holds up his head and asks, "What's the news?" as if the rest of mankind had stood his sentinels. Some give

---

[133] A system for navigating a ship at sea without the aid of the sun and stars.

[134] Germany, as Thoreau knew it during his lifetime, was an unstable grouping of states;

only in 1871 was it brought together into a national unit by Bismarck.

[135] Railroad ties.

[136] Inverting the bell by pulling it too hard.

directions to be waked every half hour, doubtless for no other purpose; and then, to pay for it, they tell what they have dreamed. After a night's sleep the news is as indispensable as the breakfast. "Pray tell me any thing new that has happened to a man any where on this globe,"—and he reads it over his coffee and rolls, that a man has had his eyes gouged out this morning on the Wachito River;[137] never dreaming the while that he lives in the dark unfathomed mammoth cave of this world, and has but the rudiment of an eye himself.

For my part, I could easily do without the post-office. I think that there are very few important communications made through it. To speak critically, I never received more than one or two letters in my life—I wrote this some years ago—that were worth the postage. The penny-post is, commonly, an institution through which you seriously offer a man that penny for his thoughts which is so often safely offered in jest. And I am sure that I never read any memorable news in a newspaper. If we read of one man robbed, or murdered, or killed by accident, or one house burned, or one vessel wrecked, or one steamboat blown up, or one cow run over on the Western Railroad, or one mad dog killed, or one lot of grasshoppers in the winter,—we never need read of another. One is enough. If you are acquainted with the principle, what do you care for a myriad instances and applications? To a philosopher all *news,* as it is called, is gossip, and they who edit and read it are old women over their tea. Yet not a few are greedy after this gossip. There was such a rush, as I hear, the other day at one of the offices to learn the foreign news by the last arrival, that several large squares of plate glass belonging to the establishment were broken by the pressure,— news which I seriously think a ready wit might write a twelvemonth or twelve years beforehand with sufficient accuracy. As for Spain, for instance, if you know how to throw in Don Carlos and the Infanta, and Don Pedro[138] and Seville and Granada, from time to time in the right proportions,—they may have changed the names a little since I saw the papers,—and serve up a bull-fight when other entertainments fail, it will be true to the letter, and give us as good an idea of the exact state or ruin of things in Spain as the most succinct and lucid reports under this head in the newspapers: and as for England, almost the last significant scrap of news from that quarter was the revolution of 1649;[139] and if you have learned the history of her crops for an average year, you never need attend to that thing again, unless your speculations are of a merely pecuniary character. If one may judge who rarely looks into the newspapers, nothing new does ever happen in foreign parts, a French revolution not excepted.

What news! how much more important to know what that is which was never old! "Kieou-pe-yu (great dignitary of the state of Wei) sent a man to Khoung-tseu[140] to know his news. Khoung-tseu caused the messenger to be seated near him, and questioned him in these terms: What is your master doing? The messenger answered with respect: My master desires to diminish the number of his faults, but he cannot accomplish it. The messenger being gone, the philosopher remarked: What a worthy messenger! What a worthy messenger!" The preacher, instead of vexing the ears of drowsy farmers on their day of rest at the end of the week,—for Sunday is the fit

---

[137] Tributary of the Red River in Arkansas.
[138] Members of the Spanish nobility.
[139] The end of the British monarchy at the hands of the Puritan Commonwealth.

[140] Confucius. The incident is described in *The Analects,* XIV, 26.

conclusion of an ill-spent week, and not the fresh and brave beginning of a new one,—with this one other draggle-tail of a sermon, should shout with thundering voice,—"Pause! Avast! Why so seeming fast, but deadly slow?"

Shams and delusions are esteemed for soundest truths, while reality is fabulous. If men would steadily observe realities only, and not allow themselves to be deluded, life, to compare it with such things as we know, would be like a fairy tale and the Arabian Nights' Entertainments. If we respected only what is inevitable and has a right to be, music and poetry would resound along the streets. When we are unhurried and wise, we perceive that only great and worthy things have any permanent and absolute existence,—that petty fears and petty pleasures are but the shadow of the reality. This is always exhilarating and sublime. By closing the eyes and slumbering, and consenting to be deceived by shows, men establish and confirm their daily life of routine and habit every where, which still is built on purely illusory foundations. Children, who play life, discern its true law and relations more clearly than men, who fail to live it worthily, but who think that they are wiser by experience, that is, by failure. I have read in a Hindoo book, that "there was a king's son, who, being expelled in infancy from his native city, was brought up by a forester, and, growing up to maturity in that state, imagined himself to belong to the barbarous race with which he lived. One of his father's ministers having discovered him, revealed to him what he was, and the misconception of his character was removed, and he knew himself to be a prince. So soul," continues the Hindoo philosopher, "from the circumstances in which it is placed, mistakes its own character, until the truth is revealed to it by some holy teacher, and then it knows itself to be *Brahme.*"[141] I perceive that we inhabitants of New England live this mean life that we do because our vision does not penetrate the surface of things. We think that that is which *appears* to be. If a man should walk through this town and see only the reality, where, think you, would the "Mill-dam"[142] go to? If he should give us an account of the realities he beheld there, we should not recognize the place in his description. Look at a meeting-house, or a court-house, or a jail, or a shop, or a dwelling-house, and say what that thing really is before a true gaze, and they would all go to pieces in your account of them. Men esteem truth remote, in the outskirts of the system, behind the farthest star, before Adam and after the last man. In eternity there is indeed something true and sublime. But all these times and places and occasions are now and here. God himself culminates in the present moment, and will never be more divine in the lapse of all the ages. And we are enabled to apprehend at all what is sublime and noble only by the perpetual instilling and drenching of the reality which surrounds us. The universe constantly and obediently answers to our conceptions; whether we travel fast or slow, the track is laid for us. Let us spend our lives in conceiving then. The poet or the artist never yet had so fair and noble a design but some of his posterity at least could accomplish it.

Let us spend one day as deliberately as Nature, and not be thrown off the track by every nutshell and mosquito's wing that falls on the rails. Let us rise early and fast, or break fast, gently and without perturbation; let company come and let company go, let the bells ring and the children cry,—determined to make a day of it. Why

[141] The foremost god in the Hindu hierarchy.
[142] Concord's town center, meeting place for idle chatter.

should we knock under and go with the stream? Let us not be upset and overwhelmed in that terrible rapid and whirlpool called a dinner, situated in the meridian shallows. Weather this danger and you are safe, for the rest of the way is down hill. With unrelaxed nerves, with morning vigor, sail by it, looking another way, tied to the mast like Ulysses.[143] If the engine whistles, let it whistle till it is hoarse for its pains. If the bell rings, why should we run? We will consider what kind of music they are like. Let us settle ourselves, and work and wedge our feet downward through the mud and slush of opinion, and prejudice, and tradition, and delusion, and appearance, that alluvion which covers the globe, through Paris and London, through New York and Boston and Concord, through church and state, through poetry and philosophy and religion, till we come to a hard bottom and rocks in place, which we can call *reality,* and say, This is, and no mistake; and then begin, having a *point d'appui,* below freshet and frost and fire, a place where you might found a wall or a state, or set a lamp-post safely, or perhaps a gauge, not a Nilometer, but a Realometer, that future ages might know how deep a freshet of shams and appearances had gathered from time to time. If you stand right fronting and face to face to a fact, you will see the sun glimmer on both its surfaces, as if it were a cimeter,[144] and feel its sweet edge dividing you through the heart and marrow, and so you will happily conclude your mortal career. Be it life or death, we crave only reality. If we are really dying, let us hear the rattle in our throats and feel cold in the extremities; if we are alive, let us go about our business.

Time is but the stream I go a-fishing in. I drink at it; but while I drink I see the sandy bottom and detect how shallow it is. Its thin current slides away, but eternity remains. I would drink deeper; fish in the sky, whose bottom is pebbly with stars. I cannot count one. I know not the first letter of the alphabet. I have always been regretting that I was not as wise as the day I was born. The intellect is a cleaver; it discerns and rifts its way into the secret of things. I do not wish to be any more busy with my hands than is necessary. My head is hands and feet. I feel all my best faculties concentrated in it. My instinct tells me that my head is an organ for burrowing, as some creatures use their snout and fore-paws, and with it I would mine and burrow my way through these hills. I think that the richest vein is somewhere hereabouts; so by the divining rod and thin rising vapors I judge; and here I will begin to mine.

Reading

With a little more deliberation in the choice of their pursuits, all men would perhaps become essentially students and observers, for certainly their nature and destiny are interesting to all alike. In accumulating property for ourselves or our posterity, in founding a family or a state, or acquiring fame even, we are mortal; but in dealing with truth we are immortal, and need fear no change nor accident. The oldest Egyptian or Hindoo philosopher raised a corner of the veil from the statue of the

[143] I.e., be able to move past dangers in safety, like Ulysses in the *Odyssey,* who had himself bound to the ship's mast so that he could both listen to the Sirens' song and resist their fatal call.   [144] Scimitar.

divinity; and still the trembling robe remains raised, and I gaze upon as fresh a glory as he did, since it was I in him that was then so bold, and it is he in me that now reviews the vision. No dust has settled on that robe; no time has elapsed since that divinity was revealed. That time which we really improve, or which is improvable, is neither past, present, nor future.

My residence was more favorable, not only to thought, but to serious reading, than a university; and though I was beyond the range of the ordinary circulating library, I had more than ever come within the influence of those books which circulate round the world, whose sentences were first written on bark, and are now merely copied from time to time on to linen paper. Says the poet Mîr Camar Uddîn Mast,[145] "Being seated to run through the region of the spiritual world; I have had this advantage in books. To be intoxicated by a single glass of wine; I have experienced this pleasure when I have drunk the liquor of the esoteric doctrines." I kept Homer's Iliad on my table through the summer, though I looked at his page only now and then. Incessant labor with my hands, at first, for I had my house to finish and my beans to hoe at the same time, made more study impossible. Yet I sustained myself by the prospect of such reading in future. I read one or two shallow books of travel in the intervals of my work, till that employment made me ashamed of myself, and I asked where it was then that *I* lived.

The student may read Homer or Æschylus[146] in the Greek without danger of dissipation or luxuriousness, for it implies that he in some measure emulate their heroes, and consecrate morning hours to their pages. The heroic books, even if printed in the character of our mother tongue, will always be in a language dead to degenerate times; and we must laboriously seek the meaning of each word and line, conjecturing a larger sense than common use permits out of what wisdom and valor and generosity we have. The modern cheap and fertile press, with all its translations, has done little to bring us nearer to the heroic writers of antiquity. They seem as solitary, and the letter in which they are printed as rare and curious, as ever. It is worth the expense of youthful days and costly hours, if you learn only some words of an ancient language, which are raised out of the trivialness of the street, to be perpetual suggestions and provocations. It is not in vain that the farmer remembers and repeats the few Latin words which he has heard. Men sometimes speak as if the study of the classics would at length make way for more modern and practical studies; but the adventurous student will always study classics, in whatever language they may be written and however ancient they may be. For what are the classics but the noblest recorded thoughts of man? They are the only oracles which are not decayed, and there are such answers to the most modern inquiry in them as Delphi and Dodona[147] never gave. We might as well omit to study Nature because she is old. To read well, that is, to read true books in a true spirit, is a noble exercise, and one that will task the reader more than any exercise which the customs of the day esteem. It requires a training such as the athletes underwent, the steady intention almost of the whole life to this object. Books must be read as deliberately and reservedly as they were written. It is not enough even to be able to speak the language of that nation by which they are written,

---

[145] Prince Qamar-urddin Minnat, eighteenth-century Persian poet.
[146] Greek dramatist (525–456 B.C.).

[147] Locations of shrines built to Apollo and Zeus by the ancient Greeks.

for there is a memorable interval between the spoken and the written language, the language heard and the language read. The one is commonly transitory, a sound, a tongue, a dialect merely, almost brutish, and we learn it unconsciously, like the brutes, of our mothers. The other is the maturity and experience of that; if that is our mother tongue, this is our father tongue, a reserved and select expression, too significant to be heard by the ear, which we must be born again in order to speak. The crowds of men who merely *spoke* the Greek and Latin tongues in the middle ages were not entitled by the accident of birth to *read* the works of genius written in those languages; for these were not written in that Greek or Latin which they knew, but in the select language of literature. They had not learned the nobler dialects of Greece and Rome, but the very materials on which they were written were waste paper to them, and they prized instead a cheap contemporary literature. But when the several nations of Europe had acquired distinct though rude written languages of their own, sufficient for the purposes of their rising literatures, then first learning revived, and scholars were enabled to discern from that remoteness the treasures of antiquity. What the Roman and Grecian multitude could not *hear,* after the lapse of ages a few scholars *read,* and a few scholars only are still reading it.

However much we may admire the orator's occasional bursts of eloquence, the noblest written words are commonly as far behind or above the fleeting spoken language as the firmament with its stars is behind the clouds. *There* are the stars, and they who can may read them. The astronomers forever comment on and observe them. They are not exhalations like our daily colloquies and vaporous breath. What is called eloquence in the forum is commonly found to be rhetoric in the study. The orator yields to the inspiration of a transient occasion, and speaks to the mob before him, to those who can *hear* him; but the writer, whose more equable life is his occasion, and who would be distracted by the event and the crowd which inspire the orator, speaks to the intellect and heart of mankind, to all in any age who can *understand* him.

No wonder that Alexander[148] carried the Iliad with him on his expeditions in a precious casket. A written word is the choicest of relics. It is something at once more intimate with us and more universal than any other work of art. It is the work of art nearest to life itself. It may be translated into every language, and not only be read but actually breathed from all human lips;—not be represented on canvas or in marble only, but be carved out of the breath of life itself. The symbol of an ancient man's thought becomes a modern man's speech. Two thousand summers have imparted to the monuments of Grecian literature, as to her marbles, only a maturer golden and autumnal tint, for they have carried their own serene and celestial atmosphere into all lands to protect them against the corrosion of time. Books are the treasured wealth of the world and the fit inheritance of generations and nations. Books, the oldest and the best, stand naturally and rightfully on the shelves of every cottage. They have no cause of their own to plead, but while they enlighten and sustain the reader his common sense will not refuse them. Their authors are a natural and irresistible aristocracy in every society, and, more than kings or emperors, exert an influence on mankind. When the illiterate and perhaps scornful trader has earned by enterprise and industry his coveted leisure and independence, and is admitted to the circles of wealth and fashion, he turns inevitably at last to those still higher but yet inaccessible circles

---

[148] Alexander the Great (356–323 B.C.).

of intellect and genius, and is sensible only of the imperfection of his culture and the vanity and insufficiency of all his riches, and further proves his good sense by the pains which he takes to secure for his children that intellectual culture whose want he so keenly feels; and thus it is that he becomes the founder of a family.

Those who have not learned to read the ancient classics in the language in which they were written must have a very imperfect knowledge of the history of the human race; for it is remarkable that no transcript of them has ever been made into any modern tongue, unless our civilization itself may be regarded as such a transcript. Homer has never yet been printed[149] in English, nor Æschylus, nor Virgil[150] even,— works as refined, as solidly done, and as beautiful almost as the morning itself; for later writers, say what we will of their genius, have rarely, if ever, equalled the elaborate beauty and finish and the life-long and heroic literary labors of the ancients. They only talk of forgetting them who never knew them. It will be soon enough to forget them when we have the learning and the genius which will enable us to attend to and appreciate them. That age will be rich indeed when those relics which we call Classics, and the still older and more than classic but even less known Scriptures of the nations, shall have still further accumulated, when the Vaticans shall be filled with Vedas and Zendavestas[151] and Bibles, with Homers and Dantes and Shakspeares, and all the centuries to come shall have successively deposited their trophies in the forum of the world. By such a pile we may hope to scale heaven at last.

The works of the great poets have never yet been read by mankind, for only great poets can read them. They have only been read as the multitude read the stars, at most astrologically, not astronomically. Most men have learned to read to serve a paltry convenience, as they have learned to cipher in order to keep accounts and not be cheated in trade; but of reading as a noble intellectual exercise they know little or nothing; yet this only is reading, in a high sense, not that which lulls us as a luxury and suffers the nobler faculties to sleep the while, but what we have to stand on tiptoe to read and devote our most alert and wakeful hours to.

I think that having learned our letters we should read the best that is in literature, and not be forever repeating our a b abs,[152] and words of one syllable, in the fourth or fifth classes, sitting on the lowest and foremost form all our lives. Most men are satisfied if they read or hear read, and perchance have been convicted by the wisdom of one good book, the Bible, and for the rest of their lives vegetate and dissipate their faculties in what is called easy reading. There is a work in several volumes in our Circulating Library entitled Little Reading, which I thought referred to a town of that name which I had not been to. There are those who, like cormorants and ostriches, can digest all sorts of this, even after the fullest dinner of meats and vegetables, for they suffer nothing to be wasted. If others are the machines to provide this provender, they are the machines to read it. They read the nine thousandth tale about Zebulon and Sephronia, and how they loved as none had ever loved before, and neither did the course of their true love run smooth,—at any rate, how it did run and stumble, and get up again and go on! how some poor unfortunate got up onto a steeple, who had better never have gone up as far as the belfry; and then, having needlessly got him up there, the happy novelist rings the bell for all the world to come together

---

[149] I.e., successfully translated.
[150] Roman poet (70–19 B.C.).

[151] Sacred texts of the Zoroastrians.
[152] Alphabet.

and hear, O dear! how he did get down again! For my part, I think that they had better metamorphose all such aspiring heroes of universal noveldom into man weathercocks, as they used to put heroes among the constellations, and let them swing round there till they are rusty, and not come down at all to bother honest men with their pranks. The next time the novelist rings the bell I will not stir though the meeting-house burn down. "The Skip of the Tip-Toe-Hop, a Romance of the Middle Ages, by the celebrated author of 'Tittle-Tol-Tan,' to appear in monthly parts; a great rush; don't all come together." All this they read with saucer eyes, and erect and primitive curiosity, and with unwearied gizzard, whose corrugations even yet need no sharpening, just as some little four-year-old bencher his two-cent gilt-covered edition of Cinderella,—without any improvement, that I can see, in the pronunciation, or accent, or emphasis, or any more skill in extracting or inserting the moral. The result is dulness of sight, a stagnation of the vital circulations, and a general deliquium[153] and sloughing off of all the intellectual faculties. This sort of gingerbread is baked daily and more sedulously than pure wheat or rye-and-Indian in almost every oven, and finds a surer market.

The best books are not read even by those who are called good readers. What does our Concord culture amount to? There is in this town, with a very few exceptions, no taste for the best or for very good books even in English literature, whose words all can read and spell. Even the college-bred and so called liberally educated men here and elsewhere have really little or no acquaintance with the English classics; and as for the recorded wisdom of mankind, the ancient classics and Bibles, which are accessible to all who will know of them, there are the feeblest efforts any where made to become acquainted with them. I know a woodchopper, of middle age, who takes a French paper, not for news as he says, for he is above that, but to "keep himself in practice," he being a Canadian by birth; and when I ask him what he considers the best thing he can do in this world, he says, beside this, to keep up and add to his English. This is about as much as the college bred generally do or aspire to do, and they take an English paper for the purpose. One who has just come from reading perhaps one of the best English books will find how many with whom he can converse about it? Or suppose he comes from reading a Greek or Latin classic in the original, whose praises are familiar even to the so called illiterate; he will find nobody at all to speak to, but must keep silence about it. Indeed, there is hardly the professor in our colleges, who, if he has mastered the difficulties of the language, has proportionally mastered the difficulties of the wit and poetry of a Greek poet, and has any sympathy to impart to the alert and heroic reader; and as for the sacred Scriptures, or Bibles of mankind, who in this town can tell me even their titles? Most men do not know that any nation but the Hebrews have had a scripture. A man, any man, will go considerably out of his way to pick up a silver dollar; but here are golden words, which the wisest men of antiquity have uttered, and whose worth the wise of every succeeding age have assured us of;—and yet we learn to read only as far as Easy Reading, the primers and classbooks, and when we leave school, the "Little Reading," and story books, which are for boys and beginners; and our reading, our conversation and thinking, are all on a very low level, worthy only of pygmies and manikins.

I aspire to be acquainted with wiser men than this our Concord soil has produced,

---

[153] Lessening.

whose names are hardly known here. Or shall I hear the name of Plato[154] and never read his book? As if Plato were my townsman and I never saw him,—my next neighbor and I never heard him speak or attended to the wisdom of his words. But how actually is it? His Dialogues, which contain what was immortal in him, lie on the next shelf, and yet I never read them. We are underbred and low-lived and illiterate; and in this respect I confess I do not make any very broad distinction between the illiterateness of my townsman who cannot read at all, and the illiterateness of him who has learned to read only what is for children and feeble intellects. We should be as good as the worthies of antiquity, but partly by first knowing how good they were. We are a race of tit-men,[155] and soar but little higher in our intellectual flights than the columns of the daily paper.

It is not all books that are as dull as their readers. There are probably words addressed to our condition exactly, which, if we could really hear and understand, would be more salutary than the morning or the spring to our lives, and possibly put a new aspect on the face of things for us. How many a man has dated a new era in his life from the reading of a book. The book exists for us perchance which will explain our miracles and reveal new ones. The at present unutterable things we may find somewhere uttered. These same questions that disturb and puzzle and confound us have in their turn occurred to all the wise men; not one has been omitted; and each has answered them, according to his ability, by his words and his life. Moreover, with wisdom we shall learn liberality. The solitary hired man on a farm in the outskirts of Concord, who has had his second birth and peculiar religious experience, and is driven as he believes into silent gravity and exclusiveness by his faith, may think it is not true; but Zoroaster, thousands of years ago, travelled the same road and had the same experience; but he, being wise, knew it to be universal, and treated his neighbors accordingly, and is even said to have invented and established worship among men. Let him humbly commune with Zoroaster then, and, through the liberalizing influence of all the worthies, with Jesus Christ himself, and let "our church" go by the board.

We boast that we belong to the nineteenth century and are making the most rapid strides of any nation. But consider how little this village does for its own culture. I do not wish to flatter my townsmen, nor to be flattered by them, for that will not advance either of us. We need to be provoked,—goaded like oxen, as we are, into a trot. We have a comparatively decent system of common schools, schools for infants only; but excepting the half-starved Lyceum[156] in the winter, and latterly the puny beginning of a library suggested by the state, no school for ourselves. We spend more on almost any article of bodily aliment or ailment than on our mental aliment. It is time that we had uncommon schools, that we did not leave off our education when we begin to be men and women. It is time that villages were universities, and their elder inhabitants the fellows of universities, with leisure—if they are indeed so well off—to pursue liberal studies the rest of their lives. Shall the world be confined to one Paris or one Oxford forever?[157] Cannot students be boarded here and get a liberal education under the skies of Concord? Can we not hire some Abelard[158] to lecture

---

[154] Greek philosopher (427?–347 B.C.).
[155] I.e., undersized.
[156] Public lectures.

[157] The universities located in those cities.
[158] Peter Abélard (1079–1142), French teacher and theologian.

to us? Alas! what with foddering the cattle and tending the store, we are kept from school too long, and our education is sadly neglected. In this country, the village should in some respects take the place of the nobleman of Europe. It should be the patron of the fine arts. It is rich enough. It wants only the magnanimity and refinement. It can spend money enough on such things as farmers and traders value, but it is thought Utopian to propose spending money for things which more intelligent men know to be of far more worth. This town has spent seventeen thousand dollars on a town-house, thank fortune or politics, but probably it will not spend so much on living wit, the true meat to put into that shell, in a hundred years. The one hundred and twenty-five dollars annually subscribed for a Lyceum in the winter is better spent than any other equal sum raised in the town. If we live in the nineteenth century, why should we not enjoy the advantages which the nineteenth century offers? Why should our life be in any respect provincial? If we will read newspapers, why not skip the gossip of Boston and take the best newspaper in the world at once?—not be sucking the pap of "neutral family" papers, or browsing "Olive-Branches"[159] here in New England. Let the reports of all the learned societies come to us, and we will see if they know any thing. Why should we leave it to Harper & Brothers and Redding & Co.[160] to select our reading? As the nobleman of cultivated taste surrounds himself with whatever conduces to his culture,—genius—learning—wit—books—paintings—statuary—music—philosophical instruments, and the like; so let the village do,—not stop short at a pedagogue, a parson, a sexton, a parish library, and three selectmen, because our pilgrim forefathers got through a cold winter once on a bleak rock with these. To act collectively is according to the spirit of our institutions; and I am confident that, as our circumstances are more flourishing, our means are greater than the nobleman's. New England can hire all the wise men in the world to come and teach her, and board them round the while, and not be provincial at all. That is the *uncommon* school we want. Instead of noblemen, let us have noble villages of men. If it is necessary, omit one bridge over the river, go round a little there, and throw one arch at least over the darker gulf of ignorance which surrounds us.

Sounds

But while we are confined to books, though the most select and classic, and read only particular written languages, which are themselves but dialects and provincial, we are in danger of forgetting the language which all things and events speak without metaphor, which alone is copious and standard. Much is published, but little printed. The rays which stream through the shutter will be no longer remembered when the shutter is wholly removed. No method nor discipline can supersede the necessity of being forever on the alert. What is a course of history, or philosophy, or poetry, no matter how well selected, or the best society, or the most admirable routine of life, compared with the discipline of looking always at what is to be seen? Will you be a reader, a student merely, or a seer? Read your fate, see what is before you, and walk on into futurity.

[159] Methodist weekly.
[160] New York publisher and Boston bookseller, respectively.

I did not read books the first summer; I hoed beans. Nay, I often did better than this. There were times when I could not afford to sacrifice the bloom of the present moment to any work, whether of the head or hands. I love a broad margin to my life. Sometimes, in a summer morning, having taken my accustomed bath, I sat in my sunny doorway from sunrise till noon, rapt in a revery, amidst the pines and hickories and sumachs, in undisturbed solitude and stillness, while the birds sang around or flitted noiseless through the house, until by the sun falling in at my west window, or the noise of some traveller's wagon on the distant highway, I was reminded of the lapse of time. I grew in those seasons like corn in the night, and they were far better than any work of the hands would have been. They were not time subtracted from my life, but so much over and above my usual allowance. I realized what the Orientals mean by contemplation and the forsaking of works. For the most part, I minded not how the hours went. The day advanced as if to light some work of mine; it was morning, and lo, now it is evening, and nothing memorable is accomplished. Instead of singing like the birds, I silently smiled at my incessant good fortune. As the sparrow had its trill, sitting on the hickory before my door, so had I my chuckle or suppressed warble which he might hear out of my nest. My days were not days of the week, bearing the stamp of any heathen deity, nor were they minced into hours and fretted by the ticking of a clock; for I lived like the Puri Indians,[161] of whom it is said that "for yesterday, to-day, and to-morrow they have only one word, and they express the variety of meaning by pointing backward for yesterday, forward for to-morrow and overhead for the passing day." This was sheer idleness to my fellow-townsmen, no doubt; but if the birds and flowers had tried me by their standard, I should not have been found wanting. A man must find his occasions in himself, it is true. The natural day is very calm, and will hardly reprove his indolence.

I had this advantage, at least, in my mode of life, over those who were obliged to look abroad for amusement, to society and the theatre, that my life itself was become my amusement and never ceased to be novel. It was a drama of many scenes and without an end. If we were always indeed getting our living, and regulating our lives according to the last and best mode we had learned, we should never be troubled with ennui. Follow your genius closely enough, and it will not fail to show you a fresh prospect every hour. Housework was a pleasant pastime. When my floor was dirty, I rose early, and, setting all my furniture out of doors on the grass, bed and bedstead making but one budget, dashed water on the floor, and sprinkled white sand from the pond on it, and then with a broom scrubbed it clean and white; and by the time the villagers had broken their fast the morning sun had dried my house sufficiently to allow me to move in again, and my meditations were almost uninterrupted. It was pleasant to see my whole household effects out on the grass, making a little pile like a gypsy's pack, and my three-legged table, from which I did not remove the books and pen and ink, standing amid the pines and hickories. They seemed glad to get out themselves, and as if unwilling to be brought in. I was sometimes tempted to stretch an awning over them and take my seat there. It was worth the while to see the sun shine on these things, and hear the free wind blow on them; so much more interesting most familiar objects look out of doors than in the house. A bird sits on the next bough, life-everlasting grows under the table, and blackberry vines run round

---

[161] Brazilian tribe.

its legs; pine cones, chestnut burs, and strawberry leaves are strewn about. It looked as if this was the way these forms came to be transferred to our furniture, to tables, chairs, and bedsteads,—because they once stood in their midst.

My house was on the side of a hill, immediately on the edge of the larger wood, in the midst of a young forest of pitch pines and hickories, and half a dozen rods from the pond, to which a narrow footpath led down the hill. In my front yard grew the strawberry, blackberry, and life-everlasting, johnswort and golden-rod, shrub-oaks and sand-cherry, blueberry and ground-nut. Near the end of May, the sand-cherry, *Cerasus pumila,* adorned the sides of the path with its delicate flowers arranged in umbels cylindrically about its short stems, which last, in the fall, weighed down with good sized and handsome cherries, fell over in wreaths like rays on every side. I tasted them out of compliment to Nature, though they were scarcely palatable. The sumach, *Rhus glabra,* grew luxuriantly about the house, pushing up through the embankment which I had made, and growing five or six feet the first season. Its broad pinnate tropical leaf was pleasant though strange to look on. The large buds, suddenly pushing out late in the spring from dry sticks which had seemed to be dead, developed themselves as by magic into graceful green and tender boughs, an inch in diameter; and sometimes, as I sat at my window, so heedlessly did they grow and tax their weak joints, I heard a fresh and tender bough suddenly fall like a fan to the ground, when there was not a breath of air stirring, broken off by its own weight. In August, the large masses of berries, which, when in flower, had attracted many wild bees, gradually assumed their bright velvety crimson hue, and by their weight again bent down and broke the tender limbs.

As I sit at my window this summer afternoon, hawks are circling about my clearing; the tantivy[162] of wild pigeons, flying by twos and threes athwart my view, or perching restless on the white-pine boughs behind my house, gives a voice to the air; a fishhawk dimples the glassy surface of the pond and brings up a fish; a mink steals out of the marsh before my door and seizes a frog by the shore; the sedge is bending under the weight of the reed-birds flitting hither and thither; and for the last half hour I have heard the rattle of railroad cars, now dying away and then reviving like the beat of a partridge, conveying travellers from Boston to the country. For I did not live so out of the world as that boy, who, as I hear, was put out to a farmer in the east part of the town, but ere long ran away and came home again, quite down at the heel and homesick. He had never seen such a dull and out-of-the-way place; the folks were all gone off; why, you couldn't even hear the whistle! I doubt if there is such a place in Massachusetts now:—

> "In truth, our village has become a butt
> For one of those fleet railroad shafts, and o'er
> Our peaceful plain its soothing sound is—Concord."[163]

The Fitchburg Railroad touches the pond about a hundred rods south of where I dwell. I usually go to the village along its causeway, and am, as it were, related to

---

[162] Sound of rapid movement.
[163] From a poem by a close acquaintance of

Thoreau, William Ellery Channing the younger (1818–1901).

society by this link. The men on the freight trains, who go over the whole length of the road, bow to me as to an old acquaintance, they pass me so often, and apparently they take me for an employee; and so I am. I too would fain be a track-repairer somewhere in the orbit of the earth.

The whistle of the locomotive penetrates my woods summer and winter, sounding like the scream of a hawk sailing over some farmer's yard, informing me that many restless city merchants are arriving within the circle of the town, or adventurous country traders from the other side. As they come under one horizon, they shout their warning to get off the track to the other, heard sometimes through the circles of two towns. Here come your groceries, country; your rations, countrymen! Nor is there any man so independent on his farm that he can say them nay. And here's your pay for them! screams the countryman's whistle; timber like long battering rams going twenty miles an hour against the city's walls, and chairs enough to seat all the weary and heavy laden that dwell within them. With such huge and lumbering civility the country hands a chair to the city. All the Indian huckleberry hills are stripped, all the cranberry meadows are raked into the city. Up comes the cotton, down goes the woven cloth; up comes the silk, down goes the woollen; up come the books, but down goes the wit that writes them.

When I meet the engine with its train of cars moving off with planetary motion, —or, rather, like a comet, for the beholder knows not if with that velocity and with that direction it will ever revisit this system, since its orbit does not look like a returning curve,—with its steam cloud like a banner streaming behind in golden and silver wreaths, like many a downy cloud which I have seen, high in the heavens, unfolding its masses to the light,—as if this travelling demigod, this cloud-compeller, would ere long take the sunset sky for the livery of his train; when I hear the iron horse make the hills echo with his snort like thunder, shaking the earth with his feet, and breathing fire and smoke from his nostrils, (what kind of winged horse or fiery dragon they will put into the new Mythology I don't know,) it seems as if the earth had got a race now worthy to inhabit it. If all were as it seems, and men made the elements their servants for noble ends! If the cloud that hangs over the engine were the perspiration of heroic deeds, or as beneficent to men as that which floats over the farmer's fields, then the elements and Nature herself would cheerfully accompany men on their errands and be their escort.

I watch the passage of the morning cars with the same feeling that I do the rising of the sun, which is hardly more regular. Their train of clouds stretching far behind and rising higher and higher, going to heaven while the cars are going to Boston, conceals the sun for a minute and casts my distant field into the shade, a celestial train beside which the petty train of cars which hugs the earth is but the barb of the spear. The stabler of the iron horse was up early this winter morning by the light of the stars amid the mountains, to fodder and harness his steed. Fire, too, was awakened thus early to put the vital heat in him and get him off. If the enterprise were as innocent as it is early! If the snow lies deep, they strap on his snow-shoes, and with the giant plow, plow a furrow from the mountains to the seaboard, in which the cars, like a following drill-barrow,[164] sprinkle all the restless men and floating merchandise in the country for seed. All day the fire-steed flies over the country, stopping only that his

---

[164] Machine for planting seed.

master may rest, and I am awakened by his tramp and defiant snort at midnight, when in some remote glen in the woods he fronts the elements incased in ice and snow; and he will reach his stall only with the morning star, to start once more on his travels without rest or slumber. Or perchance, at evening, I hear him in his stable blowing off the superfluous energy of the day, that he may calm his nerves and cool his liver and brain for a few hours of iron slumber. If the enterprise were as heroic and commanding as it is protracted and unwearied!

Far through unfrequented woods on the confines of towns, where once only the hunter penetrated by day, in the darkest night dart these bright saloons without the knowledge of their inhabitants; this moment stopping at some brilliant station-house in town or city, where a social crowd is gathered, the next in the Dismal Swamp,[165] scaring the owl and fox. The startings and arrivals of the cars are now the epochs in the village day. They go and come with such regularity and precision, and their whistle can be heard so far, that the farmers set their clocks by them, and thus one well conducted institution regulates a whole country. Have not men improved somewhat in punctuality since the railroad was invented? Do they not talk and think faster in the depot than they did in the stage-office? There is something electrifying in the atmosphere of the former place. I have been astonished at the miracles it has wrought; that some of my neighbors, who, I should have prophesied, once for all, would never get to Boston by so prompt a conveyance, were on hand when the bell rang. To do things "railroad fashion" is now the by-word; and it is worth the while to be warned so often and so sincerely by any power to get off its track. There is no stopping to read the riot act, no firing over the heads of the mob, in this case. We have constructed a fate, an *Atropos*,[166] that never turns aside. (Let that be the name of your engine.) Men are advertised that at a certain hour and minute these bolts will be shot toward particular points of the compass; yet it interferes with no man's business, and the children go to school on the other track. We live the steadier for it. We are all educated thus to be sons of Tell.[167] The air is full of invisible bolts. Every path but your own is the path of fate. Keep on your own track, then.

What recommends commerce to me is its enterprise and bravery. It does not clasp its hands and pray to Jupiter. I see these men every day go about their business with more or less courage and content, doing more even than they suspect, and perchance better employed than they could have consciously devised. I am less affected by their heroism who stood up for half an hour in the front line at Buena Vista,[168] than by the steady and cheerful valor of the men who inhabit the snow-plough for their winter quarters; who have not merely the three-o'-clock in the morning courage, which Bonaparte[169] thought was the rarest, but whose courage does not go to rest so early, who go to sleep only when the storm sleeps or the sinews of their iron steed are frozen. On this morning of the Great Snow,[170] perchance, which is still raging and chilling men's blood, I hear the muffled tone of their engine bell from out the fog bank of their chilled breath, which announces that the cars *are coming*, without long delay,

---

[165] Swamp spread across North Carolina and eastern Virginia.
[166] Controller of one's life span, in Greek myth.
[167] William Tell, Swiss patriot, shot an apple from his son's head and then slew the tyrant who had commanded that it be done.

[168] Battle of February 1847 between the Mexican army and forces of the United States.
[169] Napoleon Bonaparte (1769–1821).
[170] Possible allusion to the blizzard of February 1717.

notwithstanding the veto of a New England north-east snow storm, and I behold the ploughmen covered with snow and rime,[171] their heads peering above the mould-board[172] which is turning down other than daisies and the nests of field-mice, like bowlders of the Sierra Nevada, that occupy an outside place in the universe.

Commerce is unexpectedly confident and serene, alert, adventurous, and un-wearied. It is very natural in its methods withal, far more so than many fantastic enterprises and sentimental experiments, and hence its singular success. I am refreshed and expanded when the freight train rattles past me, and I smell the stores which go dispensing their odors all the way from Long Wharf[173] to Lake Champlain, reminding me of foreign parts, of coral reefs, and Indian oceans, and tropical climes, and the extent of the globe. I feel more like a citizen of the world at the sight of the palm-leaf which will cover so many flaxen New England heads[174] the next summer, the Manilla hemp and cocoa-nut husks, the old junk, gunny bags, scrap iron, and rusty nails. This car-load of torn sails is more legible and interesting now than if they should be wrought into paper and printed books. Who can write so graphically the history of the storms they have weathered as these rents have done? They are proof-sheets which need no correction. Here goes lumber from the Maine woods, which did not go out to sea in the last freshet, risen four dollars on the thousand because of what did go out or was split up; pine, spruce, cedar,—first, second, third and fourth qualities, so lately all of one quality, to wave over the bear, and moose, and caribou. Next rolls Thomaston lime,[175] a prime lot, which will get far among the hills before it gets slacked. These rags in bales, of all hues and qualities, the lowest condition to which cotton and linen descend, the final result of dress,—of patterns which are now no longer cried up, unless it be in Milwaukie, as those splendid articles, English, French, or American prints, ginghams, muslins, &c., gathered from all quarters both of fashion and poverty, going to become paper of one color or a few shades only, on which forsooth will be written tales of real life, high and low, and founded on fact! This closed car smells of salt fish, the strong New England and commercial scent, reminding me of the Grand Banks[176] and the fisheries. Who has not seen a salt fish, thoroughly cured for this world, so that nothing can spoil it, and putting the perseverance of the saints to the blush? with which you may sweep or pave the streets, and split your kindlings, and the teamster shelter himself and his lading against sun wind and rain behind it,—and the trader, as a Concord trader once did, hang it up by his door for a sign when he commences business, until at last his oldest customer cannot tell surely whether it be animal, vegetable, or mineral, and yet it shall be as pure as a snowflake, and if it be put into a pot and boiled, will come out an excellent dun fish[177] for a Saturday's dinner. Next Spanish hides, with the tails still preserving their twist and the angle of elevation they had when the oxen that wore them were careering over the pampas of the Spanish main,—a type of all obstinacy, and evincing how almost hopeless and incurable are all constitutional vices. I confess, that practically speaking, when I have learned a man's real disposition, I have no hopes of changing it for the better or worse in this state of existence. As the Orientals say, "A cur's tail may be

---

[171] Icy coating.
[172] Snow plow.
[173] In Boston.
[174] Hats of woven palm leaves.

[175] From town in Maine.
[176] Newfoundland fishing waters.
[177] Dried, salted fish.

warmed, and pressed, and bound round with ligatures, and after a twelve years' labor bestowed upon it, still it will retain its natural form." The only effectual cure for such inveteracies as these tails exhibit is to make glue of them, which I believe is what is usually done with them, and then they will stay put and stick. Here is a hogshead of molasses or of brandy directed to John Smith, Cuttingsville, Vermont, some trader among the Green Mountains, who imports for the farmers near his clearing, and now perchance stands over his bulk-head and thinks of the last arrivals on the coast, how they may affect the price for him, telling his customers this moment, as he has told them twenty times before this morning, that he expects some by the next train of prime quality. It is advertised in the Cuttingsville Times.

While these things go up other things come down. Warned by the whizzing sound, I look up from my book and see some tall pine, hewn on far northern hills, which has winged its way over the Green Mountains and the Connecticut,[178] shot like an arrow through the township within ten minutes, and scarce another eye beholds it; going

> "to be the mast
> Of some great ammiral."[179]

And hark! here comes the cattle-train bearing the cattle of a thousand hills, sheepcots, stables, and cowyards in the air, drovers with their sticks, and shepherd boys in the midst of their flocks, all but the mountain pastures, whirled along like leaves blown from the mountains by the September gales. The air is filled with the bleating of calves and sheep, and the hustling of oxen, as if a pastoral valley were going by. When the old bell-wether at the head rattles his bell, the mountains do indeed skip like rams and the little hills like lambs. A car-load of drovers, too, in the midst, on a level with their droves now, their vocation gone, but still clinging to their useless sticks as their badge of office. But their dogs, where are they? It is a stampede to them; they are quite thrown out; they have lost the scent. Methinks I hear them barking behind the Peterboro' Hills, or panting up the western slope of the Green Mountains.[180] They will not be in at the death. Their vocation, too, is gone. Their fidelity and sagacity are below par now. They will slink back to their kennels in disgrace, or perchance run wild and strike a league with the wolf and the fox. So is your pastoral life whirled past and away. But the bell rings, and I must get off the track and let the cars go by;—

> What's the railroad to me?
> I never go to see
> Where it ends.
> It fills a few hollows,
> And makes banks for the swallows,
> It sets the sand a-blowing,
> And the blackberries a-growing,[181]

---

[178] I.e., has traveled by way of Vermont and the Connecticut River.

[179] I.e., to be the lead ship carrying the admiral. (See John Milton's *Paradise Lost*, I, 293–294.)

[180] Peterboro' Hills: New Hampshire hills; Green Mountain: mountains extending from Massachusetts to Canada.

[181] Thoreau's own verses.

but I cross it like a cart-path in the woods. I will not have my eyes put out and my ears spoiled by its smoke and steam and hissing.

Now that the cars are gone by, and all the restless world with them, and the fishes in the pond no longer feel their rumbling, I am more alone than ever. For the rest of the long afternoon, perhaps, my meditations are interrupted only by the faint rattle of a carriage or team along the distant highway.

Sometimes, on Sundays, I heard the bells, the Lincoln, Acton, Bedford,[182] or Concord bell, when the wind was favorable, a faint, sweet, and, as it were, natural melody, worth importing into the wilderness. At a sufficient distance over the woods this sound acquires a certain vibratory hum, as if the pine needles in the horizon were the strings of a harp which it swept. All sound heard at the greatest possible distance produces one and the same effect, a vibration of the universal lyre, just as the intervening atmosphere makes a distant ridge of earth interesting to our eyes by the azure tint it imparts to it. There came to me in this case a melody which the air had strained, and which had conversed with every leaf and needle of the wood, that portion of the sound which the elements had taken up and modulated and echoed from vale to vale. The echo is, to some extent, an original sound, and therein is the magic and charm of it. It is not merely a repetition of what was worth repeating in the bell, but partly the voice of the wood; the same trivial words and notes sung by a wood-nymph.

At evening, the distant lowing of some cow in the horizon beyond the woods sounded sweet and melodious, and at first I would mistake it for the voices of certain minstrels by whom I was sometimes serenaded, who might be straying over hill and dale; but soon I was not unpleasantly disappointed when it was prolonged into the cheap and natural music of the cow. I do not mean to be satirical, but to express my appreciation of those youths' singing, when I state that I perceived clearly that it was akin to the music of the cow, and they were at length one articulation of Nature.

Regularly at half past seven, in one part of the summer, after the evening train had gone by, the whippoorwills chanted their vespers for half an hour, sitting on a stump by my door, or upon the ridge pole of the house. They would begin to sing almost with as much precision as a clock, within five minutes of a particular time, referred to the setting of the sun, every evening. I had a rare opportunity to become acquainted with their habits. Sometimes I heard four or five at once in different parts of the wood, by accident one a bar behind another, and so near me that I distinguished not only the cluck after each note, but often that singular buzzing sound like a fly in a spider's web, only proportionally louder. Sometimes one would circle round and round me in the woods a few feet distant as if tethered by a string, when probably I was near its eggs. They sang at intervals throughout the night, and were again as musical as ever just before and about dawn.

When other birds are still the screech owls take up the strain, like mourning women their ancient u-lu-lu. Their dismal scream is truly Ben Jonsonian.[183] Wise midnight hags! It is no honest and blunt tu-whit tu-who of the poets, but, without jesting, a most solemn graveyard ditty, the mutual consolations of suicide lovers remembering

---

[182] Three nearby villages.
[183] I.e., plaintive as an elegy by Ben Jonson (1573–1637), English poet and dramatist.

the pangs and the delights of supernal love in the infernal groves. Yet I love to hear their wailing, their doleful responses, trilled along the wood-side, reminding me sometimes of music and singing birds; as if it were the dark and tearful side of music, the regrets and sighs that would fain be sung. They are the spirits, the low spirits and melancholy forebodings, of fallen souls that once in human shape night-walked the earth and did the deeds of darkness, now expiating their sins with their wailing hymns or threnodies in the scenery of their transgressions. They give me a new sense of the variety and capacity of that nature which is our common dwelling. *Oh-o-o-o-o that I never had been bor-r-r-r-n!* sighs one on this side of the pond, and circles with the restlessness of despair to some new perch on the gray oaks. Then—*that I never had been bor-r-r-r-n!* echoes another on the farther side with tremulous sincerity, and—*bor-r-r-r-n!* comes faintly from far in the Lincoln woods.

I was also serenaded by a hooting owl. Near at hand you could fancy it the most melancholy sound in Nature, as if she meant by this to stereotype and make permanent in her choir the dying moans of a human being,—some poor weak relic of mortality who has left hope behind, and howls like an animal, yet with human sobs, on entering the dark valley, made more awful by a certain gurgling melodiousness,—I find myself beginning with the letters gl when I try to imitate it,—expressive of a mind which has reached the gelatinous mildewy stage in the mortification of all healthy and courageous thought. It reminded me of ghouls and idiots and insane howlings. But now one answers from far woods in a strain made really melodious by distance,—*Hoo hoo hoo, hoorer hoo;* and indeed for the most part it suggested only pleasing associations, whether heard by day or night, summer or winter.

I rejoice that there are owls. Let them do the idiotic and maniacal hooting for men. It is a sound admirably suited to swamps and twilight woods which no day illustrates, suggesting a vast and undeveloped nature which men have not recognized. They represent the stark twilight and unsatisfied thoughts which all have. All day the sun has shone on the surface of some savage swamp, where the double spruce stands hung with usnea lichens, and small hawks circulate above, and the chicadee lisps amid the evergreens, and the partridge and rabbit skulk beneath; but now a more dismal and fitting day dawns, and a different race of creatures awakes to express the meaning of Nature there.

Late in the evening I heard the distant rumbling of wagons over bridges,—a sound heard farther than almost any other at night,—the baying of dogs, and sometimes again the lowing of some disconsolate cow in a distant barn-yard. In the mean while all the shore rang with the trump of bullfrogs, the sturdy spirits of ancient wine-bibbers and wassailers, still unrepentant, trying to sing a catch[184] in their Stygian lake,[185]— if the Walden nymphs will pardon the comparison, for though there are almost no weeds, there are frogs there,—who would fain keep up the hilarious rules of their old festal tables, though their voices have waxed hoarse and solemnly grave, mocking at mirth, and the wine has lost its flavor, and become only liquor to distend their paunches, and sweet intoxication never comes to drown the memory of the past, but mere saturation and waterloggedness and distention. The most alder-

---

[184] Song.
[185] Allusion to the river Styx, of classic myth, in the land of the dead.

manic, with his chin upon a heart-leaf, which serves for a napkin to his drooling chaps, under this northern shore quaffs a deep draught of the once scorned water, and passes round the cup with the ejaculation *tr-r-r-oonk, tr-r-r-oonk, tr-r-r-oonk!* and straightway comes over the water from some distant cove the same password repeated, where the next in seniority and girth has gulped down to his mark;[186] and when this observance has made the circuit of the shores, then ejaculates the master of ceremonies, with satisfaction, *tr-r-r-oonk!* and each in his turn repeats the same down to the least distended, leakiest, and flabbiest paunched, that there be no mistake; and then the bowl goes round again and again, until the sun disperses the morning mist, and only the patriarch is not under the pond,[187] but vainly bellowing *troonk* from time to time, and pausing for a reply.

I am not sure that I ever heard the sound of cock-crowing from my clearing, and I thought that it might be worth the while to keep a cockerel for his music merely, as a singing bird. The note of this once wild Indian pheasant is certainly the most remarkable of any bird's, and if they could be naturalized without being domesticated, it would soon become the most famous sound in our woods, surpassing the clangor of the goose and the hooting of the owl; and then imagine the cackling of the hens to fill the pauses when their lords' clarions rested! No wonder that man added this bird to his tame stock,—to say nothing of the eggs and drumsticks. To walk in a winter morning in a wood where these birds abounded, their native woods, and hear the wild cockerels crow on the trees, clear and shrill for miles over the resounding earth, drowning the feebler notes of other birds,—think of it! It would put nations on the alert. Who would not be early to rise, and rise earlier and earlier every successive day of his life, till he became unspeakably healthy, wealthy, and wise? This foreign bird's note is celebrated by the poets of all countries along with the notes of their native songsters. All climates agree with brave Chanticleer. He is more indigenous even than the natives. His health is ever good, his lungs are sound, his spirits never flag. Even the sailor on the Atlantic and Pacific is awakened by his voice;[188] but its shrill sound never roused me from my slumbers. I kept neither dog, cat, cow, pig, nor hens, so that you would have said there was a deficiency of domestic sounds; neither the churn, nor the spinning wheel, nor even the singing of the kettle, nor the hissing of the urn, nor children crying, to comfort one. An old-fashioned man would have lost his senses or died of ennui before this. Not even rats in the wall, for they were starved out, or rather were never baited in,—only squirrels on the roof and under the floor, a whippoorwill on the ridge pole, a blue-jay screaming beneath the window, a hare or woodchuck under the house, a screech-owl or a cat-owl behind it, a flock of wild geese or a laughing loon on the pond, and a fox to bark in the night. Not even a lark or an oriole, those mild plantation birds, ever visited my clearing. No cockerels to crow nor hens to cackle in the yard. No yard! but unfenced Nature reaching up to your very sills. A young forest growing up under your windows, and wild sumachs and blackberry vines breaking through into your cellar; sturdy pitch-pines rubbing and creaking against the shingles for want of room, their roots reaching quite under the house. Instead of a scuttle or a blind blown off in the gale,—a pine tree snapped off or torn up by the roots behind your house for fuel. Instead of no

---

[186] Drunk his fill.
[187] Drunk; "under the table."

[188] Fowl were taken on long voyages to supply fresh eggs.

path to the front-yard gate in the Great Snow,—no gate,—no front-yard,—and no path to the civilized world!

Solitude

This is a delicious evening, when the whole body is one sense, and imbibes delight through every pore. I go and come with a strange liberty in Nature, a part of herself. As I walk along the stony shore of the pond in my shirt sleeves, though it is cool as well as cloudy and windy, and I see nothing special to attract me, all the elements are unusually congenial to me. The bullfrogs trump to usher in the night, and the note of the whippoorwill is borne on the rippling wind from over the water. Sympathy with the fluttering alder and poplar leaves almost takes away my breath; yet, like the lake, my serenity is rippled but not ruffled. These small waves raised by the evening wind are as remote from storm as the smooth reflecting surface. Though it is now dark, the wind still blows and roars in the wood, the waves still dash, and some creatures lull the rest with their notes. The repose is never complete. The wildest animals do not repose, but seek their prey now; the fox, and skunk, and rabbit, now roam the fields and woods without fear. They are Nature's watchmen,—links which connect the days of animated life.

When I return to my house I find that visitors have been there and left their cards, either a bunch of flowers, or a wreath of evergreen, or a name in pencil on a yellow walnut leaf or a chip. They who come rarely to the woods take some little piece of the forest into their hands to play with by the way, which they leave, either intentionally or accidentally. One has peeled a willow wand, woven it into a ring, and dropped it on my table. I could always tell if visitors had called in my absence, either by the bended twigs or grass, or the print of their shoes, and generally of what sex or age or quality they were by some slight trace left, as a flower dropped, or a bunch of grass plucked and thrown away, even as far off as the railroad, half a mile distant, or by the lingering odor of a cigar or pipe. Nay, I was frequently notified of the passage of a traveller along the highway sixty rods off by the scent of his pipe.

There is commonly sufficient space about us. Our horizon is never quite at our elbows. The thick wood is not just at our door, nor the pond, but somewhat is always clearing, familiar and worn by us, appropriated and fenced in some way, and reclaimed from Nature. For what reason have I this vast range and circuit, some square miles of unfrequented forest, for my privacy, abandoned to me by men? My nearest neighbor is a mile distant, and no house is visible from any place but the hill-tops within half a mile of my own. I have my horizon bounded by woods all to myself; a distant view of the railroad where it touches the pond on the one hand, and of the fence which skirts the woodland road on the other. But for the most part it is as solitary where I live as on the prairies. It is as much Asia or Africa as New England. I have, as it were, my own sun and moon and stars, and a little world all to myself. At night there was never a traveller passed my house, or knocked at my door, more than if I were the first or last man; unless it were in the spring, when at long intervals some came from the village to fish for pouts,—they plainly fished much more in the Walden Pond of their own natures, and baited their hooks with darkness,—but they soon retreated, usually with light baskets, and left "the world to darkness and to me,"[189] and the black kernel of the night was never profaned by any human neighborhood. I believe that men are generally still a little afraid of the dark, though the witches are all hung, and Christianity and candles have been introduced.

Yet I experienced sometimes that the most sweet and tender, the most innocent and encouraging society may be found in any natural object, even for the poor misanthrope and most melancholy man. There can be no very black melancholy to him who lives in the midst of Nature and has his senses still. There was never yet such a storm but it was Æolian music[190] to a healthy and innocent ear. Nothing can rightly compel a simple and brave man to a vulgar sadness. While I enjoy the friendship of the seasons I trust that nothing can make life a burden to me. The gentle rain which waters my beans and keeps me in the house to-day is not drear and melancholy, but good for me too. Though it prevents my hoeing them, it is of far more worth than my hoeing. If it should continue so long as to cause the seeds to rot in the ground and destroy the potatoes in the low lands, it would still be good for the grass on the uplands, and, being good for the grass, it would be good for me. Sometimes, when I compare myself with other men, it seems as if I were more favored by the gods than they, beyond any deserts that I am conscious of; as if I had a warrant and surety at their hands which my fellows have not, and were especially guided and guarded. I do not flatter myself, but if it be possible they flatter me. I have never felt lonesome, or in the least oppressed by a sense of solitude, but once, and that was a few weeks after I came to the woods, when, for an hour, I doubted if the near neighborhood of man was not essential to a serene and healthy life. To be alone was something unpleasant. But I was at the same time conscious of a slight insanity in my mood, and seemed to foresee my recovery. In the midst of a gentle rain while these thoughts prevailed, I was suddenly sensible of such sweet and beneficent society in Nature, in the very pattering of the drops, and in every sound and sight around my house, an infinite and unaccountable friendliness all at once like an atmosphere sustaining me, as made the fancied advantages of human neighborhood insignificant, and I have never thought of them since. Every little pine needle expanded and swelled with sympathy and befriended me. I was so distinctly made aware of the presence of something kindred to me, even in scenes which we are accustomed to call wild and dreary, and also that the nearest of blood to me and humanest was not a person nor a villager, that I thought no place could ever be strange to me again.—

> "Mourning untimely consumes the sad;
> Few are their days in the land of the living,
> Beautiful daughter of Toscar."[191]

Some of my pleasantest hours were during the long rain storms in the spring or fall, which confined me to the house for the afternoon as well as the forenoon, soothed by their ceaseless roar and pelting; when an early twilight ushered in a long evening

---

[189] From "Elegy Written in a Country Churchyard" (1751) by the English poet Thomas Gray.

[190] Music caused by the wind passing over the strings of an Aeolian harp.

[191] Lines from *Ossian* (1762) by James McPherson (1736–1796), British poet.

in which many thoughts had time to take root and unfold themselves. In those driving north-east rains which tried the village houses so, when the maids stood ready with mop and pail in front entries to keep the deluge out, I sat behind my door in my little house, which was all entry, and thoroughly enjoyed its protection. In one heavy thunder shower the lightning struck a large pitch-pine across the pond, making a very conspicuous and perfectly regular spiral groove from top to bottom, an inch or more deep, and four or five inches wide, as you would groove a walking-stick. I passed it again the other day, and was struck with awe on looking up and beholding that mark, now more distinct than ever, where a terrific and resistless bolt came down out of the harmless sky eight years ago. Men frequently say to me, "I should think you would feel lonesome down there, and want to be nearer to folks, rainy and snowy days and nights especially." I am tempted to reply to such,—This whole earth which we inhabit is but a point in space. How far apart, think you, dwell the two most distant inhabitants of yonder star, the breadth of whose disk cannot be appreciated by our instruments? Why should I feel lonely? is not our planet in the Milky Way? This which you put seems to me not to be the most important question. What sort of space is that which separates a man from his fellows and makes him solitary? I have found that no exertion of the legs can bring two minds much nearer to one another. What do we want most to dwell near to? Not to many men surely, the depot, the post-office, the bar-room, the meeting-house, the school-house, the grocery, Beacon Hill,[192] or the Five Points,[193] where men most congregate, but to the perennial source of our life, whence in all our experience we have found that to issue; as the willow stands near the water and sends out its roots in that direction. This will vary with different natures, but this is the place where a wise man will dig his cellar. . . . I one evening overtook one of my townsmen, who has accumulated what is called "a handsome property,"—though I never got a *fair* view of it,—on the Walden road, driving a pair of cattle to market, who inquired of me how I could bring my mind to give up so many of the comforts of life. I answered that I was very sure I liked it passably well; I was not joking. And so I went home to my bed, and left him to pick his way through the darkness and the mud to Brighton,—or Bright-town[194]—which place he would reach some time in the morning.

Any prospect of awakening or coming to life to a dead man makes indifferent all times and places. The place where that may occur is always the same, and indescribably pleasant to all our senses. For the most part we allow only outlying and transient circumstances to make our occasions. They are, in fact, the cause of our distraction. Nearest to all things is that power which fashions their being. *Next* to us the grandest laws are continually being executed. *Next* to us is not the workman whom we have hired, with whom we love so well to talk, but the workman whose work we are.

"How vast and profound is the influence of the subtile powers of Heaven and of Earth!"

"We seek to perceive them, and we do not see them; we seek to hear them, and we do not hear them; identified with the substance of things, they cannot be separated from them."

---

[192] Fashionable Boston residential area.
[193] A central area of New York City, known for its vices.

[194] *Bright* means "ox"; Brighton was the Boston district for slaughtering cattle.

"They cause that in all the universe men purify and sanctify their hearts, and clothe themselves in their holiday garments to offer sacrifices and oblations to their ancestors. It is an ocean of subtile intelligences. They are every where, above us, on our left, on our right; they environ us on all sides."[195]

We are the subjects of an experiment which is not a little interesting to me. Can we not do without the society of our gossips a little while under these circumstances, —have our own thoughts to cheer us? Confucius says truly, "Virtue does not remain as an abandoned orphan; it must of necessity have neighbors."[196]

With thinking we may be beside ourselves in a sane sense. By a conscious effort of the mind we can stand aloof from actions and their consequences; and all things, good and bad, go by us like a torrent. We are not wholly involved in Nature. I may be either the drift-wood in the stream, or Indra[197] in the sky looking down on it. I *may* be affected by a theatrical exhibition; on the other hand, I *may not* be affected by an actual event which appears to concern me much more. I only know myself as a human entity; the scene, so to speak, of thoughts and affections; and am sensible of a certain doubleness by which I can stand as remote from myself as from another. However intense my experience, I am conscious of the presence and criticism of a part of me, which, as it were, is not a part of me, but spectator, sharing no experience, but taking note of it; and that is no more I than it is you. When the play, it may be the tragedy, of life is over, the spectator goes his way. It was a kind of fiction, a work of the imagination only, so far as he was concerned. This doubleness may easily make us poor neighbors and friends sometimes.

I find it wholesome to be alone the greater part of the time. To be in company, even with the best, is soon wearisome and dissipating. I love to be alone. I never found the companion that was so companionable as solitude. We are for the most part more lonely when we go abroad among men than when we stay in our chambers. A man thinking or working is always alone, let him be where he will. Solitude is not measured by the miles of space that intervene between a man and his fellows. The really diligent student in one of the crowded hives of Cambridge College is as solitary as a dervish in the desert. The farmer can work alone in the field or the woods all day, hoeing or chopping, and not feel lonesome, because he is employed; but when he comes home at night he cannot sit down in a room alone, at the mercy of his thoughts, but must be where he can "see the folks," and recreate, and as he thinks remunerate himself for his day's solitude; and hence he wonders how the student can sit alone in the house all night and most of the day without ennui and "the blues;" but he does not realize that the student, though in the house, is still at work in *his* field, and chopping in *his* woods, as the farmer in his, and in turn seeks the same recreation and society that the latter does, though it may be a more condensed form of it.

Society is commonly too cheap. We meet at very short intervals, not having had time to acquire any new value for each other. We meet at meals three times a day, and give each other a new taste of that old musty cheese that we are. We have had to agree on a certain set of rules, called etiquette and politeness, to make this frequent meeting tolerable, and that we need not come to open war. We meet at the post-office,

---

[195] From *The Doctrine of the Mean* by Confucius.   [197] Hindu sky god.
[196] From Confucius' *Analects*, IV, 25.

and at the sociable, and about the fireside every night; we live thick and are in each other's way, and stumble over one another, and I think that we thus lose some respect for one another. Certainly less frequency would suffice for all important and hearty communications. Consider the girls in a factory,—never alone, hardly in their dreams.[198] It would be better if there were but one inhabitant to a square mile, as where I live. The value of a man is not in his skin, that we should touch him.

I have heard of a man lost in the woods and dying of famine and exhaustion at the foot of a tree, whose loneliness was relieved by the grotesque visions with which, owing to bodily weakness, his diseased imagination surrounded him, and which he believed to be real. So also, owing to bodily and mental health and strength, we may be continually cheered by a like but more normal and natural society, and come to know that we are never alone.

I have a great deal of company in my house; especially in the morning, when nobody calls. Let me suggest a few comparisons, that some one may convey an idea of my situation. I am no more lonely than the loon in the pond that laughs so loud, or than Walden Pond itself. What company has that lonely lake, I pray? And yet it has not the blue devils, but the blue angels in it, in the azure tint of its waters. The sun is alone, except in thick weather, when there sometimes appear to be two, but one is a mock sun. God is alone,—but the devil, he is far from being alone; he sees a great deal of company; he is legion. I am no more lonely than a single mullein or dandelion in a pasture, or a bean leaf, or sorrel, or a horsefly, or a humble-bee. I am no more lonely than the Mill Brook, or a weathercock, or the northstar, or the south wind, or an April shower, or a January thaw, or the first spider in a new house.

I have occasional visits in the long winter evenings, when the snow falls fast and the wind howls in the wood, from an old settler and original proprietor who is reported to have dug Walden Pond, and stoned it, and fringed it with pine woods; who tells me stories of old time and of new eternity; and between us we manage to pass a cheerful evening with social mirth and pleasant views of things, even without apples or cider,—a most wise and humorous friend, whom I love much, who keeps himself more secret than ever did Goffe or Whalley;[199] and though he is thought to be dead, none can show where he is buried. An elderly dame,[200] too, dwells in my neighborhood, invisible to most persons, in whose odorous herb garden I love to stroll sometimes, gathering simples and listening to her fables; for she has a genius of unequalled fertility, and her memory runs back farther than mythology, and she can tell me the original of every fable, and on what fact every one is founded, for the incidents occurred when she was young. A ruddy and lusty old dame, who delights in all weathers and seasons, and is likely to outlive all her children yet.

The indescribable innocence and beneficence of Nature,—of sun and wind and rain, of summer and winter,—such health, such cheer, they afford forever! and such sympathy have they ever with our race, that all Nature would be affected, and the

---

[198] Reference to the fact that young women working in certain New England factories were required to live in company-owned dormitories.
[199] Goffe, Whalley: English regicides who signed

Charles I's death warrant; they fled to New England in 1660 when the monarchy was restored.
[200] Mother Nature.

sun's brightness fade, and the winds would sigh humanely, and the clouds rain tears, and the woods shed their leaves and put on mourning in midsummer, if any man should ever for a just cause grieve. Shall I not have intelligence with the earth? Am I not partly leaves and vegetable mould myself?

What is the pill which will keep us well, serene, contented? Not my or thy great-grandfather's, but our great-grandmother Nature's universal, vegetable, botanic medicines, by which she has kept herself young always, outlived so many old Parrs[201] in her day, and fed her health with their decaying fatness. For my panacea, instead of one of those quack vials of a mixture dipped from Acheron[202] and the Dead Sea, which come out of those long shallow black-schooner looking wagons which we sometimes see made to carry bottles, let me have a draught of undiluted morning air. Morning air! If men will not drink of this at the fountain-head of the day, why, then, we must even bottle up some and sell it in the shops, for the benefit of those who have lost their subscription ticket to morning time in this world. But remember, it will not keep quite till noon-day even in the coolest cellar, but drive out the stopples long ere that and follow westward the steps of Aurora. I am no worshipper of Hygeia,[203] who was the daughter of that old herb-doctor Æsculapius, and who is represented on monuments holding a serpent in one hand, and in the other a cup out of which the serpent sometimes drinks; but rather of Hebe,[204] cupbearer to Jupiter, who was the daughter of Juno and wild lettuce, and who had the power of restoring gods and men to the vigor of youth. She was probably the only thoroughly sound-conditioned, healthy, and robust young lady that ever walked the globe, and wherever she came it was spring.

Visitors

I think that I love society as much as most, and am ready enough to fasten myself like a blood-sucker for the time to any full-blooded man that comes in my way. I am naturally no hermit, but might possibly sit out the sturdiest frequenter of the bar-room, if my business called me thither.

I had three chairs in my house; one for solitude, two for friendship, three for society. When visitors came in larger and unexpected numbers there was but the third chair for them all, but they generally economized the room by standing up. It is surprising how many great men and women a small house will contain. I have had twenty-five or thirty souls, with their bodies, at once under my roof, and yet we often parted without being aware that we had come very near to one another. Many of our houses, both public and private, with their almost innumerable apartments, their huge halls and their cellars for the storage of wines and other munitions of peace, appear to me extravagantly large for their inhabitants. They are so vast and magnifi-

---

[201] Thomas Parr (1483?–1635), long-lived Englishman.

[202] In Greek myth, the river that supposedly flowed into the underworld.

[203] Goddess of health, whose father Aesculapius, god of physicians, was represented by a snake that sheds its skin as a symbol of the continual renewal of life.

[204] Goddess of youth, attendant to the Greek gods; conceived by Juno as the result of eating wild lettuce.

cent that the latter seem to be only vermin which infest them. I am surprised when the herald blows his summons before some Tremont or Astor or Middlesex House,[205] to see come creeping out over the piazza for all inhabitants a ridiculous mouse, which soon again slinks into some hole in the pavement.

One inconvenience I sometimes experienced in so small a house, the difficulty of getting to a sufficient distance from my guest when we began to utter the big thoughts in big words. You want room for your thoughts to get into sailing trim and run a course or two before they make their port. The bullet of your thought must have overcome its lateral and ricochet motion and fallen into its last and steady course before it reaches the ear of the hearer, else it may plough out again through the side of his head. Also, our sentences wanted room to unfold and form their columns in the interval. Individuals, like nations, must have suitable broad and natural boundaries, even a considerable neutral ground, between them. I have found it a singular luxury to talk across the pond to a companion on the opposite side. In my house we were so near that we could not begin to hear,—we could not speak low enough to be heard; as when you throw two stones into calm water so near that they break each other's undulations. If we are merely loquacious and loud talkers, then we can afford to stand very near together, cheek by jowl, and feel each other's breath; but if we speak reservedly and thoughtfully, we want to be farther apart, that all animal heat and moisture may have a chance to evaporate. If we would enjoy the most intimate society with that in each of us which is without, or above, being spoken to, we must not only be silent, but commonly so far apart bodily that we cannot possibly hear each other's voice in any case. Referred to this standard, speech is for the convenience of those who are hard of hearing; but there are many fine things which we cannot say if we have to shout. As the conversation began to assume a loftier and grander tone, we gradually shoved our chairs farther apart till they touched the wall in opposite corners, and then commonly there was not room enough.

My "best" room, however, my withdrawing room, always ready for company, on whose carpet the sun rarely fell, was the pine wood behind my house. Thither in summer days, when distinguished guests came, I took them, and a priceless domestic swept the floor and dusted the furniture and kept the things in order.

If one guest came he sometimes partook of my frugal meal, and it was no interruption to conversation to be stirring a hasty-pudding, or watching the rising and maturing of a loaf of bread in the ashes, in the mean while. But if twenty came and sat in my house there was nothing said about dinner, though there might be bread enough for two, more than if eating were a forsaken habit; but we naturally practised abstinence; and this was never felt to be an offence against hospitality, but the most proper and considerate course. The waste and decay of physical life, which so often needs repair, seemed miraculously retarded in such a case, and the vital vigor stood its ground. I could entertain thus a thousand as well as twenty; and if any ever went away disappointed or hungry from my house when they found me at home, they may depend upon it that I sympathized with them at least. So easy is it, though many housekeepers doubt it, to establish new and better customs in the place of the old. You need not rest your reputation on the dinners you give. For my own part, I was

---

[205] Fashionable hotels in New York, Boston, and Concord, respectively.

never so effectually deterred from frequenting a man's house, by any kind of Cerberus whatever, as by the parade one made about dining me, which I took to be a very polite and roundabout hint never to trouble him so again. I think I shall never revisit those scenes. I should be proud to have for the motto of my cabin those lines of Spenser which one of my visitors inscribed on a yellow walnut leaf for a card:—

> "Arrivéd there, the little house they fill,
>   Ne looke for entertainment where none was;
> Rest is their feast, and all things at their will:
>   The noblest mind the best contentment has."[206]

When Winslow,[207] afterward governor of the Plymouth Colony, went with a companion on a visit of ceremony to Massassoit[208] on foot through the woods, and arrived tired and hungry at his lodge, they were well received by the king but nothing was said about eating that day. When the night arrived, to quote their own words, —"He laid us on the bed with himself and his wife, they at the one end and we at the other, it being only plank, laid a foot from the ground, and a thin mat upon them. Two more of his chief men, for want of room, pressed by and upon us; so that we were worse weary of our lodging than of our journey." At one o'clock the next day Massassoit "brought two fishes that he had shot," about thrice as big as a bream; "these being boiled, there were at least forty looked for a share in them. The most ate of them. This meal only we had in two nights and a day; and had not one of us bought a partridge, we had taken our journey fasting." Fearing that they would be light-headed for want of food and also sleep, owing to "the savages' barbarous singing, (for they used to sing themselves asleep,)" and that they might get home while they had strength to travel, they departed. As for lodging, it is true they were but poorly entertained, though what they found an inconvenience was no doubt intended for an honor; but as far as eating was concerned, I do not see how the Indians could have done better. They had nothing to eat themselves, and they were wiser than to think that apologies could supply the place of food to their guests; so they drew their belts tighter and said nothing about it. Another time when Winslow visited them, it being a season of plenty with them, there was no deficiency in this respect.

As for men, they will hardly fail one any where. I had more visitors while I lived in the woods than at any other period of my life; I mean that I had some. I met several there under more favorable circumstances than I could any where else. But fewer came to see me upon trivial business. In this respect, my company was winnowed by my mere distance from town. I had withdrawn so far within the great ocean of solitude, into which the rivers of society empty, that for the most part, so far as my needs were concerned, only the finest sediment was deposited around me. Beside, there were wafted to me evidences of unexplored and uncultivated continents on the other side.

Who should come to my lodge this morning but a true Homeric or Paphlagonian[209] man,—he had so suitable and poetic a name that I am sorry I cannot print it here,

---

[206] From Edmund Spenser's *The Faerie Queene*, I, i, 35.

[207] Edward Winslow (1595–1655), colonial chronicler.

[208] Indian chief (ca. 1580–1661) friendly to the colonists.

[209] Native of the mountainous region of Asia Minor; thought to be uncouth and uncivilized.

—a Canadian, a wood-chopper and post-maker, who can hole fifty posts in a day, who made his last supper on a woodchuck which his dog caught. He, too, has heard of Homer, and, "if it were not for books," would "not know what to do rainy days," though perhaps he has not read one wholly through for many rainy seasons. Some priest who could pronounce the Greek itself taught him to read his verse in the testament in his native parish far away; and now I must translate to him, while he holds the book, Achilles' reproof to Patroclus for his sad countenance.—"Why are you in tears, Patroclus, like a young girl?"—

"Or have you alone heard some news from Phthia?
They say that Menœtius lives yet, son of Actor,
And Peleus lives, son of Æacus, among the Myrmidons,
Either of whom having died, we should greatly grieve."[210]

He says, "That's good." He has a great bundle of white-oak bark[211] under his arm for a sick man, gathered this Sunday morning. "I suppose there's no harm in going after such a thing to-day," says he. To him Homer was a great writer, though what his writing was about he did not know. A more simple and natural man it would be hard to find. Vice and disease, which cast such a sombre moral hue over the world, seemed to have hardly any existence for him. He was about twenty-eight years old, and had left Canada and his father's house a dozen years before to work in the States, and earn money to buy a farm with at last, perhaps in this native country. He was cast in the coarsest mould; a stout but sluggish body, yet gracefully carried, with a thick sunburnt neck, dark bushy hair, and dull sleepy blue eyes, which were occasionally lit up with expression. He wore a flat gray cloth cap, a dingy wool-colored greatcoat, and cowhide boots. He was a great consumer of meat, usually carrying his dinner to his work a couple of miles past my house,—for he chopped all summer,—in a tin pail; cold meats, often cold woodchucks, and coffee in a stone bottle which dangled by a string from his belt; and sometimes he offered me a drink. He came along early, crossing my bean-field, though without anxiety or haste to get to his work, such as Yankees exhibit. He wasn't a-going to hurt himself. He didn't care if he only earned his board. Frequently he would leave his dinner in the bushes, when his dog had caught a woodchuck by the way, and go back a mile and a half to dress it and leave it in the cellar of the house where he boarded, after deliberating first for half an hour whether he could not sink it in the pond safely till nightfall,—loving to dwell long upon these themes. He would say, as he went by in the morning, "How thick the pigeons are! If working every day were not my trade, I could get all the meat I should want by hunting,—pigeons, woodchucks, rabbits, partridges,—by gosh! I could get all I should want for a week in one day."

He was a skilful chopper, and indulged in some flourishes and ornaments in his art. He cut his trees level and close to the ground, that the sprouts which came up afterward might be more vigorous and a sled might slide over the stumps; and instead of leaving a whole tree to support his corded wood, he would pare it away to a slender stake or splinter which you could break off with your hand at last.

He interested me because he was so quiet and solitary and so happy withal; a well

---

[210] From Homer's *Iliad*, Book XVI.   [211] Used for its medicinal properties.

of good humor and contentment which overflowed at his eyes. His mirth was without alloy. Sometimes I saw him at his work in the woods, felling trees, and he would greet me with a laugh of inexpressible satisfaction, and a salutation in Canadian French, though he spoke English as well. When I approached him he would suspend his work, and with half-suppressed mirth lie along the trunk of a pine which he had felled, and, peeling off the inner bark, roll it up into a ball and chew it while he laughed and talked. Such an exuberance of animal spirits had he that he sometimes tumbled down and rolled on the ground with laughter at any thing which made him think and tickled him. Looking round upon the trees he would exclaim,—"By George! I can enjoy myself well enough here chopping; I want no better sport." Sometimes, when at leisure, he amused himself all day in the woods with a pocket pistol, firing salutes to himself at regular intervals as he walked. In the winter he had a fire by which at noon he warmed his coffee in a kettle; and as he sat on a log to eat his dinner the chicadees would sometimes come round and alight on his arm and peck at the potato in his fingers; and he said that he "liked to have the little *fellers* about him."

In him the animal man chiefly was developed. In physical endurance and contentment he was cousin to the pine and the rock. I asked him once if he was not sometimes tired at night, after working all day; and he answered, with a sincere and serious look, "Gorrappit, I never was tired in my life." But the intellectual and what is called spiritual man in him were slumbering as in an infant. He had been instructed only in that innocent and ineffectual way in which the Catholic priests teach the aborigines, by which the pupil is never educated to the degree of consciousness, but only to the degree of trust and reverence, and a child is not made a man, but kept a child. When Nature made him, she gave him a strong body and contentment for his portion, and propped him on every side with reverence and reliance, that he might live out his threescore years and ten a child. He was so genuine and unsophisticated that no introduction would serve to introduce him, more than if you introduced a woodchuck to your neighbor. He had got to find him out as you did. He would not play any part. Men paid him wages for work, and so helped to feed and clothe him; but he never exchanged opinions with them. He was so simply and naturally humble—if he can be called humble who never aspires—that humility was no distinct quality in him, nor could he conceive of it. Wiser men were demigods to him. If you told him that such a one was coming, he did as if he thought that any thing so grand would expect nothing of himself, but take all the responsibility on itself, and let him be forgotten still. He never heard the sound of praise. He particularly reverenced the writer and the preacher. Their performances were miracles. When I told him that I wrote considerably, he thought for a long time that it was merely the handwriting which I meant, for he could write a remarkably good hand himself. I sometimes found the name of his native parish handsomely written in the snow by the highway, with the proper French accent, and knew that he had passed. I asked him if he ever wished to write his thoughts. He said that he had read and written letters for those who could not, but he never tried to write thoughts,—no, he could not, he could not tell what to put first, it would kill him, and then there was spelling to be attended to at the same time!

I heard that a distinguished wise man and reformer asked him if he did not want the world to be changed; but he answered with a chuckle of surprise in his Canadian accent, not knowing that the question had ever been entertained before, "No, I like it well enough." It would have suggested many things to a philosopher to have dealings with him. To a stranger he appeared to know nothing of things in general; yet I sometimes saw in him a man whom I had not seen before, and I did not know whether he was as wise as Shakspeare or as simply ignorant as a child, whether to suspect him of a fine poetic consciousness or of stupidity. A townsman told me that when he met him sauntering through the village in his small close-fitting cap, and whistling to himself, he reminded him of a prince in disguise.

His only books were an almanac and an arithmetic, in which last he was considerably expert. The former was a sort of cyclopædia to him, which he supposed to contain an abstract of human knowledge, as indeed it does to a considerable extent. I loved to sound him on the various reforms of the day, and he never failed to look at them in the most simple and practical light. He had never heard of such things before. Could he do without factories? I asked. He had worn the home-made Vermont gray,[212] he said, and that was good. Could he dispense with tea and coffee? Did this country afford any beverage beside water? He had soaked hemlock leaves in water and drank it, and thought that was better than water in warm weather. When I asked him if he could do without money, he showed the convenience of money in such a way as to suggest and coincide with the most philosophical accounts of the origin of this institution, and the very derivation of the word *pecunia*.[213] If an ox were his property, and he wished to get needles and thread at the store, he thought it would be inconvenient and impossible soon to go on mortgaging some portion of the creature each time to that amount. He could defend many institutions better than any philosopher, because, in describing them as they concerned him, he gave the true reason for their prevalence, and speculation had not suggested to him any other. At another time, hearing Plato's definition of a man,—a biped without feathers,—and that one exhibited a cock plucked and called it Plato's man, he thought it an important difference that the *knees* bent the wrong way. He would sometimes exclaim, "How I love to talk! By George, I could talk all day!" I asked him once, when I had not seen him for many months, if he had got a new idea this summer. "Good Lord," said he, "a man that has to work as I do, if he does not forget the ideas he has had, he will do well. May be the man you hoe with is inclined to race; then, by gorry, your mind must be there; you think of weeds." He would sometimes ask me first on such occasions, if I had made any improvement. One winter day I asked him if he was always satisfied with himself, wishing to suggest a substitute within him for the priest without, and some higher motive for living. "Satisfied!" said he; "some men are satisfied with one thing and some with another. One man, perhaps, if he has got enough, will be satisfied to sit all day with his back to the fire and his belly to the table, by George!" Yet I never, by any manœuvring, could get him to take the spiritual view of things; the highest that he appeared to conceive of was a simple expediency, such as you might expect an animal to appreciate; and this, practically, is true of most men. If I suggested any improvement in his mode of life, he merely answered, without expressing any regret, that it was too late. Yet he thoroughly believed in honesty and the like virtues.

---

[212] Homespun cloth.
[213] Latin: "money"; it is derived from the Latin word for cattle.

There was a certain positive originality, however slight, to be detected in him, and I occasionally observed that he was thinking for himself and expressing his own opinion, a phenomenon so rare that I would any day walk ten miles to observe it, and it amounted to the re-origination of many of the institutions of society. Though he hesitated, and perhaps failed to express himself distinctly, he always had a presentable thought behind. Yet his thinking was so primitive and immersed in his animal life, that, though more promising than a merely learned man's, it rarely ripened to any thing which can be reported. He suggested that there might be men of genius in the lowest grades of life, however permanently humble and illiterate, who take their own view always, or do not pretend to see at all; who are as bottomless even as Walden Pond was thought to be, though they may be dark and muddy.

Many a traveller came out of his way to see me and the inside of my house, and, as an excuse for calling, asked for a glass of water. I told them that I drank at the pond, and pointed thither, offering to lend them a dipper. Far off as I lived, I was not exempted from that annual visitation which occurs, methinks, about the first of April, when every body is on the move; and I had my share of good luck, though there were some curious specimens among my visitors. Half-witted men from the almshouse and elsewhere came to see me; but I endeavored to make them exercise all the wit they had, and make their confessions to me; in such cases making wit the theme of our conversation; and so was compensated. Indeed, I found some of them to be wiser than the so called *overseers* of the poor and selectmen of the town, and thought it was time that the tables were turned. With respect to wit, I learned that there was not much difference between the half and the whole. One day, in particular, an inoffensive, simple-minded pauper, whom with others I had often seen used as fencing stuff, standing or sitting on a bushel in the fields to keep cattle and himself from straying, visited me, and expressed a wish to live as I did. He told me, with the utmost simplicity and truth, quite superior, or rather *inferior,* to any thing that is called humility, that he was "deficient in intellect." These were his words. The Lord had made him so, yet he supposed the Lord cared as much for him as for another. "I have always been so," said he, "from my childhood; I never had much mind; I was not like other children; I am weak in the head. It was the Lord's will, I suppose." And there he was to prove the truth of his words. He was a metaphysical puzzle to me. I have rarely met a fellow-man on such promising ground,—it was so simple and sincere and so true all that he said. And, true enough, in proportion as he appeared to humble himself was he exalted. I did not know at first but it was the result of a wise policy. It seemed that from such a basis of truth and frankness as the poor weak-headed pauper had laid, our intercourse might go forward to something better than the intercourse of sages.

I had some guests from those not reckoned commonly among the town's poor, but who should be; who are among the world's poor, at any rate; guests who appeal, not to your hospitality, but to your *hospitalality;* who earnestly wish to be helped, and preface their appeal with the information that they are resolved, for one thing, never to help themselves. I require of a visitor that he be not actually starving, though he may have the very best appetite in the world, however he got it. Objects of charity are not guests. Men who did not know when their visit had terminated, though I went about my business again, answering them from greater and greater remoteness. Men of almost every degree of wit called on me in the migrating season. Some who had more wits than they knew what to do with; runaway slaves with plantation manners, who listened from time to time, like the fox in the fable, as if they heard the hounds a-baying on their track, and looked at me beseechingly, as much as to say,—

"O Christian, will you send me back?"

One real runaway slave, among the rest, whom I helped to forward toward the northstar. Men of one idea, like a hen with one chicken, and that a duckling; men of a thousand ideas, and unkempt heads, like those hens which are made to take charge of a hundred chickens, all in pursuit of one bug, a score of them lost in every morning's dew,—and become frizzled and mangy in consequence; men of ideas instead of legs, a sort of intellectual centipede that made you crawl all over. One man proposed a book in which visitors should write their names, as at the White Mountains; but, alas! I have too good a memory to make that necessary.

I could not but notice some of the peculiarities of my visitors. Girls and boys and young women generally seemed glad to be in the woods. They looked in the pond and at the flowers, and improved their time. Men of business, even farmers, thought only of solitude and employment, and of the great distance at which I dwelt from something or other; and though they said that they loved a ramble in the woods occasionally, it was obvious that they did not. Restless committed men, whose time was all taken up in getting a living or keeping it; ministers who spoke of God as if they enjoyed a monopoly of the subject, who could not bear all kinds of opinions; doctors, lawyers, uneasy housekeepers who pried into my cupboard and bed when I was out,—how came Mrs. ——— to know that my sheets were not as clean as hers? —young men who had ceased to be young, and had concluded that it was safest to follow the beaten track of the professions,—all these generally said that it was not possible to do so much good in my position. Ay! there was the rub. The old and infirm and the timid, of whatever age or sex, thought most of sickness, and sudden accident and death; to them life seemed full of danger,—what danger is there if you don't think of any?—and they thought that a prudent man would carefully select the safest position, where Dr. B.[214] might be on hand at a moment's warning. To them the village was literally a *com-munity,* a league for mutual defence, and you would suppose that they would not go a-huckleberrying without a medicine chest. The amount of it is, if a man is alive, there is always *danger* that he may die, though the danger must be allowed to be less in proportion as he is dead-and-alive to begin with. A man sits as many risks as he runs. Finally, there were the self-styled reformers, the greatest bores of all, who thought that I was forever singing,—

This is the house that I built;
This is the man that lives in the house that I built;[215]

but they did not know that the third line was,—

These are the folks that worry the man
That lives in the house that I built.

---

[214] Josiah Bartlett, the village doctor.   [215] Thoreau's version of the nursery rhyme.

I did not fear the hen-harriers,[216] for I kept no chickens; but I feared the men-harriers rather.

I had more cheering visitors than the last. Children come a-berrying, railroad men taking a Sunday morning walk in clean shirts, fishermen and hunters, poets and philosophers, in short, all honest pilgrims, who came out to the woods for freedom's sake, and really left the village behind, I was ready to greet with,—"Welcome, Englishmen! welcome, Englishmen!"[217] for I had had communication with that race.

The Bean-Field

Meanwhile my beans, the length of whose rows, added together, was seven miles already planted, were impatient to be hoed, for the earliest had grown considerably before the latest were in the ground; indeed they were not easily to be put off. What was the meaning of this so steady and self-respecting, this small Herculean labor, I knew not. I came to love my rows, my beans, though so many more than I wanted. They attached me to the earth, and so I got strength like Antæus.[218] But why should I raise them? Only Heaven knows. This was my curious labor all summer,—to make this portion of the earth's surface, which had yielded only cinquefoil, blackberries, johnswort, and the like, before, sweet wild fruits and pleasant flowers, produce instead this pulse. What shall I learn of beans or beans of me? I cherish them, I hoe them, early and late I have an eye to them; and this is my day's work. It is a fine broad leaf to look on. My auxiliaries are the dews and rains which water this dry soil, and what fertility is in the soil itself, which for the most part is lean and effete. My enemies are worms, cool days, and most of all woodchucks. The last have nibbled for me a quarter of an acre clean. But what right had I to oust johnswort and the rest, and break up their ancient herb garden? Soon, however, the remaining beans will be too tough for them, and go forward to meet new foes.

When I was four years old, as I well remember, I was brought from Boston to this my native town, through these very woods and this field, to the pond. It is one of the oldest scenes stamped on my memory. And now to-night my flute has waked the echoes over that very water. The pines still stand here older than I; or, if some have fallen, I have cooked my supper with their stumps, and a new growth is rising all around, preparing another aspect for new infant eyes. Almost the same johnswort springs from the same perennial root in this pasture, and even I have at length helped to clothe that fabulous landscape of my infant dreams, and one of the results of my presence and influence is seen in these bean leaves, corn blades, and potato vines.

I planted about two acres and a half of upland; and as it was only about fifteen years since the land was cleared, and I myself had got out two or three cords of stumps, I did not give it any manure; but in the course of the summer it appeared by the arrowheads which I turned up in hoeing, that an extinct nation had anciently dwelt here and planted corn and beans ere white men came to clear the land, and so, to some extent, had exhausted the soil for this very crop.

[216] Hawks.
[217] What the Indian Samoset supposedly said to the Pilgrims landing at Plymouth.
[218] In classic myth, the giant who received his great strength from touching Earth, his mother.

Before yet any woodchuck or squirrel had run across the road, or the sun had got above the shrub-oaks, while all the dew was on, though the farmers warned me against it,—I would advise you to do all your work if possible while the dew is on,—I began to level the ranks of haughty weeds in my bean-field and throw dust upon their heads. Early in the morning I worked barefooted, dabbling like a plastic artist in the dewy and crumbling sand, but later in the day the sun blistered my feet. There the sun lighted me to hoe beans, pacing slowly backward and forward over that yellow gravelly upland, between the long green rows, fifteen rods, the one end terminating in a shrub oak copse where I could rest in the shade, the other in a blackberry field where the green berries deepened their tints by the time I had made another bout. Removing the weeds, putting fresh soil about the bean stems, and encouraging this weed which I had sown, making the yellow soil express its summer thought in bean leaves and blossoms rather than in wormwood and piper and millet grass, making the earth say beans instead of grass,—this was my daily work. As I had little aid from horses or cattle, or hired men or boys, or improved implements of husbandry, I was much slower, and became much more intimate with my beans than usual. But labor of the hands, even when pursued to the verge of drudgery, is perhaps never the worst form of idleness. It has a constant and imperishable moral, and to the scholar it yields a classic result. A very *agricola laboriosus*[219] was I to travellers bound westward through Lincoln and Wayland to nobody knows where; they sitting at their ease in gigs, with elbows on knees, and reins loosely hanging in festoons; I the home-staying, laborious native of the soil. But soon my homestead was out of their sight and thought. It was the only open and cultivated field for a great distance on either side of the road; so they made the most of it; and sometimes the man in the field heard more of travellers' gossip and comment than was meant for his ear: "Beans so late! peas so late!"—for I continued to plant when others had begun to hoe,—the ministerial husbandman had not suspected it. "Corn, my boy, for fodder; corn for fodder." "Does he *live* there?" asks the black bonnet of the gray coat; and the hard-featured farmer reins up his grateful dobbin to inquire what you are doing where he sees no manure in the furrow, and recommends a little chip dirt, or any little waste stuff, or it may be ashes or plaster. But here were two acres and a half of furrows, and only a hoe for cart and two hands to draw it,—there being an aversion to other carts and horses,—and chip dirt far away. Fellow-travellers as they rattled by compared it aloud with the fields which they had passed, so that I came to know how I stood in the agricultural world. This was one field not in Mr. Colman's report.[220] And, by the way, who estimates the value of the crop which Nature yields in the still wilder fields unimproved by man? The crop of *English* hay is carefully weighed, the moisture calculated, the silicates and the potash; but in all dells and pond holes in the woods and pastures and swamps grows a rich and various crop only unreaped by man. Mine was, as it were, the connecting link between wild and cultivated fields; as some states are civilized, and others half-civilized, and others savage or barbarous, so my field was, though not in a bad sense, a half-cultivated field. They were beans cheerfully returning to their wild and primitive state that I cultivated, and my hoe played the *Ranz des Vaches*[221] for them.

[219] Latin: "diligent farmer."
[220] Henry Colman (1785–1849) surveyed Massachusetts agriculture in four reports (1838–1841).

[221] Song of Swiss herdsmen.

Near at hand, upon the topmost spray of a birch, sings the brown-thrasher—or red mavis, as some love to call him—all the morning, glad of your society, that would find out another farmer's field if yours were not here. While you are planting the seed, he cries,—"Drop it, drop it,—cover it up, cover it up,—pull it up, pull it up, pull it up." But this was not corn, and so it was safe from such enemies as he. You may wonder what his rigmarole, his amateur Paganini[222] performances on one string or on twenty, have to do with your planting, and yet prefer it to leached ashes or plaster. It was a cheap sort of top dressing in which I had entire faith.

As I drew a still fresher soil about the rows with my hoe, I disturbed the ashes of unchronicled nations who in primeval years lived under these heavens, and their small implements of war and hunting were brought to the light of this modern day. They lay mingled with other natural stones, some of which bore the marks of having been burned by Indian fires, and some by the sun, and also bits of pottery and glass brought hither by the recent cultivators of the soil. When my hoe tinkled against the stones, that music echoed to the woods and the sky, and was an accompaniment to my labor which yielded an instant and immeasurable crop. It was no longer beans that I hoed, nor I that hoed beans; and I remembered with as much pity as pride, if I remembered at all, my acquaintances who had gone to the city to attend the oratorios. The night-hawk circled overhead in the sunny afternoons—for I sometimes made a day of it—like a mote in the eye, or in heaven's eye, falling from time to time with a swoop and a sound as if the heavens were rent, torn at last to very rags and tatters, and yet a seamless cope remained; small imps that fill the air and lay their eggs on the ground on bare sand or rocks on the tops of hills, where few have found them; graceful and slender like ripples caught up from the pond, as leaves are raised by the wind to float in the heavens; such kindredship is in Nature. The hawk is aerial brother of the wave which he sails over and surveys, those his perfect air-inflated wings answering to the elemental unfledged pinions of the sea. Or sometimes I watched a pair of hen-hawks circling high in the sky, alternately soaring and descending, approaching and leaving one another, as if they were the imbodiment of my own thoughts. Or I was attracted by the passage of wild pigeons from this wood to that, with a slight quivering winnowing sound and carrier haste; or from under a rotten stump my hoe turned up a sluggish portentous and outlandish spotted salamander, a trace of Egypt and the Nile, yet our contemporary. When I paused to lean on my hoe, these sounds and sights I heard and saw any where in the row, a part of the inexhaustible entertainment which the country offers.

On gala days the town fires its great guns, which echo like popguns to these woods, and some waifs of martial music occasionally penetrate thus far. To me, away there in my bean-field at the other end of the town, the big guns sounded as if a puff ball had burst; and when there was a military turnout of which I was ignorant, I have sometimes had a vague sense all the day of some sort of itching and disease in the horizon, as if some eruption would break out there soon, either scarlatina or canker-rash, until at length some more favorable puff of wind, making haste over the fields and up the Wayland road, brought me information of the "trainers."[223] It seemed by the distant hum as if somebody's bees had swarmed, and that the neighbors, according to Virgil's advice, by a faint *tintinnabulum* upon the most sonorous of their domestic

---

[222] Nicolò Paganini (1782–1840), Italian violinist noted for his virtuosity.   [223] Members of the local militia.

utensils, were endeavoring to call them down into the hive again. And when the sound died quite away, and the hum had ceased, and the most favorable breezes told no tale, I knew that they had got the last drone of them all safely into the Middlesex hive, and that now their minds were bent on the honey with which it was smeared.

I felt proud to know that the liberties of Massachusetts and of our fatherland were in such safe keeping; and as I turned to my hoeing again I was filled with an inexpressible confidence, and pursued my labor cheerfully with a calm trust in the future.

When there were several bands of musicians, it sounded as if all the village was a vast bellows, and all the buildings expanded and collapsed alternately with a din. But sometimes it was a really noble and inspiring strain that reached these woods, and the trumpet that sings of fame, and I felt as if I could spit a Mexican[224] with a good relish,—for why should we always stand for trifles?—and looked round for a wood-chuck or a skunk to exercise my chivalry upon. These martial strains seemed as far away as Palestine, and reminded me of a march of crusaders in the horizon, with a slight tantivy and tremulous motion of the elm-tree tops which overhang the village. This was one of the *great* days; though the sky had from my clearing only the same everlastingly great look that it wears daily, and I saw no difference in it.

It was a singular experience that long acquaintance which I cultivated with beans, what with planting, and hoeing, and harvesting, and threshing, and picking over, and selling them,—the last was the hardest of all,—I might add eating, for I did taste. I was determined to know beans. When they were growing, I used to hoe from five o'clock in the morning till noon, and commonly spent the rest of the day about other affairs. Consider the intimate and curious acquaintance one makes with various kinds of weeds,—it will bear some iteration in the account, for there was no little iteration in the labor,—disturbing their delicate organizations so ruthlessly, and making such invidious distinctions with his hoe, levelling whole ranks of one species, and sedu-lously cultivating another. That's Roman wormwood,—that's pigweed,—that's sor-rel,—that's piper-grass,—have at him, chop him up, turn his roots upward to the sun, don't let him have a fibre in the shade, if you do he'll turn himself t'other side up and be as green as a leek in two days. A long war, not with cranes, but with weeds, those Trojans who had sun and rain and dews on their side. Daily the beans saw me come to their rescue armed with a hoe, and thin the ranks of their enemies, filling up the trenches with weedy dead. Many a lusty crest-waving Hector,[225] that towered a whole foot above his crowding comrades, fell before my weapon and rolled in the dust.

Those summer days which some of my contemporaries devoted to the fine arts in Boston or Rome, and others to contemplation in India, and others to trade in London or New York, I thus, with the other farmers of New England, devoted to husbandry. Not that I wanted beans to eat, for I am by nature a Pythagorean,[226] so far as beans are concerned, whether they mean porridge or voting,[227] and exchanged them for rice; but, perchance, as some must work in fields if only for the sake of tropes and

---

[224] As if bayoneting a soldier during the Mexican War, which was going on at the time.
[225] Hero of the Trojan War depicted in the *Iliad*.
[226] Pythagoras (582–507 B.C.), Greek philosopher

who placed beans on his list of dietary prohibitions.
[227] In ancient times beans could be used both for eating and for the casting of votes.

expression, to serve a parable-maker one day. It was on the whole a rare amusement, which, continued too long, might have become a dissipation. Though I gave them no manure, and did not hoe them all once, I hoed them unusually well as far as I went, and was paid for it in the end, "there being in truth," as Evelyn[228] says, "no compost or lætation whatsoever comparable to this continual motion, repastination, and turning of the mould with the spade." "The earth," he adds elsewhere, "especially if fresh, has a certain magnetism in it, by which it attracts the salt, power, or virtue (call it either) which gives it life, and is the logic of all the labor and stir we keep about it, to sustain us; all dungings and other sordid temperings being but the vicars succedaneous to this improvement." Moreover, this being one of those "worn-out and exhausted lay fields which enjoy their sabbath," had perchance, as Sir Kenelm Digby[229] thinks likely, attracted "vital spirits" from the air. I harvested twelve bushels of beans.

But to be more particular; for it is complained that Mr. Colman has reported chiefly the expensive experiments of gentlemen farmers; my outgoes were,—

For a hoe,	$0 54	
Ploughing, harrowing, and furrowing,	7 50,	Too much.
Beans for seed,	3 12 1/2	
Potatoes "	1 33	
Peas "	0 40	
Turnip seed,	0 06	
White line for crow fence,[230]	0 02	
Horse cultivator and boy three hours,	1 00	
Horse and cart to get crop,	0 75	
In all,	$14 72 1/2	

My income was, (patrem familias vendacem, non emacem esse oportet,)[231] from

Nine bushels and twelve quarts of beans sold,	$16 94
Five " large potatoes,	2 50
Nine " small "	2 25
Grass,	1 00
Stalks,	0 75
In all,	$23 44

Leaving a pecuniary profit, as I have elsewhere said, of .... $ 71 1/2.

This is the result of my experience in raising beans. Plant the common small white bush bean about the first of June, in rows three feet by eighteen inches apart, being careful to select fresh round and unmixed seed. First look out for worms, and supply

---

[228] John Evelyn (1620–1706), English diarist and student of natural history.
[229] English author (1603–1665) who wrote on matters of the supernatural and of natural history.

[230] Scarecrow.
[231] Quotation from Cato's work on agriculture: "The head of the household should be a seller, not a buyer."

vacancies by planting anew. Then look out for woodchucks, if it is an exposed place, for they will nibble off the earliest tender leaves almost clean as they go; and again, when the young tendrils make their appearance, they have notice of it, and will shear them off with both buds and young pods, sitting erect like a squirrel. But above all harvest as early as possible, if you would escape frosts and have a fair and saleable crop; you may save much loss by this means.

This further experience also I gained. I said to myself, I will not plant beans and corn with so much industry another summer, but such seeds, if the seed is not lost, as sincerity, truth, simplicity, faith, innocence, and the like, and see if they will not grow in this soil, even with less toil and manurance, and sustain me, for surely it has not been exhausted for these crops. Alas! I said this to myself; but now another summer is gone, and another, and another, and I am obliged to say to you, Reader, that the seeds which I planted, if indeed they *were* the seeds of those virtues, were wormeaten or had lost their vitality, and so did not come up. Commonly men will only be brave as their fathers were brave, or timid. This generation is very sure to plant corn and beans each new year precisely as the Indians did centuries ago and taught the first settlers to do, as if there were a fate in it. I saw an old man the other day, to my astonishment, making the holes with a hoe for the seventieth time at least, and not for himself to lie down in! But why should not the New Englander try new adventures, and not lay so much stress on his grain, his potato and grass crop, and his orchards?—raise other crops than these? Why concern ourselves so much about our beans for seed, and not be concerned at all about a new generation of men? We should really be fed and cheered if when we met a man we were sure to see that some of the qualities which I have named, which we all prize more than those other productions, but which are for the most part broadcast and floating in the air, had taken root and grown in him. Here comes such a subtile and ineffable quality, for instance, as truth or justice, though the slightest amount or new variety of it, along the road. Our ambassadors should be instructed to send home such seeds as these, and Congress help to distribute them over all the land. We should never stand upon ceremony with sincerity. We should never cheat and insult and banish one another by our meanness, if there were present the kernel of worth and friendliness. We should not meet thus in haste. Most men I do not meet at all, for they seem not to have time; they are busy about their beans. We would not deal with a man thus plodding ever, leaning on a hoe or a spade as a staff between his work, not as a mushroom, but partially risen out of the earth, something more than erect, like swallows alighted and walking on the ground.—

> "And as he spake, his wings would now and then
> Spread, as he meant to fly, then close again,"[232]

so that we should suspect that we might be conversing with an angel. Bread may not always nourish us; but it always does us good, it even takes stiffness out of our joints, and makes us supple and buoyant, when we knew not what ailed us, to recognize any generosity in man or Nature, to share any unmixed and heroic joy.

Ancient poetry and mythology suggest, at least, that husbandry was once a sacred

---

[232] From "The Shepheards Oracles," poem by
Francis Quarles (1592–1644).

art; but it is pursued with irreverent haste and heedlessness by us, our object being to have large farms and large crops merely. We have no festival, nor procession, nor ceremony, not excepting our Cattle-shows and so called Thanksgivings, by which the farmer expresses a sense of the sacredness of his calling, or is reminded of its sacred origin. It is the premium and the feast which tempt him. He sacrifices not to Ceres and the Terrestrial Jove, but to the infernal Plutus[233] rather. By avarice and selfishness, and a grovelling habit, from which none of us is free, of regarding the soil as property, or the means of acquiring property chiefly, the landscape is deformed, husbandry is degraded with us, and the farmer leads the meanest of lives. He knows Nature but as a robber. Cato says that the profits of agriculture are particularly pious or just, (*maximeque pius quæstus*,) and according to Varro[234] the old Romans "called the same earth Mother and Ceres, and thought that they who cultivated it led a pious and useful life, and that they alone were left of the race of King Saturn."[235]

We are wont to forget that the sun looks on our cultivated fields and on the prairies and forests without distinction. They all reflect and absorb his rays alike, and the former make but a small part of the glorious picture which he beholds in his daily course. In his view the earth is all equally cultivated like a garden. Therefore we should receive the benefit of his light and heat with a corresponding trust and magnanimity. What though I value the seed of these beans, and harvest that in the fall of the year? This broad field which I have looked at so long looks not to me as the principal cultivator, but away from me to influences more genial to it, which water and make it green. These beans have results which are not harvested by me. Do they not grow for woodchucks partly? The ear of wheat, (in Latin *spica*, obsoletely *speca*, from *spe*, hope,) should not be the only hope of the husbandman; its kernel or grain (*granum*, from *gerendo*, bearing,) is not all that it bears. How, then, can our harvest fail? Shall I not rejoice also at the abundance of the weeds whose seeds are the granary of the birds? It matters little comparatively whether the fields fill the farmer's barns. The true husbandman will cease from anxiety, as the squirrels manifest no concern whether the woods will bear chestnuts this year or not, and finish his labor with every day, relinquishing all claim to the produce of his fields, and sacrificing in his mind not only his first but his last fruits also.

The Village

After hoeing, or perhaps reading and writing, in the forenoon, I usually bathed again in the pond, swimming across one of its coves for a stint, and washed the dust of labor from my person, or smoothed out the last wrinkle which study had made, and for the afternoon was absolutely free. Every day or two I strolled to the village to hear some of the gossip which is incessantly going on there, circulating either from mouth to mouth, or from newspaper to newspaper, and which, taken in homœopathic doses,[236] was really as refreshing in its way as the rustle of leaves and the peeping of frogs. As I walked in the woods to see the birds and squirrels, so I walked in the village to see the men and boys; instead of the wind among the pines I heard

[233] Deities in the Roman pantheon: Ceres, goddess of crops; Jove, highest of the gods; and Pluto (Plutus), lord of the underworld.

[234] Quotation from *De Re Rustica*, by Marcus Terentius Varro (116–27 B.C.), Roman writer.

[235] Roman god of agriculture.

[236] Sparing amounts.

the carts rattle. In one direction from my house there was a colony of muskrats in the river meadows; under the grove of elms and buttonwoods in the other horizon was a village of busy men, as curious to me as if they had been prairie dogs, each sitting at the mouth of its burrow, or running over to a neighbor's to gossip. I went there frequently to observe their habits. The village appeared to me a great news room; and on one side, to support it, as once at Redding & Company's on State Street, they kept nuts and raisins, or salt and meal and other groceries. Some have such a vast appetite for the former commodity, that is, the news, and such sound digestive organs, that they can sit forever in public avenues without stirring, and let it simmer and whisper through them like the Etesian winds, or as if inhaling ether, it only producing numbness and insensibility to pain,—otherwise it would often be painful to hear,— without affecting the consciousness. I hardly ever failed, when I rambled through the village, to see a row of such worthies, either sitting on a ladder sunning themselves, with their bodies inclined forward and their eyes glancing along the line this way and that, from time to time, with a voluptuous expression, or else leaning against a bar with their hands in their pockets, like caryatides, as if to prop it up. They, being commonly out of doors, heard whatever was in the wind. These are the coarsest mills, in which all gossip is first rudely digested or cracked up before it is emptied into finer and more delicate hoppers within doors. I observed that the vitals of the village were the grocery, the barroom, the post-office, and the bank; and, as a necessary part of the machinery, they kept a bell, a big gun, and a fire-engine, at convenient places; and the houses were so arranged as to make the most of mankind, in lanes and fronting one another, so that every traveller had to run the gantlet, and every man, woman, and child might get a lick at him. Of course, those who were stationed nearest to the head of the line, where they could most see and be seen, and have the first blow at him, paid the highest prices for their places; and the few straggling inhabitants in the outskirts, where long gaps in the line began to occur, and the traveller could get over walls or turn aside into cow paths, and so escape, paid a very slight ground or window tax.[237] Signs were hung out on all sides to allure him; some to catch him by the appetite, as the tavern and victualling cellar; some by the fancy, as the dry goods store and the jeweller's; and others by the hair or the feet or the skirts, as the barber, the shoemaker, or the tailor. Besides, there was a still more terrible standing invitation to call at every one of these houses, and company expected about these times. For the most part I escaped wonderfully from these dangers, either by proceeding at once boldly and without deliberation to the goal, as is recommended to those who run the gantlet, or by keeping my thoughts on high things, like Orpheus, who, "loudly singing the praises of the gods to his lyre, drowned the voices of the Sirens, and kept out of danger."[238] Sometimes I bolted suddenly, and nobody could tell my where-abouts, for I did not stand much about gracefulness, and never hesitated at a gap in a fence. I was even accustomed to make an irruption into some houses, where I was well entertained, and after learning the kernels and very last sieveful of news, what had subsided, the prospects of war and peace, and whether the world was likely to hold together much longer, I was let out through the rear avenues, and so escaped to the woods again.

---

[237] Payment exacted for the number of windows in a building.

[238] Thoreau's translation of a line from Sir Francis Bacon's *De Sapientia Veterum* (1609).

It was very pleasant, when I staid late in town, to launch myself into the night, especially if it was dark and tempestuous, and set sail from some bright village parlor or lecture room, with a bag of rye or Indian meal upon my shoulder, for my snug harbor in the woods, having made all tight without and withdrawn under hatches with a merry crew of thoughts, leaving only my outer man at the helm, or even tying up the helm when it was plain sailing. I had many a genial thought by the cabin fire "as I sailed." I was never cast away nor distressed in any weather, though I encountered some severe storms. It is darker in the woods, even in common nights, than most suppose. I frequently had to look up at the opening between the trees above the path in order to learn my route, and, where there was no cart-path, to feel with my feet the faint track which I had worn, or steer by the known relation of particular trees which I felt with my hands, passing between two pines for instance, not more than eighteen inches apart, in the midst of the woods, invariably, in the darkest night. Sometimes, after coming home thus late in a dark and muggy night, when my feet felt the path which my eyes could not see, dreaming and absent-minded all the way, until I was aroused by having to raise my hand to lift the latch, I have not been able to recall a single step of my walk, and I have thought that perhaps my body would find its way home if its master should forsake it, as the hand finds its way to the mouth without assistance. Several times, when a visitor chanced to stay into evening, and it proved a dark night, I was obliged to conduct him to the cart-path in the rear of the house, and then point out to him the direction he was to pursue, and in keeping which he was to be guided rather by his feet than his eyes. One very dark night I directed thus on their way two young men who had been fishing in the pond. They lived about a mile off through the woods, and were quite used to the route. A day or two after one of them told me that they wandered about the greater part of the night, close by their own premises, and did not get home till toward morning, by which time, as there had been several showers in the mean while, and the leaves were very wet, they were drenched to their skins. I have heard of many going astray even in the village streets, when the darkness was so thick that you could cut it with a knife, as the saying is. Some who live in the outskirts, having come to town a-shopping in their wagons, have been obliged to put up for the night; and gentlemen and ladies making a call have gone half a mile out of their way, feeling the sidewalk only with their feet, and not knowing when they turned. It is a surprising and memorable, as well as valuable experience, to be lost in the woods any time. Often in a snow storm, even by day, one will come out upon a well-known road, and yet find it impossible to tell which way leads to the village. Though he knows that he has travelled it a thousand times, he cannot recognize a feature in it, but it is as strange to him as if it were a road in Siberia. By night, of course, the perplexity is infinitely greater. In our most trivial walks, we are constantly, though unconsciously, steering like pilots by certain well-known beacons and headlands, and if we go beyond our usual course we still carry in our minds the bearing of some neighboring cape; and not till we are completely lost, or turned round,—for a man needs only to be turned round once with his eyes shut in this world to be lost,—do we appreciate the vastness and strangeness of Nature. Every man has to learn the points of compass again as often as he awakes, whether from sleep or any abstraction. Not till we are lost, in other words, not till we have lost the world, do we begin to find ourselves, and realize where we are and the infinite extent of our relations.

One afternoon, near the end of the first summer, when I went to the village to get a shoe from the cobbler's, I was seized and put into jail, because, as I have elsewhere related,[239] I did not pay a tax to, or recognize the authority of, the state which buys and sells men, women, and children, like cattle at the door of its senate-house. I had gone down to the woods for other purposes. But, wherever a man goes, men will pursue and paw him with their dirty institutions, and, if they can, constrain him to belong to their desperate odd-fellow society. It is true, I might have resisted forcibly with more or less effect, might have run "amok" against society; but I preferred that society should run "amok" against me, it being the desperate party. However, I was released the next day, obtained my mended shoe, and returned to the woods in season to get my dinner of huckleberries on Fair-Haven Hill. I was never molested by any person but those who represented the state. I had no lock nor bolt but for the desk which held my papers, not even a nail to put over my latch or windows. I never fastened my door night or day, though I was to be absent several days; not even when the next fall I spent a fortnight in the woods of Maine. And yet my house was more respected than if it had been surrounded by a file of soldiers. The tired rambler could rest and warm himself by my fire, the literary amuse himself with the few books on my table, or the curious, by opening my closet door, see what was left of my dinner, and what prospect I had of a supper. Yet, though many people of every class came this way to the pond, I suffered no serious inconvenience from these sources, and I never missed any thing but one small book, a volume of Homer, which perhaps was improperly gilded, and this I trust a soldier of our camp has found by this time. I am convinced, that if all men were to live as simply as I then did, thieving and robbery would be unknown. These take place only in communities where some have got more than is sufficient while others have not enough. The Pope's Homers[240] would soon get properly distributed.——

"Nec bella fuerunt,
Faginus astabat dum scyphus ante dapes."[241]

"Nor wars did men molest,
When only beechen bowls were in request."

"You who govern public affairs, what need have you to employ punishments? Love virtue, and the people will be virtuous. The virtues of a superior man are like the wind; the virtues of a common man are like the grass; the grass, when the wind passes over it, bends."[242]

The Ponds

Sometimes, having had a surfeit of human society and gossip, and worn out all my village friends, I rambled still farther westward then I habitually dwell, into yet more

---

[239] In Thoreau's essay "Resistance to Civil Government."

[240] The epic poems by Homer that were translated by Alexander Pope (1688–1744).

[241] Lines from *Elegies* by Tibullus (ca. 54–19 B.C.), Roman poet.

[242] From *The Analects*, XII, 19, by Confucius.

unfrequented parts of the town, "to fresh woods and pastures new,"[243] or, while the sun was setting, made my supper of huckleberries and blueberries on Fair Haven Hill, and laid up a store for several days. The fruits do not yield their true flavor to the purchaser of them, nor to him who raises them for the market. There is but one way to obtain it, yet few take that way. If you would know the flavor of huckleberries, ask the cow-boy or the partridge. It is a vulgar error to suppose that you have tasted huckleberries who never plucked them. A huckleberry never reaches Boston; they have not been known there since they grew on her three hills. The ambrosial and essential part of the fruit is lost with the bloom which is rubbed off in the market cart, and they become mere provender. As long as Eternal Justice reigns, not one innocent huckleberry can be transported thither from the country's hills.

Occasionally, after my hoeing was done for the day, I joined some impatient companion who had been fishing on the pond since morning, as silent and motionless as a duck or a floating leaf, and, after practising various kinds of philosophy, had concluded commonly, by the time I arrived, that he belonged to the ancient sect of Cœnobites.[244] There was one older man, an excellent fisher and skilled in all kinds of woodcraft, who was pleased to look upon my house as a building erected for the convenience of fishermen; and I was equally pleased when he sat in my doorway to arrange his lines. Once in a while we sat together on the pond, he at one end of the boat, and I at the other; but not many words passed between us, for he had grown deaf in his later years, but he occasionally hummed a psalm, which harmonized well enough with my philosophy. Our intercourse was thus altogether one of unbroken harmony, far more pleasing to remember than if it had been carried on by speech. When, as was commonly the case, I had none to commune with, I used to raise the echoes by striking with a paddle on the side of my boat, filling the surrounding woods with circling and dilating sound, stirring them up as the keeper of a menagerie his wild beasts, until I elicited a growl from every wooded vale and hill-side.

In warm evenings I frequently sat in the boat playing the flute, and saw the perch, which I seemed to have charmed, hovering around me, and the moon travelling over the ribbed bottom, which was strewed with the wrecks of the forest. Formerly I had come to this pond adventurously, from time to time, in dark summer nights, with a companion, and making a fire close to the water's edge, which we thought attracted the fishes, we caught pouts with a bunch of worms strung on a thread; and when we had done, far in the night, threw the burning brands high into the air like skyrockets, which, coming down into the pond, were quenched with a loud hissing, and we were suddenly groping in total darkness. Through this, whistling a tune, we took our way to the haunts of men again. But now I had made my home by the shore.

Sometimes, after staying in a village parlor till the family had all retired, I have returned to the woods, and, partly with a view to the next day's dinner, spent the hours of midnight fishing from a boat by moonlight, serenaded by owls and foxes, and hearing, from time to time, the creaking note of some unknown bird close at hand. These experiences were very memorable and valuable to me,—anchored in forty feet of water, and twenty or thirty rods from the shore, surrounded sometimes by thou-

[243] From the final line of "Lycidas," the poem by John Milton.
[244] Pun by Thoreau, based on a reference to

members of a religious group; used here to describe fishermen who "see no bites."

sands of small perch and shiners, dimpling the surface with their tails in the moonlight, and communicating by a long flaxen line with mysterious nocturnal fishes which had their dwelling forty feet below, or sometimes dragging sixty feet of line about the pond as I drifted in the gentle night breeze, now and then feeling a slight vibration along it, indicative of some life prowling about its extremity, of dull uncertain blundering purpose there, and slow to make up its mind. At length you slowly raise, pulling hand over hand, some horned pout squeaking and squirming to the upper air. It was very queer, especially in dark nights, when your thoughts had wandered to vast and cosmogonal themes in other spheres, to feel this faint jerk, which came to interrupt your dreams and link you to Nature again. It seemed as if I might next cast my line upward into the air, as well as downward into this element which was scarcely more dense. Thus I caught two fishes as it were with one hook.

The scenery of Walden is on a humble scale, and, though very beautiful, does not approach to grandeur, nor can it much concern one who has not long frequented it or lived by its shore; yet this pond is so remarkable for its depth and purity as to merit a particular description. It is a clear and deep green well, half a mile long and a mile and three quarters in circumference, and contains about sixty-one and a half acres; a perennial spring in the midst of pine and oak woods, without any visible inlet or outlet except by the clouds and evaporation. The surrounding hills rise abruptly from the water to the height of forty to eighty feet, though on the south-east and east they attain to about one hundred and one hundred and fifty feet respectively, within a quarter and a third of a mile. They are exclusively woodland. All our Concord waters have two colors at least, one when viewed at a distance, and another, more proper, close at hand. The first depends more on the light, and follows the sky. In clear weather, in summer, they appear blue at a little distance, especially if agitated, and at a great distance all appear alike. In stormy weather they are sometimes of a dark slate color. The sea, however, is said to be blue one day and green another without any perceptible change in the atmosphere. I have seen our river, when, the landscape being covered with snow, both water and ice were almost as green as grass. Some consider blue "to be the color of pure water, whether liquid or solid."[245] But, looking directly down into our waters from a boat, they are seen to be of very different colors. Walden is blue at one time and green at another, even from the same point of view. Lying between the earth and the heavens, it partakes of the color of both. Viewed from a hill-top it reflects the color of the sky, but near at hand it is of a yellowish tint next the shore where you can see the sand, then a light green, which gradually deepens to a uniform dark green in the body of the pond. In some lights, viewed even from a hill-top, it is of a vivid green next the shore. Some have referred this to the reflection of the verdure; but it is equally green there against the railroad sand-bank, and in the spring, before the leaves are expanded, and it may be simply the result of the prevailing blue mixed with the yellow of the sand. Such is the color of its iris. This is that portion, also, where in the spring, the ice being warmed by the heat of the sun reflected from the bottom, and also transmitted through the earth, melts first

[245] Description of the color of glacial ice; from *Travels through the Alps of Savoy* (1843) by James D. Forbes.

and forms a narrow canal about the still frozen middle. Like the rest of our waters, when much agitated, in clear weather, so that the surface of the waves may reflect the sky at the right angle, or because there is more light mixed with it, it appears at a little distance of a darker blue than the sky itself; and at such a time, being on its surface, and looking with divided vision, so as to see the reflection, I have discerned a matchless and indescribable light blue, such as watered or changeable silks and sword blades suggest, more cerulean than the sky itself, alternating with the original dark green on the opposite sides of the waves, which last appeared but muddy in comparison. It is a vitreous greenish blue, as I remember it, like those patches of the winter sky seen through cloud vistas in the west before sundown. Yet a single glass of its water held up to the light is as colorless as an equal quantity of air. It is well known that a large plate of glass will have a green tint, owing, as the makers say, to its "body," but a small piece of the same will be colorless. How large a body of Walden water would be required to reflect a green tint I have never proved. The water of our river is black or a very dark brown to one looking directly down on it, and, like that of most ponds, imparts to the body of one bathing in it a yellowish tinge; but this water is of such crystalline purity that the body of the bather appears of an alabaster whiteness, still more unnatural, which, as the limbs are magnified and distorted withal, produces a monstrous effect, making fit studies for a Michael Angelo.

The water is so transparent that the bottom can easily be discerned at the depth of twenty-five or thirty feet. Paddling over it, you may see many feet beneath the surface the schools of perch and shiners, perhaps only an inch long, yet the former easily distinguished by their traverse bars, and you think that they must be ascetic fish that find a subsistence there. Once, in the winter, many years ago, when I had been cutting holes through the ice in order to catch pickerel, as I stepped ashore I tossed my axe back on to the ice, but, as if some evil genius had directed it, it slid four or five rods directly into one of the holes, where the water was twenty-five feet deep. Out of curiosity, I lay down on the ice and looked through the hole, until I saw the axe a little on one side, standing on its head, with its helve erect and gently swaying to and fro with the pulse of the pond; and there it might have stood erect and swaying till in the course of time the handle rotted off, if I had not disturbed it. Making another hole directly over it with an ice chisel which I had, and cutting down the longest birch which I could find in the neighborhood with my knife, I made a slip-noose, which I attached to its end, and letting it down carefully, passed it over the knob of the handle, and drew it by a line along the birch, and so pulled the axe out again.

The shore is composed of a belt of smooth rounded white stones like paving stones, excepting one or two short sand beaches, and is so steep that in many places a single leap will carry you into water over your head; and were it not for its remarkable transparency, that would be the last to be seen of its bottom till it rose on the opposite side. Some think it is bottomless. It is nowhere muddy, and a casual observer would say that there were no weeds at all in it; and of noticeable plants, except in the little meadows recently overflowed, which do not properly belong to it, a closer scrutiny does not detect a flag nor a bulrush, nor even a lily, yellow or white, but only a few small heart-leaves and potamogetons,[246] and perhaps a water-target[247] or two; all which however a bather might not perceive; and these plants are clean and bright like the

---

[246] Pond weeds.   [247] Water plant.

element they grow in. The stones extend a rod or two into the water, and then the bottom is pure sand, except in the deepest parts, where there is usually a little sediment, probably from the decay of the leaves which have been wafted on to it so many successive falls, and a bright green weed is brought up on anchors even in midwinter.

We have one other pond just like this, White Pond in Nine Acre Corner, about two and a half miles westerly; but, though I am acquainted with most of the ponds within a dozen miles of this centre, I do not know a third of this pure and well-like character. Successive nations perchance have drank at, admired, and fathomed it, and passed away, and still its water is green and pellucid as ever. Not an intermitting spring! Perhaps on that spring morning when Adam and Eve were driven out of Eden Walden Pond was already in existence, and even then breaking up in a gentle spring rain accompanied with mist and a southerly wind, and covered with myriads of ducks and geese, which had not heard of the fall, when still such pure lakes sufficed them. Even then it had commenced to rise and fall, and had clarified its waters and colored them of the hue they now wear, and obtained a patent of heaven to be the only Walden Pond in the world and distiller of celestial dews. Who knows in how many unremembered nations' literatures this has been the Castalian Fountain?[248] or what nymphs presided over it in the Golden Age?[249] It is a gem of the first water which Concord wears in her coronet.

Yet perchance the first who came to this well have left some trace of their footsteps. I have been surprised to detect encircling the pond, even where a thick wood has just been cut down on the shore, a narrow shelf-like path in the steep hill-side, alternately rising and falling, approaching and receding from the water's edge, as old probably as the race of man here, worn by the feet of aboriginal hunters, and still from time to time unwittingly trodden by the present occupants of the land. This is particularly distinct to one standing on the middle of the pond in winter, just after a light snow has fallen, appearing as a clear undulating white line, unobscured by weeds and twigs, and very obvious a quarter of a mile off in many places where in summer it is hardly distinguishable close at hand. The snow reprints it, as it were, in clear white type alto-relievo.[250] The ornamented grounds of villas which will one day be built here may still preserve some trace of this.

The pond rises and falls, but whether regularly or not, and within what period, nobody knows, though, as usual, many pretend to know. It is commonly higher in the winter and lower in the summer, though not corresponding to the general wet and dryness. I can remember when it was a foot or two lower, and also when it was at least five feet higher, than when I lived by it. There is a narrow sand-bar running into it, with very deep water on one side, on which I helped boil a kettle of chowder, some six rods from the main shore, about the year 1824, which it has not been possible to do for twenty-five years; and on the other hand, my friends used to listen with incredulity when I told them, that a few years later I was accustomed to fish from a boat in a secluded cove in the woods, fifteen rods from the only shore they knew, which place was long since converted into a meadow. But the pond has risen steadily for two years, and now, in the summer of '52, is just five feet higher than when I

[248] In classical myth, the sacred spring of the Muses.
[249] The perfect "original" state of the world.
[250] High relief.

lived there, or as high as it was thirty years ago, and fishing goes on again in the meadow. This makes a difference of level, at the outside, of six or seven feet; and yet the water shed by the surrounding hills is insignificant in amount, and this overflow must be referred to causes which affect the deep springs. This same summer the pond has begun to fall again. It is remarkable that this fluctuation, whether periodical or not, appears thus to require many years for its accomplishment. I have observed one rise and a part of two falls, and I expect that a dozen or fifteen years hence the water will again be as low as I have ever known it. Flint's Pond, a mile eastward, allowing for the disturbance occasioned by its inlets and outlets, and the smaller intermediate ponds also, sympathize with Walden, and recently attained their greatest height at the same time with the latter. The same is true, as far as my observation goes, of White Pond.

This rise and fall of Walden at long intervals serves this use at least; the water standing at this great height for a year or more, though it makes it difficult to walk round it, kills the shrubs and trees which have sprung up about its edge since the last rise, pitchpines, birches, alders, aspens, and others, and, falling again, leaves an unobstructed shore; for, unlike many ponds and all waters which are subject to a daily tide, its shore is cleanest when the water is lowest. On the side of the pond next my house, a row of pitch pines fifteen feet high has been killed and tipped over as if by a lever, and thus a stop put to their encroachments; and their size indicates how many years have elapsed since the last rise to this height. By this fluctuation the pond asserts its title to a shore, and thus the *shore* is *shorn,* and the trees cannot hold it by right of possession. These are the lips of the lake on which no beard grows. It licks its chaps from time to time. When the water is at its height, the alders, willows, and maples send forth a mass of fibrous red roots several feet long from all sides of their stems in the water, and to the height of three or four feet from the ground, in the effort to maintain themselves; and I have known the high-blueberry bushes about the shore, which commonly produce no fruit, bear an abundant crop under these circumstances.

Some have been puzzled to tell how the shore became so regularly paved. My townsmen have all heard the tradition, the oldest people tell me that they heard it in their youth, that anciently the Indians were holding a pow-wow upon a hill here, which rose as high into the heavens as the pond now sinks deep into the earth, and they used much profanity, as the story goes, though this vice is one of which the Indians were never guilty, and while they were thus engaged the hill shook and suddenly sank, and only one old squaw, named Walden, escaped, and from her the pond was named. It has been conjectured that when the hill shook these stones rolled down its side and became the present shore. It is very certain, at any rate, that once there was no pond here, and now there is one; and this Indian fable does not in any respect conflict with the account of that ancient settler whom I have mentioned, who remembers so well when he first came here with his divining rod, saw a thin vapor rising from the sward, and the hazel pointed steadily downward, and he concluded to dig a well here. As for the stones, many still think that they are hardly to be accounted for by the action of the waves on these hills; but I observe that the surrounding hills are remarkably full of the same kind of stones, so that they have been obliged to pile them up in walls on both sides of the railroad cut nearest the pond; and, moreover, there are most stones where the shore is most abrupt; so that, unfortunately, it is no longer a mystery to me. I detect the paver.[251] If the name was not derived from that of some English locality,—Saffron Walden,[252] for instance,—one might suppose that it was called, originally, *Walled-in* Pond.

The pond was my well ready dug. For four months in the year its water is as cold as it is pure at all times; and I think that it is then as good as any, if not the best, in the town. In the winter, all water which is exposed to the air is colder than springs and wells which are protected from it. The temperature of the pond water which had stood in the room where I sat from five o'clock in the afternoon till noon the next day, the sixth of March, 1846, the thermometer having been up to 65° or 70° some of the time, owing partly to the sun on the roof, was 42°, or one degree colder than the water of one of the coldest wells in the village just drawn. The temperature of the Boiling Spring the same day was 45°, or the warmest of any water tried, though it is the coldest that I know of in summer, when, beside, shallow and stagnant surface water is not mingled with it. Moreover, in summer, Walden never becomes so warm as most water which is exposed to the sun, on account of its depth. In the warmest weather I usually placed a pailful in my cellar, where it became cool in the night, and remained so during the day; though I also resorted to a spring in the neighborhood. It was as good when a week old as the day it was dipped, and had no taste of the pump. Whoever camps for a week in summer by the shore of a pond, needs only bury a pail of water a few feet deep in the shade of his camp to be independent on the luxury of ice.

There have been caught in Walden, pickerel, one weighing seven pounds, to say nothing of another which carried off a reel with great velocity, which the fisherman safely set down at eight pounds because he did not see him, perch and pouts, some of each weighing over two pounds, shiners, chivins or roach, (*Leuciscus pulchellus*,) a very few breams, (*Pomotis obesus*,) and a couple of eels, one weighing four pounds, —I am thus particular because the weight of a fish is commonly its only title to fame, and these are the only eels I have heard of here;—also, I have a faint recollection of a little fish some five inches long, with silvery sides and a greenish back, somewhat dace-like in its character, which I mention here chiefly to link my facts to fable. Nevertheless, this pond is not very fertile in fish. Its pickerel, though not abundant, are its chief boast. I have seen at one time lying on the ice pickerel of at least three different kinds; a long and shallow one, steel-colored, most like those caught in the river; a bright golden kind, with greenish reflections and remarkably deep, which is the most common here; and another, golden-colored, and shaped like the last, but peppered on the sides with small dark brown or black spots, intermixed with a few faint blood-red ones, very much like a trout. The specific name *reticulatus*[253] would not apply to this; it should be *guttatus*[254] rather. These are all very firm fish, and weigh more than their size promises. The shiners, pouts, and perch also, and indeed all the fishes which inhabit this pond, are much cleaner, handsomer, and firmer fleshed than those in the river and most other ponds, as the water is purer, and they can easily be distinguished from them. Probably many ichthyologists would make new varieties of some of them. There are also a clean race of frogs and tortoises, and a few muscles in it; muskrats and minks leave their traces about it, and occasionally a travelling

---

[251] Effect of glacial force.
[252] Near London.

[253] Netlike.
[254] Speckled.

mud-turtle visits it. Sometimes, when I pushed off my boat in the morning, I disturbed a great mud-turtle which had secreted himself under the boat in the night. Ducks and geese frequent it in the spring and fall, the white-bellied swallows (*Hirundo bicolor*) skim over it, kingfishers dart away from its coves, and the peetweets (*Totanus macularius*) "teter" along its stony shores all summer. I have sometimes disturbed a fishhawk sitting on a white-pine over the water; but I doubt if it is ever profaned by the wing of a gull, like Fair Haven. At most, it tolerates one annual loon. These are all the animals of consequence which frequent it now.

You may see from a boat, in calm weather, near the sandy eastern shore, where the water is eight or ten feet deep, and also in some other parts of the pond, some circular heaps half a dozen feet in diameter by a foot in height, consisting of small stones less than a hen's egg in size, where all around is bare sand. At first you wonder if the Indians could have formed them on the ice for any purpose, and so, when the ice melted, they sank to the bottom; but they are too regular and some of them plainly too fresh for that. They are similar to those found in rivers; but as there are no suckers nor lampreys here, I know not by what fish they could be made. Perhaps they are the nests of the chivin. These lend a pleasing mystery to the bottom.

The shore is irregular enough not to be monotonous. I have in my mind's eye the western indented with deep bays, the bolder northern, and the beautifully scalloped southern shore, where successive capes overlap each other and suggest unexplored coves between. The forest has never so good a setting, nor is so distinctly beautiful, as when seen from the middle of a small lake amid hills which rise from the water's edge; for the water in which it is reflected not only makes the best foreground in such a case, but, with its winding shore, the most natural and agreeable boundary to it. There is no rawness nor imperfection in its edge there, as where the axe has cleared a part, or a cultivated field abuts on it. The trees have ample room to expand on the water side, and each sends forth its most vigorous branch in that direction. There Nature has woven a natural selvage, and the eye rises by just gradations from the low shrubs of the shore to the highest trees. There are few traces of man's hand to be seen. The water laves the shore as it did a thousand years ago.

A lake is the landscape's most beautiful and expressive feature. It is earth's eye; looking into which the beholder measures the depth of his own nature. The fluviatile trees next the shore are the slender eyelashes which fringe it, and the wooded hills and cliffs around are its overhanging brows.

Standing on the smooth sandy beach at the east end of the pond, in a calm September afternoon, when a slight haze makes the opposite shore line indistinct, I have seen whence came the expression, "the glassy surface of a lake." When you invert your head, it looks like a thread of finest gossamer stretched across the valley, and gleaming against the distant pine woods, separating one stratum of the atmosphere from another. You would think that you could walk dry under it to the opposite hills, and that the swallows which skim over might perch on it. Indeed, they sometimes dive below the line, as it were by mistake, and are undeceived. As you look over the pond westward you are obliged to employ both your hands to defend your eyes against the reflected as well as the true sun, for they are equally bright; and if, between the two, you survey its surface critically, it is literally as smooth as glass, except where the skater insects, at equal intervals scattered over its whole extent, by their motions in the sun produce the finest imaginable sparkle on it, or, perchance, a duck plumes itself, or, as I have said, a swallow skims so low as to touch it. It may be that in the distance a fish describes an arc of three or four feet in the air, and there is one bright flash where it emerges, and another where it strikes the water; sometimes the whole silvery arc is revealed; or here and there, perhaps, is a thistle-down floating on its surface, which the fishes dart at and so dimple it again. It is like molten glass cooled but not congealed, and the few motes in it are pure and beautiful like the imperfections in glass. You may often detect a yet smoother and darker water, separated from the rest as if by an invisible cobweb, boom of the water nymphs, resting on it. From a hill-top you can see a fish leap in almost any part; for not a pickerel or shiner picks an insect from this smooth surface but it manifestly disturbs the equilibrium of the whole lake. It is wonderful with what elaborateness this simple fact is advertised,— this piscine murder will out,—and from my distant perch I distinguish the circling undulations when they are half a dozen rods in diameter. You can even detect a water-bug (*Gyrinus*) ceaselessly progressing over the smooth surface a quarter of a mile off; for they furrow the water slightly, making a conspicuous ripple bounded by two diverging lines, but the skaters glide over it without rippling it perceptibly. When the surface is considerably agitated there are no skaters nor water-bugs on it, but apparently, in calm days, they leave their havens and adventurously glide forth from the shore by short impulses till they completely cover it. It is a soothing employment, on one of those fine days in the fall when all the warmth of the sun is fully appreciated, to sit on a stump on such a height as this, overlooking the pond, and study the dimpling circles which are incessantly inscribed on its otherwise invisible surface amid the reflected skies and trees. Over this great expanse there is no disturbance but it is thus at once gently smoothed away and assuaged, as, when a vase of water is jarred, the trembling circles seek the shore and all is smooth again. Not a fish can leap or an insect fall on the pond but it is thus reported in circling dimples, in lines of beauty, as it were the constant welling up of its fountain, the gentle pulsing of its life, the heaving of its breast. The thrills of joy and thrills of pain are undistinguishable. How peaceful the phenomena of the lake! Again the works of man shine as in the spring. Ay, every leaf and twig and stone and cobweb sparkles now at mid-afternoon as when covered with dew in a spring morning. Every motion of an oar or an insect produces a flash of light; and if an oar falls, how sweet the echo!

In such a day, in September or October, Walden is a perfect forest mirror, set round with stones as precious to my eye as if fewer or rarer. Nothing so fair, so pure, and at the same time so large, as a lake, perchance, lies on the surface of the earth. Sky water. It needs no fence. Nations come and go without defiling it. It is a mirror which no stone can crack, whose quicksilver will never wear off, whose gilding Nature continually repairs; no storms, no dust, can dim its surface ever fresh;—a mirror in which all impurity presented to it sinks, swept and dusted by the sun's hazy brush, —this the light dustcloth,—which retains no breath that is breathed on it, but sends its own to float as clouds high above its surface, and be reflected in its bosom still.

A field of water betrays the spirit that is in the air. It is continually receiving new life and motion from above. It is intermediate in its nature between land and sky. On land only the grass and trees wave, but the water itself is rippled by the wind. I see where the breeze dashes across it by the streaks or flakes of light. It is remarkable that we can look down on its surface. We shall, perhaps, look down thus on the surface of air at length, and mark where a still subtler spirit sweeps over it.

The skaters and water-bugs finally disappear in the latter part of October, when the severe frosts have come; and then and in November, usually, in a calm day, there is absolutely nothing to ripple the surface. One November afternoon, in the calm at the end of a rain storm of several days' duration, when the sky was still completely overcast and the air was full of mist, I observed that the pond was remarkably smooth, so that it was difficult to distinguish its surface; though it no longer reflected the bright tints of October, but the sombre November colors of the surrounding hills. Though I passed over it as gently as possible, the slight undulations produced by my boat extended almost as far as I could see, and gave a ribbed appearance to the reflections. But, as I was looking over the surface, I saw here and there at a distance a faint glimmer, as if some skater insects which had escaped the frosts might be collected there, or, perchance, the surface, being so smooth, betrayed where a spring welled up from the bottom. Paddling gently to one of these places, I was surprised to find myself surrounded by myriads of small perch, about five inches long, of a rich bronze color in the green water, sporting there and constantly rising to the surface and dimpling it, sometimes leaving bubbles on it. In such transparent and seemingly bottomless water, reflecting the clouds, I seemed to be floating through the air as in a balloon, and their swimming impressed me as a kind of flight or hovering, as if they were a compact flock of birds passing just beneath my level on the right or left, their fins, like sails, set all around them. There were many such schools in the pond, apparently improving the short season before winter would draw an icy shutter over their broad skylight, sometimes giving to the surface an appearance as if a slight breeze struck it, or a few rain-drops fell there. When I approached carelessly and alarmed them, they made a sudden plash and rippling with their tails, as if one had struck the water with a brushy bough, and instantly took refuge in the depths. At length the wind rose, the mist increased, and the waves began to run, and the perch leaped much higher than before, half out of water, a hundred black points, three inches long, at once above the surface. Even as late as the fifth of December, one year, I saw some dimples on the surface, and thinking it was going to rain hard immediately, the air being full of mist, I made haste to take my place at the oars and row homeward; already the rain seemed rapidly increasing, though I felt none on my cheek, and I anticipated a thorough soaking. But suddenly the dimples ceased, for they were produced by the perch, which the noise of my oars had scared into the depths, and I saw their schools dimly disappearing; so I spent a dry afternoon after all.

An old man who used to frequent this pond nearly sixty years ago, when it was dark with surrounding forests, tells me that in those days he sometimes saw it all alive with ducks and other water fowl, and that there were many eagles about it. He came here a-fishing, and used an old log canoe which he found on the shore. It was made of two white-pine logs dug out and pinned together, and was cut off square at the ends. It was very clumsy, but lasted a great many years before it became water-logged and perhaps sank to the bottom. He did not know whose it was; it belonged to the pond. He used to make a cable for his anchor of strips of hickory bark tied together. An old man, a potter, who lived by the pond before the Revolution, told him once that there was an iron chest at the bottom, and that he had seen it. Sometimes it would come floating up to the shore; but when you went toward it, it would go back into deep water and disappear. I was pleased to hear of the old log canoe, which took the place of an Indian one of the same material but more graceful construction, which perchance had first been a tree on the bank, and then, as it were, fell into the water, to float there for a generation, the most proper vessel for the lake. I remember that when I first looked into these depths there were many large trunks to be seen indistinctly lying on the bottom, which had either been blown over formerly, or left on the ice at the last cutting, when wood was cheaper; but now they have mostly disappeared.

When I first paddled a boat on Walden, it was completely surrounded by thick and lofty pine and oak woods, and in some of its coves grape vines had run over the trees next the water and formed bowers under which a boat could pass. The hills which form its shores are so steep, and the woods on them were then so high, that, as you looked down from the west end, it had the appearance of an amphitheatre for some kind of sylvan spectacle. I have spent many an hour, when I was younger, floating over its surface as the zephyr willed, having paddled my boat to the middle, and lying on my back across the seats, in a summer forenoon, dreaming awake, until I was aroused by the boat touching the sand, and I arose to see what shore my fates had impelled me to; days when idleness was the most attractive and productive industry. Many a forenoon have I stolen away, preferring to spend thus the most valued part of the day; for I was rich, if not in money, in sunny hours and summer days, and spent them lavishly; nor do I regret that I did not waste more of them in the workshop or the teacher's desk. But since I left those shores the woodchoppers have still further laid them waste, and now for many a year there will be no more rambling through the aisles of the wood, with occasional vistas through which you see the water. My Muse may be excused if she is silent henceforth. How can you expect the birds to sing when their groves are cut down?

Now the trunks of trees on the bottom, and the old log canoe, and the dark surrounding woods, are gone, and the villagers, who scarcely know where it lies, instead of going to the pond to bathe or drink, are thinking to bring its water, which should be as sacred as the Ganges[255] at least, to the village in a pipe, to wash their dishes with!—to earn their Walden by the turning of a cock or drawing of a plug! That devilish Iron Horse, whose ear-rending neigh is heard throughout the town, has muddied the Boiling Spring with his foot, and he it is that has browsed off all the woods on Walden shore; that Trojan horse, with a thousand men in his belly, introduced by mercenary Greeks! Where is the country's champion, the Moore of Moore Hall,[256] to meet him at the Deep Cut[257] and thrust an avenging lance between the ribs of the bloated pest?

Nevertheless, of all the characters I have known, perhaps Walden wears best, and best preserves its purity. Many men have been likened to it, but few deserve that honor. Though the woodchoppers have laid bare first this shore and then that, and the Irish have built their sties by it, and the railroad has infringed on its border, and the ice-men have skimmed it once, it is itself unchanged, the same water which my youthful eyes fell on; all the change is in me. It has not acquired one permanent wrinkle after all its ripples. It is perennially young, and I may stand and see a swallow dip apparently to pick an insect from its surface as of yore. It struck me again tonight, as if I had not seen it almost daily for more than twenty years,—Why, here is Walden,

---

[255] River in India. [257] Where the railroad passed near the pond.
[256] Hero in an English ballad.

the same woodland lake that I discovered so many years ago; where a forest was cut down last winter another is springing up by its shore as lustily as ever; the same thought is welling up to its surface that was then; it is the same liquid joy and happiness to itself and its Maker, ay, and it *may* be to me. It is the work of a brave man surely, in whom there was no guile! He rounded this water with his hand, deepened and clarified it in his thought, and in his will bequeathed it to Concord. I see by its face that it is visited by the same reflection; and I can almost say, Walden, is it you?

> It is no dream of mine,
> To ornament a line;
> I cannot come nearer to God and Heaven
> Than I live to Walden even.
> I am its stony shore,
> And the breeze that passes o'er;
> In the hollow of my hand
> Are its water and its sand,
> And its deepest resort
> Lies high in my thought.[258]

The cars never pause to look at it; yet I fancy that the engineers and firemen and brakemen, and those passengers who have a season ticket and see it often, are better men for the sight. The engineer does not forget at night, or his nature does not, that he has beheld this vision of serenity and purity once at least during the day. Though seen but once, it helps to wash out State-street[259] and the engine's soot. One proposes that it be called "God's Drop."[260]

I have said that Walden has no visible inlet nor outlet, but it is on the one hand distantly and indirectly related to Flint's Pond, which is more elevated, by a chain of small ponds coming from that quarter, and on the other directly and manifestly to Concord River, which is lower, by a similar chain of ponds through which in some other geological period it may have flowed, and by a little digging, which God forbid, it can be made to flow thither again. If by living thus reserved and austere, like a hermit in the woods, so long, it has acquired such wonderful purity, who would not regret that the comparatively impure waters of Flint's Pond should be mingled with it, or itself should ever go to waste its sweetness in the ocean wave?

Flint's, or Sandy Pond, in Lincoln, our greatest lake and inland sea, lies about a mile east of Walden. It is much larger, being said to contain one hundred and ninety-seven acres, and is more fertile in fish; but it is comparatively shallow, and not remarkably pure. A walk through the woods thither was often my recreation. It was worth the while, if only to feel the wind blow on your cheek freely, and see the waves run, and remember the life of mariners. I went a-chestnutting there in the fall, on windy days, when the nuts were dropping into the water and were washed to my feet; and one day, as I crept along its sedgy shore, the fresh spray blowing in my face, I came upon the mouldering wreck of a boat, the sides gone, and hardly more than the

---

[258] Thoreau's own verses.   [260] Medicine for the eyes.
[259] Center of Boston's financial activities.

impression of its flat bottom left amid the rushes; yet its model was sharply defined, as if it were a large decayed pad, with its veins. It was as impressive a wreck as one could imagine on the sea-shore, and had as good a moral. It is by this time mere vegetable mould and undistinguishable pond shore, through which rushes and flags have pushed up. I used to admire the ripple marks on the sandy bottom, at the north end of this pond, made firm and hard to the feet of the wader by the pressure of the water, and the rushes which grew in Indian file, in waving lines, corresponding to these marks, rank behind rank, as if the waves had planted them. There also I have found, in considerable quantities, curious balls, composed apparently of fine grass or roots, of pipewort perhaps, from half an inch to four inches in diameter, and perfectly spherical. These wash back and forth in shallow water on a sandy bottom, and are sometimes cast on the shore. They are either solid grass, or have a little sand in the middle. At first you would say that they were formed by the action of the waves, like a pebble; yet the smallest are made of equally coarse materials, half an inch long, and they are produced only at one season of the year. Moreover, the waves, I suspect, do not so much construct as wear down a material which has already acquired consistency. They preserve their form when dry for an indefinite period.

Flint's Pond! Such is the poverty of our nomenclature. What right had the unclean and stupid farmer, whose farm abutted on this sky water, whose shores he has ruthlessly laid bare, to give his name to it? Some skin-flint, who loved better the reflecting surface of a dollar, or a bright cent, in which he could see his own brazen face; who regarded even the wild ducks which settled in it as trespassers; his fingers grown into crooked and horny talons from the long habit of grasping harpy-like;— so it is not named for me. I go not there to see him nor to hear of him; who never *saw* it, who never bathed in it, who never loved it, who never protected it, who never spoke a good word for it, nor thanked God that he had made it. Rather let it be named from the fishes that swim in it, the wild fowl or quadrupeds which frequent it, the wild flowers which grow by its shores, or some wild man or child the thread of whose history is interwoven with its own; not from him who could show no title to it but the deed which a like-minded neighbor or legislature gave him,—him who thought only of its money value; whose presence perchance cursed all the shore; who exhausted the land around it, would fain have exhausted the waters within it; who regretted only that it was not English hay or cranberry meadow,—there was nothing to redeem it, forsooth, in his eyes,—and would have drained and sold it for the mud at its bottom. It did not turn his mill, and it was no *privilege* to him to behold it. I respect not his labors, his farm where every thing has its price; who would carry the landscape, who would carry his God, to market, if he could get any thing for him; who goes to market *for* his god as it is; on whose farm nothing grows free, whose fields bear no crops, whose meadows no flowers, whose trees no fruits, but dollars; who loves not the beauty of his fruits, whose fruits are not ripe for him till they are turned to dollars. Give me the poverty that enjoys true wealth. Farmers are respectable and interesting to me in proportion as they are poor,—poor farmers. A model farm! where the house stands like a fungus in a muck-heap, chambers for men, horses, oxen, and swine, cleansed and uncleansed, all contiguous to one another! Stocked with men! A great grease-spot, redolent of manures and buttermilk! Under a high state of cultivation, being manured with the hearts and brains of men! As if you were to raise your potatoes in the church-yard! Such is a model farm.

No, no; if the fairest features of the landscape are to be named after men, let them be the noblest and worthiest men alone. Let our lakes receive as true names at least as the Icarian Sea, where "still the shore" a "brave attempt resounds."[261]

Goose Pond, of small extent, is on my way to Flint's; Fair-Haven, an expansion of Concord River, said to contain some seventy acres, is a mile southwest; and White Pond, of about forty acres, is a mile and a half beyond Fair-Haven. This is my lake country. These, with Concord River, are my water privileges; and night and day, year in year out, they grind such grist as I carry to them.

Since the woodcutters, and the railroad, and I myself have profaned Walden, perhaps the most attractive, if not the most beautiful, of all our lakes, the gem of the woods, is White Pond;—a poor name from its commonness, whether derived from the remarkable purity of its waters or the color of its sands. In these as in other respects, however, it is a lesser twin of Walden. They are so much alike that you would say they must be connected under ground. It has the same stony shore, and its waters are of the same hue. As at Walden, in sultry dog-day weather, looking down through the woods on some of its bays which are not so deep but that the reflection from the bottom tinges them, its waters are of a misty bluish-green or glaucous color. Many years since I used to go there to collect the sand by cart-loads, to make sand-paper with, and I have continued to visit it ever since. One who frequents it proposes to call it Virid[262] Lake. Perhaps it might be called Yellow-Pine Lake, from the following circumstance. About fifteen years ago you could see the top of a pitch-pine, of the kind called yellow-pine hereabouts, though it is not a distinct species, projecting above the surface in deep water, many rods from the shore. It was even supposed by some that the pond had sunk, and this was one of the primitive forest that formerly stood there. I find that even so long ago as 1792, in a "Topographical Description of the Town of Concord," by one of its citizens, in the Collections of the Massachusetts Historical Society, the author, after speaking of Walden and White Ponds, adds: "In the middle of the latter may be seen, when the water is very low, a tree which appears as if it grew in the place where it now stands, although the roots are fifty feet below the surface of the water; the top of this tree is broken off, and at the place measures fourteen inches in diameter." In the spring of '49 I talked with the man who lives nearest the pond in Sudbury, who told me that it was he who got out this tree ten or fifteen years before. As near as he could remember, it stood twelve or fifteen rods from the shore, where the water was thirty or forty feet deep. It was in the winter, and he had been getting out ice in the forenoon, and had resolved that in the afternoon, with the aid of his neighbors, he would take out the old yellow-pine. He sawed a channel in the ice toward the shore, and hauled it over and along and out on to the ice with oxen; but, before he had gone far in his work, he was surprised to find that it was wrong end upward, with the stumps of the branches pointing down, and the small end firmly fastened in the sandy bottom. It was about a foot in diameter at the big end, and he had expected to get a good saw-log, but it was so rotten as to be

---

[261] Lines from "Icarus" by William Drummond, referring to the sea where, according to classic myth, Icarus fell after attempting to soar on wings toward the sun.

[262] Green.

fit only for fuel, if for that. He had some of it in his shed then. There were marks of an axe and of woodpeckers on the but. He thought that it might have been a dead tree on the shore, but was finally blown over into the pond, and after the top had become waterlogged, while the but-end was still dry and light, had drifted out and sunk wrong end up. His father, eighty years old, could not remember when it was not there. Several pretty large logs may still be seen lying on the bottom, where, owing to the undulation of the surface, they look like huge water snakes in motion.

This pond has rarely been profaned by a boat, for there is little in it to tempt a fisherman. Instead of the white lily, which requires mud, or the common sweet flag, the blue flag (*Iris versicolor*) grows thinly in the pure water, rising from the stony bottom all around the shore, where it is visited by humming birds in June, and the color both of its bluish blades and its flowers, and especially their reflections, are in singular harmony with the glaucous water.

White Pond and Walden are great crystals on the surface of the earth, Lakes of Light. If they were permanently congealed, and small enough to be clutched, they would, perchance, be carried off by slaves, like precious stones, to adorn the heads of emperors; but being liquid, and ample, and secured to us and our successors forever, we disregard them, and run after the diamond of Kohinoor.[263] They are too pure to have a market value; they contain no muck. How much more beautiful than our lives, how much more transparent than our characters, are they! We never learned meanness of them. How much fairer than the pool before the farmer's door, in which his ducks swim! Hither the clean wild ducks come. Nature has no human inhabitant who appreciates her. The birds with their plumage and their notes are in harmony with the flowers, but what youth or maiden conspires with the wild luxuriant beauty of Nature? She flourishes most alone, far from the towns where they reside. Talk of heaven! ye disgrace earth.

Baker Farm

Sometimes I rambled to pine groves, standing like temples, or like fleets at sea, full-rigged, with wavy boughs, and rippling with light, so soft and green and shady that the Druids would have forsaken their oaks[264] to worship in them; or to the cedar wood beyond Flint's Pond, where the trees, covered with hoary blue berries, spiring higher and higher, are fit to stand before Valhalla, and the creeping juniper covers the ground with wreaths full of fruit; or to swamps where the usnea lichen hangs in festoons from the black-spruce trees, and toad-stools, round tables of the swamp gods, cover the ground, and more beautiful fungi adorn the stumps, like butterflies or shells, vegetable winkles; where the swamp-pink and dogwood grow, the red alder-berry glows like eyes of imps, the waxwork grooves and crushes the hardest woods in its folds, and the wild-holly berries make the beholder forget his home with their beauty, and he is dazzled and tempted by nameless other wild forbidden fruits, too fair for mortal taste. Instead of calling on some scholar, I paid many a visit to particular trees, of kinds which are rare in this neighborhood, standing far away in the middle of some pasture, or in the depths of a wood or swamp, or on a hill-top; such as the black-birch,

---

[263] Famous diamond.
[264] Oak groves were sacred to the Druids, the priests of Celtic Britain.

of which we have some handsome specimens two feet in diameter; its cousin the yellow-birch, with its loose golden vest, perfumed like the first; the beech, which has so neat a bole and beautifully lichen-painted, perfect in all its details, of which, excepting scattered specimens, I know but one small grove of sizeable trees left in the township, supposed by some to have been planted by the pigeons that were once baited with beech nuts near by; it is worth the while to see the silver grain sparkle when you split this wood; the bass; the hornbeam; the *Celtis occidentalis,* or false elm, of which we have but one well-grown; some taller mast of a pine, a shingle tree, or a more perfect hemlock than usual, standing like a pagoda in the midst of the woods; and many others I could mention. These were the shrines I visited both summer and winter.

Once it chanced that I stood in the very abutment of a rainbow's arch, which filled the lower stratum of the atmosphere, tinging the grass and leaves around, and dazzling me as if I looked through colored crystal. It was a lake of rainbow light, in which, for a short while, I lived like a dolphin. If it had lasted longer it might have tinged my employments and life. As I walked on the railroad causeway, I used to wonder at the halo of light around my shadow, and would fain fancy myself one of the elect. One who visited me declared that the shadows of some Irishmen before him had no halo about them, that it was only natives that were so distinguished. Benvenuto Cellini[265] tells us in his memoirs, that, after a certain terrible dream or vision which he had during his confinement in the castle of St. Angelo, a resplendent light appeared over the shadow of his head at morning and evening, whether he was in Italy or France, and it was particularly conspicuous when the grass was moist with dew. This was probably the same phenomenon to which I have referred, which is especially observed in the morning, but also at other times, and even by moonlight. Though a constant one, it is not commonly noticed, and, in the case of an excitable imagination like Cellini's, it would be basis enough for superstition. Beside, he tells us that he showed it to very few. But are they not indeed distinguished who are conscious that they are regarded at all?

I set out one afternoon to go a-fishing to Fair-Haven, through the woods, to eke out my scanty fare of vegetables. My way led through Pleasant Meadow, an adjunct of the Baker Farm, that retreat of which a poet[266] has since sung, beginning,—

> "Thy entry is a pleasant field,
> Which some mossy fruit trees yield
> Partly to a ruddy brook,
> By gliding musquash undertook,
> And mercurial trout,
> Darting about."

I thought of living there before I went to Walden. I "hooked" the apples, leaped the brook, and scared the musquash and the trout. It was one of those afternoons which seem indefinitely long before one, in which many events may happen, a large portion

---

[265] Italian artist (1500–1571).
[266] All the verses quoted in this chapter are by

William Ellery Channing the younger, a companion of Thoreau.

of our natural life, though it was already half spent when I started. By the way there came up a shower, which compelled me to stand half an hour under a pine, piling boughs over my head, and wearing my handkerchief for a shed; and when at length I had made one cast over the pickerel-weed, standing up to my middle in water, I found myself suddenly in the shadow of a cloud, and the thunder began to rumble with such emphasis that I could do no more than listen to it. The gods must be proud, thought I, with such forked flashes to rout a poor unarmed fisherman. So I made haste for shelter to the nearest hut, which stood half a mile from any road, but so much the nearer to the pond, and had long been uninhabited:—

"And here a poet builded,
    In the completed years,
  For behold a trivial cabin
      That to destruction steers."

So the Muse fables. But therein, as I found, dwelt now John Field, an Irishman, and his wife, and several children, from the broad-faced boy who assisted his father at his work, and now came running by his side from the bog to escape the rain, to the wrinkled, sibyl-like,[267] cone-headed infant that sat upon its father's knee as in the palaces of nobles, and looked out from its home in the midst of wet and hunger inquisitively upon the stranger, with the privilege of infancy, not knowing but it was the last of a noble line, and the hope and cynosure of the world, instead of John Field's poor starveling brat. There we sat together under that part of the roof which leaked the least, while it showered and thundered without. I had sat there many times of old before the ship was built that floated this family to America. An honest, hard-working, but shiftless man plainly was John Field; and his wife, she too was brave to cook so many successive dinners in the recesses of that lofty stove; with round greasy face and bare breast, still thinking to improve her condition one day; with the never absent mop in one hand, and yet no effects of it visible any where. The chickens, which had also taken shelter here from the rain, stalked about the room like members of the family, too humanized methought to roast well. They stood and looked in my eye or pecked at my shoe significantly. Meanwhile my host told me his story, how hard he worked "bogging" for a neighboring farmer, turning up a meadow with a spade or bog hoe at the rate of ten dollars an acre and the use of the land with manure for one year, and his little broad-faced son worked cheerfully at his father's side the while, not knowing how poor a bargain the latter had made. I tried to help him with my experience, telling him that he was one of my nearest neighbors, and that I too, who came a-fishing here, and looked like a loafer, was getting my living like himself; that I lived in a tight light and clean house, which hardly cost more than the annual rent of such a ruin as his commonly amounts to; and how, if he chose, he might in a month or two build himself a palace of his own; that I did not use tea, nor coffee, nor butter, nor milk, nor fresh meat, and so did not have to work to get them; again, as I did not work hard, I did not have to eat hard, and it cost me but a trifle for my food;

[267] As wizened as the Sibyl in classic myth, who
forgot to ask for perennial youth along with
eternal life.

but as he began with tea, and coffee, and butter, and milk, and beef, he had to work hard to pay for them, and when he had worked hard he had to eat hard again to repair the waste of his system,—and so it was as broad as it was long, indeed it was broader than it was long, for he was discontented and wasted his life into the bargain; and yet he had rated it as a gain in coming to America, that here you could get tea, and coffee, and meat every day. But the only true America is that country where you are at liberty to pursue such a mode of life as may enable you to do without these, and where the state does not endeavor to compel you to sustain the slavery and war and other superfluous expenses which directly or indirectly result from the use of such things. For I purposely talked to him as if he were a philosopher, or desired to be one. I should be glad if all the meadows on the earth were left in a wild state, if that were the consequence of men's beginning to redeem themselves. A man will not need to study history to find out what is best for his own culture. But alas! the culture of an Irishman is an enterprise to be undertaken with a sort of moral bog hoe. I told him, that as he worked so hard at bogging, he required thick boots and stout clothing, which yet were soon soiled and worn out, but I wore light shoes and thin clothing, which cost not half so much, though he might think that I was dressed like a gentleman, (which, however, was not the case,) and in an hour or two, without labor, but as a recreation, I could, if I wished, catch as many fish as I should want for two days, or earn enough money to support me a week. If he and his family would live simply, they might all go a-huckleberrying in the summer for their amusement. John heaved a sigh at this, and his wife stared with arms a-kimbo, and both appeared to be wondering if they had capital enough to begin such a course with, or arithmetic enough to carry it through. It was sailing by dead reckoning to them, and they saw not clearly how to make their port so; therefore I suppose they still take life bravely, after their fashion, face to face, giving it tooth and nail, not having skill to split its massive columns with any fine entering wedge, and rout it in detail;—thinking to deal with it roughly, as one should handle a thistle. But they fight at an overwhelming disadvantage,—living, John Field, alas! without arithmetic, and failing so.

"Do you ever fish?" I asked. "Oh yes, I catch a mess now and then when I am lying by; good perch I catch." "What's your bait?" "I catch shiners with fish-worms, and bait the perch with them." "You'd better go now, John," said his wife with glistening and hopeful face; but John demurred.

The shower was now over, and a rainbow above the eastern woods promised a fair evening; so I took my departure. When I had got without I asked for a drink, hoping to get a sight of the well bottom, to complete my survey of the premises; but there, alas! are shallows and quicksands, and rope broken withal, and bucket irrecoverable. Meanwhile the right culinary vessel was selected, water was seemingly distilled, and after consultation and long delay passed out to the thirsty one,—not yet suffered to cool, not yet to settle. Such gruel sustains life here, I thought; so, shutting my eyes, and excluding the motes by a skilfully directed under-current, I drank to genuine hospitality the heartiest draught I could. I am not squeamish in such cases when manners are concerned.

As I was leaving the Irishman's roof after the rain, bending my steps again to the pond, my haste to catch pickerel, wading in retired meadows, in sloughs and bog-holes, in forlorn and savage places, appeared for an instant trivial to me who had been sent to school and college; but as I ran down the hill toward the reddening west, with the rainbow over my shoulder, and some faint tinkling sounds borne to my ear through the cleansed air, from I know not what quarter, my Good Genius seemed to say,—Go fish and hunt far and wide day by day,—farther and wider,—and rest thee by many brooks and hearth-sides without misgiving. Remember thy Creator in the days of thy youth. Rise free from care before the dawn, and seek adventures. Let the noon find thee by other lakes, and the night overtake thee every where at home. There are no larger fields than these, no worthier games than may here be played. Grow wild according to thy nature, like these sedges and brakes, which will never become English hay. Let the thunder rumble; what if it threaten ruin to farmers' crops? that is not its errand to thee. Take shelter under the cloud, while they flee to carts and sheds. Let not to get a living be thy trade, but thy sport. Enjoy the land, but own it not. Through want of enterprise and faith men are where they are, buying and selling, and spending their lives like serfs.

O Baker Farm!

> "Landscape where the richest element
> Is a little sunshine innocent." * * *

> "No one runs to revel
> On thy rail-fenced lea." * * *

> "Debate with no man hast thou,
>   With questions art never perplexed,
>   As tame at the first sight as now,
>   In thy plain russet gabardine dressed." * *[268]

> "Come ye who love,
>   And ye who hate,
>   Children of the Holy Dove,
>   And Guy Faux of the state,
> And hang conspiracies
> From the tough rafters of the trees!"

Men come tamely home at night only from the next field or street, where their household echoes haunt, and their life pines because it breathes its own breath over again; their shadows morning and evening reach farther than their daily steps. We should come home from far, from adventures, and perils, and discoveries every day, with new experience and character.

Before I had reached the pond some fresh impulse had brought out John Field, with altered mind, letting go "bogging" ere this sunset. But he, poor man, disturbed only a couple of fins while I was catching a fair string, and he said it was his luck; but when we changed seats in the boat luck changed seats too. Poor John Field!—I trust he does not read this, unless he will improve by it,—thinking to live by some derivative old country mode in this primitive new country,—to catch perch with shiners. It is good bait sometimes, I allow. With his horizon all his own, yet he a poor

[268] Asterisks inserted by Thoreau.

man, born to be poor, with his inherited Irish poverty or poor life, his Adam's grandmother and boggy ways, not to rise in this world, he nor his posterity, till their wading webbed bog-trotting feet get *talaria* to their heels.[269]

Higher Laws

As I came home through the woods with my string of fish, trailing my pole, it being now quite dark, I caught a glimpse of a woodchuck stealing across my path, and felt a strange thrill of savage delight, and was strongly tempted to seize and devour him raw; not that I was hungry then, except for that wildness which he represented. Once or twice, however, while I lived at the pond, I found myself ranging the woods, like a half-starved hound, with a strange abandonment, seeking some kind of venison which I might devour, and no morsel could have been too savage for me. The wildest scenes had become unaccountably familiar. I found in myself, and still find, an instinct toward a higher, or, as it is named, spiritual life, as do most men, and another toward a primitive rank and savage one, and I reverence them both. I love the wild not less than the good. The wildness and adventure that are in fishing still recommended it to me. I like sometimes to take rank hold on life and spend my day more as the animals do. Perhaps I have owed to this employment and to hunting, when quite young, my closest acquaintance with Nature. They early introduce us to and detain us in scenery with which otherwise, at that age, we should have little acquaintance. Fishermen, hunters, woodchoppers, and others, spending their lives in the fields and woods, in a peculiar sense a part of Nature themselves, are often in a more favorable mood for observing her, in the intervals of their pursuits, than philosophers or poets even, who approach her with expectation. She is not afraid to exhibit herself to them. The traveller on the prairie is naturally a hunter, on the head waters of the Missouri and Columbia a trapper, and at the Falls of St. Mary a fisherman. He who is only a traveller learns things at second-hand and by the halves, and is poor authority. We are most interested when science reports what those men already know practically or instinctively, for that alone is a true *humanity,* or account of human experience.

They mistake who assert that the Yankee has few amusements, because he has not so many public holidays, and men and boys do not play so many games as they do in England, for here the more primitive but solitary amusements of hunting, fishing and the like have not yet given place to the former. Almost every New England boy among my contemporaries shouldered a fowling piece between the ages of ten and fourteen; and his hunting and fishing grounds were not limited like the preserves of an English nobleman, but were more boundless even than those of a savage. No wonder, then, that he did not oftener stay to play on the common. But already a change is taking place, owing, not to an increased humanity, but to an increased scarcity of game, for perhaps the hunter is the greatest friend of the animals hunted, not excepting the Humane Society.

Moreover, when at the pond, I wished sometimes to add fish to my fare for variety. I have actually fished from the same kind of necessity that the first fishers did. Whatever humanity I might conjure up against it was all factitious, and concerned

---

[269] I.e., acquire winged heels like those possessed by the Greek gods.

my philosophy more than my feelings. I speak of fishing only now, for I had long felt differently about fowling, and sold my gun before I went to the woods. Not that I am less humane than others, but I did not perceive that my feelings were much affected. I did not pity the fishes nor the worms. This was habit. As for fowling, during the last years that I carried a gun my excuse was that I was studying ornithology, and sought only new or rare birds. But I confess that I am now inclined to think that there is a finer way of studying ornithology than this. It requires so much closer attention to the habits of the birds, that, if for that reason only, I have been willing to omit the gun. Yet notwithstanding the objection on the score of humanity, I am compelled to doubt if equally valuable sports are ever substituted for these; and when some of my friends have asked me anxiously about their boys, whether they should let them hunt, I have answered, yes,—remembering that it was one of the best parts of my education,—*make* them hunters, though sportsmen only at first, if possible, mighty hunters at last, so that they shall not find game large enough for them in this or any vegetable wilderness,—hunters as well as fishers of men.[270] Thus far I am of the opinion of Chaucer's nun, who

"yave not of the text a pulled hen
That saith that hunters ben not holy men."[271]

There is a period in the history of the individual, as of the race, when the hunters are the "best men," as the Algonquins called them. We cannot but pity the boy who has never fired a gun; he is no more humane, while his education has been sadly neglected. This was my answer with respect to those youths who were bent on this pursuit, trusting that they would soon outgrow it. No humane being, past the thoughtless age of boyhood, will wantonly murder any creature, which holds its life by the same tenure that he does. The hare in its extremity cries like a child. I warn you, mothers, that my sympathies do not always make the usual phil-*anthropic* distinctions.

Such is oftenest the young man's introduction to the forest, and the most original part of himself. He goes thither at first as a hunter and fisher, until at last, if he has the seeds of a better life in him, he distinguishes his proper objects, as a poet or naturalist it may be, and leaves the gun and fish-pole behind. The mass of men are still and always young in this respect. In some countries a hunting parson is no uncommon sight. Such a one might make a good shepherd's dog, but is far from being the Good Shepherd. I have been surprised to consider that the only obvious employment, except wood-chopping, ice-cutting, or the like business, which ever to my knowledge detained at Walden Pond for a whole half day any of my fellow-citizens, whether fathers or children of the town, with just one exception, was fishing. Commonly they did not think that they were lucky, or well paid for their time, unless they got a long string of fish, though they had the opportunity of seeing the pond all the while. They might go there a thousand times before the sediment of fishing would sink to the bottom and leave their purpose pure; but no doubt such a clarifying

[270] Allusion to Jesus' words to the Galilean fishermen (Mark 1:17).
[271] The description was given by Chaucer to a monk, not a nun, in the Prologue to *The Canterbury Tales.*

process would be going on all the while. The governor and his council faintly remember the pond, for they went a-fishing there when they were boys; but now they are too old and dignified to go a-fishing, and so they know it no more forever. Yet even they expect to go to heaven at last. If the legislature regards it, it is chiefly to regulate the number of hooks to be used there; but they know nothing about the hook of hooks with which to angle for the pond itself, impaling the legislature for a bait. Thus, even in civilized communities, the embryo man passes through the hunter stage of development.

I have found repeatedly, of late years, that I cannot fish without falling a little in self-respect. I have tried it again and again. I have skill at it, and, like many of my fellows, a certain instinct for it, which revives from time to time, but always when I have done I feel that it would have been better if I had not fished. I think that I do not mistake. It is a faint intimation, yet so are the first streaks of morning. There is unquestionably this instinct in me which belongs to the lower orders of creation; yet with every year I am less a fisherman, though without more humanity or even wisdom; at present I am no fisherman at all. But I see that if I were to live in a wilderness I should again be tempted to become a fisher and hunter in earnest. Beside, there is something essentially unclean about this diet and all flesh, and I began to see where housework commences, and whence the endeavor, which costs so much, to wear a tidy and respectable appearance each day, to keep the house sweet and free from all ill odors and sights. Having been my own butcher and scullion and cook, as well as the gentleman for whom the dishes were served up, I can speak from an unusually complete experience. The practical objection to animal food in my case was its uncleanness; and, besides, when I had caught and cleaned and cooked and eaten my fish, they seemed not to have fed me essentially. It was insignificant and unnecessary, and cost more than it came to. A little bread or a few potatoes would have done as well, with less trouble and filth. Like many of my contemporaries, I had rarely for many years used animal food, or tea, or coffee, &c.; not so much because of any ill effects which I had traced to them, as because they were not agreeable to my imagination. The repugnance to animal food is not the effect of experience, but is an instinct. It appeared more beautiful to live low and fare hard in many respects; and though I never did so, I went far enough to please my imagination. I believe that every man who has ever been earnest to preserve his higher or poetic faculties in the best condition has been particularly inclined to abstain from animal food, and from much food of any kind. It is a significant fact, stated by entomologists, I find it in Kirby and Spence,[272] that "some insects in their perfect state, though furnished with organs of feeding, make no use of them;" and they lay it down as "a general rule, that almost all insects in this state eat much less than in that of larvæ. The voracious caterpillar when transformed into a butterfly," . . "and the gluttonous maggot when become a fly," content themselves with a drop or two of honey or some other sweet liquid. The abdomen under the wings of the butterfly still represents the larva. This is the tid-bit which tempts his insectivorous fate. The gross feeder is a man in the larva state; and there are whole nations in that condition, nations without fancy or imagination, whose vast abdomens betray them.

[272] William Kirby and William Spence, authors of *An Introduction to Entomology* (1815–1826).

It is hard to provide and cook so simple and clean a diet as will not offend the imagination; but this, I think, is to be fed when we feed the body; they should both sit down at the same table. Yet perhaps this may be done. The fruits eaten temperately need not make us ashamed of our appetites, nor interrupt the worthiest pursuits. But put an extra condiment into your dish, and it will poison you. It is not worth the while to live by rich cookery. Most men would feel shame if caught preparing with their own hands precisely such a dinner, whether of animal or vegetable food, as is every day prepared for them by others. Yet till this is otherwise we are not civilized, and, if gentlemen and ladies, are not true men and women. This certainly suggests what change is to be made. It may be vain to ask why the imagination will not be reconciled to flesh and fat. I am satisfied that it is not. Is it not a reproach that man is a carnivorous animal? True, he can and does live, in a great measure, by preying on other animals; but this is a miserable way,—as any one who will go to snaring rabbits, or slaughtering lambs, may learn,—and he will be regarded as a benefactor of his race who shall teach man to confine himself to a more innocent and wholesome diet. Whatever my own practice may be, I have no doubt that it is a part of the destiny of the human race, in its gradual improvement, to leave off eating animals, as surely as the savage tribes have left off eating each other when they came in contact with the more civilized.

If one listens to the faintest but constant suggestions of his genius, which are certainly true, he sees not to what extremes, or even insanity, it may lead him; and yet that way, as he grows more resolute and faithful, his road lies. The faintest assured objection which one healthy man feels will at length prevail over the arguments and customs of mankind. No man ever followed his genius till it misled him. Though the result were bodily weakness, yet perhaps no one can say that the consequences were to be regretted, for these were a life in conformity to higher principles. If the day and night are such that you greet them with joy, and life emits a fragrance like flowers and sweet-scented herbs, is more elastic, more starry, more immortal,—that is your success. All nature is your congratulation, and you have cause momentarily to bless yourself. The greatest gains and values are farthest from being appreciated. We easily come to doubt if they exist. We soon forget them. They are the highest reality. Perhaps the facts most astounding and most real are never communicated by man to man. The true harvest of my daily life is somewhat as intangible and indescribable as the tints of morning or evening. It is a little star-dust caught, a segment of the rainbow which I have clutched.

Yet, for my part, I was never unusually squeamish; I could sometimes eat a fried rat with a good relish, if it were necessary. I am glad to have drunk water so long, for the same reason that I prefer the natural sky to an opium-eater's heaven. I would fain keep sober always; and there are infinite degrees of drunkenness. I believe that water is the only drink for a wise man; wine is not so noble a liquor; and think of dashing the hopes of a morning with a cup of warm coffee, or of an evening with a dish of tea! Ah, how low I fall when I am tempted by them! Even music may be intoxicating. Such apparently slight causes destroyed Greece and Rome, and will destroy England and America. Of all ebriosity, who does not prefer to be intoxicated by the air he breathes? I have found it to be the most serious objection to coarse labors long continued, that they compelled me to eat and drink coarsely also. But to tell the truth, I find myself at present somewhat less particular in these respects. I carry less religion to the table, ask no blessing; not because I am wiser than I was, but, I am obliged to confess, because, however much it is to be regretted, with years I have grown more coarse and indifferent. Perhaps these questions are entertained only in youth, as most believe of poetry. My practice is "nowhere," my opinion is here. Nevertheless I am far from regarding myself as one of those privileged ones to whom the Ved[273] refers when it says, that "he who has true faith in the Omnipresent Supreme Being may eat all that exists," that is, is not bound to inquire what is his food, or who prepares it; and even in their case it is to be observed, as a Hindoo commentator has remarked, that the Vedant limits this privilege to "the time of distress."

Who has not sometimes derived an inexpressible satisfaction from his food in which appetite had no share? I have been thrilled to think that I owed a mental perception to the commonly gross sense of taste, that I have been inspired through the palate, that some berries which I had eaten on a hill-side had fed my genius. "The soul not being mistress of herself," says Thseng-tseu,[274] "one looks, and one does not see; one listens, and one does not hear; one eats, and one does not know the savor of food." He who distinguishes the true savor of his food can never be a glutton; he who does not cannot be otherwise. A puritan may go to his brown-bread crust with as gross an appetite as ever an alderman to his turtle. Not that food which entereth into the mouth defileth a man, but the appetite with which it is eaten. It is neither the quality nor the quantity, but the devotion to sensual savors; when that which is eaten is not a viand to sustain our animal, or inspire our spiritual life, but food for the worms that possess us. If the hunter has a taste for mud-turtles, muskrats, and other such savage tid-bits, the fine lady indulges a taste for jelly made of a calf's foot, or for sardines from over the sea, and they are even. He goes to the mill-pond, she to her preserve-pot. The wonder is how they, how you and I, can live this slimy beastly life, eating and drinking.

Our whole life is startlingly moral. There is never an instant's truce between virtue and vice. Goodness is the only investment that never fails. In the music of the harp which trembles round the world it is the insisting on this which thrills us. The harp is the travelling patterer for the Universe's Insurance Company, recommending its laws, and our little goodness is all the assessment that we pay. Though the youth at last grows indifferent, the laws of the universe are not indifferent, but are forever on the side of the most sensitive. Listen to every zephyr for some reproof, for it is surely there, and he is unfortunate who does not hear it. We cannot touch a string or move a stop but the charming moral transfixes us. Many an irksome noise, go a long way off, is heard as music, a proud sweet satire on the meanness of our lives.

We are conscious of an animal in us, which awakens in proportion as our higher nature slumbers. It is reptile and sensual, and perhaps cannot be wholly expelled; like the worms which, even in life and health, occupy our bodies. Possibly we may withdraw from it, but never change its nature. I fear that it may enjoy a certain health of its own; that we may be well, yet not pure. The other day I picked up the lower jaw of a hog, with white and sound teeth and tusks, which suggested that there was an animal health and vigor distinct from the spiritual. This creature succeeded by other

---

[273] Sacred text of the Hindus.
[274] The words of a follower of Confucius, taken from *The Great Learning*.

means than temperance and purity. "That in which men differ from brute beasts," says Mencius,[275] "is a thing very inconsiderable; the common herd lose it very soon; superior men preserve it carefully." Who knows what sort of life would result if we had attained to purity? If I knew so wise a man as could teach me purity I would go to seek him forthwith. "A command over our passions, and over the external senses of the body, and good acts, are declared by the Ved to be indispensable in the mind's approximation to God." Yet the spirit can for the time pervade and control every member and function of the body, and transmute what in form is the grossest sensuality into purity and devotion. The generative energy, which, when we are loose, dissipates and makes us unclean, when we are continent invigorates and inspires us. Chastity is the flowering of man; and what are called Genius, Heroism, Holiness, and the like, are but various fruits which succeed it. Man flows at once to God when the channel of purity is open. By turns our purity inspires and our impurity casts us down. He is blessed who is assured that the animal is dying out in him day by day, and the divine being established. Perhaps there is none but has cause for shame on account of the inferior and brutish nature to which he is allied. I fear that we are such gods or demigods only as fauns and satyrs, the divine allied to beasts, the creatures of appetite, and that, to some extent, our very life is our disgrace.—

> "How happy's he who hath due place assigned
>   To his beasts and disaforested his mind!
>
> *   *   *
>
> Can use his horse, goat, wolf, and ev'ry beast,
> And is not ass himself to all the rest!
> Else man not only is the herd of swine,
> But he's those devils too which did incline
> Them to a headlong rage, and made them worse."[276]

All sensuality is one, though it takes many forms; all purity is one. It is the same whether a man eat, or drink, or cohabit, or sleep sensually. They are but one appetite, and we only need to see a person do any one of these things to know how great a sensualist he is. The impure can neither stand nor sit with purity. When the reptile is attacked at one mouth of his burrow, he shows himself at another. If you would be chaste, you must be temperate. What is chastity? How shall a man know if he is chaste? He shall not know it. We have heard of this virtue, but we know not what it is. We speak conformably to the rumor which we have heard. From exertion come wisdom and purity; from sloth ignorance and sensuality. In the student sensuality is a sluggish habit of mind. An unclean person is universally a slothful one, one who sits by a stove, whom the sun shines on prostrate, who reposes without being fatigued. If you would avoid uncleanness, and all the sins, work earnestly, though it be at cleaning a stable. Nature is hard to be overcome, but she must be overcome. What avails it that you are Christian, if you are not purer than the heathen, if you deny

---

[275] Chinese philosopher (372?–289 B.C.), from whose *Book* this quotation is taken.

[276] From the poem by John Donne (1573–1631), "To Sir Edward Herbert, at Julyers."

yourself no more, if you are not more religious? I know of many systems of religion esteemed heathenish whose precepts fill the reader with shame, and provoke him to new endeavors, though it be to the performance of rites merely.

I hesitate to say these things, but it is not because of the subject,—I care not how obscene my *words* are,—but because I cannot speak of them without betraying my impurity. We discourse freely without shame of one form of sensuality, and are silent about another. We are so degraded that we cannot speak simply of the necessary functions of human nature. In earlier ages, in some countries, every function was reverently spoken of and regulated by law. Nothing was too trivial for the Hindoo lawgiver, however offensive it may be to modern taste. He teaches how to eat, drink, cohabit, void excrement and urine, and the like, elevating what is mean, and does not falsely excuse himself by calling these things trifles.

Every man is the builder of a temple, called his body, to the god he worships, after a style purely his own, nor can he get off by hammering marble instead. We are all sculptors and painters, and our material is our own flesh and blood and bones. Any nobleness begins at once to refine a man's features, any meanness or sensuality to imbrute them.

John Farmer sat at his door one September evening, after a hard day's work, his mind still running on his labor more or less. Having bathed he sat down to recreate his intellectual man. It was a rather cool evening, and some of his neighbors were apprehending a frost. He had not attended to the train of his thoughts long when he heard some one playing on a flute, and that sound harmonized with his mood. Still he thought of his work; but the burden of his thought was, that though this kept running in his head, and he found himself planning and contriving it against his will, yet it concerned him very little. It was no more than the scurf of his skin, which was constantly shuffled off. But the notes of the flute came home to his ears out of a different sphere from that he worked in, and suggested work for certain faculties which slumbered in him. They gently did away with the street, and the village, and the state in which he lived. A voice said to him,—Why do you stay here and live this mean moiling life, when a glorious existence is possible for you? Those same stars twinkle over other fields than these.—But how to come out of this condition and actually migrate thither? All that he could think of was to practise some new austerity, to let his mind descend into his body and redeem it, and treat himself with ever increasing respect.

Brute Neighbors

Sometimes I had a companion[277] in my fishing, who came through the village to my house from the other side of the town, and the catching of the dinner was as much a social exercise as the eating of it.

Hermit. I wonder what the world is doing now. I have not heard so much as a locust over the sweet-fern these three hours. The pigeons are all asleep upon their roosts,—no flutter from them. Was that a farmer's noon horn which sounded from

[277] William Ellery Channing the younger.

beyond the woods just now? The hands are coming in to boiled salt beef and cider and Indian bread. Why will men worry themselves so? He that does not eat need not work. I wonder how much they have reaped. Who would live there where a body can never think for the barking of Bose?[278] And O, the housekeeping! to keep bright the devil's door-knobs, and scour his tubs this bright day! Better not keep a house. Say, some hollow tree; and then for morning calls and dinner-parties! Only a woodpecker tapping. O, they swarm; the sun is too warm there; they are born too far into life for me. I have water from the spring, and a loaf of brown bread on the shelf.—Hark! I hear a rustling of the leaves. Is it some ill-fed village hound yielding to the instinct of the chase? or the lost pig which is said to be in these woods, whose tracks I saw after the rain? It comes on apace; my sumachs and sweet-briars tremble.—Eh, Mr. Poet, is it you? How do you like the world to-day?

Poet. See those clouds; how they hang! That's the greatest thing I have seen to-day. There's nothing like it in old paintings, nothing like it in foreign lands,—unless when we were off the coast of Spain. That's a true Mediterranean sky. I thought, as I have my living to get, and have not eaten to-day, that I might go a-fishing. That's the true industry for poets. It is the only trade I have learned. Come, let's along.

Hermit. I cannot resist. My brown bread will soon be gone. I will go with you gladly soon, but I am just concluding a serious meditation. I think that I am near the end of it. Leave me alone, then, for a while. But that we may not be delayed, you shall be digging the bait meanwhile. Angle-worms are rarely to be met with in these parts, where the soil was never fattened with manure; the race is nearly extinct. The sport of digging the bait is nearly equal to that of catching the fish, when one's appetite is not too keen; and this you may have all to yourself today. I would advise you to set in the spade down yonder among the ground-nuts, where you see the johnswort waving. I think that I may warrant you one worm to every three sods you turn up, if you look well in among the roots of the grass, as if you were weeding. Or, if you choose to go farther, it will not be unwise, for I have found the increase of fair bait to be very nearly as the squares of the distances.

Hermit alone. Let me see; where was I? Methinks I was nearly in this frame of mind; the world lay about at this angle. Shall I go to heaven or a-fishing? If I should soon bring this meditation to an end, would another so sweet occasion be likely to offer? I was as near being resolved into the essence of things as ever I was in my life. I fear my thoughts will not come back to me. If it would do any good, I would whistle for them. When they make us an offer, is it wise to say, We will think of it? My thoughts have left no track, and I cannot find the path again. What was it that I was thinking of? It was a very hazy day. I will just try these three sentences of Con-fut-see;[279] they may fetch that state about again. I know not whether it was the dumps or a budding ecstasy. Mem.[280] There never is but one opportunity of a kind.

Poet. How now, Hermit, is it too soon? I have got just thirteen whole ones, beside several which are imperfect or undersized; but they will do for the smaller fry; they do not cover up the hook so much. Those village worms are quite too large; a shiner may make a meal off one without finding the skewer.

---

[278] Like Fido, a common name for a dog in Thoreau's time.

[279] Confucius.
[280] Memorandum.

Hermit. Well, then, let's be off. Shall we to the Concord? There's good sport there if the water be not too high.

Why do precisely these objects which we behold make a world? Why has man just these species of animals for his neighbors; as if nothing but a mouse could have filled this crevice? I suspect that Pilpay & Co.[281] have put animals to their best use, for they are all beasts of burden, in a sense, made to carry some portion of our thoughts.

The mice which haunted my house were not the common ones, which are said to have been introduced into the country, but a wild native kind (*Mus leucopus*) not found in the village. I sent one to a distinguished naturalist, and it interested him much. When I was building, one of these had its nest underneath the house, and before I had laid the second floor, and swept out the shavings, would come out regularly at lunch time and pick up the crumbs at my feet. It probably had never seen a man before; and it soon became quite familiar, and would run over my shoes and up my clothes. It could readily ascend the sides of the room by short impulses, like a squirrel, which it resembled in its motions. At length, as I leaned with my elbow on the bench one day, it ran up my clothes, and along my sleeve, and round and round the paper which held my dinner, while I kept the latter close, and dodged and played at bo-peep with it; and when at last I held still a piece of cheese between my thumb and finger, it came and nibbled it, sitting in my hand, and afterward cleaned its face and paws, like a fly, and walked away.

A phœbe soon built in my shed, and a robin for protection in a pine which grew against the house. In June the partridge, (*Tetrao umbellus*,) which is so shy a bird, led her brood past my windows, from the woods in the rear to the front of my house, clucking and calling to them like a hen, and in all her behavior proving herself the hen of the woods. The young suddenly disperse on your approach, at a signal from the mother, as if a whirlwind had swept them away, and they so exactly resemble the dried leaves and twigs that many a traveller has placed his foot in the midst of a brood, and heard the whir of the old bird as she flew off, and her anxious calls and mewing, or seen her trail her wings to attract his attention, without suspecting their neighborhood. The parent will sometimes roll and spin round before you in such a dishabille, that you cannot, for a few moments, detect what kind of creature it is. The young squat still and flat, often running their heads under a leaf, and mind only their mother's directions given from a distance, nor will your approach make them run again and betray themselves. You may even tread on them, or have your eyes on them for a minute, without discovering them. I have held them in my open hand at such a time, and still their only care, obedient to their mother and their instinct, was to squat there without fear or trembling. So perfect is this instinct, that once, when I had laid them on the leaves again, and one accidentally fell on its side, it was found with the rest in exactly the same position ten minutes afterward. They are not callow like the young of most birds, but more perfectly developed and precocious even than chickens. The remarkably adult yet innocent expression of their open and serene eyes is very memorable. All intelligence seems reflected in them. They suggest not merely

---

[281] Makers of tales, in reference to the teller of ancient Sanskrit fables.

the purity of infancy, but a wisdom clarified by experience. Such an eye was not born when the bird was, but is coeval with the sky it reflects. The woods do not yield another such a gem. The traveller does not often look into such a limpid well. The ignorant or reckless sportsman often shoots the parent at such a time, and leaves these innocents to fall a prey to some prowling beast or bird, or gradually mingle with the decaying leaves which they so much resemble. It is said that when hatched by a hen they will directly disperse on some alarm, and so are lost, for they never hear the mother's call which gathers them again. These were my hens and chickens.

It is remarkable how many creatures live wild and free though secret in the woods, and still sustain themselves in the neighborhood of towns, suspected by hunters only. How retired the otter manages to live here! He grows to be four feet long, as big as a small boy, perhaps without any human being getting a glimpse of him. I formerly saw the raccoon in the woods behind where my house is built, and probably still heard their whinnering[282] at night. Commonly I rested an hour or two in the shade at noon, after planting, and ate my lunch, and read a little by a spring which was the source of a swamp and of a brook, oozing from under Brister's Hill, half a mile from my field. The approach to this was through a succession of descending grassy hollows, full of young pitch-pines, into a larger wood about the swamp. There, in a very secluded and shaded spot, under a spreading white-pine, there was yet a clean firm sward to sit on. I had dug out the spring and made a well of clear gray water, where I could dip up a pailful without roiling it, and thither I went for this purpose almost every day in midsummer, when the pond was warmest. Thither too the wood-cock led her brood, to probe the mud for worms, flying but a foot above them down the bank, while they ran in a troop beneath; but at last, spying me, she would leave her young and circle round and round me, nearer and nearer, till within four or five feet, pretending broken wings and legs, to attract my attention and get off her young, who would already have taken up their march, with faint wiry peep, single file through the swamp, as she directed. Or I heard the peep of the young when I could not see the parent bird. There too the turtle-doves sat over the spring, or fluttered from bough to bough of the soft white-pines over my head; or the red squirrel, coursing down the nearest bough, was particularly familiar and inquisitive. You only need sit still long enough in some attractive spot in the woods that all its inhabitants may exhibit themselves to you by turns.

I was witness to events of a less peaceful character. One day when I went out to my wood-pile, or rather my pile of stumps, I observed two large ants, the one red, the other much larger, nearly half an inch long, and black, fiercely contending with one another. Having once got hold they never let go, but struggled and wrestled and rolled on the chips incessantly. Looking farther, I was surprised to find that the chips were covered with such combatants, that it was not a *duellum,* but a *bellum,* [283] a war between two races of ants, the red always pitted against the black, and frequently two red ones to one black. The legion of these Myrmidons[284] covered all the hills and vales in my wood-yard, and the ground was already strewn with the dead and dying, both

---

[282] A sound like whining.
[283] I.e., not a duel, but a war.
[284] Since *myrmex* is the Greek word for "ant," Thoreau is able to link the battle of the ants

with the fighting done by the Myrmidons, the troops of Achilles in the Trojan War, as told in the *Iliad.*

red and black. It was the only battle which I have ever witnessed, the only battle-field I ever trod while the battle was raging; internecine war; the red republicans on the one hand, and the black imperialists on the other. On every side they were engaged in deadly combat, yet without any noise that I could hear, and human soldiers never fought so resolutely. I watched a couple that were fast locked in each other's embraces, in a little sunny valley amid the chips, now at noon-day prepared to fight till the sun went down, or life went out. The smaller red champion had fastened himself like a vice to his adversary's front, and through all the tumblings on that field never for an instant ceased to gnaw at one of his feelers near the root, having already caused the other to go by the board; while the stronger black one dashed him from side to side, and, as I saw on looking nearer, had already divested him of several of his members. They fought with more pertinacity than bull-dogs. Neither manifested the least disposition to retreat. It was evident that their battle-cry was Conquer or die. In the mean while there came along a single red ant on the hill-side of this valley, evidently full of excitement, who either had despatched his foe, or had not yet taken part in the battle; probably the latter, for he had lost none of his limbs; whose mother had charged him to return with his shield or upon it. Or perchance he was some Achilles, who had nourished his wrath apart, and had now come to avenge or rescue his Patroclus.[285] He saw this unequal combat from afar,—for the blacks were nearly twice the size of the red,—he drew near with rapid pace till he stood on his guard within half an inch of the combatants; then, watching his opportunity, he sprang upon the black warrior, and commenced his operations near the root of his right fore-leg, leaving the foe to select among his own members; and so there were three united for life, as if a new kind of attraction had been invented which put all other locks and cements to shame. I should not have wondered by this time to find that they had their respective musical bands stationed on some eminent chip, and playing their national airs the while, to excite the slow and cheer the dying combatants. I was myself excited somewhat even as if they had been men. The more you think of it, the less the difference. And certainly there is not the fight recorded in Concord history, at least, if in the history of America, that will bear a moment's comparison with this, whether for the numbers engaged in it, or for the patriotism and heroism displayed. For numbers and for carnage it was an Austerlitz or Dresden.[286] Concord Fight![287] Two killed on the patriots' side, and Luther Blanchard wounded! Why here every ant was a Buttrick,—"Fire! for God's sake fire!"—and thousands shared the fate of Davis and Hosmer. There was not one hireling[288] there. I have no doubt that it was a principle they fought for, as much as our ancestors, and not to avoid a three-penny tax on their tea; and the results of this battle will be as important and memorable to those whom it concerns as those of the battle of Bunker Hill, at least.

I took up the chip on which the three I have particularly described were struggling, carried it into my house, and placed it under a tumbler on my windowsill, in order to see the issue. Holding a microscope to the first-mentioned red ant, I saw that though he was assiduously gnawing at the near fore-leg of his enemy, having severed his

---

[285] Patroclus was Achilles' friend; when he was slain, Achilles out of wrath threw himself into the war against the Trojans.
[286] Battles fought during the wars of Napoleon.

[287] Battle of April 1775, the opening engagement of the American Revolution. The names and remarks that follow refer to that conflict.
[288] Mercenary.

remaining feeler, his own breast was all torn away, exposing what vitals he had there to the jaws of the black warrior, whose breast-plate was apparently too thick for him to pierce; and the dark carbuncles of the sufferer's eyes shone with ferocity such as war only could excite. They struggled half an hour longer under the tumbler, and when I looked again the black soldier had severed the heads of his foes from their bodies, and the still living heads were hanging on either side of him like ghastly trophies at his saddle-bow, still apparently as firmly fastened as ever, and he was endeavoring with feeble struggles, being without feelers and with only the remnant of a leg, and I know not how many other wounds, to divest himself of them; which at length, after half an hour more, he accomplished. I raised the glass, and he went off over the window-sill in that crippled state. Whether he finally survived that combat, and spent the remainder of his days in some Hotel des Invalides,[289] I do not know; but I thought that his industry would not be worth much thereafter. I never learned which party was victorious, nor the cause of the war; but I felt for the rest of that day as if I had had my feelings excited and harrowed by witnessing the struggle, the ferocity and carnage, of a human battle before my door.

Kirby and Spence tell us that the battles of ants have long been celebrated and the date of them recorded, though they say that Huber[290] is the only modern author who appears to have witnessed them. "Æneas Sylvius,"[291] say they, "after giving a very circumstantial account of one contested with great obstinacy by a great and small species on the trunk of a pear tree," adds that " 'This action was fought in the pontificate of Eugenius the Fourth,[292] in the presence of Nicholas Pistoriensis, an eminent lawyer, who related the whole history of the battle with the greatest fidelity.' A similar engagement between great and small ants is recorded by Olaus Magnus,[293] in which the small ones, being victorious, are said to have buried the bodies of their own soldiers, but left those of their giant enemies a prey to the birds. This event happened previous to the expulsion of the tyrant Christiern the Second from Sweden."[294] The battle which I witnessed took place in the Presidency of Polk, five years before the passage of Webster's Fugitive-Slave Bill.[295]

Many a village Bose, fit only to course a mud-turtle in a victualling cellar, sported his heavy quarters in the woods, without the knowledge of his master, and ineffectually smelled at old fox burrows and woodchucks' holes; led perchance by some slight cur which nimbly threaded the wood, and might still inspire a natural terror in its denizens;—now far behind his guide, barking like a canine bull toward some small squirrel which had treed itself for scrutiny, then, cantering off, bending the bushes with his weight, imagining that he is on the track of some stray member of the gerbille family. Once I was surprised to see a cat walking along the stony shore of the pond, for they rarely wander so far from home. The surprise was mutual. Nevertheless the most domestic cat, which has lain on a rug all her days, appears quite at home in the woods, and, by her sly and stealthy behavior, proves herself more native there than the regular inhabitants. Once, when berrying, I met with a cat with young kittens

---

[289] Veterans' hospital in Paris.

[290] Kirby and Spence's book on entomology includes the description of a battle among ants, taken from Huber's study of 1810.

[291] Name used by Pope Pius II (1405–1464) for his writings.

[292] Pope between 1431 and 1447.

[293] Swedish historian and churchman (1490–1557).

[294] Sixteenth-century king.

[295] Fugitive Slave Law (1850) supported by Daniel Webster, Massachusetts senator. James K. Polk was president between 1845 and 1849.

in the woods, quite wild, and they all, like their mother, had their backs up and were fiercely spitting at me. A few years before I lived in the woods there was what was called a "winged cat" in one of the farm-houses in Lincoln nearest the pond, Mr. Gilian Baker's. When I called to see her in June, 1842, she was gone a-hunting in the woods, as was her wont. (I am not sure, whether it was a male or female, and so use the more common pronoun,) but her mistress told me that she came into the neighborhood a little more than a year before, in April, and was finally taken into their house; that she was of a dark brownish-gray color, with a white spot on her throat, and white feet, and had a large bushy tail like a fox; that in the winter the fur grew thick and flattened out along her sides, forming strips ten or twelve inches long by two and a half wide, and under her chin like a muff, the upper side loose, the under matted like felt, and in the spring these appendages dropped off. They gave me a pair of her "wings," which I keep still. There is no appearance of a membrane about them. Some thought it was part flying-squirrel or some other wild animal, which is not impossible, for, according to naturalists, prolific hybrids have been produced by the union of the marten and domestic cat. This would have been the right kind of cat for me to keep, if I had kept any; for why should not a poet's cat be winged as well as his horse?[296]

In the fall the loon (*Colymbus glacialis*) came, as usual, to moult and bathe in the pond, making the woods ring with his wild laughter before I had risen. At rumor of his arrival all the Mill-dam sportsmen are on the alert, in gigs[297] and on foot, two by two and three by three, with patent rifles and conical balls and spy-glasses. They come rustling through the woods like autumn leaves, at least ten men to one loon. Some station themselves on this side of the pond, some on that, for the poor bird cannot be omnipresent; if he dive here he must come up there. But now the kind October wind rises, rustling the leaves and rippling the surface of the water, so that no loon can be heard or seen, though his foes sweep the pond with spy-glasses, and make the woods resound with their discharges. The waves generously rise and dash angrily, taking sides with all waterfowl, and our sportsmen must beat a retreat to town and shop and unfinished jobs. But they were too often successful. When I went to get a pail of water early in the morning I frequently saw this stately bird sailing out of my cove within a few rods. If I endeavored to overtake him in a boat, in order to see how he would manœuvre, he would dive and be completely lost, so that I did not discover him again, sometimes, till the latter part of the day. But I was more than a match for him on the surface. He commonly went off in a rain.

As I was paddling along the north shore one very calm October afternoon, for such days especially they settle on to the lakes, like the milkweed down, having looked in vain over the pond for a loon, suddenly one, sailing out from the shore toward the middle a few rods in front of me, set up his wild laugh and betrayed himself. I pursued with a paddle and he dived, but when he came up I was nearer than before. He dived again, but I miscalculated the direction he would take, and we were fifty rods apart when he came to the surface this time, for I had helped to widen the interval; and again he laughed long and loud, and with more reason than before. He manœuvred so cunningly that I could not get within half a dozen rods of him. Each

---

[296] Reference to Pegasus, the winged horse ridden by poets in classic myth.   [297] Light, one-horse carriages.

time, when he came to the surface, turning his head this way and that, he coolly surveyed the water and the land, and apparently chose his course so that he might come up where there was the widest expanse of water and at the greatest distance from the boat. It was surprising how quickly he made up his mind and put his resolve into execution. He led me at once to the widest part of the pond, and could not be driven from it. While he was thinking one thing in his brain, I was endeavoring to divine his thought in mine. It was a pretty game, played on the smooth surface of the pond, a man against a loon. Suddenly your adversary's checker disappears beneath the board, and the problem is to place yours nearest to where his will appear again. Sometimes he would come up unexpectedly on the opposite side of me, having apparently passed directly under the boat. So long-winded was he and so unwearible, that when he had swum farthest he would immediately plunge again, nevertheless; and then no wit could divine where in the deep pond, beneath the smooth surface, he might be speeding his way like a fish, for he had time and ability to visit the bottom of the pond in its deepest part. It is said that loons have been caught in the New York lakes eighty feet beneath the surface, with hooks set for trout,—though Walden is deeper than that. How surprised must the fishes be to see this ungainly visitor from another sphere speeding his way amid their schools! Yet he appeared to know his course as surely under water as on the surface, and swam much faster there. Once or twice I saw a ripple where he approached the surface, just put his head out to reconnoitre, and instantly dived again. I found that it was as well for me to rest on my oars and wait his reappearing as to endeavor to calculate where he would rise; for again and again, when I was straining my eyes over the surface one way, I would suddenly be startled by his unearthly laugh behind me. But why, after displaying so much cunning, did he invariably betray himself the moment he came up by that loud laugh? Did not his white breast enough betray him? He was indeed a silly loon, I thought. I could commonly hear the plash of the water when he came up, and so also detected him. But after an hour he seemed as fresh as ever, dived as willingly and swam yet farther than at first. It was surprising to see how serenely he sailed off with unruffled breast when he came to the surface, doing all the work with his webbed feet beneath. His usual note was this demoniac laughter, yet somewhat like that of a water-fowl; but occasionally, when he had balked me most successfully and come up a long way off, he uttered a long-drawn unearthly howl, probably more like that of a wolf than any bird; as when a beast puts his muzzle to the ground and deliberately howls. This was his looning,—perhaps the wildest sound that is ever heard here, making the woods ring far and wide. I concluded that he laughed in derision of my efforts, confident of his own resources. Though the sky was by this time overcast, the pond was so smooth that I could see when he broke the surface when I did not hear him. His white breast, the stillness of the air, and the smoothness of the water were all against him. At length, having come up fifty rods off, he uttered one of those prolonged howls, as if calling on the god of loons to aid him, and immediately there came a wind from the east and rippled the surface, and filled the whole air with misty rain, and I was impressed as if it were the prayer of the loon answered, and his god was angry with me; and so I left him disappearing far away on the tumultuous surface.

For hours, in fall days, I watched the ducks cunningly tack and veer and hold the middle of the pond, far from the sportsman; tricks which they will have less need to practise in Louisiana bayous. When compelled to rise they would sometimes circle round and round and over the pond at a considerable height, from which they could easily see to other ponds and the river, like black motes in the sky; and, when I thought they had gone off thither long since, they would settle down by a slanting flight of a quarter of a mile on to a distant part which was left free; but what beside safety they got by sailing in the middle of Walden I do not know, unless they love its water for the same reason that I do.

House-Warming

In October I went a-graping to the river meadows, and loaded myself with clusters more precious for their beauty and fragrance than for food. There too I admired, though I did not gather, the cranberries, small waxen gems, pendants of the meadow grass, pearly and red, which the farmer plucks with an ugly rake, leaving the smooth meadow in a snarl, heedlessly measuring them by the bushel and the dollar only, and sells the spoils of the meads to Boston and New York; destined to be *jammed,* to satisfy the tastes of lovers of Nature there. So butchers rake the tongues of bison out of the prairie grass, regardless of the torn and drooping plant. The barberry's brilliant fruit was likewise food for my eyes merely; but I collected a small store of wild apples for coddling, which the proprietor and travellers had overlooked. When chestnuts were ripe I laid up half a bushel for winter. It was very exciting at that season to roam the then boundless chestnut woods of Lincoln,—they now sleep their long sleep under the railroad,—with a bag on my shoulder, and a stick to open burrs with in my hand, for I did not always wait for the frost, amid the rustling of leaves and the loud reproofs of the red-squirrels and the jays, whose half-consumed nuts I sometimes stole, for the burrs which they had selected were sure to contain sound ones. Occasionally I climbed and shook the trees. They grew also behind my house, and one large tree which almost overshadowed it, was, when in flower, a bouquet which scented the whole neighborhood, but the squirrels and the jays got most of its fruit; the last coming in flocks early in the morning and picking the nuts out of the burrs before they fell. I relinquished these trees to them and visited the more distant woods composed wholly of chestnut. These nuts, as far as they went, were a good substitute for bread. Many other substitutes might, perhaps, be found. Digging one day for fish-worms I discovered the ground-nut (*Apios tuberosa*) on its string, the potato of the aborigines, a sort of fabulous fruit, which I had begun to doubt if I had ever dug and eaten in childhood, as I had [been] told, and had not dreamed it. I had often since seen its crimpled red velvety blossom supported by the stems of other plants, without knowing it to be the same. Cultivation has well nigh exterminated it. It has a sweetish taste, much like that of a frostbitten potato, and I found it better boiled than roasted. This tuber seemed like a faint promise of Nature to rear her own children and feed them simply here at some future period. In these days of fatted cattle and waving grainfields, this humble root, which was once the *totem* of an Indian tribe, is quite forgotten, or known only by its flowering vine; but let wild Nature reign here once more, and the tender and luxurious English grains will probably disappear before a myriad of foes, and without the care of man the crow may carry back even the last seed of corn to the great cornfield of the Indian's God in the south-west, whence he is said to have brought it; but the now almost exterminated ground-nut will perhaps revive and flourish in spite of frosts and wildness, prove itself indigenous, and resume its ancient importance and dignity as the diet of the hunter tribe. Some Indian Ceres or Minerva must have been the inventor and bestower of it; and when the reign of poetry commences here, its leaves and string of nuts may be represented on our works of art.

Already, by the first of September, I had seen two or three small maples turned scarlet across the pond, beneath where the white stems of three aspens diverged, at the point of a promontory, next the water. Ah, many a tale their color told! And gradually from week to week the character of each tree came out, and it admired itself reflected in the smooth mirror of the lake. Each morning the manager of this gallery substituted some new picture, distinguished by more brilliant or harmonious coloring, for the old upon the walls.

The wasps came by thousands to my lodge in October, as to winter quarters, and settled on my windows within and on the walls over-head, sometimes deterring visitors from entering. Each morning, when they were numbed with cold, I swept some of them out, but I did not trouble myself much to get rid of them; I even felt complimented by their regarding my house as a desirable shelter. They never molested me seriously, though they bedded with me; and they gradually disappeared, into what crevices I do not know, avoiding winter and unspeakable cold.

Like the wasps, before I finally went into winter quarters in November, I used to resort to the northeast side of Walden, which the sun, reflected from the pitch-pine woods and the stony shore, made the fire-side of the pond; it is so much pleasanter and wholesomer to be warmed by the sun while you can be, than by an artificial fire. I thus warmed myself by the still glowing embers which the summer, like a departed hunter, had left.

When I came to build my chimney I studied masonry. My bricks being second-hand ones required to be cleaned with a trowel, so that I learned more than usual of the qualities of bricks and trowels. The mortar on them was fifty years old, and was said to be still growing harder; but this is one of those sayings which men love to repeat whether they are true or not. Such sayings themselves grow harder and adhere more firmly with age, and it would take many blows with a trowel to clean an old wiseacre of them. Many of the villages of Mesopotamia are built of second-hand bricks of a very good quality, obtained from the ruins of Babylon, and the cement on them is older and probably harder still. However that may be, I was struck by the peculiar toughness of the steel which bore so many violent blows without being worn out. As my bricks had been in a chimney before, though I did not read the name of Nebuchadnezzar[298] on them, I picked out as many fire-place bricks as I could find, to save work and waste, and I filled the spaces between the bricks about the fire-place with stones from the pond shore, and also made my mortar with the white sand from the same place. I lingered most about the fire-place, as the most vital part of the house. Indeed, I worked so deliberately, that though I commenced at the ground in the morning, a course of bricks raised a few inches above the floor served for my pillow at night; yet I did not get a stiff neck for it that I remember; my stiff neck is of older

---

[298] Bricks used in the building of the palace of King Nebuchadnezzar (605–562 B.C.) were stamped with his name.

date. I took a poet to board for a fortnight about those times, which caused me to be put to it for room. He brought his own knife, though I had two, and we used to scour them by thrusting them into the earth. He shared with me the labors of cooking. I was pleased to see my work rising so square and solid by degrees, and reflected, that, if it proceeded slowly, it was calculated to endure a long time. The chimney is to some extent an independent structure, standing on the ground and rising through the house to the heavens; even after the house is burned it still stands sometimes, and its importance and independence are apparent. This was toward the end of summer. It was now November.

The north wind had already begun to cool the pond, though it took many weeks of steady blowing to accomplish it, it is so deep. When I began to have a fire at evening, before I plastered my house, the chimney carried smoke particularly well, because of the numerous chinks between the boards. Yet I passed some cheerful evenings in that cool and airy apartment, surrounded by the rough brown boards full of knots, and rafters with the bark on high overhead. My house never pleased my eye so much after it was plastered, though I was obliged to confess that it was more comfortable. Should not every apartment in which man dwells be lofty enough to create some obscurity over-head, where flickering shadows may play at evening about the rafters? These forms are more agreeable to the fancy and imagination than fresco paintings or other the most expensive furniture. I now first began to inhabit my house, I may say, when I began to use it for warmth as well as shelter. I had got a couple of old fire-dogs to keep the wood from the hearth, and it did me good to see the soot form on the back of the chimney which I had built, and I poked the fire with more right and more satisfaction than usual. My dwelling was small, and I could hardly entertain an echo in it; but it seemed larger for being a single apartment and remote from neighbors. All the attractions of a house were concentrated in one room; it was kitchen, chamber, parlor, and keeping-room;[299] and whatever satisfaction parent or child, master or servant, derive from living in a house, I enjoyed it all. Cato says, the master of a family (*patremfamilias*) must have in his rustic villa "cellam oleariam, vinariam, dolia multa, uti lubeat caritatem expectare, et rei, et virtuti, et gloriæ erit," that is, "an oil and wine cellar, many casks, so that it may be pleasant to expect hard times; it will be for his advantage, and virtue, and glory." I had in my cellar a firkin of potatoes, about two quarts of peas with the weevil in them, and on my shelf a little rice, a jug of molasses, and of rye and Indian meal a peck each.

I sometimes dream of a larger and more populous house, standing in a golden age, of enduring materials, and without ginger-bread work, which shall still consist of only one room, a vast, rude, substantial, primitive hall, without ceiling or plastering, with bare rafters and purlins supporting a sort of lower heaven over one's head—useful to keep off rain and snow; where the king and queen posts[300] stand out to receive your homage, when you have done reverence to the prostrate Saturn[301] of an older dynasty on stepping over the sill; a cavernous house, wherein you must reach up a torch upon a pole to see the roof; where some may live in the fire-place, some in the recess of

[299] Sitting room.
[300] Vertical roof supports.
[301] Those who worshiped at the temple of Saturn, legendary king of Rome, entered with bared heads.

a window, and some on settles, some at one end of the hall, some at another, and some aloft on rafters with the spiders, if they choose; a house which you have got into when you have opened the outside door, and the ceremony is over; where the weary traveller may wash, and eat, and converse, and sleep, without further journey; such a shelter as you would be glad to reach in a tempestuous night, containing all the essentials of a house, and nothing for house-keeping; where you can see all the treasures of the house at one view, and every thing hangs upon its peg that a man should use; at once kitchen, pantry, parlor, chamber, store-house, and garret; where you can see so necessary a thing as a barrel or a ladder, so convenient a thing as a cupboard, and hear the pot boil, and pay your respects to the fire that cooks your dinner and the oven that bakes your bread, and the necessary furniture and utensils are the chief ornaments; where the washing is not put out, nor the fire, nor the mistress, and perhaps you are sometimes requested to move from off the trap-door, when the cook would descend into the cellar, and so learn whether the ground is solid or hollow beneath you without stamping. A house whose inside is as open and manifest as a bird's nest, and you cannot go in at the front door and out at the back without seeing some of its inhabitants; where to be a guest is to be presented with the freedom of the house, and not to be carefully excluded from seven eighths of it, shut up in a particular cell, and told to make yourself at home there,—in solitary confinement. Nowadays the host does not admit you to *his* hearth, but has got the mason to build one for yourself somewhere in his alley, and hospitality is the art of *keeping* you at the greatest distance. There is as much secrecy about the cooking as if he had a design to poison you. I am aware that I have been on many a man's premises, and might have been legally ordered off, but I am not aware that I have been in many men's houses. I might visit in my old clothes a king and queen who lived simply in such a house as I have described, if I were going their way; but backing out of a modern palace will be all that I shall desire to learn, if ever I am caught in one.

It would seem as if the very language of our parlors would lose all its nerve and degenerate into *palaver* wholly, our lives pass at such remoteness from its symbols, and its metaphors and tropes are necessarily so far fetched, through slides and dumb-waiters, as it were; in other words, the parlor is so far from the kitchen and workshop. The dinner even is only the parable of a dinner, commonly. As if only the savage dwelt near enough to Nature and Truth to borrow a trope from them. How can the scholar, who dwells away in the North West Territory or the Isle of Man,[302] tell what is parliamentary in the kitchen?

However, only one or two of my guests were ever bold enough to stay and eat a hasty-pudding with me; but when they saw that crisis approaching they beat a hasty retreat rather, as if it would shake the house to its foundations. Nevertheless, it stood through a great many hasty-puddings.

I did not plaster till it was freezing weather. I brought over some whiter and cleaner sand for this purpose from the opposite shore of the pond in a boat, a sort of conveyance which would have tempted me to go much farther if necessary. My house had in the mean while been shingled down to the ground on every side. In lathing

---

[302] The present states of Ohio, Indiana, Illinois, Minnesota, Wisconsin, and Michigan were carved out of the area formerly known as the Northwest Territory. The Isle of Man is in the Irish Sea, between Ireland and England.

I was pleased to be able to send home each nail with a single blow of the hammer, and it was my ambition to transfer the plaster from the board to the wall neatly and rapidly. I remembered the story of a conceited fellow, who, in fine clothes, was wont to lounge about the village once, giving advice to workmen. Venturing one day to substitute deeds for words, he turned up his cuffs, seized a plasterer's board, and having loaded his trowel without mishap, with a complacent look toward the lathing overhead, made a bold gesture thitherward; and straightway, to his complete discomfiture, received the whole contents in his ruffled bosom. I admired anew the economy and convenience of plastering, which so effectually shuts out the cold and takes a handsome finish, and I learned the various casualties to which the plasterer is liable. I was surprised to see how thirsty the bricks were which drank up all the moisture in my plaster before I had smoothed it, and how many pailfuls of water it takes to christen a new hearth. I had the previous winter made a small quantity of lime by burning the shells of the *Unio fluviatilis,*[303] which our river affords, for the sake of the experiment; so that I knew where my materials came from. I might have got good limestone within a mile or two and burned it myself, if I had cared to do so.

The pond had in the mean while skimmed over[304] in the shadiest and shallowest coves, some days or even weeks before the general freezing. The first ice is especially interesting and perfect, being hard, dark, and transparent, and affords the best opportunity that ever offers for examining the bottom where it is shallow; for you can lie at your length on ice only an inch thick, like a skater insect on the surface of the water, and study the bottom at your leisure, only two or three inches distant, like a picture behind a glass, and the water is necessarily always smooth then. There are many furrows in the sand where some creature has travelled about and doubled on its tracks; and, for wrecks, it is strewn with the cases of cadis worms made of minute grains of white quartz. Perhaps these have creased it, for you find some of their cases in the furrows, though they are deep and broad for them to make. But the ice itself is the object of most interest, though you must improve the earliest opportunity to study it. If you examine it closely the morning after it freezes, you find that the greater part of the bubbles, which at first appeared to be within it, are against its under surface, and that more are continually rising from the bottom; while the ice is as yet comparatively solid and dark, that is, you see the water through it. These bubbles are from an eightieth to an eighth of an inch in diameter, very clear and beautiful, and you see your face reflected in them through the ice. There may be thirty or forty of them to a square inch. There are also already within the ice narrow oblong perpendicular bubbles about half an inch long, sharp cones with the apex upward; or oftener, if the ice is quite fresh, minute spherical bubbles one directly above another, like a string of beads. But these within the ice are not so numerous nor obvious as those beneath. I sometimes used to cast on stones to try the strength of the ice, and those which broke through carried in air with them, which formed very large and conspicuous white bubbles beneath. One day when I came to the same place forty-eight hours afterward, I found that those large bubbles were still perfect, though an inch more of ice had formed, as I could see distinctly by the seam in the edge of a cake. But as the last two days had been very warm, like an Indian summer, the ice was not now transparent,

---

[303] Fresh-water clam.

[304] Lightly frozen over.

showing the dark green color of the water, and the bottom, but opaque and whitish or gray, and though twice as thick was hardly stronger than before, for the air bubbles had greatly expanded under this heat and run together, and lost their regularity; they were no longer one directly over another, but often like silvery coins poured from a bag, one overlapping another, or in thin flakes, as if occupying slight cleavages. The beauty of the ice was gone, and it was too late to study the bottom. Being curious to know what position my great bubbles occupied with regard to the new ice, I broke out a cake containing a middling sized one, and turned it bottom upward. The new ice had formed around and under the bubble, so that it was included between the two ices. It was wholly in the lower ice, but close against the upper, and was flattish, or perhaps slightly lenticular, with a rounded edge, a quarter of an inch deep by four inches in diameter; and I was surprised to find that directly under the bubble the ice was melted with great regularity in the form of a saucer reversed, to the height of five eighths of an inch in the middle, leaving a thin partition there between the water and the bubble, hardly an eighth of an inch thick; and in many places the small bubbles in this partition had burst out downward, and probably there was no ice at all under the largest bubbles, which were a foot in diameter. I inferred that the infinite number of minute bubbles which I had first seen against the under surface of the ice were now frozen in likewise, and that each, in its degree, had operated like a burning glass on the ice beneath to melt and rot it. These are the little air-guns which contribute to make the ice crack and whoop.

At length the winter set in in good earnest, just as I had finished plastering, and the wind began to howl around the house as if it had not had permission to do so till then. Night after night the geese came lumbering in in the dark with a clangor and a whistling of wings, even after the ground was covered with snow, some to alight in Walden, and some flying low over the woods toward Fair Haven, bound for Mexico. Several times, when returning from the village at ten or eleven o'clock at night, I heard the tread of a flock of geese, or else ducks, on the dry leaves in the woods by a pond-hole behind my dwelling, where they had come up to feed, and the faint honk or quack of their leader as they hurried off. In 1845 Walden froze entirely over for the first time on the night of the 22d of December, Flint's and other shallower ponds and the river having been frozen ten days or more; in '46, the 16th; in '49, about the 31st; and in '50, about the 27th of December; in '52, the 5th of January; in '53, the 31st of December. The snow had already covered the ground since the 25th of November, and surrounded me suddenly with the scenery of winter. I withdrew yet farther into my shell, and endeavored to keep a bright fire both within my house and within my breast. My employment out of doors now was to collect the dead wood in the forest, bringing it in my hands or on my shoulders, or sometimes trailing a dead pine tree under each arm to my shed. An old forest fence which had seen its best days was a great haul for me. I sacrificed it to Vulcan, for it was past serving the god Terminus.[305] How much more interesting an event is that man's supper who has just been forth in the snow to hunt, nay, you might say, steal, the fuel to cook it with! His bread and meat are sweet. There are enough fagots and waste wood of

---

[305] Vulcan; Terminus: Roman gods of fire and of boundaries, respectively.

all kinds in the forests of most of our towns to support many fires, but which at present warm none, and, some think, hinder the growth of the young wood. There was also the drift-wood of the pond. In the course of the summer I had discovered a raft of pitch-pine logs with the bark on, pinned together by the Irish when the railroad was built. This I hauled up partly on the shore. After soaking two years and then lying high six months it was perfectly sound, though waterlogged past drying. I amused myself one winter day with sliding this piecemeal across the pond, nearly half a mile, skating behind with one end of a log fifteen feet long on my shoulder, and the other on the ice; or I tied several logs together with a birch withe, and then, with a longer birch or alder which had a hook at the end, dragged them across. Though completely waterlogged and almost as heavy as lead, they not only burned long, but made a very hot fire; nay, I thought that they burned better for the soaking, as if the pitch, being confined by the water, burned longer as in a lamp.

Gilpin,[306] in his account of the forest borderers of England, says that "the encroachments of trespassers, and the houses and fences thus raised on the borders of the forest," were "considered as great nuisances by the old forest law, and were severely punished under the name of *purprestures*,[307] as tending *ad terrorem ferarum—ad nocumentum forestæ*, &c.," to the frightening of the game and the detriment of the forest. But I was interested in the preservation of the venison and the vert[308] more than the hunters or woodchoppers, and as much as though I had been the Lord Warden[309] himself; and if any part was burned, though I burned it myself by accident, I grieved with a grief that lasted longer and was more inconsolable than that of the proprietors; nay, I grieved when it was cut down by the proprietors themselves. I would that our farmers when they cut down a forest felt some of that awe which the old Romans did when they came to thin, or let in the light to, a consecrated grove, (*lucum conlucare*,) that is, would believe that it is sacred to some god. The Roman made an expiatory offering, and prayed, Whatever god or goddess thou art to whom this grove is sacred, be propitious to me, my family, and children, &c.

It is remarkable what a value is still put upon wood even in this age and in this new country, a value more permanent and universal than that of gold. After all our discoveries and inventions no man will go by a pile of wood. It is as precious to us as it was to our Saxon and Norman ancestors. If they made their bows of it, we make our gun-stocks of it. Michaux,[310] more than thirty years ago, says that the price of wood for fuel in New York and Philadelphia "nearly equals, and sometimes exceeds, that of the best wood in Paris, though this immense capital annually requires more than three hundred thousand cords, and is surrounded to the distance of three hundred miles by cultivated plains." In this town the price of wood rises almost steadily, and the only question is, how much higher it is to be this year than it was the last. Mechanics and tradesmen who come in person to the forest on no other errand, are sure to attend the wood auction, and even pay a high price for the privilege of gleaning after the wood-chopper. It is now many years that men have resorted to the forest for fuel and the materials of the arts; the New Englander and the New

---

[306] William Gilpin (1724–1804), English writer on scenery and gardening.
[307] Wrongful seizers of land.
[308] Woodland greenery.

[309] British official in charge of protecting lands and wildlife.
[310] André Michaux (1746–1802), French botanist.

Hollander, the Parisian and the Celt, the farmer and Robinhood, Goody Blake and Harry Gill,[311] in most parts of the world the prince and the peasant, the scholar and the savage, equally require still a few sticks from the forest to warm them and cook their food. Neither could I do without them.

Every man looks at his wood-pile with a kind of affection. I loved to have mine before my window, and the more chips the better to remind me of my pleasing work. I had an old axe which nobody claimed, with which by spells in winter days, on the sunny side of the house, I played about the stumps which I had got out of my bean-field. As my driver prophesied when I was ploughing, they warmed me twice, once while I was splitting them, and again when they were on the fire, so that no fuel could give out more heat. As for the axe, I was advised to get the village blacksmith to "jump" it;[312] but I jumped him, and, putting a hickory helve from the woods into it, made it do. If it was dull, it was at least hung true.

A few pieces of fat pine were a great treasure. It is interesting to remember how much of this food for fire is still concealed in the bowels of the earth. In previous years I had often gone "prospecting" over some bare hill-side, where a pitch-pine wood had formerly stood, and got out the fat pine roots. They are almost indestructible. Stumps thirty or forty years old, at least, will still be sound at the core, though the sapwood has all become vegetable mould, as appears by the scales of the thick bark forming a ring level with the earth four or five inches distant from the heart. With axe and shovel you explore this mine, and follow the marrowy store, yellow as beef tallow, or as if you had struck on a vein of gold, deep into the earth. But commonly I kindled my fire with the dry leaves of the forest, which I had stored up in my shed before the snow came. Green hickory finely split makes the woodchopper's kindlings, when he has a camp in the woods. Once in a while I got a little of this. When the villagers were lighting their fires beyond the horizon, I too gave notice to the various wild inhabitants of Walden vale, by a smoky streamer from my chimney, that I was awake.—

Light-winged Smoke, Icarian bird,
Melting thy pinions in thy upward flight,
Lark without song, and messenger of dawn,
Circling above the hamlets as thy nest;
Or else, departing dream, and shadowy form
Of midnight vision, gathering up thy skirts;
By night star-veiling, and by day
Darkening the light and blotting out the sun;
Go thou my incense upward from this hearth,
And ask the gods to pardon this clear flame.[313]

Hard green wood just cut, though I used but little of that, answered my purpose better than any other. I sometimes left a good fire when I went to take a walk in a winter afternoon; and when I returned, three or four hours afterward, it would be

---

[311] Reference to a poem by William Wordsworth (1798) in which a poor woman is denied fuel by a wealthy landowner.   [312] Expand its cutting edge.   [313] Thoreau's verses.

still alive and glowing. My house was not empty though I was gone. It was as if I had left a cheerful housekeeper behind. It was I and Fire that lived there; and commonly my housekeeper proved trustworthy. One day, however, as I was splitting wood, I thought that I would just look in at the window and see if the house was not on fire; it was the only time I remember to have been particularly anxious on this score; so I looked and saw that a spark had caught my bed, and I went in and extinguished it when it had burned a place as big as my hand. But my house occupied so sunny and sheltered a position, and its roof was so low, that I could afford to let the fire go out in the middle of almost any winter day.

The moles nested in my cellar, nibbling every third potato, and making a snug bed even there of some hair left after plastering and of brown paper; for even the wildest animals love comfort and warmth as well as man, and they survive the winter only because they are so careful to secure them. Some of my friends spoke as if I was coming to the woods on purpose to freeze myself. The animal merely makes a bed, which he warms with his body in a sheltered place; but man, having discovered fire, boxes up some air in a spacious apartment, and warms that, instead of robbing himself, makes that his bed, in which he can move about divested of more cumbrous clothing, maintain a kind of summer in the midst of winter, and by means of windows even admit the light, and with a lamp lengthen out the day. Thus he goes a step or two beyond instinct, and saves a little time for the fine arts. Though, when I had been exposed to the rudest blasts a long time, my whole body began to grow torpid, when I reached the genial atmosphere of my house I soon recovered my faculties and prolonged my life. But the most luxuriously housed has little to boast of in this respect, nor need we trouble ourselves to speculate how the human race may be at last destroyed. It would be easy to cut their threads any time with a little sharper blast from the north. We go on dating from Cold Fridays and Great Snows; but a little colder Friday, or greater snow, would put a period to man's existence on the globe.

The next winter I used a small cooking-stove for economy, since I did not own the forest; but it did not keep fire so well as the open fire-place. Cooking was then, for the most part, no longer a poetic, but merely a chemic process. It will soon be forgotten, in these days of stoves, that we used to roast potatoes in the ashes, after the Indian fashion. The stove not only took up room and scented the house, but it concealed the fire, and I felt as if I had lost a companion. You can always see a face in the fire. The laborer, looking into it at evening, purifies his thoughts of the dross and earthiness which they have accumulated during the day. But I could no longer sit and look into the fire, and the pertinent words of a poet recurred to me with new force.—

"Never, bright flame, may be denied to me
Thy dear, life imaging, close sympathy.
What but my hopes shot upward e'er so bright?
What but my fortunes sunk so low in night?

Why art thou banished from our hearth and hall,
Thou who art welcomed and beloved by all?
Was thy existence then too fanciful
For our life's common light, who are so dull?

Did thy bright gleam mysterious converse hold
With our congenial souls? secrets too bold?
Well, we are safe and strong, for now we sit
Beside a hearth where no dim shadows flit,
Where nothing cheers nor saddens, but a fire
Warms feet and hands—nor does to more aspire;
By whose compact utilitarian heap
The present may sit down and go to sleep,
Nor fear the ghosts who from the dim past walked,
And with us by the unequal light of the old wood
    fire talked."[314]

MRS. HOOPER

Former Inhabitants; and Winter Visitors

I weathered some merry snow storms, and spent some cheerful winter evenings by my fire-side, while the snow whirled wildly without, and even the hooting of the owl was hushed. For many weeks I met no one in my walks but those who came occasionally to cut wood and sled it to the village. The elements, however, abetted me in making a path through the deepest snow in the woods, for when I had once gone through the wind blew the oak leaves into my tracks, where they lodged, and by absorbing the rays of the sun melted the snow, and so not only made a dry bed for my feet, but in the night their dark line was my guide. For human society I was obliged to conjure up the former occupants of these woods. Within the memory of many of my townsmen the road near which my house stands resounded with the laugh and gossip of inhabitants, and the woods which border it were notched and dotted here and there with their little gardens and dwellings, though it was then much more shut in by the forest than now. In some places, within my own remembrance, the pines would scrape both sides of a chaise at once, and women and children who were compelled to go this way to Lincoln alone and on foot did it with fear, and often ran a good part of the distance. Though mainly but a humble route to neighboring villages, or for the woodman's team, it once amused the traveller more than now by its variety, and lingered longer in his memory. Where now firm open fields stretch from the village to the woods, it then ran through a maple swamp on a foundation of logs, the remnants of which, doubtless, still underlie the present dusty highway, from the Stratton, now the Alms House, Farm, to Brister's Hill.

East of my bean-field, across the road, lived Cato Ingraham, slave of Duncan Ingraham, Esquire, gentleman of Concord village; who built his slave a house, and gave him permission to live in Walden Woods;—Cato, not Uticensis, but Concordiensis.[315] Some say that he was a Guinea Negro. There are a few who remember his little patch among the walnuts, which he let grow up till he should be old and need them; but a younger and whiter speculator got them at last. He too, however, occupies

---

[314] From "The Fire-Wood" by Ellen Hooper (1812–1848).

[315] That is, not the Cato born at Uticensis (the Roman statesman who lived between 95 and 46 B.C.), but his great-grandfather, whose writings on agriculture Thoreau often cited.

an equally narrow house[316] at present. Cato's half-obliterated cellar hole still remains, though known to few, being concealed from the traveller by a fringe of pines. It is now filled with the smooth sumach, (*Rhus glabra*,) and one of the earliest species of golden-rod (*Solidago stricta*) grows there luxuriantly.

Here, by the very corner of my field, still nearer to town, Zilpha, a colored woman, had her little house, where she spun linen for the townsfolk, making the Walden Woods ring with her shrill singing, for she had a loud and notable voice. At length, in the war of 1812, her dwelling was set on fire by English soldiers, prisoners on parole, when she was away, and her cat and dog and hens were all burned up together. She led a hard life, and somewhat inhumane. One old frequenter of these woods remembers, that as he passed her house one noon he heard her muttering to herself over her gurgling pot,—"Ye are all bones, bones!" I have seen bricks amid the oak copse there.

Down the road, on the right hand, on Brister's Hill, lived Brister Freeman, "a handy Negro," slave of Squire Cummings once,—there where grow still the apple-trees which Brister planted and tended; large old trees now, but their fruit still wild and ciderish to my taste. Not long since I read his epitaph in the old Lincoln burying-ground, a little on one side, near the unmarked graves of some British grenadiers who fell in the retreat from Concord—where he is styled "Sippio Brister," —Scipio Africanus[317] he had some title to be called,—"a man of color," as if he were discolored. It also told me, with staring emphasis, when he died; which was but an indirect way of informing me that he ever lived. With him dwelt Fenda, his hospitable wife, who told fortunes, yet pleasantly,—large, round, and black, blacker than any of the children of night, such a dusky orb as never rose on Concord before or since.

Farther down the hill, on the left, on the old road in the woods, are marks of some homestead of the Stratton family; whose orchard once covered all the slope of Brister's Hill, but was long since killed out by pitch-pines, excepting a few stumps, whose old roots furnish still the wild stocks of many a thrifty village tree.

Nearer yet to town, you come to Breed's location, on the other side of the way, just on the edge of the wood; ground famous for the pranks of a demon not distinctly named in old mythology, who has acted a prominent and astounding part in our New England life, and deserves, as much as any mythological character, to have his biography written one day; who first comes in the guise of a friend or hired man, and then robs and murders the whole family,—New-England Rum. But history must not yet tell the tragedies enacted here; let time intervene in some measure to assuage and lend an azure tint to them. Here the most indistinct and dubious tradition says that once a tavern stood; the well the same, which tempered the traveller's beverage and refreshed his steed. Here then men saluted one another, and heard and told the news, and went their ways again.

Breed's hut was standing only a dozen years ago, though it had long been unoccupied. It was about the size of mine. It was set on fire by mischievous boys, one Election night, if I do not mistake. I lived on the edge of the village then, and had just lost myself over Davenant's Gondibert,[318] that winter that I labored with a

---

[316] A grave.
[317] A local black named for the Roman general who defeated the Carthaginian, Hannibal.

[318] "Gondibert," a poem by William D'Avenant (1606–1668).

lethargy,—which, by the way, I never knew whether to regard as a family complaint, having an uncle who goes to sleep shaving himself, and is obliged to sprout potatoes in a cellar Sundays, in order to keep awake and keep the Sabbath, or as the consequence of my attempt to read Chalmers' collection of English poetry[319] without skipping. It fairly overcame my Nervii.[320] I had just sunk my head on this when the bells rung fire, and in hot haste the engines rolled that way, led by a straggling troop of men and boys, and I among the foremost, for I had leaped the brook. We thought it was far south over the woods,—we who had run to fires before,—barn, shop, or dwelling-house, or all together. "It's Baker's barn," cried one. "It is the Codman Place," affirmed another. And then fresh sparks went up above the wood, as if the roof fell in, and we all shouted "Concord to the rescue!" Wagons shot past with furious speed and crushing loads, bearing, perchance, among the rest, the agent of the Insurance Company, who was bound to go however far; and ever and anon the engine bell tinkled behind, more slow and sure, and rearmost of all, as it was afterward whispered, came they who set the fire and gave the alarm. Thus we kept on like true idealists, rejecting the evidence of our senses, until at a turn in the road we heard the crackling and actually felt the heat of the fire from over the wall, and realized, alas! that we were there. The very nearness of the fire but cooled our ardor. At first we thought to throw a frog-pond on to it; but concluded to let it burn, it was so far gone and so worthless. So we stood round our engine, jostled one another, expressed our sentiments through speaking trumpets, or in lower tone referred to the great conflagrations which the world has witnessed, including Bascom's shop, and, between ourselves, we thought that, were we there in season with our "tub,"[321] and a full frog-pond by, we could turn that threatened last and universal one into another flood. We finally retreated without doing any mischief,—returned to sleep and Gondibert. But as for Gondibert, I would except that passage in the preface about wit being the soul's powder,—"but most of mankind are strangers to wit, as Indians are to powder."

It chanced that I walked that way across the fields the following night, about the same hour, and hearing a low moaning at this spot, I drew near in the dark, and discovered the only survivor of the family that I know, the heir of both its virtues and its vices, who alone was interested in this burning, lying on his stomach and looking over the cellar wall at the still smouldering cinders beneath, muttering to himself, as is his wont. He had been working far off in the river meadows all day, and had improved the first moments that he could call his own to visit the home of his fathers and his youth. He gazed into the cellar from all sides and points of view by turns, always lying down to it, as if there was some treasure, which he remembered, concealed between the stones, where there was absolutely nothing but a heap of bricks and ashes. The house being gone, he looked at what there was left. He was soothed by the sympathy which my mere presence implied, and showed me, as well as the darkness permitted, where the well was covered up; which, thank Heaven, could never be burned; and he groped long about the wall to find the well-sweep[322] which his father had cut and mounted, feeling for the iron hook or staple by which a burden

---

[319] Anthology of poetry edited by Alexander Chalmers and published in 1810.
[320] Thoreau puns on the word *nerves* by citing the Nervii, a European tribe conquered by Caesar.

[321] Water pump.
[322] Pole for lifting buckets from a well.

had been fastened to the heavy end,—all that he could now cling to,—to convince me that it was no common "rider."[323] I felt it, and still remark it almost daily in my walks, for by it hangs the history of a family.

Once more, on the left, where are seen the well and lilac bushes by the wall, in the now open field, lived Nutting and Le Grosse. But to return toward Lincoln.

Farther in the woods than any of these, where the road approaches nearest to the pond, Wyman the potter squatted, and furnished his townsmen with earthen ware, and left descendants to succeed him. Neither were they rich in worldly goods, holding the land by sufferance while they lived; and there often the sheriff came in vain to collect the taxes, and "attached a chip,"[324] for form's sake, as I have read in his accounts, there being nothing else that he could lay his hands on. One day in midsummer, when I was hoeing, a man who was carrying a load of pottery to market stopped his horse against my field and inquired concerning Wyman the younger. He had long ago bought a potter's wheel of him, and wished to know what had become of him. I had read of the potter's clay and wheel in Scripture, but it had never occurred to me that the pots we use were not such as had come down unbroken from those days, or grown on trees like gourds somewhere, and I was pleased to hear that so fictile an art was ever practised in my neighborhood.

The last inhabitant of these woods before me was an Irishman, Hugh Quoil, (if I have spelt his name with coil enough,) who occupied Wyman's tenement,—Col. Quoil, he was called. Rumor said that he had been a soldier at Waterloo. If he had lived I should have made him fight his battles over again. His trade here was that of a ditcher. Napoleon went to St. Helena; Quoil came to Walden Woods. All I know of him is tragic. He was a man of manners, like one who had seen the world, and was capable of more civil speech than you could well attend to. He wore a great coat in mid-summer, being affected with the trembling delirium, and his face was the color of carmine. He died in the road at the foot of Brister's Hill shortly after I came to the woods, so that I have not remembered him as a neighbor. Before his house was pulled down, when his comrades avoided it as "an unlucky castle," I visited it. There lay his old clothes curled up by use, as if they were himself, upon his raised plank bed. His pipe lay broken on the hearth, instead a bowl broken at the fountain. The last could never have been the symbol of his death, for he confessed to me that, though he had heard of Brister's Spring, he had never seen it; and soiled cards, kings of diamonds spades and hearts, were scattered over the floor. One black chicken which the administrator could not catch, black as night and as silent, not even croaking, awaiting Reynard,[325] still went to roost in the next apartment. In the rear there was the dim outline of a garden, which had been planted but had never received its first hoeing, owing to those terrible shaking fits, though it was now harvest time. It was over-run with Roman wormwood and beggar-ticks, which last stuck to my clothes for all fruit. The skin of a woodchuck was freshly stretched upon the back of the house, a trophy of his last Waterloo; but no warm cap or mittens would he want more.

Now only a dent in the earth marks the site of these dwellings, with buried cellar stones, and strawberries, raspberries, thimble-berries, hazel-bushes, and sumachs

---

[323] Fence rail.
[324] Seized an item of little worth in order that a legal record could be made of the confiscation.

[325] Familiar name for a fox.

growing in the sunny sward there; some pitch-pine or gnarled oak occupies what was the chimney nook, and a sweet-scented black-birch, perhaps, waves where the door-stone was. Sometimes the well dent is visible, where once a spring oozed; now dry and tearless grass; or it was covered deep,—not to be discovered till some late day,—with a flat stone under the sod, when the last of the race departed. What a sorrowful act must that be,—the covering up of wells! coincident with the opening of wells of tears. These cellar dents, like deserted fox burrows, old holes, are all that is left where once were the stir and bustle of human life, and "fate, freewill, fore-knowledge absolute,"[326] in some form and dialect or other were by turns discussed. But all I can learn of their conclusions amounts to just this, that "Cato and Brister pulled wool;"[327] which is about as edifying as the history of more famous schools of philosophy.

Still grows the vivacious lilac a generation after the door and lintel and the sill are gone, unfolding its sweet-scented flowers each spring, to be plucked by the musing traveller; planted and tended once by children's hands, in front-yard plots,—now standing by wall-sides in retired pastures, and giving place to new-rising forests;—the last of that stirp, sole survivor of that family. Little did the dusky children think that the puny slip with its two eyes only, which they stuck in the ground in the shadow of the house and daily watered, would root itself so, and outlive them and house itself in the rear that shaded it, and grown man's garden and orchard, and tell their story faintly to the lone wanderer a half century after they had grown up and died,—blossoming as fair, and smelling as sweet, as in that first spring. I mark its still tender, civil, cheerful, lilac colors.

But this small village, germ of something more, why did it fail while Concord keeps its ground? Were there no natural advantages,—no water privileges, forsooth? Ay, the deep Walden Pond and cool Brister's Spring,—privilege to drink long and healthy draughts at these, all unimproved by these men but to dilute their glass. They were universally a thirsty race. Might not the basket, stable-broom, mat-making, corn-parching, linen-spinning, and pottery business have thrived here, making the wilderness to blossom like the rose, and a numerous posterity have inherited the land of their fathers? The sterile soil would at least have been proof against a low-land degeneracy. Alas! how little does the memory of these human inhabitants enhance the beauty of the landscape! Again, perhaps Nature will try, with me for a first settler, and my house raised last spring to be the oldest in the hamlet.

I am not aware that any man has ever built on the spot which I occupy. Deliver me from a city built on the site of a more ancient city, whose materials are ruins, whose gardens cemeteries. The soil is blanched and accursed there, and before that becomes necessary the earth itself will be destroyed. With such reminiscences I repeopled the woods and lulled myself asleep.

At this season I seldom had a visitor. When the snow lay deepest no wanderer ventured near my house for a week or fortnight at a time, but there I lived as snug as a meadow mouse, or as cattle and poultry which are said to have survived for a long time buried in drifts, even without food; or like that early settler's family in the town of Sutton, in this state, whose cottage was completely covered by the great snow of 1717 when

---

[326] From John Milton's *Paradise Lost*, II, 560.   [327] Cleaned the skins of animals.

he was absent, and an Indian found it only by the hole which the chimney's breath made in the drift, and so relieved the family. But no friendly Indian concerned himself about me; nor needed he, for the master of the house was at home. The Great Snow! How cheerful it is to hear of! When the farmers could not get to the woods and swamps with their teams, and were obliged to cut down the shade trees before their houses, and when the crust was harder cut off the trees in the swamps ten feet from the ground, as it appeared the next spring.

In the deepest snows, the path which I used from the highway to my house, about half a mile long, might have been represented by a meandering dotted line, with wide intervals between the dots. For a week of even weather I took exactly the same number of steps, and of the same length, coming and going, stepping deliberately and with the precision of a pair of dividers in my own deep tracks,—to such routine the winter reduces us,—yet often they were filled with heaven's own blue. But no weather interfered fatally with my walks, or rather my going abroad, for I frequently tramped eight or ten miles through the deepest snow to keep an appointment with a beech-tree, or a yellow-birch, or an old acquaintance among the pines; when the ice and snow causing their limbs to droop, and so sharpening their tops, had changed the pines into fir-trees; wading to the tops of the highest hills when the snow was nearly two feet deep on a level, and shaking down another snow-storm on my head at every step; or sometimes creeping and floundering thither on my hands and knees, when the hunters had gone into winter quarters. One afternoon I amused myself by watching a barred owl (*Strix nebulosa*) sitting on one of the lower dead limbs of a white-pine, close to the trunk, in broad daylight, I standing within a rod of him. He could hear me when I moved and cronched the snow with my feet, but could not plainly see me. When I made most noise he would stretch out his neck, and erect his neck feathers, and open his eyes wide; but their lids soon fell again, and he began to nod. I too felt a slumberous influence after watching him half an hour, as he sat thus with his eyes half open, like a cat, winged brother of the cat. There was only a narrow slit left between their lids, by which he preserved a peninsular relation to me; thus, with half-shut eyes, looking out from the land of dreams, and endeavoring to realize me, vague object or mote that interrupted his visions. At length, on some louder noise or my nearer approach, he would grow uneasy and sluggishly turn about on his perch, as if impatient at having his dreams disturbed; and when he launched himself off and flapped through the pines, spreading his wings to unexpected breadth, I could not hear the slightest sound from them. Thus, guided amid the pine boughs rather by a delicate sense of their neighborhood than by sight, feeling his twilight way as it were with his sensitive pinions, he found a new perch, where he might in peace await the dawning of his day.

As I walked over the long causeway made for the railroad through the meadows, I encountered many a blustering and nipping wind, for nowhere has it freer play; and when the frost had smitten me on one cheek, heathen as I was, I turned to it the other also.[328] Nor was it much better by the carriage road from Brister's Hill. For I came to town still, like a friendly Indian, when the contents of the broad open fields were all piled up between the walls of the Walden road, and half an hour sufficed to obliterate the tracks of the last traveller. And when I returned new drifts would have

[328] Allusion to Matthew 5:39.

formed, through which I floundered, where the busy north-west wind had been depositing the powdery snow round a sharp angle in the road, and not a rabbit's track, nor even the fine print, the small type, of a deer mouse was to be seen. Yet I rarely failed to find, even in mid-winter, some warm and springy swamp where the grass and the skunk-cabbage still put forth with perennial verdure, and some hardier bird occasionally awaited the return of spring.

Sometimes, notwithstanding the snow, when I returned from my walk at evening I crossed the deep tracks of a woodchopper leading from my door, and found his pile of whittlings on the hearth, and my house filled with the odor of his pipe. Or on a Sunday afternoon, if I chanced to be at home, I heard the cronching of the snow made by the step of a long-headed farmer, who from far through the woods sought my house, to have a social "crack;" one of the few of his vocation who are "men on their farms;" who donned a frock instead of a professor's gown, and is as ready to extract the moral out of church or state as to haul a load of manure from his barn-yard. We talked of rude and simple times, when men sat about large fires in cold bracing weather, with clear heads; and when other dessert failed, we tried our teeth on many a nut which wise squirrels have long since abandoned, for those which have the thickest shells are commonly empty.

The one who came from farthest to my lodge, through deepest snows and most dismal tempests, was a poet.[329] A farmer, a hunter, a soldier, a reporter, even a philosopher, may be daunted; but nothing can deter a poet, for he is actuated by pure love. Who can predict his comings and goings? His business calls him out at all hours, even when doctors sleep. We made that small house ring with boisterous mirth and resound with the murmur of much sober talk, making amends then to Walden vale for the long silences. Broadway was still and deserted in comparison. At suitable intervals there were regular salutes of laughter, which might have been referred indifferently to the last uttered or the forth-coming jest. We made many a "bran new" theory of life over a thin dish of gruel, which combined the advantages of conviviality with the clear-headedness which philosophy requires.

I should not forget that during my last winter at the pond there was another welcome visitor,[330] who at one time came through the village, through snow and rain and darkness, till he saw my lamp through the trees, and shared with me some long winter evenings. One of the last of the philosophers,—Connecticut gave him to the world,—he peddled first her wares, afterwards, as he declares, his brains. These he peddles still, prompting God and disgracing man, bearing for fruit his brain only, like the nut its kernel. I think that he must be the man of the most faith of any alive. His words and attitude always suppose a better state of things than other men are acquainted with, and he will be the last man to be disappointed as the ages revolve. He has no venture in the present. But though comparatively disregarded now, when his day comes, laws unsuspected by most will take effect, and masters of families and rulers will come to him for advice.—

"How blind that cannot see serenity!"

[329] The younger William Ellery Channing.
[330] Amos Bronson Alcott (1799–1888), educational reformer.

A true friend of man; almost the only friend of human progress. An Old Mortality,[331] say rather an Immortality, with unwearied patience and faith making plain the image engraven in men's bodies, the God of whom they are but defaced and leaning monuments. With his hospitable intellect he embraces children, beggars, insane, and scholars, and entertains the thought of all, adding to it commonly some breadth and elegance. I think that he should keep a caravansary on the world's highway, where philosophers of all nations might put up, and on his sign should be printed, "Entertainment for man, but not for his beast. Enter ye that have leisure and a quiet mind, who earnestly seek the right road." He is perhaps the sanest man and has the fewest crotchets of any I chance to know; the same yesterday and tomorrow. Of yore we had sauntered and talked, and effectually put the world behind us; for he was pledged to no institution in it, freeborn, *ingenuus.* Whichever way we turned, it seemed that the heavens and the earth had met together, since he enhanced the beauty of the landscape. A blue-robed man, whose fittest roof is the overarching sky which reflects his serenity. I do not see how he can ever die; Nature cannot spare him.

Having each some shingles of thought well dried, we sat and whittled them, trying our knives, and admiring the clear yellowish grain of the pumpkin pine. We waded so gently and reverently, or we pulled together so smoothly, that the fishes of thought were not scared from the stream, nor feared any angler on the bank, but came and went grandly, like the clouds which float through the western sky, and the mother-o'-pearl flocks which sometimes form and dissolve there. There we worked, revising mythology, rounding a fable here and there, and building castles in the air for which earth offered no worthy foundation. Great Looker! Great Expecter! to converse with whom was a New England Night's Entertainment. Ah! such discourse we had, hermit and philosopher, and the old settler I have spoken of,—we three,—it expanded and racked my little house; I should not dare to say how many pounds' weight there was above the atmospheric pressure on every circular inch; it opened its seams so that they had to be calked with much dulness thereafter to stop the consequent leak;—but I had enough of that kind of oakum already picked.

There was one other[332] with whom I had "solid seasons," long to be remembered, at his house in the village, and who looked in upon me from time to time; but I had no more for society there.

There too, as every where, I sometimes expected the Visitor who never comes. The Vishnu Purana[333] says, "The house-holder is to remain at eventide in his court-yard as long as it takes to milk a cow, or longer if he pleases, to await the arrival of a guest." I often performed this duty of hospitality, waited long enough to milk a whole herd of cows, but did not see the man approaching from the town.

Winter Animals

When the ponds were firmly frozen, they afforded not only new and shorter routes to many points, but new views from their surfaces of the familiar landscape around them. When I crossed Flint's Pond, after it was covered with snow, though I had often paddled about and skated over it, it was so unexpectedly wide and so strange that I

---

[331] Character in Sir Walter Scott's novel of the same name (1816).

[332] Ralph Waldo Emerson.

[333] Sacred writings of the Hindus.

could think of nothing but Baffin's Bay.[334] The Lincoln hills rose up around me at the extremity of a snowy plain, in which I did not remember to have stood before; and the fishermen, at an indeterminable distance over the ice, moving slowly about with their wolfish dogs, passed for sealers or Esquimaux, or in misty weather loomed like fabulous creatures, and I did not know whether they were giants or pygmies. I took this course when I went to lecture in Lincoln in the evening, travelling in no road and passing no house between my own hut and the lecture room. In Goose Pond, which lay in my way, a colony of muskrats dwelt, and raised their cabins high above the ice, though none could be seen abroad when I crossed it. Walden, being like the rest usually bare of snow, or with only shallow and interrupted drifts on it, was my yard, where I could walk freely when the snow was nearly two feet deep on a level elsewhere and the villagers were confined to their streets. There, far from the village street, and except at the very long intervals, from the jingle of sleigh-bells, I slid and skated, as in a vast moose-yard well trodden, overhung by oak woods and solemn pines bent down with snow or bristling with icicles.

For sounds in winter nights, and often in winter days, I heard the forlorn but melodious note of a hooting owl indefinitely far; such a sound as the frozen earth would yield if struck with a suitable plectrum, the very *lingua vernacula*[335] of Walden Wood, and quite familiar to me at last, though I never saw the bird while it was making it. I seldom opened my door in a winter evening without hearing it; *Hoo hoo hoo, hoorer hoo,* sounded sonorously, and the first three syllables accented somewhat like *how der do;* or sometimes *hoo hoo* only. One night in the beginning of winter, before the pond froze over, about nine o'clock, I was startled by the loud honking of a goose, and, stepping to the door, heard the sound of their wings like a tempest in the woods as they flew over my house. They passed over the pond toward Fair Haven, seemingly deterred from settling by my light, their commodore honking all the while with a regular beat. Suddenly an unmistakable cat-owl from very near me, with the most harsh and tremendous voice I ever heard from any inhabitant of the woods, responded at regular intervals to the goose, as if determined to expose and disgrace this intruder from Hudson's Bay by exhibiting a greater compass and volume of voice in a native, and *boo-hoo* him out of Concord horizon. What do you mean by alarming the citadel at this time of night consecrated to me? Do you think I am ever caught napping at such an hour, and that I have not got lungs and a larynx as well as yourself? *Boo-hoo, boo-hoo, boo-hoo!* It was one of the most thrilling discords I ever heard. And yet, if you had a discriminating ear, there were in it the elements of a concord such as these plains never saw nor heard.

I also heard the whooping of the ice in the pond, my great bed-fellow in that part of Concord, as if it were restless in its bed and would fain turn over, were troubled with flatulency and bad dreams; or I was waked by the cracking of the ground by the frost, as if some one had driven a team against my door, and in the morning would find a crack in the earth a quarter of a mile long and a third of an inch wide.

Sometimes I heard the foxes as they ranged over the snow crust, in moonlight nights, in search of a partridge or other game, barking raggedly and demoniacally like forest dogs, as if laboring with some anxiety, or seeking expression, struggling for light and to be dogs outright and run freely in the streets; for if we take the ages into

---

[334] In the Arctic Ocean.   [335] Latin: "ordinary language."

our account, may there not be a civilization going on among brutes as well as men? They seemed to me to be rudimental, burrowing men, still standing on their defence, awaiting their transformation. Sometimes one came near to my window, attracted by my light, barked a vulpine curse at me, and then retreated.

Usually the red squirrel (*Sciurus Hudsonius*) waked me in the dawn, coursing over the roof and up and down the sides of the house, as if sent out of the woods for this purpose. In the course of the winter I threw out half a bushel of ears of sweet-corn, which had not got ripe, on to the snow crust by my door, and was amused by watching the motions of the various animals which were baited by it. In the twilight and the night the rabbits came regularly and made a hearty meal. All day long the red squirrels came and went, and afforded me much entertainment by their manœuvres. One would approach at first warily through the shrub-oaks, running over the snow crust by fits and starts like a leaf blown by the wind, now a few paces this way, with wonderful speed and waste of energy, making inconceivable haste with his "trotters," as if it were for a wager, and now as many paces that way, but never getting on more than half a rod at a time; and then suddenly pausing with a ludicrous expression and a gratuitous somerset, as if all the eyes in the universe were fixed on him,—for all the motions of a squirrel, even in the most solitary recesses of the forest, imply spectators as much as those of a dancing girl,—wasting more time in delay and circumspection than would have sufficed to walk the whole distance,—I never saw one walk,—and then suddenly, before you could say Jack Robinson, he would be in the top of a young pitch-pine, winding up his clock and chiding all imaginary spectators, soliloquizing and talking to all the universe at the same time,—for no reason that I could ever detect, or he himself was aware of, I suspect. At length he would reach the corn, and selecting a suitable ear, frisk about in the same uncertain trigonometrical way to the top-most stick of my wood-pile, before my window, where he looked me in the face, and there sit for hours, supplying himself with a new ear from time to time, nibbling at first voraciously and throwing the half-naked cobs about; till at length he grew more dainty still and played with his food, tasting only the inside of the kernel, and the ear, which was held balanced over the stick by one paw, slipped from his careless grasp and fell to the ground, when he would look over at it with a ludicrous expression of uncertainty, as if suspecting that it had life, with a mind not made up whether to get it again, or a new one, or be off; now thinking of corn, then listening to hear what was in the wind. So the little impudent fellow would waste many an ear in a forenoon; till at last, seizing some longer and plumper one, considerably bigger than himself, and skilfully balancing it, he would set out with it to the woods, like a tiger with a buffalo, by the same zig-zag course and frequent pauses, scratching along with it as if it were too heavy for him and falling all the while, making its fall a diagonal between a perpendicular and horizontal, being determined to put it through at any rate;—a singularly frivolous and whimsical fellow;—and so he would get off with it to where he lived, perhaps carry it to the top of a pine tree forty or fifty rods distant, and I would afterwards find the cobs strewn about the woods in various directions.

At length the jays arrive, whose discordant screams were heard long before, as they were warily making their approach an eighth of a mile off, and in a stealthy and sneaking manner they flit from tree to tree, nearer and nearer, and pick up the kernels which the squirrels have dropped. Then, sitting on a pitch-pine bough, they attempt to swallow in their haste a kernel which is too big for their throats and chokes them; and after great labor they disgorge it, and spend an hour in the endeavor to crack it by repeated blows with their bills. They were manifestly thieves, and I had not much respect for them; but the squirrels, though at first shy, went to work as if they were taking what was their own.

Meanwhile also came the chicadees in flocks, which picking up the crumbs the squirrels had dropped, flew to the nearest twig, and placing them under their claws, hammered away at them with their little bills, as if it were an insect in the bark, till they were sufficiently reduced for their slender throats. A little flock of these tit-mice came daily to pick a dinner out of my wood-pile, or the crumbs at my door, with faint flitting lisping notes, like the tinkling of icicles in the grass, or else with sprightly *day day day* or more rarely, in spring-like days, a wiry summery *phe-be* from the wood-side. They were so familiar that at length one alighted on an armful of wood which I was carrying in, and pecked at the sticks without fear. I once had a sparrow alight upon my shoulder for a moment while I was hoeing in a village garden, and I felt that I was more distinguished by that circumstance than I should have been by any epaulet I could have worn. The squirrels also grew at last to be quite familiar, and occasionally stepped upon my shoe, when that was the nearest way.

When the ground was not yet quite covered, and again near the end of winter, when the snow was melted on my south hill-side and about my woodpile, the partridges came out of the woods morning and evening to feed there. Whichever side you walk in the woods the partridge bursts away on whirring wings, jarring the snow from the dry leaves and twigs on high, which comes sifting down in the sunbeams like golden dust; for this brave bird is not to be scared by winter. It is frequently covered up by drifts, and, it is said, "sometimes plunges from on wing into the soft snow, where it remains concealed for a day or two." I used to start them in the open land also, where they had come out of the woods at sunset to "bud" the wild apple-trees. They will come regularly every evening to particular trees, where the cunning sportsman lies in wait for them, and the distant orchards next the woods suffer thus not a little. I am glad that the partridge gets fed, at any rate. It is Nature's own bird which lives on buds and diet-drink.

In dark winter mornings, or in short winter afternoons, I sometimes heard a pack of hounds threading all the woods with hounding cry and yelp, unable to resist the instinct of the chase, and the note of the hunting horn at intervals, proving that man was in the rear. The woods ring again, and yet no fox bursts forth on to the open level of the pond, nor following pack pursuing their Actæon.[336] And perhaps at evening I see the hunters returning with a single brush trailing from their sleigh for a trophy, seeking their inn. They tell me that if the fox would remain in the bosom of the frozen earth he would be safe, or if he would run in a straight line away no fox-hound could overtake him; but, having left his pursuers far behind, he stops to rest and listen till they come up, and when he runs he circles round to his old haunts, where the hunters await him. Sometimes, however, he will run upon a wall many rods, and then leap off far to one side, and he appears to know that water will not retain his scent. A hunter told me that he once saw a fox pursued by hounds burst out on to Walden when the ice was covered with shallow puddles, run part way

---

[336] In classic myth, a hunter who was turned upon by his own hounds and torn to death.

across, and then return to the same shore. Ere long the hounds arrived, but here they lost the scent. Sometimes a pack hunting by themselves would pass my door, and circle round my house, and yelp and hound without regarding me, as if afflicted by a species of madness, so that nothing could divert them from the pursuit. Thus they circle until they fall upon the recent trail of a fox, for a wise hound will forsake every thing else for this. One day a man came to my hut from Lexington to inquire after his hound that made a large track, and had been hunting for a week by himself. But I fear that he was not the wiser for all I told him, for every time I attempted to answer his questions he interrupted me by asking, "What do you do here?" He had lost a dog, but found a man.

One old hunter[337] who has a dry tongue, who used to come to bathe in Walden once every year when the water was warmest, and at such times looked in upon me, told me, that many years ago he took his gun one afternoon and went out for a cruise in Walden Wood; and as he walked the Wayland road he heard the cry of hounds approaching, and ere long a fox leaped the wall into the road, and as quick as thought leaped the other wall out of the road, and his swift bullet had not touched him. Some way behind came an old hound and her three pups in full pursuit, hunting on their own account, and disappeared again in the woods. Late in the afternoon, as he was resting in the thick woods south of Walden, he heard the voice of the hounds far over toward Fair Haven still pursuing the fox; and on they came, their hounding cry which made all the woods ring sounding nearer and nearer, now from Well-Meadow, now from the Baker Farm. For a long time he stood still and listened to their music, so sweet to a hunter's ear, when suddenly the fox appeared, threading the solemn aisles with an easy coursing pace, whose sound was concealed by a sympathetic rustle of the leaves, swift and still, keeping the ground, leaving his pursuers far behind; and, leaping upon a rock amid the woods, he sat erect and listening, with his back to the hunter. For a moment compassion restrained the latter's arm; but that was a short-lived mood, and as quick as thought can follow thought his piece was levelled, and *whang!* —the fox rolling over the rock lay dead on the ground. The hunter still kept his place and listened to the hounds. Still on they came, and now the near woods resounded through all their aisles with their demoniac cry. At length the old hound burst into view with muzzle to the ground, and snapping the air as if possessed, and ran directly to the rock; but spying the dead fox she suddenly ceased her hounding, as if struck dumb with amazement, and walked round and round him in silence; and one by one her pups arrived, and, like their mother, were sobered into silence by the mystery. Then the hunter came forward and stood in their midst, and the mystery was solved. They waited in silence while he skinned the fox, then followed the brush a while, and at length turned off into the woods again. That evening a Weston Squire came to the Concord hunter's cottage to inquire for his hounds, and told how for a week they had been hunting on their own account from Weston woods. The Concord hunter told him what he knew and offered him the skin; but the other declined it and departed. He did not find his hounds that night, but the next day learned that they had crossed the river and put up at a farm-house for the night, whence, having been well fed, they took their departure early in the morning.

The hunter who told me this could remember one Sam Nutting, who used to hunt

---

[337] Probably, George Minott, the Concord farmer whom Thoreau admired for his "poetical" nature and his knowledge of local history and traditions.

bears on Fair Haven Ledges, and exchange their skins for rum in Concord village; who told him, even, that he had seen a moose there. Nutting had a famous fox-hound named Burgoyne,—he pronounced it Bugine,—which my informant used to borrow. In the "Wast Book"[338] of an old trader of this town, who was also a captain, town-clerk, and representative, I find the following entry. Jan. 18th, 1742–3, "John Melven Cr. by 1 Grey Fox 0–2–3;" they are not now found here; and in his ledger, Feb. 7th, 1743, Hezekiah Stratton has credit "by 1/2 a Catt skin 0–1–4 1/2;" of course, a wild-cat, for Stratton was a sergeant in the old French war, and would not have got credit for hunting less noble game. Credit is given for deer skins also, and they were daily sold. One man still preserves the horns of the last deer that was killed in this vicinity, and another has told me the particulars of the hunt in which his uncle was engaged. The hunters were formerly a numerous and merry crew here. I remember well one gaunt Nimrod[339] who would catch up a leaf by the road-side and play a strain on it wilder and more melodious, if my memory serves me, than any hunting horn.

At midnight, when there was a moon, I sometimes met with hounds in my path prowling about the woods, which would skulk out of my way, as if afraid, and stand silent amid the bushes till I had passed.

Squirrels and wild mice disputed for my store of nuts. There were scores of pitch-pines around my house, from one to four inches in diameter, which had been gnawed by mice the previous winter,—a Norwegian winter for them, for the snow lay long and deep, and they were obliged to mix a large proportion of pine bark with their other diet. These trees were alive and apparently flourishing at midsummer, and many of them had grown a foot, though completely girdled; but after another winter such were without exception dead. It is remarkable that a single mouse should thus be allowed a whole pine tree for its dinner, gnawing round instead of up and down it; but perhaps it is necessary in order to thin these trees, which are wont to grow up densely.

The hares (*Lepus Americanus*) were very familiar. One had her form under my house all winter, separated from me only by the flooring, and she startled me each morning by her hasty departure when I began to stir,—thump, thump, thump, striking her head against the floor timbers in her hurry. They used to come round my door at dusk to nibble the potato parings which I had thrown out, and were so nearly the color of the ground that they could hardly be distinguished when still. Sometimes in the twilight I alternately lost and recovered sight of one sitting motionless under my window. When I opened my door in the evening, off they would go with a squeak and a bounce. Near at hand they only excited my pity. One evening one sat by my door two paces from me, at first trembling with fear, yet unwilling to move; a poor wee thing, lean and bony, with ragged ears and sharp nose, scant tail and slender paws. It looked as if Nature no longer contained the breed of nobler bloods, but stood on her last toes. Its large eyes appeared young and unhealthy, almost dropsical. I took a step, and lo, away it scud with an elastic spring over the snow crust, straightening its body and its limbs into graceful length, and soon put the forest between me and itself,—the wild free venison, asserting its vigor and the dignity of Nature. Not without reason was its slenderness. Such then was its nature. (*Lepus, levipes,* light-foot, some think.)

---

[338] Diary.   [339] Hunter mentioned in Genesis 10:9.

What is a country without rabbits and partridges? They are among the most simple and indigenous animal products; ancient and venerable families known to antiquity as to modern times; of the very hue and substance of Nature, nearest allied to leaves and to the ground,—and to one another; it is either winged or it is legged. It is hardly as if you had seen a wild creature when a rabbit or a partridge bursts away, only a natural one, as much to be expected as rustling leaves. The partridge and the rabbit are still sure to thrive, like true natives of the soil, whatever revolutions occur. If the forest is cut off, the sprouts and bushes which spring up afford them concealment, and they become more numerous than ever. That must be a poor country indeed that does not support a hare. Our woods teem with them both, and around every swamp may be seen the partridge or rabbit walk, beset with twiggy fences and horse-hair snares, which some cow-boy tends.

The Pond in Winter

After a still winter night I awoke with the impression that some question had been put to me, which I had been endeavoring in vain to answer in my sleep, as what—how—when—where? But there was dawning Nature, in whom all creatures live, looking in at my broad windows with serene and satisfied face, and no question on *her* lips. I awoke to an answered question, to Nature and daylight. The snow lying deep on the earth dotted with young pines, and the very slope of the hill on which my house is placed, seemed to say, Forward! Nature puts no question and answers none which we mortals ask. She has long ago taken her resolution. "O Prince, our eyes contemplate with admiration and transmit to the soul the wonderful and varied spectacle of this universe. The night veils without doubt a part of this glorious creation; but day comes to reveal to us this great work, which extends from earth even into the plains of the ether."[340]

Then to my morning work. First I take an axe and pail and go in search of water, if that be not a dream. After a cold and snowy night it needed a divining rod to find it. Every winter the liquid and trembling surface of the pond, which was so sensitive to every breath, and reflected every light and shadow, becomes solid to the depth of a foot or a foot and a half, so that it will support the heaviest teams, and perchance the snow covers it to an equal depth, and it is not to be distinguished from any level field. Like the marmots in the surrounding hills, it closes its eye-lids and becomes dormant for three months or more. Standing on the snow-covered plain, as if in a pasture amid the hills, I cut my way first through a foot of snow, and then a foot of ice, and open a window under my feet, where, kneeling to drink, I look down into the quiet parlor of the fishes, pervaded by a softened light as through a window of ground glass, with its bright sanded floor the same as in summer; there a perennial waveless serenity reigns as in the amber twilight sky, corresponding to the cool and even temperament of the inhabitants. Heaven is under our feet as well as over our heads.

Early in the morning, while all things are crisp with frost, men come with fishing reels and slender lunch, and let down their fine lines through the snowy field to take

---

[340] From the sacred Hindu *Harivansa*. This passage is Thoreau's translation from the French version by Alexandre Langlois. The speaker is a Brahmin priest who addresses Prince Djanamedjaya.

pickerel and perch; wild men, who instinctively follow other fashions and trust other authorities than their townsmen, and by their goings and comings stitch towns together in parts where else they would be ripped. They sit and eat their luncheon in stout fear-naughts[341] on the dry oak leaves on the shore, as wise in natural lore as the citizen is in artificial. They never consulted with books, and know and can tell much less than they have done. The things which they practise are said not yet to be known. Here is one fishing for pickerel with grown perch for bait. You look into his pail with wonder as into a summer pond, as if he kept summer locked up at home, or knew where she had retreated. How, pray, did he get these in mid-winter? O, he got worms out of rotten logs since the ground froze, and so he caught them. His life itself passes deeper in Nature than the studies of the naturalist penetrate; himself a subject for the naturalist. The latter raises the moss and bark gently with his knife in search of insects; the former lays open logs to their core with his axe, and moss and bark fly far and wide. He gets his living by barking trees. Such a man has some right to fish, and I love to see Nature carried out in him. The perch swallows the grub-worm, the pickerel swallows the perch, and the fisherman swallows the pickerel; and so all the chinks in the scale of being are filled.

When I strolled around the pond in misty weather I was sometimes amused by the primitive mode which some ruder fisherman had adopted. He would perhaps have placed alder branches over the narrow holes in the ice, which were four or five rods apart and an equal distance from the shore, and having fastened the end of the line to a stick to prevent its being pulled through, have passed the slack line over a twig of the alder, a foot or more above the ice, and tied a dry oak leaf to it, which, being pulled down, would show when he had a bite. These alders loomed through the mist at regular intervals as you walked half way round the pond.

Ah, the pickerel of Walden! when I see them lying on the ice, or in the well which the fisherman cuts in the ice, making a little hole to admit the water, I am always surprised by their rare beauty, as if they were fabulous fishes, they are so foreign to the streets, even to the woods, foreign as Arabia to our Concord life. They possess a quite dazzling and transcendent beauty which separates them by a wide interval from the cadaverous cod and haddock whose fame is trumpeted in our streets. They are not green like the pines, nor gray like the stones, nor blue like the sky; but they have, to my eyes, if possible, yet rarer colors, like flowers and precious stones, as if they were the pearls, the animalized *nuclei* or crystals of the Walden water. They, of course, are Walden all over and all through; are themselves small Waldens in the animal kingdom, Waldenses.[342] It is surprising that they are caught here,—that in this deep and capacious spring, far beneath the rattling teams and chaises and tinkling sleighs that travel the Walden road, this great gold and emerald fish swims. I never chanced to see its kind in any market; it would be the cynosure of all eyes there. Easily, with a few convulsive quirks, they give up their watery ghosts, like a mortal translated before his time to the thin air of heaven.

As I was desirous to recover the long lost bottom of Walden Pond, I surveyed it carefully, before the ice broke up, early in '46, with compass and chain and sounding

---

[341] Overcoats.
[342] Twelfth-century French Protestant dissidents; used here as a pun.

line. There have been many stories told about the bottom, or rather no bottom, of this pond, which certainly had no foundation for themselves. It is remarkable how long men will believe in the bottomlessness of a pond without taking the trouble to sound it. I have visited two such Bottomless Ponds in one walk in this neighborhood. Many have believed that Walden reached quite through to the other side of the globe. Some who have lain flat on the ice for a long time, looking down through the illusive medium, perchance with watery eyes into the bargain, and driven to hasty conclusions by the fear of catching cold in their breasts, have seen vast holes "into which a load of hay might be driven," if there were any body to drive it, the undoubted source of the Styx and entrance to the Infernal Regions from these parts. Others have gone down from the village with a "fifty-six"[343] and a wagon load of inch rope, but yet have failed to find any bottom; for while the "fifty-six" was resting by the way, they were paying out the rope in the vain attempt to fathom their truly immeasurable capacity for marvellousness. But I can assure my readers that Walden has a reasonably tight bottom at a not unreasonable, though at an unusual, depth. I fathomed it easily with a cod-line and a stone weighing about a pound and a half, and could tell accurately when the stone left the bottom, by having to pull so much harder before the water got underneath to help me. The greatest depth was exactly one hundred and two feet; to which may be added the five feet which it has risen since, making one hundred and seven. This is a remarkable depth for so small an area; yet not an inch of it can be spared by the imagination. What if all ponds were shallow? Would it not react on the minds of men? I am thankful that this pond was made deep and pure for a symbol. While men believe in the infinite some ponds will be thought to be bottomless.

A factory owner, hearing what depth I had found, thought that it could not be true, for, judging from his acquaintance with dams, sand would not lie at so steep an angle. But the deepest ponds are not so deep in proportion to their area as most suppose, and, if drained, would not leave very remarkable valleys. They are not like cups between the hills; for this one, which is so unusually deep for its area, appears in a vertical section through its centre not deeper than a shallow plate. Most ponds, emptied, would leave a meadow no more hollow than we frequently see. William Gilpin, who is so admirable in all that relates to landscapes, and usually so correct, standing at the head of Loch Fyne, in Scotland, which he describes as "a bay of salt water, sixty or seventy fathoms deep, four miles in breadth," and about fifty miles long, surrounded by mountains, observes, "If we could have seen it immediately after the diluvian crash, or whatever convulsion of Nature occasioned it, before the waters gushed in, what a horrid chasm it must have appeared!"

"So high as heaved the tumid hills, so low
Down sunk a hollow bottom, broad, and deep,
Capacious bed of waters—."[344]

But if, using the shortest diameter of Loch Fyne, we apply these proportions to Walden, which, as we have seen, appears already in a vertical section only like a shallow plate, it will appear four times as shallow. So much for the *increased* horrors

---

[343] Weight of 56 pounds.   [344] From Milton's *Paradise Lost*, VII, 288–290.

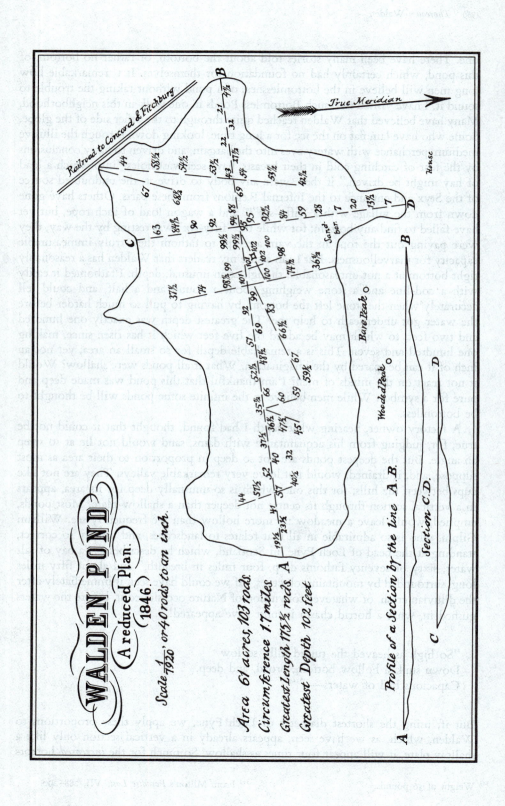

WALDEN POND
A reduced Plan.
(1846.)

Scale $\frac{1}{1020}$, or 40 rods to an inch.

Area 61 acres, 103 rods.
Circumference 1.7 miles.
Greatest Length 175½ rods.
Greatest Depth 102 feet.

True Meridian

Railroad to Concord & Fitchburg

House

Sand bar.

Bare Peak.

Wooded Peak.

Profile of a Section by the line A.B.

Section C.D.

of the chasm of Loch Fyne when emptied. No doubt many a smiling valley with its stretching cornfields occupies exactly such a "horrid chasm," from which the waters have receded, though it requires the insight and the far sight of the geologist to convince the unsuspecting inhabitants of this fact. Often an inquisitive eye may detect the shores of a primitive lake in the low horizon hills, and no subsequent elevation of the plain has been necessary to conceal their history. But it is easiest, as they who work on the highways know, to find the hollows by the puddles after a shower. The amount of it is, the imagination, give it the least license, dives deeper and soars higher than Nature goes. So, probably, the depth of the ocean will be found to be very inconsiderable compared with its breadth.

As I sounded through the ice I could determine the shape of the bottom with greater accuracy than is possible in surveying harbors which do not freeze over, and I was surprised at its general regularity. In the deepest part there are several acres more level than almost any field which is exposed to the sun wind and plough. In one instance, on a line arbitrarily chosen, the depth did not vary more than one foot in thirty rods; and generally, near the middle, I could calculate the variation for each one hundred feet in any direction beforehand within three or four inches. Some are accustomed to speak of deep and dangerous holes even in quiet sandy ponds like this, but the effect of water under these circumstances is to level all inequalities. The regularity of the bottom and its conformity to the shores and the range of the neighboring hills were so perfect that a distant promontory betrayed itself in the soundings quite across the pond, and its direction could be determined by observing the opposite shore. Cape becomes bar, and plain shoal, and valley and gorge deep water and channel.

When I had mapped the pond by the scale of ten rods to an inch, and put down the soundings, more than a hundred in all, I observed this remarkable coincidence. Having noticed that the number indicating the greatest depth was apparently in the centre of the map, I laid a rule on the map lengthwise, and then breadthwise, and found, to my surprise, that the line of greatest length intersected the line of greatest breadth *exactly* at the point of greatest depth, notwithstanding that the middle is so nearly level, the outline of the pond far from regular, and the extreme length and breadth were got by measuring into the coves; and I said to myself, Who knows but this hint would conduct to the deepest part of the ocean as well as of a pond or puddle? Is not this the rule also for the height of mountains, regarded as the opposite of valleys? We know that a hill is not highest at its narrowest part.

Of five coves, three, or all which had been sounded, were observed to have a bar quite across their mouths and deeper water within, so that the bay tended to be an expansion of water within the land not only horizontally but vertically, and to form a basin or independent pond, the direction of the two capes showing the course of the bar. Every harbor on the sea-coast, also, has its bar at its entrance. In proportion as the mouth of the cove was wider compared with its length, the water over the bar was deeper compared with that in the basin. Given, then, the length and breadth of the cove, and the character of the surrounding shore, and you have almost elements enough to make out a formula for all cases.

In order to see how nearly I could guess, with this experience, at the deepest point in a pond, by observing the outlines of its surface and the character of its shores alone, I made a plan of White Pond, which contains about forty-one acres, and, like this, has no island in it, nor any visible inlet or outlet; and as the line of greatest breadth fell very near the line of least breadth, where two opposite capes approached each other and two opposite bays receded, I ventured to mark a point a short distance from the latter line, but still on the line of greatest length, as the deepest. The deepest part was found to be within one hundred feet of this, still farther in the direction to which I had inclined, and was only one foot deeper, namely, sixty feet. Of course, a stream running through, or an island in the pond, would make the problem much more complicated.

If we knew all the laws of Nature, we should need only one fact, or the description of one actual phenomenon, to infer all the particular results at that point. Now we know only a few laws, and our result is vitiated, not, of course, by any confusion or irregularity in Nature, but by our ignorance of essential elements in the calculation. Our notions of law and harmony are commonly confined to those instances which we detect; but the harmony which results from a far greater number of seemingly conflicting, but really concurring, laws, which we have not detected, is still more wonderful. The particular laws are as our points of view, as, to the traveller, a mountain outline varies with every step, and it has an infinite number of profiles, though absolutely but one form. Even when cleft or bored through it is not comprehended in its entirety.

What I have observed of the pond is no less true in ethics. It is the law of average. Such a rule of the two diameters not only guides us toward the sun in the system and the heart in man, but draw lines through the length and breadth of the aggregate of a man's particular daily behaviors and waves of life into his coves and inlets, and where they intersect will be the height or depth of his character. Perhaps we need only to know how his shores trend and his adjacent country or circumstances, to infer his depth and concealed bottom. If he is surrounded by mountainous circumstances, an Achillean shore,[345] whose peaks overshadow and are reflected in his bosom, they suggest a corresponding depth in him. But a low and smooth shore proves him shallow on that side. In our bodies, a bold projecting brow falls off to and indicates a corresponding depth of thought. Also there is a bar across the entrance of our every cove, or particular inclination; each is our harbor for a season, in which we are detained and partially land-locked. These inclinations are not whimsical usually, but their form, size, and direction are determined by the promontories of the shore, the ancient axes of elevation. When this bar is gradually increased by storms, tides, or currents, or there is a subsidence of the waters, so that it reaches to the surface, that which was at first but an inclination in the shore in which a thought was harbored becomes an individual lake, cut off from the ocean, wherein the thought secures its own conditions, changes, perhaps, from salt to fresh, becomes a sweet sea, dead sea, or a marsh. At the advent of each individual into this life, may we not suppose that such a bar has risen to the surface somewhere? It is true, we are such poor navigators that our thoughts, for the most part, stand off and on upon a harborless coast, are conversant only with the bights of the bays of poesy, or steer for the public ports of entry, and go into the dry docks of science, where they merely refit for this world, and no natural currents concur to individualize them.

---

[345] Achilles' home in Thessaly, which is rocky and mountainous.

As for the inlet or outlet of Walden, I have not discovered any but rain and snow and evaporation, though perhaps, with a thermometer and a line, such places may be found, for where the water flows into the pond it will probably be coldest in summer and warmest in winter. When the ice-men were at work here in '46–7, the cakes sent to the shore were one day rejected by those who were stacking them up there, not being thick enough to lie side by side with the rest; and the cutters thus discovered that the ice over a small space was two or three inches thinner than elsewhere, which made them think that there was an inlet there. They also showed me in another place what they thought was a "leach hole," through which the pond leaked out under a hill into neighboring meadow, pushing me out on a cake of ice to see it. It was a small cavity under ten feet of water; but I think that I can warrant the pond not to need soldering till they find a worse leak than that. One has suggested, that if such a "leach hole" should be found, its connection with the meadow, if any existed, might be proved by conveying some colored powder or sawdust to the mouth of the hole, and then putting a strainer over the spring in the meadow, which would catch some of the particles carried through by the current.

While I was surveying, the ice, which was sixteen inches thick, undulated under a slight wind like water. It is well known that a level cannot be used on ice. At one rod from the shore its greatest fluctuation, when observed by means of a level on land directed toward a graduated staff on the ice, was three quarters of an inch, though the ice appeared firmly attached to the shore. It was probably greater in the middle. Who knows but if our instruments were delicate enough we might detect an undulation in the crust of the earth? When two legs of my level were on the shore and the third on the ice, and the sights were directed over the latter, a rise or fall of the ice of an almost infinitesimal amount made a difference of several feet on a tree across the pond. When I began to cut holes for sounding, there were three or four inches of water on the ice under a deep snow which had sunk it thus far; but the water began immediately to run into these holes, and continued to run for two days in deep streams, which wore away the ice on every side, and contributed essentially, if not mainly, to dry the surface of the pond; for, as the water ran in, it raised and floated the ice. This was somewhat like cutting a hole in the bottom of a ship to let the water out. When such holes freeze, and a rain succeeds, and finally a new freezing forms a fresh smooth ice over all, it is beautifully mottled internally by dark figures, shaped somewhat like a spider's web, what you may call ice rosettes, produced by the channels worn by the water flowing from all sides to a centre. Sometimes, also, when the ice was covered with shallow puddles, I saw a double shadow of myself, one standing on the head of the other, one on the ice, the other on the trees or hillside.

While yet it is cold January, and snow and ice are thick and solid, the prudent landlord comes from the village to get ice to cool his summer drink; impressively, even pathetically wise, to foresee the heat and thirst of July now in January,—wearing a thick coat and mittens! when so many things are not provided for. It may be that he lays up no treasures in this world which will cool his summer drink in the next. He cuts and saws the solid pond, unroofs the house of fishes, and carts off their very element and air, held fast by chains and stakes like corded wood, through the favoring winter air, to wintry cellars, to underlie the summer there. It looks like solidified azure, as, far off, it is drawn through the streets. These ice-cutters are a merry race, full of jest and sport, and when I went among them they were wont to invite me to saw pit-fashion with them, I standing underneath.

In the winter of '46–7 there came a hundred men of Hyperborean extraction[346] swoop down on to our pond one morning, with many car-loads of ungainly-looking farming tools, sleds, ploughs, drill-barrows, turf-knives, spades, saws, rakes, and each man was armed with a double-pointed pike-staff, such as is not described in the New-England Farmer or the Cultivator.[347] I did not know whether they had come to sow a crop of winter rye, or some other kind of grain recently introduced from Iceland. As I saw no manure, I judged that they meant to skim the land, as I had done, thinking the soil was deep and had lain fallow long enough. They said that a gentleman farmer, who was behind the scenes, wanted to double his money, which, as I understood, amounted to half a million already; but in order to cover each one of his dollars with another, he took off the only coat, ay, the skin itself, of Walden Pond in the midst of a hard winter. They went to work at once, ploughing, harrow-ing, rolling, furrowing, in admirable order, as if they were bent on making this a model farm; but when I was looking sharp to see what kind of seed they dropped into the furrow, a gang of fellows by my side suddenly began to hook up the virgin mould itself, with a peculiar jerk, clean down to the sand, or rather the water,—for it was a very springy soil,—indeed all the *terra firma* there was, and haul it away on sleds, and then I guessed that they must be cutting peat in a bog. So they came and went every day, with a peculiar shriek from the locomotive, from and to some point of the polar regions, as it seemed to me, like a flock of arctic snow-birds. But sometimes Squaw Walden had her revenge, and a hired man, walking behind his team, slipped through a crack in the ground down toward Tartarus,[348] and he who was so brave before suddenly became but the ninth part of a man, almost gave up his animal heat, and was glad to take refuge in my house, and acknowledged that there was some virtue in a stove; or sometimes the frozen soil took a piece of steel out of a ploughshare, or a plough got set in the furrow and had to be cut out.

To speak literally, a hundred Irishmen, with Yankee overseers, came from Cam-bridge every day to get out the ice. They divided it into cakes by methods too well known to require description, and these, being sledded to the shore, were rapidly hauled off on to an ice platform, and raised by grappling irons and block and tackle, worked by horses, on to a stack, as surely as so many barrels of flour, and there placed evenly side by side, and row upon row, as if they formed the solid base of an obelisk designed to pierce the clouds. They told me that in a good day they could get out a thousand tons, which was the yield of about one acre. Deep ruts and "cradle holes" were worn in the ice, as on *terra firma,* by the passage of the sleds over the same track, and the horses invariably ate their oats out of cakes of ice hollowed out like buckets. They stacked up the cakes thus in the open air in a pile thirty-five feet high on one side and six or seven rods square, putting hay between the outside layers to exclude the air; for when the wind, though never so cold, finds a passage through, it will wear large cavities, leaving slight supports or studs only here and there, and finally topple it down. At first it looked like a vast blue fort or Valhalla; but when they began to tuck the coarse meadow hay into the crevices, and this became covered with rime and

---

[346] Invaders from the north in classic myth; for Thoreau, they are the Irish.

[347] Farmers' journals.

[348] In classic myth, the abyss that lies below Hades.

icicles, it looked like a venerable moss-grown and hoary ruin, built of azure-tinted marble, the abode of Winter, that old man we see in the almanac,—his shanty, as if he had a design to estivate[349] with us. They calculated that not twenty-five per cent. of this would reach its destination, and that two or three per cent. would be wasted in the cars. However, a still greater part of this heap had a different destiny from what was intended; for, either because the ice was found not to keep so well as was expected, containing more air than usual, or for some other reason, it never got to market. This heap, made in the winter of '46–7 and estimated to contain ten thousand tons, was finally covered with hay and boards; and though it was unroofed the following July, and a part of it carried off, the rest remaining exposed to the sun, it stood over that summer and the next winter, and was not quite melted till September 1848. Thus the pond recovered the greater part.

Like the water, the Walden ice, seen near at hand, has a green tint, but at a distance is beautifully blue, and you can easily tell it from the white ice of the river, or the merely greenish ice of some ponds, a quarter of a mile off. Sometimes one of those great cakes slips from the ice-man's sled into the village street, and lies there for a week like a great emerald, an object of interest to all passers. I have noticed that a portion of Walden which in the state of water was green will often, when frozen, appear from the same point of view blue. So the hollows about this pond will, sometimes, in the winter, be filled with a greenish water somewhat like its own, but the next day will have frozen blue. Perhaps the blue color of water and ice is due to the light and air they contain, and the most transparent is the bluest. Ice is an interesting subject for contemplation. They told me that they had some in the ice-houses at Fresh Pond five years old which was as good as ever. Why is it that a bucket of water soon becomes putrid, but frozen remains sweet forever? It is commonly said that this is the difference between the affections and the intellect.

Thus for sixteen days I saw from my window a hundred men at work like busy husbandmen, with teams and horses and apparently all the implements of farming, such a picture as we see on the first page of the almanac; and as often as I looked out I was reminded of the fable of the lark and the reapers, or the parable of the sower, and the like; and now they are all gone, and in thirty days more, probably, I shall look from the same window on the pure sea-green Walden water there, reflecting the clouds and the trees, and sending up its evaporations in solitude, and no traces will appear that a man has ever stood there. Perhaps I shall hear a solitary loon laugh as he dives and plumes himself, or shall see a lonely fisher in his boat, like a floating leaf, beholding his form reflected in the waves, where lately a hundred men securely labored.

Thus it appears that the sweltering inhabitants of Charleston and New Orleans, of Madras and Bombay and Calcutta, drink at my well. In the morning I bathe my intellect in the stupendous and cosmogonal philosophy of the Bhagvat Geeta, since whose composition years of the gods have elapsed, and in comparison with which our modern world and its literature seem puny and trivial; and I doubt if that philosophy is not to be referred to a previous state of existence, so remote is its sublimity from our conceptions. I lay down the book and go to my well for water, and lo! there I meet the servant of the Brahmin, priest of Brahma and Vishnu and Indra,[350] who

---

[349] To spend the summer.   [350] Hindu deities.

still sits in his temple on the Ganges reading the Vedas, or dwells at the root of a tree with his crust and water jug. I meet his servant come to draw water for his master, and our buckets as it were grate together in the same well. The pure Walden water is mingled with the sacred water of the Ganges. With favoring winds it is wafted past the site of the fabulous islands of Atlantis and the Hesperides,[351] makes the periplus of Hanno,[352] and, floating by Ternate and Tidore[353] and the mouth of the Persian Gulf, melts in the tropic gales of the Indian seas, and is landed in ports of which Alexander[354] only heard the names.

Spring

The opening of large tracts by the ice-cutters commonly causes a pond to break up earlier; for the water, agitated by the wind, even in cold weather, wears away the surrounding ice. But such was not the effect on Walden that year, for she had soon got a thick new garment to take the place of the old. This pond never breaks up so soon as the others in this neighborhood, on account both of its greater depth and its having no stream passing through it to melt or wear away the ice. I never knew it to open in the course of a winter, not excepting that of '52–3, which gave the ponds so severe a trial. It commonly opens about the first of April, a week or ten days later than Flint's Pond and Fair-Haven, beginning to melt on the north side and in the shallower parts where it began to freeze. It indicates better than any water hereabouts the absolute progress of the season, being least affected by transient changes of temperature. A severe cold of a few days' duration in March may very much retard the opening of the former ponds, while the temperature of Walden increases almost uninterruptedly. A thermometer thrust into the middle of Walden on the 6th of March, 1847, stood at 32°, or freezing point; near the shore at 33°; in the middle of Flint's Pond, the same day, at 32 1/2°; at a dozen rods from the shore, in shallow water, under ice a foot thick, at 36°. This difference of three and a half degrees between the temperature of the deep water and the shallow in the latter pond, and the fact that a great proportion of it is comparatively shallow, show why it should break up so much sooner than Walden. The ice in the shallowest part was at this time several inches thinner than in the middle. In mid-winter the middle had been the warmest and the ice thinnest there. So, also, every one who has waded about the shores of a pond in summer must have perceived how much warmer the water is close to the shore, where only three or four inches deep, than a little distance out, and on the surface where it is deep, than near the bottom. In spring the sun not only exerts an influence through the increased temperature of the air and earth, but its heat passes through ice a foot or more thick, and is reflected from the bottom in shallow water, and so also warms the water and melts the under side of the ice, at the same time that it is melting it more directly above, making it uneven, and causing the air bubbles which it contains to extend themselves upward and downward until it is completely honeycombed, and at last disappears suddenly in a single spring rain. Ice has its grain as well as wood,

---

[351] Mythical islands at the westernmost ends of the known world in ancient times.
[352] Journal kept by Hanno, Carthaginian explorer of the sixth century B.C.

[353] Islands in the East Indies.
[354] Alexander the Great.

and when a cake begins to rot or "comb," that is, assume the appearance of honey-comb, whatever may be its position, the air cells are at right angles with what was the water surface. Where there is a rock or a log rising near to the surface the ice over it is much thinner, and is frequently quite dissolved by this reflected heat; and I have been told that in the experiment at Cambridge to freeze water in a shallow wooden pond, though the cold air circulated underneath, and so had access to both sides, the reflection of the sun from the bottom more than counterbalanced this advantage. When a warm rain in the middle of the winter melts off the snow-ice from Walden, and leaves a hard dark or transparent ice on the middle, there will be a strip of rotten though thicker white ice, a rod or more wide, about the shores, created by this reflected heat. Also, as I have said, the bubbles themselves within the ice operate as burning glasses to melt the ice beneath.

The phenomena of the year take place every day in a pond on a small scale. Every morning, generally speaking, the shallow water is being warmed more rapidly than the deep, though it may not be made so warm after all, and every evening it is being cooled more rapidly until the morning. The day is an epitome of the year. The night is the winter, the morning and evening are the spring and fall, and the noon is the summer. The cracking and booming of the ice indicate a change of temperature. One pleasant morning after a cold night, February 24th, 1850, having gone to Flint's Pond to spend the day, I noticed with surprise, that when I struck the ice with the head of my axe, it resounded like a gong for many rods around, or as if I had struck on a tight drum-head. The pond began to boom about an hour after sunrise, when it felt the influence of the sun's rays slanted upon it from over the hills; it stretched itself and yawned like a waking man with a gradually increasing tumult, which was kept up three or four hours. It took a short siesta at noon, and boomed once more toward night, as the sun was withdrawing his influence. In the right state of the weather a pond fires its evening gun with great regularity. But in the middle of the day, being full of cracks, and the air also being less elastic, it had completely lost its resonance, and probably fishes and muskrats could not then have been stunned by a blow on it. The fishermen say that the "thundering of the pond" scares the fishes and prevents their biting. The pond does not thunder every evening, and I cannot tell surely when to expect its thundering; but though I may perceive no difference in the weather, it does. Who would have suspected so large and cold and thick-skinned a thing to be so sensitive? Yet it has its law to which it thunders obedience when it should as surely as the buds expand in the spring. The earth is all alive and covered with papillæ. The largest pond is as sensitive to atmospheric changes as the globule of mercury in its tube.

One attraction in coming to the woods to live was that I should have leisure and opportunity to see the spring come in. The ice in the pond at length begins to be honey-combed, and I can set my heel in it as I walk. Fogs and rains and warmer suns are gradually melting the snow; the days have grown sensibly longer; and I see how I shall get through the winter without adding to my wood-pile, for large fires are no longer necessary. I am on the alert for the first signs of spring, to hear the chance note of some arriving bird, or the striped squirrel's chirp, for his stores must be now nearly exhausted, or see the woodchuck venture out of his winter quarters. On the 13th of March, after I had heard the bluebird, song-sparrow, and red-wing, the ice was still nearly a foot thick. As the weather grew warmer, it was not sensibly worn away by the water, nor broken up and floated off as in rivers, but, though it was completely melted for half a rod in width about the shore, the middle was merely honey-combed and saturated with water, so that you could put your foot through it when six inches thick; but by the next day evening, perhaps, after a warm rain followed by fog, it would have wholly disappeared, all gone off with the fog, spirited away. One year I went across the middle only five days before it disappeared entirely. In 1845 Walden was first completely open on the 1st of April; in '46, the 25th of March; in '47, the 8th of April; in '51, the 28th of March; in '52, the 18th of April, in '53, the 23d of March; in '54, about the 7th of April.

Every incident connected with the breaking up of the rivers and ponds and the settling of the weather is particularly interesting to us who live in a climate of so great extremes. When the warmer days come, they who dwell near the river hear the ice crack at night with a startling whoop as loud as artillery, as if its icy fetters were rent from end to end, and within a few days see it rapidly going out. So the alligator comes out of the mud with quakings of the earth. One old man, who has been a close observer of Nature, and seems as thoroughly wise in regard to all her operations as if she had been put upon the stocks when he was a boy, and he had helped to lay her keel,—who has come to his growth, and can hardly acquire more of natural lore if he should live to the age of Methuselah,[355]—told me, and I was surprised to hear him express wonder at any of Nature's operations, for I thought that there were no secrets between them, that one spring day he took his gun and boat, and thought that he would have a little sport with the ducks. There was ice still on the meadows, but it was all gone out of the river, and he dropped down without obstruction from Sudbury, where he lived, to Fair-Haven Pond, which he found, unexpectedly, covered for the most part with a firm field of ice. It was a warm day, and he was surprised to see so great a body of ice remaining. Not seeing any ducks, he hid his boat on the north or back side of an island in the pond, and then concealed himself in the bushes on the south side, to await them. The ice was melted for three or four rods from the shore, and there was a smooth and warm sheet of water, with a muddy bottom, such as the ducks love, within, and he thought it likely that some would be along pretty soon. After he had lain still there about an hour he heard a low and seemingly very distant sound, but singularly grand and impressive, unlike any thing he had ever heard, gradually swelling and increasing as if it would have a universal and memorable ending, a sullen rush and roar, which seemed to him all at once like the sound of a vast body of fowl coming in to settle there, and, seizing his gun, he started up in haste and excited; but he found, to his surprise, that the whole body of the ice had started while he lay there, and drifted in to the shore, and the sound he had heard was made by its edge grating on the shore,—at first gently nibbled and crumbled off, but at length heaving up and scattering its wrecks along the island to a considerable height before it came to a stand still.

At length the sun's rays have attained the right angle, and warm winds blow up mist and rain and melt the snow banks, and the sun dispersing the mist smiles on a checkered landscape of russet and white smoking with incense, through which the traveller picks his way from islet to islet, cheered by the music of a thousand tinkling

---

[355] He lived 969 years (Genesis 5:27).

rills and rivulets whose veins are filled with the blood of winter which they are
bearing off.

Few phenomena gave me more delight than to observe the forms which thawing
sand and clay assume in flowing down the sides of a deep cut on the railroad through
which I passed on my way to the village, a phenomenon not very common on so
large a scale, though the number of freshly exposed banks of the right material must
have been greatly multiplied since railroads were invented. The material was sand of
every degree of fineness and of various rich colors, commonly mixed with a little clay.
When the frost comes out in the spring, and even in a thawing day in the winter,
the sand begins to flow down the slopes like lava, sometimes bursting out through
the snow and overflowing it where no sand was to be seen before. Innumerable little
streams overlap and interlace one with another, exhibiting a sort of hybrid product,
which obeys half way the law of currents, and half way that of vegetation. As it flows
it takes the forms of sappy leaves or vines, making heaps of pulpy sprays a foot or
more in depth, and resembling, as you look down on them, the laciniated lobed and
imbricated thalluses of some lichens; or you are reminded of coral, of leopards' paws
or birds' feet, of brains or lungs or bowels, and excrements of all kinds. It is a truly
grotesque vegetation, whose forms and color we see imitated in bronze, a sort of
architectural foliage more ancient and typical than acanthus, chiccory, ivy, vine, or
any vegetable leaves; destined perhaps, under some circumstances, to become a puzzle
to future geologists. The whole cut impressed me as if it were a cave with its stalactites
laid open to the light. The various shades of the sand are singularly rich and agreeable,
embracing the different iron colors, brown, gray, yellowish, and reddish. When the
flowing mass reaches the drain at the foot of the bank it spreads out flatter into *strands,*
the separate streams losing their semi-cylindrical form and gradually becoming more
flat and broad, running together as they are more moist, till they form an almost flat
sand, still variously and beautifully shaded, but in which you can trace the original
forms of vegetation; till at length, in the water itself, they are converted into *banks,*
like those formed off the mouths of rivers, and the forms of vegetation are lost in
the ripple marks on the bottom.

The whole bank, which is from twenty to forty feet high, is sometimes overlaid
with a mass of this kind of foliage, or sandy rupture, for a quarter of a mile on one
or both sides, the produce of one spring day. What makes this sand foliage remarkable
is its springing into existence thus suddenly. When I see on the one side the inert bank,
—for the sun acts on one side first,—and on the other this luxuriant foliage, the
creation of an hour, I am affected as if in a peculiar sense I stood in the laboratory
of the Artist who made the world and me,—had come to where he was still at work,
sporting on this bank, and with excess of energy strewing his fresh designs about. I
feel as if I were nearer to the vitals of the globe, for this sandy overflow is something
such a foliaceous mass as the vitals of the animal body. You find thus in the very sands
an anticipation of the vegetable leaf. No wonder that the earth expresses itself
outwardly in leaves, it so labors with the idea inwardly. The atoms have already
learned this law, and are pregnant by it. The overhanging leaf sees here its prototype.
Internally, whether in the globe or animal body, it is a moist thick *lobe,* a word
especially applicable to the liver and lungs and the *leaves* of fat, ($\lambda\epsilon\iota\beta\omega$, *labor, lapsus,*
to flow or slip downward, a lapsing; $\lambda o\beta o\varsigma$, *globus,* lobe, globe; also lap, flap, and
many other words,) *externally* a dry thin *leaf,* even as the *f* and *v* are a pressed and

dried *b.* The radicals of lobe are *lb,* the soft mass of the *b* (single lobed, or B, double lobed,) with a liquid *l* behind it pressing it forward. In globe, *glb,* the guttural *g* adds to the meaning the capacity of the throat. The feathers and wings of birds are still drier and thinner leaves. Thus, also, you pass from the lumpish grub in the earth to the airy and fluttering butterfly. The very globe continually transcends and translates itself, and becomes winged in its orbit. Even ice begins with delicate crystal leaves, as if it had flowed into moulds which the fronds of water plants have impressed on the watery mirror. The whole tree itself is but one leaf, and rivers are still vaster leaves whose pulp is intervening earth, and towns and cities are the ova of insects in their axils.

When the sun withdraws the sand ceases to flow, but in the morning the streams will start once more and branch and branch again into a myriad of others. You here see perchance how blood vessels are formed. If you look closely you observe that first there pushes forward from the thawing mass a stream of softened sand with a drop-like point, like the ball of the finger, feeling its way slowly and blindly downward, until at last with more heat and moisture, as the sun gets higher, the most fluid portion, in its effort to obey the law to which the most inert also yields, separates from the latter and forms for itself a meandering channel or artery within that, in which is seen a little silvery stream glancing like lightning from one stage of pulpy leaves or branches to another, and ever and anon swallowed up in the sand. It is wonderful how rapidly yet perfectly the sand organizes itself as it flows, using the best material its mass affords to form the sharp edges of its channel. Such are the sources of rivers. In the silicious matter which the water deposits is perhaps the bony system, and in the still finer soil and organic matter the fleshy fibre or cellular tissue. What is man but a mass of thawing clay? The ball of the human finger is but a drop congealed. The fingers and toes flow to their extent from the thawing mass of the body. Who knows what the human body would expand and flow out to under a more genial heaven? Is not the hand a spreading *palm* leaf with its lobes and veins? The ear may be regarded, fancifully, as a lichen, *umbilicaria,* on the side of the head, with its lobe or drop. The lip (*labium* from *labor* (?)) laps or lapses from the sides of the cavernous mouth. The nose is a manifest congealed drop or stalactite. The chin is a still larger drop, the confluent dripping of the face. The cheeks are a slide from the brows into the valley of the face, opposed and diffused by the cheek bones. Each rounded lobe of the vegetable leaf, too, is a thick and now loitering drop, larger or smaller; the lobes are the fingers of the leaf; and as many lobes as it has, in so many directions it tends to flow, and more heat or other genial influences would have caused it to flow yet farther.

Thus it seemed that this one hillside illustrated the principle of all the operations of Nature. The Maker of this earth but patented a leaf. What Champollion[356] will decipher this hieroglyphic for us, that we may turn over a new leaf at last? This phenomenon is more exhilarating to me than the luxuriance and fertility of vineyards. True, it is somewhat excrementitious in its character, and there is no end to the heaps of liver lights and bowels, as if the globe were turned wrong side outward; but this suggests at least that Nature has some bowels, and there again is mother of humanity. This is the frost coming out of the ground; this is Spring. It precedes the green and

[356] Jean François Champollion (1790–1832), Frenchman who deciphered the hieroglyphics inscribed on the Rosetta Stone and thus opened up ancient Egyptian culture to contemporary knowledge.

flowery spring, as mythology precedes regular poetry. I know of nothing more purgative of winter fumes and indigestions. It convinces me that Earth is still in her swaddling clothes, and stretches forth baby fingers on every side. Fresh curls spring from the baldest brow. There is nothing inorganic. These foliaceous heaps lie along the bank like the slag of a furnace, showing that Nature is "in full blast" within. The earth is not a mere fragment of dead history, stratum upon stratum like the leaves of a book, to be studied by geologists and antiquaries chiefly, but living poetry like the leaves of a tree, which precede flowers and fruit,—not a fossil earth, but a living earth; compared with whose great central life all animal and vegetable life is merely parasitic. Its throes will heave our exuviæ from their graves. You may melt your metals and cast them into the most beautiful moulds you can; they will never excite me like the forms which this molten earth flows out into. And not only it, but the institutions upon it, are plastic like clay in the hands of the potter.

Ere long, not only on these banks, but on every hill and plain and in every hollow, the frost comes out of the ground like a dormant quadruped from its burrow, and seeks the sea with music, or migrates to other climes in clouds. Thaw with his gentle persuasion is more powerful than Thor[357] with his hammer. The one melts, the other but breaks in pieces.

When the ground was partially bare of snow, and a few warm days had dried its surface somewhat, it was pleasant to compare the first tender signs of the infant year just peeping forth with stately beauty of the withered vegetation which had withstood the winter,—life-everlasting, golden-rods, pinweeds, and graceful wild grasses, more obvious and interesting frequently than in summer even, as if their beauty was not ripe till then; even cotton-grass, cat-tails, mulleins, johnswort, hard-hack, meadow-sweet, and other strong stemmed plants, those unexhausted granaries which entertain the earliest birds,—decent weeds, at least, which widowed Nature wears. I am particularly attracted by the arching and sheaf-like top of the wool-grass; it brings back the summer to our winter memories, and is among the forms which art loves to copy, and which, in the vegetable kingdom, have the same relation to types already in the mind of man that astronomy has. It is an antique style older than Greek or Egyptian. Many of the phenomena of Winter are suggestive of an inexpressible tenderness and fragile delicacy. We are accustomed to hear this king described as a rude and boisterous tyrant; but with the gentleness of a lover he adorns the tresses of Summer.

At the approach of spring the red-squirrels got under my house, two at a time, directly under my feet as I sat reading or writing, and kept up the queerest chuckling and chirruping and vocal pirouetting and gurgling sounds that ever were heard; and when I stamped they only chirruped the louder, as if past all fear and respect in their mad pranks, defying humanity to stop them. No you don't—chickaree—chickaree. They were wholly deaf to my arguments, or failed to perceive their force, and fell into a strain of invective that was irresistible.

The first sparrow of spring! The year beginning with younger hope than ever! The faint silvery warblings heard over the partially bare and moist fields from the blue-bird, the song-sparrow, and the red-wing, as if the last flakes of winter tinkled as they fell! What at such a time are histories, chronologies, traditions, and all written

---

[357] Norse god of thunder, whose name Thoreau liked to associate with his own.

revelations? The brooks sing carols and glees to the spring. The marsh-hawk sailing low over the meadow is already seeking the first slimy life that awakes. The sinking sound of melting snow is heard in all dells, and the ice dissolves apace in the ponds. The grass flames up on the hillsides like a spring fire,—"et primitus oritur herba imbribus primoribus evocata,"[358]—as if the earth sent forth an inward heat to greet the returning sun; not yellow but green is the color of its flame;—the symbol of perpetual youth, the grass-blade, like a long green ribbon, streams from the sod into the summer, checked indeed by the frost, but anon pushing on again, lifting its spear of last year's hay with the fresh life below. It grows as steadily as the rill oozes out of the ground. It is almost identical with that, for in the growing days of June, when the rills are dry, the grass blades are their channels, and from year to year the herds drink at this perennial green stream, and the mower draws from it betimes their winter supply. So our human life but dies down to its root, and still puts forth its green blade to eternity.

Walden is melting apace. There is a canal two rods wide along the northerly and westerly sides, and wider still at the east end. A great field of ice has cracked off from the main body. I hear a song-sparrow singing from the bushes on the shore,—*olit, olit, olit,—chip, chip, chip, che char,—che wiss, wiss, wiss.* He too is helping to crack it. How handsome the great sweeping curves in the edge of the ice, answering somewhat to those of the shore, but more regular! It is unusually hard, owing to the recent severe but transient cold, and all watered or waved like a palace floor. But the wind slides eastward over its opaque surface in vain, till it reaches the living surface beyond. It is glorious to behold this ribbon of water sparkling in the sun, the bare face of the pond full of glee and youth, as if it spoke the joy of the fishes within it, and of the sands on its shore,—a silvery sheen as from the scales of a *leuciscus,*[359] as it were all one active fish. Such is the contrast between winter and spring. Walden was dead and is alive again.[360] But this spring it broke up more steadily, as I have said.

The change from storm and winter to serene and mild weather, from dark and sluggish hours to bright and elastic ones, is a memorable crisis which all things proclaim. It is seemingly instantaneous at last. Suddenly an influx of light filled my house, though the evening was at hand, and the clouds of winter still overhung it, and the eaves were dripping with sleety rain. I looked out the window, and lo! where yesterday was cold gray ice there lay the transparent pond already calm and full of hope as on a summer evening, reflecting a summer evening sky in its bosom, though none was visible overhead, as if it had intelligence with some remote horizon. I heard a robin in the distance, the first I had heard for many a thousand years, methought, whose note I shall not forget for many a thousand more,—the same sweet and powerful song of yore. O the evening robin, at the end of a New England summer day! If I could ever find the twig he sits upon! I mean *he;* I mean *the twig.* This at least is not the *Turdus migratorius.*[361] The pitch-pines and shrub-oaks about my house, which had so long drooped, suddenly resumed their several characters, looked brighter, greener, and more erect and alive, as if effectually cleansed and restored by the rain. I knew that it would not rain any more. You may tell by looking at any

---

[358] Latin: "and summonded by the early rains, the grass starts to grow." From *De Re Rustica* by Varro (116–27 B.C.).

[359] Freshwater fish.

[360] Here Thoreau echoes the language of the New Testament in the parable of the Prodigal Son, with perhaps also an allusion to Christ's resurrection.

[361] American robin.

twig of the forest, ay, at your very wood-pile, whether its winter is past or not. As it grew darker, I was startled by the *honking* of geese flying low over the woods, like weary travellers getting in late from southern lakes, and indulging at last in unrestrained complaint and mutual consolation. Standing at my door, I could hear the rush of their wings; when, driving toward my house, they suddenly spied my light, and with hushed clamor wheeled and settled in the pond. So I came in, and shut the door, and passed my first spring night in the woods.

In the morning I watched the geese from the door through the mist, sailing in the middle of the pond, fifty rods off, so large and tumultuous that Walden appeared like an artificial pond for their amusement. But when I stood on the shore they at once rose up with a great flapping of wings at the signal of their commander, and when they had got into rank circled about over my head, twenty-nine of them, and then steered straight to Canada, with a regular *honk* from the leader at intervals, trusting to break their fast in muddier pools. A "plump"[362] of ducks rose at the same time and took the route to the north in the wake of their noisier cousins.

For a week I heard the circling groping clangor of some solitary goose in the foggy mornings, seeking its companion, and still peopling the woods with the sound of a larger life than they could sustain. In April the pigeons were seen again flying express in small flocks, and in due time I heard the martins twittering over my clearing, though it had not seemed that the township contained so many that it could afford me any, and I fancied that they were peculiarly of the ancient race that dwelt in hollow trees ere white men came. In almost all climes the tortoise and the frog are among the precursors and heralds of this season, and birds fly with song and glancing plumage, and plants spring and bloom, and winds blow, to correct this slight oscillation of the poles and preserve the equilibrium of Nature.

As every season seems best to us in its turn, so the coming in of spring is like the creation of Cosmos out of Chaos and the realization of the Golden Age.—

"Eurus ad Auroram, Nabathæaque regna recessit,
    Persidaque, et radiis juga subdita matutinis."

"The East-Wind withdrew to Aurora and the
    Nabathæan kingdom,
And the Persian, and the ridges placed under
    the morning rays.
            *   *   *
Man was born. Whether that Artificer of things,
The origin of a better world, made him from
    the divine seed;
Or the earth being recent and lately sundered
    from the high
Ether, retained some seeds of cognate heaven."[363]

A single gentle rain makes the grass many shades greener. So our prospects brighten on the influx of better thoughts. We should be blessed if we lived in the present always, and took advantage of every accident that befell us, like the grass which

---

[362] Flock.   [363] From Ovid's *Metamorphoses*, Book I.

confesses the influence of the slightest dew that falls on it; and did not spend our time in atoning for the neglect of past opportunities, which we call doing our duty. We loiter in winter while it is already spring. In a pleasant spring morning all men's sins are forgiven. Such a day is a truce to vice. While such a sun holds out to burn, the vilest sinner may return. Through our own recovered innocence we discern the innocence of our neighbors. You may have known your neighbor yesterday for a thief, a drunkard, or a sensualist, and merely pitied or despised him, and despaired of the world; but the sun shines bright and warm this first spring morning, re-creating the world, and you meet him at some serene work, and see how his exhausted and debauched veins expand with still joy and bless the new day, feel the spring influence with the innocence of infancy, and all his faults are forgotten. There is not only an atmosphere of good will about him, but even a savor of holiness groping for expression, blindly and ineffectually perhaps, like a new-born instinct, and for a short hour the south hill-side echoes to no vulgar jest. You see some innocent fair shoots preparing to burst from his gnarled rind and try another year's life, tender and fresh as the youngest plant. Even he has entered into the joy of his Lord. Why the jailer does not leave open his prison doors,—why the judge does not dismiss his case,—why the preacher does not dismiss his congregation! It is because they do not obey the hint which God gives them, nor accept the pardon which he freely offers to all.

"A return to goodness produced each day in the tranquil and beneficent breath of the morning, causes that in respect to the love of virtue and the hatred of vice, one approaches a little the primitive nature of man, as the sprouts of the forest which has been felled. In like manner the evil which one does in the interval of a day prevents the germs of virtues which began to spring up again from developing themselves and destroys them.

"After the germs of virtue have thus been prevented many times from developing themselves, then the beneficent breath of evening does not suffice to preserve them. As soon as the breath of evening does not suffice longer to preserve them, then the nature of man does not differ much from that of the brute. Men seeing the nature of this man like that of the brute, think that he has never possessed the innate faculty of reason. Are those the true and natural sentiments of man?"[364]

> "The Golden Age was first created, which without
>   any avenger
> Spontaneously without law cherished fidelity and
>   rectitude.
> Punishment and fear were not; nor were threaten-
>   ing words read
> On suspended brass; nor did the suppliant crowd
>   fear
> The words of their judge; but were safe without
>   an avenger.
> Not yet the pine felled on its mountains had de-
>   scended

[364] From *The Book of Mencius*. The lines that follow are again from *Metamorphoses*, Book I.

> To the liquid waves that it might see a foreign
>   world,
> And mortals knew no shores but their own.
>   *   *   *
> There was eternal spring, and placid zephyrs with
>   warm
> Blasts soothed the flowers born without seed."

On the 29th of April, as I was fishing from the bank of th
Nine-Acre-Corner bridge, standing on the quaking grass and willow
muskrats lurk, I heard a singular rattling sound, somewhat like that of he
boys play with their fingers, when, looking up, I observed a very sli
hawk, like a night-hawk, alternately soaring like a ripple and tumblir
over and over, showing the underside of its wings, which gleamed lik
in the sun, or like the pearly inside of a shell. This sight reminded
and what nobleness and poetry are associated with that sport. The M
to me it might be called: but I care not for its name. It was the most
I had ever witnessed. It did not simply flutter like a butterfly, nor soar h
hawks, but it sported with proud reliance in the fields of air; mounting agair.
with its strange chuckle, it repeated its free and beautiful fall, turning over
like a kite, and then recovering from its lofty tumbling, as if it had never set i.
on *terra firma*. It appeared to have no companion in the universe,—sporting t.
alone,—and to need none but the morning and the ether with which it played. It w.
not lonely, but made all the earth lonely beneath it. Where was the parent which
hatched it, its kindred, and its father in the heavens? The tenant of the air, it seemed
related to the earth but by an egg hatched some time in the crevice of a crag;—or
was its native nest made in the angle of a cloud, woven of the rainbow's trimmings
and the sunset sky, and lined with some soft midsummer haze caught up from earth?
Its eyry[365] now some cliffy cloud.

Beside this I got a rare mess of golden and silver and bright cupreous fishes, which
looked like a string of jewels. Ah! I have penetrated to those meadows on the morning
of many a first spring day, jumping from hummock to hummock, from willow root
to willow root, when the wild river valley and the woods were bathed in so pure
and bright a light as would have waked the dead, if they had been slumbering in their
graves, as some suppose. There needs no stronger proof of immortality. All things must
live in such a light. O Death, where was thy sting? O Grave, where was thy victory,
then?[366]

Our village life would stagnate if it were not for the unexplored forests and
meadows which surround it. We need the tonic of wildness,—to wade sometimes in
marshes where the bittern and the meadow-hen lurk, and hear the booming of the
snipe; to smell the whispering sedge where only some wilder and more solitary fowl
builds her nest, and the mink crawls with its belly close to the ground. At the same
time that we are earnest to explore and learn all things, we require that all things be
mysterious and unexplorable, that land and sea be infinitely wild, unsurveyed and
unfathomed by us because unfathomable. We can never have enough of Nature. We

[365] Bird's nest.   [366] Allusion to 1 Corinthians 15:55.

by the sight of inexhaustible vigor, vast and Titanic features, the
must be ref wrecks, the wilderness with its living and its decaying trees, the
sea-coast nd the rain which lasts three weeks and produces freshets. We need
thunde wn limits transgressed, and some life pasturing freely where we never
to w re cheered when we observe the vulture feeding on the carrion which
wi isheartens us and deriving health and strength from the repast. There
i horse in the hollow by the path to my house, which compelled me
ce it gave me of the strong appetite and inviolable health of Nature was
ensation for this. I love to see that Nature is so rife with life that myriads
fforded to be sacrificed and suffered to prey on one another; that tender
ations can be so serenely squashed out of existence like pulp,—tadpoles which
gobble up, and tortoises and toads run over in the road; and that sometimes
rained flesh and blood! With the liability to accident, we must see how little
nt is to be made of it. The impression made on a wise man is that of universal
cence. Poison is not poisonous after all, nor are any wounds fatal. Compassion
very untenable ground. It must be expeditious. Its pleadings will not bear to be
reotyped.

Early in May, the oaks, hickories, maples, and other trees, just putting out amidst
the pine woods around the pond, imparted a brightness like sunshine to the landscape,
especially in cloudy days, as if the sun were breaking through mists and shining faintly
on the hill-sides here and there. On the third or fourth of May I saw a loon in the
pond, and during the first week of the month I heard the whippoorwill, the brown-
thrasher, the veery, the wood-pewee, the chewink, and other birds. I had heard the
wood-thrush long before. The phoebe had already come once more and looked in
at my door and window, to see if my house was cavern-like enough for her, sustaining
herself on humming wings with clinched talons, as if she held by the air, while she
surveyed the premises. The sulphur-like pollen of the pitch-pine soon covered the
pond and the stones and rotten wood along the shore, so that you could have collected
a barrel-ful. This is the "sulphur showers" we hear of. Even in Calidas' drama of
Sacontala,[367] we read of "rills dyed yellow with the golden dust of the lotus." And
so the seasons went rolling on into summer, as one rambles into higher and higher
grass.

Thus was my first year's life in the woods completed; and the second year was
similar to it. I finally left Walden September 6th, 1847.

Conclusion

To the sick the doctors wisely recommend a change of air and scenery. Thank Heaven,
here is not all the world. The buck-eye does not grow in New England, and the
mocking-bird is rarely heard here. The wild-goose is more of a cosmopolite than we;
he breaks his fast in Canada, takes a luncheon in the Ohio, and plumes himself for
the night in a southern bayou. Even the bison, to some extent, keeps pace with the
seasons, cropping the pastures of the Colorado only till a greener and sweeter grass

[367] The Sanskrit drama *Sakuntala* by the
fifth-century Hindu poet Kalidasa.

awaits him by the Yellowstone. Yet we think that if rail-fences a[*led down, and*] stone-walls piled up on our farms, bounds are henceforth set to o[*and our fates*] decided. If you are chosen town-clerk, forsooth, you cannot go [*del Fuego*] this summer: but you may go to the land of infernal fire nevertl [*e universe*] is wider than our views of it.

Yet we should oftener look over the tafferel[168] of our craft, like and not make the voyage like stupid sailors picking oakum. The oth[*engers,*] is but the home of our correspondent. Our voyaging is only great-c[*globe*] the doctors prescribe for diseases of the skin merely. One hastens t[*and*] to chase the giraffe; but surely that is not the game he would be [*a*] pray, would a man hunt giraffes if he could? Snipes and woodcock[*a*] rare sport; but I trust it would be nobler game to shoot one's self.

> "Direct your eye sight inward, and you'll find
> A thousand regions in your mind
> Yet undiscovered. Travel them, and be
> Expert in home-cosmography."[370]

What does Africa,—what does the West stand for? Is not our own interio the chart?[371] black though it may prove, like the coast, when discovered. Is t[i] of the Nile, or the Niger, or the Mississippi, or a North-West Passage aroun. continent, that we would find? Are these the problems which most concern mank. Is Franklin[372] the only man who is lost, that his wife should be so earnest to find hi. Does Mr. Grinnell[373] know where he himself is? Be rather the Mungo Park, the Lewis and Clarke and Frobisher,[374] of your own streams and oceans; explore your own higher latitudes,—with shiploads of preserved meats to support you, if they be necessary; and pile the empty cans sky-high for a sign.[375] Were preserved meats invented to preserve meat merely? Nay, be a Columbus to whole new continents and worlds within you, opening new channels, not of trade, but of thought. Every man is the lord of a realm beside which the earthly empire of the Czar[376] is but a petty state, a hummock left by the ice. Yet some can be patriotic who have no self-respect, and sacrifice the greater to the less. They love the soil which makes their graves, but have no sympathy with the spirit which may still animate their clay. Patriotism is a maggot in their heads. What was the meaning of that South-Sea Exploring Expedition,[377] with all its parade and expense, but an indirect recognition of the fact, that there are continents and seas in the moral world, to which every man is an isthmus or an inlet, yet unexplored by him, but that it is easier to sail many thousand miles through cold and storm and cannibals, in a government ship, with five hundred men and boys to assist one, than

---

168 *Rail at the ship's stern.*
369 Traveling by direct route.
370 From "To My Honoured Friend, Sir Ed. P. Knight" by William Habington (1605–1654).
371 Not yet mapped, because unexplored.
372 Sir John Franklin (1786–1847), British explorer lost on expedition to discover open route between the Atlantic and the Pacific.
373 Henry Grinnell (1799–1874), American who sponsored a rescue mission to find Franklin.

374 Leaders of various explorations: Africa (Park), the American Northwest (Lewis and Clark), and Canada (Sir Martin Frobisher).
375 A stack of cans marked one of the camps deserted by the Franklin expedition.
376 During Thoreau's lifetime Czarist Russia was the largest country.
377 Antarctic expedition (1838–1842) led by the American Charles Wilkes.

the private sea, the Atlantic and Pacific Ocean of one's being
it is to ex——
alone.—   extremos alter scrutetur Iberos.

              oet hic vitæ, plus habet ille viæ."

           wander and scrutinize the outlandish
       ralians.

          more of God, they more of the road.[378]

       worth the while to go round the world to count the cats in Zanzibar. Yet
     even till you can do better, and you may perhaps find some "Symmes' Hole"[379]
     ich to get at the inside at last. England and France, Spain and Portugal, Gold
     and Slave Coast, all front on this private sea; but no bark from them has
    ured out of sight of land, though it is without doubt the direct way to India.
   ou would learn to speak all tongues and conform to the customs of all nations,
   you would travel farther than all travellers, be naturalized in all climes, and cause
   e Sphinx to dash her head against a stone,[380] even obey the precept of the old
 philosopher, and Explore thyself. Herein are demanded the eye and the nerve. Only
the defeated and deserters go to the wars, cowards that run away and enlist. Start now
on that farthest western way, which does not pause at the Mississippi or the Pacific,
nor conduct toward a worn-out China or Japan, but leads on direct a tangent to this
sphere, summer and winter, day and night, sun down, moon down, and at last earth
down too.

It is said that Mirabeau[381] took to highway robbery "to ascertain what degree of
resolution was necessary in order to place one's self in formal opposition to the most
sacred laws of society." He declared that "a soldier who fights in the ranks does not
require half so much courage as a foot-pad,"—"that honor and religion have never
stood in the way of a well-considered and a firm resolve." This was manly, as the
world goes; and yet it was idle, if not desperate. A saner man would have found
himself often enough "in formal opposition" to what are deemed "the most sacred
laws of society," through obedience to yet more sacred laws, and so have tested his
resolution without going out of his way. It is not for a man to put himself in such
an attitude to society, but to maintain himself in whatever attitude he find himself
through obedience to the laws of his being, which will never be one of opposition
to a just government, if he should chance to meet with such.

I left the woods for as good a reason as I went there. Perhaps it seemed to me that
I had several more lives to live, and could not spare any more time for that one. It
is remarkable how easily and insensibly we fall into a particular route, and make a
beaten track for ourselves. I had not lived there a week before my feet wore a path
from my door to the pond-side; and though it is five or six years since I trod it, it

---

[378] From lines by the Roman poet Claudian, with "Australians" and "of God" replacing the original words.

[379] John Symmes (1780–1829) fostered a theory that the globe was hollow, habitable, and open at either end.

[380] In frustration over Oedipus' solving the riddle she posed to him, the Sphinx killed herself.

[381] Count de Mirabeau (1749–1791), French diplomat.

is still quite distinct. It is true, I fear that others may have fallen into it, and so helped to keep it open. The surface of the earth is soft and impressible by the feet of men; and so with the paths which the mind travels. How worn and dusty, then, must be the highways of the world, how deep the ruts of tradition and conformity! I did not wish to take a cabin passage, but rather to go before the mast and on the deck of the world, for there I could best see the moonlight amid the mountains. I do not wish to go below now.

I learned this, at least, by my experiment; that if one advances confidently in the direction of his dreams, and endeavors to live the life which he has imagined, he will meet with a success unexpected in common hours. He will put some things behind, will pass an invisible boundary; new, universal, and more liberal laws will begin to establish themselves around and within him; or the old laws be expanded, and interpreted in his favor in a more liberal sense, and he will live with the license of a higher order of beings. In proportion as he simplifies his life, the laws of the universe will appear less complex, and solitude will not be solitude, nor poverty poverty, nor weakness weakness. If you have built castles in the air, your work need not be lost; that is where they should be. Now put the foundations under them.

It is a ridiculous demand which England and America make, that you shall speak so that they can understand you. Neither men nor toad-stools grow so. As if that were important, and there were not enough to understand you without them. As if Nature could support but one order of understandings, could not sustain birds as well as quadrupeds, flying as well as creeping things, and *hush* and *who*,[382] which Bright can understand, were the best English. As if there were safety in stupidity alone. I fear chiefly lest my expression may not be *extra-vagant* enough, may not wander far enough beyond the narrow limits of my daily experience, so as to be adequate to the truth of which I have been convinced. *Extra vagance!* it depends on how you are yarded. The migrating buffalo, which seeks new pastures in another latitude, is not extravagant like the cow which kicks over the pail, leaps the cow-yard fence, and runs after her calf, in milking time. I desire to speak somewhere *without* bounds; like a man in a waking moment, to men in their waking moments; for I am convinced that I cannot exaggerate enough even to lay the foundation of a true expression. Who that has heard a strain of music feared then lest he should speak extravagantly any more forever? In view of the future or possible, we should live quite laxly and undefined in front, our outlines dim and misty on that side; as our shadows reveal an insensible perspiration toward the sun. The volatile truth of our words should continually betray the inadequacy of the residual statement. Their truth is instantly *translated;* its literal monument alone remains. The words which express our faith and piety are not definite; yet they are significant and fragrant like frankincense to superior natures.

Why level downward to our dullest perception always, and praise that as common sense? The commonest sense is the sense of men asleep, which they express by snoring. Sometimes we are inclined to class those who are once-and-a-half witted with the half-witted, because we appreciate only a third part of their wit. Some would find fault with the morning-red, if they ever got up early enough. "They pretend," as I hear, "that the verses of Kabir[383] have four different senses; illusion, spirit, intellect,

---

[382] *Hush* and *who*: commands to an ox ("Bright")   [383] Hindu mystic.
for "go" and "stop," respectively.

and the exoteric doctrine of the Vedas;" but in this part of the world it is considered a ground for complaint if a man's writings admit of more than one interpretation. While England endeavors to cure the potato-rot, will not any endeavor to cure the brain-rot, which prevails so much more widely and fatally?

I do not suppose that I have attained to obscurity, but I should be proud if no more fatal fault were found with my pages on this score than was found with the Walden ice. Southern customers objected to its blue color, which is the evidence of its purity, as if it were muddy, and preferred the Cambridge ice, which is white, but tastes of weeds. The purity men love is like the mists which envelop the earth, and not like the azure ether beyond.

Some are dinning in our ears that we Americans, and moderns generally, are intellectual dwarfs compared with the ancients, or even the Elizabethan men. But what is that to the purpose? A living dog is better than a dead lion. Shall a man go and hang himself because he belongs to the race of pygmies, and not be the biggest pygmy that he can? Let every one mind his own business, and endeavor to be what he was made.

Why should we be in such desperate haste to succeed, and in such desperate enterprises? If a man does not keep pace with his companions, perhaps it is because he hears a different drummer. Let him step to the music which he hears, however measured or far away. It is not important that he should mature as soon as an apple-tree or an oak. Shall he turn his spring into summer? If the condition of things which we were made for is not yet, what were any reality which we can substitute? We will not be shipwrecked on a vain reality. Shall we with pains erect a heaven of blue glass over ourselves, though when it is done we shall be sure to gaze still at the true ethereal heaven far above, as if the former were not?

There was an artist in the city of Kouroo[384] who was disposed to strive after perfection. One day it came into his mind to make a staff. Having considered that in an imperfect work time is an ingredient, but into a perfect work time does not enter, he said to himself, It shall be perfect in all respects, though I should do nothing else in my life. He proceeded instantly to the forest for wood, being resolved that it should not be made of unsuitable material; and as he searched for and rejected stick after stick, his friends gradually deserted him, for they grew old in their works and died, but he grew not older by a moment. His singleness of purpose and resolution, and his elevated piety, endowed him, without his knowledge, with perennial youth. As he made no compromise with Time, Time kept out of his way, and only sighed at a distance because he could not overcome him. Before he had found a stock in all respects suitable the city of Kouroo was a hoary ruin, and he sat on one of its mounds to peel the stick. Before he had given it the proper shape the dynasty of the Candahars was at an end, and with the point of the stick he wrote the name of the last of that race in the sand, and then resumed his work. By the time he had smoothed and polished the staff Kalpa was no longer the pole-star; and ere he had put on the ferrule and the head adorned with precious stones, Brahma had awoke and slumbered many times. But why do I stay to mention these things? When the finishing stroke was put to his work, it suddenly expanded before the eyes of the astonished artist into the fairest of all the creations of Brahma. He had made a new system in making a staff, a world

[384] This fable is most likely Thoreau's fabrication.

with full and fair proportions; in which, though the old cities and dynasties had passed away, fairer and more glorious ones had taken their places. And now he saw by the heap of shavings still fresh at his feet, that, for him and his work, the former lapse of time had been an illusion, and that no more time had elapsed than is required for a single scintillation from the brain of Brahma to fall on and inflame the tinder of a mortal brain. The material was pure, and his art was pure; how could the result be other than wonderful?

No face which we can give to a matter will stead us so well at last as the truth. This alone wears well. For the most part, we are not where we are, but in a false position. Through an infirmity of our natures, we suppose a case, and put ourselves into it, and hence are in two cases at the same time, and it is doubly difficult to get out. In sane moments we regard only the facts, the case that is. Say what you have to say, not what you ought. Any truth is better than make-believe. Tom Hyde, the tinker, standing on the gallows, was asked if he had any thing to say. "Tell the tailors," said he, "to remember to make a knot in their thread before they take the first stitch." His companion's prayer is forgotten.

However mean your life is, meet it and live it; do not shun it and call it hard names. It is not so bad as you are. It looks poorest when you are richest. The fault-finder will find faults even in paradise. Love your life, poor as it is. You may perhaps have some pleasant, thrilling, glorious hours, even in a poorhouse. The setting sun is reflected from the windows of the alms-house as brightly as from the rich man's abode; the snow melts before its door as early in the spring. I do not see but a quiet mind may live as contentedly there, and have as cheering thoughts, as in a palace. The town's poor seem to me often to live the most independent lives of any. May be they are simply great enough to receive without misgiving. Most think that they are above being supported by the town; but it oftener happens that they are not above supporting themselves by dishonest means, which should be more disreputable. Cultivate poverty like a garden herb, like sage. Do not trouble yourself much to get new things, whether clothes or friends. Turn the old; return to them. Things do not change; we change. Sell your clothes and keep your thoughts. God will see that you do not want society. If I were confined to a corner of a garret all my days, like a spider, the world would be just as large to me while I had my thoughts about me. The philosopher said: "From an army of three divisions one can take away its general, and put it in disorder; from the man the most abject and vulgar one cannot take away his thought." Do not seek so anxiously to be developed, to subject yourself to many influences to be played on; it is all dissipation. Humility like darkness reveals the heavenly lights. The shadows of poverty and meanness gather around us, "and lo! creation widens to our view." We are often reminded that if there were bestowed on us the wealth of Crœsus,[385] our aims must still be the same, and our means essentially the same. Moreover, if you are restricted in your range by poverty, if you cannot buy books and newspapers, for instance, you are but confined to the most significant and vital experiences; you are compelled to deal with the material which yields the most sugar and the most starch. It is life near the bone where it is sweetest. You are defended from being a trifler. No man loses ever on a lower level by magnanimity on a higher.

---

[385] Legendary king who was accounted the wealthiest man of all time.

Superfluous wealth can buy superfluities only. Money is not required to buy one necessary of the soul.

I live in the angle of a leaden wall, into whose composition was poured a little alloy of bell metal. Often, in the repose of my mid-day, there reaches my ears a confused *tintinnabulum* from without. It is the noise of my contemporaries. My neighbors tell me of their adventures with famous gentlemen and ladies, what notabilities they met at the dinner-table; but I am no more interested in such things than in the contents of the Daily Times. The interest and the conversation are about costume and manners chiefly; but a goose is a goose still, dress it as you will. They tell me of California and Texas, of England and the Indies, of the Hon. Mr. ———— of Georgia or of Massachusetts, all transient and fleeting phenomena, till I am ready to leap from their court-yard like the Mameluke bey.[386] I delight to come to my bearings, —not walk in procession with pomp and parade, in a conspicuous place, but to walk even with the Builder of the universe, if I may,—not to live in this restless, nervous, bustling, trivial Nineteenth Century, but stand or sit thoughtfully while it goes by. What are men celebrating? They are all on a committee of arrangements, and hourly expect a speech from somebody. God is only the president of the day, and Webster is his orator.[387] I love to weigh, to settle, to gravitate toward that which most strongly and rightfully attracts me;—not hang by the beam of the scale and try to weigh less, —not suppose a case, but take the case that is; to travel the only path I can, and that on which no power can resist me. It affords me no satisfaction to commence to spring an arch before I have got a solid foundation. Let us not play at kittly-benders.[388] There is a solid bottom every where. We read that the traveller asked the boy if the swamp before him had a hard bottom. The boy replied that it had. But presently the traveller's horse sank in up to the girths, and he observed to the boy, "I thought you said that this bog had a hard bottom." "So it has," answered the latter, "but you have not got half way to it yet." So it is with the bogs and quicksands of society; but he is an old boy that knows it. Only what is thought said or done at a certain rare coincidence is good. I would not be one of those who will foolishly drive a nail into mere lath and plastering; such a deed would keep me awake nights. Give me a hammer, and let me feel for the furring.[389] Do not depend on the putty. Drive a nail home and clinch it so faithfully that you can wake up in the night and think of your work with satisfaction,—a work at which you would not be ashamed to invoke the Muse. So will help you God, and so only. Every nail driven should be as another rivet in the machine of the universe, you carrying on the work.

Rather than love, than money, than fame, give me truth. I sat at a table where were rich food and wine in abundance, and obsequious attendance, but sincerity and truth were not; and I went away hungry from the inhospitable board. The hospitality was as cold as the ices. I thought that there was no need of ice to freeze them. They talked to me of the age of the wine and the fame of the vintage; but I thought of an older, a newer, and purer wine, of a more glorious vintage, which they had not got, and could not buy. The style, the house and grounds and "entertainment" pass

---

[386] The way one of the Mamelukes, a member of the Egyptian army clique, escaped being massacred in Cairo in 1811.
[387] Daniel Webster, a contemporary of Thoreau,

was considered the foremost speaker on the American political scene.
[388] Running across thin ice.
[389] Wall studs.

for nothing with me. I called on the king, but he made me wait in his hall, and conducted like a man incapacitated for hospitality. There was a man in my neighborhood who lived in a hollow tree. His manners were truly regal. I should have done better had I called on him.

How long shall we sit in our porticoes practising idle and musty virtues, which any work would make impertinent? As if one were to begin the day with long-suffering, and hire a man to hoe his potatoes; and in the afternoon go forth to practise Christian meekness and charity with goodness aforethought! Consider the China pride and stagnant self-complacency of mankind. This generation reclines a little to congratulate itself on being the last of an illustrious line; and in Boston and London and Paris and Rome, thinking of its long descent, it speaks of its progress in art and science and literature with satisfaction. There are the Records of the Philosophical Societies, and the public Eulogies of *Great Men!* It is the good Adam contemplating his own virtue. "Yes, we have done great deeds, and sung divine songs, which shall never die,"—that is, as long as *we* can remember them. The learned societies and great men of Assyria,—where are they? What youthful philosophers and experimentalists we are! There is not one of my readers who has yet lived a whole human life. These may be but the spring months in the life of the race. If we have had the seven-years' itch, we have not seen the seventeen-year locust yet in Concord. We are acquainted with a mere pellicle of the globe on which we live. Most have not delved six feet beneath the surface, nor leaped as many above it. We know not where we are. Beside, we are sound asleep nearly half our time. Yet we esteem ourselves wise, and have an established order on the surface. Truly, we are deep thinkers, we are ambitious spirits! As I stand over the insect crawling amid the pine needles on the forest floor, and endeavoring to conceal itself from my sight, and ask myself why it will cherish those humble thoughts, and hide its head from me who might perhaps be its benefactor, and impart to its race some cheering information, I am reminded of the greater Benefactor and Intelligence that stands over me the human insect.

There is an incessant influx of novelty into the world, and yet we tolerate incredible dulness. I need only suggest what kind of sermons are still listened to in the most enlightened countries. There are such words as joy and sorrow, but they are only the burden of a psalm, sung with a nasal twang, while we believe in the ordinary and mean. We think that we can change our clothes only. It is said that the British Empire is very large and respectable, and that the United States are a first-rate power. We do not believe that a tide rises and falls behind every man which can float the British Empire like a chip, if he should ever harbor it in his mind. Who knows what sort of seventeen-year locust will next come out of the ground? The government of the world I live in was not framed, like that of Britain, in after-dinner conversations over the wine.

The life in us is like the water in the river. It may rise this year higher than man has ever known it, and flood the parched uplands; even this may be the eventful year, which will drown out all our muskrats. It was not always dry land where we dwell. I see far inland the banks which the stream anciently washed, before science began to record its freshets. Every one has heard the story which has gone the rounds of New England, of a strong and beautiful bug which came out of the dry leaf of an old table of apple-tree wood, which had stood in a farmer's kitchen for sixty years, first in Connecticut, and afterward in Massachusetts,—from an egg deposited in the living tree many years earlier still, as appeared by counting the annual layers beyond it; which was heard gnawing out for several weeks, hatched perchance by the heat of an urn. Who does not feel his faith in a resurrection and immortality strengthened by hearing of this? Who knows what beautiful and winged life, whose egg has been buried for ages under many concentric layers of woodenness in the dead dry life of society, deposited at first in the alburnum of the green and living tree, which has been gradually converted into the semblance of its well-seasoned tomb,—heard perchance gnawing out now for years by the astonished family of man, as they sat round the festive board,—may unexpectedly come forth from amidst society's most trivial and handselled furniture, to enjoy its perfect summer life at last!

I do not say that John or Jonathan[390] will realize all this; but such is the character of that morrow which mere lapse of time can never make to dawn. The light which puts out our eyes is darkness to us. Only that day dawns to which we are awake. There is more day to dawn. The sun is but a morning star.

1846/1854

---

from The Maine Woods[*]

Perhaps I most fully realized that this was primeval, untamed, and forever untameable Nature, or whatever else men call it, while coming down this part of the mountain. We were passing over "Burnt Lands," burnt by lightning, perchance, though they showed no recent marks of fire, hardly so much as a charred stump, but looked rather like a natural pasture for the moose and deer, exceedingly wild and desolate, with occasional strips of timber crossing them, and low poplars springing up, and patches of blueberries here and there. I found myself traversing them familiarly, like some pasture run to waste, or partially reclaimed by man; but when I reflected what man, what brother or sister or kinsman of our race made it and claimed it, I expected the proprietor to rise up and dispute my passage. It is difficult to conceive of a region uninhabited by man. We habitually presume his presence and influence everywhere. And yet we have not seen pure Nature, unless we have seen her thus vast, and drear, and inhuman, though in the midst of cities. Nature was here something savage and awful, though beautiful. I looked with awe at the ground I trod on, to see what the Powers had made there, the form and fashion and material of their work. This was that Earth of which we have heard, made out of Chaos and Old Night. Here was no man's garden, but the unhandselled globe. It was not lawn, nor pasture, nor mead, nor woodland, nor lea, nor arable, nor waste-land. It was the fresh and natural surface of the planet Earth, as it was made forever and ever,—to be the dwelling of man,

---

[390] Common terms for a Britisher ("John Bull") and an American ("Brother Jonathan"), respectively.

[*] In 1846, 1853, and 1857 Thoreau traveled deep into the Maine wilderness in the company of Indian guides. In this passage he responds to the harsh material fact of the remote and uninhabited regions of Mount Ktaadn.

we say,—so Nature made it, and man may use it if he can. Man was not to be associated with it. It was Matter, vast, terrific,—not his Mother Earth that we have heard of, not for him to tread on, or be buried in,—no, it were being too familiar even to let his bones lie there—the home this of Necessity and Fate. There was there felt the presence of a force not bound to be kind to man. It was a place for heathenism and superstitious rites,—to be inhabited by men nearer of kin to the rocks and to wild animals than we. We walked over it with a certain awe, stopping from time to time to pick the blueberries which grew there, and had a smart and spicy taste. Perchance where *our* wild pines stand, and leaves lie on their forest floor in Concord, there were once reapers, and husbandmen planted grain; but here not even the surface had been scarred by man, but it was a specimen of what God saw fit to make this world. What is it to be admitted to a museum, to see a myriad of particular things, compared with being shown some star's surface, some hard matter in its home! I stand in awe of my body, this matter to which I am bound has become so strange to me. I fear not spirits, ghosts, of which I am one,—*that* my body might,—but I fear bodies, I tremble to meet them. What is this Titan that has possession of me? Talk of mysteries!—Think of our life in nature,—daily to be shown matter, to come in contact with it,—rocks, trees, wind on our cheeks! the *solid* earth! the *actual* world! the *common sense! Contact! Contact! Who* are we? *where* are we?

1848/1864

---

from A Week on the Concord and Merrimack Rivers

from **Wednesday**

While we float here, far from that tributary stream on whose banks our friends and kindred dwell, our thoughts, like the stars, come out of their horizon still; for there circulates a finer blood than Lavoisier[1] has discovered the laws of,—the blood, not of kindred merely, but of kindness, whose pulse still beats at any distance and forever.

> True kindness is a pure divine affinity,
> Not founded upon human consanguinity.
> It is a spirit, not a blood relation,
> Superior to family and station.[2]

After years of vain familiarity, some distant gesture or unconscious behavior, which we remember, speaks to us with more emphasis than the wisest or kindest words. We are sometimes made aware of a kindness long passed, and realize that there have been times when our friends' thoughts of us were of so pure and lofty a character that they passed over us like the winds of heaven unnoticed; when they treated us not as what

---

[1] Antoine Lavoisier (1743–1794), French chemist.   [2] Thoreau's own verses.

we were, but as what we aspired to be. There has just reached us, it may be, the nobleness of some such silent behavior, not to be forgotten, not to be remembered, and we shudder to think how it fell on us cold, though in some true but tardy hour we endeavor to wipe off these scores.

In my experience, persons, when they are made the subject of conversation, though with a friend, are commonly the most prosaic and trivial of facts. The universe seems bankrupt as soon as we begin to discuss the character of individuals. Our discourse all runs to slander, and our limits grow narrower as we advance. How is it that we are impelled to treat our old friends so ill when we obtain new ones? The housekeeper says, I never had any new crockery but I began to break the old. I say, let us speak of mushrooms and forest trees rather. Yet we can sometimes afford to remember them in private.—

Lately, alas, I knew a gentle boy,
   Whose features all were cast in Virtue's mould,
As one she had designed for Beauty's toy,
   But after manned him for her own stronghold.

On every side he open was as day,
   That you might see no lack of strength within,
For walls and ports do only serve alway
   For a pretence to feebleness and sin.

Say not that Cæsar was victorious,
   With toil and strife who stormed the
      House of Fame,
In other sense this youth was glorious,
   Himself a kingdom wheresoe'er he came.

No strength went out to get him victory,
   When all was income of its own accord;
For where he went none other was to see,
   But all were parcel of their noble lord.

He forayed like the subtil haze of summer,
   That stilly shows fresh landscapes to our eyes,
And revolutions works without a murmur,
   Or rustling of a leaf beneath the skies.

So was I taken unawares by this,
   I quite forgot my homage to confess;
Yet now am forced to know, though hard it is,
   I might have loved him had I loved him less.

Each moment as we nearer drew to each,
   A stern respect withheld us further yet,
So that we seemed beyond each other's reach,
   And less acquainted than when first we met.

We two were one while we did sympathize,
  So could we not the simplest bargain drive;
And what avails it now that we are wise,
  If absence doth this doubleness contrive?

Eternity may not the chance repeat,
  But I must tread my single way alone,
In sad remembrance that we once did meet,
  And know that bliss irrevocably gone.

The spheres henceforth my elegy shall sing,
  For elegy has other subject none;
Each strain of music in my ears shall ring
  Knell of departure from that other one.

Make haste and celebrate my tragedy;
  With fitting strain resound ye woods and fields;
Sorrow is dearer in such case to me
  Than all the joys other occasion yields.

———

Is't then too late the damage to repair?
  Distance, forsooth, from my weak grasp hath reft
The empty husk, and clutched the useless tare,
  But in my hands the wheat and kernel left.

If I but love that virtue which he is,
  Though it be scented in the morning air,
Still shall we be truest acquaintances,
  Nor mortals know a sympathy more rare.[3]

Friendship is evanescent in every man's experience, and remembered like heat lightning in past summers. Fair and flitting like a summer cloud;—there is always some vapor in the air, no matter how long the drought; there are even April showers. Surely from time to time, for its vestiges never depart, it floats through our atmosphere. It takes place, like vegetation in so many materials, because there is such a law, but always without permanent form, though ancient and familiar as the sun and moon, and as sure to come again. The heart is forever inexperienced. They silently gather as by magic, these never failing, never quite deceiving visions, like the bright and fleecy clouds in the calmest and clearest days. The Friend is some fair floating isle of palms eluding the mariner in Pacific seas. Many are the dangers to be encountered, equinoctial gales and coral reefs, ere he may sail before the constant trades. But who would not sail through mutiny and storm even over Atlantic waves, to reach the fabulous retreating shores of some continent man? The imagination still clings to the faintest tradition of

---

[3] Thoreau's own verses.

The Atlantides.[4]

The smothered streams of love, which flow
More bright than Phlegethon,[5] more low,
Island us ever, like the sea,
In an Atlantic mystery.
Our fabled shores none ever reach,
No mariner has found our beach,
Only our mirage now is seen,
And neighboring waves with floating green,
Yet still the oldest charts contain
Some dotted outline of our main;
In ancient times midsummer days
Unto the western islands' gaze,
To Teneriffe and the Azores,[6]
Have shown our faint and cloud-like shores.

But sink not yet, ye desolate isles,
Anon your coast with commerce smiles,
And richer freights ye'll furnish far
Than Africa or Malabar.
Be fair, be fertile evermore,
Ye rumored but untrodden shore,
Princes and monarchs will contend
Who first unto your land shall send,
And pawn the jewels of the crown
To call your distant soil their own.

Columbus has sailed westward of these isles by the mariner's compass, but neither
he nor his successors have found them. We are no nearer than Plato was. The earnest
seeker and hopeful discoverer of this New World always haunts the outskirts of his
time, and walks through the densest crowd uninterrupted, and as it were in a straight
line.—

Sea and land are but his neighbors,
And companions in his labors,
Who on the ocean's verge and firm land's end
Doth long and truly seek his Friend.
Many men dwell far inland,
But he alone sits on the strand.
Whether he ponders men or books,
Always still he seaward looks,
Marine news he ever reads,
And the slightest glances heeds,

---

[4] Atlantis was a fabled "lost" continent
supposedly floating somewhere in the Atlantic
Ocean. Here and in the remaining lines of his
poem, Thoreau imagines Atlantis as a group of
islands rather than one body of land.

[5] River of fire in Hades, from classic myth.
[6] Islands at the western edge of Europe.

> Feels the sea breeze on his cheek
> At each word the landsmen speak,
> In every companion's eye
> A sailing vessel doth descry;
> In the ocean's sullen roar
> From some distant port he hears,
> Of wrecks upon a distant shore,
> And the ventures of past years.

Who does not walk on the plain as amid the columns of Tadmore[7] of the desert? There is on the earth no institution which Friendship has established; it is not taught by any religion; no scripture contains its maxims. It has no temple, nor even a solitary column. There goes a rumor that the earth is inhabited, but the shipwrecked mariner has not seen a foot-print on the shore. The hunter has found only fragments of pottery and the monuments of inhabitants.

However, our fates at least are social. Our courses do not diverge; but as the web of destiny is woven it is fulled, and we are cast more and more into the centre. Men naturally, though feebly, seek this alliance, and their actions faintly foretell it. We are inclined to lay the chief stress on likeness and not on difference, and in foreign bodies we admit that there are many degrees of warmth below blood heat, but none of cold above it.

Mencius[8] says: "If one loses a fowl or a dog, he knows well how to seek them again; if one loses the sentiments of his heart, he does not know how to seek them again. . . . The duties of practical philosophy consist only in seeking after those sentiments of the heart which we have lost; that is all."

One or two persons come to my house from time to time, there being proposed to them the faint possibility of intercourse. They are as full as they are silent, and wait for my plectrum to stir the strings of their lyre. If they could ever come to the length of a sentence, or hear one, on that ground which they are dreaming of! They speak faintly, and do not obtrude themselves. They have heard some news, which none, not even they themselves, can impart. It is a wealth they can bear about them which can be expended in various ways. What came they out to seek?

No word is oftener on the lips of men than Friendship, and indeed no thought is more familiar to their aspirations. All men are dreaming of it, and its drama, which is always a tragedy, is enacted daily. It is the secret of the universe. You may thread the town, you may wander the country, and none shall ever speak of it, yet thought is every where busy about it, and the idea of what is possible in this respect affects our behavior toward all new men and women, and a great many old ones. Nevertheless, I can remember only two or three essays on this subject in all literature. No wonder that the Mythology, and Arabian Nights, and Shakspeare, and Scott's[9] novels, entertain us,—we are poets and fablers and dramatists and novelists ourselves. We are continually acting a part in a more interesting drama than any written. We are dreaming that our Friends are our *Friends,* and that we are our Friends' *Friends.* Our actual Friends are but distant relations of those to whom we are pledged. We never

---

[7] Biblical name for Palmyra, ancient Syrian city.
[8] Chinese philosopher (372?–289? B.C.), teacher of Confucianism.

[9] Sir Walter Scott (1771–1832), Scottish poet and author of romantic historical novels.

exchange more than three words with a Friend in our lives, on that level to which our thoughts and feelings almost habitually rise. One goes forth prepared to say "Sweet Friends!" and the salutation is "Damn your eyes!" But never mind; faint heart never won true Friend. O my Friend, may it come to pass, once, that when you are my Friend I may be yours.

Of what use the friendliest disposition even, if there are no hours given to Friendship, if it is forever postponed to unimportant duties and relations? Friendship is first, Friendship last. But it is equally impossible to forget our Friends, and to make them answer to our ideal. When they say farewell, then indeed we begin to keep them company. How often we find ourselves turning our backs on our actual Friends, that we may go and meet their ideal cousins. I would that I were worthy to be any man's Friend.

What is commonly honored with the name of Friendship is no very profound or powerful instinct. Men do not, after all, love their Friends greatly. I do not often see the farmers made seers and wise to the verge of insanity by their Friendship for one another. They are not often transfigured and translated by love in each other's presence. I do not observe them purified, refined, and elevated by the love of a man. If one abates a little the price of his wood, or gives a neighbor his vote at town-meeting, or a barrel of apples, or lends him his wagon frequently, it is esteemed a rare instance of Friendship. Nor do the farmers' wives lead lives consecrated to Friendship. I do not see the pair of farmer Friends of either sex prepared to stand against the world. There are only two or three couples in history. To say that a man is your Friend, means commonly no more than this, that he is not your enemy. Most contemplate only what would be the accidental and trifling advantages of Friendship, as that the Friend can assist in time of need, by his substance, or his influence, or his counsel; but he who foresees such advantages in this relation proves himself blind to its real advantage, or indeed wholly inexperienced in the relation itself. Such services are particular and menial, compared with the perpetual and all-embracing service which it is. Even the utmost good-will and harmony and practical kindness are not sufficient for Friendship, for Friends do not live in harmony merely, as some say, but in melody. We do not wish for Friends to feed and clothe our bodies,—neighbors are kind enough for that,—but to do the like office to our spirits. For this few are rich enough, however well disposed they may be. For the most part we stupidly confound one man with another. The dull distinguish only races or nations, or at most classes, but the wise man, individuals. To his Friend a man's peculiar character appears in every feature and in every action, and it is thus drawn out and improved by him.

Think of the importance of Friendship in the education of men.

"He that hath love and judgment too,
    Sees more than any other doe."[10]

It will make a man honest; it will make him a hero; it will make him a saint. It is the state of the just dealing with the just, the magnanimous with the magnanimous, the sincere with the sincere, man with man.—

And it is well said by another poet,

[10] From "An Elegie, or Friends Passion, for His Astrophill" by Matthew Royden (fl. 1580–1622).

> "Why love among the virtues is not known,
>   Is that love is them all contract in one."[11]

All the abuses which are the object of reform with the philanthropist, the statesman, and the housekeeper, are unconsciously amended in the intercourse of Friends. A Friend is one who incessantly pays us the compliment of expecting from us all the virtues, and who can appreciate them in us. It takes two to speak the truth,—one to speak, and another to hear. How can one treat with magnanimity mere wood and stone? If we dealt only with the false and dishonest, we should at last forget how to speak truth. Only lovers know the value and magnanimity of truth, while traders prize a cheap honesty, and neighbors and acquaintance a cheap civility. In our daily intercourse with men, our nobler faculties are dormant and suffered to rust. None will pay us the compliment to expect nobleness from us. Though we have gold to give, they demand only copper. We ask our neighbor to suffer himself to be dealt with truly, sincerely, nobly; but he answers no by his deafness. He does not even hear this prayer. He says practically,—I will be content if you treat me as no better than I should be, as deceitful, mean, dishonest and selfish. For the most part, we are contented so to deal and to be dealt with, and we do not think that for the mass of men there is any truer and nobler relation possible. A man may have *good* neighbors, so called, and acquaintances, and even companions, wife, parents, brothers, sisters, children, who meet himself and one another on this ground only. The State does not demand justice of its members, but thinks that it succeeds very well with the least degree of it, hardly more than rogues practise; and so do the neighborhood and the family. What is commonly called Friendship even is only a little more honor among rogues.

But sometimes we are said to *love* another, that is to stand in a true relation to him, so that we give the best to, and receive the best from, him. Between whom there is hearty truth there is love; and in proportion to our truthfulness and confidence in one another, our lives are divine and miraculous, and answer to our ideal. There are passages of affection in our intercourse with mortal men and women, such as no prophecy had taught us to expect, which transcend our earthly life, and anticipate heaven for us. What is this Love that may come right into the middle of a prosaic Goffstown[12] day, equal to any of the gods? that discovers a new world, fair and fresh and eternal, occupying the place of this old one, when to the common eye a dust has settled on the universe? which world cannot else be reached, and does not exist. What other words, we may almost ask, are memorable and worthy to be repeated than those which love has inspired? It is wonderful that they were ever uttered. They are few and rare, indeed, but, like a strain of music, they are incessantly repeated and modulated by the memory. All other words crumble off with the stucco which overlies the heart. We should not dare to repeat them now aloud. We are not competent to hear them at all times.

The books for young people say a great deal about the *selection* of Friends; it is because they really have nothing to say about *Friends*. They mean associates and confidants merely. "Know that the contrariety of foe and Friend proceeds from God." Friendship takes place between those who have an affinity for one another, and is a

---

[11] From "To the Countess of Huntingdon" by John Donne (1572–1631).

[12] Goffstown, New Hampshire, a small town near Concord.

perfectly natural and inevitable result. No professions nor advances will avail. Even speech, at first, necessarily has nothing to do with it; but it follows after silence, as the buds in the graft do not put forth into leaves till long after the graft has taken. It is a drama in which the parties have no part to act. We are all Mussulmen and fatalists in this respect.[13] Impatient and uncertain lovers think that they must say or do something kind whenever they meet; they must never be cold. But they who are Friends, do not do what they *think* they must, but what they *must.* Even their Friendship is to some extent but a sublime phenomenon to them.

The true and not despairing Friend will address his Friend in some such terms as these.

"I never asked thy leave to let me love thee,—I have a right. I love thee not as something private and personal, which is *your own,* but as something universal and worthy of love, *which I have found.* O how I think of you! You are purely good, —you are infinitely good. I can trust you forever. I did not think that humanity was so rich. Give me an opportunity to live."

"You are the fact in a fiction,—you are the truth more strange and admirable than fiction. Consent only to be what you are. I alone will never stand in your way."

"This is what I would like,—to be as intimate with you as our spirits are intimate, —respecting you as I respect my ideal. Never to profane one another by word or action, even by a thought. Between us, if necessary, let there be no acquaintance."

"I have discovered you; how can you be concealed from me?"

The Friend asks no return but that his Friend will religiously accept and wear and not disgrace his apotheosis of him. They cherish each other's hopes. They are kind to each other's dreams.

Though the poet says, "'T is the pre-eminence of Friendship to impute excellence," yet we can never praise our Friend, nor esteem him praiseworthy, nor let him think that he can please us by any *behavior,* or ever *treat* us well enough. That kindness which has so good a reputation elsewhere can least of all consist with this relation, and no such affront can be offered to a Friend, as a conscious good-will, a friendliness which is not a necessity of the Friend's nature.

The sexes are naturally most strongly attracted to one another, by constant constitutional differences, and are most commonly and surely the complements of each other. How natural and easy it is for man to secure the attention of woman to what interests himself. Men and women of equal culture, thrown together, are sure to be of a certain value to one another, more than men to men. There exists already a natural disinterestedness and liberality in such society, and I think that any man will more confidently carry his favorite books to read to some circle of intelligent women, than to one of his own sex. The visit of man to man is wont to be an interruption, but the sexes naturally expect one another. Yet Friendship is no respecter of sex; and perhaps it is more rare between the sexes, than between two of the same sex.

Friendship is, at any rate, a relation of perfect equality. It cannot well spare any

---

[13] Mohammedan believers in the idea that each person's fate is predetermined by divine edict.

outward sign of equal obligation and advantage. The nobleman can never have a Friend among his retainers, nor the king among his subjects. Not that the parties to it are in all respects equal, but they are equal in all that respects or affects their Friendship. The one's love is exactly balanced and represented by the other's. Persons are only the vessels which contain the nectar, and the hydrostatic paradox is the symbol of love's law. It finds its level and rises to its fountain-head in all breasts, and its slenderest column balances the ocean.—

> "And love as well the shepherd can
> As can the mighty nobleman."[14]

The one sex is not, in this respect, more tender than the other. A hero's love is as delicate as a maiden's.

Confucius[15] said, "Never contract Friendship with a man that is not better than thyself." It is the merit and preservation of Friendship, that it takes place on a level higher than the actual characters of the parties would seem to warrant. The rays of light come to us in such a curve that every man whom we meet appears to be taller than he actually is. Such foundation has civility. My Friend is that one whom I can associate with my choicest thought. I always assign to him a nobler employment in my absence than I ever find him engaged in; and I imagine that the hours which he devotes to me were snatched from a higher society. The sorest insult which I ever received from a Friend was, when he behaved with the license which only long and cheap acquaintance allows to one's faults, in my presence, without shame, and still addressed me in friendly accents. Beware, lest thy Friend learn at last to tolerate one frailty of thine, and so an obstacle be raised to the progress of thy love. There are times when we have had enough even of our Friends, when we begin inevitably to profane one another, and must withdraw religiously into solitude and silence, the better to prepare ourselves for a loftier intimacy. Silence is the ambrosial night in the intercourse of Friends, in which their sincerity is recruited and takes deeper root.

Friendship is never established as an understood relation. Do you demand that I be less your Friend that you may know it? Yet what right have I to think that another cherishes so rare a sentiment for me? It is a miracle which requires constant proofs. It is an exercise of the purest imagination and the rarest faith. It says by a silent but eloquent behavior,—"I will be so related to thee as thou canst imagine; even so thou mayest believe. I will spend truth,—all my wealth on thee,"—and the Friend responds silently through his nature and life, and treats his Friend with the same divine courtesy. He knows us literally through thick and thin. He never asks for a sign of love, but can distinguish it by the features which it naturally wears. We never need to stand upon ceremony with him with regard to his visits. Wait not till I invite thee, but observe that I am glad to see thee when thou comest. It would be paying too dear for thy visit to ask for it. Where my Friend lives there are all riches and every attraction, and no slight obstacle can keep me from him. Let me never have to tell thee what I have not to tell. Let our intercourse be wholly above ourselves, and draw us up to it. The language of Friendship is not words but meanings. It is an intelligence

---

[14] From "Another of His Cynthia," attributed to Fulke Greville (1554–1628).   [15] Chinese philosopher (557?–479 B.C.).

above language. One imagines endless conversations with his Friend, in which the tongue shall be loosed, and thoughts be spoken without hesitancy, or end; but the experience is commonly far otherwise. Acquaintances may come and go, and have a word ready for every occasion; but what puny word shall he utter whose very breath is thought and meaning? Suppose you go to bid farewell to your Friend who is setting out on a journey; what other outward sign do you know of than to shake his hand? Have you any palaver ready for him then? any box of salve to commit to his pocket? any particular message to send by him? any statement which you had forgotten to make?—as if you could forget any thing.—No, it is much that you take his hand and say Farewell; that you could easily omit; so far custom has prevailed. It is even painful, if he is to go, that he should linger so long. If he must go, let him go quickly. Have you any *last* words? Alas, it is only the word of words, which you have so long sought and found not; *you* have not a *first* word yet. There are few even whom I should venture to call earnestly by their most proper names. A name pronounced is the recognition of the individual to whom it belongs. He who can pronounce my name aright, he can call me, and is entitled to my love and service. Yet reserve is the freedom and abandonment of lovers. It is the reserve of what is hostile or indifferent in their natures, to give place to what is kindred and harmonious.

The violence of love is as much to be dreaded as that of hate. When it is durable it is serene and equable. Even its famous pains begin only with the ebb of love, for few are indeed lovers, though all would fain be. It is one proof of a man's fitness for Friendship that he is able to do without that which is cheap and passionate. A true Friendship is as wise as it is tender. The parties to it yield implicitly to the guidance of their love, and know no other law nor kindness. It is not extravagant and insane, but what it says is something established henceforth, and will bear to be stereotyped. It is a truer truth, it is better and fairer news, and no time will ever shame it, or prove it false. This is a plant which thrives best in a temperate zone, where summer and winter alternate with one another. The Friend is a *necessarius,* and meets his Friend on homely ground; not on carpets and cushions, but on the ground and on rocks they will sit, obeying the natural and primitive laws. They will meet without any outcry, and part without loud sorrow. Their relation implies such qualities as the warrior prizes; for it takes a valor to open the hearts of men as well as the gates of castles. It is not an idle sympathy and mutual consolation merely, but a heroic sympathy of aspiration and endeavor.

> "When manhood shall be matched so
>   That fear can take no place,
> Then weary works make warriors
>   Each other to embrace."[16]

The Friendship which Wawatam testified for Henry the fur-trader,[17] as described in the latter's "Adventures," so almost bare and leafless, yet not blossomless nor fruitless, is remembered with satisfaction and security. The stern imperturbable war-

---

[16] From "The Renuing of Love" by Richard Edwards (1524?–1566).

[17] Alexander Henry (1739–1824), Canadian fur trader.

rior, after fasting, solitude, and mortification of body, comes to the white man's lodge, and affirms that he is the white brother whom he saw in his dream, and adopts him henceforth. He buries the hatchet as it regards his friend, and they hunt and feast and make maple-sugar together. "Metals unite from fluxility; birds and beasts from motives of convenience; fools from fear and stupidity; and just men at sight." If Wawatam would taste the "white man's milk" with his tribe, or take his bowl of human broth made of the trader's fellow-countrymen, he first finds a place of safety for his Friend, whom he has rescued from a similar fate. At length, after a long winter of undisturbed and happy intercourse in the family of the chieftain in the wilderness, hunting and fishing, they return in the spring to Michilimackinac to dispose of their furs; and it becomes necessary for Wawatam to take leave of his Friend at the Isle aux Outardes, when the latter, to avoid his enemies, proceeded to the Sault de Sainte Marie,[18] supposing that they were to be separated for a short time only. "We now exchanged farewells," says Henry, "with an emotion entirely reciprocal. I did not quit the lodge without the most grateful sense of the many acts of goodness which I had experienced in it, nor without the sincerest respect for the virtues which I had witnessed among its members. All the family accompanied me to the beach; and the canoe had no sooner put off than Wawatam commenced an address to the Kichi Manito,[19] beseeching him to take care of me, his brother, till we should next meet.—We had proceeded to too great a distance to allow of our hearing his voice, before Wawatam had ceased to offer up his prayers." We never hear of him again.

Friendship is not so kind as is imagined; it has not much human blood in it, but consists with a certain disregard for men and their erections, the Christian duties and humanities, while it purifies the air like electricity. There may be the sternest tragedy in the relation of two who are more than usually innocent and true to their highest instincts. We may call it an essentially heathenish intercourse, free and irresponsible in its nature, and practising all the virtues gratuitously. It is not the highest sympathy merely, but a pure and lofty society, a fragmentary and godlike intercourse of ancient date, still kept up at intervals, which, remembering itself, does not hesitate to disregard the humbler rights and duties of humanity. It requires immaculate and godlike qualities full-grown, and exists at all only by condescension and anticipation of the remotest future. We love nothing which is merely good and not fair, if such a thing is possible. Nature puts some kind of blossom before every fruit, not simply a calix behind it. When the Friend comes out of his heathenism and superstition, and breaks his idols, being converted by the precepts of a newer testament; when he forgets his mythology, and treats his Friend like a Christian, or as he can afford; then Friendship ceases to be Friendship, and becomes charity; that principle which established the almshouse is now beginning with its charity at home, and establishing an almshouse and pauper relations there.

As for the number which this society admits, it is at any rate to be begun with one, the noblest and greatest that we know, and whether the world will ever carry it further, whether, as Chaucer affirms,

---

[18] On what is now the border between Canada and Michigan.

[19] Nature spirit revered by the Algonquin Indian tribes of the Northeastern Territories.

"There be mo sterres in the skie than a pair,"[20]

remains to be proved;—

"And certaine he is well begone
    Among a thousand that findeth one."[21]

We shall not surrender ourselves heartily to any while we are conscious that another is more deserving of our love. Yet Friendship does not stand for numbers; the Friend does not count his Friends on his fingers; they are not numerable. The more there are included by this bond, if they are indeed included, the rarer and diviner the quality of the love that binds them. I am ready to believe that as private and intimate a relation may exist by which three are embraced, as between two. Indeed we cannot have too many friends; the virtue which we appreciate we to some extent appropriate, so that thus we are made at last more fit for every relation of life. A base Friendship is of a narrowing and exclusive tendency, but a noble one is not exclusive; its very superfluity and dispersed love is the humanity which sweetens society, and sympathizes with foreign nations; for though its foundations are private, it is in effect, a public affair and a public advantage, and the Friend, more than the father of a family, deserves well of the state.

The only danger in Friendship is that it will end. It is a delicate plant though a native. The least unworthiness, even if it be unknown to one's self, vitiates it. Let the Friend know that those faults which he observes in his Friend his own faults attract. There is no rule more invariable than that we are paid for our suspicions by finding what we suspected. By our narrowness and prejudices we say, I will have so much and such of you, my Friend, no more. Perhaps there are none charitable, none disinterested, none wise, noble, and heroic enough, for a true and lasting Friendship.

I sometimes hear my Friend's complain finely that I do not appreciate their fineness. I shall not tell them whether I do or not. As if they expected a vote of thanks for every fine thing which they uttered or did. Who knows but it was finely appreciated. It may be that your silence was the finest thing of the two. There are some things which a man never speaks of, which are much finer kept silent about. To the highest communications we only lend a silent ear. Our finest relations are not simply kept silent about, but buried under a positive depth of silence, never to be revealed. It may be that we are not even yet acquainted. In human intercourse the tragedy begins, not when there is misunderstanding about words, but when silence is not understood. Then there can never be an explanation. What avails it that another loves you, if he does not understand you? Such love is a curse. What sort of companions are they who are presuming always that their silence is more expressive than yours? How foolish, and inconsiderate, and unjust, to conduct as if you were the only party aggrieved! Has not your Friend always equal ground of complaint? No doubt my Friends sometimes speak to me in vain, but they do not know what things I hear which they are not aware that they have spoken. I know that I have frequently disappointed them by not giving them words when they expected them, or such as they expected. Whenever

---

[20] From *The Parliament of Fowls* (l. 595) by Geoffrey Chaucer (1340?–1400).

[21] From Chaucer's *The Romaunt of the Rose* (ll. 5533–5534).

I see my Friend I speak to him, but the expector, the man with the ears, is not he. They will complain too that you are hard. O ye that would have the cocoa-nut wrong side outwards, when next I weep I will let you know. They ask for words and deeds, when a true relation is word and deed. If they know not of these things, how can they be informed? We often forbear to confess our feelings, not from pride, but for fear that we could not continue to love the one who required us to give such proof of our affection.

I know a woman who possesses a restless and intelligent mind, interested in her own culture, and earnest to enjoy the highest possible advantages, and I meet her with pleasure as a natural person who not a little provokes me, and I suppose is stimulated in turn by myself. Yet our acquaintance plainly does not attain to that degree of confidence and sentiment which women, which all, in fact, covet. I am glad to help her, as I am helped by her; I like very well to know her with a sort of stranger's privilege, and hesitate to visit her often, like her other Friends. My nature pauses here, I do not well know why. Perhaps she does not make the highest demand on me, a religious demand. Some, with whose prejudices or peculiar bias I have no sympathy, yet inspire me with confidence, and I trust that they confide in me also as a religious heathen at least,—a good Greek. I too have principles as well founded as their own. If this person could conceive that, without wilfulness, I associate with her as far as our destinies are coincident, as far as our Good Geniuses[22] permit, and still value such intercourse, it would be a grateful assurance to me. I feel as if I appeared careless, indifferent, and without principle to her, not expecting more, and yet not content with less. If she could know that I make an infinite demand on myself, as well as on all others, she would see that this true though incomplete intercourse, is infinitely better than a more unreserved but falsely grounded one, without the principle of growth in it. For a companion, I require one who will make an equal demand on me with my own genius. Such a one will always be rightly tolerant. It is suicide and corrupts good manners to welcome any less than this. I value and trust those who love and praise my aspiration rather than my performance. If you would not stop to look at me, but look whither I am looking and further, then my education could not dispense with your company.

My love must be as free
　　As is the eagle's wing,
Hovering o'er land and sea
　　And every thing.

I must not dim my eye
　　In thy saloon,
I must not leave my sky
　　And nightly moon.

Be not the fowler's net
　　Which stays my flight,
And craftily is set
　　T' allure the sight.

[22] Guardian spirits.

But be the favoring gale
   That bears me on,
And still doth fill my sail
   When thou art gone.

I cannot leave my sky
   For thy caprice,
True love would soar as high
   As heaven is.

The eagle would not brook
   Her mate thus won,
Who trained his eye to look
   Beneath the sun.[23]

Few things are more difficult than to help a Friend in matters which do not require the aid of Friendship, but only a cheap and trivial service, if your Friendship wants the basis of a thorough practical acquaintance. I stand in the friendliest relation, on social and spiritual grounds, to one who does not perceive what practical skill I have, but when he seeks my assistance in such matters, is wholly ignorant of that one with whom he deals; does not use my skill, which in such matters is much greater than his, but only my hands. I know another, who, on the contrary, is remarkable for his discrimination in this respect; who knows how to make use of the talents of others when he does not possess the same; knows when not to look after or oversee, and stops short at his man. It is a rare pleasure to serve him, which all laborers know. I am not a little pained by the other kind of treatment. It is as if, after the friendliest and most ennobling intercourse, your Friend should use you as a hammer and drive a nail with your head, all in good faith; notwithstanding that you are a tolerable carpenter, as well as his good Friend, and would use a hammer cheerfully in his service. This want of perception is a defect which all the virtues of the heart cannot supply.—

The Good how can we trust?
Only the Wise are just.
The Good we use,
The Wise we cannot choose.
These there are none above;
The Good they know and love,
But are not known again
By those of lesser ken.
They do not charm us with their eyes,
But they transfix with their advice;
No partial sympathy they feel
With private woe or private weal,
But with the universe joy and sigh,
Whose knowledge is their sympathy.[24]

---

[23] Thoreau's own verses.   [24] Thoreau's own verses.

Confucius said, "To contract ties of Friendship with any one, is to contract Friendship with his virtue. There ought not to be any other motive in Friendship." But men wish us to contract Friendship with their vice also. I have a Friend who wishes me to see that to be right which I know to be wrong. But if Friendship is to rob me of my eyes, if it is to darken the day, I will have none of it. It should be expansive and inconceivably liberalizing in its effects. True Friendship can afford true knowledge. It does not depend on darkness and ignorance. A want of discernment cannot be an ingredient in it. If I can see my Friend's virtues more distinctly than another's, his faults too are made more conspicuous by contrast. We have not so good a right to hate any as our Friend. Faults are not the less faults because they are invariably balanced by corresponding virtues, and for a fault there is no excuse, though it may appear greater than it is in many ways. I have never known one who could bear criticism, who could not be flattered, who would not bribe his judge, or was content that the truth should be loved always better than himself.

If two travellers would go their way harmoniously together, the one must take as true and just a view of things as the other, else their path will not be strewn with roses. Yet you can travel profitably and pleasantly even with a blind man, if he practises common courtesy, and when you converse about the scenery will remember that he is blind but that you can see; and you will not forget that his sense of hearing is probably quickened by his want of sight. Otherwise you will not long keep company. A blind man, and a man in whose eyes there was no defect, were walking together, when they came to the edge of a precipice,—"Take care! my friend," said the latter, "here is a steep precipice; go no further this way."—"I know better," said the other, and stepped off.

It is impossible to say all that we think, even to our truest Friend. We may bid him farewell forever sooner than complain, for our complaint is too well grounded to be uttered. There is not so good an understanding between any two, but the exposure by the one of a serious fault in the other will produce a misunderstanding in proportion to its heinousness. The constitutional differences which always exist, and are obstacles to a perfect Friendship, are forever a forbidden theme to the lips of Friends. They advise by their whole behavior. Nothing can reconcile them but love. They are fatally late when they undertake to explain and treat with one another like foes. Who will take an apology for a Friend? They must apologize like dew and frost, which are off again with the sun, and which all men know in their hearts to be beneficent. The necessity itself for explanation,—what explanation will atone for that? True love does not quarrel for slight reasons, such mistakes as mutual acquaintances can explain away, but alas, however slight the apparent cause, only for adequate and fatal and everlasting reasons, which can never be set aside. Its quarrel, if there is any, is ever recurring, notwithstanding the beams of affection which invariably come to gild its tears; as the rainbow, however beautiful and unerring a sign, does not promise fair weather for ever, but only for a season. I have known two or three persons pretty well, and yet I have never known advice to be of use but in trivial and transient matters. One may know what another does not, but the utmost kindness cannot impart what is requisite to make the advice useful. We must accept or refuse one another as we are. I could tame a hyena more easily than my Friend. He is a material which no tool of mine will work. A naked savage will fell an oak with a firebrand, and wear a hatchet out of the rock by friction, but I cannot hew the smallest chip out of the character of my Friend, either to beautify or deform it.

The lover learns at last that there is no person quite transparent and trustworthy, but every one has a devil in him that is capable of any crime in the long run. Yet, as an oriental philosopher has said, "Although Friendship between good men is interrupted, their principles remain unaltered. The stalk of the lotus may be broken, and the fibres remain connected."

Ignorance and bungling with love are better than wisdom and skill without. There may be courtesy, there may be even temper, and wit, and talent, and sparkling conversation, there may be good-will even,—and yet the humanest and divinest faculties pine for exercise. Our life without love is like coke and ashes. Men may be pure as alabaster and Parian Marble,[25] elegant as a Tuscan villa, sublime as Niagara, and yet if there is no milk mingled with the wine at their entertainments, better is the hospitality of Goths and Vandals. My Friend is not of some other race or family of men, but flesh of my flesh, bone of my bone. He is my real brother. I see his nature groping yonder so like mine. We do not live far apart. Have not the fates associated us in many ways? It says, in the Vishnu Purana:[26] "Seven paces together is sufficient for the friendship of the virtuous, but thou and I have dwelt together." Is it of no significance that we have so long partaken of the same loaf, drank at the same fountain, breathed the same air, summer and winter, felt the same heat and cold; that the same fruits have been pleased to refresh us both, and we have never had a thought of different fibre the one from the other!

> Nature doth have her dawn each day,
>   But mine are far between;
> Content, I cry, for sooth to say,
>   Mine brightest are I ween.
>
> For when my sun doth deign to rise,
>   Though it be her noontide,
> Her fairest field in shadow lies,
>   Nor can my light abide.
>
> Sometimes I bask me in her day,
>   Conversing with my mate,
> But if we interchange one ray,
>   Forthwith her heats abate.
>
> Through his discourse I climb and see,
>   As from some eastern hill,
> A brighter morrow rise to me
>   Than lieth in her skill.

---

[25] Fine white marble from the Greek island of Paros.

[26] Hindu sacred writings, translated by H. H. Wilson (1840).

As't were two summer days in one,
  Two Sundays come together,
Our rays united make one sun.
  With fairest summer weather.[27]

As surely as the sunset in my latest November shall translate me to the ethereal world, and remind me of the ruddy morning of youth; as surely as the last strain of music which falls on my decaying ear shall make age to be forgotten, or, in short, the manifold influences of nature survive during the term of our natural life, so surely my Friend shall forever be my Friend, and reflect a ray of God to me, and time shall foster and adorn and consecrate our Friendship, no less than the ruins of temples. As I love nature, as I love singing birds, and gleaming stubble, and flowing rivers, and morning and evening, and summer and winter, I love thee my Friend.

But all that can be said of Friendship, is like botany to flowers. How can the understanding take account of its friendliness?

Even the death of Friends will inspire us as much as their lives. They will leave consolation to the mourners, as the rich leave money to defray the expenses of their funerals, and their memories will be incrusted over with sublime and pleasing thoughts, as monuments of other men are overgrown with moss; for our Friends have no place in the graveyard.

This to our cis-Alpine and cis-Atlantic Friends.

Also this other word of entreaty and advice to the large and respectable nation of Acquaintances, beyond the mountains;—Greeting.

My most serene and irresponsible neighbors, let us see that we have the whole advantage of each other; we will be useful, at least, if not admirable, to one another. I know that the mountains which separate us are high, and covered with perpetual snow, but despair not. Improve the serene winter weather to scale them. If need be, soften the rocks with vinegar. For here lie the verdant plains of Italy ready to receive you. Nor shall I be slow on my side to penetrate to your Provence. Strike then boldly at head or heart or any vital part. Depend upon it the timber is well seasoned and tough, and will bear rough usage; and if it should crack, there is plenty more where it came from. I am no piece of crockery that cannot be jostled against my neighbor without danger of being broken by the collision, and must needs ring false and jarringly to the end of my days, when once I am cracked; but rather one of the old fashioned wooden trenchers, which one while stands at the head of the table, and at another is a milking-stool, and at another a seat for children, and finally goes down to its grave not unadorned with honorable scars, and does not die till it is worn out. Nothing can shock a brave man but dulness. Think how many rebuffs every man has experienced in his day; perhaps has fallen into a horsepond, eaten fresh-water clams, or worn one shirt for a week without washing. Indeed, you cannot receive a shock unless you have an electric affinity for that which shocks you. Use me, then, for I am useful in my way, and stand as one of many petitioners, from toadstool and henbane up to dahlia and violet, supplicating to be put to my use, if by any means

---

[27] Thoreau's own verses.

ye may find me serviceable; whether for a medicated drink or bath, as balm and lavender; or for fragrance, as verbena and geranium; or for sight, as cactus; or for thoughts, as pansy.—These humbler, at least, if not those higher uses.

Ah my dear Strangers and Enemies, I would not forget you. I can well afford to welcome you. Let me subscribe myself Yours ever and truly—your much obliged servant. We have nothing to fear from our foes; God keeps a standing army for that service; but we have no ally against our Friends, those ruthless Vandals.

Once more to one and all,

"Friends, Romans, Countrymen, and Lovers."[28]

> Let such pure hate still underprop
> Our love, that we may be
> Each other's conscience,
> And have our sympathy
> Mainly from thence.
>
> We'll one another treat like gods,
> And all the faith we have
> In virtue and in truth, bestow
> On either, and suspicion leave
> To gods below.
>
> Two solitary stars—
> Unmeasured systems far
> Between us roll,
> But by our conscious light we are
> Determined to one pole.
>
> What need confound the sphere—
> Love can afford to wait,
> For it no hour's too late
> That witnesseth one duty's end,
> Or to another doth beginning lend.
>
> It will subserve no use,
> More than the tints of flowers,
> Only the independent guest
> Frequents its bowers,
> Inherits its bequest.
>
> No speech though kind has it,
> But kinder silence doles

[28] The title of Thoreau's poem elaborates upon the opening of Marc Antony's funeral oration in Shakespeare's *Julius Caesar*, Act III, Sc. ii, l. 73.

Unto its mates,
By night consoles,
By day congratulates.

What saith the tongue to tongue?
What heareth ear of ear?
By the decrees of fate
From year to year,
Does it communicate.

Pathless the gulf of feeling yawns—
No trivial bridge of words,
Or arch of boldest span,
Can leap the moat that girds
The sincere man.

No show of bolts and bars
Can keep the foeman out,
Or 'scape his secret mine
Who entered with the doubt
That drew the line.

No warder at the gate
Can let the friendly in,
But, like the sun, o'er all
He will the castle win,
And shine along the wall.

There's nothing in the world I know
That can escape from love,
For every depth it goes below,
And every height above.

It waits as waits the sky,
Until the clouds go by,
Yet shines serenely on
With an eternal day,
Alike when they are gone,
And when they stay.

Implacable is Love,—
Foes may be bought or teazed
From their hostile intent,
But he goes unappeased,
Who is on kindness bent.

Resistance to Civil Government

I heartily accept the motto,—"That government is best which governs least;"[1] and I should like to see it acted up to more rapidly and systematically. Carried out, it finally amounts to this, which also I believe,—"That government is best which governs not at all;" and when men are prepared for it, that will be the kind of government which they will have. Government is at best but an expedient; but most governments are usually, and all governments are sometimes, inexpedient. The objections which have been brought against a standing army, and they are many and weighty, and deserve to prevail, may also at last be brought against a standing government. The standing army is only an arm of the standing government. The government itself, which is only the mode which the people have chosen to execute their will, is equally liable to be abused and perverted before the people can act through it. Witness the present Mexican war,[2] the work of comparatively a few individuals using the standing government as their tool; for, in the outset, the people would not have consented to this measure.

This American government,—what is it but a tradition, though a recent one, endeavoring to transmit itself unimpaired to posterity, but each instant losing some of its integrity? It has not the vitality and force of a single living man; for a single man can bend it to his will. It is a sort of wooden gun to the people themselves; and, if ever they should use it in earnest as a real one against each other, it will surely split. But it is not the less necessary for this; for the people must have some complicated machinery or other, and hear its din, to satisfy that idea of government which they have. Governments show thus how successfully men can be imposed on, even impose on themselves, for their own advantage. It is excellent, we must all allow; yet this government never of itself furthered any enterprise, but by the alacrity with which it got out of its way. *It* does not keep the country free. *It* does not settle the West. *It* does not educate. The character inherent in the American people has done all that has been accomplished; and it would have done somewhat more, if the government had not sometimes got in its way. For government is an expedient by which men would fain succeed in letting one another alone; and, as has been said, when it is most expedient, the governed are most let alone by it. Trade and commerce, if they were not made of India rubber, would never manage to bounce over the obstacles which legislators are continually putting in their way; and, if one were to judge these men wholly by the effects of their actions, and not partly by their intentions, they would deserve to be classed and punished with those mischievous persons who put obstructions on the railroads.

But, to speak practically and as a citizen, unlike those who call themselves no-

---

[1] Motto displayed on the masthead of the *Democratic Review,* a New York journal which, with these words, continued to support a sentiment widely upheld from the time of Thomas Jefferson.
[2] Thoreau first delivered this essay in the form of a lecture on January 26, 1848, during the height of the controversy over the Mexican War (1846–1848), which was seen by many in the North as a plan by Southern slave owners to extend the slavery system to the West.

government men, I ask for, not at once no government, but at *once* a better government. Let every man make known what kind of government would command his respect, and that will be one step toward obtaining it.

After all, the practical reason why, when the power is once in the hands of the people, a majority are permitted, and for a long period continue, to rule, is not because they are most likely to be in the right, nor because this seems fairest to the minority, but because they are physically the strongest. But a government in which the majority rule in all cases cannot be based on justice, even as far as men understand it. Can there not be a government in which majorities do not virtually decide right and wrong, but conscience?—in which majorities decide only those questions to which the rule of expediency is applicable? Must the citizen ever for a moment, or in the least degree, resign his conscience to the legislator? Why has every man a conscience, then? I think that we should be men first, and subjects afterward. It is not desirable to cultivate a respect for the law, so much as for the right. The only obligation which I have a right to assume, is to do at any time what I think right. It is truly enough said, that a corporation has no conscience; but a corporation of conscientious men is a corporation *with* a conscience. Law never made men a whit more just; and, by means of their respect for it, even the well-disposed are daily made the agents of injustice. A common and natural result of an undue respect for law is, that you may see a file of soldiers, colonel, captain, corporal, privates, powder-monkeys and all, marching in admirable order over hill and dale to the wars, against their wills, aye, against their common sense and consciences, which makes it very steep marching indeed, and produces a palpitation of the heart. They have no doubt that it is a damnable business in which they are concerned; they are all peaceably inclined. Now, what are they? Men at all? or small moveable forts and magazines, at the service of some unscrupulous man in power? Visit the Navy Yard, and behold a marine, such a man as an American government can make, or such as it can make a man with its black arts, a mere shadow and reminiscence of humanity, a man laid out alive and standing, and already, as one may say, buried under arms with funeral accompaniments, though it may be

"Not a drum was heard, not a funeral note,
     As his corse to the rampart we hurried;
Not a soldier discharged his farewell shot
     O'er the grave where our hero we buried."[3]

The mass of men serve the State thus, not as men mainly, but as machines, with their bodies. They are the standing army, and the militia, jailers, constables, *posse comitatus,*[4] &c. In most cases there is no free exercise whatever of the judgment or of the moral sense; but they put themselves on a level with wood and earth and stones, and wooden men can perhaps be manufactured that will serve the purpose as well. Such command no more respect than men of straw, or a lump of dirt. They have the same sort of worth only as horses and dogs. Yet such as these even are commonly esteemed good citizens. Others, as most legislators, politicians, lawyers, ministers, and

---

[3] Song based on "The Burial of Sir John Moore at Corunna" (1817) by Charles Wolfe (1791–1823).

[4] The Latin phrase from which the term "sheriff's posse" is derived.

officeholders, serve the State chiefly with their heads; and, as they rarely make any moral distinctions, they are as likely to serve the devil, without intending it, as God. A very few, as heroes, patriots, martyrs, reformers in the great sense, and *men,* serve the State with their consciences also, and so necessarily resist it for the most part; and they are commonly treated by it as enemies. A wise man will only be useful as a man, and will not submit to be "clay," and "stop a hole to keep the wind away,"[5] but leave that office to his dust at least:—

"I am too high-born to be propertied,
   To be a secondary at control,
   Or useful serving-man and instrument
   To any sovereign state throughout the world."[6]

He who gives himself entirely to his fellow-men appears to them useless and selfish; but he who gives himself partially to them is pronounced a benefactor and philanthropist.

How does it become a man to behave toward this American government to-day? I answer that he cannot without disgrace be associated with it. I cannot for an instant recognize that political organization as *my* government which is the *slave's* government also.

All men recognize the right of revolution; that is, the right to refuse allegiance to and to resist the government, when its tyranny or its inefficiency are great and unendurable. But almost all say that such is not the case now. But such was the case, they think, in the Revolution of '75.[7] If one were to tell me that this was a bad government because it taxed certain foreign commodities brought to its ports, it is most probable that I should not make an ado about it, for I can do without them: all machines have their friction; and possibly this does enough good to counterbalance the evil. At any rate, it is a great evil to make a stir about it. But when the friction comes to have its machine, and oppression and robbery are organized, I say, let us not have such a machine any longer. In other words, when a sixth of the population of a nation which has undertaken to be the refuge of liberty are slaves, and a whole country is unjustly overrun and conquered by a foreign army, and subjected to military law, I think that it is not too soon for honest men to rebel and revolutionize. What makes this duty the more urgent is the fact, that the country so overrun is not our own, but ours is the invading army.

Paley, a common authority with many on moral questions, in his chapter on the "Duty of Submission to Civil Government,"[8] resolves all civil obligation into expediency; and he proceeds to say, "that so long as the interest of the whole society requires it, that is, so long as the established government cannot be resisted or changed without public inconveniency, it is the will of God that the established government be obeyed, and no longer." . . . "This principle being admitted, the justice of every particular case of resistance is reduced to a computation of the quantity of the danger and grievance on the one side, and of the probability and expense of redressing it on the

---

[5] *Hamlet,* Act V, Sc. i, ll. 236–237.
[6] *King John,* Act V, Sc. ii, ll. 79–82.
[7] The American Revolution (1775–1783).

[8] From *Principles of Moral and Political Philosophy* (1785) by William Paley (1743–1805), English theologian.

other." Of this, he says, every man shall judge for himself. But Paley appears never to have contemplated those cases to which the rule of expediency does not apply, in which a people, as well as an individual, must do justice, cost what it may. If I have unjustly wrested a plank from a drowning man, I must restore it to him though I drown myself. This, according to Paley, would be inconvenient. But he that would save his life, in such a case, shall lose it.[9] This people must cease to hold slaves, and to make war on Mexico, though it cost them their existence as a people.

In their practice, nations agree with Paley; but does any one think that Massachusetts does exactly what is right at the present crisis?

> "A drab of state, a cloth-o'-silver slut,
>   To have her train borne up, and her soul trail in the dirt."[10]

Practically speaking, the opponents to a reform in Massachusetts are not a hundred thousand politicians at the South, but a hundred thousand merchants and farmers here, who are more interested in commerce and agriculture than they are in humanity, and are not prepared to do justice to the slave and to Mexico, *cost what it may.* I quarrel not with far-off foes, but with those who, near at home, co-operate with, and do the bidding of those far away, and without whom the latter would be harmless. We are accustomed to say, that the mass of men are unprepared; but improvement is slow, because the few are not materially wiser or better than the many. It is not so important that many should be as good as you, as that there be some absolute goodness somewhere; for that will leaven the whole lump.[11] There are thousands who are *in opinion* opposed to slavery and to the war, who yet in effect do nothing to put an end to them; who, esteeming themselves children of Washington and Franklin, sit down with their hands in their pockets, and say that they know not what to do, and do nothing; who even postpone the question of freedom to the question of free-trade, and quietly read the prices-current along with the latest advices[12] from Mexico, after dinner, and, it may be, fall asleep over them both. What is the price-current of an honest man and patriot to-day? They hesitate, and they regret, and sometimes they petition; but they do nothing in earnest and with effect. They will wait, well-disposed, for others to remedy the evil, that they may no longer have it to regret. At most, they give only a cheap vote, and a feeble countenance and God-speed, to the right, as it goes by them. There are nine hundred and ninety-nine patrons of virtue to one virtuous man; but it is easier to deal with the real possessor of a thing than with the temporary guardian of it.

All voting is a sort of gaming, like chequers or backgammon, with a slight moral tinge to it, a playing with right and wrong, with moral questions; and betting naturally accompanies it. The character of the voters is not staked. I cast my vote, perchance, as I think right; but I am not vitally concerned that that right should prevail. I am willing to leave it to the majority. Its obligation, therefore, never exceeds that of expediency. Even voting *for the right* is *doing* nothing for it. It is only

---

[9] Example of Thoreau's constant use of scriptural references; here, from Luke 9:24.
[10] *The Revenger's Tragedy* (1607), Act IV, Sc. iv, ll. 70–72, attributed to Cyril Tourneur (1575?–1629).
[11] Paraphrase of 1 Corinthians 5:6.
[12] News dispatches.

expressing to men feebly your desire that it should prevail. A wise man will not leave the right to the mercy of chance, nor wish it to prevail through the power of the majority. There is but little virtue in the action of masses of men. When the majority shall at length vote for the abolition of slavery, it will be because they are indifferent to slavery, or because there is but little slavery left to be abolished by their vote. *They* will then be the only slaves. Only *his* vote can hasten the abolition of slavery who asserts his own freedom by his vote.

I hear of a convention to be held at Baltimore, or elsewhere, for the selection of a candidate for the Presidency, made up chiefly of editors, and men who are politicians by profession; but I think, what is it to any independent, intelligent, and respectable man what decision they may come to, shall we not have the advantage of his wisdom and honesty, nevertheless? Can we not count upon some independent votes? Are there not many individuals in the country who do not attend conventions? But no: I find that the respectable man, so called, has immediately drifted from his position, and despairs of his country, when his country has more reason to despair of him. He forthwith adopts one of the candidates thus selected as the only *available* one, thus proving that he is himself *available* for any purposes of the demagogue. His vote is of no more worth than that of any unprincipled foreigner or hireling native, who may have been bought. Oh for a man who is a *man,* and, as my neighbor says, has a bone in his back which you cannot pass your hand through! Our statistics are at fault: the population has been returned too large. How many *men* are there to a square thousand miles in this country? Hardly one. Does not America offer any inducement for men to settle here? The American has dwindled into an Odd Fellow,[13]—one who may be known by the development of his organ of gregariousness,[14] and a manifest lack of intellect and cheerful self-reliance; whose first and chief concern, on coming into the world, is to see that the alms-houses are in good repair; and, before yet he has lawfully donned the virile garb,[15] to collect a fund for the support of the widows and orphans that may be; who, in short, ventures to live only by the aid of the mutual insurance company, which has promised to bury him decently.

It is not a man's duty, as a matter of course, to devote himself to the eradication of any, even the most enormous wrong; he may still properly have other concerns to engage him; but it is his duty, at least, to wash his hands of it, and, if he gives it no thought longer, not to give it practically his support. If I devote myself to other pursuits and contemplations, I must first see, at least, that I do not pursue them sitting upon another man's shoulders. I must get off him first, that he may pursue his contemplations too. See what gross inconsistency is tolerated. I have heard some of my townsmen say, "I should like to have them order me out to help put down an insurrection of the slaves, or to march to Mexico,—see if I would go;" and yet these very men have each, directly by their allegiance, and so indirectly, at least, by their money, furnished a substitute. The soldier is applauded who refuses to serve in an unjust war by those who do not refuse to sustain the unjust government which makes the war; is applauded by those whose own act and authority he disregards and sets

---

[13] Satiric reference to members of a secret fraternal society, the Independent Order of Odd Fellows, as part of Thoreau's argument that most Americans had fallen away from independent self-sufficiency into conformism.

[14] Phrenological term applied to persons who prefer belonging to the group.

[15] Attire that acknowledged that a Roman boy had attained adulthood.

at nought; as if the State were penitent to that degree that it hired one to scourge it while it sinned, but not to that degree that it left off sinning for a moment. Thus, under the name of order and civil government, we are all made at last to pay homage to and support our own meanness. After the first blush of sin, comes its indifference and from immoral it becomes, as it were, *unmoral,* and not quite unnecessary to that life which we have made.

The broadest and most prevalent error requires the most disinterested virtue to sustain it. The slight reproach to which the virtue of patriotism is commonly liable, the noble are most likely to incur. Those who, while they disapprove of the character and measures of a government, yield to it their allegiance and support, are undoubtedly its most conscientious supporters, and so frequently the most serious obstacles to reform. Some are petitioning the State to dissolve the Union, to disregard the requisitions of the President.[16] Why do they not dissolve it themselves,—the union between themselves and the State,—and refuse to pay their quota into its treasury? Do not they stand in the same relation to the State, that the State does to the Union? And have not the same reasons prevented the State from resisting the Union, which have prevented them from resisting the State?

How can a man be satisfied to entertain an opinion merely, and enjoy *it?* Is there any enjoyment in it, if his opinion is that he is aggrieved? If you are cheated out of a single dollar by your neighbor, you do not rest satisfied with knowing that you are cheated, or with saying that you are cheated, or even with petitioning him to pay you your due; but you take effectual steps at once to obtain the full amount, and see that you are never cheated again. Action from principle,—the perception and the performance of right,—changes things and relations; it is essentially revolutionary, and does not consist wholly with any thing which was. It not only divides states and churches, it divides families; aye, it divides the *individual,* separating the diabolical in him from the divine.

Unjust laws exist: shall we be content to obey them, or shall we endeavor to amend them, and obey them until we have succeeded, or shall we transgress them at once? Men generally, under such a government as this, think that they ought to wait until they have persuaded the majority to alter them. They think that, if they should resist, the remedy would be worse than the evil. But it is the fault of the government itself that the remedy *is* worse than the evil. *It* makes it worse. Why is it not more apt to anticipate and provide for reform? Why does it not cherish its wise minority? Why does it cry and resist before it is hurt? Why does it not encourage its citizens to be on the alert to point out its faults, and *do* better than it would have them? Why does it always crucify Christ, and excommunicate Copernicus and Luther,[17] and pronounce Washington and Franklin rebels?

One would think, that a deliberate and practical denial of its authority was the only offence never contemplated by government; else, why has it not assigned its definite, its suitable and proportionate penalty? If a man who has no property refuses

---

[16] President James K. Polk sought money and troops for the Mexican conflict over the objections of certain New England radicals who proposed breaking away from the Union in order to further their aims as abolitionists.

[17] Both the Polish astronomer Copernicus

(1473–1543) and the German head of the Protestant reformation, Martin Luther (1483–1546), were considered heretics by the Roman church. The former in fact died before he could be excommunicated.

but once to earn nine shillings[18] for the State, he is put in prison for a period unlimited by any law that I know, and determined only by the discretion of those who placed him there; but if he should steal ninety times nine shillings from the State, he is soon permitted to go at large again.

If the injustice is part of the necessary friction of the machine of government, let it go, let it go: perchance it will wear smooth,—certainly the machine will wear out. If the injustice has a spring, or a pulley, or a rope, or a crank, exclusively for itself, then perhaps you may consider whether the remedy will not be worse than the evil; but if it is of such a nature that it requires you to be the agent of injustice to another, then, I say, break the law. Let your life be a counter friction to stop the machine. What I have to do is to see, at any rate, that I do not lend myself to the wrong which I condemn.

As for adopting the ways which the State has provided for remedying the evil, I know not of such ways. They take too much time, and a man's life will be gone. I have other affairs to attend to. I came into this world, not chiefly to make this a good place to live in, but to live in it, be it good or bad. A man has not every thing to do, but something; and because he cannot do *every thing,* it is not necessary that he should do *something* wrong. It is not my business to be petitioning the governor or the legislature any more than it is theirs to petition me; and, if they should not hear my petition, what should I do then? But in this case the State has provided no way: its very Constitution is the evil. This may seem to be harsh and stubborn and unconciliatory; but it is to treat with the utmost kindness and consideration the only spirit that can appreciate or deserves it. So is all change for the better, like birth and death which convulse the body.

I do not hesitate to say, that those who call themselves abolitionists should at once effectually withdraw their support, both in person and property, from the government of Massachusetts, and not wait till they constitute a majority of one, before they suffer the right to prevail through them. I think that it is enough if they have God on their side, without waiting for that other one. Moreover, any man more right than his neighbors, constitutes a majority of one already.

I meet this American government, or its representative the State government, directly, and face to face, once a year, no more, in the person of its tax-gatherer; this is the only mode in which a man situated as I am necessarily meets it; and it then says distinctly, Recognize me; and the simplest, the most effectual, and, in the present posture of affairs, the indispensablest mode of treating with it on this head, of expressing your little satisfaction with and love for it, is to deny it then. My civil neighbor, the tax-gatherer, is the very man I have to deal with,—for it is, after all, with men and not with parchment that I quarrel,—and he has voluntarily chosen to be an agent of the government. How shall he ever know well what he is and does as an officer of the government, or as a man, until he is obliged to consider whether he shall treat me, his neighbor, for whom he has respect, as a neighbor and well-disposed man, or as a maniac and disturber of the peace, and see if he can get over this obstruction to his neighborliness without a ruder and more impetuous thought or speech corresponding with his action? I know this well, that if one thousand, if

[18] The amount of some $2, which Thoreau refused to pay in taxes.

one hundred, if ten men whom I could name,—if ten *honest* men only,—aye, if *one* HONEST man, in this State of Massachusetts, *ceasing to hold slaves,* were actually to withdraw from this copartnership, and be locked up in the county jail therefor, it would be the abolition of slavery in America. For it matters not how small the beginning may seem to be: what is once well done is done for ever. But we love better to talk about it: that we say is our mission. Reform keeps many scores of newspapers in its service, but not one man. If my esteemed neighbor, the State's ambassador,[19] who will devote his days to the settlement of the question of human rights in the Council Chamber, instead of being threatened with the prisons of Carolina, were to sit down the prisoner of Massachusetts, that State which is so anxious to foist the sin of slavery upon her sister,—though at present she can discover only an act of inhospitality to be the ground of a quarrel with her,—the Legislature would not wholly waive the subject the following winter.

Under a government which imprisons any unjustly, the true place for a just man is also a prison. The proper place to-day, the only place which Massachusetts has provided for her freer and less desponding spirits, is in her prisons, to be put out and locked out of the State by her own act, as they have already put themselves out by their principles. It is there that the fugitive slave, and the Mexican prisoner on parole, and the Indian come to plead the wrongs of his race, should find them; on that separate, but more free and honorable ground, where the State places those who are not *with* her but *against* her,—the only house in a slave-state in which a free man can abide with honor. If any think that their influence would be lost there, and their voices no longer afflict the ear of the State, that they would not be as an enemy within its walls, they do not know by how much truth is stronger than error, nor how much more eloquently and effectively he can combat injustice who has experienced a little in his own person. Cast your whole vote, not a strip of paper merely, but your whole influence. A minority is powerless while it conforms to the majority; it is not even a minority then; but it is irresistible when it clogs by its whole weight. If the alternative is to keep all just men in prison, or give up war and slavery, the State will not hesitate which to choose. If a thousand men were not to pay their tax-bills this year, that would not be a violent and bloody measure, as it would be to pay them, and enable the State to commit violence and shed innocent blood. This is, in fact, the definition of a peaceable revolution, if any such is possible. If the tax-gatherer, or any other public officer, asks me, as one has done, "But what shall I do?" my answer is, "If you really wish to do any thing, resign your office." When the subject has refused allegiance, and the officer has resigned his office, then the revolution is accomplished. But even suppose blood should flow. Is there not a sort of blood shed when the conscience is wounded? Through this wound a man's real manhood and immortality flow out, and he bleeds to an everlasting death. I see this blood flowing now.

I have contemplated the imprisonment of the offender, rather than the seizure of his goods,—though both will serve the same purpose,—because they who assert the purest right, and consequently are most dangerous to a corrupt State, commonly have

---

[19] Samuel Hoar (1778–1856) of Concord was sent by the State of Massachusetts (which he represented as senator) to South Carolina in an attempt to aid black sailors who had been taken from Massachusetts ships in Southern ports. His efforts were frustrated when he was expelled from Charleston by legal action.

not spent much time in accumulating property. To such the State renders comparatively small service, and a slight tax is wont to appear exorbitant, particularly if they
are obliged to earn it by special labor with their hands. If there were one who lived
wholly without the use of money, the State itself would hesitate to demand it of him.
But the rich man—not to make any invidious comparison—is always sold to the
institution which makes him rich. Absolutely speaking, the more money, the less
virtue; for money comes between a man and his objects, and obtains them for him;
and it was certainly no great virtue to obtain it. It puts to rest many questions which
he would otherwise be taxed to answer; while the only new question which it puts
is the hard but superfluous one, how to spend it. Thus his moral ground is taken from
under his feet. The opportunities of living are diminished in proportion as what are
called the "means" are increased. The best thing a man can do for his culture when
he is rich is to endeavour to carry out those schemes which he entertained when he
was poor. Christ answered the Herodians according to their condition. "Show me the
tribute-money," said he;—and one took a penny out of his pocket;—If you use money
which has the image of Cæsar on it, and which he has made current and valuable,
that is, *if you are men of the State,* and gladly enjoy the advantages of Cæsar's
government, then pay him back some of his own when he demands it; "Render
therefore to Cæsar that which is Cæsar's, and to God those things which are God's,"[20]
—leaving them no wiser than before as to which was which; for they did not wish
to know.

When I converse with the freest of my neighbors, I perceive that, whatever they
may say about the magnitude and seriousness of the question, and their regard for the
public tranquillity, the long and the short of the matter is, that they cannot spare the
protection of the existing government, and they dread the consequences of disobedience to it to their property and families. For my own part, I should not like to think
that I ever rely on the protection of the State. But, if I deny the authority of the State
when it presents its tax-bill, it will soon take and waste all my property, and so harass
me and my children without end. This is hard. This makes it impossible for a man
to live honestly and at the same time comfortably in outward respects. It will not
be worth the while to accumulate property; that would be sure to go again. You must
hire or squat somewhere, and raise but a small crop, and eat that soon. You must live
within yourself, and depend upon yourself, always tucked up and ready for a start,
and not have many affairs. A man may grow rich in Turkey even, if he will be in
all respects a good subject of the Turkish government. Confucius said.—"If a State
is governed by the principles of reason, poverty and misery are subjects of shame; if
a State is not governed by the principles of reason, riches and honors are the subjects
of shame."[21] No: until I want the protection of Massachusetts to be extended to me
in some distant southern port, where my liberty is endangered, or until I am bent
solely on building up an estate at home by peaceful enterprise, I can afford to refuse
allegiance to Massachusetts, and her right to my property and life. It costs me less in
every sense to incur the penalty of disobedience to the State, than it would to obey.
I should feel as if I were worth less in that case.

[20] See Matthew 22:16–22.
[21] From *The Analects* by the Chinese philosopher
Confucius (ca. 551–479 B.C.).

Some years ago, the State met me in behalf of the church, and commanded me to pay a certain sum toward the support of a clergyman whose preaching my father attended, but never I myself. "Pay it," it said, "or be locked up in the jail." I declined to pay. But, unfortunately, another man saw fit to pay it. I did not see why the schoolmaster should be taxed to support the priest, and not the priest the schoolmaster; for I was not the State's schoolmaster, but I supported myself by voluntary subscription. I did not see why the lyceum should not present its tax-bill, and have the State to back its demand, as well as the church. However, at the request of the selectmen, I condescended to make some such statement as this in writing:—"Know all men by these presents, that I, Henry Thoreau, do not wish to be regarded as a member of any incorporated society which I have not joined." This I gave to the town-clerk; and he has it. The State, having thus learned that I did not wish to be regarded as a member of that church, has never made a like demand on me since; though it said that it must adhere to its original presumption that time. If I had known how to name them, I should then have signed off in detail from all the societies which I never signed on to; but I did not know where to find a complete list.

I have paid no poll-tax for six years. I was put into a jail once on this account, for one night;[22] and, as I stood considering the walls of solid stone, two or three feet thick, the door of wood and iron, a foot thick, and the iron grating which strained the light, I could not help being struck with the foolishness of that institution which treated me as if I were mere flesh and blood and bones, to be locked up. I wondered that it should have concluded at length that this was the best use it could put me to, and had never thought to avail itself of my services in some way. I saw that, if there was a wall of stone between me and my townsmen, there was a still more difficult one to climb or break through, before they could get to be as free as I was. I did not for a moment feel confined, and the walls seemed a great waste of stone and mortar. I felt as if I alone of all my townsmen had paid my tax. They plainly did not know how to treat me, but behaved like persons who are underbred. In every threat and in every compliment there was a blunder; for they thought that my chief desire was to stand the other side of that stone wall. I could not but smile to see how industriously they locked the door on my meditations, which followed them out again without let or hinderance, and *they* were really all that was dangerous. As they could not reach me, they had resolved to punish my body; just as boys, if they cannot come at some person against whom they have a spite, will abuse his dog. I saw that the State was half-witted, that it was timid as a lone woman with her silver spoons, and that it did not know its friends from its foes, and I lost all my remaining respect for it, and pitied it.

Thus the State never intentionally confronts a man's sense, intellectual or moral, but only his body, his senses. It is not armed with superior wit or honesty, but with superior physical strength. I was not born to be forced. I will breathe after my own fashion. Let us see who is the strongest. What force has a multitude? They only can force me who obey a higher law than I. They force me to become like themselves. I do not hear of *men* being *forced* to live this way or that by masses of men. What sort of life were that to live? When I meet a government which says to me, "Your money or your life," why should I be in haste to give it my money? It may be in

[22] July 23 or 24, 1846.

a great strait, and not know what to do: I cannot help that. It must help itself; do as I do. It is not worth the while to snivel about it. I am not responsible for the successful working of the machinery of society. I am not the son of the engineer. I perceive that, when an acorn and a chestnut fall side by side, the one does not remain inert to make way for the other, but both obey their own laws, and spring and grow and flourish as best they can, till one, perchance, overshadows and destroys the other. If a plant cannot live according to its nature, it dies; and so a man.

The night in prison was novel and interesting enough. The prisoners in their shirt-sleeves were enjoying a chat and the evening air in the door-way, when I entered. But the jailer said, "Come, boys, it is time to lock up;" and so they dispersed, and I heard the sound of their steps returning into the hollow apartments. My roommate was introduced to me by the jailer, as "a first-rate fellow and a clever[23] man." When the door was locked, he showed me where to hang my hat, and how he managed matters there. The rooms were white-washed once a month; and this one, at least, was the whitest, most simply furnished, and probably the neatest apartment in the town. He naturally wanted to know where I came from, and what brought me there; and, when I had told him, I asked him in my turn how he came there, presuming him to be an honest man, of course; and, as the world goes, I believe he was. "Why," said he, "they accuse me of burning a barn; but I never did it." As near as I could discover, he had probably gone to bed in a barn when drunk, and smoked his pipe there; and so a barn was burnt. He had the reputation of being a clever man, had been there some three months waiting for his trial to come on, and would have to wait as much longer; but he was quite domesticated and contented, since he got his board for nothing, and thought that he was well treated.

He occupied one window, and I the other; and I saw, that, if one stayed there long, his principal business would be to look out the window. I had soon read all the tracts that were left there, and examined where former prisoners had broken out, and where a grate had been sawed off, and heard the history of the various occupants of that room; for I found that even here there was a history and a gossip which never circulated beyond the walls of the jail. Probably this is the only house in the town where verses are composed, which are afterward printed in a circular form, but not published. I was shown quite a long list of verses which were composed by some young men who had been detected in an attempt to escape, who avenged themselves by singing them.

I pumped my fellow-prisoner as dry as I could, for fear I should never see him again; but at length he showed me which was my bed, and left me to blow out the lamp.

It was like travelling into a far country, such as I had never expected to behold, to lie there for one night. It seemed to me that I never had heard the town-clock strike before, nor the evening sounds of the village; for we slept with the windows open, which were inside the grating. It was to see my native village in the light of the middle ages, and our Concord was turned into a Rhine stream, and visions of knights and castles passed before me. They were the voices of old burghers that I heard in the streets. I was an involuntary spectator and

---

[23] Honest.

auditor of whatever was done and said in the kitchen of the adjacent village-inn, —a wholly new and rare experience to me. It was a closer view of my native town. I was fairly inside of it. I never had seen its institutions before. This is one of its peculiar institutions; for it is a shire town.[24] I began to comprehend what its inhabitants were about.

In the morning, our breakfasts were put through the hole in the door, in small oblong-square tin pans, made to fit, and holding a pint of chocolate, with brown bread, and an iron spoon. When they called for the vessels again, I was green enough to return what bread I had left; but my comrade seized it, and said that I should lay that up for lunch or dinner. Soon after, he was let out to work at haying in a neighboring field, whither he went every day, and would not be back till noon; so he bade me good-day, saying that he doubted if he should seen me again.

When I came out of prison,—for some one interfered, and paid the tax,— I did not perceive that great changes had taken place on the common, such as he observed who went in a youth, and emerged a tottering and grayheaded man; and yet a change had to my eyes come over the scene,—the town, and State, and country,—greater than any that mere time could effect. I saw yet more distinctly the State in which I lived. I saw to what extent the people among whom I lived could be trusted as good neighbors and friends; that their friend-ship was for summer weather only; that they did not greatly purpose to do right; that they were a distinct race from me by their prejudices and superstitions, as the Chinamen and Malays are; that, in their sacrifices to humanity, they ran no risks, not even to their property; that, after all, they were not so noble but they treated the thief as he had treated them, and hoped, by a certain outward observance and a few prayers, and by walking in a particular straight though useless path from time to time, to save their souls. This may be to judge my neighbors harshly; for I believe that most of them are not aware that they have such an institution as the jail in their village.

It was formerly the custom in our village, when a poor debtor came out of jail, for his acquaintances to salute him, looking through their fingers, which were crossed to represent the grating of a jail window, "How do ye do?" My neighbors did not thus salute me, but first looked at me, and then at one another, as if I had returned from a long journey. I was put into jail as I was going to the shoemaker's to get a shoe which was mended. When I was let out the next morning, I proceeded to finish my errand, and, having put on my mended shoe, joined a huckleberry party, who were impatient to put themselves under my conduct; and in half an hour,—for the horse was soon tackled,—was in the midst of a huckleberry field, on one of our highest hills, two miles off; and then the State was nowhere to be seen.

This is the whole history of "My Prisons."[25]

I have never declined paying the highway tax, because I am as desirous of being a good neighbor as I am of being a bad subject; and, as for supporting schools, I am

[24] Country seat.
[25] Reference to a book of that title published in 1832 by Silvio Pellico, an Italian poet imprisoned by the Austrians for his revolutionary activities against their occupation of Italy.

doing my part to educate my fellow-countrymen now. It is for no particular item in the tax-bill that I refuse to pay it. I simply wish to refuse allegiance to the State, to withdraw and stand aloof from it effectually. I do not care to trace the course of my dollar, if I could, till it buys a man, or a musket to shoot one with,—the dollar is innocent,—but I am concerned to trace the effects of my allegiance. In fact, I quietly declare war with the State, after my fashion, though I will still make what use and get what advantage of her I can, as is usual in such cases.

If others pay the tax which is demanded of me, from a sympathy with the State, they do but what they have already done in their own case, or rather they abet injustice to a greater extent than the State requires. If they pay the tax from a mistaken interest in the individual taxed, to save his property or prevent his going to jail, it is because they have not considered wisely how far they let their private feelings interfere with the public good.

This, then, is my position at present. But one cannot be too much on his guard in such a case, lest his action be biassed by obstinacy, or an undue regard for the opinions of men. Let him see that he does only what belongs to himself and to the hour.

I think sometimes, Why, this people mean well; they are only ignorant; they would do better if they knew how: why give your neighbors this pain to treat you as they are not inclined to? But I think, again, this is no reason why I should do as they do, or permit others to suffer much greater pain of a different kind. Again, I sometimes say to myself, When many millions of men, without heat, without ill-will, without personal feeling of any kind, demand of you a few shillings only, without the possibility, such is their constitution, of retracting or altering their present demand, and without the possibility, on your side, of appeal to any other millions, why expose yourself to this overwhelming brute force? You do not resist cold and hunger, the winds and the waves, thus obstinately; you quietly submit to a thousand similar necessities. You do not put your head into the fire. But just in proportion as I regard this as not wholly a brute force, but partly a human force, and consider that I have relations to those millions as to so many millions of men, and not of mere brute or inanimate things, I see that appeal is possible, first and instantaneously, from them to the Maker of them, and, secondly, from them to themselves. But, if I put my head deliberately into the fire, there is no appeal to fire or to the Maker of fire, and I have only myself to blame. If I could convince myself that I have any right to be satisfied with men as they are, and to treat them accordingly, and not according, in some respects, to my requisitions and expectations of what they and I ought to be, then, like a good Mussulman[26] and fatalist, I should endeavor to be satisfied with things as they are, and say it is the will of God. And, above all, there is this difference between resisting this and a purely brute or natural force, that I can resist this with some effect; but I cannot expect, like Orpheus,[27] to change the nature of the rocks and trees and beasts.

I do not wish to quarrel with any man or nation. I do not wish to split hairs, to make fine distinctions, or set myself up as better than my neighbors. I seek rather, I may say, even an excuse for conforming to the laws of the land. I am but too ready

---

[26] Mohammedan.
[27] The poet-musician of classic myth whose powers of song were so great that he could throw a spell over beasts and natural objects.

to conform to them. Indeed I have reason to suspect myself on this head; and each year, as the tax-gatherer comes round, I find myself disposed to review the acts and position of the general and state governments, and the spirit of the people, to discover a pretext for conformity. I believe that the State will soon be able to take all my work of this sort out of my hands, and then I shall be no better a patriot than my fellow-countrymen. Seen from a lower point of view, the Constitution, with all its faults, is very good; the law and the courts are very respectable; even this State and this American government are, in many respects, very admirable and rare things, to be thankful for, such as a great many have described them; but seen from a point of view a little higher, they are what I have described them; seen from a higher still, and the highest, who shall say what they are, or that they are worth looking at or thinking of at all?

However, the government does not concern me much, and I shall bestow the fewest possible thoughts on it. It is not many moments that I live under a government, even in this world. If a man is thought-free, fancy-free, imagination-free, that which is *not* never for a long time appearing *to be* to him, unwise rulers or reformers cannot fatally interrupt him.

I know that most men think differently from myself; but those whose lives are by profession devoted to the study of these or kindred subjects, content me as little as any. Statesmen and legislators, standing so completely within the institution, never distinctly and nakedly behold it. They speak of moving society; but have no resting-place without it. They may be men of a certain experience and discrimination, and have no doubt invented ingenious and even useful systems, for which we sincerely thank them; but all their wit and usefulness lie within certain not very wide limits. They are wont to forget that the world is not governed by policy and expediency. Webster[28] never goes behind government, and so cannot speak with authority about it. His words are wisdom to those legislators who contemplate no essential reform in the existing government; but for thinkers, and those who legislate for all time, he never once glances at the subject. I know of those whose serene and wise speculations on this theme would soon reveal the limits of his mind's range and hospitality. Yet, compared with the cheap professions of most reformers, and the still cheaper wisdom and eloquence of politicians in general, his are almost the only sensible and valuable words, and we thank Heaven for him. Comparatively, he is always strong, original, and, above all, practical. Still his quality is not wisdom, but prudence. The lawyer's truth is not Truth, but consistency, or a consistent expediency. Truth is always in harmony with herself, and is not concerned chiefly to reveal the justice that may consist with wrong-doing. He well deserves to be called, as he has been called, the Defender of the Constitution. There are really no blows to be given by him but defensive ones. He is not a leader, but a follower. His leaders are the men of '87.[29] "I have never made an effort," he says, "and never propose to make an effort; I have never countenanced an effort, and never mean to countenance an effort, to disturb the arrangement as originally made, by which the

---

[28] Daniel Webster (1782–1852), influential senator from Massachusetts who was felt by the abolitionists to be a betrayer of their principles when he supported the Fugitive Slave Law, which made it possible to return slaves who had escaped to the North to their Southern masters.
[29] Drafters of the Constitution in 1787.

various States came into the Union."[30] Still thinking of the sanction which the Constitution gives to slavery, he says, "Because it was a part of the original compact, —let it stand." Notwithstanding his special acuteness and ability, he is unable to take a fact out of its merely political relations, and behold it as it lies absolutely to be disposed of by the intellect,—what, for instance, it behoves a man to do here in America to-day with regard to slavery,—but ventures, or is driven, to make some such desperate answer as the following, while professing to speak absolutely, and as a private man,—from which what new and singular code of social duties might be inferred?—"The manner," says he, "in which the governments of those States where slavery exists are to regulate it, is for their own consideration, under their responsibility to their constituents, to the general laws of propriety, humanity, and justice, and to God. Associations formed elsewhere, springing from a feeling of humanity, or any other cause, have nothing whatever to do with it. They have never received any encouragement from me, and they never will."

They who know of no purer sources of truth, who have traced up its stream no higher, stand, and wisely stand, by the Bible and the Constitution, and drink at it there with reverence and humility; but they who behold where it comes trickling into this lake or that pool, gird up their loins once more, and continue their pilgrimage toward its fountain-head.

No man with a genius for legislation has appeared in America. They are rare in the history of the world. There are orators, politicians, and eloquent men, by the thousand; but the speaker has not yet opened his mouth to speak, who is capable of settling the much-vexed questions of the day. We love eloquence for its own sake, and not for any truth which it may utter, or any heroism it may inspire. Our legislators have not yet learned the comparative value of free-trade and of freedom, of union, and of rectitude, to a nation. They have no genius or talent for comparatively humble questions of taxation and finance, commerce and manufactures and agriculture. If we were left solely to the wordy wit of legislators in Congress for our guidance, uncorrected by the seasonable experience and the effectual complaints of the people, America would not long retain her rank among the nations. For eighteen hundred years, though perchance I have no right to say it, the New Testament has been written; yet where is the legislator who has wisdom and practical talent enough to avail himself of the light which it sheds on the science of legislation?

The authority of government, even such as I am willing to submit to,—for I will cheerfully obey those who know and can do better than I, and in many things even those who neither know nor can do so well,—is still an impure one: to be strictly just, it must have the sanction and consent of the governed. It can have no pure right over my person and property but what I concede to it. The progress from an absolute to a limited monarchy, from a limited monarchy to a democracy, is a progress toward a true respect for the individual. Is a democracy, such as we know it, the last improvement possible in government? Is it not possible to take a step further towards recognizing and organizing the rights of man? There will never be a really free and enlightened State, until the State comes to recognize the individual as a higher and

---

[30] Both here and below, lines quoted from speeches delivered by Webster in 1845 and 1848. These extracts were added by Thoreau after he gave his lecture, a fact he noted when preparing the printed text of his essay.

independent power, from which all its own power and authority are derived, and treats him accordingly. I please myself with imagining a State at last which can afford to be just to all men, and to treat the individual with respect as a neighbor; which even would not think it inconsistent with its own repose, if a few were to live aloof from it, not meddling with it, nor embraced by it, who fulfilled all the duties of neighbors and fellow-men. A State which bore this kind of fruit, and suffered it to drop off as fast as it ripened, would prepare the way for a still more perfect and glorious State, which also I have imagined, but not yet anywhere seen.

1849

A Plea for Captain John Brown*

I trust that you will pardon me for being here. I do not wish to force my thoughts upon you, but I feel forced myself. Little as I know of Captain Brown,[1] I would fain do my part to correct the tone and the statements of the newspapers, and of my countrymen generally, respecting his character and actions. It costs us nothing to be just. We can at least express our sympathy with, and admiration of, him and his companions, and that is what I now propose to do.

First, as to his history.

I will endeavor to omit, as much as possible, what you have already read. I need not describe his person to you, for probably most of you have seen and will not soon forget him. I am told that his grandfather, John Brown, was an officer in the Revolution; that he himself was born in Connecticut about the beginning of this century, but early went with his father to Ohio. I heard him say that his father was a contractor who furnished beef to the army there, in the war of 1812; that he accompanied him to the camp, and assisted him in that employment, seeing a good deal of military life, more, perhaps, than if he had been a soldier, for he was often present at the councils of the officers. Especially, he learned by experience how armies are supplied and maintained in the field—a work which, he observed, requires at least as much experience and skill as to lead them in battle. He said that few persons had any conception of the cost, even the pecuniary cost, of firing a single bullet in war. He saw enough, at any rate, to disgust him with a military life, indeed to excite in him a great abhorrence of it; so much so, that though he was tempted by the offer of some petty office in the army, when he was about eighteen, he not only declined

---

* On October 16, 1859, John Brown (1800–1859) led a small group of followers in a raid on Harper's Ferry, Virginia, where a federal arsenal was located, with the intention of encouraging slaves throughout the South to revolt. Brown and his men were captured and executed shortly afterwards. Within two weeks of the raid, Thoreau wrote a lecture that he delivered first at Concord and then at Boston and at Worcester, Massachusetts. It was published early in 1860 as part of the rising antislavery campaign that quickly turned Brown into a figure of martyred heroism.

[1] Brown visited Concord twice, in 1857 and in May of 1859. On each occasion Thoreau met with him.

that, but he also refused to train when warned, and was fined for it. He then resolved that he would never have anything to do with any war, unless it were a war for liberty.

When the troubles in Kansas began,[2] he sent several of his sons thither to strengthen the party of the Free State men, fitting them out with such weapons as he had; telling them that if the troubles should increase, and there should be need of him, he would follow to assist them with his hand and counsel. This, as you all know, he soon after did; and it was through his agency, far more than any other's, that Kansas was made free.

For a part of his life he was a surveyor, and at one time he was engaged in wool-growing, and he went to Europe as an agent about that business. There, as every where, he had his eyes about him, and made many original observations. He said, for instance, that he saw why the soil of England was so rich, and that of Germany (I think it was) so poor, and he thought of writing to some of the crowned heads about it. It was because in England the peasantry live on the soil which they cultivate, but in Germany they are gathered into villages, at night. It is a pity that he did not make a book of his observations.

I should say that he was an old-fashioned man in his respect for the Constitution, and his faith in the permanence of this Union. Slavery he deemed to be wholly opposed to these, and he was its determined foe.

He was by descent and birth a New England farmer, a man of great common sense, deliberate and practical as that class is, and tenfold more so. He was like the best of those who stood at Concord Bridge once, on Lexington Common, and on Bunker Hill,[3] only he was firmer and higher principled than any that I have chanced to hear of as there. It was no abolition lecturer that converted him. Ethan Allen and Stark,[4] with whom he may in some respects be compared, were rangers in a lower and less important field. They could bravely face their country's foes, but he had the courage to face his country herself, when she was in the wrong. A Western writer says, to account for his escape from so many perils, that he was concealed under a "rural exterior;" as if, in that prairie land, a hero should, by good rights, wear a citizen's dress only.

He did not go to the college called Harvard, good old Alma Mater as she is. He was not fed on the pap that is there furnished. As he phrased it, "I know no more of grammar than one of your calves." But he went to the great university of the West, where he sedulously pursued the study of Liberty, for which he had early betrayed a fondness, and having taken many degrees, he finally commenced the public practice of Humanity in Kansas, as you all know. Such were *his humanities*, and not any study of grammar. He would have left a Greek accent slanting the wrong way, and righted up a falling man.

He was one of that class of whom we hear a great deal, but, for the most part,

---

[2] Brown went to Kansas following the passage of the 1854 Kansas-Nebraska Act, which threatened to split the frontier into a half-slave, half-free territory; there he led a massacre against Southern sympathizers in 1856, a violent incident that was given little play by abolitionist papers and of which Thoreau was probably ignorant.
[3] Battles of the American Revolution in which the colonists stood off the British troops.
[4] Ethan Allen and John Stark were heroes of the Revolution.

see nothing at all—the Puritans. It would be in vain to kill him. He died lately in the time of Cromwell,[5] but he reappeared here. Why should he not? Some of the Puritan stock are said to have come over and settled in New England. They were a class that did something else than celebrate their forefathers' day, and eat parched corn in remembrance of that time. They were neither Democrats nor Republicans, but men of simple habits, straightforward, prayerful; not thinking much of rulers who did not fear God, not making many compromises, nor seeking after available candidates.

"In his camp," as one[6] has recently written, and as I have myself heard him state, "he permitted no profanity; no man of loose morals was suffered to remain there, unless, indeed, as a prisoner of war. 'I would rather,' said he, 'have the small-pox, yellow fever, and cholera, all together in my camp, than a man without principle. . . . It is a mistake, sir, that our people make, when they think that bullies are the best fighters, or that they are the fit men to oppose these Southerners. Give me men of good principles,—God-fearing men,—men who respect themselves, and with a dozen of them I will oppose any hundred such men as these Buford[7] ruffians.'" He said that if one offered himself to be a soldier under him, who was forward to tell what he could or would do, if he could only get sight of the enemy, he had but little confidence in him.

He was never able to find more than a score or so of recruits whom he would accept, and only about a dozen, among them his sons, in whom he had perfect faith. When he was here, some years ago, he showed to a few a little manuscript book,— his "orderly book" I think he called it,—containing the names of his company in Kansas, and the rules by which they bound themselves; and he stated that several of them had already sealed the contract with their blood. When some one remarked that, with the addition of a chaplain, it would have been a perfect Cromwellian troop, he observed that he would have been glad to add a chaplain to the list, if he could have found one who could fill that office worthily. It is easy enough to find one for the United States army. I believe that he had prayers in his camp morning and evening, nevertheless.

He was a man of Spartan habits, and at sixty was scrupulous about his diet at your table, excusing himself by saying that he must eat sparingly and fare hard, as became a soldier or one who was fitting himself for difficult enterprises, a life of exposure.

A man of rare common sense and directness of speech, as of action; a transcendentalist above all, a man of ideas and principles,—that was what distinguished him. Not yielding to a whim or transient impulse, but carrying out the purpose of a life. I noticed that he did not overstate any thing, but spoke within bounds. I remember, particularly, how, in his speech here, he referred to what his family had suffered in Kansas, without ever giving the least vent to his pent-up fire. It was a volcano with an ordinary chimney-flue. Also referring to the deeds of certain Border Ruffians,[8] he said, rapidly paring away his speech, like an experienced soldier, keeping a reserve

---

[5] Oliver Cromwell (1599–1658), head of the Puritan faction during the overthrow of the British monarchy.

[6] James Redpath (1833–1891), newspaper correspondent, editor, and reformer.

[7] Jefferson Buford, whose proslavery raid into the Kansas Territory in 1856 was followed by Brown's counter-raid.

[8] Characterization by antislavery newspapers of the bands of proslavery men who crossed the border between Missouri and Kansas in a series of violent raids.

of force and meaning, "They had a perfect right to be hung." He was not in the least a rhetorician, was not talking to Buncombe[9] or his constituents any where, had no need to invent any thing, but to tell the simple truth, and communicate his own resolution; therefore he appeared incomparably strong, and eloquence in Congress and elsewhere seemed to me at a discount. It was like the speeches of Cromwell compared with those of an ordinary king.

As for his tact and prudence, I will merely say, that at a time when scarcely a man from the Free States was able to reach Kansas by any direct route, at least without having his arms taken from him, he, carrying what imperfect guns and other weapons he could collect, openly and slowly drove an ox-cart through Missouri, apparently in the capacity of a surveyor, with his surveying compass exposed in it, and so passed unsuspected, and had ample opportunity to learn the designs of the enemy. For some time after his arrival he still followed the same profession. When, for instance, he saw a knot of the ruffians on the prairie, discussing, of course, the single topic which then occupied their minds, he would, perhaps, take his compass and one of his sons, and proceed to run an imaginary line right through the very spot on which that conclave had assembled, and when he came up to them, he would naturally pause and have some talk with them, learning their news, and, at last, all their plans perfectly; and having thus completed his real survey, he would resume his imaginary one, and run on his line till he was out of sight.

When I expressed surprise that he could live in Kansas at all, with a price set upon his head, and so large a number, including the authorities, exasperated against him, he accounted for it by saying, "It is perfectly well understood that I will not be taken." Much of the time for some years he has had to skulk in swamps, suffering from poverty and from sickness, which was the consequence of exposure, befriended only by Indians and a few whites. But though it might be known that he was lurking in a particular swamp, his foes commonly did not care to go in after him. He could even come out into a town where there were more Border Ruffians than Free State men, and transact some business, without delaying long, and yet not be molested; for said he, "No little handful of men were willing to undertake it, and a large body could not be got together in season."

As for his recent failure, we do not know the facts about it. It was evidently far from being a wild and desperate attempt. His enemy, Mr. Vallandigham,[10] is compelled to say, that "it was among the best planned and executed conspiracies that ever failed."

Not to mention his other successes, was it a failure, or did it show a want of good management, to deliver from bondage a dozen human beings, and walk off with them by broad daylight, for weeks if not months, at a leisurely pace, through one State after another, for half the length of the North, conspicuous to all parties, with a price set upon his head, going into a court room on his way and telling what he had done, thus convincing Missouri that it was not profitable to try to hold slaves in his neighborhood?—and this, not because the government menials were lenient, but because they were afraid of him.

[9] Epithet for anyone given to loud and senseless political speeches.   [10] Ohio congressman and Democrat.

Yet he did not attribute his success, foolishly, to "his star," or to any magic. He said, truly, that the reason why such greatly superior numbers quailed before him, was, as one of his prisoners confessed, because they *lacked a cause*—a kind of armor which he and his party never lacked. When the time came, few men were found willing to lay down their lives in defence of what they knew to be wrong; they did not like that this should be their last act in this world.

But to make haste to *his* last act, and its effects.

The newspapers seem to ignore, or perhaps are really ignorant of the fact, that there are at least as many as two or three individuals to a town throughout the North, who think much as the present speaker does about him and his enterprise. I do not hesitate to say that they are an important and growing party. We aspire to be something more than stupid and timid chattels, pretending to read history and our bibles, but desecrating every house and every day we breathe in. Perhaps anxious politicians may prove that only seventeen white men and five negroes were concerned in the late enterprise, but their very anxiety to prove this might suggest to themselves that all is not told. Why do they still dodge the truth? They are so anxious because of a dim consciousness of the fact, which they do not distinctly face, that at least a million of the free inhabitants of the United States would have rejoiced if it had succeeded. They at most only criticise the tactics. Though we wear no crape,[11] the thought of that man's position and probable fate is spoiling many a man's day here at the North for other thinking. If any one who has seen him here can pursue successfully any other train of thought, I do not know what he is made of. If there is any such who gets his usual allowance of sleep, I will warrant him to fatten easily under any circumstances which do not touch his body or purse. I put a piece of paper and a pencil under my pillow, and when I could not sleep, I wrote in the dark.

On the whole, my respect for my fellow-men, except as one may outweigh a million, is not being increased these days. I have noticed the cold-blooded way in which newspaper writers and men generally speak of this event, as if an ordinary malefactor, though one of unusual "pluck,"—as the Governor of Virginia is reported to have said, using the language of the cock-pit, "the gamest man he ever saw,"— had been caught, and were about to be hung. He was not dreaming of his foes when the governor thought he looked so brave. It turns what sweetness I have to gall, to hear, or hear of, the remarks of some of my neighbors. When we heard at first that he was dead, one of my townsmen observed that "he died as the fool dieth;"[12] which, pardon me, for an instant suggested a likeness in him dying to my neighbor living. Others, craven-hearted, said disparagingly, that "he threw his life away," because he resisted the government. Which way have they thrown *their* lives, pray?—Such as would praise a man for attacking singly an ordinary band of thieves or murderers. I hear another ask, Yankee-like, "What will he gain by it?" as if he expected to fill his pockets by this enterprise. Such a one has no idea of gain but in this worldly sense. If it does not lead to a "surprise" party, if he does not get a new pair of boots, or a vote of thanks, it must be a failure. "But he won't gain any thing by it." Well, no, I don't suppose he could get four-and-sixpence a day for being hung, take the year round; but then he stands a chance to save a considerable part of his soul—and

---

[11] I.e., are not dressed in mourning.   [12] Allusion to 2 Samuel 3:33.

such a soul!—when *you* do not. No doubt you can get more in your market for a quart of milk than for a quart of blood, but that is not the market that heroes carry their blood to.

Such do not know that like the seed is the fruit, and that, in the moral world, when good seed is planted, good fruit is inevitable, and does not depend on our watering and cultivating; that when you plant, or bury, a hero in his field, a crop of heroes is sure to spring up. This is a seed of such force and vitality, that it does not ask our leave to germinate.

The momentary charge at Balaclava,[13] in obedience to a blundering command, proving what a perfect machine the soldier is, has, properly enough, been celebrated by a poet laureate; but the steady, and for the most part successful charge of this man, for some years, against the legions of Slavery, in obedience to an infinitely higher command, is as much more memorable than that, as an intelligent and conscientious man is superior to a machine. Do you think that that will go unsung?

"Served him right"—"A dangerous man"—"He is undoubtedly insane." So they proceed to live their sane, and wise, and altogether admirable lives, reading their Plutarch[14] a little, but chiefly pausing at that feat of Putnam,[15] who was let down into a wolf's den; and in this wise they nourish themselves for brave and patriotic deeds some time or other. The Tract Society could afford to print that story of Putnam. You might open the district schools with the reading of it, for there is nothing about Slavery or the Church in it; unless it occurs to the reader that some pastors are *wolves* in sheep's clothing. "The American Board of Commissioners for Foreign Missions" even, might dare to protest against *that* wolf. I have heard of boards, and of American boards, but it chances that I never heard of this particular lumber till lately. And yet I hear of Northern men, women, and children, by families, buying a "life member-ship" in such societies as these;—a life-membership in the grave! You can get buried cheaper than that.

Our foes are in our midst and all about us. There is hardly a house but is divided against itself, for our foe is the all but universal woodenness of both head and heart, the want of vitality in man, which is the effect of our vice; and hence are begotten fear, superstition, bigotry, persecution, and slavery of all kinds. We are mere figure-heads upon a hulk, with livers in the place of hearts. The curse is the worship of idols, which at length changes the worshipper into a stone image him-self; and the New Englander is just as much an idolater as the Hindoo. This man was an exception, for he did not set up even a political graven image between him and his God.

A church that can never have done with excommunicating Christ while it exists!

[13] In the Battle of Balaclava, during the Crimean War in 1854, the men of the British cavalry flung themselves toward death in absolute obedience to the commands of their superiors, an incident made famous by the poem *The Charge of the Light Brigade* by Alfred Tennyson, poet laureate of Great Britain.

[14] Greek (A.D. 46?–?120) known for his biographies of famous Greek and Roman leaders.

[15] Israel Putnam (1718–1790), hero of the French and Indian wars and of the Revolution; one of the legends surrounding his name was that of his bravery in killing a wolf after he was lowered into its cave-den.

Away with your broad and flat churches, and your narrow and tall churches! Take a step forward, and invent a new style of out-houses. Invent a salt that will save you,[16] and defend our nostrils.

The modern Christian is a man who has consented to say all the prayers in the liturgy, provided you will let him go straight to bed and sleep quietly afterward. All his prayers begin with "Now I lay me down to sleep," and he is forever looking forward to the time when he shall go to his "*long* rest."[17] He has consented to perform certain old established charities, too, after a fashion, but he does not wish to hear of any new-fangled ones; he doesn't wish to have any supplementary articles added to the contract, to fit it to the present time. He shows the whites of his eyes on the Sabbath, and the blacks all the rest of the week. The evil is not merely a stagnation of blood, but a stagnation of spirit. Many, no doubt, are well disposed, but sluggish by constitution and by habit, and they cannot conceive of a man who is actuated by higher motives than they are. Accordingly they pronounce this man insane, for they know that *they* could never act as he does, as long as they are themselves.

We dream of foreign countries, of other times and races of men, placing them at a distance in history or space; but let some significant event like the present occur in our midst, and we discover, often, this distance and this strangeness between us and our nearest neighbors. *They* are our Austrias, and Chinas, and South Sea Islands. Our crowded society becomes well spaced all at once, clean and handsome to the eye, a city of magnificent distances. We discover why it was that we never got beyond compliments and surfaces with them before; we become aware of as many versts between us and them as there are between a wandering Tartar and a Chinese town. The thoughtful man becomes a hermit in the thoroughfares of the market-place. Impassable seas suddenly find their level between us, or dumb steppes stretch themselves out there. It is the difference of constitution, of intelligence, and faith, and not streams and mountains, that make the true and impassable boundaries between individuals and between states. None but the like-minded can come plenipotentiary to our court.

I read all the newspapers I could get within a week after this event, and I do not remember in them a single expression of sympathy for these men. I have since seen one noble statement, in a Boston paper, not editorial. Some voluminous sheets decided not to print the full report of Brown's words to the exclusion of other matter. It was as if a publisher should reject the manuscript of the New Testament, and print Wilson's[18] last speech. The same journal which contained this pregnant news, was chiefly filled, in parallel columns, with the reports of the political conventions that were being held. But the descent to them was too steep. They should have been spared this contrast, been printed in an extra at least. To turn from the voices and deeds of earnest men to the *cackling* of political conventions! Office seekers and speech-makers, who do not so much as lay an honest egg, but wear their breasts bare upon an egg of chalk! Their great game is the game of straws,[19] or

[16] Reference to Matthew 5:13, in which "the salt of the earth" are admonished to guard against losing their savor.

[17] I.e., death.

[18] Henry Wilson, Massachusetts senator.

[19] Game of chance similar to dice.

rather that universal aboriginal game of the platter, at which the Indians cried *hub, hub!* Exclude the reports of religious and political conventions, and publish the words of a living man.

But I object not so much to what they have omitted as to what they have inserted. Even the *Liberator*[20] called it "a misguided, wild, and apparently insane . . . effort." As for the herd of newspapers and magazines, I do not chance to know an editor in the country who will deliberately print anything which he knows will ultimately and permanently reduce the number of his subscribers. They do not believe that it would be expedient. How then can they print truth? If we do not say pleasant things, they argue, nobody will attend to us. And so they do like some travelling auctioneers, who sing an obscene song in order to draw a crowd around them. Republican editors, obliged to get their sentences ready for the morning edition, and accustomed to look at every thing by the twilight of politics, express no admiration, nor true sorrow even, but call these men "deluded fanatics"—"mistaken men"—"insane," or "crazed." It suggests what a *sane* set of editors we are blessed with, *not* "mistaken men"; who know very well on which side their bread is buttered, at least.

A man does a brave and humane deed, and at once, on all sides, we hear people and parties declaring, "I didn't do it, nor countenance *him* to do it, in any conceivable way. It can't be fairly inferred from my past career." I, for one, am not interested to hear you define your position. I don't know that I ever was, or ever shall be. I think it is mere egotism, or impertinent at this time. Ye needn't take so much pains to wash your skirts of him. No intelligent man will ever be convinced that he was any creature of yours. He went and came, as he himself informs us, "under the auspices of John Brown and nobody else." The Republican party does not perceive how many his *failure* will make to vote more correctly than they would have them. They have counted the votes of Pennsylvania & Co., but they have not correctly counted Captain Brown's vote. He has taken the wind out of their sails, the little wind they had, and they may as well lie to and repair.

What though he did not belong to your clique! Though you may not approve of his method or his principles, recognize his magnanimity. Would you not like to claim kindredship with him in that, though in no other thing he is like, or likely, to you? Do you think that you would lose your reputation so? What you lost at the spile, you would gain at the bung.[21]

If they do not mean all this, then they do not speak the truth, and say what they mean. They are simply at their old tricks still.

"It was always conceded to him," *says one who calls him crazy,* "that he was a conscientious man, very modest in his demeanor, apparently inoffensive, until the subject of Slavery was introduced, when he would exhibit a feeling of indignation unparalleled."

The slave-ship is on her way, crowded with its dying victims; new cargoes are being added in mid ocean; a small crew of slaveholders, countenanced by a large body of passengers, is smothering four millions under the hatches, and yet the politician asserts that the only proper way by which deliverance is to be obtained, is by "the

[20] Abolitionist newspaper published by William Lloyd Garrison.
[21] Folk saying meaning that what is lost at one point may be regained at another. ("Spile" and "bung" refer to the openings of a cask.)

quiet diffusion of the sentiments of humanity," without any "outbreak." As if the sentiments of humanity were ever found unaccompanied by its deeds, and you could disperse them, all finished to order, the pure article, as easily as water with a watering-pot, and so lay the dust. What is that that I hear cast overboard? The bodies of the dead that have found deliverance. That is the way we are "diffusing" humanity, and its sentiments with it.

Prominent and influential editors, accustomed to deal with politicians, men of an infinitely lower grade, say, in their ignorance, that he acted "on the principle of revenge." They do not know the man. They must enlarge themselves to conceive of him. I have no doubt that the time will come when they will begin to see him as he was. They have got to conceive of a man of faith and of religious principle, and not a politician or an Indian;[22] of a man who did not wait till he was personally interfered with, or thwarted in some harmless business, before he gave his life to the cause of the oppressed.

If Walker[23] may be considered the representative of the South, I wish I could say that Brown was the representative of the North. He was a superior man. He did not value his bodily life in comparison with ideal things. He did not recognize unjust human laws, but resisted them as he was bid. For once we are lifted out of the trivialness and dust of politics into the region of truth and manhood. No man in America has ever stood up so persistently and effectively for the dignity of human nature, knowing himself for a man, and the equal of any and all governments. In that sense he was the most American of us all. He needed no babbling lawyer, making false issues, to defend him. He was more than a match for all the judges that American voters, or office-holders of whatever grade, can create. He could not have been tried by a jury of his peers, because his peers did not exist. When a man stands up serenely against the condemnation and vengeance of mankind, rising above them literally *by a whole body*,—even though he were of late the vilest murderer, who has settled that matter with himself,—the spectacle is a sublime one,—didn't ye know it, ye Liberators, ye Tribunes, ye Republicans?[24]—and we become criminal in comparison. Do yourselves the honor to recognize him. He needs none of your respect.

As for the Democratic journals, they are not human enough to affect me at all. I do not feel indignation at any thing they may say.

I am aware that I anticipate a little, that he was still, at the last accounts, alive in the hands of his foes; but that being the case, I have all along found myself thinking and speaking of him as physically dead.

I do not believe in erecting statues to those who still live in our hearts, whose bones have not yet crumbled in the earth around us, but I would rather see the statue of Captain Brown in the Massachusetts State-House yard, than that of any other man whom I know. I rejoice that I live in this age—that I am his contemporary.

What a contrast, when we turn to that political party[25] which is so anxiously shuffling him and his plot out of its way, and looking around for some available slaveholder, perhaps, to be its candidate, at least for one who will execute the

---

[22] Based on the common notion that Indians, like politicians, seek revenge.
[23] Robert J. Walker, governor of the Kansas Territory.

[24] Reference to three prominent newspapers: the Boston *Liberator,* the New York *Tribune,* and the Springfield (Massachusetts) *Republican.*
[25] I.e., the antislavery Republican party.

Fugitive Slave Law,[26] and all those other unjust laws which he took up arms to annul!

Insane! A father and six sons, and one son-in-law, and several more men besides, —as many at least as twelve disciples,—all struck with insanity at once; while the sane tyrant holds with a firmer gripe[27] than ever his four millions of slaves, and a thousand sane editors, his abettors, are saving their country and their bacon! Just as insane were his efforts in Kansas. Ask the tyrant who is his most dangerous foe, the sane man or the insane. Do the thousands who know him best, who have rejoiced at his deeds in Kansas, and have afforded him material aid there, think him insane? Such a use of this word is a mere trope with most who persist in using it, and I have no doubt that many of the rest have already in silence retracted their words.

Read his admirable answers to Mason[28] and others. How they are dwarfed and defeated by the contrast! On the one side, half brutish, half timid questioning; on the other, truth, clear as lightning, crashing into their obscene temples. They are made to stand with Pilate, and Gessler, and the Inquisition.[29] How ineffectual their speech and action! and what a void their silence! They are but helpless tools in this great work. It was no human power that gathered them about this preacher.

What have Massachusetts and the North sent a few *sane* representatives to Congress for, of late years?—to declare with effect what kind of sentiments? All their speeches put together and boiled down,—and probably they themselves will confess it,—do not match for manly directness and force, and for simple truth, the few casual remarks of crazy John Brown, on the floor of the Harper's Ferry engine house;—that man whom you are about to hang, to send to the other world, though not to represent *you* there. No, he was not our representative in any sense. He was too fair a specimen of a man to represent the like of us. Who, then, *were* his constituents? If you read his words understandingly you will find out. In his case there is no idle eloquence, no made, nor maiden speech, no compliments to the oppressor. Truth is his inspirer, and earnestness the polisher of his sentences. He could afford to lose his Sharps' rifles, while he retained his faculty of speech, a Sharps' rifle of infinitely surer and longer range.

And the *New York Herald* reports the conversation *"verbatim"!* It does not know of what undying words it is made the vehicle.

I have no respect for the penetration of any man who can read the report of that conversation, and still call the principal in it insane. It has the ring of a saner sanity than an ordinary discipline and habits of life, than an ordinary organization, secure. Take any sentence of it—"Any questions that I can honorably answer, I will; not otherwise. So far as I am myself concerned, I have told every thing truthfully. I value my word, sir." The few who talk about his vindictive spirit, while they really admire his heroism, have no test by which to detect a noble man, no amalgam to combine with his pure gold. They mix their own dross with it.

It is a relief to turn from these slanders to the testimony of his more truthful, but

---

[26] Passed in 1850, this law served to return slaves who had escaped to the free states to their original owners.
[27] Grip.
[28] James M. Mason, Virginia senator.
[29] Repressors of freedom: Pontius Pilate, Roman governor of Judea at the time of Jesus' crucifixion; Hermann Gessler, Austrian official slain by William Tell, Swiss patriot; and the Roman Catholic tribunals that persecuted those suspected of heresy from the early thirteenth to the eighteenth century.

frightened, jailers and hangmen. Governor Wise speaks far more justly and appreciat-
ingly of him than any Northern editor, or politician, or public personage, that I chance
to have heard from. I know that you can afford to hear him again on this subject.
He says: "They are themselves mistaken who take him to be a madman. . . . He is
cool, collected, and indomitable, and it is but just to him to say, that he was humane
to his prisoners. . . . And he inspired me with great trust in his integrity as a man
of truth. He is a fanatic, vain and garrulous," (I leave that part to Mr. Wise) "but
firm, truthful, and intelligent. His men, too, who survive, are like him. . . . Colonel
Washington[30] says that he was the coolest and firmest man he ever saw in defying
danger and death. With one son dead by his side, and another shot through, he felt
the pulse of his dying son with one hand, and held his rifle with the other, and
commanded his men with the utmost composure, encouraging them to be firm, and
to sell their lives as dear as they could. Of the three white prisoners, Brown, Stevens,
and Coppoc, it was hard to say which was most firm. . . ."

Almost the first Northern men whom the slaveholder has learned to respect!

The testimony of Mr. Vallandigham, though less valuable, is of the same purport,
that "it is vain to underrate either the man or his conspiracy. . . . He is the farthest
possible remove from the ordinary ruffian, fanatic, or madman."

"All is quiet at Harper's Ferry," say the journals. What is the character of that calm
which follows when the law and the slaveholder prevail? I regard this event as a
touchstone designed to bring out, with glaring distinctness, the character of this
government. We needed to be thus assisted to see it by the light of history. It needed
to see itself. When a government puts forth its strength on the side of injustice, as
ours to maintain Slavery and kill the liberators of the slave, it reveals itself a merely
brute force, or worse, a demoniacal force. It is the head of the Plug Uglies.[31] It is more
manifest than ever that tyranny rules. I see this government to be effectually allied
with France and Austria in oppressing mankind. There sits a tyrant holding fettered
four millions of slaves; here comes their heroic liberator. This most hypocritical and
diabolical government looks up from its seat on the gasping four millions, and inquires
with an assumption of innocence, "What do you assault me for? Am I not an honest
man? Cease agitation on this subject, or I will make a slave of you, too, or else hang
you."

We talk about a *representative* government; but what a monster of a government
is that where the noblest faculties of the mind, and the *whole* heart, are not *represented*.
A semi-human tiger or ox, stalking over the earth, with its heart taken out and the
top of its brain shot away. Heroes have fought well on their stumps when their legs
were shot off, but I never heard of any good done by such a government as that.

The only government that I recognize,—and it matters not how few are at the
head of it, or how small its army,—is that power that establishes justice in the land,
never that which establishes injustice. What shall we think of a government to which
all the truly brave and just men in the land are enemies, standing between it and those
whom it oppresses? A government that pretends to be Christian and crucifies a million
Christs every day!

---

[30] Great-grandnephew of George Washington,
kidnapped by Brown at the start of the
Harper's Ferry raid.

[31] Originally, big-city bullies who wore plugs, a
slang term for top hats; later, denoting any such
ruffians.

Treason! Where does such treason take its rise? I cannot help thinking of you as you deserve, ye governments. Can you dry up the fountains of thought? High treason, when it is resistance to tyranny here below, has its origin in, and is first committed by the power that makes and forever recreates man. When you have caught and hung all these human rebels, you have accomplished nothing but your own guilt, for you have not struck at the fountain head. You presume to contend with a foe against whom West Point cadets and rifled cannon *point* not. Can all the art of the cannon-founder tempt matter to turn against its maker? Is the form in which the founder thinks he casts it more essential than the constitution of it and of himself?

The United States have a coffle[32] of four millions of slaves. They are determined to keep them in this condition; and Massachusetts is one of the confederated overseers to prevent their escape. Such are not all the inhabitants of Massachusetts, but such are they who rule and are obeyed here. It was Massachusetts, as well as Virginia, that put down this insurrection at Harper's Ferry. She sent the marines there, and she will have to pay the penalty of her sin.

Suppose that there is a society in this State that out of its own purse and magnanimity saves all the fugitive slaves that run to us, and protects our colored fellow-citizens, and leaves the other work to the Government, so-called. Is not that government fast losing its occupation, and becoming contemptible to mankind? If private men are obliged to perform the offices of government, to protect the weak and dispense justice, then the government becomes only a hired man, or clerk, to perform menial or indifferent services. Of course, that is but the shadow of a government whose existence necessitates a Vigilant Committee.[33] What should we think of the oriental Cadi even, behind whom worked in secret a Vigilant Committee? But such is the character of our Northern States generally; each has its Vigilant Committee. And, to a certain extent, these crazy governments recognize and accept this relation. They say, virtually, "We'll be glad to work for you on these terms, only don't make a noise about it." And thus the government, its salary being insured, withdraws into the back shop, taking the constitution with it, and bestows most of its labor on repairing that. When I hear it at work sometimes, as I go by, it reminds me, at best, of those farmers who in winter contrive to turn a penny by following the coopering business. And what kind of spirit is their barrel made to hold? They speculate in stocks, and bore holes in mountains, but they are not competent to lay out even a decent highway. The only *free* road, the Underground Railroad,[34] is owned and managed by the Vigilant Committee. *They* have tunnelled under the whole breadth of the land. Such a government is losing its power and respectability as surely as water runs out of a leaky vessel, and is held by one that can contain it.

I hear many condemn these men because they were so few. When were the good and the brave ever in a majority? Would you have had him wait till that time came? —till you and I came over to him? The very fact that he had no rabble or troop of hirelings about him would alone distinguish him from ordinary heroes. His company was small indeed, because few could be found worthy to pass muster. Each one who there laid down his life for the poor and oppressed, was a picked man, called out of

[32] Train in the sense of a caravan or procession.
[33] In this instance, the abolitionists.
[34] The route northward taken by slaves escaping out of the South, sometimes as far as Canada, aided by abolitionists.

many thousands, if not millions; apparently a man of principle, of rare courage and devoted humanity, ready to sacrifice his life at any moment for the benefit of his fellow man. It may be doubted if there were as many more their equals in these respects in all the country—I speak of his followers only—for their leader, no doubt, scoured the land far and wide, seeking to swell his troop. These alone were ready to step between the oppressor and the oppressed. Surely, they were the very best men you could select to be hung. That was the greatest compliment which this country could pay them. They were ripe for her gallows. She has tried a long time, she has hung a good many, but never found the right one before.

When I think of him, and his six sons, and his son in law,—not to enumerate the others,—enlisted for this fight; proceeding coolly, reverently, humanely to work, for months if not years, sleeping and waking upon it, summering and wintering the thought, without expecting any reward but a good conscience, while almost all America stood ranked on the other side, I say again that it affects me as a sublime spectacle. If he had had any journal advocating *"his cause,"* any organ as the phrase is, monotonously and wearisomely playing the same old tune, and then passing round the hat, it would have been fatal to his efficiency. If he had acted in any way so as to be let alone by the government, he might have been suspected. It was the fact that the tyrant must give place to him, or he to the tyrant, that distinguished him from all the reformers of the day that I know.

It was his peculiar doctrine that a man has a perfect right to interfere by force with the slaveholder, in order to rescue the slave. I agree with him. They who are continually shocked by slavery have some right to be shocked by the violent death of the slaveholder, but no others. Such will be more shocked by his life than by his death. I shall not be forward to think him mistaken in his method who quickest succeeds to liberate the slave. I speak for the slave when I say, that I prefer the philanthropy of Captain Brown to that philanthropy which neither shoots me nor liberates me. At any rate, I do not think it is quite sane for one to spend his whole life in talking or writing about this matter, unless he is continuously inspired, and I have not done so. A man may have other affairs to attend to. I do not wish to kill nor to be killed, but I can foresee circumstances in which both these things would be by me unavoidable. We preserve the so-called "peace" of our community by deeds of petty violence every day. Look at the policeman's billy and hand cuffs! Look at the jail! Look at the gallows! Look at the chaplain of the regiment! We are hoping only to live safely on the outskirts of *this* provisional army. So we defend ourselves and our hen roosts, and maintain slavery. I know that the mass of my countrymen think that the only righteous use that can be made of Sharps' rifles and revolvers is to fight duels with them, when we are insulted by other nations, or to hunt Indians, or shoot fugitive slaves with them, or the like. I think that for once the Sharps' rifles and the revolvers were employed in a righteous cause. The tools were in the hands of one who could use them.

The same indignation that is said to have cleared the temple[35] once will clear it again. The question is not about the weapon, but the spirit in which you use it. No man has appeared in America as yet who loved his fellow man so well, and treated

---

[35] Allusion to Jesus' chasing evildoers from the temple. See Matthew 21:12–13 for the passage   Thoreau uses in the further comparison of Brown to Jesus.

him so tenderly. He lived for him. He took up his life and he laid it down for him. What sort of violence is that which is encouraged, not by soldiers but by peaceable citizens, not so much by lay-men as by ministers of the gospel, not so much by the fighting sects as by the Quakers, and not so much by Quaker men as by Quaker women?

This event advertises me that there is such a fact as death—the possibility of a man's dying. It seems as if no man had ever died in America before, for in order to die you must first have lived. I dont believe in the hearses and palls and funerals that they have had. There was no death in the case, because there had been no life; they merely rotted or sloughed off, pretty much as they had rotted or sloughed along. No temple's vail was rent,[36] only a hole dug somewhere. Let the dead bury their dead. The best of them fairly ran down like a clock. Franklin—Washington—they were let off without dying; they were merely missing one day. I hear a good many pretend that they are going to die;—or that they have died for aught that I know. Nonsense! I'll defy them to do it. They haven't got life enough in them. They'll deliquesce like fungi, and keep a hundred eulogists mopping the spot where they left off. Only half a dozen or so have died since the world began. Do you think that you are going to die, sir? No! there's no hope of you. You haven't got your lesson yet. You've got to stay after school. We make a needless ado about capital punishment—taking lives, when there is no life to take. *Memento mori!* We don't understand that sublime sentence which some worthy got sculptured on his gravestone once. We've interpreted it in a grovelling and snivelling sense; we've wholly forgotten how to die.

But be sure you do die, nevertheless. Do your work, and finish it. If you know how to begin, you will know when to end.

These men, in teaching us how to die, have at the same time taught us how to live. If this man's acts and words do not create a revival, it will be the severest possible satire on the acts and words that do. It is the best news that America has ever heard. It has already quickened the feeble pulse of the North, and infused more and more generous blood into her veins and heart, than any number of years of what is called commercial and political prosperity could. How many a man who was lately contemplating suicide has now something to live for!

One writer says that Brown's peculiar monomania made him to be "dreaded by the Missourians as a supernatural being." Sure enough, a hero in the midst of us cowards is always so dreaded. He is just that thing. He shows himself superior to nature. He has a spark of divinity in him.

> "Unless above himself he can
> Erect himself, how poor a thing is man!"[37]

Newspaper editors argue also that it is a proof of his *insanity* that he thought he was appointed to do this work which he did—that he did not suspect himself for a moment! They talk as if it were impossible that a man could be "divinely appointed" in these days to do any work whatever; as if vows and religion were out of date as connected with any man's daily work,—as if the agent to abolish Slavery could only

[36] Matthew 27:50–53 describes this occurrence at the moment of Jesus' death on the cross.

[37] From "To the Countess of Cumberland" by English poet Samuel Daniel (1562–1619).

be somebody appointed by the President, or by some political party. They talk as if a man's death were a failure, and his continued life, be it of whatever character, were a success.

When I reflect to what a cause this man devoted himself, and how religiously, and then reflect to what cause his judges and all who condemn him so angrily and fluently devote themselves, I see that they are as far apart as the heavens and earth are asunder.

The amount of it is, our *"leading men"* are a harmless kind of folk, and they know *well enough* that *they* were not divinely appointed, but elected by the votes of their party.

Who is it whose safety requires that Captain Brown be hung? Is it indispensable to any Northern man? Is there no resource but to cast these men also to the Minotaur?[38] If you do not wish it say so distinctly. While these things are being done, beauty stands veiled and music is a screeching lie. Think of him—of his rare qualities! such a man as it takes ages to make, and ages to understand; no mock hero, nor the representative of any party. A man such as the sun may not rise upon again in this benighted land. To whose making went the costliest material, the finest adamant; sent to be the redeemer of those in captivity. And the only use to which you can put him is to hang him at the end of a rope! You who pretend to care for Christ crucified, consider what you are about to do to him who offered himself to be the savior of four millions of men.

Any man knows when he is justified, and all the wits in the world cannot enlighten him on that point. The murderer always knows that he is justly punished; but when a government takes the life of a man without the consent of his conscience, it is an audacious government, and is taking a step towards its own dissolution. Is it not possible that an individual may be right and a government wrong? Are laws to be enforced simply because they were made? or declared by any number of men to be good, if they are *not* good? Is there any necessity for a man's being a tool to perform a deed of which his better nature disapproves? Is it the intention of law-makers that *good* men shall be hung ever? Are judges to interpret the law according to the letter, and not the spirit? What right have *you* to enter into a compact with yourself that you *will* do thus or so, against the light within you? Is it for *you* to *make up* your mind—to form any resolution whatever—and not accept the convictions that are forced upon you, and which ever pass your understanding? I do not believe in lawyers, in that mode of attacking or defending a man, because you descend to meet the judge on his own ground, and, in cases of the highest importance, it is of no consequence whether a man breaks a human law or not. Let lawyers decide trivial cases. Business men may arrange that among themselves. If they were the interpreters of the everlasting laws which rightfully bind man, that would be another thing. A counterfeiting law-factory, standing half in a slave land and half in a free! What kind of laws for free men can you expect from that?

I am here to plead his cause with you. I plead not for his life, but for his character —his immortal life; and so it becomes your cause wholly, and is not his in the least. Some eighteen hundred years ago Christ was crucified; this morning, perchance,

[38] Monster in classic myth that lay in wait at the center of the labyrinth in Crete, ready to devour those delivered to him in sacrifice.

Captain Brown was hung. These are the two ends of a chain which is not without its links. He is not Old Brown any longer; he is an Angel of Light.

I see now that it was necessary that the bravest and humanest man in all the country should be hung. Perhaps he saw it himself. I *almost fear* that I may yet hear of his deliverance, doubting if a prolonged life, if *any* life, can do as much good as his death.

"Misguided"! "Garrulous"! "Insane"! "Vindictive"! So ye write in your easy chairs, and thus he wounded responds from the floor of the Armory, clear as a cloudless sky, true as the voice of nature is: "No man sent me here; it was my own prompting and that of my Maker. I acknowledge no master in human form."

And in what a sweet and noble strain he proceeds, addressing his captors, who stand over him: "I think, my friends, you are guilty of a great wrong against God and humanity, and it would be perfectly right for any one to interfere with you so far as to free those you wilfully and wickedly hold in bondage."

And referring to his movement: "It is, in my opinion, the greatest service a man can render to God."

"I pity the poor in bondage that have none to help them; that is why I am here; not to gratify any personal animosity, revenge, or vindictive spirit. It is my sympathy with the oppressed and the wronged, that are as good as you, and as precious in the sight of God."

You don't know your testament when you see it.

"I want you to understand that I respect the rights of the poorest and weakest of colored people, oppressed by the slave power, just as much as I do those of the most wealthy and powerful."

"I wish to say, furthermore, that you had better, all you people at the South, prepare yourselves for a settlement of that question, that must come up for settlement sooner than you are prepared for it. The sooner you are prepared the better. You may dispose of me very easily. I am nearly disposed of now; but this question is still to be settled—this negro question, I mean; the end of that is not yet."

I foresee the time when the painter will paint that scene, no longer going to Rome for a subject; the poet will sing it; the historian record it; and, with the Landing of the Pilgrims and the Declaration of Independence, it will be the ornament of some future national gallery, when at least the present form of Slavery shall be no more here.[39] We shall then be at liberty to weep for Captain Brown. Then, and not till then, we will take our revenge.

1860

---

[39] Thoreau was correct, as proven by Thomas Hart Benton's painting, the popular marching song "John Brown's Body," Julia Ward Howe's "Battle Hymn of the Republic," the long poem on Brown by Stephen Vincent Benét (1928), and numerous historical discussions devoted to Brown's life.

Wild Apples[*]

The History of the Apple Tree

It is remarkable how closely the history of the apple tree is connected with that of man. The geologist tells us that the order of the *Rosaceae,* which includes the apple, also the true grasses, and the *Labiatae,* or mints, were introduced only a short time previous to the appearance of man on the globe.

It appears that apples made a part of the food of that unknown primitive people whose traces have lately been found at the bottom of the Swiss lakes, supposed to be older than the foundation of Rome, so old that they had no metallic implements. An entire black and shriveled crab-apple has been recovered from their stores.

Tacitus[1] says of the ancient Germans that they satisfied their hunger with wild apples (*agrestia poma*), among other things.

Niebuhr[2] observes that "the words for a house, a field, a plow, plowing, wine, oil, milk, sheep, apples, and others relating to agriculture and the gentler way of life, agree in Latin and Greek, while the Latin words for all objects pertaining to war or the chase are utterly alien from the Greek." Thus the apple tree may be considered a symbol of peace no less than the olive.

The apple was early so important, and generally distributed, that its name traced to its root in many languages signifies fruit in general. $M\eta\lambda o\nu$, in Greek, means an apple, also the fruit of other trees, also a sheep and any cattle, and finally riches in general.

The apple tree has been celebrated by the Hebrews, Greeks, Romans, and Scandinavians. Some have thought that the first human pair were tempted by its fruit. Goddesses are fabled to have contended for it, dragons were set to watch it, and heroes were employed to pluck it.

The tree is mentioned in at least three places in the Old Testament, and its fruit in two or three more. Solomon sings, "As the apple-tree among the trees of the wood, so is my beloved among the sons."[3] And again, "Stay me with flagons, comfort me with apples." The noblest part of man's noblest feature is named from this fruit, "the apple of the eye."[4]

The apple tree is also mentioned by Homer and Herodotus.[5] Ulysses saw in the glorious garden of Alcinous "pears and pomegranates, and apple trees bearing beautiful fruit" ($\kappa\alpha\grave{\iota}\ \mu\eta\lambda\acute{\epsilon}\alpha\iota\ \mathring{\alpha}\gamma\lambda\alpha\acute{o}\kappa\alpha\rho\pi o\iota$). And according to Homer, apples were among the fruits which Tantalus[6] could not pluck, the wind ever blowing their boughs away from him. Theophrastus[7] knew and described the apple tree as a botanist.

According to the Prose Edda,[8] "Iduna keeps in a box the apples which the gods,

[*] The material for this essay, first delivered as a lecture in 1860, was taken from Thoreau's Journal of 1850–1852 and of 1857–1860. The essay was published in the *Atlantic Monthly,* November 1862.
[1] Roman historian (A.D. 55?–117?).
[2] From the three-volume *Roman History* (1827–1832) by Barthold Niebuhr (1776–1831), German historian.
[3] From the Song of Songs 2:3 and 2:5.

[4] Psalms 17:8.
[5] Greek historian of the fifth century B.C.
[6] In classic myth Tantalus was doomed to stand for eternity beneath trees of fruit he was never able to reach, no matter how hungry.
[7] Greek philosopher and naturalist of the third century B.C.
[8] Medieval Icelandic literary work that summarizes the Norse myths of the gods. Iduna was the goddess of youth and springtime.

when they feel old age approaching, have only to taste of to become young again. It is in this manner that they will be kept in renovated youth until Ragnarök" (or the destruction of the gods).

I learn from Loudon[9] that "the ancient Welsh bards were rewarded for excelling in song by the token of the apple-spray;" and "in the Highlands of Scotland the apple-tree is the badge of the clan Lamont."

The apple tree (*Pyrus malus*) belongs chiefly to the northern temperate zone. Loudon says that "it grows spontaneously in every part of Europe except the frigid zone, and throughout Western Asia, China, and Japan." We have also two or three varieties of the apple indigenous in North America. The cultivated apple tree was first introduced into this country by the earliest settlers, and is thought to do as well or better here than anywhere else. Probably some of the varieties which are now cultivated were first introduced into Britain by the Romans.

Pliny, adopting the distinction of Theophrastus, says, "Of trees there are some which are altogether wild (*sylvestres*), some more civilized (*urbaniores*)."[10] Theophrastus includes the apple among the last; and, indeed, it is in this sense the most civilized of all trees. It is as harmless as a dove, as beautiful as a rose, and as valuable as flocks and herds. It has been longer cultivated than any other, and so is more humanized; and who knows but, like the dog, it will at length be no longer traceable to its wild original? It migrates with man, like the dog and horse and cow: first, perchance, from Greece to Italy, thence to England, thence to America; and our Western emigrant is still marching steadily toward the setting sun with the seeds of the apple in his pocket, or perhaps a few young trees strapped to his load. At least a million apple trees are thus set farther westward this year than any cultivated ones grew last year. Consider how the Blossom Week, like the Sabbath, is thus annually spreading over the prairies; for when man migrates, he carries with him not only his birds, quadrupeds, insects, vegetables, and his very sward, but his orchard also.

The leaves and tender twigs are an agreeable food to many domestic animals, as the cow, horse, sheep, and goat; and the fruit is sought after by the first, as well as by the hog. Thus there appears to have existed a natural alliance between these animals and this tree from the first. "The fruit of the crab in the forests of France" is said to be "a great resource for the wild boar."

Not only the Indian, but many indigenous insects, birds, and quadrupeds, welcomed the apple tree to these shores. The tent caterpillar saddled her eggs on the very first twig that was formed, and it has since shared her affections with the wild cherry; and the canker-worm also in a measure abandoned the elm to feed on it. As it grew apace, the bluebird, robin, cherry-bird, kingbird, and many more came with haste and built their nests and warbled in its boughs, and so became orchard-birds, and multiplied more than ever. It was an era in the history of their race. The downy woodpecker found such a savory morsel under its bark that he perforated it in a ring quite round the tree, before he left it,—a thing which he had never done before, to my knowledge. It did not take the partridge long to find out how sweet its buds were, and every winter eve she flew, and still flies, from the wood, to pluck them, much to the farmer's

[9] John C. Loudon (1783–1843), English naturalist, author of a study of the trees and fruits of Great Britain (1833–1838).

[10] From *The Natural History* by Pliny the Elder (A.D. 23–79), Roman naturalist.

sorrow. The rabbit, too, was not slow to learn the taste of its twigs and bark; and when the fruit was ripe, the squirrel half rolled, half carried it to his hole; and even the musquash crept up the bank from the brook at evening, and greedily devoured it, until he had worn a path in the grass there; and when it was frozen and thawed, the crow and the jay were glad to taste it occasionally. The owl crept into the first apple tree that became hollow, and fairly hooted with delight, finding it just the place for him; so, settling down into it, he has remained there ever since.

My theme being the Wild Apple, I will merely glance at some of the seasons in the annual growth of the cultivated apple, and pass on to my special province.

The flowers of the apple are perhaps the most beautiful of any tree's, so copious and so delicious to both sight and scent. The walker is frequently tempted to turn and linger near some more than usually handsome one, whose blossoms are two-thirds expanded. How superior it is in these respects to the pear, whose blossoms are neither colored nor fragrant!

By the middle of July, green apples are so large as to remind us of coddling, and of the autumn. The sward is commonly strewed with little ones which fall stillborn, as it were,—Nature thus thinning them for us. The Roman writer Palladius[11] said, "If apples are inclined to fall before their time, a stone placed in a split root will retain them." Some such notion, still surviving, may account for some of the stones which we see placed, to be overgrown, in the forks of trees. They have a saying in Suffolk, England,—

"At Michaelmas time, or a little before,
  Half an apple goes to the core."

Early apples begin to be ripe about the first of August; but I think that none of them are so good to eat as some to smell. One is worth more to scent your handkerchief with than any perfume which they sell in the shops. The fragrance of some fruits is not to be forgotten, along with that of flowers. Some gnarly apple which I pick up in the road reminds me by its fragrance of all the wealth of Pomona,[12]—carrying me forward to those days when they will be collected in golden and ruddy heaps in the orchards and about the cider-mills.

A week or two later, as you are going by orchards or gardens, especially in the evenings, you pass through a little region possessed by the fragrance of ripe apples, and thus enjoy them without price, and without robbing anybody.

There is thus about all natural products a certain volatile and ethereal quality which represents their highest value, and which cannot be vulgarized, or bought and sold. No mortal has ever enjoyed the perfect flavor of any fruit, and only the godlike among men begin to taste its ambrosial qualities. For nectar and ambrosia are only those fine flavors of every earthly fruit which our coarse palates fail to perceive,—just as we occupy the heaven of the gods without knowing it. When I see a particularly mean man carrying a load of fair and fragrant early apples to market, I seem to see a contest going on between him and his horse, on the one side, and the apples on the other,

---

[11] Rutilius Taurus Aemiliānus Palladius (fourth century A.D.) wrote a treatise on husbandry. Thoreau may have known the text from Johann

Gottlob Schneider's *Scriptores Rei Rusticae,* published 1794–1797.
[12] Roman goddess of fruits and fruit trees.

and, to my mind, the apples always gain it. Pliny says that apples are the heaviest of all things, and that the oxen begin to sweat at the mere sight of a load of them. Our driver begins to lose his load the moment he tries to transport them to where they do not belong, that is, to any but the most beautiful. Though he gets out from time to time, and feels of them, and thinks they are all there, I see the stream of their evanescent and celestial qualities going to heaven from his cart, while the pulp and skin and core only are going to market. They are not apples, but pomace. Are not these still Iduna's apples, the taste of which keeps the gods forever young? and think you that they will let Loki or Thjassi[13] carry them off to Jötunheim, while they grow wrinkled and gray? No, for Ragnarök, or the destruction of the gods, is not yet.

There is another thinning of the fruit, commonly near the end of August or in September, when the ground is strewn with windfalls; and this happens especially when high winds occur after rain. In some orchards you may see fully three quarters of the whole crop on the ground, lying in a circular form beneath the trees, yet hard and green, or, if it is a hillside, rolled far down the hill. However, it is an ill wind that blows nobody any good. All the country over, people are busy picking up the windfalls, and this will make them cheap for early apple pies.

In October, the leaves falling, the apples are more distinct on the trees. I saw one year in a neighboring town some trees fuller of fruit than I remember to have ever seen before, small yellow apples hanging over the road. The branches were gracefully drooping with their weight, like a barberry bush, so that the whole tree acquired a new character. Even the topmost branches, instead of standing erect, spread and drooped in all directions; and there were so many poles supporting the lower ones that they looked like pictures of banyan trees. As an old English manuscript says, "The mo appelen the tree bereth the more sche boweth to the folk."

Surely the apple is the noblest of fruits. Let the most beautiful or the swiftest have it. That should be the "going" price of apples.

Between the 5th and 20th of October I see the barrels lie under the trees. And perhaps I talk with one who is selecting some choice barrels to fulfill an order. He turns a specked one over many times before he leaves it out. If I were to tell what is passing in my mind, I should say that every one was specked which he had handled; for he rubs off all the bloom, and those fugacious ethereal qualities leave it. Cool evenings prompt the farmers to make haste, and at length I see only the ladders here and there left leaning against the trees.

It would be well, if we accepted these gifts with more joy and gratitude, and did not think it enough simply to put a fresh load of compost about the tree. Some old English customs are suggestive \at least. I find them described chiefly in Brand's "Popular Antiquities."[14] It appears that "on Christmas Eve the farmers and their men in Devonshire take a large bowl of cider, with a toast in it, and carrying it in state to the orchard, they salute the apple-trees with much ceremony, in order to make them bear well the next season." This salutation consists in "throwing some of the cider about the roots of the tree, placing bits of the toast on the branches," and then, "encircling one of the best bearing trees in the orchard, they drink the following toast three several times:—

---

[13] Tricksters and thiefs, figures in Norse mythology described in the Prose Edda.

[14] John Brand's *Observations on Popular Antiquities* (1777).

'Here's to thee, old apple tree,
Whence thou mayst bud, and whence thou mayst blow,
And whence thou mayst bear apples enow!
    Hats-full! caps-full!
    Bushel, bushel, sacks-full!
    And my pockets full, too! Hurra!' "

Also what was called "apple-howling" used to be practiced in various counties of England on New Year's Eve. A troop of boys visited the different orchards, and, encircling the apple trees, repeated the following words:—

"Stand fast, root! bear well, top!
Pray God send us a good howling crop:
    Every twig, apples big;
    Every bough, apples enow!"

"They then shout in chorus, one of the boys accompanying them on a cow's horn. During this ceremony they rap the trees with their sticks." This is called "wassailing" the trees, and is thought by some to be "a relic of the heathen sacrifice to Pomona." Herrick sings,[15]—

"Wassaile the trees that they may beare
You many a plum and many a peare;
For more or less fruits they will bring
As you so give them wassailing."

Our poets have as yet a better right to sing of cider than of wine; but it behooves them to sing better than English Phillips[16] did, else they will do no credit to their Muse.

So much for the more civilized apple trees (*urbaniores,* as Pliny calls them). I love better to go through the old orchards of ungrafted apple trees, at what ever season of the year,—so irregularly planted: sometimes two trees standing close together; and the rows so devious that you would think that they not only had grown while the owner was sleeping, but had been set out by him in a somnambulic state. The rows of grafted fruit will never tempt me to wander amid them like these. But I now, alas, speak rather from memory than from any recent experience, such ravages have been made!

Some soils, like a rocky tract called the Easterbrooks Country in my neighborhood, are so suited to the apple, that it will grow faster in them without any care, or if only the ground is broken up once a year, than it will in many places with any amount of care. The owners of this tract allow that the soil is excellent for fruit, but they say that it is so rocky that they have not patience to plow it, and that, together with the distance, is the reason why it is not cultivated. There are, or were recently, extensive orchards there standing without order. Nay, they spring up wild and bear

---

[15] From "Ceremonies for Christmasse" by Robert Herrick (1591–1674), English poet. [16] Perhaps a reference to Edward Phillips (1630–1696), minor English poet.

well there in the midst of pines, birches, maples, and oaks. I am often surprised to see rising amid these trees the rounded tops of apple trees glowing with red or yellow fruit, in harmony with the autumnal tints of the forest.

Going up the side of a cliff about the first of November, I saw a vigorous young apple tree, which, planted by birds or cows, had shot up amid the rocks and open woods there, and had now much fruit on it, uninjured by the frosts, when all cultivated apples were gathered. It was a rank, wild growth, with many green leaves on it still, and made an impression of thorniness. The fruit was hard and green, but looked as if it would be palatable in the winter. Some was dangling on the twigs, but more half buried in the wet leaves under the tree, or rolled far down the hill amid the rocks. The owner knows nothing of it. The day was not observed when it first blossomed, nor when it first bore fruit, unless by the chickadee. There was no dancing on the green beneath it in its honor, and now there is no hand to pluck its fruit,— which is only gnawed by squirrels, as I perceive. It has done double duty,—not only borne this crop, but each twig has grown a foot into the air. And this is *such* fruit! bigger than many berries, we must admit, and carried home will be sound and palatable next spring. What care I for Iduna's apples so long as I can get these?

When I go by this shrub thus late and hardy, and see its dangling fruit, I respect the tree, and I am grateful for Nature's bounty, even though I cannot eat it. Here on this rugged and woody hillside has grown an apple tree, not planted by man, no relic of a former orchard, but a natural growth, like the pines and oaks. Most fruits which we prize and use depend entirely on our care. Corn and grain, potatoes, peaches, melons, etc., depend altogether on our planting; but the apple emulates man's independence and enterprise. It is not simply carried, as I have said, but, like him, to some extent, it has migrated to this New World, and is even, here and there, making its way amid the aboriginal trees; just as the ox and dog and horse sometimes run wild and maintain themselves.

Even the sourest and crabbedest apple, growing in the most unfavorable position, suggests such thoughts as these, it is so noble a fruit.

The Crab

Nevertheless, *our* wild apple is wild only like myself, perchance, who belong not to the aboriginal race here, but have strayed into the woods from the cultivated stock. Wilder still, as I have said, there grows elsewhere in this country a native and aboriginal crab-apple, *Malus coronaria,* "whose nature has not yet been modified by cultivation." It is found from western New York to Minnesota, and southward. Michaux[17] says that its ordinary height "is fifteen or eighteen feet, but it is sometimes found twenty-five or thirty feet high," and that the large ones "exactly resemble the common apple tree." "The flowers are white mingled with rose color, and are collected in corymbs." They are remarkable for their delicious odor. The fruit, according to him, is about an inch and a half in diameter, and is intensely acid. Yet they make fine sweetmeats and also cider of them. He concludes that "if, on being cultivated, it does not yield new and palatable varieties, it will at least be celebrated for the beauty of its flowers, and for the sweetness of its perfume."

---

[17] André Michaux (1746–1802), French botanist, author of *North American Sylva* (1818).

I never saw the crab-apple till May, 1861. I had heard of it through Michaux, but more modern botanists, so far as I know, have not treated it as of any peculiar importance. Thus it was a half-fabulous tree to me. I contemplated a pilgrimage to the "Glades," a portion of Pennsylvania where it was said to grow to perfection. I thought of sending to a nursery for it, but doubted if they had it, or would distinguish it from European varieties. At last I had occasion to go to Minnesota,[18] and on entering Michigan I began to notice from the cars a tree with handsome rose-colored flowers. At first I thought it some variety of thorn; but it was not long before the truth flashed on me, that this was my long-sought crab-apple. It was the prevailing flowering shrub or tree to be seen from the cars at that season of the year,—about the middle of May. But the cars never stopped before one, and so I was launched on the bosom of the Mississippi without having touched one, experiencing the fate of Tantalus. On arriving at St. Anthony's Falls, I was sorry to be told that I was too far north for the crab-apple. Nevertheless I succeeded in finding it about eight miles west of the Falls; touched it and smelled it, and secured a lingering corymb of flowers for my herbarium. This must have been near its northern limit.

How the Wild Apple Grows

But though these are indigenous, like the Indians, I doubt whether they are any hardier than those backwoodsmen among the apple trees, which, though descended from cultivated stocks, plant themselves in distant fields and forests, where the soil is favorable to them. I know of no trees which have more difficulties to contend with, and which more sturdily resist their foes. These are the ones whose story we have to tell. It oftentimes reads thus:—

Near the beginning of May, we notice little thickets of apple trees just springing up in the pastures where cattle have been,—as the rocky ones of our Easterbrooks Country, or the top of Nobscot Hill, in Sudbury. One or two of these, perhaps, survive the drought and other accidents,—their very birthplace defending them against the encroaching grass and some other dangers, at first.

> In two years' time 't had thus
> Reached the level of the rocks,
> Admired the stretching world,
> Nor feared the wandering flocks.
>
> But at this tender age
> Its sufferings began:
> There came a browsing ox
> And cut it down a span.[19]

This time, perhaps, the ox does not notice it amid the grass; but the next year, when it has grown more stout, he recognizes it for a fellow-emigrant from the old country, the flavor of whose leaves and twigs he well knows; and though at first he pauses to

[18] Thoreau took a trip to Minnesota the year before his death in the hopes of regaining his health.

[19] Thoreau's verses.

welcome it, and express his surprise, and gets for answer, "The same cause that brought you here brought me," he nevertheless browses it again, reflecting, it may be, that he has some title to it.

Thus cut down annually, it does not despair; but, putting forth two short twigs for every one cut off, it spreads out low along the ground in the hollows or between the rocks, growing more stout and scrubby, until it forms, not a tree as yet, but a little pyramidal, stiff, twiggy mass, almost as solid and impenetrable as a rock. Some of the densest and most impenetrable clumps of bushes that I have ever seen, as well on account of the closeness and stubbornness of their branches as of their thorns, have been these wild apple scrubs. They are more like the scrubby fir and black spruce on which you stand, and sometimes walk, on the tops of mountains, where cold is the demon they contend with, than anything else.[20] No wonder they are prompted to grow thorns at last, to defend themselves against such foes. In their thorniness, however, there is no malice, only some malic acid.

The rocky pastures of the tract I have referred to—for they maintain their ground best in a rocky field—are thickly sprinkled with these little tufts, reminding you often of some rigid gray mosses or lichens, and you see thousands of little trees just springing up between them, with the seed still attached to them.

Being regularly clipped all around each year by the cows, as a hedge with shears, they are often of a perfect conical or pyramidal form, from one to four feet high, and more or less sharp, as if trimmed by the gardener's art. In the pastures on Nobscot Hill and its spurs, they make fine dark shadows when the sun is low. They are also an excellent covert from hawks for many small birds that roost and build in them. Whole flocks perch in them at night, and I have seen three robins' nests in one which was six feet in diameter.

No doubt many of these are already old trees, if you reckon from the day they were planted, but infants still when you consider their development and the long life before them. I counted the annual rings of some which were just one foot high, and as wide as high, and found that they were about twelve years old, but quite sound and thrifty! They were so low that they were unnoticed by the walker, while many of their contemporaries from the nurseries were already bearing considerable crops. But what you gain in time is perhaps in this case, too, lost in power,—that is, in the vigor of the tree. This is their pyramidal state.

The cows continue to browse them thus for twenty years or more, keeping them down and compelling them to spread, until at last they are so broad that they become their own fence, when some interior shoot, which their foes cannot reach, darts upward with joy: for it has not forgotten its high calling, and bears its own peculiar fruit in triumph.

Such are the tactics by which it finally defeats its bovine foes. Now, if you have watched the progress of a particular shrub, you will see that it is no longer a simple pyramid or cone, but that out of its apex there rises a sprig or two, growing more lustily perchance than an orchard-tree, since the plant now devotes the whole of its repressed energy to these upright parts. In a short time these become a small tree, an

---

[20] Thoreau's description of what he saw upon his climb to the summit of Mt. Ktaadn in Maine bears this out.

inverted pyramid resting on the apex of the other, so that the whole has now the form of a vast hour-glass. The spreading bottom, having served its purpose, finally disappears, and the generous tree permits the now harmless cows to come in and stand in its shade, and rub against and redden its trunk, which has grown in spite of them, and even to taste a part of its fruit, and so disperse the seed.

Thus the cows create their own shade and food; and the tree, its hour-glass being inverted, lives a second life, as it were.

It is an important question with some nowadays, whether you should trim young apple trees as high as your nose or as high as your eyes. The ox trims them up as high as he can reach, and that is about the right height, I think.

In spite of wandering kine, and other adverse circumstances, that despised shrub, valued only by small birds as a covert and shelter from hawks, has its blossom week at last, and in course of time its harvest, sincere, though small.

By the end of some October, when its leaves have fallen, I frequently see such a central sprig, whose progress I have watched, when I thought it had forgotten its destiny, as I had, bearing its first crop of small green or yellow or rosy fruit, which the cows cannot get at over the bushy and thorny hedge which surrounds it, and I make haste to taste the new and undescribed variety. We have all heard of the numerous varieties of fruit invented by Van Mons and Knight.[21] This is the system of Van Cow, and she has invented far more and more memorable varieties than both of them.

Through what hardships it may attain to bear a sweet fruit! Though somewhat small, it may prove equal, if not superior, in flavor to that which has grown in a garden,—will perchance be all the sweeter and more palatable for the very difficulties it has had to contend with. Who knows but this chance wild fruit, planted by a cow or a bird on some remote and rocky hillside, where it is as yet unobserved by man, may be the choicest of all its kind, and foreign potentates shall hear of it, and royal societies seek to propagate it, though the virtues of the perhaps truly crabbed owner of the soil may never be heard of,—at least, beyond the limits of his village? It was thus the Porter and the Baldwin grew.

Every wild apple shrub excites our expectation thus, somewhat as every wild child. It is, perhaps, a prince in disguise. What a lesson to man! So are human beings, referred to the highest standard, the celestial fruit which they suggest and aspire to bear, browsed on by fate; and only the most persistent and strongest genius defends itself and prevails, sends a tender scion upward at last, and drops its perfect fruit on the ungrateful earth. Poets and philosophers and statesmen thus spring up in the country pastures, and outlast the hosts of unoriginal men.

Such is always the pursuit of knowledge. The celestial fruits, the golden apples of the Hesperides,[22] are ever guarded by a hundred-headed dragon which never sleeps, so that it is an Herculean labor to pluck them.

This is one, and the most remarkable way in which the wild apple is propagated; but commonly it springs up at wide intervals in woods and swamp, and by the sides

[21] Horticulturalists; Thomas Andrew Knight (1759–1838) wrote on the cultivation of apples and pears.

[22] In classic myth, Hercules slew the dragon that watched over the golden apples in the garden of the Hesperides, the westernmost land of the ancient world.

of roads, as the soil may suit it, and grows with comparative rapidity. Those which grow in dense woods are very tall and slender. I frequently pluck from these trees a perfectly mild and tamed fruit. As Palladius says, *"Et injussu consternitur ubere mali:"*[23] And the ground is strewn with the fruit of an unbidden apple tree.

It is an old notion that, if these wild trees do not bear a valuable fruit of their own, they are the best stocks by which to transmit to posterity the most highly prized qualities of others. However, I am not in search of stocks, but the wild fruit itself, whose fierce gust has suffered no "inteneration." It is not my

> "highest plot
> To plant the Bergamot."[24]

The Fruit and Its Flavor

The time for wild apples is the last of October and the first of November. They then get to be palatable, for they ripen late, and they are still perhaps as beautiful as ever. I make a great account of these fruits, which the farmers do not think it worth the while to gather,—wild flavors of the Muse, vivacious and inspiriting. The farmer thinks that he has better in his barrels, but he is mistaken, unless he has a walker's appetite and imagination, neither of which can he have.

Such as grow quite wild, and are left out till the first of November, I presume that the owner does not mean to gather. They belong to children as wild as themselves, —to certain active boys that I know,—to the wild-eyed woman of the fields, to whom nothing comes amiss, who gleans after all the world, and, moreover, to us walkers. We have met with them, and they are ours. These rights, long enough insisted upon, have come to be an institution in some old countries, where they have learned how to live. I hear that "the custom of grippling, which may be called apple-gleaning, is, or was formerly, practiced in Herefordshire. It consists in leaving a few apples, which are called the gripples, on every tree, after the general gathering, for the boys, who go with climbing-poles and bags to collect them."[25]

As for those I speak of, I pluck them as a wild fruit, native to this quarter of the earth,—fruit of old trees that have been dying ever since I was a boy and are not yet dead, frequented only by the woodpecker and the squirrel, deserted now by the owner, who has not faith enough to look under their boughs. From the appearance of the tree-top, at a little distance, you would expect nothing but lichens to drop from it, but your faith is rewarded by finding the ground strewn with spirited fruit,—some of it, perhaps, collected at squirrel-holes, with the marks of their teeth by which they carried them,—some containing a cricket or two silently feeding within, and some, especially in damp days, a shell-less snail. The very sticks and stones lodged in the tree-top might have convinced you of the savoriness of the fruit which has been so eagerly sought after in past years.

I have seen no account of these among the "Fruits and Fruit-Trees of America,"[26] though they are more memorable to my taste than the grafted kinds; more racy and

---

[23] Actually quoted from Lucius Junius Moderatus Columella (first century A.D.), Roman writer on agriculture.
[24] From "The Horatian Ode" by the English poet Andrew Marvell (1621–1678).

[25] From Brand's *Popular Antiquities* (1777).
[26] By A. J. Downey, published 1859.

wild American flavors do they possess when October and November, when December and January, and perhaps February and March even, have assuaged them somewhat. An old farmer in my neighborhood, who always selects the right word, says that "they have a kind of bow-arrow tang."

Apples for grafting appear to have been selected commonly, not so much for their spirited flavor, as for their mildness, their size, and bearing qualities,—not so much for their beauty, as for their fairness and soundness. Indeed, I have no faith in the selected lists of pomological gentlemen. Their "Favorites" and "None-suches" and "Seek-no-farthers," when I have fruited them, commonly turn out very tame and forgettable. They are eaten with comparatively little zest, and have no real *tang* nor *smack* to them.

What if some of these wildings are acrid and puckery, genuine *verjuice,* do they not still belong to the *Pomaceæ,* which are uniformly innocent and kind to our race? I still begrudge them to the cider-mill. Perhaps they are not fairly ripe yet.

No wonder that these small and high-colored apples are thought to make the best cider. Loudon quotes from the "Herefordshire Report," that "apples of a small size are always, if equal in quality, to be preferred to those of a larger size, in order that the rind and kernel may bear the greatest proportion to the pulp, which affords the weakest and most watery juice." And he says that, "to prove this, Dr. Symonds, of Hereford, about the year 1800, made one hogshead of cider entirely from the rinds and cores of apples, and another from the pulp only, when the first was found of extraordinary strength and flavor, while the latter was sweet and insipid."

Evelyn[27] says that the "Red-strake" was the favorite cider-apple in his day; and he quotes one Dr. Newburg as saying, "In Jersey 't is a general observation, as I hear, that the more of red any apple has in its rind, the more proper it is for this use. Pale-faced apples they exclude as much as may be from their cider-vat." This opinion still prevails.

All apples are good in November. Those which the farmer leaves out as unsalable and unpalatable to those who frequent the markets are choicest fruit to the walker. But it is remarkable that the wild apple, which I praise as so spirited and racy when eaten in the fields or woods, being brought into the house has frequently a harsh and crabbed taste. The Saunterer's Apple not even the saunterer can eat in the house. The palate rejects it there, as it does haws and acorns, and demands a tamed one; for there you miss the November air, which is the sauce it is to be eaten with. Accordingly, when Titytrus, seeing the lengthening shadows, invites Melibœus to go home and pass the night with him,[28] he promises him *mild* apples and soft chestnuts,—*mitia poma, castaneæ molles.* I frequently pluck wild apples of so rich and spicy a flavor that I wonder all orchardists do not get a scion from that tree, and I fail not to bring home my pockets full. But perchance, when I take one out of my desk and taste it in my chamber, I find it unexpectedly crude,—sour enough to set a squirrel's teeth on edge and make a jay scream.

These apples have hung in the wind and frost and rain till they have absorbed the

---

[27] John Evelyn (1620–1706), English diarist, was also the author of *Sylva* (1664), dealing with the cultivation of trees and shrubs.
[28] In Virgil's *First Eclogue,* Tityrus, the householder, offers the pleasures of a domesticated repast to the wandering Meliboeus who, like Thoreau, has become accustomed to wildness.

qualities of the weather or season, and thus are highly *seasoned,* and they *pierce* and *sting* and *permeate* us with their spirit. They must be eaten in *season,* accordingly,— that is, out-of-doors.

To appreciate the wild and sharp flavors of these October fruits, it is necessary that you be breathing the sharp October or November air. The outdoor air and exercise which the walker gets give a different tone to his palate, and he craves a fruit which the sedentary would call harsh and crabbed. They must be eaten in the fields, when your system is all aglow with exercise, when the frosty weather nips your fingers, the wind rattles the bare boughs or rustles the few remaining leaves, and the jay is heard screaming around. What is sour in the house a bracing walk makes sweet. Some of these apples might be labeled, "To be eaten in the wind."

Of course no flavors are thrown away; they are intended for the taste that is up to them. Some apples have two distinct flavors, and perhaps one half of them must be eaten in the house, the other outdoors. One Peter Whitney[29] wrote from Northborough in 1782, for the Proceedings of the Boston Academy, describing an apple tree in that town "producing fruit of opposite qualities, part of the same apple being frequently sour and the other sweet;" also some all sour, and others all sweet, and this diversity on all parts of the tree.

There is a wild apple on Nawshawtuct Hill in my town which has to me a peculiarly pleasant bitter tang, not perceived till it is three-quarters tasted. It remains on the tongue. As you eat it, it smells exactly like a squash-bug. It is a sort of triumph to eat and relish it.

I hear that the fruit of a kind of plum tree in Provence is "called *Prunes sibarelles,* because it is impossible to whistle after having eaten them, from their sourness." But perhaps they were only eaten in the house and in summer, and if tried out-of-doors in a stinging atmosphere, who knows but you could whistle an octave higher and clearer?

In the fields only are the sours and bitters of Nature appreciated; just as the woodchopper eats his meal in a sunny glade, in the middle of a winter day, with content, basks in a sunny ray there, and dreams of summer in a degree of cold which, experienced in a chamber, would make a student miserable. They who are at work abroad are not cold, but rather it is they who sit shivering in houses. As with temperatures, so with flavors; as with cold and heat, so with sour and sweet. This natural raciness, the sours and bitters which the diseased palate refuses, are the true condiments.

Let your condiments be in the condition of your senses. To appreciate the flavor of these wild apples requires vigorous and healthy senses, *papillæ*[30] firm and erect on the tongue and palate, not easily flattened and tamed.

From my experience with wild apples, I can understand that there may be reason for a savage's preferring many kinds of food which the civilized man rejects. The former has the palate of an outdoor man. It takes a savage or wild taste to appreciate a wild fruit.

What a healthy out-of-door appetite it takes to relish the apple of life, the apple of the world, then!

---

[29] American author of *The History of the County of*
Worcester . . . Massachusetts. [30] Tiny, protruding cells.

"Nor is it every apple I desire,
    Nor that which pleases every palate best;
'T is not the lasting Deuxan I require,
    Nor yet the red-cheeked Greening I request,
Nor that which first beshrewed the name of wife,
Nor that whose beauty caused the golden strife:
No, no! bring me an apple from the tree of life."[31]

So there is one *thought* for the field, another for the house. I would have my thoughts, like wild apples, to be food for walkers, and will not warrant them to be palatable if tasted in the house.

Their Beauty

Almost all wild apples are handsome. They cannot be too gnarly and crabbed and rusty to look at. The gnarliest will have some redeeming traits even to the eye. You will discover some evening redness dashed or sprinkled on some protuberance or in some cavity. It is rare that the summer lets an apple go without streaking or spotting it on some part of its sphere. It will have some red stains, commemorating the mornings and evenings it has witnessed; some dark and rusty blotches, in memory of the clouds and foggy, mildewy days that have passed over it; and a spacious field of green reflecting the general face of nature,—green even as the fields; or a yellow ground, which implies a milder flavor,—yellow as the harvest, or russet as the hills.

Apples, these I mean, unspeakably fair,—apples not of Discord,[32] but of Concord! Yet not so rare but that the homeliest may have a share. Painted by the frosts, some a uniform clear bright yellow, or red, or crimson, as if their spheres had regularly revolved, and enjoyed the influence of the sun on all sides alike,—some with the faintest pink blush imaginable,—some brindled with deep red streaks like a cow, or with hundreds of fine blood-red rays running regularly from the stem-dimple to the blossom end, like meridional lines, on a straw-colored ground,—some touched with a greenish rust, like a fine lichen, here and there, with crimson blotches or eyes more or less confluent and fiery when wet,—and others gnarly, and freckled or peppered all over on the stem side with fine crimson spots on a white ground, as if accidentally sprinkled from the brush of Him who paints the autumn leaves. Others, again, are sometimes red inside, perfused with a beautiful blush, fairy food, too beautiful to eat, —apple of the Hesperides, apple of the evening sky! But like shells and pebbles on the seashore, they must be seen as they sparkle amid the withering leaves in some dell in the woods, in the autumnal air, or as they lie in the wet grass, and not when they have wilted and faded in the house.

---

[31] From *Emblems*, V, ii, 3, by Francis Quarles (1592–1644).
[32] Allusion to the story, in classic myth, of the time when Paris was asked to give a golden apple to the most beautiful goddess, from among Minerva, Hera, and Venus. The rancor caused when he chose Venus led to the outbreak of the Trojan War.

The Naming of Them

It would be a pleasant pastime to find suitable names for the hundred varieties which go to a single heap at the cider-mill. Would it not tax a man's invention,—no one to be named after a man, and all in the *lingua vernacula?*[33] Who shall stand godfather at the christening of the wild apples? It would exhaust the Latin and Greek languages, if they were used, and make the *lingua vernacula* flag. We should have to call in the sunrise and the sunset, the rainbow and the autumn woods and the wild-flowers, and the woodpecker and the purple finch and the squirrel and the jay and the butterfly, the November traveler and the truant boy, to our aid.

In 1836 there were in the garden of the London Horticultural Society more than fourteen hundred distinct sorts. But here are species which they have not in their catalogue, not to mention the varieties which our crab might yield to cultivation.

Let us enumerate a few of these. I find myself compelled, after all, to give the Latin names of some for the benefit of those who live where English is not spoken,—for they are likely to have a world-wide reputation.

There is, first of all, the Wood Apple *(Malus sylvatica)*; the Blue-Jay Apple; the Apple which grows in Dells in the Woods *(sylvestrivallis)*, also in Hollows in Pastures *(campestrivallis)*; the Apple that grows in an old Cellar-Hole *(Malus cellaris)*; the Meadow Apple; the Partridge Apple; the Truant's Apple *(cessatoris)*, which no boy will ever go by without knocking off some, however *late* it may be; the Saunterer's Apple,—you must lose yourself before you can find the way to that; the Beauty of the Air *(decus aëris)*; December-Eating; the Frozen-Thawed *(gelato-soluta)*, good only in that state; the Concord Apple, possibly the same with the *Musketaquidensis;* the Assabet Apple; the Brindled Apple; Wine of New England; the Chickaree Apple; the Green Apple *(Malus viridis)*,— this has many synonyms: in an imperfect state, it is the *choleramorbifera aut dysenterifera, puerulis dilectissima;* the Apple which Atalanta[34] stopped to pick up; the Hedge Apple *(Malus sepium)*; the Slug Apple *(lima-cea)*; the Railroad Apple, which perhaps came from a core thrown out of the cars; the Apple whose Fruit we tasted in our Youth; our Particular Apple, not to be found in any catalogue; *pedestrium solatium;* also the Apple where hangs the Forgotten Scythe; Iduna's Apples,[35] and the Apples which Loki found in the Wood; and a great many more I have on my list, too numerous to mention,—all of them good. As Bodæus[36] exclaims, referring to the cultivated kinds, and adapting Virgil to his case, so I, adapting Bodæus,—

> "Not if I had a hundred tongues, a hundred mouths,
>   An iron voice, could I describe all the forms
>   And reckon up all the names of these *wild apples.*"

[33] Latin: "common speech; native language."

[34] In classic myth, the fleet-footed Atalanta lost the race she was running when she stooped to pick up the three golden apples cast in her path by Hippomenes, her opponent. By winning the contest Hippomenes claimed her as his bride.

[35] Iduna, daughter-in-law of Odin, cared for the magical apples that restored youth to the gods when old age threatened. The wily Loki, faster brother of Odin, stole Iduna and her apples. Later, under threats of reprisal from the gods, Loki returned Iduna and the apples, and youth was once more possessed by the gods.

[36] Thoreau is probably referring to Johannes Bodaeus (d. 1636), who wrote a history of plants and was a commentator on Greek and Latin writers.

The Last Gleaning

By the middle of November the wild apples have lost some of their brilliancy, and have chiefly fallen. A great part are decayed on the ground, and the sound ones are more palatable than before. The note of the chickadee sounds now more distinct, as you wander amid the old trees, and the autumnal dandelion is half closed and tearful. But still, if you are a skillful gleaner, you may get many a pocketful even of grafted fruit, long after apples are supposed to be gone out-of-doors. I know a Blue Pearmain tree, growing within the edge of a swamp, almost as good as wild. You would not suppose that there was any fruit left there, on the first survey, but you must look according to system. Those which lie exposed are quite brown and rotten now, or perchance a few still show one blooming cheek here and there amid the wet leaves. Nevertheless, with experienced eyes, I explore amid the bare alders and the huckle-berry bushes and the withered sedge, and in the crevices of the rocks, which are full of leaves, and pry under the fallen and decaying ferns, which, with apple and alder leaves, thickly strew the ground. For I know that they lie concealed, fallen into hollows long since and covered up by the leaves of the tree itself,—a proper kind of packing. From these lurking-places, anywhere within the circumference of the tree, I draw forth the fruit, all wet and glossy, maybe nibbled by rabbits and hollowed out by crickets, and perhaps with a leaf or two cemented to it (as Curzon[37] an old manuscript from a monastery's mouldy cellar), but still with a rich bloom on it, and at least as ripe and well-kept, if not better than those in barrels, more crisp and lively than they. If these resources fail to yield anything, I have learned to look between the bases of the suckers which spring thickly from some horizontal limb, for now and then one lodges there, or in the very midst of an alder-clump, where they are covered by leaves, safe from cows which may have smelled them out. If I am sharp-set, for I do not refuse the Blue Pearmain, I fill my pockets on each side; and as I retrace my steps in the frosty eve, being perhaps four or five miles from home, I eat one first from this side, and then from that, to keep my balance.

I learn from Topsell's Gesner, whose authority appears to be Albertus,[38] that the following is the way in which the hedgehog collects and carries home his apples. He says,—"His meat is apples, worms, or grapes: when he findeth apples or grapes on the earth, he rolleth himself upon them, until he have filled all his prickles, and then carrieth them home to his den, never bearing above one in his mouth; and if it fortune that one of them fall off by the way, he likewise shaketh off all the residue, and walloweth upon them afresh, until they be all settled upon his back again. So, forth he goeth, making a noise like a cart-wheel; and if he have any young ones in his nest, they pull off his load wherewithal he is loaded, eating thereof what they please, and laying up the residue for the time to come."

[37] Robert Curzon, fourteenth Baron Zouche of Harringworth (1810–1873), discovered valuable manuscripts while on trips to Egypt, Palestine, and Greece; his account, *Visit to the Monestaries in the Levant*, was published in 1849.

[38] Edward Topsell (d. 1638?) compiled *The History of Four-Footed Beasts*, largely drawn from the works of Conrad Gesner (1516–1565), Swiss naturalist, who in turn relied upon the studies of Albertus Magnus (1193?–1280), Bavarian scholastic philosopher.

The "Frozen-Thawed" Apple

Toward the end of November, though some of the sound ones are yet more mellow and perhaps more edible, they have generally, like the leaves, lost their beauty, and are beginning to freeze. It is finger-cold, and prudent farmers get in their barreled apples, and bring you the apples and cider which they have engaged; for it is time to put them into the cellar. Perhaps a few on the ground show their red cheeks above the early snow, and occasionally some even preserve their color and soundness under the snow throughout the winter. But generally at the beginning of the winter they freeze hard, and soon, though undecayed, acquire the color of a baked apple.

Before the end of December, generally, they experience their first thawing. Those which a month ago were sour, crabbed, and quite unpalatable to the civilized taste, such at least as were frozen while sound, let a warmer sun come to thaw them,— for they are extremely sensitive to its rays,—are found to be filled with a rich, sweet cider, better than any bottled cider that I know of, and with which I am better acquainted than with wine. All apples are good in this state, and your jaws are the cider-press. Others, which have more substance, are a sweet and luscious food,—in my opinion of more worth than the pineapples which are imported from the West Indies. Those which lately even I tasted only to repent of it,—for I am semicivilized, —which the farmer willingly left on the tree, I am now glad to find have the property of hanging on like the leaves of the young oaks. It is a way to keep cider sweet without boiling. Let the frost come to freeze them first, solid as stones, and then the rain or a warm winter day to thaw them, and they will seem to have borrowed a flavor from heaven through the medium of the air in which they hang. Or perchance you find, when you get home, that those which rattled in your pocket have thawed, and the ice is turned to cider. But after the third or fourth freezing and thawing they will not be found so good.

What are the important half-ripe fruits of the torrid south, to this fruit matured by the cold of the frigid north? These are those crabbed apples with which I cheated my companion, and kept a smooth face that I might tempt him to eat. Now we both greedily fill our pockets with them,—bending to drink the cup and save our lappets from the overflowing juice,—and grow more social with their wine. Was there one that hung so high and sheltered by the tangled branches that our sticks could not dislodge it?

It is a fruit never carried to market, that I am aware of,—quite distinct from the apple of the markets, as from dried apple and cider,—and it is not every winter that produces it in perfection.

The era of the Wild Apple will soon be past. It is a fruit which will probably become extinct in New England. You may still wander through old orchards of native fruit of great extent, which for the most part went to the cider-mill, now all gone to decay. I have heard of an orchard in a distant town, on the side of a hill, where the apples rolled down and lay four feet deep against a wall on the lower side, and this the owner cut down for fear they should be made into cider. Since the temperance reform and the general introduction of grafted fruit, no native apple trees, such as I see everywhere in deserted pastures, and where the woods have grown up around them, are set out. I fear that he who walks over these fields a century hence will not know the pleasure of knocking off wild apples. Ah, poor man, there are many pleasures which he will not know! Notwithstanding the prevalence of the Baldwin and the Porter, I doubt if so extensive orchards are set out today in my town as there were a century ago, when those vast straggling cider-orchards were planted, when men both ate and drank apples, when the pomace-heap was the only nursery, and trees cost nothing but the trouble of setting them out. Men could afford then to stick a tree by every wall-side and let it take its chance. I see nobody planting trees to-day in such out of the way places, along the lonely roads and lanes, and at the bottom of dells in the wood. Now that they have grafted trees, and pay a price for them, they collect them into a plat by their houses, and fence them in,—and the end of it all will be that we shall be compelled to look for our apples in a barrel.

This is "The word of the Lord that came to Joel the son of Pethuel.[39]

"Hear this, ye old men, and give ear, all ye inhabitants of the land! Hath this been in your days, or even in the days of your fathers? . . .

"That which the palmerworm hath left hath the locust eaten; and that which the locust hath left hath the cankerworm eaten; and that which the cankerworm hath left hath the caterpillar eaten.

"Awake, ye drunkards, and weep; and howl, all ye drinkers of wine, because of the new wine; for it is cut off from your mouth.

"For a nation is come up upon my land, strong, and without number, whose teeth are the teeth of a lion, and he hath the cheek teeth of a great lion.

"He hath laid my vine waste, and barked my fig tree: he hath made it clean bare, and cast it away; the branches thereof are made white. . . .

"Be ye ashamed, O ye husbandmen; howl, O ye vinedressers. . . .

"The vine is dried up, and the fig tree languisheth; the pomegranate tree, the palm tree also, and the apple tree, even all the trees of the field, are withered: because joy is withered away from the sons of men."

1860/1862

Letter to H. G. O. Blake[*]

[December 7, 1856]

That Walt Whitman, of whom I wrote to you, is the most interesting fact to me at present. I have just read his second edition (which he gave me), and it has done me more good than any reading for a long time. Perhaps I remember best the poem of Walt Whitman, an American, and the Sun-Down Poem.[1] There are two or three pieces in the book which are disagreeable, to say the least, simply sensual. He does not celebrate love at all. It is as if the beasts spoke. I think that men have not been ashamed of themselves without reason. No doubt there have always been dens where such deeds were unblushingly recited, and it is no merit to compete with their

---

[39] Thoreau here cites Joel 1:1–2, 4–7, 11–12, in which the Old Testament prophet called upon the people of Israel to repent.

[*] This letter was written at Eagleswood, New Jersey.

[1] *Song of Myself* and *Crossing Brooklyn Ferry.*

inhabitants. But even on this side he has spoken more truth than any American or modern that I know. I have found his poem exhilarating, encouraging. As for its sensuality,—and it may turn out to be less sensual than it appears,—I do not so much wish that those parts were not written, as that men and women were so pure that they could read them without harm, that is, without understanding them. One woman told me that no woman could read it,—as if a man could read what a woman could not. Of course Walt Whitman can communicate to us no experience, and if we are shocked, whose experience is it that we are reminded of?

On the whole, it sounds to me very brave and American, after whatever deductions. I do not believe that all the sermons, so called, that have been preached in this land put together are equal to it for preaching.

We ought to rejoice greatly in him. He occasionally suggests something a little more than human. You can't confound him with the other inhabitants of Brooklyn or New York. How they must shudder when they read him! He is awfully good.

To be sure I sometimes feel a little imposed on. By his heartiness and broad generalities he puts me into a liberal frame of mind prepared to see wonders,—as it were, sets me upon a hill or in the midst of a plain,—stirs me well up, and then—throws in a thousand of brick. Though rude, and sometimes ineffectual, it is a great primitive poem,—an alarum or trumpet-note ringing through the American camp. Wonderfully like the Orientals, too, considering that when I asked him if he had read them, he answered, "No: tell me about them."

I did not get far in conversation with him,—two more being present,—and among the few things which I chanced to say, I remember that one was, in answer to him as representing America, that I did not think much of America or of politics, and so on, which may have been somewhat of a damper to him.

Since I have seen him, I find that I am not disturbed by any brag or egoism in his book. He may turn out the least of a braggart of all, having a better right to be confident.

He is a great fellow.

1856/1865

---

from The Journal

[December 19, 1837]

I observed this morning that the ice at Swamp Bridge was checkered with a kind of mosaic-work of white creases or channels; and when I examined the under side, I found it to be covered with a mass of crystallizations from three to five inches deep, standing, or rather depending, at right angles to the true ice, which was about an eighth of an inch thick. There was a yet older ice six or eight inches below this. The crystals were for the most part triangular prisms with the lower end open, though, in some cases, they had run into each other so as to form four or five sided prisms. When the ice was laid upon its smooth side, they resembled the roofs and steeples of a Gothic city, or the vessels of a crowded haven under a press of canvas.

I noticed also that where the ice in the road had melted and left the mud bare, the latter, as if crystallized, discovered countless rectilinear fissures, an inch or more in length—a continuation, as it were, of the checkered ice.

[December 23, 1837]

Dec. 23. Crossed the river to-day on the ice. Though the weather is raw and wintry and the ground covered with snow, I noticed a solitary robin, who looked as if he needed to have his services to the Babes in the Woods[1] speedily requited.

In the side of the high bank by the Leaning Hemlocks, there were some curious crystallizations. Wherever the water, or other causes, had formed a hole in the bank, its throat and outer edge, like the entrance to a citadel of the olden time, bristled with a glistening ice armor. In one place you might see minute ostrich feathers, which seemed the waving plumes of the warriors filing into the fortress, in another the glancing fan-shaped banners of the Lilliputian host,[2] and in another the needle-shaped particles, collected into bundles resembling the plumes of the pine, might pass for a phalanx of spears. The whole hill was like an immense quartz rock, with minute crystals sparkling from innumerable crannies. I tried to fancy that there was a disposition in these crystallizations to take the forms of the contiguous foliage.

[April 4, 1839]

April 4. The atmosphere of morning gives a healthy hue to our prospects. Disease is a sluggard that overtakes, never encounters, us. We have the start each day, and may fairly distance him before the dew is off; but if we recline in the bowers of noon, he will come up with us after all. The morning dew breeds no cold. We enjoy a diurnal reprieve in the beginning of each day's creation. In the morning we do not believe in expediency; we will start afresh, and have no patching, no temporary fixtures. The afternoon man has an interest in the past; his eye is divided, and he sees indifferently well either way.

Drifting in a sultry day on the sluggish waters of the pond, I almost cease to live and begin to be. A boatman stretched on the deck of his craft and dallying with the noon would be as apt an emblem of eternity for me as the serpent with his tail in his mouth. I am never so prone to lose my identity. I am dissolved in the haze.

[November 13, 1839]

Nov. 13. Make the most of your regrets; never smother your sorrow, but tend and cherish it till it comes to have a separate and integral interest. To regret deeply is to live afresh. By so doing you will be astonished to find yourself restored once more to all your emoluments.

---

[1] In the nursery tale "The Babes in the Wood" two small children are abandoned to die in a forest. The only creature to witness their plight is a robin.

[2] Diminutive people who inhabited Lilliput, described in Jonathan Swift's *Gulliver's Travels* (1726).

[November 14, 1839]

Nov. 14. There is nowhere any apology for despondency. Always there is life which, rightly lived, implies a divine satisfaction. I am soothed by the rain-drops on the door-sill; every globule that pitches thus confidently from the eaves to the ground is my life insurance. Disease and a rain-drop cannot coexist. The east wind is not itself consumptive, but has enjoyed a rare health from of old. If a fork or brand stand erect, *good* is portended by it. They are the warrant of universal innocence.

[March 21, 1840]

March 21. The world is a fit theatre to-day in which any part may be acted. There is this moment proposed to me every kind of life that men lead anywhere, or that imagination can paint. By another spring I may be a mail-carrier in Peru, or a South African planter, or a Siberian exile, or a Greenland whaler, or a settler on the Columbia River, or a Canton merchant, or a soldier in Florida, or a mackerel-fisher off Cape Sable, or a Robinson Crusoe[3] in the Pacific, or a silent navigator of any sea. So wide is the choice of parts, what a pity if the part of Hamlet be left out!

I am freer than any planet; no complaint reaches round the world. I can move away from public opinion, from government, from religion, from education, from society. Shall I be reckoned a ratable poll[4] in the county of Middlesex, or be rated at one spear under the palm trees of Guinea? Shall I raise corn and potatoes in Massachusetts, or figs and olives in Asia Minor? sit out the day in my office in State Street, or ride it out on the steppes of Tartary? For my Brobdingnag[5] I may sail to Patagonia; for my Lilliput, to Lapland. In Arabia and Persia, my day's adventures may surpass the Arabian Nights' Entertainments. I may be a logger on the head waters of the Penobscot, to be recorded in fable hereafter as an amphibious river-god, by as sounding a name as Triton or Proteus;[6] carry furs from Nootka to China, and so be more renowned than Jason[7] and his golden fleece; or go on a South Sea exploring expedition, to be hereafter recounted along with the periplus of Hanno.[8] I may repeat the adventures of Marco Polo or Mandeville.[9]

These are but few of my chances, and how many more things may I do with which there are none to be compared!

Thank Fortune, we are not rooted to the soil, and here is not all the world. The buckeye does not grow in New England; the mockingbird is rarely heard here. Why not keep pace with the day, and not allow of a sunset nor fall behind the summer and the migration of birds? Shall we not compete with the buffalo, who keeps pace with the seasons, cropping the pastures of the Colorado till a greener and sweeter grass

---

[3] Shipwrecked hero of Daniel Defoe's novel (1719). (Cape Sable is in Nova Scotia.)

[4] Taxable voter.

[5] Land of giants in *Gulliver's Travels*. (Patagonia is in southern Chile and Argentina.)

[6] I.e., a name as fine sounding as those of river-gods in Greek myths. (The Penobscot River runs through Maine.)

[7] Greek hero of classic myth who sailed forth to

find the fabled golden fleece. (Nootka Sound is a Pacific inlet in British Columbia.)

[8] The written record of the voyages of Hanno, Carthaginian navigator of ca. 500 B.C.

[9] Marco Polo: Venetian adventurer (1254?–1324?) who traveled extensively in China; Sir John Mandeville, fictitious writer of a fourteenth-century account of journeys in exotic lands.

awaits him by the Yellowstone? The wild goose is more a cosmopolite than we; he breaks his fast in Canada, takes a luncheon in the Susquehanna, and plumes himself for the night in a Louisiana bayou. The pigeon carries an acorn in his crop from the King of Holland's to Mason and Dixon's line.[10] Yet we think if rail fences are pulled down and stone walls set up on our farms, bounds are henceforth set to our lives and our fates decided. If you are chosen town clerk, forsooth, you can't go to Tierra del Fuego this summer.

But what of all this? A man may gather his limbs snugly within the shell of a mammoth squash, with his back to the northeastern boundary, and not be unusually straitened after all. Our limbs, indeed, have room enough, but it is our souls that rush in a corner. Let us migrate interiorly without intermission, and pitch our tent each day nearer the western horizon. The really fertile soils and luxuriant prairies lie on this side the Alleghanies. There has been no Hanno of the affections. Their domain is untravelled ground, to the Mogul's dominions.[11]

[February 8, 1841]

Feb. 8. All we have experienced is so much gone within us, and there lies. It is the company we keep. One day, in health or sickness, it will come out and be remembered. Neither body nor soul forgets anything. The twig always remembers the wind that shook it, and the stone the cuff it received. Ask the old tree and the sand.

To be of most service to my brother I must meet him on the most equal and even ground, the platform on which our lives are passing. But how often does politeness permit this?

I seek a man who will appeal to me when I am in fault. We will treat as gods settling the affairs of men. In his intercourse I shall be always a god to-day, who was a man yesterday. He will never confound me with my guilt, but let me be immaculate and hold up my skirts. Differences he will make haste to clear up, but leave agreements unsettled the while.

As time is measured by the lapse of ideas, we may grow of our own force, as the mussel adds new circles to its shell. My thoughts secrete the lime. We may grow old with the vigor of youth. Are we not always in youth so long as we face heaven? We may always live in the morning of our days. To him who seeks early, the sun never gets over the edge of the hill, but his rays fall slanting forever. His wise sayings are like the chopping of wood and crowing of cocks in the dawn.

My Journal is that of me which would else spill over and run to waste, gleanings from the field which in action I reap. I must not live for it, but in it for the gods. They are my correspondent, to whom daily I send off this sheet postpaid. I am clerk in their

---

[10] Boundary between Maryland and Pennsylvania, based on a survey made between 1763 and 1767 by Charles Mason and Jeremiah Dixon; it serves to distinguish the North from the South.

[11] That is, as far as India, ruled by the Mogul conquerors.

counting-room, and at evening transfer the account from day-book to ledger. It is as a leaf which hangs over my head in the path. I bend the twig and write my prayers on it; then letting it go, the bough springs up and shows the scrawl to heaven. As if it were not kept shut in my desk, but were as public a leaf as any in nature. It is papyrus by the riverside; it is vellum in the pastures; it is parchment on the hills. I find it everywhere as free as the leaves which troop along the lanes in autumn. The crow, the goose, the eagle carry my quill, and the wind blows the leaves as far as I go. Or, if my imagination does not soar, but gropes in slime and mud, then I write with a reed.

It is always a chance scrawl, and commemorates some accident,—as great as earthquake or eclipse. Like the sere leaves in yonder vase, these have been gathered far and wide. Upland and lowland, forest and field have been ransacked.

In our holiest moment our devil with a leer stands close at hand. He is a very busy devil. It gains vice some respect, I must confess, thus to be reminded how indefatigable it is. It has at least the merit of industriousness. When I go forth with zeal to some good work, my devil is sure to get his robe tucked up the first and arrives there as soon as I, with a look of sincere earnestness which puts to shame my best intent. He is as forward as I to a good work, and as disinterested. He has a winning way of recommending himself by making himself useful. How readily he comes into my best project, and does his work with a quiet and steady cheerfulness which even virtue may take pattern from.

I never was so rapid in my virtue but my vice kept up with me. It always came in by a hand, and never panting, but with a curried coolness halted, as if halting were the beginning not the end of the course. It only runs the swifter because it has no rider. It never was behind me but when I turned to look and so fell behind myself. I never did a charitable thing but there he stood, scarce in the rear, with hat in hand, partner on the same errand, ready to share the smile of gratitude. Though I shut the door never so quick and tell it to stay at home like a good dog, it will out with me, for I shut in my own legs so, and it escapes in the meanwhile and is ready to back and reinforce me in most virtuous deeds. And if I turn and say, "Get thee behind me," he then indeed turns too and takes the lead, though he seems to retire with a pensive and compassionate look, as much as to say, "Ye know not what ye do."

Just as active as I become to virtue, just so active is my remaining vice. Every time we teach our virtue a new nobleness, we teach our vice a new cunning. When we sharpen the blade it will stab better as well as whittle. The scythe that cuts will cut our legs. We are double-edged blades, and every time we whet our virtue the return stroke straps our vice. And when we cut a clear descending blow, our vice on tother edge rips up the work. Where is the skillful swordsman that can draw his blade straight back out of the wound?

[April 26, 1841]

April 26. Monday. At R. W. E.'s.[12]

The charm of the Indian to me is that he stands free and unconstrained in Nature, is her inhabitant and not her guest, and wears her easily and gracefully. But the

---

[12] R. W. E.: Ralph Waldo Emerson.

civilized man has the habits of the house. His house is a prison, in which he finds himself oppressed and confined, not sheltered and protected. He walks as if he sustained the roof; he carries his arms as if the walls would fall in and crush him, and his feet remember the cellar beneath. His muscles are never relaxed. It is rare that he overcomes the house, and learns to sit at home in it, and roof and floor and walls support themselves, as the sky and trees and earth.

It is a great art to saunter.

[May 27, 1841]

May 27. Thursday. I sit in my boat on Walden, playing the flute this evening, and see the perch, which I seem to have charmed, hovering around me, and the moon travelling over the bottom, which is strewn with the wrecks of the forest, and feel that nothing but the wildest imagination can conceive of the manner of life we are living. Nature is a wizard. The Concord nights are stranger than the Arabian nights.

We not only want elbow-room, but eye-room in this gray air which shrouds all the fields. Sometimes my eyes see over the county road by daylight to the tops of yonder birches on the hill, as at others by moonlight.

Heaven lies above, because the air is deep.

In all my life hitherto I have left nothing behind.

[August 1, 1841]

Aug. 1. Sunday. I never met a man who cast a free and healthy glance over life, but the best live in a sort of Sabbath light, a Jewish gloom. The best thought is not only without sombreness, but even without morality. The universe lies outspread in floods of white light to it. The moral aspect of nature is a jaundice reflected from man. To the innocent there are no cherubim nor angels. Occasionally we rise above the necessity of virtue into an unchangeable morning light, in which we have not to choose in a dilemma between right and wrong, but simply to live right on and breathe the circumambient air. There is no name for this life unless it be the very vitality of *vita.*[13] Silent is the preacher about this, and silent must ever be, for he who knows it will not preach.

[February 21, 1842]

Feb. 21. I must confess there is nothing so strange to me as my own body. I love any other piece of nature, almost, better.

I was always conscious of sounds in nature which my ears could never hear,—that I caught but the prelude to a strain. She always retreats as I advance. Away behind and behind is she and her meaning. Will not this faith and expectation make to itself ears at length? I never saw to the end, nor heard to the end; but the best part was unseen and unheard.

I am like a feather floating in the atmosphere; on every side is depth unfathomable. I feel as if years had been crowded into the last month, and yet the regularity of

---

[13] Latin: "life."

what we call time has been so far preserved as that I . . . will be welcome in the present. I have lived ill for the most part because too near myself. I have tripped myself up, so that there was no progress for my own narrowness. I cannot walk conveniently and pleasantly but when I hold myself far off in the horizon. And the soul dilutes the body and makes it passable. My soul and body have tottered along together of late, tripping and hindering one another like unpracticed Siamese twins. They two should walk as one, that no obstacle may be nearer than the firmament.

There must be some narrowness in the soul that compels one to have secrets.

[1845]

Thus, to try our civilization by a fair test, in the ruder states of society every family owns a shelter as good as the best, and sufficient for its ruder and simpler wants; but in modern civilized society, though the birds of the air have their nests, and wood-chucks and foxes their holes, though each one is commonly the owner of his coat and hat though never so poor, yet not more than one man in a thousand owns a shelter, but the nine hundred and ninety-nine pay an annual tax for this outside garment of all, indispensable summer and winter, which would buy a village of Indian wigwams and contributes to keep them poor as long as they live. But, answers one, by simply paying this annual tax the poorest man secures an abode which is a palace compared to the Indian's. An annual rent of from twenty to sixty or seventy dollars entitles him to the benefit of all the improvements of centuries,—Rumford fireplace, back plaster-ing, Venetian blinds, copper pump, spring lock, etc., etc. But while civilization has been improving our houses, she has not equally improved the men who should occupy them. She has created palaces, but it was not so easy to create noblemen and kings. The mason who finishes the cornice of the palace returns at night, perchance, to a hut no better than a wigwam. If she claims to have made a real advance in the welfare of man, she must show how she has produced better dwellings without making them more costly. And the cost of a thing, it will be remembered, is the amount of life it requires to be exchanged for it, immediately or in the long run. An average house costs perhaps from one thousand to fifteen hundred dollars, and to earn this sum will require from fifteen to twenty years of the day laborer's life, even if he is not incumbered with a family; so that he must spend more than half his life before a wigwam can be earned; and if we suppose he pays a rent instead, this is but a doubtful choice of evils. Would the savage have been wise to exchange his wigwam for a palace on these terms?

When I consider my neighbors, the farmers of Concord, for instance, who are at least as well off as the other classes, what are they about? For the most part I find that they have been toiling ten, twenty, or thirty years to pay for their farms, and we may set down one half of that toil to the cost of their houses; and commonly they have not yet paid for them. This is the reason they are poor; and for similar reasons we are all poor in respect to a thousand savage comforts, though surrounded by luxuries.

[July 5, 1845]

July 5. Saturday. Walden.—Yesterday I came here to live. My house makes me think of some mountain houses I have seen, which seemed to have a fresher auroral atmosphere about them, as I fancy of the halls of Olympus. I lodged at the house of a saw-miller last summer, on the Caatskill Mountains, high up as Pine Orchard, in the blueberry and raspberry region, where the quiet and cleanliness and coolness seemed to be all one,—which had their ambrosial character. He was the miller of the Kaaterskill Falls. They were a clean and wholesome family, inside and out, like their house. The latter was not plastered, only lathed, and the inner doors were not hung. The house seemed high-placed, airy, and perfumed, fit to entertain a travelling god. It was so high, indeed, that all the music, the broken strains, the waifs and accompaniments of tunes, that swept over the ridge of the Caatskills, passed through its aisles. Could not man be man in such an abode? And would he ever find out this grovelling life? It was the very light and atmosphere in which the works of Grecian art were composed, and in which they rest. They have appropriated to themselves a loftier hall than mortals ever occupy, at least on a level with the mountain-brows of the world. There was wanting a little of the glare of the lower vales, and in its place a pure twilight as became the precincts of heaven. Yet so equable and calm was the season there that you could not tell whether it was morning or noon or evening. Always there was the sound of the morning cricket.

[July 6, 1845]

July 6. I wish to meet the facts of life—the vital facts, which are the phenomena or actuality the gods meant to show us—face to face, and so I came down here. Life! who knows what it is, what it does? If I am not quite right here, I am less wrong than before; and now let us see what they will have. The preacher, instead of vexing the ears of drowsy farmers on their day of rest, at the end of the week,—for Sunday always seemed to me like a fit conclusion of an ill-spent week and not the fresh and brave beginning of a new one,—with this one other draggletail and postponed affair of a sermon, from thirdly to fifteenthly, should teach them with a thundering voice pause and simplicity. "Stop! Avast! Why so fast?" In all studies we go not forward but rather backward with redoubled pauses. We always study *antiques* with silence and reflection. Even time has a depth, and below its surface the waves do not lapse and roar. I wonder men can be so frivolous almost as to attend to the gross form of negro slavery, there are so many keen and subtle masters who subject us both. Self-emancipation in the West Indies of a man's thinking and imagining provinces, which should be more than his island territory,—one emancipated heart and intellect!

[1850]

I have been surprised to discover the amount and the various kinds of life which a single shallow swamp will sustain. On the south side of the pond, not more than a quarter of a mile from it, is a small meadow of ten or a dozen acres in the woods, considerably lower than Walden, and which by some is thought to be fed by the former by a subterranean outlet,—which is very likely, for its shores are quite springy and its supply of water is abundant and unfailing,—indeed tradition says that a sawmill once stood over its outlet, though its whole extent, including its sources, is not more than I have mentioned,—a meadow through which the Fitchburg Railroad passes by a very high causeway, which required many a carload of sand, where the laborers for a long time seemed to make no progress, for the sand settled so much in the night that by morning they were where they were the day before, and finally the weight of the sand forced upward the adjacent crust of the meadow with the trees on it many feet, and cracked it for some rods around. It is a wet and springy place throughout the summer, with a ditch-like channel, and in one part water stands the year round, with cat-o'-nine-tails[14] and tussocks and muskrats' cabins rising above it, where good cranberries may be raked if you are careful to anticipate the frost which visits this cool hollow unexpectedly early. Well, as I was saying, I heard a splashing in the shallow and muddy water and stood awhile to observe the cause of it. Again and again I heard and saw the commotion, but could not guess the cause of it,—what kind of life had its residence in that insignificant pool. We sat down on the hillside. Ere long a muskrat came swimming by as if attracted by the same disturbance, and then another and another, till three had passed, and I began to suspect that they were at the bottom of it. Still ever and anon I observed the same commotion in the waters over the same spot, and at length I observed the snout of some creature slyly raised above the surface after each commotion, as if to see if it were observed by foes, and then but a few rods distant I saw another snout above the water and began to divine the cause of the disturbance. Putting off my shoes and stockings, I crept stealthily down the hill and waded out slowly and noiselessly about a rod from the firm land, keeping behind the tussocks, till I stood behind the tussock near which I had observed the splashing. Then, suddenly stooping over it, I saw through the shallow but muddy water that there was a mud turtle there, and thrusting in my hand at once caught him by the claw, and, quicker than I can tell it, heaved him high and dry ashore; and there came out with him a large pout[15] just dead and partly devoured, which he held in his jaws. It was the pout in his flurry and the turtle in his struggles to hold him fast which had created the commotion. There he had lain, probably buried in the mud at the bottom up to his eyes, till the pout came sailing over, and then this musky lagune[16] had put forth in the direction of his ventral fins, expanding suddenly under the influence of a more than vernal heat,—there are sermons in stones, aye and mud turtles at the bottoms of the pools,—in the direction of his ventral fins, his tender white belly, where he kept no eye; and the minister squeaked his last. Oh, what an eye was there, my countrymen! buried in mud up to the lids, meditating on what? sleepless at the bottom of the pool, at the top of the bottom, directed heavenward, in no danger from motes. Pouts expect their foes not from below. Suddenly a mud volcano swallowed him up, seized his midriff; he fell into those relentless jaws from which there is no escape, which relax not their hold even in death. There the pout might calculate on remaining until nine days after the head was cut off. Sculled through Heywood's shallow meadow, not thinking of foes, looking through the water

---

[14] Cattails.
[15] Type of fish.
[16] A lake creature.

up into the sky. I saw his [the turtle's] brother sunning and airing his broad back like a ship bottom up which had been scuttled,—foundered at sea. I had no idea that there was so much going on in Heywood's meadow. . . .

It is not easy to make our lives respectable to ourselves by any course of activity. We have repeatedly to withdraw ourselves into our shells of thought like the tortoise, somewhat helplessly; and yet there is even more than philosophy in that. I do not love to entertain doubts and questions.

I am sure that my acquaintances mistake me. I am not the man they take me for. On a little nearer view they would find me out. They ask my advice on high matters, but they do not even know how poorly on't I am for hats and shoes. I have hardly a shift. Just as shabby as I am in my outward apparel,—aye, and more lamentably shabby, for nakedness is not so bad a condition after all,—am I in my inward apparel. If I should turn myself inside out, my rags and meanness would appear. I am something to him that made me, undoubtedly, but not much to any other that he has made. All I can say is that I live and breathe and have my thoughts.

What is peculiar in the life of a man consists not in his obedience, but his opposition, to his instincts. In one direction or another he strives to live a supernatural life.

Would it not be worth the while to discover Nature in Milton?[17] Be native to the universe. I, too, love Concord best, but I am glad when I discover, in oceans and wildernesses far away, the materials out of which a million Concords can be made, —indeed, unless I discover them, I am lost myself,—that there too I am at home. Nature is as far from me as God, and sometimes I have thought to go West after her. Though the city is no more attractive to me than ever, yet I see less difference between a city and some dismallest swamp than formerly. It is a swamp too dismal and dreary, however, for me. I would as lief find a few owls and frogs and mosquitoes less. I prefer even a more cultivated place, free from miasma and crocodiles, and I will take my choice.

From time to time I overlook the promised land, but I do not feel that I am travelling toward it. The moment I begin to look there, men and institutions get out of the way that I may see. I see nothing permanent in the society around me, and am not quite committed to any of its ways.

Getting into Patchogue late one night in an oyster-boat, there was a drunken Dutchman aboard whose wit reminded me of Shakespeare. When we came to leave the beach, our boat was aground, and we were detained three hours waiting for the tide. In the meanwhile two of the fishermen took an extra dram at the beach house. Then they stretched themselves on the seaweed by the shore in the sun to sleep off the effects of their debauch. One was an inconceivably broad-faced young Dutchman,—but oh! of such a peculiar breadth and heavy look, I should not know whether to call it more ridiculous or sublime. You would say that he had humbled himself so much that he was beginning to be exalted. An indescribable mynheerish[18] stupidity. I was less

---

[17] The English poet (1608–1674) or the town near Boston.
[18] Supposedly characteristic of natives of the Netherlands, where males are addressed as "Mynheer."

disgusted by their filthiness and vulgarity, because I was compelled to look on them as animals, as swine in their sty. For the whole voyage they lay flat on their backs on the bottom of the boat in the bilge-water and wet with each bailing, half insensible and wallowing in their vomit. But ever and anon, when aroused by the rude kicks or curses of the skipper, the Dutchman, who never lost his wit nor equanimity, though snoring and rolling in the vomit produced by his debauch, blurted forth some happy repartee like an illuminated swine. It was the earthiest, slimiest wit I ever heard. The countenance was one of a million. It was unmistakable Dutch. In the midst of a million faces of other races it could not be mistaken. It told of Amsterdam. I kept racking my brains to conceive how he could have been born in America, how lonely he must feel, what he did for fellowship. When we were groping up the narrow creek of Patchogue at ten o'clock at night, keeping our boat off, now from this bank, now from that, with a pole, the two inebriates roused themselves betimes. For in spite of their low estate they seemed to have all their wits as much about them as ever, aye, and all the self-respect they ever had. And the Dutchman gave wise directions to the steerer, which were not heeded. Suddenly rousing himself up where the sharpest-eyed might be bewildered in the darkness, he leaned over the side of the boat and pointed straight down into the creek, averring that that identical hole was a first-rate place for eels. And again he roused himself at the right time and declared what luck he had once had with his pots (not his cups) in another place, which we were floating over in the dark. At last he suddenly stepped on to another boat which was moored to the shore, with a divine ease and sureness, saying, "Well, good-night, take care of yourselves, I can't be with you any longer." He was one of the few remarkable men whom I have met. I have been impressed by one or two men in their cups. There was really a divinity stirred within them, so that in their case I have reverenced the drunken, as savages the insane, man. So stupid that he could never be intoxicated. When I said, "You have had a hard time of it to-day," he answered with indescribable good humor out of the very midst of his debauch, with watery eyes, "Well, it does n't happen every day." It was happening then. He had taken me aboard on his back, the boat lying a rod from the shore, before I knew his condition. In the darkness our skipper steered with a pole on the bottom, for an oysterman knows the bottom of his bay as well as the shores, and can tell where he is by the soundings. . . .

[January 10, 1851]

I have met with but one or two persons in the course of my life who understood the art of taking walks daily,—not [to] exercise the legs or body merely, nor barely to recruit the spirits, but positively to exercise both body and spirit, and to succeed to the highest and worthiest ends by the abandonment of all specific ends,—who had a genius, so to speak, for sauntering. And this word "saunter," by the way, is happily derived "from idle people who roved about the country [in the Middle Ages] and asked charity under pretence of going *à la Sainte Terre*," to the Holy Land, till, perchance, the children exclaimed, "There goes a *Sainte-Terrer*," a Holy-Lander. They who never go to the Holy Land in their walks, as they pretend, are indeed mere idlers and vagabonds.

[Perhaps I am more] than usually jealous of my freedom. I feel that my connections with and obligations to society are at present very slight and transient. Those slight labors which afford me a livelihood, and by which I am serviceable to my contemporaries, are as yet a pleasure to me, and I am not often reminded that they are a necessity. So far I am successful, and only he is successful in his business who makes that pursuit which affords him the highest pleasure sustain him. But I foresee that if my wants should be much increased the labor required to supply them would become a drudgery. If I should sell both my forenoons and afternoons to society, neglecting my peculiar calling, there would be nothing left worth living for. I trust that I shall never thus sell my birthright for a mess of pottage.[19]

[February 15, 1851]

Feb. 15. Fatal is the discovery that our friend is fallible, that he has prejudices. He is, then, only prejudiced in our favor. What is the value of his esteem who does not justly esteem another?

Alas! Alas! when my friend begins to deal in confessions, breaks silence, makes a theme of friendship (which then is always something past), and descends to merely human relations! As long as there is a spark of love remaining, cherish that alone. Only *that* can be kindled into a flame. I thought that friendship, that love was still possible between [us]. I thought that we had not withdrawn very far asunder. But now that my friend rashly, thoughtlessly, profanely speaks, *recognizing* the distance between us, that distance seems infinitely increased.

Of our friends we do not incline to speak, to complain, to others; we would not disturb the foundations of confidence that may still be.

Why should we not still continue to live with the intensity and rapidity of infants? Is not the world, are not the heavens, as unfathomed as ever? Have we exhausted any joy, any sentiment?

[April 1851]

There is such an officer, if not such a man, as the Governor of Massachusetts. What has he been about the last fortnight? He has probably had as much as he could do to keep on the fence during this moral earthquake. It seems to me that no such keen satire, no such cutting insult, could be offered to that man, as the absence of all inquiry after him in this crisis. It appears to [have] been forgotten that there was such a man or such an office. Yet no doubt he has been filling the gubernatorial chair all the while. One Mr. Boutwell,—so named, perchance, because he goes about well to suit the prevailing wind.

In '75 two or three hundred of the inhabitants of Concord assembled at one of the bridges with arms in their hands to assert the right of three millions to tax themselves, to have a voice in governing themselves.[20] About a week ago the authorities of Boston,

---

[19] What Esau gave away to his brother Jacob as the result of Jacob's conniving, Genesis 25:27–34.

[20] In 1775 a band of farmers from the Concord area met at the bridge over the Concord River to fight British troops in one of the first engagements of the Revolution, a war fought in the name of the right of the American colonists to determine matters of taxation. Thoreau sets this event in contrast to the events of the previous week, when an escaped slave was returned to his Southern master with the compliance of descendants of those Revolutionary champions of freedom.

having the sympathy of many of the inhabitants of Concord, assembled in the gray of the dawn, assisted by a still larger armed force, to send back a perfectly innocent man, and one whom they knew to be innocent, into a slavery as complete as the world ever knew. Of course it makes not the least difference—I wish you to consider this —who the man was,—whether he was Jesus Christ or another,—for inasmuch as ye did it unto the least of these his brethren ye did it unto him. Do you think *he* would have stayed here in liberty and let the black man go into slavery in his stead? They sent him back, I say, to live in slavery with other three millions—mark that—whom the same slave power, or slavish power, North and South, holds in that condition, —three millions who do not, like the first mentioned, assert the right to govern themselves but simply to run away and stay away from their prison.

Just a week afterward, those inhabitants of this town who especially sympathize with the authorities of Boston in this their deed caused the bells to be rung and the cannon to be fired to celebrate the courage and the love of liberty of those men who assembled at the bridge. As if *those* three millions had fought for the right to be free themselves, but to hold in slavery three million others. Why, gentlemen, even consistency, though it is much abused, is sometimes a virtue. Every humane and intelligent inhabitant of Concord, when he or she heard those bells and those cannon, thought not so much of the events of the 19th of April, 1775, as of the event of the 12th of April, 1851.

I wish my townsmen to consider that, whatever the human law may be, neither an individual nor a nation can ever deliberately commit the least act of injustice without having to pay the penalty for it. A government which deliberately enacts injustice, and persists in it!—it will become the laughing-stock of the world.

Much as has been said about American slavery, I think that commonly we do not yet realize what slavery is. If I were seriously to propose to Congress to make mankind into sausages, I have no doubt that most would smile at my proposition and, if any believed me to be in earnest, they would think that I proposed something much worse than Congress had ever done. But, gentlemen, if any of you will tell me that to make a man into a sausage would be much worse—would be any worse—than to make him into a slave,—than it was then to enact the fugitive slave law,—I shall here accuse him of foolishness, of intellectual incapacity, of making a distinction without a difference. The one is just as sensible a proposition as the other.

When I read the account of the carrying back of the fugitive into slavery, which was read last Sunday evening, and read also what was not read here, that the man who made the prayer on the wharf was Daniel Foster of *Concord,* I could not help feeling a slight degree of pride because, of all the towns in the Commonwealth, Concord was the only one distinctly named as being represented in that new tea-party, and, as she had a place in the first, so would have a place in this, the last and perhaps next most important chapter of the History of Massachusetts. But my second feeling, when I reflected how short a time that gentleman has resided in this town, was one of doubt and shame, because the *men* of Concord in recent times have done nothing to entitle them to the honor of having their town named in such a connection.

I hear a good deal said about trampling this law under foot. Why, one need not go out of his way to do that. This law lies not at the level of the head or the reason. Its natural habitat is in the dirt. It was bred and has its life only in the dust and mire, on a level with the feet; and he who walks with freedom, unless, with a sort of quibbling and Hindoo mercy, he avoids treading on every venomous reptile, will inevitably tread on it, and so trample it under foot.

[May 24, 1851]

May 24. Saturday. Our most glorious experiences are a kind of regret. Our regret is so sublime that we may mistake it for triumph. It is the painful, plaintively sad surprise of our Genius remembering our past lives and contemplating what is possible. It is remarkable that men commonly never refer to, never hint at, any crowning experiences when the common laws of their being were unsettled and the divine and eternal laws prevailed in them. Their lives are not revolutionary; they never recognize any other than the local and temporal authorities. It is a regret so divine and inspiring, so genuine, based on so true and distinct a contrast, that it surpasses our proudest boasts and the fairest expectations.

My most sacred and memorable life is commonly on awaking in the morning. I frequently awake with an atmosphere about me as if my unremembered dreams had been divine, as if my spirit had journeyed to its native place, and, in the act of reëntering its native body, had diffused an elysian fragrance around.

The Genius says: "Ah! That is what you were! That is what you may yet be!" It is glorious for us to be able to regret even such an existence.

A sane and growing man revolutionizes every day. What institutions of man can survive a morning experience? A single night's sleep, if we have indeed slumbered and forgotten anything and grown in our sleep, puts them behind us like the river Lethe: It is no unusual thing for him to see the kingdoms of this world pass away.

[June 14, 1851]

You feel yourself—your body, your legs,—more at night, for there is less beside to be distinctly known, and hence perhaps you think yourself more tired than you are. I see indistinctly oxen asleep in the fields, silent in majestic slumber, like the sphinx, —statuesque, Egyptian, reclining. What solid rest! How their heads are supported! A sparrow or a cricket makes more noise. From Conant's summit I hear as many as fifteen whip-poor-wills—or whip-or-I-wills—at once, the succeeding cluck sounding strangely foreign, like a hewer at work elsewhere.

The moon is accumulating yellow light and triumphing over the clouds, but still the west is suffused here and there with a slight red tinge, marking the path of the day. Though inexperienced ones might call it night, it is not yet. Dark, heavy clouds lie along the western horizon, exhibiting the forms of animals and men, while the moon is behind a cloud. Why do we detect these forms so readily?—whales or giants reclining, busts of heroes, Michael-Angelic.[21] There is the gallery of statuary, the picture gallery of man,—not a board upon an Italian's head, but these dark figures along the horizon,—the board some Titan carries on his head. What firm and heavy outlines for such soft and light material!

---

[21] After the manner of Michelangelo, known for the gigantic scale of his works.

[July 6, 1851]

There is some advantage in being the humblest, cheapest, least dignified man in the village, so that the very stable boys shall damn you. Methinks I enjoy that advantage to an unusual extent. There is many a coarsely well-meaning fellow, who knows only the skin of me, who addresses me familiarly by my Christian name. I get the whole good of him and lose nothing myself. There is "Sam," the jailer,—whom I never call Sam, however,—who exclaimed last evening: "Thoreau, are you going up the street pretty soon? Well, just take a couple of these handbills along and drop one in at Hoar's piazza[22] and one at Holbrook's, and I'll do as much for you another time." I am not above being used, aye abused, sometimes.

[July 19, 1851]

July 19. Here I am thirty-four years old, and yet my life is almost wholly unexpanded. How much is in the germ! There is such an interval between my ideal and the actual in many instances that I may say I am unborn. There is the instinct for society, but no society. Life is not long enough for one success. Within another thirty-four years that miracle can hardly take place. Methinks my seasons revolve more slowly than those of nature; I am differently timed. I am contented. This rapid revolution of nature, even of nature in me, why should it hurry me? Let a man step to the music which he hears, however measured. Is it important that I should mature as soon as an apple tree? aye, as soon as an oak? May not my life in nature, in proportion as it is supernatural, be only the spring and infantile portion of my spirit's life? Shall I turn my spring to summer? May I not sacrifice a hasty and petty completeness here to entireness there? If my curve is large, why bend it to a smaller circle? My spirit's unfolding observes not the pace of nature. The society which I was made for is not here. Shall I, then, substitute for the anticipation of that this poor reality? I would [rather] have the unmixed expectation of that than this reality. If life is a waiting, so be it. I will not be shipwrecked on a vain reality. What were any reality which I can substitute? Shall I with pains erect a heaven of blue glass over myself, though when it is done I shall be sure to gaze still on the true ethereal heaven far above, as if the former were not,—that still distant sky o'er-arching that blue expressive eye of heaven? I am enamored of the blue-eyed arch of heaven.

I did not *make* this demand for a more thorough sympathy. This is not my idiosyncrasy or disease. He that made the demand will answer the demand.

My blood flows as slowly as the waves of my native Musketaquid; yet they reach the ocean sooner, perchance, than those of the Nashua.

Already the goldenrod is budded, but I can make no haste for that.

[September 3, 1851]

As I went under the new telegraph-wire, I heard it vibrating like a harp high overhead. It was as the sound of a far-off glorious life, a supernal life, which came down to us, and vibrated the lattice-work of this life of ours.

---

[22] Large covered veranda.

[October 1, 1851]

Oct. 1. 5 P.M.—Just put a fugitive slave, who has taken the name of Henry Williams, into the cars[23] for Canada. He escaped from Stafford County, Virginia, to Boston last October; has been in Shadrach's place at the Cornhill Coffee-House; had been corresponding through an agent with his master, who is his father, about buying himself, his master asking $600, but he having been able to raise only $500. Heard that there were writs out for two Williamses, fugitives, and was informed by his fellow-servants and employer that Augerhole Burns and others of the police had called for him when he was out. Accordingly fled to Concord last night on foot, bringing a letter to our family from Mr. Lovejoy of Cambridge and another which Garrison[24] had formerly given him on another occasion. He lodged with us, and waited in the house till funds were collected with which to forward him. Intended to dispatch him at noon through to Burlington, but when I went to buy his ticket, saw one at the depot who looked and behaved so much like a Boston policeman that I did not venture that time. An intelligent and very well-behaved man, a mulatto.

[November 9, 1851]

I, too, would fain set down something beside facts. Facts should only be as the frame to my pictures; they should be material to the mythology which I am writing; not facts to assist men to make money, farmers to farm profitably, in any common sense; facts to tell who I am, and where I have been or what I have thought: as now the bell rings for evening meeting, and its volumes of sound, like smoke which rises from where a cannon is fired, make the tent in which I dwell. My facts shall be falsehoods to the common sense. I would so state facts that they shall be significant, shall be myths or mythologic. Facts which the mind perceived, thoughts which the body thought, —with these I deal. I, too, cherish vague and misty forms, vaguest when the cloud at which I gaze is dissipated quite and naught but the skyey depths are seen.

[November 12, 1851]

Nov. 12. Write often, write upon a thousand themes, rather than long at a time, not trying to turn too many feeble somersets in the air,—and so come down upon your head at last. Antæus-like,[25] be not long absent from the ground. Those sentences are good and well discharged which are like so many little resiliencies from the spring floor of our life,—a distinct fruit and kernel itself, springing from terra firma. Let there be as many distinct plants as the soil and the light can sustain. Take as many bounds in a day as possible. Sentences uttered with your back to the wall. Those are the admirable bounds when the performer has lately touched the springboard. A good bound into the air from the air [*sic*] is a good and wholesome experience, but what shall we say to a man's leaping off precipices in the attempt to fly? He comes down like lead. In the meanwhile, you have got your feet planted upon the rock, with the

---

[23] Railway cars.
[24] William Lloyd Garrison (1805–1879), leader of the Abolitionists in New England.
[25] Like Antaeus, the giant wrestler in classic myth who was finally defeated when he was lifted off the earth (his mother), from whose touch he gained all his strength.

rock also at your back, and, as in the case of King James and Roderick Dhu, can say,—

> "Come one, come all! this rock shall fly
>   From its firm base as soon as I."[26]

Such, uttered or not, is the strength of your sentence. Sentences in which there is no strain. A fluttering and inconstant and *quasi* inspiration, and ever memorable Icarian fall,[27] in which your helpless wings are expanded merely by your swift descent into the *pelagos*[28] beneath.

[November 13, 1851]

Just spent a couple of hours (eight to ten) with Miss Mary Emerson at Holbrook's. The wittiest and most vivacious woman that I know, certainly that woman among my acquaintance whom it is most profitable to meet, the least frivolous, who will most surely provoke to good conversation and the expression of what is in you. She is singular, among women at least, in being really and perseveringly interested to know what thinkers think. She relates herself surely to the intellectual where she goes. It is perhaps her greatest praise and peculiarity that she, more surely than any other woman, gives her companion occasion to utter his best thought. In spite of her own biases, she can entertain a large thought with hospitality, and is not prevented by any intellectuality in it, as women commonly are. In short, she is a genius, as woman seldom is, reminding you less often of her sex than any woman whom I know. In that sense she is capable of a masculine appreciation of poetry and philosophy. I never talked with any other woman who I thought accompanied me so far in describing a poetic experience. Miss Fuller is the only woman I think of in this connection, and of her rather from her fame than from any knowledge of her. Miss Emerson expressed to-night a singular want of respect for her own sex, saying that they were frivolous almost without exception, that woman was the weaker vessel, etc.; that into whatever family she might go, she depended more upon the "clown" for society than upon the lady of the house. Men are more likely to have opinions of their own.

[December 31, 1851]

I do not lay myself open to my friends!? The owner of the casket locks it, and unlocks it. Treat your friends for what you know them to be. Regard no surfaces. Consider not what they did, but what they intended. Be sure, as you know them you are known of them again. Last night I treated my dearest friend ill. Though I could find some excuse for myself, it is not such excuse as under the circumstances could be pleaded in so many words. Instantly I blamed myself, and sought an opportunity to make atonement, but the friend avoided me, and, with kinder feelings even than before, I

---

[26] From *The Lay of the Last Ministral* (1805) by Sir Walter Scott (1771–1832), in which the figures of King James and Roderick Dhu play major roles in a romantic tale of warfare in the Scottish Highlands.

[27] Reference to the classic myth of Icarus, who, flying too close to the sun on wings attached to his body by wax, fell to his death into the sea.
[28] Greek: "sea."

was obliged to depart. And now this morning I feel that it is too late to speak of the trifle, and, besides, I doubt now in the cool morning, if I have a right to suppose such intimate and serious relations as afford a basis for the apology I had conceived, for even magnanimity must ask this poor earth for a field. The virtues even wait for invitation. Yet I am resolved to know that one centrally, through thick and thin, and though we should be cold to one another, though we should never speak to one another, I will know that inward and essential love may exist even under a superficial cold, and that the law of attraction speaks louder than words. My true relation this instant shall be my apology for my false relation the last instant. I made haste to cast off my injustice as scurf. I own it least of anybody, for I have absolutely done with it. Let the idle and wavering and apologizing friend appropriate it. Methinks our estrangement is only like the divergence of the branches which unite in the stem.

This night I heard Mrs. S—— lecture on womanhood. The most important fact about the lecture was that a woman said it, and in that respect it was suggestive. Went to see her afterward, but the interview added nothing to the previous impression, rather subtracted. She was a woman in the too common sense after all. You had to fire small charges: I did not have a finger in once, for fear of blowing away all her works and so ending the game. You had to substitute courtesy for sense and argument. It requires nothing less than a chivalric feeling to sustain a conversation with a lady. I carried her lecture for her in my pocket wrapped in her handkerchief; my pocket exhales cologne to this moment. The championess of woman's rights still asks you to be a ladies' man. I can't fire a salute, even, for fear some of the guns may be shotted.[29] I had to unshot all the guns in truth's battery and fire powder and wadding only. Certainly the heart is only for rare occasions; the intellect affords the most unfailing entertainment. It would only do to let her feel the wind of the ball. I fear that to the last woman's lectures will demand mainly courtesy from man.

[January 30, 1852]

Nature allows of no universal secrets. The more carefully a secret is kept on one side of the globe, the larger the type it is printed in on the other. Nothing is too pointed, too personal, too immodest, for her to blazon. The relations of sex, transferred to flowers, become the study of ladies in the drawing-room. While men wear fig leaves, she grows the *Phallus impudicus* and *P. caninus* and other phallus-like fungi.

The rhymes which I used to see on the walls of privies, scribbled by boys, I have lately seen, word for word the same; in spite [of] whitewash and brick walls and admonitions they survive. They are no doubt older than Orpheus,[30] and have come down from an antiquity as remote as mythology or fable. So, too, no doubt corporations have ever struggled in vain to obtain cleanliness in those provinces. Filth and impurity are as old as cleanliness and purity. To correspond to man completely, Nature is even perhaps unchaste herself. Or perchance man's impurity begets a monster somewhere, to proclaim his sin. The poetry of the jakes,[31]—it flows as perennially as the gutter.

[29] Loaded with shot or ball and powder. [31] I.e., the graffiti found in outdoor privies.
[30] Poet-musician in classic myth.

[*February 1, 1852*]

The recent rush to California and the attitude of the world, even of its philosophers and prophets, in relation to it appears to me to reflect the greatest disgrace on mankind. That so many are ready to get their living by the lottery of gold-digging without contributing any value to society, and that the great majority who stay at home justify them in this both by precept and example! It matches the infatuation of the Hindoos who have cast themselves under the car of Juggernaut. I know of no more startling development of the morality of trade and all the modes of getting a living than the rush to California affords. Of what significance the philosophy, or poetry, or religion of a world that will rush to the lottery of California gold-digging on the receipt of the first news, to live by luck, to get the means of commanding the labor of others less lucky, *i.e.* of slaveholding, without contributing any value to society? And that is called enterprise, and the devil is only a little more enterprising! The philosophy and poetry and religion of such a mankind are not worth the dust of a puffball. The hog that *roots* his own living, and so makes manure, would be ashamed of such company. If I could command the wealth of all the worlds by lifting my finger, I would not pay such a price for it. It makes God to be a moneyed gentleman who scatters a handful of pennies in order to see mankind scramble for them. Going to California. It is only three thousand miles nearer to hell. I will resign my life sooner than live by luck. The world's raffle. A subsistence in the domains of nature a thing to be raffled for! No wonder that they gamble there. I never heard that they did anything else there. What a comment, what a satire, on our institutions! The conclusion will be that mankind will hang itself upon a tree. And who would interfere to cut it down. And have all the precepts in all the bibles taught men only this? and is the last and most admirable invention of the Yankee race only an improved muckrake?—patented too!

[*April 12, 1852*]

I am made somewhat sad this afternoon by the coarseness and vulgarity of my companion, because he is one with whom I have made myself intimate. He inclines latterly to speak with coarse jesting of facts which should always be treated with delicacy and reverence. I lose my respect for the man who can make the mystery of sex the subject of a coarse jest, yet, when you speak earnestly and seriously on the subject, is silent. I feel that this is to be truly irreligious. Whatever may befall me, I trust that I may never lose my respect for purity in others. The subject of sex is one on which I do not wish to meet a man at all unless I *can* meet him on the most inspiring ground,—if his view degrades, and does not elevate. I would preserve purity in act and thought, as I would cherish the memory of my mother. A companion can possess no worse quality than vulgarity. If I find that *he* is not habitually reverent of the fact of sex, I, even I, will not associate with [him]. I will cast this first stone. What were life without some religion of this kind? Can I walk with one who by his jests and by his habitual tone reduces the life of men and women to a level with that of cats and dogs? The man who uses such a vulgar jest describes his relation to his dearest friend. Impure as I am, I could protect and worship purity. I can have no really serious conversation with my companion. He seems not capable of it. The men whom I most esteem, when they speak at all on this subject, do not speak with sufficient reverence. They speak to men with a coarseness which they would not use in the presence of women, and I think they would feel a slight shame if a woman coming in should hear their remarks. A man's speech on this subject should, of course, be ever as reverent and chaste and simple as if it were to be heard by the ears of maidens.

[January 6, 1853]

About ten minutes before 10 A.M., I heard a very loud sound, and felt a violent jar, which made the house rock and the loose articles on my table rattle, which I knew must be either a powder-mill blown up or an earthquake. Not knowing but another and more violent might take place, I immediately ran down-stairs, but I saw from the door a vast expanding column of whitish smoke rising in the west directly over the powder-mills four miles distant. It was unfolding its volumes above, which made it widest there. In three or four minutes it had all risen and spread itself into a lengthening, somewhat copper-colored cloud parallel with the horizon from north to south, and about ten minutes after the explosion it passed over my head, being several miles long from north to south and distinctly dark and smoky toward the north, not nearly so high as the few cirrhi[32] in the sky. I jumped into a man's wagon and rode toward the mills. In a few minutes more, I saw behind me, far in the east, a faint salmon-colored cloud carrying the news of the explosion to the sea, and perchance over [the] head of the absent proprietor.

Arrived probably before half past ten. There were perhaps thirty or forty wagons there. The kernel-mill[33] had blown up first, and killed three men who were in it, said to be turning a roller with a chisel. In three seconds after, one of the mixing-houses exploded. The kernel-house was swept away, and fragments, mostly but a foot or two in length, were strewn over the hills and meadows, as if sown, for thirty rods, and the slight snow then on the ground was for the most part melted around. The mixing-house, about ten rods west, was not so completely dispersed, for most of the machinery remained, a total wreck. The press-house, about twelve rods east, had two thirds [of] its boards off, and a mixing-house next westward from that which blew up had lost some boards on the east side. The boards fell out (*i.e.* of those buildings which did not blow up), the air within apparently rushing out to fill up the vacuum occasioned by the explosions, and so, the powder being bared to the fiery particles in the air, another building explodes. The powder on the floor of the bared press-house was six inches deep in some places, and the crowd were thoughtlessly going into it. A few windows were broken thirty or forty rods off. Timber six inches square and eighteen feet long was thrown over a hill eighty feet high at least,—a dozen rods; thirty rods was about the limit of fragments. The drying-house, in which was a fire, was perhaps twenty-five rods distant and escaped. Every timber and piece of wood which was blown up was as black as if it had been dyed, except where it had broken on falling; other breakages were completely concealed by the color. I mistook what had been iron hoops in the woods for leather straps. Some of the clothes of the men

---

[32] Or *cirri*: formation of fleecy clouds, known as a "mackerel sky." [33] Where the "grains" of powder were processed.

were in the tops of the trees, where undoubtedly their bodies had been and left them. The bodies were naked and black, some limbs and bowels here and there, and a head at a distance from its trunk. The feet were bare; the hair singed to a crisp. I smelt the powder half a mile before I got there. Put the different buildings thirty rods apart, and then but one will blow up at a time.

[March 5, 1853]

The secretary of the Association for the Advancement of Science requests me, as he probably has thousands of others, by a printed circular letter from Washington the other day, to fill the blank against certain questions, among which the most important one was what branch of science I was specially interested in, using the term science in the most comprehensive sense possible. Now, though I could state to a select few that department of human inquiry which engages me, and should be rejoiced at an opportunity to do so, I felt that it would be to make myself the laughing-stock of the scientific community to describe or attempt to describe to them that branch of science which specially interests me, inasmuch as they do not believe in a science which deals with the higher law. So I was obliged to speak to their condition and describe to them that poor part of me which alone they can understand. The fact is I am a mystic, a transcendentalist, and a natural philosopher to boot. Now I think of it, I should have told them at once that I was a transcendentalist. That would have been the shortest way of telling them that they would not understand my explanations.

How absurd that, though I probably stand as near to nature as any of them, and am by constitution as good an observer as most, yet a true account of my relation to nature should excite their ridicule only! If it had been the secretary of an association of which Plato or Aristotle[34] was the president, I should not have hesitated to describe my studies at once and particularly.

[November 29, 1853]

Nov. 29. On Saturday, the 26th, a dog on whose collar the words "Milton Hill," or equivalent ones, were engraved ran through the town, having, as the story went, bitten a boy in Lincoln. He bit several dogs in this town and was finally shot. Some of the dogs bitten have been killed, and rumor now says that the boy died yesterday. People are considerably alarmed. Some years ago a boy in Lincoln was bitten by a raccoon and died of hydrophobia. I observed to Minott to-night that I did not think that our doctors knew how to cure this disease, but he said they could cure it, he had seen a man bitten who was cured. The story is worth telling, for it shows how much trouble the passage of one mad dog through the town may produce.

It was when he was a boy and lived down below the old Ben Prescott house, over the cellar-hole on what is now Hawthorne's land. The first he remembers a couple of men had got poles and were punching at a strange dog toward night under a barn in that neighborhood. The dog, which was speckled and not very large, would growl and bite the pole, and they ran a good deal of risk, but they did not know that he

---

[34] Seminal Greek philosophers who lived 427–347 B.C. and 384–322 B.C., respectively.

was mad. At length they routed him, and he took to the road and came on towards town, and Minott, keeping his distance, followed on behind. When the dog got to the old Ben Prescott place, he turned up into the yard, where there were a couple of turkeys, drove them into a corner, bit off the head of one, and carried the body off across the road into the meadow opposite. They then raised the cry of "Mad dog." He saw his mother and Aunt Prescott, two old ladies, coming down the road, while the dog was running the other way in the meadow, and he shouted to them to take care of themselves, for that dog was mad. The dog soon reëntered the road at some bars and held on toward town. Minott next saw Harry Hooper coming down the road after his cows, and he shouted to him to look out, for the dog was mad, but Harry, who was in the middle of the road, spread his arms out, one on each side, and, being short, the dog leaped right upon his open breast and made a pass at his throat, but missed it, though it frightened him a good deal; and Minott, coming up, exclaimed, "Why, you're crazy, Harry; if he'd 'a' bitten ye, 't would 'a' killed ye." When he got up as far as the red house or Curtis place, the dog was about in the middle of the road, and a large and stout old gentleman by the name of Fay, dressed in small-clothes, was coming down on the sidewalk. M. shouted to him also to take care of himself, for the dog was mad, and Fay said afterward that he heard him but he had always supposed that a mad dog would n't turn out for anything; but when this dog was nearly abreast of him, he suddenly inclined toward him, and then again inclined still more, and seized him by the left leg just below the knee, and Fay, giving him a kick with the other leg, tripped himself up; and when he was down, the dog bit him in the right leg in the same place. Being by this time well frightened, and fearing that he would spring at his throat next, Fay seized the dog himself by his throat and held him fast, and called lustily for somebody to come and kill him. A man by the name of Lewis rushed out of the red house with an old axe and began to tap on the dog's nose with it, but he was afraid to strike harder, for Fay told him not to hit him. Minott saw it all, but still kept his distance. Suddenly Fay, not knowing what he did, let go, and the man, giving the dog a blow across the back, ran into the house; but, it being a dull meat axe, the dog trotted along, still toward town.

He turned and went round the pond by Bowers's and, going down to the brook by the roadside, lapped some water. Just then, Peter coming over the bridge, the dog reared up and growled at him, and he, seeing that he was mad, made haste through the bars out of his way and cut across the fields to Reuben Brown's. The dog went on, it being now between sundown and dark, to Peter Wheeler's, and bit two cows, which afterward died of hydrophobia, and next he went to where Nathan Stow now lives, and bit a goose in the wing, and so he kept on through the town. The next that was heard of him, Black Cato, that lived at the Lee place, now Sam Wheeler's, on the river, was waked up about midnight by a noise among the pigs, and, having got up, he took a club and went out to see what was the matter. Looking over into the pen, this dog reared up at him, and he knocked him back into it, and, jumping over, mauled him till he thought he was dead and then tossed him out. In the morning he thought he [would] go out and see whose dog he had killed, but lo! he had picked himself up, and there was no dog to be found.

Cato was going out into the woods chopping that day, and as he was getting over a wall lined with brush, the same dog reared up at him once more, but this time, having heard of the mad dog, he was frightened and ran; but still the dog came on, and once or twice he knocked him aside with a large stone, till at length, the dog coming close to him, he gave him a blow which killed him; and lest he should run away again, he cut off his head and threw both head and body into the river.

In the meanwhile Fay went home (to the Dr. Heywood house), drank some spirit, then went straight over to Dr. Heywood's office and stayed there and was doctored by him for three weeks. The doctor cut out the mangled flesh and made various applications, and Fay cried like a baby, but he never experienced any further ill effects from the bite.

[December 29, 1853]

Dec. 29. We survive, in one sense, in our posterity and in the continuance of our race, but when a race of men, of Indians for instance, becomes extinct, is not that the end of the world for them? Is not the world forever beginning and coming to an end, both to men and races? Suppose we were to foresee that the Saxon race to which we belong would become extinct the present winter,—disappear from the face of the earth,—would it not look to us like the end, the dissolution of the world? Such is the prospect of the Indians.

[January 1, 1856]

On the north shore, near the railroad, I see the tracks apparently of a white rabbit, afterward many tracks of gray rabbits, and where they had squatted under or rather by the side of an alder stem or the like, and left many balls in the pure snow. Many have run in one course. In the midst of them I see the track of a large rabbit, probably a white one, which was evidently on the full spring. Its tracks are four feet apart, and, unlike the others, which are on the surface even of this light snow, these break through deep, making a hole six inches over. Why was this one in such haste? I conclude to trace him back and find out. His bounds grow greater and greater as I go back, now six feet quite, and a few rods further are the tracks of a fox (*possibly* a dog, but I think not) exactly on the trail! A little further, where the rabbit was ascending a considerable slope, through this snow nearly a foot deep, the bounds measure full seven feet, leaving the snow untouched for that space between. It appeared that the fox had started the rabbit from a bank on which it was resting, near a young hemlock, and pursued it only a dozen rods up the hill, and then gave up the chase,—and well he might, methought.

Goodwin says that the white rabbit never burrows, but the gray regularly. Yet he once knew a white one to earth itself.

In a rabbit's track the two fore feet are the furthest apart, thus:

This chase occurred probably in the night, either the last or night before, when there was not a man within a mile; but, treading on these very deep and distinct tracks, it was as if I had witnessed it, and in imagination I could see the sharp eyes of the crafty fox and the palpitating breast of the timorous rabbit, listening behind. We unwittingly traverse the scenery of what tragedies! Every square rod, perchance, was the scene of a life or death struggle last night. As you track the rabbit further off, its bounds becoming shorter and shorter, you follow also surely its changing moods from desperate terror till it walks calmly and reassured over the snow without breaking its very slight crust,—perchance till it gnaws some twig composedly,—and in the other direction you trace the retreating steps of the disappointed fox until he has forgotten this and scented some new game, maybe dreams of partridges or wild mice. Your own feelings are fluttered proportionably.

[January 9, 1856]

What a strong and hearty but reckless, hit-or-miss style had some of the early writers of New England, like Josselyn and William Wood[35] and others elsewhere in those days; as if they spoke with a relish, smacking their lips like a coach-whip, caring more to speak heartily than scientifically true. They are not to be caught napping by the wonders of Nature in a new country, and perhaps are often more ready to appreciate them than she is to exhibit them. They give you one piece of nature, at any rate, and that is themselves. (Cotton Mather,[36] too, has a rich phrase.) They use a strong, coarse, homely speech which cannot always be found in the dictionary, nor sometimes be heard in polite society, but which brings you very near to the thing itself described. The strong new soil speaks through them. I have just been reading some in Wood's "New England's Prospect." He speaks a good word for New England, indeed will come very near lying for her, and when he doubts the justness of his praise, he brings it out not the less roundly; as who cares if it is not so? we love her not the less for all that. Certainly that generation stood nearer to nature, nearer to the facts, than this, and hence their books have more life in them.

(Sometimes a lost man will be so beside himself that he will not have sense enough to trace back his own tracks in the snow.)

Expressions he uses which you now hear only in kitchens and barrooms, which therefore sound particularly fresh and telling, not book-worn. They speak like men who have backs and stomachs and bowels, with all the advantages and disadvantages that attach to them. Ready to find lions here, some having "heard such terrible roarings," "which must be either Devils or Lions; there being no other creatures which use to roar." What a gormandizing faith (or belief) he has, ready to swallow all kinds of portents and prodigies! Says the wolves have no joints from head to tail. Most admirable when they most outrage common taste and the rules of composition. Of mosquitoes he says those "that swell with their biting the first year, never swell the second."

[February 8, 1857]

And now another friendship is ended. I do not know what has made my friend doubt me, but I know that in love there is no mistake, and that every estrangement is well founded. But my destiny is not narrowed, but if possible the broader for it. The heavens withdraw and arch themselves higher. I am sensible not only of a moral, but

---

[35] John Josselyn (fl. 1638–1675) and William Wood (fl. 1629–1635), English writers and travelers during the early days of the New England settlement; best known for *An Account* *of Two Voyages to New-England* (1674) and *New Englands Prospect* (1634), respectively.

[36] Prominent New England clergyman and writer (1663–1728).

even a grand physical pain, such as gods may feel, about my head and breast, a certain ache and fullness. This rending of a tie, it is not my work nor thine. It is no accident that we mind; it is only the awards of fate that are affecting. I know of no æons, or periods, no life and death, but these meetings and separations. My life is like a stream that is suddenly dammed and has no outlet; but it rises the higher up the hills that shut it in, and will become a deep and silent lake. Certainly there is no event comparable for grandeur with the eternal separation—if we may conceive it so—from a being that we have known. I become in a degree sensible of the meaning of finite and infinite. What a grand significance the word "never" acquires! With one with whom we have walked on high ground we cannot deal on any lower ground ever after. We have tried for so many years to put each other to this immortal use, and have failed. Undoubtedly our good genii[37] have mutually found the material unsuitable. We have hitherto paid each other the highest possible compliment; we have recognized each other constantly as divine, have afforded each other that opportunity to live that no other wealth or kindness can afford. And now, for some reason inappreciable by us, it has become necessary for us to withhold this mutual aid. Perchance there is none beside who knows us for a god, and none whom we know for such. Each man and woman is a veritable god or goddess, but to the mass of their fellows disguised. There is only one in each case who sees through the disguise. That one who does not stand so near to any man as to see the divinity in him is truly alone. I am perfectly sad at parting from you. I could better have the earth taken away from under my feet, than the thought of you from my mind. One while I think that some great injury has been done, with which you are implicated, again that you are no party to it. I fear that there may be incessant tragedies, that one may treat his fellow as a god but receive somewhat less regard from him. I now almost for the first time *fear* this. Yet I believe that in the long run there is no such inequality.

[April 23, 1857]

April 23. I saw at Ricketson's a young woman, Miss Kate Brady, twenty years old, her father an Irishman, a worthless fellow, her mother a smart Yankee. The daughter formerly did sewing, but now keeps school for a livelihood. She was born at the Brady house, I think in Freetown, where she lived till twelve years old and helped her father in the field. There she rode horse to plow and was knocked off the horse by apple tree boughs, kept sheep, caught fish, etc., etc. I never heard a girl or woman express so strong a love for nature. She purposes to return to that lonely ruin, and dwell there alone, since her mother and sister will not accompany her; says that she knows all about farming and keeping sheep and spinning and weaving, though it would puzzle her to shingle the old house. There she thinks she can "live free." I was pleased to hear of her plans, because they were quite cheerful and original, not professedly reformatory, but growing out of her love for "Squire's Brook and the Middleborough ponds." A strong love for outward nature is singularly rare among both men and women. The scenery immediately about her homestead is quite ordinary, yet she appreciates and can use that part of the universe as no other being can. Her own sex, so tamely bred, only jeer at her for entertaining such an idea, but she has a strong head and a love

[37] Guardian spirits.

for good reading, which may carry her through. I would by no means discourage, nor yet particularly encourage her, for I would have her so strong as to succeed in spite of all ordinary discouragements.

[March 5, 1858]

We read the English poets; we study botany and zoölogy and geology, lean and dry as they are; and it is rare that we get a new suggestion. It is ebb-tide with the scientific reports, Professor ———— in the chair. We would fain know something more about these animals and stones and trees around us. We are ready to skin the animals alive to come at them. Our scientific names convey a very partial information only; they suggest certain thoughts only. It does not occur to me that there are other names for most of these objects, given by a people who stood between me and them, who had better senses than our race. How little I know of that *arbor-vitæ* when I have learned only what science can tell me! It is but a word. It is not a *tree* of *life*. But there are twenty words for the tree and its different parts which the Indian gave, which are not in our botanies, which imply a more practical and vital science. He used it every day. He was well acquainted with its wood, and its bark, and its leaves. No science does more than arrange what knowledge we have of any class of objects. But, generally speaking, how much more conversant was the Indian with any wild animal or plant than we are, and in his language is implied all that intimacy, as much as ours is expressed in our language. How many words in his language about a moose, or birch bark, and the like! The Indian stood nearer to wild nature than we. The wildest and noblest quadrupeds, even the largest fresh-water fishes, some of the wildest and noblest birds and the fairest flowers have actually receded as *we* advanced, and we have but the most distant knowledge of them. A rumor has come down to us that the skin of a lion was seen and his roar heard here by an early settler. But there was a race here that slept on his skin. It was a new light when my guide gave me Indian names for things for which I had only scientific ones before. In proportion as I understood the language, I saw them from a new point of view.

[March 28, 1859]

March 28. P.M.—Paddle to the Bedford line.

It is now high time to look for arrowheads, etc. I spend many hours every spring gathering the crop which the melting snow and rain have washed bare. When, at length, some island in the meadow or some sandy field elsewhere has been plowed, perhaps for rye, in the fall, I take note of it, and do not fail to repair thither as soon as the earth begins to be dry in the spring. If the spot chances never to have been cultivated before, I am the first to gather a crop from it. The farmer little thinks that another reaps a harvest which is the fruit of his toil. As much ground is turned up in a day by the plow as Indian implements could not have turned over in a month, and my eyes rest on the evidences of an aboriginal life which passed here a thousand years ago perchance. Especially if the knolls in the meadows are washed by a freshet where they have been plowed the previous fall, the soil will be taken away lower down and the stones left,—the arrowheads, etc., and soapstone pottery amid them, —somewhat as gold is washed in a dish or tom. I landed on two spots this afternoon and picked up a dozen arrowheads. It is one of the regular pursuits of the spring. As much as sportsmen go in pursuit of ducks, and gunners of musquash, and scholars of rare books, and travellers of adventures, and poets of ideas, and all men of money, I go in search of arrowheads when the proper season comes round again. So I help myself to live worthily, and loving my life as I should. It is a good collyrium[38] to look on the bare earth,—to pore over it so much, getting strength to all your senses like Antæus.[39] If I did not find arrowheads, I might, perchance, begin to pick up crockery and fragments of pipes,—the relics of a more recent man. Indeed, you can hardly name a more innocent or wholesome entertainment. As I am thus engaged, I hear the rumble of the bowling-alley's thunder, which has begun again in the village. It comes before the earliest natural thunder. But what its lightning is, and what atmospheres it purifies, I do not know. Or I might collect the various bones which I come across. They would make a museum that would delight some Owen[40] at last, and what a text they might furnish me for a course of lectures on human life or the like! I might spend my days collecting the fragments of pipes until I found enough, after all my search, to compose one perfect pipe when laid together.

I have not decided whether I had better publish my experience in searching for arrowheads in three volumes, with plates and an index, or try to compress it into one. These durable implements seem to have been suggested to the Indian mechanic with a view to my entertainment in a succeeding period. After all the labor expended on it, the bolt may have been shot but once perchance, and the shaft which was devoted to it decayed, and there lay the arrowhead, sinking into the ground, awaiting me. They lie all over the hills with like expectations, and in due time the husbandman is sent, and, tempted by the promise of corn or rye, he plows the land and turns them up to my view. Many as I have found, methinks the last one gives me about the same delight that the first did. Some time or other, you would say, it had rained arrowheads, for they lie all over the surface of America. You may have your peculiar tastes. Certain localities in your town may seem from association unattractive and uninhabitable to you. You may wonder that the land bears any money value there, and pity some poor fellow who is said to survive in that neighborhood. But plow up a new field there, and you will find the omnipresent arrow-points strewn over it, and it will appear that the red man, with other tastes and associations, lived there too. No matter how far from the modern road or meeting-house, no matter how near. They lie in the meeting-house cellar, and they lie in the distant cow-pasture. And some collections which were made a century ago by the curious like myself have been dispersed again, and they are still as good as new. You cannot tell the third-hand ones (for they are all second-hand) from the others, such is their persistent out-of-door durability; for they were chiefly made to be lost. They are sown, like a grain that is slow to germinate, broadcast over the earth. Like the dragon's teeth which bore a crop of soldiers, these bear crops of philosophers and poets, and the same seed is just as good to plant again. It is a stone fruit. Each one yields me a thought. I come nearer to the maker of it than if I found his bones. His bones would not prove any wit that wielded them, such as this work of his bones does. It is humanity inscribed on the face of the earth, patent to my eyes as soon as the snow goes off, not hidden away in some crypt or grave

---

[38] Eyewash.
[39] See footnote 25.

[40] Sir Richard Owen (1804–1892), English naturalist.

or under a pyramid. No disgusting mummy, but a clean stone, the best symbol or letter that could have been transmitted to me.

The Red Man, his mark

At every step I see it, and I can easily supply the "Tahatawan" or "Mantatuket" that might have been written if he had had a clerk. It is no single inscription on a particular rock, but a footprint—rather a mindprint—left everywhere, and altogether illegible. No vandals, however vandalic in their disposition, can be so industrious as to destroy them.

[May 28, 1859]

When I entered the interior meadow of Gowing's Swamp I heard a slight snort, and found that I had suddenly come upon a woodchuck amid the sphagnum, lambkill, *Kalmia glauca,* andromeda, cranberry, etc.,[41] there. It was only seven feet off, and, being surprised, would not run. It would only stand erect from time to time,—perfectly erect with its blackish paws held like hands near together in front,—just so as to bring its head, or eyes, above the level of the lambkill, kalmia, etc., and look round, turning now this ear toward me, then that; and every now and then it would make a short rush at me, half a foot or so, with a snort, and then draw back, and also grit its teeth —which it showed—very audibly, with a rattling sound, evidently to intimidate me. I could not drive it, but it would steadily face me and rush toward me thus. Also it made a short motion occasionally as if to bury itself by burrowing there. It impressed me as a singularly wild and grizzly [*sic*] native, survivor of the red man. He may have thought that no one but he came to Gowing's Swamp these afternoons.

Its colors were gray, reddish brown, and blackish, the gray-tipped wind hairs giving it a grizzly look above, and when it stood up its distinct rust-color beneath was seen, while the top of its head was dark-brown, becoming black at snout, as also its paws and its little rounded ears. Its head from snout to ears, when it stood up erect, made a nearly horizontal line. It did much looking round. When thus erect, its expression and posture were very bear-like, with the clumsiness of the bear. Though I drew off three or four rods, it would not retreat into the thicket (which was only a rod off) while I was there so near.

The scheuchzeria is at height or past. E. Emerson's *Calla palustris* out the 27th. *Eleocharis palustris,* R. W. E.'s[42] meadow, not long. Hear of linnæa out, the 28th. . . .

[August 28, 1859]

Aug. 28. P.M. A cool day; wind northwest. Need a half-thick coat. Thus gradually we withdraw into winter quarters. It is a clear, flashing air, and the shorn fields now look bright and yellowish and cool, tinkled and twittered over by bobolinks, goldfinches, sparrows, etc. You feel the less inclined to bathing this weather, and bathe from principle, when boys, who bathe for fun, omit it.

---

[41] Assortment of plants common to swampy areas. [42] R. W. E.: again, Ralph Waldo Emerson.

Thick fogs these mornings. We have had little or no dog-days this year, it has been so dry.

Pumpkins begin to be yellow. White cornel berries mostly fallen.

[October 19, 1859]

Oct. 19.[43] When a government puts forth its strength on the side of injustice, as ours (especially to-day) to maintain slavery and kill the liberators of the slave, what a merely brute, or worse than brute, force it is seen to be! A demoniacal force! It is more manifest than ever that tyranny rules. I see this government to be effectually allied with France and Austria in oppressing mankind.

One comment I heard of by the postmaster of this village on the news of Brown's death:[44] "He died as the fool dieth." I should have answered this man, "He did not live as the fool liveth, and he died as he lived."

Treason! where does treason take its rise? I cannot help thinking of you as you deserve, ye governments. Can you dry up the fountains of thought? High treason which is resistance to *tyranny* here below has its origin in, and is first committed by, the power that makes and forever re-creates man. When you have caught and hung all of these human rebels, you have accomplished nothing but your own guilt, for you have not struck at the fountainhead. You presume to contend with a foe against whom West Point cadets and rifled cannon *point* not. Can all the arts of the cannon-founder tempt matter to turn against its Maker? Is the form in which he casts it more essential than the constitution of it and of himself?

I see that the same journal that contains this pregnant news from Harper's Ferry is chiefly filled, in parallel columns, with the reports of the political conventions that are now being held. But the descent is too steep to them; they should have been spared this contrast. To turn from the voices and deeds of earnest men to the cackling of political conventions! Office-seekers and speechmakers, who do not so much as lay an egg, but wear their breasts bare upon an egg of chalk. Their great game is the game of straws, or rather that universal and aboriginal game of the platter, at which the Indians cried, *Hub-bub.*[45] Some of them generals forsooth.

1837–1859/1906

Edgar Allan Poe
1809–1849

There seems to be enough of Edgar Allan Poe to go around to please, or to exasperate, almost everyone. The title of Daniel Hoffman's recent study of the writer visually represents this fact: *Poe, Poe, Poe, Poe, Poe, Poe, Poe.* As Hoffman observes, there emerges from the writings "a surrogate for all of Poe's readers"—

---

[43] In this entry Thoreau makes notes for the address he delivered in Concord on October 30, extolling John Brown, who had been captured at Harper's Ferry. Brown had led an attack on October 16 against the federal arsenal in the cause of militant antislavery principles.

[44] Brown's death was mistakenly reported at the time of his capture; he was later executed, however.

[45] Game of chance during which Indians raised a tumult of noise.

the private "I" that each of holds to, and discovers in, the shadows cast by the tales and the poems. There is Poe whose horror stories scared us when we were fourteen and whom we supposed to grow away from in our maturity; but there is also the Poe who thoughts on personal epistemologies (what we know) and cosmic ontologies (what is real) awe us with their seeming profundity. There is the dissolute wastrel portrayed by Poe's first biographers— and in part by Poe himself, in the stories he spread. There is also the helpless genius who needed lots of mothering, as put forward in the swooning remembrances of the various maternal figures with which he filled his life. There is the truth sayer on the absolutes of poetry and beauty, and the diddler who took his revenge on the stupidity of his contemporaries by making fools of them for falling for his cunningly wrought hoaxes. There is the creator of the detective Dupin, whom American mystery buffs claim as the originator of "their kind" of story, the poet whom the French appropriate as the true representative of Gallic culture, and the Gothicist whom the South likes to have share its own exile from mainstream Yankee literature. Poe comes to us as drug-sodden madman or as the cool possessor of a computerlike brain that would today move him into the executive suites of IBM. He is the anarchist self we flaunt, to the extent of welcoming death when wanting to rebel against the boring routines that limit the soul. But he is also the person who sits in his dull little office as dutiful editor and reviewer, moving all his papers into the out basket. He is Poe the incomplete poet, or the precursor of the French Symbolists. He is the cheap comedown from "good" writing, or the St. John the Baptist who announces the arrival of the modern short story and short poem.

Perhaps only two warnings are in order when we approach Poe's writings, which we tend to turn into litmus tests for our own multiple selves: not to make Poe too dull (coming to him through pedantry) and not to make him too exciting (getting at him through pathology), since even the act of sensationalizing his life and writings makes them collapse boringly in on themselves).

Neat little résumés are difficult to produce when it comes to the facts of Poe's life and the development of his career as poet, writer of tales, editor, and literary critic. Too many biographers have intervened since he was found near death in a Baltimore street on an October night in 1849. But certain details have been sorted out from the slanders that attack and the legends that extol. Even so, every "normal" fact—such as his birth in Boston on January 19, 1809—is matched by something unsettling. His parents were wandering actors, members of a disreputable profession; his drunkard father decamped and his mother died by the time the child was two. Elizabeth Arnold Poe happened to die while on tour in Richmond, and when the infant Edgar and an older brother were placed with whoever would agree to care for them, a well-to-do merchant of the city, John Allan, took charge of Edgar Poe. All went well enough for the first twenty years. Although never legally adopted by the Allans, their young ward accompanied them on their travels to England (where Poe attended school) and back again to the upper-class education and social expectations of a well-bred Richmond family. But Poe's status in the Allan household was an uncertain one. He was unable to forget how shameful his antecedents were. Friction developed between Poe and John Allan—perhaps as the result of Allan's jealousy over his wife's fondness for the boy or of Poe's reluctance to go into Allan's tobacco export business. Then again, it could have been ▮▮▮ecociously romantic involvements with several young women of his ▮▮▮ the gambling debts he accumulated during his year at the University of ▮▮ginia that set him at odds with his guardian.

By 1827 the tensions were too great to bear. Po▮ left Richmond and went to Boston, where he published with his own funds hi first collection, *Tamerlane and Other Poems,* signed simply "A Bostonian." Then le vanished for a short period into the army under the pseudonym Edgar A. Perry. A brief truce between Poe and John Allan led to his discharge from the regulars and an appointment to West Point in July 1830, less than a year after the appearance of his second volume, *Al Aaraaf, Tamerlane, and Minor Poems.* Poe did not stay at West Point long. He found that he disliked the regimen and lacked the necessary allowance from John Allan that would let him live like both an officer and a gentleman. Deliberately flaunting rules about class attendance, he encouraged his own dismissal.

Meanwhile matters had again become ugly at home. The young man wished to have his position as a "son" clarified, and John Allan refused to give him that satisfaction. Allan's first wife died, and he remarried. The new wife bore him twin sons, then became pregnant again almost immediately. By the time Poe left West Point after seven months at the Academy, he realized there was no chance for him ever to be named the Allan heir; the break was complete. He was totally on his own at the age of twenty-two.

In May 1831, Poe's friends at West Point provided him with the money he needed to publish *Poems,* dedicated to "the U.S. Corps of Cadets." This collection included revisions of earlier poems and the addition of the first and best versions of "To Helen" and "Israfel." Poe decided that writing would obviously have to be the way he would earn his living and to make a "name" for himself, now that he had been denied the name Allan and the social identity of a Virginia gentleman and West Point officer. But writing poems that appeared in "little collections" was an avocation for men of independent means, not the way to lift a poor man set adrift in the shark-rich seas of an American society more interested in rewarding tobacco merchants than brilliant young poets.

Poe launched himself as an editor, a career that would sustain him, but not very well, until his death eighteen years later. He first went to Baltimore, where he lived between 1831 and 1835 with relatives from his father's side of the family. Foremost among these were his aunt, who became one of a series of "mothers" he needed to offset his lack of true "fathers," and his aunt's young daughter Virginia, whom Poe married by 1836, when she was fourteen. This threesome lived together in poverty, with Poe working with exceptional vigor.

Five of his first stories appeared in a Philadelphia newspaper during 1832. In 1833 "MS Found in a Bottle" won first prize in a story contest run by a Baltimore paper. Tales written for publication in the popular press in those days were governed by the particular demands of newspaper space and the need to achieve immediate impact; these were formulas Poe mastered quickly. By 1835, at twenty-six, he had sufficient reputation as a writer of popular fiction to win the assistant editorship of the *Southern Literary Messenger* in Richmond, but he did not keep the job long. He performed his editorial duties brilliantly, but emotionally he could not stay the course or keep his peace with the owners. The same sarcasm that gained welcome notoriety for the magazine from the reviews he wrote did not endear him to his associates. Bouts of drinking recommenced. He was fired. He had to move quickly.

He spent a few months in New York, where Harper's published his novel *The Narrative of Arthur Gordon Pym* in 1838, to no financial or critical advantage. He moved to Philadelphia in 1839. Living for a time on a diet of bread and molasses and constantly on the edge of total discouragement, Poe worked on. "Ligeia" was only the first of the major stories he wrote in 1839. It appeared, with other stories and poems, in the *American Museum* of Baltimore. Over the next few years, Poe became connected with three different magazines: *Burton's Gentleman's Magazine* (where he was coeditor from 1839 to 1840, until fired for drinking), *Graham's Magazine* (where he went in 1841 after being recommended by his former employer), and the Philadelphia weekly *Saturday Museum* in 1843. In 1842 Virginia sickened with tuberculosis (she would die at twenty-five), and Poe tried—unsuccessfully—to start a magazine of his own. But his reputation was advancing. Few readers could overlook the quality—or quantity—of his editorial writing, his critical reviews, his poems, and his stories of great impact. *Tales of the Grotesque and Arabesque* were collected in two volumes in 1840, and "The Gold Bug" won fame and the top prize of one hundred dollars in a contest sponsored by a Philadelphia newspaper.

In 1844 Poe took Virginia and his faithful aunt with him to New York, where they subsisted on the fees he earned from work on various papers and magazines. His drinking increased, gossip circulated about his eccentric behavior with various sentimental ladies who encouraged his attentions, and his sniping attacks on the literary follies he found everywhere in American letters made him the target of further vilification. Yet 1845 was a vintage year for Poe's literary career. "The Raven" appeared, and the stir it caused resulted in his giving lectures on poetry, being named the lead reviewer for the *Broadway Journal,* and being mentioned favorably by James Russell Lowell, the foremost critic of the period. Poe said proudly of "The Raven" (referring to the prize "The Gold Bug" had won him), "The bird beat the bug . . . all hollow." He made influential literary friends, and this led to the publication of *The Raven and Other Poems* by the prestigious publishing house of Wiley and Putnam. He purchased the *Broadway Journal* on credit, with the hope that the lift brought by his recent fame would bring financial success. However, by early 1846 the *Journal* had gone under, and by January 1847 Virginia was dead. What had never been a steady life now became an accelerating series of personal crises and professional disappointments.

Writing still, as ever under the compulsion to get down everything that filled his brain, Poe overextended himself even more. He attempted several editorial schemes, entered upon some fervid romances (culminating in an engagement to an old sweetheart, while writing excited letters to yet another woman), drank even more and became physically debilitated by what may have been a brain lesion. Somehow in the midst of this turmoil, enough to have unsettled a stolid man of regular habits, Poe wrote the poems "Ulalume" and "Annabel Lee," commenced the long prose poem *Eureka* in which he declared he would explain the nature of the universe, and completed the story "Hop-Frog." Despair over the loss of one's beloved, revenge on one's enemies, and exaltation over the final unification of consciousness with the cosmos—these were the themes Poe worked over in these final pieces. By now his activities were frenetic. He told tales of attempted suicides and of murder plots against his life; he gave lectures and readings of his work; he signed into a temperance group; he revisited the Richmond of his childhood. Suddenly it was over in October of 1849. On his way to Philadelphia for an editing job, he got off the train in Baltimore. He was found unconscious a few days later in the street. He died in a hospital on October 7 and was buried in Baltimore.

Poe was hardly in his grave before his biographers began to "create" a life for him. (That grave, incidently, remained unmarked for twenty-six years; when in 1875 a tombstone was placed there, the only literary representative present was Walt Whitman.) Two days after Poe's death, his literary executor and supposed friend, Rufus Griswold, attacked him in a newspaper obituary. The next year the introduction supplied by Griswold for the published collection of Poe's work contained an "exposé" of Poe's depravity—the "facts" for which Griswold obtained by falsifying Poe's letters. Griswold clearly benefited from these actions. Book sales were greatly helped by the sensationalism attending these slanders. Even Poe's aunt and Virginia's mother, Mrs. Clemm, was able to turn a profit selling copies of the edition that damned her "dear Eddie." From then on, critics, editors, and biographers have continued re-creating Poe after the images that most satisfied their own imaginations. But whether Poe was seen as a demon or as a misunderstood genius, the effect was to serve up one version or other of the Byronic hero—the most serviceable romantic image of the poet that lay at hand. It was the old story of a writer's life being substituted for his literary works as the source of the reader's interest and of having the writings evaluated according to whether one approves or disapproves of the writer. T. S. Eliot's admonition that poetry should be our "escape from personality" is not always followed. Certainly to look at the poem and not at the poet (especially if the latter happens to be Poe) can be difficult.

Critics and poets as sophisticated as Baudelaire, Mallarmé, and Valéry transformed Poe into an "honorary" Frenchman and symbolist poet, thereby accomplishing a double task: an attack on the bourgeois mentality of their own countrymen for its insensitivity to the poetic soul and an excoriation of the philistine qualities they associated with the American democratic system. In his own country, Poe was as much chastised for his literary failings as for his personal life. Emerson emerged long enough from the mental fog of his later years to characterize Poe as "the jingle man." In his memoirs, Henry James vividly recalled the excitement he and his brother William felt as boys waiting to snatch from the postman the latest issues of the magazines that contained Poe's horror tales. But James also registered his disapproval of adults who continued to take pleasure in a man whose writings were not sufficiently "about something." James knew from his own experience what Daniel Hoffman has expressed—that Poe's stories "can frighten a boy out of his pajamas." But James asked more of Poe than Poe would give. Mark Twain, D. H. Lawrence, and T. S. Eliot were also less than charitable about Poe's literary achievements. Yet through it all, Poe has been read and absorbed by almost everyone in this country, on the Continent, and in England. The roster of well-known poets and writers of fiction who have admitted the ways in which Poe's writing has colored their own imaginations is impressive. Critics of every literary persuasion find his works an inexhaustible field for cultivation. Most of all, people read Poe and respond to him with an enthusiasm that has little to do with the rise and fall of his critical status.

Poe biographies are now undergoing "domestication." The current emphasis is on a Poe snugly at home with Virginia and Aunt Clemm rather than on the drunk wandering the streets. The focus is on the orphan, not the outlaw, as one biographer, John Carl Miller, has noted. It is less on Poe's oedipal and necrophiliac fantasies than on the hours he spent at the office turning out copy for the printers. This turnabout seems sound, but it is still unwise to suggest that anyone has, or ever will, truly know Poe the man.

What seems clearer these days is the nature of Poe's literary contributions. With a total of only forty-eight poems (many of them turned out at the jingle level that Emerson referred to), Poe pointed the way toward a new kind of symbolist poetry, verses that evoke mood rather than meaning, that call attention to their own technique, and that celebrate experimentation for its own sake.

With his horror tales, Poe took over—and, in some of his best examples, transcended—the Gothic formula that had been supplying thrills to readers of popular literature for some time. Poe is credited with inventing the detective story, a form that juxtaposes the threat of anarchy (outrageous crimes whose violence and unfathomable causes upset the stability of society) with a mix of the rational (mental coolness and the application of mathematical logic) and the intuitive (emotional reactions to the illogicality of events). Poe's stories of trips to the moon, as well as his musings about the evolution and consummation of the cosmos (whether taken straight or as hoax), extended the possibilities of science fiction. Psychological literature got a boost by his tales of alter egos and outlawed urges that stalk his characters' minds. He had inherited the tradition of the romance that located terror in outward places; he relocated it, as he announced, in the soul.

In a country young in literary experience, where critical theory and the analysis of literary techniques were rude or nonexistent, Poe's reviews and essays on poetic principles set an example that would eventually bring Americans to sophistication in the arts of reading and writing. The stand Poe took against the didacticism that evaluates literary worth according to the moral truths a story demonstrates has led American literature to participate in that particular strain of Romanticism that seeks out intensity of feeling and the pleasures of beauty, not moralisms. His strictures on the merits of brevity hardly kept Walt Whitman or Hart Crane from attempting long epic poems or William Faulkner and Henry James from exploring the extended novel form, but Poe gave the American short story form the base from which it moved toward true accomplishment.

Difficulties abound, however, in the interpretation given both to the meaning of Poe's individual works and to his literary intentions. It is difficult to know whether a particular poem or story originated from an excess of feverish emotion or from calculated designs on the reader's imagination, whether it was done as a hoax or offered in sober earnestness. Much of Poe's work exists teasingly between two poles, as both *Eureka* and *The Narrative of Arthur Gordon Pym* suggest. Critics who like to tidy things up are frustrated when they find it impossible to say whether "The Fall of the House of Usher" is a bona fide tale of horror or the parody of one, or whether the decor in the tower room in "Ligeia" is intentionally vulgar or the result of the innate verbal kitsch of a man whose own tastes were deplorably déclassé. We know that Poe could work with extreme calculation to arouse his readers' feelings. His essays "How to Write a *Blackwood's* Article" and "The Philosophy of Composition" reveal the clever means by which the writer can manipulate responses. But then, perhaps these essays are at the same time exercises in leg-pulling, ways of disguising the urgency Poe felt to express his strongest passions about his literary craft.

What we finally retain from an immersion in the often nightmarish world of Poe's writings is the sense that our secret fears and desires have been touched upon: the fear of being buried alive, of being destroyed by perverse instincts that overturn the rational measures by which we protect ourselves; desires imaged in acts of revenge, cannibalism, incest, and the quest for death. It was Poe's greatest discovery that we want and yet avoid self-examination and self-knowledge. To know the secrets of the universe would be to possess will, to have power and control over our fates. Knowledge, will, power—these appear to be at the heart of Poe's authority over our imaginations. He affects us by force, not clarity. It is a lesson taken to heart by masters of the gothic romance and of the modern literary work. The example of Poe is apparent in both.

Further Reading:

G. Woodberry, *The Life of Edgar Allan Poe, Personal and Literary,* 2 vols., 1885, 1909.

H. Allen, *Israfel—The Life and Times of Edgar Allan Poe,* 2 vols., 1926, 1934.

J. Krutch, *Edgar Allan Poe,* 1926.

K. Campbell, *The Mind of Poe and Other Studies,* 1933.

A. Quinn, *Edgar Allan Poe,* 1941, 1966.

M. Bonaparte, *The Life and Works of Edgar Allan Poe: A Psycho-Analytic Interpretation,* 1949, 1971.

N. Fagin, *The Histrionic Mr. Poe,* 1949.

E. Davidson, *Poe: A Critical Study,* 1957.

V. Buranelli, *Edgar Allan Poe,* 1961, 1977.

S. Moss, *Poe's Literary Battles: The Critic in the Context of His Literary Milieu,* 1963.

E. Wagenknecht, *Edgar Allan Poe: The Man Behind the Legend,* 1963.

E. Parks, *Edgar Allan Poe,* 1967.

F. Stovall, *Edgar Allan Poe the Poet,* 1969.

R. L. Gale, *Plots and Characters in the Fiction and Poetry of Edgar Allan Poe,* 1970.

D. Hoffman, *Poe, Poe, Poe, Poe, Poe, Poe, Poe,* 1972.

Critics on Poe, ed. D. Kesterson, 1973.

J. M. Dillon, *Edgar Allan Poe: His Genius and Character,* 1974.

Poe at Work: Seven Textual Studies, ed. B. Fisher, 1978.

J. Symons, *The Tell-Tale Heart,* 1978.

D. Ketterer, *The Rationale of Deception in Poe,* 1979.

E. Phillips, *Edgar Allan Poe: An American Imagination,* 1979.

B. R. Pollin, *Poe, Creator of Words,* 1980.

Texts:

"Ligeia," "The Conversation of Eiros and Charmion," "The Fall of the House of Usher," "The Man of the Crowd," "A Descent into the Maelström," "The Murders in the Rue Morgue," "The Masque of the Red Death," "Nathaniel Hawthorne's 'Twice-Told Tales,'" "The Philosophy of Composition," and "The Poetic Principle" from *The Complete Works of Edgar Allan Poe,* 17 vols., ed. J. Harrison, 1902. "The Black Cat," "The Tell-Tale Heart," "The Purloined Letter," "The Imp of the Perverse," "The Cask of Amontillado," and poems from *Collected Works of Edgar Allan Poe,* 3 vols., ed. T. Mabbott, 1969–1978.

See also *The Works of Edgar Allan Poe,* 10 vols., ed. E. Stedman and G. Woodberry, 1894–1895, 1914.

The Complete Poems and Stories of Edgar Allan Poe, 2 vols., ed. A. Quinn and E. O'Neill, 1946.

The Letters of Edgar Allan Poe, 2 vols., ed. J. Ostrom, 1948, 1966.

Ligeia

transcendentalism

And the will therein lieth, which dieth not. Who knoweth the mysteries of the will, with its vigor? For God is but a great will pervading all things by nature of its intentness. Man doth not yield himself to the angels, nor unto death utterly, save only through the weakness of his feeble will.
Joseph Glanvill[1]

I cannot, for my soul, remember how, when, or even precisely where, I first became acquainted with the lady Ligeia. Long years have since elapsed, and my memory is feeble through much suffering. Or, perhaps, I cannot *now* bring these points to mind, because, in truth, the character of my beloved, her rare learning, her singular yet placid cast of beauty, and the thrilling and enthralling eloquence of her low musical language, made their way into my heart by paces so steadily and stealthily progressive that they have been unnoticed and unknown. Yet I believe that I met her first and most frequently in some large, old, decaying city near the Rhine. Of her family—I have surely heard her speak. That it is of a remotely ancient date cannot be doubted. Ligeia! Ligeia! Buried in studies of a nature more than all else adapted to deaden impressions of the outward world, it is by that sweet word alone—by Ligeia—that I bring before mine eyes in fancy the image of her who is no more. And now, while I write, a recollection flashes upon me that I have *never known* the paternal name of her who was my friend and my betrothed, and who became the partner of my studies, and finally the wife of my bosom. Was it a playful charge on the part of my Ligeia? or was it a test of my strength of affection, that I should institute no inquiries upon this point? or was it rather a caprice of my own—a wildly romantic offering on the shrine of the most passionate devotion? I but indistinctly recall the fact itself—what wonder that I have utterly forgotten the circumstances which originated or attended it? And, indeed, if ever that spirit which is entitled *Romance*—if ever she, the wan and the misty-winged *Ashtophet*[2] of idolatrous Egypt, presided, as they tell, over marriages ill-omened, then most surely she presided over mine.

There is one dear topic, however, on which my memory fails me not. It is the *person* of Ligeia. In stature she was tall, somewhat slender, and, in her latter days, even emaciated. I would in vain attempt to portray the majesty, the quiet ease, of her demeanor, or the incomprehensible lightness and elasticity of her footfall. She came and departed as a shadow. I was never made aware of her entrance into my closed study save by the dear music of her low sweet voice, as she placed her marble hand upon my shoulder. In beauty of face no maiden ever equalled her. It was the radiance of an opium-dream—an airy and spirit-lifting vision more wildly divine than the phantasies which hovered about the slumbering souls of the daughters of Delos.[3] Yet

floats

[1] Joseph Glanville (1636–1680), one of the Cambridge Platonists who attempted to reconcile seventeenth-century scientific thought with Christian teachings. This quotation is apparently a fabrication by Poe to suit the purposes of the narrative.

[2] Fertility goddess.

[3] Aegean island frequently mentioned in classic myth.

her features were not of that regular mould which we have been falsely taught to worship in the classical labors of the heathen. "There is no exquisite[4] beauty," says Bacon, Lord Verulam, speaking truly of all the forms and *genera* of beauty, "without some *strangeness* in the proportion." Yet, although I saw that the features of Ligeia were not of a classic regularity—although I perceived that her loveliness was indeed "exquisite," and felt that there was much of "strangeness" pervading it, yet I have tried in vain to detect the irregularity and to trace home my own perception of "the strange." I examined the contour of the lofty and pale forehead—it was faultless— how cold indeed that word when applied to a majesty so divine!—the skin rivalling the purest ivory, the commanding extent and repose, the gentle prominence of the regions above the temples; and then the raven-black, the glossy, the luxuriant and naturally-curling tresses, setting forth the full force of the Homeric epithet, "hyacin- thine!"[5] I looked at the delicate outlines of the nose—and nowhere but in the graceful medallions of the Hebrews had I beheld a similar perfection. There were the same luxurious smoothness of surface, the same scarcely perceptible tendency to the aqui- line, the same harmoniously curved nostrils speaking the free spirit. I regarded the sweet mouth. Here was indeed the triumph of all things heavenly—the magnificent turn of the short upper lip—the soft, voluptuous slumber of the under—the dimples which sported, and the color which spoke—the teeth glancing back, with a brilliancy almost startling, every ray of the holy light which fell upon them in her serene and placid, yet most exultingly radiant of all smiles. I scrutinized the formation of the chin—and here, too, I found the gentleness of breadth, the softness and the majesty, the fullness and the spirituality, of the Greek—the contour which the god Apollo revealed but in a dream, to Cleomenes,[6] the son of the Athenian. And then I peered into the large eyes of Ligeia.

For eyes we have no models in the remotely antique. It might have been, too, that in these eyes of my beloved lay the secret to which Lord Verulam alludes. They were, I must believe, far larger than the ordinary eyes of our own race. They were even fuller than the fullest of the gazelle eyes of the tribe of the valley of Nourjahad.[7] Yet it was only at intervals—in moments of intense excitement—that this peculiarity became more than slightly noticeable in Ligeia. And at such moments was her beauty —in my heated fancy thus it appeared perhaps—the beauty of beings either above or apart from the earth—the beauty of the fabulous Houri[8] of the Turk. The hue of the orbs was the most brilliant of black, and, far over them, hung jetty lashes of great length. The brows, slightly irregular in outline, had the same tint. The "strangeness," however, which I found in the eyes, was of a nature distinct from the formation, or the color, or the brilliancy of the features, and must, after all, be referred to the *expression*. Ah, word of no meaning! behind whose vast latitude of mere sound we intrench our ignorance of so much of the spiritual. The expression of the eyes of

---

[4] In his essay "Of Beauty" (1625), Francis Bacon, baron Verulam (1561–1626), used the word "excellent"; Poe substituted "exquisite." In the next line, *genera* is the Latin word for "races" or "kinds"; here it is used broadly for "species" (plural).
[5] Homer's epic poem the *Odyssey* likens the curly hair of its hero to the hyacinth.
[6] Athenian sculptor said to have created the original version of the famous statue known as the Medici Venus, inspired by Apollo, god of the arts.
[7] Virgins who await the faithful in the Mohammedan paradise, as described in *The History of Nourjahad* (1767) by Frances Sheridan.
[8] Another reference to the beauteous women of the Moslem paradise.

eyes are the window of the soul

Ligeia! How for long hours have I pondered upon it! How have I, through the whole of a midsummer night, struggled to fathom it! What *was* it—that something more profound than the well of Democritus[9]—which lay far within the pupils of my beloved? What was it? I was possessed with a passion to discover. Those eyes! those large, those shining, those divine orbs! they became to me twin stars of Leda,[10] and I to them devoutest of astrologers.

There is no point, among the many incomprehensible anomalies of the science of mind, more thrillingly exciting than the fact—never, I believe, noticed in the schools —that, in our endeavors to recall to memory something long forgotten, we often find ourselves *upon the very verge* of remembrance, without being able, in the end, to remember. And thus how frequently, in my intense scrutiny of Ligeia's eyes, have I felt approaching the full knowledge of their expression—felt it approaching—yet not quite be mine—and so at length entirely depart! And (strange, oh strangest mystery of all!) I found, in the commonest objects of the universe, a circle of analogies to that expression. I mean to say that, subsequently to the period when Ligeia's beauty passed into my spirit, there dwelling as in a shrine, I derived, from many existences in the material world, a sentiment such as I felt always aroused within me by her large and luminous orbs. Yet not the more could I define that sentiment, or analyze, or even steadily view it. I recognized it, let me repeat, sometimes in the survey of a rapidly-growing vine—in the contemplation of a moth, a butterfly, a chrysalis, a stream of running water. I have felt it in the ocean; in the falling of a meteor. I have felt it in the glances of unusually aged people. And there are one or two stars in heaven— (one especially, a star of the sixth magnitude, double and changeable, to be found near the large star in Lyra[11]) in a telescopic scrutiny of which I have been made aware of the feeling. I have been filled with it by certain sounds from stringed instruments, and not unfrequently by passages from books. Among innumerable other instances, I well remember something in a volume of Joseph Glanvill, which (perhaps merely from its quaintness—who shall say?) never failed to inspire me with the sentiment;—"And the will therein lieth, which dieth not. Who knoweth the mysteries of the will, with its vigor? For God is but a great will pervading all things by nature of its intentness. Man doth not yield him to the angels, nor unto death utterly, save only through the weakness of his feeble will."

Length of years, and subsequent reflection, have enabled me to trace, indeed, some remote connection between this passage in the English moralist and a portion of the character of Ligeia. An *intensity* in thought, action, or speech, was possibly, in her, a result, or at least an index, of that gigantic volition which, during our long intercourse, failed to give other and more immediate evidence of its existence. Of all the women whom I have ever known, she, the outwardly calm, the ever-placid Ligeia, was the most violently a prey to the tumultuous vultures of stern passion. And of such passion I could form no estimate, save by the miraculous expansion of those eyes which at once so delighted and appalled me—by the almost magical melody, modulation, distinctness and placidity of her very low voice—and by the fierce energy

[9] Greek philosopher (fifth century B.C.) who observed that truth is to be found at the bottom of a well.

[10] In the constellation Gemini; named after the twin sons of Leda, who were born of her rape by Zeus.

[11] Constellation with the brilliant star Vega.

(rendered doubly effective by contrast with her manner of utterance) of the wild words which she habitually uttered.

I have spoken of the learning of Ligeia: it was immense—such as I have never known in woman. In the classical tongues was she deeply proficient, and as far as my own acquaintance extended in regard to the modern dialects of Europe, I have never known her at fault. Indeed upon any theme of the most admired, because simply the most abstruse of the boasted erudition of the academy, have I *ever* found Ligeia at fault? How singularly—how thrillingly, this one point in the nature of my wife has forced itself, at this late period only, upon my attention! I said her knowledge was such as I have never known in woman—but where breathes the man who has traversed, and successfully, *all* the wide areas of moral, physical, and mathematical science? I saw not then what I now clearly perceive, that the acquisitions of Ligeia were gigantic, were astounding; yet I was sufficiently aware of her infinite supremacy to resign myself, with a child-like confidence, to her guidance through the chaotic world of metaphysical investigation at which I was most busily occupied during the earlier years of our marriage. With how vast a triumph—with how vivid a delight —with how much of all that is ethereal in hope—did I *feel,* as she bent over me in studies but little sought—but less known—that delicious vista by slow degrees expanding before me, down whose long, gorgeous, and all untrodden path, I might at length pass onward to the goal of a wisdom too divinely precious not to be forbidden!

How poignant, then, must have been the grief with which, after some years, I beheld my well-grounded expectations take wings to themselves and fly away! Without Ligeia I was but as a child groping benighted. Her presence, her readings alone, rendered vividly luminous the many mysteries of the transcendentalism in which we were immersed. Wanting the radiant lustre of her eyes, letters, lambent and golden, grew duller than Saturnian lead.[12] And now those eyes shone less and less frequently upon the pages over which I pored. Ligeia grew ill. The wild eyes blazed with a too—too glorious effulgence; the pale fingers became of the transparent waxen hue of the grave, and the blue veins upon the lofty forehead swelled and sank impetuously with the tides of the most gentle emotion. I saw that she must die—and I struggled desperately in spirit with the grim Azrael.[13] And the struggles of the passionate wife were, to my astonishment, even more energetic than my own. There had been much in her stern nature to impress me with the belief that, to her, death would have come without its terrors;—but not so. Words are impotent to convey any just idea of the fierceness of resistance with which she wrestled with the Shadow. I groaned in anguish at the pitiable spectacle. I would have soothed—I would have reasoned; but, in the intensity of her wild desire for life,—for life—*but* for life— solace and reason were alike the uttermost of folly. Yet not until the last instance, amid the most convulsive writhings of her fierce spirit, was shaken the external placidity of her demeanor. Her voice grew more gentle—grew more low—yet I would not wish to dwell upon the wild meaning of the quietly uttered words. My brain reeled as I hearkened entranced, to a melody more than mortal—to assumptions and aspirations which mortality had never before known.

[12] According to astrological lore the influence of Saturn (the alchemical term for lead) turns one gloomy and listless.

[13] In both Jewish and Moslem legend, the Angel of Death.

That she loved me I should not have doubted; and I might have been easily aware that, in a bosom such as hers, love would have reigned no ordinary passion. But in death only, was I fully impressed with the strength of her affection. For long hours, detaining my hand, would she pour out before me the overflowing of a heart whose more than passionate devotion amounted to idolatry. How had I deserved to be so blessed by such confessions?—how had I deserved to be so cursed with the removal of my beloved in the hour of her making them? But upon this subject I cannot bear to dilate. Let me say only, that in Ligeia's more than womanly abandonment to a love, alas! all unmerited, all unworthily bestowed, I at length recognized the principle of her longing with so wildly earnest a desire for the life which was now fleeing so rapidly away. It is this wild longing—it is this eager vehemence of desire for life—*but* for life—that I have no power to portray—no utterance capable of expressing.

At high noon of the night in which she departed, beckoning me, peremptorily, to her side, she bade me repeat certain verses composed by herself not many days before. I obeyed her.—They were these:

Lo! 't is a gala night
    Within the lonesome latter years!
An angel throng, bewinged, bedight
    In veils, and drowned in tears,
Sit in a theatre, to see
    A play of hopes and fears,
While the orchestra breathes fitfully
    The music of the spheres.

Mimes, in the form of God on high,
    Mutter and mumble low,
And hither and thither fly—
    Mere puppets they, who come and go
At bidding of vast formless things
    That shift the scenery to and fro,
Flapping from out their Condor wings
    Invisible Wo!

That motley drama!—oh, be sure
    It shall not be forgot!
With its Phantom chased forever more,
    By a crowd that seize it not,
Through a circle that ever returneth in
    To the self-same spot,
And much of Madness and more of Sin
    And Horror the soul of the plot.

But see, amid the mimic rout,
    A crawling shape intrude!
A blood-red thing that writhes from out
    The scenic solitude!

It writhes!—it writhes!—with mortal pangs
    The mimes become its food,
And the seraphs sob at vermin fangs
    In human gore imbued.

Out—out are the lights—out all!
    And over each quivering form,
The curtain, a funeral pall,
    Comes down with the rush of a storm,
And the angels, all pallid and wan,
    Uprising, unveiling, affirm
That the play is the tragedy, "Man,"
    And its hero the Conqueror Worm.

"Oh God!" half shrieked Ligeia, leaping to her feet and extending her arms aloft with a spasmodic movement, as I made an end of these lines—"O God! O Divine Father!—shall these things be undeviatingly so?—shall this Conqueror be not once conquered? Are we not part and parcel in Thee? Who—who knoweth the mysteries of the will with its vigor? Man doth not yield him to the angels, *nor unto death utterly, save only through the weakness of his feeble will.*"

And now, as if exhausted with emotion, she suffered her white arms to fall, and returned solemnly to her bed of death. And as she breathed her last sighs, there came mingled with them a low murmur from her lips. I bent to them my ear and distinguished, again, the concluding words of the passage in Glanvill—*"Man doth not yield him to the angels, nor unto death utterly, save only through the weakness of his feeble will."*

She died;—and I, crushed into the very dust with sorrow, could no longer endure the lonely desolation of my dwelling in the dim and decaying city by the Rhine. I had no lack of what the world calls wealth. Ligeia had brought me far more, very far more than ordinarily falls to the lot of mortals. After a few months, therefore, of weary and aimless wandering, I purchased, and put in some repair, an abbey, which I shall not name, in one of the wildest and least frequented portions of fair England. The gloomy and dreary grandeur of the building, the almost savage aspect of the domain, the many melancholy and time-honored memories connected with both, had much in unison with the feelings of utter abandonment which had driven me into that remote and unsocial region of the country. Yet although the external abbey, with its verdant decay hanging about it, suffered but little alteration, I gave way, with a child-like perversity, and perchance with a faint hope of alleviating my sorrows, to a display of more than regal magnificence within.—For such follies, even in child-hood, I had imbibed a taste and now they came back to me as if in the dotage of grief. Alas, I feel how much even of incipient madness might have been discovered in the gorgeous and fantastic draperies, in the solemn carvings of Egypt, in the wild cornices and furniture, in the Bedlam[14] patterns of the carpets of tufted gold! I had

---

[14] Crazed. The London lunatic asylum Bethlehem Hospital was known as "Bedlam," a contraction of the name.

become a bounden slave in the trammels of opium, and my labors and my orders had taken a coloring from my dreams. But these absurdities I must not pause to detail. Let me speak only of that one chamber, ever accursed, whither in a moment of mental alienation, I led from the altar as my bride—as the successor of the unforgotten Ligeia —the fair-haired and blue-eyed Lady Rowena Trevanion, of Tremaine.

There is no individual portion of the architecture and decoration of that bridal chamber which is not now visibly before me. Where were the souls of the haughty family of the bride, when, through thirst of gold, they permitted to pass the threshold of an apartment *so* bedecked, a maiden and a daughter so beloved? I have said that I minutely remember the details of the chamber—yet I am sadly forgetful on topics of deep moment—and here there was no system, no keeping, in the fantastic display, to take hold upon the memory. The room lay in a high turret of the castellated abbey, was pentagonal in shape, and of capacious size. Occupying the whole southern face of the pentagon was the sole window—an immense sheet of unbroken glass from Venice—a single pane, and tinted of a leaden hue, so that the rays of either the sun or moon, passing through it, fell with a ghastly lustre on the objects within. Over the upper portion of this huge window, extended the trellice-work of an aged vine, which clambered up the massy walls of the turret. The ceiling, of gloomy-looking oak, was excessively lofty, vaulted, and elaborately fretted with the wildest and most grotesque specimens of a semi-Gothic, semi-Druidical[15] device. From out the most central recess of this melancholy vaulting, depended, by a single chain of gold with long links, a huge censer of the same metal, Saracenic[16] in pattern, and with many perforations so contrived that there writhed in and out of them, as if endued with a serpent vitality, a continual succession of parti-colored fires.

Some few ottomans and golden candelabra, of Eastern figure, were in various stations about—and there was the couch, too—the bridal couch—of an Indian model, and low, and sculptured of solid ebony, with a pall-like canopy above. In each of the angles of the chamber stood on end a gigantic sarcophagus of black granite, from the tombs of the kings over against Luxor,[17] with their aged lids full of immemorial sculpture. But in the draping of the apartment lay, alas! the chief phantasy of all. The lofty walls, gigantic in height—even unproportionably so—were hung from summit to foot, in vast folds, with a heavy and massive-looking tapestry—tapestry of a material which was found alike as a carpet on the floor, as a covering for the ottomans and the ebony bed, as a canopy for the bed, and as the gorgeous volutes of the curtains which partially shaded the window. The material was the richest cloth of gold. It was spotted all over, at irregular intervals, with arabesque figures, about a foot in diameter, and wrought upon the cloth in patterns of the most jetty black. But these figures partook of the true character of the arabesque only when regarded from a single point of view. By a contrivance now common, and indeed traceable to a very remote period of antiquity, they were made changeable in aspect. To one entering the room, they bore the appearance of simple monstrosities; but upon a farther advance, this appearance gradually departed; and step by step, as the visiter moved his station in the chamber, he saw himself surrounded by an endless succession of the ghastly forms

[15] In the style of the Druids, the priestly class of Celtic Britain.   [17] City in ancient Egypt.

[16] Arabic.

which belong to the superstition of the Norman,[18] or arise in the guilty slumbers of the monk. The phantasmagoric effect was vastly heightened by the artificial introduction of a strong continual current of wind behind the draperies—giving a hideous and uneasy animation to the whole.

In halls such as these—in a bridal chamber such as this—I passed, with the Lady of Tremaine, the unhallowed hours of the first month of our marriage—passed them with but little disquietude. That my wife dreaded the fierce moodiness of my temper —that she shunned me and loved me but little—I could not help perceiving; but it gave me rather pleasure than otherwise. I loathed her with a hatred belonging more to demon than to man. My memory flew back, (oh, with what intensity of regret!) to Ligeia, the beloved, the august, the beautiful, the entombed. I revelled in recollections of her purity, of her wisdom, of her lofty, her ethereal nature, of her passionate, her idolatrous love. Now, then, did my spirit fully and freely burn with more than all the fires of her own. In the excitement of my opium dreams (for I was habitually fettered in the shackles of the drug) I would call aloud upon her name, during the silence of the night, or among the sheltered recesses of the glens by day, as if, through the wild eagerness, the solemn passion, the consuming ardor of my longing for the departed, I could restore her to the pathway she had abandoned—ah, *could* it be forever?—upon the earth.

About the commencement of the second month of the marriage, the Lady Rowena was attacked with sudden illness, from which her recovery was slow. The fever which consumed her rendered her nights uneasy; and in her perturbed state of half-slumber, she spoke of sounds, and of motions, in and about the chamber of the turret, which I concluded had no origin save in the distemper of her fancy, or perhaps in the phantasmagoric influences of the chamber itself. She became at length convalescent —finally well. Yet but a brief period elapsed, ere a second more violent disorder again threw her upon a bed of suffering; and from this attack her frame, at all times feeble, never altogether recovered. Her illnesses were, after this epoch, of alarming character, and of more alarming recurrence, defying alike the knowledge and the great exertions of her physicians. With the increase of the chronic disease which had thus, apparently, taken too sure hold upon her constitution to be eradicated by human means, I could not fail to observe a similar increase in the nervous irritation of her temperament, and in her excitability by trivial causes of fear. She spoke again, and now more frequently and pertinaciously, of the sounds—of the slight sounds—and of the unusual motions among the tapestries, to which she had formerly alluded.

One night, near the closing in of September, she pressed this distressing subject with more than usual emphasis upon my attention. She had just awakened from an unquiet slumber, and I had been watching, with feelings half of anxiety, half of vague terror, the workings of her emaciated countenance. I sat by the side of her ebony bed, upon one of the ottomans of India. She partly arose, and spoke, in an earnest low whisper, of sounds which she *then* heard, but which I could not hear—of motions which she *then* saw, but which I could not perceive. The wind was rushing hurriedly behind the tapestries, and I wished to show her (what, let me confess it, I could not *all* believe) that those almost inarticulate breathings, and those very gentle variations of the figures

[18] The Vikings who came from the North in conquest of that area of the European continent later known as French Normandy. Their crafts are noted for their intricate designs.

upon the wall, were but the natural effects of that customary rushing of the wind. But a deadly pallor, overspreading her face, had proved to me that my exertions to reassure her would be fruitless. She appeared to be fainting, and no attendants were within call. I remembered where was deposited a decanter of light wine which had been ordered by her physicians, and hastened across the chamber to procure it. But, as I stepped beneath the light of the censer, two circumstances of a startling nature attracted my attention. I had felt that some palpable although invisible object had passed lightly by my person; and I saw that there lay upon the golden carpet, in the very middle of the rich lustre thrown from the censer, a shadow—a faint, indefinite shadow of angelic aspect—such as might be fancied for the shadow of a shade. But I was wild with the excitement of an immoderate dose of opium, and heeded these things but little, nor spoke of them to Rowena. Having found the wine, I recrossed the chamber, and poured out a goblet-ful, which I held to the lips of the fainting lady. She had now partially recovered, however, and took the vessel herself, while I sank upon an ottoman near me, with my eyes fastened upon her person. It was then that I became distinctly aware of a gentle foot-fall upon the carpet, and near the couch; and in a second thereafter, as Rowena was in the act of raising the wine to her lips, I saw, or may have dreamed that I saw, fall within the goblet, as if from some invisible spring in the atmosphere of the room, three or four large drops of a brilliant and ruby colored fluid. If this I saw—not so Rowena. She swallowed the wine unhesitatingly, and I forbore to speak to her of a circumstance which must, after all, I considered, have been but the suggestion of a vivid imagination, rendered morbidly active by the terror of the lady, by the opium, and by the hour.

Yet I cannot conceal it from my own perception that, immediately subsequent to the fall of the ruby-drops, a rapid change for the worse took place in the disorder of my wife; so that, on the third subsequent night, the hands of her menials prepared her for the tomb, and on the fourth, I sat alone, with her shrouded body, in that fantastic chamber which had received her as my bride.—Wild visions, opium-engendered, flitted, shadowlike, before me. I gazed with unquiet eye upon the sarcophagi in the angles of the room, upon the varying figures of the drapery, and upon the writhing of the parti-colored fires in the censer overhead. My eyes then fell, as I called to mind the circumstances of a former night, to the spot beneath the glare of the censer where I had seen the faint traces of the shadow. It was there, however, no longer; and breathing with greater freedom, I turned my glances to the pallid and rigid figure upon the bed. Then rushed upon me a thousand memories of Ligeia—and then came back upon my heart, with the turbulent violence of a flood, the whole of that unutterable wo with which I had regarded *her* thus enshrouded. The night waned; and still, with a bosom full of bitter thoughts of the one only and supremely beloved, I remained gazing upon the body of Rowena.

It might have been midnight, or perhaps earlier, or later, for I had taken no note of time, when a sob, low, gentle, but very distinct, startled me from my revery.— I *felt* that it came from the bed of ebony—the bed of death. I listened in an agony of superstitious terror—but there was no repetition of the sound. I strained my vision to detect any motion in the corpse—but there was not the slightest perceptible. Yet I could not have been deceived. I *had* heard the noise, however faint, and my soul was awakened within me. I resolutely and perseveringly kept my attention riveted upon the body. Many minutes elapsed before any circumstance occurred tending to throw light upon the mystery. At length it became evident that a slight, a very feeble, and barely noticeable tinge of color had flushed up within the cheeks, and along the sunken small veins of the eyelids. Through a species of unutterable horror and awe, for which the language of mortality has no sufficiently energetic expression, I felt my heart cease to beat, my limbs grow rigid where I sat. Yet a sense of duty finally operated to restore my self-possession. I could no longer doubt that we had been precipitate in our preparations—that Rowena still lived. It was necessary that some immediate exertion be made; yet the turret was altogether apart from the portion of the abbey tenanted by the servants—there were none within call—I had no means of summoning them to my aid without leaving the room for many minutes—and this I could not venture to do. I therefore struggled alone in my endeavors to call back the spirit still hovering. In a short period it was certain, however, that a relapse had taken place; the color disappeared from both eyelid and cheek, leaving a wanness even more than that of marble; the lips became doubly shrivelled and pinched up in the ghastly expression of death; a repulsive clamminess and coldness overspread rapidly the surface of the body; and all the usual rigorous stiffness immediately supervened. I fell back with a shudder upon the couch from which I had been so startlingly aroused, and again gave myself up to passionate waking visions of Ligeia.

An hour thus elapsed when (could it be possible?) I was a second time aware of some vague sound issuing from the region of the bed. I listened—in extremity of horror. The sound came again—it was a sigh. Rushing to the corpse, I saw—distinctly saw—a tremor upon the lips. In a minute afterward they relaxed, disclosing a bright line of the pearly teeth. Amazement now struggled in my bosom with the profound awe which had hitherto reigned there alone. I felt that my vision grew dim, that my reason wandered; and it was only by a violent effort that I at length succeeded in nerving myself to the task which duty thus once more had pointed out. There was now a partial glow upon the forehead and upon the cheek and throat; a perceptible warmth pervaded the whole frame; there was even a slight pulsation at the heart. The lady *lived;* and with redoubled ardor I betook myself to the task of restoration. I chafed and bathed the temples and the hands, and used every exertion which experience, and no little medical reading, could suggest. But in vain. Suddenly, the color fled, the pulsation ceased, the lips resumed the expression of the dead, and, in an instant afterward, the whole body took upon itself the icy chilliness, the livid hue, the intense rigidity, the sunken outline, and all the loathsome peculiarities of that which has been, for many days, a tenant of the tomb.

And again I sunk into visions of Ligeia—and again, (what marvel that I shudder while I write?) *again* there reached my ears a low sob from the region of the ebony bed. But why shall I minutely detail the unspeakable horrors of that night? Why shall I pause to relate how, time after time, until near the period of the gray dawn, this hideous drama of revivification was repeated; how each terrific relapse was only into a sterner and apparently more irredeemable death; how each agony wore the aspect of a struggle with some invisible foe; and how each struggle was succeeded by I know not what of wild change in the personal appearance of the corpse? Let me hurry to a conclusion.

The greater part of the fearful night had worn away, and she who had been dead, once again stirred—and now more vigorously than hitherto, although arousing from a dissolution more appalling in its utter hopelessness than any. I had long ceased to struggle or to move, and remained sitting rigidly upon the ottoman, a helpless prey to a whirl of violent emotions, of which extreme awe was perhaps the least terrible, the least consuming. The corpse, I repeat, stirred, and now more vigorously than before. The hues of life flushed up with unwonted energy into the countenance—the limbs relaxed—and, save that the eyelids were yet pressed heavily together, and that the bandages and draperies of the grave still imparted their charnel character to the figure, I might have dreamed that Rowena had indeed shaken off, utterly, the fetters of Death. But if this idea was not, even then, altogether adopted, I could at least doubt no longer, when, arising from the bed, tottering, with feeble steps, with closed eyes, and with the manner of one bewildered in a dream, the thing that was enshrouded advanced boldly and palpably into the middle of the apartment.

I trembled not—I stirred not—for a crowd of unutterable fancies connected with the air, the stature, the demeanor of the figure, rushing hurriedly through my brain, had paralyzed—had chilled me into stone. I stirred not—but gazed upon the apparition. There was a mad disorder in my thoughts—a tumult unappeasable. Could it, indeed, be the *living* Rowena who confronted me? Could it indeed by Rowena *at all*—the fair-haired, the blue-eyed Lady Rowena Trevanion of Tremaine? Why, *why* should I doubt it? The bandage lay heavily about the mouth—but then might it not be the mouth of the breathing Lady of Tremaine? And the cheeks—there were the roses as in her noon of life—yes, these might indeed be the fair cheeks of the living Lady of Tremaine. And the chin, with its dimples, as in health, might it not be hers? —but *had she then grown taller since her malady?* What inexpressible madness seized me with that thought? One bound, and I had reached her feet! Shrinking from my touch, she let fall from her head, unloosened, the ghastly cerements which had confined it, and there streamed forth, into the rushing atmosphere of the chamber, huge masses of long and dishevelled hair; *it was blacker than the raven wings of the midnight!* And now slowly opened *the eyes* of the figure which stood before me. "Here, then, at least," I shrieked aloud, "can I never—can I never be mistaken—these are the full, and the black, and the wild eyes—of my lost love—of the lady—of the LADY LIGEIA."

1838

The Conversation of Eiros and Charmion

I will bring fire to thee.
Euripides, Androm.[1]

Eiros: Why do you call me Eiros?
Charmion: So henceforward will you always be called. You must forget, too, *my* earthly name, and speak to me as Charmion.

---

[1] Euripides' drama *Andromache* (427 B.C.).

Eiros: This is indeed no dream!

Charmion: Dreams are with us no more;—but of these mysteries anon. I rejoice
to see you looking life-like and rational. The film of the shadow has already
passed from off your eyes. Be of heart, and fear nothing. Your allotted days
of stupor have expired; and, to-morrow, I will myself induct you into the full
joys and wonders of your novel existence.

Eiros: True—I feel no stupor—none at all. The wild sickness and the terrible
darkness have left me, and I hear no longer that mad, rushing, horrible sound,
like the "voice of many waters." Yet my senses are bewildered, Charmion,
with the keenness of their perception of *the new.*

Charmion: A few days will remove all this;—but I fully understand you, and feel
for you. It is now ten earthly years since I underwent what you undergo—yet
the remembrance of it hangs by me still. You have now suffered all of pain,
however, which you will suffer in Aidenn.

Eiros: In Aidenn?

Charmion: In Aidenn.

Eiros: Oh God!—pity me, Charmion!—I am overburthened with the majesty of
all things—of the unknown now known—of the speculative Future merged in
the august and certain Present.

Charmion: Grapple not now with such thoughts. To-morrow we will speak of
this. Your mind wavers, and its agitation will find relief in the exercise of
simple memories. Look not around, nor forward—but back. I am burning
with anxiety to hear the details of that stupendous event which threw you
among us. Tell me of it. Let us converse of familiar things, in the old familiar
language of the world which has so fearfully perished.

Eiros: Most fearfully, fearfully!—this is indeed no dream.

Charmion: Dreams are no more. Was I much mourned, my Eiros?

Eiros: Mourned, Charmion?—oh deeply. To that last hour of all, there hung a
cloud of intense gloom and devout sorrow over your household.

Charmion: And that last hour—speak of it. Remember that, beyond the naked
fact of the catastrophe itself, I know nothing. When, coming out from among
mankind, I passed into Night through the Grave—at that period, if I
remember aright, the calamity which overwhelmed you was utterly
unanticipated. But, indeed, I knew little of the speculative philosophy of the
day.

Eiros: The individual calamity was, as you say, entirely unanticipated; but
analogous misfortunes had been long a subject of discussion with astronomers.
I need scarce tell you, my friend, that, even when you left us, men had agreed
to understand those passages in the most holy writings which speak of the final
destruction of all things by fire, as having reference to the orb of the earth
alone. But in regard to the immediate agency of the ruin, speculation had been
at fault from that epoch in astronomical knowledge in which the comets were
divested of the terrors of flame. The very moderate density of these bodies had
been well established. They had been observed to pass among the satellites of
Jupiter, without bringing about any sensible alteration either in the masses or
in the orbits of these secondary planets. We had long regarded the wanderers
as vapory creations of inconceivable tenuity, and as altogether incapable of
doing injury to our substantial globe, even in the event of contact. But

contact was not in any degree dreaded; for the elements of all the comets were accurately known. That among *them* we should look for the agency of the threatened fiery destruction had been for many years considered an inadmissible idea. But wonders and wild fancies had been, of late days, strangely rife among mankind; and, although it was only with a few of the ignorant that actual apprehension prevailed, upon the announcement by astronomers of a *new* comet, yet this announcement was generally received with I know not what of agitation and mistrust.

The elements of the strange orb were immediately calculated, and it was at once conceded by all observers, that its path, at perihelion, would bring it into very close proximity with the earth. There were two or three astronomers, of secondary note, who resolutely maintained that a contact was inevitable. I cannot very well express to you the effect of this intelligence upon the people. For a few short days they would not believe an assertion which their intellect, so long employed among worldly considerations, could not in any manner grasp. But the truth of a vitally important fact soon makes its way into the understanding of even the most stolid. Finally, all men saw that astronomical knowledge lied not, and they awaited the comet. Its approach was not, at first, seemingly rapid; nor was its appearance of very unusual character. It was of a dull red, and had little perceptible train. For seven or eight days we saw no material increase in its apparent diameter, and but a partial alteration in its color. Meantime, the ordinary affairs of men were discarded, and all interests absorbed in a growing discussion, instituted by the philosophic, in respect to the cometary nature. Even the grossly ignorant aroused their sluggish capacities to such considerations. The learned *now* gave their intellect—their soul—to no such points as the allaying of fear, or to the sustenance of loved theory. They sought—they panted for right views. They groaned for perfected knowledge. *Truth* arose in the purity of her strength and exceeding majesty, and the wise bowed down and adored.

That material injury to our globe or to its inhabitants would result from the apprehended contact, was an opinion which hourly lost ground among the wise; and the wise were now freely permitted to rule the reason and the fancy of the crowd. It was demonstrated, that the density of the comet's *nucleus* was far less than that of our rarest gas; and the harmless passage of a similar visitor among the satellites of Jupiter was a point strongly insisted upon, and which served greatly to allay terror. Theologists, with an earnestness fear-enkindled, dwelt upon the biblical prophecies, and expounded them to the people with a directness and simplicity of which no previous instance had been known. That the final destruction of the earth must be brought about by the agency of fire, was urged with a spirit that enforced everywhere conviction; and that the comets were of no fiery nature (as all men now knew) was a truth which relieved all, in a great measure, from the apprehension of the great calamity foretold. It is noticeable that the popular prejudices and vulgar errors in regard to pestilence and wars —errors which were wont to prevail upon every appearance of a comet—were now altogether unknown. As if by some sudden convulsive exertion, reason had at once hurled superstition from her throne. The feeblest intellect had derived vigor from excessive interest.

What minor evils might arise from the contact were points of elaborate question. The learned spoke of slight geological disturbances, of probable alterations in climate, and consequently in vegetation; of possible magnetic and electric influences. Many held that no visible or perceptible effect would in any manner be produced. While such discussions were going on, their subject gradually approached, growing larger in apparent diameter, and of a more brilliant lustre. Mankind grew paler as it came. All human operations were suspended.

There was an epoch in the course of the general sentiment when the comet had attained, at length, a size surpassing that of any previously recorded visitation. The people now, dismissing any lingering hope that the astronomers were wrong, experienced all the certainty of evil. The chimerical aspect of their terror was gone. The hearts of the stoutest of our race beat violently within their bosoms. A very few days sufficed, however, to merge even such feelings in sentiments more unendurable. We could no longer apply to the strange orb any *accustomed* thoughts. Its *historical* attributes had disappeared. It oppressed us with a hideous *novelty* of emotion. We saw it not as an astronomical phenomenon in the heavens, but as an incubus upon our hearts, and a shadow upon our brains. It had taken, with inconceivable rapidity, the character of a gigantic mantle of rare flame, extending from horizon to horizon.

Yet a day, and men breathed with greater freedom. It was clear that we were already within the influence of the comet; yet we lived. We even felt an unusual elasticity of frame and vivacity of mind. The exceeding tenuity of the object of our dread was apparent; for all heavenly objects were plainly visible through it. Meantime, our vegetation had perceptibly altered; and we gained faith, from this predicted circumstance, in the foresight of the wise. A wild luxuriance of foliage, utterly unknown before, burst out upon every vegetable thing.

Yet another day—and the evil was not altogether upon us. It was now evident that its nucleus would first reach us. A wild change had come over all men; and the first sense of *pain* was the wild signal for general lamentation and horror. This first sense of pain lay in a rigorous constriction of the breast and lungs, and an insufferable dryness of the skin. It could not be denied that our atmosphere was radically affected; the conformation of this atmosphere and the possible modifications to which it might be subjected, were now the topics of discussion. The result of investigation sent an electric thrill of the intensest terror through the universal heart of man.

It had been long known that the air which encircled us was a compound of oxygen and nitrogen gases, in the proportion of twenty-one measures of oxygen, and seventy-nine of nitrogen, in every one hundred of the atmosphere. Oxygen, which was the principle of combustion, and the vehicle of heat, was absolutely necessary to the support of animal life, and was the most powerful and energetic agent in nature. Nitrogen, on the contrary, was incapable of supporting either animal life or flame. An unnatural excess of oxygen would result, it had been ascertained, in just such an elevation of the animal spirits as we had latterly experienced. It was the pursuit, the extension of the idea, which had engendered awe. What would be the result of a total extraction of the nitrogen? A combustion irresistible, all-devouring, omni-prevalent, immediate;—the entire fulfilment, in all their minute and terrible details, of the fiery and horror-inspiring denunciations of the prophecies of the Holy Book.

Why need I paint, Charmion, the now disenchained frenzy of mankind? That tenuity in the comet which had previously inspired us with hope, was now the source of the bitterness of despair. In its impalpable gaseous character we clearly perceived the consummation of Fate. Meantime a day again passed —bearing away with it the last shadow of Hope. We gasped in the rapid modification of the air. The red blood bounded tumultuously through its strict channels. A furious delirium possessed all men; and, with arms rigidly outstretched towards the threatening heavens, they trembled and shrieked aloud. But the nucleus of the destroyer was now upon us;—even here in Aidenn, I shudder while I speak. Let me be brief—brief as the ruin that overwhelmed. For a moment there was a wild lurid light alone, visiting and penetrating all things. Then let us bow down, Charmion, before the excessive majesty of the great God!—then, there came a shouting and pervading sound, as if from the mouth itself of HIM; while the whole incumbent mass of ether in which we existed, burst at once into a species of intense flame, for whose surpassing brilliancy and all-fervid heat even the angels in the high Heaven of pure knowledge have no name. Thus ended all.

1839

The Fall of the House of Usher

Son cœur est un luth suspendu;
Sitôt qu'on le touche il résonne.
De Béranger[1]

During the whole of a dull, dark, and soundless day in the autumn of the year, when the clouds hung oppressively low in the heavens, I had been passing alone, on horseback, through a singularly dreary tract of country; and at length found myself, as the shades of the evening drew on, within view of the melancholy House of Usher. I know not how it was—but, with the first glimpse of the building, a sense of insufferable gloom pervaded my spirit. I say insufferable; for the feeling was un-relieved by any of that half-pleasurable, because poetic, sentiment, with which the mind usually receives even the sternest natural images of the desolate or terrible. I looked upon the scene before me—upon the mere house, and the simple landscape features of the domain—upon the bleak walls—upon the vacant eye-like windows —upon a few rank sedges—and upon a few white trunks of decayed trees—with an

---

[1] From "Le Refus" (1831) by the French poet Pierre-Jean de Béranger (1780–1857). The lines, which Poe partly altered to read "his heart" rather than "my heart," translate as "His heart is a lute, tightly strung; / The instant one touches it, it resounds."

utter depression of soul which I can compare to no earthly sensation more properly than to the after-dream of the reveller upon opium—the bitter lapse into every-day life—the hideous dropping off of the veil. There was an iciness, a sinking, a sickening of the heart—an unredeemed dreariness of thought which no goading of the imagination could torture into aught of the sublime. What was it—I paused to think—what was it that so unnerved me in the contemplation of the House of Usher? It was a mystery all insoluble; nor could I grapple with the shadowy fancies that crowded upon me as I pondered. I was forced to fall back upon the unsatisfactory conclusion, that while, beyond doubt, there *are* combinations of very simple natural objects which have the power of thus affecting us, still the analysis of this power lies among considerations beyond our depth. It was possible, I reflected, that a mere different arrangement of the particulars of the scene, of the details of the picture, would be sufficient to modify, or perhaps to annihilate its capacity for sorrowful impression; and, acting upon this idea, I reined my horse to the precipitous brink of a black and lurid tarn[2] that lay in unruffled lustre by the dwelling, and gazed down—but with a shudder even more thrilling than before—upon the remodelled and inverted images of the gray sedge, and the ghastly tree-stems, and the vacant and eye-like windows.

Nevertheless, in this mansion of gloom I now proposed to myself a sojourn of some weeks. Its proprietor, Roderick Usher, had been one of my boon companions in boyhood; but many years had elapsed since our last meeting. A letter, however, had lately reached me in a distant part of the country—a letter from him—which, in its wildly importunate nature, had admitted of no other than a personal reply. The MS. gave evidence of nervous agitation. The writer spoke of acute bodily illness—of a mental disorder which oppressed him—and of an earnest desire to see me, as his best, and indeed his only personal friend, with a view of attempting, by the cheerfulness of my society, some alleviation of his malady. It was the manner in which all this, and much more, was said—it was the apparent *heart* that went with his request— which allowed me no room for hesitation; and I accordingly obeyed forthwith what I still considered a very singular summons.

Although, as boys, we had been even intimate associates, yet I really knew little of my friend. His reserve had been always excessive and habitual. I was aware, however, that his very ancient family had been noted, time out of mind, for a peculiar sensibility of temperament, displaying itself, through long ages, in many works of exalted art, and manifested, of late, in repeated deeds of munificent yet unobtrusive charity, as well as in a passionate devotion to the intricacies, perhaps even more than to the orthodox and easily recognisable beauties, of musical science. I had learned, too, the very remarkable fact, that the stem of the Usher race, all time-honoured as it was, had put forth, at no period, any enduring branch; in other words, that the entire family lay in the direct line of descent, and had always, with very trifling and very temporary variation, so lain. It was this deficiency, I considered, while running over in thought the perfect keeping of the character of the premises with the accredited character of the people, and while speculating upon the possible influence which the one, in the long lapse of centuries, might have exercised upon the other—it was this deficiency, perhaps, of collateral issue, and the consequent undeviating transmission, from sire to son, of the patrimony with the name, which had, at length, so identified the two as

[2] Small mountain lake.

to merge the original title of the estate in the quaint and equivocal appellation of the "House of Usher"—an appellation which seemed to include, in the minds of the peasantry who used it, both the family and the family mansion.

I have said that the sole effect of my somewhat childish experiment—that of looking down within the tarn—had been to deepen the first singular impression. There can be no doubt that the consciousness of the rapid increase of my superstition —for why should I not so term it?—served mainly to accelerate the increase itself. Such, I have long known, is the paradoxical law of all sentiments having terror as a basis. And it might have been for this reason only, that, when I again uplifted my eyes to the house itself, from its image in the pool, there grew in my mind a strange fancy—a fancy so ridiculous, indeed, that I but mention it to show the vivid force of the sensations which oppressed me. I had so worked upon my imagination as really to believe that about the whole mansion and domain there hung an atmosphere peculiar to themselves and their immediate vicinity—an atmosphere which had no affinity with the air of heaven, but which had reeked up from the decayed trees, and the gray wall, and the silent tarn—a pestilent and mystic vapour, dull, sluggish, faintly discernible, and leaden-hued.

Shaking off from my spirit what *must* have been a dream, I scanned more narrowly the real aspect of the building. Its principal feature seemed to be that of an excessive antiquity. The discoloration of ages had been great. Minute fungi overspread the whole exterior, hanging in a fine tangled web-work from the eaves. Yet all this was apart from any extraordinary dilapidation. No portion of the masonry had fallen; and there appeared to be a wild inconsistency between its still perfect adaptation of parts, and the crumbling condition of the individual stones. In this there was much that reminded me of the specious totality of old wood-work which has rotted for long years in some neglected vault, with no disturbance from the breath of the external air. Beyond this indication of extensive decay, however, the fabric gave little token of instability. Perhaps the eye of a scrutinising observer might have discovered a barely perceptible fissure, which, extending from the roof of the building in front, made its way down the wall in a zigzag direction, until it became lost in the sullen waters of the tarn.

Noticing these things, I rode over a short causeway to the house. A servant in waiting took my horse, and I entered the Gothic archway of the hall. A valet, of stealthy step, thence conducted me, in silence, through many dark and intricate passages in my progress to the *studio* of his master. Much that I encountered on the way contributed, I know not how, to heighten the vague sentiments of which I have already spoken. While the objects around me—while the carvings of the ceilings, the sombre tapestries of the walls, the ebon blackness of the floors, and the phantasmagoric armorial trophies which rattled as I strode, were but matters to which, or to such as which, I had been accustomed from my infancy—while I hesitated not to acknowledge how familiar was all this—I still wondered to find how unfamiliar were the fancies which ordinary images were stirring up. On one of the staircases, I met the physician of the family. His countenance, I thought, wore a mingled expression of low cunning and perplexity. He accosted me with trepidation and passed on. The valet now threw open a door and ushered me into the presence of his master.

The room in which I found myself was very large and lofty. The windows were long, narrow, and pointed, and at so vast a distance from the black oaken floor as to be altogether inaccessible from within. Feeble gleams of encrimsoned light made their way through the trellised panes, and served to render sufficiently distinct the more prominent objects around; the eye, however, struggled in vain to reach the remoter angles of the chamber, or the recesses of the vaulted and fretted ceiling. Dark draperies hung upon the walls. The general furniture was profuse, comfortless, antique, and tattered. Many books and musical instruments lay scattered about, but failed to give any vitality to the scene. I felt that I breathed an atmosphere of sorrow. An air of stern, deep, and irredeemable gloom hung over and pervaded all.

Upon my entrance, Usher arose from a sofa on which he had been lying at full length, and greeted me with a vivacious warmth which had much in it, I at first thought, of an overdone cordiality—of the constrained effort of the *ennuyé*[3] man of the world. A glance, however, at his countenance, convinced me of his perfect sincerity. We sat down; and for some moments, while he spoke not, I gazed upon him with a feeling half of pity, half of awe. Surely, man had never before so terribly altered, in so brief a period, as had Roderick Usher! It was with difficulty that I could bring myself to admit the identity of the wan being before me with the companion of my early boyhood. Yet the character of his face had been at all times remarkable. A cadaverousness of complexion; an eye large, liquid, and luminous beyond comparison; lips somewhat thin and very pallid, but of a surpassingly beautiful curve; a nose of a delicate Hebrew model, but with a breadth of nostril unusual in similar formations; a finely moulded chin, speaking, in its want of prominence, of a want of moral energy; hair of a more than web-like softness and tenuity; these features, with an inordinate expansion above the regions of the temple, made up altogether a countenance not easily to be forgotten. And now in the mere exaggeration of the prevailing character of these features, and of the expression they were wont to convey, lay so much of change that I doubted to whom I spoke. The now ghastly pallor of the skin, and the now miraculous lustre of the eye, above all things startled and even awed me. The silken hair, too, had been suffered to grow all unheeded, and as, in its wild gossamer texture, it floated rather than fell about the face, I could not, even with effort, connect its Arabesque[4] expression with any idea of simple humanity.

In the manner of my friend I was at once struck with an incoherence—an inconsistency; and I soon found this to arise from a series of feeble and futile struggles to overcome an habitual trepidancy—an excessive nervous agitation. For something of this nature I had indeed been prepared, no less by his letter, than by reminiscences of certain boyish traits, and by conclusions deduced from his peculiar physical conformation and temperament. His action was alternately vivacious and sullen. His voice varied rapidly from a tremulous indecision (when the animal spirits seemed utterly in abeyance) to that species of energetic concision—that abrupt, weighty, unhurried, and hollow-sounding enunciation—that leaden, self-balanced and perfectly modulated guttural utterance, which may be observed in the lost drunkard, or the irreclaimable eater of opium, during the periods of his most intense excitement.

It was thus that he spoke of the object of my visit, of his earnest desire to see me, and of the solace he expected me to afford him. He entered, at some length, into what he conceived to be the nature of his malady. It was, he said, a constitutional and a family evil, and one for which he despaired to find a remedy—a mere nervous

---

[3] French: "bored." [4] Fantastic, complex.

affection, he immediately added, which would undoubtedly soon pass off. It displayed itself in a host of unnatural sensations. Some of these, as he detailed them, interested and bewildered me; although, perhaps, the terms and the general manner of the narration had their weight. He suffered much from a morbid acuteness of the senses; the most insipid food was alone endurable; he could wear only garments of certain texture; the odours of all flowers were oppressive; his eyes were tortured by even a faint light; and there were but peculiar sounds, and these from stringed instruments, which did not inspire him with horror.

To an anomalous species of terror I found him a bounden slave. "I shall perish," said he, "I *must* perish in this deplorable folly. Thus, thus, and not otherwise, shall I be lost. I dread the events of the future, not in themselves, but in their results. I shudder at the thought of any, even the most trivial, incident, which may operate upon this intolerable agitation of soul. I have, indeed, no abhorrence of danger, except in its absolute effect—in terror. In this unnerved—in this pitiable condition—I feel that the period will sooner or later arrive when I must abandon life and reason together, in some struggle with the grim phantasm, FEAR."

I learned, moreover, at intervals, and through broken and equivocal hints, another singular feature of his mental condition. He was enchained by certain superstitious impressions in regard to the dwelling which he tenanted, and whence, for many years, he had never ventured forth—in regard to an influence whose suppositious force was conveyed in terms too shadowy here to be re-stated—an influence which some peculiarities in the mere form and substance of his family mansion, had, by dint of long sufferance, he said, obtained over his spirit—an effect which the *physique* of the gray walls and turrets, and of the dim tarn into which they all looked down, had, at length, brought about upon the *morale* of his existence.

He admitted, however, although with hesitation, that much of the peculiar gloom which thus afflicted him could be traced to a more natural and far more palpable origin—to the severe and long-continued illness—indeed to the evidently approaching dissolution—of a tenderly beloved sister—his sole companion for long years—his last and only relative on earth. "Her decease," he said, with a bitterness which I can never forget, "would leave him (him the hopeless and the frail) the last of the ancient race of the Ushers." While he spoke, the lady Madeline (for so was she called) passed slowly through a remote portion of the apartment, and, without having noticed my presence, disappeared. I regarded her with an utter astonishment not unmingled with dread—and yet I found it impossible to account for such feelings. A sensation of stupor oppressed me, as my eyes followed her retreating steps. When a door, at length, closed upon her, my glance sought instinctively and eagerly the countenance of the brother—but he had buried his face in his hands, and I could only perceive that a far more than ordinary wanness had overspread the emaciated fingers through which trickled many passionate tears.

The disease of the lady Madeline had long baffled the skill of her physicians. A settled apathy, a gradual wasting away of the person, and frequent although transient affections of a partially cataleptical character, were the unusual diagnosis. Hitherto she had steadily borne up against the pressure of her malady, and had not betaken herself finally to bed; but, on the closing in of the evening of my arrival at the house, she succumbed (as her brother told me at night with inexpressible agitation) to the prostrating power of the destroyer; and I learned that the glimpse I had obtained of her person would thus probably be the last I should obtain—that the lady, at least while living, would be seen by me no more.

For several days ensuing, her name was unmentioned by either Usher or myself: and during this period I was busied in earnest endeavours to alleviate the melancholy of my friend. We painted and read together; or I listened, as if in a dream, to the wild improvisations of his speaking guitar. And thus, as a closer and still closer intimacy admitted me more unreservedly into the recesses of his spirit, the more bitterly did I perceive the futility of all attempt at cheering a mind from which darkness, as if an inherent positive quality, poured forth upon all objects of the moral and physical universe, in one unceasing radiation of gloom.

I shall ever bear about me a memory of the many solemn hours I thus spent alone with the master of the House of Usher. Yet I should fail in any attempt to convey an idea of the exact character of the studies, or of the occupations, in which he involved me, or led me the way. An excited and highly distempered ideality threw a sulphureous lustre over all. His long improvised dirges will ring forever in my ears. Among other things, I hold painfully in mind a certain singular perversion and amplification of the wild air of the last waltz of Von Weber.[5] From the paintings over which his elaborate fancy brooded, and which grew, touch by touch, into vaguenesses at which I shuddered the more thrillingly, because I shuddered knowing not why;—from these paintings (vivid as their images now are before me) I would in vain endeavour to educe more than a small portion which should lie within the compass of merely written words. By the utter simplicity, by the nakedness of his designs, he arrested and overawed attention. If ever mortal painted an idea, that mortal was Roderick Usher. For me at least—in the circumstances then surrounding me— these arose out of the pure abstractions which the hypochondriac contrived to throw upon his canvas, an intensity of intolerable awe, no shadow of which felt I ever yet in the contemplation of the certainly glowing yet too concrete reveries of Fuseli.[6]

One of the phantasmagoric conceptions of my friend, partaking not so rigidly of the spirit of abstraction, may be shadowed forth, although feebly, in words. A small picture presented the interior of an immensely long and rectangular vault or tunnel, with low walls, smooth, white, and without interruption or device. Certain accessory points of the design served well to convey the idea that this excavation lay at an exceeding depth below the surface of the earth. No outlet was observed in any portion of its vast extent, and no torch, or other artificial source of light was discernible; yet a flood of intense rays rolled throughout, and bathed the whole in a ghastly and inappropriate splendour.

I have just spoken of that morbid condition of the auditory nerve which rendered all music intolerable to the sufferer, with the exception of certain effects of stringed instruments. It was, perhaps, the narrow limits to which he thus confined himself upon the guitar, which gave birth, in great measure, to the fantastic character of his

---

[5] Karl Maria von Weber (1786–1826), German Romantic composer, who was honored by "The Last Waltz of Von Weber," written by Karl Gottlieb Reissiger (1798–1859).

[6] Henry Fuseli (1742–1825), Swiss-born artist with a long career in England, whose paintings manifest the more nightmarish side of Romanticism.

performances. But the fervid *facility* of his *impromptus* could not be so accounted for. They must have been, and were, in the notes, as well as in the words of his wild fantasias (for he not unfrequently accompanied himself with rhymed verbal improvisations), the result of that intense mental collectedness and concentration to which I have previously alluded as observable only in particular moments of the highest artificial excitement. The words of one of these rhapsodies I have easily remembered. I was, perhaps, the more forcibly impressed with it, as he gave it, because in the under or mystic current of its meaning, I fancied that I perceived, and for the first time, a full consciousness on the part of Usher, of the tottering of his lofty reason upon her throne. The verses, which were entitled "The Haunted Palace," ran very nearly, if not accurately, thus:

I.

In the greenest of our valleys,
    By good angels tenanted,
Once a fair and stately palace—
    Radiant palace—reared its head.
In the monarch Thought's dominion—
    It stood there!
Never seraph spread a pinion
    Over fabric half so fair.

II.

Banners yellow, glorious, golden,
    On its roof did float and flow;
(This—all this—was in the olden
    Time long ago)
And every gentle air that dallied,
    In that sweet day,
Along the ramparts plumed and pallid,
    A winged odour went away.

III.

Wanderers in that happy valley
    Through two luminous windows saw
Spirits moving musically
    To a lute's well-tunèd law,
Round about a throne, where sitting
    (Porphyrogene!)[7]
In state his glory well befitting,
    The ruler of the realm was seen.

[7] "Born to the purple"; that is, of royal lineage.

IV.

And all with pearl and ruby glowing
    Was the fair palace door,
Through which came flowing, flowing, flowing
    And sparkling evermore,
A troop of Echoes whose sweet duty
    Was but to sing,
In voices of surpassing beauty,
    The wit and wisdom of their king.

V.

But evil things, in robes of sorrow,
    Assailed the monarch's high estate;
(Ah, let us mourn, for never morrow
    Shall dawn upon him, desolate!)
And, round about his home, the glory
    That blushed and bloomed
Is but a dim-remembered story
    Of the old time entombed.

VI.

And travellers now within that valley,
    Through the red-litten windows, see
Vast forms that move fantastically
    To a discordant melody;
While, like a rapid ghastly river,
    Through the pale door,
A hideous throng rush out forever,
    And laugh—but smile no more.

I well remember that suggestions arising from this ballad, led us into a train of thought wherein there became manifest an opinion of Usher's which I mention not so much on account of its novelty, (for other men[8] have thought thus,) as on account of the pertinacity with which he maintained it. This opinion, in its general form, was that of the sentience of all vegetable things. But, in his disordered fancy, the idea had assumed a more daring character, and trespassed, under certain conditions, upon the kingdom of inorganization. I lack words to express the full extent, or the earnest *abandon* of his persuasion. The belief, however, was connected (as I have previously hinted) with the gray stones of the home of his forefathers. The conditions of the sentience had been here, he imagined, fulfilled in the method of collocation of these

---

[8] Poe's note: "Watson, Dr. Percival, Spallanzani, and especially the Bishop of Landaff.—See 'Chemical Essays,' vol. v." That is, Richard Watson (1737–1816), bishop of Llandaff, English theologian, chemist, and author of *Chemical Essays*; Robert Percival (1756–1839), English physician and student of chemistry; Lazzaro Spallanzani (1739–1799), Italian physiologist.

stones—in the order of their arrangement, as well as in that of the many *fungi* which overspread them, and of the decayed trees which stood around—above all, in the long undisturbed endurance of this arrangement, and in its reduplication in the still waters of the tarn. Its evidence—the evidence of the sentience—was to be seen, he said, (and I here started as he spoke,) in the gradual yet certain condensation of an atmosphere of their own about the waters and the walls. The result was discoverable, he added, in that silent, yet importunate and terrible influence which for centuries had moulded the destinies of his family, and which made *him* what I now saw him—what he was. Such opinions need no comment, and I will make none.

Our books—the books which, for years, had formed no small portion of the mental existence of the invalid—were, as might be supposed, in strict keeping with this character of phantasm. We poured together over such works as the Ververt et Chartreuse of Gresset; the Belphegor of Machiavelli; the Heaven and Hell of Swedenborg; the Subterranean Voyage of Nicholas Klimm by Holberg; the Chiromancy of Robert Flud, of Jean D'Indaginé, and of De la Chambre; the Journey into the Blue Distance of Tieck; and the City of the Sun of Campanella.[9] One favourite volume was a small octavo edition of the *Directorium Inquisitorum,* by the Dominican Eymeric de Gironne;[10] and there were passages in Pomponius Mela,[11] about the old African Satyrs and Ægipans, over which Usher would sit dreaming for hours. His chief delight, however, was found in the perusal of an exceedingly rare and curious book in quarto Gothic—the manual of a forgotten church—the *Vigiliæ Mortuorum secundum Chorum Ecclesiæ Maguntinæ.*[12]

I could not help thinking of the wild ritual of this work, and of its probable influence upon the hypochondriac, when, one evening, having informed me abruptly that the lady Madeline was no more, he stated his intention of preserving her corpse for a fortnight, (previously to its final interment,) in one of the numerous vaults within the main walls of the building. The worldly reason, however, assigned for this singular proceeding, was one which I did not feel at liberty to dispute. The brother had been led to his resolution (so he told me) by consideration of the unusual character of the malady of the deceased, of certain obtrusive and eager inquiries on the part of her medical men, and of the remote and exposed situation of the burial-ground of the family. I will not deny that when I called to mind the sinister countenance of the person whom I met upon the staircase, on the day of my arrival at the house, I had no desire to oppose what I regarded as at best but a harmless, and by no means an unnatural, precaution.[13]

[9] Usher's collection of occult lore contains actual works by a number of European and British authors spanning centuries of interest in the supernatural. His holdings include titles by Louis Gresset (1709–1777); Niccolò Machiavelli (1469–1527); Emanuel Swedenborg (1688–1772); Ludwig Holberg (1684–1754); Robert Fludd (1574–1637); Joannes Indaginé (early sixteenth century); Martin Cureau de la Chambre (1594–1669); Ludwig Tieck (1773–1853); Tommaso Campanella (1568–1639).

[10] Nicholas Eymeric de Gironne (1320?–1399), the Dominican who wrote on the tortures of the Inquisition.

[11] The Roman author, Pomponious Mela, who peopled his geography of the ancient world with fabulous beasts, including tales of satyrs and the goat-god Pan (the "Aegipan").

[12] Book written around 1500, known as *Vigils for the Dead, according to the Choir of the Church of Mayence.*

[13] To prevent Madeline's body from being stolen from its grave and sold for medical experiments, a real possibility in those days of illicit traffic in corpses.

At the request of Usher, I personally aided him in the arrangements for the temporary entombment. The body having been encoffined, we two alone bore it to its rest. The vault in which we placed it (and which had been so long unopened that our torches, half smothered in its oppressive atmosphere, gave us little opportunity for investigation) was small, damp, and entirely without means of admission for light; lying, at great depth, immediately beneath that portion of the building in which was my own sleeping apartment. It had been used, apparently, in remote feudal times, for the worst purposes of a donjon-keep, and, in later days, as a place of deposit for powder, or some other highly combustible substance, as a portion of its floor, and the whole interior of a long archway through which we reached it, were carefully sheathed with copper. The door, of massive iron, had been, also, similarly protected. Its immense weight caused an unusually sharp grating sound, as it moved upon its hinges.

Having deposited our mournful burden upon tressels within this region of horror, we partially turned aside the yet unscrewed lid of the coffin, and looked upon the face of the tenant. A striking similitude between the brother and sister now first arrested my attention; and Usher, divining, perhaps, my thoughts, murmured out some few words from which I learned that the deceased and himself had been twins, and that sympathies of a scarcely intelligible nature had always existed between them. Our glances, however, rested not long upon the dead—for we could not regard her unawed. The disease which had thus entombed the lady in the maturity of youth, had left, as usual in all maladies of a strictly cataleptical character, the mockery of a faint blush upon the bosom and the face, and that suspiciously lingering smile upon the lip which is so terrible in death. We replaced and screwed down the lid, and, having secured the door of iron, made our way, with toil, into the scarcely less gloomy apartments of the upper portion of the house.

And now, some days of bitter grief having elapsed, an observable change came over the features of the mental disorder of my friend. His ordinary manner had vanished. His ordinary occupations were neglected or forgotten. He roamed from chamber to chamber with hurried, unequal, and objectless step. The pallor of his countenance had assumed, if possible, a more ghastly hue—but the luminousness of his eye had utterly gone out. The once occasional huskiness of his tone was heard no more; and a tremulous quaver, as if of extreme terror, habitually characterized his utterance. There were times, indeed, when I thought his unceasingly agitated mind was labouring with some oppressive secret, to divulge which he struggled for the necessary courage. At times, again, I was obliged to resolve all into the mere inexplicable vagaries of madness, for I beheld him gazing upon vacancy for long hours, in an attitude of the profoundest attention as if listening to some imaginary sound. It was no wonder that his condition terrified—that it infected me. I felt creeping upon me, by slow yet certain degrees, the wild influences of his own fantastic yet impressive superstitions.

It was, especially, upon retiring to bed late in the night of the seventh or eighth day after the placing of the lady Madeline within the donjon, that I experienced the full power of such feelings. Sleep came not near my couch—while the hours waned and waned away. I struggled to reason off the nervousness which had dominion over me. I endeavoured to believe that much, if not all of what I felt, was due to the bewildering influence of the gloomy furniture of the room—of the dark and tattered draperies, which, tortured into motion by the breath of a rising tempest, swayed fitfully to and fro upon the walls, and rustled uneasily about the decorations of the bed. But my efforts were fruitless. An irrepressible tremour gradually pervaded my frame; and, at length, there sat upon my very heart an incubus of utterly causeless alarm. Shaking this off with a gasp and a struggle, I uplifted myself upon the pillows, and, peering earnestly within the intense darkness of the chamber, hearkened—I know not why, except that an instinctive spirit prompted me—to certain low and indefinite sounds which came, through the pauses of the storm, at long intervals, I knew not whence. Overpowered by an intense sentiment of horror, unaccountable yet unendurable, I threw on my clothes with haste (for I felt that I should sleep no more during the night), and endeavoured to arouse myself from the pitiable condition into which I had fallen, by pacing rapidly to and fro through the apartment.

I had taken but few turns in this manner, when a light step on an adjoining staircase arrested my attention. I presently recognised it as that of Usher. In an instant afterward he rapped, with a gentle touch, at my door, and entered, bearing a lamp. His countenance was, as usual, cadaverously wan—but, moreover, there was a species of mad hilarity in his eyes—an evidently restrained *hysteria* in his whole demeanour. His air appalled me—but anything was preferable to the solitude which I had so long endured, and I even welcomed his presence as a relief.

"And you have not seen it?" he said abruptly, after having stared about him for some moments in silence—"you have not then seen it?—but, stay! you shall." Thus speaking, and having carefully shaded his lamp, he hurried to one of the casements, and threw it freely open to the storm.

The impetuous fury of the entering gust nearly lifted us from our feet. It was, indeed, a tempestuous yet sternly beautiful night, and one wildly singular in its terror and its beauty. A whirlwind had apparently collected its force in our vicinity; for there were frequent and violent alterations in the direction of the wind; and the exceeding density of the clouds (which hung so low as to press upon the turrets of the house) did not prevent our perceiving the life-like velocity with which they flew careering from all points against each other, without passing away into the distance. I say that even their exceeding density did not prevent our perceiving this—yet we had no glimpse of the moon or stars—nor was there any flashing forth of the lightning. But the under surfaces of the huge masses of agitated vapour, as well as all terrestrial objects immediately around us, were glowing in the unnatural light of a faintly luminous and distinctly visible gaseous exhalation which hung about and enshrouded the mansion.

"You must not—you shall not behold this!" said I, shudderingly, to Usher, as I led him, with a gentle violence, from the window to a seat. "These appearances, which bewilder you, are merely electrical phenomena not uncommon—or it may be that they have their ghastly origin in the rank miasma of the tarn. Let us close this casement; —the air is chilling and dangerous to your frame. Here is one of your favourite romances. I will read, and you shall listen;—and so we will pass away this terrible night together."

The antique volume which I had taken up was the "Mad Trist"[14] of Sir Launcelot

[14] A title and narrative fabricated by Poe. "Trist" (for *tryst*) is used in the sense of an appointed meeting.

Canning; but I had called it a favourite of Usher's more in sad jest than in earnest; for, in truth, there is little in its uncouth and unimaginative prolixity which could have had interest for the lofty and spiritual ideality of my friend. It was, however, the only book immediately at hand; and I indulged a vague hope that the excitement which now agitated the hypochondriac, might find relief (for the history of mental disorder is full of similar anomalies) even in the extremeness of the folly which I should read. Could I have judged, indeed, by the wild over-strained air of vivacity with which he hearkened, or apparently hearkened, to the words of the tale, I might well have congratulated myself upon the success of my design.

I had arrived at that well-known portion of the story where Ethelred, the hero of the Trist, having sought in vain for peaceable admission into the dwelling of the hermit, proceeds to make good an entrance by force. Here, it will be remembered, the words of the narrative run thus:

"And Ethelred, who was by nature of a doughty heart, and who was now mighty withal, on account of the powerfulness of the wine which he had drunken, waited no longer to hold parley with the hermit, who, in sooth, was of an obstinate and maliceful turn, but, feeling the rain upon his shoulders, and fearing the rising of the tempest, uplifted his mace outright, and, with blows, made quickly room in the plankings of the door for his gauntleted hand; and now pulling therewith sturdily, he so cracked, and ripped, and tore all asunder, that the noise of the dry and hollow-sounding wood alarumed and reverberated throughout the forest."

At the termination of this sentence I started, and for a moment, paused; for it appeared to me (although I at once concluded that my excited fancy had deceived me)—it appeared to me that, from some very remote portion of the mansion, there came, indistinctly, to my ears, what might have been, in its exact similarity of character, the echo (but a stifled and dull one certainly) of the very cracking and ripping sound which Sir Launcelot had so particularly described. It was, beyond doubt, the coincidence alone which had arrested my attention; for, amid the rattling of the sashes of the casements, and the ordinary commingled noises of the still increasing storm, the sound, in itself, had nothing, surely, which should have interested or disturbed me. I continued the story:

"But the good champion Ethelred, now entering within the door, was sore enraged and amazed to perceive no signal of the maliceful hermit; but, in the stead thereof, a dragon of a scaly and prodigious demeanour, and of a fiery tongue, which sate in guard before a palace of gold, with a floor of silver; and upon the wall there hung a shield of shining brass with this legend enwritten—

Who entereth herein, a conqueror hath bin;
Who slayeth the dragon, the shield he shall win;

And Ethelred uplifted his mace, and struck upon the head of the dragon, which fell before him, and gave up his pesty breath, with a shriek so horrid and harsh, and withal so piercing, that Ethelred had fain to close his ears with his hands against the dreadful noise of it, the like whereof was never before heard."

Here again I paused abruptly, and now with a feeling of wild amazement—for there could be no doubt whatever that, in this instance, I did actually hear (although from what direction it proceeded I found it impossible to say) a low and apparently distant, but harsh, protracted, and most unusual screaming or grating sound—the exact counterpart of what my fancy had already conjured up for the dragon's unnatural shriek as described by the romancer.

Oppressed, as I certainly was, upon the occurrence of the second and most extraordinary coincidence, by a thousand conflicting sensations, in which wonder and extreme terror were predominant, I still retained sufficient presence of mind to avoid exciting, by any observation, the sensitive nervousness of my companion. I was by no means certain that he had noticed the sounds in question; although, assuredly, a strange alteration had, during the last few minutes, taken place in his demeanour. From a position fronting my own, he had gradually brought round his chair, so as to sit with his face to the door of the chamber; and thus I could but partially perceive his features, although I saw that his lips trembled as if he were murmuring inaudibly. His head had dropped upon his breast—yet I knew that he was not asleep, from the wide and rigid opening of the eye as I caught a glance of it in profile. The motion of his body, too, was at variance with this idea—for he rocked from side to side with a gentle yet constant and uniform sway. Having rapidly taken notice of all this, I resumed the narrative of Sir Launcelot, which thus proceeded:

"And now, the champion, having escaped from the terrible fury of the dragon, bethinking himself of the brazen shield, and of the breaking up of the enchantment which was upon it, removed the carcass from out of the way before him, and approached valorously over the silver pavement of the castle to where the shield was upon the wall; which in sooth tarried not for his full coming, but fell down at his feet upon the silver floor, with a mighty great and terrible ringing sound."

No sooner had these syllables passed my lips, than—as if a shield of brass had indeed, at the moment, fallen heavily upon a floor of silver—I became aware of a distinct, hollow, metallic, and clangorous, yet apparently muffled reverberation. Completely unnerved, I leaped to my feet; but the measured rocking movement of Usher was undisturbed. I rushed to the chair in which he sat. His eyes were bent fixedly before him, and throughout his whole countenance there reigned a stony rigidity. But, as I placed my hand upon his shoulder, there came a strong shudder over his whole person; a sickly smile quivered about his lips; and I saw that he spoke in a low, hurried, and gibbering murmur, as if unconscious of my presence. Bending closely over him, I at length drank in the hideous import of his words.

"Not hear it?—yes, I hear it, and *have* heard it. Long—long—long—many minutes, many hours, many days, have I heard it—yet I dared not—oh, pity me, miserable wretch that I am!—I dared not—I *dared* not speak! *We have put her living in the tomb!* Said I not that my senses were acute? I *now* tell you that I heard her first feeble movements in the hollow coffin. I heard them—many, many days ago—yet I dared not—*I dared not speak!* And now—to-night—Ethelred—ha! ha!—the breaking of the hermit's door, and the death-cry of the dragon, and the clangour of the shield! say, rather, the rending of her coffin, and the grating of the iron hinges of her prison, and her struggles within the coppered archway of the vault! Oh whither shall I fly? Will she not be here anon? Is she not hurrying to upbraid me for my haste? Have I not heard her footstep on the stair? Do I not distinguish that heavy and horrible beating of her heart? MADMAN!" here he sprang furiously to his feet, and shrieked out his syllables, as if in the effort he were giving up his soul—"MADMAN! I TELL YOU THAT SHE NOW STANDS WITHOUT THE DOOR!"

As if in the superhuman energy of his utterance there had been found the potency of a spell—the huge antique panels to which the speaker pointed, threw slowly back, upon the instant, their ponderous and ebony jaws. It was the work of the rushing gust —but then without those doors there did stand the lofty and enshrouded figure of the lady Madeline of Usher. There was blood upon her white robes, and the evidence of some bitter struggle upon every portion of her emaciated frame. For a moment she remained trembling and reeling to and fro upon the threshold, then, with a low moaning cry, fell heavily inward upon the person of her brother, and in her violent and now final death-agonies, bore him to the floor a corpse, and a victim to the terrors he had anticipated.

From that chamber, and from that mansion, I fled aghast. The storm was still abroad in all its wrath as I found myself crossing the old causeway. Suddenly there shot along the path a wild light, and I turned to see whence a gleam so unusual could have issued; for the vast house and its shadows were alone behind me. The radiance was that of the full, setting, and blood-red moon which now shone vividly through that once barely-discernible fissure of which I have before spoken as extending from the roof of the building, in a zigzag direction, to the base. While I gazed, this fissure rapidly widened—there came a fierce breath of the whirlwind—the entire orb of the satellite burst at once upon my sight—my brain reeled as I saw the mighty walls rushing asunder—there was a long tumultuous shouting sound like the voice of a thousand waters—and the deep and dank tarn at my feet closed sullenly and silently over the fragments of the "HOUSE OF USHER."

1839

The Man of the Crowd

Ce grand malheur, de ne pouvoir être seul.[1]
La Bruyère

It was well said of a certain German book that *"es lässt sich nicht lesen"*—it does not permit itself to be read. There are some secrets which do not permit themselves to be told. Men die nightly in their beds, wringing the hands of ghostly confessors, and looking them piteously in the eyes—die with despair of heart and convulsion of throat, on account of the hideousness of mysteries which will not *suffer themselves* to be revealed. Now and then, alas, the conscience of man takes up a burthen so heavy in horror that it can be thrown down only into the grave. And thus the essence of all crime is undivulged.

Not long ago, about the closing in of an evening in autumn, I sat at the large bow window of the D—— Coffee-House in London. For some months I had been ill in health, but was now convalescent, and, with returning strength, found my-

---

[1] "The sorrow of the inability to be alone."
From *Characters* by Jean de La Bruyère
(1645–1696).

self in one of those happy moods which are so precisely the converse of *ennui*—moods of the keenest appetency, when the film from the mental vision departs—the ἀχλὺς ἡ π ρὶυ ἐπῆ ευ[2]—and the intellect, electrified, surpasses as greatly its every-day condition, as does the vivid yet candid reason of Leibnitz,[3] the mad and flimsy rhetoric of Gorgias.[4] Merely to breathe was enjoyment; and I derived positive pleasure even from many of the legitimate sources of pain. I felt a calm but inquisitive interest in every thing. With a cigar in my mouth and a newspaper in my lap, I had been amusing myself for the greater part of the afternoon, now in poring over advertisements, now in observing the promiscuous company in the room, and now in peering through the smoky panes into the street.

This latter is one of the principal thoroughfares of the city, and had been very much crowded during the whole day. But, as the darkness came on, the throng momently increased; and, by the time the lamps were well lighted, two dense and continuous tides of population were rushing past the door. At this particular period of the evening I had never before been in a similar situation, and the tumultuous sea of human heads filled me, therefore, with a delicious novelty of emotion. I gave up, at length, all care of things within the hotel, and became absorbed in contemplation of the scene without.

At first my observations took an abstract and generalizing turn. I looked at the passengers in masses, and thought of them in their aggregate relations. Soon, however, I descended to details, and regarded with minute interest the innumerable varieties of figure, dress, air, gait, visage, and expression of countenance.

By far the greater number of those who went by had a satisfied business-like demeanor, and seemed to be thinking only of making their way through the press. Their brows were knit, and their eyes rolled quickly; when pushed against by fellow-wayfarers they evinced no symptom of impatience, but adjusted their clothes and hurried on. Others, still a numerous class, were restless in their movements, had flushed faces, and talked and gesticulated to themselves, as if feeling in solitude on account of the very denseness of the company around. When impeded in their progress, these people suddenly ceased muttering, but redoubled their gesticulations, and awaited, with an absent and overdone smile upon the lips, the course of the persons impeding them. If jostled, they bowed profusely to the jostlers, and appeared overwhelmed with confusion.—There was nothing very distinctive about these two large classes beyond what I have noted. Their habiliments belonged to that order which is pointedly termed the decent. They were undoubtedly noblemen, merchants, attorneys, tradesmen, stock-jobbers—the Eupatrids[5] and the common-places of society—men of leisure and men actively engaged in affairs of their own—conducting business upon their own responsibility. They did not greatly excite my attention.

The tribe of clerks was an obvious one; and here I discerned two remarkable divisions. There were the junior clerks of flash houses—young gentlemen with tight coats, bright boots, well-oiled hair, and supercilious lips. Setting aside a certain dapperness of carriage, which may be termed *deskism* for want of a better word, the

---

[2] From Homer's *Iliad*: "the mist that was upon it previously."
[3] Baron Gottfried Wilhelm von Leibnitz (1646–1716), German philosopher and mathematician.

[4] Greek philosopher of the fourth century B.C. noted for language that placed eloquence above reason.
[5] Individuals of the upper classes.

manner of these persons seemed to me an exact facsimile of what had been the perfection of *bon ton*[6] about twelve or eighteen months before. They wore the cast-off graces of the gentry;—and this, I believe, involves the best definition of the class.

The division of the upper clerks of staunch firms, or of the "steady old fellows," it was not possible to mistake. These were known by their coats and pantaloons of black or brown, made to sit comfortably, with white cravats and waistcoats, broad solid-looking shoes, and thick hose or gaiters.—They had all slightly bald heads, from which the right ears, long used to pen-holding, had an odd habit of standing off on end. I observed that they always removed or settled their hats with both hands, and wore watches, with short gold chains of a substantial and ancient pattern. Theirs was the affectation of respectability;—if indeed there be an affectation so honorable.

There were many individuals of dashing appearance, whom I easily understood as belonging to the race of swell pick-pockets, with which all great cities are infested. I watched these gentry with much inquisitiveness, and found it difficult to imagine how they should ever be mistaken for gentlemen by gentlemen themselves. Their voluminousness of wristband, with an air of excessive frankness, should betray them at once.

The gamblers, of whom I descried not a few, were still more easily recognisable. They wore every variety of dress, from that of the desperate thimble-rig[7] bully, with velvet waistcoat, fancy neckerchief, gilt chains, and filagreed buttons, to that of the scrupulously inornate clergyman than which nothing could be less liable to suspicion. Still all were distinguished by a certain sodden swarthiness of complexion, a filmy dimness of eye, and pallor and compression of lip. There were two other traits, moreover, by which I could always detect them;—a guarded lowness of tone in conversation, and a more than ordinary extension of the thumb in a direction at right angles with the fingers.—Very often, in company with these sharpers, I observed an order of men somewhat different in habits, but still birds of a kindred feather. They may be defined as the gentlemen who live by their wits. They seem to prey upon the public in two battalions—that of the dandies and that of the military men. Of the first grade the leading features are long locks and smiles; of the second frogged coats and frowns.

Descending in the scale of what is termed gentility, I found darker and deeper themes for speculation. I saw Jew pedlars, with hawk eyes flashing from countenances whose every other feature wore only an expression of abject humility; sturdy professional street beggars scowling upon mendicants of a better stamp, whom despair alone had driven forth into the night for charity; feeble and ghastly invalids, upon whom death had placed a sure hand, and who sidled and tottered through the mob, looking every one beseechingly in the face, as if in search of some chance consolation, some lost hope; modest young girls returning from long and late labor to a cheerless home, and shrinking more tearfully than indignantly from the glances of ruffians, whose direct contact, even, could not be avoided; women of the town of all kinds and of all ages—the unequivocal beauty in the prime of her womanhood, putting one in mind of the statue in Lucian,[8] with the surface of Parian marble, and the interior filled

---

[6] French: "stylishness."
[7] Confidence game played upon the gullible.
[8] Allusion to the play *The Cock* by Lucian, the Greek satirist (A.D. 125?–200?), which refers to the marble found on the island of Paros as being considered by sculptors to be of the finest quality.

with filth—the loathsome and utterly lost leper in rags—the wrinkled, bejewelled and paint-begrimed beldame, making a last effort at youth—the mere child of immature form, yet, from long association, an adept in the dreadful coquetries of her trade, and burning with a rabid ambition to be ranked the equal of her elders in vice; drunkards innumerable and indescribable—some in shreds and patches, reeling, inarticulate, with bruised visage and lack-lustre eyes—some in whole although filthy garments, with a slightly unsteady swagger, thick sensual lips, and hearty-looking rubicund faces— others clothed in materials which had once been good, and which even now were scrupulously well brushed—men who walked with a more than naturally firm and springy step, but whose countenances were fearfully pale, whose eyes hideously wild and red, and who clutched with quivering fingers, as they strode through the crowd, at every object which came within their reach; beside these, pie-men, porters, coal-heavers, sweeps; organ-grinders, monkey-exhibiters and ballad mongers, those who vended with those who sang; ragged artizans and exhausted laborers of every description, and all full of a noisy and inordinate vivacity which jarred discordantly upon the ear, and gave an aching sensation to the eye.

As the night deepened, so deepened to me the interest of the scene; for not only did the general character of the crowd materially alter (its gentler features retiring in the gradual withdrawal of the more orderly portion of the people, and its harsher ones coming out into bolder relief, as the late hour brought forth every species of infamy from its den,) but the rays of the gas-lamps, feeble at first in their struggle with the dying day, had now at length gained ascendancy, and threw over every thing a fitful and garish lustre. All was dark yet splendid—as that ebony to which has been likened the style of Tertullian.[9]

The wild effects of the light enchained me to an examination of individual faces; and although the rapidity with which the world of light flitted before the window, prevented me from casting more than a glance upon each visage, still it seemed that, in my then peculiar mental state, I could frequently read, even in that brief interval of a glance, the history of long years.

With my brow to the glass, I was thus occupied in scrutinizing the mob, when suddenly there came into view a countenance (that of a decrepid old man, some sixty-five or seventy years of age,)—a countenance which at once arrested and absorbed my whole attention, on account of the absolute idiosyncrasy of its expression. Any thing even remotely resembling that expression I had never seen before. I well remember that my first thought, upon beholding it, was that Retzsch,[10] had he viewed it, would have greatly preferred it to his own pictural incarnations of the fiend. As I endeavored, during the brief minute of my original survey, to form some analysis of the meaning conveyed, there arose confusedly and paradoxically within my mind, the ideas of vast mental power, of caution, of penuriousness, of avarice, of coolness, of malice, of blood-thirstiness, of triumph, of merriment, of excessive terror, of intense —of extreme despair. I felt singularly aroused, startled, fascinated. "How wild a history," I said to myself, "is written within that bosom!" Then came a craving desire to keep the man in view—to know more of him. Hurriedly putting on an overcoat, and seizing my hat and cane, I made my way into the street, and pushed through the crowd in the direction which I had seen him take; for he had already disappeared.

---

[9] Quintus Septimius Florens Tertullianus (A.D. 160?–230?), church writer and noted stylist.

[10] Moritz Retzsch (1779–1857), German artist.

With some little difficulty I at length came within sight of him, approached, and followed him closely, yet cautiously, so as not to attract his attention.

I had now a good opportunity of examining his person. He was short in stature, very thin, and apparently very feeble. His clothes, generally, were filthy and ragged; but as he came, now and then, within the strong glare of a lamp, I perceived that his linen, although dirty, was of beautiful texture; and my vision deceived me, or, through a rent in a closely-buttoned and evidently second-handed *roquelaire* which enveloped him, I caught a glimpse both of a diamond and of a dagger. These observations heightened my curiosity, and I resolved to follow the stranger whithersoever he should go.

It was now fully night-fall, and a thick humid fog hung over the city, soon ending in a settled and heavy rain. This change of weather had an odd effect upon the crowd, the whole of which was at once put into new commotion, and overshadowed by a world of umbrellas. The waver, the jostle, and the hum increased in a tenfold degree. For my own part I did not much regard the rain—the lurking of an old fever in my system rendering the moisture somewhat too dangerously pleasant. Tying a handkerchief about my mouth, I kept on. For half an hour the old man held his way with difficulty along the great thoroughfare; and I here walked close at his elbow through fear of losing sight of him. Never once turning his head to look back, he did not observe me. By and bye he passed into a cross street, which, although densely filled with people, was not quite so much thronged as the main one he had quitted. Here a change in his demeanor became evident. He walked more slowly and with less object than before—more hesitatingly. He crossed and re-crossed the way repeatedly without apparent aim; and the press was still so thick, that, at every such movement, I was obliged to follow him closely. The street was a narrow and long one, and his course lay within it for nearly an hour, during which the passengers had gradually diminished to about that number which is ordinarily seen at noon in Broadway near the Park —so vast a difference is there between a London populace and that of the most frequented American city. A second turn brought us into a square, brilliantly lighted, and overflowing with life. The old manner of the stranger re-appeared. His chin fell upon his breast, while his eyes rolled wildly from under his knit brows, in every direction, upon those who hemmed him in. He urged his way steadily and perseveringly. I was surprised, however, to find, upon his having made the circuit of the square, that he turned and retraced his steps. Still more was I astonished to see him repeat the same walk several times—once nearly detecting me as he came round with a sudden movement.

In this exercise he spent another hour, at the end of which we met with far less interruption from passengers than at first. The rain fell fast; the air grew cool; and the people were retiring to their homes. With a gesture of impatience, the wanderer passed into a by-street comparatively deserted. Down this, some quarter of a mile long, he rushed with an activity I could not have dreamed of seeing in one so aged, and which put me to much trouble in pursuit. A few minutes brought us to a large and busy bazaar, with the localities of which the stranger appeared well acquainted, and where his original demeanor again became apparent, as he forced his way to and fro, without aim, among the host of buyers and sellers.

During the hour and a half, or thereabouts, which we passed in this place, it required much caution on my part to keep him within reach without attracting his observation. Luckily I wore a pair of caoutchouc over-shoes, and could move about in perfect silence. At no moment did he see that I watched him. He entered shop after shop, priced nothing, spoke no word, and looked at all objects with a wild and vacant stare. I was now utterly amazed at his behaviour, and firmly resolved that we should not part until I had satisfied myself in some measure respecting him.

A loud-toned clock struck eleven, and the company were fast deserting the bazaar. A shop-keeper, in putting up a shutter, jostled the old man, and at the instant I saw a strong shudder come over his frame. He hurried into the street, looked anxiously around him for an instant, and then ran with incredible swiftness through many crooked and people-less lanes, until we emerged once more upon the great thorough-fare whence we had started—the street of the D———— Hotel. It no longer wore, however, the same aspect. It was still brilliant with gas; but the rain fell fiercely, and there were few persons to be seen. The stranger grew pale. He walked moodily some paces up the once populous avenue, then, with a heavy sigh, turned in the direction of the river, and, plunging through a great variety of devious ways, came out, at length, in view of one of the principal theatres. It was about being closed, and the audience were thronging from the doors. I saw the old man gasp as if for breath while he threw himself amid the crowd; but I thought that the intense agony of his countenance had, in some measure, abated. His head again fell upon his breast; he appeared as I had seen him at first. I observed that he now took the course in which had gone the greater number of the audience—but, upon the whole, I was at a loss to comprehend the waywardness of his actions.

As he proceeded, the company grew more scattered, and his old uneasiness and vacillation were resumed. For some time he followed closely a party of some ten or twelve roisterers; but from this number one by one dropped off, until three only remained together, in a narrow and gloomy lane little frequented. The stranger paused, and, for a moment, seemed lost in thought; then, with every mark of agitation, pursued rapidly a route which brought us to the verge of the city, amid regions very different from those we had hitherto traversed. It was the most noisome quarter of London, where everything wore the worst impress of the most deplorable poverty, and of the most desperate crime. By the dim light of an accidental lamp, tall, antique, worm-eaten, wooden tenements were seen tottering to their fall, in directions so many and capricious that scarce the semblance of a passage was discernible between them. The paving-stones lay at random, displaced from their beds by the rankly growing grass. Horrible filth festered in the dammed-up gutters. The whole atmosphere teemed with desolation. Yet, as we proceeded, the sounds of human life revived by sure degrees, and at length large bands of the most abandoned of a London populace were seen reeling to and fro. The spirits of the old man again flickered up, as a lamp which is near its death-hour. Once more he strode onward with elastic tread. Suddenly a corner was turned, a blaze of light burst upon our sight, and we stood before one of the huge suburban temples of Intemperance—one of the palaces of the fiend, Gin.

It was now nearly day-break; but a number of wretched inebriates still pressed in and out of the flaunting entrance. With a half shriek of joy the old man forced a passage within, resumed at once his original bearing, and stalked backward and forward, without apparent object, among the throng. He had not been thus long occupied, however, before a rush to the doors gave token that the host was closing them for the night. It was something even more intense than despair that I then observed upon the countenance of the singular being whom I had watched so pertinaciously. Yet he did not hesitate in his career, but, with a mad energy, retraced his steps at once, to the heart of the mighty London. Long and swiftly he fled, while I followed him in the wildest amazement, resolute not to abandon a scrutiny in which I now felt an interest all-absorbing. The sun arose while we proceeded, and, when we had once again reached that most thronged mart of the populous town, the street of the D——— Hotel, it presented an appearance of human bustle and activity scarcely inferior to what I had seen on the evening before. And here, long, amid the momently increasing confusion, did I persist in my pursuit of the stranger. But, as usual, he walked to and fro, and during the day did not pass from out the turmoil of that street. And, as the shades of the second evening came on, I grew wearied unto death, and, stopping fully in front of the wanderer, gazed at him steadfastly in the face. He noticed me not, but resumed his solemn walk, while I, ceasing to follow, remained absorbed in contemplation. "This old man," I said at length, "is the type and the genius of deep crime. He refuses to be alone. *He is the man of the crowd.* It will be in vain to follow; for I shall learn no more of him, nor of his deeds. The worst heart of the world is a grosser book than the 'Hortulus Animæ,'[11] and perhaps it is but one of the great mercies of God that *es lässt sich nicht lesen.*"[12]

1840

A Descent into the Maelström

The ways of God in Nature, as in Providence, are not as our ways; nor are the models that we frame any way commensurate to the vastness, profundity, and unsearchableness of His works, which have a depth in them greater than the well of Democritus.[1]
Joseph Glanville

We had now reached the summit of the loftiest crag. For some minutes the old man seemed too much exhausted to speak.

"Not long ago," said he at length, "and I could have guided you on this route as well as the youngest of my sons; but, about three years past, there happened to me an event such as never happened before to mortal man—or at least such as no man ever survived to tell of—and the six hours of deadly terror which I then endured have broken me up body and soul. You suppose me a *very* old man—but I am not. It took

---

[11] Poe's note: "The *'Hortulus Animae cum Orantiunculus Aliquibus Superadditis'* of Grünningero." This book, by the German writer John Grunninger and printed around 1500, was known to Poe for its illustrations, which were considered offensive to religious sensibilities.

[12] Repetition of the phrase used in the opening sentence of this story: "It does not permit itself to be read."

[1] From the essay "Against Confidence in Philosophy and Matters of Speculation" (1676) by Joseph Glanville (1636–1680), English philosopher. The "well of Democritus" refers to the Greek philosopher Democritus' observation that truth can be found only at the bottom of a deep well.

less than a single day to change these hairs from a jetty black to white, to weaken my limbs, and to unstring my nerves, so that I tremble at the least exertion, and am frightened at a shadow. Do you know I can scarcely look over this little cliff without getting giddy?"

The "little cliff," upon whose edge he had so carelessly thrown himself down to rest that the weightier portion of his body hung over it, while he was only kept from falling by the tenure of his elbow on its extreme and slippery edge—this "little cliff" arose, a sheer unobstructed precipice of black shining rock, some fifteen or sixteen hundred feet from the world of crags beneath us. Nothing would have tempted me to within half a dozen yards of its brink. In truth so deeply was I excited by the perilous position of my companion, that I fell at full length upon the ground, clung to the shrubs around me, and dared not even glance upward at the sky—while I struggled in vain to divest myself of the idea that the very foundations of the mountain were in danger from the fury of the winds. It was long before I could reason myself into sufficient courage to sit up and look out into the distance.

"You must get over these fancies," said the guide, "for I have brought you here that you might have the best possible view of the scene of that event I mentioned —and to tell you the whole story with the spot just under your eye."

"We are now," he continued, in that particularizing manner which distinguished him—"we are now close upon the Norwegian coast—in the sixty-eighth degree of latitude—in the great province of Nordland—and in the dreary district of Lofoden. The mountain upon whose top we sit is Helseggen, the Cloudy. Now raise yourself up a little higher—hold on to the grass if you feel giddy—so—and look out beyond the belt of vapor beneath us, into the sea."

I looked dizzily, and beheld a wide expanse of ocean, whose waters wore so inky a hue as to bring at once to my mind the Nubian geographer's account of the *Mare Tenebrarum.*[2] A panorama more deplorably desolate no human imagination can conceive. To the right and left, as far as the eye could reach, there lay outstretched, like ramparts of the world, lines of horridly black and beetling cliff, whose character of gloom was but the more forcibly illustrated by the surf which reared high up against it its white and ghastly crest, howling and shrieking for ever. Just opposite the promontory upon whose apex we were placed, and at a distance of some five or six miles out at sea, there was visible a small, bleak-looking island; or, more properly, its position was discernible through the wilderness of surge in which it was enveloped. About two miles nearer the land, arose another of smaller size, hideously craggy and barren, and encompassed at various intervals by a cluster of dark rocks.

The appearance of the ocean, in the space between the more distant island and the shore, had something very unusual about it. Although, at the time, so strong a gale was blowing landward that a brig in the remote offing lay to under a double-reefed trysail, and constantly plunged her whole hull out of sight, still there was here nothing like a regular swell, but only a short, quick, angry cross dashing of water in every direction—as well in the teeth of the wind as otherwise. Of foam there was little except in the immediate vicinity of the rocks.

"The island in the distance," resumed the old man, "is called by the Norwegians

[2] The unnamed Nubian geographer was the author of an abridgment of medieval Arabic geographical lore; *Mare Tenebrarum* is the term he used for the Atlantic Ocean.

Vurrgh. The one midway is Moskoe. That a mile to the northward is Ambaaren. Yonder are Iflesen, Hoeyholm, Kieldholm, Suarven, and Buckholm. Farther off— between Moskoe and Vurrgh—are Otterholm, Flimen, Sandflesen, and Skarholm. These are the true names of the places—but why it has been thought necessary to name them at all, is more than either you or I can understand. Do you hear any thing? Do you see any change in the water?"

We had now been about ten minutes upon the top of Helseggen, to which we had ascended from the interior of Lofoden, so that we had caught no glimpse of the sea until it had burst upon us from the summit. As the old man spoke, I became aware of a loud and gradually increasing sound, like the moaning of a vast herd of buffaloes upon an American prairie; and at the same moment I perceived that what seamen term the *chopping* character of the ocean beneath us, was rapidly changing into a current which set to the eastward. Even while I gazed, this current acquired a monstrous velocity. Each moment added to its speed—to its headlong impetuosity. In five minutes the whole sea, as far as Vurrgh, was lashed into ungovernable fury; but it was between Moskoe and the coast that the main uproar held its sway. Here the vast bed of the waters, seamed and scarred into a thousand conflicting channels, burst suddenly into phrensied convulsion—heaving, boiling, hissing—gyrating in gigantic and innumerable vortices, and all whirling and plunging on to the eastward with a rapidity which water never elsewhere assumes except in precipitous descents.

In a few minutes more, there came over the scene another radical alteration. The general surface grew somewhat more smooth, and the whirlpools, one by one, disappeared, while prodigious streaks of foam became apparent where none had been seen before. These streaks, at length, spreading out to a great distance, and entering into combination, took unto themselves the gyratory motion of the subsided vortices, and seemed to form the germ of another more vast. Suddenly—very suddenly—this assumed a distinct and definite existence, in a circle of more than half a mile in diameter. The edge of the whirl was represented by a broad belt of gleaming spray; but no particle of this slipped into the mouth of the terrific funnel, whose interior, as far as the eye could fathom it, was a smooth, shining, and jet-black wall of water, inclined to the horizon at an angle of some forty-five degrees, speeding dizzily round and round with a swaying and sweltering motion, and sending forth to the winds an appalling voice, half shriek, half roar, such as not even the mighty cataract of Niagara ever lifts up in its agony to Heaven.

The mountain trembled to its very base, and the rock rocked. I threw myself upon my face, and clung to the scant herbage in an excess of nervous agitation.

"This," said I at length, to the old man—"this *can* be nothing else than the great whirlpool of the Maelström."

"So it is sometimes termed," said he. "We Norwegians call it the Moskoe-ström, from the island of Moskoe in the midway."

The ordinary accounts of this vortex had by no means prepared me for what I saw. That of Jonas Ramus,[3] which is perhaps the most circumstantial of any, cannot impart the faintest conception either of the magnificence, or of the horror of the scene—or of the wild bewildering sense of *the novel* which confounds the beholder. I am not

---

[3] Jonas Ramus (1649–1718) wrote a description of Norway, published in 1715.

sure from what point of view the writer in question surveyed it, nor at what time; but it could neither have been from the summit of Helseggen, nor during a storm. There are some passages of his description, nevertheless, which may be quoted for their details, although their effect is exceedingly feeble in conveying an impression of the spectacle.

"Between Lofoden and Moskoe," he says, "the depth of the water is between thirty-six and forty fathoms; but on the other side, toward Ver (Vurrgh) this depth decreases so as not to afford a convenient passage for a vessel, without the risk of splitting on the rocks, which happens even in the calmest weather. When it is flood, the stream runs up the country between Lofoden and Moskoe with a boisterous rapidity; but the roar of its impetuous ebb to the sea is scarce equalled by the loudest and most dreadful cataracts; the noise being heard several leagues off, and the vortices or pits are of such an extent and depth, that if a ship comes within its attraction, it is inevitably absorbed and carried down to the bottom, and there beat to pieces against the rocks; and when the water relaxes, the fragments thereof are thrown up again. But these intervals of tranquillity are only at the turn of the ebb and flood, and in calm weather, and last but a quarter of an hour, its violence gradually returning. When the stream is most boisterous, and its fury heightened by a storm, it is dangerous to come within a Norway mile of it. Boats, yachts, and ships have been carried away by not guarding against it before they were within its reach. It likewise happens frequently, that whales come too near the stream, and are overpowered by its violence; and then it is impossible to describe their howlings and bellowings in their fruitless struggles to disengage themselves. A bear once, attempting to swim from Lofoden to Moskoe, was caught by the stream and borne down, while he roared terribly, so as to be heard on shore. Large stocks of firs and pine trees, after being absorbed by the current, rise again broken and torn to such a degree as if bristles grew upon them. This plainly shows the bottom to consist of craggy rocks, among which they are whirled to and fro. This stream is regulated by the flux and reflux of the sea—it being constantly high and low water for every six hours. In the year 1645, early in the morning of Sexagesima Sunday,[4] it raged with such noise and impetuosity that the very stones of the houses on the coast fell to the ground."

In regard to the depth of the water, I could not see how this could have been ascertained at all in the immediate vicinity of the vortex. The "forty fathoms" must have reference only to portions of the channel close upon the shore either of Moskoe or Lofoden. The depth in the centre of the Moskoe-ström must be immeasurably greater; and no better proof of this fact is necessary than can be obtained from even the side-long glance into the abyss of the whirl which may be had from the highest crag of Helseggen. Looking down from this pinnacle upon the howling Phlegethon below, I could not help smiling at the simplicity with which the honest Jonas Ramus records, as a matter difficult of belief, the anecdotes of the whales and the bears; for it appeared to me, in fact, a self-evident thing, that the largest ships of the line in existence, coming within the influence of that deadly attraction, could resist it as little as a feather the hurricane, and must disappear bodily and at once.

The attempts to account for the phenomenon—some of which, I remember, seemed

[4] The second Sunday prior to the start of the
Lenten season.

to me sufficiently plausible in perusal—now wore a very different and unsatisfactory aspect. The idea generally received is that this, as well as three smaller vortices among the Feroe islands, "have no other cause than the collision of waves rising and falling, at flux and reflux, against a ridge of rocks and shelves, which confines the water so that it precipitates itself like a cataract; and thus the higher the flood rises, the deeper must the fall be, and the natural result of all is a whirlpool or vortex, the prodigious suction of which is sufficiently known by lesser experiments."—These are the words of the Encyclopædia Britannica. Kircher[5] and others imagine that in the centre of the channel of the Maelström is an abyss penetrating the globe, and issuing in some very remote part—the Gulf of Bothnia being somewhat decidedly named in one instance. This opinion, idle in itself, was the one to which, as I gazed, my imagination most readily assented; and, mentioning it to the guide, I was rather surprised to hear him say that, although it was the view almost universally entertained of the subject by the Norwegians, it nevertheless was not his own. As to the former notion he confessed his inability to comprehend it; and here I agreed with him—for, however conclusive on paper, it becomes altogether unintelligible, and even absurd, amid the thunder of the abyss.

"You have had a good look at the whirl now," said the old man, "and if you will creep round this crag, so as to get in its lee, and deaden the roar of the water, I will tell you a story that will convince you I ought to know something of the Moskoe-ström."

I placed myself as desired, and he proceeded.

"Myself and my two brothers once owned a schooner-rigged smack of about seventy tons burthen, with which we were in the habit of fishing among the islands beyond Moskoe, nearly to Vurrgh. In all violent eddies at sea there is good fishing, at proper opportunities, if one has only the courage to attempt it; but among the whole of the Lofoden coastmen, we three were the only ones who made a regular business of going out to the islands, as I tell you. The usual grounds are a great way lower down to the southward. There fish can be got at all hours, without much risk, and therefore these places are preferred. The choice spots over here among the rocks, however, not only yield the finest variety, but in far greater abundance; so that we often got in a single day, what the more timid of the craft could not scrape together in a week. In fact, we made it a matter of desperate speculation—the risk of life standing instead of labor, and courage answering for capital.

"We kept the smack in a cove about five miles higher up the coast than this; and it was our practice, in fine weather, to take advantage of the fifteen minutes' slack to push across the main channel of the Moskoe-ström, far above the pool, and then drop down upon anchorage somewhere near Otterholm, or Sandflesen, where the eddies are not so violent as elsewhere. Here we used to remain until nearly time for slackwater again, when we weighed and made for home. We never set out upon this expedition without a steady side wind for going and coming—one that we felt sure would not fail us before our return—and we seldom made a mis-calculation upon this point. Twice, during six years, we were forced to stay all night at anchor on account of a dead calm, which is a rare thing indeed just about here; and once we

[5] Athanasius Kircher (1602–1680), writer on the scientific nature of maelstroms.

had to remain on the grounds nearly a week, starving to death, owing to a gale which blew up shortly after our arrival, and made the channel too boisterous to be thought of. Upon this occasion we should have been driven out to sea in spite of everything, (for the whirlpools threw us round and round so violently, that, at length, we fouled our anchor and dragged it) if it had not been that we drifted into one of the innumerable cross currents—here to-day and gone to-morrow—which drove us under the lee of Flimen, where, by good luck, we brought up.

"I could not tell you the twentieth part of the difficulties we encountered 'on the ground'—it is a bad spot to be in, even in good weather—but we made shift always to run the gauntlet of the Moskoe-ström itself without accident; although at times my heart has been in my mouth when we happened to be a minute or so behind or before the slack. The wind sometimes was not as strong as we thought it at starting, and then we made rather less way than we could wish, while the current rendered the smack unmanageable. My eldest brother had a son eighteen years old, and I had two stout boys of my own. These would have been of great assistance at such times, in using the sweeps, as well as afterward in fishing—but, somehow, although we ran the risk ourselves, we had not the heart to let the young ones get into the danger—for, after all said and done, it *was* a horrible danger, and that is the truth.

"It is now within a few days of three years since what I am going to tell you occurred. It was on the tenth of July, 18——, a day which the people of this part of the world will never forget—for it was one in which blew the most terrible hurricane that ever came out of the heavens. And yet all the morning, and indeed until late in the afternoon, there was a gentle and steady breeze from the south-west, while the sun shone brightly, so that the oldest seaman among us could not have foreseen what was to follow.

"The three of us—my two brothers and myself—had crossed over to the islands about two o'clock P.M., and soon nearly loaded the smack with fine fish, which, we all remarked, were more plenty that day than we had ever known them. It was just seven, *by my watch,* when we weighed and started for home, so as to make the worst of the Ström at slack water, which we knew would be at eight.

"We set out with a fresh wind on our starboard quarter, and for some time spanked along at a great rate, never dreaming of danger, for indeed we saw not the slightest reason to apprehend it. All at once we were taken aback by a breeze from over Helseggen. This was most unusual—something that had never happened to us before—and I began to feel a little uneasy, without exactly knowing why. We put the boat on the wind, but could make no headway at all for the eddies, and I was upon the point of proposing to return to the anchorage, when, looking astern, we saw the whole horizon covered with a singular copper-colored cloud that rose with the most amazing velocity.

"In the meantime the breeze that had headed us off fell away, and we were dead becalmed, drifting about in every direction. This state of things, however, did not last long enough to give us time to think about it. In less than a minute the storm was upon us—in less than two the sky was entirely overcast—and what with this and the driving spray, it became suddenly so dark that we could not see each other in the smack.

"Such a hurricane as then blew it is folly to attempt describing. The oldest seaman in Norway never experienced any thing like it. We had let our sails go by the run before it cleverly took us; but, at the first puff, both our masts went by the board as if they had been sawed off—the mainmast taking with it my youngest brother, who had lashed himself to it for safety.

"Our boat was the lightest feather of a thing that ever sat upon water. It had a complete flush deck, with only a small hatch near the bow, and this hatch it had always been our custom to batten down when about to cross the Ström, by way of precaution against the chopping seas. But for this circumstance we should have foundered at once —for we lay entirely buried for some moments. How my elder brother escaped destruction I cannot say, for I never had an opportunity of ascertaining. For my part, as soon as I had let the foresail run, I threw myself flat on deck, with my feet against the narrow gunwale of the bow, and with my hands grasping a ring-bolt near the foot of the foremast. It was mere instinct that prompted me to do this—which was undoubtedly the very best thing I could have done—for I was too much flurried to think.

"For some moments we were completely deluged, as I say, and all this time I held my breath, and clung to the bolt. When I could stand it no longer I raised myself upon my knees, still keeping hold with my hands, and thus got my head clear. Presently our little boat gave herself a shake, just as a dog does in coming out of the water, and thus rid herself, in some measure, of the seas. I was now trying to get the better of the stupor that had come over me, and to collect my senses as to see what was to be done, when I felt somebody grasp my arm. It was my elder brother, and my heart leaped for joy, for I had made sure that he was overboard—but the next moment all this joy turned into horror—for he put his mouth close to my ear, and screamed out the word '*Moskoe-ström!*'

"No one ever will know what my feelings were at that moment. I shook from head to foot as if I had had the most violent fit of the ague. I knew what he meant by that one word well enough—I knew what he wished to make me understand. With the wind that now drove us on, we were bound for the whirl of the Ström, and nothing could save us!

"You perceive that in crossing the Ström *channel,* we always went a long way up above the whirl, even in the calmest weather, and then had to wait and watch carefully for the slack—but now we were driving right upon the pool itself, and in such a hurricane as this! 'To be sure,' I thought, 'we shall get there just about the slack— there is some little hope in that'—but in the next moment I cursed myself for being so great a fool as to dream of hope at all. I knew very well that we were doomed, had we been ten times a ninety-gun ship.

"By this time the first fury of the tempest had spent itself, or perhaps we did not feel it so much, as we scudded before it, but at all events the seas, which at first had been kept down by the wind, and lay flat and frothing, now got up into absolute mountains. A singular change, too, had come over the heavens. Around in every direction it was still as black as pitch, but nearly overhead there burst out, all at once, a circular rift of clear sky—as clear as I ever saw—and of a deep bright blue—and through it there blazed forth the full moon with a lustre that I never before knew her to wear. She lit up every thing about us with the greatest distinctness—but, oh God, what a scene it was to light up!

"I now made one or two attempts to speak to my brother—but in some manner which I could not understand, the din had so increased that I could not make him hear a single word, although I screamed at the top of my voice in his ear. Presently he shook his head, looking as pale as death, and held up one of his fingers, as if to say *'listen!'*

"At first I could not make out what he meant—but soon a hideous thought flashed upon me. I dragged my watch from its fob. It was not going. I glanced at its face by the moonlight, and then burst into tears as I flung it far away into the ocean. *It had run down at seven o'clock! We were behind the time of the slack, and the whirl of the Ström was in full fury!*

"When a boat is well built, properly trimmed, and not deep laden, the waves in a strong gale, when she is going large, seem always to slip from beneath her—which appears very strange to a landsman—and this is what is called *riding,* in sea phrase.

"Well, so far we had ridden the swells very cleverly; but presently a gigantic sea happened to take us right under the counter, and bore us with it as it rose—up—up—as if into the sky. I would not have believed that any wave could rise so high. And then down we came with a sweep, a slide, and a plunge, that made me feel sick and dizzy, as if I was falling from some lofty mountain-top in a dream. But while we were up I had thrown a quick glance around—and that one glance was all sufficient. I saw our exact position in an instant. The Moskoe-ström whirlpool was about a quarter of a mile dead ahead—but no more like the every-day Moskoe-ström, than the whirl as you now see it, is like a mill-race. If I had not known where we were, and what we had to expect, I should not have recognised the place at all. As it was, I involuntarily closed my eyes in horror. The lids clenched themselves together as if in a spasm.

"It could not have been more than two minutes afterwards until we suddenly felt the waves subside, and were enveloped in foam. The boat made a sharp half turn to larboard, and then shot off in its new direction like a thunderbolt. At the same moment the roaring noise of the water was completely drowned in a kind of shrill shriek—such a sound as you might imagine given out by the water-pipes of many thousand steam-vessels, letting off their steam all together. We were now in the belt of surf that always surrounds the whirl; and I thought, of course, that another moment would plunge us into the abyss—down which we could only see indistinctly on account of the amazing velocity with which we were borne along. The boat did not seem to sink into the water at all, but to skim like an air-bubble upon the surface of the surge. Her starboard side was next the whirl, and on the larboard arose the world of ocean we had left. It stood like a huge writhing wall between us and the horizon.

"It may appear strange, but now, when we were in the very jaws of the gulf, I felt more composed than when we were only approaching it. Having made up my mind to hope no more, I got rid of a great deal of that terror which unmanned me at first. I suppose it was despair that strung my nerves.

"It may look like boasting—but what I tell you is truth—I began to reflect how magnificent a thing it was to die in such a manner, and how foolish it was in me to think of so paltry a consideration as my own individual life, in view of so wonderful a manifestation of God's power. I do believe that I blushed with shame when this idea crossed my mind. After a little while I became possessed with the keenest curiosity about the whirl itself. I positively felt a *wish* to explore its depths, even at the sacrifice I was going to make; and my principal grief was that I should never be able to tell my old companions on shore about the mysteries I should see. These, no doubt, were singular fancies to occupy a man's mind in such extremity—and I have often thought since, that the revolutions of the boat around the pool might have rendered me a little light-headed.

"There was another circumstance which tended to restore my self-possession; and this was the cessation of the wind, which could not reach us in our present situation —for, as you saw yourself, the belt of surf is considerably lower than the general bed of the ocean, and this latter now towered above us, a high, black, mountainous ridge. If you have never been at sea in a heavy gale, you can form no idea of the confusion of mind occasioned by the wind and spray together. They blind, deafen and strangle you, and take away all power of action or reflection. But we were now, in a great measure, rid of these annoyances—just as death-condemned felons in prison are allowed petty indulgences, forbidden them while their doom is yet uncertain.

"How often we made the circuit of the belt it is impossible to say. We careered round and round for perhaps an hour, flying rather than floating, getting gradually more and more into the middle of the surge, and then nearer and nearer to its horrible inner edge. All this time I had never let go of the ring-bolt. My brother was at the stern, holding on to a large empty water-cask which had been securely lashed under the coop of the counter, and was the only thing on deck that had not been swept overboard when the gale first took us. As we approached the brink of the pit he let go his hold upon this, and made for the ring, from which, in the agony of his terror, he endeavored to force my hands, as it was not large enough to afford us both a secure grasp. I never felt deeper grief than when I saw him attempt this act—although I knew he was a madman when he did it—a raving maniac through sheer fright. I did not care, however, to contest the point with him. I thought it could make no difference whether either of us held on at all; so I let him have the bolt, and went astern to the cask. This there was no great difficulty in doing; for the smack flew round steadily enough, and upon an even keel—only swaying to and fro, with the immense sweeps and swelters of the whirl. Scarcely had I secured myself in my new position, when we gave a wild lurch to starboard, and rushed headlong into the abyss. I muttered a hurried prayer to God, and thought all was over.

"As I felt the sickening sweep of the descent, I had instinctively tightened my hold upon the barrel, and closed my eyes. For some seconds I dared not open them—while I expected instant destruction, and wondered that I was not already in my death-struggles with the water. But moment after moment elapsed. I still lived. The sense of falling had ceased; and the motion of the vessel seemed much as it had been before while in the belt of foam, with the exception that she now lay more along. I took courage and looked once again upon the scene.

"Never shall I forget the sensations of awe, horror, and admiration with which I gazed about me. The boat appeared to be hanging, as if by magic, midway down, upon the interior surface of a funnel vast in circumference, prodigious in depth, and whose perfectly smooth sides might have been mistaken for ebony, but for the bewildering rapidity with which they spun around, and for the gleaming and ghastly radiance they shot forth, as the rays of the full moon, from that circular rift amid the clouds which I have already described, streamed in a flood of golden glory along the black walls, and far away down into the inmost recesses of the abyss.

"At first I was too much confused to observe anything accurately. The general burst of terrific grandeur was all that I beheld. When I recovered myself a little, however, my gaze fell instinctively downward. In this direction I was able to obtain an unobstructed view, from the manner in which the smack hung on the inclined surface of the pool. She was quite upon an even keel—that is to say, her deck lay in a plane parallel with that of the water—but this latter sloped at an angle of more than forty-five degrees, so that we seemed to be lying upon our beam-ends. I could not help observing, nevertheless, that I had scarcely more difficulty in maintaining my hold and footing in this situation, than if we had been upon a deal level; and this, I suppose, was owing to the speed at which we revolved.

"The rays of the moon seemed to search the very bottom of the profound gulf; but still I could make out nothing distinctly, on account of a thick mist in which everything there was enveloped, and over which there hung a magnificent rainbow, like that narrow and tottering bridge which Mussulmen[6] say is the only pathway between Time and Eternity. This mist, or spray, was no doubt occasioned by the clashing of the great walls of the funnel, as they all met together at the bottom—but the yell that went up to the Heavens from out of that mist, I dare not attempt to describe.

"Our first slide into the abyss itself, from the belt of foam above, had carried us to a great distance down that slope; but our farther descent was by no means proportionate. Round and round we swept—not with any uniform movement—but in dizzying swings and jerks, that sent us sometimes only a few hundred feet—sometimes nearly the complete circuit of the whirl. Our progress downward, at each revolution, was slow, but very perceptible.

"Looking about me upon the wide waste of liquid ebony on which we were thus borne, I perceived that our boat was not the only object in the embrace of the whirl. Both above and below us were visible fragments of vessels, large masses of building timber and trunks of trees, with many smaller articles, such as pieces of house furniture, broken boxes, barrels and staves. I have already described the unnatural curiosity which had taken the place of my original terrors. It appeared to grow upon me as I drew nearer and nearer to my dreadful doom. I now began to watch, with a strange interest, the numerous things that floated in our company. I *must* have been delirious—for I even sought *amusement* in speculating upon the relative velocities of their several descents toward the foam below. 'This fir tree,' I found myself at one time saying, 'will certainly be the next thing that takes the awful plunge and disappears,'—and then I was disappointed to find that the wreck of a Dutch merchant ship overtook it and went down before. At length, after making several guesses of this nature, and being deceived in all—this fact—the fact of my invariable miscalculation, set me upon a train of reflection that made my limbs again tremble, and my heart beat heavily once more.

"It was not a new terror that thus affected me, but the dawn of a more exciting *hope*. This hope arose partly from memory, and partly from present observation. I called to mind the great variety of buoyant matter that strewed the coast of Lofoden, having been absorbed and then thrown forth by the Moskoe-ström. By far the greater number of the articles were shattered in the most extraordinary way—so chafed and roughened as to have the appearance of being stuck full of splinters—but then I distinctly recollected that there were *some* of them which were not disfigured at all.

[6] Mohammedans.

Now I could not account for this difference except by supposing that the roughened fragments were the only ones which had been *completely absorbed*—that the others had entered the whirl at so late a period of the tide, or, from some reason, had descended so slowly after entering, that they did not reach the bottom before the turn of the flood came, or of the ebb, as the case might be. I conceived it possible, in either instance, that they might thus be whirled up again to the level of the ocean, without undergoing the fate of those which had been drawn in more early or absorbed more rapidly. I made, also, three important observations. The first was, that as a general rule, the larger the bodies were, the more rapid their descent;—the second, that, between two masses of equal extent, the one spherical, and the other *of any other shape,* the superiority in speed of descent was with the sphere;—the third, that, between two masses of equal size, the one cylindrical, and the other of any other shape, the cylinder was absorbed the more slowly.

Since my escape, I have had several conversations on this subject with an old school-master of the district; and it was from him that I learned the use of the words 'cylinder' and 'sphere.' He explained to me—although I have forgotten the explanation—how what I observed was, in fact, the natural consequence of the forms of the floating fragments—and showed me how it happened that a cylinder, swimming in a vortex, offered more resistance to its suction, and was drawn in with greater difficulty than an equally bulky body, of any form whatever.[7]

"There was one startling circumstance which went a great way in enforcing these observations, and rendering me anxious to turn them to account, and this was that, at every revolution, we passed something like a barrel, or else the broken yard or the mast of a vessel, while many of these things, which had been on our level when I first opened my eyes upon the wonders of the whirlpool, were now high up above us, and seemed to have moved but little from their original station.

"I no longer hesitated what to do. I resolved to lash myself securely to the water cask upon which I now held, to cut it loose from the counter, and to throw myself with it into the water. I attracted my brother's attention by signs, pointed to the floating barrels that came near us, and did everything in my power to make him understand what I was about to do. I thought at length that he comprehended my design—but, whether this was the case or not, he shook his head despairingly, and refused to move from his station by the ring-bolt. It was impossible to force him; the emergency admitted no delay; and so, with a bitter struggle, I resigned him to his fate, fastened myself to the cask by means of the lashings which secured it to the counter, and precipitated myself with it into the sea, without another moment's hesitation.

"The result was precisely what I had hoped it might be. As it is myself who now tell you this tale—as you see that I *did* escape—and as you are already in possession of the mode in which this escape was effected, and must therefore anticipate all that I have farther to say—I will bring my story quickly to conclusion. It might have been an hour, or thereabout, after my quitting the smack, when, having descended to a vast distance beneath me, it made three or four wild gyrations in rapid succession, and, bearing my loved brother with it, plunged headlong, at once and forever, into the

---

[7] Poe's note: "See Archimedes, *De Incidentibus in Fluido.*'—lib. 2." This is one of Poe's partial fabrications, designed to add a scientific aura to the explanation he gives to the story's outcome.

chaos of foam below. The barrel to which I was attached sunk very little farther than half the distance between the bottom of the gulf and the spot at which I leaped overboard, before a great change took place in the character of the whirlpool. The slope of the sides of the vast funnel became momently less and less steep. The gyrations of the whirl grew, gradually, less and less violent. By degrees, the froth and the rainbow disappeared, and the bottom of the gulf seemed slowly to uprise. The sky was clear, the winds had gone down, and the full moon was setting radiantly in the west, when I found myself on the surface of the ocean, in full view of the shores of Lofoden, and above the spot where the pool of the Moskoe-ström *had been.* It was the hour of the slack—but the sea still heaved in mountainous waves from the effects of the hurricane. I was borne violently into the channel of the Ström, and in a few minutes, was hurried down the coast into the 'grounds' of the fishermen. A boat picked me up—exhausted from fatigue—and (now that the danger was removed) speechless from the memory of its horror. Those who drew me on board were my old mates and daily companions—but they knew me no more than they would have known a traveller from the spirit-land. My hair, which had been raven-black the day before, was as white as you see it now. They say too that the whole expression of my countenance had changed. I told them my story—they did not believe it. I now tell it to *you*—and I can scarcely expect you to put more faith in it than did the merry fishermen of Lofoden.

1841

The Murders in the Rue Morgue

What song the Syrens sang, or what name Achilles assumed when he hid himself among women, although puzzling questions are not beyond all conjecture.
Sir Thomas Browne, *Urn-Burial*[1]

The mental features discoursed of as the analytical, are, in themselves, but little susceptible of analysis. We appreciate them only in their effects. We know of them, among other things, that they are always to their possessor, when inordinately possessed, a source of the liveliest enjoyment. As the strong man exults in his physical ability, delighting in such exercises as call his muscles into action, so glories the analyst in that moral activity which *disentangles.* He derives pleasure from even the most trivial occupations bringing his talents into play. He is fond of enigmas, of conundrums, of hieroglyphics; exhibiting in his solutions of each a degree of *acumen* which appears to the ordinary apprehension preternatural. His results, brought about by the very soul and essence of method, have, in truth, the whole air of intuition. The faculty of re-solution is possibly much invigorated by mathematical study, and especially by

---

[1] Sir Thomas Browne (1605–1682), English physician and essayist, wrote *Urn-Burial* in 1658; this quotation is from Chapter 5.

that highest branch of it which, unjustly, and merely on account of its retrograde operations, has been called, as if *par excellence,* analysis. Yet to calculate is not in itself to analyze. A chess-player, for example, does the one without effort at the other. It follows that the game of chess, in its effects upon mental character, is greatly misunderstood. I am not now writing a treatise, but simply prefacing a somewhat peculiar narrative by observations very much at random; I will, therefore, take occasion to assert that the higher powers of the reflective intellect are more decidedly and more usefully tasked by the unostentatious game of draughts than by all the elaborate frivolity of chess. In this latter, where the pieces have different and *bizarre* motions, with various and variable values, what is only complex is mistaken (a not unusual error) for what is profound. The *attention* is here called powerfully into play. If it flag for an instant, an oversight is committed, resulting in injury or defeat. The possible moves being not only manifold but involute, the chances of such oversights are multiplied; and in nine cases out of ten it is the more concentrative rather than the more acute player who conquers. In draughts,[2] on the contrary, where the moves are *unique* and have but little variation, the probabilities of inadvertence are diminished, and the mere attention being left comparatively unemployed, what advantages are obtained by either party are obtained by superior *acumen.* To be less abstract—Let us suppose a game of draughts where the pieces are reduced to four kings, and where, of course, no oversight is to be expected. It is obvious that here the victory can be decided (the players being at all equal) only by some *recherché*[3] movement, the result of some strong exertion of the intellect. Deprived of ordinary resources, the analyst throws himself into the spirit of his opponent, identifies himself therewith, and not unfrequently sees thus, at a glance, the sole methods (sometimes indeed absurdly simple ones) by which he may seduce into error or hurry into miscalculation.

Whist[4] has long been noted for its influence upon what is termed the calculating power; and men of the highest order of intellect have been known to take an apparently unaccountable delight in it, while eschewing chess as frivolous. Beyond doubt there is nothing of a similar nature so greatly tasking the faculty of analysis. The best chess-player in Christendom *may* be little more than the best player of chess; but proficiency in whist implies capacity for success in all these more important undertakings where mind struggles with mind. When I say proficiency, I mean that perfection in the game which includes a comprehension of *all* the sources whence legitimate advantage may be derived. These are not only manifold but multiform, and lie frequently among recesses of thought altogether inaccessible to the ordinary understanding. To observe attentively is to remember distinctly; and, so far, the concentrative chess-player will do very well at whist; while the rules of Hoyle[5] (themselves based upon the mere mechanism of the game) are sufficiently and generally comprehensible. Thus to have a retentive memory, and to proceed by "the book," are points commonly regarded as the sum total of good playing. But it is in matters beyond the limits of mere rule that the skill of the analyst is evinced. He makes, in silence, a host of observations and inferences. So, perhaps, do his companions; and the difference in the extent of the information obtained, lies not so much in the validity

---

[2] Checkers.
[3] French: "unusual."
[4] Card game, forerunner of bridge.

[5] Edmond Hoyle (1672–1769), English authority on card games.

of the inference as in the quality of the observation. The necessary knowledge is that of *what* to observe. Our player confines himself not at all; nor, because the game is the object, does he reject deductions from things external to the game. He examines the countenance of his partner, comparing it carefully with that of each of his opponents. He considers the mode of assorting the cards in each hand; often counting trump by trump, and honor by honor, through the glances bestowed by their holders upon each. He notes every variation of face as the play progresses, gathering a fund of thought from the differences in the expression of certainty, of surprise, of triumph, or chagrin. From the manner of gathering up a trick he judges whether the person taking it can make another in the suit. He recognizes what is played through feint, by the air with which it is thrown upon the table. A casual or inadvertent word; the accidental dropping or turning of a card, with the accompanying anxiety or careless-ness in regard to its concealment; the counting of the tricks, with the order of their arrangement; embarrassment, hesitation, eagerness or trepidation—all afford, to his apparently intuitive perception, indications of the true state of affairs. The first two or three rounds having been played, he is in full possession of the contents of each hand, and thenceforward puts down his cards with as absolute a precision of purpose as if the rest of the party had turned outward the faces of their own.

The analytical power should not be confounded with simple ingenuity; for while the analyst is necessarily ingenious, the ingenious man is often remarkably incapable of analysis. The constructive or combining power, by which ingenuity is usually manifested, and to which the phrenologists[6] (I believe erroneously) have assigned a separate organ, supposing it a primitive faculty, has been so frequently seen in those whose intellect bordered otherwise upon idiocy, as to have attracted general observa-tion among writers on morals. Between ingenuity and the analytic ability there exists a difference far greater, indeed, than that between the fancy and the imagination, but of a character very strictly analogous. It will be found, in fact, that the ingenious are always fanciful, and the *truly* imaginative never otherwise than analytic.

The narrative which follows will appear to the reader somewhat in the light of a commentary upon the propositions just advanced.

Residing in Paris during the spring and part of the summer of 18——, I there became acquainted with a Monsieur C. Auguste Dupin. This young gentleman was of an excellent—indeed of an illustrious family, but, by a variety of untoward events, had been reduced to such poverty that the energy of his character succumbed beneath it, and he ceased to bestir himself in the world, or to care for the retrieval of his fortunes. By courtesy of his creditors, there still remained in his possession a small remnant of his patrimony; and, upon the income arising from this, he managed, by means of a rigorous economy, to procure the necessaries of life, without troubling himself about its superfluities. Books, indeed, were his sole luxuries, and in Paris these are easily obtained.

Our first meeting was at an obscure library in the Rue Montmartre, where the accident of our both being in search of the same very rare and very remarkable volume, brought us into closer communion. We saw each other again and again. I was deeply interested in the little family history which he detailed to me with all that

[6] Advocates of phrenology, the system for the analysis of character and the development of the mental faculties by means of the study of the shape and bumps of the skull.

candor which a Frenchman indulges whenever mere self is the theme. I was astonished, too, at the vast extent of his reading; and, above all, I felt my soul enkindled within me by the wild fervor, and the vivid freshness of his imagination. Seeking in Paris the objects I then sought, I felt that the society of such a man would be to me a treasure beyond price; and this feeling I frankly confided to him. It was at length arranged that we should live together during my stay in the city; and as my worldly circumstances were somewhat less embarrassed than his own, I was permitted to be at the expense of renting, and furnishing in a style which suited the rather fantastic gloom of our common temper, a time-eaten and grotesque mansion, long deserted through superstitions into which we did not inquire, and tottering to its fall in a retired and desolate portion of the Faubourg St. Germain.

Had the routine of our life at this place been known to the world, we should have been regarded as madmen—although, perhaps, as madmen of a harmless nature. Our seclusion was perfect. We admitted no visitors. Indeed the locality of our retirement had been carefully kept a secret from my own former associates; and it had been many years since Dupin had ceased to know or be known in Paris. We existed within ourselves alone.

It was a freak of fancy in my friend (for what else shall I call it?) to be enamored of the Night for her own sake; and into this *bizarrerie,*[7] as into all his others, I quietly fell; giving myself up to his wild whims with a perfect *abandon.* The sable divinity would not herself dwell with us always; but we could counterfeit her presence. At the first dawn of the morning we closed all the massy shutters of our old building; lighted a couple of tapers which, strongly perfumed, threw out only the ghastliest and feeblest of rays. By the aid of these we then busied our souls in dreams—reading, writing, or conversing, until warned by the clock of the advent of the true Darkness. Then we sallied forth into the streets, arm and arm, continuing the topics of the day, or roaming far and wide until a late hour, seeking, amid the wild lights and shadows of the populous city, that infinity of mental excitement which quiet observation can afford.

At such times I could not help remarking and admiring (although from his rich ideality I had been prepared to expect it) a peculiar analytic ability in Dupin. He seemed, too, to take an eager delight in its exercise—if not exactly in its display—and did not hesitate to confess the pleasure thus derived. He boasted to me, with a low chuckling laugh, that most men, in respect to himself, wore windows in their bosoms, and was wont to follow up such assertions by direct and very startling proofs of his intimate knowledge of my own. His manner at these moments was frigid and abstract; his eyes were vacant in expression; while his voice, usually a rich tenor, rose into a treble which would have sounded petulantly but for the deliberateness and entire distinctness of the enunciation. Observing him in these moods, I often dwelt meditatively upon the old philosophy of the Bi-Part Soul, and amused myself with the fancy of a double Dupin—the creative and the resolvent.

Let it not be supposed, from what I have just said, that I am detailing any mystery, or penning any romance. What I have described in the Frenchman, was merely the

---

[7] French: "extravagant behavior."

result of an excited, or perhaps of a diseased intelligence. But of the character of his remarks at the periods in question an example will best convey the idea.

We were strolling one night down a long dirty street, in the vicinity of the Palais Royal. Being both, apparently, occupied with thought, neither of us had spoken a syllable for fifteen minutes at least. All at once Dupin broke forth with these words:—

"He is a very little fellow, that's true, and would do better for the *Théâtre des Variétés*."[8]

"There can be no doubt of that," I replied unwittingly, and not at first observing (so much had I been absorbed in reflection) the extraordinary manner in which the speaker had chimed in with my meditations. In an instant afterward I recollected myself, and my astonishment was profound.

"Dupin," said I, gravely, "this is beyond my comprehension. I do not hesitate to say that I am amazed, and can scarcely credit my senses. How was it possible you should know I was thinking of ———?" Here I paused, to ascertain beyond a doubt whether he really knew of whom I thought.

——— "of Chantilly," said he, "why do you pause? You were remarking to yourself that his diminutive figure unfitted him for tragedy."

This was precisely what had formed the subject of my reflections. Chantilly was a *quondam*[9] cobbler of the Rue St. Denis, who, becoming stage-mad, had attempted the *rôle* of Xerxes, in Crébillon's tragedy so called, and been notoriously Pasquinaded[10] for his pains.

"Tell me, for Heaven's sake," I exclaimed, "the method—if method there is—by which you have been enabled to fathom my soul in this matter." In fact I was even more startled than I would have been willing to express.

"It was the fruiterer," replied my friend, "who brought you to the conclusion that the mender of soles was not of sufficient height for Xerxes *et id genus omne*."[11]

"The fruiterer!—you astonish me—I know no fruiterer whomsoever."

"The man who ran up against you as we entered the street—it may have been fifteen minutes ago."

I now remembered that, in fact, a fruiterer, carrying upon his head a large basket of apples, had nearly thrown me down, by accident, as we passed from the Rue C—— into the thoroughfare where we stood; but what this had to do with Chantilly I could not possibly understand.

There was not a particle of *charlatanerie*[12] about Dupin. "I will explain," he said, "and that you may comprehend all clearly, we will first retrace the course of your meditations, from the moment in which I spoke to you until that of the *rencontre*[13] with the fruiterer in question. The larger links of the chain run thus—Chantilly, Orion, Dr. Nichols, Epicurus, Stereotomy, the street stones, the fruiterer."

There are few persons who have not, at some period of their lives, amused

[8] Vaudeville hall.
[9] Former (originally Latin).
[10] Ridiculed by means of a satiric lampoon.
Crébillon: Prosper Crébillon (1674–1762),
French dramatist.

[11] Latin: "and all that sort of thing."
[12] French: "fraudulence."
[13] French: "encounter."

themselves in retracing the steps by which particular conclusions of their own minds have been attained. The occupation is often full of interest; and he who attempts it for the first time is astonished by the apparently illimitable distance and incoherence between the starting-point and the goal. What, then, must have been my amazement when I heard the Frenchman speak what he had just spoken, and when I could not help acknowledging that he had spoken the truth. He continued:

"We had been talking of horses, if I remember aright, just before leaving the Rue C——. This was the last subject we discussed. As we crossed into this street, a fruiterer, with a large basket upon his head, brushing quickly past us, thrust you upon a pile of paving-stones collected at a spot where the causeway is undergoing repair. You stepped upon one of the loose fragments, slipped, slightly strained your ankle, appeared vexed or sulky, muttered a few words, turned to look at the pile, and then proceeded in silence. I was not particularly attentive to what you did; but observation has become with me, of late, a species of necessity.

"You kept your eyes upon the ground—glancing, with a petulant expression, at the holes and ruts in the pavement, (so that I saw you were still thinking of the stones,) until we reached the little alley called Lamartine, which has been paved, by way of experiment, with the overlapping and riveted blocks. Here your countenance brightened up, and, perceiving your lips move, I could not doubt that you murmured the word 'stereotomy,'[14] a term very affectedly applied to this species of pavement. I knew that you could not say to yourself 'stereotomy' without being brought to think of atomies,[15] and thus of the theories of Epicurus;[16] and since, when we discussed this subject not very long ago, I mentioned to you how singularly, yet with how little notice, the vague guesses of that noble Greek had met with confirmation in the late nebular cosmogony, I felt that you could not avoid casting your eyes upward to the great *nebula* in Orion,[17] and I certainly expected that you would do so. You did look up; and I was now assured that I had correctly followed your steps. But in that bitter *tirade* upon Chantilly, which appeared in yesterday's '*Musée*,'[18] the satirist, making some disgraceful allusions to the cobbler's change of name upon assuming the buskin,[19] quoted a Latin line about which we have often conversed. I mean the line

Perdidit antiquum litera prima sonum.[20]

I had told you that this was in reference to Orion, formerly written Urion; and, from certain pungencies connected with this explanation, I was aware that you could not have forgotten it. It was clear, therefore, that you would not fail to combine the two ideas of Orion and Chantilly. That you did combine them I saw by the character of

---

[14] Division of geometry that deals with the cutting of solids into sections; also, the cutting of solid blocks of stone, as in masonry or cobblestones.
[15] Particles.
[16] Greek philosopher (342?–270 B.C.) who maintained that all things are made of atoms.
[17] Constellation of stars.
[18] Literally "arts museum," here the title of a journal.

[19] High-laced boot worn by actors in classical tragedy; to wear buskins means to assume tragic roles.
[20] "The first letter has lost its original sound." This quotation is taken from Ovid's *Fasti* in allusion to the birth of Orion, whose name was originally Urion.

the smile which passed over your lips. You thought of the poor cobbler's immolation. So far, you had been stooping in your gait; but now I saw you draw yourself up to your full height. I was then sure that you reflected upon the diminutive figure of Chantilly. At this point I interrupted your meditations to remark that as, in fact, he *was* a very little fellow—that Chantilly—he would do better at the *Théâtre des Variétés.*"

Not long after this, we were looking over an evening edition of the "Gazette des Tribunaux,"[21] when the following paragraphs arrested our attention.

"EXTRAORDINARY MURDERS.—This morning, about three o'clock, the inhabitants of the Quartier St. Roch were aroused from sleep by a succession of terrific shrieks, issuing, apparently, from the fourth story of a house in the Rue Morgue, known to be in the sole occupancy of one Madame L'Espanaye, and her daughter, Mademoiselle Camille L'Espanaye. After some delay, occasioned by a fruitless attempt to procure admission in the usual manner, the gateway was broken in with a crowbar, and eight or ten of the neighbors entered, accompanied by two *gendarmes.* By this time the cries had ceased; but, as the party rushed up the first flight of stairs, two or more rough voices, in angry contention, were distinguished, and seemed to proceed from the upper part of the house. As the second landing was reached, these sounds, also, had ceased, and everything remained perfectly quiet. The party spread themselves, and hurried from room to room. Upon arriving at a large back chamber in the fourth story, (the door of which, being found locked, with the key inside, was forced open,) a spectacle presented itself which struck every one present not less with horror than with astonishment.

"The apartment was in the wildest disorder—the furniture broken and thrown about in all directions. There was only one bedstead; and from this the bed had been removed, and thrown into the middle of the floor. On a chair lay a razor, besmeared with blood. On the hearth were two or three long and thick tresses of grey human hair, also dabbled in blood, and seeming to have been pulled out by the roots. Upon the floor were found four Napoleons,[22] an ear-ring of topaz, three large silver spoons, three smaller of *métal d' Alger,*[23] and two bags, containing nearly four thousand francs in gold. The drawers of a *bureau,* which stood in one corner, were open, and had been, apparently, rifled, although many articles still remained in them. A small iron safe was discovered under the *bed* (not under the bedstead). It was open, with the key still in the door. It had no contents beyond a few old letters, and other papers of little consequence.

"Of Madame L'Espanaye no traces were here seen; but an unusual quantity of soot being observed in the fire-place, a search was made in the chimney, and (horrible to relate!) the corpse of the daughter, head downward, was dragged therefrom; it having been thus forced up the narrow aperture for a considerable distance. The body was quite warm. Upon examining it, many excoriations were perceived, no doubt occasioned by the violence with which it had been thrust up and disengaged. Upon the face were many severe scratches, and upon the throat, dark bruises, and deep indentations of finger nails, as if the deceased had been throttled to death.

"After a thorough investigation of every portion of the house, without farther

[21] French: "News of the Courts of Justice." [23] Coinage made of an inexpensive alloy.
[22] Gold pieces.

discovery, the party made its way into a small paved yard in the rear of the building, where lay the corpse of the old lady, with her throat so entirely cut that, upon an attempt to raise her, the head fell off. The body, as well as the head, was fearfully mutilated—the former so much so as scarcely to retain any semblance of humanity.

"To this horrible mystery there is not as yet, we believe, the slightest clew."

The next day's paper had these additional particulars.

"*The Tragedy in the Rue Morgue.* Many individuals have been examined in relation to this most extraordinary and frightful affair." [The word *'affaire'* has not yet, in France, that levity of import which it conveys with us,] "but nothing whatever has transpired to throw light upon it. We give below all the material testimony elicited.

"*Pauline Dubourg,* laundress, deposes that she had known both the deceased for three years, having washed for them during that period. The old lady and her daughter seemed on good terms—very affectionate towards each other. They were excellent pay. Could not speak in regard to their mode or means of living. Believed that Madame L. told fortunes for a living. Was reputed to have money put by. Never met any persons in the house when she called for the clothes or took them home. Was sure that they had no servant in employ. There appeared to be no furniture in any part of the building except in the fourth story.

"*Pierre Moreau,* tobacconist, deposes that he has been in the habit of selling small quantities of tobacco and snuff to Madame L'Espanaye for nearly four years. Was born in the neighborhood, and has always resided there. The deceased and her daughter had occupied the house in which the corpses were found, for more than six years. It was formerly occupied by a jeweller, who under-let the upper rooms to various persons. The house was the property of Madame L. She became dissatisfied with the abuse of the premises by her tenant, and moved into them herself, refusing to let any portion. The old lady was childish. Witness had seen the daughter some five or six times during the six years. The two lived an exceedingly retired life—were reputed to have money. Had heard it said among the neighbors that Madame L. told fortunes—did not believe it. Had never seen any person enter the door except the old lady and her daughter, a porter once or twice, and a physician some eight or ten times.

"Many other persons, neighbors, gave evidence to the same effect. No one was spoken of as frequenting the house. It was not known whether there were any living connexions of Madame L. and her daughter. The shutters of the front windows were seldom opened. Those in the rear were always closed, with the exception of the large back room, fourth story. The house was a good house—not very old.

"*Isidore Muset, gendarme,* deposes that he was called to the house about three o'clock in the morning, and found some twenty or thirty persons at the gateway, endeavoring to gain admittance. Forced it open, at length, with a bayonet—not with a crowbar. Had but little difficulty in getting it open, on account of its being a double or folding gate, and bolted neither at bottom nor top. The shrieks were continued until the gate was forced—and then suddenly ceased. They seemed to be screams of some person (or persons) in great agony—were loud and drawn out, not short and quick. Witness led the way up stairs. Upon reaching the first landing, heard two voices in loud and angry contention—the one a gruff voice, the other much shriller—a very strange voice. Could distinguish some words of the former, which was that of a Frenchman. Was positive that it was not a woman's voice. Could distinguish the words *'sacré'* and '*diable.*'[24] The shrill voice was that of a foreigner. Could not be sure whether it was the voice of a man or of a woman. Could not make out what was said, but believed the language to be Spanish. The state of the room and of the bodies was described by this witness as we described them yesterday.

"*Henri Duval,* a neighbor, and by trade a silversmith, deposes that he was one of the party who first entered the house. Corroborates the testimony of Musèt in general. As soon as they forced an entrance, they reclosed the door, to keep out the crowd, which collected very fast, notwithstanding the lateness of the hour. The shrill voice, the witness thinks, was that of an Italian. Was certain it was not French. Could not be sure that it was a man's voice. It might have been a woman's. Was not acquainted with the Italian language. Could not distinguish the words, but was convinced by the intonation that the speaker was an Italian. Knew Madame L. and her daughter. Had conversed with both frequently. Was sure that the shrill voice was not that of either of the deceased.

"————— *Odenheimer, restaurateur.* This witness volunteered his testimony. Not speaking French, was examined through an interpreter. Is a native of Amsterdam. Was passing the house at the time of the shrieks. They lasted for several minutes—probably ten. They were long and loud—very awful and distressing. Was one of those who entered the building. Corroborated the previous evidence in every respect but one. Was sure that the shrill voice was that of a man—of a Frenchman. Could not distinguish the words uttered. They were loud and quick—unequal—spoken apparently in fear as well as in anger. The voice was harsh—not so much shrill as harsh. Could not call it a shrill voice. The gruff voice said repeatedly '*sacré,*' '*diable*' and once '*mon Dieu.*'[25]

"*Jules Mignaud,* banker, of the firm of Mignaud et fils, Rue Deloraine. Is the elder Mignaud. Madame L'Espanaye had some property. Had opened an account with his banking house in the spring of the year ————— (eight years previously). Made frequent deposits in small sums. Had checked for nothing until the third day before her death, when she took out in person the sum of 4000 francs. This sum was paid in gold, and a clerk sent home with the money.

"*Adolphe Le Bon,* clerk to Mignaud et Fils, deposes that on the day in question, about noon, he accompanied Madame L'Espanaye to her residence with the 4000 francs, put up in two bags. Upon the door being opened, Mademoiselle L. appeared and took from his hands one of the bags, while the old lady relieved him of the other. He then bowed and departed. Did not see any person in the street at the time. It is a bye-street—very lonely.

"*William Bird,* tailor, deposes that he was one of the party who entered the house. Is an Englishman. Has lived in Paris two years. Was one of the first to ascend the stairs. Heard the voices in contention. The gruff voice was that of a Frenchman. Could make out several words, but cannot now remember all. Heard distinctly '*sacré*' and '*mon Dieu.*' There was a sound at the moment as if of several persons struggling— a scraping and scuffling sound. The shrill voice was very loud—louder than the gruff one. Is sure that it was not the voice of an Englishman. Appeared to be that of a German. Might have been a woman's voice. Does not understand German.

[24] French: "damn" and "the devil."   [25] French "My God!"

"Four of the above-named witnesses, being recalled, deposed that the door of the chamber in which was found the body of Mademoiselle L. was locked on the inside when the party reached it. Every thing was perfectly silent—no groans or noises of any kind. Upon forcing the door no person was seen. The windows, both of the back and front room, were down and firmly fastened from within. A door between the two rooms was closed, but not locked. The door leading from the front room into the passage was locked, with the key on the inside. A small room in the front of the house, on the fourth story, at the head of the passage, was open, the door being ajar. This room was crowded with old beds, boxes, and so forth. These were carefully removed and searched. There was not an inch of any portion of the house which was not carefully searched. Sweeps were sent up and down the chimneys. The house was a four story one, with garrets (*mansardes*).[26] A trap-door on the roof was nailed down very securely—did not appear to have been opened for years. The time elapsing between the hearing of the voices in contention and the breaking open of the room door, was variously stated by the witnesses. Some made it as short as three minutes —some as long as five. The door was opened with difficulty.

"*Alfonzo Garcio,* undertaker, deposes that he resides in the Rue Morgue. Is a native of Spain. Was one of the party who entered the house. Did not proceed up stairs. Is nervous, and was apprehensive of the consequences of agitation. Heard the voices in contention. The gruff voice was that of a Frenchman. Could not distinguish what was said. The shrill voice was that of an Englishman—is sure of this. Does not understand the English language, but judges by the intonation.

"*Alberto Montani,* confectioner, deposes that he was among the first to ascend the stairs. Heard the voices in question. The gruff voice was that of a Frenchman. Distinguished several words. The speaker appeared to be expostulating. Could not make out the words of the shrill voice. Spoke quick and unevenly. Thinks it the voice of a Russian. Corroborates the general testimony. Is an Italian. Never conversed with a native of Russia.

"Several witnesses, recalled, here testified that the chimneys of all the rooms on the fourth story were too narrow to admit the passage of a human being. By 'sweeps' were meant cylindrical sweeping-brushes, such as are employed by those who clean chimneys. These brushes were passed up and down every flue in the house. There is no back passage by which any one could have descended while the party proceeded up stairs. The body of Mademoiselle L'Espanaye was so firmly wedged in the chimney that it could not be got down until four or five of the party united their strength.

"*Paul Dumas,* physician, deposes that he was called to view the bodies about day-break. They were both then lying on the sacking of the bedstead in the chamber where Mademoiselle L. was found. The corpse of the young lady was much bruised and excoriated. The fact that it had been thrust up the chimney would sufficiently account for these appearances. The throat was greatly chafed. There were several deep scratches just below the chin, together with a series of livid spots which were evidently the impression of fingers. The face was fearfully discolored, and the eye-balls protruded. The tongue had been partially bitten through. A large bruise was discovered

---

[26] Top rooms, under steeply sloping roofs, in the building design revived and popularized by François Mansard (1598–1666), French architect.

upon the pit of the stomach, produced, apparently, by the pressure of a knee. In the opinion of M. Dumas, Mademoiselle L'Espanaye had been throttled to death by some person or persons unknown. The corpse of the mother was horribly mutilated. All the bones of the right leg and arm were more or less shattered. The left *tibia* much splintered, as well as all the ribs of the left side. Whole body dreadfully bruised and discolored. It was not possible to say how the injuries had been inflicted. A heavy club of wood, or a broad bar of iron—a chair—any large, heavy, and obtuse weapon would have produced such results, if wielded by the hands of a very powerful man. No woman could have inflicted the blows with any weapon. The head of the deceased, when seen by witness, was entirely separated from the body, and was also greatly shattered. The throat had evidently been cut with some very sharp instrument— probably with a razor.

"*Alexandre Etienne,* surgeon, was called with M. Dumas to view the bodies. Corroborated the testimony, and the opinions of M. Dumas.

"Nothing farther of importance was elicited, although several other persons were examined. A murder so mysterious, and so perplexing in all its particulars, was never before committed in Paris—if indeed a murder has been committed at all. The police are entirely at fault—an unusual occurrence in affairs of this nature. There is not, however, the shadow of a clew apparent."

The evening edition of the paper stated that the greatest excitement still continued in the Quartier St. Roch—that the premises in question had been carefully re-searched, and fresh examinations of witnesses instituted, but all to no purpose. A postscript, however mentioned that Adolphe Le Bon had been arrested and imprisoned —although nothing appeared to criminate him, beyond the facts already detailed.

Dupin seemed singularly interested in the progress of this affair—at least so I judged from his manner, for he made no comments. It was only after the announce-ment that Le Bon had been imprisoned, that he asked me my opinion respecting the murders.

I could merely agree with all Paris in considering them an insoluble mystery. I saw no means by which it would be possible to trace the murderer.

"We must not judge of the means," said Dupin, "by this shell of an examination. The Parisian police, so much extolled for *acumen,* are cunning, but no more. There is no method in their proceedings, beyond the method of the moment. They make a vast parade of measures; but, not unfrequently, these are so ill adapted to the objects proposed, as to put us in mind of Monsieur Jourdain's calling for his *robe-de-chambre* —*pour mieux entendre la musique.*[27] The results attained by them are not unfrequently surprising, but, for the most part, are brought about by simple diligence and activity. When these qualities are unavailing, their schemes fail. Vidocq, for example, was a good guesser, and a persevering man. But, without educated thought, he erred continually by the very intensity of his investigations. He impaired his vision by holding the object too close. He might see, perhaps, one or two points with unusual clearness, but in so doing he, necessarily, lost sight of the matter as a whole. Thus there is such a thing as being too profound. Truth is not always in a well. In fact, as regards

[27] French: "dressing-gown—the better to hear the music": Allusion to the somewhat stupid character whose behavior often fails to fit the occasion in *Le Bourgeois Gentilhomme* (Act I, Sc. ii), French comedy by Molière (1622–1673).

the more important knowledge, I do believe that she is invariably superficial. The depth lies in the valleys where we seek her, and not upon the mountain-tops where she is found. The modes and sources of this kind of error are well typified in the contemplation of the heavenly bodies. To look at a star by glances—to view it in a side-long way, by turning toward it the exterior portions of the *retina* (more susceptible of feeble impressions of light than the interior), is to behold the star distinctly—is to have the best appreciation of its lustre—a lustre which grows dim just in proportion as we turn our vision *fully* upon it. A greater number of rays actually fall upon the eye in the latter case, but, in the former, there is the more refined capacity for comprehension. By undue profundity we perplex and enfeeble thought; and it is possible to make even Venus herself vanish from the firmament by a scrutiny too sustained, too concentrated, or too direct.

"As for these murders, let us enter into some examinations for ourselves, before we make up an opinion respecting them. An inquiry will afford us amusement," [I thought this an odd term, so applied, but said nothing] "and, besides, Le Bon once rendered me a service for which I am not ungrateful. We will go and see the premises with our own eyes. I know G——, the Prefect of Police, and shall have no difficulty in obtaining the necessary permission."

The permission was obtained, and we proceeded at once to the Rue Morgue. This is one of those miserable thoroughfares which intervene between the Rue Richelieu and the Rue St. Roch. It was late in the afternoon when we reached it; as this quarter is at a great distance from that in which we resided. The house was readily found; for there were still many persons gazing up at the closed shutters, with an objectless curiosity, from the opposite side of the way. It was an ordinary Parisian house, with a gateway, on one side of which was a glazed watch-box, with a sliding panel in the window, indicating a *loge de concierge*.[28] Before going in we walked up the street, turned down an alley, and then, again turning, passed in the rear of the building— Dupin, meanwhile, examining the whole neighborhood, as well as the house, with a minuteness of attention for which I could see no possible object.

Retracing our steps, we came again to the front of the dwelling, rang, and, having shown our credentials, were admitted by the agents in charge. We went up stairs— into the chamber where the body of Mademoiselle L'Espanaye had been found, and where both the deceased still lay. The disorders of the room had, as usual, been suffered to exist. I saw nothing beyond what had been stated in the "Gazette des Tribunaux." Dupin scrutinized every thing—not excepting the bodies of the victims. We then went into the other rooms, and into the yard; a *gendarme* accompanying us through-out. The examination occupied us until dark, when we took our departure. On our way home my companion stopped in for a moment at the office of one of the daily papers.

I have said that the whims of my friend were manifold, and that *Je les menageais:*[29] —for this phrase there is no English equivalent. It was his humor, now, to decline all conversation on the subject of the murder, until about noon the next day. He then asked me, suddenly, if I had observed any thing *peculiar* at the scene of the atrocity.

There was something in his manner of emphasizing the word "peculiar," which caused me to shudder, without knowing why.

[28] French: "apartment manager's office."   [29] French: "I carefully humored them."

"No, nothing *peculiar*," I said; "nothing more, at least, than we both saw stated in the paper."

"The 'Gazette,' " he replied, "has not entered, I fear, into the unusual horror of the thing. But dismiss the idle opinions of this print. It appears to me that this mystery is considered insoluble, for the very reason which should cause it to be regarded as easy of solution—I mean for the *outré* character of its features. The police are confounded by the seeming absence of motive—not for the murder itself—but for the atrocity of the murder. They are puzzled, too, by the seeming impossibility of reconciling the voices heard in contention, with the facts that no one was discovered up stairs but the assassinated Mademoiselle L'Espanaye, and that there were no means of egress without the notice of the party ascending. The wild disorder of the room; the corpse thrust, with the head downward, up the chimney; the frightful mutilation of the body of the old lady; these considerations, with those just mentioned, and others which I need not mention, have sufficed to paralyze the powers, by putting completely at fault the boasted *acumen,* of the government agents. They have fallen into the gross but common error of confounding the unusual with the abstruse. But it is by these deviations from the plane of the ordinary, that reason feels its way, if at all, in its search for the true. In investigations such as we are now pursuing, it should not be so much asked 'what has occurred,' as 'what has occurred that has never occurred before.' In fact, the facility with which I shall arrive, or have arrived, at the solution of this mystery, is in the direct ratio of its apparent insolubility in the eyes of the police."

I stared at the speaker in mute astonishment.

"I am now awaiting," continued he, looking toward the door of our apartment —"I am now awaiting a person who, although perhaps not the perpetrator of these butcheries, must have been in some measure implicated in their perpetration. Of the worst portion of the crimes committed, it is probable that he is innocent. I hope that I am right in this supposition; for upon it I build my expectation of reading the entire riddle. I look for the man here—in this room—every moment. It is true that he may not arrive; but the probability is that he will. Should he come, it will be necessary to detain him. Here are pistols; and we both know how to use them when occasion demands their use."

I took the pistols, scarcely knowing what I did, or believing what I heard, while Dupin went on, very much as if in a soliloquy. I have already spoken of his abstract manner at such times. His discourse was addressed to myself; but his voice, although by no means loud, had that intonation which is commonly employed in speaking to some one at a great distance. His eyes, vacant in expression, regarded only the wall.

"That the voices heard in contention," he said, "by the party upon the stairs, were not the voices of the women themselves, was fully proved by the evidence. This relieves us of all doubt upon the question whether the old lady could have first destroyed the daughter, and afterward have committed suicide. I speak of this point chiefly for the sake of method; for the strength of Madame L'Espanaye would have been utterly unequal to the task of thrusting her daughter's corpse up the chimney as it was found; and the nature of the wounds upon her own person entirely preclude the idea of self-destruction. Murder, then, has been committed by some third party; and the voices of this third party were those heard in contention. Let me now advert

—not to the whole testimony respecting these voices—but to what was *peculiar* in that testimony. Did you observe anything peculiar about it?"

I remarked that, while all the witnesses agreed in supposing the gruff voice to be that of a Frenchman, there was much disagreement in regard to the shrill, or, as one individual termed it, the harsh voice.

"That was the evidence itself," said Dupin, "but it was not the peculiarity of the evidence. You have observed nothing distinctive. Yet there *was* something to be observed. The witnesses, as you remark, agreed about the gruff voice; they were here unanimous. But in regard to the shrill voice, the peculiarity is—not that they disagreed—but that, while an Italian, an Englishman, a Spaniard, a Hollander, and a Frenchman attempted to describe it, each one spoke of it as that *of a foreigner*. Each is sure that it was not the voice of one of his own countrymen. Each likens it—not to the voice of an individual of any nation with whose language he is conversant— but the converse. The Frenchman supposes it the voice of a Spaniard, and 'might have distinguished some words *had he been acquainted with the Spanish*.' The Dutchman maintains it to have been that of a Frenchman; but we find it stated that '*not understanding French this witness was examined through an interpreter*.' The Englishman thinks it the voice of a German, and '*does not understand German*.' The Spaniard 'is sure' that it was that of an Englishman, but 'judges by the intonation' altogether, '*as he has no knowledge of the English*.' The Italian believes it the voice of a Russian, but '*has never conversed with a native of Russia*.' A second Frenchman differs, moreover, with the first, and is positive that the voice was that of an Italian; but, *not being cognizant of that tongue,* is, like the Spaniard, 'convinced by the intonation.' Now, how strangely unusual must that voice have really been, about which such testimony as this *could* have been elicited!—in whose *tones,* even, denizens of the five great divisions of Europe could recognise nothing familiar! You will say that it might have been the voice of an Asiatic—of an African. Neither Asiatics nor Africans abound in Paris; but, without denying the inference, I will now merely call your attention to three points. The voice is termed by one witness 'harsh rather than shrill.' It is represented by two others to have been 'quick and *unequal*.' No words—no sounds resembling words—were by any witness mentioned as distinguishable.

"I know not," continued Dupin, "what impression I may have made, so far, upon your own understanding; but I do not hesitate to say that legitimate deductions even from this portion of the testimony—the portion respecting the gruff and shrill voices —are in themselves sufficient to engender a suspicion which should give direction to all farther progress in the investigation of the mystery. I said 'legitimate deductions;' but my meaning is not thus fully expressed. I designed to imply that the deductions are the *sole* proper ones, and that the suspicion arises *inevitably* from them as the single result. What the suspicion is, however, I will not say just yet. I merely wish you to bear in mind that, with myself, it was sufficiently forcible to give a definite form— a certain tendency—to my inquiries in the chamber.

"Let us now transport ourselves, in fancy, to this chamber. What shall we first seek here? The means of egress employed by the murderers. It is not too much to say that neither of us believe in præternatural events. Madame and Mademoiselle L'Espanaye were not destroyed by spirits. The doers of the deed were material, and escaped materially. Then how? Fortunately, there is but one mode of reasoning upon the point, and that mode *must* lead us to a definite decision.—Let us examine, each by each, the possible means of egress. It is clear that the assassins were in the room where Mademoiselle L'Espanaye was found, or at least in the room adjoining, when the party ascended the stairs. It is then only from these two apartments that we have to seek issues. The police have laid bare the floors, the ceilings, and the masonry of the walls, in every direction. No *secret* issues could have escaped their vigilance. But, not trusting to *their* eyes, I examined with my own. There were, then, *no* secret issues. Both doors leading from the rooms into the passage were securely locked, with the keys inside. Let us turn to the chimneys. These, although of ordinary width for some eight or ten feet above the hearths, will not admit, throughout their extent, the body of a large cat. The impossibility of egress, by means already stated, being thus absolute, we are reduced to the windows. Through those of the front room no one could have escaped without notice from the crowd in the street. The murderers *must* have passed, then, through those of the back room. Now, brought to this conclusion in so unequivocal a manner as we are, it is not our part, as reasoners, to reject it on account of apparent impossibilities. It is only left for us to prove that these apparent 'impossibilities' are, in reality, not such.

"There are two windows in the chamber. One of them is unobstructed by furniture, and is wholly visible. The lower portion of the other is hidden from view by the head of the unwieldy bedstead which is thrust close up against it. The former was found securely fastened from within. It resisted the utmost force of those who endeavored to raise it. A large gimlet-hole had been pierced in its frame to the left, and a very stout nail was found fitted therein, nearly to the head. Upon examining the other window, a similar nail was seen similarly fitted in it; and a vigorous attempt to raise this sash, failed also. The police were now entirely satisfied that egress had not been in these directions. And, *therefore,* it was thought a matter of supererogation to withdraw the nails and open the windows.

"My own examination was somewhat more particular, and was so for the reason I have just given—because here it was, I knew, that all apparent impossibilities *must* be proved to be not such in reality.

"I proceeded to think thus—*à posteriori.*[30] The murderers *did* escape from one of these windows. This being so, they could not have re-fastened the sashes from the inside, as they were found fastened;—the consideration which put a stop, through its obviousness, to the scrutiny of the police in this quarter. Yet the sashes *were* fastened. They *must,* then, have the power of fastening themselves. There was no escape from this conclusion. I stepped to the unobstructed casement, withdrew the nail with some difficulty, and attempted to raise the sash. It resisted all my efforts, as I had anticipated. A concealed spring must, I now knew, exist; and this corroboration of my idea convinced me that my premises, at least, were correct, however mysterious still appeared the circumstances attending the nails. A careful search soon brought to light the hidden spring. I pressed it, and, satisfied with the discovery, forebore to upraise the sash.

"I now replaced the nail and regarded it attentively. A person passing out through this window might have reclosed it, and the spring would have caught—but the nail could not have been replaced. The conclusion was plain, and again narrowed in the

---

[30] Latin: "after the fact"; generalization based on inductive reasoning.

field of my investigations. The assassins *must* have escaped through the other window. Supposing, then, the springs upon each sash to be the same, as was probable, there *must* be found a difference between the nails, or at least between the modes of their fixture. Getting upon the sacking of the bedstead, I looked over the head-board minutely at the second casement. Passing my hand down behind the board, I readily discovered and pressed the spring, which was, as I had supposed, identical in character with its neighbor. I now looked at the nail. It was as stout as the other, and apparently fitted in the same manner—driven in nearly up to the head.

"You will say that I was puzzled; but, if you think so, you must have misunderstood the nature of the inductions. To use a sporting phrase, I had not been once 'at fault.' The scene had never for an instant been lost. There was no flaw in any link of the chain. I had traced the secret to its ultimate result,—and that result was *the nail*. It had, I say, in every respect, the appearance of its fellow in the other window; but this fact was an absolute nullity (conclusive as it might seem to be) when compared with the consideration that here, at this point, terminated the clew. 'There *must* be something wrong,' I said, 'about the nail.' I touched it; and the head, with about a quarter of an inch of the shank, came off in my fingers. The rest of the shank was in the gimlet-hole, where it had been broken off. The fracture was an old one (for its edges were incrusted with rust), and had apparently been accomplished by the blow of a hammer, which had partially imbedded, in the top of the bottom sash, the head portion of the nail. I now carefully replaced this head portion in the indentation whence I had taken it, and the resemblance to a perfect nail was complete—the fissure was invisible. Pressing the spring, I gently raised the sash for a few inches; the head went up with it, remaining firm in its bed. I closed the window, and the semblance of the whole nail was again perfect.

"The riddle, so far, was now unriddled. The assassin had escaped through the window which looked upon the bed. Dropping of its own accord upon his exit (or perhaps purposely closed), it had become fastened by the spring; and it was the retention of this spring which had been mistaken by the police for that of the nail, —farther inquiry being thus considered unnecessary.

"The next question is that of the mode of descent. Upon this point I had been satisfied in my walk with you around the building. About five feet and a half from the casement in question there runs a lightning-rod. From this rod it would have been impossible for any one to reach the window itself, to say nothing of entering it. I observed, however, that the shutters of the fourth story were of the peculiar kind called by Parisian carpenters *ferrades*—a kind rarely employed at the present day, but frequently seen upon very old mansions at Lyons and Bordeaux. They are in the form of an ordinary door, (a single, not a folding door) except that the upper half is latticed or worked in open trellis—thus affording an excellent hold for the hands. In the present instance these shutters are fully three feet and a half broad. When we saw them from the rear of the house, they were both about half open—that is to say, they stood off at right angles from the wall. It is probable that the police, as well as myself, examined the back of the tenement; but, if so, in looking at these *ferrades* in the line of their breadth (as they must have done), they did not perceive this great breadth itself, or, at all events, failed to take it into due consideration. In fact, having once satisfied themselves that no egress could have been made in this quarter, they would naturally bestow here a very cursory examination. It was clear to me, however, that the shutter belonging to the window at the head of the bed, would, if swung fully back to the wall, reach to within two feet of the lightning-rod. It was also evident that, by exertion of a very unusual degree of activity and courage, an entrance into the window, from the rod, might have been thus effected.——By reaching to the distance of two feet and a half (we now suppose the shutter open to its whole extent) a robber might have taken a firm grasp upon the trellis-work. Letting go, then, his hold upon the rod, placing his feet securely against the wall, and springing boldly from it, he might have swung the shutter so as to close it, and, if we imagine the window open at the time, might even have swung himself into the room.

"I wish you to bear especially in mind that I have spoken of a *very* unusual degree of activity as requisite to success in so hazardous and so difficult a feat. It is my design to show you, first, that the thing might possibly have been accomplished:——but, secondly and *chiefly,* I wish to impress upon your understanding the *very extraordinary* —the almost præternatural character of that agility which could have accomplished it.

"You will say, no doubt, using the language of the law, that 'to make out my case' I should rather under-value, than insist upon a full estimation of the activity required in this matter. This may be the practice in law, but it is not the usage of reason. My ultimate object is only the truth. My immediate purpose is to lead you to place in juxta-position that *very unusual* activity of which I have just spoken, with that *very peculiar* shrill (or harsh) and *unequal* voice, about whose nationality no two persons could be found to agree, and in whose utterance no syllabification could be detected."

At these words a vague and half-formed conception of the meaning of Dupin flitted over my mind. I seemed to be upon the verge of comprehension, without power to comprehend—as men, at times, find themselves upon the brink of remembrance, without being able, in the end, to remember. My friend went on with his discourse.

"You will see," he said, "that I have shifted the question from the mode of egress to that of ingress. It was my design to suggest that both were effected in the same manner, at the same point. Let us now revert to the interior of the room. Let us survey the appearances here. The drawers of the bureau, it is said, had been rifled, although many articles of apparel still remained within them. The conclusion here is absurd. It is a mere guess—a very silly one—and no more. How are we to know that the articles found in the drawers were not all these drawers had originally contained? Madame L'Espanaye and her daughter lived an exceedingly retired life—saw no company—seldom went out—had little use for numerous changes of habiliment. Those found were at least of as good quality as any likely to be possessed by these ladies. If a thief had taken any, why did he not take the best—why did he not take all? In a word, why did he abandon four thousand francs in gold to encumber himself with a bundle of linen? The gold *was* abandoned. Nearly the whole sum mentioned by Monsieur Mignaud, the banker, was discovered, in bags, upon the floor. I wish you, therefore, to discard from your thoughts the blundering idea of *motive,* engendered in the brains of the police by that portion of the evidence which speaks of money delivered at the door of the house. Coincidences ten times as remarkable as this (the delivery of the money, and murder committed within three days upon the party receiving it), happen to all of us every hour of our lives, without attracting even momentary notice. Coincidences, in general, are great stumbling-blocks in the way of that class of thinkers who have been educated to know nothing of the theory of probabilities—that theory to which the most glorious objects of human research are indebted for the most glorious of illustration. In the present instance, had the gold been gone, the fact of its delivery three days before would have formed something more than a coincidence. It would have been corroborative of this idea of motive. But, under the real circumstances of the case, if we are to suppose gold the motive of this outrage, we must also imagine the perpetrator so vacillating an idiot as to have abandoned his gold and his motive together.

"Keeping now steadily in mind the points to which I have drawn your attention —that peculiar voice, that unusual agility, and that startling absence of motive in a murder so singularly atrocious as this—let us glance at the butchery itself. Here is a woman strangled to death by manual strength, and thrust up a chimney, head downward. Ordinary assassins employ no such modes of murder as this. Least of all, do they thus dispose of the murdered. In the manner of thrusting the corpse up the chimney, you will admit that there was something *excessively outré*—something altogether irreconcilable with our common notions of human action, even when we suppose the actors the most depraved of men. Think, too, how great must have been that strength which could have thrust the body *up* such an aperture so forcibly that the united vigor of several persons was found barely sufficient to drag it *down!*

"Turn, now, to other indications of the employment of a vigor most marvellous. On the hearth were thick tresses—very thick tresses—of grey human hair. These had been torn out by the roots. You are aware of the great force necessary in tearing thus from the head even twenty or thirty hairs together. You saw the locks in question as well as myself. Their roots (a hideous sight!) were clotted with fragments of the flesh of the scalp—sure token of the prodigious power which had been exerted in uprooting perhaps half a million of hairs at a time. The throat of the old lady was not merely cut, but the head absolutely severed form the body: the instrument was a mere razor. I wish you also to look at the *brutal* ferocity of these deeds. Of the bruises upon the body of Madame L'Espanaye I do not speak. Monsieur Dumas, and his worthy coadjutor[31] Monsieur Etienne, have pronounced that they were inflicted by some obtuse instrument; and so far these gentlemen are very correct. The obtuse instrument was clearly the stone pavement in the yard, upon which the victim had fallen from the window which looked in upon the bed. This idea, however simple it may now seem, escaped the police for the same reason that the breadth of these shutters escaped them—because, by the affair of the nails, their perceptions had been hermetically sealed against the possibility of the windows having ever been opened at all.

"If now, in addition to all these things, you have properly reflected upon the odd disorder of the chamber, we have gone so far as to combine the ideas of an agility astounding, a strength superhuman, a ferocity brutal, a butchery without motive, a *grotesquerie*[32] in horror absolutely alien from humanity, and a voice foreign in tone to the ears of men of many nations, and devoid of all distinct or intelligible syllabification. What result, then, has ensued? What impression have I made upon your fancy?"

I felt a creeping of the flesh as Dupin asked me the question. "A madman," I said, "has done this deed—some raving maniac, escaped from a neighboring *Maison de Santé*."[33]

[31] Assistant.
[32] French: "grotesque act."
[33] French: "insane asylum."

"In some respects," he replied, "your idea is not irrelevant. But the voices of madmen, even in their wildest paroxysms, are never found to tally with that peculiar voice heard upon the stairs. Madmen are of some nation, and their language, however incoherent in its words, has always the coherence of syllabification. Besides, the hair of a madman is not such as I now hold in my hand. I disentangled this little tuft from the rigidly clutched fingers of Madame L'Espanaye. Tell me what you can make of it."

"Dupin!" I said, completely unnerved; "this hair is most unusual—this is no *human* hair."

"I have not asserted that it is," said he; "but, before we decide this point, I wish you to glance at the little sketch I have here traced upon this paper. It is a *fac-simile* drawing of what has been described in one portion of the testimony as 'dark bruises, and deep indentations of finger nails,' upon the throat of Mademoiselle L'Espanaye, and in another, (by Messrs. Dumas and Etienne,) as a 'series of livid spots, evidently the impression of fingers.'

"You will perceive," continued my friend, spreading out the paper upon the table before us, "that this drawing gives the idea of a firm and fixed hold. There is no *slipping* apparent. Each finger has retained—possibly until the death of the victim— the fearful grasp by which it originally imbedded itself. Attempt, now, to place all your fingers, at the same time, in the respective impressions as you see them."

I made the attempt in vain.

"We are possibly not giving this matter a fair trial," he said. "The paper is spread out upon a plane surface; but the human throat is cylindrical. Here is a billet of wood, the circumference of which is about that of the throat. Wrap the drawing around it, and try the experiment again."

I did so; but the difficulty was even more obvious than before. "This," I said, "is the mark of no human hand."

"Read now," replied Dupin, "this passage from Cuvier."[34]

It was a minute anatomical and generally descriptive account of the large fulvous Ourang-Outang of the East Indian Islands. The gigantic stature, the prodigious strength and activity, the wild ferocity, and the imitative propensities of these mammalia are sufficiently well known to all. I understood the full horrors of the murder at once.

"The description of the digits," said I, as I made an end of reading, "is in exact accordance with this drawing. I see that no animal but an Ourang-Outang, of the species here mentioned, could have impressed the indentations as you have traced them. This tuft of tawny hair, too, is identical in character with that of the beast of Cuvier. But I cannot possibly comprehend the particulars of this frightful mystery. Besides, there were *two* voices heard in contention, and one of them was unquestionably the voice of a Frenchman."

"True; and you will remember an expression attributed almost unanimously, by the evidence, to this voice,—the expression, '*mon Dieu!*' This, under the circumstances, has been justly characterized by one of the witnesses (Montani, the confectioner,) as an expression of remonstrance or expostulation. Upon these two words, therefore, I

[34] The French naturalist Georges Cuvier (1769–1832) wrote about orangutans in *Règne Animal* (1817).

have mainly built my hopes of a full solution of the riddle. A Frenchman was cognizant of the murder. It is possible—indeed it is far more than probable—that he was innocent of all participation in the bloody transactions which took place. The Ourang-Outang may have escaped from him. He may have traced it to the chamber; but, under the agitating circumstances which ensued, he could never have re-captured it. It is still at large. I will not pursue these guesses—for I have no right to call them more—since the shades of reflection upon which they are based are scarcely of sufficient depth to be appreciable by my own intellect, and since I could not pretend to make them intelligible to the understanding of another. We will call them guesses then, and speak of them as such. If the Frenchman in question is indeed, as I suppose, innocent of this atrocity, this advertisement, which I left last night, upon our return home, at the office of 'Le Monde,' (a paper devoted to the shipping interest, and much sought by sailors,) will bring him to our residence."

He handed me a paper, and I read thus:

CAUGHT—In the Bois de Boulogne, early in the morning of the ———— inst., *(the morning of the murder,)* a very large, tawny Ourang-Outang of the Bornese species. The owner, (who is ascertained to be a sailor, belonging to a Maltese vessel,) may have the animal again, upon identifying it satisfactorily, and paying a few charges arising from its capture and keeping. Call at No. ————, Rue ————, Faubourg St. Germain ———— au troisième.[35]

"How was it possible," I asked, "that you should know the man to be a sailor, and belonging to a Maltese vessel?"

"I do *not* know it," said Dupin. "I am not *sure* of it. Here, however, is a small piece of ribbon, which from its form, and from its greasy appearance, has evidently been used in tying the hair in one of those long *queues*[36] of which sailors are so fond. Moreover, this knot is one which few besides sailors can tie, and is peculiar to the Maltese. I picked the ribbon up at the foot of the lightning-rod. It could not have belonged to either of the deceased. Now if, after all, I am wrong in my induction from this ribbon, that the Frenchman was a sailor belonging to a Maltese vessel, still I can have done no harm in saying what I did in the advertisement. If I am in error, he will merely suppose that I have been misled by some circumstance into which he will not take the trouble to inquire. But if I am right, a great point is gained. Cognizant although innocent of the murder, the Frenchman will naturally hesitate about replying to the advertisement—about demanding the Ourang-Outang. He will reason thus:—'I am innocent; I am poor; my Ourang-Outang is of great value—to one in my circumstances a fortune of itself—why should I lose it through idle apprehensions of danger? Here it is, within my grasp. It was found in the Bois de Boulogne—at a vast distance from the scene of that butchery. How can it ever be suspected that a brute beast should have done the deed? The police are at fault—they have failed to procure the slightest clew. Should they even trace the animal, it would be impossible to prove me cognizant of the murder, or to implicate me in guilt on account of that cognizance. Above all, *I am known.* The advertiser designates me as

---

[35] "On the third floor" in French; on what we call the fourth floor.

[36] Pigtails.

the possessor of the beast. I am not sure to what limit his knowledge may extend. Should I avoid claiming a property of so great value, which it is known that I possess, I will render the animal, at least, liable to suspicion. It is not my policy to attract attention either to myself or to the beast. I will answer the advertisement, get the Ourang-Outang, and keep it close until this matter has blown over.' "

At this moment we heard a step upon the stairs.

"Be ready," said Dupin, "with your pistols, but neither use them nor show them until at a signal from myself."

The front door of the house had been left open, and the visitor had entered, without ringing, and advanced several steps upon the staircase. Now, however, he seemed to hesitate. Presently we heard him descending. Dupin was moving quickly to the door, when we again heard him coming up. He did not turn back a second time, but stepped up with decision and rapped at the door of our chamber.

"Come in," said Dupin, in a cheerful and hearty tone.

A man entered. He was a sailor, evidently,—a tall, stout, and muscular-looking person, with a certain dare-devil expression of countenance, not altogether unprepossessing. His face, greatly sunburnt, was more than half hidden by whisker and *mustachio*. He had with him a huge oaken cudgel, but appeared to be otherwise unarmed. He bowed awkwardly, and bade us "good evening," in French accents, which, although somewhat Neufchatelish,[37] were still sufficiently indicative of a Parisian origin.

"Sit down, my friend," said Dupin. "I suppose you have called about the Ourang-Outang. Upon my word, I almost envy you the possession of him; a remarkably fine, and no doubt a very valuable animal. How old do you suppose him to be?"

The sailor drew a long breath, with the air of a man relieved of some intolerable burden, and then replied, in an assured tone:

"I have no way of telling—but he can't be more than four or five years old. Have you got him here?"

"Oh no; we had no conveniences for keeping him here. He is at a livery stable in the Rue Dubourg, just by. You can get him in the morning. Of course you are prepared to identify the property?"

"To be sure I am, sir."

"I shall be sorry to part with him," said Dupin.

"I don't mean that you should be at all this trouble for nothing, sir," said the man. "Couldn't expect it. Am very willing to pay a reward for the finding of the animal —that is to say, any thing in reason."

"Well," replied my friend, "that is all very fair, to be sure. Let me think!—what should I have? Oh! I will tell you. My reward shall be this. You shall give me all the information in your power about these murders in the Rue Morgue."

Dupin said the last words in a very low tone, and very quietly. Just as quietly, too, he walked toward the door, locked it, and put the key in his pocket. He then drew a pistol from his bosom and placed it, without the least flurry, upon the table.

The sailor's face flushed up as if he were struggling with suffocation. He started

[37] That is, in the accent of Neufchâtel, a province
of France; a way of speaking that is considered
uncouth.

to his feet and grasped his cudgel; but the next moment he fell back into his seat, trembling violently, and with the countenance of death itself. He spoke not a word. I pitied him from the bottom of my heart.

"My friend," said Dupin, in a kind tone, "you are alarming yourself unnecessarily —you are indeed. We mean you no harm whatever. I pledge you the honor of a gentleman, and of a Frenchman, that we intend you no injury. I perfectly well know that you are innocent of the atrocities in the Rue Morgue. It will not do, however, to deny that you are in some measure implicated in them. From what I have already said, you must know that I have had means of information about this matter—means of which you could never have dreamed. Now the thing stands thus. You have done nothing which you could have avoided—nothing, certainly, which renders you culpable. You were not even guilty of robbery, when you might have robbed with impunity. You have nothing to conceal. You have no reason for concealment. On the other hand, you are bound by every principle of honor to confess all you know. An innocent man is now imprisoned, charged with that crime of which you can point out the perpetrator."

The sailor had recovered his presence of mind, in a great measure, while Dupin uttered these words; but his original boldness of bearing was all gone.

"So help me God," said he, after a brief pause, "I *will* tell you all I know about this affair;—but I do not expect you to believe one half I say—I would be a fool indeed if I did. Still, I *am* innocent, and I will make a clean breast if I die for it."

What he stated was, in substance, this. He had lately made a voyage to the Indian Archipelago. A party, of which he formed one, landed at Borneo, and passed into the interior on an excursion of pleasure. Himself and a companion had captured the Ourang-Outang. This companion dying, the animal fell into his own exclusive possession. After great trouble, occasioned by the intractable ferocity of his captive during the home voyage, he at length succeeded in lodging it safely at his own residence in Paris, where, not to attract toward himself the unpleasant curiosity of his neighbors, he kept it carefully secluded, until such time as it should recover from a wound in the foot, received from a splinter on board ship. His ultimate design was to sell it.

Returning home from some sailors' frolic on the night, or rather in the morning of the murder, he found the beast occupying his own bed-room, into which it had broken from a closet adjoining, where it had been, as was thought, securely confined. Razor in hand, and fully lathered, it was sitting before a looking glass, attempting the operation of shaving, in which it had no doubt previously watched its master through the key-hole of the closet. Terrified at the sight of so dangerous a weapon in the possession of an animal so ferocious, and so well able to use it, the man, for some moments, was at a loss what to do. He had been accustomed however, to quiet the creature, even in its fiercest moods, by the use of a whip, and to this he now resorted. Upon sight of it, the Ourang-Outang sprang at once through the door of the chamber, down the stairs, and thence, through a window, unfortunately open, into the street.

The Frenchman followed in despair; the ape, razor still in hand, occasionally stopping to look back and gesticulate at its pursuer, until the latter had nearly come up with it, It then again made off. In this manner the chase continued for a long time. The streets were profoundly quiet, as it was nearly three o'clock in the morning. In passing down an alley in the rear of the Rue Morgue, the fugitive's attention was arrested by a light gleaming from the open window of Madame L'Espanaye's chamber, in the fourth story of her house. Rushing to the building, it perceived the lightning-rod, clambered up with inconceivable agility, grasped the shutter, which was thrown fully back against the wall, and, by its means, swung itself directly upon the headboard of the bed. The whole feat did not occupy a minute. The shutter was kicked open again by the Ourang-Outang as it entered the room.

The sailor, in the meantime, was both rejoiced and perplexed. He had strong hopes of now recapturing the brute, as it could scarcely escape from the trap into which it had ventured, except by the rod, where it might be intercepted as it came down. On the other hand, there was much cause for anxiety as to what it might do in the house. This latter reflection urged the man still to follow the fugitive. A lightning-rod is ascended without difficulty, especially by a sailor; but, when he had arrived as high as the window, which lay far to his left, his career was stopped; the most that he could accomplish was to reach over so as to obtain a glimpse of the interior of the room. At this glimpse he nearly fell from his hold through excess of horror. Now it was that those hideous shrieks arose upon the night, which had startled from slumber the inmates of the Rue Morgue. Madame L'Espanaye and her daughter, habited in their night clothes, had apparently been arranging some papers in the iron chest already mentioned, which had been wheeled into the middle of the room. It was open, and its contents lay beside it on the floor. The victims must have been sitting with their backs toward the window; and, from the time elapsing between the ingress of the beast and the screams, it seems probable that it was not immediately perceived. The flapping-to of the shutter would naturally have been attributed to the wind.

As the sailor looked in, the gigantic animal had seized Madame L'Espanaye by the hair, (which was loose, as she had been combing it,) and was flourishing the razor about her face, in imitation of the motions of a barber. The daughter lay prostrate and motionless; she had swooned. The screams and struggles of the old lady (during which the hair was torn from her head) had the effect of changing the probably pacific purposes of the Ourang-Outang into those of wrath. With one determined sweep of its muscular arm it nearly severed her head from her body. The sight of blood inflamed its anger into phrenzy. Gnashing its teeth, and flashing fire from its eyes, it flew upon the body of the girl, and imbedded its fearful talons in her throat, retaining its grasp until she expired. Its wandering and wild glances fell at this moment upon the head of the bed, over which the face of its master, rigid with horror, was just discernible. The fury of the beast, who no doubt bore still in mind the dreaded whip, was instantly converted into fear. Conscious of having deserved punishment, it seemed desirous of concealing its bloody deeds, and skipped about the chamber in an agony of nervous agitation; throwing down and breaking the furniture as it moved, and dragging the bed from the bedstead. In conclusion, it seized first the corpse of the daughter, and thrust it up the chimney, as it was found; then that of the old lady, which it immediately hurled through the window headlong.

As the ape approached the casement with its mutilated burden, the sailor shrank aghast to the rod, and, rather gliding than clambering down it, hurried at once home —dreading the consequences of the butchery, and gladly abandoning, in his terror, all solicitude about the fate of the Ourang-Outang. The words heard by the party upon the staircase were the Frenchman's exclamations of horror and affright, commingled with the fiendish jabberings of the brute.

I have scarcely anything to add. The Ourang-Outang must have escaped from the chamber, by the rod, just before the breaking of the door. It must have closed the window as it passed through it. It was subsequently caught by the owner himself, who obtained for it a very large sum at the *Jardin des Plantes*.[38] Le Bon was instantly released, upon our narration of the circumstances (with some comments from Dupin) at the *bureau* of the Prefect of Police. This functionary, however well disposed to my friend, could not altogether conceal his chagrin at the turn which affairs had taken, and was fain to indulge in a sarcasm or two, about the propriety of every person minding his own business.

"Let them talk," said Dupin, who had not thought it necessary to reply. "Let him discourse; it will ease his conscience. I am satisfied with having defeated him in his own castle. Nevertheless, that he failed in the solution of this mystery, is by no means that matter for wonder which he supposes it; for, in truth, our friend the Prefect is somewhat too cunning to be profound. In his wisdom is no *stamen*.[39] It is all head and no body, like the pictures of the Goddess Laverna,[40]—or, at best, all head and shoulders, like a codfish. But he is a good creature after all. I like him especially for one master stroke of cant, by which he has attained his reputation for ingenuity. I mean the way he has *'de nier ce qui est, et d'expliquer ce qui n'est pas.'* "[41]
1841

The Black Cat

For the most wild, yet most homely narrative which I am about to pen, I neither expect nor solicit belief. Mad indeed would I be to expect it, in a case where my very senses reject their own evidence. Yet, mad am I not—and very surely do I not dream. But to-morrow I die, and to-day I would unburthen my soul. My immediate purpose is to place before the world, plainly, succinctly, and without comment, a series of mere household events. In their consequences, these events have terrified—have tortured—have destroyed me. Yet I will not attempt to expound them. To me, they have presented little but Horror—to many they will seem less terrible than *barroques*.[1] Hereafter, perhaps, some intellect may be found which will reduce my phantasm to the common-place—some intellect more calm, more logical, and far less excitable than my own, which will perceive, in the circumstances I detail with awe, nothing more than an ordinary succession of very natural causes and effects.

From my infancy I was noted for the docility and humanity of my disposition. My tenderness of heart was even so conspicuous as to make me the jest of my companions. I was especially fond of animals, and was indulged by my parents with a great variety of pets. With these I spent most of my time, and never was so happy

---

[38] The botanical garden where the Paris zoo is located.
[39] Stalk; torso.
[40] Roman goddess of thievery.

[41] French: "to deny what is, and to explain what isn't"; from *La Nouvelle Héloise* by Jean Jacques Rousseau (1712–1778).
[1] Bizarre, fantastic.

as when feeding and caressing them. This peculiarity of character grew with my growth, and, in my manhood, I derived from it one of my principal sources of pleasure. To those who have cherished an affection for a faithful and sagacious dog, I need hardly be at the trouble of explaining the nature or the intensity of the gratification thus derivable. There is something in the unselfish and self-sacrificing love of a brute, which goes directly to the heart of him who has had frequent occasion to test the paltry friendship and gossamer fidelity of mere *Man*.

I married early, and was happy to find in my wife a disposition not uncongenial with my own. Observing my partiality for domestic pets, she lost no opportunity of procuring those of the most agreeable kind. We had birds, gold-fish, a fine dog, rabbits, a small monkey, and *a cat*.

This latter was a remarkably large and beautiful animal, entirely black, and sagacious to an astonishing degree. In speaking of his intelligence, my wife, who at heart was not a little tinctured with superstition, made frequent allusion to the ancient popular notion, which regarded all black cats as witches in disguise. Not that she was ever *serious* upon this point—and I mention the matter at all for no better reason than that it happens, just now, to be remembered.

Pluto[2]—this was the cat's name—was my favorite pet and play-mate. I alone fed him, and he attended me wherever I went about the house. It was even with difficulty that I could prevent him from following me through the streets.

Our friendship lasted, in this manner, for several years, during which my general temperament and character—through the instrumentality of the Fiend Intemperance —had (I blush to confess it) experienced a radical alteration for the worse. I grew, day by day, more moody, more irritable, more regardless of the feelings of others. I suffered myself to use intemperate language to my wife. At length, I even offered her personal violence. My pets, of course, were made to feel the change in my disposition. I not only neglected, but ill-used them. For Pluto, however, I still retained sufficient regard to restrain me from maltreating him, as I made no scruple of maltreating the rabbits, the monkey, or even the dog, when by accident, or through affection, they came in my way. But my disease grew upon me—for what disease is like Alcohol!—and at length even Pluto, who was now becoming old, and consequently somewhat peevish—even Pluto began to experience the effects of my ill temper.

One night, returning home, much intoxicated, from one of my haunts about town, I fancied that the cat avoided my presence. I seized him; when, in his fright at my violence, he inflicted a slight wound upon my hand with his teeth. The fury of a demon instantly possessed me. I knew myself no longer. My original soul seemed, at once, to take its flight from my body; and a more than fiendish malevolence, gin-nurtured, thrilled every fibre of my frame. I took from my waistcoat-pocket a pen-knife, opened it, grasped the poor beast by the throat, and deliberately cut one of its eyes from the socket! I blush, I burn, I shudder, while I pen the damnable atrocity.

When reason returned with the morning—when I had slept off the fumes of the night's debauch—I experienced a sentiment half of horror, half of remorse, for the

[2] Ruler of the underworld and lord of the dead in classic myth.

crime of which I had been guilty; but it was, at best, a feeble and equivocal feeling, and the soul remained untouched. I again plunged into excess, and soon drowned in wine all memory of the deed.

In the meantime the cat slowly recovered. The socket of the lost eye presented, it is true, a frightful appearance, but he no longer appeared to suffer any pain. He went about the house as usual, but, as might be expected, fled in extreme terror at my approach. I had so much of my old heart left, as to be at first grieved by this evident dislike on the part of a creature which had once so loved me. But this feeling soon gave place to irritation. And then came, as if to my final and irrevocable overthrow, the spirit of PERVERSENESS. Of this spirit philosophy takes no account. Yet I am not more sure that my soul lives, than I am that perverseness is one of the primitive impulses of the human heart—one of the indivisible primary faculties, or sentiments, which give direction to the character of Man. Who has not, a hundred times, found himself committing a vile or a silly action, for no other reason than because he knows he should *not*? Have we not a perpetual inclination, in the teeth of our best judgment, to violate that which is *Law,* merely because we understand it to be such? This spirit of perverseness, I say, came to my final overthrow. It was this unfathomable longing of the soul to *vex itself*—to offer violence to its own nature —to do wrong for the wrong's sake only—that urged me to continue and finally to consummate the injury I had inflicted upon the unoffending brute. One morning, in cold blood, I slipped a noose about its neck and hung it to the limb of a tree;—hung it with the tears streaming from my eyes, and with the bitterest remorse at my heart; —hung it *because* I knew that it had loved me, and *because* I felt it had given me no reason of offence;—hung it *because* I knew that in so doing I was committing a sin—a deadly sin that would so jeopardize my immortal soul as to place it—if such a thing were possible—even beyond the reach of the infinite mercy of the Most Merciful and Most Terrible God.

On the night of the day on which this cruel deed was done, I was aroused from sleep by the cry of fire. The curtains of my bed were in flames. The whole house was blazing. It was with great difficulty that my wife, a servant, and myself, made our escape from the conflagration. The destruction was complete. My entire worldly wealth was swallowed up, and I resigned myself thenceforward to despair.

I am above the weakness of seeking to establish a sequence of cause and effect, between the disaster and the atrocity. But I am detailing a chain of facts—and wish not to leave even a possible link imperfect. On the day succeeding the fire, I visited the ruins. The walls, with one exception, had fallen in. This exception was found in a compartment wall, not very thick, which stood about the middle of the house, and against which had rested the head of my bed. The plastering had here, in great measure, resisted the action of the fire—a fact which I attributed to its having been recently spread. About this wall a dense crowd were collected, and many persons seemed to be examining a particular portion of it with very minute and eager attention. The words "strange!" "singular!" and other similar expressions, excited my curiosity. I approached and saw, as if graven in *bas relief* upon the white surface, the figure of a gigantic *cat.* The impression was given with an accuracy truly marvellous. There was a rope about the animal's neck.

When I first beheld this apparition—for I could scarcely regard it as less—my wonder and my terror were extreme. But at length reflection came to my aid. The cat, I remembered, had been hung in a garden adjacent to the house. Upon the alarm of fire, this garden had been immediately filled by the crowd—by some one of whom the animal must have been cut from the tree and thrown, through an open window, into my chamber. This had probably been done with the view of arousing me from sleep. The falling of other walls had compressed the victim of my cruelty into the substance of the freshly-spread plaster; the lime of which, with the flames, and the *ammonia* from the carcass, had then accomplished the portraiture as I saw it.

Although I thus readily accounted to my reason, if not altogether to my conscience, for the startling fact just detailed, it did not the less fail to make a deep impression upon my fancy. For months I could not rid myself of the phantasm of the cat; and, during this period, there came back into my spirit a half-sentiment that seemed, but was not, remorse. I went so far as to regret the loss of the animal, and to look about me, among the vile haunts which I now habitually frequented, for another pet of the same species, and of somewhat similar appearance, with which to supply its place.

One night as I sat, half stupified, in a den of more than infamy, my attention was suddenly drawn to some black object, reposing upon the head of one of the immense hogsheads[3] of Gin, or of Rum, which constituted the chief furniture of the apartment. I had been looking steadily at the top of this hogshead for some minutes, and what now caused me surprise was the fact that I had not sooner perceived the object thereupon. I approached it, and touched it with my hand. It was a black cat—a very large one—fully as large as Pluto, and closely resembling him in every respect but one. Pluto had not a white hair upon any portion of his body; but this cat had a large, although indefinite splotch of white, covering nearly the whole region of the breast.

Upon my touching him, he immediately arose, purred loudly, rubbed against my hand and appeared delighted with my notice. This, then, was the very creature of which I was in search. I at once offered to purchase it of the landlord; but this person made no claim to it—knew nothing of it—had never seen it before.

I continued my caresses, and, when I prepared to go home, the animal evinced a disposition to accompany me. I permitted it to do so; occasionally stooping and patting it as I proceeded. When it reached the house it domesticated itself at once, and became immediately a great favorite with my wife.

For my own part, I soon found a dislike to it arising within me. This was just the reverse of what I had anticipated; but—I know not how or why it was—its evident fondness for myself rather disgusted and annoyed. By slow degrees, these feelings of disgust and annoyance rose into the bitterness of hatred. I avoided the creature; a certain sense of shame, and the remembrance of my former deed of cruelty, preventing me from physically abusing it. I did not, for some weeks, strike, or otherwise violently ill use it; but gradually—very gradually—I came to look upon it with unutterable loathing, and to flee silently from its odious presence, as from the breath of a pestilence.

What added, no doubt, to my hatred of the beast, was the discovery, on the morning after I brought it home, that, like Pluto, it also had been deprived of one of its eyes. This circumstance, however, only endeared it to my wife, who, as I have already said, possessed, in a high degree, that humanity of feeling which had once been my distinguishing trait, and the source of many of my simplest and purest pleasures.

With my aversion to this cat, however, its partiality for myself seemed to increase. It followed my footsteps with a pertinacity which it would be difficult to make the

[3] Large barrels or casks.

reader comprehend. Whenever I sat, it would crouch beneath my chair, or spring upon my knees, covering me with its loathsome caresses. If I arose to walk it would get between my feet and thus nearly throw me down, or, fastening its long and sharp claws in my dress, clamber, in this manner, to my breast. At such times, although I longed to destroy it with a blow, I was yet withheld from so doing, partly by a memory of my former crime, but chiefly—let me confess it at once—by absolute *dread* of the beast.

This dread was not exactly a dread of physical evil—and yet I should be at a loss how otherwise to define it. I am almost ashamed to own—yes, even in this felon's cell, I am almost ashamed to own—that the terror and horror with which the animal inspired me, had been heightened by one of the merest chimæras it would be possible to conceive. My wife had called my attention, more than once, to the character of the mark of white hair, of which I have spoken, and which constituted the sole visible difference between the strange beast and the one I had destroyed. The reader will remember that this mark, although large, had been originally very indefinite; but, by slow degrees—degrees nearly imperceptible, and which for a long time my Reason struggled to reject as fanciful—it had, at length, assumed a rigorous distinctness of outline. It was now the representation of an object that I shudder to name—and for this, above all, I loathed, and dreaded, and would have rid myself of the monster *had I dared*—it was now, I say, the image of a hideous—of a ghastly thing—of the GALLOWS!—oh, mournful and terrible engine of Horror and of Crime—of Agony and of Death!

And now was I indeed wretched beyond the wretchedness of mere Humanity. And *a brute beast*—whose fellow I had contemptuously destroyed—*a brute beast* to work out for *me*—for me a man, fashioned in the image of the High God—so much of insufferable wo! Alas! neither by day nor by night knew I the blessing of Rest any more! During the former the creature left me no moment alone; and, in the latter, I started, hourly, from dreams of unutterable fear, to find the hot breath of *the thing* upon my face, and its vast weight—an incarnate Night-Mare that I had no power to shake off—incumbent eternally upon my *heart!*

Beneath the pressure of torments such as these, the feeble remnant of the good within me succumbed. Evil thoughts became my sole intimates—the darkest and most evil of thoughts. The moodiness of my usual temper increased to hatred of all things and of all mankind; while, from the sudden, frequent, and ungovernable outbursts of a fury to which I now blindly abandoned myself, my uncomplaining wife, alas! was the most usual and most patient of sufferers.

One day she accompanied me, upon some household errand, into the cellar of the old building which our poverty compelled us to inhabit. The cat followed me down the steep stairs, and, nearly throwing me headlong, exasperated me to madness. Uplifting an axe, and forgetting, in my wrath, the childish dread which had hitherto stayed my hand, I aimed a blow at the animal which, of course, would have proved instantly fatal had it descended as I wished. But this blow was arrested by the hand of my wife. Goaded, by the interference, into a rage more than demoniacal, I withdrew my arm from her grasp and buried the axe in her brain. She fell dead upon the spot, without a groan.

This hideous murder accomplished, I set myself forthwith, and with entire deliberation, to the task of concealing the body. I knew that I could not remove it from the house, either by day or by night, without the risk of being observed by the neighbors.

Many projects entered my mind. At one period I thought of cutting the corpse into minute fragments, and destroying them by fire. At another, I resolved to dig a grave for it in the floor of the cellar. Again, I deliberated about casting it in the well in the yard—about packing it in a box, as if merchandize, with the usual arrangements, and so getting a porter to take it from the house. Finally I hit upon what I considered a far better expedient than either of these. I determined to wall it up in the cellar— as the monks of the middle ages are recorded to have walled up their victims.

For a purpose such as this the cellar was well adapted. Its walls were loosely constructed, and had lately been plastered throughout with a rough plaster, which the dampness of the atmosphere had prevented from hardening. Moreover, in one of the walls was a projection, caused by a false chimney, or fireplace, that had been filled up, and made to resemble the rest of the cellar. I made no doubt that I could readily displace the bricks at this point, insert the corpse, and wall the whole up as before, so that no eye could detect any thing suspicious.

And in this calculation I was not deceived. By means of a crowbar I easily dislodged the bricks, and, having carefully deposited the body against the inner wall, I propped it in that position, while, with little trouble, I re-laid the whole structure as it originally stood. Having procured mortar, sand, and hair, with every possible precaution, I prepared a plaster which could not be distinguished from the old, and with this I very carefully went over the new brick-work. When I had finished, I felt satisfied that all was right. The wall did not present the slightest appearance of having been disturbed. The rubbish on the floor was picked up with the minutest care. I looked around triumphantly, and said to myself—: "Here at least, then, my labor has not been in vain."

My next step was to look for the beast which had been the cause of so much wretchedness; for I had, at length, firmly resolved to put it to death. Had I been able to meet with it, at the moment, there could have been no doubt of its fate; but it appeared that the crafty animal had been alarmed at the violence of my previous anger, and forebore to present itself in my present mood. It is impossible to describe, or to imagine, the deep, the blissful sense of relief which the absence of the detested creature occasioned in my bosom. It did not make its appearance during the night—and thus for one night at least, since its introduction into the house, I soundly and tranquilly slept; aye, *slept* even with the burden of murder upon my soul!

The second and the third day passed, and still my tormentor came not. Once again I breathed as a freeman. The monster, in terror, had fled the premises forever! I should behold it no more! My happiness was supreme! The guilt of my dark deed disturbed me but little. Some few inquiries had been made, but these had been readily answered. Even a search had been instituted—but of course nothing was to be discovered. I looked upon my future felicity as secured.

Upon the fourth day of the assassination, a party of the police came, very unexpectedly, into the house, and proceeded again to make rigorous investigation of the premises. Secure, however, in the inscrutability of my place of concealment, I felt no embarrassment whatever. The officers bade me accompany them in their search. They left no nook or corner unexplored. At length, for the third or fourth time, they descended into the cellar. I quivered not in a muscle. My heart beat calmly as that of one who slumbers in innocence. I walked the cellar from end to end. I folded my arms upon my bosom, and roamed easily to and fro. The police were thoroughly satisfied and prepared to depart. The glee at my heart was too strong to be restrained.

I burned to say if but one word, by way of triumph, and to render doubly sure their assurance of my guiltlessness.

"Gentlemen," I said at last, as the party ascended the steps, "I delight to have allayed your suspicions. I wish you all health, and a little more courtesy. By the bye, gentlemen, this—this is a very well constructed house." [In the rabid desire to say something easily, I scarcely knew what I uttered at all.]—"I may say an *excellently* well constructed house. These walls—are you going, gentlemen?—these walls are solidly put together;" and here, through the mere phrenzy of bravado, I rapped heavily, with a cane which I held in my hand, upon that very portion of the brick-work behind which stood the corpse of the wife of my bosom.

But may God shield and deliver me from the fangs of the Arch-Fiend! No sooner had the reverberation of my blows sunk into silence, then I was answered by a voice from within the tomb!—by a cry, at first muffled and broken, like the sobbing of a child, and then quickly swelling into one long, loud, and continuous scream, utterly anomalous and inhuman—a howl—a wailing shriek, half of horror and half of triumph, such as might have arisen only out of hell, conjointly from the throats of the damned in their agony and of the demons that exult in the damnation.

Of my own thoughts it is folly to speak. Swooning, I staggered to the opposite wall. For one instant the party upon the stairs remained motionless, through extremity of terror and of awe. In the next, a dozen stout arms were toiling at the wall. It fell bodily. The corpse, already greatly decayed and clotted with gore, stood erect before the eyes of the spectators. Upon its head with red extended mouth and solitary eye of fire, sat the hideous beast whose craft had seduced me into murder, and whose informing voice had consigned me to the hangman. I had walled the monster up within the tomb!

1843

The Masque of the Red Death

The "Red Death" had long devastated the country. No pestilence had ever been so fatal, or so hideous. Blood was its Avatar[1] and its seal—the redness and the horror of blood. There were sharp pains, and sudden dizziness, and then profuse bleeding at the pores, with dissolution. The scarlet stains upon the body and especially upon the face of the victim, were the pest ban which shut him out from the aid and from the sympathy of his fellow-men. And the whole seizure, progress and termination of the disease, were the incidents of half an hour.

But the Prince Prospero was happy and dauntless and sagacious. When his dominions were half de-populated, he summoned to his presence a thousand hale and light-hearted friends from among the knights and dames of his court, and with these retired to the deep seclusion of one of his castellated abbeys. This was an extensive

[1] Embodiment.

and magnificent structure, the creation of the prince's own eccentric yet august taste. A strong and lofty wall girdled it in. This wall had gates of iron. The courtiers, having entered, brought furnaces and massy hammers and welded the bolts. They resolved to leave means neither of ingress or egress to the sudden impulses of despair or of frenzy from within. The abbey was amply provisioned. With such precautions the courtiers might bid defiance to contagion. The external world could take care of itself. In the meantime it was folly to grieve, or to think. The prince had provided all the appliances of pleasure. There were buffoons, there were improvisatori,[2] there were ballet-dancers, there were musicians, there was Beauty, there was wine. All these and security were within. Without was the "Red Death."

It was toward the close of the fifth or sixth month of his seclusion, and while the pestilence raged most furiously abroad, that the Prince Prospero entertained his thousand friends at a masked ball of the most unusual magnificence.

It was a voluptuous scene, that masquerade. But first let me tell of the rooms in which it was held. There were seven—an imperial suite. In many palaces, however, such suites form a long and straight vista, while the folding doors slide back nearly to the walls on either hand, so that the view of the whole extent is scarcely impeded. Here the case was very different; as might have been expected from the duke's love of the *bizarre*. The apartments were so irregularly disposed that the vision embraced but little more than one at a time. There was a sharp turn at every twenty or thirty yards, and at each turn a novel effect. To the right and left, in the middle of each wall, a tall and narrow Gothic window looked out upon a closed corridor which pursued the windings of the suite. These windows were of stained glass whose color varied in accordance with the prevailing hue of the decorations of the chamber into which it opened. That at the eastern extremity was hung, for example, in blue—and vividly blue were its windows. The second chamber was purple in its ornaments and tapestries, and here the panes were purple. The third was green throughout, and so were the casements. The fourth was furnished and lighted with orange—the fifth with white—the sixth with violet. The seventh apartment was closely shrouded in black velvet tapestries that hung all over the ceiling and down the walls, falling in heavy folds upon a carpet of the same material and hue. But in this chamber only, the color of the windows failed to correspond with the decorations. The panes here were scarlet —a deep blood color. Now in no one of the seven apartments was there any lamp or candelabrum, amid the profusion of golden ornaments that lay scattered to and fro or depended from the roof. There was no light of any kind emanating from lamp or candle within the suite of chambers. But in the corridors that followed the suite, there stood, opposite to each window, a heavy tripod, bearing a brazier of fire that projected its rays through the tinted glass and so glaringly illumined the room. And thus were produced a multitude of gaudy and fantastic appearances. But in the western or black chamber the effect of the fire-light that streamed upon the dark hangings through the blood-tinted panes, was ghastly in the extreme, and produced so wild a look upon the countenances of those who entered, that there were few of the company bold enough to set foot within its precincts at all.

It was in this apartment, also, that there stood against the western wall, a gigantic clock of ebony. Its pendulum swung to and fro with a dull, heavy, monotonous clang;

[2] Improvisers.

and when the minute-hand made the circuit of the face, and the hour was to be stricken, there came from the brazen lungs of the clock a sound which was clear and loud and deep and exceedingly musical, but of so peculiar a note and emphasis that, at each lapse of an hour, the musicians of the orchestra were constrained to pause, momentarily, in their performance, to hearken to the sound; and thus the waltzers perforce ceased their evolutions; and there was a brief disconcert of the whole gay company; and, while the chimes of the clock yet rang, it was observed that the giddiest grew pale, and the more aged and sedate passed their hands over their brows as if in confused reverie or meditation. But when the echoes had fully ceased, a light laughter at once pervaded the assembly; the musicians looked at each other and smiled as if at their own nervousness and folly, and made whispering vows, each to the other, that the next chiming of the clock should produce in them no similar emotion; and then, after the lapse of sixty minutes, (which embrace three thousand and six hundred seconds of the Time that flies,) there came yet another chiming of the clock, and then were the same disconcert and tremulousness and meditation as before.

But, in spite of these things, it was a gay and magnificent revel. The tastes of the duke were peculiar. He had a fine eye for colors and effects. He disregarded the *decora*[3] of mere fashion. His plans were bold and fiery, and his conceptions glowed with barbaric lustre. There are some who would have thought him mad. His followers felt that he was not. It was necessary to hear and see and touch him to be *sure* that he was not.

He had directed, in great part, the moveable embellishments of the seven chambers, upon occasion of this great *fête;* and it was his own guiding taste which had given character to the masqueraders. Be sure they were grotesque. There were much glare and glitter and piquancy and phantasm—much of what has been since seen in "Hernani."[4] There were arabesque figures with unsuited limbs and appointments. There were delirious fancies such as the madman fashions. There was much of the beautiful, much of the wanton, much of the *bizarre,* something of the terrible, and not a little of that which might have excited disgust. To and fro in the seven chambers there stalked, in fact, a multitude of dreams. And these—the dreams—writhed in and about, taking hue from the rooms, and causing the wild music of the orchestra to seem as the echo of their steps. And, anon, there strikes the ebony clock which stands in the hall of the velvet. And then, for a moment, all is still, and all is silent save the voice of the clock. The dreams are stiff-frozen as they stand. But the echoes of the chime die away—they have endured but an instant—and a light, half-subdued laughter floats after them as they depart. And now again the music swells, and the dreams live, and writhe to and fro more merrily than ever, taking hue from the many-tinted windows through which stream the rays from the tripods. But to the chamber which lies most westwardly of the seven, there are now none of the maskers who venture; for the night is waning away; and there flows a ruddier light through the blood-colored panes; and the blackness of the sable drapery appals; and to him whose foot falls upon the sable carpet, there comes from the near clock of ebony a muffled peal more solemnly emphatic than any which reaches *their* ears who indulge in the more remote gaieties of the other apartments.

[3] Rules.
[4] Play (1830) by Victor Hugo (1802–1885),
French poet, novelist, and dramatist.

But these other apartments were densely crowded, and in them beat feverishly the heart of life. And the revel went whirlingly on, until at length there commenced the sounding of midnight upon the clock. And then the music ceased, as I have told; and the evolutions of the waltzers were quieted; and there was an uneasy cessation of all things as before. But now there were twelve strokes to be sounded by the bell of the clock; and thus it happened, perhaps, that more of thought crept, with more of time, into the meditations of the thoughtful among those who revelled. And thus, too, it happened, perhaps, that before the last echoes of the last chime had utterly sunk into silence, there were many individuals in the crowd who had found leisure to become aware of the presence of a masked figure which had arrested the attention of no single individual before. And the rumor of this new presence having spread itself whisperingly around, there arose at length from the whole company a buzz, or murmur, expressive of disapprobation and surprise—then, finally, of terror, of horror, and of disgust.

In an assembly of phantasms such as I have painted, it may well be supposed that no ordinary appearance could have excited such sensation. In truth the masquerade license of the night was nearly unlimited; but the figure in question had out-Heroded Herod,[5] and gone beyond the bounds of even the prince's indefinite decorum. There are chords in the hearts of the most reckless which cannot be touched without emotion. Even with the utterly lost, to whom life and death are equally jests, there are matters of which no jest can be made. The whole company, indeed, seemed now deeply to feel that in the costume and bearing of the stranger neither wit nor propriety existed. The figure was tall and gaunt, and shrouded from head to foot in the habiliments of the grave. The mask which concealed the visage was made so nearly to resemble the countenance of a stiffened corpse that the closest scrutiny must have had difficulty in detecting the cheat. And yet all this might have been endured, if not approved, by the mad revellers around. But the mummer had gone so far as to assume the type of the Red Death. His vesture was dabbled in *blood*—and his broad brow, with all the features of the face, was besprinkled with the scarlet horror.

When the eyes of Prince Prospero fell upon this spectral image (which with a slow and solemn movement, as if more fully to sustain its *rôle,* stalked to and fro among the waltzers) he was seen to be convulsed, in the first moment with a strong shudder either of terror or distaste; but, in the next, his brow reddened with rage.

"Who dares?" he demanded hoarsely of the courtiers who stood near him—"who dares insult us with this blasphemous mockery? Seize him and unmask him—that we may know whom we have to hang at sun-rise, from the battlements!"

It was in the eastern or blue chamber in which stood the Prince Prospero as he uttered these words. They rang throughout the seven rooms loudly and clearly—for the prince was a bold and robust man, and the music had become hushed at the waving of his hand.

It was in the blue room where stood the prince, with a group of pale courtiers by his side. At first, as he spoke, there was a slight rushing movement of this group in the direction of the intruder, who at the moment was also near at hand, and now,

---

[5] Excessive behavior traditionally associated with Herod, the king of Judea who sought to destroy the infant Jesus by ordering the slaughter of all children of the region, and who fell into a rage upon learning of Jesus' escape. In *Hamlet,* Act 3, Sc. ii, Shakespeare refers to actors who "out-Herod Herod" as an entrenched stage convention.

with deliberate and stately step, made closer approach to the speaker. But from a certain nameless awe with which the mad assumptions of the mummer had inspired the whole party, there were found none who put forth hand to seize him; so that, unimpeded, he passed within a yard of the prince's person; and, while the vast assembly, as if with one impulse, shrank from the centres of the rooms to the walls, he made his way uninterruptedly, but with the same solemn and measured step which had distinguished him from the first, through the blue chamber to the purple—through the purple to the green—through the green to the orange—through this again to the white—and even thence to the violet, ere a decided movement had been made to arrest him. It was then, however, that the Prince Prospero, maddening with rage and the shame of his own momentary cowardice, rushed hurriedly through the six chambers, while none followed him on account of a deadly terror that had seized upon all. He bore aloft a drawn dagger, and had approached, in rapid impetuosity, to within three or four feet of the retreating figure, when the latter, having attained the extremity of the velvet apartment, turned suddenly and confronted his pursuer. There was a sharp cry—and the dagger dropped gleaming upon the sable carpet, upon which, instantly afterwards, fell prostrate in death the Prince Prospero. Then, summoning the wild courage of despair, a throng of the revellers at once threw themselves into the black apartment, and, seizing the mummer, whose tall figure stood erect and motionless within the shadow of the ebony clock, gasped in unutterable horror at finding the grave-cerements and corpse-like mask which they handled with so violent a rudeness, untenanted by any tangible form.

And now was acknowledged the presence of the Red Death. He had come like a thief in the night. And one by one dropped the revellers in the blood-bedewed halls of their revel, and died each in the despairing posture of his fall. And the life of the ebony clock went out with that of the last of the gay. And the flames of the tripods expired. And Darkness and Decay and the Red Death held illimitable dominion over all.

1843

---

from Nathaniel Hawthorne's *Twice-Told Tales**

We said a few hurried words about Mr. Hawthorne in our last number, with the design of speaking more fully in the present. We are still, however, pressed for room, and must necessarily discuss his volumes more briefly and more at random than their high merits deserve.

---

* In the April 1842 issue of *Graham's Magazine,* Poe briefly noted Hawthorne's collection of tales. He followed in May with a more extensive examination of Hawthorne's writings, the review from which this selection is extracted.

The book professes to be a collection of *tales,* yet is, in two respects, misnamed.
These pieces are now in their third publication, and, of course, are thrice-told.[1]
Moreover, they are by no means *all* tales, either in the ordinary or in the legitimate
understanding of the term. Many of them are pure essays; for example, "Sights from
a Steeple," "Sunday at Home," "Little Annie's Ramble," "A Rill from the Town
Pump," "The Toll-Gatherer's Day," "The Haunted Mind," "The Sister Years,"
"Snow-Flakes," "Night-Sketches," and "Foot-Prints on the Sea-Shore." We mention
these matters chiefly on account of their discrepancy with that marked precision and
finish by which the body of the work is distinguished.

Of the essays just named, we must be content to speak in brief. They are each
and all beautiful, without being characterised by the polish and adaptation so visible in the tales proper. A painter would at once note their leading or predominant
feature, and style it *repose.* There is no attempt at effect. All is quiet, thoughtful,
subdued. Yet this repose may exist simultaneously with high originality of
thought; and Mr. Hawthorne has demonstrated the fact. At every turn we meet
with novel combinations; yet these combinations never surpass the limits of the
quiet. We are soothed as we read; and withal is a calm astonishment that ideas so
apparently obvious have never occurred or been presented to us before. Herein our
author differs materially from Lamb or Hunt or Hazlitt[2]—who, with vivid originality of manner and expression, have less of the true novelty of thought than is
generally supposed, and whose originality, at best, has an uneasy and meretricious
quaintness, replete with startling effects unfounded in nature, and inducing trains
of reflection which lead to no satisfactory result. The Essays of Hawthorne have
much of the character of Irving,[3] with more of originality, and less of finish;
while, compared with the Spectator,[4] they have a vast superiority at all points. The
Spectator, Mr. Irving, and Mr. Hawthorne have in common that tranquil and subdued manner which we have chosen to denominate *repose;* but, in the case of the
two former, this repose is attained rather by the absence of novel combination, or
of originality, than otherwise, and consists chiefly in the calm, quiet, unostentatious
expression of commonplace thoughts, in an unambitious, unadulterated Saxon. In
them, by strong effort, we are made to conceive the absence of all. In the essays
before us the absence of effort is too obvious to be mistaken, and a strong under-
current of *suggestion* runs continuously beneath the upper stream of the tranquil
thesis. In short, these effusions of Mr. Hawthorne are the product of a truly imaginative intellect, restrained, and in some measure repressed, by fastidiousness of taste,
by constitutional melancholy and by indolence.

But it is of his tales that we desire principally to speak. The tale proper, in our
opinion, affords unquestionably the fairest field for the exercise of the loftiest talent,
which can be afforded by the wide domains of mere prose. Were we bidden to say

[1] Poe here notes that Hawthorne's tales had first
appeared in various magazines, were then
collected and published in a volume in 1837,
and were published again in an 1842 edition
(the "thrice-told" version that he is reviewing).

[2] Three English essayists: Charles Lamb
(1775–1834), Leigh Hunt (1784–1859), and
William Hazlitt (1778–1830).

[3] Washington Irving (1783–1859), whose *Tales of
a Traveller* (1824) had been compared with
Hawthorne's tales in Poe's April review.

[4] That is, with material that appeared in the
eighteenth-century English magazine *Spectator,*
edited by Richard Steele (1672–1729) and
Joseph Addison (1672–1719).

1596 The Literature of the American Renaissance

how the highest genius could be most advantageously employed for the best display of its own powers, we should answer, without hesitation—in the composition of a rhymed poem, not to exceed in length what might be perused in an hour. Within this limit alone can the highest order of true poetry exist. We need only here say, upon this topic, that, in almost all classes of composition, the unity of effect or impression is a point of the greatest importance. It is clear, moreover, that this unity cannot be thoroughly preserved in productions whose perusal cannot be completed at one sitting. We may continue the reading of a prose composition, from the very nature of prose itself, much longer than we can persevere, to any good purpose, in the perusal of a poem. This latter, if truly fulfilling the demands of the poetic sentiment, induces an exaltation of the soul which cannot be long sustained. All high excitements are necessarily transient. Thus a long poem is a paradox. And, without unity of impression, the deepest effects cannot be brought about. Epics were the offspring of an imperfect sense of Art, and their reign is no more. A poem *too* brief may produce a vivid, but never an intense or enduring impression. Without a certain continuity of effort—without a certain duration or repetition of purpose—the soul is never deeply moved. There must be the dropping of the water upon the rock. De Béranger[5] has wrought brilliant things—pungent and spirit-stirring—but, like all immassive[6] bodies, they lack *momentum,* and thus fail to satisfy the Poetic Sentiment. They sparkle and excite, but, from want of continuity, fail deeply to impress. Extreme brevity will degenerate into epigrammatism; but the sin of extreme length is even more unpardonable. *In medio tutissimus ibis.*[7]

Were we called upon, however, to designate that class of composition which, next to such a poem as we have suggested, should best fulfill the demands of high genius —should offer it the most advantageous field of exertion—we should unhesitatingly speak of the prose tale, as Mr. Hawthorne has here exemplified it. We allude to the short prose narrative, requiring from a half-hour to one or two hours in its perusal. The ordinary novel is objectionable, from its length, for reasons already stated in substance. As it cannot be read at one sitting, it deprives itself, of course, of the immense force derivable from *totality.* Worldly interests intervening during the pauses of perusal, modify, annul, or counteract, in a greater or less degree, the impressions of the book. But simple cessation in reading, would, of itself, be sufficient to destroy the true unity. In the brief tale, however, the author is enabled to carry out the fulness of his intention, be it what it may. During the hour of perusal the soul of the reader is at the writer's control. There are no external or extrinsic influences—resulting from weariness or interruption.

A skilful literary artist has constructed a tale. If wise, he has not fashioned his thoughts to accommodate his incidents; but having conceived, with deliberate care, a certain unique or single *effect* to be wrought out, he then invents such incidents— he then combines such events as may best aid him in establishing this preconceived effect. If his very initial sentence tend not to the outbringing of this effect, then he has failed in his first step. In the whole composition there should be no word written, of which the tendency, direct or indirect, is not to the one pre-established design. And

[5] French poet Pierre-Jean de Béranger (1780–1857).
[6] Without mass.

[7] Latin: "You will go most safely in the middle way."

by such means, with such care and skill, a picture is at length painted which leaves in the mind of him who contemplates it with a kindred art, a sense of the fullest satisfaction. The idea of the tale has been presented unblemished, because undisturbed; and this is an end unattainable by the novel. Undue brevity is just as exceptionable here as in the poem; but undue length is yet more to be avoided.

We have said that the tale has a point of superiority even over the poem. In fact, while the *rhythm* of this latter is an essential aid in the development of the poet's highest idea—the idea of the Beautiful—the artificialities of this rhythm are an inseparable bar to the development of all points of thought or expression which have their basis in *Truth*. But Truth is often, and in very great degree, the aim of the tale. Some of the finest tales are tales of ratiocination. Thus the field of this species of composition, if not in so elevated a region on the mountain of Mind, is a table-land of far vaster extent than the domain of the mere poem. Its products are never so rich, but infinitely more numerous, and more appreciable by the mass of mankind. The writer of the prose tale, in short, may bring to his theme a vast variety of modes or inflections of thought and expression—(the ratiocinative, for example, the sarcastic, or the humorous) which are not only antagonistical to the nature of the poem, but absolutely forbidden by one of its most peculiar and indispensable adjuncts; we allude, of course, to rhythm. It may be added here, *par parenthèse,* [8] that the author who aims at the purely beautiful in a prose tale is laboring at great disadvantage. For Beauty can be better treated in the poem. Not so with terror, or passion, or horror, or a multitude of such other points. And here it will be seen how full of prejudice are the usual animadversions against those *tales of effect,* many fine examples of which were found in the earlier numbers of Blackwood.[9] The impressions produced were wrought in a legitimate sphere of action, and constituted a legitimate although sometimes an exaggerated interest. They were relished by every man of genius: although there were found many men of genius who condemned them without just ground. The true critic will but demand that the design intended be accomplished, to the fullest extent, by the means most advantageously applicable.

We have very few American tales of real merit—we may say, indeed, none, with the exception of "The Tales of a Traveller" of Washington Irving, and these "Twice-Told Tales" of Mr. Hawthorne. Some of the pieces of Mr. John Neal[10] abound in vigor and originality; but in general, his compositions of this class are excessively diffuse, extravagant, and indicative of an imperfect sentiment of Art. Articles at random are, now and then, met with in our periodicals which might be advantageously compared with the best effusions of the British Magazines; but, upon the whole, we are far behind our progenitors in this department of literature.

Of Mr. Hawthorne's Tales we would say, emphatically, that they belong to the highest region of Art—an Art subservient to genius of a very lofty order. We had supposed, with good reason for so supposing, that he had been thrust into his present position by one of the impudent *cliques* which beset our literature, and whose pretensions it is our full purpose to expose at the earliest opportunity; but we have been most agreeably mistaken. We know of few compositions which the critic can

[8] French: "parenthetically."
[9] Blackwood's *Edinburgh Magazine,* a British monthly, made a speciality of the gothic tale.
[10] American writer (1793–1876).

more honestly commend than these "Twice-Told Tales." As Americans, we felt proud of the book.

Mr. Hawthorne's distinctive trait is invention, creation, imagination, originality— a trait which, in the literature of fiction, is positively worth all the rest. But the nature of originality, so far as regards its manifestation in letters, is but imperfectly under- stood. The inventive or original mind as frequently displays itself in novelty of *tone* as in novelty of matter. Mr. Hawthorne is original at *all* points. . . .

In the way of objection we have scarcely a word to say of these tales. There is, perhaps, a somewhat too general or prevalent *tone*—a tone of melancholy and mysticism. The subjects are insufficiently varied. There is not so much of *versatility* evinced as we might well be warranted in expecting from the high powers of Mr. Hawthorne. But beyond these trivial exceptions we have really none to make. The style is purity itself. Force abounds. High imagination gleams from every page. Mr. Hawthorne is a man of the truest genius. We only regret that the limits of our Magazine will not permit us to pay him that full tribute of commendation, which, under other circumstances, we should be so eager to pay.

1842

The Tell-Tale Heart

True!—nervous—very, very dreadfully nervous I had been and am; but why *will* you say that I am mad? The disease had sharpened my senses—not destroyed—not dulled them. Above all was the sense of hearing acute. I heard all things in the heaven and in the earth. I heard many things in hell. How, then, am I mad? Hearken! and observe how healthily—how calmly I can tell you the whole story.

It is impossible to say how first the idea entered my brain; but, once conceived, it haunted me day and night. Object there was none. Passion there was none. I loved the old man. He had never wronged me. He had never given me insult. For his gold I had no desire. I think it was his eye! yes, it was this! One of his eyes resembled that of a vulture—a pale blue eye, with a film over it. Whenever it fell upon me, my blood ran cold; and so by degrees—very gradually—I made up my mind to take the life of the old man, and thus rid myself of the eye forever.

Now this is the point. You fancy me mad. Madmen know nothing. But you should have seen *me*. You should have seen how wisely I proceeded—with what caution— with what foresight—with what dissimulation I went to work! I was never kinder to the old man than during the whole week before I killed him. And every night, about midnight, I turned the latch of his door and opened it—oh, so gently! And then, when I had made an opening sufficient for my head, I put in a dark lantern, all closed, closed, so that no light shone out, and then I thrust in my head. Oh, you would have laughed to see how cunningly I thrust it in! I moved it slowly—very, very slowly, so that I might not disturb the old man's sleep. It took me an hour to place my whole head within the opening so far that I could see him as he lay upon his bed. Ha!—would a madman have been so wise as this? And then, when my head was well in the room, I undid the lantern cautiously—oh, so cautiously—cautiously (for the hinges creaked)—I undid it just so much that a single thin ray fell upon the vulture eye. And this I did for seven long nights—every night just at midnight—but I found the eye always closed; and so it was impossible to do the work; for it was not the old man who vexed me, but his Evil Eye. And every morning, when the day broke, I went boldly into the chamber and spoke courageously to him, calling him by name in a hearty tone, and inquiring how he had passed the night. So you see he would have been a very profound old man, indeed, to suspect that every night, just at twelve, I looked in upon him while he slept.

Upon the eighth night I was more than usually cautious in opening the door. A watch's minute hand moves more quickly than did mine. Never, before that night, had I *felt* the extent of my own powers—of my sagacity. I could scarcely contain my feelings of triumph. To think that there I was, opening the door, little by little, and he not even to dream of my secret deeds or thoughts. I fairly chuckled at the idea; and perhaps he heard me; for he moved on the bed suddenly, as if startled. Now you may think that I drew back—but no. His room was as black as pitch with the thick darkness, (for the shutters were close fastened, through fear of robbers,) and so I knew that he could not see the opening of the door, and I kept pushing it on steadily, steadily.

I had my head in, and was about to open the lantern, when my thumb slipped upon the tin fastening, and the old man sprang up in the bed, crying out—"Who's there?"

I kept quite still and said nothing. For a whole hour I did not move a muscle, and in the meantime I did not hear him lie down. He was still sitting up in the bed, listening;—just as I have done, night after night, hearkening to the death-watches in the wall.

Presently I heard a slight groan, and I knew it was the groan of mortal terror. It was not a groan of pain or of grief—oh, no!—it was the low stifled sound that arises from the bottom of the soul when overcharged with awe. I knew the sound well. Many a night, just at midnight, when all the world slept, it has welled up from my own bosom, deepening, with its dreadful echo, the terrors that distracted me. I say I knew it well. I knew what the old man felt, and pitied him, although I chuckled at heart. I knew that he had been lying awake ever since the first slight noise, when he had turned in the bed. His fears had been ever since growing upon him. He had been trying to fancy them causeless, but could not. He had been saying to himself —"It is nothing but the wind in the chimney—it is only a mouse crossing the floor," or "it is merely a cricket which has made a single chirp." Yes, he has been trying to comfort himself with these suppositions: but he had found all in vain. *All in vain;* because Death, in approaching him, had stalked with his black shadow before him, and enveloped the victim. And it was the mournful influence of the unperceived shadow that caused him to feel—although he neither saw nor heard—to *feel* the presence of my head within the room.

When I had waited a long time, very patiently, without hearing him lie down, I resolved to open a little—a very, very little crevice in the lantern. So I opened it —you cannot imagine how stealthily, stealthily—until, at length, a single dim ray, like the thread of the spider, shot from out the crevice and fell upon the vulture eye.

It was open—wide, wide open—and I grew furious as I gazed upon it. I saw it with perfect distinctness—all a dull blue, with a hideous veil over it that chilled the very marrow in my bones; but I could see nothing else of the old man's face or person: for I had directed the ray as if by instinct, precisely upon the damned spot.

And now—have I not told you that what you mistake for madness is but over acuteness of the senses?—now, I say there came to my ears a low, dull, quick sound, such as a watch makes when enveloped in cotton. I knew *that* sound well, too, It was the beating of the old man's heart. It increased my fury, as the beating of a drum stimulates the soldier into courage.

But even yet I refrained and kept still. I scarcely breathed. I held the lantern motionless. I tried how steadily I could maintain the ray upon the eye. Meantime the hellish tattoo of the heart increased. It grew quicker and quicker, and louder and louder every instant. The old man's terror *must* have been extreme! It grew louder, I say, louder every moment!—do you mark me well? I have told you that I am nervous: so I am. And now at the dead hour of the night, amid the dreadful silence of that old house, so strange a noise as this excited me to uncontrollable terror. Yet, for some minutes longer I refrained and stood still. But the beating grew louder, louder! I thought the heart must burst. And now a new anxiety seized me—the sound would be heard by a neighbor! The old man's hour had come! With a loud yell, I threw open the lantern and leaped into the room. He shrieked once—once only. In an instant I dragged him to the floor, and pulled the heavy bed over him. I then smiled gaily, to find the deed so far done. But, for many minutes, the heart beat on with a muffled sound. This, however, did not vex me; it would not be heard through the wall. At length it ceased. The old man was dead. I removed the bed and examined the corpse. Yes, he was stone, stone dead. I placed my hand upon the heart and held it there many minutes. There was no pulsation. He was stone dead. His eye would trouble me no more.

If still you think me mad, you will think so no longer when I describe the wise precautions I took for the concealment of the body. The night waned, and I worked hastily, but in silence. First of all I dismembered the corpse. I cut off the head and the arms and the legs.

I then took up three planks from the flooring of the chamber, and deposited all between the scantlings. I then replaced the boards so cleverly, so cunningly, that no human eye—not even *his*— could have detected anything wrong. There was nothing to wash out—no stain of any kind—no blood-spot whatever. I had been too wary for that. A tub had caught all—ha! ha!

When I had made an end of these labors it was four o'clock—still dark as midnight. As the bell sounded the hour, there came a knocking at the street door. I went down to open it with a light heart,—for what had I *now* to fear? There entered three men, who introduced themselves, with perfect suavity, as officers of the police. A shriek had been heard by a neighbor during the night; suspicion of foul play had been aroused; information had been lodged at the police office, and they (the officers) had been deputed to search the premises.

I smiled,—for *what* had I to fear? I bade the gentlemen welcome. The shriek, I said, was my own in a dream. The old man, I mentioned, was absent in the country. I took my visitors all over the house. I bade them search—search *well*. I led them, at length, to *his* chamber. I showed them his treasures, secure, undisturbed. In the enthusiasm of my confidence, I brought chairs into the room and desired them *here* to rest from their fatigues, while I myself, in the wild audacity of my perfect triumph, placed my own seat upon the very spot beneath which reposed the corpse of the victim.

The officers were satisfied. My *manner* had convinced them. I was singularly at ease. They sat, and while I answered cheerily, they chatted of familiar things. But, ere long, I felt myself getting pale and wished them gone. My head ached, and I fancied a ringing in my ears: but still they sat and still they chatted. The ringing became more distinct;—it continued and became more distinct: I talked more freely to get rid of the feeling: but it continued and gained definitiveness—until, at length, I found that the noise was *not* within my ears.

No doubt I now grew *very* pale;—but I talked more fluently, and with a heightened voice. Yet the sound increased—and what could I do? It was *a low, dull, quick sound—much such a sound as a watch makes when enveloped in cotton.* I gasped for breath —and yet the officers heard it not. I talked more quickly—more vehemently; but the noise steadily increased. I arose and argued about trifles, in a high key and with violent gesticulations; but the noise steadily increased. Why *would* they not be gone? I paced the floor to and fro with heavy strides, as if excited to fury by the observations of the men—but the noise steadily increased. Oh God! what *could* I do? I foamed—I raved—I swore! I swung the chair upon which I had been sitting, and grated it upon the boards, but the noise arose over all and continually increased. It grew louder— louder—*louder!* And still the men chatted pleasantly, and smiled. Was it possible they heard not? Almighty God!—no, no! They heard!—they suspected!—they *knew!*— they were making a mockery of my horror!—this I thought, and this I think. But anything was better than this agony! Anything was more tolerable than this derision! I could bear those hypocritical smiles no longer! I felt that I must scream or die!— and now—again!—hark! louder! louder! louder! *louder!*—

"Villains!" I shrieked, "dissemble no more! I admit the deed!—tear up the planks! —here, here!—it is the beating of his hideous heart!"

1843

The Purloined Letter

At Paris, just after dark one gusty evening in the autumn of 18——, I was enjoying the twofold luxury of meditation and a meerschaum, in company with my friend C. Auguste Dupin, in his little back library, or book-closet, *au troisième,* [1] *No. 33, Rue Dunôt, Faubourg St. Germain.* For one hour at least we had maintained a profound silence; while each, to any casual observer, might have seemed intently and exclusively

---

[1] "On the third floor" (not counting the ground floor) in French; thus, on what we call the fourth floor.

occupied with the curling eddies of smoke that oppressed the atmosphere of the chamber. For myself, however, I was mentally discussing certain topics which had formed matter for conversation between us at an earlier period of the evening; I mean the affair of the Rue Morgue, and the mystery attending the murder of Marie Rogêt.[2] I looked upon it, therefore, as something of a coincidence, when the door of our apartment was thrown open and admitted our old acquaintance, Monsieur G——, the Prefect of the Parisian police.

We gave him a hearty welcome; for there was nearly half as much of the entertaining as of the contemptible about the man, and we had not seen him for several years. We had been sitting in the dark, and Dupin now arose for the purpose of lighting a lamp, but sat down again, without doing so, upon G.'s saying that he had called to consult us, or rather to ask the opinion of my friend, about some official business which had occasioned a great deal of trouble.

"If it is any point requiring reflection," observed Dupin, as he forebore to enkindle the wick, "we shall examine it to better purpose in the dark."

"That is another of your odd notions," said the Prefect, who had a fashion of calling every thing "odd" that was beyond his comprehension, and thus lived amid an absolute legion of "oddities."

"Very true," said Dupin, as he supplied his visiter with a pipe, and rolled towards him a comfortable chair.

"And what is the difficulty now?" I asked. "Nothing more in the assassination way, I hope?"

"Oh no; nothing of that nature. The fact is, the business is *very* simple indeed, and I make no doubt that we can manage it sufficiently well ourselves; but then I thought Dupin would like to hear the details of it, because it is so excessively *odd.*"

"Simple and odd," said Dupin.

"Why, yes; and not exactly that, either. The fact is, we have all been a good deal puzzled because the affair is so simple, and yet baffles us altogether."

"Perhaps it is the very simplicity of the thing which puts you at fault," said my friend.

"What nonsense you *do* talk!" replied the Prefect, laughing heartily.

"Perhaps the mystery is a little *too* plain," said Dupin.

"Oh, good heavens! who ever heard of such an idea?"

"A little *too* self-evident."

"Ha! ha! ha!—ha! ha! ha!—ho! ho! ho!" roared our visiter, profoundly amused, "oh, Dupin, you will be the death of me yet!"

"And what, after all, *is* the matter on hand?" I asked.

"Why, I will tell you," replied the Prefect, as he gave a long, steady, and contemplative puff, and settled himself in his chair. "I will tell you in a few words; but, before I begin, let me caution you that this is an affair demanding the greatest secrecy, and that I should most probably lose the position I now hold, were it known that I confided it to any one."

"Proceed," said I.

"Or not," said Dupin.

"Well, then; I have received personal information, from a very high quarter, that

---

[2] Two earlier cases solved by Dupin.

a certain document of the last importance, has been purloined from the royal apartments. The individual who purloined it is known; this beyond a doubt; he was seen to take it. It is known, also, that it still remains in his possession."

"How is this known?" asked Dupin.

"It is clearly inferred," replied the Prefect, "from the nature of the document, and from the non-appearance of certain results which would at once arise from its passing *out* of the robber's possession;—that is to say, from his employing it as he must design in the end to employ it."

"Be a little more explicit," I said.

"Well, I may venture so far as to say that the paper gives its holder a certain power in a certain quarter where such power is immensely valuable." The Prefect was fond of the cant of diplomacy.

"Still I do not quite understand," said Dupin.

"No? Well; the disclosure of the document to a third person, who shall be nameless, would bring in question the honor of a personage of most exalted station; and this fact gives the holder of the document an ascendancy over the illustrious personage whose honor and peace are so jeopardized."

"But this ascendancy," I interposed, "would depend upon the robber's knowledge of the loser's knowledge of the robber. Who would dare—"

"The thief," said G., "is the Minister D——, who dares all things, those unbecoming as well as those becoming a man. The method of the theft was not less ingenious than bold. The document in question—a letter, to be frank—had been received by the personage robbed while alone in the royal *boudoir.* During its perusal she was suddenly interrupted by the entrance of the other exalted personage from whom especially it was her wish to conceal it. After a hurried and vain endeavor to thrust it in a drawer, she was forced to place it, open as it was, upon a table. The address, however, was uppermost, and, the contents thus unexposed, the letter escaped notice. At this juncture enters the Minister D——. His lynx eye immediately perceives the paper, recognises the handwriting of the address, observes the confusion of the personage addressed, and fathoms her secret. After some business transactions, hurried through in his ordinary manner, he produces a letter somewhat similar to the one in question, opens it, pretends to read it, and then places it in close juxtaposition to the other. Again he converses, for some fifteen minutes, upon the public affairs. At length, in taking leave, he takes also from the table the letter to which he had no claim. Its rightful owner saw, but, of course, dared not call attention to the act, in the presence of the third personage who stood at her elbow. The minister decamped; leaving his own letter—one of no importance—upon the table."

"Here, then," said Dupin to me, "you have precisely what you demand to make the ascendancy complete—the robber's knowledge of the loser's knowledge of the robber."

"Yes," replied the Prefect; "and the power thus attained has, for some months past, been wielded, for political purposes, to a very dangerous extent. The personage robbed is more thoroughly convinced, every day, of the necessity of reclaiming her letter. But this, of course, cannot be done openly. In fine, driven to despair, she has committed the matter to me."

"Than whom," said Dupin, amid a perfect whirlwind of smoke, "no more sagacious agent could, I suppose, be desired, or even imagined."

"You flatter me," replied the Prefect; "but it is possible that some such opinion may have been entertained."

"It is clear," said I, "as you observe, that the letter is still in possession of the minister; since it is this possession, and not any employment of the letter, which bestows the power. With the employment the power departs."

"True," said G.; "and upon this conviction I proceeded. My first care was to make thorough search of the minister's hotel;[3] and here my chief embarrassment lay in the necessity of searching without his knowledge. Beyond all things, I have been warned of the danger which would result from giving him reason to suspect our design."

"But," said I, "you are quite *au fait*[4] in these investigations. The Parisian police have done this thing often before."

"O yes; and for this reason I did not despair. The habits of the minister gave me, too, a great advantage. He is frequently absent from home all night. His servants are by no means numerous. They sleep at a distance from their master's apartment, and, being chiefly Neapolitans, are readily made drunk. I have keys, as you know, with which I can open any chamber or cabinet in Paris. For three months a night has not passed, during the greater part of which I have not been engaged, personally, in ransacking the D—— Hotel. My honor is interested, and, to mention a great secret, the reward is enormous. So I did not abandon the search until I had become fully satisfied that the thief is a more astute man than myself. I fancy that I have investigated every nook and corner of the premises in which it is possible that the paper can be concealed."

"But is it not possible," I suggested, "that although the letter may be in possession of the minister, as it unquestionably is, he may have concealed it elsewhere than upon his own premises?"

"This is barely possible," said Dupin. "The present peculiar condition of affairs at court, and especially of those intrigues in which D—— is known to be involved, would render the instant availability of the document—its susceptibility of being produced at a moment's notice—a point of nearly equal importance with its possession."

"Its susceptibility of being produced?" said I.

"That is to say, of being *destroyed*," said Dupin.

"True," I observed; "the paper is clearly then upon the premises. As for its being upon the person of the minister, we may consider that as out of the question."

"Entirely," said the Prefect. "He has been twice waylaid, as if by footpads, and his person rigorously searched under my own inspection."

"You might have spared yourself this trouble," said Dupin. "D——, I presume, is not altogether a fool, and, if not, must have anticipated these waylayings, as a matter of course."

"Not *altogether* a fool," said G., "but then he's a poet, which I take to be only one remove from a fool."

"True," said Dupin, after a long and thoughtful whiff from his meerschaum, "although I have been guilty of certain doggrel myself."

"Suppose you detail," said I, "the particulars of your search."

"Why the fact is, we took our time, and we searched *every where*. I have had long

---

[3] Large private residence.   [4] French: "accomplished."

experience in these affairs. I took the entire building, room by room; devoting the nights of a whole week to each. We examined, first, the furniture of each apartment. We opened every possible drawer; and I presume you know that, to a properly trained police agent, such a thing as a *secret* drawer is impossible. Any man is a dolt who permits a 'secret' drawer to escape him in a search of this kind. The thing is *so* plain. There is a certain amount of bulk—of space—to be accounted for in every cabinet. Then we have accurate rules. The fiftieth part of a line could not escape us. After the cabinets we took the chairs. The cushions we probed with fine long needles you have seen me employ. From the tables we removed the tops."

"Why so?"

"Sometimes the top of a table, or other similarly arranged piece of furniture, is removed by the person wishing to conceal an article; then the leg is excavated, the article deposited within the cavity, and the top replaced. The bottoms and tops of bedposts are employed in the same way."

"But could not the cavity be detected by sounding?" I asked.

"By no means, if, when the article is deposited, a sufficient wadding of cotton be placed around it. Besides, in our case, we were obliged to proceed without noise."

"But you could not have removed—you could not have taken to pieces *all* articles of furniture in which it would have been possible to make a deposit in the manner you mention. A letter may be compressed into a thin spiral roll, not differing much in shape or bulk from a large knitting-needle, and in this form it might be inserted into the rung of a chair, for example, You did not take to pieces all the chairs?"

"Certainly not; but we did better—we examined the rungs of every chair in the hotel, and, indeed, the jointings of every description of furniture, by the aid of a most powerful microscope.[5] Had there been any traces of recent disturbance we should not have failed to detect it instantly. A single grain of gimlet-dust, for example, would have been as obvious as an apple. Any disorder in the glueing—any unusual gaping in the joints—would have sufficed to insure detection."

"I presume you looked to the mirrors, between the boards and the plates, and you probed the beds and the bed-clothes, as well as the curtains and carpets."

"That of course; and when we had absolutely completed every particle of the furniture in this way, then we examined the house itself. We divided its entire surface into compartments, which we numbered, so that none might be missed; then we scrutinized each individual square inch throughout the premises, including the two houses immediately adjoining, with the microscope, as before."

"The two houses adjoining!" I exclaimed; "you must have had a great deal of trouble."

"We had; but the reward offered is prodigious."

"You include the *grounds* about the houses?"

"All the grounds are paved with brick. They gave us comparatively little trouble. We examined the moss between the bricks, and found it undisturbed."

"You looked among D——'s papers, of course, and into the books of the library?"

"Certainly; we opened every package and parcel; we not only opened every book, but we turned over every leaf in each volume, not contenting ourselves with a mere shake, according to the fashion of some of our police officers. We also measured the

---

[5] Magnifying glass.

thickness of every book-*cover,* with the most accurate admeasurement, and applied to each the most jealous scrutiny of the microscope. Had any of the bindings been recently meddled with, it would have been utterly impossible that the fact should have escaped observation. Some five or six volumes, just from the hand of the binder, we carefully probed, longitudinally, with the needles."

"You explored the floors beneath the carpets?"

"Beyond doubt. We removed every carpet, and examined the boards with the microscope."

"And the paper on the walls?"

"Yes."

"You looked into the cellars?"

"We did."

"Then," I said, "you have been making a miscalculation, and the letter is *not* upon the premises, as you suppose."

"I fear you are right there," said the Prefect. "And now, Dupin, what would you advise me to do?"

"To make a thorough re-search of the premises."

"That is absolutely needless," replied G———. "I am not more sure that I breathe than I am that the letter is not at the Hotel."

"I have no better advice to give you," said Dupin. "You have, of course, an accurate description of the letter?"

"Oh yes!"—And here the Prefect, producing a memorandum-book, proceeded to read aloud a minute account of the internal, and especially of the external appearance of the missing document. Soon after finishing the perusal of this description, he took his departure, more entirely depressed in spirits than I had ever known the good gentleman before.

In about a month afterwards he paid us another visit, and found us occupied very nearly as before. He took a pipe and a chair and entered into some ordinary conversation. At length I said,—

"Well, but G———, what of the purloined letter? I presume you have at last made up your mind that there is no such thing as overreaching the Minister?"

"Confound him, say I—yes; I made the re-examination, however, as Dupin suggested—but it was all labor lost, as I knew it would be."

"How much was the reward offered, did you say?" asked Dupin.

"Why a very great deal—a *very* liberal reward—I don't like to say how much, precisely; but one thing I *will* say, that I wouldn't mind giving my individual check for fifty thousand francs to any one who could obtain me that letter. The fact is, it is becoming of more and more importance every day; and the reward has been lately doubled. If it were trebled, however, I could do no more than I have done."

"Why, yes," said Dupin, drawlingly, between the whiffs of his meerschaum, "I really—think, G———, you have not exerted yourself—to the utmost in this matter. You might—do a little more, I think, eh?"

"How?—in what way?"

"Why—puff, puff—you might—puff, puff—employ counsel in the matter, eh? —puff, puff, puff. Do you remember the story they tell of Abernethy?"[6]

---

[6] John Abernethy, English surgeon (1764–1831).

"No; hang Abernethy!"

"To be sure! hang him and welcome. But, once upon a time, a certain rich miser conceived the design of spunging upon this Abernethy for a medical opinion. Getting up, for this purpose, an ordinary conversation in a private company, he insinuated his case to the physician, as that of an imaginary individual.

" 'We will suppose,' said the miser, 'that his symptoms are such and such; now, doctor, what would *you* have directed him to take?'

" 'Take!' said Abernethy, 'why, take *advice,* to be sure.' "

"But," said the Prefect, a little discomposed, "I am *perfectly* willing to take advice, and to pay for it. I would *really* give fifty thousand francs to any one who would aid me in the matter."

"In that case," replied Dupin, opening a drawer, and producing a check-book, "you may as well fill me up a check for the amount mentioned. When you have signed it, I will hand you the letter."

I was astounded. The Prefect appeared absolutely thunder-stricken. For some minutes he remained speechless and motionless, looking incredulously at my friend with open mouth, and eyes that seemed starting from their sockets; then, apparently recovering himself in some measure, he seized a pen, and after several pauses and vacant stares, finally filled up and signed a check for fifty thousand francs, and handed it across the table to Dupin. The latter examined it carefully and deposited it in his pocketbook; then, unlocking an *escritoire,*[7] took thence a letter and gave it to the Prefect. This functionary grasped it in a perfect agony of joy, opened it with a trembling hand, cast a rapid glance at its contents, and then, scrambling and struggling to the door, rushed at length unceremoniously from the room and from the house, without having uttered a syllable since Dupin had requested him to fill up the check.

When he had gone, my friend entered into some explanations.

"The Parisian police," he said, "are exceedingly able in their way. They are persevering, ingenious, cunning, and thoroughly versed in the knowledge which their duties seem chiefly to demand. Thus, when G—— detailed to us his mode of searching the premises at the Hotel D——, I felt entire confidence in his having made a satisfactory investigation—so far as his labors extended."

"So far as his labors extended?" said I.

"Yes," said Dupin. "The measures adopted were not only the best of their kind, but carried out to absolute perfection. Had the letter been deposited within the range of their search, these fellows would, beyond a question, have found it."

I merely laughed—but he seemed quite serious in all that he said.

"The measures, then," he continued, "were good in their kind, and well executed; their defect lay in their being inapplicable to the case, and to the man. A certain set of highly ingenious resources are, with the Prefect, a sort of Procrustean bed,[8] to which he forcibly adapts his designs. But he perpetually errs by being too deep or too shallow, for the matter in hand; and many a school-boy is a better reasoner than he. I knew one about eight years of age, whose success at guessing in the game of 'even and odd' attracted universal admiration. This game is simple, and is played with

[7] French: "writing desk."
[8] I.e., an unyielding system. Procrustes, robber in classic myth, forced his victims to fit the bed to which he tied them by cutting off their legs if they were too long or by stretching them if too short.

marbles. One player holds in his hand a number of these toys, and demands of another whether that number is even or odd. If the guess is right, the guesser wins one; if wrong, he loses one. The boy to whom I allude won all the marbles of the school. Of course he had some principle of guessing; and this lay in mere observation and admeasurement of the astuteness of his opponents. For example, an arrant simpleton is his opponent, and, holding up his closed hand, asks, 'are they even or odd?' Our schoolboy replies, 'odd,' and loses; but upon the second trial he wins, for he then says to himself, "the simpleton had them even upon the first trial, and his amount of cunning is just sufficient to make him have them odd upon the second; I will therefore guess odd;—he guesses odd, and wins. Now, with a simpleton a degree above the first, he would have reasoned thus: 'This fellow finds that in the first instance I guessed odd, and, in the second, he will propose to himself, upon the first impulse, a simple variation from even to odd, as did the first simpleton; but then a second thought will suggest that this is too simple a variation, and finally he will decide upon putting it even as before. I will therefore guess even;'—he guesses even, and wins. Now this mode of reasoning in the schoolboy, whom his fellows termed 'lucky,'—what, in its last analysis, is it?"

"It is merely," I said, "an identification of the reasoner's intellect with that of his opponent."

"It is," said Dupin; "and, upon inquiring of the boy by what means he effected the *thorough* identification in which his success consisted, I received answer as follows: 'When I wish to find out how wise, or how stupid, or how good, or how wicked is any one, or what are his thoughts at the moment, I fashion the expression of my face, as accurately as possible, in accordance with the expression of his, and then wait to see what thoughts or sentiments arise in my mind or heart, as if to match or correspond with the expression.' This response of the schoolboy lies at the bottom of all the spurious profundity which has been attributed to Rochefoucault, to La Bruyère, to Machiavelli, and to Campanella."[9]

"And the identification," I said, "of the reasoner's intellect with that of his opponent, depends, if I understand you aright, upon the accuracy with which the opponent's intellect is admeasured."

"For its practical value it depends upon this," replied Dupin; "and the Prefect and his cohort fail so frequently, first, by default of this identification, and, secondly, by ill-admeasurement, or rather through non-admeasurement, of the intellect with which they are engaged. They consider only their *own* ideas of ingenuity; and, in searching for anything hidden, advert only to the modes in which *they* would have hidden it. They are right in this much—that their own ingenuity is a faithful representative of that of *the mass;* but when the cunning of the individual felon is diverse in character from their own, the felon foils them, of course. This always happens when it is above their own, and very usually when it is below. They have no variation of principle in their investigations; at best, when urged by some unusual emergency—by some extraordinary reward—they extend or exaggerate their old modes of *practice,* without touching their principles. What, for example, in this case of D——, has been done to vary the principle of action? What is all this boring, and probing, and sounding,

⁹ French and Italian moralists and philosophers of the fifteenth to seventeenth centuries.

and scrutinizing with the microscope, and dividing the surface of the building into registered square inches—what is it all but an exaggeration *of the application* of the one principle or set of principles of search, which are based upon the one set of notions regarding human ingenuity, to which the Prefect, in the long routine of his duty, has been accustomed? Do you not see he has taken it for granted that *all* men proceed to conceal a letter,—not exactly in a gimlet-hole bored in a chair-leg—but, at least, in *some* out-of-the-way hole or corner suggested by the same tenor of thought which would urge a man to secrete a letter in a gimlet-hole bored in a chair-leg? And do you not see also, that such *recherchés*[10] nooks for concealment are adapted only for ordinary occasions, and would be adopted only by ordinary intellects; for, in all cases of concealment, a disposal of the article concealed—a disposal of it in this *recherché* manner,—is, in the very first instance, presumable and presumed; and thus its discovery depends, not at all upon the acumen, but altogether upon the mere care, patience, and determination of the seekers; and where the case is of importance—or, what amounts to the same thing in the policial eyes, when the reward is of magnitude,— the qualities in question have *never* been known to fail. You will now understand what I meant in suggesting that, had the purloined letter been hidden any where within the limits of the Prefect's examination—in other words, had the principle of its concealment been comprehended within the principles of the Prefect—its discovery would have been a matter altogether beyond question. This functionary, however, has been thoroughly mystified; and the remote source of his defeat lies in the supposition that the Minister is a fool, because he has acquired renown as a poet. All fools are poets; this the Prefect *feels;* and he is merely guilty of a *non distributio medii*[11] in thence inferring that all poets are fools."

"But is this really the poet?" I asked. "There are two brothers, I know; and both have attained reputation in letters. The Minister I believe has written learnedly on the Differential Calculus. He is a mathematician, and no poet."

"You are mistaken; I know him well; he is both. As poet *and* mathematician, he would reason well; as mere mathematician, he could not have reasoned at all, and thus would have been at the mercy of the Prefect."

"You surprise me," I said, "by these opinions, which have been contradicted by the voice of the world. You do not mean to set at naught the well-digested idea of centuries. The mathematical reason has long been regarded as *the* reason *par excellence.*"[12]

" '*Il y a à parier,*' " replied Dupin, quoting from Chamfort, " '*que toute idée publique, toute convention reçue, est une sottise, car elle a convenu au plus grand nombre.*'[13] The mathematicians, I grant you, have done their best to promulgate the popular error to which you allude, and which is none the less an error for its promulgation as truth. With an art worthy a better cause, for example, they have insinuated the term 'analysis' into application to algebra. The French are the originators of this particular deception; but if a term is of any importance—if words derive any value from applicability—then 'analysis' conveys 'algebra' about as much as, in Latin, '*ambitus*'

---

[10] French: "unusual."
[11] Latin: "undistributed middle." A term in logic that indicates faulty reasoning.
[12] French: "the very best."
[13] A maxim from the eighteenth-century French moralist Sebastien Chamfort: "There's a good chance that every generally accepted notion, every commonly received convention, is nonsense, exactly because it pleased the majority view."

implies 'ambition,' *'religio'* 'religion,' or *'homines honesti,'* a set of *honorable* men."

"You have a quarrel on hand, I see," said I, "with some of the algebraists of Paris; but proceed."

"I dispute the availability, and thus the value, of that reason which is cultivated in any especial form other than the abstractly logical. I dispute, in particular, the reason educed by mathematical study. The mathematics are the science of form and quantity; mathematical reasoning is merely logic applied to observation upon form and quantity. The great error lies in supposing that even the truths of what is called *pure* algebra, are abstract or general truths. And this error is so egregious that I am confounded at the universality with which it has been received. Mathematical axioms are *not* axioms of general truth. What is true of *relation*—of form and quantity—is often grossly false in regard to morals, for example. In this latter science it is very usually *un*true that the aggregated parts are equal to the whole. In chemistry also the axiom fails. In the consideration of motive it fails; for two motives, each of a given value, have not, necessarily, a value when united, equal to the sum of their values apart. There are numerous other mathematical truths which are only truths within the limits of *relation*. But the mathematician argues, from his *finite truths,* through habit, as if they were of an absolutely general applicability—as the world indeed imagines them to be. Bryant,[14] in his very learned 'Mythology,' mentions an analogous source of error, when he says that 'although the Pagan fables are not believed, yet we forget ourselves continually, and make inferences from them as existing realities.' With the algebraists, however, who are Pagans themselves, the 'Pagan fables' *are* believed, and the inferences are made, not so much through lapse of memory, as through an unaccountable addling of the brains. In short, I never yet encountered the mere mathematician who could be trusted out of equal roots, or one who did not clandestinely hold it as a point of his faith that x^2+px was absolutely and unconditionally equal to q. Say to one of these gentlemen, by way of experiment, if you please, that you believe occasions may occur where x^2+px is *not* altogether equal to q, and, having made him understand what you mean, get out of his reach as speedily as convenient, for, beyond doubt, he will endeavor to knock you down.

"I mean to say," continued Dupin, while I merely laughed at his last observations, "that if the Minister had been no more than a mathematician, the Prefect would have been under no necessity of giving me this check. I knew him, however, as both mathematician and poet, and my measures were adapted to his capacity, with reference to the circumstances by which he was surrounded. I knew him as a courtier, too, and as a bold *intriguant.*[15] Such a man, I considered, could not fail to be aware of the ordinary policial modes of action. He could not have failed to anticipate—and events have proved that he did not fail to anticipate—the waylayings to which he was subjected. He must have foreseen, I reflected, the secret investigations of his premises. His frequent absences from home at night, which were hailed by the Prefect as certain aids to his success, I regarded only as *ruses,* to afford opportunity for thorough search to the police, and thus the sooner to impress them with the conviction to which G——, in fact, did finally arrive—the conviction that the letter was not upon the

[14] Jacob Bryant (1715–1804), whose *A New System, or an Analysis of Antient Mythology* was published between 1774 and 1776.

[15] French: "conniver."

premises. I felt, also, that the whole train of thought, which I was at some pains in detailing to you just now, concerning the invariable principle of policial action in searches for articles concealed—I felt that this whole train of thought would necessarily pass through the mind of the Minister. It would imperatively lead him to despise all the ordinary *nooks* of concealment. *He* could not, I reflected, be so weak as not to see that the most intricate and remote recess of his hotel would be as open as his commonest closets to the eyes, to the probes, to the gimlets, and to the microscopes of the Prefect. I saw, in fine, that he would be driven, as a matter of course, to *simplicity,* if not deliberately induced to it as a matter of choice. You will remember, perhaps, how desperately the Prefect laughed when I suggested, upon our first interview, that it was just possible this mystery troubled him so much on account of its being so *very* self-evident."

"Yes," said I, "I remember his merriment well. I really thought he would have fallen into convulsions."

"The material world," continued Dupin, "abounds with very strict analogies to the immaterial; and thus some color of truth has been given to the rhetorical dogma, that metaphor, or simile, may be made to strengthen an argument, as well as to embellish a description. The principle of the *vis inertiæ,* [16] for example, seems to be identical in physics and metaphysics. It is not more true in the former, that a large body is with more difficulty set in motion than a smaller one, and that its subsequent *momentum* is commensurate with this difficulty, than it is, in the latter, that intellects of the vaster capacity, while more forcible, more constant, and more eventful in their movements than those of inferior grade, are yet the less readily moved, and more embarrassed and full of hesitation in the first few steps of their progress. Again: have you ever noticed which of the street signs, over the shop-doors, are the most attractive of attention?"

"I have never given the matter a thought," I said.

"There is a game of puzzles," he resumed, "which is played upon a map. One party playing requires another to find a given word—the name of town, river, state or empire—any word, in short, upon the motley and perplexed surface of the chart. A novice in the game generally seeks to embarrass his opponents by giving them the most minutely lettered names; but the adept selects such words as stretch, in large characters, from one end of the chart to the other. These, like the over-largely lettered signs and placards of the street, escape observation by dint of being excessively obvious; and here the physical oversight is precisely analogous with the moral inapprehension by which the intellect suffers to pass unnoticed those considerations which are too obtrusively and too palpably self-evident. But this is a point, it appears, somewhat above or beneath the understanding of the Prefect. He never once thought it probable, or possible, that the Minister had deposited the letter immediately beneath the nose of the whole world, by way of best preventing any portion of that world from perceiving it.

"But the more I reflected upon the daring, dashing, and discriminating ingenuity of D——; upon the fact that the document must always have been *at hand,* if he intended to use it to good purpose; and upon the decisive evidence, obtained by the Prefect, that it was not hidden within the limits of that dignitary's ordinary search —the more satisfied I became that, to conceal this letter, the Minister had resorted

---

[16] Latin: "power of inertia."

to the comprehensive and sagacious expedient of not attempting to conceal it at all.

"Full of these ideas, I prepared myself with a pair of green spectacles, and called one fine morning, quite by accident at the Ministerial hotel. I found D—— at home, yawning, lounging, and dawdling, as usual, and pretending to be in the last extremity of *ennui*. He is, perhaps, the most really energetic human being now alive—but that is only when nobody sees him.

"To be even with him, I complained of my weak eyes, and lamented the necessity of the spectacles, under cover of which I cautiously and thoroughly surveyed the apartment, while seemingly intent only upon the conversation of my host.

"I paid especial attention to a large writing-table near which he sat, and upon which lay confusedly, some miscellaneous letters and other papers, with one or two musical instruments and a few books. Here, however, after a long and very deliberate scrutiny, I saw nothing to excite particular suspicion.

"At length my eyes, in going the circuit of the room, fell upon a trumpery fillagree card-rack of pasteboard, that hung dangling by a dirty blue ribbon from a little brass knob just beneath the middle of the mantel-piece. In this rack, which had three or four compartments, were five or six visiting cards and a solitary letter. This last was much soiled and crumpled. It was torn nearly in two, across the middle—as if a design, in the first instance, to tear it entirely up as worthless, had been altered, or stayed, in the second. It had a large black seal, bearing the D—— cipher *very* conspicuously, and was addressed, in a diminutive female hand, to D——, the minister, himself. It was thrust carelessly, and even, as it seemed, contemptuously, into one of the upper divisions of the rack.

"No sooner had I glanced at this letter, than I concluded it to be that of which I was in search. To be sure, it was, to all appearance, radically different from the one of which the Prefect had read us so minute a description Here the seal was large and black, with the D—— cipher; there it was small and red, with the ducal arms of the S—— family. Here, the address, to the Minister, was diminutive and feminine; there the superscription, to a certain royal personage, was markedly bold and decided; the size alone formed a point of correspondence. But, then, the *radicalness* of these differences, which was excessive; the dirt; the soiled and torn condition of the paper, so inconsistent with the *true* methodical habits of D——, and so suggestive of a design to delude the beholder into an idea of the worthlessness of the document; these things, together with the hyperobtrusive situation of this document, full in the view of every visiter, and thus exactly in accordance with the conclusions to which I had previously arrived; these things, I say, were strongly corroborative of suspicion, in one who came with the intention to suspect.

"I protracted my visit as long as possible, and, while I maintained a most animated discussion with the Minister, on a topic which I knew well had never failed to interest and excite him, I kept my attention really riveted upon the letter. In this examination, I committed to memory its external appearance and arrangement in the rack; and also fell, at length, upon a discovery which set at rest whatever trivial doubt I might have entertained. In scrutinizing the edges of the paper, I observed them to be more *chafed* than seemed necessary. They presented the *broken* appearance which is manifested when a stiff paper, having been once folded and pressed with a folder, is refolded in a reversed direction, in the same creases or edges which had formed the original fold.

This discovery was sufficient. It was clear to me that the letter had been turned, as a glove, inside out, re-directed, and re-sealed. I bade the Minister good morning, and took my departure at once, leaving a gold snuff-box upon the table.

"The next morning I called for the snuff-box, when we resumed, quite eagerly, the conversation of the preceding day. While thus engaged, however, a loud report, as if of a pistol, was heard immediately beneath the windows of the hotel, and was succeeded by a series of fearful screams, and the shoutings of a mob. D—— rushed to a casement, threw it open, and looked out. In the meantime, I stepped to the card-rack, took the letter, put it in my pocket, and replaced it by a *fac-simile,* (so far as regards externals,) which I had carefully prepared at my lodgings; imitating the D—— cipher, very readily, by means of a seal formed of bread.

"The disturbance in the street had been occasioned by the frantic behavior of a man with a musket. He had fired it among a crowd of women and children. It proved, however, to have been without ball, and the fellow was suffered to go his way as a lunatic or a drunkard. When he had gone, D—— came from the window, whither I had followed him immediately upon securing the object in view. Soon afterwards I bade him farewell. The pretended lunatic was a man in my own pay."

"But what purpose had you," I asked, "in replacing the letter by a *fac-simile?* Would it not have been better, at the first visit, to have seized it openly, and departed?"

"D——," replied Dupin, "is a desperate man, and a man of nerve. His hotel, too, is not without attendants devoted to his interests. Had I made the wild attempt you suggest, I might never have left the Ministerial presence alive. The good people of Paris might have heard of me no more. But I had an object apart from these considerations. You know my political prepossessions. In this matter, I act as a partisan of the lady concerned. For eighteen months the Minister has had her in his power. She has now him in hers; since, being unaware that the letter is not in his possession, he will proceed with his exactions as if it was. Thus will he inevitably commit himself, at once, to his political destruction. His downfall, too, will not be more precipitate than awkward. It is all very well to talk about the *facilis descensus Averni;*[17] but in all kinds of climbing, as Catalani[18] said of singing, it is far more easy to get up than to come down. In the present instance I have no sympathy—at least no pity—for him who descends. He is that *monstrum horrendum,*[19] an unprincipled man of genius. I confess, however, that I should like very well to know the precise character of his thoughts, when, being defied by her whom the Prefect terms 'a certain personage,' he is reduced to opening the letter which I left for him in the card-rack."

"How? did you put any thing particular in it?"

"Why—it did not seem altogether right to leave the interior blank—that would have been insulting. D——, at Vienna once, did me an evil turn, which I told him, quite good-humoredly, that I should remember. So, as I knew he would feel some curiosity in regard to the identity of the person who had outwitted him, I thought it a pity not to give him a clue. He is well acquainted with my MS., and I just copied into the middle of the blank sheet the words—

---

[17] Paraphrase from Virgil's *Aeneid:* "The way down to Hell is easy."

[18] Angelica Catalani (1780–1849), Italian soprano.
[19] "Latin: "hideous monstrosity."

—Un dessein si funeste,
S'il n'est digne d'Atrée, est digne de Thyeste.

They are to be found in Crébillon's 'Atrée.' "[20]
1844

The Imp of the Perverse

In the consideration of the faculties and impulses—of the *prima mobilia*[1] of the human soul, the phrenologists[2] have failed to make room for a propensity which, although obviously existing as a radical, primitive, irreducible sentiment, has been equally over-looked by all the moralists who have preceded them. In the pure arrogance of the reason, we have all overlooked it. We have suffered its existence to escape our senses, solely through want of belief—of faith;—whether it be faith in Revelation, or faith in the Kabbala.[3] The idea of it has never occurred to us, simply because of its supererogation.[4] We saw no *need* of the impulse—for the propensity. We could not perceive its necessity. We could not understand, that is to say, we could not have understood, had the notion of this *primum mobile* ever obtruded itself;—we could not have understood in what manner it might be made to further the objects of humanity, either temporal or eternal. It cannot be denied that phrenology and, in great measure, all metaphysicianism have been concocted *à priori*.[5] The intellectual or logical man, rather than the understanding or observant man, set himself to imagine designs—to dictate purposes to God. Having thus fathomed, to his satisfaction, the intentions of Jehovah, out of these intentions he built his innumerable systems of mind. In the matter of phrenology, for example, we first determined, naturally enough, that it was the design of the Deity that man should eat. We then assigned to man an organ[6] of alimentiveness, and this organ is the scourge with which the Deity compels man, will-I nill-I, into eating. Secondly, having settled it to be God's will that man should continue his species, we discovered an organ of amativeness, forthwith. And so with combativeness, with ideality, with causality, with constructiveness,—so, in short, with every organ, whether representing a propensity, a moral sentiment, or a faculty of

---

[20] The drama *Atrée et Thyeste* (1770) by Prosper de Crébillon (1674–1762), based on the classic myth of the revenge of Atreus. Having seduced Atreus' wife, Thyestes is served a feast prepared from the bodies of his sons, whom Atreus has murdered. The quotation states: "So dire a scheme, / Though unworthy of Atreus, is worthy of Thyestes."

[1] Latin: "prime mover."

[2] Advocates of phrenology, the system popular during the mid-nineteenth century by which character is analyzed by the study of the shape of the skull.

[3] Revelation and Kabbala (or Cabala): Christian and Jewish writings given mystical, occult interpretation.

[4] Superfluousness.

[5] Derived by means of theory, not experience.

[6] According to phrenology, the human mind is divided into various faculties, each located in different parts of the brain and detectable by the skilled observer through the protuberances of the skull. Among them were the six "organs" Poe itemizes here which "determine" individuals to pursue certain kinds of behavior.

the pure intellect. And in these arrangements of the *principia* of human action, the Spurzheimites,[7] whether right or wrong, in part, or upon the whole, have but followed, in principle, the footsteps of their predecessors; deducing and establishing every thing from the preconceived destiny of man, and upon the ground of the objects of his Creator.

It would have been wiser, it would have been safer to classify, (if classify we must,) upon the basis of what man usually or occasionally did, and was always occasionally doing, rather than upon the basis of what we took it for granted the Deity intended him to do. If we cannot comprehend God in his visible works, how then in his inconceivable thoughts, that call the works into being? If we cannot understand him in his objective creatures, how then in his substantive moods and phases of creation?

Induction, *à posteriori*,[8] would have brought phrenology to admit, as an innate and primitive principle of human action, a paradoxical something, which we may call *perverseness*, for want of a more characteristic term. In the sense I intend, it is, in fact, a *mobile*[9] without motive, a motive not *motivirt*.[10] Through its promptings we act without comprehensible object; or, if this shall be understood as a contradiction in terms, we may so far modify the proposition as to say, that through its promptings we act, for the reason that we should *not*. In theory, no reason can be more unreasonable; but, in fact, there is none more strong. With certain minds, under certain conditions, it becomes absolutely irresistible. I am not more certain that I breathe, than that the assurance of the wrong or error of any action is often the one unconquerable *force* which impels us, and alone impels us to its prosecution. Nor will this overwhelming tendency to do wrong for the wrong's sake, admit of analysis, or resolution into ulterior elements. It is a radical, a primitive impulse—elementary. It will be said, I am aware, that when we persist in acts because we feel we should *not* persist in them, our conduct is but a modification of that which ordinarily springs from the *combativeness* of phrenology. But a glance will show the fallacy of this idea. The phrenological combativeness has for its essence, the necessity of self-defence. It is our safeguard against injury. Its principle regards our well-being; and thus the desire to be well is excited simultaneously with its development. It follows, that the desire to be well must be excited simultaneously with any principle which shall be merely a modification of combativeness, but in the case of that something which I term *perverseness*, the desire to be well is not only not aroused, but a strongly antagonistical sentiment exists.

An appeal to one's own heart is, after all, the best reply to the sophistry just noticed. No one who trustingly consults and thoroughly questions his own soul, will be disposed to deny the entire radicalness of the propensity in question. It is not more incomprehensible than distinctive. There lives no man who at some period has not been tormented, for example, by an earnest desire to tantalize a listener by circumlocution. The speaker is aware that he displeases; he has every intention to please; he is usually curt, precise, and clear; the most laconic and luminous language is struggling for utterance upon his tongue; it is only with difficulty that he restrains himself from giving it flow; he dreads and deprecates the anger of him whom he addresses; yet, the thought strikes him, that by certain involutions and parentheses, this anger may be

---

[7] Followers of the German phrenologist Johann Spurzheim (1776–1832).
[8] The opposite of deductive or a priori reasoning.

[9] Something movable.
[10] Without motivation.

engendered. That single thought is enough. The impulse increases to a wish, the wish to a desire, the desire to an uncontrollable longing, and the longing, (to the deep regret and mortification of the speaker, and in defiance of all consequences,) is indulged.

We have a task before us which must be speedily performed. We know that it will be ruinous to make delay. The most important crisis of our life calls, trumpet-tongued, for immediate energy and action. We glow, we are consumed with eagerness to commence the work, with the anticipation of whose glorious results our whole souls are on fire. It must, it shall be undertaken to-day, and yet we put it off until to-morrow; and why? There is no answer, except that we feel *perverse,* using the word with no comprehension of the principle. To-morrow arrives, and with it a more impatient anxiety to do our duty, but with this very increase of anxiety arrives, also, a nameless, a positively fearful because unfathomable, craving for delay. This craving gathers strength as the moments fly. The last hour for action is at hand. We tremble with the violence of the conflict within us,—of the definite with the indefinite—of the substance with the shadow. But, if the contest have proceeded thus far, it is the shadow which prevails,—we struggle in vain. The clock strikes, and is the knell of our welfare. At the same time, it is the chanticleer-note to the ghost[11] that has so long overawed us. It flies—it disappears—we are free. The old energy returns. We will labor *now.* Alas, it is *too late!*

We stand upon the brink of a precipice. We peer into the abyss—we grow sick and dizzy. Our first impulse is to shrink from the danger. Unaccountably we remain. By slow degrees our sickness, and dizziness, and horror, become merged in a cloud of unnameable feeling. By gradations, still more imperceptible, this cloud assumes shape, as did the vapor from the bottle out of which arose the genius[12] in the Arabian Nights. But out of this *our* cloud upon the precipice's edge, there grows into palpability, a shape, far more terrible than any genius, or any demon of a tale, and yet it is but a thought, although a fearful one, and one which chills the very marrow of our bones with the fierceness of the delight of its horror. It is merely the idea of what would be our sensations during the sweeping precipitancy of a fall from such a height. And this fall—this rushing annihilation—for the very reason that it involves that one most ghastly and loathsome of all the most ghastly and loathsome images of death and suffering which have ever presented themselves to our imagination— for this very cause do we now the most vividly desire it. And because our reason violently deters us from the brink, *therefore,* do we the more impetuously approach it. There is no passion in nature so demoniacally impatient, as that of him, who shuddering upon the edge of a precipice, thus meditates a plunge. To indulge for a moment, in any attempt at *thought,* is to be inevitably lost; for reflection but urges us to forbear, and *therefore* it is, I say, that we *cannot.* If there be no friendly arm to check us, or if we fail in a sudden effort to prostrate ourselves backward from the abyss, we plunge, and are destroyed.

Examine these and similar actions as we will, we shall find them resulting solely from the spirit of the *Perverse.* We perpetrate them merely because we feel that we

---

[11] Perhaps a reference to the ghost of Hamlet's father, which disappears, as in folklore, at the coming of dawn, announced by the cock's crow.

[12] The supernatural spirit, or genie, that escaped from the bottle in which it had been held captive.

should *not.* Beyond or behind this, there is no intelligible principle: and we might, indeed, deem this perverseness a direct instigation of the arch-fiend,[13] were it not occasionally known to operate in furtherance of good.

I have said thus much, that in some measure I may answer your question—that I may explain to you why I am here—that I may assign to you something that shall have at least the faint aspect of a cause for my wearing these fetters, and for my tenanting this cell of the condemned. Had I not been thus prolix, you might either have misunderstood me altogether, or, with the rabble, have fancied me mad. As it is, you will easily perceive that I am one of the many uncounted victims of the Imp of the Perverse.

It is impossible that any deed could have been wrought with a more thorough deliberation. For weeks, for months, I pondered upon the means of the murder. I rejected a thousand schemes, because their accomplishment involved a *chance* of detection. At length, in reading some French memoirs, I found an account of a nearly fatal illness that occurred to Madame Pilau, through the agency of a candle accidentally poisoned. The idea struck my fancy at once. I knew my victim's habit of reading in bed. I knew, too, that his apartment was narrow and ill-ventilated. But I need not vex you with impertinent details. I need not describe the easy artifices by which I substituted, in his bed-room candlestand, a wax-light of my own making, for the one which I there found. The next morning he was discovered dead in his bed, and the coroner's verdict was,—"Death by the visitation of God."

Having inherited his estate, all went well with me for years. The idea of detection never once entered my brain. Of the remains of the fatal taper, I had myself carefully disposed. I had left no shadow of a clue by which it would be possible to convict, or even to suspect me of the crime. It is inconceivable how rich a sentiment of satisfaction arose in my bosom as I reflected upon my absolute security. For a very long period of time, I was accustomed to revel in this sentiment. It afforded me more real delight than all the mere worldly advantages accruing from my sin. But there arrived at length an epoch, from which the pleasurable feeling grew, by scarcely perceptible gradations, into a haunting and harassing thought. It harassed because it haunted. I could scarcely get rid of it for an instant. It is quite a common thing to be thus annoyed with the ringing in our ears, or rather in our memories, of the burthen of some ordinary song, or some unimpressive snatches from an opera. Nor will we be less tormented if the song in itself be good, or the opera air meritorious. In this manner, at last, I would perpetually catch myself pondering upon my security, and repeating, in a low, under-tone, the phrase, "I am safe."

One day, whilst sauntering along the streets, I arrested myself in the act of murmuring, half aloud, these customary syllables. In a fit of petulance, I re-modelled them thus:—"I am safe—I am safe—yes—if I be not fool enough to make open confession!"

No sooner had I spoken these words, than I felt an icy chill creep to my heart. I had had some experience in these fits of perversity, (whose nature I have been at some trouble to explain,) and I remembered well, that in no instance, I had successfully resisted their attacks. And now my own casual self-suggestion, that I might possibly be fool enough to confess the murder of which I had been guilty, confronted

[13] Satan.

me, as if the very ghost of him whom I had murdered—and beckoned me on to death.

At first, I made an effort to shake off this nightmare of the soul. I walked vigorously —faster—still faster—at length I ran. I felt a maddening desire to shriek aloud. Every succeeding wave of thought overwhelmed me with new terror, for, alas! I well, too well understood that, to *think* in my situation, was to be lost. I still quickened my pace. I bounded like a madman through the crowded thoroughfares. At length, the populace took the alarm, and pursued me. I felt *then* the consummation of my fate. Could I have torn out my tongue, I would have done it—but a rough voice resounded in my ears—a rougher grasp seized me by the shoulder. I turned—I gasped for breath. For a moment, I experienced all the pangs of suffocation; I became blind, and deaf, and giddy; and then, some invisible fiend, I thought, struck me with his broad palm upon the back. The long-imprisoned secret burst forth from my soul.

They say that I spoke with a distinct enunciation, but with marked emphasis and passionate hurry, as if in dread of interruption before concluding the brief but pregnant sentences that consigned me to the hangman and to hell.

Having related all that was necessary for the fullest judicial conviction, I fell prostrate in a swoon.

But why shall I say more? To-day I wear these chains, and am *here*. To-morrow I shall be fetterless!—*but where?*

1845

The Cask of Amontillado

The thousand injuries of Fortunato I had borne as I best could; but when he ventured upon insult, I vowed revenge. You, who so well know the nature of my soul, will not suppose, however, that I gave utterance to a threat. *At length* I would be avenged; this was a point definitively settled—but the very definitiveness with which it was resolved precluded the idea of risk. I must not only punish, but punish with impunity. A wrong is unredressed when retribution overtakes its redresser. It is equally unredressed when the avenger fails to make himself felt as such to him who has done the wrong.

It must be understood that neither by word nor deed had I given Fortunato cause to doubt my good will. I continued, as was my wont, to smile in his face, and he did not perceive that my smile *now* was at the thought of his immolation.

He had a weak point—this Fortunato—although in other regards he was a man to be respected and even feared. He prided himself on his connoisseurship in wine. Few Italians have the true virtuoso spirit. For the most part their enthusiasm is adopted to suit the time and opportunity—to practice imposture upon the British and Austrian *millionaires*. In painting and gemmary[1] Fortunato, like his countrymen, was a quack

---

[1] Knowledge of precious gems.

—but in the matter of old wines he was sincere. In this respect I did not differ from him materially; I was skilful in the Italian vintages myself, and bought largely whenever I could.

It was about dusk, one evening during the supreme madness of the carnival season, that I encountered my friend. He accosted me with excessive warmth, for he had been drinking much. The man wore motley. He had on a tight-fitting parti-striped dress, and his head was surmounted by the conical cap and bells. I was so pleased to see him that I thought I should never have done wringing his hand.

I said to him—"My dear Fortunato, you are luckily met. How remarkably well you are looking to-day! But I have received a pipe of what passes for Amontillado, and I have my doubts."

"How?" said he. "Amontillado? A pipe? Impossible! And in the middle of the carnival!"

"I have my doubts," I replied; "and I was silly enough to pay the full Amontillado price without consulting you in the matter. You were not to be found, and I was fearful of losing a bargain."

"Amontillado!"

"I have my doubts."

"Amontillado!"

"And I must satisfy them."

"Amontillado!"

"As you are engaged, I am on my way to Luchesi. If any one has a critical turn, it is he. He will tell me—"

"Luchesi cannot tell Amontillado from Sherry."

"And yet some fools will have it that his taste is a match for your own."

"Come, let us go."

"Whither?"

"To your vaults."

"My friend, no; I will not impose upon your good nature. I perceive you have an engagement. Luchesi—"

"I have no engagement;—come."

"My friend, no. It is not the engagement, but the severe cold with which I perceive you are afflicted. The vaults are insufferably damp. They are encrusted with nitre."

"Let us go, nevertheless. The cold is merely nothing. Amontillado! You have been imposed upon. And as for Luchesi, he cannot distinguish Sherry from Amontillado."

Thus speaking, Fortunato possessed himself of my arm. Putting on a mask of black silk, and drawing a *roquelaire* closely about my person, I suffered him to hurry me to my palazzo.[2]

There were no attendants at home; they had absconded to make merry in honor of the time. I had told them that I should not return until the morning, and had given them explicit orders not to stir from the house. These orders were sufficient, I well knew, to insure their immediate disappearance, one and all, as soon as my back was turned.

I took from their sconces two flambeaux, and giving one to Fortunato, bowed him through several suites of rooms to the archway that led into the vaults. I passed down

[2] Large residence.

a long and winding staircase, requesting him to be cautious as he followed. We came at length to the foot of the descent, and stood together on the damp ground of the catacombs of the Montresors.

The gait of my friend was unsteady, and the bells upon his cap jingled as he strode.

"The pipe," said he.

"It is farther on," said I; "but observe the white web-work which gleams from these cavern walls."

He turned towards me, and looked into my eyes with two filmy orbs that distilled the rheum of intoxication.

"Nitre?" he asked, at length.

"Nitre," I replied. "How long have you had that cough?"

"Ugh! ugh! ugh!—ugh! ugh! ugh!—ugh! ugh! ugh!—ugh! ugh! ugh!—ugh! ugh! ugh!"

My poor friend found it impossible to reply for many minutes.

"It is nothing," he said, at last.

"Come," I said, with decision, "we will go back; your health is precious. You are rich, respected, admired, beloved; you are happy, as once I was. You are a man to be missed. For me it is no matter. We will go back; you will be ill, and I cannot be responsible. Besides, there is Luchesi—"

"Enough," he said; "the cough is a mere nothing; it will not kill me. I shall not die of a cough."

"True—true," I replied; "and, indeed, I had no intention of alarming you unnecessarily—but you should use all proper caution. A draught of this Medoc will defend us from the damps."

Here I knocked off the neck of a bottle which I drew from a long row of its fellows that lay upon the mould.

"Drink" I said, presenting him the wine.

He raised it to his lips with a leer. He paused and nodded to me familiarly, while his bells jingled.

"I drink," he said, "to the buried that repose around us."

"And I to your long life."

He again took my arm, and we proceeded.

"These vaults," he said, "are extensive."

"The Montresors," I replied, "were a great and numerous family."

"I forget your arms."

"A huge human foot d'or, in a field azure;[3] the foot crushes a serpent rampant whose fangs are imbedded in the heel."

"And the motto?"

"*Nemo me impune lacessit.*"[4]

"Good!" he said.

The wine sparkled in his eyes and the bells jingled. My own fancy grew warm with the Medoc. We had passed through walls of piled bones, with casks and

---

[3] Heraldic terms describing a golden foot laid upon a blue background.

[4] "No one may insult me without fearing punishment."

puncheons intermingling, into the inmost recesses of the catacombs. I paused again, and this time I made bold to seize Fortunato by an arm above the elbow.

"The nitre!" I said; "see, it increases. It hangs like moss upon the vaults. We are below the river's bed. The drops of moisture trickle among the bones. Come, we will go back ere it is too late. Your cough—"

"It is nothing," he said; "let us go on. But first, another draught of the Medoc."

I broke and reached him a flaçon of De Grâve.[5] He emptied it at a breath. His eyes flashed with a fierce light. He laughed and threw the bottle upwards with a gesticulation I did not understand.

I looked at him in surprise. He repeated the movement—a grotesque one.

"You do not comprehend?" he said.

"Not I," I replied.

"Then you are not of the brotherhood."

"How?"

"You are not of the masons."

"Yes, yes," I said, "yes, yes."

"You? Impossible! A mason?"

"A mason," I replied.

"A sign," he said.

"It is this," I answered, producing a trowel from beneath the folds of my *roquelaire*.

"You jest," he exclaimed, recoiling a few paces. "But let us proceed to the Amontillado."

"Be it so," I said, replacing the tool beneath the cloak, and again offering him my arm. He leaned upon it heavily. We continued our route in search of the Amontillado. We passed through a range of low arches, descended, passed on, and descending again, arrived at a deep crypt, in which the foulness of the air caused our flambeaux rather to glow than flame.

At the most remote end of the crypt there appeared another less spacious. Its walls had been lined with human remains, piled to the vault overhead, in the fashion of the great catacombs of Paris. Three sides of this interior crypt were still ornamented in this manner. From the fourth the bones had been thrown down, and lay promiscuously upon the earth, forming at one point a mound of some size. Within the wall thus exposed by the displacing of the bones, we perceived a still interior recess, in depth about four feet, in width three, in height six or seven. It seemed to have been constructed for no especial use within itself, but formed merely the interval between two of the colossal supports of the roof of the catacombs, and was backed by one of their circumscribing walls of solid granite.

It was in vain that Fortunato, uplifting his dull torch, endeavored to pry into the depth of the recess. Its termination the feeble light did not enable us to see.

"Proceed," I said; "herein is the Amontillado. As for Luchesi—"

"He is an ignoramus," interrupted my friend, as he stepped unsteadily forward, while I followed immediately at his heels. In an instant he had reached the extremity of the niche, and finding his progress arrested by the rock, stood stupidly bewildered.

---

[5] White wine from Bordeaux.

A moment more and I had fettered him to the granite. In its surface were two iron staples, distant from each other about two feet, horizontally. From one of these depended a short chain, from the other a padlock. Throwing the links about his waist, it was but the work of a few seconds to secure it. He was too much astounded to resist. Withdrawing the key I stepped back from the recess.

"Pass your hand," I said, "over the wall; you cannot help feeling the nitre. Indeed it is *very* damp. Once more let me *implore* you to return. No? Then I must positively leave you. But I must first render you all the little attentions in my power."

"The Amontillado!" ejaculated my friend, not yet recovered from his astonishment.

"True," I replied; "the Amontillado."

As I said these words I busied myself among the pile of bones of which I have before spoken. Throwing them aside, I soon uncovered a quantity of building stone and mortar With these materials and with the aid of my trowel, I began vigorously to wall up the entrance of the niche.

I had scarcely laid the first tier of the masonry when I discovered that the intoxication of Fortunato had in a great measure worn off. The earliest indication I had of this was a low moaning cry from the depth of the recess. It was *not* the cry of a drunken man. There was then a long and obstinate silence. I laid the second tier, and the third, and the fourth; and then I heard the furious vibrations of the chain. The noise lasted for several minutes, during which, that I might hearken to it with the more satisfaction, I ceased my labors and sat down upon the bones. When at last the clanking subsided, I resumed the trowel, and finished without interruption the fifth, the sixth, and the seventh tier. The wall was now nearly upon a level with my breast. I again paused, and holding the flambeaux over the mason-work, threw a few feeble rays upon the figure within.

A succession of loud and shrill screams, bursting suddenly from the throat of the chained form, seemed to thrust me violently back. For a brief moment I hesitated— I trembled. Unsheathing my rapier, I began to grope with it about the recess: but the thought of an instant reassured me. I placed my hand upon the solid fabric of the catacombs, and felt satisfied. I reapproached the wall. I replied to the yells of him who clamored. I re-echoed—I aided—I surpassed them in volume and in strength. I did this, and the clamorer grew still.

It was now midnight, and my task was drawing to a close. I had completed the eighth, the ninth, and the tenth tier. I had finished a portion of the last and the eleventh; there remained but a single stone to be fitted and plastered in. I struggled with its weight; I placed it partially in its destined position. But now there came from out the niche a low laugh that erected the hairs upon my head. It was succeeded by a sad voice, which I had difficulty in recognising as that of the noble Fortunato. The voice said—

"Ha! ha? ha?—he! he!—a very good joke indeed—an excellent jest. We will have many a rich laugh about it at the palazzo—he! he! he!—over our wine—he! he! he!"

"The Amontillado!" I said.

"He! he! he!—he! he! he!—yes, the Amontillado. But is it not getting late? Will not they be awaiting us at the palazzo, the Lady Fortunato and the rest? Let us be gone."

"Yes," I said, "let us be gone."

"For the love of God, Montresor!"

"Yes," I said, "for the love of God!"

But to these words I hearkened in vain for a reply. I grew impatient. I called aloud—

"Fortunato!"

No answer. I called again—

"Fortunato!"

No answer still. I thrust a torch through the remaining aperture and let it fall within. There came forth in return only a jingling of the bells. My heart grew sick —on account of the dampness of the catacombs. I hastened to make an end of my labor. I forced the last stone into its position; I plastered it up. Against the new masonry I re-erected the old rampart of bones. For the half of a century no mortal has disturbed them. *In pace requiescat!*[6]

1846

The Philosophy of Composition

Charles Dickens, in a note now lying before me, alluding to an examination I once made of the mechanism of "Barnaby Rudge,"[1] says—"By the way, are you aware that Godwin wrote his 'Caleb Williams' backwards?[2] He first involved his hero in a web of difficulties, forming the second volume and then, for the first, cast about him for some mode of accounting for what had been done."

I cannot think this the *precise* mode of procedure on the part of Godwin—and indeed what he himself acknowledges, is not altogether in accordance with Mr. Dickens' idea—but the author of "Caleb Williams" was too good an artist not to perceive the advantage derivable from at least a somewhat similar process. Nothing is more clear than that every plot, worth the name, must be elaborated to its *dénouement* before anything be attempted with the pen. It is only with the *dénouement* constantly in view that we can give a plot its indispensable air of consequence, or causation, by making the incidents, and especially the tone at all points, tend to the development of the intention.

There is a radical error, I think, in the usual mode of constructing a story. Either history affords a thesis—or one is suggested by an incident of the day—or, at best, the author sets himself to work in the combination of striking events to form merely the basis of his narrative—designing, generally, to fill in with description, dialogue, or autorial comment, whatever crevices of fact, or action, may, from page to page, render themselves apparent.

---

[6] "Rest in peace!"

[1] While the opening chapters of Dickens's novel were appearing in serialized form during 1841, Poe wrote an essay in which he conjectured about the conclusion to the extent of correctly naming the murderer.

[2] The 1832 preface which William Godwin wrote for his novel, first published in 1794, makes the assertion that he wrote it from end to beginning.

I prefer commencing with the consideration of an *effect*. Keeping originality *always* in view—for he is false to himself who ventures to dispense with so obvious and so easily attainable a source of interest—I say to myself, in the first place, "Of the innumerable effects, or impressions, of which the heart, the intellect, or (more generally) the soul is susceptible, what one shall I, on the present occasion, select?" Having chosen a novel, first, and secondly a vivid effect, I consider whether it can be best wrought by incident or tone—whether by ordinary incidents and peculiar tone, or the converse, or by peculiarity both of incident and tone—afterward looking about me (or rather within) for such combinations of event, or tone, as shall best aid me in the construction of the effect.

I have often thought how interesting a magazine paper might be written by any author who would—that is to say who could—detail, step by step, the processes by which any one of his compositions attained its ultimate point of completion. Why such a paper has never been given to the world, I am much at a loss to say—but, perhaps, the autorial vanity has had more to do with the omission that any one other cause. Most writers—poets in especial—prefer having it understood that they compose by a species of fine frenzy—an ecstatic intuition—and would positively shudder at letting the public take a peep behind the scenes, at the elaborate and vacillating crudities of thought—at the true purposes seized only at the last moment—at the innumerable glimpses of idea that arrived not at the maturity of full view—at the fully matured fancies discarded in despair as unmanageable—at the cautious selections and rejections—at the painful erasures and interpolations—in a word, at the wheels and pinions—the tackle for scene-shifting—the step-ladders and demon-traps—the cock's feathers, the red paint and the black patches, which, in ninety-nine cases out of the hundred, constitute the properties of the literary *histrio*.[3]

I am aware, on the other hand, that the case is by no means common, in which an author is at all in condition to retrace the steps by which his conclusions have been attained. In general, suggestions, having arisen pell-mell, are pursued and forgotten in a similar manner.

For my own part, I have neither sympathy with the repugnance alluded to, nor, at any time the least difficulty in recalling to mind the progressive steps of any of my compositions; and, since the interest of an analysis, or reconstruction, such as I have considered a *desideratum,* is quite independent of any real or fancied interest in the thing analyzed, it will not be regarded as a breach of decorum on my part to show the *modus operandi* by which some one of my own works was put together. I select "The Raven," as most generally known. It is my design to render it manifest that no one point in its composition is referrible either to accident or intuition—that the work proceeded, step by step, to its completion with the precision and rigid consequence of a mathematical problem.

Let us dismiss, as irrelevant to the poem, *per se,* the circumstance—or say the necessity—which, in the first place, gave rise to the intention of composing a poem that should suit at once the popular and the critical taste.

We commence, then, with this intention.

The initial consideration was that of extent. If any literary work is too long to be read at one sitting, we must be content to dispense with the immensely important

---

[3] Performer.

effect derivable from unity of impression—for, if two sittings be required, the affairs of the world interfere, and every thing like totality is at once destroyed. But since, *ceteris paribus,*[4] no poet can afford to dispense with *any thing* that may advance his design, it but remains to be seen whether there is, in extent, any advantage to counterbalance the loss of unity which attends it. Here I say no, at once. What we term a long poem is, in fact, merely a succession of brief ones—that is to say, of brief poetical effects. It is needless to demonstrate that a poem is such, only inasmuch as it intensely excites, by elevating, the soul; and all intense excitements are, through a psychal[5] necessity, brief. For this reason, at least one half of the "Paradise Lost"[6] is essentially prose—a succession of poetical excitements interspersed, *inevitably,* with corresponding depressions—the whole being deprived, through the extremeness of its length, of the vastly important artistic element, totality, or unity, of effect.

It appears evident, then, that there is a distinct limit, as regards length, to all works of literary art—the limit of a single sitting—and that, although in certain classes of prose composition, such as "Robinson Crusoe,"[7] (demanding no unity,) this limit may be advantageously overpassed, it can never properly be overpassed in a poem. Within this limit, the extent of a poem may be made to bear mathematical relation to its merit—in other words, to the excitement or elevation—again in other words, to the degree of the true poetical effect which it is capable of inducing; for it is clear that the brevity must be in direct ratio of the intensity of the intended effect:—this, with one proviso—that a certain degree of duration is absolutely requisite for the production of any effect at all.

Holding in view these considerations, as well as that degree of excitement which I deemed not above the popular, while not below the critical, taste, I reached at once what I conceived the proper *length* for my intended poem—a length of about one hundred lines. It is, in fact, a hundred and eight.

My next thought concerned the choice of an impression, or effect, to be conveyed: and here I may as well observe that, throughout the construction, I kept steadily in view the design of rendering the work *universally* appreciable. I should be carried too far out of my immediate topic were I to demonstrate a point upon which I have repeatedly insisted, and which, with the poetical, stands not in the slightest need of demonstration—the point, I mean, that Beauty is the sole legitimate province of the poem. A few words, however, in elucidation of my real meaning, which some of my friends have evinced a disposition to misrepresent. That pleasure which is at once the most intense, the most elevating, and the most pure, is, I believe, found in the contemplation of the beautiful. When, indeed, men speak of Beauty, they mean, precisely, not a quality, as is supposed, but an effect—they refer, in short, just to that intense and pure elevation of *soul—not* of intellect, or of heart—upon which I have commented, and which is experienced in consequence of contemplating "the beautiful." Now I designate Beauty as the province of the poem, merely because it is an obvious rule of Art that effects should be made to spring from direct causes—that objects should be attained through means best adapted for their attainment—no one

[4] Latin: "other things being equal."
[5] Emotional or spiritual.
[6] This epic poem by John Milton is an example of the extreme length Poe sought to reject.

[7] Lengthy novel by Daniel Defoe, published in 1719.

as yet having been weak enough to deny that the peculiar elevation alluded to is *most readily* attained in the poem. Now the object, Truth, or the satisfaction of the intellect, and the object Passion, or the excitement of the heart, are, although attainable, to a certain extent, in poetry, far more readily attainable in prose. Truth, in fact, demands a precision, and Passion a *homeliness* (the truly passionate will comprehend me) which are absolutely antagonistic to that Beauty which, I maintain, is the excitement, or pleasurable elevation, of the soul. It by no means follows from any thing here said, that passion, or even truth, may not be introduced, and even profitably introduced, into a poem—for they may serve in elucidation, or aid the general effect, as do discords in music, by contrast—but the true artist will always contrive, first, to tone them into proper subservience to the predominant aim, and, secondly, to enveil them, as far as possible, in that Beauty which is the atmosphere and the essence of the poem.

Regarding, then, Beauty as my province, my next question referred to the *tone* of its highest manifestation—and all experience has shown that this tone is one of *sadness.* Beauty of whatever kind, in its supreme development, invariably excites the sensitive soul to tears. Melancholy is thus the most legitimate of all the poetical tones.

The length, the province, and the tone, being thus determined, I betook myself to ordinary induction, with the view of obtaining some artistic piquancy which might serve me as a key-note in the construction of the poem—some pivot upon which the whole structure might turn. In carefully thinking over all the usual artistic effects— or more properly *points,* in the theatrical sense—I did not fail to perceive immediately that no one had been so universally employed as that of the *refrain.* The universality of its employment sufficed to assure me of its intrinsic value, and spared me the necessity of submitting it to analysis. I considered it, however, with regard to its susceptibility of improvement, and soon saw it to be in a primitive condition. As commonly used, the *refrain,* or burden, not only is limited to lyric verse, but depends for its impression upon the force of monotone—both in sound and thought. The pleasure is deduced solely from the sense of identity—of repetition. I resolved to diversify, and so heighten, the effect, by adhering, in general, to the monotone of sound, while I continually varied that of thought: that is to say, I determined to produce continuously novel effects, by the variation *of the application* of the *refrain* —the *refrain* itself remaining, for the most part, unvaried.

These points being settled, I next bethought me of the *nature* of my *refrain.* Since its application was to be repeatedly varied, it was clear that the *refrain* itself must be brief, for there would have been an insurmountable difficulty in frequent variations of application in any sentence of length. In proportion to the brevity of the sentence, would, of course, be the facility of the variation. This led me at once to a single word as the best *refrain.*

The question now arose as to the *character* of the word. Having made up my mind to a *refrain,* the division of the poem into stanzas was, of course, a corollary: the *refrain* forming the close of each stanza. That such a close, to have force, must be sonorous and susceptible of protracted emphasis, admitted no doubt: and these considerations inevitably led me to the long *o* as the most sonorous vowel, in connection with *r* as the most producible consonant.

The sound of the *refrain* being thus determined, it became necessary to select a word embodying this sound, and at the same time in the fullest possible keeping with that melancholy which I had predetermined as the tone of the poem. In such a search it would have been absolutely impossible to overlook the word "Nevermore." In fact, it was the very first which presented itself.

The next *desideratum* was a pretext for the continuous use of the word "nevermore." In observing the difficulty which I at once found in inventing a sufficiently plausible reason for its continuous repetition, I did not fail to perceive that this difficulty arose solely from the pre-assumption that the word was to be so continuously or monotonously spoken by a *human* being—I did not fail to perceive, in short, that the difficulty lay in the reconciliation of this monotony with the exercise of reason on the part of the creature repeating the word. Here, then, immediately arose the idea of a *non-*reasoning creature capable of speech; and, very naturally, a parrot, in the first instance, suggested itself, but was superseded forthwith by a Raven, as equally capable of speech, and infinitely more in keeping with the intended *tone*.

I had now gone so far as the conception of a Raven—the bird of ill omen—monotonously repeating the one word, "Nevermore," at the conclusion of each stanza, in a poem of melancholy tone, and in length about one hundred lines. Now, never losing sight of the object *supremeness,* or perfection, at all points, I asked myself—"Of all melancholy topics, what, according to the *universal* understanding of mankind, is the *most* melancholy?" Death—was the obvious reply. "And when," I said, "is this most melancholy of topics most poetical?" From what I have already explained at some length, the answer, here also, is obvious—"When it most closely allies itself to *Beauty:* the death, then, of a beautiful woman is, unquestionably, the most poetical topic in the world—and equally is it beyond doubt that the lips best suited for such topic are those of a bereaved lover."

I had now to combine the two ideas, of a lover lamenting his deceased mistress and a Raven continuously repeating the word "Nevermore."—I had to combine these, bearing in mind my design of varying, at every turn, the *application* of the word repeated; but the only intelligible mode of such combination is that of imagining the Raven employing the word in answer to the queries of the lover. And here it was that I saw at once the opportunity afforded for the effect on which I had been depending—that is to say, the effect of the *variation of application.* I saw that I could make the first query propounded by the lover—the first query to which the Raven should reply "Nevermore"—that I could make this first query a commonplace one —the second less so—the third still less, and so on—until at length the lover, startled from his original *nonchalance* by the melancholy character of the word itself—by its frequent repetition—and by a consideration of the ominous reputation of the fowl that uttered it—is at length excited to superstition, and wildly propounds queries of a far different character—queries whose solution he has passionately at heart—propounds them half in superstition and half in that species of despair which delights in self-torture—propounds them not altogether because he believes in the prophetic or demoniac character of the bird (which, reason assures him, is merely repeating a lesson learned by rote) but because he experiences a phrenzied pleasure in so modeling his questions as to receive from the *expected* "Nevermore" the most delicious because the most intolerable of sorrow. Perceiving the opportunity thus afforded me—or, more strictly, thus forced upon me in the progress of the construction—I first established in mind the climax, or concluding query—that query to which "Nevermore" should be in the last place an answer—that in reply to which this word "Nevermore" should involve the utmost conceivable amount of sorrow and despair.

Here then the poem may be said to have its beginning—at the end, where all works of art should begin—for it was here, at this point of my preconsiderations, that I first put pen to paper in the composition of the stanza:

"Prophet," said I, "thing of evil! prophet still if bird or devil!
By that heaven that bends above us—by that God we both adore,
Tell this soul with sorrow laden, if within the distant Aidenn,
It shall clasp a sainted maiden whom the angels name Lenore—
Clasp a rare and radiant maiden whom the angels name Lenore."
    Quoth the raven "Nevermore."

I composed this stanza, at this point, first that, by establishing the climax, I might the better vary and graduate, as regards seriousness and importance, the preceding queries of the lover—and, secondly, that I might definitely settle the rhythm, the metre, and the length and general arrangement of the stanza—as well as graduate the stanzas which were to precede, so that none of them might surpass this in rhythmical effect. Had I been able, in the subsequent composition, to construct more vigorous stanzas, I should, without scruple, have purposely enfeebled them, so as not to interfere with the climacteric effect.

And here I may as well say a few words of the versification. My first object (as usual) was originality. The extent to which this has been neglected, in versification, is one of the most unaccountable things in the world. Admitting that there is little possibility of variety in mere *rhythm,* it is still clear that the possible varieties of metre and stanza are absolutely infinite—and yet, *for centuries, no man, in verse, has ever done, or ever seemed to think of doing, an original thing.* The fact is, that originality (unless in minds of very unusual force) is by no means a matter, as some suppose, of impulse or intuition. In general, to be found, it must be elaborately sought, and although a positive merit of the highest class, demands in its attainment less of invention than negation.

Of course, I pretend to no originality in either the rhythm or metre of the "Raven." The former is trochaic—the latter is octameter acatalectic, alternating with heptameter catalectic repeated in the *refrain* of the fifth verse, and terminating with tetrameter catalectic. Less pedantically—the feet employed throughout (trochees) consist of a long syllable followed by a short: the first line of the stanza consists of eight of these feet—the second of seven and a half (in effect two-thirds)—the third of eight—the fourth of seven and a half—the fifth the same—the sixth three and a half. Now, each of these lines, taken individually, has been employed before, and what originality the "Raven" has, is in their *combination into stanza;* nothing even remotely approaching this combination has ever been attempted. The effect of this originality of combination is aided by other unusual, and some altogether novel effects, arising from an extension of the application of the principles of rhyme and alliteration.

The next point to be considered was the mode of bringing together the lover and the Raven—and the first branch of this consideration was the *locale.* For this the most natural suggestion might seem to be a forest, or the fields—but it has always appeared to me that a close *circumscription of space* is absolutely necessary to the effect of insulated incident:—it has the force of a frame to a picture. It has an indisputable moral power in keeping concentrated the attention, and, of course, must not be confounded with mere unity of place.

I determined, then, to place the lover in his chamber—in a chamber rendered sacred to him by memories of her who had frequented it. The room is represented as richly furnished—this in mere pursuance of the ideas I have already explained on the subject of Beauty, as the sole true poetical thesis.

The *locale* being thus determined, I had now to introduce the bird—and the thought of introducing him through the window, was inevitable. The idea of making the lover suppose, in the first instance, that the flapping of the wings of the bird against the shutter, is a "tapping" at the door, originated in a wish to increase, by prolonging, the reader's curiosity, and in a desire to admit the incidental effect arising from the lover's throwing open the door, finding all dark, and thence adopting the half-fancy that it was the spirit of his mistress that knocked.

I made the night tempestuous, first, to account for the Raven's seeking admission, and secondly, for the effect of contrast with the (physical) serenity within the chamber.

I made the bird alight on the bust of Pallas,[8] also for the effect of contrast between the marble and the plumage—it being understood that the bust was absolutely *suggested* by the bird—the bust of *Pallas* being chosen, first, as most in keeping with the scholarship of the lover, and, secondly, for the sonorousness of the word, Pallas, itself.

About the middle of the poem, also, I have availed myself of the force of contrast, with a view of deepening the ultimate impression. For example, an air of the fantastic —approaching as nearly to the ludicrous as was admissible—is given to the Raven's entrance. He comes in "with many a flirt and flutter."

Not the *least obeisance made he*—not a moment stopped or stayed he,
But with mien of lord or lady, perched above my chamber door.

In the two stanzas which follow, the design is more obviously carried out:—

Then this ebony bird beguiling my sad fancy into smiling
By the *grave and stern decorum of the countenance it wore,*
"Though thy *crest be shorn and shaven* thou," I said, "art sure no craven,
Ghastly grim and ancient Raven wandering from the nightly shore—
Tell me what thy lordly name is on the Night's Plutonian shore?"
              Quoth the Raven "Nevermore."

Much I marvelled *this ungainly fowl* to hear discourse so plainly
Though its answer little meaning—little relevancy bore;
For we cannot help agreeing that no living human being
Ever yet was blessed with seeing bird above his chamber door—
Bird or beast upon the sculptured bust above his chamber door,
              With such name as "Nevermore."

---

[8] Marble bust of Pallas Athena, goddess of
wisdom in classic myth.

The effect of the *dénouement* being thus provided for, I immediately drop the fantastic for a tone of the most profound seriousness:—this tone commencing in the stanza directly following the one last quoted, with the line,

But the Raven, sitting lonely on that placid bust, spoke only, etc.

From this epoch the lover no longer jests—no longer sees any thing even of the fantastic in the Raven's demeanor. He speaks of him as a "grim, ungainly, ghastly, gaunt, and ominous bird of yore," and feels the "fiery eyes" burning into his "bosom's core." This revolution of thought, or fancy, on the lover's part, is intended to induce a similar one on the part of the reader—to bring the mind into a proper frame for the *dénouement*—which is now brought about as rapidly and as *directly* as possible.

With the *dénouement* proper—with the Raven's reply, "Nevermore," to the lover's final demand if he shall meet his mistress in another world—the poem, in its obvious phase, that of a simple narrative, may be said to have its completion. So far, every thing is within the limits of the accountable—of the real. A raven, having learned by rote the single word "Nevermore," and having escaped from the custody of its owner, is driven at midnight, through the violence of a storm, to seek admission at a window from which a light still gleams—the chamber-window of a student, occupied half in pouring over a volume, half in dreaming of a beloved mistress deceased. The casement being thrown open at the fluttering of the bird's wings, the bird itself perches on the most convenient seat out of the immediate reach of the student, who, amused by the incident and the oddity of the visitor's demeanor, demands of it, in jest and without looking for a reply, its name. The raven addressed, answers with its customary word, "Nevermore"—a word which finds immediate echo in the melancholy heart of the student, who, giving utterance aloud to certain thoughts suggested by the occasion, is again startled by the fowl's repetition of "Nevermore." The student now guesses the state of the case, but is impelled, as I have before explained, by the human thirst for self-torture, and in part by superstition, to propound such queries to the bird as will bring him, the lover, the most of the luxury of sorrow, through the anticipated answer "Nevermore." With the indulgence, to the extreme, of this self-torture, the narration, in what I have termed its first or obvious phase, has a natural termination, and so far there has been no overstepping of the limits of the real.

But in subjects so handled, however skilfully, or with however vivid an array of incident, there is always a certain hardness or nakedness, which repels the artistical eye. Two things are invariably required—first, some amount of complexity, or more properly, adaptation; and, secondly, some amount of suggestiveness—some undercurrent, however indefinite, of meaning. It is this latter, in especial, which imparts to a work of art so much of that *richness* (to borrow from colloquy a forcible term) which we are too fond of confounding with *the ideal*. It is the *excess* of the suggested meaning—it is the rendering this the upper instead of the under current of the theme —which turns into prose (and that of the very flattest kind) the so called poetry of the so called transcendentalists.

Holding these opinions, I have added the two concluding stanzas of the poem— their suggestiveness being thus made to pervade all the narrative which has preceded them. The under-current of meaning is rendered first apparent in the lines—

"Take thy beak from out *my heart,* and take thy form from off
    my door!"
                    Quoth the Raven "Nevermore!"

It will be observed that the words, "from out my heart," involve the first metaphorical expression in the poem. They, with the answer, "Nevermore," dispose the
mind to seek a moral in all that has been previously narrated. The reader begins now
to regard the Raven as emblematical—but it is not until the very last line of the very
last stanza, that the intention of making him emblematical of *Mournful and Never-
ending Remembrance* is permitted distinctly to be seen:

And the Raven, never flitting, still is sitting, still is sitting,
On the pallid bust of Pallas, just above my chamber door;
And his eyes have all the seeming of a demon's that is dreaming,
And the lamplight o'er him streaming throws his shadow on the floor;
And my soul *from out that shadow* that lies floating on the floor
              Shall be lifted—nevermore.

1846

---

from The Poetic Principle

In speaking of the Poetic Principle, I have no design to be either thorough or
profound.[1] While discussing, very much at random, the essentiality of what we call
Poetry, my principal purpose will be to cite for consideration, some few of those
minor English or American poems which best suit my own taste, or which, upon my
own fancy, have left the most definite impression. By "minor poems" I mean, of
course, poems of little length. And here, in the beginning, permit me to say a few
words in regard to a somewhat peculiar principle, which, whether rightfully or
wrongfully, has always had its influence in my own critical estimate of the poem. I
hold that a long poem does not exist. I maintain that the phrase, "a long poem," is
simply a flat contradiction in terms.

I need scarcely observe that a poem deserves its title only inasmuch as it excites,
by elevating the soul. The value of the poem is in the ratio of this elevating
excitement. But all excitements are, through a psychal necessity, transient. That degree
of excitement which would entitle a poem to be so called at all, cannot be sustained
throughout a composition of any great length. After the lapse of half an hour, at the

[1] Poe originally intended this analysis as a lecture;
it was first printed the year after his death, in
1850.

very utmost, it flags—fails—a revulsion ensues—and then the poem is, in effect, and in fact, no longer such.

There are, no doubt, many who have found difficulty in reconciling the critical dictum that the "Paradise Lost" is to be devoutly admired throughout, with the absolute impossibility of maintaining for it, during perusal, the amount of enthusiasm which that critical dictum would demand. This great work, in fact, is to be regarded as poetical, only when, losing sight of that vital requisite in all works of Art, Unity, we view it merely as a series of minor poems. If, to preserve its Unity—its totality of effect or impression—we read it (as would be necessary) at a single sitting, the result is but a constant alternation of excitement and depression. After a passage of what we feel to be true poetry, there follows, inevitably, a passage of platitude which no critical pre-judgment can force us to admire; but if, upon completing the work, we read it again; omitting the first book—that is to say, commencing with the second—we shall be surprised at now finding that admirable which we before condemned—that damnable which we had previously so much admired. It follows from all this that the ultimate, aggregate, or absolute effect of even the best epic under the sun, is a nullity:—and this is precisely the fact.

In regard to the Iliad, we have, if not positive proof, at least very good reason, for believing it intended as a series of lyrics; but, granting the epic intention, I can say only that the work is based in an imperfect sense of art. The modern epic is, of the supposititious ancient model, but an inconsiderate and blindfold imitation. But the day of these artistic anomalies is over. If, at any time, any very long poem *were* popular in reality, which I doubt, it is at least clear that no very long poem will ever be popular again.

That the extent of a poetical work is, *ceteris paribus,* the measure of its merit, seems undoubtedly, when we thus state it, a proposition sufficiently absurd—yet we are indebted for it to the Quarterly Reviews. Surely there can be nothing in mere *size,* abstractly considered—there can be nothing in mere *bulk,* so far as a volume is concerned, which has so continuously elicited admiration from these saturnine pamphlets! A mountain, to be sure, by the mere sentiment of physical magnitude which it conveys, *does* impress us with a sense of the sublime—but no man is impressed after *this* fashion by the material grandeur of even "The Columbiad."[2] Even the Quarterlies have not instructed us to be so impressed by it. *As yet,* they have not *insisted* on our estimating Lamartine[3] by the cubic foot, or Pollok[4] by the pound—but what else are we to *infer* from their continual prating about "sustained effort?" If, by "sustained effort," any little gentleman has accomplished an epic, let us frankly commend him for the effort—if this indeed be a thing commendable—but let us forbear praising the epic on the effort's account. It is to be hoped that common sense, in the time to come, will prefer deciding upon a work of art, rather by the impression it makes, by the effect it produces, than by the time it took to impress the effect or by the amount of "sustained effort" which had been found necessary in effecting the impression. The fact is, that perseverance is one thing, and genius quite another—nor can all the

---

[2] Joel Barlow (1754–1812) intended this long poem about the vision of Columbus (finished in 1807) to stand as the great American epic.
[3] Alphonse de Lamartine (1790–1869), French writer of Romantic poetry.

[4] Scottish poet Robert Pollok (1798–1827), author of yet another long poem, "The Course of Time" (1827).

Quarterlies in Christendom confound them. By-and-by, this proposition, with many which I have been just urging, will be received as self-evident. In the meantime, by being generally condemned as falsities, they will not be essentially damaged as truths.

On the other hand, it is clear that a poem may be improperly brief. Undue brevity degenerates into mere epigrammatism. A *very* short poem, while now and then producing a brilliant or vivid, never produces a profound or enduring effect. . . .

While the epic mania—while the idea that, to merit in poetry, prolixity is indispensable—has, for some years past, been gradually dying out of the public mind, by mere dint of its own absurdity—we find it succeeded by a heresy too palpably false to be long tolerated, but one which, in the brief period it has already endured, may be said to have accomplished more in the corruption of our Poetical Literature than all its other enemies combined. I allude to the heresy of *The Didactic.* It has been assumed, tacitly and avowedly, directly and indirectly, that the ultimate object of all Poetry is Truth. Every poem, it is said, should inculcate a moral; and by this moral is the poetical merit of the work to be adjudged. We Americans especially have patronised this happy idea; and we Bostonians, very especially, have developed it in full. We have taken it into our heads that to write a poem simply for the poem's sake, and to acknowledge such to have been our design, would be to confess ourselves radically wanting in the true Poetic dignity and force:—but the simple fact is, that, would we but permit ourselves to look into our own souls, we should immediately there discover that under the sun there neither exists nor *can* exist any work more thoroughly dignified—more supremely noble than this very poem—this poem *per se* —this poem which is a poem and nothing more—this poem written solely for the poem's sake.

With as deep a reverence for the True as ever inspired the bosom of man, I would, nevertheless, limit, in some measure, its modes of inculcation. I would limit to enforce them. I would not enfeeble them by dissipation. The demands of Truth are severe. She has no sympathy with the myrtles.[5] All *that* which is so indispensable in Song, is precisely all *that* with which *she* has nothing whatever to do. It is but making her a flaunting paradox, to wreathe her in gems and flowers. In enforcing a truth, we need severity rather than efflorescence of language. We must be simple, precise, terse. We must be cool, calm, unimpassioned. In a word, we must be in that mood which, as nearly as possible, is the exact converse of the poetical. *He* must be blind, indeed, who does not perceive the radical and chasmal differences between the truthful and the poetical modes of inculcation. He must be theory-mad beyond redemption who, in spite of these differences, shall still persist in attempting to reconcile the obstinate oils and waters of Poetry and Truth.

Dividing the world of mind into its three most immediately obvious distinctions, we have the Pure Intellect, Taste, and the Moral Sense. I place Taste in the middle, because it is just this position which, in the mind, it occupies. It holds intimate relations with either extreme; but from the Moral Sense is separated by so faint a difference that Aristotle has not hesitated to place some of its operations among the virtues themselves. Nevertheless, we find the *offices* of the trio marked with a sufficient distinction. Just as the Intellect concerns itself with Truth, so Taste informs us of the

---

[5] In classic times the myrtle was associated with
Venus, the goddess of love.

Beautiful while the Moral Sense is regardful of Duty. Of this latter, while Conscience teaches the obligation, and Reason the expediency, Taste contents herself with display-ing the charms:—waging war upon Vice solely on the ground of her deformity—her disproportion—her animosity to the fitting, to the appropriate, to the harmonious—in a word, to Beauty.

An immortal instinct, deep within the spirit of man, is thus, plainly, a sense of the Beautiful. This it is which administers to his delight in the manifold forms, and sounds, and odours, and sentiments amid which he exists. And just as the lily is repeated in the lake, or the eyes of Amaryllis[6] in the mirror, so is the mere oral or written repetition of these forms, and sounds, and colours, and odours, and sentiments, a duplicate source of delight. But this mere repetition is not poetry. He who shall simply sing, with however glowing enthusiasm, or with however vivid a truth of description, of the sights, and sounds, and odours, and colours, and sentiments, which greet *him* in common with all mankind—he, I say, has yet failed to prove his divine title. There is still a something in the distance which he has been unable to attain. We have still a thirst unquenchable, to allay which he has not shown us the crystal springs. This thirst belongs to the immortality of Man. It is at once a consequence and an indication of his perennial existence. It is the desire of the moth for the star. It is no mere appreciation of the Beauty before us—but a wild effort to reach the Beauty above. Inspired by an ecstatic prescience of the glories beyond the grave, we struggle, by multiform combinations among the things and thoughts of Time, to attain a portion of that Loveliness whose very elements, perhaps, appertain to eternity alone. And thus when by Poetry—or when by Music, the most entrancing of the Poetic moods—we find ourselves melted into tears—we weep then—not as the Abbate Gravina[7] supposes—through excess of pleasure, but through a certain, petulant, impatient sorrow at our inability to grasp *now,* wholly, here on earth, at once and for ever, those divine and rapturous joys, of which *through* the poem, or *through* the music, we attain to but brief and indeterminate glimpses.

The struggle to apprehend the supernal Loveliness—this struggle, on the part of souls fittingly constituted—has given to the world all *that* which it (the world) has ever been enabled at once to understand and *to feel* as poetic.

The Poetic Sentiment, of course, may develope itself in various modes—in Painting, in Sculpture, in Architecture, in the Dance—very especially in Music—and very peculiarly, and with a wide field, in the composition of the Landscape Garden. Our present theme, however, has regard only to its manifestation in words. And here let me speak briefly on the topic of rhythm. Contenting myself with the certainty that Music, in its various modes of metre, rhythm, and rhyme, is of so vast a moment in Poetry as never to be wisely rejected—is so vitally important an adjunct, that he is simply silly who declines its assistance, I will not now pause to maintain its absolute essentiality. It is in Music, perhaps, that the soul most nearly attains the great end for which, when inspired by the Poetic Sentiment, it struggles—the creation of supernal Beauty. It *may* be, indeed, that here this sublime end is, now and then, attained *in fact.* We are often made to feel, with a shivering delight,

---

[6] In Theocritus' pastoral poem *Idyls,* the shepherdess Amaryllis is described as "the Nymph of the pretty glance."

[7] Gian Vincenzo Gravina (1664–1718), Italian writer.

that from an earthly harp are stricken notes which *cannot* have been unfamiliar to the angels. And thus there can be little doubt that in the union of Poetry with Music in its popular sense, we shall find the widest field for the Poetic development. The old Bards and Minnesingers[8] had advantages which we do not possess—and Thomas Moore,[9] singing his own songs, was, in the most legitimate manner, perfecting them as poems.

To recapitulate, then:—I would define, in brief, the Poetry of words as *The Rhythmical Creation of Beauty.* Its sole arbiter is Taste. With the Intellect or with the Conscience, it has only collateral relations. Unless incidentally, it has no concern whatever either with Duty or with Truth.

A few words, however, in explanation. *That* pleasure which is at once the most pure, the most elevating, and the most intense, is derived, I maintain, from the contemplation of the Beautiful. In the contemplation of Beauty we alone find it possible to attain that pleasurable elevation, or excitement, *of the soul,* which we recognise as the Poetic Sentiment, and which is so easily distinguished from Truth, which is the satisfaction of the Reason, or from Passion, which is the excitement of the heart. I make Beauty, therefore—using the word as inclusive of the sublime— I make Beauty the province of the poem, simply because it is an obvious rule of Art that effects should be made to spring as directly as possible from their causes:—no one as yet having been weak enough to deny that the peculiar elevation in question is at least *most readily* attainable in the poem. It by no means follows, however, that the incitements of Passion, or the precepts of Duty, or even the lessons of Truth, may not be introduced into a poem, and with advantage; for they may subserve, incidentally, in various ways, the general purposes of the work:—but the true artist will always contrive to tone them down in proper subjection to that *Beauty* which is the atmosphere and the real essence of the poem. . . .[10]

Thus, although in a very cursory and imperfect manner, I have endeavoured to convey to you my conception of the Poetic Principle. It has been my purpose to suggest that, while this Principle itself is, strictly and simply, the Human Aspiration for Supernal Beauty, the manifestation of the Principle is always found in *an elevating excitement of the Soul*—quite independent of that passion which is the intoxication of the Heart—or of that Truth which is the satisfaction of the Reason. For, in regard to Passion, alas! its tendency is to degrade, rather than to elevate the Soul. Love, on the contrary—Love—the true, the divine Eros—the Uranian, as distinguished from the Dionæan Venus[11]—is unquestionably the purest and truest of all poetical themes. And in regard to Truth—if, to be sure, through the attainment of a truth, we are led to perceive a harmony where none was apparent before, we experience, at once, the true poetical effect—but this effect is referable to the harmony alone, and not in the least degree to the truth which merely served to render the harmony manifest.

We shall reach, however, more immediately a distinct conception of what the true Poetry is, by mere reference to a few of the simple elements which induce in the Poet

---

[8] Medieval poets and musicians.
[9] Irish poet (1778–1852).
[10] Omitted is a series of verses from poems by Longfellow, Bryant, Tennyson, Byron, and others, used by Poe to illustrate his theories of poetry.

[11] The Uranian Eros represented divine love to the ancient Romans, whereas the Dionaean Venus was the goddess of earthly passion.

himself the true poetical effect. He recognises the ambrosia which nourishes his soul, in the bright orbs that shine in Heaven—in the volutes of the flower—in the clustering of low shrubberies—in the waving of the grain-fields—in the slanting of tall, Eastern trees—in the blue distance of mountains—in the grouping of clouds—in the twinkling of half-hidden brooks—in the gleaming of silver rivers—in the repose of sequestered lakes—in the star-mirroring depths of lonely wells. He perceives it in the songs of birds—in the harp of Æolus[12]—in the sighing of the night-wind—in the repining voice of the forest—in the surf that complains to the shore—in the fresh breath of the woods—in the scent of the violet—in the voluptuous perfume of the hyacinth—in the suggestive odour that comes to him, at eventide, from far-distant, undiscovered islands, over dim oceans, illimitable and unexplored. He owns it in all noble thoughts—in all unworldly motives—in all holy impulses—in all chivalrous, generous, and self-sacrificing deeds. He feels it in the beauty of woman—in the grace of her step—in the lustre of her eye—in the melody of her voice—in her soft laughter—in her sigh—in the harmony of the rustling of her robes. He deeply feels it in her winning endearments—in her burning enthusiasms—in her gentle charities—in her meek and devotional endurances—but above all—ah, far above all—he kneels to it—he worships it in the faith, in the purity, in the strength, in the altogether divine majesty—of her *love*. . . .

1850

Sonnet—to Science

Science! true daughter of Old Time thou art!
 Who alterest all things with thy peering eyes.
Why preyest thou thus upon the poet's heart,
 Vulture, whose wings are dull realities?
How should he love thee? or how deem thee wise.   5
 Who wouldst not leave him in his wandering
To seek for treasure in the jewelled skies.
 Albeit he soared with an undaunted wing?
Hast thou not dragged Diana from her car?
 And driven the Hamadryad from the wood   10
To seek a shelter in some happier star?
 Hast thou not torn the Naiad from her flood,
The Elfin from the green grass, and from me
 The summer dream beneath the tamarind tree?

1829

---

[12] Aeolus was the god of winds in classic myth. The Aeolian harp is a stringed instrument that makes musical sounds when the wind blows across it.

The City in the Sea*

Lo! Death has reared himself a throne
In a strange city lying alone
Far down within the dim West,
Where the good and the bad and the worst and the best
Have gone to their eternal rest.   5
There shrines and palaces and towers
(Time-eaten towers that tremble not!)
Resemble nothing that is ours.
Around, by lifting winds forgot,
Resignedly beneath the sky   10
The melancholy waters lie.

No rays from the holy heaven come down
On the long night-time of that town;
But light from out the lurid sea
Streams up the turrets silently—   15
Gleams up the pinnacles far and free
Up domes—up spires—up kingly halls—
Up fanes—up Babylon-like¹ walls—
Up shadowy long-forgotten bowers
Of sculptured ivy and stone flowers—   20
Up many and many a marvellous shrine
Whose wreathéd friezes intertwine
The viol, the violet, and the vine.

Resignedly beneath the sky
The melancholy waters lie.   25
So blend the turrets and shadows there
That all seem pendulous in air,
While from a proud tower in the town
Death looks gigantically down.

There open fanes and gaping graves   30
Yawn level with the luminous waves;
But not the riches there that lie
In each idol's diamond eye—
Not the gaily-jewelled dead
Tempt the waters from their bed;   35
For no ripples curl, alas!

---

* This poem was first published as "The Doomed   ¹ The city of ancient Babylon was famous for its
City," in 1831. It was revised and retitled in   immense towers and walls.
1845.

Along that wilderness of glass—
No swellings tell that winds may be
Upon some far-off happier sea—
No heavings hint that winds have been   40
On seas less hideously serene.

But lo, a stir is in the air!
The wave—there is a movement there!
As if the towers had thrust aside,
In slightly sinking, the dull tide—   45
As if their tops had feebly given
A void within the filmy Heaven.
The waves have now a redder glow—
The hours are breathing faint and low—
And when, amid no earthly moans,   50
Down, down that town shall settle hence,
Hell, rising from a thousand thrones,
Shall do it reverence.

1831–1845

To Helen[*]

Helen,[1] thy beauty is to me
   Like those Nicéan[2] barks of yore,
That gently, o'er a perfumed sea,
   The weary, way-worn wanderer bore
     To his own native shore.   5

On desperate seas long wont to roam,
   Thy hyacinth[3] hair, thy classic face,
Thy Naiad[4] airs have brought me home
   To the glory that was Greece,
   And the grandeur that was Rome.   10

Lo! in yon brilliant window-niche
   How statue-like I see thee stand,

---

[*] This poem first appeared in 1831 but was rewritten over the next 12 years. This version was included in the 1845 edition of *The Raven and Other Poems.*
[1] Helen of Troy, considered the most beautiful woman of ancient times, was celebrated in the Homeric epic the *Iliad.* She was considered the cause of the Trojan War.
[2] Probably derived from Nike, the Greek goddess of Victory; thus, "victorious."
[3] Lustrous, curling hair.
[4] Water nymph.

> The agate lamp within thy hand!
> Ah, Psyche,[5] from the regions which
> Are Holy-Land![6]   15

1831–1843

The Raven[*]

Once upon a midnight dreary, while I pondered, weak and weary,
Over many a quaint and curious volume of forgotten lore—
While I nodded, nearly napping, suddenly there came a tapping,
As of some one gently rapping, rapping at my chamber door—
" 'Tis some visiter," I muttered, "tapping at my chamber door—   5
      Only this and nothing more."

Ah, distinctly I remember it was in the bleak December;
And each separate dying ember wrought its ghost upon the floor.
Eagerly I wished the morrow;—vainly I had sought to borrow
From my books surcease of sorrow—sorrow for the lost Lenore—   10
For the rare and radiant maiden whom the angels name Lenore—
      Nameless *here* for evermore.

And the silken, sad, uncertain rustling of each purple curtain
Thrilled me—filled me with fantastic terrors never felt before;
So that now, to still the beating of my heart, I stood repeating   15
" 'Tis some visiter entreating entrance at my chamber door—
Some late visiter entreating entrance at my chamber door;—
      This it is and nothing more."

Presently my soul grew stronger; hesitating then no longer,
"Sir," said I, "or Madam, truly your forgiveness I implore;   20
But the fact is I was napping, and so gently you came rapping,
And so faintly you came tapping, tapping at my chamber door,
That I scarce was sure I heard you"—here I opened wide the door;——
      Darkness there and nothing more.

Deep into that darkness peering, long I stood there wondering, fearing,   25
Doubting, dreaming dreams no mortal ever dared to dream before;
But the silence was unbroken, and the stillness gave no token,
And the only word there spoken was the whispered word, "Lenore?"

---

[5] Greek word for soul.
[6] If Palestine is a religious holy land, Greece is the sacred place of art.

[*] This poem was probably written during 1844. It was first published in January 1845. This version was published in September 1849.

This I whispered, and an echo murmured back the word, "Lenore!"
      Merely this and nothing more.   30

Back into the chamber turning, all my soul within me burning,
Soon again I heard a tapping somewhat louder than before.
"Surely," said I, "surely that is something at my window lattice;
Let me see, then, what thereat is, and this mystery explore—
Let my heart be still a moment and this mystery explore;—   35
      'Tis the wind and nothing more!"

Open here I flung the shutter, when with many a flirt and flutter,
In there stepped a stately Raven of the saintly days of yore;
Not the least obeisance made he; not a minute stopped or stayed he;
But, with mien of lord or lady, perched above my chamber door—   40
Perched upon a bust of Pallas[1] just above my chamber door—
      Perched, and sat, and nothing more.

Then this ebony bird beguiling my sad fancy into smiling,
By the grave and stern decorum of the countenance it wore,
"Though thy crest be shorn and shaven, thou," I said, "art sure no craven,   45
Ghastly grim and ancient Raven wandering from the Nightly shore—
Tell me what thy lordly name is on the Night's Plutonian[2] shore!"
      Quoth the Raven "Nevermore."

Much I marvelled this ungainly fowl to hear discourse so plainly,
Though its answer little meaning—little relevancy bore;   50
For we cannot help agreeing that no living human being
Ever yet was blessed with seeing bird above his chamber door—
Bird or beast upon the sculptured bust above his chamber door,
      With such name as "Nevermore."

But the Raven, sitting lonely on the placid bust, spoke only   55
That one word, as if his soul in that one word he did outpour.
Nothing farther then he uttered—not a feather then he fluttered—
Till I scarcely more than muttered "Other friends have flown before—
On the morrow *he* will leave me, as my Hopes have flown before."
      Then the bird said "Nevermore."   60

Startled at the stillness broken by reply so aptly spoken,
"Doubtless," said I, "what it utters is its only stock and store
Caught from some unhappy master whom unmerciful Disaster
Followed fast and followed faster till his songs one burden bore—
Till the dirges of his Hope that melancholy burden bore   65
      Of 'Never—nevermore.' "

[1] Athena, in classic myth the goddess of wisdom.
[2] I.e., as black as the region of the underworld
ruled over by Pluto in mythology.

But the Raven still beguiling my sad fancy into smiling,
Straight I wheeled a cushioned seat in front of bird, and bust and door;
Then, upon the velvet sinking, I betook myself to linking
Fancy unto fancy, thinking what this ominous bird of yore—   70
What this grim, ungainly, ghastly, gaunt, and ominous bird of yore
      Meant in croaking "Nevermore."

This I sat engaged in guessing, but no syllable expressing
To the fowl whose fiery eyes now burned into my bosom's core;
This and more I sat divining, with my head at ease reclining   75
On the cushion's velvet lining that the lamp-light gloated³ o'er,
But whose velvet-violet lining with the lamp-light gloating o'er,
      She shall press, ah, nevermore!

Then, methought, the air grew denser, perfumed from an unseen censer
Swung by seraphim whose foot-falls tinkled on the tufted floor.   80
"Wretch," I cried, "thy God hath lent thee—by these angels he hath sent
   thee
Respite—respite and nepenthe from thy memories of Lenore;
Quaff, oh quaff this kind nepenthe and forget this lost Lenore!"
      Quoth the Raven "Nevermore."

"Prophet!" said I, "thing of evil!—prophet still, if bird, or devil!—   85
Whether Tempter sent, or whether tempest tossed thee here ashore,
Desolate yet all undaunted, on this desert land enchanted—
On this home by Horror haunted—tell me truly, I implore—
Is there—*is* there balm in Gilead?⁴—tell me—tell me, I implore!"
      Quoth the Raven "Nevermore."   90

"Prophet!" said I, "thing of evil!—prophet still, if bird or devil!
By that Heaven that bends above us—by that God we both adore—
Tell this soul with sorrow laden if, within the distant Aidenn,⁵
It shall clasp a sainted maiden whom the angels name Lenore—
Clasp a rare and radiant maiden whom the angels name Lenore."   95
      Quoth the Raven "Nevermore."

"Be that word our sign of parting, bird or fiend!" I shrieked, upstarting—
"Get thee back into the tempest and the Night's Plutonian shore!
Leave no black plume as a token of that lie thy soul hath spoken!
Leave my loneliness unbroken!—quit the bust above my door!   100
Take thy beak from out my heart, and take thy form from off my door!"
      Quoth the Raven "Nevermore."

---

³ Here meaning both glowed and relished with malicious pleasure.
⁴ Reference to lines from Jeremiah 8:22, which speak ironically of the healing medicinal resin taken from evergreen trees in the region of Gilead in Jordan.
⁵ Of Arabic derivation, suggesting Eden.

And the Raven, never flitting, still is sitting, *still* is sitting
On the pallid bust of Pallas just above my chamber door;
And his eyes have all the seeming of a demon's that is dreaming,   105
And the lamp-light o'er him streaming throws his shadow on the floor;
And my soul from out that shadow that lies floating on the floor
      Shall be lifted—nevermore!

1844–1849

Ulalume—a Ballad[*]

    The skies they were ashen and sober;
        The leaves they were crispéd and sere—
        The leaves they were withering and sere:
    It was night, in the lonesome October
        Of my most immemorial[1] year: 5
    It was hard by the dim lake of Auber,
        In the misty mid region of Weir:—
    It was down by the dank tarn[2] of Auber,
        In the ghoul-haunted woodland of Weir.

    Here once, through an alley Titanic,   10
        Of cypress, I roamed with my Soul—
        Of cypress, with Psyche, my Soul.
    These were days when my heart was volcanic
        As the scoriac[3] rivers that roll—
        As the lavas that restlessly roll   15
    Their sulphurous currents down Yaanek,
        In the ultimate climes of the Pole[4]—
    That groan as they roll down Mount Yaanek,
        In the realms of the Boreal[5] Pole.

    Our talk had been serious and sober.   20
        By our thoughts they were palsied and sere—
        Our memories were treacherous and sere;
    For we knew not the month was October,
        And we marked not the night of the year—
        (Ah, night of all nights in the year!)[6]   25
    We noted not the dim lake of Auber,

---

[*] This poem was first written and published in 1847. This version is from a revision written in 1849.
[1] Memorable.
[2] Mountain lake.
[3] Lavalike.
[4] The South Pole.
[5] Here, the direction of the south magnetic pole.
[6] All Saints' Eve.

(Though once we had journeyed down here)
  We remembered not the dank tarn of Auber,
    Nor the ghoul-haunted woodland of Weir.

And now, as the night was senescent,   30
  And star-dials pointed to morn—
    As the star-dials hinted of morn—
At the end of our path a liquescent
  And nebulous lustre was born,
Out of which a miraculous crescent   35
  Arose with a duplicate horn—
Astarte's[7] bediamonded crescent,
  Distinct with its duplicate horn.

And I said—"She is warmer than Dian;[8]
  She rolls through an ether of sighs—   40
    She revels in a region of sighs.
She has seen that the tears are not dry on
  These cheeks where the worm never dies,
And has come past the stars of the Lion,[9]
  To point us the path to the skies—   45
    To the Lethean[10] peace of the skies—
Come up, in despite of the Lion,
  To shine on us with her bright eyes—
Come up, through the lair of the Lion,
  With love in her luminous eyes."   50

But Psyche, uplifting her finger,
  Said—"Sadly this star I mistrust—
    Her pallor I strangely mistrust—
Ah, hasten!—ah, let us not linger!
  Ah, fly!—let us fly!—for we must."   55
In terror she spoke; letting sink her
  Wings till they trailed in the dust—
In agony sobbed; letting sink her
  Plumes till they trailed in the dust—
    Till they sorrowfully trailed in the dust.   60

I replied—"This is nothing but dreaming.
  Let us on, by this tremulous light!
    Let us bathe in this crystalline light!
Its Sibyllio[11] splendor is beaming
  With Hope and in Beauty to-night—   65

---

[7] Astarte: Phoenician fertility goddess, patroness of carnal love.
[8] Diana, virgin goddess of the moon.
[9] The constellation Leo, sign of uneasy love.

[10] Forgetfulness, caused by drinking from the river Lethe in Hades.
[11] In classic myth, the Sibyls prophesied the future.

See!—it flickers up the sky through the night!
Ah, we safely may trust to its gleaming
    And be sure it will lead us aright—
We surely may trust to a gleaming
    That cannot but guide us aright   70
Since it flickers up to Heaven through the night."

Thus I pacified Psyche and kissed her,
    And tempted her out of her gloom—
    And conquered her scruples and gloom;
And we passed to the end of the vista—   75
    But were stopped by the door of a tomb—
    By the door of a legended tomb:—
And I said—"What is written, sweet sister.
    On the door of this legended tomb?"
She replied—"Ulalume—Ulalume!—   80
    'Tis the vault of thy lost Ulalume!"

Then my heart it grew ashen and sober
    As the leaves that were crispéd and sere—
    As the leaves that were withering and sere—
And I cried—"It was surely October,   85
    On *this* very night of last year,
That I journeyed—I journeyed down here!—
    That I brought a dread burden down here—
    On this night, of all nights in the year,
Ah, what demon hath tempted me here?   90
Well I know, now, this dim lake of Auber—
    This misty mid region of Weir:—
Well I know, now, this dank tarn of Auber—
    This ghoul-haunted woodland of Weir."

Said we, then—the two, then—"Ah, can it   95
    Have been that the woodlandish ghouls—
    The pitiful, the merciful ghouls,
To bar up our way and to ban it
    From the secret that lies in these wolds—
    From the thing that lies hidden in these wolds—   100
Have drawn up the spectre of a planet
    From the limbo[12] of lunary souls—

This sinfully scintillant planet
    From the Hell of the planetary souls?"

1847–1849

---

[12] The resting place of the unbaptized on the
fringes of hell.

A Dream Within a Dream

Take this kiss upon the brow!
And, in parting from you now,
Thus much let me avow—
You are not wrong, who deem
That my days have been a dream;   5
Yet if hope has flown away
In a night, or in a day,

In a vision, or in none,
Is it therefore the less *gone?*
All that we see or seem   10
Is but a dream within a dream.

I stand amid the roar
Of a surf-tormented shore,
And I hold within my hand
Grains of the golden sand—   15
How few! yet how they creep
Through my fingers to the deep,
While I weep—while I weep!
O God! can I not grasp
Them with a tighter clasp?   20
O God! can I not save
One from the pitiless wave?
Is *all* that we see or seem
But a dream within a dream?

1849

Annabel Lee

It was many and many a year ago,
    In a kingdom by the sea,
That a maiden there lived whom you may know
    By the name of Annabel Lee;—
And this maiden she lived with no other thought   5
    Than to love and be loved by me.

I was a child and *she* was a child,
　In this kingdom by the sea;
But we loved with a love that was more than love—
　I and my Annabel Lee—　　　　　　　　　　　　　　10
With a love that the wingéd seraphs in Heaven
　Coveted her and me.

And this was the reason that, long ago,
　In this kingdom by the sea,
A wind blew out of a cloud, chilling　　　　　　　　15
　My beautiful Annabel Lee;
So that her high-born kinsmen came
　And bore her away from me,
To shut her up in a sepulchre,
　In this kingdom by the sea.　　　　　　　　　　　20

The angels, not half so happy in Heaven,
　Went envying her and me—
Yes!—that was the reason (as all men know,
　In this kingdom by the sea)
That the wind came out of the cloud by night,　　　25
　Chilling and killing my Annabel Lee.

But our love it was stronger by far than the love
　Of those who were older than we—
　Of many far wiser than we—
And neither the angels in Heaven above,　　　　　30
　Nor the demons down under the sea,
Can ever dissever my soul from the soul
　Of the beautiful Annabel Lee:—

For the moon never beams, without bringing me dreams
　Of the beautiful Annabel Lee;　　　　　　　　　35
And the stars never rise, but I feel the bright eyes
　Of the beautiful Annabel Lee:—
And so, all the night-tide, I lie down by the side
Of my darling—my darling—my life and my bride,
　In her sepulchre there by the sea—　　　　　　40
　In her tomb by the sounding sea.

1849

Nathaniel Hawthorne
1804–1864

Nathaniel Hawthorne rarely seemed at ease with himself, his work, or his place in American literary history. The author of America's most famous novel of religious conscience, he nevertheless professed to be unmoved by any form of religion. He characterized his regularly enforced attendance at the services at Salem's Meeting House, where his ancestors had worshiped for nearly two centuries, as "the frozen purgatory of my childhood." A writer who spent twelve years in self-imposed retirement from the world, ensconced in the literary solitude of a small room tucked under the eaves of the family house in Salem, he nevertheless yearned to participate in what he called "the opaque substance of today." Consider the letter he wrote to his sister Louisa shortly before his graduation from college. In it, Hawthorne solemnly announced: "I have thought much upon the subject and have finally come to the conclusion that I shall never make a distinguished figure in the world, and all I hope or wish is to plod along with the multitude."

This constant struggle between the private and public self, the real and the imagined self, also marked Hawthorne's attitude toward his writing. He seemed interested in creating a literary world abstracted from reality, yet he also noted that "the most desirable mode of existence might be that of a spiritualized Paul Pry, hovering invisible round men and women, witnessing their deeds, searching their hearts, borrowing brightness from their felicity and shade from their sorrow, and retaining no emotion peculiar to himself." Henry James, in his celebrated study of the writer, perceptively identified this as Hawthorne's paradoxical mixture of "evasive and inquisitive tendencies."

Hawthorne's literary ambition was often at odds with what he regarded as his accomplishments. He criticized himself, for example, for not having transcribed the reality of Puritan New England accurately enough, yet his genius transformed it into what later readers called classic fiction. Hawthorne drew his strength as a writer from his ample reserves of self-doubt. And while the circumstances of his life may appear uneventful, the drama in his life—much like the conflict in his fiction—took place in the private moral and psychic recesses of this complex individual.

Nathaniel Hawthorne was born on July 4, 1804, in Salem, Massachusetts. His Puritan ancestors were among the first settlers in the state and included two prominent judges, one active in the persecution of the Quakers in the 1650s, the other in the witch trials of the 1690s. By Hawthorne's time, however, the family had receded from public eminence. Both his father and his grandfather were captains of merchant ships. In 1808 his father died of yellow fever in Dutch Guiana (now Surinam), leaving his widow with three children: Nathaniel; an older sister, Elizabeth; and a younger sister, Louisa. Taking the customs of Puritan bereavement to an unusual extreme, the mother moved with her children back into the household of her parents and rarely left her room for the 40 remaining years of her life, eating nearly all her meals alone. Her grief,

Hawthorne later noted, "outlasted its vitality, and grew to be merely a torpid habit."

Hawthorne attended school in Salem but at the age of nine was hurt playing ball. Partially lame for three years, he was tutored at home, where his devotion to reading Spenser, Shakespeare, Milton, Thomson, and Bunyan's *The Pilgrim's Progress* first showed itself. (The first book he bought with his own money was *The Faerie Queene.*) He did not remain entirely inactive, however. His mother's family owned some land and houses in Raymond, Maine, a settlement in the middle of dense and broad forests. Hawthorne made several lengthy visits there, one lasting a year. "I lived in Maine like a bird of the air, so perfect was the freedom I enjoyed. But it was there I first got my cursed habits of solitude."

In 1821 he entered Bowdoin College in Maine, and some aspects of his career there suggest that his habits of solitude were temporarily modified. He joined, for example, a literary society, a card-playing club, and a student militia led by his friend Franklin Pierce, who was to become the fourteenth president of the United States. Hawthorne described himself during this period as an "idle student," one who was "negligent of college rules and the Procrustean details of academic life, rather choosing to nurse my own fancies than to dig into Greek roots." He took up tobacco chewing and, like many of his fellow undergraduates, was fined on more than one occasion for drinking and gambling. An unusually handsome and charming young man, he participated in social activities; yet full of self-effacement and reserve, he avoided drawing attention to himself. His classmates described him as aloof when in company, and one remarked at the time: "I love Hawthorne; I admire him; but I do not know him. He lives in a mysterious world of thought and imagination which he never permits me to enter." Hawthorne graduated in 1825, an undistinguished eighteenth in a class of 38.

Returning to Salem, he lived with his mother and sisters and settled once again into a solitary way of life. With no immediate need to work for pay, he was able to read widely, showing a special interest in the history of Puritan New England, in Gothic romances, and in the great novelists of the eighteenth century, especially Fielding, Smollett, and Richardson. He also took long walks along the seashore and, after dark, through town. But he was also at work writing. In 1828 his first novel, *Fanshawe,* was published anonymously. The story, set in a rural American college (said to resemble the Bowdoin of Hawthorne's day) is one of abduction: A villain enters the scene and makes off with the ward of the college president. She is rescued by Fanshawe, described as a handsome, brave, yet reclusive student, someone "unconnected with the world, unconnected in its feelings, and uninfluenced by it in any of his pursuits. In this respect he probably deceived himself. If his inmost heart could have been laid open, there would have been discovered that dream of undying fame, which dream as it is, is more powerful than a thousand realities." She is willing to marry her rescuer, but Fanshawe declines the opportunity and, being "a hard scholar," reads himself into an early grave. Though generally regarded as a minor work, *Fanshawe* is an accomplished performance for a twenty-four-year-old author, one that reflected the styles of Fielding and Scott. However, the novel did not sell many copies, and Hawthorne soon became dissatisfied with it himself. He never later acknowledged it as his work.

Hawthorne's first short stories were published in the early 1830s. They appeared in "gift-books," a kind of magazine published annually that printed poems, stories, and essays, usually with no attribution to the author. In such stories as "The Hollow of the Three Hills," "The Wives of the Dead," and "Young Goodman Brown," a strong narrative voice presents mysterious or puzzling incidents. Yet, as the stories unfold, Hawthorne often suppresses that narrative voice to achieve a dramatic mode that frequently leaves the puzzles unresolved. During this period, he also worked for six months in Boston as the editor of *The American Magazine of Useful and Entertaining Knowledge,* for which he and his sister Elizabeth wrote nearly all the material. When a fire pushed the magazine to the brink of bankruptcy, Hawthorne resigned and wrote a history of the world for children. The volume sold well over a million copies, yet Hawthorne had signed a contract that earned him only a $100 fee.

In 1837 *Twice-Told Tales,* his first acknowledged book, was published. Of it, Hawthorne reported in a letter to Henry Wadsworth Longfellow, a former fellow student at Bowdoin, "I have . . . great difficulty in the lack of materials, for I have seen so little of the world that I have nothing but thin air to concoct my stories of, and it is not easy to give a life-like semblance to such shadowy stuff." Hawthorne began to address this problem in one way by keeping a notebook and filling it with telling observations of daily life—many of which were incorporated into his fiction. *Twice-Told Tales* contained about half of his stories that had appeared by that time. The collection received favorable reviews and sold steadily for many months, gradually earning him a considerable reputation, if not Fanshawe's secretly desired "undying fame."

At the same time, Hawthorne began to mix in the society of Salem, most notably with the Peabody family. Sophia Peabody, seven years younger, was a well-educated, talented artist and a near invalid. Their love grew quickly, and by the end of 1838 they were secretly engaged. Looking forward to supporting a family, Hawthorne turned to work that would be more remunerative than writing stories for magazines. In 1839, through the political influence of old friends, he obtained a position as an inspector at the Boston Custom House, weighing and measuring the goods shipped in and out of the harbor. He composed some short tales for children in these years, but he was distracted from doing any more substantial literary work. Increasingly displeased by the working conditions at the port, Hawthorne was glad to be relieved of the job when the political administration changed in 1841.

He moved almost immediately to the Brook Farm Institute of Agriculture and Education, a communal experiment founded by a group of writers and thinkers associated with Transcendentalism. There he intended to "establish a mode of life which shall combine the enchantments of poetry with the facts of daily experience." He worked conscientiously on the farm but gradually judged the chores disagreeable and his fellow workers troublesome and intrusive. He left after eight months. "I can best attain the higher ends of my life by retaining the ordinary relation to society," he announced in a letter at the time.

Yet Hawthorne's life-style after Brook Farm seems only slightly more ordinary. He married Sophia Peabody in 1842, and soon afterward they took up residence at Concord in the Old Manse, a house built by Ralph Waldo Emerson's grandfather. Hawthorne's daily routine there is charmingly described in the preface to *Mosses from an Old Manse* (1846) and in his journals. He gardened, took on many of the housekeeping chores, boated on the river in summer, and skated in the winter. Occasionally, he wrote. He also mixed, sometimes, with such illustrious neighbors as Emerson, Margaret Fuller, Ellery Channing, Amos Bronson Alcott, and Henry David Thoreau. His conversations with Emerson and Fuller were awkward at best. Emerson, Hawthorne noted, was "a great searcher for facts; but they seem to melt away and become unsubstantial in his grasp." (Henry James explained the incompatibility from a more distant and generous perspective: "Emerson, as a spiritual sun-worshipper, could have attached but a moderate value to Hawthorne's catlike faculty of seeing in the dark.") Hawthorne seemed unable—perhaps finally unwilling—to share Emerson's cosmic optimism and his Transcendentalist belief in the salvific qualities of experience. The young Herman Melville, in reviewing *Mosses from an Old Manse,* had also recognized Hawthorne's "Calvinistic sense of Innate Depravity and Original Sin, from whose visitations . . . no deeply thinking mind is always and wholly free."

Despite this social awkwardness and the fact that during their stay at the Old Manse Nathaniel and Sophia Hawthorne lived rather meagerly on their savings and on the small payments Hawthorne received for his writing, they always referred to these years as an extremely happy period of their lives. The birth of their first child, a daughter named Una, in 1844 only augmented the spiritual self-sufficiency of their household.

Eventually, however, the family needed more income. In 1846 Hawthorne moved his family back into his mother's house and began a three-year stint as surveyor of customs, under conditions he described fully in the essay "The Custom-House," printed as a preface to *The Scarlet Letter.* Although he published very little during this time, an extraordinary period of creative work was to follow. As before, Hawthorne's job had been a political appointment, and he lost it when the presidential administration changed in 1849. Soon after, his mother died. Through the summer and autumn of that year, his family living on money Sophia had saved and from unsolicited loans from friends, Hawthorne composed *The Scarlet Letter,* generally considered his greatest work.

The central idea of the novel—a woman sentenced to wear a lettered badge as punishment for adultery—had been conceived by Hawthorne more than a decade earlier in his short story "Endicott and the Red Cross" (1838). Usually rather desultory in his writing habits, Hawthorne threw himself into drafting *The Scarlet Letter,* writing "immensely," as his wife said—up to nine hours a day. He had originally planned it to be a tale, somewhat longer than usual, to be included in his next collection. But his publisher, James T. Fields, read the manuscript, praised it highly, and urged him to expand the work and issue it as a single volume. He did so, completing it in February 1850.

Hawthorne judged the book to be "positively a hell-fired story, into which I found it almost impossible to throw a cheering light," and he feared it would not be well received. He described in his notebook his experience as he read the final scene aloud to his wife—or "tried to read it, rather, for my voice swelled and heaved, as if I were tossed up and down on an ocean as it subsided after a storm. But I was in a very nervous state, then, having gone through a great diversity and severity of emotion, for many months past." His anxiety was short lived. On the day following the incident he was able to write to a friend in a very different tone to describe his wife's experience: "It broke her heart and sent her to bed with a grievous headache—which I look upon as a triumphant success! Judging from its effects on her and the publisher, I may calculate on what bowlers call a ten-strike!" He had calculated correctly, for the first edition sold out in ten days, and reviewers variously classed him with Alexander Pope, Sir Walter Scott, Charles Lamb, and Charles Dickens.

In the spring of 1850, Hawthorne moved with his wife and children (a son, Julian, had been born in 1846) to Lenox, Massachussetts, at the time a rural community where many literary people spent the summer. Characteristically, Hawthorne was found by many to be an aloof, even reluctant member of the community. During this time, he and Melville saw each other often, usually at Melville's suggestion. With the success of *The Scarlet Letter*, Hawthorne began work on a new romance, *The House of the Seven Gables*, which he intended to be more varied in tone and less uniformly somber than *The Scarlet Letter*. He finished the new book in 1851, and, against his expectations, it proved to be as popular as its predecessor. Other new work included another volume of stories for children, *Tanglewood Tales for Boys and Girls* (1851), a new edition of *Twice-Told Tales* (1851), and another collection of stories, *The Snow-Image, and Other Twice-Told Tales* (1851). For the first time Hawthorne was earning enough from his writing to support his family. (A daughter, Rose, was born in 1852.) Looking for a less rustic environment than Lenox, the family moved to West Newton, a suburb of Boston. Here Hawthorne began *The Blithedale Romance* (1852), a book satirizing the pretensions and delusions of social reformers.

Acclaimed in both America and Britain as one of the preeminent writers of the day, Hawthorne could finally afford to buy a permanent home for his family. In 1852 he bought The Wayside, the former house of Bronson Alcott in Concord, and once again entered the neighborhood of Emerson, Fuller, Channing, and Thoreau. Here he worked on a final volume of children's stories as well as on a campaign biography of his college friend Franklin Pierce, who had been unexpectedly chosen the Democratic candidate for president. Soon after Pierce's election, he appointed Hawthorne American consul at Liverpool, England.

Hawthorne served as consul from 1853 to 1857. Following the pattern he had established at the customhouses in Boston and Salem, Hawthorne soon grew to dislike the job. Once again he composed no fiction while employed, but he wrote copiously in his notebooks. And though he traveled widely through the English countryside, he did not seek out the company of literary people. As the title of his published recollections of this time, *Our Old Home*, suggests, he felt a certain hereditary connection to the culture of England. Yet as an American he felt a more immediate link to the increasingly distinct culture of America. England for Hawthorne was "our *old* home," not simply "our home."

Hawthorne's relation to America in the years immediately preceding the Civil War was, however, still uneasy. "It sickens me to look back at America," he wrote in a letter from England. "I am sick to death of the continual fuss and tumult and excitement and bad blood which we keep up about political topics." It is easy to imagine how the intensely factional climate at home would have repulsed Hawthorne, a naturally reserved man who, largely for reasons of friendship rather than ideology, supported Pierce, then being villified as a proslavery leader.

When Hawthorne left the consulate in 1857, he moved his family to Italy. They settled eventually in the countryside near Florence, not far from Robert and Elizabeth Barrett Browning, with whom they had become friendly. Here Hawthorne began work, slowly, on his last completed romance, *The Marble Faun,* which treats the conflict between American and Old World values. He remained in Italy two years, writing and visiting the American and British artists residing there. On the journey home the family stopped again in England, where Hawthorne finished *The Marble Faun.* He returned to The Wayside in June 1860.

Though he supported the Union during the Civil War, Hawthorne maintained a fairly evenhanded view of the conflict. He shared little of the abolitionist zeal of many of his neighbors in New England. (On the occasion of John Brown's execution, Hawthorne remarked, "Nobody was ever more justly hanged.") During this period, he felt increasingly out of touch with the nation that had gone to war with itself. Henry James, Sr., the novelist's father, described Hawthorne at the time as having the look "of a rogue who suddenly finds himself in the company of detectives." Hawthorne continued to work, revising his English notebooks for publication and sketching new romances, but he found it difficult to complete these drafts, and finally he abandoned them.

By the spring of 1864, Hawthorne's health had mysteriously and rapidly declined. Though mentally alert, he was quite feeble. He could hardly hold the pen as he wrote. Oliver Wendell Holmes, visiting him at the time, inferred that he had a brain tumor. Pierce proposed to take him on a trip to the seacoast of Maine, hoping this might revive his health and spirit. But on May 19, soon after they reached Plymouth, New Hampshire, Hawthorne died quietly in his sleep. His body was returned to Concord, where he was buried at Sleepy Hollow cemetery.

At a time when, as Emerson said, "things are in the saddle," Hawthorne devoted himself to a more aesthetic purpose—to explore the territory "where the Actual and the Imaginary might meet." And the setting Hawthorne most often chose for this encounter was Puritan New England, a place of "dark necessity," as he called it, an overbearing, threatening world where the responsibility for moral order remained with individuals who were themselves seriously flawed. His interests were humanistic and literary. He drew on Puritan orthodoxy not to study theology but to examine individual and collective consciousness under the pressures of anguish and suffering. He sought to dramatize the relation between society and powerful individuals; to probe such themes as the individual's relation to sin, guilt, and retribution; to explore the mysteries of the human heart; to examine characters caught in the grip of the past or in the need for greater experience and knowledge. His writing is marked by its introspective depth, by its urge to get inside the characters he created. In this respect, Hawthorne is one of the first major American writers of fiction to focus on the interior lives of his characters, to explore what Henry James would later call "the deeper psychology of art."

More generally, the compelling energy of Hawthorne's fiction derives from his fascination with the interplay of characters living in extremes and absolutes—be they a community of Puritans obsessed with uncovering sin or a scientist, artist, or idealist preoccupied with perfecting the world by pressing beyond the boundaries of mortal action. Hawthorne's work suggests that the imagination might reconcile such extremes and establish a more balanced, less dehumanized view of individual action and moral responsibility. But he was not always confident that this was possible. He leaves us with a fictional world in which, as in reality, the consequences of trying to transcend the mortal and the moral remain all too painfully apparent.

Hawthorne never stopped studying his own techniques as a writer. Perhaps this is one reason so many other major writers were so attracted to his work. Poe admired him, as did Henry James, Thomas Hardy, and D. H. Lawrence. And Herman Melville dedicated *Moby-Dick* to Hawthorne "in token of my admiration for his genius." And yet it may be most fitting to turn to one of Hawthorne's own early sketches for a projection of his contribution to an indigenous American literature. In "A Select Party," Hawthorne creates a character, not unlike himself in appearance, manner, and aspiration, who is "as yet unhonored" by those around him but "for whom our country is looking anxiously into the mist of Time, as destined to fulfill the great mission of creating an American literature, as it were, out of our intellectual quarries." The enduring strength of Hawthorne's writing suggests that he accomplished that mission.

Further Reading:

H. James, *Hawthorne*, 1879.
J. Hawthorne, *Nathaniel Hawthorne and His Wife*, 2 vols., 1884, 1968.
G. Woodberry, *Nathaniel Hawthorne*, 1902.
D. H. Lawrence, *Studies in Classic American Literature*, 1923.
F. O. Matthiessen, *The American Renaissance*, 1941.
H. Levin, *The Power of Blackness*, 1958, 1980.
A. Turner, *Nathaniel Hawthorne. An Introduction and Interpretation*, 1961.
Hawthorne Centenary Essays, ed. R. H. Pearce, 1964.
F. Crews, *The Sins of the Fathers, Hawthorne's Psychological Themes*, 1966.
Hawthorne: A Collection of Critical Essays, ed. A. Kaul, 1966.
Hawthorne Among His Contemporaries, ed. K. Cameron, 1968.
J. C. Stubbs, *The Pursuit of Form: A Study of Hawthorne and the Romance*, 1970.
N. F. Doubleday, *Hawthorne's Early Tales: A Critical Study*, 1972.
R. H. Brodhead, *Hawthorne, Melville, and the Novel*, 1976.
A. Turner, *Nathaniel Hawthorne: A Biography*, 1980.
J. Mellows, *Nathaniel Hawthorne in His Times*, 1980.
T. Martin, *Nathaniel Hawthorne*, 1983.

Texts:

Stories, novels, and "Abraham Lincoln" from *The Complete Works of Nathaniel Hawthorne*, 12 vols., 1883.
The American Notebooks, ed. R. Stewart, 1932.
The English Notebooks, ed. R. Stewart, 1941.
Letter to H. W. Longfellow from *The Portable Hawthorne*, ed. M. Cowley, 1969.
Letters to S. Peabody from *Love Letters of Nathaniel Hawthorne*, 1907.
See also *Nathaniel Hawthorne: Tales and Sketches*, ed. R. H. Pearce, 1982.
Nathaniel Hawthorne: Novels, ed. M. Bell, 1983.

My Kinsman, Major Molineux

After the kings of Great Britain had assumed the right of appointing the colonial governors,[1] the measures of the latter seldom met with the ready and general approbation which had been paid to those of their predecessors, under the original charters. The people looked with most jealous scrutiny to the exercise of power which did not emanate from themselves, and they usually rewarded their rulers with slender gratitude for the compliances by which, in softening their instructions from beyond the sea, they had incurred the reprehension of those who gave them. The annals of Massachusetts Bay will inform us, that of six governors in the space of about forty years from the surrender of the old charter, under James II., two were imprisoned by a popular insurrection; a third, as Hutchinson[2] inclines to believe, was driven from the province by the whizzing of a musket-ball; a fourth, in the opinion of the same historian, was hastened to his grave by continual bickerings with the House of Representatives; and the remaining two, as well as their successors, till the Revolution, were favored with few and brief intervals of peaceful sway. The inferior members of the court party,[3] in times of high political excitement, led scarcely a more desirable life. These remarks may serve as a preface to the following adventures, which chanced upon a summer night, not far from a hundred years ago. The reader, in order to avoid a long and dry detail of colonial affairs, is requested to dispense with an account of the train of circumstances that had caused much temporary inflammation of the popular mind.

It was near nine o'clock of a moonlight evening, when a boat crossed the ferry with a single passenger, who had obtained his conveyance at that unusual hour by the promise of an extra fare. While he stood on the landing-place, searching in either pocket for the means of fulfilling his agreement, the ferryman lifted a lantern, by the aid of which, and the newly risen moon, he took a very accurate survey of the stranger's figure. He was a youth of barely eighteen years, evidently country-bred, and now, as it should seem, upon his first visit to town. He was clad in a coarse gray coat, well worn, but in excellent repair; his under garments were durably constructed of leather, and fitted tight to a pair of serviceable and well-shaped limbs; his stockings of blue yarn were the incontrovertible work of a mother or a sister; and on his head was a three-cornered hat, which in its better days had perhaps sheltered the graver brow of the lad's father. Under his left arm was a heavy cudgel formed of an oak sapling, and retaining a part of the hardened root; and his equipment was completed by a wallet,[4] not so abundantly stocked as to incommode the vigorous shoulders on which it hung. Brown, curly hair, well-shaped features, and bright, cheerful eyes were nature's gifts, and worth all that art could have done for his adornment.

The youth, one of whose names was Robin, finally drew from his pocket the half

---

[1] The first royal governor of Massachusetts was appointed in 1685 by James II, after the Massachusetts Charter had been annulled.
[2] Thomas Hutchinson (1711–1780), the last royal governor of Massachusetts, was also a historian

and author of *The History of the Colony and Province of Massachusetts-Bay* (1764, 1767).
[3] The pro-royal party.
[4] Knapsack.

of a little province bill[5] of five shillings, which, in the depreciation in that sort of currency, did but satisfy the ferryman's demand, with the surplus of a sexangular piece of parchment, valued at three pence. He then walked forward into the town, with as light a step as if his day's journey had not already exceeded thirty miles, and with as eager an eye as if he were entering London city, instead of the little metropolis of a New England colony. Before Robin had proceeded far, however, it occurred to him that he knew not whither to direct his steps; so he paused, and looked up and down the narrow street, scrutinizing the small and mean wooden buildings that were scattered on either side.

"This low hovel cannot be my kinsman's dwelling," thought he, "nor yonder old house, where the moonlight enters at the broken casement; and truly I see none hereabouts that might be worthy of him. It would have been wise to inquire my way of the ferryman, and doubtless he would have gone with me, and earned a shilling from the Major for his pains. But the next man I meet will do as well."

He resumed his walk, and was glad to perceive that the street now became wider, and the houses more respectable in their appearance. He soon discerned a figure moving on moderately in advance, and hastened his steps to overtake it. As Robin drew nigh, he saw that the passenger was a man in years, with a full periwig of gray hair, a wide-skirted coat of dark cloth, and silk stockings rolled above his knees. He carried a long and polished cane, which he struck down perpendicularly before him at every step; and at regular intervals he uttered two successive hems, of a peculiarly solemn and sepulchral intonation. Having made these observations, Robin laid hold of the skirt of the old man's coat, just when the light from the open door and windows of a barber's shop fell upon both their figures.

"Good evening to you," honored sir, said he, making a low bow, and still retaining his hold of the skirt. "I pray you tell me whereabouts is the dwelling of my kinsman, Major Molineux."

The youth's question was uttered very loudly; and one of the barbers, whose razor was descending on a well-soaped chin, and another who was dressing a Ramillies wig,[6] left their occupations, and came to the door. The citizen, in the mean time, turned a long-favored countenance upon Robin, and answered him in a tone of excessive anger and annoyance. His two sepulchral hems, however, broke into the very centre of his rebuke, with most singular effect, like a thought of the cold grave obtruding among wrathful passions.

"Let go my garment, fellow! I tell you, I know not the man you speak of. What! I have authority, I have—hem, hem—authority; and if this be the respect you show for your betters, your feet shall be brought acquainted with the stocks[7] by daylight, tomorrow morning!"

Robin released the old man's skirt, and hastened away, pursued by an ill-mannered roar of laughter from the barber's shop. He was at first considerably surprised by the result of his question, but, being a shrewd youth, soon thought himself able to account for the mystery.

"This is some country representative," was his conclusion, "who has never seen the

---

[5] Colonial paper money.
[6] Elaborately braided wig named for a British victory at Ramillies, Belgium.

[7] Heavy wooden instruments, used for public punishment, that lock around the ankles and sometimes the wrists.

inside of my kinsman's door, and lacks the breeding to answer a stranger civilly. The man is old, or verily—I might be tempted to turn back and smite him on the nose. Ah, Robin, Robin! even the barber's boys laugh at you for choosing such a guide! You will be wiser in time, friend Robin."

He now became entangled in a succession of crooked and narrow streets, which crossed each other, and meandered at no great distance from the water-side. The smell of tar was obvious to his nostrils, the masts of vessels pierced the moonlight above the tops of the buildings, and the numerous signs, which Robin paused to read, informed him that he was near the centre of business. But the streets were empty, the shops were closed, and lights were visible only in the second stories of a few dwelling-houses. At length, on the corner of a narrow lane, through which he was passing, he beheld the broad countenance of a British hero swinging before the door[8] of an inn, whence proceeded the voices of many guests. The casement of one of the lower windows was thrown back, and a very thin curtain permitted Robin to distinguish a party at supper, round a well-furnished table. The fragrance of the good cheer steamed forth into the outer air, and the youth could not fail to recollect that the last remnant of his travelling stock of provision had yielded to his morning appetite, and that noon had found and left him dinnerless.

"Oh, that a parchment three-penny might give me a right to sit down at yonder table!" said Robin, with a sigh. "But the Major will make me welcome to the best of his victuals; so I will even step boldly in, and inquire my way to his dwelling."

He entered the tavern, and was guided by the murmur of voices and the fumes of tobacco to the public-room. It was a long and low apartment, with oaken walls, grown dark in the continual smoke, and a floor which was thickly sanded, but of no immaculate purity. A number of persons—the larger part of whom appeared to be mariners, or in some way connected with the sea—occupied the wooden benches, or leather-bottomed chairs, conversing on various matters, and occasionally lending their attention to some topic of general interest. Three or four little groups were draining as many bowls of punch, which the West India trade had long since made a familiar drink in the colony. Others, who had the appearance of men who lived by regular and laborious handicraft, preferred the insulated bliss of an unshared potation, and became more taciturn under its influence. Nearly all, in short, evinced a predilection for the Good Creature[9] in some of its various shapes, for this is a vice to which, as Fast Day[10] sermons of a hundred years ago will testify, we have a long hereditary claim. The only guests to whom Robin's sympathies inclined him were two or three sheepish countrymen, who were using the inn somewhat after the fashion of a Turkish caravansary,[11] they had gotten themselves into the darkest corner of the room, and heedless of the Nicotian[12] atmosphere, were supping on the bread of their own ovens, and the bacon cured in their own chimney-smoke. But though Robin felt a sort of brotherhood with these strangers, his eyes were attracted from them to a person who stood near the door, holding whispered conversation with a group of ill-dressed associates. His features were separately striking almost to grotesqueness, and the whole

---

[8] I.e., on a signboard.
[9] See 1 Timothy 4:4: "For every creature of God is good and nothing to be refused, if it be received with Thanksgiving."
[10] A day for public penitence.

[11] Inn built to accommodate caravans.
[12] Smoke-filled from tobacco. Jean Nicot (hence "nicotine") brought the first tobacco to France from Lisbon.

face left a deep impression on the memory. The forehead bulged out into a double prominence, with a vale between; the nose came boldly forth in an irregular curve, and its bridge was of more than a finger's breadth; the eyebrows were deep and shaggy, and the eyes glowed beneath them like fire in a cave.

While Robin deliberated of whom to inquire respecting his kinsman's dwelling, he was accosted by the innkeeper, a little man in a stained white apron, who had come to pay his professional welcome to the stranger. Being in the second generation from a French Protestant, he seemed to have inherited the courtesy of his parent nation; but no variety of circumstances was ever known to change his voice from the one shrill note in which he now addressed Robin.

"From the country, I presume, sir?" said he, with a profound bow. "Beg leave to congratulate you on your arrival, and trust you intend a long stay with us. Fine town here, sir, beautiful buildings, and much that may interest a stranger. May I hope for the honor of your commands in respect to supper?"

"The man sees a family likeness! the rogue has guessed that I am related to the Major!" thought Robin, who had hitherto experienced little superfluous civility.

All eyes were now turned on the country lad, standing at the door, in his worn three-cornered hat, gray coat, leather breeches, and blue yarn stockings, leaning on an oaken cudgel, and bearing a wallet on his back.

Robin replied to the courteous innkeeper, with such an assumption of confidence as befitted the Major's relative. "My honest friend," he said, "I shall make it a point to patronize your house on some occasion, when"—here he could not help lowering his voice—"when I may have more than a parchment three-pence in my pocket. My present business," continued he, speaking with lofty confidence, "is merely to inquire my way to the dwelling of my kinsman, Major Molineux."

There was a sudden and general movement in the room, which Robin interpreted as expressing the eagerness of each individual to become his guide. But the innkeeper turned his eyes to a written paper on the wall, which he read, or seemed to read, with occasional recurrences to the young man's figure.

"What have we here?" said he, breaking his speech into little dry fragments. " 'Left the house of the subscriber, bounden servant,[13] Hezekiah Mudge,—had on, when he went away, gray coat, leather breeches, master's third-best hat. One pound currency reward to whosoever shall lodge him in any jail of the province.' Better trudge, boy; better trudge!"

Robin had begun to draw his hand towards the lighter end of the oak cudgel, but a strange hostility in every countenance induced him to relinquish his purpose of breaking the courteous innkeeper's head. As he turned to leave the room, he encountered a sneering glance from the bold-featured personage whom he had before noticed; and no sooner was he beyond the door, than he heard a general laugh, in which the innkeeper's voice might be distinguished, like the dropping of small stones into a kettle.

"Now, is it not strange," thought Robin, with his usual shrewdness,—"is it not strange that the confession of an empty pocket should outweigh the name of my

---

[13] Person bound to servitude (indentured) for a specific period, usually in exchange for transportation to the colonies.

kinsman, Major Molineux? Oh, if I had one of those grinning rascals in the woods, where I and my oak sapling grew up together, I would teach him that my arm is heavy though my purse be light!"

On turning the corner of the narrow lane, Robin found himself in a spacious street, with an unbroken line of lofty houses on each side, and a steepled building at the upper end, whence the ringing of a bell announced the hour of nine. The light of the moon, and the lamps from the numerous shop-windows, discovered people promenading on the pavement, and amongst them Robin hoped to recognize his hitherto inscrutable relative. The result of his former inquiries made him unwilling to hazard another, in a scene of such publicity, and he determined to walk slowly and silently up the street, thrusting his face close to that of every elderly gentleman, in search of the Major's lineaments. In his progress, Robin encountered many gay and gallant figures. Embroidered garments of showy colors, enormous periwigs, gold-laced hats, and silver-hilted swords glided past him and dazzled his optics. Travelled youths, imitators of the European fine gentlemen of the period, trod jauntily along, half dancing to the fashionable tunes which they hummed, and making poor Robin ashamed of his quiet and natural gait. At length, after many pauses to examine the gorgeous display of goods in the shop-windows, and after suffering some rebukes for the impertinence of his scrutiny into people's faces, the Major's kinsman found himself near the steepled building, still unsuccessful in his search. As yet, however, he had seen only one side of the thronged street; so Robin crossed, and continued the same sort of inquisition down the opposite pavement, with stronger hopes than the philosopher seeking an honest man,[14] but with no better fortune. He had arrived about midway towards the lower end, from which his course began, when he overheard the approach of some one who struck down a cane on the flag-stones at every step, uttering, at regular intervals, two sepulchral hems.

"Mercy on us!" quoth Robin, recognizing the sound.

Turning a corner, which chanced to be close at his right hand, he hastened to pursue his researches in some other part of the town. His patience now was wearing low, and he seemed to feel more fatigue from his rambles since he crossed the ferry, than from his journey of several days on the other side. Hunger also pleaded loudly within him, and Robin began to balance the propriety of demanding, violently, and with lifted cudgel, the necessary guidance from the first solitary passenger whom he should meet. While a resolution to this effect was gaining strength, he entered a street of mean appearance, on either side of which a row of ill-built houses was straggling towards the harbor. The moonlight fell upon no passenger along the whole extent, but in the third domicile which Robin passed there was a half-opened door, and his keen glance detected a woman's garment within.

"My luck may be better here," said he to himself.

Accordingly, he approached the door, and beheld it shut closer as he did so; yet an open space remained, sufficing for the fair occupant to observe the stranger, without a corresponding display on her part. All that Robin could discern was a strip of scarlet petticoat, and the occasional sparkle of an eye, as if the moon-beams were trembling on some bright thing.

[14] Diogenes, Greek Cynic philosopher (412?–323 B.C.), supposedly roamed the world in search of an honest man.

"Pretty mistress," for I may call her so with a good conscience, thought the shrewd youth, since I know nothing to the contrary,—"my sweet pretty mistress, will you be kind enough to tell me whereabouts I must seek the dwelling of my kinsman, Major Molineux?"

Robin's voice was plaintive and winning, and the female, seeing nothing to be shunned in the handsome country youth, thrust open the door, and came forth into the moonlight. She was a dainty little figure, with a white neck, round arms, and a slender waist, at the extremity of which her scarlet petticoat jutted out over a hoop, as if she were standing in a balloon. Moreover, her face was oval and pretty, her hair dark beneath the little cap, and her bright eyes possessed a sly freedom, which triumphed over those of Robin.

"Major Molineux dwells here," said this fair woman.

Now, her voice was the sweetest Robin had heard that night, the airy counterpart of a stream of melted silver; yet he could not help doubting whether that sweet voice spoke Gospel truth. He looked up and down the mean street, and then surveyed the house before which they stood. It was a small, dark edifice of two stories, the second of which projected over the lower floor, and the front apartment had the aspect of a shop for petty commodities.

"Now, truly, I am in luck," replied Robin, cunningly, "and so indeed is my kinsman, the Major, in having so pretty a housekeeper. But I prithee trouble him to step to the door; I will deliver him a message from his friends in the country, and then go back to my lodgings at the inn."

"Nay, the Major has been abed this hour or more," said the lady of the scarlet petticoat; "and it would be to little purpose to disturb him to-night, seeing his evening draught was of the strongest. But he is a kind-hearted man, and it would be as much as my life's worth to let a kinsman of his turn away from the door. You are the good old gentleman's very picture, and I could swear that was his rainy-weather hat. Also he has garments very much resembling those leather small-clothes. But come in, I pray, for I bid you hearty welcome in his name."

So saying, the fair and hospitable dame took our hero by the hand; and the touch was light, and the force was gentleness, and though Robin read in her eyes what he did not hear in her words, yet the slender-waisted woman in the scarlet petticoat proved stronger than the athletic country youth. She had drawn his half-willing footsteps nearly to the threshold, when the opening of a door in the neighborhood startled the Major's housekeeper, and, leaving the Major's kinsman, she vanished speedily into her own domicile. A heavy yawn preceded the appearance of a man, who, like the Moonshine of Pyramus and Thisbe,[15] carried a lantern, needlessly aiding his sister luminary in the heavens. As he walked sleepily up the street, he turned his broad, dull face on Robin, and displayed a long staff, spiked at the end.

"Home, vagabond, home!" said the watchman, in accents that seemed to fall asleep as soon as they were uttered. "Home, or we'll set you in the stocks by peep of day!"

"This is the second hint of the kind," thought Robin. "I wish they would end my difficulties, by setting me there to-night."

Nevertheless, the youth felt an instinctive antipathy towards the guardian of midnight order, which at first prevented him from asking his usual question. But just

---

[15] Moonshine appears in a bumbling enactment of the story of Pyramus and Thisbe by characters in Shakespeare's play *A Midsummer Night's Dream*.

when the man was about to vanish behind the corner, Robin resolved not to lose the opportunity, and shouted lustily after him,—

"I say, friend! will you guide me to the house of my kinsman, Major Molineux?"

The watchman made no reply, but turned the corner and was gone; yet Robin seemed to hear the sound of drowsy laughter stealing along the solitary street. At that moment, also, a pleasant titter saluted him from the open window above his head; he looked up, and caught the sparkle of a saucy eye; a round arm beckoned to him, and next he heard light footsteps descending the staircase within. But Robin, being of the household of a New England clergyman, was a good youth, as well as a shrewd one; so he resisted temptation, and fled away.

He now roamed desperately, and at random, through the town, almost ready to believe that a spell was on him, like that by which a wizard of his country had once kept three pursuers wandering, a whole winter night, within twenty paces of the cottage which they sought. The streets lay before him, strange and desolate, and the lights were extinguished in almost every house. Twice, however, little parties of men, among whom Robin distinguished individuals in outlandish attire, came hurrying along; but, though on both occasions they paused to address him, such intercourse did not at all enlighten his perplexity. They did but utter a few words in some language of which Robin knew nothing, and perceiving his inability to answer, bestowed a curse upon him in plain English and hastened away. Finally, the lad determined to knock at the door of every mansion that might appear worthy to be occupied by his kinsman, trusting that perseverance would overcome the fatality that had hitherto thwarted him. Firm in this resolve, he was passing beneath the walls of a church, which formed the corner of two streets, when, as he turned into the shade of its steeple, he encountered a bulky stranger, muffled in a cloak. The man was proceeding with the speed of earnest business, but Robin planted himself full before him, holding the oak cudgel with both hands across his body as a bar to further passage.

"Halt, honest man, and answer me a question," said he, very resolutely. "Tell me, this instant, whereabouts is the dwelling of my kinsman, Major Molineux!"

"Keep your tongue between your teeth, fool, and let me pass!" said a deep, gruff voice, which Robin partly remembered. "Let me pass, I say, or I'll strike you to the earth!"

"No, no, neighbor!" cried Robin, flourishing his cudgel, and then thrusting its larger end close to the man's muffled face. "No, no, I'm not the fool you take me for, nor do you pass till I have an answer to my question. Whereabouts is the dwelling of my kinsman, Major Molineux?"

The stranger, instead of attempting to force his passage, stepped back into the moonlight, unmuffled his face, and stared full into that of Robin.

"Watch here an hour, and Major Molineux will pass by," said he.

Robin gazed with dismay and astonishment on the unprecedented physiognomy of the speaker. The forehead with its double prominence, the broad hooked nose, the shaggy eyebrows, and fiery eyes were those which he had noticed at the inn, but the man's complexion had undergone a singular, or, more properly, a twofold change. One side of the face blazed an intense red, while the other was black as midnight, the division line being in the broad bridge of the nose; and a mouth which seemed to extend from ear to ear was black or red, in contrast to the color of the cheek. The effect was as if two individual devils, a fiend of fire and a fiend of darkness, had united themselves to form this infernal visage. The stranger grinned in Robin's face, muffled his party-colored features, and was out of sight in a moment.

"Strange things we travellers see!" ejaculated Robin.

He seated himself, however, upon the steps of the church-door, resolving to wait the appointed time for his kinsman. A few moments were consumed in philosophical speculations upon the species of man who had just left him; but having settled this point shrewdly, rationally, and satisfactorily, he was compelled to look elsewhere for his amusement. And first he threw his eyes along the street. It was of more respectable appearance than most of those into which he had wandered; and the moon, creating, like the imaginative power, a beautiful strangeness in familiar objects, gave something of romance to a scene that might not have possessed it in the light of day. The irregular and often quaint architecture of the houses, some of whose roofs were broken into numerous little peaks, while others ascended, steep and narrow, into a single point, and others again were square; the pure snow-white of some of their complexions, the aged darkness of others, and the thousand sparklings, reflected from bright substances in the walls of many; these matters engaged Robin's attention for a while, and then began to grow wearisome. Next he endeavored to define the forms of distant objects, starting away, with almost ghostly indistinctness, just as his eye appeared to grasp them; and finally he took a minute survey of an edifice which stood on the opposite side of the street, directly in front of the church-door, where he was stationed. It was a large, square mansion, distinguished from its neighbors by a balcony, which rested on tall pillars, and by an elaborate Gothic window, communicating therewith.

"Perhaps this is the very house I have been seeking," thought Robin.

Then he strove to speed away the time, by listening to a murmur which swept continually along the street, yet was scarcely audible, except to an unaccustomed ear like his; it was a low, dull, dreamy sound, compounded of many noises, each of which was at too great a distance to be separately heard. Robin marvelled at this snore of a sleeping town, and marvelled more whenever its continuity was broken by now and then a distant shout, apparently loud where it originated. But altogether it was a sleep-inspiring sound, and, to shake off its drowsy influence, Robin arose, and climbed a window-frame, that he might view the interior of the church. There the moonbeams came trembling in, and fell down upon the deserted pews, and extended along the quiet aisles. A fainter yet more awful radiance was hovering around the pulpit, and one solitary ray had dared to rest upon the open page of the great Bible. Had nature, in that deep hour, become a worshipper in the house which man had builded? Or was that heavenly light the visible sanctity of the place,—visible because no earthly and impure feet were within the walls? The scene made Robin's heart shiver with a sensation of loneliness stronger than he had ever felt in the remotest depths of his native woods; so he turned away and sat down again before the door. There were graves around the church, and now an uneasy thought obtruded into Robin's breast. What if the object of his search, which had been so often and so strangely thwarted, were all the time mouldering in his shroud? What if his kinsman should glide through yonder gate, and nod and smile to him in dimly passing by?

"Oh that any breathing thing were here with me!" said Robin.

Recalling his thoughts from this uncomfortable track, he sent them over forest, hill, and stream, and attempted to imagine how that evening of ambiguity and weariness had been spent by his father's household. He pictured them assembled at the door, beneath the tree, the great old tree, which had been spared for its huge twisted trunk and venerable shade, when a thousand leafy brethren fell. There, at the going down of the summer sun, it was his father's custom to perform domestic worship, that the neighbors might come and join with him like brothers of the family, and that the wayfaring man might pause to drink at that fountain, and keep his heart pure by freshening the memory of home. Robin distinguished the seat of every individual of the little audience; he saw the good man in the midst, holding the Scriptures in the golden light that fell from the western clouds; he beheld him close the book and all rise up to pray. He heard the old thanksgivings for daily mercies, the old supplications for their continuance, to which he had so often listened in weariness, but which were now among his dear remembrances. He perceived the slight inequality of his father's voice when he came to speak of the absent one; he noted how his mother turned her face to the broad and knotted trunk; how his elder brother scorned, because the beard was rough upon his upper lip, to permit his features to be moved; how the younger sister drew down a low hanging branch before her eyes; and how the little one of all, whose sports had hitherto broken the decorum of the scene, understood the prayer for her playmate, and burst into clamorous grief. Then he saw them go in at the door; and when Robin would have entered also, the latch tinkled into its place, and he was excluded from his home.

"Am I here, or there?" cried Robin, starting; for all at once, when his thoughts had become visible and audible in a dream, the long, wide, solitary street shone out before him.

He aroused himself, and endeavored to fix his attention steadily upon the large edifice which he had surveyed before. But still his mind kept vibrating between fancy and reality; by turns, the pillars of the balcony lengthened into the tall, bare stems of pines, dwindled down to human figures, settled again into their true shape and size, and then commenced a new succession of changes. For a single moment, when he deemed himself awake, he could have sworn that a visage—one which he seemed to remember, yet could not absolutely name as his kinsman's—was looking towards him from the Gothic window. A deeper sleep wrestled with and nearly overcame him, but fled at the sound of footsteps along the opposite pavement. Robin rubbed his eyes, discerned a man passing at the foot of the balcony, and addressed him in a loud, peevish, and lamentable cry.

"Hallo, friend! must I wait here all night for my kinsman, Major Molineux?"

The sleeping echoes awoke, and answered the voice; and the passenger, barely able to discern a figure sitting in the oblique shade of the steeple, traversed the street to obtain a nearer view. He was himself a gentleman in his prime, of open, intelligent, cheerful, and altogether prepossessing countenance. Perceiving a country youth, apparently homeless and without friends, he accosted him in a tone of real kindness, which had become strange to Robin's ears.

"Well, my good lad, who are you sitting here?" inquired he. "Can I be of service to you in any way?"

"I am afraid not, sir," replied Robin, despondingly; "yet I shall take it kindly, if you'll answer me a single question. I've been searching, half the night, for one Major Molineux; now, sir, is there really such a person in these parts, or am I dreaming?"

"Major Molineux! The name is not altogether strange to me," said the gentleman, smiling. "Have you any objection to telling me the nature of your business with him?"

Then Robin briefly related that his father was a clergyman, settled on a small salary, at a long distance back in the country, and that he and Major Molineux were brothers' children. The Major, having inherited riches, and acquired civil and military rank, had visited his cousin, in great pomp, a year or two before; had manifested much interest in Robin and an elder brother, and, being childless himself, had thrown out hints respecting the future establishment of one of them in life. The elder brother was destined to succeed to the farm which his father cultivated in the interval of sacred duties; it was therefore determined that Robin should profit by his kinsman's generous intentions, especially as he seemed to be rather the favorite, and was thought to possess other necessary endowments.

"For I have the name of being a shrewd youth," observed Robin, in this part of his story.

"I doubt not you deserve it," replied his new friend, good-naturedly; "but pray proceed."

"Well, sir, being nearly eighteen years old, and well grown, as you see," continued Robin, drawing himself up to his full height, "I thought it high time to begin the world. So my mother and sister put me in handsome trim, and my father gave me half the remnant of his last year's salary, and five days ago I started for this place, to pay the Major a visit. But, would you believe it, sir! I crossed the ferry a little after dark, and have yet found nobody that would show me the way to his dwelling; only, an hour or two since, I was told to wait here, and Major Molineux would pass by."

"Can you describe the man who told you this?" inquired the gentleman.

"Oh, he was a very ill-favored fellow, sir," replied Robin, "with two great bumps on his forehead, a hook nose, fiery eyes; and, what struck me as the strangest, his face was of two different colors. Do you happen to know such a man, sir?"

"Not intimately," answered the stranger, "but I chanced to meet him a little time previous to your stopping me. I believe you may trust his word, and that the Major will very shortly pass through this street. In the mean time, as I have a singular curiosity to witness your meeting, I will sit down here upon the steps and bear you company."

He seated himself accordingly, and soon engaged his companion in animated discourse. It was but of brief continuance, however, for a noise of shouting, which had long been remotely audible, drew so much nearer that Robin inquired its cause.

"What may be the meaning of this uproar?" asked he. "Truly, if your town be always as noisy, I shall find little sleep while I am an inhabitant."

"Why, indeed, friend Robin, there do appear to be three or four riotous fellows abroad to-night," replied the gentleman. "You must not expect all the stillness of your native woods here in our streets. But the watch will shortly be at the heels of these lads and"—

"Ay, and set them in the stocks by peep of day," interrupted Robin, recollecting his own encounter with the drowsy lantern-bearer. "But, dear sir, if I may trust my ears, an army of watchmen would never make head against such a multitude of rioters. There were at least a thousand voices went up to make that one shout."

"May not a man have several voices, Robin, as well as two complexions?" said his friend.

"Perhaps a man may; but Heaven forbid that a woman should!" responded the shrewd youth, thinking of the seductive tones of the Major's housekeeper.

The sounds of a trumpet in some neighboring street now became so evident and continual, that Robin's curiosity was strongly excited. In addition to the shouts, he heard frequent bursts from many instruments of discord, and a wild and confused laughter filled up the intervals. Robin rose from the steps, and looked wistfully towards a point whither people seemed to be hastening.

"Surely some prodigious merry-making is going on," exclaimed he. "I have laughed very little since I left home, sir, and should be sorry to lose an opportunity. Shall we step round the corner by that darkish house, and take our share of the fun?"

"Sit down again, sit down, good Robin," replied the gentleman, laying his hand on the skirt of the gray coat. "You forget that we must wait here for your kinsman; and there is reason to believe that he will pass by, in the course of a very few moments."

The near approach of the uproar had now disturbed the neighborhood; windows flew open on all sides: and many heads, in the attire of the pillow, and confused by sleep suddenly broken, were protruded to the gaze of whoever had leisure to observe them. Eager voices hailed each other from house to house, all demanding the explanation, which not a soul could give. Half-dressed men hurried towards the unknown commotion, stumbling as they went over the stone steps that thrust themselves into the narrow foot-walk. The shouts, the laughter, and the tuneless bray, the antipodes of music, came onwards with increasing din, till scattered individuals, and then denser bodies, began to appear round a corner at the distance of a hundred yards.

"Will you recognize your kinsman, if he passes in this crowd?" inquired the gentleman.

"Indeed, I can't warrant it, sir; but I'll take my stand here, and keep a bright lookout," answered Robin, descending to the outer edge of the pavement.

A mighty stream of people now emptied into the street, and came rolling slowly towards the church. A single horseman wheeled the corner in the midst of them, and close behind him came a band of fearful wind-instruments, sending forth a fresher discord now that no intervening buildings kept it from the ear. Then a redder light disturbed the moonbeams, and a dense multitude of torches shone along the street, concealing, by their glare, whatever object they illuminated. The single horseman, clad in a military dress, and bearing a drawn sword, rode onward as the leader, and, by his fierce and variegated countenance, appeared like war personified; the red of one cheek was an emblem of fire and sword; the blackness of the other betokened the mourning that attends them. In his train were wild figures in the Indian dress, and many fantastic shapes without a model, giving the whole march a visionary air, as if a dream had broken forth from some feverish brain, and were sweeping visibly through the midnight streets. A mass of people, inactive, except as applauding spectators, hemmed the procession in; and several women ran along the sidewalk, piercing the confusion of heavier sounds with their shrill voices of mirth or terror.

"The double-faced fellow has his eye upon me," muttered Robin, with an indefinite but an uncomfortable idea that he was himself to bear a part in the pageantry.

The leader turned himself in the saddle, and fixed his glance full upon the country youth, as the steed went slowly by. When Robin had freed his eyes from those fiery ones, the musicians were passing before him, and the torches were close at hand; but the unsteady brightness of the latter formed a veil which he could not penetrate. The rattling of wheels over the stones sometimes found its way to his ear, and confused traces of a human form appeared at intervals, and then melted into the vivid light.

A moment more, and the leader thundered a command to halt: the trumpets vomited a horrid breath, and then held their peace; the shouts and laughter of the people died away, and there remained only a universal hum, allied to silence. Right before Robin's eyes was an uncovered cart. There the torches blazed the brightest, there the moon shone out like day, and there, in tar-and-feathery dignity, sat his kinsman, Major Molineux!

He was an elderly man, of large and majestic person, and strong, square features, betokening a steady soul; but steady as it was, his enemies had found means to shake it. His face was pale as death, and far more ghastly; the broad forehead was contracted in his agony, so that his eyebrows formed one grizzled line; his eyes were red and wild, and the foam hung white upon his quivering lip. His whole frame was agitated by a quick and continual tremor, which his pride strove to quell, even in those circumstances of overwhelming humiliation. But perhaps the bitterest pang of all was when his eyes met those of Robin; for he evidently knew him on the instant, as the youth stood witnessing the foul disgrace of a head grown gray in honor. They stared at each other in silence, and Robin's knees shook, and his hair bristled, with a mixture of pity and terror. Soon, however, a bewildering excitement began to seize upon his mind; the preceding adventures of the night, the unexpected appearance of the crowd, the torches, the confused din and the hush that followed, the spectre of his kinsman reviled by that great multitude,—all this, and, more than all, a perception of tremendous ridicule in the whole scene, affected him with a sort of mental inebrity. At that moment a voice of sluggish merriment saluted Robin's ears; he turned instinctively, and just behind the corner of the church stood the lantern-bearer, rubbing his eyes, and drowsily enjoying the lad's amazement. Then he heard a peal of laughter like the ringing of silvery bells; a woman twitched his arm, a saucy eye met his, and he saw the lady of the scarlet petticoat. A sharp, dry cachinnation[16] appealed to his memory, and, standing on tiptoe in the crowd, with his white apron over his head, he beheld the courteous little innkeeper. And lastly, there sailed over the heads of the multitude a great, broad laugh, broken in the midst by two sepulchral hems; thus, "Haw, haw, haw,—hem, hem,—haw, haw, haw, haw!"

The sound proceeded from the balcony of the opposite edifice, and thither Robin turned his eyes. In front of the Gothic window stood the old citizen, wrapped in a wide gown, his gray periwig exchanged for a nightcap, which was thrust back from his forehead, and his silk stockings hanging about his legs. He supported himself on his polished cane in a fit of convulsive merriment, which manifested itself on his solemn old features like a funny inscription on a tomb-stone. Then Robin seemed to hear the voices of the barbers, of the guests of the inn, and of all who had made sport of him that night. The contagion was spreading among the multitude, when all at once, it seized upon Robin, and he sent forth a shout of laughter that echoed through the street,—every man shook his sides, every man emptied his lungs, but Robin's shout was the loudest there. The cloud-spirits peeped from their silvery islands, as the congregated mirth went roaring up the sky! The Man in the Moon heard the far bellow. "Oho," quoth he, "the old earth is frolicsome to-night!"

When there was a momentary calm in that tempestuous sea of sound, the leader gave the sign, the procession resumed its march. On they went, like fiends that throng

---

[16] Laugh.

in mockery around some dead potentate, mighty no more, but majestic still in his agony. On they went, in counterfeited pomp, in senseless uproar, in frenzied merriment, trampling all on an old man's heart. On swept the tumult, and left a silent street behind. . . .

"Well, Robin, are you dreaming?" inquired the gentleman, laying his hand on the youth's shoulder.

Robin started, and withdrew his arm from the stone post to which he had instinctively clung, as the living stream rolled by him. His cheek was somewhat pale, and his eye not quite as lively as in the earlier part of the evening.

"Will you be kind enough to show me the way to the ferry?" said he, after a moment's pause.

"You have, then, adopted a new subject of inquiry?" observed his companion, with a smile.

"Why, yes, sir," replied Robin, rather dryly. "Thanks to you, and to my other friends, I have at last met my kinsman, and he will scarce desire to see my face again. I begin to grow weary of a town life, sir. Will you show me the way to the ferry?"

"No, my good friend Robin,—not to-night, at least," said the gentleman. "Some few days hence, if you wish it, I will speed you on your journey. Or, if you prefer to remain with us, perhaps, as you are a shrewd youth, you may rise in the world without the help of your kinsman, Major Molineux."

1832

Young Goodman Brown

Young Goodman[1] Brown came forth at sunset into the street at Salem village; but put his head back, after crossing the threshold, to exchange a parting kiss with his young wife. And Faith, as the wife was aptly named, thrust her own pretty head into the street, letting the wind play with the pink ribbons of her cap while she called to Goodman Brown.

"Dearest heart," whispered she, softly and rather sadly, when her lips were close to his ear, "prithee put off your journey until sunrise and sleep in your own bed to-night. A lone woman is troubled with such dreams and such thoughts that she's afeard of herself sometimes. Pray tarry with me this night, dear husband, of all nights in the year."

"My love and my Faith," replied young Goodman Brown, "of all nights in the year, this one night must I tarry away from thee. My journey, as thou callest it, forth and back again, must needs be done 'twixt now and sunrise. What, my sweet, pretty wife, *dost thou doubt me already,* and we but three months married?"

[1] Polite term of address for a man of humble standing.

"Then God bless you!" said Faith, with the pink ribbons; "and may you find all well when you come back."

"Amen!" cried Goodman Brown. "Say thy prayers, dear Faith, and go to bed at dusk, and no harm will come to thee."

So they parted; and the young man pursued his way until, being about to turn the corner by the meeting-house, he looked back and saw the head of Faith still peeping after him with a melancholy air, in spite of her pink ribbons.

"Poor little Faith!" thought he, for his heart smote him. "What a wretch am I to leave her on such an errand! She talks of dreams, too. Methought as she spoke there was trouble in her face, as if a dream had warned her what work is to be done tonight. But no, no; 't would kill her to think it. Well, she's a blessed angel on earth; and after this one night I'll cling to her skirts and follow her to heaven."

With this excellent resolve for the future, Goodman Brown felt himself justified in making more haste on his present evil purpose. He had taken a dreary road, darkened by all the gloomiest trees of the forest, which barely stood aside to let the narrow path creep through, and closed immediately behind. It was all as lonely as could be; and there is this peculiarity in such a solitude, that the traveller knows not who may be concealed by the innumerable trunks and the thick boughs overhead; so that with lonely footsteps he may yet be passing through an unseen multitude.

"There may be a devilish Indian behind every tree," said Goodman Brown to himself; and he glanced fearfully behind him as he added, "What if the devil himself should be at my very elbow!"

His head being turned back, he passed a crook of the road, and, looking forward again, beheld the figure of a man, in grave and decent attire, seated at the foot of an old tree. He arose at Goodman Brown's approach and walked onward side by side with him.

"You are late, Goodman Brown," said he. "The clock of the Old South[2] was striking as I came through Boston, and that is full fifteen minutes agone."

"Faith kept me back a while," replied the young man, with a tremor in his voice, caused by the sudden appearance of his companion, though not wholly unexpected.

It was now deep dusk in the forest, and deepest in that part of it where these two were journeying. As nearly as could be discerned, the second traveller was about fifty years old, apparently in the same rank of life as Goodman Brown, and bearing a considerable resemblance to him, though perhaps more in expression than features. Still they might have been taken for father and son. And yet, though the elder person was as simply clad as the younger, and as simple in manner too, he had an indescribable air of one who knew the world, and who would not have felt abashed at the governor's dinner table or in King William's[3] court, were it possible that his affairs should call him thither. But the only thing about him that could be fixed upon as remarkable was his staff, which bore the likeness of a great black snake, so curiously wrought that it might almost be seen to twist and wriggle itself like a living serpent. This, of course, must have been an ocular deception, assisted by the uncertain light.

---

[2] Famous church in Boston.
[3] William III ruled England jointly with Queen Mary II from 1689 to 1702.

"Come, Goodman Brown," cried his fellow-traveller, "this is a dull pace for the beginning of a journey. Take my staff, if you are so soon weary."

"Friend," said the other, exchanging his slow pace for a full stop, "having kept covenant by meeting thee here, it is my purpose now to return whence I came. I have scruples touching the matter thou wot'st[4] of."

"Sayest thou so?" replied he of the serpent, smiling apart. "Let us walk on, nevertheless, reasoning as we go; and if I convince thee not thou shalt turn back. We are but a little way in the forest yet."

"Too far! too far!" exclaimed the goodman, unconsciously resuming his walk. "My father never went into the woods on such an errand, nor his father before him. We have been a race of honest men and good Christians since the days of the martyrs;[5] and shall I be the first of the name of Brown that ever took this path and kept"—

"Such company, thou wouldst say," observed the elder person, interpreting his pause. "Well said, Goodman Brown! I have been as well acquainted with your family as with ever a one among the Puritans; and that's no trifle to say. I helped your grandfather, the constable, when he lashed the Quaker woman so smartly through the streets of Salem; and it was I that brought your father a pitch-pine knot, kindled at my own hearth, to set fire to an Indian village, in King Philip's war.[6] They were my good friends, both; and many a pleasant walk have we had along this path, and returned merrily after midnight. I would fain be friends with you for their sake."

"If it be as thou sayest," replied Goodman Brown, "I marvel they never spoke of these matters; or, verily, I marvel not, seeing that the least rumor of the sort would have driven them from New England. We are a people of prayer, and good works to boot, and abide no such wickedness."

"Wickedness or not," said the traveller with the twisted staff, "I have a very general acquaintance here in New England. The deacons of many a church have drunk the communion wine with me; the selectmen of divers towns make me their chairman; and a majority of the Great and General Court[7] are firm supporters of my interest. The governor and I, too—But these are state secrets."

"Can this be so?" cried Goodman Brown, with a stare of amazement at his undisturbed companion. "Howbeit, I have nothing to do with the governor and council; they have their own ways, and are no rule for a simple husbandman[8] like me. But, were I to go on with thee, how should I meet the eye of that good old man, our minister, at Salem village? Oh, his voice would make me tremble both Sabbath day and lecture day."[9]

Thus far the elder traveller had listened with due gravity; but now burst into a fit of irrepressible mirth, shaking himself so violently that his snake-like staff actually seemed to wriggle in sympathy.

---

[4] Knowest.
[5] Allusion to the treatment of Protestants in England under the Catholic monarch Mary Tudor (1553–1558).
[6] War waged (1675–1676) against the New England colonists by the Indian leader Metacomset, also known as "King Philip."

[7] Legislature of the Puritan colony.
[8] Most often a farmer, but here a man of ordinary standing.
[9] Midweek sermon day, either Wednesday or Thursday.

"Ha! ha! ha!" shouted he again and again; then composing himself, "Well, go on, Goodman Brown, go on; but, prithee, don't kill me with laughing."

"Well, then, to end the matter at once," said Goodman Brown, considerably nettled, "there is my wife, Faith. It would break her dear little heart; and I'd rather break my own."

"Nay, if that be the case," answered the other, "e'en go thy ways, Goodman Brown. I would not for twenty old women like the one hobbling before us that Faith should come to any harm."

As he spoke he pointed his staff at a female figure on the path, in whom Goodman Brown recognized a very pious and exemplary dame, who had taught him his catechism in youth, and was still his moral and spiritual adviser, jointly with the minister and Deacon Gookin.

"A marvel, truly, that Goody[10] Cloyse[11] should be so far in the wilderness at nightfall," said he. "But with your leave, friend, I shall take a cut through the woods until we have left this Christian woman behind. Being a stranger to you, she might ask whom I was consorting with and whither I was going."

"Be it so," said his fellow-traveller. "Betake you to the woods, and let me keep the path."

Accordingly the young man turned aside, but took care to watch his companion, who advanced softly along the road until he had come within a staff's length of the old dame. She, meanwhile, was making the best of her way, with singular speed for so aged a woman, and mumbling some indistinct words—a prayer, doubtless—as she went. The traveller put forth his staff and touched her withered neck with what seemed the serpent's tail.

"The devil!" screamed the pious old lady.

"Then Goody Cloyse knows her old friend?" observed the traveller, confronting her and leaning on his writhing stick.

"Ah, forsooth, and is it your worship indeed?" cried the good dame. "Yea, truly is it, and in the very image of my old gossip, Goodman Brown, the grandfather of the silly fellow that now is. But—would your worship believe it?—my broomstick hath strangely disappeared, stolen, as I suspect, by that unhanged witch, Goody Cory, and that, too, when I was all anointed with the juice of smallage, and cinquefoil, and wolf's bane"[12]—

"Mingled with fine wheat and the fat of a new-born babe," said the shape of old Goodman Brown.

"Ah, your worship knows the recipe," cried the old lady, cackling aloud. "So, as I was saying, being all ready for the meeting, and no horse to ride on, I made up my mind to foot it; for they tell me there is a nice young man to be taken into communion to-night. But now your good worship will lend me your arm, and we shall be there in a twinkling."

"That can hardly be," answered her friend. "I may not spare you my arm, Goody Cloyse; but here is my staff, if you will."

---

[10] Contraction of "goodwife" and a polite term for a married woman of humble standing.

[11] Hawthorne uses given names (such as Cloyse and Cory) of people involved in the Salem witch trials.

[12] The plants mentioned here were associated with magic and witchcraft.

So saying, he threw it down at her feet, where, perhaps, it assumed life, being one of the rods which its owner had formerly lent to the Egyptian magi.[13] Of this fact, however, Goodman Brown could not take cognizance. He had cast up his eyes in astonishment, and, looking down again, beheld neither Goody Cloyse nor the serpentine staff, but his fellow-traveller alone, who waited for him as calmly as if nothing had happened.

"That old woman taught me my catechism," said the young man; and there was a world of meaning in this simple comment.

They continued to walk onward, while the elder traveller exhorted his companion to make good speed and persevere in the path, discoursing so aptly that his arguments seemed rather to spring up in the bosom of his auditor than to be suggested by himself. As they went, he plucked a branch of maple to serve for a walking stick, and began to strip it of the twigs and little boughs, which were wet with evening dew. The moment his fingers touched them they became strangely withered and dried up as with a week's sunshine. Thus the pair proceeded, at a good free pace, until suddenly, in a gloomy hollow of the road, Goodman Brown sat himself down on the stump of a tree and refused to go any farther.

"Friend," said he, stubbornly, "my mind is made up. Not another step will I budge on this errand. What if a wretched old woman do choose to go to the devil when I thought she was going to heaven: is that any reason why I should quit my dear Faith and go after her?"

"You will think better of this by and by," said his acquaintance, composedly. "Sit here and rest yourself a while; and when you feel like moving again, there is my staff to help you along."

Without more words, he threw his companion the maple stick, and was as speedily out of sight as if he had vanished into the deepening gloom. The young man sat a few moments by the roadside, applauding himself greatly, and thinking with how clear a conscience he should meet the minister in his morning walk, nor shrink from the eye of good old Deacon Gookin. And what calm sleep would be his that very night, which was to have been spent so wickedly, but so purely and sweetly now, in the arms of Faith! Amidst these pleasant and praiseworthy meditations, Goodman Brown heard the tramp of horses along the road, and deemed it advisable to conceal himself within the verge of the forest, conscious of the guilty purpose that had brought him thither, though now so happily turned from it.

On came the hoof tramps and the voices of the riders, two grave old voices, conversing soberly as they drew near. These mingled sounds appeared to pass along the road, within a few yards of the young man's hiding-place; but, owing doubtless to the depth of the gloom at that particular spot, neither the travellers nor their steeds were visible. Though their figures brushed the small boughs by the wayside, it could not be seen that they intercepted, even for a moment, the faint gleam from the strip of bright sky athwart which they must have passed. Goodman Brown alternately crouched and stood on tiptoe, pulling aside the branches and thrusting forth his head as far as he durst without discerning so much as a shadow. It vexed him the more, because he could have sworn, were such a thing possible, that he recognized the voices

[13] See Exodus 7 for a description of the Egyptian magicians who turned their rods into serpents.

of the minister and Deacon Gookin, jogging along quietly, as they were wont to do, when bound to some ordination or ecclesiastical council. While yet within hearing, one of the riders stopped to pluck a switch.

"Of the two, reverend sir," said the voice like the deacon's, "I had rather miss an ordination dinner than to-night's meeting. They tell me that some of our community are to be here from Falmouth[14] and beyond, and others from Connecticut and Rhode Island, besides several of the Indian powwows,[15] who, after their fashion, know almost as much deviltry as the best of us. Moreover, there is a goodly young woman to be taken into communion."

"Mighty well, Deacon Gookin!" replied the solemn old tones of the minister. "Spur up, or we shall be late. Nothing can be done, you know, until I get on the ground."

The hoofs clattered again; and the voices, talking so strangely in the empty air, passed on through the forest, where no church had ever been gathered or solitary Christian prayed. Whither, then, could these holy men be journeying so deep into the heathen wilderness? Young Goodman Brown caught hold of a tree for support, being ready to sink down on the ground, faint and overburdened with the heavy sickness of his heart. He looked up to the sky, doubting whether there really was a heaven above him. Yet there was the blue arch, and the stars brightening in it.

"With heaven above and Faith below, I will yet stand firm against the devil!" cried Goodman Brown.

While he still gazed upward into the deep arch of the firmament and had lifted his hands to pray, a cloud, though no wind was stirring, hurried across the zenith and hid the brightening stars. The blue sky was still visible, except directly overhead, where this black mass of cloud was sweeping swiftly northward. Aloft in the air, as if from the depths of the cloud, came a confused and doubtful sound of voices. Once the listener fancied that he could distinguish the accents of towns-people of his own, men and women, both pious and ungodly, many of whom he had met at the communion table, and had seen others rioting at the tavern. The next moment, so indistinct were the sounds, he doubted whether he had heard aught but the murmur of the old forest, whispering without a wind. Then came a stronger swell of those familiar tones, heard daily in the sunshine at Salem village, but never until now from a cloud of night. There was one voice, of a young woman, uttering lamentations, yet with an uncertain sorrow, and entreating for some favor, which, perhaps, it would grieve her to obtain; and all the unseen multitude, both saints and sinners, seemed to encourage her onward.

"Faith!" shouted Goodman Brown, in a voice of agony and desperation; and the echoes of the forest mocked him, crying, "Faith! Faith!" as if bewildered wretches were seeking her all through the wilderness.

The cry of grief, rage, and terror was yet piercing the night, when the unhappy husband held his breath for a response. There was a scream, drowned immediately in a louder murmur of voices, fading into far-off laughter, as the dark cloud swept away, leaving the clear and silent sky above Goodman Brown. But something fluttered

---

[14] Town on Cape Cod, 70 miles from Salem, Massachusetts.   [15] Medicine men.

lightly down through the air and caught on the branch of a tree. The young man seized it, and beheld a pink ribbon.

"My Faith is gone!" cried he, after one stupefied moment. "There is no good on earth; and sin is but a name. Come, devil; for to thee is this world given."

And, maddened with despair, so that he laughed loud and long, did Goodman Brown grasp his staff and set forth again, at such a rate that he seemed to fly along the forest path rather than to walk or run. The road grew wilder and drearier and more faintly traced, and vanished at length, leaving him in the heart of the dark wilderness, still rushing onward with the instinct that guides mortal man to evil. The whole forest was peopled with frightful sounds—the creaking of the trees, the howling of wild beasts, and the yell of Indians; while sometimes the wind tolled like a distant church bell, and sometimes gave a broad roar around the traveller, as if all Nature were laughing him to scorn. But he was himself the chief horror of the scene, and shrank not from its other horrors.

"Ha! ha! ha!" roared Goodman Brown when the wind laughed at him. "Let us hear which will laugh loudest. Think not to frighten me with your deviltry. Come witch, come wizard, come Indian powwow, come devil himself, and here comes Goodman Brown. You may as well fear him as he fear you."

In truth, all through the haunted forest there could be nothing more frightful than the figure of Goodman Brown. On he flew among the black pines, brandishing his staff with frenzied gestures, now giving vent to an inspiration of horrid blasphemy, and now shouting forth such laughter as set all the echoes of the forest laughing like demons around him. The fiend in his own shape is less hideous than when he rages in the breast of man. Thus sped the demoniac on his course, until, quivering among the trees, he saw a red light before him, as when the felled trunks and branches of a clearing have been set on fire, and throw up their lurid blaze against the sky, at the hour of midnight. He paused, in a lull of the tempest that had driven him onward, and heard the swell of what seemed a hymn, rolling solemnly from a distance with the weight of many voices. He knew the tune; it was a familiar one in the choir of the village meeting-house. The verse died heavily away, and was lengthened by a chorus, not of human voices, but of all the sounds of the benighted wilderness pealing in awful harmony together. Goodman Brown cried out, and his cry was lost to his own ear by its unison with the cry of the desert.

In the interval of silence he stole forward until the light glared full upon his eyes. At one extremity of an open space, hemmed in by the dark wall of the forest, arose a rock, bearing some rude, natural resemblance either to an altar or a pulpit, and surrounded by four blazing pines, their tops aflame, their stems untouched, like candles at an evening meeting. The mass of foliage that had overgrown the summit of the rock was all on fire, blazing high into the night and fitfully illuminating the whole field. Each pendent twig and leafy festoon was in a blaze. As the red light arose and fell, a numerous congregation alternately shone forth, then disappeared in shadow, and again grew, as it were, out of the darkness, peopling the heart of the solitary woods at once.

"A grave and dark-clad company," quoth Goodman Brown.

In truth they were such. Among them, quivering to and fro between gloom and splendor, appeared faces that would be seen next day at the council board of the province, and others which, Sabbath after Sabbath, looked devoutly heavenward, and benignantly over the crowded pews, from the holiest pulpits in the land. Some affirm that the lady of the governor was there. At least there were high dames well known to her, and wives of honored husbands, and widows, a great multitude, and ancient maidens, all of excellent repute, and fair young girls, who trembled lest their mothers should espy them. Either the sudden gleams of light flashing over the obscure field bedazzled Goodman Brown, or he recognized a score of the church members of Salem village famous for their especial sanctity. Good old Deacon Gookin had arrived, and waited at the skirts of that venerable saint, his revered pastor. But, irreverently consorting with these grave, reputable, and pious people, these elders of the church, these chaste dames and dewy virgins, there were men of dissolute lives and women of spotted fame, wretches given over to all mean and filthy vice, and suspected even of horrid crimes. It was strange to see that the good shrank not from the wicked, nor were the sinners abashed by the saints. Scattered also among their pale-faced enemies were the Indian priests, or powwows, who had often scared their native forest with more hideous incantations than any known to English witchcraft.

"But where is Faith?" thought Goodman Brown; and, as hope came into his heart, he trembled.

Another verse of the hymn arose, a slow and mournful strain, such as the pious love, but joined to words which expressed all that our nature can conceive of sin, and darkly hinted at far more. Unfathomable to mere mortals is the lore of fiends. Verse after verse was sung; and still the chorus of the desert swelled between like the deepest tone of a mighty organ; and with the final peal of that dreadful anthem there came a sound, as if the roaring wind, the rushing streams, the howling beasts, and every other voice of the unconcerted wilderness were mingling and according with the voice of guilty man in homage to the prince of all. The four blazing pines threw up a loftier flame, and obscurely discovered shapes and visages of horror on the smoke wreaths above the impious assembly. At the same moment the fire on the rock shot redly forth and formed a glowing arch above its base, where now appeared a figure. With reverence be it spoken, the figure bore no slight similitude, both in garb and manner, to some grave divine of the New England churches.

"Bring forth the converts!" cried a voice that echoed through the field and rolled into the forest.

At the word, Goodman Brown stepped forth from the shadow of the trees and approached the congregation, with whom he felt a loathful brotherhood by the sympathy of all that was wicked in his heart. He could have well-nigh sworn that the shape of his own dead father beckoned him to advance, looking downward from a smoke wreath, while a woman, with dim features of despair, threw out her hand to warn him back. Was it his mother? But he had no power to retreat one step, nor to resist, even in thought, when the minister and good old Deacon Gookin seized his arms and led him to the blazing rock. Thither came also the slender form of a veiled female, led between Goody Cloyse, that pious teacher of the catechism, and Martha Carrier,[16] who had received the devil's promise to be queen of hell. A rampant hag was she. And there stood the proselytes beneath the canopy of fire.

"Welcome, my children," said the dark figure, "to the communion of your race.

---

[16] Woman hanged in Salem in 1697 for claiming the devil had appointed her queen of hell.

You have found thus young your nature and your destiny. My children, look behind you!"

They turned; and flashing forth, as it were, in a sheet of flame, the fiend worshippers were seen; the smile of welcome gleamed darkly on every visage.

"There," resumed the sable form, "are all whom ye have reverenced from youth. Ye deemed them holier than yourselves, and shrank from your own sin, contrasting it with their lives of righteousness and prayerful aspirations heavenward. Yet here are they all in my worshipping assembly. This night it shall be granted you to know their secret deeds: how hoary-bearded elders of the church have whispered wanton words to the young maids of their households; how many a woman, eager for widows' weeds, has given her husband a drink at bedtime and let him sleep his last sleep in her bosom; how beardless youths have made haste to inherit their fathers' wealth; and how fair damsels—blush not, sweet ones—have dug little graves in the garden, and bidden me, the sole guest, to an infant's funeral. By the sympathy of your human hearts for sin ye shall scent out all the places—whether in church, bed-chamber, street, field, or forest—where crime has been committed, and shall exult to behold the whole earth one stain of guilt, one mighty blood spot. Far more than this. It shall be yours to penetrate, in every bosom, the deep mystery of sin, the fountain of all wicked arts, and which inexhaustibly supplies more evil impulses than human power—than my power at its utmost—can make manifest in deeds. And now, my children, look upon each other."

They did so; and, by the blaze of the hell-kindled torches, the wretched man beheld his Faith, and the wife her husband, trembling before that unhallowed altar.

"Lo, there ye stand, my children," said the figure, in a deep and solemn tone, almost sad with its despairing awfulness, as if his once angelic nature could yet mourn for our miserable race. "Depending upon one another's hearts, ye had still hoped that virtue were not all a dream. Now are ye undeceived. Evil is the nature of mankind. Evil must be your only happiness. Welcome again, my children, to the communion of your race."

"Welcome," repeated the fiend worshippers, in one cry of despair and triumph.

And there they stood, the only pair, as it seemed, who were yet hesitating on the verge of wickedness in this dark world. A basin was hollowed, naturally, in the rock. Did it contain water, reddened by the lurid light? or was it blood? or, perchance, a liquid flame? Herein did the shape of evil dip his hand and prepare to lay the mark of baptism upon their foreheads, that they might be partakers of the mystery of sin, more conscious of the secret guilt of others, both in deed and thought, than they could now be of their own. The husband cast one look at his pale wife, and Faith at him. What polluted wretches would the next glance show them to each other, shuddering alike at what they disclosed and what they saw!

"Faith! Faith!" cried the husband, "look up to heaven, and resist the wicked one."

Whether Faith obeyed he knew not. Hardly had he spoken when he found himself amid calm night and solitude, listening to a roar of the wind which died heavily away through the forest. He staggered against the rock, and felt it chill and damp; while a hanging twig, that had been all on fire, besprinkled his cheek with the coldest dew.

The next morning young Goodman Brown came slowly into the street of Salem village, staring around him like a bewildered man. The good old minister was taking a walk along the graveyard to get an appetite for breakfast and meditate his sermon, and bestowed a blessing, as he passed, on Goodman Brown. He shrank from the venerable saint as if to avoid an anathema. Old Deacon Gookin was at domestic worship, and the holy words of his prayer were heard through the open window. "What God doth the wizard pray to?" quoth Goodman Brown. Goody Cloyse, that excellent old Christian, stood in the early sunshine at her own lattice, catechizing a little girl who had brought her a pint of morning's milk. Goodman Brown snatched away the child as from the grasp of the fiend himself. Turning the corner by the meeting-house, he spied the head of Faith, with the pink ribbons, gazing anxiously forth, and bursting into such joy at sight of him that she skipped along the street and almost kissed her husband before the whole village. But Goodman Brown looked sternly and sadly into her face, and passed on without a greeting.

Had Goodman Brown fallen asleep in the forest and only dreamed a wild dream of a witch-meeting?

Be it so if you will; but, alas! it was a dream of evil omen for young Goodman Brown. A stern, a sad, a darkly meditative, a distrustful, if not a desperate man did he become from the night of that fearful dream. On the Sabbath day, when the congregation were singing a holy psalm, he could not listen because an anthem of sin rushed loudly upon his ear and drowned all the blessed strain. When the minister spoke from the pulpit with power and fervid eloquence, and, with his hand on the open Bible, of the sacred truths of our religion, and of saint-like lives and triumphant deaths, and of future bliss or misery unutterable, then did Goodman Brown turn pale, dreading lest the roof should thunder down upon the gray blasphemer and his hearers. Often, awaking suddenly at midnight, he shrank from the bosom of Faith; and at morning or eventide, when the family knelt down at prayer, he scowled and muttered to himself, and gazed sternly at his wife, and turned away. And when he had lived long, and was borne to his grave a hoary corpse, followed by Faith, an aged woman, and children and grandchildren, a goodly procession, besides neighbors not a few, they carved no hopeful verse upon his tombstone, for his dying hour was gloom.

1835

Wakefield

In some old magazine or newspaper I recollect a story, told as truth, of a man—let us call him Wakefield—who absented himself for a long time from his wife. The fact, thus abstractedly stated, is not very uncommon, nor—without a proper distinction of circumstances—to be condemned either as naughty or nonsensical. Howbeit, this, though far from the most aggravated, is perhaps the strangest, instance on record, of marital delinquency; and, moreover, as remarkable a freak as may be found in the whole list of human oddities. The wedded couple lived in London. The man, under pretence of going a journey, took lodgings in the next street to his own house, and there, unheard of by his wife or friends, and without the shadow of a reason for such self-banishment, dwelt upwards of twenty years. During that period, he beheld his home every day, and frequently the forlorn Mrs. Wakefield. And after so great a gap in his matrimonial felicity—when his death was reckoned certain, his estate settled, his name dismissed from memory, and his wife, long, long ago, resigned to her autumnal widowhood—he entered the door one evening, quietly, as from a day's absence, and became a loving spouse till death.

This outline is all that I remember. But the incident, though of the purest originality, unexampled, and probably never to be repeated, is one, I think, which appeals to the generous sympathies of mankind. We know, each for himself, that none of us would perpetrate such a folly, yet feel as if some other might. To my own contemplations, at least, it has often recurred, always exciting wonder, but with a sense that the story must be true, and a conception of its hero's character. Whenever any subject so forcibly affects the mind, time is well spent in thinking of it. If the reader choose, let him do his own meditation; or if he prefer to ramble with me through the twenty years of Wakefield's vagary, I bid him welcome; trusting that there will be a pervading spirit and a moral, even should we fail to find them, done up neatly, and condensed into the final sentence. Thought has always its efficacy, and every striking incident its moral.

What sort of a man was Wakefield? We are free to shape out our own idea, and call it by his name. He was now in the meridian of life; his matrimonial affections, never violent, were sobered into a calm, habitual sentiment; of all husbands, he was likely to be the most constant, because a certain sluggishness would keep his heart at rest, wherever it might be placed. He was intellectual, but not actively so; his mind occupied itself in long and lazy musings, that ended to no purpose, or had not vigor to attain it; his thoughts were seldom so energetic as to seize hold of words. Imagination, in the proper meaning of the term, made no part of Wakefield's gifts. With a cold but not depraved nor wandering heart, and a mind never feverish with riotous thoughts, nor perplexed with originality, who could have anticipated that our friend would entitle himself to a foremost place among the doers of eccentric deeds? Had his acquaintances been asked, who was the man in London the surest to perform nothing to-day which should be remembered on the morrow, they would have thought of Wakefield. Only the wife of his bosom might have hesitated. She, without having analyzed his character, was partly aware of a quiet selfishness, that had rusted into his inactive mind; of a peculiar sort of vanity, the most uneasy attribute about him; of a disposition to craft, which had seldom produced more positive effects than the keeping of petty secrets, hardly worth revealing; and, lastly, of what she called a little strangeness, sometimes, in the good man. This latter quality is indefinable, and perhaps non-existent.

Let us now imagine Wakefield bidding adieu to his wife. It is the dusk of an October evening. His equipment is a drab great-coat, a hat covered with an oilcloth, top-boots, an umbrella in one hand and a small portmanteau in the other. He has informed Mrs. Wakefield that he is to take the night coach into the country. She would fain inquire the length of his journey, its object, and the probable time of his return; but, indulgent to his harmless love of mystery, interrogates him only by a look. He tells her not to expect him positively by the return coach, nor to be alarmed should he tarry three or four days; but, at all events, to look for him at supper on Friday evening. Wakefield himself, be it considered, has no suspicion of what is before him. He holds out his hand, she gives her own, and meets his parting kiss in the matter-of-course way of a ten years' matrimony; and forth goes the middle-aged Mr. Wakefield, almost resolved to perplex his good lady by a whole week's absence. After the door has closed behind him, she perceives it thrust partly open, and a vision of her husband's face, through the aperture, smiling on her, and gone in a moment. For the time, this little incident is dismissed without a thought. But, long afterwards, when she has been more years a widow than a wife, that smile recurs, and flickers across all her reminiscences of Wakefield's visage. In her many musings, she surrounds the original smile with a multitude of fantasies, which make it strange and awful: as, for instance, if she imagines him in a coffin, that parting look is frozen on his pale features; or, if she dreams of him in heaven, still his blessed spirit wears a quiet and crafty smile. Yet, for its sake, when all others have given him up for dead, she sometimes doubts whether she is a widow.

But our business is with the husband. We must hurry after him along the street, ere he lose his individuality, and melt into the great mass of London life. It would be vain searching for him there. Let us follow close at his heels, therefore, until, after several superfluous turns and doublings, we find him comfortably established by the fireside of a small apartment, previously bespoken. He is in the next street to his own, and at his journey's end. He can scarcely trust his good fortune, in having got thither unperceived—recollecting that, at one time, he was delayed by the throng, in the very focus of a lighted lantern; and, again, there were footsteps that seemed to tread behind his own, distinct from the multitudinous tramp around him; and, anon, he heard a voice shouting afar, and fancied that it called his name. Doubtless, a dozen busybodies had been watching him, and told his wife the whole affair. Poor Wakefield! Little knowest thou thine own insignificance in this great world! No mortal eye but mine has traced thee. Go quietly to thy bed, foolish man; and, on the morrow, if thou wilt be wise, get thee home to good Mrs. Wakefield, and tell her the truth. Remove not thyself, even for a little week, from thy place in her chaste bosom. Were she, for a single moment, to deem thee dead, or lost, or lastingly divided from her, thou wouldst be wofully conscious of a change in thy true wife forever after. It is perilous to make a chasm in human affections; not that they gape so long and wide—but so quickly close again!

Almost repenting of his frolic, or whatever it may be termed, Wakefield lies down betimes, and starting from his first nap, spreads forth his arms into the wide and solitary waste of the unaccustomed bed. "No,"—thinks he, gathering the bedclothes about him,—"I will not sleep alone another night."

In the morning he rises earlier than usual, and sets himself to consider what he really means to do. Such are his loose and rambling modes of thought that he has taken this very singular step with the consciousness of a purpose, indeed, but without being able to define it sufficiently for his own contemplation. The vagueness of the project, and the convulsive effort with which he plunges into the execution of it, are equally characteristic of a feeble-minded man. Wakefield sifts his ideas, however, as minutely as he may, and finds himself curious to know the progress of matters at home—how his exemplary wife will endure her widowhood of a week; and, briefly, how the little sphere of creatures and circumstances, in which he was a central object, will be affected by his removal. A morbid vanity, therefore, lies nearest the bottom of the affair. But, how is he to attain his ends? Not, certainly, by keeping close in this comfortable lodging, where, though he slept and awoke in the next street to his home, he is as effectually abroad as if the stage-coach had been whirling him away all night. Yet, should he reappear, the whole project is knocked in the head. His poor brains being hopelessly puzzled with this dilemma, he at length ventures out, partly resolving to cross the head of the street, and send one hasty glance towards his forsaken domicile. Habit—for he is a man of habits—takes him by the hand, and guides him, wholly unaware, to his own door, where, just at the critical moment, he is aroused by the scraping of his foot upon the step. Wakefield! whither are you going?

At that instant his fate was turning on the pivot. Little dreaming of the doom to which his first backward step devotes him, he hurries away, breathless with agitation hitherto unfelt, and hardly dares turn his head at the distant corner. Can it be that nobody caught sight of him? Will not the whole household—the decent Mrs. Wakefield, the smart maid servant, and the dirty little footboy—raise a hue and cry, through London streets, in pursuit of their fugitive lord and master? Wonderful escape! He gathers courage to pause and look homeward, but is perplexed with a sense of change about the familiar edifice, such as affects us all, when, after a separation of months or years, we again see some hill or lake, or work of art, with which we were friends of old. In ordinary cases, this indescribable impression is caused by the comparison and contrast between our imperfect reminiscences and the reality. In Wakefield, the magic of a single night has wrought a similar transformation, because, in that brief period, a great moral change has been effected. But this is a secret from himself. Before leaving the spot, he catches a far and momentary glimpse of his wife, passing athwart the front window, with her face turned towards the head of the street. The crafty nincompoop takes to his heels, scared with the idea that, among a thousand such atoms of mortality, her eye must have detected him. Right glad is his heart, though his brain be somewhat dizzy, when he finds himself by the coal fire of his lodgings.

So much for the commencement of this long whim-wham. After the initial conception, and the stirring up of the man's sluggish temperament to put it in practice, the whole matter evolves itself in a natural train. We may suppose him, as the result of deep deliberation, buying a new wig, of reddish hair, and selecting sundry garments, in a fashion unlike his customary suit of brown, from a Jew's old-clothes bag. It is accomplished. Wakefield is another man. The new system being now established, a retrograde movement to the old would be almost as difficult as the step that placed him in his unparalleled position. Furthermore, he is rendered obstinate by a sulkiness occasionally incident to his temper, and brought on at present by the inadequate sensation which he conceives to have been produced in the bosom of Mrs. Wakefield. He will not go back until she be frightened half to death. Well; twice or thrice has she passed before his sight, each time with a heavier step, a paler cheek, and more anxious brow; and in the third week of his non-appearance he detects a portent of evil entering the house, in the guise of an apothecary. Next day the knocker is muffled. Towards nightfall comes the chariot of a physician, and deposits its big-wigged and solemn burden at Wakefield's door, whence, after a quarter of an hour's visit, he emerges, perchance the herald of a funeral. Dear woman! Will she die? By this time, Wakefield is excited to something like energy of feeling, but still lingers away from his wife's bedside, pleading with his conscience that she must not be disturbed at such a juncture. If aught else restrains him, he does not know it. In the course of a few weeks she gradually recovers; the crisis is over; her heart is sad, perhaps, but quiet; and, let him return soon or late, it will never be feverish for him again. Such ideas glimmer through the mist of Wakefield's mind, and render him indistinctly conscious that an almost impassable gulf divides his hired apartment from his former home. "It is but in the next street!" he sometimes says. Fool! it is in another world. Hitherto, he has put off his return from one particular day to another; henceforward, he leaves the precise time undetermined. Not to-morrow—probably next week—pretty soon. Poor man! The dead have nearly as much chance of revisiting their earthly homes as the self-banished Wakefield.

Would that I had a folio to write, instead of an article of a dozen pages! Then might I exemplify how an influence beyond our control lays its strong hand on every deed which we do, and weaves its consequences into an iron tissue of necessity. Wakefield is spell-bound. We must leave him, for ten years or so, to haunt around his house, without once crossing the threshold, and to be faithful to his wife, with all the affection of which his heart is capable, while he is slowly fading out of hers. Long since, it must be remarked, he had lost the perception of singularity in his conduct.

Now for a scene! Amid the throng of a London street we distinguish a man, now waxing elderly, with few characteristics to attract careless observers, yet bearing, in his whole aspect, the handwriting of no common fate, for such as have the skill to read it. He is meagre; his low and narrow forehead is deeply wrinkled; his eyes, small and lustreless, sometimes wander apprehensively about him, but oftener seem to look inward. He bends his head, and moves with an indescribable obliquity of gait, as if unwilling to display his full front to the world. Watch him long enough to see what we have described, and you will allow that circumstances—which often produce remarkable men from nature's ordinary handiwork—have produced one such here. Next, leaving him to sidle along the footwalk, cast your eyes in the opposite direction, where a portly female, considerably in the wane of life, with a prayer-book in her hand, is proceeding to yonder church. She has the placid mien of settled widowhood. Her regrets have either died away, or have become so essential to her heart, that they would be poorly exchanged for joy. Just as the lean man and well-conditioned woman are passing, a slight obstruction occurs, and brings these two figures directly in contact. Their hands touch; the pressure of the crowd forces her bosom against his shoulder; they stand, face to face, staring into each other's eyes. After a ten years' separation, thus Wakefield meets his wife!

The throng eddies away, and carries them asunder. The sober widow, resuming her former pace, proceeds to church, but pauses in the portal, and throws a perplexed glance along the street. She passes in, however, opening her prayer-book as she goes. And the man! with so wild a face that busy and selfish London stands to gaze after him, he hurries to his lodgings, bolts the door, and throws himself upon the bed. The latent feelings of years break out; his feeble mind acquires a brief energy from their strength; all the miserable strangeness of his life is revealed to him at a glance: and he cries out, passionately, "Wakefield! Wakefield! You are mad!"

Perhaps he was so. The singularity of his situation must have so moulded him to himself, that, considered in regard to his fellow-creatures and the business of life, he could not be said to possess his right mind. He had contrived, or rather he had happened, to dissever himself from the world—to vanish—to give up his place and privileges with living men, without being admitted among the dead. The life of a hermit is nowise parallel to his. He was in the bustle of the city, as of old; but the crowd swept by and saw him not; he was, we may figuratively say, always beside his wife and at his hearth, yet must never feel the warmth of the one nor the affection of the other. It was Wakefield's unprecedented fate to retain his original share of human sympathies, and to be still involved in human interests, while he had lost his reciprocal influence on them. It would be a most curious speculation to trace out the effect of such circumstances on his heart and intellect, separately, and in unison. Yet, changed as he was, he would seldom be conscious of it, but deem himself the same man as ever; glimpses of the truth, indeed, would come, but only for the moment; and still he would keep saying, "I shall soon go back!"—nor reflect that he had been saying so for twenty years.

I conceive, also, that these twenty years would appear, in the retrospect, scarcely longer than the week to which Wakefield had at first limited his absence. He would look on the affair as no more than an interlude in the main business of his life. When, after a little while more, he should deem it time to reënter his parlor, his wife would clap her hands for joy, on beholding the middle-aged Mr. Wakefield. Alas, what a mistake! Would Time but await the close of our favorite follies, we should be young men, all of us, and till Doomsday.

One evening, in the twentieth year since he vanished, Wakefield is taking his customary walk towards the dwelling which he still calls his own. It is a gusty night of autumn, with frequent showers that patter down upon the pavement, and are gone before a man can put up his umbrella. Pausing near the house, Wakefield discerns, through the parlor windows of the second floor, the red glow and the glimmer and fitful flash of a comfortable fire. On the ceiling appears a grotesque shadow of good Mrs. Wakefield. The cap, the nose and chin, and the broad waist, form an admirable caricature, which dances, moreover, with the up-flickering and down-sinking blaze, almost too merrily for the shade of an elderly widow. At this instant a shower chances to fall, and is driven, by the unmannerly gust, full into Wakefield's face and bosom. He is quite penetrated with its autumnal chill. Shall he stand, wet and shivering here, when his own hearth has a good fire to warm him, and his own wife will run to fetch the gray coat and small-clothes, which, doubtless, she has kept carefully in the closet of their bed chamber? No! Wakefield is no such fool. He ascends the steps—heavily! —for twenty years have stiffened his legs since he came down—but he knows it not. Stay, Wakefield! Would you go to the sole home that is left you? Then step into your grave! The door opens. As he passes in, we have a parting glimpse of his visage, and recognize the crafty smile, which was the precursor of the little joke that he has ever since been playing off at his wife's expense. How unmercifully has he quizzed the poor woman! Well, a good night's rest to Wakefield!

This happy event—supposing it to be such—could only have occurred at an unpremeditated moment. We will not follow our friend across the threshold. He has left us much food for thought, a portion of which shall lend its wisdom to a moral, and be shaped into a figure. Amid the seeming confusion of our mysterious world, individuals are so nicely adjusted to a system, and systems to one another and to a whole, that, by stepping aside for a moment, a man exposes himself to a fearful risk of losing his place forever. Like Wakefield, he may become, as it were, the Outcast of the Universe.

1835

The Maypole of Merry Mount[1]

There is an admirable foundation for a philosophic romance in the curious history of the early settlement of Mount Wollaston, or Merry Mount. In the slight sketch here attempted, the facts, recorded on the grave pages of our New England annalists, have wrought themselves, almost spontaneously, into a sort of allegory. The masques, mummeries, and festive customs, described in the text, are in accordance with the manners of the age. Authority on these points may be found in Strutt's Book of English Sports and Pastimes.[2]

Bright were the days at Merry Mount, when the Maypole[3] was the banner staff of that gay colony! They who reared it, should their banner be triumphant, were to pour sunshine over New England's rugged hills, and scatter flower seeds throughout the soil. Jollity and gloom were contending for an empire. Midsummer eve[4] had come, bringing deep verdure to the forest, and roses in her lap, of a more vivid hue than the tender buds of Spring. But May, or her mirthful spirit, dwelt all the year round at Merry Mount, sporting with the Summer months, and revelling with Autumn, and basking in the glow of Winter's fireside. Through a world of toil and care she flitted with a dreamlike smile, and came hither to find a home among the lightsome hearts of Merry Mount.

Never had the Maypole been so gayly decked as at sunset on midsummer eve. This venerated emblem was a pine-tree, which had preserved the slender grace of youth, while it equalled the loftiest height of the old wood monarchs. From its top streamed a silken banner, colored like the rainbow. Down nearly to the ground the pole was dressed with birchen boughs, and others of the liveliest green, and some with silvery leaves, fastened by ribbons that fluttered in fantastic knots of twenty different colors, but no sad ones. Garden flowers, and blossoms of the wilderness, laughed gladly forth amid the verdure, so fresh and dewy that they must have grown by magic on that happy pinetree. Where this green and flowery splendor terminated, the shaft of the Maypole was stained with the seven brilliant hues of the banner at its top. On the lowest green bough hung an abundant wreath of roses, some that had been gathered in the sunniest spots of the forest, and others, of still richer blush, which the colonists had reared from English seed. O, people of the Golden Age, the chief of your husbandry was to raise flowers!

But what was the wild throng that stood hand in hand about the Maypole? It could not be that the fauns and nymphs, when driven from their classic groves and homes of ancient fable, had sought refuge, as all the persecuted did, in the fresh woods of the West. These were Gothic monsters, though perhaps of Grecian ancestry. On the shoulders of a comely youth uprose the head and branching antlers of a stag; a second, human in all other points, had the grim visage of a wolf; a third, still with the trunk

---

[1] For additional information on the colony of Merry Mount, see William Bradford's *Of Plymouth Plantation.*

[2] Joseph Strutt, *The Sports and Pastimes of the People of England* (1801).

[3] The tall, flower-wreathed pole that is the chief symbol of May Day. Participants in May Day celebrations dressed in outlandish paganlike costumes and wore animal masks; the Puritans condemned these activities as licentious.

[4] The evening before Midsummer Day (June 24), which is the celebration of the nativity of John the Baptist.

and limbs of a mortal man, showed the beard and horns of a venerable he-goat. There was the likeness of a bear erect, brute in all but his hind legs, which were adorned with pink silk stockings. And here again, almost as wondrous, stood a real bear of the dark forest, lending each of his fore paws to the grasp of a human hand, and as ready for the dance as any in that circle. His inferior nature rose half way, to meet his companions as they stooped. Other faces wore the similitude of man or woman, but distorted or extravagant, with red noses pendulous before their mouths, which seemed of awful depth, and stretched from ear to ear in an eternal fit of laughter. Here might be seen the Salvage Man,[5] well known in heraldry, hairy as a baboon, and girdled with green leaves. By his side, a noble figure, but still a counterfeit, appeared an Indian hunter, with feathery crest and wampum belt. Many of this strange company wore foolscaps, and had little bells appended to their garments, tinkling with a silvery sound, responsive to the inaudible music of their gleesome spirits. Some youths and maidens were of soberer garb, yet well maintained their places in the irregular throng by the expression of wild revelry upon their features. Such were the colonists of Merry Mount, as they stood in the broad smile of sunset round their venerated Maypole.

Had a wanderer, bewildered in the melancholy forest, heard their mirth, and stolen a half-affrighted glance, he might have fancied them the crew of Comus,[6] some already transformed to brutes, some midway between man and beast, and the others rioting in the flow of tipsy jollity that foreran the change. But a band of Puritans, who watched the scene, invisible themselves, compared the masques to those devils and ruined souls with whom their superstition peopled the black wilderness.

Within the ring of monsters appeared the two airiest forms that had ever trodden on any more solid footing than a purple and golden cloud. One was a youth in glistening apparel, with a scarf of the rainbow pattern crosswise on his breast. His right hand held a gilded staff, the ensign[7] of high dignity among the revellers, and his left grasped the slender fingers of a fair maiden, not less gayly decorated than himself. Bright roses glowed in contrast with the dark and glossy curls of each, and were scattered round their feet, or had sprung up spontaneously there. Behind this lightsome couple, so close to the Maypole that its boughs shaded his jovial face, stood the figure of an English priest, canonically dressed, yet decked with flowers, in heathen fashion, and wearing a chaplet[8] of the native vine leaves. By the riot of his rolling eye, and the pagan decorations of his holy garb, he seemed the wildest monster there, and the very Comus of the crew.

"Votaries[9] of the Maypole," cried the flower-decked priest, "merrily, all day long, have the woods echoed to your mirth. But be this your merriest hour, my hearts! Lo, here stand the Lord and Lady of the May, whom I, a clerk[10] of Oxford, and high priest of Merry Mount, am presently to join in holy matrimony. Up with your nimble spirits, ye morris-dancers, green men, and glee maidens,[11] bears and wolves, and horned gentlemen! Come; a chorus now, rich with the old mirth of Merry England, and the wilder glee of this fresh forest; and then a dance, to show the youthful pair what life

---

[5] Someone dressed in foliage to represent a savage.
[6] The classical god of merrymaking, here associated with John Milton's poem "Comus."
[7] Symbolic emblem or flag.
[8] Wreath.

[9] Devotees.
[10] One who assists the clergyman.
[11] Morris dancers, green men, and glee maidens were all part of the traditional May Day celebrations.

is made of, and how airily they should go through it! All ye that love the Maypole, lend your voices to the nuptial song of the Lord and Lady of the May!"

This wedlock was more serious than most affairs of Merry Mount, where jest and delusion, trick and fantasy, kept up a continual carnival. The Lord and Lady of the May, though their titles must be laid down at sunset, were really and truly to be partners for the dance of life, beginning the measure that same bright eve. The wreath of roses, that hung from the lowest green bough of the Maypole, had been twined for them, and would be thrown over both their heads, in symbol of their flowery union. When the priest had spoken, therefore, a riotous uproar burst from the rout of monstrous figures.

"Begin you the stave,[12] reverend Sir," cried they all; "and never did the woods ring to such a merry peal as we of the Maypole shall send up!"

Immediately a prelude of pipe, cithern,[13] and viol, touched with practised minstrelsy, began to play from a neighboring thicket, in such a mirthful cadence that the boughs of the Maypole quivered to the sound. But the May Lord, he of the gilded staff, chancing to look into his Lady's eyes, was wonder struck at the almost pensive glance that met his own.

"Edith, sweet Lady of the May," whispered he reproachfully, "is yon wreath of roses a garland to hang above our graves, that you look so sad? O, Edith, this is our golden time! Tarnish it not by any pensive shadow of the mind; for it may be that nothing of futurity will be brighter than the mere remembrance of what is now passing."

"That was the very thought that saddened me! How came it in your mind too?" said Edith, in a still lower tone than he, for it was high treason to be sad at Merry Mount. "Therefore do I sigh amid this festive music. And besides, dear Edgar, I struggle as with a dream, and fancy that these shapes of our jovial friends are visionary, and their mirth unreal, and that we are no true Lord and Lady of the May. What is the mystery in my heart?"

Just then, as if a spell had loosened them, down came a little shower of withering rose leaves from the Maypole. Alas, for the young lovers! No sooner had their hearts glowed with real passion than they were sensible of something vague and unsubstantial in their former pleasures, and felt a dreary presentiment of inevitable change. From the moment that they truly loved, they had subjected themselves to earth's doom of care and sorrow, and troubled joy, and had no more a home at Merry Mount. That was Edith's mystery. Now leave we the priest to marry them, and the masquers to sport round the Maypole, till the last sunbeam be withdrawn from its summit, and the shadows of the forest mingle gloomily in the dance. Meanwhile, we may discover who these gay people were.

Two hundred years ago, and more, the old world and its inhabitants became mutually weary of each other. Men voyaged by thousands to the West: some to barter glass beads, and such like jewels, for the furs of the Indian hunter; some to conquer virgin empires; and one stern band to pray. But none of these motives had much weight with the colonists of Merry Mount. Their leaders were men who had sported so long with life, that when Thought and Wisdom came, even these unwelcome guests were led astray by the crowd of vanities which they should have put to flight. Erring

---

[12] Stanza.　　　　　　　　　　　　[13] Cittern or lute.

Thought and perverted Wisdom were made to put on masques, and play the fool. The men of whom we speak, after losing the heart's fresh gayety, imagined a wild philosophy of pleasure, and came hither to act out their latest day-dream. They gathered followers from all that giddy tribe whose whole life is like the festal[14] days of soberer men. In their train were minstrels, not unknown in London streets: wandering players, whose theatres had been the halls of noblemen; mummers,[15] rope-dancers, and mountebanks,[16] who would long be missed at wakes, church ales, and fairs; in a word, mirth makers of every sort, such as abounded in that age, but now began to be discountenanced by the rapid growth of Puritanism. Light had their footsteps been on land, and as lightly they came across the sea. Many had been maddened by their previous troubles into a gay despair; others were as madly gay in the flush of youth, like the May Lord and his Lady; but whatever might be the quality of their mirth, old and young were gay at Merry Mount. The young deemed themselves happy. The elder spirits, if they knew that mirth was but the counterfeit of happiness, yet followed the false shadow wilfully, because at least her garments glittered brightest. Sworn triflers of a lifetime, they would not venture among the sober truths of life not even to be truly blest.

All the hereditary pastimes of Old England were transplanted hither. The King of Christmas was duly crowned, and the Lord of Misrule[17] bore potent sway. On the Eve of St. John,[18] they felled whole acres of the forest to make bonfires, and danced by the blaze all night, crowned with garlands, and throwing flowers into the flame. At harvest time, though their crop was of the smallest, they made an image with the sheaves of Indian corn, and wreathed it with autumnal garlands, and bore it home triumphantly. But what chiefly characterized the colonists of Merry Mount was their veneration for the Maypole. It has made their true history a poet's tale. Spring decked the hallowed emblem with young blossoms and fresh green boughs; Summer brought roses of the deepest blush, and the perfected foli-age of the forest; Autumn enriched it with that red and yellow gorgeousness which converts each wildwood leaf into a painted flower; and Winter silvered it with sleet, and hung it round with icicles, till it flashed in the cold sunshine, itself a frozen sunbeam. Thus each alternate season did homage to the Maypole, and paid it a tribute of its own richest splendor. Its votaries danced round it, once, at least, in every month; sometimes they called it their religion, or their altar; but always, it was the banner staff of Merry Mount.

Unfortunately, there were men in the new world of a sterner faith than these Maypole worshippers. Not far from Merry Mount was a settlement of Puritans, most dismal wretches, who said their prayers before daylight, and then wrought in the forest or the cornfield till evening made it prayer time again. Their weapons were always at hand to shoot down the straggling savage. When they met in conclave, it was never to keep up the old English mirth, but to hear sermons three hours long, or to proclaim bounties on the heads of wolves and the scalps of Indians. Their festivals were fast days, and their chief pastime the singing of psalms. Woe to the youth or maiden who did but dream of a dance! The selectman nodded to the constable; and there sat the

---

[14] Festive.
[15] Costumed revelers.
[16] Street venders who peddle quack medicines.

[17] Leader of Christmas revelry.
[18] June 23, Midsummer's Eve.

light-heeled reprobate in the stocks; or if he danced, it was round the whipping-post, which might be termed the Puritan Maypole.

A party of these grim Puritans, toiling through the difficult woods, each with a horseload of iron armor to burden his footsteps, would sometimes draw near the sunny precincts of Merry Mount. There were the silken colonists, sporting round their Maypole; perhaps teaching a bear to dance, or striving to communicate their mirth to the grave Indian; or masquerading in the skins of deer and wolves, which they had hunted for that especial purpose. Often, the whole colony were playing at blindman's buff, magistrates and all, with their eyes bandaged, except a single scapegoat, whom the blinded sinners pursued by the tinkling of the bells at his garments. Once, it is said, they were seen following a flower-decked corpse, with merriment and festive music, to his grave. But did the dead man laugh? In their quietest times, they sang ballads and told tales, for the edification of their pious visitors; or perplexed them with juggling tricks; or grinned at them through horse collars; and when sport itself grew wearisome, they made game of their own stupidity, and began a yawning match. At the very least of these enormities, the men of iron shook their heads and frowned so darkly that the revellers looked up, imagining that a momentary cloud had overcast the sunshine, which was to be perpetual there. On the other hand, the Puritans affirmed that, when a psalm was pealing from their place of worship, the echo which the forest sent them back seemed often like the chorus of a jolly catch, closing with a roar of laughter. Who but the fiend, and his bond slaves, the crew of Merry Mount, had thus disturbed them? In due time, a feud arose, stern and bitter on one side, and as serious on the other as anything could be among such light spirits as had sworn allegiance to the Maypole. The future complexion of New England was involved in this important quarrel. Should the grizzly saints establish their jurisdiction over the gay sinners, then would their spirits darken all the clime, and make it a land of clouded visages, of hard toil, of sermon and psalm forever. But should the banner staff of Merry Mount be fortunate, sunshine would break upon the hills, and flowers would beautify the forest, and late posterity do homage to the Maypole.

After these authentic passages from history, we return to the nuptials of the Lord and Lady of the May. Alas! we have delayed too long, and must darken our tale too suddenly. As we glance again at the Maypole, a solitary sunbeam is fading from the summit, and leaves only a faint, golden tinge blended with the hues of the rainbow banner. Even that dim light is now withdrawn, relinquishing the whole domain of Merry Mount to the evening gloom, which has rushed so instantaneously from the black surrounding woods. But some of these black shadows have rushed forth in human shape.

Yes, with the setting sun, the last day of mirth had passed from Merry Mount. The ring of gay masquers was disordered and broken; the stag lowered his antlers in dismay; the wolf grew weaker than a lamb; the bells of the morris-dancers tinkled with tremulous affright. The Puritans had played a characteristic part in the Maypole mummeries. Their darksome figures were intermixed with the wild shapes of their foes, and made the scene a picture of the moment, when waking thoughts start up amid the scattered fantasies of a dream. The leader of the hostile party stood in the centre of the circle, while the route of monsters cowered around him, like evil spirits in the presence of a dread magician. No fantastic foolery could look him in the face. So stern was the energy of his aspect, that the whole man, visage, frame, and soul, seemed wrought of iron, gifted with life and thought, yet all of one substance with his headpiece and breastplate. It was the Puritan of Puritans; it was Endicott[19] himself!

"Stand off, priest of Baal!"[20] said he, with a grim frown, and laying no reverent hand upon the surplice. "I know thee, Blackstone![21] Thou art the man who couldst not abide the rule even of thine own corrupted church,[22] and hast come hither to preach iniquity, and to give example of it in thy life. But now shall it be seen that the Lord hath sanctified this wilderness for his peculiar people. Woe unto them that would defile it! And first, for this flower-decked abomination, the altar of thy worship!"

And with his keen sword Endicott assaulted the hallowed Maypole. Nor long did it resist his arm. It groaned with a dismal sound; it showered leaves and rosebuds upon the remorseless enthusiast; and finally, with all its green boughs and ribbons and flowers, symbolic of departed pleasures, down fell the banner staff of Merry Mount. As it sank, tradition says, the evening sky grew darker, and the woods threw forth a more sombre shadow.

"There," cried Endicott, looking triumphantly on his work, "there lies the only Maypole in New England! The thought is strong within me that, by its fall, is shadowed forth the fate of light and idle mirth makers, amongst us and our posterity. Amen, saith John Endicott."

"Amen!" echoed his followers.

But the votaries of the Maypole gave one groan for their idol. At the sound, the Puritan leader glanced at the crew of Comus, each a figure of broad mirth, yet, at this moment, strangely expressive of sorrow and dismay.

"Valiant captain," quoth Peter Palfrey, the Ancient[23] of the band, "what order shall be taken with the prisoners?"

"I thought not to repent me of cutting down a Maypole," replied Endicott, "yet now I could find in my heart to plant it again, and give each of these bestial pagans one other dance round their idol. It would have served rarely for a whipping-post!"

"But there are pine-trees enow," suggested the lieutenant.

"True, good Ancient," said the leader. "Wherefore, bind the heathen crew, and bestow on them a small matter of stripes apiece, as earnest of our future justice. Set some of the rogues in the stocks to rest themselves, so soon as Providence shall bring us to one of our own well-ordered settlements, where such accommodations may be found. Further penalties, such as branding and cropping of ears, shall be thought of hereafter."

"How many stripes for the priest?" inquired Ancient Palfrey.

"None as yet," answered Endicott, bending his iron frown upon the culprit. "It must be for the Great and General Court to determine, whether stripes and long imprisonment, and other grievous penalty, may atone for his transgressions. Let him look to himself! For such as violate our civil order, it may be permitted us to show mercy. But woe to the wretch that troubleth our religion!"

---

[19] John Endicott (1589–1665), governor of the colony of Massachusetts.
[20] Fertility god (see 1 Kings 18).
[21] Hawthorne's note: "Did Governor Endicott speak less positively, we should suspect a mistake here. The Reverend Blackstone, though an eccentric, is not known to have been an immoral man. We rather doubt his identity with the priest of Merry Mount."
[22] I.e., the Church of England.
[23] Bearer of an emblem or flag.

"And this dancing bear," resumed the officer. "Must he share the stripes of his fellows?"

"Shoot him through the head!" said the energetic Puritan. "I suspect witchcraft in the beast."

"Here be a couple of shining ones," continued Peter Palfrey, pointing his weapon at the Lord and Lady of the May. "They seem to be of high station among these misdoers. Methinks their dignity will not be fitted with less than a double share of stripes."

Endicott rested on his sword, and closely surveyed the dress and aspect of the hapless pair. There they stood, pale, downcast, and apprehensive. Yet there was an air of mutual support, and of pure affection, seeking aid and giving it, that showed them to be man and wife, with the sanction of a priest upon their love. The youth, in the peril of the moment, had dropped his gilded staff, and thrown his arm about the Lady of the May, who leaned against his breast, too lightly to burden him, but with weight enough to express that their destinies were linked together, for good or evil. They looked first at each other, and then into the grim captain's face. There they stood, in the first hour of wedlock, while the idle pleasures, of which their companions were the emblems, had given place to the sternest cares of life, personified by the dark Puritans. But never had their youthful beauty seemed so pure and high as when its glow was chastened by adversity.

"Youth," said Endicott, "ye stand in an evil case thou and thy maiden wife. Make ready presently, for I am minded that ye shall both have a token to remember your wedding day!"

"Stern man," cried the May Lord, "how can I move thee? Were the means at hand, I would resist to the death. Being powerless, I entreat! Do with me as thou wilt, but let Edith go untouched!"

"Not so," replied the immitigable zealot. "We are not wont to show an idle courtesy to that sex, which requireth the stricter discipline. What sayest thou, maid? Shall thy silken bridegroom suffer thy share of the penalty, besides his own?"

"Be it death," said Edith, "and lay it all on me!"

Truly, as Endicott had said, the poor lovers stood in a woful case. Their foes were triumphant, their friends captive and abased, their home desolate, the benighted wilderness around them, and a rigorous destiny, in the shape of the Puritan leader, their only guide. Yet the deepening twilight could not altogether conceal that the iron man was softened; he smiled at the fair spectacle of early love; he almost sighed for the inevitable blight of early hopes.

"The troubles of life have come hastily on this young couple," observed Endicott. "We will see how they comport themselves under their present trials ere we burden them with greater. If, among the spoil, there be any garments of a more decent fashion, let them be put upon this May Lord and his Lady, instead of their glistening vanities. Look to it, some of you."

"And shall not the youth's hair be cut?" asked Peter Palfrey, looking with abhorrence at the lovelock and long glossy curls of the young man.

"Crop it forthwith, and that in the true pumpkin-shell[24] fashion," answered the captain. "Then bring them along with us, but more gently than their fellows. There

[24] The Puritan style of closely cropped hair.

be qualities in the youth, which may make him valiant to fight, and sober to toil, and pious to pray; and in the maiden, that may fit her to become a mother in our Israel,[25] bringing up babes in better nurture than her own hath been. Nor think ye, young ones, that they are the happiest, even in our lifetime of a moment, who misspend it in dancing round a Maypole!"

And Endicott, the severest Puritan of all who laid the rock foundation of New England, lifted the wreath of roses from the ruin of the Maypole, and threw it, with his own gauntleted hand, over the heads of the Lord and Lady of the May. It was a deed of prophecy. As the moral gloom of the world overpowers all systematic gayety, even so was their home of wild mirth made desolate amid the sad forest. They returned to it no more. But as their flowery garland was wreathed of the brightest roses that had grown there, so, in the tie that united them, were intertwined all the purest and best of their early joys. They went heavenward, supporting each other along the difficult path which it was their lot to tread, and never wasted one regretful thought on the vanities of Merry Mount.

1836

The Minister's Black Veil

A Parable[1]

The sexton stood in the porch of Milford meeting house, pulling *lustily* busily at the bell-rope. The old people of the village came stooping along the street. Children, with bright faces, tripped merrily beside their parents, or mimicked a graver gait, in the conscious dignity of their Sunday clothes. Spruce bachelors looked sidelong at the pretty maidens, and fancied that the Sabbath sunshine made them prettier than on week days. When the throng had mostly streamed into the porch, the sexton began to toll the bell, keeping his eye on the Reverend Mr. Hooper's door. The first glimpse of the clergyman's figure was the signal for the bell to cease its summons.

"But what has good Parson Hooper got upon his face?" cried the sexton in astonishment.

All within hearing immediately turned about, and beheld the semblance of Mr. Hooper, pacing slowly his meditative way towards the meeting-house. With one accord they started, expressing more wonder than if some strange minister were coming to dust the cushions of Mr. Hooper's pulpit.

"Are you sure it is our parson?" inquired Goodman Gray of the sexton.

"Of a certainty it is good Mr. Hooper," replied the sexton. "He was to have

---

[25] Puritan name for the promised land, envisioned as America.

[1] Hawthorne's note: "Another clergyman in New England, Mr. Joseph Moody, of York, Maine, who died about eighty years since made himself remarkable by the same eccentricity that is here related of the Reverend Mr. Hooper. In this case, however, the symbol had a different import. In early life he had accidentally killed a beloved friend; and from that day till the hour of his own death, he hid his face from men."

exchanged pulpits with Parson Shute, of Westbury; but Parson Shute sent to excuse himself yesterday, being to preach a funeral sermon."

The cause of so much amazement may appear sufficiently slight. Mr. Hooper, a gentlemanly person, of about thirty, though still a bachelor, was dressed with due clerical neatness, as if a careful wife had starched his band, and brushed the weekly dust from his Sunday's garb. There was but one thing remarkable in his appearance. Swathed about his forehead, and hanging down over his face, so low as to be shaken by his breath, Mr. Hooper had on a black veil. On a nearer view it seemed to consist of two folds of crape, which entirely concealed his features, except the mouth and chin, but probably did not intercept his sight, further than to give a darkened aspect to all living and inanimate things. With this gloomy shade before him, good Mr. Hooper walked onward, at a slow and quiet pace, stooping somewhat, and looking on the ground, as is customary with abstracted men, yet nodding kindly to those of his parishioners who still waited on the meeting-house steps. But so wonder-struck were they that his greeting hardly met with a return.

"I can't really feel as if good Mr. Hooper's face was behind that piece of crape," said the sexton.

"I don't like it," muttered an old woman, as she hobbled into the meeting-house. "He has changed himself into something awful, only by hiding his face."

"Our parson has gone mad!" cried Goodman Gray, following him across the threshold.

A rumor of some unaccountable phenomenon had preceded Mr. Hooper into the meeting-house, and set all the congregation astir. Few could refrain from twisting their heads towards the door; many stood upright, and turned directly about; while several little boys clambered upon the seats, and came down again with a terrible racket. There was a general bustle, a rustling of the women's gowns and shuffling of the men's feet, greatly at variance with that hushed repose which should attend the entrance of the minister. But Mr. Hooper appeared not to notice the perturbation of his people. He entered with an almost noiseless step, bent his head mildly to the pews on each side, and bowed as he passed his oldest parishioner, a white-haired great-grandsire, who occupied an arm-chair in the centre of the aisle. It was strange to observe how slowly this venerable man became conscious of something singular in the appearance of his pastor. He seemed not fully to partake of the prevailing wonder, till Mr. Hooper had ascended the stairs, and showed himself in the pulpit, face to face with his congregation, except for the black veil. That mysterious emblem was never once withdrawn. It shook with his measured breath, as he gave out the psalm; it threw its obscurity between him and the holy page, as he read the Scriptures; and while he prayed, the veil lay heavily on his uplifted countenance. Did he seek to hide it from the dread Being whom he was addressing?

Such was the effect of this simple piece of crape, that more than one woman of delicate nerves was forced to leave the meeting-house. Yet perhaps the pale-faced congregation was almost as fearful a sight to the minister, as his black veil to them.

Mr. Hooper had the reputation of a good preacher, but not an energetic one: he strove to win his people heavenward by mild, persuasive influences, rather than to drive them thither by the thunders of the Word. The sermon which he now delivered was marked by the same characteristics of style and manner as the general series of his pulpit oratory. But there was something, either in the sentiment of the discourse itself, or in the imagination of the auditors, which made it greatly the most powerful effort that they had ever heard from their pastor's lips. It was tinged, rather more darkly than usual, with the gentle gloom of Mr. Hooper's temperament. The subject had reference to secret sin, and those sad mysteries which we hide from our nearest and dearest, and would fain conceal from our own consciousness, even forgetting that the Omniscient can detect them. A subtle power was breathed into his words. Each member of the congregation, the most innocent girl, and the man of hardened breast, felt as if the preacher had crept upon them, behind his awful veil, and discovered their hoarded iniquity of deed or thought. Many spread their clasped hands on their bosoms. There was nothing terrible in what Mr. Hooper said, at least, no violence; and yet, with every tremor of his melancholy voice, the hearers quaked. An unsought pathos came hand in hand with awe. So sensible were the audience of some unwonted attribute in their minister, that they longed for a breath of wind to blow aside the veil, almost believing that a stranger's visage would be discovered, though the form, gesture, and voice were those of Mr. Hooper.

At the close of the services, the people hurried out with indecorous confusion, eager to communicate their pent-up amazement, and conscious of lighter spirits the moment they lost sight of the black veil. Some gathered in little circles, huddled closely together, with their mouths all whispering in the centre; some went homeward alone, wrapt in silent meditation; some talked loudly, and profaned the Sabbath day with ostentatious laughter. A few shook their sagacious heads, intimating that they could penetrate the mystery; while one or two affirmed that there was no mystery at all, but only that Mr. Hooper's eyes were so weakened by the midnight lamp, as to require a shade. After a brief interval, forth came good Mr. Hooper also, in the rear of his flock. Turning his veiled face from one group to another, he paid due reverence to the hoary heads, saluted the middle aged with kind dignity as their friend and spiritual guide, greeted the young with mingled authority and love, and laid his hands on the little children's heads to bless them. Such was always his custom on the Sabbath day. Strange and bewildered looks repaid him for his courtesy. None, as on former occasions, aspired to the honor of walking by their pastor's side. Old Squire Saunders, doubtless by an accidental lapse of memory, neglected to invite Mr. Hooper to his table, where the good clergyman had been wont to bless the food, almost every Sunday since his settlement. He returned, therefore, to the parsonage, and, at the moment of closing the door, was observed to look back upon the people, all of whom had their eyes fixed upon the minister. A sad smile gleamed faintly from beneath the black veil, and flickered about his mouth, glimmering as he disappeared.

"How strange," said a lady, "that a simple black veil, such as any woman might wear on her bonnet, should become such a terrible thing on Mr. Hooper's face!"

"Something must surely be amiss with Mr. Hooper's intellects," observed her husband, the physician of the village. "But the strangest part of the affair is the effect of this vagary, even on a sober-minded man like myself. The black veil, though it covers only our pastor's face, throws its influence over his whole person, and makes him ghostlike from head to foot. Do you not feel it so?"

"Truly do I," replied the lady; "and I would not be alone with him for the world. I wonder he is not afraid to be alone with himself!"

"Men sometimes are so," said her husband.

The afternoon service was attended with similar circumstances. At its conclusion, the bell tolled for the funeral of a young lady. The relatives and friends were assembled in the house, and the more distant acquaintances stood about the door, speaking of the good qualities of the deceased, when their talk was interrupted by the appearance of Mr. Hooper, still covered with his black veil. It was now an appropriate emblem. The clergyman stepped into the room where the corpse was laid, and bent over the coffin, to take a last farewell of his deceased parishioner. As he stooped, the veil hung straight down from his forehead, so that, if her eyelids had not been closed forever, the dead maiden might have seen his face. Could Mr. Hooper be fearful of her glance, that he so hastily caught back the black veil? A person who watched the interview between the dead and living, scrupled not to affirm, that, at the instant when the clergyman's features were disclosed, the corpse had slightly shuddered, rustling the shroud and muslin cap, though the countenance retained the composure of death. A superstitious old woman was the only witness of this prodigy. From the coffin Mr. Hooper passed into the chamber of the mourners, and thence to the head of the staircase, to make the funeral prayer. It was a tender and heart-dissolving prayer, full of sorrow, yet so imbued with celestial hopes, that the music of a heavenly harp, swept by the fingers of the dead, seemed faintly to be heard among the saddest accents of the minister. The people trembled, though they but darkly understood him when he prayed that they, and himself, and all of mortal race, might be ready, as he trusted this young maiden had been, for the dreadful hour that should snatch the veil from their faces. The bearers went heavily forth, and the mourners followed, saddening all the street, with the dead before them, and Mr. Hooper in his black veil behind.

"Why do you look back?" said one in the procession to his partner.

"I had a fancy," replied she, "that the minister and the maiden's spirit were walking hand in hand."

"And so had I, at the same moment," said the other.

That night, the handsomest couple in Milford village were to be joined in wedlock. Though reckoned a melancholy man, Mr. Hooper had a placid cheerfulness for such occasions, which often excited a sympathetic smile where livelier merriment would have been thrown away. There was no quality of his disposition which made him more beloved than this. The company at the wedding awaited his arrival with impatience, trusting that the strange awe, which had gathered over him throughout the day, would now be dispelled. But such was not the result. When Mr. Hooper came, the first thing that their eyes rested on was the same horrible black veil, which had added deeper gloom to the funeral, and could portend nothing but evil to the wedding. Such was its immediate effect on the guests that a cloud seemed to have rolled duskily from beneath the black crape, and dimmed the light of the candles. The bridal pair stood up before the minister. But the bride's cold fingers quivered in the tremulous hand of the bridegroom, and her deathlike paleness caused a whisper that the maiden who had been buried a few hours before was come from her grave to be married. If ever another wedding were so dismal, it was that famous one where they tolled the wedding knell. After performing the ceremony, Mr. Hooper raised a glass of wine to his lips, wishing happiness to the new-married couple in a strain of mild pleasantry that ought to have brightened the features of the guests, like a cheerful gleam from the hearth. At that instant, catching a glimpse of his figure in the looking-glass, the black veil involved his own spirit in the horror with which it overwhelmed all others. His frame shuddered, his lips grew white, he spilt the untasted wine upon the carpet, and rushed forth into the darkness. For the Earth, too, had on her Black Veil.

The next day, the whole village of Milford talked of little else than Parson Hooper's black veil. That, and the mystery concealed behind it, supplied a topic for discussion between acquaintances meeting in the street, and good women gossiping at their open windows. It was the first item of news that the tavernkeeper told to his guests. The children babbled of it on their way to school. One imitative little imp covered his face with an old black handkerchief, thereby so affrighting his playmates that the panic seized himself, and he well-nigh lost his wits by his own waggery.

It was remarkable that of all the busybodies and impertinent people in the parish, not one ventured to put the plain question to Mr. Hooper, wherefore he did this thing. Hitherto, whenever there appeared the slightest call for such interference, he had never lacked advisers, nor shown himself averse to be guided by their judgment. If he erred at all, it was by so painful a degree of self-distrust, that even the mildest censure would lead him to consider an indifferent action as a crime. Yet, though so well acquainted with this amiable weakness, no individual among his parishioners chose to make the black veil a subject of friendly remonstrance. There was a feeling of dread, neither plainly confessed nor carefully concealed, which caused each to shift the responsibility upon another, till at length it was found expedient to send a deputation of the church, in order to deal with Mr. Hooper about the mystery, before it should grow into a scandal. Never did an embassy so ill discharge its duties. The minister received them with friendly courtesy, but became silent, after they were seated, leaving to his visitors the whole burden of introducing their important business. The topic, it might be supposed, was obvious enough. There was the black veil swathed round Mr. Hooper's forehead, and concealing every feature above his placid mouth, on which, at times, they could perceive the glimmering of a melancholy smile. But that piece of crape, to their imagination, seemed to hang down before his heart, the symbol of a fearful secret between him and them. Were the veil but cast aside, they might speak freely of it, but not till then. Thus they sat a considerable time, speechless, confused, and shrinking uneasily from Mr. Hooper's eye, which they felt to be fixed upon them with an invisible glance. Finally, the deputies returned abashed to their constituents, pronouncing the matter too weighty to be handled, except by a council of the churches, if, indeed, it might not require a general synod.

But there was one person in the village unappalled by the awe with which the black veil had impressed all beside herself. When the deputies returned without an explanation, or even venturing to demand one, she, with the calm energy of her character, determined to chase away the strange cloud that appeared to be settling round Mr. Hooper, every moment more darkly than before. As his plighted wife, it should be her privilege to know what the black veil concealed. At the minister's first visit, therefore, she entered upon the subject with a direct simplicity, which made the task easier both for him and her. After he had seated himself, she fixed her eyes steadfastly upon the veil, but could discern nothing of the dreadful gloom that had so overawed the multitude: it was but a double fold of crape, hanging down from his forehead to his mouth, and slightly stirring with his breath.

"No," said she aloud, and smiling, "there is nothing terrible in this piece of crape, except that it hides a face which I am always glad to look upon. Come, good sir, let the sun shine from behind the cloud. First lay aside your black veil: then tell me why you put it on."

Mr. Hooper's smile glimmered faintly.

"There is an hour to come," said he, "when all of us shall cast aside our veils. Take it not amiss, beloved friend, if I wear this piece of crape till then."

"Your words are a mystery, too," returned the young lady. "Take away the veil from them, at least."

"Elizabeth, I will," said he, "so far as my vow may suffer me. Know, then, this veil is a type and a symbol, and I am bound to wear it ever, both in light and darkness, in solitude and before the gaze of multitudes, and as with strangers, so with my familiar friends. No mortal eye will see it withdrawn. This dismal shade must separate me from the world: even you, Elizabeth, can never come behind it!"

"What grievous affliction hath befallen you," she earnestly inquired, "that you should thus darken your eyes forever?"

"If it be a sign of mourning," replied Mr. Hooper, "I, perhaps, like most other mortals, have sorrows dark enough to be typified by a black veil."

"But what if the world will not believe that it is the type of an innocent sorrow?" urged Elizabeth. "Beloved and respected as you are, there may be whispers that you hide your face under the consciousness of secret sin. For the sake of your holy office, do away this scandal!"

The color rose into her cheeks as she intimated the nature of the rumors that were already abroad in the village. But Mr. Hooper's mildness did not forsake him. He even smiled again—that same sad smile, which always appeared like a faint glimmering of light, proceeding from the obscurity beneath the veil.

"If I hide my face for sorrow, there is cause enough," he merely replied; "and if I cover it for secret sin, what mortal might not do the same?"

And with this gentle, but unconquerable obstinacy did he resist all her entreaties. At length Elizabeth sat silent. For a few moments she appeared lost in thought, considering, probably, what new methods might be tried to withdraw her lover from so dark a fantasy, which, if it had no other meaning, was perhaps a symptom of mental disease. Though of a firmer character than his own, the tears rolled down her cheeks. But, in an instant, as it were, a new feeling took the place of sorrow: her eyes were fixed insensibly on the black veil, when, like a sudden twilight in the air, its terrors fell around her. She arose, and stood trembling before him.

"And do you feel it then, at last?" said he mournfully.

She made no reply, but covered her eyes with her hand, and turned to leave the room. He rushed forward and caught her arm.

"Have patience with me, Elizabeth!" cried he, passionately. "Do not desert me, though this veil must be between us here on earth. Be mine, and hereafter there shall be no veil over my face, no darkness between our souls! It is but a mortal veil—it is not for eternity! O! you know not how lonely I am, and how frightened, to be alone behind my black veil. Do not leave me in this miserable obscurity forever!"

"Lift the veil but once, and look me in the face," said she.

"Never! It cannot be!" replied Mr. Hooper.

"Then farewell!" said Elizabeth.

She withdrew her arm from his grasp, and slowly departed, pausing at the door, to give one long shuddering gaze, that seemed almost to penetrate the mystery of the black veil. But, even amid his grief, Mr. Hooper smiled to think that only a material emblem had separated him from happiness, though the horrors, which it shadowed forth, must be drawn darkly between the fondest of lovers.

From that time no attempts were made to remove Mr. Hooper's black veil, or, by a direct appeal, to discover the secret which it was supposed to hide. By persons who claimed a superiority to popular prejudice, it was reckoned merely an eccentric whim, such as often mingles with the sober actions of men otherwise rational, and tinges them all with its own semblance of insanity. But with the multitude, good Mr. Hooper was irreparably a bugbear. He could not walk the street with any peace of mind, so conscious was he that the gentle and timid would turn aside to avoid him, and that others would make it a point of hardihood to throw themselves in his way. The impertinence of the latter class compelled him to give up his customary walk at sunset to the burial ground; for when he leaned pensively over the gate, there would always be faces behind the gravestones, peeping at his black veil. A fable went the rounds that the stare of the dead people drove him thence. It grieved him, to the very depth of his kind heart, to observe how the children fled from his approach, breaking up their merriest sports, while his melancholy figure was yet afar off. Their instinctive dread caused him to feel more strongly than aught else, that a preternatural horror was interwoven with the threads of the black crape. In truth, his own antipathy to the veil was known to be so great, that he never willingly passed before a mirror, nor stooped to drink at a still fountain, lest, in its peaceful bosom, he should be affrighted by himself. This was what gave plausibility to the whispers, that Mr. Hooper's conscience tortured him for some great crime too horrible to be entirely concealed, or otherwise than so obscurely intimated. Thus, from beneath the black veil, there rolled a cloud into the sunshine, an ambiguity of sin or sorrow, which enveloped the poor minister, so that love or sympathy could never reach him. It was said that ghost and fiend consorted with him there. With self-shudderings and outward terrors, he walked continually in its shadow, groping darkly within his own soul, or gazing through a medium that saddened the whole world. Even the lawless wind, it was believed, respected his dreadful secret, and never blew aside the veil. But still good Mr. Hooper sadly smiled at the pale visages of the worldly throng as he passed by.

Among all its bad influences, the black veil had the one desirable effect, of making its wearer a very efficient clergyman. By the aid of his mysterious emblem—for there was no other apparent cause—he became a man of awful power over souls that were in agony for sin. His converts always regarded him with a dread peculiar to themselves, affirming, though but figuratively, that, before he brought them to celestial light, they had been with him behind the black veil. Its gloom, indeed, enabled him to sympathize with all dark affections. Dying sinners cried aloud for Mr. Hooper, and would not yield their breath till he appeared; though ever, as he stooped to whisper consolation, they shuddered at the veiled face so near their own. Such were the terrors of the black veil, even when Death had bared his visage! Strangers came long distances to attend service at his church, with the mere idle purpose of gazing at his figure, because it was forbidden them to behold his face. But many were made to quake ere they departed! Once, during Governor Belcher's administration,[2] Mr. Hooper was appointed to preach the election sermon.[3] Covered with his black veil, he stood before the chief magistrate, the council, and the representatives, and wrought so deep an

---

[2] Jonathan Belcher (1682–1757) was governor of Massachusetts and New Hampshire from 1730 to 1741.

[3] It was an honor to be chosen to preach the special sermon at the inauguration of a new governor.

He is very — Eliz. left
Alone   him.

people come to him w/ their
problems.

impression, that the legislative measures of that year were characterized by all the gloom and piety of our earliest ancestral sway.

In this manner Mr. Hooper spent a long life, irreproachable in outward act, yet shrouded in dismal suspicions; kind and loving, though unloved, and dimly feared; a man apart from men, shunned in their health and joy, but ever summoned to their aid in mortal anguish. As years wore on, shedding their snows above his sable veil, he acquired a name throughout the New England churches, and they called him Father Hooper. Nearly all his parishioners, who were of mature age when he was settled, had been borne away by many a funeral: he had one congregation in the church, and a more crowded one in the churchyard; and having wrought so late into the evening, and done his work so well, it was now good Father Hooper's turn to rest.

Several persons were visible by the shaded candlelight, in the death chamber of the old clergyman. Natural connections he had none. But there was the decorously grave, though unmoved physician, seeking only to mitigate the last pangs of the patient whom he could not save. There were the deacons, and other eminently pious members of his church. There, also, was the Reverend Mr. Clark, of Westbury, a young and zealous divine, who had ridden in haste to pray by the bedside of the expiring minister. There was the nurse, no hired handmaiden of death, but one whose calm affection had endured thus long in secrecy, in solitude, amid the chill of age, and would not perish, even at the dying hour. Who, but Elizabeth! And there lay the hoary head of good Father Hooper upon the death pillow, with the black veil still swathed about his brow, and reaching down over his face, so that each more difficult gasp of his faint breath caused it to stir. All through life that piece of crape had hung between him and the world: it had separated him from cheerful brotherhood and woman's love, and kept him in that saddest of all prisons, his own heart; and still it lay upon his face, as if to deepen the gloom of his darksome chamber, and shade him from the sunshine of eternity.

For some time previous, his mind had been confused, wavering doubtfully between the past and the present, and hovering forward, as it were, at intervals, into the indistinctness of the world to come. There had been feverish turns, which tossed him from side to side, and wore away what little strength he had. But in his most convulsive struggles, and in the wildest vagaries of his intellect, when no other thought retained its sober influence, he still showed an awful solicitude lest the black veil should slip aside. Even if his bewildered soul could have forgotten, there was a faithful woman at his pillow, who, with averted eyes, would have covered that aged face, which she had last beheld in the comeliness of manhood. At length the death-stricken old man lay quietly in the torpor of mental and bodily exhaustion, with an imperceptible pulse, and breath that grew fainter and fainter, except when a long, deep, and irregular inspiration seemed to prelude the flight of his spirit.

The minister of Westbury approached the bedside.

"Venerable Father Hooper," said he, "the moment of your release is at hand. Are you ready for the lifting of the veil that shuts in time from eternity?"

Father Hooper at first replied merely by a feeble motion of his head; then, apprehensive, perhaps, that his meaning might be doubtful, he exerted himself to speak.

"Yea," said he, in faint accents, "my soul hath a patient weariness until that veil be lifted."

"And is it fitting," resumed the Reverend Mr. Clark, "that a man so given to prayer, of such a blameless example, holy in deed and thought, so far as mortal judgment may pronounce; is it fitting that a father in the church should leave a shadow on his memory, that may seem to blacken a life so pure? I pray you, my venerable brother, let not this thing be! Suffer us to be gladdened by your triumphant aspect as you go to your reward. Before the veil of eternity be lifted, let me cast aside this black veil from your face!"

And thus speaking, the Reverend Mr. Clark bent forward to reveal the mystery of so many years. But, exerting a sudden energy, that made all the beholders stand aghast, Father Hooper snatched both his hands from beneath the bedclothes, and pressed them strongly on the black veil, resolute to struggle, if the minister of Westbury would contend with a dying man.

"Never!" cried the veiled clergyman. "On earth, never!"

"Dark old man!" exclaimed the affrighted minister, "with what horrible crime upon your soul are you now passing to the judgment?"

Father Hooper's breath heaved; it rattled in his throat; but, with a mighty effort, grasping forward with his hands, he caught hold of life, and held it back till he should speak. He even raised himself in bed; and there he sat, shivering with the arms of death around him, while the black veil hung down, awful, at that last moment, in the gathered terrors of a lifetime. And yet the faint, sad smile, so often there, now seemed to glimmer from its obscurity, and linger on Father Hooper's lips.

"Why do you tremble at me alone?" cried he, turning his veiled face round the circle of pale spectators. "Tremble also at each other! Have men avoided me, and women shown no pity, and children screamed and fled, only for my black veil? What, but the mystery which it obscurely typifies, has made this piece of crape so awful? When the friend shows his inmost heart to his friend; the lover to his best beloved; when man does not vainly shrink from the eye of his Creator, loathsomely treasuring up the secret of his sin; then deem me a monster, for the symbol beneath which I have lived, and die! I look around me, and, lo! on every visage a Black Veil!"

While his auditors shrank from one another, in mutual affright, Father Hooper fell back upon his pillow, a veiled corpse, with a faint smile lingering on the lips. Still veiled, they laid him in his coffin, and a veiled corpse they bore him to the grave. The grass of many years has sprung up and withered on that grave, the burial stone is moss-grown, and good Mr. Hooper's face is dust; but awful is still the thought that it mouldered beneath the Black Veil!

1836

The Artist of the Beautiful

An elderly man, with his pretty daughter on his arm, was passing along the street, and emerged from the gloom of the cloudy evening into the light that fell across the pavement from the window of a small shop. It was a projecting window; and on the inside were suspended a variety of watches, pinchbeck,[1] silver, and one or two of gold, all with their faces turned from the streets, as if churlishly disinclined to inform the wayfarers what o'clock it was. Seated within the shop, sidelong to the window, with his pale face bent earnestly over some delicate piece of mechanism on which was thrown the concentrated lustre of a shade lamp, appeared a young man.

"What can Owen Warland be about?" muttered old Peter Hovenden, himself a retired watchmaker, and the former master of this same young man whose occupation he was now wondering at. "What can the fellow be about? These six months past I have never come by his shop without seeing him just as steadily at work as now. It would be a flight beyond his usual foolery to seek for the perpetual motion;[2] and yet I know enough of my old business to be certain that what he is now so busy with is no part of the machinery of a watch."

"Perhaps, father," said Annie, without showing much interest in the question, "Owen is inventing a new kind of timekeeper. I am sure he has ingenuity enough."

"Poh, child! He has not the sort of ingenuity to invent anything better than a Dutch toy," answered her father, who had formerly been put to much vexation by Owen Warland's irregular genius. "A plague on such ingenuity! All the effect that ever I knew of it was to spoil the accuracy of some of the best watches in my shop. He would turn the sun out of its orbit and derange the whole course of time, if, as I said before, his ingenuity could grasp anything bigger than a child's toy!"

"Hush, father! He hears you!" whispered Annie, pressing the old man's arm. "His ears are as delicate as his feelings; and you know how easily disturbed they are. Do let us move on."

So Peter Hovenden and his daughter Annie plodded on without further conversation, until in a by-street of the town they found themselves passing the open door of a blacksmith's shop. Within was seen the forge, now blazing up and illuminating the high and dusky roof, and now confining its lustre to a narrow precinct of the coal-strewn floor, according as the breath of the bellows was puffed forth or again inhaled into its vast leathern lungs. In the intervals of brightness it was easy to distinguish objects in remote corners of the shop and the horseshoes that hung upon the wall; in the momentary gloom the fire seemed to be glimmering amidst the vagueness of unenclosed space. Moving about in this red glare and alternate dusk was the figure of the blacksmith, well worthy to be viewed in so picturesque an aspect of light and shade, where the bright blaze struggled with the black night, as if each would have snatched his comely strength from the other. Anon he drew a white-hot bar of iron from the coals, laid it on the anvil, uplifted his arm of might, and was soon enveloped in the myriads of sparks which the strokes of his hammer scattered into the surrounding gloom.

"Now, that is a pleasant sight," said the old watchmaker. "I know what it is to work in gold; but give me the worker in iron after all is said and done. He spends his labor upon a reality. What say you, daughter Annie?"

"Pray don't speak so loud, father," whispered Annie, "Robert Danforth will hear you."

---

[1] Copper and zinc alloy made to imitate gold.
[2] I.e., to try to invent a perpetual-motion machine.

"And what if he should hear me?" said Peter Hovenden. "I say again, it is a good and a wholesome thing to depend upon main strength and reality, and to earn one's bread with the bare and brawny arm of a blacksmith. A watchmaker gets his brain puzzled by his wheels within a wheel, or loses his health or the nicety of his eyesight, as was my case, and finds himself at middle age, or a little after, past labor at his own trade and fit for nothing else, yet too poor to live at his ease. So I say once again, give me main strength for my money. And then, how it takes the nonsense out of a man! Did you ever hear of a blacksmith being such a fool as Owen Warland yonder?"

"Well said, uncle Hovenden!" shouted Robert Danforth from the forge, in a full, deep, merry voice, that made the roof reëcho. "And what says Miss Annie to that doctrine? She, I suppose, will think it a genteeler business to tinker up a lady's watch than to forge a horseshoe or make a gridiron."

Annie drew her father onward without giving him time for reply.

But we must return to Owen Warland's shop, and spend more meditation upon his history and character than either Peter Hovenden, or probably his daughter Annie, or Owen's old school-fellow, Robert Danforth, would have thought due to so slight a subject. From the time that his little fingers could grasp a penknife, Owen had been remarkable for a delicate ingenuity, which sometimes produced pretty shapes in wood, principally figures of flowers and birds, and sometimes seemed to aim at the hidden mysteries of mechanism. But it was always for purposes of grace, and never with any mockery of the useful. He did not, like the crowd of school-boy artisans, construct little windmills on the angle of a barn or watermills across the neighboring brook. Those who discovered such peculiarity in the boy as to think it worth their while to observe him closely, sometimes saw reason to suppose that he was attempting to imitate the beautiful movements of Nature as exemplified in the flight of birds or the activity of little animals. It seemed, in fact, a new development of the love of the beautiful, such as might have made him a poet, a painter, or a sculptor, and which was as completely refined from all utilitarian coarseness as it could have been in either of the fine arts. He looked with singular distaste at the stiff and regular processes of ordinary machinery. Being once carried to see a steam-engine, in the expectation that his intuitive comprehension of mechanical principles would be gratified, he turned pale and grew sick, as if something monstrous and unnatural had been presented to him. This horror was partly owing to the size and terrible energy of the iron laborer; for the character of Owen's mind was microscopic, and tended naturally to the minute, in accordance with his diminutive frame and the marvellous smallness and delicate power of his fingers. Not that his sense of beauty was thereby diminished into a sense of prettiness. The beautiful idea has no relation to size, and may be as perfectly developed in a space too minute for any but microscopic investigation as within the ample verge that is measured by the arc of the rainbow. But, at all events, this characteristic minuteness in his objects and accomplishments made the world even more incapable than it might otherwise have been of appreciating Owen Warland's genius. The boy's relatives saw nothing better to be done—as perhaps there was not —than to bind him apprentice to a watchmaker, hoping that his strange ingenuity might thus be regulated and put to utilitarian purposes.

Peter Hovenden's opinion of his apprentice has already been expressed. He could make nothing of the lad. Owen's apprehension of the professional mysteries, it is true, was inconceivably quick; but he altogether forgot or despised the grand object of a watchmaker's business, and cared no more for the measurement of time than if it had been merged into eternity. So long, however, as he remained under his old master's care, Owen's lack of sturdiness made it possible, by strict injunctions and sharp oversight, to restrain his creative eccentricity within bounds; but when his apprenticeship was served out, and he had taken the little shop which Peter Hovenden's failing eyesight compelled him to relinquish, then did people recognize how unfit a person was Owen Warland to lead old blind Father Time along his daily course. One of his most rational projects was to connect a musical operation with the machinery of his watches, so that all the harsh dissonances of life might be rendered tuneful, and each flitting moment fall into the abyss of the past in golden drops of harmony. If a family clock was intrusted to him for repair,—one of those tall, ancient clocks that have grown nearly allied to human nature by measuring out the lifetime of many generations,—he would take upon himself to arrange a dance or funeral procession of figures across its venerable face, representing twelve mirthful or melancholy hours. Several freaks of this kind quite destroyed the young watchmaker's credit with that steady and matter-of-fact class of people who hold the opinion that time is not to be trifled with, whether considered as the medium of advancement and prosperity in this world or preparation for the next. His custom rapidly diminished—a misfortune, however, that was probably reckoned among his better accidents by Owen Warland, who was becoming more and more absorbed in a secret occupation which drew all his science and manual dexterity into itself, and likewise gave full employment to the characteristic tendencies of his genius. This pursuit had already consumed many months.

After the old watchmaker and his pretty daughter had gazed at him out of the obscurity of the street, Owen Warland was seized with a fluttering of the nerves, which made his hand tremble too violently to proceed with such delicate labor as he was now engaged upon.

"It was Annie herself!" murmured he. "I should have known it, by this throbbing of my heart, before I heard her father's voice. Ah, how it throbs! I shall scarcely be able to work again on this exquisite mechanism to-night. Annie! dearest Annie! thou shouldst give firmness to my heart and hand, and not shake them thus; for if I strive to put the very spirit of beauty into form and give it motion, it is for thy sake alone. O throbbing heart, be quiet! If my labor be thus thwarted, there will come vague and unsatisfied dreams which will leave me spiritless to-morrow."

As he was endeavoring to settle himself again to his task, the shop door opened and gave admittance to no other than the stalwart figure which Peter Hovenden had paused to admire, as seen amid the light and shadow of the blacksmith's shop. Robert Danforth had brought a little anvil of his own manufacture, and peculiarly constructed, which the young artist had recently bespoken. Owen examined the article and pronounced it fashioned according to his wish.

"Why, yes," said Robert Danforth, his strong voice filling the shop as with the sound of a bass viol, "I consider myself equal to anything in the way of my own trade; though I should have made but a poor figure at yours with such a fist as this," added he, laughing, as he laid his vast hand beside the delicate one of Owen. "But what then? I put more main strength into one blow of my sledge hammer than all that you have expended since you were a 'prentice. Is not that the truth?"

"Very probably," answered the low and slender voice of Owen. "Strength is an earthly monster. I make no pretensions to it. My force, whatever there may be of it, is altogether spiritual."

"Well, but, Owen, what are you about?" asked his old school-fellow, still in such a hearty volume of tone that it made the artist shrink, especially as the question related to a subject so sacred as the absorbing dream of his imagination. "Folks do say that you are trying to discover the perpetual motion."

"The perpetual motion? Nonsense!" replied Owen Warland, with a movement of disgust; for he was full of little petulances. "It can never be discovered. It is a dream that may delude men whose brains are mystified with matter, but not me. Besides, if such a discovery were possible, it would not be worth my while to make it only to have the secret turned to such purposes as are now effected by steam and water power. I am not ambitious to be honored with the paternity of a new kind of cotton machine."

"That would be droll enough!" cried the blacksmith, breaking out into such an uproar of laughter that Owen himself and the bell glasses on his work-board quivered in unison. "No, no, Owen! No child of yours will have iron joints and sinews. Well, I won't hinder you any more. Good night, Owen, and success, and if you need any assistance, so far as a downright blow of hammer upon anvil will answer the purpose, I'm your man."

And with another laugh the man of main strength left the shop.

"How strange it is," whispered Owen Warland to himself, leaning his head upon his hand, "that all my musings, my purposes, my passion for the beautiful, my consciousness of power to create it,—a finer, more ethereal power, of which this earthly giant can have no conception,—all, all, look so vain and idle whenever my path is crossed by Robert Danforth! He would drive me mad were I to meet him often. His hard, brute force darkens and confuses the spiritual element within me; but I, too, will be strong in my own way. I will not yield to him."

He took from beneath a glass a piece of minute machinery, which he set in the condensed light of his lamp, and, looking intently at it through a magnifying glass, proceeded to operate with a delicate instrument of steel. In an instant, however, he fell back in his chair and clasped his hands, with a look of horror on his face that made its small features as impressive as those of a giant would have been.

"Heaven! What have I done?" exclaimed he. "The vapor, the influence of that brute force,—it has bewildered me and obscured my perception. I have made the very stroke—the fatal stroke—that I have dreaded from the first. It is all over—the toil of months, the object of my life. I am ruined!"

And there he sat, in strange despair, until his lamp flickered in the socket and left the Artist of the Beautiful in darkness.

Thus it is that ideas, which grow up within the imagination and appear so lovely to it and of a value beyond whatever men call valuable, are exposed to be shattered and annihilated by contact with the practical. It is requisite for the ideal artist to possess a force of character that seems hardly compatible with its delicacy; he must keep his faith in himself while the incredulous world assails him with its utter disbelief; he must stand up against mankind and be his own sole disciple, both as respects his genius and the objects to which it is directed.

For a time Owen Warland succumbed to this severe but inevitable test. He spent a few sluggish weeks with his head so continually resting in his hands that the towns-people had scarcely an opportunity to see his countenance. When at last it was again uplifted to the light of day, a cold, dull, nameless change was perceptible upon it. In the opinion of Peter Hovenden, however, and that order of sagacious understandings who think that life should be regulated, like clockwork, with leaden weights, the alteration was entirely for the better. Owen now, indeed, applied himself to business with dogged industry. It was marvellous to witness the obtuse gravity with which he would inspect the wheels of a great old silver watch; thereby delighting the owner, in whose fob it had been worn till he deemed it a portion of his own life, and was accordingly jealous of its treatment. In consequence of the good report thus acquired, Owen Warland was invited by the proper authorities to regulate the clock in the church steeple. He succeeded so admirably in this matter of public interest that the merchants gruffly acknowledged his merits on 'Change;[3] the nurse whispered his praises as she gave the potion in the sick-chamber; the lover blessed him at the hour of appointed interview; and the town in general thanked Owen for the punctuality of dinner time. In a word, the heavy weight upon his spirits kept everything in order, not merely within his own system, but wheresoever the iron accents of the church clock were audible. It was a circumstance, though minute, yet characteristic of his present state, that, when employed to engrave names or initials on silver spoons, he now wrote the requisite letters in the plainest possible style, omitting a variety of fanciful flourishes that had heretofore distinguished his work in this kind.

One day, during the era of this happy transformation, old Peter Hovenden came to visit his former apprentice.

"Well, Owen," said he, "I am glad to hear such good accounts of you from all quarters, and especially from the town clock yonder, which speaks in your commendation every hour of the twenty-four. Only get rid altogether of your nonsensical trash about the beautiful, which I nor nobody else, nor yourself to boot, could ever understand,—only free yourself of that, and your success in life is as sure as daylight. Why, if you go on in this way, I should even venture to let you doctor this precious old watch of mine; though, except my daughter, Annie, I have nothing else so valuable in the world."

"I should hardly dare touch it, sir," replied Owen, in a depressed tone; for he was weighed down by his old master's presence.

"In time," said the latter,—"in time, you will be capable of it."

The old watchmaker, with the freedom naturally consequent on his former authority, went on inspecting the work which Owen had in hand at the moment, together with other matters that were in progress. The artist, meanwhile, could scarcely lift his head. There was nothing so antipodal to his nature as this man's cold, unimaginative sagacity, by contact with which everything was converted into a dream except the densest matter of the physical world. Owen groaned in spirit and prayed fervently to be delivered from him.

"But what is this?" cried Peter Hovenden abruptly, taking up a dusty bell glass, beneath which appeared a mechanical something, as delicate and minute as the system of a butterfly's anatomy. "What have we here? Owen! Owen! there is witchcraft in

---

[3] Place of business similar to the modern stock exchange.

these little chains, and wheels, and paddles. See! with one pinch of my finger and thumb I am going to deliver you from all future peril."

"For Heaven's sake," screamed Owen Warland, springing up with wonderful energy, "as you would not drive me mad, do not touch it! The slightest pressure of your finger would ruin me forever."

"Aha, young man! And is it so?" said the old watchmaker, looking at him with just enough of penetration to torture Owen's soul with the bitterness of worldly criticism. "Well, take your own course; but I warn you again that in this small piece of mechanism lives your evil spirit. Shall I exorcise him?"

"You are my evil spirit," answered Owen, much excited,—"you and the hard, coarse world! The leaden thoughts and the despondency that you fling upon me are my clogs, else I should long ago have achieved the task that I was created for."

Peter Hovenden shook his head, with the mixture of contempt and indignation which mankind, of whom he was partly a representative, deem themselves entitled to feel towards all simpletons who seek other prizes than the dusty one along the highway. He then took his leave, with an uplifted finger and a sneer upon his face that haunted the artist's dreams for many a night afterwards. At the time of his old master's visit, Owen was probably on the point of taking up the relinquished task; but, by this sinister event, he was thrown back into the state whence he had been slowly emerging.

But the innate tendency of his soul had only been accumulating fresh vigor during its apparent sluggishness. As the summer advanced he almost totally relinquished his business, and permitted Father Time, so far as the old gentleman was represented by the clocks and watches under his control, to stray at random through human life, making infinite confusion among the train of bewildered hours. He wasted the sunshine, as people said, in wandering through the woods and fields and along the banks of streams. There, like a child, he found amusement in chasing butterflies or watching the motions of water insects. There was something truly mysterious in the intentness with which he contemplated these living playthings as they sported on the breeze or examined the structure of an imperial insect whom he had imprisoned. The chase of butterflies was an apt emblem of the ideal pursuit in which he had spent so many golden hours; but would the beautiful idea ever be yielded to his hand like the butterfly that symbolized it? Sweet, doubtless, were these days, and congenial to the artist's soul. They were full of bright conceptions, which gleamed through his intellectual world as the butterflies gleamed through the outward atmosphere, and were real to him, for the instant, without the toil, and perplexity, and many disappointments of attempting to make them visible to the sensual eye. Alas that the artist, whether in poetry, or whatever other material, may not content himself with the inward enjoyment of the beautiful, but must chase the flitting mystery beyond the verge of his ethereal domain, and crush its frail being in seizing it with a material grasp. Owen Warland felt the impulse to give external reality to his ideas as irresistibly as any of the poets or painters who have arrayed the world in a dimmer and fainter beauty, imperfectly copied from the richness of their visions.

The night was now his time for the slow progress of re-creating the one idea to which all his intellectual activity referred itself. Always at the approach of dusk he stole into the town, locked himself within his shop, and wrought with patient delicacy of touch for many hours. Sometimes he was startled by the rap of the watchman, who, when all the world should be asleep, had caught the gleam of lamplight through the crevices of Owen Warland's shutters. Daylight, to the morbid sensibility of his mind, seemed to have an intrusiveness that interfered with his pursuits. On cloudy and inclement days, therefore, he sat with his head upon his hands, muffling, as it were, his sensitive brain in a mist of indefinite musings; for it was a relief to escape from the sharp distinctness with which he was compelled to shape out his thoughts during his nightly toil.

From one of these fits of torpor he was aroused by the entrance of Annie Hovenden, who came into the shop with the freedom of a customer, and also with something of the familiarity of a childish friend. She had worn a hole through her silver thimble, and wanted Owen to repair it.

"But I don't know whether you will condescend to such a task," said she, laughing, "now that you are so taken up with the notion of putting spirit into machinery."

"Where did you get that idea, Annie?" said Owen, starting in surprise.

"Oh, out of my own head," answered she, "and from something that I heard you say, long ago, when you were but a boy and I a little child. But come; will you mend this poor thimble of mine?"

"Anything for your sake, Annie," said Owen Warland,—"anything, even were it to work at Robert Danforth's forge."

"And that would be a pretty sight!" retorted Annie, glancing with imperceptible slightness at the artist's small and slender frame. "Well; here is the thimble."

"But that is a strange idea of yours," said Owen, "about the spiritualization of matter."

And then the thought stole into his mind that this young girl possessed the gift to comprehend him better than all the world besides. And what a help and strength would it be to him in his lonely toil if he could gain the sympathy of the only being whom he loved! To persons whose pursuits are insulated from the common business of life—who are either in advance of mankind or apart from it—there often comes a sensation of moral cold that makes the spirit shiver as if it had reached the frozen solitudes around the pole. What the prophet, the poet, the reformer, the criminal, or any other man with human yearnings, but separated from the multitude by a peculiar lot, might feel, poor Owen felt.

"Annie," cried he, growing pale as death at the thought, "how gladly would I tell you the secret of my pursuit! You, methinks, would estimate it rightly. You, I know, would hear it with a reverence that I must not expect from the harsh, material world."

"Would I not? to be sure I would!" replied Annie Hovenden, lightly laughing. "Come; explain to me quickly what is the meaning of this little whirligig, so delicately wrought that it might be a plaything for Queen Mab.[4] See! I will put it in motion."

"Hold!" exclaimed Owen, "hold!"

Annie had but given the slightest possible touch, with the point of a needle, to the same minute portion of complicated machinery which has been more than once mentioned, when the artist seized her by the wrist with a force that made her scream aloud. She was affrighted at the convulsion of intense rage and anguish that writhed across his features. The next instant he let his head sink upon his hands.

"Go, Annie," murmured he; "I have deceived myself, and must suffer for it. I

[4] Legendary fairy queen who reigns over dreams.

yearned for sympathy, and thought, and fancied, and dreamed that you might give it me; but you lack the talisman, Annie, that should admit you into my secrets. That touch has undone the toil of months and the thought of a lifetime! It was not your fault, Annie; but you have ruined me!"

Poor Owen Warland! He had indeed erred, yet pardonably; for if any human spirit could have sufficiently reverenced the processes so sacred in his eyes, it must have been a woman's. Even Annie Hovenden, possibly, might not have disappointed him had she been enlightened by the deep intelligence of love.

The artist spent the ensuing winter in a way that satisfied any persons who had hitherto retained a hopeful opinion of him that he was, in truth, irrevocably doomed to inutility as regarded the world, and to an evil destiny on his own part. The decease of a relative had put him in possession of a small inheritance. Thus freed from the necessity of toil, and having lost the steadfast influence of a great purpose,—great, at least, to him,—he abandoned himself to habits from which it might have been supposed the mere delicacy of his organization would have availed to secure him. But when the ethereal portion of a man of genius is obscured, the earthly part assumes an influence the more uncontrollable, because the character is now thrown off the balance to which Providence had so nicely adjusted it, and which, in coarser natures, is adjusted by some other method. Owen Warland made proof of whatever show of bliss may be found in riot. He looked at the world through the golden medium of wine, and contemplated the visions that bubble up so gayly around the brim of the glass, and that people the air with shapes of pleasant madness, which so soon grow ghostly and forlorn. Even when this dismal and inevitable change had taken place, the young man might still have continued to quaff the cup of enchantments, though its vapor did but shroud life in gloom and fill the gloom with spectres that mocked at him. There was a certain irksomeness of spirit, which, being real, and the deepest sensation of which the artist was now conscious, was more intolerable than any fantastic miseries and horrors that the abuse of wine could summon up. In the latter case he could remember, even out of the midst of his trouble, that all was but a delusion; in the former, the heavy anguish was his actual life.

From this perilous state he was redeemed by an incident which more than one person witnessed, but of which the shrewdest could not explain or conjecture the operation on Owen Warland's mind. It was very simple. On a warm afternoon of spring, as the artist sat among his riotous companions with a glass of wine before him, a splendid butterfly flew in at the open window and fluttered about his head.

"Ah," exclaimed Owen, who had drank freely, "are you alive again, child of the sun and playmate of the summer breeze, after your dismal winter's nap? Then it is time for me to be at work!"

And, leaving his unemptied glass upon the table, he departed and was never known to sip another drop of wine.

And now, again, he resumed his wanderings in the woods and fields. It might be fancied that the bright butterfly, which had come so spirit-like into the window as Owen sat with the rude revellers, was indeed a spirit commissioned to recall him to the pure, ideal life that had so etherealized him among men. It might be fancied that he went forth to seek this spirit in its sunny haunts; for still, as in the summer time gone by, he was seen to steal gently up wherever a butterfly had alighted, and lose himself in contemplation of it. When it took flight his eyes followed the winged vision, as if its airy track would show the path to heaven. But what could be the purpose of the unseasonable toil, which was again resumed, as the watchman knew by the lines of lamplight through the crevices of Owen Warland's shutters? The towns-people had one comprehensive explanation of all these singularities. Owen Warland had gone mad! How universally efficacious—how satisfactory, too, and soothing to the injured sensibility of narrowness and dulness—is this easy method of accounting for whatever lies beyond the world's most ordinary scope! From St. Paul's[5] days down to our poor little Artist of the Beautiful, the same talisman had been applied to the elucidation of all mysteries in the words or deeds of men who spoke or acted too wisely or too well. In Owen Warland's case the judgment of his towns-people may have been correct. Perhaps he was mad. The lack of sympathy— that contrast between himself and his neighbors which took away the restraint of example—was enough to make him so. Or possibly he had caught just so much of ethereal radiance as served to bewilder him, in an earthly sense, by its intermixture with the common daylight.

One evening, when the artist had returned from a customary ramble and had just thrown the lustre of his lamp on the delicate piece of work so often interrupted, but still taken up again, as if his fate were embodied in its mechanism, he was surprised by the entrance of old Peter Hovenden. Owen never met this man without a shrinking of the heart. Of all the world he was most terrible, by reason of a keen understanding which saw so distinctly what it did see, and disbelieved so uncompromisingly in what it could not see. On this occasion the old watchmaker had merely a gracious word or two to say.

"Owen, my lad," said he, "we must see you at my house to-morrow night."

The artist began to mutter some excuse.

"Oh, but it must be so," quoth Peter Hovenden, "for the sake of the days when you were one of the household. What, my boy! don't you know that my daughter Annie is engaged to Robert Danforth? We are making an entertainment, in our humble way, to celebrate the event."

"Ah!" said Owen.

That little monosyllable was all he uttered; its tone seemed cold and unconcerned to an ear like Peter Hovenden's; and yet there was in it the stifled outcry of the poor artist's heart, which he compressed within him like a man holding down an evil spirit. One slight outbreak, however, imperceptible to the old watchmaker, he allowed himself. Raising the instrument with which he was about to begin his work, he let it fall upon the little system of machinery that had, anew, cost him months of thought and toil. It was shattered by the stroke!

Owen Warland's story would have been no tolerable representation of the troubled life of those who strive to create the beautiful, if, amid all other thwarting influences, love had not interposed to steal the cunning from his hand. Outwardly he had been no ardent or enterprising lover; the career of his passion had confined its tumults and vicissitudes so entirely within the artist's imagination that Annie herself had scarcely more than a woman's intuitive perception of it; but, in Owen's view, it covered the whole field of his life. Forgetful of the time when she had shown herself incapable

---

[5] Reference to the apostle Paul (d. ca. A.D. 67).
(See Acts 26:24.)

of any deep response, he had persisted in connecting all his dreams of artistical success with Annie's image; she was the visible shape in which the spiritual power that he worshipped, and on whose altar he hoped to lay a not unworthy offering, was made manifest to him. Of course he had deceived himself; there were no such attributes in Annie Hovenden as his imagination had endowed her with. She, in the aspect which she wore to his inward vision, was as much a creature of his own as the mysterious piece of mechanism would be were it ever realized. Had he become convinced of his mistake through the medium of successful love,—had he won Annie to his bosom, and there beheld her fade from angel into ordinary woman,—the disappointment might have driven him back, with concentrated energy, upon his sole remaining object. On the other hand, had he found Annie what he fancied, his lot would have been so rich in beauty that out of its mere redundancy he might have wrought the beautiful into many a worthier type than he had toiled for; but the guise in which his sorrow came to him, the sense that the angel of his life had been snatched away and given to a rude man of earth and iron, who could neither need nor appreciate her ministrations,—this was the very perversity of fate that makes human existence appear too absurd and contradictory to be the scene of one other hope or one other fear. There was nothing left for Owen Warland but to sit down like a man that had been stunned.

He went through a fit of illness. After his recovery his small and slender frame assumed an obtuser garniture of flesh than it had ever before worn. His thin cheeks became round; his delicate little hand, so spiritually fashioned to achieve fairy task-work, grew plumper than the hand of a thriving infant. His aspect had a childishness such as might have induced a stranger to pat him on the head—pausing, however, in the act, to wonder what manner of child was here. It was as if the spirit had gone out of him, leaving the body to flourish in a sort of vegetable existence. Not that Owen Warland was idiotic. He could talk, and not irrationally. Somewhat of a babbler, indeed, did people begin to think him; for he was apt to discourse at wearisome length of marvels of mechanism that he had read about in books, but which he had learned to consider as absolutely fabulous. Among them he enumerated the Man of Brass, constructed by Albertus Magnus, and the Brazen Head of Friar Bacon;[6] and, coming down to later times, the automata of a little coach and horses, which it was pretended had been manufactured for the Dauphin of France;[7] together with an insect that buzzed about the ear like a living fly, and yet was but a contrivance of minute steel springs. There was a story, too, of a duck that waddled, and quacked, and ate; though, had any honest citizen purchased it for dinner, he would have found himself cheated with the mere mechanical apparition of a duck.

"But all these accounts," said Owen Warland, "I am now satisfied are mere impositions."

Then, in a mysterious way, he would confess that he once thought differently. In his idle and dreamy days he had considered it possible, in a certain sense, to spiritualize machinery, and to combine with the new species of life and motion thus produced a beauty that should attain to the ideal which Nature has proposed to herself in all

[6] St. Albert the Great (German, 1193?–1280) and Roger Bacon (English, 1214–1294) were scientists and philosophers thought to have supernatural powers to bring life to mere metal.

[7] Title given the eldest son of the French king.

her creatures, but has never taken pains to realize. He seemed, however, to retain no very distinct perception either of the process of achieving this object or of the design itself.

"I have thrown it all aside now," he would say. "It was a dream such as young men are always mystifying themselves with. Now that I have acquired a little common sense, it makes me laugh to think of it."

Poor, poor and fallen Owen Warland! These were the symptoms that he had ceased to be an inhabitant of the better sphere that lies unseen around us. He had lost his faith in the invisible, and now prided himself, as such unfortunates invariably do, in the wisdom which rejected much that even his eye could see, and trusted confidently in nothing but what his hand could touch. This is the calamity of men whose spiritual part dies out of them and leaves the grosser understanding to assimilate them more and more to the things of which alone it can take cognizance; but in Owen Warland the spirit was not dead nor passed away; it only slept.

How it awoke again is not recorded. Perhaps the torpid slumber was broken by a convulsive pain. Perhaps, as in a former instance, the butterfly came and hovered about his head and reinspired him,—as indeed this creature of the sunshine had always a mysterious mission for the artist,—reinspired him with the former purpose of his life. Whether it were pain or happiness that thrilled through his veins, his first impulse was to thank Heaven for rendering him again the being of thought, imagination, and keenest sensibility that he had long ceased to be.

"Now for my task," said he. "Never did I feel such strength for it as now."

Yet, strong as he felt himself, he was incited to toil the more diligently by an anxiety lest death should surprise him in the midst of his labors. This anxiety, perhaps, is common to all men who set their hearts upon anything so high, in their own view of it, that life becomes of importance only as conditional to its accomplishment. So long as we love life for itself, we seldom dread the losing it. When we desire life for the attainment of an object, we recognize the frailty of its texture. But, side by side with this sense of insecurity, there is a vital faith in our invulnerability to the shaft of death while engaged in any task that seems assigned by Providence as our proper thing to do, and which the world would have cause to mourn for should we leave it unaccomplished. Can the philosopher, big with the inspiration of an idea that is to reform mankind, believe that he is to be beckoned from this sensible existence at the very instant when he is mustering his breath to speak the word of light? Should he perish so, the weary ages may pass away—the world's, whose life sand may fall,[8] drop by drop—before another intellect is prepared to develop the truth that might have been uttered then. But history affords many an example where the most previous spirit, at any particular epoch manifested in human shape, has gone hence untimely, without space allowed him, so far as mortal judgment could discern, to perform his mission on the earth. The prophet dies, and the man of torpid heart and sluggish brain lives on. The poet leaves his song half sung, or finishes it, beyond the scope of mortal ears, in a celestial choir. The painter—as Allston[9] did—leaves half his conception on the canvas to sadden us with its imperfect beauty, and goes to picture forth the whole, if it be no irreverence to say so, in the hues of heaven. But rather such incomplete

---

[8] I.e., as the sand falls in an hourglass.
[9] The American painter Washington Allston

(1779–1843) died before finishing *Belshazzar's Feast.*

designs of this life will be perfected nowhere. This so frequent abortion of man's dearest projects must be taken as a proof that the deeds of earth, however etherealized by piety or genius, are without value, except as exercises and manifestations of the spirit. In heaven, all ordinary thought is higher and more melodious than Milton's song. Then, would he add another verse to any strain that he had left unfinished here?

But to return to Owen Warland. It was his fortune, good or ill, to achieve the purpose of his life. Pass we over a long space of intense thought, yearning effort, minute toil, and wasting anxiety, succeeded by an instant of solitary triumph: let all this be imagined; and then behold the artist, on a winter evening, seeking admittance to Robert Danforth's fireside circle. There he found the man of iron, with his massive substance thoroughly warmed and attempered by domestic influences. And there was Annie, too, now transformed into a matron, with much of her husband's plain and sturdy nature, but imbued, as Owen Warland still believed, with a finer grace, that might enable her to be the interpreter between strength and beauty. It happened, likewise, that old Peter Hovenden was a guest this evening at his daughter's fireside; and it was his well-remembered expression of keen, cold criticism that first encountered the artist's glance.

"My old friend Owen!" cried Robert Danforth, starting up, and compressing the artist's delicate fingers with a hand that was accustomed to gripe bars of iron. "This is kind and neighborly to come to us at last. I was afraid your perpetual motion had bewitched you out of the remembrance of old times."

"We are glad to see you," said Annie, while a blush reddened her matronly cheek. "It was not like a friend to stay from us so long."

"Well, Owen," inquired the old watchmaker, as his first greeting, "how comes on the beautiful? Have you created it at last?"

The artist did not immediately reply, being startled by the apparition of a young child of strength that was tumbling about on the carpet,—a little personage who had come mysteriously out of the infinite, but with something so sturdy and real in his composition that he seemed moulded out of the densest substance which earth could supply. This hopeful infant crawled towards the new-comer, and setting himself on end, as Robert Danforth expressed the posture, stared at Owen with a look of such sagacious observation that the mother could not help exchanging a proud glance with her husband. But the artist was disturbed by the child's look, as imagining a resemblance between it and Peter Hovenden's habitual expression. He could have fancied that the old watchmaker was compressed into this baby shape, and looking out of those baby eyes, and repeating, as he now did, the malicious question:—

"The beautiful, Owen! How comes on the beautiful? Have you succeeded in creating the beautiful?"

"I have succeeded," replied the artist, with a momentary light of triumph in his eyes and a smile of sunshine, yet steeped in such depth of thought that it was almost sadness. "Yes, my friends, it is the truth. I have succeeded."

"Indeed!" cried Annie, a look of maiden mirthfulness peeping out of her face again. "And is it lawful, now, to inquire what the secret is?"

"Surely; it is to disclose it that I have come," answered Owen Warland. "You shall know, and see, and touch, and possess the secret! For, Annie,—if by that name I may still address the friend of my boyish years,—Annie, it is for your bridal gift that I have wrought this spiritualized mechanism, this harmony of motion, this mystery of beauty. It comes late, indeed; but it is as we go onward in life, when objects begin to lose their freshness of hue and our souls their delicacy of perception, that the spirit of beauty is most needed. If,—forgive me, Annie,—if you know how to value this gift, it can never come too late."

He produced, as he spoke, what seemed a jewel box. It was carved richly out of ebony by his own hand, and inlaid with a fanciful tracery of pearl, representing a boy in pursuit of a butterfly, which, elsewhere, had become a winged spirit, and was flying heavenward; while the boy, or youth, had found such efficacy in his strong desire that he ascended from earth to cloud, and from cloud to celestial atmosphere, to win the beautiful. This case of ebony the artist opened, and bade Annie place her finger on its edge. She did so, but almost screamed as a butterfly fluttered forth, and, alighting on her finger's tip, sat waving the ample magnificence of its purple and gold-speckled wings, as if in prelude to a flight. It is impossible to express by words the glory, the splendor, the delicate gorgeousness which were softened into the beauty of this object. Nature's ideal butterfly was here realized in all its perfection; not in the pattern of such faded insects as flit among earthly flowers, but of those which hover across the meads of paradise for child-angels and the spirits of departed infants to disport themselves with. The rich down was visible upon its wings; the lustre of its eyes seemed instinct with spirit. The firelight glimmered around this wonder—the candles gleamed upon it; but it glistened apparently by its own radiance, and illuminated the finger and outstretched hand on which it rested with a white gleam like that of precious stones. In its perfect beauty, the consideration of size was entirely lost. Had its wings overreached the firmament, the mind could not have been more filled or satisfied.

"Beautiful! beautiful!" exclaimed Annie. "Is it alive? Is it alive?"

"Alive? To be sure it is," answered her husband. "Do you suppose any mortal has skill enough to make a butterfly, or would put himself to the trouble of making one, when any child may catch a score of them in a summer's afternoon? Alive? Certainly! But this pretty box is undoubtedly of our friend Owen's manufacture; and really it does him credit."

At this moment the butterfly waved its wings anew, with a motion so absolutely lifelike that Annie was startled, and even awestricken; for, in spite of her husband's opinion, she could not satisfy herself whether it was indeed a living creature or a piece of wondrous mechanism.

"Is it alive?" she repeated, more earnestly than before.

"Judge for yourself," said Owen Warland, who stood gazing in her face with fixed attention.

The butterfly now flung itself upon the air, fluttered round Annie's head, and soared into a distant region of the parlor, still making itself perceptible to sight by the starry gleam in which the motion of its wings enveloped it. The infant on the floor followed its course with his sagacious little eyes. After flying about the room, it returned in a spiral curve and settled again on Annie's finger.

"But is it alive?" exclaimed she again; and the finger on which the gorgeous mystery had alighted was so tremulous that the butterfly was forced to balance himself with his wings. "Tell me if it be alive, or whether you created it."

"Wherefore ask who created it, so it be beautiful?" replied Owen Warland. "Alive? Yes, Annie; it may well be said to possess life, for it has absorbed my own being into itself; and in the secret of that butterfly, and in its beauty,—which is not merely outward, but deep as its whole system,—is represented the intellect, the imagination, the sensibility, the soul of an Artist of the Beautiful! Yes; I created it. But"—and here his countenance somewhat changed—"this butterfly is not now to me what it was when I beheld it afar off in the daydreams of my youth."

"Be it what it may, it is a pretty plaything," said the blacksmith, grinning with childlike delight. "I wonder whether it would condescend to alight on such a great clumsy finger as mine? Hold it hither, Annie."

By the artist's direction, Annie touched her finger's tip to that of her husband; and, after a momentary delay, the butterfly fluttered from one to the other. It preluded a second flight by a similar, yet not precisely the same, waving of wings as in the first experiment; then, ascending from the blacksmith's stalwart finger, it rose in a gradually enlarging curve to the ceiling, made one wide sweep around the room, and returned with an undulating movement to the point whence it had started.

"Well, that does beat all nature!" cried Robert Danforth, bestowing the heartiest praise that he could find expression for; and, indeed, had he paused there, a man of finer words and nicer perception could not easily have said more. "That goes beyond me, I confess. But what then? There is more real use in one downright blow of my sledge hammer than in the whole five years' labor that our friend Owen has wasted on this butterfly."

Here the child clapped his hands and made a great babble of indistinct utterance, apparently demanding that the butterfly should be given him for a plaything.

Owen Warland, meanwhile, glanced sidelong at Annie, to discover whether she sympathized in her husband's estimate of the comparative value of the beautiful and the practical. There was, amid all her kindness towards himself, amid all the wonder and admiration with which she contemplated the marvellous work of his hands and incarnation of his idea, a secret scorn—too secret, perhaps, for her own consciousness, and perceptible only to such intuitive discernment as that of the artist. But Owen, in the latter stages of his pursuit, had risen out of the region in which such a discovery might have been torture. He knew that the world, and Annie as the representative of the world, whatever praise might be bestowed, could never say the fitting word nor feel the fitting sentiment which should be the perfect recompense of an artist who, symbolizing a lofty moral by a material trifle,—converting what was earthly to spiritual gold,—had won the beautiful into his handiwork. Not at this latest moment was he to learn that the reward of all high performance must be sought within itself, or sought in vain. There was, however, a view of the matter which Annie and her husband, and even Peter Hovenden, might fully have understood, and which would have satisfied them that the toil of years had here been worthily bestowed. Owen Warland might have told them that this butterfly, this plaything, this bridal gift of a poor watchmaker to a blacksmith's wife, was, in truth, a gem of art that a monarch would have purchased with honors and abundant wealth, and have treasured it among the jewels of his kingdom as the most unique and wondrous of them all. But the artist smiled and kept the secret to himself.

"Father," said Annie, thinking that a word of praise from the old watchmaker might gratify his former apprentice, "do come and admire this pretty butterfly."

"Let us see," said Peter Hovenden, rising from his chair, with a sneer upon his face that always made people doubt, as he himself did, in everything but a material existence. "Here is my finger for it to alight upon. I shall understand it better when once I have touched it."

But, to the increased astonishment of Annie, when the tip of her father's finger was pressed against that of her husband, on which the butterfly still rested, the insect drooped its wings and seemed on the point of falling to the floor. Even the bright spots of gold upon its wings and body, unless her eyes deceived her, grew dim, and the glowing purple took a dusky hue, and the starry lustre that gleamed around the blacksmith's hand became faint and vanished.

"It is dying! it is dying!" cried Annie, in alarm.

"It has been delicately wrought," said the artist, calmly. "As I told you, it has imbibed a spiritual essence—call it magnetism, or what you will. In an atmosphere of doubt and mockery its exquisite susceptibility suffers torture, as does the soul of him who instilled his own life into it. It has already lost its beauty; in a few moments more its mechanism would be irreparably injured."

"Take away your hand, father!" entreated Annie, turning pale. "Here is my child; let it rest on his innocent hand. There, perhaps, its life will revive and its colors grow brighter than ever."

Her father, with an acrid smile, withdrew his finger. The butterfly then appeared to recover the power of voluntary motion, while its hues assumed much of their original lustre, and the gleam of starlight, which was its most ethereal attribute, again formed a halo round about it. At first, when transferred from Robert Danforth's hand to the small finger of the child, this radiance grew so powerful that it positively threw the little fellow's shadow back against the wall. He, meanwhile, extended his plump hand as he had seen his father and mother do, and watched the waving of the insect's wings with infantine delight. Nevertheless, there was a certain odd expression of sagacity that made Owen Warland feel as if here were old Peter Hovenden, partially, and but partially, redeemed from his hard scepticism into childish faith.

"How wise the little monkey looks!" whispered Robert Danforth to his wife.

"I never saw such a look on a child's face," answered Annie, admiring her own infant, and with good reason, far more than the artistic butterfly. "The darling knows more of the mystery than we do."

As if the butterfly, like the artist, were conscious of something not entirely congenial in the child's nature, it alternately sparkled and grew dim. At length it arose from the small hand of the infant with an airy motion that seemed to bear it upward without an effort, as if the ethereal instincts with which its master's spirit had endowed it impelled this fair vision involuntarily to a higher sphere. Had there been no obstruction, it might have soared into the sky and grown immortal. But its lustre gleamed upon the ceiling; the exquisite texture of its wings brushed against that earthly medium; and a sparkle or two, as of stardust, floated downward and lay glimmering on the carpet. Then the butterfly came fluttering down, and, instead of returning to the infant, was apparently attracted towards the artist's hand.

"Not so! not so!" murmured Owen Warland, as if his handiwork could have understood him. "Thou hast gone forth out of thy master's heart. There is no return for thee."

With a wavering movement, and emitting a tremulous radiance, the butterfly struggled, as it were, towards the infant, and was about to alight upon his finger; but while it still hovered in the air, the little child of strength, with his grandsire's sharp and shrewd expression in his face, made a snatch at the marvellous insect and compressed it in his hand. Annie screamed. Old Peter Hovenden burst into a cold and scornful laugh. The blacksmith, by main force, unclosed the infant's hand, and found within the palm a small heap of glittering fragments, whence the mystery of beauty had fled forever. And as for Owen Warland, he looked placidly at what seemed the ruin of his life's labor, and which was yet no ruin. He had caught a far other butterfly than this. When the artist rose high enough to achieve the beautiful, the symbol by which he made it perceptible to mortal senses became of little value in his eyes while his spirit possessed itself in the enjoyment of the reality.

1844

Rappaccini's Daughter

(From the writings of Aubépine.[1])

We do not remember to have seen any translated specimens of the productions of M. de l'Aubépine—a fact the less to be wondered at, as his very name is unknown to many of his own countrymen as well as to the student of foreign literature. As a writer, he seems to occupy an unfortunate position between the Transcendentalists (who, under one name or another, have their share in all the current literature of the world) and the great body of pen-and-ink men who address the intellect and sympathies of the multitude. If not too refined, at all events too remote, too shadowy, and unsubstantial in his modes of development to suit the taste of the latter class, and yet too popular to satisfy the spiritual or metaphysical requisitions of the former, he must necessarily find himself without an audience, except here and there an individual or possibly an isolated clique. His writings, to do them justice, are not altogether destitute of fancy and originality; they might have won him greater reputation but for an inveterate love of allegory, which is apt to invest his plots and characters with the aspect of scenery and people in the clouds, and to steal away the human warmth out of his conceptions. His fictions are sometimes historical, sometimes of the present day, and sometimes, so far as can be discovered, have little or no reference either to time or space. In any case, he generally contents himself with a very slight embroidery of outward manners,—the faintest possible counterfeit of real life,—and endeavors to create an interest by some less obvious peculiarity of the subject. Occasionally a breath of Nature, a raindrop of pathos and tenderness, or a gleam of humor, will find its way into the midst of his fantastic imagery, and make us feel as if, after all, we were yet within the limits of our native earth. We will only add to this very cursory notice that M. de l'Aubépine's productions, if the reader chance to take them in precisely the proper point of view, may amuse a leisure hour as well as those of a brighter man; if otherwise, they can hardly fail to look excessively like nonsense.

Our author is voluminous; he continues to write and publish with as much praiseworthy and indefatigable prolixity as if his efforts were crowned with the

---

[1] French: "Hawthorne."

brilliant success that so justly attends those of Eugene Sue.[2] His first appearance was by a collection of stories in a long series of volumes entitled "Contes deux fois racontées."[3] The titles of some of his more recent works (we quote from memory) are as follows: "Le Voyage Céleste à Chemin de Fer," 3 tom., 1838; "Le nouveau Père Adam et la nouvelle Mère Eve," 2 tom., 1839; "Roderic; ou le Serpent à l'estomac," 2 tom., 1840; "Le Culte du Feu," a folio volume of ponderous research into the religion and ritual of the old Persian Ghebers, published in 1841; "La Soirée du Chateau en Espagne," 1 tom., 8vo, 1842; and "L'Artiste du Beau; ou le Papillon Mécanique," 5 tom., 4to, 1843.[4] Our somewhat wearisome perusal of this startling catalogue of volumes has left behind it a certain personal affection and sympathy, though by no means admiration, for M. de l'Aubépine; and we would fain do the little in our power towards introducing him favorably to the American public. The ensuing tale is a translation of his "Beatrice; ou la Belle Empoisonneuse," recently published in "La Revue Anti-Aristocratique." This journal, edited by the Comte de Bearhaven,[5] has for some years past led the defence of liberal principles and popular rights with a faithfulness and ability worthy of all praise.

A young man, named Giovanni Guasconti, came, very long ago, from the more southern region of Italy, to pursue his studies at the University of Padua. Giovanni, who had but a scanty supply of gold ducats in his pocket, took lodgings in a high and gloomy chamber of an old edifice which looked not unworthy to have been the palace of a Paduan noble, and which, in fact, exhibited over its entrance the armorial bearings of a family long since extinct. The young stranger, who was not unstudied in the great poem of his country, recollected that one of the ancestors of this family, and perhaps an occupant of this very mansion, had been pictured by Dante as a partaker of the immortal agonies of his Inferno. These reminiscences and associations, together with the tendency to heartbreak natural to a young man for the first time out of his native sphere, caused Giovanni to sigh heavily as he looked around the desolate and ill-furnished apartment.

"Holy Virgin, signor!" cried old Dame Lisabetta, who, won by the youth's remarkable beauty of person, was kindly endeavoring to give the chamber a habitable air, "what a sigh was that to come out of a young man's heart! Do you find this old mansion gloomy? For the love of Heaven, then, put your head out of the window, and you will see as bright sunshine as you have left in Naples."

Guasconti mechanically did as the old woman advised, but could not quite agree with her that the Paduan sunshine was as cheerful as that of southern Italy. Such as it was, however, it fell upon a garden beneath the window and expended its fostering influences on a variety of plants, which seemed to have been cultivated with exceeding care.

"Does this garden belong to the house?" asked Giovanni.

"Heaven forbid, signor, unless it were fruitful of better pot herbs than any that grow there now," answered old Lisabetta. "No; that garden is cultivated by the own

---

[2] Popular French novelist (1804–1857).
[3] I.e., Hawthorne's *Twice-Told Tales* (1837).
[4] Mock bibliographic references, including the supposed volume ("tom"), octavo ("8vo"), and quarto ("4to") of each work.
[5] John O'Sullivan, editor of *The Democractic Review.*

hands of Signor Giacomo Rappaccini, the famous doctor, who, I warrant him, has been heard of as far as Naples. It is said that he distils these plants into medicines that are as potent as a charm. Oftentimes you may see the signor doctor at work, and perchance the signora, his daughter, too, gathering the strange flowers that grow in the garden."

The old woman had now done what she could for the aspect of the chamber; and, commending the young man to the protection of the saints, took her departure.

Giovanni still found no better occupation than to look down into the garden beneath his window. From its appearance, he judged it to be one of those botanic gardens which were of earlier date in Padua than elsewhere in Italy or in the world. Or, not improbably, it might once have been the pleasure-place of an opulent family; for there was the ruin of a marble fountain in the centre, sculptured with rare art, but so wofully shattered that it was impossible to trace the original design from the chaos of remaining fragments. The water, however, continued to gush and sparkle into the sunbeams as cheerfully as ever. A little gurgling sound ascended to the young man's window, and made him feel as if the fountain were an immortal spirit that sung its song unceasingly and without heeding the vicissitudes around it, while one century imbodied it in marble and another scattered the perishable garniture on the soil. All about the pool into which the water subsided grew various plants, that seemed to require a plentiful supply of moisture for the nourishment of gigantic leaves, and, in some instances, flowers gorgeously magnificent. There was one shrub in particular, set in a marble vase in the midst of the pool, that bore a profusion of purple blossoms, each of which had the lustre and richness of a gem; and the whole together made a show so resplendent that it seemed enough to illuminate the garden, even had there been no sunshine. Every portion of the soil was peopled with plants and herbs, which, if less beautiful, still bore tokens of assiduous care, as if all had their individual virtues, known to the scientific mind that fostered them. Some were placed in urns, rich with old carving, and others in common garden pots; some crept serpent-like along the ground or climbed on high, using whatever means of ascent was offered them. One plant had wreathed itself round a statue of Vertumnus,[6] which was thus quite veiled and shrouded in a drapery of hanging foliage, so happily arranged that it might have served a sculptor for a study.

While Giovanni stood at the window he heard a rustling behind a screen of leaves, and became aware that a person was at work in the garden. His figure soon emerged into view, and showed itself to be that of no common laborer, but a tall, emaciated, sallow, and sickly-looking man, dressed in a scholar's garb of black. He was beyond the middle term of life, with gray hair, a thin, gray beard, and a face singularly marked with intellect and cultivation, but which could never, even in his more youthful days, have expressed much warmth of heart.

Nothing could exceed the intentness with which this scientific gardener examined every shrub which grew in his path: it seemed as if he was looking into their inmost nature, making observations in regard to their creative essence, and discovering why one leaf grew in this shape and another in that, and wherefore such and such flowers differed among themselves in hue and perfume. Nevertheless, in spite of this deep intelligence on his part, there was no approach to intimacy between himself and these

[6] Mythic god who controlled plant growth by presiding over the seasons.

vegetable existences. On the contrary, he avoided their actual touch or the direct inhaling of their odors with a caution that impressed Giovanni most disagreeably; for the man's demeanor was that of one walking among malignant influences, such as savage beasts, or deadly snakes, or evil spirits, which, should he allow them one moment of license, would wreak upon him some terrible fatality. It was strangely frightful to the young man's imagination to see this air of insecurity in a person cultivating a garden, that most simple and innocent of human toils, and which had been alike the joy and labor of the unfallen parents of the race. Was this garden, then, the Eden of the present world? And this man, with such a perception of harm in what his own hands caused to grow,—was he the Adam?

The distrustful gardener, while plucking away the dead leaves or pruning the too luxuriant growth of the shrubs, defended his hands with a pair of thick gloves. Nor were these his only armor. When, in his walk through the garden, he came to the magnificent plant that hung its purple gems beside the marble fountain, he placed a kind of mask over his mouth and nostrils, as if all this beauty did but conceal a deadlier malice; but, finding his task still too dangerous, he drew back, removed the mask, and called loudly, but in the infirm voice of a person affected with inward disease,—

"Beatrice! Beatrice!"

"Here am I, my father. What would you?" cried a rich and youthful voice from the window of the opposite house—a voice as rich as a tropical sunset, and which made Giovanni, though he knew not why, think of deep hues of purple or crimson and of perfumes heavily delectable. "Are you in the garden?"

"Yes, Beatrice," answered the gardener, "and I need your help."

Soon there emerged from under a sculptured portal the figure of a young girl, arrayed with as much richness of taste as the most splendid of the flowers, beautiful as the day, and with a bloom so deep and vivid that one shade more would have been too much. She looked redundant with life, health, and energy; all of which attributes were bound down and compressed, as it were, and girdled tensely, in their luxuriance, by her virgin zone.[7] Yet Giovanni's fancy must have grown morbid while he looked down into the garden; for the impression which the fair stranger made upon him was as if here were another flower, the human sister of those vegetable ones, as beautiful as they, more beautiful than the richest of them, but still to be touched only with a glove, nor to be approached without a mask. As Beatrice came down the garden path, it was observable that she handled and inhaled the odor of several of the plants which her father had most sedulously avoided.

"Here, Beatrice," said the latter, "see how many needful offices require to be done to our chief treasure. Yet, shattered as I am, my life might pay the penalty of approaching it so closely as circumstances demand. Henceforth, I fear, this plant must be consigned to your sole charge."

"And gladly will I undertake it," cried again the rich tones of the young lady, as she bent towards the magnificent plant and opened her arms as if to embrace it. "Yes, my sister, my splendor, it shall be Beatrice's task to nurse and serve thee; and thou shalt reward her with thy kisses and perfumed breath, which to her is as the breath of life."

Then, with all the tenderness in her manner that was so strikingly expressed in her

[7] Belt or girdle customarily worn by unmarried women.

words, she busied herself with such attentions as the plant seemed to require; and Giovanni, at his lofty window, rubbed his eyes and almost doubted whether it were a girl tending her favorite flower, or one sister performing the duties of affection to another. The scene soon terminated. Whether Dr. Rappaccini had finished his labors in the garden, or that his watchful eye had caught the stranger's face, he now took his daughter's arm and retired. Night was already closing in; oppressive exhalations seemed to proceed from the plants and steal upward past the open window; and Giovanni, closing the lattice, went to his couch and dreamed of a rich flower and beautiful girl. Flower and maiden were different, and yet the same, and fraught with some strange peril in either shape.

But there is an influence in the light of morning that tends to rectify whatever errors of fancy, or even of judgment, we may have incurred during the sun's decline, or among the shadows of the night, or in the less wholesome glow of moonshine. Giovanni's first movement, on starting from sleep, was to throw open the window and gaze down into the garden which his dreams had made so fertile of mysteries. He was surprised and a little ashamed to find how real and matter-of-fact an affair it proved to be, in the first rays of the sun which gilded the dew-drops that hung upon leaf and blossom, and, while giving a brighter beauty to each rare flower, brought everything within the limits of ordinary experience. The young man rejoiced that, in the heart of the barren city, he had the privilege of overlooking this spot of lovely and luxuriant vegetation. It would serve, he said to himself, as a symbolic language to keep him in communion with Nature. Neither the sickly and thought-worn Dr. Giacomo Rappaccini, it is true, nor his brilliant daughter, were now visible; so that Giovanni could not determine how much of the singularity which he attributed to both was due to their own qualities and how much to his wonder-working fancy; but he was inclined to take a most rational view of the whole matter.

In the course of the day he paid his respects to Signor Pietro Baglioni, professor of medicine in the university, a physician of eminent repute, to whom Giovanni had brought a letter of introduction. The professor was an elderly personage, apparently of genial nature, and habits that might almost be called jovial. He kept the young man to dinner, and made himself very agreeable by the freedom and liveliness of his conversation, especially when warmed by a flask or two of Tuscan wine. Giovanni, conceiving that men of science, inhabitants of the same city, must needs be on familiar terms with one another, took an opportunity to mention the name of Dr. Rappaccini. But the professor did not respond with so much cordiality as he had anticipated.

"Ill would it become a teacher of the divine art of medicine," said Professor Pietro Baglioni, in answer to a question of Giovanni, "to withhold due and well-considered praise of a physician so eminently skilled as Rappaccini; but, on the other hand, I should answer it but scantily to my conscience were I to permit a worthy youth like yourself, Signor Giovanni, the son of an ancient friend, to imbibe erroneous ideas respecting a man who might hereafter chance to hold your life and death in his hands. The truth is, our worshipful Dr. Rappaccini has as much science as any member of the faculty—with perhaps one single exception—in Padua, or all Italy; but there are certain grave objections to his professional character."

"And what are they?" asked the young man.

"Has my friend Giovanni any disease of body or heart, that he is so inquisitive about physicians?" said the professor, with a smile. "But as for Rappaccini, it is said of him—and I, who know the man well, can answer for its truth—that he cares infinitely more for science than for mankind. His patients are interesting to him only as subjects for some new experiment. He would sacrifice human life, his own among the rest, or whatever else was dearest to him, for the sake of adding so much as a grain of mustard seed to the great heap of his accumulated knowledge."

"Methinks he is an awful man indeed," remarked Guasconti, mentally recalling the cold and purely intellectual aspect of Rappaccini. "And yet, worshipful professor, is it not a noble spirit? Are there many men capable of so spiritual a love of science?"

"God forbid," answered the professor, somewhat testily; "at least, unless they take sounder views of the healing art than those adopted by Rappaccini. It is his theory that all medicinal virtues are comprised within those substances which we term vegetable poisons. These he cultivates with his own hands, and is said even to have produced new varieties of poison, more horribly deleterious than Nature, without the assistance of this learned person, would ever have plagued the world withal. That the signor doctor does less mischief than might be expected with such dangerous substances is undeniable. Now and then, it must be owned, he has effected, or seemed to effect, a marvellous cure; but, to tell you my private mind, Signor Giovanni, he should receive little credit for such instances of success,—they being probably the work of chance,—but should be held strictly accountable for his failures, which may justly be considered his own work."

The youth might have taken Baglioni's opinions with many grains of allowance had he known that there was a professional warfare of long continuance between him and Dr. Rappaccini, in which the latter was generally thought to have gained the advantage. If the reader be inclined to judge for himself, we refer him to certain black-letter tracts on both sides, preserved in the medical department of the University of Padua.

"I know not, most learned professor," returned Giovanni, after musing on what had been said of Rappaccini's exclusive zeal for science,—"I know not how dearly this physician may love his art; but surely there is one object more dear to him. He has a daughter."

"Aha!" cried the professor, with a laugh. "So now our friend Giovanni's secret is out. You have heard of this daughter, whom all the young men in Padua are wild about, though not half a dozen have ever had the good hap to see her face. I know little of the Signora Beatrice save that Rappaccini is said to have instructed her deeply in his science, and that, young and beautiful as fame reports her, she is already qualified to fill a professor's chair. Perchance her father destines her for mine! Other absurd rumors there be, not worth talking about or listening to. So now, Signor Giovanni, drink off your glass of lachryma."[8]

Guasconti returned to his lodgings somewhat heated with the wine he had quaffed, and which caused his brain to swim with strange fantasies in reference to Dr. Rappaccini and the beautiful Beatrice. On his way, happening to pass by a florist's, he bought a fresh bouquet of flowers.

Ascending to his chamber, he seated himself near the window, but within the shadow thrown by the depth of the wall, so that he could look down into the garden

---

[8] I.e., Lachryma Christi ("Tears of Christ"), an Italian wine produced near Vesuvius.

with little risk of being discovered. All beneath his eye was a solitude. The strange plants were basking in the sunshine, and now and then nodding gently to one another, as if in acknowledgment of sympathy and kindred. In the midst, by the shattered fountain, grew the magnificent shrub, with its purple gems clustering all over it; they glowed in the air, and gleamed back again out of the depths of the pool, which thus seemed to overflow with colored radiance from the rich reflection that was steeped in it. At first, as we have said, the garden was a solitude. Soon, however,—as Giovanni had half hoped, half feared, would be the case,—a figure appeared beneath the antique sculptured portal, and came down between the rows of plants, inhaling their various perfumes as if she were one of those beings of old classic fable that lived upon sweet odors. On again beholding Beatrice, the young man was even startled to perceive how much her beauty exceeded his recollection of it; so brilliant, so vivid, was its character, that she glowed amid the sunlight, and, as Giovanni whispered to himself, positively illuminated the more shadowy intervals of the garden path. Her face being now more revealed than on the former occasion, he was struck by its expression of simplicity and sweetness,—qualities that had not entered into his idea of her character, and which made him ask anew what manner of mortal she might be. Nor did he fail again to observe, or imagine, an analogy between the beautiful girl and the gorgeous shrub that hung its gemlike flowers over the fountain,—a resemblance which Beatrice seemed to have indulged a fantastic humor in heightening, both by the arrangement of her dress and the selection of its hues.

Approaching the shrub, she threw open her arms, as with a passionate ardor, and drew its branches into an intimate embrace—so intimate that her features were hidden in its leafy bosom and her glistening ringlets all intermingled with the flowers.

"Give me thy breath, my sister," exclaimed Beatrice; "for I am faint with common air. And give me this flower of thine, which I separate with gentlest fingers from the stem and place it close beside my heart."

With these words the beautiful daughter of Rappaccini plucked one of the richest blossoms of the shrub, and was about to fasten it in her bosom. But now, unless Giovanni's draughts of wine had bewildered his senses, a singular incident occurred. A small orange-colored reptile, of the lizard or chameleon species, chanced to be creeping along the path, just at the feet of Beatrice. It appeared to Giovanni,—but, at the distance from which he gazed, he could scarcely have seen anything so minute, —it appeared to him, however, that a drop or two of moisture from the broken stem of the flower descended upon the lizard's head. For an instant the reptile contorted itself violently, and then lay motionless in the sunshine. Beatrice observed this remarkable phenomenon, and crossed herself, sadly, but without surprise; nor did she therefore hesitate to arrange the fatal flower in her bosom. There it blushed, and almost glimmered with the dazzling effect of a precious stone, adding to her dress and aspect the one appropriate charm which nothing else in the world could have supplied. But Giovanni, out of the shadow of his window, bent forward and shrank back, and murmured and trembled.

"Am I awake? Have I my senses?" said he to himself. "What is this being? Beautiful shall I call her, or inexpressibly terrible?"

Beatrice now strayed carelessly through the garden, approaching closer beneath Giovanni's window, so that he was compelled to thrust his head quite out of its concealment in order to gratify the intense and painful curiosity which she excited.

At this moment there came a beautiful insect over the garden wall; it had, perhaps, wandered through the city, and found no flowers or verdure among those antique haunts of men until the heavy perfumes of Dr. Rappaccini's shrubs had lured it from afar. Without alighting on the flowers, this winged brightness seemed to be attracted by Beatrice, and lingered in the air and fluttered about her head. Now, here it could not be but that Giovanni Guasconti's eyes deceived him. Be that as it might, he fancied that, while Beatrice was gazing at the insect with childish delight, it grew faint and fell at her feet; its bright wings shivered; it was dead—from no cause that he could discern, unless it were the atmosphere of her breath. Again Beatrice crossed herself and sighed heavily as she bent over the dead insect.

An impulsive movement of Giovanni drew her eyes to the window. There she beheld the beautiful head of the young man—rather a Grecian than an Italian head, with fair, regular features, and a glistening of gold among his ringlets—gazing down upon her like a being that hovered in mid air. Scarcely knowing what he did, Giovanni threw down the bouquet which he had hitherto held in his hand.

"Signora," said he, "there are pure and healthful flowers. Wear them for the sake of Giovanni Guasconti."

"Thanks, signor," replied Beatrice, with her rich voice, that came forth as it were like a gush of music, and with a mirthful expression half childish and half woman-like. "I accept your gift, and would fain recompense it with this precious purple flower; but if I toss it into the air it will not reach you. So Signor Guasconti must even content himself with my thanks."

She lifted the bouquet from the ground, and then, as if inwardly ashamed at having stepped aside from her maidenly reserve to respond to a stranger's greeting, passed swiftly homeward through the garden. But few as the moments were, it seemed to Giovanni, when she was on the point of vanishing beneath the sculptured portal, that his beautiful bouquet was already beginning to wither in her grasp. It was an idle thought; there could be no possibility of distinguishing a faded flower from a fresh one at so great a distance.

For many days after this incident the young man avoided the window that looked into Dr. Rappaccini's garden, as if something ugly and monstrous would have blasted his eyesight had he been betrayed into a glance. He felt conscious of having put himself, to a certain extent, within the influence of an unintelligible power by the communication which he had opened with Beatrice. The wisest course would have been, if his heart were in any real danger, to quit his lodgings and Padua itself at once; the next wiser, to have accustomed himself, as far as possible, to the familiar and daylight view of Beatrice—thus bringing her rigidly and systematically within the limits of ordinary experience. Least of all, while avoiding her sight, ought Giovanni to have remained so near this extraordinary being that the proximity and possibility even of intercourse should give a kind of substance and reality to the wild vagaries which his imagination ran riot continually in producing. Guasconti had not a deep heart—or, at all events, its depths were not sounded now; but he had a quick fancy, and an ardent southern temperament, which rose every instant to a higher fever pitch. Whether or no Beatrice possessed those terrible attributes, that fatal breath, the affinity with those so beautiful and deadly flowers which were indicated by what Giovanni had witnessed, she had at least instilled a fierce and subtle poison into his system. It was not love, although her rich beauty was a madness to him; nor horror, even while he fancied her spirit to be imbued with the same baneful essence that seemed to pervade her physical frame; but a wild offspring of both love and horror that had each parent in it, and burned like one and shivered like the other. Giovanni knew not what to dread; still less did he know what to hope; yet hope and dread kept a continual warfare in his breast, alternately vanquishing one another and starting up afresh to renew the contest. Blessed are all simple emotions, be they dark or bright! It is the lurid intermixture of the two that produces the illuminating blaze of the infernal regions.

Sometimes he endeavored to assuage the fever of his spirit by a rapid walk through the streets of Padua or beyond its gates: his footsteps kept time with the throbbings of his brain, so that the walk was apt to accelerate itself to a race. One day he found himself arrested; his arm was seized by a portly personage, who had turned back on recognizing the young man and expended much breath in overtaking him.

"Signor Giovanni! Stay, my young friend!" cried he. "Have you forgotten me? That might well be the case if I were as much altered as yourself."

It was Baglioni, whom Giovanni had avoided ever since their first meeting, from a doubt that the professor's sagacity would look too deeply into his secrets. Endeavoring to recover himself, he stared forth wildly from his inner world into the outer one and spoke like a man in a dream.

"Yes; I am Giovanni Guasconti. You are Professor Pietro Baglioni. Now let me pass!"

"Not yet, not yet, Signor Giovanni Guasconti," said the professor, smiling, but at the same time scrutinizing the youth with an earnest glance. "What! did I grow up side by side with your father? and shall his son pass me like a stranger in these old streets of Padua? Stand still, Signor Giovanni; for we must have a word or two before we part."

"Speedily, then, most worshipful professor, speedily," said Giovanni, with feverish impatience. "Does not your worship see that I am in haste?"

Now, while he was speaking there came a man in black along the street, stooping and moving feebly like a person in inferior health. His face was all overspread with a most sickly and sallow hue, but yet so pervaded with an expression of piercing and active intellect that an observer might easily have overlooked the merely physical attributes and have seen only this wonderful energy. As he passed, this person exchanged a cold and distant salutation with Baglioni, but fixed his eyes upon Giovanni with an intentness that seemed to bring out whatever was within him worthy of notice. Nevertheless, there was a peculiar quietness in the look, as if taking merely a speculative, not a human, interest in the young man.

"It is Dr. Rappaccini!" whispered the professor when the stranger had passed. "Has he ever seen your face before?"

"Not that I know," answered Giovanni, starting at the name.

"He *has* seen you! he must have seen you!" said Baglioni, hastily. "For some purpose or other, this man of science is making a study of you. I know that look of his! It is the same that coldly illuminates his face as he bends over a bird, a mouse, or a butterfly, which, in pursuance of some experiment, he has killed by the perfume of a flower; a look as deep as Nature itself, but without Nature's warmth of love. Signor Giovanni, I will stake my life upon it, you are the subject of one of Rappaccini's experiments!"

"Will you make a fool of me?" cried Giovanni, passionately. "*That*, signor professor, were an untoward experiment."

"Patience! patience!" replied the imperturbable professor. "I tell thee, my poor Giovanni, that Rappaccini has a scientific interest in thee. Thou hast fallen into fearful hands! And the Signora Beatrice,—what part does she act in this mystery?"

But Guasconti, finding Baglioni's pertinacity intolerable, here broke away, and was gone before the professor could again seize his arm. He looked after the young man intently and shook his head.

"This must not be," said Baglioni to himself. "The youth is the son of my old friend, and shall not come to any harm from which the arcana of medical science can preserve him. Besides, it is too insufferable an impertinence in Rappaccini, thus to snatch the lad out of my own hands, as I may say, and make use of him for his infernal experiments. This daughter of his! It shall be looked to. Perchance, most learned Rappaccini, I may foil you where you little dream of it!"

Meanwhile Giovanni had pursued a circuitous route, and at length found himself at the door of his lodgings. As he crossed the threshold he was met by old Lisabetta, who smirked and smiled, and was evidently desirous to attract his attention; vainly, however, as the ebullition of his feelings had momentarily subsided into a cold and dull vacuity. He turned his eyes full upon the withered face that was puckering itself into a smile, but seemed to behold it not. The old dame, therefore, laid her grasp upon his cloak.

"Signor! signor!" whispered she, still with a smile over the whole breadth of her visage, so that it looked not unlike a grotesque carving in wood, darkened by centuries. "Listen, signor! There is a private entrance into the garden!"

"What do you say?" exclaimed Giovanni, turning quickly about, as if an inanimate thing should start into feverish life. "A private entrance into Dr. Rappaccini's garden?"

"Hush! hush! not so loud!" whispered Lisabetta, putting her hand over his mouth. "Yes; into the worshipful doctor's garden, where you may see all his fine shrubbery. Many a young man in Padua would give gold to be admitted among those flowers."

Giovanni put a piece of gold into her hand.

"Show me the way," said he.

A surmise, probably excited by his conversation with Baglioni, crossed his mind, that this interposition of old Lisabetta might perchance be connected with the intrigue, whatever were its nature, in which the professor seemed to suppose that Dr. Rappaccini was involving him. But such a suspicion, though it disturbed Giovanni, was inadequate to restrain him. The instant that he was aware of the possibility of approaching Beatrice, it seemed an absolute necessity of his existence to do so. It mattered not whether she were angel or demon; he was irrevocably within her sphere, and must obey the law that whirled him onward, in ever-lessening circles, towards a result which he did not attempt to foreshadow; and yet, strange to say, there came across him a sudden doubt whether this intense interest on his part were not delusory; whether it were really of so deep and positive a nature as to justify him in now thrusting himself into an incalculable position; whether it were not merely the fantasy of a young man's brain, only slightly or not at all connected with his heart.

He paused, hesitated, turned half about, but again went on. His withered guide led him along several obscure passages, and finally undid a door, through which, as it was opened, there came the sight and sound of rustling leaves, with the broken sunshine glimmering among them. Giovanni stepped forth, and, forcing himself through the entanglement of a shrub that wreathed its tendrils over the hidden entrance, stood beneath his own window in the open area of Dr. Rappaccini's garden.

How often is it the case that, when impossibilities have come to pass and dreams have condensed their misty substance into tangible realities, we find ourselves calm, and even coldly self-possessed, amid circumstances which it would have been a delirium of joy or agony to anticipate! Fate delights to thwart us thus. Passion will choose his own time to rush upon the scene, and lingers sluggishly behind when an appropriate adjustment of events would seem to summon his appearance. So was it now with Giovanni. Day after day his pulses had throbbed with feverish blood at the improbable idea of an interview with Beatrice, and of standing with her, face to face, in this very garden, basking in the Oriental sunshine of her beauty, and snatching from her full gaze the mystery which he deemed the riddle of his own existence. But now there was a singular and untimely equanimity within his breast. He threw a glance around the garden to discover if Beatrice or her father were present, and, perceiving that he was alone, began a critical observation of the plants.

The aspect of one and all of them dissatisfied him; their gorgeousness seemed fierce, passionate, and even unnatural. There was hardly an individual shrub which a wanderer, straying by himself through a forest, would not have been startled to find growing wild, as if an unearthly face had glared at him out of the thicket. Several also would have shocked a delicate instinct by an appearance of artificialness indicating that there had been such commixture, and, as it were, adultery, of various vegetable species, that the production was no longer of God's making, but the monstrous offspring of man's depraved fancy, glowing with only an evil mockery of beauty. They were probably the result of experiment, which in one or two cases had succeeded in mingling plants individually lovely into a compound possessing the questionable and ominous character that distinguished the whole growth of the garden. In fine, Giovanni recognized but two or three plants in the collection, and those of a kind that he well knew to be poisonous. While busy with these contemplations he heard the rustling of a silken garment, and, turning, beheld Beatrice emerging from beneath the sculptured portal.

Giovanni had not considered with himself what should be his deportment; whether he should apologize for his intrusion into the garden, or assume that he was there with the privity at least, if not by the desire, of Dr. Rappaccini or his daughter; but Beatrice's manner placed him at his ease, though leaving him still in doubt by what agency he had gained admittance. She came lightly along the path and met him near the broken fountain. There was surprise in her face, but brightened by a simple and kind expression of pleasure.

"You are a connoisseur in flowers, signor," said Beatrice, with a smile, alluding to the bouquet which he had flung her from the window. "It is no marvel, therefore, if the sight of my father's rare collection has tempted you to take a nearer view. If he were here, he could tell you many strange and interesting facts as to the nature and habits of these shrubs; for he has spent a lifetime in such studies, and this garden is his world."

"And yourself, lady," observed Giovanni, "if fame says true,—you likewise are deeply skilled in the virtues indicated by these rich blossoms and these spicy perfumes. Would you deign to be my instructress, I should prove an apter scholar than if taught by Signor Rappaccini himself."

"Are there such idle rumors?" asked Beatrice, with the music of a pleasant laugh. "Do people say that I am skilled in my father's science of plants? What a jest is there! No; though I have grown up among these flowers, I know no more of them than their hues and perfume; and sometimes methinks I would fain rid myself of even that small knowledge. There are many flowers here, and those not the least brilliant, that shock and offend me when they meet my eye. But pray, signor, do not believe these stories about my science. Believe nothing of me save what you see with your own eyes."

"And must I believe all that I have seen with my own eyes?" asked Giovanni, pointedly, while the recollection of former scenes made him shrink. "No, signora; you demand too little of me. Bid me believe nothing save what comes from your own lips."

It would appear that Beatrice understood him. There came a deep flush to her cheek; but she looked full into Giovanni's eyes, and responded to his gaze of uneasy suspicion with a queenlike haughtiness.

"I do so bid you, signor," she replied. "Forget whatever you may have fancied in regard to me. If true to the outward senses, still it may be false in its essence; but the words of Beatrice Rappaccini's lips are true from the depths of the heart outward. Those you may believe."

A fervor glowed in her whole aspect and beamed upon Giovanni's consciousness like the light of truth itself; but while she spoke there was a fragrance in the atmosphere around her, rich and delightful, though evanescent, yet which the young man, from an indefinable reluctance, scarcely dared to draw into his lungs. It might be the odor of the flowers. Could it be Beatrice's breath which thus embalmed her words with a strange richness, as if by steeping them in her heart? A faintness passed like a shadow over Giovanni and flitted away; he seemed to gaze through the beautiful girl's eyes into her transparent soul, and felt no more doubt or fear.

The tinge of passion that had colored Beatrice's manner vanished; she became gay, and appeared to derive a pure delight from her communion with the youth not unlike what the maiden of a lonely island might have felt conversing with a voyager from the civilized world. Evidently her experience of life had been confined within the limits of that garden. She talked now about matters as simple as the daylight or summer clouds, and now asked questions in reference to the city, or Giovanni's distant home, his friends, his mother, and his sisters—questions indicating such seclusion, and such lack of familiarity with modes and forms, that Giovanni responded as if to an infant. Her spirit gushed out before him like a fresh rill that was just catching its first glimpse of the sunlight and wondering at the reflections of earth and sky which were flung into its bosom. There came thoughts, too, from a deep source, and fantasies of a gemlike brilliancy, as if diamonds and rubies sparkled upward among the bubbles of the fountain. Ever and anon there gleamed across the young man's mind a sense of wonder that he should be walking side by side with the being who had so wrought upon his imagination, whom he had idealized in such hues of terror, in whom he had positively witnessed such manifestations of dreadful attributes,—that he should be conversing with Beatrice like a brother, and should find her so human and so maidenlike. But such reflections were only momentary; the effect of her character was too real not to make itself familiar at once.

In this free intercourse they had strayed through the garden, and now, after many turns among its avenues, were come to the shattered fountain, beside which grew the magnificent shrub, with its treasury of glowing blossoms. A fragrance was diffused from it which Giovanni recognized as identical with that which he had attributed to Beatrice's breath, but incomparably more powerful. As her eyes fell upon it, Giovanni beheld her press her hand to her bosom as if her heart were throbbing suddenly and painfully.

"For the first time in my life," murmured she, addressing the shrub, "I had forgotten thee."

"I remember, signora," said Giovanni, "that you once promised to reward me with one of these living gems for the bouquet which I had the happy boldness to fling to your feet. Permit me now to pluck it as a memorial of this interview."

He made a step towards the shrub with extended hand; but Beatrice darted forward, uttering a shriek that went through his heart like a dagger. She caught his hand and drew it back with the whole force of her slender figure. Giovanni felt her touch thrilling through his fibers.

"Touch it not!" exclaimed she, in a voice of agony. "Not for thy life! It is fatal!"

Then, hiding her face, she fled from him and vanished beneath the sculptured portal. As Giovanni followed her with his eyes, he beheld the emaciated figure and pale intelligence of Dr. Rappaccini, who had been watching the scene, he knew not how long, within the shadow of the entrance.

No sooner was Guasconti alone in his chamber than the image of Beatrice came back to his passionate musings, invested with all the witchery that had been gathering around it ever since his first glimpse of her, and now likewise imbued with a tender warmth of girlish womanhood. She was human; her nature was endowed with all gentle and feminine qualities; she was worthiest to be worshipped; she was capable, surely, on her part, of the height and heroism of love. Those tokens which he had hitherto considered as proofs of a frightful peculiarity in her physical and moral system were now either forgotten, or, by the subtle sophistry of passion transmitted into a golden crown of enchantment, rendering Beatrice the more admirable by so much as she was the more unique. Whatever had looked ugly was now beautiful; or, if incapable of such a change, it stole away and hid itself among those shapeless half ideas which throng the dim region beyond the daylight of our perfect consciousness. Thus did he spend the night, nor fell asleep until the dawn had begun to awake the slumbering flowers in Dr. Rappaccini's garden, whither Giovanni's dreams doubtless led him. Up rose the sun in his due season, and, flinging his beams upon the young man's eyelids, awoke him to a sense of pain. When thoroughly aroused, he became sensible of a burning and tingling agony in his hand—in his right hand—the very hand which Beatrice had grasped in her own when he was on the point of plucking one of the gemlike flowers. On the back of that hand there was now a purple print like that of four small fingers, and the likeness of a slender thumb upon his wrist.

Oh, how stubbornly does love,—or even that cunning semblance of love which flourishes in the imagination, but strikes no depth of root into the heart,—how stubbornly does it hold its faith until the moment comes when it is doomed to vanish into thin mist! Giovanni wrapped a handkerchief about his hand and wondered what evil thing had stung him, and soon forgot his pain in a reverie of Beatrice.

After the first interview, a second was in the inevitable course of what we call fate. A third; a fourth; and a meeting with Beatrice in the garden was no longer an incident in Giovanni's daily life, but the whole space in which he might be said to live; for the anticipation and memory of that ecstatic hour made up the remainder. Nor was it otherwise with the daughter of Rappaccini. She watched for the youth's appearance, and flew to his side with confidence as unreserved as if they had been playmates from early infancy—as if they were such playmates still. If, by any unwonted chance, he failed to come at the appointed moment, she stood beneath the window and sent up the rich sweetness of her tones to float around him in his chamber and echo and reverberate throughout his heart: "Giovanni! Giovanni! Why tarriest thou? Come down!" And down he hastened into that Eden of poisonous flowers.

But, with all this intimate familiarity, there was still a reserve in Beatrice's demeanor, so rigidly and invariably sustained that the idea of infringing it scarcely occurred to his imagination. By all appreciable signs, they loved; they had looked love with eyes that conveyed the holy secret from the depths of one soul into the depths of the other, as if it were too sacred to be whispered by the way; they had even spoken love in those gushes of passion when their spirits darted forth in articulated breath like tongues of long-hidden flame; and yet there had been no seal of lips, no clasp of hands, nor any slightest caress such as love claims and hallows. He had never touched one of the gleaming ringlets of her hair; her garment—so marked was the physical barrier between them—had never been waved against him by a breeze. On the few occasions when Giovanni had seemed tempted to overstep the limit, Beatrice grew so sad, so stern, and withal wore such a look of desolate separation, shuddering at itself, that not a spoken word was requisite to repel him. At such times he was startled at the horrible suspicions that rose, monster-like, out of the caverns of his heart and stared him in the face; his love grew thin and faint as the morning mist, his doubts alone had substance. But, when Beatrice's face brightened again after the momentary shadow, she was transformed at once from the mysterious, questionable being whom he had watched with so much awe and horror; she was now the beautiful and unsophisticated girl whom he felt that his spirit knew with a certainty beyond all other knowledge.

A considerable time had now passed since Giovanni's last meeting with Baglioni. One morning, however, he was disagreeably surprised by a visit from the professor, whom he had scarcely thought of for whole weeks, and would willingly have forgotten still longer. Given up as he had long been to a pervading excitement, he could tolerate no companions except upon condition of their perfect sympathy with his present state of feeling. Such sympathy was not to be expected from Professor Baglioni.

The visitor chatted carelessly for a few moments about the gossip of the city and the university, and then took up another topic.

"I have been reading an old classic author lately," said he, "and met with a story[9] that strangely interested me. Possibly you may remember it. It is of an Indian prince, who sent a beautiful woman as a present to Alexander the Great. She was as lovely as the dawn and gorgeous as the sunset; but what especially distinguished her was a certain rich perfume in her breath—richer than a garden of Persian roses. Alexander,

[9] See *Vulgar Errors* (1646) by Sir Thomas Browne (1605–1682), English physician and author.

as was natural to a youthful conqueror, fell in love at first sight with this magnificent stranger; but a certain sage physician, happening to be present, discovered a terrible secret in regard to her."

"And what was that?" asked Giovanni, turning his eyes downward to avoid those of the professor.

"That this lovely woman," continued Baglioni, with emphasis, "had been nourished with poisons from her birth upward, until her whole nature was so imbued with them that she herself had become the deadliest poison in existence. Poison was her element of life. With that rich perfume of her breath she blasted the very air. Her love would have been poison—her embrace death. Is not this a marvellous tale?"

"A childish fable," answered Giovanni, nervously starting from his chair. "I marvel how your worship finds time to read such nonsense among your graver studies."

"By the by," said the professor, looking uneasily about him, "what singular fragrance is this in your apartment? Is it the perfume of your gloves? It is faint, but delicious; and yet, after all, by no means agreeable. Were I to breathe it long, methinks it would make me ill. It is like the breath of a flower; but I see no flowers in the chamber."

"Nor are there any," replied Giovanni, who had turned pale as the professor spoke; "nor, I think, is there any fragrance except in your worship's imagination. Odors, being a sort of element combined of the sensual and the spiritual, are apt to deceive us in this manner. The recollection of a perfume, the bare idea of it, may easily be mistaken for a present reality."

"Ay; but my sober imagination does not often play such tricks," said Baglioni; "and, were I to fancy any kind of odor, it would be that of some vile apothecary drug, wherewith my fingers are likely enough to be imbued. Our worshipful friend Rappaccini, as I have heard, tinctures his medicaments with odors richer than those of Araby. Doubtless, likewise, the fair and learned Signora Beatrice would minister to her patients with draughts as sweet as a maiden's breath; but woe to him that sips them!"

Giovanni's face evinced many contending emotions. The tone in which the professor alluded to the pure and lovely daughter of Rappaccini was a torture to his soul; and yet the intimation of a view of her character, opposite to his own, gave instantaneous distinctness to a thousand dim suspicions, which now grinned at him like so many demons. But he strove hard to quell them and to respond to Baglioni with a true lover's perfect faith.

"Signor professor," said he, "you were my father's friend; perchance, too, it is your purpose to act a friendly part towards his son. I would fain feel nothing towards you save respect and deference; but I pray you to observe, signor, that there is one subject on which we must not speak. You know not the Signora Beatrice. You cannot, therefore, estimate the wrong—the blasphemy, I may even say—that is offered to her character by a light or injurious word."

"Giovanni! my poor Giovanni!" answered the professor, with a calm expression of pity, "I know this wretched girl far better than yourself. You shall hear the truth in respect to the poisoner Rappaccini and his poisonous daughter; yes, poisonous as she is beautiful. Listen; for, even should you do violence to my gray hairs, it shall not silence me. That old fable of the Indian woman has become a truth by the deep and deadly science of Rappaccini and in the person of the lovely Beatrice."

Giovanni groaned and hid his face.

"Her father," continued Baglioni, "was not restrained by natural affection from offering up his child in this horrible manner as the victim of his insane zeal for science; for, let us do him justice, he is as true a man of science as ever distilled his own heart in an alembic.[10] What, then, will be your fate? Beyond a doubt you are selected as the material of some new experiment. Perhaps the result is to be death; perhaps a fate more awful still. Rappaccini, with what he calls the interest of science before his eyes, will hesitate at nothing."

"It is a dream," muttered Giovanni to himself; "surely it is a dream."

"But," resumed the professor, "be of good cheer, son of my friend. It is not yet too late for the rescue. Possibly we may even succeed in bringing back this miserable child within the limits of ordinary nature, from which her father's madness has estranged her. Behold this little silver vase! It was wrought by the hands of the renowned Benvenuto Cellini,[11] and is well worthy to be a love gift to the fairest dame in Italy. But its contents are invaluable. One little sip of this antidote would have rendered the most virulent poisons of the Borgias[12] innocuous. Doubt not that it will be as efficacious against those of Rappaccini. Bestow the vase, and the precious liquid within it, on your Beatrice, and hopefully await the result."

Baglioni laid a small, exquisitely wrought silver vial on the table and withdrew, leaving what he had said to produce its effect upon the young man's mind.

"We will thwart Rappaccini yet," thought he, chuckling to himself, as he descended the stairs; "but, let us confess the truth of him, he is a wonderful man—a wonderful man indeed; a vile empiric, however, in his practice, and therefore not to be tolerated by those who respect the good old rules of the medical profession."

Throughout Giovanni's whole acquaintance with Beatrice, he had occasionally, as we have said, been haunted by dark surmises as to her character; yet so thoroughly had she made herself felt by him as a simple, natural, most affectionate, and guileless creature, that the image now held up by Professor Baglioni looked as strange and incredible as if it were not in accordance with his own original conception. True, there were ugly recollections connected with his first glimpses of the beautiful girl; he could not quite forget the bouquet that withered in her grasp, and the insect that perished amid the sunny air, by no ostensible agency save the fragrance of her breath. These incidents, however, dissolving in the pure light of her character, had no longer the efficacy of facts, but were acknowledged as mistaken fantasies, by whatever testimony of the senses they might appear to be substantiated. There is something truer and more real than what we can see with the eyes and touch with the finger. On such better evidence had Giovanni founded his confidence in Beatrice, though rather by the necessary force of her high attributes than by any deep and generous faith on his part. But now his spirit was incapable of sustaining itself at the height to which the early enthusiasm of passion had exalted it; he fell down, grovelling among earthly doubts, and defiled therewith the pure whiteness of Beatrice's image. Not that he gave her up; he did but distrust. He resolved to institute some decisive test that should satisfy him, once for all, whether there were those dreadful peculiarities in her physical nature

---

[10] Laboratory device for distillation of substances.
[11] Italian artisan, artist, and writer Benvenuto Cellini (1500–1571).

[12] Aristocratic Italian family influential in Renaissance religion and politics, and notorious for its cruelty and licentiousness.

which could not be supposed to exist without some corresponding monstrosity of soul. His eyes, gazing down afar, might have deceived him as to the lizard, the insect, and the flowers; but if he could witness, at the distance of a few paces, the sudden blight of one fresh and healthful flower in Beatrice's hand, there would be room for no further question. With this idea he hastened to the florist's and purchased a bouquet that was still gemmed with the morning dew-drops.

It was now the customary hour of his daily interview with Beatrice. Before descending into the garden, Giovanni failed not to look at his figure in the mirror, —a vanity to be expected in a beautiful young man, yet, as displaying itself at that troubled and feverish moment, the token of a certain shallowness of feeling and insincerity of character. He did gaze, however, and said to himself that his features had never before possessed so rich a grace, nor his eyes such vivacity, nor his cheeks so warm a hue of super-abundant life.

"At least," thought he, "her poison has not yet insinuated itself into my system. I am no flower to perish in her grasp."

With that thought he turned his eyes on the bouquet, which he had never once laid aside from his hand. A thrill of indefinable horror shot through his frame on perceiving that those dewy flowers were already beginning to droop; they wore the aspect of things that had been fresh and lovely yesterday. Giovanni grew white as marble, and stood motionless before the mirror, staring at his own reflection there as at the likeness of something frightful. He remembered Baglioni's remark about the fragrance that seemed to pervade the chamber. It must have been the poison in his breath! Then he shuddered—shuddered at himself. Recovering from his stupor, he began to watch with curious eye a spider that was busily at work hanging its web from the antique cornice of the apartment, crossing and recrossing the artful system of interwoven lines—as vigorous and active a spider as ever dangled from an old ceiling. Giovanni bent towards the insect, and emitted a deep, long breath. The spider suddenly ceased its toil; the web vibrated with a tremor originating in the body of the small artisan. Again Giovanni sent forth a breath, deeper, longer, and imbued with a venomous feeling out of his heart: he knew not whether he were wicked, or only desperate. The spider made a convulsive gripe with his limbs and hung dead across the window.

"Accursed! accursed!" muttered Giovanni, addressing himself. "Hast thou grown so poisonous that this deadly insect perishes by thy breath?"

At that moment a rich, sweet voice came floating up from the garden.

"Giovanni! Giovanni! It is past the hour! Why tarriest thou? Come down!"

"Yes," muttered Giovanni again. "She is the only being whom my breath may not slay! Would that it might!"

He rushed down, and in an instant was standing before the bright and loving eyes of Beatrice. A moment ago his wrath and despair had been so fierce that he could have desired nothing so much as to wither her by a glance; but with her actual presence there came influences which had too real an existence to be at once shaken off: recollections of the delicate and benign power of her feminine nature, which had so often enveloped him in a religious calm; recollections of many a holy and passionate outgush of her heart, when the pure fountain had been unsealed from its depths and made visible in its transparency to his mental eye; recollections which, had Giovanni known how to estimate them, would have assured him that all this ugly mystery was but an earthly illusion, and that, whatever mist of evil might seem to have gathered over her, the real Beatrice was a heavenly angel. Incapable as he was of such high faith, still her presence had not utterly lost its magic. Giovanni's rage was quelled into an aspect of sullen insensibility. Beatrice, with a quick spiritual sense, immediately felt that there was a gulf of blackness between them which neither he nor she could pass. They walked on together, sad and silent, and came thus to the marble fountain and to its pool of water on the ground, in the midst of which grew the shrub that bore gem-like blossoms. Giovanni was affrighted at the eager enjoyment—the appetite, as it were—with which he found himself inhaling the fragrance of the flowers.

"Beatrice," asked he, abruptly, "whence came this shrub?"

"My father created it," answered she, with simplicity.

"Created it! created it!" repeated Giovanni. "What mean you, Beatrice?"

"He is a man fearfully acquainted with the secrets of Nature," replied Beatrice; "and, at the hour when I first drew breath, this plant sprang from the soil, the offspring of his science, of his intellect, while I was but his earthly child. Approach it not!" continued she, observing with terror that Giovanni was drawing nearer to the shrub. "It has qualities that you little dream of. But I, dearest Giovanni,—I grew up and blossomed with the plant and was nourished with its breath. It was my sister, and I loved it with a human affection; for, alas!—hast thou not suspected it?—there was an awful doom."

Here Giovanni frowned so darkly upon her that Beatrice paused and trembled. But her faith in his tenderness reassured her, and made her blush that she had doubted for an instant.

"There was an awful doom," she continued, "the effect of my father's fatal love of science, which estranged me from all society of my kind. Until Heaven sent thee, dearest Giovanni, oh, how lonely was thy poor Beatrice!"

"Was it a hard doom?" asked Giovanni, fixing his eyes upon her.

"Only of late have I known how hard it was," answered she, tenderly. "Oh, yes; but my heart was torpid, and therefore quiet."

Giovanni's rage broke forth from his sullen gloom like a lightning flash out of a dark cloud.

"Accursed one!" cried he, with venomous scorn and anger. "And, finding thy solitude wearisome, thou hast severed me likewise from all the warmth of life and enticed me into thy region of unspeakable horror!"

"Giovanni!" exclaimed Beatrice, turning her large bright eyes upon his face. The force of his words had not found its way into her mind; she was merely thunderstruck.

"Yes, poisonous thing!" repeated Giovanni, beside himself with passion. "Thou hast done it! Thou hast blasted me! Thou hast filled my veins with poison! Thou hast made me as hateful, as ugly, as loathsome and deadly a creature as thyself—a world's wonder of hideous monstrosity! Now, if our breath be happily as fatal to ourselves as to all others, let us join our lips in one kiss of unutterable hatred, and so die!"

"What has befallen me?" murmured Beatrice, with a low moan out of her heart. "Holy Virgin, pity me, a poor heart-broken child!"

"Thou,—dost thou pray?" cried Giovanni, still with the same fiendish scorn. "Thy very prayers, as they come from thy lips, taint the atmosphere with death. Yes, yes; let us pray! Let us to church and dip our fingers in the holy water at the portal! They that come after us will perish as by a pestilence! Let us sign crosses in the air! It will be scattering curses abroad in the likeness of holy symbols!"

"Giovanni," said Beatrice, calmly, for her grief was beyond passion, "why dost thou join thyself with me thus in those terrible words? I, it is true, am the horrible thing thou namest me. But thou,—what hast thou to do, save with one other shudder at my hideous misery to go forth out of the garden and mingle with thy race, and forget that there ever crawled on earth such a monster as poor Beatrice?"

"Dost thou pretend ignorance?" asked Giovanni, scowling upon her. "Behold! this power have I gained from the pure daughter of Rappaccini."

There was a swarm of summer insects flitting through the air in search of the food promised by the flower odors of the fatal garden. They circled round Giovanni's head, and were evidently attracted towards him by the same influence which had drawn them for an instant within the sphere of several of the shrubs. He sent forth a breath among them, and smiled bitterly at Beatrice as at least a score of the insects fell dead upon the ground.

"I see it! I see it!" shrieked Beatrice. "It is my father's fatal science! No, no, Giovanni; it was not I! Never! never! I dreamed only to love thee and be with thee a little time, and so to let thee pass away, leaving but thine image in mine heart; for, Giovanni, believe it, though my body be nourished with poison, my spirit is God's creature, and craves love as its daily food. But my father,—he has united us in this fearful sympathy. Yes; spurn me, tread upon me, kill me! Oh, what is death after such words as thine? But it was not I. Not for a world of bliss would I have done it."

Giovanni's passion had exhausted itself in its outburst from his lips. There now came across him a sense, mournful, and not without tenderness, of the intimate and peculiar relationship between Beatrice and himself. They stood, as it were, in an utter solitude, which would be made none the less solitary by the densest throng of human life. Ought not, then, the desert of humanity around them to press this insulated pair closer together? If they should be cruel to one another, who was there to be kind to them? Besides, thought Giovanni, might there not still be a hope of his returning within the limits of ordinary nature, and leading Beatrice, the redeemed Beatrice, by the hand? O, weak, and selfish, and unworthy spirit, that could dream of an earthly union and earthly happiness as possible, after such deep love had been so bitterly wronged as was Beatrice's love by Giovanni's blighting words! No, no; there could be no such hope. She must pass heavily, with that broken heart, across the borders of Time—she must bathe her hurts in some fount of paradise, and forget her grief in the light of immortality, and *there* be well.

But Giovanni did not know it.

"Dear Beatrice," said he, approaching her, while she shrank away as always at his approach, but now with a different impulse, "dearest Beatrice, our fate is not yet so desperate. Behold! there is a medicine, potent, as a wise physician has assured me, and almost divine in its efficacy. It is composed of ingredients the most opposite to those by which thy awful father has brought this calamity upon thee and me. It is distilled of blessed herbs. Shall we not quaff it together, and thus be purified from evil?"

"Give it me!" said Beatrice, extending her hand to receive the little silver vial which Giovanni took from his bosom. She added, with a peculiar emphasis, "I will drink; but do thou await the result."

She put Baglioni's antidote to her lips; and, at the same moment, the figure of Rappaccini emerged from the portal and came slowly towards the marble fountain. As he drew near, the pale man of science seemed to gaze with a triumphant expression at the beautiful youth and maiden, as might an artist who should spend his life in achieving a picture or a group of statuary and finally be satisfied with his success. He paused; his bent form grew erect with conscious power; he spread out his hands over them in the attitude of a father imploring a blessing upon his children; but those were the same hands that had thrown poison into the stream of their lives. Giovanni trembled. Beatrice shuddered nervously, and pressed her hand upon her heart.

"My daughter," said Rappaccini, "thou art no longer lonely in the world. Pluck one of those precious gems from thy sister shrub and bid thy bridegroom wear it in his bosom. It will not harm him now. My science and the sympathy between thee and him have so wrought within his system that he now stands apart from common men, as thou dost, daughter of my pride and triumph, from ordinary women. Pass on, then, through the world, most dear to one another and dreadful to all besides!"

"My father," said Beatrice, feebly,—and still as she spoke she kept her hand upon her heart,—"wherefore didst thou inflict this miserable doom upon thy child?"

"Miserable!" exclaimed Rappaccini. "What mean you, foolish girl? Dost thou deem it misery to be endowed with marvellous gifts against which no power nor strength could avail an enemy—misery, to be able to quell the mightiest with a breath —misery, to be as terrible as thou art beautiful? Wouldst thou, then, have preferred the condition of a weak woman, exposed to all evil and capable of none?"

"I would fain have been loved, not feared," murmured Beatrice, sinking down upon the ground. "But now it matters not. I am going, father, where the evil which thou hast striven to mingle with my being will pass away like a dream—like the fragrance of these poisonous flowers, which will no longer taint my breath among the flowers of Eden. Farewell, Giovanni! Thy words of hatred are like lead within my heart; but they, too, will fall away as I ascend. Oh, was there not, from the first, more poison in thy nature than in mine?"

To Beatrice,—so radically had her earthly part been wrought upon by Rappaccini's skill,—as poison had been life, so the powerful antidote was death; and thus the poor victim of man's ingenuity and of thwarted nature, and of the fatality that attends all such efforts of perverted wisdom, perished there, at the feet of her father and Giovanni. Just at that moment Professor Pietro Baglioni looked forth from the window, and called loudly, in a tone of triumph mixed with horror, to the thunderstricken man of science,—

"Rappaccini! Rappaccini! and is *this* the upshot of your experiment!"

1844

Ethan Brand
A Chapter from an Abortive Romance

Bartram the lime-burner,[1] a rough, heavy-looking man, begrimed with charcoal, sat watching his kiln at nightfall, while his little son played at building houses with the scattered fragments of marble, when, on the hill-side below them, they heard a roar

---

[1] One who burns limestone in the making of cement.

of laughter, not mirthful, but slow, and even solemn, like a wind shaking the boughs of the forest.

"Father, what is that?" asked the little boy, leaving his play, and pressing betwixt his father's knees.

"Oh, some drunken man, I suppose," answered the lime-burner; "some merry fellow from the bar-room in the village, who dared not laugh loud enough within doors lest he should blow the roof of the house off. So here he is, shaking his jolly sides at the foot of Graylock."[2]

"But, father," said the child, more sensitive than the obtuse, middle-aged clown, "he does not laugh like a man that is glad. So the noise frightens me!"

"Don't be a fool, child!" cried his father, gruffly. "You will never make a man, I do believe; there is too much of your mother in you. I have known the rustling of a leaf startle you. Hark! Here comes the merry fellow now. You shall see that there is no harm in him."

Bartram and his little son, while they were talking thus, sat watching the same lime-kiln that had been the scene of Ethan Brand's solitary and meditative life, before he began his search for the Unpardonable Sin. Many years, as we have seen, had now elapsed, since that portentous night when the IDEA was first developed. The kiln, however, on the mountain-side, stood unimpaired, and was in nothing changed since he had thrown his dark thoughts into the intense glow of its furnace, and melted them, as it were, into the one thought that took possession of his life. It was a rude, round, tower-like structure about twenty feet high, heavily built of rough stones, and with a hillock of earth heaped about the larger part of its circumference; so that the blocks and fragments of marble might be drawn by cart-loads, and thrown in at the top. There was an opening at the bottom of the tower, like an oven-mouth, but large enough to admit a man in a stooping posture, and provided with a massive iron door. With the smoke and jets of flame issuing from the chinks and crevices of this door, which seemed to give admittance into the hill-side, it resembled nothing so much as the private entrance to the infernal regions, which the shepherds of the Delectable Mountains were accustomed to show to pilgrims.[3]

There are many such lime-kilns in that tract of country, for the purpose of burning the white marble which composes a large part of the substance of the hills. Some of them, built years ago, and long deserted, with weeds growing in the vacant round of the interior, which is open to the sky, and grass and wildflowers rooting themselves into the chinks of the stones, look already like relics of antiquity, and may yet be overspread with the lichens of centuries to come. Others, where the lime-burner still feeds his daily and night-long fire, afford points of interest to the wanderer among the hills, who seats himself on a log of wood or a fragment of marble, to hold a chat with the solitary man. It is a lonesome, and, when the character is inclined to thought, may be an intensely thoughtful occupation; as it proved in the case of Ethan Brand, who had mused to such strange purpose, in days gone by, while the fire in this very kiln was burning.

The man who now watched the fire was of a different order, and troubled himself

---

[2] Mt. Graylock in the Berkshires has the highest elevation in the state of Massachusetts.
[3] In John Bunyan's novel *The Pilgrim's Progress*

(1678, 1684), the pilgrims were taken to the top of the Delectable Mountains to view the gates of both Heaven and Hell.

with no thoughts save the very few that were requisite to his business. At frequent intervals, he flung back the clashing weight of the iron door, and, turning his face from the insufferable glare, thrust in huge logs of oak, or stirred the immense brands with a long pole. Within the furnace were seen the curling and riotous flames, and the burning marble, almost molten with the intensity of heat; while without, the reflection of the fire quivered on the dark intricacy of the surrounding forest, and showed in the foreground a bright and ruddy little picture of the hut, the spring beside its door, the athletic and coal-begrimed figure of the lime-burner, and the half-frightened child, shrinking into the protection of his father's shadow. And when, again, the iron door was closed, then reappeared the tender light of the half-full moon, which vainly strove to trace out the indistinct shapes of the neighboring mountains; and, in the upper sky, there was a flitting congregation of clouds, still faintly tinged with the rosy sunset, though thus far down into the valley the sunshine had vanished long and long ago.

The little boy now crept still closer to his father, as footsteps were heard ascending the hill-side, and a human form thrust aside the bushes that clustered beneath the trees.

"Halloo! who is it?" cried the lime-burner, vexed at his son's timidity, yet half infected by it. "Come forward, and show yourself, like a man, or I'll fling this chunk of marble at your head!"

"You offer me a rough welcome," said a gloomy voice, as the unknown man drew nigh. "Yet I neither claim nor desire a kinder one, even at my own fireside."

To obtain a distincter view, Bartram threw open the iron door of the kiln, whence immediately issued a gush of fierce light, that smote full upon the stranger's face and figure. To a careless eye there appeared nothing very remarkable in his aspect, which was that of a man in a coarse, brown, country-made suit of clothes, tall and thin, with the staff and heavy shoes of a wayfarer. As he advanced, he fixed his eyes—which were very bright—intently upon the brightness of the furnace, as if he beheld, or expected to behold, some object worthy of note within it.

"Good evening, stranger," said the lime-burner; "whence come you, so late in the day?"

"I come from my search," answered the wayfarer; "for, at last, it is finished."

"Drunk!—or crazy!" muttered Bartram to himself. "I shall have trouble with the fellow. The sooner I drive him away, the better."

The little boy, all in a tremble, whispered to his father, and begged him to shut the door of the kiln, so that there might not be so much light; for that there was something in the man's face which he was afraid to look at, yet could not look away from. And, indeed, even the lime-burner's dull and torpid sense began to be impressed by an indescribable something in that thin, rugged, thoughtful visage, with the grizzled hair hanging wildly about it, and those deeply sunken eyes, which gleamed like fires within the entrance of a mysterious cavern. But, as he closed the door, the stranger turned towards him, and spoke in a quiet, familiar way, that made Bartram feel as if he were a sane and sensible man, after all.

"Your task draws to an end, I see," said he. "This marble has already been burning three days. A few hours more will convert the stone to lime."

"Why, who are you?" exclaimed the lime-burner. "You seem as well acquainted with my business as I am myself."

"And well I may be," said the stranger; "for I followed the same craft many a long year, and here, too, on this very spot. But you are a new-comer in these parts. Did you never hear of Ethan Brand?"

"The man that went in search of the Unpardonable Sin?" asked Bartram, with a laugh.

"The same," answered the stranger. "He has found what he sought, and therefore he comes back again."

"What! then you are Ethan Brand himself?" cried the lime-burner, in amazement. "I am a new-comer here, as you say, and they call it eighteen years since you left the foot of Graylock. But, I can tell you, the good folks still talk about Ethan Brand, in the village yonder, and what a strange errand took him away from his lime-kiln. Well, and so you have found the Unpardonable Sin?"

"Even so!" said the stranger, calmly.

"If the question is a fair one," proceeded Bartram, "where might it be?"

Ethan Brand laid his finger on his own heart.

"Here!" replied he.

And then, without mirth in his countenance, but as if moved by an involuntary recognition of the infinite absurdity of seeking throughout the world for what was the closest of all things to himself, and looking into every heart, save his own, for what was hidden in no other breast, he broke into a laugh of scorn. It was the same slow, heavy laugh, that had almost appalled the lime-burner when it heralded the wayfarer's approach.

The solitary mountain-side was made dismal by it. Laughter, when out of place, mistimed, or bursting forth from a disordered state of feeling, may be the most terrible modulation of the human voice. The laughter of one asleep, even if it be a little child, —the madman's laugh,—the wild, screaming laugh of a born idiot,—are sounds that we sometimes tremble to hear, and would always willingly forget. Poets have imagined no utterance of fiends or hobgoblins so fearfully appropriate as a laugh. And even the obtuse lime-burner felt his nerves shaken, as this strange man looked inward at his own heart, and burst into laughter that rolled away into the night, and was indistinctly reverberated among the hills.

"Joe," said he to his little son, "scamper down to the tavern in the village, and tell the jolly fellows there that Ethan Brand has come back, and that he has found the Unpardonable Sin!"

The boy darted away on his errand, to which Ethan Brand made no objection, nor seemed hardly to notice it. He sat on a log of wood, looking steadfastly at the iron door of the kiln. When the child was out of sight, and his swift and light footsteps ceased to be heard treading first on the fallen leaves and then on the rocky mountain-path, the lime-burner began to regret his departure. He felt that the little fellow's presence had been a barrier between his guest and himself, and that he must now deal, heart to heart, with a man who, on his own confession, had committed the one only crime for which Heaven could afford no mercy. That crime, in its indistinct blackness, seemed to overshadow him. The lime-burner's own sins rose up within him, and made his memory riotous with a throng of evil shapes that asserted their kindred with the Master Sin, whatever it might be, which it was within the scope of man's corrupted nature to conceive and cherish. They were all of one family; they went to and fro between his breast and Ethan Brand's, and carried dark greetings from one to the other.

Then Bartram remembered the stories which had grown traditionary in reference to this strange man, who had come upon him like a shadow of the night, and was making himself at home in his old place, after so long absence, that the dead people, dead and buried for years, would have had more right to be at home, in any familiar spot, than he. Ethan Brand, it was said, had conversed with Satan himself in the lurid blaze of this very kiln. The legend had been matter of mirth heretofore, but looked grisly now. According to this tale, before Ethan Brand departed on his search, he had been accustomed to evoke a fiend from the hot furnace of the lime-kiln, night after night, in order to confer with him about the Unpardonable Sin; the man and the fiend each laboring to frame the image of some mode of guilt which could neither be atoned for nor forgiven. And, with the first gleam of light upon the mountain-top, the fiend crept in at the iron door, there to abide the intensest element of fire until again summoned forth to share in the dreadful task of extending man's possible guilt beyond the scope of Heaven's else infinite mercy.

While the lime-burner was struggling with the horror of these thoughts, Ethan Brand rose from the log, and flung open the door of the kiln. The action was in such accordance with the idea in Bartram's mind, that he almost expected to see the Evil One issue forth, red-hot, from the raging furnace.

"Hold! hold!" cried he, with a tremulous attempt to laugh; for he was ashamed of his fears, although they overmastered him. "Don't, for mercy's sake, bring out your Devil now!"

"Man!" sternly replied Ethan Brand, "what need have I of the Devil? I have left him behind me, on my track. It is with such half-way sinners as you that he busies himself. Fear not, because I open the door. I do but act by old custom, and am going to trim your fire, like a lime-burner, as I was once."

He stirred the vast coals, thrust in more wood, and bent forward to gaze into the hollow prison-house of the fire, regardless of the fierce glow that reddened upon his face. The lime-burner sat watching him, and half suspected this strange guest of a purpose, if not to evoke a fiend, at least to plunge bodily into the flames, and thus vanish from the sight of man. Ethan Brand, however, drew quietly back, and closed the door of the kiln.

"I have looked," said he, "into many a human heart that was seven times hotter with sinful passions than yonder furnace is with fire. But I found not there what I sought. No, not the Unpardonable Sin!"

"What is the Unpardonable Sin?" asked the lime-burner; and then he shrank farther from his companion, trembling lest his question should be answered.

"It is a sin that grew within my own breast," replied Ethan Brand, standing erect, with a pride that distinguishes all enthusiasts of his stamp. "A sin that grew nowhere else! The sin of an intellect that triumphed over the sense of brotherhood with man and reverence for God, and sacrificed everything to its own mighty claims! The only sin that deserves a recompense of immortal agony! Freely, were it to do again, would I incur the guilt. Unshrinkingly I accept the retribution!"

"The man's head is turned," muttered the lime-burner to himself. "He may be a sinner like the rest of us,—nothing more likely,—but, I'll be sworn, he is a madman too."

Nevertheless, he felt uncomfortable at his situation, alone with Ethan Brand on the wild mountain-side, and was right glad to hear the rough murmur of tongues, and the footsteps of what seemed a pretty numerous party, stumbling over the stones and rustling through the underbrush. Soon appeared the whole lazy regiment that was wont to infest the village tavern, comprehending three or four individuals who had drunk flip[4] beside the bar-room fire through all the winters, and smoked their pipes beneath the stoop through all the summers, since Ethan Brand's departure. Laughing boisterously, and mingling all their voices together in unceremonious talk, they now burst into the moonshine and narrow streaks of firelight that illuminated the open space before the lime-kiln. Bartram set the door ajar again, flooding the spot with light, that the whole company might get a fair view of Ethan Brand, and he of them.

There, among other old acquaintances, was a once ubiquitous man, now almost extinct, but whom we were formerly sure to encounter at the hotel of every thriving village throughout the country. It was the stage-agent. The present specimen of the genus was a wilted and smoke-dried man, wrinkled and red-nosed, in a smartly cut, brown, bobtailed coat, with brass buttons, who, for a length of time unknown, had kept his desk and corner in the bar-room, and was still puffing what seemed to be the same cigar that he had lighted twenty years before. He had great fame as a dry joker, though, perhaps, less on account of any intrinsic humor than from a certain flavor of brandy-toddy and tobacco-smoke, which impregnated all his ideas and expressions, as well as his person. Another well-remembered, though strangely altered, face was that of Lawyer Giles, as people still called him in courtesy; an elderly ragamuffin, in his soiled shirt-sleeves and tow-cloth[5] trousers. This poor fellow had been an attorney, in what he called his better days, a sharp practitioner, and in great vogue among the village litigants; but flip, and sling, and toddy, and cocktails, imbibed at all hours, morning, noon, and night, had caused him to slide from intellectual to various kinds and degrees of bodily labor, till at last, to adopt his own phrase, he slid into a soap-vat. In other words, Giles was now a soap-boiler, in a small way. He had come to be but the fragment of a human being, a part of one foot having been chopped off by an axe, and an entire hand torn away by the devilish grip of a steam-engine. Yet, though the corporeal hand was gone, a spiritual member remained; for, stretching forth the stump, Giles steadfastly averred that he felt an invisible thumb and fingers with as vivid a sensation as before the real ones were amputated. A maimed and miserable wretch he was; but one, nevertheless, whom the world could not trample on, and had no right to scorn, either in this or any previous stage of his misfortunes, since he had still kept up the courage and spirit of a man, asked nothing in charity, and with his one hand—and that the left one—fought a stern battle against want and hostile circumstances.

Among the throng, too, came another personage, who, with certain points of similarity to Lawyer Giles, had many more of difference. It was the village doctor; a man of some fifty years, whom, at an earlier period of his life, we introduced as paying a professional visit to Ethan Brand during the latter's supposed insanity. He was now a purple-visaged, rude, and brutal, yet half-gentlemanly figure, with something wild, ruined, and desperate in his talk, and in all the details of his gesture and manners. Brandy possessed this man like an evil spirit, and made him as surly and savage as a wild beast, and as miserable as a lost soul; but there was supposed to be in him such wonderful skill, such native gifts of healing, beyond any which medical

---

[4] A spicy, sweet beer or ale.　　[5] Coarse fabric.

science could impart, that society caught hold of him, and would not let him sink out of its reach. So, swaying to and fro upon his horse, and grumbling thick accents at the bedside, he visited all the sick-chambers for miles about among the mountain towns, and sometimes raised a dying man, as it were; by miracle, or quite as often, no doubt, sent his patient to a grave that was dug many a year too soon. The doctor had an everlasting pipe in his mouth, and, as somebody said, in allusion to his habit of swearing, it was always alight with hell-fire.

These three worthies pressed forward, and greeted Ethan Brand each after his own fashion, earnestly inviting him to partake of the contents of a certain black bottle, in which, as they averred, he would find something far better worth seeking for than the Unpardonable Sin. No mind, which has wrought itself by intense and solitary meditation into a high state of enthusiasm, can endure the kind of contact with low and vulgar modes of thought and feeling to which Ethan Brand was now subjected. It made him doubt—and, strange to say, it was a painful doubt—whether he had indeed found the Unpardonable Sin, and found it within himself. The whole question on which he had exhausted life, and more than life, looked like a delusion.

"Leave me," he said bitterly, "ye brute beasts, that have made yourselves so, shrivelling up your souls with fiery liquors! I have done with you. Years and years ago, I groped into your hearts and found nothing there for my purpose. Get ye gone!"

"Why, you uncivil scoundrel," cried the fierce doctor, "is that the way you respond to the kindness of your best friends? Then let me tell you the truth. You have no more found the Unpardonable Sin than yonder boy Joe has. You are but a crazy fellow,—I told you so twenty years ago,—neither better nor worse than a crazy fellow, and the fit companion of old Humphrey, here!"

He pointed to an old man, shabbily dressed, with long white hair, thin visage, and unsteady eyes. For some years past this aged person had been wandering about among the hills, inquiring of all travellers whom he met for his daughter. The girl, it seemed, had gone off with a company of circus-performers, and occasionally tidings of her came to the village, and fine stories were told of her glittering appearance as she rode on horseback in the ring, or performed marvellous feats on the tight-rope.

The white-haired father now approached Ethan Brand, and gazed unsteadily into his face.

"They tell me you have been all over the earth," said he, wringing his hands with earnestness. "You must have seen my daughter, for she makes a grand figure in the world, and everybody goes to see her. Did she send any word to her old father, or say when she was coming back?"

Ethan Brand's eye quailed beneath the old man's. That daughter, from whom he so earnestly desired a word of greeting, was the Esther of our tale, the very girl whom, with such cold and remorseless purpose, Ethan Brand had made the subject of a psychological experiment, and wasted, absorbed, and perhaps annihilated her soul, in the process.

"Yes," murmured he, turning away from the hoary wanderer, "it is no delusion. There is an Unpardonable Sin!"

While these things were passing, a merry scene was going forward in the area of cheerful light, beside the spring and before the door of the hut. A number of the youth of the village, young men and girls, had hurried up the hill-side, impelled by curiosity to see Ethan Brand, the hero of so many a legend familiar to their childhood. Finding nothing, however, very remarkable in his aspect,—nothing but a sunburnt wayfarer, in plain garb and dusty shoes, who sat looking into the fire as if he fancied pictures among the coals,—these young people speedily grew tired of observing him. As it happened, there was other amusement at hand. An old German Jew travelling with a diorama[6] on his back, was passing down the mountain-road towards the village just as the party turned aside from it, and, in hopes of eking out the profits of the day, the showman had kept them company to the lime-kiln.

"Come, old Dutchman," cried one of the young men, "let us see your pictures, if you can swear they are worth looking at!"

"Oh yes, Captain," answered the Jew,—whether as a matter of courtesy or craft, he styled everybody Captain,—"I shall show you, indeed, some very superb pictures!"

So, placing his box in a proper position, he invited the young men and girls to look through the glass orifices of the machine, and proceeded to exhibit a series of the most outrageous scratchings and daubings, as specimens of the fine arts, that ever an itinerant showman had the face to impose upon his circle of spectators. The pictures were worn out, moreover, tattered, full of cracks and wrinkles, dingy with tobacco-smoke, and otherwise in a most pitiable condition. Some purported to be cities, public edifices, and ruined castles in Europe; others represented Napoleon's battles and Nelson's[7] sea-fights; and in the midst of these would be seen a gigantic, brown, hairy hand,—which might have been mistaken for the Hand of Destiny, though, in truth, it was only the showman's,—pointing its forefinger to various scenes of the conflict, while its owner gave historical illustrations. When, with much merriment at its abominable deficiency of merit, the exhibition was concluded, the German bade little Joe put his head into the box. Viewed through the magnifying-glasses, the boy's round, rosy visage assumed the strangest imaginable aspect of an immense Titanic child, the mouth grinning broadly, and the eyes and every other feature overflowing with fun at the joke. Suddenly, however, that merry face turned pale, and its expression changed to horror, for this easily impressed and excitable child had become sensible that the eye of Ethan Brand was fixed upon him through the glass.

"You make the little man to be afraid, Captain," said the German Jew, turning up the dark and strong outline of his visage from his stooping posture. "But look again, and, by chance, I shall cause you to see somewhat that is very fine, upon my word!"

Ethan Brand gazed into the box for an instant, and then starting back, looked fixedly at the German. What had he seen? Nothing, apparently; for a curious youth, who had peeped in almost at the same moment, beheld only a vacant space of canvas.

"I remember you now," muttered Ethan Brand to the showman.

"Ah, Captain, whispered the Jew of Nuremburg, with a dark smile, "I find it to be a heavy matter in my show-box,—this Unpardonable Sin! By my faith, Captain, it has wearied my shoulders, this long day, to carry it over the mountain."

"Peace," answered Ethan Brand, sternly, "or get thee into the furnace yonder!"

The Jew's exhibition had scarcely concluded, when a great, elderly dog—who seemed to be his own master, as no person in the company laid claim to him—saw fit to render himself the object of public notice. Hitherto, he had shown himself a

---

[6] Box or chamber used for viewing inserted pictures.   [7] Horatio Nelson (1758–1805), British admiral.

very quiet, well-disposed old dog, going round from one to another, and, by way of being sociable, offering his rough head to be patted by any kindly hand that would take so much trouble. But now, all of a sudden, this grave and venerable quadruped, of his own mere motion, and without the slightest suggestion from anybody else, began to run round after his tail, which, to heighten the absurdity of the proceeding, was a great deal shorter than it should have been. Never was seen such headlong eagerness in pursuit of an object that could not possibly be attained; never was heard such a tremendous outbreak of growling, snarling, barking, and snapping,—as if one end of the ridiculous brute's body were at deadly and most unforgivable enmity with the other. Faster and faster, round about went the cur; and faster and still faster fled the unapproachable brevity of his tail; and louder and fiercer grew his yells of rage and animosity; until, utterly exhausted, and as far from the goal as ever, the foolish old dog ceased his performance as suddenly as he had begun it. The next moment he was as mild, quiet, sensible, and respectable in his deportment, as when he first scraped acquaintance with the company.

As may be supposed, the exhibition was greeted with universal laughter, clapping of hands, and shouts of encore, to which the canine performer responded by wagging all that there was to wag of his tail, but appeared totally unable to repeat his very successful effort to amuse the spectators.

Meanwhile, Ethan Brand had resumed his seat upon the log, and moved, it might be, by a perception of some remote analogy between his own case and that of this self-pursuing cur, he broke into the awful laugh, which, more than any other token, expressed the condition of his inward being. From that moment, the merriment of the party was at an end; they stood aghast, dreading lest the inauspicious sound should be reverberated around the horizon, and that mountain would thunder it to mountain, and so the horror be prolonged upon their ears. Then, whispering one to another that it was late,—that the moon was almost down,—that the August night was growing chill,—they hurried homewards, leaving the lime-burner and little Joe to deal as they might with their unwelcome guest. Save for these three human beings, the open space on the hill-side was a solitude, set in a vast gloom of forest. Beyond that darksome verge, the firelight glimmered on the stately trunks and almost black foliage of pines, intermixed with the lighter verdure of sapling oaks, maples, and poplars, while here and there lay the gigantic corpses of dead trees, decaying on the leaf-strewn soil. And it seemed to little Joe—a timorous and imaginative child—that the silent forest was holding its breath until some fearful thing should happen.

Ethan Brand thrust more wood into the fire, and closed the door of the kiln; then looking over his shoulder at the lime-burner and his son, he bade, rather than advised, them to retire to rest.

"For myself, I cannot sleep," said he. "I have matters that it concerns me to meditate upon. I will watch the fire, as I used to do in the old time."

"And call the Devil out of the furnace to keep you company, I suppose," muttered Bartram, who had been making intimate acquaintance with the black bottle above mentioned. "But watch, if you like, and call as many devils as you like! For my part, I shall be all the better for a snooze. Come, Joe!"

As the boy followed his father into the hut, he looked back at the wayfarer, and the tears came into his eyes, for his tender spirit had an intuition of the bleak and terrible loneliness in which this man had enveloped himself.

When they had gone, Ethan Brand sat listening to the crackling of the kindled wood, and looking at the little spirts of fire that issued through the chinks of the door. These trifles, however, once so familiar, had but the slightest hold of his attention, while deep within his mind he was reviewing the gradual but marvelous change that had been wrought upon him by the search to which he had devoted himself. He remembered how the night dew had fallen upon him,—how the dark forest had whispered to him,—how the stars had gleamed upon him,—a simple and loving man, watching his fire in the years gone by, and ever musing as it burned. He remembered with what tenderness, with what love and sympathy for mankind, and what pity for human guilt and woe, he had first begun to contemplate those ideas which afterwards became the inspiration of his life; with what reverence he had then looked into the heart of man, viewing it as a temple originally divine, and, however desecrated, still to be held sacred by a brother; with what awful fear he had deprecated the success of his pursuit, and prayed that the Unpardonable Sin might never be revealed to him. Then ensued that vast intellectual development, which, in its progress, disturbed the counterpoise between his mind and heart. The Idea that possessed his life had operated as a means of education; it had gone on cultivating his powers to the highest point of which they were susceptible; it had raised him from the level of an unlettered laborer to stand on a star-lit eminence, whither the philosophers of the earth, laden with the lore of universities, might vainly strive to clamber after him. So much for the intellect! But where was the heart? That, indeed, had withered,—had contracted, —had hardened,—had perished! It had ceased to partake of the universal throb. He had lost his hold of the magnetic chain of humanity. He was no longer a brother-man, opening the chambers or the dungeons of our common nature by the key of holy sympathy, which gave him a right to share in all its secrets; he was now a cold observer, looking on mankind as the subject of his experiment, and, at length, converting man and woman to be his puppets, and pulling the wires that moved them to such degrees of crime as were demanded for his study.

Thus Ethan Brand became a fiend. He began to be so from the moment that his moral nature had ceased to keep the pace of improvement with his intellect. And now, as his highest effort and inevitable development,—as the bright and gorgeous flower, and rich, delicious fruit of his life's labor,—he had produced the Unpardonable Sin!

"What more have I to seek? what more to achieve?" said Ethan Brand to himself. "My task is done, and well done!"

Starting from the log with a certain alacrity in his gait and ascending the hillock of earth that was raised against the stone circumference of the lime-kiln, he thus reached the top of the structure. It was a space of perhaps ten feet across, from edge to edge, presenting a view of the upper surface of the immense mass of broken marble with which the kiln was heaped. All these innumerable blocks and fragments of marble were red-hot and vividly on fire, sending up great spouts of blue flame, which quivered aloft and danced madly, as within a magic circle, and sank and rose again, with continual and multitudinous activity. As the lonely man bent forward over this terrible body of fire, the blasting heat smote up against his person with a breath that, it might be supposed, would have scorched and shrivelled him up in a moment.

Ethan Brand stood erect, and raised his arms on high. The blue flames played upon his face, and imparted the wild and ghastly light which alone could have suited its expression; it was that of a fiend on the verge of plunging into his gulf of intensest torment.

"O Mother Earth," cried he, "who art no more my Mother, and into whose bosom this frame shall never be resolved! O mankind, whose brotherhood I have cast off, and trampled thy great heart beneath my feet! O stars of heaven, that shone on me of old, as if to light me onward and upward!—farewell all, and forever. Come, deadly element of Fire,—henceforth my familiar friend! Embrace me, as I do thee!"

That night the sound of a fearful peal of laughter rolled heavily through the sleep of the lime-burner and his little son; dim shapes of horror and anguish haunted their dreams, and seemed still present in the rude hovel, when they opened their eyes to the day-light.

"Up, boy, up!" cried the lime-burner, staring about him. "Thank Heaven, the night is gone, at last; and rather than pass such another, I would watch my lime-kiln, wide awake, for a twelvemonth. This Ethan Brand, with his humbug of an Unpardonable Sin, has done me no such mighty favor, in taking my place!"

He issued from the hut, followed by little Joe, who kept fast hold of his father's hand. The early sunshine was already pouring its gold upon the mountaintops, and though the valleys were still in shadow, they smiled cheerfully in the promise of the bright day that was hastening onward. The village, completely shut in by hills, which swelled away gently about it, looked as if it had rested peacefully in the hollow of the great hand of Providence. Every dwelling was distinctly visible; the little spires of the two churches pointed upwards, and caught a fore-glimmering of brightness from the sun-gilt skies upon their gilded weather-cocks. The tavern was astir, and the figure of the old, smoke-dried stage-agent, cigar in mouth, was seen beneath the stoop. Old Graylock was glorified with a golden cloud upon his head. Scattered likewise over the breasts of the surrounding mountains, there were heaps of hoary mist, in fantastic shapes, some of them far down into the valley, others high up towards the summits, and still others, of the same family of mist or cloud, hovering in the gold radiance of the upper atmosphere. Stepping from one to another of the clouds that rested on the hills, and thence to the loftier brotherhood that sailed in air, it seemed almost as if a mortal man might thus ascend into the heavenly regions. Earth was so mingled with sky that it was a day-dream to look at it.

To supply that charm of the familiar and homely, which Nature so readily adopts into a scene like this, the stage-coach was rattling down the mountain-road, and the driver sounded his horn, while Echo[8] caught up the notes, and intertwined them into a rich and varied and elaborate harmony, of which the original performer could lay claim to little share. The great hills played a concert among themselves, each contributing a strain of airy sweetness.

Little Joe's face brightened at once.

"Dear father," cried he, skipping cheerily to and fro, "that strange man is gone, and the sky and the mountains all seem glad of it!"

"Yes," growled the lime-burner, with an oath, "but he has let the fire go down, and no thanks to him if five hundred bushels of lime are not spoiled. If I catch the fellow hereabouts again, I shall feel like tossing him into the furnace!"

With his long pole in his hand, he ascended to the top of the kiln. After a moment's pause, he called to his son.

[8] In classical mythology, the nymph Echo was turned into a voice that could only repeat what was said to her.

"Come up here, Joe!" said he.

So little Joe ran up the hillock, and stood by his father's side. The marble was all burnt into perfect, snow-white lime. But on its surface, in the midst of the circle,—snow-white too, and thoroughly converted into lime,—lay a human skeleton, in the attitude of a person who, after long toil, lies down to long repose. Within the ribs—strange to say—was the shape of a human heart.

"Was the fellow's heart made of marble?" cried Bartram, in some perplexity at this phenomenon. "At any rate, it is burnt into what looks like special good lime; and, taking all the bones together, my kiln is half a bushel the richer for him."

So saying, the rude lime-burner lifted his pole, and, letting it fall upon the skeleton, the relics of Ethan Brand were crumbled into fragments.

1850

The Old Manse

The Author Makes the Reader Acquainted with His Abode

Between two tall gateposts of rough-hewn stone (the gate itself having fallen from its hinges at some unknown epoch) we beheld the gray front of the old parsonage terminating the vista of an avenue of black ash-trees. It was now a twelvemonth since the funeral procession of the venerable clergyman,[1] its last inhabitant, had turned from that gateway towards the village burying-ground. The wheel-track leading to the door, as well as the whole breadth of the avenue, was almost overgrown with grass, affording dainty mouthfuls to two or three vagrant cows and an old white horse who had his own living to pick up along the roadside. The glimmering shadows that lay half asleep between the door of the house and the public highway were a kind of spiritual medium, seen through which the edifice had not quite the aspect of belonging to the material world. Certainly it had little in common with those ordinary abodes which stand so imminent upon the road that every passer-by can thrust his head, as it were, into the domestic circle. From these quiet windows the figures of passing travellers looked too remote and dim to disturb the sense of privacy. In its near retirement and accessible seclusion it was the very spot for the residence of a clergyman,—a man not estranged from human life, yet enveloped in the midst of it with a veil woven of intermingled gloom and brightness. It was worthy to have been one of the time-honored parsonages of England in which, through many generations, a succession of holy occupants pass from youth to age, and bequeath each an inheritance of sanctity to pervade the house and hover over it as with an atmosphere.

Nor, in truth, had the Old Manse ever been profaned by a lay occupant until that memorable summer afternoon when I entered it as my home. A priest[2] had built it;

---

[1] The Reverend Ezra Ripley.
[2] The Reverend William Emerson, Ralph Waldo Emerson's grandfather, who built the house in 1765.

a priest had succeeded to it; other priestly men from time to time had dwelt in it; and children born in its chambers had grown up to assume the priestly character. It was awful to reflect how many sermons must have been written there. The latest inhabitant alone—he by whose translation to paradise the dwelling was left vacant —had penned nearly three thousand discourses, besides the better, if not the greater, number that gushed living from his lips. How often, no doubt, had he paced to and fro along the avenue, attuning his meditations to the sighs and gentle murmurs, and deep and solemn peals of the wind among the lofty tops of the trees! In that variety of natural utterances he could find something accordant with every passage of his sermon, were it of tenderness or reverential fear. The boughs over my head seemed shadowy with solemn thoughts as well as with rustling leaves. I took shame to myself for having been so long a writer of idle stories, and ventured to hope that wisdom would descend upon me with the falling leaves of the avenue, and that I should light upon an intellectual treasure in the Old Manse well worth those hoards of long-hidden gold which people seek for in moss-grown houses. Profound treatises of morality; a layman's unprofessional and therefore unprejudiced views of religion; histories (such as Bancroft[3] might have written had he taken up his abode here as he once purposed) bright with picture, gleaming over a depth of philosophic thought,—these were the works that might fitly have flowed from such a retirement. In the humblest event I resolved at least to achieve a novel that should evolve some deep lesson and should possess physical substance enough to stand alone.

In furtherance of my design, and as if to leave me no pretext for not fulfilling it, there was in the rear of the house the most delightful little nook of a study that ever afforded its snug seclusion to a scholar. It was here that Emerson wrote Nature; for he was then an inhabitant of the Manse, and used to watch the Assyrian dawn and Paphian sunset and moonrise from the summit of our eastern hill. When I first saw the room its walls were blackened with the smoke of unnumbered years, and made still blacker by the grim prints of Puritan ministers that hung around. These worthies looked strangely like bad angels, or at least like men who had wrestled so continually and so sternly with the devil that some what of his sooty fierceness had been imparted to their own visages. They had all vanished now; a cheerful coat of paint and golden-tinted paper-hangings lighted up the small apartment; while the shadow of a willow-tree that swept against the overhanging eaves attempered the cheery western sunshine. In place of the grim prints there was the sweet and lovely head of one of Raphael's Madonnas and two pleasant little pictures of the Lake of Como. The only other decorations were a purple vase of flowers, always fresh, and a bronze one containing graceful ferns. My books (few, and by no means choice; for they were chiefly such waifs as chance had thrown in my way) stood in order about the room, seldom to be disturbed.

The study had three windows, set with little, old-fashioned panes of glass, each with a crack across it. The two on the western side looked, or rather peeped, between the willow branches down into the orchard, with glimpses of the river through the trees. The third, facing northward, commanded a broader view of the river at a spot where its hitherto obscure waters gleam forth into the light of history. It was at this window

[3] George Bancroft (1800–1891), author of *History of the United States* (1834–1875).

that the clergyman who then dwelt in the Manse stood watching the outbreak of a long and deadly struggle between two nations; he saw the irregular array of his parishioners on the farther side of the river and the glittering line of the British on the hither bank. He awaited in an agony of suspense the rattle of the musketry. It came, and there needed but a gentle wind to sweep the battle smoke around this quiet house.

Perhaps the reader, whom I cannot help considering as my guest in the Old Manse and entitled to all courtesy in the way of sight-showing,—perhaps he will choose to take a nearer view of the memorable spot. We stand now on the river's brink. It may well be called the Concord, the river of peace and quietness; for it is certainly the most unexcitable and sluggish stream that ever loitered imperceptibly towards its eternity—the sea. Positively, I had lived three weeks beside it before it grew quite clear to my perception which way the current flowed. It never has a vivacious aspect except when a northwestern breeze is vexing its surface on a sunshiny day. From the incurable indolence of its nature, the stream is happily incapable of becoming the slave of human ingenuity, as is the fate of so many a wild, free mountain torrent. While all things else are compelled to subserve some useful purpose, it idles its sluggish life away in lazy liberty, without turning a solitary spindle or affording even water-power enough to grind the corn that grows upon its banks. The torpor of its movement allows it nowhere a bright, pebbly shore, nor so much as a narrow strip of glistening sand, in any part of its course. It slumbers between broad prairies, kissing the long meadow grass, and bathes the overhanging boughs of elder bushes and willows or the roots of elms and ash-trees and clumps of maples. Flags and rushes grow along its plashy shore; the yellow water-lily spreads its broad, flat leaves on the margin; and the fragrant white pond-lily abounds, generally selecting a position just so far from the river's brink that it cannot be grasped save at the hazard of plunging in.

It is a marvel whence this perfect flower derives its loveliness and perfume, springing as it does from the black mud over which the river sleeps, and where lurk the slimy eel and speckled frog and the mud turtle, whom continual washing cannot cleanse. It is the very same black mud out of which the yellow lily sucks its obscene life and noisome odor. Thus we see, too, in the world that some persons assimilate only what is ugly and evil from the same moral circumstances which supply good and beautiful results—the fragrance of celestial flowers—to the daily life of others.

The reader must not, from any testimony of mine, contract a dislike towards our slumberous stream. In the light of a calm and golden sunset it becomes lovely beyond expression; the more lovely for the quietude that so well accords with the hour, when even the wind, after blustering all day long, usually hushes itself to rest. Each tree and rock, and every blade of grass, is distinctly imaged, and, however unsightly in reality, assumes ideal beauty in the reflection. The minutest things of earth and the broad aspect of the firmament are pictured equally without effort and with the same felicity of success. All the sky glows downward at our feet; the rich clouds float through the unruffled bosom of the stream like heavenly thoughts through a peaceful heart. We will not, then, malign our river as gross and impure while it can glorify itself with so adequate a picture of the heaven that broods above it; or, if we remember its tawny hue and the muddiness of its bed, let it be a symbol that the earthliest human soul has an infinite spiritual capacity and may contain the better world within its depths. But, indeed, the same lesson might be drawn out of any mud puddle in the streets of a city; and, being taught us everywhere, it must be true.

Come, we have pursued a somewhat devious track in our walk to the battle-ground. Here we are, at the point where the river was crossed by the old bridge, the possession of which was the immediate object of the contest. On the hither side grow two or three elms, throwing a wide circumference of shade, but which must have been planted at some period within the threescore years and ten that have passed since the battle day. On the farther shore, overhung by a clump of elder bushes, we discern the stone abutment of the bridge. Looking down into the river, I once discovered some heavy fragments of the timbers, all green with half a century's growth of water moss; for during that length of time the tramp of horses and human footsteps has ceased along this ancient highway. The stream has here about the breadth of twenty strokes of a swimmer's arm,—a space not too wide when the bullets were whistling across. Old people who dwell hereabouts will point out the very spots on the western bank where our countrymen fell down and died; and on this side of the river an obelisk of granite has grown up from the soil that was fertilized with British blood. The monument, not more than twenty feet in height, is such as it befitted the inhabitants of a village to erect in illustration of a matter of local interest rather than what was suitable to commemorate an epoch of national history. Still, by the fathers of the village this famous deed was done; and their descendants might rightfully claim the privilege of building a memorial.

A humbler token of the fight, yet a more interesting one than the granite obelisk, may be seen close under the stone-wall which separates the battle-ground from the precincts of the parsonage. It is the grave—marked by a small, mossgrown fragment of stone at the head and another at the foot—the grave of two British soldiers who were slain in the skirmish, and have ever since slept peacefully where Zechariah Brown and Thomas Davis buried them. Soon was their warfare ended; a weary night march from Boston, a rattling volley of musketry across the river, and then these many years of rest. In the long procession of slain invaders who passed into eternity from the battle-fields of the revolution, these two nameless soldiers led the way.

Lowell, the poet, as we were once standing over this grave, told me a tradition in reference to one of the inhabitants below. The story has something deeply impressive, though its circumstances cannot altogether be reconciled with probability. A youth in the service of the clergyman happened to be chopping wood, that April morning, at the back door of the Manse, and when the noise of battle rang from side to side of the bridge he hastened across the intervening field to see what might be going forward. It is rather strange, by the way, that this lad should have been so diligently at work when the whole population of town and country were startled out of their customary business by the advance of the British troops. Be that as it might, the tradition says that the lad now left his task and hurried to the battle-field with the axe still in his hand. The British had by this time retreated, the Americans were in pursuit; and the late scene of strife was thus deserted by both parties. Two soldiers lay on the ground—one was a corpse; but, as the young New Englander drew nigh, the other Briton raised himself painfully upon his hands and knees and gave a ghastly stare into his face. The boy,—it must have been a nervous impulse, without purpose, without thought, and betokening a sensitive and impressible nature rather than a hardened one,—the boy uplifted his axe and dealt the wounded soldier a fierce and fatal blow upon the head.

I could wish that the grave might be opened; for I would fain know whether either of the skeleton soldiers has the mark of an axe in his skull. The story comes home to me like truth. Oftentimes, as an intellectual and moral exercise, I have sought to follow that poor youth through his subsequent career, and observe how his soul was tortured by the blood stain, contracted as it had been before the long custom of war had robbed human life of its sanctity, and while it still seemed murderous to slay a brother man. This one circumstance has borne more fruit for me than all that history tells us of the fight.

Many strangers come in the summer time to view the battle-ground. For my own part, I have never found my imagination much excited by this or any other scene of historic celebrity; nor would the placid margin of the river have lost any of its charm for me had men never fought and died there. There is a wilder interest in the tract of land—perhaps a hundred yards in breadth—which extends between the battle-field and the northern face of our Old Manse, with its contiguous avenue and orchard. Here, in some unknown age, before the white man came, stood an Indian village, convenient to the river, whence its inhabitants must have drawn so large a part of their subsistence. The site is identified by the spear and arrow heads, the chisels, and other implements of war, labor, and the chase, which the plough turns up from the soil. You see a splinter of stone, half hidden beneath a sod; it looks like nothing worthy of note; but, if you have faith enough to pick it up, behold a relic! Thoreau, who has a strange faculty of finding what the Indians have left behind them, first set me on the search; and I afterwards enriched myself with some very perfect specimens, so rudely wrought that it seemed almost as if chance had fashioned them. Their great charm consists in this rudeness and in the individuality of each article, so different from the productions of civilized machinery, which shapes everything on one pattern. There is exquisite delight, too, in picking up for one's self an arrowhead that was dropped centuries ago and has never been handled since, and which we thus receive directly from the hand of the red hunter, who purposed to shoot it at his game or at an enemy. Such an incident builds up again the Indian village and its encircling forest, and recalls to life the painted chiefs and warriors, the squaws at their household toil, and the children sporting among the wigwams, while the little wind-rocked pappoose swings from the branch of the tree. It can hardly be told whether it is a joy or a pain, after such a momentary vision, to gaze around in the broad day-light of reality and see stone fences, white houses, potato fields, and men doggedly hoeing in their shirt-sleeves and homespun pantaloons. But this is nonsense. The Old Manse is better than a thousand wigwams.

The Old Manse! We had almost forgotten it, but will return thither through the orchard. This was set out by the last clergyman, in the decline of his life, when the neighbors laughed at the hoary-headed man for planting trees from which he could have no prospect of gathering fruit. Even had that been the case, there was only so much the better motive for planting them, in the pure and unselfish hope of benefiting his successors,—an end so seldom achieved by more ambitious efforts. But the old minister, before reaching his patriarchal age of ninety, ate the apples from this orchard during many years, and added silver and gold to his annual stipend by disposing of the superfluity. It is pleasant to think of him walking among the trees in the quiet afternoons of early autumn and picking up here and there a windfall, while he observes how heavily the branches are weighed down, and computes the number of empty flour barrels that will be filled by their burden. He loved each tree, doubtless, as if it had been his own child. An orchard has a relation to mankind, and readily connects itself with matters of the heart. The trees possess a domestic character; they have lost the wild nature of their forest kindred, and have grown humanized by receiving the care of man as well as by contributing to his wants. There is so much individuality of character, too, among apple-trees that it gives them an additional claim to be the objects of human interest. One is harsh and crabbed in its manifestations; another gives us fruit as mild as charity. One is churlish and illiberal, evidently grudging the few apples that it bears; another exhausts itself in free-hearted benevolence. The variety of grotesque shapes into which apple-trees contort themselves has its effect on those who get acquainted with them: they stretch out their crooked branches, and take such hold of the imagination that we remember them as humorists and odd-fellows. And what is more melancholy than the old apple-trees that linger about the spot where once stood a homestead, but where there is now only a ruined chimney rising out of a grassy and weed-grown cellar? They offer their fruit to every wayfarer,—apples that are bitter sweet with the moral of Time's vicissitude.

I have met with no other such pleasant trouble in the world as that of finding myself, with only the two or three mouths which it was my privilege to feed, the sole inheritor of the old clergyman's wealth of fruits. Throughout the summer there were cherries and currants; and then came autumn, with his immense burden of apples, dropping them continually from his overladen shoulders as he trudged along. In the stillest afternoon, if I listened, the thump of a great apple was audible, falling without a breath of wind, from the mere necessity of perfect ripeness. And, besides, there were pear-trees, that flung down bushels upon bushels of heavy pears; and peach-trees, which, in a good year, tormented me with peaches, neither to be eaten nor kept, nor, without labor and perplexity, to be given away. The idea of an infinite generosity and exhaustless bounty on the part of our Mother Nature was well worth obtaining through such cares as these. That feeling can be enjoyed in perfection only by the natives of summer islands, where the bread-fruit, the cocoa, the palm, and the orange grow spontaneously and hold forth the ever-ready meal; but likewise almost as well by a man long habituated to city life, who plunges into such a solitude as that of the Old Manse, where he plucks the fruit of trees that he did not plant, and which therefore, to my heterodox taste, bear the closest resemblance to those that grew in Eden. It has been an apothegm these five thousand years, that toil sweetens the bread it earns. For my part (speaking from hard experience, acquired while belaboring the rugged furrows of Brook Farm), I relish best the free gifts of Providence.

Not that it can be disputed that the light toil requisite to cultivate a moderately-sized garden imparts such zest to kitchen vegetables as is never found in those of the market gardener. Childless men, if they would know something of the bliss of paternity, should plant a seed,—be it squash, bean, Indian corn, or perhaps a mere flower or worthless weed,—should plant it with their own hands, and nurse it from infancy to maturity altogether by their own care. If there be not too many of them, each individual plant becomes an object of separate interest. My garden, that skirted the avenue of the Manse, was of precisely the right extent. An hour or two of morning labor was all that it required. But I used to visit and revisit it a dozen times a day, and stand in deep contemplation over my vegetable progeny with a love that nobody could share or conceive of who had never taken part in the process of creation. It was one of the most bewitching sights in the world to observe a hill of beans thrusting aside the soil, or a row of early peas just peeping forth sufficiently to trace a line of delicate green. Later in the season the humming-birds were attracted by the blossoms of a peculiar variety of bean; and they were a joy to me, those little spiritual visitants, for deigning to sip airy food out of my nectar cups. Multitudes of bees used to bury themselves in the yellow blossoms of the summer squashes. This, too, was a deep satisfaction; although when they had laden themselves with sweets they flew away to some unknown hive, which would give back nothing in requital of what my garden had contributed. But I was glad thus to fling a benefaction upon the passing breeze with the certainty that somebody must profit by it, and that there would be a little more honey in the world to allay the sourness and bitterness which mankind is always complaining of. Yes, indeed; my life was the sweeter for that honey.

Speaking of summer squashes, I must say a word of their beautiful and varied forms. They presented an endless diversity of urns and vases, shallow or deep, scalloped or plain, moulded in patterns which a sculptor would do well to copy, since Art has never invented anything more graceful. A hundred squashes in the garden were worthy, in my eyes at least, of being rendered indestructible in marble. If ever Providence (but I know it never will) should assign me a superfluity of gold, part of it shall be expended for a service of plate, or most delicate porcelain, to be wrought into the shapes of summer squashes gathered from vines which I will plant with my own hands. As dishes for containing vegetables they would be peculiarly appropriate.

But not merely the squeamish love of the beautiful was gratified by my toil in the kitchen garden. There was a hearty enjoyment, likewise, in observing the growth of the crook-necked winter squashes, from the first little bulb, with the withered blossom adhering to it, until they lay strewn upon the soil, big, round fellows, hiding their heads beneath the leaves, but turning up their great yellow rotundities to the noontide sun. Gazing at them, I felt that by my agency something worth living for had been done. A new substance was born into the world. They were real and tangible existences, which the mind could seize hold of and rejoice in. A cabbage, too,— especially the early Dutch cabbage, which swells to a monstrous circumference, until its ambitious heart often bursts asunder,—is a matter to be proud of when we can claim a share with the earth and sky in producing it. But, after all, the hugest pleasure is reserved until these vegetable children of ours are smoking on the table, and we, like Saturn, make a meal of them.

What with the river, the battle-field, the orchard and the garden, the reader begins to despair of finding his way back into the Old Manse. But in agreeable weather it is the truest hospitality to keep him out-of-doors. I never grew quite acquainted with my habitation till a long spell of sulky rain had confined me beneath its roof. There could not be a more sombre aspect of external Nature than as then seen from the windows of my study. The great willow-tree had caught and retained among its leaves a whole cataract of water, to be shaken down at intervals by the frequent gusts of wind. All day long, and for a week together, the rain was drip-drip-dripping and splash-splash-splashing from the eaves, and bubbling and foaming into the tubs beneath the spouts. The old, unpainted shingles of the house and out-buildings were black with moisture; and the mosses of ancient growth upon the walls looked green and fresh, as if they were the newest things and afterthought of Time. The usually mirrored surface of the river was blurred by an infinity of raindrops; the whole landscape had a completely water-soaked appearance, conveying the impression that the earth was wet through like a sponge; while the summit of a wooded hill, about a mile distant, was enveloped in a dense mist, where the demon of the tempest seemed to have his abiding-place and to be plotting still direr inclemencies.

Nature has no kindness, no hospitality, during a rain. In the fiercest heat of sunny days she retains a secret mercy, and welcomes the wayfarer to shady nooks of the woods whither the sun cannot penetrate; but she provides no shelter against her storms. It makes us shiver to think of those deep, umbrageous recesses, those overshadowing banks, where we found such enjoyment during the sultry afternoons. Not a twig of foilage there but would dash a little shower into our faces. Looking reproachfully towards the impenetrable sky,—if sky there be above that dismal uniformity of cloud, —we are apt to murmur against the whole system of the universe, since it involves the extinction of so many summer days in so short a life by the hissing and spluttering rain. In such spells of weather—and it is to be supposed such weather came—Eve's bower in paradise must have been but a cheerless and aguish kind of shelter, nowise comparable to the old parsonage, which had resources of its own to beguile the week's imprisonment. The idea of sleeping on a couch of wet roses!

Happy the man who in a rainy day can betake himself to a huge garret, stored, like that of the Manse, with lumber that each generation has left behind it from a period before the revolution. Our garret was an arched hall, dimly illuminated through small and dusty windows; it was but a twilight at the best; and there were nooks, or rather caverns, of deep obscurity, the secrets of which I never learned, being too reverent of their dust and cobwebs. The beams and rafters, roughly hewn and with strips of bark still on them, and the rude masonry of the chimneys, made the garret look wild and uncivilized,—an aspect unlike what was seen elsewhere in the quiet and decorous old house. But on one side there was a little whitewashed apartment which bore the traditionary title of the Saint's Chamber, because holy men in their youth had slept and studied and prayed there. With its elevated retirement, its one window, its small fireplace, and its closet, convenient for an oratory, it was the very spot where a young man might inspire himself with solemn enthusiasm and cherish saintly dreams. The occupants, at various epochs, had left brief records and ejaculations inscribed upon the walls. There, too, hung a tattered and shrivelled roll of canvas, which on inspection proved to be the forcibly wrought picture of a clergyman, in wig, band, and gown, holding a Bible in his hand. As I turned his face towards the light he eyed me with an air of authority such as men of his profession seldom assume in our days. The original had been pastor of the parish more than a century ago, a friend of Whitefield,[4] and almost his equal in fervid eloquence. I bowed before the effigy of the dignified divine, and felt as if I had now met face to face with the ghost by whom, as there was reason to apprehend, the Manse was haunted.

Houses of any antiquity in New England are so invariably possessed with spirits that the matter seems hardly worth alluding to. Our ghost used to heave deep sighs in a particular corner of the parlor, and sometimes rustled paper, as if he were turning over a sermon in the long upper entry,—where nevertheless he was invisible in spite of the bright moonshine that fell through the eastern window. Not improbably he wished me to edit and publish a selection from a chest full of manuscript discourses

---

[4] The "original," Reverend Daniel Bliss, had invited the English evangelist George Whitefield (1714–1770) to Concord to preach.

that stood in the garret. Once, while Hillard[5] and other friends sat talking with us in the twilight, there came a rustling noise as of a minister's silk gown, sweeping through the very midst of the company so closely as almost to brush against the chairs. Still there was nothing visible. A yet stranger business was that of a ghostly servant maid, who used to be heard in the kitchen at deepest midnight, grinding coffee, cooking, ironing,—performing, in short, all kinds of domestic labor,—although no traces of anything accomplished could be detected the next morning. Some neglected duty of her servitude—some ill-starched ministerial band—disturbed the poor damsel in her grave and kept her at work without any wages.

But to return from this digression. A part of my predecessor's library was stored in the garret,—no unfit receptacle indeed for such dreary trash as comprised the greater number of volumes. The old books would have been worth nothing at an auction. In this venerable garret, however, they possessed an interest, quite apart from their literary value, as heirlooms, many of which had been transmitted down through a series of consecrated hands from the days of the mighty Puritan divines. Autographs of famous names were to be seen in faded ink on some of their flyleaves; and there were marginal observations or interpolated pages closely covered with manuscript in illegible shorthand, perhaps concealing matter of profound truth and wisdom. The world will never be the better for it. A few of the books were Latin folios, written by Catholic authors; others demolished Papistry, as with a sledge-hammer, in plain English. A dissertation on the book of Job—which only Job himself could have had patience to read—filled at least a score of small, thickset quartos, at the rate of two or three volumes to a chapter. Then there was a vast folio body of divinity—too corpulent a body, it might be feared, to comprehend the spiritual element of religion. Volumes of this form dated back two hundred years or more, and were generally bound in black leather, exhibiting precisely such an appearance as we should attribute to books of enchantment. Others equally antique were of a size proper to be carried in the large waistcoat pockets of old times,—diminutive, but as black as their bulkier brethren, and abundantly interfused with Greek and Latin quotations. These little old volumes impressed me as if they had been intended for very large ones, but had been unfortunately blighted at an early stage of their growth.

The rain pattered upon the roof and the sky gloomed through the dusty garret windows, while I burrowed among these venerable books in search of any living thought which should burn like a coal of fire, or glow like an inextinguishable gem, beneath the dead trumpery that had long hidden it. But I found no such treasure; all was dead alike; and I could not but muse deeply and wonderingly upon the humiliating fact that the works of man's intellect decay like those of his hands. Thought grows mouldy. What was good and nourishing food for the spirits of one generation affords no sustenance for the next. Books of religion, however, cannot be considered a fair test of the enduring and vivacious properties of human thought, because such books so seldom really touch upon their ostensible subject, and have, therefore, so little business to be written at all. So long as an unlettered soul can attain to saving grace, there would seem to be no deadly error in holding theological libraries to be accumulations of, for the most part, stupendous impertinence.

---

[5] George Stillman Hillard (1808–1879), a Boston lawyer and Hawthorne's friend.

Many of the books had accrued in the latter years of the last clergyman's lifetime. These threatened to be of even less interest than the elder works, a century hence, to any curious inquirer who should then rummage them as I was doing now. Volumes of the "Liberal Preacher" and "Christian Examiner,"[6] occasional sermons, controversial pamphlets, tracts, and other productions of a like fugitive nature took the place of the thick and heavy volumes of past time. In a physical point of view there was much the same difference as between a feather and a lump of lead; but, intellectually regarded, the specific gravity of old and new was about upon a par. Both also were alike frigid. The elder books, nevertheless, seemed to have been earnestly written, and might be conceived to have possessed warmth at some former period; although, with the lapse of time, the heated masses had cooled down even to the freezing point. The frigidity of the modern productions, on the other hand, was characteristic and inherent, and evidently had little to do with the writer's qualities of mind and heart. In fine, of this whole dusty heap of literature I tossed aside all the sacred part, and felt myself none the less a Christian for eschewing it. There appeared no hope of either mounting to the better world on a Gothic staircase of ancient folios or of flying thither on the wings of a modern tract.

Nothing, strange to say, retained any sap except what had been written for the passing day and year without the remotest pretension or idea of permanence. There were a few old newspapers, and still older almanacs, which reproduced to my mental eye the epochs when they had issued from the press with a distinctness that was altogether unaccountable. It was as if I had found bits of magic looking-glass among the books, with the images of a vanished century in them. I turned my eyes towards the tattered picture above mentioned, and asked of the austere divine wherefore it was that he and his brethren, after the most painful rummaging and groping into their minds, had been able to produce nothing half so real as these newspaper scribblers and almanac makers had thrown off in the effervescence of a moment. The portrait responded not; so I sought an answer for myself. It is the age itself that writes newspapers and almanacs, which, therefore, have a distinct purpose and meaning at the time, and a kind of intelligible truth for all times; whereas most other works— being written by men who, in the very act, set themselves apart from their age—are likely to possess little significance when new, and none at all when old. Genius, indeed, melts many ages into one, and thus effects something permanent, yet still with a similarity of office to that of the more ephemeral writer. A work of genius is but the newspaper of a century, or perchance of a hundred centuries.

Lightly as I have spoken of these old books, there yet lingers with me a superstitious reverence for literature of all kinds. A bound volume has a charm in my eyes similar to what scraps of manuscript possess for the good Mussulman. He imagines that those wind-wafted records are perhaps hallowed by some sacred verse; and I, that every new book or antique one may contain the "open sesame,"—the spell to disclose treasures hidden in some unsuspected cave of Truth. Thus it was not without sadness that I turned away from the library of the Old Manse.

Blessed was the sunshine when it came again at the close of another stormy day, beaming from the edge of the western horizon; while the massive firmament of clouds

---

[6] Religious periodicals published between 1824 and 1869.

threw down all the gloom it could, but served only to kindle the golden light into a more brilliant glow by the strongly contrasted shadows. Heaven smiled at the earth, so long unseen, from beneath its heavy eyelid. To-morrow for the hill-tops and the wood paths.

Or it might be that Ellery Channing[7] came up the avenue to join me in a fishing excursion on the river. Strange and happy times were those when we cast aside all irksome forms and strait-laced habitudes, and delivered ourselves up to the free air, to live like the Indians or any less conventional race during one bright semicircle of the sun. Rowing our boat against the current, between wide meadows, we turned aside into the Assabeth. A more lovely stream than this, for a mile above its junction with the Concord, has never flowed on earth,—nowhere, indeed, except to lave the interior regions of a poet's imagination. It is sheltered from the breeze by woods and a hill-side; so that elsewhere there might be a hurricane, and here scarcely a ripple across the shaded water. The current lingers along so gently that the mere force of the boatsman's will seems sufficient to propel his craft against it. It comes flowing softly through the midmost privacy and deepest heart of a wood which whispers it to be quiet; while the stream whispers back again from its sedgy borders, as if river and wood were hushing one another to sleep. Yes; the river sleeps along its course and dreams of the sky and of the clustering foliage, amid which fall showers of broken sunlight, imparting specks of vivid cheerfulness, in contrast with the quiet depth of the prevailing tint. Of all this scene, the slumbering river has a dream picture in its bosom. Which, after all, was the most real—the picture, or the original?—the objects palpable to our grosser senses, or their apotheosis in the stream beneath? Surely the disembodied images stand in closer relation to the soul. But both the original and the reflection had here an ideal charm; and, had it been a thought more wild, I could have fancied that this river had strayed forth out of the rich scenery of my companion's inner world; only the vegetation along its banks should then have had an Oriental character.[8]

Gentle and unobtrusive as the river is, yet the tranquil woods seem hardly satisfied to allow it passage. The trees are rooted on the very verge of the water, and dip their pendent branches into it. At one spot there is a lofty bank, on the slope of which grow some hemlocks, declining across the stream with out-stretched arms, as if resolute to take the plunge. In other places the banks are almost on a level with the water; so that the quiet congregation of trees set their feet in the flood, and are fringed with foliage down to the surface. Cardinal flowers kindle their spiral flames and illuminate the dark nooks among the shrubbery. The pond-lily grows abundantly along the margin—that delicious flower, which, as Thoreau tells me, opens its virgin bosom to the first sunlight and perfects its being through the magic of that genial kiss. He has beheld beds of them unfolding in due succession as the sunrise stole gradually from flower to flower—a sight not to be hoped for unless when a poet adjusts his inward eye to a proper focus with the outward organ. Grape-vines here and there twine themselves around shrub and tree and hang their clusters over the water within reach of the boat-man's hand. Oftentimes they unite two trees of alien race in an inextricable twine, marrying the hemlock and the maple against their will, and enriching them

[7] William Ellery Channing (1818–1901), Transcendentalist poet.

[8] Allusion to the interest the Transcendentalists were taking in Eastern philosophy.

with a purple offspring of which neither is the parent. One of these ambitious parasites has climbed into the upper branches of a tall, white pine, and is still ascending from bough to bough, unsatisfied till it shall crown the tree's airy summit with a wreath of its broad foliage and a cluster of its grapes.

The winding course of the stream continually shut out the scene behind us, and revealed as calm and lovely a one before. We glided from depth to depth, and breathed new seclusion at every turn. The shy kingfisher flew from the withered branch close at hand to another at a distance, uttering a shrill cry of anger or alarm. Ducks that had been floating there since the preceding eve were startled at our approach, and skimmed along the glassy river, breaking its dark surface with a bright streak. The pickerel leaped from among the lily-pads. The turtle, sunning itself upon a rock or at the root of a tree, slid suddenly into the water with a plunge. The painted Indian who paddled his canoe along the Assabeth three hundred years ago could hardly have seen a wilder gentleness displayed upon its banks and reflected in its bosom than we did. Nor could the same Indian have prepared his noontide meal with more simplicity. We drew up our skiff at some point where the overarching shade formed a natural bower, and there kindled a fire with the pine cones and decayed branches that lay strewn plentifully around. Soon the smoke ascended among the trees, impregnated with a savory incense, not heavy, dull, and surfeiting, like the steam of cookery within doors, but sprightly and piquant. The smell of our feast was akin to the woodland odors with which it mingled: there was no sacrilege committed by our intrusion there: the sacred solitude was hospitable, and granted us free leave to cook and eat in the recess that was at once our kitchen and banqueting hall. It is strange what humble offices may be performed in a beautiful scene without destroying its poetry. Our fire, red gleaming among the trees, and we beside it, busied with culinary rites and spreading out our meal on a mossgrown log, all seemed in unison with the river gliding by and the foliage rustling over us. And, what was strangest, neither did our mirth seem to disturb the propriety of the solemn woods; although the hobgoblins of the old wilderness and the will-of-the-wisps that glimmered in the marshy places might have come trooping to share our table talk, and have added their shrill laughter to our merriment. It was the very spot in which to utter the extremest nonsense or the profoundest wisdom, or that ethereal product of the mind which partakes of both, and may become one or the other, in correspondence with the faith and insight of the auditor.

So amid sunshine and shadow, rustling leaves and sighing waters, up gushed our talk like the babble of a fountain. The evanescent spray was Ellery's; and his, too, the lumps of golden thought that lay glimmering in the fountain's bed and brightened both our faces by the reflection. Could he have drawn out that virgin gold and stamped it with the mint mark that alone gives currency, the world might have had the profit, and he the fame. My mind was the richer merely by the knowledge that it was there. But the chief profit of those wild days to him and me lay, not in any definite idea, not in any angular or rounded truth, which we dug out of the shapeless mass of problematical stuff, but in the freedom which we thereby won from all custom and conventionalism and fettering influences of man on man. We were so free to-day that it was impossible to be slaves again to-morrow. When we crossed the threshold of the house or trod the thronged pavements of a city, still the leaves of the trees that overhang the Assabeth were whispering to us, "Be free! be free!" Therefore along that shady river-bank there are spots, marked with a heap of ashes and half-consumed brands, only less sacred in my remembrance than the hearth of a household fire.

And yet how sweet, as we floated homeward adown the golden river at sunset, —how sweet was it to return within the system of human society, not as to a dungeon and a chain, but as to a stately edifice, whence we could go forth at will into statelier simplicity! How gently, too, did the sight of the Old Manse, best seen from the river, overshadowed with its willow and all environed about with the foliage of its orchard and avenue,—how gently did its gray, homely aspect rebuke the speculative extravagances of the day! It had grown sacred in connection with the artificial life against which we inveighed; it had been a home for many years in spite of all; it was my home too; and, with these thoughts, it seemed to me that all the artifice and conventionalism of life was but an impalpable thinness upon its surface, and that the depth below was none the worse for it. Once, as we turned our boat to the bank, there was a cloud, in the shape of an immensely gigantic figure of a hound, couched above the house, as if keeping guard over it. Gazing at this symbol, I prayed that the upper influences might long protect the institutions that had grown out of the heart of mankind.

If ever my readers should decide to give up civilized life, cities, houses, and whatever moral or material enormities in addition to these the perverted ingenuity of our race has contrived, let it be in the early autumn. Then Nature will love him better than at any other season, and will take him to her bosom with a more motherly tenderness. I could scarcely endure the roof of the old house above me in those first autumnal days. How early in the summer, too, the prophecy of autumn comes! Earlier in some years than in others; sometimes even in the first weeks of July. There is no other feeling like what is caused by this faint, doubtful, yet real perception—if it be not rather a foreboding—of the year's decay, so blessedly sweet and sad in the same breath.

Did I say that there was no feeling like it? Ah, but there is a half-acknowledged melancholy like to this when we stand in the perfected vigor of our life and feel that Time has now given us all his flowers, and that the next work of his never idle fingers must be to steal them one by one away.

I have forgotten whether the song of the cricket be not as early a token of autumn's approach as any other,—that song which may be called an audible stillness; for though very loud and heard afar, yet the mind does not take note of it as a sound, so completely is its individual existence merged among the accompanying characteristics of the season. Alas for the pleasant summer time! In August the grass is still verdant on the hills and in the valleys; the foliage of the trees is as dense as ever, and as green; the flowers gleam forth in richer abundance along the margin of the river, and by the stone walls, and deep among the woods; the days, too, are as fervid now as they were a month ago; and yet in every breath of wind and in every beam of sunshine we hear the whispered farewell and behold the parting smile of a dear friend. There is a coolness amid all the heat, a mildness in the blazing noon. Not a breeze can stir but it thrills us with the breath of autumn. A pensive glory is seen in the far golden gleams, among the shadows of the trees. The flowers—even the brightest of them, and they are the most gorgeous of the year—have this gentle sadness wedded to their pomp, and typify the character of the delicious time each within itself. The brilliant cardinal flower has never seemed gay to me.

Still later in the season Nature's tenderness waxes stronger. It is impossible not to be fond of our mother now; for she is so fond of us! At other periods she does not make this impression on me, or only at rare intervals; but in those genial days of autumn, when she has perfected her harvests and accomplished every needful thing that was given her to do, then she overflows with a blessed superfluity of love. She has leisure to caress her children now. It is good to be alive at such times. Thank Heaven for breath—yes, for mere breath—when it is made up of a heavenly breeze like this! It comes with a real kiss upon our cheeks; it would linger fondly around us if it might; but, since it must be gone, it embraces us with its whole kindly heart and passes onward to embrace likewise the next thing that it meets. A blessing is flung abroad and scattered far and wide over the earth, to be gathered up by all who choose. I recline upon the still unwithered grass and whisper to myself, "O perfect day! O beautiful world! O beneficent God!" And it is the promise of a blessed eternity; for our Creator would never have made such lovely days and have given us the deep hearts to enjoy them, above and beyond all thought, unless we were meant to be immortal. This sunshine is the golden pledge thereof. It beams through the gates of paradise and shows us glimpses far inward.

By and by, in a little time, the outward world puts on a drear austerity. On some October morning there is a heavy hoar-frost on the grass and along the tops of the fences; and at sunrise the leaves fall from the trees of our avenue without a breath of wind, quietly descending by their own weight. All summer long they have murmured like the noise of waters; they have roared loudly while the branches were wrestling with the thunder gust; they have made music both glad and solemn; they have attuned my thoughts by their quiet sound as I paced to and fro beneath the arch of intermingling boughs. Now they can only rustle under my feet. Henceforth the gray parsonage begins to assume a larger importance, and draws to its fireside,—for the abomination of the air-tight stove is reserved till wintry weather,—draws closer and closer to its fireside the vagrant impulses that had gone wandering about through the summer.

When summer was dead and buried the Old Manse became as lonely as a hermitage. Not that ever—in my time at least—it had been thronged with company; but, at no rare intervals, we welcomed some friend out of the dusty glare and tumult of the world, and rejoiced to share with him the transparent obscurity that was floating over us. In one respect our precincts were like the Enchanted Ground through which the pilgrim travelled on his way to the Celestial City![9] The guests, each and all, felt a slumberous influence upon them; they fell asleep in chairs, or took a more deliberate siesta on the sofa, or were seen stretched among the shadows of the orchard, looking up dreamily through the boughs. They could not have paid a more acceptable compliment to my abode, nor to my own qualities as a host. I held it as a proof that they left their cares behind them as they passed between the stone gate-posts at the entrance of our avenue, and that the so powerful opiate was the abundance of peace

[9] Reference to the protagonist's travels in John Bunyan's *The Pilgrim's Progress* (1678).

and quiet within and all around us. Others could give them pleasure and amusement or instruction—these could be picked up anywhere; but it was for me to give them rest—rest in a life of trouble. What better could be done for those weary and world-worn spirits?—for him[10] whose career of perpetual action was impeded and harassed by the rarest of his powers and the richest of his acquirements?—for another[11] who had thrown his ardent heart from earliest youth into the strife of politics, and now, perchance, began to suspect that one lifetime is too brief for the accomplishment of any lofty aim?—for her[12] on whose feminine nature had been imposed the heavy gift of intellectual power, such as a strong man might have staggered under, and with it the necessity to act upon the world?—in a word, not to multiply instances, what better could be done for anybody who came within our magic circle than to throw the spell of a tranquil spirit over him? And when it had wrought its full effect, then we dismissed him, with but misty reminiscences, as if he had been dreaming of us.

Were I to adopt a pet idea, as so many people do, and fondle it in my embraces to the exclusion of all others, it would be, that the great want which mankind labors under at this present period is sleep. The world should recline its vast head on the first convenient pillow and take an age-long nap. It has gone distracted through a morbid activity, and, while preternaturally wide awake, is nevertheless tormented by visions that seem real to it now, but would assume their true aspect and character were all things once set right by an interval of sound repose. This is the only method of getting rid of old delusions and avoiding new ones; of regenerating our race, so that it might in due time awake as an infant out of dewy slumber; of restoring to us the simple perception of what is right, and the single-hearted desire to achieve it, both of which have long been lost in consequence of this weary activity of brain and torpor or passion of the heart that now afflict the universe. Stimulants, the only mode of treatment hitherto attempted, cannot quell the disease; they do but heighten the delirium.

Let not the above paragraph ever be quoted against the author; for, though tinctured with its modicum of truth, it is the result and expression of what he knew, while he was writing, to be but a distorted survey of the state and prospects of mankind. There were circumstances around me which made it difficult to view the world precisely as it exists; for, severe and sober as was the Old Manse, it was necessary to go but a little way beyond its threshold before meeting with stranger moral shapes of men than might have been encountered elsewhere in a circuit of a thousand miles.

These hobgoblins of flesh and blood were attracted thither by the widespreading influence of a great original thinker, who had his earthly abode at the opposite extremity of our village. His mind acted upon other minds of a certain constitution with wonderful magnetism, and drew many men upon long pilgrimages to speak with him face to face. Young visionaries—to whom just so much of insight had been imparted as to make life all a labyrinth around them—came to seek the clew that should guide them out of their self-involved bewilderment. Grayheaded theorists—whose systems, at first air, had finally imprisoned them in an iron frame-work—

[10] Horatio Bridge (1806–1893), Hawthorne's lifelong friend, who had just finished his *Journal of an African Cruiser* (1845).
[11] Franklin Pierce (1804–1869), another lifelong friend, who became the fourteenth president in 1853.
[12] Margaret Fuller Ossoli (1810–1850), American critic and reformer.

travelled painfully to his door, not to ask deliverance, but to invite the free spirit into their own thraldom. People that had lighted on a new thought, or a thought that they fancied new, came to Emerson, as the finder of a glittering gem hastens to a lapidary, to ascertain its quality and value. Uncertain, troubled, earnest wanderers through the midnight of the moral world beheld his intellectual fire as a beacon burning on a hill-top, and, climbing the difficult ascent, looked forth into the surrounding obscurity more hopefully than hitherto. The light revealed objects unseen before,—mountains, gleaming lakes, glimpses of a creation among the chaos; but, also, as was unavoidable, it attracted bats and owls and the whole host of night birds, which flapped their dusky wings against the gazer's eyes, and sometimes were mistaken for fowls of angelic feather. Such delusions always hover nigh whenever a beacon fire of truth is kindled.

For myself, there had been epochs of my life when I, too, might have asked of this prophet the master word that should solve me the riddle of the universe; but now, being happy, I felt as if there were no question to be put, and therefore admired Emerson as a poet of deep beauty and austere tenderness, but sought nothing from him as a philosopher. It was good, nevertheless, to meet him in the woodpaths, or sometimes in our avenue, with that pure intellectual gleam diffused about his presence like the garment of a shining one; and he so quiet, so simple, so without pretension, encountering each man alive as if expecting to receive more than he could impart. And, in truth, the heart of many an ordinary man had, perchance, inscriptions which he could not read. But it was impossible to dwell in his vicinity without inhaling more or less the mountain atmosphere of his lofty thought, which, in the brains of some people, wrought a singular giddiness,—new truth being as heady as new wine. Never was a poor little country village infested with such a variety of queer, strangely-dressed, oddly-behaved mortals, most of whom took upon themselves to be important agents of the world's destiny, yet were simply bores of a very intense water. Such, I imagine, is the invariable character of persons who crowd so closely about an original thinker as to draw in his unuttered breath and thus become imbued with a false originality. This triteness of novelty is enough to make any man of common sense blaspheme at all ideas of less than a century's standing, and pray that the world may be petrified and rendered immovable in precisely the worst moral and physical state that it ever yet arrived at, rather than be benefited by such schemes of such philosophers.

And now I begin to feel—and perhaps should have sooner felt—that we have talked enough of the Old Manse. Mine honored reader, it may be, will vilify the poor author as an egotist for babbling through so many pages about a mossgrown country parsonage, and his life within its walls and on the river and in the woods, and the influences that wrought upon him from all these sources. My conscience, however, does not reproach me with betraying anything too sacredly individual to be revealed by a human spirit to its brother or sister spirit. How narrow—how shallow and scanty too—is the stream of thought that has been flowing from my pen, compared with the broad tide of dim emotions, ideas, and associations which swell around me from that portion of my existence! How little have I told! and of that little, how almost nothing is even tinctured with any quality that makes it exclusively my own! Has the reader gone wandering, hand in hand with me, through the inner passages of my being? and have we groped together into all its chambers and examined their treasures or their rubbish? Not so. We have been standing on the greensward, but just within the cavern's mouth, where the common sunshine is free to penetrate, and where every footstep is therefore free to come. I have appealed to no sentiment or sensibilities save such as are diffused among us all. So far as I am a man of really individual attributes I veil my face; nor am I, nor have I ever been, one of those supremely hospitable people who serve up their own hearts, delicately fried, with brain sauce, as a tidbit for their beloved public.

Glancing back over what I have written, it seems but the scattered reminiscences of a single summer. In fairyland there is no measurement of time; and, in a spot so sheltered from the turmoil of life's ocean, three years hastened away with a noiseless flight, as the breezy sunshine chases the cloud shadows across the depths of a still valley. Now came hints, growing more and more distinct, that the owner of the old house was pining for his native air. Carpenters next appeared, making a tremendous racket among the out-buildings, strewing the green grass with pine shavings and chips of chestnut joists, and vexing the whole antiquity of the place with their discordant renovations. Soon, moreover, they divested our abode of the veil of woodbine which had crept over a large portion of its southern face. All the aged mosses were cleared unsparingly away; and there were horrible whispers about brushing up the external walls with a coat of paint—a purpose as little to my taste as might be that of roughing the venerable cheeks of one's grandmother. But the hand that renovates is always more sacrilegious than that which destroys. In fine, we gathered up our household goods, drank a farewell cup of tea in our pleasant little breakfast room,—delicately fragrant tea, an unpurchasable luxury, one of the many angel gifts that had fallen like dew upon us,—and passed forth between the tall stone gateposts as uncertain as the wandering Arabs where our tent might next be pitched. Providence took me by the hand, and—an oddity of dispensation which, I trust, there is no irreverence in smiling at—has led me, as the newspapers announce while I am writing, from the Old Manse into a custom house. As a story teller, I have often contrived strange vicissitudes for my imaginary personages, but none like this.

The treasure of intellectual good which I hoped to find in our secluded dwelling had never come to light. No profound treatise of ethics, no philosophic history, no novel even, that could stand unsupported on its edges. All that I had to show, as a man of letters, were these few tales and essays, which had blossomed out like flowers in the calm summer of my heart and mind. Save editing (an easy task) the journal of my friend of many years, the African Cruiser, I had done nothing else. With these idle weeds and withering blossoms I have intermixed some that were produced long ago,—old, faded things, reminding me of flowers pressed between the leaves of a book,—and now offer the bouquet, such as it is, to any whom it may please. These fitful sketches, with so little of external life about them, yet claiming no profundity of purpose,—so reserved, even while they sometimes seem so frank,—often but half in earnest, and never, even when most so, expressing satisfactorily the thoughts which they profess to image,—such trifles, I truly feel, afford no solid basis for a literary reputation. Nevertheless, the public—if my limited number of readers, whom I venture to regard rather as a circle of friends, may be termed a public—will receive them the more kindly, as the last offering, the last collection, of this nature which it is my purpose ever to put forth. Unless I could do better, I have done enough in this kind. For myself the book will always retain one charm—as reminding me of the river, with its delightful solitudes, and of the avenue, the garden, and the orchard, and especially the dear old Manse, with the little study on its western side, and the sunshine glimmering through the willow branches while I wrote.

Let the reader, if he will do me so much honor, imagine himself my guest, and that, having seen whatever may be worthy of notice within and about the Old Manse, he has finally been ushered into my study. There, after seating him in an antique elbow chair, an heirloom of the house, I take forth a roll of manuscript and entreat his attention to the following tales—an act of personal inhospitality, however, which I never was guilty of, nor ever will be, even to my worst enemy.

1846

The Scarlet Letter[*]

The Custom-House

Introductory to "The Scarlet Letter"

It is a little remarkable, that—though disinclined to talk overmuch of myself and my affairs at the fireside, and to my personal friends—an autobiographical impulse should twice in my life have taken possession of me, in addressing the public. The first time was three or four years since, when I favored the reader—inexcusably, and for no earthly reason, that either the indulgent reader or the intrusive author could imagine —with a description of my way of life in the deep quietude of an Old Manse.[1] And now—because, beyond my deserts, I was happy enough to find a listener or two on the former occasion—I again seize the public by the button, and talk of my three years' experience in a Custom-House. The example of the famous "P. P.,"[2] Clerk of this Parish," was never more faithfully followed. The truth seems to be, however, that, when he casts his leaves forth upon the wind, the author addresses, not the many who will fling aside his volume, or never take it up, but the few who will understand him, better than most of his schoolmates and lifemates. Some authors, indeed, do far more than this, and indulge themselves in such confidential depths of revelation as could fittingly be addressed, only and exclusively, to the one heart and mind of perfect sympathy; as if the printed book, thrown at large on the wide world, were certain to find out the divided segment of the writer's own nature, and complete his circle

---

[*] In 1846 President James K. Polk, a Democrat, appointed Hawthorne surveyor of the U. S. Customhouse in Salem, Massachusetts, a post that required him to evaluate taxable goods. In 1849, soon after Zachary Taylor was elected president, Hawthorne was dismissed. He then began writing *The Scarlet Letter*, which was completed in February 1850 and published in Boston the following month. Hawthorne wrote *The Custom-House* as an introduction to *The Scarlet Letter* to add realism to the novel, to express his views of the writing of fiction at that time, and to attack the Whig politicians who had caused his dismissal from his post.

[1] From 1842 to 1845, Hawthorne lived in the Old Manse in Concord, Massachusetts, where he finished a collection of tales and sketches, *Mosses from an Old Manse* (1846), which contains the autobiographical essay, "The Author Makes the Reader Acquainted with His Abode."

[2] *The Memoirs of P. P., Clerk of this Parish,* a mock eighteenth-century autobiography that satirizes the tedious and egocentric Bishop Gilbert Burnet's *A History of His Own Times* (1723).

of existence by bringing him into communion with it. It is scarcely decorous, however, to speak all, even where we speak impersonally. But—as thoughts are frozen and utterance benumbed, unless the speaker stand in some true relation with his audience—it may be pardonable to imagine that a friend, a kind and apprehensive, though not the closest friend, is listening to our talk; and then, a native reserve being thawed by this genial consciousness, we may prate of the circumstances that lie around us, and even of ourself, but still keep the inmost Me behind its veil. To this extent and within these limits, an author, methinks, may be autobiographical, without violating either the reader's rights or his own.

It will be seen, likewise, that this Custom-House sketch has a certain propriety, of a kind always recognized in literature, as explaining how a large portion of the following pages came into my possession, and as offering proofs of the authenticity of a narrative therein contained. This, in fact,—a desire to put myself in my true position as editor, or very little more, of the most prolix among the tales that make up my volume,[3]—this, and no other, is my true reason for assuming a personal relation with the public. In accomplishing the main purpose, it has appeared allowable, by a few extra touches, to give a faint representation of a mode of life not heretofore described, together with some of the characters that move in it, among whom the author happened to make one.

In my native town of Salem, at the head of what, half a century ago, in the days of old King Derby,[4] was a bustling wharf,—but which is now burdened with decayed wooden warehouses, and exhibits few or no symptoms of commercial life; except, perhaps, a bark or brig, half-way down its melancholy length, discharging hides; or, nearer at hand, a Nova Scotia schooner, pitching out her cargo of firewood,—at the head, I say, of this dilapidated wharf, which the tide often overflows, and along which, at the base and in the rear of the row of buildings, the track of many languid years is seen in a border of unthrifty grass,—here, with a view from its front windows adown this not very enlivening prospect, and thence across the harbour, stands a spacious edifice of brick. From the loftiest point of its roof, during precisely three and a half hours of each forenoon, floats or droops, in breeze or calm, the banner of the republic; but with the thirteen stripes turned vertically, instead of horizontally, and thus indicating that a civil, and not a military post of Uncle Sam's government, is here established. Its front is ornamented with a portico of half a dozen wooden pillars, supporting a balcony, beneath which a flight of wide granite steps descends towards the street. Over the entrance hovers an enormous specimen of the American eagle, with outspread wings, a shield before her breast, and, if I recollect aright, a bunch of intermingled thunderbolts and barbed arrows in each claw. With the customary infirmity of temper that characterizes this unhappy fowl, she appears, by the fierceness of her beak and eye and the general truculency of her attitude, to threaten mischief to the inoffensive community; and especially to warn all citizens, careful of their safety, against intruding on the premises which she overshadows with her wings. Nevertheless, vixenly as she looks, many people are seeking, at this very moment, to shelter themselves under the wing of the federal eagle; imagining, I presume, that her

---

[3] Originally several other shorter tales and sketches were to be included in *The Scarlet Letter*.

[4] E. H. Derby (1739–1799), nicknamed "Old King Derby," was a wealthy Salem shipowner and merchant.

bosom has all the softness and snugness of an eider-down pillow. But she has no great tenderness, even in her best of moods, and, sooner or later,—oftener soon than late, —is apt to fling off her nestlings with a scratch of her claw, a dab of her beak, or a rankling wound from her barbed arrows.

The pavement round about the above-described edifice—which we may as well name at once as the Custom-House of the port—has grass enough growing in its chinks to show that it has not, of late days, been worn by any multitudinous resort of business. In some months of the year, however, there often chances a forenoon when affairs move onward with a livelier tread. Such occasions might remind the elderly citizen of that period, before the last war with England,[5] when Salem was a port by itself; not scorned, as she is now, by her own merchants and ship-owners, who permit her wharves to crumble to ruin, while their ventures go to swell, needlessly and imperceptibly, the mighty flood of commerce at New York or Boston. On some such morning, when three or four vessels happen to have arrived at once,—usually from Africa or South America,—or to be on the verge of their departure thitherward, there is a sound of frequent feet, passing briskly up and down the granite steps. Here, before his own wife has greeted him, you may greet the sea-flushed ship-master, just in port, with his vessel's papers under his arm in a tarnished tin box. Here, too, comes his owner, cheerful or sombre, gracious or in the sulks, accordingly as his scheme of the now accomplished voyage has been realized in merchandise that will readily be turned to gold, or has buried him under a bulk of incommodities, such as nobody will care to rid him of. Here, likewise,—the germ of the wrinkle-browed, grizzly-bearded, careworn merchant,—we have the smart young clerk, who gets the taste of traffic as a wolf-cub does of blood, and already sends adventures in his master's ships, when he had better be sailing mimic boats upon a mill-pond. Another figure in the scene is the outward-bound sailor, in quest of a protection;[6] or the recently arrived one, pale and feeble, seeking a passport to the hospital. Nor must we forget the captains of the rusty little schooners that bring firewood from the British provinces; a rough-looking set of tarpaulins, without the alertness of the Yankee aspect, but contributing an item of no slight importance to our decaying trade.

Cluster all these individuals together, as they sometimes were, with other miscellaneous ones to diversify the group, and, for the time being, it made the Custom-House a stirring scene. More frequently, however, on ascending the steps, you would discern —in the entry, if it were summer time, or in their appropriate rooms, if wintry or inclement weather—a row of venerable figures, sitting in old-fashioned chairs, which were tipped on their hind legs back against the wall. Oftentimes they were asleep, but occasionally might be heard talking together, in voices between speech and a snore, and with that lack of energy that distinguishes the occupants of alms-houses, and all other human beings who depend for subsistence on charity, on monopolized labor, or any thing else but their own independent exertions. These old gentlemen—seated, like Matthew,[7] at the receipt of custom, but not very liable to be summoned thence, like him, for apostolic errands—were Custom-House officers.

Furthermore, on the left hand as you enter the front door, is a certain room or office, about fifteen feet square, and of a lofty height; with two of its arched windows

---

[5] The War of 1812.
[6] Document verifying citizenship.
[7] The apostle Matthew was a customs officer,

"sitting at the receipt of custom," when first seen by Jesus. (See Matthew 9:9.)

commanding a view of the aforesaid dilapidated wharf, and the third looking across a narrow lane, and along a portion of Derby Street. All three give glimpses of the shops of grocers, block-makers, slop-sellers, and ship-chandlers;[8] around the doors of which are generally to be seen, laughing and gossiping, clusters of old salts, and such other wharf-rats as haunt the Wapping[9] of a seaport. The room itself is cobwebbed, and dingy with old paint; its floor is strewn with gray sand, in a fashion that has elsewhere fallen into long disuse; and it is easy to conclude, from the general slovenliness of the place, that this is a sanctuary into which womankind, with her tools of magic, the broom and mop, has very infrequent access. In the way of furniture, there is a stove with a voluminous funnel; an old pine desk, with a three-legged stool beside it; two or three wooden-bottom chairs, exceedingly decrepit and infirm; and,—not to forget the library,—on some shelves, a score or two of volumes of the Acts of Congress, and a bulky Digest of the Revenue Laws. A tin pipe ascends through the ceiling, and forms a medium of vocal communication with other parts of the edifice. And here, some six months ago,—pacing from corner to corner, or lounging on the long-legged stool, with his elbow on the desk, and his eyes wandering up and down the columns of the morning newspaper,—you might have recognized, honored reader, the same individual who welcomed you into his cheery little study, where the sunshine glimmered so pleasantly through the willow branches, on the western side of the Old Manse. But now, should you go thither to seek him, you would inquire in vain for the Loco-foco[10] Surveyor. The besom[11] of reform has swept him out of office; and a worthier successor wears his dignity and pockets his emoluments.

This old town of Salem—my native place, though I have dwelt much away from it, both in boyhood and maturer years—possesses, or did possess, a hold on my affections, the force of which I have never realized during my seasons of actual residence here. Indeed, so far as its physical aspect is concerned, with its flat, unvaried surface, covered chiefly with wooden houses, few or none of which pretend to architectural beauty,—its irregularity, which is neither picturesque nor quaint, but only tame,—its long and lazy street, lounging wearisomely through the whole extent of the peninsula, with Gallows Hill[12] and New Guinea at one end, and a view of the alms-house at the other,—such being the features of my native town, it would be quite as reasonable to form a sentimental attachment to a disarranged checkerboard. And yet, though invariably happiest elsewhere, there is within me a feeling for old Salem, which, in lack of a better phrase, I must be content to call affection. The sentiment is probably assignable to the deep and aged roots which my family has struck into the soil. It is now nearly two centuries and a quarter since the original Briton, the earliest emigrant of my name,[13] made his appearance in the wild and forest-bordered

---

8 Manufacturers and distributors of general shipping equipment and clothing.
9 Originally London's ancient run-down dock area; subsequently a term applied to the slums of any wharf district.
10 Conservative Democrats disrupted the 1835 convention by extinguishing the lights in the meeting hall. The radical faction relit the lamps with friction matches, called "locofocos," which then quickly became a popular term for Democrats.

11 Broom.
12 The Salem "witches" were reputed to have been executed on Gallows Hill.
13 William Hathorne (1607–1681) immigrated to Massachusetts from England in 1630. His son John (1641–1717) served as a judge during the Salem witch trials of 1692. John Hathorne was the great-grandfather of Nathaniel Hathorne (1775–1808), the novelist's father, who added a w to his surname as a youth.

settlement, which has since become a city. And here his descendants have been born and died, and have mingled their earthy substance with the soil; until no small portion of it must necessarily be akin to the mortal frame wherewith, for a little while, I walk the streets. In part, therefore, the attachment which I speak of is the mere sensuous sympathy of dust for dust. Few of my countrymen can know what it is; nor, as frequent transplantation is perhaps better for the stock, need they consider it desirable to know.

But the sentiment has likewise its moral quality. The figure of that first ancestor, invested by family tradition with a dim and dusky grandeur, was present to my boyish imagination, as far back as I can remember. It still haunts me, and induces a sort of home-feeling with the past, which I scarcely claim in reference to the present phase of the town. I seem to have a stronger claim to a residence here on account of this grave, bearded, sable-cloaked, and steeple-crowned progenitor,—who came so early, with his Bible and his sword, and trode the unworn street with such a stately port, and made so large a figure, as a man of war and peace,—a stronger claim than for myself, whose name is seldom heard and my face hardly known. He was a soldier, legislator, judge; he was a ruler in the Church; he had all the Puritanic traits, both good and evil. He was likewise a bitter persecutor; as witness the Quakers, who have remembered him in their histories, and relate an incident of his hard severity towards a woman of their sect, which will last longer, it is to be feared, than any record of his better deeds, although these were many. His son, too, inherited the persecuting spirit, and made himself so conspicuous in the martyrdom of the witches, that their blood may fairly be said to have left a stain upon him. So deep a stain, indeed, that his old dry bones, in the Charter Street burial-ground, must still retain it, if they have not crumbled utterly to dust! I know not whether these ancestors of mine bethought themselves to repent, and ask pardon of Heaven for their cruelties; or whether they are now groaning under the heavy consequences of them, in another state of being. At all events, I, the present writer, as their representative, hereby take shame upon myself for their sakes, and pray that any curse incurred by them—as I have heard, and as the dreary and unprosperous condition of the race, for many a long year back, would argue to exist—may be now and henceforth removed.

Doubtless, however, either of these stern and black-browed Puritans would have thought it quite a sufficient retribution for his sins, that, after so long a lapse of years, the old trunk of the family tree, with so much venerable moss upon it, should have borne, as its topmost bough, an idler like myself. No aim, that I have ever cherished, would they recognize as laudable; no success of mine—if my life, beyond its domestic scope, had ever been brightened by success—would they deem otherwise than worthless, if not positively disgraceful. "What is he?" murmurs one gray shadow of my forefathers to the other. "A writer of story-books! What kind of a business in life, —what mode of glorifying God, or being serviceable to mankind in his day and generation,—may that be? Why, the degenerate fellow might as well have been a fiddler!" Such are the compliments bandied between my great-grandsires and myself, across the gulf of time! And yet, let them scorn me as they will, strong traits of their nature have intertwined themselves with mine.

Planted deep, in the town's earliest infancy and childhood, by these two earnest and energetic men, the race has ever since subsisted here; always, too, in respectability; never, so far as I have known, disgraced by a single unworthy member; but seldom or never, on the other hand, after the first two generations, performing any memorable deed, or so much as putting forward a claim to public notice. Gradually, they have sunk almost out of sight; as old houses, here and there about the streets, get covered half-way to the eaves by the accumulation of new soil. From father to son, for above a hundred years, they followed the sea; a gray-headed shipmaster, in each generation, retiring from the quarter-deck to the homestead, while a boy of fourteen took the hereditary place before the mast, confronting the salt spray and the gale, which had blustered against his sire and grandsire. The boy, also, in due time, passed from the forecastle to the cabin,[14] spent a tempestuous manhood, and returned from his world-wanderings, to grow old, and die, and mingle his dust with the natal earth. This long connection of a family with one spot, as its place of birth and burial, creates a kindred between the human being and the locality, quite independent of any charm in the scenery or moral circumstances that surround him. It is not love, but instinct. The new inhabitant—who came himself from a foreign land, or whose father or grandfather came—has little claim to be called a Salemite; he has no conception of the oyster-like tenacity with which an old settler, over whom his third century is creeping, clings to the spot where his successive generations have been imbedded. It is no matter that the place is joyless for him; that he is weary of the old wooden houses, the mud and dust, the dead level of site and sentiment, the chill east wind, and the chillest of social atmospheres;—all these, and whatever faults besides he may see or imagine, are nothing to the purpose. The spell survives, and just as powerfully as if the natal spot were an earthly paradise. So has it been in my case. I felt it almost as a destiny to make Salem my home; so that the mould of features and cast of character which had all along been familiar here—ever, as one representative of the race lay down in his grave, another assuming, as it were, his sentry-march along the Main Street—might still in my little day be seen and recognized in the old town. Nevertheless, this very sentiment is an evidence that the connection, which has become an unhealthy one, should at last be severed. Human nature will not flourish, any more than a potato, if it be planted and replanted, for too long a series of generations, in the same worn-out soil. My children have had other birth-places, and, so far as their fortunes may be within my control, shall strike their roots into unaccustomed earth.

On emerging from the Old Manse, it was chiefly this strange, indolent, unjoyous attachment for my native town, that brought me to fill a place in Uncle Sam's brick edifice,[15] when I might as well, or better, have gone somewhere else. My doom was on me. It was not the first time, nor the second, that I had gone away,—as it seemed, permanently,—but yet returned, like the bad half-penny; or as if Salem were for me the inevitable centre of the universe. So, one fine morning, I ascended the flight of granite steps, with the President's commission in my pocket, and was introduced to the corps of gentlemen who were to aid me in my weighty responsibility, as chief executive officer of the Custom-House.[16]

I doubt greatly—or rather, I do not doubt at all—whether any public functionary of the United States, either in the civil or military line, has ever had such a patriarchal body of veterans under his orders as myself. The whereabouts of the Oldest Inhabitant

---

[14] I.e., moved from the crew's quarters to the captain's.
[15] The customhouse in Salem.

[16] Hawthorne was the surveyor in the Salem Custom-House from 1846 to 1849.

was at once settled, when I looked at them. For upwards of twenty years before this epoch, the independent position of the Collector had kept the Salem Custom-House out of the whirlpool of political vicissitude, which makes the tenure of office generally so fragile. A soldier,—New England's most distinguished soldier,—he stood firmly on the pedestal of his gallant services; and, himself secure in the wise liberality of the successive administrations through which he had held office, he had been the safety of his subordinates in many an hour of danger and heart-quake. General Miller[17] was radically conservative; a man over whose kindly nature habit had no slight influence; attaching himself strongly to familiar faces, and with difficulty moved to change, even when change might have brought unquestionable improvement. Thus, on taking charge of my department, I found few but aged men. They were ancient sea-captains, for the most part, who, after being tost on every sea, and standing up sturdily against life's tempestuous blast, had finally drifted into this quiet nook; where, with little to disturb them, except the periodical terrors of a Presidential election, they one and all acquired a new lease of existence. Though by no means less liable than their fellow-men to age and infirmity, they had evidently some talisman or other that kept death at bay. Two or three of their number, as I was assured, being gouty and rheumatic, or perhaps bed-ridden, never dreamed of making their appearance at the Custom-House, during a large part of the year; but, after a torpid winter, would creep out into the warm sunshine of May or June, go lazily about what they termed duty, and, at their own leisure and convenience, betake themselves to bed again. I must plead guilty to the charge of abbreviating the official breath of more than one of these venerable servants of the republic. They were allowed, on my representation, to rest from their arduous labors, and soon afterwards—as if their sole principle of life had been zeal for their country's service; as I verily believe it was—withdrew to a better world. It is a pious consolation to me, that, through my interference, a sufficient space was allowed them for repentance of the evil and corrupt practices, into which, as a matter of course, every Custom-House officer must be supposed to fall. Neither the front nor the back entrance of the Custom-House opens on the road to Paradise.

The greater part of my officers were Whigs.[18] It was well for their venerable brotherhood, that the new Surveyor was not a politician, and, though a faithful Democrat in principle, neither received nor held his office with any reference to political services. Had it been otherwise,—had an active politician been put into this influential post, to assume the easy task of making head against a Whig Collector, whose infirmities withheld him from the personal administration of his office,— hardly a man of the old corps would have drawn the breath of official life, within a month after the exterminating angel had come up the Custom-House steps. According to the received code in such matters, it would have been nothing short of duty, in a politician, to bring every one of those white heads under the axe of the guillotine. It was plain enough to discern, that the old fellows dreaded some such discourtesy at my hands. It pained, and at the same time amused me, to behold the terrors that attended my advent; to see a furrowed cheek, weather-beaten by half a

---

[17] General James F. Miller (1776–1851), a hero of the War of 1812 and governor of Arkansas from 1819 to 1825, was chief officer of the Salem Custom-House from 1825 to 1849.

[18] Political party (1834–1852) opposed to the Democrats.

century of storm, turn ashy pale at the glance of so harmless an individual as myself; to detect, as one or another addressed me, the tremor of a voice, which, in long-past days, had been wont to bellow through a speaking-trumpet, hoarsely enough to frighten Boreas[19] himself to silence. They knew, these excellent old persons, that, by all established rule,—and, as regarded some of them, weighed by their own lack of efficiency for business,—they ought to have given place to younger men, more orthodox in politics, and altogether fitter than themselves to serve our common Uncle. I knew it too, but could never quite find in my heart to act upon the knowledge. Much and deservedly to my own discredit, therefore, and considerably to the detriment of my official conscience, they continued, during my incumbency, to creep about the wharves, and loiter up and down the Custom-House steps. They spent a good deal of time, also, asleep in their accustomed corners, with their chairs tilted back against the wall; awaking, however, once or twice in a forenoon, to bore one another with the several thousandth repetition of old sea-stories, and mouldy jokes, that had grown to be pass-words and countersigns among them.

The discovery was soon made, I imagine, that the new Surveyor had no great harm in him. So, with lightsome hearts, and the happy consciousness of being usefully employed,—in their own behalf, at least, if not for our beloved country,—these good old gentlemen went through the various formalities of office. Sagaciously, under their spectacles, did they peep into the holds of vessels! Mighty was their fuss about little matters, and marvellous, sometimes, the obtuseness that allowed greater ones to slip between their fingers! Whenever such a mischance occurred,—when a wagon-load of valuable merchandise had been smuggled ashore, at noonday, perhaps, and directly beneath their unsuspicious noses,—nothing could exceed the vigilance and alacrity with which they proceeded to lock, and double-lock, and secure with tape and sealing-wax, all the avenues of the delinquent vessel. Instead of a reprimand for their previous negligence, the case seemed rather to require an eulogium on their praise-worthy caution, after the mischief had happened; a grateful recognition of the promp-titude of their zeal, the moment that there was no longer any remedy!

Unless people are more than commonly disagreeable, it is my foolish habit to contract a kindness for them. The better part of my companion's character, if it have a better part, is that which usually comes uppermost in my regard, and forms the type whereby I recognize the man. As most of these old Custom-House officers had good traits, and as my position in reference to them, being paternal and protective, was favorable to the growth of friendly sentiments, I soon grew to like them all. It was pleasant, in the summer forenoons,—when the fervent heat, that almost liquefied the rest of the human family, merely communicated a genial warmth to their half-torpid systems,—it was pleasant to hear them chatting in the back entry, a row of them all tipped against the wall, as usual; while the frozen witticisms of past generations were thawed out, and came bubbling with laughter from their lips. Externally, the jollity of aged men has much in common with the mirth of children; the intellect, any more than a deep sense of humor, has little to do with the matter; it is, with both, a gleam that plays upon the surface, and imparts a sunny and cheery aspect alike to the green branch, and gray, mouldering trunk. In one case, however, it is real sunshine; in the other, it more resembles the phosphorescent glow of decaying wood.

[19] In Greek mythology, god of the north wind.

It would be sad injustice, the reader must understand, to represent all my excellent old friends as in their dotage. In the first place, my coadjutors were not invariably old; there were men among them in their strength and prime, of marked ability and energy, and altogether superior to the sluggish and dependent mode of life on which their evil stars had cast them. Then, moreover, the white locks of age were sometimes found to be the thatch of an intellectual tenement in good repair. But, as respects the majority of my corps of veterans, there will be no wrong done, if I characterize them generally as a set of wearisome old souls, who had gathered nothing worth preservation from their varied experience of life. They seemed to have flung away all the golden grain of practical wisdom, which they had enjoyed so many opportunities of harvesting, and most carefully to have stored their memories with the husks. They spoke with far more interest and unction of their morning's breakfast, or yesterday's, today's, or to-morrow's dinner, than of the shipwreck of forty or fifty years ago, and all the world's wonders which they had witnessed with their youthful eyes.

The father of the Custom-House—the patriarch, not only of this little squad of officials, but, I am bold to say, of the respectable body of tide-waiters[20] all over the United States—was a certain permanent Inspector. He might truly be termed a legitimate son of the revenue system, dyed in the wool, or rather, born in the purple; since his sire, a Revolutionary colonel, and formerly collector of the port, had created an office for him, and appointed him to fill it, at a period of the early ages which few living men can now remember. This Inspector, when I first knew him, was a man of fourscore years, or thereabouts, and certainly one of the most wonderful specimens of winter-green that you would be likely to discover in a lifetime's search. With his florid cheek, his compact figure, smartly arrayed in a bright-buttoned blue coat, his brisk and vigorous step, and his hale and hearty aspect, altogether, he seemed—not young, indeed—but a kind of new contrivance of Mother Nature in the shape of man, whom age and infirmity had no business to touch. His voice and laugh, which perpetually reëchoed through the Custom-House, had nothing of the tremulous quaver and cackle of an old man's utterance; they came strutting out of his lungs, like the crow of a cock, or the blast of a clarion. Looking at him merely as an animal, —and there was very little else to look at,—he was a most satisfactory object, from the thorough healthfulness and wholesomeness of his system, and his capacity, at that extreme age, to enjoy all, or nearly all, the delights which he had ever aimed at, or conceived of. The careless security of his life in the Custom-House, on a regular income, and with but slight and infrequent apprehensions of removal, had no doubt contributed to make time pass lightly over him. The original and more potent causes, however, lay in the rare perfection of his animal nature, the moderate proportion of intellect, and the very trifling admixture of moral and spiritual ingredients; these latter qualities, indeed, being in barely enough measure to keep the old gentleman from walking on all-fours. He possessed no power of thought, no depth of feeling, no troublesome sensibilities; nothing, in short, but a few commonplace instincts, which, aided by the cheerful temper that grew inevitably out of his physical well-being, did duty very respectably, and to general acceptance, in lieu of a heart. He had been the husband of three wives, all long since dead; the father of twenty children, most of

---

[20] I.e., customs officials who boarded an incoming ship to direct the unloading of its cargo.

whom, at every age of childhood or maturity, had likewise returned to dust. Here, one would suppose, might have been sorrow enough to imbue the sunniest disposition, through and through, with a sable tinge. Not so with our old Inspector! One brief sigh sufficed to carry off the entire burden of these dismal reminiscences. The next moment, he was as ready for sport as any unbreeched infant; far readier than the Collector's junior clerk, who, at nineteen years, was much the elder and graver man of the two.

I used to watch and study this patriarchal personage with, I think, livelier curiosity than any other form of humanity there presented to my notice. He was, in truth, a rare phenomenon; so perfect in one point of view; so shallow, so delusive, so impalpable, such an absolute nonentity, in every other. My conclusion was that he had no soul, no heart, no mind; nothing, as I have already said, but instincts; and yet, withal, so cunningly had the few materials of his character been put together, that there was no painful perception of deficiency, but, on my part, an entire contentment with what I found in him. It might be difficult—and it was so—to conceive how he should exist hereafter, so earthy and sensuous did he seem; but surely his existence here, admitting that it was to terminate with his last breath, had been not unkindly given; with no higher moral responsibilities than the beasts of the field, but with a larger scope of enjoyment than theirs, and with all their blessed immunity from the dreariness and duskiness of age.

One point, in which he had vastly the advantage over his four-footed brethren, was his ability to recollect the good dinners which it had made no small portion of the happiness of his life to eat. His gourmandism was a highly agreeable trait; and to hear him talk of roast-meat was as appetizing as a pickle or an oyster. As he possessed no higher attribute, and neither sacrificed nor vitiated any spiritual endowment by devoting all his energies and ingenuities to subserve the delight and profit of his maw, it always pleased and satisfied me to hear him expatiate on fish, poultry, and butcher's meat, and the most eligible methods of preparing them for the table. His reminiscences of good cheer, however ancient the date of the actual banquet, seemed to bring the savor of pig or turkey under one's very nostrils. There were flavors on his palate, that had lingered there not less than sixty or seventy years, and were still apparently as fresh as that of the mutton-chop which he had just devoured for his breakfast. I have heard him smack his lips over dinners, every guest at which, except himself, had long been food for worms. It was marvelous to observe how the ghosts of bygone meals were continually rising up before him; not in anger or retribution, but as if grateful for his former appreciation, and seeking to reduplicate an endless series of enjoyment, at once shadowy and sensual. A tenderloin of beef, a hind-quarter of veal, a spare-rib of pork, a particular chicken, or a remarkably praiseworthy turkey, which had perhaps adorned his board in the days of the elder Adams,[21] would be remembered; while all the subsequent experience of our race, and all the events that brightened or darkened his individual career, had gone over him with as little permanent effect as the passing breeze. The chief tragic event of the old man's life, so far as I could judge, was his mishap with a certain goose, which lived and died some twenty or forty years ago;

[21] John Adams (1735–1826), second president of the United States and father of John Quincy Adams (1767–1848), sixth president.

a goose of most promising figure, but which, at table, proved so inveterately tough that the carving-knife would make no impression on its carcass; and it could only be divided with an axe and handsaw.

But it is time to quit this sketch; on which, however, I should be glad to dwell at considerably more length, because, of all men whom I have ever known, this individual was fittest to be a Custom-House officer. Most persons, owing to causes which I may not have space to hint at, suffer moral detriment from this peculiar mode of life. The old Inspector was incapable of it, and, were he to continue in office to the end of time, would be just as good as he was then, and sit down to dinner with just as good an appetite.

There is one likeness, without which my gallery of Custom-House portraits would be strangely incomplete; but which my comparatively few opportunities for observation enable me to sketch only in the merest outline. It is that of the Collector, our gallant old General,[22] who, after his brilliant military service, subsequently to which he had ruled over a wild Western territory, had come hither, twenty years before, to spend the decline of his varied and honorable life. The brave soldier had already numbered, nearly or quite, his threescore years and ten, and was pursuing the remainder of his earthly march, burdened with infirmities which even the martial music of his own spirit-stirring recollections could do little towards lightening. The step was palsied now, that had been foremost in the charge. It was only with the assistance of a servant, and by leaning his hand heavily on the iron balustrade, that he could slowly and painfully ascend the Custom-House steps, and, with a toilsome progress across the floor, attain his customary chair beside the fireplace. There he used to sit, gazing with a somewhat dim serenity of aspect at the figures that came and went; amid the rustle of papers, the administering of oaths, the discussion of business, and the casual talk of the office; all which sounds and circumstances seemed but indistinctly to impress his senses, and hardly to make their way into his inner sphere of contemplation. His countenance, in this repose, was mild and kindly. If his notice was sought, an expression of courtesy and interest gleamed out upon his features; proving that there was light within him, and that it was only the outward medium of the intellectual lamp that obstructed the rays in their passage. The closer you penetrated to the substance of his mind, the sounder it appeared. When no longer called upon to speak, or listen, either of which operations cost him an evident effort, his face would briefly subside into its former not uncheerful quietude. It was not painful to behold this look; for, though dim, it had not the imbecility of decaying age. The framework of his nature, originally strong and massive, was not yet crumbled into ruin.

To observe and define his character, however, under such disadvantages, was as difficult a task as to trace out and build up anew, in imagination, an old fortress, like Ticonderoga,[23] from a view of its gray and broken ruins. Here and there, perchance, the walls may remain almost complete; but elsewhere may be only a shapeless mound, cumbrous with its very strength, and overgrown, through long years of peace and neglect, with grass and alien weeds.

Nevertheless, looking at the old warrior with affection,—for, slight as was the

---

[22] General James F. Miller (see note 17 above).
[23] Fort Ticonderoga, New York, was captured from the British in 1775.

communication between us, my feeling towards him, like that of all bipeds and quadrupeds who knew him, might not improperly be termed so,—I could discern the main points of his portrait. It was marked with the noble and heroic qualities which showed it to be not by a mere accident, but of good right, that he had won a distinguished name. His spirit could never, I conceive, have been characterized by an uneasy activity; it must, at any period of his life, have required an impulse to set him in motion; but, once stirred up, with obstacles to overcome, and an adequate object to be attained, it was not in the man to give out or fail. The heat that had formerly pervaded his nature, and which was not yet extinct, was never of the kind that flashes and flickers in a blaze, but, rather, a deep, red glow, as of iron in a furnace. Weight, solidity, firmness; this was the expression of his repose, even in such decay as had crept untimely over him, at the period of which I speak. But I could imagine, even then, that, under some excitement which should go deeply into his consciousness,—roused by a trumpet-peal, loud enough to awaken all of his energies that were not dead, but only slumbering,—he was yet capable of flinging off his infirmities like a sick man's gown, dropping the staff of age to seize a battle-sword, and starting up once more a warrior. And, in so intense a moment, his demeanour would have still been calm. Such an exhibition, however, was but to be pictured in fancy; not to be anticipated, nor desired. What I saw in him—as evidently as the indestructible ramparts of Old Ticonderoga, already cited as the most appropriate simile—were the features of stubborn and ponderous endurance, which might well have amounted to obstinacy in his earlier days; of integrity, that, like most of his other endowments, lay in a somewhat heavy mass, and was just as unmalleable and unmanageable as a ton of iron ore; and of benevolence, which, fiercely as he led the bayonets on at Chippewa or Fort Erie,[24] I take to be of quite as genuine a stamp as what actuates any or all the polemical philanthropists of the age. He had slain men with his own hand, for aught I know;—certainly, they had fallen, like blades of grass at the sweep of the scythe, before the charge to which his spirit imparted its triumphant energy;—but, be that as it might, there was never in his heart so much cruelty as would have brushed the down off a butterfly's wing. I have not known the man, to whose innate kindliness I would more confidently make an appeal.

Many characteristics—and those, too, which contribute not the least forcibly to impart resemblance in a sketch—must have vanished, or been obscured, before I met the General. All merely graceful attributes are usually the most evanescent; nor does Nature adorn the human ruin with blossoms of new beauty, that have their roots and proper nutriment only in the chinks and crevices of decay, as she sows wall-flowers over the ruined fortress of Ticonderoga. Still, even in respect of grace and beauty, there were points well worth noting. A ray of humor, now and then, would make its way through the veil of dim obstruction, and glimmer pleasantly upon our faces. A trait of native elegance, seldom seen in the masculine character after childhood or early youth, was shown in the General's fondness for the sight and fragrance of flowers. An old soldier might be supposed to prize only the bloody laurel on his brow; but here was one, who seemed to have a young girl's appreciation of the floral tribe.

There, beside the fireplace, the brave old General used to sit; while the Surveyor

---

[24] Significant battles that occurred on the Niagara frontier in 1814.

—though seldom, when it could be avoided, taking upon himself the difficult task of engaging him in conversation—was fond of standing at a distance, and watching his quiet and almost slumberous countenance. He seemed away from us, although we saw him but a few yards off; remote, though we passed close beside his chair; unattainable, though we might have stretched forth our hands and touched his own. It might be, that he lived a more real life within his thoughts, than amid the unappropriate environment of the Collector's office. The evolutions of the parade; the tumult of the battle; the flourish of old, heroic music, heard thirty years before;—such scenes and sounds, perhaps, were all alive before his intellectual sense. Meanwhile, the merchants and ship-masters, the spruce clerks, and uncouth sailors, entered and departed; the bustle of this commercial and Custom-House life kept up its little murmur roundabout him; and neither with the men nor their affairs did the General appear to sustain the most distant relation. He was as much out of place as an old sword —now rusty, but which had flashed once in the battle's front, and showed still a bright gleam along its blade—would have been, among the inkstands, paper-folders, and mahogany rulers, on the Deputy Collector's desk.

There was one thing that much aided me in renewing and re-creating the stalwart soldier of the Niagara frontier,—the man of true and simple energy. It was the recollection of those memorable words of his,—"I'll try, Sir!"[25]—spoken on the very verge of a desperate and heroic enterprise, and breathing the soul and spirit of New England hardihood, comprehending all perils, and encountering all. If, in our country, valor were rewarded by heraldic honor, this phrase—which it seems so easy to speak, but which only he, with such a task of danger and glory before him, has ever spoken —would be the best and fittest of all mottoes for the General's shield of arms.

It contributes greatly towards a man's moral and intellectual health, to be brought into habits of companionship with individuals unlike himself, who care little for his pursuits, and whose sphere and abilities he must go out of himself to appreciate. The accidents of my life have often afforded me this advantage, but never with more fulness and variety than during my continuance in office. There was one man, especially, the observation of whose character gave me a new idea of talent. His gifts were emphatically those of a man of business; prompt, acute, clear-minded; with an eye that saw through all perplexities, and a faculty of arrangement that made them vanish, as by the waving of an enchanter's wand. Bred up from boyhood in the Custom-House, it was his proper field of activity; and the many intricacies of business, so harassing to the interloper, presented themselves before him with the regularity of a perfectly comprehended system. In my contemplation, he stood as the ideal of his class. He was, indeed, the Custom-House in himself; or, at all events, the main-spring that kept its variously revolving wheels in motion; for, in an institution like this, where its officers are appointed to subserve their own profit and convenience, and seldom with a leading reference to their fitness for the duty to be performed, they must perforce seek elsewhere the dexterity which is not in them. Thus, by an inevitable necessity, as a magnet attracts steel-filings, so did our man of business draw to himself the difficulties which everybody met with. With an easy condescension, and kind

---

[25] General James Miller's response to General Winfield Scott's order to capture a British battery at Lundy's Lane near Niagara Falls.

forbearance towards our stupidity,—which, to his order of mind, must have seemed little short of crime,—would he forthwith, by the merest touch of his finger, make the incomprehensible as clear as daylight. The merchants valued him not less than we, his esoteric friends. His integrity was perfect; it was a law of nature with him, rather than a choice or a principle; nor can it be otherwise than the main condition of an intellect so remarkably clear and accurate as his, to be honest and regular in the administration of affairs. A stain on his conscience, as to any thing that came within the range of his vocation, would trouble such a man very much in the same way, though to a far greater degree, than an error in the balance of an account, or an ink-blot on the fair page of a book of record. Here, in a word,—and it is a rare instance in my life,—I had met with a person thoroughly adapted to the situation which he held.

Such were some of the people with whom I now found myself connected. I took it in good part at the hands of Providence, that I was thrown into a position so little akin to my past habits; and set myself seriously to gather from it whatever profit was to be had. After my fellowship of toil and impracticable schemes, with the dreamy brethren of Brook Farm;[26] after living for three years within the subtile influence of an intellect like Emerson's;[27] after those wild, free days on the Assabeth, indulging fantastic speculations beside our fire of fallen boughs, with Ellery Channing; after talking with Thoreau about pine-trees and Indian relics, in his hermitage at Walden; after growing fastidious by sympathy with the classic refinement of Hillard's culture; after becoming imbued with poetic sentiment at Longfellow's hearth-stone;—it was time, at length, that I should exercise other faculties of my nature, and nourish myself with food for which I had hitherto had little appetite. Even the old Inspector was desirable, as a change of diet, to a man who had known Alcott. I looked upon it as an evidence, in some measure, of a system naturally well balanced, and lacking no essential part of a thorough organization, that, with such associates to remember, I could mingle at once with men of altogether different qualities, and never murmur at the change.

Literature, its exertions and objects, were now of little moment in my regard. I cared not, at this period, for books; they were apart from me. Nature,—except it were human nature,—the nature that is developed in earth and sky, was, in one sense, hidden from me; and all the imaginative delight, wherewith it had been spiritualized, passed away out of my mind. A gift, a faculty, if it had not departed, was suspended and inanimate within me. There would have been something sad, unutterably dreary, in all this, had I not been conscious that it lay at my own option to recall whatever was valuable in the past. It might be true, indeed, that this was a life which could not, with impunity, be lived too long; else, it might make me permanently other than I had been, without transforming me into any shape which it would be worth my while to take. But I never considered it as other than a transitory life. There was always

---

[26] Thinking that he could do a great deal of writing there, Hawthorne participated in Brook Farm, a Transcendentalist commune near Boston in 1841. He left within less than a year, married, and moved to the Old Manse in Concord, Massachusetts. His experiences at Brook Farm provided the basis of his third novel, *The Blithedale Romance* (1852).

[27] When Hawthorne lived in Concord (1842–1845), he associated with Ralph Waldo Emerson (1803–1882), Henry David Thoreau (1817–1862), Ellery Channing (1818–1901), and Amos Bronson Alcott (1799–1888), the most prominent Transcendentalists. While living in Boston his neighbors included his attorney, George Hillard (1808–1879), and the poet Henry Wadsworth Longfellow (1807–1882).

a prophetic instinct, a low whisper in my ear, that, within no long period, and whenever a new change of custom should be essential to my good, a change would come.

Meanwhile, there I was, a Surveyor of the Revenue, and, so far as I have been able to understand, as good a Surveyor as need be. A man of thought, fancy, and sensibility, (had he ten times the Surveyor's proportion of those qualities,) may, at any time, be a man of affairs, if he will only choose to give himself the trouble. My fellow-officers, and the merchants and sea-captains with whom my official duties brought me into any manner of connection, viewed me in no other light, and probably knew me in no other character. None of them, I presume, had ever read a page of my inditing, or would have cared a fig the more for me, if they had read them all; nor would it have mended the matter, in the least, had those same unprofitable pages been written with a pen like that of Burns[28] or of Chaucer,[29] each of whom was a Custom-House officer in his day, as well as I. It is a good lesson—though it may often be a hard one—for a man who has dreamed of literary fame, and of making for himself a rank among the world's dignitaries by such means, to step aside out of the narrow circle in which his claims are recognized, and to find how utterly devoid of significance, beyond that circle, is all that he achieves, and all he aims at. I know not that I especially needed the lesson, either in the way of warning or rebuke; but, at any rate, I learned it thoroughly; nor, it gives me pleasure to reflect, did the truth, as it came home to my perception, ever cost me a pang, or require to be thrown off in a sigh. In the way of literary talk, it is true, the Naval Officer—an excellent fellow, who came into office with me, and went out only a little later—would often engage me in a discussion about one or the other of his favorite topics, Napoleon or Shakespeare. The Collector's junior clerk, too,—a young gentleman who, it was whispered, occasionally covered a sheet of Uncle Sam's letter-paper with what, (at the distance of a few yards,) looked very much like poetry,—used now and then to speak to me of books, as matters with which I might possibly be conversant. This was my all of lettered intercourse; and it was quite sufficient for my necessities.

No longer seeking nor caring that my name should be blazoned abroad on title-pages, I smiled to think that it had now another kind of vogue. The Custom-House marker imprinted it, with a stencil and black paint, on pepper-bags, and baskets of anatto,[30] and cigar-boxes, and bales of all kinds of dutiable merchandise, in testimony that these commodities had paid the impost,[31] and gone regularly through the office. Borne on such queer vehicle of fame, a knowledge of my existence, so far as a name conveys it, was carried where it had never been before, and, I hope, will never go again.

But the past was not dead. Once in a great while, the thoughts, that had seemed so vital and so active, yet had been put to rest so quietly, revived again. One of the most remarkable occasions, when the habit of bygone days awoke in me, was that which brings it within the law of literary propriety to offer the public the sketch which I am now writing.

---

[28] The Scottish poet Robert Burns (1759–1796) served as an excise-tax collector from 1789 to 1791.
[29] The poet Geoffrey Chaucer (1340?–1400) was a controller of customs in London from 1374 to 1386.

[30] Tropical American tree yielding a yellowish-red dye.
[31] Tax on imported goods.

In the second story of the Custom-House, there is a large room, in which the brick-work and naked rafters have never been covered with panelling and plaster. The edifice—originally projected on a scale adapted to the old commercial enterprise of the port, and with an idea of subsequent prosperity destined never to be realized—contains far more space than its occupants know what to do with. This airy hall, therefore, over the Collector's apartments, remains unfinished to this day, and, in spite of the aged cobwebs that festoon its dusky beams, appears still to await the labor of the carpenter and mason. At one end of the room, in a recess, were a number of barrels, piled one upon another, containing bundles of official documents. Large quantities of similar rubbish lay lumbering[32] the floor. It was sorrowful to think how many days, and weeks, and months, and years of toil, had been wasted on these musty papers, which were now only an encumbrance on earth, and were hidden away in this forgotten corner, never more to be glanced at by human eyes. But, then, what reams of other manuscripts—filled, not with the dulness of official formalities, but with the thought of inventive brains and the rich effusion of deep hearts—had gone equally to oblivion; and that, moreover, without serving a purpose in their day, as these heaped-up papers had, and—saddest of all—without purchasing for their writers the comfortable livelihood which the clerks of the Custom-House had gained by these worthless scratchings of the pen! Yet not altogether worthless, perhaps, as materials of local history. Here, no doubt, statistics of the former commerce of Salem might be discovered, and memorials of her princely merchants,—old King Derby,—old Billy Gray,—old Simon Forrester,[33]—and many another magnate in his day; whose powdered head, however, was scarcely in the tomb, before his mountain-pile of wealth began to dwindle. The founders of the greater part of the families which now compose the aristocracy of Salem might here be traced, from the petty and obscure beginnings of their traffic, at periods generally much posterior to the Revolution, upward to what their children look upon as long-established rank.

Prior to the Revolution, there is a dearth of records; the earlier documents and archives of the Custom-House having, probably, been carried off to Halifax, when all the King's officials accompanied the British army in its flight from Boston.[34] It has often been a matter of regret with me; for, going back, perhaps, to the days of the Protectorate,[35] those papers must have contained many references to forgotten or remembered men, and to antique customs, which would have affected me with the same pleasure as when I used to pick up Indian arrow-heads in the field near the Old Manse.

But, one idle and rainy day, it was my fortune to make a discovery of some little interest. Poking and burrowing into the heaped-up rubbish in the corner; unfolding one and another document, and reading the names of vessels that had long ago foundered at sea or rotted at the wharves, and those of merchants, never heard of now on 'Change,[36] nor very readily decipherable on their mossy tombstones; glancing at

---

[32] Cluttering.

[33] William Gray (1750–1825) and Simon Forrester (1776–1851) were wealthy merchants of Salem. (For "King Derby," see note 4 above.)

[34] Washington attacked the British forces in January 1776, causing them to evacuate to Nova Scotia.

[35] Oliver Cromwell (1599–1658) and his son Richard (1626–1712) ruled as lords protector of England from 1653 to 1660.

[36] Exchange, a center for business transactions similar to the modern stock exchange.

such matters with the saddened, weary, half-reluctant interest which we bestow on the corpse of dead activity,—and exerting my fancy, sluggish with little use, to raise up from these dry bones an image of the old town's brighter aspect, when India was a new region, and only Salem knew the way thither,—I chanced to lay my hand on a small package, carefully done up in a piece of ancient yellow parchment. This envelope had the air of an official record of some period long past, when clerks engrossed their stiff and formal chirography on more substantial materials than at present. There was something about it that quickened an instinctive curiosity, and made me undo the faded red tape, that tied up the package, with the sense that a treasure would here be brought to light. Unbending the rigid folds of the parchment cover, I found it to be a commission, under the hand and seal of Governor Shirley,[37] in favor of one Jonathan Pue,[38] as Surveyor of his Majesty's Customs for the port of Salem, in the Province of Massachusetts Bay. I remembered to have read (probably in Felt's Annals) a notice of the decease of Mr. Surveyor Pue, about fourscore years ago; and likewise, in a newspaper of recent times, an account of the digging up of his remains in the little grave yard of St. Peter's Church,[39] during the renewal of that edifice. Nothing, if I rightly call to mind, was left of my respected predecessor, save an imperfect skeleton, and some fragments of apparel, and a wig of majestic frizzle; which, unlike the head that it once adorned, was in very satisfactory preservation. But, on examining the papers which the parchment commission served to envelop, I found more traces of Mr. Pue's mental part, and the internal operations of his head, than the frizzled wig had contained of the venerable skull itself.

They were documents, in short, not official, but of a private nature, or, at least, written in his private capacity, and apparently with his own hand. I could account for their being included in the heap of Custom-House lumber only by the fact, that Mr. Pue's death had happened suddenly; and that these papers, which he probably kept in his official desk, had never come to the knowledge of his heirs, or were supposed to relate to the business of the revenue. On the transfer of the archives to Halifax, this package, proving to be of no public concern, was left behind, and had remained ever since unopened.

The ancient Surveyor—being little molested, I suppose, at that early day, with business pertaining to his office—seems to have devoted some of his many leisure hours to researches as a local antiquarian, and other inquisitions of a similar nature. These supplied material for petty activity to a mind that would otherwise have been eaten up with rust. A portion of his facts, by the by, did me good service in the preparation of the article entitled "MAIN STREET," included in the present volume.[40] The remainder may perhaps be applied to purposes equally valuable, hereafter; or not impossibly may be worked up, so far as they go, into a regular history of Salem, should my veneration for the natal soil ever impel me to so pious a task. Meanwhile, they

---

[37] William Shirley (1694–1771), governor of Massachusetts from 1741 to 1749 and from 1753 to 1756.

[38] Jonathan Pue was Salem's customs surveyor in 1752. His death is recorded in Joseph B. Felt's *The Annals of Salem, from Its First Settlement* (1827), a text Hawthorne used for much of the background information for *The Scarlet Letter*.

[39] Salem's first Anglican church, established in 1633.

[40] "Main Street" was one of the stories and sketches Hawthorne initially had planned to publish along with *The Scarlet Letter*. Later it was included in *The Snow-Image, and Other Twice-Told Tales* (1852).

shall be at the command of any gentleman, inclined, and competent, to take the unprofitable labor off my hands. As a final disposition, I contemplate depositing them with the Essex Historical Society.[41]

But the object that most drew my attention, in the mysterious package, was a certain affair of fine red cloth, much worn and faded. There were traces about it of gold embroidery, which, however, was greatly frayed and defaced; so that none, or very little, of the glitter was left. It had been wrought, as was easy to perceive, with wonderful skill of needlework; and the stitch (as I am assured by ladies conversant with such mysteries) gives evidence of a now forgotten art, not to be recovered even by the process of picking out the threads. This rag of scarlet cloth,—for time, and wear, and a sacrilegious moth, had reduced it to little other than a rag,—on careful examination, assumed the shape of a letter. It was the capital letter A. By an accurate measurement, each limb proved to be precisely three inches and a quarter in length. It had been intended, there could be no doubt, as an ornamental article of dress; but how it was to be worn, or what rank, honor, and dignity, in by-past times, were signified by it, was a riddle which (so evanescent are the fashions of the world in these particulars) I saw little hope of solving. And yet it strangely interested me. My eyes fastened themselves upon the old scarlet letter, and would not be turned aside. Certainly, there was some deep meaning in it, most worthy of interpretation, and which, as it were, streamed forth from the mystic symbol, subtly communicating itself to my sensibilities, but evading the analysis of my mind. *(Poe, mystical about scarlet letter)*

While thus perplexed,—and cogitating, among other hypotheses, whether the letter might not have been one of those decorations which the white men used to contrive, in order to take the eyes of Indians,—I happened to place it on my breast. It seemed to me,—the reader may smile, but must not doubt my word,—it seemed to me, then, that I experienced a sensation not altogether physical, yet almost so, as of burning heat; and as if the letter were not of red cloth, but red-hot iron. I shuddered, and involuntarily let it fall upon the floor. *Romance w/ fact, its fiction.*

In the absorbing contemplation of the scarlet letter, I had hitherto neglected to examine a small roll of dingy paper, around which it had been twisted. This I now opened, and had the satisfaction to find, recorded by the old Surveyor's pen, a reasonably complete explanation of the whole affair. There were several foolscap sheets,[42] containing many particulars respecting the life and conversation of one Hester Prynne, who appeared to have been rather a noteworthy personage in the view of our ancestors. She had flourished during a period between the early days of Massachusetts and the close of the seventeenth century. Aged persons, alive in the time of Mr. Surveyor Pue, and from whose oral testimony he had made up his narrative, remembered her, in their youth, as a very old, but not decrepit woman, of a stately and solemn aspect. It had been her habit, from an almost immemorial date, to go about the country as a kind of voluntary nurse, and doing whatever miscellaneous good she might; taking upon herself, likewise, to give advice in all matters, especially those of the heart; by which means, as a person of such propensities inevitably must, she gained

---

[41] Although Hawthorne had read widely among the colonial records of the Essex Historical Society, the documents referred to here are fictional.

[42] Paper sheets watermarked with a cap and bells, traditional symbols of the fool or jester, often a prominent figure in medieval royal entourages.

from many people the reverence due to an angel, but, I should imagine, was looked upon by others as an intruder and a nuisance. Prying farther into the manuscript, I found the record of other doings and sufferings of this singular woman, for most of which the reader is referred to the story entitled "THE SCARLET LETTER"; and it should be borne carefully in mind, that the main facts of that story are authorized and authenticated by the document of Mr. Surveyor Pue. The original papers, together with the scarlet letter itself,—a most curious relic,—are still in my possession, and shall be freely exhibited to whomsoever, induced by the great interest of the narrative, may desire a sight of them. I must not be understood as affirming, that, in the dressing up of the tale, and imagining the motives and modes of passion that influenced the characters who figure in it, I have invariably confined myself within the limits of the old Surveyor's half a dozen sheets of foolscap. On the contrary, I have allowed myself, as to such points, nearly or altogether as much license as if the facts had been entirely of my own invention. What I contend for is the authenticity of the outline.

This incident recalled my mind, in some degree, to its old track. There seemed to be here the groundwork of a tale. It impressed me as if the ancient Surveyor, in his garb of a hundred years gone by, and wearing his immortal wig,—which was buried with him, but did not perish in the grave,—had met me in the deserted chamber of the Custom-House. In his port was the dignity of one who had borne his Majesty's commission, and who was therefore illuminated by a ray of the splendor that shone so dazzlingly about the throne. How unlike, alas! the hang-dog look of a republican official, who, as the servant of the people, feels himself less than the least, and below the lowest, of his masters. With his own ghostly hand, the obscurely seen, but majestic, figure had imparted to me the scarlet symbol, and the little roll of explanatory manuscript. With his own ghostly voice, he had exhorted me, on the sacred consideration of my filial duty and reverence towards him,—who might reasonably regard himself as my official ancestor,—to bring his mouldy and moth-eaten lucubrations[43] before the public. "Do this," said the ghost of Mr. Surveyor Pue, emphatically nodding the head that looked so imposing within its memorable wig, "do this, and the profit shall be all your own! You will shortly need it; for it is not in your days as it was in mine, when a man's office was a life-lease, and oftentimes an heirloom. But, I charge you, in this matter of old Mistress Prynne, give to your predecessor's memory the credit which will be rightfully its due!" And I said to the ghost of Mr. Surveyor Pue,—"I will!"

On Hester Prynne's story, therefore, I bestowed much thought. It was the subject of my meditations for many an hour, while pacing to and fro across my room, or traversing, with a hundredfold repetition, the long extent from the front-door of the Custom-House to the side-entrance, and back again. Great were the weariness and annoyance of the old Inspector and the Weighers and Gaugers, whose slumbers were disturbed by the unmercifully lengthened tramp of my passing and returning foot-steps. Remembering their own former habits, they used to say that the Surveyor was walking the quarter-deck. They probably fancied that my sole object—and, indeed, the sole object for which a sane man could ever put himself into voluntary motion —was, to get an appetite for dinner. And to say the truth, an appetite, sharpened by the east-wind that generally blew along the passage, was the only valuable result of

---

[43] Laborious work or writing.

so much indefatigable exercise. So little adapted is the atmosphere of a Custom-House to the delicate harvest of fancy and sensibility, that, had I remained there through ten Presidencies yet to come, I doubt whether the tale of "The Scarlet Letter" would ever have been brought before the public eye. My imagination was a tarnished mirror. It would not reflect, or only with miserable dimness, the figures with which I did my best to people it. The characters of the narrative would not be warmed and rendered malleable, by any heat that I could kindle at my intellectual forge. They would take neither the glow of passion nor the tenderness of sentiment, but retained all the rigidity of dead corpses, and stared me in the face with a fixed and ghastly grin of contemptuous defiance. "What have you to do with us?" that expression seemed to say. "The little power you might once have possessed over the tribe of unrealities is gone! You have bartered it for a pittance of the public gold. Go, then, and earn your wages!" In short, the almost torpid creatures of my own fancy twitted me with imbecility, and not without fair occasion.

It was not merely during the three hours and a half which Uncle Sam claimed as his share of my daily life, that this wretched numbness held possession of me. It went with me on my sea-shore walks and rambles into the country, whenever—which was seldom and reluctantly—I bestirred myself to seek that invigorating charm of Nature, which used to give me such freshness and activity of thought, the moment that I stepped across the threshold of the Old Manse. The same torpor, as regarded the capacity for intellectual effort, accompanied me home, and weighed upon me in the chamber which I most absurdly termed my study. Nor did it quit me, when, late at night, I sat in the deserted parlour, lighted only by the glimmering coal-fire and the moon, striving to picture forth imaginary scenes, which, the next day, might flow out on the brightening page in many-hued description.

If the imaginative faculty refused to act at such an hour, it might well be deemed a hopeless case. Moonlight, in a familiar room, falling so white upon the carpet, and showing all its figures so distinctly,—making every object so minutely visible, yet so unlike a morning or noontide visibility,—is a medium the most suitable for a romance-writer to get acquainted with his illusive guests. There is the little domestic scenery of the well-known apartment; the chairs, with each its separate individuality; the centre-table, sustaining a work-basket, a volume or two, and an extinguished lamp; the sofa; the book-case; the picture on the wall;—all these details, so completely seen, are so spiritualized by the unusual light, that they seem to lose their actual substance, and become things of intellect. Nothing is too small or too trifling to undergo this change, and acquire dignity thereby. A child's shoe; the doll, seated in her little wicker carriage; the hobby-horse;—whatever, in a word, has been used or played with, during the day, is now invested with a quality of strangeness and remoteness, though still almost as vividly present as by daylight. Thus, therefore, the floor of our familiar room has become a neutral territory, somewhere between the real world and fairy-land, where the Actual and the Imaginary may meet, and each imbue itself with the nature of the other. Ghosts might enter here, without affrighting us. It would be too much in keeping with the scene to excite surprise, were we to look about us and discover a form, beloved, but gone hence, now sitting quietly in a streak of this magic moonshine, with an aspect that would make us doubt whether it had returned from afar, or had never once stirred from our fireside.

The somewhat dim coal-fire has an essential influence in producing the effect which

I would describe. It throws its unobtrusive tinge throughout the room, with a faint ruddiness upon the walls and ceiling, and a reflected gleam from the polish of the furniture. This warmer light mingles itself with the cold spirituality of the moon-beams, and communicates, as it were, a heart and sensibilities of human tenderness to the forms which fancy summons up. It converts them from snow-images into men and women. Glancing at the looking-glass, we behold—deep within its haunted verge —the smouldering glow of the half-extinguished anthracite, the white moonbeams on the floor, and a repetition of all the gleam and shadow of the picture, with one remove farther from the actual, and nearer to the imaginative. Then, at such an hour, and with this scene before him, if a man, sitting all alone, cannot dream strange things, and make them look like truth, he need never try to write romances.

But, for myself, during the whole of my Custom-House experience, moonlight and sunshine, and the glow of firelight, were just alike in my regard; and neither of them was of one whit more avail than the twinkle of a tallow-candle. An entire class of susceptibilities, and a gift connected with them,—of no great richness or value, but the best I had,—was gone from me.

It is my belief, however, that, had I attempted a different order of composition, my faculties would not have been found so pointless and inefficacious. I might, for instance, have contented myself with writing out the narratives of a veteran shipmas-ter, one of the Inspectors, whom I should be most ungrateful not to mention; since scarcely a day passed that he did not stir me to laughter and admiration by his marvellous gifts as a story-teller. Could I have preserved the picturesque force of his style, and the humorous coloring which nature taught him how to throw over his descriptions, the result, I honestly believe, would have been something new in litera-ture. Or I might readily have found a more serious task. It was a folly, with the materiality of this daily life pressing so intrusively upon me, to attempt to fling myself back into another age; or to insist on creating the semblance of a world out of airy matter, when, at every moment, the impalpable beauty of my soap-bubble was broken by the rude contact of some actual circumstance. The wiser effort would have been, to diffuse thought and imagination through the opaque substance of to-day, and thus to make it a bright transparency; to spiritualize the burden that began to weigh so heavily; to seek, resolutely, the true and indestructible value that lay hidden in the petty and wearisome incidents, and ordinary characters, with which I was now conversant. The fault was mine. The page of life that was spread out before me seemed dull and commonplace, only because I had not fathomed its deeper import. A better book than I shall ever write was there; leaf after leaf presenting itself to me, just as it was written out by the reality of the flitting hour, and vanishing as fast as written, only because my brain wanted the insight and my hand the cunning to transcribe it. At some future day, it may be, I shall remember a few scattered fragments and broken paragraphs, and write them down, and find the letters turn to gold upon the page.

These perceptions have come too late. At the instant, I was only conscious that what would have been a pleasure once was now a hopeless toil. There was no occasion to make much moan about this state of affairs. I had ceased to be a writer of tolerably poor tales and essays, and had become a tolerably good Surveyor of the Customs. That was all. But, nevertheless, it is any thing but agreeable to be haunted by a suspicion that one's intellect is dwindling away; or exhaling, without your consciousness, like ether out of a phial; so that, at every glance, you find a smaller and less volatile residuum. Of the fact, there could be no doubt; and, examining myself and others, I was led to conclusions in reference to the effect of public office on the character, not very favorable to the mode of life in question. In some other form, perhaps, I may hereafter develop these effects. Suffice it here to say, that a Custom-House officer, of long continuance, can hardly be a very praiseworthy or respectable personage, for many reasons; one of them, the tenure by which he holds his situation, and another, the very nature of his business, which—though, I trust, an honest one—is of such a sort that he does not share in the united effort of mankind.

An effect—which I believe to be observable, more or less, in every individual who has occupied the position—is, that, while he leans on the mighty arm of the Republic, his own proper strength departs from him. He loses, in an extent proportioned to the weakness or force of his original nature, the capability of self-support. If he possess an unusual share of native energy, or the enervating magic of place do not operate too long upon him, his forfeited powers may be redeemable. The ejected officer— fortunate in the unkindly shove that sends him forth betimes, to struggle amid a struggling world—may return to himself, and become all that he has ever been. But this seldom happens. He usually keeps his ground just long enough for his own ruin, and is then thrust out, with sinews all unstrung, to totter along the difficult footpath of life as he best may. Conscious of his own infirmity,—that his tempered steel and elasticity are lost,—he for ever afterwards looks wistfully about him in quest of support external to himself. His pervading and continual hope—a hallucination, which, in the face of all discouragement, and making light of impossibilities, haunts him while he lives, and, I fancy, like the convulsive throes of the cholera, torments him for a brief space after death—is, that, finally, and in no long time, by some happy coincidence of circumstances, he shall be restored to office. This faith, more than any thing else, steals the pith and availability out of whatever enterprise he may dream of undertaking. Why should he toil and moil, and be at so much trouble to pick himself up out of the mud, when, in a little while hence, the strong arm of his Uncle will raise and support him? Why should he work for his living here, or go to dig gold in California, when he is so soon to be made happy, at monthly intervals, with a little pile of glittering coin out of his Uncle's pocket? It is sadly curious to observe how slight a taste of office suffices to infect a poor fellow with this singular disease. Uncle Sam's gold—meaning no disrespect to the worthy old gentleman—has, in this respect, a quality of enchantment like that of the Devil's wages. Whoever touches it should look well to himself, or he may find the bargain to go hard against him, involving, if not his soul, yet many of its better attributes; its sturdy force, its courage and constancy, its truth, its self-reliance, and all that gives the emphasis to manly character.

Here was a fine prospect in the distance! Not that the Surveyor brought the lesson home to himself, or admitted that he could be so utterly undone, either by continuance in office, or ejectment. Yet my reflections were not the most comfortable. I began to grow melancholy and restless; continually prying into my mind, to discover which of its poor properties were gone, and what degree of detriment had already accrued to the remainder. I endeavoured to calculate how much longer I could stay in the Custom-House, and yet go forth a man. To confess the truth, it was my greatest apprehension,—as it would never be a measure of policy to turn out so quiet an

individual as myself, and it being hardly in the nature of a public officer to resign,
—it was my chief trouble, therefore, that I was likely to grow gray and decrepit in
the Surveyorship, and become much such another animal as the old Inspector. Might
it not, in the tedious lapse of official life that lay before me, finally be with me as
it was with this venerable friend,—to make the dinner-hour the nucleus of the day,
and to spend the rest of it, as an old dog spends it, asleep in the sunshine or the shade?
A dreary look-forward this, for a man who felt it to be the best definition of happiness
to live throughout the whole range of his faculties and sensibilities! But, all this while,
I was giving myself very unnecessary alarm. Providence had meditated better things
for me than I could possibly imagine for myself.

A remarkable event of the third year of my Surveyorship—to adopt the tone of
"P.P."—was the election of General Taylor to the Presidency.[44] It is essential, in order
to form a complete estimate of the advantages of official life, to view the incumbent
at the in-coming of a hostile administration. His position is then one of the most
singularly irksome, and, in every contingency, disagreeable, that a wretched mortal
can possibly occupy; with seldom an alternative of good, on either hand, although
what presents itself to him as the worst event may very probably be the best. But it
is a strange experience, to a man of pride and sensibility, to know that his interests
are within the control of individuals who neither love nor understand him, and by
whom, since one or the other must needs happen, he would rather be injured than
obliged. Strange, too, for one who has kept his calmness throughout the contest, to
observe the bloodthirstiness that is developed in the hour of triumph, and to be
conscious that he is himself among its objects! There are few uglier traits of human
nature than this tendency—which I now witnessed in men no worse than their
neighbours—to grow cruel, merely because they possessed the power of inflicting
harm. If the guillotine, as applied to office-holders, were a literal fact, instead of one
of the most apt of metaphors, it is my sincere belief, that the active members of the
victorious party were sufficiently excited to have chopped off all our heads, and have
thanked Heaven for the opportunity! It appears to me—who have been a calm and
curious observer, as well in victory as defeat—that this fierce and bitter spirit of malice
and revenge has never distinguished the many triumphs of my own party as it now
did that of the Whigs. The Democrats take the offices, as a general rule, because they
need them, and because the practice of many years has made it the law of political
warfare, which, unless a different system be proclaimed, it were weakness and cowardice to murmur at. But the long habit of victory has made them generous. They know
how to spare, when they see occasion; and when they strike, the axe may be sharp,
indeed, but its edge is seldom poisoned with ill-will; nor is it their custom ignominiously to kick the head which they have just struck off.

In short, unpleasant as was my predicament, at best, I saw much reason to congratulate myself that I was on the losing side, rather than the triumphant one. If, heretofore,
I had been none of the warmest of partisans, I began now, at this season of peril and
adversity, to be pretty acutely sensible with which party my predilections lay; nor
was it without something like regret and shame, that, according to a reasonable

---

[44] Zachary Taylor (1784–1850) was elected
president in 1848 on the Whig ticket, an event
that led to Hawthorne's dismissal from the
customhouse.

calculation of chances, I saw my own prospect of retaining office to be better than those of my Democratic brethren.[45] But who can see an inch into futurity, beyond his nose? My own head was the first that fell!

The moment when a man's head drops off is seldom or never, I am inclined to think, precisely the most agreeable of his life. Nevertheless, like the greater part of our misfortunes, even so serious a contingency brings its remedy and consolation with it, if the sufferer will but make the best, rather than the worst, of the accident which has befallen him. In my particular case, the consolatory topics were close at hand, and, indeed, had suggested themselves to my meditations a considerable time before it was requisite to use them. In view of my previous weariness of office, and vague thoughts of resignation, my fortune somewhat resembled that of a person who should entertain an idea of committing suicide, and, altogether beyond his hopes, meet with the good hap to be murdered. In the Custom-House, as before in the Old Manse, I had spent three years; a term long enough to rest a weary brain; long enough to break off old intellectual habits, and make room for new ones; long enough, and too long, to have lived in an unnatural state, doing what was really of no advantage nor delight to any human being, and withholding myself from toil that would, at least, have stilled an unquiet impulse in me. Then, moreover, as regarded his unceremonious ejectment, the late Surveyor was not altogether ill-pleased to be recognized by the Whigs as an enemy; since his inactivity in political affairs,—his tendency to roam, at will, in that broad and quiet field where all mankind may meet, rather than confine himself to those narrow paths where brethren of the same household must diverge from one another, —had sometimes made it questionable with his brother Democrats whether he was a friend. Now, after he had won the crown of martyrdom, (though with no longer a head to wear it on,) the point might be looked upon as settled. Finally, little heroic as he was, it seemed more decorous to be overthrown in the downfall of the party with which he had been content to stand, than to remain a forlorn survivor, when so many worthier men were falling; and, at last, after subsisting for four years on the mercy of a hostile administration, to be compelled then to define his position anew, and claim the yet more humiliating mercy of a friendly one.

Meanwhile, the press had taken up my affair, and kept me, for a week or two, careering[46] through the public prints, in my decapitated state, like Irving's Headless Horseman;[47] ghastly and grim, and longing to be buried, as a politically dead man ought. So much for my figurative self. The real human being, all this time, with his head safely on his shoulders, had brought himself to the comfortable conclusion, that every thing was for the best; and, making an investment in ink, paper, and steel-pens, had opened his long-disused writing-desk, and was again a literary man.

Now it was, that the lucubrations of my ancient predecessor, Mr. Surveyor Pue, came into play. Rusty through long idleness, some little space was requisite before my intellectual machinery could be brought to work upon the tale, with an effect in any degree satisfactory. Even yet, though my thoughts were ultimately much absorbed in the task, it wears, to my eye, a stern and sombre aspect; too much

---

[45] A Democrat, Hawthorne enjoyed bipartisan support for his appointment as surveyor and believed his position was safe regardless of governmental changes. His dismissal brought considerable sympathy and drew great attention

to *The Scarlet Letter* when it was published in 1850.
[46] Running; rushing.
[47] In Washington Irving's *The Legend of Sleepy Hollow* (1819).

ungladdened by genial sunshine; too little relieved by the tender and familiar influences which soften almost every scene of nature and real life, and, undoubtedly, should soften every picture of them. This uncaptivating effect is perhaps due to the period of hardly accomplished revolution, and still seething turmoil, in which the story shaped itself. It is no indication, however, of a lack of cheerfulness in the writer's mind; for he was happier, while straying through the gloom of these sunless fantasies, than at any time since he had quitted the Old Manse. Some of the briefer articles, which contribute to make up the volume, have likewise been written since my involuntary withdrawal from the toils and honors of public life, and the remainder are gleaned from annuals and magazines, of such antique date that they have gone round the circle, and come back to novelty again.[48] Keeping up the metaphor of the political guillotine, the whole may be considered as the POSTHUMOUS PAPERS OF A DECAPITATED SURVEYOR; and the sketch which I am now bringing to a close, if too autobiographical for a modest person to publish in his lifetime, will readily be excused in a gentleman who writes from beyond the grave. Peace be with all the world! My blessing on my friends! My forgiveness to my enemies! For I am in the realm of quiet!

The life of the Custom-House lies like a dream behind me. The old Inspector,—who, by the by, I regret to say, was overthrown and killed by a horse, some time ago; else he would certainly have lived for ever,—he, and all those other venerable personages who sat with him at the receipt of custom, are but shadows in my view; white-headed and wrinkled images, which my fancy used to sport with, and has now flung aside for ever. The merchants,—Pingree, Phillips, Shepard, Upton, Kimball, Bertram, Hunt,—these, and many other names, which had such a classic familiarity for my ear six months ago,—these men of traffic, who seemed to occupy so important a position in the world,—how little time has it required to disconnect me from them all, not merely in act, but recollection! It is with an effort that I recall the figures and appellations of these few. Soon, likewise, my old native town will loom upon me through the haze of memory, a mist brooding over and around it; as if it were no portion of the real earth, but an overgrown village in cloud-land, with only imaginary inhabitants to people its wooden houses, and walk its homely lanes, and the unpicturesque prolixity of its main street. Henceforth, it ceases to be a reality of my life. I am a citizen of somewhere else. My good townspeople will not much regret me; for—though it has been as dear an object as any, in my literary efforts, to be of some importance in their eyes, and to win myself a pleasant memory in this abode and burial-place of so many of my forefathers—there has never been, for me, the genial atmosphere which a literary man requires, in order to ripen the best harvest of his mind. I shall do better amongst other faces; and these familiar ones, it need hardly be said, will do just as well without me.

It may be, however,—O, transporting and triumphant thought!—that the great-grandchildren of the present race may sometimes think kindly of the scribbler of bygone days, when the antiquary of days to come, among the sites memorable in the town's history, shall point out the locality of THE TOWN-PUMP![49]

The Scarlet Letter

I: The Prison-Door

A throng of bearded men, in sad-colored garments and gray, steeple-crowned hats, intermixed with women, some wearing hoods, and others bareheaded, was assembled in front of a wooden edifice, the door of which was heavily timbered with oak, and studded with iron spikes.

The founders of a new colony, whatever Utopia of human virtue and happiness they might originally project, have invariably recognized it among their earliest practical necessities to allot a portion of the virgin soil as a cemetery, and another portion as the site of a prison. In accordance with this rule, it may safely be assumed that the forefathers of Boston had built the first prison-house, somewhere in the vicinity of Cornhill, almost as seasonably as they marked out the first burial-ground, on Isaac Johnson's lot,[50] and round about his grave, which subsequently became the nucleus of all the congregated sepulchres in the old church-yard of King's Chapel.[51] Certain it is, that, some fifteen or twenty years after the settlement of the town,[52] the wooden jail was already marked with weather-stains and other indications of age, which gave a yet darker aspect to its beetle-browed and gloomy front. The rust on the ponderous iron-work of its oaken door looked more antique than any thing else in the new world. Like all that pertains to crime, it seemed never to have known a youthful era. Before this ugly edifice, and between it and the wheel-track of the street, was a grass-plot, much overgrown with burdock, pig-weed, apple-peru, and such unsightly vegetation, which evidently found something congenial in the soil that had so early borne the black flower of civilized society, a prison. But, on one side of the portal, and rooted almost at the threshold, was a wild rose-bush, covered, in this month of June, with its delicate gems, which might be imagined to offer their fragrance and fragile beauty to the prisoner as he went in, and to the condemned criminal as he came forth to his doom, in token that the deep heart of Nature could pity and be kind to him.

This rose-bush, by a strange chance, has been kept alive in history; but whether it had merely survived out of the stern old wilderness, so long after the fall of the gigantic pines and oaks that originally overshadowed it,—or whether, as there is fair authority for believing, it had sprung up under the footsteps of the sainted Ann Hutchinson,[53] as she entered the prison-door,—we shall not take upon us to determine. Finding it so directly on the threshold of our narrative, which is now about to issue from that inauspicious portal, we could hardly do otherwise than pluck one of its flowers and present it to the reader. It may serve, let us hope, to symbolize some sweet moral blossom, that may be found along the track, or relieve the darkening close of a tale of human frailty and sorrow.

---

[50] Isaac Johnson (1601–1630), Puritan immigrant to New England, whose land went to public use after his death.

[51] Boston's first Anglican church, built in 1688.

[52] The events of the novel occur between 1642 and 1649.

[53] Anne Hutchinson (1591–1643) was banished from the Massachusetts colony for advocating religious principles the Puritans judged seditious. Eventually she became a symbol of Puritan repression of individual religious belief.

Type

II: *The Market-Place*

The grass-plot before the jail, in Prison Lane, on a certain summer morning, not less than two centuries ago, was occupied by a pretty large number of the inhabitants of Boston; all with their eyes intently fastened on the iron-clamped oaken door. Amongst any other population, or at a later period in the history of New England, the grim rigidity that petrified the bearded physiognomies of these good people would have augured some awful business in hand. It could have betokened nothing short of the anticipated execution of some noted culprit, on whom the sentence of a legal tribunal had but confirmed the verdict of public sentiment. But, in that early severity of the Puritan character, an inference of this kind could not so indubitably be drawn. It might be that a sluggish bond-servant, or an undutiful child, whom his parents had given over to the civil authority, was to be corrected at the whipping-post. It might be, that an Antinomian, a Quaker, or other heterodox religionist, was to be scourged out of the town, or an idle and vagrant Indian, whom the white man's fire-water had made riotous about the streets, was to be driven with stripes[54] into the shadow of the forest. It might be, too, that a witch, like old Mistress Hibbins, the bitter-tempered widow of the magistrate, was to die upon the gallows.[55] In either case, there was very much the same solemnity of demeanour on the part of the spectators; as befitted a people amongst whom religion and law were almost identical, and in whose character both were so thoroughly interfused, that the mildest and the severest acts of public discipline were alike made venerable and awful. Meagre, indeed, and cold, was the sympathy that a transgressor might look for, from such bystanders at the scaffold. On the other hand, a penalty which, in our days, would infer a degree of mocking infamy and ridicule, might then be invested with almost as stern a dignity as the punishment of death itself.   Religion ——— law identical.

It was a circumstance to be noted, on the summer morning when our story begins its course, that the women, of whom there were several in the crowd, appeared to take a peculiar interest in whatever penal infliction might be expected to ensue. The age had not so much refinement, that any sense of impropriety restrained the wearers of petticoat and farthingale[56] from stepping forth into the public ways, and wedging their not unsubstantial persons, if occasion were, into the throng nearest to the scaffold at an execution. Morally, as well as materially, there was a coarser fibre in those wives and maidens of old English birth and breeding, than in their fair descendants, separated from them by a series of six or seven generations; for, throughout that chain of ancestry, every successive mother has transmitted to her child a fainter bloom, a more delicate and briefer beauty, and a slighter physical frame, if not a character of less force and solidity, than her own. The women, who were now standing about the prison-door, stood within less than half a century of the period when the man-like Elizabeth[57] had been the not altogether unsuitable representative of the sex. They were her countrywomen; and the beef and ale of their native land, with a moral diet not a whit more refined, entered largely into their composition. The bright morning sun, there-fore, shone on broad shoulders and well-developed busts, and on round and ruddy

---

[54] Banished by whipping.
[55] Ann Hibbins was tried for witchcraft and later executed.
[56] Hoop skirt.
[57] Queen Elizabeth I (1533–1603), who ruled England from 1558 to 1603.

cheeks, that had ripened in the far-off island, and had hardly yet grown paler or thinner in the atmosphere of New England. There was, moreover, a boldness and rotundity of speech among these matrons, as most of them seemed to be, that would startle us at the present day, whether in respect to its purport or its volume of tone.

"Goodwives," said a hard-featured dame of fifty, "I'll tell ye a piece of my mind. It would be greatly for the public behoof, if we women, being of mature age and church-members in good repute, should have the handling of such malefactresses as this Hester Prynne. What think ye, gossips?[58] If the hussy stood up for judgment before us five, that are now here in a knot together, would she come off with such a sentence as the worshipful magistrates have awarded? Marry, I trow[59] not!"

"People say," said another, "that the Reverend Master Dimmesdale, her godly pastor, takes it very grievously to heart that such a scandal should have come upon his congregation."

"The magistrates are God-fearing gentlemen, but merciful overmuch,—that is a truth," added a third autumnal matron. "At the very least, they should have put the brand of a hot iron on Hester Prynne's forehead. Madam Hester would have winced at that, I warrant me. But she,—the naughty baggage,—little will she care what they put upon the bodice of her gown! Why, look you, she may cover it with a brooch, or such like heathenish adornment, and so walk the streets as brave as ever!"

"Ah, but," interposed, more softly, a young wife, holding a child by the hand, "let her cover the mark as she will, the pang of it will be always in her heart."

"What do we talk of marks and brands, whether on the bodice of her gown, or the flesh of her forehead?" cried another female, the ugliest as well as the most pitiless of these self-constituted judges. "This woman has brought shame upon us all, and ought to die. Is there not law for it? Truly there is, both in the Scripture[60] and the statute-book. Then let the magistrates, who have made it of no effect, thank themselves if their own wives and daughters go astray!"

"Mercy on us, goodwife," exclaimed a man in the crowd, "is there no virtue in woman, save what springs from a wholesome fear of the gallows? That is the hardest word yet! Hush, now, gossips; for the lock is turning in the prison-door, and here comes Mistress Prynne herself."

The door of the jail being flung open from within, there appeared, in the first place, like a black shadow emerging into the sunshine, the grim and grisly presence of the town-beadle,[61] with a sword by his side and his staff of office in his hand. This personage prefigured and represented in his aspect the whole dismal severity of the Puritanic code of law, which it was his business to administer in its final and closest application to the offender. Stretching forth the official staff in his left hand, he laid his right upon the shoulder of a young woman, whom he thus drew forward; until, on the threshold of the prison-door, she repelled him, by an action marked with natural dignity and force of character, and stepped into the open air, as if by her own free-will. She bore in her arms a child, a baby of some three months old, who winked and turned aside its little face from the too vivid light of day; because its existence,

---

[58] Female companions or friends.
[59] Believe.
[60] "Thou shalt not commit adultery" (Exodus 20:14) and "The adulterer and the adulteress shall surely be put to death" (Leviticus 20:10)

are biblical passages that influenced Puritan laws permitting public humiliation, whipping, branding, and even the execution of violators.
[61] Constable.

heretofore, had brought it acquainted only with the gray twilight of a dungeon, or other darksome apartment of the prison.

When the young woman—the mother of this child—stood fully revealed before the crowd, it seemed to be her first impulse to clasp the infant closely to her bosom; not so much by an impulse of motherly affection, as that she might thereby conceal a certain token, which was wrought or fastened into her dress. In a moment, however, wisely judging that one token of her shame would but poorly serve to hide another, she took the baby on her arm, and, with a burning blush, and yet a haughty smile, and a glance that would not be abashed, looked around at her townspeople and neighbours. On the breast of her gown, in fine red cloth, surrounded with an elaborate embroidery and fantastic flourishes of gold thread, appeared the letter A. It was so artistically done, and with so much fertility and gorgeous luxuriance of fancy, that it had all the effect of a last and fitting decoration to the apparel which she wore; and which was of a splendor in accordance with the taste of the age, but greatly beyond what was allowed by the sumptuary regulations of the colony.

The young woman was tall, with a figure of perfect elegance, on a large scale. She had dark and abundant hair, so glossy that it threw off the sunshine with a gleam, and a face which, besides being beautiful from regularity of feature and richness of complexion, had the impressiveness belonging to a marked brow and deep black eyes. She was lady-like, too, after the manner of the feminine gentility of those days; characterized by a certain state and dignity, rather than by the delicate, evanescent, and indescribable grace, which is now recognized as its indication. And never had Hester Prynne appeared more lady-like, in the antique interpretation of the term, than as she issued from the prison. Those who had before known her, and had expected to behold her dimmed and obscured by a disastrous cloud, were astonished, and even startled, to perceive how her beauty shone out, and made a halo of the misfortune and ignominy in which she was enveloped. It may be true, that, to a sensitive observer, there was something exquisitely painful in it. Her attire, which, indeed, she had wrought for the occasion, in prison, and had modelled much after her own fancy, seemed to express the attitude of her spirit, the desperate recklessness of her mood, by its wild and picturesque peculiarity. But the point which drew all eyes, and, as it were, transfigured the wearer,—so that both men and women, who had been familiarly acquainted with Hester Prynne, were now impressed as if they beheld her for the first time,—was that SCARLET LETTER, so fantastically embroidered and illuminated upon her bosom. It had the effect of a spell, taking her out of the ordinary relations with humanity, and inclosing her in a sphere by herself.

"She hath good skill at her needle, that's certain," remarked one of the female spectators; "but did ever a woman, before this brazen hussy, contrive such a way of showing it! Why, gossips, what is it but to laugh in the faces of our godly magistrates, and makes a pride out of what they, worthy gentlemen, meant for a punishment?"

"It were well," muttered the most iron-visaged of the old dames, "if we stripped Madam Hester's rich gown off her dainty shoulders; and as for the red letter, which she hath stitched so curiously, I'll bestow a rag of mine own rheumatic flannel, to make a fitter one!"

"O, peace, neighbours, peace!" whispered their youngest companion. "Do not let her hear you! Not a stitch in that embroidered letter, but she has felt it in her heart."

The grim beadle now made a gesture with his staff.

"Make way, good people, make way, in the King's name," cried he. "Open a passage; and, I promise ye, Mistress Prynne shall be set where man, woman, and child may have a fair sight of her brave apparel, from this time till an hour past meridian. A blessing on the righteous Colony of the Massachusetts, where iniquity is dragged out into the sunshine! Come along, Madam Hester, and show your scarlet letter in the market-place!"

A lane was forthwith opened through the crowd of spectators. Preceded by the beadle, and attended by an irregular procession of stern-browed men and unkindly-visaged women, Hester Prynne set forth towards the place appointed for her punishment. A crowd of eager and curious schoolboys, understanding little of the matter in hand, except that it gave them a half-holiday, ran before her progress, turning their heads continually to stare into her face, and at the winking baby in her arms, and at the ignominious letter on her breast. It was no great distance, in those days, from the prison-door to the market-place. Measured by the prisoner's experience, however, it might be reckoned a journey of some length; for, haughty as her demeanour was, she perchance underwent an agony from every footstep of those that thronged to see her, as if her heart had been flung into the street for them all to spurn and trample upon. In our nature, however, there is a provision, alike marvellous and merciful, that the sufferer should never know the intensity of what he endures by its present torture, but chiefly by the pang that rankles after it. With almost a serene deportment, therefore, Hester Prynne passed through this portion of her ordeal, and came to a sort of scaffold, at the western extremity of the market-place. It stood nearly beneath the eaves of Boston's earliest church, and appeared to be a fixture there.

In fact, this scaffold constituted a portion of a penal machine, which now, for two or three generations past, has been merely historical and traditionary among us, but was held, in the old time, to be as effectual an agent in the promotion of good citizenship, as ever was the guillotine among the terrorists of France.[62] It was, in short, the platform of the pillory; and above it rose the framework of that instrument of discipline, so fashioned as to confine the human head in its tight grasp, and thus hold it up to the public gaze. The very ideal of ignominy was embodied and made manifest in this contrivance of wood and iron. There can be no outrage, methinks, against our common nature,—whatever be the delinquencies of the individual,—no outrage more flagrant than to forbid the culprit to hide his face for shame; as it was the essence of this punishment to do. In Hester Prynne's instance, however, as not unfrequently in other cases, her sentence bore, that she should stand a certain time upon the platform, but without undergoing that gripe about the neck and confinement of the head, the proneness to which was the most devilish characteristic of this ugly engine. Knowing well her part, she ascended a flight of wooden steps, and was thus displayed to the surrounding multitude, at about the height of a man's shoulders above the street.

Had there been a Papist among the crowd of Puritans, he might have seen in this beautiful woman, so picturesque in her attire and mien, and with the infant at her bosom, an object to remind him of the image of Divine Maternity, which so many illustrious painters have vied with one another to represent; something which should remind him, indeed, but only by contrast, of that sacred image of sinless motherhood,

---

[62] Reference to the Reign of Terror in France (1793–1794).

whose infant was to redeem the world. Here, there was the taint of deepest sin in the most sacred quality of human life, working such effect, that the world was only the darker for this woman's beauty, and the more lost for the infant that she had borne.

The scene was not without a mixture of awe, such as must always invest the spectacle of guilt and shame in a fellow-creature, before society shall have grown corrupt enough to smile, instead of shuddering, at it. The witnesses of Hester Prynne's disgrace had not yet passed beyond their simplicity. They were stern enough to look upon her death, had that been the sentence, without a murmur at its severity, but had none of the heartlessness of another social state, which would find only a theme for jest in an exhibition like the present. Even had there been a disposition to turn the matter into ridicule, it must have been repressed and overpowered by the solemn presence of men no less dignified than the Governor, and several of his counsellors, a judge, a general, and the ministers of the town; all of whom sat or stood in a balcony of the meeting-house, looking down upon the platform. When such personages could constitute a part of the spectacle, without risking the majesty or reverence of rank and office, it was safely to be inferred that the infliction of a legal sentence would have an earnest and effectual meaning. Accordingly, the crowd was sombre and grave. The unhappy culprit sustained herself as best a woman might, under the heavy weight of a thousand unrelenting eyes, all fastened upon her, and concentred at her bosom. It was almost intolerable to be borne. Of an impulsive and passionate nature, she had fortified herself to encounter the stings and venomous stabs of public contumely, wreaking itself in every variety of insult; but there was a quality so much more terrible in the solemn mood of the popular mind, that she longed rather to behold all those rigid countenances contorted with scornful merriment, and herself the object. Had a roar of laughter burst from the multitude,—each man, each woman, each little shrill-voiced child, contributing their individual parts,—Hester Prynne might have repaid them all with a bitter and disdainful smile. But, under the leaden infliction which it was her doom to endure, she felt, at moments, as if she must needs shriek out with the full power of her lungs, and cast herself from the scaffold down upon the ground, or else go mad at once.

Yet there were intervals when the whole scene, in which she was the most conspicuous object, seemed to vanish from her eyes, or, at least, glimmered indistinctly before them, like a mass of imperfectly shaped and spectral images. Her mind, and especially her memory, was preternaturally active, and kept bringing up other scenes than this roughly hewn street of a little town, on the edge of the Western wilderness; other faces than were lowering upon her from beneath the brims of those steeple-crowned hats. Reminiscences, the most trifling and immaterial, passages of infancy and school-days, sports, childish quarrels, and the little domestic traits of her maiden years, came swarming back upon her, intermingled with recollections of whatever was gravest in her subsequent life; one picture precisely as vivid as another; as if all were of similar importance, or all alike a play. Possibly, it was an instinctive device of her spirit, to relieve itself, by the exhibition of these phantasmagoric forms, from the cruel weight and hardness of the reality.

Be that as it might, the scaffold of the pillory was a point of view that revealed to Hester Prynne the entire track along which she had been treading, since her happy infancy. Standing on that miserable eminence, she saw again her native village, in Old England, and her paternal home; a decayed house of gray stone, with a poverty-stricken aspect, but retaining a half-obliterated shield of arms over the portal, in token of antique gentility. She saw her father's face, with its bald brow, and reverend white beard, that flowed over the old-fashioned Elizabethan ruff; her mother's, too, with the look of heedful and anxious love which it always wore in her remembrance, and which, even since her death, had so often laid the impediment of a gentle remonstrance in her daughter's pathway. She saw her own face, glowing with girlish beauty, and illuminating all the interior of the dusky mirror in which she had been wont to gaze at it. There she beheld another countenance, of a man well stricken in years, a pale, thin, scholar-like visage, with eyes dim and bleared by the lamp-light that had served them to pore over many ponderous books. Yet those same bleared optics had a strange, penetrating power, when it was their owner's purpose to read the human soul. This figure of the study and the cloister, as Hester Prynne's womanly fancy failed not to recall, was slightly deformed, with the left shoulder a trifle higher than the right. Next rose before her, in memory's picture-gallery, the intricate and narrow thoroughfares, the tall, gray houses, the huge cathedrals, and the public edifices, ancient in date and quaint in architecture, of a Continental city;[63] where a new life had awaited her, still in connection with the misshapen scholar; a new life, but feeding itself on time-worn materials, like a tuft of green moss on a crumbling wall. Lastly, in lieu of these shifting scenes, came back the rude market-place of the Puritan settlement, with all the townspeople assembled and levelling their stern regards at Hester Prynne,—yes, at herself,—who stood on the scaffold of the pillory, an infant on her arm, and the letter A, in scarlet, fantastically embroidered with gold thread, upon her bosom!

Could it be true? She clutched the child so fiercely to her breast, that it sent forth a cry; she turned her eyes downward at the scarlet letter, and even touched it with her finger, to assure herself that the infant and the shame were real. Yes!—these were her realities,—all else had vanished!

III: The Recognition

From this intense consciousness of being the object of severe and universal observation, the wearer of the scarlet letter was at length relieved by discerning, on the outskirts of the crowd, a figure which irresistibly took possession of her thoughts. An Indian, in his native garb, was standing there; but the red men were not so infrequent visitors of the English settlements, that one of them would have attracted any notice from Hester Prynne, at such a time; much less would he have excluded all other objects and ideas from her mind. By the Indian's side, and evidently sustaining a companionship with him, stood a white man, clad in a strange disarray of civilized and savage costume.

He was small in stature, with a furrowed visage, which, as yet, could hardly be termed aged. There was a remarkable intelligence in his features, as of a person who had so cultivated his mental part that it could not fail to mould the physical to itself, and become manifest by unmistakable tokens. Although, by a seemingly careless arrangement of his heterogeneous garb, he had endeavoured to conceal or abate the

[63] English Separatists and Puritans gathered in Amsterdam, the Continental City, before migrating to the New World.

peculiarity, it was sufficiently evident to Hester Prynne, that one of this man's shoulders rose higher than the other. Again, at the first instant of perceiving that thin visage, and the slight deformity of the figure, she pressed her infant to her bosom, with so convulsive a force that the poor babe uttered another cry of pain. But the mother did not seem to hear it.

At his arrival in the market-place, and some time before she saw him, the stranger had bent his eyes on Hester Prynne. It was carelessly, at first, like a man chiefly accustomed to look inward, and to whom external matters are of little value and import, unless they bear relation to something within his mind. Very soon, however, his look became keen and penetrative. A writhing horror twisted itself across his features, like a snake gliding swiftly over them, and making one little pause, with all its wreathed intervolutions in open sight. His face darkened with some powerful emotion, which, nevertheless, he so instantaneously controlled by an effort of his will, that, save at a single moment, its expression might have passed for calmness. After a brief space, the convulsion grew almost imperceptible, and finally subsided into the depths of his nature. When he found the eyes of Hester Prynne fastened on his own, and saw that she appeared to recognize him, he slowly and calmly raised his finger, made a gesture with it in the air, and laid it on his lips.

Then, touching the shoulder of a townsman who stood next to him, he addressed him in a formal and courteous manner.

"I pray you, good Sir," said he, "who is this woman?—and wherefore is she here set up to public shame?"

"You must needs be a stranger in this region, friend," answered the townsman, looking curiously at the questioner and his savage companion; "else you would surely have heard of Mistress Hester Prynne, and her evil doings. She hath raised a great scandal, I promise you, in godly Master Dimmesdale's church."

"You say truly," replied the other. "I am a stranger, and have been a wanderer, sorely against my will. I have met with grievous mishaps by sea and land, and have been long held in bonds among the heathen-folk, to the southward; and am now brought hither by this Indian, to be redeemed out of my captivity. Will it please you, therefore, to tell me of Hester Prynne's,—have I her name rightly?—of this woman's offences, and what has brought her to yonder scaffold?"

"Truly, friend, and methinks it must gladden your heart, after your troubles and sojourn in the wilderness," said the townsman, "to find yourself, at length, in a land where iniquity is searched out, and punished in the sight of rulers and people; as here in our godly New England. Yonder woman, Sir, you must know, was the wife of a certain learned man, English by birth, but who had long dwelt in Amsterdam, whence, some good time agone, he was minded to cross over and cast in his lot with us of the Massachusetts. To this purpose, he sent his wife before him, remaining himself to look after some necessary affairs. Marry, good Sir, in some two years, or less, that the woman has been a dweller here in Boston, no tidings have come of this learned gentleman, Master Prynne; and his young wife, look you, being left to her own misguidance—"

"Ah!—aha!—I conceive you," said the stranger, with a bitter smile. "So learned a man as you speak of should have learned this too in his books. And who, by your favor, Sir, may be the father of yonder babe—it is some three or four months old, I should judge—which Mistress Prynne is holding in her arms?"

"Of a truth, friend, that matter remaineth a riddle; and the Daniel[64] who shall expound it is yet a-wanting," answered the townsman. "Madam Hester absolutely refuseth to speak, and the magistrates have laid their heads together in vain. Peradventure the guilty one stands looking on at this sad spectacle, unknown of man, and forgetting that God sees him."

"The learned man," observed the stranger, with another smile, "should come himself to look into the mystery."

"It behooves him well, if he be still in life," responded the townsman. "Now, good Sir, our Massachusetts magistracy, bethinking themselves that this woman is youthful and fair, and doubtless was strongly tempted to her fall;—and that, moreover, as is most likely, her husband may be at the bottom of the sea;—they have not been bold to put in force the extremity of our righteous law against her. The penalty thereof is death. But, in their great mercy and tenderness of heart, they have doomed Mistress Prynne to stand only a space of three hours on the platform of the pillory, and then and thereafter, for the remainder of her natural life, to wear a mark of shame upon her bosom."

"A wise sentence!" remarked the stranger, gravely bowing his head. "Thus she will be a living sermon against sin, until the ignominious letter be engraved upon her tombstone. It irks me, nevertheless, that the partner of her iniquity should not, at least, stand on the scaffold by her side. But he will be known!—he will be known!—he will be known!"

He bowed courteously to the communicative townsman, and, whispering a few words to his Indian attendant, they both made their way through the crowd.

While this passed, Hester Prynne had been standing on her pedestal, still with a fixed gaze towards the stranger; so fixed a gaze, that, at moments of intense absorption, all other objects in the visible world seemed to vanish, leaving only him and her. Such an interview, perhaps, would have been more terrible than even to meet him as she now did, with the hot, midday sun burning down upon her face, and lighting up its shame; with the scarlet token of infamy on her breast; with the sin-born infant in her arms; with a whole people, drawn forth as to a festival, staring at the features that should have been seen only in the quiet gleam of the fireside, in the happy shadow of a home, or beneath a matronly veil, at church. Dreadful as it was, she was conscious of a shelter in the presence of these thousand witnesses. It was better to stand thus, with so many betwixt him and her, than to greet him, face to face, they two alone. She fled for refuge, as it were, to the public exposure, and dreaded the moment when its protection should be withdrawn from her. Involved in these thoughts, she scarcely heard a voice behind her, until it had repeated her name more than once, in a loud and solemn tone, audible to the whole multitude.

"Hearken unto me, Hester Prynne!" said the voice.

It has already been noticed, that directly over the platform on which Hester Prynne stood was a kind of balcony, or open gallery, appended to the meeting-house. It was the place whence proclamations were wont to be made, amidst an assemblage of the magistracy, with all the ceremonial that attended such public observances in those

[64] In the Old Testament, Daniel interpreted the handwriting on the wall at Belshazzar's feast. (See Daniel 5.)

days. Here, to witness the scene which we are describing, sat Governor Bellingham[65] himself, with four sergeants about his chair, bearing halberds,[66] as a guard of honor. He wore a dark feather in his hat, a border of embroidery on his cloak, and a black velvet tunic beneath; a gentleman advanced in years, and with a hard experience written in his wrinkles. He was not ill fitted to be the head and representative of a community, which owed its origin and progress, and its present state of development, not to the impulses of youth, but to the stern and tempered energies of manhood, and the sombre sagacity of age; accomplishing so much, precisely because it imagined and hoped so little. The other eminent characters, by whom the chief ruler was surrounded, were distinguished by a dignity of mien, belonging to a period when the forms of authority were felt to possess the sacredness of divine institutions. They were, doubtless, good men, just, and sage. But, out of the whole human family, it would not have been easy to select the same number of wise and virtuous persons, who should be less capable of sitting in judgment on an erring woman's heart, and disentangling its mesh of good and evil, than the sages of rigid aspect towards whom Hester Prynne now turned her face. She seemed conscious, indeed, that whatever sympathy she might expect lay in the larger and warmer heart of the multitude; for, as she lifted her eyes towards the balcony, the unhappy woman grew pale and trembled.

The voice which had called her attention was that of the reverend and famous John Wilson,[67] the eldest clergyman of Boston, a great scholar, like most of his contemporaries in the profession, and withal a man of kind and genial spirit. This last attribute, however, had been less carefully developed than his intellectual gifts, and was, in truth, rather a matter of shame than self-congratulation with him. There he stood, with a border of grizzled locks beneath his skull-cap; while his gray eyes, accustomed to the shaded light of his study, were winking, like those of Hester's infant, in the unadulterated sunshine. He looked like the darkly engraved portraits which we see prefixed to old volumes of sermons; and had no more right than one of those portraits would have, to step forth, as he now did, and meddle with a question of human guilt, passion, and anguish.

"Hester Prynne," said the clergyman, "I have striven with my young brother here, under whose preaching of the word you have been privileged to sit,"—here Mr. Wilson laid his hand on the shoulder of a pale young man beside him,—"I have sought, I say, to persuade this godly youth, that he should deal with you, here in the face of Heaven, and before these wise and upright rulers, and in hearing of all the people, as touching the vileness and blackness of your sin. Knowing your natural temper better than I, he could the better judge what arguments to use, whether of tenderness or terror, such as might prevail over your hardness and obstinacy; insomuch that you should no longer hide the name of him who tempted you to this grievous fall. But he opposes to me, (with a young man's oversoftness, albeit wise beyond his years,) that it were wronging the very nature of woman to force her to lay open her heart's secrets in such broad daylight, and in presence of so great a multitude. Truly, as I sought to convince him, the shame lay in the commission of the sin, and not in

---

[65] Richard Bellingham (1592–1672), governor of Massachusetts in 1641 and 1654 and from 1665 to 1672.
[66] Halberd: weapon of the fifteenth and sixteenth centuries that combined a spear and an ax-head

on a long handle. Later, a ceremonial symbol of honor guards.
[67] Puritan minister (ca. 1591–1667) who immigrated to Boston with the earliest settlers in 1630.

the showing of it forth. What say you to it, once again, brother Dimmesdale? Must it be thou or I that shall deal with this poor sinner's soul?"

There was a murmur among the dignified and reverend occupants of the balcony; and Governor Bellingham gave expression to its purport, speaking in an authoritative voice, although tempered with respect towards the youthful clergyman whom he addressed.

"Good Master Dimmesdale," said he, "the responsibility of this woman's soul lies greatly with you. It behooves you, therefore, to exhort her to repentance, and to confession, as a proof and consequence thereof."

The directness of this appeal drew the eyes of the whole crowd upon the Reverend Mr. Dimmesdale; a young clergyman, who had come from one of the great English universities, bringing all the learning of the age into our wild forest-land. His eloquence and religious fervor had already given the earnest of high eminence in his profession. He was a person of very striking aspect, with a white, lofty, and impending brow, large, brown, melancholy eyes, and a mouth which, unless when he forcibly compressed it, was apt to be tremulous, expressing both nervous sensibility and a vast power of self-restraint. Notwithstanding his high native gifts and scholar-like attainments, there was an air about this young minister,—an apprehensive, a startled, a half-frightened look,—as of a being who felt himself quite astray and at a loss in the pathway of human existence, and could only be at ease in some seclusion of his own. Therefore, so far as his duties would permit, he trode in the shadowy by-paths, and thus kept himself simple and childlike; coming forth, when occasion was, with a freshness, and fragrance, and dewy purity of thought, which, as many people said, affected them like the speech of an angel.

Such was the young man whom the Reverend Mr. Wilson and the Governor had introduced so openly to the public notice, bidding him speak, in the hearing of all men, to that mystery of a woman's soul, so sacred even in its pollution. The trying nature of his position drove the blood from his cheek, and made his lips tremulous.

"Speak to the woman, my brother," said Mr. Wilson. "It is of moment to her soul, and therefore, as the worshipful Governor says, momentous to thine own, in whose charge hers is. Exhort her to confess the truth!"

The Reverend Mr. Dimmesdale bent his head, in silent prayer, as it seemed, and then came forward.

"Hester Prynne," said he, leaning over the balcony, and looking down stedfastly into her eyes, "thou hearest what this good man says, and seest the accountability under which I labor. If thou feelest it to be for thy soul's peace, and that thy earthly punishment will thereby be made more effectual to salvation, I charge thee to speak out the name of thy fellow-sinner and fellow-sufferer! Be not silent from any mistaken pity and tenderness for him; for, believe me, Hester, though he were to step down from a high place, and stand there beside thee, on thy pedestal of shame, yet better were it so, than to hide a guilty heart through life. What can thy silence do for him, except it tempt him—yea, compel him, as it were—to add hypocrisy to sin? Heaven hath granted thee an open ignominy, that thereby thou mayest work out an open triumph over the evil within thee, and the sorrow without. Take heed how thou deniest to him—who, perchance, hath not the courage to grasp it for himself—the bitter, but wholesome, cup that is now presented to thy lips!"

The young pastor's voice was tremulously sweet, rich, deep, and broken. The feeling that it so evidently manifested, rather than the direct purport of the words, caused it to vibrate within all hearts, and brought the listeners into one accord of sympathy. Even the poor baby, at Hester's bosom, was affected by the same influence; for it directed its hitherto vacant gaze towards Mr. Dimmesdale, and held up its little arms, with a half pleased, half plaintive murmur. So powerful seemed the minister's appeal, that the people could not believe but that Hester Prynne would speak out the guilty name; or else that the guilty one himself, in whatever high or lowly place he stood, would be drawn forth by an inward and inevitable necessity, and compelled to ascend the scaffold.

Hester shook her head.

"Woman, transgress not beyond the limits of Heaven's mercy!" cried the Reverend Mr. Wilson, more harshly than before. "That little babe hath been gifted with a voice, to second and confirm the counsel which thou hast heard. Speak out the name! That, and thy repentance, may avail to take the scarlet letter off thy breast."

"Never!" replied Hester Prynne, looking, not at Mr. Wilson, but into the deep and troubled eyes of the younger clergyman. "It is too deeply branded. Ye cannot take it off. And would that I might endure his agony, as well as mine!"

"Speak, woman!" said another voice, coldly and sternly, proceeding from the crowd about the scaffold. "Speak; and give your child a father!"

"I will not speak!" answered Hester, turning pale as death, but responding to this voice, which she too surely recognized. "And my child must seek a heavenly Father; she shall never know an earthly one!"

"She will not speak!" murmured Mr. Dimmesdale, who, leaning over the balcony, with his hand upon his heart, had awaited the result of his appeal. He now drew back, with a long respiration. "Wondrous strength and generosity of a woman's heart! She will not speak!"

Discerning the impracticable state of the poor culprit's mind, the elder clergyman, who had carefully prepared himself for the occasion, addressed to the multitude a discourse on sin, in all its branches, but with continual reference to the ignominious letter. So forcibly did he dwell upon this symbol, for the hour or more during which his periods were rolling over the people's heads, that it assumed new terrors in their imagination, and seemed to derive its scarlet hue from the flames of the infernal pit. Hester Prynne, meanwhile, kept her place upon the pedestal of shame, with glazed eyes, and an air of weary indifference. She had borne, that morning, all that nature could endure; and as her temperament was not of the order that escapes from too intense suffering by a swoon, her spirit could only shelter itself beneath a stony crust of insensibility, while the faculties of animal life remained entire. In this state, the voice of the preacher thundered remorselessly, but unavailingly, upon her ears. The infant, during the latter portion of her ordeal, pierced the air with its wailings and screams; she strove to hush it, mechanically, but seemed scarcely to sympathize with its trouble. With the same hard demeanour, she was led back to prison, and vanished from the public gaze within its iron-clamped portal. It was whispered, by those who peered after her, that the scarlet letter threw a lurid gleam along the dark passage-way of the interior.

IV: The Interview

After her return to the prison, Hester Prynne was found to be in a state of nervous excitement that demanded constant watchfulness, lest she should perpetrate violence on herself, or do some half-frenzied mischief to the poor babe. As night approached, it proving impossible to quell her insubordination by rebuke or threats of punishment, Master Brackett, the jailer, thought fit to introduce a physician. He described him as a man of skill in all Christian modes of physical science, and likewise familiar with whatever the savage people could teach, in respect to medicinal herbs and roots that grew in the forest. To say the truth, there was much need of professional assistance, not merely for Hester herself, but still more urgently for the child; who, drawing its sustenance from the maternal bosom, seemed to have drank in with it all the turmoil, the anguish, and despair, which pervaded the mother's system. It now writhed in convulsions of pain, and was a forcible type,[68] in its little frame, of the moral agony which Hester Prynne had borne throughout the day.

Closely following the jailer into the dismal apartment, appeared that individual, of singular aspect, whose presence in the crowd had been of such deep interest to the wearer of the scarlet letter. He was lodged in the prison, not as suspected of any offence, but as the most convenient and suitable mode of disposing of him, until the magistrates should have conferred with the Indian sagamores[69] respecting his ransom. His name was announced as Roger Chillingworth. The jailer, after ushering him into the room, remained a moment, marvelling at the comparative quiet that followed his entrance; for Hester Prynne had immediately become as still as death, although the child continued to moan.

"Prithee, friend, leave me alone with my patient," said the practitioner. "Trust me, good jailer, you shall briefly have peace in your house; and, I promise you, Mistress Prynne shall hereafter be more amenable to just authority than you may have found her heretofore."

"Nay, if your worship can accomplish that," answered Master Brackett, "I shall own you for a man of skill indeed! Verily, the woman hath been like a possessed one; and there lacks little, that I should take in hand to drive Satan out of her with stripes."

The stranger had entered the room with the characteristic quietude of the profession to which he announced himself as belonging. Nor did his demeanour change, when the withdrawal of the prison-keeper left him face to face with the woman, whose absorbed notice of him, in the crowd, had intimated so close a relation between himself and her. His first care was given to the child; whose cries, indeed, as she lay writhing on the trundle-bed, made it of peremptory necessity to postpone all other business to the task of soothing her. He examined the infant carefully, and then proceeded to unclasp a leathern case, which he took from beneath his dress. It appeared to contain certain medical preparations, one of which he mingled with a cup of water.

"My old studies in alchemy," observed he, "and my sojourn, for above a year past, among a people well versed in the kindly properties of simples,[70] have made a better physician of me than many that claim the medical degree. Here, woman! The child

---

[68] Forcible type: forceful symbol.
[69] Chiefs.

[70] Drugs derived from plants.

is yours,—she is none of mine,—neither will she recognize my voice or aspect as a father's. Administer this draught, therefore, with thine own hand."

Hester repelled the offered medicine, at the same time gazing with strongly marked apprehension into his face.

"Wouldst thou avenge thyself on the innocent babe?" whispered she.

"Foolish woman!" responded the physician, half coldly, half soothingly. "What should ail me to harm this misbegotten and miserable babe? The medicine is potent for good; and were it my child,—yea, mine own, as well as thine!—I could do no better for it."

As she still hesitated, being, in fact, in no reasonable state of mind, he took the infant in his arms, and himself administered the draught. It soon proved its efficacy, and redeemed the leech's[71] pledge. The moans of the little patient subsided; its convulsive tossings gradually ceased; and in a few moments, as is the custom of young children after relief from pain, it sank into a profound and dewy slumber. The physician, as he had a fair right to be termed, next bestowed his attention on the mother. With calm and intent scrutiny, he felt her pulse, looked into her eyes,—a gaze that made her heart shrink and shudder, because so familiar, and yet so strange and cold,—and, finally, satisfied with his investigation, proceeded to mingle another draught.

"I know not Lethe nor Nepenthe,"[72] remarked he; "but I have learned many new secrets in the wilderness, and here is one of them,—a recipe that an Indian taught me, in requital of some lessons of my own, that were as old as Paracelsus.[73] Drink it! It may be less soothing than a sinless conscience. That I cannot give thee. But it will calm the swell and heaving of thy passion, like oil thrown on the waves of a tempestuous sea."

He presented the cup to Hester, who received it with a slow, earnest look into his face; not precisely a look of fear, yet full of doubt and questioning, as to what his purposes might be. She looked also at her slumbering child.

"I have thought of death," said she,—"have wished for it,—would even have prayed for it, were it fit that such as I should pray for any thing. Yet, if death be in this cup, I bid thee think again, ere thou beholdest me quaff it. See! It is even now at my lips."

"Drink, then," replied he, still with the same cold composure. "Dost thou know me so little, Hester Prynne? Are my purposes wont to be so shallow? Even if I imagine a scheme of vengeance, what could I do better for my object than to let thee live, —than to give thee medicines against all harm and peril of life,—so that this burning shame may still blaze upon thy bosom?"—As he spoke, he laid his long forefinger on the scarlet letter, which forthwith seemed to scorch into Hester's breast, as if it had been red-hot. He noticed her involuntary gesture, and smiled.—"Live, therefore, and bear about thy doom with thee, in the eyes of men and women,—in the eyes of him whom thou didst call thy husband,—in the eyes of yonder child! And, that thou mayest live, take off this draught."

Without further expostulation or delay, Hester Prynne drained the cup, and, at the

---

[71] Leech: common name for a doctor, after the blood-sucking aquatic worms prescribed for illnesses.

[72] In classical mythology, Lethe and Nepenthe induced oblivion and the alleviation of pain.

[73] Swiss alchemist and physician (1493–1541).

motion of the man of skill, seated herself on the bed where the child was sleeping; while he drew the only chair which the room afforded, and took his own seat beside her. She could not but tremble at these preparations; for she felt that—having now done all that humanity, or principle, or, if so it were, a refined cruelty, impelled him to do, for the relief of physical suffering—he was next to treat with her as the man whom she had most deeply and irreparably injured.

"Hester," said he, "I ask not wherefore, nor how, thou hast fallen into the pit, or say rather, thou hast ascended to the pedestal of infamy, on which I found thee. The reason is not far to seek. It was my folly, and thy weakness. I,—a man of thought, —the book-worm of great libraries,—a man already in decay, having given my best years to feed the hungry dream of knowledge,—what had I to do with youth and beauty like thine own! Misshapen from my birth-hour, how could I delude myself with the idea that intellectual gifts might veil physical deformity in a young girl's fantasy! Men call me wise. If sages were ever wise in their own behoof, I might have foreseen all this. I might have known that, as I came out of the vast and dismal forest, and entered this settlement of Christian men, the very first object to meet my eyes would be thyself, Hester Prynne, standing up, a statue of ignominy, before the people. Nay, from the moment when we came down the old church-steps together, a married pair, I might have beheld the bale-fire[74] of that scarlet letter blazing at the end of our path!"

"Thou knowest," said Hester,—for, depressed as she was, she could not endure this last quiet stab at the token of her shame,—"thou knowest that I was frank with thee. I felt no love, nor feigned any."

"True!" replied he. "It was my folly! I have said it. But, up to that epoch of my life, I had lived in vain. The world had been so cheerless! My heart was a habitation large enough for many guests, but lonely and chill, and without a household fire. I longed to kindle one! It seemed not so wild a dream,—old as I was, and sombre as I was, and misshapen as I was,—that the simple bliss, which is scattered far and wide, for all mankind to gather up, might yet be mine. And so, Hester, I drew thee into my heart, into its innermost chamber, and sought to warm thee by the warmth which thy presence made there!"

"I have greatly wronged thee," murmured Hester.

"We have wronged each other," answered he. "Mine was the first wrong, when I betrayed thy budding youth into a false and unnatural relation with my decay. Therefore, as a man who has not thought and philosophized in vain, I seek no vengeance, plot no evil against thee. Between thee and me, the scale hangs fairly balanced. But, Hester, the man lives who has wronged us both! Who is he?"

"Ask me not!" replied Hester Prynne, looking firmly into his face. "That thou shalt never know!"

"Never, sayest thou?" rejoined he, with a smile of dark and self-relying intelligence. "Never know him! Believe me, Hester, there are few things,—whether in the outward world, or, to a certain depth, in the invisible sphere of thought,—few things hidden from the man, who devotes himself earnestly and unreservedly to the solution of a mystery. Thou mayest cover up thy secret from the prying multitude. Thou mayest conceal it, too, from the ministers and magistrates, even as thou didst this day, when

[74] Often, a signal fire.

they sought to wrench the name out of thy heart, and give thee a partner on thy pedestal. But, as for me, I come to the inquest with other senses than they possess. I shall seek this man, as I have sought truth in books; as I have sought gold in alchemy. There is a sympathy that will make me conscious of him. I shall see him tremble. I shall feel myself shudder, suddenly and unawares. Sooner or later, he must needs be mine!"

The eyes of the wrinkled scholar glowed so intensely upon her, that Hester Prynne clasped her hands over her heart, dreading lest he should read the secret there at once.

"Thou wilt not reveal his name? Not the less he is mine," resumed he, with a look of confidence, as if destiny were at one with him. "He bears no letter of infamy wrought into his garment, as thou dost; but I shall read it on his heart. Yet fear not for him! Think not that I shall interfere with Heaven's own method of retribution, or, to my own loss, betray him to the gripe[75] of human law. Neither do thou imagine that I shall contrive aught against his life; no, nor against his fame, if, as I judge, he be a man of fair repute. Let him live! Let him hide himself in outward honor, if he may! Not the less he shall be mine!"

"Thy acts are like mercy," said Hester, bewildered and appalled. "But thy words interpret thee as a terror!"

"One thing, thou that wast my wife, I would enjoin upon thee," continued the scholar. "Thou hast kept the secret of thy paramour. Keep, likewise, mine! There are none in this land that know me. Breathe not, to any human soul, that thou didst ever call me husband! Here, on this wild outskirt of the earth, I shall pitch my tent; for, elsewhere a wanderer, and isolated from human interests, I find here a woman, a man, a child, amongst whom and myself there exist the closest ligaments. No matter whether of love or hate; no matter whether of right or wrong! Thou and thine, Hester Prynne, belong to me. My home is where thou art, and where he is. But betray me not!"

"Wherefore dost thou desire it?" inquired Hester, shrinking, she hardly knew why, from this secret bond. "Why not announce thyself openly, and cast me off at once?"

"It may be," he replied, "because I will not encounter the dishonor that besmirches the husband of a faithless woman. It may be for other reasons. Enough, it is my purpose to live and die unknown. Let, therefore, thy husband be to the world as one already dead, and of whom no tidings shall ever come. Recognize me not, by word, by sign, by look! Breathe not the secret, above all, to the man thou wottest[76] of. Shouldst thou fail me in this, beware! His fame, his position, his life, will be in my hands. Beware!"

"I will keep thy secret, as I have his," said Hester.

"Swear it!" rejoined he.

And she took the oath.

"And now, Mistress Prynne," said old Roger Chillingworth, as he was hereafter to be named. "I leave thee alone; alone with thy infant, and the scarlet letter! How is it, Hester? Doth thy sentence bind thee to wear the token in thy sleep? Art thou not afraid of nightmares and hideous dreams?"

"Why dost thou smile so at me?" inquired Hester, troubled at the expression of

---

[75] Variant spelling of *grip*.   [76] Knowest.

his eyes. "Art thou like the Black Man[77] that haunts the forest round about us? Hast thou enticed me into a bind that will prove the ruin of my soul?"

"Not thy soul," he answered, with another smile. "No, not thine!"

V: Hester at Her Needle

Hester Prynne's term of confinement was now at an end. Her prison-door was thrown open, and she came forth into the sunshine, which, falling on all alike, seemed, to her sick and morbid heart, as if meant for no other purpose than to reveal the scarlet letter on her breast. Perhaps there was a more real torture in her first unattended footsteps from the threshold of the prison, than even in the procession and spectacle that have been described, where she was made the common infamy, at which all mankind was summoned to point its finger. Then, she was supported by an unnatural tension of the nerves, and by all the combative energy of her character, which enabled her to convert the scene into a kind of lurid triumph. It was, moreover, a separate and insulated event, to occur but once in her lifetime, and to meet which, therefore, reckless of economy, she might call up the vital strength that would have sufficed for many quiet years. The very law that condemned her—a giant of stern features, but with vigor to support, as well as to annihilate, in his iron arm—had held her up, through the terrible ordeal of her ignominy. But now, with this unattended walk from her prison-door, began the daily custom, and she must either sustain and carry it forward by the ordinary resources of her nature, or sink beneath it. She could no longer borrow from the future, to help her through the present grief. To-morrow would bring its own trial with it; so would the next day, and so would the next; each its own trial, and yet the very same that was now so unutterably grievous to be borne. The days of the far-off future would toil onward, still with the same burden for her to take up, and bear along with her, but never to fling down; for the accumulating days, and added years, would pile up their misery upon the heap of shame. Throughout them all, giving up her individuality, she would become the general symbol at which the preacher and moralist might point, and in which they might vivify and embody their images of woman's frailty and sinful passion. Thus the young and pure would be taught to look at her, with the scarlet letter flaming on her breast,—at her, the child of honorable parents,—at her, the mother of a babe, that would hereafter be a woman,—at her, who had once been innocent,—as the figure, the body, the reality of sin. And over her grave, the infamy that she must carry thither would be her only monument.

It may seem marvellous, that, with the world before her,—kept by no restrictive clause of her condemnation within the limits of the Puritan settlement, so remote and so obscure,—free to return to her birthplace, or to any other European land, and there hide her character and identity under a new exterior, as completely as if emerging into another state of being,—and having also the passes of the dark, inscrutable forest open to her, where the wildness of her nature might assimilate itself with a people whose customs and life were alien from the law that had condemned her,—it may seem marvellous, that this woman should still call that place her home, where, and where only, she must needs be the type of shame. But there is a fatality, a feeling so

[77] Name given the Devil, or Satan, in folklore.

irresistible and inevitable that it has the force of doom, which almost invariably compels human beings to linger around and haunt, ghost-like, the spot where some great and marked event has given the color to their lifetime; and still the more irresistibly, the darker the tinge that saddens it. Her sin, her ignominy, were the roots which she had struck into the soil. It was as if a new birth, with stronger assimilations than the first, had converted the forest-land, still so uncongenial to every other pilgrim and wanderer, into Hester Prynne's wild and dreary, but life-long home. All other scenes of earth—even that village of rural England, where happy infancy and stainless maidenhood seemed yet to be in her mother's keeping, like garments put off long ago —were foreign to her, in comparison. The chain that bound her here was of iron links, and galling to her inmost soul, but never could be broken. *she doesn't think she's bad.*

It might be, too,—doubtless it was so, although she hid the secret from herself, and grew pale whenever it struggled out of her heart, like a serpent from its hole, —it might be that another feeling kept her within the scene and pathway that had been so fatal. There dwelt, there trode the feet of one with whom she deemed herself connected in a union, that, unrecognized on earth, would bring them together before the bar of final judgment, and make that their marriage-altar, for a joint futurity of endless retribution. Over and over again, the tempter of souls had thrust this idea upon Hester's contemplation, and laughed at the passionate and desperate joy with which she seized, and then strove to cast it from her. She barely looked the idea in the face, and hastened to bar it in its dungeon. What she compelled herself to believe,—what, finally, she reasoned upon, as her motive for continuing a resident of New England, —was half a truth, and half a self-delusion. Here, she said to herself, had been the scene of her guilt, and here should be the scene of her earthly punishment; and so, perchance, the torture of her daily shame would at length purge her soul, and work out another purity than that which she had lost; more saint-like, because the result of martyrdom.

Hester Prynne, therefore, did not flee. On the outskirts of the town, within the verge of the peninsula, but not in close vicinity to any other habitation, there was a small thatched cottage. It had been built by an earlier settler, and abandoned, because the soil about it was too sterile for cultivation, while its comparative remoteness put it out of the sphere of that social activity which already marked the habits of the emigrants. It stood on the shore, looking across a basin of the sea at the forest-covered hills, towards the west. A clump of scrubby trees, such as alone grew on the peninsula, did not so much conceal the cottage from view, as seem to denote that here was some object which would fain have been, or at least ought to be, concealed. In this little, lonesome dwelling, with some slender means that she possessed, and by the license of the magistrates, who still kept an inquisitorial watch over her, Hester established herself, with her infant child. A mystic shadow of suspicion immediately attached itself to the spot. Children, too young to comprehend wherefore this woman should be shut out from the sphere of human charities, would creep nigh enough to behold her plying her needle at the cottage-window, or standing in the door-way, or laboring in her little garden, or coming forth along the pathway that led townward; and, discerning the scarlet letter on her breast, would scamper off, with a strange, conta- gious fear.

Lonely as was Hester's situation, and without a friend on earth who dared to show himself, she, however, incurred no risk of want. She possessed an art that sufficed, even in a land that afforded comparatively little scope for its exercise, to supply food for her thriving infant and herself. It was the art—then, as now, almost the only one within a woman's grasp—of needle-work. She bore on her breast, in the curiously embroidered letter, a specimen of her delicate and imaginative skill, of which the dames of a court might gladly have availed themselves, to add the richer and more spiritual adornment of human ingenuity to their fabrics of silk and gold. Here, indeed, in the sable simplicity that generally characterized the Puritanic modes of dress, there might be an infrequent call for the finer productions of her handiwork. Yet the taste of the age, demanding whatever was elaborate in compositions of this kind, did not fail to extend its influence over our stern progenitors, who had cast behind them so many fashions which it might seem harder to dispense with. Public ceremonies, such as ordinations, the installation of magistrates, and all that could give majesty to the forms in which a new government manifested itself to the people, were, as a matter of policy, marked by a stately and well-conducted ceremonial, and a sombre, but yet a studied magnificence. Deep ruffs, painfully wrought bands, and gorgeously embroidered gloves, were all deemed necessary to the official state of men assuming the reins of power; and were readily allowed to individuals dignified by rank or wealth, even while sumptuary laws[78] forbade these and similar extravagances to the plebeian order. In the array of funerals, too,—whether for the apparel of the dead body, or to typify, by manifold emblematic devices of sable[79] cloth and snowy lawn,[80] the sorrow of the survivors,—there was a frequent and characteristic demand for such labor as Hester Prynne could supply. Baby-linen—for babies then wore robes of state—afforded still another possibility of toil and emolument.

By degrees, nor very slowly, her handiwork became what would now be termed the fashion. Whether from commiseration for a woman of so miserable a destiny; or from the morbid curiosity that gives a fictitious value even to common or worthless things; or by whatever other intangible circumstance was then, as now, sufficient to bestow, on some persons, what others might seek in vain; or because Hester really filled a gap which must otherwise have remained vacant; it is certain that she had ready and fairly requited employment for as many hours as she saw fit to occupy with her needle. Vanity, it may be, chose to mortify itself, by putting on, for ceremonials of pomp and state, the garments that had been wrought by her sinful hands. Her needle-work was seen on the ruff of the Governor; military men wore it on their scarfs, and the minister on his band; it decked the baby's little cap; it was shut up, to be mildewed and moulder away, in the coffins of the dead. But it is not recorded that, in a single instance, her skill was called in aid to embroider the white veil which was to cover the pure blushes of a bride. The exception indicated the ever relentless vigor with which society frowned upon her sin.

Hester sought not to acquire any thing beyond a subsistence, of the plainest and most ascetic description, for herself, and a simple abundance for her child. Her own dress was of the coarsest materials and the most sombre hue; with only that one ornament,—the scarlet letter,—which it was her doom to wear. The child's attire, on the other hand, was distinguished by a fanciful, or, we might rather say, a fantastic ingenuity, which served, indeed, to heighten the airy charm that early began to develop itself in the little girl, but which appeared to have also a deeper meaning.

---

[78] Laws prescribing standards of dress.
[79] Black or dark.
[80] Type of fine fabric.

We may speak further of it hereafter. Except for that small expenditure in the decoration of her infant, Hester bestowed all her superfluous means in charity, on wretches less miserable than herself, and who not unfrequently insulted the hand that fed them. Much of the time, which she might readily have applied to the better efforts of her art, she employed in making coarse garments for the poor. It is probable that there was an idea of penance in this mode of occupation, and that she offered up a real sacrifice of enjoyment, in devoting so many hours to such rude handiwork. She had in her nature a rich, voluptuous, Oriental characteristic,—a taste for the gorgeously beautiful, which, save in the exquisite productions of her needle, found nothing else, in all the possibilities of her life, to exercise itself upon. Women derive a pleasure, incomprehensible to the other sex, from the delicate toil of the needle. To Hester Prynne it might have been a mode of expressing, and therefore soothing, the passion of her life. Like all other joys, she rejected it as sin. This morbid meddling of conscience with an immaterial matter betokened, it is to be feared, no genuine and stedfast penitence, but something doubtful, something that might be deeply wrong, beneath.

In this manner, Hester Prynne came to have a part to perform in the world. With her native energy of character, and rare capacity, it could not entirely cast her off, although it had set a mark upon her, more intolerable to a woman's heart than that which branded the brow of Cain.[81] In all her intercourse with society, however, there was nothing that made her feel as if she belonged to it. Every gesture, every word, and even the silence of those with whom she came in contact, implied, and often expressed, that she was banished, and as much alone as if she inhabited another sphere, or communicated with the common nature by other organs and senses than the rest of human kind. She stood apart from mortal interests, yet close beside them, like a ghost that revisits the familiar fireside, and can no longer make itself seen or felt; no more smile with the household joy, nor mourn with the kindred sorrow; or, should it succeed in manifesting its forbidden sympathy, awakening only terror and horrible repugnance. These emotions, in fact, and its bitterest scorn besides, seemed to be the sole portion that she retained in the universal heart. It was not an age of delicacy; and her position, although she understood it well, and was in little danger of forgetting it, was often brought before her vivid self-perception, like a new anguish, by the rudest touch upon the tenderest spot. The poor, as we have already said, whom she sought out to be the objects of her bounty, often reviled the hand that was stretched forth to succor them. Dames of elevated rank, likewise, whose doors she entered in the way of her occupation, were accustomed to distil drops of bitterness into her heart; sometimes through that alchemy of quiet malice, by which women can concoct a subtile poison from ordinary trifles; and sometimes, also, by a coarser expression, that fell upon the sufferer's defenceless breast like a rough blow upon an ulcerated wound. Hester had schooled herself long and well; she never responded to these attacks, save by a flush of crimson that rose irrepressibly over her pale cheek, and again subsided into the depths of her bosom. She was patient,—a martyr, indeed, —but she forbore to pray for her enemies; lest, in spite of her forgiving aspirations, the words of the blessing should stubbornly twist themselves into a curse.

Continually, and in a thousand other ways, did she feel the innumerable throbs of

[81] Genesis 4:15: "And the Lord sat a mark upon Cain, lest any finding him should kill him."

anguish that had been so cunningly contrived for her by the undying, the ever-active sentence of the Puritan tribunal. Clergymen paused in the street to address words of exhortation, that brought a crowd, with its mingled grin and frown, around the poor, sinful woman. If she entered a church, trusting to share the Sabbath smile of the Universal Father, it was often her mishap to find herself the text of the discourse. She grew to have a dread of children; for they had imbibed from their parents a vague idea of something horrible in this dreary woman, gliding silently through the town, with never any companion but one only child. Therefore, first allowing her to pass, they pursued her at a distance with shrill cries, and the utterance of a word that had no distinct purport to their own minds, but was none the less terrible to her, as proceeding from lips that babbled it unconsciously. It seemed to argue so wide a diffusion of her shame, that all nature knew of it; it could have caused her no deeper pang, had the leaves of the trees whispered the dark story among themselves,—had the summer breeze murmured about it,—had the wintry blast shrieked it aloud! Another peculiar torture was felt in the gaze of a new eye. When strangers looked curiously at the scarlet letter,—and none ever failed to do so,—they branded it afresh into Hester's soul; so that, oftentimes, she could scarcely refrain, yet always did refrain, from covering the symbol with her hand. But then, again, an accustomed eye had likewise its own anguish to inflict. Its cool stare of familiarity was intolerable. From first to last, in short, Hester Prynne had always this dreadful agony in feeling a human eye upon the token; the spot never grew callous; it seemed, on the contrary, to grow more sensitive with daily torture.

But sometimes, once in many days, or perchance in many months, she felt an eye—a human eye—upon the ignominious brand, that seemed to give a momentary relief, as if half of her agony were shared. The next instant, back it all rushed again, with still a deeper throb of pain; for, in that brief interval, she had sinned anew. Had Hester sinned alone?

Her imagination was somewhat affected, and, had she been of a softer moral and intellectual fibre, would have been still more so, by the strange and solitary anguish of her life. Walking to and fro, with those lonely footsteps, in the little world with which she was outwardly connected, it now and then appeared to Hester,—if altogether fancy, it was nevertheless too potent to be resisted,—she felt or fancied, then, that the scarlet letter had endowed her with a new sense. She shuddered to believe, yet could not help believing, that it gave her a sympathetic knowledge of the hidden sin in other hearts. She was terror-stricken by the revelations that were thus made. What were they? Could they be other than the insidious whispers of the bad angel,[82] who would fain have persuaded the struggling woman, as yet only half his victim, that the outward guise of purity was but a lie, and that, if truth were everywhere to be shown, a scarlet letter would blaze forth on many a bosom besides Hester Prynne's? Or, must she receive those intimations—so obscure, yet so distinct—as truth? In all her miserable experience, there was nothing else so awful and so loathsome as this sense. It perplexed, as well as shocked her, by the irreverent inopportuneness of the occasions that brought it into vivid action. Sometimes, the red infamy upon her breast would give a sympathetic throb, as she passed near a venerable minister or magistrate, the model of piety and justice, to whom that age of antique reverence looked up, as to a mortal man in fellowship with angels. "What evil thing is at hand?"

[82] Satan or Lucifer.

would Hester say to herself. Lifting her reluctant eyes, there would be nothing human within the scope of view, save the form of this earthly saint! Again, a mystic sisterhood would contumaciously assert itself, as she met the sanctified frown of some matron, who, according to the rumor of all tongues, had kept cold snow within her bosom throughout life. That unsunned snow in the matron's bosom, and the burning shame on Hester Prynne's,—what had the two in common? Or, once more, the electric thrill would give her warning,—"Behold, Hester, here is a companion!"—and, looking up, she would detect the eyes of a young maiden glancing at the scarlet letter, shyly and aside, and quickly averted, with a faint, chill crimson in her cheeks; as if her purity were somewhat sullied by that momentary glance. O Fiend, whose talisman was that fatal symbol, wouldst thou leave nothing, whether in youth or age, for this poor sinner to revere?—Such loss of faith is ever one of the saddest results of sin. Be it accepted as a proof that all was not corrupt in this poor victim of her own frailty, and man's hard law, that Hester Prynne yet struggled to believe that no fellow-mortal was guilty like herself.

The vulgar, who, in those dreary old times, were always contributing a grotesque horror to what interested their imaginations, had a story about the scarlet letter which we might readily work up into a terrific legend. They averred, that the symbol was not mere scarlet cloth, tinged in an earthly dye-pot, but was red-hot with infernal fire, and could be seen glowing all alight, whenever Hester Prynne walked abroad in the night-time. And we must needs say, it seared Hester's bosom so deeply, that perhaps there was more truth in the rumor than our modern incredulity may be inclined to admit.

VI: Pearl

We have as yet hardly spoken of the infant; that little creature, whose innocent life had sprung, by the inscrutable decree of Providence, a lovely and immortal flower, out of the rank luxuriance of a guilty passion. How strange it seemed to the sad woman, as she watched the growth, and the beauty that became every day more brilliant, and the intelligence that threw its quivering sunshine over the tiny features of this child! Her Pearl!—For so had Hester called her; not as a name expressive of her aspect, which had nothing of the calm, white, unimpassioned lustre that would be indicated by the comparison. But she named the infant "Pearl," as being of great price,[83]—purchased with all she had,—her mother's only treasure! How strange, indeed! Man had marked this woman's sin by a scarlet letter, which had such potent and disastrous efficacy that no human sympathy could reach her, save it were sinful like herself. God, as a direct consequence of the sin which man thus punished, had given her a lovely child, whose place was on that same dishonored bosom, to connect her parent for ever with the race and descent of mortals, and to be finally a blessed soul in heaven! Yet these thoughts affected Hester Prynne less with hope than apprehension. She knew that her deed had been evil; she could have no faith, therefore, that its result would be for good. Day after day, she looked fearfully into the child's

[83] Matthew 13:45–46: "The kingdom of heaven is like unto a merchant man seeking goodly pearls: Who, when he had found one pearl of great price, went out and sold all he had, and bought it."

expanding nature; ever dreading to detect some dark and wild peculiarity, that should correspond with the guiltiness to which she owed her being.

Certainly, there was no physical defect. By its perfect shape, its vigor, and its natural dexterity in the use of all its untried limbs, the infant was worthy to have been brought forth in Eden; worthy to have been left there, to be the plaything of the angels, after the world's first parents were driven out. The child had a native grace which does not invariably coexist with faultless beauty; its attire, however simple, always impressed the beholder as if it were the very garb that precisely became it best. But little Pearl was not clad in rustic weeds. Her mother, with a morbid purpose that may be better understood hereafter, had bought the richest tissues that could be procured, and allowed her imaginative faculty its full play in the arrangement and decoration of the dresses which the child wore, before the public eye. So magnificent was the small figure, when thus arrayed, and such was the splendor of Pearl's own proper beauty, shining through the gorgeous robes which might have extinguished a paler loveliness, that there was an absolute circle of radiance around her, on the darksome cottage-floor. And yet a russet gown, torn and soiled with the child's rude play, made a picture of her just as perfect. Pearl's aspect was imbued with a spell of infinite variety; in this one child there were many children, comprehending the full scope between the wild-flower prettiness of a peasant-baby, and the pomp, in little, of an infant princess. Throughout all, however, there was a trait of passion, a certain depth of hue, which she never lost; and if, in any of her changes, she had grown fainter or paler, she would have ceased to be herself;—it would have been no longer Pearl!

This outward mutability indicated, and did not more than fairly express, the various properties of her inner life. Her nature appeared to possess depth, too, as well as variety; but—or else Hester's fears deceived her—it lacked reference and adaptation to the world into which she was born. The child could not be made amenable to rules. In giving her existence, a great law had been broken; and the result was a being, whose elements were perhaps beautiful and brilliant, but all in disorder; or with an order peculiar to themselves, amidst which the point of variety and arrangement was difficult or impossible to be discovered. Hester could only account for the child's character—and even then, most vaguely and imperfectly—by recalling what she herself had been, during that momentous period while Pearl was imbibing her soul from the spiritual world, and her bodily frame from its material of earth. The mother's impassioned state had been the medium through which were transmitted to the unborn infant the rays of its moral life; and, however white and clear originally, they had taken the deep stains of crimson and gold, the fiery lustre, the black shadow, and the untempered light, of the intervening substance. Above all, the warfare of Hester's spirit, at that epoch, was perpetuated in Pearl. She could recognize her wild, desperate, defiant mood, the flightiness of her temper, and even some of the very cloud-shapes of gloom and despondency that had brooded in her heart. They were now illuminated by the morning radiance of a young child's disposition, but, later in the day of earthly existence, might be prolific of the storm and whirlwind.

The discipline of the family, in those days, was of a far more rigid kind than now. The frown, the harsh rebuke, the frequent application of the rod, enjoined by Scriptural authority,[84] were used, not merely in the way of punishment for actual

---

[84] Proverbs 13:24: "He that spareth his rod hateth his son: but he that loveth him chasteneth him betimes."

offences, but as a wholesome regimen for the growth and promotion of all childish virtues. Hester Prynne, nevertheless, the lonely mother of this one child, ran little risk of erring on the side of undue severity. Mindful, however, of her own errors and misfortunes, she early sought to impose a tender, but strict, control over the infant immortality that was committed to her charge. But the task was beyond her skill. After testing both smiles and frowns, and proving that neither mode of treatment possessed any calculable influence, Hester was ultimately compelled to stand aside, and permit the child to be swayed by her own impulses. Physical compulsion or restraint was effectual, of course, while it lasted. As to any other kind of discipline, whether addressed to her mind or heart, little Pearl might or might not be within its reach, in accordance with the caprice that ruled the moment. Her mother, while Pearl was yet an infant, grew acquainted with a certain peculiar look, that warned her when it would be labor thrown away to insist, persuade, or plead. It was a look so intelligent, yet inexplicable, so perverse, sometimes so malicious, but generally accompanied by a wild flow of spirits, that Hester could not help questioning, at such moments, whether Pearl was a human child. She seemed rather an airy sprite, which, after playing its fantastic sports for a little while upon the cottage-floor, would flit away with a mocking smile. Whenever that look appeared in her wild, bright, deeply black eyes, it invested her with a strange remoteness and intangibility; it was as if she were hovering in the air and might vanish, like a glimmering light that comes we know not whence, and goes we know not whither. Beholding it, Hester was constrained to rush towards the child,—to pursue the little elf in the flight which she invariably began,—to snatch her to her bosom, with a close pressure and earnest kisses,—not so much from overflowing love, as to assure herself that Pearl was flesh and blood, and not utterly delusive. But Pearl's laugh, when she was caught, though full of merriment and music, made her mother more doubtful than before.

Heart-smitten at this bewildering and baffling spell, that so often came between herself and her sole treasure, whom she had bought so dear, and who was all her world, Hester sometimes burst into passionate tears. Then, perhaps,—for there was no foreseeing how it might affect her,—Pearl would frown, and clench her little fist, and harden her small features into a stern, unsympathizing look of discontent. Not seldom, she would laugh anew, and louder than before, like a thing incapable and unintelligent of human sorrow. Or—but this more rarely happened—she would be convulsed with a rage of grief, and sob out her love for her mother, in broken words, and seem intent on proving that she had a heart, by breaking it. Yet Hester was hardly safe in confiding herself to that gusty tenderness; it passed, as suddenly as it came. Brooding over all these matters, the mother felt like one who has evoked a spirit, but, by some irregularity in the process of conjuration, has failed to win the master-word that should control this new and incomprehensible intelligence. Her only real comfort was when the child lay in the placidity of sleep. Then she was sure of her, and tasted hours of quiet, sad, delicious happiness; until—perhaps with that perverse expression glimmering from beneath her opening lids—little Pearl awoke!

How soon—with what strange rapidity, indeed!—did Pearl arrive at an age that was capable of social intercourse, beyond the mother's ever-ready smile and nonsense-words! And then what a happiness would it have been, could Hester Prynne have heard her clear, bird-like voice mingling with the uproar of other childish voices, and have distinguished and unravelled her own darling's tones, amid all the entangled outcry of a group of sportive children! But this could never be. Pearl was a born outcast of the infantile world. An imp of evil, emblem and product of sin, she had no right among christened infants. Nothing was more remarkable than the instinct, as it seemed, with which the child comprehended her loneliness; the destiny that had drawn an inviolable circle round about her; the whole peculiarity, in short, of her position in respect to other children. Never, since her release from prison, had Hester met the public gaze without her. In all her walks about the town, Pearl, too, was there; first as the babe in arms, and afterwards as the little girl, small companion of her mother, holding a forefinger with her whole grasp, and tripping along at the rate of three or four footsteps to one of Hester's. She saw the children of the settlement, on the grassy margin of the street, or at the domestic thresholds, disporting themselves in such grim fashion as the Puritanic nurture would permit; playing at going to church, perchance; or at scourging Quakers; or taking scalps in a sham-fight with the Indians; or scaring one another with freaks of imitative witchcraft. Pearl saw, and gazed intently, but never sought to make acquaintance. If spoken to, she would not speak again. If the children gathered about her, as they sometimes did, Pearl would grow positively terrible in her puny wrath, snatching up stones to fling at them, with shrill, incoherent exclamations that made her mother tremble, because they had so much the sound of a witch's anathemas in some unknown tongue.

The truth was, that the little Puritans, being of the most intolerant brood that ever lived, had got a vague idea of something outlandish, unearthly, or at variance with ordinary fashions, in the mother and child; and therefore scorned them in their hearts, and not unfrequently reviled them with their tongues. Pearl felt the sentiment, and requited it with the bitterest hatred that can be supposed to rankle in a childish bosom. These outbreaks of a fierce temper had a kind of value, and even comfort, for her mother; because there was at least an intelligible earnestness in the mood, instead of the fitful caprice that so often thwarted her in the child's manifestations. It appalled her, nevertheless, to discern here, again, a shadowy reflection of the evil that had existed in herself. All this enmity and passion had Pearl inherited, by inalienable right, out of Hester's heart. Mother and daughter stood together in the same circle of seclusion from human society; and in the nature of the child seemed to be perpetuated those unquiet elements that had distracted Hester Prynne before Pearl's birth, but had since begun to be soothed away by the softening influences of maternity.

At home, within and around her mother's cottage, Pearl wanted not a wide and various circle of acquaintance. The spell of life went forth from her ever creative spirit, and communicated itself to a thousand objects, as a torch kindles a flame wherever it may be applied. The unlikeliest materials, a stick, a bunch of rags, a flower, were the puppets of Pearl's witchcraft, and, without undergoing any outward change, became spiritually adapted to whatever drama occupied the stage of her inner world. Her one baby-voice served a multitude of imaginary personages, old and young, to talk withal. The pine-trees, aged, black, and solemn, and flinging groans and other melancholy utterances on the breeze, needed little transformation to figure as Puritan elders; the ugliest weeds of the garden were their children, whom Pearl smote down and uprooted, most unmercifully. It was wonderful, the vast variety of forms into which she threw her intellect, with no continuity, indeed, but darting up and dancing, always in a state of preternatural activity,—soon sinking down, as if exhausted by so rapid and feverish a tide of life,—and succeeded by other shapes of a similar wild energy. It was like nothing so much as the phantasmagoric play of the northern lights. In the mere exercise of the fancy, however, and the sportiveness of a growing mind, there might be little more than was observable in other children of bright faculties; except as Pearl, in the dearth of human playmates, was thrown more upon the visionary throng which she created. The singularity lay in the hostile feelings with which the child regarded all these offspring of her own heart and mind. She never created a friend, but seemed always to be sowing broadcast the dragon's teeth,[85] whence sprung a harvest of armed enemies, against whom she rushed to battle. It was inexpressibly sad—then what depth of sorrow to a mother, who felt in her own heart the cause!—to observe, in one so young, this constant recognition of an adverse world, and so fierce a training of the energies that were to make good her cause, in the contest that must ensue.

Gazing at Pearl, Hester Prynne often dropped her work upon her knees, and cried out, with an agony which she would fain have hidden, but which made utterance for itself, betwixt speech and a groan,—"O Father in Heaven,—if Thou art still my Father,—what is this being which I have brought into the world!" And Pearl, overhearing the ejaculation, or aware, through some more subtile channel, of those throbs of anguish, would turn her vivid and beautiful little face upon her mother, smile with sprite-like intelligence, and resume her play.

One peculiarity of the child's deportment remains yet to be told. The very first thing which she had noticed, in her life, was—what?—not the mother's smile, responding to it, as other babies do, by that faint, embryo smile of the little mouth, remembered so doubtfully afterwards, and with such fond discussion whether it were indeed a smile. By no means! But that first object of which Pearl seemed to become aware was—shall we say it?—the scarlet letter on Hester's bosom! One day, as her mother stooped over the cradle, the infant's eyes had been caught by the glimmering of the gold embroidery about the letter; and, putting up her little hand, she grasped at it, smiling, not doubtfully, but with a decided gleam that gave her face the look of a much older child. Then, gasping for breath, did Hester Prynne clutch the fatal token, instinctively endeavouring to tear it away; so infinite was the torture inflicted by the intelligent touch of Pearl's baby-hand. Again, as if her mother's agonized gesture were meant only to make sport for her, did little Pearl look into her eyes, and smile! From that epoch, except when the child was asleep, Hester had never felt a moment's safety; not a moment's calm enjoyment of her. Weeks, it is true, would sometimes elapse, during which Pearl's gaze might never once be fixed upon the scarlet letter; but then, again, it would come at unawares, like the stroke of sudden death, and always with that peculiar smile, and odd expression of the eyes.

Once, this freakish, elfish cast came into the child's eyes, while Hester was looking at her own image in them, as mothers are fond of doing; and, suddenly,—for women in solitude, and with troubled hearts, are pestered with unaccountable delusions,— she fancied that she beheld, not her own miniature portrait, but another face in the small black mirror of Pearl's eye. It was a face, fiend-like, full of smiling malice, yet bearing the semblance of features that she had known full well, though seldom with

---

[85] In Greek mythology, Cadmus slew a dragon and planted its teeth, which sprouted into an army.

a smile, and never with malice, in them. It was as if an evil spirit possessed the child, and had just then peeped forth in mockery. Many a time afterwards had Hester been tortured, though less vividly, by the same illusion.

In the afternoon of a certain summer's day, after Pearl grew big enough to run about, she amused herself with gathering handfuls of wild-flowers, and flinging them, one by one, at her mother's bosom; dancing up and down, like a little elf, whenever she hit the scarlet letter. Hester's first motion had been to cover her bosom with her clasped hands. But, whether from pride or resignation, or a feeling that her penance might best be wrought out by this unutterable pain, she resisted the impulse, and sat erect, pale as death, looking sadly into little Pearl's wild eyes. Still came the battery of flowers, almost invariably hitting the mark, and covering the mother's breast with hurts for which she could find no balm in this world, nor knew how to seek it in another. At last, her shot being all expended, the child stood still and gazed at Hester, with that little, laughing image of a fiend peeping out—or, whether it peeped or no, her mother so imagined it—from the unsearchable abyss of her black eyes.

"Child, what art thou?" cried the mother.

"O, I am your little Pearl!" answered the child.

But, while she said it, Pearl laughed and began to dance up and down, with the humorsome gesticulation of a little imp, whose next freak[86] might be to fly up the chimney.

"Art thou my child, in very truth?" asked Hester.

Nor did she put the question altogether idly, but, for the moment, with a portion of genuine earnestness; for, such was Pearl's wonderful intelligence, that her mother half doubted whether she were not acquainted with the secret spell of her existence, and might not now reveal herself.

"Yes; I am little Pearl!" repeated the child, continuing her antics.

"Thou art not my child! Thou art no Pearl of mine!" said the mother, half playfully; for it was often the case that a sportive impulse came over her, in the midst of her deepest suffering. "Tell me, then, what thou art, and who sent thee hither?"

"Tell me, mother!" said the child, seriously, coming up to Hester, and pressing herself close to her knees. "Do thou tell me!"

"Thy Heavenly Father sent thee!" answered Hester Prynne.

But she said it with a hesitation that did not escape the acuteness of the child. Whether moved only by her ordinary freakishness, or because an evil spirit prompted her, she put up her small forefinger, and touched the scarlet letter.

"He did not send me!" cried she, positively. "I have no Heavenly Father!"

"Hush, Pearl, hush! Thou must not talk so!" answered the mother, suppressing a groan. "He sent us all into this world. He sent even me, thy mother. Then, much more, thee! Or, if not, thou strange and elfish child, whence didst thou come?"

"Tell me! Tell me!" repeated Pearl, no longer seriously, but laughing, and capering about the floor. "It is thou that must tell me!"

But Hester could not resolve the query, being herself in a dismal labyrinth of doubt.

---

[86] Prank.

She remembered—betwixt a smile and a shudder—the talk of the neighbouring townspeople; who, seeking vainly elsewhere for the child's paternity, and observing some of her odd attributes, had given out that poor little Pearl was a demon offspring; such as, ever since old Catholic times,[87] had occasionally been seen on earth, through the agency of their mothers' sin, and to promote some foul and wicked purpose. Luther,[88] according to the scandal of his monkish enemies, was a brat of that hellish breed; nor was Pearl the only child to whom this inauspicious origin was assigned, among the New England Puritans.

VII: The Governor's Hall

Hester Prynne went, one day, to the mansion of Governor Bellingham, with a pair of gloves, which she had fringed and embroidered to his order, and which were to be worn on some great occasion of state; for, though the chances of a popular election had caused this former ruler to descend a step or two from the highest rank, he still held an honorable and influential place among the colonial magistracy.[89]

Another and far more important reason than the delivery of a pair of embroidered gloves impelled Hester, at this time, to seek an interview with a personage of so much power and activity in the affairs of the settlement. It had reached her ears, that there was a design on the part of some of the leading inhabitants, cherishing the more rigid order of principles in religion and government, to deprive her of her child. On the supposition that Pearl, as already hinted, was of demon origin, these good people not unreasonably argued that a Christian interest in the mother's soul required them to remove such a stumbling-block from her path. If the child, on the other hand, were really capable of moral and religious growth, and possessed the elements of ultimate salvation, then, surely, it would enjoy all the fairer prospect of these advantages by being transferred to wiser and better guardianship than Hester Prynne's. Among those who promoted the design, Governor Bellingham was said to be one of the most busy. It may appear singular, and, indeed, not a little ludicrous, that an affair of this kind, which, in later days, would have been referred to no higher jurisdiction than that of the selectmen of the town, should then have been a question publicly discussed, and on which statesmen of eminence took sides. At that epoch of pristine simplicity, however, matters of even slighter public interest, and of far less intrinsic weight than the welfare of Hester and her child, were strangely mixed up with the deliberations of legislators and acts of state. The period was hardly, if at all, earlier than that of our story, when a dispute concerning the right of property in a pig, not only caused a fierce and bitter contest in the legislative body of the colony, but resulted in an important modification of the framework itself of the legislature.[90]

Full of concern, therefore,—but so conscious of her own right, that it seemed scarcely an unequal match between the public, on the one side, and a lonely woman,

---

[87] I.e., before the Reformation of the Church of England in the sixteenth century.

[88] Martin Luther (1483–1546), German Protestant reformer.

[89] Bellingham became a magistrate in 1642, after having completed his first term as governor.

[90] *Sherman* v. *Keayne* (1642–1643), called "the Sow Case," led to the division of the Massachusetts legislature into two houses.

backed by the sympathies of nature, on the other,—Hester Prynne set forth from her solitary cottage. Little Pearl, of course, was her companion. She was now of an age to run lightly along by her mother's side, and, constantly in motion from morn till sunset, could have accomplished a much longer journey than that before her. Often, nevertheless, more from caprice than necessity, she demanded to be taken up in arms, but was soon as imperious to be set down again, and frisked onward before Hester on the grassy pathway, with many a harmless trip and tumble. We have spoken of Pearl's rich and luxuriant beauty; a beauty that shone with deep and vivid tints; a bright complexion, eyes possessing intensity both of depth and glow, and hair already of a deep, glossy brown, and which, in after years, would be nearly akin to black. There was fire in her and throughout her; she seemed the unpremeditated offshoot of a passionate moment. Her mother, in contriving the child's garb, had allowed the gorgeous tendencies of her imagination their full play; arraying her in a crimson velvet tunic, of a peculiar cut, abundantly embroidered with fantasies and flourishes of gold thread. So much strength of coloring, which must have given a wan and pallid aspect to cheeks of a fainter bloom, was admirably adapted to Pearl's beauty, and made her the very brightest little jet of flame that ever danced upon the earth.

But it was a remarkable attribute of this garb, and, indeed, of the child's whole appearance, that it irresistibly and inevitably reminded the beholder of the token which Hester Prynne was doomed to wear upon her bosom. It was the scarlet letter in another form; the scarlet letter endowed with life! The mother herself—as if the red ignominy were so deeply scorched into her brain, that all her conceptions assumed its form—had carefully wrought out the similitude; lavishing many hours of morbid ingenuity, to create an analogy between the object of her affection, and the emblem of her guilt and torture. But, in truth, Pearl was the one, as well as the other; and only in consequence of that identity had Hester contrived so perfectly to represent the scarlet letter in her appearance.

As the two wayfarers came within the precincts of the town, the children of the Puritans looked up from their play,—or what passed for play with those sombre little urchins,—and spake gravely one to another:—

"Behold, verily, there is the woman of the scarlet letter; and, of a truth, moreover, there is the likeness of the scarlet letter running along by her side! Come, therefore, and let us fling mud at them!"

But Pearl, who was a dauntless child, after frowning, stamping her foot, and shaking her little hand with a variety of threatening gestures, suddenly made a rush at the knot of her enemies, and put them all to flight. She resembled, in her fierce pursuit of them, an infant pestilence,—the scarlet fever, or some such half-fledged angel of judgment,—whose mission was to punish the sins of the rising generation. She screamed and shouted, too, with a terrific volume of sound, which doubtless caused the hearts of the fugitives to quake within them. The victory accomplished, Pearl returned quietly to her mother, and looked up smiling into her face.

Without further adventure, they reached the dwelling of Governor Bellingham. This was a large wooden house, built in a fashion of which there are specimens still extant in the streets of our elder towns; now moss-grown, crumbling to decay, and melancholy at heart with the many sorrowful or joyful occurrences, remembered or forgotten, that have happened, and passed away, within their dusky chambers. Then, however, there was the freshness of the passing year on its exterior, and the cheerfulness, gleaming forth from the sunny windows, of a human habitation into which death had never entered. It had indeed a very cheery aspect; the walls being overspread with a kind of stucco, in which fragments of broken glass were plentifully intermixed; so that, when the sunshine fell aslant-wise over the front of the edifice, it glittered and sparkled as if diamonds had been flung against it by the double handful. The brilliancy might have befitted Aladdin's[91] palace, rather than the mansion of a grave old Puritan ruler. It was further decorated with strange and seemingly cabalistic[92] figures and diagrams, suitable to the quaint taste of the age, which had been drawn in the stucco when newly laid on, and had now grown hard and durable, for the admiration of after times.

Pearl, looking at this bright wonder of a house, began to caper and dance, and imperatively required that the whole breadth of sunshine should be stripped off its front, and given her to play with.

"No, my little Pearl!" said her mother. "Thou must gather thine own sunshine. I have none to give thee!"

They approached the door; which was of an arched form, and flanked on each side by a narrow tower or projection of the edifice, in both of which were lattice-windows, with wooden shutters to close over them at need. Lifting the iron hammer that hung at the portal, Hester Prynne gave a summons, which was answered by one of the Governor's bond-servants; a free-born Englishman, but now a seven years' slave. During that term he was to be the property of his master, and as much a commodity of bargain and sale as an ox, or a joint-stool. The serf wore the blue coat, which was the customary garb of serving-men at that period, and long before, in the old hereditary halls of England.

"Is the worshipful Governor Bellingham within?" inquired Hester.

"Yea, forsooth," replied the bond-servant, staring with wide-open eyes at the scarlet letter, which, being a new-comer in the country, he had never before seen. "Yea, his honorable worship is within. But he hath a godly minister or two with him, and likewise a leech. Ye may not see his worship now."

"Nevertheless, I will enter," answered Hester Prynne; and the bond-servant, perhaps judging from the decision of her air and the glittering symbol in her bosom, that she was a great lady in the land, offered no opposition.

So the mother and little Pearl were admitted into the hall of entrance. With many variations, suggested by the nature of his building-materials, diversity of climate, and a different mode of social life, Governor Bellingham had planned his new habitation after the residences of gentlemen of fair estate in his native land. Here, then, was a wide and reasonably lofty hall, extending through the whole depth of the house, and forming a medium of general communication, more or less directly, with all the other apartments. At one extremity, this spacious room was lighted by the windows of the two towers, which formed a small recess on either side of the portal. At the other end, though partly muffled by a curtain, it was more powerfully illuminated by one of those embowed hall-windows which we read of in old books, and which was provided with a deep and cushioned seat. Here, on the cushion, lay a folio tome, probably of the Chronicles of England,[93] or other such substantial literature; even as, in our own days, we scatter gilded volumes on the centre-table, to be turned over

---

[91] Aladdin: character in *The Arabian Nights* who finds a magic ring and lamp.
[92] Occult.

[93] *Chronicles of England, Scotland, and Ireland* (1577) by Raphael Holinshed.

by the casual guest. The furniture of the hall consisted of some ponderous chairs, the backs of which were elaborately carved with wreaths of oaken flowers; and likewise a table in the same taste; the whole being of the Elizabethan age, or perhaps earlier, and heirlooms, transferred hither from the Governor's paternal home. On the table —in token that the sentiment of old English hospitality had not been left behind— stood a large pewter tankard, at the bottom of which, had Hester or Pearl peeped into it, they might have seen the frothy remnant of a recent draught of ale.

On the wall hung a row of portraits, representing the forefathers of the Bellingham lineage, some with armour on their breasts, and others with stately ruffs and robes of peace. All were characterized by the sternness and severity which old portraits so invariably put on; as if they were the ghosts, rather than the pictures, of departed worthies, and were gazing with harsh and intolerant criticism at the pursuits and enjoyments of living men.

At about the centre of the oaken panels, that lined the hall, was suspended a suit of mail, not, like the pictures, an ancestral relic, but of the most modern date; for it had been manufactured by a skilful armorer in London, the same year in which Governor Bellingham came over to New England. There was a steel head-piece, a cuirass, a gorget, and greaves,[94] with a pair of gauntlets and a sword hanging beneath; all, and especially the helmet and breastplate, so highly burnished as to glow with white radiance, and scatter an illumination everywhere about upon the floor. This bright panoply was not meant for mere idle show, but had been worn by the Governor on many a solemn muster and training field, and had glittered, moreover, at the head of a regiment in the Pequod war.[95] For, though bred a lawyer, and accustomed to speak of Bacon, Coke, Noye, and Finch,[96] as his professional associates, the exigencies of this new country had transformed Governor Bellingham into a soldier, as well as a statesman and ruler.

Little Pearl—who was as greatly pleased with the gleaming armour as she had been with the glittering frontispiece of the house—spent some time looking into the polished mirror of the breastplate.

"Mother," cried she, "I see you here. Look! Look!"

Hester looked, by way of humoring the child; and she saw that, owing to the peculiar effect of this convex mirror, the scarlet letter was represented in exaggerated and gigantic proportions, so as to be greatly the most prominent feature of her appearance. In truth, she seemed absolutely hidden behind it. Pearl pointed upward, also, at a similar picture in the headpiece; smiling at her mother, with the elfish intelligence that was so familiar an expression on her small physiognomy. That look of naughty merriment was likewise reflected in the mirror, with so much breadth and intensity of effect, that it made Hester Prynne feel as if it could not be the image of her own child, but of an imp who was seeking to mould itself into Pearl's shape.

"Come along, Pearl!" said she, drawing her away. "Come and look into this fair garden. It may be, we shall see flowers there; more beautiful ones than we find in the woods."

---

[94] Cuirass: chest armor; gorget: neck armor; greaves: shin armor.

[95] The Pequots, an Indian tribe who controlled eastern Connecticut, were virtually destroyed by the English in 1637.

[96] Sir Francis Bacon (1561–1626), Sir Edward Coke (1552–1634), William Noye (1577–1634), and Sir John Finch (1584–1660) were all English barristers.

Pearl, accordingly, ran to the bow-window, at the farther end of the hall, and looked along the vista of a garden-walk, carpeted with closely shaven grass, and bordered with some rude and immature attempt at shrubbery. But the proprietor appeared already to have relinquished, as hopeless, the effort to perpetuate on this side of the Atlantic, in a hard soil and amid the close struggle for subsistence, the native English taste for ornamental gardening. Cabbages grew in plain sight; and a pumpkin vine, rooted at some distance, had run across the intervening space, and deposited one of its gigantic products directly beneath the hall-window; as if to warn the Governor that this great lump of vegetable gold was as rich an ornament as New England earth would offer him. There were a few rose-bushes, however, and a number of apple-trees, probably the descendants of those planted by the Reverend Mr. Blackstone,[97] the first settler of the peninsula; that half mythological personage who rides through our early annals, seated on the back of a bull.

Pearl, seeing the rose-bushes, began to cry for a red rose, and would not be pacified.

"Hush, child, hush!" said her mother earnestly. "Do not cry, dear little Pearl! I hear voices in the garden. The Governor is coming, and gentlemen along with him!"

In fact, adown the vista of the garden-avenue, a number of persons were seen approaching towards the house. Pearl, in utter scorn of her mother's attempt to quiet her, gave an eldritch[98] scream, and then became silent; not from any notion of obedience, but because the quick and mobile curiosity of her disposition was excited by the appearance of these new personages.

VIII: The Elf-Child and the Minister

Governor Bellingham, in a loose gown and easy cap,—such as elderly gentlemen loved to indue themselves with, in their domestic privacy,—walked foremost, and appeared to be showing off his estate, and expatiating on his projected improvements. The wide circumference of an elaborate ruff, beneath his gray beard, in the antiquated fashion of King James's reign,[99] caused his head to look not a little like that of John the Baptist in a charger.[100] The impression made by his aspect, so rigid and severe, and frost-bitten with more than autumnal age, was hardly in keeping with the appliances of worldly enjoyment wherewith he had evidently done his utmost to surround himself. But it is an error to suppose that our grave forefathers—though accustomed to speak and think of human existence as a state merely of trial and warfare, and though unfeignedly prepared to sacrifice goods and life at the behest of duty—made it a matter of conscience to reject such means of comfort, or even luxury, as lay fairly within their grasp. This creed was never taught, for instance, by the venerable pastor, John Wilson, whose beard, white as a snow-drift, was seen over Governor Belling-ham's shoulder; while its wearer suggested that pears and peaches might yet be naturalized in the New England climate, and that purple grapes might possibly be compelled to flourish, against the sunny garden-wall. The old clergyman, nurtured at the rich bosom of the English Church, had a long established and legitimate taste

---

[97] After the arrival of the Puritans in 1630, and in the face of disputes with them, William Blackstone, Boston's Anglican minister, left the colony to join Indian settlements in Rhode Island.

[98] Uncanny or strange.

[99] James I (1566–1625) was king of England from 1603 to 1625.

[100] Platter. (See Matthew 14:6–11.)

for all good and comfortable things; and however stern he might show himself in the pulpit, or in his public reproof of such transgressions as that of Hester Prynne, still, the genial benevolence of his private life had won him warmer affection than was accorded to any of his professional contemporaries.

Behind the Governor and Mr. Wilson came two other guests; one, the Reverend Arthur Dimmesdale, whom the reader may remember, as having taken a brief and reluctant part in the scene of Hester Prynne's disgrace; and, in close companionship with him, old Roger Chillingworth, a person of great skill in physic, who, for two or three years past, had been settled in the town. It was understood that this learned man was the physician as well as friend of the young minister, whose health had severely suffered, of late, by his too unreserved self-sacrifice to the labors and duties of the pastoral relation.

The Governor, in advance of his visitors, ascended one or two steps, and throwing open the leaves of the great hall window, found himself close to little Pearl. The shadow of the curtain fell on Hester Prynne, and partially concealed her.

"What have we here?" said Governor Bellingham, looking with surprise at the scarlet little figure before him. "I profess, I have never seen the like, since my days of vanity, in old King James's time, when I was wont to esteem it a high favor to be admitted to a court mask! There used to be a swarm of these small apparitions, in holiday-time; and we called them children of the Lord of Misrule.[101] But how gat such a guest into my hall?"

"Ay, indeed!" cried good old Mr. Wilson. "What little bird of scarlet plumage may this be? Methinks I have seen just such figures, when the sun has been shining through a richly painted window, and tracing out the golden and crimson images across the floor. But that was in the old land. Prithee, young one, who art thou, and what has ailed thy mother to bedizen thee in this strange fashion? Art thou a Christian child,—ha? Dost know thy catechism? Or art thou one of those naughty elfs or fairies, whom we thought to have left behind us, with other relics of Papistry, in merry old England?"

"I am mother's child," answered the scarlet vision, "and my name is Pearl!"

"Pearl?—Ruby, rather!—or Coral!—or Red Rose, at the very least, judging from thy hue!" responded the old minister, putting forth his hand in a vain attempt to pat little Pearl on the cheek. "But where is this mother of thine? Ah! I see," he added; and, turning to Governor Bellingham, whispered,—"This is the selfsame child of whom we have held speech together; and behold here the unhappy woman, Hester Prynne, her mother!"

"Sayest thou so?" cried the Governor. "Nay, we might have judged that such a child's mother must needs be a scarlet woman, and a worthy type of her of Babylon![102] But she comes at a good time; and we will look into this matter forthwith."

Governor Bellingham stepped through the window into the hall, followed by his three guests.

"Hester Prynne," said he, fixing his naturally stern regard on the wearer of the

---

[101] Traditional figure who was leader of the Christmas celebrations in England before the rise of the Puritans.

[102] Biblical reference to the "scarlet woman" of Babylon. (See Revelations 17:3–5.)

scarlet letter, "there hath been much question concerning thee, of late. The point hath been weightily discussed, whether we, that are of authority and influence, do well discharge our consciences by trusting an immortal soul, such as there is in yonder child, to the guidance of one who hath stumbled and fallen, amid the pitfalls of this world. Speak thou, the child's own mother! Were it not, thinkest thou, for thy little one's temporal and eternal welfare, that she be taken out of thy charge, and clad soberly, and disciplined strictly, and instructed in the truths of heaven and earth? What canst thou do for the child, in this kind?"

"I can teach my little Pearl what I have learned from this!" answered Hester Prynne, laying her finger on the red token.

"Woman, it is thy badge of shame!" replied the stern magistrate. "It is because of the stain which that letter indicates, that we would transfer thy child to other hands."

"Nevertheless," said the mother calmly, though growing more pale, "this badge hath taught me,—it daily teaches me,—it is teaching me at this moment,—lessons whereof my child may be the wiser and better, albeit they can profit nothing to myself."

"We will judge warily," said Bellingham, "and look well what we are about to do. Good Master Wilson, I pray you, examine this Pearl,—since that is her name,—and see whether she hath had such Christian nurture as befits a child of her age."

The old minister seated himself in an arm-chair, and made an effort to draw Pearl betwixt his knees. But the child, unaccustomed to the touch or familiarity of any but her mother, escaped through the open window and stood on the upper step, looking like a wild, tropical bird, of rich plumage, ready to take flight into the upper air. Mr. Wilson, not a little astonished at this outbreak,—for he was a grandfatherly sort of personage, and usually a vast favorite with children,—essayed, however, to proceed with the examination.

"Pearl," said he, with great solemnity, "thou must take heed to instruction, that so, in due season, thou mayest wear in thy bosom the pearl of great price.[103] Canst thou tell me, my child, who made thee?"

Now Pearl knew well enough who made her; for Hester Prynne, the daughter of a pious home, very soon after her talk with the child about her Heavenly Father, had begun to inform her of those truths which the human spirit, at whatever stage of immaturity, imbibes with such eager interest. Pearl, therefore, so large were the attainments of her three years' lifetime, could have borne a fair examination in the New England Primer,[104] or the first column of the Westminster Catechism,[105] although unacquainted with the outward form of either of those celebrated works. But that perversity, which all children have more or less of, and of which little Pearl had a tenfold portion, now, at the most inopportune moment, took thorough possession of her, and closed her lips, or impelled her to speak words amiss. After putting her finger in her mouth, with many ungracious refusals to answer good Mr. Wilson's question, the child finally announced that she had not been made at all, but had been plucked by her mother off the bush of wild roses, that grew by the prison-door.

[103] The "pearl of great price" is associated with godliness in Matthew 13:46.
[104] Highly moralistic school text used in colonial New England.
[105] Catechism drafted by the Westminster Assembly (1645–1647) and used to teach Christian principles.

This fantasy was probably suggested by the near proximity of the Governor's red roses, as Pearl stood outside of the window; together with her recollection of the prison rose-bush, which she had passed in coming hither.

Old Roger Chillingworth, with a smile on his face, whispered something in the young clergyman's ear. Hester Prynne looked at the man of skill, and even then, with her fate hanging in the balance, was startled to perceive what a change had come over his features,—how much uglier they were,—how his dark complexion seemed to have grown duskier, and his figure more misshapen,—since the days when she had familiarly known him. She met his eyes for an instant, but was immediately constrained to give all her attention to the scene now going forward.

"This is awful!" cried the Governor, slowly recovering from the astonishment into which Pearl's response had thrown him. "Here is a child of three years old, and she cannot tell who made her! Without question, she is equally in the dark as to her soul, its present depravity, and future destiny! Methinks, gentlemen, we need inquire no further."

Hester caught hold of Pearl, and drew her forcibly into her arms, confronting the old Puritan magistrate with almost a fierce expression. Alone in the world, cast off by it, and with this sole treasure to keep her heart alive, she felt that she possessed indefeasible rights against the world, and was ready to defend them to the death.

"God gave me the child!" cried she. "He gave her, in requital of all things else, which ye had taken from me. She is my happiness!—she is my torture, none the less! Pearl keeps me here in life! Pearl punishes me too! See ye not, she is the scarlet letter, only capable of being loved, and so endowed with a million-fold the power of retribution for my sin? Ye shall not take her! I will die first!"

"My poor woman," said the not unkind old minister, "the child shall be well cared for!—far better than thou canst do it."

"God gave her into my keeping," repeated Hester Prynne, raising her voice almost to a shriek. "I will not give her up!"—And here, by a sudden impulse, she turned to the young clergyman, Mr. Dimmesdale, at whom, up to this moment, she had seemed hardly so much as once to direct her eyes.—"Speak thou for me!" cried she. "Thou wast my pastor, and hadst charge of my soul, and knowest me better than these men can. I will not lose the child! Speak for me! Thou knowest,—for thou hast sympathies which these men lack!—thou knowest what is in my heart, and what are a mother's rights, and how much the stronger they are, when that mother has but her child and the scarlet letter! Look thou to it! I will not lose the child! Look to it!"

At this wild and singular appeal, which indicated that Hester Prynne's situation had provoked her to little less than madness, the young minister at once came forward, pale, and holding his hand over his heart, as was his custom whenever his peculiarly nervous temperament was thrown into agitation. He looked now more careworn and emaciated than as we described him at the scene of Hester's public ignominy; and whether it were his failing health, or whatever the cause might be, his large dark eyes had a world of pain in their troubled and melancholy depth.

"There is truth in what she says," began the minister, with a voice sweet, tremulous, but powerful, insomuch that the hall reëchoed, and the hollow armour rang with it, —"truth in what Hester says, and in the feeling which inspires her! God gave her the child, and gave her, too, an instinctive knowledge of its nature and requirements, —both seemingly so peculiar,—which no other mortal being can possess. And, moreover, is there not a quality of awful sacredness in the relation between this mother and this child?"

"Ay!—how is that, good Master Dimmesdale?" interrupted the Governor. "Make that plain, I pray you!"

"It must be even so," resumed the minister. "For, if we deem it otherwise, do we not thereby say that the Heavenly Father, the Creator of all flesh, hath lightly recognized a deed of sin, and made of no account the distinction between unhallowed lust and holy love? This child of its father's guilt and its mother's shame hath come from the hand of God, to work in many ways upon her heart, who pleads so earnestly, and with such bitterness of spirit, the right to keep her. It was meant for a blessing; for the one blessing of her life! It was meant, doubtless, as the mother herself hath told us, for a retribution too; a torture, to be felt at many an unthought of moment; a pang, a sting, an ever-recurring agony, in the midst of a troubled joy! Hath she not expressed this thought in the garb of the poor child, so forcibly reminding us of that red symbol which sears her bosom?"

"Well said, again!" cried good Mr. Wilson. "I feared the woman had no better thought than to make a mountebank of her child!"

"O, not so!—not so!" continued Mr. Dimmesdale. "She recognizes, believe me, the solemn miracle which God hath wrought, in the existence of that child. And may she feel, too,—what, methinks, is the very truth,—that this boon was meant, above all things else, to keep the mother's soul alive, and to preserve her from blacker depths of sin into which Satan might else have sought to plunge her! Therefore it is good for this poor, sinful woman that she hath an infant immortality, a being capable of eternal joy or sorrow, confided to her care,—to be trained up by her to righteousness, —to remind her, at every moment, of her fall,—but yet to teach her, as it were by the Creator's sacred pledge, that, if she bring the child to heaven, the child also will bring its parent thither! Herein is the sinful mother happier than the sinful father. For Hester Prynne's sake, then, and no less for the poor child's sake, let us leave them as Providence hath seen fit to place them!"

"You speak, my friend, with a strange earnestness," said old Roger Chillingworth, smiling at him.

"And there is weighty import in what my young brother hath spoken," added the Reverend Mr. Wilson. "What say you, worshipful Master Bellingham? Hath he not pleaded well for the poor woman?"

"Indeed hath he," answered the magistrate, "and hath adduced such arguments, that we will even leave the matter as it now stands; so long, at least, as there shall be no further scandal in the woman. Care must be had, nevertheless, to put the child to due and stated examination in the catechism at thy hands or Master Dimmesdale's. More-over, at a proper season, the tithing-men[106] must take heed that she go both to school and to meeting."

The young minister, on ceasing to speak, had withdrawn a few steps from the group, and stood with his face partially concealed in the heavy folds of the window-curtain; while the shadow of his figure, which the sunlight cast upon the floor, was tremulous with the vehemence of his appeal. Pearl, that wild and flighty little elf, stole softly towards him, and, taking his hand in the grasp of both her own, laid her cheek

---

[106] Parish law officers.

against it; a caress so tender, and withal so unobtrusive, that her mother, who was looking on, asked herself,—"Is that my Pearl?" Yet she knew that there was love in the child's heart, although it mostly revealed itself in passion, and hardly twice in her lifetime had been softened by such gentleness as now. The minister,—for, save the long-sought regards of woman, nothing is sweeter than these marks of childish preference, accorded spontaneously by a spiritual instinct, and therefore seeming to imply in us something truly worthy to be loved,—the minister looked round, laid his hand on the child's head, hesitated an instant, and then kissed her brow. Little Pearl's unwonted mood of sentiment lasted no longer; she laughed, and went capering down the hall, so airily, that old Mr. Wilson raised a question whether even her tiptoes touched the floor.

"The little baggage hath witchcraft in her, I profess," said he to Mr. Dimmesdale. "She needs no old woman's broomstick to fly withal!"

"A strange child!" remarked old Roger Chillingworth. "It is easy to see the mother's part in her. Would it be beyond a philosopher's research, think ye, gentlemen, to analyze that child's nature, and, from its make and mould, to give a shrewd guess at the father?"

"Nay; it would be sinful, in such a question, to follow the clew of profane philosophy," said Mr. Wilson. "Better to fast and pray upon it; and still better, it may be, to leave the mystery as we find it, unless Providence reveal it of its own accord. Thereby, every good Christian man hath a title to show a father's kindness towards the poor, deserted babe."

The affair being so satisfactorily concluded, Hester Prynne, with Pearl, departed from the house. As they descended the steps, it is averred that the lattice of a chamber-window was thrown open, and forth into the sunny day was thrust the face of Mistress Hibbins, Governor Bellingham's bitter-tempered sister, and the same who, a few years later, was executed as a witch.

"Hist, hist!" said she, while her ill-omened physiognomy seemed to cast a shadow over the cheerful newness of the house. "Wilt thou go with us to-night? There will be a merry company in the forest; and I wellnigh promised the Black Man that comely Hester Prynne should make one."

"Make my excuse to him, so please you!" answered Hester, with a triumphant smile. "I must tarry at home, and keep watch over my little Pearl. Had they taken her from me, I would willingly have gone with thee into the forest, and signed my name in the Black Man's book too, and that with mine own blood!"

"We shall have thee there anon!" said the witch-lady, frowning, as she drew back her head.

But here—if we suppose this interview betwixt Mistress Hibbins and Hester Prynne to be authentic, and not a parable—was already an illustration of the young minister's argument against sundering the relation of a fallen mother to the offspring of her frailty. Even thus early had the child saved her from Satan's snare.

IX: The Leech

Under the appellation of Roger Chillingworth, the reader will remember, was hidden another name, which its former wearer had resolved should never more be spoken. It has been related, how, in the crowd that witnessed Hester Prynne's ignominious exposure, stood a man, elderly, travel-worn, who, just emerging from the perilous wilderness, beheld the woman, in whom he hoped to find embodied the warmth and cheerfulness of home, set up as a type of sin before the people. Her matronly fame was trodden under all men's feet. Infamy was babbling around her in the public market-place. For her kindred, should the tidings ever reach them, and for the companions of her unspotted life, there remained nothing but the contagion of her dishonor; which would not fail to be distributed in strict accordance and proportion with the intimacy and sacredness of their previous relationship. Then why—since the choice was with himself—should the individual, whose connection with the fallen woman had been the most intimate and sacred of them all, come forward to vindicate his claim to an inheritance so little desirable? He resolved not to be pilloried beside her on her pedestal of shame. Unknown to all but Hester Prynne, and possessing the lock and key of her silence, he chose to withdraw his name from the roll of mankind, and, as regarded his former ties and interests, to vanish out of life as completely as if he indeed lay at the bottom of the ocean, whither rumor had long ago consigned him. This purpose once effected, new interests would immediately spring up, and likewise a new purpose; dark, it is true, if not guilty, but of force enough to engage the full strength of his faculties.

In pursuance of this resolve, he took up his residence in the Puritan town, as Roger Chillingworth, without other introduction than the learning and intelligence of which he possessed more than a common measure. As his studies, at a previous period of his life, had made him extensively acquainted with the medical science of the day, it was as a physician that he presented himself, and as such was cordially received. Skilful men, of the medical and chirurgical[107] profession, were of rare occurrence in the colony. They seldom, it would appear, partook of the religious zeal that brought other emigrants across the Atlantic. In their researches into the human frame, it may be that the higher and more subtile faculties of such men were materialized, and that they lost the spiritual view of existence amid the intricacies of that wondrous mechanism, which seemed to involve art enough to comprise all of life within itself. At all events, the health of the good town of Boston, so far as medicine had aught to do with it, had hitherto lain in the guardianship of an aged deacon and apothecary, whose piety and godly deportment were stronger testimonials in his favor, than any that he could have produced in the shape of a diploma. The only surgeon was one who combined the occasional exercise of that noble art with the daily and habitual flourish of a razor. To such a professional body Roger Chillingworth was a brilliant acquisition. He soon manifested his familiarity with the ponderous and imposing machinery of antique physic; in which every remedy contained a multitude of far-fetched and heterogeneous ingredients, as elaborately compounded as if the proposed result had been the Elixir of Life. In his Indian captivity, moreover, he had gained much knowledge of the properties of native herbs and roots; nor did he conceal from his patients, that these simple medicines, Nature's boon to the untutored savage, had quite as large a share of his own confidence as the European pharmacopœia,[108] which so many learned doctors had spent centuries in elaborating.

This learned stranger was exemplary, as regarded at least the outward forms of a religious life, and, early after his arrival, had chosen for his spiritual guide the

---

[107] Surgical.

[108] Manual of approved medicines and chemicals.

Reverend Mr. Dimmesdale. The young divine, whose scholar-like renown still lived in Oxford, was considered by his more fervent admirers as little less than a heaven-ordained apostle, destined, should he live and labor for the ordinary term of life, to do as great deeds for the now feeble New England Church, as the early Fathers had achieved for the infancy of the Christian faith. About this period, however, the health of Mr. Dimmesdale had evidently begun to fail. By those best acquainted with his habits, the paleness of the young minister's cheek was accounted for by his too earnest devotion to study, his scrupulous fulfilment of parochial duty, and, more than all, by the fasts and vigils of which he made a frequent practice, in order to keep the grossness of this earthly state from clogging and obscuring his spiritual lamp. Some declared, that, if Mr. Dimmesdale were really going to die, it was cause enough, that the world was not worthy to be any longer trodden by his feet. He himself, on the other hand, with characteristic humility, avowed his belief, that, if Providence should see fit to remove him, it would be because of his own unworthiness to perform its humblest mission here on earth. With all this difference of opinion as to the cause of his decline, there could be no question of the fact. His form grew emaciated; his voice, though still rich and sweet, had a certain melancholy prophecy of decay in it; he was often observed, on any slight alarm or other sudden accident, to put his hand over his heart, with first a flush and then a paleness, indicative of pain.

Such was the young clergyman's condition, and so imminent the prospect that his dawning light would be extinguished, all untimely, when Roger Chillingworth made his advent to the town. His first entry on the scene, few people could tell whence, dropping down, as it were, out of the sky, or starting from the nether earth, had an aspect of mystery, which was easily heightened to the miraculous. He was now known to be a man of skill; it was observed that he gathered herbs, and the blossoms of wild-flowers, and dug up roots and plucked off twigs from the forest-trees, like one acquainted with hidden virtues in what was valueless to common eyes. He was heard to speak of Sir Kenelm Digby,[109] and other famous men,—whose scientific attainments were esteemed hardly less than supernatural,—as having been his correspondents or associates. Why, with such rank in the learned world, had he come hither? What could he, whose sphere was in great cities, be seeking in the wilderness? In answer to this query, a rumor gained ground,—and, however absurd, was entertained by some very sensible people,—that Heaven had wrought an absolute miracle, by transporting an eminent Doctor of Physic, from a German university, bodily through the air, and setting him down at the door of Mr. Dimmesdale's study! Individuals of wiser faith, indeed, who knew that Heaven promotes its purposes without aiming at the stage-effect of what is called miraculous interposition, were inclined to see a providential hand in Roger Chillingworth's so opportune arrival.

This idea was countenanced by the strong interest which the physician ever manifested in the young clergyman; he attached himself to him as a parishioner, and sought to win a friendly regard and confidence from his naturally reserved sensibility. He expressed great alarm at his pastor's state of health, but was anxious to attempt the cure, and, if early undertaken, seemed not despondent of a favorable result. The elders, the deacons, the motherly dames, and the young and fair maidens, of Mr.

[109] English scientist (1603–1665).

Dimmesdale's flock, were alike importunate that he should make trial of the physician's frankly offered skill. Mr. Dimmesdale gently repelled their entreaties.

"I need no medicine," said he.

But how could the young minister say so, when, with every successive Sabbath, his cheek was paler and thinner, and his voice more tremulous than before,—when it had now become a constant habit, rather than a casual gesture, to press his hand over his heart? Was he weary of his labors? Did he wish to die? These questions were solemnly propounded to Mr. Dimmesdale by the elder ministers of Boston and the deacons of his church, who, to use their own phrase, "dealt with him" on the sin of rejecting the aid which Providence so manifestly held out. He listened in silence, and finally promised to confer with the physician.

"Were it God's will," said the Reverend Mr. Dimmesdale, when, in fulfilment of this pledge, he requested old Roger Chillingworth's professional advice, "I could be well content, that my labors, and my sorrows, and my sins, and my pains, should shortly end with me, and what is earthly of them be buried in my grave, and the spiritual go with me to my eternal state, rather than that you should put your skill to the proof in my behalf."

"Ah," replied Roger Chillingworth, with that quietness which, whether imposed or natural, marked all his deportment, "it is thus that a young clergyman is apt to speak. Youthful men, not having taken a deep root, give up their hold of life so easily! And saintly men, who walk with God on earth, would fain be away, to walk with him on the golden pavements of the New Jerusalem."

"Nay," rejoined the young minister, putting his hand to his heart, with a flush of pain flitting over his brow, "were I worthier to walk there, I could be better content to toil here."

"Good men ever interpret themselves too meanly," said the physician.

In this manner, the mysterious old Roger Chillingworth became the medical adviser of the Reverend Mr. Dimmesdale. As not only the disease interested the physician, but he was strongly moved to look into the character and qualities of the patient, these two men, so different in age, came gradually to spend much time together. For the sake of the minister's health, and to enable the leech to gather plants with healing balm in them, they took long walks on the sea-shore, or in the forest; mingling various talk with the plash and murmur of the waves, and the solemn wind-anthem among the tree-tops. Often, likewise, one was the guest of the other, in his place of study and retirement. There was a fascination for the minister in the company of the man of science, in whom he recognized an intellectual cultivation of no moderate depth or scope; together with a range and freedom of ideas, that he would have vainly looked for among the members of his own profession. In truth, he was startled, if not shocked, to find this attribute in the physician. Mr. Dimmesdale was a true priest, a true religionist, with the reverential sentiment largely developed, and an order of mind that impelled itself powerfully along the track of a creed, and wore its passage continually deeper with the lapse of time. In no state of society would he have been what is called a man of liberal views; it would always be essential to his peace to feel the pressure of a faith about him, supporting, while it confined him within its iron framework. Not the less, however, though with a tremulous enjoyment, did he feel the occasional relief of looking at the universe through the medium of another kind of intellect than those with which he habitually held converse. It was as if a window were thrown open, admitting a freer atmosphere into the close and stifled study, where his life was wasting itself away, amid lamp-light, or obstructed day-beams, and the musty fragrance, be it sensual or moral, that exhales from books. But the air was too fresh and chill to be long breathed, with comfort. So the minister, and the physician with him, withdrew again within the limits of what their church defined as orthodox.

Thus Roger Chillingworth scrutinized his patient carefully, both as he saw him in his ordinary life, keeping an accustomed pathway in the range of thoughts familiar to him, and as he appeared when thrown amidst other moral scenery, the novelty of which might call out something new to the surface of his character. He deemed it essential, it would seem, to know the man, before attempting to do him good. Wherever there is a heart and an intellect, the diseases of the physical frame are tinged with the peculiarities of these. In Arthur Dimmesdale, thought and imagination were so active, and sensibility so intense, that the bodily infirmity would be likely to have its groundwork there. So Roger Chillingworth—the man of skill, the kind and friendly physician—strove to go deep into his patient's bosom, delving among his principles, prying into his recollections, and probing every thing with a cautious touch, like a treasure-seeker in a dark cavern. Few secrets can escape an investigator, who has opportunity and license to undertake such a quest, and skill to follow it up. A man burdened with a secret should especially avoid the intimacy of his physician. If the latter possess native sagacity, and a nameless something more,—let us call it intuition; if he show no intrusive egotism, nor disagreeably prominent characteristics of his own; if he have the power, which must be born with him, to bring his mind into such affinity with his patient's, that this last shall unawares have spoken what he imagines himself only to have thought; if such revelations be received without tumult, and acknowledged not so often by an uttered sympathy, as by silence, an inarticulate breath, and here and there a word, to indicate that all is understood; if, to these qualifications of a confidant be joined the advantages afforded by his recognized character as a physician;—then, at some inevitable moment, will the soul of the sufferer be dissolved, and flow forth in a dark, but transparent stream, bringing all its mysteries into the daylight.

Roger Chillingworth possessed all, or most, of the attributes above enumerated. Nevertheless, time went on; a kind of intimacy, as we have said, grew up between these two cultivated minds, which had as wide a field as the whole sphere of human thought and study, to meet upon; they discussed every topic of ethics and religion, of public affairs, and private character; they talked much, on both sides, of matters that seemed personal to themselves; and yet no secret, such as the physician fancied must exist there, ever stole out of the minister's consciousness into his companion's ear. The latter had his suspicions, indeed, that even the nature of Mr. Dimmesdale's bodily disease had never fairly been revealed to him. It was a strange reserve!

After a time, at a hint from Roger Chillingworth, the friends of Mr. Dimmesdale effected an arrangement by which the two were lodged in the same house; so that every ebb and flow of the minister's life-tide might pass under the eye of his anxious and attached physician. There was much joy throughout the town, when this greatly desirable object was attained. It was held to be the best possible measure for the young clergyman's welfare; unless, indeed, as often urged by such as felt authorized to do so, he had selected some one of the many blooming damsels, spiritually devoted to him, to become his devoted wife. This latter step, however, there was no present prospect that Arthur Dimmesdale would be prevailed upon to take; he rejected all suggestions of the kind, as if priestly celibacy were one of his articles of church-discipline. Doomed by his own choice, therefore, as Mr. Dimmesdale so evidently was, to eat his unsavory morsel always at another's board, and endure the life-long chill which must be his lot who seeks to warm himself only at another's fireside, it truly seemed that this sagacious, experienced, benevolent, old physician, with his concord of paternal and reverential love for the young pastor, was the very man, of all mankind, to be constantly within reach of his voice.

The new abode of the two friends was with a pious widow, of good social rank, who dwelt in a house covering pretty nearly the site on which the venerable structure of King's Chapel has since been built. It had the grave-yard, originally Isaac Johnson's home-field, on one side, and so was well adapted to call up serious reflections, suited to their respective employments, in both minister and man of physic. The motherly care of the good widow assigned to Mr. Dimmesdale a front apartment, with a sunny exposure, and heavy window-curtains to create a noontide shadow, when desirable. The walls were hung round with tapestry, said to be from the Gobelin looms,[110] and, at all events, representing the Scriptural story of David and Bathsheba, and Nathan the Prophet,[111] in colors still unfaded, but which made the fair woman of the scene almost as grimly picturesque as the woe-denouncing seer. Here, the pale clergyman piled up his library, rich with parchment-bound folios of the Fathers,[112] and the lore of Rabbis, and monkish erudition, of which the Protestant divines, even while they vilified and decried that class of writers, were yet constrained often to avail themselves. On the other side of the house, old Roger Chillingworth arranged his study and laboratory; not such as a modern man of science would reckon even tolerably complete, but provided with a distilling apparatus, and the means of compounding drugs and chemicals, which the practised alchemist knew well how to turn to purpose. With such commodiousness of situation, these two learned persons sat themselves down, each in his own domain, yet familiarly passing from one apartment to the other, and bestowing a mutual and not incurious inspection into one another's business.

And the Reverend Arthur Dimmesdale's best discerning friends, as we have intimated, very reasonably imagined that the hand of Providence had done all this, for the purpose—besought in so many public, and domestic, and secret prayers—of restoring the young minister to health. But—it must now be said—another portion of the community had latterly begun to take its own view of the relation betwixt Mr. Dimmesdale and the mysterious old physician. When an uninstructed multitude attempts to see with its eyes, it is exceedingly apt to be deceived. When, however, it forms its judgment, as it usually does, on the intuitions of its great and warm heart, the conclusions thus attained are often so profound and so unerring, as to possess the character of truths supernaturally revealed. The people, in the case of which we speak, could justify its prejudice against Roger Chillingworth by no fact or argument

---

[110] The Gobelins were a famous tapestry-making family in sixteenth-century Paris.
[111] David and Bathsheba's marriage and Nathan's prophecies are recounted in 2 Samuel 11–12.

[112] Early Christian teachers and writers who developed the doctrines of the church.

worthy of serious refutation. There was an aged handicraftsman, it is true, who had been a citizen of London at the period of Sir Thomas Overbury's murder,[113] now some thirty years agone; he testified to having seen the physician, under some other name, which the narrator of the story had now forgotten, in company with Doctor Forman, the famous old conjurer, who was implicated in the affair of Overbury. Two or three individuals hinted, that the man of skill, during his Indian captivity, had enlarged his medical attainments by joining in the incantations of the savage priests; who were universally acknowledged to be powerful enchanters, often performing seemingly miraculous cures by their skill in the black art. A large number—and many of these were persons of such sober sense and practical observation, that their opinions would have been valuable, in other matters—affirmed that Roger Chillingworth's aspect had undergone a remarkable change while he had dwelt in town, and especially since his abode with Mr. Dimmesdale. At first, his expression had been calm, meditative, scholar-like. Now, there was something ugly and evil in his face, which they had not previously noticed, and which grew still the more obvious to sight, the oftener they looked upon him. According to the vulgar idea, the fire in his laboratory had been brought from the lower regions, and was fed with infernal fuel; and so, as might be expected, his visage was getting sooty with the smoke.

To sum up the matter, it grew to be a widely diffused opinion, that the Reverend Arthur Dimmesdale, like many other personages of especial sanctity, in all ages of the Christian world, was haunted either by Satan himself, or Satan's emissary, in the guise of old Roger Chillingworth. This diabolical agent had the Divine permission, for a season, to burrow into the clergyman's intimacy, and plot against his soul. No sensible man, it was confessed, could doubt on which side the victory would turn. The people looked, with an unshaken hope, to see the minister come forth out of the conflict, transfigured with the glory which he would unquestionably win. Meanwhile, nevertheless, it was sad to think of the perchance mortal agony through which he must struggle towards his triumph.

Alas, to judge from the gloom and terror in the depths of the poor minister's eyes, the battle was a sore one, and the victory any thing but secure!

X: The Leech and His Patient

Old Roger Chillingworth, throughout life, had been calm in temperament, kindly, though not of warm affections, but ever, and in all his relations with the world, a pure and upright man. He had begun an investigation, as he imagined, with the severe and equal integrity of a judge, desirous only of truth, even as if the question involved no more than the air-drawn lines and figures of a geometrical problem, instead of human passions, and wrongs inflicted on himself. But, as he proceeded, a terrible fascination, a kind of fierce, though still calm, necessity seized the old man within its gripe, and never set him free again, until he had done all its bidding. He now dug into the poor clergyman's heart, like a miner searching for gold; or, rather, like a sexton delving into a grave, possibly in quest of a jewel that had been buried on the

[113] Sir Thomas Overbury (1581–1613) was poisoned by Ann Turner at the command of the countess of Essex because he opposed her marriage to his patron, Viscount Rochester. Dr. Simon Forman (1552–1611) had conspired with Overbury's murderers before his own death.

dead man's bosom, but likely to find nothing save mortality and corruption. Alas for his own soul, if these were what he sought!

Sometimes, a light glimmered out of the physician's eyes, burning blue and ominous, like the reflection of a furnace, or, let us say, like one of those gleams of ghastly fire that darted from Bunyan's awful door-way in the hill-side,[114] and quivered on the pilgrim's face. The soil where this dark miner was working had perchance shown indications that encouraged him.

"This man," said he, at one such moment, to himself, "pure as they deem him,— all spiritual as he seems,—hath inherited a strong animal nature from his father or his mother. Let us dig a little farther in the direction of this vein!"

Then, after long search into the minister's dim interior, and turning over many precious materials, in the shape of high aspirations for the welfare of his race, warm love of souls, pure sentiments, natural piety, strengthened by thought and study, and illuminated by revelation,—all of which invaluable gold was perhaps no better than rubbish to the seeker,—he would turn back, discouraged, and begin his quest towards another point. He groped along as stealthily, with as cautious a tread, and as wary an outlook, as a thief entering a chamber where a man lies only half asleep,—or, it may be, broad awake,—with purpose to steal the very treasure which this man guards as the apple of his eye. In spite of his premediated carefulness, the floor would now and then creak; his garments would rustle; the shadow of his presence, in a forbidden proximity, would be thrown across his victim. In other words, Mr. Dimmesdale, whose sensibility of nerve often produced the effect of spiritual intuition, would become vaguely aware that something inimical to his peace had thrust itself into relation with him. But old Roger Chillingworth, too, had perceptions that were almost intuitive; and when the minister threw his startled eyes towards him, there the physician sat; his kind, watchful, sympathizing, but never intrusive friend.

Yet Mr. Dimmesdale would perhaps have seen this individual's character more perfectly, if a certain morbidness, to which sick hearts are liable, had not rendered him suspicious of all mankind. Trusting no man as his friend, he could not recognize his enemy when the latter actually appeared. He therefore still kept up a familiar intercourse with him, daily receiving the old physician in his study; or visiting the laboratory, and, for recreation's sake, watching the processes by which weeds were converted into drugs of potency.

One day, leaning his forehead on his hand, and his elbow on the sill of the open window, that looked towards the graveyard, he talked with Roger Chillingworth, while the old man was examining a bundle of unsightly plants.

"Where," asked he, with a look askance at them,—for it was the clergyman's peculiarity that he seldom, now-a-days, looked straightforth at any object, whether human or inanimate,—"where, my kind doctor, did you gather those herbs, with such a dark, flabby leaf?"

"Even in the grave-yard, here at hand," answered the physician, continuing his employment. "They are new to me. I found them growing on a grave, which bore no tombstone, nor other memorial of the dead man, save these ugly weeds that have

---

[114] In John Bunyan's *The Pilgrim's Progress* (1678),
the gates of Hell stood flaming on the hillside
trail to the Celestial City.

taken upon themselves to keep him in remembrance. They grew out of his heart, and typify, it may be, some hideous secret that was buried with him, and which he had done better to confess during his lifetime."

"Perchance," said Mr. Dimmesdale, "he earnestly desired it, but could not."

"And wherefore?" rejoined the physician. "Wherefore not; since all the powers of nature call so earnestly for the confession of sin, that these black weeds have sprung up out of a buried heart, to make manifest an unspoken crime?"

"That, good Sir, is but a fantasy of yours," replied the minister. "There can be, if I forebode aright, no power, short of the Divine mercy, to disclose, whether by uttered words, or by type or emblem, the secrets that may be buried with a human heart. The heart, making itself guilty of such secrets, must perforce hold them, until the day when all hidden things shall be revealed. Nor have I so read or interpreted Holy Writ, as to understand that the disclosure of human thoughts and deeds, then to be made, is intended as a part of the retribution. That, surely, were a shallow view of it. No; these revelations, unless I greatly err, are meant merely to promote the intellectual satisfaction of all intelligent beings, who will stand waiting, on that day,[115] to see the dark problem of this life made plain. A knowledge of men's hearts will be needful to the completest solution of that problem. And I conceive, moreover, that the hearts holding such miserable secrets as you speak of will yield them up, at that last day, not with reluctance, but with a joy unutterable."

"Then why not reveal them here?" asked Roger Chillingworth, glancing quietly aside at the minister. "Why should not the guilty ones sooner avail themselves of this unutterable solace?"

"They mostly do," said the clergyman, griping hard at his breast, as if afflicted with an importunate throb of pain. "Many, many a poor soul hath given its confidence to me, not only on the death-bed, but while strong in life, and fair in reputation. And ever, after such an outpouring, O, what a relief have I witnessed in those sinful brethren! even as in one who at last draws free air, after long stifling with his own polluted breath. How can it be otherwise? Why should a wretched man, guilty, we will say, of murder, prefer to keep the dead corpse buried in his own heart, rather than fling it forth at once, and let the universe take care of it!"

"Yet some men bury their secrets thus," observed the calm physician.

"True; there are such men," answered Mr. Dimmesdale. "But, not to suggest more obvious reasons, it may be that they are kept silent by the very constitution of their nature. Or,—can we not suppose it?—guilty as they may be, retaining, nevertheless, a zeal for God's glory and man's welfare, they shrink from displaying themselves black and filthy in the view of men; because, thenceforward, no good can be achieved by them; no evil of the past be redeemed by better service. So, to their own unutterable torment, they go about among their fellow-creatures, looking pure as new-fallen snow; while their hearts are all speckled and spotted with iniquity of which they cannot rid themselves."

"These men deceive themselves," said Roger Chillingworth, with somewhat more emphasis than usual, and making a slight gesture with his forefinger. "They fear to take up the shame that rightfully belongs to them. Their love for man, their zeal for God's service,—these holy impulses may or may not coexist in their hearts with the

---

[115] I.e., Judgment Day.

evil inmates to which their guilt has unbarred the door, and which must needs propagate a hellish breed within them. But, if they seek to glorify God, let them not lift heavenward their unclean hands! If they would serve their fellow-men, let them do it by making manifest the power and reality of conscience, in constraining them to penitential self-abasement! Wouldst thou have me to believe, O wise and pious friend, that a false show can be better—can be more for God's glory, or man's welfare —than God's own truth? Trust me, such men deceive themselves!"

"It may be so," said the young clergyman indifferently, as waiving a discussion that he considered irrelevant or unseasonable. He had a ready faculty, indeed, of escaping from any topic that agitated his too sensitive and nervous temperament.— "But, now, I would ask of my well-skilled physician, whether, in good sooth, he deems me to have profited by his kindly care of this weak frame of mine?"

Before Roger Chillingworth could answer, they heard the clear, wild laughter of a young child's voice, proceeding from the adjacent burial-ground. Looking instinctively from the open window,—for it was summer-time,—the minister beheld Hester Prynne and little Pearl passing along the footpath that traversed the inclosure. Pearl looked as beautiful as the day, but was in one of those moods of perverse merriment which, whenever they occurred, seemed to remove her entirely out of the sphere of sympathy or human contact. She now skipped irreverently from one grave to another; until, coming to the broad, flat, armorial tombstone of a departed worthy,—perhaps of Isaac Johnson himself,—she began to dance upon it. In reply to her mother's command and entreaty that she would behave more decorously, little Pearl paused to gather the prickly burrs from a tall burdock, which grew beside the tomb. Taking a handful of these, she arranged them along the lines of the scarlet letter that decorated the maternal bosom, to which the burrs, as their nature was, tenaciously adhered. Hester did not pluck them off.

Roger Chillingworth had by this time approached the window, and smiled grimly down.

"There is no law, nor reverence for authority, no regard for human ordinances or opinions, right or wrong, mixed up with that child's composition," remarked he, as much to himself as to his companion. "I saw her, the other day, bespatter the Governor himself with water, at the cattle-trough in Spring Lane. What, in Heaven's name, is she? Is the imp altogether evil? Hath she affections? Hath she any discoverable principle of being?"

"None,—save the freedom of a broken law," answered Mr. Dimmesdale, in a quiet way, as if he had been discussing the point within himself. "Whether capable of good, I know not."

The child probably overheard their voices; for, looking up to the window, with a bright, but naughty smile of mirth and intelligence, she threw one of the prickly burrs at the Reverend Mr. Dimmesdale. The sensitive clergyman shrunk, with nervous dread, from the light missile. Detecting his emotion, Pearl clapped her little hands in the most extravagant ecstasy. Hester Prynne, likewise, had involuntarily looked up; and all these four persons, old and young, regarded one another in silence, till the child laughed aloud, and shouted,—"Come away, mother! Come away, or yonder old Black Man will catch you! He hath got hold of the minister already. Come away, mother, or he will catch you! But he cannot catch little Pearl!"

So she drew her mother away, skipping, dancing, and frisking fantastically among the hillocks of the dead people, like a creature that had nothing in common with a bygone and buried generation, nor owned herself akin to it. It was as if she had been made afresh, out of new elements, and must perforce be permitted to live her own life, and be a law unto herself, without her eccentricities being reckoned to her for a crime.

"There goes a woman," resumed Roger Chillingworth, after a pause, "who, be her demerits what they may, hath none of that mystery of hidden sinfulness which you deem so grievous to be borne. Is Hester Prynne the less miserable, think you, for that scarlet letter on her breast?"

"I do verily believe it," answered the clergyman. "Nevertheless, I cannot answer for her. There was a look of pain in her face, which I would gladly have been spared the sight of. But still, methinks, it must needs better for the sufferer to be free to show his pain, as this poor woman Hester is, than to cover it all up in his heart."

There was another pause; and the physician began anew to examine and arrange the plants which he had gathered.

"You inquired of me, a little time agone," said he, at length, "my judgment as touching your health."

"I did," answered the clergyman, "and would gladly learn it. Speak frankly, I pray you, be it for life or death."

"Freely, then, and plainly," said the physician, still busy with his plants, but keeping a wary eye on Mr. Dimmesdale, "the disorder is a strange one; not so much in itself, nor as outwardly manifested,—in so far, at least, as the symptoms have been laid open to my observation. Looking daily at you, my good Sir, and watching the tokens of your aspect, now for months gone by, I should deem you a man sore sick, it may be, yet not so sick but that an instructed and watchful physician might well hope to cure you. But—I know not what to say—the disease is what I seem to know, yet know it not."

"You speak in riddles, learned Sir," said the pale minister, glancing aside out of the window.

"Then, to speak more plainly," continued the physician, "and I crave pardon, Sir, —should it seem to require pardon,—for this needful plainness of my speech. Let me ask,—as your friend,—as one having charge, under Providence, of your life and physical well-being,—hath all the operation of this disorder been fairly laid open and recounted to me?"

"How can you question it?" asked the minister. "Surely, it were child's play to call in a physician, and then hide the sore!"

"You would tell me, then, that I know all?" said Roger Chillingworth, deliberately, and fixing an eye, bright with intense and concentrated intelligence, on the minister's face. "Be it so! But, again! He to whom only the outward and physical evil is laid open knoweth, oftentimes, but half the evil which he is called upon to cure. A bodily disease, which we look upon as whole and entire within itself, may, after all, be but a symptom of some ailment in the spiritual part. Your pardon, once again, good Sir, if my speech give the shadow of offence. You, Sir, of all men whom I have known, are he whose body is the closest conjoined, and imbued, and identified, so to speak, with the spirit whereof it is the instrument."

"Then I need ask no further," said the clergyman, somewhat hastily rising from his chair. "You deal not, I take it, in medicine for the soul!"

"Thus, a sickness," continued Roger Chillingworth, going on, in an unaltered tone, without heeding the interruption,—but standing up, and confronting the emaciated and whitecheeked minister with his low, dark, and misshapen figure,—"a sickness, a sore place, if we may so call it, in your spirit, hath immediately its appropriate manifestation in your bodily frame. Would you, therefore, that your physician heal the bodily evil? How may this be, unless you first lay open to him the wound or trouble in your soul?"

"No!—not to thee!—not to an earthly physician!" cried Mr. Dimmesdale, passionately, and turning his eyes, full and bright, and with a kind of fierceness, on old Roger Chillingworth. "Not to thee! But, if it be the soul's disease, then do I commit myself to the one Physician of the soul! He, if it stand with his good pleasure, can cure; or he can kill! Let him do with me as, in his justice and wisdom, he shall see good. But who are thou, that meddlest in this matter?—that dares thrust himself between the sufferer and his God?"

With a frantic gesture, he rushed out of the room.

"It is as well to have made this step," said Roger Chillingworth to himself, looking after the minister with a grave smile. "There is nothing lost. We shall be friends again anon. But see, now, how passion takes hold upon this man, and hurrieth him out of himself! As with one passion, so with another! He hath done a wild thing ere now, this pious Master Dimmesdale, in the hot passion of his heart!"

It proved not difficult to reëstablish the intimacy of the two companions, on the same footing and in the same degree as heretofore. The young clergyman, after a few hours of privacy, was sensible that the disorder of his nerves had hurried him into an unseemly outbreak of temper, which there had been nothing in the physician's words to excuse or palliate. He marvelled, indeed, at the violence with which he had thrust back the kind old man, when merely proffering the advice which it was his duty to bestow, and which the minister himself had expressly sought. With these remorseful feelings, he lost no time in making the amplest apologies, and besought his friend still to continue the care, which, if not successful in restoring him to health, had, in all probability, been the means of prolonging his feeble existence to that hour. Roger Chillingworth readily assented, and went on with his medical supervision of the minister; doing his best for him, in all good faith, but always quitting the patient's apartment, at the close of a professional interview, with a mysterious and puzzled smile upon his lips. This expression was invisible in Mr. Dimmesdale's presence, but grew strongly evident as the physician crossed the threshold.

"A rare case!" he muttered. "I must needs look deeper into it. A strange sympathy betwixt soul and body! Were it only for the art's sake, I must search this matter to the bottom!"

It came to pass, not long after the scene above recorded, that the Reverend Mr. Dimmesdale, at noonday, and entirely unawares, fell into a deep, deep slumber, sitting in his chair, with a large black-letter[116] volume open before him on the table. It must have been a work of vast ability in the somniferous school of literature. The profound depth of the minister's repose was the more remarkable; inasmuch as he was one of those persons whose sleep, ordinarily, is as light, as fitful, and as easily scared away, as a small bird hopping on a twig. To such an unwonted remoteness, however, had

---

[116] Old English or Gothic printing type.

his spirit now withdrawn into itself, that he stirred not in his chair, when old Roger Chillingworth, without any extraordinary precaution, came into the room. The physician advanced directly in front of his patient, laid his hand upon his bosom, and thrust aside the vestment, that, hitherto, had always covered it even from the professional eye.

Then, indeed, Mr. Dimmesdale shuddered, and slightly stirred.

After a brief pause, the physician turned away.

But with what a wild look of wonder, joy, and horror! With what a ghastly rapture, as it were, too mighty to be expressed only by the eye and features, and therefore bursting forth through the whole ugliness of his figure, and making itself even riotously manifest by the extravagant gestures with which he threw up his arms towards the ceiling, and stamped his foot upon the floor! Had a man seen old Roger Chillingworth, at that moment of his ecstasy, he would have had no need to ask how Satan comports himself, when a precious human soul is lost to heaven, and won into his kingdom.

But what distinguished the physician's ecstasy from Satan's was the trait of wonder in it!

XI: *The Interior of a Heart*

After the incident last described, the intercourse between the clergyman and the physician, though externally the same, was really of another character than it had previously been. The intellect of Roger Chillingworth had now a sufficiently plain path before it. It was not, indeed, precisely that which he had laid out for himself to tread. Calm, gentle, passionless, as he appeared, there was yet, we fear, a quiet depth of malice, hitherto latent, but active now, in this unfortunate old man, which led him to imagine a more intimate revenge than any mortal had ever wreaked upon an enemy. To make himself the one trusted friend, to whom should be confided all the fear, the remorse, the agony, the ineffectual repentance, the backward rush of sinful thoughts, expelled in vain! All that guilty sorrow, hidden from the world, whose great heart would have pitied and forgiven, to be revealed to him, the Pitiless, to him, the Unforgiving! All that dark treasure to be lavished on the very man, to whom nothing else could so adequately pay the debt of vengeance!

The clergyman's shy and sensitive reserve had balked this scheme. Roger Chillingworth, however, was inclined to be hardly, if at all, less satisfied with the aspect of affairs, which Providence—using the avenger and his victim for its own purposes, and, perchance, pardoning, where it seemed most to punish—had substituted for his black devices. A revelation, he could almost say, had been granted to him. It mattered little, for his object, whether celestial, or from what other region. By its aid, in all the subsequent relations betwixt him and Mr. Dimmesdale, not merely the external presence, but the very inmost soul of the latter seemed to be brought out before his eyes, so that he could see and comprehend its every movement. He became, thenceforth, not a spectator only, but a chief actor, in the poor minister's interior world. He could play upon him as he chose. Would he arouse him with a throb of agony? The victim was for ever on the rack; it needed only to know the spring that controlled the engine;—and the physician knew it well! Would he startle him with sudden fear? As at the waving of a magician's wand, uprose a grisly phantom,—uprose a thousand phantoms,—in many shapes, of death, or more awful shame, all flocking roundabout the clergyman, and pointing with their fingers at his breast!

All this was accomplished with a subtlety so perfect, that the minister, though he had constantly a dim perception of some evil influence watching over him, could never gain a knowledge of its actual nature. True, he looked doubtfully, fearfully, —even, at times, with horror and the bitterness of hatred,—at the deformed figure of the old physician. His gestures, his gait, his grizzled beard, his slightest and most indifferent acts, the very fashion of his garments, were odious in the clergyman's sight; a token, implicitly to be relied on, of a deeper antipathy in the breast of the latter than he was willing to acknowledge to himself. For, as it was impossible to assign a reason for such distrust and abhorrence, so Mr. Dimmesdale, conscious that the poison of one morbid spot was infecting his heart's entire substance, attributed all his presentiments to no other cause. He took himself to task for his bad sympathies in reference to Roger Chillingworth, disregarded the lesson that he should have drawn from them, and did his best to root them out. Unable to accomplish this, he neverthe-less, as a matter of principle, continued his habits of social familiarity with the old man, and thus gave him constant opportunities for perfecting the purpose to which —poor, forlorn creature that he was, and more wretched than his victim—the avenger had devoted himself.

While thus suffering under bodily disease, and gnawed and tortured by some black trouble of the soul, and given over to the machinations of his deadliest enemy, the Reverend Mr. Dimmesdale had achieved a brilliant popularity in his sacred office. He won it, indeed, in great part, by his sorrows. His intellectual gifts, his moral percep-tions, his power of experiencing and communicating emotion, were kept in a state of preternatural activity by the prick and anguish of his daily life. His fame, though still on its upward slope, already overshadowed the soberer reputations of this fellow-clergymen, eminent as several of them were. There were scholars among them, who had spent more years in acquiring abstruse lore, connected with the divine profession, than Mr. Dimmesdale had lived; and who might well, therefore, be more profoundly versed in such solid and valuable attainments than their youthful brother. There were men, too, of a sturdier texture of mind than his, and endowed with a far greater share of shrewd, hard, iron or granite understanding; which, duly mingled with a fair proportion of doctrinal ingredient, constitutes a highly respectable, efficacious, and unamiable variety of the clerical species. There were others, again, true saintly fathers, whose faculties had been elaborated by weary toil among their books, and by patient thought, and etherealized, moreover, by spiritual communications with the better world, into which their purity of life had almost introduced these holy personages, with their garments of mortality still clinging to them. All that they lacked was the gift that descended upon the chosen disciples, at Pentecost, in tongues of flame;[117] symbolizing, it would seem, not the power of speech in foreign and unknown languages, but that of addressing the whole human brotherhood in the heart's native language. These fathers, otherwise so apostolic, lacked Heaven's last and rarest attesta-tion of their office, the Tongue of Flame. They would have vainly sought—had they

[117] On Pentecost, the Holy Spirit came to the apostles and enabled them to speak foreign languages. (See Acts 2:1–8.)

ever dreamed of seeking—to express the highest truths through the humblest medium of familiar words and images. Their voices came down, afar and indistinctly, from the upper heights where they habitually dwelt.

Not improbably, it was to this latter class of men that Mr. Dimmesdale, by many of his traits of character, naturally belonged. To their high mountain-peaks of faith and sanctity he would have climbed, had not the tendency been thwarted by the burden, whatever it might be, of crime or anguish, beneath which it was his doom to totter. It kept him down, on a level with the lowest; him, the man of ethereal attributes, whose voice the angels might else have listened to and answered! But this very burden it was, that gave him sympathies so intimate with the sinful brotherhood of mankind; so that his heart vibrated in unison with theirs, and received their pain into itself, and sent its own throb of pain through a thousand other hearts, in gushes of sad, persuasive eloquence. Oftenest persuasive, but sometimes terrible! The people knew not the power that moved them thus. They deemed the young clergyman a miracle of holiness. They fancied him the mouthpiece of Heaven's messages of wisdom, and rebuke, and love. In their eyes, the very ground on which he trod was sanctified. The virgins of his church grew pale around him, victims of a passion so imbued with religious sentiment that they imagined it to be all religion, and brought it openly, in their white bosoms, as their most acceptable sacrifice before the altar. The aged members of his flock, beholding Mr. Dimmesdale's frame so feeble, while they were themselves so rugged in their infirmity, believed that he would go heaven-ward before them, and enjoined it upon their children, that their old bones should be buried close to their young pastor's holy grave. And, all this time, perchance, when poor Mr. Dimmesdale was thinking of his grave, he questioned with himself whether the grass would ever grow on it, because an accursed thing must there be buried!

It is inconceivable, the agony with which this public veneration tortured him! It was his genuine impulse to adore the truth, and to reckon all things shadow-like, and utterly devoid of weight or value, that had not its divine essence as the life within their life. Then, what was he?—a substance?—or the dimmest of all shadows? He longed to speak out, from his own pulpit, at the full height of his voice, and tell the people what he was. "I, whom you behold in these black garments of the priesthood, —I, who ascend the sacred desk, and turn my pale face heavenward, taking upon myself to hold communion, in your behalf, with the Most High Omniscience,—I, in whose daily life you discern the sanctity of Enoch,[118]—I, whose footsteps, as you suppose, leave a gleam along my earthly track, whereby the pilgrims that shall come after me may be guided to the regions of the blest,—I, who have laid the hand of baptism upon your children,—I, who have breathed the parting prayer over your dying friends, to whom the Amen sounded faintly from a world which they had quitted,—I, your pastor, whom you so reverence and trust, am utterly a pollution and a lie!"

More than once, Mr. Dimmesdale had gone into the pulpit, with a purpose never to come down its steps, until he should have spoken words like the above. More than once, he had cleared his throat, and drawn in the long, deep, and tremulous breath,

[118] In Genesis 5:21–24, "Enoch walked with God" and was said to have been "translated" to Heaven without dying.

which, when sent forth again, would come burdened with the black secret of his soul. More than once—nay, more than a hundred times—he had actually spoken! Spoken! But how? He had told his hearers that he was altogether vile, a viler companion of the vilest, the worst of sinners, an abomination, a thing of unimaginable iniquity; and that the only wonder was, that they did not see his wretched body shrivelled up before their eyes, by the burning wrath of the Almighty! Could there be plainer speech than this? Would not the people start up in their seats, by a simultaneous impulse, and tear him down out of the pulpit which he defiled? Not so, indeed! They heard it all, and did but reverence him the more. They little guessed what deadly purport lurked in those self-condemning words. "The godly youth!" said they among themselves. "The saint on earth! Alas, if he discern such sinfulness in his own white soul, what horrid spectacle would he behold in thine or mine!" The minister well knew—subtle, but remorseful hypocrite that he was!—the light in which his vague confession would be viewed. He had striven to put a cheat[119] upon himself by making the avowal of a guilty conscience, but had gained only one other sin, and a self-acknowledged shame, without the momentary relief of being self-deceived. He had spoken the very truth, and transformed it into the veriest falsehood. And yet, by the constitution of his nature, he loved the truth, and loathed the lie, as few men ever did. Therefore, above all things else, he loathed his miserable self!

His inward trouble drove him to practices, more in accordance with the old, corrupted faith of Rome, than with the better light of the church in which he had been born and bred. In Mr. Dimmesdale's secret closet, under lock and key, there was a bloody scourge.[120] Oftentimes, this Protestant and Puritan divine had plied it on his own shoulders; laughing bitterly at himself the while, and smiting so much the more pitilessly, because of that bitter laugh. It was his custom, too, as it has been that of many other pious Puritans, to fast,—not, however, like them, in order to purify the body and render it the fitter medium of celestial illumination,—but rigorously, and until his knees trembled beneath him, as an act of penance. He kept vigils, likewise, night after night, sometimes in utter darkness; sometimes with a glimmering lamp; and sometimes, viewing his own face in a looking-glass, by the most powerful light which he could throw upon it. He thus typified the constant introspection wherewith he tortured, but could not purify, himself. In these lengthened vigils, his brain often reeled, and visions seemed to flit before him; perhaps seen doubtfully, and by a faint light of their own, in the remote dimness of the chamber, or more vividly, and close beside him, within the looking-glass. Now it was a herd of diabolic shapes, that grinned and mocked at the pale minister, and beckoned him away with them; now a group of shining angels, who flew upward heavily, as sorrow-laden, but grew more ethereal as they rose. Now came the dead friends of his youth, and his white-bearded father, with a saint-like frown, and his mother, turning her face away as she passed by. Ghost of a mother,—thinnest fantasy of a mother,—methinks she might yet have thrown a pitying glance towards her son! And now, through the chamber which these spectral thoughts had made so ghastly, glided Hester Prynne, leading along little Pearl, in her scarlet garb, and pointing her forefinger, first, at the scarlet letter on her bosom, and then at the clergyman's own breast.

None of these visions ever quite deluded him. At any moment, by an effort of his

---

[119] I.e., to delude or excuse. [120] Whip.

will, he could discern substances through their misty lack of substance, and convince himself that they were not solid in their nature, like yonder table of carved oak, or that big, square, leathern-bound and brazen-clasped volume of divinity. But, for all that, they were, in one sense, the truest and most substantial things which the poor minister now dealt with. It is the unspeakable misery of a life so false as his, that it steals the pith and substance out of whatever realities there are around us, and which were meant by Heaven to be the spirit's joy and nutriment. To the untrue man, the whole universe is false,—it is impalpable,—it shrinks to nothing within his grasp. And he himself, in so far as he shows himself in a false light, becomes a shadow, or, indeed, ceases to exist. The only truth, that continued to give Mr. Dimmesdale a real existence on this earth, was the anguish in his inmost soul, and the undissembled expression of it in his aspect. Had he once found power to smile, and wear a face of gayety, there would have been no such man!

On one of those ugly nights, which we have faintly hinted at, but forborne to picture forth, the minister started from his chair. A new thought had struck him. There might be a moment's peace in it. Attiring himself with as much care as if it had been for public worship, and precisely in the same manner, he stole softly down the staircase, undid the door, and issued forth.

XII: The Minister's Vigil

Walking in the shadow of a dream, as it were, and perhaps actually under the influence of a species of somnambulism, Mr. Dimmesdale reached the spot, where, now so long since, Hester Prynne had lived through her first hour of public ignominy. The same platform or scaffold, black and weather-stained with the storm or sunshine of seven long years, and foot-worn, too, with the tread of many culprits who had since ascended it, remained standing beneath the balcony of the meeting-house. The minister went up the steps.

It was an obscure night of early May. An unvaried pall of cloud muffled the whole expanse of sky from zenith to horizon. If the same multitude which had stood as eyewitnesses while Hester Prynne sustained her punishment could now have been summoned forth, they would have discerned no face above the platform, nor hardly the outline of a human shape, in the dark gray of the midnight. But the town was all asleep. There was no peril of discovery. The minister might stand there, if it so pleased him, until morning should redden in the east, without other risk than that the dank and chill night-air would creep into his frame, and stiffen his joints with rheumatism, and clog his throat with catarrh and cough; thereby defrauding the expectant audience of to-morrow's prayer and sermon. No eye could see him, save that ever-wakeful one which had seen him in his closet, wielding the bloody scourge. Why, then, had he come hither? Was it but the mockery of penitence? A mockery, indeed, but in which his soul trifled with itself! A mockery at which angels blushed and wept, while fiends rejoiced, with jeering laughter! He had been driven hither by the impulse of that Remorse which dogged him everywhere, and whose own sister and closely linked companion was that Cowardice which invariably drew him back, with her tremulous gripe, just when the other impulse had hurried him to the verge of a disclosure. Poor, miserable man! what right had infirmity like his to burden itself with crime? Crime is for the iron-nerved, who have their choice either to endure it, or, if it press too hard, to exert their fierce and savage strength for a good purpose, and fling it off at once! This feeble and most sensitive of spirits could do neither, yet continually did one thing or another, which intertwined, in the same inextricable knot, the agony of heaven-defying guilt and vain repentance.

And thus, while standing on the scaffold, in this vain show of expiation, Mr. Dimmesdale was overcome with a great horror of mind, as if the universe were gazing at a scarlet token on his naked breast, right over his heart. On that spot, in very truth, there was, and there had long been, the gnawing and poisonous tooth of bodily pain. Without any effort of his will, or power to restrain himself, he shrieked aloud; an outcry that went pealing through the night, and was beaten back from one house to another, and reverberated from the hills in the background; as if a company of devils, detecting so much misery and terror in it, had made a plaything of the sound, and were bandying it to and fro.

"It is done!" muttered the minister, covering his face with his hands. "The whole town will awake, and hurry forth, and find me here!"

But it was not so. The shriek had perhaps sounded with a far greater power, to his own startled ears, than it actually possessed. The town did not awake; or, if it did, the drowsy slumberers mistook the cry either for something frightful in a dream, or for the noise of witches; whose voices, at that period, were often heard to pass over the settlements or lonely cottages, as they rode with Satan through the air. The clergyman, therefore, hearing no symptoms of disturbance, uncovered his eyes and looked about him. At one of the chamber-windows of Governor Bellingham's mansion, which stood at some distance, on the line of another street, he beheld the appearance of the old magistrate himself, with a lamp in his hand, a white night-cap on his head, and a long white gown enveloping his figure. He looked like a ghost, evoked unseasonably from the grave. The cry had evidently startled him. At another window of the same house, moreover, appeared old Mistress Hibbins, the Governor's sister, also with a lamp, which, even thus far off, revealed the expression of her sour and discontented face. She thrust forth her head from the lattice, and looked anxiously upward. Beyond the shadow of a doubt, this venerable witch-lady had heard Mr. Dimmesdale's outcry, and interpreted it, with its multitudinous echoes and reverberations, as the clamor of the fiends and night-hags, with whom she was well known to make excursions into the forest.

Detecting the gleam of Governor Bellingham's lamp, the old lady quickly extinguished her own, and vanished. Possibly, she went up among the clouds. The minister saw nothing further of her motions. The magistrate, after a wary observation of the darkness—into which, nevertheless, he could see but little farther than he might into a mill-stone—retired from the window.

The minister grew comparatively calm. His eyes, however, were soon greeted by a little, glimmering light, which, at first a long way off, was approaching up the street. It threw a gleam of recognition on here a post, and there a garden-fence, and here a latticed window-pane, and there a pump, with its full trough of water, and here, again, an arched door of oak, with an iron knocker, and a rough log for the door-step. The Reverend Mr. Dimmesdale noted all these minute particulars, even while firmly convinced that the doom of his existence was stealing onward, in the footsteps which he now heard; and that the gleam of the lantern would fall upon him, in a few moments more, and reveal his long-hidden secret. As the light drew nearer, he beheld, within its illuminated circle, his brother clergyman,—or, to speak more accurately, his professional father, as well as highly valued friend,—the Reverend Mr. Wilson; who, as Mr. Dimmesdale now conjectured, had been praying at the bedside of some dying man. And so he had. The good old minister came freshly from the death-chamber of Governor Winthrop,[121] who had passed from earth to heaven within that very hour. And now, surrounded, like the saint-like personages of olden times, with a radiant halo, that glorified him amid this gloomy night of sin,—as if the departed Governor had left him an inheritance of his glory, or as if he had caught upon himself the distant shine of the celestial city, while looking thitherward to see the triumphant pilgrim pass within its gates,—now, in short, good Father Wilson was moving homeward, aiding his footsteps with a lighted lantern! The glimmer of this luminary suggested the above conceits to Mr. Dimmesdale, who smiled,—nay, almost laughed at them,—and then wondered if he were going mad.

As the Reverend Mr. Wilson passed beside the scaffold, closely muffling his Geneva cloak[122] about him with one arm, and holding the lantern before his breast with the other, the minister could hardly restrain himself from speaking.

"A good evening to you, venerable Father Wilson! Come up hither, I pray you, and pass a pleasant hour with me!"

Good heavens! Had Mr. Dimmesdale actually spoken? For one instant, he believed that these words had passed his lips. But they were uttered only within his imagination. The venerable Father Wilson continued to step slowly onward, looking carefully at the muddy pathway before his feet, and never once turning his head towards the guilty platform. When the light of the glimmering lantern had faded quite away, the minister discovered, by the faintness which came over him, that the last few moments had been a crisis of terrible anxiety; although his mind had made an involuntary effort to relieve itself by a kind of lurid playfulness.

Shortly afterwards, the like grisly sense of the humorous again stole in among the solemn phantoms of his thought. He felt his limbs growing stiff with the unaccustomed chilliness of the night, and doubted whether he should be able to descend the steps of the scaffold. Morning would break, and find him there. The neighborhood would begin to rouse itself. The earliest riser, coming forth in the dim twilight, would perceive a vaguely defined figure aloft on the place of shame; and, half crazed betwixt alarm and curiosity, would go, knocking from door to door, summoning all the people to behold the ghost—as he needs must think it—of some defunct transgressor. A dusky tumult would flap its wings from one house to another. Then—the morning light still waxing stronger—old patriarchs would rise up in great haste, each in his flannel gown, and matronly dames, without pausing to put off their night-gear. The whole tribe of decorous personages, who had never heretofore been seen with a single hair of their heads awry, would start into public view, with the disorder of a nightmare in their aspects. Old Governor Bellingham would come grimly forth, with his King James's ruff fastened askew; and Mistress Hibbins, with some twigs of the forest clinging to her skirts, and looking sourer than ever, as having hardly got a wink of sleep after her night ride; and good Father Wilson, too, after spending half the night

---

[121] John Winthrop (1588–1649) actually died in March. He was one of the founders of the Massachusetts Bay Colony.

[122] Loose, black clerical robe named for the Calvinist preachers in Geneva, Switzerland, who wore it.

at a death-bed, and liking ill to be disturbed, thus early, out of his dreams about the glorified saints. Hither, likewise, would come the elders and deacons of Mr. Dimmesdale's church, and the young virgins who so idolized their minister, and had made a shrine for him in their white bosoms; which, now, by the by, in their hurry and confusion, they would scantly have given themselves time to cover with their kerchiefs. All people, in a word, would come stumbling over their thresholds, and turning up their amazed and horror-stricken visages around the scaffold. Whom would they discern there, with the red eastern light upon his brow? Whom, but the Reverend Arthur Dimmesdale, half frozen to death, overwhelmed with shame, and standing where Hester Prynne had stood!

Carried away by the grotesque horror of this picture, the minister, unawares, and to his own infinite alarm, burst into a great peal of laughter. It was immediately responded to by a light, airy, childish laugh, in which, with a thrill of the heart,—but he knew not whether of exquisite pain, or pleasure as acute,—he recognized the tones of little Pearl.

"Pearl! Little Pearl!" cried he, after a moment's pause; then, suppressing his voice,—"Hester! Hester Prynne! Are you there?"

"Yes; it is Hester Prynne!" she replied, in a tone of surprise; and the minister heard her footsteps approaching from the sidewalk, along which she had been passing.—"It is I, and my little Pearl."

"Whence come you, Hester?" asked the minister. "What sent you hither?"

"I have been watching at a death-bed," answered Hester Prynne;—"at Governor Winthrop's death-bed, and have taken his measure for a robe, and am now going homeward to my dwelling."

"Come up hither, Hester, thou and little Pearl," said the Reverend Mr. Dimmesdale. "Ye have both been here before, but I was not with you. Come up hither once again, and we will stand all three together!"

She silently ascended the steps, and stood on the platform, holding little Pearl by the hand. The minister felt for the child's other hand, and took it. The moment that he did so, there came what seemed a tumultuous rush of new life, other life than his own, pouring like a torrent into his heart, and hurrying through all his veins, as if the mother and the child were communicating their vital warmth to his half-torpid system. The three formed an electric chain.

"Minister!" whispered little Pearl.

"What wouldst thou say, child?" asked Mr. Dimmesdale.

"Wilt thou stand here with mother and me, to-morrow noontide?" inquired Pearl.

"Nay; not so, my little Pearl!" answered the minister; for, with the new energy of the moment, all the dread of public exposure, that had so long been the anguish of his life, had returned upon him; and he was already trembling at the conjunction in which—with a strange joy, nevertheless—he now found himself. "Not so, my child. I shall, indeed, stand with thy mother and thee one other day, but not to-morrow!"

Pearl laughed, and attempted to pull away her hand. But the minister held it fast.

"A moment longer, my child!" said he.

"But wilt thou promise," asked Pearl, "to take my hand, and mother's hand, to-morrow noontide?"

"Not then, Pearl," said the minister, "but another time!"

"And what other time?" persisted the child.

"At the great judgment day!" whispered the minister,—and, strangely enough, the sense that he was a professional teacher of the truth impelled him to answer the child so. "Then, and there, before the judgment-seat, thy mother, and thou, and I, must stand together! But the daylight of this world shall not see our meeting!"

Pearl laughed again.

But, before Mr. Dimmesdale had done speaking, a light gleamed far and wide over all the muffled sky. It was doubtless caused by one of those meteors, which the night-watcher may so often observe burning out to waste, in the vacant regions of the atmosphere. So powerful was its radiance, that it thoroughly illuminated the dense medium of cloud betwixt the sky and earth. The great vault brightened, like the dome of an immense lamp. It showed the familiar scene of the street, with the distinctness of mid-day, but also with the awfulness that is always imparted to familiar objects by an unaccustomed light. The wooden houses, with their jutting stories and quaint gable-peaks; the doorsteps and thresholds, with the early grass springing up about them; the garden-plots, black with freshly turned earth; the wheel-track, little worn, and, even in the market-place, margined with green on either side;—all were visible, but with a singularity of aspect that seemed to give another moral interpretation to the things of this world than they had ever borne before. And there stood the minister, with his hand over his heart; and Hester Prynne, with the embroidered letter glimmering on her bosom; and little Pearl, herself a symbol, and the connecting link between those two. They stood in the noon of that strange and solemn splendor, as if it were the light that is to reveal all secrets, and the daybreak that shall unite all who belong to one another.

There was witchcraft in little Pearl's eyes; and her face, as she glanced upward at the minister, wore that naughty smile which made its expression frequently so elfish. She withdrew her hand from Mr. Dimmesdale's, and pointed across the street. But he clasped both his hands over his breast, and cast his eyes towards the zenith.

Nothing was more common, in those days, than to interpret all meteoric appearances, and other natural phenomena, that occurred with less regularity than the rise and set of sun and moon, as so many revelations from a supernatural source. Thus, a blazing spear, a sword of flame, a bow, or a sheaf of arrows, seen in the midnight sky, prefigured Indian warfare. Pestilence was known to have been foreboded by a shower of crimson light. We doubt whether any marked event, for good or evil, ever befell New England, from its settlement down to Revolutionary times, of which the inhabitants had not been previously warned by some spectacle of this nature. Not seldom, it had been seen by multitudes. Oftener, however, its credibility rested on the faith of some lonely eyewitness, who beheld the wonder through the colored, magnifying, and distorting medium of his imagination, and shaped it more distinctly in his after-thought. It was, indeed, a majestic idea, that the destiny of nations should be revealed, in these awful hieroglyphics, on the cope[123] of heaven. A scroll so wide might not be deemed too expansive for Providence to write a people's doom upon. The belief was a favorite one with our forefathers, as betokening that their infant commonwealth was under a celestial guardianship of peculiar intimacy and strictness. But what shall we say, when an individual discovers a revelation, addressed to himself alone,

[123] Canopy.

on the same vast sheet of record! In such a case, it could only be the symptom of a highly disordered mental state, when a man, rendered morbidly self-contemplative by long, intense, and secret pain, had extended his egotism over the whole expanse of nature, until the firmament itself should appear no more than a fitting page for his soul's history and fate.

We impute it, therefore, solely to the disease in his own eye and heart, that the minister, looking upward to the zenith, beheld there the appearance of an immense letter,—the letter A,—marked out in lines of dull red light. Not but the meteor may have shown itself at that point, burning duskily through a veil of cloud; but with no such shape as his guilty imagination gave it; or, at least, with so little definiteness, that another's guilt might have seen another symbol in it.

There was a singular circumstance that characterized Mr. Dimmesdale's psychological state, at this moment. All the time that he gazed upward to the zenith, he was, nevertheless, perfectly aware that little Pearl was pointing her finger towards old Roger Chillingworth, who stood at no great distance from the scaffold. The minister appeared to see him, with the same glance that discerned the miraculous letter. To his features, as to all other objects, the meteoric light imparted a new expression; or it might well be that the physician was not careful then, as at all other times, to hide the malevolence with which he looked upon his victim. Certainly, if the meteor kindled up the sky, and disclosed the earth, with an awfulness that admonished Hester Prynne and the clergyman of the day of judgment, then might Roger Chillingworth have passed with them for the arch-fiend, standing there, with a smile and scowl, to claim his own. So vivid was the expression, or so intense the minister's perception of it, that it seemed still to remain painted on the darkness, after the meteor had vanished, with an effect as if the street and all things else were at once annihilated.

"Who is that man, Hester?" gasped Mr. Dimmesdale, overcome with terror. "I shiver at him! Dost thou know the man? I hate him, Hester!"

She remembered her oath, and was silent.

"I tell thee, my soul shivers at him," muttered the minister again. "Who is he? Who is he? Canst thou do nothing for me? I have a nameless horror of the man."

"Minister," said little Pearl, "I can tell thee who he is!"

"Quickly, then, child!" said the minister, bending his ear close to her lips. "Quickly—and as low as thou canst whisper."

Pearl mumbled something into his ear, that sounded, indeed, like human language, but was only such gibberish as children may be heard amusing themselves with, by the hour together. At all events, if it involved any secret information in regard to old Roger Chillingworth, it was in a tongue unknown to the erudite clergyman, and did but increase the bewilderment of his mind. The elfish child then laughed aloud.

"Dost thou mock me now?" said the minister.

"Thou wast not bold!—thou wast not true!" answered the child. "Thou wouldst not promise to take my hand, and mother's hand, to-morrow noontide!"

"Worthy Sir," said the physician, who had now advanced to the foot of the platform. "Pious Master Dimmesdale! can this be you? Well, well, indeed! We men of study, whose heads are in our books, have need to be straitly looked after! We dream in our waking moments, and walk in our sleep. Come, good Sir, and my dear friend, I pray you, let me lead you home!"

"How knewest thou that I was here?" asked the minister, fearfully.

"Verily, and in good faith," answered Roger Chillingworth, "I knew nothing of the matter. I had spent the better part of the night at the bedside of the worshipful Governor Winthrop, doing what my poor skill might to give him ease. He going home to a better world, I, likewise, was on my way homeward, when this strange light shone out. Come with me, I beseech you, Reverend Sir; else you will be poorly able to do Sabbath duty to-morrow. Aha! see now, how they trouble the brain,— these books!—these books! You should study less, good Sir, and take a little pastime; or these night-whimseys will grow upon you!"

"I will go home with you," said Mr. Dimmesdale.

With a chill despondency, like one awaking, all nerveless, from an ugly dream, he yielded himself to the physician, and was led away.

The next day, however, being the Sabbath, he preached a discourse which was held to be the richest and most powerful, and the most replete with heavenly influences, that had ever proceeded from his lips. Souls, it is said, more souls than one, were brought to the truth by the efficacy of that sermon, and vowed within themselves to cherish a holy gratitude towards Mr. Dimmesdale throughout the long hereafter. But, as he came down the pulpit-steps, the gray-bearded sexton met him, holding up a black glove, which the minister recognized as his own.

"It was found," said the sexton, "this morning, on the scaffold, where evil-doers are set up to public shame. Satan dropped it there, I take it, intending a scurrilous jest against your reverence. But, indeed, he was blind and foolish, as he ever and always is. A pure hand needs no glove to cover it!"

"Thank you, my good friend," said the minister gravely, but startled at heart; for, so confused was his remembrance, that he had almost brought himself to look at the events of the past night as visionary. "Yes, it seems to be my glove indeed!"

"And, since Satan saw fit to steal it, your reverence must needs handle him without gloves, henceforward," remarked the old sexton, grimly smiling. "But did your reverence hear of the portent that was seen last night? A great red letter in the sky, —the letter A,—which we interpret to stand for Angel. For, as our good Governor Winthrop was made an angel this past night, it was doubtless held fit that there should be some notice thereof!"

"No," answered the minister. "I had not heard of it."

XIII: *Another View of Hester*

In her late singular interview with Mr. Dimmesdale, Hester Prynne was shocked at the condition to which she found the clergyman reduced. His nerve seemed absolutely destroyed. His moral force was abased into more than childish weakness. It grovelled helpless on the ground, even while his intellectual faculties retained their pristine strength, or had perhaps acquired a morbid energy, which disease only could have given them. With her knowledge of a train of circumstances hidden from all others, she could readily infer, that, besides the legitimate action of his own conscience, a terrible machinery had been brought to bear, and was still operating, on Mr. Dimmesdale's well-being and repose. Knowing what this poor, fallen man had once been, her whole soul was moved by the shuddering terror with which he had appealed to her, —the outcast woman,—for support against his instinctively discovered enemy. She decided, moreover, that he had a right to her utmost aid. Little accustomed, in her long seclusion from society, to measure her ideas of right and wrong by any standard external to herself, Hester saw—or seemed to see—that there lay a responsibility upon her, in reference to the clergyman, which she owed to no other, nor to the whole world besides. The links that united her to the rest of human kind—links of flowers, or silk, or gold, or whatever the material—had all been broken. Here was the iron link of mutual crime, which neither he nor she could break. Like all other ties, it brought along with it its obligations.

Hester Prynne did not now occupy precisely the same position in which we beheld her during the earlier periods of her ignominy. Years had come, and gone. Pearl was now seven years old. Her mother, with the scarlet letter on her breast, glittering in its fantastic embroidery, had long been a familiar object to the townspeople. As is apt to be the case when a person stands out in any prominence before the community, and, at the same time, interferes neither with public nor individual interests and convenience, a species of general regard had ultimately grown up in reference to Hester Prynne. It is to the credit of human nature, that, except where its selfishness is brought into play, it loves more readily than it hates. Hatred, by a gradual and quiet process, will even be transformed to love, unless the change be impeded by a continually new irritation of the original feeling of hostility. In this matter of Hester Prynne, there was neither irritation nor irksomeness. She never battled with the public, but submitted uncomplainingly to its worst usage; she made no claim upon it, in requital for what she suffered; she did not weigh upon its sympathies. Then, also, the blameless purity of her life, during all these years in which she had been set apart to infamy, was reckoned largely in her favor. With nothing now to lose, in the sight of mankind, and with no hope, and seemingly no wish, of gaining any thing, it could only be a genuine regard for virtue that had brought back the poor wanderer to its paths.

It was perceived, too, that, while Hester never put forward even the humblest title to share in the world's privileges,—farther than to breathe the common air, and earn daily bread for little Pearl and herself by the faithful labor of her hands,—she was quick to acknowledge her sisterhood with the race of man, whenever benefits were to be conferred. None so ready as she to give of her little substance to every demand of poverty; even though the bitter-hearted pauper threw back a gibe in requital of the food brought regularly to his door, or the garments wrought for him by the fingers that could have embroidered a monarch's robe. None so self-devoted as Hester, when pestilence stalked through the town. In all seasons of calamity, indeed, whether general or of individuals, the outcast of society at once found her place. She came, not as a guest, but as a rightful inmate, into the household that was darkened by trouble; as if its gloomy twilight were a medium in which she was entitled to hold intercourse with her fellow-creatures. There glimmered the embroidered letter, with comfort in its unearthly ray. Elsewhere the token of sin, it was the taper of the sick-chamber. It had even thrown its gleam, in the sufferer's hard extremity, across the verge of time. It had shown him where to set his foot, while the light of earth was fast becoming dim, and ere the light of futurity could reach him. In such emergencies, Hester's nature showed itself warm and rich; a well-spring of human tenderness, unfailing to every real demand, and inexhaustible by the largest. Her breast, with its badge of shame, was but the softer pillow for the head that needed one. She was self-ordained a Sister of Mercy; or, we may rather say, the world's heavy hand had so ordained her, when neither the world nor she looked forward to this result. The letter was the symbol of her calling. Such helpfulness was found in her,—so much power to do, and power to sympathize,—that many people refused to interpret the scarlet A by its original signification. They said that it meant Able; so strong was Hester Prynne, with a woman's strength.

It was only the darkened house that could contain her. When sunshine came again, she was not there. Her shadow had faded across the threshold. The helpful inmate had departed, without one backward glance to gather up the meed[124] of gratitude, if any were in the hearts of those whom she had served so zealously. Meeting them in the street, she never raised her head to receive their greeting. If they were resolute to accost her, she laid her finger on the scarlet letter, and passed on. This might be pride, but was so like humility, that it produced all the softening influence of the latter quality on the public mind. The public is despotic in its temper; it is capable of denying common justice, when too strenuously demanded as a right; but quite as frequently it awards more than justice, when the appeal is made, as despots love to have it made, entirely to its generosity. Interpreting Hester Prynne's deportment as an appeal of this nature, society was inclined to show its former victim a more benign countenance than she cared to be favored with, or, perchance, than she deserved.

The rulers, and the wise and learned men of the community, were longer in acknowledging the influence of Hester's good qualities than the people. The prejudices which they shared in common with the latter were fortified in themselves by an iron framework of reasoning, that made it a far tougher labor to expel them. Day by day, nevertheless, their sour and rigid wrinkles were relaxing into something which, in the due course of years, might grow to be an expression of almost benevolence. Thus it was with the men of rank, on whom their eminent position imposed the guardianship of the public morals. Individuals in private life, meanwhile, had quite forgiven Hester Prynne for her frailty; nay, more, they had begun to look upon the scarlet letter as the token, not of that one sin, for which she had borne so long and dreary a penance, but of her many good deeds since. "Do you see that woman with the embroidered badge?" they would say to strangers. "It is our Hester,—the town's own Hester,— who is so kind to the poor, so helpful to the sick, so comfortable to the afflicted!" Then, it is true, the propensity of human nature to tell the very worst of itself, when embodied in the person of another, would constrain them to whisper the black scandal of bygone years. It was none the less a fact, however, that, in the eyes of the very men who spoke thus, the scarlet letter had the effect of the cross on a nun's bosom. It imparted to the wearer a kind of sacredness, which enabled her to walk securely amid all peril. Had she fallen among thieves, it would have kept her safe. It was reported, and believed by many, that an Indian had drawn his arrow against the badge, and that the missile struck it, but fell harmless to the ground.

The effect of the symbol—or rather, of the position in respect to society that was indicated by it—on the mind of Hester Prynne herself, was powerful and peculiar. All the light and graceful foliage of her character had been withered up by this red-hot brand, and had long ago fallen away, leaving a bare and harsh outline, which might have been repulsive, had she possessed friends or companions to be repelled by it. Even the attractiveness of her person had undergone a similar change. It might be partly owing to the studied austerity of her dress, and partly owing to the lack of demonstra-

[124] Reward.

tion in her manners. It was a sad transformation, too, that her rich and luxuriant hair had either been cut off, or was so completely hidden by a cap, that not a shining lock of it ever once gushed into the sunshine. It was due in part to all these causes, but still more to something else, that there seemed to be no longer any thing in Hester's face for Love to dwell upon; nothing in Hester's form, though majestic and statue-like, that Passion would ever dream of clasping in its embrace; nothing in Hester's bosom, to make it ever again the pillow of Affection. Some attribute had departed from her, the permanence of which had been essential to keep her a woman. Such is frequently the fate, and such the stern development, of the feminine character and person, when the woman has encountered, and lived through, an experience of peculiar severity. If she be all tenderness, she will die. If she survive, the tenderness will either be crushed out of her, or—and the outward semblance is the same—crushed so deeply into her heart that it can never show itself more. The latter is perhaps the truest theory. She who has once been woman, and ceased to be so, might at any moment become a woman again, if there were only the magic touch to effect the transfiguration. We shall see whether Hester Prynne were ever afterwards so touched, and so transfigured.

Much of the marble coldness of Hester's impression was to be attributed to the circumstance that her life had turned, in a great measure, from passion and feeling, to thought. Standing alone in the world,—alone, as to any dependence on society, and with little Pearl to be guided and protected,—alone, and hopeless of retrieving her position, even had she not scorned to consider it desirable,—she cast away the fragments of a broken chain. The world's law was no law for her mind. It was an age in which the human intellect, newly emancipated, had taken a more active and a wider range than for many centuries before. Men of the sword had overthrown nobles and kings. Men bolder than these had overthrown and rearranged—not actually, but within the sphere of theory, which was their most real abode—the whole system of ancient prejudice, wherewith was linked much of ancient principle. Hester Prynne imbibed this spirit. She assumed a freedom of speculation, then common enough on the other side of the Atlantic, but which our forefathers, had they known of it, would have held to be a deadlier crime than that stigmatized by the scarlet letter. In her lonesome cottage, by the sea-shore, thoughts visited her, such as dared to enter no other dwelling in New England; shadowy guests, that would have been as perilous as demons to their entertainer, could they have been seen so much as knocking at her door.

It is remarkable, that persons who speculate the most boldly often conform with the most perfect quietude to the external regulations of society. The thought suffices them, without investing itself in the flesh and blood of action. So it seemed to be with Hester. Yet, had little Pearl never come to her from the spiritual world, it might have been far otherwise. Then, she might have come down to us in history, hand in hand with Ann Hutchinson, as the foundress of a religious sect. She might, in one of her phases, have been a prophetess. She might, and not improbably would, have suffered death from the stern tribunals of the period, for attempting to undermine the foundations of the Puritan establishment. But, in the education of her child, the mother's enthusiasm of thought had something to wreak itself upon. Providence, in the person of this little girl, had assigned to Hester's charge the germ and blossom of womanhood, to be cherished and developed amid a host of difficulties. Every thing was against her. The world was hostile. The child's own nature had something wrong in it, which continually betokened that she had been born amiss,—the effluence of her mother's lawless passion,—and often impelled Hester to ask, in bitterness of heart, whether it were for ill or good that the poor little creature had been born at all.

Indeed, the same dark question often rose into her mind, with reference to the whole race of womanhood. Was existence worth accepting, even to the happiest among them? As concerned her own individual existence, she had long ago decided in the negative, and dismissed the point as settled. A tendency to speculation, though it may keep woman quiet, as it does man, yet makes her sad. She discerns, it may be, such a hopeless task before her. As a first step, the whole system of society is to be torn down, and built up anew. Then, the very nature of the opposite sex, or its long hereditary habit, which has become like nature, is to be essentially modified, before woman can be allowed to assume what seems a fair and suitable position. Finally, all other difficulties being obviated, woman cannot take advantage of these preliminary reforms, until she herself shall have undergone a still mightier change; in which, perhaps, the ethereal essence, wherein she has her truest life, will be found to have evaporated. A woman never overcomes these problems by any exercise of thought. They are not to be solved, or only in one way. If her heart chance to come uppermost, they vanish. Thus, Hester Prynne, whose heart had lost its regular and healthy throb, wandered without a clew in the dark labyrinth of mind; now turned aside by an insurmountable precipice; now starting back from a deep chasm. There was wild and ghastly scenery all around her, and a home and comfort nowhere. At times, a fearful doubt strove to possess her soul, whether it were not better to send Pearl at once to heaven, and go herself to such futurity as Eternal Justice should provide.

The scarlet letter had not done its office.

Now, however, her interview with the Reverend Mr. Dimmesdale, on the night of his vigil, had given her a new theme of reflection, and held up to her an object that appeared worthy of any exertion and sacrifice for its attainment. She had witnessed the intense misery beneath which the minister struggled, or, to speak more accurately, had ceased to struggle. She saw that he stood on the verge of lunacy, if he had not already stepped across it. It was impossible to doubt, that, whatever painful efficacy there might be in the secret sting of remorse, a deadlier venom had been infused into it by the hand that proffered relief. A secret enemy had been continually by his side, under the semblance of a friend and helper, and had availed himself of the opportunities thus afforded for tampering with the delicate springs of Mr. Dimmesdale's nature. Hester could not but ask herself, whether there had not originally been a defect of truth, courage, and loyalty, on her own part, in allowing the minister to be thrown into a position where so much evil was to be foreboded, and nothing auspicious to be hoped. Her only justification lay in the fact, that she had been able to discern no method of rescuing him from a blacker ruin than had overwhelmed herself, except by acquiescing in Roger Chillingworth's scheme of disguise. Under that impulse, she had made her choice, and had chosen, as it now appeared, the more wretched alternative of the two. She determined to redeem her error, so far as it might yet be possible. Strengthened by years of hard and solemn trial, she felt herself no longer so inadequate to cope with Roger Chillingworth as on that night, abased by sin, and half maddened by the ignominy that was still new, when they had talked together in the prison-chamber. She had climbed her way, since then, to a higher point. The old man, on the other hand, had brought himself nearer to her level, or perhaps below it, by the revenge which he had stooped for.

In fine, Hester Prynne resolved to meet her former husband, and do what might be in her power for the rescue of the victim on whom he had so evidently set his gripe. The occasion was not long to seek. One afternoon, walking with Pearl in a retired part of the peninsula, she beheld the old physician, with a basket on one arm, and a staff in the other hand, stooping along the ground, in quest of roots and herbs to concoct his medicines withal.

XIV: Hester and the Physician

Hester bade little Pearl run down to the margin of the water, and play with the shells and tangled seaweed, until she should have talked awhile with yonder gatherer of herbs. So the child flew away like a bird, and, making bare her small white feet, went pattering along the moist margin of the sea. Here and there, she came to a full stop, and peeped curiously into a pool, left by the retiring tide as a mirror for Pearl to see her face in. Forth peeped at her, out of the pool, with dark, glistening curls around her head, and an elf-smile in her eyes, the image of a little maid, whom Pearl, having no other playmate, invited to take her hand and run a race with her. But the visionary little maid, on her part, beckoned likewise, as if to say,—"This is a better place! Come thou into the pool!" And Pearl, stepping in, mid-leg deep, beheld her own white feet at the bottom; while, out of a still lower depth, came the gleam of a kind of fragmentary smile, floating to and fro in the agitated water.

Meanwhile, her mother had accosted the physician.

"I would speak a word with you," said she,—"a word that concerns us much."

"Aha! And is it Mistress Hester that has a word for old Roger Chillingworth?" answered he, raising himself from his stooping posture. "With all my heart! Why, Mistress, I hear good tidings of you on all hands! No longer ago than yestereve, a magistrate, a wise and godly man, was discoursing of your affairs, Mistress Hester, and whispered me that there had been question concerning you in the council. It was debated whether or no, with safety to the common weal, yonder scarlet letter might be taken off your bosom. On my life, Hester, I made my entreaty to the worshipful magistrate that it might be done forthwith!"

"It lies not in the pleasure of the magistrates to take off this badge," calmly replied Hester. "Were I worthy to be quit of it, it would fall away of its own nature, or be transformed into something that should speak a different purport."

"Nay, then, wear it, if it suit you better," rejoined he. "A woman must needs follow her own fancy, touching the adornment of her person. The letter is gayly embroidered, and shows right bravely on your bosom!"

All this while, Hester had been looking steadily at the old man, and was shocked, as well as wonder-smitten, to discern what a change had been wrought upon him within the past seven years. It was not so much that he had grown older; for though the traces of advancing life were visible, he bore his age well, and seemed to retain a wiry vigor and alertness. But the former aspect of an intellectual and studious man, calm and quiet, which was what she best remembered in him, had altogether vanished, and been succeeded by an eager, searching, almost fierce, yet carefully guarded look. It seemed to be his wish and purpose to mask this expression with a smile; but the latter played him false, and flickered over his visage so derisively, that the spectator could see his blackness all the better for it. Ever and anon, too, there came a glare of red light out of his eyes; as if the old man's soul were on fire, and kept on smouldering duskily within his breast, until, by some casual puff of passion, it was blown into a momentary flame. This he repressed as speedily as possible, and strove to look as if nothing of the kind had happened.

In a word, old Roger Chillingworth was a striking evidence of man's faculty of transforming himself into a devil, if he will only, for a reasonable space of time, undertake a devil's office. This unhappy person had effected such a transformation by devoting himself, for seven years, to the constant analysis of a heart full of torture, and deriving his enjoyment thence, and adding fuel to those fiery tortures which he analyzed and gloated over.

The scarlet letter burned on Hester Prynne's bosom. Here was another ruin, the responsibility of which came partly home to her.

"What see you in my face," asked the physician, "that you look at it so earnestly?"

"Something that would make me weep, if there were any tears bitter enough for it," answered she. "But let it pass! It is of yonder miserable man that I would speak."

"And what of him?" cried Roger Chillingworth eagerly, as if he loved the topic, and were glad of an opportunity to discuss it with the only person of whom he could make a confidant. "Not to hide the truth, Mistress Hester, my thoughts happen just now to be busy with the gentleman. So speak freely; and I will make answer."

"When we last spake together," said Hester, "now seven years ago, it was your pleasure to extort a promise of secrecy, as touching the former relation betwixt yourself and me. As the life and good fame of yonder man were in your hands, there seemed no choice to me, save to be silent, in accordance with your behest. Yet it was not without heavy misgivings that I thus bound myself; for, having cast off all duty towards other human beings, there remained a duty towards him; and something whispered me that I was betraying it, in pledging myself to keep your counsel. Since that day, no man is so near to him as you. You tread behind his every footstep. You are beside him, sleeping and waking. You search his thoughts. You burrow and rankle in his heart! Your clutch is on his life, and you cause him to die daily a living death; and still he knows you not. In permitting this, I have surely acted a false part by the only man to whom the power was left me to be true!"

"What choice had you?" asked Roger Chillingworth. "My finger, pointed at this man, would have hurled him from his pulpit into a dungeon,—thence, peradventure, to the gallows!"

"It had been better so!" said Hester Prynne.

"What evil have I done the man?" asked Roger Chillingworth again. "I tell thee, Hester Prynne, the richest fee that ever physician earned from monarch could not have bought such care as I have wasted on this miserable priest! But for my aid, his life would have burned away in torments, within the first two years after the perpetration of his crime and thine. For, Hester, his spirit lacked the strength that could have borne up, as thine has, beneath a burden like thy scarlet letter. O, I could reveal a goodly secret! But enough! What art can do, I have exhausted on him. That he now breathes, and creeps about on earth, is owing all to me!"

"Better he had died at once!" said Hester Prynne.

"Yea, woman, thou sayest truly!" cried old Roger Chillingworth, letting the lurid fire of his heart blaze out before her eyes. "Better had he died at once! Never did mortal suffer what this man has suffered. And all, all, in the sight of his worst enemy! He has been conscious of me. He has felt an influence dwelling always upon him like a curse. He knew, by some spiritual sense,—for the Creator never made another being so sensitive as this,—he knew that no friendly hand was pulling at his heart-strings, and that an eye was looking curiously into him, which sought only evil, and found it. But he knew not that the eye and hand were mine! With the superstition common to his brotherhood, he fancied himself given over to a fiend, to be tortured with frightful dreams, and desperate thoughts, the sting of remorse, and despair of pardon; as a foretaste of what awaits him beyond the grave. But it was the constant shadow of my presence!—the closest propinquity of the man whom he had most vilely wronged!—and who had grown to exist only by this perpetual poison of the direst revenge! Yea, indeed!—he did not err!—there was a fiend at his elbow! A mortal man, with once a human heart, has become a fiend for his especial torment!"

The unfortunate physician, while uttering these words, lifted his hands with a look of horror, as if he had beheld some frightful shape, which he could not recognize, usurping the place of his own image in a glass. It was one of those moments—which sometimes occur only at the interval of years—when a man's moral aspect is faithfully revealed to his mind's eye. Not improbably, he had never before viewed himself as he did now.

"Hast thou not tortured him enough?" said Hester, noticing the old man's look. "Has he not paid thee all?"

"No!—no!—He has but increased the debt!" answered the physician; and, as he proceeded, his manner lost its fiercer characteristics, and subsided into gloom. "Dost thou remember me, Hester, as I was nine years agone? Even then, I was in the autumn of my days, nor was it the early autumn. But all my life had been made up of earnest, studious, thoughtful, quiet years, bestowed faithfully for the increase of mine own knowledge, and faithfully, too, though this latter object was but casual to the other, —faithfully for the advancement of human welfare. No life had been more peaceful and innocent than mine; few lives so rich with benefits conferred. Dost thou remember me? Was I not, though you might deem me cold, nevertheless a man thoughtful for others, craving little for himself,—kind, true, just, and of constant, if not warm affections? Was I not all this?"

"All this, and more," said Hester.

"And what am I now?" demanded he, looking into her face, and permitting the whole evil within him to be written on his features. "I have already told thee what I am! A fiend! Who made me so?"

"It was myself!" cried Hester, shuddering. "It was I, not less than he. Why hast thou not avenged thyself on me?"

"I have left thee to the scarlet letter," replied Roger Chillingworth. "If that have not avenged me, I can do no more!"

He laid his finger on it, with a smile.

"It has avenged thee!" answered Hester Prynne.

"I judged no less," said the physician. "And now, what wouldst thou with me touching this man?"

"I must reveal the secret," answered Hester, firmly. "He must discern thee in thy true character. What may be the result, I know not. But this long debt of confidence, due from me to him, whose bane and ruin I have been, shall at length be paid. So far as concerns the overthrow or preservation of his fair fame and his earthly state, and perchance his life, he is in thy hands. Nor do I,—whom the scarlet letter has disciplined to truth, though it be the truth of red-hot iron, entering into the soul,—nor do I perceive such advantage in his living any longer a life of ghastly emptiness, that I shall stoop to implore thy mercy. Do with him as thou wilt! There is no good for him,—no good for me,—no good for thee! There is no good for little Pearl! There is no path to guide us out of this dismal maze!"

"Woman, I could wellnigh pity thee!" said Roger Chillingworth, unable to restrain a thrill of admiration too; for there was a quality almost majestic in the despair which she expressed. "Thou hadst great elements. Peradventure, hadst thou met earlier with a better love than mine, this evil had not been. I pity thee, for the good that has been wasted in thy nature!"

"And I thee," answered Hester Prynne, "for the hatred that has transformed a wise and just man to a fiend! Wilt thou yet purge it out of thee, and be once more human? If not for his sake, then doubly for thine own! Forgive, and leave his further retribution to the Power that claims it! I said, but now, that there could be no good event for him, or thee, or me, who are here wandering together in this gloomy maze of evil, and stumbling, at every step, over the guilt wherewith we have strewn our path. It is not so! There might be good for thee, and thee alone, since thou hast been deeply wronged, and hast it at thy will to pardon. Wilt thou give up that only privilege? Wilt thou reject that priceless benefit?"

"Peace, Hester, peace!" replied the old man, with gloomy sternness. "It is not granted me to pardon. I have no such power as thou tellest me of. My old faith, long forgotten, comes back to me, and explains all that we do, and all we suffer. By thy first step awry, thou didst plant the germ of evil; but, since that moment, it has all been a dark necessity. Ye that have wronged me are not sinful, save in a kind of typical illusion; neither am I fiend-like, who have snatched a fiend's office from his hands. It is our fate. Let the black flower blossom as it may! Now go thy ways, and deal as thou wilt with yonder man."

He waved his hand, and betook himself again to his employment of gathering herbs.

XV: Hester and Pearl

So Roger Chillingworth—a deformed old figure, with a face that haunted men's memories longer than they liked—took leave of Hester Prynne, and went stooping away along the earth. He gathered here and there an herb, or grubbed up a root, and put it into the basket on his arm. His gray beard almost touched the ground, as he crept onward. Hester gazed after him a little while, looking with a half-fantastic curiosity to see whether the tender grass of early spring would not be blighted beneath him, and show the wavering track of his footsteps, sere and brown, across its cheerful verdure. She wondered what sort of herbs they were, which the old man was so sedulous to gather. Would not the earth, quickened to an evil purpose by the sympathy of his eye, greet him with poisonous shrubs, of species hitherto unknown, that would start up under his fingers? Or might it suffice him, that every wholesome growth should be converted into something deleterious and malignant at his touch? Did the sun, which shone so brightly everywhere else, really fall upon him? Or was there, as it rather seemed, a circle of ominous shadow moving along with his deformity, whichever way he turned himself? And whither was he now going? Would he not suddenly sink into the earth, leaving a barren and blasted spot, where, in due course of time, would be seen deadly nightshade, dogwood, henbane,[125] and whatever else of vegetable wickedness the climate could produce, all flourishing with hideous luxuriance? Or would he spread bat's wings and flee away, looking so much the uglier, the higher he rose towards heaven?

"Be it sin or no," said Hester Prynne bitterly, as she still gazed after him, "I hate the man!"

She upbraided herself for the sentiment, but could not overcome or lessen it. Attempting to do so, she thought of those long-past days, in a distant land, when he used to emerge at eventide from the seclusion of his study, and sit down in the fire-light of their home, and in the light of her nuptial smile. He needed to bask himself in that smile, he said, in order that the chill of so many lonely hours among his books might be taken off the scholar's heart. Such scenes had once appeared not otherwise than happy, but now, as viewed through the dismal medium of her subsequent life, they classed themselves among her ugliest remembrances. She marvelled how such scenes could have been! She marvelled how she could ever have been wrought upon to marry him! She deemed it her crime most to be repented of, that she had ever endured, and reciprocated, the lukewarm grasp of his hand, and had suffered the smile of her lips and eyes to mingle and melt into his own. And it seemed a fouler offence committed by Roger Chillingworth, than any which had since been done him, that, in the time when her heart knew no better, he had persuaded her to fancy herself happy by his side.

"Yes, I hate him!" repeated Hester, more bitterly than before. "He betrayed me! He has done me worse wrong than I did him!"

Let men tremble to win the hand of woman, unless they win along with it the utmost passion of her heart! Else it may be their miserable fortune, as it was Roger Chillingworth's, when some mightier touch than their own may have awakened all her sensibilities, to be reproached even for the calm content, the marble image of happiness, which they will have imposed upon her as the warm reality. But Hester ought long ago to have done with this injustice. What did it betoken? Had seven long years, under the torture of the scarlet letter, inflicted so much of misery, and wrought out no repentance?

The emotions of that brief space, while she stood gazing after the crooked figure of old Roger Chillingworth, threw a dark light on Hester's state of mind, revealing much that she might not otherwise have acknowledged to herself.

He being gone, she summoned back her child.

"Pearl! Little Pearl! Where are you?"

Pearl, whose activity of spirit never flagged, had been at no loss for amusement while her mother talked with the old gatherer of herbs. At first, as already told, she had flirted fancifully with her own image in a pool of water, beckoning the phantom forth, and—as it declined to venture—seeking a passage for herself into its sphere of impalpable earth and unattainable sky. Soon finding, however, that either she or the image was unreal, she turned elsewhere for better pastime. She made little boats out

---

[125] Three poisonous plants associated with witchcraft.

of birch-bark, and freighted them with snail-shells, and sent out more ventures on the mighty deep than any merchant in New England; but the larger part of them foundered near the shore. She seized a live horse-shoe[126] by the tail, and made prize of several five-fingers,[127] and laid out a jelly-fish to melt in the warm sun. Then she took up the white foam, that streaked the line of the advancing tide, and threw it upon the breeze, scampering after it with winged footsteps, to catch the great snow-flakes ere they fell. Perceiving a flock of beach-birds, that fed and fluttered along the shore, the naughty child picked up her apron full of pebbles, and, creeping from rock to rock after these small sea-fowl, displayed remarkable dexterity in pelting them. One little gray bird, with a white breast, Pearl was almost sure, had been hit by a pebble, and fluttered away with a broken wing. But then the elf-child sighed, and gave up her sport; because it grieved her to have done harm to a little being that was as wild as the sea-breeze, or as wild as Pearl herself.

Her final employment was to gather sea-weed, of various kinds, and make herself a scarf, or mantle, and a head-dress, and thus assume the aspect of a little mermaid. She inherited her mother's gift for devising drapery and costume. As the last touch to her mermaid's garb, Pearl took some eel-grass, and imitated, as best she could, on her own bosom, the decoration with which she was so familiar on her mother's. A letter,—the letter A,—but freshly green, instead of scarlet! The child bent her chin upon her breast, and contemplated this device with strange interest; even as if the one only thing for which she had been sent into the world was to make out its hidden import.

"I wonder if mother will ask me what it means!" thought Pearl.

Just then, she heard her mother's voice, and, flitting along as lightly as one of the little sea-birds, appeared before Hester Prynne, dancing, laughing, and pointing her finger to the ornament upon her bosom.

"My little Pearl," said Hester, after a moment's silence, "the green letter, and on thy childish bosom, has no purport. But dost thou know, my child, what this letter means which thy mother is doomed to wear?"

"Yes, mother," said the child. "It is the great letter A. Thou hast taught it me in the horn-book."[128]

Hester looked steadily into her little face; but, though there was that singular expression which she had so often remarked in her black eyes, she could not satisfy herself whether Pearl really attached any meaning to the symbol. She felt a morbid desire to ascertain the point.

"Dost thou know, child, wherefore thy mother wears this letter?"

"Truly do I!" answered Pearl, looking brightly into her mother's face. "It is for the same reason that the minister keeps his hand over his heart!"

"And what reason is that?" asked Hester, half smiling at the absurd incongruity of the child's observation; but, on second thoughts, turning pale. "What has the letter to do with any heart, save mine?"

"Nay, mother, I have told all I know," said Pearl, more seriously than she was wont to speak. "Ask yonder old man whom thou hast been talking with! It may be he can

---

[126] Horseshoe crab.
[127] Starfish.
[128] Child's primer for spelling; its single page was covered with a protective sheet of transparent horn.

tell. But in good earnest now, mother dear, what does this scarlet letter mean?—and why dost thou wear it on thy bosom?—and why does the minister keep his hand over his heart?"

She took her mother's hand in both her own, and gazed into her eyes with an earnestness that was seldom seen in her wild and capricious character. The thought occurred to Hester, that the child might really be seeking to approach her with childlike confidence, and doing what she could, and as intelligently as she knew how, to establish a meeting-point of sympathy. It showed Pearl in an unwonted aspect. Heretofore, the mother, while loving her child with the intensity of a sole affection, had schooled herself to hope for little other return than the waywardness of an April breeze; which spends its time in airy sport, and has its gusts of inexplicable passion, and is petulant in its best of moods, and chills oftener than caresses you, when you take it to your bosom; in requital of which misdemeanours, it will sometimes, of its own vague purpose, kiss your cheek with a kind of doubtful tenderness, and play gently with your hair, and then begone about its other idle business, leaving a dreamy pleasure at your heart. And this, moreover, was a mother's estimate of the child's disposition. Any other observer might have seen few but unamiable traits, and have given them a far darker coloring. But now the idea came strongly into Hester's mind, that Pearl, with her remarkable precocity and acuteness, might already have approached the age when she could be made a friend, and intrusted with as much of her mother's sorrows as could be imparted, without irreverence either to the parent or the child. In the little chaos of Pearl's character, there might be seen emerging—and could have been, from the very first—the stedfast principles of an unflinching courage,—an uncontrollable will,—a sturdy pride, which might be disciplined into self-respect,—and a bitter scorn of many things, which, when examined, might be found to have the taint of falsehood in them. She possessed affections, too, though hitherto acrid and disagreeable, as are the richest flavors of unripe fruit. With all these sterling attributes, thought Hester, the evil which she inherited from her mother must be great indeed, if a noble woman do not grow out of this elfish child.

Pearl's inevitable tendency to hover about the enigma of the scarlet letter seemed an innate quality of her being. From the earliest epoch of her conscious life, she had entered upon this as her appointed mission. Hester had often fancied that Providence had a design of justice and retribution, in endowing the child with this marked propensity; but never, until now, had she bethought herself to ask, whether, linked with that design, there might not likewise be a purpose of mercy and beneficence. If little Pearl were entertained with faith and trust, as a spirit-messenger no less than an earthly child, might it not be her errand to soothe away the sorrow that lay cold in her mother's heart, and converted it into a tomb?—and to help her to overcome the passion, once so wild, and even yet neither dead nor asleep, but only imprisoned within the same tomb-like heart?

Such were some of the thoughts that now stirred in Hester's mind, with as much vivacity of impression as if they had actually been whispered into her ear. And there was little Pearl, all this while, holding her mother's hand in both her own, and turning her face upward, while she put these searching questions, once, and again, and still a third time.

"What does the letter mean, mother?—and why dost thou wear it?—and why does the minister keep his hand over his heart?"

"What shall I say?" thought Hester to herself.—"No! If this be the price of the child's sympathy, I cannot pay it!"

Then she spoke aloud.

"Silly Pearl," said she, "what questions are these? There are many things in this world that a child must not ask about. What know I of the minister's heart? And as for the scarlet letter, I wear it for the sake of its gold thread!"

In all the seven bygone years, Hester Prynne had never before been false to the symbol on her bosom. It may be that it was the talisman of a stern and severe, but yet a guardian spirit, who now forsook her; as recognizing that, in spite of his strict watch over her heart, some new evil had crept into it, or some old one had never been expelled. As for little Pearl, the earnestness soon passed out of her face.

But the child did not see fit to let the matter drop. Two or three times, as her mother and she went homeward, and as often at supper-time, and while Hester was putting her to bed, and once after she seemed to be fairly asleep, Pearl looked up, with mischief gleaming in her black eyes.

"Mother," said she, "what does the scarlet letter mean?"

And the next morning, the first indication the child gave of being awake was by popping up her head from the pillow, and making that other inquiry, which she had so unaccountably connected with her investigations about the scarlet letter:—

"Mother!—Mother!—Why does the minister keep his hand over his heart?"

"Hold thy tongue, naughty child!" answered her mother, with an asperity that she had never permitted to herself before. "Do not tease me; else I shall shut thee into the dark closet!"

XVI: *A Forest Walk*

Hester Prynne remained constant in her resolve to make known to Mr. Dimmesdale, at whatever risk of present pain or ulterior consequences, the true character of the man who had crept into his intimacy. For several days, however, she vainly sought an opportunity of addressing him in some of the meditative walks which she knew him to be in the habit of taking, along the shores of the peninsula, or on the wooded hills of the neighbouring country. There would have been no scandal, indeed, nor peril to the holy whiteness of the clergyman's good fame, had she visited him in his own study; where many a penitent, ere now, had confessed sins of perhaps as deep a dye as the one betokened by the scarlet letter. But, partly that she dreaded the secret or undisguised interference of old Roger Chillingworth, and partly that her conscious heart imputed suspicion where none could have been felt, and partly that both the minister and she would need the whole wide world to breathe in, while they talked together,—for all these reasons, Hester never thought of meeting him in any narrower privacy than beneath the open sky.

At last, while attending in a sick-chamber, whither the Reverend Mr. Dimmesdale had been summoned to make a prayer, she learnt that he had gone, the day before, to visit the Apostle Eliot,[129] among his Indian converts. He would probably return, by a certain hour, in the afternoon of the morrow. Betimes, therefore, the next day,

---

[129] John Eliot (1604–1690), a Puritan missionary to the Indians.

Hester took little Pearl,—who was necessarily the companion of all her mother's expeditions, however inconvenient her presence,—and set forth.

The road, after the two wayfarers had crossed from the peninsula to the mainland, was no other than a footpath. It straggled onward into the mystery of the primeval forest. This hemmed it in so narrowly, and stood so black and dense on either side, and disclosed such imperfect glimpses of the sky above, that, to Hester's mind, it imaged not amiss the moral wilderness in which she had so long been wandering. The day was chill and sombre. Overhead was a gray expanse of cloud, slightly stirred, however, by a breeze; so that a gleam of flickering sunshine might now and then be seen at its solitary play along the path. This flitting cheerfulness was always at the farther extremity of some long vista through the forest. The sportive sunlight—feebly sportive, at best, in the predominant pensiveness of the day and scene—withdrew itself as they came nigh, and left the spots where it had danced the drearier, because they had hoped to find them bright.

"Mother," said little Pearl, "the sunshine does not love you. It runs away and hides itself, because it is afraid of something on your bosom. Now, see! There it is, playing, a good way off. Stand you here, and let me run and catch it. I am but a child. It will not flee from me; for I wear nothing on my bosom yet!"

"Nor ever will, my child, I hope," said Hester.

"And why not, mother?" asked Pearl, stopping short, just at the beginning of her race. "Will not it come of its own accord, when I am a woman grown?"

"Run away, child," answered her mother, "and catch the sunshine! It will soon be gone."

Pearl set forth, at a great pace, and, as Hester smiled to perceive, did actually catch the sunshine, and stood laughing in the midst of it, all brightened by its splendor, and scintillating with the vivacity excited by rapid motion. The light lingered about the lonely child, as if glad of such a playmate, until her mother had drawn almost nigh enough to step into the magic circle too.

"It will go now!" said Pearl, shaking her head.

"See!" answered Hester, smiling. "Now I can stretch out my hand, and grasp some of it."

As she attempted to do so, the sunshine vanished; or, to judge from the bright expression that was dancing on Pearl's features, her mother could have fancied that the child had absorbed it into herself, and would give it forth again, with a gleam about her path, as they should plunge into some gloomier shade. There was no other attribute that so much impressed her with a sense of new and untransmitted vigor in Pearl's nature, as this never-failing vivacity of spirits; she had not the disease of sadness, which almost all children, in these latter days, inherit, with the scrofula,[130] from the troubles of their ancestors. Perhaps this too was a disease, and but the reflex of the wild energy with which Hester had fought against her sorrows, before Pearl's birth. It was certainly a doubtful charm, imparting a hard, metallic lustre to the child's character. She wanted—what some people want throughout life—a grief that should deeply touch her, and thus humanize and make her capable of sympathy. But there was time enough yet for little Pearl!

"Come, my child!" said Hester, looking about her, from the spot where Pearl had

---

[130] Type of tuberculosis usually found in children.

stood still in the sunshine. "We will sit down a little way within the wood, and rest ourselves."

"I am not aweary, mother," replied the little girl. "But you may sit down, if you will tell me a story meanwhile."

"A story, child!" said Hester. "And about what?"

"O, a story about the Black Man!" answered Pearl, taking hold of her mother's gown, and looking up, half earnestly, half mischievously, into her face. "How he haunts this forest, and carries a book with him,—a big, heavy book, with iron clasps; and how this ugly Black Man offers his book and an iron pen to every body that meets him here among the trees; and they are to write their names with their own blood. And then he sets his mark on their bosoms! Didst thou ever meet the Black Man, mother?"

"And who told you this story, Pearl?" asked her mother, recognizing a common superstition of the period.

"It was the old dame in the chimney-corner, at the house where you watched last night," said the child. "But she fancied me asleep while she was talking of it. She said that a thousand and a thousand people had met him here, and had written in his book, and have his mark on them. And that ugly-tempered lady, old Mistress Hibbins, was one. And, mother, the old dame said that this scarlet letter was the Black Man's mark on thee, and that it glows like a red flame when thou meetest him at midnight, here in the dark wood. Is it true, mother? And dost thou go to meet him in the nighttime?"

"Didst thou ever awake, and find thy mother gone?" asked Hester.

"Not that I remember," said the child. "If thou fearest to leave me in our cottage, thou mightest take me along with thee. I would very gladly go! But, mother, tell me now! Is there such a Black Man? And didst thou ever meet him? And is this his mark?"

"Wilt thou let me be at peace, if I once tell thee?" asked her mother.

"Yes, if thou tellest me all," answered Pearl.

"Once in my life I met the Black Man!" said her mother. "This scarlet letter is his mark!"

Thus conversing, they entered sufficiently deep into the wood to secure themselves from the observation of any casual passenger along the forest-track. Here they sat down on a luxuriant heap of moss; which, at some epoch of the preceding century, had been a gigantic pine, with its roots and trunk in the darksome shade, and its head aloft in the upper atmosphere. It was a little dell where they had seated themselves, with a leaf-strewn bank rising gently on either side, and a brook flowing through the midst, over a bed of fallen and drowned leaves. The trees impending over it had flung down great branches, from time to time, which choked up the current, and compelled it to form eddies and black depths at some points; while, in its swifter and livelier passages, there appeared a channel-way of pebbles, and brown, sparkling sand. Letting the eyes follow along the course of the stream, they could catch the reflected light from its water, at some short distance within the forest, but soon lost all traces of it amid the bewilderment of tree-trunks and underbrush, and here and there a huge rock, covered over with gray lichens. All these giant trees and boulders of granite seemed intent on making a mystery of the course of this small brook; fearing, perhaps, that, with its never-ceasing loquacity, it should whisper tales out of the heart of the old forest whence it flowed, or mirror its revelations on the smooth surface of a pool. Continually, indeed, as it stole onward, the streamlet kept up a babble, kind, quiet, soothing, but melancholy, like the voice of a young child that was spending its infancy without playfulness, and knew not how to be merry among sad acquaintance and events of sombre hue.

"O brook! O foolish and tiresome little brook!" cried Pearl, after listening awhile to its talk. "Why art thou so sad? Pluck up a spirit, and do not be all the time sighing and murmuring!"

But the brook, in the course of its little lifetime among the forest-trees, had gone through so solemn an experience that it could not help talking about it, and seemed to have nothing else to say. Pearl resembled the brook, inasmuch as the current of her life gushed from a well-spring as mysterious, and had flowed through scenes shadowed as heavily with gloom. But, unlike the little stream, she danced and sparkled, and prattled airily along her course.

"What does this sad little brook say, mother?" inquired she.

"If thou hadst a sorrow of thine own, the brook might tell thee of it," answered her mother, "even as it is telling me of mine! But now, Pearl, I hear a footstep along the path, and the noise of one putting aside the branches. I would have thee betake thyself to play, and leave me to speak with him that comes yonder."

"Is it the Black Man?" asked Pearl.

"Wilt thou go and play, child?" repeated her mother. "But do not stray far into the wood. And take heed that thou come at my first call."

"Yes, mother," answered Pearl. "But, if it be the Black Man, wilt thou not let me stay a moment, and look at him, with his big book under his arm?"

"Go, silly child!" said her mother, impatiently. "It is no Black Man! Thou canst see him now through the trees. It is the minister!"

"And so it is!" said the child. "And, mother, he has his hand over his heart! Is it because, when the minister wrote his name in the book, the Black Man set his mark in that place? But why does he not wear it outside his bosom, as thou dost, mother?"

"Go now, child, and thou shalt tease me as thou wilt another time!" cried Hester Prynne. "But do not stray far. Keep where thou canst hear the babble of the brook."

The child went singing away, following up the current of the brook, and striving to mingle a more lightsome cadence with its melancholy voice. But the little stream would not be comforted, and still kept telling its unintelligible secret of some very mournful mystery that had happened—or making a prophetic lamentation about something that was yet to happen—within the verge of the dismal forest. So Pearl, who had enough of shadow in her own little life, chose to break off all acquaintance with this repining brook. She set herself, therefore, to gathering violets and wood-anemones, and some scarlet columbines that she found growing in the crevices of a high rock.

When her elf-child had departed, Hester Prynne made a step or two towards the track that led through the forest, but still remained under the deep shadow of the trees. She beheld the minister advancing along the path, entirely alone, and leaning on a staff which he had cut by the way-side. He looked haggard and feeble, and betrayed a nerveless despondency in his air, which had never so remarkably characterized him in his walks about the settlement, nor in any other situation where he deemed himself liable to notice. Here it was wofully visible, in this intense seclusion of the forest, which of itself would have been a heavy trial to the spirits. There was a listlessness in his gait; as if he saw no reason for taking one step farther, nor felt any desire to do so, but would have been glad, could he be glad of any thing, to fling himself down at the root of the nearest tree, and lie there passive for evermore. The leaves might bestrew him, and the soil gradually accumulate and form a little hillock over his frame, no matter whether there were life in it or no. Death was too definite an object to be wished for, or avoided.

To Hester's eye, the Reverend Mr. Dimmesdale exhibited no symptom of positive and vivacious suffering, except that, as little Pearl had remarked, he kept his hand over his heart.

XVII: The Pastor and His Parishioner

Slowly as the minister walked, he had almost gone by, before Hester Prynne could gather voice enough to attract his observation. At length, she succeeded.

"Arthur Dimmesdale!" she said, faintly at first; then louder, but hoarsely. "Arthur Dimmesdale!"

"Who speaks?" answered the minister.

Gathering himself quickly up, he stood more erect, like a man taken by surprise in a mood to which he was reluctant to have witnesses. Throwing his eyes anxiously in the direction of the voice, he indistinctly beheld a form under the trees, clad in garments so sombre, and so little relieved from the gray twilight into which the clouded sky and the heavy foliage had darkened the noontide, that he knew not whether it were a woman or a shadow. It may be, that his pathway through life was haunted thus, by a spectre that had stolen out from among his thoughts.

He made a step nigher, and discovered the scarlet letter.

"Hester! Hester Prynne!" said he. "Is it thou? Art thou in life?"

"Even so!" she answered. "In such life as has been mine these seven years past! And thou, Arthur Dimmesdale, dost thou yet live?"

It was no wonder that they thus questioned one another's actual and bodily existence, and even doubted of their own. So strangely did they meet, in the dim wood, that it was like the first encounter, in the world beyond the grave, of two spirits who had been intimately connected in their former life, but now stood coldly shuddering, in mutual dread; as not yet familiar with their state, nor wonted to the companionship of disembodied beings. Each a ghost, and awe-stricken at the other ghost! They were awe-stricken likewise at themselves; because the crisis flung back to them their consciousness, and revealed to each heart its history and experience, as life never does, except at such breathless epochs. The soul beheld its features in the mirror of the passing moment. It was with fear, and tremulously, and, as it were, by a slow, reluctant necessity, that Arthur Dimmesdale put forth his hand, chill as death, and touched the chill hand of Hester Prynne. The grasp, cold as it was, took away what was dreariest in the interview. They now felt themselves, at least, inhabitants of the same sphere.

Without a word more spoken—neither he nor she assuming the guidance, but with an unexpressed consent,—they glided back into the shadow of the woods, whence Hester had emerged, and sat down on the heap of moss where she and Pearl had before been sitting. When they found voice to speak, it was, at first, only to utter remarks and inquiries such as any two acquaintance might have made, about the gloomy sky, the threatening storm, and, next, the health of each. Thus they went onward, not boldly, but step by step, into the themes that were brooding deepest in their hearts. So long estranged by fate and circumstances, they needed something slight and casual to run before, and throw open the doors of intercourse, so that their real thoughts might be led across the threshold.

After a while, the minister fixed his eyes on Hester Prynne's.

"Hester," said he, "hast thou found peace?"

She smiled drearily, looking down upon her bosom.

"Hast thou?" she asked.

"None!—nothing but despair!" he answered. "What else could I look for, being what I am, and leading such a life as mine? Were I an atheist,—a man devoid of conscience,—a wretch with coarse and brutal instincts,—I might have found peace, long ere now. Nay, I never should have lost it! But, as matters stand with my soul, whatever of good capacity there originally was in me, all of God's gifts that were the choicest have become the ministers of spiritual torment. Hester, I am most miserable!"

"The people reverence thee," said Hester. "And surely thou workest good among them! Doth this bring thee no comfort?"

"More misery, Hester!—only the more misery!" answered the clergyman, with a bitter smile. "As concerns the good which I may appear to do, I have no faith in it. It must needs be a delusion. What can a ruined soul, like mine, effect towards the redemption of other souls?—or a polluted soul, towards their purification? And as for the people's reverence, would that it were turned to scorn and hatred! Canst thou deem it, Hester, a consolation, that I must stand up in my pulpit, and meet so many eyes turned upward to my face, as if the light of heaven were beaming from it!— must see my flock hungry for the truth, and listening to my words as if a tongue of Pentecost were speaking!—and then look inward, and discern the black reality of what they idolize? I have laughed, in bitterness and agony of heart, at the contrast between what I seem and what I am! And Satan laughs at it!"

"You wrong yourself in this," said Hester, gently. "You have deeply and sorely repented. Your sin is left behind you, in the days long past. Your present life is not less holy, in very truth, than it seems in people's eyes. Is there no reality in the penitence thus sealed and witnessed by good works? And wherefore should it not bring you peace?"

"No, Hester, no!" replied the clergyman. "There is no substance in it! It is cold and dead, and can do nothing for me! Of penance I have had enough! Of penitence there has been none! Else, I should long ago have thrown off these garments of mock holiness, and have shown myself to mankind as they will see me at the judgment-seat. Happy are you, Hester, that wear the scarlet letter openly upon your bosom! Mine burns in secret! Thou little knowest what a relief it is, after the torment of a seven years' cheat, to look into an eye that recognizes me for what I am! Had I one friend, —or were it my worst enemy!—to whom, when sickened with the praises of all other men, I could daily betake myself, and be known as the vilest of all sinners, methinks my soul might keep itself alive thereby. Even thus much of truth would save me! But, now, it is all falsehood!—all emptiness!—all death!"

Hester Prynne looked into his face, but hesitated to speak. Yet, uttering his long-restrained emotions so vehemently as he did, his words here offered her the very point of circumstances in which to interpose what she came to say. She conquered her fears, and spoke.

"Such a friend as thou hast even now wished for," said she, "with whom to weep over thy sin, thou hast in me, the partner of it!"—Again she hesitated, but brought out the words with an effort.—"Thou hast long had such an enemy, and dwellest with him under the same roof!"

The minister started to his feet, gasping for breath, and clutching at his heart as if he would have torn it out of his bosom.

"Ha! What sayest thou?" cried he. "An enemy! And under mine own roof! What mean you?"

Hester Prynne was now fully sensible of the deep injury for which she was responsible to this unhappy man, in permitting him to lie for so many years, or, indeed, for a single moment, at the mercy of one, whose purposes could not be other than malevolent. The very contiguity of his enemy, beneath whatever mask the latter might conceal himself, was enough to disturb the magnetic sphere of a being so sensitive as Arthur Dimmesdale. There had been a period when Hester was less alive to this consideration; or, perhaps, in the misanthropy of her own trouble, she left the minister to bear what she might picture to herself as a more tolerable doom. But of late, since the night of his vigil, all her sympathies towards him had been both softened and invigorated. She now read his heart more accurately. She doubted not, that the continual presence of Roger Chillingworth,—the secret poison of his malignity, infecting all the air about him,—and his authorized interference, as a physician, with the minister's physical and spiritual infirmities,—that these bad opportunities had been turned to a cruel purpose. By means of them, the sufferer's conscience had been kept in an irritated state, the tendency of which was, not to cure by wholesome pain, but to disorganize and corrupt his spiritual being. Its result, on earth, could hardly fail to be insanity, and hereafter, that eternal alienation from the Good and True, of which madness is perhaps the earthly type.

Such was the ruin to which she had brought the man, once,—nay, why should we not speak it?—still so passionately loved! Hester felt that the sacrifice of the clergyman's good name, and death itself, as she had already told Roger Chillingworth, would have been infinitely preferable to the alternative which she had taken upon herself to choose. And now, rather than have had this grievous wrong to confess, she would gladly have lain down on the forest-leaves, and died there, at Arthur Dimmesdale's feet.

"O Arthur," cried she, "forgive me! In all things else, I have striven to be true! Truth was the one virtue which I might have held fast, and did hold fast through all extremity; save when thy good,—thy life,—thy fame,—were put in question! Then I consented to a deception. But a lie is never good, even though death threaten on the other side! Dost thou not see what I would say? That old man!—the physician! —he whom they call Roger Chillingworth!—he was my husband!"

The minister looked at her, for an instant, with all that violence of passion, which —intermixed, in more shapes than one, with his higher, purer, softer qualities—was, in fact, the portion of him which the Devil claimed, and through which he sought to win the rest. Never was there a blacker or a fiercer frown, than Hester now encountered. For the brief space that it lasted, it was a dark transfiguration. But his character had been so much enfeebled by suffering, that even its lower energies were incapable of more than a temporary struggle. He sank down on the ground, and buried his face in his hands.

"I might have known it!" murmured he. "I did know it! Was not the secret told me in the natural recoil of my heart, at the first sight of him, and as often as I have seen him since? Why did I not understand? O Hester Prynne, thou little, little knowest all the horror of this thing! And the shame!—the indelicacy!—the horrible ugliness of this exposure of a sick and guilty heart to the very eye that would gloat over it! Woman, woman, thou art accountable for this! I cannot forgive thee!"

"Thou shalt forgive me!" cried Hester, flinging herself on the fallen leaves beside him. "Let God punish! Thou shalt forgive!"

With sudden and desperate tenderness, she threw her arms around him, and pressed his head against her bosom; little caring though his cheek rested on the scarlet letter. He would have released himself, but strove in vain to do so. Hester would not set him free, lest he should look her sternly in the face. All the world had frowned on her,—for seven long years had it frowned upon this lonely woman,—and still she bore it all, nor ever once turned away her firm, sad eyes. Heaven, likewise, had frowned upon her, and she had not died. But the frown of this pale, weak, sinful, and sorrow-stricken man was what Hester could not bear, and live!

"Wilt thou yet forgive me?" she repeated, over and over again. "Wilt thou not frown? Wilt thou forgive?"

"I do forgive you, Hester," replied the minister, at length, with a deep utterance out of an abyss of sadness, but no anger. "I freely forgive you now. May God forgive us both! We are not, Hester, the worst sinners in the world. There is one worse than even the polluted priest! That old man's revenge has been blacker than my sin. He has violated, in cold blood, the sanctity of a human heart. Thou and I, Hester, never did so!"

"Never, never!" whispered she. "What we did had a consecration of its own. We felt it so! We said so to each other! Hast thou forgotten it?"

"Hush, Hester!" said Arthur Dimmesdale, rising from the ground. "No; I have not forgotten!"

They sat down again, side by side, and hand clasped in hand, on the mossy trunk of the fallen tree. Life had never brought them a gloomier hour; it was the point whither their pathway had so long been tending, and darkening ever, as it stole along; —and yet it inclosed a charm that made them linger upon it, and claim another, and another, and, after all, another moment. The forest was obscure around them, and creaked with a blast that was passing through it. The boughs were tossing heavily above their heads; while one solemn old tree groaned dolefully to another, as if telling the sad story of the pair that sat beneath, or constrained to forebode evil to come.

And yet they lingered. How dreary looked the forest-track that led backward to the settlement, where Hester Prynne must take up again the burden of her ignominy, and the minister the hollow mockery of his good name! So they lingered an instant longer. No golden light had ever been so precious as the gloom of this dark forest. Here, seen only by his eyes, the scarlet letter need not burn into the bosom of the fallen woman! Here, seen only by her eyes, Arthur Dimmesdale, false to God and man, might be, for one moment, true!

He started at a thought that suddenly occurred to him.

"Hester," cried he, "here is a new horror! Roger Chillingworth knows your purpose to reveal his true character. Will he continue, then, to keep our secret? What will now be the course of his revenge?"

"There is a strange secrecy in his nature," replied Hester, thoughtfully; "and it has grown upon him by the hidden practices of his revenge. I deem it not likely that he will betray the secret. He will doubtless seek other means of satiating his dark passion."

"And I!—how am I to live longer, breathing the same air with this deadly enemy?" exclaimed Arthur Dimmesdale, shrinking within himself, and pressing his hand nervously against his heart,—a gesture that had grown involuntary with him. "Think for me, Hester! Thou art strong. Resolve for me!"

"Thou must dwell no longer with this man," said Hester, slowly and firmly. "Thy heart must be no longer under his evil eye!"

"It were far worse than death!" replied the minister. "But how to avoid it? What choice remains to me? Shall I lie down again on these withered leaves, where I cast myself when thou didst tell me what he was? Must I sink down there, and die at once?"

"Alas, what a ruin has befallen thee!" said Hester, with the tears gushing into her eyes. "Wilt thou die for very weakness? There is no other cause!"

"The judgment of God is on me," answered the conscience-stricken priest. "It is too mighty for me to struggle with!"

"Heaven would show mercy," rejoined Hester, "hadst thou but the strength to take advantage of it."

"Be thou strong for me!" answered he. "Advise me what to do."

"Is the world then so narrow?" exclaimed Hester Prynne, fixing her deep eyes on the minister's, and instinctively exercising a magnetic power over a spirit so shattered and subdued, that it could hardly hold itself erect. "Doth the universe lie within the compass of yonder town, which only a little time ago was but a leaf-strewn desert, as lonely as this around us? Whither leads yonder forest-track? Backward to the settlement, thou sayest! Yes; but onward, too! Deeper it goes, and deeper, into the wilderness, less plainly to be seen at every step; until, some few miles hence, the yellow leaves will show no vestige of the white man's tread. There thou art free! So brief a journey would bring thee from a world where thou hast been most wretched, to one where thou mayest still be happy! Is there not shade enough in all this boundless forest to hide thy heart from the gaze of Roger Chillingworth?"

"Yes, Hester; but only under the fallen leaves!" replied the minister, with a sad smile.

"Then there is the broad pathway of the sea!" continued Hester. "It brought thee hither. If thou so choose, it will bear thee back again. In our native land, whether in some remote rural village or in vast London,—or, surely, in Germany, in France, in pleasant Italy,—thou wouldst be beyond his power and knowledge! And what hast thou to do with all these iron men, and their opinions? They have kept thy better part in bondage too long already!"

"It cannot be!" answered the minister, listening as if he were called upon to realize a dream. "I am powerless to go. Wretched and sinful as I am, I have had no other thought than to drag on my earthly existence in the sphere where Providence hath placed me. Lost as my own soul is, I would still do what I may for other human souls! I dare not quit my post, though an unfaithful sentinel, whose sure reward is death and dishonor, when his dreary watch shall come to an end!"

"Thou art crushed under this seven years' weight of misery," replied Hester, fervently resolved to buoy him up with her own energy. "But thou shalt leave it all behind thee! It shall not cumber thy steps, as thou treadest along the forest-path; neither shalt thou freight the ship with it, if thou prefer to cross the sea. Leave this wreck and ruin here where it hath happened! Meddle no more with it! Begin all anew! Hast thou exhausted possibility in the failure of this one trial? Not so! The future is yet full of trial and success. There is happiness to be enjoyed! There is good to be done! Exchange this false life of thine for a true one. Be, if thy spirit summon thee to such a mission, the teacher and apostle of the red men. Or,—as is more thy nature, —be a scholar and a sage among the wisest and the most renowned of the cultivated world. Preach! Write! Act! Do any thing, save to lie down and die! Give up this name of Arthur Dimmesdale, and make thyself another, and a high one, such as thou canst wear without fear or shame. Why shouldst thou tarry so much as one other day in the torments that have so gnawed into thy life!—that have made thee feeble to will and to do!—that will leave thee powerless even to repent! Up, and away!"

"O Hester!" cried Arthur Dimmesdale, in whose eyes a fitful light, kindled by her enthusiasm, flashed up and died away, "thou tellest of running a race to a man whose knees are tottering beneath him! I must die here. There is not the strength or courage left me to venture into the wide, strange, difficult world, alone!"

It was the last expression of the despondency of a broken spirit. He lacked energy to grasp the better fortune that seemed within his reach.

He repeated the word.

"Alone, Hester!"

"Thou shalt not go alone!" answered she, in a deep whisper.

Then, all was spoken!

XVIII: A Flood of Sunshine

Arthur Dimmesdale gazed into Hester's face with a look in which hope and joy shone out, indeed, but with fear betwixt them, and a kind of horror at her boldness, who had spoken what he vaguely hinted at, but dared not speak.

But Hester Prynne, with a mind of native courage and activity, and for so long a period not merely estranged, but outlawed, from society, had habituated herself to such latitude of speculation as was altogether foreign to the clergyman. She had wandered, without rule or guidance, in a moral wilderness; as vast, as intricate and shadowy, as the untamed forest, amid the gloom of which they were now holding a colloquy that was to decide their fate. Her intellect and heart had their home, as it were, in desert places, where she roamed as freely as the wild Indian in his woods. For years past she had looked from this estranged point of view at human institutions, and whatever priests or legislators had established; criticizing all with hardly more reverence than the Indian would feel for the clerical band, the judicial robe, the pillory, the gallows, the fireside, or the church. The tendency of her fate and fortunes had been to set her free. The scarlet letter was her passport into regions where other women dared not tread. Shame, Despair, Solitude! These had been her teachers,—stern and wild ones,—and they had made her strong, but taught her much amiss.

The minister, on the other hand, had never gone through an experience calculated to lead him beyond the scope of generally received laws; although, in a single instance, he had so fearfully transgressed one of the most sacred of them. But this had been a sin of passion, not of principle, nor even purpose. Since that wretched epoch, he had watched, with morbid zeal and minuteness, not his acts,—for those it was easy to arrange,—but each breath of emotion, and his every thought. At the head of the social system, as the clergymen of that day stood, he was only the more trammelled by its regulations, its principles, and even its prejudices. As a priest, the framework of his order inevitably hemmed him in. As a man who had once sinned, but who kept his conscience all alive and painfully sensitive by the fretting of an unhealed wound, he might have been supposed safer within the line of virtue, than if he had never sinned at all.

Thus, we seem to see that, as regarded Hester Prynne, the whole seven years of outlaw and ignominy had been little other than a preparation for this very hour. But Arthur Dimmesdale! Were such a man once more to fall, what plea could be urged in extenuation of his crime? None; unless it avail him somewhat, that he was broken down by long and exquisite suffering; that his mind was darkened and confused by the very remorse which harrowed it; that, between fleeing as an avowed criminal, and remaining as a hypocrite, conscience might find it hard to strike the balance; that it was human to avoid the peril of death and infamy, and the inscrutable machinations of an enemy; that, finally, to this poor pilgrim, on his dreary and desert path, faint, sick, miserable, there appeared a glimpse of human affection and sympathy, a new life, and a true one, in exchange for the heavy doom which he was now expiating. And be the stern and sad truth spoken, that the breach which guilt has once made into the human soul is never, in this mortal state, repaired. It may be watched and guarded; so that the enemy shall not force his way again into the citadel, and might even, in his subsequent assaults, select some other avenue, in preference to that where he had formerly succeeded. But there is still the ruined wall, and, near it, the stealthy tread of the foe that would win over again his unforgotten triumph.

The struggle, if there were one, need not be described. Let it suffice, that the clergyman resolved to flee, and not alone.

"If, in all these past seven years," thought he, "I could recall one instant of peace or hope, I would yet endure, for the sake of that earnest of Heaven's mercy. But now, —since I am irrevocably doomed,—wherefore should I not snatch the solace allowed to the condemned culprit before his execution? Or, if this be the path to a better life, as Hester would persuade me, I surely give up no fairer prospect by pursuing it! Neither can I any longer live without her companionship; so powerful is she to sustain, —so tender to soothe! O Thou to whom I dare not lift mine eyes, wilt Thou yet pardon me!"

"Thou wilt go!" said Hester calmly, as he met her glance.

The decision once made, a glow of strange enjoyment threw its flickering brightness over the trouble of his breast. It was the exhilarating effect—upon a prisoner just escaped from the dungeon of his own heart—of breathing the wild, free atmosphere of an unredeemed, unchristianized, lawless region. His spirit rose, as it were, with a bound, and attained a nearer prospect of the sky, than throughout all the misery which had kept him grovelling on the earth. Of a deeply religious temperament, there was inevitably a tinge of the devotional in his mood.

"Do I feel joy again?" cried he, wondering at himself. "Methought the germ of it was dead in me! O Hester, thou art my better angel! I seem to have flung myself —sick, sin-stained, and sorrow-blackened—down upon these forest-leaves, and to have risen up all made anew, and with new powers to glorify Him that hath been merciful! This is already the better life! Why did we not find it sooner?"

"Let us not look back," answered Hester Prynne. "The past is gone! Wherefore should we linger upon it now? See! With this symbol, I undo it all, and make it as it had never been!"

So speaking, she undid the clasp that fastened the scarlet letter, and, taking it from her bosom, threw it to a distance among the withered leaves. The mystic token alighted on the hither verge of the stream. With a hand's breadth farther flight it would have fallen into the water, and have given the little brook another woe to carry onward, besides the unintelligible tale which it still kept murmuring about. But there lay the embroidered letter, glittering like a lost jewel, which some ill-fated wanderer might pick up, and thenceforth be haunted by strange phantoms of guilt, sinkings of the heart, and unaccountable misfortune.

The stigma gone, Hester heaved a long, deep sigh, in which the burden of shame and anguish departed from her spirit. O exquisite relief! She had not known the weight, until she felt the freedom! By another impulse, she took off the formal cap that confined her hair; and down it fell upon her shoulders, dark and rich, with at once a shadow and a light in its abundance, and imparting the charm of softness to her features. There played around her mouth, and beamed out of her eyes, a radiant and tender smile, that seemed gushing from the very heart of womanhood. A crimson flush was glowing on her cheek, that had been long so pale. Her sex, her youth, and the whole richness of her beauty, came back from what men call the irrevocable past, and clustered themselves, with her maiden hope, and a happiness before unknown, within the magic circle of this hour. And, as if the gloom of the earth and sky had been but the effluence of these two mortal hearts, it vanished with their sorrow. All at once, as with a sudden smile of heaven, forth burst the sunshine, pouring a very flood into the obscure forest, gladdening each green leaf, transmuting the yellow fallen ones to gold, and gleaming adown the gray trunks of the solemn trees. The objects that had made a shadow hitherto, embodied the brightness now. The course of the little brook might be traced by its merry gleam afar into the wood's heart of mystery, which had become a mystery of joy.

Such was the sympathy of Nature—that wild, heathen Nature of the forest, never subjugated by human law, nor illumined by higher truth—with the bliss of these two spirits! Love, whether newly born, or aroused from a deathlike slumber, must always create a sunshine, filling the heart so full of radiance, that it overflows upon the outward world. Had the forest still kept its gloom, it would have been bright in Hester's eyes, and bright in Arthur Dimmesdale's!

Hester looked at him with the thrill of another joy.

"Thou must know Pearl!" said she. "Our little Pearl! Thou hast seen her,—yes, I know it!—but thou wilt see her now with other eyes. She is a strange child! I hardly comprehend her! But thou wilt love her dearly, as I do, and wilt advise me how to deal with her."

"Dost thou think the child will be glad to know me?" asked the minister, somewhat uneasily. "I have long shrunk from children, because they often show a distrust,—a backwardness to be familiar with me. I have even been afraid of little Pearl!"

"Ah, that was sad!" answered the mother. "But she will love thee dearly, and thou her. She is not far off. I will call her! Pearl! Pearl!"

"I see the child," observed the minister. "Yonder she is, standing in a streak of sunshine, a good way off, on the other side of the brook. So thou thinkest the child will love me?"

Hester smiled, and again called to Pearl, who was visible, at some distance, as the minister had described her, like a bright-apparelled vision, in a sunbeam, which fell down upon her through an arch of boughs. The ray quivered to and fro, making her figure dim or distinct,—now like a real child, now like a child's spirit,—as the splendor went and came again. She heard her mother's voice, and approached slowly through the forest.

Pearl had not found the hour pass wearisomely, while her mother sat talking with the clergyman. The great black forest—stern as it showed itself to those who brought the guilt and troubles of the world into its bosom—became the playmate of the lonely infant, as well as it knew how. Sombre as it was, it put on the kindest of its moods to welcome her. It offered her the partridge-berries, the growth of the preceding autumn, but ripening only in the spring, and now red as drops of blood upon the withered leaves. These Pearl gathered, and was pleased with their wild flavor. The small denizens of the wilderness hardly took pains to move out of her path. A partridge, indeed, with a brood of ten behind her, ran forward threateningly, but soon repented of her fierceness, and clucked to her young ones not to be afraid. A pigeon, alone on a low branch, allowed Pearl to come beneath, and uttered a sound as much of greeting as alarm. A squirrel, from the lofty depths of his domestic tree, chattered either in anger or merriment,—for a squirrel is such a choleric and humorous little personage that it is hard to distinguish between his moods,—so he chattered at the child, and flung down a nut upon her head. It was a last year's nut, and already gnawed by his sharp tooth. A fox, startled from his sleep by her light footstep on the leaves, looked inquisitively at Pearl, as doubting whether it were better to steal off, or renew his nap on the same spot. A wolf, it is said,—but here the tale has surely lapsed into the improbable,—came up, and smelt of Pearl's robe, and offered his savage head to be patted by her hand. The truth seems to be, however, that the mother-forest, and these wild things which it nourished, all recognized a kindred wildness in the human child.

And she was gentler here than in the grassy-margined streets of the settlement, or in her mother's cottage. The flowers appeared to know it; and one and another whispered, as she passed, "Adorn thyself with me, thou beautiful child, adorn thyself with me!"—and, to please them, Pearl gathered the violets, and anemones, and columbines, and some twigs of the freshest green, which the old trees held down before her eyes. With these she decorated her hair, and her young waist, and became a nymph-child, or an infant dryad,[131] or whatever else was in closest sympathy with the antique wood. In such guise had Pearl adorned herself, when she heard her mother's voice, and came slowly back.

Slowly; for she saw the clergyman!

XIX: The Child at the Brook-Side

"Thou wilt love her dearly," repeated Hester Prynne, as she and the minister sat watching little Pearl. "Dost thou not think her beautiful? And see with what natural

---

[131] Wood nymph in Greek mythology.

skill she has made those simple flowers adorn her! Had she gathered pearls, and diamonds, and rubies, in the wood, they could not have become her better. She is a splendid child! But I know whose brow she has!"

"Dost thou know, Hester," said Arthur Dimmesdale, with an unquiet smile, "that this dear child, tripping about always at thy side, hath caused me many an alarm? Methought—O Hester, what a thought is that, and how terrible to dread it!—that my own features were partly repeated in her face, and so strikingly that the world might see them! But she is mostly thine!"

"No, no! Not mostly!" answered the mother with a tender smile. "A little longer, and thou needest not to be afraid to trace whose child she is. But how strangely beautiful she looks, with those wild flowers in her hair! It is as if one of the fairies, whom we left in our dear old England, had decked her out to meet us."

It was with a feeling which neither of them had ever before experienced, that they sat and watched Pearl's slow advance. In her was visible the tie that united them. She had been offered to the world, these seven years past, as the living hieroglyphic, in which was revealed the secret they so darkly sought to hide,—all written in this symbol,—all plainly manifest,—had there been a prophet or magician skilled to read the character of flame! And Pearl was the oneness of their being. Be the foregone evil what it might, how could they doubt that their earthly lives and future destinies were conjoined, when they beheld at once the material union, and the spiritual idea, in whom they met, and were to dwell immortally together? Thoughts like these—and perhaps other thoughts, which they did not acknowledge or define—threw an awe about the child, as she came onward.

"Let her see nothing strange—no passion nor eagerness—in thy way of accosting her," whispered Hester. "Our Pearl is a fitful and fantastic little elf, sometimes. Especially, she is seldom tolerant of emotion, when she does not fully comprehend the why and wherefore. But the child hath strong affections! She loves me, and will love thee!"

"Thou canst not think," said the minister, glancing aside at Hester Prynne, "how my heart dreads this interview, and yearns for it! But, in truth, as I already told thee, children are not readily won to be familiar with me. They will not climb my knee, nor prattle in my ear, nor answer to my smile; but stand apart, and eye me strangely. Even little babes, when I take them in my arms, weep bitterly. Yet Pearl, twice in her little lifetime, hath been kind to me! The first time,—thou knowest it well! The last was when thou ledst her with thee to the house of yonder stern old Governor."

"And thou didst plead so bravely in her behalf and mine!" answered the mother. "I remember it; and so shall little Pearl. Fear nothing! She may be strange and shy at first, but will soon learn to love thee!"

By this time Pearl had reached the margin of the brook, and stood on the farther side, gazing silently at Hester and the clergyman, who still sat together on the mossy tree-trunk, waiting to receive her. Just where she had paused the brook chanced to form a pool, so smooth and quiet that it reflected a perfect image of her little figure, with all the brilliant picturesqueness of her beauty, in its adornment of flowers and wreathed foliage, but more refined and spiritualized than the reality. This image, so nearly identical with the living Pearl, seemed to communicate somewhat of its own shadowy and intangible quality to the child herself. It was strange, the way in which Pearl stood, looking so stedfastly at them through the dim medium of the forest-gloom; herself, meanwhile, all glorified with a ray of sunshine, that was attracted thitherward as by a certain sympathy. In the brook beneath stood another child,—another and the same,—with likewise its ray of golden light. Hester felt herself, in some indistinct and tantalizing manner, estranged from Pearl; as if the child, in her lonely ramble through the forest, had strayed out of the sphere in which she and her mother dwelt together, and was now vainly seeking to return to it.

There was both truth and error in the impression; the child and mother were estranged, but through Hester's fault, not Pearl's. Since the latter rambled from her side, another inmate had been admitted within the circle of the mother's feelings, and so modified the aspect of them all, that Pearl, the returning wanderer, could not find her wonted place, and hardly knew where she was.

"I have a strange fancy," observed the sensitive minister, "that this brook is the boundary between two worlds, and that thou canst never meet thy Pearl again. Or is she an elfish spirit, who, as the legends of our childhood taught us, is forbidden to cross a running stream? Pray hasten her; for this delay has already imparted a tremor to my nerves."

"Come, dearest child!" said Hester encouragingly, and stretching out both her arms. "How slow thou art! When hast thou been so sluggish before now? Here is a friend of mine, who must be thy friend also. Thou wilt have twice as much love, henceforward, as thy mother alone could give thee! Leap across the brook and come to us. Thou canst leap like a young deer!"

Pearl, without responding in any manner to these honey-sweet expressions, remained on the other side of the brook. Now she fixed her bright, wild eyes on her mother, now on the minister, and now included them both in the same glance; as if to detect and explain to herself the relation which they bore to one another. For some unaccountable reason, as Arthur Dimmesdale felt the child's eyes upon himself, his hand—with that gesture so habitual as to have become involuntary—stole over his heart. At length, assuming a singular air of authority, Pearl stretched out her hand, with the small forefinger extended, and pointing evidently towards her mother's breast. And beneath, in the mirror of the brook, there was the flower-girdled and sunny image of little Pearl, pointing her small forefinger too.

"Thou strange child, why dost thou not come to me?" exclaimed Hester.

Pearl still pointed with her forefinger; and a frown gathered on her brow; the more impressive from the childish, the almost baby-like aspect of the features that conveyed it. As her mother still kept beckoning to her, and arraying her face in a holiday suit of unaccustomed smiles, the child stamped her foot with a yet more imperious look and gesture. In the brook, again, was the fantastic beauty of the image, with its reflected frown, its pointed finger, and imperious gesture, giving emphasis to the aspect of little Pearl.

"Hasten, Pearl; or I shall be angry with thee!" cried Hester Prynne, who, however inured to such behaviour on the elf-child's part at other seasons, was naturally anxious for a more seemly deportment now. "Leap across the brook, naughty child, and run hither! Else I must come to thee!"

But Pearl, not a whit startled at her mother's threats, any more than mollified by her entreaties, now suddenly burst into a fit of passion, gesticulating violently, and throwing her small figure into the most extravagant contortions. She accompanied this wild outbreak with piercing shrieks, which the woods reverberated on all sides; so that, alone as she was in her childish and unreasonable wrath, it seemed as if a hidden multitude were lending her their sympathy and encouragement. Seen in the brook, once more, was the shadowy wrath of Pearl's image, crowned and girdled with flowers, but stamping its foot, wildly gesticulating, and, in the midst of all, still pointing its small forefinger at Hester's bosom!

"I see what ails the child," whispered Hester to the clergyman, and turning pale in spite of a strong effort to conceal her trouble and annoyance. "Children will not abide any, the slightest, change in the accustomed aspect of things that are daily before their eyes. Pearl misses something which she has always seen me wear!"

"I pray you," answered the minister, "if thou hast any means of pacifying the child, do it forthwith! Save it were the cankered wrath of an old witch, like Mistress Hibbins," added he, attempting to smile, "I know nothing that I would not sooner encounter than this passion in a child. In Pearl's young beauty, as in the wrinkled witch, it has a preternatural effect. Pacify her, if thou lovest me!"

Hester turned again towards Pearl, with a crimson blush upon her cheek, a conscious glance aside at the clergyman, and then a heavy sigh; while, even before she had time to speak, the blush yielded to a deadly pallor.

"Pearl," said she, sadly, "look down at thy feet! There!—before thee!—on the hither side of the brook!"

The child turned her eyes to the point indicated; and there lay the scarlet letter, so close upon the margin of the stream, that the gold embroidery was reflected in it.

"Bring it hither!" said Hester.

"Come thou and take it up!" answered Pearl.

"Was ever such a child!" observed Hester aside to the minister. "O, I have much to tell thee about her. But, in very truth, she is right as regards this hateful token. I must bear its torture yet a little longer,—only a few days longer,—until we shall have left this region, and look back hither as to a land which we have dreamed of. The forest cannot hide it! The mid-ocean shall take it from my hand, and swallow it up for ever!"

With these words, she advanced to the margin of the brook, took up the scarlet letter, and fastened it again into her bosom. Hopefully, but a moment ago, as Hester had spoken of drowning it in the deep sea, there was a sense of inevitable doom upon her, as she thus received back this deadly symbol from the hand of fate. She had flung it into infinite space!—she had drawn an hour's free breath!—and here again was the scarlet misery, glittering on the old spot! So it ever is, whether thus typified or no, that an evil deed invests itself with the character of doom. Hester next gathered up the heavy tresses of her hair, and confined them beneath her cap. As if there were a withering spell in the sad letter, her beauty, the warmth and richness of her womanhood, departed, like fading sunshine; and a gray shadow seemed to fall across her.

When the dreary change was wrought, she extended her hand to Pearl.

"Dost thou know thy mother now, child?" asked she, reproachfully, but with a subdued tone. "Wilt thou come across the brook, and own thy mother, now that she has her shame upon her,—now that she is sad?"

"Yes; now I will!" answered the child, bounding across the brook, and clasping Hester in her arms. "Now thou art my mother indeed! And I am thy little Pearl!"

In a mood of tenderness that was not usual with her, she drew down her mother's head, and kissed her brow and both her cheeks. But then—by a kind of necessity that always impelled this child to alloy whatever comfort she might chance to give with a throb of anguish—Pearl put up her mouth, and kissed the scarlet letter too!

"That was not kind!" said Hester. "When thou hast shown me a little love, thou mockest me!"

"Why doth the minister sit yonder?" asked Pearl.

"He waits to welcome thee," replied her mother. "Come thou, and entreat his blessing! He loves thee, my little Pearl, and loves thy mother too. Wilt thou not love him? Come! he longs to greet thee!"

"Doth he love us?" said Pearl, looking up with acute intelligence into her mother's face. "Will he go back with us, hand in hand, we three together, into the town?"

"Not now, dear child," answered Hester. "But in days to come he will walk hand in hand with us. We will have a home and fireside of our own; and thou shalt sit upon his knee; and he will teach thee many things, and love thee dearly. Thou wilt love him; wilt thou not?"

"And will he always keep his hand over his heart?" inquired Pearl.

"Foolish child, what a question is that!" exclaimed her mother. "Come and ask his blessing!"

But, whether influenced by the jealousy that seems instinctive with every petted child towards a dangerous rival, or from whatever caprice of her freakish nature, Pearl would show no favor to the clergyman. It was only by an exertion of force that her mother brought her up to him, hanging back, and manifesting her reluctance by odd grimaces; of which, ever since her babyhood, she had possessed a singular variety, and could transform her mobile physiognomy into a series of different aspects, with a new mischief in them, each and all. The minister—painfully embarrassed, but hoping that a kiss might prove a talisman to admit him into the child's kindlier regards—bent forward, and impressed one on her brow. Hereupon, Pearl broke away from her mother, and, running to the brook, stooped over it, and bathed her forehead, until the unwelcome kiss was quite washed off, and diffused through a long lapse of the gliding water. She then remained apart, silently watching Hester and the clergyman; while they talked together, and made such arrangements as were suggested by their new position, and the purposes soon to be fulfilled.

And now this fateful interview had come to a close. The dell was to be left a solitude among its dark, old trees, which, with their multitudinous tongues, would whisper long of what had passed there, and no mortal be the wiser. And the melancholy brook would add this other tale to the mystery with which its little heart was already overburdened, and whereof it still kept up a murmuring babble, with not a whit more cheerfulness of tone than for ages heretofore.

XX: The Minister in a Maze

As the minister departed, in advance of Hester Prynne and little Pearl, he threw a backward glance; half expecting that he should discover only some faintly traced features or outline of the mother and the child, slowly fading into the twilight of the woods. So great a vicissitude in his life could not at once be received as real. But there was Hester, clad in her gray robe, still standing beside the tree-trunk, which some blast had overthrown a long antiquity ago, and which time had ever since been covering with moss, so that these two fated ones, with earth's heaviest burden on them, might there sit down together, and find a single hour's rest and solace. And there was Pearl, too, lightly dancing from the margin of the brook,—now that the intrusive third person was gone,—and taking her old place by her mother's side. So the minister had not fallen asleep, and dreamed!

In order to free his mind from this indistinctness and duplicity of impression, which vexed it with a strange disquietude, he recalled and more thoroughly defined the plans which Hester and himself had sketched for their departure. It had been determined between them, that the Old World, with its crowds and cities, offered them a more eligible shelter and concealment than the wilds of New England, or all America, with its alternatives of an Indian wigwam, or the few settlements of Europeans, scattered thinly along the seaboard. Not to speak of the clergyman's health, so inadequate to sustain the hardships of a forest life, his native gifts, his culture, and his entire development would secure him a home only in the midst of civilization and refinement; the higher the state, the more delicately adapted to it the man. In furtherance of this choice, it so happened that a ship lay in the harbour; one of those questionable cruisers, frequent at that day, which, without being absolutely outlaws of the deep, yet roamed over its surface with a remarkable irresponsibility of character. This vessel had recently arrived from the Spanish Main, and, within three days' time, would sail for Bristol.[132] Hester Prynne—whose vocation, as a self-enlisted Sister of Charity, had brought her acquainted with the captain and crew—could take upon herself to secure the passage of two individuals and a child, with all the secrecy which circumstances rendered more than desirable.

The minister had inquired of Hester, with no little interest, the precise time at which the vessel might be expected to depart. It would probably be on the fourth day from the present. "That is most fortunate!" he had then said to himself. Now, why the Reverend Mr. Dimmesdale considered it so very fortunate, we hesitate to reveal. Nevertheless,—to hold nothing back from the reader,—it was because, on the third day from the present, he was to preach the Election Sermon;[133] and, as such an occasion formed an honorable epoch in the life of a New England clergyman, he could not have chanced upon a more suitable mode and time of terminating his professional career. "At least, they shall say of me," thought this exemplary man, "that I leave no public duty unperformed, nor ill performed!" Sad, indeed, that an introspection so profound and acute as this poor minister's should be so miserably deceived! We have had, and may still have, worse things to tell of him; but none, we apprehend, so pitiably weak; no evidence, at once so slight and irrefragable, of a subtle disease, that had long since begun to eat into the real substance of his character. No man, for any considerable period, can wear one face to himself, and another to the multitude, without finally getting bewildered as to which may be the true.

The excitement of Mr. Dimmesdale's feelings, as he returned from his interview with Hester, lent him unaccustomed physical energy, and hurried him townward at a rapid pace. The pathway among the woods seemed wilder, more uncouth with its rude natural obstacles, and less trodden by the foot of man, than he remembered it on his outward journey. But he leaped across the plashy places, thrust himself through

---

[132] Seaport in southwest England.
[133] Sermon delivered at the inauguration of the newly elected colonial governor.

the clinging underbrush, climbed the ascent, plunged into the hollow, and overcame, in short, all the difficulties of the track, with an unweariable activity that astonished him. He could not but recall how feebly, and with what frequent pauses for breath, he had toiled over the same ground only two days before. As he drew near the town, he took an impression of change from the series of familiar objects that presented themselves. It seemed not yesterday, not one, nor two, but many days, or even years ago, since he had quitted them. There, indeed, was each former trace of the street, as he remembered it, and all the peculiarities of the houses, with the due multitude of gable-peaks, and a weathercock at every point where his memory suggested one. Not the less, however, came this importunately obtrusive sense of change. The same was true as regarded the acquaintances whom he met, and all the well-known shapes of human life, about the little town. They looked neither older nor younger, now; the beards of the aged were no whiter, nor could the creeping babe of yesterday walk on his feet to-day; it was impossible to describe in what respect they differed from the individuals on whom he had so recently bestowed a parting glance; and yet the minister's deepest sense seemed to inform him of their mutability. A similar impression struck him most remarkably, as he passed under the walls of his own church. The edifice had so very strange, and yet so familiar, an aspect, that Mr. Dimmesdale's mind vibrated between two ideas; either that he had seen it only in a dream hitherto, or that he was merely dreaming about it now.

This phenomenon, in the various shapes which it assumed, indicated no external change, but so sudden and important a change in the spectator of the familiar scene, that the intervening space of a single day had operated on his consciousness like the lapse of years. The minister's own will, and Hester's will, and the fate that grew between them, had wrought this transformation. It was the same town as heretofore; but the same minister returned not from the forest. He might have said to the friends who greeted him,—"I am not the man for whom you take me! I left him yonder in the forest, withdrawn into a secret dell, by a mossy tree-trunk, and near a melancholy brook! Go, seek your minister, and see if his emaciated figure, his thin cheek, his white, heavy, pain-wrinkled brow, be not flung down there like a cast-off garment!" His friends, no doubt, would still have insisted with him,—"Thou art thyself the man!"—but the error would have been their own, not his.

Before Mr. Dimmesdale reached home, his inner man gave him other evidences of a revolution in the sphere of thought and feeling. In truth, nothing short of a total change of dynasty and moral code, in that interior kingdom, was adequate to account for the impulses now communicated to the unfortunate and startled minister. At every step he was incited to do some strange, wild, wicked thing or other, with a sense that it would be at once involuntary and intentional; in spite of himself, yet growing out of a profounder self than that which opposed the impulse. For instance, he met one of his own deacons. The good old man addressed him with the paternal affection and patriarchal privilege, which his venerable age, his upright and holy character, and his station in the Church, entitled him to use; and, conjoined with this, the deep, almost worshipping respect, which the minister's professional and private claims alike demanded. Never was there a more beautiful example of how the majesty of age and wisdom may comport with the obeisance and respect enjoined upon it, as from a lower social rank and inferior order of endowment, towards a higher. Now, during a conversation of some two or three moments between the Reverend Mr. Dimmesdale and this excellent and hoary-bearded deacon, it was only by the most careful self-control that the former could refrain from uttering certain blasphemous suggestions that rose into his mind, respecting the communion-supper. He absolutely trembled and turned pale as ashes, lest his tongue should wag itself, in utterance of these horrible matters, and plead his own consent for so doing, without his having fairly given it. And, even with this terror in his heart, he could hardly avoid laughing to imagine how the sanctified old patriarchal deacon would have been petrified by his minister's impiety!

Again, another incident of the same nature. Hurrying along the street, the Reverend Mr. Dimmesdale encountered the eldest female member of his church; a most pious and exemplary old dame; poor, widowed, lonely, and with a heart as full of reminiscences about her dead husband and children, and her dead friends of long ago, as a burial-ground is full of storied grave-stones. Yet all this, which would else have been such heavy sorrow, was made almost a solemn joy to her devout old soul by religious consolations and the truths of Scripture, wherewith she had fed herself continually for more than thirty years. And, since Mr. Dimmesdale had taken her in charge, the good grandam's chief earthly comfort—which, unless it had been likewise a heavenly comfort, could have been none at all—was to meet her pastor, whether casually, or of set purpose, and be refreshed with a word of warm, fragrant, heaven-breathing Gospel truth from his beloved lips into her dulled, but rapturously attentive ear. But, on this occasion, up to the moment of putting his lips to the old woman's ear, Mr. Dimmesdale, as the great enemy of souls would have it, could recall no text of Scripture, nor aught else, except a brief, pithy, and, as it then appeared to him, unanswerable argument against the immortality of the human soul. The instilment thereof into her mind would probably have caused this aged sister to drop down dead, at once, as by the effect of an intensely poisonous infusion. What he really did whisper, the minister could never afterwards recollect. There was, perhaps, a fortunate disorder in his utterance, which failed to impart any distinct idea to the good widow's comprehension, or which Providence interpreted after a method of its own. Assuredly, as the minister looked back, he beheld an expression of divine gratitude and ecstasy that seemed like the shine of the celestial city on her face, so wrinkled and ashy pale.

Again, a third instance. After parting from the old church-member, he met the youngest sister of them all. It was a maiden newly won—and won by the Reverend Mr. Dimmesdale's own sermon, on the Sabbath after his vigil—to barter the transitory pleasures of the world for the heavenly hope, that was to assume brighter substance as life grew dark around her, and which would gild the utter gloom with final glory. She was fair and pure as a lily that had bloomed in Paradise. The minister knew well that he was himself enshrined within the stainless sanctity of her heart, which hung its snowy curtains about his image, imparting to religion the warmth of love, and to love a religious purity. Satan, that afternoon, had surely led the poor young girl away from her mother's side, and thrown her into the pathway of this sorely tempted, or—shall we not rather say?—this lost and desperate man. As she drew nigh, the arch-fiend whispered him to condense into small compass and drop into her tender bosom a germ of evil that would be sure to blossom darkly soon, and bear black fruit betimes. Such was his sense of power over this virgin soul, trusting him as she did, that the minister felt potent to blight all the field of innocence with but one wicked look, and develop all its opposite with but a word. So—with a mightier struggle than he had yet sustained—he held his Geneva cloak before his face, and hurried onward, making no sign of recognition, and leaving the young sister to digest his rudeness as she might. She ransacked her conscience,—which was full of harmless little matters, like her pocket or her work-bag,—and took herself to task, poor thing, for a thousand imaginary faults; and went about her household duties with swollen eyelids the next morning.

Before the minister had time to celebrate his victory over this last temptation, he was conscious of another impulse, more ludicrous, and almost as horrible. It was,—we blush to tell it,—it was to stop short in the road, and teach some very wicked words to a knot of little Puritan children who were playing there, and had but just begun to talk. Denying himself this freak, as unworthy of his cloth, he met a drunken seaman, one of the ship's crew from the Spanish Main. And, here, since he had so valiantly forborne all other wickedness, poor Mr. Dimmesdale longed, at least, to shake hands with the tarry blackguard, and recreate himself with a few improper jests, such as dissolute sailors so abound with, and a volley of good, round, solid, satisfactory, and heaven-defying oaths! It was not so much a better principle, as partly his natural good taste, and still more his buckramed[134] habit of clerical decorum, that carried him safely through the latter crisis.

"What is it that haunts and tempts me thus?" cried the minister to himself, at length, pausing in the street, and striking his hand against his forehead. "Am I mad? or am I given over utterly to the fiend? Did I make a contract with him in the forest, and sign it with my blood? And does he now summon me to its fulfilment, by suggesting the performance of every wickedness which his most foul imagination can conceive?"

At the moment when the Reverend Mr. Dimmesdale thus communed with himself, and struck his forehead with his hand, old Mistress Hibbins, the reputed witch-lady, is said to have been passing by. She made a very grand appearance; having on a high head-dress, a rich gown of velvet, and a ruff done up with the famous yellow starch, of which Ann Turner, her especial friend, had taught her the secret, before this last good lady had been hanged for Sir Thomas Overbury's murder. Whether the witch had read the minister's thoughts, or no, she came to a full stop, looked shrewdly into his face, smiled craftily, and—though little given to converse with clergymen—began a conversation.

"So, reverend Sir, you have made a visit into the forest," observed the witch-lady, nodding her high head-dress at him. "The next time, I pray you to allow me only a fair warning, and I shall be proud to bear you company. Without taking overmuch upon myself, my good word will go far towards gaining any strange gentleman a fair reception from yonder potentate you wot of!"

"I profess, madam," answered the clergyman, with a grave obeisance, such as the lady's rank demanded, and his own good-breeding made imperative,—"I profess, on my conscience and character, that I am utterly bewildered as touching the purport of your words! I went not into the forest to seek a potentate; neither do I, at any future time, design a visit thither, with a view to gaining the favor of such personage. My one sufficient object was to greet that pious friend of mine, the Apostle Eliot, and rejoice with him over the many precious souls he hath won from heathendom!"

"Ha, ha, ha!" cackled the old witch-lady, still nodding her high head-dress at the minister. "Well, well, we must needs talk thus in the daytime! You carry it off like

---

[134] I.e., stiff like the fabric buckram.

an old hand! But at midnight, and in the forest, we shall have other talk together!"

She passed on with her aged stateliness, but often turning back her head and smiling at him, like one willing to recognize a secret intimacy of connection.

"Have I then sold myself," thought the minister, "to the fiend whom, if men say true, this yellow-starched and velveted old hag has chosen for her prince and master!"

The wretched minister! He had made a bargain very like it! Tempted by a dream of happiness, he had yielded himself with deliberate choice, as he had never done before, to what he knew was deadly sin. And the infectious poison of that sin had been thus rapidly diffused throughout his moral system. It had stupefied all blessed impulses, and awakened into vivid life the whole brotherhood of bad ones. Scorn, bitterness, unprovoked malignity, gratuitous desire of ill, ridicule of whatever was good and holy, all awoke, to tempt, even while they frightened him. And his encounter with old Mistress Hibbins, if it were a real incident, did but show his sympathy and fellowship with wicked mortals and the world of perverted spirits.

He had by this time reached his dwelling, on the edge of the burial-ground, and, hastening up the stairs, took refuge in his study. The minister was glad to have reached this shelter, without first betraying himself to the world by any of those strange and wicked eccentricities to which he had been continually impelled while passing through the streets. He entered the accustomed room, and looked around him on its books, its windows, its fireplace, and the tapestried comfort of the walls, with the same perception of strangeness that had haunted him throughout his walk from the forest-dell into the town, and thitherward. Here he had studied and written; here, gone through fast and vigil, and come forth half alive; here, striven to pray; here, borne a hundred thousand agonies! There was the Bible, in its rich old Hebrew, with Moses and the Prophets speaking to him, and God's voice through all! There, on the table, with the inky pen beside it, was an unfinished sermon, with a sentence broken in the midst, where his thoughts had ceased to gush out upon the page two days before. He knew that it was himself, the thin and white-cheeked minister, who had done and suffered these things, and written thus far into the Election Sermon! But he seemed to stand apart, and eye this former self with scornful, pitying, but half-envious curiosity. That self was gone! Another man had returned out of the forest; a wiser one; with a knowledge of hidden mysteries which the simplicity of the former never could have reached. A bitter kind of knowledge that!

While occupied with these reflections, a knock came at the door of the study, and the minister said, "Come in!"—not wholly devoid of an idea that he might behold an evil spirit. And so he did! It was old Roger Chillingworth that entered. The minister stood, white and speechless, with one hand on the Hebrew Scriptures, and the other spread upon his breast.

"Welcome home, reverend Sir!" said the physician. "And how found you that godly man, the Apostle Eliot? But methinks, dear Sir, you look pale; as if the travel through the wilderness had been too sore for you. Will not my aid be requisite to put you in heart and strength to preach your Election Sermon?"

"Nay, I think not so," rejoined the Reverend Mr. Dimmesdale. "My journey, and the sight of the holy Apostle yonder, and the free air which I have breathed, have done me good, after so long confinement in my study. I think to need no more of your drugs, my kind physician, good though they be, and administered by a friendly hand."

All this time, Roger Chillingworth was looking at the minister with the grave and intent regard of a physician towards his patient. But, in spite of this outward show, the latter was almost convinced of the old man's knowledge, or, at least, his confident suspicion, with respect to his own interview with Hester Prynne. The physician knew, then, that, in the minister's regard, he was no longer a trusted friend, but his bitterest enemy. So much being known, it would appear natural that a part of it should be expressed. It is singular, however, how long a time often passes before words embody things; and with what security two persons, who choose to avoid a certain subject, may approach its very verge, and retire without disturbing it. Thus, the minister felt no apprehension that Roger Chillingworth would touch, in express words, upon the real position which they sustained towards one another. Yet did the physician, in his dark way, creep frightfully near the secret.

"Were it not better," said he, "that you use my poor skill to-night? Verily, dear Sir, we must take pains to make you strong and vigorous for this occasion of the Election discourse. The people look for great things from you; apprehending that another year may come about, and find their pastor gone."

"Yea, to another world," replied the minister, with pious resignation. "Heaven grant it be a better one; for, in good sooth, I hardly think to tarry with my flock through the flitting seasons of another year! But, touching your medicine, kind Sir, in my present frame of body I need it not."

"I joy to hear it," answered the physician. "It may be that my remedies, so long administered in vain, begin now to take due effect. Happy man were I, and well deserving of New England's gratitude, could I achieve this cure!"

"I thank you from my heart, most watchful friend," said the Reverend Mr. Dimmesdale, with a solemn smile. "I thank you, and can but requite your good deeds with my prayers."

"A good man's prayers are golden recompense!" rejoined old Roger Chillingworth, as he took his leave. "Yea, they are the current gold coin of the New Jerusalem, with the King's own mint-mark on them!"

Left alone, the minister summoned a servant of the house, and requested food, which, being set before him, he ate with ravenous appetite. Then, flinging the already written pages of the Election Sermon into the fire, he forthwith began another, which he wrote with such an impulsive flow of thought and emotion, that he fancied himself inspired; and only wondered that Heaven should see fit to transmit the grand and solemn music of its oracles through so foul an organ-pipe as he. However, leaving that mystery to solve itself, or go unsolved for ever, he drove his task onward, with earnest haste and ecstasy. Thus the night fled away, as if it were a winged steed, and he careering on it; morning came, and peeped blushing through the curtains; and at last sunrise threw a golden beam into the study, and laid it right across the minister's bedazzled eyes. There he was, with the pen still between his fingers, and a vast, immeasurable tract of written space behind him!

XXI: *The New England Holiday*

Betimes in the morning of the day on which the new Governor was to receive his office at the hands of the people, Hester Prynne and little Pearl came into the market-place. It was already thronged with the craftsmen and other plebeian inhabitants of the town, in considerable numbers; among whom, likewise, were many rough figures, whose attire of deer-skins marked them as belonging to some of the forest settlements, which surrounded the little metropolis of the colony.

On this public holiday, as on all other occasions, for seven years past, Hester was clad in a garment of coarse gray cloth. Not more by its hue than by some indescribable peculiarity in its fashion, it had the effect of making her fade personally out of sight and outline; while, again, the scarlet letter brought her back from this twilight indistinctness, and revealed her under the moral aspect of its own illumination. Her face, so long familiar to the townspeople, showed the marble quietude which they were accustomed to behold there. It was like a mask; or rather, like the frozen calmness of a dead woman's features; owing this dreary resemblance to the fact that Hester was actually dead, in respect to any claim of sympathy, and had departed out of the world with which she still seemed to mingle.

It might be, on this one day, that there was an expression unseen before, nor, indeed, vivid enough to be detected now; unless some preternaturally gifted observer should have first read the heart, and have afterwards sought a corresponding development in the countenance and mien. Such a spiritual seer might have conceived, that, after sustaining the gaze of the multitude through seven miserable years as a necessity, a penance, and something which it was a stern religion to endure, she now, for one last time more, encountered it freely and voluntarily, in order to convert what had so long been agony into a kind of triumph. "Look your last on the scarlet letter and its wearer!"—the people's victim and life-long bond-slave, as they fancied her, might say to them. "Yet a little while, and she will be beyond your reach! A few hours longer, and the deep, mysterious ocean will quench and hide for ever the symbol which ye have caused to burn upon her bosom!" Nor were it an inconsistency too improbable to be assigned to human nature, should we suppose a feeling of regret in Hester's mind, at the moment when she was about to win her freedom from the pain which had been thus deeply incorporated with her being. Might there not be an irresistible desire to quaff a last, long, breathless draught of the cup of wormwood and aloes, with which nearly all her years of womanhood had been perpetually flavored? The wine of life, henceforth to be presented to her lips, must be indeed rich, delicious, and exhilarating, in its chased and golden beaker; or else leave an inevitable and weary languor, after the lees of bitterness wherewith she had been drugged, as with a cordial of intensest potency.

Pearl was decked out with airy gayety. It would have been impossible to guess that this bright and sunny apparition owed its existence to the shape of gloomy gray; or that a fancy, at once so gorgeous and so delicate as must have been requisite to contrive the child's apparel, was the same that had achieved a task perhaps more difficult, in imparting so distinct a peculiarity to Hester's simple robe. The dress, so proper was it to little Pearl, seemed an effluence, or inevitable development and outward manifestation of her character, no more to be separated from her than the many-hued brilliancy from a butterfly's wing, or the painted glory from the leaf of a bright flower. As with these, so with the child; her garb was all of one idea with her nature. On this eventful day, moreover, there was a certain singular inquietude and excitement in her mood, resembling nothing so much as the shimmer of a diamond, that sparkles and flashes with the varied throbbings of the breast on which it is displayed. Children have always a sympathy in the agitations of those connected with them; always, especially, a sense of any trouble or impending revolution, of whatever kind, in domestic circumstances; and therefore Pearl, who was the gem on her mother's unquiet bosom, betrayed, by the very dance of her spirits, the emotions which none could detect in the marble passiveness of Hester's brow.

This effervescence made her flit with a bird-like movement, rather than walk by her mother's side. She broke continually into shouts of a wild, inarticulate, and sometimes piercing music. When they reached the market-place, she became still more restless, on perceiving the stir and bustle that enlivened the spot; for it was usually more like the broad and lonesome green before a village meeting-house, than the centre of a town's business.

"Why, what is this, mother?" cried she. "Wherefore have all the people left their work to-day? Is it a play-day for the whole world? See, there is the blacksmith! He has washed his sooty face, and put on his Sabbath-day clothes, and looks as if he would gladly be merry, if any kind body would only teach him how! And there is Master Brackett, the old jailer, nodding and smiling at me. Why does he do so, mother?"

"He remembers thee a little babe, my child," answered Hester.

"He should not nod and smile at me, for all that,—the black, grim, ugly-eyed old man!" said Pearl. "He may nod at thee if he will; for thou art clad in gray, and wearest the scarlet letter. But, see, mother, how many faces of strange people, and Indians among them, and sailors! What have they all come to do here in the market-place?"

"They wait to see the procession pass," said Hester. "For the Governor and the magistrates are to go by, and the ministers, and all the great people and good people, with the music, and the soldiers marching before them."

"And will the minister be there?" asked Pearl. "And will he hold out both his hands to me, as when thou ledst me to him from the brook-side?"

"He will be there, child," answered her mother. "But he will not greet thee to-day; nor must thou greet him."

"What a strange, sad man is he!" said the child, as if speaking partly to herself. "In the dark night-time, he calls us to him, and holds thy hand and mine, as when we stood with him on the scaffold yonder! And in the deep forest, where only the old trees can hear, and the strip of sky see it, he talks with thee, sitting on a heap of moss! And he kisses my forehead, too, so that the little brook would hardly wash it off! But here in the sunny day, and among all the people, he knows us not; nor must we know him! A strange, sad man is he, with his hand always over his heart!"

"Be quiet, Pearl! Thou understandest not these things," said her mother. "Think not now of the minister, but look about thee, and see how cheery is every body's face to-day. The children have come from their schools, and the grown people from their workshops and their fields, on purpose to be happy. For, to-day, a new man is beginning to rule over them; and so—as has been the custom of mankind ever since a nation was first gathered—they make merry and rejoice; as if a good and golden year were at length to pass over the poor old world!"

It was as Hester said, in regard to the unwonted jollity that brightened the faces of the people. Into this festal season of the year—as it already was, and continued to be during the greater part of two centuries—the Puritans compressed whatever mirth and public joy they deemed allowable to human infirmity; thereby so far dispelling the customary cloud, that, for the space of a single holiday, they appeared scarcely more grave than most other communities at a period of general affliction.

But we perhaps exaggerate the gray or sable tinge, which undoubtedly characterized the mood and manners of the age. The persons now in the market-place of Boston had not been born to an inheritance of Puritanic gloom. They were native Englishmen, whose fathers had lived in the sunny richness of the Elizabethan epoch; a time when the life of England, viewed as one great mass, would appear to have been as stately, magnificent, and joyous, as the world has ever witnessed. Had they followed their hereditary taste, the New England settlers would have illustrated all events of public importance by bonfires, banquets, pageantries, and processions. Nor would it have been impracticable, in the observance of majestic ceremonies, to combine mirthful recreation with solemnity, and give, as it were, a grotesque and brilliant embroidery to the great robe of state, which a nation, at such festivals, puts on. There was some shadow of an attempt of this kind in the mode of celebrating the day on which the political year of the colony commenced. The dim reflection of a remembered splendor, a colorless and manifold diluted repetition of what they had beheld in proud old London,—we will not say at a royal coronation, but at a Lord Mayor's show,[135] —might be traced in the customs which our forefathers instituted, with reference to the annual installation of magistrates. The fathers and founders of the commonwealth —the statesman, the priest, and the soldier—deemed it a duty then to assume the outward state and majesty, which, in accordance with antique style, was looked upon as the proper garb of public or social eminence. All came forth, to move in procession before the people's eye, and thus impart a needed dignity to the simple framework of a government so newly constructed.

Then, too, the people were countenanced, if not encouraged, in relaxing the severe and close application to their various modes of rugged industry, which, at all other times, seemed of the same piece and material with their religion. Here, it is true, were none of the appliances which popular merriment would so readily have found in the England of Elizabeth's time, or that of James;[136]—no rude shows of a theatrical kind; no minstrel with his harp and legendary ballad, nor gleeman, with an ape dancing to his music; no juggler, with his tricks of mimic witchcraft; no Merry Andrew,[137] to stir up the multitude with jests, perhaps hundreds of years old, but still effective, by their appeals to the very broadest sources of mirthful sympathy. All such professors of the several branches of jocularity would have been sternly repressed, not only by the rigid discipline of law, but by the general sentiment which gives law its vitality. Not the less, however, the great, honest face of the people smiled, grimly, perhaps, but widely too. Nor were sports wanting, such as the colonists had witnessed, and shared in, long ago, at the country fairs and on the village-greens of England; and which it was thought well to keep alive on this new soil, for the sake of the courage and manliness that were essential in them. Wrestling-matches, in the differing fashions of Cornwall and Devonshire, were seen here and there about the market-place; in one corner, there was a friendly bout at quarterstaff;[138] and—what attracted most interest of all—on the platform of the pillory, already so noted in our pages, two masters of defence were commencing an exhibition with the buckler[139] and broadsword. But, much to the disappointment of the crowd, this latter business was broken off by the

---

[135] Annual ceremonies of the inauguration of the Lord Mayor of London.
[136] Elizabeth I reigned from 1558 to 1603 and James I from 1603 to 1625, the years before the Puritans' rise to power.
[137] Clown.
[138] I.e., a set-to with a long, wooden staff.
[139] Shield.

interposition of the town beadle, who had no idea of permitting the majesty of the law to be violated by such an abuse of one of its consecrated places.

It may not be too much to affirm, on the whole, (the people being then in the first stages of joyless deportment, and the offspring of sires who had known how to be merry, in their day,) that they would compare favorably, in point of holiday keeping, with their descendants, even at so long an interval as ourselves. Their immediate posterity, the generation next to the early emigrants, wore the blackest shade of Puritanism, and so darkened the national visage with it, that all the subsequent years have not sufficed to clear it up. We have yet to learn again the forgotten art of gayety.

The picture of human life in the market-place, though its general tint was the sad gray, brown, or black of the English emigrants, was yet enlivened by some diversity of hue. A party of Indians—in their savage finery of curiously embroidered deer-skin robes, wampum-belts, red and yellow ochre, and feathers, and armed with the bow and arrow and stone-headed spear—stood apart, with countenances of inflexible gravity, beyond what even the Puritan aspect could attain. Nor, wild as were these painted barbarians, were they the wildest feature of the scene. This distinction could more justly be claimed by some mariners,—a part of the crew of the vessel from the Spanish Main,—who had come ashore to see the humors of Election Day. They were rough-looking desperadoes, with sun-blackened faces, and an immensity of beard; their wide, short trousers were confined about the waist by belts, often clasped with a rough plate of gold, and sustaining always a long knife, and, in some instances, a sword. From beneath their broad-brimmed hats of palm-leaf, gleamed eyes which, even in good nature and merriment, had a kind of animal ferocity. They transgressed, without fear or scruple, the rules of behaviour that were binding on all others; smoking tobacco under the beadle's very nose, although each whiff would have cost a townsman a shilling; and quaffing, at their pleasure, draughts of wine or aqua-vitæ[140] from pocket-flasks, which they freely tendered to the gaping crowd around them. It remarkably characterized the incomplete morality of the age, rigid as we call it, that a license was allowed the seafaring class, not merely for their freaks on shore, but for far more desperate deeds on their proper element. The sailor of that day would go near to be arraigned as a pirate in our own. There could be little doubt, for instance, that this very ship's crew, though no unfavorable specimens of the nautical brotherhood, had been guilty, as we should phrase it, of depredations on the Spanish commerce, such as would have perilled all their necks in a modern court of justice.

But the sea, in those old times, heaved, swelled, and foamed very much at its own will, or subject only to the tempestuous wind, with hardly any attempts at regulation by human law. The buccaneer on the wave might relinquish his calling, and become at once, if he chose, a man of probity and piety on land; nor, even in the full career of his reckless life, was he regarded as a personage with whom it was disreputable to traffic, or casually associate. Thus, the Puritan elders, in their black cloaks, starched bands, and steeple-crowned hats, smiled not unbenignantly at the clamor and rude deportment of these jolly seafaring men; and it excited neither surprise nor animadversion when so reputable a citizen as old Roger Chillingworth, the physician, was seen to enter the market-place, in close and familiar talk with the commander of the questionable vessel.

---

[140] Brandy.

The latter was by far the most showy and gallant figure, so far as apparel went, anywhere to be seen among the multitude. He wore a profusion of ribbons on his garment, and gold lace on his hat, which was also encircled by a gold chain, and surmounted with a feather. There was a sword at his side, and a sword-cut on his forehead, which, by the arrangement of his hair, he seemed anxious rather to display than hide. A landsman could hardly have worn this garb and shown this face, and worn and shown them both with such a galliard[141] air, without undergoing stern question before a magistrate, and probably incurring fine or imprisonment, or perhaps an exhibition in the stocks. As regarded the shipmaster, however, all was looked upon as pertaining to the character, as to a fish his glistening scales.

After parting from the physician, the commander of the Bristol ship strolled idly through the market-place; until, happening to approach the spot where Hester Prynne was standing, he appeared to recognize, and did not hesitate to address her. As was usually the case wherever Hester stood, a small, vacant area—a sort of magic circle —had formed itself about her, into which, though the people were elbowing one another at a little distance, none ventured, or felt disposed to intrude. It was a forcible type of the moral solitude in which the scarlet letter enveloped its fated wearer; partly by her own reserve, and partly by the instinctive, though no longer so unkindly, withdrawal of her fellow-creatures. Now, if never before, it answered a good purpose, by enabling Hester and the seaman to speak together without risk of being overheard; and so changed was Hester Prynne's repute before the public, that the matron in town most eminent for rigid morality could not have held such intercourse with less result of scandal than herself.

"So, mistress," said the mariner, "I must bid the steward make ready one more berth than you bargained for! No fear of scurvy or ship-fever, this voyage! What with the ship's surgeon and this other doctor, our only danger will be from drug or pill; more by token, as there is a lot of apothecary's stuff aboard, which I traded for with a Spanish vessel."

"What mean you?" inquired Hester, startled more than she permitted to appear. "Have you another passenger?"

"Why, know you not," cried the shipmaster, "that this physician here—Chilling-worth, he calls himself—is minded to try my cabin-fare with you? Ay, ay, you must have known it; for he tells me he is of your party, and a close friend to the gentleman you spoke of,—he that is in peril from these sour old Puritan rulers!"

"They know each other well, indeed," replied Hester, with a mien of calmness, though in the utmost consternation. "They have long dwelt together."

Nothing further passed between the mariner and Hester Prynne. But, at that instant, she beheld old Roger Chillingworth himself, standing in the remotest corner of the market-place, and smiling on her; a smile which—across the wide and bustling square, and through all the talk and laughter, and various thoughts, moods, and interests of the crowd—conveyed secret and fearful meaning.

XXII: *The Procession*

Before Hester Prynne could call together her thoughts, and consider what was practicable to be done in this new and startling aspect of affairs, the sound of military

---

[141] Gay or lively.

music was heard approaching along a contiguous street. It denoted the advance of the procession of magistrates and citizens, on its way towards the meeting-house; where, in compliance with a custom thus early established, and ever since observed, the Reverend Mr. Dimmesdale was to deliver an Election Sermon.

Soon the head of the procession showed itself, with a slow and stately march, turning a corner, and making its way across the market-place. First came the music. It comprised a variety of instruments, perhaps imperfectly adapted to one another, and played with no great skill, but yet attaining the great object for which the harmony of drum and clarion addresses itself to the multitude,—that of imparting a higher and more heroic air to the scene of life that passes before the eye. Little Pearl at first clapped her hands, but then lost, for an instant, the restless agitation that had kept her in a continual effervescence throughout the morning; she gazed silently, and seemed to be borne upward, like a floating sea-bird, on the long heaves and swells of sound. But she was brought back to her former mood by the shimmer of the sunshine on the weapons and bright armour of the military company, which followed after the music, and formed the honorary escort of the procession. This body of soldiery[142]—which still sustains a corporate existence, and marches down from past ages with an ancient and honorable fame—was composed of no mercenary materials. Its ranks were filled with gentlemen, who felt the stirrings of martial impulse, and sought to establish a kind of College of Arms,[143] where, as in an association of Knights Templars,[144] they might learn the science, and, so far as peaceful exercise would teach them, the practices of war. The high estimation then placed upon the military character might be seen in the lofty port of each individual member of the company. Some of them, indeed, by their services in the Low Countries and on other fields of European warfare, had fairly won their title to assume the name and pomp of soldiership. The entire array, moreover, clad in burnished steel, and with plumage nodding over their bright morions,[145] had a brilliancy of effect which no modern display can aspire to equal.

And yet the men of civil eminence, who came immediately behind the military escort, were better worth a thoughtful observer's eye. Even in outward demeanour they showed a stamp of majesty that made the warrior's haughty stride look vulgar, if not absurd. It was an age when what we call talent had far less consideration than now, but the massive materials which produce stability and dignity of character a great deal more. The people possessed, by hereditary right, the quality of reverence; which, in their descendents, if it survive at all, exists in smaller proportion, and with a vastly diminished force in the selection and estimate of public men. The change may be for good or ill, and is partly, perhaps, for both. In that old day, the English settler on these rude shores,—having left king, nobles, and all degrees of awful rank behind, while still the faculty and necessity of reverence were strong in him,—bestowed it on the white hair and venerable brow of age; on long-tried integrity; on solid wisdom and sad-colored experience; on endowments of that grave and weighty order, which

[142] The Ancient and Honorable Artillery Company of Massachusetts, the first military unit in the colonies, founded in 1638.
[143] In the fifteenth century a corporation, the Herald's College of England, was established to keep records of genealogies and coats of arms.
[144] Military-religious order founded during the Crusades of the twelfth century.
[145] High-crested Spanish helmets.

gives the idea of permanence, and comes under the general definition of respectability. These primitive statesmen, therefore,—Bradstreet, Endicott, Dudley, Bellingham,[146] and their compeers,—who were elevated to power by the early choice of the people, seem to have been not often brilliant, but distinguished by a ponderous sobriety, rather than activity of intellect. They had fortitude and self-reliance, and, in time of difficulty or peril, stood up for the welfare of the state like a line of cliffs against a tempestuous tide. The traits of character here indicated were well represented in the square cast of countenance and large physical development of the new colonial magistrates. So far as a demeanour of natural authority was concerned, the mother country need not have been ashamed to see these foremost men of an actual democracy adopted into the House of Peers,[147] or made the Privy Council of the sovereign.

Next in order to the magistrates came the young and eminently distinguished divine, from whose lips the religious discourse of the anniversary was expected. His was the profession, at that era, in which intellectual ability displayed itself far more than in political life; for—leaving a higher motive out of the question—it offered inducements powerful enough, in the almost worshipping respect of the community, to win the most aspiring ambition into its service. Even political power—as in the case of Increase Mather[148]—was within the grasp of a successful priest.

It was the observation of those who beheld him now, that never, since Mr. Dimmesdale first set his foot on the New England shore, had he exhibited such energy as was seen in the gait and air with which he kept his pace in the procession. There was no feebleness of step, as at other times; his frame was not bent; nor did his hand rest ominously upon his heart. Yet, if the clergyman were rightly viewed, his strength seemed not of the body. It might be spiritual, and imparted to him by angelic ministrations. It might be the exhilaration of that potent cordial, which is distilled only in the furnace-glow of earnest and long-continued thought. Or, perchance, his sensitive temperament was invigorated by the loud and piercing music, that swelled heavenward, and uplifted him on its ascending wave. Nevertheless, so abstracted was his look, it might be questioned whether Mr. Dimmesdale even heard the music. There was his body, moving onward, and with an unaccustomed force. But where was his mind? Far and deep in its own region, busying itself, with preternatural activity, to marshal a procession of stately thoughts that were soon to issue thence; and so he saw nothing, heard nothing, knew nothing, of what was around him; but the spiritual element took up the feeble frame, and carried it along, unconscious of the burden, and converting it to spirit like itself. Men of uncommon intellect, who have grown morbid, possess this occasional power of mighty effort, into which they throw the life of many days, and then are lifeless for as many more.

Hester Prynne, gazing stedfastly at the clergyman, felt a dreary influence come over her, but wherefore or whence she knew not; unless that he seemed so remote from her own sphere, and utterly beyond her reach. One glance of recognition, she had imagined, must needs pass between them. She thought of the dim forest, with its little dell of solitude, and love, and anguish, and the mossy tree-trunk, where, sitting hand

---

[146] Four early governors of Massachusetts: Simon Bradstreet (1603–1697), husband of Anne Bradstreet; John Endicott (ca. 1589–1665); Thomas Dudley (1576–1653); and Richard Bellingham (1592–1672).

[147] British Parliament's House of Lords.
[148] Puritan minister (1639–1723) and father of Cotton Mather (1663–1728).

in hand, they had mingled their sad and passionate talk with the melancholy murmur of the brook. How deeply had they known each other then! And was this the man? She hardly knew him now! He, moving proudly past, enveloped, as it were, in the rich music, with the procession of majestic and venerable fathers; he, so unattainable in his worldly position, and still more so in that far vista of his unsympathizing thoughts, through which she now beheld him! Her spirit sank with the idea that all must have been a delusion, and that, vividly as she had dreamed it, there could be no real bond betwixt the clergyman and herself. And thus much of woman was there in Hester, that she could scarcely forgive him,—least of all now, when the heavy footstep of their approaching Fate might be heard, nearer, nearer, nearer!—for being able so completely to withdraw himself from their mutual world; while she groped darkly, and stretched forth her cold hands, and found him not.

Pearl either saw and responded to her mother's feelings, or herself felt the remoteness and intangibility that had fallen around the minister. While the procession passed, the child was uneasy, fluttering up and down, like a bird on the point of taking flight. When the whole had gone by, she looked up into Hester's face.

"Mother," said she, "was that the same minister that kissed me by the brook?"

"Hold thy peace, dear little Pearl!" whispered her mother. "We must not always talk in the market-place of what happens to us in the forest."

"I could not be sure that it was he; so strange he looked," continued the child. "Else I would have run to him, and bid him kiss me now, before all the people; even as he did yonder among the dark old trees. What would the minister have said, mother? Would he have clapped his hand over his heart, and scowled on me, and bid me begone?"

"What should he say, Pearl," answered Hester, "save that it was no time to kiss, and that kisses are not to be given in the market-place? Well for thee, foolish child, that thou didst not speak to him!"

Another shade of the same sentiment, in reference to Mr. Dimmesdale, was expressed by a person whose eccentricities—or insanity, as we should term it—led her to do what few of the townspeople would have ventured on; to begin a conversation with the wearer of the scarlet letter, in public. It was Mistress Hibbins, who, arrayed in great magnificence, with a triple ruff, a broidered stomacher, a gown of rich velvet, and a gold-headed cane, had come forth to see the procession. As this ancient lady had the renown (which subsequently cost her no less a price than her life) of being a principal actor in all the works of necromancy that were continually going forward, the crowd gave way before her, and seemed to fear the touch of her garment, as if it carried the plague among its gorgeous folds. Seen in conjunction with Hester Prynne,—kindly as so many now felt towards the latter,—the dread inspired by Mistress Hibbins was doubled, and caused a general movement from that part of the market-place in which the two women stood.

"Now, what mortal imagination could conceive it!" whispered the old lady confidentially to Hester. "Yonder divine man! That saint on earth, as the people uphold him to be, and as—I must needs say—he really looks! Who, now, that saw him pass in the procession, would think how little while it is since he went forth out of his study,—chewing a Hebrew text of Scripture in his mouth, I warrant,—to take an airing in the forest! Aha! we know what that means, Hester Prynne! But, truly, forsooth, I find it hard to believe him the same man. Many a church-member saw

I, walking behind the music, that has danced in the same measure with me, when Somebody was fiddler, and, it might be, an Indian powwow[149] or a Lapland wizard changing hands with us! That is but a trifle, when a woman knows the world. But this minister! Couldst thou surely tell, Hester, whether he was the same man that encountered thee on the forest-path!"

"Madam, I know not of what you speak," answered Hester Prynne, feeling Mistress Hibbins to be of infirm mind; yet strangely startled and awe-stricken by the confidence with which she affirmed a personal connection between so many persons (herself among them) and the Evil One. "It is not for me to talk lightly of a learned and pious minister of the Word, like the Reverend Mr. Dimmesdale!"

"Fie, woman, fie!" cried the old lady, shaking her finger at Hester. "Dost thou think I have been to the forest so many times, and have yet no skill to judge who else has been there? Yea; though no leaf of the wild garlands, which they wore while they danced, be left in their hair! I know thee, Hester; for I behold the token. We may all see it in the sunshine; and it glows like a red flame in the dark. Thou wearest it openly; so there need be no question about that. But this minister! Let me tell thee in thine ear! When the Black Man sees one of his own servants, signed and sealed, so shy of owning to the bond as is the Reverend Mr. Dimmesdale, he hath a way of ordering matters so that the mark shall be disclosed in open daylight to the eyes of all the world! What is it that the minister seeks to hide, with his hand always over his heart? Ha, Hester Prynne!"

"What is it, good Mistress Hibbins?" eagerly asked little Pearl. "Hast thou seen it?"

"No matter, darling!" responded Mistress Hibbins, making Pearl a profound reverence. "Thou thyself wilt see it, one time or another. They say, child, thou art of the lineage of the Prince of the Air![150] Wilt thou ride with me, some fine night, to see thy father? Then thou shalt know wherefore the minister keeps his hand over his heart!"

Laughing so shrilly that all the market-place could hear her, the weird old gentlewoman took her departure.

By this time the preliminary prayer had been offered in the meeting-house, and the accents of the Reverend Mr. Dimmesdale were heard commencing his discourse. An irresistible feeling kept Hester near the spot. As the sacred edifice was too much thronged to admit another auditor, she took up her position close beside the scaffold of the pillory. It was in sufficient proximity to bring the whole sermon to her ears, in the shape of an indistinct, but varied, murmur and flow of the minister's very peculiar voice.

This vocal organ was in itself a rich endowment; insomuch that a listener, comprehending nothing of the language in which the preacher spoke, might still have been swayed to and fro by the mere tone and cadence. Like all other music, it breathed passion and pathos, and emotions high or tender, in a tongue native to the human heart, wherever educated. Muffled as the sound was by its passage through the church-walls, Hester Prynne listened with such intentness, and sympathized so intimately, that the sermon had throughout a meaning for her, entirely apart from its indistinguishable words. These, perhaps, if more distinctly heard, might have been

---

[149] Medicine man.   [150] Satan. (See Ephesians 2:2.)

only a grosser medium, and have clogged the spiritual sense. Now she caught the low undertone, as of the wind sinking down to repose itself; then ascended with it, as it rose through progressive gradations of sweetness and power, until its volume seemed to envelop her with an atmosphere of awe and solemn grandeur. And yet, majestic as the voice sometimes became, there was for ever in it an essential character of plaintiveness. A loud or low expression of anguish,—the whisper, or the shriek, as it might be conceived, of suffering humanity, that touched a sensibility in every bosom! At times this deep strain of pathos was all that could be heard, and scarcely heard, sighing amid a desolate silence. But even when the minister's voice grew high and commanding,—when it gushed irrepressibly upward,—when it assumed its utmost breadth and power, so overfilling the church as to burst its way through the solid walls, and diffuse itself in the open air,—still, if the auditor listened intently, and for the purpose, he could detect the same cry of pain. What was it? The complaint of a human heart, sorrow-laden, perchance guilty, telling its secret, whether of guilt or sorrow, to the great heart of mankind; beseeching its sympathy or forgiveness,—at every moment,—in each accent,—and never in vain! It was this profound and continual undertone that gave the clergyman his most appropriate power.

During all this time Hester stood, statue-like, at the foot of the scaffold. If the minister's voice had not kept her there, there would nevertheless have been an inevitable magnetism in that spot, whence she dated the first hour of her life of ignominy. There was a sense within her,—too ill-defined to be made a thought, but weighing heavily on her mind,—that her whole orb of life, both before and after, was connected with this spot, as with the one point that gave it unity.

Little Pearl, meanwhile, had quitted her mother's side, and was playing at her own will about the market-place. She made the sombre crowd cheerful by her erratic and glistening ray; even as a bird of bright plumage illuminates a whole tree of dusky foliage by darting to and fro, half seen and half concealed, amid the twilight of the clustering leaves. She had an undulating, but, oftentimes, a sharp and irregular movement. It indicated the restless vivacity of her spirit, which to-day was doubly indefatigable in its tiptoe dance, because it was played upon and vibrated with her mother's disquietude. Whenever Pearl saw any thing to excite her ever active and wandering curiosity, she flew thitherward, and, as we might say, seized upon that man or thing as her own property, so far as she desired it; but without yielding the minutest degree of control over her motions in requital. The Puritans looked on, and, if they smiled, were none the less inclined to pronounce the child a demon offspring, from the indescribable charm of beauty and eccentricity that shone through her little figure, and sparkled with its activity. She ran and looked the wild Indian in the face; and he grew conscious of a nature wilder than his own. Thence, with native audacity, but still with a reserve as characteristic, she flew into the midst of a group of mariners, the swarthy-cheeked wild men of the ocean, as the Indians were of the land; and they gazed wonderingly and admiringly at Pearl, as if a flake of the sea-foam had taken the shape of a little maid, and were gifted with a soul of the seafire, that flashes beneath the prow in the night-time.

One of these seafaring men—the shipmaster, indeed, who had spoken to Hester Prynne—was so smitten with Pearl's aspect, that he attempted to lay hands upon her, with purpose to snatch a kiss. Finding it as impossible to touch her as to catch a humming-bird in the air, he took from his hat the gold chain that was twisted about it, and threw it to the child. Pearl immediately twined it around her neck and waist, with such happy skill, that, once seen there, it became a part of her, and it was difficult to imagine her without it.

"Thy mother is yonder woman with the scarlet letter," said the seaman. "Wilt thou carry her a message from me?"

"If the message pleases me I will," answered Pearl.

"Then tell her," rejoined he, "that I spake again with the black-a-visaged, hump-shouldered old doctor, and he engages to bring his friend, the gentleman she wots of, aboard with him. So let thy mother take no thought, save for herself and thee. Wilt thou tell her this, thou witch-baby?"

"Mistress Hibbins says my father is the Prince of the Air!" cried Pearl, with her naughty smile. "If thou callest me that ill name, I shall tell him of thee; and he will chase thy ship with a tempest!"

Pursuing a zigzag course across the market-place, the child returned to her mother, and communicated what the mariner had said. Hester's strong, calm, stedfastly endur-ing spirit almost sank, at last, on beholding this dark and grim countenance of an inevitable doom, which—at the moment when a passage seemed to open for the minister and herself out of their labyrinth of misery—showed itself, with an unrelent-ing smile, right in the midst of their path.

With her mind harassed by the terrible perplexity in which the shipmaster's intelligence involved her, she was also subjected to another trial. There were many people present, from the country roundabout, who had often heard of the scarlet letter, and to whom it had been made terrific by a hundred false or exaggerated rumors, but who had never beheld it with their own bodily eyes. These, after exhausting other modes of amusement, now thronged about Hester Prynne with rude and boorish intrusiveness. Unscrupulous as it was, however, it could not bring them nearer than a circuit of several yards. At that distance they accordingly stood, fixed there by the centrifugal force of the repugnance which the mystic symbol inspired. The whole gang of sailors, likewise, observing the press of spectators, and learning the purport of the scarlet letter, came and thrust their sunburnt and desperado-looking faces into the ring. Even the Indians were affected by a sort of cold shadow of the white man's curiosity, and, gliding through the crowd, fastened their snake-like black eyes on Hester's bosom; conceiving, perhaps, that the wearer of this brilliantly embroidered badge must needs be a personage of high dignity among her people. Lastly, the inhabitants of the town (their own interest in this worn-out subject languidly reviving itself, by sympathy with what they saw others feel) lounged idly to the same quarter, and tormented Hester Prynne, perhaps more than all the rest, with their cool, well-acquainted gaze at her familiar shame. Hester saw and recognized the self-same faces of that group of matrons, who had awaited her forthcoming from the prison-door, seven years ago; all save one, the youngest and only compassionate among them, whose burial-robe she had since made. At the final hour, when she was so soon to fling aside the burning letter, it had strangely become the centre of more remark and excitement, and was thus made to sear her breast more painfully, than at any time since the first day she put it on.

While Hester stood in that magic circle of ignominy, where the cunning cruelty of her sentence seemed to have fixed her for ever, the admirable preacher was looking down from the sacred pulpit upon an audience, whose very inmost spirits had yielded to his control. The sainted minister in the church! The woman of the scarlet letter in the market-place! What imagination would have been irreverent enough to surmise that the same scorching stigma was on them both?

XXIII: The Revelation of the Scarlet Letter

The eloquent voice, on which the souls of the listening audience had been borne aloft, as on the swelling waves of the sea, at length came to a pause. There was a momentary silence, profound as what should follow the utterance of oracles. Then ensued a murmur and half-hushed tumult; as if the auditors, released from the high spell that had transported them into the region of another's mind, were returning into themselves, with all their awe and wonder still heavy on them. In a moment more, the crowd began to gush forth from the doors of the church. Now that there was an end, they needed other breath, more fit to support the gross and earthly life into which they relapsed, than that atmosphere which the preacher had converted into words of flame, and had burdened with the rich fragrance of his thought.

In the open air their rapture broke into speech. The street and the market-place absolutely babbled, from side to side, with applauses of the minister. His hearers could not rest until they had told one another of what each knew better than he could tell or hear. According to their united testimony, never had man spoken in so wise, so high, and so holy a spirit, as he that spake this day; nor had inspiration ever breathed through mortal lips more evidently than it did through his. Its influence could be seen, as it were, descending upon him, and possessing him, and continually lifting him out of the written discourse that lay before him, and filling him with ideas that must have been as marvellous to himself as to his audience. His subject, it appeared, had been the relation between the Deity and the communities of mankind, with a special reference to the New England which they were here planting in the wilderness. And, as he drew towards the close, a spirit as of prophecy had come upon him, constraining him to its purpose as mightily as the old prophets of Israel were constrained; only with this difference, that, whereas the Jewish seers had denounced judgments and ruin on their country, it was his mission to foretell a high and glorious destiny for the newly gathered people of the Lord. But, throughout it all, and through the whole discourse, there had been a certain deep, sad undertone of pathos, which could not be interpreted otherwise than as the natural regret of one soon to pass away. Yes; their minister whom they so loved—and who so loved them all, that he could not depart heavenward without a sigh—had the foreboding of untimely death upon him, and would soon leave them in their tears! This idea of his transitory stay on earth gave the last emphasis to the effect which the preacher had produced; it was as if an angel, in his passage to the skies, had shaken his bright wings over the people for an instant, —at once a shadow and a splendor,—and had shed down a shower of golden truths upon them.

Thus, there had come to the Reverend Mr. Dimmesdale—as to most men, in their various spheres, though seldom recognized until they see it far behind them—an epoch of life more brilliant and full of triumph than any previous one, or than any which could hereafter be. He stood, at this moment, on the very proudest eminence of superiority, to which the gifts of intellect, rich lore, prevailing eloquence, and a reputation of whitest sanctity, could exalt a clergyman in New England's earliest days, when the professional character was of itself a lofty pedestal. Such was the position which the minister occupied, as he bowed his head forward on the cushions of the pulpit, at the close of his Election Sermon. Meanwhile, Hester Prynne was standing beside the scaffold of the pillory, with the scarlet letter still burning on her breast!

Now was heard again the clangor of the music, and the measured tramp of the military escort, issuing from the church-door. The procession was to be marshalled thence to the town-hall, where a solemn banquet would complete the ceremonies of the day.

Once more, therefore, the train of venerable and majestic fathers was seen moving through a broad pathway of the people, who drew back reverently, on either side, as the Governor and magistrates, the old and wise men, the holy ministers, and all that were eminent and renowned, advanced into the midst of them. When they were fairly in the market-place, their presence was greeted by a shout. This—though doubtless it might acquire additional force and volume from the childlike loyalty which the age awarded to its rulers—was felt to be an irrepressible outburst of the enthusiasm kindled in the auditors by that high strain of eloquence which was yet reverberating in their ears. Each felt the impulse in himself, and, in the same breath, caught it from his neighbour. Within the church, it had hardly been kept down; beneath the sky, it pealed upward to the zenith. There were human beings enough, and enough of highly wrought and symphonious feeling, to produce that more impressive sound than the organ-tones of the blast, or the thunder, or the roar of the sea; even that mighty swell of many voices, blended into one great voice by the universal impulse which makes likewise one vast heart out of the many. Never, from the soil of New England, had gone up such a shout! Never, on New England soil, had stood the man so honored by his mortal brethren as the preacher!

How fared it with him then? Were there not the brilliant particles of a halo in the air about his head? So etherealized by spirit as he was, and so apotheosized by worshipping admirers, did his footsteps in the procession really tread upon the dust of earth?

As the ranks of military men and civil fathers moved onward, all eyes were turned towards the point where the minister was seen to approach among them. The shout died into a murmur, as one portion of the crowd after another obtained a glimpse of him. How feeble and pale he looked amid all his triumph! The energy—or say, rather, the inspiration which had held him up, until he should have delivered the sacred message that brought its own strength along with it from heaven—was withdrawn, now that it had so faithfully performed its office. The glow, which they had just before beheld burning on his cheek, was extinguished, like a flame that sinks down hopelessly among the late-decaying embers. It seemed hardly the face of a man alive, with such a deathlike hue; it was hardly a man with life in him, that tottered on his path so nervelessly, yet tottered, and did not fall!

One of his clerical brethren,—it was the venerable John Wilson,—observing the state in which Mr. Dimmesdale was left by the retiring wave of intellect and sensibility, stepped forward hastily to offer his support. The minister tremulously, but decidedly, repelled the old man's arm. He still walked onward, if that movement could be so described, which rather resembled the wavering effort of an infant, with its mother's arms in view, outstretched to tempt him forward. And now, almost imperceptible as were the latter steps of his progress, he had come opposite the well-remembered and weather-darkened scaffold, where, long since, with all that dreary lapse of time between, Hester Prynne had encountered the world's ignominious stare. There stood Hester, holding little Pearl by the hand! And there was the scarlet letter on her breast! The minister here made a pause; although the music still played the stately and rejoicing march to which the procession moved. It summoned him onward, —onward to the festival!—but here he made a pause.

Bellingham, for the last few moments, had kept an anxious eye upon him. He now left his own place in the procession, and advanced to give assistance; judging from Mr. Dimmesdale's aspect that he must otherwise inevitably fall. But there was something in the latter's expression that warned back the magistrate, although a man not readily obeying the vague intimations that pass from one spirit to another. The crowd, meanwhile, looked on with awe and wonder. This earthly faintness was, in their view, only another phase of the minister's celestial strength; nor would it have seemed a miracle too high to be wrought for one so holy, had he ascended before their eyes, waxing dimmer and brighter, and fading at last into the light of heaven!

He turned towards the scaffold, and stretched forth his arms.

"Hester," said he, "come hither! Come, my little Pearl!"

It was a ghastly look with which he regarded them; but there was something at once tender and strangely triumphant in it. The child, with the bird-like motion which was one of her characteristics, flew to him, and clasped her arms about his knees. Hester Prynne—slowly, as if impelled by inevitable fate, and against her strongest will— likewise drew near, but paused before she reached him. At this instant old Roger Chillingworth thrust himself through the crowd,—or, perhaps, so dark, disturbed, and evil was his look, he rose up out of some nether region,—to snatch back his victim from what he sought to do! Be that as it might, the old man rushed forward and caught the minister by the arm.

"Madman, hold! What is your purpose?" whispered he. "Wave back that woman! Cast off this child! All shall be well! Do not blacken your fame, and perish in dishonor! I can yet save you! Would you bring infamy on your sacred profession?"

"Ha, tempter! Methinks thou art too late!" answered the minister, encountering his eye, fearfully, but firmly. "Thy power is not what it was! With God's help, I shall escape thee now!"

He again extended his hand to the woman of the scarlet letter.

"Hester Prynne," cried he, with a piercing earnestness, "in the name of Him, so terrible and so merciful, who gives me grace, at this last moment, to do what—for my own heavy sin and miserable agony—I withheld myself from doing seven years ago, come hither now, and twine thy strength about me! Thy strength, Hester; but let it be guided by the will which God hath granted me! This wretched and wronged old man is opposing it with all his might!—with all his own might and the fiend's! Come, Hester, come! Support me up yonder scaffold!"

The crowd was in a tumult. The men of rank and dignity, who stood more immediately around the clergyman, were so taken by surprise, and so perplexed as to the purport of what they saw,—unable to receive the explanation which most readily presented itself, or to imagine any other,—that they remained silent and inactive spectators of the judgment which Providence seemed about to work. They beheld the minister, leaning on Hester's shoulder and supported by her arm around him, approach the scaffold, and ascend its steps; while still the little hand of the sin-born child was clasped in his. Old Roger Chillingworth followed, as one intimately connected with the drama of guilt and sorrow in which they had all been actors, and well entitled, therefore, to be present at its closing scene.

"Hadst thou sought the whole earth over," said he, looking darkly at the clergyman, "there was no one place so secret,—no high place nor lowly place, where thou couldst have escaped me,—save on this very scaffold!"

"Thanks be to Him who hath led me hither!" answered the minister.

Yet he trembled, and turned to Hester with an expression of doubt and anxiety in his eyes, not the less evidently betrayed, that there was a feeble smile upon his lips.

"Is not this better," murmured he, "than what we dreamed of in the forest?"

"I know not! I know not!" she hurriedly replied. "Better? Yea; so we may both die, and little Pearl die with us!"

"For thee and Pearl, be it as God shall order," said the minister; "and God is merciful! Let me now do the will which he hath made plain before my sight. For, Hester, I am a dying man. So let me make haste to take my shame upon me."

Partly supported by Hester Prynne, and holding one hand of little Pearl's, the Reverend Mr. Dimmesdale turned to the dignified and venerable rulers; to the holy ministers, who were his brethren; to the people, whose great heart was thoroughly appalled, yet overflowing with tearful sympathy, as knowing that some deep life-matter—which, if full of sin, was full of anguish and repentance likewise—was now to be laid open to them. The sun, but little past its meridian, shone down upon the clergyman, and gave a distinctness to his figure, as he stood out from all the earth to put in his plea of guilty at the bar of Eternal Justice.

"People of New England!" cried he, with a voice that rose over them, high, solemn, and majestic,—yet had always a tremor through it, and sometimes a shriek, struggling up out of a fathomless depth of remorse and woe,—"ye, that have loved me!—ye, that have deemed me holy!—behold me here, the one sinner of the world! At last!—at last!—I stand upon the spot where, seven years since, I should have stood; here, with this woman, whose arm, more than the little strength wherewith I have crept hitherward, sustains me, at this dreadful moment, from grovelling down upon my face! Lo, the scarlet letter which Hester wears! Ye have all shuddered at it! Wherever her walk hath been,—wherever, so miserably burdened, she may have hoped to find repose,—it hath cast a lurid gleam of awe and horrible repugnance roundabout her. But there stood one in the midst of you, at whose brand of sin and infamy ye have not shuddered!"

It seemed, at this point, as if the minister must leave the remainder of his secret undisclosed. But he fought back the bodily weakness,—and, still more, the faintness of heart,—that was striving for the mastery with him. He threw off all assistance, and stepped passionately forward a pace before the woman and the child.

"It was on him!" he continued, with a kind of fierceness; so determined was he to speak out the whole. "God's eye beheld it! The angels were for ever pointing at it! The Devil knew it well, and fretted it continually with the touch of his burning finger! But he hid it cunningly from men, and walked among you with the mien of a spirit, mournful, because so pure in a sinful world!—and sad, because he missed his heavenly kindred! Now, at the death-hour, he stands up before you! He bids you look again at Hester's scarlet letter! He tells you, that, with all its mysterious horror, it is but the shadow of what he bears on his own breast, and that even this, his own red stigma, is no more than the type of what has seared his inmost heart! Stand any here that question God's judgment on a sinner? Behold! Behold a dreadful witness of it!"

With a convulsive motion he tore away the ministerial band from before his breast. It was revealed! But it were irreverent to describe that revelation. For an instant the gaze of the horror-stricken multitude was concentred on the ghastly miracle; while the minister stood with a flush of triumph in his face, as one who, in the crisis of acutest pain, had won a victory. Then, down he sank upon the scaffold! Hester partly raised him, and supported his head against her bosom. Old Roger Chillingworth knelt down beside him, with a blank, dull countenance, out of which the life seemed to have departed.

"Thou hast escaped me!" he repeated more than once. "Thou hast escaped me!"

"May God forgive thee!" said the minister. "Thou, too, hast deeply sinned!"

He withdrew his dying eyes from the old man, and fixed them on the woman and the child.

"My little Pearl," said he feebly,—and there was a sweet and gentle smile over his face, as of a spirit sinking into deep repose; nay, now that the burden was removed, it seemed almost as if he would be sportive with the child,—"dear little Pearl, wilt thou kiss me now? Thou wouldst not yonder, in the forest! But now thou wilt?"

Pearl kissed his lips. A spell was broken. The great scene of grief, in which the wild infant bore a part, had developed all her sympathies; and as her tears fell upon her father's cheek, they were the pledge that she would grow up amid human joy and sorrow, nor for ever do battle with the world, but be a woman in it. Towards her mother, too, Pearl's errand as a messenger of anguish was all fulfilled.

"Hester," said the clergyman, "farewell!"

"Shall we not meet again?" whispered she, bending her face down close to his. "Shall we not spend our immortal life together? Surely, surely, we have ransomed one another, with all this woe! Thou lookest far into eternity, with those bright dying eyes! Then tell me what thou seest?"

"Hush, Hester, hush!" said he, with tremulous solemnity. "The law we broke!— the sin here so awfully revealed!—let these alone be in thy thoughts! I fear! I fear! It may be, that, when we forgot our God,—when we violated our reverence each for the other's soul,—it was thenceforth vain to hope that we could meet hereafter, in an everlasting and pure reunion. God knows; and He is merciful! He hath proved his mercy, most of all, in my afflictions. By giving me this burning torture to bear upon my breast! By sending yonder dark and terrible old man, to keep the torture always at red-heat! By bringing me hither, to die this death of triumphant ignominy before the people! Had either of these agonies been wanting, I had been lost for ever! Praised be his name! His will be done! Farewell!"

That final word came forth with the minister's expiring breath. The multitude, silent till then, broke out in a strange, deep voice of awe and wonder, which could not as yet find utterance, save in this murmur that rolled so heavily after the departed spirit.

XXIV: Conclusion

After many days, when time sufficed for the people to arrange their thoughts in reference to the foregoing scene, there was more than one account of what had been witnessed on the scaffold.

Most of the spectators testified to having seen, on the breast of the unhappy minister, a SCARLET LETTER—the very semblance of that worn by Hester Prynne—imprinted in the flesh. As regarded its origin, there were various explanations, all of which must necessarily have been conjectural. Some affirmed that the Reverend Mr. Dimmesdale, on the very day when Hester Prynne first wore her ignominious badge, had begun a course of penance,—which he afterwards, in so many futile methods, followed out,—by inflicting a hideous torture on himself. Others contended that the stigma had not been produced until a long time subsequent, when old Roger Chillingworth, being a potent necromancer, had caused it to appear, through the agency of magic and poisonous drugs. Others, again,—and those best able to appreciate the minister's peculiar sensibility, and the wonderful operation of his spirit upon the body,—whispered their belief, that the awful symbol was the effect of the ever active tooth of remorse, gnawing from the inmost heart outwardly, and at last manifesting Heaven's dreadful judgment by the visible presence of the letter. The reader may choose among these theories. We have thrown all the light we could acquire upon the portent, and would gladly, now that it has done its office, erase its deep print out of our own brain; where long meditation has fixed it in very undesirable distinctness.

It is singular, nevertheless, that certain persons, who were spectators of the whole scene, and professed never once to have removed their eyes from the Reverend Mr. Dimmesdale, denied that there was any mark whatever on his breast, more than on a new-born infant's. Neither, by their report, had his dying words acknowledged, nor even remotely implied, any, the slightest connection, on his part, with the guilt for which Hester Prynne had so long worn the scarlet letter. According to these highly respectable witnesses, the minister, conscious that he was dying,—conscious, also, that the reverence of the multitude placed him already among saints and angels,—had desired, by yielding up his breath in the arms of that fallen woman, to express to the world how utterly nugatory is the choicest of man's own righteousness. After exhausting life in his efforts for mankind's spiritual good, he had made the manner of his death a parable, in order to impress on his admirers the mighty and mournful lesson, that, in the view of Infinite Purity, we are sinners all alike. It was to teach them, that the holiest among us has but attained so far above his fellows as to discern more clearly the Mercy which looks down, and repudiate more utterly the phantom of human merit, which would look aspiringly upward. Without disputing a truth so momentous, we must be allowed to consider this version of Mr. Dimmesdale's story as only an instance of that stubborn fidelity with which a man's friends—and especially a clergyman's—will sometimes uphold his character; when proofs, clear as the mid-day sunshine on the scarlet letter, establish him a false and sin-stained creature of the dust.

The authority which we have chiefly followed—a manuscript of old date, drawn up from the verbal testimony of individuals, some of whom had known Hester Prynne, while others had heard the tale from contemporary witnesses—fully confirms the view taken in the foregoing pages. Among many morals which press upon us from the poor minister's miserable experience, we put only this into a sentence:—"Be true! Be true! Be true! Show freely to the world, if not your worst, yet some trait whereby the worst may be inferred!"

Nothing was more remarkable than the change which took place, almost immediately after Mr. Dimmesdale's death, in the appearance and demeanour of the old man known as Roger Chillingworth. All his strength and energy—all his vital and intellectual force—seemed at once to desert him; insomuch that he positively withered up, shrivelled away, and almost vanished from mortal sight, like an uprooted weed that lies wilting in the sun. This unhappy man had made the very principle of his life to consist in the pursuit and systematic exercise of revenge; and when, by its completest triumph and consummation, that evil principle was left with no further material to support it,—when, in short, there was no more devil's work on earth for him to do, it only remained for the unhumanized mortal to betake himself whither his Master would find him tasks enough, and pay him his wages duly. But, to all these shadowy beings, so long our near acquaintances,—as well Roger Chillingworth as his companions,—we would fain be merciful. It is a curious subject of observation and inquiry, whether hatred and love be not the same thing at bottom. Each, in its utmost development, supposes a high degree of intimacy and heart-knowledge; each renders one individual dependent for the food of his affections and spiritual life upon another; each leaves the passionate lover, or the no less passionate hater, forlorn and desolate by the withdrawal of his object. Philosophically considered, therefore, the two passions seem essentially the same, except that one happens to be seen in a celestial radiance, and the other in a dusky and lurid glow. In the spiritual world, the old physician and the minister—mutual victims as they have been—may, unawares, have found their earthly stock of hatred and antipathy transmuted into golden love.

Leaving this discussion apart, we have a matter of business to communicate to the reader. At old Roger Chillingworth's decease (which took place within the year), and by his last will and testament, of which Governor Bellingham and the Reverend Mr. Wilson were executors, he bequeathed a very considerable amount of property, both here and in England, to little Pearl, the daughter of Hester Prynne.

So Pearl—the elf-child,—the demon offspring, as some people, up to that epoch, persisted in considering her—became the richest heiress of her day, in the New World. Not improbably, this circumstance wrought a very material change in the public estimation; and, had the mother and child remained here, little Pearl, at a marriageable period of life, might have mingled her wild blood with the lineage of the devoutest Puritan among them all. But, in no long time after the physician's death, the wearer of the scarlet letter disappeared, and Pearl along with her. For many years, though a vague report would now and then find its way across the sea,—like a shapeless piece of driftwood tost ashore, with the initials of a name upon it,—yet no tidings of them unquestionably authentic were received. The story of the scarlet letter grew into a legend. Its spell, however, was still potent, and kept the scaffold awful where the poor minister had died, and likewise the cottage by the sea-shore, where Hester Prynne had dwelt. Near this latter spot, one afternoon, some children were at play, when they beheld a tall woman, in a gray robe, approach the cottage-door. In all those years it had never once been opened; but either she unlocked it, or the decaying wood and iron yielded to her hand, or she glided shadow-like through these impediments,— and, at all events, went in.

On the threshold she paused,—turned partly round,—for, perchance, the idea of entering, all alone, and all so changed, the home of so intense a former life, was more dreary and desolate than even she could bear. But her hesitation was only for an instant, though long enough to display a scarlet letter on her breast.

And Hester Prynne had returned, and taken up her long-forsaken shame. But where was little Pearl? If still alive, she must now have been in the flush and bloom of early womanhood. None knew—nor ever learned, with the fulness of perfect certainty—

whether the elf-child had gone thus untimely to a maiden grave; or whether her wild, rich nature had been softened and subdued, and made capable of a woman's gentle happiness. But, through the remainder of Hester's life, there were indications that the recluse of the scarlet letter was the object of love and interest with some inhabitant of another land. Letters came, with armorial seals upon them, though of bearings unknown to English heraldry. In the cottage there were articles of comfort and luxury, such as Hester never cared to use, but which only wealth could have purchased, and affection have imagined for her. There were trifles, too, little ornaments, beautiful tokens of a continual remembrance, that must have been wrought by delicate fingers, at the impulse of a fond heart. And, once, Hester was seen embroidering a baby-garment, with such a lavish richness of golden fancy as would have raised a public tumult, had any infant, thus apparelled, been shown to our sombre-hued community.

In fine, the gossips of that day believed,—and Mr. Surveyor Pue, who made investigations a century later, believed,—and one of his recent successors in office, moreover, faithfully believes,—that Pearl was not only alive, but married, and happy, and mindful of her mother; and that she would most joyfully have entertained that sad and lonely mother at her fireside.

But there was a more real life for Hester Prynne, here, in New England, than in that unknown region where Pearl had found a home. Here had been her sin; here, her sorrow; and here was yet to be her penitence. She had returned, therefore, and resumed,—of her own free will, for not the sternest magistrate of that iron period would have imposed it,—resumed the symbol of which we have related so dark a tale. Never afterwards did it quit her bosom. But, in the lapse of the toilsome, thoughtful, and self-devoted years that made up Hester's life, the scarlet letter ceased to be a stigma which attracted the world's scorn and bitterness, and became a type of something to be sorrowed over, and looked upon with awe, yet with reverence too. And, as Hester Prynne had no selfish ends, nor lived in any measure for her own profit and enjoyment, people brought all their sorrows and perplexities, and besought her counsel, as one who had herself gone through a mighty trouble. Women, more especially,—in the continually recurring trials of wounded, wasted, wronged, mis-placed, or erring and sinful passion,—or with the dreary burden of a heart unyielded, because unvalued and unsought,—came to Hester's cottage, demanding why they were so wretched, and what the remedy! Hester comforted and counselled them, as best she might. She assured them, too, of her firm belief, that, at some brighter period, when the world should have grown ripe for it, in Heaven's own time, a new truth would be revealed, in order to establish the whole relation between man and woman on a surer ground of mutual happiness. Earlier in life, Hester had vainly imagined that she herself might be the destined prophetess, but had long since recognized the impossibility that any mission of divine and mysterious truth should be confided to a woman stained with sin, bowed down with shame, or even burdened with a life-long sorrow. The angel and apostle of the coming revelation must be a woman, indeed, but lofty, pure, and beautiful; and wise, moreover, not through dusky grief, but the ethereal medium of joy; and showing how sacred love should make us happy, by the truest test of a life successful to such an end!

So said Hester Prynne, and glanced her sad eyes downward at the scarlet letter. And, after many, many years, a new grave was delved, near an old and sunken one, in that burial-ground beside which King's Chapel has since been built. It was near that old and sunken grave, yet with a space between, as if the dust of the two sleepers had no right to mingle. Yet one tombstone served for both. All around, there were monuments carved with armorial bearings; and on this simple slab of slate—as the curious investigator may still discern, and perplex himself with the purport—there appeared the semblance of an engraved escutcheon.[151] It bore a device, a herald's wording of which might serve for a motto and brief description of our now concluded legend; so sombre is it, and relieved only by one ever-glowing point of light gloomier than the shadow:—

"ON A FIELD, SABLE, THE LETTER A, GULES."[152]

1850

Preface to *Twice-Told Tales*

The Author of "Twice-Told Tales" has a claim to one distinction, which, as none of his literary brethren will care about disputing it with him, he need not be afraid to mention. He was, for a good many years, the obscurest man of letters in America.

These stories were published in magazines and annuals, extending over a period of ten or twelve years, and comprising the whole of the writer's young manhood, without making (so far as he has ever been aware) the slightest impression on the public. One or two among them, the "Rill from the Town Pump," in perhaps a greater degree than any other, had a pretty wide newspaper circulation; as for the rest, he had no grounds for supposing that, on their first appearance, they met with the good or evil fortune to be read by anybody. Throughout the time above specified, he had no incitement to literary effort in a reasonable prospect of reputation or profit, nothing but the pleasure itself of composition—an enjoyment not at all amiss in its way, and perhaps essential to the merit of the work in hand, but which, in the long run, will hardly keep the chill out of a writer's heart, or the numbness out of his fingers. To this total lack of sympathy, at the age when his mind would naturally have been most effervescent, the public owe it (and it is certainly an effect not to be regretted on either part) that the Author can show nothing for the thought and industry of that portion of his life, save the forty sketches, or thereabouts, included in these volumes.

Much more, indeed, he wrote; and some very small part of it might yet be rummaged out (but it would not be worth the trouble) among the dingy pages of fifteen-or-twenty-year-old periodicals, or within the shabby morocco covers of faded souvenirs. The remainder of the works alluded to had a very brief existence, but, on the score of brilliancy, enjoyed a fate vastly superior to that of their brotherhood, which succeeded in getting through the press. In a word, the Author burned them without mercy or remorse, and, moreover, without any subsequent regret, and had

---

[151] Shield.   [152] The heraldic color red.

more than one occasion to marvel that such very dull stuff, as he knew his condemned manuscripts to be, should yet have possessed inflammability enough to set the chimney on fire!

After a long while the first collected volume of the "Tales" was published. By this time, if the Author had ever been greatly tormented by literary ambition (which he does not remember or believe to have been the case), it must have perished, beyond resuscitation, in the dearth of nutriment. This was fortunate; for the success of the volume was not such as would have gratified a craving desire for notoriety. A moderate edition was "got rid of" (to use the publisher's very significant phrase) within a reasonable time, but apparently without rendering the writer or his productions much more generally known than before. The great bulk of the reading public probably ignored the book altogether. A few persons read it, and liked it better than it deserved. At an interval of three or four years, the second volume was published, and encountered much the same sort of kindly, but calm, and very limited reception. The circulation of the two volumes was chiefly confined to New England; nor was it until long after this period, if it even yet be the case, that the Author could regard himself as addressing the American public, or, indeed, any public at all. He was merely writing to his known or unknown friends.

As he glances over these long-forgotten pages, and considers his way of life while composing them, the Author can very clearly discern why all this was so. After so many sober years, he would have reason to be ashamed if he could not criticize his own work as fairly as another man's; and, though it is little his business, and perhaps still less his interest, he can hardly resist a temptation to achieve something of the sort. If writers were allowed to do so, and would perform the task with perfect sincerity and unreserve, their opinions of their own productions would often be more valuable and instructive than the works themselves.

At all events, there can be no harm in the Author's remarking that he rather wonders how the "Twice-Told Tales" should have gained what vogue they did than that it was so little and so gradual. They have the pale tint of flowers that blossomed in too retired a shade,—the coolness of a meditative habit, which diffuses itself through the feeling and observation of every sketch. Instead of passion there is sentiment; and, even in what purport to be pictures of actual life, we have allegory, not always so warmly dressed in its habiliments of flesh and blood as to be taken into the reader's mind without a shiver. Whether from lack of power, or an unconquerable reserve, the Author's touches have often an effect of tameness; the merriest man can hardly contrive to laugh at his broadest humor; the tenderest woman, one would suppose, will hardly shed warm tears at his deepest pathos. The book, if you would see anything in it, requires to be read in the clear, brown, twilight atmosphere in which it was written; if opened in the sunshine, it is apt to look exceedingly like a volume of blank pages.

With the foregoing characteristics, proper to the production of a person in retirement (which happened to be the Author's category at the time), the book is devoid of others that we should quite as naturally look for. The sketches are not, it is hardly necessary to say, profound; but it is rather more remarkable that they seldom, if ever, show any design on the writer's part to make them so. They have none of the abstruseness of idea, or obscurity of expression, which mark the written communications of a solitary mind with itself. They never need translation. It is, in fact, the style of a man of society. Every sentence, so far as it embodies thought or sensibility, may be understood and felt by anybody who will give himself the trouble to read it, and will take up the book in a proper mood.

This statement of apparently opposite peculiarities leads us to a perception of what the sketches truly are. They are not the talk of a secluded man with his own mind and heart (had it been so, they could hardly have failed to be more deeply and permanently valuable), but his attempts, and very imperfectly successful ones, to open an intercourse with the world.

The Author would regret to be understood as speaking sourly or querulously of the slight mark made by his earlier literary efforts on the Public at large. It is so far the contrary, that he has been moved to write this Preface chiefly as affording him an opportunity to express how much enjoyment he has owed to these volumes, both before and since their publication. They are the memorials of very tranquil and not unhappy years. They failed, it is true,—nor could it have been otherwise,—in winning an extensive popularity. Occasionally, however, when he deemed them entirely forgotten, a paragraph or an article, from a native or foreign critic, would gratify his instincts of authorship with unexpected praise,—too generous praise, indeed, and too little alloyed with censure, which, therefore, he learned the better to inflict upon himself. And, by the by, it is a very suspicious symptom of a deficiency of the popular element in a book when it calls forth no harsh criticism. This has been particularly the fortune of the "TWICE-TOLD TALES." They made no enemies, and were so little known and talked about that those who read, and chanced to like them, were apt to conceive the sort of kindness for the book which a person naturally feels for a discovery of his own.

This kindly feeling (in some cases, at least) extended to the Author, who, on the internal evidence of his sketches, came to be regarded as a mild, shy, gentle, melancholic, exceedingly sensitive, and not very forcible man, hiding his blushes under an assumed name, the quaintness of which was supposed, somehow or other, to symbolize his personal and literary traits. He is by no means certain that some of his subsequent productions have not been influenced and modified by a natural desire to fill up so amiable an outline, and to act in consonance with the character assigned to him; nor, even now, could he forfeit it without a few tears of tender sensibility. To conclude, however: these volumes have opened the way to most agreeable associations, and to the formation of imperishable friendships; and there are many golden threads interwoven with his present happiness, which he can follow up more or less directly, until he finds their commencement here; so that his pleasant pathway among realities seems to proceed out of the Dreamland of his youth, and to be bordered with just enough of its shadowy foliage to shelter him from the heat of the day. He is therefore satisfied with what the "TWICE-TOLD TALES" have done for him and feels it to be far better than fame.

LENOX, *January* 11, 1851.
1851/1851

from The House of the Seven Gables

Preface

When a writer calls his work a Romance, it need hardly be observed that he wishes to claim a certain latitude, both as to its fashion and material, which he would not have felt himself entitled to assume had he professed to be writing a Novel. The latter form of composition is presumed to aim at a very minute fidelity, not merely to the possible, but to the probable and ordinary course of man's experience. The former —while, as a work of art, it must rigidly subject itself to laws, and while it sins unpardonably so far as it may swerve aside from the truth of the human heart—has fairly a right to present that truth under circumstances, to a great extent, of the writer's own choosing or creation. If he think fit, also, he may so manage his atmospherical medium as to bring out or mellow the lights and deepen and enrich the shadows of the picture. He will be wise, no doubt, to make a very moderate use of the privileges here stated, and, especially, to mingle the Marvellous rather as a slight, delicate, and evanescent flavor, than as any portion of the actual substance of the dish offered to the public. He can hardly be said, however, to commit a literary crime even if he disregard this caution.

In the present work, the author has proposed to himself—but with what success, fortunately, it is not for him to judge—to keep undeviatingly within his immunities. The point of view in which this tale comes under the Romantic definition lies in the attempt to connect a bygone time with the very present that is flitting away from us. It is a legend prolonging itself, from an epoch now gray in the distance, down into our own broad daylight, and bringing along with it some of its legendary mist, which the reader, according to his pleasure, may either disregard, or allow it to float almost imperceptibly about the characters and events for the sake of a picturesque effect. The narrative, it may be, is woven of so humble a texture as to require this advantage, and, at the same time, to render it the more difficult of attainment.

Many writers lay very great stress upon some definite moral purpose, at which they profess to aim their works. Not to be deficient in this particular, the author has provided himself with a moral,—the truth, namely, that the wrong-doing of one generation lives into the successive ones, and, divesting itself of every temporary advantage, becomes a pure and uncontrollable mischief; and he would feel it a singular gratification if this romance might effectually convince mankind—or, indeed, any one man—of the folly of tumbling down an avalanche of ill-gotten gold, or real estate, on the heads of an unfortunate posterity, thereby to maim and crush them, until the accumulated mass shall be scattered abroad in its original atoms. In good faith, however, he is not sufficiently imaginative to flatter himself with the slightest hope of this kind. When romances do really teach anything, or produce any effective operation, it is usually through a far more subtle process than the ostensible one. The author has considered it hardly worth his while, therefore, relentlessly to impale the story with its moral as with an iron rod,—or, rather, as by sticking a pin through a butterfly,—thus at once depriving it of life, and causing it to stiffen in an ungainly and unnatural attitude. A high truth, indeed, fairly, finely, and skilfully wrought out, brightening at every step, and crowning the final development of a work of fiction, may add an artistic glory, but is never any truer, and seldom any more evident, at the last page than at the first.

The reader may perhaps choose to assign an actual locality to the imaginary events of this narrative. If permitted by the historical connection,—which, though slight, was essential to his plan,—the author would very willingly have avoided anything of this nature. Not to speak of other objections, it exposes the romance to an inflexible and exceedingly dangerous species of criticism, by bringing his fancy-pictures almost into positive contact with the realities of the moment. It has been no part of his object, however, to describe local manners, nor in any way to meddle with the characteristics of a community for whom he cherishes a proper respect and a natural regard. He trusts not to be considered as unpardonably offending by laying out a street that infringes upon nobody's private rights, and appropriating a lot of land which had no visible owner, and building a house of materials long in use for constructing castles in the air. The personages of the tale—though they give themselves out to be of ancient stability and considerable prominence—are really of the author's own making, or, at all events, of his own mixing; their virtues can shed no lustre, nor their defects redound, in the remotest degree, to the discredit of the venerable town[1] of which they profess to be inhabitants. He would be glad, therefore, if—especially in the quarter to which he alludes—the book may be read strictly as a Romance, having a great deal more to do with the clouds over head than with any portion of the actual soil of the County of Essex.

LENOX, January 27, 1851.

1851/1851

from The Marble Faun

Preface

It is now seven or eight years (so many, at all events, that I cannot precisely remember the epoch) since the author of this romance last appeared before the Public. It had grown to be a custom with him to introduce each of his humble publications with a familiar kind of preface, addressed nominally to the Public at large, but really to a character with whom he felt entitled to use far greater freedom. He meant it for that one congenial friend,—more comprehensive of his purposes, more appreciative of his success, more indulgent of his shortcomings, and, in all respects, closer and kinder than a brother,—that all-sympathizing critic, in short, whom an author never actually meets, but to whom he implicitly makes his appeal whenever he is conscious of having done his best.

The antique fashion of Prefaces recognized this genial personage as the "Kind Reader," the "Gentle Reader," the "Beloved," the "Indulgent," or, at coldest, the "Honored Reader," to whom the prim old author was wont to make his preliminary

[1] Salem, Massachusetts.

explanations and apologies, with the certainty that they would be favorably received. I never personally encountered, nor corresponded through the post with this representative essence of all delightful and desirable qualities which a reader can possess. But, fortunately for myself, I never therefore concluded him to be merely a mythic character. I had always a sturdy faith in his actual existence, and wrote for him year after year, during which the great eye of the Public (as well it might) almost utterly overlooked my small productions.

Unquestionably, this gentle, kind, benevolent, indulgent, and most beloved and honored Reader did once exist for me, and (in spite of the infinite chances against a letter's reaching its destination without a definite address) duly received the scrolls which I flung upon whatever wind was blowing, in the faith that they would find him out. But, is he extant now? In these many years, since he last heard from me, may he not have deemed his earthly task accomplished, and have withdrawn to the paradise of gentle readers, wherever it may be, to the enjoyments of which his kindly charity on my behalf must surely have entitled him? I have a sad foreboding that this may be the truth. The "Gentle Reader," in the case of any individual author, is apt to be extremely short-lived; he seldom outlasts a literary fashion, and, except in very rare instances, closes his weary eyes before the writer has half done with him. If I find him at all, it will probably be under some mossy gravestone, inscribed with a half-obliterated name which I shall never recognize.

Therefore, I have little heart or confidence (especially, writing as I do, in a foreign land, and after a long, long absence[1] from my own) to presume upon the existence of that friend of friends, that unseen brother of the soul, whose apprehensive sympathy has so often encouraged me to be egotistical in my prefaces, careless though unkindly eyes should skim over what was never meant for them. I stand upon ceremony now; and, after stating a few particulars about the work which is here offered to the Public, must make my most reverential bow, and retire behind the curtain.

This Romance was sketched out during a residence of considerable length in Italy, and has been rewritten and prepared for the press in England. The author proposed to himself merely to write a fanciful story, evolving a thoughtful moral, and did not purpose attempting a portraiture of Italian manners and character. He has lived too long abroad not to be aware that a foreigner seldom acquires that knowledge of a country at once flexible and profound, which may justify him in endeavoring to idealize its traits.

Italy, as the site of his Romance, was chiefly valuable to him as affording a sort of poetic or fairy precinct, where actualities would not be so terribly insisted upon as they are, and must needs be, in America. No author, without a trial, can conceive of the difficulty of writing a romance about a country where there is no shadow, no antiquity, no mystery, no picturesque and gloomy wrong, nor anything but a commonplace prosperity, in broad and simple daylight, as is happily the case with my dear native land. It will be very long, I trust, before romance-writers may find congenial and easily handled themes, either in the annals of our stalwart republic, or in any characteristic and probable events of our individual lives. Romance and poetry, ivy, lichens, and wall-flowers, need ruin to make them grow.

In rewriting these volumes, the author was somewhat surprised to see the extent

---

[1] Hawthorne lived abroad from 1853 to 1860.

to which he had introduced descriptions of various Italian objects, antique, pictorial, and statuesque. Yet these things fill the mind everywhere in Italy, and especially in Rome, and cannot easily be kept from flowing out upon the page when one writes freely, and with self-enjoyment. And, again, while reproducing the book, on the broad and dreary sands of Redcar, with the gray German Ocean tumbling in upon me, and the northern blast always howling in my ears, the complete change of scene made these Italian reminiscences shine out so vividly that I could not find it in my heart to cancel them.

An act of justice remains to be performed towards two men of genius with whose productions the author has allowed himself to use a quite unwarrantable freedom. Having imagined a sculptor in this Romance, it was necessary to provide him with such works in marble as should be in keeping with the artistic ability which he was supposed to possess. With this view, the author laid felonious hands upon a certain bust of Milton, and a statute of a pearl-diver, which he found in the studio of Mr. PAUL AKERS, and secretly conveyed them to the premises of his imaginary friend, in the Via Frezza. Not content even with these spoils, he committed a further robbery upon a magnificent statute of Cleopatra, the production of Mr. WILLIAM W. STORY, an artist whom his country and the world will not long fail to appreciate. He had thoughts of appropriating, likewise, a certain door of bronze by Mr. RANDOLPH ROGERS, representing the history of Columbus in a series of admirable bas-reliefs, but was deterred by an unwillingness to meddle with public property. Were he capable of stealing from a lady, he would certainly have made free with Miss HOSMER'S admirable statute of Zenobia.

He now wishes to restore the above-mentioned beautiful pieces of sculpture to their proper owners, with many thanks, and the avowal of his sincere admiration. What he has said of them in the Romance does not partake of the fiction in which they are imbedded, but expresses his genuine opinion, which, he has little doubt, will be found in accordance with that of the Public. It is, perhaps, unnecessary to say, that, while stealing their designs, the Author has not taken a similar liberty with the personal characters of either of these gifted sculptors; his own man of marble being entirely imaginary.

LEAMINGTON, *December* 15, 1859.

1859/1860

---

from The American Notebooks

[Remarkable Characters]

JULY 29th.

REMARKABLE characters:—a disagreeable figure, waning from middle-age, clad in a pair of tow homespun pantaloons and very dirty shirt, bare-foot, and with one of his feet maimed by an axe; also, an arm amputated two or three inches below the elbow. His beard of a week's growth, grim and grisly, with a general effect of black; —altogether a filthy and disgusting object. Yet he has signs of having been a handsome man in his idea; though now such a beastly figure that, probably, no living thing but his great dog would touch him without an effort. Coming to the stoop, where several persons were sitting,—"Good morning, gentlemen," said the wretch. Nobody answered for a time, till at last one said, "I don't know who you speak to;—not me, I'm sure;" meaning that he did not claim to be a gentleman. "Why, I thought you all speak at once," replied the figure laughing. So he sat himself down on the lower step of the stoop, and began to talk; and the conversation being turned upon his bare feet, by one of the company, he related the story of his losing his toes by the glancing aside of an axe, and with what grim fortitude he bore it. Then he made a transition to the loss of his arm; and setting his teeth and drawing in his breath, said that the pain was dreadful; but this, too, he seems to have borne like an Indian; and a person testified to his fortitude by saying that he did not suppose that there was any feeling in him, from observing how he bore it. The man spoke of the pain of cutting the muscles, and the particular agony at one moment, while the bone was being sawed asunder; and there was a strange expression of remembered agony, as he shrugged his half-limb, and described the matter. Afterwards, in a reply to a question of mine whether he still seemed to feel the hand that had been amputated, he answered that he did, always—and baring the stump, he moved the severed muscles, saying, "There is the thumb, there the forefinger &c." Then he talked to me about phrenology,[1] of which he seems a firm believer and skilful practitioner, telling how he had hit upon the true characters of many people. There was a great deal of sense and acuteness in his talk, and something of elevation in his expression; perhaps a studied elevation— and a sort of courtesy in his manner; but his sense had something out of the way in it; something wild, and ruined, and desperate, in his talk, though I can hardly say what it was. There was something of the gentleman and man of intellect in his deep degradation; and a pleasure in intellectual pursuits, and an acuteness and trained judgment, which bespoke a mind once strong and cultivated. "My study is man," said he. And looking at me "I do not know your name," said he, "but there is something of the hawk-eye about you too." This man was formerly a lawyer in good practice, but taking to drinking, was reduced to this lowest state. Yet not the lowest; for, after the amputation of his arm, being advised by divers persons to throw himself upon the public for support, he told them that, even if he should lose his other arm, he would still be able to support himself and a waiter. Certainly he is a strong minded and iron-constitutioned man; but, looking at the stump of his arm, he said "that the pain of the mind was a thousand times greater than the pain of the body—"That hand could make the pen go fast," said he. Among people in general, he does not seem to have any greater consideration in his ruin, for the sake of his former standing in society. He supports himself by making soap; and on account of the offals used in that business, there is probably rather an evil smell in his domicile. Talking about a dead horse, near his house, he said that he could not bear the scent of it. "I should not think you could smell carrion in that house," said a stage-agent. Whereupon the soap-maker dropped his head, with a little snort, as it were, of wounded feeling; but immediately said that he took all in good part. There was an old squire of the village, a lawyer probably, whose demeanor was different—with a distance, yet a kindliness; for he

---

[1] Study of the human skull as an indicator of mental faculties and character traits. Considered today a pseudoscience, phrenology was much in vogue during the mid-nineteenth century and was endorsed by many prestigious figures, including Walt Whitman.

remembered the times when they met on equal terms. "You and I," said the squire, alluding to their respective troubles and sicknesses, "would have died long ago, if we had not had the courage to live." The poor devil kept talking to me long after everybody else had left the stoop, giving vent to much practical philosophy and just observation on the ways of men, mingled with rather more assumption of literature and cultivation, than belonged to the present condition of his mind. Meantime his great dog—a cleanly looking, and not ill-bred dog, being the only decent attribute appertaining to his master—a well natured dog, too, and receiving civilly any demonstration of courtesy from other people, though preserving a certain distance of deportment—this great dog grew weary of his master's lengthy talk, and expressed his impatience to be gone, by thrusting himself between his legs, rolling over on his back, seizing his ragged trowsers, or playfully taking his maimed bare foot into his mouth—using, in short, the kindly and humorous freedom of a friend, with a wretch to whom all are free enough, but none other kind. His master rebuked him, but with kindness too, and not so that the dog felt himself bound to desist, though he seemed willing to allow his master all the time that could possibly be spared. And, at last, having said many times that he must go and shave and dress himself—and as his beard had been at least a week growing, it might have seemed almost a week's work to get rid of it—he rose from the stoop, and went his way, a forlorn and miserable thing in the light of the cheerful summer Sabbath morning. Yet he seems to keep his spirits up, and still preserves himself a man among men, asking nothing from them—nor is it clearly perceptible what right they have to scorn him, though he seems to acquiesce, in a sort, in their doing so. And yet he cannot wholly have lost his self-respect; and doubtless there were persons on the stoop more grovelling than himself.

Another character—a blacksmith of fifty or upwards; a corpulent figure, big in the belly, and enormous in the backsides; yet there is such an appearance of strength and robustness in his frame, that his corpulence appears very proper and necessary to him. A pound of flesh could not be spared from his abundance, any more than from the leanest man; and he walks about briskly, without any panting, or symptom of labor and pain in his motion. He has a round jolly face, always mirthful and humorous, and shrewd—and the air of a man well to do, and well-respected, yet not caring much about the opinions of men, because his independence is sufficient to itself. Nobody would take him for other than a man of some importance in the community, though his summer dress is a tow cloth pair of pantaloons, a shirt not of the cleanest, open at the breast, and the sleeves rolled up at the elbows, and a straw hat. There is not such a vast difference between this costume and that of lawyer Haynes, above-mentioned—yet never was there a greater diversity of appearance than between these two men; and a glance at them, would be sufficient to mark the difference. The blacksmith loves his glass, and comes to the tavern for it, whenever it seems good to him, not calling for it slily and shyly, but marching sturdily to the bar, or calling across the room for it to be prepared. He speaks with great bitterness against the new license law,[2] and vows if it be not repealed by fair means, it shall be by violence, and that he will be as ready to cock his rifle for such a cause as for any other. On this

[2] Statute of July 1, 1838, geared to "regulate the sale of spiritous liquors." Pubkeepers who received their licenses after July 1 were prohibited from selling liquor in amounts less than 15 gallons.

subject his talk is really fierce; but as to all other matters he is good-natured, and good-hearted, fond of joke, and shaking his jolly sides with frequent laughter. His conversation has much strong, unlettered sense, imbued with humor, as everybody's talk is, in New-England. He takes a queer position sometimes—queer for his figure, particularly—straddling across a chair, facing the back, with his arms resting thereon, and his chin on them, for the benefit of conversing closely with some one. When he has spent as much time in the bar-room, or under the stoop, as he chooses to spare, he gets up at once and goes off with a brisk, vigorous pace. He owns a mill, and seems to be well to do in the world. I know no man who seems more like a man—more indescribably human—than this sturdy blacksmith. 9 1/4[3]

A respectable, elderly man in grey homespun in cloth, who arrived in a wagon, I believe, and began to inquire, after supper, about a certain new kind of mill machinery. Being referred to the blacksmith, who owned one of these mills, the stranger said that he had come from Vermont to learn about the matter. "What may I call your name?" said he to the blacksmith. "My name is Hodge replied the latter. "I believe I have heard of you," said the stranger. Then they colloqued at much length about the various peculiarities and merits of the new invention. The stranger continued here two or three days, making his researches, and forming acquaintance with several mill-wrights and others. He was a man evidently of influence in his neighborhood, and the tone of his conversation was in the style of one accustomed to be heard with deference—though all in a plain and homely way. Lawyer Haynes took notice of this manner; for the talk being about the nature of soap, and the evil smell arising from that process, the stranger joined in. "There need not be any disagreeable smell in making soap," said he. "Now we are to receive a lesson," said Haynes; and the remark was particularly apropos to the large wisdom of the stranger's tone and air. Then he gave an account of the process in his domestic establishment, saying that he threw away the whole offals of the hog, as not producing any soap, and preserved the skins of the intestines for sausages. He seemed to be hospitable, inviting those with whom he did business to take "a mouthful of dinner" with him, and treating them; for he was not an ultra temperance man, though moderate in his potations. I suspect he would turn out a pattern character of the upper class of New-England yeomen, if I had an opportunity of studying him. Doubtless he has been selectman, representative, justice, and filled all but weighty offices. He was highly pleased with the new mill-contrivance, and expressed his opinion, that, when his neighbors saw the success of his, it would be extensively introduced into that vicinity.

Mem—The hostlers, at taverns, call the money given them "Pergasus"—corrupted from perquisites. Otherwise "knock-down money."

[Mr. Edmund Hosmer]

About nine o'clock, Hillard[4] and I set out for a walk to Walden Pond, calling by the way at Mr. Emerson's, to obtain his guidance or directions. He, from a scruple of his external conscience, detained us till after the people had got into church, and then accompanied us in his own illustrious person. We turned aside a little from our way to visit a Mr. Edmund Hosmer, a yeoman of whose homely and self-acquired

[3] Probably referring to the time of morning, i.e., 9:15.

[4] George Hillard, a Boston lawyer and lifelong friend of Hawthorne's.

wisdom Mr. Emerson has a very high opinion. We found him walking in his fields —a short, but stalwart and sturdy personage of middle age, somewhat uncouth and ugly to look at, but with a face of shrewd and kind expression, and manners of natural courtesy. He seemed to have a very free flow of talk, and not much diffidence about his own opinions; for, with a little induction from Mr. Emerson, he began to discourse about the state of the nation, agriculture, and business in general—uttering thoughts that had come to him at the plough, and which had a sort of flavor and smell of the fresh earth about them. I was not impressed with any remarkable originality in his views; but they were sensible and characteristic, and had grown in the soil where we found them. Methought, however, the good yeoman was not quite so natural as he may have been at a former period; the simplicity of his character has probably suffered, in some degree, by his detecting the impression which he makes on those around him. There is a circle, I suppose, who look up to him as an oracle; and so he inevitably assumes the oracular manner, and speaks as if truth and wisdom were uttering themselves by his voice. Mr. Emerson has risked the doing him much mischief, by putting him in print[5]—a trial which few persons can sustain, without losing their unconsciousness. But, after all, a man gifted with thought and expression, whatever his rank in life, and his mode of uttering himself, whether by pen or tongue, cannot be expected to go through the world, without finding himself out—and as all such self-discoveries are partial and imperfect, they do more harm than good to the character. Mr. Hosmer is more natural than ninety-nine men out of a hundred; and he is certainly a man of intellectual and moral substance, a sturdy fact, a reality, something to be felt and touched. It would be amusing to draw a parallel between him and his admirer, Mr. Emerson—the mystic, stretching his hand out of cloud-land, in vain search for something real, and the man of sturdy sense, all whose ideas seem to be dug out of his mind, hard and substantial, as he digs potatoes, beets, carrots, and turnips, out of the earth. Mr. Emerson is a great searcher for facts; but they seem to melt away and become unsubstantial in his grasp.

After leaving Mr. Hosmer, we proceeded through woodpaths to Walden Pond, picking blackberries of enormous size along the way. The pond itself was beautiful and refreshing to my soul, after such long and exclusive familiarity with our tawny and sluggish river. It lies embosomed among wooded hills, not very extensive, but large enough for waves to dance upon its surface, and to look like a piece of blue firmament, earth-encircled. The shore has a narrow, pebbly strand, which it was worth a day's journey to look at, for the sake of the contrast between it and the weedy, slimy, oozy margin of the river. Farther within its depths, you perceive a bottom of pure white sand, sparkling through the transparent water, which, methought, was the very purest liquid in the world. After Mr. Emerson left us, Hillard and I bathed in the pond; and it does really seem as if not only my corporeal person, but my moral self, had received a cleansing from that bath. A good deal of mud and river-slime had accumulated on my soul; but these bright waters washed it all away.

---

[5] Emerson recounted a number of Hosmer's observations in his essay "Agriculture in Massachusetts."

[Margaret Fuller and Ralph Waldo Emerson]

I took a walk through the woods, yesterday afternoon, to Mr. Emerson's, with a book which Margaret Fuller had left behind her, after a call on Saturday eve. I missed the nearest way, and wandered into a very secluded portion of the forest—for forest it might justly be called, so dense and sombre was the shade of oaks and pines. Once I wandered into a tract so overgrown with bushes and underbrush that I could scarcely force a passage through. Nothing is more annoying than a walk of this kind—to be tormented to death by an innumerable host of petty impediments; it incenses and depresses me at the same time. Always when I flounder into the midst of a tract of bushes, which cross and intertwine themselves about my legs, and brush my face, and seize hold of my clothes with a multitudinous gripe—always, in such a difficulty, I feel as if it were almost as well to lie down and die in rage and despair, as to go one step further. It is laughable, after I have got out of the scrape, to think how miserably it affected me for the moment; but I had better learn patience betimes; for there are many such bushy tracts in this vicinity, on the margins of meadows; and my walks will often lead me into them. Escaping from the bushes, I soon came to an open space among the woods—a very lonely spot, with the tall old trees standing around, as quietly as if nobody had intruded there throughout the whole summer. A company of crows were holding their sabbath in the tops of some of the trees; apparently they felt themselves injured or insulted by my presence; for, with one consent, they began to caw—caw—caw—and launching themselves sullenly on the air, took flight to some securer solitude. Mine, probably, was the first human shape that they had seen, all day long—at least, if they had been stationary in that spot; but perhaps they had winged their way over miles and miles of country—had breakfasted on the summit of Graylock, and dined at the base of Wachusett, and were merely come to sup and sleep among the quiet woods of Concord. But it was my impression, at the time, that they had sat still and silent in the tops of the trees, all through the Sabbath-day; and I felt like one who should unawares disturb an assembly of worshippers. A crow, however, has no real pretensions to religion, in spite of their gravity of mien and black attire;—they are certainly thieves, and probably infidels. Nevertheless, their voices, yesterday, were in admirable accordance with the influences of the quiet, sunny, warm, yet autumnal afternoon; they were so far above my head, that their loud clamor added to the quiet of the scene, instead of disturbing it. There was no other sound, except the song of the crickets, which is but an audible stillness; for though it be very loud, and heard afar, yet the mind does not take note of it as a sound, so entirely does it mingle and lose its individuality among the other characteristics of coming Autumn. Alas, for the summer! The grass is still verdant on the hills and in the vallies; the foliage of the trees is as dense as ever, and as green; the flowers are abundant along the margin of the river, and in the hedge-rows, and deep among the woods; the days, too, are as fervid as they were a month ago—and yet, in every breath of wind, and in every beam of sunshine, there is an autumnal influence. I know not how to describe it;— methinks there is a sort of coolness amid all the heat, and a mildness in the brightest of the sunshine. A breeze cannot stir, without thrilling me with the breath of autumn; and I behold its pensive glory in the far golden gleams among the long shadows of the trees. The flowers—even the brightest of them—the Golden-Rod, and the gorgeous cardinals, all the most glorious flowers of the year, have this gentle sadness amid their pomp. Pensive autumn is expressed in the glow of every one of them. I have felt this influence earlier in some years than in others—sometimes Autumn may be perceived even in the early days of July. There is no other feeling like what is caused by this faint, doubtful, yet real perception, or rather prophecy, of the year's decay —so deliciously sweet and sad in the same breath.

After leaving the book at Mr. Emerson's, I returned through the woods, and entering Sleepy Hollow, I perceived a lady reclining near the path which bends along its verge. It was Margaret herself. She had been there the whole afternoon, meditating or reading; for she had a book in her hand, with some strange title, which I did not understand and have forgotten. She said that nobody had broken her solitude, and was just giving utterance to a theory that no inhabitant of Concord ever visited Sleepy Hollow, when we saw a whole group of people entering the sacred precincts. Most of them followed a path that led them remote from us; but an old man passed near us, and smiled to see Margaret lying on the ground, and me sitting by her side. He made some remark about the beauty of the afternoon, and withdrew himself into the shadow of the wood. Then we talked about Autumn—and about the pleasures of getting lost in the woods—and about the crows, whose voices Margaret had heard —and about the experiences of early childhood, whose influence remains upon the character after the recollection of them has passed away—and about the sight of mountains from a distance, and the view from their summits—and about other matters of high and low philosophy. In the midst of our talk, we heard footsteps above us, on the high bank; and while the intruder was still hidden among the trees, he called to Margaret, of whom he had gotten a glimpse. Then he emerged from the green shade; and behold, it was Mr. Emerson, who, in spite of his clerical consecration, had found no better way of spending the Sabbath than to ramble among the woods. He appeared to have had a pleasant time; for he said that there were Muses in the woods to-day, and whispers to be heard in the breezes. It being now nearly six o'clock, we separated, Mr. Emerson and Margaret towards his home, and I towards mine, where my little wife was very busy getting tea. By the bye, Mr. Emerson gave me an invitation to dinner to-day, to be complied with or not, as might suit my convenience at the time; and it happens not to suit. He likewise communicated an invitation from Mrs. Ripley of Waltham for my wife and me to attend a party at her house, next Thursday evening—an annual party, I believe, on the evening after the Φ. B. K.[6] celebration. If my wife chooses, she shall go, and stay all night, away from her poor desolate husband.

Last evening there was the most beautiful moonlight that ever hallowed this earthly world; and when I went to bathe in the river, which was as calm as death, it seemed like plunging down into the sky. But I had rather be on earth than even in the seventh Heaven, just now.

[Henry David Thoreau]

SEPT 1ST. THURSDAY.

Mr. Thorow dined with us yesterday. He is a singular character—a young man with much of wild original nature still remaining in him; and so far as he is sophisticated, it is in a way and method of his own. He is as ugly as sin, long-nosed,

[6] Phi Beta Kappa, the honor society.

queer-mouthed, and with uncouth and somewhat rustic, although courteous manners, corresponding very well with such an exterior. But his ugliness is of an honest and agreeable fashion, and becomes him much better than beauty. He was educated, I believe, at Cambridge, and formerly kept school in this town; but for two or three years back, he has repudiated all regular modes of getting a living, and seems inclined to lead a sort of Indian life among civilized men—an Indian life, I mean, as respects the absence of any systematic effort for a livelihood. He has been for sometime an inmate of Mr. Emerson's family; and, in requital, he labors in the garden, and performs such other offices as may suit him—being entertained by Mr. Emerson for the sake of what true manhood there is in him. Mr. Thorow is a keen and delicate observer of nature—a genuine observer, which, I suspect, is almost as rare a character as even an original poet; and Nature, in return for his love, seems to adopt him as her especial child, and shows him secrets which few others are allowed to witness. He is familiar with beast, fish, fowl, and reptile, and has strange stories to tell of adventures, and friendly passages with these lower brethren of mortality. Herb and flower, likewise, whenever they grow, whether in garden, or wild wood, are his familiar friends. He is also on intimate terms with the clouds, and can tell the portents of storms. It is a characteristic trait, that he has a great regard for the memory of the Indian tribes, whose wild life would have suited him so well; and strange to say, he seldom walks over a ploughed field without picking up an arrow-point, a spear-head, or other relic of the red men—as if their spirits willed him to be the inheritor of their simple wealth.

With all this he has more than a tincture of literature—a deep and true taste for poetry, especially the elder poets, although more exclusive than is desirable, like all other Transcendentalists, so far as I am acquainted with them. He is a good writer —at least, he has written one good article, a rambling disquisition on Natural History in the last Dial,[7]—which, he says, was chiefly made up from journals of his own observations. Methinks this article gives a very fair image of his mind and character —so true, minute, and literal in observation, yet giving the spirit as well as letter of what he sees, even as a lake reflects its wooded banks, showing every leaf, yet giving the wild beauty of the whole scene;—then there are passages in the article of cloudy and dreamy metaphysics, partly affected, and partly the natural exhalations of his intellect;—and also passages where his thoughts seem to measure and attune themselves into spontaneous verse, as they rightfully may, since there is real poetry in him. There is a basis of good sense and moral truth, too, throughout the article, which also is a reflection of his character; for he is not unwise to think and feel, however imperfect in his own mode of action. On the whole, I find him a healthy and wholesome man to know.

After dinner (at which we cut the first water-melon and musk melon that our garden has ripened) Mr. Thorow and I walked up the bank of the river; and, at a certain point, he shouted for his boat. Forthwith, a young man paddled it across the river, and Mr. Thorow and I voyaged further up the stream, which soon became more beautiful than any picture, with its dark and quiet sheet of water, half shaded, half sunny, between high and wooded banks. The late rains have swollen the stream so much, that many trees are standing up to their knees, as it were, in the water; and boughs, which lately swung high in air, now dip and drink deep of the passing wave.

[7] Prestigious journal of the time, originally edited by Ralph Waldo Emerson and Margaret Fuller.

As to the poor cardinals, which glowed upon the bank, a few days since, I could see only a few of their scarlet caps, peeping above the water. Mr. Thorow managed the boat so perfectly, either with two paddles or with one, that it seemed instinct with his own will, and to require no physical effort to guide it. He said that, when some Indians visited Concord a few years since, he found that he had acquired, without a teacher, their precise method of propelling and steering a canoe. Nevertheless, being in want of money, the poor fellow was desirous of selling the boat, of which he is so fit a pilot, and which was built by his own hands; so I agreed to give him his price (only seven dollars) and accordingly became possessor of the Musketaquid.[8] I wish I could acquire the aquatic skill of its original owner at as a reaonable rate.

SEPT 2d. FRIDAY.

Yesterday afternoon, while my wife, and Louisa, and I, were gathering the wind-fallen apples in our orchard, Mr. Thorow arrived with the boat. The adjacent meadow being overflowed by the rise of the stream, he had rowed directly to the foot of the orchard, and landed at the bars, after floating over forty or fifty yards of water, where people were making hay, a week or two since. I entered the boat with him, in order to have the benefit of a lesson in rowing and paddling. My little wife, who was looking on, cannot feel very proud of her husband's proficiency. I managed, indeed, to propel the boat by rowing with two oars; but the use of the single paddle is quite beyond my present skill. Mr. Thorow had assured me that it was only necessary to will the boat to go in any particular direction, and she would immediately take that course, as if imbued with the spirit of the steersman. It may be so with him, but certainly not with me; the boat seemed to be bewitched, and turned its head to every point of the compass except the right one. He then took the paddle himself, and though I could observe nothing peculiar in his management of it, the Musketaquid immediately became as docile as a trained steed. I suspect that she has not yet transferred her affections from her old master to her new one. By and bye, when we are better acquainted, she will grow more tractable; especially after she shall have had the honor of bearing my little wife, who is loved by all things, living or inanimate. We propose to change her name from Musketaquid (the Indian name of Concord river, meaning the river of meadows) to the Pond Lily—which will be very beautiful and appropriate, as, during the summer season, she will bring home many a cargo of pond lilies from along the river's weedy shore. It is not very likely that I shall make such long voyages in her as Mr. Thorow has. He once followed our river down to the Merrimack, and thence, I believe, to Newburyport—a voyage of about eighty miles, in this little vessel.

[Walden Pond]

OCTOBER 6th. FRIDAY.

Yesterday afternoon (leaving wifie with my sister Louisa, who has been with us two or three days) I took a solitary walk to Walden Pond. It was a cool, north-west

---

[8] Canoe built by Thoreau and his brother John.
In 1839, they used it in their extensive travels
along the Concord and Merrimack rivers.

windy day, with heavy clouds rolling and tumbling about the sky, but still a prevalence of genial autumn sunshine. The fields are still green, and the great masses of the
woods have not yet assumed their many-colored garments; but here and there, are
solitary oaks of a deep, substantial red, or maples of a more brilliant hue, or chestnuts,
either yellow or of a tenderer green than in summer. Some trees seem to return to
their hue of May or early June, before they put on the brighter autumnal tints. In
some places, along the borders of low and moist land, a whole range of trees were
clothed in the perfect gorgeousness of autumn, of all shades of brilliant color, looking
like the palette on which Nature was arranging the tints wherewith to paint a picture.
These hues appeared to be thrown together without design; and yet there was perfect
harmony among them, and a softness and delicacy made up of a thousand different
brightnesses. There is not, I think, so much contrast among these colors as might at
first appear; the more you consider them, the more they seem to have one element
among them all—which is the reason that the most brilliant display of them soothes
the observer, instead of exciting him. And I know not whether it be more a moral
effect, or a physical one operating merely on the eye, but it is a pensive gaiety, which
causes a sigh often, but never a smile. We never fancy, for instance, that these
gaily-clad trees should be changed into young damsels in holiday attire, and betake
themselves to dancing on the plain. If they were to undergo such a transformation,
they would surely arrange themselves in a funeral procession, and go sadly along with
their purple, and scarlet, and golden garments trailing over the withering grass. When
the sunshine falls upon them, they seem to smile; but it is as if they were heartbroken.
But it is in vain for me to attempt to describe these autumnal brilliancies, or to convey
the impression which they make on me. I have tried a thousand times, and always
without the slightest self-satisfaction. Luckily, there is no need of such a record; for
Nature renews the scene, year after year; and even when we shall have passed away
from the world, we can spiritually create these scenes; so that we may dispense now
and hereafter with all further efforts to put them into words.

Walden Pond was clear and beautiful, as usual. It tempted me to bathe; and though
the water was thrillingly cold, it was like the thrill of a happy death. Never was there
such transparent water as this. I threw sticks into it, and saw them float suspended on
an almost invisible medium; it seemed as if the pure air was beneath them, as well
as above. If I were to be baptized, it should be in this pond; but then one would not
wish to pollute it by washing off his sins into it. None but angels should bathe there.
It would be a fit bathing-place for my little wife; and sometime or other, I hope, our
blessed baby[9] shall be dipt into its bosom.

In a small and secluded dell, that opens upon the most beautiful cove of the whole
lake, there is a little hamlet of huts or shanties, inhabited by the Irish people who are
at work upon the rail-road. There are three or four of these habitations, the very
rudest, I should imagine, that civilized men ever made for themselves, constructed of
rough boards, with protruding ends. Against some of them the earth is heaped up to
the roof, or nearly so; and when the grass has had time to sprout upon them, they
will look like small natural hillocks, or a species of ant-hill, or something in which
Nature has a larger share than man. These huts are placed beneath the trees, (oaks,

---

[9] The Hawthornes' first child, Una, born March
3, 1844.

walnuts, and white pines) wherever the trunks give them space to stand; and by thus adapting themselves to natural interstices instead of making new ones, they do not break or disturb the solitude and seclusion of the place. Voices are heard, and the shouts and laughter of children, who play about like the sun-beams that come down through the branches. Women are washing beneath the trees, and long lines of whitened clothes are extended from tree to tree, fluttering and gambolling in the breeze. A pig, in a stye even more extemporary than the shanties, is grunting, and poking his snout through the clefts of his habitation. The household pots and kettles are seen at the doors, and a glance within shows the rough benches that serve for chairs, and the bed upon the floor. The visiter's nose takes note of the fragrance of a pipe. And yet, with all these homely items, the repose and sanctity of the old wood do not seem to be destroyed or prophaned; she overshadows these poor people, and assimilates them, somehow or other, to the character of her natural inhabitants. Their presence did not shock me, any more than if I had merely discovered a squirrel's nest in a tree. To be sure, it is a torment to see the great, high, ugly embankment of the railroad, which is here protruding itself into the lake, or along its margin, in close vicinity to this picturesque little hamlet. I have seldom seen anything more beautiful than the cove, on the border of which the huts are situated; and the more I looked, the lovelier it grew. The trees overshadowed it deeply; but on one side there was some brilliant shrubbery which seemed to light up the whole picture with the effect of a sweet and melancholy smile. I felt as if spirits were there—or as if these shrubs had a spiritual life—in short, the impression was undefinable; and after gazing and musing a good while, I retraced my steps through the Irish hamlet, and plodded on along a wood-path.

According to my invariable custom, I mistook my way, and emerging upon a road, I turned my back, instead of my face, towards Concord, and walked on very diligently, till a guide-board informed me of my mistake. I then turned about, and was shortly overtaken by an old yeoman in a chaise, who kindly offered me a ride, and shortly set me down in the village.

[Sketches and Scenes for Stories]

What is the price of a day's labor in Lapland, where the sun never sets for six months?

Miss Asphyxia Dennis.

A life generally of a grave hue, may be said to be *embroidered* with occasional sports and fantasies.

A Father Confessor—his reflections on character, and the contrast of the inward man with the outward, as he looks round on his congregation—all whose secret sins are known to him.

A person with an ice-cold hand—his right hand; which people ever afterwards remember, when once they have grasped it

A stove possessed by a Devil

A physician for the cure of moral diseases.

Fancy pictures of familiar places, which one has never been in—as the green-room of a theatre &c.

The famous characters of history—to imagine their spirits now extant on earth, in the guise of various public or private personages.

The case quoted in Combe's Physiology,[10] from Pinel, of a young man of great talents and profound knowledge of chemistry, who had in view some new discovery of importance. In order to put his mind into the highest possible activity, he shut himself up, for several successive days, and used various methods of excitement; he had a singing girl with him; he drank spirits; smelled penetrating odors, sprinkled cologne-water round the room &c. &c. Eight days thus passed, when he was seized with a fit of frenzy, which terminated in mania.

Flesh and Blood—a firm of butchers.
Miss Polly Syllable—a schoolmistress
Mankind are earthen jugs with spirit in them
Tender Love, Tough Love, which is better.
A spendthrift—in one sense he has his money's worth, by the purchase of large lots of repentance and other dolorous commodities.
Men's accidents are God's purposes. S.A.H.[11]
To sit at the gate of Heaven, and watch persons, as they apply for admittance, some gaining it, others being thrust away.
To point out the moral slavery of one who deems himself a freeman.

A stray leaf from the book of Fate, picked up in the street.

The streak of sunshine journeying through the prisoner's cell; it may be considered as something sent from heaven to keep the soul alive and glad within him. And there is something equivalent to this sunbeam in the darkest circumstances; as flowers, which figuratively grew in Paradise, in the dusky room of a poor maiden in a great city; the child, with its sunny smile, is a cherub. God does not let us live anywhere or anyhow on earth, without placing something of Heaven close at hand, by rightly using and considering which, the earthly darkness or trouble will vanish, and all be Heaven.

A moral philosopher to buy a slave, or otherwise get possession of a human being, and to use him for the sake of experiment, by trying the operation of a certain vice on him.

When the reformation of the world is complete, a fire shall be made of the gallows; and the Hangman shall come and sit down by it, in solitude and despair. To him shall

[10] *The Principles of Physiology* (1836) by Andrew Combe.
[11] Initials of Hawthorne's wife, Sophia. Her

quotations are similarly identified throughout the notebooks.

come the Last Thief, the Last Prostitute, the Last Drunkard, and other representatives of past crime and vice; and they shall hold a dismal merrymaking, quaffing the contents of the Drunkard's last Brandy Bottle.

The human Heart to be allegorized as a cavern; at the entrance there is sunshine, and flowers growing about it. You step within, but a short distance, and begin to find yourself surrounded with a terrible gloom, and monsters of divers kinds; it seems like Hell itself. You are bewildered, and wander long without hope. At last a light strikes upon you. You peep towards it, and find yourself in a region that seems, in some sort, to reproduce the flowers and sunny beauty of the entrance, but all perfect. These are the depths of the heart, or of human nature, bright and peaceful; the gloom and terror may lie deep; but deeper still is the eternal beauty.

A man, in his progress through life, picks up various matters, time, care, habit, riches &c. until at last he staggers along under a heavy burden.

To have a life-long desire for a certain object, which shall appear to be the one thing essential to happiness. At last that object is attained, but proves to be merely incidental to a more important affair; and that affair is the greatest evil fortune that can occur. For instance, all through the winter I had wished to sit in the dusk of evening, by the flickering firelight, with my wife, instead of beside a dismal stove. At last, this has come to pass; but it was owing to her illness, and our having no chamber with a stove, fit to receive her.

Generosity is the flower of Justice. S.A.H.

Madame Calderon de la B (in Life in Mexico)[12] speaks of persons who have been inoculated with the venom of rattlesnakes, by pricking them in various places with the tooth. These persons are thus secured forever after against the bite of any venomous reptile. They have the power of calling snakes, and feel great pleasure in playing with and handling them. Their own bite becomes poisonous to people not inoculated in the same manner. Thus a part of the serpent's nature appears to be transfused into them.

An Auction (perhaps in Vanity Fair) of offices, honors, and all sorts of things considered desirable by mankind; together with things eternally valuable, which shall be considered by most people as worthless lumber.

An examination of wits and poets at a police-court; and they to be sentenced by the Judge to various penalties, or fines, the house of correction, whipping &c. according to the worst offenses of which they were guilty.

A volume bound in cowhide. It should treat of breeding cattle, or some other coarse subject.

A young girl inherits a family grave-yard—that being all that remains of rich hereditary possessions.

[12] *Life in Mexico* (1843) by Mme. Calderon de la Barca.

An interview between General Charles Lee, of the Revolution, and his sister,[13] the Foundress and Mother of the sect of Shakers.

For a child's sketch, perhaps, the life of a city Dove; or perhaps of a flock of doves, flying about the streets, and sometimes alighting on church steeples; on the eaves of lofty houses &c.

The greater picturesqueness and reality of back-yards, and everything appertaining to the rear of a house; as compared with the front, which is fitted up for the public eye. There is much to be learnt, always, by getting a glimpse at rears. When the direction of a road has been altered, so as to pass the rear of farm-houses, instead of the front, a very noticeable aspect is presented.

A sketch—the devouring of the old country residences by the overgrown monster of a city. For instance, Mr. Beekman's ancestral residence was originally several miles from the city of New-York; but the pavements kept creeping nearer and nearer; till now the house is removed, and a street runs directly through what was once its hall.

The print in blood of a naked foot to be traced through the street of a town.

An essay on various kinds of death, together with the just-before and just-after.

The majesty of death to be exemplified in a beggar, who, after being seen, humble and cringing, in the streets of a city, for many years, at length, by some means or other, gets admittance into a rich man's mansion, and there dies—assuming state, and striking awe into the breasts of those who had looked down upon him.

To write a dream, which shall resemble the real course of a dream, with all its inconsistency, its strange transformations, which are all taken as a matter of course, its eccentricities and aimlessness—with nevertheless a leading idea running through the whole. Up to this old age of the world, no such thing ever has been written.

To allegorize life with a masquerade, and represent mankind generally as masquers. Here and there, a natural face may appear.

Sketch of a personage with the malignity of a witch, and doing the mischief attributed to one—but by natural means; breaking off love-affairs, teaching children vices, ruining men of wealth, &c.

With an emblematical divining-rod to seek for emblematic gold—that is for Truth —for what of Heaven is left on earth.

A task for a subjugated fiend—to gather up all the fallen autumnal leaves of a forest, apart them, and affix each one to the twig where it originally grew.

---

[13] Hawthorne mistakenly assumes Charles Lee (1731–1782) and Ann Lee (1736–1784) to be siblings.

A vision of Grub-street,[14] forming an allegory of the literary world.

The emerging from their lurking-places of evil-characters, on some occasion suited to their action—they having been quite unknown to the world hitherto. For instance, the French Revolution brought out such wretches.

The advantages of a longer life than is allotted to mortals—the many things that might then be accomplished;—to which one life-time is inadequate, and for which the time spent is therefore lost; a successor being unable to take up the task when we drop it.

George First had promised the Duchess of Kendall, his mistress, that, if possible, he would pay her a visit, after Death. Accordingly, a large raven flew into the window of her villa at Isleworth. She believed it to be his soul, and treated it ever after with all respect and tenderness, till either she or the bird died.

Walpole's Reminiscences[15]

The history of an Alms-House in a country village, from the eve of its foundation downward—a record of the remarkable occupants of it; and extracts from interesting portions of its annals. The rich of one generation might, in the next, seek for a home there, either in their own persons or those of their representatives. Perhaps the son and heir of the founder might have no better refuge. There should be occasional sunshine let into the story; for instance, the good fortune of some nameless infant, educated there, and discovered finally to be the child of wealthy parents.

Ladislaus, King of Naples, beseiging the city of Florence, agreed to show mercy, provided the inhabitants would deliver to him a certain virgin of famous beauty, the daughter of a physician of the city. When she was sent to the king—every one contributing something to adorn her in the richest manner—her father gave her a perfumed handkerchief, at that time a universal decoration, richly wrought. This handkerchief was poisoned with his utmost art; and in their first embrace, the poison being received into their pores, opened by heat,—it killed them both—"converting their warm sweat into a cold sweat, they presently died in one another's arms."

Cotton's Montaigne.[16]

Pearl—the English of Margaret—a pretty name for a girl in a story.

The conversation of the steeples of a city, when the bells are ringing on Sunday —Calvinist, Episcopalian, Unitarian &c.

Of a bitter satirist—of Swift, for instance—it might be said, that the person or thing, on which his satire fell, shrivelled up, as if the Devil had spit on it.

Allston's picture of Belshazzar's Feast[17]—with reference to the advantages, or otherwise, of having life assured to us, till we could finish important tasks on which we were engaged.

---

[14] London street known in the eighteenth century as a center for writers, publishers, and copyists. In modern usage, it is a pejorative term for any group or community of hack writers or ghostwriters.

[15] *The Works of Horatio Walpole, Earl of Orford* (1798).

[16] *Essays of Michel Seigneur de Montaigne,* translated in 1686 by Charles Cotton.

[17] American painter Washington Allston (1779–1843) worked on the painting for 26 years but died before completing it.

Visits to Castles in the Air—Chateaus en Espagne &c—with remarks on that sort of architecture.

To consider a piece of gold as a sort of talisman—or as containing within itself all the forms of enjoyment that it can purchase—so that they might appear, by some fantastical chemical process, as visions.

To personify If—But—And—Though—&c.

The fount of Tears—a traveller to discover it, and other similar localities.

Benvenuto Cellini[18] saw a salamander in the household fire. It was shown him by his father, in his childhood.

A man seeks for something excellent, and seeks it in the wrong way, and in a wrong spirit, and finds something horrible—as for instance, he seeks for treasure, and finds a dead body—for the gold that somebody has hidden, and brings to light his accumulated sins.

An auction of second hands—then moralizing how the fashion of this world passeth away.

Noted people in a town:—as the town-crier—the old fruit-man—the constable—the oyster-seller—the fish-man—the scissors-grinder—&c &c &c

The Magic Play of Sunshine, for a child's story—the sunshine circling round through a prisoner's cell, from his high and narrow window. He keeps his soul alive and cheerful by means of it, it typyfying cheerfulness; and when he is released, he takes up the ray of sunshine and carries it away with him; and it enables him to discover treasures all over the world, in places where nobody else would think of looking for any.

A young man finds a portion of the skeleton of a Mammoth; he begins by degrees to become interested in completing it; searches round the world for the means of doing so; spends youth and manhood in the pursuit; and in old age has nothing to show for his life, but this skeleton.

For the Virtuoso's Collection—the pen with which Faust signed away his salvation, with a drop of blood dried on it.

For a child's sketch—a meeting with all the personages mentioned in Mother Goose's Melodies, and other juvenile stories.

   Great Expectation to be entertained in the allegorical Grub-street of the appearance of the great American writer. Or a search warrant to be sent thither to catch a poet.

---

[18] Italian artisan, artist, and author (1500–1571).
Hawthorne recalls a passage from Cellini's
Autobiography.

On the former supposition, he shall be discovered under some most unlikely form; or shall be supposed to have lived and died unrecognized.

An old man to promise a youth a treasure of gold;—and to keep his promise by teaching him practically a Golden Rule.

A valuable jewel to be buried in the grave of a beloved person, or thrown over with a corpse at sea, or deposited under the foundation-stone of an edifice—and to be afterward met with by the former owner, in the possession of some one.

In moods of heavy despondency, one feels as if it would be delightful to sink down in some quiet spot, and lie there forever, letting the soil gradually accumulate and form a little hillock over us, and the grass and perhaps flowers gather over it. At such times, death is too much of an event to be wished for;—we have not spirits to encounter it; but choose to pass out of existence in this sluggish way.

A noted gambler had acquired such self-command, that, in the most desperate circumstances of his game, no change of feature ever betrayed him;—only there was a slight scar upon his forehead, which, at such moments, assumed a deep blood-red hue. Thus, in playing at Brag, for instance, his antagonist could judge from this index, when he had a bad hand. At last, discovering what it was that betrayed him, he covered the scar with a green silk shade.

A dream, the other night, that the world had become dissatisfied with the inaccurate manner in which facts are reported, and had employed me, with a salary of a thousand dollars, to relate things of public importance exactly as they happen.

A person who has all the qualities of a friend, except that he invariably fails you at the pinch.
1868

from The English Notebooks

[Herman Melville]

NOVEMBER 20TH, THURSDAY.

A week ago last Monday, Herman Melville came to see me at the Consulate, looking much as he used to do (a little paler, and perhaps a little sadder), in a rough outside coat, and with his characteristic gravity and reserve of manner. He had crossed from New York to Glasgow in a screw steamer, about a fortnight before, and had since been seeing Edinburgh and other interesting places. I felt rather awkward at first; because this is the first time I have met him since my ineffectual attempt to get him a consular appointment from General Pierce. However, I failed only from real lack of power to serve him; so there was no reason to be ashamed, and we soon found ourselves on pretty much our former terms of sociability and confidence. Melville has not been well, of late; he has been affected with neuralgic complaints in his head and limbs, and no doubt has suffered from too constant literary occupation, pursued without much success, latterly; and his writings, for a long while past, have indicated a morbid state of mind. So he left his place at Pittsfield, and has established his wife and family, I believe, with his father-in-law in Boston, and is thus far on his way to Constantinople. I do not wonder that he found it necessary to take an airing through the world, after so many years of toilsome pen-labor and domestic life, following upon so wild and adventurous a youth as his was. I invited him to come and stay with us at Southport, as long as he might remain in this vicinity; and, accordingly, he did come, the next day, taking with him, by way of baggage, the least little bit of a bundle, which, he told me, contained a night-shirt and a tooth-brush. He is a person of very gentlemanly instincts in every respect, save that he is a little heterodox in the matter of clean linen.

He stayed with us from Tuesday till Thursday; and, on the intervening day, we took a pretty long walk together, and sat down in a hollow among the sand hills (sheltering ourselves from the high, cool wind) and smoked a cigar. Melville, as he always does, began to reason of Providence and futurity, and of everything that lies beyond human ken, and informed me that he had "pretty much made up his mind to be annihilated"; but still he does not seem to rest in that anticipation; and, I think, will never rest until he gets hold of a definite belief. It is strange how he persists— and has persisted ever since I knew him, and probably long before—in wandering to-and-fro over these deserts, as dismal and monotonous as the sand hills amid which we were sitting. He can neither believe, nor be comfortable in his unbelief; and he is too honest and courageous not to try to do one or the other. If he were a religious man, he would be one of the most truly religious and reverential; he has a very high and noble nature, and better worth immortality than most of us. . . .

We left Chester at about four o'clock; and I took the rail for Southport at half-past six, parting from Melville at a street-corner in Liverpool, in the rainy evening. I saw him again on Monday, however. He said that he already felt much better than in America; but observed that he did not anticipate much pleasure in his rambles, for that the spirit of adventure is gone out of him. He certainly is much overshadowed since I saw him last; but I hope he will brighten as he goes onward. He sailed from Liverpool in a steamer on Tuesday, leaving his trunk behind him at my consulate, and taking only a carpet-bag to hold all his travelling-gear. This is the next best thing to going naked; and as he wears his beard and moustache, and so needs no dressing-case —nothing but a tooth-brush—I do not know a more independent personage. He learned his travelling habits by drifting about, all over the South Sea, with no other clothes or equipage than a red flannel shirt and a pair of duck trowsers. Yet we seldom see men of less criticizable manners than he.

1870

---

from Abraham Lincoln

[*from* **March–April 1862**]

By and by there was a little stir on the staircase and in the passage-way, and in lounged a tall, loose-jointed figure, of an exaggerated Yankee port and demeanor, whom (as being about the homeliest man I ever saw, yet by no means repulsive or disagreeable) it was impossible not to recognize as Uncle Abe.

Unquestionably, Western man though he be, and Kentuckian by birth, President Lincoln is the essential representative of all Yankees, and the veritable specimen, physically, of what the world seems determined to regard as our characteristic qualities. It is the strangest and yet the fittest thing in the jumble of human vicissitudes, that he, out of so many millions, unlooked for, unselected by any intelligible process that could be based upon his genuine qualities, unknown to those who chose him, and unsuspected of what endowments may adapt him for his tremendous responsibility, should have found the way open for him to fling his lank personality into the chair of state,—where, I presume, it was his first impulse to throw his legs on the council-table, and tell the Cabinet Ministers a story. There is no describing his lengthy awkwardness, nor the uncouthness of his movement; and yet it seemed as if I had been in the habit of seeing him daily, and had shaken hands with him a thousand times in some village street; so true was he to the aspect of the pattern American, though with a certain extravagance which, possibly, I exaggerated still further by the delighted eagerness with which I took it in. If put to guess his calling and livelihood, I should have taken him for a country schoolmaster as soon as anything else. He was dressed in a rusty black frock-coat and pantaloons, unbrushed, and worn so faithfully that the suit had adapted itself to the curves and angularities of his figure, and had grown to be an outer skin of the man. He had shabby slippers on his feet. His hair was black, still unmixed with gray, stiff, somewhat bushy, and had apparently been acquainted with neither brush nor comb that morning, after the disarrangement of the pillow; and as to a nightcap, Uncle Abe probably knows nothing of such effeminacies. His complexion is dark and sallow, betokening, I fear, an insalubrious atmosphere around the White House; he has thick black eyebrows and an impending brow; his nose is large, and the lines about his mouth are very strongly defined.

The whole physiognomy is as coarse a one as you would meet anywhere in the length and breadth of the States; but, withal, it is redeemed, illuminated, softened, and brightened by a kindly though serious look out of his eyes, and an expression of homely sagacity, that seems weighted with rich results of village experience. A great deal of native sense; no bookish cultivation, no refinement; honest at heart, and thoroughly so, and yet, in some sort, sly,—at least, endowed with a sort of tact and wisdom that are akin to craft, and would impel him, I think, to take an antagonist in flank, rather than to make a bull-run at him right in front. But, on the whole, I liked this sallow, queer, sagacious visage, with the homely human sympathies that warmed it; and, for my small share in the matter, would as lief have Uncle Abe for a ruler as any man whom it would have been practicable to put in his place. . . .

Letter to Henry Wadsworth Longfellow*

[June 4, 1837]

Salem, June 4th, 1837

Dear Sir,

Not to burthen you with my correspondence, I have delayed a rejoinder to your very kind and cordial letter, until now. It gratifies me to find that you have occasionally felt an interest in my situation; but your quotation from Jean Paul,[1] about the "lark's nest," makes me smile. You would have been nearer the truth if you had pictured me as dwelling in an owl's nest; for mine is about as dismal; and, like the owl I seldom venture abroad till after dark. By some witchcraft or other—for I really cannot assign any reasonable why and wherefore—I have been carried apart from the main current of life, and find it impossible to get back again. Since we last met— which, I remember, was in Sawtell's[2] room, where you read a farewell poem to the relics of the class—ever since that time, I have secluded myself from society; and yet I never meant any such thing, nor dreamed what sort of life I was going to lead. I have made a captive of myself and put me into a dungeon and now I cannot find the key to let myself out—and if the door were open, I should be almost afraid to come out. You tell me that you have met with troubles and changes. I know not what they may have been; but I can assure you that trouble is the next best thing to enjoyment, and that there is no fate in this work so horrible as to have no share in either its joys or sorrows. For the last ten years, I have not lived, but only dreamed about living. It may be true that there have been some unsubstantial pleasures here in the shade, which I should have missed in the sunshine, but you cannot conceive how utterly devoid of satisfaction all my retrospects[3] are. I have laid up no treasure of pleasant remembrances, against old age; but there is some comfort in thinking that my future years can hardly fail to be more varied, and therefore more tolerable, than the past.

You give me more credit than I deserve, in supposing that I have led a studious life. I have, indeed, turned over a good many books, but in so desultory a way that it cannot be called study, nor has it left me the fruits of study. As to my literary efforts, I do not think much of them—neither is it worth while to be ashamed of them. They would have been better, I trust, if written under more favorable circumstances. I have had no external excitement—no consciousness that the public would like what I wrote, nor much hope nor a very passionate desire that they should do so. Nevertheless, having nothing else to be ambitious of, I have felt considerably interested in literature; and if my writings had made any decided impression, I should probably

---

* Longfellow (1807–1882), who had known Hawthorne at Bowdoin as a classmate rather than a close friend, had recently been appointed Smith Professor of Modern Languages at Harvard. The occasion for Hawthorne's writing was the publication of his *Twice-Told Tales*.

[1] Pseudonym of Johann Paul Friedrich Richter (1763–1825), German novelist.

[2] Cullen Sawtelle (1805–1887): Hawthorne's classmate at Bowdoin and later a member of Congress.

[3] Memories; recollections.

have been stimulated to greater exertions; but there has been no warmth of approbation, so that I have always written with benumbed fingers. I have another great difficulty, in the lack of materials; for I have seen so little of the world, that I have nothing but thin air to concoct my stories of, and it is not easy to give a lifelike semblance to such shadowy stuff. Sometimes, through a peep-hole, I have caught a glimpse of the real world; and the two or three articles in which I have portrayed such glimpses, please me better than the others. I have now, or shall soon have, one sharp spur to exertion, which I lacked at an earlier period; for I see little prospect but that I must scribble for a living. But this troubles me much less than you would suppose. I can turn my pen to all sorts of drudgery, such as children's books, etc., and by and by, I shall get some editorship that will answer my purpose. Frank Pierce, who was with us at college, offered me his influence to obtain an office in the Exploring Expedition; but I believe that he was mistaken in supposing that a vacancy existed. If such a post were attainable, I should certainly accept it; for, though fixed so long to one spot, I have always had a desire to run around the world.

The copy of my Tales⁴ was sent to Mr. Owen's, the bookseller's in Cambridge.⁵ I am glad to find that you had read and liked some of the stories. To be sure, you could not well help flattering me a little; but I value your praise too highly not to have faith in its sincerity. When I last heard from the publisher—which was not very recently—the book was doing pretty well. Six or seven hundred copies had been sold. I suppose, however, these awful times have now stopped the sale.

I intend in a week or two to come out of my owl's nest, and not return to it till late in the summer—employing the interval in making a tour somewhere in New England. You, who have the dust of distant countries on your "sandal-shoon,"⁶ cannot imagine how much enjoyment I shall have in this little excursion. Whenever I get abroad, I feel just as young as I did, ten years ago. What a letter I am inflicting on you! I trust you will answer it.

Yours sincerely,
Nath. Hawthorne.

1837/1969

Letters to Sophia Peabody

[October 4, 1840]

Salem, Oct. 4ᵗʰ, 1840— 1/2 past 10 A.M.

Mine ownest,

Here sits thy husband¹ in his old accustomed chamber, where he used to sit in years gone by, before his soul became acquainted with thine. Here I have written many tales —many that have been burned to ashes—many that doubtless deserved the same fate. This deserves to be called a haunted chamber, for thousands upon thousands of visions

---

⁴ Hawthorne's *Twice-Told Tales*.
⁵ Cambridge, Massachusetts.
⁶ Sandals or shoes.
¹ Hawthorne and Sophia were not yet married.

have appeared to me in it; and some few of them have become visible to the world. If ever I should have a biographer, he ought to make great mention of this chamber in my memoirs, because so much of my lonely youth was wasted here, and here my mind and character were formed: and here I have been glad and hopeful, and here I have been despondent; and here I sat a long, long time, waiting patiently for the world to know me, and sometimes wondering why it did not know me sooner, or whether it would ever know me at all—at least, till I were in my grave. And sometimes (for I had no wife then to keep my heart warm) it seemed as if I were already in the grave, with only life enough to be chilled and benumbed. But oftener I was happy—at least as happy as I then knew how to be, or was aware of the possibility of being. By and bye, the world found me out in my lonely chamber, and called me forth—not, indeed, with a loud roar of acclamation, but rather with a still, small voice; and forth I went, but found nothing in the world that I thought preferable to my old solitude, till at length a certain Dove[2] was revealed to me, in the shadow of a seclusion as deep as my own had been. And I drew nearer and nearer to the Dove, and opened my bosom to her, and she flitted into it, and closed her wings there— and there she nestles now and forever, keeping my heart warm, and renewing my life with her own. So now I begin to understand why I was imprisoned so many years in this lonely chamber, and why I could never break through the viewless bolts and bars; for if I had sooner made my escape into the world, I should have grown hard and rough, and been covered with earthly dust, and my heart would have become callous by rude encounters with the multitude; so that I should have been all unfit to shelter a heavenly Dove in my arms. But living in solitude till the fulness of time was come, I still kept the dew of my youth and the freshness of my heart, and had these to offer to my Dove.

Well, dearest, I had no notion what I was going to write, when I began, and indeed I doubted whether I should write anything at all; for after such communion as that of our last blissful evening, it seems as if a sheet of paper could only be a veil betwixt us. Ownest, in the times that I have been speaking of, I used to think that I could imagine all passions, all feelings, all states of the heart and mind; but how little did I know what it is to be mingled with another's being! Thou only hast taught me that I have a heart—thou only hast thrown a light deep downward, and upward, into my soul. Thou only hast revealed me to myself; for without thy aid, my best knowledge of myself would have been merely to know my own shadow—to watch it flickering on the wall, and mistake its fantasies for my own real actions. Indeed, we are but shadows—we are not endowed with real life, and all that seems most real about us is but the thinnest substance of a dream—till the heart is touched. That touch creates us—then we begin to be—thereby we are beings of reality, and inheritors of eternity. Now, dearest, dost thou comprehend what thou hast done for me? And is it not a somewhat fearful thought, that a few slight circumstances might have prevented us from meeting, and then I should have returned to my solitude, sooner or later (probably now, when I have thrown down my burthen of coal and salt) and never should [have] been created at all! But this is an idle speculation. If the whole world had stood between us, we must have met—if we had been born in different ages, we could not have been sundered.

---

[2] I.e., Sophia.

Belovedest, how dost thou do? If I mistake not, it was a southern rain yesterday, and, next to the sunshine of Paradise, *that* seems to be thy element.[3] . . .

Miss Sophia A. Peabody,
    Care of Dr. N. Peabody,
        Boston, Mass.

1840/1907

[April 13, 1841][4]

Oak Hill, April 13th, 1841

Ownest love,

Here is thy poor husband in a polar Paradise! I know not how to interpret this aspect of Nature—whether it be of good or evil omen to our enterprise. But I reflect that the Plymouth pilgrims arrived in the midst of storm and stept ashore upon mountain snow-drifts; and nevertheless they prospered, and became a great people— and doubtless it will be the same with us. I laud my stars, however, that thou wilt not have thy first impressions of our future home from such a day as this. Thou wouldst shiver all thy life afterwards, and never realise that there could be bright skies, and green hills and meadows, and trees heavy with foliage, when now the whole scene is a great snow-bank, and the sky full of snow likewise. Through faith, I persist in believing that spring and summer will come in their due season; but the unregenerated man shivers within me, and suggests a doubt whether I may not have wandered within the precincts of the Arctic circle, and chosen my heritage among everlasting snows. Dearest, provide thyself with a good stock of furs; and if thou canst obtain the skin of a polar bear, thou wilt find it a very suitable summer dress for this region. Thou must not hope ever to walk abroad, except upon snow-shoes, nor to find any warmth, save in thy husband's heart.

Belovedest, I have not yet taken my first lesson in agriculture, as thou mayst well suppose—except that I went to see our cows foddered, yesterday afternoon. We have eight of our own; and the number is now increased by a transcendental heifer, belonging to Miss Margaret Fuller.[5] She is very fractious, I believe, and apt to kick over the milk pail. Thou knowest best, whether in these traits of character, she resembles her mistress. Thy husband intends to convert himself into a milk-maid, this evening; but I pray heaven that Mr. Ripley[6] may be moved to assign him the kindliest cow in the herd—otherwise he will perform his duty with fear and trembling:

Ownest wife, I like my brethren in affliction very well; and couldst thou see us sitting round our table, at meal-times, before the great kitchen-fire, thou wouldst call it a cheerful sight. Mrs. Parker is a most comfortable woman to behold; she looks as if her ample person were stuffed full of tenderness—indeed, as if she were all one great, kind heart. Wert thou here, I should ask for nothing more—not even for sunshine and summer weather; for thou wouldst be both, to thy husband. And how is that cough of thine, my belovedest? Hast thou thought of me, in my perils and wanderings?

---

[3] The final eight lines of the letter are missing.
[4] This letter was written on the day after Hawthorne's arrival at Brook Farm, the utopian community founded by George Ripley.
[5] Margaret Fuller (1810–1850), editor of *The Dial*

(1840–1842) and author of *Women in the Nineteenth Century* (1845).
[6] The Reverend George Ripley (1802–1880), Massachusetts religious thinker, idealist, and reformer.

I trust that thou dost muse upon me with hope and joy; not with repining. Think that I am gone before, to prepare a home for my Dove, and will return for her, all in good time.

Thy husband has the best chamber in the house, I believe; and though not quite so good as the apartment I have left, it will do very well. I have hung up thy two pictures; and they give me a glimpse of summer and of thee. The vase I intended to have brought in my arms, but could not very conveniently do it yesterday; so that it still remains at Mrs. Hillard's,[7] together with my carpet. I shall bring them [at] the next opportunity.

Now farewell, for the present, most beloved. I have been writing this in my chamber; but the fire is getting low, and the house is old and cold: so that the warmth of my whole person has retreated to my heart, which burns with love for thee. I must run down to the kitchen or parlor hearth, when thy image shall sit beside me—yea, be pressed to my breast. At bed-time, thou shalt have a few lines more. Now I think of it, dearest, wilt thou give Mrs. Ripley a copy of Grandfather's Chair and Liberty Tree; she wants them for some boys here. I have several copies of Famous Old People.

April 14th, 10 A.M. Sweetest, I did not milk the cows last night, because Mr. Ripley was afraid to trust them to my hands, or me to their horns—I know not which. But this morning, I have done wonders. Before breakfast, I went out to the barn, and began to chop hay for the cattle; and with such "righteous vehemence" (as Mr. Ripley says) did I labor, that in the space of ten minutes, I broke the machine. Then I brought wood and replenished the fires; and finally sat down to breakfast and ate up a huge mound of buckwheat cakes. After breakfast, Mr. Ripley put a four-pronged instrument into my hands, which he gave me to understand was called a pitch-fork; and he and Mr. Farley[8] being armed with similar weapons, we all then commenced a gallant attack upon a heap of manure. This office being concluded, and thy husband having purified himself, he sits down to finish this letter to his most beloved wife. Dearest, I will never consent that thou come within half a mile of me, after such an encounter as that of this morning. Pray Heaven that his letter retain none of the fragrance with which the writer was imbued. As for thy husband himself, he is peculiarly partial to the odor; but that whimsical little nose of thine might chance to quarrel with it.

Belovedest, Miss Fuller's cow hooks the other cows, and has made herself ruler of the herd, and behaves in a very tyrannical manner. Sweetest, I know not when I shall see thee; but I trust it will not be longer than the end of next week. I love thee! I love thee! I wouldst thou wert with me; for then would my labor be joyful—and even now it is not sorrowful. Dearest, I shall make an excellent husbandman. I feel the original Adam reviving within me.

Miss Sophia A. Peabody,
    13 West street,
        Boston.

1841/1907

---

[7] Mrs. Hilliard: Susan Howe Hillard, a friend of the Peabodys and with whom Hawthorne lived for a time.

[8] Frank Farley, a fellow resident of Brook Farm.

Herman Melville
1819–1891

The twentieth century recognizes Herman Melville as a major American writer, but in his lifetime Melville was regarded only as an exciting and once-popular travel writer whose strange fiction cast doubt on his sanity. Melville traced his ancestry to two Revolutionary War figures. His mother was the daughter of Albany's wealthy General Peter Gansvoort, and his father, Allan, was a New York City merchant-importer. The family took pride in its ties to American history. Typical of their educated, merchant class, they enrolled Herman, the third child of eight, at the New York Male High School at the age of seven. Evidently his parents foresaw a career in business for him, perhaps the very business that enabled the Melville family to prosper. That situation changed drastically in 1830, however, when the overextended business of young Herman's father collapsed, forcing him into bankruptcy. The family moved to Albany, where for a time Allan Melville recovered financially. Herman and his two brothers attended the Albany Academy, where the boy saw his older brother, Gansvoort, distinguish himself in prestigious classical subjects while young Herman pursued the commercial course. But once again Allan Melville suffered business reverses, which led to the mental and physical breakdown that preceded his death in 1832. These family experiences would ultimately emerge in *Pierre.*

Melville's next years were a scramble for a career. Forced to leave school, he became successively a bank clerk, a farmhand on the western Massachusetts acreage of his uncle Thomas, a store clerk and bookkeeper for his successful older brother Gansvoort, and, when Gansvoort's business failed, a country schoolmaster. In 1838 the family moved to Lansingburgh, in upstate New York, where they lived thriftily with aid from a wealthy relative. Hoping—in vain, as it turned out—for work on the new Erie Canal, Melville enrolled in a course in engineering and surveying at the local academy. When no job materialized, Melville looked downstate, toward New York City, where a packet to Liverpool had a berth for him. Melville later developed that maritime experience into the novel *Redburn.* Back in the United States in 1840, the young man traveled West to Illinois. Though his trip included a Mississippi riverboat ride later crucial to the novel *The Confidence-Man,* it yielded no immediate career prospects. Early the next year, doubtless feeling desperate, Melville shipped out from New Bedford, Massachusetts, on the whaling ship *Acushnet,* bound for the South Pacific.

Melville's maritime adventures have been well documented. The *Acushnet* killed few whales, and morale sank as dissension mounted between the captain and the officers. With a shipmate, Melville jumped ship in summer 1842 and lived with a native tribe in the Marquesas for several weeks. Picked up by an Australian whaler, he participated in a revolt that landed him in a Tahiti prison along with a physician-companion, who later helped him explore the flora and fauna of Tahiti and Eimeo, where Melville shipped aboard a Nantucket whaler. Discharged at Honolulu, Melville stayed in Hawaii for a few months as a beachcomber, then signed onto the frigate *United States.* That ship's captain of the maintop, John J. ("Jack") Chase, proved to be a Melvillian hero. (He appears as a character in *White-Jacket,* a novel on the severity of maritime discipline, and *Billy Budd* is dedicated to him.) The *United States* toured the Pacific before sailing for Boston, arriving in autumn 1844, when Melville was twenty-five years old and, after drawing his pay, an unemployed sailor.

A few months later, again living at home, Melville began sorting out the meaning of his adventures and his life. His introspection led to the psychological unfolding he graphed in all his writings. "Until I was twenty-five," he later wrote to his friend and fellow writer, Nathaniel Hawthorne, "I had no development at all. From my twenty-fifth year I date my life."

Melville's self-styled birth occurred when he wrote fictionalized versions of his South Sea adventures. *Typee* (1846) and *Omoo* (1847) were popular successes with American and English readers eager for tales of exotic places. Some close readers were offended by Melville's critique of the missionaries who "evangelized" and "civilized" the islanders into "draft horses" or "beasts of burden," but prospects were generally bright for the young author. Washington Irving, American literature's patriarchal figure, thought *Typee* brilliant, and even at the end of the century the writer Henry Adams consulted it in preparation for his South Sea voyage.

Largely on the strength of his prospects as a professional author, Melville married Elizabeth Shaw and settled in New York City in a house that also accommodated his younger brother Allan and Allan's new bride, Melville's mother, and his unmarried sisters. He soon took his place in the New York literary life dominated by the prominent editor and writer Evert Duyckinck, for whose *Literary World* Melville wrote reviews. Unknown to the young author, his career was about to reach a critical point. Had he continued to write adventure stories in the mold of his early books, he might have been a financially successful "pen-and-ink man" and a footnote in literary history. Instead, Melville's third novel, *Mardi,* took a radical midway departure into philosophy, satire, fantasy, and allegory. The young writer had discovered the works of Robert Burton, Sir Thomas Browne, François Rabelais, and others and, encouraged by their example, broke the bounds of conventional form. He was taken aback when the public spurned his effort and reviewers urged him to resume the style and structure of his adventure narratives.

Melville now faced the terrible problem common to American writers from the eighteenth century into the twentieth. To earn a living from the sale of his books, he needed to win the very readers whose professed values and beliefs he attacked. How could he possibly find favor with a public that wished only to be entertained, when he offered probing, experimental, critical writings in the face of social complacency? The issue was especially pressing because Melville now had an infant son, Malcolm, to support. Chastened, he wrote two novels intended to satisfy popular taste, *Redburn* (1849) and *White-Jacket* (1850), based respectively on his youthful Liverpool voyage and on his South Pacific tour. The style of both is gently ironic, though Melville felt constrained by both efforts and called them the literary equivalent of "sawing wood." Determined to realize maximal profits from his literary slave labor, Melville carried proofs of *White-Jacket* to

England personally to arrange terms with his London publisher. After brief visits to France and Germany, he returned home, pleased when his books earned critical acclaim and sold well.

A newly confident Melville now began his whaling book. Initially he may have intended once again to write an adventure story based on his experience on whaling ships. But Melville had been rereading Shakespeare and the works of Thomas Carlyle. He also had made the acquaintance of Nathaniel Hawthorne, whom he would soon call an American Shakespeare in a review-essay entitled "Hawthorne and His Mosses," a survey of the state of American writers in the English-speaking world. In *Moby-Dick,* Melville continued to unfold his psyche, and the style and structure of the new work embodied the change. He was relentlessly speculative, posing challenge to the literary and social status quo, probing society's hypocrisies, its complacency, its contradictions.

Meanwhile, the crowded conditions of the New York City household made it necessary for Melville to move his family. Western Massachusetts had become a summer resort for American writers, who picnicked together in an occasional "pleasure party." Doubtless anticipating the seasonal literary comradeship, Melville moved his family in autumn 1850 to a 160-acre farm called Arrowhead, purchased in part with a loan from the formidable Judge Lemuel Shaw, Melville's father-in-law. By winter Melville had completed his book on whaling, which he revised in the study whose window looked out upon Mt. Greylock, its peak shaped rather like the outline of a whale. Customarily Melville wrote into the afternoon, then read and gathered materials in the evening and at night. His meals were sometimes served on trays left at his study door. Beyond the door and walls he could hear all household noises.

Moby-Dick (1851) was published to a mixed reception, and sales were disappointing. This masculine, experimental novel did not appeal to a novel-reading public principally comprising women. By now Melville was financially pressed, in debt to his publisher, Harper, for advances, and responsible for a household that included his mother, his sisters, one small child, and a pregnant wife. Once again he attempted to capture a popular audience, this time with a deliberately sentimental gothic novel. Melville promised "a rural bowl of milk" in *Pierre,* the story of a young landed gentleman. Instead the novel became a dark exploration of sexuality, identity, depravity, tragic and inevitable destruction, and, covertly, the plight of the American artist. The manuscript was long, and Harper offered poor royalties. The reception of the book was hostile. Reviewers attacked Melville personally. Everett Duyckinck, a reviewer who had thought *Moby-Dick* immoral, was scandalized and concluded that Melville had gone insane.

Under severe strain, Melville managed to keep apace of his farm work, though the family feared that his health was in jeopardy. And financial problems were less important that the public's repudiation of his work. With the election of Franklin Pierce, Melville's well-connected relatives (as well as Pierce's onetime classmate Hawthorne) tried to secure him a political appointment, but their efforts were unsuccessful. Thereafter Melville turned to short fiction (such as "Bartleby, the Scrivener"), which he wrote for such magazines as *Harper's* and

Putnam's, and cast in a style intended to be accessible to a large readership. The short novel *Israel Potter* was written along such lines. A fire at Harper's destroyed an inventory of Melville's work, and to meet his obligations, including debts to the publisher, he continued to write stories and sketches into the mid-1850s. These include "The Paradise of Bachelors and the Tartarus of Maids," a commentary on industrial conditions and on men's and women's lives. He also worked on "Benito Cereno."

In April 1856, Melville sold half of his farm. He saw *The Piazza Tales* published in that year, and he also prepared for publication a new novel, *The Confidence-Man* (1857), which criticized American culture and its corrupt language. The work satirized several American writers, including Ralph Waldo Emerson and Henry David Thoreau. But it lacked conventional action and plot, and sales were dismal. Melville, now thirty-seven, was tired and frustrated. The writings he most cared about were met with public indifference, while his potboilers brought meager returns. He needed to find another occupation.

Melville went abroad alone in 1856 for his health under the financial sponsorship of his family. He toured Scotland, then went on to Liverpool, England, where he renewed his friendship with Hawthorne, the U.S. consul. In the Mediterranean, Melville visited Malta, Greece, and Egypt. In 1857, he toured the Holy Land, which became the setting for his long poem *Clarel.* After hasty tours of Italy, Switzerland, Germany, and the Netherlands, he returned to England and sailed for home. For two seasons Melville earned a living of sorts by giving lectures on topics like "Statues in Rome" and "The South Seas." In 1860 he traveled again briefly, to San Francisco. The death of his father-in-law and the inheritance of a portion of the estate enabled Melville to move to New York City. In 1866 Harper published his Civil War poems, *Battle-Pieces,* though that work, too, was soon forgotten. Melville seemed destined, as he once observed to Hawthorne, to be known as "the man who lived among the cannibals." Considered a failure by his in-laws, Melville at last obtained a political job in 1866 as deputy inspector of customs in New York City. Through the 1860s and 1870s he worked on *Clarel,* which became an eighteen-thousand-line poem in which this "pondering man," as Melville called himself, explored the relation between religious faith and skepticism in the age of Darwinian theory.

Melville's last years were tragic and ironic. Several bequests left him and his wife materially comfortable, but his first child, Malcolm, had committed suicide in 1867, and his second, Stanwix, had become a drifter; Stanwix died in San Francisco in 1886. One of his daughters, Bessie, was severely arthritic, and the second, Frances, felt only bitterness toward her father. In the late 1880s Melville wrote *Billy Budd,* a work perhaps motivated by the suicide of his son and found nearly complete among his papers after his death. *Billy Budd* was published in 1924 and stands as a major achievement in American literature. When Melville died, a newspaper obituary speculated that "his own generation has long thought him dead." Hawthorne had already offered a fitting epitaph: "He has a very high and noble nature, and better worth immortality than most of us."

Further Reading:
R. Chase, *Herman Melville: A Critical Study*,
1949.
N. Arvin, *Herman Melville*, 1950, 1957.
J. Leyda, *The Melville Log*, 2 vols., 1951, 1969.
L. Howard, *Herman Melville*, 1951, 1958.
The Letters of Herman Melville, ed. M. Davis
and W. Gilman, 1960.
E. Dryden, *Melville's Thematics of Form*, 1969.
J. Seelye, *Melville: The Ironic Diagram*, 1970.
R. B. Bickley, *The Method of Melville's Short
Fiction*, 1975.
T. Herbert, *Marquesan Encounters*, 1981.

Texts:
"Hawthorne and His Mosses" from *The Portable
Melville*, ed. J. Leyda, 1952.
Moby-Dick, 1851.
"Bartleby" and "Benito Cerino" from *The
Piazza Tales*, ed. E. Oliver, 1962.
"The Paradise of Bachelors . . ." from
Complete Stories of Herman Melville, ed.
J. Leyda, 1948.
Billy Budd, Sailor, ed. H. Hayford and
M. Sealts, 1962.
Battle Pieces and Aspects of the War, 1866.
Remaining selections from *The Collected Poems*,
ed. H. P. Vincent, 1948, 1981.
See also *The Works of Herman Melville*, 16
vols., 1922–1924, 1963.
Complete Works of Herman Melville, 14 vols.
projected, 7 published, ed. H. Vincent,
1947–1969, superseded by the ongoing *Writings
of Herman Melville*, 16 vols. projected, ed.
H. Hayford, 1968–.
Selected Poems of Herman Melville, ed.
H. Cohen, 1964.

---

from Hawthorne and His Mosses

*By a Virginian Spending July in Vermont**

A papered chamber in a fine old farm-house—a mile from any other dwelling, and
dipped to the eaves in foliage—surrounded by mountains, old woods, and Indian
ponds—this, surely, is the place to write of Hawthorne. Some charm is in this northern
air, for love and duty seem both impelling to the task. A man of a deep and noble
nature has seized me in this seclusion. His wild, witch voice rings through me; or,
in softer cadences, I seem to hear it in the songs of the hillside birds that sing in the
larch trees at my window. . . .

   It is curious, how a man may travel along a country road, and yet miss the grandest
or sweetest of prospects, by reason of an intervening hedge so like all other hedges
as in no way to hint of the wide landscape beyond. So has it been with me concerning
the enchanting landscape in the soul of this Hawthorne, this most excellent Man of
Mosses. His *Old Manse* has been written now four years, but I never read it till a day
or two since. I had seen it in the bookstores—heard of it often—even had it
recommended to me by a tasteful friend, as a rare, quiet book, perhaps too deserving
of popularity to be popular. But there are so many books called "excellent," and so
much unpopular merit, that amid the thick stir of other things, the hint of my tasteful

---

* Hawthorne's collection of tales and sketches
Mosses from an Old Manse was published in
1846. Melville read the collection in 1850 and
wrote the review after meeting Hawthorne in
an outing in the Berkshire Mountains of
western Massachusetts in August 1850. Melville,
perhaps sensitive about his emotional tone of
voice, disguised himself as a visiting Virginian.

friend was disregarded; and for four years the Mosses on the Old Manse never refreshed me with their perennial green. It may be, however, that all this while, the book, like wine, was only improving in flavor and body. At any rate, it so chanced that this long procrastination eventuated in a happy result. At breakfast the other day, a mountain girl, a cousin of mine, who for the last two weeks has every morning helped me to strawberries and raspberries—which, like the roses and pearls in the fairy-tale, seemed to fall into the saucer from those strawberry-beds, her cheeks—this delightful creature, this charming Cherry, says to me—"I see you spend your mornings in the haymow; and yesterday I found there Dwight's *Travels in New England.*[1] Now I have something far better than that—something more congenial to our summer on these hills. Take these raspberries, and then I will give you some moss." —"Moss!" said I.—"Yes, and you must take it to the barn with you, and good-by to 'Dwight.'"

With that she left me, and soon returned with a volume, verdantly bound, and garnished with a curious frontispiece in green—nothing less than a fragment of real moss cunningly pressed to a flyleaf.—"Why this," said I, spilling my raspberries, "this is the *Mosses from an Old Manse.*" "Yes," said cousin Cherry, "yes, it is that flowering Hawthorne."—"Hawthorne and Mosses," said I, "no more: it is morning: it is July in the country: and I am off for the barn."

Stretched on that new-mown clover, the hillside breeze blowing over me through the wide barn door, and soothed by the hum of the bees in the meadows around, how magically stole over me this Mossy Man! And how amply, how bountifully, did he redeem that delicious promise to his guests in the Old Manse, of whom it is written: "Others could give them pleasure and amusement, or instruction—these could be picked up anywhere—but it was for me to give them rest. Rest, in a life of trouble! What better could be done for those weary and world-worn spirits? . . . what better could be done for anybody, who came within our magic circle, than to throw the spell of a magic spirit over him?"[2]—So all that day, half-buried in the new clover, I watched this Hawthorne's "Assyrian dawn and Paphian sunset and moonrise, from the summit of our eastern hill."

The soft ravishments of the man spun me round about in a web of dreams, and when the book was closed, when the spell was over, this wizard "dismissed me, with but misty reminiscences, as if I had been dreaming of him."

What a wild moonlight of contemplative humor bathes that Old Manse!—the rich and rare distillment of a spicy and slowly oozing heart. No rollicking rudeness, no gross fun fed on fat dinners, and bred in the lees of wine—but a humor so spiritually gentle, so high, so deep, and yet so richly relishable, that it were hardly inappropriate in an angel. It is the very religion of mirth; for nothing so human but it may be advanced to that. The orchard of the Old Manse seems the visible type of the fine mind that has described it. Those twisted and contorted old trees that "stretch out their crooked branches, and take such hold of the imagination, that we remember them as humorists and odd fellows." And then, as surrounded by these grotesque forms, and

---

[1] *Travels in New-England and New York,* by Timothy Dwight, appeared in 1821 and 1822.
[2] From Hawthorne's introduction to *The Old* Manse. Throughout his review-essay Melville intersperses titles and quotations from Hawthorne's book.

hushed in the noon-day repose of this Hawthorne's spell, how aptly might the still fall of his ruddy thoughts into your soul be symbolized by "the thump of a great apple, in the stillest afternoon, falling without a breath of wind, from the mere necessity of perfect ripeness!" For no less ripe than ruddy are the apples of the thoughts and fancies in this sweet Man of Mosses.

"Buds and Bird-Voices"—What a delicious thing is that!—"Will the world ever be so decayed, that spring may not renew its greenness?"—And the "Fire-Worship." Was ever the hearth so glorified into an altar before? The mere title of that piece is better than any common work in fifty folio volumes. How exquisite is this:

> Nor did it lessen the charm of his soft, familiar courtesy and helpfulness, that the mighty spirit, were opportunity offered him, would run riot through the peaceful house, wrap its inmates in his terrible embrace, and leave nothing of them save their whitened bones. This possibility of mad destruction only made his domestic kindness the more beautiful and touching. It was so sweet of him, being endowed with such power, to dwell, day after day, and one long, lonesome night after another, on the dusky hearth, only now and then betraying his wild nature, by thrusting his red tongue out of the chimney-top! True, he had done much mischief in the world, and was pretty certain to do more; but his warm heart atoned for all. He was kindly to the race of man. . . .

But he has still other apples, not quite so ruddy, though full as ripe—apples that have been left to wither on the tree, after the pleasant autumn gathering is past. The sketch of "The Old Apple-Dealer" is conceived in the subtlest spirit of sadness; he whose "subdued and nerveless boyhood prefigured his abortive prime, which, likewise, contained within itself the prophecy and image of his lean and torpid age." Such touches as are in this piece cannot proceed from any common heart. They argue such a depth of tenderness, such a boundless sympathy with all forms of being, such an omnipresent love, that we must needs say that this Hawthorne is here almost alone —in his generation at least—in the artistic manifestation of these things. Still more. Such touches as these—and many, very many similar ones, all through his chapters —furnish clues, whereby we enter a little way into the intricate, profound heart where they originated. And we see that suffering, some time or other and in some shape or other—this only can enable any man to depict it in others. All over him, Hawthorne's melancholy rests like an Indian summer, which, though bathing a whole country in one softness, still reveals the distinctive hue of every towering hill, and each far-winding vale.

But it is the least part of genius that attracts admiration. Where Hawthorne is known, he seems to be deemed a pleasant writer, with a pleasant style—a sequestered, harmless man, from whom any deep and weighty thing would hardly be anticipated: a man who means no meanings. But there is no man, in whom humor and love, like mountain peaks, soar to such a rapt height, as to receive the irradiations of the upper skies; there is no man in whom humor and love are developed in that high form called genius—no such man can exist without also possessing, as the indispensable complement of these, a great, deep intellect, which drops down into the universe like a plummet. Or, love and humor are only the eyes, through which such an intellect views this world. The great beauty in such a mind is but the product of its strength. What, to all readers, can be more charming than the piece entitled "Monsieur du Miroir";[3] and to a reader at all capable of fully fathoming it, what, at the same time, can possess more mystical depth of meaning?—Yes, there he sits, and looks at me—this "shape of mystery," this "identical Monsieur du Miroir."—"Methinks I should tremble now, were his wizard power, of gliding through all impediments in search of me, to place him suddenly before my eyes."

How profound, nay, appalling, is the moral evolved by the "Earth's Holocaust," where—beginning with the hollow follies and affectations of the world—all vanities and empty theories and forms are, one after another, and by an admirably graduated, growing comprehensiveness, thrown into the allegorical fire, till, at length, nothing is left but the all-engendering heart of man; which remaining still unconsumed, the great conflagration is naught.

Of a piece with this is "The Intelligence Office," a wondrous symbolizing of the secret workings in men's souls. There are other sketches, still more charged with ponderous import.

"The Christmas Banquet" and "The Bosom Serpent" would be fine subjects for a curious and elaborate analysis, touching the conjectural parts of the mind that produced them. For spite of all the Indian-summer sunlight on the hither side of Hawthorne's soul, the other side—like the dark half of the physical sphere—is shrouded in a blackness, ten times black. But this darkness but gives more effect to the ever-moving dawn, that forever advances through it, and circumnavigates his world. Whether Hawthorne has simply availed himself of this mystical blackness as a means to the wondrous effects he makes it to produce in his lights and shades; or whether there really lurks in him, perhaps unknown to himself, a touch of Puritanic gloom—this, I cannot altogether tell. Certain it is, however, that this great power of blackness in him derives its force from its appeals to that Calvinistic sense of Innate Depravity and Original Sin, from whose visitations, in some shape or other, no deeply thinking mind is always and wholly free. For, in certain moods, no man can weigh this world, without throwing in something, somehow like Original Sin, to strike the uneven balance. At all events, perhaps no writer has ever wielded this terrific thought with greater terror than this same harmless Hawthorne. Still more: this black conceit pervades him, through and through. You may be witched by his sunlight, transported by the bright gildings in the skies he builds over you, but there is the blackness of darkness beyond; and even his bright gildings but fringe and play upon the edges of thunder-clouds.—In one word, the world is mistaken in this Nathaniel Hawthorne. He himself must often have smiled at its absurd misconception of him. He is immeasurably deeper than the plummet of the mere critic. For it is not the brain that can test such a man; it is only the heart. You cannot come to know greatness by inspecting it; there is no glimpse to be caught of it, except by intuition; you need not ring it, you but touch it, and you find it is gold.

Now it is that blackness in Hawthorne, of which I have spoken, that so fixes and fascinates me. It may be, nevertheless, that it is too largely developed in him. Perhaps he does not give us a ray of his light for every shade of his dark. But however this

---

[3] French: "Gentleman of the Mirror." The phrases
in quotation marks are the titles of stories in
Hawthorne's book.

may be, this blackness it is that furnishes the infinite obscure of his background—that background, against which Shakespeare plays his grandest conceits, the things that have made for Shakespeare his loftiest but most circumscribed renown, as the profoundest of thinkers. For by philosophers Shakespeare is not adored as the great man of tragedy and comedy.—"Off with his head! so much for Buckingham!"[4] This sort of rant, interlined by another hand, brings down the house—those mistaken souls, who dream of Shakespeare as a mere man of Richard-the-Third humps, and Macbeth daggers. But it is those deep far-away things in him; those occasional flashings-forth of the intuitive Truth in him; those short, quick probings at the very axis of reality; —these are the things that make Shakespeare Shakespeare. Through the mouths of the dark characters of Hamlet, Timon, Lear, and Iago, he craftily says, or sometimes insinuates, the things which we feel to be so terrifically true that it were all but madness for any good man, in his own proper character, to utter, or even hint of them. Tormented into desperation, Lear the frantic king tears off the mask, and speaks the sane madness of vital truth. But, as I before said, it is the least part of genius that attracts admiration. And so, much of the blind, unbridled admiration that has been heaped upon Shakespeare has been lavished upon the least part of him. And few of his endless commentators and critics seem to have remembered, or even perceived, that the immediate products of a great mind are not so great as that undeveloped, and sometimes undevelopable yet dimly discernible greatness, to which these immediate products are but the infallible indices. In Shakespeare's tomb lies infinitely more than Shakespeare ever wrote. And if I magnify Shakespeare, it is not so much for what he did do, as for what he did not do, or refrained from doing. For in this world of lies, Truth is forced to fly like a scared white doe in the woodlands; and only by cunning glimpses will she reveal herself, as in Shakespeare and other masters of the great Art of Telling the Truth—even though it be covertly, and by snatches.

But if this view of the all-popular Shakespeare be seldom taken by his readers, and if very few who extol him have ever read him deeply, or, perhaps, only have seen him on the tricky stage (which alone made, and is still making, him his mere mob renown)—if few men have time, or patience, or palate, for the spiritual truth as it is in that great genius—it is, then, no matter of surprise that in a contemporaneous age, Nathaniel Hawthorne is a man as yet almost utterly mistaken among men. Here and there, in some quiet armchair in the noisy town, or some deep nook among the noiseless mountains, he may be appreciated for something of what he is. But unlike Shakespeare, who was forced to the contrary course by circumstances, Hawthorne (either from simple disinclination, or else from inaptitude) refrains from all the popularizing noise and show of broad farce, and blood-besmeared tragedy; content with the still, rich utterances of a great intellect in repose, and which sends few thoughts into circulation, except they be arterialized at his large warm lungs, and expanded in his honest heart.

Nor need you fix upon that blackness in him, if it suit you not. Nor, indeed, will all readers discern it, for it is, mostly, insinuated to those who may best understand it, and account for it; it is not obtruded upon every one alike.

Some may start to read of Shakespeare and Hawthorne on the same page. They

---

[4] From a corrupted version of Shakespeare's
Richard III.

may say, that if an illustration were needed, a lesser light might have sufficed to elucidate this Hawthorne, this small man of yesterday. But I am not, willingly, one of those who, as touching Shakespeare at least, exemplify the maxim of Roche-foucauld,[5] that "we exalt the reputation of some, in order to depress that of others"; who, to teach all noble-souled aspirants that there is no hope for them, pronounce Shakespeare absolutely unapproachable. But Shakespeare has been approached. There are minds that have gone as far as Shakespeare into the universe. And hardly a mortal man, who, at some time or other, has not felt as great thoughts in him as any you will find in *Hamlet.* We must not inferentially malign mankind for the sake of any one man, whoever he may be. This is too cheap a purchase of contentment for conscious mediocrity to make. Besides, this absolute and unconditional adoration of Shakespeare has grown to be a part of our Anglo-Saxon superstitions. The Thirty-Nine Articles[6] are now Forty. Intolerance has come to exist in this matter. You must believe in Shakespeare's unapproachability, or quit the country. But what sort of a belief is this for an American, a man who is bound to carry republican progressiveness into Literature, as well as into Life? Believe me, my friends, that men not very much inferior to Shakespeare are this day being born on the banks of the Ohio. And the day will come when you shall say; who reads a book by an Englishman that is a modern?[7] The great mistake seems to be that even with those Americans who look forward to the coming of a great literary genius among us, they somehow fancy he will come in the costume of Queen Elizabeth's day, be a writer of dramas founded upon old English history, or the tales of Boccaccio.[8] Whereas great geniuses are parts of the times; they themselves are the times, and possess a correspondent coloring. It is of a piece with the Jews, who, while their Shiloh[9] was meekly walking in their streets, were still praying for his magnificent coming; looking for him in a chariot, who was already among them on an ass. Nor must we forget that, in his own lifetime, Shakespeare was not Shakespeare, but only Master William Shakespeare of the shrewd, thriving business firm of Condell, Shakespeare & Co., proprietors of the Globe Theatre in London, and by a courtly author, of the name of Chettle,[10] was looked at as an "upstart crow" beautified "with other birds' feathers." For, mark it well, imitation is often the first charge brought against real originality. Why this is so, there is not space to set forth here. You must have plenty of sea-room to tell the Truth in; especially when it seems to have an aspect of newness, as America did in 1492, though it was then just as old, and perhaps older than Asia, only those sagacious philosophers, the common sailors, had never seen it before, swearing it was all water and moonshine there.

Now, I do not say that Nathaniel of Salem is a greater than William of Avon,[11] or as great. But the difference between the two men is by no means immeasurable. Not a very great deal more, and Nathaniel were verily William.

This, too, I mean—that if Shakespeare has not been equaled, give the world time,

---

[5] François de la Rochefoucauld (1613–1680), French moralist.
[6] Protestant tenets.
[7] The Scottish critic Sydney Smith had insulted American writers, saying, "In the four quarters of the globe, who reads an American book?" (1820).
[8] Giovanni Boccaccio (1313–1375), Italian author of the *Decameron.*
[9] Christ or Messiah.
[10] Melville errs in attributing to Henry Chettle Robert Greene's derisions of the young Shakespeare in 1592.
[11] I.e., Shakespeare.

and he is sure to be surpassed, in one hemisphere or the other. Nor will it at all do to say that the world is getting gray and grizzled now, and has lost that fresh charm which she wore of old, and by virtue of which the great poets of past times made themselves what we esteem them to be. Not so. The world is as young today as when it was created and this Vermont morning dew is as wet to my feet as Eden's dew to Adam's. Nor has Nature been all over ransacked by our progenitors, so that no new charms and mysteries remain for this latter generation to find. Far from it. The trillionth part has not yet been said, and all that has been said but multiplies the avenues to what remains to be said. It is not so much paucity as superabundance of material that seems to incapacitate modern authors.

Let America then prize and cherish her writers; yea, let her glorify them. They are not so many in number as to exhaust her good will. And while she has good kith and kin of her own, to take to her bosom, let her not lavish her embraces upon the household of an alien. For believe it or not, England, after all, is, in many things, an alien to us. China has more bowels of real love for us than she. But even were there no strong literary individualities among us, as there are some dozen at least, nevertheless, let America first praise mediocrity even, in her own children, before she praises (for everywhere, merit demands acknowledgment from every one) the best excellence in the children of any other land. Let her own authors, I say, have the priority of appreciation. I was much pleased with a hot-headed Carolina cousin of mine, who once said, "If there were no other American to stand by, in Literature— why, then, I would stand by Pop Emmons and his *Fredoniad*,[12] and till a better epic came along, swear it was not very far behind the *Iliad*." Take away the words, and in spirit he was sound.

Not that American genius needs patronage in order to expand. For that explosive sort of stuff will expand though screwed up in a vise, and burst it, though it were triple steel. It is for the nation's sake, and not for her authors' sake, that I would have America be heedful of the increasing greatness among her writers. For how great the shame, if other nations should be before her, in crowning her heroes of the pen! But this is almost the case now. American authors have received more just and discriminating praise (however loftily and ridiculously given, in certain cases) even from some Englishmen, than from their own countrymen. There are hardly five critics in America; and several of them are asleep. As for patronage, it is the American author who now patronizes his country, and not his country him. And if at times some among them appeal to the people for more recognition, it is not always with selfish motives, but patriotic ones.

It is true that but few of them as yet have evinced that decided originality which merits great praise. But that graceful writer,[13] who perhaps of all Americans has received the most plaudits from his own country for his productions—that very popular and amiable writer, however good, and self-reliant in many things, perhaps owes his chief reputation to the self-acknowledged imitation of a foreign model, and to the studied avoidance of all topics but smooth ones. But it is better to fail in originality than to succeed in imitation. He who has never failed somewhere, that man can not be great. Failure is the true test of greatness. And if it be said that continual

---

[12] Poem by Richard Emmons commemorating the War of 1812.　[13] Washington Irving.

success is a proof that a man wisely knows his powers, it is only to be added that, in that case, he knows them to be small. Let us believe it, then, once for all, that there is no hope for us in these smooth, pleasing writers that know their powers. Without malice, but to speak the plain fact, they but furnish an appendix to Goldsmith,[14] and other English authors. And we want no American Goldsmiths; nay, we want no American Miltons.[15] It were the vilest thing you could say of a true American author, that he were an American Tompkins.[16] Call him an American, and have done; for you cannot say a nobler thing of him.—But it is not meant that all American writers should studiously cleave to nationality in their writings; only this, no American writer should write like an Englishman, or a Frenchman; let him write like a man, for then he will be sure to write like an American. Let us away with this leaven of literary flunkyism towards England. If either must play the flunky in this thing, let England do it, not us. While we are rapidly preparing for that political supremacy among the nations, which prophetically awaits us at the close of the present century, in a literary point of view we are deplorably unprepared for it, and we seem studious to remain so. Hitherto, reasons might have existed why this should be; but no good reason exists now. And all that is requisite to amendment in this matter is simply this: that, while freely acknowledging all excellence, everywhere, we should refrain from unduly lauding foreign writers and, at the same time, duly recognize the meritorious writers that are our own; those writers who breathe that unshackled, democratic spirit of Christianity in all things, which now takes the practical lead in this world, though at the same time led by ourselves—us Americans. Let us boldly contemn all imitation, though it comes to us graceful and fragrant as the morning, and foster all originality, though, at first, it be crabbed and ugly as our own pine knots. And if any of our authors fail, or seem to fail, then, in the words of my enthusiastic Carolina cousin, let us clap him on the shoulder, and back him against all Europe for his second round. The truth is that, in our point of view, this matter of a national literature has come to such a pass with us that in some sense we must turn bullies, else the day is lost, or superiority so far beyond us, that we can hardly say it will ever be ours.

And now, my countrymen, as an excellent author, of your own flesh and blood —an unimitating, and, perhaps, in his way, an inimitable man—whom better can I commend to you, in the first place, than Nathaniel Hawthorne. He is one of the new and far better generation of your writers. The smell of your beeches and hemlocks is upon him; your own broad prairies are in his soul; and if you travel away inland into his deep and noble nature, you will hear the far roar of his Niagara. Give not over to future generations the glad duty of acknowledging him for what he is. Take that joy to yourself, in your own generation; and so shall he feel those grateful impulses in him that may possibly prompt him to the full flower of some still greater achievement in your eyes. And by confessing him, you thereby confess others; you brace the whole brotherhood. For genius, all over the world, stands hand in hand, and one shock of recognition runs the whole circle round.

In treating of Hawthorne, or rather of Hawthorne in his writings (for I never saw the man, and in the chances of a quiet plantation life, remote from his haunts, perhaps never shall); in treating of his works, I say, I have thus far omitted all mention of

---

[14] Oliver Goldsmith (1728–1774), British poet, playwright, and novelist.   [15] John Milton (1607–1674), English poet.   [16] Colloquial term for subordinate or flunky.

his *Twice-Told Tales,* and *The Scarlet Letter.* Both are excellent, but full of such manifold, strange, and diffusive beauties, that time would all but fail me to point the half of them out. But there are things in those two books which, had they been written in England a century ago, Nathaniel Hawthorne had utterly displaced many of the bright names we now revere on authority. But I am content to leave Hawthorne to himself, and to the infallible finding of posterity; and however great may be the praise I have bestowed upon him, I feel, that in so doing, I have more served and honored myself than him. For, at bottom, great excellence is praise enough to itself; but the feeling of a sincere and appreciative love and admiration towards it—this is relieved by utterance; and warm, honest praise ever leaves a pleasant flavor in the mouth; and it is an honorable thing to confess to what is honorable in others.

But I cannot leave my subject yet. No man can read a fine author, and relish him to his very bones, while he reads, without subsequently fancying to himself some ideal image of the man and his mind. And if you rightly look for it, you will almost always find that the author himself has somewhere furnished you with his own picture. For poets (whether in prose or verse), being painters of Nature, are like their brethren of the pencil, the true portrait painters, who, in the multitude of likenesses to be sketched, do not invariably omit their own; and in all high instances, they paint them without any vanity, though, at times, with a lurking something, that would take several pages to properly define.

I submit it, then, to those best acquainted with the man personally, whether the following is not Nathaniel Hawthorne; and to himself, whether something involved in it does not express the temper of his mind—that lasting temper of all true, candid men—a seeker, not a finder yet:

A man now entered, in neglected attire, with the aspect of a thinker, but somewhat too rough-hewn and brawny for a scholar. His face was full of sturdy vigor, with some finer and keener attribute beneath; though harsh at first, it was tempered with the glow of a large, warm heart, which had force enough to heat his powerful intellect through and through. He advanced to the Intelligencer, and looked at him with a glance of such stern sincerity, that perhaps few secrets were beyond its scope.

"I seek for Truth," said he.

Twenty-four hours have elapsed since writing the foregoing. I have just returned from the haymow, charged more and more with love and admiration of Hawthorne. For I have just been gleaning through the *Mosses,* picking up many things here and there that had previously escaped me. And I found that but to glean after this man is better than to be in at the harvest of others. To be frank (though, perhaps, rather foolish), notwithstanding what I wrote yesterday of these Mosses, I had not then culled them all; but had, nevertheless, been sufficiently sensible of the subtle essences in them as to write as I did. To what infinite height of loving wonder and admiration I may yet be borne, when by repeatedly banqueting on these Mosses, I shall have thoroughly incorporated their whole stuff into my being—that, I can not tell. But already I feel that this Hawthorne has dropped germinous seeds into my soul. He expands and deepens down, the more I contemplate him; and further, and further, shoots his strong New England roots into the hot soil of my Southern soul. . . .

1850

from Moby-Dick

Chapter 23: The Lee Shore

Some chapters back, one Bulkington was spoken of, a tall, new-landed mariner, encountered in New Bedford at the inn.

When on that shivering winter's night, the Pequod thrust her vindictive bows into the cold malicious waves, who should I see standing at her helm but Bulkington! I looked with sympathetic awe and fearfulness upon the man, who in mid-winter just landed from a four years' dangerous voyage, could so unrestingly push off again for still another tempestuous term. The land seemed scorching to his feet. Wonderfullest things are ever the unmentionable; deep memories yield no epitaphs; this six-inch chapter is the stoneless grave of Bulkington. Let me only say that it fared with him as with the storm-tossed ship, that miserably drives along the leeward land. The port would fain give succor; the port is pitiful; in the port is safety, comfort, hearthstone, supper, warm blankets, friends, all that's kind to our mortalities. But in that gale, the port, the land, is that ship's direst jeopardy, she must fly all hospitality, one touch of land though it but graze the keel, would make her shudder through and through. With all her might she crowds all sail off shore; in so doing, fights 'gainst the very winds that fain would blow her homeward; seeks all the lashed sea's landlessness again; for refuge's sake forlornly rushing into peril; her only friend her bitterest foe!

Know ye, now, Bulkington? Glimpses do ye seem to see of that mortally intolerable truth; that all deep, earnest thinking is but the intrepid effort of the soul to keep the open independence of her sea; while the wildest winds of heaven and earth conspire to cast her on the treacherous, slavish shore?

But as in landlessness alone resides the highest truth, shoreless, indefinite as God —so, better is it to perish in that howling infinite, than be ingloriously dashed upon the lee, even if that were safety! For worm-like, then, oh! who would craven crawl to land! Terrors of the terrible! is all this agony so vain? Take heart, take heart, O Bulkington! Bear thee grimly, demigod! Up from the spray of thy ocean-perishing —straight up, leaps thy apotheosis!

Chapter 26: Knights and Squires

The chief mate of the Pequod was Starbuck, a native of Nantucket, and a Quaker by descent. He was a long, earnest man, and though born on an icy coast, seemed well adapted to endure hot latitudes, his flesh being hard as twice-baked biscuit. Transported to the Indies, his live blood would not spoil like bottled ale. He must have been born in some time of general drought and famine, or upon one of those fast days for which his state is famous. Only some thirty arid summers had he seen; those summers had dried up all his physical superfluousness. But this, his thinness, so to speak, seemed no more the token of wasting anxieties and cares, than it seemed the indication of any bodily blight. It was merely the condensation of the man. He was by no means ill-looking; quite the contrary. His pure tight skin was an excellent fit; and closely wrapped up in it, and embalmed with inner health and strength, like a revivified Egyptian, this Starbuck seemed prepared to endure for long ages to come, and to endure always, as now; for be it Polar snow or torrid sun, like a patent chronometer, his interior vitality was warranted to do well in all climates. Looking into his eyes, you seemed to see there the yet lingering images of those thousand-fold perils he had calmly confronted through life. A staid, steadfast man, whose life for the most part was a telling pantomime of action, and not a tame chapter of sounds. Yet, for all his hardy sobriety and fortitude, there were certain qualities in him which at times affected, and in some cases seemed well nigh to overbalance all the rest. Uncommonly conscientious for a seaman, and endued with a deep natural reverence, the wild watery loneliness of his life did therefore strongly incline him to superstition; but to that sort of superstition, which in some organizations seems rather to spring, somehow, from intelligence than from ignorance. Outward portents and inward presentiments were his. And if at times these things bent the welded iron of his soul, much more did his far-away domestic memories of his young Cape wife and child, tend to bend him still more from the original ruggedness of his nature, and open him still further to those latent influences which, in some honest-hearted men, restrain the gush of dare-devil daring, so often evinced by others in the more perilous vicissitudes of the fishery. "I will have no man in my boat," said Starbuck, "who is not afraid of a whale." By this, he seemed to mean, not only that the most reliable and useful courage is that which arises from the fair estimation of the encountered peril, but that an utterly fearless man is a far more dangerous comrade than a coward.

"Aye, aye," said Stubb, the second mate, "Starbuck, there, is as careful a man as you'll find anywhere in this fishery." But we shall ere long see what that word "careful" precisely means when used by a man like Stubb, or almost any other whale hunter.

Starbuck was no crusader after perils; in him courage was not a sentiment; but a thing simply useful to him, and always at hand upon all mortally practical occasions. Besides, he thought, perhaps, that in this business of whaling, courage was one of the great staple outfits of the ship, like her beef and her bread, and not to be foolishly wasted. Wherefore he had no fancy for lowering for whales after sun-down; nor for persisting in fighting a fish that too much persisted in fighting him. For, thought Starbuck, I am here in this critical ocean to kill whales for my living, and not to be killed by them for theirs; and that hundreds of men had been so killed Starbuck well knew. What doom was his own father's? Where, in the bottomless deeps, could he find the torn limbs of his brother?

With memories like these in him, and, moreover, given to a certain superstitiousness, as has been said; the courage of this Starbuck which could, nevertheless, still flourish, must indeed have been extreme. But it was not in reasonable nature that a man so organized, and with such terrible experiences and remembrances as he had; it was not in nature that these things should fail in latently engendering an element in him, which, under suitable circumstances, would break out from its confinement, and burn all his courage up. And brave as he might be, it was that sort of bravery, chiefly visible in some intrepid men, which, while generally abiding firm in the conflict with seas, or winds, or whales, or any of the ordinary irrational horrors of the world, yet cannot withstand those more terrific, because more spiritual terrors, which sometimes menace you from the concentrating brow of an enraged and mighty man.

But were the coming narrative to reveal, in any instance, the complete abasement of poor Starbuck's fortitude, scarce might I have the heart to write it; for it is a thing most sorrowful, nay shocking, to expose the fall of valor in the soul. Men may seem detestable as joint stock-companies and nations; knaves, fools, and murderers there may be; men may have mean and meagre faces; but man, in the ideal, is so noble and so sparkling, such a grand and glowing creature, that over any ignominious blemish in him all his fellows should run to throw their costliest robes. That immaculate manliness we feel within ourselves, so far within us, that it remains intact though all the outer character seem gone; bleeds with keenest anguish at the undraped spectacle of a valor-ruined man. Nor can piety itself, at such a shameful sight, completely stifle her upbraidings against the permitting stars. But this august dignity I treat of, is not the dignity of kings and robes, but that abounding dignity which has no robed investiture. Thou shalt see it shining in the arm that wields a pick or drives a spike; that democratic dignity which, on all hands, radiates without end from God; Himself! The great God absolute! The centre and circumference of all democracy! His omnipresence, our divine equality!

If, then, to meanest mariners, and renegades and castaways, I shall hereafter ascribe high qualities, though dark; weave round them tragic graces; if even the most mournful, perchance the most abased, among them all, shall at times lift himself to the exalted mounts; if I shall touch that workman's arm with some ethereal light; if I shall spread a rainbow over his disastrous set of sun; then against all mortal critics bear me out in it, thou just Spirit of Equality, which hast spread one royal mantle of humanity over all my kind! Bear me out in it, thou great democratic God! who didst not refuse to the swart convict, Bunyan,[1] the pale, poetic pearl; Thou who didst clothe with doubly hammered leaves of finest gold, the stumped and paupered arm of old Cervantes;[2] Thou who didst pick up Andrew Jackson[3] from the pebbles; who didst hurl him upon a warhorse; who didst thunder him higher than a throne! Thou who, in all Thy mighty earthly marchings, ever cullest Thy selectest champions from the kingly commons; bear me out in it, O God!

Chapter 27: Knights and Squires

Stubb was the second mate. He was a native of Cape Cod; and hence, according to local usage, was called a Cape-Codman. A happy-go-lucky; neither craven nor valiant; taking perils as they came with an indifferent air; and while engaged in the most imminent crisis of the chase, toiling away, calm and collected as a journeyman joiner engaged for the year. Good-humored, easy, and careless, he presided over his whale-boat as if the most deadly encounter were but a dinner, and his crew all invited guests. He was as particular about the comfortable arrangement of his part of the boat, as an old stage-driver is about the snugness of his box. When close to the whale, in the very death-lock of the fight, he handled his unpitying lance coolly and off-handedly, as a whistling tinker his hammer. He would hum over his old rigadig tunes[4] while

---

[1] John Bunyan (1628–1688), religious mystic and author of *The Pilgrim's Progress,* served almost 12 years in an English prison for religious heresy.

[2] Miguel de Cervantes Saavedra (1547–1616), author of *Don Quixote,* lost the use of his left arm in the naval battle of Lepanto in 1571.

[3] Jackson (1767–1845), seventh president of the United States, was known for violence both in his professional life as a soldier and in his personal life.

[4] Jiglike whaling songs.

flank and flank with the most exasperated monster. Long usage had, for this Stubb, converted the jaws of death into an easy chair. What he thought of death itself, there is no telling. Whether he ever thought of it at all, might be a question; but, if he ever did chance to cast his mind that way after a comfortable dinner, no doubt, like a good sailor, he took it to be a sort of call of the watch to tumble aloft, and bestir themselves there, about something which he would find out when he obeyed the order, and not sooner.

What, perhaps, with other things, made Stubb such an easy going, unfearing man, so cheerily trudging off with the burden of life in a world full of grave peddlers, all bowed to the ground with their packs; what helped to bring about that almost impious good humor of his; that thing must have been his pipe. For, like his nose, his short, black little pipe was one of the regular features of his face. You would almost as soon have expected him to turn out of his bunk without his nose as without his pipe. He kept a whole row of pipes there ready loaded, stuck in a rack, within easy reach of his hand; and, whenever he turned in, he smoked them all out in succession, lighting one from the other to the end of the chapter; then loading them again to be in readiness anew. For, when Stubb dressed, instead of first putting his legs into his trowsers, he put his pipe into his mouth.

I say this continual smoking must have been one cause, at least, of his peculiar disposition; for every one knows that this earthly air, whether ashore or afloat, is terribly infected with the nameless miseries of the numberless mortals who have died exhaling it; and as in time of the cholera, some people go about with a camphorated handkerchief to their mouths; so, likewise, against all mortal tribulations, Stubb's tobacco smoke might have operated as a sort of disinfecting agent.

The third mate was Flask, a native of Tisbury, in Martha's Vineyard. A short, stout, ruddy young fellow, very pugnacious concerning whales, who somehow seemed to think that the great Leviathans had personally and hereditarily affronted him; and therefore it was a sort of point of honor with him, to destroy them whenever encountered. So utterly lost was he to all sense of reverence for the many marvels of their majestic bulk and mystic ways; and so dead to anything like an apprehension of any possible danger from encountering them; that in his poor opinion, the won-drous whale was but a species of magnified mouse, or at least water-rat, requiring only a little circumvention and some small application of time and trouble in order to kill and boil. This ignorant, unconscious fearlessness of his made him a little waggish in the matter of whales; he followed these fish for the fun of it; and a three years' voyage round Cape Horn was only a jolly joke that lasted that length of time. As a carpenter's nails are divided into wrought nails and cut nails; so mankind may be similarly divided. Little Flask was one of the wrought ones; made to clinch tight and last long. They called him King-Post on board of the Pequod; because, in form, he could be well likened to the short, square timber known by that name in Arctic whalers; and which by the means of many radiating side timbers inserted into it, serves to brace the ship against the icy concussions of those battering seas.

Now these three mates—Starbuck, Stubb, and Flask, were momentous men. They it was who by universal prescription commanded three of the Pequod's boats as headsmen. In that grand order of battle in which Captain Ahab would probably marshal his forces to descend on the whales, these three headsmen were as captains of companies. Or, being armed with their long keen whaling spears, they were as a picked trio of lancers; even as the harpooneers were flingers of javelins.

And since in this famous fishery, each mate or headsman, like a Gothic Knight of old, is always accompanied by his boat-steerer or harpooneer, who in certain conjectures provides him with a fresh lance, when the former one has been badly twisted, or elbowed in the assault; and moreover, as there generally subsists between the two, a close intimacy and friendliness; it is therefore but meet, that in this place we set down who the Pequod's harpooneers were, and to what headsman each of them belonged.

First of all was Queequeg, whom Starbuck, the chief mate, had selected for his squire. But Queequeg is already known.

Next was Tashtego, an unmixed Indian from Gay Head, the most westerly promontory of Martha's Vineyard, where there still exists the last remnant of a village of red men, which has long supplied the neighboring island of Nantucket with many of her most daring harpooneers. In the fishery, they usually go by the generic name of Gay-Headers. Tashtego's long, lean, sable hair, his high cheek bones, and black rounding eyes—for an Indian, Oriental in their largeness, but Antarctic in their glittering expression—all this sufficiently proclaimed him an inheritor of the unvitiated blood of those proud warrior hunters, who, in quest of the great New England moose, had scoured, bow in hand, the aboriginal forests of the main. But no longer snuffing in the trail of the wild beasts of the woodland, Tashtego now hunted in the wake of the great whales of the sea; the unerring harpoon of the son fitly replacing the infallible arrow of the sires. To look at the tawny brawn of his lithe snaky limbs, you would almost have credited the superstitions of some of the earlier Puritans, and half believed this wild Indian to be a son of the Prince of the Powers of the Air.[5] Tashtego was Stubb the second mate's squire.

Third among the harpooneers was Daggoo, a gigantic, coal-black negro-savage, with a lion-like tread—an Ahasuerus[6] to behold. Suspended from his ears were two golden hoops, so large that the sailors called them ring-bolts, and would talk of securing the topsail halyards to them. In his youth Daggoo had voluntarily shipped on board of a whaler, lying in a lonely bay on his native coast. And never having been anywhere in the world but in Africa, Nantucket, and the pagan harbors most frequented by whalemen; and having now led for many years the bold life of the fishery in the ships of owners uncommonly heedful of what manner of men they shipped; Daggoo retained all his barbaric virtues, and erect as a giraffe, moved about the decks in all the pomp of six feet five in his socks. There was a corporeal humility in looking up at him; and a white man standing before him seemed a white flag come to beg truce of a fortress. Curious to tell, this imperial negro, Ahasuerus Daggoo, was the Squire of little Flask, who looked like a chess-man beside him. As for the residue of the Pequod's company, be it said, that at the present day not one in two of the many thousand men before the mast employed in the American whale fishery, are Americans born, though pretty nearly all the officers are. Herein it is the same with the American whale fishery as with the American army and military and merchant navies, and the engineering forces employed in the construction of the American Canals and Railroads. The same, I say, because in all these cases the native American liberally provides the brains, the rest of the world as generously supplying the muscles. No small number of these whaling seamen belong to the Azores, where the outward bound Nantucket whalers frequently touch to augment their crews from the hardy

[5] The devil. (See Ephesians 2:2.)
[6] In the biblical Book of Esther, Persian king said to have ruled over lands "from India even unto Ethiopia."

peasants of those rocky shores. In like manner, the Greenland whalers sailing out of Hull or London, put in at the Shetland Islands, to receive the full complement of their crew. Upon the passage homewards, they drop them there again. How it is, there is no telling, but Islanders seem to make the best whalemen. They were nearly all Islanders in the Pequod, *Isolatoes* too, I call such, not acknowledging the common continent of men, but each *Isolato* living on a separate continent of his own. Yet now, federated along one keel, what a set these Isolatoes were! An Anacharsis Clootz deputation[7] from all the isles of the sea, and all the ends of the earth, accompanying Old Ahab in the Pequod to lay the world's grievances before that bar from which not very many of them ever came back. Black Little Pip—he never did! Poor Alabama boy! On the grim Pequod's forecastle, ye shall ere long see him, beating his tambourine; prelusive of the eternal time, when sent for, to the great quarter-deck on high, he was bid strike in with angels, and beat his tambourine in glory; called a coward here, hailed a hero there!

Chapter 28: Ahab

For several days after leaving Nantucket, nothing above hatches was seen of Captain Ahab. The mates regularly relieved each other at the watches, and for aught that could be seen to the contrary, they seemed to be the only commanders of the ship; only they sometimes issued from the cabin with orders so sudden and peremptory, that after all it was plain they but commanded vicariously. Yes, their supreme lord and dictator was there, though hitherto unseen by any eyes not permitted to penetrate into the now sacred retreat of the cabin.

Every time I ascended to the deck from my watches below, I instantly gazed aft to mark if any strange face were visible; for my first vague disquietude touching the unknown captain, now in the seclusion of the sea, became almost a perturbation. This was strangely heightened at times by the ragged Elijah's[8] diabolical incoherences uninvitedly recurring to me, with a subtle energy I could not have before conceived of. But poorly could I withstand them, much as in other moods I was almost ready to smile at the solemn whimsicalities of that outlandish prophet of the wharves. But whatever it was of apprehensiveness or uneasiness—to call it so—which I felt, yet whenever I came to look about me in the ship, it seemed against all warranty to cherish such emotions. For though the harpooneers, with the great body of the crew, were a far more barbaric, heathenish, and motley set than any of the tame merchant-ship companies which my previous experiences had made me acquainted with, still I ascribed this—and rightly ascribed it—to the fierce uniqueness of the very nature of that wild Scandinavian vocation in which I had so abandonedly embarked. But it was especially the aspect of the three chief officers of the ship, the mates, which was most forcibly calculated to allay these colorless misgivings, and induce confidence and cheerfulness in every presentment of the voyage. Three better, more likely sea-officers and men, each in his own different way, could not readily be found, and they were

---

[7] I.e., made up of men of various countries and races, like the group with which Clootz appeared at the French National Assembly in 1790 to signify worldwide support of the French Revolution.

[8] Elijah: a derelict who haunts the Nantucket docks. He detains Ishmael and Queequeg at the beginning of the novel and prophesies the fate of the *Pequod* and her crew.

every one of them Americans; a Nantucketer, a Vineyarder, a Cape man. Now, it being Christmas when the ship shot from out her harbor, for a space we had biting Polar weather, though all the time running away from it to the southward; and by every degree and minute of latitude which we sailed, gradually leaving that merciless winter, and all its intolerable weather behind us. It was one of those less lowering, but still grey and gloomy enough mornings of the transition, when with a fair wind the ship was rushing through the water with a vindictive sort of leaping and melancholy rapidity, that as I mounted to the deck at the call of the forenoon watch, so soon as I levelled my glance towards the taffrail, forboding shivers ran over me. Reality outran apprehension; Captain Ahab stood upon his quarter-deck.

There seemed no sign of common bodily illness about him, nor of the recovery from any. He looked like a man cut away from the stake, when the fire has overrunningly wasted all the limbs without consuming them, or taking away one particle from their compacted aged robustness. His whole high, broad form, seemed made of solid bronze, and shaped in an unalterable mould, like Cellini's cast Perseus.[9] Threading its way out from among his grey hairs, and continuing right down one side of his tawny scorched face and neck, till it disappeared in his clothing, you saw a slender rod-like mark, lividly whitish. It resembled that perpendicular seam sometimes made in the straight, lofty trunk of a great tree, when the upper lightning tearingly darts down it, and without wrenching a single twig, peels and grooves out the bark from top to bottom, ere running off into the soil, leaving the tree still greenly alive, but branded. Whether that mark was born with him, or whether it was the scar left by some desperate wound, no one could certainly say. By some tacit consent, throughout the voyage little or no allusion was made to it, especially by the mates. But once Tashtego's senior, an old Gay-Head Indian among the crew, superstitiously asserted that not till he was forty years old did Ahab become that way branded, and then it came upon him, not in the fury of any mortal fray, but in an elemental strife at sea. Yet, this wild hint seemed inferentially negatived, by what a grey Manxman[10] insinuated, an old sepulchral man, who, having never before sailed out of Nantucket, had never ere this laid eye upon wild Ahab. Nevertheless, the old sea-traditions, the immemorial credulities, popularly invested this old Manxman with preternatural powers of discernment. So that no white sailor seriously contradicted him when he said that if ever Captain Ahab should be tranquilly laid out—which might hardly come to pass, so he muttered—then, whoever should do that last office for the dead, would find a birth-mark on him from crown to sole.

So powerfully did the whole grim aspect of Ahab affect me, and the livid brand which streaked it, that for the first few moments I hardly noted that not a little of this overbearing grimness was owing to the barbaric white leg upon which he partly stood. It had previously come to me that this ivory leg had at sea been fashioned from the polished bone of the sperm whale's jaw. "Aye, he was dismasted off Japan," said the old Gay-Head Indian once, "but like his dismasted craft, he shipped another mast without coming home for it. He has a quiver of 'em."

I was struck with the singular posture he maintained. Upon each side of the

[9] Melville alludes here to the bronze sculpture of Perseus holding the slain Medusa's head, executed by Benvenuto Cellini (1500–1571).

[10] Native of the Isle of Man.

Pequod's quarter deck, and pretty close to the mizen shrouds, there was an auger hole, bored about half an inch or so, into the plank. His leg bone steadied in that hole; one arm elevated, and holding by a shroud; Captain Ahab stood erect, looking straight out beyond the ship's ever-pitching prow. There was an infinity of firmest fortitude, a determinate, unsurrenderable wilfulness, in the fixed and fearless, forward dedication of that glance. Not a word he spoke; nor did his officers say aught to him; though by all their minutest gestures and expressions, they plainly showed the uneasy, if not painful, consciousness of being under a troubled master-eye. And not only that, but moody stricken Ahab stood before them with a crucifixion in his face; in all the nameless regal over-bearing dignity of some mighty woe.

Ere long, from his first visit in the air, he withdrew into his cabin. But after that morning, he was every day visible to the crew; either standing in his pivot-hole, or seated upon an ivory stool he had; or heavily walking the deck. As the sky grew less gloomy; indeed, began to grow a little genial, he became still less and less a recluse; as if, when the ship had sailed from home, nothing but the dead wintry bleakness of the sea had then kept him so secluded. And, by and by, it came to pass, that he was almost continually in the air; but, as yet, for all that he said, or perceptibly did, on the at last sunny deck, he seemed as unnecessary there as another mast. But the Pequod was only making a passage now; not regularly cruising; nearly all whaling preparatives needing supervision the mates were fully competent to, so that there was little or nothing, out of himself to employ or excite Ahab, now; and thus chase away, for that one interval, the clouds that layer upon layer were piled upon his brow, as ever all clouds choose the loftiest peaks to pile themselves upon.

Nevertheless, ere long, the warm, warbling persuasiveness of the pleasant, holiday weather we came to, seemed gradually to charm him from his mood. For, as when the red-cheeked, dancing girls, April and May, trip home to the wintry, misanthropic woods; even the barest, ruggedest, most thunder-cloven old oak will at least send forth some few green sprouts, to welcome such gladhearted visitants; so Ahab did, in the end, a little respond to the playful allurings of that girlish air. More than once did he put forth the faint blossom of a look, which, in any other man, would have soon flowered out in a smile.

Chapter 36: The Quarter-Deck

(Enter Ahab: Then, all.)

It was not a great while after the affair of the pipe, that one morning shortly after breakfast, Ahab, as was his wont, ascended the cabin-gangway to the deck. There most sea-captains usually walk at that hour, as country gentlemen, after the same meal, take a few turns in the garden.

Soon his steady, ivory stride was heard, as to and fro he paced his old rounds, upon planks so familiar to his tread, that they were all over dented, like geological stones, with the peculiar mark of his walk. Did you fixedly gaze, too, upon that ribbed and dented brow; there also, you would see still stranger foot-prints—the foot-prints of his one unsleeping, ever-pacing thought.

But on the occasion in question, those dents looked deeper, even as his nervous step that morning left a deeper mark. And, so full of his thought was Ahab, that at every uniform turn that he made, now at the main-mast and now at the binnacle, you could almost see that thought turn in him as he turned, and pace in him as he paced; so completely possessing him, indeed, that it all but seemed the inward mould of every outer movement.

"D'ye mark him, Flask?" whispered Stubb; "the chick that's in him pecks the shell. 'Twill soon be out."

The hours wore on;—Ahab now shut up within his cabin; anon, pacing the deck, with the same intense bigotry of purpose[11] in his aspect.

It drew near the close of day. Suddenly he came to a halt by the bulwarks, and inserting his bone leg into the auger-hole there, and with one hand grasping a shroud, he ordered Starbuck to send everybody aft.

"Sir!" said the mate, astonished at an order seldom or never given on ship-board except in some extraordinary case.

"Send everybody aft," repeated Ahab. "Mast-heads, there! come down!"

When the entire ship's company were assembled, and with curious and not wholly unapprehensive faces, were eyeing him, for he looked not unlike the weather horizon when a storm is coming up, Ahab, after rapidly glancing over the bulwarks, and then darting his eyes among the crew, started from his stand-point; and as though not a soul were nigh him resumed his heavy turns upon the deck. With bent head and half-slouched hat he continued to pace, unmindful of the wondering whisperings among the men; till Stubb cautiously whispered to Flask, that Ahab must have summoned them there for the purpose of witnessing a pedestrian feat. But this did not last long. Vehemently pausing, he cried:—

"What do ye do when ye see a whale, men?"

"Sing out for him!" was the impulsive rejoinder from a score of clubbed voices.

"Good!" cried Ahab, with a wild approval in his tones; observing the hearty animation into which his unexpected question had so magnetically thrown them.

"And what do ye next, men?"

"Lower away, and after him!"

"And what tune is it ye pull to, men?"

"A dead whale or a stove boat!"

More and more strangely and fiercely glad and approving, grew the countenance of the old man at every shout; while the mariners began to gaze curiously at each other, as if marvelling how it was that they themselves became so excited at such seemingly purposeless questions.

But, they were all eagerness again, as Ahab, now half-revolving in his pivot-hole, with one hand reaching high up a shroud, and tightly, almost convulsively grasping it, addressed them thus:—

"All ye mast-headers have before now heard me give orders about a white whale. Look ye! d'ye see this Spanish ounce of gold?"—holding up a broad bright coin to the sun—"it is a sixteen dollar piece, men,—a doubloon. D'ye see it? Mr. Starbuck, hand me yon top-maul."

While the mate was getting the hammer, Ahab, without speaking, was slowly rubbing the gold piece against the skirts of his jacket, as if to heighten its lustre, and without using any words was meanwhile lowly humming to himself, producing a

[11] Single-mindedness of intent; monomania.

sound so strangely muffled and inarticulate that it seemed the mechanical humming of the wheels of his vitality in him.

Receiving the top-maul from Starbuck, he advanced towards the main-mast with the hammer uplifted in one hand, exhibiting the gold with the other, and with a high raised voice exclaiming: "Whosoever of ye raises me a white-headed whale with a wrinkled brow and a crooked jaw; whosoever of ye raises me that white-headed whale, with three holes punctured in his starboard fluke—look ye, whosoever of ye raises me that same white whale, he shall have this gold ounce, my boys!"

"Huzza! huzza!" cried the seamen, as with swinging tarpaulins they hailed the act of nailing the gold to the mast.

"It's a white whale, I say," resumed Ahab, as he threw down the top-maul; "a white whale. Skin your eyes for him, men; look sharp for white water; if ye see but a bubble, sing out."

All this while Tashtego, Daggoo, and Queequeg had looked on with even more intense interest and surprise than the rest, and at the mention of the wrinkled brow and crooked jaw they had started as if each was separately touched by some specific recollection.

"Captain Ahab," said Tashtego, "that white whale must be the same that some call Moby Dick."

"Moby Dick?" shouted Ahab. "Do ye know the white whale then, Tash?"

"Does he fan-tail a little curious, sir, before he goes down?" said the Gay-Header deliberately.

"And has he a curious spout, too," said Daggoo, "very bushy, even for a parma-cetty, and mighty quick, Captain Ahab?"

"And he have one, two, tree—oh! good many iron in him hide, too, Captain," cried Queequeg disjointedly, "all twiske-tee be-twist, like him—him—" faltering hard for a word, and screwing his hand round and round as though uncorking a bottle —"like him—him—"

"Corkscrew!" cried Ahab, "aye, Queequeg, the harpoons lie all twisted and wrenched in him; aye, Daggoo, his spout is a big one, like a whole shock of wheat, and white as a pile of our Nantucket wool after the great annual sheep-shearing; aye, Tashtego, and he fan-tails like a split jib in a squall. Death and devils! men, it is Moby Dick ye have seen—Moby Dick—Moby Dick!"

"Captain Ahab," said Starbuck, who, with Stubb and Flask, had thus far been eyeing his superior with increasing surprise, but at last seemed struck with a thought which somewhat explained all the wonder. "Captain Ahab, I have heard of Moby Dick—but it was not Moby Dick that took off thy leg?"

"Who told thee that?" cried Ahab; then pausing, "Aye, Starbuck; aye, my hearties all round; it was Moby Dick that dismasted me; Moby Dick that brought me to this dead stump I stand on now. Aye, Aye," he shouted with a terrific, loud, animal sob, like that of a heart-stricken moose; "Aye, aye! it was that accursed white whale that razeed[12] me; made a poor pegging lubber of me for ever and a day!" Then tossing both arms, with measureless imprecations he shouted out: "Aye, aye! and I'll chase him round Good Hope, and round the Horn, and round the Norway Maelstrom, and

---

[12] Razee: literally, to reduce the size of a ship by cutting away its upper deck.

round perdition's flames before I give him up. And this is what ye have shipped for, men! to chase that white whale on both sides of land, and over all sides of earth, till he spouts black blood and rolls fin out. What say ye, men, will ye splice hands on it, now? I think ye do look brave."

"Aye, aye!" shouted the harpooneers and seamen, running closer to the excited old man: "A sharp eye for the White Whale; a sharp lance for Moby Dick!"

"God bless ye," he seemed to half sob and half shout. "God bless ye, men. Steward! go draw the great measure of grog. But what's this long face about, Mr. Starbuck; wilt thou not chase the white whale? art not game for Moby Dick?"

"I am game for his crooked jaw, and for the jaws of Death too, Captain Ahab, if it fairly comes in the way of the business we follow; but I came here to hunt whales, not my commander's vengeance. How many barrels will thy vengeance yield thee even if thou gettest it, Captain Ahab? it will not fetch thee much in our Nantucket market!"

"Nantucket market! Hoot! But come closer, Starbuck; thou requirest a little lower layer. If money's to be the measurer, man, and the accountants have computed their great counting-house the globe, by girdling it with guineas, one to every three parts of an inch; then, let me tell thee, that my vengeance will fetch a great premium *here!*"

"He smites his chest," whispered Stubb, "what's that for? methinks it rings most vast, but hollow."

"Vengeance on a dumb brute!" cried Starbuck, "that simply smote thee from blindest instinct! Madness! To be enraged with a dumb thing, Captain Ahab, seems blasphemous."

"Hark ye yet again,—the little lower layer. All visible objects, man, are but as pasteboard masks. But in each event—in the living act, the undoubted deed—there, some unknown but still reasoning thing puts forth the mouldings of its features from behind the unreasoning mask. If man will strike, strike through the mask! How can the prisoner reach outside except by thrusting through the wall? To me, the white whale is that wall, shoved near to me. Sometimes I think there's naught beyond. But 'tis enough. He tasks me; he heaps me; I see in him outrageous strength, with an inscrutable malice sinewing it. That inscrutable thing is chiefly what I hate; and be the white whale agent, or be the white whale principal, I will wreak that hate upon him. Talk not to me of blasphemy, man; I'd strike the sun if it insulted me. For could the sun do that, then could I do the other; since there is ever a sort of fair play herein, jealousy presiding over all creations. But not my master, man, is even that fair play. Who's over me? Truth hath no confines. Take off thine eye! more intolerable than fiends' glarings is a doltish stare! So, so; thou reddenest and palest; my heat has melted thee to anger-glow. But look ye, Starbuck, what is said in heat, that thing unsays itself. There are men from whom warm words are small indignity. I meant not to incense thee. Let it go. Look! see yonder Turkish cheeks of spotted tawn—living, breathing pictures painted by the sun. The Pagan leopards—the unrecking and unworshipping things, that live; and seek, and give no reasons for the torrid life they feel! The crew, man, the crew! Are they not one and all with Ahab, in this matter of the whale? See Stubb! he laughs! See yonder Chilean! he snorts to think of it. Stand up amid the general hurricane, thy one tost sapling cannot, Starbuck! And what is it? Reckon it. 'Tis but to help strike a fin; no wondrous feat for Starbuck. What is it more? From this one poor hunt, then, the best lance out of all Nantucket, surely he will not hang back, when every foremast-hand has clutched a whetstone? Ah! constrainings seize thee; I see! the billow lifts thee! Speak, but speak!—Aye, aye! thy silence, then, *that* voices thee. *(Aside)* Something shot from my dilated nostrils, he has inhaled it in his lungs. Starbuck now is mine; cannot oppose me now, without rebellion."

"God keep me!—keep us all!" murmured Starbuck, lowly.

But in his joy at the enchanted, tacit acquiescence of the mate, Ahab did not hear his foreboding invocation; nor yet the low laugh from the hold; nor yet the presaging vibrations of the winds in the cordage; nor yet the hollow flap of the sails against the masts, as for a moment their hearts sank in. For again Starbuck's downcast eyes lighted up with the stubbornness of life; the subterranean laugh died away; the winds blew on; the sails filled out; the ship heaved and rolled as before. Ah, ye admonitions and warnings! why stay ye not when ye come? But rather are ye predictions than warnings, ye shadows! Yet not so much predictions from without, as verifications of the foregoing things within. For with little external to constrain us, the innermost necessities in our being, these still drive us on.

"The measure! the measure!" cried Ahab.

Receiving the brimming pewter, and turning to the harpooneers, he ordered them to produce their weapons. Then ranging them before him near the capstan, with their harpoons in their hands, while his three mates stood at his side with their lances, and the rest of the ship's company formed a circle round the group; he stood for an instant searchingly eyeing every man of his crew. But those wild eyes met his, as the bloodshot eyes of the prairie wolves meet the eye of their leader, ere he rushes on at their head in the trail of the bison; but, alas! only to fall into the hidden snare of the Indian.

"Drink and pass!" he cried, handing the heavy charged flagon to the nearest seaman. "The crew alone now drink. Round with it, round! Short draughts—long swallows, men; 'tis hot as Satan's hoof. So, so; it goes round excellently. It spiralizes in ye; forks out at the serpent-snapping eye. Well done; almost drained. That way it went, this way it comes. Hand it me—here's a hollow! Men, ye seem the years; so brimming life is gulped and gone. Steward, refill!

"Attend now, my braves. I have mustered ye all round this capstan; and ye mates, flank me with your lances; and ye harpooneers, stand there with your irons; and ye, stout mariners, ring me in, that I may in some sort revive a noble custom of my fisherman fathers before me. O men, you will yet see that—Ha! boy, come back? bad pennies come not sooner. Hand it me. Why, now, this pewter had run brimming again, wert not thou St. Vitus' imp—away, thou ague!

"Advance, ye mates! Cross your lances full before me. Well done! Let me touch the axis." So saying, with extended arm, he grasped the three level, radiating lances at their crossed centre; while so doing, suddenly and nervously twitched them; meanwhile, glancing intently from Starbuck to Stubb; from Stubb to Flask. It seemed as though, by some nameless, interior volition, he would fain have shocked into them the same fiery emotion accumulated within the Leyden jar[13] of his own magnetic life. The three mates qualified before his strong, sustained, and mystic aspect. Stubb and Flask looked sideways from him; the honest eye of Starbuck fell downright.

"In vain!" cried Ahab; "but, maybe, 'tis well. For did ye three but once take the

---

[13] Early type of electrical capacitor.

full-forced shock, then mine own electric thing, *that* had perhaps expired from out me. Perchance, too, it would have dropped ye dead. Perchance ye need it not. Down lances! And now, ye mates, I do appoint ye three cup-bearers to my three pagan kinsmen there—yon three most honorable gentlemen and noblemen, my valiant harpooneers. Disdain the task? What, when the great Pope washes the feet of beggars, using his tiara for ewer? Oh, my sweet cardinals! your own condescension, *that* shall bend ye to it. I do not order ye; ye will it. Cut your seizings and draw the poles, ye harpooneers!"

Silently obeying the order, the three harpooneers now stood with the detached iron part of their harpoons, some three feet long, held, barbs up, before him.

"Stab me not with that keen steel! Cant them; cant them over! know ye not the goblet end? Turn up the socket! So, so; now, ye cup-bearers, advance. The irons! take them; hold them while I fill!" Forthwith, slowly going from one officer to the other, he brimmed the harpoon sockets with the fiery waters from the pewter.

"Now, three to three, ye stand. Commend the murderous chalices! Bestow them, ye who are now made parties to this indissoluble league. Ha! Starbuck! but the deed is done! Yon ratifying sun now waits to sit upon it. Drink, ye harpooneers! drink and swear, ye men that man the deathful whaleboat's bow—Death to Moby Dick! God hunt us all, if we do not hunt Moby Dick to his death!" The long, barbed steel goblets were lifted; and to cries and maledictions against the white whale, the spirits were simultaneously quaffed down with a hiss. Starbuck paled, and turned, and shivered. Once more, and finally, the replenished pewter went the rounds among the frantic crew; when, waving his free hand to them, they all dispersed; and Ahab retired within his cabin.

1851

Bartleby, the Scrivener

I am a rather elderly man. The nature of my avocations, for the last thirty years, has brought me into more than ordinary contact with what would seem an interesting and somewhat singular set of men, of whom, as yet, nothing, that I know of, has ever been written—I mean, the law-copyists, or scriveners. I have known very many of them, professionally and privately, and, if I pleased, could relate divers histories, at which good-natured gentlemen might smile, and sentimental souls might weep. But I waive the biographies of all other scriveners, for a few passages in the life of Bartleby, who was a scrivener, the strangest I ever saw, or heard of. While, of other law-copyists, I might write the complete life, of Bartleby nothing of that sort can be done. I believe that no materials exist, for a full and satisfactory biography of this man. It is an irreparable loss to literature. Bartleby was one of those beings of whom nothing is ascertainable, except from the original sources, and, in his case, those are very small. What my own astonished eyes saw of Bartleby, *that* is all I know of him, except, indeed, one vague report, which will appear in the sequel.

Ere introducing the scrivener, as he first appeared to me, it is fit I make some mention of myself, my *employés,* my business, my chambers, and general surroundings; because some such description is indispensable to an adequate understanding of the chief character about to be presented. Imprimis: I am a man who, from his youth upwards, has been filled with a profound conviction that the easiest way of life is the best. Hence, though I belong to a profession proverbially energetic and nervous, even to turbulence, at times, yet nothing of that sort have I ever suffered to invade my peace. I am one of those unambitious lawyers who never addresses a jury, or in any way draws down public applause; but, in the cool tranquillity of a snug retreat, do a snug business among rich men's bonds, and mortgages, and title-deeds. All who know me, consider me an eminently *safe* man. The late John Jacob Astor, a personage little given to poetic enthusiasm, had no hesitation in pronouncing my first grand point to be prudence; my next, method. I do not speak it in vanity, but simply record the fact, that I was not unemployed in my profession by the late John Jacob Astor; a name which, I admit, I love to repeat; for it hath a rounded and orbicular sound to it, and rings like unto bullion. I will freely add, that I was not insensible to the late John Jacob Astor's good opinion.

Some time prior to the period at which this little history begins, my avocations had been largely increased. The good old office, now extinct in the State of New York, of a Master in Chancery, had been conferred upon me. It was not a very arduous office, but very pleasantly remunerative. I seldom lose my temper; much more seldom indulge in dangerous indignation at wrongs and outrages; but, I must be permitted to be rash here, and declare, that I consider the sudden and violent abrogation of the office of Master in Chancery, by the new Constitution, as a—premature act; inasmuch as I had counted upon a life-lease of the profits, whereas I only received those of a few short years. But this is by the way.

My chambers were up stairs, at No. ——— Wall Street. At one end, they looked upon the white wall of the interior of a spacious sky-light shaft, penetrating the building from top to bottom.

This view might have been considered rather tame than otherwise, deficient in what landscape painters call "life." But, if so, the view from the other end of my chambers offered, at least, a contrast, if nothing more. In that direction, my windows commanded an unobstructed view of a lofty brick wall, black by age and everlasting shade; which wall required no spy-glass to bring out its lurking beauties, but, for the benefit of all near-sighted spectators, was pushed up to within ten feet of my window panes. Owing to the great height of the surrounding buildings, and my chambers being on the second floor, the interval between this wall and mine not a little resembled a huge square cistern.

At the period just preceding the advent of Bartleby, I had two persons as copyists in my employment, and a promising lad as an office-boy. First, Turkey; second, Nippers; third, Ginger Nut. These may seem names, the like of which are not usually found in the Directory. In truth, they were nicknames, mutually conferred upon each other by my three clerks, and were deemed expressive of their respective persons or characters. Turkey was a short, pursy[1] Englishman, of about my own age—that is, somewhere not far from sixty. In the morning, one might say, his face was of a fine

[1] Short-winded, especially from fatness.

florid hue, but after twelve o'clock, meridian—his dinner hour—it blazed like a grate full of Christmas coals; and continued blazing—but, as it were, with a gradual wane—till six o'clock, P.M., or thereabouts; after which, I saw no more of the proprietor of the face, which, gaining its meridian with the sun, seemed to set with it, to rise, culminate, and decline the following day, with the like regularity and undiminished glory. There are many singular coincidences I have known in the course of my life, not the least among which was the fact, that, exactly when Turkey displayed his fullest beams from his red and radiant countenance, just then, too, at that critical moment, began the daily period when I considered his business capacities as seriously disturbed for the remainder of the twenty-four hours. Not that he was absolutely idle, or averse to business, then; far from it. The difficulty was, he was apt to be altogether too energetic. There was a strange, inflamed, flurried, flighty recklessness of activity about him. He would be incautious in dipping his pen into his inkstand. All his blots upon my documents were dropped there after twelve o'clock, meridian. Indeed, not only would he be reckless, and sadly given to making blots in the afternoon, but, some days, he went further, and was rather noisy. At such times, too, his face flamed with augmented blazonry, as if cannel coal had been heaped on anthracite. He made an unpleasant racket with his chair; spilled his sand-box; in mending his pens, impatiently split them all to pieces, and threw them on the floor in a sudden passion; stood up, and leaned over his table, boxing his papers about in a most indecorous manner, very sad to behold in an elderly man like him. Nevertheless, as he was in many ways a most valuable person to me, and all the time before twelve o'clock, meridian, was the quickest, steadiest creature, too, accomplishing a great deal of work in a style not easily to be matched—for these reasons, I was willing to overlook his eccentricities, though, indeed, occasionally, I remonstrated with him. I did this very gently, however, because, though the civilest, nay, the blandest and most reverential of men in the morning, yet, in the afternoon, he was disposed, upon provocation, to be slightly rash with his tongue—in fact, insolent. Now, valuing his morning services as I did, and resolved not to lose them—yet, at the same time, made uncomfortable by his inflamed ways after twelve o'clock—and being a man of peace, unwilling by my admonitions to call forth unseemly retorts from him, I took upon me, one Saturday noon (he was always worse on Saturdays) to hint to him, very kindly, that, perhaps, now that he was growing old, it might be well to abridge his labors; in short, he need not come to my chambers after twelve o'clock, but, dinner over, had best go home to his lodgings, and rest himself till tea-time. But no; he insisted upon his afternoon devotions. His countenance became intolerably fervid, as he oratorically assured me—gesticulating with a long ruler at the other end of the room—that if his services in the morning were useful, how indispensable, then, in the afternoon?

"With submission, sir," said Turkey, on this occasion, "I consider myself your right-hand man. In the morning I but marshal and deploy my columns; but in the afternoon I put myself at their head, and gallantly charge the foe, thus"—and he made a violent thrust with the ruler.

"But the blots, Turkey," intimated I.

"True; but, with submission, sir, behold these hairs! I am getting old. Surely, sir, a blot or two of a warm afternoon is not to be severely urged against gray hairs. Old age—even if it blot the page—is honorable. With submission, sir, we *both* are getting old."

This appeal to my fellow-feeling was hardly to be resisted. At all events, I saw that go he would not. So, I made up my mind to let him stay, resolving, nevertheless, to see to it that, during the afternoon, he had to do with my less important papers.

Nippers, the second on my list, was a whiskered, sallow, and, upon the whole, rather piratical-looking young man, of about five and twenty. I always deemed him the victim of two evil powers—ambition and indigestion. The ambition was evinced by a certain impatience of the duties of a mere copyist, an unwarrantable usurpation of strictly professional affairs, such as the original drawing up of legal documents. The indigestion seemed betokened in an occasional nervous testiness and grinning irritability, causing the teeth to audibly grind together over mistakes committed in copying; unnecessary maledictions, hissed, rather than spoken, in the heat of business; and especially by a continual discontent with the height of the table where he worked. Though of a very ingenious mechanical turn, Nippers could never get this table to suit him. He put chips under it, blocks of various sorts, bits of pasteboard, and at last went so far as to attempt an exquisite adjustment, by final pieces of folded blotting-paper. But no invention would answer. If, for the sake of easing his back, he brought the table lid at a sharp angle well up towards his chin, and wrote there like a man using the steep roof of a Dutch house for his desk, then he declared that it stopped the circulation in his arms. If now he lowered the table to his waistbands, and stooped over it in writing, then there was a sore aching in his back. In short, the truth of the matter was, Nippers knew not what he wanted. Or, if he wanted anything, it was to be rid of a scrivener's table altogether. Among the manifestations of his diseased ambition was a fondness he had for receiving visits from certain ambiguous-looking fellows in seedy coats, whom he called his clients. Indeed, I was aware that not only was he, at times, considerable of a ward-politician, but he occasionally did a little business at the Justices' courts, and was not unknown on the steps of the Tombs. I have good reason to believe, however, that one individual who called upon him at my chambers, and who, with a grand air, he insisted was his client, was no other than a dun,[2] and the alleged title-deed, a bill. But, with all his failings, and the annoyances he caused me, Nippers, like his compatriot Turkey, was a very useful man to me; wrote a neat, swift hand; and, when he chose, was not deficient in a gentlemanly sort of deportment. Added to this, he always dressed in a gentlemanly sort of way; and so, incidentally, reflected credit upon my chambers. Whereas, with respect to Turkey, I had much ado to keep him from being a reproach to me. His clothes were apt to look oily, and smell of eating-houses. He wore his pantaloons very loose and baggy in summer. His coats were execrable; his hat not to be handled. But while the hat was a thing of indifference to me, inasmuch as his natural civility and deference, as a dependent Englishman, always led him to doff it the moment he entered the room, yet his coat was another matter. Concerning his coats, I reasoned with him; but with no effect. The truth was, I suppose, that a man with so small an income could not afford to sport such a lustrous face and a lustrous coat at one and the same time. As Nippers once observed, Turkey's money went chiefly for red ink. One winter day, I presented Turkey with a highly respectable-looking coat of my own—a padded gray coat, of a most comfortable warmth, and which buttoned straight up from the knee to the neck. I thought Turkey would appreciate the favor, and abate his rashness and

[2] Bill collector.

obstreperousness of afternoons. But no; I verily believe that buttoning himself up in so downy and blanket-like a coat had a pernicious effect upon him—upon the same principle that too much oats are bad for horses. In fact, precisely as a rash, restive horse is said to feel his oats, so Turkey felt his coat. It made him insolent. He was a man whom prosperity harmed.

Though, concerning the self-indulgent habits of Turkey, I had my own private surmises, yet, touching Nippers, I was well persuaded that, whatever might be his faults in other respects, he was, at least, a temperate young man. But, indeed, nature herself seemed to have been his vintner, and, at his birth, charged him so thoroughly with an irritable, brandy-like disposition, that all subsequent potations were needless. When I consider how, amid the stillness of my chambers, Nippers would sometimes impatiently rise from his seat, and stooping over his table, spread his arms wide apart, seize the whole desk, and move it, and jerk it, with a grim, grinding motion on the floor, as if the table were a perverse voluntary agent, intent on thwarting and vexing him, I plainly perceive that, for Nippers, brandy-and-water were altogether superfluous.

It was fortunate for me that, owing to its peculiar cause—indigestion—the irritability and consequent nervousness of Nippers were mainly observable in the morning, while in the afternoon he was comparatively mild. So that, Turkey's paroxysms only coming on about twelve o'clock, I never had to do with their eccentricities at one time. Their fits relieved each other, like guards. When Nippers's was on, Turkey's was off; and *vice versa*. This was a good natural arrangement, under the circumstances.

Ginger Nut, the third on my list, was a lad, some twelve years old. His father was a car-man, ambitious of seeing his son on the bench instead of a cart, before he died. So he sent him to my office, as student at law, errand-boy, cleaner and sweeper, at the rate of one dollar a week. He had a little desk to himself, but he did not use it much. Upon inspection, the drawer exhibited a great array of the shells of various sorts of nuts. Indeed, to this quick-witted youth, the whole noble science of the law was contained in a nutshell. Not the least among the employments of Ginger Nut, as well as one which he discharged with the most alacrity, was his duty as cake and apple purveyor for Turkey and Nippers. Copying law-papers being proverbially a dry, husky sort of business, my two scriveners were fain to moisten their mouths very often with Spitzenbergs,[3] to be had at the numerous stalls nigh the Custom House and Post Office. Also, they sent Ginger Nut very frequently for that peculiar cake —small, flat, round, and very spicy—after which he had been named by them. Of a cold morning, when business was but dull, Turkey would gobble up scores of these cakes, as if they were mere wafers—indeed, they sell them at the rate of six or eight for a penny—the scrape of his pen blending with the crunching of the crisp particles in his mouth. Of all the fiery afternoon blunders and flurried rashnesses of Turkey, was his once moistening a ginger-cake between his lips, and clapping it on to a mortgage, for a seal. I came within an ace of dismissing him then. But he mollified me by making an oriental bow, and saying—

"With submission, sir, it was generous of me to find you in stationery on my own account."

Now my original business—that of a conveyancer and title hunter, and drawer-up

[3] Apples.

of recondite documents of all sorts[4]—was considerably increased by receiving the master's office. There was now great work for scriveners. Not only must I push the clerks already with me, but I must have additional help.

In answer to my advertisement, a motionless young man one morning stood upon my office threshold, the door being open, for it was summer. I can see that figure now —pallidly neat, pitiably respectable, incurably forlorn! It was Bartleby.

After a few words touching his qualifications, I engaged him, glad to have among my corps of copyists a man of so singularly sedate an aspect, which I thought might operate beneficially upon the flighty temper of Turkey, and the fiery one of Nippers.

I should have stated before that ground glass folding-doors divided my premises into two parts, one of which was occupied by my scriveners, the other by myself. According to my humor, I threw open these doors, or closed them. I resolved to assign Bartleby a corner by the folding-doors, but on my side of them, so as to have this quiet man within easy call, in case any trifling thing was to be done. I placed his desk close up to a small side-window in that part of the room, a window which originally had afforded a lateral view of certain grimy back-yards and bricks, but which, owing to subsequent erections, commanded at present no view at all, though it gave some light. Within three feet of the panes was a wall, and the light came down from far above, between two lofty buildings, as from a very small opening in a dome. Still further to a satisfactory arrangement, I procured a high green folding screen, which might entirely isolate Bartleby from my sight, though not remove him from my voice. And thus, in a manner, privacy and society were conjoined.

At first, Bartleby did an extraordinary quantity of writing. As if long famishing for something to copy, he seemed to gorge himself on my documents. There was no pause for digestion. He ran a day and night line, copying by sun-light and by candle-light. I should have been quite delighted with his application, had he been cheerfully industrious. But he wrote on silently, palely, mechanically.

It is, of course, an indispensable part of a scrivener's business to verify the accuracy of his copy, word by word. Where there are two or more scriveners in an office, they assist each other in this examination, one reading from the copy, the other holding the original. It is a very dull, wearisome, and lethargic affair. I can readily imagine that, to some sanguine temperaments, it would be altogether intolerable. For example, I cannot credit that the mettlesome poet, Byron, would have contentedly sat down with Bartleby to examine a law document of, say five hundred pages, closely written in a crimpy hand.

Now and then, in the haste of business, it had been my habit to assist in comparing some brief document myself, calling Turkey or Nippers for this purpose. One object I had, in placing Bartleby so handy to me behind the screen, was, to avail myself of his services on such trivial occasions. It was on the third day, I think, of his being with me, and before any necessity had arisen for having his own writing examined, that, being much hurried to complete a small affair I had in hand, I abruptly called to Bartleby. In my haste and natural expectancy of instant compliance, I sat with my head bent over the original on my desk, and my right hand sideways, and somewhat nervously extended with the copy, so that, immediately upon emerging from his retreat, Bartleby might snatch it and proceed to business without the least delay.

[4] Legal work beyond ordinary knowledge, such as drawing up deeds for property transfers or checking records to ascertain that there are no prior claims on property to be transferred.

In this very attitude did I sit when I called to him, rapidly stating what it was I wanted him to do—namely, to examine a small paper with me. Imagine my surprise, nay, my consternation, when, without moving from his privacy, Bartleby, in a singularly mild, firm voice, replied, "I would prefer not to."

I sat awhile in perfect silence, rallying my stunned faculties. Immediately it occurred to me that my ears had deceived me, or Bartleby had entirely misunderstood my meaning. I repeated my request in the clearest tone I could assume; but in quite as clear a one came the previous reply, "I would prefer not to."

"Prefer not to," echoed I, rising in high excitement, and crossing the room with a stride. "What do you mean? Are you moon-struck? I want you to help me compare this sheet here—take it," and I thrust it towards him.

"I would prefer not to," said he.

I looked at him steadfastly. His face was leanly composed; his gray eye dimly calm. Not a wrinkle of agitation rippled him. Had there been the least uneasiness, anger, impatience or impertinence in his manner; in other words, had there been any thing ordinarily human about him, doubtless I should have violently dismissed him from the premises. But as it was, I should have as soon thought of turning my pale plaster-of-paris bust of Cicero[5] out of doors. I stood gazing at him awhile, as he went on with his own writing, and then reseated myself at my desk. This is very strange, thought I. What had one best do? But my business hurried me. I concluded to forget the matter for the present, reserving it for my future leisure. So calling Nippers from the other room, the paper was speedly examined.

A few days after this, Bartleby concluded four lengthy documents, being quadruplicates of a week's testimony taken before me in my High Court of Chancery. It became necessary to examine them. It was an important suit, and great accuracy was imperative. Having all things arranged, I called Turkey, Nippers, and Ginger Nut, from the next room, meaning to place the four copies in the hands of my four clerks, while I should read from the original. Accordingly, Turkey, Nippers, and Ginger Nut had taken their seats in a row, each with his document in his hand, when I called to Bartleby to join this interesting group.

"Bartleby! quick, I am waiting."

I heard a slow scrape of his chair legs on the uncarpeted floor, and soon he appeared standing at the entrance of his hermitage.

"What is wanted?" said he, mildly.

"The copies, the copies," said I, hurriedly. "We are going to examine them. There"—and I held towards him the fourth quadruplicate.

"I would prefer not to," he said, and gently disappeared behind the screen.

For a few moments I was turned into a pillar of salt,[6] standing at the head of my seated column of clerks. Recovering myself, I advanced towards the screen, and demanded the reason for such extraordinary conduct.

"*Why* do you refuse?"

"I would prefer not to."

With any other man I should have flown outright into a dreadful passion, scorned all further words, and thrust him ignominiously from my presence. But there was something about Bartleby that not only strangely disarmed me, but, in a wonderful manner, touched and disconcerted me. I began to reason with him.

---

[5] Roman statesman and orator (106–42 B.C.).   [6] Like Lot's disobedient wife (Genesis 19:26).

"These are your own copies we are about to examine. It is labor saving to you, because one examination will answer for your four papers. It is common usage. Every copyist is bound to help examine his copy. Is it not so? Will you not speak? Answer!"

"I prefer not to," he replied in a flutelike tone. It seemed to me that, while I had been addressing him, he carefully revolved every statement that I made; fully comprehended the meaning; could not gainsay the irresistible conclusion; but, at the same time, some paramount consideration prevailed with him to reply as he did.

"You are decided, then, not to comply with my request—a request made according to common usage and common sense?"

He briefly gave me to understand, that on that point my judgment was sound. Yes: his decision was irreversible.

It is not seldom the case that, when a man is browbeaten in some unprecedented and violently unreasonable way, he begins to stagger in his own plainest faith. He begins, as it were, vaguely to surmise that, wonderful as it may be, all the justice and all the reason is on the other side. Accordingly, if any disinterested persons are present, he turns to them for some reinforcement of his own faltering mind.

"Turkey," said I, "what do you think of this? Am I not right?"

"With submission, sir," said Turkey, in his blandest tone, "I think that you are."

"Nippers," said I, "what do *you* think of it?"

"I think I should kick him out of the office."

(The reader, of nice perceptions, will here perceive that, it being morning, Turkey's answer is couched in polite and tranquil terms, but Nippers replies in ill-tempered ones. Or, to repeat a previous sentence, Nippers's ugly mood was on duty, and Turkey's off.)

"Ginger Nut," said I, willing to enlist the smallest suffrage in my behalf, "what do *you* think of it?"

"I think, sir, he's a little *luny*," replied Ginger Nut, with a grin.

"You hear what they say," said I, turning towards the screen, "come forth and do your duty."

But he vouchsafed no reply. I pondered a moment in sore perplexity. But once more business hurried me. I determined again to postpone the consideration of this dilemma to my future leisure. With a little trouble we made out to examine the papers without Bartleby, though at every page or two Turkey deferentially dropped his opinion, that this proceeding was quite out of the common; while Nippers, twitching in his chair with a dyspeptic nervousness, ground out, between his set teeth, occasional hissing maledictions against the stubborn oaf behind the screen. And for his (Nippers's) part, this was the first and the last time he would do another man's business without pay.

Meanwhile Bartleby sat in his hermitage, oblivious to everything but his own peculiar business there.

Some days passed, the scrivener being employed upon another lengthy work. His late remarkable conduct led me to regard his ways narrowly. I observed that he never went to dinner; indeed, that he never went anywhere. As yet I had never, of my personal knowledge, known him to be outside of my office. He was a perpetual sentry in the corner. At about eleven o'clock though, in the morning, I noticed that Ginger Nut would advance toward the opening in Bartleby's screen, as if silently beckoned thither by a gesture invisible to me where I sat. The boy would then leave the office, jingling a few pence, and reappear with a handful of ginger-nuts, which he delivered in the hermitage, receiving two of the cakes for his trouble.

He lives, then, on ginger-nuts, thought I; never eats a dinner, properly speaking; he must be a vegetarian, then; but no; he never eats even vegetables, he eats nothing but ginger-nuts. My mind then ran on in reveries concerning the probable effects upon the human constitution of living entirely on ginger-nuts. Ginger-nuts are so called, because they contain ginger as one of their peculiar constituents, and the final flavoring one. Now, what was ginger? A hot, spicy thing. Was Bartleby hot and spicy? Not at all. Ginger, then, had no effect upon Bartleby. Probably he preferred it should have none.

Nothing so aggravates an earnest person as a passive resistance. If the individual so resisted be of a not inhumane temper, and the resisting one perfectly harmless in his passivity, then, in the better moods of the former, he will endeavor charitably to construe to his imagination what proves impossible to be solved by his judgment. Even so, for the most part, I regarded Bartleby and his ways. Poor fellow! thought I, he means no mischief; it is plain he intends no insolence; his aspect sufficiently evinces that his eccentricities are involuntary. He is useful to me. I can get along with him. If I turn him away, the chances are he will fall in with some less-indulgent employer, and then he will be rudely treated, and perhaps driven forth miserably to starve. Yes. Here I can cheaply purchase a delicious self-approval. To befriend Bartleby; to humor him in his strange willfulness, will cost me little or nothing, while I lay up in my soul what will eventually prove a sweet morsel for my conscience. But this mood was not invariable with me. The passiveness of Bartleby sometimes irritated me. I felt strangely goaded on to encounter him in new opposition—to elicit some angry spark from him answerable to my own. But, indeed, I might as well have essayed to strike fire with my knuckles against a bit of Windsor soap. But one afternoon the evil impulse in me mastered me, and the following little scene ensued:

"Bartleby," said I, "when those papers are all copied, I will compare them with you."

"I would prefer not to."

"How? Surely you do not mean to persist in that mulish vagary?"

No answer.

I threw open the folding-doors near by, and, turning upon Turkey and Nippers, exclaimed:

"Bartleby a second time says, he won't examine his papers. What do you think of it, Turkey?"

It was afternoon, be it remembered. Turkey sat glowing like a brass boiler; his bald head steaming; his hands reeling among his blotted papers.

"Think of it?" roared Turkey; "I think I'll just step behind his screen, and black his eyes for him!"

So saying, Turkey rose to his feet and threw his arms into a pugilistic position. He was hurrying away to make good his promise, when I detained him, alarmed at the effect of incautiously rousing Turkey's combativeness after dinner.

"Sit down, Turkey," said I, "and hear what Nippers has to say. What do you think of it, Nippers? Would I not be justified in immediately dismissing Bartleby?"

"Excuse me, that is for you to decide, sir. I think his conduct quite unusual, and, indeed, unjust, as regards Turkey and myself. But it may only be a passing whim."

"Ah," exclaimed I, "you have strangely changed your mind, then—you speak very gently of him now."

"All beer," cried Turkey; "gentleness is effects of beer—Nippers and I dined together to-day. You see how gentle *I* am, sir. Shall I go and black his eyes?"

"You refer to Bartleby, I suppose. No, not to-day, Turkey," I replied; "pray, put up your fists."

I closed the doors, and again advanced towards Bartleby. I felt additional incentives tempting me to my fate. I burned to be rebelled against again. I remembered that Bartleby never left the office.

"Bartleby," said I, "Ginger Nut is away; just step around to the Post Office, won't you? (it was but a three minutes' walk), and see if there is anything for me."

"I would prefer not to."

"You *will* not?"

"I *prefer* not."

I staggered to my desk, and sat there in a deep study. My blind inveteracy returned. Was there any other thing in which I could procure myself to be ignominiously repulsed by this lean, penniless wight?—my hired clerk? What added thing is there, perfectly reasonable, that he will be sure to refuse to do?

"Bartleby!"

No answer.

"Bartleby," in a louder tone.

No answer.

"Bartleby," I roared.

Like a very ghost, agreeably to the laws of magical invocation, at the third summons, he appeared at the entrance of his hermitage.

"Go to the next room, and tell Nippers to come to me."

"I prefer not to," he respectfully and slowly said, and mildly disappeared.

"Very good, Bartleby," said I, in a quiet sort of serenely-severe self-possessed tone, intimating the unalterable purpose of some terrible retribution very close at hand. At the moment I half intended something of the kind. But upon the whole, as it was drawing towards my dinner-hour, I thought it best to put on my hat and walk home for the day, suffering much from perplexity and distress of mind.

Shall I acknowledge it? The conclusion of this whole business was, that it soon became a fixed fact of my chambers, that a pale young scrivener, by the name of Bartleby, had a desk there; that he copied for me at the usual rate of four cents a folio (one hundred words); but he was permanently exempt from examining the work done by him, that duty being transferred to Turkey and Nippers, out of compliment, doubtless, to their superior acuteness; moreover, said Bartleby was never, on any account, to be dispatched on the most trivial errand of any sort; and that even if entreated to take upon him such a matter, it was generally understood that he would "prefer not to"—in other words, that he would refuse point-blank.

As days passed on, I became considerably reconciled to Bartleby. His steadiness, his freedom from all dissipation, his incessant industry (except when he chose to throw himself into a standing revery behind his screen), his great stillness, his unalterableness of demeanor under all circumstances, made him a valuable acquisition. One prime thing was this—*he was always there*—first in the morning, continually through the day, and the last at night. I had a singular confidence in his honesty. I felt my most precious papers perfectly safe in his hands. Sometimes, to be sure, I could not, for the very soul of me, avoid falling into sudden spasmodic passions with him. For it was exceeding difficult to bear in mind all the time those strange peculiarities, privileges, and unheard of exemptions, forming the tacit stipulations on Bartleby's part under which he remained in my office. Now and then, in the eagerness of dispatching pressing business, I would inadvertently summon Bartleby, in a short, rapid tone, to put his finger, say, on the incipient tie of a bit of red tape with which I was about compressing some papers. Of course, from behind the screen the usual answer, "I prefer not to," was sure to come; and then, how could a human creature, with the common infirmities of our nature, refrain from bitterly exclaiming upon such perverseness— such unreasonableness. However, every added repulse of this sort which I received only tended to lessen the probability of my repeating the inadvertence.

Here it must be said, that according to the custom of most legal gentlemen occupying chambers in densely-populated law buildings, there were several keys to my door. One was kept by a woman residing in the attic, which person weekly scrubbed and daily swept and dusted my apartments. Another was kept by Turkey for convenience sake. The third I sometimes carried in my own pocket. The fourth I knew not who had.

Now, one Sunday morning I happened to go to Trinity Church, to hear a celebrated preacher, and finding myself rather early on the ground I thought I would walk around to my chambers for a while. Luckily I had my key with me; but upon applying it to the lock, I found it resisted by something inserted from the inside. Quite surprised, I called out; when to my consternation a key was turned from within; and thrusting his lean visage at me, and holding the door ajar, the apparition of Bartleby appeared, in his shirt sleeves, and otherwise in a strangely tattered deshabille, saying quietly that he was sorry, but he was deeply engaged just then, and—preferred not admitting me at present. In a brief word or two, he moreover added, that perhaps I had better walk around the block two or three times, and by that time he would probably have concluded his affairs.

Now, the utterly unsurmised appearance of Bartleby, tenanting my law-chambers of a Sunday morning, with his cadaverously gentlemanly *nonchalance,* yet withal firm and self-possessed, had such a strange effect upon me, that incontinently I slunk away from my own door, and did as desired. But not without sundry twinges of impotent rebellion against the mild effrontery of this unaccountable scrivener. Indeed, it was his wonderful mildness chiefly, which not only disarmed me, but unmanned me as it were. For I consider that one, for the time, is a sort of unmanned when he tranquilly permits his hired clerk to dictate to him, and order him away from his own premises. Furthermore, I was full of uneasiness as to what Bartleby could possibly be doing in my office in his shirt sleeves, and in an otherwise dismantled condition of a Sunday morning. Was anything amiss going on? Nay, that was out of the question. It was not to be thought of for a moment that Bartleby was an immoral person. But what could he be doing there?—copying? Nay again, whatever might be his eccentricities, Bartleby was an eminently decorous person. He would be the last man to sit down to his desk in any state approaching to nudity. Besides, it was Sunday; and there was something about Bartleby that forbade the supposition that he would by any secular occupation violate the proprieties of the day.

Nevertheless, my mind was not pacified; and full of a restless curiosity, at last I returned to the door. Without hindrance I inserted my key, opened it, and entered. Bartleby was not to be seen. I looked round anxiously, peeped behind his screen; but it was very plain that he was gone. Upon more closely examining the place, I surmised that for an indefinite period Bartleby must have ate, dressed, and slept in my office, and that, too without plate, mirror, or bed. The cushioned seat of a rickety old sofa in one corner bore the faint impress of a lean, reclining form. Rolled away under his desk, I found a blanket; under the empty grate, a blacking box and brush; on a chair, a tin basin, with soap and a ragged towel; in a newspaper a few crumbs of ginger-nuts and a morsel of cheese. Yes, thought I, it is evident enough that Bartleby has been making his home here, keeping bachelor's hall all by himself. Immediately then the thought came sweeping across me, what miserable friendlessness and loneliness are here revealed! His poverty is great; but his solitude, how horrible! Think of it. Of a Sunday, Wall Street is deserted as Petra;[7] and every night of every day it is an emptiness. This building, too, which of week-days hums with industry and life, at nightfall echoes with sheer vacancy, and all through Sunday is forlorn. And here Bartleby makes his home; sole spectator of a solitude which he has seen all populous —a sort of innocent and transformed Marius brooding among the ruins of Carthage![8]

For the first time in my life a feeling of over-powering stinging melancholy seized me. Before, I had never experienced aught but a not unpleasing sadness. The bond of a common humanity now drew me irresistibly to gloom. A fraternal melancholy! For both I and Bartleby were sons of Adam. I remembered the bright silks and sparkling faces I had seen that day, in gala trim, swan-like sailing down the Mississippi of Broadway; and I contrasted them with the pallid copyist, and thought to myself, Ah, happiness courts the light, so we deem the world is gay; but misery hides aloof, so we deem that misery there is none. These sad fancyings—chimeras, doubtless, of a sick and silly brain—led on to other and more special thoughts, concerning the eccentricities of Bartleby. Presentiments of strange discoveries hovered round me. The scrivener's pale form appeared to me laid out, among uncaring strangers, in its shivering winding sheet.

Suddenly I was attracted by Bartleby's closed desk, the key in open sight left in the lock.

I mean no mischief, seek the gratification of no heartless curiosity, thought I; besides, the desk is mine, and its contents, too, so I will make bold to look within. Everything was methodically arranged, the papers smoothly placed. The pigeon holes were deep, and removing the files of documents, I groped into their recesses. Presently I felt something there, and dragged it out. It was an old bandanna handkerchief, heavy and knotted. I opened it, and saw it was a savings's bank.

I now recalled all the quiet mysteries which I had noted in the man. I remembered that he never spoke but to answer; that, though at intervals he had considerable time to himself, yet I had never seen him reading—no, not even a newspaper; that for long periods he would stand looking out, at his pale window behind the screen, upon the dead brick wall; I was quite sure he never visited any refectory or eating house; while his pale face clearly indicated that he never drank beer like Turkey, or tea and coffee even, like other men; that he never went anywhere in particular that I could learn;

---

[7] Ruins of ancient city on Mt. Hor, Jordan.
[8] Marius: Gaius Marius (157–86 B.C.), Roman general; Carthage: commercial empire destroyed by Rome in the Third Punic War.

never went out for a walk, unless, indeed, that was the case at present; that he had declined telling who he was, or whence he came, or whether he had any relatives in the world; that though so thin and pale, he never complained of ill health. And more than all, I remembered a certain unconscious air of pallid—how shall I call it?—of pallid haughtiness, say, or rather an austere reserve about him, which had positively awed me into my tame compliance with his eccentricities, when I had feared to ask him to do the slightest incidental thing for me, even though I might know, from his long-continued motionlessness, that behind his screen he must be standing in one of those dead-wall reveries of his.

Revolving all these things, and coupling them with the recently discovered fact, that he made my office his constant abiding place and home, and not forgetful of his morbid moodiness; revolving all these things, a prudential feeling began to steal over me. My first emotions had been those of pure melancholy and sincerest pity; but just in proportion as the forlornness of Bartleby grew and grew to my imagination, did that same melancholy merge into fear, that pity into repulsion. So true it is, and so terrible, took that up to a certain point the thought or sight of misery enlists our best affections; but, in certain special cases, beyond that point it does not. They err who would assert that invariably this is owing to the inherent selfishness of the human heart. It rather proceeds from a certain hopelessness of remedying excessive and organic ill. To a sensitive being, pity is not seldom pain. And when at last it is perceived that such pity cannot lead to effectual succor, common sense bids the soul be rid of it. What I saw that morning persuaded me that the scrivener was the victim of innate and incurable disorder. I might give alms to his body; but his body did not pain him; it was his soul that suffered, and his soul I could not reach.

I did not accomplish the purpose of going to Trinity Church that morning. Somehow, the things I had seen disqualified me for the time from church-going. I walked homeward, thinking what I would do with Bartleby. Finally, I resolved upon this—I would put certain calm questions to him the next morning, touching his history, etc., and if he declined to answer them openly and unreservedly (and I supposed he would prefer not), then to give him a twenty dollar bill over and above whatever I might owe him, and tell him his services were no longer required; but that if in any other way I could assist him, I would be happy to do so, especially if he desired to return to his native place, wherever that might be, I would willingly help to defray the expenses. Moreover, if, after reaching home, he found himself at any time in want of aid, a letter from him would be sure of a reply.

The next morning came.

"Bartleby," said I, gently calling to him behind his screen.

No reply.

"Bartleby," said I, in a still gentler tone, "come here; I am not going to ask you to do anything you would prefer not to do—I simply wish to speak to you."

Upon this he noiselessly slid into view.

"Will you tell me, Bartleby, where you were born?"

"I would prefer not to."

"Will you tell me *anything* about yourself?"

"I would prefer not to."

"But what reasonable objection can you have to speak to me? I feel friendly towards you."

He did not look at me while I spoke, but kept his glance fixed upon my bust of Cicero, which, as I then sat, was directly behind me, some six inches above my head.

"What is your answer, Bartleby," said I, after waiting a considerable time for a reply, during which his countenance remained immovable, only there was the faintest conceivable tremor of the white attenuated mouth.

"At present I prefer to give no answer," he said, and retired into his hermitage.

It was rather weak in me I confess, but his manner, on this occasion, nettled me. Not only did there seem to lurk in it a certain calm disdain, but his perverseness seemed ungrateful, considering the undeniable good usage and indulgence he had received from me.

Again I sat ruminating what I should do. Mortified as I was at his behavior, and resolved as I had been to dismiss him when I entered my office, nevertheless I strangely felt something superstitious knocking at my heart, and forbidding me to carry out my purpose, and denouncing me for a villain if I dared to breathe one bitter word against this forlornest of mankind. At last, familiarly drawing my chair behind his screen, I sat down and said: "Bartleby, never mind, then, about revealing your history; but let me entreat you, as a friend, to comply as far as may be with the usages of this office. Say now, you will help to examine papers to-morrow or next day: in short, say now, that in a day or two you will begin to be a little reasonable:—say so, Bartleby."

"At present I would prefer not to be a little reasonable," was his mildly cadaverous reply.

Just then the folding-doors opened, and Nippers approached. He seemed suffering from an unusually bad night's rest, induced by severer indigestion than common. He overheard those final words of Bartleby.

"*Prefer not*, eh?" gritted Nippers—"I'd *prefer* him, if I were you, sir," addressing me—"I'd *prefer* him; I'd give him preferences, the stubborn mule! What is it, sir, pray, that he *prefers* not to do now?"

Bartleby moved not a limb.

"Mr. Nippers," said I, "I'd prefer that you would withdraw for the present."

Somehow, of late, I had got into the way of involuntarily using this word "prefer" upon all sorts of not exactly suitable occasions. And I trembled to think that my contact with the scrivener had already and seriously affected me in a mental way. And what further and deeper aberration might it not yet produce? This apprehension had not been without efficacy in determining me to summary measures.

As Nippers, looking very sour and sulky, was departing, Turkey blandly and deferentially approached.

"With submission, sir," said he, "yesterday I was thinking about Bartleby here, and I think that if he would but prefer to take a quart of good ale every day, it would do much towards mending him, and enabling him to assist in examining his papers."

"So you have got the word, too," said I, slightly excited.

"With submission, what word, sir," asked Turkey, respectfully crowding himself into the contracted space behind the screen, and by so doing, making me jostle the scrivener. "What word, sir?"

"I would prefer to be left alone here," said Bartleby, as if offended at being mobbed in his privacy.

"*That's* the word, Turkey," said I—"*that's* it."

"Oh, *prefer?* oh yes—queer word. I never use it myself. But, sir, as I was saying, if he would but prefer—"

"Turkey," interrupted I, "you will please withdraw."

"Oh, certainly, sir, if you prefer that I should."

As he opened the folding-door to retire, Nippers at his desk caught a glimpse of me, and asked whether I would prefer to have a certain paper copied on blue paper or white. He did not in the least roguishly accent the word prefer. It was plain that it involuntarily rolled from his tongue. I thought to myself, surely I must get rid of a demented man, who already has in some degree turned the tongues, if not the heads of myself and clerks. But I thought it prudent not to break the dismission at once.

The next day I noticed that Bartleby did nothing but stand at his window in his dead-wall revery. Upon asking him why he did not write, he said that he had decided upon doing no more writing.

"Why, how now? what next?" exclaimed I, "do no more writing?"

"No more."

"And what is the reason?"

"Do you not see the reason for yourself," he indifferently replied.

I looked steadfastly at him, and perceived that his eyes looked dull and glazed. Instantly it occurred to me, that his unexampled diligence in copying by his dim window for the first few weeks of his stay with me might have temporarily impaired his vision.

I was touched. I said something in condolence with him. I hinted that of course he did wisely in abstaining from writing for a while; and urged him to embrace that opportunity of taking wholesome exercise in the open air. This, however, he did not do. A few days after this, my other clerks being absent, and being in a great hurry to dispatch certain letters by the mail, I thought that, having nothing else earthly to do, Bartleby would surely be less inflexible than usual, and carry these letters to the post-office. But he blankly declined. So, much to my inconvenience, I went myself.

Still added days went by. Whether Bartleby's eyes improved or not, I could not say. To all appearance, I thought they did. But when I asked him if they did, he vouchsafed no answer. At all events, he would do no copying. At last, in reply to my urgings, he informed me that he had permanently given up copying.

"What!" exclaimed I; "suppose your eyes should get entirely well—better than ever before—would you not copy then?"

"I have given up copying," he answered, and slid aside.

He remained as ever, a fixture in my chamber. Nay—if that were possible—he became still more of a fixture than before. What was to be done? He would do nothing in the office; why should he stay there? In plain fact, he had now become a millstone to me, not only useless as a necklace, but afflictive to bear. Yet I was sorry for him. I speak less than truth when I say that, on his own account, he occasioned me uneasiness. If he would but have named a single relative or friend, I would instantly have written, and urged their taking the poor fellow away to some convenient retreat. But he seemed alone, absolutely alone in the universe. A bit of wreck in the mid Atlantic. At length, necessities connected with my business tyrannized over all other considerations. Decently as I could, I told Bartleby that in six days time he must unconditionally leave the office. I warned him to take measures, in the interval, for procuring some other abode. I offered to assist him in this endeavor, if he himself would but take the first step towards a removal. "And when you finally quit me, Bartleby," added I, "I shall see that you go not away entirely unprovided. Six days from this hour, remember."

At the expiration of that period, I peeped behind the screen, and lo! Bartleby was there.

I buttoned up my coat, balanced myself; advanced slowly towards him, touched his shoulder, and said, "The time has come; you must quit this place; I am sorry for you; here is money; but you must go."

"I would prefer not," he replied, with his back still towards me.

"You *must*."

He remained silent.

Now I had an unbounded confidence in this man's common honesty. He had frequently restored to me sixpences and shillings carelessly dropped upon the floor, for I am apt to be very reckless in such shirt-button affairs. The proceeding, then, which followed will not be deemed extraordinary.

"Bartleby," said I, "I owe you twelve dollars on account; here are thirty-two; the odd twenty are yours—Will you take it?" and I handed the bills towards him.

But he made no motion.

"I will leave them here, then," putting them under a weight on the table. Then taking my hat and cane and going to the door, I tranquilly turned and added—"After you have removed your things from these offices, Bartleby, you will of course lock the door—since every one is now gone for the day but you—and if you please, slip your key underneath the mat, so that I may have it in the morning. I shall not see you again; so good-by to you. If, hereafter, in your new place of abode, I can be of any service to you, do not fail to advise me by letter. Good-by, Bartleby, and fare you well."

But he answered not a word; like the last column of some ruined temple, he remained standing mute and solitary in the middle of the otherwise deserted room.

As I walked home in a pensive mood, my vanity got the better of my pity. I could not but highly plume myself on my masterly management in getting rid of Bartleby. Masterly I call it, and such it must appear to any dispassionate thinker. The beauty of my procedure seemed to consist in its perfect quietness. There was no vulgar bullying, no bravado of any sort, no choleric hectoring, and striding to and fro across the apartment, jerking out vehement commands for Bartleby to bundle himself off with his beggarly traps. Nothing of the kind. Without loudly bidding Bartleby depart —as an inferior genius might have done—I *assumed* the ground that depart he must; and upon that assumption built all I had to say. The more I thought over my procedure, the more I was charmed with it. Nevertheless, next morning, upon awakening, I had my doubts—I had somehow slept off the fumes of vanity. One of the coolest and wisest hours a man has, is just after he awakes in the morning. My procedure seemed as sagacious as ever—but only in theory. How it would prove in practice—there was the rub. It was truly a beautiful thought to have assumed Bartleby's departure; but, after all, that assumption was simply my own, and none of Bartleby's. The great point was, not whether I had assumed that he would quit me, but whether he would prefer so to do. He was more a man of preferences than assumptions.

After breakfast, I walked down town, arguing the probabilities *pro* and *con*. One moment I thought it would prove a miserable failure, and Bartleby would be found all alive at my office as usual; the next moment it seemed certain that I should find his chair empty. And so I kept veering about. At the corner of Broadway and Canal Street, I saw quite an excited group of people standing in earnest conversation.

"I'll take odds he doesn't," said a voice as I passed.

"Doesn't go?—done!" said I, "put up your money."

I was instinctively putting my hand in my pocket to produce my own, when I remembered that this was an election day. The words I had overheard bore no reference to Bartleby, but to the success or non-success of some candidate for the mayoralty. In my intent frame of mind, I had, as it were, imagined that all Broadway shared in my excitement, and were debating the same question with me. I passed on, very thankful that the uproar of the street screened my momentary absent-mindedness.

As I had intended, I was earlier than usual at my office door. I stood listening for a moment. All was still. He must be gone. I tried the knob. The door was locked. Yes, my procedure had worked to a charm; he indeed must be vanished. Yet a certain melancholy mixed with this: I was almost sorry for my brilliant success. I was fumbling under the door mat for the key, which Bartleby was to have left there for me, when accidentally my knee knocked against a panel, producing a summoning sound, and in response a voice came to me from within—"Not yet; I am occupied."

It was Bartleby.

I was thunderstruck. For an instant I stood like the man who, pipe in mouth, was killed one cloudless afternoon long ago in Virginia, by summer lightning; at his own warm open window he was killed, and remained leaning out there upon the dreamy afternoon, till some one touched him, when he fell.

"Not gone!" I murmured at last. But again obeying that wondrous ascendancy which the inscrutable scrivener had over me, and from which ascendancy, for all my chafing, I could not completely escape, I slowly went down stairs and out into the street, and while walking round the block, considered what I should next do in this unheard-of perplexity. Turn the man out by an actual thrusting I could not; to drive him away by calling him hard names would not do; calling in the police was an unpleasant idea; and yet, permit him to enjoy his cadaverous triumph over me—this, too, I could not think of. What was to be done? or, if nothing could be done, was there anything further that I could *assume* in the matter? Yes, as before I had prospectively assumed that Bartleby would depart, so now I might retrospectively assume that departed he was. In the legitimate carrying out of this assumption, I might enter my office in a great hurry, and pretending not to see Bartleby at all, walk straight against him as if he were air. Such a proceeding would in a singular degree have the appearance of a home-thrust. It was hardly possible that Bartleby could withstand such an application of the doctrine of assumptions. But upon second thoughts the success of the plan seemed rather dubious. I resolved to argue the matter over with him again.

"Bartleby," said I, entering the office, with a quietly severe expression, "I am seriously displeased. I am pained, Bartleby. I had thought better of you. I had imagined you of such a gentlemanly organization, that in any delicate dilemma a slight hint would suffice—in short, an assumption. But it appears I am deceived. Why," I added, unaffectedly starting, "you have not even touched that money yet," pointing to it, just where I had left it the evening previous.

He answered nothing.

"Will you, or will you not, quit me?" I now demanded in a sudden passion, advancing close to him.

"I would prefer *not* to quit you," he replied, gently emphasizing the *not.*

"What earthly right have you to stay here? Do you pay any rent? Do you pay my taxes? Or is this property yours?"

He answered nothing.

"Are you ready to go on and write now? Are your eyes recovered? Could you copy a small paper for me this morning? or help examine a few lines? or step round to the post-office? In a word, will you do anything at all, to give a coloring to your refusal to depart the premises?"

He silently retired into his hermitage.

I was now in such a state of nervous resentment that I thought it but prudent to check myself at present from further demonstrations. Bartleby and I were alone. I remembered the tragedy of the unfortunate Adams and the still more unfortunate Colt in the solitary office of the latter; and how poor Colt, being dreadfully incensed by Adams, and imprudently permitting himself to get wildly excited, was at unawares hurried into his fatal act—an act which certainly no man could possibly deplore more than the actor himself.[9] Often it had occurred to me in my ponderings upon the subject, that had that altercation taken place in the public street, or at a private residence, it would not have terminated as it did. It was the circumstance of being alone in a solitary office, up stairs, of a building entirely unhallowed by humanizing domestic associations—an uncarpeted office, doubtless, of a dusty, haggard sort of appearance—this it must have been, which greatly helped to enhance the irritable desperation of the hapless Colt.

But when this old Adam of resentment rose in me and tempted me concerning Bartleby, I grappled him and threw him. How? Why, simply by recalling the divine injunction: "A new commandment give I unto you, that ye love one another." Yes, this it was that saved me. Aside from higher considerations, charity often operates as a vastly wise and prudent principle—a great safeguard to its possessor. Men have committed murder for jealousy's sake, and anger's sake, and hatred's sake, and selfishness' sake, and spiritual pride's sake; but no man, that ever I heard of, ever committed a diabolical murder for sweet charity's sake. Mere self-interest, then, if no better motive can be enlisted, should, especially with high-tempered men, prompt all beings to charity and philanthropy. At any rate, upon the occasion in question, I strove to drown my exasperated feelings towards the scrivener by benevolently construing his conduct. Poor fellow, poor fellow! thought I, he don't mean anything; and besides, he has seen hard times, and ought to be indulged.

I endeavored, also, immediately to occupy myself, and at the same time to comfort my despondency. I tried to fancy, that in the course of the morning, at such time as might prove agreeable to him, Bartleby, of his own free accord, would emerge from his hermitage and take up some decided line of march in the direction of the door. But no. Half-past twelve o'clock came; Turkey began to glow in the face, overturn his inkstand, and become generally obstreperous; Nippers abated down into quietude and courtesy; Ginger Nut munched his noon apple; and Bartleby remained standing

[9] In 1841 John C. Colt axe-murdered his creditor, Samuel Adams, and committed suicide following his conviction for the crime, which was widely publicized.

at his window in one of his profoundest dead-wall reveries. Will it be credited? Ought I to acknowledge it? That afternoon I left the office without saying one further word to him.

Some days now passed, during which, at leisure intervals I looked a little into "Edwards on the Will," and "Priestly on Necessity."[10] Under the circumstances, those books induced a salutary feeling. Gradually I slid into the persuasion that these troubles of mine, touching the scrivener, had been all predestinated from eternity, and Bartleby was billeted upon me for some mysterious purpose of an allwise Providence, which it was not for a mere mortal like me to fathom. Yes, Bartleby, stay there behind your screen, thought I; I shall persecute you no more; you are harmless and noiseless as any of these old chairs; in short, I never feel so private as when I know you are here. At last I see it, I feel it; I penetrate to the predestinated purpose of my life. I am content. Others may have loftier parts to enact; but my mission in this world, Bartleby, is to furnish you with office-room for such period as you may see fit to remain.

I believe that this wise and blessed frame of mind would have continued with me, had it not been for the unsolicited and uncharitable remarks obtruded upon me by my professional friends who visited the rooms. But thus it often is, that the constant friction of illiberal minds wears out at last the best resolves of the more generous. Though to be sure, when I reflected upon it, it was not strange that people entering my office should be struck by the peculiar aspect of the unaccountable Bartleby, and so be tempted to throw out some sinister observations concerning him. Sometimes an attorney, having business with me, and calling at my office, and finding no one but the scrivener there, would undertake to obtain some sort of precise information from him touching my whereabouts; but without heeding his idle talk, Bartleby would remain standing immovable in the middle of the room. So after contemplating him in that position for a time, the attorney would depart, no wiser than he came.

Also, when a reference[11] was going on, and the room full of lawyers and witnesses, and business driving fast, some deeply-occupied legal gentleman present, seeing Bartleby wholly unemployed, would request him to run round to his (the legal gentleman's) office and fetch some papers for him. Thereupon, Bartleby would tranquilly decline, and yet remain idle as before. Then the lawyer would give a great stare, and turn to me. And what could I say? At last I was made aware that all through the circle of my professional acquaintance, a whisper of wonder was running round, having reference to the strange creature I kept at my office. This worried me very much. And as the idea came upon me of his possibly turning out a long-lived man, and keep occupying my chambers, and denying my authority; and perplexing my visitors; and scandalizing my professional reputation; and casting a general gloom over the premises; keeping soul and body together to the last upon his savings (for doubtless he spent but half a dime a day), and in the end perhaps outlive me, and claim possession of my office by right of his perpetual occupancy: as all these dark anticipations crowded upon me more and more, and my friends continually intruded their relentless remarks upon the apparition in my room; a great change was wrought in me. I resolved to gather all my faculties together, and forever rid me of this intolerable incubus.

---

[10] Both the Puritan theologian Jonathan Edwards and the English scientist Joseph Priestly concluded that the will is not free.

[11] The referring of disputes to arbitrators.

Ere revolving any complicated project, however, adapted to this end, I first simply suggested to Bartleby the propriety of his permanent departure. In a calm and serious tone, I commended the idea to his careful and mature consideration. But, having taken three days to meditate upon it, he apprised me, that his original determination remained the same; in short, that he still preferred to abide with me.

What shall I do? I now said to myself, buttoning up my coat to the last button. What shall I do? what ought I to do? what does conscience say I *should* do with this man, or, rather, ghost. Rid myself of him, I must; go, he shall. But how? You will not thrust him, the poor, pale, passive mortal—you will not thrust such a helpless creature out of your door? you will not dishonor yourself by such cruelty? No, I will not, I cannot do that. Rather would I let him live and die here, and then mason up his remains in the wall. What, then, will you do? For all your coaxing, he will not budge. Bribes he leaves under your own paper-weight on your table; in short, it is quite plain that he prefers to cling to you.

Then something severe, something unusual must be done. What! surely you will not have him collared by a constable, and commit his innocent pallor to the common jail? And upon what ground could you procure such a thing to be done?—a vagrant, is he? What! he a vagrant, a wanderer, who refuses to budge? It is because he will *not* be a vagrant, then, that you seek to count him *as* a vagrant. That is too absurd. No visible means of support: there I have him. Wrong again: for indubitably he *does* support himself, and that is the only unanswerable proof that any man can show of his possessing the means so to do. No more, then. Since he will not quit me, I must quit him. I will change my offices; I will move elsewhere, and give him fair notice, that if I find him on my new premises I will then proceed against him as a common trespasser.

Acting accordingly, next day I thus addressed him: "I find these chambers too far from the City Hall; the air is unwholesome. In a word, I propose to remove my offices next week, and shall no longer require your services. I tell you this now, in order that you may seek another place."

He made no reply, and nothing more was said.

On the appointed day I engaged carts and men, proceeded to my chambers, and, having but little furniture, everything was removed in a few hours. Throughout, the scrivener remained standing behind the screen, which I directed to be removed the last thing. It was withdrawn; and, being folded up like a huge folio, left him the motion-less occupant of a naked room. I stood in the entry watching him a moment, while something from within me upbraided me.

I re-entered, with my hand in my pocket—and—and my heart in my mouth.

"Good-by, Bartleby; I am going—good-by, and God some way bless you; and take that," slipping something in his hand. But it dropped upon the floor, and then—strange to say—I tore myself from him whom I had so longed to be rid of.

Established in my new quarters, for a day or two I kept the door locked, and started at every footfall in the passages. When I returned to my rooms, after any little absence, I would pause at the threshold for an instant, and attentively listen, ere applying my key. But these fears were needless. Bartleby never came nigh me.

I thought all was going well, when a perturbed-looking stranger visited me, inquiring whether I was the person who had recently occupied rooms at No. ———— Wall Street.

Full of forebodings, I replied that I was.

"Then, sir," said the stranger, who proved a lawyer, "you are responsible for the man you left there. He refuses to do any copying; he refuses to do anything; he says he prefers not to; and he refuses to quit the premises."

"I am very sorry, sir," said I, with assumed tranquillity, but an inward tremor, "but, really, the man you allude to is nothing to me—he is no relation or apprentice of mine, that you should hold me responsible for him."

"In mercy's name, who is he?"

"I certainly cannot inform you. I know nothing about him. Formerly I employed him as a copyist; but he has done nothing for me now for some time past."

"I shall settle him, then—good morning, sir."

Several days passed, and I heard nothing more; and, though I often felt a charitable prompting to call at the place and see poor Bartleby, yet a certain squeamishness, of I know not what, withheld me.

All is over with him, by this time, thought I, at last, when, through another week, no further intelligence reached me. But, coming to my room the day after, I found several persons waiting at my door in a high state of nervous excitement.

"That's the man—here he comes," cried the foremost one, whom I recognized as the lawyer who had previously called upon me alone.

"You must take him away, sir, at once," cried a portly person among them, advancing upon me, and whom I knew to be the landlord of No. ———— Wall Street. "These gentlemen, my tenants, cannot stand it any longer; Mr. B——," pointing to the lawyer, "has turned him out of his room, and he now persists in haunting the building generally, sitting upon the banisters of the stairs by day, and sleeping in the entry by night. Everybody is concerned; clients are leaving the offices; some fears are entertained of a mob; something you must do, and that without delay."

Aghast at this torrent, I fell back before it, and would fain have locked myself in my new quarters. In vain I persisted that Bartleby was nothing to me—no more than to any one else. In vain—I was the last person known to have anything to do with him, and they held me to the terrible account. Fearful, then, of being exposed in the papers (as one person present obscurely threatened), I considered the matter, and, at length, said, that if the lawyer would give me a confidential interview with the scrivener, in his (the lawyer's) own room, I would, that afternoon, strive my best to rid them of the nuisance they complained of.

Going up stairs to my old haunt, there was Bartleby silently sitting upon the banister at the landing.

"What are you doing here, Bartleby?" said I.

"Sitting upon the banister," he mildly replied.

I motioned him into the lawyer's room, who then left us.

"Bartleby," said I, "are you aware that you are the cause of great tribulation to me, by persisting in occupying the entry after being dismissed from the office?"

No answer.

"Now one of two things must take place. Either you must do something, or something must be done to you. Now what sort of business would you like to engage in? Would you like to re-engage in copying for some one?"

"No; I would prefer not to make any change."

"Would you like a clerkship in a dry-goods store?"

"There is too much confinement about that. No, I would not like a clerkship; but I am not particular."

"Too much confinement," I cried, "why you keep yourself confined all the time!"

"I would prefer not to take a clerkship," he rejoined, as if to settle that little item at once.

"How would a bar-tender's business suit you? There is no trying of the eye-sight in that."

"I would not like it at all; though, as I said before, I am not particular."

His unwonted wordiness inspirited me. I returned to the charge.

"Well, then, would you like to travel through the country collecting bills for the merchants? That would improve your health."

"No, I would prefer to be doing something else."

"How, then, would going as a companion to Europe, to entertain some young gentleman with your conversation—how would that suit you?"

"Not at all. It does not strike me that there is anything definite about that. I like to be stationary. But I am not particular."

"Stationary you shall be, then," I cried, now losing all patience, and, for the first time in all my exasperating connection with him, fairly flying into a passion. "If you do not go away from these premises before night, I shall feel bound—indeed, I *am* bound—to—to—to quit the premises myself!" I rather absurdly concluded, knowing not with what possible threat to try to frighten his immobility into compliance. Despairing of all further efforts, I was precipitately leaving him, when a final thought occurred to me—one which had not been wholly unindulged before.

"Bartleby," said I, in the kindest tone I could assume under such exciting circumstances, "will you go home with me now—not to my office, but my dwelling—and remain there till we can conclude upon some convenient arrangement for you at our leisure? Come, let us start now, right away."

"No: at present I would prefer not to make any change at all."

I answered nothing; but, effectually dodging every one by the suddenness and rapidity of my flight, rushed from the building, ran up Wall Street towards Broadway, and, jumping into the first omnibus, was soon removed from pursuit. As soon as tranquillity returned, I distinctly perceived that I had now done all that I possibly could, both in respect to the demands of the landlord and his tenants, and with regard to my own desire and sense of duty, to benefit Bartleby, and shield him from rude persecution. I now strove to be entirely care-free and quiescent; and my conscience justified me in the attempt; though, indeed, it was not so successful as I could have wished. So fearful was I of being again hunted out by the incensed landlord and his exasperated tenants, that, surrendering my business to Nippers, for a few days, I drove about the upper part of the town and through the suburbs, in my rockaway;[12] crossed over to Jersey City and Hoboken, and paid fugitive visits to Manhattanville and Astoria. In fact, I almost lived in my rockaway for the time.

When again I entered my office, lo, a note from the landlord lay upon the desk. I opened it with trembling hands. It informed me that the writer had sent to the police, and had Bartleby removed to the Tombs as a vagrant. Moreover, since I knew more about him than any one else, he wished me to appear at that place, and make a suitable statement of the facts. These tidings had a conflicting effect upon me. At first I was

---

[12] Carriage.

indignant; but, at last, almost approved. The landlord's energetic, summary disposition, had led him to adopt a procedure which I do not think I would have decided upon myself; and yet, as a last resort, under such peculiar circumstances, it seemed the only plan.

As I afterwards learned, the poor scrivener, when told that he must be conducted to the Tombs, offered not the slightest obstacle; but, in his pale, unmoving way, silently acquiesced.

Some of the compassionate and curious bystanders joined the party; and headed by one of the constables arm in arm with Bartleby, the silent procession filed its way through all the noise, and heat, and joy of the roaring thoroughfares at noon.

The same day I received the note, I went to the Tombs, or, to speak more properly, the Halls of Justice. Seeking the right officer, I stated the purpose of my call, and was informed that the individual I described was, indeed, within. I then assured the functionary that Bartleby was a perfectly honest man, and greatly to be compassionated, however unaccountably eccentric. I narrated all I knew, and closed by suggesting the idea of letting him remain in as indulgent confinement as possible, till something less harsh might be done—though, indeed, I hardly knew what. At all events, if nothing else could be decided upon, the alms-house must receive him. I then begged to have an interview.

Being under no disgraceful charge, and quite serene and harmless in all his ways, they had permitted him freely to wander about the prison, and, especially, in the inclosed grass-platted yards thereof. And so I found him there, standing all alone in the quietest of the yards, his face towards a high wall, while all around, from the narrow slits of the jail windows, I thought I saw peering out upon him the eyes of murderers and thieves.

"Bartleby!"

"I know you," he said, without looking around—"and I want nothing to say to you."

"It was not I that brought you here, Bartleby," said I, keenly pained at his implied suspicion. "And to you, this should not be so vile a place. Nothing reproachful attaches to you by being here. And see, it is not so sad a place as one might think. Look, there is the sky, and here is the grass."

"I know where I am," he replied, but would say nothing more, and so I left him.

As I entered the corridor again, a broad meat-like man, in an apron, accosted me, and, jerking his thumb over his shoulder, said—"Is that your friend?"

"Yes."

"Does he want to starve? If he does, let him live on the prison fare, that's all."

"Who are you?" asked I, not knowing what to make of such an unofficially speaking person in such a place.

"I am the grub-man. Such gentlemen as have friends here, hire me to provide them with something good to eat."

"Is this so?" said I, turning to the turnkey.

He said it was.

"Well, then," said I, slipping some silver into the grub-man's hands (for so they called him), "I want you to give particular attention to my friend there; let him have the best dinner you can get. And you must be as polite to him as possible."

"Introduce me, will you?" said the grub-man, looking at me with an expression which seemed to say he was all impatience for an opportunity to give a specimen of his breeding.

Thinking it would prove of benefit to the scrivener, I acquiesced; and, asking the grub-man his name, went up with him to Bartleby.

"Bartleby, this is a friend; you will find him very useful to you."

"Your sarvant, sir, your sarvant," said the grub-man, making a low salutation behind his apron. "Hope you find it pleasant here, sir; nice grounds—cool apartments —hope you'll stay with us sometime—try to make it agreeable. What will you have for dinner to-day?"

"I prefer not to dine to-day," said Bartleby, turning away. "It would disagree with me; I am unused to dinners." So saying, he slowly moved to the other side of the inclosure, and took up a position fronting the dead-wall.

"How's this?" said the grub-man, addressing me with a stare of astonishment. "He's odd, ain't he?"

"I think he is a little deranged," said I, sadly.

"Deranged? deranged is it? Well, now, upon my word, I thought that friend of yourn was a gentleman forger; they are always pale and genteel-like, them forgers. I can't help pity 'em—can't help it, sir. Did you know Monroe Edwards?"[13] he added, touchingly, and paused. Then, laying his hand piteously on my shoulder, sighed, "he died of consumption at Sing-Sing. So you weren't acquainted with Monroe?"

"No, I was never socially acquainted with any forgers. But I cannot stop longer. Look to my friend yonder. You will not lose by it. I will see you again."

Some few days after this, I again obtained admission to the Tombs, and went through the corridors in quest of Bartleby; but without finding him.

"I saw him coming from his cell not long ago," said a turnkey, "may be he's gone to loiter in the yards."

So I went in that direction.

"Are you looking for the silent man?" said another turnkey, passing me. "Yonder he lies—sleeping in the yard there. 'Tis not twenty minutes since I saw him lie down."

The yard was entirely quiet. It was not accessible to the common prisoners. The surrounding walls, of amazing thickness, kept off all sounds behind them. The Egyptian character of the masonry weighed upon me with its gloom. But a soft imprisoned turf grew under foot. The heart of the eternal pyramids, it seemed, wherein, by some strange magic, through the clefts, grass-seed, dropped by birds, had sprung.

Strangely huddled at the base of the wall, his knees drawn up, and lying on his side, his head touching the cold stones, I saw the wasted Bartleby. But nothing stirred. I paused; then went close up to him; stooped over, and saw that his dim eyes were open; otherwise he seemed profoundly sleeping. Something prompted me to touch him. I felt his hand, when a tingling shiver ran up my arm and down my spine to my feet.

The round face of the grub-man peered upon me now. "His dinner is ready. Won't he dine to-day, either? Or does he live without dining?"

"Lives without dining," said I, and closed the eyes.

"Eh!—He's asleep, ain't he?"

---

[13] Financier convicted in 1842 of forgery and swindle.

"With kings and counselors,"[14] murmured I.

There would seem little need for proceeding further in this history. Imagination will readily supply the meagre recital of poor Bartleby's interment. But, ere parting with the reader, let me say, that if this little narrative has sufficiently interested him, to awaken curiosity as to who Bartleby was, and what manner of life he led prior to the present narrator's making his acquaintance, I can only reply, that in such curiosity I fully share, but am wholly unable to gratify it. Yet here I hardly know whether I should divulge one little item of rumor, which came to my ear a few months after the scrivener's decease. Upon what basis it rested, I could never ascertain; and hence, how true it is I cannot now tell. But, inasmuch as this vague report has not been without a certain suggestive interest to me, however sad, it may prove the same with some others; and so I will briefly mention it. The report was this: that Bartleby had been a subordinate clerk in the Dead Letter Office at Washington, from which he had been suddenly removed by a change in the administration. When I think over this rumor, hardly can I express the emotions which seize me. Dead letters! does it not sound like dead men? Conceive a man by nature and misfortune prone to a pallid hopelessness, can any business seem more fitted to heighten it than that of continually handling these dead letters, and assorting them for the flames? For by the cart-load they are annually burned. Sometimes from out the folded paper the pale clerk takes a ring—the finger it was meant for, perhaps, moulders in the grave; a bank-note sent in swiftest charity—he whom it would relieve, nor eats nor hungers any more; pardon for those who died despairing; hope for those who died unhoping; good tidings for those who died stifled by unrelieved calamities. On errands of life, these letters speed to death.

Ah, Bartleby! Ah, humanity!

1853/1856

The Paradise of Bachelors
and the Tartarus of Maids

I: The Paradise of Bachelors

It lies not far from Temple Bar.[1]

Going to it, by the usual way, is like stealing from a heated plain into some cool, deep glen, shady among harboring hills.

Sick with the din and soiled with the mud of Fleet Street—where the Benedick[2] tradesmen are hurrying by, with ledger-lines ruled along their brows, thinking upon rise of bread and fall of babies—you adroitly turn a mystic corner—not a street—

---

[14] Job 3:14.
[1] Chambers principally of barristers or attorneys in London; also name of the gateway closing the entrance to the City of London (removed in 1878).

[2] Determined bachelor in Shakespeare's comedy *Much Ado About Nothing* (ca. 1598).

glide down a dim, monastic way, flanked by dark, sedate, and solemn piles, and still wending on, give the whole care-worn world the slip, and, disentangled, stand beneath the quiet cloisters of the Paradise of Bachelors.

Sweet are the oases in Sahara; charming the isle-groves of August prairies; delectable pure faith amidst a thousand perfidies; but sweeter, still more charming, most delectable, the dreamy Paradise of Bachelors, found in the stony heart of stunning London.

In mild meditation pace the cloisters; take your pleasure, sip your leisure, in the garden waterward; go linger in the ancient library; go worship in the sculptured chapel; but little have you seen, just nothing do you know, not the sweet kernel have you tasted, till you dine among the banded Bachelors, and see their convivial eyes and glasses sparkle. Not dine in bustling commons, during term-time, in the hall; but tranquilly, by private hint, at a private table; some fine Templar's[3] hospitably invited guest.

Templar? That's a romantic name. Let me see. Brian de Bois-Guilbert was a Templar, I believe. Do we understand you to insinuate that those famous Templars still survive in modern London? May the ring of their armed heels be heard, and the rattle of their shields, as in mailed prayer the monk-knights kneel before the consecrated Host? Surely a monk-knight were a curious sight picking his way along the Strand, his gleaming corselet[4] and snowy surcoat spattered by an omnibus. Long-bearded, too, according to his order's rule; his face fuzzy as a pard's;[5] how would the grim ghost look among the crop-haired, close-shaven citizens? We know indeed— sad history recounts it—that a moral blight tainted at last this sacred Brotherhood. Though no sworded foe might outskill them in the fence, yet the worm of luxury crawled beneath their guard, gnawing the core of knightly troth, nibbling the monastic vow, till at last the monk's austerity relaxed to wassailing, and the sworn knights-bachelors grew to be but hypocrites and rakes.

But for all this, quite unprepared were we to learn that Knights-Templars (if at all in being) were so entirely secularized as to be reduced from carving out immortal fame in glorious battling for the Holy Land, to the carving of roast-mutton at a dinner-board. Like Anacreon,[6] do these degenerate Templars now think it sweeter far to fall in banquet than in war? Or, indeed, how can there be any survival of that famous order? Templars in modern London! Templars in their red-cross mantles smoking cigars at the Divan! Templars crowded in a railway train, till, stacked with steel helmet, spear, and shield, the whole train looks like one elongated locomotive!

No. The genuine Templar is long since departed. Go view the wondrous tombs in the Temple Church; see there the rigidly-haughty forms stretched out, with crossed arms upon their stilly hearts, in everlasting and undreaming rest. Like the years before the flood, the bold Knights-Templars are no more. Nevertheless, the name remains, and the nominal society, and the ancient grounds, and some of the ancient edifices.

---

[3] Member of a military and religious order founded in 1118 for the protection of the Holy Sepulchre and of Christian pilgrims visiting the Holy Land.

[4] Suit of light armor over which an embroidered outer coat, or surcoat, was often worn.

[5] Pard: medieval word for leopard.

[6] Sixth-century Greek lyric poet of love and wine.

But the iron heel is changed to a boot of patent-leather; the long two-handed sword to a one-handed quill; the monk-giver of gratuitous ghostly counsel now counsels for a fee; the defender of the sarcophagus (if in good practice with his weapon) now has more than one case to defend; the vowed opener and clearer of all highways leading to the Holy Sepulchre, now has it in particular charge to check, to clog, to hinder, and embarrass all the courts and avenues of Law; the knight-combatant of the Saracen,[7] breasting spear-points at Acre, now fights law-points in Westminster Hall. The helmet is a wig. Struck by Time's enchanter's wand, the Templar is to-day a Lawyer.

But, like many others tumbled from proud glory's height—like the apple, hard on the bough but mellow on the ground—the Templar's fall has but made him all the finer fellow.

I dare say those old warrior-priests were but gruff and grouty at the best; cased in Birmingham[8] hardware, how could their crimped arms give yours or mine a hearty shake? Their proud, ambitious, monkish souls clasped shut, like horn-book missals; their very faces clapped in bomb-shells; what sort of genial men were these? But best of comrades, most affable of hosts, capital diner is the modern Templar. His wit and wine are both of sparkling brands.

The church and cloisters, courts and vaults, lanes and passages, banquet-halls, refectories, libraries, terraces, gardens, broad walks, domiciles, and dessert-rooms, covering a very large space of ground, and all grouped in central neighborhood, and quite sequestered from the old city's surrounding din; and everything about the place being kept in most bachelor-like particularity, no part of London offers to a quiet wight so agreeable a refuge.

The Temple is, indeed, a city by itself. A city with all the best appurtenances, as the above enumeration shows. A city with a park to it, and flower-beds, and a river-side—the Thames flowing by as openly, in one part, as by Eden's primal garden flowed the mild Euphrates. In what is now the Temple Garden the old Crusaders used to exercise their steeds and lances; the modern Templars now lounge on the benches beneath the trees, and, switching their patent-leather boots, in gay discourse exercise at repartee.

Long lines of stately portraits in the banquet-halls, show what great men of mark —famous nobles, judges, and Lord Chancellors—have in their time been Templars. But all Templars are not known to universal fame; though, if the having warm hearts and warmer welcomes, full minds and fuller cellars, and giving good advice and glorious dinners, spiced with rare divertisements of fun and fancy, merit immortal mention, set down, ye muses, the names of R. F. C. and his imperial brother.

Though to be a Templar, in the one true sense, you must needs be a lawyer, or a student at the law, and be ceremoniously enrolled as member of the order, yet as many such, though Templars, do not reside within the Temple's precincts, though they may have their offices there, just so, on the other hand, there are many residents of the hoary old domiciles who are not admitted Templars. If being, say, a lounging gentleman and bachelor, or a quiet, unmarried, literary man, charmed with the soft seclusion of the spot, you much desire to pitch your shady tent among the rest in this

---

[7] Member of Muslim nomadic tribes on the Syrian borders of the Roman Empire.

[8] English city noted for manufacture of steel and armaments.

serene encampment, then you must make some special friend among the order, and procure him to rent, in his name but at your charge, whatever vacant chamber you may find to suit.

Thus, I suppose, did Dr. Johnson,[9] that nominal Benedick and widower but virtual bachelor, when for a space he resided here. So, too, did that undoubted bachelor and rare good soul, Charles Lamb.[10] And hundreds more, of sterling spirits, Brethren of the Order of Celibacy, from time to time have dined, and slept, and tabernacled here. Indeed, the place is all a honey-comb of offices and domiciles. Like any cheese, it is quite perforated through and through in all directions with the snug cells of bachelors. Dear, delightful spot! Ah! when I bethink me of the sweet hours there passed, enjoying such genial hospitalities beneath those time-honored roofs, my heart only finds due utterance through poetry; and, with a sigh, I softly sing, "Carry me back to old Virginny!"

Such then, at large, is the Paradise of Bachelors. And such I found it one pleasant afternoon in the smiling month of May, when, sallying from my hotel in Trafalgar Square, I went to keep my dinner-appointment with that fine Barrister, Bachelor, and Bencher, R. F. C. (he *is* the first and second, and *should be* the third; I hereby nominate him), whose card I kept fast pinched between my gloved forefinger and thumb, and every now and then snatched still another look at the pleasant address inscribed beneath the name, "No——, Elm Court, Temple."

At the core he was a right bluff, care-free, right comfortable, and most companionable Englishman. If on a first acquaintance he seemed reserved, quite icy in his air— patience; this Champagne will thaw. And if it never do, better frozen Champagne than liquid vinegar.

There were nine gentlemen, all bachelors, at the dinner. One was from "No. ———, King's Bench Walk, Temple"; a second, third, and fourth, and fifth, from various courts or passages christened with some similarly rich resounding syllables. It was, indeed, a sort of Senate of the Bachelors, sent to this dinner from widely scattered districts, to represent the general celibacy of the Temple. Nay, it was, by representation, a Grand Parliament of the best Bachelors in universal London; several of those present being from distant quarters of the town, noted immemorial seats of lawyers and unmarried men—Lincoln's Inn, Furnival's Inn; and one gentleman, upon whom I looked with a sort of collateral awe, hailed from the spot where Lord Verulam once abode a bachelor—Gray's Inn.[11]

The apartment was well up toward heaven. I know not how many strange old stairs I climbed to get to it. But a good dinner, with famous company, should be well earned. No doubt our host had his dining-room so high with a view to secure the prior exercise necessary to the due relishing and digesting of it.

The furniture was wonderfully unpretending, old, and snug. No new shining mahogany, sticky with undried varnish; no uncomfortably luxurious ottomans, and sofas too fine to use, vexed you in this sedate apartment. It is a thing which every sensible American should learn from every sensible Englishman, that glare and glitter, gim-cracks and gewgaws, are not indispensable to domestic solacement. The American

[9] Samuel Johnson (1709–1784), English writer and lexicographer.
[10] English essayist and critic (1775–1834).

[11] Lincoln's Inn, Furnival's Inn, and Grey's Inn were legal societies

Benedick snatches, down-town, a tough chop in a gilded show-box; the English bachelor leisurely dines at home on that incomparable South Down of his, off a plain deal board.

The ceiling of the room was low. Who wants to dine under the dome of St. Peter's? High ceilings! If that is your demand, and the higher the better, and you be so very tall, then go dine out with the topping giraffe in the open air.

In good time the nine gentlemen sat down to nine covers, and soon were fairly under way.

If I remember right, ox-tail soup inaugurated the affair. Of a rich russet hue, its agreeable flavor dissipated my first confounding of its main ingredient with teamsters' gads and the raw-hides[12] of ushers. (By way of interlude, we here drank a little claret.) Neptune's[13] was the next tribute rendered—turbot coming second; snow-white, flaky, and just gelatinous enough, not too turtleish in its unctuousness.

(At this point we refreshed ourselves with a glass of sherry.) After these light skirmishers had vanished, the heavy artillery of the feast marched in, led by that well-known English generalissimo, roast beef. For aides-de-camp we had a saddle of mutton, a fat turkey, a chicken-pie, and endless other savory things; while for avant-couriers came nine silver flagons of humming ale. This heavy ordnance having departed on the track of the light skirmishers, a picked brigade of game-fowl encamped upon the board, their camp-fires lit by the ruddiest of decanters.

Tarts and puddings followed, with innumerable niceties; then cheese and crackers. (By way of ceremony, simply, only to keep up good old fashions, we here each drank a glass of good old port.)

The cloth was now removed; and, like Blucher's[14] army coming in at the death on the field of Waterloo, in marched a fresh detachment of bottles, dusty with their hurried march.

All these manoeuvrings of the forces were superintended by a surprising old field-marshal (I can not school myself to call him by the inglorious name of waiter), with snowy hair and napkin, and a head like Socrates. Amidst all the hilarity of the feast, intent on important business, he disdained to smile. Venerable man!

I have above endeavored to give some slight schedule of the general plan of operations. But any one knows that a good, genial dinner is a sort of pell-mell, indiscriminate affair, quite baffling to detail in all particulars. Thus, I spoke of taking a glass of claret, and a glass of sherry, and a glass of port, and a mug of ale—all at certain specific periods and times. But those were merely the state bumpers,[15] so to speak. Innumerable impromptu glasses were drained between the periods of those grand imposing ones.

The nine bachelors seemed to have the most tender concern for each other's health. All the time, in flowing wine, they most earnestly expressed their sincerest wishes for the entire well-being and lasting hygiene of the gentleman on the right and on the left. I noticed that when one of these kind bachelors desired a little more wine (just for his stomach's sake, like Timothy,[16]) he would not help himself to it unless some

---

[12] Whips.

[13] I.e., for the Roman god of the sea; hence the fish, turbot.

[14] Gebhart von Blucher (1742–1819), Prussian field marshal.

[15] Cups or glasses filled to the brim.

[16] Disciple and companion of the Apostle Paul, to whom Paul addressed two Epistles, 1 Timothy and 2 Timothy.

other bachelor would join him. It seemed held something indelicate, selfish, and unfraternal, to be seen taking a lonely, unparticipated glass. Meantime, as the wine ran apace, the spirits of the company grew more and more to perfect genialness and unconstraint. They related all sorts of pleasant stories. Choice experiences in their private lives were now brought out, like choice brands of Moselle or Rhenish, only kept for particular company. One told us how mellowly he lived when a student at Oxford; with various spicy anecdotes of most frank-hearted noble lords, his liberal companions. Another bachelor, a gray-headed man, with a sunny face, who, by his own account, embraced every opportunity of leisure to cross over into the Low Countries, on sudden tours of inspection of the fine old Flemish architecture there —this learned, white-haired, sunny-faced old bachelor excelled in his descriptions of the elaborate splendors of those old guild-halls, town-halls, and stadthold-houses, to be seen in the land of the ancient Flemings. A third was a great frequenter of the British Museum, and knew all about scores of wonderful antiquities, of Oriental manuscripts, and costly books without a duplicate. A fourth had lately returned from a trip to Old Granada, and, of course, was full of Saracenic scenery. A fifth had a funny case in law to tell. A sixth was erudite in wines. A seventh had a strange characteristic anecdote of the private life of the Iron Duke, never printed, and never before announced in any public or private company. An eighth had lately been amusing his evenings, now and then, with translating a comic poem of Pulci's. He quoted for us the more amusing passages.

And so the evening slipped along, the hours told, not by a water-clock, like King Alfred's, but a wine-chronometer. Meantime the table seemed a sort of Epsom Heath;[17] a regular ring, where the decanters galloped round. For fear one decanter should not with sufficient speed reach his destination, another was sent express after him to hurry him; and then a third to hurry the second; and so on with a fourth and fifth. And throughout all this nothing loud, nothing unmannerly, nothing turbulent. I am quite sure, from the scrupulous gravity and austerity of his air, that had Socrates, the field-marshal, perceived aught of indecorum in the company he served, he would have forthwith departed without giving warning. I afterward learned that, during the repast, an invalid bachelor in an adjoining chamber enjoyed his first sound refreshing slumber in three long, weary weeks.

It was the very perfection of quiet absorption of good living, good drinking, good feeling, and good talk. We were a band of brothers. Comfort—fraternal, household comfort, was the grand trait of the affair. Also, you could plainly see that these easy-hearted men had no wives or children to give an anxious thought. Almost all of them were travelers, too; for bachelors alone can travel freely, and without any twinges of their consciences touching desertion of the fireside.

The thing called pain, the bugbear styled trouble—those two legends seemed preposterous to their bachelor imaginations. How could men of liberal sense, ripe scholarship in the world, and capacious philosophical and convivial understandings —how could they suffer themselves to be imposed upon by such monkish fables? Pain! Trouble! As well talk of Catholic miracles. No such thing.—Pass the sherry, sir.— Pooh, pooh! Can't be!—The port, sir, if you please. Nonsense; don't tell me so.— The decanter stops with you, sir, I believe.

[17] Racetrack.

And so it went.

Not long after the cloth was drawn our host glanced significantly upon Socrates, who, solemnly stepping to a stand, returned with an immense convolved horn, a regular Jericho horn,[18] mounted with polished silver, and otherwise chased and curiously enriched; not omitting two life-like goats' heads, with four more horns of solid silver, projecting from opposite sides of the mouth of the noble main horn.

Not having heard that our host was a performer on the bugle, I was surprised to see him lift this horn from the table, as if he were about to blow an inspiring blast. But I was relieved from this, and set quite right as touching the purposes of the horn, by his now inserting his thumb and forefinger into its mouth; whereupon a slight aroma was stirred up, and my nostrils were greeted with the smell of some choice Rappee. It was a mull of snuff. It went the rounds. Capital idea this, thought I, of taking snuff about this juncture. This goodly fashion must be introduced among my countrymen at home, further ruminated I.

The remarkable decorum of the nine bachelors—a decorum not to be affected by any quantity of wine—a decorum unassailable by any degree of mirthfulness—this was again set in a forcible light to me, by now observing that, though they took snuff very freely, yet not a man so far violated the proprieties, or so far molested the invalid bachelor in the adjoining room as to indulge himself in a sneeze. The snuff was snuffed silently, as if it had been some fine innoxious powder brushed off the wings of butterflies.

But fine though they be, bachelors' dinners, like bachelors' lives, can not endure forever. The time came for breaking up. One by one the bachelors took their hats, and two by two, and arm-in-arm they descended, still conversing, to the flagging of the court; some going to their neighboring chambers to turn over the *Decameron* ere retiring for the night; some to smoke a cigar, promenading in the garden on the cool river-side; some to make for the street, call a hack, and be driven snugly to their distant lodgings.

I was the last lingerer.

"Well," said my smiling host, "what do you think of the Temple here, and the sort of life we bachelors make out to live in it?"

"Sir," said I, with a burst of admiring candor—"Sir, this is the very Paradise of Bachelors!"

II: The Tartarus[19] of Maids

It lies not far from Woedolor Mountain in New England. Turning to the East, right out from among bright farms and sunny meadows, nodding in early June with odorous grasses, you enter ascendingly among bleak hills. These gradually close in upon a dusky pass, which, from the violent Gulf Stream of air unceasingly driving between its cloven walls of haggard rock, as well as from the tradition of a crazy spinster's hut having long ago stood somewhere hereabouts, is called the Mad Maid's Bellows-pipe.

Winding along at the bottom of the gorge is a dangerously narrow wheel-road, occupying the bed of a former torrent. Following this road to its highest point, you

[18] Ram's horn made into a wind instrument.   [19] In Greek myth, a sunless abyss below Hades.

stand as within a Dantean[20] gateway. From the steepness of the walls here, their strangely ebon hue, and the sudden contraction of the gorge, this particular point is called the Black Notch. The ravine now expandingly descends into a great, purple, hopper-shaped hollow, far sunk among many Plutonian,[21] shaggy-wooded mountains. By the country people this hollow is called the Devil's Dungeon. Sounds of torrents fall on all sides upon the ear. These rapid waters unite at last in one turbid brick-colored stream, boiling through a flume among enormous boulders. They call this strange-colored torrent Blood River. Gaining a dark precipice it wheels suddenly to the West, and makes one maniac spring of sixty feet into the arms of a stunted wood of gray-haired pines, between which it thence eddies on its further way down to the invisible low-lands.

Conspicuously crowning a rocky bluff high to one side, at the cataract's verge, is the ruin of an old saw-mill, built in those primitive times when vast pines and hemlocks superabounded throughout the neighboring region. The black-mossed bulk of those immense, rough-hewn, and spike-knotted logs, here and there tumbled all together, in long abandonment and decay, or left in solitary, perilous projection over the cataract's gloomy brink, impart to this rude wooden ruin not only much of the aspect of one of rough-quarried stone, but also a sort of feudal, Rhineland, and Thurmberg[22] look, derived from the pinnacled wildness of the neighboring scenery.

Not far from the bottom of the Dungeon stands a large whitewashed building, relieved, like some great whited sepulchre, against the sullen background of mountain-side firs, and other hardy evergreens, inaccessibly rising in grim terraces for some two thousand feet.

The building is a paper-mill.

Having embarked on a large scale in the seedsman's business (so extensively and broadcast, indeed, that at length my seeds were distributed through all the Eastern and Northern States, and even fell into the far soil of Missouri and the Carolinas), the demand for paper at my place became so great, that the expenditure soon amounted to a most important item in the general account. It need hardly be hinted how paper comes into use with seedsmen, as envelopes. These are mostly made of yellowish paper, folded square; and when filled, are all but flat, and being stamped, and superscribed with the nature of the seeds contained, assume not a little the appearance of business-letters ready for the mail. Of these small envelopes I used an incredible quantity—several hundreds of thousands in a year. For a time I had purchased my paper from the wholesale dealers in a neighboring town. For economy's sake, and partly for the adventure of the trip, I now resolved to cross the mountains, some sixty miles, and order my future paper at the Devil's Dungeon paper-mill.

The sleighing being uncommonly fine toward the end of January, and promising to hold so for no small period, in spite of the bitter cold I started one gray Friday noon in my pung,[23] well fitted with buffalo and wolf robes; and, spending one night on the road, next noon came in sight of Woedolor Mountain.

The far summit fairly smoked with frost; white vapors curled up from its white-

---

[20] Dante Alighieri (1265–1321), Italian poet of whose allegorical epic poem, *Divine Comedy*, the *Inferno* is a part.
[21] In Greek myth, Pluto or Hades is the god of the underworld or region of the dead.

[22] German forest lands.
[23] Boxlike sleigh on runners.

wooded top, as from a chimney. The intense congelation made the whole country look like one petrifaction.[24] The steel shoes of my pung craunched and gritted over the vitreous, chippy snow, as if it had been broken glass. The forests here and there skirting the route, feeling the same all-stiffening influence, their inmost fibres penetrated with the cold, strangely groaned—not in the swaying branches merely, but likewise in the vertical trunk—as the fitful gusts remorselessly swept through them. Brittle with excessive frost, many colossal tough-grained maples, snapped in twin like pipestems, cumbered the unfeeling earth.

Flaked all over with frozen sweat, white as a milky ram, his nostrils at each breath sending forth two horn-shaped shoots of heated respiration, Black, my good horse, but six years old, started at a sudden turn, where, right across the track—not ten minutes fallen—an old distorted hemlock lay, darkly undulatory as an anaconda.

Gaining the Bellows-pipe, the violent blast, dead from behind, all but shoved my high-backed pung up-hill. The gust shrieked through the shivered pass, as if laden with lost spirits bound to the unhappy world. Ere gaining the summit, Black, my horse, as if exasperated by the cutting wind, slung out with his strong hind legs, tore the light pung straight up-hill, and sweeping grazingly through the narrow notch, sped downward madly past the ruined saw-mill. Into the Devil's Dungeon horse and cataract rushed together.

With might and main, quitting my seat and robes, and standing backward, with one foot braced against the dashboard, I rasped and churned the bit, and stopped him just in time to avoid collision, at a turn, with the bleak nozzle of a rock, couchant like a lion in the way—a roadside rock.

At first I could not discover the paper-mill.

The whole hollow gleamed with the white, except, here and there, where a pinnacle of granite showed one wind-swept angle bare. The mountains stood pinned in shrouds—a pass of Alpine corpses. Where stands the mill? Suddenly a whirring, humming sound broke upon my ear. I looked, and there, like an arrested avalanche, lay the large whitewashed factory. It was subordinately surrounded by a cluster of other and smaller buildings, some of which, from their cheap, blank air, great length, gregarious windows, and comfortless expression, no doubt were boarding-houses of the operatives.[25] A snow-white hamlet amidst the snows. Various rude, irregular squares and courts resulted from the somewhat picturesque clusterings of these buildings, owing to the broken, rocky nature of the ground, which forbade all method in their relative arrangement. Several narrow lanes and alleys, too, partly blocked with snow fallen from the roof, cut up the hamlet in all directions.

When, turning from the traveled highway, jingling with bells of numerous farmers —who, availing themselves of the fine sleighing, were dragging their wood to market —and frequently diversified with swift cutters dashing from inn to inn of the scattered villages—when, I say, turning from that bustling main-road, I by degrees wound into the Mad Maid's Bellows-pipe, and saw the grim Black Notch beyond, then something latent, as well as something obvious in the time and scene, strangely brought back to my mind my first sight of dark and grimy Temple Bar. And when Black, my horse, went darting through the Notch, perilously grazing its rocky wall, I remembered being in a runaway London omnibus, which in much the same sort of style, though

---

[24] I.e., in the process of petrifying.   [25] Factory workers.

by no means at an equal rate, dashed through the ancient arch of Wren.[26] Though the two objects did by no means completely correspond, yet this partial inadequacy but served to tinge the similitude not less with the vividness than the disorder of a dream. So that, when upon reining up at the protruding rock I at last caught sight of the quaint groupings of the factory-buildings, and with the traveled highway and the Notch behind, found myself all alone, silently and privily stealing through deep-cloven passages into this sequestered spot, and saw the long, high-gabled main factory edifice, with a rude tower—for hoisting heavy boxes—at one end, standing among its crowded outbuildings and boarding-houses, as the Temple Church amidst the surrounding offices and dormitories, and when the marvelous retirement of this mysterious mountain nook fastened its whole spell upon me, then, what memory lacked, all tributary imagination furnished, and I said to myself, "This is the very counterpart of the Paradise of Bachelors, but snowed upon, and frost-painted to a sepulchre."

Dismounting and warily picking my way down the dangerous declivity—horse and man both sliding now and then upon the icy ledges—at length I drove, or the blast drove me, into the largest square, before one side of the main edifice. Piercingly and shrilly the shotted blast blew by the corner; and redly and demoniacally boiled Blood River at one side. A long wood-pile, of many scores of cords, all glittering in mail of crusted ice, stood crosswise in the square. A row of horse-posts, their north sides plastered with adhesive snow, flanked the factory wall. The bleak frost packed and paved the square as with some ringing metal.

The inverted similitude recurred—"The sweet, tranquil Temple garden, with the Thames bordering its green beds," strangely mediated I.

But where are the gay bachelors?

Then, as I and my horse stood shivering in the wind-spray, a girl ran from a neighboring dormitory door, and throwing her thin apron over her bare head, made for the opposite building.

"One moment, my girl; is there no shed hereabouts which I may drive into?"

Pausing, she turned upon me a face pale with work, and blue with cold; an eye supernatural with unrelated misery.

"Nay," faltered I, "I mistook you. Go on; I want nothing."

Leading my horse close to the door from which she had come, I knocked. Another pale, blue girl appeared, shivering in the doorway as, to prevent the blast, she jealously held the door ajar.

"Nay, I mistake again. In God's name shut the door. But hold, is there no man about?"

That moment a dark-complexioned, well-wrapped personage passed, making for the factory door, and spying him coming, the girl rapidly closed the other one.

"Is there no horse-shed here, sir?"

"Yonder, to the wood-shed," he replied, and disappeared inside the factory.

With much ado I managed to wedge in horse and pung between the scattered piles of wood all sawn and split. Then, blanketing my horse, and piling my buffalo on the blanket's top, and tucking in its edges well around the breast-band and breeching, so

[26] Sir Christopher Wren (1632–1723), noted
English architect.

that the wind might not strip him bare, I tied him fast, and ran lamely for the factory door, stiff with frost, and cumbered with my driver's dread-naught.

Immediately I found myself standing in a spacious place, intolerably lighted by long rows of windows, focusing inward the snowy scene without.

At rows of blank-looking counters sat rows of blank-looking girls, with blank, white folders in their blank hands, all blankly folding blank paper.

In one corner stood some huge frame of ponderous iron, with a vertical thing like a piston periodically rising and falling upon a heavy wooden block. Before it—its tame minister—stood a tall girl, feeding the iron animal with half-quires[27] of rose-hued note-paper which, at every downward dab of the piston-like machine, received in the corner the impress of a wreath of roses. I looked from the rosy paper to the pallid cheek, but said nothing.

Seated before a long apparatus, strung with long, slender strings like any harp, another girl was feeding it with foolscap[28] sheets which, so soon as they curiously traveled from her on the cords, were withdrawn at the opposite end of the machine by a second girl. They came to the first girl blank; they went to the second girl ruled.

I looked upon the first girl's brow, and saw it was young and fair; I looked upon the second girl's brow, and saw it was ruled and wrinkled. Then, as I still looked, the two—for some small variety to the monotony—changed places; and where had stood the young, fair brow, now stood the ruled and wrinkled one.

Perched high upon a narrow platform, and still higher upon a high stool crowning it, sat another figure serving some other iron animal; while below the platform sat her mate in some sort of reciprocal attendance.

Not a syllable was breathed. Nothing was heard but the low, steady overruling hum of the iron animals. The human voice was banished from the spot. Machinery —that vaunted slave of humanity—here stood menially served by human beings, who served mutely and cringingly as the slave serves the Sultan. The girls did not so much seem accessory wheels to the general machinery as mere cogs to the wheels.

All this scene around me was instantaneously taken in at one sweeping glance— even before I had proceeded to unwind the heavy fur tippet[29] from around my neck. But as soon as this fell from me, the dark-complexioned man, standing close by, raised a sudden cry, and seizing my arm, dragged me out into the open air, and without pausing for a word instantly caught up some congealed snow and began rubbing both my cheeks.

"Two white spots like the whites of your eyes," he said; "man, your cheeks are frozen."

"That may well be," muttered I; " 'tis some wonder the frost of the Devil's Dungeon strikes in no deeper. Rub away."

Soon a horrible, tearing pain caught at my reviving cheeks. Two gaunt blood-hounds, one on each side, seemed mumbling them. I seemed Actaeon.[30]

Presently, when all was over, I re-entered the factory, made known my business, concluded it satisfactorily, and then begged to be conducted throughout the place to view it.

---

[27] Sets of uniform sheets of paper.
[28] A size (13 1/2 × 17 inches) of drawing or printing paper.

[29] Neck scarf.
[30] In Greek myth, hunter who was changed into a stag and torn to pieces by his own hounds.

"Cupid is the boy for that," said the dark-complexioned man. "Cupid!" and by this odd fancy-name calling a dimpled, red-cheeked, spirited-looking, forward little fellow, who was rather impudently, I thought, gliding about among the passive-looking girls—like a gold-fish through hueless waves—yet doing nothing in particular that I could see, the man bade him lead the stranger through the edifice.

"Come first and see the water-wheel," said this lively lad, with the air of boyishly-brisk importance.

Quitting the folding-room, we crossed some damp, cold boards, and stood beneath a great wet shed, incessantly showering with foam, like the green barnacled bow of some East Indiaman in a gale. Round and round here went the enormous revolutions of the dark colossal water-wheel, grim with its one immutable purpose.

"This sets our whole machinery a-going, sir; in every part of all these buildings; where the girls work and all."

I looked, and saw that the turbid waters of Blood River had not changed their hue by coming under the use of man.

"You make only blank paper; no printing of any sort, I suppose? All blank paper, don't you?"

"Certainly; what else should a paper-factory make?"

The lad here looked at me as if suspicious of my commonsense.

"Oh, to be sure!" said I, confused and stammering; "it only struck me as so strange that red waters should turn out pale chee—— paper, I mean."

He took me up a wet and rickety stair to a great light room, furnished with no visible thing but rude, manger-like receptacles running all round its sides; and up to these mangers, like so many mares haltered to the rack, stood rows of girls. Before each was vertically thrust up a long, glittering scythe, immovably fixed at bottom to the manger-edge. The curve of the scythe, and its having no snath to it, made it look exactly like a sword. To and fro, across the sharp edge, the girls forever dragged long strips of rags, washed white, picked from baskets at one side; thus ripping asunder every seam, and converting the tatters almost into lint. The air swam with the fine, poisonous particles, which from all sides darted, subtilely, as motes in sunbeams, into the lungs.

"This is the rag-room," coughed the boy.

"You find it rather stifling here," coughed I, in answer; "but the girls don't cough."

"Oh, they are used to it."

"Where do you get such hosts of rags?" picking up a handful from a basket.

"Some from the country round about; some from far over sea—Leghorn and London."

" 'Tis not unlikely, then," murmured I, "that among these heaps of rags there may be some old shirts, gathered from the dormitories of the Paradise of Bachelors. But the buttons are all dropped off. Pray, my lad, do you ever find any bachelors' buttons hereabouts?"

"None grow in this part of the country. The Devil's Dungeon is no place for flowers."

"Oh! you mean the *flowers* so called—the Bachelor's Buttons?"

"And was not that what you asked about? Or did you mean the gold bosom-buttons of our boss, Old Bach, as our whispering girls all call him?"

"The man, then, I saw below is a bachelor, is he?"

"Oh, yes, he's a Bach."

"The edges of those swords, they are turned outward from the girls, if I see right; but their rags and fingers fly so, I can not distinctly see."

"Turned outward."

Yes, murmured I to myself; I see it now; turned outward; and each erected sword is so borne, edge-outward, before each girl. If my reading fails me not, just so, of old, condemned state-prisoners went from the hall of judgment to their doom: an officer before, bearing a sword, its edge turned outward, in significance of their fatal sentence. So, through consumptive pallors of this blank, raggy life, go these white girls to death.

"Those scythes look very sharp," again turning toward the boy.

"Yes; they have to keep them so. Look!"

That moment two of the girls, dropping their rags, plied each a whet-stone up and down the sword-blade. My unaccustomed blood curdled at the sharp shriek of the tormented steel.

Their own executioners; themselves whetting the very swords that slay them; meditated I.

"What makes those girls so sheet-white, my lad?"

"Why"—with a roguish twinkle, pure ignorant drollery, not knowing heartlessness—"I suppose the handling of such white bits of sheets all the time makes them so sheety."

"Let us leave the rag-room now, my lad."

More tragical and more inscrutably mysterious than any mystic sight, human or machine, throughout the factory, was the strange innocence of cruel-heartedness in this usage-hardened boy.

"And now," said he, cheerily, "I suppose you want to see our great machine, which cost us twelve thousand dollars only last autumn. That's the machine that makes the paper, too. This way, sir."

Following him, I crossed a large, bespattered place, with two great round vats in it, full of a white, wet, woolly-looking stuff, not unlike the albuminous part of an egg, soft-boiled.

"There," said Cupid, tapping the vats carelessly, "these are the first beginnings of the paper, this white pulp you see. Look how it swims bubbling round and round, moved by the paddle here. From hence it pours from both vats into that one common channel yonder, and so goes, mixed up and leisurely, to the great machine. And now for that."

He led me into a room, stifling with a strange, blood-like, abdominal heat, as if here, true enough, were being finally developed the germinous particles lately seen.

Before me, rolled out like some long Eastern manuscript, lay stretched one continuous length of iron frame-word—multitudinous and mystical, with all sorts of rollers, wheels, and cylinders, in slowly-measured and unceasing motion.

"Here first comes the pulp now," said Cupid, pointing to the nighest end of the machine. "See; first it pours out and spreads itself upon this wide, sloping board; and then—look—slides, thin and quivering, beneath the first roller there. Follow on now, and see it as it slides from under that to the next cylinder. There; see how it has become just a very little less pulpy now. One step more, and it grows still more to some slight consistence. Still another cylinder, and it is so knitted—though as yet mere dragon-fly wing—that it forms an air-bridge here, like a suspended cobweb, between two more separated rollers; and flowing over the last one, and under again, and doubling about there out of sight for a minute among all those mixed cylinders you indistinctly see, it reappears here, looking now at last a little less like pulp and more like paper, but still quite delicate and defective yet awhile. But—a little further onward, sir, if you please—here now, at this further point, it puts on something of a real look, as if it might turn out to be something you might possibly handle in the end. But it's not yet done, sir. Good way to travel yet, and plenty more of cylinders must roll it."

"Bless my soul!" said I, amazed at the elongation, interminable convolutions, and deliberate slowness of the machine; "it must take a long time for the pulp to pass from end to end, and come out paper."

"Oh! not so long," smiled the precocious lad, with a superior and patronizing air; "only nine minutes. But look; you may try it for yourself. Have you a bit of paper? Ah! here's a bit on the floor. Now mark that with any word you please, and let me dab it on here, and we'll see how long before it comes out at the other end."

"Well, let me see," said I, taking out my pencil; "come, I'll mark it with your name."

Bidding me take out my watch, Cupid adroitly dropped the inscribed slip on an exposed part of the incipient mass.

Instantly my eye marked the second-hand on my dial-plate.

Slowly I followed the slip, inch by inch; sometimes pausing for full half a minute as it disappeared beneath inscrutable groups of the lower cylinders, but only gradually to emerge again; and so, on, and on, and on—inch by inch; now in open sight, sliding along like a freckle on the quivering sheet; and then again wholly vanished; and so, on, and on, and on—inch by inch; all the time the main sheet growing more and more to final firmness—when, suddenly, I saw a sort of paper-fall, not wholly unlike a water-fall; a scissory sound smote my ear, as of some cord being snapped; and down dropped an unfolded sheet of perfect foolscap, with my "Cupid" half faded out of it, and still moist and warm.

My travels were at an end, for here was the end of the machine.

"Well, how long was it?" said Cupid.

"Nine minutes to a second," replied I, watch in hand.

"I told you so."

For a moment a curious emotion filled me, not wholly unlike that which one might experience at the fulfillment of some mysterious prophecy. But how absurd, thought I again; the thing is a mere machine, the essence of which is unvarying punctuality and precision.

Previously absorbed by the wheels and cylinders, my attention was now directed to a sad-looking woman standing by.

"That is rather an elderly person so silently tending the machine-end here. She would not seem wholly used to it either."

"Oh," knowingly whispered Cupid, through the din, "she only came last week. She was a nurse formerly. But the business is poor in these parts, and she's left it. But look at the paper she is piling there."

"Aye, foolscap," handling the piles of moist, warm sheets, which continually were being delivered into the woman's waiting hands. "Don't you turn out anything but foolscap at this machine?"

"Oh, sometimes, but not often, we turn out finer work—cream-laid and royal sheets, we call them. But foolscap being in chief demand, we turn out foolscap most."

It was very curious. Looking at that blank paper continually dropping, dropping,

dropping, my mind ran on in wonderings of those strange uses to which those thousand sheets eventually would be put. All sorts of writings would be writ on those now vacant things—sermons, lawyers' briefs, physicians' prescriptions, love-letters, marriage certificates, bills of divorce, registers of births, death-warrants, and so on, without end. Then, recurring back to them as they here lay all blank, I could not but bethink me of that celebrated comparison of John Locke,[31] who, in demonstration of his theory that man had no innate ideas, compared the human mind at birth to a sheet of blank paper; something destined to be scribbled on, but what sort of characters no soul might tell.

Pacing slowly to and fro along the involved machine, still humming with its play, I was struck as well by the inevitability as the evolvement-power in all its motions.

"Does that thin cobweb there," said I, pointing to the sheet in its more imperfect stage, "does that never tear or break? It is marvelous fragile, and yet this machine it passes through is so mighty."

"It never is known to tear a hair's point."

"Does it never stop—get clogged?"

"No. It *must* go. The machinery makes it go just so; just that very way, and at that very pace you there plainly *see* it go. The pulp can't help going."

Something of awe now stole over me, as I gazed upon this inflexible iron animal. Always, more or less, machinery of this ponderous, elaborate sort strikes, in some moods, strange dread into the human heart, as some living, panting Behemoth might. But what made the thing I saw so specially terrible to me was the metallic necessity, the unbudging fatality which governed it. Though, here and there, I could not follow the thin, gauzy vail of pulp in the course of its more mysterious or entirely invisible advance, yet it was indubitable that, at those points where it eluded me, it still marched on in unvarying docility to the autocratic cunning of the machine. A fascination fastened on me. I stood spell-bound and wandering in my soul. Before my eyes—there, passing in slow procession along the wheeling cylinders, I seemed to see, glued to the pallid incipience of the pulp, the yet more pallid faces of all the pallid girls I had eyed that heavy day. Slowly, mournfully, beseechingly, yet unresistingly, they gleamed along, their agony dimly outlined on the imperfect paper, like the print of the tormented face on the handkerchief of Saint Veronica.[32]

"Halloa! the heat of the room is too much for you," cried Cupid, staring at me.

"No—I am rather chill, if anything."

"Come out, sir—out—out," and, with the protecting air of a careful father, the precocious lad hurried me outside.

In a few moments, feeling revived a little, I went into the folding-room—the first room I had entered, and where the desk for transacting business stood, surrounded by the blank counters and blank girls engaged at them.

"Cupid here has led me a strange tour," said I to the dark-complexioned man before mentioned, whom I had ere this discovered not only to be an old bachelor, but also the principal proprietor. "Yours is a most wonderful factory. Your great machine is a miracle of inscrutable intricacy."

"Yes, all our visitors think it so. But we don't have many. We are in a very

[31] English philosopher (1632–1704).
[32] A woman of Jerusalem who wiped the brow of
Jesus as he carried the cross to Calvary.

out-of-the-way corner here. Few inhabitants, too. Most of our girls come from far-off villages."

"The girls," echoed I, glancing round at their silent forms. "Why is it, sir, that in most factories, female operatives, of whatever age, are indiscriminately called girls, never women?"

"Oh! as to that—why, I suppose, the fact of their being generally unmarried—that's the reason, I should think. But it never struck me before. For our factory here, we will not have married women; they are apt to be off-and-on too much. We want none but steady workers: twelve hours to the day, day after day, through the three hundred and sixty-five days, excepting Sundays, Thanksgiving, and Fast-days. That's our rule. And so, having no married women, what females we have are rightly enough called girls."

"Then these are all maids," said I, while some pained homage to their pale virginity made me involuntarily bow.

"All maids."

Again the strange emotion filled me.

"Your cheeks look whitish yet, sir," said the man, gazing at me narrowly. "You must be careful going home. Do they pain you at all now? It's a bad sign, if they do."

"No doubt, sir," answered I, "when once I have got out of the Devil's Dungeon, I shall feel them mending."

"Ah, yes; the winter air in valleys, or gorges, or any sunken place, is far colder and more bitter than elsewhere. You would hardly believe it now, but it is colder here than at the top of Woedolor Mountain."

"I dare say it is, sir. But time presses me; I must depart."

With that, remuffling myself in dread-naught and tippet, thrusting my hands into my huge seal-skin mittens, I sallied out into the nipping air, and found poor Black, my horse, all cringing and doubled up with the cold.

Soon, wrapped in furs and meditations, I ascended from the Devil's Dungeon.

At the Black Notch I paused, and once more bethought me of Temple Bar. Then, shooting through the pass, all alone with inscrutable nature, I exclaimed—Oh! Paradise of Bachelors! and oh! Tartarus of Maids!

1835

Benito Cereno

In the year 1799, Captain Amasa Delano, of Duxbury, in Massachusetts, commanding a large sealer and general trader, lay at anchor with a valuable cargo, in the harbor of St. Maria—a small, desert, uninhabited island toward the southern extremity of the long coast of Chili. There he had touched for water.[1]

---

[1] Melville based his plot on portions of Captain Amasa Delano's *Narrative of the Voyages and Travels in the Northern and Southern Hemispheres* (Boston, 1817), including documents printed in Delano and used in the "deposition" section toward the end of *Benito Cereno*.

On the second day, not long after dawn, while lying in his berth, his mate came below, informing him that a strange sail was coming into the bay. Ships were then not so plenty in those waters as now. He rose, dressed, and went on deck.

The morning was one peculiar to that coast. Everything was mute and calm; everything gray. The sea, though undulated into long roods of swells, seemed fixed, and was sleeked at the surface like waved lead that has cooled and set in the smelter's mould. The sky seemed a gray surtout.[2] Flights of troubled gray fowl, kith and kin with flights of troubled gray vapors among which they were mixed, skimmed low and fitfully over the waters, as swallows over meadows before storms. Shadows present, foreshadowing deeper shadows to come.

To Captain Delano's surprise, the stranger, viewed through the glass, showed no colors; though to do so upon entering a haven, however uninhabited in its shores, where but a single other ship might be lying, was the custom among peaceful seamen of all nations. Considering the lawlessness and loneliness of the spot, and the sort of stories, at that day, associated with those seas, Captain Delano's surprise might have deepened into some uneasiness had he not been a person of a singularly undistrustful good nature, not liable, except on extraordinary and repeated incentives, and hardly then, to indulge in personal alarms, any way involving the imputation of malign evil in man. Whether, in view of what humanity is capable, such a trait implies, along with a benevolent heart, more than ordinary quickness and accuracy of intellectual perception, may be left to the wise to determine.

But whatever misgivings might have obtruded on first seeing the stranger, would almost, in any seaman's mind, have been dissipated by observing that, the ship, in navigating into the harbor, was drawing too near the land; a sunken reef making out off her bow. This seemed to prove her a stranger, indeed, not only to the sealer, but the island; consequently, she could be no wonted freebooter on that ocean. With no small interest, Captain Delano continued to watch her—a proceeding not much facilitated by the vapors partly mantling the hull, through which the far matin[3] light from her cabin streamed equivocally enough; much like the sun—by this time hemisphered on the rim of the horizon, and, apparently, in company with the strange ship entering the harbor—which, wimpled by the same low, creeping clouds, showed not unlike a Lima intriguante's one sinister eye peering across the Plaza from the Indian loop-hole of her dusk *saya-y-manta*.[4]

It might have been but a deception of the vapors, but, the longer the stranger was watched the more singular appeared her manoeuvres. Ere long it seemed hard to decide whether she meant to come in or no—what she wanted, or what she was about. The wind, which had breezed up a little during the night, was now extremely light and baffling, which the more increased the apparent uncertainty of her movements.

Surmising, at last, that it might be a ship in distress, Captain Delano ordered his whale-boat to be dropped, and, much to the wary opposition of his mate, prepared to board her, and, at the least, pilot her in. On the night previous, a fishing-party of the seamen had gone a long distance to some detached rocks out of sight from the sealer, and, an hour or two before daybreak, had returned, having met with no small success. Presuming that the stranger might have been long off sound-

---

[2] Overcoat.
[3] Morning.

[4] Skirt-and-cloak combination concealing the entire body.

ings, the good captain put several baskets of the fish, for presents, into his boat, and so pulled away. From her continuing too near the sunken reef, deeming her in danger, calling to his men, he made all haste to apprise those on board of their situation. But, some time ere the boat came up, the wind, light though it was, having shifted, had headed the vessel off, as well as partly broken the vapors from about her.

Upon gaining a less remote view, the ship, when made signally visible on the verge of the leaden-hued swells, with the shreds of fog here and there raggedly furring her, appeared like a white-washed monastery after a thunder-storm, seen perched upon some dun cliff among the Pyrenees. But it was no purely fanciful resemblance which now, for a moment, almost led Captain Delano to think that nothing less than a ship-load of monks was before him. Peering over the bulwarks were what really seemed, in the hazy distance, throngs of dark cowls; while, fitfully revealed through the open port-holes, other dark moving figures were dimly described, as of Black Friars pacing the cloisters.[5]

Upon a still nigher approach, this appearance was modified, and the true character of the vessel was plain—a Spanish merchantman of the first class, carrying negro slaves, amongst other valuable freight, from one colonial port to another. A very large, and, in its time, a very fine vessel, such as in those days were at intervals encountered along that main; sometimes superseded Acapulco treasure-ships, or retired frigates of the Spanish king's navy, which, like superannuated Italian palaces, still, under a decline of masters, preserved signs of former state.

As the whale-boat drew more and more nigh, the cause of the peculiar pipe-clayed aspect of the stranger was seen in the slovenly neglect pervading her. The spars, ropes, and great part of the bulwarks, looked woolly, from long unacquaintance with the scraper, tar, and the brush. Her keel seemed laid, her ribs put together, and she launched, from Ezekiel's Valley of Dry Bones.[6]

In the present business in which she was engaged, the ship's general model and rig appeared to have undergone no material change from their original warlike and Froissart[7] pattern. However, no guns were seen.

The tops were large, and were railed about with what had once been octagonal net-work, all now in sad disrepair. These tops hung overhead like three ruinous aviaries, in one of which was seen perched, on a ratlin,[8] a white noddy, a strange fowl, so called from its lethargic, somnambulistic character, being frequently caught by hand at sea. Battered and mouldy, the castellated forecastle seemed some ancient turret, long ago taken by assault, and then left to decay. Toward the stern, two high-raised quarter galleries—the balustrades here and there covered with dry, tindery sea-moss—opening out from the unoccupied state-cabin, whose dead-lights, for all the mild weather, were hermetically closed and calked—these tenantless balconies hung over the sea as if it were the grand Venetian canal. But the principal relic of faded grandeur was the ample oval of the shield-like stern-piece, intricately carved with the arms of Castile and Leon,[9] medallioned about by groups of mythological or symbolical devices; upper-

---

[5] Place of religious seclusion.
[6] See Ezekiel 37:1.
[7] Jean Froissart (1337–1410), historian of English and of French wars.

[8] "Step" of a rope ladder.
[9] Insignia of Spanish kingdoms.

most and central of which was a dark satyr in a mask, holding his foot on the prostrate neck of a writhing figure, likewise masked.

Whether the ship had a figure-head, or only a plain beak, was not quite certain, owing to canvas wrapped about that part, either to protect it while undergoing a re-furbishing, or else decently to hide its decay. Rudely painted or chalked, as in a sailor freak, along the forward side of a sort of pedestal below the canvas, was the sentence, *"Seguid vuestro jefe,"* (follow your leader); while upon the tarnished head-boards, near by, appeared, in stately capitals, once gilt, the ship's name, "SAN DOMINICK," each letter streakingly corroded with tricklings of copper-spike rust; while, like mourning weeds, dark festoons of sea-grass slimily swept to and fro over the name, with every hearse-like roll of the hull.

As, at last, the boat was hooked from the bow along toward the gangway amidship, its keel, while yet some inches separated from the hull, harshly grated as on a sunken coral reef. It proved a huge bunch of conglobated barnacles adhering below the water to the side like a wen—a token of baffling airs and long calms passed somewhere in those seas.

Climbing the side, the visitor was at once surrounded by a clamorous throng of whites and blacks, but the latter outnumbering the former more than could have been expected, negro transportation-ship as the stranger in port was. But, in one language, and as with one voice, all poured out a common tale of suffering; in which the negresses, of whom there were not a few, exceeded the others in their dolorous vehemence. The scurvy, together with the fever, had swept off a great part of their number, more especially the Spaniards. Off Cape Horn they had narrowly escaped shipwreck; then, for days together, they had lain tranced without wind; their provisions were low; their water next to none; their lips that moment were baked.

While Captain Delano was thus made the mark of all eager tongues, his one eager glance took in all faces, with every other object about him.

Always upon first boarding a large and populous ship at sea, especially a foreign one, with a nondescript crew such as Lascars or Manilla men,[10] the impression varies in a peculiar way from that produced by first entering a strange house with strange inmates in a strange land. Both house and ship—the one by its walls and blinds, the other by its high bulwarks like ramparts—hoard from view their interiors till the last moment: but in the case of the ship there is this addition; that the living spectacle it contains, upon its sudden and complete disclosure, has, in contrast with the blank ocean which zones it, something of the effect of enchantment. The ship seems unreal; these strange costumes, gestures, and faces, but a shadowy tableau just emerged from the deep, which directly must receive back what it gave.

Perhaps it was some such influence, as above is attempted to be described, which, in Captain Delano's mind, heightened whatever, upon a staid scrutiny, might have seemed unusual; especially the conspicuous figures of four elderly grizzled negroes, their heads like black, doddered willow tops, who, in venerable contrast to the tumult below them, were couched, sphynx-like, one on the starboard cat-head,[11] another on the larboard, and the remaining pair face to face on the opposite bulwarks above the main-chains. They each had bits of unstranded old junk in their hands, and, with a

---

[10] From East India or the Philippines.
[11] Projecting timber, often carved as the head of a cat, to which the anchor is secured at the front or bow of the ship.

sort of stoical self-content, were picking the junk into oakum,[12] a small heap of which lay by their sides. They accompanied the task with a continuous, low, monotonous chant; droning and druling away like so many gray-headed bag-pipers playing a funeral march.

The quarter-deck rose into an ample elevated poop, upon the forward verge of which, lifted, like the oakum-pickers, some eight feet above the general throng, sat along in a row, separated by regular spaces, the cross-legged figures of six other blacks; each with a rusty hatchet in his hand, which, with a bit of brick and a rag, he was engaged like a scullion in scouring; while between each two was a small stack of hatchets, their rusted edges turned forward awaiting a like operation. Though occasionally the four oakum-pickers would briefly address some person or persons in the crowd below, yet the six hatchet-polishers neither spoke to others, nor breathed a whisper among themselves, but sat intent upon their task, except at intervals, when, with the peculiar love in negroes of uniting industry with pastime, two and two they sideways clashed their hatchets together, like cymbals, with a barbarous din. All six, unlike the generality, had the raw aspect of unsophisticated Africans.

But that first comprehensive glance which took in those ten figures, with scores less conspicuous, rested but an instant upon them, as, impatient of the hubbub of voices, the visitor turned in quest of whomsoever it might be that commanded the ship.

But as if not unwilling to let nature make known her own case among his suffering charge, or else in despair of restraining it for the time, the Spanish captain, a gentlemanly, reserved-looking, and rather young man to a stranger's eye, dressed with singular richness, but bearing plain traces of recent sleepless cares and disquietudes, stood passively by, leaning against the main-mast, at one moment casting a dreary, spiritless look upon his excited people, at the next an unhappy glance toward his visitor. By his side stood a black of small stature, in whose rude face, as occasionally, like a shepherd's dog, he mutely turned it up into the Spaniard's, sorrow and affection were equally blended.

Struggling through the throng, the American advanced to the Spaniard, assuring him of his sympathies, and offering to render whatever assistance might be in his power. To which the Spaniard returned for the present but grave and ceremonious acknowledgments, his national formality dusked by the saturnine mood of ill-health.

But losing no time in mere compliments, Captain Delano, returning to the gangway, had his basket of fish brought up; and as the wind still continued light, so that some hours at least must elapse ere the ship could be brought to the anchorage, he bade his men return to the sealer, and fetch back as much water as the whale-boat could carry, with whatever soft bread the steward might have, all the remaining pumpkins on board, with a box of sugar, and a dozen of his private bottles of cider.

Not many minutes after the boat's pushing off, to the vexation of all, the wind entirely died away, and the tide turning, began drifting back the ship helplessly seaward. But trusting this would not long last, Captain Delano sought, with good hopes, to cheer up the strangers, feeling no small satisfaction that, with persons in their condition, he could—thanks to his frequent voyages along the Spanish main— converse with some freedom in their native tongue.

[12] Loose strands of worn-out rope (called junk)
used for calking.

While left alone with them, he was not long in observing some things tending to heighten his first impressions; but surprise was lost in pity, both for the Spaniards and blacks, alike evidently reduced from scarcity of water and provisions; while long-continued suffering seemed to have brought out the less good-natured qualities of the negroes, besides, at the same time, impairing the Spaniard's authority over them. But, under the circumstances, precisely this condition of things was to have been anticipated. In armies, navies, cities, or families, in nature herself, nothing more relaxes good order than misery. Still, Captain Delano was not without the idea, that had Benito Cereno been a man of greater energy, misrule would hardly have come to the present pass. But the debility, constitutional or induced by hardships, bodily and mental, of the Spanish captain, was too obvious to be overlooked. A prey to settled dejection, as if long mocked with hope he would not now indulge it, even when it had ceased to be a mock, the prospect of that day, or evening at furthest, lying at anchor, with plenty of water for his people, and a brother captain to counsel and befriend, seemed in no perceptible degree to encourage him. His mind appeared unstrung, if not still more seriously affected. Shut up in these oaken walls, chained to one dull round of command, whose unconditionality cloyed him, like some hypochondriac abbot he moved slowly about, at times suddenly pausing, starting, or staring, biting his lip, biting his finger-nail, flushing, paling, twitching his beard, with other symptoms of an absent or moody mind. This distempered spirit was lodged, as before hinted, in as distempered a frame. He was rather tall, but seemed never to have been robust, and now with nervous suffering was almost worn to a skeleton. A tendency to some pulmonary complaint appeared to have been lately confirmed. His voice was like that of one with lungs half gone—hoarsely suppressed, a husky whisper. No wonder that, as in this state he tottered about, his private servant apprehensively followed him. Sometimes the negro gave his master his arm, or took his handkerchief out of his pocket for him; performing these and similar offices with that affectionate zeal which transmutes into something filial or fraternal acts in themselves but menial; and which has gained for the negro the repute of making the most pleasing body-servant in the world; one, too, whom a master need be on no stiffly superior terms with, but may treat with familiar trust; less a servant than a devoted companion.

Marking the noisy indocility of the blacks in general, as well as what seemed the sullen inefficiency of the whites it was not without humane satisfaction that Captain Delano witnessed the steady good conduct of Babo.

But the good conduct of Babo, hardly more than the ill-behavior of others, seemed to withdraw the half-lunatic Don Benito from his cloudy languor. Not that such precisely was the impression made by the Spaniard on the mind of his visitor. The Spaniard's individual unrest was, for the present, but noted as a conspicuous feature in the ship's general affliction. Still, Captain Delano was not a little concerned at what he could not help taking for the time to be Don Benito's unfriendly indifference towards himself. The Spaniard's manner, too, conveyed a sort of sour and gloomy disdain, which he seemed at no pains to disguise. But this the American in charity ascribed to the harrassing effects of sickness, since, in former instances, he had noted that there are peculiar natures on whom prolonged physical suffering seems to cancel every social-instinct of kindness; as if, forced to black bread themselves, they deemed it but equity that each person coming nigh them should, indirectly, by some slight or affront, be made to partake of their fare.

But ere long Captain Delano bethought him that, indulgent as he was at the first, in judging the Spaniard, he might not, after all, have exercised charity enough. At bottom it was Don Benito's reserve which displeased him; but the same reserve was shown towards all but his faithful personal attendant. Even the formal reports which, according to sea-usage, were, at stated times, made to him by some petty underling, either a white, mulatto or black, he hardly had patience enough to listen to, without betraying contemptuous aversion. His manner upon such occasions was, in its degree, not unlike that which might be supposed to have been his imperial countryman's, Charles V., just previous to the anchoritish retirement of that monarch from the throne.[13]

This splenetic disrelish of his place was evinced in almost every function pertaining to it. Proud as he was moody, he condescended to no personal mandate. Whatever special orders were necessary, their delivery was delegated to his body-servant, who in turn transferred them to their ultimate destination, through runners, alert Spanish boys or slave boys, like pages or pilot-fish within easy call continually hovering round Don Benito. So that to have beheld this undemonstrative invalid gliding about, apathetic and mute, no landsman could have dreamed that in him was lodged a dictatorship beyond which, while at sea, there was no earthly appeal.

Thus, the Spaniard, regarded in his reserve, seemed the involuntary victim of mental disorder. But, in fact, his reserve might, in some degree, have proceeded from design. If so, then here was evinced the unhealthy climax of that icy though conscientious policy, more or less adopted by all commanders of large ships, which, except in signal emergencies, obliterates alike the manifestation of sway with every trace of sociality; transforming the man into a block, or rather into a loaded cannon, which, until there is call for thunder, has nothing to say.

Viewing him in this light, it seemed but a natural token of the perverse habit induced by a long course of such hard self-restraint, that, notwithstanding the present condition of his ship, the Spaniard should still persist in a demeanor, which, however harmless, or, it may be, appropriate, in a well-appointed vessel, such as the San Dominick might have been at the outset of the voyage, was anything but judicious now. But the Spaniard, perhaps, thought that it was with captains as with gods: reserve, under all events, must still be their cue. But probably this appearance of slumbering dominion might have been but an attempted disguise to conscious imbecility—not deep policy, but shallow device. But be all this as it might, whether Don Benito's manner was designed or not, the more Captain Delano noted its pervading reserve, the less he felt uneasiness at any particular manifestation of that reserve towards himself.

Neither were his thoughts taken up by the captain alone. Wonted to the quiet orderliness of the sealer's comfortable family of a crew, the noisy confusion of the San Dominick's suffering host repeatedly challenged his eye. Some prominent breaches, not only of discipline but of decency, were observed. These Captain Delano could not but ascribe, in the main, to the absence of those subordinate deck-officers to whom, along with higher duties, is intrusted what may be styled the police department of a populous ship. True, the old oakum-pickers appeared at times to act the part of monitorial constables to their countrymen, the blacks; but though occasion-

---

[13] Charles V (1500–1558), king of Spain, spent his last years in a monastery while keeping claim to political power and property.

ally succeeding in allaying trifling outbreaks now and then between man and man, they could do little or nothing toward establishing general quiet. The San Dominick was in the condition of a transatlantic emigrant ship, among whose multitude of living freight are some individuals, doubtless, as little troublesome as crates and bales; but the friendly remonstrances of such with their ruder companions are of not so much avail as the unfriendly arm of the mate. What the San Dominick wanted was, what the emigrant ship has, stern superior officers. But on these decks not so much as a fourth-mate was to be seen.

The visitor's curiosity was roused to learn the particulars of those mishaps which had brought about such absenteeism, with its consequences; because, though deriving some inkling of the voyage from the wails which at the first moment had greeted him, yet of the details no clear understanding had been had. The best account would, doubtless, be given by the captain. Yet at first the visitor was loth to ask it, unwilling to provoke some distant rebuff. But plucking up courage, he at last accosted Don Benito, renewing the expression of his benevolent interest, adding, that did he (Captain Delano) but know the particulars of the ship's misfortunes, he would, perhaps, be better able in the end to relieve them. Would Don Benito favor him with the whole story.

Don Benito faltered; then, like some somnambulist suddenly interfered with, vacantly stared at his visitor, and ended by looking down on the deck. He maintained this posture so long, that Captain Delano, almost equally disconcerted, and involuntarily almost as rude, turned suddenly from him, walking forward to accost one of the Spanish seamen for the desired information. But he had hardly gone five paces, when, with a sort of eagerness, Don Benito invited him back, regretting his momentary absence of mind, and professing readiness to gratify him.

While most part of the story was being given, the two captains stood on the after part of the main-deck, a privileged spot, no one being near but the servant.

"It is now a hundred and ninety days," began the Spaniard, in his husky whisper, "that this ship, well officered and well manned, with several cabin passengers—some fifty Spaniards in all—sailed from Buenos Ayres bound to Lima, with a general cargo, hardware, Paraguay tea and the like—and," pointing forward, "that parcel of negroes, now not more than a hundred and fifty, as you see, but then numbering over three hundred souls. Off Cape Horn we had heavy gales. In one moment, by night, three of my best officers, with fifteen sailors, were lost, with the main-yard; the spar snapping under them in the slings, as they sought, with heavers, to beat down the icy sail. To lighten the hull, the heavier sacks of mata[14] were thrown into the sea, with most of the water-pipes[15] lashed on deck at the time. And this last necessity it was, combined with the prolonged detentions afterwards experienced, which eventually brought about our chief causes of suffering. When—"

Here there was a sudden fainting attack of his cough, brought on, no doubt, by his mental distress. His servant sustained him, and drawing a cordial from his pocket placed it to his lips. He a little revived. But unwilling to leave him unsupported while yet imperfectly restored, the black with one arm still encircled his master, at the same time keeping his eye fixed on his face, as if to watch for the first sign of complete restoration, or relapse, as the event might prove.

The Spaniard proceeded, but brokenly and obscurely, as one in a dream.

---

[14] Cotton.   [15] Casks.

—"Oh, my God! rather than pass through what I have, with joy I would have hailed the most terrible gales; but—"

His cough returned and with increased violence; this subsiding, with reddened lips and closed eyes he fell heavily against his supporter.

"His mind wanders. He was thinking of the plague that followed the gales," plaintively sighed the servant; "my poor, poor master!" wringing one hand, and with the other wiping the mouth. "But be patient, Señor," again turning to Captain Delano, "these fits do not last long; master will soon be himself."

Don Benito reviving, went on; but as this portion of the story was very brokenly delivered, the substance only will here be set down.

It appeared that after the ship had been many days tossed in storms off the Cape, the scurvy broke out, carrying off numbers of the whites and blacks. When at last they had worked round into the Pacific, their spars and sails were so damaged, and so inadequately handled by the surviving mariners, most of whom were become invalids, that, unable to lay her northerly course by the wind, which was powerful, the unmanageable ship, for successive days and nights, was blown northwestward, where the breeze suddenly deserted her, in unknown waters, to sultry calms. The absence of the water-pipes now proved as fatal to life as before their presence had menaced it. Induced, or at least aggravated, by the more than scanty allowance of water, a malignant fever followed the scurvy; with the excessive heat of the length-ened calm, making such short work of it as to sweep away, as by billows, whole families of the Africans, and a yet larger number, proportionably, of the Spaniards, including, by a luckless fatality, every remaining officer on board. Consequently, in the smart west winds eventually following the calm, the already rent sails, having to be simply dropped, not furled, at need, had been gradually reduced to the beggars' rags they were now. To procure substitutes for his lost sailors, as well as supplies of water and sails, the captain, at the earliest opportunity, had made for Baldivia, the southernmost civilized port of Chili and South America; but upon nearing the coast the thick weather had prevented him from so much as sighting that harbor. Since which period, almost without a crew, and almost without canvas and almost without water, and, at intervals, giving its added dead to the sea, the San Dominick had been battle-dored[16] about by contrary winds, inveigled by currents, or grown weedy in calms. Like a man lost in woods, more than once she had doubled upon her own track.

"But throughout these calamities," huskily continued Don Benito, painfully turn-ing in the half embrace of his servant, "I have to thank those negroes you see, who, though to your inexperienced eyes appearing unruly, have, indeed, conducted them-selves with less of restlessness than even their owner could have thought possible under such circumstances."

Here he again fell faintly back. Again his mind wandered; but he rallied, and less obscurely proceeded.

"Yes, their owner was quite right in assuring me that no fetters would be needed with his blacks; so that while, as is wont in this transportation, those negroes have always remained upon deck—not thrust below, as in the Guinea-men—they have, also, from the beginning, been freely permitted to range within given bounds, at their pleasure."

---

[16] Tossed back and forth.

Once more the faintness returned—his mind roved—but, recovering, he resumed:

"But it is Babo here to whom, under God, I owe not only my own preservation, but likewise to him, chiefly, the merit is due, of pacifying his more ignorant brethren, when at intervals tempted to murmurings."

"Ah, master," sighed the black, bowing his face, "don't speak of me; Babo is nothing; what Babo has done was but duty."

"Faithful fellow!" cried Captain Delano. "Don Benito, I envy you such a friend; slave I cannot call him."

As master and man stood before him, the black upholding the white, Captain Delano could not but bethink him of the beauty of that relationship which could present such a spectacle of fidelity on the one hand and confidence on the other. The scene was heightened by the contrast in dress, denoting their relative positions. The Spaniard wore a loose Chili jacket of dark velvet; white small-clothes and stockings, with silver buckles at the knee and instep; a high-crowned sombrero, of fine grass; a slender sword, silver mounted, hung from a knot in his sash—the last being an almost invariable adjunct, more for utility than ornament, of a South American gentleman's dress to this hour. Excepting when his occasional nervous contortions brought about disarray, there was a certain precision in his attire curiously at variance with the unsightly disorder around; especially in the belittered Ghetto, forward of the main-mast, wholly occupied by the blacks.

The servant wore nothing but wide trowsers, apparently, from their coarseness and patches, made out of some old topsail; they were clean, and confined at the waist by a bit of unstranded rope, which, with his composed, deprecatory air at times, made him look something like a begging friar of St. Francis.

However unsuitable for the time and place, at least in the blunt-thinking American's eyes, and however strangely surviving in the midst of all his afflictions, the toilette of Don Benito might not, in fashion at least, have gone beyond the style of the day among South Americans of his class. Though on the present voyage sailing from Buenos Ayres, he had avowed himself a native and resident of Chili, whose inhabitants had not so generally adopted the plain coat and once plebeian pantaloons; but, with a becoming modification, adhered to their provincial costume, picturesque as any in the world. Still, relatively to the pale history of the voyage, and his own pale face, there seemed something so incongruous in the Spaniard's apparel, as almost to suggest the image of an invalid courtier tottering about London streets in the time of the plague.

The portion of the narrative which, perhaps, most excited interest, as well as some surprise, considering the latitudes in question, was the long calms spoken of, and more particularly the ship's so long drifting about. Without communicating the opinion, of course, the American could not but impute at least part of the detentions both to clumsy seamanship and faulty navigation. Eying Don Benito's small, yellow hands, he easily inferred that the young captain had not got into command at the hawse-hole, but the cabin-window;[17] and if so, why wonder at incompetence, in youth, sickness, and gentility united?

But drowning criticism in compassion, after a fresh repetition of his sympathies, Captain Delano, having heard out his story, not only engaged, as in the first place,

---

[17] I.e., had not started his career from the bottom.

to see Don Benito and his people supplied in their immediate bodily needs, but, also, now further promised to assist him in procuring a large permanent supply of water, as well as some sails and rigging; and, though it would involve no small embarrassment to himself, yet he would spare three of his best seamen for temporary deck officers; so that without delay the ship might proceed to Conception, there fully to refit for Lima, her destined port.

Such generosity was not without its effect, even upon the invalid. His face lighted up; eager and hectic, he met the honest glance of his visitor. With gratitude he seemed overcome.

"This excitement is bad for master," whispered the servant, taking his arm, and with soothing words gently drawing him aside.

When Don Benito returned, the American was pained to observe that his hopefulness, like the sudden kindling in his cheek, was but febrile and transient.

Ere long, with a joyless mien, looking up towards the poop, the host invited his guest to accompany him there, for the benefit of what little breath of wind might be stirring.

As, during the telling of the story, Captain Delano had once or twice started at the occasional cymballing of the hatchet-polishers, wondering why such an interruption should be allowed, especially in that part of the ship, and in the ears of an invalid; and moreover, as the hatchets had anything but an attractive look, and the handlers of them still less so, it was, therefore, to tell the truth, not without some lurking reluctance, or even shrinking, it may be, that Captain Delano, with apparent complaisance, acquiesced in his host's invitation. The more so, since, with an untimely caprice of punctillo, rendered distressing by his cadaverous aspect, Don Benito, with Castilian bows, solemnly insisted upon his guest's preceding him up the ladder leading to the elevation; where, one on each side of the last step, sat for armorial supporters and sentries two of the ominous file. Gingerly enough stepped good Captain Delano between them, and in the instant of leaving them behind, like one running the gauntlet, he felt an apprehensive twitch in the calves of his legs.

But when, facing about, he saw the whole file, like so many organ-grinders, still stupidly intent on their work, unmindful of everything beside, he could not but smile at his late fidgety panic.

Presently, while standing with his host, looking forward upon the decks below, he was struck by one of those instances of insubordination previously alluded to. Three black boys, with two Spanish boys, were sitting together on the hatches, scraping a rude wooden platter, in which some scanty mess had recently been cooked. Suddenly, one of the black boys, enraged at a word dropped by one of his white companions, seized a knife, and, though called to forebear by one of the oakum-pickers, struck the lad over the head, inflicting a gash from which blood flowed.

In amazement, Captain Delano inquired what this meant. To which the pale Don Benito dully muttered, that it was merely the sport of the lad.

"Pretty serious sport, truly," rejoined Captain Delano. "Had such a thing happened on board the Bachelor's Delight, instant punishment would have followed."

At these words the Spaniard turned upon the American one of his sudden, staring, half-lunatic looks; then, relapsing into his torpor, answered, "Doubtless, doubtless, Señor."

Is it, thought Captain Delano, that this hapless man is one of those paper captains

I've known, who by policy wink at what by power they cannot put down? I know no sadder sight than a commander who has little of command but the name.

"I should think, Don Benito," he now said, glancing towards the oakum-picker who had sought to interfere with the boys, "that you would find it advantageous to keep all your blacks employed, especially the younger ones, no matter at what useless task, and no matter what happens to the ship. Why, even with my little band, I find such a course indispensable. I once kept a crew on my quarter-deck thrumming mats[18] for my cabin, when, for three days, I had given up my ship—mats, men, and all— for a speedy loss, owing to the violence of a gale, in which we could do nothing but helplessly drive before it."

"Doubtless, doubtless," muttered Don Benito.

"But," continued Captain Delano, again glancing upon the oakum-pickers and then at the hatchet-polishers, near by, "I see you keep some, at least, of your host employed."

"Yes," was again the vacant response.

"Those old men there, shaking their pows[19] from their pulpits," continued Captain Delano, pointing to the oakum-pickers, "seem to act the part of old dominies to the rest, little heeded as their admonitions are at times. Is this voluntary on their part, Don Benito, or have you appointed them shepherds to your flock of black sheep?"

"What posts they fill, I appointed them," rejoined the Spaniard, in an acrid tone, as if resenting some supposed satiric reflection.

"And these others, these Ashantee[20] conjurors here," continued Captain Delano, rather uneasily eyeing the brandished steel of the hatchet-polishers, where, in spots, it had been brought to a shine, "this seems a curious business they are at, Don Benito?"

"In the gales we met," answered the Spaniard, "what of our general cargo was not thrown overboard was much damaged by the brine. Since coming into calm weather, I have had several cases of knives and hatchets daily brought up for overhauling and cleaning."

"A prudent idea, Don Benito. You are part owner of ship and cargo, I presume; but none of the slaves, perhaps?"

"I am owner of all you see," impatiently returned Don Benito, "except the main company of blacks, who belonged to my late friend, Alexandro Aranda."

As he mentioned this name, his air was heart-broken; his knees shook; his servant supported him.

Thinking he divined the cause of such unusual emotion, to confirm his surmise, Captain Delano, after a pause, said: "And may I ask, Don Benito, whether—since awhile ago you spoke of some cabin passengers—the friend, whose loss so afflicts you, at the outset of the voyage accompanied his blacks?"

"Yes."

"But died of the fever?"

"Died of the fever. Oh, could I but—"

Again quivering, the Spaniard paused.

"Pardon me," said Captain Delano, lowly, "but I think that, by a sympathetic experience, I conjecture, Don Benito, what it is that gives the keener edge to your

---

[18] Weaving rope into canvas.   [20] West African tribe.
[19] Heads.

grief. It was once my hard fortune to lose, at sea, a dear friend, my own brother, then supercargo. Assured of the welfare of his spirit, its departure I could have borne like a man; but that honest eye, that honest hand—both of which had so often met mine —and that warm heart; all, all—like scraps to the dogs—to throw all to the sharks! It was then I vowed never to have for fellow-voyager a man I loved, unless, unbeknown to him, I had provided every requisite, in case of a fatality, for embalming his mortal part for interment on shore. Were your friend's remains now on board this ship, Don Benito, not thus strangely would the mention of his name affect you."

"On board this ship?" echoed the Spaniard. Then, with horrified gestures, as directed against some spectre, he unconsciously fell into the ready arms of his attendant, who, with a silent appeal toward Captain Delano, seemed beseeching him not again to broach a theme so unspeakably distressing to his master.

This poor fellow now, thought the pained American, is the victim of that sad superstition which associates goblins with the deserted body of man, as ghosts with an abandoned house. How unlike are we made! What to me, in like case, would have been a solemn satisfaction, the bare suggestion, even, terrifies the Spaniard into this trance. Poor Alexandro Aranda! what would you say could you here see your friend —who, on former voyages, when you, for months, were left behind, has, I dare say, often longed, and longed, for one peep at you—now transported with terror at the least thought of having you anyway nigh him.

At this moment, with a dreary grave-yard toll, betokening a flaw, the ship's forecastle bell, smote by one of the grizzled oakum-pickers, proclaimed ten o'clock, through the leaden calm; when Captain Delano's attention was caught by the moving figure of a gigantic black, emerging from the general crowd below, and slowly advancing towards the elevated poop. An iron collar was about his neck, from which depended a chain, thrice wound round his body; the terminating links padlocked together at a broad band of iron, his girdle.

"How like a mute Atufal moves," murmured the servant.

The black mounted the steps of the poop, and, like a brave prisoner, brought up to receive sentence, stood in unquailing muteness before Don Benito, now recovered from his attack.

At the first glimpse of his approach, Don Benito had started, a resentful shadow swept over his face; and, as with the sudden memory of bootless rage, his white lips glued together.

This is some mulish mutineer, thought Captain Delano, surveying, not without a mixture of admiration, the colossal form of the negro.

"See, he waits your question, master," said the servant.

Thus reminded, Don Benito, nervously averting his glance, as if shunning, by anticipation, some rebellious response, in a disconcerted voice, thus spoke:—

"Atufal, will you ask my pardon, now?"

The black was silent.

"Again, master," murmured the servant, with bitter upbraiding eyeing his countryman, "Again, master; he will bend to master yet."

"Answer," said Don Benito, still averting his glance, "say but the one word, *pardon*, and your chains shall be off."

Upon this, the black, slowly raising both arms, let them lifelessly fall, his links clanking, his head bowed; as much as to say, "no, I am content."

"Go," said Don Benito, with inkept and unknown emotion.

Deliberately as he had come, the black obeyed.

"Excuse me, Don Benito," said Captain Delano, "but this scene surprises me; what means it, pray?"

"It means that that negro alone, of all the band, has given me peculiar cause of offense. I have put him in chains; I—"

Here he paused; his hand to his head, as if there were a swimming there, or a sudden bewilderment of memory had come over him; but meeting his servant's kindly glance seemed reassured, and proceeded:—

"I could not scourge such a form. But I told him he must ask my pardon. As yet he has not. At my command, every two hours he stands before me."

"And how long has this been?"

"Some sixty days."

"And obedient in all else? And respectful?"

"Yes."

"Upon my conscience, then," exclaimed Captain Delano, impulsively, "he has a royal spirit in him, this fellow."

"He may have some right to it," bitterly returned Don Benito, "he says he was king in his own land."

"Yes," said the servant, entering a word, "those slits in Atufal's ears once held wedges of gold; but poor Babo here, in his own land, was only a poor slave; a black man's slave was Babo, who now is the white's."

Somewhat annoyed by these conversational familiarities, Captain Delano turned curiously upon the attendant, then glanced inquiringly at his master; but, as if long wonted to these little informalities, neither master nor man seemed to understand him.

"What, pray, was Atufal's offense, Don Benito?" asked Captain Delano; "if it was not something very serious, take a fool's advice, and, in view of his general docility, as well as in some natural respect for his spirit, remit him his penalty."

"No, no, master never will do that," here murmured the servant to himself, "proud Atufal must first ask master's pardon. The slave there carries the padlock, but master here carries the key."

His attention thus directed, Captain Delano now noticed for the first, that, suspended by a slender silken cord, from Don Benito's neck, hung a key. At once, from the servant's muttered syllables, divining the key's purpose, he smiled and said:—"So, Don Benito—padlock and key—significant symbols, truly."

Biting his lip, Don Benito faltered.

Though the remark of Captain Delano, a man of such native simplicity as to be incapable of satire or irony, had been dropped in playful allusion to the Spaniard's singularly evidenced lordship over the black; yet the hypochondriac seemed some way to have taken it as a malicious reflection upon his confessed inability thus far to break down, at least, on a verbal summons, the entrenched will of the slave. Deploring this supposed misconception, yet despairing of correcting it, Captain Delano shifted the subject; but finding his companion more than ever withdrawn, as if still sourly digesting the lees of the presumed affront above-mentioned, by-and-by Captain Delano likewise became less talkative, oppressed, against his own will, by what seemed the secret vindictiveness of the morbidly sensitive Spaniard. But the good sailor, himself of a quite contrary disposition, refrained, on his part, alike from the appearance as from the feeling of resentment, and if silent, was only so from contagion.

Presently the Spaniard, assisted by his servant somewhat discourteously crossed over from his guest; a procedure which, sensibly enough, might have been allowed to pass for idle caprice of ill-humor, had not master and man, lingering round the corner of the elevated skylight, began whispering together in low voices. This was unpleasing. And more; the moody air of the Spaniard, which at times had not been without a sort of valetudinarian stateliness, now seemed anything but dignified; while the menial familiarity of the servant lost its original charm of simple-hearted attachment.

In his embarrassment, the visitor turned his face to the other side of the ship. By so doing, his glance accidentally fell on a young Spanish sailor, a coil of rope in his hand, just stepped from the deck to the first round of the mizzenrigging. Perhaps the man would not have been particularly noticed, were it not that, during his ascent to one of the yards, he, with a sort of covert intentness, kept his eye fixed on Captain Delano, from whom, presently, it passed, as if by a natural sequence, to the two whisperers.

His own attention thus redirected to that quarter, Captain Delano gave a slight start. From something in Don Benito's manner just then, it seemed as if the visitor had, at least partly, been the subject of the withdrawn consultation going on—a conjecture as little agreeable to the guest as it was little flattering to the host.

The singular alternations of courtesy and ill-breeding in the Spanish captain were unaccountable, except on one of two suppositions—innocent lunacy, or wicked imposture.

But the first idea, though it might naturally have occurred to an indifferent observer, and, in some respect, had not hitherto been wholly a stranger to Captain Delano's mind, yet, now that, in an incipient way, he began to regard the stranger's conduct something in the light of an intentional affront, of course the idea of lunacy was virtually vacated. But if not a lunatic, what then? Under the circumstances, would a gentleman, nay, any honest boor, act the part now acted by his host? The man was an imposter. Some low-born adventurer, masquerading as an oceanic grandee; yet so ignorant of the first requisites of mere gentlemanhood as to be betrayed into the present remarkable indecorum. That strange ceremoniousness, too, at other times evinced, seemed not uncharacteristic of one playing a part above his real level. Benito Cereno—Don Benito Cereno—a sounding name. One, too, at that period, not unknown, in the surname, to supercargoes and sea captains trading along the Spanish Main, as belonging to one of the most enterprising and extensive mercantile families in all those provinces; several members of it having titles; a sort of Castilian Rothschild,[21] with a noble brother, or cousin, in every great trading town of South America. The alleged Don Benito was in early manhood, about twenty-nine or thirty. To assume a sort of roving cadetship in the maritime affairs of such a house, what more likely scheme for a young knave of talent and spirit? But the Spaniard was a pale invalid. Never mind. For even to the degree of simulating mortal disease, the craft of some tricksters had been known to attain. To think that, under the aspect of infantile weakness, the most savage energies might be couched—those velvets of the Spaniard but the silky paw to his fangs.

[21] I.e., a Spanish counterpart of the famous German banking family.

From no train of thought did these fancies come; not from within, but from without; suddenly, too, and in one throng, like hoar frost; yet as soon to vanish as the mild sun of Captain Delano's good-nature regained its meridian.

Glancing over once more towards his host—whose side-face, revealed above the skylight, was now turned towards him—he was struck by the profile, whose clearness of cut was refined by the thinness, incident to ill-health, as well as ennobled about the chin by the beard. Away with suspicion. He was a true off-shoot of a true hidalgo Cereno.

Relieved by these and other better thoughts, the visitor, lightly humming a tune, now began indifferently pacing the poop, so as not to betray to Don Benito that he had at all mistrusted incivility, much less duplicity; for such mistrust would yet be proved illusory, and by the event; though, for the present, the circumstance which had provoked that distrust remained unexplained. But when that little mystery should have been cleared up, Captain Delano thought he might extremely regret it, did he allow Don Benito to become aware that he had indulged in ungenerous surmises. In short, to the Spaniard's black-letter text, it was best, for awhile, to leave open margin.[22]

Presently, his pale face twitching and overcast, the Spaniard, still supported by his attendant, moved over towards his guest, when, with even more than his usual embarrassment, and a strange sort of intriguing intonation in his husky whisper, the following conversation began:—

"Señor, may I ask how long you have lain at this isle?"

"Oh, but a day or two, Don Benito."

"And from what port are you last?"

"Canton."

"And there, Señor, you exchanged your sealskins for teas and silks, I think you said?"

"Yes. Silks, mostly."

"And the balance you took in specie, perhaps?"

Captain Delano, fidgeting a little, answered—

"Yes; some silver; not a very great deal, though."

"Ah—well. May I ask how many men have you, Señor?"

Captain Delano slightly started, but answered—

"About five-and-twenty, all told."

"And at present, Señor, all on board, I suppose?"

"All on board, Don Benito," replied the Captain, now with satisfaction.

"And will be to-night, Señor?"

At this last question, following so many pertinacious ones, for the soul of him Captain Delano could not but look very earnestly at the questioner, who, instead of meeting the glance, with every token of craven discomposure dropped his eyes to the deck; presenting an unworthy contrast to his servant, who, just then, was kneeling at his feet, adjusting a loose shoe-buckle; his disengaged face meantime, with humble curiosity, turned openly up into his master's downcast one.

The Spaniard, still with a guilty shuffle, repeated his question:

"And—and will be to-night, Señor?"

[22] To reserve judgment.

"Yes, for aught I know," returned Captain Delano—"but nay," rallying himself into fearless truth, "some of them talked of going off on another fishing party about midnight."

"Your ships generally go—go more or less armed, I believe, Señor?"

"Oh, a six-pounder or two, in case of emergency," was the intrepidly indifferent reply, "with a small stock of muskets, sealing-spears, and cutlasses, you know."

As he thus responded, Captain Delano again glanced at Don Benito, but the latter's eyes were averted; while abruptly and awkwardly shifting the subject, he made some peevish allusion to the calm, and then, without apology, once more, with his attendant, withdrew to the opposite bulwarks, where the whispering was resumed.

At this moment, and ere Captain Delano could cast a cool thought upon what had just passed, the young Spanish sailor, before mentioned, was seen descending from the rigging. In act of stooping over to spring inboard to the deck, his voluminous, unconfined frock, or shirt, of coarse woolen, much spotted with tar, opened out far down the chest, revealing a soiled under garment of what seemed the finest linen, edged, about the neck, with a narrow blue ribbon, sadly faded and worn. At this moment the young sailor's eye was again fixed on the whisperers, and Captain Delano thought he observed a lurking significance in it, as if silent signs, of some Freemason[23] sort, had that instant been interchanged.

This once more impelled his own glance in the direction of Don Benito, and, as before, he could not but infer that himself formed the subject of the conference. He paused. The sound of the hatchet-polishing fell on his ears. He cast another swift side-look at the two. They had the air of conspirators. In connection with the late questionings, and the incident of the young sailor, these things now begat such return of involuntary suspicion, that the singular guilelessness of the American could not endure it. Plucking up a gay and humorous expression, he crossed over to the two rapidly, saying:—"Ha, Don Benito, your black here seems high in your trust; a sort of privy-counselor, in fact."

Upon this, the servant looked up with a good-natured grin, but the master started as from a venomous bite. It was a moment or two before the Spaniard sufficiently recovered himself to reply; which he did, at last, with cold constraint:—"Yes, Señor, I have trust in Babo."

Here Babo, changing his previous grin of mere animal humor into an intelligent smile, not ungratefully eyed his master.

Finding that the Spaniard now stood silent and reserved, as if involuntarily, or purposely giving hint that his guest's proximity was inconvenient just then, Captain Delano, unwilling to appear uncivil even to incivility itself, made some trivial remark and moved off; again and again turning over in his mind the mysterious demeanor of Don Benito Cereno.

He had descended from the poop, and, wrapped in thought, was passing near a dark hatchway, leading down into the steerage, when, perceiving motion there, he looked to see what moved. The same instant there was a sparkle in the shadowy hatchway, and he saw one of the Spanish sailors, prowling there, hurriedly placing his hand in the bosom of his frock, as if hiding something. Before the man could have been certain

---

[23] Men's secret society feared for presumed political plotting.

who it was that was passing, he slunk below out of sight. But enough was seen of him to make it sure that he was the same young sailor before noticed in the rigging.

What was that which so sparkled? thought Captain Delano. It was no lamp—no match—no live coal. Could it have been a jewel? But how come sailors with jewels? —or with silk-trimmed under-shirts either? Has he been robbing the trunks of the dead cabin-passengers? But if so, he would hardly wear one of the stolen articles on board ship here. Ah, ah—if, now, that was, indeed, a secret sign I saw passing between this suspicious fellow and his captain awhile since; if I could only be certain that, in my uneasiness, my senses did not deceive me, then—

Here, passing from one suspicious thing to another, his mind revolved the strange questions put to him concerning his ship.

By a curious coincidence, as each point was recalled, the black wizards of Ashantee would strike up with their hatchets, as in ominous comment on the white stranger's thoughts. Pressed by such enigmas and portents, it would have been almost against nature, had not, even into the least distrustful heart, some ugly misgivings obtruded.

Observing the ship, now helplessly fallen into a current, with enchanted sails, drifting with increased rapidity seaward; and noting that, from a lately intercepted projection of the land, the sealer was hidden, the stout mariner began to quake at thoughts which he barely durst confess to himself. Above all, he began to feel a ghostly dread of Don Benito. And yet, when he roused himself, dilated his chest, felt himself strong on his legs, and coolly considered it—what did all these phantoms amount to?

Had the Spaniard any sinister scheme, it must have reference not so much to him (Captain Delano) as to his ship (the Bachelor's Delight). Hence the present drifting away of the one ship from the other, instead of favoring any such possible scheme, was, for the time, at least, opposed to it. Clearly any suspicion, combining such contradictions, must need be delusive. Beside, was it not absurd to think of a vessel in distress—a vessel by sickness almost dismanned of her crew—a vessel whose inmates were parched for water—was it not a thousand times absurd that such a craft should, at present, be of a piratical character; or her commander, either for himself or those under him, cherish any desire but for speedy relief and refreshment? But then, might not general distress, and thirst in particular, be affected? And might not that same undiminished Spanish crew, alleged to have perished off to a remnant, be at that very moment lurking in the hold? On heart-broken pretense of entreating a cup of cold water, fiends in human form had got into lonely dwellings, nor retired until a dark deed had been done. And among the Malay pirates, it was no unusual thing to lure ships after them into their treacherous harbors, or entice boarders from a declared enemy at sea, by the spectacle of thinly manned or vacant decks, beneath which prowled a hundred spears with yellow arms ready to upthrust them through the mats. Not that Captain Delano had entirely credited such things. He had heard of them— and now, as stories, they recurred. The present destination of the ship was the anchorage. There she would be near his own vessel. Upon gaining that vicinity, might not the San Dominick, like a slumbering volcano, suddenly let loose energies now hid?

He recalled the Spaniard's manner while telling his story. There was a gloomy hesitancy and subterfuge about it. It was just the manner of one making up his tale for evil purposes, as he goes. But if that story was not true, what was the truth? That the ship had unlawfully come into the Spaniard's possession? But in many of its details, especially in reference to the more calamitous parts, such as the fatalities among the seamen, the consequent prolonged beating about, the past sufferings from obstinate calms, and still continued suffering from thirst; in all these points, as well as others, Don Benito's story had corroborated not only the wailing ejaculations of the indiscriminate multitude, white and black, but likewise—what seemed impossible to be counterfeit—by the very expression and play of every human feature, which Captain Delano saw. If Don Benito's story was, throughout, an invention, then every soul on board, down to the youngest negress, was his carefully drilled recruit in the plot: an incredible inference. And yet, if there was ground for mistrusting his veracity, that inference was a legitimate one.

But those questions of the Spaniard. There, indeed, one might pause. Did they not seem put with much the same object with which the burglar or assassin, by day-time, reconnoitres the walls of a house? But, with ill purposes, to solicit such information openly of the chief person endangered, and so, in effect, setting him on his guard; how unlikely a procedure was that? Absurd, then, to suppose that those questions had been prompted by evil designs. Thus, the same conduct, which, in this instance, had raised the alarm, served to dispel it. In short, scarce any suspicion or uneasiness, however apparently reasonable at the time, which was not now, with equal apparent reason, dismissed.

At last he began to laugh at his former forebodings; and laugh at the strange ship for, in its aspect, someway siding with them, as it were; and laugh, too, at the odd-looking blacks, particularly those old scissors-grinders, the Ashantees; and those bed-ridden old knitting women, the oakum-pickers; and almost at the dark Spaniard himself, the central hobgoblin of all.

For the rest, whatever in a serious way seemed enigmatical, was now good-naturedly explained away by the thought that, for the most part, the poor invalid scarcely knew what he was about; either sulking in black vapors, or putting idle questions without sense or object. Evidently, for the present, the man was not fit to be intrusted with the ship. On some benevolent plea withdrawing the command from him, Captain Delano would yet have to send her to Conception, in charge of his second mate, a worthy person and good navigator—a plan not more convenient for the San Dominick than for Don Benito; for, relieved from all anxiety, keeping wholly to his cabin, the sick man, under the good nursing of his servant, would, probably, by the end of the passage, be in a measure restored to health, and with that he should also be restored to authority.

Such were the American's thoughts. They were tranquilizing. There was a difference between the idea of Don Benito's darkly pre-ordaining Captain Delano's fate, and Captain Delano's lightly arranging Don Benito's. Nevertheless, it was not without something of relief that the good seaman presently perceived his whale-boat in the distance. Its absence had been prolonged by unexpected detention at the sealer's side, as well as its returning trip lengthened by the continual recession of the goal.

The advancing speck was observed by the blacks. Their shouts attracted the attention of Don Benito, who, with a return of courtesy, approaching Captain Delano, expressed satisfaction at the coming of some supplies, slight and temporary as they must necessarily prove.

Captain Delano responded; but while doing so, his attention was drawn to something passing on the deck below: among the crowd climbing the landward bulwarks, anxiously watching the coming boat, two blacks, to all appearances accidentally incommoded by one of the sailors, violently pushed him aside, which the sailor someway resenting, they dashed him to the deck, despite the earnest cries of the oakum-pickers.

"Don Benito," said Captain Delano quickly, "do you see what is going on there? Look!"

But, seized by his cough, the Spaniard staggered, with both hands to his face, on the point of falling. Captain Delano would have supported him, but the servant was more alert, who, with one hand sustaining his master, with the other applied the cordial. Don Benito restored, the black withdrew his support, slipping aside a little, but dutifully remaining within call of a whisper. Such discretion was here evinced as quite wiped away, in the visitor's eyes, any blemish of impropriety which might have attached to the attendant, from the indecorous conferences before mentioned; showing, too, that if the servant were to blame, it might be more the master's fault than his own, since, when left to himself, he could conduct thus well.

His glance called away from the spectacle of disorder to the more pleasing one before him, Captain Delano could not avoid again congratulating his host upon possessing such a servant, who, though perhaps a little too forward now and then, must upon the whole be invaluable to one in the invalid's situation.

"Tell me, Don Benito," he added, with a smile—"I should like to have your man here, myself—what will you take for him? Would fifty doubloons be any object?"

"Master wouldn't part with Babo for a thousand doubloons," murmured the black, overhearing the offer, and taking it in earnest, and, with the strange vanity of a faithful slave, appreciated by his master, scorning to hear so paltry a valuation put upon him by a stranger. But Don Benito, apparently hardly yet completely restored, and again interrupted by his cough, made but some broken reply.

Soon his physical distress became so great, affecting his mind, too, apparently, that, as if to screen the sad spectacle, the servant gently conducted his master below.

Left to himself, the American, to while away the time till his boat should arrive, would have pleasantly accosted some one of the few Spanish seamen he saw; but recalling something that Don Benito had said touching their ill conduct, he refrained; as a shipmaster indisposed to countenance cowardice or unfaithfulness in seamen.

While, with these thoughts, standing with eye directed forward towards that handful of sailors, suddenly he thought that one or two of them returned the glance and with a sort of meaning. He rubbed his eyes, and looked again; but again seemed to see the same thing. Under a new form, but more obscure than any previous one, the old suspicions recurred, but, in the absence of Don Benito, with less of panic than before. Despite the bad account given of the sailors, Captain Delano resolved forthwith to accost one of them. Descending the poop, he made his way through the blacks, his movement drawing a queer cry from the oakum-pickers, prompted by whom, the negroes, twitching each other aside, divided before him; but, as if curious to see what was the object of this deliberate visit to their Ghetto, closing in behind, in tolerable order, followed the white stranger up. His progress thus proclaimed as by mounted kings-at-arms, and escorted as by a Caffre[24] guard of honor, Captain Delano, assuming a good-humored, off-handed air, continued to advance; now and then saying a blithe

[24] South African tribe.

word to the negroes, and his eye curiously surveying the white faces, here and there sparsely mixed in with the blacks, like stray white pawns venturously involved in the ranks of the chess-men opposed.

While thinking which of them to select for his purpose, he chanced to observe a sailor seated on the deck engaged in tarring the strap of a large block, a circle of blacks squatted round him inquisitively eyeing the process.

The mean employment of the man was in contrast with something superior in his figure. His hand, black with continually thrusting it into the tar-pot held for him by a negro, seemed not naturally allied to his face, a face which would have been a very fine one but for its haggardness. Whether this haggardness had aught to do with criminality, could not be determined; since, as intense heat and cold, though unlike, produce like sensations, so innocence and guilt, when, through casual association with mental pain, stamping any visible impress, use one seal—a hacked one.

Not again that this reflection occurred to Captain Delano at the time, charitable man as he was. Rather another idea. Because observing so singular a haggardness combined with a dark eye, averted as in trouble and shame, and then again recalling Don Benito's confessed ill opinion of his crew, insensibly he was operated upon by certain general notions which, while disconnecting pain and abashment from virtue, invariably link them with vice.

If, indeed, there be any wickedness on board this ship, thought Captain Delano, be sure that man there has fouled his hand in it, even as now he fouls it in the pitch. I don't like to accost him. I will speak to this other, this old Jack here on the windlass.

He advanced to an old Barcelona tar, in ragged red breeches and dirty night-cap, cheeks trenched and bronzed, whiskers dense as thorn hedges. Seated between two sleepy-looking Africans, this mariner, like his younger shipmate, was employed upon some rigging—splicing a cable—the sleepy-looking blacks performing the inferior function of holding the outer parts of the ropes for him.

Upon Captain Delano's approach, the man at once hung his head below its previous level; the one necessary for business. It appeared as if he desired to be thought absorbed, with more than common fidelity, in his task. Being addressed, he glanced up, but with what seemed a furtive, diffident air, which sat strangely enough on his weather-beaten visage, much as if a grizzly bear, instead of growling and biting, should simper and cast sheep's eyes. He was asked several questions concerning the voyage—questions purposely referring to several particulars in Don Benito's narrative, not previously corroborated by those impulsive cries greeting the visitor on first coming on board. The questions were briefly answered, confirming all that remained to be confirmed of the story. The negroes about the windlass joined in with the old sailor; but, as they became talkative, he by degrees became mute, and at length quite glum, seemed morosely unwilling to answer more questions, and yet, all the while, this ursine air was somehow mixed with his sheepish one.

Despairing of getting into unembarrassed talk with such a centaur, Captain Delano, after glancing round for a more promising countenance, but seeing none, spoke pleasantly to the blacks to make way for him; and so, amid various grins and grimaces, returned to the poop, feeling a little strange at first, he could hardly tell why, but upon the whole with regained confidence in Benito Cereno.

How plainly, thought he, did that old whiskerando yonder betray a consciousness of ill desert. No doubt, when he saw me coming, he dreaded lest I, apprised by his

Captain of the crew's general misbehavior, came with sharp words for him, and so down with his head. And yet—and yet, now that I think of it, that very old fellow, if I err not, was one of those who seemed so earnestly eyeing me here awhile since. Ah, these currents spin one's head round almost as much as they do the ship. Ha, there now's a pleasant sort of sunny sight; quite sociable, too.

His attention had been drawn to a slumbering negress, partly disclosed through the lace-work of some rigging, lying, with youthful limbs carelessly disposed, under the lee of the bulwarks, like a doe in the shade of a woodland rock. Sprawling at her lapped breasts, was her wide-awake fawn, stark naked, its black little body half lifted from the deck, crosswise with its dam's; its hands, like two paws, clambering upon her; its mouth and nose ineffectually rooting to get at the mark; and meantime giving a vexatious half-grunt, blending with the composed snore of the negress.

The uncommon vigor of the child at length roused the mother. She started up, at a distance facing Captain Delano. But as if not at all concerned at the attitude in which she had been caught, delightedly she caught the child up, with maternal transports, covering it with kisses.

There's naked nature, now; pure tenderness and love, thought Captain Delano, well pleased.

This incident prompted him to remark the other negresses more particularly than before. He was gratified with their manners: like most uncivilized women, they seemed at once tender of heart and tough of constitution; equally ready to die for their infants or fight for them. Unsophisticated as leopardesses; loving as doves. Ah! thought Captain Delano, these, perhaps, are some of the very women whom Ledyard[25] saw in Africa, and gave such a noble account of.

These natural sights somehow insensibly deepened his confidence and ease. At last he looked to see how his boat was getting on; but it was still pretty remote. He turned to see if Don Benito had returned; but he had not.

To change the scene, as well as to please himself with a leisurely observation of the coming boat, stepping over into the mizzen-chains, he clambered his way into the starboard quarter-gallery—one of those abandoned Venetian-looking water-balconies previously mentioned—retreats cut off from the deck. As his foot pressed the half-damp, half-dry sea-mosses matting the place, and a chance phantom cats-paw—an islet of breeze, unheralded, unfollowed—as this ghostly cats-paw came fanning his cheek; as his glance fell upon the row of small, round dead-lights—all closed like coppered eyes of the coffined—and the state-cabin door, once connecting with the gallery, even as the dead-lights had once looked out upon it, but now calked fast like a sarcophagus lid; and to a purple-black tarred-over, panel, threshold, and post; and he bethought him of the time, when that state-cabin and this state-balcony had heard the voices of the Spanish king's officers, and the forms of the Lima viceroy's daughters had perhaps leaned where he stood—as these and other images flitted through his mind, as the cats-paw through the calm, gradually he felt rising a dreamy inquietude, like that of one who alone on the prairie feels unrest from the repose of the noon.

He leaned against the carved balustrade, again looking off toward his boat; but found his eye falling upon the ribbon grass, trailing along the ship's water-line, straight

[25] John Ledyard (1752–1789), American travel writer on Africa.

as a border of green box; and parterres[26] of sea-weed, broad ovals and crescents, floating nigh and far, with what seemed long formal alleys between, crossing the terraces of swells, and sweeping round as if leading to the grottoes below. And overhanging all was the balustrate by his arm, which, partly stained with pitch and partly embossed with moss, seemed the charred ruin of some summer-house in a grand garden long running to waste.

Trying to break one charm, he was but becharmed anew. Though upon the wide sea, he seemed in some far inland country; prisoner in some deserted cheau, left to stare at empty grounds, and peer out at vague roads, where never wagon or wayfarer passed.

But these enchantments were a little disenchanted as his eye fell on the corroded main-chains. Of an ancient style, massy and rusty in link, shackle and bolt, they seemed even more fit for the ship's present business than the one for which she had been built.

Presently he thought something moved nigh the chains. He rubbed his eyes, and looked hard. Groves of rigging were about the chains; and there, peering from behind a great stay, like an Indian from behind a hemlock, a Spanish sailor, a marlingspike in his hand, was seen, who made what seemed an imperfect gesture towards the balcony, but immediately, as if alarmed by some advancing step along the deck within, vanished into the recesses of the hempen forest, like a poacher.

What meant this? Something the man had sought to communicate, unbeknown to any one, even to his captain. Did the secret involve aught unfavorable to his captain? Were those previous misgivings of Captain Delano's about to be verified? Or, in his haunted mood at the moment, had some random, unintentional motion of the man, while busy with the stay, as if repairing it, been mistaken for a significant beckoning?

Not unbewildered, again he gazed off for his boat. But it was temporarily hidden by a rocky spur of the isle. As with some eagerness he bent forward, watching for the first shooting view of its beak, the balustrade gave way before him like charcoal. Had he not clutched an outreaching rope he would have fallen into the sea. The crash, though feeble, and the fall, though hollow, of the rotten fragments, must have been overheard. He glanced up. With sober curiosity peering down upon him was one of the old oakum-pickers, slipped from his perch to an outside boom; while below the old negro, and, invisible to him, reconnoitering from a port-hole like a fox from the mouth of its den, crouched the Spanish sailor again. From something suddenly suggested by the man's air, the mad idea now darted into Captain Delano's mind, that Don Benito's plea of indisposition, in withdrawing below, was but a pretence: that he was engaged there maturing his plot, of which the sailor, by some means gaining an inkling, had a mind to warn the stranger against; incited, it may be, by gratitude for a kind word on first boarding the ship. Was it from foreseeing some possible interference like this, that Don Benito had, beforehand, given such a bad character of his sailors, while praising the negroes; though, indeed, the former seemed as docile as the latter the contrary? The whites, too, by nature, were the shrewder race. A man with some evil design, would he not be likely to speak well of that stupidity which was blind to his depravity, and malign that intelligence from which it might not be hidden? Not unlikely, perhaps. But if the whites had dark secrets concerning Don Benito, could then Don Benito be any way in complicity with the blacks? But they

---

[26] Ornamental gardens.

were too stupid. Besides, who ever heard of a white so far a renegade as to apostatize[27] from his very species almost, by leaguing in against it with negroes? These difficulties recalled former ones. Lost in their mazes, Captain Delano, who had now regained the deck, was uneasily advancing along it, when he observed a new face; an aged sailor seated cross-legged near the main hatchway. His skin was shrunk up with wrinkles like a pelican's empty pouch; his hair frosted; his countenance grave and composed. His hands were full of ropes, which he was working into a large knot. Some blacks were about him obligingly dipping the strands for him, here and there, as the exigencies of the operation demanded.

Captain Delano crossed over to him, and stood in silence surveying the knot; his mind, by a not uncongenial transition, passing from its own entanglements to those of the hemp. For intricacy, such a knot he had never seen in an American ship, nor indeed any other. The old man looked like an Egyptian priest, making Gordian knots for the temple of Ammon.[28] The knot seemed a combination of double-bowline-knot, treble-crown-knot, back-handed-well-knot, knot-in-and-out-knot, and jamming-knot.

At last, puzzled to comprehend the meaning of such a knot, Captain Delano addressed the knotter:—

"What are you knotting there, my man?"

"The knot," was the brief reply, without looking up.

"So it seems; but what is it for?"

"For some one else to undo," muttered back the old man, plying his fingers harder than ever, the knot being now nearly completed.

While Captain Delano stood watching him, suddenly the old man threw the knot towards him, saying in broken English—the first heard in the ship—something to this effect: "Undo it, cut it, quick." It was said lowly, but with such condensation of rapidity, that the long, slow words in Spanish, which had preceded and followed, almost operated as covers to the brief English between.

For a moment, knot in hand, and knot in head, Captain Delano stood mute; while, without further heeding him, the old man was now intent upon other ropes. Presently there was a slight stir behind Captain Delano. Turning, he saw the chained negro, Atufal, standing quietly there. The next moment the old sailor rose, muttering, and, followed by his subordinate negros, removed to the forward part of the ship, where in the crowd he disappeared.

An elderly negro, in a clout like an infant's, and with a pepper and salt head, and a kind of attorney air, now approached Captain Delano. In tolerable Spanish, and with a good-natured, knowing wink, he informed him that the old knotter was simple-witted, but harmless; often playing his odd tricks. The negro concluded by begging the knot, for of course the stranger would not care to be troubled with it. Unconsciously, it was handed to him. With a sort of congé,[29] the negro received it, and, turning his back, ferreted into it like a detective custom-house officer after smuggled laces. Soon, with some African word, equivalent to pshaw, he tossed the knot overboard.

---

[27] Renounce.
[28] The temple oracle predicted that whoever undid King Gordius' knot would become master of Asia. Alexander the Great simply cut the Gordian knot with his sword.
[29] Bow of farewell.

All this is very queer now, thought Captain Delano, with a qualmish sort of emotion; but, as one feeling incipient sea-sickness, he strove, by ignoring the symptoms, to get rid of the malady. Once more he looked off for his boat. To his delight, it was now again in view, leaving the rocky spur astern.

The sensation here experienced, after at first relieving his uneasiness, with unforeseen efficacy soon began to remove it. The less distant sight of that well-known boat—showing it, not as before, half blended with the haze, but with outline defined, so that its individuality, like a man's, was manifest; that boat, Rover by name, which, though now in strange seas, had often pressed the beach of Captain Delano's home, and, brought to its threshold for repairs, had familiarly lain there, as a Newfoundland dog; the sight of that household boat evoked a thousand trustful associations, which, contrasted with previous suspicions, filled him not only with lightsome confidence, but somehow with half humorous self-reproaches at his former lack of it.

"What, I, Amasa Delano—Jack of the Beach, as they called me when a lad—I, Amasa; the same that, duck-satchel in hand, used to paddle along the water-side to the school-house made from the old hulk—I, little Jack of the Beach, that used to go berrying with cousin Nat and the rest; I to be murdered here at the ends of the earth, on board a haunted pirate-ship by a horrible Spaniard? Too nonsensical to think of! Who would murder Amasa Delano? His conscience is clean. There is some one above. Fie, fie, Jack of the Beach! you are a child indeed; a child of the second childhood, old boy; you are beginning to dote and drule, I'm afraid."

Light of heart and foot, he stepped aft, and there was met by Don Benito's servant, who, with a pleasing expression, responsive to his own present feelings, informed him that his master had recovered from the effects of his coughing fit, and had just ordered him to go present his compliments to his good guest, Don Amasa, and say that he (Don Benito) would soon have the happiness to rejoin him.

There now, do you mark that? again thought Captain Delano, walking the poop. What a donkey I was. This kind gentleman who here sends me his kind compliments, he, but ten minutes ago, dark-lantern in hand, was dodging round some old grindstone in the hold, sharpening a hatchet for me, I thought. Well, well; these long calms have a morbid effect on the mind, I've often heard, though I never believed it before. Ha! glancing towards the boat; there's Rover; good dog; a white bone in her mouth. A pretty big bone though, seems to me.—What? Yes, she has fallen afoul of the bubbling tide-rip there. It sets her the other way, too, for the time. Patience.

It was now about noon, though, from the grayness of everything, it seemed to be getting towards dusk.

The calm was confirmed. In the far distance, away from the influence of land, the leaden ocean seemed laid out and leaded up, its course finished, soul gone, defunct. But the current from landward, where the ship was, increased; silently sweeping her further and further towards the tranced waters beyond.

Still, from his knowledge of those latitudes, cherishing hopes of a breeze, and a fair and fresh one, at any moment, Captain Delano, despite present prospects, buoyantly counted upon bringing the San Dominick safely to anchor ere night. The distance swept over was nothing; since, with a good wind, ten minutes' sailing would retrace more than sixty minutes, drifting. Meantime, one moment turning to mark "Rover" fighting the tide-rip, and the next to see Don Benito approaching, he continued walking the poop.

Gradually he felt a vexation arising from the delay of his boat; this soon merged into uneasiness; and at last—his eye falling continually, as from a stage-box into the pit, upon the strange crowd before and below him, and, by-and-by, recognizing there the face—now composed to indifference—of the Spanish sailor who had seemed to beckon from the main-chains—something of his old trepidations returned.

Ah, thought he—gravely enough—this is like the ague: because it went off, it follows not that it won't come back.

Though ashamed of the relapse, he could not altogether subdue it; and so, exerting his good-nature to the utmost, insensibly he came to a compromise.

Yes, this is a strange craft; a strange history, too, and strange folks on board. But—nothing more.

By way of keeping his mind out of mischief till the boat should arrive, he tried to occupy it with turning over and over, in a purely speculative sort of way, some lesser peculiarities of the captain and crew. Among others, four curious points recurred:

First, the affair of the Spanish lad assailed with a knife by the slave boy; an act winked at by Don Benito. Second, the tyranny in Don Benito's treatment of Atufal, the black; as if a child should lead a bull of the Nile by the ring in his nose. Third, the trampling of the sailor by the two negroes; a piece of insolence passed over without so much as a reprimand. Fourth, the cringing submission to their master, of all the ship's underlings, mostly blacks; as if by the least inadvertence they feared to draw down his despotic displeasure.

Coupling these points, they seemed somewhat contradictory. But what then, thought Captain Delano, glancing towards his now nearing boat—what then? Why, Don Benito is a very capricious commander. But he is not the first of the sort I have seen; though it's true he rather exceeds any other. But as a nation—continued he in his reveries—these Spaniards are all an odd set; the very word Spaniard has a curious, conspirator, Guy-Fawkish[30] twang to it. And yet, I dare say, Spaniards in the main are as good folks as any in Duxbury, Massachusetts. Ah good! At last "Rover" has come.

As, with its welcome freight, the boat touched the side, the oakum-pickers, with venerable gestures, sought to restrain the blacks, who, at the sight of three gurried[31] water-casks in its bottom, and a pile of wilted pumpkins in its bow, hung over the bulwarks in disorderly raptures.

Don Benito, with his servant, now appeared; his coming, perhaps, hastened by hearing the noise. Of him Captain Delano sought permission to serve out the water, so that all might share alike, and none injure themselves by unfair excess. But sensible, and, on Don Benito's account, kind as this offer was, it was received with what seemed impatience; as if aware that he lacked energy as a commander, Don Benito, with the true jealousy of weakness, resented as an affront any interference. So, at least, Captain Delano inferred.

In another moment the casks were being hoisted in, when some of the eager negroes accidentally jostled Captain Delano, where he stood by the gangway; so that, unmind-

---

30 Guy Fawkes (1570–1606) was a Catholic conspirator who plotted to blow up the English Parliament.

31 Slimy.

ful of Don Benito, yielding to the impulse of the moment, with good-natured authority he bade the blacks stand back; to enforce his words making use of a half-mirthful, half-menacing gesture. Instantly the blacks paused, just where they were, each negro and negress suspended in his or her posture, exactly as the word had found them—for a few seconds continuing so—while, as between the responsive posts of a telegraph, an unknown syllable ran from man to man among the perched oakum-pickers. While the visitor's attention was fixed by this scene, suddenly the hatchet-polishers half rose, and a rapid cry came from Don Benito.

Thinking that at the signal of the Spaniard he was about to be massacred, Captain Delano would have sprung for his boat, but paused, as the oakum-pickers, dropping down into the crowd with earnest exclamations, forced every white and every negro back, at the same moment, with gestures friendly and familiar, almost jocose, bidding him, in substance, not be a fool. Simultaneously the hatchet-polishers resumed their seats, quietly as so many tailors, and at once, as if nothing had happened, the work of hoisting in the casks was resumed, whites and blacks singing at the tackle.

Captain Delano glanced towards Don Benito. As he saw his meagre form in the act of recovering itself from reclining in the servant's arms, into which the agitated invalid had fallen, he could not but marvel at the panic by which himself had been surprised, on the darting supposition that such a commander, who, upon a legitimate occasion, so trivial, too, as it now appeared, could lose all self-command, was, with energetic iniquity, going to bring about his murder.

The casks being on deck, Captain Delano was handed a number of jars and cups by one of the steward's aids, who, in the name of his captain, entreated him to do as he had, proposed—dole out the water. He complied, with republican impartiality as to this republican element, which always seeks one level, serving the oldest white no better than the youngest black; excepting, indeed, poor Don Benito, whose condition, if not rank, demanded an extra allowance. To him, in the first place, Captain Delano presented a fair pitcher of the fluid; but, thirsting as he was for it, the Spaniard quaffed not a drop until after several grave bows and salutes. A reciprocation of courtesies which the sight-loving Africans hailed with clapping of hands.

Two of the less wilted pumpkins being reserved for the cabin table, the residue were minced up on the spot for the general regalement. But the soft bread, sugar, and bottled cider, Captain Delano would have given the whites alone, and in chief Don Benito; but the latter objected; which disinterestedness not a little pleased the American; and so mouthfuls all around were given alike to whites and blacks; excepting one bottle of cider, which Babo insisted upon setting aside for his master.

Here it may be observed that as, on the first visit of the boat, the American had not permitted his men to board the ship, neither did he now; being unwilling to add to the confusion of the decks.

Not uninfluenced by the peculiar good-humor at present prevailing, and for the time oblivious of any but benevolent thoughts, Captain Delano, who, from recent indications, counted upon a breeze within an hour or two at furthest, dispatched the boat back to the sealer, with orders for all the hands that could be spared immediately to set about rafting casks to the watering-place and filling them. Likewise he bade word be carried to his chief officer, that if, against present expectation, the ship was not brought to anchor by sunset, he need be under no concern; for as there was to be a full moon that night, he (Captain Delano) would remain on board ready to play the pilot, come the wind soon or late.

As the two Captains stood together, observing the departing boat—the servant, as it happened, having just spied a spot on his master's velvet sleeve, and silently engaged rubbing it out—the American expressed his regrets that the San Dominick had no boats; none, at least, but the unseaworthy old hulk of the long-boat, which, warped as a camel's skeleton in the desert, and almost as bleached, lay pot-wise inverted amidships, one side a little tipped, furnishing a subterraneous sort of den for family groups of the blacks, mostly women and small children; who, squatting on old mats below, or perched above in the dark dome, on the elevated seats, were described, some distance within, like a social circle of bats, sheltering in some friendly cave; at intervals, ebon flights of naked boys and girls, three or four years old, darting in and out of the den's mouth.

"Had you three or four boats now, Don Benito," said Captain Delano, "I think that, by tugging at the oars, your negroes here might help along matters some. Did you sail from port without boats, Don Benito?"

"They were stove in the gales, Señor."

"That was bad. Many men, too, you lost then. Boats and men. Those must have been hard gales, Don Benito."

"Past all speech," cringed the Spaniard.

"Tell me, Don Benito," continued his companion with increased interest, "tell me, were these gales immediately off the pitch of Cape Horn?"

"Cape Horn?—who spoke of Cape Horn?"

"Yourself did, when giving me an account of your voyage," answered Captain Delano, with almost equal astonishment at this eating of his own words, even as he ever seemed eating his own heart, on the part of the Spaniard. "You yourself, Don Benito, spoke of Cape Horn," he emphatically repeated.

The Spaniard turned, in a sort of stooping posture, pausing an instant, as one about to make a plunging exchange of elements, as from air to water.

At this moment a messenger-boy, a white, hurried by, in the regular performance of his function carrying the last expired half hour forward to the forecastle, from the cabin time-piece, to have it struck at the ship's large bell.

"Master," said the servant, discontinuing his work on the coat sleeve, and addressing the rapt Spaniard with a sort of timid apprehensiveness, as one charged with a duty, the discharge of which, it was foreseen, would prove irksome to the very person who had imposed it, and for whose benefit it was intended, "master told me never mind where he was, or how engaged, always to remind him, to a minute, when shaving-time comes. Miguel has gone to strike the half-hour afternoon. It is *now* master. Will master go into the cuddy?"

"Ah—yes," answered the Spaniard, starting, as from dreams into realities; then turning upon Captain Delano, he said that ere long he would resume the conversation.

"Then if master means to talk more to Don Amasa," said the servant, "why not let Don Amasa sit by master in the cuddy, and master can talk, and Don Amasa can listen, while Babo here lathers and strops."

"Yes," said Captain Delano, not unpleased with this sociable plan, "yes, Don Benito, unless you had rather not, I will go with you."

"Be it so, Señor."

As the three passed aft, the American could not but think it another strange instance of his host's capriciousness, this being shaved with such uncommon punctuality in the middle of the day. But he deemed it more than likely that the servant's anxious fidelity had something to do with the matter; inasmuch as the timely interruption served to rally his master from the mood which had evidently been coming upon him.

The place called the cuddy was a light deck-cabin formed by the poop, a sort of attic to the large cabin below. Part of it had formerly been the quarters of the officers; but since their death all the partitionings had been thrown down, and the whole interior converted into one spacious and airy marine hall; for absence of fine furniture and picturesque disarray of odd appurtenances, somewhat answering to the wide, cluttered hall of some eccentric bachelor-squire in the country, who hangs his shooting-jacket and tobacco-pouch on deer antlers, and keeps his fishing-rod, tongs, and walking-stick in the same corner.

The similitude was heightened, if not originally suggested, by glimpses of the surrounding sea; since, in one aspect, the country and the ocean seem cousins-german.

The floor of the cuddy was matted. Overhead, four or five old muskets were stuck into horizontal holes along the beams. On one side was a claw-footed old table lashed to the deck; a thumbed missal on it, and over it a small, meagre crucifix attached to the bulk-head. Under the table lay a dented cutlass or two, with a hacked harpoon, among some melancholy old rigging, like a heap of poor friars' girdles. There were also two long, sharp-ribbed settees of Malacca cane, black with age, and uncomfortable to look at as inquisitors' racks, with a large, misshapen arm-chair, which, furnished with a rude barber's crotch[32] at the back, working with a screw, seemed some grotesque engine of torment. A flag locker was in one corner, open, exposing various colored bunting, some rolled up, others half unrolled, still others tumbled. Opposite was a cumbrous washstand, of black mahogany, all of one block, with a pedestal, like a font, and over it a railed shelf, containing combs, brushes, and other implements of the toilet. A torn hammock of stained grass swung near; the sheets tossed, and the pillow wrinkled up like a brow, as if whoever slept here slept but illy, with alternate visitations of sad thoughts and bad dreams.

The further extremity of the cuddy, overhanging the ship's stern, was pierced with three openings, windows or port-holes, according as men or cannon might peer, socially or unsocially, out of them. At present neither men nor cannon were seen, though huge ring-bolts and other rusty iron fixtures of the wood-work hinted of twenty-four-pounders.

Glancing towards the hammock as he entered, Captain Delano said, "You sleep here, Don Benito?"

"Yes, Señor; since we got into mild weather."

"This seems a sort of dormitory, sitting-room, sail-loft, chapel, armory, and private closet all together, Don Benito," added Captain Delano, looking round.

"Yes, Señor; events have not been favorable to much order in my arrangements."

Here the servant, napkin on arm, made a motion as if waiting his master's good pleasure. Don Benito signified his readiness, when, seating him in the Malacca arm-chair, and for the guest's convenience drawing opposite one of the settees, the servant commenced operations by throwing back his master's collar and loosening his cravat.

There is something in the negro which, in a peculiar way, fits him for avocations about one's person. Most negroes are natural valets and hair-dressers; taking to the comb and brush congenially as to the castinets, and flourishing them apparently with

---

[32] Headrest.

almost equal satisfaction. There is, too, a smooth tact about them in this employment, with a marvelous, noiseless, gliding briskness, not ungraceful in its way, singularly pleasing to behold, and still more so to be the manipulated subject of. And above all is the great gift of good-humor. Not the mere grin or laugh is here meant. Those were unsuitable. But a certain easy cheerfulness, harmonious in every glance and gesture; as though God had set the whole negro to some pleasant tune.

When to this is added the docility arising from the unaspiring contentment of a limited mind, and that susceptibility of bland attachment sometimes inhering in indisputable inferiors, one readily perceives why those hypochondriacs, Johnson and Byron—it may be, something like the hypochondriac Benito Cereno—took to their hearts, almost to the exclusion of the entire white race, their serving men, the negroes, Barber and Fletcher.[33] But if there be that in the negro which exempts him from the inflicted sourness of the morbid or cynical mind, how, in his most prepossessing aspects, must he appear to a benevolent one? When at ease with respect to exterior things, Captain Delano's nature was not only benign, but familiarly and humorously so. At home, he had often taken rare satisfaction in sitting in his door, watching some free man of color at his work or play. If on a voyage he chanced to have a black sailor, invariably he was on chatty and half-gamesome terms with him. In fact, like most men of a good, blithe heart, Captain Delano took to negroes, not philanthropically, but genially, just as other men to Newfoundland dogs.

Hitherto, the circumstances in which he found the San Dominick had repressed the tendency. But in the cuddy, relieved from his former uneasiness, and, for various reasons, more sociably inclined than at any previous period of the day, and seeing the colored servant, napkin on arm, so debonair about his master, in a business so familiar as that of shaving, too, all his old weakness for negroes returned.

Among other things, he was amused with an odd instance of the African love of bright colors and fine shows, in the black's informally taking from the flag-locker a great piece of bunting of all hues, and lavishly tucking it under his master's chin for an apron.

The mode of shaving among the Spaniards is a little different from what it is with other nations. They have a basin, specifically called a barber's basin, which on one side is scooped out, so as accurately to receive the chin, against which it is closely held in lathering; which is done, not with a brush, but with soap dipped in the water of the basin and rubbed on the face.

In the present instance salt-water was used for lack of better; and the parts lathered were only the upper lip, and low down under the throat, all the rest being cultivated beard.

The preliminaries being somewhat novel to Captain Delano, he sat curiously eying them, so that no conversation took place, nor, for the present, did Don Benito appear disposed to renew any.

Setting down his basin, the negro searched among the razors, as for the sharpest, and having found it, gave it an additional edge by expertly strapping it on the firm, smooth, oily skin of his open palm; he then made a gesture as if to begin, but midway stood suspended for an instant, one hand elevating the razor, the other professionally

[33] Samuel Johnson and Lord Byron both left generous bequests to loyal black servants.

dabbling among the bubbling suds on the Spaniard's lank neck. Not unaffected by the close sight of the gleaming steel, Don Benito nervously shuddered; his usual ghastliness was heightened by the lather, which lather, again, was intensified in its hue by the contrasting sootiness of the negro's body. Altogether the scene was somewhat peculiar, at least to Captain Delano, nor, as he saw the two thus postured, could he resist the vagary, that in the black he saw a headsman, and in the white a man at the block. But this was one of those antic conceits, appearing and vanishing in a breath, from which, perhaps, the best regulated mind is not always free.

Meantime the agitation of the Spaniard had a little loosened the bunting from around him, so that one broad fold swept curtain-like over the chair-arm to the floor, revealing, amid a profusion of armorial bars and ground-colors—black, blue, and yellow—a closed castle in a blood-red field diagonal with a lion rampant in a white.

"The castle and the lion," exclaimed Captain Delano—"why, Don Benito, this is the flag of Spain you use here. It's well it's only I, and not the King, that sees this," he added, with a smile, "but"—turning towards the black—"it's all one, I suppose, so the colors be gay;" which playful remark did not fail somewhat to tickle the negro.

"Now, master," he said, readjusting the flag, and pressing the head gently further back into the crotch of the chair; "now, master," and the steel glanced nigh the throat.

Again Don Benito faintly shuddered.

"You must not shake so, master. See, Don Amasa, master always shakes when I shave him. And yet master knows I never yet have drawn blood, though it's true, if master will shake so, I may some of these times. Now master," he continued. "And now, Don Amasa, please go on with your talk about the gale, and all that; master can hear, and, between times, master can answer."

"Ah yes, these gales," said Captain Delano; "but the more I think of your voyage, Don Benito, the more I wonder, not at the gales, terrible as they must have been, but at the disastrous interval following them. For here, by your account, have you been these two months and more getting from Cape Horn to St. Maria, a distance which I myself, with a good wind, have sailed in a few days. True, you had calms, and long ones, but to be becalmed for two months, that is, at least, unusual. Why, Don Benito, had almost any other gentleman told me such a story, I should have been half disposed to a little incredulity."

Here an involuntary expression came over the Spaniard, similar to that just before on the deck, and whether it was the start he gave, or a sudden gawky roll of the hull in the calm, or a momentary unsteadiness of the servant's hand, however it was, just then the razor drew blood, spots of which stained the creamy lather under the throat: immediately the black barber drew back his steel, and, remaining in his professional attitude, back to Captain Delano, and face to Don Benito, held up the trickling razor, saying, with a sort of half humorous sorrow, "See, master—you shook so—here's Babo's first blood."

No sword drawn before James the First of England, no assassination in that timid King's presence,[34] could have produced a more terrified aspect than was now presented by Don Benito.

---

[34] James I (1566–1625) was terrified of assassination.

Poor fellow, thought Captain Delano, so nervous he can't even bear the sight of barber's blood; and this unstrung, sick man, is it credible that I should have imagined he meant to spill all my blood, who can't endure the sight of one little drop of his own? Surely, Amasa Delano, you have been beside yourself this day. Tell it not when you get home, sappy Amasa. Well, well, he looks like a murderer, doesn't he? More like as if himself were to be done for. Well, well, this day's experience shall be a good lesson.

Meantime, while these things were running through the honest seaman's mind, the servant had taken the napkin from his arm, and to Don Benito had said—"But answer Don Amasa, please, master, while I wipe this ugly stuff off the razor, and strop it again."

As he said the words, his face was turned half round, so as to be alike visible to the Spaniard and the American, and seemed, by its expression, to hint, that he was desirous, by getting his master to go on with the conversation, considerably to withdraw his attention from the recent annoying accident. As if glad to snatch the offered relief, Don Benito resumed, rehearsing to Captain Delano, that not only were the calms of unusual duration, but the ship had fallen in with obstinate currents; and other things he added, some of which were but repetitions of former statements, to explain how it came to pass that the passage from Cape Horn to St. Maria had been so exceedingly long; now and then mingling with his words, incidental praises, less qualified than before, to the blacks, for their general good conduct. These particulars were not given consecutively, the servant, at convenient times, using his razor, and so, between the intervals of shaving, the story and panegyric went on with more than usual huskiness.

To Captain Delano's imagination, now again not wholly at rest, there was something so hollow in the Spaniard's manner, with apparently some reciprocal hollowness in the servant's dusky comment of silence, that the idea flashed across him, that possibly master and man, for some unknown purpose, were acting out, both in word and deed, nay, to the very tremor of Don Benito's limbs, some juggling play before him. Neither did the suspicion of collusion lack apparent support, from the fact of those whispered conferences before mentioned. But then, what could be the object of enacting this play of the barber before him? At last, regarding the notion as a whimsy, insensibly suggested, perhaps, by the theatrical aspect of Don Benito in his harlequin ensign, Captain Delano speedily banished it.

The shaving over, the servant bestirred himself with a small bottle of scented waters, pouring a few drops on the head, and then diligently rubbing; the vehemence of the exercise causing the muscles of his face to twitch rather strangely.

His next operation was with comb, scissors, and brush; going round and round, smoothing a curl here, clipping an unruly whisker-hair there, giving a graceful sweep to the temple-lock, with other impromptu touches evincing the hand of a master; while, like any resigned gentleman in barber's hands, Don Benito bore all, much less uneasily, at least, than he had done the razoring; indeed, he sat so pale and rigid now, that the negro seemed a Nubian sculptor finishing off a white statue-head.

All being over at last, the standard of Spain removed, tumbled up, and tossed back into the flag-locker, the negro's warm breath blowing away any stray hair which might have lodged down his master's neck; collar and cravat readjusted; a speck of lint whisked off the velvet lapel; all this being done; backing off a little space, and pausing with an expression of subdued self-complacency, the servant for a moment surveyed his master, as, in toilet at least, the creature of his own tasteful hands.

Captain Delano playfully complimented him upon his achievement; at the same time congratulating Don Benito.

But neither sweet waters, nor shampooing, nor fidelity, nor sociality, delighted the Spaniard. Seeing him relapsing into forbidding gloom, and still remaining seated, Captain Delano, thinking that his presence was undesired just then, withdrew, on pretense of seeing whether, as he had prophesied, any signs of a breeze were visible.

Walking forward to the main-mast, he stood awhile thinking over the scene, and not without some undefined misgivings, when he heard a noise near the cuddy, and turning, saw the negro, his hand to his cheek. Advancing, Captain Delano perceived that the cheek was bleeding. He was about to ask the cause, when the negro's wailing soliloquy enlightened him.

"Ah, when will master get better from his sickness; only the sour heart that sour sickness breeds made him serve Babo so; cutting Babo with the razor, because, only by accident, Babo had given master one little scratch; and for the first time in so many a day, too. Ah, ah, ah," holding his hand to his face.

Is it possible, thought Captain Delano; was it to wreak in private his Spanish spite against this poor friend of his, that Don Benito, by his sullen manner, impelled me to withdraw? Ah, this slavery breeds ugly passions in man.——Poor fellow!

He was about to speak in sympathy to the negro, but with a timid reluctance he now re-entered the cuddy.

Presently master and man came forth; Don Benito leaning on his servant as if nothing had happened.

But a sort of love-quarrel, after all, thought Captain Delano.

He accosted Don Benito, and they slowly walked together. They had gone but a few paces, when the steward—a tall, rajah-looking mulatto, orientally set off with a pagoda turban formed by three or four Madras handkerchiefs wound about his head, tier on tier—approaching with a saalam, announced lunch in the cabin.

On their way thither, the two captains were preceded by the mulatto, who, turning round as he advanced, with continual smiles and bows, ushered them on, a display of elegance which quite completed the insignificance of the small bare-headed Babo, who, as if not unconscious of inferiority, eyed askance the graceful steward. But in part, Captain Delano imputed his jealous watchfulness to that peculiar feeling which the full-blooded African entertains for the adulterated one. As for the steward, his manner, if not bespeaking much dignity or self-respect, yet evidenced his extreme desire to please; which is doubly meritorious, as at once Christian and Chesterfieldian.[35]

Captain Delano observed with interest that while the complexion of the mulatto was hybrid, his physiognomy was European—classically so.

"Don Benito," whispered he, "I am glad to see this usher-of-the-golden-rod of yours; the sight refutes an ugly remark once made to me by a Barbadoes planter; that

[35] Philip Dormer of Stanhope, the fourth earl of Chesterfield (1694–1773), advocated a worldly code of conduct.

when a mulatto has a regular European face, look out for him; he is a devil. But see, your steward here has features more regular than King George's of England; and yet there he nods, and bows, and smiles; a king, indeed—the king of kind hearts and polite fellows. What a pleasant voice he has, too?"

"He has, Señor."

"But tell me, has he not, so far as you have known him, always proved a good, worthy fellow?" said Captain Delano, pausing, while with a final genuflexion the steward disappeared into the cabin; "come, for the reason just mentioned, I am curious to know."

"Francesco is a good man," a sort of sluggishly responded Don Benito, like a phlegmatic appreciator, who would neither find fault nor flatter.

"Ah, I thought so. For it were strange, indeed, and not very creditable to us white-skins, if a little of our blood mixed with the African's, should, far from improving the latter's quality, have the sad effect of pouring vitriolic acid into black broth; improving the hue, perhaps, but not the wholesomeness."

"Doubtless, doubtless, Señor, but"—glancing at Babo—"not to speak of negroes, your planter's remark I have heard applied to the Spanish and Indian intermixtures in our provinces. But I know nothing about the matter," he listlessly added.

And here they entered the cabin.

The lunch was a frugal one. Some of Captain Delano's fresh fish and pumpkins, biscuit and salt beef, the reserved bottle of cider, and the San Dominick's last bottle of Canary.

As they entered, Francesco, with two or three colored aids, was hovering over the table giving the last adjustments. Upon perceiving their master they withdrew, Francesco making a smiling congé, and the Spaniard, without condescending to notice it, fastidiously remarking to his companion that he relished not superfluous attendance.

Without companions, host and guest sat down, like a childless married couple, at opposite ends of the table, Don Benito waving Captain Delano to his place, and, weak as he was, insisting upon that gentleman being seated before himself.

The negro placed a rug under Don Benito's feet, and a cushion behind his back, and then stood behind, not his master's chair, but Captain Delano's. At first, this a little surprised the latter. But it was soon evident that, in taking his position, the black was still true to his master; since by facing him he could the more readily anticipate his slightest want.

"This in an uncommonly intelligent fellow of yours, Don Benito," whispered Captain Delano across the table.

"You say true, Señor."

During the repast, the guest again reverted to parts of Don Benito's story, begging further particulars here and there. He inquired how it was that the scurvy and fever should have committed such wholesale havoc upon the whites, while destroying less than half of the blacks. As if this question reproduced the whole scene of plague before the Spaniard's eyes, miserably reminding him of his solitude in a cabin where before he had had so many friends and officers round him, his hand shook, his face became hueless, broken words escaped; but directly the sane memory of the past seemed replaced by insane terrors of the present. With starting eyes he stared before him at vacancy. For nothing was to be seen but the hand of his servant pushing the Canary over towards him. At length a few sips served partially to restore him. He made random reference to the different constitution of races, enabling one to offer more resistance to certain maladies than another. The thought was new to his companion.

Presently Captain Delano, intending to say something to his host concerning the pecuniary part of the business he had undertaken for him, especially—since he was strictly accountable to his owners—with reference to the new suit of sails, and other things of that sort; and naturally preferring to conduct such affairs in private, was desirous that the servant should withdraw; imagining that Don Benito for a few minutes could dispense with his attendance. He, however, waited awhile; thinking that, as the conversation proceeded, Don Benito, without being prompted, would perceive the propriety of the step.

But it was otherwise. At last catching his host's eye, Captain Delano, with a slight backward gesture of his thumb, whispered, "Don Benito, pardon me, but there is an interference with the full expression of what I have to say to you."

Upon this the Spaniard changed countenance; which was imputed to his resenting the hint, as in some way a reflection upon his servant. After a moment's pause, he assured his guest that the black's remaining with them could be of no disservice; because since losing his officers he had made Babo (whose original office, it now appeared, had been captain of the slaves) not only his constant attendant and companion, but in all things his confidant.

After this, nothing more could be said; though, indeed, Captain Delano could hardly avoid some little tinge of irritation upon being left ungratified in so inconsiderable a wish, by one, too, for whom he intended such solid services. But it is only his querulousness, thought he; and so filling his glass he proceeded to business.

The price of the sails and other matters was fixed upon. But while this was being done, the American observed that, though his original offer of assistance had been hailed with hectic animation, yet now when it was reduced to a business transaction, indifference and apathy were betrayed. Don Benito, in fact, appeared to submit to hearing the details more out of regard to common propriety, than from any impression that weighty benefit to himself and his voyage was involved.

Soon, his manner became still more reserved. The effort was vain to seek to draw him into social talk. Gnawed by his splenetic mood, he sat twitching his beard, while to little purpose the hand of his servant, mute as that on the wall, slowly pushed over the Canary.

Lunch being over, they sat down on the cushioned transom; the servant placing a pillow behind his master. The long continuance of the calm had now affected the atmosphere. Don Benito sighed heavily, as if for breath.

"Why not adjourn to the cuddy," said Captain Delano; "there is more air there." But the host sat silent and motionless.

Meantime his servant knelt before him, with a large fan of feathers. And Francesco coming in on tiptoes, handed the negro a little cup of aromatic waters, with which at intervals he chafed his master's brow; smoothing the hair along the temples as a nurse does a child's. He spoke no word. He only rested his eye on his master's, as if, amid all Don Benito's distress, a little to refresh his spirit by the silent sight of fidelity.

Presently the ship's bell sounded two o'clock; and through the cabin windows a slight rippling of the sea was discerned; and from the desired direction.

"There," exclaimed Captain Delano, "I told you so, Don Benito, look!"

He had risen to his feet, speaking in a very animated tone, with a view the more to rouse his companion. But though the crimson curtain of the stern-window near him that moment fluttered against his pale cheek, Don Benito seemed to have even less welcome for the breeze than the calm.

Poor fellow, thought Captain Delano, bitter experience has taught him that one ripple does not make a wind, any more than one swallow a summer. But he is mistaken for once. I will get his ship in for him, and prove it.

Briefly alluding to his weak condition, he urged his host to remain quietly where he was, since he (Captain Delano) would with pleasure take upon himself the responsibility of making the best use of the wind.

Upon gaining the deck, Captain Delano started at the unexpected figure of Atufal, monumentally fixed at the threshold, like one of those sculptured porters of black marble guarding the porches of Egyptian tombs.

But this time the start was, perhaps, purely physical. Atufal's presence, singularly attesting docility even in sullenness, was contrasted with that of the hatchet-polishers, who in patience evinced their industry; while both spectacles showed, that lax as Don Benito's general authority might be, still, whenever he chose to exert it, no man so savage or colossal but must, more or less, bow.

Snatching a trumpet which hung from the bulwarks, with a free step Captain Delano advanced to the forward edge of the poop, issuing his orders in his best Spanish. The few sailors and many negroes, all equally pleased, obediently set about heading the ship towards the harbor.

While giving some directions about setting a lower stu'n'-sail, suddenly Captain Delano heard a voice faithfully repeating his orders. Turning, he saw Babo, now for the time acting, under the pilot, his original part of captain of the slaves. This assistance proved valuable. Tattered sails and warped yards were soon brought into some trim. And no brace or halyard was pulled but to the blithe songs of the inspirited negroes.

Good fellows, thought Captain Delano, a little training would make fine sailors of them. Why see, the very women pull and sing too. These must be some of those Ashantee negresses that make such capital soldiers, I've heard. But who's at the helm. I must have a good hand there.

He went to see.

The San Dominick steered with a cumbrous tiller, with large horizontal pullies attached. At each pulley-end stood a subordinate black, and between them, at the tiller-head, the responsible post, a Spanish seaman, whose countenance evinced his due share in the general hopefulness and confidence at the coming of the breeze.

He proved the same man who had behaved with so shame-faced an air on the windlass.

"Ah,—it is you, my man," exclaimed Captain Delano—"well, no more sheep's-eyes now;—look straight forward and keep the ship so. Good hand, I trust? And want to get into the harbor, don't you?"

The man assented with an inward chuckle, grasping the tiller-head firmly. Upon this, unperceived by the American, the two blacks eyed the sailor intently.

Finding all right at the helm, the pilot went forward to the forecastle, to see how matters stood there.

The ship now had way enough to breast the current. With the approach of evening, the breeze would be sure to freshen.

Having done all that was needed for the present, Captain Delano, giving his last orders to the sailors, turned aft to report affairs to Don Benito in the cabin; perhaps additionally incited to rejoin him by the hope of snatching a moment's private chat while the servant was engaged upon deck.

From opposite sides, there were, beneath the poop, two approaches to the cabin; one further forward than the other, and consequently communicating with a longer passage. Marking the servant still above, Captain Delano, taking the nighest entrance —the one last named, and at whose porch Atufal still stood—hurried on his way, till, arrived at the cabin threshold, he paused an instant, a little to recover from his eagerness. Then, with the words of his intended business upon his lips, he entered. As he advanced toward the seated Spaniard, he heard another footstep, keeping time with his. From the opposite door, a salver in hand, the servant was likewise advancing.

"Confound the faithful fellow," thought Captain Delano; "what a vexatious coincidence."

Possibly, the vexation might have been something different, were it not for the brisk confidence inspired by the breeze. But even as it was, he felt a slight twinge, from a sudden indefinite association in his mind of Babo with Atufal.

"Don Benito," said he, "I give you joy; the breeze will hold, and will increase. By the way, your tall man and time-piece, Atufal, stands without. By your order, of course?"

Don Benito recoiled, as if at some bland satirical touch, delivered with such adroit garnish of apparent good breeding as to present no handle for retort.

He is like one flayed alive, thought Captain Delano; where may one touch him without causing a shrink?

The servant moved before his master, adjusting a cushion; recalled to civility, the Spaniard stiffly replied: "you are right. The slave appears where you saw him, according to my command; which is, that if at the given hour I am below, he must take his stand and abide my coming."

"Ah now, pardon me, but that is treating the poor fellow like an ex-king indeed. Ah, Don Benito," smiling, "for all the license you permit in some things, I fear lest, at bottom, you are a bitter hard master."

Again Don Benito shrank; and this time, as the good sailor thought, from a genuine twinge of his conscience.

Again conversation became constrained. In vain Captain Delano called attention to the now perceptible motion of the keel gently cleaving the sea; with lack-lustre eye, Don Benito returned words few and reserved.

By-and-by, the wind having steadily risen, and still blowing right into the harbor, bore the San Dominick swiftly on. Rounding a point of land, the sealer at distance came into open view.

Meantime Captain Delano had again repaired to the deck, remaining there sometime. Having at last altered the ship's course, so as to give the reef a wide berth, he returned for a few moments below.

I will cheer up my poor friend, this time, thought he.

"Better and better, Don Benito," he cried as he blithely re-entered: "there will soon be an end to your cares, at least for awhile. For when, after a long, sad voyage, you know, the anchor drops into the haven, all its vast weight seems lifted from the captain's heart. We are getting on famously, Don Benito. My ship is in sight. Look through this side-light here; there she is; all a-taunt-o! The Bachelor's Delight, my good friend. Ah, how this wind braces one up. Come, you must take a cup of coffee with me this evening. My old steward will give you as fine a cup as ever any sultan tasted. What say you, Don Benito, will you?"

At first, the Spaniard glanced feverishly up, casting a longing look towards the sealer, while with mute concern his servant gazed into his face. Suddenly the old ague of coldness returned, and dropping back to his cushions he was silent.

"You do not answer. Come, all day you have been my host; would you have hospitality all on one side?"

"I cannot go," was the response.

"What? it will not fatigue you. The ships will lie together as near as they can, without swinging foul. It will be little more than stepping from deck to deck; which is but as from room to room. Come, come, you must not refuse me."

"I cannot go," decisively and repulsively repeated Don Benito.

Renouncing all but the last appearance of courtesy, with a sort of cadaverous sullenness, and biting his thin nails to the quick, he glanced, almost glared, at his guest, as if impatient that a stranger's presence should interfere with the full indulgence of his morbid hour. Meantime the sound of the parted waters came more and more gurglingly and merrily in at the windows; as reproaching him for his dark spleen; as telling him that, sulk as he might, and go mad with it, nature cared not a jot; since, whose fault was it, pray?

But the foul mood was now at its depth, as the fair wind at its height.

There was something in the man so far beyond any mere unsociality or sourness previously evinced, that even the forbearing good-nature of his guest could no longer endure it. Wholly at a loss to account for such demeanor, and deeming sickness with eccentricity, however extreme, no adequate excuse, well satisfied, too, that nothing in his own conduct could justify it, Captain Delano's pride began to be roused. Himself became reserved. But all seemed one to the Spaniard. Quitting him, therefore, Captain Delano once more went to the deck.

The ship was now within less than two miles of the sealer. The whale-boat was seen darting over the interval.

To be brief, the two vessels, thanks to the pilot's skill, ere long in neighborly style lay anchored together.

Before returning to his own vessel, Captain Delano had intended communicating to Don Benito the smaller details of the proposed services to be rendered. But, as it was, unwilling anew to subject himself to rebuffs, he resolved, now that he had seen the San Dominick safely moored, immediately to quit her, without further allusion to hospitality or business. Indefinitely postponing his ulterior plans, he would regulate his future actions according to future circumstances. His boat was ready to receive him; but his host still tarried below. Well, thought Captain Delano, if he has little breeding, the more need to show mine. He descended to the cabin to bid a ceremonious, and, it may be, tacitly rebukeful adieu. But to his great satisfaction, Don Benito, as if he began to feel the weight of that treatment with which his slighted guest had, not indecorously, retaliated upon him, now supported by his servant, rose to his feet, and grasping Captain Delano's hand, stood tremulous; too much agitated to speak. But the good augury hence drawn was suddenly dashed, by his resuming all his previous reserve, with augmented gloom, as, with half-averted eyes, he silently reseated himself on his cushions. With a corresponding return of his own chilled feelings, Captain Delano bowed and withdrew.

He was hardly midway in the narrow corridor, dim as a tunnel, leading from the cabin to the stairs, when a sound, as of the tolling for execution in some jail-yard, fell on his ears. It was the echo of the ship's flawed bell, striking the hour, drearily reverberated in this subterranean vault. Instantly, by a fatality not to be withstood, his mind, responsive to the portent, swarmed with superstitious suspicions. He paused. In images far swifter than these sentences, the minutest details of all his former distrusts swept through him.

Hitherto, credulous good-nature had been too ready to furnish excuses for reasonable fears. Why was the Spaniard, so superfluously punctilious at times, now heedless of common propriety in not accompanying to the side his departing guest? Did indisposition forbid? Indisposition had not forbidden more irksome exertion that day. His last equivocal demeanor recurred. He had risen to his feet, grasped his guest's hand, motioned toward his hat; then, in an instant, all was eclipsed in sinister muteness and gloom. Did this imply one brief, repentant relenting at the final moment, from some iniquitous plot, followed by remorseless return to it? His last glance seemed to express a calamitous, yet acquiescent farewell to Captain Delano forever. Why decline the invitation to visit the sealer that evening? Or was the Spaniard less hardened than the Jew, who refrained not from supping at the board of him whom the same night he meant to betray?[36] What imported all those day-long enigmas and contradictions, except they were intended to mystify, preliminary to some stealthy blow? Atufal, the pretended rebel, but punctual shadow, that moment lurked by the threshold without. He seemed a sentry, and more. Who, by his own confession, had stationed him there? Was the negro now lying in wait?

The Spaniard behind—his creature before: to rush from darkness to light was the involuntary choice.

The next moment, with clenched jaw and hand, he passed Atufal, and stood unharmed in the light. As he saw his trim ship lying peacefully at anchor, and almost within ordinary call; as he saw his household boat, with familiar faces in it, patiently rising and falling on the short waves by the San Dominick's side; and then, glancing about the decks where he stood, saw the oakum-pickers still gravely plying their fingers; and heard the low, buzzing whistle and industrious hum of the hatchet-polishers, still bestirring themselves over their endless occupation; and more than all, as he saw the benign aspect of nature, taking her innocent repose in the evening; the screened sun in the quiet camp of the west shining out like the mild light from Abraham's tent; as charmed eye and ear took in all these, with the chained figure of the black, clenched jaw and hand relaxed. Once again he smiled at the phantoms which had mocked him, and felt something like a tinge of remorse, that, by harboring them even for a moment, he should, by implication, have betrayed an atheist doubt of the ever-watchful Providence above.

There was a few minutes' delay, while, in obedience to his orders, the boat was being hooked along to the gangway. During this interval, a sort of saddened satisfaction stole over Captain Delano, at thinking of the kindly offices he had that day

[36] Reference to Judas' betrayal of Jesus.

discharged for a stranger. Ah, thought he, after good actions one's conscience is never ungrateful, however much so the benefited party may be.

Presently, his foot, in the first act of descent into the boat, pressed the first round of the side-ladder, his face presented inward upon the deck. In the same moment, he heard his name courteously sounded; and, to his pleased surprise, saw Don Benito advancing—an unwonted energy in his air, as if, at the last moment, intent upon making amends for his recent discourtesy. With instinctive good feeling, Captain Delano, withdrawing his foot, turned and reciprocally advanced. As he did so, the Spaniard's nervous eagerness increased, but his vital energy failed; so that, the better to support him, the servant, placing his master's hand on his naked shoulder, and gently holding it there, formed himself into a sort of crutch.

When the two captains met, the Spaniard again fervently took the hand of the American, at the same time casting an earnest glance into his eyes, but, as before, too much overcome to speak.

I have done him wrong, self-reproachfully thought Captain Delano; his apparent coldness has deceived me; in no instance has he meant to offend.

Meantime, as if fearful that the continuance of the scene might too much unstring his master, the servant seemed anxious to terminate it. And so, still presenting himself as a crutch, and walking between the two captains, he advanced with them towards the gangway; while still, as if full of kindly contrition, Don Benito would not let go the hand of Captain Delano, but retained it in his, across the black's body.

Soon they were standing by the side, looking over into the boat, whose crew turned up their curious eyes. Waiting a moment for the Spaniard to relinquish his hold, the now embarrassed Captain Delano lifted his foot, to overstep the threshold of the open gangway; but still Don Benito would not let go his hand. And yet, with an agitated tone, he said, "I can go no further; here I must bid you adieu. Adieu, my dear, dear Don Amasa. Go—go!" suddenly tearing his hand loose, "go, and God guard you better than me, my best friend."

Not unaffected, Captain Delano would now have lingered; but catching the meekly admonitory eye of the servant, with a hasty farewell he descended into his boat, followed by the continual adieus of Don Benito, standing rooted in the gangway.

Seating himself in the stern, Captain Delano, making a last salute, ordered the boat shoved off. The crew had their oars on end. The bowsmen pushed the boat a sufficient distance for the oars to be lengthwise dropped. The instant that was done, Don Benito sprang over the bulwarks, falling at the feet of Captain Delano; at the same time calling towards his ship, but in tones so frenzied, that none in the boat could understand him. But, as if not equally obtuse, three sailors, from three different and distant parts of the ship, splashed into the sea, swimming after their captain, as if intent upon his rescue.

The dismayed officer of the boat eagerly asked what this meant. To which, Captain Delano, turning a disdainful smile upon the unaccountable Spaniard, answered that, for his part, he neither knew nor cared; but it seemed as if Don Benito had taken it into his head to produce the impression among his people that the boat wanted to kidnap him. "Or else—give way for your lives," he wildly added, starting at a clattering hubbub in the ship, above which rang the tocsin of the hatchet-polishers; and seizing Don Benito by the throat he added, "this plotting pirate means murder!" Here, in apparent verification of the words, the servant, a dagger in his hand, was seen on the rail overhead, poised, in the act of leaping, as if with desperate fidelity to befriend his master to the last; while, seemingly to aid the black, the three white sailors were trying to clamber into the hampered bow. Meantime, the whole host of negroes, as if inflamed at the sight of their jeopardized captain, impended in one sooty avalanche over the bulwarks.

All this, with what preceded, and what followed, occurred with such involutions of rapidity, that past, present, and future seemed one.

Seeing the negro coming, Captain Delano had flung the Spaniard aside, almost in the very act of clutching him, and, by the unconscious recoil, shifting his place, with arms thrown up, so promptly grappled the servant in his descent, that with dagger presented at Captain Delano's heart, the black seemed of purpose to have leaped there as to his mark. But the weapon was wrenched away, and the assailant dashed down into the bottom of the boat, which now, with disentangled oars, began to speed through the sea.

At this juncture, the left hand of Captain Delano, on one side, again clutched the half-reclined Don Benito, heedless that he was in a speechless faint, while his right foot, on the other side, ground the prostrate negro; and his right arm pressed for added speed on the after oar, his eye bent forward, encouraging his men to their utmost.

But here, the officer of the boat, who had at last succeeded in beating off the towing sailors, and was now, with face turned aft, assisting the bowsman at his oar, suddenly called to Captain Delano, to see what the black was about; while a Portuguese oarsman shouted to him to give heed to what the Spaniard was saying.

Glancing down at his feet, Captain Delano saw the freed hand of the servant aiming with a second dagger—a small one, before concealed in his wool—with this he was snakishly writhing up from the boat's bottom, at the heart of his master, his countenance lividly vindictive, expressing the centred purpose of his soul; while the Spaniard, half-choked, was vainly shrinking way, with husky words, incoherent to all but the Portuguese.

That moment, across the long-benighted mind of Captain Delano, a flash of revelation swept, illuminating, in unanticipated clearness, his host's whole mysterious demeanor, with every enigmatic event of the day, as well as the entire past voyage of the San Dominick. He smote Babo's hand down, but his own heart smote him harder. With infinite pity he withdrew his hold from Don Benito. Not Captain Delano, but Don Benito, the black, in leaping into the boat, had intended to stab.

Both the black's hands were held, as, glancing up towards the San Dominick, Captain Delano, now with scales dropped from his eyes, saw the negroes, not in misrule, not in tumult, not as if frantically concerned for Don Benito, but with mask torn away, flourishing hatchets and knives, in ferocious piratical revolt. Like delirious black dervishes, the six Ashantees danced on the poop. Prevented by their foes from springing into the water, the Spanish boys were hurrying up to the topmost spars, while such of the few Spanish sailors, not already in the sea, less alert, were described, helplessly mixed in, on deck, with the blacks.

Meantime Captain Delano hailed his own vessel, ordering the ports up, and the guns run out. But by this time the cable of the San Dominick had been cut; and the fag-end, in lashing out, whipped away the canvas shroud about the beak, suddenly revealing, as the bleached hull swung round towards the open ocean, death for the figure-head, in a human skeleton; chalky comment on the chalked words below, *"Follow your leader."*

At the sight, Don Benito, covering his face, wailed out: " 'Tis he, Aranda! my murdered, unburied friend!"

Upon reaching the sealer, calling for ropes, Captain Delano bound the negro, who made no resistance, and had him hoisted to the deck. He would then have assisted the now almost helpless Don Benito up the side; but Don Benito, wan as he was, refused to move, or be moved, until the negro should have been first put below out of view. When, presently assured that it was done, he no more shrank from the ascent.

The boat was immediately dispatched back to pick up the three swimming sailors. Meantime, the guns were in readiness, though, owing to the San Dominick having glided somewhat astern of the sealer, only the aftermost one could be brought to bear. With this, they fired six times; thinking to cripple the fugitive ship by bringing down her spars. But only a few inconsiderable ropes were shot away. Soon the ship was beyond the gun's range, steering broad out of the bay; the blacks thickly clustering round the bowsprit, one moment with taunting cries towards the whites, the next with upthrown gestures hailing the now dusky moors of ocean—cawing crows escaped from the hand of the fowler.

The first impulse was to slip the cables and give chase. But, upon second thoughts, to pursue with whale-boat and yawl seemed more promising.

Upon inquiring of Don Benito what fire-arms they had on board the San Dominick, Captain Delano was answered that they had none that could be used; because, in the earlier stages of the mutiny, a cabin-passenger, since dead, had secretly put out of order the locks of what few muskets there were. But with all his remaining strength, Don Benito entreated the American not to give chase, either with ship or boat; for the negroes had already proved themselves such desperadoes, that, in case of a present assault, nothing but a total massacre of the whites could be looked for. But, regarding this warning as coming from one whose spirit had been crushed by misery the American did not give up his design.

The boats were got ready and armed. Captain Delano ordered his men into them. He was going himself when Don Benito grasped his arm.

"What! have you saved my life, Señor, and are you now going to throw away your own?"

The officers also, for reasons connected with their interests and those of the voyage, and a duty owing to the owners, strongly objected against their commander's going. Weighing their remonstrances a moment, Captain Delano felt bound to remain; appointing his chief mate—an athletic and resolute man, who had been a privateer's-man[37]—to head the party. The more to encourage the sailors, they were told, that the Spanish captain considered his ship good as lost; that she and her cargo, including some gold and silver, were worth more than a thousand doubloons. Take her, and no small part should be theirs. The sailors replied with a shout.

The fugitives had now almost gained an offing. It was nearly night; but the moon

[37] I.e., had served on a privateer, a ship commissioned by a government to prey upon other nations' shipping.

was rising. After hard, prolonged pulling, the boats came up on the ship's quarters, at a suitable distance laying upon their oars to discharge their muskets. Having no bullets to return, the negroes sent their yells. But, upon the second volley, Indian-like, they hurtled their hatchets. One took off a sailor's fingers. Another struck the whale-boat's bow, cutting off the rope there, and remaining stuck in the gunwale like a woodman's axe. Snatching it, quivering from its lodgment, the mate hurled it back. The returned gauntlet now stuck in the ship's broken quarter-gallery, and so remained.

The negroes giving too hot a reception, the whites kept a more respectful distance. Hovering now just out of reach of the hurtling hatchets, they, with a view to the close encounter which must soon come, sought to decoy the blacks into entirely disarming themselves of their most murderous weapons in a hand-to-hand fight, by foolishly flinging them, as missiles, short of the mark, into the sea. But, ere long, perceiving the stratagem, the negroes desisted, though not before many of them had to replace their lost hatchets with handspikes; an exchange which, as counted upon, proved, in the end, favorable to the assailants.

Meantime, with a strong wind, the ship still clove the water; the boats alternately falling behind, and pulling up, to discharge fresh volleys.

The fire was mostly directed towards the stern, since there, chiefly, the negroes, at present, were clustering. But to kill or maim the negroes was not the object. To take them, with the ship, was the object. To do it, the ship must be boarded; which could not be done by boats while she was sailing so fast.

A thought now struck the mate. Observing the Spanish boys still aloft, high as they could get, he called to them to descend to the yards, and cut adrift the sails. It was done. About this time, owning to causes hereafter to be shown, two Spaniards, in the dress of sailors, and conspicuously showing themselves, were killed; not by volleys, but by deliberate marksman's shots; while, as it afterwards appeared, by one of the general discharges, Atufal, the black, and the Spaniard at the helm likewise were killed. What now, with the loss of the sails, and loss of leaders, the ship became unmanageable to the negroes.

With creaking masts, she came heavily round to the wind; the prow slowly swinging into view of the boats, its skeleton gleaming in the horizontal moonlight, and casting a gigantic ribbed shadow upon the water. One extended arm of the ghost seemed beckoning the whites to avenge it.

"Follow your leader!" cried the mate; and, one on each bow, the boats boarded. Sealing-spears and cutlasses crossed hatchets and hand-spikes. Huddled upon the long-boat amidships, the negresses raised a wailing chant, whose chorus was the clash of the steel.

For a time, the attack wavered; the negroes wedging themselves to beat it back; the half-repelled sailors, as yet unable to gain a footing, fighting as troopers in the saddle, one leg sideways flung over the bulwarks, and one without, plying their cutlasses like carters' whips. But in vain. They were almost overborne, when, rallying themselves into a squad as one man, with a huzza, they sprang inboard, where, entangled, they involuntarily separated again. For a few breaths' space, there was a vague, muffled, inner sound, as of submerged sword-fish rushing hither and thither through shoals of black-fish. Soon, in a reunited band, and joined by the Spanish seamen, the whites came to the surface, irresistibly driving the negroes toward the stern. But a barricade of casks and sacks, from side to side, had been thrown up by the mainmast. Here the negroes faced about, and though scorning peace or truce, yet fain would have had respite. But, without pause, overleaping the barrier, the unflagging sailors again closed. Exhausted, the blacks now fought in despair. Their red tongues lolled, wolf-like, from their black mouths. But the pale sailors' teeth were set; not a word was spoken; and, in five minutes more, the ship was won.

Nearly a score of the negroes were killed. Exclusive of those by the balls, many were mangled; their wounds—mostly inflicted by the long-edged sealing-spears, resembling those shaven ones of the English at Preston Pans, made by the poled scythes of the Highlanders.[38] On the other side, none were killed, though several were wounded; some severely, including the mate. The surviving negroes were temporarily secured, and the ship, towed back into the harbor at midnight, once more lay anchored.

Omitting the incidents and arrangements ensuing, suffice it that, after two days spent in refitting, the ships sailed in company for Conception, in Chili, and thence for Lima, in Peru; where, before the vice-regal courts, the whole affair, from the beginning, underwent investigation.

Though, midway on the passage, the ill-fated Spaniard, relaxed from constraint, showed some signs of regaining health with free-will; yet, agreeably to his own foreboding, shortly before arriving at Lima, he relapsed, finally becoming so reduced as to be carried ashore in arms. Hearing of his story and plight, one of the many religious institutions of the City of Kings opened an hospitable refuge to him, where both physician and priest were his nurses, and a member of the order volunteered to be his one special guardian and consoler, by night and by day.

The following extracts, translated from one of the official Spanish documents, will, it is hoped, shed light on the preceding narrative, as well as, in the first place, reveal the true port of departure and true history of the San Dominick's voyage, down to the time of her touching at the island of St. Maria.

But, ere the extracts come, it may be well to preface them with a remark.

The document selected, from among many others, for partial translation, contains the deposition of Benito Cereno; the first taken in the case. Some disclosures therein were, at the time, held dubious for both learned and natural reasons. The tribunal inclined to the opinion that the deponent, not undisturbed in his mind by recent events, raved of some things which could never have happened. But subsequent depositions of the surviving sailors, bearing out the revelations of their captain in several of the strangest particulars, gave credence to the rest. So that the tribunal, in its final decision, rested its capital sentences upon statements which, had they lacked confirmation, it would have deemed it but duty to reject.

————

I, Don Jose de Abos and Padilla, His Majesty's Notary for the Royal Revenue, and Register of this Province, and Notary Public of the Holy Crusade of this Bishopric, etc.

Do certify and declare, as much as is requisite in law, that, in the criminal cause commenced the twenty-fourth of the month of September, in the year seventeen

---

[38] Scythes fastened to long poles were used successfully by Scotsmen in the Battle of Prestan Pans (1745).

hundred and ninety-nine, against the negroes of the ship San Dominick, the following declaration before me was made:

Declaration of the first witness, DON BENITO CERENO.

The same day, and month, and year, His Honor, Doctor Juan Martinez de Rozas, Councilor of the Royal Audience of this Kingdom, and learned in the law of this Intendency, ordered the captain of the ship San Dominick, Don Benito Cereno, to appear; which he did in his litter, attended by the monk Infelez; of whom he received the oath, which he took by God, our Lord, and a sign of the Cross; under which he promised to tell the truth of whatever he should know and should be asked;—and being interrogated agreeably to the tenor of the act commencing the process, he said, that on the twentieth of May last, he set sail with his ship from the port of Valparaiso, bound to that of Callao; loaded with the produce of the country beside thirty cases of hardware and one hundred and sixty blacks, of both sexes, mostly belonging to Don Alexandro Aranda, gentleman, of the city of Mendoza; that the crew of the ship consisted of thirty-six men, beside the persons who went as passengers; that the negroes were in part as follows:

[Here, in the original, follows a list of some fifty names, descriptions, and ages, compiled from certain recovered documents of Aranda's, and also from recollections of the deponent, from which portions only are extracted.]

—One, from about eighteen to nineteen years, named José, and this was the man that waited upon his master, Don Alexandro, and who speaks well the Spanish, having served him four or five years; * * * a mulatto, named Francesco, the cabin steward, of a good person and voice, having sung in the Valparaiso churches, native of the province of Buenos Ayres, aged about thirty-five years. * * * A smart negro, named Dago, who had been for many years a gravedigger among the Spaniards, aged forty-six years. * * * Four old negroes, born in Africa, from sixty to seventy, but sound, calkers by trade, whose names are as follows:—the first was named Muri, and he was killed (as was also his son named Diamelo); the second, Nacta; the third, Yola, likewise killed; the fourth, Ghofan; and six full-grown negroes, aged from thirty to forty-five, all raw, and born among the Ashantees—Matiluqui, Yan, Lecbe, Mapenda, Yambaio, Akim; four of whom were killed; * * * a powerful negro named Atufal, who being supposed to have been a chief in Africa, his owner set great store by him. * * * And a small negro of Senegal, but some years among the Spaniards, aged about thirty, which negro's name was Babo; * * * that he does not remember the names of the others, but that still expecting the residue of Don Alexandro's papers will be found, will then take due account of them all, and remit to the court; * * * and thirty-nine women and children of all ages.

[The catalogue over, the deposition goes on.]

* * * That all the negroes slept upon deck, as is customary in this navigation, and none wore fetters, because the owner, his friend Aranda, told him that they were all tractable; * * * that on the seventh day after leaving port, at three o'clock in the morning, all the Spaniards being asleep except the two officers on the watch, who were the boatswain, Juan Robles, and the carpenter, Juan Bautista Gayete, and the helmsman and his boy, the negroes revolted suddenly, wounded dangerously the boatswain and the carpenter, and successively killed eighteen men of those who were sleeping upon deck, some with hand-spikes and hatchets, and others by throwing them alive overboard, after tying them; that of the Spaniards upon deck, they left about

seven, as he thinks, alive and tied, to manœuvre the ship, and three or four more, who hid themselves, remained also alive. Although in the act of revolt the negroes made themselves masters of the hatchway, six or seven wounded went through it to the cockpit, without any hindrance on their part; that during the act of revolt, the mate and another person, whose name he does not recollect, attempted to come up through the hatchway, but being quickly wounded, were obliged to return to the cabin; that the deponent resolved at break of day to come up the companion-way, where the negro Babo was, being the ring-leader, and Atufal, who assisted him, and having spoken to them, exhorted them to cease committing such atrocities, asking them, at the same time, what they wanted and intended to do, offering, himself, to obey their commands; that notwithstanding this, they threw, in his presence, three men, alive and tied, overboard; that they told the deponent to come up, and that they would not kill him; which having done, the negro Babo asked him whether there were in those seas any negro countries where they might be carried, and he answered them, No; that the negro Babo afterwards told him to carry them to Senegal, or to the neighboring islands of St. Nicholas; and he answered, that this was impossible, on account of the great distance, the necessity involved of rounding Cape Horn, the bad condition of the vessel, the want of provisions, sails, and water; but that the negro Babo replied to him he must carry them in any way; that they would do and conform themselves to everything the deponent should require as to eating and drinking; that after a long conference, being absolutely compelled to please them, for they threatened to kill all the whites if they were not, at all events, carried to Senegal, he told them, that what was most wanting for the voyage was water; that they would go near the coast to take it, and thence they would proceed on their course; that the negro Babo agreed to it; and the deponent steered towards the intermediate ports, hoping to meet some Spanish or foreign vessel that would save them; that within ten or eleven days they saw the land, and continued their course by it in the vicinity of Nasca; that the deponent observed that the negroes were now restless and mutinous, because he did not effect the taking in of water, the negro Babo having required, with threats, that it should be done, without fail, the following day; he told him he saw plainly that the coast was steep, and the rivers designated in the maps were not to be found, with other reasons suitable to the circumstances; that the best way would be to go to the island of Santa Maria, where they might water easily, it being a solitary island, as the foreigners did; that the deponent did not go to Pisco, that was near, nor make any other port of the coast, because the negro Babo had intimated to him several times, that he would kill all the whites the very moment he should perceive any city, town, or settlement of any kind on the shores to which they should be carried: that having determined to go to the island of Santa Maria, as the deponent had planned, for the purpose of trying whether, on the passage or near the island itself, they could find any vessel that should favor them, or whether he could escape from it in a boat to the neighboring coast of Arruco, to adopt the necessary means he immediately changed his course, steering for the island; that the negroes Babo and Atufal held daily conferences, in which they discussed what was necessary for their design of returning to Senegal, whether they were to kill all the Spaniards, and particularly the deponent; that eight days after parting from the coast of Nasca, the deponent being on the watch a little after day-break, and soon after the negroes had their meeting, the negro Babo came to the place where the deponent was, and told him that he had determined to kill his master, Don Alexandro Aranda, both because he and his companions could not otherwise be sure of their liberty, and that to keep the seamen in subjection, he wanted to prepare a warning of what road they should be made to take did they or any of them oppose him; and that, by means of the death of Don Alexandro, that warning would best be given; but, that what this last meant, the deponent did not at the time comprehend, nor could not, further than that the death of Don Alexandro was intended; and moreover the negro Babo proposed to the deponent to call the mate Raneds, who was sleeping in the cabin, before the thing was done, for fear, as the deponent understood it, that the mate, who was a good navigator, should be killed with Don Alexandro and the rest; that the deponent, who was the friend, from youth, of Don Alexandro, prayed and conjured, but all was useless; for the negro Babo answered him that the thing could not be prevented, and that all the Spaniards risked their death if they could attempt to frustrate his will in this matter, or any other; that, in this conflict, the deponent called the mate, Raneds, who was forced to go apart, and immediately the negro Babo commanded the Ashantee Martinqui and the Ashantee Lecbe to go and commit the murder; that those two went down with hatchets to the berth of Don Alexandro; that, yet half alive and mangled, they dragged him on deck; that they were going to throw him overboard in that state, but the negro Babo stopped them, bidding the murder be completed on the deck before him, which was done, when, by his orders, the body was carried below, forward; that nothing more was seen of it by the deponent for three days; * * * that Don Alonzo Sidonia, an old man, long resident at Valparaiso, and lately appointed to a civil office in Peru, whither he had taken passage, was at the time sleeping in the berth opposite Don Alexandro's; that awakening at his cries, surprised by them, and at the sight of the negroes with their bloody hatchets in their hands, he threw himself into the sea through a window which was near him, and was drowned, without it being in the power of the deponent to assist or take him up; * * * that a short time after killing Aranda, they brought upon deck his german-cousin, of middle-age, Don Francisco Masa, of Mendoza, and the young Don Joaquin, Marques de Aramboalaza, then lately from Spain, with his Spanish servant Ponce, and the three young clerks of Aranda, José Mozairi, Lorenzo Bargas, and Hermenegildo Gandix, all of Cadiz; that Don Joaquin and Hermenegildo Gandix, the negro Babo, for purposes hereafter to appear, preserved alive; but Don Francisco Masa, José Mozairi, and Lorenzo Bargas, with Ponce the servant, beside the boatswain, Juan Robles, the boatswain's mates, Manual Viscaya and Roderigo Hurta, and four of the sailors, the negro Babo ordered to be thrown alive into the sea, although they made no resistance, nor begged for anything else but mercy; that the boatswain, Juan Robles, who knew how to swim, kept the longest above water, making acts of contrition, and, in the last words he uttered, charged this deponent to cause mass to be said for his soul to our Lady of Succor: * * * that, during the three days which followed, the deponent, uncertain what fate had befallen the remains of Don Alexandro, frequently asked the negro Babo where they were, and, if still on board, whether they were to be preserved for interment ashore, entreating him so to order it; that the negro Babo answered nothing till the fourth day, when at sunrise, the deponent coming on deck, the negro Babo showed him a skeleton, which had been substituted for the ship's proper figure-head—the image of Christopher Colon, the discoverer of the New World; that the negro Babo asked him whose skeleton that was, and whether, from its whiteness, he should not think it a white's; that, upon discovering his face, the negro Babo, coming close, said words to this effect: "Keep faith with the blacks from here to Senegal, or you shall in spirit, as now in body, follow your leader," pointing to the prow; * * * that the same morning the negro Babo took by succession each Spaniard forward, and asked him whose skeleton that was, and whether, from its whiteness, he should not think it a white's; that each Spaniard covered his face; that then to each the negro Babo repeated the words in the first place said to the deponent; * * * that they (the Spaniards), being then assembled aft, the negro Babo harangued them, saying that he had now done all; that the deponent (as navigator for the negroes) might pursue his course, warning him and all of them that they should, soul and body, go the way of Don Alexandro, if he saw them (the Spaniards) speak or plot anything against them (the negroes)—a threat which was repeated every day; that, before the events last mentioned, they had tied the cook to throw him overboard, for it is not known what thing they heard him speak, but finally the negro Babo spared his life, at the request of the deponent; that a few days after, the deponent, endeavoring not to omit any means to preserve the lives of the remaining whites, spoke to the negroes of peace and tranquillity, and agreed to draw up a paper, signed by the deponent and the sailors who could write, as also by the negro Babo, for himself and all the blacks, in which the deponent obliged himself to carry them to Senegal, and they not to kill any more, and he formally to make over to them the ship, with the cargo, with which they were for that time satisfied and quieted. * * * But the next day, the more surely to guard against the sailors' escape, the negro Babo commanded all the boats to be destroyed but the long-boat, which was unseaworthy, and another, a cutter in good condition, which knowing it would yet be wanted for towing the water casks, he had it lowered down into the hold.

* *

[Various particulars of the prolonged and perplexed navigation ensuing here follow, with incidents of a calamitous calm, from which portion one passage is extracted, to wit:]—That on the fifth day of the calm, all on board suffering much from the heat, and want of water, and five having died in fits, and mad, the negroes became irritable, and for a chance gesture, which they deemed suspicious—though it was harmless—made by the mate, Raneds, to the deponent in the act of handing a quadrant, they killed him; but that for this they afterwards were sorry, the mate being the only remaining navigator on board, except the deponent.

* *

—That omitting other events, which daily happened, and which can only serve uselessly to recall past misfortunes and conflicts, after seventy-three days' navigation, reckoned from the time they sailed from Nasca, during which they navigated under a scanty allowance of water, and were afflicted with the calms before mentioned, they at last arrived at the island of Santa Maria, on the seventeenth of the month of August, at about six o'clock in the afternoon, at which hour they cast anchor very near the American ship, Bachelor's Delight, which lay in the same bay, commanded by the generous Captain Amasa Delano; but at six o'clock in the morning, they had already described the port, and the negroes became uneasy, as soon as at distance they saw the ship, not having expected to see one there; that the negro Babo pacified them, assuring them that no fear need be had; that straightway he ordered the figure on the bow to be covered with canvas, as for repairs, and had the decks a little set in order; that for a time the negro Babo and the negro Atufal conferred; that the negro Atufal was for sailing away, but the negro Babo would not, and, by himself, cast about what to do; that at last he came to the deponent, proposing to him to say and do all that the deponent declares to have said and done to the American captain;

* *

that the negro Babo warned him that if he varied in the least, or uttered any word, or gave any look that should give the least intimation of the past events or present state, he would instantly kill him, with all his companions, showing a dagger, which he carried hid, saying something which, as he understood it, meant that that dagger would be alert as his eye; that the negro Babo then announced the plan to all his companions, which pleased them; that he then, the better to disguise the truth, devised many expedients, in some of them uniting deceit and defense; that of this sort was the device of the six Ashantees before named, who were his bravoes;[39] that them he stationed on the break of the poop, as if to clean certain hatchets (in cases, which were part of the cargo), but in reality to use them, and distribute them at need, and at a given word he told them; that, among other devices, was the device of presenting Atufal, his right hand man, as chained, though in a moment the chains could be dropped; that in every particular he informed the deponent what part he was expected to enact in every device, and what story he was to tell on every occasion, always threatening him with instant death if he varied in the least: that, conscious that many of the negroes would be turbulent, the negro Babo appointed the four aged negroes, who were calkers, to keep what domestic order they could on the decks; that again and again he harangued the Spaniards and his companions, informing them of his intent, and of his devices, and of the invented story that this deponent was to tell; charging them lest any of them varied from that story; that these arrangements were made and matured during the interval of two or three hours, between their first sighting the ship and the arrival on board of Captain Amasa Delano; that this happened about half-past seven o'clock in the morning, Captain Amasa Delano coming in his boat, and all gladly receiving him; that the deponent, as well as he could force himself, acting then the part of principal owner, and a free captain of the ship, told Captain Amasa Delano, when called upon, that he came from Buenos Ayres, bound to Lima, with three hundred negroes; that off Cape Horn, and in a subsequent fever, many negroes had died; that also, by similar casualties, all the sea officers and the greatest part of the crew had died.

* *

[And so the deposition goes on, circumstantially recounting the fictitious story dictated to the deponent by Babo, and through the deponent imposed upon Captain Delano; and also recounting the friendly offers of Captain Delano, with other things, but all of which is here omitted. After the fictitious story, etc. the deposition proceeds:]

* *

—that the generous Captain Amasa Delano remained on board all the day, till he left the ship anchored at six o'clock in the evening, deponent speaking to him always of his pretended misfortunes, under the fore-mentioned principles, without having had it in his power to tell a single word, or give him the least hint, that he might know

---

[39] Henchmen.

the truth and state of things; because the negro Babo, performing the office of an officious servant with all the appearance of submission of the humble slave, did not leave the deponent one moment; that this was in order to observe the deponent's actions and words, for the negro Babo understands well the Spanish; and besides, there were thereabout some others who were constantly on the watch, and likewise understood the Spanish; *** that upon one occasion, while deponent was standing on the deck conversing with Amasa Delano, by a secret sign the negro Babo drew him (the deponent) aside, the act appearing as if originating with the deponent; that then, he being drawn aside, the negro Babo proposed to him to gain from Amasa Delano full particulars about his ship, and crew, and arms; that the deponent asked "For what?" that the negro Babo answered he might conceive; that, grieved at the prospect of what might overtake the generous Captain Amasa Delano, the deponent at first refused to ask the desired questions, and used every argument to induce the negro Babo to give up this new design; that the negro Babo showed the point of his dagger; that, after the information had been obtained the negro Babo again drew him aside, telling him that that very night he (the deponent) would be captain of two ships, instead of one, for that, great part of the American's ship's crew being to be absent fishing, the six Ashantees, without any one else, would easily take it; that at this time he said other things to the same purpose; that no entreaties availed; that, before Amasa Delano's coming on board, no hint had been given touching the capture of the American ship: that to prevent this project the deponent was powerless; * * *—that in some things his memory is confused, he cannot distinctly recall every event; * * *—that as soon as they had cast anchor at six of the clock in the evening, as has before been stated, the American Captain took leave, to return to his vessel; that upon a sudden impulse, which the deponent believes to have come from God and his angels, he, after the farewell had been said, followed the generous Captain Amasa Delano as far as the gunwale, where he stayed, under pretense of taking leave, until Amasa Delano should have been seated in his boat; that on shoving off, the deponent sprang from the gunwale into the boat, and fell into it, he knows not how, God guarding him; that—

* * * * * * * * * * * * * * * * * * * *

[Here, in the original, follows the account of what further happened at the escape, and how the San Dominick was retaken, and of the passage to the coast; including in the recital many expressions of "eternal gratitude" to the "generous Captain Amasa Delano." The deposition then proceeds with recapitulatory remarks, and a partial renumeration of the negroes, making record of their individual part in the past events, with a view to furnishing, according to command of the court, the data whereon to found the criminal sentences to be pronounced. From this portion is the following;]

—That he believes that all the negroes, though not in the first place knowing to the design of revolt, when it was accomplished, approved it. * * * That the negro, José, eighteen years old, and in the personal service of Don Alexandro, was the one who communicated the information to the negro Babo, about the state of things in the cabin, before the revolt; that this is known, because, in the preceding midnight, he use to come from his berth, which was under his master's, in the cabin, to the deck where the ringleader and his associates were, and had secret conversations with the negro Babo, in which he was several times seen by the mate; that, one night, the mate drove him away twice; * * * that this same negro

José was the one who, without being commanded to do so by the negro Babo, as Lecbe and Martinqui were, stabbed his master, Don Alexandro, after he had been dragged half-lifeless to the deck; * * * that the mulatto steward, Francesco, was of the first band of revolters, that he was, in all things, the creature and tool of the negro Babo; that, to make his court, he, just before a repast in the cabin, proposed, to the negro Babo, poisoning a dish for the generous Captain Amasa Delano; this is known and believed, because the negroes have said it; but that the negro Babo, having another design, forbade Francesco; * * * that the Ashantee Lecbe was one of the worst of them; for that, on the day the ship was retaken, he assisted in the defense of her, with a hatchet in each hand, with one of which he wounded, in the breast, the chief mate of Amasa Delano, in the first act of boarding; this all knew; that, in sight of the deponent, Lecbe struck, with a hatchet, Don Francisco Masa, when, by the negro Babo's orders, he was carrying him to throw him over-board, alive, beside participating in the murder, before mentioned, of Don Alexan-dro Aranda, and others of the cabin-passengers; that, owing to the fury with which the Ashantees fought in the engagement with the boats, but this Lecbe and Yan survived; that Yan was bad as Lecbe; that Yan was the man who, by Babo's com-mand, willingly prepared the skeleton of Don Alexandro, in a way the negroes afterwards told the deponent, but which he, so long as reason is left him, can never divulge; that Yan and Lecbe were the two who, in a calm by night, riveted the skeleton to the bow; this also the negroes told him; that the negro Babo was he who traced the inscription below it; that the negro Babo was the plotter from first to last; he ordered every murder, and was the helm and keel of the revolt; that Atufal was his lieutenant in all; but Atufal, with his own hand, committed no murder; nor did the negro Babo; * * * that Atufal was shot, being killed in the fight with the boats, ere boarding; * * * that the negresses, of age, were knowing to the revolt, and testified themselves satisfied at the death of their master, Don Alexandro; that, had the negroes not restrained them, they would have tortured to death, instead of simply killing, the Spaniards slain by command of the negro Babo; that the negresses used their utmost influence to have the deponent made away with; that, in the various acts of murder, they sang songs and danced—not gaily, but solemnly; and before the engagement with the boats, as well as during the action, they sang melancholy songs to the negroes, and that this melancholy tone was more inflaming than a different one would have been, and was so in-tended; that all this is believed, because the negroes have said it.—that of the thirty-six men of the crew, exclusive of the passengers (all of whom are now dead), which the deponent had knowledge of, six only remained alive, with four cabin-boys and ship-boys, not included with the crew; * * *—that the negroes broke an arm of one of the cabin-boys and gave him strokes with hatchets.

[Then follow various random disclosures referring to various periods of time. The following are extracted;]

—That during the presence of Captain Amasa Delano on board, some attempts were made by the sailors, and one by Hermenegildo Gandix, to convey hints to him of the true state of affairs; but that these attempts were ineffectual, owing to fear of incurring death, and, furthermore, owing to the devices which offered contradictions to the true state of affairs, as well as owing to the generosity and piety of Amasa Delano incapable of sounding such wickedness; * * * that Luys Galgo, a sailor about sixty years of age, and formerly of the king's navy, was one of those who sought to convey tokens to Captain Amasa Delano; but his intent, though undiscovered, being suspected, he was, on a pretense, made to retire out of sight, and at last into the hold, and there was made away with. This the negroes have since said; * * * that one of the ship-boys feeling, from Captain Amasa Delano's presence, some hopes of release, and not having enough prudence, dropped some chance-word respecting his expectations, which being overheard and understood by a slave-boy with whom he was eating at the time, the latter struck him on the head with a knife, inflicting a bad wound, but of which the boy is now healing; that likewise, not long before the ship was brought to anchor, one of the seamen, steering at the time, endangered himself by letting the blacks remark some expression in his countenance, arising from a cause similar to the above; but this sailor, by his heedful after conduct, escaped; * * * that these statements are made to show the court that from the beginning to the end of the revolt, it was impossible for the deponent and his men to act otherwise than they did; * * *—that the third clerk, Hermenegildo Gandix, who before had been forced to live among the seamen, wearing a seaman's habit, and in all respects appearing to be one for the time; he, Gandix, was killed by a musket ball fired through mistake from the boats before boarding; having in his fright run up the mizzen-rigging, calling to the boats—"don't board," lest upon their boarding the negroes should kill him; that this inducing the Americans to believe he some way favored the cause of the negroes, they fired two balls at him, so that he fell wounded from the rigging, and was drowned in the sea; * * *—that the young Don Joaquin, Marques de Aramboalaza, like Hermenegildo Gandix, the third clerk, was degraded to the office and appearance of a common seaman; that upon one occasion when Don Joaquin shrank, the negro Babo commanded the Ashantee Lecbe to take tar and heat it, and pour it upon Don Joaquin's hands; * * *—that Don Joaquin was killed owing to another mistake of the Americans, but one impossible to be avoided, as upon the approach of the boats, Don Joaquin, with a hatchet tied edge out and upright to his hand, was made by the negroes to appear on the bulwarks; whereupon, seen with arms in his hands and in a questionable attitude, he was shot for a renegade seaman; * * *—that on the person of Don Joaquin was found secreted a jewel, which, by papers that were discovered, proved to have been meant for the shrine of our Lady of Mercy in Lima; a votive offering, beforehand prepared and guarded, to attest his gratitude, when he should have landed in Peru, his last destination, for the safe conclusion of his entire voyage from Spain; * * *—that the jewel, with the other effects of the late Don Joaquin, is in the custody of the brethren of the Hospital de Sacerdotes, awaiting the disposition of the honorable court; * * *—that, owing to the condition of the deponent, as well as the haste in which the boats departed for the attack, the Americans were not forewarned that there were, among the apparent crew, a passenger and one of the clerks disguised by the negro Babo; * * *—that, beside the negroes killed in the action, some were killed after the capture and re-anchoring at night, when shackled to the ring-bolts on deck; that these deaths were committed by the sailors, ere they could be prevented. That so soon as informed of it, Captain Amasa Delano used all his authority, and, in particular with his own hand, struck down Martinez Gola, who, having found a razor in the pocket of an old jacket of his, which one of the shackled negroes had on, was aiming it at the negro's throat; that the noble Captain Amasa Delano also wrenched from the hand of Bartholomew Barlo a dagger, secreted at the time of the massacre of the whites, with which he was in the act of stabbing a shackled negro, who, the same day, with another negro, had thrown him down and jumped upon him; * * *—that, for all the events, befalling through so long a time, during which the ship was in the hands of the negro Babo, he cannot here give account; but that, what he has said is the most substantial of what occurs to him at present, and is the truth under the oath which he has taken; which declaration he affirmed and ratified, after hearing it read to him.

He said that he is twenty-nine years of age, and broken in body and mind; that when finally dismissed by the court, he shall not return home to Chili, but betake himself to the monastery on Mount Agonia without; and signed with his honor, and crossed himself, and, for the time, departed as he came, in his litter, with the monk Infelez, to the Hospital de Sacerdotes.

Benito Cereno.

Doctor Rozas.

If the Deposition have served as the key to fit into the lock of the complications which precede it, then, as a vault whose door has been flung back, the San Dominick's hull lies open to-day.

Hitherto the nature of this narrative, besides rendering the intricacies in the beginning unavoidable, has more or less required that many things, instead of being set down in the order of occurrence, should be retrospectively, or irregularly given; this last is the case with the following passages, which will conclude the account:

During the long, mild voyage to Lima, there was, as before hinted, a period during which the sufferer a little recovered his health, or, at least in some degree, his tranquillity. Ere the decided relapse which came, the two captains had many cordial conversations—their fraternal unreserve in singular contrast with former withdrawments.

Again and again it was repeated, how hard it had been to enact the part forced on the Spaniard by Babo.

"Ah, my dear friend," Don Benito once said, "at those very times when you thought me so morose and ungrateful, nay, when, as you now admit, you half thought me plotting your murder, at those very times my heart was frozen; I could not look at you, thinking of what, both on board this ship and your own, hung, from other hands, over my kind benefactor. And as God lives, Don Amasa, I know not whether desire for my own safety alone could have nerved me to that leap into your boat, had it not been for the thought that, did you, unenlightened, return to your ship, you, my best friend, with all who might be with you, stolen upon, that night, in your hammocks, would never in this world have wakened again. Do but think how you walked this deck, how you sat in this cabin, every inch of ground mined into honey-combs under you. Had I dropped the least hint, made the least advance towards an understanding between us, death, explosive death—yours as mine—would have ended the scene."

"True, true," cried Captain Delano, starting, "you have saved my life, Don Benito, more than I yours; saved it, too, against my knowledge and will."

"Nay, my friend," rejoined the Spaniard, courteous even to the point of religion, "God charmed your life, but you saved mine. To think of some things you did— those smilings and chattings, rash pointings and gesturings. For less than these, they slew my mate, Raneds; but you had the Prince of Heaven's safe-conduct through all ambuscades."

"Yes, all is owing to Providence, I know: but the temper of my mind that morning was more than commonly pleasant, while the sight of so much suffering, more apparent than real, added to my good-nature, compassion, and charity, happily interweaving the three. Had it been otherwise, doubtless, as you hint, some of my interferences might have ended unhappily enough. Besides, those feelings I spoke of enabled me to get the better of momentary distrust, at times when acuteness might have cost me my life, without saving another's. Only at the end did my suspicions get the better of me, and you know how wide of the mark they then proved."

"Wide, indeed," said Don Benito, sadly; "you were with me all day; stood with me, sat with me, talked with me, looked at me, ate with me, drank with me; and yet, your last act was to clutch for a monster, not only an innocent man, but the most pitiable of all men. To such degree may malign machinations and deceptions impose. So far may even the best man err, in judging the conduct of one with the recesses of whose condition he is not acquainted. But you were forced to it; and you were in time undeceived. Would that, in both respects, it was so ever, and with all men."

"You generalize, Don Benito; and mournfully enough. But the past is passed; why moralize upon it? Forget it. See, yon bright sun has forgotten it all, and the blue sea, and the blue sky; these have turned over new leaves."

"Because they have no memory," he dejectedly replied; "because they are not human."

"But these mild trades[40] that now fan your cheek, do they not come with a human-like healing to you? Warm friends, steadfast friends are the trades."

"With their steadfastness they but waft me to my tomb, Señor," was the foreboding response.

"You are saved," cried Captain Delano, more and more astonished and pained; "you are saved: what has cast such a shadow upon you?"

"The negro."

There was silence, while the moody man sat, slowly and unconsciously gathering his mantle about him, as if it were a pall.

There was no more conversation that day.

But if the Spaniard's melancholy sometimes ended in muteness upon topics like the above, there were others upon which he never spoke at all; on which, indeed, all his old reserves were piled. Pass over the worst, and, only to elucidate, let an item or two of these be cited. The dress, so precise and costly, worn by him on the day whose events have been narrated, had not willingly been put on. And that silver-mounted sword, apparent symbol of despotic command, was not, indeed, a sword, but the ghost of one. The scabbard, artificially stiffened, was empty.

As for the black—whose brain, not body, had schemed and led the revolt, with the plot—his slight frame, inadequate to that which it held, had at once yielded to the superior muscular strength of his captor, in the boat. Seeing all was over, he uttered no sound, and could not be forced to. His aspect seemed to say, since I cannot do deeds, I will not speak words. Put in irons in the hold, with the rest, he was car-

---

[40] Tradewinds.

ried to Lima. During the passage, Don Benito did not visit him. Nor then, nor at any time after, would he look at him. Before the tribunal he refused. When pressed by the judges he fainted. On the testimony of the sailors alone rested the legal identity of Babo.

Some months after, dragged to the gibbet at the tail of a mule, the black met his voiceless end. The body was burned to ashes; but for many days, the head, that hive of subtlety, fixed on a pole in the Plaza, met, unabashed, the gaze of the whites; and across the Plaza looked towards St. Bartholomew's church, in whose vaults slept then, as now, the recovered bones of Aranda: and across the Rimac bridge looked towards the monastery, on Mount Agonia without; where, three months after being dismissed by the court, Benito Cereno, borne on the bier, did, indeed, follow his leader.

1855–1856

Billy Budd, Sailor

(An Inside Narrative)*

Dedicated
to
JACK CHASE
Englishman
Wherever that great heart may now be
Here on Earth or harbored in Paradise.
Captain of the Maintop
in the year 1843
in the U.S. Frigate
United States[1]

1

In the time before steamships, or then more frequently than now, a stroller along the docks of any considerable seaport would occasionally have his attention arrested by a group of bronzed mariners, man-of-war's men or merchant sailors in holiday attire, ashore on liberty. In certain instances they would flank, or like a bodyguard quite

---

* Melville's mysterious phrase has been interpreted in several ways. Historically *Billy Budd* is based upon a 1797 mutiny in the British Navy, yet it also is the insider's version of an 1842 mutiny on the *Somers,* an American naval ship. Psychologically, *Billy Budd* may represent Melville's private, inner life. And the narrative, which on one level is an adventure story, also yields deeper, "inside" meanings. *Billy Budd* was written in the late 1880s, then found in manuscript among Melville's belongings after his death, and finally published in 1924.

[1] Jack Chase, Melville's shipmate on the *United States,* appeared in Melville's novel *White-Jacket* (1850) as the leader of the skilled crew assigned to the top of the mainmast.

surround, some superior figure of their own class, moving along with them like Aldebaran[2] among the lesser lights of his constellation. That signal object was the "Handsome Sailor" of the less prosaic time alike of the military and merchant navies. With no perceptible trace of the vain-glorious about him, rather with the offhand unaffectedness of natural regality, he seemed to accept the spontaneous homage of his shipmates.

A somewhat remarkable instance recurs to me. In Liverpool, now half a century ago, I saw under the shadow of the great dingy street-wall of Prince's Dock (an obstruction long since removed) a common sailor so intensely black that he must needs have been a native African of the unadulterate blood of Ham[3]—a symmetric figure much above the average height. The two ends of a gay silk handkerchief thrown loose about the neck danced upon the displayed ebony of his chest, in his ears were big hoops of gold, and a Highland bonnet with a tartan band set off his shapely head. It was a hot noon in July; and his face, lustrous with perspiration, beamed with barbaric good humor. In jovial sallies right and left, his white teeth flashing into view, he rollicked along, the center of a company of his shipmates. These were made up of such an assortment of tribes and complexions as would have well fitted them to be marched up by Anacharsis Cloots[4] before the bar of the first French Assembly as Representatives of the Human Race. At each spontaneous tribute rendered by the wayfarers to this black pagod[5] of a fellow—the tribute of a pause and stare, and less frequently an exclamation—the motley retinue showed that they took that sort of pride in the evoker of it which the Assyrian priests doubtless showed for their grand sculptured Bull when the faithful prostrated themselves.

To return. If in some cases a bit of a nautical Murat[6] in setting forth his person ashore, the Handsome Sailor of the period in question evinced nothing of the dandified Billy-be-Dam, an amusing character all but extinct now, but occasionally to be encountered, and in a form yet more amusing than the original, at the tiller of the boats on the tempestuous Erie Canal or, more likely, vaporing in the groggeries along the towpath.[7] Invariably a proficient in his perilous calling, he was also more or less of a mighty boxer or wrestler. It was strength and beauty. Tales of his prowess were recited. Ashore he was the champion; afloat the spokesman; on every suitable occasion always foremost. Close-reefing topsails in a gale, there he was, astride the weather yardarm-end, foot in the Flemish horse as stirrup,[8] both hands tugging at the earing as at a bridle, in very much the attitude of young Alexander curbing the fiery Bucephalus.[9] A superb figure, tossed up as by the horns of Taurus against the thunderous sky, cheerily hallooing to the strenuous file along the spar.

The moral nature was seldom out of keeping with the physical make. Indeed,

---

[2] The brightest star and "eye" of the constellation Taurus, the Bull.

[3] Noah's curse on his son Ham, in Genesis 9:22–25, was assumed to result in black skin in Ham's descendants.

[4] Revolutionary Prussian (1755–1794) who demonstrated the variety and unity of mankind by parading men of different classes and nationalities before the French National Assembly.

[5] Idol.

[6] Joachim Murat (1767–1815), a dandy and king of Naples.

[7] I.e., boasting in the saloons, the placid Erie Canal being hardly tempestuous.

[8] I.e., he was lowering sails and fastening them to a yardarm or spar while braced in the foot rope on the end of the yardarm on the windward side.

[9] Horse of Alexander the Great (356–323 B.C.).

except as toned by the former, the comeliness and power, always attractive in masculine conjunction, hardly could have drawn the sort of honest homage the Handsome Sailor in some examples received from his less gifted associates.

Such a cynosure, at least in aspect, and something such too in nature, though with important variations made apparent as the story proceeds, was welkin-eyed[10] Billy Budd—or Baby Budd, as more familiarly, under circumstances hereafter to be given, he at last came to be called—aged twenty-one, a foretopman[11] of the British fleet toward the close of the last decade of the eighteenth century. It was not very long prior to the time of the narration that follows that he had entered the King's service, having been impressed on the Narrow Seas[12] from a homeward-bound English merchantman into a seventy-four[13] outward bound, H.M.S. *Bellipotent;* which ship, as was not unusual in those hurried days, having been obliged to put to sea short of her proper complement of men. Plump upon Billy at first sight in the gangway the boarding officer, Lieutenant Ratcliffe, pounced, even before the merchantman's crew was formally mustered on the quarter-deck for his deliberate inspection. And him only he elected. For whether it was because the other men when ranged before him showed to ill advantage after Billy, or whether he had some scruples in view of the merchantman's being rather short-handed, however it might be, the officer contented himself with his first spontaneous choice. To the surprise of the ship's company, though much to the lieutenant's satisfaction, Billy made no demur. But, indeed, any demur would have been as idle as the protest of a goldfinch popped into a cage.

Noting this uncomplaining acquiescence, all but cheerful, one might say, the shipmaster turned a surprised glance of silent reproach at the sailor. The shipmaster was one of those worthy mortals found in every vocation, even the humbler ones— the sort of person whom everybody agrees in calling "a respectable man." And—nor so strange to report as it may appear to be—though a ploughman of the troubled waters, lifelong contending with the intractable elements, there was nothing this honest soul at heart loved better than simple peace and quiet. For the rest, he was fifty or thereabouts, a little inclined to corpulence, a prepossessing face, unwhiskered, and of an agreeable color—a rather full face, humanely intelligent in expression. On a fair day with a fair wind and all going well, a certain musical chime in his voice seemed to be the veritable unobstructed outcome of the innermost man. He had much prudence, much conscientiousness, and there were occasions when these virtues were the cause of overmuch disquietude in him. On a passage, so long as his craft was in any proximity to land, no sleep for Captain Graveling. He took to heart those serious responsibilities not so heavily borne by some shipmasters.

Now while Billy Budd was down in the forecastle[14] getting his kit together, the *Bellipotent's* lieutenant, burly and bluff, nowise disconcerted by Captain Graveling's omitting to proffer the customary hospitalities on an occasion so unwelcome to him, an omission simply caused by preoccupation of thought, unceremoniously invited himself into the cabin, and also to a flask from the spirit locker, a receptacle which his experienced eye instantly discovered. In fact he was one of those sea dogs in whom

---

[10] Blue-eyed.
[11] Crewman assigned to the top of the foretop mast.
[12] Forced into naval service on the channels separating England from Ireland and Europe.

[13] Battleship of an impressive 74 guns.
[14] Crew's quarters in the forward part of the ship.

all the hardship and peril of naval life in the great prolonged wars of his time never impaired the natural instinct for sensuous enjoyment. His duty he always faithfully did; but duty is sometimes a dry obligation, and he was for irrigating its aridity, whensoever possible, with a fertilizing decoction of strong waters. For the cabin's proprietor there was nothing left but to play the part of the enforced host with whatever grace and alacrity were practicable. As necessary adjuncts to the flask, he silently placed tumbler and water jug before the irrepressible guest. But excusing himself from partaking just then, he dismally watched the unembarrassed officer deliberately diluting his grog a little, then tossing it off in three swallows, pushing the empty tumbler away, yet not so far as to be beyond easy reach, at the same time settling himself in his seat and smacking his lips with high satisfaction, looking straight at the host.

These proceedings over, the master broke the silence; and there lurked a rueful reproach in the tone of his voice: "Lieutenant, you are going to take my best man from me, the jewel of 'em."

"Yes, I know," rejoined the other, immediately drawing back the tumbler preliminary to a replenishing. "Yes, I know. Sorry."

"Beg pardon, but you don't understand, Lieutenant. See here, now. Before I shipped that young fellow, my forecastle was a rat-pit of quarrels. It was black times, I tell you, aboard the *Rights* here. I was worried to that degree my pipe had no comfort for me. But Billy came; and it was like a Catholic priest striking peace in an Irish shindy.[15] Not that he preached to them or said or did anything in particular; but a virtue went out of him, sugaring the sour ones. They took to him like hornets to treacle; all but the buffer[16] of the gang, the big shaggy chap with the fire-red whiskers. He indeed, out of envy, perhaps, of the newcomer, and thinking such a "sweet and pleasant fellow," as he mockingly designated him to the others, could hardly have the spirit of a gamecock, must needs bestir himself in trying to get up an ugly row with him. Billy forebore with him and reasoned with him in a pleasant way—he is something like myself, Lieutenant, to whom aught like a quarrel is hateful —but nothing served. So, in the second dogwatch one day, the Red Whiskers in presence of the others, under pretense of showing Billy just whence a sirloin steak was cut—for the fellow had once been a butcher—insultingly gave him a dig under the ribs. Quick as lightning Billy let fly his arm. I dare say he never meant to do quite as much as he did, but anyhow he gave the burly fool a terrible drubbing. It took about half a minute, I should think. And, lord bless you, the lubber was astonished at the celerity. And will you believe it, Lieutenant, the Red Whiskers now really loves Billy—loves him, or is the biggest hypocrite that ever I heard of. But they all love him. Some of 'em do his washing, darn his old trousers for him; the carpenter is at odd times making a pretty little chest of drawers for him. Anybody will do anything for Billy Budd; and it's the happy family here. But now, Lieutenant, if that young fellow goes—I know how it will be aboard the *Rights*. Not again very soon shall I, coming up from dinner, lean over the capstan smoking a quiet pipe—no, not very soon again, I think. Ay, Lieutenant, you are going to take away the jewel of 'em; you are going to take away my peacemaker!" And with that the good soul had really some ado in checking a rising sob.

[15] Brawl.   [16] Bully.

"Well," said the lieutenant, who had listened with amused interest to all this and now was waxing merry with his tipple; "well, blessed are the peacemakers, especially the fighting peacemakers. And such are the seventy-four beauties some of which you see poking their noses out of the portholes of yonder warship lying to for me," pointing through the cabin window at the *Bellipotent*. "But courage! Don't look so downhearted, man. Why, I pledge you in advance the royal approbation. Rest assured that His Majesty will be delighted to know that in a time when his hardtack is not sought for by sailors with such avidity as should be, a time also when some shipmasters privily resent the borrowing from them a tar or two for the service; His Majesty, I say, will be delighted to learn that *one* shipmaster at least cheerfully surrenders to the King the flower of his flock, a sailor who with equal loyalty makes no dissent.—But where's my beauty? Ah," looking through the cabin's open door, "here he comes; and, by Jove, lugging along his chest—Apollo with his portmanteau!—My man," stepping out to him, "you can't take that big box aboard a warship. The boxes there are mostly shot boxes. Put your duds in a bag, lad. Boot and saddle for the cavalryman, bag and hammock for the man-of-war's man."

The transfer from chest to bag was made. And, after seeing his man into the cutter and then following him down, the lieutenant pushed off from the *Rights-of-Man*.[17] That was the merchant ship's name, though by her master and crew abbreviated in sailor fashion into the *Rights*. The hardheaded Dundee owner[18] was a staunch admirer of Thomas Paine, whose book in rejoinder to Burke's arraignment of the French Revolution had then been published for some time and had gone everywhere. In christening his vessel after the title of Paine's volume the man of Dundee was something like his contemporary shipowner, Stephen Girard[19] of Philadelphia, whose sympathies, alike with his native land and its liberal philosophers, he evinced by naming his ships after Voltaire, Diderot, and so forth.

But now, when the boat swept under the merchantman's stern, and officer and oarsmen were noting—some bitterly and others with a grin—the name emblazoned there; just then it was that the new recruit jumped up from the bow where the coxswain[20] had directed him to sit, and waving hat to his silent shipmates sorrowfully looking over at him from the taffrail,[21] bade the lads a genial good-bye. Then, making a salutation as to the ship herself, "And good-bye to you too, old *Rights-of-Man*."

"Down, sir!" roared the lieutenant, instantly assuming all the rigor of his rank, though with difficulty repressing a smile.

To be sure, Billy's action was a terrible breach of naval decorum. But in that decorum he had never been instructed; in consideration of which the lieutenant would hardly have been so energetic in reproof but for the concluding farewell to the ship. This he rather took as meant to convey a covert sally on the new recruit's part, a sly slur at impressment in general, and that of himself in especial. And yet, more likely, if satire it was in effect, it was hardly so by intention, for Billy, though happily endowed with the gaiety of high health, youth, and a free heart, was yet by no means

---

[17] Thomas Paine's *The Rights of Man* (1791–1792) argued for individual human rights. It was a direct response to Edmund Burke's *Reflections on the Revolution in France* (1790), which stated that human rights are best preserved through strong social and political institutions.

[18] Scotsman from the seaport of Dundee.

[19] Merchant and shipper who admired the views of the French philosophers Voltaire (1694–1778) and Denis Diderot (1713–1784).

[20] Boat steersman.

[21] Rail at ship's rear or stern.

of a satirical turn. The will to it and the sinister dexterity were alike wanting. To deal in double meanings and insinuations of any sort was quite foreign to his nature.

As to his enforced enlistment, that he seemed to take pretty much as he was wont to take any vicissitude of weather. Like the animals, though no philosopher, he was, without knowing it, practically a fatalist. And it may be that he rather liked this adventurous turn in his affairs, which promised an opening into novel scenes and martial excitements.

Aboard the *Bellipotent* our merchant sailor was forthwith rated as an able seaman and assigned to the starboard watch of the foretop. He was soon at home in the service, not at all disliked for his unpretentious good looks and a sort of genial happy-go-lucky air. No merrier man in his mess: in marked contrast to certain other individuals included like himself among the impressed portion of the ship's company; for these when not actively employed were sometimes, and more particularly in the last dogwatch[22] when the drawing near of twilight induced revery, apt to fall into a saddish mood which in some partook of sullenness. But they were not so young as our foretopman, and no few of them must have known a hearth of some sort, others may have had wives and children left, too probably, in uncertain circumstances, and hardly any but must have had acknowledged kith and kin, while for Billy, as will shortly be seen, his entire family was practically invested in himself.

2

Though our new-made foretopman was well received in the top and on the gun decks, hardly here was he that cynosure he had previously been among those minor ship's companies of the merchant marine, with which companies only had he hitherto consorted.

He was young; and despite his all but fully developed frame, in aspect looked even younger than he really was, owing to a lingering adolescent expression in the as yet smooth face all but feminine in purity of natural complexion but where, thanks to his seagoing, the lily was quite suppressed and the rose had some ado visibly to flush through the tan.

To one essentially such a novice in the complexities of factitious life, the abrupt transition from his former and simpler sphere to the ampler and more knowing world of a great warship; this might well have abashed him had there been any conceit or vanity in his composition. Among her miscellaneous multitude, the *Bellipotent* mustered several individuals who however inferior in grade were of no common natural stamp, sailors more signally susceptive of that air which continuous martial discipline and repeated presence in battle can in some degree impart even to the average man. As the Handsome Sailor, Billy Budd's position aboard the seventy-four was something analogous to that of a rustic beauty transplanted from the provinces and brought into competition with the highborn dames of the court. But this change of circumstances he scarce noted. As little did he observe that something about him provoked an ambiguous smile in one or two harder faces among the blue jackets. Nor less unaware

---

22 A two-hour watch between 4 and 8 P.M. Billy's
assignment as foretopman and rating as an
able-bodied seaman indicate his skills as a sailor.

was he of the peculiar favorable effect his person and demeanor had upon the more intelligent gentlemen of the quarter-deck.[23] Nor could this well have been otherwise. Cast in a mold peculiar to the finest physical examples of those Englishmen in whom the Saxon strain would seem not at all to partake of any Norman or other admixture, he showed in face that humane look of reposeful good nature which the Greek sculptor in some instances gave to his heroic strong man, Hercules. But this again was subtly modified by another and pervasive quality. The ear, small and shapely, the arch of the foot, the curve in mouth and nostril, even the indurated hand dyed to the orange-tawny of the toucan's bill, a hand telling alike of the halyards and tar bucket; but, above all, something in the mobile expression, and every chance attitude and movement, something suggestive of a mother eminently favored by Love and the Graces; all this strangely indicated a lineage in direct contradiction to his lot. The mysteriousness here became less mysterious through a matter of fact elicited when Billy at the capstan was being formally mustered into the service. Asked by the officer, a small, brisk little gentleman as it chanced, among other questions, his place of birth, he replied, "Please, sir, I don't know."

"Don't know where you were born? Who was your father?"

"God knows, sir."

Struck by the straightforward simplicity of these replies, the officer next asked, "Do you know anything about your beginning?"

"No, sir. But I have heard that I was found in a pretty silk-lined basket hanging one morning from the knocker of a good man's door in Bristol."

"*Found,* say you? Well," throwing back his head and looking up and down the new recruit; "well, it turns out to have been a pretty good find. Hope they'll find some more like you, my man; the fleet sadly needs them."

Yes, Billy Budd was a foundling, a presumable by-blow,[24] and, evidently, no ignoble one. Noble descent was as evident in him as in a blood horse.

For the rest, with little or no sharpness of faculty or any trace of the wisdom of the serpent, nor yet quite a dove,[25] he possessed that kind and degree of intelligence going along with the unconventional rectitude of a sound human creature, one to whom not yet has been proffered the questionable apple of knowledge. He was illiterate; he could not read, but he could sing, and like the illiterate nightingale was sometimes the composer of his own song.

Of self-consciousness he seemed to have little or none, or about as much as we may reasonably impute to a dog of Saint Bernard's breed.

Habitually living with the elements and knowing little more of the land than as a beach, or, rather, that portion of the terraqueous globe providentially set apart for dance-houses, doxies, and tapsters, in short what sailors call a "fiddler's green,"[26] his simple nature remained unsophisticated by those moral obliquities which are not in every case incompatible with that manufactured thing known as respectability. But are sailors, frequenters of fiddlers' greens, without vices? No; but less often than with landsmen do their vices, so called, partake of crookedness of heart, seeming less to

---

[23] Rear section of the main deck, customarily reserved for officers.

[24] Bastard.

[25] Matthew 10:16: "Behold, I send you forth as sheep in the midst of wolves; be ye therefore wise as serpents and harmless as doves."

[26] Doxies: wenches; tapsters: bartenders; "fiddler's green": a sailors' pleasureground.

proceed from viciousness than exuberance of vitality after long constraint: frank manifestations in accordance with natural law. By his original constitution aided by the co-operating influences of his lot, Billy in many respects was little more than a sort of upright barbarian, much such perhaps as Adam presumably might have been ere the urbane Serpent wriggled himself into his company.

And here be it submitted that apparently going to corroborate the doctrine of man's Fall,[27] a doctrine now popularly ignored, it is observable that where certain virtues pristine and unadulterate peculiarly characterize anybody in the external uniform of civilization, they will upon scrutiny seem not to be derived from custom or convention, but rather to be out of keeping with these, as if indeed exceptionally transmitted from a period prior to Cain's city[28] and citified man. The character marked by such qualities has to an unvitiated taste an untampered-with flavor like that of berries, while the man thoroughly civilized, even in a fair specimen of the breed, has to the same moral palate a questionable smack as of a compounded wine. To any stray inheritor of these primitive qualities found, like Caspar Hauser,[29] wandering dazed in any Christian capital of our time, the good-natured poet's famous invocation, near two thousand years ago, of the good rustic out of his latitude in the Rome of the Caesars, still appropriately holds:

> Honest and poor, faithful in word and thought,
> What hath thee, Fabian, to the city brought?[30]

Though our Handsome Sailor had as much of masculine beauty as one can expect anywhere to see; nevertheless, like the beautiful woman in one of Hawthorne's minor tales,[31] there was just one thing amiss in him. No visible blemish indeed, as with the lady; no, but an occasional liability to a vocal defect. Though in the hour of elemental uproar or peril he was everything that a sailor should be, yet under sudden provocation of strong heart-feeling his voice, otherwise singularly musical, as if expressive of the harmony within, was apt to develop an organic hesitancy, in fact more or less of a stutter or even worse. In this particular Billy was a striking instance that the arch interferer, the envious marplot of Eden, still has more or less to do with every human consignment to this planet of Earth. In every case, one way or another he is sure to slip in his little card, as much as to remind us—I too have a hand here.

The avowal of such an imperfection in the Handsome Sailor should be evidence not alone that he is not presented as a conventional hero, but also that the story in which he is the main figure is no romance.

3

At the time of Billy Budd's arbitrary enlistment into the *Bellipotent* that ship was on her way to join the Mediterranean fleet. No long time elapsed before the junction was effected. As one of that fleet the seventy-four participated in its movements,

---

[27] Human downfall caused by Adam and Eve's sin.
[28] See Genesis 4:16–17. Cain killed his brother, Abel, and then "went out from the presence of the Lord. . . . And he builded a city."

[29] German boy (1812?–1833) of mysterious origins, supposed to be of noble birth and to exhibit an innocent nature.
[30] Martial, *Epigrams,* I, iv.
[31] Hawthorne's "The Birthmark."

though at times on account of her superior sailing qualities, in the absence of frigates, dispatched on separate duty as a scout and at times on less temporary service. But with all this the story has little concernment, restricted as it is to the inner life of one particular ship and the career of an individual sailor.

It was the summer of 1797. In the April of that year had occurred the commotion at Spithead followed in May by a second and yet more serious outbreak in the fleet at the Nore.[32] The latter is known, and without exaggeration in the epithet, as "the Great Mutiny." It was indeed a demonstration more menacing to England than the contemporary manifestoes and conquering and proselyting armies of the French Directory.[33] To the British Empire the Nore Mutiny was what a strike in the fire brigade would be to London threatened by general arson. In a crisis when the kingdom might well have anticipated the famous signal[34] that some years later published along the naval line of battle what it was that upon occasion England expected of Englishmen; *that* was the time when at the mastheads of the three-deckers and seventy-fours moored in her own roadstead—a fleet the right arm of a Power then all but the sole free conservative one of the Old World—the bluejackets, to be numbered by thousands, ran up with huzzas the British colors with the union and cross wiped out; by that cancellation transmuting the flag of founded law and freedom defined, into the enemy's red meteor of unbridled and unbounded revolt. Reasonable discontent growing out of practical grievances in the fleet had been ignited into irrational combustion as by live cinders blown across the Channel from France in flames.

The event converted into irony for a time those spirited strains of Dibdin[35]—as a song-writer no mean auxiliary to the English government at that European conjuncture—strains celebrating, among other things, the patriotic devotion of the British tar: "And as for my life, 'tis the King's!"

Such an episode in the Island's grand naval story her naval historians naturally abridge, one of them (William James) candidly acknowledging that fain would he pass it over did not "impartiality forbid fastidiousness." And yet his mention is less a narration than a reference, having to do hardly at all with details. Nor are these readily to be found in the libraries. Like some other events in every age befalling states everywhere, including America, the Great Mutiny was of such character that national pride along with views of policy would fain shade it off into the historical background. Such events cannot be ignored, but there is a considerate way of historically treating them. If a well-constituted individual refrains from blazoning aught amiss or calamitous in his family, a nation in the like circumstance may without reproach be equally discreet.

Though after parleyings between government and the ringleaders, and concessions by the former as to some glaring abuses, the first uprising—that at Spithead—with difficulty was put down, or matters for the time pacified; yet at the Nore the unforeseen renewal of insurrection on a yet larger scale, and emphasized in the conferences that ensued by demands deemed by the authorities not only inadmissible but aggressively insolent, indicated—if the Red Flag[36] did not sufficiently do so— what was the spirit animating the men. Final suppression, however, there was; but only

---

[32] Spithead and Nore were locations in which British seamen mutinied.

[33] Post-Revolutionary French governing body (1795–1799).

[34] Reference to British Admiral Nelson's famous

signal, "England expects every man to do his duty," prior to the Battle of Trafalgar (1805).

[35] Charles Dibdin (1745–1815), English writer of patriotic songs.

[36] Traditional banner of revolution.

made possible perhaps by the unswerving loyalty of the marine corps[37] and a voluntary resumption of loyalty among influential sections of the crews.

To some extent the Nore Mutiny may be regarded as analogous to the distempering irruption of contagious fever in a frame constitutionally sound, and which anon throws it off.

At all events, of these thousands of mutineers were some of the tars who not so very long afterwards—whether wholly prompted thereto by patriotism, or pugnacious instinct, or by both—helped to win a coronet for Nelson at the Nile, and the naval crown of crowns for him at Trafalgar. To the mutineers, those battles and especially Trafalgar were a plenary absolution and a grand one. For all that goes to make up scenic naval display and heroic magnificence in arms, those battles, especially Trafalgar, stand unmatched in human annals.

4

In this matter of writing, resolve as one may to keep to the main road, some bypaths have an enticement not readily to be withstood. I am going to err into such a bypath. If the reader will keep me company I shall be glad. At the least, we can promise ourselves that pleasure which is wickedly said to be in sinning, for a literary sin the divergence will be.

Very likely it is no new remark that the inventions of our time have at last brought about a change in sea warfare in degree corresponding to the revolution in all warfare effected by the original introduction from China into Europe of gunpowder. The first European firearm, a clumsy contrivance, was, as is well known, scouted by no few of the knights as a base implement, good enough peradventure for weavers too craven to stand up crossing steel with steel in frank fight. But as ashore knightly valor, though shorn of its blazonry, did not cease with the knights, neither on the seas—though nowadays in encounters there a certain kind of displayed gallantry be fallen out of date as hardly applicable under changed circumstances—did the nobler qualities of such naval magnates as Don John of Austria, Doria, Van Tromp, Jean Bart, the long line of British admirals, and the American Decaturs of 1812 become obsolete with their wooden walls.[38]

Nevertheless, to anybody who can hold the Present at its worth without being inappreciative of the Past, it may be forgiven, if to such an one the solitary old hulk at Portsmouth, Nelson's *Victory,* seems to float there, not alone as the decaying monument of a fame incorruptible, but also as a poetic reproach, softened by its picturesqueness, to the *Monitors* and yet mightier hulls of the European ironclads.[39] And this not altogether because such craft are unsightly, unavoidably lacking the symmetry and grand lines of the old battleships, but equally for other reasons.

There are some, perhaps, who while not altogether inaccessible to that poetic

---

[37] Marines were stationed on men-of-war and often had an antagonistic relation to the crew.

[38] Don Juan of Austria (1547–1578) led a fleet to defeat Turkey (1571); Andrea Doria (1466–1560) was renowned as admiral of the Genoese and French fleet; Maarten Van Tromp (1597–1653) commanded Dutch fleets against Britain and Spain; Jean Bart (1651?–1702) led

French privateers against the Dutch; Stephen Decatur (1779–1820) led American naval ships against Tripoli pirates and against Britain in the War of 1812.

[39] The *Victory* was Nelson's flagship at Trafalgar, where he died; the iron-clad Union *Monitor* defeated the Confederate *Merrimac* in the American Civil War.

reproach just alluded to, may yet on behalf of the new order be disposed to parry it; and this to the extent of iconoclasm, if need be. For example, prompted by the sight of the star inserted in the *Victory*'s quarter-deck designating the spot where the Great Sailor fell, these martial utilitarians may suggest considerations implying that Nelson's ornate publication of his person in battle was not only unnecessary, but not military, nay, savored of foolhardiness and vanity. They may add, too, that at Trafalgar it was in effect nothing less than a challenge to death; and death came; and that but for his bravado the victorious admiral might possibly have survived the battle, and so, instead of having his sagacious dying injunctions overruled by his immediate successor in command, he himself when the contest was decided might have brought his shattered fleet to anchor, a proceeding which might have averted the deplorable loss of life by shipwreck in the elemental tempest that followed the martial one.

Well, should we set aside the more than disputable point whether for various reasons it was possible to anchor the fleet, then plausibly enough the Benthamites[40] of war may urge the above. But the *might-have-been* is but boggy ground to build on. And, certainly, in foresight as to the larger issue of an encounter, and anxious preparations for it—buoying the deadly way and mapping it out, as at Copenhagen[41] —few commanders have been so painstakingly circumspect as this same reckless declarer of his person in fight.

Personal prudence, even when dictated by quite other than selfish considerations, surely is no special virtue in a military man; while an excessive love of glory, impassioning a less burning impulse, the honest sense of duty, is the first. If the name *Wellington* is not so much of a trumpet to the blood as the simpler name *Nelson,* the reason for this may perhaps be inferred from the above. Alfred[42] in his funeral ode on the victor of Waterloo ventures not to call him the greatest soldier of all time, though in the same ode he invokes Nelson as "the greatest sailor since our world began."

At Trafalgar Nelson on the brink of opening the fight sat down and wrote his last brief will and testament. If under the presentiment of the most magnificent of all victories to be crowned by his own glorious death, a sort of priestly motive led him to dress his person in the jewelled vouchers of his own shining deeds; if thus to have adorned himself for the altar and the sacrifice were indeed vainglory, then affectation and fustian is each more heroic line in the great epics and dramas, since in such lines the poet but embodies in verse those exaltations of sentiment that a nature like Nelson, the opportunity being given, vitalizes into acts.

5

Yes, the outbreak at the Nore was put down. But not every grievance was redressed. If the contractors, for example, were no longer permitted to ply some practices peculiar to their tribe everywhere, such as providing shoddy cloth, rations not sound, or false in the measure; not the less impressment, for one thing, went on. By custom sanctioned for centuries, and judicially maintained by a Lord Chancellor as late as

[40] Followers of Jeremy Bentham (1748–1832), English advocate of utilitarianism.
[41] Reference to Nelson's careful preparations for the Battle of Copenhagen (1801).

[42] Alfred, Lord Tennyson (1809–1892) commemorated the English victory over Napoleon at Waterloo (1815) in "Ode on the Death of the Duke of Wellington."

Mansfield,[43] that mode of manning the fleet, a mode now fallen into a sort of abeyance but never formally renounced, it was not practicable to give up in those years. Its abrogation would have crippled the indispensable fleet, one wholly under canvas, no steam power, its innumerable sails and thousands of cannon, everything in short, worked by muscle alone; a fleet the more insatiate in demand for men, because then multiplying its ships of all grades against contingencies present and to come of the convulsed Continent.

Discontent foreran the Two Mutinies, and more or less it lurkingly survived them. Hence it was not unreasonable to apprehend some return of trouble sporadic or general. One instance of such apprehensions: In the same year with this story, Nelson, then Rear Admiral Sir Horatio, being with the fleet off the Spanish coast, was directed by the admiral in command to shift his pennant from the *Captain* to the *Theseus;* and for this reason: that the latter ship having newly arrived on the station from home, where it had taken part in the Great Mutiny, danger was apprehended from the temper of the men; and it was thought that an officer like Nelson was the one, not indeed to terrorize the crew into base subjection, but to win them, by force of his mere presence and heroic personality, back to an allegiance if not as enthusiastic as his own yet as true.

So it was that for a time, on more than one quarter-deck, anxiety did exist. At sea, precautionary vigilance was strained against relapse. At short notice an engagement might come on. When it did, the lieutenants assigned to batteries felt it incumbent on them, in some instances, to stand with drawn swords behind the men working the guns.

6

But on board the seventy-four in which Billy now swung his hammock, very little in the manner of the men and nothing obvious in the demeanor of the officers would have suggested to an ordinary observer that the Great Mutiny was a recent event. In their general bearing and conduct the commissioned officers of a warship naturally take their tone from the commander, that is if he have that ascendancy of character that ought to be his.

Captain the Honorable Edward Fairfax Vere, to give his full title, was a bachelor of forty or thereabouts, a sailor of distinction even in a time prolific of renowned seamen. Though allied to the higher nobility, his advancement had not been altogether owing to influences connected with that circumstance. He had seen much service, been in various engagements, always acquitting himself as an officer mindful of the welfare of his men, but never tolerating an infraction of discipline; thoroughly versed in the science of his profession, and intrepid to the verge of temerity, though never injudiciously so. For his gallantry in the West Indian waters as flag lieutenant under Rodney in that admiral's crowning victory over De Grasse,[44] he was made a post captain.

Ashore, in the garb of a civilian, scarce anyone would have taken him for a sailor, more especially that he never garnished unprofessional talk with nautical terms, and grave in his bearing, evinced little appreciation of mere humor. It was not out of

---

[43] William Murray, the earl of Mansfield (1705–1793), authorized impressment, virtual kidnapping, to secure sailors for the naval fleet.

[44] British Admiral George Rodney (1719–1792) defeated French admiral François Paul DeGrasse (1722–1788) in the West Indies in 1782.

keeping with these traits that on a passage when nothing demanded his paramount action, he was the most undemonstrative of men. Any landsman observing this gentleman not conspicuous by his stature and wearing no pronounced insignia, emerging from his cabin to the open deck, and noting the silent deference of the officers retiring to leeward, might have taken him for the King's guest, a civilian aboard the King's ship, some highly honorable discreet envoy on his way to an important post. But in fact this unobtrusiveness of demeanor may have proceeded from a certain unaffected modesty of manhood sometimes accompanying a resolute nature, a modesty evinced at all times not calling for pronounced action, which shown in any rank of life suggests a virtue aristocratic in kind. As with some others engaged in various departments of the world's more heroic activities, Captain Vere though practical enough upon occasion would at times betray a certain dreaminess of mood. Standing alone on the weather side of the quarter-deck, one hand holding by the rigging, he would absently gaze off at the black sea. At the presentation to him then of some minor matter interrupting the current of his thoughts, he would show more or less irascibility; but instantly he would control it.

In the navy he was popularly known by the appellation "Starry Vere." How such a designation happened to fall upon one who whatever his sterling qualities was without any brilliant ones, was in this wise: A favorite kinsman, Lord Denton, a freehearted fellow, had been the first to meet and congratulate him upon his return to England from his West Indian cruise; and but the day previous turning over a copy of Andrew Marvell's poems had lighted, not for the first time, however, upon the lines entitled "Appleton House," the name of one of the seats of their common ancestor, a hero in the German wars of the seventeenth century, in which poem occur the lines:

> This 'tis to have been from the first
> In a domestic heaven nursed,
> Under the discipline severe
> Of Fairfax and the starry Vere.[45]

And so, upon embracing his cousin fresh from Rodney's great victory wherein he had played so gallant a part, brimming over with just family pride in the sailor of their house, he exuberantly exclaimed, "Give ye joy, Ed; give ye joy, my starry Vere!" This got currency, and the novel prefix serving in familiar parlance readily to distinguish the *Bellipotent*'s captain from another Vere his senior, a distant relative, an officer of like rank in the navy, it remained permanently attached to the surname.

7

In view of the part that the commander of the *Bellipotent* plays in scenes shortly to follow, it may be well to fill out that sketch of him outlined in the previous chapter.

Aside from his qualities as a sea officer Captain Vere was an exceptional character. Unlike no few of England's renowned sailors, long and arduous service with signal devotion to it had not resulted in absorbing and *salting* the entire man. He had a

---

[45] The poet Andrew Marvell's lines refer to Ann Vere, wife of Lord Fairfax (1612–1671); Melville adapts the material to his own fictional uses here.

marked leaning toward everything intellectual. He loved books, never going to sea without a newly replenished library, compact but of the best. The isolated leisure, in some cases so wearisome, falling at intervals to commanders even during a war cruise, never was tedious to Captain Vere. With nothing of that literary taste which less heeds the thing conveyed than the vehicle, his bias was toward those books to which every serious mind of superior order occupying any active post of authority in the world naturally inclines: books treating of actual men and events no matter of what era—history, biography, and unconventional writers like Montaigue, who, free from cant and convention, honestly and in the spirit of common sense philosophize upon realities. In this line of reading he found confirmation of his own more reserved thoughts—confirmation which he had vainly sought in social converse, so that as touching most fundamental topics, there had got to be established in him some positive convictions which he forefelt would abide in him essentially unmodified so long as his intelligent part remained unimpaired. In view of the troubled period in which his lot was cast, this was well for him. His settled convictions were as a dike against those invading waters of novel opinion social, political, and otherwise, which carried away as in a torrent no few minds in those days, minds by nature not inferior to his own. While other members of that aristocracy to which by birth he belonged were incensed at the innovators mainly because their theories were inimical to the privileged classes, Captain Vere disinterestedly opposed them not alone because they seemed to him insusceptible of embodiment in lasting institutions, but at war with the peace of the world and the true welfare of mankind.

With minds less stored than his and less earnest, some officers of his rank, with whom at times he would necessarily consort, found him lacking in the companionable quality, a dry and bookish gentleman, as they deemed. Upon any chance withdrawal from their company one would be apt to say to another something like this: "Vere is a noble fellow, Starry Vere. 'Spite the gazettes,[46] Sir Horatio" (meaning him who became Lord Nelson) "is at bottom scarce a better seaman or fighter. But between you and me now, don't you think there is a queer streak of the pedantic running through him? Yes, like the King's yarn[47] in a coil of navy rope?"

Some apparent ground there was for this sort of confidential criticism; since not only did the captain's discourse never fall into the jocosely familiar, but in illustrating of any point touching the stirring personages and events of the time he would be as apt to cite some historic character or incident of antiquity as he would be to cite from the moderns. He seemed unmindful of the circumstance that to his bluff company such remote allusions, however pertinent they might really be, were altogether alien to men whose reading was mainly confined to the journals. But considerateness in such matters is not easy to natures constituted like Captain Vere's. Their honesty prescribes to them directness, sometimes far-reaching like that of a migratory fowl that in its flight never heeds when it crosses a frontier.

8

The lieutenants and other commissioned gentlemen forming Captain Vere's staff it is not necessary here to particularize, nor needs it to make any mention of any of the warrant officers. But among the petty officers was one who, having much to do with

---

[46] Despite newspaper reports.   [47] Noticeable thread in a length of rope.

the story, may as well be forthwith introduced. His portrait I essay, but shall never hit it. This was John Claggart, the master-at-arms. But that sea title may to landsmen seem somewhat equivocal. Originally, doubtless, that petty officer's function was the instruction of the men in the use of arms, sword or cutlass. But very long ago, owing to the advance in gunnery making hand-to-hand encounters less frequent and giving to niter and sulphur the pre-eminence over steel,[48] that function ceased; the master-at-arms of a great warship becoming a sort of chief of police charged among other matters with the duty of preserving order on the populous lower gun decks.

Claggart was a man about five-and-thirty, somewhat spare and tall, yet of no ill figure upon the whole. His hand was too small and shapely to have been accustomed to hard toil. The face was a notable one, the features all except the chin cleanly cut as those on a Greek medallion; yet the chin, beardless as Tecumseh's,[49] had something of strange protuberant broadness in its make that recalled the prints of the Reverend Dr. Titus Oates, the historic deponent with the clerical drawl in the time of Charles II and the fraud of the alleged Popish Plot.[50] It served Claggart in his office that his eye could cast a tutoring glance. His brow was of the sort phrenologically associated with more than average intellect; silken jet curls partly clustering over it, making a foil to the pallor below, a pallor tinged with a faint shade of amber akin to the hue of time-tinted marbles of old. This complexion, singularly contrasting with the red or deeply bronzed visages of the sailors, and in part the result of his official seclusion from the sunlight, though it was not exactly displeasing, nevertheless seemed to hint of something defective or abnormal in the constitution and blood. But his general aspect and manner were so suggestive of an education and career incongruous with his naval function that when not actively engaged in it he looked like a man of high quality, social and moral, who for reasons of his own was keeping incog.[51] Nothing was known of his former life. It might be that he was an Englishman; and yet there lurked a bit of accent in his speech suggesting that possibly he was not such by birth, but through naturalization in early childhood. Among certain grizzled sea gossips of the gun decks and forecastle went a rumor perdue that the master-at-arms was a *chevalier*[52] who had volunteered into the King's navy by way of compounding for some mysterious swindle whereof he had been arraigned at the King's Bench.[53] The fact that nobody could substantiate this report was, of course, nothing against its secret currency. Such a rumor once started on the gun decks in reference to almost anyone below the rank of a commissioned officer would, during the period assigned to this narrative, have seemed not altogether wanting in credibility to the tarry old wiseacres of a man-of-war crew. And indeed a man of Claggart's accomplishments, without prior nautical experience entering the navy at mature life, as he did, and necessarily allotted at the start to the lowest grade in it; a man too who never made allusion to his previous life ashore; these were circumstances which in the dearth of exact knowledge as to his true antecedents opened to the invidious a vague field for unfavorable surmise.

But the sailors' dogwatch gossip concerning him derived a vague plausibility from

---

[48] Gunpowder formed by mixture of charcoal, sulphur, and potassium nitrate.
[49] Tecumseh: Shawnee Indian chief (1768?–1813).
[50] The perjurer Oates (1649–1705) accused Catholics of plotting to murder English Protestants and King Charles II, and to burn London.
[51] Incognito.
[52] Adventurer.
[53] Court of law.

the fact that now for some period the British navy could so little afford to be squeamish in the matter of keeping up the muster rolls, that not only were press gangs notoriously abroad both afloat and ashore, but there was little or no secret about another matter, namely, that the London police were at liberty to capture any able-bodied suspect, any questionable fellow at large, and summarily ship him to the dockyard or fleet. Furthermore, even among voluntary enlistments there were instances where the motive thereto partook neither of patriotic impulse nor yet of a random desire to experience a bit of sea life and martial adventure. Insolvent debtors of minor grade, together with the promiscuous lame ducks of morality, found in the navy a convenient and secure refuge, secure because, once enlisted aboard a King's ship, they were as much in sanctuary as the transgressor of the Middle Ages harboring himself under the shadow of the altar. Such sanctioned irregularities, which for obvious reasons the government would hardly think to parade at the time and which consequently, and as affecting the least influential class of mankind, have all but dropped into oblivion, lend color to something for the truth whereof I do not vouch, and hence have some scruple in stating; something I remember having seen in print though the book I cannot recall; but the same thing was personally communicated to me now more than forty years ago by an old pensioner in a cocked hat with whom I had a most interesting talk on the terrace at Greenwich, a Baltimore Negro, a Trafalgar man. It was to this effect: In the case of a warship short of hands whose speedy sailing was imperative, the deficient quota, in lack of any other way of making it good, would be eked out by drafts culled direct from the jails. For reasons previously suggested it would not perhaps be easy at the present day directly to prove or disprove the allegation. But allowed as a verity, how significant would it be of England's straits at the time confronted by those wars[54] which like a flight of harpies rose shrieking from the din and dust of the fallen Bastille. That era appears measurably clear to us who look back at it, and but read of it. But to the grandfathers of us graybeards, the more thoughtful of them, the genius of it presented an aspect like that of Camoëns'[55] Spirit of the Cape, an eclipsing menace mysterious and prodigious. Not America was exempt from apprehension. At the height of Napoleon's unexampled conquests, there were Americans who had fought at Bunker Hill who looked forward to the possibility that the Atlantic might prove no barrier against the ultimate schemes of this French portentous upstart from the revolutionary chaos who seemed in act of fulfilling judgment prefigured in the Apocalypse.

But the less credence was to be given to the gun-deck talk touching Claggart, seeing that no man holding his office in a man-of-war can ever hope to be popular with the crew. Besides, in derogatory comments upon anyone against whom they have a grudge, or for any reason or no reason mislike, sailors are much like landsmen: they are apt to exaggerate or romance it.

About as much was really known to the *Bellipotent*'s tars of the master-at-arms' career before entering the service as an astronomer knows about a comet's travels prior to its first observable appearance in the sky. The verdict of the sea quidnuncs[56] has

---

[54] I.e., the Napoleonic wars (1796–1815).
[55] Luis de Camoëns (1524–1580), Portuguese epic poet of Vasco da Gama's voyage to India via the treacherous Cape of Good Hope.

[56] Gossips.

been cited only by way of showing what sort of moral impression the man made upon rude uncultivated natures whose conceptions of human wickedness were necessarily of the narrowest, limited to ideas of vulgar rascality—a thief among the swinging hammocks during a night watch, or the man-brokers and land-sharks of the seaports.

It was no gossip, however, but fact that though, as before hinted, Claggart upon his entrance into the navy was, as a novice, assigned to the least honorable section of a man-of-war's crew, embracing the drudgery, he did not long remain there. The superior capacity he immediately evinced, his constitutional sobriety, an ingratiating deference to superiors, together with a peculiar ferreting genius manifested on a singular occasion; all this, capped by a certain austere patriotism, abruptly advanced him to the position of master-at-arms.

Of this maritime chief of police the ship's corporals, so called, were the immediate subordinates, and compliant ones; and this, as is to be noted in some business departments ashore, almost to a degree inconsistent with entire moral volition. His place put various converging wires of underground influence under the chief's control, capable when astutely worked through his understrappers of operating to the mysterious discomfort, if nothing worse, of any of the sea commonalty.

9

Life in the foretop well agreed with Billy Budd. There, when not actually engaged on the yards yet higher aloft, the topmen, who as such had been picked out for youth and activity, constituted an aerial club lounging at ease against the smaller stun'sails rolled up into cushions, spinning yarns like the lazy gods, and frequently amused with what was going on in the busy world of the decks below. No wonder then that a young fellow of Billy's disposition was well content in such society. Giving no cause of offense to anybody, he was always alert at a call. So in the merchant service it had been with him. But now such a punctiliousness in duty was shown that his topmates would sometimes good-naturedly laugh at him for it. This heightened alacrity had its cause, namely, the impression made upon him by the first formal gangway-punishment he had ever witnessed, which befell the day following his impressment. It had been incurred by a little fellow, young, a novice afterguardsman absent from his assigned post when the ship was being put about; a dereliction resulting in a rather serious hitch to that maneuver, one demanding instantaneous promptitude in letting go and making fast. When Billy saw the culprit's naked back under the scourge, gridironed with red welts and worse, when he marked the dire expression in the liberated man's face as with his woolen shirt flung over him by the executioner he rushed forward from the spot to bury himself in the crowd, Billy was horrified. He resolved that never through remissness would he make himself liable to such a visitation or do or omit aught that might merit even verbal reproof. What then was his surprise and concern when ultimately he found himself getting into petty trouble occasionally about such matters as the stowage of his bag or something amiss in his hammock, matters under the police oversight of the ship's corporals of the lower decks, and which brought down on him a vague threat from one of them.

So heedful in all things as he was, how could this be? He could not understand it, and it more than vexed him. When he spoke to his young topmates about it they were either lightly incredulous or found something comical in his unconcealed anxiety. "Is it your bag, Billy?" said one. "Well, sew yourself up in it, bully boy, and then you'll be sure to know if anybody meddles with it."

Now there was a veteran aboard who because his years began to disqualify him for more active work had been recently assigned duty as mainmastman in his watch, looking to the gear belayed at the rail roundabout that great spar near the deck. At off-times the foretopman had picked up some acquaintance with him, and now in his trouble it occurred to him that he might be the sort of person to go to for wise counsel. He was an old Dansker[57] long anglicized in the service, of few words, many wrinkles, and some honorable scars. His wizened face, time-tinted and weather-stained to the complexion of an antique parchment, was here and there peppered blue by the chance explosion of a gun cartridge in action.

He was an *Agamemnon* man, some two years prior to the time of this story having served under Nelson when still captain in that ship immortal in naval memory, which dismantled and in part broken up to her bare ribs is seen a grand skeleton in Haden's etching.[58] As one of a boarding party from the *Agamemnon* he had received a cut slantwise along one temple and cheek leaving a long pale scar like a streak of dawn's light falling athwart the dark visage. It was on account of that scar and the affair in which it was known that he had received it, as well as from his blue-peppered complexion, that the Dansker went among the *Bellipotent*'s crew by the name of "Board-Her-in-the-Smoke."

Now the first time that his small weasel eyes happened to light on Billy Budd, a certain grim internal merriment set all his ancient wrinkles into antic play. Was it that his eccentric unsentimental old sapience, primitive in its kind, saw or thought it saw something which in contrast with the warship's environment looked oddly incongruous in the Handsome Sailor? But after slyly studying him at intervals, the old Merlin's[59] equivocal merriment was modified; for now when the twain would meet, it would start in his face a quizzing sort of look, but it would be but momentary and sometimes replaced by an expression of speculative query as to what might eventually befall a nature like that, dropped into a world not without some mantraps and against whose subtleties simple courage lacking experience and address, and without any touch of defensive ugliness, is of little avail; and where such innocence as man is capable of does yet in a moral emergency not always sharpen the faculties or enlighten the will.

However it was, the Dansker in his ascetic way rather took to Billy. Nor was this only because of a certain philosophic interest in such a character. There was another cause. While the old man's eccentricities, sometimes bordering on the ursine, repelled the juniors, Billy, undeterred thereby, revering him as a salt hero, would make advances, never passing the old *Agamemnon* man without a salutation marked by that respect which is seldom lost on the aged, however crabbed at times or whatever their station in life.

There was a vein of dry humor, or what not, in the mastman; and, whether in freak

[57] Dane.
[58] Francis Seymour Haden's (1818–1910) popular etching *The Breaking Up of Ole Agamemnon* (1870).
[59] Merlin: Magician in the legends of King Arthur.

of patriarchal irony touching Billy's youth and athletic frame, or for some other and more recondite reason, from the first in addressing him he always substituted *Baby* for Billy, the Dansker in fact being the originator of the name by which the foretopman eventually became known aboard ship.

Well then, in his mysterious little difficulty going in quest of the wrinkled one, Billy found him off duty in a dogwatch ruminating by himself, seated on a shot box of the upper gun deck, now and then surveying with a somewhat cynical regard certain of the more swaggering promenaders there. Billy recounted his trouble, again wondering how it all happened. The salt seer attentively listened, accompanying the foretopman's recital with queer twitchings of his wrinkles and problematical little sparkles of his small ferret eyes. Making an end of his story, the foretopman asked, "And now, Dansker, do tell me what you think of it."

The old man, shoving up the front of his tarpaulin[60] and deliberately rubbing the long slant scar at the point where it entered the thin hair, laconically said, "Baby Budd, *Jemmy Legs*" (meaning the master-at-arms) "is down on you."

"*Jemmy Legs!*" ejaculated Billy, his welkin eyes expanding. "What for? Why, he calls me 'the sweet and pleasant young fellow,' they tell me."

"Does he so?" grinned the grizzled one; then said, "Ay, Baby had, a sweet voice has Jemmy Legs."

"No, not always. But to me he has. I seldom pass him but there comes a pleasant word."

"And that's because he's down upon you, Baby Budd."

Such reiteration, along with the manner of it, incomprehensible to a novice, disturbed Billy almost as much as the mystery for which he had sought explanation. Something less unpleasantly oracular he tried to extract; but the old sea Chiron,[61] thinking perhaps that for the nonce he had sufficiently instructed his young Achilles, pursed his lips, gathered all his wrinkles together, and would commit himself to nothing further.

Years, and those experiences which befall certain shrewder men subordinated lifelong to the will of superiors, all this had developed in the Dansker the pithy guarded cynicism that was his leading characteristic.

10

The next day an incident served to confirm Billy Budd in his incredulity as to the Dansker's strange summing up of the case submitted. The ship at noon, going large before the wind, was rolling on her course, and he below at dinner and engaged in some sportful talk with the members of his mess, chanced in a sudden lurch to spill the entire contents of his soup pan upon the new-scrubbed deck. Claggart, the master-at-arms, official rattan[62] in hand, happened to be passing along the battery in a bay of which the mess was lodged, and the greasy liquid streamed just across his path. Stepping over it, he was proceeding on his way without comment, since the matter was nothing to take notice of under the circumstances, when he happened to observe who it was that had done the spilling. His countenance changed. Pausing, he was about to ejaculate something hasty at the sailor, but checked himself, and pointing

---

[60] Waterproof hat.
[61] Teacher of Achilles in Greek myth.
[62] Cane.

down to the streaming soup, playfully tapped him from behind with his rattan, saying in a low musical voice peculiar to him at times, "Handsomely done, my lad! And handsome is as handsome did it, too!" And with that passed on. Not noted by Billy as not coming within his view was the involuntary smile, or rather grimace, that accompanied Claggart's equivocal words. Aridly it drew down the thin corners of his shapely mouth. But everybody taking his remark as meant for humorous, and at which therefore as coming from a superior they were bound to laugh "with counter-feited glee,"[63] acted accordingly; and Billy, tickled, it may be, by the allusion to his being the Handsome Sailor, merrily joined in; then addressing his messmates ex-claimed, "There now, who says that Jemmy Legs is down on me!"

"And who said he was, Beauty?" demanded one Donald with some surprise. Whereat the foretopman looked a little foolish, recalling that it was only one person, Board-Her-in-the-Smoke, who had suggested what to him was the smoky idea that this master-at-arms was in any peculiar way hostile to him. Meantime that function-ary, resuming his path, must have momentarily worn some expression less guarded than that of the bitter smile, usurping the face from the heart—some distorting expression perhaps, for a drummer-boy heedlessly frolicking along from the opposite direction and chancing to come into light collision with his person was strangely disconcerted by his aspect. Nor was the impression lessened when the official, impetu-ously giving him a sharp cut with the rattan, vehemently exclaimed, "Look where you go!"

11

What was the matter with the master-at-arms? And, be the matter what it might, how could it have direct relation to Billy Budd, with whom prior to the affair of the spilled soup he had never come into any special contact official or otherwise? What indeed could the trouble have to do with one so little inclined to give offense as the merchant-ship's "peacemaker," even him who in Claggart's own phrase was "the sweet and pleasant young fellow"? Yes, why should Jemmy Legs, to borrow the Dansker's expression, be "down" on the Handsome Sailor? But, at heart and not for nothing, as the late chance encounter may indicate to the discerning, down on him, secretly down on him, he assuredly was.

Now to invent something touching the more private career of Claggart, something involving Billy Budd, of which something the latter should be wholly ignorant, some romantic incident implying that Claggart's knowledge of the young blue-jacket began at some period anterior to catching sight of him on board the seventy-four—all this, not so difficult to do, might avail in a way more or less interesting to account for whatever of enigma may appear to lurk in the case. But in fact there was nothing of the sort. And yet the cause necessarily to be assumed as the sole one assignable is in its very realism as much charged with that prime element of Radcliffian romance, the mysterious, as any that the ingenuity of the author of *The Mysteries of Udolpho* could devise.[64] For what can more partake of the mysterious than an antipathy

---

[63] In Oliver Goldsmith's poem "The Deserted Village" (1770), the school children laugh "with counterfeited glee" at the jokes of the tyrannical schoolmaster.

[64] Ann Radcliffe (1764–1823) wrote *The Mysteries of Udolpho* (1794) and other gothic novels.

spontaneous and profound such as is evoked in certain exceptional mortals by the mere aspect of some other mortal, however harmless he may be, if not called forth by this very harmlessness itself?

Now there can exist no irritating juxtaposition of dissimilar personalities comparable to that which is possible aboard a great warship fully manned and at sea. There, every day among all ranks, almost every man comes into more or less of contact with almost every other man. Wholly there to avoid even the sight of an aggravating object one must needs give it Jonah's toss[65] or jump overboard himself. Imagine how all this might eventually operate on some peculiar human creature the direct reverse of a saint!

But for the adequate comprehending of Claggart by a normal nature these hints are insufficient. To pass from a normal nature to him one must cross "the deadly space between." And this is best done by indirection.

Long ago an honest scholar, my senior, said to me in reference to one who like himself is now no more, a man so unimpeachably respectable that against him nothing was ever openly said though among the few something was whispered, "Yes, X—— is a nut not to be cracked by the tap of a lady's fan. You are aware that I am the adherent of no organized religion, much less of any philosophy built into a system. Well, for all that, I think that to try and get into X——, enter his labyrinth and get out again, without a clue derived from some source other than what is known as 'knowledge of the world'—that were hardly possible, at least for me."

"Why," said I, "X——, however singular a study to some, is yet human, and knowledge of the world assuredly implies the knowledge of human nature, and in most of its varieties."

"Yes, but a superficial knowledge of it, serving ordinary purposes. But for anything deeper, I am not certain whether to know the world and to know human nature be not two distinct branches of knowledge, which while they may coexist in the same heart, yet either may exist with little or nothing of the other. Nay, in an average man of the world, his constant rubbing with it blunts that finer spiritual insight indispensable to the understanding of the essential in certain exceptional characters, whether evil ones or good. In a matter of some importance I have seen a girl wind an old lawyer about her little finger. Nor was it the dotage of senile love. Nothing of the sort. But he knew law better than he knew the girl's heart. Coke and Blackstone[66] hardly shed so much light into obscure spiritual places as the Hebrew prophets. And who were they? Mostly recluses."

At the time, my inexperience was such that I did not quite see the drift of all this. It may be that I see it now. And, indeed, if that lexicon which is based on Holy Writ were any longer popular, one might with less difficulty define and denominate certain phenomenal men. As it is, one must turn to some authority not liable to the charge of being tinctured with the biblical element.

In a list of definitions included in the authentic translation of Plato, a list attributed to him, occurs this: "Natural Depravity: a depravity according to nature," a definition

[65] Jonah 1:15: "So they took up Jonah, and cast him forth into the sea" (i.e., threw him overboard).

[66] Sir Edward Coke (1552–1634) and Sir William Blackstone (1723–1780) were renowned British jurists.

which, though savoring of Calvinism, by no means involves Calvin's dogma as to total mankind.[67] Evidently its intent makes it applicable but to individuals. Not many are the examples of this depravity which the gallows and jail supply. At any rate, for notable instances, since these have no vulgar alloy of the brute in them, but invariably are dominated by intellectuality, one must go elsewhere. Civilization, especially if of the austerer sort, is suspicious to it. It folds itself in the mantle of respectability. It has its certain negative virtues serving as silent auxiliaries. It never allows wine to get within its guard. It is not going too far to say that it is without vices or small sins. There is a phenomenal pride in it that excludes them. It is never mercenary or avaricious. In short, the depravity here meant partakes nothing of the sordid or sensual. It is serious, but free from acerbity. Though no flatterer of mankind it never speaks ill of it.

But the thing which in eminent instances signalizes so exceptional a nature is this: Though the man's even temper and discreet bearing would seem to intimate a mind peculiarly subject to the law of reason, not the less in heart he would seem to riot in complete exemption from that law, having apparently little to do with reason further than to employ it as an ambidexter implement for effecting the irrational. That is to say: Toward the accomplishment of an aim which in wantonness of atrocity would seem to partake of the insane, he will direct a cool judgment sagacious and sound. These men are madmen, and of the most dangerous sort, for their lunacy is not continuous, but occasional, evoked by some special object; it is protectively secretive, which is as much as to say it is self-contained, so that when, moreover, most active it is to the average mind not distinguishable from sanity, and for the reason above suggested: that whatever its aims may be—and the aim is never declared—the method and the outward proceeding are always perfectly rational.

Now something such an one was Claggart, in whom was the mania of an evil nature, not engendered by vicious training or corrupting books or licentious living, but born with him and innate, in short "a depravity according to nature."

Dark sayings are these, some will say. But why? Is it because they somewhat savor of Holy Writ in its phrase "mystery of iniquity?"[68] If they do, such savor was far enough from being intended, for little will it commend these pages to many a reader of today.

The point of the present story turning on the hidden nature of the master-at-arms has necessitated this chapter. With an added hint or two in connection with the incident at the mess, the resumed narrative must be left to vindicate, as it may, its own credibility.

12

That Claggart's figure was not amiss, and his face, save the chin, well molded, has already been said. Of these favorable points he seemed not insensible, for he was not only neat but careful in his dress. But the form of Billy Budd was heroic; and if his face was without the intellectual look of the pallid Claggart's, not the less was it lit,

---

[67] The theologian John Calvin (1509–1564) emphasized that all mankind is born depraved as a consequence of the sin of Adam and Eve.

[68] See 2 Thessalonians 2:7: ". . . the mystery of iniquity doth already work."

like his, from within, though from a different source. The bonfire in his heart made luminous the rose-tan in his cheek.

In view of the marked contrast between the persons of the twain, it is more than probable that when the master-at-arms in the scene last given applied to the sailor the proverb "Handsome is as handsome does," he there let escape an ironic inkling, not caught by the young sailors who heard it, as to what it was that had first moved him against Billy, namely, his significant personal beauty.

Now envy and antipathy, passions irreconcilable in reason, nevertheless in fact may spring conjoined like Chang and Eng[69] in one birth. Is Envy then such a monster? Well, though many an arraigned mortal has in hopes of mitigated penalty pleaded guilty to horrible actions, did ever anybody seriously confess to envy? Something there is in it universally felt to be more shameful than even felonious crime. And not only does everybody disown it, but the better sort are inclined to incredulity when it is in earnest imputed to an intelligent man. But since its lodgment is in the heart not the brain, no degree of intellect supplies a guarantee against it. But Claggart's was no vulgar form of the passion. Nor, as directed toward Billy Budd, did it partake of that streak of apprehensive jealousy that marred Saul's visage perturbedly brooding on the comely young David.[70] Claggart's envy struck deeper. If askance he eyed the good looks, cheery health, and frank enjoyment of young life in Billy Budd, it was because these went along with a nature that, as Claggart magnetically felt, had in its simplicity never willed malice or experienced the reactionary bite of that serpent. To him, the spirit lodged within Billy, and looking out from his welkin eyes as from windows, that ineffability it was which made the dimple in his dyed cheek, suppled his joints, and dancing in his yellow curls made him pre-eminently the Handsome Sailor. One person excepted, the master-at-arms was perhaps the only man in the ship intellectually capable of adequately appreciating the moral phenomenon presented in Billy Budd. And the insight but intensified his passion, which assuming various secret forms within him, at times assumed that of cynic disdain, disdain of innocence—to be nothing more than innocent! Yet in an aesthetic way he saw the charm of it, the courageous free-and-easy temper of it, and fain would have shared it, but he despaired of it.

With no power to annul the elemental evil in him, though readily enough he could hide it; apprehending the good, but powerless to be it; a nature like Claggart's, surcharged with energy as such natures almost invariably are, what recourse is left to it but to recoil upon itself and, like the scorpion for which the Creator alone is responsible, act out to the end the part allotted it.

13

Passion, and passion in its profoundest, is not a thing demanding a palatial stage whereon to play its part. Down among the groundlings, among the beggars and rakers of the garbage, profound passion is enacted. And the circumstances that provoke it,

---

[69] Famous Siamese twins displayed by P. T. Barnum in the United States.

[70] Saul's jealousy of David, recounted in 1 Samuel 16, 18.

however trivial or mean, are no measure of its power. In the present instance the stage is a scrubbed gun deck, and one of the external provocations a man-of-war's man's spilled soup.

Now when the master-at-arms noticed whence came that greasy fluid streaming before his feet, he must have taken it—to some extent wilfully, perhaps—not for the mere accident it assuredly was, but for the sly escape of a spontaneous feeling on Billy's part more or less answering to the antipathy on his own. In effect a foolish demonstration, he must have thought, and very harmless, like the futile kick of a heifer, which yet were the heifer a shod stallion would not be so harmless. Even so was it that into the gall of Claggart's envy he infused the vitriol of his contempt. But the incident confirmed to him certain telltale reports purveyed to his ear by "Squeak," one of his more cunning corporals, a grizzled little man, so nicknamed by the sailors on account of his squeaky voice and sharp visage ferreting about the dark corners of the lower decks after interlopers, satirically suggesting to them the idea of a rat in a cellar.

From his chief's employing him as an implicit tool in laying little traps for the worriment of the foretopman—for it was from the master-at-arms that the petty persecutions heretofore adverted to had proceeded—the corporal, having naturally enough concluded that his master could have no love for the sailor, made it his business, faithful understrapper that he was, to foment the ill blood by perverting to his chief certain innocent frolics of the good-natured foretopman, besides inventing for his mouth sundry contumelious epithets he claimed to have overheard him let fall. The master-at-arms never suspected the veracity of these reports, more especially as to the epithets, for he well knew how secretly unpopular may become a master-at-arms, at least a master-at-arms of those days, zealous in his function, and how the bluejackets shoot at him in private their raillery and wit; the nickname by which he goes among them (Jemmy Legs) implying under the form of merriment their cherished disrespect and dislike. But in view of the greediness of hate for pabulum[71] it hardly needed a purveyor to feed Claggart's passion.

An uncommon prudence is habitual with the subtler depravity, for it has everything to hide. And in case of an injury but suspected, its secretiveness voluntarily cuts it off from enlightenment or disillusion; and, not unreluctantly, action is taken upon surmise as upon certainty. And the retaliation is apt to be in monstrous disproportion to the supposed offense; for when in anybody was revenge in its exactions aught else but an inordinate usurer? But how with Claggart's conscience? For though consciences are unlike as foreheads, every intelligence, not excluding the scriptural devils who "believe and tremble,"[72] has one. But Claggart's conscience being but the lawyer to his will, made ogres of trifles, probably arguing that the motive imputed to Billy in spilling the soup just when he did, together with the epithets alleged, these, if nothing more, made a strong case against him; nay, justified animosity into a sort of retributive righteousness. The Pharisee is the Guy Fawkes[73] prowling in the hid chambers underlying some natures like Claggart's. And they can really form no conception of an unreciprocated malice. Probably the master-at-arms' clandestine persecution of Billy

[71] Food.
[72] James 2:19.

[73] Conspirator in the Gunpowder Plot to blow up Parliament.

was started to try the temper of the man; but it had not developed any quality in him that enmity could make official use of or even pervert into plausible self-justification; so that the occurrence at the mess, petty if it were, was a welcome one to that peculiar conscience assigned to be the private mentor of Claggart; and, for the rest, not improbably it put him upon new experiments.

14

Not many days after the last incident narrated, something befell Billy Budd that more graveled him than aught that had previously occurred.

It was a warm night for the latitude; and the foretopman, whose watch at the time was properly below, was dozing on the uppermost deck whither he had ascended from his hot hammock, one of hundreds suspended so closely wedged together over a lower gun deck that there was little or no swing to them. He lay as in the shadow of a hillside, stretched under the lee of the booms, a piled ridge of spare spars amidships between foremast and mainmast among which the ship's largest boat, the launch, was stowed. Alongside of three other slumberers from below, he lay near that end of the booms which approaches the foremast; his station aloft on duty as a foretopman being just over the deck-station of the forecastlemen, entitling him according to usage to make himself more or less at home in that neighborhood.

Presently he was stirred into semiconsciousness by somebody, who must have previously sounded the sleep of the others, touching his shoulder, and then, as the foretopman raised his head, breathing into his ear in a quick whisper, "Slip into the lee forechains, Billy; there is something in the wind. Don't speak. Quick, I will meet you there," and disappearing.

Now Billy, like sundry other essentially good-natured ones, had some of the weaknesses inseparable from essential good nature; and among these was a reluctance, almost an incapacity of plumply saying *no* to an abrupt proposition not obviously absurd on the face of it, nor obviously unfriendly, nor iniquitous. And being of warm blood, he had not the phlegm[74] tacitly to negative any proposition by unresponsive inaction. Like his sense of fear, his apprehension as to aught outside of the honest and natural was seldom very quick. Besides, upon the present occasion, the drowse from his sleep still hung upon him.

However it was, he mechanically rose and, sleepily wondering what could be in the wind, betook himself to the designated place, a narrow platform, one of six, outside of the high bulwarks and screened by the great deadeyes and multiple co-lumned lanyards of the shrouds and backstays; and, in a great warship of that time, of dimensions commensurate to the hull's magnitude; a tarry balcony in short, over-hanging the sea, and so secluded that one mariner of the *Bellipotent,* a Nonconformist old tar of a serious turn, made it even in daytime his private oratory.[75]

In this retired nook the stranger soon joined Billy Budd. There was no moon as yet; a haze obscured the starlight. He could not distinctly see the stranger's face. Yet from something in the outline and carriage, Billy took him, and correctly, for one of the afterguard.

---

[74] Cool self-control.   [75] Place for prayer.

"Hist! Billy," said the man, in the same quick cautionary whisper as before. "You were impressed, weren't you? Well, so was I"; and he paused, as to mark the effect. But Billy, not knowing exactly what to make of this, said nothing. Then the other: "We are not the only impressed ones, Billy. There's a gang of us.—Couldn't you—help—at a pinch?"

"What do you mean?" demanded Billy, here thoroughly shaking off his drowse.

"Hist, hist!" the hurried whisper now growing husky. "See here," and the man held up two small objects faintly twinkling in the night-light; "see, they are yours, Billy, if you'll only—"

But Billy broke in, and in his resentful eagerness to deliver himself his vocal infirmity somewhat intruded. "D—d—damme, I don't know what you are d—d—driving at, or what you mean, but you had better g—g—go where you belong!" For the moment the fellow, as confounded, did not stir; and Billy, springing to his feet, said, "If you d—don't start, I'll t—t—toss you back over the r—rail!" There was no mistaking this, and the mysterious emissary decamped, disappearing in the direction of the mainmast in the shadow of the booms.[76]

"Hallo, what's the matter?" here came growling from a forecastleman awakened from his deck-doze by Billy's raised voice. And as the foretopman reappeared and was recognized by him: "Ah, Beauty, is it you? Well, something must have been the matter, for you st—st—stuttered."

"Oh," rejoined Billy, now mastering the impediment, "I found an afterguardsman in our part of the ship here, and I bid him be off where he belongs."

"And is that all you did about it, Foretopman?" gruffly demanded another, an irascible old fellow of brick-colored visage and hair who was known to his associate forecastlemen as "Red Pepper." "Such sneaks I should like to marry to the gunner's daughter!"—by that expression meaning that he would like to subject them to disciplinary castigation over a gun.

However, Billy's rendering of the matter satisfactorily accounted to these inquirers for the brief commotion, since of all the sections of a ship's company the forecastlemen, veterans for the most part and bigoted in their sea prejudices, are the most jealous in resenting territorial encroachments, especially on the part of any of the afterguard, of whom they have but a sorry opinion—chiefly landsmen, never going aloft except to reef or furl the mainsail, and in no wise competent to handle a marlinspike or turn in a deadeye,[77] say.

15

This incident sorely puzzled Billy Budd. It was an entirely new experience, the first time in his life that he had ever been personally approached in underhand intriguing fashion. Prior to this encounter he had known nothing of the afterguardsman, the two men being stationed wide apart, one forward and aloft during his watch, the other on deck and aft.

What could it mean? And could they really be guineas, those two glittering objects

---

[76] Horizontal poles for extending the feet or bottoms of sails.

[77] I.e., to use a rope-splicing tool or a rope-threaded wood block as a pulley.

the interloper had held up to his (Billy's) eyes? Where could the fellow get guineas? Why, even spare buttons are not so plentiful at sea. The more he turned the matter over, the more he was nonplussed, and made uneasy and discomfited. In his disgustful recoil from an overture which, though he but ill comprehended, he instinctively knew must involve evil of some sort, Billy Budd was like a young horse fresh from the pasture suddenly inhaling a vile whiff from some chemical factory, and by repeated snortings trying to get it out of his nostrils and lungs. This frame of mind barred all desire of holding further parley with the fellow, even were it but for the purpose of gaining some enlightenment as to his design in approaching him. And yet he was not without natural curiosity to see how such a visitor in the dark would look in broad day.

He espied him the following afternoon in his first dogwatch below, one of the smokers on that forward part of the upper gun deck allotted to the pipe. He recognized him by his general cut and build more than by his round freckled face and glassy eyes of pale blue, veiled with lashes all but white. And yet Billy was a bit uncertain whether indeed it were he—yonder chap about his own age chatting and laughing in freehearted way, leaning against a gun; a genial young fellow enough to look at, and something of a rattlebrain, to all appearance. Rather chubby too for a sailor, even an afterguardsman. In short, the last man in the world, one would think, to be overburdened with thoughts, especially those perilous thoughts that must needs belong to a conspirator in any serious project, or even to the underling of such a conspirator.

Although Billy was not aware of it, the fellow, with a sidelong watchful glance, had perceived Billy first, and then noting that Billy was looking at him, thereupon nodded a familiar sort of friendly recognition as to an old acquaintance, without interrupting the talk he was engaged in with the group of smokers. A day or two afterwards, chancing in the evening promenade on a gun deck to pass Billy, he offered a flying word of good-fellowship, as it were, which by its unexpectedness, and equivocalness under the circumstances, so embarrassed Billy that he knew not how to respond to it, and let it go unnoticed.

Billy was now left more at a loss than before. The ineffectual speculations into which he was led were so disturbingly alien to him that he did his best to smother them. It never entered his mind that here was a matter which, from its extreme questionableness, it was his duty as a loyal bluejacket to report in the proper quarter. And, probably, had such a step been suggested to him, he would have been deterred from taking it by the thought, one of novice magnanimity, that it would savor overmuch of the dirty work of a telltale. He kept the thing to himself. Yet upon one occasion he could not forbear a little disburdening himself to the old Dansker, tempted thereto perhaps by the influence of a balmy night when the ship lay becalmed; the twain, silent for the most part, sitting together on deck, their heads propped against the bulwarks. But it was only a partial and anonymous account that Billy gave, the unfounded scruples above referred to preventing full disclosure to anybody. Upon hearing Billy's version, the sage Dansker seemed to divine more than he was told; and after a little meditation, during which his wrinkles were pursed as into a point, quite effacing for the time that quizzing expression his face sometimes wore: "Didn't I say so, Baby Budd?"

"Say what?" demanded Billy.

"Why, *Jemmy Legs* is *down* on you."

"And what," rejoined Billy in amazement, "has *Jemmy Legs* to do with that cracked afterguardsman?"

"Ho, it was an afterguardsman, then. A cat's-paw, a cat's-paw!" And with that exclamation, whether it had reference to a light puff of air just then coming over the calm sea, or a subtler relation to the afterguardsman, there is no telling, the old Merlin gave a twisting wrench with his black teeth at his plug of tobacco, vouchsafing no reply to Billy's impetuous question, though now repeated, for it was his wont to relapse into grim silence when interrogated in skeptical sort as to any of his sententious oracles, not always very clear ones, rather partaking of that obscurity which invests most Delphic deliverances[78] from any quarter.

Long experience had very likely brought this old man to that bitter prudence which never interferes in aught and never gives advice.

16

Yes, despite the Dansker's pithy insistence as to the master-at-arms being at the bottom of these strange experiences of Billy on board the *Bellipotent,* the young sailor was ready to ascribe them to almost anybody but the man who, to use Billy's own expression, "always had a pleasant word for him." This is to be wondered at. Yet not so much to be wondered at. In certain matters, some sailors even in mature life remain unsophisticated enough. But a young seafarer of the disposition of our athletic foretopman is much of a child-man. And yet a child's utter innocence is but its blank ignorance, and the innocence more or less wanes as intelligence waxes. But in Billy Budd intelligence, such as it was, had advanced while yet his simple-mindedness remained for the most part unaffected. Experience is a teacher indeed; yet did Billy's years make his experience small. Besides, he had none of that intuitive knowledge of the bad which in natures not good or incompletely so foreruns experience, and therefore may pertain, as in some instances it too clearly does pertain, even to youth.

And what could Billy know of man except of man as a mere sailor? And the old-fashioned sailor, the veritable man before the mast, the sailor from boyhood up, he, though indeed of the same species as a landsman, is in some respects singularly distinct from him. The sailor is frankness, the landsman is finesse. Life is not a game with the sailor, demanding the long head—no intricate game of chess where few moves are made in straightforwardness and ends are attained by indirection, an oblique, tedious, barren game hardly worth that poor candle burnt out in playing it.

Yes, as a class, sailors are in character a juvenile race. Even their deviations are marked by juvenility, this more especially holding true with the sailors of Billy's time. Then too, certain things which apply to all sailors do more pointedly operate here and there upon the junior one. Every sailor, too, is accustomed to obey orders without debating them; his life afloat is externally ruled for him; he is not brought into that promiscuous commerce with mankind where unobstructed free agency on equal terms —equal superficially, at least—soon teaches one that unless upon occasion he exercise a distrust keen in proportion to the fairness of the appearance, some foul turn may be served him. A ruled undemonstrative distrustfulness is so habitual, not with

---

[78] Prophesies of the priests at the shrine of Apollo at Delphi in Greece.

businessmen so much as with men who know their kind in less shallow relations than business, namely, certain men of the world, that they come at last to employ it all but unconsciously; and some of them would very likely feel real surprise at being charged with it as one of their general characteristics.

17

But after the little matter at the mess Billy Budd no more found himself in strange trouble at times about his hammock or his clothes bag or what not. As to that smile that occasionally sunned him, and the pleasant passing word, these were, if not more frequent, yet if anything more pronounced than before.

But for all that, there were certain other demonstrations now. When Claggart's unobserved glance happened to light on belted Billy rolling along the upper gun deck in the leisure of the second dogwatch, exchanging passing broadsides of fun with other young promenaders in the crowd, that glance would follow the cheerful sea Hyperion[79] with a settled meditative and melancholy expression, his eyes strangely suffused with incipient feverish tears. Then would Claggart look like the man of sorrows.[80] Yes, and sometimes the melancholy expression would have in it a touch of soft yearning, as if Claggart could even have loved Billy but for fate and ban. But this was an evanescence, and quickly repented of, as it were, by an immitigable look, pinching and shriveling the visage into the momentary semblance of a wrinkled walnut. But sometimes catching sight in advance of the foretopman coming in his direction, he would, upon their nearing, step aside a little to let him pass, dwelling upon Billy for the moment with the glittering dental satire of a Guise.[81] But upon any abrupt unforeseen encounter a red light would flash forth from his eye like a spark from an anvil in a dusk smithy. That quick, fierce light was a strange one, darted from orbs which in repose were of a color nearest approaching a deeper violet, the softest of shades.

Though some of these caprices of the pit could not but be observed by their object, yet were they beyond the construing of such a nature. And the thews of Billy were hardly compatible with that sort of sensitive spiritual organization which in some cases instinctively conveys to ignorant innocence an admonition of the proximity of the malign. He thought the master-at-arms acted in a manner rather queer at times. That was all. But the occasional frank air and pleasant word went for what they purported to be, the young sailor never having heard as yet of the "too fair-spoken man."

Had the foretopman been conscious of having done or said anything to provoke the ill will of the official, it would have been different with him, and his sight might have been purged if not sharpened. As it was, innocence was his blinder.

So was it with him in yet another matter. Two minor officers, the armorer and captain of the hold, with whom he had never exchanged a word, his position in the ship not bringing him into contact with them, these men now for the first began to cast upon Billy, when they chanced to encounter him, that peculiar glance which evidences that the man from whom it comes has been some way tampered with, and to the prejudice of him upon whom the glance lights. Never did it occur to Billy

[79] Titan in Greek myth.
[80] See Isaiah 53:3.

[81] French family known for villainies masked by smiles.

as a thing to be noted or a thing suspicious, though he well knew the fact, that the armorer and captain of the hold, with the ship's yeoman, apothecary, and others of that grade, were by naval usage messmates of the master-at-arms, men with ears convenient to his confidential tongue.

But the general popularity that came from our Handsome Sailor's manly forwardness upon occasion and irresistible good nature, indicating no mental superiority tending to excite an invidious feeling, this good will on the part of most of his shipmates made him the less to concern himself about such mute aspects toward him as those whereto allusion has just been made, aspects he could not so fathom as to infer their whole import.

As to the afterguardsman, though Billy for reasons already given necessarily saw little of him, yet when the two did happen to meet, invariably came the fellow's offhand cheerful recognition, sometimes accompanied by a passing pleasant word or two. Whatever that equivocal young person's original design may really have been, or the design of which he might have been the deputy, certain it was from his manner upon these occasions that he had wholly dropped it.

It was as if his precocity of crookedness (and every vulgar villain is precocious) had for once deceived him, and the man he had sought to entrap as a simpleton had through his very simplicity ignominiously baffled him.

But shrewd ones may opine that it was hardly possible for Billy to refrain from going up to the afterguardsman and bluntly demanding to know his purpose in the initial interview so abruptly closed in the forechains. Shrewd ones may also think it but natural in Billy to set about sounding some of the other impressed men of the ship in order to discover what basis, if any, there was for the emissary's obscure suggestions as to plotting disaffection abroad. Yes, shrewd ones may so think. But something more, or rather something else than mere shrewdness is perhaps needful for the due understanding of such a character as Billy Budd's.

As to Claggart, the monomania in the man—if that indeed it were—as involuntarily disclosed by starts in the manifestations detailed, yet in general covered over by his self-contained and rational demeanor; this, like a subterranean fire, was eating its way deeper and deeper in him. Something decisive must come of it.

18

After the mysterious interview in the forechains, the one so abruptly ended there by Billy, nothing especially germane to the story occurred until the events now about to be narrated.

Elsewhere it has been said that in the lack of frigates (of course better sailers than line-of-battleships) in the English squadron up the Straits at that period, the *Bellipotent* 74 was occasionally employed not only as an available substitute for a scout, but at times on detached service of more important kind. This was not alone because of her sailing qualities, not common in a ship of her rate, but quite as much, probably, that the character of her commander, it was thought, specially adapted him for any duty where under unforeseen difficulties a prompt initiative might have to be taken in some matter demanding knowledge and ability in addition to those qualities implied in good seamanship. It was on an expedition of the latter sort, a somewhat distant one, and when the *Bellipotent* was almost at her furthest remove from the fleet, that in the latter part of an afternoon watch she unexpectedly came in sight of a ship of the enemy. It proved to be a frigate. The latter, perceiving through the glass that the weight of men and metal would be heavily against her, invoking her light heels crowded sail to get away. After a chase urged almost against hope and lasting until about the middle of the first dogwatch, she signally succeeded in effecting her escape.

Not long after the pursuit had been given up, and ere the excitement incident thereto had altogether waned away, the master-at-arms, ascending from his cavernous sphere, made his appearance cap in hand by the mainmast respectfully waiting the notice of Captain Vere, then solitary walking the weather side of the quarter-deck, doubtless somewhat chafed at the failure of the pursuit. The spot where Claggart stood was the place allotted to men of lesser grades seeking some more particular interview either with the officer of the deck or the captain himself. But from the latter it was not often that a sailor or petty officer of those days would seek a hearing; only some exceptional cause would, according to established custom, have warranted that.

Presently, just as the commander, absorbed in his reflections, was on the point of turning aft in his promenade, he became sensible of Claggart's presence, and saw the doffed cap held in deferential expectancy. Here be it said that Captain Vere's personal knowledge of this petty officer had only begun at the time of the ship's last sailing from home, Claggart then for the first, in transfer from a ship detained for repairs, supplying on board the *Bellipotent* the place of a previous master-at-arms disabled and ashore.

No sooner did the commander observe who it was that now deferentially stood awaiting his notice than a peculiar expression came over him. It was not unlike that which uncontrollably will flit across the countenance of one at unawares encountering a person who, though known to him indeed, has hardly been long enough known for thorough knowledge, but something in whose aspect nevertheless now for the first provokes a vaguely repellent distaste. But coming to a stand and resuming much of his wonted official manner, save that a sort of impatience lurked in the intonation of the opening word, he said "Well? What is it, Master-at-arms?"

With the air of a subordinate grieved at the necessity of being a messenger of ill tidings, and while conscientiously determined to be frank yet equally resolved upon shunning overstatement, Claggart at this invitation, or rather summons to disburden, spoke up. What he said, conveyed in the language of no uneducated man, was to the effect following, if not altogether in these words, namely, that during the chase and preparations for the possible encounter he had seen enough to convince him that at least one sailor aboard was a dangerous character in a ship mustering some who not only had taken a guilty part in the late serious troubles, but others also who, like the man in question, had entered His Majesty's service under another form than enlistment.

At this point Captain Vere with some impatience interrupted him: "Be direct, man; say *impressed men.*"

Claggart made a gesture of subservience, and proceeded. Quite lately he (Claggart) had begun to suspect that on the gun decks some sort of movement prompted by the sailor in question was covertly going on, but he had not thought himself warranted in reporting the suspicion so long as it remained indistinct. But from what he had that afternoon observed in the man referred to, the suspicion of something clandestine going on had advanced to a point less removed from certainty. He deeply felt, he added, the serious responsibility assumed in making a report involving such possible consequences to the individual mainly concerned, besides tending to augment those natural anxieties which every naval commander must feel in view of extraordinary outbreaks so recent as those which, he sorrowfully said it, it needed not to name.

Now at the first broaching of the matter Captain Vere, taken by surprise, could not wholly dissemble his disquietude. But as Claggart went on, the former's aspect changed into restiveness under something in the testifier's manner in giving his testimony. However, he refrained from interrupting him. And Claggart, continuing, concluded with this: "God forbid, your honor, that the *Bellipotent*'s should be the experience of the—"

"Never mind that!" here peremptorily broke in the superior, his face altering with anger, instinctively divining the ship that the other was about to name, one in which the Nore Mutiny had assumed a singularly tragical character that for a time jeopardized the life of its commander. Under the circumstances he was indignant at the purposed allusion. When the commissioned officers themselves were on all occasions very heedful how they referred to the recent events in the fleet, for a petty officer unnecessarily to allude to them in the presence of his captain, this struck him as a most immodest presumption. Besides, to his quick sense of self-respect it even looked under the circumstances something like an attempt to alarm him. Nor at first was he without some surprise that one who so far as he had hitherto come under his notice had shown considerable tact in his function should in this particular evince such lack of it.

But these thoughts and kindred dubious ones flitting across his mind were suddenly replaced by an intuitional surmise which, though as yet obscure in form, served practically to affect his reception of the ill tidings. Certain it is that, long versed in everything pertaining to the complicated gun-deck life, which like every other form of life has its secret mines and dubious side, the side popularly disclaimed, Captain Vere did not permit himself to be unduly disturbed by the general tenor of his subordinate's report.

Furthermore, if in view of recent events prompt action should be taken at the first palpable sign of recurring insubordination, for all that, not judicious would it be, he thought, to keep the idea of lingering disaffection alive by undue forwardness in crediting an informer, even if his own subordinate and charged among other things with police surveillance of the crew. This feeling would not perhaps have so prevailed with him were it not that upon a prior occasion that patriotic zeal officially evinced by Claggart had somewhat irritated him as appearing rather supersensible and strained. Furthermore, something even in the official's self-possessed and somewhat ostentatious manner in making his specifications strangely reminded him of a bandsman, a perjurous witness in a capital case before a court-martial ashore of which when a lieutenant he (Captain Vere) had been a member.

Now the peremptory check given to Claggart in the matter of the arrested allusion was quickly followed up by this: "You say that there is at least one dangerous man aboard. Name him."

"William Budd, a foretopman, your honor."

"William Budd!" repeated Captain Vere with unfeigned astonishment. "And mean you the man that Lieutenant Ratcliffe took from the merchantman not very long ago, the young fellow who seems to be so popular with the men—Billy, the Handsome Sailor, as they call him?"

"The same, your honor; but for all his youth and good looks, a deep one. Not for nothing does he insinuate himself into the good will of his shipmates, since at the least they will at a pinch say—all hands will—a good word for him, and at all hazards. Did Lieutenant Ratcliffe happen to tell your honor of that adroit fling of Budd's, jumping up in the cutter's bow under the merchantman's stern when he was being taken off? It is even masked by that sort of good-humored air that at heart he resents his impressment. You have but noted his fair cheek. A mantrap may be under the ruddy-tipped daisies."

Now the Handsome Sailor as a signal figure among the crew had naturally enough attracted the captain's attention from the first. Though in general not very demonstrative to his officers, he had congratulated Lieutenant Ratcliffe upon his good fortune in lighting on such a fine specimen of the *genus homo,* who in the nude might have posed for a statue of young Adam before the Fall. As to Billy's adieu to the ship *Rights-of-Man,* which the boarding lieutenant had indeed reported to him, but, in a deferential way, more as a good story than aught else, Captain Vere, though mistakenly understanding it as a satiric sally, had but thought so much the better of the impressed man for it; as a military sailor, admiring the spirit that could take an arbitrary enlistment so merrily and sensibly. The foretopman's conduct, too, so far as it had fallen under the captain's notice, had confirmed the first happy augury, while the new recruit's qualities as a "sailor-man" seemed to be such that he had thought of recommending him to the executive officer for promotion to a place that would more frequently bring him under his own observation, namely, the captaincy of the mizzentop, replacing there in the starboard watch a man not so young whom partly for that reason he deemed less fitted for the post. Be it parenthesized here that since the mizzentopmen have not to handle such breadths of heavy canvas as the lower sails on the mainmast and foremast, a young man if of the right stuff not only seems best adapted to duty there, but in fact is generally selected for the captaincy of that top, and the company under him are light hands and often but striplings. In sum, Captain Vere had from the beginning deemed Billy Budd to be what in the naval parlance of the time was called a "King's bargain": that is to say, for His Britannic Majesty's navy a capital investment at small outlay or none at all.

After a brief pause, during which the reminiscences above mentioned passed vividly through his mind and he weighed the import of Claggart's last suggestion conveyed in the phrase "mantrap under the daisies," and the more he weighed it the less reliance he felt in the informer's good faith, suddenly he turned upon him and in a low voice demanded: "Do you come to me, Master-at-arms, with so foggy a tale? As to Budd, cite me an act or spoken word of his confirmatory of what you in general charge against him. Stay," drawing nearer to him; "heed what you speak. Just now, and in a case like this, there is a yardarm-end[82] for the false witness."

"Ah, your honor!" sighed Claggart, mildly shaking his shapely head as in sad depreciation of such unmerited severity of tone. Then, bridling—erecting himself as in virtuous self-assertion—he circumstantially alleged certain words and acts which collectively, if credited, led to presumptions mortally inculpating Budd. And for some of these averments, he added, substantiating proof was not far.

With gray eyes impatient and distrustful essaying to fathom to the bottom Claggart's calm violet ones, Captain Vere again heard him out; then for the moment stood

---

[82] I.e., hanging.

ruminating. The mood he evinced, Claggart—himself for the time liberated from the other's scrutiny—steadily regarded with a look difficult to render: a look curious of the operation of his tactics, a look such as might have been that of the spokesman of the envious children of Jacob deceptively imposing upon the troubled patriarch the blood-dyed coat of young Joseph.[83]

Though something exceptional in the moral quality of Captain Vere made him, in earnest encounter with a fellow man, a veritable touchstone of that man's essential nature, yet now as to Claggart and what was really going on in him his feeling partook less of intuitional conviction than of strong suspicion clogged by strange dubieties. The perplexity he evinced proceeded less from aught touching the man informed against—as Claggart doubtless opined—than from considerations how best to act in regard to the informer. At first, indeed, he was naturally for summoning that substantiation of his allegations which Claggart said was at hand. But such a proceeding would result in the matter at once getting abroad, which in the present stage of it, he thought, might undesirably affect the ship's company. If Claggart was a false witness—that closed the affair. And therefore, before trying the accusation, he would first practically test the accuser; and he thought this could be done in a quiet, undemonstrative way.

The measure he determined upon involved a shifting of the scene, a transfer to a place less exposed to observation than the broad quarter-deck. For although the few gun-room officers there at the time had, in due observance of naval etiquette, withdrawn to leeward the moment Captain Vere had begun his promenade on the deck's weather side; and though during the colloquy with Claggart they of course ventured not to diminish the distance; and though throughout the interview Captain Vere's voice was far from high, and Claggart's silvery and low; and the wind in the cordage and the wash of the sea helped the more to put them beyond earshot; nevertheless, the interview's continuance already had attracted observation from some topmen aloft and other sailors in the waist or further forward.

Having determined upon his measures, Captain Vere forthwith took action. Abruptly turning to Claggart, he asked, "Master-at-arms, is it now Budd's watch aloft?"

"No, your honor."

Whereupon, "Mr. Wilkes!" summoning the nearest midshipman. "Tell Albert to come to me." Albert was the captain's hammock-boy, a sort of sea valet in whose discretion and fidelity his master had much confidence. The lad appeared.

"You know Budd, the foretopman?"

"I do, sir."

"Go find him. It is his watch off. Manage to tell him out of earshot that he is wanted aft. Contrive it that he speaks to nobody. Keep him in talk yourself. And not till you get well aft here, not till then let him know that the place where he is wanted is my cabin. You understand. Go.—Master-at-arms, show yourself on the decks below, and when you think it time for Albert to be coming with his man, stand by quietly to follow the sailor in."

[83] In Genesis 37:31–32, Joseph's brothers use the coat, stained with a goat's blood, to convince their father, Jacob, that Joseph is dead.

19

Now when the foretopman found himself in the cabin, closeted there, as it were, with the captain and Claggart, he was surprised enough. But it was a surprise unaccompanied by apprehension or distrust. To an immature nature essentially honest and humane, forewarning intimations of subtler danger from one's kind come tardily if at all. The only thing that took shape in the young sailor's mind was this: Yes, the captain, I have always thought, looks kindly upon me. Wonder if he's going to make me his coxswain.[84] I should like that. And may be now he is going to ask the master-at-arms about me.

"Shut the door there, sentry," said the commander; "stand without, and let nobody come in.—Now, Master-at-arms, tell this man to his face what you told of him to me," and stood prepared to scrutinize the mutually confronting visages.

With the measured step and calm collected air of an asylum physician approaching in the public hall some patient beginning to show indications of a coming paroxysm, Claggart deliberately advanced within short range of Billy and, mesmerically looking him in the eye, briefly recapitulated the accusation.

Not at first did Billy take it in. When he did, the rose-tan of his cheek looked struck as by white leprosy. He stood like one impaled and gagged. Meanwhile the accuser's eyes, removing not as yet from the blue dilated ones, underwent a phenomenal change, their wonted rich violet color blurring into a muddy purple. Those lights of human intelligence, losing human expression, were gelidly protruding like the alien eyes of certain uncatalogued creatures of the deep. The first mesmeristic glance was one of serpent fascination; the last was as the paralyzing lurch of the torpedo fish.[85]

"Speak, man!" said Captain Vere to the transfixed one, struck by his aspect even more than by Claggart's. "Speak! Defend yourself!" Which appeal caused but a strange dumb gesturing and gurgling in Billy; amazement at such an accusation so suddenly sprung on inexperienced nonage; this, and, it may be, horror of the accuser's eyes, serving to bring out his lurking defect and in this instance for the time intensifying it into a convulsed tongue-tie; while the intent head and entire form straining forward in an agony of ineffectual eagerness to obey the injunction to speak and defend himself, gave an expression to the face like that of a condemned vestal priestess in the moment of being buried alive, and in the first struggle against suffocation.

Though at the time Captain Vere was quite ignorant of Billy's liability to vocal impediment, he now immediately divined it, since vividly Billy's aspect recalled to him that of a bright young schoolmate of his whom he had once seen struck by much the same startling impotence in the act of eagerly rising in the class to be foremost in response to a testing question put to it by the master. Going close up to the young sailor, and laying a soothing hand on his shoulder, he said, "There is no hurry, my boy. Take your time, take your time." Contrary to the effect intended, these words so fatherly in tone, doubtless touching Billy's heart to the quick, prompted yet more violent efforts at utterance—efforts soon ending for the time in confirming the paralysis, and bringing to his face an expression which was as a crucifixion to behold. The next instant, quick as the flame from a discharged cannon at night, his right arm

---

[84] Steerer and crew leader of the captain's own boat.

[85] Fish that stuns its prey with electrical shocks.

shot out, and Claggart dropped to the deck. Whether intentionally or but owing to the young athlete's superior height, the blow had taken effect full upon the forehead, so shapely and intellectual-looking a feature in the master-at-arms; so that the body fell over lengthwise, like a heavy plank tilted from erectness. A gasp or two, and he lay motionless.

"Fated boy," breathed Captain Vere in tone so low as to be almost a whisper, "what have you done! But here, help me."

The twain raised the felled one from the loins up into a sitting position. The spare form flexibly acquiesced, but inertly. It was like handling a dead snake. They lowered it back. Regaining erectness, Captain Vere with one hand covering his face stood to all appearance as impassive as the object at his feet. Was he absorbed in taking in all the bearings of the event and what was best not only now at once to be done, but also in the sequel? Slowly he uncovered his face; and the effect was as if the moon emerging from eclipse should reappear with quite another aspect than that which had gone into hiding. The father in him, manifested towards Billy thus far in the scene, was replaced by the military disciplinarian. In his official tone he bade the foretopman retire to a stateroom aft (pointing it out), and there remain till thence summoned. This order Billy in silence mechanically obeyed. Then going to the cabin door where it opened on the quarter-deck, Captain Vere said to the sentry without, "Tell somebody to send Albert here." When the lad appeared, his master so contrived it that he should not catch sight of the prone one. "Albert," he said to him, "tell the surgeon I wish to see him. You need not come back till called."

When the surgeon entered—a self-poised character of that grave sense and experience that hardly anything could take him aback—Captain Vere advanced to meet him, thus unconsciously intercepting his view of Claggart, and, interrupting the other's wonted cermonious salutation, said, "Nay. Tell me how it is with yonder man," directing his attention to the prostrate one.

The surgeon looked, and for all his self-command somewhat started at the abrupt revelation. On Claggart's always pallid complexion, thick black blood was now oozing from nostril and ear. To the gazer's professional eye it was unmistakably no living man that he saw.

"Is it so, then?" said Captain Vere, intently watching him. "I thought it. But verify it." Whereupon the customary tests confirmed the surgeon's first glance, who now, looking up in unfeigned concern, cast a look of intense inquisitiveness upon his superior. But Captain Vere, with one hand to his brow, was standing motionless. Suddenly, catching the surgeon's arm convulsively, he exclaimed, pointing down to the body, "It is the divine judgment on Ananias![86] Look!"

Disturbed by the excited manner he had never before observed in the *Bellipotent*'s captain, and as yet wholly ignorant of the affair, the prudent surgeon nevertheless held his peace, only again looking an earnest interrogatory as to what it was that had resulted in such a tragedy.

But Captain Vere was now again motionless, standing absorbed in thought. Again starting, he vehemently exclaimed, "Struck dead by an angel of God! Yet the angel must hang!"

---

[86] According to Acts 5:3–5, Ananias dropped dead when told he had lied to God.

At these passionate interjections, mere incoherences to the listener as yet unapprised of the antecedents, the surgeon was profoundly discomposed. But now, as recollecting himself, Captain Vere in less passionate tone briefly related the circumstances leading up to the event. "But come; we must dispatch," he added. "Help me to remove him" (meaning the body) "to yonder compartment," designating one opposite that where the foretopman remained immured. Anew disturbed by a request that, as implying a desire for secrecy, seemed unaccountably strange to him, there was nothing for the subordinate to do but comply.

"Go now," said Captain Vere with something of his wonted manner. "Go now. I presently shall call a drumhead court.[87] Tell the lieutenants what has happened, and tell Mr. Mordant" (meaning the captain of marines), "and charge them to keep the matter to themselves."

20

Full of disquietude and misgiving, the surgeon left the cabin. Was Captain Vere suddenly affected in his mind, or was it but a transient excitement, brought about by so strange and extraordinary a tragedy? As to the drumhead court, it struck the surgeon as impolitic, if nothing more. The thing to do, he thought, was to place Billy Budd in confinement, and in a way dictated by usage, and postpone further action in so extraordinary a case to such time as they should rejoin the squadron, and then refer it to the admiral. He recalled the unwonted agitation of Captain Vere and his excited exclamations, so at variance with his normal manner. Was he unhinged?

But assuming that he is, it is not so susceptible of proof. What then can the surgeon do? No more trying situation is conceivable than that of an officer subordinate under a captain whom he suspects to be not mad, indeed, but yet not quite unaffected in his intellects. To argue his order to him would be insolence. To resist him would be mutiny.

In obedience to Captain Vere, he communicated what had happened to the lieutenants and captain of marines, saying nothing as to the captain's state. They fully shared his own surprise and concern. Like him too, they seemed to think that such a matter should be referred to the admiral.

21

Who in the rainbow can draw the line where the violet tint ends and the orange tint begins? Distinctly we see the difference of the colors, but where exactly does the one first blendingly enter into the other? So with sanity and insanity. In pronounced cases there is no question about them. But in some supposed cases, in various degrees supposedly less pronounced, to draw the exact line of demarcation few will undertake, though for a fee becoming considerate some professional experts will. There is nothing namable but that some men will, or undertake to, do it for pay.

Whether Captain Vere, as the surgeon professionally and privately surmised, was really the sudden victim of any degree of aberration, every one must determine for himself by such light as this narrative may afford.

[87] Court-martial.

That the unhappy event which has been narrated could not have happened at a worse juncture was but too true. For it was close on the heel of the suppressed insurrections, an aftertime very critical to naval authority, demanding from every English sea commander two qualities not readily interfusable—prudence and rigor. Moreover, there was something crucial in the case.

In the jugglery of circumstances preceding and attending the event on board the *Bellipotent,* and in the light of that martial code whereby it was formally to be judged, innocence and guilt personified in Claggart and Budd in effect changed places. In a legal view the apparent victim of the tragedy was he who had sought to victimize a man blameless; and the indisputable deed of the latter, navally regarded, constituted the most heinous of military crimes. Yet more. The essential right and wrong involved in the matter, the clearer that might be, so much the worse for the responsibility of a loyal sea commander, inasmuch as he was not authorized to determine the matter on that primitive basis.

Small wonder then that the *Bellipotent*'s captain, though in general a man of rapid decision, felt that circumspectness not less than promptitude was necessary. Until he could decide upon his course, and in each detail; and not only so, but until the concluding measure was upon the point of being enacted, he deemed it advisable, in view of all the circumstances, to guard as much as possible against publicity. Here he may or may not have erred. Certain it is, however, that subsequently in the confidential talk of more than one or two gun rooms and cabins he was not a little criticized by some officers, a fact imputed by his friends and vehemently by his cousin Jack Denton to professional jealousy of Starry Vere. Some imaginative ground for invidious comment there was. The maintenance of secrecy in the matter, the confining all knowledge of it for a time to the place where the homicide occurred, the quarter-deck cabin; in these particulars lurked some resemblance to the policy adopted in those tragedies of the palace which have occurred more than once in the capital founded by Peter the Barbarian.[88]

The case indeed was such that fain would the *Bellipotent*'s captain have deferred taking any action whatever respecting it further than to keep the foretopman a close prisoner till the ship rejoined the squadron and then submitting the matter to the judgment of his admiral.

But a true military officer is in one particular like a true monk. Not with more of self-abnegation will the latter keep his vows of monastic obedience than the former his vows of allegiance to martial duty.

Feeling that unless quick action was taken on it, the deed of the foretopman, so soon as it should be known on the gun decks, would tend to awaken any slumbering embers of the Nore among the crew, a sense of the urgency of the case overruled in Captain Vere every other consideration. But though a conscientious disciplinarian, he was no lover of authority for mere authority's sake. Very far was he from embracing opportunities for monopolizing to himself the perils of moral responsibility, none at least that could properly be referred to an official superior or shared with him by his official equals or even subordinates. So thinking, he was glad it would not be at variance with usage to turn the matter over to a summary court of his own officers,

[88] Peter the Great of Russia (1672–1725), founder of St. Petersburg (now Leningrad).

reserving to himself, as the one on whom the ultimate accountability would rest, the right of maintaining a supervision of it, or formally or informally interposing at need. Accordingly a drumhead court was summarily convened, he electing the individuals composing it: the first lieutenant, the captain of marines, and the sailing master.

In associating an officer of marines with the sea lieutenant and the sailing master in a case having to do with a sailor, the commander perhaps deviated from general custom. He was prompted thereto by the circumstance that he took that soldier to be a judicious person, thoughtful, and not altogether incapable of grappling with a difficult case unprecedented in his prior experience. Yet even as to him he was not without some latent misgiving, for withal he was an extremely good-natured man, an enjoyer of his dinner, a sound sleeper, and inclined to obesity—a man who though he would always maintain his manhood in battle might not prove altogether reliable in a moral dilemma involving aught of the tragic. As to the first lieutenant and the sailing master, Captain Vere could not but be aware that though honest natures, of approved gallantry upon occasion, their intelligence was mostly confined to the matter of active seamanship and the fighting demands of their profession.

The court was held in the same cabin where the unfortunate affair had taken place. This cabin, the commander's, embraced the entire area under the poop deck. Aft, and on either side, was a small stateroom, the one now temporarily a jail and the other a dead-house, and a yet smaller compartment, leaving a space between expanding forward into a goodly oblong of length coinciding with the ship's beam. A skylight of moderate dimension was overhead, and at each end of the oblong space were two sashed porthole windows easily convertible back into embrasures for short carronades.[89]

All being quickly in readiness, Billy Budd was arraigned, Captain Vere necessarily appearing as the sole witness in the case, and as such temporarily sinking his rank, though singularly maintaining it in a matter apparently trivial, namely, that he testified from the ship's weather side, with that object having caused the court to sit on the lee side. Concisely he narrated all that had led up to the catastrophe, omitting nothing in Claggart's accusation and deposing as to the manner in which the prisoner had received it. At this testimony the three officers glanced with no little surprise at Billy Budd, the last man they would have suspected either of the mutinous design alleged by Claggart or the undeniable deed he himself had done. The first lieutenant, taking judicial primacy and turning toward the prisoner, said, "Captain Vere has spoken. Is it or is it not as Captain Vere says?"

In response came syllables not so much impeded in the utterance as might have been anticipated. They were these: "Captain Vere tells the truth. It is just as Captain Vere says, but it is not as the master-at-arms said. I have eaten the King's bread and I am true to the King."

"I believe you, my man," said the witness, his voice indicating a suppressed emotion not otherwise betrayed.

"God will bless you for that, your honor!" not without stammering said Billy, and all but broke down. But immediately he was recalled to self-control by another question, to which with the same emotional difficulty of utterance he said, "No, there

---

[89] Cannon.

was no malice between us. I never bore malice against the master-at-arms. I am sorry that he is dead. I did not mean to kill him. Could I have used my tongue I would not have struck him. But he foully lied to my face and in presence of my captain, and I had to say something, and I could only say it with a blow, God help me!"

In the impulsive aboveboard manner of the frank one the court saw confirmed all that was implied in words that just previously had perplexed them, coming as they did from the testifier to the tragedy and promptly following Billy's impassioned disclaimer of mutinous intent—Captain Vere's words, "I believe you, my man."

Next it was asked of him whether he knew of or suspected aught savoring of incipient trouble (meaning mutiny, though the explicit term was avoided) going on in any section of the ship's company.

The reply lingered. This was naturally imputed by the court to the same vocal embarrassment which had retarded or obstructed previous answers. But in main it was otherwise here, the question immediately recalling to Billy's mind the interview with the afterguardsman in the forechains. But an innate repugnance to playing a part at all approaching that of an informer against one's own shipmates—the same erring sense of uninstructed honor which had stood in the way of his reporting the matter at the time, though as a loyal man-of-war's man it was incumbent on him, and failure so to do, if charged against him and proven, would have subjected him to the heaviest of penalties; this, with the blind feeling now his that nothing really was being hatched, prevailed with him. When the answer came it was a negative.

"One question more," said the officer of marines, now first speaking and with a troubled earnestness. "You tell us that what the master-at-arms said against you was a lie. Now why should he have so lied, so maliciously lied, since you declare there was no malice between you?"

At that question, unintentionally touching on a spiritual sphere wholly obscure to Billy's thoughts, he was nonplussed, evincing a confusion indeed that some observers, such as can readily be imagined, would have construed into involuntary evidence of hidden guilt. Nevertheless, he strove some way to answer, but all at once relinquished the vain endeavor, at the same time turning an appealing glance towards Captain Vere as deeming him his best helper and friend. Captain Vere, who had been seated for a time, rose to his feet, addressing the interrogator. "The question you put to him comes naturally enough. But how can he rightly answer it?—or anybody else, unless indeed it be he who lies within there," designating the compartment where lay the corpse. "But the prone one there will not rise to our summons. In effect, though, as it seems to me, the point you make is hardly material. Quite aside from any conceivable motive actuating the master-at-arms, and irrespective of the provocation to the blow, a martial court must needs in the present case confine its attention to the blow's consequence, which consequence justly is to be deemed not otherwise than as the striker's deed."

This utterance, the full significance of which it was not at all likely that Billy took in, nevertheless caused him to turn a wistful interrogative look toward the speaker, a look in its dumb expressiveness not unlike that which a dog of generous breed might turn upon his master, seeking in his face some elucidation of a previous gesture ambiguous to the canine intelligence. Nor was the same utterance without marked effect upon the three officers, more especially the soldier. Couched in it seemed to them a meaning unanticipated, involving a prejudgment on the speaker's part. It served to augment a mental disturbance previously evident enough.

The soldier once more spoke, in a tone of suggestive dubiety addressing at once his associates and Captain Vere: "Nobody is present—none of the ship's company, I mean—who might shed lateral light, if any is to be had, upon what remains mysterious in this matter."

"That is thoughtfully put," said Captain Vere; "I see your drift. Ay, there is a mystery; but, to use a scriptural phrase, it is a 'mystery of iniquity,' a matter for psychologic theologians to discuss. But what has a military court to do with it? Not to add that for us any possible investigation of it is cut off by the lasting tongue-tie of—him—in yonder," again designating the mortuary sateroom. "The prisoner's deed —with that alone we have to do."

To this, and particularly the closing reiteration, the marine soldier, knowing not how aptly to reply, sadly abstained from saying aught. The first lieutenant, who at the outset had not unnaturally assumed primacy in the court, now overrulingly instructed by a glance from Captain Vere, a glance more effective than words, resumed that primacy. Turning to the prisoner, "Budd," he said, and scarce in equable tones, "Budd, if you have aught further to say for yourself, say it now."

Upon this the young sailor turned another quick glance toward Captain Vere; then, as taking a hint from that aspect, a hint confirming his own instinct that silence was now best, replied to the lieutenant, "I have said all, sir."

The marine—the same who had been the sentinel without the cabin door at the time that the foretopman, followed by the master-at-arms, entered it—he, standing by the sailor throughout these judicial proceedings, was now directed to take him back to the after compartment originally assigned to the prisoner and his custodian. As the twain disappeared from view, the three officers, as partially liberated from some inward constraint associated with Billy's mere presence, simultaneously stirred in their seats. They exchanged looks of troubled indecision, yet feeling that decide they must and without long delay. For Captain Vere, he for the time stood—unconsciously with his back toward them, apparently in one of his absent fits—gazing out from a sashed porthole to windward upon the monotonous blank of the twilight sea. But the court's silence continuing, broken only at moments by brief consultations, in low earnest tones, this served to arouse him and energize him. Turning, he to-and-fro paced the cabin athwart; in the returning ascent to windward climbing the slant deck in the ship's lee roll, without knowing it symbolizing thus in his action a mind resolute to surmount difficulties even if against primitive instincts strong as the wind and the sea. Presently he came to a stand before the three. After scanning their faces he stood less as mustering his thoughts for expression than as one inly deliberating how best to put them to well-meaning men not intellectually mature, men with whom it was necessary to demonstrate certain principles that were axioms to himself. Similar impatience as to talking is perhaps one reason that deters some minds from addressing any popular assemblies.

When speak he did, something, both in the substance of what he said and his manner of saying it, showed the influence of unshared studies modifying and tempering the practical training of an active career. This, along with his phraseology, now and then was suggestive of the grounds whereon rested that imputation of a certain pedantry socially alleged against him by certain naval men of wholly practical cast, captains who nevertheless would frankly concede that His Majesty's navy mustered no more efficient officer of their grade than Starry Vere.

What he said was to this effect: "Hitherto I have been but the witness, little more; and I should hardly think now to take another tone, that of your coadjutor for the time, did I not perceive in you—at the crisis too—a troubled hesitancy, proceeding, I doubt not, from the clash of military duty with moral scruple—scruple vitalized by compassion. For the compassion, how can I otherwise than share it? But, mindful of paramount obligations, I strive against scruples that may tend to enervate decision. Not, gentlemen, that I hide from myself that the case is an exceptional one. Speculatively regarded, it well might be referred to a jury of casuists. But for us here, acting not as casuists or moralists, it is a case practical, and under martial law practically to be dealt with.

"But your scruples: do they move as in a dusk? Challenge them. Make them advance and declare themselves. Come now; do they import something like this: If, mindless of palliating circumstances, we are bound to regard the death of the master-at-arms as the prisoner's deed, then does that deed constitute a capital crime whereof the penalty is a mortal one. But in natural justice is nothing but the prisoner's overt act to be considered? How can we adjudge to summary and shameful death a fellow creature innocent before God, and whom we feel to be so?—Does that state it aright? You sign sad assent. Well, I too feel that, the full force of that. It is Nature. But do these buttons that we wear attest that our allegiance is to Nature? No, to the King. Though the ocean, which is inviolate Nature primeval, though this be the element where we move and have our being as sailors, yet as the King's officers lies our duty in a sphere correspondingly natural? So little is that true, that in receiving our commissions we in the most important regards ceased to be natural free agents. When war is declared are we the commissioned fighters previously consulted? We fight at command. If our judgments approve the war, that is but coincidence. So in other particulars. So now. For suppose condemnation to follow these present proceedings. Would it be so much we ourselves that would condemn as it would be martial law operating through us? For that law and the rigor of it, we are not responsible. Our vowed responsibility is in this: That however pitilessly that law may operate in any instances, we nevertheless adhere to it and administer it.

"But the exceptional in the matter moves the hearts within you. Even so too is mine moved. But let not warm hearts betray heads that should be cool. Ashore in a criminal case, will an upright judge allow himself off the bench to be waylaid by some tender kinswoman of the accused seeking to touch him with her tearful plea? Well, the heart here, sometimes the feminine in man, is as that piteous woman, and hard though it be, she must here be ruled out."

He paused, earnestly studying them for a moment; then resumed.

"But something in your aspect seems to urge that it is not solely the heart that moves in you, but also the conscience, the private conscience. But tell me whether or not, occupying the position we do, private conscience should not yield to that imperial one formulated in the code under which alone we officially proceed?"

Here the three men moved in their seats, less convinced than agitated by the course of an argument troubling but the more the spontaneous conflict within.

Perceiving which, the speaker paused for a moment; then abruptly changing his tone, went on.

"To steady us a bit, let us recur to the facts.—In wartime at sea a man-of-war's man strikes his superior in grade, and the blow kills. Apart from its effect the blow itself is, according to the Articles of War, a capital crime. Furthermore—"

"Ay, sir," emotionally broke in the officer of marines, "in one sense it was. But surely Budd purposed neither mutiny nor homicide."

"Surely not, my good man. And before a court less arbitrary and more merciful than a martial one, that plea would largely extenuate. At the Last Assizes[90] it shall acquit. But how here? We proceed under the law of the Mutiny Act. In feature no child can resemble his father more than that Act resembles in spirit the thing from which it derives—War. In His Majesty's service—in this ship, indeed—there are Englishmen forced to fight for the King against their will. Against their conscience, for aught we know. Though as their fellow creatures some of us may appreciate their position, yet as navy officers what reck we of it? Still less recks the enemy. Our impressed men he would fain cut down in the same swath with our volunteers. As regards the enemy's naval conscripts, some of whom may even share our own abhorrence of the regicidal French Directory, it is the same on our side. War looks but to the frontage, the appearance. And the Mutiny Act, War's child, takes after the father. Budd's intent or non-intent is nothing to the purpose.

"But while, put to it by those anxieties in you which I cannot but respect, I only repeat myself—while thus strangely we prolong proceedings that should be summary—the enemy may be sighted and an engagement result. We must do; and one of two things must we do—condemn or let go."

"Can we not convict and yet mitigate the penalty?" asked the sailing master, here speaking, and falteringly, for the first.

"Gentlemen, were that clearly lawful for us under the circumstances, consider the consequences of such clemency. The people" (meaning the ship's company) "have native sense; most of them are familiar with our naval usage and tradition; and how would they take it? Even could you explain to them—which our official position forbids—they, long molded by arbitrary discipline, have not that kind of intelligent responsiveness that might qualify them to comprehend and discriminate. No, to the people the foretopman's deed, however it be worded in the announcement, will be plain homicide committed in a flagrant act of mutiny. What penalty for that should follow, they know. But it does not follow. *Why?* they will ruminate. You know what sailors are. Will they not revert to the recent outbreak at the Nore? Ay. They know the well-founded alarm—the panic it struck throughout England. Your clement sentence they would account pusillanimous. They would think that we flinch, that we are afraid of them—afraid of practicing a lawful rigor singularly demanded at this juncture, lest it should provoke new troubles. What shame to us such a conjecture on their part, and how deadly to discipline. You see then, whither, prompted by duty and the law, I steadfastly drive. But I beseech you, my friends, do not take me amiss. I feel as you do for this unfortunate boy. But did he know our hearts, I take him to be of that generous nature that he would feel even for us on whom in this military necessity so heavy a compulsion is laid."

---

[90] On Judgment Day.

With that, crossing the deck he resumed his place by the sashed porthole, tacitly leaving the three to come to a decision. On the cabin's opposite side the troubled court sat silent. Loyal lieges, plain and practical, though at bottom they dissented from some points Captain Vere had put to them, they were without the faculty, hardly had the inclination, to gainsay one whom they felt to be an earnest man, one too not less their superior in mind than in naval rank. But it is not improbable that even such of his words as were not without influence over them, less came home to them than his closing appeal to their instinct as sea officers: in the forethought he threw out as to the practical consequences to discipline, considering the unconfirmed tone of the fleet at the time, should a man-of-war's man's violent killing at sea of a superior in grade be allowed to pass for aught else than a capital crime demanding prompt infliction of the penalty.

Not unlikely they were brought to something more or less akin to that harassed frame of mind which in the year 1842 actuated the commander of the U.S. brig-of-war *Somers* to resolve, under the so-called Articles of War, Articles modeled upon the English Mutiny Act, to resolve upon the execution at sea of a midshipman and two sailors as mutineers designing the seizure of the brig. Which resolution was carried out though in a time of peace and within not many days' sail of home. An act vindicated by a naval court of inquiry subsequently convened ashore. History, and here cited without comment. True, the circumstances on board the *Somers* were different from those on board the *Bellipotent*. But the urgency felt, well-warranted or otherwise, was much the same.

Says a writer whom few know,[91] "Forty years after a battle it is easy for a noncombatant to reason about how it ought to have been fought. It is another thing personally and under fire to have to direct the fighting while involved in the obscuring smoke of it. Much so with respect to other emergencies involving considerations both practical and moral, and when it is imperative promptly to act. The greater the fog the more it imperils the steamer, and speed is put on though at the hazard of running somebody down. Little ween[92] the snug card players in the cabin of the responsibilities of the sleepless man on the bridge."

In brief, Billy Budd was formally convicted and sentenced to be hung at the yardarm in the early morning watch, it being now night. Otherwise, as is customary in such cases, the sentence would forthwith have been carried out. In wartime on the field or in the fleet, a mortal punishment decreed by a drumhead court—on the field sometimes decreed by but a nod from the general—follows without delay on the heel of conviction, without appeal.

22

It was Captain Vere himself who of his own motion communicated the finding of the court to the prisoner, for that purpose going to the compartment where he was in custody and bidding the marine there to withdraw for the time.

Beyond the communication of the sentence, what took place at this interview was never known. But in view of the character of the twain briefly closeted in that stateroom, each radically sharing in the rarer qualities of our nature—so rare indeed

[91] Melville is perhaps referring to himself.   [92] Think.

as to be all but incredible to average minds however much cultivated—some conjectures may be ventured.

It would have been in consonance with the spirit of Captain Vere should he on this occasion have concealed nothing from the condemned one—should he indeed have frankly disclosed to him the part he himself had played in bringing about the decision, at the same time revealing his actuating motives. On Billy's side it is not improbable that such a confession would have been received in much the same spirit that prompted it. Not without a sort of joy, indeed, he might have appreciated the brave opinion of him implied in his captain's making such a confidant of him. Nor, as to the sentence itself, could he have been insensible that it was imparted to him as to one not afraid to die. Even more may have been. Captain Vere in end may have developed the passion sometimes latent under an exterior stoical or indifferent. He was old enough to have been Billy's father. The austere devotee of military duty, letting himself melt back into what remains primeval in our formalized humanity, may in end have caught Billy to his heart, even as Abraham may have caught young Isaac on the brink of resolutely offering him up in obedience to the exacting behest.[93] But there is no telling the sacrament, seldom if in any case revealed to the gadding world, wherever under circumstances at all akin to those here attempted to be set forth two of great Nature's nobler order embrace. There is privacy at the time, inviolable to the survivor; and holy oblivion, the sequel to each diviner magnanimity, providentially covers all at last.

The first to encounter Captain Vere in act of leaving the compartment was the senior lieutenant. The face he beheld, for the moment one expressive of the agony of the strong, was to that officer, though a man of fifty, a startling revelation. That the condemned one suffered less than he who mainly had effected the condemnation was apparently indicated by the former's exclamation in the scene soon perforce to be touched upon.

23

Of a series of incidents within a brief term rapidly following each other, the adequate narration may take up a term less brief, especially if explanation or comment here and there seem requisite to the better understanding of such incidents. Between the entrance into the cabin of him who never left it alive, and him who when he did leave it left it as one condemned to die; between this and the closeted interview just given, less than an hour and a half had elapsed. It was an interval long enough, however, to awaken speculations among no few of the ship's company as to what it was that could be detaining in the cabin the master-at-arms and the sailor; for a rumor that both of them had been seen to enter it and neither of them had been seen to emerge, this rumor had got abroad upon the gun decks and in the tops, the people of a great warship being in one respect like villagers, taking microscopic note of every outward movement or non-movement going on. When therefore, in weather not at all tempestuous, all hands were called in the second dogwatch, a summons under such circumstances not usual in those hours, the crew were not wholly unprepared for some

---

[93] See Genesis 22:1–18. God tested Abraham by commanding him to sacrifice his son Isaac. At the moment of sacrifice, God withdrew the command.

announcement extraordinary, one having connection too with the continued absence of the two men from their wonted haunts.

There was a moderate sea at the time; and the moon, newly risen and near to being at its full, silvered the white spar deck wherever not blotted by the clear-cut shadows horizontally thrown of fixtures and moving men. On either side the quarterdeck the marine guard under arms was drawn up; and Captain Vere, standing in his place surrounded by all the wardroom officers, addressed his men. In so doing, his manner showed neither more nor less than that properly pertaining to his supreme position aboard his own ship. In clear terms and concise he told them what had taken place in the cabin: that the master-at-arms was dead, that he who had killed him had been already tried by a summary court and condemned to death, and that the execution would take place in the early morning watch. The word *mutiny* was not named in what he said. He refrained too from making the occasion an opportunity for any preachment as to the maintenance of discipline, thinking perhaps that under existing circumstances in the navy the consequence of violating discipline should be made to speak for itself.

Their captain's announcement was listened to by the throng of standing sailors in a dumbness like that of a seated congregation of believers in hell listening to the clergyman's announcement of his Calvinistic text.

At the close, however, a confused murmur went up. It began to wax. All but instantly, then, at a sign, it was pierced and suppressed by shrill whistles of the boatswain and his mates. The word was given to about ship.

To be prepared for burial Claggart's body was delivered to certain petty officers of his mess. And here, not to clog the sequel with lateral matters, it may be added that at a suitable hour, the master-at-arms was committed to the sea with every funeral honor properly belonging to his naval grade.

In this proceeding as in every public one growing out of the tragedy strict adherence to usage was observed. Nor in any point could it have been at all deviated from, either with respect to Claggart or Billy Budd, without begetting undesirable speculations in the ship's company, sailors, and more particularly men-of-war's men, being of all men the greatest sticklers for usage. For similar cause, all communication between Captain Vere and the condemned one ended with the closeted interview already given, the latter being now surrendered to the ordinary routine preliminary to the end. His transfer under guard from the captain's quarters was effected without unusual precautions—at least no visible ones. If possible, not to let the men so much as surmise that their officers anticipate aught amiss from them is the tacit rule in a military ship. And the more that some sort of trouble should really be apprehended, the more do the officers keep that apprehension to themselves, though not the less unostentatious vigilance may be augmented. In the present instance, the sentry placed over the prisoner had strict orders to let no one have communication with him but the chaplain. And certain unobtrusive measures were taken absolutely to insure this point.

24

In a seventy-four of the old order the deck known as the upper gun deck was the one covered over by the spar deck, which last, though not without its armament, was for the most part exposed to the weather. In general it was at all hours free from hammocks; those of the crew swinging on the lower gun deck and berth deck, the latter being not only a dormitory but also the place for the stowing of the sailors' bags, and on both sides lined with the large chests or movable pantries of the many messes of the men.

On the starboard side of the *Bellipotent*'s upper gun deck, behold Billy Budd under sentry lying prone in irons in one of the bays formed by the regular spacing of the guns comprising the batteries on either side. All these pieces were of the heavier caliber of that period. Mounted on lumbering wooden carriages, they were hampered with cumbersome harness of breeching and strong side-tackles for running them out. Guns and carriages, together with the long rammers and shorter linstocks[94] lodged in loops overhead—all these, as customary, were painted black; and the heavy hempen breechings, tarred to the same tint, wore the like livery of the undertakers. In contrast with the funereal hue of these surroundings, the prone sailor's exterior apparel, white jumper and white duck trousers, each more or less soiled, dimly glimmered in the obscure light of the bay like a patch of discolored snow in early April lingering at some upland cave's black mouth. In effect he is already in his shroud, or the garments that shall serve him in lieu of one. Over him but scarce illuminating him, two battle lanterns swing from two massive beams of the deck above. Fed with the oil supplied by the war contractors (whose gains, honest or otherwise, are in every land an anticipated portion of the harvest of death), with flickering splashes of dirty yellow light they pollute the pale moonshine all but ineffectually struggling in obstructed flecks through the open ports from which the tampioned[95] cannon protrude. Other lanterns at intervals serve but to bring out somewhat the obscurer bays which, like small confessionals or side-chapels in a cathedral, branch from the long dim-vistaed broad aisle between the two batteries of that covered tier.

Such was the deck where now lay the Handsome Sailor. Through the rose-tan of his complexion no pallor could have shown. It would have taken days of sequestration from the winds and the sun to have brought about the effacement of that. But the skeleton in the cheekbone at the point of its angle was just beginning delicately to be defined under the warm-tinted skin. In fervid hearts self-contained, some brief experiences devour our human tissue as secret fire in a ship's hold consumes cotton in the bale.

But now lying between the two guns, as nipped in the vice of fate, Billy's agony, mainly proceeding from a generous young heart's virgin experience of the diabolical incarnate and effective in some men—the tension of that agony was over now. It survived not the something healing in the closeted interview with Captain Vere. Without movement, he lay as in a trance, that adolescent expression previously noted as his taking on something akin to the look of a slumbering child in the cradle when the warm hearth-glow of the still chamber at night plays on the dimples that at whiles mysteriously form in the cheek, silently coming and going there. For now and then in the gyved[96] one's trance a serene happy light born of some wandering reminiscence or dream would diffuse itself over his face, and then wane away only anew to return.

The chaplain, coming to see him and finding him thus, and perceiving no sign that

---

[94] Sticks that hold the match used to fire cannon.   [96] Shackled.
[95] Plugged.

he was conscious of his presence, attentively regarded him for a space, then slipping aside, withdrew for the time, peradventure feeling that even he, the minister of Christ though receiving his stipend from Mars, had no consolation to proffer which could result in a peace transcending that which he beheld. But in the small hours he came again. And the prisoner, now awake to his surroundings, noticed his approach, and civilly, all but cheerfully, welcomed him. But it was to little purpose that in the interview following, the good man sought to bring Billy Budd to some godly understanding that he must die, and at dawn. True, Billy himself freely referred to his death as a thing close at hand; but it was something in the way that children will refer to death in general, who yet among their other sports will play a funeral with hearse and mourners.

Not that like children Billy was incapable of conceiving what death really is. No, but he was wholly without irrational fear of it, a fear more prevalent in highly civilized communities than those so-called barbarous ones which in all respects stand nearer to unadulterate Nature. And, as elsewhere said, a barbarian Billy radically was —as much so, for all the costume, as his countrymen the British captives, living trophies, made to march in the Roman triumph of Germanicus.[97] Quite as much so as those later barbarians, young men probably, and picked specimens among the earlier British converts to Christianity, at least nominally such, taken to Rome (as today converts from lesser isles of the sea may be taken to London), of whom the Pope[98] of that time, admiring the strangeness of their personal beauty so unlike the Italian stamp, their clear ruddy complexion and curled flaxen locks, exclaimed, "Angles" (meaning *English,* the modern derivative), "Angels, do you call them? And is it because they look so like angels?" Had it been later in time, one would think that the Pope had in mind Fra Angelico's[99] seraphs, some of whom, plucking apples in gardens of the Hesperides,[100] have the faint rosebud complexion of the more beautiful English girls.

If in vain the good chaplain sought to impress the young barbarian with ideas of death akin to those conveyed in the skull, dial, and crossbones on old tombstones, equally futile to all appearance were his efforts to bring home to him the thought of salvation and a Savior. Billy listened, but less out of awe or reverence, perhaps, than from a certain natural politeness, doubtless at bottom regarding all that in much the same way that most mariners of his class take any discourse abstract or out of the common tone of the workaday world. And this sailor way of taking clerical discourse is not wholly unlike the way in which the primer of Christianity, full of transcendent miracles, was received long ago on tropic isles by any superior *savage,* so called— a Tahitian, say, of Captain Cook's[101] time or shortly after that time. Out of natural courtesy he received, but did not appropriate. It was like a gift placed in the palm of an outreached hand upon which the fingers do not close.

But the *Bellipotent*'s chaplain was a discreet man possessing the good sense of a good heart. So he insisted not in his vocation here. At the instance of Captain Vere, a lieutenant had apprised him of pretty much everything as to Billy; and since he felt

---

[97] Germanicus Caesar (15 B.C.–A.D. 19), whose military victories were celebrated in Rome.
[98] Gregory the Great (540–604).
[99] Fra Angelico: Italian painter (1387–1455).

[100] In Greek myth, gardens in which golden apples grow.
[101] James Cook (1728–1779), English explorer of the Pacific.

that innocence was even a better thing than religion wherewith to go to Judgment, he reluctantly withdrew; but in his emotion not without first performing an act strange enough in an Englishman, and under the circumstances yet more so in any regular priest. Stooping over, he kissed on the fair cheek his fellow man, a felon in martial law, one whom though on the confines of death he felt he could never convert to a dogma; nor for all that did he fear for his future.

Marvel not that having been made acquainted with the young sailor's essential innocence the worthy man lifted not a finger to avert the doom of such a martyr to martial discipline. So to do would not only have been as idle as invoking the desert, but would also have been an audacious transgression of the bounds of his function, one as exactly prescribed to him by military law as that of the boatswain or any other naval officer. Bluntly put, a chaplain is the minister of the Prince of Peace serving in the host of the God of War—Mars. As such, he is as incongruous as a musket would be on the altar at Christmas. Why, then, is he there? Because he indirectly subserves the purpose attested by the cannon; because too he lends the sanction of the religion of the meek to that which practically is the abrogation of everything but brute Force.

25

The night so luminous on the spar deck, but otherwise on the cavernous ones below, levels so like the tiered galleries in a coal mine—the luminous night passed away. But like the prophet in the chariot disappearing in heaven and dropping his mantle to Elisha,[102] the withdrawing night transferred its pale robe to the breaking day. A meek, shy light appeared in the East, where stretched a diaphanous fleece of white furrowed vapor. That light slowly waxed. Suddenly *eight bells* was struck aft, responded to by one louder metallic stroke from forward. It was four o'clock in the morning. Instantly the silver whistles were heard summoning all hands to witness punishment. Up through the great hatchways rimmed with racks of heavy shot the watch below came pouring, overspreading with the watch already on deck the space between the main-mast and foremast including that occupied by the capacious launch and the black booms tiered on either side of it, boat and booms making a summit of observation for the powder-boys and younger tars. A different group comprising one watch of topmen leaned over the rail of that sea balcony, no small one in a seventy-four, looking down on the crowd below. Man or boy, none spake but in whisper, and few spake at all. Captain Vere—as before, the central figure among the assembled commis-sioned officers—stood nigh the break of the poop deck[103] facing forward. Just below him on the quarter-deck the marines in full equipment were drawn up much as at the scene of the promulgated sentence.

At sea in the old time, the execution by halter of a military sailor was generally from the foreyard. In the present instance, for special reasons the mainyard was assigned. Under an arm of that yard the prisoner was presently brought up, the chaplain attending him. It was noted at the time, and remarked upon afterwards, that

---

[102] In 2 Kings 2:11–13, the prophet Elijah, ascending to heaven, drops his mantle, which Elisha then takes up.

[103] Raised deck at ship's stern.

in this final scene the good man evinced little or nothing of the perfunctory. Brief speech indeed he had with the condemned one, but the genuine Gospel was less on his tongue than in his aspect and manner towards him. The final preparations personal to the latter being speedily brought to an end by two boatswain's mates, the consummation impended. Billy stood facing aft. At the penultimate moment, his words, his only ones, words wholly unobstructed in the utterance, were these: "God bless Captain Vere!" Syllables so unanticipated coming from one with the ignominious hemp about his neck—a conventional felon's benediction directed aft towards the quarters of honor; syllables too delivered in the clear melody of a singing bird on the point of launching from the twig—had a phenomenal effect, not unenhanced by the rare personal beauty of the young sailor, spiritualized now through late experiences so poignantly profound.

Without volition, as it were, as if indeed the ship's populace were but the vehicles of some vocal current electric, with one voice from alow and aloft came a resonant sympathetic echo: "God bless Captain Vere!" And yet at that instant Billy alone must have been in their hearts, even as in their eyes.

At the pronounced words and the spontaneous echo that voluminously rebounded them, Captain Vere, either through stoic self-control or a sort of momentary paralysis induced by emotional shock, stood erectly rigid as a musket in the ship-armorer's rack.

The hull, deliberately recovering from the periodic roll to leeward, was just regaining an even keel when the last signal, a preconcerted dumb one, was given. At the same moment it chanced that the vapory fleece hanging low in the East was shot through with a soft glory as of the fleece of the Lamb of God seen in mystical vision, and simultaneously therewith, watched by the wedged mass of upturned faces, Billy ascended; and, ascending, took the full rose of the dawn.

In the pinioned figure arrived at the yard-end, to the wonder of all no motion was apparent, none save that created by the slow roll of the hull in moderate weather, so majestic in a great ship ponderously cannoned.

26

When some days afterwards, in reference to the singularity just mentioned, the purser,[104] a rather ruddy, rotund person more accurate as an accountant than profound as a philosopher, said at mess to the surgeon, "What testimony to the force lodged in will power," the latter, saturnine, spare, and tall, one in whom a discreet causticity went along with a manner less genial than polite, replied, "Your pardon, Mr. Purser. In a hanging scientifically conducted—and under special orders I myself directed how Budd's was to be effected—any movement following the completed suspension and originating in the body suspended, such movement indicates mechanical spasm in the muscular system. Hence the absence of that is no more attributable to will power, as you call it, than to horsepower—begging your pardon."

"But this muscular spasm you speak of, is not that in a degree more or less invariable in these cases?"

"Assuredly so, Mr. Purser."

"How then, my good sir, do you account for its absence in this instance?"

---

[104] Ship's financial officer.

"Mr. Purser, it is clear that your sense of the singularity in this matter equals not mine. You account for it by what you call will power—a term not yet included in the lexicon of science. For me, I do not, with my present knowledge, pretend to account for it at all. Even should we assume the hypothesis that at the first touch of the halyards the action of Budd's heart, intensified by extraordinary emotion at its climax, abruptly stopped—much like a watch when in carelessly winding it up you strain at the finish, thus snapping the chain—even under that hypothesis how account for the phenomenon that followed?"

"You admit, then, that the absence of spasmodic movement was phenomenal."

"It was phenomenal, Mr. Purser, in the sense that it was an appearance the cause of which is not immediately to be assigned."

"But tell me, my dear sir," pertinaciously continued the other, "was the man's death effected by the halter, or was it a species of euthanasia?"[105]

"*Euthanasia,* Mr. Purser, is something like your *will power:* I doubt its authenticity as a scientific term—begging your pardon again. It is at once imaginative and metaphysical—in short, Greek.—But," abruptly changing his tone, "there is a case in the sick bay that I do not care to leave to my assistants. Beg your pardon, but excuse me." And rising from the mess he formally withdrew.

27

The silence at the moment of execution and for a moment or two continuing thereafter, a silence but emphasized by the regular wash of the sea against the hull or the flutter of a sail caused by the helmsman's eyes being tempted astray, this emphasized silence was gradually disturbed by a sound not easily to be verbally rendered. Whoever has heard the freshet-wave of a torrent suddenly swelled by pouring showers in tropical mountains, showers not shared by the plain; whoever has heard the first muffled murmur of its sloping advance through precipitous woods may form some conception of the sound now heard. The seeming remoteness of its source was because of its murmurous indistinctness, since it came from close by, even from the men massed on the ship's open deck. Being inarticulate, it was dubious in significance further than it seemed to indicate some capricious revulsion of thought or feeling such as mobs ashore are liable to, in the present instance possibly implying a sullen revocation on the men's part of their involuntary echoing of Billy's benediction. But ere the murmur had time to wax into clamor it was met by a strategic command, the more telling that it came with abrupt unexpectedness: "Pipe down the starboard watch, Boatswain, and see that they go."

Shrill as the shriek of the sea hawk, the silver whistles of the boatswain and his mates pierced that ominous low sound, dissipating it; and yielding to the mechanism of discipline the throng was thinned by one-half. For the remainder, most of them were set to temporary employments connected with trimming the yards and so forth, business readily to be got up to serve occasion by any officer of the deck.

Now each proceeding that follows a mortal sentence pronounced at sea by a drumhead court is characterized by promptitude not perceptibly merging into hurry, though bordering that. The hammock, the one which had been Billy's bed when alive,

[105] Mercy-killing.

having already been ballasted with shot and otherwise prepared to serve for his canvas coffin, the last offices of the sea undertakers, the sailmaker's mates, were now speedily completed. When everything was in readiness a second call for all hands, made necessary by the strategic movement before mentioned, was sounded, now to witness burial.

The details of this closing formality it needs not to give. But when the tilted plank let slide its freight into the sea, a second strange human murmur was heard, blended now with another inarticulate sound proceeding from certain larger seafowl who, their attention having been attracted by the peculiar commotion in the water resulting from the heavy sloped dive of the shotted hammock into the sea, flew screaming to the spot. So near the hull did they come, that the stridor or bony creak of their gaunt double-jointed pinions was audible. As the ship under light airs passed on, leaving the burial spot astern, they still kept circling it low down with the moving shadow of their outstretched wings and the croaked requiem of their cries.

Upon sailors as superstitious as those of the age preceding ours, men-of-war's men too who had just beheld the prodigy of repose in the form suspended in air, and now foundering in the deeps; to such mariners the action of the seafowl, though dictated by mere animal greed for prey, was big with no prosaic significance. An uncertain movement began among them, in which some encroachment was made. It was tolerated but for a moment. For suddenly the drum beat to quarters, which familiar sound happening at least twice every day, had upon the present occasion a signal peremptoriness in it. True martial discipline long continued superinduces in average man a sort of impulse whose operation at the official word of command much resembles in its promptitude the effect of an instinct.

The drumbeat dissolved the multitude, distributing most of them along the batteries of the two covered gun decks. There, as wonted, the guns' crews stood by their respective cannon erect and silent. In due course the first officer, sword under arm and standing in his place on the quarter-deck, formally received the successive reports of the sworded lieutenants commanding the sections of batteries below; the last of which reports being made, the summed report he delivered with the customary salute to the commander. All this occupied time, which in the present case was the object in beating to quarters at an hour prior to the customary one. That such variance from usage was authorized by an officer like Captain Vere, a martinet as some deemed him, was evidence of the necessity for unusual action implied in what he deemed to be temporarily the mood of his men. "With mankind," he would say, "forms, measured forms, are everything; and that is the import couched in the story of Orpheus[106] with his lyre spellbinding the wild denizens of the wood." And this he once applied to the disruption of forms going on across the Channel and the consequences thereof.

At this unwonted muster at quarters, all proceeded as at the regular hour. The band on the quarter-deck played a sacred air, after which the chaplain went through the customary morning service. That done, the drum beat the retreat; and toned by music and religious rites subserving the discipline and purposes of war, the men in their wonted orderly manner dispersed to the places allotted them when not at the guns.

And now it was full day. The fleece of low-hanging vapor had vanished, licked

---

[106] In Greek myth, the poet whose music charmed wild beasts.

up by the sun that late had so glorified it. And the circumambient air in the clearness of its serenity was like smooth white marble in the polished block not yet removed from the marble-dealer's yard.

28

The symmetry of form attainable in pure fiction cannot so readily be achieved in a narration essentially having less to do with fable than with fact. Truth uncompromisingly told will always have its ragged edges; hence the conclusion of such a narration is apt to be less finished than an architectural finial.

How it fared with the Handsome Sailor during the year of the Great Mutiny has been faithfully given. But though properly the story ends with his life, something in way of sequel will not be amiss. Three brief chapters will suffice.

In the general rechristening under the Directory of the craft originally forming the navy of the French monarchy, the *St. Louis* line-of-battle ship was named the *Athée* (the *Atheist*). Such a name, like some other substituted ones in the Revolutionary fleet, while proclaiming the infidel audacity of the ruling power, was yet, though not so intended to be, the aptest name, if one consider it, ever given to a warship; far more so indeed than the *Devastation,* the *Erebus* (the *Hell*), and similar names bestowed upon fighting ships.

On the return passage to the English fleet from the detached cruise during which occurred the events already recorded, the *Bellipotent* fell in with the *Athée*. An engagement ensued, during which Captain Vere, in the act of putting his ship alongside the enemy with a view of throwing his boarders across her bulwarks, was hit by a musket ball from a porthole of the enemy's main cabin. More than disabled, he dropped to the deck and was carried below to the same cockpit where some of his men already lay. The senior lieutenant took command. Under him the enemy was finally captured, and though much crippled was by rare good fortune successfully taken into Gibraltar, an English port not very distant from the scene of the fight. There, Captain Vere with the rest of the wounded was put ashore. He lingered for some days, but the end came. Unhappily he was cut off too early for the Nile and Trafalgar.[107] The spirit that 'spite its philosophic austerity may yet have indulged in the most secret of all passions, ambition, never attained to the fulness of fame.

Not long before death, while lying under the influence of that magical drug which, soothing the physical frame, mysteriously operates on the subtler element in man, he was heard to murmur words inexplicable to his attendant: "Billy Budd, Billy Budd." That these were not the accents of remorse would seem clear from what the attendant said to the *Bellipotent*'s senior officer of marines, who, as the most reluctant to condemn of the members of the drumhead court, too well knew, though here he kept the knowledge to himself, who Billy Budd was.

29

Some few weeks after the execution, among other matters under the head of "News from the Mediterranean," there appeared in a naval chronicle of the time, an author-

[107] Subsequent battles (Nile, 1798; Trafalgar, 1805).

ized weekly publication, an account of the affair. It was doubtless for the most part written in good faith, though the medium, partly rumor, through which the facts must have reached the writer served to deflect and in part falsify them. The account was as follows:

"On the tenth of the last month a deplorable occurrence took place on board H.M.S. *Bellipotent*. John Claggart, the ship's master-at-arms, discovering that some sort of plot was incipient among an inferior section of the ship's company, and that the ringleader was one William Budd; he, Claggart, in the act of arraigning the man before the captain, was vindictively stabbed to the heart by the suddenly drawn sheath knife of Budd.

"The deed and the implement employed sufficiently suggest that though mustered into the service under an English name the assassin was no Englishman, but one of those aliens adopting English cognomens whom the present extraordinary necessities of the service have caused to be admitted into it in considerable numbers.

"The enormity of the crime and the extreme depravity of the criminal appear the greater in view of the character of the victim, a middle-aged man respectable and discreet, belonging to that minor official grade, the petty officers, upon whom, as none know better than the commissioned gentlemen, the efficiency of His Majesty's navy so largely depends. His function was a responsible one, at once onerous and thankless; and his fidelity in it the greater because of his strong patriotic impulse. In this instance as in so many other instances in these days, the character of this unfortunate man signally refutes, if refutation were needed, that peevish saying attributed to the late Dr. Johnson,[108] that patriotism is the last refuge of a scoundrel.

"The criminal paid the penalty of his crime. The promptitude of the punishment has proved salutary. Nothing amiss is now apprehended aboard H.M.S. *Bellipotent.*"

The above, appearing in a publication now long ago superannuated and forgotten, is all that hitherto has stood in human record to attest what manner of men respectively were John Claggart and Billy Budd.

30

Everything is for a term venerated in navies. Any tangible object associated with some striking incident of the service is converted into a monument. The spar from which the foretopman was suspended was for some few years kept trace of by the bluejackets. Their knowledges followed it from ship to dockyard and again from dockyard to ship, still pursuing it even when at last reduced to a mere dockyard boom. To them a chip of it was as a piece of the Cross. Ignorant though they were of the secret facts of the tragedy, and not thinking but that the penalty was somehow unavoidably inflicted from the naval point of view, for all that, they instinctively felt that Billy was a sort of man as incapable of mutiny as of wilful murder. They recalled the fresh young image of the Handsome Sailor, that face never deformed by a sneer or subtler vile freak of the heart within. This impression of him was doubtless deepened by the fact that he was gone, and in a measure mysteriously gone. On the gun decks of the *Bellipotent* the general estimate of his nature and its unconscious simplicity eventually found rude utterance from another foretopman, one of his own watch, gifted, as some

---

[108] The lexicographer Samuel Johnson (1709–1784).

sailors are, with an artless *poetic* temperament. The tarry hand made some lines which, after circulating among the shipboard crews for a while, finally got rudely printed at Portsmouth as a ballad. The title given to it was the sailor's.

BILLY IN THE DARBIES[109]

Good of the chaplain to enter Lone Bay
And down on his marrowbones here and pray
For the likes just o' me, Billy Budd.—But, look:
Through the port comes the moonshine astray!
It tips the guard's cutlass and silvers this nook;
But 'twill die in the dawning of Billy's last day.
A jewel-block they'll make of me tomorrow,
Pendant pearl from the yardarm-end
Like the eardrop I gave to Bristol Molly—
O, 'tis me, not the sentence they'll suspend.
Ay, ay, all is up; and I must up too,
Early in the morning, aloft from alow.
On an empty stomach now never it would do.
They'll give me a nibble—bit o' biscuit ere I go.
Sure, a messmate will reach me the last parting cup;
But, turning heads away from the hoist and the belay.
Heaven knows who will have the running of me up!
No pipe to those halyards.—But aren't it all sham?
A blur's in my eyes; it is dreaming that I am.
A hatchet to my hawser? All adrift to go?
The drum roll to grog, and Billy never know?
But Donald he has promised to stand by the plank;
So I'll shake a friendly hand ere I sink.
But—no! It is dead then I'll be, come to think.
I remember Taff the Welshman when he sank.
And his cheek it was like the budding pink.
But me they'll lash in hammock, drop me deep.
Fathoms down, fathoms down, how I'll dream fast asleep.
I feel it stealing now. Sentry, are you there?
Just ease these darbies at the wrist,
And roll me over fair!
I am sleepy, and the oozy weeds about me twist.

1924

---

[109] Handcuffs.

from Battle Pieces and Aspects of the War

The Portent
(1859)

Hanging from the beam,
   Slowly swaying (such the law),
Gaunt the shadow on your green,
   Shenandoah!
The cut is on the crown   5
   (Lo, John Brown),[1]
And the stabs shall heal no more.

Hidden in the cap[2]
   Is the anguish none can draw;
So your future veils its face,   10
   Shenandoah!
But the streaming beard is shown
   (Weird John Brown),
The meteor of the war.

1866

The March into Virginia
Ending in the First Manassas
(July, 1861)[3]

Did all the lets[4] and bars appear
   To every just or larger end,
Whence should come the trust and cheer?
   Youth must its ignorant impulse lend—
Age finds place in the rear.   5
   All wars are boyish, and are fought by boys,
   The champions and enthusiasts of the state:
   Turbid ardors and vain joys
   Not barrenly abate—

---

[1] In 1859 the bearded abolitionist John Brown was hanged for treason after he had incited a slave rebellion and led an attack on a Federal arsenal at Harpers Ferry, Virginia. He had received a scalp wound when captured.
[2] Hood placed over the head of the condemned man.

[3] At Bull Run, near Manassas, Virginia, Confederate troops defeated Union forces in July 1861.
[4] Obstacles.

Stimulants to the power mature,   10
    Preparatives of fate.

Who here forecasteth the event?
What heart but spurns at precedent
And warnings of the wise,
Contemned foreclosures of surprise?   15
The banners play, the bugles call,
The air is blue and prodigal.
    No berrying party, pleasure-wooed,
No picnic party in the May,
Ever went less loth than they   20
    Into that leafy neighborhood.
In Bacchic glee[5] they file toward Fate,
Moloch's[6] uninitiate;
Expectancy, and glad surmise
Of battle's unknown mysteries.   25

All they feel is this: 'tis glory,
A rapture sharp, though transitory,
Yet lasting in belaureled story.
So they gayly go to fight,
Chatting left and laughing right.   30

But some who this blithe mood present,
    As on in lightsome files they fare,
Shall die experienced ere three days be spent—
    Perish, enlightened by the vollied glare;
Or shame survive, and, like to adamant,   35
    The throe of Second Manassas[7] share.

1866

A Utilitarian View of the Monitor's Fight[8]

Plain be the phrase, yet apt the verse,
    More ponderous than nimble;
For since grimed War here laid aside
His Orient pomp, 'twould ill befit
    Overmuch to ply   5
    The rhyme's barbaric cymbal.

---

[5] Revels of the kind inspired by Bacchus, Roman god of wine.

[6] Moloch: Ancient Semitic god to whom worshippers sacrificed children.

[7] In the Second Battle of Manassas (August 1862), Union forces were once again defeated.

[8] One of the two ironclad vessels that battled in May 1862, at Hampton Roads, Virginia. The *Monitor* belonged to the Union navy, and its adversary was the Confederate *Merrimack*.

Hail to victory without the gaud
Of glory; zeal that needs no fans
Of banners; plain mechanic power
Plied cogently in War now placed—   10
Where War belongs—
Among the trades and artisans.

Yet this was battle, and intense—
Beyond the strife of fleets heroic;
Deadlier, closer, calm 'mid storm;   15
No passion; all went on by crank,
Pivot, and screw,
And calculations of caloric.

Needless to dwell; the story's known.
The ringing of those plates on plates   20
Still ringeth round the world—
The clangor of that blacksmiths' fray.
The anvil-din
Resounds this message from the Fates:

War yet shall be, and to the end;   25
But war-paint shows the streaks of weather;
War yet shall be, but warriors
Are now but operatives;[9] War's made
Less grand than Peace,
And a singe runs through lace and feather.   30

1866

Shiloh[10]
A Requiem

(April, 1862)

Skimming lightly, wheeling still,
The swallows fly low
Over the field in clouded days,
The forest-field of Shiloh—
Over the field where April rain   5
Solaced the parched ones stretched in pain
Through the pause of night
That followed the Sunday fight
Around the church of Shiloh—
The church so lone, the log-built one,   10

[9] Factory workers.
[10] Site of battle and Union victory over
Confederate forces in northwestern Tennessee,
April 1862.

That echoed to many a parting groan
    And natural prayer
      Of dying foemen mingled there—
    Foemen at morn, but friends at eve—
      Fame or country least their care: 15
    (What like a bullet can undeceive!)
      But now they lie low,
    While over them the swallows skim,
      And all is hushed at Shiloh.

1866

---

from John Marr and Other Sailors

The Tuft of Kelp

All dripping in tangles green,
    Cast up by a lonely sea
If purer for that, O Weed,
    Bitterer, too, are 'ye?

1888

The Maldive Shark

About the Shark, phlegmatical one,
Pale sot of the Maldive sea,[1]
The sleek little pilot-fish, azure and slim,
How alert in attendance be.
From his saw-pit of mouth, from his charnel of maw   5
They have nothing of harm to dread,
But liquidly glide on his ghastly flank
Or before his Gorgonian[2] head;
Or lurk in the port of serrated teeth
In white triple tiers of glittering gates,   10
And there find a haven when peril's abroad,
An asylum in jaws of the Fates!

They are friends; and friendly they guide him to prey,
Yet never partake of the treat—
Eyes and brains to the dotard lethargic and dull,   15
Pale ravener of horrible meat.

1888

---

[1] Indian Ocean near the Maldive Islands, southwest of the southern end of India.

[2] Able to turn the beholder to stone, as the Gorgon's head did in Greek mythology.

from Timoleon, Etc.

After the Pleasure Party
Lines Traced Under an Image of Amor Threatening[1]

Fear me, virgin whosoever
Taking pride from love exempt,
Fear me, slighted. Never, never
Brave me, nor my fury tempt:
Downy wings, but wroth they beat
Tempest even in reason's seat.

Behind the house the upland falls
With many an odorous tree—
White marbles gleaming through green halls,
Terrace by terrace, down and down,
And meets the starlit Mediterranean Sea.   5

'Tis Paradise. In such an hour
Some pangs that rend might take release.
Nor less perturbed who keeps this bower
Of balm, nor finds balsamic peace?
From whom the passionate words in vent   10
After long revery's discontent?

Tired of the homeless deep,
Look how their flight yon hurrying billows urge,
Hitherward but to reap
Passive repulse from the iron-bound verge!   15
Insensate, can they never know
'Tis mad to wreck the impulsion so?

An art of memory is, they tell:
But to forget! forget the glade
Wherein Fate sprung Love's ambuscade,   20
To flout pale years of cloistral life
And flush me in this sensuous strife.
'Tis Vesta struck with Sappho's smart.[2]
No fable her delirious leap:
With more of cause in desperate heart,   25
Myself could take it—but to sleep!

Now first I feel, what all may ween,
That soon or late, if faded e'en,

---

[1] Amor, or Cupid, positioned with bow and arrow.
[2] Priestesses of Vesta, the Roman goddess of hearth and household, were required to be virgins. Here Melville imagines Vesta possessed by the sexual drives that preoccupied Sappho, the Greek woman lyric poet of the seventh century B.C.

One's sex asserts itself. Desire,
The dear desire through love to sway,   30
Is like the Geysers that aspire—
Through cold obstruction win their fervid way.
But baffled here—to take disdain,
To feel rule's instinct, yet not reign;
To dote, to come to this drear shame—   35
Hence the winged blaze that sweeps my soul
Like prairie fires that spurn control,
Where withering weeds incense the flame.

    And kept I long heaven's watch for this,
Contemning love, for this, even this?   40
O terrace chill in Northern air,
O reaching ranging tube I placed
Against yon skies, and fable chased
Till, fool, I hailed for sister there
Starred Cassiopea in Golden Chair.[3]   45
In dream I throned me, nor I saw
In cell the idiot crowned with straw.

    And yet, ah yet scarce ill I reigned,
Through self-illusion self-sustained,
When now—enlightened, undeceived—   50
What gain I barrenly bereaved!
Than this can be yet lower decline—
Envy and spleen, can these be mine?

    The pleasant girl demure that trod
Beside our wheels that climbed the way,   55
And bore along a blossoming rod
That looked the sceptre of May-Day—
On her—to fire this petty hell,
His softened glance how moistly fell!
The cheat! on briars her buds were strung;   60
And wiles peeped forth from mien how meek.
The innocent bare-foot! young, so young!
To girls, strong man's a novice weak.
To tell such beads! And more remain,
Sad rosary of belittling pain.   65

    When after lunch and sallies gay,
Like the Decameron folk[4] we lay
In sylvan groups; and I—let be!

---

[3] The constellation Cassiopeia is a queen seated in a golden chair or throne.
[4] In *The Decameron,* by the Italian Giovanni Boccaccio (1313–1375), characters amuse one another by telling stories.

O, dreams he, can he dream that one
Because not roseate feels no sun? 70
The plain lone bramble thrills with Spring
As much as vines that grapes shall bring.

Me now fair studies charm no more.
Shall great thoughts writ, or high themes sung
Damask wan cheeks—unlock his arm 75
About some radiant ninny flung?
How glad with all my starry lore,
I'd buy the veriest wanton's rose
Would but my bee therein repose.

Could I remake me! or set free 80
This sexless bound in sex, then plunge
Deeper than Sappho, in a lunge
Piercing Pan's[5] paramount mystery!
For, Nature, in no shallow surge
Against thee either sex may urge, 85
Why hast thou made us but in halves—
Co-relatives?[6] This makes us slaves.
If these co-relatives never meet
Self-hood itself seems incomplete
And such the dicing of blind fate 90
Few matching halves here meet and mate.
What Cosmic jest or Anarch blunder
The human integral clove asunder
And shied the fractions through life's gate?

Ye stars that long your votary knew 95
Rapt in her vigil, see me here!
Whither is gone the spell ye threw
When rose before me Cassiopea?
Usurped on by love's stronger reign—
But lo, your very selves do wane: 100
Light breaks—truth breaks! Silvered no more,
But chilled by dawn that brings the gale
Shivers yon bramble above the vale,
And disillusion opens all the shore.

One knows not if Urania[7] yet 105
The pleasure-party may forget;
Or whether she lived down the strain

---

[5] Pan: in Greek myth, the half-man, half-goat
who is god of woods, fields, and flocks.
[6] Plato's *Symposium* contains the legend that man
was once split in two and ever after has sought
reunification through sex.

[7] In Greek myth, the muse of astronomy. Here,
the modern woman.

Of turbulent heart and rebel brain;
For Amor so resents a slight,
And her's had been such haught disdain,   110
He long may wreak his boyish spite,
And boy-like, little reck the pain.

One knows not, no. But late in Rome
(For queens discrowned a congruous home)
Entering Albani's[8] porch she stood   115
Fixed by an antique pagan stone
Colossal carved. No anchorite seer,
Not Thomas a Kempis,[9] monk austere,
Religious more are in their tone;
Yet far, how far from Christian heart   120
That form august of heathen Art.
Swayed by its influence, long she stood,
Till surged emotion seething down,
She rallied and this mood she won:

Languid in frame for me,   125
To-day by Mary's convent shrine,
Touched by her picture's moving plea
In that poor nerveless hour of mine,
I mused—A wanderer still must grieve.
Half I resolved to kneel and believe,   130
Believe and submit, the veil take on.
But thee, armed Virgin![10] less benign,
Thee now I invoke, thou mightier one.
Helmeted woman—if such term
Befit thee, far from strife   135
Of that which makes the sexual feud
And clogs the aspirant life—
O self-reliant, strong and free,
Thou in whom power and peace unite,
Transcender! raise me up to thee,   140
Raise me and arm me!

Fond appeal.
For never passion peace shall bring,
Nor Art inanimate for long
Inspire. Nothing may help or heal   145
While Amor incensed remembers wrong.
Vindictive, not himself he'll spare;
For scope to give his vengeance play
Himself he'll blaspheme and betray.

---

[8] Melville visited the Villa Albani in 1857.   [10] I.e., Athena, Greek goddess of wisdom.
[9] German theologian (1380–1471).

Then for Urania, virgins everywhere,   150
O pray! Example take too, and have care.
1891

Monody[11]

To have known him, to have loved him
    After loneness long;
And then to be estranged in life,
    And neither in the wrong;
And now for death to set his seal—   5
    Ease me, a little ease, my song!

By wintry hills his hermit-mound
    The sheeted snow-drifts drape,
And houseless there the snow-bird flits
    Beneath the fir-trees' crape: 10
Glazed now with ice the cloistral vine
    That hid the shyest grape.
1891

Art

In placid hours well-pleased we dream
Of many a brave unbodied scheme.
But form to lend, pulsed life create,
What unlike things must meet and mate:
A flame to melt—a wind to freeze;   5
Sad patience—joyous energies;
Humility—yet pride and scorn;
Instinct and study; love and hate;
Audacity—reverence. These must mate,
And fuse with Jacob's[12] mystic heart,   10
To wrestle with the angel—Art.
1891

Greek Architecture

Not magnitude, not lavishness,
But Form—the Site;
Not innovating wilfulness,
But reverence for the Archetype.
1891

---

[11] Ode, elegy, or dirge sung by one voice.
"Monody" is thought to be a lament for
Melville's fellow writer, Nathaniel Hawthorne.

[12] According to Genesis 32:24–30, Jacob wrestled
with an angel.

Richard Henry Dana, Jr.
1815–1882

Years after completing a voyage as a young man of nineteen on a sailing ship around the Cape to the Pacific shores of Spanish California, Richard Henry Dana commented, "My great success—my book—was a boy's book." In one sense, everything this active Massachusetts lawyer and politician accomplished after that voyage was an anticlimax to the months he spent in 1834 "before the mast," serving as a common seaman abroad the *Pilgrim*.

The son of a prominent New England family, Dana was born in Cambridge, Massachusetts. He entered Harvard in 1831, but he was afflicted while an undergraduate with a severe case of measles that left his eyesight seriously impaired. To regain his health, he left college in 1834 and signed on a ship bound for California to take on a cargo of hides for the New England shoe trade. Dana's experiences resulted in *Two Years Before the Mast,* published to wide public acclaim in 1840. Maritime literature held great interest for readers in those final days of long sailing voyages and splendid ships, an enthusiasm also reflected in the popular sea narratives of James Fenimore Cooper and Herman Melville.

Dana gained particular attention for the realism with which he evoked both life on board ship and in the Spanish colony of California in the days before the American seizure of the territory and the Gold Rush. But equal to the impact of the book on his readers was the effect of his experiences on his own mind. Reared according to upper-class conventions and biases, Dana found himself appalled by the harsh treatment sailors often suffered under the unchecked authority of the ships' captains. The sympathy he felt for his comrades at sea led him to write an article on cruelty to seamen for the *American Jurist* in 1839 and *The Seaman's Friend* in 1841. Both were intended to arouse public indignation over the ordinary seaman's lack of legal rights.

Dana reentered Harvard upon his return to New England in 1836 and went on to graduate first in his class. He took up the study of law and was admitted to the bar in 1840, the same year his "boy's work" was published. His professional life was long and busy, but also frustrating. Although he was active in forming the Free Soil Party (which eventually became the liberal Republican Party), Dana never received official recognition as a political force. He served as attorney for slaves held under the Fugitive Slave Law and acted as United States Attorney for Massachusetts during the Civil War. But Dana failed to win a Congressional race in 1868 or to get his appointment as minister to England approved by the Senate in 1876.

Dana's happiest times as an adult were during his extensive travels, including two trips around the world, in 1859 and 1860. He died in Rome in 1882 before he was able to complete his definitive study of international law. The details of Dana's distinguished but somewhat abortive professional career are overlooked in the light of the single book for which he is rightly famous. He is best remembered for the keen, dense vivacity of spirit with which, as a young man of nineteen, he responded to his adventures on sea and shore.

Further Reading:
C. Adams, *Richard Henry Dana: A Biography*, 1890.
B. Perry, *Richard Henry Dana, 1851–1931*, 1933.
S. Shapiro, *Richard Henry Dana, Jr., 1815–1882*, 1961.
R. Gale, *Richard Henry Dana, Jr.*, 1969.

Text:
Two Years Before the Mast, 1840.

from Two Years Before the Mast

Chapter XVIII[1]

The next Sunday was Easter Sunday, and as there had been no liberty at San Pedro, it was our turn to go ashore and misspend another Sabbath. Soon after breakfast, a large boat, filled with men in blue jackets, scarlet caps, and various colored under-clothes, bound ashore on liberty, left the Italian ship, and passed under our stern; the men singing beautiful Italian boat-songs, all the way, in fine, full chorus. Among the songs I recognized the favorite "O Pescator dell' onda."[2] It brought back to my mind piano-fortes, drawing-rooms, young ladies singing, and a thousand other things which as little befitted me, in my situation, to be thinking upon. Supposing that the whole day would be too long a time to spend ashore, as there was no place to which we could take a ride, we remained quietly on board until after dinner. We were then pulled ashore in the stern of the boat, and, with orders to be on the beach at sun-down, we took our way for the town. There, everything wore the appearance of a holyday. The people were all dressed in their best; the men riding about on horseback among the houses, and the women sitting on carpets before the doors. Under the piazza of a "pulperia,"[3] two men were seated, decked out with knots of ribands and bouquets, and playing the violin and the Spanish guitar. These are the only instruments, with the exception of the drums and trumpets at Monterey, that I ever heard in California; and I suspect they play upon no others, for at a great *fandango*[4] at which I was afterwards present, and where they mustered all the music they could find, there were three violins and two guitars, and no other instruments. As it was now too near the middle of the day to see any dancing, and hearing that a bull was expected down from the country, to be baited in the presidio square, in the course of an hour or two, we took a stroll among the houses. Inquiring for an American who, we had been told, had married in the place, and kept a shop, we were directed to a long, low building, at the end of which was a door, with a sign over it, in Spanish. Entering the shop, we found no one in it, and the whole had an empty, deserted appearance. In a few minutes the man made his appearance, and apologized for having nothing to entertain us with, saying that he had had a fandango at his house the night before, and the people had eaten and drunk up everything.

---

[1] Dana and his crew have gone ashore along the southern coast of California, then under the rule of the Spanish crown.
[2] Italian: "O fisherman of the wave."
[3] Spanish: "store for provisions."
[4] Animated Spanish dance characterized by variations in rhythm.

"Oh yes!" said I, "Easter holydays!"

"No!" said he, with a singular expression to his face; "I had a little daughter die the other day, and that's the custom of the country."

Here I felt a little strangely, not knowing what to say, or whether to offer consolation or no, and was beginning to retire, when he opened a side door and told us to walk in. Here I was no less astonished; for I found a large room, filled with young girls, from three or four years of age up to fifteen and sixteen, dressed all in white, with wreaths of flowers on their heads, and bouquets in their hands. Following our conductor through all these girls, who were playing about in high spirits, we came to a table, at the end of the room, covered with a white cloth, on which lay a coffin, about three feet long, with the body of his child. The coffin was lined on the outside with white cloth, and on the inside with white satin, and was strewed with flowers. Through an open door we saw, in another room, a few elderly people in common dresses; while the benches and tables thrown up in a corner, and the stained walls, gave evident signs of the last night's "high go." Feeling, like Garrick,[5] between tragedy and comedy, an uncertainty of purpose and a little awkwardness, I asked the man when the funeral would take place, and being told that it would move toward the mission in about an hour, took my leave.

To pass away the time, we took horses and rode down to the beach, and there found three or four Italian sailors, mounted, and riding up and down, on the hard sand, at a furious rate. We joined them, and found it fine sport. The beach gave us a stretch of a mile or more, and the horses flew over the smooth, hard sand, apparently invigorated and excited by the salt sea-breeze, and by the continual roar and dashing of the breakers. From the beach we returned to the town, and finding that the funeral procession had moved, rode on and overtook it, about half way to the mission. Here was as peculiar a sight as we had seen before in the house; the one looking as much like a funeral procession as the other did like a house of mourning. The little coffin was borne by eight girls, who were continually relieved by others, running forward from the procession and taking their places. Behind it came a straggling company of girls, dressed as before, in white and flowers, and including, I should suppose by their numbers, nearly all the girls between five and fifteen in the place. They played along on the way, frequently stopping and running all together to talk to some one, or to pick up a flower, and then running on again to overtake the coffin. There were a few elderly women in common colors; and a herd of young men and boys, some on foot and others mounted, followed them, or walked or rode by their side, frequently interrupting them by jokes and questions. But the most singular thing of all was, that two men walked, one on each side of the coffin, carrying muskets in their hands, which they continually loaded, and fired into the air. Whether this was to keep off the evil spirits or not, I do not know. It was the only interpretation that I could put upon it.

As we drew near the mission, we saw the great gate thrown open, and the padre standing on the steps, with a crucifix in hand. The mission is a large and deserted-looking place, the out-buildings going to ruin, and everything giving one the impression of decayed grandeur. A large stone fountain threw out pure water, from four

[5] David Garrick (1717–1779), versatile English actor who played both comic and tragic roles.

mouths, into a basin, before the church door; and we were on the point of riding up to let our horses drink, when it occurred to us that it might be consecrated, and we forbore. Just at this moment, the bells set up their harsh, discordant clang; and the procession moved into the court. I was anxious to follow, and see the ceremony, but the horse of one of my companions had become frightened, and was tearing off toward the town; and having thrown his rider, and got one of his feet caught in the saddle, which had slipped, was fast dragging and ripping it to pieces. Knowing that my shipmate could not speak a word of Spanish, and fearing that he would get into difficulty, I was obliged to leave the ceremony and ride after him. I soon overtook him, trudging along, swearing at the horse, and carrying the remains of the saddle, which he had picked up on the road. Going to the owner of the horse, we made a settlement with him, and found him surprisingly liberal. All parts of the saddle were brought back, and being capable of repair, he was satisfied with six *reals*.[6] We thought it would have been a few dollars. We pointed to the horse, which was now halfway up one of the mountains; but he shook his head, saying, "No importe!"[7] and giving us to understand that he had plenty more.

Having returned to the town, we saw a great crowd collected in the square before the principal pulperia, and riding up, found that all these people—men, women, and children—had been drawn together by a couple of bantam cocks. The cocks were in full tilt, springing into one another, and the people were as eager, laughing and shouting, as though the combatants had been men. There had been a disappointment about the bull; he had broken his bail, and taken himself off, and it was too late to get another; so the people were obliged to put up with a cock-fight. One of the bantams having been knocked in the head, and had an eye put out, he gave in, and two monstrous prize-cocks were brought on. These were the object of the whole affair; the two bantams having been merely served up as a first course, to collect the people together. Two fellows came into the ring holding the cocks in their arms, and stroking them, and running about on all fours, encouraging and setting them on. Bets ran high, and, like most other contests, it remained for some time undecided. They both showed great pluck, and fought probably better and longer than their masters would. Whether, in the end, it was the white or the red that beat, I do not recollect; but whichever it was, he strutted off with the true veni-vidi-vici look, leaving the other lying panting on his beam-ends.

This matter having been settled, we heard some talk about *"caballos"* and *"carréra,"*[8] and seeing the people all streaming off in one direction, we followed, and came upon a level piece of ground, just out of the town, which was used as a race-course. Here the crowd soon became thick again, the ground was marked off; the judges stationed; and the horses led up to one end. Two fine-looking old gentle-men—Don Carlos and Don Domingo, so called—held the stakes, and all was now ready. We waited some time, during which we could just see the horses twisting round and turning, until, at length, there was a shout along the lines, and on they came—heads stretched out and eyes starting;—working all over, both man and beast. The steeds came by us like a couple of chain-shot—neck and neck; and now we could see nothing but their backs, and their hind hoofs flying in the air. As fast

---

[6] Spanish coins.
[7] Spanish: "No matter!"

[8] Spanish: "horses" and "race."

as the horses passed, the crowd broke up behind them, and ran to the goal. When we got there, we found the horses returning on a slow walk, having run far beyond the mark, and heard that the long, bony one had come in head and shoulders before the other. The riders were light-built men; had handkerchiefs tied round their heads; and were bare-armed and bare-legged. The horses were noble-looking beasts, not so sleek and combed as our Boston stable horses, but with fine limbs and spirited eyes. After this had been settled, and fully talked over, the crowd scattered again and flocked back to the town.

Returning to the large pulperia, we found the violin and guitar screaming and twanging away under the piazza, where they had been all day. As it was now sun-down, there began to be some dancing. The Italian sailors danced, and one of our crew exhibited himself in a sort of West India shuffle, much to the amusement of the bystanders, who cried out, "Bravo!" "Otra vez!"[9] and "Vivan los marineros!" but the dancing did not become general, as the women and the "gente de razón"[10] had not yet made their appearance. We wished very much to stay and see the style of dancing; but, although we had had our own way during the day, yet we were, after all, but 'foremost Jacks;'[11] and having been ordered to be on the beach by sun-down, did not venture to be more than an hour behind the time; so we took our way down. We found the boat just pulling ashore through the breakers, which were running high, there having been a heavy fog outside, which, from some cause or other, always brings on or precedes a heavy sea. Liberty-men are privileged from the time they leave the vessel until they step on board again; so we took our places in the stern sheets, and were congratulating ourselves upon getting off dry, when a great comber[12] broke fore and aft the boat, and wet us through and through, filling the boat half full of water. Having lost her buoyancy by the weight of the water, she dropped heavily into every sea that struck her, and by the time we had pulled out of the surf into deep water, she was but just afloat, and we were up to our knees. By the help of a small bucket and our hats, we bailed her out, got on board, hoisted the boats, ate our supper, changed our clothes, gave (as is usual) the whole history of our day's adventures to those who had staid on board, and having taken a night-smoke, turned-in. Thus ended our second day's liberty on shore.

On Monday morning, as an offset to our day's sport, we were all set to work "tarring down" the rigging. Some got girt-lines up for riding down the stays and back-stays, and others tarred the shrouds, lifts, etc., laying out on the yards, and coming down the rigging. We overhauled our bags and took out our old tarry trowsers and frocks, which we had used when we tarred down before, and were all at work in the rigging by sun-rise. After breakfast, we had the satisfaction of seeing the Italian ship's boat go ashore, filled with men, gaily dressed, as on the day before, and singing their barcarollas. The Easter holydays are kept up on shore during three days; and being a Catholic vessel, the crew had the advantage of them. For two successive days, while perched up in the rigging, covered with tar and engaged in our disagreeable work, we saw these fellows going ashore in the morning, and coming off again at night, in high spirits. So much for being Protestants. There's no danger of Catholicism's spreading in New England; Yankees can't afford the time to be Catholics. American shipmasters get nearly three weeks more labor out of their crews,

---

[9] Spanish: "Again!" and "Long live the seamen."
[10] Spanish: "educated folk."
[11] Simple seamen.
[12] Ocean breaker.

in the course of a year, than the masters of vessels from Catholic countries. Yankees don't keep Christmas, and ship-masters at sea never know when Thanksgiving comes, so Jack has no festival at all.

About noon, a man aloft called out "Sail ho!" and looking round, we saw the head sails of a vessel coming round the point. As she drew round, she showed the broadside of a full-rigged brig, with the Yankee ensign at her peak. We ran up our stars and stripes, and knowing that there was no American brig on the coast but ourselves, expected to have news from home. She rounded-to and let go her anchor, but the dark faces on her yards, when they furled the sails, and the Babel[13] on deck, soon made known that she was from the Islands. Immediately afterwards, a boat's crew came aboard, bringing her skipper, and from them we learned that she was from Oahu, and was engaged in the same trade with the *Ayacucho, Loriotte,* etc., between the coast, the Sandwich Islands,[14] and the leeward coast of Peru and Chili. Her captain and officers were Americans, and also a part of her crew; the rest were Islanders. She was called the *Catalina,* and, like all the other vessels in that trade, except the *Ayacucho,* her papers and colors were from Uncle Sam. They, of course, brought us no news, and we were doubly disappointed, for we had thought, at first, it might be the ship which we were expecting from Boston.

After lying here about a fortnight, and collecting all the hides the place afforded, we set sail again for San Pedro. There we found the brig which we had assisted in getting off, lying at anchor, with a mixed crew of Americans, English, Sandwich Islanders, Spaniards, and Spanish Indians; and though much smaller than we, yet she had three times the number of men; and she needed them, for her officers were Californians. No vessels in the world go so poorly manned as American and English; and none do so well. A Yankee brig of that size would have had a crew of four men, and would have worked round and round her. The Italian ship had a crew of thirty men; nearly three times as many as the *Alert,* which was afterwards on the coast, and was of the same size; yet the *Alert* would get under weigh and come-to in half the time, and get two anchors, while they were all talking at once—jabbering like a parcel of "Yahoos," and running about decks to find their cat-block.

There was only one point in which they had the advantage over us, and that was in lightening their labors in the boats by their songs. The Americans are a time and money saving people, but have not yet, as a nation, learned that music may be "turned to account." We pulled the long distances to and from the shore, with our loaded boats, without a word spoken, and with discontented looks, while they not only lightened the labor of rowing, but actually made it pleasant and cheerful, by their music. So true is it, that—

> "For the tired slave, song lifts the languid oar,
>   And bids it aptly fall, with chime
> That beautifies the fairest shore,
>   And mitigates the harshest clime."[15]

---

[13] I.e., mixture of many languages. The allusion here is to the biblical story of Babel, the city whose residents God caused to speak in a confusing variety of tongues because of their vainglorious attempt to erect a tower up to heaven.

[14] Former name of the Hawaiian islands.

[15] From "On the Power of Sound" by the English poet William Wordsworth (1770–1850).

We lay about a week in San Pedro, and got under weigh for San Diego, intending to stop at San Juan, as the southeaster season was nearly over, and there was little or no danger.

This being the spring season, San Pedro, as well as all the other open ports upon the coast, was filled with whales, that had come in to make their annual visit upon soundings. For the first few days that we were here and at Santa Barbara, we watched them with great interest—calling out "there she blows!" every time we saw the spout of one breaking the surface of the water; but they soon became so common that we took little notice of them. They often "broke" very near us, and one thick, foggy night, during a dead calm, while I was standing anchor-watch, one of them rose so near, that he struck our cable, and made all surge again. He did not seem to like the encounter much himself, for he sheered off, and spouted at a good distance. We once came very near running one down in the gig, and should probably have been knocked to pieces and blown sky-high. We had been on board the little Spanish brig, and were returning, stretching out well at our oars, the little boat going like a swallow; our backs were forward (as is always the case in pulling), and the captain, who was steering, was not looking ahead, when, all at once, we heard the spout of a whale directly ahead. "Back water! back water, for your lives!" shouted the captain; and we backed our blades in the water and brought the boat to in a smother of foam. Turning our heads, we saw a great, rough, hump-backed whale, slowly crossing our fore foot, within three or four yards of the boat's stem. Had we not backed water just as we did, we should inevitably have gone smash upon him, striking him with our stem just about amidships. He took no notice of us, but passed slowly on, and dived a few yards beyond us, throwing his tail high in the air. He was so near that we had a perfect view of him, and, as may be supposed, had no desire to see him nearer. He was a disgusting creature; with a skin rough, hairy, and of an iron-grey color. This kind differs much from the sperm, in color and skin, and is said to be fiercer. We saw a few sperm whales; but most of the whales that come upon the coast are fin-backs, hump-backs, and right-whales, which are more difficult to take, and are said not to give oil enough to pay for the trouble. For this reason, whale-ships do not come upon the coast after them. Our captain, together with Captain Nye of the *Loriotte,* who had been in a whale-ship, thought of making an attempt upon one of them with two boats' crews, but as we had only two harpoons and no proper lines, they gave it up.

During the months of March, April, and May, these whales appear in great numbers in the open ports of Santa Barbara, San Pedro, etc., and hover off the coast, while a few find their way into the close harbors of San Diego and Monterey. They are all off again before midsummer, and make their appearance on the "off-shore ground." We saw some fine "schools" of sperm whales, which are easily distinguished by their spout, blowing away, a few miles to windward, on our passage to San Juan.

Coasting along on the quiet shore of the Pacific, we came to anchor, in twenty fathoms' water, almost out at sea, as it were, and directly abreast of a steep hill which overhung the water, and was twice as high as our royal-mast-head. We had heard much of this place from the *Lagoda's* crew, who said it was the worst place in California. The shore is rocky, and directly exposed to the south-east, so that vessels are obliged to slip and run for their lives on the first sign of a gale; and late as it was in the season, we got up our slip-rope and gear, though we meant to stay only twenty-four hours. We pulled the agent ashore, and were ordered to wait for him, while he took a circuitous way round the hill to the mission, which was hidden behind it. We were glad of the opportunity to examine this singular place, and hauling the boat up and making her well fast, took different directions up and down the beach, to explore it.

San Juan is the only romantic spot in California. The country here for several miles is high table-land, running boldly to the shore, and breaking off in a steep hill, at the foot of which the waters of the Pacific are constantly dashing. For several miles the water washes the very base of the hill, or breaks upon ledges and fragments of rocks which run out into the sea. Just where we landed was a small cove, or "bight," which gave us, at high tide, a few square feet of sand-beach between the sea and the bottom of the hill. This was the only landing-place. Directly before us, rose the perpendicular height of four or five hundred feet. How we were to get hides down, or goods up, upon the table-land on which the mission was situated, was more than we could tell. The agent had taken a long circuit, and yet had frequently to jump over breaks, and climb up steep places, in the ascent. No animal but a man or a monkey could get up it. However, that was not our look-out; and knowing that the agent would be gone an hour or more, we strolled about, picking up shells, and following the sea where it tumbled in, roaring and spouting, among the crevices of the great rocks. What a sight, thought I, must this be in a south-easter! The rocks were as large as those of Nahant or Newport,[16] but, to my eye, more grand and broken. Beside, there was a grandeur in everything around, which gave almost a solemnity to the scene: a silence and solitariness which affected everything! Not a human being but ourselves for miles; and no sound heard but the pulsations of the great Pacific! and the great steep hill rising like a wall, and cutting us off from all the world, but the "world of waters!" I separated myself from the rest, and sat down on a rock, just where the sea ran in and formed a fine spouting horn. Compared with the plain, dull sand-beach of the rest of the coast, this grandeur was as refreshing as a great rock in a weary land. It was almost the first time that I had been positively alone—free from the sense that human beings were at my elbow, if not talking with me—since I had left home. My better nature returned strong upon me. Everything was in accordance with my state of feeling, and I experienced a glow of pleasure at finding that what of poetry and romance I ever had in me, had not been entirely deadened by the laborious and frittering life I had led. Nearly an hour did I sit, almost lost in the luxury of this entire new scene of the play in which I had been so long acting, when I was aroused by the distant shouts of my companions, and saw that they were collecting together, as the agent had made his appearance, on his way back to our boat.

We pulled aboard, and found the long-boat hoisted out, and nearly laden with goods; and after dinner, we all went on shore in the quarter-boat, with the long-boat in tow. As we drew in, we found an ox-cart and a couple of men standing directly on the brow of the hill; and having landed, the captain took his way round the hill, ordering me and one other to follow him. We followed, picking our way out, and jumping and scrambling up, walking over briers and prickly pears, until we came to

[16] Nahant, Massachusetts, and Newport, Rhode Island, were seaports "back home" in the States.

the top. Here the country stretched out for miles, as far as the eye could reach, on a level, table surface; and the only habitation in sight was the small white mission of San Juan Campestrano, with a few Indian huts about it, standing in a small hollow, about a mile from where we were. Reaching the brow of the hill where the cart stood, we found several piles of hides, and Indians sitting round them. One or two other carts were coming slowly on from the mission, and the captain told us to begin and throw the hides down. This, then, was the way they were to be got down: thrown down, one at a time, a distance of four hundred feet! This was doing the business on a great scale. Standing on the edge of the hill and looking down the perpendicular height, the sailors,

> —"That walked upon the beach,
> Appeared like mice; and *our* tall anchoring bark
> Diminished to her cock; her cock a buoy
> Almost too small for sight."[17]

Down this height we pitched the hides, throwing them as far out into the air as we could; and as they were all large, stiff, and doubled, like the cover of a book, the wind took them, and they swayed and eddied about, plunging and rising in the air, like a kite when it has broken its string. As it was now low tide, there was no danger of their falling into the water, and as fast as they came to ground, the men below picked them up, and taking them on their heads, walked off with them to the boat. It was really a picturesque sight: the great height; the scaling of the hides; and the continual walking to and fro of the men, who looked like mites, on the beach! This was the romance of high-droghing![18]

Some of the hides lodged in cavities which were under the bank and out of our sight, being directly under us; but by sending others down in the same direction, we succeeded in dislodging them. Had they remained there, the captain said he should have sent on board for a couple of pair of long halyards, and got some one to have gone down for them. It was said that one of the crew of an English brig went down in the same way, a few years before. We looked over, and thought it would not be a welcome task, especially for a few paltry hides; but no one knows what he can do until he is called upon; for, six months afterwards, I went down the same place by a pair of top-gallant studding-sail halyards, to save a half a dozen hides which had lodged there.

Having thrown them all down, we took our way back again, and found the boat loaded and ready to start. We pulled off; took the hides all aboard; hoisted in the boats; hove up our anchor; made sail; and before sun-down, were on our way to San Diego.

Friday, May 8th, 1835. Arrived at San Diego. Here we found the little harbor deserted. The *Lagoda, Ayacucho, Loriotte,* and all, had left the coast, and we were nearly alone. All the hide-houses on the beach, but ours, were shut up, and the Sandwich Islanders, a dozen or twenty in number, who had worked for the other vessels and been paid off when they sailed, were living on the beach, keeping up a grand carnival.

[17] Adapted from Shakespeare's tragedy *King Lear,*   [18] The carrying of cargo onto small coastal vessels.
Act IV, Sc. vi, ll. 17–20.

A Russian discovery-ship, which had been in this port a few years before, had built a large oven for baking bread, and went away, leaving it standing. This, the Sandwich Islanders took possession of, and had kept, ever since, undisturbed. It was big enough to hold six or eight men—that is, it was as large as a ship's forecastle; had a door at the side, and a vent-hole at top. They covered it with Oahu mats, for a carpet; stopped up the vent-hole in bad weather, and made it their headquarters. It was now inhabited by as many as a dozen or twenty men, who lived there in complete idleness—drinking, playing cards, and carousing in every way. They bought a bullock once a week, which kept them in meat, and one of them went up to the town every day to get fruit, liquor, and provisions. Besides this, they had bought a cask of ship-bread, and a barrel of flour from the *Lagoda,* before she sailed. There they lived, having a grand time, and caring for nobody. Captain T—— was anxious to get three or four of them to come on board the *Pilgrim,* as we were so much diminished in numbers; and went up to the oven, and spent an hour or two trying to negotiate with them. One of them,—a finely built, active, strong and intelligent fellow,—who was a sort of king among them, acted as spokesman. He was called Mannini,—or rather, out of compliment to his known importance and influence, *Mr.* Mannini,—and was known all over California. Through him, the captain offered them fifteen dollars a month, and one month's pay in advance; but it was like throwing pearls before swine, or, rather, carrying coals to Newcastle. So long as they had money, they would not work for fifty dollars a month, and when their money was gone, they would work for ten.

"What do you do here, Mr. Mannini?"[19] said the captain.

"Oh, we play cards, get drunk, smoke—do anything we're a mind to."

"Don't you want to come aboard and work?"

"*Aole! aole make make makou i ka hana.* Now, got plenty money; no good, work. *Mamule,* money *pau*—all gone. Ah! very good, work!—*maikai, hana hana nui!*"

"But you'll spend all your money in this way," said the captain.

"Aye! me know that. By-'em-by money *pau*—all gone; then Kanaka[20] work plenty."

This was a hopeless case, and the captain left them, to wait patiently until their money was gone.

We discharged our hides and tallow, and in about a week were ready to set sail again for the windward. We unmoored, and got everything ready, when the captain made another attempt upon the oven. This time he had more regard to the "mollia tempora fandi,"[21] and succeeded very well. He got Mr. Mannini in his interest, and as the shot was getting low in the locker, prevailed upon him and three others to come on board with their chests and baggage, and sent a hasty summons to me and the boy to come ashore with our things, and join the gang at the hide-house. This was unexpected to me; but anything in the way of variety I liked; so we got ready, and were pulled ashore. I stood on the beach while the brig got under weigh, and watched her until she rounded the point, and then went up to the hide-house to take up my quarters for a few months.

1840

---

[19] Dana's note: "The letter *i* in the Sandwich Island language is sounded like *e* in the English."

[20] The name natives of Hawaii applied to themselves and others from the South Seas, as distinguished from the term given to whites: "Haole."

[21] Italian: "favorable occasions for speaking."

Henry Wadsworth Longfellow
1807–1882

Henry Wadsworth Longfellow belonged to the "New England triumvirate" of ruling poets, which included James Russell Lowell and John Greenleaf Whittier. Their works graced the Victorian parlors and the rude outland cabins of western frontier America. Longfellow proved that the poetry of an American could be hailed on both sides of the Atlantic: He was awarded an honorary doctoral degree by Oxford and Cambridge universities and honored with a bust in the Poets' Corner of Westminster Abbey. Longfellow symbolized the respectability, culture, and learning that signified a mature America. In the Revolutionary era John Adams had predicted that it would take three generations before citizens of the new nation could "give their children a right to study . . . Poetry." Longfellow's success meant that the time had come.

Longfellow was born in Portland, Maine, at the time a part of Massachusetts. His parents traced their ancestry to the *Mayflower.* Henry was a sports-minded boy who grew up with access to his father's library, which contained the works of Shakespeare, Milton, Pope, and classical authors. At the age of thirteen he saw his own verse published in the *Portland Gazette,* and in the following year he was admitted to Bowdoin College, though he waited another year before beginning his studies there. A classmate remembers Henry as "genial, sociable, and agreeable," "free from envy and every corroding passion and vice," and "always a gentleman in his deportment." Fortunately Longfellow, a classmate of Nathaniel Hawthorne, found a faculty mentor who guided his work in language and literature. He continued to write poems, placing some in reputable Boston and Philadelphia periodicals.

Opposed to his father's proposal that he study law, Henry argued for a career in publishing after graduate study in languages at Harvard, quoting the saying that "as many languages as a person acquires, so many times is he a man." In a happy convergence of circumstances, the young man had the opportunity to hold college positions in the then-new field of modern foreign languages, first at Bowdoin and then at Harvard, where he became a professor in 1836. Both colleges sent Longfellow abroad for intense study of languages. From 1826 to 1829 and again from 1835 to 1836 he sojourned in Europe, making the acquaintance of scholars and poets and acquiring habits of dress that made him a dandified figure back in America. In 1831 he married a Portland girl, Mary Storer Potter, who died just four years later. Longfellow referred obliquely to her death as "sorrow, and a care that almost killed."

Professor Longfellow taught responsibly but without great enthusiasm. He confided to his journal, "Perhaps the worst thing in a College Life is this having your mind constantly a play-mate for boys." He finally resigned from teaching in 1854. By then he had earned a considerable reputation for such poems as "Psalm of Life," which Whittier called the "moral enginery of an age of action." His first book of poems, *Voices of the Night* (1839), had sold an impressive 43,000 copies, and he later published *Ballads and Other Poems* (1841) and *Poems on Slavery* (1842). Longfellow had also remarried. Frances Appleton was the daughter of one of Boston's wealthiest merchants, whose wedding gift was Craigie House, once General Washington's headquarters and now a literary landmark. In 1861 Frances Appleton Longfellow, the mother of four children, died in a house fire. "The Cross of Snow," one of Longfellow's most moving poems, was occasioned by her death and was found among the poet's personal effects after his own death.

Longfellow's genius lay in the expression of American values and yearnings. He mixed moral statement with hymns to the work ethic, family relationships, and nature. In a nation still primitive in material conditions he sought to "clothe the real with the ideal and make actual and common things radiant with poetic beauty."

In large part that clothing was a masterful prosody seldom equaled in American literature. Longfellow's metrics bear the closest scrutiny, and the variety of his verse forms, from ballad to sonnet, is astonishing. In an era that valued smoothly flowing rhythms, uplifting sentiment, and poetic statement close to the surface of each stanza, Longfellow's work became the standard against which poetry and poetic success were measured. In addition, in works like *Evangeline* (1847), *Hiawatha* (1855), and *The Courtship of Miles Standish* (1858), Longfellow gave Americans a poetry of "native materials." He also brought the long ago and far away to his nineteenth-century readers in such works as *The Belfry of Bruges and Other Poems* (1845) and *Tales of a Wayside Inn* (1863), modeled on *The Decameron,* a story collection of the Italian Renaissance poet Boccaccio. These works gratified Americans eager to believe in their nation's achievement in the fine arts, which many judged by European standards. Longfellow's work conferred the mantle of European legitimacy on America. The writer Henry James understood this, remarking that he found Longfellow engaging because his " 'European' culture and his native kept house together."

Further Reading:
S. Longfellow, *The Life of Henry Wadsworth Longfellow,* 3 vols., 1886.
L. Thompson, *Young Longfellow,* 1938.
N. Arvin, *Longfellow: His Life and Work,* 1963.
C. Williams, *Henry Wadsworth Longfellow,* 1964.
E. Wagenknecht, *Henry Wadsworth Longfellow: Portrait of an American Humanist,* 1966.

Text:
The Complete Poetical Works of Henry Wadsworth Longfellow, 1922.

A Psalm of Life

*What the Heart of the Young Man Said
to the Psalmist*

Tell me not, in mournful numbers,
　　Life is but an empty dream!—
For the soul is dead that slumbers,
　　And things are not what they seem.

Life is real! Life is earnest!   5
    And the grave is not its goal;
Dust thou art, to dust returnest,
    Was not spoken of the soul.

Not enjoyment, and not sorrow,
    Is our destined end or way;   10
But to act, that each to-morrow
    Find us farther than to-day.

Art is long, and Time is fleeting,
    And our hearts, though stout and brave,
Still, like muffled drums, are beating   15
    Funeral marches to the grave.

In the world's broad field of battle,
    In the bivouac of Life,
Be not like dumb, driven cattle!
    Be a hero in the strife!   20

Trust no Future, howe'er pleasant!
    Let the dead Past bury its dead!
Act,—act in the living Present!
    Heart within, and God o'erhead!

Lives of great men all remind us   25
    We can make our lives sublime,
And, departing, leave behind us
    Footprints on the sands of time;

Footprints, that perhaps another,
    Sailing o'er life's solemn main,   30
A forlorn and shipwrecked brother,
    Seeing, shall take heart again.

Let us, then, be up and doing,
    With a heart for any fate;
Still achieving, still pursuing,   35
    Learn to labor and to wait.
1838

The Arsenal at Springfield

This is the Arsenal. From floor to ceiling,
    Like a huge organ, rise the burnished arms;
But from their silent pipes no anthem pealing
    Startles the villages with strange alarms.

Ah! what a sound will rise, how wild and dreary,   5
    When the death-angel touches those swift keys!
What loud lament and dismal Miserere
    Will mingle with their awful symphonies!

I hear even now the infinite fierce chorus,
    The cries of agony, the endless groan,   10
Which, through the ages that have gone before us,
    In long reverberations reach our own.

On helm and harness rings the Saxon hammer,
    Through Cimbric forest roars the Norseman's song,
And loud, amid the universal clamor,   15
    O'er distant deserts sounds the Tartar gong.

I hear the Florentine, who from his palace
    Wheels out his battle-bell with dreadful din,
And Aztec priests upon their teocallis[1]
    Beat the wild war-drums made of serpent's skin;   20

The tumult of each sacked and burning village;
    The shout that every prayer for mercy drowns;
The soldiers' revels in the midst of pillage;
    The wail of famine in beleaguered towns;

The bursting shell, the gateway wrenched asunder,   25
    The rattling musketry, the clashing blade;
And ever and anon, in tones of thunder
    The diapason[2] of the cannonade.

Is it, O man, with such discordant noises,
    With such accursed instruments as these.   30
Thou drownest Nature's sweet and kindly voices,
    And jarrest the celestial harmonies?

---

[1] Low, terraced pyramid.
[2] Full tonal range.

Were half the power that fills the world with terror,
   Were half the wealth bestowed on camps and courts,
Given to redeem the human mind from error,   35
   There were no need of arsenals or forts:

The warrior's name would be a name abhorrèd!
   And every nation, that should lift again
Its hand against a brother, on its forehead
   Would wear forevermore the curse of Cain!   40

Down the dark future, through long generations,
   The echoing sounds grow fainter and then cease ;
And like a bell, with solemn, sweet vibrations,
   I hear once more the voice of Christ say, "Peace!"

Peace! and no longer from its brazen portals   45
   The blast of War's great organ shakes the skies!
But beautiful as songs of the immortals,
   The holy melodies of love arise.

1844

The Fire of Drift-wood

Devereux Farm near Marblehead

We sat within the farm-house old,
   Whose windows, looking o'er the bay,
Gave to the sea-breeze damp and cold
   An easy entrance, night and day.

Not far away we saw the port,   5
   The strange, old-fashioned, silent town,
The lighthouse, the dismantled fort,
   The wooden houses, quaint and brown.

We sat and talked until the night,
   Descending, filled the little room;   10
Our faces faded from the sight,
   Our voices only broke the gloom.

We spake of many a vanished scene,
   Of what we once had thought and said,
Of what had been, and might have been,   15
   And who was changed, and who was dead;

And all that fills the hearts of friends,
   When first they feel, with secret pain,
Their lives thenceforth have separate ends,
   And never can be one again;   20

The first slight swerving of the heart,
   That words are powerless to express,
And leave it still unsaid in part,
   Or say it in too great excess.

The very tones in which we spake   25
   Had something strange, I could but mark;
The leaves of memory seemed to make
   A mournful rustling in the dark.

Oft died the words upon our lips,
   As suddenly, from out the fire   30
Built of the wreck of stranded ships,
   The flames would leap and then expire.

And, as their splendor flashed and failed,
   We thought of wrecks upon the main,
Of ships dismasted, that were hailed   35
   And sent no answer back again.

The windows, rattling in their frames,
   The ocean, roaring up the beach,
The gusty blast, the bickering flames,
   All mingled vaguely in our speech;   40

Until they made themselves a part
   Of fancies floating through the brain,
The long-lost ventures of the heart,
   That send no answers back again.

O flames that glowed! O hearts that yearned!   45
They were indeed too much akin,
The drift-wood fire without that burned,
   The thoughts that burned and glowed within.

1849

The Jewish Cemetery at Newport

How strange it seems! These Hebrews in their graves,
    Close by the street of this fair seaport town,
Silent beside the never-silent waves,
    At rest in all this moving up and down!

The trees are white with dust, that o'er their sleep   5
    Wave their broad curtains in the south-wind's breath,
While underneath these leafy tents they keep
    The long, mysterious Exodus of Death.

And these sepulchral stones, so old and brown,
    That pave with level flags their burial-place,   10
Seem like the tablets of the Law, thrown down
    And broken by Moses at the mountain's base.

The very names recorded here are strange,
    Of foreign accent, and of different climes;
Alvares and Rivera interchange   15
    With Abraham and Jacob of old times.

"Blessed be God, for he created Death!"
The mourners said, "and Death is rest and peace";
Then added, in the certainty of faith,
"And giveth Life that nevermore shall cease."   20

Closed are the portals of their Synagogue,
    No Psalms of David now the silence break,
No Rabbi reads the ancient Decalogue[1]
    In the grand dialect the Prophets spake.

Gone are the living, but the dead remain,   25
    And not neglected; for a hand unseen,
Scattering its bounty, like a summer rain,
    Still keeps their graves and their remembrance green.

How came they here? What burst of Christian hate,
    What persecution, merciless and blind,   30
Drove o'er the sea—that desert desolate—
    These Ishmaels and Hagars of mankind?

---

[1] The Ten Commandments (see Exodus 20:1–17).

They lived in narrow streets and lanes obscure,
  Ghetto and Judenstrass, in mirk and mire;
Taught in the school of patience to endure   35
  The life of anguish and the death of fire.

All their lives long, with the unleavened bread
  And bitter herbs of exile and its fears,
The wasting famine of the heart they fed,
  And slaked its thirst with marah[2] of their tears.   40

Anathema maranatha![3] was the cry
  That rang from town to town, from street to street:
At every gate the accursed Mordecai[4]
  Was mocked and jeered, and spurned by Christian feet.

Pride and humiliation hand in hand   45
  Walked with them through the world where'er they went;
Trampled and beaten were they as the sand,
  And yet unshaken as the continent.

For in the background figures vague and vast
  Of patriarchs and of prophets rose sublime,   50
And all the great traditions of the Past
  They saw reflected in the coming time.

And thus forever with reverted look
  The mystic volume of the world they read,
Spelling it backward, like a Hebrew book,   55
  Till life became a Legend of the Dead.

But ah! what once has been shall be no more!
  The groaning earth in travail and in pain
Brings forth its races, but does not restore,
  And the dead nations never rise again.   60

1854

---

[2] Hebrew: "bitter."
[3] A vile curse of the early Christians applied to
the Jews.

[4] Foster father of Esther, wife of the Persian king
Xerxes.

Aftermath

When the summer fields are mown,
When the birds are fledged and flown,
   And the dry leaves strew the path:
With the falling of the snow,
With the cawing of the crow,   5
Once again the fields we mow
   And gather in the aftermath.

Not the sweet, new grass with flowers
Is this harvesting of ours;
   Not the upland clover bloom;   10
But the rowen mixed with weeds,
Tangled tufts from marsh and meads,
Where the poppy drops its seeds
   In the silence and the gloom.

1873

Chaucer

An old man in a lodge[1] within a park;
   The chamber walls depicted all around
   With portraitures of huntsman, hawk, and hound,
   And the hurt deer. He listeneth to the lark,
Whose song comes with the sunshine through the dark   5
   Of painted glass in leaden lattice bound;
   He listeneth and he laugheth at the sound,
   Then writeth in a book like any clerk.
He is the poet of the dawn, who wrote
   The Canterbury Tales, and his old age   10
   Made beautiful with song; and as I read
I hear the crowing cock, I hear the note
   Of lark and linnet, and from every page
   Rise odors of ploughed field or flowery mead.

1875

---

[1] I.e., a hunting lodge.

Milton

I pace the sounding sea-beach and behold
  How the voluminous billows roll and run.
  Upheaving and subsiding, while the sun
Shines through their sheeted emerald far unrolled,
And the ninth wave, slow gathering fold by fold   5
  All its loose-flowing garments into one,
  Plunges upon the shore, and floods the dun
Pale reach of sands, and changes them to gold.
So in majestic cadence rise and fall
  The mighty undulations of thy song,   10
  O sightless bard, England's Mæonides![1]
And ever and anon, high over all
  Uplifted, a ninth wave superb and strong,
  Floods all the soul with its melodious seas.

1875

Keats

The young Endymion sleeps Endymion's sleep;
  The shepherd-boy whose tale was left half told!
  The solemn grove uplifts its shield of gold
To the red rising moon, and loud and deep
The nightingale is singing from the steep;   5
  It is midsummer, but the air is cold;
  Can it be death? Alas, beside the fold
A shepherd's pipe lies shattered near his sheep.
Lo! in the moonlight gleams a marble white,
  On which I read: "Here lieth one whose name   10
  Was writ in water." And was this the meed
Of his sweet singing? Rather let me write:
  "The smoking flax before it burst to flame
  Was quenched by death, and broken the bruised reed."

1875

---

[1] Pseudonym for the Greek poet Homer.

Nature

As a fond mother, when the day is o'er,
   Leads by the hand her little child to bed,
   Half willing, half reluctant to be led,
   And leave his broken playthings on the floor,
Still gazing at them through the open door,   5
   Nor wholly reassured and comforted
   By promises of others in their stead,
   Which, though more splendid, may not please him more:
So Nature deals with us, and takes away
   Our playthings one by one, and by the hand   10
   Leads us to rest so gently, that we go
Scarce knowing if we wish to go or stay,
   Being too full of sleep to understand
   How far the unknown transcends the what we know.

1875

The Cross of Snow

In the long, sleepless watches of the night,
   A gentle face—the face of one long dead—
   Looks at me from the wall, where round its head
   The night-lamp casts a halo of pale light.
Here in this room she died; and soul more white   5
   Never through martyrdom of fire was led
   To its repose; nor can in books be read
   The legend of a life more benedight.[1]
There is a mountain in the distant West
   That, sun-defying, in its deep ravines   10
   Displays a cross of snow upon its side.
Such is the cross I wear upon my breast
   These eighteen years, through all the changing scenes
   And seasons, changeless since the day she died.

1886

---

[1] Blessed.

John Greenleaf Whittier
1807–1892

A century-old, hand-hewn oak cabin north of Boston, near the seacoast town of
Haverhill, Massachusetts, provided the unassuming setting for John Greenleaf
Whittier's birth in 1807. The son of devout and industrious Quaker farmers,
Whittier was limited by his daily chores and frail health to irregular attendance
at the local country school. There he was introduced to the works of Robert
Burns, which he described as "about the first poetry I had ever read" and which
"had a lasting influence upon me." Reflecting on the modest circumstances of his
childhood, Whittier noted somewhat wistfully, "I had at that time a great thirst
for knowledge and little means to gratify it. The beauty of outward nature early
impressed me, and the moral and spiritual beauty of the holy lives I read of in
the Bible and other books also affected me with a sense of my falling short and
longing for a better life." Whittier quickly discovered in poetry an appropriate
outlet for his idyllic vision of the American experience. His verse remains
preindustrial America's most ardent expression of such rustic values as simplicity,
independence, and moral certitude.

Whittier nourished his youthful "thirst for knowledge" both by reading the
"few books within my reach," most notably such staples of the Quaker tradition
as the Bible and Bunyan's *Pilgrim's Progress,* as well as by writing what he later
called "wood hymns" devoted to nature and country folklore. His older sister,
confident of his ability, sent several of these poems to local newspapers, one of
which, the Newburyport *Free Press,* was edited by the youthful, but not yet
zealous, abolitionist William Lloyd Garrison. Delighted with what he read,
Garrison published the first of many of Whittier's poems in 1826 and soon
traveled to the Whittier farm to encourage this young poet and to urge his
father to provide his son with "every facility for the development of his
remarkable genius"—to which the senior Whittier quickly replied, "Sir, poetry
will not give him bread." An "over-wearied child," too slender for the heavy
work required of him, Whittier enrolled, with his father's reluctant permission, at
nearby Haverhill Academy and supported himself through two terms with odd
jobs, including service as a cobbler. Unable to afford a college education,
Whittier worked as a country journalist and editorial assistant at several minor
newspapers in Boston and Hartford while continuing to circulate his verse. In the
years that followed, the public recognition his poetry earned him was invariably
offset by his poor health, which often forced him to resign his newspaper work
and return to the family farm to recuperate.

As a young adult, Whittier suffered through several years of personal turmoil
filled with depression, self-pity, and insomnia and marked by a series of
unrequited loves. (He was to remain a lifelong bachelor.) During this period he
began to gain considerable attention as his poetry reached a wider audience.
Conscious both of what he called his own "slumbering powers" and of his
neighbors' confidence in him, Whittier began to speak out on public issues and to
participate in local politics. At the age of thirty, he was elected to the

Massachusetts state legislature and reelected the following year. He declined another term, responding instead to Garrison's call that he devote his energies to the abolition of slavery: "The cause is worthy of Gabriel, yea, the God of hosts places himself at its head. Whittier enlist!—Your talents, zeal, influence—all are needed."

Resolving to knock "Pegasus on the head," Whittier began what would be a distinguished three-decade career as an abolitionist poet and editorialist when he published at his own expense a pamphlet entitled *Justice and Expediency* (1833). In that same year, he represented the state of Massachusetts at the first meeting of the American Anti-Slavery Society. He later declared that having drafted and then signed the resolutions of that convention meant more to him than having his name on any book he had written. Throughout these years, Whittier sustained himself as a full-time political activist and a part-time editor of several abolitionist newspapers, including the *Pennsylvania Freeman* and *The National Era,* which would later publish Harriet Beecher Stowe's *Uncle Tom's Cabin* as a serial. Whittier drew his abolitionist zeal primarily from his Quaker heritage, most eloquently expressed in the late-eighteenth-century work of John Woolman. But, as he explained in a letter to E. L. Godkin, then editor of *The Nation,* altruism, modesty, and a recognition of the personal "costs" of a literary life also reinforced his commitment to abolitionist causes: "I can not be sufficiently grateful to the Divine Providence that so early called my attention to the great interests of humanity, saving me from the poor ambitions and miserable jealousies of a selfish pursuit of literary reputation, the pain of disappointment and the temptation to envy." Nathaniel Hawthorne later noted, "Strictly speaking, Whittier did not care much for literature."

Whittier quickly became the most eloquent voice in the abolitionist movement by publishing in virtually every major newspaper and periodical sympathetic to the cause. He first gathered the work of this period in a volume entitled *Poems Written During the Progress of the Abolition Question* (1837). Subsequent volumes included *Lays of My Home* (1843), *Voices of Freedom* (1846), *Songs of Labor and Other Poems* (1850), *The Chapel of the Hermits and Other Poems* (1853), and *The Panorama and Other Poems* (1856). Describing himself as a "silent, shy, peace-loving man," Whittier was an early advocate of organized nonviolence and always hoped that reform rather than war could resolve the slavery issue. Yet Whittier eventually aligned himself, as did such writers as James Russell Lowell, with several of the more extreme positions of the abolitionists, including their willingness to see the Union dissolve if that were necessary to end the injustice of slavery. After the Civil War, Whittier wrote of his abolitionist verse, "They were written with no expectation that they would survive the occasions which called them forth: they were protests, alarm signals, trumpet-calls to actions, words wrung from the writer's heart, forged at white heat, and of course lacking the finish and careful word-selection which reflection and patient brooding might have given." Yet several of the poems of this period, including "Massachusetts to Virginia" and "Letter from a Missionary," contain a lyric vitality that carries them beyond the limitations of the specific political contexts in which they were written.

Whittier's prominence during his three-decade struggle to defeat slavery did

not prevent him from quietly continuing to write reflective verse focusing on
New England's rustic life. The first volume in this series, *Legends of New England*
(1831), consists of eleven poems and seven prose pieces on local country lore.
Like Cooper, Longfellow, and Hawthorne, Whittier frequently turned to the
New England past, an interest reflected in such volumes as *Moll Pitcher* (1832),
Mogg Megone (1836), and a historical novel, *Leaves from Margaret Smith's Journal*
(1849), a richly textured tale of Quaker life in colonial New England told in the
form of a young girl's diary. He also published a collection of essays titled
Literary Recreations and Miscellanies (1854). But it was not until 1857, when James
Russell Lowell, the editor of the newly founded *Atlantic Monthly,* invited
Whittier to contribute regularly to the magazine, that he enjoyed some measure
of financial security.

Widespread recognition for the quality of Whittier's verse came late—when,
after the Emancipation Proclamation, he could turn from engaging in polemic
battles over slavery to devoting more time to cultivating his literary talents. In
1866, the same year that Herman Melville published *Battle-Pieces* in relative
obscurity, Whittier published "Snow-Bound" to critical acclaim. "Snow-Bound"
remains universally regarded as his most significant work. The poem offers in
direct, simple, concrete, and sincere terms an idyllic vision of American life that
the war-torn nation could take great comfort in. And as the nation became
increasingly swept up in the rush toward industrialization in the decades that
followed, new generations continued to find Whittier's Edenic view of village
and farm life singularly appealing.

In the post–Civil War years, Whittier published several more volumes,
including *Among the Hills and Other Poems* (1869) and *Ballads of New England*
(1870), each replete with charming poetic renditions of local folklore and
superstition. Whittier remained fascinated with childhood innocence,
individualism, moral righteousness, social equality, and honest emotions
throughout his career. Yet in his later years, his poetic interests broadened to
include religious humanism; he became preoccupied as much with the possibility
of moral perfection as with the prospect of political and social reform. His poems
quickly became schoolroom classics. Venerated as a public figure, he celebrated
his seventieth birthday at a public reception in the company of nearly every
major American writer, from the elderly William Cullen Bryant to the feisty
Mark Twain. Each came to sing his praises.

Whittier delighted in the public adulation. Like Walt Whitman, he began to
manage his public image. He interviewed himself for publication; he wrote a
flattering entry for himself in an encyclopedia of biography; he provided
photographers with numerous opportunities to portray him in his favorite rural
settings. In his later years, he rarely ventured from the family home that he had
inherited. After years of illness, he died at home of a stroke in 1892, the same
year as Whitman. Whittier's final volume, *At Sundown,* was published shortly
before his death.

In the prelude to his volume *The Tent on the Beach and Other Poems* (1867),
Whittier described himself as a "dreamer" who had "a mission to fulfill," a
writer who had "left the Muses' haunts to turn / The crank of an
opinion-mill, / Making his rustic reed of song / A weapon in the war with

wrong." He readily recognized his own limitations as a poet. In a letter to Francis H. Underwood, who had begun work on Whittier's biography, the old poet endorsed James Russell Lowell's assessment of him in "A Fable for Critics": Whittier's was "a fervor of mind which knows no separation / 'Twixt simple excitement and pure inspiration." Yet the best of Whittier's poetry focuses on the place he knew best—rural New England. His lifelong interest in rendering the universal qualities of the everyday experiences of commonplace people remains an eloquent response to Ralph Waldo Emerson's plea in "The American Scholar" that American writers embrace "the near, the low, the common."

Further Reading:

S. T. Pickard, *The Life and Letters of John Greenleaf Whittier*, 2 vols., 1894, 1907.

A. Mordell, *Quaker Militant: John Greenleaf Whittier*, 1933.

W. T. Scott, "Poetry in America: A New Consideration of Whittier's Verse," *New England Quarterly* 7, 1934.

T. F. Currier, *A Bibliography of John Greenleaf Whittier*, 1937.

W. Bennett, *Whittier, Bard of Freedom*, 1941. *Whittier on Writers and Writing*, ed. E. H. Cady and H. H. Clark, 1950.

G. Arms, *The Fields Were Green*, 1953.

J. B. Pickard, *John Greenleaf Whittier: An Introduction and Interpretation*, 1961.

L. Leary, *John Greenleaf Whittier*, 1961.

E. Wagenknecht, *John Greenleaf Whittier: A Portrait in Paradox*, 1967.

R. P. Warren, *John Greenleaf Whittier's Poetry: An Appraisal and a Selection*, 1971.

W. J. Linton, *Life of Whittier*, 1972.

D. C. Freeman, J. B. Pickard, and R. C. Woodwell, *Whittier and Whittierland: Portrait of a Poet and His World*, 1976.

Critical Essays on John Greenleaf Whittier, ed. J. K. Kribbs, 1980.

Text:
The Complete Poetical Works of John Greenleaf Whittier, ed. H. E. Scudder, 1892.

Massachusetts to Virginia[*]

The blast from Freedom's Northern hills, upon its Southern way,
Bears greeting to Virginia from Massachusetts Bay:
No word of haughty challenging, nor battle bugle's peal,
Nor steady tread of marching files, nor clang of horsemen's steel.

No trains of deep-mouthed cannon along our highways go;   5
Around our silent arsenals untrodden lies the snow;
And to the land-breeze of our ports, upon their errands far,
A thousand sails of commerce swell, but none are spread for war.

[*] Whittier's note: "Written on reading an account of the proceedings of the citizens of Norfolk, Va., in reference to George Latimer, the alleged fugitive slave, who was seized in Boston without warrant at the request of James B. Grey, of Norfolk, claiming to be his master. The case caused great excitement North and South, and led to the presentation of a petition to Congress, signed by more than fifty thousand citizens of Massachusetts, calling for such laws and proposed amendments to the Constitution as should relieve the Commonwealth from all further participation in the crime of oppression. George Latimer himself was finally given free papers for the sum of four hundred dollars."

We hear thy threats, Virginia! thy stormy words and high
Swell harshly on the Southern winds which melt along our sky;   10
Yet, not one brown, hard hand foregoes its honest labor here,
No hewer of our mountain oaks suspends his axe in fear.

Wild are the waves which lash the reefs along St. George's bank;[1]
Cold on the shores of Labrador the fog lies white and dank;
Through storm, and wave, and blinding mist, stout are the hearts which man   15
The fishing-smacks of Marblehead, the seaboats of Cape Ann.[2]

The cold north light and wintry sun glare on their icy forms,
Bent grimly o'er their straining lines or wrestling with the storms;
Free as the winds they drive before, rough as the waves they roam,
They laugh to scorn the slaver's threat against their rocky home.   20

What means the Old Dominion?[3] Hath she forgot the day
When o'er her conquered valleys swept the Briton's steel array?
How side by side, with sons of hers, the Massachusetts men
Encountered Tarleton's charge of fire, and stout Cornwallis,[4] then?

Forgets she how the Bay State,[5] in answer to the call   25
Of her old House of Burgesses,[6] spoke out from Faneuil Hall?[7]
When, echoing back her Henry's cry,[8] came pulsing on each breath
Of Northern winds the thrilling sounds of "Liberty or Death!"

What asks the Old Dominion? If now her sons have proved
False to their fathers' memory, false to the faith they loved;   30
If she can scoff at Freedom, and its great charter[9] spurn,
Must we of Massachusetts from truth and duty turn?

We hunt your bondmen,[10] flying from Slavery's hateful hell;
Our voices, at your bidding, take up the bloodhound's yell;
We gather, at your summons, above our fathers' graves,   35
From Freedom's holy altar-horns[11] to tear your wretched slaves!

Thank God! not yet so vilely can Massachusetts bow;
The spirit of her early time is with her even now;

---

[1] Off Newfoundland.
[2] On the Massachusetts coast.
[3] Nickname for the state of Virginia.
[4] General Charles Cornwallis (1738–1805), commander of British forces in Virginia during the American Revolution.
[5] Massachusetts.
[6] Lower house of Virginia's colonial legislature.
[7] Boston meeting hall.
[8] Reference to Patrick Henry's speech at the Virginia convention.
[9] I.e., the Declaration of Independence.
[10] The Northern states were required by the fugitive slave laws to capture and return escaped slaves to the South.
[11] Horns projecting from the corners of Hebrew altars offered sanctuary to fugitives. (See 1 Kings 1:50–53 and 2:28.)

Dream not because her Pilgrim blood moves slow and calm and cool,
She thus can stoop her chainless neck, a sister's slave and tool!   40

All that a sister State should do, all that a free State may,
Heart, hand, and purse we proffer, as in our early day;
But that one dark loathsome burden ye must stagger with alone,
And reap the bitter harvest which ye yourselves have sown!

Hold, while ye may, your struggling slaves, and burden God's free air   45
With woman's shriek beneath the lash, and manhood's wild despair;
Cling closer to the "cleaving curse"[12] that writes upon your plains
The blasting of Almighty wrath against a land of chains.

Still shame your gallant ancestry, the cavaliers of old,
By watching round the shambles[13] where human flesh is sold;   50
Gloat o'er the new-born child, and count his market value, when
The maddened mother's cry of woe shall pierce the slaver's den!

Lower than plummet[14] soundeth, sink the Virginia name;
Plant, if ye will, your fathers' graves with rankest weeds of shame;
Be, if ye will, the scandal of God's fair universe;   55
We wash our hands forever of your sin and shame and curse.

A voice from lips whereon the coal from Freedom's shrine hath been,[15]
Thrilled, as but yesterday, the hearts of Berkshire's[16] mountain men:
The echoes of that solemn voice are sadly lingering still
In all our sunny valleys, on every windswept hill.   60

And when the prowling man-thief[17] came hunting for his prey
Beneath the very shadow of Bunker's shaft[18] of gray,
How, through the free lips of the son, the father's warning spoke;
How, from its bonds of trade and sect, the Pilgrim city broke!

A hundred thousand right arms were lifted up on high,   65
A hundred thousand voices sent back their loud reply;
Through the thronged towns of Essex the startling summons rang,
And up from bench and loom and wheel her young mechanics sprang!

---

[12] Some slavery advocates asserted that as Cain's descendants blacks bore a curse "cleaving" them from the human race. (See Genesis 4:11–12.)
[13] Meat market and slaughterhouse.
[14] Lead weight for measuring depths (as in Shakespeare's *The Tempest*, Act III, Sc. iii, ll. 101–102: "I'll seek him deeper than the plummet soundeth / and with him there lie mudded").
[15] Isaiah 6:6–7: "Then flew one of the seraphims unto me, having a live coal in his hand, which he had taken with tongs from off the altar: And he laid it upon my mouth, and said, Lo, this hath touched thy lips; and thine iniquity is taken away, and thy sin purged."
[16] Berkshire: a county in Massachusetts, along with Essex, Middlesex, Norfolk, Plymouth, Worcester, Barnstable, Bristol, Hampden, and Hampshire in the lines that follow.
[17] Slave catcher.
[18] Monument commemorating the Battle of Bunker Hill in the American Revolution.

The voice of free, broad Middlesex, of thousands as of one,
The shaft of Bunker calling to that of Lexington;   70
From Norfolk's ancient villages, from Plymouth's rocky bound
To where Nantucket[19] feels the arms of ocean close her round;

From rich and rural Worcester, where through the calm repose
Of cultured vales and fringing woods the gentle Nashua flows,[20]
To where Wachuset's[21] wintry blasts the mountain larches stir,   75
Swelled up to Heaven the thrilling cry of "God save Latimer!"

And sandy Barnstable rose up, wet with the salt sea spray;
And Bristol sent her answering shout down Narragansett Bay!
Along the broad Connecticut[22] old Hampden felt the thrill,
And the cheer of Hampshire's woodmen swept down from Holyoke Hill.   80

The voice of Massachusetts! Of her free sons and daughters,
Deep calling unto deep aloud, the sound of many waters![23]
Against the burden of that voice what tyrant power shall stand?
No fetters in the Bay State! No slave upon her land!

Look to it well, Virginians! In calmness, we have borne,   85
In answer to our faith and trust, your insult and your scorn;
You've spurned our kindest counsels; you've hunted for our lives;
And shaken round our hearths and homes your manacles and gyves!

We wage no war, we lift no arm, we fling no torch within
The fire-damps[24] of the quaking mine beneath your soil of sin;   90
We leave ye with your bondmen, to wrestle, while ye can,
With the strong upward tendencies and godlike soul of man!

But for us and for our children, the vow which we have given
For freedom and humanity is registered in heaven;
No slave-hunt in our borders,—no pirate on our strand!   95
No fetters in the Bay State,—no slave upon our land!

1843

---

[19] Island off the coast of Massachusetts.
[20] River in Massachusetts.
[21] Mountain in Massachusetts.
[22] River flowing through Massachusetts.

[23] Psalms 42:7: "Deep calleth unto deep at the noise of thy water spouts"; Ezekiel 43:2: "His voice was like a noise of many waters."
[24] Explosive gases formed in mines.

Ichabod[*]

So fallen! so lost! the light withdrawn
    Which once he wore!
The glory from his gray hairs gone
    Forevermore!

Revile him not, the Tempter hath   5
    A snare for all;
And pitying tears, not scorn and wrath,
    Befit his fall!

Oh, dumb be passion's stormy rage,
    When he who might   10
Have lighted up and led his age,
    Falls back in night.

Scorn! would the angels laugh, to mark
    A bright soul driven,
Fiend-goaded, down the endless dark,   15
    From hope and heaven!

Let not the land once proud of him
    Insult him now,
Nor brand with deeper shame his dim,
    Dishonored brow.   20

But let its humbled sons, instead,
    From sea to lake,
A long lament, as for the dead,
    In sadness make.

[*] The title is from 1 Samuel 4:21: "And she named the child Ichabod, saying the glory is departed from Israel." Whittier's note: "This poem was the outcome of the surprise and grief and forecast of evil consequences which I felt on reading the seventh of March speech of Daniel Webster in support of the 'compromise,' and the Fugitive Slave Law. No partisan or personal enmity dictated it. On the contrary my admiration of the splendid personality and intellectual power of the great Senator was never stronger than when I laid down his speech, and, in one of the saddest moments of my life, penned my protest. I saw, as I wrote, with painful clearness its sure results,—the Slave Power arrogant and defiant, strengthened and encouraged to carry out its scheme for the extension of its baleful system, or the dissolution of the Union, the guaranties of personal liberty in the free States broken down, and the whole country made the hunting-ground of slave-catchers. In the horror of such a vision, so soon fearfully fulfilled, if one spoke at all, he could only speak in tones of stern and sorrowful rebuke.

But death softens all resentments, and the consciousness of a common inheritance of frailty and weakness modifies the severity of judgment. Years after, in *The Lost Occasion*, I gave utterance to an almost universal regret that the great statesman did not live to see the flag which he loved trampled under the feet of Slavery, and, in view of this desecration, make his last days glorious in defence of 'Liberty and Union, one and inseparable.' "

Of all we loved and honored, naught   25
   Save power remains;
A fallen angel's pride of thought,
   Still strong in chains.

All else is gone; from those great eyes
   The soul has fled;   30
When faith is lost, when honor dies,
   The man is dead!

Then, pay the reverence of old days
   To his dead fame;
Walk backward, with averted gaze,   35
   And hide the shame!

1850

First-day Thoughts[1]

In calm and cool and silence, once again
   I find my old accustomed place among
My brethren, where, perchance, no human tongue
Shall utter words; where never hymn is sung,
Nor deep-toned organ blown, nor censer swung,   5
Nor dim light falling through the pictured pane![2]
There, syllabled by silence, let me hear
The still small voice which reached the prophet's ear;
Read in my heart a still diviner law
Than Israel's leader on his tables saw![3]   10
There let me strive with each besetting sin,
   Recall my wandering fancies, and restrain
   The sore disquiet of a restless brain;
   And, as the path of duty is made plain,
May grace be given that I may walk therein,   15
   Not like the hireling, for his selfish gain,
With backward glances and reluctant tread,
Making a merit of his coward dread,

---

[1] The Quakers called the days of the week by number to avoid reference to the pagan gods for which the days are named. "First-day" is Sunday.

[2] Fellowship was emphasized in the Society of Friends (Quakers), and communal silence was observed rather than the use of music and images.

[3] Reference to Moses and the tablets containing the Ten Commandments. (See Exodus 31:18, 20.)

But, cheerful, in the light around me thrown,
  Walking as one to pleasant service led;   20
Doing God's will as if it were my own,
Yet trusting not in mine, but in His strength alone!

1853

Letter*
From a Missionary of the Methodist Episcopal Church South, in Kansas, to a Distinguished Politician

Douglas Mission, *August,* 1854.

  Last week—the Lord be praised for all His mercies
To His unworthy servant!—I arrived
Safe at the Mission, via Westport where
I tarried over night, to aid in forming
A Vigilance Committee, to send back,   5
In shirts of tar, and feather-doublets quilted
With forty stripes save one, all Yankee comers,
Uncircumcised and Gentile, aliens from
The Commonwealth of Israel, who despise
The prize of the high calling of the saints,   10
Who plant amidst this heathen wilderness
Pure gospel institutions, sanctified
By patriarchal use. The meeting opened
With prayer, as was most fitting. Half an hour,
Or thereaway, I groaned, and strove, and wrestled,   15
As Jacob did at Penuel,[1] till the power
Fell on the people, and they cried "Amen!"
"Glory to God!" and stamped and clapped their hands;
And the rough river boatmen wiped their eyes;
"Go it, old hoss!" they cried, and cursed the niggers—   20

---

* This poem recalls the struggle in the 1850s between the "Free-Soilers" and the Southern immigrants for control of the Kansas territory. The conflict set the stage for the Civil War and produced several particularly violent episodes, the two most noted being the burning of Lawrence, Kansas, by Southern raiders and the massacre perpetrated by John Brown and his sons at Pottawatomie.

[1] Site where Jacob wrestled with God (see Genesis 32:22–31).

Fulfilling thus the word of prophecy,
"Cursëd be Canaan."[2] After prayer, the meeting
Chose a committee—good and pious men—
A Presbyterian Elder, Baptist deacon,
A local preacher, three or four class-leaders,   25
Anxious inquirers, and renewed backsliders,
A score in all—to watch the river ferry,
(As they of old did watch the fords of Jordan,)
And cut off all whose Yankee tongues refuse
The Shibboleth of the Nebraska bill.[3]   30
And then, in answer to repeated calls,
I gave a brief account of what I saw
In Washington; and truly many hearts
Rejoiced to know the President, and you
And all the Cabinet regularly hear   35
The gospel message of a Sunday morning,
Drinking with thirsty souls of the sincere
Milk of the Word. Glory! Amen, and Selah![4]

  Here, at the Mission, all things have gone well:
The brother who, throughout my absence, acted   40
As overseer, assures me that the crops
Never were better. I have lost one negro,
A first-rate hand, but obstinate and sullen.
He ran away some time last spring, and hid
In the river timber. There my Indian converts   45
Found him, and treed and shot him. For the rest,
The heathens round about begin to feel
The influence of our pious ministrations
And works of love; and some of them already
Have purchased negroes, and are settling down   50
As sober Christians! Bless the Lord for this!
I know it will rejoice you. You, I hear,
Are on the eve of visiting Chicago,
To fight with the wild beasts of Ephesus,[5]
Long John,[6] and Dutch Free-Soilers. May your arm   55
Be clothed with strength, and on your tongue be found

---

[2] In Genesis 9:25 Ham, the son of Noah, shames his father. Noah in turn curses Ham's son Canaan and declares that Canaan will be a servant to his brothers. In Whittier's time, Canaan was considered to be the ancestor of all blacks.
[3] The Kansas-Nebraska Act, passed in May 1854, which allowed the settlers in the American territories to make their own decisions regarding slavery.

[4] Hebrew term of uncertain meaning, found in the text of the Psalms.
[5] In A.D. 431 at Ephesus in Asia Minor, the General Council, involving Rome, Alexandria, Jerusalem, and Thessalonica, erupted into brutal violence over a heretical controversy.
[6] John P. Hale (1806–1873), zealous opponent of slavery in the U.S. Senate and a presidential candidate for the Free-Soil party.

The sweet oil of persuasion. So desires
Your brother and co-laborer. Amen!

   P.S. All's lost. Even while I write these lines,
The Yankee abolitionists are coming   60
Upon us like a flood—grim, stalwart men,
Each face set like a flint of Plymouth Rock
Against our institutions—staking out
Their farm lots on the wooded Wakarusa,[7]
Or squatting by the mellow-bottomed Kansas;[8]   65
The pioneers of mightier multitudes,
The small rain-patter, ere the thunder shower
Drowns the dry prairies. Hope from man is not.
Oh, for a quiet berth at Washington,
Snug naval chaplaincy, or clerkship, where   70
These rumors of free labor and free soil
Might never meet me more. Better to be
Door-keeper in the White House, than to dwell
Amidst these Yankee tents, that, whitening, show
On the green prairie like a fleet becalmed.   75
Methinks I hear a voice come up the river
From those far bayous where the alligators
Mount guard around the camping filibusters:
"Shake off the dust of Kansas. Turn to Cuba[9]—
(That golden orange just about to fall,   80
O'er-ripe, into the Democratic lap;)
Keep pace with Providence, or, as we say,
Manifest destiny. Go forth and follow
The message of *our* gospel, thither borne
Upon the point of Quitman's bowie knife,   85
And the persuasive lips of Colt's revolvers.
There may'st thou, underneath thy vine and fig-tree,
Watch thy increase of sugar cane and negroes,
Calm as a patriarch in his eastern tent!"
Amen: So mote it be. So prays your friend.   90
1854

---

[7] River in northeast Kansas.
[8] I.e., the Kansas River.
[9] Cuba had been declared indispensable for the
security of slavery, through opportunistic use of

the sugar industry. The Democrats in power
were thus actively seeking its acquisition from
Spain.

Song of Slaves in the Desert[*]

Where are we going? where are we going,
    Where are we going, Rubee?
Lord of peoples, lord of lands,
Look across these shining sands,
Through the furnace of the moon,   5
Through the white light of the moon.
Strong the Ghiblee wind is blowing,
Strange and large the world is growing!
Speak and tell us where we are going,
    Where are we going, Rubee?   10

Bornou land was rich and good,
Wells of water, fields of food,
Dourra fields, and bloom of bean,
And the palm-tree cool and green:
Bornou land we see no longer,   15
Here we thirst and here we hunger,
Here the Moor-man smites in anger:
    Where are we going, Rubee?

When we went from Bornou land,
We were like the leaves and sand,   20
We were many, we are few;
Life has one, and death has two:
Whitened bones our path are showing,
Thou All-seeing, thou All-knowing!
Hear us, tell us, where are we going,   25
    Where are we going, Rubee?

Moons of marches from our eyes
Bornou land behind us lies;

[*] Whittier's note: "Sebah, Oasis of Fezzan, 10th March, 1846. This evening the female slaves were unusually excited in singing, and I had the curiosity to ask my negro servant Said, what they were singing about. As many of them were natives of his own country, he had no difficulty in translating the Manara or Bornou language. I had often asked the Moors to translate their songs for me, but got no satisfactory account from them. Said at first said, 'Oh, they sing of Rubee' (God). 'What do you mean?' I replied, impatiently. 'Oh, don't you know?' he continued, 'they asked God to give them their Atka' (certificate of freedom). I inquired, 'Is that all?' Said: 'No; they say, "Where are we going? The world is large. O God! Where are we going? O God!"' I inquired, 'What else?' Said: 'They remember their country, Bornou, and say, "Bornou was a pleasant country, full of good things, but this is a bad country, and we are miserable!"' 'Do they say anything else?' Said: 'No; they repeat these words over and over again, and add, "O God! give us our Atka, and let us return again to our dear home!"'—Richardson's Journal in Africa."

Stranger round us day by day
Bends the desert circle gray;   30
Wild the waves of sand are flowing,
Hot the winds above them blowing,—
Lord of all things! where are we going?
    Where are we going, Rubee?

We are weak, but Thou art strong;   35
Short our lives, but Thine is long;
We are blind, but Thou hast eyes;
We are fools, but Thou art wise!
Thou, our morrow's pathway knowing
Through the strange world round us growing,   40
Hear us, tell us where are we going,
    Where are we going, Rubee?

1856

Skipper Ireson's Ride*

Of all the rides since the birth of time,
Told in story or sung in rhyme,—
On Apuleius's Golden Ass,[1]
Or one-eyed Calender's horse of brass,[2]
Witch astride of a human back,   5
Islam's prophet on Al-Borák,[3]—
The strangest ride that ever was sped
Was Ireson's, out from Marblehead![4]
    Old Floyd Ireson, for his hard heart,
    Tarred and feathered and carried in a cart   10
    By the women of Marblehead!

Body of turkey, head of owl,
Wings a-droop like a rained-on fowl,

---

* Whittier claims that this ballad "was founded solely on a fragment of rhyme which I heard from one of my early schoolmates, a native of Marblehead." The fragment is presumably the refrain sung by either the women escorting Captain Ireson in his cart or by the skipper himself. This record of events is "pure fancy," as Whittier declared in his note for the 1888 edition, and not according to the facts about the case presented in *History of Marblehead* (1879) by Samuel Roads.

[1] Roman satirist Lucius Apuleius (second century B.C.) tells of the metamorphosis of Aman into an "excellent" ass in *The Golden Ass*.
[2] In the *Arabian Nights* tale, "the story of the third royal mendicant," a calender (or dervish) slew the owner of a horse of brass and later lost an eye.
[3] In one legend, Mohammed was carried to highest heaven by a supernatural winged animal.
[4] Massachusetts seaport.

Feathered and ruffled in every part,
Skipper Ireson stood in the cart.   15
Scores of women, old and young,
Strong of muscle, and glib of tongue,
Pushed and pulled up the rocky lane,
Shouting and singing the shrill refrain:
"Here's Flud Oirson, fur his horrd horrt,   20
    Torr'd an' futherr'd an' corr'd in a corrt
    By the women o' Morble'ead!"[5]

Wrinkled scolds with hands on hips,
Girls in bloom of cheek and lips,
Wild-eyed, free-limbed, such as chase   25
Bacchus[6] round some antique vase,
Brief of skirt, with ankles bare,
Loose of kerchief and loose of hair,
With conch-shells blowing and fish-horns'[7] twang,
Over and over the Mænads sang: 30
"Here's Flud Oirson, fur his horrd horrt,
    Torr'd an' futherr'd an' corr'd in a corrt
    By the women o' Morble'ead!"

Small pity for him!—He sailed away
From a leaking ship in Chaleur Bay,[8]—   35
Sailed away from a sinking wreck,
With his own town's-people on her deck!
"Lay by! lay by!" they called to him.
Back he answered, "Sink or swim!
Brag of your catch of fish again!"   40
And off he sailed through the fog and rain!
    Old Floyd Ireson, for his hard heart,
    Tarred and feathered and carried in a cart
    By the women of Marblehead!

Fathoms deep in dark Chaleur   45
That wreck shall lie forevermore.
Mother and sister, wife and maid,
Looked from the rocks of Marblehead
Over the moaning and rainy sea,—
Looked for the coming that might not be!   50
What did the winds and the sea-birds say
Of the cruel captain who sailed away?—

---

[5] James Russell Lowell, Whittier's editor, suggested that the Marblehead dialect be used for the refrain in stanzas 2, 3, 6, and 7 in contrast to the standard English used in the refrain in stanzas 1, 4, 5, 8, and 9.

[6] Roman god of wine, usually depicted as surrounded by frenetic women known as maenads.
[7] Fish peddler's horns.
[8] In the Gulf of St. Lawrence.

Old Floyd Ireson, for his hard heart,
Tarred and feathered and carried in a cart
   By the women of Marblehead!   55

Through the street, on either side,
Up flew windows, doors swung wide;
Sharp-tongued spinsters, old wives gray,
Treble lent the fish-horn's bray.
Sea-worn grandsires, cripple-bound,   60
Hulks of old sailors run aground,
Shook head, and fist, and hat, and cane,
And cracked with curses the hoarse refrain:
"Here's Flud Oirson, fur his horrd horrt,
Torr'd an' futherr'd an' corr'd in a corrt   65
   By the women o' Morble'ead!"

Sweetly along the Salem road
Bloom of orchard and lilac showed.
Little the wicked skipper knew
Of the fields so green and the sky so blue.   70
Riding there in his sorry trim,
Like an Indian idol glum and grim,
Scarcely he seemed the sound to hear
Of voices shouting, far and near:
"Here's Flud Oirson, fur his horrd horrt,   75
Torr'd an' futherr'd an' corr'd in a corrt
   By the women o' Morble'ead!"

"Hear me, neighbors!" at last he cried,—
"What to me is this noisy ride?
What is the shame that clothes the skin
To the nameless horror that lives within?   80
Waking or sleeping, I see a wreck,
And hear a cry from a reeling deck!
Hate me and curse me,—I only dread
The hand of God and the face of the dead!"
   Said old Floyd Ireson, for his hard heart,   85
   Tarred and feathered and carried in a cart
   By the women of Marblehead!

Then the wife of the skipper lost at sea
Said, "God has touched him! why should we!"   90
Said an old wife mourning her only son,
"Cut the rogue's tether and let him run!"
So with soft relentings and rude excuse,
Half scorn, half pity, they cut him loose,
And gave him a cloak to hide him in,   95

And left him alone with his shame and sin.
   Poor Floyd Ireson, for his hard heart,
   Tarred and feathered and carried in a cart
      By the women of Marblehead!

1857

Telling the Bees[1]

Here is the place; right over the hill
   Runs the path I took;
You can see the gap in the old wall still,
   And the stepping-stones in the shallow brook.

There is the house, with the gate red-barred,   5
   And the poplars tall;
And the barn's brown length, and the cattle-yard,
   And the white horns tossing above the wall.

There are the beehives ranged in the sun;
   And down by the brink   10
Of the brook are her poor flowers, weed-o'errun,
   Pansy and daffodil, rose and pink.

A year has gone, as the tortoise goes,
   Heavy and slow;
And the same rose blows, and the same sun glows,   15
   And the same brook sings of a year ago.

There's the same sweet clover-smell in the breeze;
   And the June sun warm
Tangles his wings of fire in the trees,
   Setting, as then, over Fernside farm.   20

I mind me how with a lover's care
   From my Sunday coat
I brushed off the burrs, and smoothed my hair,
   And cooled at the brookside my brow and throat.

[1] Whittier's note: "A remarkable custom, brought from the Old Country, formerly prevailed in the rural districts of New England. On the death of a member of the family, the bees were at once informed of the event, and their hives dressed in mourning. This ceremonial was supposed to be necessary to prevent the swarms from leaving their hives and seeking a new home."

Since we parted, a month had passed,—   25
   To love, a year;
Down through the beeches I looked at last
   On the little red gate and the well-sweep near.

I can see it all now,—the slantwise rain
   Of light through the leaves,   30
The sundown's blaze on her window-pane,
   The bloom of her roses under the eaves.

Just the same as a month before,—
   The house and the trees,
The barn's brown gable, the vine by the door,—   35
   Nothing changed but the hives of bees.

Before them, under the garden wall,
   Forward and back,
Went drearily singing the chore-girl small,
   Draping each hive with a shred of black.   40

Trembling, I listened: the summer sun
   Had the chill of snow;
For I knew she was telling the bees of one
   Gone on the journey we all must go!

Then I said to myself, "My Mary weeps   45
   For the dead to-day:
Haply her blind old grandsire sleeps
   The fret and the pain of his age away."

But her dog whined low; on the doorway sill,
   With his cane to his chin,
The old man sat; and the chore-girl still   50
   Sung to the bees stealing out and in.

And the song she was singing ever since
   In my ear sounds on:—
"Stay at home, pretty bees, fly not hence!
   Mistress Mary is dead and gone!"   55

1858

Laus Deo[1]

It is done!
Clang of bell and roar of gun
Send the tidings up and down.
How the belfries rock and reel!
How the great guns, peal on peal,   5
Fling the joy from town to town!

Ring, O bells!
Every stroke exulting tells
Of the burial hour of crime.
Loud and long, that all may hear,   10
Ring for every listening ear
Of Eternity and Time!

Let us kneel:
God's own voice is in that peal,
And this spot is holy ground.[2]   15
Lord, forgive us! What are we,
That our eyes this glory see,
That our ears have heard the sound!

For the Lord
On the whirlwind is abroad;   20
In the earthquake He has spoken;
He has smitten with His thunder[3]
The iron walls asunder,
And the gates of brass are broken!

Loud and long   25
Lift the old exulting song;
Sing with Miriam by the sea,
He has cast the mighty down;
Horse and rider sink and drown;
"He hath triumphed gloriously!"[4]   30

---

[1] The title of the poem translates from the Latin as "Praise Be to God." Whittier's note: "On hearing the bells ring on the passage of the constitutional amendment abolishing slavery. The resolution was adopted by Congress, January 31, 1865. Ratification by the requisite number of States was announced December 18, 1865."

[2] In Exodus 3:4–5, God instructs Moses to take off his shoes "for the place whereon thou standest is holy ground."

[3] Job 37:2–12 describes how "God thundereth marvelously with his voice; great things doeth he which we cannot comprehend."

[4] Exodus 15:21: "And Miriam answered them, sing ye to the Lord, for he hath triumphed gloriously; the horse and his rider he hath thrown into the sea."

Did we dare,
In our agony of prayer,[5]
Ask for more than He has done?
When was ever His right hand
Over any time or land   35
Stretched as now beneath the sun?[6]

How they pale,
Ancient myth and song and tale,
In this wonder of our days,
When the cruel rod of war   40
Blossoms white with righteous law,[7]
And the wrath of man is praise!

Blotted out!
All within and all about
Shall a fresher life begin;   45
Freer breathe the universe
As it rolls its heavy curse
On the dead and buried sin!

It is done!
In the circuit of the sun   50
Shall the sound thereof go forth.
It shall bid the sad rejoice,
It shall give the dumb a voice,
It shall belt with joy the earth![8]

Ring and swing,   55
Bells of joy! On morning's wing
Send the song of praise abroad!
With a sound of broken chains
Tell the nations that He reigns,
Who alone is Lord and God!   60

1865

---

[5] Luke 22:44: "And being in an agony he prayed more earnestly: and his sweat was as it were great drops of blood falling down to the ground."

[6] Regarding God's wrath and God's mercy, Isaiah uses the phrase "But his hand is stretched out still." (See Isaiah 5:25, 14:27, 9:12–13, 10:4.)

[7] Reference to Aaron's rod of war (as in Exodus 7:8–17) and his rod of law (as in Numbers 17:8–10).

[8] In Isaiah 35:4–8, the prophet proclaims "then shall . . . the tongue of the dumb sing . . . and come to Zion with songs and everlasting joy upon their heads."

Snow-Bound

A Winter Idyl

To the memory of the household[1] it describes, this
poem is dedicated by the author

> *"As the Spirits of Darkness be stronger in the dark, so Good*
> *Spirits, which be Angels of Light, are augmented not only by the*
> *Divine light of the Sun, but also by our common Wood Fire: and*
> *as the Celestial Fire drives away dark spirits, so also this our Fire*
> *of Wood doth the same."*
> Cor. Agrippa,[2] *Occult Philosophy*, Book I. ch. v

> *"Announced by all the trumpets of the sky,*
> *Arrives the snow, and, driving o'er the fields,*
> *Seems nowhere to alight: the whited air*
> *Hides hills and woods, the river and the heaven,*
> *And veils the farm-house at the garden's end.*
> *The sled and traveller stopped, the courier's feet*
> *Delayed, all friends shut out, the housemates sit*
> *Around the radiant fireplace, enclosed*
> *In a tumultuous privacy of storm."*
> Emerson, *The Snow Storm*

The sun that brief December day
Rose cheerless over hills of gray,
And, darkly circled, gave at noon
A sadder light than waning moon.
Slow tracing down the thickening sky   5
Its mute and ominous prophecy,
A portent seeming less than threat,
It sank from sight before it set.
A chill no coat, however stout,
Of homespun stuff could quite shut out,   10
A hard, dull bitterness of cold,

---

[1] Whittier's note: "The inmates of the family at
the Whittier homestead who are referred to in
the poem were my father, mother, my brother
and two sisters, and my uncle and aunt both
unmarried. In addition, there was the district
school-master who boarded with us. The 'not
unfeared, half-welcome guest' was Harriet
Livermore, daughter of Judge Livermore, of
New Hampshire, a young woman of fine
natural ability, enthusiastic, eccentric, with
slight control over her violent temper. . . . She
early embraced the doctrine of the Second
Advent, and felt it her duty to proclaim the
Lord's speedy coming. With this message she
crossed the Atlantic and spent the greater part
of a long life travelling over Europe and Asia.
She lived some time with Lady Hester
Stanhope, a woman as fantastic and mentally
strained as herself, on the slope of Mt.
Lebanon. . . . "

[2] Heinrich Cornelius Agrippa (1486–1535),
German physician, theologian, and student of
the occult.

That checked, mid-vein, the circling race
Of life-blood in the sharpened face,
The coming of the snow-storm told.
The wind blew east;[3] we heard the roar   15
Of Ocean on his wintry shore,
And felt the strong pulse throbbing there
Beat with low rhythm our inland air.

Meanwhile we did our nightly chores,—
Brought in the wood from out of doors,   20
Littered the stalls, and from the mows
Raked down the herd's-grass[4] for the cows:
Heard the horse whinnying for his corn;
And, sharply clashing horn on horn,
Impatient down the stanchion rows   25
The cattle shake their walnut bows;[5]
While, peering from his early perch
Upon the scaffold's pole of birch,
The cock his crested helmet bent
And down his querulous challenge sent.   30

Unwarmed by any sunset light
The gray day darkened into night,
A night made hoary with the swarm,
And whirl-dance of the blinding storm,
As zigzag, wavering to and fro,   35
Crossed and recrossed the wingèd snow:
And ere the early bedtime came
The white drift piled the window-frame,
And through the glass the clothes-line posts
Looked in like tall and sheeted ghosts.   40

So all night long the storm roared on:
The morning broke without a sun;
In tiny spherule traced with lines
Of Nature's geometric signs,
In starry flake, and pellicle,   45
All day the hoary meteor fell;
And, when the second morning shone,
We looked upon a world unknown,
On nothing we could call our own.
Around the glistening wonder bent   50
The blue walls of the firmament,
No cloud above, no earth below,—
A universe of sky and snow!

---

[3] I.e., from the Atlantic coast.   [5] Bows: yokes; scaffold (line 28): loft of a barn.
[4] Used as fodder.

The old familiar sights of ours
Took marvellous shapes; strange domes and towers   55
Rose up where sty or corn-crib stood,
Or garden-wall, or belt of wood;
A smooth white mound the brush-pile showed,
A fenceless drift what once was road;
The bridle-post an old man sat   60
With loose-flung coat and high cocked hat;
The well-curb had a Chinese roof;
And even the long sweep, high aloof,
In its slant splendor, seemed to tell
Of Pisa's leaning miracle.[6]   65

A prompt, decisive man, no breath
Our father wasted: "Boys, a path!"
Well pleased, (for when did farmer boy
Count such a summons less than joy?)
Our buskins on our feet we drew;   70
With mittened hands, and caps drawn low,
To guard our necks and ears from snow,
We cut the solid whiteness through.
And, where the drift was deepest, made
A tunnel walled and overlaid   75
With dazzling crystal: we had read
Of rare Aladdin's wondrous cave,
And to our own his name we gave,
With many a wish the luck were ours
To test his lamp's supernal powers.   80
We reached the barn with merry din,
And roused the prisoned brutes within.
The old horse thrust his long head out,
And grave with wonder gazed about;
The cock his lusty greeting said,   85
And forth his speckled harem led;
The oxen lashed their tails, and hooked,
And mild reproach of hunger looked;
The hornëd patriarch of the sheep,
Like Egypt's Amun[7] roused from sleep,   90
Shook his sage head with gesture mute,
And emphasized with stamp of foot.

All day the gusty north-wind bore
The loosening drift its breath before;
Low circling round its southern zone,   95

---

[6] The leaning tower of Pisa in Italy.
[7] Ammon, Egyptian god who had the head of a
ram.

The sun through dazzling snow-mist shone.
No church-bell lent its Christian tone
To the savage air, no social smoke
Curled over woods of snow-hung oak.
A solitude made more intense   100
By dreary-voicèd elements,
The shrieking of the mindless wind,
The moaning tree-boughs swaying blind,
And on the glass the unmeaning beat
Of ghostly finger-tips of sleet.   105
Beyond the circle of our hearth
No welcome sound of toil or mirth
Unbound the spell, and testified
Of human life and thought outside.
We minded that the sharpest ear   110
The buried brooklet could not hear,
The music of whose liquid lip
Had been to us companionship,
And, in our lonely life, had grown
To have an almost human tone.   115

As night drew on, and, from the crest
Of wooded knolls that ridged the west,
The sun, a snow-blown traveller, sank
From sight beneath the smothering bank,
We piled, with care, our nightly stack   120
Of wood against the chimney-back,—
The oaken log, green, huge, and thick,
And on its top the stout back-stick;
The knotty forestick laid apart,
And filled between with curious art   125
The ragged brush; then, hovering near,
We watched the first red blaze appear,
Heard the sharp crackle, caught the gleam
On whitewashed wall and sagging beam,
Until the old, rude-furnished room   130
Burst, flower-like, into rosy bloom;
While radiant with a mimic flame
Outside the sparkling drift became,
And through the bare-boughed lilac-tree
Our own warm hearth seemed blazing free.   135
The crane and pendent trammels showed,
The Turks' heads[8] on the andirons glowed;
While childish fancy, prompt to tell
The meaning of the miracle,

[8] Ornaments in wrought iron resembling turbans.

Whispered the old rhyme: *"Under the tree,*   140
When fire outdoors burns merrily,
There the witches are making tea."

The moon above the eastern wood
Shone at its full; the hill-range stood
Transfigured in the silver flood,   145
Its blown snows flashing cold and keen,
Dead white, save where some sharp ravine
Took shadow, or the sombre green
Of hemlocks turned to pitchy black
Against the whiteness at their back.   150
For such a world and such a night
Most fitting that unwarming light,
Which only seemed where'er it fell
To make the coldness visible.

Shut in from all the world without,   155
We sat the clean-winged hearth about,
Content to let the north-wind roar
In baffled rage at pane and door,
While the red logs before us beat
The frost-line back with tropic heat;   160
And ever, when a louder blast
Shook beam and rafter as it passed,
The merrier up its roaring draught
The great throat of the chimney laughed;
The house-dog on his paws outspread   165
Laid to the fire his drowsy head,
The cat's dark silhouette on the wall
A couchant tiger's seemed to fall;
And, for the winter fireside meet,
Between the andirons' straddling feet,   170
The mug of cider simmered slow,
The apples sputtered in a row,
And, close at hand, the basket stood
With nuts from brown October's wood.

What matter how the night behaved?   175
What matter how the north-wind raved?
Blow high, blow low, not all its snow
Could quench our hearth-fire's ruddy glow.
O Time and Change!—with hair as gray
As was my sire's that winter day,   180
How strange it seems, with so much gone
Of life and love, to still live on!

Ah, brother![9] only I and thou
Are left of all that circle now,—
The dear home faces whereupon   185
That fitful firelight paled and shone.
Henceforward, listen as we will,
The voices of that hearth are still;
Look where we may, the wide earth o'er
Those lighted faces smile no more.   190
We tread the paths their feet have worn,
    We sit beneath their orchard trees,
    We hear, like them, the hum of bees
And rustle of the bladed corn;
We turn the pages that they read,   195
    Their written words we linger o'er,
But in the sun they cast no shade,
No voice is heard, no sign is made,
    No step is on the conscious floor!
Yet Love will dream, and Faith will trust,   200
(Since He who knows our need is just,)
That somehow, somewhere, meet we must.
Alas for him who never sees
The stars shine through his cypress-trees!
Who, hopeless, lays his dead away,   205
Nor looks to see the breaking day
Across the mournful marbles[10] play!
Who hath not learned, in hours of faith,
    The truth to flesh and sense unknown,
That Life is ever lord of Death,   210
    And Love can never lose its own!

We sped the time with stories old,
Wrought puzzles out, and riddles told,
Or stammered from our school-book lore
"The Chief of Gambia's golden shore."[11]   215
How often since, when all the land
Was clay in Slavery's shaping hand,
As if a far-blown trumpet stirred
The languorous sin-sick air, I heard:
"Does not the voice of reason cry,   220
    Claim the first right which Nature gave,
From the red scourge of bondage fly,
    Nor deign to live a burdened slave!"
Our father rode again his ride

---

[9] Matthew Whittier (1812–1883).
[10] Gravestones.
[11] Quotations in this stanza are from an abolitionist poem, "The African Chief," by

Sarah Wentworth Morton (1759–1846). Whittier inaccurately cites the author as Mercy Warren.

On Memphremagog's[12] wooded side;   225
Sat down again to moose and samp[13]
In trapper's hut and Indian camp;
Lived o'er the old idyllic ease
Beneath St. François'[14] hemlock-trees;
Again for him the moonlight shone   230
On Norman cap[15] and bodiced zone;
Again he heard the violin play
Which led the village dance away,
And mingled in its merry whirl
The grandam and the laughing girl.   235
Or, nearer home, our steps he led
Where Salisbury's[16] level marshes spread
  Mile-wide as flies the laden bee;
Where merry mowers, hale and strong,
Swept, scythe on scythe, their swaths along   240
  The low green prairies of the sea.
We shared the fishing off Boar's Head,[17]
  And round the rocky Isles of Shoals[18]
The hake-broil[19] on the drift-wood coals;
The chowder on the sand-beach made,   245
Dipped by the hungry, steaming hot,
With spoons of clam-shell from the pot.
We heard the tales of witchcraft old,
And dream and sign and marvel told
To sleepy listeners as they lay   250
Stretched idly on the salted hay,
Adrift along the winding shores,
When favoring breezes deigned to blow
The square sail of the gundelow[20]
And idle lay the useless oars.   255

Our mother, while she turned her wheel
Or run the new-knit stocking-heel,
Told how the Indian hordes came down
At midnight on Cocheco town,[21]
And how her own great-uncle bore   260
His cruel scalp-mark to fourscore.
Recalling, in her fitting phrase,
  So rich and picturesque and free,

---

[12] Memphremagog: lake on the border of
   Vermont and Quebec.
[13] Hominy or cornmeal mush.
[14] Village north of Lake Memphremagog.
[15] Cap worn by women in French-Canadian
   settlements.
[16] Salisbury: town in Massachusetts.

[17] Headland on the New England coast.
[18] Islands off the coast of New Hampshire.
[19] A fish.
[20] Flat-bottomed boat.
[21] Village near Dover, New Hampshire, on the
   Cocheco River.

(The common unrhymed poetry
Of simple life and country ways,)   265
The story of her early days,—
She made us welcome to her home;
Old hearths grew wide to give us room;
We stole with her a frightened look
At the gray wizard's conjuring-book,   270
The fame whereof went far and wide
Through all the simple country side;
We heard the hawks at twilight play,
The boat-horn on Piscataqua,[22]
The loon's weird laughter far away;   275
We fished her little trout-brook, knew
What flowers in wood and meadow grew,
What sunny hillsides autumn-brown
She climbed to shake the ripe nuts down,
Saw where in sheltered cover and bay   280
The ducks' black squadron anchored lay,
And heard the wild-geese calling loud
Beneath the gray November cloud.

Then, haply, with a look more grave,
And soberer tone, some tale she gave   285
From painful Sewell's ancient tome,[23]
Beloved in every Quaker home,
Of faith fire-winged by martyrdom,
Or Chalkley's Journal,[24] old and quaint,—
Gentlest of skippers, rare sea-saint!—   290
Who, when the dreary calms prevailed,
And water-butt and bread-cask failed,
And cruel, hungry eyes pursued
His portly presence mad for food,
With dark hints muttered under breath   295
Of casting lots for life or death,
Offered, if Heaven withheld supplies,
To be himself the sacrifice.
Then, suddenly, as if to save
The good man from his living grave,   300
A ripple on the water grew,
A school of porpoise flashed in view.
"Take, eat,"[25] he said, "and be content;
These fishes in my stead are sent

---

[22] River in New Hampshire.
[23] *History of the Rise, Increase and Progress of the People Called Quakers* (1717–1725) by William Sewell (1650–1725).
[24] The *Journal* (1747) of Thomas Chalkley (1675–1741), Quaker sea captain.
[25] In Matthew 26:26, Jesus gives bread to his disciples and says, "Take, eat; this is my body."

By Him who gave the tangled ram   305
To spare the child of Abraham."[26]

Our uncle, innocent of books,
Was rich in lore of fields and brooks,
The ancient teachers never dumb
Of Nature's unhoused lyceum.   310
In moons and tides and weather wise,
He read the clouds as prophecies,
And foul or fair could well divine,
By many an occult hint and sign,
Holding the cunning-warded[27] keys   315
To all the woodcraft mysteries;
Himself to Nature's heart so near
That all her voices in his ear
Of beast or bird had meanings clear,
Like Apollonius[28] of old,   320
Who knew the tales the sparrows told,
Or Hermes[29] who interpreted
What the sage cranes of Nilus[30] said;
Content to live where life began;
A simple, guileless, childlike man,   325
Strong only on his native grounds,
The little world of sights and sounds
Whose girdle was the parish bounds,
Whereof his fondly partial pride
The common features magnified,   330
As Surrey hills to mountains grew
In White[31] of Selborne's loving view,—
He told how teal and loon he shot,
And how the eagle's eggs he got,
The feats on pond and river done,   335
The prodigies of rod and gun;
Till, warming with the tales he told,
Forgotten was the outside cold,
The bitter wind unheeded blew,
From ripening corn the pigeons flew,   340
The partridge drummed i' the wood, the mink
Went fishing down the river-brink.

[26] In Genesis 22:8–13, Abraham finds a ram caught in a thicket and sacrifices it to God in place of his son, Isaac.
[27] Skillfully or cleverly shaped.
[28] Mystic Greek philosopher of the first century A.D.
[29] Hermes Trismegistus, mythical Egyptian author of third-century books of magic.
[30] The Nile.
[31] Gilbert White (1720–1793), English naturalist who lived in the English county of Surrey; author of *The Natural History and Antiquities of Selborne* (1789).

In fields with bean or clover gay,
The woodchuck, like a hermit gray,
  Peered from the doorway of his cell;   345
The muskrat plied the mason's trade,
And tier by tier his mud-walls laid;
And from the shagbark overhead
  The grizzled squirrel dropped his shell.

Next, the dear aunt, whose smile of cheer   350
And voice in dreams I see and hear,—
The sweetest woman ever Fate
Perverse denied a household mate,
Who, lonely, homeless, not the less
Found peace in love's unselfishness,   355
And welcome wheresoe'er she went,
A calm and gracious element,
Whose presence seemed the sweet income
And womanly atmosphere of home,—
Called up her girlhood memories,   360
The huskings and the apple-bees,
The sleigh-rides and the summer sails,
Weaving through all the poor details
And homespun warp of circumstance
A golden woof-thread of romance.   365
For well she kept her genial mood
And simple faith of maidenhood;
Before her still a cloud-land lay,
The mirage loomed across her way;
The morning dew, that dries so soon   370
With others, glistened at her noon;
Through years of toil and soil and care,
From glossy tress to thin gray hair,
All unprofaned she held apart
The virgin fancies of the heart.   375
Be shame to him of woman born
Who hath for such but thought of scorn.

There, too, our elder sister plied
Her evening task the stand beside;
A full, rich nature, free to trust,   380
Truthful and almost sternly just,
Impulsive, earnest, prompt to act,
And make her generous thought a fact,
Keeping with many a light disguise
The secret of self-sacrifice.   385
O heart sore-tired! thou hast the best
That Heaven itself could give thee,—rest,

Rest from all bitter thoughts and things!
　How many a poor one's blessing went
　With thee beneath the low green tent　　　　390
Whose curtain never outward swings!

As one who held herself a part
　Of all she saw, and let her heart
　Against the household bosom lean,
Upon the motley-braided mat　　　　395
Our youngest and our dearest sat,
Lifting her large, sweet, asking eyes,
　Now bathed in the unfading green
And holy peace of Paradise.
Oh, looking from some heavenly hill,　　　　400
　Or from the shade of saintly palms,
　Or silver reach of river calms,
Do those large eyes behold me still?
With me one little year ago:—
The chill weight of the winter snow　　　　405
　For months upon her grave has lain;
And now, when summer south-winds blow
　And brier and harebell bloom again,
I tread the pleasant paths we trod,
I see the violet-sprinkled sod　　　　410
Whereon she leaned, too frail and weak
The hillside flowers she loved to seek,
Yet following me where'er I went
With dark eyes full of love's content.
The birds are glad; the brier-rose fills　　　　415
The air with sweetness; all the hills
Stretch green to June's unclouded sky;
But still I wait with ear and eye
For something gone which should be nigh,
A loss in all familiar things,　　　　420
In flower that blooms, and bird that sings.
And yet, dear heart! remembering thee,
　Am I not richer than of old?
Safe in thy immortality,
　What change can reach the wealth I hold?　　　　425
　What chance can mar the pearl and gold
Thy love hath left in trust with me?
And while in life's late afternoon,
　Where cool and long the shadows grow,
I walk to meet the night that soon　　　　430
　Shall shape and shadow overflow,
I cannot feel that thou art far,
Since near at need the angels are;

And when the sunset gates unbar,
    Shall I not see thee waiting stand,   435
And, white against the evening star,
    The welcome of thy beckoning hand?

Brisk wielder of the birch and rule,
The master of the district school
Held at the fire his favored place,   440
Its warm glow lit a laughing face
Fresh-hued and fair, where scarce appeared
The uncertain prophecy of beard.
He teased the mitten-blinded cat,
Played cross-pins[32] on my uncle's hat,   445
Sang songs, and told us what befalls
In classic Dartmouth's college halls.
Born the wild Northern hills among,
From whence his yeoman father wrung
By patient toil subsistence scant,   450
Not competence and yet not want,
He early gained the power to pay
His cheerful, self-reliant way;
Could doff at ease his scholar's gown
To peddle wares from town to town;   455
Or through the long vacation's reach
In lonely lowland districts teach,
Where all the droll experience found
At stranger hearths in boarding round,
The moonlit skater's keen delight,   460
The sleigh-drive through the frosty night,
The rustic party, with its rough
Accompaniment of blind-man's-buff,
And whirling plate,[33] and forfeits paid,
His winter task a pastime made.   465
Happy the snow-locked homes wherein
He tuned his merry violin,
Or played the athlete in the barn,
Or held the good dame's winding-yarn,
Or mirth-provoking versions told   470
Of classic legends rare and old,
Wherein the scenes of Greece and Rome
Had all the commonplace of home,
And little seemed at best the odds
'Twixt Yankee pedlers and old gods;   475
Where Pindus-born Arachthus[34] took

---

[32] Children's game.
[33] Contest to see who can spin a plate on edge the longest.
[34] Greek river beginning in the Pindus Mountains.

The guise of any grist-mill brook,
And dread Olympus at his will
Became a huckleberry hill.

A careless boy that night he seemed;   480
　　But at his desk he had the look
And air of one who wisely schemed,
　　And hostage from the future took
　　In trainëd thought and lore of book.
Large-brained, clear-eyed, of such as he   485
Shall Freedom's young apostles be,
Who, following in War's bloody trail,[35]
Shall every lingering wrong assail;
All chains from limb and spirit strike,
Uplift the black and white alike;   490
Scatter before their swift advance
The darkness and the ignorance,
The pride, the lust, the squalid sloth,
Which nurtured Treason's monstrous growth,
Made murder pastime, and the hell   495
Of prison-torture possible;
The cruel lie of caste refute,
Old forms remould, and substitute
For Slavery's lash the freeman's will,
For blind routine, wise-handed skill;   500
A school-house plant on every hill,
Stretching in radiate nerve-lines thence
The quick wires of intelligence;[36]
Till North and South together brought
Shall own the same electric thought,   505
In peace a common flag salute,
And, side by side in labor's free
And unresentful rivalry,
Harvest the fields wherein they fought.

Another guest[37] that winter night   510
Flashed back from lustrous eyes the light.
Unmarked by time, and yet not young,
The honeyed music of her tongue
And words of meekness scarcely told
A nature passionate and bold,   515
Strong, self-concentred, spurning guide,
Its milder features dwarfed beside
Her unbent will's majestic pride.
She sat among us, at the best,

---

[35] "Snow-Bound" was completed in 1865, shortly after the American Civil War ended.

[36] I.e., the telegraph.

[37] Harriet Livermore. (See Whittier's note.)

A not unfeared, half-welcome guest,   520
Rebuking with her cultured phrase
Our homeliness of words and ways.
A certain pard-like,[38] treacherous grace
  Swayed the lithe limbs and dropped the lash,
Lent the white teeth their dazzling flash;   525
And under low brows, black with night,
Rayed out at times a dangerous light;
The sharp heat-lightnings of her face
Presaging ill to him whom Fate
Condemned to share her love or hate.   530
A woman tropical, intense
In thought and act, in soul and sense,
She blended in a like degree
The vixen and the devotee,
Revealing with each freak or feint   535
  The temper of Petruchio's Kate,[39]
The raptures of Siena's saint.[40]
Her tapering hand and rounded wrist
Had facile power to form a fist;
The warm, dark languish of her eyes   540
Was never safe from wrath's surprise.
Brows saintly calm and lips devout
Knew every change of scowl and pout;
And the sweet voice had notes more high
And shrill for social battle-cry.   545

Since then what old cathedral town
Has missed her pilgrim staff and gown,
What convent-gate has held its lock
Against the challenge of her knock!
Through Smyrna's plague-hushed thoroughfares,   550
Up sea-set Malta's rocky stairs,
Gray olive slopes of hills that hem
  Thy tombs and shrines, Jerusalem,
Or startling on her desert throne
The crazy Queen of Lebanon[41]   555
With claims fantastic as her own,
Her tireless feet have held their way;
And still, unrestful, bowed, and gray,
She watches under Eastern skies,
  With hope each day renewed and fresh,   560
The Lord's quick coming in the flesh,
Whereof she dreams and prophesies!

[38] Leopardlike.   [40] St. Catherine of Siena (1347–1380).
[39] Ill-tempered heroine subdued by Petruchio in   [41] Lady Hester Stanhope. (See Whittier's note.)
Shakespeare's The Taming of the Shrew.

Where'er her troubled path may be,
The Lord's sweet pity with her go!
The outward wayward life we see,   565
The hidden springs we may not know.
Nor is it given us to discern
What threads the fatal sisters[42] spun,
Through what ancestral years has run
The sorrow with the woman born,   570
What forged her cruel chain of moods,
What set her feet in solitudes,
And held the love within her mute,
What mingled madness in the blood,
A life-long discord and annoy,   575
Water of tears with oil of joy,
And hid within the folded bud
Perversities of flower and fruit.
It is not ours to separate
The tangled skein of will and fate,   580
To show what metes and bounds should stand
Upon the soul's debatable land,
And between choice and Providence
Divide the circle of events;
But He who knows our frame is just,   585
Merciful and compassionate,
And full of sweet assurances
And hope for all the language is,
That He remembereth we are dust![43]

At last the great logs, crumbling low,   590
Sent out a dull and duller glow,
The bull's-eye watch[44] that hung in view,
Ticking its weary circuit through,
Pointed with mutely warning sign
Its black hand to the hour of nine.   595
That sign the pleasant circle broke:
My uncle ceased his pipe to smoke,
Knocked from its bowl the refuse gray,
And laid it tenderly away,
Then roused himself to safely cover   600
The dull red brands with ashes over.
And while, with care, our mother laid
The work aside, her steps she stayed
One moment, seeking to express
Her grateful sense of happiness   605

---

[42] In Greek myth, the goddesses of destiny who spun the thread of life, measured its length, and cut it off.

[43] Psalms 103:14: "For he knoweth our frame; he remembereth that we are dust."

[44] Globular watch with a thick glass face.

For food and shelter, warmth and health,
And love's contentment more than wealth,
With simple wishes (not the weak,
Vain prayers which no fulfilment seek,
But such as warm the generous heart,   610
O'er-prompt to do with Heaven its part)
That none might lack, that bitter night,
For bread and clothing, warmth and light.

Within our beds awhile we heard
The wind that round the gables roared,   615
With now and then a ruder shock,
Which made our very bedsteads rock.
We heard the loosened clapboards tost,
The board-nails snapping in the frost;
And on us, through the unplastered wall,   620
Felt the light sifted snow-flakes fall.
But sleep stole on, as sleep will do
When hearts are light and life is new;
Faint and more faint the murmurs grew,
Till in the summer-land of dreams   625
They softened to the sound of streams,
Low stir of leaves, and dip of oars,
And lapsing waves on quiet shores.

Next morn we wakened with the shout
Of merry voices high and clear;   630
And saw the teamsters drawing near
To break the drifted highways out.
Down the long hillside treading slow
We saw the half-buried oxen go,
Shaking the snow from heads uptost,   635
Their straining nostrils white with frost.
Before our door the straggling train
Drew up, an added team to gain.
The elders threshed their hands a-cold,
Passed, with the cider-mug, their jokes   640
From lip to lip; the younger folks
Down the loose snow-banks, wrestling, rolled,
Then toiled again the cavalcade
O'er windy hill, through clogged ravine,
And woodland paths that wound between   645
Low drooping pine-boughs winter-weighed.
From every barn a team afoot,
At every house a new recruit,
Where, drawn by Nature's subtlest law
Haply the watchful young men saw   650

Sweet doorway pictures of the curls
And curious eyes of merry girls,
Lifting their hands in mock defence
Against the snow-ball's compliments,
And reading in each missive tost   655
The charm with Eden never lost.

We heard once more the sleigh-bells' sound;
   And, following where the teamsters led,
The wise old Doctor went his round,
Just pausing at our door to say,   660
   In the brief autocratic way
Of one who, prompt at Duty's call,
Was free to urge her claim on all,
   That some poor neighbor sick abed
At night our mother's aid would need.   665
For, one in generous thought and deed,
   What mattered in the sufferer's sight
   The Quaker matron's inward light,
The Doctor's mail of Calvin's creed?[45]
All hearts confess the saints elect   670
   Who, twain in faith, in love agree,
And melt not in an acid sect
   The Christian pearl of charity!
So days went on: a week had passed
Since the great world was heard from last.   675
The Almanac we studied o'er,
Read and reread our little store,
Of books and pamphlets, scarce a score;
One harmless novel, mostly hid
From younger eyes, a book forbid,   680
And poetry, (or good or bad,
A single book was all we had,)
Where Ellwood's[46] meek, drab-skirted Muse,
   A stranger to the heathen Nine,[47]
   Sang, with a somewhat nasal whine,   685
The wars of David and the Jews.
At last the floundering carrier bore
The village paper to our door.
Lo! broadening outward as we read,
To warmer zones the horizon spread;   690
In panoramic length unrolled

---

[45] Reference to John Calvin's doctrine of
predestination as being impregnable like the
"whole armour of God," which Paul beseeches
the Christians to wear in Ephesians 6:11–17.

[46] Thomas Ellwood (1639–1714), English Quaker
and author of the *Davideis* (1712), an epic poem
about a drab hero.
[47] I.e., the nine muses of Greek mythology.

We saw the marvels that it told.
Before us passed the painted Creeks,[48]
And daft McGregor[49] on his raids
In Costa Rica's everglades.   695
And up Taygetos winding slow
Rode Ypsilanti's Mainote Greeks,[50]
A Turk's head at each saddle-bow!
Welcome to us its week-old news,
Its corner for the rustic Muse,   700
    Its monthly gauge of snow and rain,
Its record, mingling in a breath
The wedding bell and dirge of death;
Jest, anecdote, and love-lorn tale,
The latest culprit sent to jail;   705
Its hue and cry of stolen and lost,
Its vendue[51] sales and goods at cost,
    And traffic calling loud for gain.
We felt the stir of hall and street,
The pulse of life that round us beat;   710
The chill embargo of the snow
Was melted in the genial glow;
Wide swung again our ice-locked door,
And all the world was ours once more!

Clasp, Angel of the backward look   715
    And folded wings of ashen gray
    And voice of echoes far away,
The brazen covers of thy book;
The weird palimpsest[52] old and vast,
Wherein thou hid'st the spectral past;   720
Where, closely mingling, pale and glow
The characters of joy and woe;
The monographs of outlived years,
Or smile-illumed or dim with tears,
    Green hills of life that slope to death,   725
And haunts of home, whose vistaed trees
Shade off to mournful cypresses
    With the white amaranths[53] underneath.
Even while I look, I can but heed
The restless sands' incessant fall,   730

---

[48] Alabama tribe of American Indians defeated in the Creek War (1813–1814) and forced to resettle in present-day Oklahoma.
[49] The Scottish adventurer Sir Gregor MacGregor failed to establish a colony in Costa Rica in 1819.
[50] Greek soldiers from Maina, led by Alexander

Ypsilanti (1792–1828), fought against the Turks to gain independence and achieved a salient victory at Mount Taygetos in Greece.
[51] Auction.
[52] Reused parchment.
[53] Imaginary flowers symbolic of immortality.

Importunate hours that hours succeed,
Each clamorous with its own sharp need,
   And duty keeping pace with all.
Shut down and clasp the heavy lids;
I hear again the voice that bids   735
The dreamer leave his dream midway
For larger hopes and graver fears:
Life greatens in these later years,
The century's aloe[54] flowers to-day!
Yet, haply, in some lull of life,   740
Some Truce of God which breaks its strife,
The worldling's eyes shall gather dew,
   Dreaming in throngful city ways
Of winter joys his boyhood knew;
And dear and early friends—the few   745
Who yet remain—shall pause to view
   These Flemish pictures[55] of old days;
Sit with me by the homestead hearth,
And stretch the hands of memory forth
   To warm them at the wood-fire's blaze! 750
And thanks untraced to lips unknown
Shall greet me like the odors blown
From unseen meadows newly mown,
Or lilies floating in some pond,
Wood-fringed, the wayside gaze beyond; 755
The traveller owns the grateful sense
Of sweetness near, he knows not whence,
And, pausing, takes with forehead bare
The benediction of the air.

1864–1865/1866

Abraham Davenport[1]

In the old days (a custom laid aside
With breeches and cocked hats) the people sent
Their wisest men to make the public laws.
And so, from a brown homestead, where the Sound

[54] In legend, plant that blooms once each century.
[55] I.e., Flemish seventeenth-century art portraying domestic realism.
[1] Whittier's note: "The famous Dark Day of New England, May 19, 1780, was a physical puzzle for many years to our ancestors, but its occurrence brought something more than philosophical speculation into the minds of those who passed through it. The incident of Colonel Abraham Davenport's sturdy protest is a matter of history."

Drinks the small tribute of the Mianas,   5
Waved over by the woods of Rippowams,
And hallowed by pure lives and tranquil deaths,
Stamford[2] sent up to the councils of the State
Wisdom and grace in Abraham Davenport.

'Twas on a May-day of the far old year   10
Seventeen hundred eighty, that there fell
Over the bloom and sweet life of the Spring,
Over the fresh earth and the heaven of noon,
A horror of great darkness, like the night
In day of which the Norland sagas tell,—   15
The Twilight of the Gods.[3] The low-hung sky
Was black with ominous clouds, save where its rim
Was fringed with a dull glow, like that which climbs
The crater's sides from the red hell below.
Birds ceased to sing, and all the barn-yard fowls   20
Roosted; the cattle at the pasture bars
Lowed, and looked homeward; bats on leathern wings
Flitted abroad; the sounds of labor died;
Men prayed, and women wept; all ears grew sharp
To hear the doom-blast of the trumpet[4] shatter   25
The black sky, that the dreadful face of Christ
Might look from the rent clouds, not as he looked
A loving guest at Bethany,[5] but stern
As Justice and inexorable Law.

Meanwhile in the old State House, dim as ghosts,   30
Sat the lawgivers of Connecticut,
Trembling beneath their legislative robes.
"It is the Lord's Great Day! Let us adjourn,"
Some said; and then, as if with one accord,
All eyes were turned to Abraham Davenport.   35
He rose, slow cleaving with his steady voice
The intolerable hush. "This well may be
The Day of Judgment which the world awaits;
But be it so or not, I only know
My present duty, and my Lord's command   40
To occupy till He come.[6] So at the post
Where He hath set me in His providence,
I choose, for one, to meet Him face to face,—

---

[2] City in southern Connecticut on the Long
Island Sound.
[3] As in the *Götterdämerung,* Norse and Germanic
myths of the last judgment and destruction.
[4] The trumpet of Judgment Day in 1 Corinthians
15:52–53.

[5] In Matthew 26:6–13, Jesus was a guest of
Simon the Leper at Bethany.
[6] Luke 19:13: "And he called his ten servants, and
delivered them ten pounds, and said unto them,
occupy till I come."

No faithless servant frightened from my task,
But ready when the Lord of the harvest[7] calls;   45
And therefore, with all reverence, I would say,
Let God do His work, we will see to ours.
Bring in the candles." And they brought them in.

　　Then by the flaring lights the Speaker read,
Albeit with husky voice and shaking hands,   50
An act to amend an act to regulate
The shad and alewive fisheries. Whereupon
Wisely and well spake Abraham Davenport,
Straight to the question, with no figures of speech
Save the ten Arab signs,[8] yet not without   55
The shrewd dry humor natural to the man:
His awe-struck colleagues listening all the while,
Between the pauses of his argument,
To hear the thunder of the wrath of God
Break from the hollow trumpet of the cloud.   60

　　And there he stands in memory to this day,
Erect, self-poised, a rugged face, half seen
Against the background of unnatural dark,
A witness to the ages as they pass,
That simple duty hath no place for fear.   65
1866

At Last

When on my day of life the night is falling,
　　And, in the winds from unsunned spaces blown,
I hear far voices out of darkness calling
　　My feet to paths unknown,

Thou who hast made my home of life so pleasant,   5
　　Leave not its tenant when its walls decay;
O Love Divine, O Helper ever present,
　　Be Thou my strength and stay!

---

[7] Luke 10:2: "Therefore said he unto them, the harvest truly is great, but the labourers are few: Pray ye therefore the Lord of the Harvest, that he would send forth labourers into his harvest."

[8] I.e., the Arabic numerals.

Be near me when all else is from me drifting;
   Earth, sky, home's pictures, days of shade and shine,   10
And kindly faces to my own uplifting
   The love which answers mine.

I have but Thee, my Father! let Thy spirit
   Be with me then to comfort and uphold;
No gate of pearl, no branch of palm I merit,   15
   Nor street of shining gold.

Suffice it if—my good and ill unreckoned,
   And both forgiven through Thy abounding grace—
I find myself by hands familiar beckoned
   Unto my fitting place.   20

Some humble door among Thy many mansions,
   Some sheltering shade where sin and striving cease,
And flows forever through heaven's green expansions
   The river of Thy peace.

There, from the music round about me stealing,   25
   I fain would learn the new and holy song,
And find at last, beneath Thy trees of healing,
   The life for which I long.

1882

Oliver Wendell Holmes
1809–1894

Dr. Oliver Wendell Holmes was born in 1809, exactly one hundred years after the major English literary figure Dr. Samuel Johnson—a coincidence Holmes enjoyed immensely, as he strived to emulate Johnson's Neoclassical approach to life. "It was for me," Holmes said of the bond he felt with Johnson, "a kind of unison between two instruments, both playing that old familiar air, 'Life'—one a bassoon . . . the other an oaten pipe. . . . At last the thinner thread of sound is heard by itself, and its deep accompaniment rolls out its thunder no more." Compared to Johnson's robust proportions, Holmes's five-foot two-inch slender frame made a thin pipe indeed. And his seemingly gentle, colloquial style matched his physique, just as Johnson's orotund style matched his. Yet Holmes's self-deprecation of both his intellectual and physical stature as well as his occasionally overly sentimental style belies the impregnable core of honesty at the center of his writing. That core enabled him to reject the Calvinist heritage of his father, the Reverend Abiel Holmes, an orthodox Congregationalist minister, just as his own son and namesake, Justice Oliver Wendell Holmes, would eventually reject his father's conservatism. Dr. Holmes's own self-criticisms to the contrary, such honesty in his poems, essays, novels, lectures, and conversations made him as eminent a man of letters in his time as Johnson was in his. Even more than Johnson, who was assuredly a dilettante in many intellectual spheres, Holmes spread his considerable talents far beyond his avocation for literature, making a name for himself as a prominent medical man, a scientist, an inventor, a teacher, a moralist, and finally as a kind of elder statesman for Boston, the town that he called home and that, in Holmes's provincial and patriotic estimation at least, he celebrated as "the hub of the solar system."

In the popular opinion of the time, Oliver Wendell Holmes was the brightest star of what was undeniably the cultural hub of the nation, if not quite the solar system. Holmes may seem today to have been eclipsed by his son, the Justice, but such a judgment is more the result of changing tastes and literary fashions than any actual intrinsic literary skill. Although many modern readers regard Holmes primarily as a writer of congenial occasional verse, his literary and moral influence was far vaster. Surrounded by a constellation of dazzling literary luminaries that included Ralph Waldo Emerson, Nathaniel Hawthorne, Henry Wadsworth Longfellow, James Russell Lowell, and William Dean Howells, Holmes's chief claim to literary fame was, as Dr. Johnson's had been, a remarkable conversational wit. That wit first achieved notoriety in 1831, when Holmes was only twenty-two and attending medical school. In a series of essays for the *New England Magazine* titled "The Autocrat of the Breakfast Table," Holmes displayed a virtuosity at monologue at once entertaining and acerbic. More than twenty-five years later, he resumed this series for the *Atlantic Monthly,* a periodical whose considerable reputation both here and abroad he helped establish and ensure. By this time Holmes did not merely hold his own among the literary giants of the Saturday Club when they met once a month. More often, he monopolized and mesmerized them with a verbal barrage so intense that he occasionally felt compelled to apologize: "I came to listen and then I talked too much again." Such enthusiasm proved equally Holmes's success and his undoing as he struggled with a wider and wider range of interests.

As a student at Harvard, Holmes excelled both academically and socially. Elected to Phi Beta Kappa, he also wrote less than genteel poetry for the satiric wits who belonged to the Hasty Pudding Club, along with several sophomoric satires of the faculty, thereby ingratiating himself with his fellow students. He was the class poet in 1829, the year he graduated. Holmes spent the following year studying law, only to discover himself apparently unsuited for the profession.

The year 1830 also brought Holmes literary recognition. His poetry achieved national prominence with the publication in the *Boston Daily Advertiser* of "Old Ironsides," an indignant, rousing poem patriotically protesting the scrapping of the frigate *Constitution,* a Boston-built ship that had served the nation well in many battles. Typically, the unassuming Holmes signed this poem simply "H." In favor of pursuing still another vocation, medicine, Holmes ignored the favorable critical reception of this early poem and another, "The Last Leaf," which Edgar Allan Poe pronounced "an excellent well conceived and well managed specimen of versification." Yet literature would remain Holmes's lifelong interest.

Religious beliefs, like vocational choices, created dilemmas for Holmes. Though he remained outwardly loyal to his father's preaching, privately he agreed with the more liberal members of his father's congregation, who eventually rejected Abiel Holmes's rather puritanical brand of Calvinism, forcing the minister to form a new parish. In a similar vein, Holmes remembered that as a young boy he had viewed John Bunyan's *Pilgrim's Progress* "more like the hunting of sinners with a pack of demons for the amusement of the lord of the terrestrial manor than like the tender care of a father for his offspring." This is, perhaps, the first inkling of what in later essays and lectures would stir considerable controversy. In these writings Holmes risked his moral reputation by claiming that the chief end of man could not be prescribed by religious dogma since that end varied with the individual.

Doubtless Holmes's own difficulty in settling on a chief end for himself helped prompt such liberal views. Yet he remained far more comfortable in the role of one of the most prominent cultural conservatives of his time. Finding the Romantically inspired thinking of his Transcendental contemporaries superfluous —and rather too difficult to understand—Holmes preferred the relative surety of science, keeping even his literary forays into the study of human conduct mainly within the realm of what he regarded as the practical.

Holmes had begun to study medicine in Boston in 1830, and in 1833 he left for Paris, where experimental techniques were revolutionizing the profession. He returned to Harvard in 1836, taking a degree in medicine a year after his first volume, *Poems,* was published. Holmes's three years of medical study in Paris gave him a clear and strong sense of purpose. Before he left, American doctors still relied on what were considered archaic remedies: leeches, blistering, and emetics. When he returned, Holmes helped change these primitive practices. After two years as professor of anatomy at Dartmouth (1838–1840), Holmes settled into private practice in Boston and married.

Teaching and medical writing gradually had become his chief professional interests. In *Homeopathy and Its Kindred Delusions* (1842) Holmes advocated a reduction in primitive medical treatments, and in *The Contagiousness of Puerperal Fever* (1843) he argued for cleanliness among doctors and midwives to inhibit the spread of infection at childbirth. In 1847 he was named Parkman Professor of Anatomy and Physiology at the Harvard Medical School, where he remained for nearly forty years. During his tenure there, Holmes introduced the microscopic study of tissues, advocated such radical practices as the use of anesthesia and antisepsis, and helped found the American Medical Association. Yet such devotion to science kept Holmes distant from the social causes of his time. He remained secure in his identity as a respectable citizen—a conservative culturally and a humanitarian professionally.

Writing was his favorite, steady avocation. He published volumes of poetry in 1846, 1849, 1852, and 1854. In 1857 he helped found the *Atlantic Monthly,* which he named. He helped set the distinctive tone of that magazine with the publication of his *Autocrat* essays, for which he soon earned national recognition. The first collected edition of these conversational essays was published in 1858 as *The Autocrat of the Breakfast Table.* Later volumes appeared as *The Professor of the Breakfast Table* (1860), *The Poet at the Breakfast Table* (1872), and *Over the Teacups* (1891). Over these same decades, Holmes continued to cultivate his interest in verse. Marked by a delightful mixture of urbane wit and comic sensibility, Holmes's reflective and occasional poems were published principally in the *Atlantic Monthly.* Several of these poems (including "Old Ironsides," "The Chambered Nautilus," and "The Deacon's Masterpiece, or 'The One-Hoss Shay' ") eventually became schoolroom classics.

Holmes's novels brought him far less attention and praise. *Elsie Venner: A Romance of Destiny* (1861), *The Guardian Angel* (1867), and *A Moral Antipathy* (1885) blend social commentary and character analysis but lack mastery of fictional technique and a strong narrative line. Self-styled "medicated" novels by Holmes, each traces a character's psychological reaction, as it would be called today, to the events that shaped his or her life. Holmes's point in these novels is less to demonstrate literary excellence than to explore alternatives to a strictly theological explanation for human behavior. In *Elsie Venner,* for instance, a pregnant woman is bitten by a rattlesnake. At birth, the child embodies the snakelike characteristics of that prenatal influence. Thus the novel remains, as Holmes recognized it would be, more a curious early psychological study than a first-rate literary effort. In their attention to such issues as moral responsibility, hereditary influence, and mental trauma, these novels anticipate a good deal of later, more technically sophisticated fiction.

Holmes was in great demand as a lecturer at medical meetings, and he wrote several treatises, along with three biographical studies, the most widely known of which focuses on his friend Ralph Waldo Emerson. Like his novels, Holmes's study of Emerson for the *American Men of Letters* series (1885) attempted to treat only those aspects of character and behavior Holmes felt sure he understood. He did not capture Emerson the literary theorist as well as he presented Emerson the person, the friend he knew from their meetings at the Saturday Club and from their mutual literary acquaintances.

By the 1870s, Holmes had became one of America's most respected public figures, renowned as a medical practitioner, a respected author of humorous witty essays and whimsical verse for special occasions, and the late nineteenth century's most celebrated after-dinner speaker. Holmes's writing represented the epitome of what he dubbed the "Brahmin Caste of New England," the "harmless, inoffensive, untitled aristocracy" that is "merely the richer part of the community, that live in the tallest houses, drive real carriages (not 'kerridges') . . . and have a provokingly easy way of dressing, walking, talking, and nodding to people." For eighty-five years, Oliver Wendell Holmes practiced that easy way, to everyone's delight.

Further Reading:
Life and Letters of Oliver Wendell Holmes, ed. J. T. Morse, Jr., 2 vols., 1896.
M. A. D. Howe, *Holmes of the Breakfast Table,* 1939, 1972.
Oliver Wendell Holmes, ed. S. I. Hayakawa and H. M. Jones, 1939.
M. Tilton, *Amiable Autocrat: A Biography of Oliver Wendell Holmes,* 1947.
E. P. Hoyt, *The Improper Bostonian: Dr. Oliver Wendell Holmes,* 1979.

Text:
The Complete Poetical Works of Oliver Wendell Holmes, ed. H. E. Scudder, 1895.

Old Ironsides[*]

Ay, tear her tattered ensign down!
   Long has it waved on high,
And many an eye has danced to see
   That banner in the sky;
Beneath it rung the battle shout,   5
   And burst the cannon's roar;—
The meteor of the ocean air
   Shall sweep the clouds no more.

Her deck, once red with heroes' blood,
   Where knelt the vanquished foe,   10
When winds were hurrying o'er the flood,
   And waves were white below,
No more shall feel the victor's tread,
   Or know the conquered knee;—
The harpies[1] of the shore shall pluck   15
   The eagle of the sea!

Oh, better that her shattered hulk
   Should sink beneath the wave;
Her thunders shook the mighty deep,
   And there should be her grave;   20
Nail to the mast her holy flag,
   Set every threadbare sail,
And give her to the god of storms,
   The lightning and the gale!

1830

---

[*] This poem was written in response to an announcement in the Boston *Daily Advertiser* for September 14, 1830, that the frigate *Constitution,* which had defeated the British *Guerrière* in the War of 1812, was to be dismantled. Holmes's poem appeared in the *Daily Advertiser* two days later, was widely circulated, and help saved Old Ironsides, the popular name for the *Constitution.*

[1] Harpy: mythological monster, half bird and half woman, that was said to carry off the souls of the dead.

The Last Leaf*

I saw him once before,
As he passed by the door,
   And again
The pavement stones resound,
As he totters o'er the ground   5
   With his cane.

They say that in his prime,
Ere the pruning-knife of Time
   Cut him down,
Not a better man was found   10
By the Crier on his round
   Through the town.

But now he walks the streets,
And he looks at all he meets
   Sad and wan,   15
And he shakes his feeble head,
That it seems as if he said,
   "They are gone."

The mossy marbles rest
On the lips that he has prest   20
   In their bloom,
And the names he loved to hear
Have been carved for many a year
   On the tomb.

My grandmamma has said—   25
Poor old lady, she is dead
   Long ago—
That he had a Roman nose,
And his cheek was like a rose
   In the snow;   30

* Holmes's note: "This poem was suggested by the sight of a figure well known to Bostonians, that of Major Thomas Melville, 'the last of the cocked hats,' as he was often pointed at as one of the 'Indians' of the famous 'Boston Tea Party' of 1774. His aspect among the crowds of a late generation reminded me of a withered leaf which has held to its stem through the storms of autumn and winter, and finds itself still clinging to its bough while the new growths of spring are bursting their buds and spreading their foliage all around it." Major Thomas Melville was Herman Melville's grandfather.

But now his nose is thin,
And it rests upon his chin
    Like a staff,
And a crook is in his back,
And a melancholy crack   35
    In his laugh.

I know it is a sin
For me to sit and grin
    At him here;
But the old three-cornered hat,   40
And the breeches, and all that,
    Are so queer!

And if I should live to be
The last leaf upon the tree
    In the spring,   45
Let them smile, as I do now,
At the old forsaken bough
    Where I cling.

1831

My Aunt

My aunt! my dear unmarried aunt!
    Long years have o'er her flown;
Yet still she strains the aching clasp[1]
    That binds her virgin zone;
I know it hurts her,—though she looks   5
    As cheerful as she can;
Her waist is ampler than her life,
    For life is but a span.

My aunt! my poor deluded aunt!
    Her hair is almost gray;   10
Why will she train that winter curl
    In such a spring-like way?
How can she lay her glasses down,
    And say she reads as well,
When through a double convex lens   15
    She just makes out to spell?

[1] Broad ornamental belt.

Her father—grandpapa! forgive
   This erring lip its smiles—
Vowed she should make the finest girl
   Within a hundred miles;   20
He sent her to a stylish school;
   'T was in her thirteenth June;
And with her, as the rules required,
   "Two towels and a spoon."

They braced my aunt against a board,   25
   To make her straight and tall;
They laced her up, they starved her down,
   To make her light and small;
They pinched her feet, they singed her hair,
   They screwed it up with pins;—   30
Oh, never mortal suffered more
   In penance for her sins.

So, when my precious aunt was done,
   My grandsire brought her back;
(By daylight, lest some rabid youth   35
   Might follow on the track;)
"Ah!" said my grandsire, as he shook
   Some powder in his pan,[2]
"What could this lovely creature do
   Against a desperate man!"   40

Alas! nor chariot, nor barouche,[3]
   Nor bandit cavalcade,
Tore from the trembling father's arms
   His all-accomplished maid.
For her how happy had it been!   45
   And Heaven had spared to me
To see one sad, ungathered rose
   On my ancestral tree.

   1831

---

[2] Hollow in the lock of a musket where priming powder was placed.   [3] Four-wheeled carriage fashionable at the time.

The Chambered Nautilus*

This is the ship of pearl,¹ which, poets feign,
    Sails the unshadowed main,—
      The venturous bark that flings
On the sweet summer wind its purpled wings
In gulfs enchanted, where the Siren² sings,
    And coral reefs lie bare,   5
Where the cold sea-maids rise to sun their streaming hair.

Its webs of living gauze no more unfurl;
    Wrecked is the ship of pearl!
      And every chambered cell,   10
Where its dim dreaming life was wont to dwell,
As the frail tenant shaped his growing shell,
    Before thee lies revealed,—
Its irised ceiling rent, its sunless crypt unsealed!

Year after year beheld the silent toil   15
    That spread his lustrous coil;
      Still, as the spiral grew,
He left the past year's dwelling for the new,
Stole with soft step its shining archway through,
    Built up its idle door,   20
Stretched in his last-found home, and knew the old no more.

Thanks for the heavenly message brought by thee,
    Child of the wandering sea,
      Cast from her lap, forlorn!
From thy dead lips a clearer note is born
Than ever Triton³ blew from wreathèd horn!   25
    While on mine ear it rings,
Through the deep caves of thought I hear a voice that sings:—

Build thee more stately mansions, O my soul,
    As the swift seasons roll!   30
    Leave thy low-vaulted past!
Let each new temple, nobler than the last,

---

* This poem, published as part of *The Autocrat of
the Breakfast-Table,* first appeared in the *Atlantic
Monthly* in February 1858.
¹ The "chambered" or pearly nautilus is a South
Pacific and Indian Ocean mollusk that builds a
spiral shell by adding a compartment each year.

The Greeks thought it capable of moving over
the water using its membrane as a sail.
² Mythical sea nymph who lures sailors to
destruction with her song.
³ In Greek myth, the sea god who ruled the
waves with a conch-shell trumpet.

Shut thee from heaven with a dome more vast,
    Till thou at length art free,
Leaving thine outgrown shell by life's unresting sea!   35
1858

The Deacon's Masterpiece
Or, The Wonderful "One-Hoss Shay"[1]

A Logical Story

Have you heard of the wonderful one-hoss shay,
That was built in such a logical way
It ran a hundred years to a day,
And then, of a sudden, it—ah, but stay,
I'll tell you what happened without delay,   5
Scaring the parson into fits,
Frightening people out of their wits,—
Have you ever heard of that, I say?

Seventeen hundred and fifty-five.
Georgius Secundus[2] was then alive,—   10
Snuffy old drone from the German hive.
That was the year when Lisbon-town
Saw the earth open and gulp her down,[3]
And Braddock's[4] army was done so brown,
Left without a scalp to its crown.   15
It was on the terrible Earthquake-day
That the Deacon finished the one-hoss shay.

Now in building of chaises, I tell you what,
There is always *somewhere* a weakest spot,—
In hub, tire, felloe, in spring or thill,[5]   20
In panel, or crossbar, or floor, or sill,
In screw, bolt, thoroughbrace,[6]—lurking still,
Find it somewhere you must and will,—

[1] Light, open, two-wheeled, horse-drawn carriage.
[2] German-born George II, king of England from 1727 to 1760.
[3] Reference to the devastating Lisbon earthquake of 1755.
[4] The British general Edward Braddock (1695–1755) was killed during the defeat of his army in the French and Indian War.
[5] Felloe: outer wooden rim of a wheel; thill: the two thin shafts between which a horse is harnessed.
[6] Leather strap that fastens the carriage body to the springs.

Above or below, or within or without,—
And that's the reason, beyond a doubt,   25
That a chaise *breaks down,* but does n't *wear out.*

But the Deacon swore (as Deacons do,
With an "I dew vum,"[7] or an "I tell *yeou*")
He would build one shay to beat the taown
'N' the keounty 'n' all the kentry raoun';   30
It should be so built that it *could n'* break daown:
"Fur," said the Deacon, "'t's mighty plain
Thut the weakes' place mus' stan' the strain;
'N' the way t' fix it, uz I maintain,
                    Is only jest   35
T' make that place uz strong uz the rest."

So the Deacon inquired of the village folk
Where he could find the strongest oak,
That could n't be split nor bent nor broke,—
That was for spokes and floor and sills;   40
He sent for lancewood to make the thills;
The crossbars were ash, from the straightest trees,
The panels of white-wood, that cuts like cheese,
But lasts like iron for things like these;
The hubs of logs from the "Settler's ellum,"[8]—   45
Last of its timber,—they could n't sell 'em,

Never an axe had seen their chips,
And the wedges flew from between their lips,
Their blunt ends frizzled like celery-tips;
Step and prop-iron, bolt and screw,   50
Spring, tire, axle, and linchpin[9] too,
Steel of the finest, bright and blue;
Thoroughbrace bison-skin, thick and wide;
Boot, top, dasher,[10] from tough old hide
Found in the pit when the tanner died.   55
That was the way he "put her through."
"There!" said the Deacon, "naow she'll dew!"

Do! I tell you, I rather guess
She was a wonder, and nothing less!
Colts grew horses, beards turned gray,   60
Deacon and deaconess dropped away,
Children and grandchildren—where were they?

---

[7] "I do vow."
[8] "Settler's ellum": elm dating back to the first
settlers in New England.

[9] Similar to a modern cotter pin, a linchpin
secured the wheel to the axle.
[10] Dashboard.

But there stood the stout old one-hoss shay
As fresh as on Lisbon-earthquake-day!

EIGHTEEN HUNDRED;—it came and found   65
The Deacon's masterpiece strong and sound.
Eighteen hundred increased by ten;—
"Hahnsum kerridge" they called it then.
Eighteen hundred and twenty came;—
Running as usual; much the same.   70
Thirty and forty at last arrive,
And then come fifty, and FIFTY-FIVE.

Little of all we value here
Wakes on the morn of its hundredth year
Without both feeling and looking queer.   75
In fact, there's nothing that keeps its youth,
So far as I know, but a tree and truth.
(This is a moral that runs at large;
Take it.—You're welcome.—No extra charge.)

FIRST OF NOVEMBER,—the Earthquake-day,—   80
There are traces of age in the one-hoss shay,
A general flavor of mild decay,
But nothing local, as one may say.
There could n't be,—for the Deacon's art
Had made it so like in every part   85
That there was n't a chance for one to start.
For the wheels were just as strong as the thills,
And the floor was just as strong as the sills,
And the panels just as strong as the floor,
And the whipple-tree[11] neither less nor more,   90
And the back crossbar as strong as the fore,
And spring and axle and hub *encore.*
And yet, *as a whole,* it is past a doubt
In another hour it will be *worn out!*

First of November, 'Fifty-five!   95
This morning the parson takes a drive.
Now, small boys, get out of the way!
Here comes the wonderful one-hoss shay,
Drawn by a rat-tailed, ewe-necked bay.
"Huddup!" said the parson.—Off went they.   100
The parson was working his Sunday's text,—

[11] Pivoted bar on the frame behind the horse, to
which the harness is attached.

Had got to *fifthly*,[12] and stopped perplexed
At what the—Moses—was coming next.
All at once the horse stood still,
Close by the meet'n'-house on the hill.   105
First a shiver, and then a thrill,
Then something decidedly like a spill,—
And the parson was sitting upon a rock,
At half past nine by the meet'n'-house clock,—
Just the hour of the Earthquake shock!   110
What do you think the parson found,
When he got up and stared around?
The poor old chaise in a heap or mound,
As if it had been to the mill and ground!
You see, of course, if you're not a dunce,   115
How it went to pieces all at once,—
All at once, and nothing first,—
Just as bubbles do when they burst.

End of the wonderful one-hoss shay.
Logic is logic. That's all I say.   120
1858

Dorothy Q[1]

Grandmother's mother: her age, I guess,
Thirteen summers, or something less;
Girlish bust, but womanly air;
Smooth, square forehead with uprolled hair;
Lips that lover has never kissed;   5
Taper fingers and slender wrist;
Hanging sleeves of stiff brocade;
So they painted the little maid.

On her hand a parrot green
Sits unmoving and broods serene.   10
Hold up the canvas full in view,—
Look! there's a rent the light shines through,

---

[12] I.e., fifth application of that day's biblical text.
(The text was presented and then applied to the
lives of the congregation.)

[1] Holmes's note: "Dorothy was the daughter of
Judge Edmund Quincy, and the niece of Josiah
Quincy, Jr., the young patriot and orator who
died just before the American Revolution, of
which he was one of the most eloquent and
effective promoters." Dorothy was Holmes's
maternal great-grandmother.

Dark with a century's fringe of dust,—
That was a Red-Coat's rapier-thrust!
Such is the tale the lady old,   15
Dorothy's daughter's daughter, told.

Who the painter was none may tell,—
One whose best was not over well;
Hard and dry, it must be confessed,
Flat as a rose that has long been pressed;   20
Yet in her cheek the hues are bright,
Dainty colors of red and white,
And in her slender shape are seen
Hint and promise of stately mien.

Look not on her with eyes of scorn,—   25
Dorothy Q. was a lady born!
Ay! since the galloping Normans came,
England's annals have known her name;[2]
And still to the three-hilled[3] rebel town
Dear is that ancient name's renown,   30
For many a civic wreath they won,
The youthful sire and the gray-haired son.

O Damsel Dorothy ! Dorothy Q.!
Strange is the gift that I owe to you;
Such a gift as never a king   35
Save to daughter or son might bring,—
All my tenure of heart and hand,
All my title to house and land;
Mother and sister and child and wife
And joy and sorrow and death and life!   40

What if a hundred years ago
Those close-shut lips had answered No,
When forth the tremulous question came
That cost the maiden her Norman name,
And under the folds that look so still   45
The bodice swelled with the bosom's thrill?
Should I be I, or would it be
One tenth another, to nine tenths me?

Soft is the breath of a maiden's YES:
Not the light gossamer stirs with less;   50

---

[2] The Norman invasion of 1066 introduced many   [3] Boston was built on three hills.
French names into English genealogy. *Quincy* is
one example.

But never a cable that holds so fast
Through all the battles of wave and blast,
And never an echo of speech or song
That lives in the babbling air so long!
There were tones in the voice that whispered then   55
You may hear to-day in a hundred men.

O lady and lover, how faint and far
Your images hover,—and here we are,
Solid and stirring in flesh and bone,—
Edward's and Dorothy's—all their own,—   60
A goodly record for Time to show
Of a syllable spoken so long ago!—
Shall I bless you, Dorothy, or forgive
For the tender whisper that bade me live?

It shall be a blessing, my little maid!   65
I will heal the stab of the Red-Coat's blade,[4]
And freshen the gold of the tarnished frame,
And gild with a rhyme your household name;
So you shall smile on us brave and bright
As first you greeted the morning's light,   70
And live untroubled by woes and fears
Through a second youth of a hundred years.

1871

Harriet Beecher Stowe
1811–1896

Harriet Beecher Stowe was the daughter of a New England Congregational
preacher, the sister of five preachers, and the wife of another. Born in Litchfield,
Connecticut, on June 14, 1811, she was raised in a family whose members had
devoted themselves to Christian purpose, self-abnegation, and spiritual rebirth, "a
kind of moral heaven, replete with moral oxygen—fully charged with
intellectual electricity." She was educated at a local school for girls and in 1824
graduated from—and then taught at—the Hartford Female Seminary, founded by
her famous sister Catherine, a pioneer in women's education. When her father
accepted an appointment to head the Lane Theological Seminary in 1832, she
moved with her family to Cincinnati, a town at the border of North and South,
East and West and at the center of increasing antislavery sentiment. While

---

[4] Holmes's note: "The canvas of the painting was so much decayed that it had to be replaced by a new one, in doing which the rapier thrust was of course filled up."

working at Catherine's newly founded Western Female Institute, Harriet Beecher began writing sketches and stories for literary and evangelical periodicals. In 1836 she married the Reverend Calvin Ellis Stowe, a preacher and a professor of biblical literature at Lane Theological Seminary. The demands of raising their seven children forced Mrs. Stowe to set aside the idea of a literary career. Yet during what would amount to nearly fifteen years, she wrote, when she could find the time, mostly to help support their large family. And she came to realize that she was a woman writer drawn to a provocative subject: the moral, political, and ethical issues surrounding the slavery question.

The moral principles that guided her life infused her thinking and writing. Her views on slavery derived from reading both slave narratives and abolitionist tracts, visiting slaveholding plantations in Kentucky, and feeling moral revulsion at the passage of the Fugitive Slave Law (1850), which legally obliged residents of free states to return fugitives to their "rightful owners." Her plans to write a moral "epic of negro bondage" crystallized in a vision of a slave's suffering and death she had in a church in Brunswick, Maine, where the family had moved in 1850. Years later, Stowe described her state of mind at the time: "My heart was bursting with the anguish excited by the cruelty and injustice our nation was showing to the slave, and praying to God to let me do a little and to cause my cry for them to be heard." Eventually, she came to believe that she was simply God's instrument for writing *Uncle Tom's Cabin,* a book she hoped would "make this whole nation feel what an accursed thing slavery is."

With an incomplete draft in hand, Stowe approached *The National Era,* a Washington, D.C., antislavery weekly, with plans to publish her novel in three or four installments. The success of this serial led in 1852 to the publication in two volumes of what was originally titled *Uncle Tom's Cabin, or The Man That Was a Thing.* It was a historic event in publishing: Ten thousand copies were sold in the first week, over three hundred thousand in the first year. By the outbreak of the Civil War that number had soared beyond three million. The book was translated into thirty-seven languages. Praise poured in from all over the world. Ralph Waldo Emerson spoke for many when he hailed Stowe's ability to create a book that at once could enjoy popular success, speak "to the universal heart," and be "read with equal interest to three audiences, namely, in the parlor, in the kitchen, and in the nursery of every house." Suddenly, Harriet Beecher Stowe found herself the most famous literary figure in America and an international celebrity. She toured England and met many of the leading literary figures there and on the Continent. Several years later, when the diminutive Stowe met the towering president, Lincoln is reported to have said, "So this is the little lady who made this big war!"

A powerful but controversial instrument of reform, *Uncle Tom's Cabin* had an extraordinary impact on the culture and politics of its time. Its publication helped change public opinion and sway political action. Its message—that the slave, the master, and their respective families are destroyed by slavery—stirred the nation. And its principal characters—Simon Legree, Eliza, Little Eva, and Uncle Tom— became archetypes in the national literary consciousness. The book not only inspired southern writers to respond in print but also sparked intense debates among politicians and readers on both sides of the Mason-Dixon line. In 1853 Stowe published *Key to Uncle Tom's Cabin,* in which she defended herself against widespread charges that she had distorted the reality of slave life. Stowe's reliance on slave narratives as her primary sources and her correspondence with Frederick Douglass to verify the accuracy of her presentation of Tom made *Uncle Tom's Cabin* a significant early example of black literature's influence on a mainstream American novel. In a similar manner, Stowe's second novel on slavery, *Dred* (1856), drew heavily on the widely circulated slave narrative *Confessions of Nat Turner* (1831) but enjoyed no comparable popular success.

Harriet Beecher Stowe applied her considerable literary skills to subjects other than the moral and social reform advocated in her novels about slavery. And whether it was a gripping potboiler or a polemic essay on domestic affairs, a sentimental romance or a delightful sketch of the rural New England she knew so well, a piece of journalism or a letter to a friend, Harriet Beecher Stowe wrote immensely readable prose. She had an excellent ear for local idiom and a practiced eye for telling details. Her local-color fiction constitutes, in the words of Edmund Wilson, the celebrated literary critic, "a kind of encyclopedia of old New England institutions, characters, customs and points of view." She wrote at least one book in each of the years between 1862 and 1884, and many—including *The Minister's Wooing* (1859), *The Pearl of Orr's Island* (1862), and *Oldtown Fireside Stories* (1872)—captured domestic life and local color and vividness. Stowe called *Oldtown Folks* (1869) "my résumé of the whole spirit and body of New England" and described her technique and purpose in these terms: "to make my mind as still and passive as a looking-glass, or a mountain lake, and then to give you merely the images reflected there." In this respect, her novels anticipate much of the local-color realism of Mary Wilkins Freeman and especially Sarah Orne Jewett, who acknowledged her indebtedness to Stowe.

Within Stowe's lifetime, the characters over whom half the world had anguished were gradually refashioned into stereotypes and burlesqued on stage and in literature. Aunt Chloe was transformed into Aunt Jemima, and Uncle Tom, once the focus of compassion, became an object of derision, a symbol of the foot-shuffling, servile black. An era of new sensibilities challenged the misconceptions of even the best-intentioned social reformers, activists, and writers. Yet there was little in Stowe's later years that turned out the way she would have preferred. One of her children died from alcoholism, another from drug addiction, a third from drowning, a fourth from cholera. She received none of the foreign and theatrical royalties due her for *Uncle Tom's Cabin,* and most of what she did receive was lost in mismanaged real estate investments. The adultery trial of her brother Henry Ward Beecher, one of the most famous preachers in the nineteenth century, greatly affected her. And her friendship with Lady Byron —and her exposé in the *Atlantic Monthly* of the Lord Byron–Augusta Leigh incest episode—cost the magazine nearly fifteen thousand subscribers and caused many readers of her fiction to regard her as a spiteful gossip. Stowe spent her later years in Hartford, the winters in Florida. She died in 1896, several years after senility had taken its toll. At her funeral her coffin was draped with a wreath from a group of Boston blacks. The note read, "The Children of Uncle Tom."

Further Reading:
*The Life of Harriet Beecher Stowe from Her
Letters and Journals,* ed. C. E. Stowe, 1889.
F. Wilson, *Crusader in Crinoline: The Life of
Harriet Beecher Stowe,* 1941.
J. Baldwin, "Everybody's Protest Novel,"
Partisan Review 16, 1949.
C. H. Foster, *The Rungless Ladder: Harriet
Beecher Stowe and New England Puritanism,*
1954.

E. Wilson, *Patriotic Gore,* 1962.
J. R. Adams, *Harriet Beecher Stowe,* 1963.
E. Wagenknecht, *Harriet Beecher Stowe: The
Known and the Unknown,* 1965.
A. Crozier, *The Novels of Harriet Beecher Stowe,*
1970.
E. B. Kirkham, *The Building of "Uncle Tom's
Cabin,"* 1977.

Text:
The Writings of Harriet Beecher Stowe, 16 vols.,
1896.

from Uncle Tom's Cabin;
Or, Life Among the Lowly

*Chapter V: Showing the Feelings of Living
Property on Changing Owners*

Mr. and Mrs. Shelby had retired to their apartment for the night. He was lounging
in a large easy-chair, looking over some letters that had come in the afternoon mail,
and she was standing before her mirror, brushing out the complicated braids and curls
in which Eliza had arranged her hair; for, noticing her pale cheeks and haggard eyes,
she had excused her attendance that night, and ordered her to bed. The employment,
naturally enough, suggested her conversation with the girl in the morning; and,
turning to her husband, she said carelessly,—

"By the bye, Arthur, who was that low-bred fellow that you lugged in to our
dinner-table to-day?"

"Haley is his name," said Shelby, turning himself rather uneasily in his chair, and
continuing with his eyes fixed on a letter.

"Haley! Who is he, and what may be his business here, pray?"

"Well, he's a man that I transacted some business with, last time I was at Natchez,"
said Mr. Shelby.

"And he presumed on it to make himself quite at home, and call and dine here,
ay?"

"Why, I invited him; I had some accounts with him," said Shelby.

"Is he a negro-trader?" said Mrs. Shelby, noticing a certain embarrassment in her
husband's manner.

"Why, my dear, what put that into your head?" said Shelby, looking up.

"Nothing,—only Eliza came in here, after dinner, in a great worry, crying and
taking on, and said you were talking with a trader, and that she heard him make an
offer for her boy,—the ridiculous little goose!"

"She did, hey?" said Mr. Shelby, returning to his paper, which he seemed for a few moments quite intent upon, not perceiving that he was holding it bottom upwards.

"It will have to come out," said he mentally; "as well now as ever."

"I told Eliza," said Mrs. Shelby, as she continued brushing her hair, "that she was a little fool for her pains, and that you never had anything to do with that sort of persons. Of course, I knew you never meant to sell any of our people,—least of all, to such a fellow."

"Well, Emily," said her husband, "so I have always felt and said; but the fact is that my business lies so that I cannot get on without. I shall have to sell some of my hands."

"To that creature? Impossible! Mr. Shelby, you cannot be serious."

"I'm sorry to say that I am," said Mr. Shelby. "I've agreed to sell Tom."

"What! our Tom?—that good, faithful creature!—been your faithful servant from a boy! Oh, Mr. Shelby!—and you have promised him his freedom, too,—you and I have spoken to him a hundred times of it. Well, I can believe anything now,—I can believe *now* that you could sell little Harry, poor Eliza's only child!" said Mrs. Shelby, in a tone between grief and indignation.

"Well, since you must know all, it is so. I have agreed to sell Tom and Harry both; and I don't know why I am to be rated, as if I were a monster, for doing what every one does every day."

"But why, of all others, choose these?" said Mrs. Shelby. "Why sell them, of all on the place, if you must sell at all?"

"Because they will bring the highest sum of any,—that's why. I could choose another, if you say so. The fellow made me a high bid on Eliza, if that would suit you any better," said Mr. Shelby.

"The wretch!" said Mrs. Shelby vehemently.

"Well, I didn't listen to it, a moment,—out of regard to your feelings, I wouldn't; —so give me some credit."

"My dear," said Mrs. Shelby, recollecting herself, "forgive me; I have been hasty. I was surprised, and entirely unprepared for this;—but surely you will allow me to intercede for these poor creatures. Tom is a noble-hearted, faithful fellow, if he is black. I do believe, Mr. Shelby, that if he were put to it, he would lay down his life for you."

"I know it,—I dare say;—but what's the use of all this?—I can't help myself."

"Why not make a pecuniary sacrifice? I'm willing to bear my part of the inconvenience. Oh, Mr. Shelby, I have tried—tried most faithfully, as a Christian woman should—to do my duty to these poor, simple, dependent creatures. I have cared for them, instructed them, watched over them, and known all their little cares and joys, for years; and how can I ever hold up my head again among them if, for the sake of a little paltry gain, we sell such a faithful, excellent, confiding creature as poor Tom, and tear from him in a moment all we have taught him to love and value? I have taught them the duties of the family, of parent and child, and husband and wife; and how can I bear to have this open acknowledgment that we care for no tie, no duty, no relation, however sacred, compared with money? I have talked with Eliza about her boy,—her duty to him as a Christian mother, to watch over him, pray for him, and bring him up in a Christian way; and now what can I say, if you tear him away, and sell him, soul and body, to a profane, unprincipled man, just to save a little money? I have told her that one soul is worth more than all the money in the world; and how will she believe me when she sees us turn round and sell her child?—sell him, perhaps, to certain ruin of body and soul!"

"I'm sorry you feel so about it, Emily,—indeed I am," said Mr. Shelby; "and I respect your feelings, too, though I don't pretend to share them to their full extent; but I tell you now, solemnly, it's of no use,—I can't help myself. I didn't mean to tell you this, Emily; but in plain words, there is no choice between selling these two and selling everything. Either they must go, or *all* must. Haley has come into possession of a mortgage which, if I don't clear off with him directly, will take everything before it. I've raked, and scraped, and borrowed, and all but begged,—and the price of these two was needed to make up the balance, and I had to give them up. Haley fancied the child; he agreed to settle the matter that way and no other. I was in his power, and *had* to do it. If you feel so to have them sold, would it be any better to have *all* sold?"

Mrs. Shelby stood like one stricken. Finally, turning to her toilet, she rested her face in her hands, and gave a sort of groan.

"This is God's curse on slavery!—a bitter, bitter, most accursed thing!—a curse to the master and a curse to the slave! I was a fool to think I could make anything good out of such a deadly evil. It is a sin to hold a slave under laws like ours,—I always felt it was,—I always thought so when I was a girl,—I thought so still more after I joined the church; but I thought I could gild it over,—I thought, by kindness, and care, and instruction, I could make the condition of mine better than freedom, —fool that I was!"

"Why, wife, you are getting to be an abolitionist, quite."

"Abolitionist! if they knew all I know about slavery they *might* talk! We don't need them to tell us; you know I never thought that slavery was right,—never felt willing to own slaves."

"Well, therein you differ from many wise and pious men," said Mr. Shelby. "You remember Mr. B.'s sermon, the other day?"

"I don't want to hear such sermons; I never wish to hear Mr. B. in our church again. Ministers can't help the evil, perhaps,—can't cure it, any more than we can, — but defend it!—it always went against my common sense. And I think you didn't think much of that sermon, either."

"Well," said Shelby, "I must say these ministers sometimes carry matters further than we poor sinners would exactly dare to do. We men of the world must wink pretty hard at various things, and get used to a deal that is n't the exact thing. But we don't quite fancy, when women and ministers come out broad and square, and go beyond us in matters of either modesty or morals, that's a fact. But now, my dear, I trust you see the necessity of the thing, and you see that I have done the very best that circumstances would allow."

"Oh, yes, yes!" said Mrs. Shelby, hurriedly and abstractedly fingering her gold watch,—"I have n't any jewelry of any amount," she added thoughtfully; "but would not this watch do something?—it was an expensive one when it was bought. If I could only at least save Eliza's child, I would sacrifice anything I have."

"I'm sorry, very sorry, Emily," said Mr. Shelby. "I'm sorry this takes hold of you so; but it will do no good. The fact is, Emily, the thing's done; the bills of sale are already signed, and in Haley's hands; and you must be thankful it is no worse. That man has had it in his power to ruin us all,—and now he is fairly off. If you knew the man as I do, you'd think that we had had a narrow escape."

"Is he so hard, then?"

"Why, not a cruel man, exactly, but a man of leather,— a man alive to nothing but trade and profit,—cool, and unhesitating, and unrelenting, as death and the grave. He'd sell his own mother at a good percentage,—not wishing the old woman any harm, either."

"And this wretch owns that good, faithful Tom and Eliza's child!"

"Well, my dear, the fact is that this goes rather hard with me; it's a thing I hate to think of. Haley wants to drive matters, and take possession to-morrow. I'm going to get out my horse bright and early, and be off. I can't see Tom, that's a fact; and you had better arrange a drive somewhere, and carry Eliza off. Let the thing be done when she is out of sight."

"No, no," said Mrs. Shelby; "I'll be in no sense accomplice or help in this cruel business. I'll go and see poor old Tom, God help him, in his distress! They shall see, at any rate, that their mistress can feel for and with them. As to Eliza, I dare not think about it. The Lord forgive us! What have we done, that this cruel necessity should come on us?"

There was one listener to this conversation whom Mr. and Mrs. Shelby little suspected.

Communicating with their apartment was a large closet, opening by a door into the outer passage. When Mrs. Shelby had dismissed Eliza for the night, her feverish and excited mind had suggested the idea of this closet; and she had hidden herself there, and, with her ear pressed close against the crack of the door, had lost not a word of the conversation.

When the voices died into silence, she rose and crept stealthily away. Pale, shivering, with rigid features and compressed lips, she looked an entirely altered being from the soft and timid creature she had been hitherto. She moved cautiously along the entry, paused one moment at her mistress's door and raised her hands in mute appeal to Heaven, and then turned and glided into her own room. It was a quiet, neat apartment, on the same floor with her mistress. There was the pleasant sunny window, where she had often sat singing at her sewing; there, a little case of books, and various little fancy articles, ranged by them, the gifts of Christmas holidays; there was her simple wardrobe in the closet and in the drawers:—here was, in short, her home; and, on the whole, a happy one it had been to her. But there, on the bed, lay her slumbering boy, his long curls falling negligently around his unconscious face, his rosy mouth half open, his little fat hands thrown out over the bedclothes, and a smile spread like a sunbeam over his whole face.

"Poor boy! poor fellow!" said Eliza; "they have sold you! but your mother will save you yet!"

No tear dropped over that pillow; in such straits as these the heart has no tears to give,—it drops only blood, bleeding itself away in silence. She took a piece of paper and a pencil, and wrote hastily,—

"Oh, Missis! dear Missis! don't think me ungrateful,—don't think hard of me, anyway,—I heard all you and Master said to-night. I am going to try to save my boy,—you will not blame me! God bless and reward you for all your kindness!"

Hastily folding and directing this, she went to a drawer and made up a little package of clothing for her boy, which she tied with a handkerchief firmly round her waist; and, so fond is a mother's remembrance that, even in the terrors of that hour, she did not forget to put in the little package one or two of his favorite toys, reserving a gayly painted parrot to amuse him, when she should be called on to awaken him. It was some trouble to arouse the little sleeper; but, after some effort, he sat up, and was playing with his bird, while his mother was putting on her bonnet and shawl.

"Where are you going, mother?" said he, as she drew near the bed, with his little coat and cap.

His mother drew near, and looked so earnestly into his eyes that he at once divined that something unusual was the matter.

"Hush, Harry," she said; "mustn't speak loud, or they will hear us. A wicked man was coming to take little Harry away from his mother, and carry him 'way off in the dark; but mother won't let him,—she's going to put on her little boy's cap and coat, and run off with him, so the ugly man can't catch him."

Saying these words, she had tied and buttoned on the child's simple outfit, and, taking him in her arms, she whispered to him to be very still; and, opening a door in her room which led into the outer veranda, she glided noiselessly out.

It was a sparkling, frosty, starlight night, and the mother wrapped the shawl close round her child, as, perfectly quiet with vague terror, he clung round her neck.

Old Bruno, a great Newfoundland, who slept at the end of the porch, rose, with a low growl, as she came near. She gently spoke his name, and the animal, an old pet and playmate of hers, instantly, wagging his tail, prepared to follow her, though apparently revolving much, in his simple dog's head, what such an indiscreet midnight promenade might mean. Some dim ideas of imprudence or impropriety in the measure seemed to embarrass him considerably; for he often stopped, as Eliza glided forward, and looked wistfully, first at her and then at the house, and then, as if reassured by reflection, he pattered along after her again. A few minutes brought them to the window of Uncle Tom's cottage, and Eliza, stopping, tapped lightly on the window-pane.

The prayer-meeting at Uncle Tom's had, in the order of hymn-singing, been protracted to a very late hour; and, as Uncle Tom had indulged himself in a few lengthy solos afterwards, the consequence was that, although it was now between twelve and one o'clock, he and his worthy helpmeet were not yet asleep.

"Good Lord! what's that?" said Aunt Chloe, starting up and hastily drawing the curtain. "My sakes alive, if it ain't Lizy! Get on your clothes, old man, quick! —there's old Bruno, too, a-pawin' round. What on airth—I'm gwine to open the door."

And, suiting the action to the word, the door flew open, and the light of the tallow candle, which Tom had hastily lighted, fell on the haggard face and dark, wild eyes of the fugitive.

"Lord bless you!—I'm skeered to look at ye, Lizy! Are ye tuck sick, or what's come over ye?"

"I'm running away,—Uncle Tom and Aunt Chloe,—carrying off my child,— Master sold him!"

"Sold him?" echoed both, lifting up their hands in dismay.

"Yes, sold him!" said Eliza firmly. "I crept into the closet by Mistress's door to-night, and I heard Master tell Missis that he had sold my Harry, and you, Uncle Tom, both to a trader; and that he was going off this morning on his horse, and that the man was to take possession to-day."

Tom had stood, during the speech, with his hands raised, and his eyes dilated, like a man in a dream. Slowly and gradually, as its meaning came over him, he collapsed, rather than seated himself, on his old chair, and sunk his head down upon his knees.

"The good Lord have pity on us!" said Aunt Chloe. "Oh, it don't seem as if it was true! What has he done, that Mas'r should sell *him?*"

"He hasn't done anything,—it is n't for that. Master don't want to sell; and Missis, —she's always good. I heard her plead and beg for us; but he told her 't was no use; that he was in this man's debt, and that this man had got the power over him; and that if he didn't pay him off clear, it would end in his having to sell the place and all the people, and move off. Yes, I heard him say there was no choice between selling these two and selling all, the man was driving him so hard. Master said he was sorry; but oh, Missis,—you ought to have heard her talk! If she ain't a Christian and an angel, there never was one. I'm a wicked girl to leave her so; but, then, I can't help it. She said, herself, one soul was worth more than the world; and this boy has a soul, and if I let him be carried off, who knows what'll become of it? It must be right; but, if it ain't right, the Lord forgive me, for I can't help doing it!"

"Well, old man!" said Aunt Chloe, "why don't you go, too? Will you wait to be toted down river, where they kill niggers with hard work and starving? I'd a heap rather die than go there, any day! There's time for ye,—be off with Lizy,—you've got a pass to come and go any time. Come, bustle up, and I'll get your things together."

Tom slowly raised his head, and looked sorrowfully but quietly around, and said,—

"No, no,—I ain't going. Let Eliza go,—it's her right! I wouldn't be the one to say no,—'t ain't in *natur* for her to stay; but you heard what she said! If I must be sold, or all the people on the place, and everything go to rack, why, let me be sold. I s'pose I can b'ar it as well as any on 'em," he added, while something like a sob and a sigh shook his broad, rough chest convulsively. "Mas'r always found me on the spot,—he always will. I never have broke trust, nor used my pass noways contrary to my word, and I never will. It's better for me alone to go, than to break up the place and sell all. Mas'r ain't to blame, Chloe, and he'll take care of you and the poor"—

Here he turned to the rough trundle-bed full of little woolly heads, and broke fairly down. He leaned over the back of the chair, and covered his face with his large hands. Sobs, heavy, hoarse, and loud, shook the chair, and great tears fell through his fingers on the floor: just such tears, sir, as you dropped into the coffin where lay your firstborn son; such tears, woman, as you shed when you heard the cries of your dying babe. For, sir, he was a man,—and you are but another man. And, woman, though dressed in silk and jewels, you are but a woman, and, in life's great straits and mighty griefs, ye feel but one sorrow!

"And now," said Eliza, as she stood in the door, "I saw my husband only this afternoon, and I little knew then what was to come. They have pushed him to the very last standing-place, and he told me, to-day, that he was going to run away. Do try, if you can, to get word to him. Tell him how I went, and why I went; and tell him I'm going to try and find Canada. You must give my love to him, and tell him, if I never see him again,"—she turned away, and stood with her back to them for a moment, and then added, in a husky voice,—"tell him to be as good as he can, and try and meet me in the kingdom of heaven."

"Call Bruno in there," she added. "Shut the door on him, poor beast! He must n't go with me!"

A few last words and tears, a few simple adieus and blessings, and, clasping her wondering and affrighted child in her arms, she glided noiselessly away.

1851–1852

---

from Oldtown Folks

Author's Preface

GENTLE READER,—It is customary to omit prefaces. I beg you to make an exception in my particular case; I have something I really want to say. I have an object in this book, more than the mere telling of a story, and you can always judge of a book better if you compare it with the author's object. My object is to interpret to the world the New England life and character in that particular time of its history which may be called the seminal period. I would endeavor to show you New England in its *seed-bed,* before the hot suns of modern progress had developed its sprouting germs into the great trees of to-day.

New England has been to these United States what the Dorian hive[1] was to Greece. It has always been a capital country to emigrate from, and North, South, East, and West have been populated largely from New England, so that the seed-bed of New England was the seed-bed of this great American Republic, and of all that is likely to come of it.

New England people cannot be thus interpreted without calling into view many grave considerations and necessitating some serious thinking.

In doing this work, I have tried to make my mind as still and passive as a looking-glass, or a mountain lake, and then to give you merely the images reflected there. I desire that you should see the characteristic persons of those times, and hear them talk; and sometimes I have taken an author's liberty of explaining their characters to you, and telling you why they talked and lived as they did.

My studies for this object have been Pre-Raphaelite,[2]—taken from real characters, real scenes, and real incidents. And some of those things in the story which may

---

[1] The Dorians were an ancient Hellenic people who completed the overthrow of Mycenaean civilization and settled especially in Peloponnesus and Crete ca. 1100–1000 B.C. The Dorian conquerors subsequently merged with the subject peoples and migrated into surrounding areas.

[2] Nineteenth-century literary and artistic movement that strove to present the "real" in the manner of the artists of the early Renaissance.

appear most romantic and like fiction are simple renderings and applications of facts.

Any one who may be curious enough to consult Rev. Elias Nason's book, called "Sir Charles Henry Frankland, or Boston in the Colonial Times," will there see a full description of the old manor-house which in this story is called the Dench House. It was by that name I always heard it spoken of in my boyhood.

In portraying the various characters which I have introduced, I have tried to maintain the part simply of a sympathetic spectator. I propose neither to teach nor preach through them, any farther than any spectator of life is preached to by what he sees of the workings of human nature around him.

Though Calvinist, Arminian, High-Church Episcopalian,[3] skeptic, and simple believer all speak in their turn, I merely listen, and endeavor to understand and faithfully represent the inner life of each. I myself am but the observer and reporter, seeing much, doubting much, questioning much, and believing with all my heart in only a very few things.

And so I take my leave of you.

Horace Holyoke.[4]

Chapter IV: The Village Do-nothing[5]

"Wal, naow, Horace, don't ye cry so. Why, I'm railly concerned for ye. Why, don't you s'pose your daddy's better off? Why, sartin *I* do. Don't cry, there's a good boy, now. I'll give ye my jack-knife, now."

This was addressed to me the day after my father's death, while the preparations for the funeral hung like a pall over the house, and the terror of the last cold mystery, the tears of my mother, and a sort of bustling dreariness on the part of my aunts and grandmother, all conspired to bear down on my childish nerves with fearful power. It was a doctrine of those good old times, no less than of many in our present days, that a house invaded by death should be made as forlorn as hands could make it. It should be rendered as cold and stiff, as unnatural, as dead and corpse-like as possible, by closed shutters, looking-glasses pinned up in white sheets, and the locking up and hiding out of sight of any pleasant little familiar object which would be thought out of place in a sepulchre. This work had been driven through with unsparing vigor by Aunt Lois, who looked like one of the Fates as she remorselessly cleared away every little familiar object belonging to my father, and reduced every room to the shrouded stillness of a well-kept tomb.

Of course no one thought of looking after me. It was not the fashion of those days to think of children, if only they would take themselves off out of the way of the movements of the grown people; and so I had run out into the orchard back of the house, and, throwing myself down on my face under an apple-tree in the tall clover, I gave myself up to despair, and was sobbing aloud in a nervous paroxysm of agony, when these words were addressed to me. The speaker was a tall, shambling, loose-

---

[3] The Arminian religious movement rebuked the doctrine of predestination in Calvinism. High-church Episcopalians adopted a Roman interpretation of Anglican doctrine.

[4] Fictional narrator of *Oldtown Folks*.

[5] This chapter introduces Sam Lawson, who became one of Stowe's most popular characters.

jointed man, with a long, thin visage, prominent watery blue eyes, very fluttering and seedy habiliments, who occupied the responsible position of first do-nothing-in-ordinary in our village of Oldtown, and as such I must introduce him to my readers' notice.

Every New England village, if you only think of it, must have its do-nothing as regularly as it has its school-house or meeting-house. Nature is always wide-awake in the matter of compensation. Work, thrift, and industry are such an incessant steam-power in Yankee life, that society would burn itself out with intense friction were there not interposed here and there the lubricating power of a decided do-nothing,—a man who won't be hurried, and won't work, and will take his ease in his own way, in spite of the whole protest of his neighborhood to the contrary. And there is on the face of the whole earth no do-nothing whose softness, idleness, general inaptitude to labor, and everlasting, universal shiftlessness can compare with that of this worthy, as found in a brisk Yankee village.

Sam Lawson filled this post with ample honor in Oldtown. He was a fellow dear to the souls of all "us boys" in the village, because, from the special nature of his position, he never had anything more pressing to do than croon and gossip with us. He was ready to spend hours in tinkering a boy's jack-knife, or mending his skate, or start at the smallest notice to watch at a woodchuck's hole, or give incessant service in tending a dog's sprained paw. He was always on hand to go fishing with us on Saturday afternoons; and I have known him to sit hour after hour on the bank, surrounded by a troop of boys, baiting our hooks and taking off our fish. He was a soft-hearted old body, and the wrigglings and contortions of our prey used to disturb his repose so that it was a regular part of his work to kill the fish by breaking their necks when he took them from the hook.

"Why, lordy massy, boys," he would say, "I can't bear to see no kind o' critter in torment. These 'ere pouts ain't to blame for bein' fish, and ye ought to put 'em out of their misery. Fish hes their rights as well as any on us."

Nobody but Sam would have thought of poking through the high grass and clover on our back lot to look me up, as I lay sobbing under the old apple-tree, the most insignificant little atom of misery that ever bewailed the inevitable.

Sam was of respectable family, and not destitute of education. He was an expert in at least five or six different kinds of handicraft, in all of which he had been pronounced by the knowing ones to be a capable workman, "if only he would stick to it." He had a blacksmith's shop, where, when the fit was on him, he would shoe a horse better than any man in the county. No one could supply a missing screw, or apply a timely brace, with more adroitness. He could mend cracked china so as to be almost as good as new; he could use carpenter's tools as well as a born carpenter, and would doctor a rheumatic door or a shaky window better than half the professional artisans in wood. No man could put a refractory clock to rights with more ingenuity than Sam, —that is, if you would give him his time to be about it.

I shall never forget the wrath and dismay which he roused in my Aunt Lois's mind by the leisurely way in which, after having taken our own venerable kitchen clock to pieces, and strewn the fragments all over the kitchen, he would roost over it in endless incubation, telling stories, entering into long-winded theological discussions, smoking pipes, and giving histories of all the other clocks in Oldtown, with occasional memoirs of those in Needmore, the North Parish, and Podunk, as placidly indifferent to all her volleys of sarcasm and contempt, her stinging expostulations and philippies, as the sailing old moon is to the frisky, animated barking of some puppy dog of earth.

"Why, ye see, Miss Lois," he would say, "clocks can't be druv; that's jest what they can't. Some things can be druv, and then agin some things can't, and clocks is that kind. They's jest got to be humored. Now this 'ere's a 'mazin' good clock; give me my time on it, and I'll have it so 't will keep straight on to the Millennium."[6]

"Millennium!" says Aunt Lois, with a snort of infinite contempt.

"Yes, the Millennium," says Sam, letting fall his work in a contemplative manner. "That 'ere's an interestin' topic now. Parson Lothrop, he don't think the Millennium will last a thousand years. What's your 'pinion on that pint, Miss Lois?"

"My opinion is," said Aunt Lois, in her most nipping tones, "that if folks don't mind their own business, and do with their might what their hand finds to do, the Millennium won't come at all."

"Wal, you see, Miss Lois, it's just here,—one day is with the Lord as a thousand years, and a thousand years as one day."

"I should think you thought a day was a thousand years, the way you work," said Aunt Lois.

"Wal," says Sam, sitting down with his back to his desperate litter of wheels, weights, and pendulums, and meditatively caressing his knee as he watched the sailing clouds in abstract meditation, "ye see, ef a thing's ordained, why it's got to be, ef you don't lift a finger. That 'ere's *so*, now, ain't it?"

"Sam Lawson, you are about the most aggravating creature I ever had to do with. Here you've got our clock all to pieces, and have been keeping up a perfect hurrah's nest in our kitchen for three days, and there you sit maundering and talking with your back to your work, fussin' about the Millennium, which is none of your business, or mine, as I know of! Do either put that clock together or let it alone!"

"Don't you be a grain uneasy, Miss Lois. Why, I'll have your clock all right in the end, but I can't be druv. Wal, I guess I'll take another spell on't to-morrow or Friday."

Poor Aunt Lois, horror-stricken, but seeing herself actually in the hands of the imperturbable enemy, now essayed the task of concilation. "Now do, Lawson, just finish up this job, and I'll pay you down, right on the spot; and you need the money."

"I'd like to 'blige ye, Miss Lois; but ye see money ain't everything in this world. Ef I work tew long on one thing, my mind kind o' gives out, ye see; and besides, I've got some 'sponsibilities to 'tend to. There's Mrs. Captain Brown, she made me promise to come to-day and look at the nose o' that 'ere silver teapot o' her'n; it's kind o' sprung a leak. And then I 'greed to split a little oven-wood for the Widdah Pedee, that lives up on the Shelburn road. Must visit the widdahs in their affliction, Scriptur' says. And then there's Hepsy: she's allers a-castin' it up at me that I don't do nothing for her and the chil'en; but then, lordy massy, Hepsy hain't no sort o' patience. Why, jest this mornin' I was a-tellin' her to count up her marcies,[7] and I

[6] According to ancient prediction, thousand-year period on earth during which Christ will reign and holiness will prevail.   [7] Blessings.

'clare for't if I didn't think she'd a throwed the tongs at me. That 'ere woman's temper railly makes me consarned. Wal, good day, Miss Lois. I'll be along again to-morrow or Friday, or the first o' next week." And away he went with long, loose strides down the village street, while the leisurely wail of an old fuguing tune floated back after him,—

"Thy years are an
    Eternal day,
Thy years are an
    Eternal day."

"An eternal torment," said Aunt Lois, with a snap. "I'm sure, if there's a mortal creature on this earth that I pity, it's Hepsy Lawson. Folks talk about her scolding, —that Sam Lawson is enough to make the saints in Heaven fall from grace. And you can't *do* anything with him; it's like charging bayonet into a woolsack."

Now, the Hepsy thus spoken of was the luckless woman whom Sam's easy temper, and a certain youthful reputation for being a capable fellow, had led years before into the snares of matrimony with him, in consequence of which she was encumbered with the bringing up of six children on very short rations. She was a gnarly, compact, efficient little pepper-box of a woman, with snapping black eyes, pale cheeks, and a mouth always at half-cock, ready to go off with some sharp crack of reproof at the shoreless, bottomless, and tideless inefficiency of her husband. It seemed to be one of those facts of existence that she could not get used to, nor find anywhere in her brisk, fiery little body a grain of cool resignation for. Day after day she fought it with as bitter and intense a vigor, and with as much freshness of objurgation, as if it had come upon her for the first time,—just as a sharp, wiry little terrier will bark and bark from day to day, with never-ceasing pertinacity, into an empty squirrel-hole. She seemed to have no power within her to receive and assimilate the great truth that her husband was essentially, and was to be, and always would be, only a do-nothing.

Poor Hepsy was herself quite as essentially a do-something,—an early-rising, bustling, driving, neat, efficient, capable little body,—who contrived, by going out to day's works,—washing, scrubbing, cleaning,—by making vests for the tailor, or closing and binding shoes for the shoemaker, by hoeing corn and potatoes in the garden at most unseasonable hours, actually to find bread to put into the mouths of the six young ravens aforesaid, and to clothe them decently. This might all do very well; but when Sam, who believed with all his heart in the modern doctrines of woman's rights so far as to have no sort of objection to Hepsy's sawing wood or hoeing potatoes if she chose, would make the small degree of decency and prosperity the family had attained by these means a text on which to preach resignation, cheerfulness, and submission, then Hepsy's last cobweb of patience gave out, and she often became, for the moment, really dangerous, so that Sam would be obliged to plunge hastily out of doors to avoid a strictly personal encounter.

It was not to be denied that poor Hepsy really was a scold, in the strong old Saxon acceptation of the word. She had fought life single-handed, tooth and nail, with all the ferocity of outraged sensibilities, and had come out of the fight scratched and disheveled, with few womanly graces. The good wives of the village, versed in the outs and ins of their neighbors' affairs, while they admitted that Sam was not all he should be, would sometimes roll up the whites of their eyes mysteriously, and say, "But then, poor man, what could you expect when he hasn't a happy home? Hepsy's temper is, you know," etc., etc.

The fact is, that Sam's softly easy temper and habits of miscellaneous handiness caused him to have a warm corner in most of the households. No mothers ever are very hard on a man who always pleases the children; and every one knows the welcome of a universal gossip, who carries round a district a wallet of choice bits of neighborhood information.

Now Sam knew everything about everybody. He could tell Mrs. Major Broad just what Lady Lothrop gave for her best parlor carpet, that was brought over from England, and just on what occasions she used the big silver tankard, and on what they were content with the little one, and how many pairs of long silk stockings the minister had, and how many rows of stitching there were on the shoulders of his Sunday shirts. He knew just all that was in Deacon Badger's best room, and how many silver table-spoons and teaspoons graced the beaufet[8] in the corner; and when each of his daughters was born, and just how Miss Susy came to marry as she did, and who wanted to marry her and couldn't. He knew just the cost of Major Broad's scarlet cloak and shoe-buckles, and how Mrs. Major had a real *Ingy* shawl[9] up in her "camphire"[10] trunk, that cost nigh as much as Lady Lothrop's. Nobody had made love, or married, or had children born, or been buried, since Sam was able to perambulate the country, without his informing himself minutely of every available particular; and his unfathomable knowledge on these subjects was an unfailing source of popularity.

Besides this, Sam was endowed with no end of idle accomplishments. His indolence was precisely of a turn that enjoyed the excitement of an occasional odd bit of work with which he had clearly no concern, and which had no sort of tendency toward his own support or that of his family. Something so far out of the line of practical utility as to be in a manner an artistic labor would awaken all the energies of his soul. His shop was a perfect infirmary for decayed articles of *vertu*[11] from all the houses for miles around. Cracked china, lame teapots, broken shoe-buckles, rickety tongs, and decrepit fire-irons, all stood in melancholy proximity, awaiting Sam's happy hours of inspiration; and he was always happy to sit down and have a long, strictly confidential conversation concerning any of these with the owner, especially if Hepsy were gone out washing, or on any other work which kept her at a safe distance.

Sam could shave and cut hair as neatly as any barber, and was always in demand up and down the country to render these offices to the sick. He was ready to go for miles to watch with invalids, and a very acceptable watcher he made, beguiling the night hours with endless stories and legends. He was also an expert in psalmody, having in his youth been the pride of the village singing-school. In those days he could perform reputably on the bass-viol in the choir of a Sunday with a dolefulness and solemnity of demeanor in the highest degree edifying,—though he was equally ready of a week-evening in scraping on a brisk little fiddle, if any of the thoughtless ones

---

[8] Buffet.
[9] Ingy shawl: shawl from India.
[10] Obsolete spelling for camphor.

[11] Art objects; curiosities (*vertu*: French for "value").

wanted a performer at a husking or a quilting frolic. Sam's obligingness was many-sided, and he was equally prepared at any moment to raise a funeral psalm or whistle the time of a double-shuffle.

But the more particular delight of Sam's heart was in funerals. He would walk miles on hearing the news of a dangerous illness, and sit roosting on the fence of the premises, delighted to gossip over the particulars, but ready to come down at any moment to do any of the odd turns which sickness in a family makes necessary; and when the last earthly scene was over, Sam was more than ready to render those final offices from which the more nervous and fastidious shrink, but in which he took almost a professional pride.

The business of an undertaker is a refinement of modern civilization. In simple old days neighbors fell into one another's hands for all the last wants of our poor mortality; and there were men and women of note who took a particular and solemn pride in these mournful offices. Sam had in fact been up all night in our house, and having set me up in the clover, and comforted me with a jack-knife, he proceeded to inform me of the particulars.

"Why, ye see, Horace, I ben up with 'em pretty much all night; and I laid yer father out myself, and I never see a better-lookin' corpse. It's a 'mazin' pity your daddy hed such feelin's 'bout havin' people come to look at him, 'cause he does look beautiful, and it's been a long time since we've had a funeral, anyway, and everybody was expectin' to come to his'n, and they'll all be dissipinted if the corpse ain't show'd; but then, lordy massy, folks ought n't to think hard on 't ef folks hes their own way 'bout their own funeral. That 'ere's what I've been a-tellin' on 'em all, over to the tavern and round to the store. Why, you never see such a talk as there was about it. There was Aunt Sally Morse, and Betsey and Patsy Sawin, and Mis' Zeruiah Bacon, come over early to look at the corpse, and when they was n't let in, you never heerd sich a jawin'. Betsey and Patsy Sawin said that they allers suspected your father was an infidel, or some sich, and now they was clear; and Aunt Sally, she asked who made his shroud, and when she heerd there was n't to be none, he was laid out in his clothes, she said she never heerd such unchristian doin's, —that she always had heerd he had strange opinions, but she never thought it would come to that."

"My father is n't an infidel, and I wish I could kill 'em for talking so," said I, clenching my jack-knife in my small fist, and feeling myself shake with passion.

"Wal, wal, I kind o' spoke up to 'em about it. I was n't a-goin' to hear no sich jaw; and says I, 'I think ef there is anybody that knows what's what about funerals I'm the man, for I don't s'pose there's a man in the county that's laid out more folks, and set up with more corpses, and ben sent for fur and near, than I have; and my opinion is that mourners must always follow the last directions gi'n to 'em by the person. Ef a man has n't a right to have the say about his own body, what hes he a right to?' Wal, they said that it was putty well of me to talk so, when I had the privilege of sittin' up with him, and seein' all that was to be seen. 'Lordy massy,' says I, 'I don't see why ye need envi me; 't ain't my fault that folks thinks it's agreeable to have me round. As to bein' buried in his clothes, why, lordy massy, 't ain't nothin' so extraordinary. In the old country great folks is very often laid out in their clothes. 'Member, when I was a boy, old Mr. Sanger, the minister in Deerbrook, was laid out in his gown and bands, with a Bible in his hands, and he looked as nateral as a pictur.

I was at Parson Rider's funeral, down to Wrentham. He was laid out in white flannel. But then there was old Captain Bigelow, down to the Pint there, he was laid out regular in his rigimentals, jest as he wore 'em in the war, epaulets and all.' Wal now, Horace, your daddy looks jest as peaceful as a psalm-tune. Now, you don't know, —jest as nateral as if he'd only jest gone to sleep. So ye may set your heart at rest 'bout him."

It was one of those beautiful serene days of October, when the earth lies as bright and still as anything one can dream of in the New Jerusalem, and Sam's homely expressions of sympathy had quieted me somewhat. Sam, tired of his discourse, lay back in the clover, with his hands under his head, and went on with his moralizing.

"Lordy massy, Horace, to think on't,—it's so kind o' solemnizin'! It's one's turn to-day, and another's to-morrow. We never know when our turn'll come." And Sam raised a favorite stave,—

"And must these active limbs of mine
Lie moulderin' in the clay?"

"Active limbs! I guess so!" said a sharp voice, which came through the clover-heads like the crack of a rifle.

"Well, I've found you at last. Here you be, Sam Lawson, lyin' flat on your back at eleven o'clock in the morning, and not a potato dug, and not a stick of wood cut to get dinner with; and I won't cut no more if we never have dinner. It's no use a-humorin' you,—doin' your work for you. The more I do, the more I may do; so come home, won't you?"

"Lordy massy, Hepsy," said Sam, slowly erecting himself out of the grass, and staring at her with white eyes, "you don't ought to talk so. I ain't to blame. I hed to sit up with Mr. Holyoke all night, and help 'em lay him out at four o'clock this mornin'."

"You're always everywhere but where you've business to be," said Hepsy; "and helpin' and doin' for everybody but your own. For my part, I think charity ought to begin at home. You're everywhere, up and down and round,—over to Shelbun, down to Podunk, up to North Parish; and here Abram and Kiah Stebbins have been waitin' all the morning with a horse they brought all the way from Boston to get you to shoe."

"Wal now, that 'ere shows they know what's what. I told Kiah that ef they'd bring that 'ere hoss to me I'd 'tend to his huffs."

"And be off lying in the mowing, like a patridge, when they come after ye. That's one way to do business," said Hepsy.

"Hepsy, I was just a miditatin'. Ef we don't miditate sometimes on all these 'ere things, it'll be wus for us by and by."

"Meditate! I'll help your meditations in a way you won't like, if you don't look out. So now you come home, and stop your meditatin', and go to doin' somethin'. I told 'em to come back this afternoon, and I'd have you on the spot if 't was a possible thing," said the very practical Hepsy, laying firm hold of Sam's unresisting arm, and leading him away captive.

I stole into the darkened, silent room where my father had lain so long. Its desolate neatness struck a chill to my heart. Not even a bottle remained of the many familiar ones that used to cover the stand and the mantelpiece; but he, lying in his threadbare Sunday coat, looked to me as I had often seen him in later days, when he had come from school exhausted, and fallen asleep on the bed. I crept to his side and nestled down on the floor as quietly as a dog lies down by the side of his master.

1869

from Oldtown Fireside Stories

X: How to Fight the Devil

"Look here, boys," said Sam, "don't you want to go with me up to the Devil's Den this afternoon?"

"Where is the Devil's Den?" said I, with a little awe.

"Wal, it's a longer tramp than I've ever took ye. It's clear up past the pickerel pond, and beyond old Skunk John's pasture lot. It's a 'mazin' good place for raspberries; should n't wonder if we should get two three quarts there. Great rocks there higher'n yer head; kinder solemn, 't is."

This was a delightful and seductive account, and we arranged for a walk that very afternoon.

In almost every New England village the personality of Satan has been acknowledged by calling by his name some particular rock or cave, or other natural object whose singularity would seem to suggest a more than mortal occupancy. "The Devil's Punch-Bowl," "The Devil's Wash-Bowl," "The Devil's Kettle," "The Devil's Pulpit," and "The Devil's Den," have been designations that marked places or objects of some striking natural peculiarity. Often these are found in the midst of the most beautiful and romantic scenery, and the sinister name seems to have no effect in lessening its attractions. To me, the very idea of going to the Devil's Den was full of a pleasing horror. When a boy, I always lived in the shadowy edge of that line which divides spirit land from mortal life, and it was my delight to walk among its half lights and shadows. The old graveyard, where, side by side, mouldered the remains of Indian sachems and the ancients of English blood, was my favorite haunt. I loved to sit on the graves while the evening mists arose from them, and to fancy cloudy forms waving and beckoning. To me, this spirit land was my only refuge from the dry details of a hard, prosaic life. The schoolroom—with its hard seats rudely fashioned from slabs of rough wood, with its clumsy desks, hacked and ink-stained, with its unintelligible text-books and its unsympathetic teacher—was to me a prison out of whose weary windows I watched the pomp and glory of nature,—the free birds singing, the clouds sailing, the trees waving and whispering,—and longed, as earnestly as ever did the Psalmist, to flee far away, and wander in the wilderness.

Hence, no joy of after life—nothing that the world has now to give—can equal that joyous sense of freedom and full possession which came over me on Saturday afternoons, when I started off on a tramp with the world all before me,—the mighty, unexplored world of mysteries and possibilities, bounded only by the horizon. Ignorant alike of all science, neither botanist nor naturalist, I was studying at first-hand all that lore out of which science is made. Every plant and flower had a familiar face to me, and said something to my imagination. I knew where each was to be found, its time of coming and going, and met them year after year as returning friends.

So it was with joyous freedom that we boys rambled off with Sam this afternoon, intent to find the Devil's Den. It was a ledge of granite rocks rising in the midst of a grove of pines and white birches. The ground was yellow and slippery with the fallen needles of the pines of other days, and the glistening white stems of the birches shone through the shadows like ivory pillars. Underneath the great granite ledges, all sorts of roots and plants grappled and kept foothold; and whole armies of wild raspberries matured their fruit, rounder and juicier for growing in the shade.

In one place yawned a great rift, or cavern, as if the rocks had been violently twisted and wrenched apart, and a mighty boulder lodging in the rift had roofed it over, making a cavern of most seductive darkness and depth. This was the Devil's Den; and after we had picked our pail full of berries, we sat down there to rest.

"Sam, do you suppose the Devil ever was here?" said I. "What do they call this his den for?"

"Massy, child! that 'ere was in old witch times. There used to be witch meetin's held here, and awful doin's; they used to have witch sabba' days and witch sacraments, and sell their souls to the old boy."

"What should they want to do that for?"

"Wal, sure enough; what was it for? I can't make out that the Devil ever gin 'em anything, any on 'em. They wa'n't no richer, nor did n't get no more 'n this world than the rest; and they was took and hung; and then ef they went to torment after that, they hed a pretty bad bargain on 't, I say."

"Well, people don't do such things any more, do they?" said I.

"No," said Sam. "Since the great fuss and row-de-dow about it, it's kind o' died out; but there's those, I s'pose, that hez dealin's with the old boy. Folks du say that old Ketury was a witch, and that ef 't ben in old times, she'd 'a' hed her neck stretched; but she lived and died in peace."

"But do you think," said I, now proposing the question that lay nearest my heart, "that the Devil can hurt us?"

"That depends consid'able on how you take him," said Sam. "Ye see, come to a straight out-an'-out fight with him, he'll git the better on yer."

"But," said I, "Christian did fight Apollyon,[1] and got him down too."

I had no more doubt in those days that this was an historic fact than I had of the existence of Romulus and Remus and the wolf.[2]

"Wal, that 'ere wa'n't jest like real things: they say that 'ere's an allegory. But I'll tell ye how old Sarah Bunganuck fit the Devil, when he 'peared to her. Ye see, old Sarah she was one of the converted Injuns, and a good old critter she was too; worked hard and got her livin' honest. She made baskets, and she made brooms, and she used

---

[1] One of the various names of the devil.
[2] In Roman mythology, Romulus and Remus were the twin sons of Mars and Rea Silva. Rea's uncle, Amulius, did not want to lose his ill-gotten throne to her heirs, so he imprisoned her and had her babies exposed in a basket on the Tiber River. The basket floated to shore, where the infants were suckled by a she-wolf and fed by a woodpecker. The twins grew to be strong and bold and eventually killed the tyrannical Amulius.

to pick young wintergreen and tie it up in bunches, and dig sassafras and ginsing to make beer; and she got her a little bit o' land, right alongside o' old Black Hoss John's white-birch wood-lot.

"Now, I've heerd some o' these 'ere modern ministers that come down from Cambridge college, and are larnt about everything in creation, they say there ain't no devil, and the reason on 't is, 'cause there can't be none. These 'ere fellers is so sort o' green!—they don't mean no harm, but they don't know nothin' about nobody that does. If they'd ha' known old Black Hoss John, they'd ha' been putty sure there was a devil. He was jest the crossest, ugliest critter that ever ye see, and he was ugly jest for the sake o' ugliness. He could n't bear to let the boys pick huckleberries in his paster lots, when he did n't pick 'em himself; and he was allers jawin' me 'cause I would go trout-fishin' in one o' his pasters. Jest ez if the trout that swims wa'n't the Lord's, and jest ez much mine as his. He grudged every critter everything; and if he 'd ha' hed his will and way, every bird would ha' fell down dead that picked up a worm on his grounds. He was jest as nippin' as a black frost. Old Black Hoss did n't git drunk in a regerlar way, like Uncle Eph and Toddy Whitney, and the rest o' them boys. But he jest sot at home, a-soakin' on cider, till he was crosser 'n a bear with a sore head. Old Black Hoss hed a special spite agin old Sarah. He said she was an old witch and an old thief, and that she stole things off'n his grounds, when everybody knew that she was a regerlar church member, and as decent an old critter as there was goin'. As to her stealin', she did n't do nothin' but pick huckleberries and grapes, and git chesnuts and wannuts and butternuts, and them 'ere wild things that's the Lord's, grow on whose land they will, and is free to all. I've hearn 'em tell that, over in the old country, the poor was kept under so that they could n't shoot a bird, nor ketch a fish, nor gather no nuts, nor do nothin' to keep from starvin', 'cause the quality folks they thought they owned everything, 'way down to the middle of the earth and clear up to the stars. We never hed no sech doin's this side of the water, thank the Lord! We've allers been free to have the chesnuts and the wannuts and the grapes and the huckleberries and the strawberries ef we could git 'em, and ketch fish when and where we was a mind to. Lordy massy! your grandthur's old Cæsar he used to call the pond his pork-pot. He'd jest go down and throw in a line and ketch his dinner. Wal, old Black Hoss he knowed the law was so, and he could n't do nothin' agin her by law; but he sarved her out every mean trick he could think of. He used to go and stan' and lean over her garden-gate and jaw at her an hour at a time; but old Sarah she had the Injun in her; she did n't run to talk much: she used to jest keep on with her weedin' and her work, jest 's if he wa'n't there, and that made old Black Hoss madder 'n ever; and he thought he'd try and frighten her off'n the ground, by makin' on her believe he was the Devil. So one time, when he'd been killin' a beef critter, they took off the skin with the horns and all on; and old Black Hoss he says to Toddy and Eph and Loker, 'You jest come up to-night, and see how I'll frighten old Sarah Bunganuck.'

"Wal, Toddy and Eph and Loker, they hed n't no better to do, and they thought they 'd jest go round and see. Ye see, 't was a moonlight night, and old Sarah—she was an industrious critter—she was cuttin' white-birch brush for brooms in the paster lot. Wal, old Black Hoss he wrapped the critter's skin round him, with the horns on his head, and come and stood by the fence, and begun to roar and make a noise. Old Sarah she kept right on with her work, cuttin' her brush and pilin' on 't up, and jest let him roar. Wal, old Black Hoss felt putty foolish, 'specially ez the fellers were waitin' to see how she took it. So he calls out in a grum voice,—

" 'Woman, don't ye know who I be?'

" 'No,' says she quite quiet, 'I don't know who yer be.'

" 'Wal, I'm the Devil,' sez he.

" 'Ye be?' says old Sarah. 'Poor old critter, how I pity ye!' and she never gin him another word, but jest bundled up her broom-stuff, and took it on her back and walked off, and old Black Hoss he stood there mighty foolish with his skin and horns; and so he had the laugh agin him, 'cause Eph and Loker they went and told the story down to the tavern, and he felt awful cheap to think old Sarah had got the upper hands on him.

"Wal, ye see boys, that 'ere's jest the way to fight the Devil. Jest keep straight on with what ye're doin', and don't ye mind him, and he can't do nothing to ye."

1872

Jones Very
1813–1880

An acquaintance described Jones Very as he approached his fortieth birthday: "tall, thin, quiet, reserved, silent, serene, with somewhat the aspect of an extinct crater; he looked as if he belonged to another sphere." At once a fragile figure and a spiritually rapturous poet, Jones Very, more than any other nineteenth-century American writer, made mysticism—the belief in direct communication with God through contemplation and ecstasy and without human reasoning—the central element in his life and work.

Jones Very's life was as ascetic as his verse. He was born in Salem, Massachusetts, in 1813, the eldest of six children and a descendant of zealous and austere Puritans. He spent a good deal of his youth on and near the sea with his father, who had privateered during the War of 1812 and later captained a Boston merchant ship. But few events mark Jones Very's adult years. He entered Harvard as a sophomore, where he displayed his devotion to classical and English literature, read extensively in philosophy and theology, and experienced what he later called a *"change of heart,* which tells us that all we have belongs to God and that we ought to have no *will* of our own." He graduated with honors in 1836 and stayed on for nearly two years tutoring in Greek while attending the Divinity School. In 1836 he was asked to withdraw when he claimed he had beheld visions, and he spent a month in a nearby asylum. Over the next several years, Very lived the Bible and wrote over seven hundred intensely religious poems. Lacking a divinity degree, he was licensed to preach by the Cambridge Association in 1843, and for nearly the next forty years he quietly preached more than a hundred sermons and briefly held pastorates in Maine, Rhode Island, and Massachusetts. He settled into retirement with his sisters in Salem and occasionally contributed essays to local newspapers and did genealogical research for the Essex Institute.

Jones Very's life and verse were bound, as he noted, by "but one thought, the immanence of God; but one emotion, a desire that the spirit might be intrepid and confessed; but one interest, that men should turn their eyes toward the light." His poems eloquently express the Christian paradox of total passivity as a condition for complete religious fulfillment. In this respect, he regarded himself as an instrument of a higher will, and having recounted blissful states of religious awareness, Very would say, "I value these verses, not because they are *mine*, but because they are *not*." His austere poems feature minor variations on the Shakespearean sonnet, his syntax and diction the pervasive influence of the Bible.

Ralph Waldo Emerson admired the efforts of this man, whom he called a "brave saint," to communicate his religious beliefs in verse. In 1839 Emerson selected and edited the work for Very's first book, *Essays and Poems*. His delicate and recondite verse captured little public attention but earned the praise of the leading literary figures of the day, including Margaret Fuller, Bronson Alcott, and Richard Henry Dana. William Cullen Bryant found in Very's poems "extraordinary grace and originality" and judged them "among the finest in the language." Even Nathaniel Hawthorne, although he disliked Very, called him "a poet whose voice is scarcely heard . . . by reason of its depth." But perhaps the most astute nineteenth-century judgment of Very's work was offered by Charles Eliot Norton: "The work of an exquisite spirit: some are as if written by a George Herbert who had studied Shakespeare, read Wordsworth, and lived in America." Yet despite the publication of two volumes of his work within a few years of his death in 1880, Jones Very all but disappeared from literary histories and anthologies until the mid-twentieth century, when his meditational sonnets were reclaimed as luminous enactments of the Transcendental exhortation to discover one's own inner divinity.

Further Reading:
Y. Winters, *Maules Curse: Seven Studies in the History of American Obscurantism*, 1938.
W. I. Bartlett, *Jones Very, Emerson's "Brave Saint,"* 1942.
E. Gittleman, *Jones Very: The Effective Years, 1833–1840*, 1967.

Text:
Jones Very: Selected Poems, ed. N. Lyons, 1966.

The Hand and Foot

The hand and foot that stir not, they shall find
Sooner than all the rightful place to go:
Now in their motion free as roving wind,
Though first no snail so limited and slow;
I mark them full of labor all the day,   5
Each active motion made in perfect rest;

They cannot from their path mistaken stray,
Though 'tis not theirs, yet in it they are blest;
The bird has not their hidden track found out,
The cunning fox though full of art he be;   10
It is the way unseen, the certain route,
Where ever bound, yet thou art ever free;
The path of Him, whose perfect law of love
Bids spheres and atoms in just order move.
1833

The Garden

I saw the spot where our first parents dwelt;
And yet it wore to me no face of change,
For while amid its fields and groves, I felt
As if I had not sinned, nor thought it strange;
My eye seemed but a part of every sight,   5
My ear heard music in each sound that rose,
Each sense forever found a new delight,
Such as the spirit's vision only knows;
Each act some new and ever-varying joy
Did by my Father's love for me prepare;   10
To dress the spot my ever fresh employ,
And in the glorious whole with Him to share;
No more without the flaming gate to stray,
No more for sin's dark stain the debt of death to
    pay.
1839

The Dead

I see them, crowd on crowd they walk the earth
Dry, leafless trees no autumn wind laid bare;
And in their nakedness find cause for mirth,
And all unclad would winter's rudeness dare;
No sap doth through their clattering branches flow,   5
Whence springing leaves and blossoms bright appear;

Their hearts the living God have ceased to know,
Who gives the springtime to th'expectant year;
They mimic life, as if from him to steal
His glow of health to paint the livid cheek;   10
They borrow words for thoughts they cannot feel,
That with a seeming heart their tongue may speak;
And in their show of life more dead they live
Than those that to the earth with many tears they give.

1839

The Presence

I sit within my room and joy to find
That Thou who always loves art with me here,
That I am never left by Thee behind,
But by Thyself Thou keep'st me ever near;
The fire turns brighter when with Thee I look,   5
And seems a kinder servant sent to me;
With gladder heart I read Thy holy book,
Because Thou art the eyes by which I see;
This aged chair, that table, watch, and door
Around in ready service ever wait;   10
Nor can I ask of Thee a menial more
To fill the measure of my large estate,
For Thou Thyself, with all a Father's care,
Where'er I turn, art ever with me there.

1839

Thy Brother's Blood

I have no brother,—they who meet me now
Offer a hand with their own wills defiled,
And, while they wear a smooth unwrinkled brow,
Know not that Truth can never be beguiled;
Go wash the hand that still betrays thy guilt;—   5
Before the spirit's gaze what stain can hide?

Abel's red blood' upon the earth is spilt,
And by thy tongue it cannot be denied;
I hear not with the ear,—the heart doth tell
Its secret deeds to me untold before;   10
Go, all its hidden plunder quickly sell,
Then shalt thou cleanse thee from thy brother's gore,
Then will I take thy gift;—that bloody stain
Shall not be seen upon thy hand again.

1839

Morning

The light will never open sightless eyes,
It comes to those who willingly would see;
And every object, hill, and stream, and skies,
Rejoice within th' encircling line to be;
'Tis day—the field is filled with busy hands,   5
The shop resounds with noisy workmen's din,
The traveler with his staff already stands
His yet unmeasured journey to begin;
The light breaks gently, too, within the breast—
Yet there no eye awaits the crimson morn,   10
The forge and noisy anvil are at rest,
Nor men nor oxen tread the fields of corn,
Nor pilgrim lifts his staff—it is no day
To those who find on earth their place to stay.

1839

George Washington Harris
1814–1869

George Washington Harris was born on March 20, 1814, in Alleghany City,
Pennsylvania. When he was five, his half brother took him to live in Knoxville,
Tennessee, where he later served an apprenticeship as a metalworker. Harris
worked at a variety of jobs: A steamboat captain at nineteen, he also operated his
own metalworking shop, ran a large farm in the foothills of the Great Smoky

---

' Abel, a son of Adam and Eve, was killed by his
brother, Cain.

Mountains, managed a sawmill, supervised a glassworks factory, and spent time in the copper mines of southeastern Tennessee. In 1839 he began contributing political pieces to the Knoxville *Argus.* He also wrote articles for *The Scientific American.*

By the late 1850s, Harris, a Jacksonian Democrat, became increasingly absorbed in secessionist politics. He served as a delegate to the Southern Commercial Convention at Savannah, Georgia, and in 1859, after moving to Nashville, was elected to the Democratic State Central Committee. Anti-Lincoln, anti-Republican, and anti-Yankee in general, Harris fled Nashville with his wife and family to escape the Union army, and for the duration of the Civil War he lived in various southern cities. In December 1869, while arranging for the publication of his second book, *High Times and Hard Times,* Harris mysteriously died en route to Knoxville; his manuscript was never found.

In 1845 Harris began writing sketches "illustrative of manners and customs of East Tennessee." He contributed "sporting epistles" to William T. Porter's popular *Spirit of the Times* (which also printed Thorpe's "The Big Bear of Arkansas") in the 1850s under the pseudonym "Mr. Free." Both before and after the war he also fired off an abundance of vituperative antinorthern articles to local newspapers.

Harris published only one book in his lifetime. But the sheer comic power of that collection of twenty-four tales, *Sut Lovingood. Yarns Spun by a "Nat'ral Born Durn'd Fool"* (1867), entitles Harris to a permanent place in American literature. Sut, loosely based on a character Harris met in the southeastern Tennessee mountains, is a crude, illiterate, shiftless, lecherous nineteen-year-old hillbilly whose noblest pursuits in life are hard whisky, young widows, and devastating practical jokes. In its oral cadences and exaggerated similes, Harris's writing typifies frontier humor at its best, though his unrelenting use of dialect and phonetic spelling makes his style seem at times nearly impenetrable. The Lovingood yarns, like most writing that relies on oral traditions, are intended to be *heard:* Words that look strange on the page become familiar once they are sounded.

Harris's writing, however, goes beyond the formulas of regional humor. Sut's antichivalric and antisentimental code is clearly Harris's visceral response to conventionally romanticized, idyllic versions of southern life. Sut's practical jokes, too, appear to have an extra touch of ferocity in them; he seems to live in a constant state of repressed anger and misdirected hostility. In tale after tale, he is violently about to "break up" some ceremonious occasion—a funeral, a wedding, a prayer meeting, or, as in the story below, a traditional quilting—either for revenge or simply for the "fun" of it. It was undoubtedly this uncontrollable comic rage that endeared *Sut Lovingood's Yarns* to such staunch observers of the human comedy as Mark Twain and William Faulkner.

Further Reading:
M. Rickels, *George Washington Harris,* 1965.
L. Ziff, *Literary Democracy,* 1981.

Text:
Sut Lovingood. Yarns Spun by a "Nat'ral Born Durn'd Fool." Warped and Wove for Public Wear, 1867.
See also *High Times and Hard Times,* ed. M. T. Inge, 1967.

Mrs. Yardley's Quilting

"Thar's one durn'd nasty muddy job, an' I is jis' glad enuf tu take a ho'n' ur two, on the straingth ove hit."

"What have you been doing, Sut?"

"Helpin tu salt ole Missis Yardley down."

"What do you mean by that?"

"Fixin her fur rotten cumfurtably, kiverin[2] her up wif sile, tu keep the buzzards frum cheatin the wurms."

"Oh, you have been helping to bury a woman."

"That's hit, by golly! Now why the devil can't I 'splain mysef like yu? I ladles out my words at random, like a calf kickin at yaller-jackids; yu jis' rolls em out tu the pint, like a feller a-layin bricks—every one fits. How is it that bricks fits so clost enyhow? Rocks won't ni du hit."

"Becaze they'se all ove a size," ventured a man with a wen[3] over his eye.

"The devil yu say, hon'ey-head! haint reapin-mersheens ove a size? I'd like tu see two ove em fit clost. Yu wait until yu sprouts tuther ho'n, afore yu venters to 'splain mix'd questions. George, did yu know ole Missis Yardley?"

"No."

"Well, she wer a curious 'oman in her way, an' she wore shiney specks. Now jis' listen: Whenever yu see a ole 'oman ahine a par ove *shiney* specks, yu keep yer eye skinn'd; they am dang'rus in the extreme. Thar is jis' no knowin what they ken du. I hed one a-stradil ove me onst, fur kissin her gal. She went fur my har, an' she went fur my skin, ontil I tho't she ment tu kill me, an' wud a-dun hit, ef my hollerin hadent fotch ole Dave Jordan, a *bacheler,* tu my aid. He, like a durn'd fool, cotch her by the laig, an' drug her back'ards ofen me. She jis' kivered him, an' I run, by golly! The nex time I seed him he wer bald headed, an' his face looked like he'd been a-fitin wildcats.

"Ole Missis Yardley wer a great noticer ove littil things, that nobody else ever seed. She'd say right in the middil ove sumbody's serious talk: 'Law sakes! thar goes that yaller slut ove a hen, a-flingin straws over her shoulder; she's arter settin now, an' haint laid but seven aigs. I'll disapint *her,* see ef I don't; I'll put a punkin in her nes', an' a feather in her nose. An' bless my soul! jis' look at that cow wif the wilted ho'n, a-flingin up dirt an' a-smellin the place whar hit cum frum, wif the rale ginuine still-wurim[4] twis' in her tail, too; what upon the face ove the yeath kin she be arter now, the ole fool? watch her, Sally. An' sakes alive! jis' look at that ole sow; she's a-gwine in a fas' trot, wif her empty bag a-floppin agin her sides. Thar, she hes stop't, an's a-listenin! massy on us! what a long yearnis[5] grunt she gin; hit cum frum way back ove her kidneys. Thar she goes agin; she's arter no good, sich kerryin on means no good.'

"An' so she wud gabble, no odds who wer a-listenin. She looked like she mout

---

[1] Horn; i.e., a drink.
[2] Covering.
[3] A benign skin tumor; Sut makes fun of this "horn" in the next paragraph.

[4] Still worm; i.e., the coiled condensing tubes of a whiskey still.
[5] Earnest.

been made at fust 'bout four foot long, an' the common thickness ove wimen when they's at tharsefs,[6] an' then had her har tied tu a stump, a par ove steers hitched to her heels, an' then straiched out a-mos' two foot more—mos' ove the straichin cumin outen her laigs an' naik. Her stockins, a-hangin on the clothes–line tu dry, looked like a par ove sabre scabbards, an' her naik looked like a dry beef shank smoked, an' mout been ni ontu es tough. I never felt hit mysef, I didn't, I jis' jedges by looks. Her darter Sal wer bilt at fust 'bout the laingth ove her mam, but wer never straiched eny by a par ove steers, an' she wer fat enuf tu kill; she wer taller lyin down than she wer a-standin up. Hit wer her who gin me the 'hump shoulder.' Jis' look at me; haint I'se got a tech ove the dromedary back thar bad? haint I humpy? Well, a-stoopin tu kiss that squatty lard-stan[7] ove a gal is what dun hit tu me. She wer the fairest-lookin gal I ever seed. She allers wore thick woolin stockins 'bout six inches too long fur her laig; they rolled down over her garters, lookin like a par ove life–presarvers up thar. I tell yu she wer a tarin gal enyhow. Luved kissin, wrastlin, an' biled cabbige, an' hated tite clothes, hot weather, an' suckit-riders.[8] B'leved strong in married folk's ways, cradles, an' the remishun ove sins, an' didn't b'leve in corsets, fleas, peaners,[9] nur the fashun plates."

"What caused the death of Mrs. Yardley, Sut?"

"Nuffin, only her heart stop't beatin 'bout losin a nine dimunt[10] quilt. True, she got a skeer'd hoss tu run over her, but she'd a-got over that ef a quilt hadn't been mix'd up in the catastrophy. Yu see quilts wer wun ove her speshul gifts; she run strong on the bed-kiver question. Irish chain, star ove Texas, sun-flower, nine dimunt, saw teeth, checker board, an' shell quilts; blue, an' white, an' yaller an' black coverlids, an' callickercumfurts reigned triumphan' 'bout her hous'. They wer packed in drawers, layin in shelfs full, wer hung four dubbil on lines in the lof, packed in chists, piled on cheers, an' wer everywhar, even ontu the beds, an' wer changed every bed-makin. She told everybody she cud git tu listen tu hit that she ment tu give every durn'd one ove them tu Sal when she got married. Oh, lordy! what es fat a gal es Sal Yardley cud ever du wif half ove em, an' sleepin wif a husbun at that, is more nor I ever cud see through. Jis' think ove her onder twenty layer ove quilts in July, an' yu in thar too. Gewhillikins! George, look how I is sweatin' now, an' this is December. I'd 'bout es lief be shet up in a steam biler wif a three hundred pound bag ove lard, es tu make a bisiness ove sleepin wif that gal—'twould kill a glass-blower.

"Well, tu cum tu the serious part ove this conversashun, that is how the old quilt-mersheen an' coverlid-loom cum tu stop operashuns on this yeath. She hed narrated hit thru the neighborhood that nex Saterday she'd gin a quiltin—three quilts an' one cumfurt tu tie.[11] 'Goblers, fiddils, gals, an' whisky,' wer the words she sent tu the men-folk, an' more tetchin ur wakenin words never drap't ofen an 'oman's tongue. She sed tu the gals, 'Sweet toddy, huggin, dancin, an' huggers in 'bundunce.' Them words struck the gals rite in the pit ove the stumick, an' spread a ticklin sensashun bof ways, until they scratched thar heads wif one han, an' thar heels wif tuther.

"Everybody, he an' she, what wer baptized b'levers in the righteousnes ove quiltins

---

wer thar, an' hit jis' so happen'd that everybody in them parts, frum fifteen summers tu fifty winters, wer unannamus b'levers. Strange, warn't hit? Hit wer the bigges' quiltin ever Missis Yardley hilt, an' she hed hilt hundreds; everybody wer thar, 'scept the constibil an' suckit-rider, two dam easily-spared pussons; the numbers ni ontu even too; jis' a few more boys nur gals; that made hit more exhitin, fur hit gin the gals a chance tu kick an' squeal a littil, wifout running eny risk ove not gittin kissed at all, an' hit gin reasonabil grouns fur a few scrimmages amung the he's. Now es kissin an' fitin am the pepper an' salt ove all soshul getherins, so hit wer more espishully wif this ove ours. Es I swung my eyes over the crowd, George, I thought quiltins, managed in a morril an' sensibil way, truly am good things—good fur free drinkin, good fur free eatin, good fur free huggin, good fur free dancin, good fur free fitin, an' goodest ove all fur poperlatin a country fas'.

"Thar am a fur-seein wisdum in quiltins, ef they hes proper trimmins: 'vittils, fiddils, an' sperrits[12] in 'bundunce.' One holesum quiltin am wuf three old pray'r-meetins on the poperlashun pint, purtickerly ef hits hilt in the dark ove the moon, an' runs intu the night a few hours, an' April ur May am the time chosen. The moon don't suit quiltins whar everybody is well acquainted an' already fur along in courtin. She dus help pow'ful tu begin a courtin match onder, but when hit draws ni ontu a head, nobody wants a moon but the ole mammys.

"The mornin cum, still, saft, sunshiney; cocks crowin, hens singin, birds chirpin, tuckeys gobblin—jis' the day tu sun quilts, kick, kiss, squeal, an' make love.

"All the plow-lines an' clothes-lines wer straiched tu every post an' tree. Quilts purvailed. Durn my gizzard ef two acres roun that ar house warn't jis' one solid quilt, all out a-sunnin, an' tu be seed. They dazzled the eyes, skeered the hosses, gin wimen the heart-burn, an' perdominated.

"To'ards sundown the he's begun tu drap in. Yearnis' needil-drivin cummenced tu lose groun; threads broke ofen, thimbils got los', an' quilts needed anuther roll. Gigglin, winkin, whisperin, smoofin ove har, an' gals a-ticklin one anuther, wer a-gainin every inch ove groun what the needils los'. Did you ever notis, George, at all soshul getherins, when the he's begin tu gather, that the young she's begin tu tickil one anuther an' the ole maids swell thar tails, roach[13] up thar backs, an' sharpen thar nails ontu the bed-posts an' door jams, an' spit an' groan sorter like cats a-courtin? Dus hit mean *rale* rath,[14] ur is hit a dare tu the he's, sorter kivered up wif the outside signs ove danger? I honestly b'leve that the young shes' ticklin means, 'Cum an' take this job ofen our hans.' But that swellin I jis' don't onderstan; dus yu? Hit looks skeery, an' I never tetch one ove em when they am in the swellin way. I may be mistaken'd 'bout the ticklin bisiness too; hit may be dun like a feller chaws poplar bark when he haint got eny terbacker, a-sorter better nur nun make-shif. I dus know one thing tu a certainty: that is, when the he's take hold the ticklin quits, an' ef yu gits one ove the ole maids out tu herself, then she subsides an' is the smoofes, sleekes, saft thing yu ever seed, an' dam ef yu can't hear her purr, jis' es plain!

"But then, George, gals an' ole maids haint the things tu fool time away on. Hits widders, by golly, what am the rale sensibil, steady-goin, never-skeerin, never-kickin, willin, sperrited, smoof pacers. They cum clost up tu the hoss-block,[15] standin still wif

---

[12] Spirits; i.e., hard liquor.
[13] Arch.

[14] Real wrath.
[15] Hitching post.

thar purty silky years playin, an' the naik-veins a-throbbin, an' waits fur the word, which ove course yu gives, arter yu finds yer feet well in the stirrup, an' away they moves like a cradil on cushioned rockers, ur a spring buggy runnin in damp san'. A tetch ove the bridil, an' they knows yu wants em tu turn, an' they dus hit es willin es ef the idear wer thar own. I be dod rabbited ef a man can't 'propriate happiness by the skinful ef he is in contack wif sumbody's widder, an' is smart. Gin me a willin widder, the yeath over: what they don't know, haint worth larnin. They hes all been tu Jamakey an' larnt how sugar's made, an' knows how tu sweeten wif hit; an' by golly, they is always ready tu use hit. All yu hes tu du is tu find the spoon, an' then drink cumfort till yer blind. Nex tu good sperrits an' my laigs, I likes a twenty-five year ole widder, wif roun ankils, an' bright eyes, honestly an' squarly lookin intu yurn, an' sayin es plainly es a partrige sez 'Bob White,' 'Don't be afraid ove me; I hes been thar; yu know hit ef yu hes eny sense, an' thar's no use in eny humbug, ole feller—cum ahead!'

"Ef yu onderstans widder nater, they ken save yu a power ove troubil, onsartinty, an' time, an' ef yu is interprisin yu gits mons'rous well paid fur hit. The very soun ove thar littil shoe-heels speak full trainin, an' hes a knowin click as they tap the floor; an' the rustil ove thar dress sez, 'I dar yu tu ax[16] me.'

"When yu hes made up yer mind tu court one, jis' go at hit like hit wer a job ove rail-maulin.[17] Ware yer workin close, use yer common, every-day moshuns an' words, an' abuv all, fling away yer cinamint ile[18] vial an' burn all yer love songs. No use in tryin tu fool em, fur they sees plum thru yu, a durn'd sight plainer than they dus thru thar veils. No use in a pasted[19] shut; she's been thar. No use in borrowin a cavortin fat hoss; she's been thar. No use in har-dye; she's been thar. No use in cloves, tu kill whisky breff; she's been thar. No use in buyin clost curtains fur yer bed, fur she has been thar. Widders am a speshul means, George, fur ripenin green men, killin off weak ones, an makin 'ternally happy the soun ones.

"Well, es I sed afore, I flew the track an' got ontu the widders. The fellers begun tu ride up an' walk up, sorter slow, like they warn't in a hurry, the durn'd 'saitful[20] raskils, hitchin thar critters tu enything they cud find. One red-comb'd, long-spurr'd, dominecker feller, frum town, in a red an' white grid-iron[21] jackid an' patent leather gaiters, hitched his hoss, a wild, skeery, wall-eyed devil, inside the yard palins, tu a cherry tree lim'. Thinks I, that hoss hes a skeer intu him big enuf tu run intu town, an' perhaps beyant hit, ef I kin only tetch hit off; so I sot intu thinkin.

"One aind ove a long clothes-line, wif nine dimunt quilts ontu hit, wer tied tu the same cherry tree that the hoss wer. I tuck my knife and socked hit thru every quilt, 'bout the middil, an' jis' below the rope, an' tied them thar wif bark, so they cudent slip. Then I went tu the back aind, an' ontied hit frum the pos', knottin in a hoe-handil, by the middil, tu keep the quilts frum slippin off ef my bark strings failed, an' laid hit on the groun. Then I went tu the tuther aind: thar wer 'bout ten foot tu spar, a-lyin on the groun arter tyin tu the tree. I tuck hit atwix Wall-eye's hine laigs, an' tied hit fas' tu bof stirrups, an' then cut the cherry tree lim' betwix his bridil an' the

---

[16] Ask.
[17] Rail splitting.
[18] Cinnamon-oil perfume.
[19] Starched.

[20] Deceitful.
[21] Dressed up like a Dominique, an American red-and-white chicken. (A grid iron is a cross-hatched pattern.)

tree, almos' off. Now, mine yu thar wer two ur three uther ropes full ove quilts atween me an' the hous', so I wer purty well hid frum thar. I jis' tore off a palin frum the fence, an' tuck hit in bof hans, an' arter raisin hit 'way up yander, I fotch hit down, es hard es I cud, flatsided to'ards the groun, an' hit acksidentally happen'd tu hit Wall-eye, 'bout nine inches ahead ove the root ove his tail. Hit landed so hard that hit made my hans tingle, an' then busted intu splinters. The first thing I did, wer tu feel ove mysef, on the same spot whar hit hed hit the hoss. I cudent help duin hit tu save my life, an' I swar I felt sum ove Wall-eye's sensashun, jis' es plain. The fust thing he did, wer tu tare down the lim' wif a twenty footjump, his head to'ards the hous. Thinks I, now yu hev dun hit, yu durn'd wall-eyed fool! tarin down that lim' wer the beginin ove all the troubil, an' the hoss did hit hissef; my conshuns felt clar es a mountain spring, an' I wer in a frame ove mine tu obsarve things es they happen'd, an' they soon begun tu happen purty clost arter one anuther rite then, an' thar, an' tharabouts, clean ontu town, thru hit, an' still wer a-happenin, in the woods beyant thar ni ontu eleven mile frum ole man Yardley's gate, an' four beyant town.

"The fust line ove quilts he tried tu jump, but broke hit down; the nex one he ran onder; the rope cotch ontu the ho'n ove the saddil, broke at bof ainds, an' went along wif the hoss, the cherry tree lim' an' the fust line ove quilts, what I hed proverdensally tied fas' tu the rope. That's what I calls foresight, George. Right furnint[22] the frunt door he cum in contack wif ole Missis Yardley herself, an' anuther ole 'oman; they wer a-holdin a nine dimunt quilt spread out, a-'zaminin hit, an' a-praisin hits purfeckshuns. The durn'd onmanerly, wall eyed fool run plum over Missis Yardley, frum ahine, stompt one hine foot through the quilt, takin hit along, a-kickin ontil he made hits corners snap like a whip. The gals screamed, the men hollered wo! an' the ole 'oman wer toted intu the hous' limber es a wet string, an' every word she sed wer, 'Oh, my preshus nine dimunt quilt!'

"Wall-eye busted thru the palins, an' Dominicker sed 'im, made a mortal rush fur his bitts, wer too late fur them, but in good time fur the strings ove flyin quilts, got tangled amung em, an' the gridiron jackid patren wer los' tu my sight amung star an' Irish chain quilts; he went frum that quiltin at the rate ove thuty miles tu the hour. Nuffin lef on the lot ove the hole consarn, but a nine biler hat, a par ove gloves, an' the jack ove hearts.

"What a onmanerly, suddin way ove leavin places sum folks hev got, enyhow.

"Thinks I, well, that fool hoss, tarin down that cherry tree lim', hes dun sum good, enyhow; hit hes put the ole 'oman outen the way fur the balance ove the quiltin, an' tuck Dominicker outen the way an' outen danger, fur that gridiron jackid wud a-bred a scab on his nose afore midnite; hit wer morrily boun tu du hit.

"Two months arterwards, I tracked the route that hoss tuck in his kalamatus skeer, by quilt rags, tufts ove cotton, bunches ove har, (human an' hoss,) an' scraps ove a gridiron jackid stickin ontu the bushes, an' plum at the aind ove hit, whar all signs gin out, I foun a piece ove watch chain an' a hosses head. The places what know'd Dominicker, know'd 'im no more.

"Well, arter they'd tuck the ole 'oman up stairs an' camfired[23] her tu sleep, things begun tu work agin. The widders broke the ice, an' arter a littil gigilin, goblin, an'

---

[22] In front of. [23] Camphored.

gabblin, the kissin begun. *Smack!*—'Thar, now,' a widder sed that. *Pop!*—'Oh, don't!' *Pfip!*—'Oh, yu quit!' *Plosh!*—'Go *way* yu awkerd critter, yu kissed me in the eye!' anuther widder sed that. *Bop!* 'Now yu ar satisfied, I recon, big mouf!' *Vip!*—'That haint fair!' *Spat!*—'Oh, lordy! May, cum pull Bill away; he's a-tanglin my har.' *Thut!* —"I jis' d-a-r-e yu tu du that agin!' a widder sed that, too. Hit sounded all 'roun that room like poppin co'n in a hot skillet, an' wer pow'ful sujestif.

"Hit kep on ontil I be durn'd ef *my* bristils didn't begin tu rise, an' sumthin like a cold buckshot wud run down the marrow in my back-bone 'bout every ten secons, an' then run up agin, tolerabil hot. I kep a swallerin wif nuthin tu swaller, an' my face felt swell'd; an' yet I wer fear'd tu make a bulge. Thinks I, I'll ketch one out tu herse'f torreckly,[24] an' then I guess we'll rastil.[25] Purty soon Sal Yardley started fur the smoke 'hous, so I jis' gin my head I few short shakes, let down one ove my wings a-trailin, an' sirkiled roun her wif a side twis' in my naik, steppin sidewise, an' a-fetchin up my hinmos' foot wif a sorter jerkin slide at every step. Sez I, 'Too coo-took a-too." She onderstood hit, an stopt, sorter spreadin her shoulders. An' jis' es I hed pouch'd out my mouf, an' wer a-reachin forrid wif hit, fur the article hitse'f, sunthin interfared wif me, hit did. George, wer yu ever ontu yer hans an' knees, an' let a hell-tarin big, mad ram, wif a ten-yard run, but[26] yu yearnis'ly, jis' onst, right squar ontu the pint ove yer back-bone?"

"No, you fool; why do you ask?"

"Kaze I wanted tu know ef yu cud hev a realizin' noshun ove my shock. Hits scarcely worth while tu try tu make yu onderstan the case by words only, onless yu hev been tetched in that way. Gr-eat golly! the fust thing I felt, I tuck hit tu be a back-ackshun yeathquake; an' the fust thing I seed wer my chaw'r terbacker a-flyin over Sal's head like a skeer'd bat. My mouf wer pouch'd out, ready fur the article hitse'f, yu know, an' hit went outen the roun hole like the wad outen a pop-gun— thug! an' the fust thing I know'd, I wer a flyin over Sal's head too, an' a-gainin on the chaw'r terbacker fast. I wer straitened out strait, toes hinemos', middil finger-nails foremos', an' the fust thing I hearn wer, "Yu dam Shanghi!"[27] Great Jerus-a-lam! I lit ontu my all fours jis' in time tu but the yard gate ofen hits hinges, an' skeer loose sum more hosses—kep on in a four-footed gallop, clean acrost the lane afore I cud straiten up, an' yere I cotch up wif my chaw'r terbacker, stickin flat agin a fence-rail. I hed got so good a start that I thot hit a pity tu spile hit, so I jis' jump'd the fence an' tuck thru the orchurd. I tell yu I dusted these yere close,[28] fur I tho't hit wer arter me.

"Arter runnin a spell, I ventured tu feel roun back thar, fur sum sings ove what hed happened tu me. George, arter two pow'ful hardtugs, I pull'd out the vamp[29] an' sole ove one ove ole man Yardley's big brogans,[30] what he hed los' amung my coat-tails. Dre'-ful! dre'ful! Arter I got hit away frum thar, my flesh went fas' asleep, frum abuv my kidneys tu my knees; about now, fur the fust time, the idear struck me, what hit wer that hed interfar'd wif me, an' los' me the kiss. Hit wer ole Yardley

[24] Directly.
[25] Wrestle.
[26] Butt.
[27] A long-legged chicken.
[28] Clothes.
[29] Portion of a shoe.
[30] Large, heavy workshoes.

hed kicked me. I walked fur a month like I wer straddlin a thorn hedge. Sich a shock, at sich a time, an' on sich a place—jis' think ove hit! hit am tremenjus, haint hit? The place feels num, right now."

"Well, Sut, how did the quilting come out?"

"How the hell du yu 'speck me tu know? I warn't thar eny more."

1867

Thomas Bangs Thorpe
1815–1875

"Our eyes will be turned westward," Emerson wrote in 1843, "and a new and stronger tone in literature will be the result." Emerson was not thinking here of James Fenimore Cooper and Washington Irving, writers who had helped launch American literature's western movement yet who clearly felt more at home in European capitals than in frontier towns. Instead, Emerson envisioned a western American literature arising from a new generation of frontier writers whose work was steeped in an authentic idiom: "The Kentucky stump-oratory, the exploits of Boone and David Crockett, the journals of western pioneers, agriculturalists and socialists . . . are genuine growths, which are sought with avidity in Europe, where our European-like books are of no value." Daniel Boone's legendary adventures first appeared in print in 1784, and Davy—Emerson's own distance from the frontier is apparent in his use of "David"—Crockett's distinctive blend of backwoods humor and self-promotion made for exciting reading throughout the 1830s. By the next decade, a sizable body of writing from the Midwest and Old Southwest had begun to attract the attention of eastern writers and editors.

One of these editors was William T. Porter, a Vermonter who had moved to New York City and in 1831 founded *Spirit of the Times,* a racy "Chronicle of the Turf, Agriculture, Field Sports, Literature, and the Stage." With a nationwide circulation of over forty thousand, *Spirit of the Times* soon grew to be a leading organ of southwestern humor, printing such classics as the Sut Lovingood tales of George Washington Harris. In 1841 Porter published what would become one of the most famous tall tales of American frontier literature, Thomas Bangs Thorpe's "The Big Bear of Arkansas." Arkansas (known as the "Bear State" until 1923) had been admitted into the Union as the twenty-fifth state in 1836. Public interest in the region had been especially fueled by an enormously popular humor book, *The Arkansas Traveler* (1840). Thorpe's tale is as much a piece of self-conscious regional boosterism for "the creation state, the finishing-up country" as it is an enduring frontier myth about an "unhuntable bar."

Thomas Bangs Thorpe was born in Westfield, Massachusetts, on March 1, 1815. He grew up in New York City, where he studied painting with John Quidon, a fine early American historical and figure painter who derived many of his themes from the work of Washington Irving. Thorpe attended Wesleyan University in Middletown, Connecticut, from 1834 to 1836 but because of ill health moved to Louisiana. He lived there from 1837 to 1853, painting portraits and landscapes as well as contributing tales and hunting sketches to Porter's *Spirit of the Times*. In 1846 Thorpe published a collection of his stories, *The Mysteries of the Backwoods,* and in the same year wrote and illustrated a book on the Mexican War, *Our Army on the Rio Grande*. Thorpe returned to New York City in 1854; he published a second collection of backwoods tales, *The Hive of "The Bee-Hunter"* (1854), and after Porter's death in 1858 took over *Spirit of the Times* until it folded in 1861. As a colonel in the Union army, Thorpe served as city administrator of New Orleans during the occupation. From 1869 until his death in 1878, he worked at the customs house in New York City and continued to write for various magazines. But never again did he capture the American literary imagination as he did with that one short sketch of Jim Doggett and his pursuit of the fabulous bear.

Further Reading:
W. Blair, "The Technique of 'The Big Bear of Arkansas,'" *Southwest Review,* Summer 1943.
M. Rickels, *Thomas Bangs Thorpe: Humorist of the Old Southwest,* 1962.

Text:
The Big Bear of Arkansas, and Other Sketches Illustrative of Characters and Incidents in the South and South-West, ed. W. T. Porter, 1845.

The Big Bear of Arkansas

As the author of "Tom Owen the Bee Hunter," and other tales and sketches, Mr. THORPE has acquired a distinguished reputation on both sides of the Atlantic. Though by profession a painter, his time for several years past has been about equally divided between the brush and the pen. He is now engaged in the publication of the "Concordia Intelligencer," a journal of unusual ability, issued weekly in the pleasant little village situated directly opposite the city of Natchez. The New York "Spirit of the Times" was the medium through which Mr. T. first appeared before the world of letters; and his inimitable delineations of South-western characters, incidents, and scenery, soon attracted attention. Now, wherever the language is spoken, he is deemed
        —"Great in mouths of wisest censure."
It is understood to be his intention to publish, at an early day, a collection of his writings, original and selected, to be illustrated by himself. As he is alike felicitous in the use of crayon, brush, or pen, we anticipate a brace or two of volumes of the highest pictorial and literary interest. The story annexed will give the reader an idea of his peculiar style in hitting off the original "characters" frequently met with in the great valley of the Mississippi.

A steamboat on the Mississippi frequently, in making her regular trips, carries between places varying from one to two thousand miles apart; and as these boats advertise to land passengers and freight at "all intermediate landings," the heterogeneous character of the passengers of one of these up-country boats can scarcely be imagined by one who has never seen it with his own eyes. Starting from New Orleans in one of these boats, you will find yourself associated with men from every state in the Union, and from every portion of the globe; and a man of observation need not lack for amusement or instruction in such a crowd, if he will take the trouble to read the great book of character so favourably opened before him. Here may be seen jostling together the wealthy Southern planter, and the pedler of tin-ware from New England—the Northern merchant, and the Southern jockey—a venerable bishop, and a desperate gambler—the land speculator, and the honest farmer—professional men of all creeds and characters—Wolvereens, Suckers, Hoosiers, Buckeyes, and Corn-crackers,[1] beside a "plentiful sprinkling" of the half-horse and half-alligator species of men,[2] who are peculiar to "old Mississippi," and who appear to gain a livelihood simply by going up and down the river. In the pursuit of pleasure or business, I have frequently found myself in such a crowd.

On one occasion, when in New Orleans, I had occasion to take a trip of a few miles up the Mississippi, and I hurried on board the well-known "high-pressure-and-beat-every-thing" steamboat "Invincible," just as the last note of the last bell was sounding; and when the confusion and bustle that is natural to a boat's getting under way had subsided, I discovered that I was associated in as heterogeneous a crowd as was ever got together. As my trip was to be of a few hours' duration only, I made no endeavours to become acquainted with my fellow passengers, most of whom would be together many days. Instead of this, I took out of my pocket the "latest paper," and more critically than usual examined its contents; my fellow passengers at the same time disposed of themselves in little groups. While I was thus busily employed in reading, and my companions were more busily still employed in discussing such subjects as suited their humours best, we were startled most unexpectedly by a loud Indian whoop, uttered in the "social hall," that part of the cabin fitted off for a bar; then was to be heard a loud crowing, which would not have continued to have interested us—such sounds being quite common in that *place of spirits*—had not the hero of these windy accomplishments stuck his head into the cabin and hallooed out, "Hurra for the Big Bar of Arkansaw!" and then might be heard a confused hum of voices, unintelligible, save in such broken sentences as "horse," "screamer,"[3] "lightning is slow," &c. As might have been expected, this continued interruption attracted the attention of every one in the cabin; all conversation dropped, and in the midst of this surprise the "Big Bar" walked into the cabin, took a chair, put his feet on the stove, and looking back over his shoulder, passed the general and familiar salute of "Strangers, how are you?" He then expressed himself as much at home as if he had been at "the Forks of Cypress," and "prehaps a little more so." Some of the company at this familiarity looked a little angry, and some astonished; but in a moment every face was wreathed in a smile. There was something about the intruder that won the heart on sight. He appeared to be a man enjoying perfect health and contentment: his eyes

---

[1] Nicknames for the inhabitants of Michigan, Illinois, Indiana, Ohio, and Kentucky, respectively.

[2] Popular expression for the breed of noisy, boasting Mississippi River raftsmen and backwoodsmen. Washington Irving: "It is an old remark that persons of Indian mixture are half civilized, half savage, and half devil—a third half being provided for their particular convenience. It is for similar reasons, and probably with equal truth, that the backwoodsmen of Kentucky are styled half man, half horse, and half alligator, by the settlers on the Mississippi, and held accordingly in great respect and abhorrence."

[3] Slang expression for a burly, noisy, bragging backwoodsman; i.e., a "Kentucky Screamer."

were as sparkling as diamonds, and good-natured to simplicity. Then his perfect confidence in himself was irresistibly droll. "Prehaps," said he, "gentlemen," running on without a person speaking, "prehaps you have been to New Orleans often; I never made *the first visit before,* and I don't intend to make another in a crow's life. I am thrown away in that ar place, and useless, that ar a fact. Some of the gentlemen thar called me *green*—well, prehaps I am, said I, *but I arn't so at home;* and if I aint off my trail much, the heads of them perlite chaps themselves wern't much the hardest; for according to my notion, they were *real know-nothings,* green as a pumpkin-vine —could'nt, in farming, I'll bet, raise a crop of turnips: and as for shooting, they'd miss a barn if the door was swinging, and that, too, with the best rifle in the country. And then they talked to me 'bout hunting, and laughed at my calling the principal game in Arkansaw poker, and high-low-jack. 'Prehaps,' said I, 'you prefer, chickens and rolette;'[4] at this they laughed harder than ever, and asked me if I lived in the woods, and didn't know what *game* was? At this I rather think I laughed. 'Yes,' I roared, and says, 'Strangers, if you'd asked me *how we got our meat* in Arkansaw, I'd a told you at once, and given you a list of varmints that would make a caravan, beginning with the bar, and ending off with the cat; that's *meat* though, not game.' Game, indeed, that's what city folks call it; and with them it means chippen-birds and shite-pokes;[5] maybe such trash live in my diggins, but I arn't noticed them yet: a bird any way is too trifling. I never did shoot at but one, and I'd never forgiven myself for that, had it weighed less than forty pounds. I wouldn't draw a rifle on any thing less than that; and when I meet with another wild turkey of the same weight I will drap him."

"A wild turkey weighing forty pounds!" exclaimed twenty voices in the cabin at once.

"Yes, strangers, and wasn't it a whopper? You see, the thing was so fat that it couldn't fly far; and when he fell out of the tree, after I shot him, on striking the ground he bust open behind, and the way the pound gobs of tallow rolled out of the opening was perfectly beautiful."

"Where did all that happen?" asked a cynical-looking Hoosier.

"Happen! happened in Arkansaw: where else could it have happened, but in the creation state, the finishing-up country—a state where the *sile* runs down to the centre of the 'arth, and government gives you a title to every inch of it? Then its airs— just breathe them, and they will make you snort like a horse. It's a state without a fault, it is."

"Excepting mosquitoes," cried the Hoosier.

"Well, stranger, except them; for it ar a fact that they are rather *enormous,* and do push themselves in somewhat troublesome. But, stranger, they never stick twice in the same place; and give them a fair chance for a few months, and you will get as much above noticing them as an alligator. They can't hurt my feelings, for they lay under the skin; and I never knew but one case of injury resulting from them, and that was to a Yankee: and they take worse to foreigners, any how, than they do to natives. But the way they used that fellow up! first they punched him until he swelled up and busted; then he sup-per-a-ted, as the doctor called it, until he was as raw as beef;

---

[4] "Chickens" is probably a misprint for "checkers"; "rolette": roulette.

[5] Chirping sparrows and herons, respectively.

then he took the ager,[6] owing to the warm weather, and finally he took a steamboat and left the country. He was the only man that ever took mosquitoes at heart that I know of. But mosquitoes is natur, and I never find fault with her. If they ar large, Arkansaw is large, her varmints ar large, her trees ar large, her rivers ar large, and a small mosquitoe would be of no more use in Arkansaw than preaching in a cane-brake."

This knock-down argument in favour of big mosquitoes used the Hoosier up, and the logician started on a new track, to explain how numerous bear were in his "diggins," where he represented them to be "about as plenty as blackberries, and a little plentifuler."

Upon the utterance of this assertion, a timid little man near me inquired if the bear in Arkansaw ever attacked the settlers in numbers.

"No," said our hero, warming with the subject, "no, stranger, for you see it ain't the natur of bar to go in droves; but the way they squander about in pairs and single ones is edifying. And then the way I hunt them—the old black rascals know the crack of my gun as well as they know a pig's squealing. They grow thin in our parts, it frightens them so, and they do take the noise dreadfully, poor things. That gun of mine is a perfect *epidemic among bar:* if not watched closely, it will go off as quick on a warm scent as my dog Bowie-knife[7] will: and then that dog—whew! why the fellow thinks that the world is full of bar, he finds them so easy. It's lucky he don't talk as well as think; for with his natural modesty, if he should suddenly learn how much he is acknowledged to be ahead of all other dogs in the universe, he would be astonished to death in two minutes. Strangers, that dog knows a bar's way as well as a horse-jockey knows a woman's: he always barks at the right time, bites at the exact place, and whips without getting a scratch. I never could tell whether he was made expressly to hunt bar, or whether bar was made expressly for him to hunt: any way, I believe they were ordained to go together as naturally as Squire Jones says a man and woman is, when he moralizes in marrying a couple. In fact, Jones once said, said he, 'Marriage according to law is a civil contract of divine origin; it's common to all countries as well as Arkansaw, and people take to it as naturally as Jim Doggett's Bowie-knife takes to bar.' "

"What season of the year do your hunts take place?" inquired a gentlemanly foreigner, who, from some peculiarities of his baggage, I suspected to be an Englishman, on some hunting expedition, probably at the foot of the Rocky mountains.

"The season for bar hunting, stranger," said the man of Arkansaw, "is generally all the year round, and the hunts take place about as regular. I read in history that varmints have their fat season, and their lean season. That is not the case in Arkansaw, feeding as they do upon the *spontenacious* productions of the sile, they have one continued fat season the year round: though in winter things in this way is rather more greasy than in summer, I must admit. For that reason bar with us run in warm weather, but in winter they only waddle. Fat, fat! it's an enemy to speed; it tames every thing that has plenty of it. I have seen wild turkeys, from its influence, as gentle as chickens. Run a bar in this fat condition, and the way it improves the critter for eating is

---

[6] Fever and chills; ague.
[7] Famous knife named for the frontiersman and soldier James Bowie (1799–1836).

amazing; it sort of mixes the ile up with the meat, until you can't tell t'other from which. I've done this often. I recollect one perty morning in particular, of putting an old he fellow on the stretch, and considering the weight he carried, he run well. But the dogs soon tired him down, and when I came up with him wasn't he in a beautiful sweat—I might say fever; and then to see his tongue sticking out of his mouth a feet,[8] and his sides sinking and opening like a bellows, and his cheeks so fat he couldn't look cross. In this fix I blazed at him, and pitch me naked into a briar patch if the steam didn't come out of the bullet-hole ten foot in a straight line. The fellow, I reckon, was made on the high-pressure system, and the lead sort of bust his biler."

"That column of steam was rather curious, or else the bear must have been warm," observed the foreigner, with a laugh.

"Stranger, as you observe, that bar was WARM, and the blowing off of the steam show'd it, and also how hard the varmint had been run. I have no doubt if he had kept on two miles farther his insides would have been stewed; and I expect to meet with a varmint yet of extra bottom, who will run himself into a skinfull of bar's grease: it is possible; much onlikelier things have happened."

"Whereabouts are these bears so abundant?" inquired the foreigner, with increasing interest.

"Why, stranger, they inhabit the neighbourhood of my settlement, one of the prettiest places on old Mississippi—a perfect location, and no mistake; a place that had some defects until the river made the 'cut-off' at 'Shirt-tail bend,' and that remedied the evil, as it brought my cabin on the edge of the river—a great advantage in wet weather, I assure you, as you can now roll a barrel of whiskey into my yard in high water from a boat, as easy as falling off a log. It's a great improvement, as toting it by land in a jug, as I used to do, *evaporated* it too fast, and it became expensive. Just stop with me, stranger, a month or two, or a year if you like, and you will appreciate my place. I can give you plenty to eat; for beside hog and hominy, you can have bar-ham, and bar-sausages, and a mattrass of bar-skins to sleep on, and a wildcat-skin, pulled off hull, stuffed with corn-shucks, for a pillow. That bed would put you to sleep if you had the rheumatics in every joint in your body. I call that ar bed a *quietus*.[9] Then look at my land—the government ain't got another such a piece to dispose of. Such timber, and such bottom land, why you can't preserve any thing natural you plant in it unless you pick it young, things thar will grow out of shape so quick. I once planted in those diggins a few potatoes and beets: they took a fine start, and after that an ox team couldn't have kept them from growing. About that time I went off to old Kentuck on bisiness, and did not hear from them things in three months, when I accidentally stumbled on a fellow who had stopped at my place, with an idea of buying me out. 'How did you like things?' said I. 'Pretty well,' said he; 'the cabin is convenient, and the timber land is good; but that bottom land ain't worth the first red cent.' 'Why?' said I. ' 'Cause,' said he. ' 'Cause what?' said I. ' 'Cause it's full of cedar stumps and Indian mounds,' said he, 'and *it can't be cleared.*' 'Lord,' said I, 'them ar "cedar stumps" is beets, and them ar "Indian mounds" ar tater hills.' As I expected, the crop was overgrown and useless: the sile is too rich, *and planting in Arkansaw is dangerous.* I had a good-sized sow killed in that same bottom

---

[8] Probably misprint for "foot."   [9] Final release from all cares; i.e., death.

land. The old thief stole an ear of corn, and took it down where she slept at night to eat. Well, she left a grain or two on the ground, and lay down on them: before morning the corn shot up, and the percussion killed her dead. I don't plant any more: natur intended Arkansaw for a hunting ground, and I go according to natur."

The questioner who thus elicited the description of our hero's settlement, seemed to be perfectly satisfied, and said no more; but the "Big Bar of Arkansaw" rambled on from one thing to another with a volubility perfectly astonishing, occasionally disputing with those around him, particularly with a "live Sucker" from Illinois, who had the daring to say that our Arkansaw friend's stories "smelt rather tall."

In this manner the evening was spent; but conscious that my own association with so singular a personage would probably end before morning, I asked him if he would not give me a description of some particular bear hunt; adding, that I took great interest in such things, though I was no sportsman. The desire seemed to please him, and he squared himself round towards me, saying, that he could give me an idea of a bar hunt that was never beat in this world, or in any other. His manner was so singular, that half of his story consisted in his excellent way of telling it, the great peculiarity of which was, the happy manner he had of emphasizing the prominent parts of his conversation. As near as I can recollect, I have italicized them, and given the story in his own words.

"Stranger," said he, "in bar hunts *I am numerous,* and which particular one, as you say, I shall tell, puzzles me. There was the old she devil I shot at the Hurricane last fall—then there was the old hog thief I popped over at the Bloody Crossing, and then—Yes, I have it! I will give you an idea of a hunt, in which the greatest bar was killed that ever lived, *none excepted;* about an old fellow that I hunted, more or less, for two or three years; and if that ain't a *particular bar hunt,* I ain't got one to tell. But in the first place, stranger, let me say, I am pleased with you, because you ain't ashamed to gain information by asking, and listening; and that's what I say to Countess's pups every day when I'm home; and I have got great hopes of them ar pups, because they are continually *nosing* about; and though they stick it sometimes in the wrong place, they gain experience any how, and may learn something useful to boot. Well, as I was saying about this big bar, you see when I and some more first settled in our region, we were drivin to hunting naturally; we soon liked it, and after that we found it an easy matter to make the thing our business. One old chap who had pioneered 'afore us, gave us to understand that we had settled in the right place. He dwelt upon its merits until it was affecting, and showed us, to prove his assertions, more marks on the sassafras trees than I ever saw on a tavern door 'lection time.[10] 'Who keeps that ar reckoning?' said I. 'The bar,' said he. 'What for?' said I. 'Can't tell,' said he; 'but so it is: the bar bite the bark and wood too, at the highest point from the ground they can reach, and you can tell, by the marks,' said he, 'the length of the bar to an inch.' 'Enough,' said I; 'I've learned something here a'ready, and I'll put it in practice.'

"Well, stranger, just one month from that time I killed a bar, and told its exact length before I measured it, by those very marks; and when I did that, I swelled up

---

[10] Drinking was notoriously heavy at election time, and the reckonings of bills were marked on the doors of taverns.

considerable—I've been a prouder man ever since. So I went on, larning something every day, until I was reckoned a buster,[11] and allowed to be decidedly the best bar hunter in my district; and that is a reputation as much harder to earn than to be reckoned first man in Congress, as an iron ramrod is harder than a toad-stool. Did the varmints grow over-cunning by being fooled with by green-horn hunters, and by this means get troublesome, they send for me as a matter of course; and thus I do my own hunting, and most of my neighbours'. I walk into the varmints though, and it has become about as much the same to me as drinking. It is told in two sentences —a bar is started, and he is killed. The thing is somewhat monotonous now—I know just how much they will run, where they will tire, how much they will growl, and what a thundering time I will have in getting them home. I could give you this history of the chase with all the particulars at the commencement, I know the signs so well —*Stranger, I'm certain.* Once I met with a match though, and I will tell you about it; for a common hunt would not be worth relating.

"On a fine fall day, long time ago, I was trailing about for bar, and what should I see but fresh marks on the sassafras trees, about eight inches above any in the forests that I knew of. Says I, 'them marks is a hoax, or it indicates the d——t bar that was ever grown.' In fact, stranger, I couldn't believe it was real, and I went on. Again I saw the same marks, at the same height, and *I knew the thing lived.* That conviction came home to my soul like an earthquake. Says I, 'here is something a-purpose for me: that bar is mine, or I give up the hunting business.' The very next morning what should I see but a number of buzzards hovering over my corn-field. 'The rascal has been there,' said I, 'for that sign is certain:' and, sure enough, on examining, I found the bones of what had been as beautiful a hog the day before, as was ever raised by a Buckeye. Then I tracked the critter out of the field to the woods, and all the marks he left behind, showed me that he was *the bar.*

"Well, stranger, the first fair chase I ever had with that big critter, I saw him no less than three distinct times at a distance: the dogs run him over eighteen miles and broke down, my horse gave out, and I was as nearly used up as a man can be, made on *my* principle, *which is patent.* Before this adventure, such things were unknown to me as possible; but, strange as it was, that bar got me used to it before I was done with him; for he got so at last, that he would leave me on a long chase *quite easy.* How he did it, I never could understand. That a bar runs at all, is puzzling; but how this one could tire down and bust up a pack of hounds and a horse, that were used to overhauling everything they started after in no time, was past my understanding. Well, stranger, that bar finally got so sassy, that he used to help himself to a hog off my premises whenever he wanted one; the buzzards followed after what he left, and so, between *bar and buzzard,* I rather think I was *out of pork.*

"Well, missing that bar so often took hold of my vitals, and I wasted away. The thing had been carried too far, and it reduced me in flesh faster than an ager. I would see that bar in every thing I did: *he hunted me,* and that, too, like a devil, which I began to think he was. While in this fix, I made preparations to give him a last brush, and be done with it. Having completed every thing to my satisfaction, I started at sunrise, and to my great joy, I discovered from the way the dogs run, that they were near him; finding his trail was nothing, for that had become as

[11] Slang for a big, roaring fellow.

plain to the pack as a turnpike road. On we went, and coming to an open country, what should I see but the bar very leisurely ascending a hill, and the dogs close at his heels, either a match for him this time in speed, or else he did not care to get out of their way—I don't know which. But wasn't he a beauty, though? I loved him like a brother.

"On he went, until he came to a tree, the limbs of which formed a crotch about six feet from the ground. Into this crotch he got and seated himself, the dogs yelling all around it; and there he sat eyeing them as quiet as a pond in low water. A green-horn friend of mine, in company, reached shooting distance before me, and blazed away, hitting the critter in the centre of his forehead. The bar shook his head as the ball struck it, and then walked down from that tree as gently as a lady would from a carriage. 'Twas a beautiful sight to see him do that—he was in such a rage that he seemed to be as little afraid of the dogs as if they had been sucking pigs; and the dogs warn't slow in making a ring around him at a respectful distance, I tell you; even Bowie-knife, himself, stood off. Then the way his eyes flashed—why the fire of them would have singed a cat's hair; in fact that bar was in a *wrath all over*. Only one pup came near him, and he was brushed out so totally with the bar's left paw, that he entirely disappeared; and that made the old dogs more cautious still. In the mean time, I came up, and taking deliberate aim as a man should do, at his side, just back of his foreleg, if *my gun did not snap*,[12] call me a coward, and I won't take it personal. Yes, stranger, *it snapped*, and I could not find a cap[13] about my person. While in this predicament, I turned round to my fool friend—says I, 'Bill,' says I, 'you're an ass—you're a fool—you might as well have tried to kill that bar by barking the tree under his belly, as to have done it by hitting him in the head. Your shot has made a tiger of him, and blast me, if a dog gets killed or wounded when they come to blows, I will stick my knife into your liver, I will ————, my wrath was up. I had lost my caps, my gun had snapped, the fellow with me had fired at the bar's head, and I expected every moment to see him close in with the dogs, and kill a dozen of them at least. In this thing I was mistaken, for the bar leaped over the ring formed by the dogs, and giving a fierce growl, was off—the pack, of course, in full cry after him. The run this time was short, for coming to the edge of a lake the varmint jumped in, and swam to a little island in the lake, which it reached just a moment before the dogs. 'I'll have him now,' said I, for I had found my caps in the *lining of my coat*—so, rolling a log into the lake, I paddled myself across to the island, just as the dogs had cornered the bar in a thicket. I rushed up and fired—at the same time the critter leaped over the dogs and came within three feet of me, running like mad; he jumped into the lake, and tried to mount the log I had just deserted, but every time he got half his body on it, it would roll over and send him under; the dogs, too, got around him, and pulled him about, and finally Bowie-knife clenched with him, and they sunk into the lake together. Stranger, about this time I was excited, and I stripped off my coat, drew my knife, and intended to have taken a part with Bowie-knife myself, when the bar rose to the surface. But the varmint staid under—Bowie-knife came up alone, more dead than alive, and with the pack came ashore. 'Thank God,' said I, 'the old villain has got his deserts at last.' Determined to have the body, I cut a grape-vine for a rope, and dove down where I could see the bar in the water, fastened

---

[12] Misfire.   [13] Percussion cap.

my queer rope to his leg, and fished him, with great difficulty, asho. I be chawed to death by young alligators, if the thing I looked at wa. *and not the old critter after all.* The way matters got mixed on that island was onaccou ably curious, and thinking of it made me more than ever convinced that I was hunting the devil himself. I went home that night and took to my bed—the thing was killing me. The entire team of Arkansaw in bar-hunting, acknowledged himself used up, and the fact sunk into my feelings like a snagged boat will in the Mississippi. I grew as cross as a bar with two cubs and a sore tail. The thing got out 'mong my neighbours, and I was asked how come on that individ-u-al that never lost a bar when once started? and if that same individ-u-al didn't wear telescopes when he turned a she bar, of ordinary size, into an old he one, a little larger than a horse? 'Prehaps,' said I, 'friends' —getting wrathy—'prehaps you want to call somebody a liar.' 'Oh, no,' said they, 'we only heard such things as being *rather common* of late, but we don't believe one word of it; oh, no,'—and then they would ride off and laugh like so many hyenas over a dead nigger. It was too much, and I determined to catch that bar, go to Texas, or die,—and I made my preparations accordin'. I had the pack shut up and rested. I took my rifle to pieces, and iled it. I put caps in every pocket about my person, *for fear of the lining.* I then told my neighbours, that on Monday morning—naming the day—I would start THAT BAR, and bring him home with me, or they might divide my settlement among them, the owner having disappeared. Well, stranger, on the morning previous to the great day of my hunting expedition, I went into the woods near my house, taking my gun and Bowie-knife along, just *from habit,* and there sitting down also from habit,[14] what should I see, getting over my fence, but *the bar!* Yes, the old varmint was within a hundred yards of me, and the way he walked over that fence—stranger, he loomed up like a *black mist,* he seemed so large, and he walked right towards me. I raised myself, took deliberate aim, and fired. Instantly the varmint wheeled, gave a yell, and *walked through the fence* like a falling tree would through a cobweb. I started after, but was tripped up by my inexpressibles,[15] which either from habit, or the excitement of the moment, were about my heels, and before I had really gathered myself up, I heard the old varmint groaning in a thicket near by, like a thousand sinners, and by the time I reached him he was a corpse. Stranger, it took five niggers and myself to put that carcase on a mule's back, and old long-ears waddled under his load, as if he was foundered in every leg of his body, and with a common whopper of a bar, he would have trotted off, and enjoyed himself. 'Twould astonish you to know how big he was: I made a *bed-spread of his skin,* and the way it used to cover my bar mattress, and leave several feet on each side to tuck up, would have delighted you. It was in fact a creation bar, and if it had lived in Samson's[16] time, and had met him, in a fair fight, it would have licked him in the twinkling of a dice-box. But, stranger, I never liked the way I hunted him, *and missed him.* There is something curious about it, I could never understand,—and I never was satisfied at his giving in so *easy at last.* Prehaps, he had heard of my preparations to hunt him the next day, so he jist come in, like Capt. Scott's coon,[17] to save his wind to grunt

---

[14] I.e., habitual morning bowel movement.
[15] Euphemism for trousers. Doggett had lowered them from "habit."
[16] Samson: Biblical hero famous for his great strength (Judges 13–16).

[17] Allusion to a popular anecdote in which a raccoon, seeing that it is about to be shot, wisely gives up.

with in dying; but that ain't likely. My private opinion is, that that bar was an *unhuntable bar, and died when his time come.*"

When the story was ended, our hero sat some minutes with his auditors in a grave silence; I saw there was a mystery to him connected with the bear whose death he had just related, that had evidently made a strong impression on his mind. It was also evident that there was some superstitious awe connected with the affair,—a feeling common with all "children of the wood," when they meet with any thing out of their everyday experience. He was the first one, however, to break the silence, and jumping up, he asked all present to "liquor" before going to bed,—a thing which he did, with a number of companions, evidently to his heart's content.

Long before day, I was put ashore at my place of destination, and I can only follow with the reader, in imagination, our Arkansas friend, in his adventures at the "Forks of Cypress" on the Mississippi.

1841

Frederick Douglass
1817?–1895

This black man, who did not know his birthday or who his father was, who rarely saw his mother after he was taken from her as an infant, created a life for himself out of the nothingness his slave status had conferred upon him and his race. At twenty-one Frederick Bailey escaped from the Maryland plantation where he had spent most of his young life. He arrived in 1838 in New Bedford, Massachusetts, where he changed his name to Douglass, ostensibly to throw his pursuers off his trail but also to forge an identity for himself as a free man.

Douglass taught himself to read and write, then launched himself into the thick of the abolitionist movement. By 1841 he was recognized as one of the most eloquent speakers for the Massachusetts Anti-Slavery Society. Writing and lecturing took Douglass across the northern states and to England. Purchasing his freedom in 1847, he added editing to his other activities by founding the *North Star* and *Douglass' Monthly*. During the Civil War he recruited blacks for service in the Union Army. His active life included serving as a United States Marshal and an appointment as Consul General to the Haitian Republic as well as speaking out for women's rights, antilynching laws, and the betterment of the lives of poor tenant farmers in the postwar South.

It was natural for Douglass to thrust himself into the center of public attention on heated issues, but the ugliest kind of controversy surrounded him when he married a white woman and, later, when he was reputed to have supported John Brown's raid on the Harpers Ferry arsenal—a false accusation that caused him, prudently, to leave the country until the facts were made clear. But it was as a writer of autobiography that he achieved his greatest fame.

The first version of Douglass's memoirs appeared in 1845 under the title *Narrative of the Life of Frederick Douglass.* Later revisions and additions led to *My*

Bondage and My Freedom, published in 1855. Two much later revisions resulted in the *Life and Times of Frederick Douglass,* brought out in 1881 and 1892. In these accounts, Douglass borrows, with irony, the autobiographical form of the young man on his way to fame and fortune that Benjamin Franklin made a central motif in American letters. Douglass joined it, however, to another literary tradition: slave narratives that recounted the oppression of a people who were not considered human enough to have the rights of autobiography. As the final title of his book indicates, Douglass's life is also a powerful examination of the times that he made and that made him. Douglass's autobiography now stands as one of the most memorable of the exemplary lives written by self-created Americans.

Further Reading:

C. Chesnutt, *Frederick Douglass,* 1899, 1970.
B. Washington, *Frederick Douglass,* 1906, 1969.
E. Fuller, *A Star Pointed North,* 1946.
S. Graham, *There Once Was a Slave,* 1947.
B. Quarles, *Frederick Douglass,* 1968.
J. Gregory, *Frederick Douglass, The Orator,* 1969.
F. Holland, *Frederick Douglass: The Colored Orator,* 1969.
C. Hoexter, *Black Crusader: Frederick Douglass,* 1970.
A. Bontemps, *Free at Last: The Life of Frederick Douglass,* 1971.

Frederick Douglass on Women's Rights, ed. P. Foner, 1976.
The Frederick Douglass Papers, 2 vols., ed. J. Blassingame, 1979.
N. I. Huggins, *Slave and Citizen: The Life of Frederick Douglass,* 1980.
D. Preston, *Young Frederick Douglass: The Maryland Years,* 1980.
W. E. Martin, Jr., *The Mind of Frederick Douglass,* 1985.
D. J. Preston, *Young Frederick Douglass: The Maryland Years,* 1985.

Texts:

The *Life and Times of Frederick Douglass,* 1892. Letter to Thomas Auld, "At Home Again," and "Prejudice Against Color" from *The Life and*

Writings of Frederick Douglass, 4 vols., ed. P. Foner, 1950–1955.

---

from Life and Times of Frederick Douglass[*]

Chapter XIII: Covey, the Negro-Breaker

In the region of the bay there was a farm renter named Edward Covey who was said to be a first-rate hand at breaking young Negroes. Mr. Covey had the most fiery farm helpers of the neighborhood at little cost to himself because he could be depended upon to return them to their owners well broken. While I could not look forward to going to him with pleasure I was glad to get away from St. Michaels. I believed I would get enough to eat at Covey's, even if I suffered in other respects.

Eight or ten years had now passed since I had been taken from my grandmother's cabin in Tuckahoe. For the most part I had spent these years in Baltimore where I

---

[*] The full title of this 1892 version—the final and complete version—of Douglass's autobiography is *Life and Times of Frederick Douglass: his early life as a slave, his escape and*

bondage, and his complete history, written by himself. Previous but markedly different versions of the autobiography had been published in 1845, 1855, and 1881.

was treated with comparative tenderness. I was now about to sound profounder depths of slave life.

The morning of January 1, 1834, found me on the road to Covey's. The chilling wind and pinching frost matched the winter of my own mind as I trudged along. At last I came in sight of a small wooden building about a mile from the main road. From the description I had received, I recognized it as my new home. The little house stood on the banks of Chesapeake Bay, which was now white with foam raised by a heavy northwest wind. The good clothes I had brought with me from Baltimore were now worn thin and had not been replaced. I was glad to find shelter of any kind, even with the dreaded Covey, and I hurried on to the house.

The family consisted of Mr. and Mrs. Covey; Mrs. Kemp (a broken-backed woman), sister to Mrs. Covey; William Hughes, cousin to Mr. Covey; Caroline, the cook; Bill Smith, a hired man; and myself. For the first time in my life I was now to be a field hand. Bill Smith, Bill Hughes, and I were the working force of the farm, which was three or four hundred acres in size.

I had been in my new home only three days before Mr. Covey gave me a bitter foretaste of what was in store for me. At daybreak I was ordered to get a load of wood from a forest about two miles from the house. To perform this work, Mr. Covey gave me a pair of unbroken oxen. He knew what I had yet to discover, that though tame and docile when well trained, oxen are the most sullen and intractable of animals when half broken to the yoke. Mr. Covey took a rope about ten feet long and one inch thick and placed one end of it around the horns of one of the oxen and gave the other end to me. He told me that if the oxen started to run away (as he knew they would) I must hold onto the rope and stop them. I afterwards learned that even Covey himself would not have taken the oxen to the woods without first driving them for some time in the open field. At the time, however, I had no directions other than the ones he had given me, and I started for the woods anxious to perform my first exploit in a creditable manner.

I had never driven oxen before, and I was as awkward a driver as it is possible to imagine. Yet the first mile, from the house to the gate at the woods, was passed over with little difficulty. The animals ran, but I was fast enough in the open field to keep up with them. On reaching the woods, my situation took a turn for the worse. The animals became frightened and started off ferociously. As I held the rope I expected every moment to be crushed between the cart and the huge trees. After running for several minutes, my oxen were finally brought to a halt by a tree. Wild and enraged, they dashed themselves against it with such violence that they became entangled in some young saplings. The body of the cart was flung in one direction and the wheels and tongue in another, all in the greatest confusion.

I stood a few minutes surveying the damage and wondering how best to put it all right again. I took one end of the cart body and by an extra outlay of strength succeeded in getting it in its place on the axle tree. The cart was provided with an ax, a tool which I had learned to use in the shipyard at Baltimore. With this I cut down the saplings and freed my oxen. I again pursued my journey with my heart in my mouth lest the beasts cut up another caper. On reaching the part of the forest where I had been chopping wood the day before, I filled the cart with a heavy load.

Half the day was gone, and I had not yet started home. I knew that such an apparent waste of time would not be overlooked by Covey, and I hurried back through the woods. On reaching the edge of the field, I let go the end of the rope to open the gate. Once the gate was opened in front of them, my oxen charged through full tilt. They caught the huge gate between the wheel and the cart body, crushing it to splinters and coming within a few inches of crushing me with it.

When I went to Covey to explain about the casualties of my trip, his sharp face became intensely ferocious.

"Go back to the woods again," he said, muttering something about wasting time.

I obeyed, and looking over my shoulder, I saw that he was following me. On reaching the woods, Covey told me that he would now teach me how to break gates and idle away my time. He went to a large black gum tree, the young shoots of which are generally used for ox goads because they are exceedingly tough. He cut off three of these goads, from four to six feet long, and trimmed them up with his large jackknife. This done, he ordered me to take off my clothes. I made no reply, but by ignoring his order I indicated my determination to do no such thing.

"If you beat me," I thought, "you shall do so over my clothes."

After many threats he rushed at me with the savage fierceness of a wolf, tore off the few thin clothes I had on, and proceeded to wear out on my back the heavy goads which he had cut from the gum tree.

This was the first of a series of floggings I received while at Covey's. It was less severe than many which came after it, and these for offenses far lighter than the gate-breaking. I remained with Mr. Covey one year, and during the first six months there I was whipped, either with sticks or a cowhide whip, every week. Aching bones and a sore back were my constant companions. From the dawn of day in the morning till complete darkness in the evening, I was kept hard at work in the field or the woods. He had in his life been an overseer, and he well understood the business of slave driving. There was no deceiving him. He knew just what a man or boy could do and he held both to strict account.

It was, however, scarcely necessary for Mr. Covey to be present in the field to have his work go on industriously. We never knew when we were being watched. He would creep in the gullies and hide behind bushes. We were never secure. He would sometimes mount his horse and make believe he was going to St. Michaels. But thirty minutes afterwards we might find his horse tied in the woods. A short distance away, Covey might be seen lying flat in the ditch with his head lifted above its edge, watching every movement of the slaves. He did not seem conscious that such spying had anything contemptible about it. It was part of an important system with him, essential to the relation of master and slave.

Mr. Edward Covey was a poor but ambitious man. He was just beginning to lay the foundation of his fortune, and in a slave state that meant owning human property. He had acquired one slave of his own, a woman named Caroline, whom he had bought "as a breeder." Covey and his wife were ecstatic with joy when twins were born at the end of the year. No one reproached the woman or found fault with the hired man, Bill Smith, the father of the children. Mr. Covey had locked the two up together every night to bring about this result.

If at any one time of my life more than another I was made to drink the bitterest dregs of slavery, that time was during the first six months of my stay with this man Covey. We worked all weathers. It was never too hot or too cold. It could never rain, blow, snow, or hail too hard for us to work in the field. Work, work, work was as much the order of the night as the order of the day. I had neither time to eat nor time to sleep. I was somewhat unmanageable at first, but a few months of Covey's discipline tamed me. He succeeded in breaking me in body, soul, and spirit. My natural elasticity was crushed, my intellect languished, the wish to read departed, and the dark night of slavery closed in upon me.

Sunday was my only leisure time. I spent this in a sort of beast-like stupor, between sleeping and waking, under some large tree. I was sometimes tempted to take my life and that of Covey but was prevented by a combination of hope and fear. My sufferings, as I remember them now, seem like a dream rather than a stern reality.

Chapter XIV: The Beginning of the End

One hot day in August of that year I was at work in what was called the "treading yard," where wheat was threshed from the straw by the horses' feet. The work required strength and activity rather than skill. Our force consisted of Bill Hughes, Bill Smith, and a slave by the name of Eli who had been hired for the occasion. I was bringing wheat to the "fan" while Bill Smith was feeding.

About three o'clock, while the sun poured down its burning rays and not a breeze stirred, I suddenly broke down. My strength failed me. I was seized with a violent headache, dizziness, and trembling. Knowing that it would never do to stop work, I nerved myself up and tried to stagger on. But at last I fell by the side of the wheat fan, bringing the entire work to a standstill. There was work for four. Each of us had his part to perform, and each part depended on the other; when one stopped, all were compelled to stop. Covey, who had become my dread, was at the house about a hundred yards from where we were working. Instantly, upon hearing the work cease, he came down to the treading yard. Bill Smith told him I was sick and that I was unable to bring wheat to the fan any longer.

By this time I had crawled to a place in the shade and was exceedingly ill. The intense heat of the sun, the heavy dust rising from the fan, and the continual stooping to take up the wheat from the yard had caused a rush of blood to my head. Covey stood over me and asked what was the matter. I told him as well as I could, for it was difficult for me to speak. He gave me a savage kick in the side which jarred my whole frame, and commanded me to get up. He had obtained complete control over me, and if he had commanded me to do any possible thing, I would have tried to obey. I made an effort to rise but fell back before getting to my feet. He gave me another heavy kick and again told me to rise. I again tried and succeeded in standing up. But when I stooped to get the tub with which I was feeding the fan I again staggered and fell to the ground. If I had been threatened with a hundred bullets I could not have gotten up.

"If you have got the headache, I'll cure you," he said.

He took up a hickory slab and with the edge of it dealt me a heavy blow on my head which made a large gash and caused the blood to run freely. He ordered me again to rise, but I made no effort to do so. I had now made up my mind that it was useless and the villain could do no worse than kill me and put me out of my misery.

Finding me unable to rise, or rather giving up hope of my doing so, Covey left to get on with the work without me. I was bleeding freely, and my face was soon covered with blood. Cruel as the blow was, the wound was a fortunate one for me. The pain in my head quickly abated, and I was soon able to rise. I asked myself if I should return to my work or should I find my way to St. Michaels, show Capt. Auld the results of Covey's cruelty, and beseech him to get me another master? Remembering Capt. Thomas Auld's behavior of the past, there was little ground to hope that he would receive me favorably. Nevertheless, I thought he might interfere on my behalf from selfish considerations.

"He cannot," I thought, "allow his property to be thus bruised and battered, marred, and defaced, and I will go to him about the matter."

In order to get to St. Michaels by the most direct road I had to walk seven miles, and this, in my sad condition, was no easy thing to do. However, I watched my chance while Covey was looking in another direction and started off across the field for St. Michaels. I was halfway across the field toward the woods when Covey saw me.

"Come back! Come back!" he shouted, with threats of what he would do if I did not return instantly.

But I disregarded his calls and threats and hurried on toward the woods as fast as my feeble state would allow. Seeing no signs of my stopping, he had his horse brought out and saddled as if he intended to pursue me. I reached the woods where I kept away from the road. If he followed me, I did not see or hear him.

I had not gone far among the trees before my strength failed me again and I was obliged to lie down. The blood was still oozing from the wound in my head, and for a time I suffered more than I can describe. I was afraid I might bleed to death. The thought of dying in the woods all alone and being torn to pieces by the buzzards was not a tolerable one. I was glad when the shade of the trees and the cool evening breeze stopped the flow of blood and I could again take up my journey to St. Michaels. I was five hours in going the seven or eight miles, partly because of the difficulties of the route I took and partly because of the feebleness induced by my illness, bruises, and loss of blood.

On reaching my master's, I found I had jumped from a sinking ship into the sea. I told him the circumstances as well as I could. At first Master Thomas walked the floor, agitated by my story and the spectacle I presented. But soon it was his turn to talk. He said that he had no doubt I deserved the treatment I had received from Covey. He did not believe I was sick but that I was only trying to get out of work. He asked what I wanted him to do. I told him I wished him to let me find a new master. I told him that I was sure if I went back again to live with Mr. Covey that I would be killed or, if not that, that I would be ruined for future service.

Master Thomas regarded this as "nonsense." He said that Mr. Covey was a good man, industrious and religious.

"Besides," he said, "if you leave Covey now with your year only half over, I will lose your wages for the entire year. You belong to Mr. Covey for one year, and you must go back to him come what will. You must not trouble me with any more stories. If you don't go back to Covey's house immediately, I'll give you a whipping myself."

"But sir," I said, "I am sick and tired, and I cannot get home tonight."

He finally allowed me to spend the night but made me swallow a huge dose of Epsom salts, which was about the only medicine ever administered to slaves.

Chapter XV: The Last Flogging

Sleep does not always come to the relief of the weary in body and broken in spirit. I remained, but did not sleep, all that Friday night at St. Michaels. In the morning I set off feeling that I had no friend on earth and doubting if I had one in heaven. I reached the field at Covey's house about nine o'clock. True to his snakish habits Covey darted out at me from a fence corner where he had hidden himself for the purpose of capturing me. He had a cowhide whip and a rope, and he evidently intended to tie me up and wreak his vengeance on me to the fullest extent. I would have been easy prey had he gotten his hands upon me. I had taken no food since noon the day before, and this, with the other trying circumstances, had greatly reduced my strength. However, I darted back into the woods before he could reach me and buried myself in a thicket. He was much chagrined that I escaped him, as I could see by his angry movements as he returned to the house.

I was alone in the woods, buried in somber gloom, shut in with nature, and I wanted to pray. But the sham religion which I saw everywhere made me doubt that my prayers would be of any help.

Night came. I was still in the woods and had not yet made up my mind whether to remain in the woods and starve or return to Covey and have my flesh torn off. I lay down in the leaves to rest. I had been watching for hunters all day, but not having seen them during the day, I expected no disturbance from them during the night. I had come to the conclusion that Covey believed I would be driven home by hunger, and in this I believe I was correct, for he made no effort to catch me after the morning.

During the night I heard the step of a man in the woods. He was coming toward the place where I lay. I hid myself in the leaves to prevent discovery. But as the stranger drew nearer, I found him to be a friend, not an enemy. He was a slave of Mr. William Groomes of Easton, a kindhearted fellow named "Sandy." Sandy lived with Mr. Kemp about four miles from St. Michaels. He, like myself, had been hired out that year, but not to be broken. He was the husband of a free woman who lived not far away and he was now on his way through the woods to spend Sunday with her.

As soon as I discovered that the intruder was the goodnatured Sandy I came out from my hiding place. I explained the circumstances of the past two days which had driven me to the woods, and he deeply sympathized with me. Sandy knew Covey well, for Mrs. Covey was the daughter of Mrs. Kemp. Sandy had heard of the barbarous treatment to which I had been subjected, and he wanted to do something for me. I did not ask him to shelter me. Had I been found in his slave quarters, he would have suffered thirty-nine lashes on his bare back, if not something worse. But Sandy was too generous to leave me to my fate. He took me with him to the home of his free wife, who owned her house and lot. It was about midnight, but his wife was called up, a fire was made, some Indian meal was mixed with salt and water, and an ash cake was baked to relieve my hunger. Since that night I have partaken of banquets. But my supper on ash cake and cold water with these two fine people was the meal of all my life most sweet to my taste and most vivid to my memory.

Both Sandy and his wife seemed to think it a privilege to help me. I was hated by Covey and by my master, but I was the only slave in that region who could read or write, and my knowledge was the pride of my brother slaves. No doubt Sandy felt something of the general interest in me on that account.

In Sandy at least I found an old adviser. He was not only a religious man but a genuine African and had inherited some of the so-called magical powers said to be possessed by those from the eastern nations. He told me that there was an herb which possessed all the powers required for my protection. He told me further that if I would take the root of the herb and wear it on my right side it would be impossible for a white man to whip me. He said he had carried it for years and that he had fully tested its virtues. He had never received a blow from a slaveholder since he carried it.

All this talk about the root was, to me, ridiculous, if not positively sinful. I did not propose to load up my pockets with "magic roots" and felt the whole notion was beneath my intelligence. But Sandy was more than a match for me.

"Your book learning," he said, "has not protected you from Covey." I confess this was a powerful argument just then. He entreated me to try the root. Sandy was so confident that, to please him, I took the roots and placed them in my right-hand pocket.

Sunday morning dawned, and Sandy woke me and urged me to hurry home. He advised me to walk up to the house as though nothing had happened. I started off toward Covey's, as directed. Just as I entered the yard gate I met Covey and his wife dressed in their Sunday best. Smiling like a pair of angels, they were on their way to church. Covey inquired how I was and told me that the pigs had got into the lot and he wished me to go drive them out. I was amazed to see the change in him, but I suspected that the Sabbath, not the root, was the real cause. His religion kept him from breaking the Sabbath but not from breaking my skin on any other day than Sunday.

Long before daylight on Monday I was called and told to go feed, rub, and curry the horses. I obeyed, for I had resolved to obey every order, however unreasonable. But I had made up my mind that if Mr. Covey tried to beat me in spite of my best efforts to please him, I would defend and protect myself to the best of my ability. A bitter but wonderful thing had happened to me. I was no longer afraid to die.

I went to the barn to get the horses ready for the field. But as I was climbing the ladder to the stable loft, Covey sneaked into the stable and seized me suddenly by the leg. He tried to slip a rope around my legs before I could draw up my feet. As soon as I found what he was up to I gave a sudden spring (my two days' rest had been of much help to me) and he brought me to the floor, giving my newly-mended body a terrible jar. He seemed to think he had me securely in his power. Two days before Covey could, with his slightest word, have made me tremble like a leaf in a storm, but no more. The fighting madness was upon me, and I found my strong fingers firmly attached to his throat, heedless of consequences. The color of the man was forgotten. I felt supple as a cat, ready for him at every turn. Every blow of his was parried, although I dealt no blows in return. I was determined to prevent him from injuring me. I flung him on the ground several times when he meant to have hurled me there. I held him so firmly by the throat that his blood followed my nails. He held me and I held him.

All was fair so far, and the contest was about equal. Covey was taken back by my unexpected resistance.

"Are you going to resist, you scoundrel?" said he.

"Yes, sir," I politely replied, steadily gazing him in the eye.

But the conflict did not long remain equal. Covey cried lustily for help, not because I was getting the best of him but because he was making no progress in getting the best of me. He called for his cousin, Bill Hughes, to come help him, and I saw the tide was about to turn against me. I was now compelled to give blows as well as ward them off. Since I expected to suffer anyway, because I was resisting, I felt that I might as well be hanged for an old sheep as a lamb. On his first approach, Hughes tried to catch and tie my right hand. I stopped him by giving him a kick which sent him staggering away in pain, all the while holding Covey with a firm hand.

Taken by surprise, Covey stood puffing for a moment, unable to deliver words or blows. When he saw Hughes half bent with pain he asked if I meant to continue to resist. I told him I did mean to resist, come what might. I said that I had been treated like a brute during the last six months and would stand it no longer. With that he gave me a shake and tried to drag me toward a stick of wood lying just outside the stable door. He meant to knock me down with it. Just as he leaned over to get the stick of wood, I seized him by the collar. With a vigorous and sudden snatch I threw him full length on the not over-clean ground of the cow yard. He picked the place for the fight, and I thought it was only right that he would enjoy its advantages, foul-smelling though those advantages might be.

By this time Bill, the hired man, came home. Covey and I had been fighting since before daybreak, and we were still at it. I could not see where the matter was to end. Covey called Bill to help him, and the scene became comical. Bill, who knew perfectly well what Covey wished him to do, pretended that he did not.

"What shall I do, Master Covey?" said Bill

"Take hold of him! Take hold of him!" cried Covey.

"Indeed, Master Covey, I want to go to work."

"This is your work," shouted Covey. "Take hold of him!"

"My master hired me here to work," Bill replied with spirit, "and not to help you whip Frederick."

It was my turn to speak. "Bill," said I, "don't put your hands on me."

"My God, Frederick," he whined. "I ain't goin' to tech ye," and he walked off, leaving Covey and myself to settle our differences as best we might.

My advantage was again threatened when I saw Caroline, the slave woman, coming to the cow yard to milk. She was a powerful woman and could overcome me easily, exhausted as I was.

As soon as she came near, Covey ordered her to help him. Strangely and fortunately, Caroline was in no humor to take a hand in any such sport. She answered Covey's command to take hold of me much as Bill had done. Caroline endangered herself more than Bill, however, for she was the slave of Covey and he could do what he pleased with her. It was not so with Bill, and Bill knew it. Samuel Harris, Bill's owner, did not allow his slaves to be beaten unless they were guilty of some crime which the law would punish. But poor Caroline, like myself, was at Covey's mercy.

On this occasion, indeed, she did not escape the results of her refusal. Covey gave her several sharp blows.

At last, after two hours had gone by, Covey gave up. Letting go of me, puffing and blowing at a great rate, he said, "Now, you scoundrel, go to your work. I would not have whipped you half so hard if you had not resisted."

The fact was, he had not whipped me at all. I was the one who had drawn blood from him, not the other way around.

During the months I lived with Covey after this episode, he never again laid his finger on me in anger. Occasionally he would say he "did not want to have to get hold of me again," and I had no trouble believing this statement. I silently answered, "You had better not wished to get hold of me again because you will be likely to come off worse in a second fight than you did in the first."

This battle with Mr. Covey was the turning point in my life as a slave. I was a changed being after that fight. I was nothing before; I was a man now. It inspired me with a renewed determination to be a free man.

The reader may like to know why Mr. Covey did not turn me over to the authorities. I myself expected it. By the law of Maryland, at that time, a slave who resisted his master was sentenced to the gallows. The probable reason is that Covey was ashamed to have it known that he had lost a fight to a boy of sixteen. His reputation as a first-rate overseer and Negro-breaker enabled him to procure his farm hands cheaply and easily. His interest and his pride would both suggest the wisdom of silence.

I am not altogether proud to say that after this conflict I did, at times, purposely try to provoke him to attack me again by refusing to keep with the other hands in the field. But I could never bully him into another battle.

1892

Letter to Thomas Auld[*]

[September 3, 1848]

September 3d, 1848

Sir:

The long and intimate, though by no means friendly relation which unhappily subsisted between you and myself, leads me to hope that you will easily account for the great liberty which I now take in addressing you in this open and public manner. The same fact may possibly remove any disagreeable surprise which you may experience on again finding your name coupled with mine, in any other way than in an

---

[*] This letter is addressed to the man who was Douglass's former master on the tenth anniversary of Douglass's escape from slavery; it was added to the 1855 version of the Douglass autobiography. The two men eventually met in 1881 as Auld lay dying, and Douglass was able to comment afterwards that both of them had been victims of their times.

advertisement, accurately describing my person, and offering a large sum for arrest. In thus dragging you again before the public, I am aware that I shall subject myself to no inconsiderable amount of censure. I shall probably be charged with an unwarrantable, if not a wanton and reckless disregard of the rights and proprieties of private life. There are those North as well as South who entertain a much higher respect for rights which are merely conventional, than they do for rights which are personal and essential. Not a few there are in our country, who, while they have no scruples against robbing the laborer of the hard earned results of his *patient industry,* will be shocked by the extremely indelicate manner of bringing your name before the public. Believing this to be the case, and wishing to meet every reasonable or plausible objection to my conduct, I will frankly state the ground upon which I justify myself in this instance, as well as on former occasions when I have thought proper to mention your name in public. All will agree that a man guilty of theft, robbery, or murder, has forfeited the right to concealment and private life; that the community have a right to subject such persons to the most complete exposure. However much they may desire retirement, and aim to conceal themselves and their movements from the popular gaze, the public have a right to ferret them out, and bring their conduct before the proper tribunals of the country for investigation. Sir, you will undoubtedly make the proper application of these generally admitted principles, and will easily see the light in which you are regarded by me. I will not therefore manifest ill temper, by calling you hard names. I know you to be a man of some intelligence, and can readily determine the precise estimate which I entertain of your character. I may therefore indulge in language which may seem to others indirect and ambiguous, and yet be quite well understood by yourself.

I have selected this day on which to address you, because it is the anniversary of my emancipation; and knowing of no better way, I am led to this as the best mode of celebrating that truly important event. Just ten years ago this beautiful September morning, yon bright sun beheld me a slave—a poor, degraded chattel—trembling at the sound of your voice, lamenting that I was a man, and wishing myself a brute. The hopes which I had treasured up for weeks of a safe and successful escape from your grasp, were powerfully confronted at this last hour by dark clouds of doubt and fear, making my person shake and my bosom to heave with the heavy contest between hope and fear. I have no words to describe to you the deep agony of soul which I experienced on that never to be forgotten morning—(for I left by daylight). I was making a leap in the dark. The probabilities, so far as I could by reason determine them, were stoutly against the undertaking. The preliminaries and precautions I had adopted previously, all worked badly. I was like one going to war without weapons—ten chances of defeat to one of victory. One in whom I had confided, and one who had promised me assistance, appalled by fear at the trial hour, deserted me, thus leaving the responsibility of success or failure solely with myself. You, sir, can never know my feelings. As I look back to them, I can scarcely realize that I have passed through a scene so trying. Trying however as they were, and gloomy as was the prospect, thanks be to the Most High, who is ever the God of the oppressed, at the moment which was to determine my whole earthly career. His grace was sufficient, my mind was made up. I embraced the golden opportunity, took the morning tide at the flood, and a free man, young, active and strong, is the result.

I have often thought I should like to explain to you the grounds upon which I have justified myself in running away from you. I am almost ashamed to do so now, for by this time you may have discovered them yourself. I will, however, glance at them. When yet but a child about six years old, I imbibed the determination to run away. The very first mental effort that I now remember on my part, was an attempt to solve the mystery, Why am I a slave? and with this question my youthful mind was troubled for many days, pressing upon me more heavily at times than others. When I saw the slave-driver whip a slave woman, cut the blood out of her neck, and heard her piteous cries, I went away into the corner of the fence, wept and pondered over the mystery. I had, through some medium, I know not what, got some idea of God, the Creator of all mankind, the black and the white, and that he had made the blacks to serve the whites as slaves. How he could do this and be *good,* I could not tell. I was not satisfied with this theory, which made God responsible for slavery, for it pained me greatly, and I have wept over it long and often. At one time, your first wife, Mrs. Lucretia, heard me singing and saw me shedding tears, and asked of me the matter, but I was afraid to tell her. I was puzzled with this question, till one night, while sitting in the kitchen, I heard some of the old slaves talking of their parents having been stolen from Africa by white men, and were sold here as slaves. The whole mystery was solved at once. Very soon after this my aunt Jinny and uncle Noah ran away, and the great noise made about it by your father-in-law, made me for the first time acquainted with the fact, that there were free States as well as slave States. From that time, I resolved that I would some day run away. The morality of the act, I dispose as follows: I am myself; you are yourself; we are two distinct persons, equal persons. What you are, I am. You are a man, and so am I. God created both, and made us separate beings. I am not by nature bound to you, or you to me. Nature does not make your existence depend upon me, or mine to depend upon yours. I cannot walk upon your legs, or you upon mine. I cannot breathe for you, or you for me; I must breathe for myself, and you for yourself. We are distinct persons, and are each equally provided with faculties necessary to our individual existence. In leaving you, I took nothing but what belonged to me, and in no way lessened your means for obtaining an *honest* living. Your faculties remained yours, and mine became useful to their rightful owner. I therefore see no wrong in any part of the transaction. It is true, I went off secretly, but that was more your fault than mine. Had I let you into the secret, you would have defeated the enterprise entirely; but for this, I should have been really glad to have made you acquainted with my intentions to leave.

You may perhaps want to know how I like my present condition. I am free to say, I greatly prefer it to that which I occupied in Maryland. I am, however, by no means prejudiced against the State as such. Its geography, climate, fertility and products, are such as to make it a very desirable abode for any man; and but for the existence of slavery there, it is not impossible that I might again take up my abode in that State. It is not that I love Maryland less, but freedom more. You will be surprised to learn that people at the North labor under the strange delusion that if the slaves were emancipated at the South, they would flock to the North. So far from this being the case, in that event, you would see many old and familiar faces back again to the South. The fact is, there are few here who would not return to the South in the event of emancipation. We want to live in the land of our birth, and to lay our bones by the side of our fathers'; and nothing short of an intense love of personal freedom keeps us from the South. For the sake of this, most of us would live on a crust of bread and a cup of cold water.

Since I left you, I have had a rich experience. I have occupied stations which I never dreamed of when a slave. Three out of the ten years since I left you, I spent as a common laborer on the wharves of New Bedford, Massachusetts. It was there I earned my first free dollar. It was mine. I could spend it as I pleased. I could buy hams or herring with it, without asking any odds of any body. That was a precious dollar to me. You remember when I used to make seven or eight, or even nine dollars a week in Baltimore, you would take every cent of it from me every Saturday night, saying that I belonged to you, and my earnings also. I never liked this conduct on your part —to say the best, I thought it a little mean. I would not have served you so. But let that pass. I was a little awkward about counting money in New England fashion when I first landed in New Bedford. I like to have betrayed myself several times. I caught myself saying phip, for fourpence; and at one time a man actually charged me with being a runaway, whereupon I was silly enough to become one by running away from him, for I was greatly afraid he might adopt measures to get me again into slavery, a condition I then dreaded more than death.

I soon, however, learned to count money, as well as to make it, and got on swimmingly. I married soon after leaving you: in fact, I was engaged to be married before I left you; and instead of finding my companion a burden, she was truly a helpmeet. She went to live at service, and I to work on the wharf, and though we toiled hard the first winter, we never lived more happily. After remaining in New Bedford for three years, I met with Wm. Lloyd Garrison,[1] a person of whom you have *possibly* heard, as he is pretty generally known among slaveholders. He put it into my head that I might make myself serviceable to the cause of the slave by devoting a portion of my time to telling my own sorrows, and those of other slaves which had come under my observation. This was the commencement of a higher state of existence than any to which I had ever aspired. I was thrown into society the most pure, enlightened and benevolent that the country affords. Among these I have never forgotten you, but have invariably made you the topic of conversation—thus giving you all the notoriety I could do. I need not tell you that the opinion formed of you in these circles, is far from being favorable. They have little respect for your honesty, and less for your religion.

But I was going on to relate to you something of my interesting experience. I had not long enjoyed the excellent society to which I have referred, before the light of its excellence exerted a beneficial influence on my mind and heart. Much of my early dislike of white persons was removed, and their manners, habits and customs, so entirely unlike what I had been used to in the kitchen-quarters on the plantations of the South, fairly charmed me, and gave me a strong disrelish for the coarse and degrading customs of my former condition. I therefore made an effort so to improve my mind and deportment, as to be somewhat fitted to the station to which I seemed almost providentially called. The transition from degradation to respectability was indeed great, and to get from one to the other without carrying some marks of one's former condition, is truly a difficult matter. I would not have you think that I am

---

[1] Garrison (1805–1879) was an important spokesman for the antislavery cause.

now entirely clear of all plantation peculiarities, but my friends here, while they entertain the strongest dislike to them, regard me with that charity to which my past life somewhat entitles me, so that my condition in this respect is exceedingly pleasant. So far as my domestic affairs are concerned, I can boast of as comfortable a dwelling as your own. I have an industrious and neat companion, and four dear children—the oldest a girl of nine years, and three fine boys, the oldest eight, the next six, and the youngest four years old. The three oldest are now going regularly to school—two can read and write, and the other can spell with tolerable correctness words of two syllables: Dear fellows! they are all in comfortable beds, and are sound asleep, perfectly secure under my own roof. There are no slaveholders here to rend my heart by snatching them from my arms, or blast a mother's dearest hopes by tearing them from her bosom. These dear children are ours—not to work up into rice, sugar and tobacco, but to watch over, regard, and protect, and to rear them up in the nurture and admonition of the gospel—to train them up in the paths of wisdom and virtue, and, as far as we can to make them useful to the world and to themselves. Oh! sir, a slaveholder never appears to me so completely an agent of hell, as when I think of and look upon my dear children. It is then that my feelings rise above my control. I meant to have said more with respect to my own prosperity and happiness, but thoughts and feelings which this recital has quickened unfits me to proceed further in that direction. The grim horrors of slavery rise in all their ghastly terror before me, the wails of millions pierce my heart, and chill my blood. I remember the chain, the gag, the bloody whip, the death-like gloom overshadowing the broken spirit of the fettered bondman, the appalling liability of his being torn away from wife and children, and sold like a beast in the market. Say not that this is a picture of fancy. You well know that I wear stripes on my back inflicted by your direction; and that you, while we were brothers in the same church, caused this right hand, with which I am now penning this letter, to be closely tied to my left, and my person dragged at the pistol's mouth, fifteen miles from the Bay side to Easton to be sold like a beast in the market, for the alleged crime of intending to escape from your possession. All this and more you remember, and know to be perfectly true, not only of yourself, but of nearly all of the slaveholders around you.

At this moment, you are probably the guilty holder of at least three of my own dear sisters, and my only brother in bondage. These you regard as your property. They are recorded on your ledger, or perhaps have been sold to human flesh mongers, with a view to filling your own ever-hungry purse. Sir, I desire to know how and where these dear sisters are. Have you sold them? or are they still in your possession? What has become of them? are they living or dead? And my dear old grand-mother, whom you turned out like an old horse, to die in the woods—is she still alive? Write and let me know all about them. If my grandmother be still alive, she is of no service to you, for by this time she must be nearly eighty years old—too old to be cared for by one to whom she has ceased to be of service, send her to me at Rochester, or bring her to Philadelphia, and it shall be the crowning happiness of my life to take care of her in her old age. Oh! she was to me a mother, and a father, so far as hard toil for my comfort could make her such. Send me my grandmother! that I may watch over and take care of her in her old age. And my sisters, let me know all about them. I would write to them, and learn all I want to know of them, without disturbing you in any way, but that, through your unrighteous conduct, they have been entirely deprived of the power to read and write. You have kept them in utter ignorance, and have therefore robbed them of the sweet enjoyments of writing or receiving letters from absent friends and relatives. Your wickedness and cruelty committed in this respect on your fellow-creatures, are greater than all the stripes you have laid upon my back, or theirs. It is an outrage upon the soul—a war upon the immortal spirit, and one for which you must give account at the bar of our common Father and Creator.

The responsibility which you have assumed in this regard is truly awful—and how you could stagger under it these many years is marvellous. Your mind must have become darkened, your heart hardened, your conscience seared and petrified, or you would have long since thrown off the accursed load and sought relief at the hands of a sin-forgiving God. How, let me ask, would you look upon me, were I some dark night in company with a band of hardened villains, to enter the precincts of your elegant dwelling and seize the person of your own lovely daughter Amanda, and carry her off from your family, friends and all the loved ones of her youth—make her my slave—compel her to work, and I take her wages—place her name on my ledger as property—disregard her personal rights—fetter the powers of her immortal soul by denying her the right and privilege of learning to read and write—feed her coarsely —clothe her scantily, and whip her on the naked back occasionally; more and still more horrible, leave her unprotected—a degraded victim to the brutal lust of fiendish overseers, who would pollute, blight, and blast her fair soul—rob her of all dignity —destroy her virtue, and annihilate all in her person the graces that adorn the character of virtuous womanhood? I ask how would you regard me, if such were my conduct? Oh! the vocabulary of the damned would not afford a word sufficiently infernal, to express your idea of my God-provoking wickedness. Yet sir, your treatment of my beloved sisters is in all essential points, precisely like the case I have now supposed. Damning as would be such a deed on my part, it would be no more so than that which you have committed against me and my sisters.

I will now bring this letter to a close, you shall hear from me again unless you let me hear from you. I intend to make use of you as a weapon with which to assail the system of slavery—as a means of concentrating public attention on the system, and deepening their horror of trafficking in the souls and bodies of men. I shall make use of you as a means of exposing the character of the American church and clergy —and as a means of bringing this guilty nation with yourself to repentance. In doing this I entertain no malice towards you personally. There is no roof under which you would be more safe than mine, and there is nothing in my house which you might need for your comfort, which I would not readily grant. Indeed, I should esteem it a privilege, to set you an example as to how mankind ought to treat each other.

I am your fellow man, but not your slave,

Frederick Douglass

1848

At Home Again[*]

Having been, during the past few weeks, the special object of attack, marked out by a corrupt and fiendish Press, for assassination, the victim of a continuous train of almost unprecedented abuse—harassed and dogged from day to day by the furious blood-hounds of American Slavery,—I should be something more than a Stoic,[1] if I did not feel and acknowledge a sense of profound gratitude to the God of the oppressed, that I am again permitted safely to occupy my editorial chair. Never since the day I entered the field of public effort in the cause of my enslaved brethren, have I been called to endure persecution more bitter, insults more brutal, violence more fierce, scorn and contempt more malicious and demoniacal, than that heaped upon me in the city of New York, during the past three weeks. I have been made to feel keenly that I am in an enemy's land—surrounded on all sides by hardships, difficulties and dangers—that on the side of the oppressor there is power, and that there are few to take up the cause of my deeply injured and down-trodden people. These things grieve, but do not appal me. Not an inch will I retreat—not one jot of zeal will I abate—not one word will I retract; and, in the strength of God, while the red current of life flows through my veins, I will continue to labor for the downfall of slavery and the freedom of my race. I am denounced as an offender. I am not ignorant of my offences. I plead guilty to the worst of those laid to my charge. Amplified as they have been, enormous as they are alleged to be, I do not shrink from looking them full in the face, and glorying in having committed them. My *crime* is, that I have assumed to be a man, entitled to all the rights, privileges and dignity, which belong to human nature—that color is no crime, and that all men are brothers. I have acted on this presumption. The very "head and front of my offending hath this extent—no more." I have not merely talked of human brotherhood and human equality, but have reduced that talk to practice. This I have done in broad open day, scorning concealment. I have walked through the streets of New York, in company with white persons, not as a menial, but as an equal. This was done with no purpose to inflame the public mind; not to provoke popular violence; not to make a display of my contempt for public opinion; but simply as a matter of course, and because it was right so to do. The right to associate with my fellow worms of the dust, on terms of equality, without regard to color, is a right which I will yield only with my latest breath.

My readers will have observed, in the *North Star* of last week, an account of a most cowardly assault made upon me in the Battery[2] at New York. Like most other statements which emanate from the American press, this one (though partly true) is false in several particulars. It is not true that I walked down Broadway[3] with two white females resting on my arm, in the case alluded to, although I *insist* upon the

---

[*] Printed in Douglass's newspaper *The North Star* on May 30, 1850.
[1] Follower of the Greek philosopher Zeno (fl. ca. 300 B.C.), who held that events are determined by divine will and that mortals must therefore calmly accept whatever happens to them without undue emotion.
[2] The harbor area at the southern tip of Manhattan.
[3] Fashionable street in mid-Manhattan.

right to do so. It is not true that the ladies in company with me placed themselves under the care of the gentleman (ruffian?) who assaulted me, nor any of the villainous party, nor of anybody else. It is not true that I sneered or spoke to the loafing assailants. The facts briefly are these. Myself and friends were going to Philadelphia, and supposing that the "John Porter" departed from New York at twelve o'clock, we rode down a quarter before twelve but found on our arrival, that we had been mistaken; the time of starting being half-past one o'clock. The interval, therefore, we passed in the Battery. When about to leave for the Steamer, five or six men surrounded us, assailing us with all sorts of coarse and filthy language, and two of them finally struck the ladies on the head, while another attacked me. I warded off the blows with my umbrella, and the cowardly creatures left without doing any personal harm. Thinking that we should not be disturbed by them again we walked slowly toward the Steamer, one of the mob observing that I was off my guard, ran up behind me and before I could put myself in a position to ward off the assassin's blow, I was struck in the face. These are the whole facts in the case. I never was more calm or self-possessed than when under his beastly assault. I felt no indignation toward the poor miserable wretches who committed the outrage. They were but executing upon me the behests of the proslavery church and the clergy of the land; doing the dirty work of the men who despise them, and who have no more respect for them in reality than they have for me.

1850

Prejudice Against Color[*]

Let no one imagine that we are about to give undue prominence to this subject. Regarding, as we do, the feeling named above to be the greatest of all obstacles in the way of the anti-slavery cause, we think there is little danger of making the subject of it too prominent. The heartless apathy which prevails in this community on the subject of slavery—the cold-blooded indifference with which the wrongs of the perishing and heart-broken slave are regarded—the contemptuous, slanderous, and malicious manner in which the names and characters of Abolitionists are handled by the American pulpit and press generally, may be traced mainly to the *malign* feeling which passes under the name of prejudice against color. Every step in our experience in this country since we commenced our anti-slavery labors, has been marked by facts demonstrative of what we have just said. The day that we started on our first anti-slavery journey to Nantucket, now nine years ago, the steamer was detained at the wharf in New Bedford two hours later than the usual time of starting, in an attempt on the part of the captain to compel the colored passengers to separate from the white passengers, and to go on the forward deck of that steamer; and during this time, the most savage feelings were evinced towards every colored man who asserted his right to enjoy equal privileges with other passengers.—Aside from the twenty

[*] Printed in *The North Star* on June 13, 1850.

months which we spent in England, (where color is no crime, and where a man's fitness for respectable society is measured by his moral and intellectual worth,) we do not remember to have made a single anti-slavery tour in any direction in this country, when we have not been assailed by this mean spirit of caste. A feeling so universal and so powerful for evil, cannot well be too much commented upon. We have used the term prejudice against color to designate the feeling to which we allude, not because it expresses correctly what that feeling is, but simply because that *innocent* term is usually employed for that purpose.

Properly speaking, *prejudice against color* does not exist in this country. The feeling (or whatever it is) which we call *prejudice,* is no less than a *murderous, hell-born hatred* of every virtue which may adorn the character of a *black man.* It is not the black man's color which makes him the object of brutal treatment. When he is drunken, idle, ignorant and vicious, *"Black Bill"* is a source of amusement: he is called a good-natured fellow; he is the first to [give] service in holding his horse, or blacking his boots. The white gentleman tells the landlord to give "Bill" *"something to drink,"* and actually drinks with "Bill" himself!—While poor black "Bill" will minister to the pride, vanity and laziness of white American gentlemen—while he consents to play the buffoon for their sport, he will share their regard. But let him cease to be what we have described him to be—let him shake off the filthy rags that cover him—let him abandon drunkenness for sobriety, industry for indolence, ignorance for intelligence, and give up his menial occupation for respectable employment—let him quit the hotel and go to the church, and assume there the rights and privileges of one for whom the Son of God died, and he will be pursued with the fiercest hatred. His name will be cast out as evil; and his life will be embittered with all the venom which hate and malice can generate. Thousands of colored men can bear witness to the truth of this representation. While we are servants, we are never offensive to the whites, or marks of popular displeasure. We have been often dragged or driven from the tables of hotels where colored men were officiating acceptably as waiters; and from steamboat cabins where twenty or thirty colored men in light jackets and white aprons were frisking about as servants among the whites in every direction. On the very day we were brutally assaulted in New York for riding down Broadway in company with ladies, we saw several white ladies riding with *black servants.* These servants were well-dressed, proud looking men, evidently living on the fat of the land—yet they were servants. They rode not for their own, but for the pleasure and convenience of white persons. They were not in those carriages as friends or equals.—They were there as appendages; they constituted a part of the magnificent equipages.—They were there as the fine black horses which they drove were there—to minister to the pride and splendor of their employers. As they passed down Broadway, they were observed with admiration by the multitude; and even the *poor* wretches who assaulted us might have said in their hearts, as they looked upon such splendor, "We would do so too if we could." We repeat, then, that color is not the cause of our persecution; that is, it *is not our color* which makes our proximity to white men disagreeable. The evil lies deeper than prejudice against color. It is, as we have said, an intense hatred of the colored man when he is distinguished for any ennobling qualities of head or heart. If the feeling which persecutes us were prejudice against color, the colored servant would be as obnoxious as the colored gentleman, for the color is the same in both cases; and being the same in both cases, it would produce the *same* result in both cases.

We are then a persecuted people; not because we are *colored,* but simply because that color has for a series of years been coupled in the public mind with the degradation of slavery and servitude. In these conditions, we are thought to be in our place; and to aspire to anything above them, is to contradict the established views of the community—to get out of our sphere, and commit the provoking sin of *impudence.* Just here is our sin: we have been a slave; we have passed through all the grades of servitude, and have, under God, secured our freedom; and if we have become the special object of attack, it is because we speak and act among our fellow-men without the slightest regard to their or our own complexion;—and further, because we claim and exercise the right to associate with just such persons as are willing to associate with us, and who are agreeable to our tastes, and suited to our moral and intellectual tendencies, without reference to the color of their skin, and without giving ourselves the slightest trouble to inquire whether the world are pleased or displeased by our conduct. We believe in human equality; that character, not color, should be the criterion by which to choose associates; and we pity the pride of the poor pale dust and ashes which would erect any other standard of social fellowship.

This doctrine of human equality is the bitterest yet taught by the abolitionists. It is swallowed with more difficulty than all the other points of the anti-slavery creed put together. "What, make a Negro equal to a *white* man? No, we will never consent to that! No, that won't do!" But stop a moment; don't be in a passion; keep cool. What *is* a white man that you do so revolt at the idea of making a Negro equal with him? Who made . . .[1] an angel of a man? "A man." Very well, he is a man, and nothing but a man—possessing the same weaknesses, liable to the same diseases, and under the same necessities to which a black man is subject. Wherein does the white man differ from the black? Why, one is white and the other is black. Well, what of that? Does the sun shine more brilliantly upon the one than it does upon the other? Is nature more lavish with her gifts toward the one than toward the other? Do earth, sea and air yield their united treasures to the one more readily than to the other? In a word, "have we not all one Father?" Why then do you revolt at that equality which God and nature instituted?

The very apprehension which the American people betray on this point, is proof of the fitness of treating all men equally. The fact that they fear an acknowledgment of our equality, shows that they see a fitness in such an acknowledgment. Why are they not apprehensive lest the horse should be placed on an equality with man? Simply because the horse is not a man; and no amount of reasoning can convince the world, against its common sense, that the horse is anything else than a horse. So here all can repose without fear. But not so with the Negro. He stands erect. Upon his brow he bears the seal of manhood, from the hand of the living God. Adopt any mode of reasoning you please with respect to him, he is a man, possessing an immortal soul, illuminated by intellect, capable of heavenly aspirations, and in all things pertaining to manhood, he is at once self-evidently a man, and therefore entitled to all the rights and privileges which belong to human nature.

1850

[1] Philip S. Foner, editor of *The Life and Writings of Frederick Douglass. Early Years (1817–1849),* notes here that several words are illegible in the original copy of the paper.

Henry Timrod
1828–1867

It may at first seem odd that Henry Timrod, described by his contemporaries as
at once "timid, reserved, unready if taken by surprise" and as someone who
"shrank from noisy debate, and the wordy clash of argument," should serve as
the poetic voice for the Confederacy during the Civil War. But to know the
circumstances of Timrod's life is to recognize the connections between his career
and the fate of the South during this nation's war with itself.

Henry Timrod was born in 1828 in Charleston, South Carolina, the son of a
Scots-Irish bookbinder and a Swiss-English homemaker who imbued him with a
love of nature. An ambitious, active, yet frail child, Henry Timrod attended
Charleston's German Friendly Society School and later studied at the nearby
Classical School of Christopher Cotes, where he developed a lifelong friendship
with the writer Paul Hamilton Hayne.

In January 1845 Timrod entered the University of Georgia as a sophomore and
diligently studied literature and the classics, only to withdraw a year later
without taking a degree because of ill health and insufficient funds. But that year
provided him with the opportunity to exercise his fledgling poetic talents. "A
large part of my leisure at college was occupied in the composition of love
verses, frantic or tender. Every pretty girl's face I met acted upon me like an
inspiration!" Several of the wittiest of these poems were published in the
Charleston Evening News over the signature "T.W." From 1847 to 1849, while
preparing himself for a university appointment teaching classics, Timrod worked
in the law office of James L. Petigru, who judged him "too wholly a poet to
keep company with so exacting a mistress as the law." During this period
Timrod also began contributing to the *Southern Literary Messenger* under the
psuedonym "Aglaus." With no professorship forthcoming, Timrod spent virtually
the full decade of the 1850s working as a tutor on various plantations. During
this period he returned as often as possible to Charleston to join the lively
conversations of a small group of literary friends headed by the novelist William
Gilmore Simms. From these "little suppers," as Timrod called them, came the
impetus to found a new southern literary periodical, *Russell's Magazine*
(1857–1860), in which Timrod published several literary essays and many of his
best poems. In 1860 Ticknor and Fields, one of Boston's prestigious publishing
houses, printed Timrod's small collection, *Poems,* which earned him favorable
reviews in both the North and the South. But attention to the volume was
quickly diverted by the rush of events leading to the Civil War.

Henry Timrod wrote movingly of both the impending hostilities and the
outbreak of the war. His stirring series of war poems earned him an international
audience and increasing acclaim; the popular press endorsed Alfred Lord
Tennyson's suggestion that he be dubbed "the laureate of the South." Timrod
spent the first year of the war in Charleston, tending to his poor health. In
March 1862 he enlisted as a private in the Confederate Army and served as a
clerk and then a war correspondent on the western front before being discharged
that December because of ill health. Timrod reenlisted in July 1863, but a severe

hemorrhage forced him to resign again, this time after a single day of service. Soon after, he worked as the assistant editor of the Charleston *Mercury,* leaving in January 1864 to become the associate editor of the Columbia *Daily South Carolinian.* He wrote most of that newspaper's editorials until the city was captured and burned by Union troops in February 1865. His livelihood destroyed, his infant son dead, his health weakened, Timrod summarized his misfortunes in a letter to his friend Hayne:

> I can embody it all in a few words: *beggary, starvation, death, bitter grief, utter want of hope. . . .* We have lived for a long period, and are still living, on the proceeds of the gradual sale of furniture and plate. . . . I not only feel that I can write no more verse, but I am perfectly indifferent to the fate of what I have already composed. I would consign every line of it to eternal oblivion for—*one hundred dollars in hand.*

In the three remaining years of his life following the Civil War, Timrod struggled with his deteriorating health to work temporarily as a journalist, teacher, and part-time secretary to South Carolina governor J. L. Orr. Henry Timrod died on October 7, 1867, after yet another bout with tuberculosis, before seeing the bulk of his work in print. Paul Hamilton Hayne collected Timrod's poems and published them, along with a memoir, in 1873.

Despite the sickness, anguish, and violence that crowded his later years, Henry Timrod managed to write highly balanced and carefully controlled poetry. These "classical" tendencies were nurtured by his wide reading among eighteenth-century English poets, but not at the expense of his fondness for those of the early nineteenth century, including Byron, Tennyson, Browning, and especially Wordsworth, whose influence is everywhere apparent in Timrod's poetry and literary criticism. His declamatory verse has remained most memorable. Its clear vision, vigorous imagery, irrepressible sincerity, and oratorical elegance expressed the collective hopes of the South during the Civil War and earned him the praise of his contemporaries as "the ablest poet the South has yet produced."

Further Reading:
G. P. Voigt, "New Light on Timrod's 'Memorial Ode,'" *American Literature,* January 1933.
J. B. Hubbell, *The Last Years of Henry Timrod,* 1941.
E. W. Parks, *Henry Timrod,* 1964.

Text:
Poems of Henry Timrod, 1899.
See also *The Uncollected Poems of Henry Timrod,* ed. G. A. Coldwell, Jr., 1942.

The Cotton Boll

While I recline
At ease beneath
This immemorial pine,
Small sphere!
(By dusky fingers brought this morning here   5
And shown with boastful smiles),
I turn thy cloven sheath,
Through which the soft white fibres peer,
That, with their gossamer bands,
Unite, like love, the sea-divided lands,   10
And slowly, thread by thread,
Draw forth the folded strands,
Than which the trembling line,
By whose frail help yon startled spider fled
Down the tall spear-grass from his swinging bed,   15
Is scarce more fine;
And as the tangled skein
Unravels in my hands,
Betwixt me and the noonday light,
A veil seems lifted, and for miles and miles   20
The landscape broadens on my sight,
As, in the little boll, there lurked a spell
Like that which, in the ocean shell,
With mystic sound,
Breaks down the narrow walls that hem us round,   25
And turns some city lane
Into the restless main,
With all his capes and isles!

Yonder bird,
Which floats, as if at rest,   30
In those blue tracts above the thunder, where
No vapors cloud the stainless air,
And never sound is heard,
Unless at such rare time
When, from the City of the Blest,[1]   35
Rings down some golden chime,
Sees not from his high place
So vast a cirque of summer space

[1] City of heaven or the "new Jerusalem"
(Revelation 21, 22).

As widens round me in one mighty field,
Which, rimmed by seas and sands,   40
Doth hail its earliest daylight in the beams
Of gray Atlantic dawns;
And, broad as realms made up of many lands,
Is lost afar
Behind the crimson hills and purple lawns   45
Of sunset, among plains which roll their streams
Against the Evening Star!
And lo!
To the remotest point of sight,
Although I gaze upon no waste of snow,   50
The endless field is white;
And the whole landscape glows,
For many a shining league away,
With such accumulated light
As Polar lands would flash beneath a tropic day!   55
Nor lack there (for the vision grows,
And the small charm within my hands—
More potent even than the fabled one,
Which oped whatever golden mystery
Lay hid in fairy wood or magic vale,   60
The curious ointment of the Arabian tale²—
Beyond all mortal sense
Doth stretch my sight's horizon, and I see,
Beneath its simple influence,
As if with Uriel's³ crown,   65
I stood in some great temple of the Sun,
And looked, as Uriel, down!)
Nor lack there pastures rich and fields all green
With all the common gifts of God,
For temperate airs and torrid sheen   70
Weave Edens of the sod;
Through lands which look one sea of billowy gold
Broad rivers wind their devious ways;
A hundred isles in their embraces fold
A hundred luminous bays;   75
And through yon purple haze
Vast mountains lift their plumed peaks cloud-crowned;
And, save where up their sides the ploughman creeps,
An unhewn forest girds them grandly round,
In whose dark shades a future navy sleeps!   80
Ye Stars, which, though unseen, yet with me gaze
Upon this loveliest fragment of the earth!

² I.e., the *Arabian Nights*.
³ Uriel: an archangel. (See John Milton's *Paradise
Lost*, III, 621–724.)

Thou Sun, that kindlest all thy gentlest rays
Above it, as to light a favorite hearth!
Ye Clouds, that in your temples in the West   85
See nothing brighter than its humblest flowers!
And you, ye Winds, that on the ocean's breast
Are kissed to coolness ere ye reach its bowers!
Bear witness with me in my song of praise,
And tell the world that, since the world began,   90
No fairer land hath fired a poet's lays,
Or given a home to man!

But these are charms already widely blown!
His be the meed whose pencil's trace
Hath touched our very swamps with grace,   95
And round whose tuneful way
All Southern laurels bloom;
The Poet of "The Woodlands,"[4] unto whom
Alike are known
The flute's low breathing and the trumpet's tone, 100
And the soft west wind's sighs;
But who shall utter all the debt,
O Land wherein all powers are met
That bind a people's heart,
The world doth owe thee at this day,   105
And which it never can repay,
Yet scarcely deigns to own!
Where sleeps the poet who shall fitly sing
The source wherefrom doth spring
That mighty commerce which, confined   110
To the mean channels of no selfish mart,
Goes out to every shore
Of this broad earth, and throngs the sea with ships
That bear no thunders; hushes hungry lips
In alien lands;   115
Joins with a delicate web remotest strands;
And gladdening rich and poor,
Doth gild Parisian domes,
Or feed the cottage-smoke of English homes,
And only bounds its blessings by mankind!   120
In offices like these, thy mission lies,
My Country! and it shall not end
As long as rain shall fall and Heaven bend
In blue above thee; though thy foes be hard
And cruel as their weapons, it shall guard   125
Thy hearth-stones as a bulwark; make thee great

[4] William Gilmore Simms (1806–1870), poet and
novelist.

In white and bloodless state;
And haply, as the years increase—
Still working through its humbler reach
With that large wisdom which the ages teach—   130
Revive the half-dead dream of universal peace!
As men who labor in that mine
Of Cornwall, hollowed out beneath the bed
Of ocean, when a storm rolls overhead,
Hear the dull booming of the world of brine   135
Above them, and a mighty muffled roar
Of winds and waters, yet toil calmly on,
And split the rock, and pile the massive ore,
Or carve a niche, or shape the archèd roof;
So I, as calmly, weave my woof   140
Of song, chanting the days to come,
Unsilenced, though the quiet summer air
Stirs with the bruit of battles, and each dawn
Wakes from its starry silence to the hum
Of many gathering armies. Still,   145
In that we sometimes hear,
Upon the Northern winds, the voice of woe
Not wholly drowned in triumph, though I know
The end must crown us, and a few brief years
Dry all our tears,   150
I may not sing too gladly. To Thy will
Resigned, O Lord! we cannot all forget
That there is much even Victory must regret.
And, therefore, not too long
From the great burthen of our country's wrong   155
Delay our just release!
And, if it may be, save
These sacred fields of peace
From stain of patriot or of hostile blood!
Oh, help us, Lord! to roll the crimson flood   160
Back on its course, and, while our banners wing
Northward, strike with us! till the Goth[5] shall cling
To his own blasted altar-stones, and crave
Mercy; and we shall grant it, and dictate
The lenient future of his fate   165
There, where some rotting ships and crumbling quays
Shall one day mark the Port which ruled the Western seas.

1861

---

[5] The Goths, a Teutonic people, were considered
barbarians by the Romans.

Charleston

Calm as that second summer which precedes
   The first fall of the snow,
In the broad sunlight of heroic deeds,
   The City bides the foe.

As yet, behind their ramparts stern and proud,   5
   Her bolted thunders sleep—
Dark Sumter, like a battlemented cloud,
   Looms o'er the solemn deep.

No Calpe[1] frowns from lofty cliff or scar
   To guard the holy strand;   10
But Moultrie[2] holds in leash her dogs of war
   Above the level sand.

And down the dunes a thousand guns lie couched,
   Unseen, beside the flood—
Like tigers in some Orient jungle crouched   15
   That wait and watch for blood.

Meanwhile, through streets still echoing with trade,
   Walk grave and thoughtful men,
Whose hands may one day wield the patriot's blade
   As lightly as the pen.   20

And maidens, with such eyes as would grow dim
   Over a bleeding hound,
Seem each one to have caught the strength of him
   Whose sword she sadly bound.

Thus girt without and garrisoned at home,   25
   Day patient following day,
Old Charleston looks from roof, and spire, and dome,
   Across her tranquil bay.

Ships, through a hundred foes, from Saxon lands
   And spicy Indian ports,   30
Bring Saxon steel and iron to her hands,
   And Summer to her courts.

[1] Gibraltar.
[2] Fort on Sullivan's Island named for General
William Moultrie.

But still, along yon dim Atlantic line,
  The only hostile smoke
Creeps like a harmless mist above the brine,   35
  From some frail, floating oak.

Shall the Spring dawn, and she still clad in smiles,
  And with an unscathed brow,
Rest in the strong arms of her palm-crowned isles,
  As fair and free as now?   40

We know not; in the temple of the Fates
  God has inscribed her doom;
And, all untroubled in her faith, she waits
  The triumph or the tomb.

1862

Spring

Spring, with that nameless pathos in the air
Which dwells with all things fair,
Spring, with her golden suns and silver rain,
Is with us once again.

Out in the lonely woods the jasmine burns   5
Its fragrant lamps, and turns
Into a royal court with green festoons
The banks of dark lagoons.

In the deep heart of every forest tree
The blood is all aglee,   10
And there's a look about the leafless bowers
As if they dreamed of flowers.

Yet still on every side we trace the hand
Of Winter in the land,
Save where the maple reddens on the lawn,   15
Flushed by the season's dawn;

Or where, like those strange semblances we find
That age to childhood bind,
The elm puts on, as if in Nature's scorn,
The brown of Autumn corn.   20

As yet the turf is dark, although you know
That, not a span below,
A thousand germs are groping through the gloom,
And soon will burst their tomb.

Already, here and there, on frailest stems   25
Appear some azure gems,
Small as might deck, upon a gala day,
The forehead of a fay.

In gardens you may note amid the dearth
The crocus breaking earth;   30
And near the snowdrop's tender white and green,
The violet in its screen.

But many gleams and shadows need must pass
Along the budding grass,
And weeks go by, before the enamored South   35
Shall kiss the rose's mouth.

Still there's a sense of blossoms yet unborn
In the sweet airs of morn;
One almost looks to see the very street
Grow purple at his feet.   40

At times a fragrant breeze comes floating by,
And brings, you know not why,
A feeling as when eager crowds await
Before a palace gate

Some wondrous pageant; and you scarce would
    start,   45
If from a beech's heart,
A blue-eyed Dryad, stepping forth, should say,
"Behold me! I am May!"

Ah! who would couple thoughts of war and crime
With such a blessèd time!   50
Who in the west wind's aromatic breath
Could hear the call of Death!

Yet not more surely shall the Spring awake
The voice of wood and brake,
Than she shall rouse, for all her tranquil charms, 55
A million men to arms.

There shall be deeper hues upon her plains
Than all her sunlit rains,

And every gladdening influence around,
  Can summon from the ground.   60

Oh! standing on this desecrated mould,
  Methinks that I behold,
Lifting her bloody daisies up to God,
  Spring kneeling on the sod,

And calling, with the voice of all her rills,   65
  Upon the ancient hills
To fall and crush the tyrants and the slaves
  Who turn her meads to graves.
1863

Ode

Sung on the occasion of decorating the graves of the
Confederate dead at Magnolia Cemetery, Charleston,
S. C., 1866

Sleep sweetly in your humble graves,
  Sleep, martyrs of a fallen cause!—
Though yet no marble column craves
  The pilgrim here to pause.

In seeds of laurels in the earth,   5
  The garlands of your fame are sown;
And, somewhere, waiting for its birth,
  The shaft is in the stone.

Meanwhile, your sisters for the years
  Which hold in trust your storied tombs,   10
Bring all they now can give you—tears,
  And these memorial blooms.

Small tributes, but your shades will smile
  As proudly on these wreaths to-day,
As when some cannon-moulded pile   15
  Shall overlook this Bay.

Stoop, angels, hither from the skies!
  There is no holier spot of ground,
Than where defeated valor lies
  By mourning beauty crowned.   20
1866

James Russell Lowell
1819–1891

The Lowells trace their New England heritage to 1639. Over the course of 350 years, this distinguished American family has produced an impressive number of eminent religious, political, business, and literary figures, including most recently the poets Amy and Robert Lowell. James Russell Lowell enhanced the reputation of this family, already renowned for its accomplishments and tradition. As a poet, critic, essayist, editor, linguist, teacher, reformer, and diplomat, he was was widely regarded as one of the most versatile and respected literary figures in America in the second half of the nineteenth century.

James Russell Lowell was born in 1819 at Elmwood, the family's large, pre-Revolutionary house prominently situated on a street called Tory Row near the Charles River in Cambridge. His background and education reflect what Oliver Wendell Holmes called the "Brahmin caste." His father maintained a large library, and Lowell very early developed a taste for literature, especially Spenser's *Faerie Queene* and the novels of Sir Walter Scott. In 1834 Lowell enrolled at Harvard, where, from at least an official point of view, he proved to be a rather weak student who habitually missed class and chapel exercises, preferring to immerse himself in classical, Renaissance, and modern literature—"nearly everything," he later noted, "except the books prescribed by the faculty." He also held two posts—secretary of the Hasty Pudding Club and editor of the college magazine—that afforded him the opportunity to publish his own writing. One measure of his success among this small audience was his election as class poet.

When Lowell graduated in 1838, he had not yet settled on a career. He had also experienced an unhappy love affair and for a considerable time lost the cheerfulness that characterized the rest of his life. "I remember in '39," he wrote some years later, "putting a cocked pistol to my forehead and being afraid to pull the trigger." With some misgivings, he studied law and obtained his degree in 1840. In that same year he became engaged to Maria White, the sister of a classmate. A poet herself, she was well educated and idealistic and introduced Lowell to "the Band," a group of young people committed to various humanitarian causes and social reforms. Lowell soon spoke out in favor of temperance and woman suffrage and became a strong, vocal, but not extreme, abolitionist. (He was not willing, for example, to see the Union dissolved in order to end slavery, as were such more ardent compatriots as William Lloyd Garrison and John Greenleaf Whittier.)

Lowell cultivated his interests in poetry and literary essays while practicing law. His first volume of verse, *A Year's Life* (1841), earned critical acclaim. Soon after, he abandoned his law practice to found and edit a literary magazine replete with Lowell's faith in the prospects for serious literature in America. Yet despite the best of intentions—and the contributions of Edgar Allan Poe, Hawthorne, and Whittier—Lowell could not keep *The Pioneer* in print beyond its first three issues. In 1843 he published *Poems,* which contained a great deal of topical verse on political and social issues and received uniformly favorable reviews. He and Maria White married in 1844, living in part by selling poems and essays to magazines and in part by writing blistering editorials for such abolitionist newspapers as the *Pennsylvania Freeman.* His literary essays and frequent contributions to antislavery periodicals brought him a good deal of attention. In 1845 he published a collection of critical essays, *Conversations on Some of the Old Poets,* before returning to Elmwood a celebrated author in 1846.

In that year Lowell published the first of *The Biglow Papers,* a newspaper series that eventually extended to nine numbers. The success of this satire depended as much on Lowell's literary skills as on his fierce opposition to the Mexican War, which he thought at least partially motivated by southern interests in extending the boundaries of slavery. Hosea Biglow's clever and amusing observations in these "letters" represent one of the earliest and most artful uses of local dialect and humor for satirical political purposes. An eager student of language, Lowell spoke of an American anxiety in the literature of the period to be formally correct, if not elegant, in the use of English. ("We use it," Lowell said, "not as if it belonged to us, but as if wished to prove that we belong to it.") In *The Biglow Papers,* from which "The Courtin' " is extracted, he attempted what he called a "Yankee pastoral," employing vernacular American speech for poetic ends.

The year 1848 was perhaps the most remarkable year in Lowell's literary career. He published what were to be his major works: *Poems: Second Series,* the collected two-volume edition of his verse; *The Vision of Sir Launfal,* a Christian allegory popular for many years in schools; the collected first series of *The Biglow Papers;* as well as his most famous work, *A Fable for Critics.* His *Fable* represents the best features of Lowell's writing throughout what became a long and highly respected career. Similar to his other light verse, *Fable* demonstrates his facility and wit in rhyming. And, similar to his later criticism and academic work, the poem is grounded in his thorough familiarity with works of classical and modern literature. Finally, similar to his criticism and even his later conduct as a diplomat, *Fable* expresses a supreme confidence in his own ability to evaluate the achievements and actions of others, to identify their strengths, and to expose their pretensions. Given its comic deflation of several distinguished American literary reputations, *A Fable for Critics* was also a rather bold poetic venture. Only a writer with Lowell's urbane wit, judicious taste, and quiet confidence could have carried it off as effectively as he did. Wisely, Lowell chose not to exempt himself from his own good-natured criticism; he presented himself in the poem as someone "Who's striving Parnassus to climb / With a whole bale of *isms* tied together with rhyme."

Lowell's lifelong success as a writer did not exempt him from misery. Between 1847 and 1853, his domestic life was ravaged by the deaths of three of his four children, his wife, and his mother. But after a trip to Europe he resumed his work, writing travel sketches and essays on his trip abroad as well as lecturing on the major English poets. In 1855 he was chosen to succeed Henry Wadsworth Longfellow as Smith Professor of Modern Languages and Literature at Harvard. Lowell prepared for this appointment by traveling for a year in Europe to strengthen his command of foreign languages and literature. Soon after his return, he married Frances Dunlap, the governess of his remaining child, and settled into sixteen years of what from all reports were dazzling lectures on literature at Harvard.

An eager conversationalist, Lowell became identified with several social groups, including the famous Saturday Club, that brought him into the company of the most distinguished writers in New England, including Ralph Waldo Emerson, Nathaniel Hawthorne, Henry Wadsworth Longfellow, John Greenleaf Whittier, Dr. Oliver Wendell Holmes, the geologist Louis Agassiz, and the historian William Hickling Prescott. (Henry David Thoreau is said to have refused to attend the Saturday Club because he could not tolerate their smoking at the meetings; Lowell would later criticize Thoreau as one who "watched Nature like a detective.") Lowell's prominence in Boston's most prestigious literary circles made him this group's choice for editor when they collectively launched the *Atlantic Monthly* in 1857. Lowell resigned this post after a few years, but in 1864 he took on the same responsibilities at the *North American Review*. But he had already helped set a standard for American literary journalism.

During the Civil War, Lowell promoted the northern cause through essays in the *Atlantic Monthly* and a second series of *Biglow Papers*. But his most celebrated writing about the Civil War was not composed until after it was over. In 1865 he was invited to contribute a poem to the memorial service held at Harvard for its graduates who were killed during the war, including three of Lowell's beloved nephews. The poem he read that day expresses his deep and unwavering belief in democratic principles and his opposition to slavery. His reputation as a poet and literary critic soon took on international dimensions; on a trip to England from 1872 to 1874 he was awarded honorary degrees from Oxford and Cambridge.

Various social and political issues—especially corruption in the civil service— continued to attract Lowell's attention in the decade after the Civil War. He attacked political bosses in print and wrote speeches for candidates who shared his zeal for reform. He also published two additional volumes of poetry, *Under the Willows* (1869) and *The Cathedral* (1869 but dated 1870), as well as two more collections of essays, *Among My Books* (1870) and *My Study Windows* (1871). In 1877 he was appointed ambassador to Spain (a post Washington Irving had also held), and in 1880 ambassador to England, where he lectured widely on American culture. "During my reign," Queen Victoria noted of Lowell, "no ambassador or minister has created so much interest or won so much regard." Returning to the United States in 1885, soon after the death of his second wife, Lowell spent his last years lecturing on literature and politics as well as collecting his essays and speeches for publication. He died at Elmwood on August 12, 1891.

A few years after Lowell's death, Henry James offered a judicious estimate of Lowell's importance in American literary history. Having reread his work, James noted: "He looms, in such a renewed impression, very large and ripe and sane. . . . He was strong without narrowness; he was wise without bitterness and bright without folly. That appears for the most part the clearest ideal of those who handle the English form, and he was altogether in the straight tradition."

Further Reading:
H. James, "James Russell Lowell," in *Essays in London and Elsewhere*, 1893.
W. D. Howells, "Studies of Lowell," in *Literary Friends and Acquaintances*, 1900.
H. E. Scudder, *James Russell Lowell: A Biography*, 2 vols., 1901.
F. Greenslet, *James Russell Lowell: His Life and Work*, 1905, 1969.
L. Howard, *Victorian Knight-Errant: A Study of the Early Literary Career of James Russell Lowell*, 1952.
M. Duberman, *James Russell Lowell*, 1966.
C. McGlinchee, *James Russell Lowell*, 1967.
E. Wagenknecht, *James Russell Lowell: A Portrait of a Many-Sided Man*, 1971.
C. David Heymann, *American Aristocracy: The Lives and Times of James Russell, Amy, & Robert Lowell*, 1980.

Text:
The Writings of James Russell Lowell, 10 vols., 1890.
See also *Letters of James Russell Lowell*, ed. C. E. Norton, 3 vols., 1894.
New Letters of James Russell Lowell, ed. M. A. D. Howe, 1932.
James Russell Lowell's The Biglow Papers, 1st series, ed. T. Wortham, 1977.

---

from The Biglow Papers, First Series[*]

No. I: A Letter

From Mr. Ezekiel Biglow of Jaalam to the Hon. Joseph T. Buckingham, Editor of the Boston Courier, inclosing a poem of his son, Mr. Hosea Biglow.

JAYLEM, june 1846.

MISTER EDDYTER:—Our Hosea wuz down to Boston last week, and he see a cruetin Sarjunt[1] a struttin round as popler as a hen with 1 chicking, with 2 fellers a drummin and fifin arter him like all nater.[2] the sarjunt he thout Hosea hed n't gut his i teeth cut cos he looked a kindo's though he'd jest com down,[3] so he cal'lated to hook him in, but Hosy wood n't take none o' his sarse[4] for all he hed much as 20 Rooster's tales stuck onto his hat and eenamost enuf brass a bobbin up and down on his shoulders and figureed onto his coat and trousis, let alone wut nater hed sot in his featers, to make a 6 pounder[5] out on.

wal, Hosea he com home considerabal riled, and arter I'd gone to bed I heern Him

---

[*] The Boston *Courier* of June 17, 1846, printed a letter to the editor, reputedly from a New England farmer, Ezekiel Biglow, along with a poem of his son Hosea Biglow. Thus began the first series of *The Biglow Papers* (1846–1848), protesting the Mexican War (1846–1847) and the expansion of slavery. H.W., the pedantic Rev. Homer Wilbur, Hosea's parson, supposedly edited *The Biglow Papers.* The Civil War brought Biglow back into print, this time in the *Atlantic Monthly*, as a staunch supporter

of the Union. *The Biglow Papers, Second Series* was published in England in 1862. An American edition followed in 1867.
[1] Recruiting sergeant. To fight the Mexican War, the federal government called out fifty thousand volunteers. The recruiting sergeants used numerous inducements to meet their quotas.
[2] Nature.
[3] I.e., just come down from the country.
[4] Lowell's note: "Sarse: abuse, impertinence."
[5] Brass cannon.

a thrashin round like a short-tailed Bull in fli-time. The old Woman ses she to me ses she, Zekle, ses she, our Hosee's gut the chollery[6] or suthin anuther ses she, don't you Bee skeered, ses I, he's oney amakin pottery[7] ses i, he 's ollers on hand at that ere busynes like Da & martin,[8] and shure enuf, cum mornin, Hosy he cum down stares full chizzle,[9] hare on eend and cote tales flyin, and sot rite of to go reed his varses to Parson Wilbur bein he haint aney grate shows o' book larnin himself, bimeby he cum back and sed the parson wuz dreffle tickled with 'em as i hoop you will Be, and said they wuz True grit.

Hosea ses taint hardly fair to call 'em hisn now, cos the parson kind o' slicked off sum o' the last varses, but he told Hosee he did n't want to put his ore in to tetch to the Rest on 'em, bein they wuz verry well As thay wuz, and then Hosy ses he sed suthin a nuther about Simplex Mundishes[10] or sum sech feller, but I guess Hosea kind o' did n't hear him, for I never hearn o' nobody o' that name in this villadge, and I've lived here man and boy 76 year cum next tater diggin, and thair aint no wheres a kitting spryer 'n I be.

If you print 'em I wish you'd jest let folks know who hosy's father is, cos my ant Keziah used to say it's nater to be curus ses she, she aint livin though and he's a likely kind o' lad.

EZEKIEL BIGLOW.

THRASH away, you'll *hev* to rattle
　　On them kittle-drums o' yourn,—
　　'Taint a knowin' kind o' cattle
　　Thet is ketched with mouldy corn;
Put in stiff, you fifer feller,　　　　　　　　　　　5
　　Let folks see how spry you be,—
Guess you'll toot till you are yeller
　　'Fore you git ahold o' me!

Thet air flag's a leetle rotten,
　　Hope it aint your Sunday's best;—　　　　　10
Fact! it takes a sight o' cotton
　　To stuff out a soger's[11] chest:
Sence we farmers hev to pay fer 't,
　　Ef you must wear humps like these,
S'posin' you should try salt hay fer 't,　　　　15
　　It would du ez slick ez grease.

'T would n't suit them Southun fellers,
　　They 're a dreffle graspin' set,

---

[6] Choleric; out of humor.
[7] Lowell's note: *"Aut insanit, aut versas facit.—* H.W." This is a slight misquotation from Horace's *Satires,* in which the poet's slave says of his master, "He is either mad, or is making verses."
[8] Day and Martin, makers of shoe blacking, advertised their product in rhymed verses.
[9] At full chisel; i.e., at full speed.
[10] Mispronunciation of "simplex mundities" (Latin: "simple neatness"), from Horace's *Odes,* I, v, 5.
[11] Soldier's. Lowell's note: "Sogerin', soldiering: a barbarous amusement common among men in the savage state."

We must ollers blow the bellers
Wen they want their irons het;   20
May be it 's all right ez preachin',
But *my* narves it kind o' grates,
Wen I see the overreachin'
O' them nigger-drivin' States.

Them thet rule us, them slave-traders,   25
Haint they cut a thunderin' swarth
(Helped by Yankee renegaders),
Thru the vartu o' the North!
We begin to think it 's nater
To take sarse an' not be riled;—   30
Who 'd expect to see a tater
All on eend at bein' biled?

Ez fer war, I call it murder,—
There you hev it plain an' flat;
I don't want to go no furder   35
Than my Testyment fer that;
God hez sed so plump an' fairly,
It 's ez long ez it is broad,
An' you 've gut to git up airly
Ef you want to take in God.   40

'Taint your eppyletts an' feathers
Make the thing a grain more right;
'Taint afollerin' your bell-wethers[12]
Will excuse ye in His sight;
Ef you take a sword an' dror it,   45
An' go stick a feller thru,
Guv'ment aint to answer for it,
God 'll send the bill to you.

Wut's the use o' meetin'-goin'
Every Sabbath, wet or dry,   50
Ef it 's right to go amowin'
Feller-men like oats an' rye?
I dunno but wut it 's pooty
Trainin' round in bobtail coats,—
But it 's curus Christian dooty   55
This 'ere cuttin' folks's throats.

They may talk o' Freedom's airy[13]
Tell they're pupple in the face,—
It 's a grand gret cemetary

---

[12] Rams that lead the flock; hence, leaders.   [13] Lowell's note: "airy: area."

Fer the barthrights of our race;   60
They jest want this Californy
So 's to lug new slave-states in[14]
To abuse ye, an' to scorn ye,
An' to plunder ye like sin.

Aint it cute to see a Yankee   65
Take sech everlastin' pains,
All to git the Devil's thankee
Helpin' on 'em weld their chains?
Wy, it's jest ez clear ez figgers,
Clear exz one an' one make two,   70
Chaps thet make black slaves o' niggers
Want to make wite slaves o' you.

Tell ye jest the eend I've come to
Arter cipherin' plaguy smart,
An' it makes a handy sum, tu,   75
Any gump[15] could larn by heart;
Laborin' man an' laborin' woman
Hev one glory an' one shame.
Ev'y thin' thet's done inhuman
Injers all on 'em the same.   80

'Taint by turnin' out to hack folks
You 're agoin' to git your right,
Nor by lookin' down on black folks
Coz you 're put upon by wite;
Slavery aint o' nary color,   85
'Taint the hide thet makes it wus,
All it keers fer in a feller
'S jest to make him fill its pus.[16]

Want to tackle *me* in, du ye?
I expect you 'll hev to wait;   90
Wen cold lead puts daylight thru ye
You'll begin to kal'late;[17]
S'pose the crows wun't fall to pickin'
All the carkiss from your bones,
Cox you helped to give a lickin'   95
To them poor half-Spanish drones?[18]

---

[14] The abolitionists feared that California would be admitted to the Union as a slave state. The Compromise of 1850 resolved the issue, admitting California as a free state.

[15] Lowell's note: "gump: a foolish fellow, a dullard."

[16] Lowell's note: "pus: purse."

[17] Calculate; consider.

[18] I.e., the Mexicans.

Jest go home an' ask our Nancy
 Wether I 'd be sech a goose
Ex to jine ye,—guess you 'd fancy
 The etarnal bung[19] wuz loose!   100
She wants me fer home consumption,
 Let alone the hay 's to mow,—
Ef you 're arter folks o' gumption,
 You 've a darned long row to hoe.

Take them editors thet 's crowin'   105
 Like a cockerel three months old,—
Don't ketch any on 'em goin',
 Though they *be* so blasted bold;
Aint they a prime lot o' fellers?
 'Fore they think on 't guess they'll sprout 110
(Like a peach thet 's got the yellers),[20]
 With the meanness bustin' out.

Wal, go 'long to help 'em stealin'
 Bigger pens to cram with slaves,
Help the men thet's ollers dealin'   115
 Insults on your fathers' graves;
Help the strong to grind the feeble,
 Help the many agin the few,
Help the men thet call your people
 Witewashed slaves an' peddlin' crew! 120

Massachusetts, God forgive her,
 She 's akneelin' with the rest,[21]
She, thet ough' to ha' clung ferever
 In her grand old eagle-nest;
She thet ough' to stand so fearless   125
 W'ile the wracks[22] are round her hurled,
Holdin' up a beacon peerless
 To the oppressed of all the world!

Ha'n't they sold your colored seamen?
 Ha'n't they made your env'ys w'iz?[23] 130
Wut 'll make ye act like freemen?
 Wut 'll git your dander riz?
Come, I 'll tell ye wut I 'm thinkin'
 Is our dooty in this fix,
They 'd ha' done 't ez quick ez winkin' 135
 In the days o' seventy-six.

---

[19] The darned plug.
[20] A disease of peach trees.
[21] Representatives of Massachusetts had voted to declare war with Mexico.

[22] Misfortunes.
[23] Envoys sent to the South to protest the enslavement of free Negroes from Massachusetts were forced to "w'iz" (whiz), that is, to flee.

Clang the bells in every steeple,
    Call all true men to disown
The tradoocers of our people,
    The enslavers o' their own;
Let our dear old Bay State proudly
    Put the trumpet to her mouth,
Let her ring this messidge loudly
    In the ears of all the South:—   140

"I'll return ye good for evil   145
    Much ez we frail mortils can,
But I wun't go help the Devil
    Makin' man the cus o' man;
Call me coward, call me traiter,
    Jest ez suits your mean idees,—   150
Here I stand a tyrant-hater,
    An' the friend o' God an' Peace!"

Ef I'd *my* way I hed ruther
    We should go to work an' part,
They take one way, we take t' other,   155
    Guess it would n't break my heart;
Man hed ough' to put asunder
    Them thet God has noways jined;
An' I should n't gretly wonder
    Ef there's thousands o' my mind.   160

[The first recruiting sergeant on record I conceive to have been that individual[24] who is mentioned in the Book of Job as *going to and fro in the earth, and
walking up and down in it.* Bishop Latimer[25] will have him to have been a bishop,
but to me that other calling would appear more congenial. The sect of Cainites[26]
is not yet extinct, who esteemed the first-born of Adam to be the most worthy,
not only because of that privilege of primogeniture, but inasmuch as he was able
to overcome and slay his younger brother. That was a wise saying of the famous
Marquis Pescara[27] to the Papal Legate, that *it was impossible for men to serve Mars
and Christ at the same time.* Yet in time past the profession of arms was judged
to be κατ' εξοχήν[28] that of a gentleman, nor does this opinion want for
strenuous upholders even in our day. Must we suppose, then, that the profession
of Christianity was only intended for losers, or, at best, to afford an opening
for plebeian ambition? Or shall we hold with that nicely metaphysical
Pomeranian, Captain Vratz,[29] who was Count Königsmark's chief instrument in
the murder of Mr. Thynne, that the Scheme of Salvation has been arranged with
an especial eye to the necessities of the upper classes, and that "God would

[24] The "individual" here is Satan. (See Job 1:17.)
[25] Hugh Latimer, bishop of Worcester
(1485?–1555) and defender of the English
Reformation, who was martyred during the
reign of Queen Mary.

[26] Second-century religious sect that honored evil
characters in the Old Testament.
[27] Spanish soldier (1489–1525).
[28] Greek: "particularly."
[29] Murderer executed in 1682.

consider a *gentleman* and deal with him suitably to the condition and profession he had placed him in"? It may be said of us all, *Exemplo plus quam ratione vivimus.*[30]—*H. W.*][31]

1846

---

from A Fable for Critics

Reader! walk up at once (it will soon be too late),
and buy at a perfectly ruinous rate

A FABLE FOR CRITICS:

OR, BETTER,

(I LIKE, AS A THING THAT THE READER'S FIRST FANCY MAY STRIKE,

AN OLD-FASHIONED TITLE-PAGE,

SUCH AS PRESENTS A TABULAR VIEW OF THE VOLUME'S CONTENTS),

A GLANCE AT A FEW OF OUR LITERARY PROGENIES

(MRS. MALAPROP'S[1] WORD)

FROM THE TUB OF DIOGENES;[2]

A VOCAL AND MUSICAL MEDLEY,

THAT IS,

A SERIES OF JOKES

By A Wonderful Quiz,

WHO ACCOMPANIES HIMSELF WITH A RUB-A-DUB-DUB, FULL OF SPIRIT AND GRACE,

ON THE TOP OF THE TUB.

Set forth in October, the 31st day,
In the year '48, G. P. Putnam, Broadway.

---

[30] Latin: "We live more by example than by reason."
[31] The fictional Reverend Homer Wilbur, Lowell's creation.
[1] Mrs. Malaprop, a character in Richard Brinsley Sheridan's play *The Rivals* (1775), was noted for her misuse of words.
[2] Greek philospher (412?–323 B.C.) who purportedly lived in a tub and from there criticized society.

It being the commonest mode of procedure, I premise a few candid remarks
To The Reader:—

This trifle, begun to please only myself and my own private fancy, was laid on
the shelf. But some friends, who had seen it, induced me, by dint of saying they liked
it, to put it in print. That is, having come to that very conclusion, I asked their advice
when 't would make no confusion. For though (in the gentlest of ways) they had
hinted it was scarce worth the while, I should doubtless have printed it.

I began it, intending a Fable, a frail, slender thing, rhyme-ywinged, with a sting
in its tail. But, by addings and alterings not previously planned, digressions chance-
hatched, like birds' eggs in the sand, and dawdlings to suit every whimsey's demand
(always freeing the bird which I held in my hand, for the two perched, perhaps out
of reach, in the tree),—it grew by degrees to the size which you see. I was like the
old woman that carried the calf, and my neighbors, like hers, no doubt, wonder and
laugh; and when, my strained arms with their grown burthen full, I call it my Fable,
they call it a bull.[3]

Having scrawled at full gallop (as far as that goes) in a style that is neither good
verse nor bad prose, and being a person whom nobody knows, some people will say
I am rather more free with my readers than it is becoming to be, that I seem to expect
them to wait on my leisure in following wherever I wander at pleasure, that, in short,
I take more than a young author's lawful ease, and laugh in a queer way so like
Mephistopheles,[4] that the Public will doubt, as they grope through my rhythm, if in
truth I am making fun *of* them or *with* them.

So the excellent Public is hereby assured that the sale of my book is already secured.
For there is not a poet throughout the whole land but will purchase a copy or two
out of hand, in the fond expectation of being amused in it, by seeing his betters cut
up and abused in it. Now, I find, by a pretty exact calculation, there are something
like ten thousand bards in the nation, of that special variety whom the Review and
Magazine critics call *lofty* and *true,* and about thirty thousand (*this* tribe is increasing)
of the kinds who are termed *full of promise* and *pleasing.* The Public will see by a glance
at this schedule, that they cannot expect me to be over-sedulous about courting *them,*
since it seems I have got enough fuel made sure of for boiling my pot.

As for such of our poets as find not their names mentioned once in my pages, with
praises or blames, let them SEND IN THEIR CARDS, without further DELAY, to my friend
G. P. Putnam, Esquire, in Broadway, where a LIST will be kept with the strictest
regard to the day and the hour of receiving the card. Then, taking them up as I chance
to have time (that is, if their names can be twisted in rhyme), I will honestly give
each his PROPER POSITION, at the rate of ONE AUTHOR to each new EDITION. Thus a
PREMIUM is offered sufficiently HIGH (as the magazines say when they tell their best
lie) to induce bards to CLUB their resources and buy the balance of every edition, until
they have all of them fairly been run through the mill.

One word to such readers (judicious and wise) as read books with something
behind the mere eyes, of whom in the country, perhaps, there are two, including
myself, gentle reader, and you. All the characters sketched in this slight *jeu d'esprit,*[5]
though, it may be, they seem, here and there, rather free, and drawn from a somewhat
too cynical standpoint, are *meant* to be faithful, for that is the grand point, and none

---

[3] Jest or linguistic blunder.
[4] One of the seven fallen archangels; Satan.
[5] French: "witty jest."

but an owl would feel sore at a rub from a jester who tells you, without any subterfuge, that he sits in Diogenes' tub.

[from **Emerson**]

"There comes Emerson[6] first, whose rich words, every one,
Are like gold nails[7] in temples to hang trophies on,
Whose prose is grand verse, while his verse, the Lord knows,
Is some of it pr—— No, 't is not even prose;
I'm speaking of metres; some poems have welled   5
From those rare depths of soul that have ne'er been excelled;
They 're not epics, but that does n't matter a pin,
In creating, the only hard thing 's to begin;
A grass-blade 's no easier to make than an oak;
If you 've once found the way, you 've achieved the grand stroke;   10
In the worst of his poems are mines of rich matter,
But thrown in a heap with a crash and a clatter;
Now it is not one thing nor another alone
Makes a poem, but rather the general tone,
The something pervading, uniting the whole,   15
The before unconceived, unconceivable soul,
So that just in removing this trifle or that, you
Take away, as it were, a chief limb of the statue;
Roots, wood, bark, and leaves singly perfect may be,
But, clapt hodge-podge together, they don't make a tree.   20

"But, to come back to Emerson (whom, by the way,
I believe we left waiting),—his is, we may say,
A Greek head on right Yankee shoulders, whose range
Has Olympus for one pole, for t' other the Exchange;[8]
He seems, to my thinking (although I'm afraid   25
The comparison must, long ere this, have been made),
A Plotinus-Montaigne,[9] where the Egyptian's gold mist
And the Gascon's shrewd wit cheek-by-jowl coexist;
All admire, and yet scarcely six converts he's got
To I don't (nor they either) exactly know what;   30
For though he builds glorious temples, 't is odd
He leaves never a doorway to get in a god.
'T is refreshing to old-fashioned people like me
To meet such a primitive Pagan as he,

---

[6] Ralph Waldo Emerson (1803–1882).
[7] Ecclesiastes 12:11: "The words of the wise are as goads, and as nails fastened by the masters of assemblies, which are given from one shepherd."
[8] Olympus: dwelling place of the Greek gods; Exchange: the stock exchange.

[9] Plotinus (205?–?270): Roman Neoplatonic philosopher born in Egypt; Michel de Montaigne (1533–1592): skeptical French essayist.

In whose mind all creation is duly respected   35
As parts of himself—just a little projected;
And who 's willing to worship the stars and the sun,
A convert to—nothing but Emerson.
So perfect a balance there is in his head,
That he talks of things sometimes as if they were dead;   40
Life, nature, love, God, and affairs of that sort,
He looks at as merely ideas; in short,
As if they were fossils stuck round in a cabinet,
Of such vast extent that our earth's a mere dab in it;
Composed just as he is inclined to conjecture her,   45
Namely, one part pure earth, ninety-nine parts pure lecturer;
You are filled with delight at his clear demonstration,
Each figure, word, gesture, just fits the occasion,
With the quiet precision of science he 'll sort 'em,
But you can't help suspecting the whole a *post mortem*.   50

"There are persons, mole-blind to the soul's make and style,
Who insist on a likeness 'twixt him and Carlyle;[10]
To compare him with Plato[11] would be vastly fairer,
Carlyle's the more burly, but E. is the rarer;
He sees fewer objects, but clearlier, truelier,   55
If C. 's as original, E. 's more peculiar;
That he 's more of a man you might say of the one,
Of the other he 's more of an Emerson;
C. 's the Titan,[12] as shaggy of mind as of limb,—
E. the clear-eyed Olympian, rapid and slim;   60
The one 's two thirds Norseman, the other half Greek,
Where the one 's most abounding, the other 's to seek;
C.'s generals require to be seen in the mass,—
E.'s specialties gain if enlarged by the glass;
C. gives nature and God his own fits of the blues,   65
And rims common-sense things with mystical hues,—
E. sits in a mystery calm and intense,
And looks coolly around him with sharp commonsense;
C. shows you how every-day matters unite
With the dim transdiurnal recesses of night,—   70
While E., in a plain, preternatural way,
Makes mysteries matters of mere every day;
C. draws all his characters quite *à la* Fuseli,[13]—
Not sketching their bundles of muscles and thews illy,

---

[10] Thomas Carlyle (1795–1881), English essayist
and friend of Ralph Waldo Emerson.
[11] The Greek philosopher (427–347 B.C.).
[12] One of the primitive gods, the children of
heaven and earth, who were overthrown by the
Olympian gods.

[13] In the manner of Johann Heinrich Fuseli
(1741–1825), Swiss-born painter of extravagant,
distorted figures.

He paints with a brush so untamed and profuse, 75
They seem nothing but bundles of muscles and thews;
E. is rather like Flaxman,[14] lines strait and severe,
And a colorless outline, but full, round, and clear;—
To the men he thinks worthy he frankly accords
The design of a white marble statue in words. 80
C. labors to get at the centre, and then
Take a reckoning from there of his actions and men;
E. calmly assumes the said centre as granted,
And, given himself, has whatever is wanted.

"He has imitators in scores, who omit 85
No part of the man but his wisdom and wit,—
Who go carefully o'er the sky-blue of his brain,
And when he has skimmed it once, skim it again;
If at all they resemble him, you may be sure it is
Because their shoals mirror his mists and obscurities, 90
As a mud-puddle seems deep as heaven for a minute,
While a cloud that floats o'er is reflected within it.
. . . .

1848

[from **Channing**]

"There comes ————,[15] for instance; to see him 's rare sport,
Tread in Emerson's tracks with legs painfully short;
How he jumps, how he strains, and gets red in the face,
To keep step with the mystagogue's natural pace!
He follows as close as a stick to a rocket,[16] 5
His fingers exploring the prophet's each pocket.
Fie, for shame, brother bard; with good fruit of your own,
Can't you let Neighbor Emerson's orchards alone?
Besides, 't is no use, you'll not find e'en a core,— 10
————[17] has picked up all the windfalls before.
They might strip every tree, and E. never would catch 'em,
His Hesperides[18] have no rude dragon to watch 'em;
When they send him a dishful, and ask him to try 'em,
He never suspects how the sly rogues came by 'em; 15
He wonders why 't is there are none such his trees on,
And thinks 'em the best he has tasted this season.

[14] John Flaxman (1755–1826), English sculptor and illustrator, celebrated for his drawings of Homer's and Dante's epics.
[15] Leon Howard, in his book on Lowell entitled *Victorian Knight-Errant,* identifies this figure as William Ellery Channing (1818–1901), poet and a friend of Henry David Thoreau.
[16] Fireworks device.
[17] According to Howard, Thoreau. Windfalls: unexpected legacies.
[18] The Isles of the Blest, containing the Garden of the Golden Apples.

"Yonder, calm as a cloud, Alcott[19] stalks in a dream,
And fancies himself in thy groves, Academe,[20]
With the Parthenon nigh, and the olive-trees o'er him,   20
And never a fact to perplex him or bore him,
With a snug room at Plato's when night comes, to walk to,
And people from morning till midnight to talk to,
And from midnight till morning, nor snore in their listening;—
So he muses, his face with the joy of it glistening,   25
For his highest conceit of a happiest state is
Where they'd live upon acorns, and hear him talk gratis;
And indeed, I believe, no man ever talked better,—
Each sentence hangs perfectly poised to a letter;
He seems piling words, but there's royal dust hid   30
In the heart of each sky-piercing pyramid.
While he talks he is great, but goes out like a taper,
If you shut him up closely with pen, ink, and paper;
Yet his fingers itch for 'em from morning till night,
And he thinks he does wrong if he don't always write;   35
In this, as in all things, a lamb among men,
He goes to sure death when he goes to his pen.
. . . .

1848

[from *Bryant*]

"There is Bryant,[21] as quiet, as cool, and as dignified,
As a smooth, silent iceberg, that never is ignified,
Save when by reflection 't is kindled o' nights
With a semblance of flame by the chill Northern Lights.
He may rank (Griswold[22] says so) first bard of your nation   5
(There's no doubt that he stands in supreme iceolation),
Your topmost Parnassus[23] he may set his heel on,
But no warm applauses come, peal following peal on,—
He 's too smooth and too polished to hang any zeal on:
Unqualified merits, I'll grant, if you choose, he has 'em,   10
But he lacks the one merit of kindling enthusiasm;
If he stir you at all, it is just, on my soul,
Like being stirred up with the very North Pole.

"He is very nice reading in summer, but *inter
Nos,*[24] we don't want *extra* freezing in winter;   15
Take him up in the depth of July, my advice is,

[19] Bronson Alcott (1799–1888), transcendentalist
and innovative educator.
[20] Plato and his followers conducted philosophical
discussions in this Athenian olive grove near the
Parthenon.
[21] William Cullen Bryant (1794–1878).

[22] Rufus Griswold (1815–1857), editor of the
popular *Poets and Poetry of America* (1842).
[23] Greek mountain, sacred to the gods, whose peak
exceeded the height of the waves in the Flood.
[24] Latin: "between us" or "among ourselves."

When you feel an Egyptian devotion to ices.[25]
But, deduct all you can, there 's enough that 's right good in him,
He has a true soul for field, river, and wood in him;
And his heart, in the midst of brick walls, or where'er it is,   20
Glows, softens, and thrills with the tenderest charities—
To you mortals that delve in this trade-ridden planet?
No, to old Berkshire's hills, with their limestone and granite.
If you 're one who *in loco* (add *foco* here) *desipis*,[26]
You will get of his outermost heart (as I guess) a piece;   25
But you 'd get deeper down if you came as a precipice,
And would break the last seal of its inwardest fountain,
If you only could palm yourself off for a mountain.
Mr. Quivis,[27] or somebody quite as discerning,
Some scholar who 's hourly expecting his learning,   30
Calls B. the American Wordsworth; but Wordsworth
May be rated at more than your whole tuneful herd 's worth.
No, don't be absurd, he 's an excellent Bryant;
But, my friends, you 'll endanger the life of your client,
By attempting to stretch him up into a giant: 35
If you choose to compare him, I think there are two per-
sons fit for a parallel—Thomson and Cowper;[28]
I don't mean exactly,—there's something of each,
There's T.'s love of nature, C.'s penchant to preach;
Just mix up their minds so that C.'s spice of craziness   40
Shall balance and neutralize T.'s turn for laziness,
And it gives you a brain cool, quite frictionless, quiet,
Whose internal police nips the buds of all riot,—
A brain like a permanent strait-jacket put on
The heart that strives vainly to burst off a button,—   45
A brain which, without being slow or mechanic,
Does more than a larger less drilled, more volcanic;
He's a Cowper condensed, with no craziness bitten,
And the advantage that Wordsworth before him had written.

  "But, my dear little bardlings, don't prick up your ears   50
Nor suppose I would rank you and Bryant as peers;
If I call him an iceberg, I don't mean to say
There is nothing in that which is grand in its way;

---

[25] Pun on Isis, the Egyptian fertility goddess.
[26] Cf. Horace, *Odes*, IV, xii, 28: "dulce est desipere in loco." ("It's pleasant at times to engage in trifling.") Lowell also puns here on the political term "Locofoco," epithet for a radical faction of the New York Democratic party that responded to its conservative opponents' efforts to turn off the gaslights by lighting the locofocos, the newly invented "lucifer matches."

[27] Mr. Whoever or Mr. Anyone.
[28] Thomson: James Thomson (1700–1748), Scottish poet and author of *The Seasons* (1730); Cowper: William Cowper (1731–1800), author of *Olney Hymns* (1779) and *The Task* (1785). Lowell's note: "To demonstrate quickly and easily how per- / versely absurd 'tis to sound this name *Cowper,* / As people in general call him named *super,* / I remark that he rhymes it himself with horse-trooper."

He is almost the one of your poets that knows
How much grace, strength, and dignity lie in Repose;   55
If he sometimes fall short, he is too wise to mar
His thought's modest fulness by going too far;
'T would be well if your authors should all make a trial
Of what virtue there is in severe self-denial,
And measure their writings by Hesiod's[29] staff,   60
Which teaches that all has less value than half.

· ·

1848

[from **Whittier**]

"There is Whittier,[30] whose swelling and vehement heart
Strains the strait-breasted drab of the Quaker apart,
And reveals the live Man, still supreme and erect,
Underneath the bemummying wrappers of sect;
There was ne'er a man born who had more of the swing   5
Of the true lyric bard and all that kind of thing;
And his failures arise (though he seem not to know it)
From the very same cause that has made him a poet,—
A fervor of mind which knows no separation
'Twixt simple excitement and pure inspiration,   10
As my Pythoness[31] erst sometimes erred from not knowing
If 't were I or mere wind through her tripod was blowing;
Let his mind once get head in its favorite direction
And the torrent of verse bursts the dams of reflection,
While, borne with the rush of the metre along,   15
The poet may chance to go right or go wrong,
Content with the whirl and delirium of song;
Then his grammar 's not always correct, nor his rhymes,
And he's prone to repeat his own lyrics sometimes,
Not his best, though, for those are struck off at white-heats   20
When the heart in his breast like a trip-hammer beats,
And can ne'er be repeated again any more
Than they could have been carefully plotted before:
Like old what's-his-name[32] there at the battle of Hastings
(Who, however, gave more than mere rhythmical bastings),   25
Our Quaker leads off metaphorical fights
For reform and whatever they call human rights,
Both singing and striking in front of the war,

---

[29] Hesiod: Greek didactic poet of the eighth
century B.C. "Hesiod's staff" refers to a poetic
line. (See Hesiod's *Works and Days*, l. 40: "the
half is better than the whole.")
[30] John Greenleaf Whittier (1807–1892).

[31] Priestess of Apollo who delivered inspired
prophecies while seated on a tripod.
[32] The minstrel Taillefer, who led the charge of
William the Conquerer's cavalry at the Battle
of Hastings (1066).

And hitting his foes with the mallet of Thor;[33]
Anne haec, one exclaims, on beholding his knocks,
Vestis filii tui,[34] O leather-clad Fox?   30
Can that be thy son, in the battle's mid din,
Preaching brotherly love and then driving it in
To the brain of the tough old Goliath[35] of sin,
With the smoothest of pebbles from Castaly's spring[36]   35
Impressed on his hard moral sense with a sling?

    "All honor and praise to the right-hearted bard
Who was true to The Voice when such service was hard,
Who himself was so free he dared sing for the slave
When to look but a protest in silence was brave;   40
All honor and praise to the women and men
Who spoke out for the dumb and the down-trodden then!
It needs not to name them, already for each
I see History preparing the statue and niche;
They were harsh, but shall *you* be so shocked at hard words   45
Who have beaten your pruning-hooks up into swords,[37]
Whose rewards and hurrahs men are surer to gain
By the reaping of men and of women than grain?
Why should *you* stand aghast at their fierce wordy war, if
You scalp one another for Bank or for Tariff?[38]   50
Your calling them cut-throats and knaves all day long
Does n't prove that the use of hard language is wrong;
While the World's heart beats quicker to think of such men
As signed Tyranny's doom with a bloody steel-pen,
While on Fourth-of-Julys beardless orators fright one   55
With hints at Harmodius and Aristogeiton,[39]
You need not look shy at your sisters and brothers
Who stab with sharp words for the freedom of others;—
No, a wreath, twine a wreath for the loyal and true
Who, for sake of the many, dared stand with the few,   60
Not of blood-spattered laurel for enemies braved,
But of broad, peaceful oak-leaves for citizens saved!
. . . .

1848

---

[33] Norse god of thunder.
[34] Latin translation of Genesis 37:32: "This we
have found: know now whether it be thy son's
coat or no." (Asked by Jacob's deceitful sons,
who show him a bloodied coat to suggest that
Joseph, his favorite son, is dead.) Fox: George
Fox (1624–1691), founder of the Quakers,
known for wearing leather breeches.
[35] The giant Goliath, slain by a rock from David's
slingshot. (See 1 Samuel 17.)

[36] Castaly's spring: tributary at the base of Mount
Parnassus from which poets drink for
inspiration.
[37] Allusion to mobilizing for the Mexican War.
[38] Two controversial issues of the time were the
creation of a national bank and whether to raise
or lower tariffs.
[39] Greek assassins of the Athenian tyrant
Hipparchus in the sixth century B.C., regarded as
heroes after their execution.

[from **Hawthorne**]

"There is Hawthorne,[40] with genius so shrinking and rare
That you hardly at first see the strength that is there;
A frame so robust, with a nature so sweet,
So earnest, so graceful, so lithe and so fleet,
Is worth a descent from Olympus to meet;   5
'Tis as if a rough oak that for ages had stood,
With his gnarled bony branches like ribs of the wood,
Should bloom, after cycles of struggle and scathe,
With a single anemone trembly and rathe;
His strength is so tender, his wildness so meek,   10
That a suitable parallel sets one to seek,—
He's a John Bunyan Fouqué, a Puritan Tieck;[41]
When Nature was shaping him, clay was not granted
For making so full-sized a man as she wanted,
So, to fill out her model, a little she spared   15
From some finer-grained stuff for a woman prepared,
And she could not have hit a more excellent plan
For making him fully and perfectly man.

. . . .

1848

[from **Cooper**]

"Here's Cooper,[42] who's written six volumes to show
He 's as good as a lord: well, let's grant that he's so;
If a person prefer that description of praise,
Why, a coronet 's certainly cheaper than bays;
But he need take no pains to convince us he 's not   5
(As his enemies say) the American Scott.[43]
Choose any twelve men, and let C. read aloud
That one of his novels of which he's most proud,
And I 'd lay any bet that, without ever quitting
Their box,[44] they'd be all, to a man, for acquitting.   10
He has drawn you one character, though, that is new,
One wildflower he 's plucked that is wet with the dew
Of this fresh Western world, and, the thing not to mince,
He has done naught but copy it ill ever since;
His Indians, with proper respect be it said,   15

[40] Nathaniel Hawthorne (1804–1864).
[41] I.e., Hawthorne is seen as both a Puritan and a
   romantic: a combination of John Bunyan
   (1628–1688), Puritan author of *The Pilgrim's
   Progress* (1678); Friedrich Heinrich Karl La
   Motte-Fouqué (1777–1843), German author of
   the romantic *Undine* (1811); and Ludwig Tieck
   (1773–1853), German romanticist.

[42] James Fenimore Cooper (1789–1851).
[43] Sir Walter Scott (1771–1832), English novelist
   after whom Cooper patterned some of his early
   fiction.
[44] I.e., the jury box where jurors sit.

Are just Natty Bumppo,[45] daubed over with red,
And his very Long Toms[46] are the same useful Nat,
Rigged up in duck pants and a sou'wester hat
(Though once in a Coffin, a good chance was found
To have slipped the old fellow away underground).   20
All his other men-figures are clothes upon sticks,
The *dernière chemise*[47] of a man in a fix
(As a captain besieged, when his garrison 's small,
Sets up caps upon poles to be seen o'er the wall);
And the women he draws from one model don't vary,   25
All sappy as maples and flat as a prairie.
When a character 's wanted, he goes to the task
As a cooper would do in composing a cask;
He picks out the staves, of their qualities heedful,
Just hoops them together as tight as is needful,   30
And, if the best fortune should crown the attempt, he
Has made at the most something wooden and empty.

    "Don't suppose I would underrate Cooper's abilities;
If I thought you 'd do that, I should feel very ill at ease;
The men who have given to *one* character life   35
And objective existence are not very rife;
You may number them all, both prose-writers and singers,
Without overrunning the bounds of your fingers,
And Natty won't go to oblivion quicker
Than Adams the parson or Primrose the vicar.[48]   40

    "There is one thing in Cooper I like, too, and that is
That on manners he lectures his countrymen gratis;
Not precisely so either, because, for a rarity,
He is paid for his tickets in unpopularity.
Now he may overcharge his American pictures,   45
But you'll grant there 's a good deal of truth in his strictures;
And I honor the man who is willing to sink
Half his present repute for the freedom to think,
And, when he has thought, be his cause strong or weak,
Will risk t' other half for the freedom to speak,   50
Caring naught for what vengeance the mob has in store,
Let that mob be the upper ten thousand or lower.

    "There are truths you Americans need to be told,
And it never 'll refute them to swagger and scold;

---

[45] Hero of Cooper's *Leather-Stocking Tales*.
[46] Long Tom Coffin, hero of Cooper's novel *The Pilot* (1823).
[47] French: "last shirt."

[48] Adams: parson in Henry Fielding's *Joseph Andrews* (1742); Primrose: Dr. Primrose in Oliver Goldsmith's *The Vicar of Wakefield* (1766).

John Bull, looking o'er the Atlantic, in choler   55
At your aptness for trade, says you worship the dollar;
But to scorn such eye-dollar-try 's what very few do,
And John goes to that church as often as you do.
No matter what John says, don't try to outcrow him,
'T is enough to go quietly on and outgrow him;   60
Like most fathers, Bull hates to see Number One
Displacing himself in the mind of his son,
And detests the same faults in himself he 'd neglected
When he sees them again in his child's glass reflected;
To love one another you 're too like by half;   65
If he is a bull, you 're a pretty stout calf,
And tear your own pasture for naught but to show
What a nice pair of horns you 're beginning to grow.

"There are one or two things I should just like to hint,
For you don't often get the truth told you in print;   70
The most of you (this is what strikes all beholders)
Have a mental and physical stoop in the shoulders;
Though you ought to be free as the winds and the waves,
You 've the gait and the manners of runaway slaves;
Though you brag of your New World, you don't half believe in it;   75
And as much of the Old as is possible weave in it;
Your goddess of freedom, a tight, buxom girl,
With lips like a cherry and teeth like a pearl,
With eyes bold as Herë's,[49] and hair floating free,
And full of the sun as the spray of the sea,   80
Who can sing at a husking or romp at a shearing,
Who can trip through the forests alone without fearing,
Who can drive home the cows with a song through the grass,
Keeps glancing aside into Europe's cracked glass,
Hides her red hands in gloves, pinches up her lithe waist,   85
And makes herself wretched with transmarine taste;
She loses her fresh country charm when she takes
Any mirror except her own rivers and lakes.

"You steal Englishmen's books[50] and think Englishmen's thought,
With their salt on her tail your wild eagle is caught;   90
Your literature suits its each whisper and motion
To what will be thought of it over the ocean;
The cast clothes of Europe your statesmanship tries
And mumbles again the old blarneys and lies;—
Forget Europe wholly, your veins throb with blood,   95
To which the dull current in hers is but mud;

---

[49] Herë: Hera, Olympian goddess and wife of Zeus.

[50] Foreign authors could not copyright their works in the United States at this time.

Let her sneer, let her say your experiment fails,
In her voice there's a tremble e'en now while she rails,
And your shore will soon be in the nature of things
Covered thick with gilt drift-wood of castaway kings,   100
Where alone, as it were in a Longfellow's Waif,[51]
Her fugitive pieces will find themselves safe.
O my friends, thank your god, if you have one, that he
'Twixt the Old World and you set the gulf of a sea;
Be strong-backed, brown-handed, upright as your pines,   105
By the scale of a hemisphere shape your designs,
Be true to yourselves and this new nineteenth age,
As a statue by Powers, or a picture by Page,[52]
Plough, sail, forge, build, carve, paint, make all over new,
To your own New-World instincts contrive to be true,   110
Keep your ears open wide to the Future's first call,
Be whatever you will, but yourselves first of all,
Stand fronting the dawn on Toil's heaven-scaling peaks,
And become my new race of more practical Greeks.—   115
Hem! your likeness at present, I shudder to tell o't,
Is that you have your slaves, and the Greek had his helot."[53]

. . . .

1848

[from *Poe*]

"There comes Poe,[54] with his raven, like Barnaby Rudge,[55]
Three fifths of him genius and two fifths sheer fudge,
Who talks like a book of iambs and pentameters,
In a way to make people of common sense damn metres,
Who has written some things quite the best of their kind,   5
But the heart somehow seems all squeezed out by the mind.
Who—But hey-day! What's this? Messieurs Mathews[56] and Poe,
You must n't fling mud-balls at Longfellow so,
Does it make a man worse that his character 's such
As to make his friends love him (as you think) too much?   10
Why, there is not a bard at this moment alive
More willing than he that his fellows should thrive;
While you are abusing him thus, even now
He would help either one of you out of a slough;

[51] Anthology of poetry published by Henry Wadsworth Longfellow in 1845.
[52] Powers: Hiram Powers (1805–1873), sculptor of such political figures as Calhoun and Jackson; Page: William Page (1811–1885), painter of American historical scenes.
[53] Spartan serf who, unlike the American slave, could not be sold and could be freed by the state.
[54] Edgar Allan Poe (1809–1849).
[55] Central character in Charles Dickens's novel *Barnaby Rudge* (1841); Rudge owned a raven.
[56] Cornelius Mathews (1817–1889), editor, novelist, and magazine writer who joined Poe in criticizing Longfellow's work.

You may say that he 's smooth and all that till you 're hoarse,   15
But remember that elegance also is force;
After polishing granite as much as you will,
The heart keeps its tough old persistency still;
Deduct all you can, *that* still keeps you at bay;
Why, he 'll live till men weary of Collins and Gray.[57]   20
I 'm not over-fond of Greek metres in English,[58]
To me rhyme's a gain, so it be not too jinglish,
And your modern hexameter verses are no more
Like Greek ones than sleek Mr. Pope is like Homer;[59]
As the roar of the sea to the coo of a pigeon is,   25
So, compared to your moderns, sounds old Melesigenes;
I may be too partial, the reason, perhaps, o't is
That I've heard the old blind man recite his own rhapsodies,
And my ear with that music impregnate may be,
Like the poor exiled shell with the soul of the sea,   30
Or as one can't bear Strauss when his nature is cloven
To its deeps within deeps by the stroke of Beethoven;[60]
But, set that aside, and 't is truth that I speak,
Had Theocritus[61] written in English, not Greek,
I believe that his exquisite sense would scarce change a line   35
In that rare, tender, virgin-like pastoral Evangeline.
That's not ancient nor modern, its place is apart
Where time has no sway, in the realm of pure Art,
'Tis a shrine of retreat from Earth's hubbub and strife
As quiet and chaste as the author's own life.   40

. . . .

1848

[from **Irving**]

"What! Irving? thrice welcome, warm heart and fine brain,
You bring back the happiest spirit from Spain,[62]
And the gravest sweet humor, that ever were there
Since Cervantes[63] met death in his gentle despair;
Nay, don't be embarrassed, nor look so beseeching,   5
I sha'n't run directly against my own preaching,

---

[57] Collins: William Collins (1721–1759), English author of odes and elegies; Gray: Thomas Gray (1716–1771), English author of "Elegy Written in a Country Churchyard" (1751).

[58] Longfellow adapted the hexameter of Greek epic poetry in his *Evangeline, A Tale of Arcadie* (1847).

[59] Alexander Pope (1688–1744) translated Homer's *Iliad* and *Odyssey* into English heroic couplets. "Old Melesigenes," the "old blind man" below, is Homer, who was supposedly born in Melos.

[60] Strauss: Johann Strauss (1804–1849), Austrian composer famous for his waltzes; Beethoven: Ludwig van Beethoven (1770–1827), German composer.

[61] Greek pastoral poet of the third century B.C.

[62] Washington Irving (1783–1859) had served as minister to Spain in the early 1840s. He also had written a history of Granada (1829) and *The Legend of the Alhambra* (1832).

[63] Miguel de Cervantes Saavedra (1547–1616), author of *Don Quixote* (1605; 1615).

And, having just laughed at their Raphaels and Dantes,
Go to setting you up beside matchless Cervantes;
But allow me to speak what I honestly feel,—
To a true poet-heart add the fun of Dick Steele,[64]   10
Throw in all of Addison, *minus* the chill,
With the whole of that partnership's stock and good-will,
Mix well, and while stirring, hum o'er, as a spell,
The fine *old* English Gentleman,[65] simmer it well,
Sweeten just to your own private liking, then strain,   15
That only the finest and clearest remain,
Let it stand out of doors till a soul it receives
From the warm lazy sun loitering down through green leaves,
And you 'll find a choice nature, not wholly deserving
A name either English or Yankee,—just Irving.   20

. . . .

1848

[from *Holmes*]

"There 's Holmes,[66] who is matchless among you for wit;
A Leyden-jar[67] always full-charged, from which flit
The electrical tingles of hit after hit;
In long poems 't is painful sometimes, and invites
A thought of the way the new Telegraph writes,[68]   5
Which pricks down its little sharp sentences spitefully
As if you got more than you 'd title to rightfully,
And you find yourself hoping its wild father Lightning
Would flame in for a second and give you a fright'ning.
He has perfect sway of what *I* call a sham metre,   10
But many admire it, the English pentameter,
And Campbell,[69] I think, wrote most commonly worse,
With less nerve, swing, and fire in the same kind of verse,
Nor e'er achieved aught in 't so worthy of praise
As the tribute of Holmes to the grand *Marseillaise*.[70]   15
You went crazy last year over Bulwer's New Timon;[71]—
Why, if B., to the day of his dying, should rhyme on,
Heaping verses on verses and tomes upon tomes,
He could ne'er reach the best point and vigor of Holmes.
His are just the fine hands, too, to weave you a lyric   20

[64] Richard Steele (1672–1729), English essayist; collaborator with Joseph Addison (1672–1719) on the periodical *The Spectator*.

[65] Allusion to "The English Country Gentleman," an essay in Irving's *Bracebridge Hall* (1822).

[66] Oliver Wendell Holmes (1809–1894).

[67] Glass jar used as one of the earliest electrical condensers.

[68] The telegraph, demonstrated by Samuel F. B.

Morse (1791–1872) in 1844, was in service between Washington and New York City by 1846.

[69] Thomas Campbell (1777–1844), Scottish poet.

[70] French national anthem. Cf. Holmes, "Poetry: A Metrical Essay" (1836).

[71] *The New Timon: A Romance of London* by Edward Bulwer-Lytton (1803–1873).

Full of fancy, fun, feeling, or spiced with satiric
In a measure so kindly, you doubt if the toes
That are trodden upon are your own or your foes'.
. . . .

1848

[from **Lowell**]

"There is Lowell, who's striving Parnassus to climb
With a whole bale of *isms* tied together with rhyme,
He might get on alone, spite of brambles and boulders,
But he can't with that bundle he has on his shoulders,
The top of the hill he will ne'er come nigh reaching   5
Till he learns the distinction 'twixt singing and preaching;
His lyre has some chords that would ring pretty well,
But he 'd rather by half make a drum of the shell,
And rattle away till he 's old as Methusalem,[72]
At the head of a march to the last new Jerusalem.   10
. . . .

1848

Ode Recited at the Harvard Commemoration[*]

July 21, 1865

I.

Weak-winged is song,
Nor aims at that clear-ethered height
Whither the brave deed climbs for light:
        We seem to do them wrong,
Bringing our robin's-leaf to deck their hearse   5
Who in warm life-blood wrote their nobler verse,
Our trivial song to honor those who come
With ears attuned to strenuous trump and drum,

---

[72] Methuselah is said to have lived 969 years. (See Genesis 5:27.)

[*] Lowell read this poem at Harvard College on July 21, 1865, to honor the Harvard men who had fought in the Civil War. (Three of Lowell's nephews had died in the war.) He noted to a friend: "The poem was written with a vehement speed, which I thought I had lost in the skirts of my professor's gown. Till within two days of the celebration I was hopelessly dumb, and then it all came with a rush, literally making me lean . . . and so nervous that I was weeks in getting over it."

And shaped in squadron-strophes their desire,
Live battle-odes whose lines were steel and fire: 10
    Yet sometimes feathered words are strong,
A gracious memory to buoy up and save
From Lethe's¹ dreamless ooze, the common grave
    Of the unventurous throng.

II.

To-day our Reverend Mother² welcomes back   15
    Her wisest Scholars, those who understood
The deeper teaching of her mystic tome,
    And offered their fresh lives to make it good:
        No lore of Greece or Rome,
No science peddling with the names of things,   20
Or reading stars to find inglorious fates,
        Can lift our life with wings
Far from Death's idle gulf that for the many waits,
        And lengthen out our dates
With that clear fame whose memory sings   25
In manly hearts to come, and nerves them and dilates:
Nor such thy teaching, Mother of us all!
        Not such the trumpet-call
        Of thy diviner mood,
        That could thy sons entice   30
From happy homes and toils, the fruitful nest
Of those half-virtues which the world calls best,
        Into War's tumult rude;
        But rather far that stern device
The sponsors chose that round thy cradle stood   35
        In the dim, unventured wood,
        The VERITAS³ that lurks beneath
        The letter's unprolific sheath,
    Life of whate'er makes life worth living,
Seed-grain of high emprise, immortal food,   40
    One heavenly thing whereof earth hath the giving.

III.

Many loved Truth, and lavished life's best oil
    Amid the dust of books to find her,
Content at last, for guerdon of their toil,
    With the cast mantle she hath left behind her.   45

---

¹ Lethe, a river of Hades, offered forgetfulness of
the past to those who drank from it.
² I.e., their alma mater, Harvard College.

³ "Truth," the motto imprinted on the Harvard
seal.

Many in sad faith sought for her,
Many with crossed hands sighed for her;
But these, our brothers, fought for her;
At life's dear peril wrought for her,
So loved her that they died for her,   50
Tasting the raptured fleetness
Of her divine completeness:
    Their higher instinct knew
Those love her best who to themselves are true,
And what they dare to dream of, dare to do;   55
    They followed her and found her
    Where all may hope to find,
Not in the ashes of the burnt-out mind,
But beautiful, with danger's sweetness round her.
    Where faith made whole with deed   60
    Breathes its awakening breath
    Into the lifeless creed,
    They saw her plumed and mailed,
    With sweet, stern face unveiled,
And all-repaying eyes, look proud on them in death.   65

IV.

Our slender life runs rippling by, and glides
    Into the silent hollow of the past;
        What is there that abides
    To make the next age better for the last?
        Is earth too poor to give us   70
    Something to live for here that shall outlive us?
        Some more substantial boon
Than such as flows and ebbs with Fortune's fickle moon?
        The little that we see
        From doubt is never free;   75
        The little that we do
        Is but half-nobly true;
        With our laborious hiving
What men call treasure, and the gods call dross,
    Life seems a jest of Fate's contriving,   80
    Only secure in every one's conniving,
A long account of nothings paid with loss,
Where we poor puppets, jerked by unseen wires,
    After our little hour of strut and rave,
With all our pasteboard passions and desires,   85
Loves, hates, ambitions, and immortal fires,
    Are tossed pell-mell together in the grave.
    But stay! no age was e'er degenerate,
    Unless men held it at too cheap a rate,

For in our likeness still we shape our fate.   90
  Ah, there is something here
Unfathomed by the cynic's sneer,
Something that gives our feeble light
A high immunity from Night,
Something that leaps life's narrow bars   95
To claim its birthright with the hosts of heaven;
 A seed of sunshine that can leaven
Our earthy dulness with the beams of stars,
  And glorify our clay
With light from fountains elder than the Day;   100
 A conscience more divine than we,
 A gladness fed with secret tears,
 A vexing, forward-reaching sense
Of some more noble permanence;
  A light across the sea,   105
Which haunts the soul and will not let it be,
Still beaconing from the heights of undegenerate years.

V.

  Whither leads the path
  To ampler fates that leads?
  Not down through flowery meads,   110
  To reap an aftermath
  Of youth's vainglorious weeds,
  But up the steep, amid the wrath
  And shock of deadly-hostile creeds,
  Where the world's best hope and stay   115
By battle's flashes gropes a desperate way,
And every turf the fierce foot clings to bleeds.
  Peace hath her not ignoble wreath,
  Ere yet the sharp, decisive word
Light the black lips of cannon, and the sword   120
  Dreams in its easeful sheath;
But some day the live coal behind the thought,
  Whether from Baäl's stone[4] obscene,
  Or from the shrine serene
  Of God's pure altar brought,   125
Bursts up in flame; the war of tongue and pen
Learns with what deadly purpose it was fraught,
And, helpless in the fiery passion caught,
Shakes all the pillared state with shock of men:
Some day the soft Ideal that we wooed   130

---

[4] Pagan idol worshiped by the priest of Baäl.
(Cf. 1 Kings 18.)

Confronts us fiercely, foe-beset, pursued,
And cries reproachful: "Was it, then, my praise,
And not myself was loved? Prove now thy truth;
I claim of thee the promise of thy youth;
Give me thy life, or cower in empty phrase,   135
The victim of thy genius, not its mate!"
    Life may be given in many ways,
    And loyalty to Truth be sealed
As bravely in the closet as the field,
      So bountiful is Fate;   140
      But then to stand beside her,
      When craven churls deride her,
To front a lie in arms and not to yield,
        This shows, methinks, God's plan
        And measure of a stalwart man,   145
        Limbed like the old heroic breeds,
      Who stands self-poised on manhood's solid earth,
Not forced to frame excuses for his birth,
Fed from within with all the strength he needs.

VI.

Such was he, our Martyr-Chief,[5]   150
    Whom late the Nation he had led,
    With ashes on her head,
Wept with the passion of an angry grief;
Forgive me, if from present things I turn
To speak what in my heart will beat and burn,   155
And hang my wreath on his world-honored urn.
      Nature, they say, doth dote,
      And cannot make a man
      Save on some worn-out plan,
      Repeating us by rote: 160
For him her Old-World moulds aside she threw,
    And, choosing sweet clay from the breast
    Of the unexhausted West,
With stuff untainted shaped a hero new,
Wise, steadfast in the strength of God, and true.   165
      How beautiful to see
Once more a shepherd of mankind indeed,
Who loved his charge, but never loved to lead;
One whose meek flock the people joyed to be,
      Not lured by any cheat of birth,   170
      But by his clear-grained human worth,

[5] Abraham Lincoln. This stanza was added after
the poem's recital at Harvard.

And brave old wisdom of sincerity!
    They knew that outward grace is dust;
    They could not choose but trust
In that sure-footed mind's unfaltering skill,   175
      And supple-tempered will
That bent like perfect steel to spring again and thrust.
    His was no lonely mountain-peak of mind,
    Thrusting to thin air o'er our cloudy bars,
    A sea-mark now, now lost in vapors blind;   180
    Broad prairie rather, genial, level-lined,
    Fruitful and friendly for all human kind,
Yet also nigh to heaven and loved of loftiest stars.
      Nothing of Europe here,
Or, then, of Europe fronting mornward still,   185
      Ere any names of Serf and Peer
    Could Nature's equal scheme deface
    And thwart her genial will;
    Here was a type of the true elder race,
And one of Plutarch's men[6] talked with us face to face.   190
    I praise him not; it were too late;
And some innative weakness there must be
In him who condescends to victory
Such as the Present gives, and cannot wait,
    Safe in himself as in a fate.   195
      So always firmly he:
      He knew to bide his time,
      And can his fame abide,
Still patient in his simple faith sublime,
      Till the wise years decide.   200
  Great captains, with their guns and drums,
    Disturb our judgment for the hour,
    But at last silence comes;
These all are gone, and, standing like a tower,
Our children shall behold his fame,   205
    The kindly-earnest, brave, foreseeing man,
Sagacious, patient, dreading praise, not blame,
    New birth of our new soil, the first American.

VII.

    Long as man's hope insatiate can discern
      Or only guess some more inspiring goal   210
      Outside of Self, enduring as the pole,

---

[6] I.e., someone comparable to the heroes of
ancient Greece and Rome commemorated by
Plutarch (A.D. 46?–120) in his *Parallel Lives*.

Along whose course the flying axles burn
Of spirits bravely-pitched, earth's manlier brood;
   Long as below we cannot find
The meed that stills the inexorable mind;   215
So long this faith to some ideal Good,
Under whatever mortal names it masks,
Freedom, Law, Country, this ethereal mood
That thanks the Fates for their severer tasks,
   Feeling its challenged pulses leap,   220
   While others skulk in subterfuges cheap,
And, set in Danger's van, has all the boon it asks,
   Shall win man's praise and woman's love,
   Shall be a wisdom that we set above
All other skills and gifts to culture dear,   225
   A virtue round whose forehead we inwreathe
   Laurels that with a living passion breathe
When other crowns grow, while we twine them, sear.
   What brings us thronging these high rites to pay,
And seal these hours the noblest of our year,   230
   Save that our brothers found this better way?

VIII.

We sit here in the Promised Land
   That flows with Freedom's honey and milk;[7]
   But 't was they won it, sword in hand,
Making the nettle danger soft for us as silk.   235
   We welcome back our bravest and our best;—
   Ah me! not all! some come not with the rest,
Who went forth brave and bright as any here!
I strive to mix some gladness with my strain,
      But the sad strings complain,   240
      And will not please the ear:
I sweep them for a pæan, but they wane
      Again and yet again
Into a dirge, and die away, in pain.
In these brave ranks I only see the gaps,   245
Thinking of dear ones whom the dumb turf wraps,
Dark to the triumph which they died to gain:
   Fitlier may others greet the living,
   For me the past is unforgiving;
      I with uncovered head   250
      Salute the sacred dead,
Who went, and who return not.—Say not so!
'T is not the grapes of Canaan[8] that repay,

---

[7] See Exodus 3:8.   [8] See Numbers 13:23–27.

But the high faith that failed not by the way;
Virtue treads paths that end not in the grave;   255
No bar of endless night exiles the brave;
            And to the saner mind
We rather seem the dead that stayed behind.
Blow, trumpets, all your exultations blow!
For never shall their aureoled presence lack: 260
I see them muster in a gleaming row,
With ever-youthful brows that nobler show;
We find in our dull road their shining track;
            In every nobler mood
We feel the orient of their spirit glow,   265
Part of our life's unalterable good,
Of all our saintlier aspiration;
            They come transfigured back,
Secure from change in their high-hearted ways,
Beautiful evermore, and with the rays   270
Of morn on their white Shields of Expectation!

IX.

            But is there hope to save
    Even this ethereal essence from the grave?
    What ever 'scaped Oblivion's subtle wrong
Save a few clarion names, or golden threads of song?   275
            Before my musing eye
        The mighty ones of old sweep by,
    Disvoicèd now and insubstantial things,
    As noisy once as we; poor ghosts of kings,
    Shadows of empire wholly gone to dust,   280
    And many races, nameless long ago,
    To darkness driven by that imperious gust
    Of ever-rushing Time that here doth blow:
    O visionary world, condition strange,
    Where naught abiding is but only Change,   285
Where the deep-bolted stars themselves still shift and range!
    Shall we to more continuance make pretence?
Renown builds tombs; a life-estate is Wit;
            And, bit by bit,
The cunning years steal all from us but woe;   290
    Leaves are we, whose decays no harvest sow.
        But, when we vanish hence,
    Shall they lie forceless in the dark below,
    Save to make green their little length of sods,
    Or deepen pansies for a year or two,   295
    Who now to us are shining-sweet as gods?
    Was dying all they had the skill to do?

That were not fruitless: but the Soul resents
Such short-lived service, as if blind events
Ruled without her, or earth could so endure;   300
She claims a more divine investiture
Of longer tenure than Fame's airy rents;
Whate'er she touches doth her nature share;
Her inspiration haunts the ennobled air,
  Gives eyes to mountains blind,   305
Ears to the deaf earth, voices to the wind,
And her clear trump sings succor everywhere
By lonely bivouacs to the wakeful mind;
For soul inherits all that soul could dare:
  Yea, Manhood hath a wider span   310
And larger privilege of life than man.
The single deed, the private sacrifice,
So radiant now through proudly-hidden tears,
Is covered up erelong from mortal eyes
With thoughtless drift of the deciduous years;   315
But that high privilege that makes all men peers,
That leap of heart whereby a people rise
  Up to a noble anger's height,
And, flamed on by the Fates, not shrink, but grow more bright,
  That swift validity in noble veins,   320
  Of choosing danger and disdaining shame,
   Of being set on flame
By the pure fire that flies all contact base,
But wraps its chosen with angelic might,
  These are imperishable gains,   325
 Sure as the sun, medicinal as light,
 These hold great futures in their lusty reins
And certify to earth a new imperial race.

X.

  Who now shall sneer?
  Who dare again to say we trace   330
  Our lines to a plebeian race?
  Roundhead and Cavalier![9]
Dumb are those names erewhile in battle loud;
Dream-footed as the shadow of a cloud,
  They flit across the ear: 335
That is best blood that hath most iron in 't.
To edge resolve with, pouring without stint

[9] The Roundhead represents the Puritans
(Northerners), the Cavalier the followers of
Charles I (Southerners).

For what makes manhood dear.
   Tell us not of Plantagenets,[10]
Hapsburgs, and Guelfs,[11] whose thin bloods crawl   340
Down from some victor in a border-brawl!
   How poor their outworn coronets,
Matched with one leaf of that plain civic wreath
Our brave for honor's blazon shall bequeath,
   Through whose desert a rescued Nation sets   345
Her heel on treason, and the trumpet hears
Shout victory, tingling Europe's sullen ears
   With vain resentments and more vain regrets!

XI.

      Not in anger, not in pride,
      Pure from passion's mixture rude   350
      Ever to base earth allied,
      But with far-heard gratitude,
      Still with heart and voice renewed,
To heroes living and dear martyrs dead,
The strain should close that consecrates our brave.   355
   Lift the heart and lift the head!
      Lofty be its mood and grave,
      Not without a martial ring,
      Not without a prouder tread
      And a peal of exultation: 360
      Little right has he to sing
      Through whose heart in such an hour
      Beats no march of conscious power,
      Sweeps no tumult of elation!
      'T is no Man we celebrate,   365
      By his country's victories great,
   A hero half, and half the whim of Fate,
      But the pith and marrow of a Nation
      Drawing force from all her men,
      Highest, humblest, weakest, all,   370
      For her time of need, and then
      Pulsing it again through them,
Till the basest can no longer cower,
Feeling his soul spring up divinely tall,
Touched but in passing by her mantle-hem.   375
Come back, then, noble pride, for 't is her dower!
      How could poet ever tower,

---

[10] Line of English kings from Henry II (1154) to Richard III (1485).
[11] Hapsburgs: rulers of the Holy Roman Empire from the mid-fifteenth to the eighteenth centuries; Guelfs: the papal party in medieval Italy.

If his passions, hopes, and fears,
If his triumphs and his tears,
Kept not measure with his people?   380
Boom, cannon, boom to all the winds and waves!
Clash out, glad bells, from every rocking steeple!
Banners, adance with triumph, bend your staves!
    And from every mountain-peak
    Let beacon-fire to answering beacon speak,   385
Katahdin tell Monadnock, Whiteface[12] he,
And so leap on in light from sea to sea,
    Till the glad news be sent
    Across a kindling continent,
Making earth feel more firm and air breathe braver: 390
"Be proud! for she is saved, and all have helped to save her!
She that lifts up the manhood of the poor,
She of the open soul and open door,
With room about her hearth for all mankind!
The fire is dreadful in her eyes no more;   395
From her bold front the helm she doth unbind,
Sends all her handmaid armies back to spin,
And bids her navies, that so lately hurled
Their crashing battle, hold their thunders in,
Swimming like birds of calm along the unharmful shore.   400
No challenge sends she to the elder world,
That looked askance and hated; a light scorn
Plays o'er her mouth, as round her mighty knees
She calls her children back, and waits the morn
Of nobler day, enthroned between her subject seas."   405

XII.

Bow down, dear Land, for thou hast found release!
    Thy God, in these distempered days,
    Hath taught thee the sure wisdom of His ways,
And through thine enemies hath wrought thy peace!
    Bow down in prayer and praise!   410
No poorest in thy borders but may now
Lift to the juster skies a man's enfranchised brow.
O Beautiful! my Country! ours once more!
Smoothing thy gold of war-dishevelled hair
O'er such sweet brows as never other wore,   415
    And letting thy set lips,
    Freed from wrath's pale eclipse,
The rosy edges of their smile lay bare,

[12] Mountains in Maine, New Hampshire, and New
York, respectively.

What words divine of lover or of poet
Could tell our love and make thee know it,   420
Among the Nations bright beyond compare?
     What were our lives without thee?
     What all our lives to save thee?
     We reck not what we gave thee;
     We will not dare to doubt thee,   425
But ask whatever else, and we will dare!
1865

---

from The Biglow Papers, Second Series

from **Introduction**

THE COURTIN'*

God makes sech nights, all white an' still
    Fur 'z you can look or listen,
Moonshine an' snow on field an' hill,
    All silence an' all glisten.

Zekle crep' up quite unbeknown   5
    An' peeked in thru' the winder,
An' there sot Huldy all alone,
    'ith no one nigh to hender.

A fireplace filled the room's one side
    With half a cord o' wood in—   10
There warn't no stoves (tell comfort died)
    To bake ye to a puddin'.

---

* A brief version of 44 lines of the poem appeared in *The Biglow Papers, First Series* (1848). In the introduction to the *Second Series,* Lowell explains why and how he expanded it: "The only attempt I had ever made at anything like a pastoral (if that may be called an attempt which was the result almost of pure accident) was in 'The Courtin.'" While the Introduction to the First Series was going through the press, I received word from the printer that there was a blank page left which must be filled. I sat down at once and improvised another fictitious 'notice of the press,' in which, because verse would fill up space more cheaply than prose, I inserted an extract from a supposed ballad of Mr. Biglow. I kept no copy of it, and the printer, as directed, cut it off when the gap was filled. Presently I began to receive letters asking for the rest of it, sometimes for the *balance* of it. I had none, but to answer such demands, I patched a conclusion upon it in a later edition. Those who had only the first continued to importune me. Afterward, being asked to write it out as an autograph for the Baltimore Sanitary Commission Fair, I added other verses, into some of which I infused a little more sentiment in a homely way, and after a fashion completed it by sketching in the characters and making a connected story. Most likely I have spoiled it, but I shall put it at the end of this Introduction to answer once for all those kindly importunings."

The wa'nut logs shot sparkles out
    Towards the pootiest, bless her,
An' leetle flames danced all about 15
    The chiny on the dresser.

Agin the chimbley crook-necks[1] hung,
    An' in amongst 'em rusted
The ole queen's-arm[2] thet gran'ther Young
    Fetched back f'om Concord busted. 20

The very room, coz she was in,
    Seemed warm f'om floor to ceilin',
An' she looked full ez rosy agin
    Ez the apples she was peelin'.

'T was kin' o' kingdom-come to look 25
    On sech a blessed cretur,
A dogrose blushin' to a brook
    Ain't modester nor sweeter.

He was six foot o' man, A 1,
    Clear grit an' human natur', 30
None could n't quicker pitch a ton
    Nor dror a furrer straighter.

He 'd sparked it with full twenty gals,
    Hed squired 'em, danced 'em, druv 'em,
Fust this one, an' then thet, by spells— 35
    All is, he could n't love 'em.

But long o' her his veins 'ould run
    All crinkly like curled maple,
The side she breshed felt full o' sun
    Ez a south slope in Ap'il. 40

She thought no v'ice hed sech a swing
    Ez hisn in the choir;
My! when he made Ole Hunderd[3] ring,
    She *knowed* the Lord was nigher.

An' she 'd blush scarlit, right in prayer, 45
    When her new meetin'-bunnet
Felt somehow thru' its crown a pair
    O' blue eyes sot upun it.

[1] Gourds.
[2] Revolutionary War musket.
[3] I.e., Psalm 100. A psalm.

Thet night, I tell ye, she looked *some!*
She seemed to 've gut a new soul,
For she felt sartin-sure he 'd come,
Down to her very shoe-sole.   50

She heered a foot, an' knowed it tu,
A-raspin' on the scraper,—
All ways to once her feelins flew   55
Like sparks in burnt-up paper.

He kin' o' l'itered on the mat,
Some doubtfle o' the sekle,[4]
His heart kep' goin' pity-pat,
But hern went pity Zekle.   60

An' yit she gin her cheer a jerk
Ez though she wished him furder,
An' on her apples kep' to work,
Parin' away like murder.

"You want to see my Pa, I s'pose?"   65
"Wal . . . no . . . I come dasignin' "
"To see my Ma? She 's sprinklin' clo'es
Agin to-morrer's i'nin'."

To say why gals acts so or so,
Or don't, 'ould be presumin';
Mebby to mean *yes* an' say *no*   70
Comes nateral to women.

He stood a spell on one foot fust,
Then stood a spell on t' other,
An' on which one he felt the wust   75
He could n't ha' told ye nuther.

Says he, "I'd better call agin";
Says she, "Think likely, Mister":
Thet last word pricked him like a pin,
An' . . . Wal, he up an' kist her.   80

When Ma bimeby upon 'em slips,
Huldy sot pale ez ashes,
All kin' o' smily roun' the lips
An' teary roun' the lashes.

[4] Sequel.

For she was jes' the quiet kind 85
Whose naturs never vary,
Like streams that keep a summer mind
Snowhid in Jenooary.

The blood clost roun' her heart felt glued
Too tight for all expressin', 90
Tell mother see how metters stood,
An' gin 'em both her blessin'.

Then her red come back like the tide
Down to the Bay o' Fundy,
An' all I know is they was cried 95
In meetin' come nex' Sunday.[5]

1848/1867

Frederick Goddard Tuckerman
1821–1873

Frederick Goddard Tuckerman spent most of his adult life in retirement in rural
western Massachusetts, quietly cultivating his chief interests—literature, botany,
and astronomy. He acquired a modest reputation as an authority on the local
fauna and occasionally published observations on meteorology and eclipses. A
single collection of Tuckerman's poems was published in his lifetime; although
several of his poems earned the praise of his contemporaries, none was included
in the literary anthologies of the next several decades. After Tuckerman's sonnets
had been discovered in the mid-twentieth century and promoted by the writer N.
Scott Momaday, the critic Edmund Wilson could rightly note, "Tuckerman has
emerged at last from the obscurity which the retirement of his life invited."

Frederick Goddard Tuckerman was the third of four children born to Sophia
May and Edward Tuckerman, a prosperous Boston merchant, whose family had
long distinguished itself in literature and science. Frederick Tuckerman attended
the Boston Latin School, enrolled at Harvard, and graduated with a law degree
in 1842. Although he was admitted to the bar, he never practiced law, finding it
distasteful. With an ample inheritance from his father's business, Tuckerman
settled in Greenfield, Massachusetts, in 1847 and married Hannah Lucinda Jones,
who died ten years later, a week after the birth of their third child. With the
exception of two holidays in Europe, Tuckerman lived in virtual seclusion until
his death in 1873.

Tuckerman's contacts with the most respected literary figures of the day were
made largely through his having sent them his privately printed *Poems* (1860),

---

[5] I.e., the wedding was announced in church the
following Sunday.

along with a letter of introduction. Ralph Waldo Emerson was the first to respond, noting that the volume "has given me great pleasure,—more than I dared hoped for in opening it" and urging him to submit several of the poems to the *Atlantic Monthly*. Henry Wadsworth Longfellow graciously acknowledged the volume but expressed little enthusiasm for it. Nathaniel Hawthorne, in the first of what became a fairly extensive exchange of letters, called the volume "remarkable" but questioned whether Tuckerman's poems would ever have a wide audience:

> Their merit does not lie upon the surface, but must be looked for with faith and sympathy, and a kind of insight as when you look into a carbuncle to discover its hidden fire. . . . The greatest difficulty with you will be to get yourself read at all; if you could be read twice, the book might be a success.

Although he continued to write until his death, and his *Poems* was published in England in 1863 and in Boston in 1864 and 1869, Tuckerman hardly seemed interested in exposing his work to public view again. His seclusion and diffidence about his poems recall the life and attitude of another literary recluse, Emily Dickinson, who lived at the same time in nearby Amherst, Massachusetts.

Witter Bynner discovered a large cache of Tuckerman's unpublished poems through correspondence with the poet's granddaughter, and in 1931 he published an edition of Tuckerman's sonnets, now generally regarded as his finest work. "Never did a man write poetry more straightly to himself," Bynner observed in his introduction, "with nothing fictitious. He is isolated in an intense integrity toward nature." Tuckerman's verse indeed reflects the American Romantic tradition of self-reliance in a world whose vital force is nature. And Tuckerman's scientific eye made him a more focused and precise observer of nature than either of that tradition's chief voices, Ralph Waldo Emerson and Walt Whitman. Tuckerman's poetry reflects neither their transcendent urges nor the mystic rapture of Jones Very, his former tutor at Harvard. In contrast, Tuckerman's topics are far more local and personal. His is poetry that begins in observation and ends in meditation—usually on the enigmatic beauty of nature.

Further Reading:
W. Bynner, *The Sonnets of Frederick Goddard Tuckerman*, 1931.
S. Golden, *Frederick Goddard Tuckerman: An American Sonneteer*, 1952.
E. Wilson, *Patriotic Gore*, 1962.
S. Golden, *Frederick Goddard Tuckerman*, 1966.

Text:
The Complete Poems of Frederick Tuckerman, ed. N. S. Momaday, 1965.

from Sonnets

from **First Series**

X

An upper chamber in a darkened house,
Where, ere his footsteps reached ripe manhood's brink,
Terror and anguish were his lot to drink;
I cannot rid the thought nor hold it close
But dimly dream upon that man alone: 5
Now though the autumn clouds most softly pass,
The cricket chides beneath the doorstep stone
And greener than the season grows the grass.
Nor can I drop my lids nor shade my brows,
But there he stands beside the lifted sash;   10
And with a swooning of the heart, I think
Where the black shingles slope to meet the boughs
And, shattered on the roof like smallest snows,
The tiny petals of the mountain ash.
1860

XXVI

For Nature daily through her grand design
Breathes contradiction where she seems most clear,
For I have held of her the gift to hear
And felt indeed endowed of sense divine
When I have found by guarded insight fine,   5
Cold April flowers in the green end of June,
And thought myself possessed of Nature's ear
When by the lonely mill-brook into mine,
Seated on slab or trunk asunder sawn,
The night-hawk blew his horn at summer noon;   10
And in the rainy midnight I have heard
The ground sparrow's long twitter from the pine,
And the catbird's silver song, the wakeful bird
That to the lighted window sings for dawn.
1860

from **Second Series**

XVI

Under the mountain, as when first I knew
Its low dark roof and chimney creeper-twined,
The red house stands; and yet my footsteps find,
Vague in the walks, waste balm and feverfew.
But they are gone: no soft-eyed sisters trip   5
Across the porch or lintels; where, behind,
The mother sat, sat knitting with pursed lip.
The house stands vacant in its green recess,
Absent of beauty as a broken heart.
The wild rain enters, and the sunset wind   10
Sighs in the chambers of their loveliness
Or shakes the pane—and in the silent noons
The glass falls from the window, part by part,
And ringeth faintly in the grassy stones.
1860

XVIII

And change with hurried hand has swept these scenes:
The woods have fallen, across the meadow-lot
The hunter's trail and trap-path is forgot,
And fire has drunk the swamps of evergreens;
Yet for a moment let my fancy plant   5
These autumn hills again: the wild dove's haunt,
The wild deer's walk. In golden umbrage shut,
The Indian river runs, Quonecktacut![1]
Here, but a lifetime back, where falls tonight
Behind the curtained pane a sheltered light   10
On buds of rose or vase of violet
Aloft upon the marble mantel set,
Here in the forest-heart, hung blackening
The wolfbait on the bush beside the spring.
1860

XXII

Put off thy bark from shore, though near the night,
And leaving home and friends and hope behind,
Sail down the lights. Thou scarce canst fail to find,

[1] The Connecticut River.

O desolate one, the morning breaking white,
Some shore of rest beyond the laboring wave.　　5
Ah, 'tis for this I mourn: too long I have
Wandered in tears along life's stormy way
Where day to day no haven or hope reveals.
Yet on the bound my weary sight I keep
As one who sails, a landsman on the deep,　　10
And longing for the land, day after day
Sees the horizon rise and fall and feels
His heart die out, still riding restlessly
Between the sailing cloud and the seasick sea.
1860

from **Fourth Series**

X

Hast thou seen reversed the prophet's miracle—
The worm that, touched, a twig-like semblance takes?
Or hast thou mused what giveth the craft that makes
The twirling spider at once invisible,
And the spermal odor to the barberry flower,　　5
Or heard the singing sand by the cold coast foam,
Or late—in inland autumn groves afar—
Hast thou ever plucked the little chick-wintergreen star
And tasted the sour of its leaf? Then come
With me betimes, and I will show thee more　　10
Than these, of nature's secrecies the least:
In the first morning, overcast and chill,
And in the day's young sunshine, seeking still
For earliest flowers and gathering to the east.
1931

from **Fifth Series**

II

Nor, though she seem to cast with backward hand
Strange measure, sunny cold or cloudy heat,
Or break with stamping rain the farmer's wheat,
Yet in such waste no waste the soul descries,
Intent to glean by barrenest sea and land.　　5
For whoso waiteth, long and patiently,
Will see a movement stirring at his feet—
If he but wait nor think himself much wise.

Nay, from the mind itself a glimpse will rest
Upon the dark; summoning from vacancy   10
Dim shapes about his intellectual lamp,
Calling these in and causing him to see;
As the night-heron waking in the swamp
Lights up the pools with her phosphoric breast.

1931

The Cricket

I

The humming bee purrs softly o'er his flower;
  From lawn and thicket
The dogday locust singeth in the sun
  From hour to hour:
Each has his bard, and thou, ere day be done,   5
  Shalt have no wrong.
So bright that murmur mid the insect crowd,
Muffled and lost in bottom-grass, or loud
  By pale and picket:
Shall I not take to help me in my song   10
  A little cooing cricket?

II

The afternoon is sleepy; let us lie
Beneath these branches whilst the burdened brook,
Muttering and moaning to himself, goes by;
And mark our minstrel's carol whilst we look   15
Toward the faint horizon swooning blue.
  Or in a garden bower,
Trellised and trammeled with deep drapery
  Of hanging green,
  Light glimmering through—   20
There let the dull hop be,
Let bloom, with poppy's dark refreshing flower:
Let the dead fragrance round our temples beat,
Stunning the sense to slumber, whilst between
The falling water and fluttering wind   25
  Mingle and meet,
  Murmur and mix,

No few faint pipings from the glades behind,
   Or alder-thicks:
But louder as the day declines,   30
From tingling tassel, blade, and sheath,
Rising from nets of river vines,
    Winrows and ricks,
     Above, beneath,
      At every breath,   35
At hand, around, illimitably
Rising and falling like the sea,
    Acres of crickets!

III

Dear to the child who hears thy rustling voice
Cease at his footstep, though he hears thee still,   40
Cease and resume with vibrance crisp and shrill,
Thou sittest in the sunshine to rejoice.
Night lover too; bringer of all things dark
And rest and silence; yet thou bringest to me
Always that burthen of the unresting Sea,   45
The moaning cliffs, the low rocks blackly stark;
These upland inland fields no more I view,
But the long flat seaside beach, the wild seamew,[1]
    And the overturning wave!
Thou bringest too, dim accents from the grave   50
To him who walketh when the day is dim,
Dreaming of those who dream no more of him,
With edged remembrances of joy and pain;
And heyday looks and laughter come again:
Forms that in happy sunshine lie and leap,   55
With faces where but now a gap must be,
Renunciations, and partitions deep
And perfect tears, and crowning vacancy!
And to thy poet at the twilight's hush,
No chirping touch of lips with laugh and blush,   60
But wringing arms, hearts wild with love and woe,
Closed eyes, and kisses that would not let go!

IV

So wert thou loved in that old graceful time
   When Greece was fair,
While god and hero hearkened to thy chime;   65
   Softly astir

---

[1] Sea gull.

Where the long grasses fringed Caÿster's lip;[2]
Long-drawn, with glimmering sails of swan and ship,
    And ship and swan;
    Or where
    Reedy Eurotas[3] ran.   70
Did that low warble teach thy tender flute
    Xenaphyle?[4]
Its breathings mild? say! did the grasshopper
Sit golden in thy purple hair   75
    O Psammathe?[5]
    Or wert thou mute,
Grieving for Pan[6] amid the alders there?
And by the water and along the hill
That thirsty tinkle in the herbage still,
Though the lost forest wailed to horns of Arcady?[7]   80

V

Like the Enchanter[8] old—
Who sought mid the dead water's weeds and scum
For evil growths beneath the moonbeam cold,
    Or mandrake or dorcynium;[9]
And touched the leaf that opened both his ears,   85
So that articulate voices now he hears
In cry of beast, or bird, or insect's hum,—
Might I but find thy knowledge in thy song!
    That twittering tongue,
Ancient as light, returning like the years.   90
    So might I be,
Unwise to sing, thy true interpreter
Through denser stillness and in sounder dark,
Than ere thy notes have pierced to harrow me.   95
    So might I stir
    The world to hark
    To thee my lord and lawgiver,
And cease my quest:
Content to bring thy wisdom to the world;   100
Content to gain at last some low applause,
    Now low, now lost
Like thine from mossy stone, amid the stems and straws,

---

[2] The Cayster River empties into the Aegean Sea near the ancient port of Ephesus in Asia Minor.
[3] River in the Peloponnesus.
[4] Xenophilos, ancient Greek musician.
[5] Mother of Linus, hero in Greek myth.
[6] Greek god of fields, forests, and animals, and inventor of the flute.
[7] Ancient pastoral area in the Peloponnesus, where believers in the god Pan claimed to hear him piping in the woods.
[8] Melampus, a prophet in Greek myth who could comprehend the language of birds and animals.
[9] Mandrake; dorcynium: plants thought to possess human attributes and magical powers.

Or garden gravemound tricked and dressed—
  Powdered and pearled   105
    By stealing frost—
In dusky rainbow beauty of euphorbias!
For larger would be less indeed, and like
The ceaseless simmer in the summer grass
To him who toileth in the windy field,   110
  Or where the sunbeams strike,
Naught in innumerable numerousness.
    So might I much possess,
    So much must yield;
But failing this, the dell and grassy dike,   115
The water and the waste shall still be dear,
And all the pleasant plots and places
  Where thou hast sung, and I have hung
    To ignorantly hear.
Then Cricket, sing thy song! or answer mine!   120
Thine whispers blame, but mine has naught but praises.
It matters not. Behold! the autumn goes,
  The shadow grows,
The moments take hold of eternity;
Even while we stop to wrangle or repine   125
  Our lives are gone—
  Like thinnest mist,
Like yon escaping color in the tree;
Rejoice! rejoice! whilst yet the hours exist—
Rejoice or mourn, and let the world swing on   130
Unmoved by cricket song of thee or me.
1950

Under the Locust Blossoms

Under the locust blossoms
That hung and smelt like grapes:
Under the honey-locust blossoms,—
Faintly their breath escapes
And smites my heart; though years have passed since I   5
Beheld those clusters swinging silently,
Silver racemes against that sunset sky:

A sky all over rosy.
I waited for the night

Till the crickets tinkled drowsy   10
In their beds of clover white
Or fell silent at my footfall, one by one.
Did I wait? Did I wander there alone,
Under shadow, in that garden not my own?

'Tis but a shade of odour,   15
A recollected breath,
And I stand, a dark intruder
The swaying flowers beneath,
Alone, and peering on through anxious gloom
For a motion, for a glimmer; did it come?   20
Oh that moment! Oh that breath of locust bloom!

1965

Abraham Lincoln
1809–1865

Abraham Lincoln came to the presidency from a successful law practice and
exercised unprecedented executive authority during a civil war far bloodier and
longer than anyone had foreseen. Midway through the war, Whitman described
Lincoln:

> He has a face like a hoosier Michael Angelo, so awful ugly it becomes beautiful,
> with its strange mouth, its deep cut, cris-cross lines, and its doughnut complex-
> ion. . . . He has shown, I sometimes think, an almost supernatural tack in keeping
> the ship afloat at all, with head steady, not only not going down, and now
> certain not to, but with proud and resolute spirit, and flag flying in sight of the
> world, menacing and high as ever.

Lincoln's "idiomatic western genius," as Whitman called it, was above all
conspicuous in his spoken and written prose, a supple middle style that was lofty
and colloquial, beautiful and homely, and always got to the point. Lincoln's
prose showed that the basic forms of American humor, including the tall tale and
the anecdote, were appropriate in statecraft as well as literature. For the
thirty-year-old Mark Twain, Lincoln's "With malice toward none" address
proved that simplicity was one of the secrets of eloquence.

Only Andrew Jackson among the presidents was as true a child of the frontier
as Lincoln, though many others claimed birth in a log cabin. Born in a clearing
in Hardin County, Kentucky, to illiterate parents, Lincoln had a harsh father and

a loving mother whom he lost when he was nine. Largely self-educated, Lincoln was deeply read in the few books he could find, including the Bible and Shakespeare, two major sources he drew on in preparing his public addresses.

It was Lincoln's destiny to lead the disunited states through the fire of a civil war that established the Union as we know it. His addresses have passed beyond literature into the heritage, character, and soul of the nation. The style was the man, a powerful genius of a politician joined to the mystical sensitivity of a poet.

Further Reading:
C. B. Strozier, *Lincoln's Quest for Union,* 1982.
S. B. Oates, *Abraham Lincoln: The Man Behind the Myths,* 1984.
G. Vidal, *Lincoln,* 1984.

Text:
R. P. Basler et al., *The Collected Works of Abraham Lincoln,* 9 vols., 1953.

Farewell Address at Springfield, Illinois*

February 11, 1861

My Friends:

No one, not in my situation, can appreciate my feeling of sadness at this parting. To this place, and the kindness of these people, I owe everything. Here I have lived a quarter of a century, and have passed from a young to an old man. Here my children have been born, and one is buried. I now leave, not knowing when or whether ever I may return, with a task before me greater than that which rested upon Washington. Without the assistance of that Divine Being who ever attended him, I cannot succeed. With that assistance, I cannot fail. Trusting in Him who can go with me, and remain with you, and be everywhere for good, let us confidently hope that all will yet be well. To His care commending you, as I hope in your prayers you will commend me, I bid you an affectionate farewell.

1861

---

* Of several slightly differing contemporary printed versions of Lincoln's address on departing Springfield for his inauguration, the one here appeared in *Harper's Weekly.* Lincoln was 52 at the time.

First Inaugural Address[*]

March 4, 1861

Fellow-citizens of the United States:

In compliance with a custom as old as the government itself, I appear before you to address you briefly, and to take, in your presence, the oath prescribed by the Constitution of the United States, to be taken by the President "before he enters on the execution of his office."

I do not consider it necessary at present for me to discuss those matters of administration about which there is no special anxiety or excitement.

Apprehension seems to exist among the people of the Southern States, that by the accession of a Republican Administration, their property, and their peace, and personal security, are to be endangered. There has never been any reasonable cause for such apprehension. Indeed, the most ample evidence to the contrary has all the while existed, and been open to their inspection. It is found in nearly all the published speeches of him who now addresses you. I do but quote from one of those speeches when I declare that "I have no purpose, directly or indirectly, to interfere with the institution of slavery in the States where it exists. I believe I have no lawful right to do so, and I have no inclination to do so." Those who nominated and elected me did so with full knowledge that I had made this, and many similar declarations, and had never recanted them. And more than this, they placed in the platform, for my acceptance, and as a law to themselves, and to me, the clear and emphatic resolution which I now read:

> "*Resolved,* That the maintenance inviolate of the rights of the States, and especially the right of each State to order and control its own domestic institutions according to its own judgment exclusively, is essential to that balance of power on which the perfection and endurance of our political fabric depend; and we denounce the lawless invasion by armed force of the soil of any State or Territory, no matter under what pretext, as among the gravest of crimes."

I now reiterate these sentiments: and in doing so, I only press upon the public attention the most conclusive evidence of which the case is susceptible, that the property, peace and security of no section are to be in any wise endangered by the now incoming Administration. I add too, that all the protection which, consistently with the Constitution and the laws, can be given, will be cheerfully given to all the States when lawfully demanded, for whatever cause—as cheerfully to one section as to another.

[*] South Carolina had seceded from the Union in December 1860, demanding the withdrawal of Federal troops from Fort Moultrie and Fort Sumter at Charleston (South Carolina) Harbor. The rest of the South was in the process of secession as Lincoln was being sworn in. His strategy in dealing with this overwhelming crisis was to treat the session ordinances as unconstitutional and hence of no effect. The seceded states, subject to the police power of national government, were nevertheless assured of all the guarantees of the Constitution.

There is much controversy about the delivering up of fugitives from service or labor. The clause I now read is as plainly written in the Constitution as any other of its provisions:

"No person held to service or labor in one State, under the laws thereof, escaping into another, shall, in consequence of any law or regulation therein, be discharged from such service or labor, but shall be delivered up on claim of the party to whom such service or labor may be due."

It is scarcely questioned that this provision was intended by those who made it, for the reclaiming of what we call fugitive slaves; and the intention of the law-giver is the law. All members of Congress swear their support to the whole Constitution—to this provision as much as to any other. To the proposition, then, that slaves whose cases come within the terms of this clause, "shall be delivered up," their oaths are unanimous. Now, if they would make the effort in good temper, could they not, with nearly equal unanimity, frame and pass a law, by means of which to keep good that unanimous oath?

There is some difference of opinion whether this clause should be enforced by national or by state authority; but surely that difference is not a very material one. If the slave is to be surrendered, it can be of but little consequence to him, or to others, by which authority it is done. And should any one, in any case, be content that his oath shall go unkept, on a merely unsubstantial controversy as to *how* it shall be kept?

Again, in any law upon this subject, ought not all the safeguards of liberty known in civilized and humane jurisprudence to be introduced, so that a free man be not, in any case, surrendered as a slave? And might it not be well, at the same time to provide by law for the enforcement of that clause in the Constitution which guarantees that "the citizens of each State shall be entitled to all privileges and immunities of citizens in the several States"?

I take the official oath to-day, with no mental reservations, and with no purpose to construe the Constitution or laws, by any hypercritical rules. And while I do not choose now to specify particular acts of Congress as proper to be enforced, I do suggest that it will be much safer for all, both in official and private stations, to conform to, and abide by, all those acts which stand unrepealed, than to violate any of them, trusting to find impunity in having them held to be unconstitutional.

It is seventy-two years since the first inauguration of a President under our national Constitution. During that period fifteen different and greatly distinguished citizens, have, in succession, administered the executive branch of the government. They have conducted it through many perils; and, generally, with great success. Yet, with all this scope for [of] precedent, I now enter upon the same task for the brief constitutional term of four years, under great and peculiar difficulty. A disruption of the Federal Union, heretofore only menaced, is now formidably attempted.

I hold, that in contemplation of universal law, and of the Constitution, the Union of these States is perpetual. Perpetuity is implied, if not expressed, in the fundamental law of all national governments. It is safe to assert that no government proper, ever had a provision in its organic law for its own termination. Continue to execute all the express provisions of our national Constitution, and the Union will endure forever —it being impossible to destroy it, except by some action not provided for in the instrument itself.

Again, if the United States be not a government proper, but an association of States in the nature of contract merely, can it, as a contract, be peaceably unmade, by less than all the parties who made it? One party to a contract may violate it—break it, so to speak; but does it not require all to lawfully rescind it?

Descending from these general principles, we find the proposition that, in legal contemplation, the Union is perpetual, confirmed by the history of the Union itself. The Union is much older than the Constitution. It was formed in fact, by the Articles of Association in 1774. It was matured and continued by the Declaration of Independence in 1776. It was further matured and the faith of all the then thirteen States expressly plighted and engaged that it should be perpetual, by the Articles of Confederation in 1778. And finally, in 1787, one of the declared objects for ordaining and establishing the Constitution, was *"to form a more perfect Union."*

But if [the] destruction of the Union, by one, or by a part only, of the States, be lawfully possible, the Union is *less* perfect than before the Constitution, having lost the vital element of perpetuity.

It follows from these views that no State, upon its own mere motion, can lawfully get out of the Union,—that *resolves* and *ordinances* to that effect are legally void, and that acts of violence, within any State or States, against the authority of the United States, are insurrectionary or revolutionary, according to circumstances.

I therefore consider that in view of the Constitution and the laws, the Union is unbroken; and to the extent of my ability I shall take care, as the Constitution itself expressly enjoins upon me, that the laws of the Union be faithfully executed in all the States. Doing this I deem to be only a simple duty on my part; and I shall perform it, so far as practicable, unless my rightful masters, the American people, shall withhold the requisite means, or, in some authoritative manner, direct the contrary. I trust this will not be regarded as a menace, but only as the declared purpose of the Union that it will constitutionally defend and maintain itself.

In doing this there needs to be no bloodshed or violence; and there shall be none, unless it be forced upon the national authority. The power confided to me will be used to hold, occupy, and possess the property and places belonging to the government, and to collect the duties and imposts; but beyond what may be necessary for these objects, there will be no invasion—no using of force against or among the people anywhere. Where hostility to the United States, in any interior locality, shall be so great and so universal, as to prevent competent resident citizens from holding the Federal offices, there will be no attempt to force obnoxious strangers among the people for that object. While the strict legal right may exist in the government to enforce the exercise of these offices, the attempt to do so would be so irritating, and so nearly impracticable with all, that I deem it better to forego, for the time, the uses of such offices.

The mails, unless repelled, will continue to be furnished in all parts of the Union. So far as possible, the people everywhere shall have that sense of perfect security which is most favorable to calm thought and reflection. The course here indicated will be followed, unless current events and experience shall show a modification or change to be proper; and in every case and exigency my best discretion will be exercised according to circumstances actually existing, and with a view and a hope of a peaceful solution of the national troubles, and the restoration of fraternal sympathies and affections.

That there are persons in one section or another who seek to destroy the Union at all events, and are glad of any pretext to do it, I will neither affirm or deny; but if there be such, I need address no word to them. To those, however, who really love the Union, may I not speak?

Before entering upon so grave a matter as the destruction of our national fabric, with all its benefits, its memories and its hopes, would it not be wise to ascertain precisely why we do it? Will you hazard so desperate a step, while there is any possibility that any portion of the ills you fly from have no real existence? Will you, while the certain ills you fly to, are greater than all the real ones you fly from? Will you risk the commission of so fearful a mistake?

All profess to be content in the Union, if all constitutional rights can be maintained. Is it true, then, that any right, plainly written in the Constitution, has been denied? I think not. Happily the human mind is so constituted, that no party can reach to the audacity of doing this. Think, if you can, of a single instance in which a plainly written provision of the Constitution has ever been denied. If, by the mere force of numbers, a majority should deprive a minority of any clearly written constitutional right, it might, in a moral point of view, justify revolution—certainly would, if such a right were a vital one. But such is not our case. All the vital rights of minorities, and of individuals, are so plainly assured to them, by affirmations and negations, guarantees and prohibitions, in the Constitution, that controversies never arise concerning them. But no organic law can ever be framed with a provision specifically applicable to every question which may occur in practical administration. No foresight can anticipate, nor any document of reasonable length contain express provisions for all possible questions. Shall fugitives from labor be surrendered by national or by State authority? The Constitution does not expressly say. *May* Congress prohibit slavery in the territories? The Constitution does not expressly say. *Must* Congress protect slavery in the territories? The Constitution does not expressly say.

From questions of this class spring all our constitutional controversies, and we divide upon them into majorities and minorities. If the minority will not acquiesce, the majority must, or the government must cease. There is no other alternative; for continuing the government, is acquiescence on one side or the other. If a minority, in such case, will secede rather than acquiesce, they make a precedent which, in turn, will divide and ruin them; for a minority of their own will secede from them whenever a majority refuses to be controlled by such minority. For instance, why may not any portion of a new confederacy, a year or two hence, arbitrarily secede again, precisely as portions of the present Union now claim to secede from it? All who cherish disunion sentiments, are now being educated to the exact temper of doing this.

Is there such perfect identity of interests among the States to compose a new Union, as to produce harmony only, and prevent renewed secession?

Plainly, the central idea of secession, is the essence of anarchy. A majority, held in restraint by constitutional checks and limitations, and always changing easily with deliberate changes of popular opinions and sentiments is the only true sovereign of a free people. Whoever rejects it, does, of necessity, fly to anarchy or to despotism. Unanimity is impossible; the rule of a minority, as a permanent arrangement, is wholly inadmissible; so that, rejecting the majority principle, anarchy or despotism in some form is all that is left.

I do not forget the position assumed by some, that constitutional questions are to be decided by the Supreme Court; nor do I deny that such decisions must be binding in any case, upon the parties to a suit, as to the object of that suit, while they are also entitled to very high respect and consideration in all parallel cases by all other departments of the government. And while it is obviously possible that such decision may be erroneous in any given case, still the evil effect following it, being limited to that particular case, with the chance that it may be over-ruled, and never become a precedent for other cases, can better be borne than could the evils of a different practice. At the same time, the candid citizen must confess that if the policy of the government upon vital questions, affecting the whole people, is to be irrevocably fixed by decisions of the Supreme Court, the instant they are made, in ordinary litigation between parties, in personal actions, the people will have ceased to be their own rulers, having to that extent practically resigned their government into the hands of that eminent tribunal. Nor is there in this view any assault upon the court or the judges. It is a duty from which they may not shrink, to decide cases properly brought before them; and it is no fault of theirs if others seek to turn their decisions to political purposes.

One section of our country believes slavery is *right,* and ought to be extended, while the other believes it is *wrong,* and ought not to be extended. This is the only substantial dispute. The fugitive slave clause of the Constitution, and the law for the suppression of the foreign slave trade, are each as well enforced, perhaps, as any law can ever be in a community where the moral sense of the people imperfectly supports the law itself. The great body of the people abide by the dry legal obligation in both cases, and a few break over in each. This, I think, cannot be perfectly cured; and it would be worse in both cases *after* the separation of the sections, than before. The foreign slave trade, now imperfectly suppressed, would be ultimately revived without restriction, in one section; while fugitive slaves, now only partially surrendered, would not be surrendered at all, by the other.

Physically speaking, we cannot separate. We cannot remove our respective sections from each other, nor build an impassable wall between them. A husband and wife may be divorced, and go out of the presence, and beyond the reach of each other; but the different parts of our country cannot do this. They cannot but remain face to face; and intercourse, either amicable or hostile, must continue between them. Is it possible, then, to make that intercourse more advantageous or more satisfactory, *after* separation than *before?* Can aliens make treaties easier than friends can make laws? Can treaties be more faithfully enforced between aliens than laws can among friends? Suppose you go to war, you cannot fight always; and when, after much loss on both sides, and no gain on either, you cease fighting, the identical old questions, as to terms of intercourse, are again upon you.

This country, with its institutions, belongs to the people who inhabit it. Whenever they shall grow weary of the existing government, they can exercise their *constitutional* right of amending it, or their *revolutionary* right to dismember or overthrow it. I cannot be ignorant of the fact that many worthy and patriotic citizens are desirous of having the national Constitution amended. While I make no recommendation of amendments, I fully recognize the rightful authority of the people over the whole

2309 *Lincoln* · First Inaugural Address

subject to be exercised in either of the modes prescribed in the instrument itself; and I should under existing circumstances favor rather than oppose a fair opportunity being afforded the people to act upon it.

I will venture to add that to me the Convention mode seems preferable, in that it allows amendments to originate with the people themselves, instead of only permitting them to take or reject propositions, originated by others, not especially chosen for the purpose, and which might not be precisely such as they would wish to either accept or refuse. I understand a proposed amendment to the Constitution, which amendment, however, I have not seen, has passed Congress, to the effect that the federal government shall never interfere with the domestic institutions of the States, including that of persons held to service. To avoid misconstruction of what I have said, I depart from my purpose not to speak of particular amendments, so far as to say that holding such a provision to now be implied constitutional law, I have no objection to its being made express and irrevocable.

The Chief Magistrate derives all his authority from the people, and they have conferred none upon him to fix terms for the separation of the States. The people themselves can do this also if they choose; but the executive, as such, has nothing to do with it. His duty is to administer the present government, as it came to his hands, and to transmit it, unimpaired by him, to his successor.

Why should there not be a patient confidence in the ultimate justice of the people? Is there any better or equal hope, in the world? In our present differences, is either party without faith of being in the right? If the Almighty Ruler of nations, with his eternal truth and justice, be on your side of the North or on yours of the South, that truth, and that justice, will surely prevail, by the judgment of this great tribunal, the American people.

By the frame of the government under which we live, this same people have wisely given their public servants but little power for mischief; and have, with equal wisdom, provided for the return of that little to their own hands at very short intervals.

While the people retain their virtue and vigilance, no administration, by any extreme of wickedness or folly, can very seriously injure the government in the short space of four years.

My countrymen, one and all, think calmly and *well,* upon this whole subject. Nothing valuable can be lost by taking time. If there be an object to *hurry* any of you, in hot haste, to a step which you would never take *deliberately,* that object will be frustrated by taking time; but no good object can be frustrated by it. Such of you as are now dissatisfied, still have the old Constitution unimpaired, and, on the sensitive point, the laws of your own framing under it; while the new administration will have no immediate power, if it would, to change either. If it were admitted that you who are dissatisfied, hold the right side in the dispute, there still is no single good reason for precipitate action. Intelligence, patriotism, Christianity, and a firm reliance on Him, who has never yet forsaken this favored land, are still competent to adjust, in the best way, all our present difficulty.

In *your* hands, my dissatisfied fellow countrymen, and not in *mine,* is the momentous issue of civil war. The government will not assail *you.* You can have no conflict, without being yourselves the aggressors. *You* have no oath registered in Heaven to destroy the government, while *I* shall have the most solemn one to "preserve, protect and defend" it.

I am loth to close. We are not enemies, but friends. We must not be enemies. Though passion may have strained, it must not break our bonds of affection. The mystic chords of memory, stretching from every battle-field, and patriot grave, to every living heart and hearth-stone, all over this broad land, will yet swell the chorus of the Union, when again touched, as surely they will be, by the better angels of our nature.

1861

Letter to General Joseph Hooker[*]

[January 26, 1863]

Executive Mansion,
Washington, January 26, 1863.

Major-General Hooker:
General.

I have placed you at the head of the Army of the Potomac. Of course I have done this upon what appear to me to be sufficient reasons. And yet I think it best for you to know that there are some things in regard to which, I am not quite satisfied with you. I believe you to be a brave and skilful soldier, which, of course, I like. I also believe you do not mix politics with your profession, in which you are right. You have confidence in yourself, which is a valuable, if not an indispensable quality. You are ambitious, which, within reasonable bounds, does good rather than harm. But I think that during Gen. Burnside's command of the Army, you have taken counsel of your ambition, and thwarted him as much as you could, in which you did a great wrong to the country, and to a most meritorious and honorable brother officer. I have heard, in such a way as to believe it, of your recently saying that both the Army and the Government needed a Dictator. Of course it was not *for* this, but in spite of it, that I have given you the command. Only those generals who gain successes, can set up dictators. What I now ask of you is military success, and I will risk the dictatorship. The government will support you to the utmost of its ability, which is neither more nor less than it has done and will do for all commanders. I much fear that the spirit which you have aided to infuse into the Army, of criticizing their Commander, and withholding confidence from him, will now turn upon you. I shall assist you as far as I can, to put it down. Neither you, nor Napoleon, if he were alive again, could get any good out of an army, while such a spirit prevails in it.

---

[*] As the Civil War began, Winfield Scott, in his seventies and a hero of the Mexican War, was commander of the Union army. Then followed between 1861 and 1863 a long and rapid succession of unsuccessful generals as Lincoln sought a competent battlefield strategist: McDowell, McClellan, Pope, McClellan again, Burnside, Hooker, and Meade. Joseph Hooker was Lincoln's choice after Burnside's disaster at Fredericksburg, Virginia. (Lincoln's frank tone and cool personal appraisal are unique in high military annals.) Hooker was defeated, however, in Robert E. Lee's most "elegant" victory, at Chancellorsville, Virginia, in May 1863, and resigned his command less than a month later. Hooker later fought well under General Ulysses S. Grant at Chattanooga, Tennessee.

And now, beware of rashness. Beware of rashness, but with energy, and sleepless vigilance, go forward, and give us victories.

Yours very truly

A. Lincoln.

1863

Address Delivered at the Dedication of the Cemetery at Gettysburg[*]

November 19, 1863

Four score and seven years ago our fathers brought forth on this continent, a new nation, conceived in Liberty, and dedicated to the proposition that all men are created equal.

Now we are engaged in a great civil war, testing whether that nation, or any nation so conceived and so dedicated, can long endure. We are met on a great battle-field of that war. We have come to dedicate a portion of that field, as a final resting place for those who here gave their lives that that nation might live. It is altogether fitting and proper that we should do this.

But, in a larger sense, we can not dedicate—we can not consecrate—we can not hallow—this ground. The brave men, living and dead, who struggled here, have consecrated it, far above our poor power to add or detract. The world will little note, nor long remember what we say here, but it can never forget what they did here. It is for us the living, rather, to be dedicated here to the unfinished work which they who fought here have thus far so nobly advanced. It is rather for us to be here dedicated to the great task remaining before us—that from these honored dead we take increased devotion to that cause for which they gave the last full measure of devotion—that we here highly resolve that these dead shall not have died in vain—that this nation, under God, shall have a new birth of freedom—and that government of the people, by the people, for the people, shall not perish from the earth.

Abraham Lincoln.

November 19, 1863.

1863

---

[*] Only four months before Lincoln's address, Robert E. Lee, with 70,000 Southern troops, had engaged George Gordon Meade, with an army of 90,000, in a three-day battle resulting in over 6,000 deaths and many thousands of injuries. (Meade, to Lincoln's private disgust, failed to pursue the retreating Lee, who led his army safely back to Virginia.) The Union dead were buried on Cemetery Hill, where Lincoln spoke. Lee's defeat at Gettysburg, Pennsylvania, coming on the same day Ulysses Grant took Vicksburg, 1,000 miles to the southwest (and thus cutting the Confederacy in two), spelled the end of the South's realistic chances for world recognition as an independent country, ensured the preservation of the Union, and guaranteed the final abolition of slavery. These prospects notwithstanding, the war was to continue for nearly another two years.

Second Inaugural Address[*]

March 4, 1865

At this second appearing to take the oath of the presidential office, there is less occasion for an extended address than there was at the first. Then a statement, somewhat in detail, of a course to be pursued, seemed fitting and proper. Now, at the expiration of four years, during which public declarations have been constantly called forth on every point and phase of the great contest which still absorbs the attention, and engrosses the energies of the nation, little that is new could be presented. The progress of our arms, upon which all else chiefly depends, is as well known to the public as to myself; and it is, I trust, reasonably satisfactory and encouraging to all. With high hope for the future, no prediction in regard to it is ventured.

On the occasion corresponding to this four years ago, all thoughts were anxiously directed to an impending civil war. All dreaded it—all sought to avert it. While the inaugural address was being delivered from this place, devoted altogether to *saving* the Union without war, insurgent agents were in the city seeking to *destroy* it without war—seeking to dissolve the Union, and divide effects, by negotiation. Both parties deprecated war; but one of them would *make* war rather than let the nation survive; and the other would *accept* war rather than let it perish. And the war came.

One eighth of the whole population were colored slaves, not distributed generally over the Union, but localized in the Southern part of it. These slaves constituted a peculiar and powerful interest. All knew that this interest was, somehow, the cause of the war. To strengthen, perpetuate, and extend this interest was the object for which the insurgents would rend the Union, even by war; while the government claimed no right to do more than to restrict the territorial enlargement of it. Neither party expected for the war, the magnitude, or the duration, which it has already attained. Neither anticipated that the *cause* of the conflict might cease with, or even before, the conflict itself should cease. Each looked for an easier triumph, and a result less fundamental and astounding. Both read the same Bible, and pray to the same God and each invokes His aid against the other. It may seem strange that any men should dare to ask a just God's assistance in wringing their bread from the sweat of other men's faces; but let us judge not that we be not judged. The prayers of both could not be answered; that of neither has been answered fully. The Almighty has his own purposes. "Woe unto the world because of offences! for it must needs be that offences come; but woe to that man by whom the offence cometh!"[1] If we shall suppose that American Slavery is one of those offences which, in the providence of God, must needs come, but which, having continued through His appointed time, He now wills to remove, and that He gives to both North and South, this terrible war, as the woe due

[*] Delivered a month before the Union victories at Petersburg and Richmond (Virginia) and 35 days before the decisive surrender of General Robert E. Lee to the Union commander, Ulysses S. Grant, at Appomattox. On April 14, only weeks before the war ended, Lincoln was fatally shot; he died the following day. In its reason and compassion the Second Inaugural Address is considered to rank in world literature with Pericles' funeral oration to the Athenians.

[1] Matthew 18:7.

to those by whom the offence came, shall we discern therein any departure from those divine attributes which the believers in a Living God always ascribe to Him? Fondly do we hope—fervently do we pray—that this mighty scourge of war may speedily pass away. Yet, if God wills that it continue, until all the wealth piled by the bond-man's two hundred and fifty years of unrequited toil shall be sunk, and until every drop of blood drawn with the lash, shall be paid by another drawn with the sword, as was said three thousand years ago, so still it must be said "the judgments of the Lord, are true and righteous altogether."[2]

With malice toward none; with charity for all; with firmness in the right, as God gives us to see the right, let us strive on to finish the work we are in; to bind up the nation's wounds; to care for him who shall have borne the battle, and for his widow, and his orphan—to do all which may achieve and cherish a just and lasting peace, among ourselves, and with all nations.

1865

Walt Whitman
1819–1892

Whitman is the great bridge figure of nineteenth-century American literature. He links the era of Hawthorne and Thoreau to that of Mark Twain and Henry James. He fulfilled the promise of romanticism while pointing to the open road of modernist form, vision, and experiment. His powerful, imperial presence continues to assert itself in the work of Wallace Stevens, William Carlos Williams, Ezra Pound, Hart Crane, and the generation of Allen Ginsberg. Whitman once said that his leading trait was caution and that there was "something in my nature *furtive* like an old hen." Still, he worshiped boldness, contradiction, and change, shocked contemporaries with his candor about sexuality, and created a radical poetry voicing a radical consciousness: "For I confront peace, security, and all the settled laws, to unsettle them." He was the most ardent of nationalists and said that his book "could not possibly have emerged or been fashion'd or completed, from any other era than the latter half of the Nineteenth Century, nor from any other land than democratic America." Yet he was also America's chief poet of international standing, with followers in the British Isles, Europe, and Scandinavia. Today his work is read in Chinese, Japanese, Russian, and every other major tongue.

When Whitman was born in 1819, in a farmhouse on eastern Long Island, New York, the United States was rural and relatively isolated. The President, James Monroe, had fought in the Revolution and still wore knee breeches. When Whitman died in 1892, in a working-class neighborhood of Camden, New Jersey, a corporation lawyer, Benjamin Harrison, occupied the White House and the United States was a world power.

[2] Psalms 19:9.

During the poet's early years, the Whitmans, descendants of early Dutch and English settlers, fell on hard times and moved from the country districts to Brooklyn, then a thriving, independent city. They were in psychic as well as economic disarray. A failure at farming and business, Walter Whitman, Sr., was "addicted to alcohol," according to his son, and frequently depressed. Of his eight children who survived infancy, four were disturbed or incompetent, but one went on to celebrate "physiology from top to toe . . . Life immense in passion, pulse, and power."

Walt Whitman's dependent childhood, along with all the formal schooling he was ever to have, came to an end when he was about twelve. Like Benjamin Franklin, Mark Twain, and William Dean Howells, he learned the printing trade and in the printing office, the poor-boy's college for many Americans, began to acquire a miscellaneous literary and intellectual culture. He worked in Brooklyn and New York and on Long Island as a typesetter, schoolteacher, newspaper editor, free-lance journalist, storekeeper, and housebuilder. During the 1840s he published a novel, *Franklin Evans,* about the evils of drink, at least sixteen conventional poems, and about two dozen stories and sketches, most of them imitative or hackwork, that nevertheless anticipate many of the themes and images of his mature work.

The poet, Whitman was to say, "must flood himself with the immediate age as with vast oceanic tides." He absorbed the Emersonian gospel of self-trust and the infinitude of the private man; oratory; the writings of George Sand and Thomas Carlyle; science, art, and philosophy; the Free Soil movement; the vibrant life of Broadway and "million-footed Manhattan." He studied linguistics and the American vernacular, believing that "a perfect writer would make words sing, dance, kiss, do the male and female act, bear children . . . or do any thing that man or woman or the natural powers can do." Whitman's discovery of grand opera, which was then enjoying its first vogue in the United States, released his emotions, suggested poetic equivalents for recitative and aria, and helped free him from conventional forms and meters. Although he may have reasoned his way to the right conclusions by using the wrong data, phrenology and other pseudosciences and improving regimens revealed a creative potential within himself that he believed was as large as the American continent. He saw the continent itself and democratic vistas of city and wilderness in a five-thousand-mile journey he took in 1848 from New York to New Orleans and back. Egyptology and Eastern wisdom-writing opened up other vistas of time and space.

"I was simmering, simmering, simmering." In his early thirties Whitman at last found a supreme purpose, to be "a master after my own kind, making the poems of emotions, as they pass or stay, the poems of freedom, and the exposé of personality—singing in high tones democracy and the New World of it through These States." He intended *Leaves of Grass* to be nothing less than a "new Bible" for the new age of democracy and science. A pre-1855 verse fragment suggests the inner drama of Whitman's transformation: "I cannot be awake, for nothing looks to me as it did before, / Or else I am awake for the first time, and all before has been a mean sleep."

Leaves

of

Grass.

Brooklyn, New York:
1855.

Photograph courtesy of the Library of Congress

In July 1855, "after many MS. doings and undoings—(I had great trouble in leaving out the stock 'poetical' touches—but succeeded at last)," Whitman issued the first edition of *Leaves of Grass,* here reprinted in its entirety. A slim volume, with its title stamped on the cloth cover in tendriled letters, Whitman's ninety-six-page book opened with an uncaptioned frontispiece portrait of a bearded man wearing a broad-brimmed hat and an open-necked shirt. The facing title page did not give the author's name. An eccentrically punctuated prose preface, the most decisive of Whitman's critical manifestos, introduced twelve as yet untitled poems, at first glance clusters of prose sentences set up like Bible verses. Not until page twenty-nine did the author declare his identity: "Walt Whitman, An American, one of the roughs, a kosmos, / Disorderly, fleshy and sensual."

Leaves of Grass came into a largely indifferent world in 1855 not as a trial venture, not as a greatly "promising" book, but as a stylistically and substantively achieved masterpiece. "I find it the most extraordinary piece of wit and wisdom that America has yet contributed," Emerson wrote to the new poet. "I give you joy of your free and brave thought. I have great joy in it. I find incomparable things said incomparably well, as they must be. I find the courage of treatment which so delights us, and which large perception only can inspire. I greet you at the beginning of a great career, which yet must have had a long foreground somewhere, for such a start." Emerson's celebrated letter remains unequaled for the generosity, force, and simple justice of its understanding.

Leaves of Grass changed and grew over the next four decades. Whitman wished to endow it with the scope and structure of something monumental, a great tree with many growth rings, a cathedral, a modern city like his million-footed Manhattan. His second edition (1856) added twenty new poems, among them "Crossing Brooklyn Ferry"; his third (1860) added 146, including

"Out of the Cradle Endlessly Rocking" and two cycles, or "clusters," "Calamus" (treating "manly love," or "the love of comrades") and "Children of Adam" (treating heterosexual love); his fourth (1867) added the Civil War cycle "Drum-Taps" and the majestic poem of mourning for Abraham Lincoln, "When Lilacs Last in the Dooryard Bloom'd." By the time Whitman issued his final ("deathbed") edition of 1891–1892, the original ninety-six printed pages of 1855 had grown to 438. After the late 1850s, a markedly tragic element tempered his early, lyric celebrations. Still later, his diction, once assertively American and vernacular, tended to become somewhat denatured, even transatlantic, and he vacillated between a poetry of precise observation and a poetry of ideas and large declarations.

"The proof of a poet," Whitman declared in his preface, "is that his country absorbs him as affectionately as he has absorbed it." Years later he was to concede, "I have not gain'd the acceptance of my time." While he lived, his most fervent readers as a group turned out to be not the working-class American men and women—the democratic leaven—he had hoped to reach but another class altogether, even another nationality: highly cultivated foreign writers and intellectuals like William Michael Rossetti, Oscar Wilde, Algernon Charles Swinburne, Robert Louis Stevenson, Gerard Manley Hopkins, poet laureate Alfred Tennyson, John Addington Symonds, and Professor Edward Dowden of Trinity College, Dublin. One English admirer, Anne Gilchrist, wrote an important appreciation, fell in love with Whitman, and came to America with the hope of marrying him. But aside from his attachments to semiliterate younger men, it was Whitman's book that remained his sole heart's companion, the center of his life. He was willing to go to any length to preserve, protect, and defend it.

Whitman's effective exploitation of Emerson's private letter (he circulated it without permission and used it as promotional material) distressed the Concord sage and his friends. But this episode only marked the beginning of Whitman's unremitting campaign to assure *Leaves of Grass* a breathing space in the world. Like Mark Twain a brilliant publicist, he reviewed his own book on several occasions, planted newspaper stories about his doings and whereabouts, interviewed himself, collaborated with the authors of biographies, polemics, and encomiums, and eagerly sat for hundreds of photographs and portraits that called attention to his trademark flowing beard and open-necked shirts. One unsigned article by Whitman, published in a Camden paper in 1876, touched off a noisy Anglo-American controversy over the extent to which he was allegedly neglected by his compatriots.

For a few years after 1855, Whitman made a living as a newspaper editor and freelance journalist. During the Civil War, having vowed to live a "purged" and "cleansed" life, he turned his back on New York's literary and artistic bohemia and moved to beleaguered Washington. There, supporting himself by part-time clerking in the army paymaster's office, he served as volunteer nurse and comforter—"wound-dresser"—in the military hospitals. This caring for the sick, wounded, and dying may have been the most intense emotional experience of his middle and later years. In 1865 he was appointed to a full-time government clerkship, a job that paid him about $1,600 a year until 1874. By then he was an invalid, having suffered a paralytic stroke the year before, and had moved, permanently, from Washington to Camden. With the major exceptions of trips to Colorado and Canada in 1879 and 1880, he spent the rest of his life in Camden, first as a paying guest in his brother's house and finally as the owner of 328 Mickle Street, "a little old shanty of my own" that he bought for $1,750. Whitman managed to live in frugal comfort, and even build an imposing tomb, on money derived from direct sales of books, fees and honoraria, and gifts from admirers. His average annual income from 1876 to 1892 was $1,270. During those years, as for most of his career, he mainly isolated himself from professional literary people in New York, Philadelphia, and Boston, preferring the company of the small band of disciples that had formed around him and celebrated his birthdays with eucharistic feasts.

An important prose writer as well as a poet, Whitman published *Democratic Vistas* (1871), a searching essay on American society and ideals, and *Specimen Days* (1882), a loosely structured autobiography focusing on the Civil War period. His history after 1855, however, is largely the history of *Leaves of Grass* in its successive editions and collisions with guardians of public taste and morals. Despite Emerson's endorsement, early reviewers called Whitman's poetry "a mass of stupid filth" and its author a pig rooting "among a rotten garbage of licentious thoughts." In 1865 the secretary of the Interior fired Whitman from his clerkship on the grounds that *Leaves of Grass* violated "the rules of decorum and propriety prescribed by a Christian Civilization." Whitman was quickly transferred to an equivalent post in the attorney general's office, but in the hands of supporters like William Douglas O'Connor, Whitman's dismissal became a cause célèbre and served an important purpose in his developing reputation: No longer "one of the roughs," he was now, in O'Connor's words, "The Good Gray Poet," sage, martyr, and redeemer. Fifteen years later a district attorney in Boston found *Leaves of Grass* actionable under "the Public Statutes respecting obscene literature" and in effect forced Whitman's publishers there to withdraw the book. *Leaves of Grass* moved to Philadelphia for its final editions. Such "bruises" and "buffetings" did not discourage its author. Whitman believed that his book was "a candidate for the future" and that its value would be "decided by time."

Further Reading:

H. Traubel, *With Walt Whitman in Camden*, 6 vols., 1906–1982.
N. Arvin, *Whitman*, 1938.
H. S. Canby, *Walt Whitman, An American*, 1943.
R. D. Faner, *Walt Whitman and Opera*, 1951.
R. Chase, *Walt Whitman Reconsidered*, 1955.
Leaves of Grass One Hundred Years After, ed. M. Hindus, 1955.
J. E. Miller, Jr., *A Critical Guide to Leaves of Grass*, 1957.
R. Asselineau, *The Evolution of Walt Whitman*, 2 vols., 1960, 1962.
Whitman: A Collection of Critical Essays, ed. R. H. Pearce, 1962.
G. W. Allen, *The Solitary Singer*, 1967.
E. H. Miller, *Walt Whitman's Poetry: A Psychological Journey*, 1968.
G. W. Allen, *The New Walt Whitman Handbook*, 1975.
S. Black, *Whitman's Journey into Chaos*, 1975.
J. Kaplan, *Walt Whitman: A Life*, 1980.
P. Zweig, *Walt Whitman: The Making of the Poet*, 1984.

Text:

Leaves of Grass, 1855.
See also *The Collected Writings of Walt Whitman*, ed. G. W. Allen and S. Bradley, 1963–.

Leaves of Grass [1855]

*[Preface]**

America does not repel the past or what it has produced under its forms or amid other politics or the idea of castes or the old religions . . . . accepts the lesson with calmness . . . is not so impatient as has been supposed that the slough still sticks to opinions and manners and literature while the life which served its requirements has passed into the new life of the new forms . . . perceives that the corpse is slowly borne from the eating and sleeping rooms of the house . . . perceives that it waits a little while in the door . . . that it was fittest for its days . . . that its action has descended to the stalwart and wellshaped heir who approaches . . . and that he shall be fittest for his days.

The Americans of all nations at any time upon the earth have probably the fullest poetical nature. The United States themselves are essentially the greatest poem. In the history of the earth hitherto the largest and most stirring appear tame and orderly to their ampler largeness and stir. Here at last is something in the doings of man that corresponds with the broadcast doings of the day and night. Here is not merely a nation but a teeming nation of nations. Here is action untied from strings necessarily blind to particulars and details magnificently moving in vast masses. Here is the hospitality which forever indicates heroes . . . . Here are the roughs and beards and space and ruggedness and nonchalance that the soul loves. Here the performance disdaining the trivial unapproached in the tremendous audacity of its crowds and groupings and the push of its perspective spreads with crampless and flowing breadth and showers its prolific and splendid extravagance. One sees it must indeed own the riches of the summer and winter, and need never be bankrupt while corn grows from the ground or the orchards drop apples or the bays contain fish or men beget children upon women.

Other states indicate themselves in their deputies . . . . but the genius of the United States is not best or most in its executives or legislatures, nor in its ambassadors or authors or colleges or churches or parlors, nor even in its newspapers or inventors . . . but always most in the common people. Their manners speech dress friendships —the freshness and candor of their physiognomy—the picturesque looseness of their carriage . . . their deathless attachment to freedom—their aversion to anything indecorous or soft or mean—the practical acknowledgment of the citizens of one state by the citizens of all other states—the fierceness of their roused resentment—their curiosity and welcome of novelty—their self-esteem and wonderful sympathy—their susceptibility to a slight—the air they have of persons who never knew how it felt to stand in the presence of superiors—the fluency of their speech—their delight in music, the sure symptom of manly tenderness and native elegance of soul . . . their good temper and open-handedness—the terrible significance of their elections—the President's taking off his hat to them not they to him—these too are unrhymed poetry. It awaits the gigantic and generous treatment worthy of it.

---

* Untitled in 1855 and omitted from subsequent editions.

The largeness of nature or the nation were monstrous without a corresponding largeness and generosity of the spirit of the citizen. Not nature nor swarming states nor streets and steamships nor prosperous business nor farms nor capital nor learning may suffice for the ideal of man . . . nor suffice the poet. No reminiscences may suffice either. A live nation can always cut a deep mark and can have the best authority the cheapest . . . namely from its own soul. This is the sum of the profitable uses of individuals or states and of present action and grandeur and of the subjects of poets. —As if it were necessary to trot back generation after generation to the eastern records! As if the beauty and sacredness of the demonstrable must fall behind that of the mythical! As if men do not make their mark out of any times! As if the opening of the western continent by discovery and what has transpired since in North and South America were less than the small theatre of the antique or the aimless sleepwalking of the middle ages! The pride of the United States leaves the wealth and finesse of the cities and all returns of commerce and agriculture and all the magnitude of geography or shows of exterior victory to enjoy the breed of fullsized men or one fullsized man unconquerable and simple.

The American poets are to enclose old and new for America is the race of races. Of them a bard is to be commensurate with a people. To him the other continents arrive as contributions . . . he gives them reception for their sake and his own sake. His spirit responds to his country's spirit . . . . he incarnates its geography and natural life and rivers and lakes. Mississippi with annual freshets and changing chutes, Missouri and Columbia and Ohio and Saint Lawrence with the falls and beautiful masculine Hudson, do not embouchure where they spend themselves more than they embouchure into him. The blue breadth over the inland sea of Virginia and Maryland and the sea off Massachusetts and Maine and over Manhattan bay and over Champlain and Erie and over Ontario and Huron and Michigan and Superior, and over the Texan and Mexican and Floridian and Cuban seas and over the seas off California and Oregon, is not tallied by the blue breadth of the waters below more than the breadth of above and below is tallied by him. When the long Atlantic coast stretches longer and the Pacific coast stretches longer he easily stretches with them north or south. He spans between them also from east to west and reflects what is between them. On him rise solid growths that offset the growths of pine and cedar and hemlock and liveoak and locust and chestnut and cypress and hickory and limetree and cottonwood and tuliptree and cactus and wildvine and tamarind and persimmon . . . . and tangles as tangled as any canebrake or swamp . . . . and forests coated with transparent ice and icicles hanging from the boughs and crackling in the wind . . . . and sides and peaks of mountains . . . . and pasturage sweet and free as savannah or upland or prairie . . . . with flights and songs and screams that answer those of the wildpigeon and highhold and orchard-oriole and coot and surf-duck and redshouldered-hawk and fish-hawk and white-ibis and indian-hen and cat-owl and water-pheasant and qua-bird and piedsheldrake and blackbird and mockingbird and buzzard and condor and night-heron and eagle. To him the hereditary countenance descends both mother's and father's. To him enter the essences of the real things and past and present events— of the enormous diversity of temperature and agriculture and mines—the tribes of red aborigines—the weatherbeaten vessels entering new ports or making landings on rocky coasts—the first settlements north or south—the rapid stature and muscle—the haughty defiance of '76, and the war and peace and formation of the constitution

. . . . the union always surrounded by blatherers and always calm and impregnable —the perpetual coming of immigrants—the wharfhem'd cities and superior marine —the unsurveyed interior—the loghouses and clearings and wild animals and hunters and trappers . . . . the free commerce—the fisheries and whaling and gold-digging —the endless gestation of new states—the convening of Congress every December, the members duly coming up from all climates and the uttermost parts . . . . the noble character of the young mechanics and of all free American workmen and workwomen . . . . the general ardor and friendliness and enterprise—the perfect equality of the female with the male . . . . the large amativeness—the fluid movement of the population—the factories and mercantile life and laborsaving machinery—the Yankee swap—the New-York firemen and the target excursion—the southern plantation life —the character of the northeast and of the northwest and southwest—slavery and the tremulous spreading of hands to protect it, and the stern opposition to it which shall never cease till it ceases or the speaking of tongues and the moving of lips cease. For such the expression of the American poet is to be transcendant and new. It is to be indirect and not direct or descriptive or epic. Its quality goes through these to much more. Let the age and wars of other nations be chanted and their eras and characters be illustrated and that finish the verse. Not so the great psalm of the republic. Here the theme is creative and has vista. Here comes one among the wellbeloved stonecutters and plans with decision and science and sees the solid and beautiful forms of the future where there are now no solid forms.

Of all nations the United States with veins full of poetical stuff most need poets and will doubtless have the greatest and use them the greatest. Their Presidents shall not be their common referee so much as their poets shall. Of all mankind the great poet is the equable man. Not in him but off from him things are grotesque or eccentric or fail of their sanity. Nothing out of its place is good and nothing in its place is bad. He bestows on every object or quality its fit proportions neither more nor less. He is the arbiter of the diverse and he is the key. He is the equalizer of his age and land . . . . he supplies what wants supplying and checks what wants checking. If peace is the routine out of him speaks the spirit of peace, large, rich, thrifty, building vast and populous cities, encouraging agriculture and the arts and commerce—lighting the study of man, the soul, immortality—federal, state or municipal government, marriage, health, freetrade, intertravel by land and sea . . . . nothing too close, nothing too far off . . . the stars not too far off. In war he is the most deadly force of the war. Who recruits him recruits horse and foot . . . he fetches parks of artillery the best that engineer ever knew. If the time becomes slothful and heavy he knows how to arouse it . . . he can make every word he speaks draw blood. Whatever stagnates in the flat of custom or obedience or legislation he never stagnates. Obedience does not master him, he masters it. High up out of reach he stands turning a concentrated light . . . he turns the pivot with his finger . . . he baffles the swiftest runners as he stands and easily overtakes and envelops them. The time straying toward infidelity and confections and persiflage he withholds by his steady faith . . . he spreads out his dishes . . . he offers the sweet firmfibred meat that grows men and women. His brain is the ultimate brain. He is no arguer . . . he is judgment. He judges not as the judge judges but as the sun falling around a helpless thing. As he sees the farthest he has the most faith. His thoughts are the hymns of the praise of things. In the talk on the soul and eternity and God off of his equal plane he is silent. He sees eternity less like a play with a prologue and denouement . . . . he sees eternity in men and women . . . he does not see men and women as dreams or dots. Faith is the antiseptic of the soul . . . it pervades the common people and preserves them . . . they never give up believing and expecting and trusting. There is that indescribable freshness and unconsciousness about an illiterate person that humbles and mocks the power of the noblest expressive genius. The poet sees for a certainty how one not a great artist may be just as sacred and perfect as the greatest artist. . . . . . . The power to destroy or remould is freely used by him but never the power of attack. What is past is past. If he does not expose superior models and prove himself by every step he takes he is not what is wanted. The presence of the greatest poet conquers . . . not parleying or struggling or any prepared attempts. Now he has passed that way see after him! there is not left any vestige of despair or misanthropy or cunning or exclusiveness or the ignominy of a nativity or color or delusion of hell or the necessity of hell . . . . . and no man thenceforward shall be degraded for ignorance or weakness or sin.

The greatest poet hardly knows pettiness or triviality. If he breathes into any thing that was before thought small it dilates with the grandeur and life of the universe. He is a seer . . . . he is individual . . . he is complete in himself . . . . the others are as good as he, only he sees it and they do not. He is not one of the chorus . . . . he does not stop for any regulation . . . he is the president of regulation. What the eyesight does to the rest he does to the rest. Who knows the curious mystery of the eyesight? The other senses corroborate themselves, but this is removed from any proof but its own and foreruns the identities of the spiritual world. A single glance of it mocks all the investigations of man and all the instruments and books of the earth and all reasoning. What is marvellous? what is unlikely? what is impossible or baseless or vague? after you have once just opened the space of a peachpit and given audience to far and near and to the sunset and had all things enter with electric swiftness softly and duly without confusion or jostling or jam.

The land and sea, the animals fishes and birds, the sky of heaven and the orbs, the forests mountains and rivers, are not small themes . . . but folks expect of the poet to indicate more than the beauty and dignity which always attach to dumb real objects . . . . they expect him to indicate the path between reality and their souls. Men and women perceive the beauty well enough . . probably as well as he. The passionate tenacity of hunters, woodmen, early risers, cultivators of gardens and orchards and fields, the love of healthy women for the manly form, seafaring persons, drivers of horses, the passion for light and the open air, all is an old varied sign of the unfailing perception of beauty and of a residence of the poetic in outdoor people. They can never be assisted by poets to perceive . . . some may but they never can. The poetic quality is not marshalled in rhyme or uniformity or abstract addresses to things nor in melancholy complaints or good precepts, but is the life of these and much else and is in the soul. The profit of rhyme is that it drops seeds of a sweeter and more luxuriant rhyme, and of uniformity that it conveys itself into its own roots in the ground out of sight. The rhyme and uniformity of perfect poems show the free growth of metrical laws and bud from them as unerringly and loosely as lilacs or roses on a bush, and take shapes as compact as the shapes of chestnuts and oranges and melons and pears, and shed the perfume impalpable to form. The fluency and ornaments of the finest poems or music or orations or recitations are not independent but dependent. All beauty comes from beautiful blood and a beautiful brain. If the greatnesses are in conjunction in a man or woman it is enough . . . . the fact will prevail through the universe . . . . but the gaggery and gilt of a million years will not prevail. Who troubles himself about his ornaments or fluency is lost. This is what you shall do: Love the earth and sun and the animals, despise riches, give alms to every one that asks, stand up for the stupid and crazy, devote your income and labor to others, hate tyrants, argue not concerning God, have patience and indulgence toward the people, take off your hat to nothing known or unknown or to any man or number of men, go freely with powerful uneducated persons and with the young and with the mothers of families, read these leaves in the open air every season of every year of your life, re-examine all you have been told at school or church or in any book, dismiss whatever insults your own soul, and your very flesh shall be a great poem and have the richest fluency not only in its words but in the silent lines of its lips and face and between the lashes of your eyes and in every motion and joint of your body . . . . The poet shall not spend his time in unneeded work. He shall know that the ground is always ready ploughed and manured . . . . others may not know it but he shall. He shall go directly to the creation. His trust shall master the trust of everything he touches . . . . and shall master all attachment.

The known universe has one complete lover and that is the greatest poet. He consumes an eternal passion and is indifferent which chance happens and which possible contingency of fortune or misfortune and persuades daily and hourly his delicious pay. What balks or breaks others is fuel for his burning progress to contact and amorous joy. Other proportions of the reception of pleasure dwindle to nothing to his proportions. All expected from heaven or from the highest he is rapport with in the sight of the daybreak or a scene of the winter woods or the presence of children playing or with his arm round the neck of a man or woman. His love above all love has leisure and expanse . . . . he leaves room ahead of himself. He is no irresolute or suspicious lover . . . he is sure . . . he scorns intervals. His experience and the showers and thrills are not for nothing. Nothing can jar him . . . . suffering and darkness cannot —death and fear cannot. To him complaint and jealousy and envy are corpses buried and rotten in the earth . . . . he saw them buried. The sea is not surer of the shore or the shore of the sea than he is of the fruition of his love and of all perfection and beauty.

The fruition of beauty is no chance of hit or miss . . . it is inevitable as life . . . . it is exact and plumb as gravitation. From the eyesight proceeds another eyesight and from the hearing proceeds another hearing and from the voice proceeds another voice eternally curious of the harmony of things with man. To these respond perfections not only in the committees that were supposed to stand for the rest but in the rest themselves just the same. These understand the law of perfection in masses and floods . . . that its finish is to each for itself and onward from itself . . . that it is profuse and impartial . . . that there is not a minute of the light or dark nor an acre of the earth or sea without it—nor any direction of the sky nor any trade or employment nor any turn of events. This is the reason that about the proper expression of beauty there is precision and balance . . . one part does not need to be thrust above another. The best singer is not the one who has the most lithe and powerful organ . . . the pleasure of poems is not in them that take the handsomest measure and similes and sound.

Without effort and without exposing in the least how it is done the greatest poet brings the spirit of any or all events and passions and scenes and persons some more and some less to bear on your individual character as you hear or read. To do this well is to compete with the laws that pursue and follow time. What is the purpose must surely be there and the clue of it must be there . . . . and the faintest indication is the indication of the best and then becomes the clearest indication. Past and present and future are not disjoined but joined. The greatest poet forms the consistence of what is to be from what has been and is. He drags the dead out of their coffins and stands them again on their feet . . . . he says to the past, Rise and walk before me that I may realize you. He learns the lesson . . . . he places himself where the future becomes present. The greatest poet does not only dazzle his rays over character and scenes and passions . . . he finally ascends and finishes all . . . he exhibits the pinnacles that no man can tell what they are for or what is beyond . . . . he glows a moment on the extremest verge. He is most wonderful in his last half-hidden smile or frown . . . by that flash of the moment of parting the one that sees it shall be encouraged or terrified afterward for many years. The greatest poet does not moralize or make applications of morals . . . he knows the soul. The soul has that measureless pride which consists in never acknowledging any lessons but its own. But it has sympathy as measureless as its pride and the one balances the other and neither can stretch too far while it stretches in company with the other. The inmost secrets of art sleep with the twain. The greatest poet has lain close betwixt both and they are vital in his style and thoughts.

The art of art, the glory of expression and the sunshine of the light of letters is simplicity. Nothing is better than simplicity . . . . nothing can make up for excess or for the lack of definiteness. To carry on the heave of impulse and pierce intellectual depths and give all subjects their articulations are powers neither common nor very uncommon. But to speak in literature with the perfect rectitude and insousiance of the movements of animals and the unimpeachableness of the sentiment of trees in the woods and grass by the roadside is the flawless triumph of art. If you have looked on him who has achieved it you have looked on one of the masters of the artists of all nations and times. You shall not contemplate the flight of the graygull over the bay or the mettlesome action of the blood horse or the tall leaning of sunflowers on their stalk or the appearance of the sun journeying through heaven or the appearance of the moon afterward with any more satisfaction than you shall contemplate him. The greatest poet has less a marked style and is more the channel of thoughts and things without increase or diminution, and is the free channel of himself. He swears to his art, I will not be meddlesome, I will not have in my writing any elegance or effect or originality to hang in the way between me and the rest like curtains. I will have nothing hang in the way, not the richest curtains. What I tell I tell for precisely what it is. Let who may exalt or startle or fascinate or soothe I will have purposes as health or heat or snow has and be as regardless of observation. What I experience or portray shall go from my composition without a shred of my composition. You shall stand by my side and look in the mirror with me.

The old red blood and stainless gentility of great poets will be proved by their unconstraint. A heroic person walks at his ease through and out of that custom or precedent or authority that suits him not. Of the traits of the brotherhood of writers savans musicians inventors and artists nothing is finer than silent defiance advancing from new free forms. In the need of poems philosophy politics mechanism science behaviour, the craft of art, an appropriate native grand-opera, shipcraft, or any craft, he is greatest forever and forever who contributes the greatest original practical example. The cleanest expression is that which finds no sphere worthy of itself and makes one.

The messages of great poets to each man and woman are, Come to us on equal terms, Only then can you understand us, We are no better than you, What we enclose you enclose, What we enjoy you may enjoy. Did you suppose there could be only one Supreme? We affirm there can be unnumbered Supremes, and that one does not countervail another any more than one eyesight countervails another .. and that men can be good or grand only of the consciousness of their supremacy within them. What do you think is the grandeur of storms and dismemberments and the deadliest battles and wrecks and the wildest fury of the elements and the power of the sea and the motion of nature and of the throes of human desires and dignity and hate and love? It is that something in the soul which says, Rage on, Whirl on, I tread master here and everywhere, Master of the spasms of the sky and of the shatter of the sea, Master of nature and passion and death, And of all terror and all pain.

The American bards shall be marked for generosity and affection and for encouraging competitors .. They shall be kosmos .. without monopoly or secrecy .. glad to pass any thing to any one .. hungry for equals night and day. They shall not be careful of riches and privilege . . . . they shall be riches and privilege . . . . they shall perceive who the most affluent man is. The most affluent man is he that confronts all the shows he sees by equivalents out of the stronger wealth of himself. The American bard shall delineate no class of persons nor one or two out of the strata of interests nor love most nor truth most nor the soul most nor the body most . . . . and not be for the eastern states more than the western or the northern states more than the southern.

Exact science and its practical movements are no checks on the greatest poet but always his encouragement and support. The outset and remembrance are there .. there the arms that lifted him first and brace him best . . . . there he returns after all his goings and comings. The sailor and traveler . . the anatomist chemist astronomer geologist phrenologist spiritualist mathematician historian and lexicographer are not poets, but they are the lawgivers of poets and their construction underlies the structure of every perfect poem. No matter what rises or is uttered they sent the seed of the conception of it . . . of them and by them stand the visible proofs of souls . . . . . always of their fatherstuff must be begotten the sinewy races of bards. If there shall be love and content between the father and the son and if the greatness of the son is the exuding of the greatness of the father there shall be love between the poet and the man of demonstrable science. In the beauty of poems are the tuft and final applause of science.

Great is the faith of the flush of knowledge and of the investigation of the depths of qualities and things. Cleaving and circling here swells the soul of the poet yet is president of itself always. The depths are fathomless and therefore calm. The innocence and nakedness are resumed . . . they are neither modest nor immodest. The whole theory of the special and supernatural and all that was twined with it or educed out of it departs as a dream. What has ever happened . . . . what happens and whatever may or shall happen, the vital laws enclose all . . . . they are sufficient for any case and for all cases . . . none to be hurried or retarded . . . . any miracle of affairs or persons inadmissible in the vast clear scheme where every motion and every spear of grass and the frames and spirits of men and women and all that concerns them are unspeakably perfect miracles all referring to all and each distinct and in its place. It is also not consistent with the reality of the soul to admit that there is anything in the known universe more divine than men and women.

Men and women and the earth and all upon it are simply to be taken as they are, and the investigation of their past and present and future shall be unintermitted and shall be done with perfect candor. Upon this basis philosophy speculates ever looking toward the poet, ever regarding the eternal tendencies of all toward happiness never inconsistent with what is clear to the senses and to the soul. For the eternal tendencies of all toward happiness make the only point of sane philosophy. Whatever comprehends less than that . . . whatever is less than the laws of light and of astronomical motion . . . or less than the laws that follow the thief the liar the glutton and the drunkard through this life and doubtless afterward . . . . . . or less than vast stretches of time or the slow formation of density or the patient upheaving of strata—is of no account. Whatever would put God in a poem or system of philosophy as contending against some being or influence is also of no account. Sanity and ensemble characterise the great master . . . spoilt in one principle all is spoilt. The great master has nothing to do with miracles. He sees health for himself in being one of the mass . . . . he sees the hiatus in singular eminence. To the perfect shape comes common ground. To be under the general law is great for that is to correspond with it. The master knows that he is unspeakably great and that all are unspeakably great . . . . that nothing for instance is greater than to conceive children and bring them up well . . . that to be is just as great as to perceive or tell.

In the make of the great masters the idea of political liberty is indispensable. Liberty takes the adherence of heroes wherever men and women exist . . . . but never takes any adherence or welcome from the rest more than from poets. They are the voice and exposition of liberty. They out of ages are worthy the grand idea . . . . to them it is confided and they must sustain it. Nothing has precedence of it and nothing can warp or degrade it. The attitude of great poets is to cheer up slaves and horrify despots. The turn of their necks, the sound of their feet, the motions of their wrists, are full of hazard to the one and hope to the other. Come nigh them awhile and though they neither speak or advise you shall learn the faithful American lesson. Liberty is poorly served by men whose good intent is quelled from one failure or two failures or any number of failures, or from the casual indifference or ingratitude of the people, or from the sharp show of the tushes of power, or the bringing to bear soldiers and cannon or any penal statutes. Liberty relies upon itself, invites no one, promises nothing, sits in calmness and light, is positive and composed, and knows no discouragement. The battle rages with many a loud alarm and frequent advance and retreat . . . . the enemy triumphs . . . . the prison, the handcuffs, the iron necklace and anklet, the scaffold, garrote and leadballs do their work . . . . the cause is asleep . . . . the strong throats are choked with their own blood . . . . the young men drop their eyelashes toward the ground when they pass each other . . . . and is liberty gone out of that place? No never. When liberty goes it is not the first to go nor the second or third to go . . it waits for all the rest to go . . it is the last . . . When the memories of the old martyrs are faded utterly away . . . . when the large names of patriots are laughed at in the public halls from the lips of the orators . . . . when the boys are

no more christened after the same but christened after tyrants and traitors instead
.... when the laws of the free are grudgingly permitted and laws for informers and
bloodmoney are sweet to the taste of the people .... when I and you walk abroad
upon the earth stung with compassion at the sight of numberless brothers answering
our equal friendship and calling no man master—and when we are elated with noble
joy at the sight of slaves .... when the soul retires in the cool communion of the
night and surveys its experience and has much extasy over the word and deed that
put back a helpless innocent person into the gripe of the gripers or into any cruel
inferiority .... when those in all parts of these states who could easier realize the
true American character but do not yet—when the swarms of cringers, suckers,
doughfaces, lice of politics, planners of sly involutions for their own preferment to
city offices or state legislatures or the judiciary or congress or the presidency, obtain
a response of love and natural deference from the people whether they get the offices
or no .... when it is better to be a bound booby and rogue in office at a high salary
than the poorest free mechanic or farmer with his hat unmoved from his head and
firm eyes and a candid and generous heart .... and when servility by town or state
or the federal government or any oppression on a large scale or small scale can be
tried on without its own punishment following duly after in exact proportion against
the smallest chance of escape .... or rather when all life and all the souls of men
and women are discharged from any part of the earth—then only shall the instinct
of liberty be discharged from that part of the earth.

As the attributes of the poets of the kosmos concentre in the real body and soul
and in the pleasure of things they possess the superiority of genuineness over all fiction
and romance. As they emit themselves facts are showered over with light .... the
daylight is lit with more volatile light .... also the deep between the setting and
rising sun goes deeper many fold. Each precise object or condition or combination
or process exhibits a beauty .... the multiplication table its—old age its—the
carpenter's trade its—the grand-opera its .... the hugehulled cleanshaped New-York
clipper at sea under steam or full sail gleams with unmatched beauty .... the American
circles and large harmonies of government gleam with theirs .... and the commonest
definite intentions and actions with theirs. The poets of the kosmos advance through
all interpositions and coverings and turmoils and stratagems to first principles. They
are of use .... they dissolve poverty from its need and riches from its conceit. You
large proprietor they say shall not realize or perceive more than any one else. The
owner of the library is not he who holds a legal title to it having bought and paid
for it. Any one and every one is owner of the library who can read the same through
all the varieties of tongues and subjects and styles, and in whom they enter with ease
and take residence and force toward paternity and maternity, and make supple and
powerful and rich and large. . . . . These American states strong and healthy
and accomplished shall receive no pleasure from violations of natural models and must
not permit them. In paintings or mouldings or carvings in mineral or wood, or in
the illustrations of books or newspapers, or in any comic or tragic prints, or in the
patterns of woven stuffs or any thing to beautify rooms or furniture or costumes, or
to put upon cornices or monuments or on the prows or sterns of ships, or to put
anywhere before the human eye indoors or out, that which distorts honest shapes or
which creates unearthly beings or places or contingencies is a nuisance and revolt. Of
the human form especially it is so great it must never be made ridiculous. Of

ornaments to a work nothing outre can be allowed . . but those ornaments can be allowed that conform to the perfect facts of the open air and that flow out of the nature of the work and come irrepressibly from it and are necessary to the completion of the work. Most works are most beautiful without ornament. . . Exaggerations will be revenged in human physiology. Clean and vigorous children are jetted and conceived only in those communities where the models of natural forms are public every day. . . . . Great genius and the people of these states must never be demeaned to romances. As soon as histories are properly told there is no more need of romances.

The great poets are also to be known by the absence in them of tricks and by the justification of perfect personal candor. Then folks echo a new cheap joy and a divine voice leaping from their brains: How beautiful is candor! All faults may be forgiven of him who has perfect candor. Henceforth let no man of us lie, for we have seen that openness wins the inner and outer world and that there is no single exception, and that never since our earth gathered itself in a mass have deceit or subterfuge or prevarication attracted its smallest particle or the faintest tinge of a shade—and that through the enveloping wealth and rank of a state or the whole republic of states a sneak or sly person shall be discovered and despised . . . . and that the soul has never been once fooled and never can be fooled . . . . and thrift without the loving nod of the soul is only a fœtid puff . . . . and there never grew up in any of the continents of the globe nor upon any planet or satellite or star, nor upon the asteroids, nor in any part of ethereal space, nor in the midst of density, nor under the fluid wet of the sea, nor in that condition which precedes the birth of babes, nor at any time during the changes of life, nor in that condition that follows what we term death, nor in any stretch of abeyance or action afterward of vitality, nor in any process of formation or reformation anywhere, a being whose instinct hated the truth.

Extreme caution or prudence, the soundest organic health, large hope and comparison and fondness for women and children, large alimentiveness and destructiveness and causality, with a perfect sense of the oneness of nature and the propriety of the same spirit applied to human affairs . . these are called up of the float of the brain of the world to be parts of the greatest poet from his birth out of his mother's womb and from her birth out of her mother's. Caution seldom goes far enough. It has been thought that the prudent citizen was the citizen who applied himself to solid gains and did well for himself and his family and completed a lawful life without debt or crime. The greatest poet sees and admits these economies as he sees the economies of food and sleep, but has higher notions of prudence than to think he gives much when he gives a few slight attentions at the latch of the gate. The premises of the prudence of life are not the hospitality of it or the ripeness and harvest of it. Beyond the independence of a little sum laid aside for burial-money, and of a few clapboards around and shingles overhead on a lot of American soil owned, and the easy dollars that supply the year's plain clothing and meals, the melancholy prudence of the abandonment of such a great being as a man is to the toss and pallor of years of moneymaking with all their scorching days and icy nights and all their stifling deceits and underhanded dodgings, or infinitessimals of parlors, or shameless stuffing while others starve . . and all the loss of the bloom and odor of the earth and of the flowers and atmosphere and of the sea and of the true taste of the women and men you pass or have to do with in youth or middle age, and the issuing sickness and desperate revolt at the close of a life without elevation or naivete, and the ghastly chatter of a death without serenity or majesty, is the great fraud upon modern civilization and fore-thought, blotching the surface and system which civilization undeniably drafts, and moistening with tears the immense features it spreads and spreads with such velocity before the reached kisses of the soul. . . Still the right explanation remains to be made about prudence. The prudence of the mere wealth and respectability of the most esteemed life appears too faint for the eye to observe at all when little and large alike drop quietly aside at the thought of the prudence suitable for immortality. What is wisdom that fills the thinness of a year or seventy or eighty years to wisdom spaced out by ages and coming back at a certain time with strong reinforcements and rich presents and the clear faces of wedding-guests as far as you can look in every direction running gaily toward you? Only the soul is of itself . . . . all else has reference to what ensues. All that a person does or thinks is of consequence. Not a move can a man or woman make that affects him or her in a day or a month or any part of the direct lifetime or the hour of death but the same affects him or her onward afterward through the indirect lifetime. The indirect is always as great and real as the direct. The spirit receives from the body just as much as it gives to the body. Not one name of word or deed . . not of venereal sores or discolorations . . not the privacy of the onanist . . not of the putrid veins of gluttons or rumdrinkers . . . not peculation or cunning or betrayal or murder . . no serpentine poison of those that seduce women . . not the foolish yielding of women . . not prostitution . . not of any depravity of young men . . not of the attainment of gain by discreditable means . . not any nastiness of appetite . . not any harshness of officers to men or judges to prisoners or fathers to sons or sons to fathers or of husbands to wives or bosses to their boys . . not of greedy looks or malignant wishes . . . nor any of the wiles practised by people upon themselves . . . ever is or ever can be stamped on the programme but it is duly realized and returned, and that returned in further performances . . . and they returned again. Nor can the push of charity or personal force ever be any thing else than the profoundest reason, whether it brings arguments to hand or no. No specification is necessary . . to add or subtract or divide is in vain. Little or big, learned or unlearned, white or black, legal or illegal, sick or well, from the first inspiration down the windpipe to the last expiration out of it, all that a male or female does that is vigorous and benevolent and clean is so much sure profit to him or her in the unshakable order of the universe and through the whole scope of it forever. If the savage or felon is wise it is well . . . . if the greatest poet or savan is wise it is simply the same . . if the President or chief justice is wise it is the same . . . if the young mechanic or farmer is wise it is no more or less . . if the prostitute is wise it is no more nor less. The interest will come round . . all will come round. All the best actions of war and peace . . . all help given to relatives and strangers and the poor and old and sorrowful and young children and widows and the sick, and to all shunned persons . . all furtherance of fugitives and of the escape of slaves . . all the self-denial that stood steady and aloof on wrecks and saw others take the seats of the boats . . . all offering of substance or life for the good old cause, or for a friend's sake or opinion's sake . . . all pains of enthusiasts scoffed at by their neighbors . . all the vast sweet love and precious suffering of mothers . . . all honest men baffled in strifes recorded or unrecorded . . . . all the grandeur and good of the few ancient nations whose fragments of annals we inherit . . and all the good of the hundreds of far mightier and more ancient nations unknown to us by name or date or location . . . . all that was ever manfully begun, whether it succeeded or no . . . . all that has at any time been well suggested out of the divine heart of man or by the divinity of his mouth or by the shaping of his great hands . . and all that is well thought or done this day on any part of the surface of the globe . . or on any of the wandering stars or fixed stars by those there as we are here . . or that is henceforth to be well thought or done by you whoever you are, or by any one—these singly and wholly inured at their time and inure now and will inure always to the identities from which they sprung or shall spring. . . Did you guess any of them lived only its moment? The world does not so exist . . no parts palpable or impalpable so exist . . . no result exists now without being from its long antecedent result, and that from its antecedent, and so backward without the farthest mentionable spot coming a bit nearer the beginning than any other spot. . . . . Whatever satisfies the soul is truth. The prudence of the greatest poet answers at last the craving and glut of the soul, is not contemptuous of less ways of prudence if they conform to its ways, puts off nothing, permits no let-up for its own case or any case, has no particular sabbath or judgment-day, divides not the living from the dead or the righteous from the unrighteous, is satisfied with the present, matches every thought or act by its correlative, knows no possible forgiveness or deputed atonement . . knows that the young man who composedly periled his life and lost it has done exceeding well for himself, while the man who has not periled his life and retains it to old age in riches and ease has perhaps achieved nothing for himself worth mentioning . . and that only that person has no great prudence to learn who has learnt to prefer real longlived things, and favors body and soul the same, and perceives the indirect assuredly following the direct, and what evil or good he does leaping onward and waiting to meet him again—and who in his spirit in any emergency whatever neither hurries or avoids death.

The direct trial of him who would be the greatest poet is today. If he does not flood himself with the immediate age as with vast oceanic tides . . . . . and if he does not attract his own land body and soul to himself and hang on its neck with incomparable love and plunge his semitic muscle into its merits and demerits . . . and if he be not himself the age transfigured . . . . and if to him is not opened the eternity which gives similitude to all periods and locations and processes and animate and inanimate forms, and which is the bond of time, and rises up from its inconceivable vagueness and infiniteness in the swimming shape of today, and is held by the ductile anchors of life, and makes the present spot the passage from what was to what shall be, and commits itself to the representation of this wave of an hour and this one of the sixty beautiful children of the wave—let him merge in the general run and wait his development. . . . . Still the final test of poems or any character or work remains. The prescient poet projects himself centuries ahead and judges performer or performance after the changes of time. Does it live through them? Does it still hold on untired? Will the same style and the direction of genius to similar points be satisfactory now? Has no new discovery in science or arrival at superior planes of thought and judgment and behaviour fixed him or his so that either can be looked down upon? Have the marches of tens and hundreds and thousands of years made willing detours to the right hand and the left hand for his sake? Is he beloved long and long after he is buried? Does the young man think often of him? and the young woman think often of him? and do the middleaged and the old think of him?

A great poem is for ages and ages in common and for all degrees and complexions and all departments and sects and for a woman as much as a man and a man as much as a woman. A great poem is no finish to a man or woman but rather a beginning. Has any one fancied he could sit at last under some due authority and rest satisfied with explanations and realize and be content and full? To no such terminus does the greatest poet bring . . . he brings neither cessation or sheltered fatness and ease. The touch of him tells in action. Whom he takes he takes with firm sure grasp into live regions previously unattained . . . . thenceforward is no rest . . . . they see the space and ineffable sheen that turn the old spots and lights into dead vacuums. The companion of him beholds the birth and progress of stars and learns one of the meanings. Now there shall be a man cohered out of tumult and chaos . . . . the elder encourages the younger and shows him how . . . they two shall launch off fearlessly together till the new world fits an orbit for itself and looks unabashed on the lesser orbits of the stars and sweeps through the ceaseless rings and shall never be quiet again.

There will soon be no more priests. Their work is done. They may wait awhile . . perhaps a generation or two . . dropping off by degrees. A superior breed shall take their place . . . . the gangs of kosmos and prophets en masse shall take their place. A new order shall arise and they shall be the priests of man, and every man shall be his own priest. The churches built under their umbrage shall be the churches of men and women. Through the divinity of themselves shall the kosmos and the new breed of poets be interpreters of men and women and of all events and things. They shall find their inspiration in real objects today, symptoms of the past and future . . . . They shall not deign to defend immortality or God or the perfection of things or liberty or the exquisite beauty and reality of the soul. They shall arise in America and be responded to from the remainder of the earth.

The English language befriends the grand American expression . . . . it is brawny enough and limber and full enough. On the tough stock of a race who through all change of circumstance was never without the idea of political liberty, which is the animus of all liberty, it has attracted the terms of daintier and gayer and subtler and more elegant tongues. It is the powerful language of resistance . . . it is the dialect of common sense. It is the speech of the proud and melancholy races and of all who aspire. It is the chosen tongue to express growth faith self-esteem freedom justice equality friendliness amplitude prudence decision and courage. It is the medium that shall well nigh express the inexpressible.

No great literature nor any like style of behaviour or oratory or social intercourse or household arrangements or public institutions or the treatment by bosses of employed people, nor executive detail or detail of the army or navy, nor spirit of legislation or courts or police or tuition or architecture or songs or amusements or the costumes of young men, can long elude the jealous and passionate instinct of American standards. Whether or no the sign appears from the mouths of the people, it throbs a live interrogation in every freeman's and freewoman's heart after that which passes by or this built to remain. Is it uniform with my country? Are its disposals without ignominious distinctions? Is it for the evergrowing communes of brothers and lovers, large, well-united, proud beyond the old models, generous beyond all models? Is it something grown fresh out of the fields or drawn from the sea for use to me today here? I know that what answers for me an American must answer for any individual or nation that serves for a part of my materials. Does this answer? or is it without reference to universal needs? or sprung of the needs of the less developed society of special ranks? or old needs of pleasure overlaid by modern science and forms? Does this acknowledge liberty with audible and absolute acknowledgement, and set slavery at nought for life and death? Will it help breed one goodshaped and wellhung man, and a woman to be his perfect and independent mate? Does it improve manners? Is it for the nursing of the young of the republic? Does it solve readily with the sweet milk of the nipples of the breasts of the mother of many children? Has it too the old ever-fresh forbearance and impartiality? Does it look with the same love on the last born and on those hardening toward stature, and on the errant, and on those who disdain all strength of assault outside of their own?

The poems distilled from other poems will probably pass away. The coward will surely pass away. The expectation of the vital and great can only be satisfied by the demeanor of the vital and great. The swarms of the polished deprecating and reflectors and the polite float off and leave no remembrance. America prepares with composure and goodwill for the visitors that have sent word. It is not intellect that is to be their warrant and welcome. The talented, the artist, the ingenious, the editor, the statesman, the erudite . . they are not unappreciated . . they fall in their place and do their work. The soul of the nation also does its work. No disguise can pass on it . . no disguise can conceal from it. It rejects none, it permits all. Only toward as good as itself and toward the like of itself will it advance half-way. An individual is as superb as a nation when he has the qualities which make a superb nation. The soul of the largest and wealthiest and proudest nation may well go half-way to meet that of its poets. The signs are effectual. There is no fear of mistake. If the one is true the other is true. The proof of a poet is that his country absorbs him as affectionately as he has absorbed it.

[Song of Myself]*

[1]

I celebrate myself,
And what I assume you shall assume,
For every atom belonging to me as good belongs to you.

I loafe and invite my soul,
I lean and loafe at my ease . . . . observing a spear of summer grass.   5

looking at nature,

[2]

Houses and rooms are full of perfumes . . . . the shelves are crowded with
    perfumes,
I breathe the fragrance myself, and know it and like it,
The distillation would intoxicate me also, but I shall not let it.

---

* In the 1855 edition of *Leaves of Grass* the poem was untitled and unsectioned. The final title was supplied in 1881. Earlier titles were "Poem of Walt Whitman, an American" and "Walt Whitman."

nature better than the perfumes (atmosphere)

The atmosphere is not a perfume . . . . it has no taste of the distillation . . . . it
   is odorless,
It is for my mouth forever . . . . I am in love with it,   10
I will go to the bank by the wood and become undisguised and naked,
I am mad for it to be in contact with me.

The smoke of my own breath,
Echos, ripples, and buzzed whispers . . . . loveroot, silkthread, crotch and vine,
My respiration and inspiration . . . . the beating of my heart . . . . the passing
   of blood and air through my lungs,   15
The sniff of green leaves and dry leaves, and of the shore and darkcolored
   sea-rocks, and of hay in the barn,
The sound of the belched words of my voice . . . . words loosed to the eddies
   of the wind,
A few light kisses . . . . a few embraces . . . . a reaching around of arms,
The play of shine and shade on the trees as the supple boughs wag,
The delight alone or in the rush of the streets, or along the fields and hillsides,   20
The feeling of health . . . . the full-noon trill . . . . the song of me rising from
   bed and meeting the sun.
Have you reckoned a thousand acres much? Have you reckoned the earth much?
Have you practiced so long to learn to read?
Have you felt so proud to get at the meaning of poems?

Stop this day and night with me and you shall possess the origin of all poems,   25
You shall possess the good of the earth and sun . . . . there are millions of suns
   left,
You shall no longer take things at second or third hand . . . . nor look through
   the eyes of the dead . . . . nor feed on the spectres in books,
You shall not look through my eyes either, nor take things from me,
You shall listen to all sides and filter them from yourself.

learn for yourself.

[3]

I have heard what the talkers were talking . . . . the talk of the beginning and
   the end,   30
But I do not talk of the beginning or the end.

There was never any more inception than there is now,
Nor any more youth or age than there is now;
And will never be any more perfection than there is now,
Nor any more heaven or hell than there is now.   35

Urge and urge and urge,
Always the procreant urge of the world.

Out of the dimness opposite equals advance . . . . Always substance and
   increase,
Always a knit of identity . . . . always distinction . . . . always a breed of life.

To elaborate is no avail . . . . Learned and unlearned feel that it is so.   40

Sure as the most certain sure . . . . plumb in the uprights, well entretied,[1] braced
   in the beams,
Stout as a horse, affectionate, haughty, electrical,
I and this mystery here we stand.
Clear and sweet is my soul . . . . and clear and sweet is all that is not my soul.

Lack one lacks both . . . . and the unseen is proved by the seen,   45
Till that becomes unseen and receives proof in its turn.

Showing the best and dividing it from the worst, age vexes age,
Knowing the perfect fitness and equanimity of things, while they discuss I am
   silent, and go bathe and admire myself.

Welcome is every organ and attribute of me, and of any man hearty and clean,
Not an inch nor a particle of an inch is vile, and none shall be less familiar
   than the rest.   50

I am satisfied . . . . I see, dance, laugh, sing;
As God comes a loving bedfellow and sleeps at my side all night and close on
   the peep of the day,
And leaves for me baskets covered with white towels bulging the house with
   their plenty,
Shall I postpone my acceptation and realization and scream at my eyes,
That they turn from gazing after and down the road,   55
And forthwith cipher and show me to a cent,
Exactly the contents of one, and exactly the contents of two, and which is
   ahead?

[4]

Trippers and askers surround me,
People I meet . . . . . the effect upon me of my early life . . . . of the ward
   and city I live in . . . . of the nation,
The latest news . . . . discoveries, inventions, societies . . . . authors old and
   new,   60
My dinner, dress, associates, looks, business, compliments, dues,
The real or fancied indifference of some man or woman I love,

---

[1] Cross-braced.   *both beautiful*

The sickness of one of my folks—or of myself . . . . or ill-doing . . . . or loss
    or lack of money . . . . or depressions or exaltations,
They come to me days and nights and go from me again,
But they are not the Me myself.   65

Apart from the pulling and hauling stands what I am,
Stands amused, complacent, compassionating, idle, unitary,
Looks down, is erect, bends an arm on an impalpable certain rest,
Looks with its sidecurved head curious what will come next,
Both in and out of the game, and watching and wondering at it.   70

Backward I see in my own days where I sweated through fog with linguists
    and contenders,
I have no mockings or arguments . . . . I witness and wait.

[5]

I believe in you my soul . . . . the other I am must not abase itself to you,
And you must not be abased to the other.

Loafe with me on the grass . . . . loose the stop from your throat,   75
Not words, not music or rhyme I want . . . . not custom or lecture, not even
    the best,
Only the lull I like, the hum of your valved voice.

I mind how we lay in June, such a transparent summer morning;
You settled your head athwart my hips and gently turned over upon me,
And parted the shirt from my bosom-bone, and plunged your tongue to my
    barestript heart,   80
And reached till you felt my beard, and reached till you held my feet.

Swiftly arose and spread around me the peace and joy and knowledge that pass
    all the art and argument of the earth;
And I know that the hand of God is the elderhand of my own,
And I know that the spirit of God is the eldest brother of my own,
And that all the men ever born are also my brothers . . . . and the women my
    sisters and lovers,   85
And that a kelson[2] of the creation is love;
And limitless are leaves stiff or drooping in the fields,
And brown ants in the little wells beneath them,
And mossy scabs of the wormfence, and heaped stones, and elder and mullen
    and pokeweed.

---

rstructure of a ship's keel.

[6]

A child said, What is the grass? fetching it to me with full hands;   90
How could I answer the child? . . . . I do not know what it is any more than
 he.

I guess it must be the flag of my disposition, out of hopeful green stuff woven.

Or I guess it is the handkerchief of the Lord,
A scented gift and remembrancer designedly dropped,
Bearing the owner's name someway in the corners, that we may see and remark,
 and say Whose?   95

Or I guess the grass is itself a child . . . . the produced babe of the vegetation.

Or I guess it is a uniform hieroglyphic,
And it means, Sprouting alike in broad zones and narrow zones,
Growing among black folks as among white,
Kanuck,[3] Tuckahoe,[4] Congressman, Cuff,[5] I give them the same, I receive them
 the same.   100.

And now it seems to me the beautiful uncut hair of graves.

Tenderly will I use you curling grass,
It may be you transpire from the breasts of young men,
It may be if I had known them I would have loved them;
It may be you are from old people and from women, and from offspring taken
 soon out of their mothers' laps,   105
And here you are the mothers' laps.
This grass is very dark to be from the white heads of old mothers,
Darker than the colorless beards of old men,
Dark to come from under the faint red roofs of mouths.

O I perceive after all so many uttering tongues!   110
And I perceive they do not come from the roofs of mouths for nothing.

I wish I could translate the hints about the dead young men and women,
And the hints about old men and mothers, and the offspring taken soon out of
 their laps.

What do you think has become of the young and old men?
And what do you think has become of the women and children?   115

[3] French Canadian.   [5] Black.
[4] Native of tidewater Virginia.

They are alive and well somewhere;
The smallest sprout shows there is really no death,
And if ever there was it led forward life, and does not wait at the end to arrest
    it,
And ceased the moment life appeared.

All goes onward and outward . . . . and nothing collapses,   120
And to die is different from what any one supposed, and luckier.

[7]

Has any one supposed it lucky to be born?
I hasten to inform him or her it is just as lucky to die, and I know it.

I pass death with the dying, and birth with the new-washed babe . . . . and am
    not contained between my hat and boots,
And peruse manifold objects, no two alike, and every one good,   125
The earth good, and the stars good, and their adjuncts all good.
I am not an earth nor an adjunct of an earth,
I am the mate and companion of people, all just as immortal and fathomless as
    myself;
They do not know how immortal, but I know.

Every kind for itself and its own . . . . for me mine male and female,   130
For me all that have been boys and that love women,
For me the man that is proud and feels how it stings to be slighted,
For me the sweetheart and the old maid . . . . for me mothers and the mothers
    of mothers,
For me lips that have smiled, eyes that have shed tears,
For me children and the begetters of children.   135

Who need be afraid of the merge?
Undrape . . . . you are not guilty to me, nor stale nor discarded,
I see through the broadcloth and gingham whether or no,
And am around, tenacious, acquisitive, tireless . . . . and can never be shaken
    away.

[8]

The little one sleeps in its cradle,   140
I lift the gauze and look a long time, and silently brush away flies with my
    hand.

The youngster and the redfaced girl turn aside up the bushy hill,
I peeringly view them from the top.

The suicide sprawls on the bloody floor of the bedroom.
It is so . . . . I witnessed the corpse . . . . there the pistol had fallen.   145

The blab of the pave . . . . the tires of carts and sluff of bootsoles and talk of
    the promenaders,
The heavy omnibus, the driver with his interrogating thumb, the clank of the
    shod horses on the granite floor,
The carnival of sleighs, the clinking and shouted jokes and pelts of snowballs;
The hurrahs for popular favorites . . . . the fury of roused mobs,
The flap of the curtained litter—the sick man inside, borne to the hospital,   150
The meeting of enemies, the sudden oath, the blows and fall,
The excited crowd—the policeman with his star quickly working his passage to
    the centre of the crowd;
The impassive stones that receive and return so many echoes,
The souls moving along . . . . are they invisible while the least atom of the
    stones is visible?
What groans of overfed or half-starved who fall on the flags sunstruck or in
    fits,   155
What exclamations of women taken suddenly, who hurry home and give birth
    to babes,
What living and buried speech is always vibrating here . . . . what howls
    restrained by decorum,
Arrests of criminals, slights, adulterous offers made, acceptances, rejections with
    convex lips,
I mind them or the resonance of them . . . . I come again and again.

[9]

The big doors of the country-barn stand open and ready,   160
The dried grass of the harvest-time loads the slow-drawn wagon,
The clear light plays on the brown gray and green intertinged,
The armfuls are packed to the sagging mow:
I am there . . . . I help . . . . I came stretched atop of the load,
I felt its soft jolts . . . . one leg reclined on the other,   165
I jump from the crossbeams, and seize the clover and timothy,
And roll head over heels, and tangle my hair full of wisps.

[10]

Alone far in the wilds and mountains I hunt,
Wandering amazed at my own lightness and glee,
In the late afternoon choosing a safe spot to pass the night,   170
Kindling a fire and broiling the freshkilled game,
Soundly falling asleep on the gathered leaves, my dog and gun by my side.
The Yankee clipper is under her three skysails . . . . she cuts the sparkle and
    scud,

My eyes settle the land . . . . I bend at her prow or shout joyously from the deck.

The boatmen and clamdiggers arose early and stopped for me,   175
I tucked my trowser-ends in my boots and went and had a good time,
You should have been with us that day round the chowder-kettle.

I saw the marriage of the trapper in the open air in the far-west . . . . the bride
  was a red girl,
Her father and his friends sat near by crosslegged and dumbly smoking . . . .
  they had moccasins to their feet and large thick blankets hanging from their
  shoulders;
On a bank lounged the trapper . . . . he was dressed mostly in skins . . . . his
  luxuriant beard and curls protected his neck,   180
One hand rested on his rifle . . . . the other hand held firmly the wrist of the
  red girl,
She had long eyelashes . . . . her head was bare . . . . her coarse straight locks
  descended upon her voluptuous limbs and reached to her feet.

The runaway slave came to my house and stopped outside,
I heard his motions crackling the twigs of the woodpile,
Through the swung half-door of the kitchen I saw him limpsey and weak,   185
And went where he sat on a log, and led him in and assured him,
And brought water and filled a tub for his sweated body and bruised feet,
And gave him a room that entered from my own, and gave him some coarse
  clean clothes,
And remember perfectly well his revolving eyes and his awkwardness,
And remember putting plasters on the galls of his neck and ankles;   190
He staid with me a week before he was recuperated and passed north,
I had him sit next me at table . . . . my firelock leaned in the corner.

[11]

Twenty-eight young men bathe by the shore,
Twenty-eight young men, and all so friendly,
Twenty-eight years of womanly life, and all so lonesome.   195

She owns the fine house by the rise of the bank,
She hides handsome and richly drest aft the blinds of the window.

Which of the young men does she like the best?
Ah the homeliest of them is beautiful to her.

Where are you off to, lady? for I see you,   200
You splash in the water there, yet stay stock still in your room.

Dancing and laughing along the beach came the twenty-ninth bather,
The rest did not see her, but she saw them and loved them.

The beards of the young men glistened with wet, it ran from their long hair,
Little streams passed all over their bodies.   205

An unseen hand also passed over their bodies,
It descended tremblingly from their temples and ribs.

The young men float on their backs, their white bellies swell to the sun . . . .
    they do not ask who siezes fast to them,
They do not know who puffs and declines with pendant and bending arch,
They do not think whom they souse with spray.   210

[12]

The butcher-boy puts off his killing-clothes, or sharpens his knife at the stall in
    the market,
I loiter enjoying his repartee and his shuffle[6] and breakdown.[7]
Blacksmiths with grimed and hairy chests environ the anvil,
Each has his main-sledge . . . . they are all out . . . . there is a great heat in the
    fire.

From the cinder-strewed threshold I follow their movements,   215
The lithe sheer of their waists plays even with their massive arms,
Overhand the hammers roll—overhand so slow—overhand so sure,
They do not hasten, each man hits in his place.

[13]

The negro holds firmly the reins of his four horses . . . . the block swags
    underneath on its tied-over chain,
The negro that drives the huge dray of the stoneyard . . . . steady and tall he
    stands poised on one leg on the stringpiece,[8]   220
His blue shirt exposes his ample neck and breast and loosens over his hipband,
His glance is calm and commanding . . . . he tosses the slouch of his hat away
    from his forehead,
The sun falls on his crispy hair and moustache . . . . falls on the black of his
    polish'd and perfect limbs.

I behold the picturesque giant and love him . . . . and I do not stop there,
I go with the team also.   225

---

[6] Slow dance.   [8] Connective or supporting timber.
[7] Rollicking dance.

In me the caresser of life wherever moving . . . . backward as well as forward
  slueing,
To niches aside and junior bending, *not a person or object missing*
absorbing all to myself and for the song.
Oxen that rattle the yoke or halt in the shade, what is that you express in your
  eyes?
It seems to me more than all the print I have read in my life.

My tread scares the wood-drake and wood-duck on my distant and daylong
  ramble,   230
They rise together, they slowly circle around.
. . . . I believe in those winged purposes,
And acknowledge the red yellow and white playing within me,
And consider the green and violet and the tufted crown intentional;
And do not call the tortoise unworthy because she is not something else,   235
And the mockingbird in the swamp never studied the gamut, yet trills pretty
  well to me,
And the look of the bay mare shames silliness out of me.

[14]
The wild gander leads his flock through the cool night,
Ya-honk! he says, and sounds it down to me like an invitation;
The pert may suppose it meaningless, but I listen closer,   240
I find its purpose and place up there toward the November sky.

The sharphoofed moose of the north, the cat on the housesill, the chickadee, the
  prairie-dog,
The litter of the grunting sow as they tug at her teats,
The brood of the turkeyhen, and she with her halfspread wings,
I see in them and myself the same old law.   245

The press of my foot to the earth springs a hundred affections,
They scorn the best I can do to relate them.

I am enamoured of growing outdoors,
Of men that live among cattle or taste of the ocean or woods,
Of the builders and steerers of ships, of the wielders of axes and mauls, of the
  drivers of horses,   250
I can eat and sleep with them week in and week out.

What is commonest and cheapest and nearest and easiest is Me,
Me going in for my chances, spending for vast returns,
Adorning myself to bestow myself on the first that will take me,
Not asking the sky to come down to my goodwill,   255
Scattering it freely forever.

[15]

The pure contralto sings in the organloft,
The carpenter dresses his plank . . . . the tongue of his foreplane whistles its
   wild ascending lisp,
The married and unmarried children ride home to their thanksgiving dinner,
The pilot seizes the king-pin, he heaves down with a strong arm,   260
The mate stands braced in the whaleboat, lance and harpoon are ready,
The duck-shooter walks by silent and cautious stretches,
The deacons are ordained with crossed hands at the altar,
The spinning-girl retreats and advances to the hum of the big wheel,
The farmer stops by the bars of a Sunday and looks at the oats and rye,   265
The lunatic is carried at last to the asylum a confirmed case,
He will never sleep any more as he did in the cot in his mother's bedroom;
The jour printer[9] with gray head and gaunt jaws works at his case,
He turns his quid of tobacco, his eyes get blurred with the manuscript;
The malformed limbs are tied to the anatomist's table,   270
What is removed drops horribly in a pail;
The quadroon girl is sold at the stand . . . . the drunkard nods by the barroom
   stove,
The machinist rolls up his sleeves . . . . the policeman travels his beat . . . . the
   gate-keeper marks who pass,
The young fellow drives the express-wagon . . . . I love him though I do not
   know him;
The half-breed straps on his light boots to compete in the race,   275
The western turkey-shooting draws old and young . . . . some lean on their
   rifles, some sit on logs,
Out from the crowd steps the marksman and takes his position and levels his
   piece;
The groups of newly-come immigrants cover the wharf or levee,
The woollypates hoe in the sugarfield, the overseer views them from his saddle;
The bugle calls in the ballroom, the gentlemen run for their partners, the
   dancers bow to each other;   280
The youth lies awake in the cedar-roofed garret and harks to the musical rain,
The Wolverine[10] sets traps on the creek that helps fill the Huron,
The reformer ascends the platform, he spouts with his mouth and nose,
The company returns from its excursion, the darkey brings up the rear and
   bears the well-riddled target,
The squaw wrapt in her yellow-hemmed cloth is offering moccasins and
   beadbags for sale,   285
The connoisseur peers along the exhibition-gallery with halfshut eyes bent
   sideways,
The deckhands make fast the steamboat, the plank is thrown for the shoregoing
   passengers,

---

[9] Journeyman or working printer (from French   [10] Native of Michigan.
jour: "day").

The young sister holds out the skein, the elder sister winds it off in a ball and
  stops now and then for the knots,
The one-year wife is recovering and happy, a week ago she bore her first child,
The cleanhaired Yankee girl works with her sewing-machine or in the factory
  or mill,   290
The nine months' gone is in the parturition chamber, her faintness and pains are
  advancing;
The pavingman leans on his twohanded rammer—the reporter's lead flies swiftly
  over the notebook—the signpainter is lettering with red and gold,
The canal-boy trots on the towpath—the bookkeeper counts at his desk—the
  shoemaker waxes his thread,
The conductor beats time for the band and all the performers follow him,
The child is baptised—the convert is making the first professions,   295
The regatta is spread on the bay . . . . how the white sails sparkle!
The drover watches his drove, he sings out to them that would stray,
The pedlar sweats with his pack on his back—the purchaser higgles about the
  odd cent,
The camera and plate are prepared, the lady must sit for her daguerreotype,
The bride unrumples her white dress, the minutehand of the clock moves
  slowly,   300
The opium eater reclines with rigid head and just-opened lips,
The prostitute draggles her shawl, her bonnet bobs on her tipsy and pimpled
  neck,
The crowd laugh at her blackguard oaths, the men jeer and wink to each other,
(Miserable! I do not laugh at your oaths nor jeer you,)
The President holds a cabinet council, he is surrounded by the great secretaries, 305
On the piazza walk five friendly matrons with twined arms;
The crew of the fish-smack pack repeated layers of halibut in the hold,
The Missourian crosses the plains toting his wares and his cattle,
The fare-collector goes through the train—he gives notice by the jingling of
  loose change,
The floormen are laying the floor—the tinners are tinning the roof—the masons
  are calling for mortar,   310
In single file each shouldering his hod pass onward the laborers;
Seasons pursuing each other the indescribable crowd is gathered . . . . it is the
  Fourth of July . . . . what salutes of cannon and small arms!
Seasons pursuing each other the plougher ploughs and the mower mows and the
  wintergrain falls in the ground;
Off on the lakes the pikefisher watches and waits by the hole in the frozen
  surface,
The stumps stand thick round the clearing, the squatter strikes deep with his axe, 315
The flatboatmen make fast toward dusk near the cottonwood or pekantrees,
The coon-seekers go now through the regions of the Red river, or through
  those drained by the Tennessee, or through those of the Arkansas,
The torches shine in the dark that hangs on the Chattahoochee or Altamahaw;
Patriarchs sit at supper with sons and grandsons and great grandsons around
  them,

In walls of adobe, in canvass tents, rest hunters and trappers after their day's
    sport,   320
The city sleeps and the country sleeps,
The living sleep for their time . . . . the dead sleep for their time,
The old husband sleeps by his wife and the young husband sleeps by his wife;
And these one and all tend inward to me, and I tend outward to them,
And such as it is to be of these more or less I am.   325

*And of these one and all I weave the
                song of myself.*

[16]

I am of old and young, of the foolish as much as the wise,
Regardless of others, ever regardful of others,
Maternal as well as paternal, a child as well as a man,
Stuffed with the stuff that is coarse, and stuffed with the stuff that is fine,
One of the great nation, the nation of many nations—the smallest the same and
    the largest the same,   330
A southerner soon as a northerner, a planter nonchalant and hospitable,
A Yankee bound my own way . . . . ready for trade . . . . my joints the
    limberest joints on earth and the sternest joints on earth.
A Kentuckian walking the vale of the Elkhorn in my deerskin leggings,
A boatman over the lakes or bays or along coasts . . . . a Hoosier, a Badger, a
    Buckeye,[11]
A Louisianian or Georgian, a poke-easy from sandhills and pines,   335
At home on Canadian snowshoes or up in the bush, or with fishermen off
    Newfoundland,
At home in the fleet of iceboats, sailing with the rest and tacking,
At home on the hills of Vermont or in the woods of Maine or the Texan
    ranch,
Comrade of Californians . . . . comrade of free northwesterners, loving their
    big proportions,
Comrade of raftsmen and coalmen—comrade of all who shake hands and
    welcome to drink and meat;   340
A learner with the simplest, a teacher of the thoughtfulest,
A novice beginning experient of myriads of seasons,
Of every hue and trade and rank, of every caste and religion,
Not merely of the New World but of Africa Europe or Asia . . . . a
    wandering savage,
A farmer, mechanic, or artist . . . . a gentleman, sailor, lover or quaker,   345
A prisoner, fancy-man, rowdy, lawyer, physician or priest.

I resist anything better than my own diversity,
And breathe the air and leave plenty after me,
And am not stuck up, and am in my place.

---

[11] Hoosier; Badger; Buckeye: natives, respectively,
of Indiana, Wisconsin, and Ohio.

The moth and the fisheggs are in their place, 350
The suns I see and the suns I cannot see are in their place,
The palpable is in its place and the impalpable is in its place.

[17]

These are the thoughts of all men in all ages and lands, they are not original
    with me,
If they are not yours as much as mine they are nothing or next to nothing,
If they do not enclose everything they are next to nothing, 355
If they are not the riddle and the untying of the riddle they are nothing,
If they are not just as close as they are distant they are nothing.

This is the grass that grows wherever the land is and the water is,
This is the common air that bathes the globe.

This is the breath of laws and songs and behaviour, 360
This is the the tasteless water of souls . . . . this is the true sustenance,
It is for the illiterate . . . . it is for the judges of the supreme court . . . . it is
    for the federal capitol and the state capitols,
It is for the admirable communes of literary men and composers and singers and
    lecturers and engineers and savans,
It is for the endless races of working people and farmers and seamen.

[18]

This is the trill of a thousand clear cornets and scream of the octave flute and
    strike of triangles. 365

I play not a march for victors only . . . . I play great marches for conquered
    and slain persons.

Have you heard that it was good to gain the day?
I also say it is good to fall . . . . battles are lost in the same spirit in which
    they are won.

I sound triumphal drums for the dead . . . . I fling through my embouchures[12]
    the loudest and gayest music to them,
Vivas to those who have failed, and to those whose war vessels sank in the sea,
    and those themselves who sank in the sea, 370
And to all generals that lost engagements, and all overcome heroes, and the
    numberless unknown heroes equal to the greatest heroes known.

---

[12] Mouthpieces of wind instruments.

[*19*]

This is the meal pleasantly set . . . . this is the meat and drink for natural
    hunger,
It is for the wicked just the same as the righteous . . . . I make appointments
    with all,
I will not have a single person slighted or left away,
The keptwoman and sponger and thief are hereby invited . . . . the
    heavy-lipped slave is invited . . . . the venerealee is invited,   375
There shall be no difference between them and the rest.

This is the press of a bashful hand . . . . this is the float and odor of hair,
This is the touch of my lips to yours . . . . this is the murmur of yearning,
This is the far-off depth and height reflecting my own face,
This is the thoughtful merge of myself and the outlet again.   380
Do you guess I have some intricate purpose?
Well I have . . . . for the April rain has, and the mica on the side of a rock
    has.

Do you take it I would astonish?
Does the daylight astonish? or the early redstart twittering through the woods?
Do I astonish more than they?   385

This hour I tell things in confidence,
I might not tell everybody but I will tell you.

[*20*]

Who goes there! hankering, gross, mystical, nude?
How is it I extract strength from the beef I eat?

What is a man anyhow? What am I? and what are you?   390
All I mark as my own you shall offset it with your own,
Else it were time lost listening to me.
I do not snivel that snivel the world over,
That months are vacuums and the ground but wallow and filth,
That life is a suck and a sell, and nothing remains at the end but threadbare
    crape and tears.   395

Whimpering and truckling fold with powders for invalids. . . . conformity goes
    to the fourth-removed,
I cock my hat as I please indoors or out.

Shall I pray? Shall I venerate and be ceremonious?

I have pried through the strata and analyzed to a hair,
And counselled with doctors and calculated close and found no sweeter fat than
   sticks to my own bones.   400

In all people I see myself, none more and not one a barleycorn less,
And the good or bad I say of myself I say of them.

And I know I am solid and sound,
To me the converging objects of the universe perpetually flow,
All are written to me, and I must get what the writing means.   405

And I know I am deathless,
I know this orbit of mine cannot be swept by a carpenter's compass,
I know I shall not pass like a child's carlacue[13] cut with a burnt stick at night.

I know I am august,
I do not trouble my spirit to vindicate itself or be understood,   410
I see that the elementary laws never apologize,
I reckon I behave no prouder than the level I plant my house by after all.

I exist as I am, that is enough,
If no other in the world be aware I sit content,
And if each and all be aware I sit content.   415

One world is aware, and by far the largest to me, and that is myself,
And whether I come to my own today or in ten thousand or ten million years,
I can cheerfully take it now, or with equal cheerfulness I can wait.

My foothold is tenoned and mortised in granite,
I laugh at what you call dissolution,   420
And I know the amplitude of time.

[21]

I am the poet of the body,
And I am the poet of the soul.

The pleasures of heaven are with me, and the pains of hell are with me,
The first I graft and increase upon myself . . . . the latter I translate into a new
   tongue.   425

I am the poet of the woman the same as the man,
And I say it is as great to be a woman as to be a man,
And I say there is nothing greater than the mother of men.
I chant a new chant of dilation or pride,

---

[13] Curlicue.

We have had ducking and deprecating about enough,   430
I show that size is only developement.

Have you outstript the rest? Are you the President?
It is a trifle . . . . they will more than arrive there every one, and still pass on.

I am he that walks with the tender and growing night;
I call to the earth and sea half-held by the night.   435

Press close barebosomed night! Press close magnetic nourishing night!
Night of south winds! Night of the large few stars!
Still nodding night! Mad naked summer night!

Smile O voluptuous coolbreathed earth!
Earth of the slumbering and liquid trees!   440
Earth of departed sunset! Earth of the mountains misty-topt!
Earth of the vitreous pour of the full moon just tinged with blue!
Earth of shine and dark mottling the tide of the river!
Earth of the limpid gray of clouds brighter and clearer for my sake!
Far-swooping elbowed earth! Rich apple-blossomed earth!   445
Smile, for your lover comes!

Prodigal! you have given me love! . . . . therefore I to you give love!
O unspeakable passionate love!

Thruster holding me tight and that I hold tight!
We hurt each other as the bridegroom and the bride hurt each other.   450

[22]

You sea! I resign myself to you also . . . . I guess what you mean,
I behold from the beach your crooked inviting fingers,
I believe you refuse to go back without feeling of me;
We must have a turn together . . . . I undress . . . . hurry me out of sight of
    the land,
Cushion me soft . . . . rock me in billowy drowse,   455
Dash me with amorous wet . . . . I can repay you.

Sea of stretched ground-swells!
Sea breathing broad and convulsive breaths!
Sea of the brine of life! Sea of unshovelled and always-ready graves!
Howler and scooper of storms! Capricious and dainty sea!   460
I am integral with you . . . . I too am of one phase and of all phases.

Partaker of influx and efflux . . . . extoler of hate and conciliation,
Extoler of amies and those that sleep in each others' arms.

I am he attesting sympathy;
Shall I make my list of things in the house and skip the house that supports
   them?   465

I am the poet of commonsense and of the demonstrable and of immortality;
And am not the poet of goodness only . . . . I do not decline to be the poet of
   wickedness also.

Washes and razors for foofoos[14] . . . . for me freckles and a bristling beard.

What blurt is it about virtue and about vice?
Evil propels me, and reform of evil propels me . . . . I stand indifferent,   470
My gait is no faultfinder's or rejecter's gait,
I moisten the roots of all that has grown.

Did you fear some scrofula out of the unflagging pregnancy?
Did you guess the celestial laws are yet to be worked over and rectified?

I step up to say that what we do is right and what we affirm is right . . . . and
   some is only the ore of right,   475
Witnesses of us . . . . one side a balance and the antipodal side a balance,
Soft doctrine as steady help as stable doctrine,
Thoughts and deeds of the present our rouse and early start.

This minute that comes to me over the past decillions,
There is no better than it and now.   480

What behaved well in the past or behaves well today is not such a wonder,
The wonder is always and always how there can be a mean man or an infidel.

[23]

Endless unfolding of words of ages!
And mine a word of the modern . . . . a word en masse.

A word of the faith that never balks,
One time as good as another time . . . . here or henceforward it is all the same
   to me.   485

A word of reality . . . . materialism first and last imbueing.

Hurrah for positive science! Long live exact demonstration!
Fetch stonecrop and mix it with cedar and branches of lilac;
This is the lexicographer or chemist . . . . this made a grammar of the old
   cartouches,   490

[14] Inconsequential people; "small potatoes."

These mariners put the ship through dangerous unknown seas,
This is the geologist, and this works with the scalpel, and this is a
  mathematician.

Gentlemen I receive you, and attach and clasp hands with you,
The facts are useful and real . . . . they are not my dwelling . . . . I enter by
  them to an area of the dwelling.

I am less the reminder of property or qualities, and more the reminder of life,   495
And go on the square for my own sake and for others' sakes,
And make short account of neuters and geldings, and favor men and women
  fully equipped,
And beat the gong of revolt, and stop with fugitives and them that plot and
  conspire.

Talking about self or creating a persona?

[24]

Walt Whitman, an American, one of the roughs, a kosmos,
Disorderly fleshy and sensual . . . . eating drinking and breeding,   500
No sentimentalist . . . . no stander above men and women or apart from them
  . . . . no more modest than immodest.

*egoist, more than
himself, he is everybody
cosmos - universe
unto himself but
not more
than anyone
else*

Unscrew the locks from the doors!
Unscrew the doors themselves from their jambs!

Whoever degrades another degrades me . . . . and whatever is done or said
  returns at last to me,
And whatever I do or say I also return.   505

Through me the afflatus surging and surging . . . . through me the current and
  index.

I speak the password primeval . . . . I give the sign of democracy;
By God! I will accept nothing which all cannot have their counterpart of on
  the same terms.

Through me many long dumb voices,
Voices of the interminable generations of slaves,   510
Voices of prostitutes and of deformed persons,
Voices of the diseased and despairing, and of thieves and dwarfs,
Voices of cycles of preparation and accretion,
And of the threads that connect the stars—and of wombs, and of the fatherstuff,
And of the rights of them the others are down upon,   515
Of the trivial and flat and foolish and despised,
Of fog in the air and beetles rolling balls of dung.

Through me forbidden voices,
Voices of sexes and lusts . . . . voices veiled, and I remove the veil,
Voices indecent by me clarified and transfigured.   520
I do not press my finger across my mouth,
I keep as delicate around the bowels as around the head and heart,
Copulation is no more rank to me than death is.

I believe in the flesh and the appetites,
Seeing hearing and feeling are miracles, and each part and tag of me is a
   miracle.   525

Divine am I inside and out, and I make holy whatever I touch or am touched
   from;
The scent of these arm-pits is aroma finer than prayer,
This head is more than churches or bibles or creeds.

If I worship any particular thing it shall be some of the spread of my body;
Translucent mould of me it shall be you,   530
Shaded ledges and rests, firm masculine coulter, it shall be you,
Whatever goes to the tilth of me it shall be you,
You my rich blood, your milky stream pale strippings of my life;
Breast that presses against other breasts it shall be you,
My brain it shall be your occult convolutions,   535
Root of washed sweet-flag, timorous pond-snipe, nest of guarded duplicate eggs,
   it shall be you,
Mixed tussled hay of head and beard and brawn it shall be you,
Trickling sap of maple, fibre of manly wheat, it shall be you;
Sun so generous it shall be you,
Vapors lighting and shading my face it shall be you,   540
You sweaty brooks and dews it shall be you,
Winds whose soft-tickling genitals rub against me it shall be you,
Broad muscular fields, branches of liveoak, loving lounger in my winding paths,
   it shall be you,
Hands I have taken, face I have kissed, mortal I have ever touched, it shall be
   you.

I dote on myself . . . . there is that lot of me, and all so luscious,   545
Each moment and whatever happens thrills me with joy.
I cannot tell how my ankles bend . . . . nor whence the cause of my faintest
   wish,
Nor the cause of the friendship I emit . . . . nor the cause of the friendship I
   take again.

To walk up my stoop is unaccountable . . . . I pause to consider if it really be,
That I eat and drink is spectacle enough for the great authors and schools,   550
A morning-glory at my window satisfies me more than the metaphysics of
   books.

To behold the daybreak!
The little light fades the immense and diaphanous shadows,
The air tastes good to my palate.

Hefts of the moving world at innocent gambols, silently rising, freshly exuding,   555
Scooting obliquely high and low.

Something I cannot see puts upward libidinous prongs,
Seas of bright juice suffuse heaven.

The earth by the sky staid with . . . . the daily close of their junction,
The heaved challenge from the east that moment over my head,   560
The mocking taunt, See then whether you shall be master!

[25]

Dazzling and tremendous how quick the sunrise would kill me,
If I could not now and always send sunrise out of me.

We also ascend dazzling and tremendous as the sun,
We found our own my soul in the calm and cool of the daybreak.   565

My voice goes after what my eyes cannot reach,
With the twirl of my tongue I encompass worlds and volumes of worlds.
Speech is the twin of my vision . . . . it is unequal to measure itself.

It provokes me forever,
It says sarcastically, Walt, you understand enough . . . . why don't you let it
    out then?   570

Come now I will not be tantalized . . . . you conceive too much of
    articulation.

Do you not know how the buds beneath are folded?
Waiting in gloom protected by frost,
The dirt receding before my prophetical screams,
I underlying causes to balance them at last,   575
My knowledge my live parts . . . . it keeping tally with the meaning of things,
Happiness . . . . which whoever hears me let him or her set out in search of
    this day.

My final merit I refuse you . . . . I refuse putting from me the best I am.

Encompass worlds but never try to encompass me,
I crowd your noisiest talk by looking toward you.   580

Writing and talk do not prove me,
I carry the plenum of proof and every thing else in my face,
With the hush of my lips I confound the topmost skeptic.

[26]

I think I will do nothing for a long time but listen,
And accrue what I hear into myself . . . . and let sounds contribute toward me.   585

I hear the bravuras of birds . . . . the bustle of growing wheat . . . . gossip of
   flames . . . . clack of sticks cooking my meals.

I hear the sound of the human voice . . . . a sound I love,
I hear all sounds as they are tuned to their uses . . . . sounds of the city and
   sounds out of the city . . . . sounds of the day and night;
Talkative young ones to those that like them . . . . the recitative of fish-pedlars
   and fruit-pedlars . . . . the loud laugh of workpeople at their meals,
The angry base of disjointed friendship . . . . the faint tones of the sick,   590
The judge with hands tight to the desk, his shaky lips pronouncing a
   death-sentence,
The heave'e'yo of stevedores unlading ships by the wharves . . . . the refrain of
   the anchor-lifters;
The ring of alarm-bells . . . . the cry of fire . . . . the whirr of swift-streaking
   engines and hose-carts with premonitory tinkles and colored lights,
The steam-whistle . . . . the solid roll of the train of approaching cars;
The slow-march played at night at the head of the association,   595
They go to guard some corpse . . . . the flag-tops are draped with black muslin.

I hear the violincello or man's heart's complaint,
And hear the keyed cornet or else the echo of sunset.

I hear the chorus . . . . it is a grand-opera . . . . this indeed is music!

A tenor large and fresh as the creation fills me,   600
The orbic flex of his mouth is pouring and filling me full.

I hear the trained soprano . . . . she convulses me like the climax of my
   love-grip;
The orchestra whirls me wider than Uranus flies,
It wrenches unnamable ardors from my breast,
It throbs me to gulps of the farthest down horror,   605
It sails me . . . . I dab with bare feet . . . . they are licked by the indolent
   waves,
I am exposed . . . . cut by bitter and poisoned hail,
Steeped amid honeyed morphine . . . . my windpipe squeezed in the fakes of
   death,
Let up again to feel the puzzle of puzzles,
And that we call Being.   610

[27]

To be in any form, what is that?
If nothing lay more developed the quahaug and its callous shell were enough.

Mine is no callous shell,
I have instant conductors all over me whether I pass or stop,
They seize every object and lead it harmlessly through me.   615

I merely stir, press, feel with my fingers, and am happy,
To touch my person to some one else's is about as much as I can stand.

[28]

Is this then a touch? . . . . quivering me to a new identity,
Flames and ether making a rush for my veins,
Treacherous tip of me reaching and crowding to help them,   620
My flesh and blood playing out lightning, to strike what is hardly different
    from myself,
On all sides prurient provokers stiffening my limbs,
Straining the udder of my heart for its withheld drip,
Behaving licentious toward me, taking no denial,
Depriving me of my best as for a purpose,   625
Unbuttoning my clothes and holding me by the bare waist,
Deluding my confusion with the calm of the sunlight and pasture fields,
Immodestly sliding the fellow-senses away,
They bribed to swap off with touch, and go and graze at the edges of me,
No consideration, no regard for my draining strength or my anger,   630
Fetching the rest of the herd around to enjoy them awhile,
Then all uniting to stand on a headland and worry me.

The sentries desert every other part of me,
They have left me helpless to a red marauder,
They all come to the headland to witness and assist against me.   635
I am given up by traitors;
I talk wildly . . . . I have lost my wits . . . . I and nobody else am the greatest
    traitor,
I went myself first to the headland . . . . my own hands carried me there.

You villain touch! what are you doing? . . . . my breath is tight in its throat;
Unclench your floodgates! you are too much for me.   640

[29]

Blind loving wrestling touch! Sheathed hooded sharptoothed touch!
Did it make you ache so leaving me?

Parting tracked by arriving . . . . perpetual payment of the perpetual loan,
Rich showering rain, and recompense richer afterward.

Sprouts take and accumulate . . . . stand by the curb prolific and vital,   645
Landscapes projected masculine full-sized and golden.

[30]

All truths wait in all things,
They neither hasten their own delivery nor resist it,
They do not need the obstetric forceps of the surgeon,
The insignificant is as big to me as any,   650
What is less or more than a touch?

Logic and sermons never convince,
The damp of the night drives deeper into my soul.

Only what proves itself to every man and woman is so,
Only what nobody denies is so.   655

A minute and a drop of me settle my brain;
I believe the soggy clods shall become lovers and lamps,
And a compend of compends is the meat of a man or woman,
And a summit and flower there is the feeling they have for each other,
And they are to branch boundlessly out of that lesson until it becomes omnific,   660
And until every one shall delight us, and we them.

[31]

I believe a leaf of grass is no less than the journeywork of the stars,
And the pismire is equally perfect, and a grain of sand, and the egg of the
    wren,
And the tree-toad is a chef-d'ouvre for the highest,
And the running blackberry would adorn the parlors of heaven,   665
And the narrowest hinge in my hand puts to scorn all machinery,
And the cow crunching with depressed head surpasses any statue,
And a mouse is miracle enough to stagger sextillions of infidels,
And I could come every afternoon of my life to look at the farmer's girl
    boiling her iron tea-kettle and baking shortcake.

I find I incorporate gneiss and coal and long-threaded moss and fruits and grains
    and esculent roots,   670
And am stucco'd with quadrupeds and birds all over,
And have distanced what is behind me for good reasons,
And call any thing close again when I desire it.

In vain the speeding or shyness,
In vain the plutonic rocks send their old heat against my approach,   675

In vain the mastadon retreats beneath its own powdered bones,
In vain objects stand leagues off and assume manifold shapes,
In vain the ocean settling in hollows and the great monsters lying low,
In vain the buzzard houses herself with the sky,
In vain the snake slides through the creepers and logs,   680
In vain the elk takes to the inner passes of the woods,
In vain the razorbilled auk sails far north to Labrador,
I follow quickly . . . . I ascend to the nest in the fissure of the cliff.

[32]

I think I could turn and live awhile with the animals . . . . they are so placid
    and self-contained,
I stand and look at them sometimes half the day long.   685

They do not sweat and whine about their condition,
They do not lie awake in the dark and weep for their sins,
They do not make me sick discussing their duty to God,
Not one is dissatisfied . . . . not one is demented with the mania of owning
    things,
Not one kneels to another nor to his kind that lived thousands of years ago, 690
Not one is respectable or industrious over the whole earth.

So they show their relations to me and I accept them;
They bring me tokens of myself . . . . they evince them plainly in their
    possession.

I do not know where they got those tokens,
I must have passed that way untold times ago and negligently dropt them,   695
Myself moving forward then and now and forever,
Gathering and showing more always and with velocity,
Infinite and omnigenous[15] and the like of these among them;
Not too exclusive toward the reachers of my remembrancers,
Picking out here one that shall be my amie,   700
Choosing to go with him on brotherly terms.

A gigantic beauty of a stallion, fresh and responsive to my caresses,
Head high in the forehead and wide between the ears,
Limbs glossy and supple, tail dusting the ground,
Eyes well apart and full of sparkling wickedness . . . . ears finely cut and
    flexibly moving.   705

His nostrils dilate . . . . my heels embrace him . . . . his well built limbs
    tremble with pleasure . . . . we speed around and return.
I but use you a moment and then I resign you stallion . . . . and do not need
    your paces, and outgallop them,
And myself as I stand or sit pass faster than you.

---

[15] Of all kinds.

[33]

Swift wind! Space! My Soul! Now I know it is true what I guessed at;
What I guessed when I loafed on the grass,   710
What I guessed while I lay alone in my bed . . . . and again as I walked the
  beach under the paling stars of the morning.

My ties and ballasts leave me . . . . I travel . . . . I sail . . . . my elbows rest in
  the sea-gaps,
I skirt the sierras . . . . my palms cover continents,
I am afoot with my vision.

By the city's quadrangular houses . . . . in log-huts, or camping with
  lumbermen,   715
Along the ruts of the turnpike . . . . along the dry gulch and rivulet bed,
Hoeing my onion-patch, and rows of carrots and parsnips . . . crossing savannas
  . . . trailing in forests,
Prospecting . . . . gold-digging . . . . girdling the trees of a new purchase,
Scorched ankle-deep by the hot sand . . . . hauling my boat down the shallow
  river;
Where the panther walks to and fro on a limb overhead . . . . where the buck
  turns furiously at the hunter,   720
Where the rattlesnake suns his flabby length on a rock . . . . where the otter is
  feeding on fish,
Where the alligator in his tough pimples sleeps by the bayou,
Where the black bear is searching for roots or honey . . . . where the beaver
  pats the mud with his paddle-tail;
Over the growing sugar . . . . over the cottonplant . . . . over the rice in its
  low moist field;
Over the sharp-peaked farmhouse with its scalloped scum and slender shoots
  from the gutters;   725
Over the western persimmon . . . . over the longleaved corn and the delicate
  blueflowered flax;
Over the white and brown buckwheat, a hummer and a buzzer there with the
  rest,
Over the dusky green of the rye as it ripples and shades in the breeze;
Scaling mountains . . . . pulling myself cautiously up . . . . holding on by low
  scragged limbs,
Walking the path worn in the grass and beat through the leaves of the brush;   730
Where the quail is whistling betwixt the woods and the wheatlot,
Where the bat flies in the July eve . . . . where the great goldbug drops
  through the dark;
Where the flails keep time on the barn floor,
Where the brook puts out of the roots of the old tree and flows to the
  meadow,
Where cattle stand and shake away flies with the tremulous shuddering of their
  hides,   735

Where the cheese-cloth hangs in the kitchen, and andirons straddle the
    hearth-slab, and cobwebs fall in festoons from the rafters;
Where triphammers crash . . . . where the press is whirling its cylinders;
Wherever the human heart beats with terrible throes out of its ribs;
Where the pear-shaped balloon is floating aloft . . . . floating in it myself and
    looking composedly down;
Where the life-car is drawn on the slipnoose . . . . where the heat hatches
    pale-green eggs in the dented sand,   740
Where the she-whale swims with her calves and never forsakes them,
Where the steamship trails hindways its long pennant of smoke,
Where the ground-shark's fin cuts like a black chip out of the water,
Where the half-burned brig is riding on unknown currents,
Where shells grow to her slimy deck, and the dead are corrupting below;   745
Where the striped and starred flag is borne at the head of the regiments;
Approaching Manhattan, up by the long-stretching island,
Under Niagara, the cataract falling like a veil over my countenance;
Upon a door-step . . . . upon the horse-block of hard wood outside,
Upon the race-course, or enjoying pic-nics or jigs or a good game of base-ball,   750
At he-festivals with blackguard jibes and ironical license and bull-dances and
    drinking and laughter,
At the cider-mill, tasting the sweet of the brown sqush . . . . sucking the juice
    through a straw,
At apple-pealings, wanting kisses for all the red fruit I find,
At musters and beach-parties and friendly bees and huskings and house-raisings;
Where the mockingbird sounds his delicious gurgles, and crackles and screams
    and weeps,   755
Where the hay-rick stands in the barnyard, and the dry-stalks are scattered, and
    the brood cow waits in the hovel,
Where the bull advances to do his masculine work, and the stud to the mare,
    and the cock is treading the hen,
Where the heifers browse, and the geese nip their food with short jerks;
Where the sundown shadows lengthen over the limitless and lonesome prairie,
Where the herds of buffalo make a crawling spread of the square miles far and
    near;   760
Where the hummingbird shimmers . . . . where the neck of the longlived swan
    is curving and winding;
Where the laughing-gull scoots by the slappy shore and laughs her near-human
    laugh;
Where beehives range on a gray bench in the garden half-hid by the high
    weeds;
Where the band-necked partridges roost in a ring on the ground with their
    heads out;
Where burial coaches enter the arched gates of a cemetery;   765
Where winter wolves bark amid wastes of snow and icicled trees;
Where the yellow-crowned heron comes to the edge of the marsh at night and
    feeds upon small crabs;
Where the splash of swimmers and divers cools the warm noon;

Where the katydid works her chromatic reed on the walnut-tree over the well;
Through patches of citrons and cucumbers with silver-wired leaves,   770
Through the salt-lick or orange glade . . . . or under conical firs;
Through the gymnasium . . . . through the curtained saloon . . . . through the
    office or public hall;
Pleased with the native and pleased with the foreign . . . . pleased with the new
    and old,
Pleased with women, the homely as well as the handsome,
Pleased with the quakeress as she puts off her bonnet and talks melodiously,   775
Pleased with the primitive tunes of the choir of the whitewashed church,
Pleased with the earnest words of the sweating Methodist preacher, or any
    preacher . . . . looking seriously at the camp-meeting;
Looking in at the shop-windows in Broadway the whole forenoon . . . .
    pressing the flesh of my nose to the thick plate-glass,
Wandering the same afternoon with my face turned up to the clouds;
My right and left arms round the sides of two friends and I in the middle;   780
Coming home with the bearded and dark-cheeked bush-boy . . . . riding behind
    him at the drape of the day;
Far from the settlements studying the print of animals' feet, or the moccasin
    print;
By the cot in the hospital reaching lemonade to a feverish patient,
By the coffined corpse when all is still, examining with a candle;
Voyaging to every port to dicker and adventure;   785
Hurrying with the modern crowd, as eager and fickle as any,
Hot toward one I hate, ready in my madness to knife him;
Solitary at midnight in my back yard, my thoughts gone from me a long
    while,
Walking the old hills of Judea with the beautiful gentle god by my side;
Speeding through space . . . . speeding through heaven, and the stars,   790
Speeding amid the seven satellites and the broad ring and the diameter of eighty
    thousand miles,
Speeding with tailed meteors . . . . throwing fire-balls like the rest,
Carrying the crescent child that carries its own full mother in its belly;
Storming enjoying planning loving cautioning,
Backing and filling, appearing and disappearing,   795
I tread day and night such roads.

I visit the orchards of God and look at the spheric product,
And look at quintillions ripened, and look at quintillions green.

I fly the flight of the fluid and swallowing soul,
My course runs below the soundings of plummets.   800

I help myself to material and immaterial,
No guard can shut me off, no law can prevent me.

I anchor my ship for a little while only,
My messengers continually cruise away or bring their returns to me.

I go hunting polar furs and the seal . . . . leaping chasms with a pike-pointed
    staff . . . . clinging to topples of brittle and blue.   805

I ascend to the foretruck . . . . I take my place late at night in the crow's nest
    . . . . we sail through the arctic sea . . . . it is plenty light enough,
Through the clear atmosphere I stretch around on the wonderful beauty,
The enormous masses of ice pass me and I pass them . . . . the scenery is plain
    in all directions,
The white-topped mountains point up in the distance . . . . I fling out my
    fancies toward them;
We are about approaching some great battlefield in which we are soon to be
    engaged,   810
We pass the colossal outposts of the encampments . . . . we pass with still feet
    and caution;
Or we are entering by the suburbs some vast and ruined city . . . . the blocks
    and fallen architecture more than all the living cities of the globe.

I am a free companion . . . . I bivouac by invading watchfires.

I turn the bridegroom out of bed and stay with the bride myself,
And tighten her all night to my thighs and lips.   815

My voice is the wife's voice, the screech by the rail of the stairs,
They fetch my man's body up dripping and drowned.

I understand the large hearts of heroes,
The courage of present times and all times;
How the skipper saw the crowded and rudderless wreck of the steamship, and
    death chasing it up and down the storm,   820
How he knuckled tight and gave not back one inch, and was faithful of days
    and faithful of nights,
And chalked in large letters on a board, Be of good cheer, We will not desert
    you;
How he saved the drifting company at last,
How the lank loose-gowned women looked when boated from the side of their
    prepared graves,
How the silent old-faced infants, and the lifted sick, and the sharp-lipped
    unshaved men;   825
All this I swallow and it tastes good . . . . I like it well, and it becomes mine,
I am the man . . . . I suffered . . . . I was there.

The disdain and calmness of martyrs,
The mother condemned for a witch and burnt with dry wood, and her children
    gazing on;

The hounded slave that flags in the race and leans by the fence, blowing and
    covered with sweat,   830
The twinges that sting like needles his legs and neck,
The murderous buckshot and the bullets,
All these I feel or am.

I am the hounded slave . . . . I wince at the bite of the dogs,
Hell and despair are upon me . . . . crack and again crack the marksmen,   835
I clutch the rails of the fence . . . . my gore dribs thinned with the ooze of my
    skin,
I fall on the weeds and stones,
The riders spur their unwilling horses and haul close,
They taunt my dizzy ears . . . . they beat me violently over the head with their
    whip-stocks.

Agonies are one of my changes of garments;   840
I do not ask the wounded person how he feels . . . . I myself become the
    wounded person,
My hurt turns livid upon me as I lean on a cane and observe.

I am the mashed fireman with breastbone broken . . . . tumbling walls buried
    me in their debris,
Heat and smoke I inspired . . . . I heard the yelling shouts of my comrades,
I heard the distant click of their picks and shovels;   845
They have cleared the beams away . . . . they tenderly lift me forth.

I lie in the night air in my red shirt . . . . the pervading hush is for my sake,
Painless after all I lie, exhausted but not so unhappy,
White and beautiful are the faces around me . . . . the heads are bared of their
    fire-caps,
The kneeling crowd fades with the light of the torches.   850

Distant and dead resuscitate,
They show as the dial or move as the hands of me . . . . and I am the clock
    myself.
I am an old artillerist, and tell of some fort's bombardment . . . . and am there
    again.

Again the reveille of drummers . . . . again the attacking cannon and mortars
    and howitzers,
Again the attacked send their cannon responsive.   855

I take part . . . . I see and hear the whole,
The cries and curses and roar . . . . the plaudits for well aimed shots,
The ambulanza[16] slowly passing and trailing its red drip,
Workmen searching after damages and to make indispensible repairs,

---

[16] Italian: "ambulance."

The fall of grenades through the rent roof . . . . the fan-shaped explosion,   860
The whizz of limbs heads stone wood and iron high in the air.

Again gurgles the mouth of my dying general . . . . he furiously waves with
  his hand,
He gasps through the clot . . . . Mind not me . . . . mind . . . . the
  entrenchments.

[34]

I tell not the fall of Alamo . . . . not one escaped to tell the fall of Alamo,
The hundred and fifty are dumb yet at Alamo.   865

Hear now the tale of a jetblack sunrise,
Hear of the murder in cold blood of four hundred and twelve young men.

Retreating they had formed in a hollow square with their baggage for
  breastworks,
Nine hundred lives out of the surrounding enemy's nine times their number was
  the price they took in advance,
Their colonel was wounded and their ammunition gone,   870
They treated for an honorable capitulation, received writing and seal, gave up
  their arms, and marched back prisoners of war.
They were the glory of the race of rangers,
Matchless with a horse, a rifle, a song, a supper or a courtship,
Large, turbulent, brave, handsome, generous, proud and affectionate,
Bearded, sunburnt, dressed in the free costume of hunters,   875
Not a single one over thirty years of age.

The second Sunday morning they were brought out in squads and massacred
  . . . . it was beautiful early summer,
The work commenced about five o'clock and was over by eight.

None obeyed the command to kneel,
Some made a mad and helpless rush . . . . some stood stark and straight,   880
A few fell at once, shot in the temple or heart . . . . the living and dead lay
  together,
The maimed and mangled dug in the dirt . . . . the newcomers saw them there;
Some half-killed attempted to crawl away,
These were dispatched with bayonets or battered with the blunts of muskets;
A youth not seventeen years old seized his assassin till two more came to release
  him,   885
The three were all torn, and covered with the boy's blood.

At eleven o'clock began the burning of the bodies;
And that is the tale of the murder of the four hundred and twelve young men,
And that was a jetblack sunrise.

[35]

Did you read in the seabooks of the oldfashioned frigate-fight?   890
Did you learn who won by the light of the moon and stars?

Our foe was no skulk in his ship, I tell you,
His was the English pluck, and there is no tougher or truer, and never was, and
    never will be;
Along the lowered eve he came, horribly raking us.
We closed with him . . . . the yards entangled . . . . the cannon touched,   895
My captain lashed fast with his own hands.

We had received some eighteen-pound shots under the water,
On our lower-gun-deck two large pieces had burst at the first fire, killing all
    around and blowing up overhead.

Ten o'clock at night, and the full moon shining and the leaks on the gain, and
    five feet of water reported,
The master-at-arms loosing the prisoners confined in the after-hold to give them
    a chance for themselves.   900

The transit to and from the magazine was now stopped by the sentinels,
They saw so many strange faces they did not know whom to trust.

Our frigate was afire . . . . the other asked if we demanded quarters? if our
    colors were struck and the fighting done?

I laughed content when I heard the voice of my little captain,
We have not struck, he composedly cried, We have just begun our part of the
    fighting.   905

Only three guns were in use,
One was directed by the captain himself against the enemy's mainmast,
Two well-served with grape and canister silenced his musketry and cleared his
    decks.

The tops alone seconded the fire of this little battery, especially the maintop,
They all held out bravely during the whole of the action.   910

Not a moment's cease,
The leaks gained fast on the pumps . . . . the fire eat toward the
    powder-magazine,
One of the pumps was shot away . . . . it was generally thought we were
    sinking.
Serene stood the little captain,
He was not hurried . . . . his voice was neither high nor low,   915
His eyes gave more light to us than our battle-lanterns.

Toward twelve at night, there in the beams of the moon they surrendered to us.

[36]

Stretched and still lay the midnight,
Two great hulls motionless on the breast of the darkness,
Our vessel riddled and slowly sinking . . . . preparations to pass to the one we
    had conquered,   920
The captain on the quarter deck coldly giving his orders through a countenance
    white as a sheet,
Near by the corpse of the child that served in the cabin,
The dead face of an old salt with long white hair and carefully curled whiskers,
The flames spite of all that could be done flickering aloft and below,
The husky voices of the two or three officers yet fit for duty,   925
Formless stacks of bodies and bodies by themselves . . . . dabs of flesh upon the
    masts and spars,
The cut of cordage and dangle of rigging . . . . the slight shock of the soothe
    of waves,
Black and impassive guns, and litter of powder-parcels, and the strong scent,
Delicate sniffs of the seabreeze . . . . smells of sedgy grass and fields by the
    shore . . . . death-messages given in charge to survivors,
The hiss of the surgeon's knife and the gnawing teeth of his saw,   930
The wheeze, the cluck, the swash of falling blood . . . . the short wild scream,
    the long dull tapering groan,
These so . . . . these irretrievable.

[37]

O Christ! My fit is mastering me!
What the rebel said gaily adjusting his throat to the rope-noose,
What the savage at the stump, his eye-sockets empty, his mouth spirting
    whoops and defiance,   935
What stills the traveler come to the vault at Mount Vernon,
What sobers the Brooklyn boy as he looks down the shores of the Wallabout
    and remembers the prison ships,
What burnt the gums of the redcoat at Saratoga when he surrendered his
    brigades,
These become mine and me every one, and they are but little,
I become as much more as I like.   940

I become any presence or truth of humanity here,
And see myself in prison shaped like another man,
And feel the dull unintermitted pain.

For me the keepers of convicts shoulder their carbines and keep watch,
It is I let out in the morning and barred at night.   945

Not a mutineer walks handcuffed to the jail, but I am handcuffed to him and
    walk by his side,

I am less the jolly one there, and more the silent one with sweat on my
 twitching lips.

Not a youngster is taken for larceny, but I go up too and am tried and
 sentenced.

Not a cholera patient lies at the last gasp, but I also lie at the last gasp,
My face is ash-colored, my sinews gnarl . . . . away from me people retreat.   950

Askers embody themselves in me, and I am embodied in them,
I project my hat and sit shamefaced and beg.

[38]

I rise extatic through all, and sweep with the true gravitation,
The whirling and whirling is elemental within me.

Somehow I have been stunned. Stand back!   955
Give me a little time beyond my cuffed head and slumbers and dreams and
 gaping,
I discover myself on a verge of the usual mistake.

That I could forget the mockers and insults!
That I could forget the trickling tears and the blows of the bludgeons and
 hammers!
That I could look with a separate look on my own crucifixion and bloody
 crowning!   960

I remember . . . . I resume the overstaid fraction,
The grave of rock multiplies what has been confided to it . . . . or to any
 graves,
The corpses rise . . . . the gashes heal . . . . the fastenings roll away.

I troop forth replenished with supreme power, one of an average unending
 procession,
We walk the roads of Ohio and Massachusetts and Virginia and Wisconsin and
 New York and New Orleans and Texas and Montreal and San Francisco and
 Charleston and Savannah and Mexico,   965
Inland and by the seacoast and boundary lines . . . . and we pass the boundary
 lines.

Our swift ordinances are on their way over the whole earth,
The blossoms we wear in our hats are the growth of two thousand years.

Eleves[17] I salute you,
I see the approach of your numberless gangs . . . . I see you understand
 yourselves and me,   970

[17] Pupils or disciples (from French *élève:*
 "student").

And know that they who have eyes are divine, and the blind and lame are
    equally divine,
And that my steps drag behind yours yet go before them,
And are aware how I am with you no more than I am with everybody.

[39]

The friendly and flowing savage . . . . Who is he?
Is he waiting for civilization or past it and mastering it?   975

Is he some southwesterner raised outdoors? Is he Canadian?
Is he from the Mississippi country? or from Iowa, Oregon or California? or
    from the mountains? or prairie life or bush-life? or from the sea?
Wherever he goes men and women accept and desire him,
They desire he should like them and touch them and speak to them and stay
    with them.

Behaviour lawless as snow-flakes . . . . words simple as grass . . . . uncombed
    head and laughter and naivete;   980
Slowstepping feet and the common features, and the common modes and
    emanations,
They descend in new forms from the tips of his fingers,
They are wafted with the odor of his body or breath . . . . they fly out of the
    glance of his eyes.

[40]

Flaunt of the sunshine I need not your bask . . . . lie over,
You light surfaces only . . . . I force the surfaces and the depths also.   985

Earth! you seem to look for something at my hands,
Say old topknot![18] what do you want?

Man or woman! I might tell how I like you, but cannot,
And might tell what it is in me and what it is in you, but cannot,
And might tell the pinings I have . . . . the pulse of my nights and days.   990

Behold I do not give lectures or a little charity,
What I give I give out of myself.

You there, impotent, loose in the knees, open your scarfed chops till I blow
    grit within you,
Spread your palms and lift the flaps of your pockets,
I am not to be denied . . . . I compel . . . . I have stores plenty and to spare,   995
And any thing I have I bestow.

---

[18] An Indian.

I do not ask who you are . . . . that is not important to me,
You can do nothing and be nothing but what I will infold you.

To a drudge of the cottonfields or emptier of privies I lean . . . . on his right
    cheek I put the family kiss,
And in my soul I swear I never will deny him.   1000
On women fit for conception I start bigger and nimbler babes,
This day I am jetting the stuff of far more arrogant republics.

To any one dying . . . . thither I speed and twist the knob of the door,
Turn the bedclothes toward the foot of the bed,
Let the physician and the priest go home.   1005

I seize the descending man . . . . I raise him with resistless will.

O despairer, here is my neck,
By God! you shall not go down! Hang your whole weight upon me.

I dilate you with tremendous breath . . . . I buoy you up;
Every room of the house do I fill with an armed force . . . . lovers of me,
    bafflers of graves: 1010
Sleep! I and they keep guard all night;
Not doubt, not decease shall dare to lay finger upon you,
I have embraced you, and henceforth possess you to myself,
And when you rise in the morning you will find what I tell you is so.

[41]

I am he bringing help for the sick as they pant on their backs,   1015
And for strong upright men I bring yet more needed help.

I heard what was said of the universe,
Heard it and heard of several thousand years;
It is middling well as far as it goes . . . . but is that all?

Magnifying and applying come I,   1020
Outbidding at the start the old cautious hucksters,
The most they offer for mankind and eternity less than a spirt of my own
    seminal wet,
Taking myself the exact dimensions of Jehovah and laying them away,
Lithographing Kronos and Zeus his son, and Hercules[19] his grandson,
Buying drafts of Osiris and Isis and Belus and Brahma[20] and Adonai,[21]   1025

---

[19] Kronos; Zeus; Hercules: divinities in Greek   [21] In Hebrew, another name for God.
mythology.
[20] Osiris and Isis; Belus and Brahma: Egyptian and
Hindu deities, respectively.

In my portfolio placing Manito[22] loose, and Allah[23] on a leaf, and the crucifix
    engraved,
With Odin,[24] and the hideous-faced Mexitli,[25] and all idols and images,
Honestly taking them all for what they are worth, and not a cent more,
Admitting they were alive and did the work of their day,
Admitting they bore mites as for unfledged birds who have now to rise and fly
    and sing for themselves,   1030
Accepting the rough deific sketches to fill out better in myself . . . . bestowing
    them freely on each man and woman I see,
Discovering as much or more in a framer framing a house,
Putting higher claims for him there with his rolled-up sleeves, driving the
    mallet and chisel;
Not objecting to special relevations . . . . considering a curl of smoke or a hair
    on the back of my hand as curious as any relevation;
Those ahold of fire-engines and hook-and-ladder ropes more to me than the
    gods of the antique wars,   1035
Minding their voices peal through the crash of destruction,
Their brawny limbs passing safe over charred laths . . . . their white foreheads
    whole and unhurt out of the flames;
By the mechanic's wife with her babe at her nipple interceding for every person
    born;
Three scythes at harvest whizzing in a row from three lusty angels with shirts
    bagged out at their waists;
The snag-toothed hostler with red hair redeeming sins past and to come,   1040
Selling all he possesses and traveling on foot to fee lawyers for his brother and
    sit by him while he is tried for forgery:
What was strewn in the amplest strewing the square rod about me, and not
    filling the square rod then;
The bull and the bug never worshipped half enough,
Dung and dirt more admirable than was dreamed,
The supernatural of no account . . . . myself waiting my time to be one of the
    supremes,   1045
The day getting ready for me when I shall do as much good as the best, and be
    as prodigious,
Guessing when I am it will not tickle me much to receive puffs out of pulpit
    or print;
By my life-lumps! becoming already a creator!
Putting myself here and now to the ambushed womb of the shadows!

[42]

 . . . . A call in the midst of the crowd,   1050
My own voice, orotund sweeping and final.

---

[22] Algonquin Indian nature spirit.   [24] Norse god of war.
[23] Moslem supreme being.   [25] Aztec god of war.

Come my children,
Come my boys and girls, and my women and household and intimates,
Now the performer launches his nerve . . . . he has passed his prelude on the
    reeds within.

Easily written loosefingered chords! I feel the thrum of their climax and close.   1055

My head evolves on my neck,
Music rolls, but not from the organ . . . . folks are around me, but they are no
    household of mine.

Ever the hard and unsunk ground,
Ever the eaters and drinkers . . . . ever the upward and downward sun . . . .
    ever the air and the ceaseless tides,
Ever myself and my neighbors, refreshing and wicked and real,   1060
Ever the old inexplicable query . . . . ever that thorned thumb—that breath of
    itches and thirsts,
Ever the vexer's hoot! hoot! till we find where the sly one hides and bring him
    forth;
Ever love . . . . ever the sobbing liquid of life,
Ever the bandage under the chin . . . . ever the tressels of death.

Here and there with dimes on the eyes walking,   1065
To feed the greed of the belly the brains liberally spooning,
Tickets buying or taking or selling, but in to the feast never once going;
Many sweating and ploughing and thrashing, and then the chaff for payment
    receiving,
A few idly owning, and they the wheat continually claiming.

This is the city . . . . and I am one of the citizens;   1070
Whatever interests the rest interests me . . . . politics, churches, newspapers,
    schools,
Benevolent societies, improvements, banks, tariffs, steamships, factories, markets,
Stocks and stores and real estate and personal estate.

They who piddle and patter here in collars and tailed coats . . . . I am aware
    who they are . . . . and that they are not worms or fleas,
I acknowledge the duplicates of myself under all the scrape-lipped and
    pipe-legged concealments.   1075

The weakest and shallowest is deathless with me,
What I do and say the same waits for them,
Every thought that flounders in me the same flounders in them.

I know perfectly well my own egotism,
And know my omniverous words, and cannot say any less,   1080
And would fetch you whoever you are flush with myself.

My words are words of a questioning, and to indicate reality;
This printed and bound book . . . . but the printer and the printing-office boy?
The marriage estate and settlement . . . . but the body and mind of the
    bridegroom? also those of the bride?
The panorama of the sea . . . . but the sea itself?   1085
The well-taken photographs . . . . but your wife or friend close and solid in
    your arms?
The fleet of ships of the line and all the modern improvements . . . . but the
    craft and pluck of the admiral?
The dishes and fare and furniture . . . . but the host and hostess, and the look
    out of their eyes?
The sky up there . . . . yet here or next door or across the way?
The saints and sages in history . . . . but you yourself?   1090
Sermons and creeds and theology . . . . but the human brain, and what is called
    reason, and what is called love, and what is called life?

[43]

I do not despise you priests;
My faith is the greatest of faiths and the least of faiths,
Enclosing all worship ancient and modern, and all between ancient and modern,
Believing I shall come again upon the earth after five thousand years,   1095
Waiting responses from oracles . . . . honoring the gods . . . . saluting the sun,
Making a fetish of the first rock or stump . . . . powowing with sticks in the
    circle of obis,[26]
Helping the lama or brahmin as he trims the lamps of the idols,
Dancing yet through the streets in a phallic procession . . . . rapt and austere in
    the woods, a gymnosophist,[27]
Drinking mead from the skull-cup . . . to shasta[28] and vedas admirant . . . .
    minding the koran,   1100
Walking the teokallis,[29] spotted with gore from the stone and knife—beating
    the serpent-skin drum;
Accepting the gospels, accepting him that was crucified, knowing assuredly that
    he is divine,
To the mass kneeling—to the puritan's prayer rising—sitting patiently in a pew,
Ranting and frothing in my insane crisis—waiting dead-like till my spirit
    arouses me;
Looking forth on pavement and land, and outside of pavement and land,   1105
Belonging to the winders of the circuit of circuits.

One of that centripetal and centrifugal gang,
I turn and talk like a man leaving charges before a journey.
Down-hearted doubters, dull and excluded,

---

[26] I.e., obeah, referring to West African witchcraft
and sorcery.
[27] Hindu ascetic.
[28] I.e., Shastra, a Hindu sacred writing (cf. the
Vedas).
[29] Aztec temples.

Frivolous sullen moping angry affected disheartened atheistical,   1110
I know every one of you, and know the unspoken interrogatories,
By experience I know them.

How the flukes splash!
How they contort rapid as lightning, with spasms and spouts of blood!

Be at peace bloody flukes of doubters and sullen mopers,   1115
I take my place among you as much as among any;
The past is the push of you and me and all precisely the same,
And the night is for you and me and all,
And what is yet untried and afterward is for you and me and all.

I do not know what is untried and afterward,   1120
But I know it is sure and alive, and sufficient.

Each who passes is considered, and each who stops is considered, and not a
      single one can it fail.

It cannot fail the young man who died and was buried,
Nor the young woman who died and was put by his side,
Nor the little child that peeped in at the door and then drew back and was
      never seen again,   1125
Nor the old man who has lived without purpose, and feels it with bitterness
      worse than gall,
Nor him in the poorhouse tubercled by rum and the bad disorder,
Nor the numberless slaughtered and wrecked . . . . nor the brutish koboo,[30]
      called the ordure of humanity,
Nor the sacs merely floating with open mouths for food to slip in,
Nor any thing in the earth, or down in the oldest graves of the earth,   1130
Nor any thing in the myriads of spheres, nor one of the myriads of myriads
      that inhabit them,
Nor the present, nor the least wisp that is known.

[44]
It is time to explain myself . . . . let us stand up.

What is known I strip away . . . . I launch all men and women forward with
      me into the unknown.

The clock indicates the moment . . . . but what does eternity indicate?   1135

Eternity lies in bottomless reservoirs . . . . its buckets are rising forever and
      ever,
They pour and they pour and they exhale away.

---

[30] Sumatran savage.

We have thus far exhausted trillions of winters and summers;
There are trillions ahead, and trillions ahead of them.

Births have brought us richness and variety,   1140
And other births will bring us richness and variety.

I do not call one greater and one smaller,
That which fills its period and place is equal to any.

Were mankind murderous or jealous upon you my brother or my sister?
I am sorry for you . . . . they are not murderous or jealous upon me;   1145
All has been gentle with me . . . . . . I keep no account with lamentation;
What have I to do with lamentation?

I am an acme of things accomplished, and I an encloser of things to be.

My feet strike an apex of the apices of the stairs,
On every step bunches of ages, and larger bunches between the steps,   1150
All below duly traveled—and still I mount and mount.

Rise after rise bow the phantoms behind me,
Afar down I see the huge first Nothing, the vapor from the nostrils of death,
I know I was even there . . . . I waited unseen and always,
And slept while God carried me through the lethargic mist,   1155
And took my time . . . . and took no hurt from the fœtid carbon.

Long I was hugged close . . . . long and long.

Immense have been the preparations for me,
Faithful and friendly the arms that have helped me.

Cycles ferried my cradle, rowing and rowing like cheerful boatmen;   1160
For room to me stars kept aside in their own rings,
They sent influences to look after what was to hold me.

Before I was born out of my mother generations guided me,
My embryo has never been torpid . . . . nothing could overlay it;
For it the nebula cohered to an orb . . . . the long slow strata piled to rest it
     on . . . . vast vegetables gave it sustenance,   1165
Monstrous sauroids[31] transported it in their mouths and deposited it with care.

All forces have been steadily employed to complete and delight me,
Now I stand on this spot with my soul.

[31] Prehistoric reptiles.

[45]

Span of youth! Ever-pushed elasticity! Manhood balanced and florid and full!

My lovers suffocate me!   1170
Crowding my lips, and thick in the pores of my skin,
Jostling me through streets and public halls . . . . coming naked to me at night,
Crying by day Ahoy from the rocks of the river . . . . swinging and chirping
    over my head,
Calling my name from flowerbeds or vines or tangled underbrush,
Or while I swim in the bath . . . . or drink from the pump at the corner . . . .
    or the curtain is down at the opera . . . . or I glimpse at a woman's face in
    the railroad car;   1175
Lighting on every moment of my life,
Bussing my body with soft and balsamic busses,
Noiselessly passing handfuls out of their hearts and giving them to be mine.

Old age superbly rising! Ineffable grace of dying days!

Every condition promulges[32] not only itself . . . . it promulges what grows after
    and out of itself,   1180
And the dark hush promulges as much as any.

I open my scuttle at night and see the far-sprinkled systems,
And all I see, multiplied as high as I can cipher, edge but the rim of the farther
    systems.

Wider and wider they spread, expanding and always expanding,
Outward and outward and forever outward.   1185

My sun has his sun, and round him obediently wheels,
He joins with his partners a group of superior circuit,
And greater sets follow, making specks of the greatest inside them.

There is no stoppage, and never can be stoppage;
If I and you and the worlds and all beneath or upon their surfaces, and all the
    palpable life, were this moment reduced back to a pallid float, it would not
    avail in the long run,   1190
We should surely bring up again where we now stand,
And as surely go as much farther, and then farther and farther.

A few quadrillions of eras, a few octillions of cubic leagues, do not hazard the
    span, or make it impatient,
They are but parts . . . . any thing is but a part.

---

[32] Promulgates.

See ever so far . . . . there is limitless space outside of that,   1195
Count ever so much . . . . there is limitless time around that.
Our rendezvous is fitly appointed . . . . God will be there and wait till we
    come.

[46]

I know I have the best of time and space—and that I was never measured, and
    never will be measured.

I tramp a perpetual journey,
My signs are a rain-proof coat and good shoes and a staff cut from the woods;   1200
No friend of mine takes his ease in my chair,
I have no chair, nor church nor philosophy;
I lead no man to a dinner-table or library or exchange,
But each man and each woman of you I lead upon a knoll,
My left hand hooks you round the waist,   1205
My right hand points to landscapes of continents, and a plain public road.

Not I, not any one else can travel that road for you,
You must travel it for yourself.

It is not far . . . . it is within reach,
Perhaps you have been on it since you were born, and did not know,   1210
Perhaps it is every where on water and on land.

Shoulder your duds, and I will mine, and let us hasten forth;
Wonderful cities and free nations we shall fetch as we go.

If you tire, give me both burdens, and rest the chuff[33] of your hand on my hip,
And in due time you shall repay the same service to me;   1215
For after we start we never lie by again.

This day before dawn I ascended a hill and looked at the crowded heaven,
And I said to my spirit, When we become the enfolders of those orbs and the
    pleasure and knowledge of every thing in them, shall we be filled and
    satisfied then?
And my spirit said No, we level that lift to pass and continue beyond.
You are also asking me questions, and I hear you;   1220
I answer that I cannot answer . . . . you must find out for yourself.

Sit awhile wayfarer,
Here are biscuits to eat and here is milk to drink,
But as soon as you sleep and renew yourself in sweet clothes I will certainly
    kiss you with my goodbye kiss and open the gate for your egress hence.

[33] Heel.

Long enough have you dreamed contemptible dreams,   1225
Now I wash the gum from your eyes,
You must habit yourself to the dazzle of the light and of every moment of
　your life.

Long have you timidly waded, holding a plank by the shore,
Now I will you to be a bold swimmer,
To jump off in the midst of the sea, and rise again and nod to me and shout,
　and laughingly dash with your hair.   1230

[47]

I am the teacher of athletes,
He that by me spreads a wider breast than my own proves the width of my
　own,
He most honors my style who learns under it to destroy the teacher.

The boy I love, the same becomes a man not through derived power but in his
　own right,
Wicked, rather than virtuous out of conformity or fear,   1235
Fond of his sweetheart, relishing well his steak,
Unrequited love or a slight cutting him worse than a wound cuts,
First rate to ride, to fight, to hit the bull's eye, to sail a skiff, to sing a song or
　play on the banjo,
Preferring scars and faces pitted with smallpox over all latherers and those that
　keep out of the sun.

I teach straying from me, yet who can stray from me?   1240
I follow you whoever you are from the present hour;
My words itch at your ears till you understand them.
I do not say these things for a dollar, or to fill up the time while I wait for a
　boat;
It is you talking just as much as myself . . . . . I act as the tongue of you,
It was tied in your mouth . . . . . in mine it begins to be loosened.   1245

I swear I will never mention love or death inside a house,
And I swear I never will translate myself at all, only to him or her who
　privately stays with me in the open air.

If you would understand me go to the heights or water-shore,
The nearest gnat is an explanation and a drop or the motion of waves a key,
The maul the oar and the handsaw second my words.   1250

No shuttered room or school can commune with me,
But roughs and little children better than they.

The young mechanic is closest to me . . . . he knows me pretty well,
The woodman that takes his axe and jug with him shall take me with him all
    day,
The farmboy ploughing in the field feels good at the sound of my voice,   1255
In vessels that sail my words must sail . . . . I go with fishermen and seamen,
    and love them,
My face rubs to the hunter's face when he lies down alone in his blanket,
The driver thinking of me does not mind the jolt of his wagon,
The young mother and old mother shall comprehend me,
The girl and the wife rest the needle a moment and forget where they are,   1260
They and all would resume what I have told them.

[48]

I have said that the soul is not more than the body,
And I have said that the body is not more than the soul,
And nothing, not God, is greater to one than one's-self is,
And whoever walks a furlong without sympathy walks to his own funeral,
    dressed in his shroud,   1265
And I or you pocketless of a dime may purchase the pick of the earth,
And to glance with an eye or show a bean in its pod confounds the learning of
    all times,
And there is no trade or employment but the young man following it may
    become a hero,
And there is no object so soft but it makes a hub for the wheeled universe,
And any man or woman shall stand cool and supercilious before a million
    universes.   1270

And I call to mankind, Be not curious about God,
For I who am curious about each am not curious about God,
No array of terms can say how much I am at peace about God and about
    death.   *Knows God is there*
I hear and behold God in every object, yet I understand God not in the least,
Nor do I understand who there can be more wonderful than myself.   1275

Why should I wish to see God better than this day?   *Celebrate self*
I see something of God each hour of the twenty-four, and each moment then,
In the faces of men and women I see God, and in my own face in the glass;
I find letters from God dropped in the street, and every one is signed by God's
    name,
And I leave them where they are, for I know that others will punctually come
    forever and ever.   1280

[49]

And as to you death, and you bitter hug of mortality . . . . it is idle to try to
    alarm me.

To his work without flinching the accoucheur[34] comes,
I see the elderhand pressing receiving supporting,
I recline by the sills of the exquisite flexible doors . . . . and mark the outlet,
    and mark the relief and escape.
And as to you corpse I think you are good manure, but that does not offend
    me,   1285
I smell the white roses sweetscented and growing,
I reach to the leafy lips . . . . I reach to the polished breasts of melons.

And as to you life, I reckon you are the leavings of many deaths,
No doubt I have died myself ten thousand times before.

I hear you whispering there O stars of heaven,   1290
O suns . . . . O grass of graves . . . . O perpetual transfers and promotions
    . . . . if you do not say anything how can I say anything?

Of the turbid pool that lies in the autumn forest,
Of the moon that descends the steeps of the soughing twilight,
Toss, sparkles of day and dusk . . . . toss on the black stems that decay in the
    muck,
Toss to the moaning gibberish of the dry limbs.   1295

I ascend from the moon . . . . I ascend from the night,
And perceive of the ghastly glitter the sunbeams reflected,
And debouch to the steady and central from the offspring great or small.

[50]

There is that in me . . . I do not know what it is . . . . but I know it is in me.

Wrenched and sweaty . . . . calm and cool and then my body becomes;   1300
I sleep . . . . I sleep long.

I do not know it . . . . it is without name . . . . it is a word unsaid,
It is not in any dictionary or utterance or symbol.

Something it swings on more than the earth I swing on,
To it the creation is the friend whose embracing awakes me.   1305
Perhaps I might tell more . . . . Outlines! I plead for my brothers and sisters.

---

[34] Midwife.

Do you see O my brothers and sisters?
It is not chaos or death . . . . it is form and union and plan . . . . it is eternal
    life . . . . it is happiness.

[51]

The past and present wilt . . . . I have filled them and emptied them,
And proceed to fill my next fold of the future.   1310

Listener up there! Here you . . . . what have you to confide to me?
Look in my face while I snuff the sidle of evening,
Talk honestly, for no one else hears you, and I stay only a minute longer.

Do I contradict myself?
Very well then . . . I contradict myself;   1315
I am large . . . . I contain multitudes.

I concentrate toward them that are nigh . . . . I wait on the door-slab.

Who has done his day's work and will soonest be through with his supper?
Who wishes to walk with me?

Will you speak before I am gone? Will you prove already too late?   1320

[52]

The spotted hawk swoops by and accuses me . . . . he complains of my gab and
    my loitering.

I too am not a bit tamed . . . . I too am untranslatable,
I sound my barbaric yawp over the roofs of the world.

The last scud of day holds back for me,
It flings my likeness after the rest and true as any on the shadowed wilds,   1325
It coaxes me to the vapor and the dusk.
I depart as air . . . . I shake my white locks at the runaway sun,
I effuse my flesh in eddies and drift it in lacy jags.

I bequeath myself to the dirt to grow from the grass I love,
If you want me again look for me under your bootsoles.   1330

You will hardly know who I am or what I mean,
But I shall be good health to you nevertheless,
And filter and fibre your blood.

Failing to fetch me at first keep encouraged,
Missing me one place search another,   1335
I stop some where waiting for you

1855

[A Song for Occupations]*

Come closer to me,
Push close my lovers and take the best I possess,
Yield closer and closer and give me the best you possess.

This is unfinished business with me . . . . how is it with you?
I was chilled with the cold types and cylinder and wet paper between us.   5

I pass so poorly with paper and types . . . . I must pass with the contact of
    bodies and souls.

I do not thank you for liking me as I am, and liking the touch of me I
    know that it is good for you to do so.

Were all educations practical and ornamental well displayed out of me, what
    would it amount to?
Were I as the head teacher or charitable proprietor or wise statesman, what
    would it amount to?
Were I to you as the boss employing and paying you, would that satisfy you?   10

The learned and virtuous and benevolent, and the usual terms;
A man like me, and never the usual terms.

Neither a servant nor a master am I,
I take no sooner a large price than a small price . . . . I will have my own
    whoever enjoys me,
I will be even with you, and you shall be even with me.   15

If you are a workman or workwoman I stand as nigh as the nighest that works
    in the same shop,
If you bestow gifts on your brother or dearest friend, I demand as good as your
    brother or dearest friend,
If your lover or husband or wife is welcome by day or night, I must be
    personally as welcome;
If you have become degraded or ill, then I will become so for your sake;
If you remember your foolish and outlawed deeds, do you think I cannot
    remember my foolish and outlawed deeds?   20
If you carouse at the table I say I will carouse at the opposite side of the table;

---

* Final title supplied in 1881.

If you meet some stranger in the street and love him or her, do I not often
    meet strangers in the street and love them?
If you see a good deal remarkable in me I see just as much remarkable in you.

Why what have you thought of yourself?
Is it you then that thought yourself less?   25
Is it you that thought the President greater than you? or the rich better off than
    you? or the educated wiser than you?

Because you are greasy or pimpled—or that you was once drunk, or a thief, or
    diseased, or rheumatic, or a prostitute—or are so now—or from frivolity or
    impotence—or that you are no scholar, and never saw your name in print
    . . . . do you give in that you are any less immortal?

Souls of men and women! it is not you I call unseen, unheard, untouchable and
    untouching;
It is not you I go argue pro and con about, and to settle whether you are alive
    or no;
I own publicly who you are, if nobody else owns . . . . and see and hear you,
    and what you give and take;   30
What is there you cannot give and take?

I see not merely that you are polite or whitefaced . . . . married or single . . . .
    citizens of old states or citizens of new states . . . . eminent in some
    profession . . . . a lady or gentleman in a parlor . . . . or dressed in the jail
    uniform . . . . or pulpit uniform,
Not only the free Utahan, Kansian, or Arkansian . . . . not only the free Cuban
    . . . not merely the slave . . . . not Mexican native, or Flatfoot, or negro
    from Africa,
Iroquois eating the warflesh—fishtearer in his lair of rocks and sand . . . .
    Esquimaux in the dark cold snowhouse . . . . Chinese with his transverse eyes
    . . . . Bedowee—or wandering nomad—or tabounschik at the head of his
    droves,
Grown, half-grown, and babe—of this country and every country, indoors and
    outdoors I see . . . . and all else is behind or through them.   35

The wife—and she is not one jot less than the husband,
The daughter—and she is just as good as the son,
The mother—and she is every bit as much as the father.

Offspring of those not rich—boys apprenticed to trades,
Young fellows working on farms and old fellows working on farms;   40
The naive . . . . the simple and hardy . . . . he going to the polls to vote . . . .
    he who has a good time, and he who has a bad time;
Mechanics, southerners, new arrivals, sailors, mano'warsmen, merchantmen,
    coasters,
All these I see . . . . but nigher and farther the same I see;
None shall escape me, and none shall wish to escape me.

I bring what you much need, yet always have, 45
I bring not money or amours or dress or eating. . . . but I bring as good;
And send no agent or medium . . . . and offer no representative of value—but offer the value itself.

There is something that comes home to one now and perpetually,
It is not what is printed or preached or discussed . . . . it eludes discussion and print,
It is not to be put in a book . . . . it is not in this book, 50
It is for you whoever you are . . . . it is no farther from you than your hearing and sight are from you,
It is hinted by nearest and commonest and readiest . . . . it is not them, though it is endlessly provoked by them . . . . What is there ready and near you now?
You may read in many languages and read nothing about it;
You may read the President's message and read nothing about it there,
Nothing in the reports from the state department or treasury department. . . . or in the daily papers, or the weekly papers, 55
Or in the census returns or assessors' returns or prices current or any accounts of stock.

The sun and stars that float in the open air . . . . the appleshaped earth and we upon it . . . . surely the drift of them is something grand;
I do not know what it is except that it is grand, and that it is happiness,
And that the enclosing purport of us here is not a speculation, or bon-mot or reconnoissance,
And that it is not something which by luck may turn out well for us, and without luck must be a failure for us, 60
And not something which may yet be retracted in a certain contingency.

The light and shade—the curious sense of body and identity—the greed that with perfect complaisance devours all things—the endless pride and outstretching of man—unspeakable joys and sorrows,
The wonder every one sees in every one else he sees . . . . and the wonders that fill each minute of time forever and each acre of surface and space forever,
Have you reckoned them as mainly for a trade or farmwork? or for the profits of a store? or to achieve yourself a position? or to fill a gentleman's leisure or a lady's leisure?

Have you reckoned the landscape took substance and form that it might be painted in a picture?
65
Or men and women that they might be written of, and songs sung?
Or the attraction of gravity and the great laws and harmonious combinations and the fluids of the air as subjects for the savans?[35]
Or the brown land and the blue sea for maps and charts?

[35] Savants.

Or the stars to be put in constellations and named fancy names?
Or that the growth of seeds is for agricultural tables or agriculture itself?   70

Old institutions . . . . these arts libraries legends collections—and the practice
    handed along in manufactures . . . . will we rate them so high?
Will we rate our prudence and business so high? . . . . I have no objection,
I rate them as high as the highest . . . . but a child born of a woman and man I
    rate beyond all rate.

We thought our Union grand and our Constitution grand;
I do not say they are not grand and good—for they are,   75
I am this day just as much in love with them as you,
But I am eternally in love with you and with all my fellows upon the earth.

We consider the bibles and religions divine . . . . I do not say they are not
    divine,
I say they have all grown out of you and may grow out of you still,
It is not they who give the life . . . . it is you who give the life;   80
Leaves are not more shed from the trees or trees from the earth than they are
    shed out of you.

The sum of all known value and respect I add up in you whoever you are;
The President is up there in the White House for you . . . . it is not you who
    are here for him,
The Secretaries act in their bureaus for you . . . . not you here for them,
The Congress convenes every December for you,   85
Laws, courts, the forming of states, the charters of cities, the going and coming
    of commerce and mails are all for you.

All doctrines, all politics and civilization exurge from you,
All sculpture and monuments and anything inscribed anywhere are tallied in
    you,
The gist of histories and statistics as far back as the records reach is in you this
    hour—and myths and tales the same;
If you were not breathing and walking here where would they all be?   90
The most renowned poems would be ashes . . . . orations and plays would be
    vacuums.

All architecture is what you do to it when you look upon it;
Did you think it was in the white or gray stone? or the lines of the arches and
    cornices?

All music is what awakens from you when you are reminded by the
    instruments,
It is not the violins and the cornets . . . . it is not the oboe nor the beating
    drums—nor the notes of the baritone singer singing his sweet romanza . . . .
    nor those of the men's chorus, nor those of the women's chorus,   95
It is nearer and farther than they.

Will the whole come back then?

Can each see the signs of the best by a look in the lookingglass? Is there
    nothing greater or more?

Does all sit there with you and here with me?

The old forever new things . . . . you foolish child! . . . . the closest simplest   100
    things—this moment with you,

Your person and every particle that relates to your person,

The pulses of your brain waiting their chance and encouragement at every deed
    or sight;

Anything you do in public by day, and anything you do in secret
    betweendays,

What is called right and what is called wrong . . . . what you behold or touch
    . . . . what causes your anger or wonder,

The anklechain of the slave, the bed of the bedhouse, the cards of the gambler,
    the plates of the forger;   105

What is seen or learned in the street, or intuitively learned,

What is learned in the public school—spelling, reading, writing and ciphering
    . . . . the blackboard and the teacher's diagrams:

The panes of the windows and all that appears through them . . . . the going
    forth in the morning and the aimless spending of the day;

(What is it that you made money? what is it that you got what you wanted?)

The usual routine . . . . the workshop, factory, yard, office, store, or desk;   110

The jaunt of hunting or fishing, or the life of hunting or fishing,

Pasturelife, foddering, milking and herding, and all the personnel and usages;

The plum-orchard and apple-orchard . . . . gardening . . seedlings, cuttings,
    flowers and vines,

Grains and manures . . marl, clay, loam . . the subsoil plough . . the shovel and
    pick and rake and hoe . . irrigation and draining;

The currycomb . . the horse-cloth . . the halter and bridle and bits . . the very
    wisps of straw,   115

The barn and barn-yard . . the bins and mangers . . the mows and racks:

Manufactures . . commerce . . engineering . . the building of cities, and every
    trade carried on there . . and the implements of every trade,

The anvil and tongs and hammer . . the axe and wedge . . the square and mitre
    and jointer and smoothingplane;

The plumbob and trowel and level . . the wall-scaffold, and the work of walls
    and ceilings . . or any mason-work:

The ship's compass . . the sailor's tarpaulin . . the stays and lanyards, and the
    ground-tackle for anchoring or mooring,   120

The sloop's tiller . . the pilot's wheel and bell . . the yacht or fish-smack . . the
    great gay-pennanted three-hundred-foot steamboat under full headway, with
    her proud fat breasts and her delicate swift-flashing paddles;

The trail and line and hooks and sinkers . . the seine, and hauling the seine;

Smallarms and rifles . . . . the powder and shot and caps and wadding . . . . the
    ordnance for war . . . . the carriages:

Everyday objects . . . . the housechairs, the carpet, the bed and the counterpane
 of the bed, and him or her sleeping at night, and the wind blowing, and the
 indefinite noises:

The snowstorm or rainstorm . . . . the tow-trowsers . . . . the lodge-hut in the
 woods, and the still-hunt: 125

City and country . . fireplace and candle . . gaslight and heater and aqueduct;

The message of the governor, mayor, or chief of police . . . . the dishes of
 breakfast or dinner or supper;

The bunkroom, the fire-engine, the string-team, and the car or truck behind;

The paper I write on or you write on . . and every word we write . . and
 every cross and twirl of the pen . . and the curious way we write what we
 think . . . . yet very faintly;

The directory, the detector, the ledger . . . . the books in ranks or the
 bookshelves . . . . the clock attached to the wall,   130

The ring on your finger . . the lady's wristlet . . the hammers of stonebreakers
 or coppersmiths . . the druggist's vials and jars;

The etui of surgical instruments, and the etui of oculist's or aurist's instruments,
 or dentist's instruments;

Glassblowing, grinding of wheat and corn . . casting, and what is cast . .
 tinroofing, shingledressing,

Shipcarpentering, flagging of sidewalks by flaggers . . dockbuilding, fishcuring,
 ferrying;

The pump, the piledriver, the great derrick . . the coalkiln and brickkiln, 135

Ironworks or whiteleadworks . . the sugarhouse . . steamsaws, and the great
 mills and factories;

The cottonbale . . the stevedore's hook . . the saw and buck of the sawyer . .
 the screen of the coalscreener . . the mould of the moulder . . the
 workingknife of the butcher;

The cylinder press . . the handpress . . the frisket and tympan . . the
 compositor's stick and rule,

The implements for daguerreotyping . . . . the tools of the rigger or grappler or
 sailmaker or blockmaker,

Goods of guttapercha or papiermache . . . . colors and brushes . . . . glaziers'
 implements,   140

The veneer and gluepot . . the confectioner's ornaments . . the decanter and
 glasses . . the shears and flatiron;

The awl and kneestrap . . the pint measure and quart measure . . the counter
 and stool . . the writingpen of quill or metal;

Billiards and tenpins . . . . the ladders and hanging ropes of the gymnasium, and
 the manly exercises;

The designs for wallpapers or oilcloths or carpets . . . . the fancies for goods for
 women . . . . the bookbinder's stamps;

Leatherdressing, coachmaking, boilermaking, ropetwisting, distilling,
 signpainting, limeburning, coopering, cottonpicking,   145

The walkingbeam of the steam-engine . . the throttle and governors, and the up
 and down rods,

Stavemachines and plainingmachines . . . . the cart of the carman . . the
  omnibus . . the ponderous dray;
The snowplough and two engines pushing it . . . . the ride in the express train
  of only one car . . . . the swift go through a howling storm:
The bearhunt or coonhunt . . . . the bonfire of shavings in the open lot in the
  city . . the crowd of children watching;
The blows of the fighting-man . . the upper cut and one-two-three;   150
The shopwindows . . . . the coffins in the sexton's wareroom . . . . the fruit on
  the fruitstand . . . . the beef on the butcher's stall,
The bread and cakes in the bakery . . . . the white and red pork in the
  pork-store;
The milliner's ribbons . . the dressmaker's patterns . . . . the tea-table . . the
  homemade sweetmeats:
The column of wants in the one-cent paper . . the news by telegraph . . . . the
  amusements and operas and shows:
The cotton and woolen and linen you wear . . . . the money you make and
  spend;   155
Your room and bedroom . . . . your piano-forte . . . . the stove and cookpans,
The house you live in . . . . the rent . . . . the other tenants . . . . the deposite
  in the savings-bank . . . . the trade at the grocery,
The pay on Saturday night . . . . the going home, and the purchases;
In them the heft of the heaviest . . . . in them far more than you estimated, and
  far less also,
In them, not yourself . . . . you and your soul enclose all things, regardless of
  estimation,   160
In them your themes and hints and provokers . . if not, the whole earth has no
  themes or hints or provokers, and never had.

I do not affirm what you see beyond is futile . . . . I do not advise you to stop,
I do not say leadings you thought great are not great,
But I say that none lead to greater or sadder or happier than those lead to.

Will you seek afar off? You surely come back at last,   165
In things best known to you finding the best or as good as the best,
In folks nearest to you finding also the sweetest and strongest and lovingest,
Happiness not in another place, but this place . . not for another hour, but this
  hour,
Man in the first you see or touch . . . . always in your friend or brother or
  nighest neighbor . . . . Woman in your mother or lover or wife,
And all else thus far known giving place to men and women.   170

When the psalm sings instead of the singer,
When the script preaches instead of the preacher,
When the pulpit descends and goes instead of the carver that carved the
  supporting desk,
When the sacred vessels or the bits of the eucharist, or the lath and plast,

procreate as effectually as the young silversmiths or bakers, or the masons in
their overalls,
When a university course convinces like a slumbering woman and child
convince,   175
When the minted gold in the vault smiles like the nightwatchman's daughter,
When warrantee deeds loafe in chairs opposite and are my friendly companions,
I intend to reach them my hand and make as much of them as I do of men and
women.

1855

[To Think of Time]*

To think of time . . . . to think through the retrospection,
To think of today . . and the ages continued henceforward.

Have you guessed you yourself would not continue? Have you dreaded those
earth-beetles?
Have you feared the future would be nothing to you?

Is today nothing? Is the beginningless past nothing?   5
If the future is nothing they are just as surely nothing.

To think that the sun rose in the east . . . . that men and women were flexible
and real and alive . . . . that every thing was real and alive;
To think that you and I did not see feel think nor bear our part,
To think that we are now here and bear our part.

Not a day passes . . not a minute or second without an accouchement;   10
Not a day passes . . not a minute or second without a corpse.

When the dull nights are over, and the dull days also,
When the soreness of lying so much in bed is over,
When the physician, after long putting off, gives the silent and terrible look for
an answer,
When the children come hurried and weeping, and the brothers and sisters have
been sent for,   15
When medicines stand unused on the shelf, and the camphor-smell has pervaded
the rooms,
When the faithful hand of the living does not desert the hand of the dying,
When the twitching lips press lightly on the forehead of the dying,
When the breath ceases and the pulse of the heart ceases,
Then the corpse-limbs stretch on the bed, and the living look upon them,   20
They are palpable as the living are palpable.

---
* Final title supplied in 1871.

The living look upon the corpse with their eyesight,
But without eyesight lingers a different living and looks curiously on the
    corpse.

To think that the rivers will come to flow, and the snow fall, and fruits ripen
    . . and act upon others as upon us now . . . . yet not act upon us;
To think of all these wonders of city and country . . and others taking great
    interest in them . . and we taking small interest in them.   25

To think how eager we are in building our houses,
To think others shall be just as eager . . and we quite indifferent.

I see one building the house that serves him a few years . . . . or seventy or
    eighty years at most;
I see one building the house that serves him longer than that.

Slowmoving and black lines creep over the whole earth . . . . they never cease
    . . . . they are the burial lines,   30
He that was President was buried, and he that is now President shall surely be
    buried.

Cold dash of waves at the ferrywharf,
Posh and ice in the river . . . . half-frozen mud in the streets,
A gray discouraged sky overhead . . . . the short last daylight of December,
A hearse and stages . . . . other vehicles give place,   35
The funeral of an old stagedriver . . . . the cortege mostly drivers.

Rapid the trot to the cemetery,
Duly rattles the deathbell . . . . the gate is passed . . . . the grave is halted at
    . . . . the living alight . . . . the hearse uncloses,
The coffin is lowered and settled . . . . the whip is laid on the coffin,
The earth is swiftly shovelled in . . . . a minute . . no one moves or speaks
    . . . . it is done,   40
He is decently put away . . . . is there anything more?

He was a goodfellow,
Freemouthed, quicktempered, not badlooking, able to take his own part,
Witty, sensitive to a slight, ready with life or death for a friend,
Fond of women, . . played some . . eat hearty and drank hearty,   45
Had known what it was to be flush . . grew lowspirited toward the last . .
    sickened . . was helped by a contribution,
Died aged forty-one years . . and that was his funeral.

Thumb extended or finger uplifted,
Apron, cape, gloves, strap . . . . wetweather clothes . . . . whip carefully chosen
    . . . . boss, spotter, starter, and hostler,

Somebody loafing on you, or you loafing on somebody . . . . headway . . . .
    man before and man behind,   50
Good day's work or bad day's work . . . . pet stock or mean stock . . . . first
    out or last out . . . . turning in at night,
To think that these are so much and so nigh to other drivers . . and he there
    takes no interest in them.

The markets, the government, the workingman's wages . . . . to think what
    account they are through our nights and days;
To think that other workingmen will make just as great account of them . . yet
    we make little or no account.

The vulgar and the refined . . . . what you call sin and what you call goodness
    . . to think how wide a difference;   55
To think the difference will still continue to others, yet we lie beyond the
    difference.

To think how much pleasure there is!
Have you pleasure from looking at the sky? Have you pleasure from poems?
Do you enjoy yourself in the city? or engaged in business? or planning a
    nomination and election? or with your wife and family?
Or with your mother and sisters? or in womanly housework? or the beautiful
    maternal cares?   60

These also flow onward to others . . . . you and I flow onward;
But in due time you and I shall take less interest in them.

Your farm and profits and crops . . . . to think how engrossed you are;
To think there will still be farms and profits and crops . yet for you of what
    avail?

What will be will be well—for what is is well,   65
To take interest is well, and not to take interest shall be well.

The sky continues beautiful . . . . the pleasure of men with women shall never
    be sated . . nor the pleasure of women with men . . nor the pleasure from
    poems;
The domestic joys, the daily housework or business, the building of houses—
    they are not phantasms . . they have weight and form and location;
The farms and profits and crops . . the markets and wages and government . .
    they also are not phantasms;
The difference between sin and goodness is no apparition;   70
The earth is not an echo . . . . man and his life and all the things of his life are
    well-considered.

You are not thrown to the winds . . you gather certainly and safely around
    yourself,

Yourself! Yourself! Yourself forever and ever!
It is not to diffuse you that you were born of your mother and father—it is to
    identify you,
It is not that you should be undecided, but that you should be decided;   75
Something long preparing and formless is arrived and formed in you,
You are thenceforth secure, whatever comes or goes.

The threads that were spun are gathered . . . . the weft crosses the warp. . . .
    the pattern is systematic.

The preparations have every one been justified;
The orchestra have tuned their instruments sufficiently . . . . the baton has given
    the signal.   80

The guest that was coming . . . . he waited long for reasons . . . . he is now
    housed,
He is one of those who are beautiful and happy . . . . he is one of those that to
    look upon and be with is enough.

The law of the past cannot be eluded.
The law of the present and future cannot be eluded,
The law of the living cannot be eluded . . . . it is eternal,   85
The law of promotion and transformation cannot be eluded,
The law of heroes and good-doers cannot be eluded,
The law of drunkards and informers and mean persons cannot be eluded.

Slowmoving and black lines go ceaselessly over the earth,
Northerner goes carried and southerner goes carried . . . . and they on the
    Atlantic side and they on the Pacific, and they between, and all through the
    Mississippi country . . . . and all over the earth.   90

The great masters and kosmos are well as they go . . . . the heroes and
    good-doers are well,
The known leaders and inventors and the rich owners and pious and
    distinguished may be well,
But there is more account than that . . . . there is strict account of all.
The interminable hordes of the ignorant and wicked are not nothing,
The barbarians of Africa and Asia are not nothing,   95
The common people of Europe are not nothing . . . . the American aborigines
    are not nothing,
A zambo or a foreheadless Crowfoot or a Camanche is not nothing,
The infected in the immigrant hospital are not nothing . . . . the murderer or
    mean person is not nothing,
The perpetual succession of shallow people are not nothing as they go,
The prostitute is not nothing . . . . the mocker of religion is not nothing as he
    goes.   100

I shall go with the rest . . . . we have satisfaction:
I have dreamed that we are not to be changed so much . . . . nor the law of us
    changed;
I have dreamed that heroes and good-doers shall be under the present and past
    law,
And that murderers and drunkards and liars shall be under the present and past
    law;
For I have dreamed that the law they are under now is enough.   105

And I have dreamed that the satisfaction is not so much changed . . . . and that
    there is no life without satisfaction;
What is the earth? what are body and soul without satisfaction?

I shall go with the rest,
We cannot be stopped at a given point . . . . that is no satisfaction;
To show us a good thing or a few good things for a space of time—that is no
    satisfaction;   110
We must have the indestructible breed of the best, regardless of time.

If otherwise, all these things came but to ashes of dung;
If maggots and rats ended us, then suspicion and treachery and death.
Do you suspect death? If I were to suspect death I should die now,
Do you think I could walk pleasantly and well-suited toward annihilation?   115

Pleasantly and well-suited I walk,
Whither I walk I cannot define, but I know it is good,
The whole universe indicates that it is good,
The past and the present indicate that it is good.

How beautiful and perfect are the animals! How perfect is my soul!   120
How perfect the earth, and the minutest thing upon it!
What is called good is perfect, and what is called sin is just as perfect;
The vegetables and minerals are all perfect . . and the imponderable fluids are
    perfect;
Slowly and surely they have passed on to this, and slowly and surely they will
    yet pass on.

O my soul! if I realize you I have satisfaction,   125
Animals and vegetables! if I realize you I have satisfaction,
Laws of the earth and air! if I realize you I have satisfaction.

I cannot define my satisfaction . . yet it is so,
I cannot define my life . . yet it is so.

I swear I see now that every thing has an eternal soul!   130
The trees have, rooted in the ground . . . . the weeds of the sea have . . . . the
    animals.

I swear I think there is nothing but immortality!
That the exquisite scheme is for it, and the nebulous float is for it, and the
    cohering is for it,
And all preparation is for it . . and identity is for it . . and life and death are
    for it.

1855

[The Sleepers]*

I wander all night in my vision,
Stepping with light feet . . . . swiftly and noiselessly stepping and stopping,
Bending with open eyes over the shut eyes of sleepers;
Wandering and confused . . . . lost to myself . . . . ill-assorted . . . .
    contradictory,
Pausing and gazing and bending and stopping.   5

How solemn they look there, stretched and still;
How quiet they breathe, the little children in their cradles.

The wretched features of ennuyees, the white features of corpses, the livid faces
    of drunkards, the sick-gray faces of onanists,
The gashed bodies on battlefields, the insane in their strong-doored rooms, the
    sacred idiots,
The newborn emerging from gates and the dying emerging from gates,   10
The night pervades them and enfolds them.

The married couple sleep calmly in their bed, he with his palm on the hip of
    the wife, and she with her palm on the hip of the husband,
The sisters sleep lovingly side by side in their bed,
The men sleep lovingly side by side in theirs,
And the mother sleeps with her little child carefully wrapped.   15

The blind sleep, and the deaf and dumb sleep,
The prisoner sleeps well in the prison . . . . the runaway son sleeps,
The murderer that is to be hung next day . . . . how does he sleep?
And the murdered person . . . . how does he sleep?
The female that loves unrequited sleeps,   20
And the male that loves unrequited sleeps;
The head of the moneymaker that plotted all day sleeps,
And the enraged and treacherous dispositions sleep.

I stand with drooping eyes by the worstsuffering and restless,
I pass my hands soothingly to and fro a few inches from them;   25
The restless sink in their beds . . . . they fitfully sleep.

* Final title supplied in 1871.

The earth recedes from me into the night,
I saw that it was beautiful . . . . and I see that what is not the earth is
    beautiful.

I go from bedside to bedside . . . . I sleep close with the other sleepers, each in
    turn;
I dream in my dream all the dreams of the other dreamers,   30
And I become the other dreamers.

I am a dance . . . . Play up there! the fit is whirling me fast.

I am the everlaughing . . . . it is new moon and twilight,
I see the hiding of douceurs[36] . . . . I see nimble ghosts whichever way I look,
Cache[37] and cache again deep in the ground and sea, and where it is neither
    ground or sea.   35

Well do they do their jobs, those journeymen divine,
Only from me can they hide nothing and would not if they could;
I reckon I am their boss, and they make me a pet besides,
And surround me, and lead me and run ahead when I walk,
And lift their cunning covers and signify me with stretched arms, and resume
    the way;   40
Onward we move, a gay gang of blackguards with mirthshouting music and
    wildflapping pennants of joy.

I am the actor and the actress . . . . the voter . . the politician,
The emigrant and the exile . . the criminal that stood in the box,
He who has been famous, and he who shall be famous after today,
The stammerer . . . . the wellformed person . . the wasted or feeble person. 45

I am she who adorned herself and folded her hair expectantly,
My truant lover has come and it is dark.

Double yourself and receive me darkness,
Receive me and my lover too . . . . he will not let me go without him.

I roll myself upon you as upon a bed . . . . I resign myself to the dusk.   50

He whom I call answers me and takes the place of my lover,
He rises with me silently from the bed.

Darkness you are gentler than my lover . . . . his flesh was sweaty and panting,
I feel the hot moisture yet that he left me.

---

[36] French: "delights."   [37] Hide (from French *cacher*: "to hide").

My hands are spread forth . . I pass them in all directions,   55
I would sound up the shadowy shore to which you are journeying.

Be careful, darkness . . . . already, what was it touched me?
I thought my lover had gone . . . . else darkness and he are one,
I hear the heart-beat . . . . I follow . . I fade away.

O hotcheeked and blushing! O foolish hectic!   60
O for pity's sake, no one must see me now! . . . . my clothes were stolen while
    I was abed,
Now I am thrust forth, where shall I run?

Pier that I saw dimly last night when I looked from the windows,
Pier out from the main, let me catch myself with you and stay . . . . I will not
    chafe you;
I feel ashamed to go naked about the world,   65
And am curious to know where my feet stand . . . . and what is this flooding
    me, childhood or manhood . . . . and the hunger that crosses the bridge
    between.

The cloth laps a first sweet eating and drinking,
Laps life-swelling yolks . . . . laps ear of rose-corn, milky and just ripened:
The white teeth stay, and the boss-tooth advances in darkness,
And liquor is spilled on lips and bosoms by touching glasses, and the best liquor
    afterward.   70

I descend my western course . . . . my sinews are flaccid,
Perfume and youth course through me, and I am their wake.

It is my face yellow and wrinkled instead of the old woman's,
I sit low in a strawbottom chair and carefully darn my grandson's stockings.

It is I too . . . . the sleepless widow looking out on the winter midnight,   75
I see the sparkles of starshine on the icy and pallid earth.

A shroud I see—and I am the shroud . . . . I wrap a body and lie in the coffin;
It is dark here underground . . . . it is not evil or pain here . . . . it is blank
    here, for reasons.

It seems to me that everything in the light and air ought to be happy;
Whoever is not in his coffin and the dark grave, let him know he has enough.   80

I see a beautiful gigantic swimmer swimming naked through the eddies of the
    sea,
His brown hair lies close and even to his head . . . . he strikes out with
    courageous arms . . . . he urges himself with his legs.
I see his white body . . . . I see his undaunted eyes;
I hate the swift-running eddies that would dash him headforemost on the rocks.

What are you doing you ruffianly red-trickled waves?   85
Will you kill the courageous giant? Will you kill him in the prime of his
    middle age?

Steady and long he struggles;
He is baffled and banged and bruised . . . . he holds out while his strength holds
    out,
The slapping eddies are spotted with his blood . . . . they bear him away . . . .
    they roll him and swing him and turn him:
His beautiful body is borne in the circling eddies . . . . it is continually bruised
    on rocks,   90
Swiftly and out of sight is borne the brave corpse.

I turn but do not extricate myself;
Confused . . . . a pastreading . . . . another, but with darkness yet.

The beach is cut by the razory ice-wind . . . . the wreck-guns sound,
The tempest lulls and the moon comes floundering through the drifts.   95

I look where the ship helplessly heads end on . . . . I hear the burst as she
    strikes . . I hear the howls of dismay . . . . they grow fainter and fainter.

I cannot aid with my wringing fingers;
I can but rush to the surf and let it drench me and freeze upon me.

I search with the crowd . . . . not one of the company is washed to us alive;
In the morning I help pick up the dead and lay them in rows in a barn.   100
Now of the old war-days . . the defeat at Brooklyn;[38]
Washington stands inside the lines . . he stands on the entrenched hills amid a
    crowd of officers,
His face is cold and damp . . . . he cannot repress the weeping drops . . . . he
    lifts the glass perpetually to his eyes . . . . the color is blanched from his
    cheeks,
He sees the slaughter of the southern braves confided to him by their parents.

The same at last and at last when peace is declared,   105
He stands in the room of the old tavern[39] . . . . the wellbeloved soldiers all pass
    through,
The officers speechless and slow draw near in their turns,
The chief encircles their necks with his arm and kisses them on the cheek,
He kisses lightly the wet cheeks one after another . . . . he shakes hands and
    bids goodbye to the army.

Now I tell what my mother told me today as we sat at dinner together,   110
Of when she was a nearly grown girl living home with her parents on the old
    homestead.

[38] In the Battle of Long Island, August 1776.   [39] Fraunces Tavern in New York City.

A red squaw came one breakfasttime to the old homestead,
On her back she carried a bundle of rushes for rushbottoming chairs;
Her hair straight shiny coarse black and profuse halfenveloped her face,
Her step was free and elastic . . . . her voice sounded exquisitely as she spoke.   115

My mother looked in delight and amazement at the stranger,
She looked at the beauty of her tallborne face and full and pliant limbs,
The more she looked upon her she loved her,
Never before had she seen such wonderful beauty and purity;
She made her sit on a bench by the jamb of the fireplace . . . . she cooked food
     for her,   120
She had no work to give her but she gave her remembrance and fondness.

The red squaw staid all the forenoon, and toward the middle of the afternoon
     she went away;
O my mother was loth to have her go away,
All the week she thought of her . . . . she watched for her many a month,
She remembered her many a winter and many a summer,   125
But the red squaw never came nor was heard of there again.

Now Lucifer was not dead . . . . or if he was I am his sorrowful terrible heir;
I have been wronged . . . . I am oppressed . . . . I hate him that oppresses me,
I will either destroy him, or he shall release me.

Damn him! how he does defile me,   130
How he informs against my brother and sister and takes pay for their blood,
How he laughs when I look down the bend after the steamboat that carries
     away my woman.

Now the vast dusk bulk that is the whale's bulk . . . . it seems mine,
Warily, sportsman! though I lie so sleepy and sluggish, my tap is death.

A show of the summer softness . . . . a contact of something unseen . . . . an
     amour of the light and air;   135
I am jealous and overwhelmed with friendliness,
And will go gallivant with the light and the air myself,
And have an unseen something to be in contact with them also.

O love and summer! you are in the dreams and in me,
Autumn and winter are in the dreams . . . . the farmer goes with his thrift,   140
The droves and crops increase . . . . the barns are wellfilled.
Elements merge in the night . . . . ships make tacks in the dreams . . . . the
     sailor sails . . . . the exile returns home,
The fugitive returns unharmed . . . . the immigrant is back beyond months and
     years;
The poor Irishman lives in the simple house of his childhood, with the
     wellknown neighbors and faces,

They warmly welcome him . . . . he is barefoot again . . . . he forgets he is
    welloff;   145
The Dutchman voyages home, and the Scotchman and Welchman voyage home
    . . and the native of the Mediterranean voyages home;
To every port of England and France and Spain enter wellfilled ships;
The Swiss foots it toward his hills . . . . the Prussian goes his way, and the
    Hungarian his way, and the Pole goes his way,
The Swede returns, and the Dane and Norwegian return.

The homeward bound and the outward bound,   150
The beautiful lost swimmer, the ennuyee, the onanist, the female that loves
    unrequited, the moneymaker,
The actor and actress . . those through with their parts and those waiting to
    commence,
The affectionate boy, the husband and wife, the voter, the nominee that is
    chosen and the nominee that has failed,
The great already known, and the great anytime after to day,
The stammerer, the sick, the perfectformed, the homely,   155
The criminal that stood in the box, the judge that sat and sentenced him, the
    fluent lawyers, the jury, the audience,
The laugher and weeper, the dancer, the midnight widow, the red squaw,
The consumptive, the erysipalite, the idiot, he that is wronged,
The antipodes, and every one between this and them in the dark,
I swear they are averaged now . . . . one is no better than the other,   160
The night and sleep have likened them and restored them.
I swear they are all beautiful,
Every one that sleeps is beautiful . . . . every thing in the dim night is
    beautiful,
The wildest and bloodiest is over and all is peace.

Peace is always beautiful,   165
The myth of heaven indicates peace and night.

The myth of heaven indicates the soul;
The soul is always beautiful . . . . it appears more or it appears less . . . . it
    comes or lags behind,
It comes from its embowered garden and looks pleasantly on itself and encloses
    the world;
Perfect and clean the genitals previously jetting, and perfect and clean the
    womb cohering,   170
The head wellgrown and proportioned and plumb, and the bowels and joints
    proportioned and plumb.

The soul is always beautiful,
The universe is duly in order . . . . every thing is in its place,
What is arrived is in its place, and what waits is in its place;
The twisted skull waits . . . . the watery or rotten blood waits,   175

The child of the glutton or venerealee waits long, and the child of the
    drunkard waits long, and the drunkard himself waits long,
The sleepers that lived and died wait . . . . the far advanced are to go on in
    their turns, and the far behind are to go on in their turns,
The diverse shall be no less diverse, but they shall flow and unite . . . . they
    unite now.

The sleepers are very beautiful as they lie unclothed,
They flow hand in hand over the whole earth from east to west as they lie
    unclothed;   180
The Asiatic and African are hand in hand . . . . the European and American are
    hand in hand,
Learned and unlearned are hand in hand . . and male and female are hand in
    hand;
The bare arm of the girl crosses the bare breast of her lover . . . . they press
    close without lust . . . . his lips press her neck,
The father holds his grown or ungrown son in his arms with measureless
    love . . . . and the son holds the father in his arms with measureless love,
The white hair of the mother shines on the white wrist of the daughter,   185
The breath of the boy goes with the breath of the man . . . . friend is inarmed
    by friend,
The scholar kisses the teacher and the teacher kisses the scholar . . . . the
    wronged is made right,
The call of the slave is one with the master's call . . and the master salutes the
    slave,
The felon steps forth from the prison . . . . the insane becomes sane . . . . the
    suffering of sick persons is relieved,
The sweatings and fevers stop . . the throat that was unsound is sound . . the
    lungs of the consumptive are resumed . . the poor distressed head is free,   190
The joints of the rheumatic move as smoothly as ever, and smoother than ever,
Stiflings and passages open . . . . the paralysed become supple,
The swelled and convulsed and congested awake to themselves in condition,
They pass the invigoration of the night and the chemistry of the night and
    awake.

I too pass from the night;   195
I stay awhile away O night, but I return to you again and love you;
Why should I be afraid to trust myself to you?
I am not afraid . . . . I have been well brought forward by you;
I love the rich running day, but I do not desert her in whom I lay so long;
I know not how I came of you, and I know not where I go with you . . . .
    but I know I came well and shall go well.   200
I will stop only a time with the night . . . . and rise betimes.

I will duly pass the day O my mother and duly return to you;
Not you will yield forth the dawn again more surely than you will yield forth
    me again,

Not the womb yields the babe in its time more surely than I shall be yielded
    from you in my time.

1855

[I Sing the Body Electric]*

The bodies of men and women engirth me, and I engirth them,
They will not let me off nor I them till I go with them and respond to them
    and love them.

Was it dreamed whether those who corrupted their own live bodies could
    conceal themselves?
And whether those who defiled the living were as bad as they who defiled the
    dead?

The expression of the body of man or woman balks account,   5
The male is perfect and that of the female is perfect.

The expression of a wellmade man appears not only in his face,
It is in his limbs and joints also . . . . it is curiously in the joints of his hips and
    wrists,
It is in his walk . . the carriage of his neck . . the flex of his waist and knees
    . . . . dress does not hide him,
The strong sweet supple quality he has strikes through the cotton and flannel;   10
To see him pass conveys as much as the best poem . . perhaps more,
You linger to see his back and the back of his neck and shoulderside.

The sprawl and fulness of babes . . . . the bosoms and heads of women . . . .
    the folds of their dress . . . . their style as we pass in the street . . . . the
    contour of their shape downwards;
The swimmer naked in the swimmingbath . . seen as he swims through the salt
    transparent greenshine, or lies on his back and rolls silently with the heave of
    the water;
Framers bare-armed framing a house . . hoisting the beams in their places . . or
    using the mallet and mortising-chisel,   15
The bending forward and backward of rowers in rowboats . . . . the horseman
    in his saddle;
Girls and mothers and housekeepers in all their exquisite offices,
The group of laborers seated at noontime with their open dinnerkettles, and
    their wives waiting,
The female soothing a child . . . . the farmer's daughter in the garden or
    cowyard,

---

* Final title supplied in 1867, by which time the
poem, revised and augmented, opened with the
line: "I sing the body electric."

The woodman rapidly swinging his axe in the woods . . . . the young fellow
    hoeing corn . . . . the sleighdriver guiding his six horses through the crowd,   20
The wrestle of wrestlers . . two apprentice-boys, quite grown, lusty,
    goodnatured, nativeborn, out on the vacant lot at sundown after work,
The coats vests and caps thrown down . . the embrace of love and resistance,
The upperhold and underhold—the hair rumpled over and blinding the eyes;
The march of firemen in their own costumes—the play of the masculine muscle
    through cleansetting trowsers and waistbands,
The slow return from the fire . . . . the pause when the bell strikes suddenly
    again—the listening on the alert,   25
The natural perfect and varied attitudes . . . . the bent head, the curved neck,
    the counting:
Suchlike I love . . . . I loosen myself and pass freely . . . . and am at the
    mother's breast with the little child,
And swim with the swimmer, and wrestle with wrestlers, and march in line
    with the firemen, and pause and listen and count.

I knew a man . . . . he was a common farmer . . . . he was the father of five
    sons . . . and in them were the fathers of sons . . . and in them were the
    fathers of sons.

This man was of wonderful vigor and calmness and beauty of person;   30
The shape of his head, the richness and breadth of his manners, the pale yellow
    and white of his hair and beard, the immeasurable meaning of his black eyes,
These I used to go and visit him to see . . . . He was wise also,
He was six feet tall . . . . he was over eighty years old . . . . his sons were
    massive clean bearded tanfaced and handsome,
They and his daughters loved him . . . all who saw him loved him . . . they
    did not love him by allowance . . . they loved him with personal love;
He drank water only . . . . the blood showed like scarlet through the clear
    brown skin of his face;   35
He was a frequent gunner and fisher . . . he sailed his boat himself . . . he had
    a fine one presented to him by a shipjoiner . . . . he had fowling-pieces,
    presented to him by men that loved him;
When he went with his five sons and many grandsons to hunt or fish you
    would pick him out as the most beautiful and vigorous of the gang,
You would wish long and long to be with him . . . . you would wish to sit by
    him in the boat that you and he might touch each other.

I have perceived that to be with those I like is enough,
To stop in company with the rest at evening is enough,
To be surrounded by beautiful curious breathing laughing flesh is enough,   40
To pass among them . . to touch any one . . . . to rest my arm ever so lightly
    round his or her neck for a moment . . . . what is this then?
I do not ask any more delight . . . . I swim in it as in a sea.

There is something in staying close to men and women and looking on them
   and in the contact and odor of them that pleases the soul well,
All things please the soul, but these please the soul well.   45

This is the female form,
A divine nimbus exhales from it from head to foot,
It attracts with fierce undeniable attraction,
I am drawn by its breath as if I were no more than a helpless vapor . . . . all
   falls aside but myself and it,
Books, art, religion, time . . the visible and solid earth . . the atmosphere and
   the fringed clouds . . what was expected of heaven or feared of hell are now
   consumed,   50
Mad filaments, ungovernable shoots play out of it . . the response likewise
   ungovernable,
Hair, bosom, hips, bend of legs, negligent falling hands—all diffused . . . . mine
   too diffused,
Ebb stung by the flow, and flow stung by the ebb . . . . loveflesh swelling and
   deliciously aching,
Limitless limpid jets of love hot and enormous . . . . quivering jelly of love
   . . . white-blow and delirious juice,
Bridegroom-night of love working surely and softly into the prostrate dawn,   55
Undulating into the willing and yielding day,
Lost in the cleave of the clasping and sweetfleshed day.

This is the nucleus . . . after the child is born of woman the man is born of
   woman,
This is the bath of birth . . . this is the merge of small and large and the outlet
   again.

Be not ashamed women . . your privilege encloses the rest . . it is the exit of
   the rest,   60
You are the gates of the body and you are the gates of the soul.

The female contains all qualities and tempers them . . . . she is in her place
   . . . . she moves with perfect balance,
She is all things duly veiled . . . . she is both passive and active . . . . she is to
   conceive daughters as well as sons and sons as well as daughters.

As I see my soul reflected in nature . . . . as I see through a mist one with
   inexpressible completeness and beauty . . . . see the bent head and arms
   folded over the breast . . . . the female I see,
I see the bearer of the great fruit which is immortality . . . . the good thereof
   is not tasted by roues, and never can be.   65

The male is not less the soul, nor more . . . . he too is in his place,
He too is all qualities . . . . he is action and power . . . . the flush of the
   known universe is in him,

Scorn becomes him well and appetite and defiance become him well,
The fiercest largest passions . . bliss that is utmost and sorrow that is utmost
    become him well . . . . pride is for him,
The fullspread pride of man is calming and excellent to the soul;   70
Knowledge becomes him . . . . he likes it always . . . . he brings everything to
    the test of himself,
Whatever the survey . . whatever the sea and the sail, he strikes soundings at
    last only here,
Where else does he strike soundings except here?

The man's body is sacred and the woman's body is sacred . . . . it is no matter
    who,
Is it a slave? Is it one of the dullfaced immigrants just landed on the wharf?   75

Each belongs here or anywhere just as much as the welloff . . . . just as much as
    you,
Each has his or her place in the procession.

All is a procession,
The universe is a procession with measured and beautiful motion.

Do you know so much that you call the slave or the dullface ignorant?   80
Do you suppose you have a right to a good sight . . . and he or she has no
    right to a sight?
Do you think matter has cohered together from its diffused float, and the soil is
    on the surface and water runs and vegetation sprouts for you . . and not for
    him and her?

A slave at auction!
I help the auctioneer . . . . the sloven does not half know his business.

Gentlemen look on this curious creature,   85
Whatever the bids of the bidders they cannot be high enough for him,
For him the globe lay preparing quintillions of years without one animal or
    plant,
For him the revolving cycles truly and steadily rolled.

In that head the allbaffling brain,
In it and below it the making of the attributes of heroes.   90

Examine these limbs, red black or white . . . . they are very cunning in tendon
    and nerve;
They shall be stript that you may see them.

Exquisite senses, lifelit eyes, pluck, volition,
Flakes of breastmuscle, pliant backbone and neck, flesh not flabby, goodsized
    arms and legs,
And wonders within there yet.   95

Within there runs his blood . . . . the same old blood . . the same red running
  blood;
There swells and jets his heart . . . . There all passions and desires . . all
  reachings and aspirations:
Do you think they are not there because they are not expressed in parlors and
  lecture-rooms?

This is not only one man . . . . he is the father of those who shall be fathers in
  their turns,
In him the start of populous states and rich republics,   100
Of him countless immortal lives with countless embodiments and enjoyments.

How do you know who shall come from the offspring of his offspring through
  the centuries?
Who might you find you have come from yourself if you could trace back
  through the centuries?

A woman at auction,
She too is not only herself . . . . she is the teeming mother of mothers,   105
She is the bearer of them that shall grow and be mates to the mothers.

Her daughters or their daughters' daughters . . who knows who shall mate with
  them?
Who knows through the centuries what heroes may come from them?

In them and of them natal love . . . . in them the divine mystery . . . . the
  same old beautiful mystery.

Have you ever loved a woman?   110
Your mother . . . . is she living? . . . . Have you been much with her? and has
  she been much with you?
Do you not see that these are exactly the same to all in all nations and times all
  over the earth?

If life and the soul are sacred the human body is sacred;
And the glory and sweet of a man is the token of manhood untainted,
And in man or woman a clean strong firmfibred body is beautiful as the most
  beautiful face.   115

Have you seen the fool that corrupted his own live body? or the fool that
  corrupted her own live body?
For they do not conceal themselves, and cannot conceal themselves.

Who degrades or defiles the living human body is cursed,
Who degrades or defiles the body of the dead is not more cursed.

1855

[Faces]*

Sauntering the pavement or riding the country byroad here then are faces,
Faces of friendship, precision, caution, suavity, ideality,
The spiritual prescient face, the always welcome common benevolent face,
The face of the singing of music, the grand faces of natural lawyers and judges
    broad at the backtop,
The faces of hunters and fishers, bulged at the brows . . . . the shaved blanched
    faces of orthodox citizens,   5
The pure extravagant yearning questioning artist's face,
The welcome ugly face of some beautiful soul . . . . the handsome detested or
    despised face,
The sacred faces of infants . . . . the illuminated face of the mother of many
    children,
The face of an amour . . . . the face of veneration,
The face as of a dream . . . . the face of an immobile rock,   10
The face withdrawn of its good and bad . . a castrated face,
A wild hawk . . his wings clipped by the clipper,
A stallion that yielded at last to the thongs and knife of the gelder.

Sauntering the pavement or crossing the ceaseless ferry, here then are faces;
I see them and complain not and am content with all.   15

Do you suppose I could be content with all if I thought them their own finale?

This now is too lamentable a face for a man;
Some abject louse asking leave to be . . cringing for it,
Some milknosed maggot blessing what lets it wrig⁴⁰ to its hole.

This face is a dog's snout sniffing for garbage;   20
Snakes nest in that mouth . . I hear the sibilant threat.
This face is a haze more chill than the arctic sea,
Its sleepy and wobbling icebergs crunch as they go.

This is a face of bitter herbs . . . . this an emetic . . . . they need no label,
And more of the drugshelf . . laudanum, caoutchouc, or hog's lard.   25

This face is an epilepsy advertising and doing business . . . . its wordless tongue
    gives out the unearthly cry,
Its veins down the neck distend . . . . its eyes roll till they show nothing but
    their whites,
Its teeth grit . . the palms of the hands are cut by the turned-in nails,
The man falls struggling and foaming to the ground while he speculates well.

---

* Final title supplied in 1871.   ⁴⁰ Wriggle.

This face is bitten by vermin and worms,   30
And this is some murderer's knife with a halfpulled scabbard.

This face owes to the sexton his dismalest fee,
An unceasing deathbell tolls there.

Those are really men! . . . . the bosses and tufts of the great round globe.

Features of my equals, would you trick me with your creased and cadaverous
    march?   35
Well then you cannot trick me.

I see your rounded never-erased flow,
I see neath the rims of your haggard and mean disguises.

Splay and twist as you like . . . . poke with the tangling fores of fishes or rats,
You'll be unmuzzled . . . . you certainly will.   40

I saw the face of the most smeared and slobbering idiot they had at the asylum,
And I knew for my consolation what they knew not;
I knew of the agents that emptied and broke my brother,
The same wait to clear the rubbish from the fallen tenement;
And I shall look again in a score or two of ages,   45
And I shall meet the real landlord perfect and unharmed, every inch as good as
    myself.

The Lord advances and yet advances:
Always the shadow in front . . . . always the reached hand bringing up the
    laggards.

Out of this face emerge banners and horses . . . . O superb! . . . . I see what is
    coming,
I see the high pioneercaps . . . . I see the staves of runners clearing the way,   50
I hear victorious drums.

This face is a lifeboat;
This is the face commanding and bearded . . . . it asks no odds of the rest;
This face is flavored fruit ready for eating;
This face of a healthy honest boy is the programme of all good.   55

These faces bear testimony slumbering or awake,
They show their descent from the Master himself.

Off the word I have spoken I except not one . . . . red white or black, all are
    deific,
In each house is the ovum . . . . it comes forth after a thousand years.

Spots or cracks at the windows do not disturb me,   60
Tall and sufficient stand behind and make signs to me;
I read the promise and patiently wait.

This is a fullgrown lily's face,
She speaks to the limber-hip'd man near the garden pickets,
Come here, she blushingly cries . . . . Come nigh to me limber-hip'd man and
     give me your finger and thumb,   65
Stand at my side till I lean as high as I can upon you,
Fill me with albescent honey . . . . bend down to me,
Rub to me with your chafing beard . . rub to my breast and shoulders.

The old face of the mother of many children:
Whist! I am fully content.   70

Lulled and late is the smoke of the Sabbath morning,
It hangs low over the rows of trees by the fences,
It hangs thin by the sassafras, the wildcherry and the catbrier under them.

I saw the rich ladies in full dress at the soiree,
I heard what the run of poets were saying so long,   75
Heard who sprang in crimson youth from the white froth and the water-blue.

Behold a woman!
She looks out from her quaker cap . . . . her face is clearer and more beautiful
     than the sky.

She sits in an armchair under the shaded porch of the farmhouse,
The sun just shines on her old white head.   80

Her ample gown is of creamhued linen,
Her grandsons raised the flax, and her granddaughters spun it with the distaff
     and the wheel.

The melodious character of the earth!
The finish beyond which philosophy cannot go and does not wish to go!
The justified mother of men!   85

1855

[Song of the Answerer]*

A young man came to me with a message from his brother,
How should the young man know the whether and when of his brother?
Tell him to send me the signs.

---

* Final title supplied in 1889, by which time the
poem had been substantially augmented.

And I stood before the young man face to face, and took his right hand in my
    left hand and his left hand in my right hand,
And I answered for his brother and for men . . . . and I answered for the poet,
    and sent these signs.   5

Him all wait for . . . . him all yield up to . . . . his word is decisive and final,
Him they accept . . . . in him lave . . . . in him perceive themselves as amid
    light,
Him they immerse, and he immerses them.

Beautiful women, the haughtiest nations, laws, the landscape, people and
    animals,
The profound earth and its attributes, and the unquiet ocean,   10
All enjoyments and properties, and money, and whatever money will buy,
The best farms . . . . others toiling and planting, and he unavoidably reaps,
The noblest and costliest cities . . . . others grading and building, and he
    domiciles there;
Nothing for any one but what is for him . . . . near and far are for him,
The ships in the offing . . . . the perpetual shows and marches on land are for
    him if they are for any body.   15

He puts things in their attitudes,
He puts today out of himself with plasticity and love,
He places his own city, times, reminiscences, parents, brothers and sisters,
    associations employment and politics, so that the rest never shame them
    afterward, nor assume to command them.

He is the answerer,
What can be answered he answers, and what cannot be answered he shows how
    it cannot be answered.   20

A man is a summons and challenge,
It is vain to skulk . . . . Do you hear that mocking and laughter? Do you hear
    the ironical echoes?

Books friendships philosophers priests action pleasure pride beat up and down
    seeking to give satisfaction;
He indicates the satisfaction, and indicates them that beat up and down also.

Whichever the sex . . . whatever the season or place he may go freshly and
    gently and safely by day or by night,   25
He has the passkey of hearts . . . . to him the response of the prying of hands
    on the knobs.

His welcome is universal . . . . the flow of beauty is not more welcome or
    universal than he is,
The person he favors by day or sleeps with at night is blessed.

Every existence has its idiom . . . . every thing has an idiom and tongue;

He resolves all tongues into his own, and bestows it upon men . . and any man
    translates . . and any man translates himself also: 30

One part does not counteract another part . . . . He is the joiner . . he sees how
    they join.

He says indifferently and alike, How are you friend? to the President at his
    levee,

And he says Good day my brother, to Cudge[41] that hoes in the sugarfield;

And both understand him and know that his speech is right.

He walks with perfect ease in the capitol,   35

He walks among the Congress . . . . and one representative says to another,
    Here is our equal appearing and new.

Then the mechanics take him for a mechanic,

And the soldiers suppose him to be a captain . . . . and the sailors that he has
    followed the sea,

And the authors take him for an author . . . . and the artists for an artist,

And the laborers perceive he could labor with them and love them;   40

No matter what the work is, that he is one to follow it or has followed it,

No matter what the nation, that he might find his brothers and sisters there.

The English believe he comes of their English stock,

A Jew to the Jew he seems . . . . a Russ to the Russ . . . . usual and near . .
    removed from none.

Whoever he looks at in the traveler's coffeehouse claims him,   45

The Italian or Frenchman is sure, and the German is sure, and the Spaniard is
    sure . . . . and the island Cuban is sure.

The engineer, the deckhand on the great lakes or on the Mississippi or St
    Lawrence or Sacramento or Hudson or Delaware claims him.

The gentleman of perfect blood acknowledges his perfect blood,

The insulter, the prostitute, the angry person, the beggar, see themselves in the
    ways of him . . . . he strangely transmutes them,

They are not vile any more . . . . they hardly know themselves, they are so
    grown.   50

You think it would be good to be the writer of melodious verses,

Well it would be good to be the writer of melodious verses;

But what are verses beyond the flowing character you could have? . . . . or
    beyond beautiful manners and behaviour?

Or beyond one manly or affectionate deed of an apprenticeboy? . . or old
    woman? . . or man that has been in prison or is likely to be in prison?

1855

---

[41] Black field hand.

[Europe the 72d and 73d Years of These States]*

Suddenly out of its stale and drowsy lair, the lair of slaves,
Like lightning Europe le'pt forth[42] . . . . half startled at itself,
Its feet upon the ashes and the rags . . . . Its hands tight to the throats of kings.

O hope and faith! O aching close of lives! O many a sickened heart!
Turn back unto this day, and make yourselves afresh.   5

And you, paid to defile the People . . . . you liars mark:
Not for numberless agonies, murders, lusts,
For court thieving in its manifold mean forms,
Worming from his simplicity the poor man's wages;
For many a promise sworn by royal lips, And broken, and laughed at in the
    breaking,   10
Then in their power not for all these did the blows strike of personal revenge
    . . or the heads of the nobles fall;
The People scorned the ferocity of kings.

But the sweetness of mercy brewed bitter destruction, and the frightened rulers
    come back:
Each comes in state with his train . . . . hangman, priest and tax-gatherer . . . .
    soldier, lawyer, jailer and sycophant.

Yet behind all, lo, a Shape,   15
Vague as the night, draped interminably, head front and form in scarlet folds,
Whose face and eyes none may see,
Out of its robes only this . . . . the red robes, lifted by the arm,
One finger pointed high over the top, like the head of a snake appears.

Meanwhile corpses lie in new-made graves . . . . bloody corpses of young men: 20
The rope of the gibbet hangs heavily . . . . the bullets of princes are flying
    . . . . the creatures of power laugh aloud,
And all these things bear fruits . . . . and they are good.

Those corpses of young men,
Those martyrs that hang from the gibbets . . . those hearts pierced by the gray
    lead,
Cold and motionless as they seem . . live elsewhere with unslaughter'd vitality.   25

They live in other young men, O kings,
They live in brothers, again ready to defy you:
They were purified by death . . . . They were taught and exalted.

---

* Final title supplied in 1860. The poem was first   [42] I.e., in the revolutions of 1848.
published as "Resurgemus" in the New York
Daily Tribune, June 21, 1850.

Not a grave of the murdered for freedom but grows seed for freedom . . . . in
   its turn to bear seed,
Which the winds carry afar and re-sow, and the rains and the snows nourish.   30

Not a disembodied spirit can the weapons of tyrants let loose,
But it stalks invisibly over the earth . . whispering counseling cautioning.

Liberty let others despair of you . . . . I never despair of you.

Is the house shut? Is the master away?
Nevertheless be ready . . . . be not weary of watching,   35
He will soon return . . . . his messengers come anon.

1855

[A Boston Ballad]*

Clear the way there Jonathan!
Way for the President's marshal! Way for the government cannon!
Way for the federal foot and dragoons . . . . and the phantoms afterward.

I rose this morning early to get betimes in Boston town;
Here's a good place at the corner . . . . I must stand and see the show.   5

I love to look on the stars and stripes . . . . I hope the fifes will play Yankee
   Doodle.

How bright shine the foremost with cutlasses,
Every man holds his revolver . . . . marching stiff through Boston town.

A fog follows . . . . antiques of the same come limping,
Some appear wooden-legged and some appear bandaged and bloodless.   10

Why this is a show! It has called the dead out of the earth,
The old graveyards of the hills have hurried to see;
Uncountable phantoms gather by flank and rear of it,
Cocked hats of mothy mould and crutches made of mist,
Arms in slings and old men leaning on young men's shoulders.   15

What troubles you, Yankee phantoms? What is all this chattering of bare gums?
Does the ague convulse your limbs? Do you mistake your crutches for firelocks,
   and level them?

---

* Final title supplied in 1871. The poem refers to
the events of June 2, 1854, when a fugitive
slave, Anthony Burns, was marched through the
streets of Boston to the harbor to be returned
to his Southern owner.

If you blind your eyes with tears you will not see the President's marshal,
If you groan such groans you might balk the government cannon.

For shame old maniacs! . . . . Bring down those tossed arms, and let your white
    hair be;   20
Here gape your smart grandsons . . . . their wives gaze at them from the
    windows,
See how well-dressed . . . . see how orderly they conduct themselves.

Worse and worse . . . . Can't you stand it? Are you retreating?
Is this hour with the living too dead for you?

Retreat then! Pell-mell! . . . . Back to the hills, old limpers!   25
I do not think you belong here anyhow.

But there is one thing that belongs here . . . . Shall I tell you what it is,
    gentlemen of Boston?

I will whisper it to the Mayor . . . . he shall send a committee to England,
They shall get a grant from the Parliament, and go with a cart to the royal
    vault,
Dig out King George's coffin . . . . unwrap him quick from the graveclothes
    . . . . box up his bones for a journey: 30
Find a swift Yankee clipper . . . . here is freight for you blackbellied clipper,
Up with your anchor! shake out your sails! . . . . steer straight toward Boston
    bay.

Now call the President's marshal again, and bring out the government cannon,
And fetch home the roarers from Congress, and make another procession and
    guard it with foot and dragoons.

Here is a centrepiece for them: 35
Look! all orderly citizens . . . . look from the windows women.

The committee open the box and set up the regal ribs and glue those that will
    not stay,
And clap the skull on top of the ribs, and clap a crown on top of the skull.

You have got your revenge old buster! . . . . The crown is come to its own
    and more than its own.

Stick your hands in your pockets Jonathan . . . . you are a made man from this
    day,   40
You are mighty cute . . . . and here is one of your bargains.

1855

[There Was a Child Went Forth]*

There was a child went forth every day,
And the first object he looked upon and received with wonder or pity or love
   or dread, that object he became,
And that object became part of him for the day or a certain part of the day
   .... or for many years or stretching cycles of years.

The early lilacs became part of this child,
And grass, and white and red morningglories, and white and red clover, and the
   song of the phœbe-bird,   5
And the March-born lambs, and the sow's pink-faint litter, and the mare's foal,
   and the cow's calf, and the noisy brood of the barnyard or by the mire of
   the pond-side .. and the fish suspending themselves so curiously below there
   .. and the beautiful curious liquid .. and the water-plants with their
   graceful flat heads .. all became part of him.

And the field-sprouts of April and May became part of him .... wintergrain
   sprouts, and those of the light-yellow corn, and of the esculent roots of the
   garden,
And the appletrees covered with blossoms, and the fruit afterward .... and
   woodberries .. and the commonest weeds by the road;
And the old drunkard staggering home from the outhouse of the tavern whence
   he had lately risen,
And the schoolmistress that passed on her way to the school .. and the friendly
   boys that passed .. and the quarrelsome boys .. and the tidy and
   freshcheeked girls .. and the barefoot negro boy and girl,   10
And all the changes of city and country wherever he went.

His own parents .. he that had propelled the fatherstuff at night, and fathered
   him .. and she that conceived him in her womb and birthed him .... they
   gave this child more of themselves than that,
They gave him afterward every day .... they and of them became part of
   him.
The mother at home quietly placing the dishes on the suppertable,
The mother with mild words .... clean her cap and gown .... a wholesome
   odor falling off her person and clothes as she walks by: 15
The father, strong, selfsufficient, manly, mean, angered, unjust,
The blow, the quick loud word, the tight bargain, the crafty lure,
The family usages, the language, the company, the furniture .... the yearning
   and swelling heart,
Affection that will not be gainsayed .... The sense of what is real .... the
   thought if after all it should prove unreal,
The doubts of daytime and the doubts of nighttime ... the curious whether
   and how,   20

* Final title supplied in 1871.

Whether that which appears so is so . . . . Or is it all flashes and specks?

Men and women crowding fast in the streets . . if they are not flashes and specks what are they?

The streets themselves, and the facades of houses . . . . the goods in the windows,

Vehicles . . teams . . the tiered wharves, and the huge crossing at the ferries;

The village on the highland seen from afar at sunset . . . . the river between,   25

Shadows . . aureola and mist . . light falling on roofs and gables of white or brown, three miles off,

The schooner near by sleepily dropping down the tide . . the little boat slacktowed astern,

The hurrying tumbling waves and quickbroken crests and slapping;

The strata of colored clouds . . . . the long bar of maroontint away solitary by itself . . . . the spread of purity it lies motionless in,

The horizon's edge, the flying seacrow, the fragrance of saltmarsh and shoremud;   30

These became part of that child who went forth every day, and who now goes and will always go forth every day,

And these become of him or her that peruses them now.

1855

[Who Learns My Lesson Complete?]*

Who learns my lesson complete?

Boss and journeyman and apprentice? . . . . churchman and atheist?

The stupid and the wise thinker . . . . parents and offspring . . . . merchant and clerk and porter and customer . . . . editor, author, artist and schoolboy?

Draw nigh and commence,

It is no lesson . . . . it lets down the bars to a good lesson,   5

And that to another . . . . and every one to another still.

The great laws take and effuse without argument,

I am of the same style, for I am their friend,

I love them quits and quits . . . . I do not halt and make salaams.

I lie abstracted and hear beautiful tales of things and the reasons of things,   10

They are so beautiful I nudge myself to listen.

I cannot say to any person what I hear . . . . I cannot say it to myself . . . . it is very wonderful.

It is no little matter, this round and delicious globe, moving so exactly in its orbit forever and ever, without one jolt or the untruth of a single second;

---

* Final title supplied in 1871.

I do not think it was made in six days, nor in ten thousand years, nor ten
 decillions of years,
Nor planned and built one thing after another, as an architect plans and builds a
 house.   15

I do not think seventy years is the time of a man or woman,
Nor that seventy millions of years is the time of a man or woman,
Nor that years will ever stop the existence of me or any one else.
Is it wonderful that I should be immortal? as every one is immortal,
I know it is wonderful . . . . but my eyesight is equally wonderful . . . . and
 how I was conceived in my mother's womb is equally wonderful,   20
And how I was not palpable once but am now . . . . and was born on the last
 day of May 1819 . . . . and passed from a babe in the creeping trance of
 three summers and three winters to articulate and walk . . . . are all equally
 wonderful.

And that I grew six feet high . . . . and that I have become a man thirty-six
 years old in 1855 . . . . and that I am here anyhow—are all equally
 wonderful;
And that my soul embraces you this hour, and we affect each other without
 ever seeing each other, and never perhaps to see each other, is every bit as
 wonderful:
And that I can think such thoughts as these is just as wonderful,
And that I can remind you, and you think them and know them to be true is
 just as wonderful,   25
And that the moon spins round the earth and on with the earth is equally
 wonderful,
And that they balance themselves with the sun and stars is equally wonderful.

Come I should like to hear you tell me what there is in yourself that is not just
 as wonderful,
And I should like to hear the name of anything between Sunday morning and
 Saturday night that is not just as wonderful.

1855

[Great Are the Myths]*

Great are the myths . . . . I too delight in them,
Great are Adam and Eve . . . . I too look back and accept them;
Great the risen and fallen nations, and their poets, women, sages, inventors,
 rulers, warriors and priests.

Great is liberty! Great is equality! I am their follower,
Helmsmen of nations, choose your craft . . . . where you sail I sail,   5

* Final title supplied in 1867. From 1881 on, the
poem was omitted from *Leaves of Grass*.

Yours is the muscle of life or death . . . . yours is the perfect science . . . . in
   you I have absolute faith.

Great is today, and beautiful,
It is good to live in this age . . . . there never was any better.

Great are the plunges and throes and triumphs and falls of democracy,
Great the reformers with their lapses and screams,   10
Great the daring and venture of sailors on new explorations.

Great are yourself and myself,
We are just as good and bad as the oldest and youngest or any,
What the best and worst did we could do,
What they felt . . do not we feel it in ourselves?   15
What they wished . . do we not wish the same?

Great is youth, and equally great is old age . . . . great are the day and night;
Great is wealth and great is poverty . . . . great is expression and great is
   silence.

Youth large lusty and loving . . . . youth full of grace and force and
   fascination,
Do you know that old age may come after you with equal grace and force and
   fascination?   20
Day fullblown and splendid . . . . day of the immense sun, and action and
   ambition and laughter,
The night follows close, with millions of suns, and sleep and restoring darkness.

Wealth with the flush hand and fine clothes and hospitality:
But then the soul's wealth—which is candor and knowledge and pride and
   enfolding love:
Who goes for men and women showing poverty richer than wealth?   25

Expression of speech . . in what is written or said forget not that silence is also
   expressive,
That anguish as hot as the hottest and contempt as cold as the coldest may be
   without words,
That the true adoration is likewise without words and without kneeling.

Great is the greatest nation . . the nation of clusters of equal nations.

Great is the earth, and the way it became what it is,   30
Do you imagine it is stopped at this? . . . . and the increase abandoned?
Understand then that it goes as far onward from this as this is from the times
   when it lay in covering waters and gases.

Great is the quality of truth in man,
The quality of truth in man supports itself through all changes,
It is inevitably in the man . . . . He and it are in love, and never leave each
    other. 35

The truth in man is no dictum . . . . it is vital as eyesight,
If there be any soul there is truth . . . . if there be man or woman there is
    truth . . . . If there be physical or moral there is truth,
If there be equilibrium or volition there is truth . . . . if there be things at all
    upon the earth there is truth.
O truth of the earth! O truth of things! I am determined to press the whole
    way toward you,
Sound your voice! I scale mountains or dive in the sea after you. 40

Great is language . . . . it is the mightiest of the sciences,
It is the fulness and color and form and diversity of the earth . . . . and of men
    and women . . . . and of all qualities and processes;
It is greater than wealth . . . . it is greater than buildings or ships or religions
    or paintings or music.

Great is the English speech . . . . What speech is so great as the English?
Great is the English brood . . . . What brood has so vast a destiny as the
    English? 45
It is the mother of the brood that must rule the earth with the new rule,
The new rule shall rule as the soul rules, and as the love and justice and
    equality that are in the soul rule.

Great is the law . . . . Great are the old few landmarks of the law . . . . they
    are the same in all times and shall not be disturbed.

Great are marriage, commerce, newspapers, books, freetrade, railroads, steamers,
    international mails and telegraphs and exchanges.

Great is Justice; 50
Justice is not settled by legislators and laws . . . . it is in the soul,
It cannot be varied by statutes any more than love or pride or the attraction of
    gravity can,
It is immutable . . it does not depend on majorities . . . . majorities or what not
    come at last before the same passionless and exact tribunal.

For justice are the grand natural lawyers and perfect judges . . . . it is in their
    souls,
It is well asserted . . . . they have not studied for nothing . . . . the great
    includes the less,
They rule on the highest grounds . . . . they oversee all eras and states and
    administrations. 55

The perfect judge fears nothing . . . . he could go front to front before God,
Before the perfect judge all shall stand back . . . . life and death shall stand
    back . . . . heaven and hell shall stand back.

Great is goodness;
I do not know what it is any more than I know what health is . . . . but I
    know it is great.   60

Great is wickedness . . . . I find I often admire it just as much as I admire
    goodness:
Do you call that a paradox? It certainly is a paradox.

The eternal equilibrium of things is great, and the eternal overthrow of things
    is great,
And there is another paradox.

Great is life . . and real and mystical . . wherever and whoever,   65
Great is death . . . . Sure as life holds all parts together, death holds all parts
    together;
Sure as the stars return again after they merge in the light, death is great as life.
1855

Acknowledgments

Abigail Adams: From *The Adams–Jefferson Letters*, by Lester J. Cappon. Copyright the University of North Carolina Press 1959. Published for the Institute of Early American History and Culture, Williamsburg. Used with permission of the Publisher.

Abigail and John Adams: Reprinted by permission of the publishers from *The Book of Abigail and John: Selected Letters of the Adams Family*, edited by L. H. Butterfield, Marc Friedlaender and Mary-Jo Kline, Cambridge, Mass.: Harvard University Press, Copyright © 1975 by the Massachusetts Historical Society.

John Adams: From *The Adams–Jefferson Letters*, by Lester J. Cappon. Copyright the University of North Carolina Press 1959. Published for the Institute of Early American History and Culture, Williamsburg. Used with permission of the Publisher. Reprinted by permission of the publishers from *Diary and Autobiography of John Adams*, Vols. 1–4, edited by L. H. Butterfield, Cambridge, Mass.: Harvard University Press, Copyright © 1961 by the Massachusetts Historical Society.

Anon.: Adapted from *The Book of Chilam Balam of Chumayel*, by Ralph L. Roys, with an Introduction by J. Eric S. Thompson. New edition copyright 1967 by the University of Oklahoma Press.

Anon.: From "Prayer of the First Night Male Shooting Chant Evil: A Navajo Evil-Chasing Chant" from *Prayer: The Compulsive Word*, by Gladys A. Reichard. Monographs of the American Ethnologic Society, No. 7. Reprinted by permission of University of Washington Press.

Joel Barlow: "Advice to a Raven in Russia." Huntington manuscript BN46. Text reprinted with the permission of the Henry E. Huntington Library and Art Gallery from Leon Howard, "Joel Barlow and Napoleon," *Huntington Library Quarterly* 2 (1938): 49–50.

William Bartram: "The Alligators" from *The Travels of William Bartram*, edited by Francis Harper. Reprinted by permission of Yale University Press.

William Ralganal Benson: "The Facts of the Stone and Kelsey Massacre in Lake County, California." Reprinted by permission of the California Historical Society and The Bancroft Library, University of California, Berkeley.

Robert Beverley: From *The History and Present State of Virginia*, by Robert Beverley. Ed. by Louis B. Wright. Copyright 1947 by the University of North Carolina Press. Published for the Institute of Early American History and Culture, Williamsburg. Used with permission of the publisher.

William Bradford: From *Of Plymouth Plantation*, by William Bradford, edited by Samuel Eliot Morison. Copyright 1952 by Samuel Eliot Morison and renewed 1980 by Emily M. Beck. Reprinted by permission of Alfred A. Knopf, Inc.

Anne Bradstreet: Reprinted by permission of the publishers of *The Works of Anne Bradstreet*, edited by Jeannine Hensley, Cambridge, Mass.: The Belknap Press of Harvard University Press. Copyright © 1967 by the President and Fellows of Harvard College.

William Hill Brown: Reprinted from *The Power of Sympathy*, ed. by William S. Osborne. College & University Press Services, Inc.

William Byrd II: Reprinted by permission of the publishers from *The Prose Works of William Byrd of Westover*, edited by Louis B. Wright, Cambridge, Mass.: The Belknap Press of Harvard University Press, Copyright © 1966 by the President and Fellows of Harvard College.

Columbus: From *The Columbus Journals,* ed. by Samuel Eliot Morison. Copyright © 1964 by Samuel Eliot Morison. Reprinted by permission of Curtis Brown, Ltd.

Giovanni da Verrazzano: From *Letter to the King.* Reprinted by permission of The Pierpont Morgan Library.

Michele de Cuneo: "The Second Voyage," translated by Elissa B. Weaver. Reprinted by permission of Elissa B. Weaver.

Frederick Douglass: From *The Life and Writings of Frederick Douglass,* ed. by Philip S. Foner. © 1950, Ren. 1978 International Publishers Co., Inc., New York. Chapters 13–15 from *Life and Times,* by Frederick Douglass (New York: Macmillan/Collier Books, 1962).

Timothy Dwight: Reprinted by permission of the publishers from *Travels in New England and New York,* by Timothy Dwight, edited by Barbara Miller Solomon, Cambridge, Mass.: The Belknap Press of Harvard University Press, Copyright © 1969 by the President and Fellows of Harvard College.

Jonathan Edwards: Letter to Rev. Dr. B. Coleman from *The Great Awakening,* edited by C. C. Goen. Copyright © 1972 by Yale University. Reprinted by permission of the publisher, Yale University Press.

Ralph Waldo Emerson: From *The Correspondence of Emerson and Carlyle,* ed. by Joseph Slater. © 1964 Columbia University Press. From *The Letters of Ralph Waldo Emerson,* ed. by Ralph L. Rusk. Both reprinted by permission of Columbia University Press and the Ralph Waldo Emerson Memorial Association. Reprinted by permission of the publishers from *Journals and Miscellaneous Notebooks* of Ralph Waldo Emerson, edited by William H. Gilman, et al. Cambridge, Mass.: The Belknap Press of Harvard University Press, Copyright © 1960, 1961, 1965, 1966, 1969, 1970, 1971, 1973, 1975, 1976, 1977, 1978, 1982 by the President and Fellows of Harvard College. Reprinted by permission of the publishers from *The Collected Works of Ralph Waldo Emerson,* Volume I: *Nature, Addresses, and Lectures,* edited by R. E. Spiller and A. R. Ferguson. Cambridge, Mass.: The Belknap Press of Harvard University Press, Copyright © 1971 by the President and Fellows of Harvard College. Reprinted by permission from the publishers from *The Collected Works of Ralph Waldo Emerson,* Volume II: *Essays.: First Series,* edited by J. Slater, A. R. Ferguson and J. F. Carr. Cambridge, Mass.: The Belknap Press of Harvard University Press, Copyright © 1979 by the President and Fellows of Harvard College.

Benjamin Franklin: Autobiography of Benjamin Franklin as edited by Leonard W. Labaree, et al.

for Yale University Press, 1964 [Parts I & II]. HM 9999. Reprinted by permission of The Huntington Library, San Marino, California. "On Literary Style" reprinted courtesy of Historical Society of Pennsylvania. "Preface" to *Poor Richard Improved* (1758), by Benjamin Franklin from *The Papers of Benjamin Franklin,* ed. by Labaree et al. Reprinted by permission by Yale University Library.

Philip Freneau: "To a New England Poet" from *The Last Poems of Philip Freneau,* edited by Lewis Leary. Copyright 1945 by The Trustees of Rutgers College in New Jersey. "To a Honey Bee," "To Crispin O'Conner" from *The Poems of Philip Freneau,* vol. 3, ed. by Fred L. Pattee. Reprinted by permission of Princeton University Library.

Margaret Fuller: From *The Writings of Margaret Fuller,* edited by Mason Wade. Copyright 1941, renewed © 1968 by The Viking Press, Inc. Reprinted by permission of Viking Penguin Inc.

Richard Hakluyt: "The First New England" from *The Principal Navigations, Voyages, Traffiques, and Discoveries of the English Nation,* Second Edition, 1598–1600. Ed. and Abridged by Jack Beeching (Penguin Books, 1972).

Nathaniel Hawthorne: Reprinted by permission of the Modern Language Association of America from *The English Notebooks,* by Nathaniel Hawthorne, edited by Randall Stewart. The passages from *The American Notebooks,* by Nathaniel Hawthorne, are from the edition by Claude M. Simpson published as Volume VIII of the Centenary Edition of the Works of Nathaniel Hawthorne, edited by William Charvat, Roy Harvey Pearce, and Claude M. Simpson, and are copyright © 1982, 1960, and 1972 by the Ohio State University Press. All rights are reserved.

Thomas Jefferson: From *The Adams–Jefferson Letters,* by Lester J. Cappon. Copyright the University of North Carolina Press 1959. Published for the Institute of Early American History and Culture, Williamsburg. Used with permission of the Publisher. From *Notes on the State of Virginia,* by Thomas Jefferson. Ed. by William Peden. Copyright 1954 by the University of North Carolina Press. Published for the Institute of Early American History and Culture, Williamsburg. Used with permission of the Publisher.

Charles H. Lincoln: Excerpted from "A Narrative of the Captivity and Restoration of Mrs. Mary Rowlandson" from *Narratives of the Indian Wars 1675–1699.* Copyright 1913 Charles Scribner's Sons; copyright renewed 1941. Reprinted with permission of Charles Scribner's Sons.

John Logan: [Speech at the End of Lord Dunmore's War.] Reprinted from *Great Documents in American Indian History,* copyright by Praeger Publishers 1973.

Cotton Mather: Reprinted by permission of the publishers from *Bonifacius, An Essay upon the Good,* by Cotton Mather, edited by David Levin. Cambridge, Mass.: The Belknap Press of Harvard University Press, Copyright © 1966 by the President and Fellows of Harvard College.

Herman Melville: "Greek Architecture," "Art," "Monody," "After the Pleasure Party," "The Maldive Shark," "The Tuft of Kelp," "Benito Cereno," and "Bartleby the Scrivener." Reprinted by permission of Hendricks House, Inc., Putney, Vermont 05346. *Billy Budd, Sailor,* by Herman Melville. Edited by Harrison Hayford and Merton M. Sealts, Jr. © 1962 by The University of Chicago. Reprinted by permission of the University of Chicago Press.

Samuel Eliot Morison: From *The European Discovery of America: The Southern Voyages 1492–1616,* by Samuel Eliot Morison. Copyright © 1974 by Samuel Eliot Morison. Reprinted by permission of Oxford University Press.

Thomas Paine: *The Age of Reason, The American Crisis,* and *Common Sense* from *The Complete Writings of Thomas Paine.* Ed. by Philip S. Foner. Published by arrangement with Lyle Stuart.

Edgar Allan Poe: Reprinted by permission of the publishers from *The Collected Works of Edgar Allan Poe,* edited by Thomas Ollive Mabbott. Cambridge, Mass.: The Belknap Press of Harvard University Press, Copyright © 1969 (vol. I, Poems) and © 1978 (vols. II and III, Tales and Sketches) by the President and Fellows of Harvard College.

John Ridge: "Essay on Cherokee Civilization," transcribed by William Sturtevant first appeared in *Journal of Cherokee Studies,* Vol. VI, No. 2. Reprinted by permission of the Museum of the Cherokee Indian and William Sturtevant.

Samuel Sewall: Excerpts from *The Diary of Samuel Sewall 1674–1729,* edited by M. Halsey Thomas. Copyright © 1973 by Farrar, Straus and Giroux, Inc. Reprinted by permission of Farrar, Straus and Giroux, Inc.

Edward Taylor: From *The Poems of Edward Taylor,* edited by Donald E. Stanford. Copyright © 1960 by Donald E. Stanford. Reprinted by permission of Donald E. Stanford.

Tecumseh: "We all belong to one family." From *Native American Testimony.* Crowell. 1978. pp. 118–120. Reprinted by permission of Peter Nabokov.

Henry David Thoreau: "The Ascent of Ktaadn" from Joseph J. Moldenhauer, ed., *The Maine Woods, The Writings of Henry D. Thoreau.* Copyright © 1972 by Princeton University Press. Selection from "Wednesday" from Carl F. Hovde, William L. Howarth, Elizabeth Hale Witherell, eds., *A Week on the Concord and Merrimack Rivers: The Writings of Henry D. Thoreau.* Copyright © 1980 by Princeton University Press. "Resistance to Civil Government," "Paradise (to Be) Regained," "A Plea for Captain John Brown" from Wendell Glick, *The Writings of Henry D. Thoreau: Reform Papers.* Copyright © 1973 by Princeton University Press. J. Lyndon Stanley, ed., *Henry D. Thoreau: Walden.* Copyright © 1971 by Princeton University Press. All reprinted by permission of Princeton University Press. Henry D. Thoreau, *Journal,* Vol. 1: *1837–1844,* ed. Elizabeth Hall Witherell. Copyright © 1981 by Princeton University Press. Selections reprinted by permission of Princeton University Press.

Frederick Goddard Tuckerman: "The Cricket." Copyright 1950 by Margaret Tuckerman Clark. Reprinted by permission of the Cummington Press. From *The Complete Poems of Frederick Tuckerman,* edited by N. Scott Momaday. Copyright © 1965 by Oxford University Press, Inc. Reprinted by permission.

Phillis Wheatley: "On the Death of the Rev. Mr. George Whitefield, 1770," "On Being Brought from Africa to America," "On Imagination," "To S.M. A Young African Painter, on Seeing His Works," and "To His Excellency General Washington" from *The Poems of Phillis Wheatley.* Edited with an Introduction by Julian D. Mason, Jr., Copyright 1966 The University of North Carolina Press. By permission of the publisher.

Roger Williams: "What Habacuck once spake, mine eyes," "The Courteous Pagan shall condemne," "Truth is a Native, Naked Beauty," in the Narragansett Edition of Roger Williams, edited by J. Hammond Trumbull, et al. (1899), reprinted from Volume 1 of *The Complete Writings of Roger Williams,* edited by Perry Miller (New York: Russell & Russell, 1963).

John Winthrop: "A Model of Christian Charity." Courtesy Massachusetts Historical Society.

John Woolman: From *The Journal and Major Essays of John Woolman,* edited by Phillips P. Moulton. Oxford University Press, 1971. Reprinted by permission of Phillips P. Moulton.

Index of Authors, Titles, and First Lines of Poems